Happy Gardening!

Love,
Mom

Flora Americana

A Gardener's Encyclopedia of Plants, Trees, and Shrubs for the American Garden

Flora Americana

A Gardener's Encyclopedia of Plants, Trees, and Shrubs for the American Garden

Chief Consultant: Sean Hogan

First published in 2016 by
Global Book Publishing Pty Ltd
Part of The Quarto Group
Level One, Ovest House,
58 West Street, Brighton, BN1 2RA, UK

ISBN 978-0-85762-473-4

A Global Book

Printed and Bound in China

Conceived, designed and produced by Global Book Publishing

Design: Tony Seddon

Chief consultant: Sean Hogan

Horticultural editor: Katie Elzer-Peters

Contributors:
David Austin, David Banks, Cathy Wilkinson Barash, Matthew Biggs, Don Blaxell, David Bond, Peter Brownless, Geoff Bryant, Kate Bryant, Cole Burrell, Derek Butcher, Jerry Coleby-Williams, Ian Connor, Penny Dunn, Lorraine Flanigan, Jim Folsom, Richard Francis, Jo Ann Gardner, William Grant, Ken Grapes, Sarah Guest, Keith Hammett, Patricia Hanbidge, Ian Hay, Terry Hewitt, Geoff Hodge, Mark Kane, Ruth Kiew, Melanie Kinsey, Isobyl la Croix, Todd Lasseigne, Tony Lord, David Mabberley, Lawrie Metcalf, Valda Paddison, Helene Pizzi, Lee Reich, Martyn Rix, Tony Rodd, Bruce Rutherford, Stephen Ryan, Donald Schnell, Patrick Seymour, Julie Silk, Geoff Stebbings, Wendy Thomas, David Tomlinson, John Trager, R. G. Turner Jr., Marion Tyree, Rachel Vogan, Scott Williams

Cover images:
© photolinc/Shutterstock; © Whatafoto/Shutterstock; © wjarek/ Shutterstock

Photographs:
Pages 3–4 © Gita Kunlinitch Studio/Shutterstock, page 5 © motorolka/ Shutterstock, pages 6–7 © Kathie Nichols/Shutterstock, pages 10–11 © JPL Designs/Shutterstock.
Page 44 top, 45 top, 46 bottom, 49 both, all © Art Archive.
Page 359 (*Nassella tenuissima)* © Stan Shebs

All other photographs and illustrations from the Global Photo Library, © Global Book Publishing Pty Ltd

Contents

How This Book Works

Flora Americana provides a wealth of up-to-date information on a huge variety of plants. Selection has been based on those most significant in horticulture, and most suitable for growing in the varied climate zones of North America. It is expected that most readers will be interested in the plants found and grown in gardens and parks rather than in the wild. And because the great majority of garden enthusiasts live in the temperate zones, there is proportionately a more complete coverage of temperate plants than of tropical species.

The book is composed of three sections. The first section introduces the book and looks at plants in general terms: how they differ from each other, environmental factors that affect their growth, classification, human uses, and cultivations. A color-coded map showing plant hardiness zones, and detailed explanation of each of those zones, is also included.

The second section, the major part of the book, is arranged in alphabetical order according to genus. The symbol × before a genus or

Lampranthus glaucus

Lamprocapnos spectabilis 'Alba'

Lantana camara var. *crocea*

Species entry

Symbols (see listings at right)

Hardiness zones

Genus entry

Family name

Place of origin

Cultivation

Flora award

Synonym

Common name

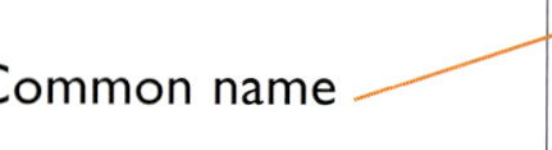

Forms (variants, subspecies or cultivars)

Lamium orvala
↔40 in (100 cm)
↑40 in (100 cm)
Bushy perennial found from southern to central Europe. Leaves are toothed, pointed oval, to 6 in (15 cm) long. Flowerheads consist of a few pinkish red to purple flowers, ¾ in (18 mm) long, appear in summer. Zones 6–10.

LAMPRANTHUS
This genus of some 155 species belonging to the iceplant (Aizoaceae) family is found from southern Namibia to South Africa's Eastern Cape; there is also one species possibly native to Australia. They are creeping, sometimes erect subshrubs. The succulent leaves are linear to club-shaped, often triangular in section. The flowers are commonly large and brightly colored and produced profusely over long periods in spring–summer, making them useful for summer bedding and containers in temperate regions. A few are frost hardy, and can be grown all year round in sheltered sites. Some species formerly placed here have now been reclassified as *Oscularia*.
CULTIVATION: These plants need full sun and thrive in poor well-drained soils. They are very easily propagated from stem cuttings, which can be rooted at almost any time of the year.

Lampranthus aurantiacus ★
syn. *Mesembryanthemum aurantiacum*
ICE PLANT
↔8–18 in (20–45 cm)
↑6–12 in (15–30 cm)
Succulent perennial with upright stems becoming prostrate with age. Leaves bluish green, tapering, minutely rough and spotted. Bears profuse daisy-like bright yellow or orange flowers in the late spring. 'Sunman', golden yellow flowers. Zones 9–11.

Lampranthus filicaulis
syn. *Mesembryanthemum filicaule*
TRAILING ICE PLANT
↔18–36 in (45–90 cm)
↑12–24 in (30–60 cm)
Succulent perennial. Weak, delicate, creeping or prostrate stems. Leaves are crowded, tapering, curved, and about 1 in (25 mm) long. Reddish flowers are borne on long stalks. Zones 8–11.

Lampranthus glaucus
NOON FLOWER
↔12–24 in (30–60 cm)
↑12–24 in (30–60 cm)
Bushy, low-spreading, succulent perennial with roughly dotted, flattened, 3-angled, gray-green leaves, to 1 in (25 mm) long. The soft, sulfur yellow, daisy-like flowers appear in late spring. The fruit is a dry capsule. Zones 9–11.

Lampranthus productus
PURPLE ICE PLANT
↔12–24 in (30–60 cm)
↑12–24 in (30–60 cm)
Much-branched succulent perennial with narrow leaves, to 1½ in (35 mm) long, covered with fine dots. Groups of 3 or 5 pale rose pink flowers, each 1 in (25 mm) across. Zones 9–11.

Lampranthus roseus
syns *Lampranthus multiradiatus*, *Mesembryanthemum roseum*
↔12–20 in (30–50 cm)
↑12–20 in (30–50 cm)
Short-lived, erect, shrubby, succulent perennial, sometimes grown as an annual, with slender branches and narrow curved leaves. Clusters of rose pink to reddish violet daisy-like flowers, with a slightly peppery smell, in mid-spring–early summer. Zones 9–11.

Lampranthus specta
syn. *Mesembryanthemum s*
ICE PLANT
↔20–30 in (50–75 cm)
↑6–20 in (15–50 cm)
Prostrate, trailing, succul
Branching stems, moun
habit. Fleshy, bright gr
green, curved leaves w
keeled and triangular i
Profuse glossy, pink to pur
daisy-like flowers, 2–3 i
across, in spring–summ
Apricot', apricot flowers;
Brilliant', magenta flower
Red', fiery red flowers. Z

LAMPROCAPNOS
The sole species in this ge
better known under its f
of *Dicentra spectabilis*. I
most popular of the blee
is now in a genus of its o
the poppy (Papaveraceae)
a woodland perennial wit
blue-green foliage and a
below which from mid
graceful, heart-shaped flo
CULTIVATION: Thrives i
compost-rich, well-drai
to dappled shade. Delicate
but tough and adaptable.
from seed, by division, o
cuttings of non-flowerin

Lamprocapnos spec
syn. *Dicentra spectabilis*
BLEEDING HEART
↔20–40 in (50
↑40–56 in (100–140 cm)
Perennial from Japan,
China, and Russia's far e
grower with leaves coarse
Strongly upright, often
flower stems carry up t
heart-shaped flowers w
protruding white inner
pure white flowers. Zone

the Flora award

full sun

half sun

shade

fully hardy

frost hardy

half hardy

frost tender

height

spread

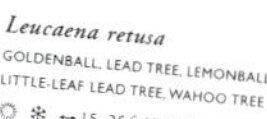

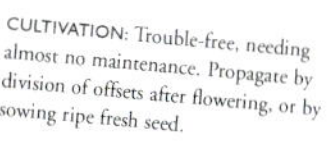

PAGE HEADINGS
help you locate a particular plant. Headings on each double-page spread name the first genus described on the left-hand page, and the last genus described on the right-hand page.

THUMB TABS
are colored alphabetical tabs in the margin that help you find the plant you are looking for.

CAPTIONS
indicate the plant's botanical name.

GENUS ENTRY
contains information about the group as a whole, including geographical range, and cultivation and propagation requirements.

SPECIES ENTRY
contains detailed information on particular species and forms, and includes hardiness rating by zones.

species name usually indicates a hybrid genus or species. The genus entries give the family to which the plant belongs, as well as geographical range, number of species, distinguishing features, commercial uses, and propagation and cultivation requirements of the genus as a whole. Under every genus entry are species entries (including synonym and common name, if applicable), each containing the growth habit, flowering season, flower color, forms, and hardiness zones, with symbols denoting aspect, hardiness, width, and height. The width and height given apply to a mature plant in cultivation. The hardiness zones show the climatic areas in which plants can be grown. However, for annuals the minimum zone is that in which the plant can be raised and planted out over the spring to autumn period, disregarding winter hardiness.

Many plant entries have a photograph—each one is captioned with its botanical name.

Flora awards, indicated with a star, show the plants recommended by our consultants as outstanding in their group. Usually the award appears next to the plant name.

The third section includes five pages of color illustrations, depicting flower and leaf structure, shape, and arrangement, and fruit types; a comprehensive glossary; and finally an index that lists botanical names, common names, and synonyms.

CLOSE-UP PHOTOGRAPHS
zoom in on a leaf, flower, fruit, or bark to help you appreciate the plant's unique qualities.

"IN THE WILD" PHOTOGRAPHS
show plants in their natural habitat.

The World
of Plants

The Gardening Tradition

Below: This 700-year-old Douglas fir (Pseudotsuga menziesii) *has established itself among the rocks of Canyon National Park, Utah. This hardy tree can grow to 150 ft (45 m) tall.*

Never before have so many plants been available to North American gardeners. Ease of travel and communication, as well as the internet, have conspired to allow exotic introductions from the farthest reaches of the planet to appear with increasing frequency in local garden centers. A growing awareness of our own gardening conditions, including factors such as climate and soil, has given us a new appreciation for what we can do in our own backyards. In addition, we've been able to learn more about what others do in other parts of the country, not to mention in the rest of the world. The consequence of so much detailed information is a changing understanding and a greater appreciation of what it means to garden in North America.

Gardening in North America

The native peoples on the North American continent taught settlers in the New World about many growing techniques and new plants. For the early settlers, gardens were a necessity focused on food production, with the occasional decorative plant carefully nurtured from seed brought lovingly from the Old Country. As economics allowed, gardens evolved, often harking back to the styles left behind. Along the immediate West Coast and in the Southwest, gardens have been influenced not only by the practicality of the frontier life, but also by settlers from Europe, most notably Britain and Spain, and Asia.

Formal gardens, following the designs of the great European estates, for example, still influence gardening, especially in eastern parts of the USA, and many of the desired classical characteristics, such as ideas of balancing masses of plants and designing view corridors and corners into even much smaller gardens, still provide useful elements in garden design.

Gradually, local styles evolved that included more indigenous plant materials, as well as newly discovered plant species from around the world, and, most recently, more informal plantings influenced by wild surroundings. In the American West, gardening developed from frontier practicality where, at one point, the closest thing to horticulture, other than the essential vegetable garden, might have been the one lilac kept alive at a kitchen door with the excess dishwater. Today, however, a sense of regionalism exists that incorporates not only the area's specific plants, but also the types of plants that grow well in nearby environs, into design and plantings.

Origins of North American flora

The natural flora that surrounds us has been influenced by many factors, including the geological development of the continents themselves. Over time, with the movement of landmasses—separating and coming back together again, natural bridges forming and disappearing—plants have evolved in North America at times independently and at other periods intermingled with the flora of other continents.

Millions of years ago, the continents of North America, Europe, and Asia were connected, sharing plant life as well as broad climatic characteristics and soil types. Even after the continents drifted apart, large areas of North America remained lowland, with fairly similar rainfall patterns over the entire continent, so that much of the flora corresponded to that found in the similar

Right: Nyssa, Betula, *and* Celtis *species produce glorious red and gold autumn displays in Blue Ridge Parkway, near the Great Smoky Mountain National Park of North Carolina.*

climates of Europe and Asia. (By contrast, the vegetation of the Southern Hemisphere, which developed in isolation, is markedly different.) Gradually, however, the flora of North America developed in unique ways, as it responded to an increasingly dry landscape, caused by both climate change and the rain shadows of emerging mountains, and to increasing isolation.

In damper areas of the USA, old links to the flora of other northern continents can still be seen. For example, in areas such as the East Coast, many species, including numerous forest trees, are closely related to species in Europe and Asia. Liquidambars, inhabiting the summer-wet forests of Mexico and the eastern USA, have counterpart species in Asia; hollies, such as *Ilex aquifolium* in Europe, are related to *I. opaca* found on the East Coast. Indeed, some species remain nearly identical to those found in Europe and Asia. In the far north, plants like *Juniperus communis* are known as circumboreal, meaning that the same species can be found inhabiting similar niches in all three of the major northern hemisphere landmasses.

In contrast, areas of North America with unique or isolated rock formations, soil types, or climates, especially those that appeared after the landmasses separated, now possess flora known as endemic, or unique to the area. The cactus family, for example, began its formation in the West, in the dry rain shadow areas of mountains or the early North American deserts, and is found only within the new worlds of North and South America.

This oversimplified version of millions of years of geological history serves principally to illustrate that in every region of the country, when we look out of our windows, each of us sees a different landscape, with specific plants and associations. Each one, however, is integrally connected with all the rest.

Fire and ice

The North America we garden has been shaped by many forces, especially the fire and ice—the cyclical cooling and heating, drying and wetting—of the Ice Ages. In much of the North—in the Puget Sound, the northern states, and New England—the glaciers of the last Ice Ages scraped away the top soil, leaving bare stone or heavy blue clay with (as gardeners in these places often complain) nothing in between. The Great Plains, by contrast, escaped glaciation and are enriched with fine deep soils. Here, gardeners can grow prize peonies and lilacs but are limited by intrusions of Arctic air.

Above: The Great Plains, with their rich soil and favorable growing conditions, are key agricultural areas for the USA. In Middleton, Indiana, fields of corn (Zea mays) *stretch to the horizon.*

Rising mountains, rain shadow deserts, and the mitigating effects of large bodies of water have also shaped growing conditions. In the Mountain States, winter cold, as well as the shortness of the frost-free period, limits some plantings but allows exquisite alpines and cushion plants. In the deserts of the West and Southwest, the heat and persistent water shortages dictate that many lawns are of stone but are compensated for by the succulent and drought-adapted flora that can flourish there. Along the immediate West Coast are North America's Mediterranean climes. Although the rainfall varies from abundant to nearly non-existent, the entire region west of the Cascade and Sierra Nevada Mountain ranges can rely on rainless summers. Thus, for most natives there, the growing season is winter, with plants going into dormancy when the spring or summer drought hits. Especially in areas most influenced by the Pacific Ocean, gardeners are treated to mild and often frost-free winters, though they must contend with very little summer heat accumulation. In contrast, the Southeast, with its abundant rainfall and high humidity, allows near-perfect subtropicals but is without the cool summer nights required by many Southern Hemisphere and Mediterranean plants.

Left: Cacti, bromeliads, and succulents such as the agaves and yuccas have evolved quite independent forms in North America. Carnegiea gigantea *is the only species in its genus. It is native to the deserts of California, Arizona, and western Mexico.*

Right: Hibiscus are one of the classic subtropical and tropical plants. The hybrid cultivar Hibiscus rosa-sinensis *'Eileen McMullen' is grown for its stunning red and gold blooms.*

Plants indigenous to any specific region change during any prolonged dry period or wet period, during change in geology or an inundation, but the greatest changes probably occur during ice ages, when the flora of whole regions is pushed to the south in search of warmth, many individual species not surviving at all. As the ice sheets retreat, the opposite occurs, and plants quickly spread north. As a result of these movements, botanists have identified an interesting phenomenon, known as the nunatack. When great ice sheets covered much of North America, some mountain peaks remained above the ice, harboring plants that would later recolonize surrounding areas or remain in place as endemics. In some regions, unencumbered by steep mountains or other obstacles, the newly released flora of these mountaintop sanctuaries quickly spread, covering large areas. One good example of this is the single-leaf pinyon pine (*Pinus monophylla*) in Great Basin West. Records indicate that, at the end of the last ice age, only 10,000 or 11,000 years ago, the plant was confined almost entirely to what is now Mexico. Today, however, the plant inhabits many hundreds of desert mountain ranges as far north as the Oregon/Nevada border, its bird-carried seeds easily skipping the more arid valleys below.

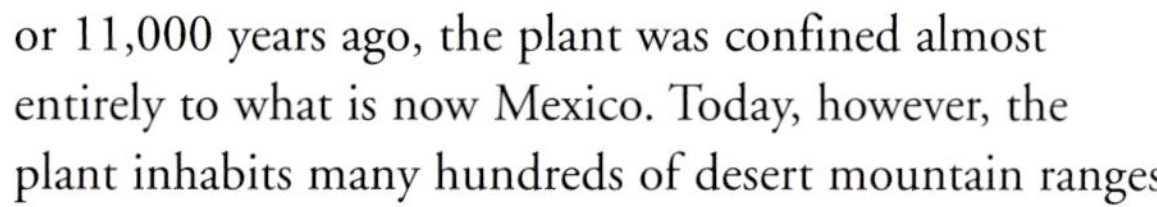

Microclimates

In some areas the climatic regions are broad, changing little over hundreds of miles. But in other places, such as areas close to large bodies of water or where mountainous terrain prevails, conditions can change within a matter of feet, creating very distinct microclimates. On the West Coast, for example, moisture-laden storms bring plentiful moisture in the winter, though this moisture decreases sharply as the storm moves inland, shedding its water to the west and leaving desert to the east. This may happen within as little as thirty miles. Even within the one rainfall zone, rainfall can vary greatly depending on the impact of hills, or elevation; often, lee sides of promontories are in a mini-rain shadow area whereas higher slopes catch more clouds and moisture.

Elevation and exposure can play a role in shaping temperature. We might expect temperatures to increase or decrease as we move south or north over great distances, but even locally, the smallest valley can trap cold air, causing overnight temperatures to be as much as ten degrees colder where, in the same vicinity, a couple of hundred feet of elevation allows cold air to drain away, raising overnight temperatures. There, as well, wind exposure is often greater, keeping air stirred up and preventing the coldest air from reaching ground level. An example of this is the citrus belt, which lies a few hundred feet up in the foothills surrounding California's San Joaquin Valley.

Areas adjacent to large bodies of water can also benefit from warmer temperatures. This includes coastal areas, and also areas around the Great Lakes, which may be, in some cases, a full zone above neighboring inland areas.

For gardeners, larger areas such as those influenced by the factors above are noted and designated as warmer winter locals on the Zone maps. Though no one map could include all the climatic factors that influence one spot on the planet, the USDA Zone maps included here provide, at the least, the average minimum temperatures experienced throughout these broad-ranging climates. However, with so many local influences on weather,

Above left: Pinus monophylla *occurs from Nevada, USA, to Baja California, Mexico, and is favored by Native Americans for its highly nutritious nuts. The cultivar 'Glauca' is popular for its bluish foliage.*

Left: Maples such as Acer saccharum *and* A. rubrum *are typical features of eastern North American forests and contribute to the spectacular color display seen there.*

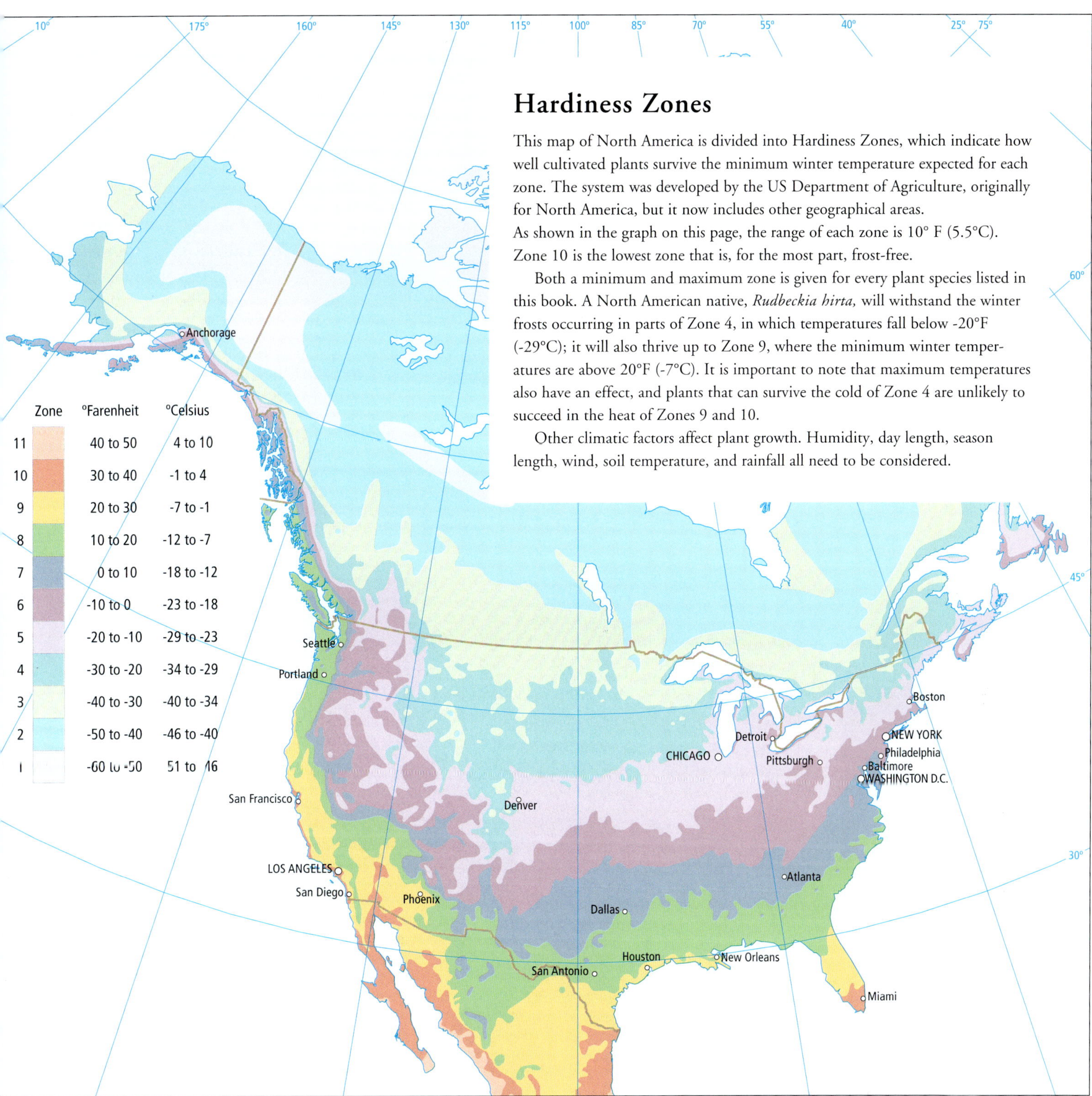

Hardiness Zones

This map of North America is divided into Hardiness Zones, which indicate how well cultivated plants survive the minimum winter temperature expected for each zone. The system was developed by the US Department of Agriculture, originally for North America, but it now includes other geographical areas.
As shown in the graph on this page, the range of each zone is 10° F (5.5°C). Zone 10 is the lowest zone that is, for the most part, frost-free.

Both a minimum and maximum zone is given for every plant species listed in this book. A North American native, *Rudbeckia hirta,* will withstand the winter frosts occurring in parts of Zone 4, in which temperatures fall below -20°F (-29°C); it will also thrive up to Zone 9, where the minimum winter temperatures are above 20°F (-7°C). It is important to note that maximum temperatures also have an effect, and plants that can survive the cold of Zone 4 are unlikely to succeed in the heat of Zones 9 and 10.

Other climatic factors affect plant growth. Humidity, day length, season length, wind, soil temperature, and rainfall all need to be considered.

especially temperature, it is still wise to become familiar with your own microclimates. The first step is often as simple as observing what is growing well—or not so well—in the neighbor's garden.

Regional identification

The term "indicator plant" is often used to describe botanically what might be found native to specific regions or soil types, but the idea of indicator plants can also be used in the observation of neighbors' gardens and of other plants in our neighborhoods. Carefully noting which plants flourish in an area provides valuable information about local conditions. Broadly, if one lives along the eastern seaboard and sees on the horizon thickets of red maples (*Acer rubrum*) and birches, it can be assumed that there is wet ground, or at least general moisture to work with. If, however, in the same area, there are oaks and kalmia, than it's safe to say wet spots won't be a problem, though there might be rocks to contend with.

In the West, along the Pacific Coast, if western red cedars (*Thuja plicata*) abound and there are rhododendrons in full sun, either rainfall is high, or the garden is protected by the coolness and moisture of the coast, or your neighbors have been particularly daring. Taking the time to notice what's growing well in a neighbor's garden or on a nearby hillside is a wonderful shortcut to discovering what might be successful in your immediate area.

Left: Whatever the size of your garden, great pleasure can be gained from it. Here, the garden becomes an extra room, one that is particularly suited to relaxation and conversation.

Above: Increasingly, today, gardening competes with myriad activities for our time. Don't overlook the simple, however. This container of bulbs brings a stylish splash of color to the garden for little effort.

Right: The nine species of Echinacea *are all native to the USA, and they were among the earliest American genera to enter European cultivation.* E. purpurea *'White Swan' is one of various cultivars, valued for its vivid blooms.*

Emerging trends

When talking about trends, it is important to differentiate between trendiness—which depicts the fad of the moment, possibly "here one year and gone the next"—and trends themselves. Trends we recognize over time and, we hope, tend to move in an improving direction. A number of trends are emerging among gardeners in North America, including those listed below.

Rediscovering the act of gardening

In a time when so many people used to "garden" by hiring a mow-blow-and-go, the greatest change seems to be a rediscovery of the act of gardening itself and the pleasure obtained by the simple act of nurture. This includes large gardens with dramatic themes or a single avocado pit on the windowsill.

With so many plants available and, increasingly, good information accompanying them, it is natural that more imagination is being used when introducing them into our gardens. New plants, encouraging inspired combinations of color and texture, have lifted gardens to the level of fine art. This same act of nurturing our gardens has also had increased impact on nurturing our communities. With gardens come conversation, sharing, and enhanced connection amongst those with whom we share our small corners of the world.

Sustainable gardening

Though overused and possibly even a bit clichéd, the term "sustainable," by definition, denotes another important recent trend. It suggests understanding both the plants and what is achievable in one's own climate or situation without having to resort to excess use of energy (one's own or manufactured), excess use of water (a crucial consideration in areas in which it is scarce), or the use of chemicals that have either proven to have, or may potentially have, harmful effects. This trend is evidenced by the large number of organically grown nursery products available, along with the many organic foods now in our grocery stores.

Native planting and restoration

Along with considering the sustainability of our gardens, we are giving new thought to the natural landscape around us, restoration of native areas, and ways of using both local and regional native plants in our landscapes. Increasingly, nurseries are carrying local flora. One word of caution: especially in western areas of the USA, where land types and climates change quickly over quite short distances, the term "native" can be a bit confusing. The well-researched gardener is learning to tell between a "native" plant that prefers the edge of a creek and the one found several miles away on a stony hillside. As well, many plants were, at one time, collected whole from wild areas. In many places this is no longer allowed and we, as gardeners, now know to ask, helping to ensure the plant was grown from seeds or cuttings, rather than coming from the wild.

Our new information and awareness makes us conscious, as well, of the few remaining wild areas around us and increasingly protective of their safety. With greater knowledge of our natural surroundings, gardeners are getting a better grip on restoring areas that have been disturbed and that we would like to see returned to as natural a state as possible.

Exotic plants

With so many new plants at our disposal and the ease of getting them from one part of the world to the next, the responsibility for ensuring they are not too happy in their new home falls on each of us. Kudzu in the South, loosestrife in much of the nation's wetlands, and broom and Himalayan blackberries on the West Coast, are jarring examples of the speed with which a weedy plant can invade the landscape. Along with increased efforts to rid our fragile landscapes of already established thugs, we must be, and increasingly have been, wary of plants newly introduced from foreign lands. Local agriculture departments, universities, nursery people, and we, as plant collectors, all share the responsibility. We want the new and the unusual but a few rules of thumb can be applied when obtaining the unfamiliar: ask whether the plant reseeds itself quickly; is it impervious to our drought and cold cycles; did it come from waste places in its original home; does it have close relatives that are already a problem; and, of course, did it leap the neighbor's fence within the first two weeks of planting?

These few cautions aside, the following pages offer more ingredients for our individual gardening recipes than we could probably ever use. Each entry describes both the physical characteristics of each plant and the best situations for them in our gardens. Though we can't have them all, learning about them sparks our enthusiasm and gives us a broader idea of the possibilities. In this manner, each of us is contributing to the trends of the future.

All horticulture is local

If there is one defining truth about gardening in the USA, it is that there is no defining garden. Known as a nation of lawn lovers, possibly even responsible for the invention of the suburban lawn (with the help of some grazing sheep), it is simply not possible for many parts of the country to share in this gardening dream. Similarly, though our gardening styles have been heavily influenced by Western Europe, local climate and geography have dictated that certain plants or gardening styles are just not going to work.

Our own stereotype of big machines endlessly mowing vast properties is fading in favor of mellower, more naturalistic landscapes that promote greater interest and diversity in the garden, as well as serving to attract wildlife. Increasing urbanization, where lack of space means that gardens are more often growing up rather than out, is also demanding a more imaginative response to gardening. This is particularly true for the coasts and large cities, where gardens are increasingly seen as places of sanctuary, rather than simply a way of taming the world around into a decorative landscape.

Summing it up

Fortified with good information, we can not only compare and contrast potential plants for our gardens but also judge the conditions they might need, essentially allowing us to fit what conditions we have to the plant, rather than insisting a new addition to our collection fit one condition we *might* have. With the use of the many microclimates, we might achieve success with growing our hostas on the north side of a wall, or succeed with a palm, thought too tender, cloistered against the south side of a house. In this book we find plants both tried and true and many more worthy of a place in our gardening imaginations. Some we can grow and some we can't, but all expand our understanding of the many possibilities and provide new inspiration.

Bottom: In the twentieth century, our gardens were often defined by the suburban block and front lawn. Today, while many of us still value lawns as a play area, we are exploring other ways of creating harmonious gardens.

Below: A wider choice of plants is bringing nature back into our gardens in more ways than one. Creatures great and small are attracted by the feast of a varied landscape.

Global Hardiness Zones

Each region of the world has its own set of physical conditions. Topography, levels of precipitation and evaporation, amount and arrival of heat and cold, days of frost, and length of growing season are all factors that help create our individual climates. Ways of quantifying and charting the weather have been the preoccupation of scientists, farmers, and zealous gardeners down the centuries.

The system employed in *Flora Americana* follows the map developed in the 1960s by the United States Department of Agriculture (USDA), which divides North America into twelve designated hardiness zones. Each zone is separated by 10°F (5.5°C), beginning with the Arctic at -50°F (-46°C) and ending in the equatorial tropics at +50°F (10°C). These average minimum temperatures for each hardiness zone are based on the minimum temperature recorded each winter season over a period of 20 years.

The zones are not uniform. There are cooler and warmer areas within a zone depending on its most northerly or southerly part. Topographical features such as mountain ranges, plains, and proximity to the coast all affect temperature, and therefore, whether that area falls in one zone or another. For this reason, a zone on a map may suddenly dip into an area surrounded by a warmer zone, or curve up in a thin line along a coast.

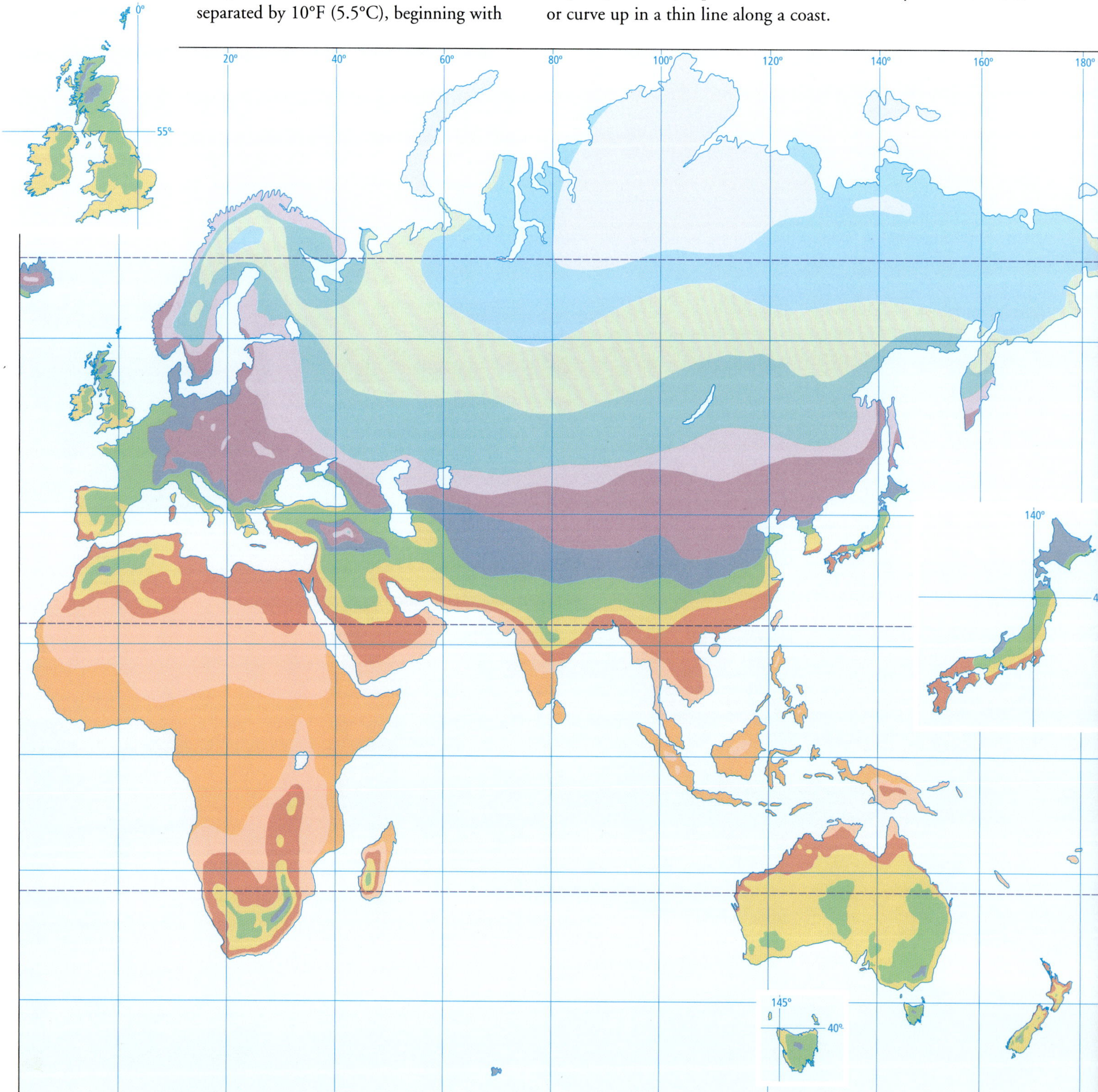

The main purpose of the USDA map is to tell us what zone we are in, and therefore indicate what plants can be grown in our part of the world. Secondly, it allows us to look at other regions or countries in the same zone, and also surrounding zones, and see what plants do well in those areas. Essentially, climate zones provide an indication of a plant's "hardiness", that is, its ability to survive cold weather, including frost and ice.

The zones are based on average low temperatures only, and do not provide additional information about extremes and variations in low temperatures for a region. In some regions temperatures can be much warmer and much colder than the average from year to year. Other factors also need to be considered. For example, if a garden is in or near an urban center, situated on a hillside above a valley floor where cold air is likely to settle, or tends to experience breezes when other areas are still, winter minimums are likely to be a bit warmer than surrounding areas. The opposite is true if a garden is situated at a valley bottom out of the wind. Here, temperatures are likely to fall during the night. These are all characteristics of what is called a microclimate and can be taken advantage of.

It is important to reiterate that the zone maps only indicate the average lowest temperatures. When a plant in this book is rated to a specific zone, it means that horticulturists have succeeded in that zone, even with the reasonable yearly fluctuations in winter lows.

Factors to consider

People garden for the future, but, of course, they also garden for the moment. On occasion, a winter cold spell brings temperatures well below the zone's averages, damaging or even killing a plant normally expected to perform well. Reactions to these possibilities are down to the individual gardener. Those who like to live life on the wild side might acquire plants knowing they will not be permanent but might try to minimize risk by planting in an area where they can be protected from full sun or frost.

Caution might be best employed where the size and structure of the plant is a consideration. To ensure a long life, a tree or any other anchoring plant could be chosen from a colder zone than the garden it is to be planted in, thereby overcoming the rigors of cold it may experience as a sapling.

Other factors to consider when choosing plants are: length of the frost-free season; whether cold lasts for weeks or months, and, in colder zones, the amount of snowfall, which can act as an insulating blanket for roots. Another factor is the amount of heat received over the warm season. Areas of high summer temperatures, especially when combined with humidity, are best suited to heat-loving plants that need to reach full maturity quickly, in preparation for possibly lower temperatures in the winter. Areas receiving warmth accompanied by cool summer nights are better off with Mediterranean and Southern Hemisphere treasures that would otherwise melt in high summer heat. Soil conditions and rainfall must be taken into consideration as well, along with the need for mulching, or less water, or drier air.

The more knowledge we have about what kinds of temperatures and other conditions our plants are likely to tolerate, the more our gardens will flourish. The more, also, we can then keep our special needs plants and proclaim with satisfaction to an envious neighbor that this supposed tender creature has been in our garden for years.

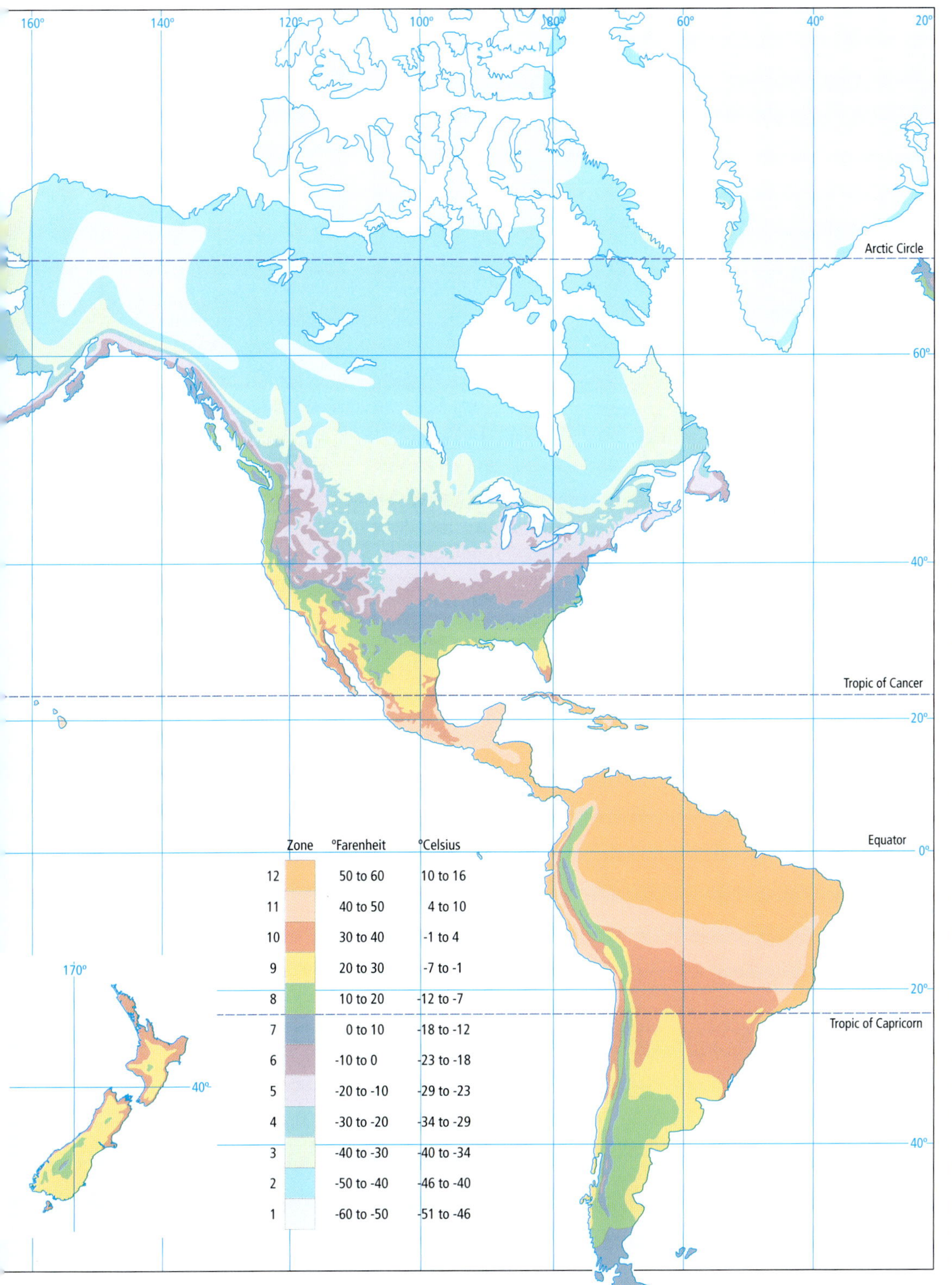

Zone 1 -60 to -50°F (-51 to -46°C)

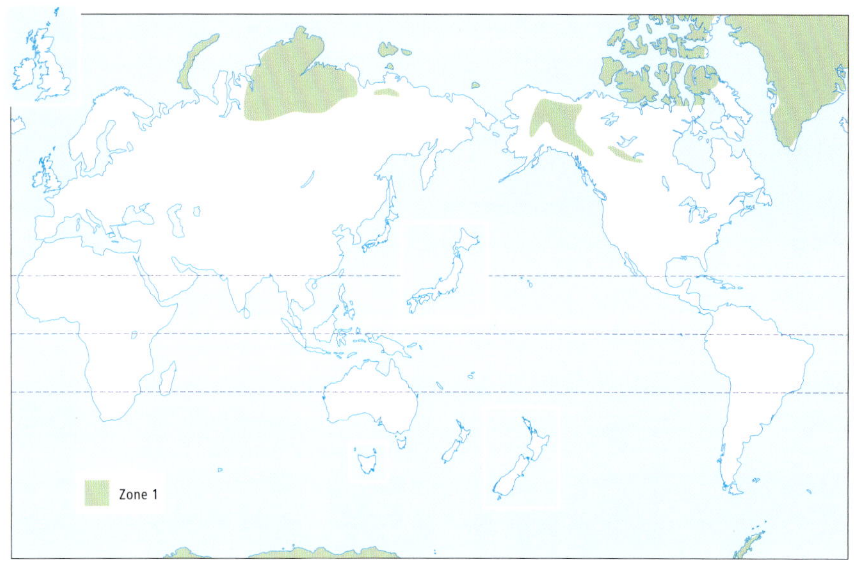

Far right: The Arctic contains the largest areas of remaining wilderness in the Northern Hemisphere. The Svalbard Islands, north of Norway, feature mostly sparse tundra and large caribou populations.

It is no small matter to say that the flora of Zone 1 is shaped by the patterns and variations of the climate. The climate is characterized by severity, seasonality, and unpredictable variability. Winter temperatures of -50°F (-46°C) and less—the coldest temperature ever recorded was -87°F (-66°C)—coupled with cool summers, challenge even the hardiest plant material. The summers, lasting for just two brief months from July to August, are so cool that the determining factor behind differing vegetative regions within the zone is not the extreme cold of winter but the amount of warmth received during summer. Precipitation is also limited, with some areas receiving less than 2 in (50 mm) per year. The long days at this time (24 hours of daylight) compensate for the rigors of the short summers and cold conditions.

Below: In the northern tundra, a smooth carpet of plant growth is usually a collection of lichens and mosses, and a few tiny and hardy plants like sedge and cotton grass.

In the Southern Hemisphere, Zone 1 includes only the Antarctic continent, which is uninhabited and has very few species of flowering plant. These are confined to the Antarctic peninsula. In the remaining area, there are only lichens and mosses. There is greater diversity in the Northern Hemisphere, where the Arctic landscapes range from bare rock to swamp, glacier to meadow, and mountain to lowland plain. The key feature of most land areas in this zone is permafrost. This permanently frozen ground reaches depths of 1,640 yards (1,500 m) in Siberia, and extends under most land areas. Because of the permafrost, plant roots are closer to the surface and are exposed to more severe cold. Plants need to be able to withstand solid freezing for many months. For seven to 10 months every year, plants are in a state of quasi-hibernation. During the remaining couple of months, they run through their entire growth cycle.

Zone 1 plants survive these extreme conditions in many ways. The severity of the climate means that the major biomass of the plants exists below ground. This reduces the desiccation (drying out) due to prevalent strong winds that result in much sand/soil abrasion. The reproductive cycle of the vascular plants is often carried out over a period of years. For example, buds formed one year will be generally covered in hair to increase insulation, and then will often lie beneath the soil surface until the following year when they complete their reproductive cycle. This survival mechanism also allows plants to miraculously bloom within hours of the snow cover melting. Many plants use unique means to ensure survival. *Dryas integrifolia*, a dwarf, creeping, slightly woody shrub of the rose family which also grows in Zone 2, has flowers in the shape of a curved reflector. This allows them to follow the sun and to focus the sun's rays on their reproductive structures to raise the temperature of these organs several degrees on a sunny day. Many Zone 1 plants will retain dense mats of dead or persistent leaves that can produce a rise of as much as 30°F (as much as 16°C).

Survival in the tundra

The landmass known as the tundra is a true indicator of a Zone 1 climate. It is a treeless barren area occurring south of the polar ice cap worldwide. The tundra flora becomes progressively impoverished (sparser) the closer it is to the ice cap, creating bands of differing vegetation. The tundra "trees" consist of dwarf willow *(Salix)*, birch *(Betula)*, and heaths. The heath (Ericaceae) family—which includes familiar plants like rhododendrons, azaleas, heather, and mountain laurel *(Kalmia latifolia)*—is represented in this zone by dwarf shrubs such as labrador tea *(Ledum)*. They are characterized by small, thick, evergreen leaves and shallow root systems that are particularly well adapted to the acidic, boggy conditions of low Arctic tundra. Some *Vaccinium* species occur throughout the Arctic Circle (the circumpolar north) in all but the highest Arctic areas, including lingonberry *(V. vitis-idaea)*, blueberry *(V. angustifolium)*, and cranberry *(V. macrocarpon)*.

As elevation or latitude increases, the scrub brush peters out and the flora now consists of sedges, grasses, and herbs. This vegetative zone is considered to be sedge meadows. The flora in these meadows belongs to two major genera only, *Eriophorum* and *Carex*, and they are very variable in species: cotton grass *(Eriophorum vaginatum)* is the major, single most abundant plant in the low Arctic, closely followed by a true sedge, *Carex aquatilis*. As climatic conditions vary, as one moves away from the Arctic, the genus remains the same with only the species changing.

A wildflower wonderland

Areas within the sedge meadows can experience slightly different climatic conditions, which produce a different type of vegetation, termed the mesic tundra. The mesic (not too wet and not too dry) tundra is the rock garden of this climatic zone. Grasses are common but the most conspicuous feature of the mesic or grassy tundra is the wild flowers. Nothing on earth compares seeing over 100 species in flower simultaneously along a short walk.

Snowbeds are a particular type of mesic tundra where snow drifts deeply into a hollow. The snow lies late in the spring, which shortens the growing season for the plants under and around it, but also provides a steady source of moisture throughout the growing season. The snow also provides a comparatively warm, moist, protected environment for over wintering plants. Many snowbed species burst into flower within hours of being freed from the drifted snow. Some of our early flowering spring bulbs are derived from snowbed species with this habit. Examples include Siberian fritillary *(Fritillaria pallidiflora)* and Siberian squill *(Scilla siberica)*.

Plants of mesic tundra areas are not circumpolar in their distribution patterns. They often appear to have originated in alpine areas and to have migrated into the Arctic secondarily and locally. Therefore, while some tundra plants may be indistinguishable by locality, the mesic tundra plants will vary with the region.

As the latitude or elevation continues to increase, the last vegetation zone found is the polar desert. This area is largely bare ground or rock, with the last vestiges of plant life being mostly lichens. The polar desert dominates most of the high Arctic areas.

Zone 1 flora consists of distinctive and highly adaptive species. Plants must eke out an existence in a few meager inches of earth, their roots confined by unwieldy bedrock or permafrost that is never far from the surface. Plants are mostly small, prostrate, and always straddling the tenuous line between wakefulness and dormancy. It is not uncommon to find woody plant material that is hundreds of years old yet no thicker than a person's thumb. While hardy species in more temperate latitudes easily succumb to freak frosts, the flora of Zone 1 can be completely frozen one minute and thawed the next. This physiological ability of Arctic plants to be able to freeze with impunity is still a mystery to scientists.

Below: As one moves closer to the pole, the terrain is known as polar desert. These areas lack sufficient moisture and warmth to sustain any significant amount of higher plant life.

Zone 2 -50 to -40°F (-46 to -40°C)

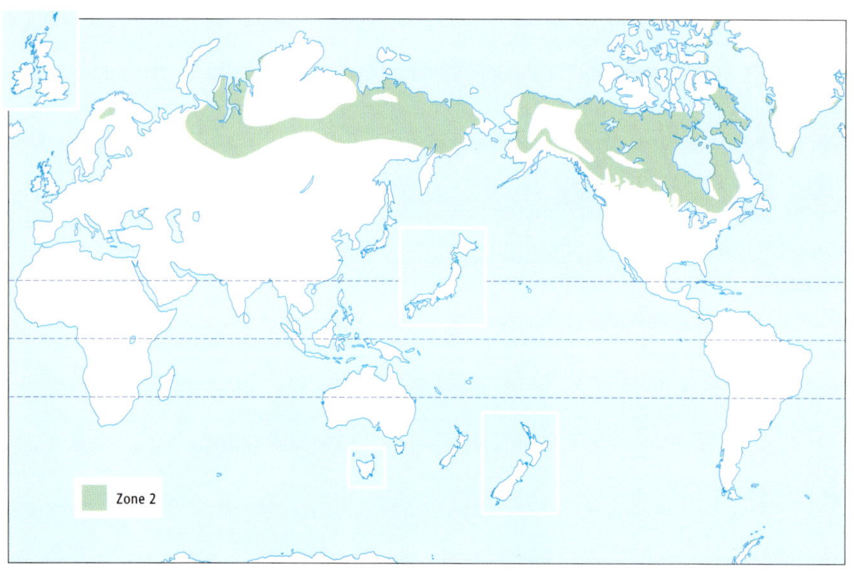

Zone 2 is the world's largest hardiness zone and extends in a band across the Northern Hemisphere, just south of the Artic Circle. It covers a vast area of sparsely populated, predominantly cool, coniferous woodland which is replaced by swamp and then tundra further north. In North America this woodland area is ecologically described as boreal forest while in northern Europe and across Asiatic Russia this area is known as taiga.

The zone has a cold but not arctic climate, with an average minimum winter temperature of -50 to -40°F (-46 to -40°C) with over 40 in (100 cm) of precipitation in a wet year and 20 in (50 cm) in a dry year. The ground is snow covered for up to eight months of the year in the most northerly parts of the zone. As the land nears the Arctic Ocean, the summers become shorter, cooler, drier and the winters longer and colder.

The southernmost section of this zone includes some plains, with some forested areas in the mid-zone. As the forest progresses northward the trees gradually reduce in size and thin out. The ground progressively becomes more waterlogged and the tree cover declines and is replaced by an almost continuous band of swamp, known as "muskeg" in North America. This ground supports only limited tree growth. Moving further northward, approaching the Arctic Ocean, the ground becomes drier. At the extreme north of the zone the subsoil becomes permanently frozen, forming a layer of permafrost that can be several feet deep. Here the muskeg is in its turn replaced by stony barren ground and treeless tundra.

North of this lies Zone 1, which has a uniform cold dry climate. Winters are colder than in Zone 2 and annual precipitation is often as low as 5–10 in (12–25 cm) a year and summer temperatures rarely exceed 50°F (10°C). Plants found in Zone 1 are sparsely distributed, xerophytic in habit (adapted to low levels of water), low growing, and are mainly found on sheltered slopes or in depressions where snow accumulates in winter.

Effects of climate on plant life

The boreal forest and taiga are mainly coniferous, however, they do support some deciduous trees. Evergreens dominate because they do not renew their foliage annually and are more efficient in utilizing scarce nutrients and minerals on infertile soils. Due to its northern location diversity within the forest is restricted to less than a dozen tree species. In the Canadian boreal forest coniferous trees include tamarack *(Larix laricina),* white spruce *(Picea glauca),* black spruce *(Picea mariana),* and jack pine *(Pinus banksiana).* Deciduous species such as white birch *(Betula papyrifera),* trembling aspen *(Populus tremuloides),* and balsam poplar *(P. balsamifera)* also occur. A similar group of related tree species inhabit Alaska and the taiga of Northern Europe and Siberia.

Many of these tree species are widely distributed and can be grown much further south. This also applies to some of the boreal forest shrubs and herbaceous perennial plants that are found in the zone. Most successful are those that grow in profusion following a forest fire: choke cherry *(Prunus virginiana),* pin cherry *(P. pensylvanica),* red osier dogwood *(Cornus sericea),* and herbaeous perennials like fireweed *(Epilobium angustifolium),* though fireweed can become a major thug in the garden. More desirable, delicate shade plants like twin flower *(Linnaea borealis)* are challenging to horticulturists further south due to the difficulty of recreating their cool mossy habitat. Twin flower, like most Zone 2 plants, is best grown from seed that requires a 6 to 8 week cold period at 40°F (4°C) to ensure germination.

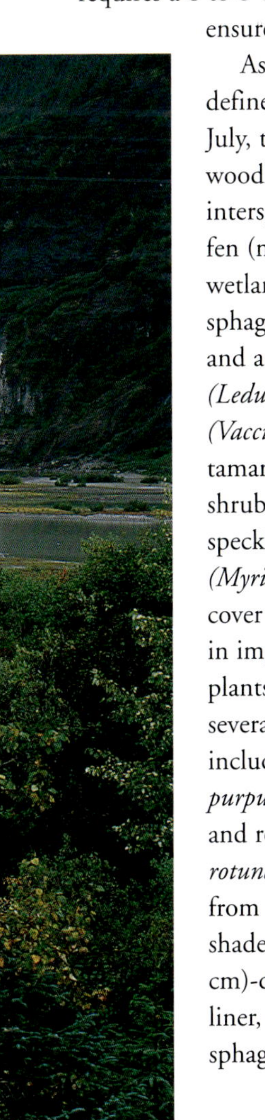

As the forest nears the tree line, generally defined by the 50°F (10°C) isotherm in mid-July, the trees thin and open lichen-rich woodland dominates dry sites. These are interspersed by vast areas of muskeg bog and fen (marsh). These poorly drained, peaty wetlands often support continuous sheets of sphagnum moss, with scattered black spruce and a heath layer that includes Labrador tea *(Ledum groenlandicum)* and bog blueberry *(Vaccinium uliginosum).* On less acid fens, tamarack replaces the black spruce and the shrub layer is mainly willow *(Salix* species*),* speckled alder *(Alnus rugosa),* and bog myrtle *(Myrica gale)* with an herbaceous ground cover of mainly sedges *(Carex* species*).* Even in impoverished wetlands such as these, plants will adapt and this area supports several species of insectivorous plants, including northern pitcher plant *(Sarracenia purpurea),* butterwort *(Pinguicula vulgaris),* and round-leafed sundew *(Drosera rotundifolia).* These and other plant species from muskeg bogs can be grown in semi-shade as far south as Zone 7, in 18 in (45 cm)-deep beds lined with a rubber pond liner, filled with a mixture of 50 percent sphagnum peat and 50 percent sand.

Closer to the Arctic Ocean, even when the surface of the permafrost thaws, this thawing often reaches only a few inches deep by mid-August, and the remaining permafrost layer prevents the rainfall and melting snow from draining. However, if it were not for this trapped moisture, flowering plants would be rare in the near desertlike conditions of the Arctic. As a result of low temperatures and few nutrients, stony barrens and tundra, plants are dwarf in size and starved, and frequently drought-tolerant in habit. Vegetation in the far north of the zone is confined to a few tough plants such as alpine bearberry *(Arctostaphylos alpina),* mountain cranberry *(Vaccinium vitis-idaea),* Lapland rosebay *(Rhododendron lapponicum),* and *Dryas integrifolia.*

Above: Betula papyrifera *is found throughout the Canadian boreal forest. In warmer zones, it is valued for its elegant habit, but this apparent fragility belies its ability to withstand the cold and even drought of Zone 2.*

On moist tundra the vegetation often forms a continuous low mat of sedges such as cotton grass *(Eriophorum angustifolium),* grasses, and dwarf shrub willow, with unusual plants like *Cassiope tetragona,* lousewort *(Pedicularis lapponica),* and the pink-flowered tufted moss campion *(Silene acaulis).* Some of these tundra plants, particularly those from dry gravel or rocky locations, can be grown in a traditional rock-garden alpine scree, as long as these are constructed with an infertile fast-draining gravel soil. Most of the more unusual tundra plants are very difficult to grow successfully further south where high soil temperatures are usually fatal. Perhaps the only way to succeed is grow them in an alpine house in a refrigerated planting bed.

Left: Mendenhall Glacier *near Juneau, Alaska. Most of Alaska is wilderness. Due to its northern location, only a limited range of coniferous and deciduous trees thrive.*

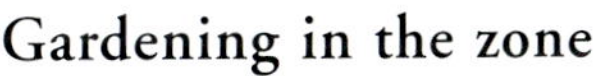

Gardening in the zone

Because gardeners have only half the year to work in they really concentrate their efforts then, and the longer days give plenty of time.

Every year, more hardy plants are introduced into the colder zones. There are even rhododendrons and roses that are now grown successfully in Zones 2 and 3. The limiting factor is the dryness rather than the cold. Even in the far north of the zone, where soils are quite infertile, plants will grow. When a small boy, the doyen of arctic and subarctic botany, A. E. Porsild, lived in the Arctic and planted a small garden. Later he revisited the area and was surprised to see the outline of his garden still visible. He noticed a patch of lush green grass and realized this was where he had spilled some goat manure. The effects of the manure were still apparent 34 years later.

Provided the garden is placed in a sheltered location, has good snow cover, and the ground is manured, fertilized, and limed, there is no reason why some perennial plants from Zones 3 and 4 could not be grown.

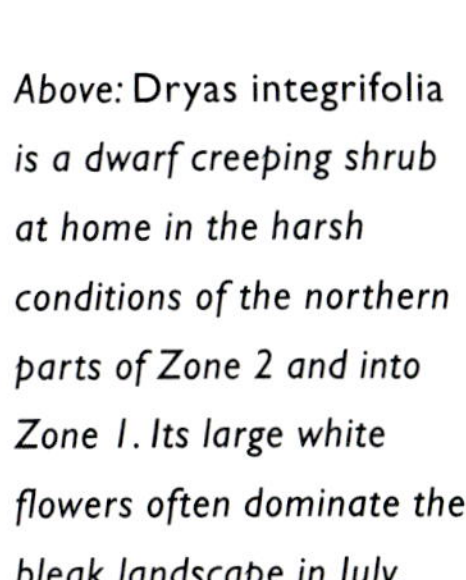

Above: Dryas integrifolia *is a dwarf creeping shrub at home in the harsh conditions of the northern parts of Zone 2 and into Zone 1. Its large white flowers often dominate the bleak landscape in July.*

Zone 3 -40 to -30°F (-40 to -34°C)

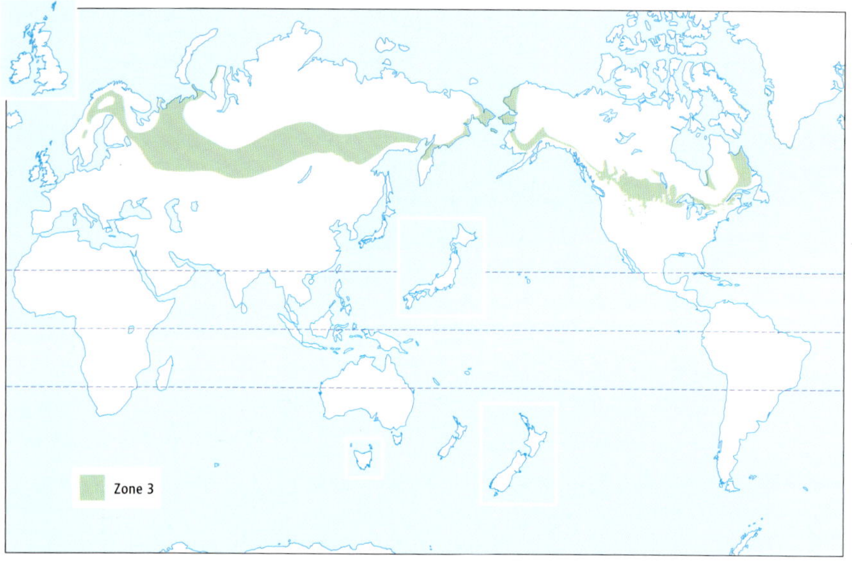

Long cold winters are the foremost characteristic of this climatic zone which forms an arc of varying width around the Northern Hemisphere. In North America, from as far north as Point Hope on the Arctic Ocean in Alaska, well above the Arctic Circle, this zone swings south to the center of the continent. Here it straddles the Canadian/US border and dips as far south as a few isolated mountain ranges in Colorado and New Mexico in the mid 30s latitude. It then rises northward again as it approaches the Atlantic Ocean and eventually reaches Ungava Bay in northern Quebec. Zone 3 forms a similar arc in Eurasia and due largely to the influence of the Gulf Stream, it extends further into northern Scandinavia than would perhaps be expected. As the distance from the ocean increases, winter temperatures become colder and summer temperatures become warmer. In climatic terms, this effect is known as continentality, and it plays a major role in shaping the climate of these large continents and explains why Zone 3 reaches so far south into both these landmasses.

Below: Arctostaphylos uva-ursi, *bearberry—also known as kinnikinick—is hardy in areas where snow cover offers protection. White flowers, flushed pink, are followed by bright red fruit.*

Temperatures and rainfall

Zone 3 is a typical continental climate and the average annual lowest temperature ranges between -40 and -30°F (-40 and -34°C), while the average summer highs can range between 86 and 100°F (30 and 38°C). This climate evokes images of blizzards and frostbite, blowing snow and whiteouts, but this tells only half the story. It is actually a place with dramatically different seasons. Summer can be quite pleasant and often the majority of the precipitation falls at this time during thunderstorms, promoting a rich growing season. Spring and fall are typically short and often variable. Often, one week in either of these seasons can experience extreme temperature swings. The growing season (frost-free days) varies from under 60 days to more than 120 days. Precipitation in Zone 3 varies. Mountainous regions of British Columbia can experience above 80 in (200 cm) of rainfall per year whereas the driest areas of the prairies receive well under 20 in (50 cm). The amount roughly determines the type of flora present in an area. In very general terms, areas that receive over 25 in (62 cm) annually are forested; those with less are grassland.

Landscape and soil

In North America, Zone 3 includes varying terrain. In the west, moist conifer-covered mountains with thin, acidic soil are prevalent. From the mountains it spills out onto the vast drier prairies where it widens, encompassing the northern regions of this rich rolling prairie, skirting along the southern extent of the boreal forest. It then swings north again through the boreal forest of central Canada north of the Great Lakes where the ground is smooth glaciated bedrock supporting only thin acidic soil again. In winter, the ground freezes solid in all areas of Zone 3 to at least 24 in (60 cm) below the soil surface and often to 36 in (90 cm).

Effects of climate on plant life

Despite the cold winters, many plants are well adapted to the conditions. Plants that thrive in the zone are able to completely freeze (roots and all) and stay dormant for several months with little or no long-term damage. Snow cover is an important factor for plant hardiness as it is excellent insulation for root systems below the ground as well as for the branches above. Areas with reliably heavy snow cover usually have a higher diversity of plants compared to areas with unreliable snow cover as it protects plants from the harsh cold temperatures and desiccating winds.

Despite harsh winters, Zone 3 regions can be rich in flora and many well-known genera are represented by their hardier species. In general, broadleaf evergreen trees or shrubs cannot survive here as they do not grow higher than the usual snow cover. However, low-growing evergreens like mosses such as *Pleurozium schreberi*, clubmoss *(Lycopodium clavatum)*, and wintergreen *(Gaultheria procumbens)* that are covered by winter snow are prevalent. These blanket the ground along with deciduous shrubs and perennials including raspberries *(Rubus* species*)*, blueberries *(Vaccinium myrtilloides)*, scarlet sumac *(Rhus glabra)*, bog myrtle *(Myrica gale)*, red osier dogwood *(Cornus sericea)*, and alum root *(Heuchera* species*)*, and evening primrose *(Oenothera biennis)* in the glades of the boreal forest floor surrounded by endless stands of primarily conifers.

In the drier areas where prairies dominate the landscape, small deciduous forests appear like scattered islands in an endless sea of grasses, perennials, and

Right: Populus tremuloides *is an extremely hardy North American tree. It reaches near-dominance in Zones 4 and 5 but can be found in areas as cold as Zone 1.*

annuals. The flora here is very different than that of the boreal forest due to richer deeper soil and less precipitation. The diminutive, slow-growing forest dwellers can't compete against the faster-growing deciduous plants of the prairie. Few conifers are seen in the prairies, instead, deciduous species such as maple *(Acer* species*)*, willows *(Salix)*, Saskatoon *(Amelanchier alnifolia)*, white birch *(Betula papyrifera)*, ninebark *(Physocarpus opulifolius)*, aspen *(Populus tremuloides)*, choke cherry *(Prunus virginiana)*, oak *(Quercus rubra)*, and mountain ash *(Sorbus* species*)* provide a brief but spectacular fall color display. During the short growing season, these small trees and shrubs rush to flower and bear fruit and, in the spring and summer, the prairie forests are alive with their modest blooms and they provide a feast for birds and animals that rely on them to carry them through the long cold winters.

Cacti may not initially come to mind, but ball cactus *(Escobaria vivipara)* and plains prickly pear *(Opuntia polyacantha)*, as well as other desert plants, are native to the driest prairie areas and do extend into this region.

Areas within Zone 3 with warm summers and reasonably long growing seasons are able to produce excellent cereal, vegetable, and fruit crops. In Canada and Russia, the so-called "bread basket" regions envelop Zone 3. Much of their domestic and export crops are grown in these rich fertile plains. Wheat *(Triticum)*, barley *(Hordeum vulgare)*, canola *(Brassica)*, flax *(Linum usitatissimum)*, and sunflower *(Helianthus)* all grow very well in this climate. Similarly, carrots *(Daucus carota* subsp. *sativus)*, beets *(Beta)*, spinach *(Spinacia)*, even tomatoes *(Lycopersicon)* and other vegetable crops thrive.

Gardening in the zone

The gardening season is short as the only time when the ground is not frozen is generally from May to October. It can be very expensive to heat greenhouses, so few operate all winter long. Annual growers begin production in early March, six to eight weeks before the last frosts. Nurseries are usually closed in winter and stock is often imported from warmer climates in April. Summer annuals are widely used and bulbs and tuberous plants such as canna, gladiola, and dahlia are planted in spring then dug up in autumn (to protect them from the cold and kept in frost-free conditions for replanting the following spring). Indoor plants are popular, but low winter humidity is a problem, so plants suited to dry conditions are successful. This includes varieties of *Dieffenbachia, Monstera, Philodendron, Crassula (C. arborescens)*, and *Ficus benjamina*, as well as African violets *(Saintpaulia* cultivars*)* and begonias.

Perennials are often overlooked in Zone 3, although some gardeners successfully grow a great variety. Many perennials listed in nursery catalogues as Zone 4 and 5 have never been tried in Zone 3. This zone is home to many wonderful species too numerous to list, but many genera familiar to horticulture have species native to Zone 3 and many other non-native varieties will grow here, as well. For example, species of lily (such as *Lilium columbianum*), most hostas, and daylilies *(Hemerocallis)* survive and even flourish in Zone 3.

The zone is home to highly acclaimed plants such as sought-after delicate orchids like pink and yellow lady slippers *(Cypripedium aucale* and *C. parviflorum)*, as well as the dainty fairy slipper *(Calypso bulbosa)*.

There are many plants no one has ever attempted to grow here. It is a horticultural frontier as plants are always being introduced and bred for hardiness. There will always be new plants that will thrive in Zone 3.

Above: Salix reptans *is native to the far north of Asia and European Russia. It is a small shrub with green to red branchlets that are covered in dense hairs. The erect catkins, also covered in long hairs, grow to 2 in (5 cm) long.*

Zone 4 -30 to -20°F (-34 to -29°C)

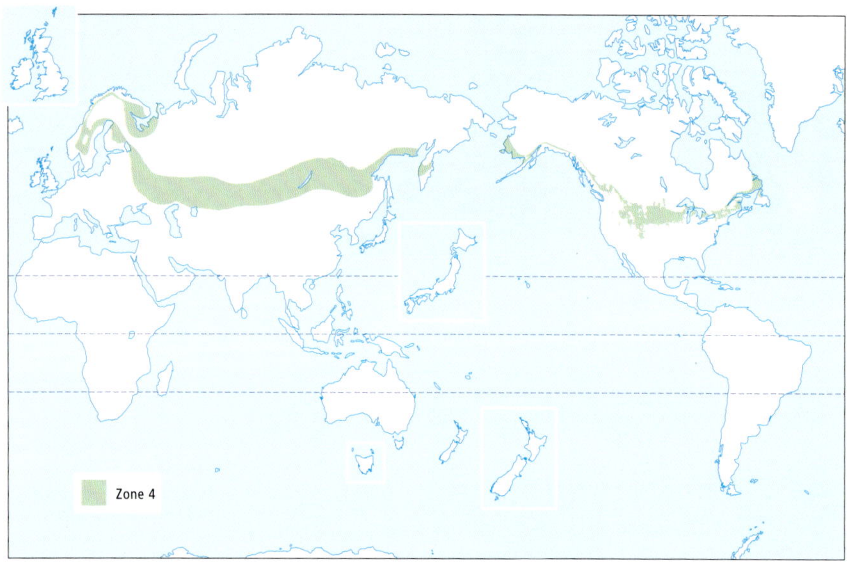

Top right: Willow trees (Salix species) cover vast areas of North America. This genus is a large and varied one, consisting of around 400 species, with the majority occurring in cold and temperate areas.

Right: Native to southern Scandinavia and other parts of Europe, Picea abies is the most commonly cultivated spruce in Europe. It has thick reddish brown bark, dark green leaves, and long, slender, light brown cones.

The geographic regions and plant communities covered by Zone 4 are many and varied, however, they have one thing in common: cold winters that make selection of hardy plants a challenge for gardeners. Most areas within the zone were subject to the effects of glaciers in the most recent, or Pleistocene glaciation. When the glaciers retreated to the polar regions some 10,000 to 12,000 years ago, they left behind a clean slate of mostly deep, rich till (post-glacial) soils. In many places, however, bare bedrock was left exposed. By 4,000 to 6,000 years ago, the post-glacial soils were stabilized, and the broad vegetation patterns that persist to this day were established.

The zone covers a vast area of the Northern Hemisphere (moving in a wide band across the top of the USA and around the Great Lakes, through China and Russia, and over to the Scandinavian countries). The climate is one of extremes. The winter temperature can drop to -30°F (-34°C) for weeks on end. Polar blasts as cold as -45°F (-43°C) are possible. Summer temperatures may soar to around 95°F (35°C), pushed by dry breezes that gain heat over large continental landmasses. Mean annual rainfall can range from 10 to 40 in (250 to 1,000 mm). Where rainfall exceeds evapotranspiration, forests dominate. Grasslands occupy areas where there is insufficient summer moisture for trees.

Colder regions of the zone

Forests in the colder reaches of the zone are predominately a mix of deciduous and coniferous trees. These forests are mostly composed of aspen *(Populus)* when young, and maples *(Acer)*, linden *(Tilia)*, fir *(Abies)*, and spruce *(Picea)* at maturity. At higher altitudes, hardy deciduous species like aspen are the pioneers that make up the young plant community before conifers become established. On poor or thin mineral soils over bedrock, pine *(Pinus)*, fir, and spruce usually dominate.

In the rain shadows of mountain ranges, such as the Rockies, herbaceous grasslands dominate. Excessive summer heat, persistent winds, and low average precipitation, along with fire, make it difficult for trees to thrive in these areas. The nature of these herbaceous grasslands differs from more familiar woodland landscapes in several significant ways. Grasses have extensive underground networks of fibrous roots that probe deeply and thoroughly for moisture. In fact, most of the body (biomass) of both grasses and prairie wildflowers is below the ground. In times of plenty, growth is lush and flowers are exuberant. During drought cycles, plants may remain in a semi-dormant condition during the growing season to conserve resources. Trees, with their comparatively massive bodies, are not as flexible, and therefore most trees do not survive in this part of the zone.

Warmer regions of the zone

In the warmer reaches of Zone 4, deciduous forests dominate in areas where there is sufficient rainfall. This is a vast area with a variety of soils, and a topography that varies dramatically from ancient mountains and foothills to gently undulating plains. This diverse landscape hosts many plant associations, which will also change over time. In the Northern Hemisphere, moist soils support forests of mixed oak *(Quercus)* and ash *(Fraxinus)* when young, and later beech *(Fagus)*, maple or linden communities. The drier sites with leaner soils support communities of oak and hickory *(Carya)*, or pines. Floodplains have a distinctive association of flood and drought-tolerant species such as silver maple *(Acer saccharinum)* in North America, and aspen *(Populus)* and willow *(Salix)* throughout the Northern Hemisphere. The forest floor is carpeted with showy herbaceous plants such as bellwort *(Uvularia)*, Solomon's plume *(Smilacina)*, and liverleaf *(Hepatica)*.

Deciduous plants with bloom cycles tied to the availability of light and moisture put on brief but dazzling displays of spring wildflowers. As warm spring sunshine pours through the bare branches of the trees and the days lengthen, tree buds break and the burst of leaf growth begins to form a veil of shade on the forest floor. Within a few short weeks the canopy provides cooling shade. Woodland plants grow and bloom early in the spring to take advantage of this brief contact with the sun's rays. For gardeners, this means a glorious, though short-lived, flower display.

Many species of the zone are hardy plants adapted to cold temperatures, and many also tolerate periods of summer drought by becoming dormant and relying on their specialized water-storage organs, such as bulbs and fleshy underground stems, until the dry period passes. There are a number of exceptions, however: wildflowers such as wood lilies *(Trillium),* bloodroot *(Sanguinaria),* and cranesbill *(Geranium)* spread wide foliage to absorb summer's light, instead of becoming dormant. Late blooming plants like asters and goldenrods *(Solidago)* produce a flush of lush foliage early in the year, but flower in the autumn. These varied blooming times are useful to gardeners for year-round interest.

Grassland such as the North American prairie and the European steppe are dominated by grasses and a number of colorful wildflowers, in particular legumes and daisies. Dozens of popular perennial plants originate in the North American prairies, such as *Liatris*, coneflower *(Echinacea),* and sunflower *(Helianthus)*. The steppes give us peony *(Paeonia)* and *Perovskia.*

Wetlands are common in the zone, especially on areas of shallow bedrock such as are found on the Canadian Shield, and in grasslands such as the North American prairies. Forested wetlands include swamps and bogs, and are filled in with sphagnum mosses, heathlike shrubs, and grasses. Prairie potholes and other marshes are shallow and broad and are dominated by sedges *(Carex).* Wetlands offer gardeners a variety of ornamental plants including the familiar iris and marsh marigold *(Caltha palustris).*

The zone produces wheat *(Triticum),* oats *(Avena),* and other cereal crops; a variety of vegetables such as beets *(Beta)* and potatoes *(Solanum tuberosum);* and fruits such as apples *(Malus)* and cherries *(Prunus).*

Gardening in the zone

Gardening in the zone can be a challenge. The intense winter cold, often high summer heat, and periodic drought produce stressful conditions for plants.

However, winters in the northern reaches of the region generally have consistent snow cover that makes gardening with herbaceous plants easier than for more southern neighbors in Zone 5. Consistent winter snows protect plants from the worst of the cold, so perennial and vegetable gardeners are happy, especially in areas where it is moister and the soil is richer. On the down side, the growing season is shorter, on average 160 to 180 days. The number of woody ornamental species, especially flowering trees and shrubs, is dramatically less than that available in warmer zones. But what must be given up in woody species, can often be gained in herbaceous plants. Many plants thrive in the cooler conditions, especially cooler night temperatures, and in the reduced humidity. Insect and disease problems are fewer than in warmer zones. Lilacs *(Syringa),* viburnums, crabapples *(Malus),* iris, daylilies *(Hemerocallis),* and hostas are just a few of the plants that are popular in Zone 4.

Above: Wildflowers form a vibrant, if brief, carpet of color across the prairie landscape. This scene features red-flowering Castilleja *species, cream-flowered* Persicaria bistorta, *and* Pedicularis groenlandica *with its maroon flower heads.*

Zone 5 -20 to -10°F (-29 to -23°C)

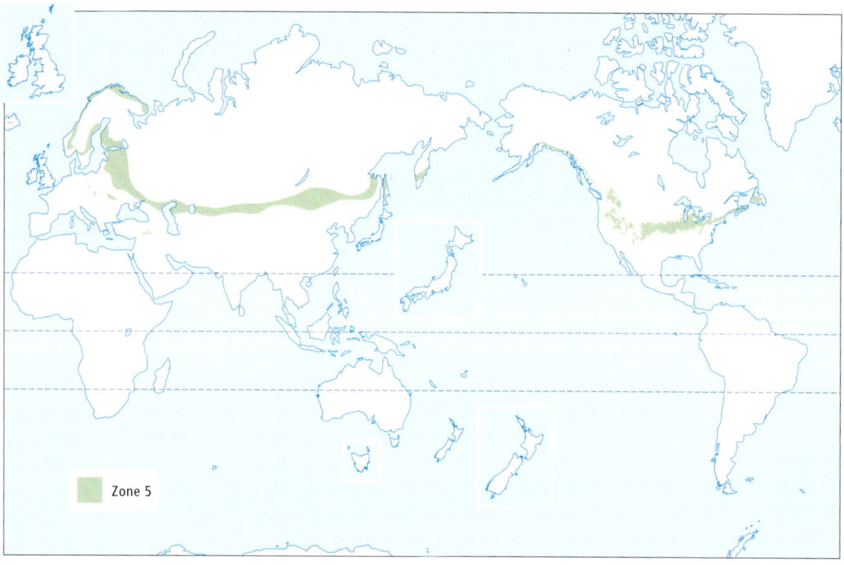

Below: Ulmus × hollandica *has given rise to a wide range of cultivars, including 'Modolina', shown here, which is a tall and vigorous-growing tree. It makes a suitable landscape subject in Zone 5 and warmer.*

The many climates—wet, dry, maritime, continental, and alpine—of Zone 5 worldwide have in common their position between vast regions of much colder and much warmer temperatures. In short, Zone 5 is in the middle.

Nominally, the climates of this zone are united by low average winter temperatures in the range of -20 to -10°F (-29 to -23°C), but this masks the extremes. The greater portion of the zone runs east-west across the continents of Russia, Asia, and North America at roughly 40 degrees latitude. On these continental landmasses, away from maritime influences, waves of polar air frequently rush southward to the zone with little high ground to hinder them, sometimes driving the temperature well below -20°F (-29°C). During such episodes of deep cold, even hardy plants suffer severe damage and sometimes death.

Rainfall, snow, and soils vary widely across Zone 5. In North America the western plains are dry, with 12–20 in (30–50 cm) of rain a year and snowfalls that do not provide winter-long cover. Unleached by rain, the soils tend to be alkaline. Eastward, rainfall increases, the soils turn neutral or basic, and the prairie ecology of the plains gives way to forest. In Europe, the rainfall is highest in the west and declines to the east, with similar changes in the soils.

Winter varies widely in intensity. Some years temperatures can linger for a month or more at below freezing. Other years, the entire winter passes without dropping this low. In times of protracted cold, the weather is typically dry and windy—a combination that desiccates even tough needle-leafed evergreens such as spruce *(Picea),* and leaves them brown in spring, while broad-leafed evergreens such as rhododendrons may lose leaves, buds, and twigs.

In eastern North America, winter vagaries are followed by vagaries of heat and humidity when warm moist air from southern regions spreads northward in the summer. Conifers such as larch *(Larix),* hemlock *(Tsuga),* and fir *(Abies)* from colder zones do not tolerate this heat and grow poorly. Instead, southern conifers such as shortleaf pine *(Pinus echinata)* and pitch pine *(P. rigida)* take their place.

Zone 5 is also found running in thin bands at elevations of roughly 5,000 to 8,000 ft (1,525 to 2,440 m). All plants in these high grounds must endure rapid and severe changes of temperature in summer and winter, as well as intense sunlight. Here, penstemons are common perennials, while spruce and pines are familiar trees.

Long cold spells and occasional polar weather limit the viability of broad-leafed evergreens in this zone. *Pieris, Leucothoe,* and even *Kalmia,* among others, do not thrive unless trees shelter them. Other plants, such as heaths *(Erica)* and heathers *(Calluna),* thrive only in the maritime climates of the zone, where the sea buffers outbreaks of polar air and provides moisture. Only a few rhododendron cultivars, such as *Rhododendron* 'Nova Zembla' and *R.* 'PJM', and the hardier species like *R. yakushimanum, R. maximum,* and *R. viscosum,* are reliable. However, even the toughest rhododendrons may suffer damage in this zone. Their performance in spring is acceptable, not perfect. Only the deciduous azaleas reliably escape damage.

Needle-leafed evergreens, such as white pine *(Pinus strobus)* for example, are prominent only where summers are moist and cool, and scarce where the summers are hot and humid, or hot and arid. In the west of North America, native spruces like *Picea pungens,* junipers *(Juniperus),* and pinyon *(Pinus edulis)* are the common evergreens, adapted to alkaline soils and aridity.

Sudden cold snaps and late freezes

On average, the first hard freeze of autumn arrives in mid-October, but it can come a month earlier or later. An early hard freeze, with temperatures at 27°F (-3°C), will burn the still-green leaves of woody and herbaceous perennials, and even damage the twigs of shrubs and trees that have not yet begun hardening. The last hard freeze of winter falls in mid-May, but some years it arrives as early as March and other years as late as June.

Furthermore, false springs and tardy winters bracket

Right: This deciduous tree, Fagus sylvatica, *is native to Europe and southern England. It is a valued garden tree, both for its ornamental uses and its capacity to conserve the productiveness of the soil.*

the growing season. Surges of southern air can arrive anytime from midwinter to spring, lulling shrubs, trees, and herbaceous perennials partially out of dormancy. Once started, they lose hardiness. When a new wave of cold arrives, as it usually does, it can kill plants outright. Even temperatures considerably warmer than the average low for the zone can cause damage. In areas where snow is heavy, herbaceous perennials are usually spared from premature awakenings. Where snow is sparse, as it often is on the plains, exotic species such as daffodils *(Narcissus)* that are not adapted to false springs often emerge too soon and are burned by the return of deep cold.

In the areas of Zone 5 with adequate rainfall, the main crops are soybeans, corn, wheat, and oil seeds such as sunflowers. The hardier tree fruits such as apples and pears are grown, but require frequent spraying for the insects and disease that can thrive.

Gardening in the zone

Many plants are adapted to winters in the zone. Among trees and shrubs, some of the toughest are blueberry *(Vaccinium)*, hawthorn *(Crataegus)*, and apple *(Malus)*. Areas with dependable summer rainfall support deciduous shrubs and trees, including maples *(Acer)*, oaks *(Quercus)*, beeches *(Fagus)*, elms *(Ulmus)*, locusts *(Gleditsia)*, ashes *(Fraxinus)*, cherries *(Prunus)*, and more. Some exotics do well. The Chinese dawn redwood *(Metasequoia glyptostroboides)* is hardy in the wetter parts of the zone in North America, as is *Parrotia persica* in areas with cooler summers. Smoke bush *(Cotinus)* is widely adapted and so are the dogwoods, such as *Cornus alternifolia*, *C. kousa*, and *C. mas*. Daphnes are hardy, as are many species of honeysuckle, like *Lonicera* × *heckrottii*, some so rampant they are pests.

Among herbaceous perennials, the plains, steppes, and low mountains of the zone offer exceedingly tough species, adapted to cold and heat, drought and downpour. They include coreopsis *(Coreopsis)*, black-eyed Susans *(Rudbeckia)*, sunflowers *(Helianthus)*, cup plant *(Silphium perfoliatum)*, species of stachys, and succulents such as sedums, as well as a large group of grasses such as the graceful pennisetums, short fescues *(Festuca)*, and hair grasses *(Deschampsia)*. In areas with rainfall of 24 in (600 mm) or more, the hostas, the low pachysandras, lobelias, asters, thistley eryngiums, violets, astilbes, and epimediums, notable for their ability to grow in dry shade, will all do well.

Though much prized, English ivy and boxwood are ill adapted to Zone 5. English yew *(Taxus baccata)* is also not entirely suitable. However, yews such as *T. canadensis* and *T. media* are fully hardy.

Magnolia × *soulangeana* is fairly hardy, but in central North America may fail to open its chalicelike flowers three years in five if late cold spells nip the opening buds. Many other magnolias are hardy but unreliable bloomers.

Although the climate can be testing, gardeners of Zone 5 nonetheless have a wide choice of dependable, desirable plants, both woody and herbaceous, and the pleasure of three seasons in the garden. Spring is sudden and intense. Crabapples cover themselves in white and daffodils flower yellow at their feet, while the herbaceous perennials burst from the ground and race into bloom. Within two months the show segues into the summer display of sunflowers and grasses. Autumn bloomers like anemone cannot match the paintbox of spring, but then the maples turn red and the garden season ends ablaze.

Above: Witch hazel, Hamamelis virginiana, *is one of the earliest to flower of the trees and shrubs in the zone, but is almost never harmed by the cold. The serviceberries* (Amelanchier *spp.*) *are another early-bloomer.*

Zone 6 -10 to 0°F (-23 to -18°C)

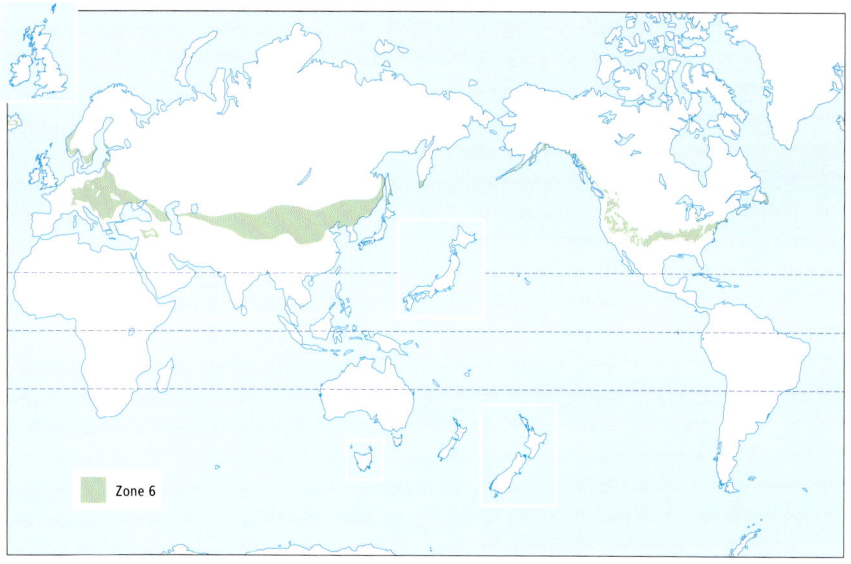

In Zone 6, the average low temperature in winter ranges from -10 to 0°F (-23 to -18°C). It ranges throughout the Northern Hemisphere, making a wide U-shaped curve through the USA from New York City on the east, down through the Midwest and Southwest, and up to Washington and parts of British Columbia. Off the northeastern coast of North America, the warming effects of the Gulf Stream place unlikely areas such as parts of Newfoundland in the zone. Also in this zone's northern tier are areas of Norway, Sweden, Denmark, and Finland.

Zone 6 cuts a path through much of central and eastern Europe, from Germany to Greece and northern Croatia; moving into Asia via the Caspian Sea, and narrowing into a small swathe through Afghanistan and into China. Its sole presence in the Southern Hemisphere is two small regions in Argentina.

Below: Bulbs are a favorite of gardeners throughout Zone 6. Crocus speciosus offers welcome color in autumn.

Topographically, Zone 6 covers many landscapes: coastal regions, flood plains, lowlands, mountains, prairies, plains, and even some high desert, and the vegetation varies accordingly. Among plants that will grow in wet coastal areas, along riversides and marshes, are giant reed plants *(Phragmites australis)* and cat tail *(Typha latifolia)*. The dry sandy Pine Barrens of New Jersey, USA, support plants that need fire to survive, such as scrub pine *(Pinus virginiana)*, northern pitch pine *(Pinus rigida)*, bearberry *(Arctostaphylos uva-ursi)*, and sweet pepper bush *(Clethra alnifolia)*.

Lowland mountain ranges, such as the Blue Ridge Mountains of USA, and some of the mountains in Europe give rise to dogwoods: among them, the green osier *(Cornus alternifolia)*, the native American flowering dogwood *(C. florida)*, the European and western Asian Cornelian cherry *(C. mas)*, and the giant dogwood *(C. controversa)*.

The plains and prairies of Zone 6 are home to plants that not only survive winter cold, but also often heat and drought (but flooding some years) over summer. These plants include the coneflowers *(Echinacea)* and sunflowers *(Helianthus)*. The genus *Leucanthemum* (shasta and ox-eye daisies) straddles Zone 6, growing in grasslands, rocky meadows, and wastelands of Europe and temperate Asia.

Seasonal displays

Spring can be beautifully long (and moist in places), arriving early and staying late—especially in the warmer ranges of the zone. Snowdrops *(Galanthus nivalis)* and *Crocus tommasinianus* can put on a spring preview in late winter. Adding to the show are some deciduous shrubs such as forsythia, Chinese witch hazel *(Hamamelis mollis)*, and winter hazels *(Corylopsis)*, as these can shed the snow and keep on blooming. Other woodland and scrub region shrubs and small trees, such as firethorn *(Pyracantha)* and Japanese flowering crab-apples *(Malus floribunda)*, retain colorful berries from autumn. In moist regions of northwestern North America and northeastern Asia, skunk cabbage *(Lysichiton* species*)* actually creates heat as it rises up from the earth in early spring, melting any snow around it. However, early blooming trees, especially magnolias—*Magnolia denudata* from China, the Japanese *Magnolia kobus*, and others—are often hit with a late blast of cold or snow that browns out their blossoms. Shrubs are more forgiving, and it is common to see hardy shrubs such as Korean rhododendron *(Rhododendron mucronulatum)* unaffected by late chills and snows.

Within weeks, spring brings a riot of colors from bulbs, many of which many originated in western Asia and southeastern Europe, such as tulips *(Tulipa)*, daffodils *(Narcissus)*, squill *(Scilla)*, and grape hyacinths *(Muscari)*. Dozens of woodland wildflowers add to the beauty: European forget-me-nots *(Myosotis sylvatica)* and lungwort *(Pulmonaria)*, mayapple *(Podophyllum)*, and columbine *(Aquilegia canadensis)*. Not to be forgotten are the perennials such as lupins *(Lupinus)*, bleeding heart *(Dicentra spectabilis)*,and peonies *(Paeonia)*. Acid-loving woodland shrubs abound, adding to the colors of late spring: rhododendrons and azaleas from around the world, hollies *(Ilex)*, mountain laurel *(Kalmia latifolia)*, viburnums *(Viburnum)*, and blueberries *(Vaccinium)*.

Summer brings another burst of color from daylilies *(Hemerocallis)*, which seemingly defy nature by growing anywhere, lilies that originated in Asia, and perennials such as native American prairie plants: bee balm *(Monarda didyma)*, black-eyed Susan *(Rudbeckia)*, and purple coneflower *(Echinacea purpurea)*. The tough shrubs of summer include shrubby cinquefoil *(Potentilla fruticosa)*, butterfly bush *(Buddleja davidii)*, and the hardy cluster-flowered (floribunda) roses.

Woodland areas contribute to summer beauty. Even without its airy blooms, purple smokebush *(Cotinus coggyria* 'Purpureus') adds a bold note to the garden with its deep burgundy leaves. Trees such as dove tree *(Davidia involucrata),* sweetspire *(Itea virginica),* and sorrel tree *(Oxydendron arboreum),* with its white blooms, add to the delight of summer.

For many, autumn is a favorite season as Zone 6 is favored with a last burst of color before trees shed their leaves. Maples abound, from the sugar maple *(Acer saccharum)* to red maple *(A. rubrum)* and the numerous Japanese maples *(A. palmatum, A. japonicum,* and cultivars*)* with their foliage ranging in color from yellow to orange, crimson to burgundy, and almost everything in between. Sweet gum *(Liquidambar styraciflua)* and burning bush *(Euonymus alatus)* are stunning as their leaves turn flaming red, while the eastern North American staghorn sumac *(Rhus typhina)* turns yellow to orange. Sweet autumn clematis *(Clematis ternifolia)* lives up to its name with fragrant white blooms that evolve into magnificent daintily twirled seed heads that often last through the winter. Even autumn bulbs put on a show, for example, the large lavender autumn crocus native to Europe *(Colchicum autumnale)* and autumn daffodil *(Sternbergia lutea)*. In acidic areas, hollies *(Ilex* species and cultivars*)* are king of the broadleaf evergreens. Their berries color in autumn and persist through the winter.

Above: Zone 6 is particularly blessed with an abundance of deciduous trees and shrubs, which mark autumn in reds and golds.

Growing in the zone

Zone 6 could be considered a crossover zone, and as such it is able to sustain a larger range of woody plants of varying hardiness than most other zones. Many gardeners use this to their advantage, especially within microclimates in their own properties, growing Zone 7 plants along the south side of the house or in a protected area, and growing plants from cooler zones, in more exposed or north-facing spaces. The range of plants to grow in Zone 6 seems limitless, and includes many trees, shrubs, woody perennials and annuals. If you also make use of the microclimates around your property, you will find thousands of plants suitable for your garden. The choices are up to you.

Above: Acer species are valued throughout the Northern Hemisphere for their beautiful autumn colors. This, combined with their elegant foliage and growth habit, make them very useful to gardeners.

Zone 7 0 to 10°F (-18 to -12°C)

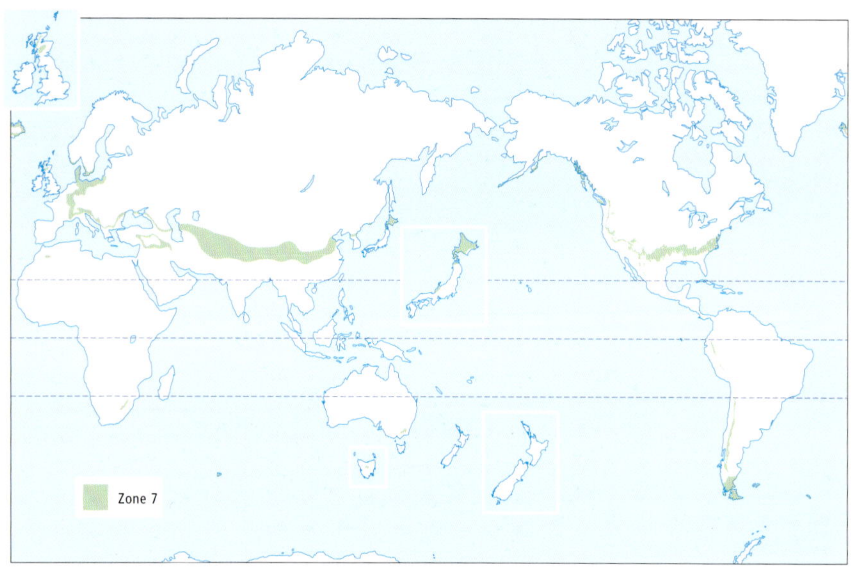

Below: Pinus strobus, Populus tremuloides, Betula, *and* Acer *species combine to beautiful effect in New York State, USA.*

Zone 7 is found mainly across the middle lattitudes of the Northern Hemisphere temperate regions, with only odd patches in the Southern Hemisphere, in mountain areas. In North America, the zone runs in an arc across the southern states of USA, from Virginia through northern Texas, Arizona, and the mountains of California, coming to a northernmost tail in the maritime region of western Canada and the Alaskan Panhandle. In Europe it occupies a north-south belt through central Europe, from Denmark to the Balkans, and also occurs in the Scottish Highlands. From the eastern Mediterranean, it runs in a broad belt through parts of the Caucasus and Turkey and through much of the Himalayas and northern China. Northern Japan is also in this zone. In the Southern Hemisphere, the largest occurrences of Zone 7 are in the higher Andes of South America—dropping almost to sea level in the far south—in the Drakensberg of eastern South Africa, and in the higher mountains of New Zealand's South Island.

A zone of diverse climates

Most parts of this zone experience medium to high rainfall, without any severe dry season. In the continental interiors, for example in central Asia and the American Southwest, this zone is pushed toward lower latitudes by cold air masses expanding from the north in winter. As a result, summers are long and hot and humidity is low for much of the year. These continental climates have more sharply defined seasons and more predictable winter temperatures than those of regions bordering the oceans, where, generally speaking, summers are milder and more humid. Zone 7 is the highest zone in which the soil is likely to be frozen for any length of time in winter, which precludes the growth of many subtropical plants, most notably palms (family Arecaceae).

A point worth considering is that climates change and plants may be caught in a climate warmer or colder than the one in which they originally evolved. It often happens that plants can tolerate more cold or heat than is now recorded in their native homes. Recent winters have been warmer than in the past 10,000 years, so plants found wild in Zone 7 can generally grow in Zones 5 or 6.

Flora of the Northern Hemisphere

Woody plants are more sensitive indicators of this zone than herbaceous plants, being less easily protected from heavy frost by soil or snow cover. Unlike their deciduous counterparts, many temperate evergreens have their cold limit at or around Zone 7. One such is *Magnolia grandiflora,* a typical Zone 7 tree from the southern USA, and widely planted elsewhere in the world. Similarly, many of the Chinese evergreen *Rhododendron* species are not hardy below Zone 7.

Certain plants are readily grown right across the zone, others are much more sensitive to climatic factors such as summer temperatures, rainfall, and humidity. For example, some plants that are hardy down to Zone 6 or even Zone 5 in hot dry continental regions will hardly cope with winter in oceanic climates of Zone 7, such as those of southwestern Canada and Scotland, because they enter the winter with their aerial growth less hardened and their root systems wetter. Rose of Sharon *(Hibiscus syriacus)* is one such example.

For the same reason, the Scottish Highlands and the Pacific Northwest (of North America) are excellent for trees and shrubs from the cold wet parts of Chile and New Zealand, or from Himalayan areas with wet summers. The British horticulturist Ken Beckett, who has made several studies of plant hardiness, considers that gardeners in British Isles should choose plants rated to one zone more hardy than that in which they garden.

The greatest horticultural wealth for the zone is to be found in the plants from the mountains of Japan, China, and the Himalayas. Native to this region are the many hardy rhododendron species, which have given rise to a multitude of hybrids, and the magnificent flowering cherries *(Prunus),* developed mainly in Japan although some of their wild progenitors may have come from China.

In the southern interior of the USA, there is a wealth of native plant life for gardeners, in particular, annuals and perennials of the daisy family. Examples include *Helianthus, Rudbeckia, Cosmos,* and *Coreopsis.* Some of the many colorful perennials and subshrubs in the genus *Penstemon* are also centered in Zone 7.

Alpine plants from the south

In the Southern Hemisphere, with its stronger oceanic influence on climates, Zone 7 is restricted to mountainous areas. In Australia, the hardy snow gum *(Eucalyptus pauciflora* subsp. *niphophila)* and cider gum *(E. gunnii),* as well as shrubs such as the candle heath *(Richea continentis),* which will survive in warmer parts of Zone 7 in Europe, are only found above 5,000 ft (1,500 m) in New South Wales, Victoria, and Tasmania.

In Africa, only the highlands of Lesotho above 6,500 ft (2,000 m) have Zone 7 winters. Garden plants from this area are mostly bulbs or corms. They are tolerant of fire, which means they can lose their tops to frost and still survive. *Moraea alticola, Kniphofia caulescens,* and the deciduous *Agapanthus campanulatus* subsp. *patens* can grow at altitudes of 8,200 ft (2,500 m).

Zone 7 covers extensive areas of the mountains in the South Island of New Zealand where there is a distinct lack of summer heat. The evergreen *Celmisia* species, from the alpine grasslands, thrive on sandy acid soil with good drainage and the cool summers of eastern Scotland.

Commercial crops

Crops in this zone depend mainly on summer temperatures: maize *(Zea mays)* is grown in warm wet areas, and wheat *(Triticum)* where summers are drier. Few places in Zone 7 have a long enough growing season to produce two crops in a year. In the coldest areas of the Himalayas above 6,560 ft (2,000 m), buckwheat *(Fragopyrum esculentum)* is grown as a grain in place of wheat.

Most fruit trees thrive, and the rather delicate Japanese apricot *(Prunus mume)* can be grown. Figs *(Ficus carica)* will need wall protection and will lose their fruit buds in the coldest winters. Grape vines will survive in many parts of Zone 7 but for high-quality wine they require warm sunny microclimates, such as in the valleys of the Rhine and the Moselle in Germany.

Above: This yellow-flowering Senecio *species, with the brown-red flowers of a* Buddleja *species peeping through, is at home in the temperate conditions of Central Sichuan, China.*

Top: A native of China, Lagerstroemia indica *makes a highly attractive tree for gardeners in Zones 7 and 8. It has a widespreading habit; white, pink, or purple flowers; and dark green leaves that turn orange-red in autumn.*

Zone 8 10 to 20°F (-12 to -7°C)

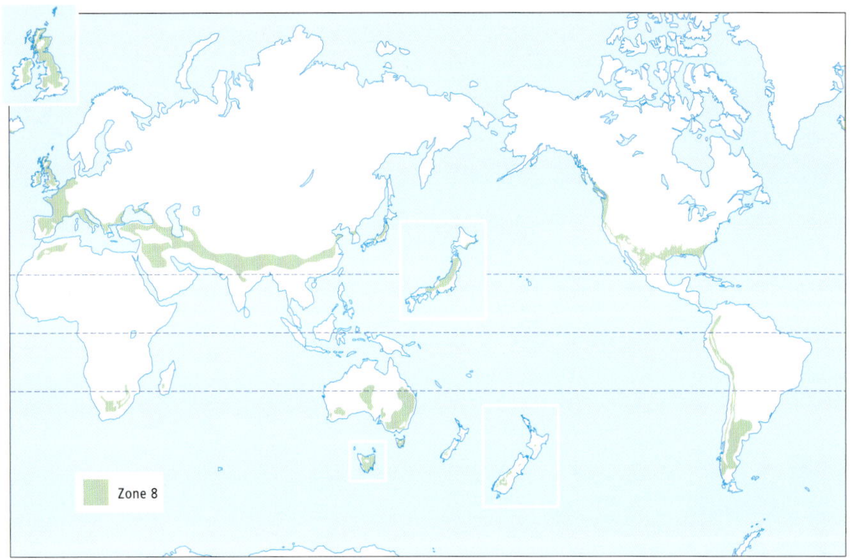

Mother Nature has provided a vast selection of plants hardy to Zone 8, and humans have done a mostly admirable job of carting them all over the world, adding, swapping, and enriching the panorama of flora available.

Characterized by four definite seasons, Zone 8 has mild winters with a sporadic snowfall that doesn't last. Temperatures can plunge from 20 to 10°F (-7 to -12°C). The first frosts begin in November and end in March in the Northern Hemisphere, whereas in the Southern Hemisphere frosts can last from April to as late as November.

Some of the world's most spectacular gardens can be found in this favorable zone. Most of the British Isles and central Ireland lies within the zone. A good part of France, and a large portion of Spain, are also Zone 8. The vast rich agriculture area of the Po River Valley in northern Italy, famous for its many Renaissance gardens, is also in this hardiness zone. North America's Zone 8, on the other hand, sweeps across the southern part of the USA, taking in the Californian foothill regions of the Sierra and the Northwest coast. South of the equator, Zone 8 moves inland, down the coast of Peru and Chile, and covers much of inland Argentina, part of the Tierra del Fuego, and the Falkland Islands.

On the opposite side of the world, eastern Australia, most of Tasmania, and some of New Zealand lie in Zone 8. In Asia, the zone includes large areas of Japan, and parts of China and Myanmar. The only region of Africa that lies in the zone is at the far south, in a small crescent shaped area that touches Lesotho.

Below: Parts of New Zealand's South Island boast a mild Zone 8 climate. Conditions are ideal for commercial grape cultivation, and numerous vineyards exist.

Zone 8 worldwide is temperate, with long summer daylight hours that guarantee plants at least six hours of sun per day. As "hardiness" describes places, not plants, variations do occur. Continental regions of this zone have long hot summers that help the plants to mature and tolerate cold better, with some rain. Heavy winter rainfalls follow summer, along with some snow in winter. Maritime regions have mostly cool wet summers, with winters bringing more rain. Mediterranean climates have hot dry summers that are followed by winter rains.

Winter dormancy across the zone lasts three to four months, and in this favorable mild climate plants may bloom for up to ten months. In hot dry places, some plants will have summer dormancy as well.

Common methods of propagation apply in the zone: budding, grafting, and cuttings. Some plants normally tender to Zone 8 may be successfully grown in microclimate situations. Perfect examples of this are the olive *(Olea europaea)* and citrus trees that grow in the open on the south side of the Alps, protected from the icy north winds by the mountains.

Rosemary *(Rosmarinus)* and lavender *(Lavandula),* native to the Mediterranean and spread by the Romans, are intolerant to excessive winter wet yet thrive in the British Isles in soil with good drainage. Often, keeping tender plants in place and dry during winter improves their chances for survival. Lavender cotton *(Santolina),* lavender, and butcher's broom *(Ruscus)*—called *pungitopo,* "pricks mice" in Italy—are all Zone 8 plants.

Plants are amazingly adaptable, even to different elevations. English walnuts *(Juglans regia)* will grow to elevations of 4,920 ft (1,500 m), and yet the plants—the famous *noce di Sorrento* of Italy—hug the Tyrrhenian coast. The common bearded iris *(Iris germanica)* will grow from sea level to 3,940 ft (1,200 m). Grapes *(Vitis vinifera)* grow from 0 to 2,620 ft (800 m). Microclimates within Zone 8, influenced by elevation, a diversity of soil, and local climatic conditions, will determine what plant will grow where. A more tender plant, ideal for Zone 9, may thrive in a protected spot in Zone 8, whereas in a windy area, perhaps with poor drainage, a plant usually hardy to this zone may die. Observation is a good garden tool.

Indicator plants

Most roses thrive in Zone 8, requiring a mild winter to perform best. Tender roses, however, such as the double white banksia rose *(Rosa banksiae banksiae),* Teas, and Noisettes may need to be planted in sheltered spots. Hardy plants such as stonecrop *(Sedum),* iris, columbine *(Aquilegia),* bugle *(Ajuga),* some pinks *(Dianthus),* and other cold climate plants, grow at a leisurely pace, almost doubling their leafed-out period in a Zone 8 climate.

The wonderful trees of this zone include one of the oldest and tallest trees on earth; the Californian redwood *(Sequoia sempervirens).* The magnificent giant sequoias *(Sequoiadendron),* also from California, have larger trunks but do not grow so tall.

Nearly 2,000 years ago, Pliny described the oriental plane tree *(Platanus orientalis)* growing in one of his Tuscany gardens with ivy *(Hedera)* entwining the trunks for contrasting foliage. These plants are still familiar features of the zone. From China and Japan the crape myrtle *(Lagerstroemia indica)*, has migrated worldwide, has been overloved, overgrown, and is now overshunned as being common. Little do those in Zone 8 know how cold climate gardeners envy and covet this beautiful elegant little tree.

Apples, a favorite fruit crop today, have been discovered in Swiss and Austrian Stone Age dwellings. Nut crops include chestnut *(Castanea sativa)*, grown in southern Europe, and the much sought after pine nut produced from the Mediterranean umbrella pine *(Pinus pinea)*. Hazelnuts *(Corylus avellana)* have been grown since humans can remember, and the walnut is also grown for oil. Olives are commercially grown in some warmer protected areas of the zone. Grape crops are grown across Europe—curiously, over the same area that the Roman Empire occupied in the second century AD—and in California, Australia, and New Zealand.

Above: In ideal conditions—which include fog, rain, and cool summer winds—Sequoia sempervirens can reach 360 ft (110 m).

Some problem plants

Humans have caused the spread of some very invasive weeds. The noxious free-floating aquatic fern *Salvinia molesta* has recently invaded areas of Zone 8 worldwide. Faithful to its name *molesta*, this native of southeastern Brazil grows vigorously from sea level to 1,000 ft (300 m), multiplies rapidly, and has already clogged major waterways everywhere, causing serious problems.

Rosa multiflora, introduced into the USA from Japan and China, has "escaped" and is now considered a noxious weed, as pasturing cows eat this rose and the prickles rip their intestines. Yellow wood sorrel *(Oxalis exilis)*, from New Zealand and Australia, has become a farmer's nightmare in many places and it is almost impossible to remove. On the other hand, nettle *(Urtica dioica)* might be considered a friendly weed as it enriches the soil and can be harvested to eat. Everyone (except farmers) loves the red Flanders poppy *(Papaver rhoeas)*, which regularly survives the crop weed killers by growing along field edges, and in unsprayed areas.

True floral globalization has made hundreds of good (and bad, alas) "discovered" treasures from around the world available in this zone.

Gardening in the zone

With the mild winter temperatures, Zone 8 gardeners have paradise at their fingertips and can choose from a vast selection of plants. Stately fragrant *Magnolia grandiflora* can share garden space with richly perfumed Mexican orange *(Choisya ternata)*, Japanese pittosporum *(Pittosporum tobira)*, and flowering trees such as flowering dogwood *(Cornus florida)* and the elegant lacy silk tree *(Albizia julibrissin)*. The stunning evergreen shrub Oregon holly grape *(Mahonia aquifolium)* and the deciduous flowering-quince *(Chaenomeles speciosa)* bloom in the winter, alongside the cheerful yellow winter jasmine *(Jasminum nudiflorum)*. The superb ground covers lily-turf *(Liriope spicata)* and mondo grass *(Ophiopogon japonicus)* grow well in Zone 8.

Gardeners in Zone 8 are destined to suffer great temptations (there is always that plant you don't have) and great satisfactions.

Left: Roses should abound in Zone 8 gardens, as almost every type of rose can be grown, including those that can only survive mild winters, and tender classics like 'Mutabilis', 'Lady Hillingdon', and 'Mme Alfred Carrière', left.

Zone 9 20 to 30°F (-7 to -1°C)

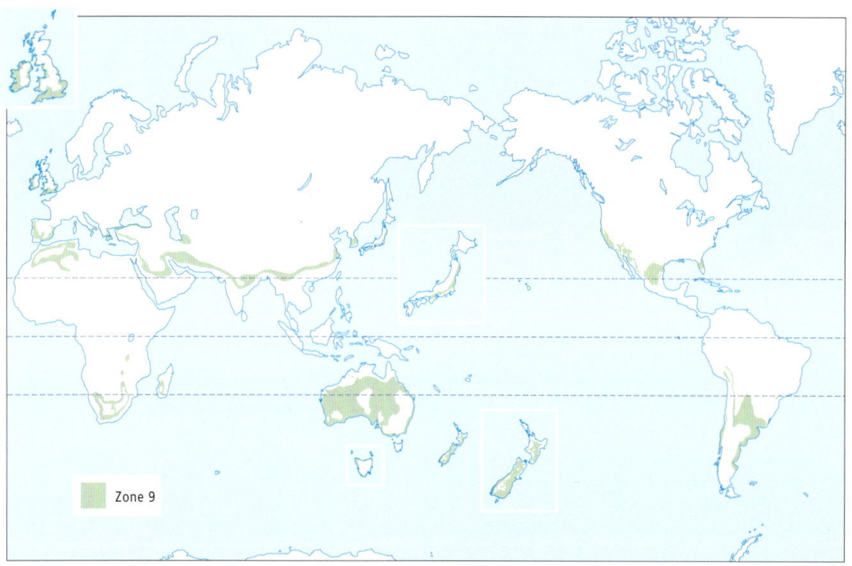

The minimum winter temperature in Zone 9 ranges between 20 and 30°F (-7 to -1°C) and the bulk of the garden plants are from the Mediterranean basin, the Cape region of South Africa, the coastal areas of Oregon and California to Arizona, southern Texas and deep south coast of the USA, Chile in South America, and central and parts of southern Australia and neighboring areas. Although hardiness zones relate to areas with similarities of climate rather than to plants that are similar biologically, plants from different regions in the same zone frequently share common characteristics. Cultivation of the plants also has many similarities.

Above: Protea cynaroides, *known as king protea, is the floral emblem of South Africa, and is native to the lower mountain slopes and heathlands of the Cape region. Its striking flowers appear from midwinter to early summer.*

In the main, the native vegetation in these parts of the world is grouped as "Mediterranean," from the vegetation found in southern Europe, Turkey, Israel, Lebanon, and North Africa. This vegetation was the subject of the earliest Western study of plants. Plants with a true Mediterranean distribution include rosemary *(Rosmarinus officinalis),* the strawberry tree *(Arbutus unedo),* and the rock-rose (Cistaceae) family.

Adaptations to fire and drought

The Mediterranean climate is characterized by mild wet winters and long dry summers, summer being defined as the three months when the days are the longest, hottest, and driest. Plants have become adapted to these hot dry summers in several ways. Some avoid the dry weather by being short-lived and surviving as seeds (annuals), others die down to below ground level and survive as corms, bulbs, or fleshy stems: tulips do this. Woody plants such as kermes oak *(Quercus coccifera)* in the Mediterranean tend to have tough leathery leaves, or, as with many ice plants (family Aizoaceae) from southern Africa, succulent leaves or stems. These features help the plant withstand water stress during the summer.

All such plants that have parts above ground in the hottest time of the year have adaptations to deter grazing animals. These adaptations can be in the form of tough leaves and stems, spines and thorns (such as many legume species like gorse, *Ulex europaeus,* in the Mediterranean), or leaves that are foul-smelling or -tasting (such as many pelargonium), or through camouflage, so that the plant resembles little stones (like the "living stones," *Lithops*).

Many Mediterranean regions are prone to fires, both natural and induced by humans, and so many of the plants are also adapted to fire. Some, such as cork oak *(Quercus suber),* have thick burn-tolerant bark, while others, like *Cistus salviifolius,* sucker from the base once the existing shoot structure has been killed. Others, as is the case with many Australian plants like banksias and hakeas, will only germinate after fire has cleared an area of competing plants.

The horticultural significance of these features is that the great majority of succulent plants, many "bulbs," and many plants with spines and strong aromatic leaves turn out to be Zone 9 plants. The trees, which formerly dominated much of these Zone 9 ecosystems, were some of the first evergreens brought into cultivation.

The first Mediterranean plants grown as ornamentals were from southern Europe and, in northern countries, they had to be overwintered in buildings called orangeries. Later, plants of the eastern Mediterranean and the North African coast were introduced.

An extensive floral kingdom

Most significant, though, was the bringing into cultivation of the Cape region flora of South Africa. Although grouped under "Mediterranean," it is botanically so distinctive as to be considered one of the world's six floral kingdoms, with some 9,000 species of seed plants and plants that are without seeds and flowers (pteridophytes), of which 69 percent are found only there. It has provided many of the world's most important ornamentals for Zone 9, and accommodating them in the horticulture of northern Europe led to improved greenhouse design, allowing the cultivation of many succulents and winter-flowering heaths *(Erica)*. The introduction of Cape plants also led to the increased use of outside "summer" bulbs in the form of gladioli *(Gladiolus)*, corn lily *(Ixia)*, montbretia *(Crocosmia)*, harlequin flower *(Sparaxis)*, and freesias. Also important was the introduction of half-hardy annuals, such as lobelia, nemesia, and Livingstone daisies *(Dorotheanthus)*, used in summer bedding. The beds often included South African "geraniums" (pelargoniums) that had been overwintered indoors. These species of pelargonium, like many succulent plants from the Cape, were to become some of the most widely grown pot plants and were seen decorating windowsills of even the humblest cottages in northern Europe.

Later, other floras in the zone were explored and their plants introduced into other countries. These included California poppy *(Eschscholzia californica)* and species of *Clarkia*, to be grown as half-hardy annuals. From South America came the slipper flower *(Calceolaria)*, and from southern Australia came golden everlastings *(Xerochrysum bracteatum)* and, more importantly, hordes of species of wattle *(Acacia)* and gum *(Eucalyptus)*. Plantations of both have transformed the landscape of many parts of Zone 9 throughout the world.

Below: The red flowers of the candelabra flower, Brunsvigia orientalis, *brighten the southern African landscape, where it is endemic, in autumn. When the flowerhead dries out, the seeds are dispersed across the land.*

Because of their native climate regimes, many plants in this zone are dormant in the hot summer months. Many of them require a baking to flower the following season and will rot if moistened during this time. This means that many of the succulent plants such as those from the Cape region must be grown in greenhouses even in warm climates, merely to keep off rain. Other perennial plants from the zone would die if left outside in cooler climates and are often treated as annuals, though in mild winters some, such as gazanias, will survive to flower the next year. Most of the evergreen trees will not stand the cool dank winters of the north, though in sheltered urban spots, such as at the Chelsea Physic Garden in London, even olive trees *(Olea europaea)* grow unprotected.

Many Zone 9 plants are important to the cut flower industry in this zone and in other warm and temperate countries. Other commercial crops grown include citrus, peaches *(Prunus persica)* and other stone fruit, melons and other cucurbits, strawberries *(Fragaria)*, figs *(Ficus)*, avocados *(Persea americana)*, olives, and wine grapes *(Vitis vinifera)*. In plastic greenhouses with little other protection, tropical crops can also be grown successfully: papayas *(Carica)*, bananas *(Musa)*, and custard apples *(Annona squamosa)*.

Introducing Zone 9 plants to other parts of the world has led to major weed problems in several areas. South African Cape dandelion *(Arctotheca calendula)*, pigface *(Carpobrotus)*, gladioli, and *Watsonia* are weeds in the Mediterranean, California and Oregon in the USA, and Australia. And species of wattle *(Acacia)* and *Hakea* from Australia are pests in the Mediterranean and in South Africa, though some of them are now being kept in check using biological control measures.

Left: From southeastern Australia, Xanthorrhoea australis *has a dense rosette of long, narrow, arching leaves, with sweetly fragrant spring flowers clustered on long "spears."*

Zone 10 30 to 40°F (-1 to 4°C)

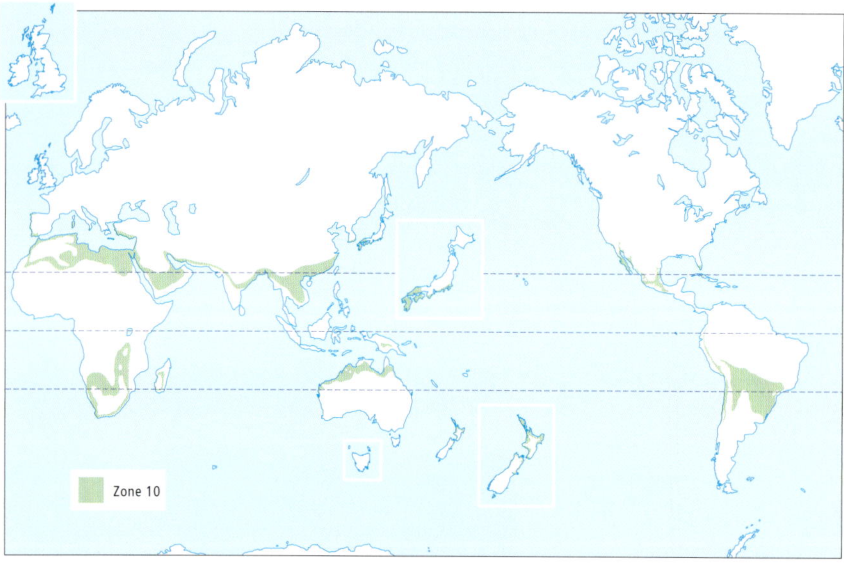

Zone 10 offers the adventurous horticulturist great possibilities. To many gardeners it is horticultural Mecca. The mild climate is influenced both by moist maritime air and dry continental air, resulting in a complex patchwork of microclimates that support a remarkable diversity of plants. Everything seems to grow here with ease.

This zone is characterized by cool wet winters and hot dry summers. It is the climate found around parts of the Mediterranean Sea in Europe and North Africa, and four other regions of the world: southern California in the USA, central Chile in South America, northwestern Australia, and southern areas of South Africa. Mountains provide a buffer from the cold continental air of Zone 9, and distance from the equator diminishes the moist tropical air that brings summer storms to Zone 11. Nevertheless, Zone 10, if based strictly on minimum winter temperatures, does includes some regions with summer monsoons: southern Florida in the USA, northern Australia, eastern South Africa, and parts of South America and Mexico.

Right: The many-petalled red flowers of Opuntia ficus-indica *appear all year round, making this an attractive species, as well as useful; its fruit are an important source of food in some African countries.*

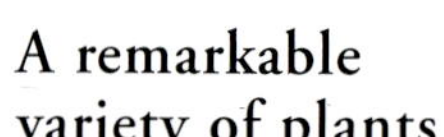

Below: Cistus ladanifer *is native to the southwestern Mediterranean region and North Africa. Ladanum is exuded through the leaves, leaving them sticky; hence its name gum cistus.*

A remarkable variety of plants

There are a number of reasons for the staggering variety of Zone 10 plants. The major factor is climate, an understanding of which can be invaluable in their successful cultivation in the garden. The climate of this zone is far from homogeneous. Diverse topography interacting with latitude and elevation, as well as varying degrees of maritime or continental influence, result in a multitude of climate variations that are characterized by average minimum temperatures of 30 to 40°F (-1 to 4°C). Such variation allows the cultivation of temperate trees like beeches and birches alongside tropical-looking philodendrons and cannas, if one is so inclined.

Along the coast and in isolated thermal belts (that is, neither in the cold sinks of the valleys nor the exposed higher elevations) frost is rare, restricted to cold spells in cycles of 10, 20, or even 50 years. Further inland, even just 10 or 15 miles (16 or 24 km), several light frosts a year may be typical. However, these are rarely below 30°F (-1°C) and don't last more than an hour or two in the predawn. Along the coast, summer temperatures normally peak between 70 and 86°F (21 and 30°C). In the inland valleys, highs of more than 95°F (35°C) or 100°F (38°C) are not uncommon. Rare heat spells bring temperatures of 113°F (45°C) or higher.

Rainfall in the zone varies from desert levels (under 5 in/12 cm per year) in the shadow of coastal mountain ranges to coastal areas that receive about 15 in (38 cm) per year. Parts of northern Australia and South America in this zone can receive considerably more than this. Humidity decreases with distance from the coast, though fingers of fog can creep many miles inland and can be a vital source of moisture. Cool drizzly days can be followed by scorching ones, with high atmospheric pressure, dry winds, and temperatures of 90°F (32°C) or more. Clearly, plants that demand more uniform conditions are not happy outside of protective greenhouses or shade structures.

Predominant growth forms

The range of possible adaptations for survival in Zone 10 is manifest in four predominant growth forms: annuals, geophytes, xeromorphic woody plants, and succulents.There are thousands of species of annuals native to the zone, and the California poppy *(Eschscholzia californica)* is a well known representative of Zones 9 and 10. As an ecological strategy, annuals are masters of avoidance, surviving the characteristic long dry season of most Zone 10 climates in the form of seed. This seed easily endures a few months of drought until rains return. In some cases, seeds can survive for years to outlive longer cycles of drought. African daisies *(Dimorphotheca)*, godetias *(Clarkia)*, *Nemesia*, and *Schizanthus* include some of the loveliest examples of the annual strategy.

Geophytes are a group of plants that survive prolonged drought by means of perennial underground bulbs, tubers, or fleshy stems. This group reaches the zenith of its diversity in Zone 10. An example is the iris (Iridaceae) family, especially diverse in South Africa, which is spectacular in its variety of form and color. This family includes some of the most distinctive floral forms

Right: Live oaks, Quercus virginiana, *are valued for their heavy, hard, and strong timber. Spanish moss,* Tillandsia usneoides, *an epiphytic rootless plant, hangs from their branches—a common sight in the Deep South of the USA.*

in the plant kingdom: irises, moraeas, gladioli, and more.

An ubiquitous plant from this zone is the oleander *(Nerium).* Native to a broad range of regions from the Mediterranean to Japan, *Nerium oleander* is representative of the dominant growth form of Zone 10: that is, a woody shrub with one or more water-conserving (xeromorphic) adaptations that aid in surviving drought. Some trees also have these adaptations. Other distinctive examples of Zone 10 shrubs include *Ceanothus, Alyogyne* and rosemary.

Other woody plants display different designs for reducing water loss: felty or waxy leaves, water-storing spongy wood, prickly armature for protection, photosynthetic stems, or thick corky bark—an adaptation taken to the extreme in the cork oak, *Quercus suber.*

A fourth universally known Zone 10 growth form is the succulent. Succulents represent a conspicuously different variation on the theme of drought adaptation. The jade plant *(Crassula ovata)* is much loved by windowsill gardeners throughout the temperate Northern Hemisphere, but it is native to Zone 10 in South Africa. There, and in similar climates, the jade plant can grow as tall as a person. Other familiar succulents include the aeoniums and the kalanchoes.

Among succulents, too, adaptations are often combined for best advantage. Succulent leaves with a thick waxy cuticle give some echeverias a magical quality when they capture mercurial-looking droplets of water in their waxy-leafed rosettes. Other species display various protective coverings of hairs or spines and photosynthetic stems (the universally recognized cacti and their look-alike convergent euphorbias); tuberous roots and swollen stems (caudiciforms from more than a dozen different plant families); and a specialized physiology that allows them to keep their pores closed during the heat of the day to avoid water loss found in all succulents including the bromeliads and many orchids.

Gardening in the zone

Soils are as diverse as topography and rock types, but are typically neutral to basic in pH. This means soils may require acidification for plants such as azaleas. Neutral to basic soils can pose a problem for some Australian species that are, paradoxically, adapted to acid soils *and* drought. However, normal soil-building practices using organic matter are usually ample for most plants.

Careful microclimate selection can afford success with some of the more challenging plants for this zone, such as *Lithodora diffusa* from North Africa and Mediterranean Europe with its gentian-blue star-shaped flowers. Members of the Proteaceae family from South Africa and western Australia may require generous application of iron sulfate or other acidifying measures in the garden. Plant pests and diseases are rarely a problem these days given proper culture and selection of appropriate disease-resistant varieties.

Above: Andalusia, Spain, is characterized by hot temperatures and rivers that habitually dry up in the summer. Despite its semi-arid climate, its chalk-rich soil makes this a suitable area for wine-production.

Zone 11 40 to 50°F (4 to 10°C)

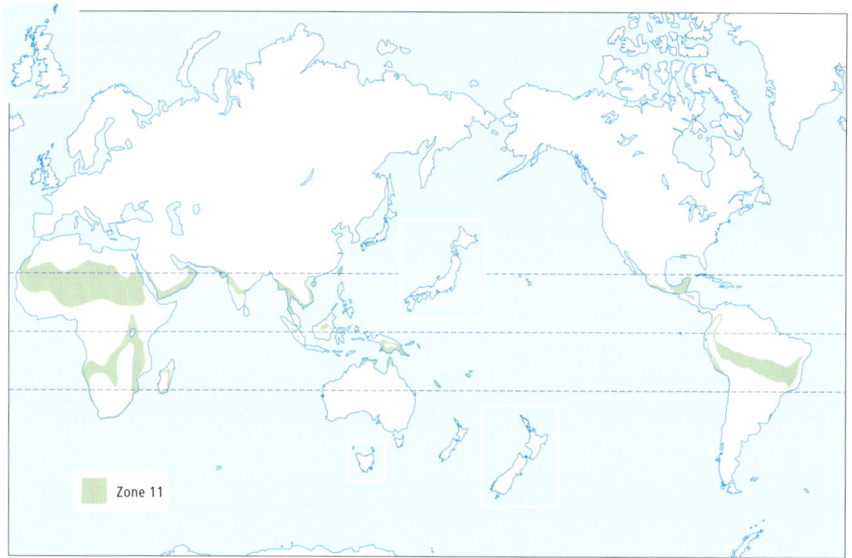

Of the twelve hardiness zones, Zones 11 and 12 represent tropical areas where frost, or even severe chilling, are never issues. Zone 11 is distinguished from its warmer counterpart, however, by the potential for very cool weather, where it is not astonishing for temperatures to fall below 50°F (10°C).

As this zone covers the transition from warm temperate and subtropical climates to tropical equatorial, its climate and plant life are far from uniform. Zone 11 includes three distinct regional types: cooler montane areas near the equator; cool tropical lowlands more distant from the equator (nearer the Tropic of Capricorn in the South and the Tropic of Cancer in the North); and certain oceanic islands outside the tropics. Consequently, vegetation native to Zone 11 has many biogeographic affinities, and varies greatly: from plants characteristic of wet tropical rainforest found near the equator, to those more at home in desert and scrub, such as is found along the 20th parallel of Africa.

Below: This remarkable plant is a member of the Nepenthes *genus, commonly known as pitcher plants. These carnivorous plants have large specialized leaves, "pitchers", whose rim is covered with slippery wax.*

Mountainous tropics

In equatorial mountain areas such as Nairobi, Kenya and Caracas, Venezuela, the day to night temperature differential will be significant; as much as 18 to 22°F (10 to 12°C). For example, in Caracas, the January average daily maximum of 75°F (24°C) yields to an average daily minimum of 56°F (13°C); in Nairobi the difference is equally as marked. The average high for January is 77°F (25°C), while the average low is 54°F (12°C). However, the temperature tends to be moderate throughout the year. In many equatorial mountain areas, rainfall may be high, but in many places patterns of rainfall will often create a distinct "summer"—that is, dry season.

If accompanied by high rainfall throughout the year, such as in the sub-mountain and mountainous areas of Central and South America, the vegetation can be rife with epiphytic orchids such as *Miltoniopsis*, *Sobralia*, and *Odontoglossum,* as well as bromeliads such as *Guzmania* and *Aechmea.* These habitats frequently involve cloud forest (areas drenched by mist and condensation from low clouds), which further increases the density of epiphytes. Cloud forests also occur in limited areas of Africa, though epiphytes are less evident. In Tanzania, for example, the African violet is a native of the mountain regions of the zone. Though not as moist, the high ground of Ethiopia is the native habitat for coffee *(Coffea arabica),* the cultivation or which characterizes both Zones 10 and 11 today.

Cool tropical lowlands

On the nonequatorial edges of the zone, the climate is subtropical and warm-temperate. Unlike the mountain equatorial zones that have a moderate climate and moisture regimen, the cooler temperatures near the Tropic of Cancer or the Tropic of Capricorn arrive seasonally. This cooler tropical climate also occurs away from the equator where maritime influence is great, especially on islands, such as Malta (35°N), and Bermuda and Madeira (32°N).

Areas of the zone closer to the cooler tropics are often characterized by marked dry seasons, as in Calcutta in India. One expects seasonal forest to be less layered and not as tall as wet forest, with a higher presence of deciduous material.

Many locations classified as Zone 11 receive sparse or no rainfall and are desert, as in parts of tropical Africa, such as Faya-Largeau in Chad, and Khartoum in Sudan, Namibia in southwest Africa, or Antofagasto in Chile. From the desert of southern Saudi Arabia come frankincense *(Boswellia sacra)* and myrrh *(Commiphora myrrha),* and one encounters the fabulous *Welwitschia mirabilis* in Namibia, along the southwestern coast of Africa where the heat of this zone is cooled by ocean currents.

Right: Pandanus aquaticus *is found in much of northern Australia. Turtles eat the fruit yet pass the seeds intact, aiding in their dispersal.*

Gardening in the zone

Horticulturally (as contrasted with the warmer Zone 12), one recognizes wet areas of Zone 11 for their ability to support cultivation of some temperate garden plants. Roses, evergreen azaleas *(Rhodendron* spp.*)*, and hydrangeas survive but are not at their best, while nasturtiums *(Tropaeolum)* and impatiens, which do not thrive in Zone 12, will perform well. Cool-crop vegetable production and cut flower production begin in Zone 11, both industries developing yet more thoroughly in cooler zones at yet higher altitudes. Dry climates in Zone 11 will support a Mediterranean plant palette, or succulent plants and dryland gardening such as one encounters in more subtropical areas.

Being transitional, Zone 11 is best identified in contrast with Zones 10 and 12. Tropical plants that can be cultivated successfully in Zone 10 (at the risk of an occasional killing frost) should thrive in Zone 11. Plants from dry tropical and subtropical climates will likely thrive in this zone as compared to Zone 12.

However, the most cool-sensitive of lowland tropical plants, especially plants that benefit from warm nights, like cocoa *(Theobroma cacao)* or breadfruit *(Artocarpus)*, or even vanilla *(Vanilla planifolia)* and the various spice trees, are not at their best in this zone. One would not plan to grow true Zone 12 plants such as sealing-wax palm *(Cyrtostachys renda)* or pride of Burma *(Amherstia nobilis)* in the landscape. On the other hand, Zone 11 gardeners can bask in the glory of fuchsias and sensational aroids, such as the *Anthurium veitchii* and *A. warocqueanum,* sometimes referred to as the king and queen anthuriums, respectively, due to their magnificent foliage.

For those who have a moist climate, this is truly the orchid and epiphyte zone, where thousands of species and cultivars of orchids and bromeliads can be grown with modest effort. Gardeners in drier areas can enjoy the pleasure of growing many succulents and honorary succulents that are problematic in more temperate climates, such as *Adansonia.* Landscapes with good rainfall, but a strong dry season, would well support material from the seasonal savannas of Africa (such as *Cussonia* species and *Coccinea*) and South America *(Tabebuia, Jacaranda),* as well as Mexico and into Central America *(Cochlospermum)*—much of which is easily found in the trade.

Even though an incredibly wide range of plant material exists that is completely appropriate for Zone 11, comparatively little effort has been dedicated to "bringing plants into cultivation." It would be exciting and practical to see more work dedicated to the logical and sensitive development of a variety of appropriate plant palates and horticultural techniques for this zone.

Left: The large dramatic spathes of Anthurium andraeanum *make it popular for cultivation in tropical areas. In cooler areas, anthuriums can be grown indoors. The spathes are mostly glossy red, but pink varieties also exist.*

Zone 12 50 to 60°F (10 to 16°C)

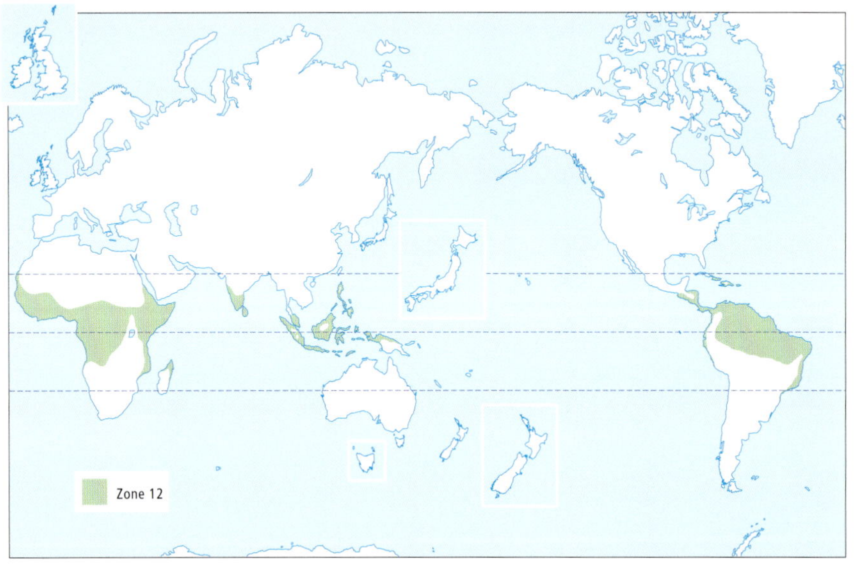

Zone 12 covers much of the area north and south of the equator to latitude 20°. It includes vast regions in the tropical lowlands of South America, the Caribbean, Africa, northern Madagascar, tropical Asia, and Hawaii. Of all the zones, it is the most conducive to plant growth, experiencing neither frosts nor severe dry seasons. Maximum temperature ranges from 79 to 100°F (26 to 38°C) and minimum temperature ranges from a pleasant 50 to 60°F (10 to 16°C). Relative humidity averages at about 80 percent, dropping to around 60 percent in the drier months during the day. Night temperatures often remain above 50°F (10°C) in the lowlands, but drop below this in mountainous regions, which thus are rated Zone 11.

Annual rainfall in the ever-wet tropics exceeds 80 in (200 cm). Although monthly averages vary from year to year, the driest months have not less than 24 in (60 cm) of rain and the dry season usually does not persist for more than three or four consecutive months. Rainfall patterns vary with topography, prevailing winds, and distance from the coast, as well as yearly fluctuations.

Below: This bromeliad Tillandsia lieboldiana, produces purple and red flowers. It is shown here at the Jardîn Botânico Lankester, near Cartago, Costa Rica.

A combination of high rainfall and high temperatures results in heavily weathered soils (frequently red earth laterites) with low fertility. The exception is volcanic soils, which, for example, support intensive wet rice culture in Java and the Philippines.

A vibrant and rich ecosystem

The forests in Zone 12 are some of the most species-rich ecosystems in the world, being home to an estimated one-third of the world's 249,500 species of flowering plants, with many species yet to be found. Vegetation types are primarily determined by water regime and soil and can vary from swamp forests and rainforest in areas of year-round rain, to more open semi-deciduous forest in areas with a pronounced dry season.

Most plants are evergreen but few plants are truly aseasonal, that is, grow at a continuous rate, exceptions being papaya *(Carica papaya),* pineapple *(Ananas comosus),* and banana *(Musa* cultivars*),* among the tropical fruits. Even for herbs, perennial rather than annual is the norm. The exception are weeds, some of which are super-annuals with life cycles as short as eight weeks, so six to seven generations exist in a year. Weeds, however, depend on humans to create ephemeral disturbed conditions. Only a handful can compete in the rainforest.

Although there are broad similarities between the plant families of South America, Africa, and tropical Asia, at the genus and particularly at the species level there are more differences than similarities. The mahogany, the rubber tree, sapodillas, and fig families are found in tropical rainforests across the zone, as are the myrtle, laurel, and nutmeg families, although Africa has fewer examples of plants in these last three families. Shrubs belonging to the acanthus and tibouchina families and herbs like the aroid, African violet, orchids, fern, and spikemoss families also grow across the zone. Each continent has more of some families than others: for example, South America has more bromeliads and heliconias; Asia is noted for dipterocarps and gingers, and Africa for the cacao family.

Reaching for the light

Most of the plants above grow in the multilayered tropical rainforests. The topmost layer is formed of scattered giant emergent trees, such as the dipterocarps, which grow 100–165 ft (30–50 m) tall. Underneath is the continuous high to middle tree-canopy layer with trees of 35–80 ft (10–24 m) tall, which include fruit and nut trees like durian, rambutan, and the brazil nut, followed by a third canopy layer of smaller and immature trees of the upper canopy. Characteristic of these rainforest trees are giant buttress roots that anchor them to the ground and those that flower and fruit from the trunk, such as the jackfruit and cannonball tree, which have weighty fruits too heavy to be borne on twigs.

Conditions below the tree canopy are extremely uniform for the shrub and herb layers. Here temperatures are about 5 degrees lower than outside the forest, and the relative humidity is frequently 100 percent. Little wind and only about 1–3 percent of sunlight penetrates to the forest floor. Hundreds of species with brilliantly colored or variegated leaves, like begonias, calatheas, and peperomias, thrive in the damp and deep shade.

Large woody climbers (lianas), such as the jade vine or garlic vine, whose thick woody vinelike stems carry photosynthesizing leaf growth up into the canopy, and strangler figs, add to the complexity. So do the epiphytes, which includes many orchids (a large tropical family that comprises about 10 percent of all flowering plant species) and ferns growing in the high canopy. Characteristic, too, are the giant monocots, such as the palms, pandangs *(Pandanus),* bananas, and heliconias.

In semideciduous forest, the emergent trees are smaller (up to 100 ft/30 m tall) and less frequent than in rainforest. About a quarter of them are deciduous for periods of a few weeks. In some areas, the canopy is open with grasses and herbs in the ground layer. Several tree species, like teak and *Albizia,* also grow in monsoon regions.

Many plantation crops of the zone are grown outside their native regions to escape indigenous pests and diseases. For example, the major world production of oil palm *(Elaeis guineensis),* a native of West Africa, and rubber *(Hevea brasiliensis),* a native from South America, is in Asia. Bananas and cloves *(Syzygium aromaticum)* from Asia are more widely grown in the Caribbean and Zanzibar, respectively.

A zone to think big

Gardeners in Zone 12 can think big with majestic flowering trees, massive climbers, giant palms, and a superb display of herbs. Plants from South America such as the rain tree *(Albizia saman)* and royal palms *(Roystonea)* are grown across the zone. So, too, are the African tulip tree *(Spathodea campanulata)* from Africa, the yellow flame tree *(Peltophorum pterocarpum)* and queen crape myrtle *(Lagerstroemia speciosa)* from Asia, and the royal poinciana *(Delonix regia)* from Madagascar.

Canopy plants such as orchids can be grown in shade houses. Most understory forest plants, such as aroids, need deep shade. Provided understory plants adapt to low humidity, they also make ideal house plants and the spectacular foliage of begonias and monsteras, for example, provide year-round interest.

Heavy rain and high temperatures can lead to heavy nutrient-depleted soil. Trees help to mitigate the beating of raindrops on the soil and so reduce runoff. Organic fertilizers and mulch also help to maintain soil fertility.

Plants that require a distinct dry season, such as jacaranda *(Jacaranda mimosifolia)* and Indian senna *(Cassia fistula)* will not give a showy flowering display. Hybridization has overcome this in bougainvilleas.

Plants that require a dry resting season, such as *Curcuma* species, may not flower or even survive beyond the first season. For cacti, a clear roof and free draining soil is necessary to prevent their roots rotting in high rainfall conditions.

Outside the zone, greenhouses are needed in frost regions, as well as lighting to compensate for shorter daylight hours, the lack of which accounts for the spindly growth of some tropical plants, such as papaya.

Above: Dipterocarp trees, in the wild, Borneo. Some of these remarkable trees can grow to 200 ft (60 m) in the wild. They are important in Malaysia, where they provide the country's main source of timber.

Left: Plumeria rubra *is native to Central America, Mexico, and Venezuela. It makes a lovely specimen tree in tropical zones, and there are numerous cultivars. 'Rosy Dawn', shown here, bears yellow flowers flushed with pink.*

Plant Nomenclature

It is remarkable that a naming system devised over 250 years ago should still be the best way for people around the world to talk about a plant, confident in the knowledge that everyone will know exactly which plant is being discussed. Common names, though often very evocative, are not reliable as they vary from place to place, country to country, and language to language. For example, in the British Isles, the plant called the bluebell in Scotland is not the same as the bluebell of England. The only unambiguous and reliable name for any plant is its Latin-based botanical name.

Right: Carolus Linnaeus, 1707–1778, Swedish botanist, naturalist, and explorer. His Species Plantarum *established the use of a binomial naming system that could be applied to all species, including humans. Portrait by Johan Henrik Scheffel, 1690–1781.*

The history of botanical nomenclature

Early in human history it was found useful to know which plants were good for food, which were poisonous, and so on. And it was soon noticed that these plants possessed certain consistent features by which they could be recognized. To begin with this information was passed on by word of mouth but eventually it began to be written down. When the first printed books appeared in Europe Latin was the international language used by scholars. By the eighteenth century the Latin names of plants had generally become short descriptions that enabled people to recognize plants and distinguish one from another. For instance, the famous Swedish biologist Carolus Linnaeus gave a *Gladiolus* species the name *Gladiolus foliis linearibus, floribus distantibus, coroallarum tubo limbis longiore* (Gladiolus with very narrow leaves, flowers widely spaced, and the tube of the corolla longer than the width of the upper spreading part). At the time this brief description was sufficient to distinguish this plant from all other known species of *Gladiolus*. However, even Linnaeus soon found this convention cumbersome when speaking about plants and also very awkward when compiling indices to his books. In an attempt to simplify the matter he gave each plant a number, so that students, scientists, and others could refer to it simply. For instance, the *Gladiolus* mentioned above became *'Gladiolus* no. 4', but numbers in general are harder to remember than words and, in any case, the scheme was of no use to anyone who did not have Linnaeus's book. His next step was to add a second word instead of a number, often taking the word from the Latin descriptive phrase. In the case of *Gladiolus* no. 4 it was *angustus*, a Latin word meaning narrow in reference to its leaves. Thus *'Gladiolus'* is the name of the genus and *'angustus,'* is known as the 'specific' epithet.

The plant thus acquired a two-word or binomial name, *Gladiolus angustus*, and although he was not the first to use such binomials, Linnaeus used them from 1745 onward, before applying them consistently to the whole of the plant kingdom known to him in his *Species Plantarum* of 1753. The principal object of this book, however, was not to introduce binomial nomenclature but to provide a concise usable survey of all known plants. By writing in Latin he made his work known immediately to the whole learned world of his day. Had he written in Swedish his work would probably have passed unnoticed.

And a success his system proved to be. In the tenth edition of his *Systema Naturae*, published in 1758, he gave binomials to all known animal species including us, *Homo sapiens*, "man the wise."

Botanical names of plants are printed in italics or at least in a typeface different from that of the rest of the text. Also, if there is no chance of confusion, the name of the genus is abbreviated to the initial letter the second and subsequent times the name is used. The name of the genus should always have a capital initial letter and that of the specific epithet should be in lower case, even when derived from a proper noun or a person's name.

Below: The conventions of the binomial system are simple and few: Rosa banksiae, *the parent of this cultivar 'Lutea', was named after Lady Banks, the wife of Sir Joseph Banks. Though a proper noun, the specific epithet is always in lower case.*

Linnaeus worked at a time when exploration and colonialism had made it possible for him to examine plants and animals from many parts of the world. Even then the task was immense and, in all, he coined Latin or Latin-form names for roughly 4,400 species of animals and 7,700 species of plants. Had he lived today, when over 800,000 animal species and more than 260,000 vascular plants (plants with internal conducting systems) have been described and named in accordance with his unambiguous and internationally understandable system, the whole enterprise would have been impossible for one man to complete. As it was, he had planned to share the task of making known what he considered all the works of the Maker in an orderly manner with his friend Petrus Artede. They divided up the work, entering into a pact that if one died the other would finish the task. As it turned out Artede fell into a canal in Amsterdam in 1736 and drowned, with only a book on the fishes published, leaving Linnaeus to deal with everything else.

Above: Though Linnaeus aspired to classify all living things, the task was done by many—with inevitable overlaps. For 100 years this plant was known as Rhododendron aucklandii, *the name given it by J. D. Hooker in his* Rhododendrons of the Sikkim Himalayas, *published in 1851. It was later discovered, however, that a surgeon in India,* Robert Wight, *had published a description of the plant in 1847, and named it* R. griffithianum, *by which it is now known.*

How the naming system works

Linnaeus's writings are therefore the starting point for the nomenclature of many groups of organisms, plants being just one. As well as establishing the recognized system for naming and describing them, Linnaeus also discussed a hierarchy of groups or ranks that share common characters, but he never really used them. Subsequently naturalists have not only grouped the species into genera, but also the genera into families, the families into orders, the orders into classes, and the classes into kingdoms. More categories have been interpolated into this hierarchy as is shown below for the classification of a well-known *Rhododendron* species.

Not surprisingly, considering the scientific advances of the past 250 years, the vascular plants are now classified on the basis of characteristics very different from those employed by Linnaeus. They are divided into two major groups, the Spermatophyta, the seed plants, and the Pteridophyta, plants that reproduce by means of spores. The Spermatophyta in turn are divided into two, the Angiospermae (usually loosely referred to as flowering plants), with 249,500 species in over 13,100 genera in 405 families, and the Gymnospermae, containing some 840 species in 86 genera in 17 families. The Gymnospermae, a diverse group of plants whose seeds are not enclosed in carpels and so do not produce flowers, are divided into four groups: the Pinopsida (conifers), Cycadopsida (cycads), Ginkgoopsida *(Ginkgo)* and the Gnetopsida *(Ephedra, Gnetum,* and *Welwitschia).* The Pteridophyta—spore-producing plants—with 9,800 species in 230 or so genera in 38 families include the Filicopsida (ferns), Lycopsida (clubmosses), Psilotopsida (psilophytes), and Equisetopsida (horsetails).

Kingdom	Plantae
Division	Angiospermae
Class	Dicotyledonae
Subclass	Rosidae
Order	Ericales
Family	Ericaceae
Subfamily	Rhododendroideae
Tribe	Rhododendreae
Genus	*Rhododendron*
Subgenus	Hymenanthes
Section	Ponticum
Subsection	Arborea
Species	*Rhododendron arboreum*
Subspecies	*Rhododendron arboreum* subsp. *delavayi*
Variety	*Rhododendron arboreum* subsp. *delavayi* var. *delavayi*

Below: Rhododendron arboreum *subsp.* delavayi

Left: Gladiolus murielae *was previously known as* Acidanthera bicolor *var.* murielae. *Among its common names are Abyssinian sword lily, fragrant gladiolus, and peacock flower.*

On the whole it is only the names of genera, species, and sometimes the families that are of interest to most horticulturists. At times, though, the ranks below that of species are of significance from a horticultural point of view. A species may be divided into subspecies when its characters vary noticeably across a wide geographic range, as in the case of *Rhododendron arboreum* given previously. Likewise, a variety differs in a minor but distinct way from the typical species. The lowest rank of all is that known as "form." It is rarely used nowadays but in the past has been applied to plants showing very minor differences from the typical species, such as variations in flower or leaf color.

Below: Citrus × aurantium. *Convention states that the name of a plant known to be a hybrid between two species should always include the symbol '×' in front of the species name.*

Cumbersome though it might appear, it sometimes, though mercifully rarely, happens that names in all three of these minor categories are used in order of rank in the name of a plant.

In order for a plant name to be accepted it must be of Latin form and be published in a recognized journal or book along with a description in Latin based on a particular specimen, known as the type specimen, which must be preserved in a recognized museum or herbarium. This ensures that there can never be any doubt as to the plant to which the name applies. The type specimens of plants are therefore almost invariably dried specimens kept in a herbarium. This is why taxonomic botanists often have to spend more time with dead dried specimens than with living plants.

Horticulturists, gardeners, and others are disturbed upon discovering that the name by which they have known a plant for years has been changed. The naming of plants is governed by *The International Code of Botanical Nomenclature*, the aim of which is to provide a stable method of naming plant groups, avoiding and rejecting the use of names that may cause error and ambiguity. Among the principles of the *Code* are those which state that each plant or group of plants may have only one correct name and that where more than one botanical name has been applied, it is the earliest to have been published in print that is correct.

Botanical names may appear to change if it turns out that a plant in cultivation has been misidentified. As an example, for many years a South African composite grown in European rock gardens was called *Euryops evansii*. But when it was examined critically it was found not to be that species at all, but really *Euryops acraeus*, which is the name used for it today. Names also change when research reveals that plants should be classified differently. For example, names change if a species is moved from the genus in which it was originally placed, or when two formerly recognized species are shown not to be sufficiently distinct and are merged, or when it has been shown that one species should be split into two or more. Recent work on the iris family has shown that species of *Acidanthera* are really species of *Gladiolus* and that species of *Anomatheca* belong in *Freesia*. Nowadays the use of DNA sequencing is giving taxonomic botanists a more reliable picture of the relationships between plants and will undoubtedly have a major effect on the future naming of plants.

In the case of the well-known plant names that have been widely and unambiguously used for many years, such that changing of them would be costly as well as destabilizing, exceptions can be made, and a name conserved. For example, a striking example of where international agreement has had happy consequences concerns plants originally placed in the genus *Chrysanthemum,* which have been undergone various classifications and names since the time of Linnaeus. The most confronting of these changes came from the discovery 30 or so years ago that the perennial garden chrysanthemums did not belong in the same genus as the cultivated annual species. This meant that if the annuals were still to be called *Chrysanthemum*, then the perennials would have to be placed in a separate genus, for which the earliest correct name is *Dendranthema*.

Reflecting widespread concern over this, the committee accepted that the name *Chrysanthemum* should accommodate the perennial garden plants, much to the relief of gardeners everywhere. But the unavoidable consequence of this is that the annual species, which still have to be put in a separate genus, have to be renamed *Xanthophthalmum,* the earliest name for them outside *Chrysanthemum.*

Naming hybrids and cultivars

The names of hybrid plants in the wild or in cultivation (where their parentage is known), have an "×" inserted between the generic and specific epithets. For example, oranges and grapefruits are hybrids between the shaddock or pomelo *(Citrus maxima)* and the mandarin *(Citrus reticulata)* and are included under the hybrid name, *Citrus* × *aurantium.* There are other conventions for the names of plants found only in cultivation. These plants are variants of wild species or plants of hybrid origin and are known collectively as cultivated varieties or cultivars. The use of the word "variety" for these plants must be avoided as this is used for a category in the accepted hierarchy of botanical classification outlined above.

To avoid confusion in the naming of cultivars, any person thinking of giving a name to a new cultivar should consult the *International Code for the Nomenclature of Cultivated Plants*, a set of recommendations along the lines of the *International Code of Botanical Nomenclature.* Under the rules of this *Code*, the full name of a cultivar is the accepted Latin botanical name of the plant followed by what is known as the cultivar epithet. To distinguish them from botanical names, cultivar epithets are not written in italics and are enclosed within single quotation marks, for example *Gardenia augusta* 'Magnifica'. Double quotation marks or the abbreviations "cv." and "var." should not be used to distinguish cultivar names.

It is usual for all words, with the exception of articles or prepositions, in the cultivar name to have an initial capital letter, for example *Rhododendron* 'Beauty of Littleworth'. Amongst its other recommendations, the *Code* also proposes that new cultivar names should consist of no more than ten syllables and no more than 30 characters overall, excluding spaces and demarcation marks.

These simple practices can be used by breeders everywhere. Unfortunately, some nurserymen tend not to use recognized cultivar names when they consider them to be unsuitable for selling purposes and give trade names to their plants instead.

While these trade names may help with sales, they can also be confusing. There are many instances of the same plant appearing in different catalogs under several names, as unsatisfactory as using common names outside of anything but a small area. Hopefully, with increased awareness of the work of Linnaeus and the *International Code for the Nomenclature of Cultivated Plants,* greater appreciation will develop for this remarkable system.

Left: Tulipa, *Lily-flowered Group, 'Queen of Sheba'. Owing to the thousands of cultivars now available, tulips are divided into 15 broad groups, such as Lily-flowered, as well as given a specific cultivar name.*

Below: Gardenia augusta *'Magnifica'. The cultivar name differs from a botanical epithet in its style of printing. It has initial capitals, is in a different typeface, and is usually enclosed in single quotation marks.*

Plant Geography, Discovery, and Classification

Right: In medieval times, inconsistencies such as the problem of "extinct" plants and animals known only from fossils were explained away by suggestions that they had merely changed their distribution and would be found alive again once the world had been fully explored.

Below: Spore-producing plants include horsetails like Equisetum arvense, *ferns, and club mosses.*

In medieval times it was widely thought that the world's animals and plants were stable entities, unchanging over time and place. Many attempts were made to match local European plants with those in the Bible, for example. With greater traveling, however, it was found that no such homogeneity existed. Since that time, evolutionary theories, allowing for change in time and space, have been proposed. Darwin's theory of evolution by natural selection, formulated in the 1850s, is now accepted so that, although there is still much to learn, we can now interpret fossils and modern plant distributions to explain the history of groups of plants.

Origin of ferns and seed plants

The oldest known land plants with vascular systems are fossils from the Devonian period (some 370 million years ago). Traces of their form can still be seen in some modern ferns, notably species of *Psilotum* found in tropical and other warm parts of the world. Today's ferns, like those ancient plants, still reproduce by spores spread by wind. It was not the ferns that were to form the ecosystems in which humans evolved, however, but those plants derived from ancient fernlike groups: the seed-producing plants.

A seed, in essence, is a tiny plant in suspended animation sealed up in an environment-proof coat. It is formed from fertilization of an egg in an ovule held on an adult plant. In contrast, fertilization of the egg of a spore plant takes place in the open and requires water for the sperms to travel to it. This crucial evolutionary difference gave seed plants the edge. Though many seed plant groups have died out, modern seed plants appear to be more closely related to one another than they are to modern spore plants. Today, the most significant, both ecologically and economically, of the seed plants are the conifers and, above all, the angiosperms, or the "flowering plants."

Left: The genus Liriodendron *has only two species.* L. tulipifera, *left, is found east of the Mississippi River, USA, while* L. chinense *is native to China.*

Plant distribution

The shearing apart in the Cretaceous Period (about 100 million years ago) of what are now the continents of Australia and Antarctica and what was to become India and finally Africa, from South America, coincided with the divergence of the angiosperms away from other seed plants and into a number of lineages. From this time, there are fossils of plants, which, if they occurred today, could be put in families we now recognize in the world's flora.

The effect of these continental movements on plant distribution is only now being fully assessed, but it is clear that, despite their seed-dispersal mechanisms, some groups of plants failed to reach some of the receding continents. Certain families are found, for example, only in the Americas or with very few recent extensions to Africa, as is the case with Cactaceae and Bromeliaceae. Even very widespread families like Asteraceae have scarcely reached New Caledonia.

On to these basic patterns is superimposed the effects of climatic change of more recent times, notably those of the advancing and contracting ice sheets. These have pushed apart, and then allowed to come back together again in some cases, whole assemblages of plants. The apparent similarity of species of *Liriodendron* and *Magnolia* in the floras of the eastern USA and of East Asia can be explained in this way.

Classification

To comprehend the great diversity of the world's flora, past and present, a system of classification is essential. The great age of cataloging the world's animals and plants was during the eighteenth century, which saw, among other things, the publication of Linnaeus's great system of binomial plant classification, *Species Plantarum*, in 1753.

The system of classification established by Linnaeus hinged on the numbers of stamens and pistils in the flowers. It contains several groupings of plants we recognize today, for example, most temperate legumes (Fabaceae) fall into Decandria Monogynia (ten stamens and one pistil). However, also in that group are many other plants we would not now consider closely allied. The reason is that this

Left: Improved greenhouse technology in the nineteenth century led to the scouring of tropical regions for orchids, ferns, and other exotica. This engraving from that century is of The Victoria Glasshouse, Van Houtte Gardens, Netherlands.

"artificial" system is based on the overriding importance of two basic features of the plants and, at this level of classification, ignores all other evidence. This system was never fully acceptable to the French school of science, which maintained "natural" systems invented before Linnaeus's time.

These natural systems attempted to assess all features of the plants. For example, many tropical plants in the family Fabaceae have different numbers of stamens but the "look" of the plants strongly suggests they belong together. Michel Adanson (1727–1806), and his fellow countryman, Adrien de Jussieu, based in Paris, established improved natural systems. By this time, most of the northern European flora had been discovered and named. From the sixteenth century onward, plants had been preserved as herbarium specimens and, therefore, it was no longer necessary to have to describe a new species from a living plant. The number of descriptions grew: from dried and living plants from the Mediterranean, Caribbean and North America, the Near East, Russia, and North and South Africa. In fact, European herbaria contained materials from tropical Southeast Asia and China, and even Australia, before 1700.

Plant introductions

People were interested in importing plants to grow as well as to classify. As living plants of the new species were introduced throughout the nineteenth century, there were horticultural fashions for North American plants, for Cape plants, Australian and, later, Chinese. By the end of that century, plants from almost every country in the world were being grown commercially in North America and Europe.

The First World War brought an end to this great accumulation. Introductions were now concentrated on hardy plants and more focused on the mass market rather than the exclusive connoisseur. Nonetheless, the rich and vainglorious, as well as public institutions, continued to support horticultural expeditions, especially to China and the Himalayas, the Andes, and the Near East.

Above: Charles Darwin, 1809–1882, English naturalist and author of On the Origin of Species, *which established the theory of natural selection. (Painting, 1858.)*

Hybridization

Throughout the great period of introductions, gardeners were selecting forms of plants with bigger or more brightly colored flowers or for larger or better-flavored fruits and so on. Although considered to be tampering with the work of the Maker, hybridization was championed by the Reverend William Herbert, Dean of Manchester, UK.

He was an important influence on the young Charles Darwin who made many hybrids himself and wrote about them at length in his *On the Origin of Species* (1859). In fact, Darwin's discussions with breeders gave him much evidence for his theory of natural selection, and he considered "artificial" selection as merely an extension of an all-pervading phenomenon.

What remains to be done?

Despite all this botanical and horticultural effort, new plants are still being introduced into horticulture all the time. But there are also plants not only to be introduced but also to be found. In developing countries, there are thousands of species of angiosperms still to be described. Many are known just as herbarium specimens and, no doubt, some of them will become extinct due to clearing of their native habitats before they are even named.

Botanists, skilled horticulturists, patrons, and gardeners are needed to help collect, describe, and thereby preserve, the world's plants for the benefit of all.

A

A

ABELIA

This decorative genus from the woodbine (Caprifoliaceae) family has about 30 ornamental shrubs, both evergreen and deciduous, and occurs across the Northern Hemisphere from eastern Asia to Mexico. Named after Dr Clarke Abel, a British physician and plant collector, the main features are glossy opposite leaves and funnelform or tubular flowers, white or pinkish, sometimes with orange blotches, through summer. Some species also have persistent reddish sepals which provide an additional ornamental feature after the flowers have faded. In the garden they can be planted singly in a shrub border or as a low informal hedge.

CULTIVATION: Propagate by soft-tip cuttings in spring or summer, or half-hardened cuttings in late autumn or winter. Plant in any well-drained, moderately fertile soil, in a sunny spot. Moderately frost hardy, prune in winter, removing some of the basal shoots to make room for new growth, plus the cane ends. Care should be taken to preserve the plant's naturally arching habit.

Abelia chinensis

☼ ❄ ↔8 ft (2.4 m) ↑6 ft (1.8 m)

From central and eastern China, a medium deciduous shrub with glossy green leaves. Moderately fragrant white flowers, tinted with rose, in late summer–autumn. Similar to the commonly grown *A.* × *grandiflora.* Zones 8–10.

Abelia 'Edward Goucher'

☼ ❄ ↔6 ft (1.8 m) ↑5 ft (1.5 m)

Raised in 1911, this hybrid between *A.* × *grandiflora* and *A. schumannii* is from USA. It is a small semi-evergreen shrub with bright glossy leaves, bronzed tinged when young. Lilac-pink flowers appear in summer–autumn. Pink calyces, 2-lobed. Zones 7–10.

Abelia floribunda

☼ ❄ ↔6 ft (1.8 m) ↑6 ft (1.8 m)

From Mexico. Evergreen, open habit. Leaves smaller, less glossy than *A.* × *grandiflora.* Pendulous clusters of pale rose to deep red flowers in summer–autumn. Persistent sepals. Zones 9–11.

Abelia × *grandiflora* ★

GLOSSY ABELIA

☼ ❄ ↔6 ft (1.8 m) ↑6 ft (1.8 m)

Evergreen shrub with arching canes, a hybrid between *A. chinensis* and *A. uniflora.* Reddish brown stems. Leaves dark green, turning red to orange in winter. Perfumed flowers flushed mauve-pink. **'Frances Mason'**, leaves heavily margined and suffused with yellow; **'Kaleidoscope'**, gold-edged leaves, bronze new growth, red stems, mounding to 5 ft (1.5 m) high and wide; **'Prostrata'**, low growing, to 24 in (60 cm) high; **'Sherwoodii'**, compact habit, to 4 ft (1.2 m) high; **'Snow Showers'**, cream-edged foliage, pink tinted in winter, white flowers, to 3 ft (0.9 m) high; **'Sunrise'**, to 6 ft (1.8 m) tall, attractive autumn foliage color. Zones 7–10.

Abelia chinensis

Abelia × *grandiflora,* in summer

Abelia schumannii

syn. *Abelia longituba*

SCHUMANN'S ABELIA

☼ ❄ ↔8 ft (2.4 m) ↑4 ft (1.2 m)

From China, this nearly evergreen shrub has pale green to dull green leaves, and pale rosy mauve flowers in clusters, with a broad white stripe and some orange spots on the lower lobe, produced summer–autumn. Zones 7–10.

ABELIOPHYLLUM

The name of this genus, of the olive (Oleaceae) family, is derived from *Abelia,* which it is said to resemble. It contains just one species of small deciduous shrub, closely related to *Forsythia,* bearing similar flowers in white. The shrub is native to the mountains of Korea, where it is becoming scarce.

CULTIVATION: The species will grow in a range of soil conditions but in cool temperate climates should be given a warm site. It can be trained against a wall if desired. Less vigorous old canes should be cut out. Prune every 2 to 3 years to maintain shape. Propagation is usually by half-hardened cuttings taken in summer or by layering in spring or autumn.

Abeliophyllum distichum

WHITE FORSYTHIA

☼ ✱ ↔6 ft (1.8 m) ↑3 ft (0.9 m)

This arching, straggly, deciduous shrub from Korea can be trained up a wall. Late winter, bare branches are smothered in fragrant, white, forsythia-like flowers that burst from pink-tinged buds. In some forms buds are a deeper shade with flowers emerging pale pink. Zones 5–10.

ABELMOSCHUS

This genus in the mallow (Malvaceae) family consists of about 15 species of annuals, perennials, and soft-wooded shrubs native to warmer parts of Asia and Africa. Closely allied to *Hibiscus,* it is distinguished by having flowers with a single bract wrapping around the base of the sepals, splitting down one side as the flower expands. Leaves usually maple-like or divided into finger-like lobes. Flowers often showy, in shades of pink, red, or yellow, and followed by elongated pods. An annual species grown as a vegetable is okra (or gumbo) *(A. esculentus).* Leafy young shoots of most *Abelmoschus* species can also be used as pot greens.

CULTIVATION: They like a sunny position sheltered from strong winds, and well-drained soil, fertilized in summer. Propagation is possible from basal cuttings as well as from seed sown as soon as weather is warm enough in late spring.

Abelmoschus manihot

syn. *Hibiscus manihot*

AIBIKA

☼ ❄ ↔3 ft (0.9 m) ↑3–6 ft (0.9–1.8 m)

Shrubby Southeast Asian perennial. Large, deeply lobed leaves. Pale yellow flowers with a dark purplish eye at the branch tips in summer. Zones 9–12.

ABIES

This genus in the pine (Pinaceae) family consists of about 50 species, occurring in the northern temperate zones of Europe, North Africa, Asia, and North America. Mostly long lived and medium to very tall, these evergreen conifers have long, narrow, smooth leaves in whorls on the

Abeliophyllum distichum

branches. Leaves are mid- to dark green, often with a grayish white band. Female cones are carried erect on upper branches, while the hanging male cones grow throughout the crown. Fully hardy, although frost damage can occur on juvenile foliage.
CULTIVATION: Best in neutral to acid, moist, fertile soil with good drainage in full sun; most tolerate some shade. Some, including *A. pinsapo*, tolerate alkaline soils. Some juvenile trees need shelter from cold winds. Adelgids and honey fungus can be a problem. Sow seed as it ripens, but needs to be stratified for 3 weeks for better germination. Graft cultivars in winter.

Abies amabilis, in the wild, in North Cascades National Park, Washington State, USA

Abies amabilis

BEAUTIFUL FIR, PACIFIC FIR

☼ ✱ ↔12–20 ft (3.5–6 m) ↑100 ft (30 m)

This conifer has glossy green leaves with grayish white stripes beneath, to 1 in (25 mm) long. Cones are egg-shaped, red to deep purple ripening to brown. Grows best in a cool moist climate and acid soil. Zones 5–9.

Abies balsamea

BALSAM FIR, DWARF BALSAM FIR

☼ ✱ ↔15 ft (4.5 m) ↑50 ft (15 m)

Conical tree with sleek gray bark and fragrant resin. Leaves dark green with whitish undersides. Cones cylindrical, purplish blue in color. A source of wood pulp in Canada, it is fairly short lived in gardens. Dwarf cultivars include **'Nana'** and the members of the **Hudsonia Group**. Zones 3–8.

Abies cephalonica

syn. *Abies apollinis*

GREEK FIR

☼ ✱ ↔25 ft (8 m) ↑100 ft (30 m)

Native to central and southern Greece, this pyramidal tree has dark green, rigid, slightly curved leaves with greenish white undersides. Cylindrical greenish brown cones are resinous. **'Meyer's Dwarf'**, with shorter leaves, forms a mound, only 20 in (50 cm) high, with a diameter to 10 ft (3 m). Zones 7–10.

Abies concolor

BLUE FIR, COLORADO WHITE FIR, SILVER FIR, WHITE FIR

☼ ✱ ↔25 ft (8 m) ↑120 ft (36 m)

Growing in western USA down to northern Mexico, this statuesque tree with a pyramidal crown has dull greenish gray leaves with mid-green to brown cylindrical cones. Cultivars include **'Compacta'**, **'Masonic Broom'**, and **Violacea Group** ★. Dwarf cultivars grow no more than 30 in (75 cm) in height and spread. Zones 5–9.

Abies firma

syn. *Abies bifida*

JAPANESE FIR

☼ ✱ ↔20 ft (6 m) ↑100 ft (30 m)

Originally from southern Japan. Shiny deep green leaves. Brown egg-shaped cones up to 6 in (15 cm) long. Susceptible to spring frost damage. Zones 6–9.

Abies fraseri

☼ ✱ ↔20 ft (6 m) ↑60 ft (18 m)

Pyramidal tree, native to southwestern Virginia, western North Carolina, and eastern Tennessee, USA. Leaves are 1 in (25 mm) long, mid- to dark green with a silvery to greenish white band on the underside. Cylindrical cones are green to dark purple, ripening to brown, pronounced bracts. Zones 6–9.

Abies grandis

GIANT FIR

☼ ✱ ↔25 ft (8 m) ↑300 ft (90 m)

Giant conical to columnar tree from western North America. Dark green, soft, shiny leaves, with whitish banding on undersides. Cones smallish, ripening to gray-brown. Timber of this tree is used in construction work. **'Johnsonii'** reaches a height of 60–70 ft (18–21 m). Zones 6–9.

Abies homolepis

syn. *Abies brachyphylla*

MANCHURIAN FIR, NIKKO FIR

☼ ✱ ↔25 ft (8 m) ↑80 ft (24 m)

A conical tree that is native to southern and central Japan. Leaves are dull grayish green with silver banding. Branches are tiered up the trunk. Cones are cylindrical and violet-blue, turning brown with age. This species is tolerant of urban pollution. Zones 5–9.

Abies koreana ★

KOREAN FIR

☼ ✱ ↔5 ft (1.5 m) ↑50 ft (15 m)

From the mountains of South Korea, this fir is a formal, narrow, pyramid-shaped, slow-growing tree with striking purple cones. Leaves are dark green above and shiny white beneath. Cultivars include **'Flava'**; **'Compact Dwarf'**, a popular bonsai subject; and **'Silberlocke'** (syn. 'Horstmann's Silberlocke'), a compact tree, new growth white beneath. Zones 5–8.

Abies lasiocarpa

ALPINE FIR, ROCKY MOUNTAIN FIR, SUBALPINE FIR

☼ ✱ ↔12 ft (3.5 m) ↑60 ft (18 m)

Conical tree found up to the tree line in the Rocky Mountains, North America. Gray-green leaves dense and spiky with bluish stripes on both sides. Oblong cylindrical cones turn from dark purple to brown as they ripen. A. l. **var. *arizonica***, silver-gray leaves. **'Compacta'** is a popular cultivar to 10 ft (3 m) high. Zones 4–9.

Abies nordmanniana

CAUCASIAN FIR

☼ ✱ ↔20 ft (6 m) ↑180 ft (55 m)

This species is found in mountain forests in the western Caucasus. The tree forms an elegant conical spire, with foliage that is deep glossy green in distinct rows with 2 white bands underneath. Cones are cylindrical in shape and green in color, ripening to purple-brown. **'Golden Spreader'** ★ is a handsome cultivar. Zones 4–8.

Abies koreana

Abies pinsapo

SPANISH FIR

↔ 15 ft (4.5 m) ↑ 80 ft (24 m)

From the dry mountain slopes of southern Spain, this tree adds distinction to a garden. Foliage is a series of rigid, short, linear, dark green leaves. The cylindrical cones are purplish brown. Cultivars include: **'Glauca'**, with gray-blue leaves; and **'Kelleriis'**, a robust dwarf. Zones 6–8.

Abies procera

syn. *Abies nobilis*

NOBLE FIR

↔ 30 ft (9 m) ↑ 150 (45 m)

Native to the high rainfall areas of western USA, this pyramidal tree becomes broader with age. Leaves gray-green to blue-silver, banded gray underneath. Barrel-shaped green cones ripen to brown. The **Glauca Group** features cultivars (including **'Glauca Prostrata'**), with blue leaves. Zones 4–9.

Abies veitchii

↔ 20 ft (6 m) ↑ 60 ft (18 m)

This fast-growing pyramidal tree native to Japan has smooth dark green leaves with silvery undersides. Bright gray-blue cylindrical cones ripen to a brown color. A. v. var. sikokiana has smaller leaves. Zones 6–9.

ABRONIA

SAND VERBENA

Although it is known as verbena, this genus is in the four-o-clock (Nyctaginaceae) family and not in the family to which the true verbenas be-long. There are 33 species of annuals and perennials occurring in southwestern USA and northern Mexico, from sandy seashores to sandy and gravelly habitats further inland. All the species have terminal heads of small tubular flowers, ranging in color from pale pink to yellow, and tend to be prostrate, sprawling, or scrambling plants. The dried and powdered roots of some species were eaten by the indigenous people.

CULTIVATION: Propagate from seed and cuttings, preferably using new growth from the stem tips after flowering. Full sun in well-draining sandy or gravelly soils gives best results. Some of the species are tolerant of salt-affected coastal locations.

Abronia umbellata

Abronia umbellata

BEACH SAND VERBENA

↔ 8–36 in (20–90 cm) ↑ up to 36 in (90 cm)

Native to the North American west coast, from Washington, USA, south to Baja California, Mexico, along the coastal fringe, occasionally further inland. A prostrate perennial with succulent leaves and showy, rose-colored, fragrant flowers. Can be deciduous under stress. Zones 8–10.

ABUTILON

CHINESE LANTERN

This genus of the mallow (Malvaceae) family is represented in warmer parts of the world. Species come from South or Central America, Australia, and Africa. Most are shrubs with slender tough-barked twigs but a few are annuals, perennials, or even small trees. Leaves vary from heart-shaped to jaggedly lobed with toothed margins. The common name alludes to the pendent bell-shaped flowers with 5 petals. Colors range from white through pink, and from yellow and orange to deep bronzy red. Fruit is a capsule. In mild climates they flower almost throughout the year, in cooler climates from spring to autumn.

CULTIVATION: Plant in well-drained moderately fertile soil, in light shade or bright sun. Extra water is needed if in an exposed position. In cool climates keep indoors until the worst frosts are past, then plant out for summer display; newer dwarf cultivars are suitable for this purpose. Prune leading shoots in late winter for a compact form, although some cultivars display their blooms best on long arching branches. Propagate from tip cuttings in late summer.

Abutilon × *hybridum*

CHINESE LANTERN, GARDEN ABUTILON

↔ 5–10 ft (1.5–3 m) ↑ 2½–15 ft (0.75–4.5 m)

This is a wide-ranging group of hybrids with unclear origins, although most show *A. pictum* influence. Leaves are usually dark green, smooth, 3–6 in (8–15 cm) long, toothed or with up to 5 lobes. Flowers to 3 in (8 cm) wide, one per leaf axil, mainly yellow, orange, and red shades, appear most of the year. Popular hybrids include: **'Apricot'**, open habit, terracotta flowers; **'Ashford Red'**, brilliant red flowers; **'Bartley Schwartz'**, drooping growth with golden to orange-yellow flowers; **'Boule de Neige'**, an older cultivar, flowers white flushed pink; **'Canary Bird'**, bright yellow flowers; **'Cannington Carol'**, dwarf, dense variegated foliage, flowers bright orange; **'Cannington Skies'**, similar to 'Cannington Carol', red flowers; **'Cerise Queen'**, flowers dark pink; **'Clementine'**, compact plant with bright red flowers; **'Crimson Belle'**, bright sealing wax red flowers; **'Dwarf Red'**, upright and bushy, small leaves, massed small bright red flowers; **'Golden Bell'**, bright yellow flowers, 32 in (80 cm) tall; **'Halo'**, red-veined yellow flowers, compact; **'Kentish Belle'**, glowing orange flowers; **'Linda Vista Peach'**, upright, peach pink flowers with bronze calyces; **'Mobile Pink'**, large downy leaves and wide open soft pink flowers; **'Moonchimes'**, compact habit, pale yellow flowers; **'Moritz'**, very dark leaves and pendulous orange flowers; **'Nabob'** ★, tall, flowers dark purple-red, leaves purple-tinged; **'Souvenir de Bonn'**, tall, narrow leaf lobes edged cream, pendulous orange bells; **'Summer Sherbet'**, compact seedling strain for summer bedding, wide color range; and **'Wakehurst'** (syn. 'Wisley Red'), dark red bell-shaped flowers. Zones 8–11.

Abutilon × *hybridum* 'Apricot'

Abutilon megapotamicum

syn. *Abutilon vexillarum*

CHINESE LANTERN, TRAILING ABUTILON

↔ 8 ft (2.4 m) ↑ 8 ft (2.4 m)

A native of southern Brazil. Has several forms, from an erect shrub with arching branches to an almost prostrate form. Flowers bell-shaped with red calyx contrasting with pale yellow petals. **'Marianne'**, vividly colored flowers; **'Variegatum'**, **yellow mottled leaves**; **'Victory'** ★, smaller, with darker yellow leaves. Zones 8–10.

Abutilon pictum

CHINESE LANTERN

↔ 8 ft (2.4 m) ↑ 15 ft (4.5 m)

A native of southern Brazil, this evergreen species is the most important parent of hybrid abutilons. This lanky shrub has scrambling branches, deeply divided dark green leaves, and flowers with orange petals netted with dark red veins. **'Thompsonii'**, leaves spattered with pale yellow (a virus variegation), and larger flowers. Zones 9–12.

ACACIA

From the mimosa subfamily of legumes (Fabaceae), *Acacia* used to contain at least 1,200 species, but recent revisions have seen the species found outside Australia reclassified in new genera. *Acacia* as it now stands comprises a wide range of evergreen shrubs and trees commonly known as wattles. Flowers are densely crowded into spikes or globular heads in colors of yellow or cream, rarely white or purple-tinted. Leaf structure is basically bipinnate—but in many species the leaves change to phyllodes. The acacia fruit is a typical legume pod, splitting open when ripe to reveal a row of hard seeds. A prominent feature of the Australian bush, fast growing wattles enrich the soils by converting nitrogen from the air into soil nitrogen.

CULTIVATION: Most acacias require well-drained soil and full sun. In mild climates they can become environmental weeds. They are often short-lived. Propagate from seed, treated to soften the hard coating. Cultivars may be propagated from half-hardened cuttings. Give a light prune after flowering.

Acacia aneura

MULGA

↔12 ft (3.5 m) ↕10–30 ft (3–9 m)

Shrubby tree from dry inland Australia, thrives in arid gardens. Phyllodes gray-green. Golden yellow flowers in winter–spring after good rain. Mulga is the Aboriginal Australian word for the long narrow shield made from the wood. Zones 9–10.

Acacia baileyana

COOTAMUNDRA WATTLE

↔20 ft (6 m) ↕6–20 ft (1.8–6 m)

Widely naturalized in most Australia States, this small elegant tree occurs naturally around Cootamundra, New South Wales. Leaves feathery silver-gray. Flowers bright yellow, globular, in racemes, winter–spring. **'Purpurea'** has attractive purplish foliage and new growth. Zones 9–10.

Acacia boormanii

↔7 ft (2 m) ↕6–12 ft (1.8–3.5 m)

From the Snowy River region of southeastern Australia. Erect bushy shrub, slender branches, dark green narrow phyllodes. Bright yellow ball-shaped flowerheads, axillary racemes, late winter–early spring. Zones 8–11.

Acacia burkittii

PINBUSH WATTLE

↔15 ft (4.5 m) ↕3–15 ft (0.9–4.5 m)

Tall spreading shrub, occurs naturally in semi-arid regions of southern Australia. Phyllodes long and fine. Bright yellow flowers, in short oblong spikes, borne in late winter–spring. Zones 8–10.

Acacia cognata

NARROW-LEAF BOWER WATTLE

↔8 ft (2.4 m) ↕10–25 ft (3–8 m)

Small resinous tree, native of southeastern Australia. Pendulous branches and bright green narrow phyllodes. Short stemmed, golden yellow, ball-shaped flowers in late winter to spring. Prefers moist conditions. Has recently been developed to produce a range of cultivars, including: **'Bower Beauty'**, very compact plant forming a dense foliage mound; **'Copper Tips'**, bright green with copper-red to purple-bronze young foliage; **'Lime Magik'**, strongly pendulous habit, small tree; **'Mini Cog'** (syn. 'Cousin Itt'), compact, forms a mound of weeping foliage; **'Waterfall'**, a cascading ground cover, creamy yellow flowers. Zones 9–11.

Acacia baileyana

Acacia covenyi

BLUE BUSH

↔10 ft (3 m) ↕20 ft (6 m)

Rare species from southern tablelands of New South Wales, Australia. Large shrub or small tree. Narrow blue-green phyllodes. Clusters of small heads of bright yellow flowers in spring. Seed pods up to 3 in (8 cm) long. Zones 9–11.

Acacia cultriformis

KNIFE-LEAF WATTLE, PLOUGHSHARE WATTLE

↔6–10 ft (1.8–3 m) ↕6–10 ft (1.8–3 m)

This widely cultivated tall shrub comes from eastern Australia. Drooping branches with blue-gray almost triangular phyllodes. Perfumed, bright yellow, globular flowers on long sprays. Excellent for hedging. **'Cascade'** (syn. 'Austraflora Cascade'), prostrate habit, flowers similar in size and color to the species. Zones 8–11.

Acacia dealbata ★

MIMOSA, SILVER WATTLE

↔25 ft (8 m) ↕50 ft (15 m)

From Tasmania, Australia. Trunk has dark gray to black bark, silvery branchlets, gray-green bipinnate leaves. In late winter–spring has pale lemon to bright yellow globular flowers on extended racemes. Known in Europe as mimosa. Cultivars include: **'Gaulois Astier'**, deep green foliage; **'Kambah Karpet'**, dense, prostrate habit. Drought tolerant. Zones 8–10.

Acacia cultriformis

Acacia decurrens

BLACK WATTLE

↔15 ft (4.5 m) ↕15–50 ft (4.5–15 m)

This erect tree comes from the coast and tablelands of New South Wales, Australia. Dark gray furrowed bark, deep green bipinnate leaves with widely spaced leaflets. Fragrant, brilliant yellow, ball-shaped flowers in winter–early spring. Zones 9–10.

Acacia glaucoptera

CLAY-BUSH WATTLE

↔10 ft (3 m) ↕5 ft (1.5 m)

From Western Australia, this attractive dome-shaped shrub has unusual, flat, gray-green phyllodes overlapping along zigzagging stems. The tree has large deep yellow flower balls in winter–spring. Needs good drainage. Zones 9–11.

Acacia melanoxylon

BLACKWOOD

↔20 ft (6 m) ↕100 ft (30 m)

From mainland eastern Australia and Tasmania. Spreading bushy crown of dull green phyllodes with longitudinal veins. Clusters of pale yellow globular flowers, late winter–early spring. Best in a moist sheltered situation. Considered a weed in South Africa. Zones 8–11.

Acacia pendula

BOREE, WEEPING MYALL

↔20 ft (6 m) ↕40 ft (12 m)

Weeping tree widespread in low-rainfall areas of eastern Australia. Narrow silvery phyllodes. Small lemon yellow flower balls are inconspicuous. Timber used for wood-turning. Zones 9–11.

Acacia podalyriifolia

QUEENSLAND WATTLE

↔15 ft (4.5 m) ↕10–15 ft (3–4.5 m)

Native to coastal areas of southern Queensland, Australia. This large shrub or slender small tree is widely cultivated for its decorative, rounded, silvery phyllodes and profuse, fragrant, golden flower balls, in clusters, in early winter–spring. Zones 9–11.

Acacia pravissima ★

OVENS WATTLE, WEDGE-LEAFED WATTLE

↔10 ft (3 m) ↕10–25 ft (3–8 m)

Native to hilly country in southeastern Australia. Spreading shrub or small tree, drooping branches and small, roughly triangular, olive green phyllodes. Profuse, golden yellow, globular flowers in racemes, in spring. **'Golden Carpet'**, spreads to 15 ft (4.5 m). Zones 8–10.

Acalypha reptans

Acacia redolens

☼ ❄ ↔ 10–25 ft (3–8 m)
↑ 3–15 ft (0.9–4.5 m)

Small spreading shrub with gray-green or bluish green phyllodes with 3 to 4 prominent longitudinal veins, sweetly scented. Yellow flowerheads are borne in spring. Pods narrow. Occurs in southwestern Australia. Zones 8–9.

Acacia stenophylla

EUMONG, NATIVE WILLOW, RIVER COOBA

☼ ❄ ↔ 10–20 ft (3–6 m)
↑ 15–50 ft (4.5–15 m)

Found along inland streams of all mainland States of Australia, this is a dense tree, often weeping, with rough dark bark. The tree has thick, pendulous, gray-green phyllodes, up to 16 in (40 cm) long, with many longitudinal veins. Clusters of creamy colored flowerheads appear in autumn–winter. Pods are straight but wrinkled. Zones 8–10.

Acacia vestita

WEEPING BOREE

☼ ❄ ↔ 6–15 ft (1.8–4.5 m)
↑ 6–15 ft (1.8–4.5 m)

From eastern Australia. Dense shrub, widely cultivated, attractive pendulous branches, green phyllodes. Masses of golden yellow ball-shaped flowers, in clusters, in spring. Good screen, hedge, or low windbreak. Prune after flowering to maintain shape. Zones 9–11.

ACALYPHA

This pantropical genus of the spurge or euphorbia (Euphorbiaceae) family contains over 400 species of perennials, shrubs, and trees best known for their long catkins or spikes of flowers, often bright magenta to red shades. Their leaves are simple, fairly large, oval-shaped with toothed edges. The foliage of *A. amentacea* subsp. *wilkesiana* has showy variegations, though mostly the plants are grown for their flowers. Individually these are minute, but those of female plants form densely packed catkins that in some species can be up to 18 in (45 cm) long.

CULTIVATION: Warm, almost frost-free conditions are essential as is plenty of moisture during the growing season. Plant in moist, humus-rich, well-drained soil, and feed well to keep the foliage lush and the plants flowering freely. Pinch back the young shoots and deadhead the flowers to keep the growth compact; otherwise little pruning is required. Propagate from cuttings and, if growing indoors, watch for mealybugs and white flies.

Acalypha amentacea subsp. *wilkesiana*

syn. *Acalypha wilkesiana*

COPPERLEAF, FIJIAN FIRE PLANT, JACOB'S COAT

☼ ❄ ↔ 10 ft (3 m) ↑ 10 ft (3 m)

From Fiji and nearby Pacific islands. Shrub with striking foliage colors and patterns. Colors range from green to bronze, and in tapestries of pink, rosy red, cream, or yellow, sometimes with contrasting margins that are coarsely serrated. Flowers in summer–autumn are upstaged by the foliage. **'Ceylon'**, bronze-purple leaves, edged in pink or white; **'Marginata'**, coppery leaves edged in red. Zones 10–12.

Acanthus spinosus 'Lady Moore'

Acalypha hispida

CHENILLE PLANT, RED-HOT CAT-TAIL

◐ ✢ ↔ 5 ft (1.5 m) ↑ 12 ft (3.5 m)

Famed for its long tassels of blood red flowers, this species is most likely a native of tropical East Asia. Leaves are bright green, with toothed edges, and covered in fine hairs. Excellent in hanging baskets where the tassels can be seen from below. Zones 11–12.

Acalypha reptans

RED CAT-TAILS

◐ ❄ ↔ 12 in (30 cm) ↑ 12 in (30 cm)

Often grown as a hanging basket plant, this native of Florida, USA, and nearby Caribbean islands has soft light to mid-green leaves. Its flower catkins are deep pink to pale red in summer, spot flowering at other times. Zones 10–12.

ACANTHUS

BEAR'S BREECHES

From the acanthus (Acanthaceae) family, this genus includes 30 species of perennials and subshrubs from the temperate and tropical Old World regions. Cultivated species are valued for their bold, often near-evergreen foliage and upright flower spikes. The leaves, which form a basal clump, are usually large, glossy, and pinnately lobed, the lobes being toothed or spiny. The flowers are tubular, tend to be mauve and white, and are partially enclosed within conspicuous bracts. May self-sow freely and can sucker. Large, but not especially attractive, seed pods follow. The acanthus leaf is the basis for many classical Greek and Roman designs, often featured atop columns and along friezes. It can also be found in Coptic, Byzantine, Celtic, and Baroque art. Early Christians adopted the leaf as a symbol of heaven.

CULTIVATION: Species mostly cold tolerant but prefer mild winters. Plant in moist, well-drained, humus-rich soil in sun or half-sun. Many have heavy roots and divide easily, otherwise raise from spring-sown seed.

Acanthus mollis

BEAR'S BREECHES

☼/◐ ✱ ↔ 40–60 in (100–150 cm)
↑ 7 ft (2 m)

Found in southern Europe and northwest Africa. Deep lustrous green, deeply toothed, soft-spined, pinnate or doubly pinnate leaves up to 36 in (90 cm) long. White flowers flushed pale purple in toothed mauve bracts on stems up to 7 ft (2 m) tall, in summer. **'Candelabrus'**, large-lobed flowers on sometimes branching flower stems; **'Hollard's Gold'**, golden yellow spring foliage; **'Rue Ledan'**, white flowers in mainly green bracts; **'Tasmanian Angel'**, boldly variegated cream and creamy white foliage, red-stemmed cream and pink flowerheads. Zones 6–10.

Acanthus spinosus

☼/◐ ✱ ↔ 40–60 in (100–150 cm)
↑ 36 in (90 cm)

Found around the Mediterranean. Similar to *A. mollis* but with leaves more deeply divided, broader and spinier. White, sometimes mauve-tinted flowers in spiny bracts. **'Lady Moore'** (Spinosissimus Group), variegated leaves and purple and white flowers. Zones 6–10.

ACCA

syn. *Feijoa*

This South American genus of the myrtle (Myrtaceae) family consists of 6 species of evergreen shrubs and small trees that bear a guava-like fruit. Simple, smooth-edged leaves are paler on the underside. The attractive single flowers have fleshy petals and conspicuous stamens. Only one species, *A. sellowiana* (syn. *Feijoa sellowiana*), is commonly cultivated, for its tasty fruit or for ornament, and is grown in the same kinds of warm-temperate climates that suit oranges.

CULTIVATION: The feijoa likes a sunny position and well-drained soil of moderate fertility. It is tolerant of exposure and even salt-laden winds, and can be clipped to form a dense hedge. Mature plants tolerate moderate winter frosts but in cooler climates will thrive better against a wall that traps the sun's heat. Cross-pollination, preferably by another plant not of the same clone, is needed for good fruit production. Named varieties are propagated from cuttings or grafting, but seed-raised plants are just as ornamental, if lacking fruit quality, and are more reliable pollinators.

Acca sellowiana ★

syn. *Feijoa sellowiana*

FEIJOA, PINEAPPLE GUAVA

☼ ❄ ↔10 ft (3 m) ↑10 ft (3 m)

Native from southern Brazil to northern Argentina, the feijoa has leathery, oval, glossy green leaves, whitish beneath. Flowers have cupped petals, pale carmine, with dark crimson stamens. Fruit is elliptical with sweet, aromatic, cream flesh. Cultivars include: '**Beechwood**', with smooth-skinned fruit; '**Coolidge**', bearing abundant fruit; '**Mammoth**', bearing large wrinkled-skinned fruit; '**Nazemetz**', bearing large fruit to 4 in (10 cm) long; and '**Trask**', with thick-skinned fruit. Zones 8–10.

ACER

MAPLE

This mostly deciduous tree genus of the soapberry (Sapindaceae) family has many species valued for their ornamental qualities. It consists of around 120 species, most from the Northern Hemisphere. Maples are forest or woodland trees of moist climates. The majority have simple leaves, mostly toothed or lobed, borne on slender leaf stalks attached to the twigs in opposite pairs. A small number have compound leaves with 3, 5, or 7 leaflets. Flowers are small, in clusters or dense spikes. Fruits consists of two small nuts (samaras), joined where attached to the flower stalk, each terminating in an elongated wing.

CULTIVATION: Maples thrive best in cooler temperate climates with adequate rainfall, aided by warm humid summers and sharply demarcated winters. Best in deep well-drained soil with permanent subsoil moisture. Some need dappled shade to preserve their foliage from summer scorching, but some can tolerate exposure to drying winds. Propagation of species is from seed, cultivars by grafting.

Acer buergerianum

TRIDENT MAPLE

☼ ✱ ↔25 ft (8 m) ↑30 ft (9 m)

From eastern China and Korea. Usually seen as a sturdy small tree, and a popular bonsai subject. Leaves have 3 short lobes, turning yellowish often flushed with red in autumn. Bark flaky, pale gray. Winged fruits persist through winter. Zones 6–11.

Acer campbellii

syns *Acer sinense, A. wilsonii*

☼ ❄ ↔8–15 ft (2.4–4.5 m) ↑15–40 ft (4.5–12 m)

From China, Indochina, and the eastern Himalayas, this is a variable species divided into 4 subspecies. Leaves have 5 to 7 lobes. New foliage is bronzy red, and autumn color is golden yellow to brilliant red. A. c. subsp. flabellatum is a smaller hardier tree with a twiggy habit and large shiny leaves, while A. c. subsp. wilsonii has smaller, 3-lobed leaves. Zones 7–10.

Acer capillipes

RED SNAKEBARK MAPLE

☼ ✱ ↔35 ft (10 m) ↑40 ft (12 m)

This species from Japan has interesting bark and attractive foliage. Its young stems are bright pinkish red ageing to white-striped green-brown bark. Leaves are dark green with serrated edges and prominent red stalks. Zones 5–9.

Acer circinatum

Acer carpinifolium

HORNBEAM MAPLE

☼ ✱ ↔30 ft (9 m) ↑30 ft (9 m)

From the mountain forests of Japan. Either a tree or large shrub. Densely branched. Unlobed corrugated leaves with serrated margins, turning gold in autumn. Winged fruits are curved. A slow-growing plant. Zones 4–8.

Acer circinatum

VINE MAPLE

☼ ✱ ↔15 ft (4.5 m) ↑15 ft (4.5 m)

Native to western North America, this shrub or low-branching tree is noted for its spectacular color. Leaves rounded with 7 to 9 lobes turn orange-scarlet to deep red in autumn. Purple flowers. Red horizontal winged fruits. '**Monroe**' has deeply cut leaves. Zones 6–9.

Acer cissifolium

VINE-LEAF MAPLE

☼ ✱ ↔35 ft (10 m) ↑30 ft (9 m)

From Japan, this small tree or shrub has a spreading crown, smooth gray bark, and compound leaves. The 3 bronze-tinted leaflets with serrated margins turn yellow, orange, or red in autumn. Seeds in clusters. Needs acid soil. Zones 5–8.

Acer × *conspicuum*

☼ ✱ ↔20–30 ft (6–9 m) ↑30 ft (9 m)

This is a hybrid between the 2 snakebark maples *A. davidii* and *A. pensylvanicum*, first found in England in the 1960s. A vigorous tree, it has leaves with 3 or 5 lobes. The original clone is '**Silver Vein**', with very large leaves and bark more conspicuously striped than any other maple. Zones 5–9.

Acer crataegifolium

☼ ✱ ↔25 ft (8 m) ↑25 ft (8 m)

From Japan. Leaves resemble hawthorn *(Crataegus)*. Leaves 3-lobed or almost unlobed, to 3 in (8 cm) long, dark green to bluish green, wavy margins, purplish stalks. Small winged fruits, ¾ in (18 mm) across. Needs summer moisture. Zones 6–8.

Acer davidii ★

PERE DAVID'S MAPLE

☼ ✱ ↔25 ft (8 m) ↑30 ft (9 m)

Elegant fast-growing tree from central and western China. Open habit with arching branches, striped greenish bark. Leaves pointed, toothed, some with small lobes near base. Small reddish fruits in long pendent spikes. Cultivars include: '**Ernest Wilson**', a compact tree with narrow orange leaves; '**George Forrest**', with dark red young foliage, almost unlobed leaves; and '**Serpentine**', smaller-leafed than the species. Zones 5–9.

Acer × *freemanii*

☼ ✱ ↔20–40 ft (6–12 m) ↑50 ft (15 m)

This cross between *A. rubrum* and *A. saccharinum* was raised at the US National Arboretum in 1930, and the two species frequently interbreed in the wild. The resultant plants are quick-growing round-topped trees with 5-lobed leaves. The foliage often develops brilliant autumn colors. Cultivars include: '**Armstrong**', with orange-yellow autumn color; Autumn Blaze/'**Jeffersred**' ★ (syn. *A. rubrum* 'Autumn Blaze'), with intense orange and red autumn foliage; Celebration/'**Celzam**', fairly compact, with red and gold autumn color; and '**Marmo**', with an oval-shaped foliage head and red to maroon autumn color. Zones 5–9.

Acer griseum

CHINESE PAPERBARK MAPLE, PAPERBARK MAPLE

☼ ✱ ↔35 ft (10 m) ↑40 ft (12 m)

From central and western China, this species is an attractive slender tree. Its outstanding feature is the texture and color of the bark. Leaves turn orange, scarlet, and crimson in autumn. The tree's winged fruits have large seeds. Zones 4–8.

Acer henryi

☼ ✱ ↔30 ft (9 m) ↑30 ft (9 m)

From mountain forests in central China, this spreading dome-shaped tree has bluish olive green, 3-part, compound leaves, and bark with bluish striations. Yellow flowers. Clusters of winged fruits. Zones 6–8.

Acer japonicum

FULL-MOON MAPLE

☼ ✱ ↔30 ft (9 m) ↑30 ft (9 m)

A broadly spreading small tree from the mostly dry and sunny mountain forests of Japan. Leaves are rounded with 7 to 11 sharply toothed, pointed lobes turning yellow, orange and crimson in autumn. Cultivars include: '**Aconitifolium**', leaves deeply dissected and toothed turning crimson in autumn; and '**Vitifolium**', large leaves, bronzy when young. Zones 6–8.

A

Acer macrophyllum

OREGON MAPLE

☼ ✱ ↔ 80 ft (24 m) ↑ 80 ft (24 m)

From western North America this striking species has the largest leaves of all maples. Tall broadly columnar tree. Leaves 5-lobed, dark green, glossy, turning bright orange in autumn. Large pendulous fruit clusters. Zones 7–9.

Acer mono

☼ ✱ ↔ 50 ft (15 m) ↑ 50 ft (15 m)

From central and northern China to Mongolia, eastern Siberia, Korea, and Japan. Variable species, often found as a spreading dome-shaped tree, but can be shrub-like. Leaves 5- or 7-lobed, turn yellow to orange in autumn. Variegated cultivars can revert. Zones 5–8.

Acer monspessulanum

MONTPELIER MAPLE

☼ ✱ ↔ 35 ft (10 m) ↑ 40 ft (12 m)

Sometimes confused with *A. campestre,* this species from the Mediterranean region is a small tidy tree or large shrub with smooth gray bark and 3-lobed, smooth, leathery leaves. Pendulous clusters of winged fruits. Zones 6–8.

Acer negundo

BOX ELDER, BOX ELDER MAPLE, MANITOBA MAPLE

☼ ✱ ↔ 30 ft (9 m) ↑ 60 ft (18 m)

From eastern North America. This fast-growing hardy tree has several popular variegated forms. The green species is a rounded to broadly columnar tree. Colored forms are smaller and less vigorous. All have compound leaves with 3 to 5 or 7 large leaflets. A. n. var. violaceum bears red to purple flowers on dark colored branches. Cultivars include: A. n. **'Aureovariegatum'**, gold-edged leaflets; **'Elegans'**, broad gold margin, male clone; **'Flamingo'**, pink-margined in early spring, fading to white; **'Sensation'**, rich pink autumn color; and **'Variegatum'** ★, a white-margined, sterile, female clone. Zones 5–9.

Acer palmatum

GREENLEAF JAPANESE MAPLE, JAPANESE MAPLE

◐ ✱ ↔ 25 ft (8 m) ↑ 20 ft (6 m)

With its species name alluding to the lobed leaves resembling a hand, this tree from Japan, Korea, and China has produced more than 1,000 cultivars; it is by far the most prolific of all maples. Best in rich, moist, well-drained loams, sheltered from drying or freezing winds. The 5- to 7-lobed leaves turn yellow, amber, crimson, and purple. Cultivars must be propagated by grafting or cuttings to be true to type. A. p. var. coreanum **'Korean Gem'** has black bark and spectacular autumn foliage.

Many cultivars belong to A. p. var. dissectum (syns *A. p.* 'Dissectum' and *A. p.* Dissectum Group), which consists of shrubs with narrow leaf lobes, which themselves are strongly lobed. Most are low growing with cascading branches, giving mature plants an umbrella-like or dome-like form. Further subdivisions of this variety are the **Dissectum Viride Group** with mid-green foliage, and the **Dissectum Atropurpureum Group** with deep purple-red spring foliage that becomes more greenish in summer and often takes on yellow tones in autumn; **'Crimson Queen'**, vigorous growth, bright red autumn foliage; **'Dissectum Nigrum'** (syn. **'Ever Red'**), bright red in autumn; **'Inabe-shidare'**, burgundy foliage; **'Ornatum'**, deeply dissected leaves, turning red, amber, and gold in autumn.

Acer palmatum, in autumn

Cultivars include: A. p. **'Akaji-nishiki'** (syn. 'Bonfire'), pinkish foliage in spring and autumn; **'Atrolineare'** (syns 'Filiferum Purpureum', 'Linearilobium Rubrum'), with 5-lobed red leaves, becoming greenish in summer; **'Atropurpureum'**, leaves of 5 to 7 lobes, vibrant red in autumn; **'Bloodgood'**, dark red leaves of 5 to 7 lobes, vibrant red in autumn; **'Burgundy Lace'**, purple-bronze deeply cut leaves; **'Butterfly'**, vase-shaped with cream-white margined 5-lobed leaves; **'Chishio'**, spring foliage shrimp pink becoming greenish; **'Chitoseyama'**, purple-red 7-lobed leaves; **'Garnet'**, deep red spring foliage turning fiery red in autumn; **'Heptalobum Rubrum'**, wine purple spring foliage; **'Higasayama'**, cream and pink variegated leaves; **'Katsura'**, a spectacular shrubby tree; **'Kotohime'**, dwarf to 5 ft (1.5 m) high, green-brown leaves turning golden in autumn; **'Linearilobum'**, also known as **'Scolopendrifolium'**; **'Moonfire'**, claret-colored 7-lobed leaves that mature to purple; **'Nicholsonii'**, a much-branched shrub with leaves olive-bronze in spring, coloring brilliant gold to brilliant crimson; **'Nigrum'**, a very dark purple shrub with light green winged fruits; **'Osakazuki'**, 7-lobed brown-green leaves, turning russet in autumn; **'Red Dragon'**, rich purple foliage; **'Red Filigree Lace'**, with the most finely divided leaves of all maples of this type; **'Red Pygmy'**, 5-lobed purple-brown leaves; **'Shigitatsu-sawa'** ('Reticulatum'), 7-lobed leaves green with a white net-like patterning; **'Sango-kaku'**, remarkable for its glowing red bark in winter; **'Seiryu'**, distinctive vigorous growth and upright habit; **'Shindeshojo'**, fresh spring growth an eye-catching scarlet; **'Shishigashira'**, known as the "lion's head maple," good for seaside gardens; **'Suminagashi'**, 7-lobed purplish leaves cut almost to the midrib, turning crimson in autumn; **'Trompenburg'**, unique among maples for its mature foliage; **'Villa Taranto'**, vase shaped; and **'Waterfall'**, a classic, cascading, dome-shaped shrub. Zones 6–9.

Acer saccharinum 'Beebe's Cutleaf Weeping'

Acer pensylvanicum

GOOSEFOOT, MAPLE, MOOSEWOOD, STRIPED MAPLE

◐ ✱ ↔ 35 ft (10 m) ↑ 30 ft (9 m)

The only North American snakebark maple, with branches marked like markings found on the garter snake. From moist woodlands, it is a broadly columnar tree. White and red-brown stripes pattern green bark on the species. **'Erythrocladum'**, winter bark is coral to salmon red, striped white. Leaves turn golden amber. Zones 4–9.

Acer rubrum

CANADIAN MAPLE, RED MAPLE, SCARLET MAPLE, SWAMP MAPLE

☼ ✱ ↔ 35 ft (10 m) ↑ 100 ft (30 m)

A native of eastern North America, this large tree is appreciated for its fast growth, spectacular autumn color, and tolerance of wet soils and atmospheric pollution. Its leaves are 3- to 5-lobed, dark green in color, bluish beneath, changing to yellow, amber, or fiery red. Dense red flower clusters are formed. Red winged fruit. A. r. var. drummondii varies from the typical species in that it has larger flowers and thicker leaves, whitish beneath. Cultivars and hybrids include: A. r. **'Autumn Flame'**, with a dense rounded crown and crimson autumn foliage; **'Gerling'**, with a broad conical shape and fiery red autumn color; **'October Glory'**, a spectacular 'Lipstick' tree; **'Scanlon'**, with leaves turning gold-orange and speckled crimson in autumn; **'Scarsen'**, with an upright habit and yellow-orange to vivid red color in autumn; and **'Sunshine'**. Zones 4–8.

Acer saccharinum

RIVER MAPLE, SILVER MAPLE, SOFT MAPLE, WHITE MAPLE

☼ ✱ ↔ 80 ft (24 m) ↑ 100 ft (30 m)

From eastern North America, a large tree found on moist riverbanks. Fast-growing but can be short-lived, easily damaged by wind. Deep angularly lobed leaves, silvery beneath, turn clear yellow in autumn. Coppery green winged fruits fall early. A. s. f. lutescens, yellow spring foliage turns light green then yellow in autumn; A. s. f. pyramidale, a narrower form with deeply cut leaves, ideal street tree. Cultivars include: A. s. **'Beebe's Cutleaf Weeping'** and **'Skinneri'**. Zones 4–9.

Acer saccharum

HARD MAPLE, ROCK MAPLE, SUGAR MAPLE

☼ ✱ ↔40 ft (12 m) ↕100 ft (30 m)

This North American species produces the best sap, which is extracted to make maple syrup. The tree and foliage resemble *A. platanoides*. Leaves turn yellow-orange and crimson in autumn. A stylized interpretation of the leaf is the national symbol of Canada. A. s. subsp. grandidentatum (syn. *A. grandidentatum*) grows 35–40 ft (10–12 m) high; A. s. subsp. leucoderme (syn. *A. leucoderme*) grows to 25 ft (8 m) high; and A. s. subsp. nigrum (syn. *A. nigrum*) is known as the black maple for its black bark; **'Green Column'**, light green foliage turning yellow to apricot orange in autumn; **'Temple's Upright'** is a narrow upright form. Cultivars include: A. s. **'Flax Hill Majesty'**, **'Green Mountain'**, **'Legacy'**, and **'Seneca Chief'**. Zones 4–9.

Acer shirasawanum

◑ ✱ ↔20 ft (6 m) ↕20 ft (6 m)

Leaves 9- to 13-lobed, lime green spring foliage, turns yellowish, then crimson in autumn. Red winged fruits. **'Aureum'** (syn. *A. japonicum* 'Aureum'), a popular cultivar; **'Microphyllum'** (syn. *A. japonicum* 'Microphyllum'), slightly smaller leaves. Zones 6–9.

Acer 'Silver Cardinal'

☼ ✱ ↔10–20 ft (3–6 m) ↕10–25 ft (3–8 m)

Previously thought to be a form of *A.* × *conspicuum*. Silver-striped maroon bark. Mottled green and cream leaves, pink veins, red leaf stalks. Zones 5–9.

Acer spicatum

MOUNTAIN MAPLE

☼ ✱ ↔15 ft (4.5 m) ↕30 ft (9 m)

From central and eastern North America, this is usually a large shrub and occasionally a spreading tree with dense branch structure and greenish bark. The 3- to 5-lobed leaves are sharply serrated turning amber color in autumn. Zones 4–8.

Acer tataricum

AMUR MAPLE, TATARIAN MAPLE

☼ ✱ ↔25 ft (8 m) ↕35 ft (10 m)

From China, Japan, and Korea, this is a small, fast-growing, broadly spreading tree or shrub. Its leaves have 3 glossy toothed lobes, and color brilliantly amber and crimson in autumn. Fruits have broad red wings. A. t. subsp. ginnala (syn. *A. ginnala*), the most commonly seen subspecies, has given risen to several cultivars, including: **'Burgundy'**, rich autumn color; **'Compactum'**, to 8 ft (2.4 m) tall, vivid red autumn color; and **'Durand Dwarf'**, to 24 in (60 cm) tall. Zones 4–8.

Acer tegmentosum

☼ ✱ ↔35 ft (10 m) ↕30 ft (9 m)

From moist soils in Russia, North Korea, and northeastern China, this shrub or tree is appreciated for its green bark, distinctly striped white. Foliage and young shoots are bluish; autumn foliage is gold. Flowers and fruits hang in pendulous clusters. Zones 5–8.

Acer triflorum

THREE-FLOWER MAPLE

☼/◑ ✱ ↔20–30 ft (6–9 m) ↕20–30 ft (6–9 m)

A small, upright tree from north-eastern China and Korea. Its dark green trifoliate leaves become rich yellow or red in autumn. Flaking bark gives winter interest. This maple has greenish yellow flowers in clusters of 3, giving rise to its common name. Zones 5–8.

Acer truncatum

SHANTUNG MAPLE

☼ ✱ ↔18–25 ft (6–8 m) ↕25–35 ft (8–10 m)

Upright oval-shaped tree from northern and northeastern China and Korea. Smooth branches tinged with purple when young. Bright green deeply lobed leaves to 4 in (10 cm) long. Zones 5–8.

ACHILLEA

MILFOIL, YARROW

This genus of about 100 species of clumping or mat-forming perennial plants is a member of the large daisy (Asteraceae) family. They are found throughout Europe and northern and western Asia in a range of habitats, including alpine. Some species can be invasive. The foliage is usually finely divided with a fern-like appearance and is often aromatic. Usually grouped in flat corymbs, the small flowerheads are white and pale cream, lemon, and pink, and many cultivars in brighter colors extend the range. The genus is named after Achilles, the hero of Greek mythology, who is said to have known of its wound-healing qualities. CULTIVATION: Most yarrows can easily be grown in well-drained soil in full sun. They can tolerate quite poor conditions and are frost hardy to 5°F (–15°C). Alpine species require perfect drainage and protection from winter rain if downy-leafed. Propagation is by division or from seed.

Achillea × *kellereri*

Achillea × *lewisii* 'King Edward'

Achillea millefolium

Achillea ageratifolia

☼ ✱ ↔18 in (45 cm) ↕6 in (15 cm)

A slow-growing alpine species from the Balkans. Downy silver foliage. Smothered in small white flowers in late spring. Zones 3–9.

Achillea clypeolata

☼ ✱ ↔12–18 in (30–45 cm) ↕18–24 in (45–60 cm)

Mat-forming species from eastern Europe. Fern-like foliage is grayish green. Corymbs 2–3 in (5–8 cm) across are crowded with small bright yellow flowerheads in summer. Zones 6–10.

Achillea filipendulina

☼ ✱ ↔24–48 in (60–120 cm) ↕24–48 in (60–120 cm)

Robust species from central and western Asia. Divided, hairy, aromatic leaves up to 8 in (20 cm) long. Tiny gold flowers are crowded in flattened flowerheads, up to 4 in (10 cm) across, in summer. **'Cloth of Gold'**, **'Gold Plate'**, and **'Parker's Variety'** are improved cultivars growing 4–6 ft (1.2–1.8 m) high with bright golden flowerheads up to 6 in (15 cm) across. **'Schwellenburg'** grows to about 18 in (45 cm) high and has lemon yellow flowers. Zones 5–10.

Achillea × *kellereri*

☼ ✱ ↔10 in (25 cm) ↕6 in (15 cm)

Garden hybrid of *A. clypeolata* and *A. ageratifolia*. This plant forms mats of ferny gray foliage. Small creamy white daisy-like flowerheads, pale yellow centers, in summer. Suits rock garden. Zones 5–10.

Achillea × *lewisii* 'King Edward'

☼ ✱ ↔10 in (25 cm) ↕4 in (10 cm)

Garden hybrid of *A. clavennae* and *A. clypeolata*. Feathery silvery gray foliage in tight clumps. Small flat heads of pale yellow flowers in summer. Suits rock garden. Zones 5–10.

Achillea millefolium

MILFOIL, YARROW

☼ ✱ ↔18–30 in (45–75 cm) ↕12–30 in (30–75 cm)

Weedy species from western Asia and Europe. Naturalized in temperate regions, too invasive for most gardens. Fern-like leaves. Flat sprays of small dull white flowerheads in summer–autumn. Herbal anti-inflammatory. **'Cerise Queen'**, cherry red, vigorous. Zones 3–10.

Acinos alpinus

Achillea ptarmica

SNEEZEWORT

↔30 in (75 cm) ↑30 in (75 cm)

From Europe. Vigorous spreading mats of dark green, narrow, serrated leaves. Loose heads of small white flowers are borne in summer. Tolerant of damp sites. **'The Pearl'** bears double white flowers in profusion. Zones 6–10.

Achillea tomentosa

↔12–18 in (30–45 cm)
↑6–10 in (15–25 cm)

Mat-forming alpine species, native to central Europe. Soft woolly foliage. Bright yellow flowers in summer. **'King George'**, lemon yellow flowers in spring. Zones 3–9.

Achillea Hybrid Cultivars

↔18–30 in (45–75 cm)
↑12–40 in (30–100 cm)

Numerous cultivars in bright shades, make excellent border plants. Cultivars include: Anthea/**'Anblo'**, pale yellow flowers, silvery foliage; **'Apfelblüte' (syn. Apple Blossom)**, rose pink flowers; **'Coronation Gold'**, to 40 in (100 cm) high, bright yellow flowers; **'Fanal'** (syn. 'The Beacon'), crimson-red, yellow centers; **'Heidi'**, bright salmon, yellow centers; **'Lachsschönheit'**, salmon fading to pale pink; **'Moonshine'**, bright yellow flowerheads, silvery foliage; and **'Paprika'**, bright red, yellow centers. Quick to flower from seed are **'Taygetea'**, gray foliage, lemon yellow flowers; **'Terracotta'**, rusty orange; **'Walther Funcke'**, red with yellow centers; **'Wesersandstein'**, salmon fading to cream. Zones 3–10.

ACINOS

BASIL THYME, CALAMINTHA, SATUREJA

This Eurasian genus of 10 species of annuals and perennials belongs to the mint (Lamiaceae) family. They may be low and spreading or more upright and bushy. The leaves, opposite on the stems, are simple pointed ellipses, sometimes toothed and/or downy. Flower stems with whorls of simple, small, 2-lipped, tubular, pale mauve to purple-pink flowers appear in summer. Interestingly, the common names reflect some confusion—basil thyme suggests a strongly aromatic culinary herb, which it is not, though it can be used as a garnish, while *Satureja* and *Calamintha* are the proper names for two closely related herb genera: savory and calamint, a genus in which some species were formerly included.

CULTIVATION: *Acinos* species are easily grown in any temperate climate that is not extremely hot and dry in summer. Plant in moist, humus-rich, well-drained soil in part shade. Remove spent flowerheads to keep compact and tidy. Propagate from seed or base cuttings.

Acinos alpinus

ALPINE CALAMINT

↔8–12 in (20–30 cm)
↑4–8 in (10–20 cm)

Found in southern and central European mountains. Compact, bushy, downy-leafed perennial. Toothed leaves around ½ in (12 mm) long. Heads of ½ in (12 mm) long violet flowers marked white on the lower lip. Zones 5–9.

ACONITUM

BADGER'S BANE, MONKSHOOD, WOLFSBANE

This buttercup (Ranunculaceae) family genus of around 100 species of often tuberous biennials and perennials is found in northern temperate zones. Completely dormant over winter, they quickly develop a clump of deeply lobed fan-shaped leaves from which emerge erect stems bearing racemes of hooded or helmet-shaped flowers, usually white, creamy yellow, or mauve-blue to purple in color. Summer to autumn is the main flowering season. Monkshood sap contains several highly toxic alkaloids, principally aconitine, and has a long history of use as a poison, especially in animal traps, hence its common names of wolfsbane and badger's bane. Aconitine causes paralysis of the nerves and eventually the heart, and is used medicinally in controlled doses to slow the heart rate.

CULTIVATION: *Aconitum* species are mostly very hardy and easily grown in full sun or half-sun in moist, humus-rich, well-drained soil. Propagation is by division when dormant or they can be raised from seed.

Aconitum carmichaelii

↔24–36 in (60–90 cm)
↑7 ft (2 m)

From China. Upright growth with dark green, 3- to 5-lobed, toothed, leathery leaves with pale undersides. Dense spikes of white to mauve helmet-shaped flowers that are deep purple inside. Popular cultivars include: **'Arendsii'**, deep blue flowers; and **'Kelmscott'** (Wilsonii Group) ★, light purple-blue flowers. Zones 3–9.

Aconitum lycoctonum

syn. *Aconitum septentrionale*

BADGER'S BANE, WOLFSBANE

↔2–3 ft (0.6–0.9 m)
↑5–7 ft (1.5–2 m)

Found in Europe and into North Africa. Erect perennial with rounded often hairy leaves divided into 5 to 7 toothed lobes. Flowers are white, yellow, or purple, and may be downy. Zones 3–9.

Aconitum napellus

FRIAR'S CAP, HELMET FLOWER, MONKSHOOD

↔24–32 in (60–80 cm)
↑5–6 ft (1.5–1.8 m)

Found in Europe and temperate Asia. Upright perennial with dark green slightly hairy leaves with 5 to 7 toothed lobes. Bright purple-blue helmet-shaped flowers in dense heads atop tall stems, late summer–autumn. Zones 5–9.

Aconitum carmichaelii

Aconitum Hybrid Cultivars

↔24 in (60 cm) ↑4 ft (1.2 m)

Several hybrid monkshoods, varying in size, color, and flowering season, are sometimes listed under the name *A.* × *cammarum* (*A. variegatum* × *A. napellus*), but as they are not all of this parentage this grouping seems inappropriate. Popular hybrids include: **'Bressingham Spire'**, strongly upright, with long spikes of purple-blue flowers; *A.* × *cammarum* **'Grandiflorum Album'**, large heads of white flowers; **'Ivorine'**, with creamy white flowers; **'Spark's Variety'**, tall, non-twining, open plant, bright purple-blue flowers; and **'Stainless Steel'**, gray-green foliage and white-centered metallic blue flowers. Zones 4–9.

Aconitum napellus

Aconitum, Hybrid Cultivar, 'Stainless Steel'

ACORUS

SWEET FLAG

Making up the family Acoraceae, this rather sedge-like genus of 2 evergreen perennial species occurs around pond margins in temperate East Asia and southeast USA. The narrow iris-like leaves in fans are often variegated in the cultivated forms. In summer they produce flowers in which the typically showy arum spathe is leaf-like and inconspicuous. The flowerhead (spadix) is pronounced but not a feature. The stout, aromatic rhizomes contain compounds sometimes used in perfumes or to make a digestive tonic. Extracts or candied fleshy stems of *A. calamus* are used widely in herbal medicines.

CULTIVATION: *Acorus* species are tough and easily grown. Plant in damp or boggy soil, preferably by a pond, and cut back or divide occasionally to encourage fresh young leaves. Propagation is by division or from seed if available.

Acorus calamus

CALAMUS, FLAGROOT, MYRTLE FLAG, SWEET CALAMUS, SWEET FLAG

☼/◐ ✱ ↔3–7 ft (0.9–2 m) ↑4 ft (1.2 m)

Originally from temperate Eurasia and eastern North America but now widely naturalized in the Northern Hemisphere. Has iris-like leaves to 5 ft (1.5 m) long and a narrow yellow-green spadix to 4 in (10 cm) long. **'Variegatus'** ★ has cream and yellow variegated leaves. Zones 3–10.

Acorus gramineus

☼/◐ ✱ ↔18–36 in (45–90 cm)
↑16 in (40 cm)

From Japan and possibly nearby mainland Asia, very similar to *A. calamus* but smaller grassy leaves, to 18 in (45 cm) long. Spadix broad and up to 3 in (8 cm) long. Several foliage cultivars, including: **'Hakuro-nishiki'**, compact, yellow-green foliage; **'Ôgon'** (syn. 'Wogon'), bright yellow-green and cream variegation; **'Pusillus'**, dwarf, leaves 3 in (8 cm) long; and **'Variegatus'** (syn. 'Aureovariegatus'), golden yellow and cream variegation. Zones 5–10.

ACTAEA

With over 30 species, this is a genus of the buttercup (Ranunculaceae) family, and occurs in temperate regions of the Northern Hemisphere as fleshy-stemmed woodland perennials with divided toothed leaves. Terminal heads of white flowers are followed by white, red, or black poisonous berries.

CULTIVATION: Propagate from seed or by division. Full to part-shade in a friable loamy soil will give good results.

Actaea rubra

RED BANEBERRY, RED COHOSH, SNAKEBERRY

◐ ✱ ↔24–36 in (60–90 cm)
↑12–24 in (30–60 cm)

From North America, this is a bushy perennial for woodland settings. Dark green divided leaves. Clusters of small white flowers in spring. Round red berries appear in summer. All parts, including berries, poisonous if eaten. Zones 3–9.

Actaea spicata

syn. *Actaea alba*

DOLL'S EYES, WHITE BANEBERRY

☼/◐ ✱ ↔20–24 in (50–60 cm)
↑36 in (90 cm)

From woodlands of eastern North America. Divided leaves, up to 24 in (60 cm) long, composed of 3–12 leaflets, arise from a fleshy stem. In late spring–early summer, white flowers are produced in terminal heads, 1–2 in (2.5–5 cm) long. Tiny, globular, white berries. Each berry has a black "eye," hence the common name. Zones 5–9.

Acorus gramineus 'Hakuro-nishiki'

Actinidia deliciosa 'Hayward'

Actinidia kolomikta

ACTINIDIA

This genus of about 60 species of evergreen and deciduous twining climbers from East Asia belongs to the family Actinidiaceae. The species are grown for their handsome foliage and often scented creamy white flowers in spring. The fruit of some is edible, but both male and female plants are needed to produce these. As decorative climbers, they can be used to cover walls, pergolas and dead or unattractive trees. The name *Actinidia* comes from the Greek *aktin* (ray), alluding to the rayed stigmas of the female flowers. The most famous is *A. deliciosa,* the Chinese gooseberry or kiwi fruit, which isn't a gooseberry nor does it come from New Zealand!

CULTIVATION: Plant in full sun to partial shade in any well-drained loamy soil that should not dry out. Prune in winter as necessary. Vigor suggests strong support needed as vines become heavy, with little need for fertilizer. Propagate from seed sown in spring or autumn, from half-hardened cuttings, or by layering in late autumn or winter. Vines of both sexes are required for fruiting of most varieties.

Actinidia arguta

BOWER ACTINIDIA, BOWER VINE, COCKTAIL KIWI, DESSERT KIWI, HARDY KIWI, KOKUWA, SIBERIAN GOOSEBERRY, TARA VINE, YANG-TAO

☼ ✱ ↔20–30 ft (6–9 m)
↑20–30 ft (6–9 m)

Vigorous twining vine of variable habit from Japan, Korea, and northeastern China. It has fragrant white flowers that are tinged with green, with purple anthers, from mid- to late summer. Leaves to 6 in (15 cm) long, oval, smooth and serrated. Abundant yellow-green, hairless fruit that has a slightly acid flavor. **'Ananasnaya'** (syn. 'Anna') is a vigorous female cultivar that has large clusters of small sweet-smelling flowers; **'Issai'** is a self- pollinating form. Zones 4–9.

Actinidia chinensis

CHINESE GOOSEBERRY

☼ ❄ ↔15–30 ft (4.5–9 m)
↑10–20 ft (3–6 m)

Long cultivated in southern China, native region uncertain. Resembles the better known *A. deliciosa* in habit, foliage, and flowers but fruit is smaller, tapering more to a point, almost hairless when ripe, with bright yellow to reddish flesh of a rich, sweet aromatic flavor. Prefers a long frost-free season. Zones 7–10.

Actinidia deliciosa ★

syn. *Actinidia chinensis of gardens*

CHINESE GOOSEBERRY, KIWI FRUIT, YANTAO

☼ ❄ ↔35 ft (10 m) ↑35 ft (10 m)

Vigorous climber from China. Large, furry, green leaves to 8 in (20 cm) long. Scented cream flowers in spring are followed by tasty, brown, fuzzy fruit with green flesh and black seeds that ripen in early winter. **'Hayward'**, large-fruited commercial form bred in New Zealand. Zones 7–10.

Actinidia kolomikta

syn. *Trochostigma kolomikta*

◐ ✱ ↔17–20 ft (5–6 m)
↑20–35 ft (6–10 m)

A climber from East Asia. Grown for its handsome leaves, green or tipped with white or pink. This strange variegation develops as the plant grows, rarely evident in very young plants. Not produced commercially but, if both male and female plants present, fruit is edible. **'September Sun'**, richer variegated foliage. Zones 4–9.

A

Adenium obesum subsp. *swazicum*

Adenophora polyantha

Adiantum tenerum

ADENIUM

The current view is that this genus, which belongs to the dogbane (Apocynaceae) family, consists of a single variable species ranging from southern Arabia through eastern and central Africa to northeastern South Africa. There are a number of subspecies, some with swollen succulent stems. The less succulent forms are popular ornamentals in tropical gardens around the world, displaying their striking trumpet-shaped blooms. When cut or broken, the milky sap is believed to be poisonous. The fleshy leaves, widest toward the apex, are spirally arranged rather than opposite or whorled.
CULTIVATION: Adeniums are grown outdoors in the tropics, in containers or well-drained garden beds. In warm-temperate climates they can be grown against a hot sunny wall but in cool climates they require a greenhouse or conservatory with high light levels. They are very drought and heat tolerant. Watering through summer and autumn promotes leaf growth and prolongs flowering. Propagation is from seed (if obtainable) or cuttings allowed to callus before planting.

Adenium obesum

syn. *Adenium multiflorum*

DESERT ROSE, IMPALA LILY, SABI STAR

☼ ❄ ↔5 ft (1.5 m) ↑5 ft (1.5 m)

Usually a shrub, branching into multiple stems with age, the impala lily can be more tree-like, reaching a height of 15 ft (4.5 m) or more. Growing on sunny rock outcrops, roots are swollen and succulent, as are the stem bases. The forms grown for showy flowers all belong to A. o. subsp. obesum ★; flower color of cultivars varies from pink to deep crimson, commonly with a white or paler zone, late summer–autumn. A. o. subsp. oleifolium, tuberous and largely underground; A. o. subsp. somaliense, small tree, smooth hairless leaves; A. o. subsp. swazicum, also largely underground. Zones 10–12.

ADENOPHORA

GARLAND FLOWER, LADYBELLS

Found from Europe to Japan, this genus of around 40 species of perennials is closely related to the bellflowers (*Campanula*) and is included in that family (Campanulaceae). They have fleshy roots and may colonize freely in loose open soil in partial shade. Whorls of oblong to pointed oval leaves form at the base of the plants, from which emerge upright flower stems, usually quite narrow and wiry, around which are tiers of tubular to bell-shaped, blue, violet, or pink flowers, opening mainly in summer and autumn.
CULTIVATION: Plant in cool, moist, humus-rich, well-drained soil with shade from the hottest summer sun. Water and feed well during the growing season. Propagate from seed or by division when dormant.

Adenophora liliifolia

syns *Adenophora communis, A. stylosa*

LADYBELLS, LILYLEAF LADYBELLS

☼/◐ ✱ ↔24 in (60 cm)
↑18–24 in (45–60 cm)

From East Asia and central Europe. Erect perennial. Rounded green foliage. Fragrant, pale blue, bell-shaped flowers hang downward along the stem; resemble campanula flower; blooms appear early–mid-summer. Zones 4–8.

Adenophora polyantha

◐ ❄ ↔12–16 in (30–40 cm)
↑36 in (90 cm)

Native to Korea and nearby parts of China. Leaves and flowers in whorls. The flowers are bright blue and closely clustered. Zones 7–9.

ADIANTUM

MAIDENHAIR FERN

Large genus of about 200 terrestrial fern species distributed worldwide; members of the maidenhair-fern (Adiantaceae) family. From the Greek word *adiantos* (dry, unmoistened, or unwettable), because the leaflets appear to be waterproof. Wide range of frond colors: pink and red new fronds, changing to shades of green, including variegated types, on maturity. Pinnules borne on thin, shiny, black or brown stalks, with oblong or fan-shaped leaflets.
CULTIVATION: Organically rich loams, kept moist but not soggy, with surface mulching in humid semi-shaded situations. Soil pH varies according to species. Protect from wind. Allow abundant light but shelter from hot sun. Propagate from spores or by division.

Adiantum aethiopicum

COMMON MAIDENHAIR FERN

◐/● ❄ ↔10–36 in (25–90 cm)
↑8–32 in (20–80 cm)

This widely distributed clumping fern comes from a range of climates in Africa, Australia, and New Zealand. Creeping rhizomes produce clusters of spreading, pinnate, lacy, light green fronds on shiny black stalks. Zones 7–11.

Adiantum capillus-veneris

COMMON MAIDENHAIR, SOUTHERN MAIDENHAIR, TRUE MAIDENHAIR, VENUS MAIDENHAIR, VENUS-HAIR FERN, VENUS'S HAIR

◐/● ❄ ↔12–24 in (30–60 cm)
↑12–24 in (30–60 cm)

Robust wiry fern found worldwide in warm-temperate to tropical climates. Creeping rhizomes produce clusters of many fronds on circular black stalks. Deeply dissected triangular blades give a lacy appearance. Bronze pink new growth. Zones 8–11.

Adiantum hispidulum

◐/● ❄ ↔12–20 in (30–50 cm)
↑12–20 in (30–50 cm)

ROUGH MAIDENHAIR FERN, ROSY MAIDENHAIR FERN, FIVE-FINGERED JACK

Small, clump-forming fern, native to Africa, southern Asia, Australia, and the south Pacific. Fronds have pinkish bronze new growth and overlapping pinnules. Creeping rhizomes. Young fronds initially red becoming light green, then dark green with maturity. Zones 9–12.

Adiantum jordanii

CALIFORNIAN MAIDENHAIR

◐/● ❄ ↔12–24 in (30–60 cm)
↑12–24 in (30–60 cm)

Clump-forming fern native from Baja, Mexico, to Oregon USA. Fronds have triangular pinnate blades of finely toothed pinnules. Flushes of new growth in early spring and again in autumn. Zones 7–10.

Adiantum pedatum

AMERICAN MAIDENHAIR FERN, EASTERN MAIDENHAIR, FIVE-FINGERED MAIDENHAIR FERN

● ✱ ↔12–24 in (30–60 cm)
↑12–24 in (30–60 cm)

Fern from temperate North America and East Asia. Bears pinnate fronds, with primary divisions to 12 in (30 cm) long and green triangular or oblong pinnules. Deciduous in cooler climates. A. p. subsp. calderi, small, clump-forming, upright form from

Adiantum pedatum 'Imbricatum'

northwestern North America with bluish green fronds and small pinnules. A. p. var. aleuticum, deciduous and clump-forming variety from Alaska, USA, Canada, and the Aleutian Islands with pale green fronds, new fronds occasionally flushed with pink. A. p. var. subpumilum, wind-tolerant dwarf variety from northwestern North America, bluish green fronds and overlapping pinnules, yellowish green new growth. **A. p. 'Asiaticum'**, drooping fronds; **'Imbricatum'**, crowded, stiffly erect, green fronds; **'Japonicum'**, pinkish bronze new growth; **'Laceratum'**, deeply cut pinnules; **'Miss Sharples'**, golden green lobed fronds; **'Montanum'**, compact form. Zones 4–9.

Adiantum raddianum

DELTA MAIDENHAIR FERN

↔ 18–24 in (45–60 cm)
↑ 18–24 in (45–60 cm)

This is a widely cultivated clump-forming fern that comes from tropical regions of Uruguay, Brazil, and Paraguay. Clusters of green pinnate fronds with triangular blades and wedge-shaped pinnules are borne on purplish black stalks. This species has numerous cultivars, including: **'Bridal Veil'**, with drooping fronds with small tear-drop segments; **'Deflexum'**, hardy more open form with black stems, triangular fronds, segments smaller than species; **'Elegans'**, with hardy, triangular fronds with heart-shaped segments; **'Fragrantissimum'**, vigorous form with deep green fronds and toothed segments; **'Fritz Luth'**, with triangular, bright green, erect fronds with overlapping segments; **'Gracillimum'**, has pendulous divided fronds with pink new growth; **'Lawsonianum'**, a strong grower with delicate lacy fronds; **'Tinctum'**, from the Andes, with triangular fronds and large, overlapping, wedge-shaped pinnules; and **'Waltonii'**, considered by some to be a cultivar of *Adiantum excisum*. Zones 10–12.

Adiantum tenerum

BRITTLE MAIDENHAIR FERN, FAN MAIDENHAIR FERN

↔ 12–36 in (30–90 cm)
↑ 12–36 in (30–90 cm)

This species of fern is found in tropical to subtropical regions of southwestern USA, the West Indies, and Central America. It has a creeping rhizome and clusters of pinnate fronds with rounded or diamond-shaped blades, borne on glossy maroon-black stalks. Cultivars of this species include: **'Farleyense'**, arching or drooping pinnate fronds, to 36 in (90 cm) long, with large ruffled segments and sharp edges; **'Gloriosum Roseum'**, arching or pendulous fronds with wavy segments and pink new growth; **'Japonicum'**, fronds 6–8 in (15–20 cm) long, with large, deeply lobed, overlapping pinnules on thin wiry stalks; and **'Lady M. Lyalle'**, pale green fronds 12–24 in (30–60 cm) long, with large, deeply incised, fan-like segments. Zones 10–12.

Adiantum venustum

EVERGREEN MAIDENHAIR, HIMALAYAN MAIDENHAIR

↔ 12–48 in (30–120 cm)
↑ 8–32 in (20–80 cm)

Native to high altitudes of Afghanistan, the Himalayas, India, and Canada. Deciduous in cooler climates. It has a creeping rhizome,

Adonis annua

and fronds up to 32 in (80 cm) long with triangular blades and toothed pinnules borne on stalks that extend to 10 in (25 cm) long. Zones 4–9.

ADONIS

This genus, which is a member of the buttercup (Ranunculaceae) family, consists of about 20 species of annual and perennial herbs. It is found in mountain meadows in Europe and Asia. Plants grow to about 16 in (40 cm) with bipinnately divided foliage that is feathery in some species. The white, yellow, or red flowers provide a bright splash in spring. They are up to 3 in (8 cm) across and have 3 to 30 petals. The genus is named after the beautiful youth of Greek mythology who was killed by a wild boar and changed into a flower by Aphrodite.
CULTIVATION: These are plants for the rock garden or front of border, where they require moist but well-drained soil in a sunny or partially shaded site. They are best suited to cooler climates. Propagation can be from fresh seed in summer or by divisions, which may be quite difficult to re-establish, in early spring or autumn.

Adonis aestivalis

PHEASANT'S EYE

↔ 12 in (30 cm) ↑ 18 in (45 cm)

From Europe, this is an annual species with finely divided foliage. Solitary terminal flowers are about 1 in (25 mm) across with 5 to 8 deep blood-red petals with a black base or "eye." Zones 5–9.

Adonis amurensis

PHEASANT'S EYE

↔ 12 in (30 cm) ↑ 12 in (30 cm)

From Asia. Perennial for use in borders, open woodland, and rock gardens. Green, ferny, deeply dissected leaves. Yellow flowers similar to buttercups appear in early spring. **'Sandanzaki'**, a rare and expensive cultivar, grows in deep shade, deep yellow and green petals. Zones 3–9.

Adonis annua

syn. *Adonis autumnalis*

PHEASANT'S EYE

↔ 12 in (30 cm) ↑ 16 in (40 cm)

Found from southern Europe to southwestern Asia and naturalized in the UK and northern Europe. A summer-flowering annual very similar to *A. aestivalis*. Has fine ferny foliage on upright branching stems. Flowers are blood red in color with a black base. Zones 3–9.

AEGOPODIUM

The 5 perennial herbs in this genus in the carrot (Apiaceae) family grow from creeping rhizomes. They are native to Europe and western Asia. Umbels of compound flowers are borne in spring and summer. Fruit are 2-winged or ribbed nuts that separate on ripening.
CULTIVATION: These frost-hardy plants prefer moist well-drained soil in an open sunny position. They are drought tender. Can be invasive and are regarded as weeds in some areas. Propagate from seed.

Aegopodium podagraria

ASH WEED, BISHOP'S WEED, GOUTWEED, GROUND ASH, GROUND ELDER, HERB GERARD

↔ 10–36 in (25–90 cm)
↑ 10–36 in (25–90 cm)

From Europe, naturalized in North America. Leaves usually with 3 oval lobes. Creeping, branching, aromatic, rhizomes and fibrous roots. Large compound umbels of numerous white, pink, or cream flowers in early summer. Oval ribbed fruit. This species was introduced into England during the Norman Conquest and was used as a cure for gout. Young leaves contain high amounts of vitamin C and can be used in salads. **'Variegatum'** has off-white splotches on the edges and surface of its leaves. Zones 3–9.

Aegopodium podagraria 'Variegatum'

AEONIUM

This genus, a member of the stonecrop (Crassulaceae) family, contains around 30 species of often shrubby and woody-stemmed succulents with terminal rosettes of fleshy leaves. Mainly from the Canary Islands and Madeira, they can also be found in eastern and northern Africa, parts of the Mediterranean, and the Middle East. Their brittle branches, often arranged rather like a multi-headed candlestick, are covered with a papery bark. Pyramidal inflorescences of small flowers, which are usually yellow but sometimes red, pink, or white, develop in the centers of the rosettes, usually in spring, followed by brown seed heads.

CULTIVATION: As with most succulents, aeoniums are very drought tolerant once established. They demand full sun and perfect drainage, and in the wild can often be found on precipitous slopes with their roots anchored in the crevices between rocks. They are easily propagated by removing rooted basal suckers, by treating the rosettes as cuttings, or by raising from seed.

Aeonium arboreum

↔ 4 ft (1.2 m) ↑ 6 ft (1.8 m)

From the west coast of Morocco, this heavily branching species has bright green sometimes red tinted leaves in rosettes 6–8 in (15–20 cm) wide. Large conical heads of yellow flowers in spring. A. a. var. holochrysum, 7 ft (2 m) tall, very showy sprays of yellow flowers in summer; A. a. **'Atropurpureum'** ★, deep purple-bronze leaves; and the cream-variegated **'Variegatum'**. Zones 9–11.

Aeonium canariense

CANARY ISLANDS AEONIUM, GIANT VELVET ROSE, VELVET ROSE

↔ 20–48 in (50–120 cm)
↑ 8–24 in (20–60 cm)

Canary Islands native with short-stemmed rosettes up to 18 in (45 cm) across. Individual leaflets spoon-shaped, downy, gray-green, with red or yellow edges. Stems multiple but usually unbranched. Yellow-green flowerheads in spring, at 2–3 years. Whole plant monocarpic (dies after flowering), not just stems. Zones 9–11.

Aeonium decorum ★

↔ 12–36 in (30–90 cm)
↑ 16–24 in (40–60 cm)

Shrubby and branching. Relatively small rosettes with glossy blue-green leaves to 2 in (5 cm) long, often brown-marked and red-edged. Yellow flowers from mid-spring to mid-summer. A. d. var. mascaense (syn. *A. mascaense*) is a compact densely branching plant with succulent, red-marked, bright green leaves. A. d. **'Tricolor'** ★ has green, cream, and pink variegated foliage. Zones 9–11.

Aeonium arboreum

Aeonium glandulosum

↔ 32 in (80 cm) ↑ 20 in (50 cm)

Biennial or perennial from Madeira. Shrubby habit with flat wide rosettes of aromatic light green leaves to 5 in (12 cm) long. Yellow or white flower sprays, up to 12 in (30 cm) long, in summer. Often monocarpic (dies after flowering). Zones 9–11.

Aeonium haworthii

PINWHEEL

↔ 32 in (80 cm) ↑ 24 in (60 cm)

Mounding subshrub, occasionally branching stems with aerial roots, from the Canary Islands. Small rosettes with red-edged blue-green leaves to slightly over 2 in (5 cm) long. Pink-flushed pale yellow flowers from spring. Drops much foliage while flowering. **'Variegatum'** ★ has cream variegated foliage that develops pink tints. Zones 9–11.

Aeonium lindleyi

↔ 27 in (70 cm) ↑ 20 in (50 cm)

Spreading subshrub from the Canary Islands. Small rosettes of aromatic, thickly succulent, broad leaves to around 2 in (5 cm) long. Leaves have fine hairs and are sticky. Yellow flowers from spring. Rosette dies after flowering. Zones 10–11.

Aeonium nobile

↔ 36 in (90 cm) ↑ 24 in (60 cm)

Canary Islands perennial with erect unbranched stems, each bearing a cup-shaped rosette to 20 in (50 cm) wide. Brown-tinted leaves to 12 in (30 cm) long, edged with fine hairs, sticky when young. Tiny yellow flowers in dome-shaped inflorescences. Zones 9–11.

Aeonium sedifolium

↔ 16 in (40 cm) ↑ 16 in (40 cm)

Small shrubby perennial from the Canary Islands. Branching stems and small rosettes of a few thickly succulent mid-green leaves, sometimes with red to brown stripes, each less than 1 in (25 mm) long. Leaves sticky when young. Zones 9–11.

Aeonium spathulatum

↔ 24 in (60 cm) ↑ 24 in (60 cm)

From the Canary Islands, Madeira, and nearby Atlantic Islands. Has branching upright stems with 2 in (5 cm) wide rosettes of bright green to gray-green, 1 in (25 mm) long leaves with a brown mid-stripe. Small sprays of yellow flowers from spring. Zones 9–11.

Aeonium tabuliforme ★

↔ 24 in (60 cm) ↑ 12 in (30 cm)

Low spreading biennial or perennial from the Canary Islands. Has flat rosettes to 16 in (40 cm) wide, densely packed with spirals of pale green. Leaves are often red-tinted and hair-fringed, to 8 in (20 cm) long. Flower stems tall and branching, with yellow flowers. Usually monocarpic (dies after flowering). Zones 9–11.

Aeonium undulatum

SAUCER PLANT

↔ 24 in (60 cm) ↑ 12 in (30 cm)

From the Canary Islands, this plant forms clumps of usually unbranched upright stems bearing huge cup-shaped rosettes of deep green brown-edged leaves, around 6 in (15 cm) long but sometimes larger, curved inward. Yellow flowers in spring. Zones 9–11.

Aeonium urbicum

↔ 3–6 ft (0.9–1.8 m)
↑ 3–6 ft (0.9–1.8 m)

From the Canary Islands. Upright unbranched stems with densely foliaged cup-shaped rosettes of blue-green leaves to 6 in (15 cm) long, fleshy at the base. Creamy yellow flowers through the warmer months. Usually monocarpic (dies after flowering). Zones 9–11.

Aeonium Hybrid Cultivars

↔ 8–24 in (20–60 cm)
↑ 12–24 in (30–60 cm)

A number of cultivars have arisen from either deliberate or accidental crosses between *Aeonium* species. They feature more colorful foliage (bronze or variegated), or larger, more brightly colored flowers. Cultivars include: **'Plum Purdy'**, rosettes of maroon leaves; **'Sunburst'** ★, symmetrical rosettes of pale green leaves with clearly defined creamy yellow edges that often develop pink tints; **'Zwartkop'** ★, rosettes of shiny reddish black leaves. Zones 9–11.

AESCULUS

BUCKEYE, HORSE CHESTNUT

There are about 15 species of deciduous shrubs to tall trees in this genus, a member of the soapberry (Sapindaceae) family. Half are native to North America, commonly called buckeye; the remainder spread from Asia to southeastern Europe. Growing in sheltered valleys they have large compound leaves of 5 to 11 leaflets palmately arranged, and in spring to summer showy upright panicles of cream to reddish flowers are borne. The inedible fruits are held in big seed capsules that vary from smooth to spiny and give rise to the other common name, horse chestnut.

CULTIVATION: These trees do best in cool-temperate climates with marked differences in summer and winter temperatures. The larger species suit parks and open landscapes where their pyramidal crowns can develop fully. They need a deep, fertile, and moisture-retentive soil. Propagation is by seed, which is best sown fresh, and cultivars are grafted in late winter.

Aesculus californica

CALIFORNIA BUCKEYE

↔ 30 ft (9 m) ↑ 15 ft (4.5 m)

From California and Oregon, USA. Spreading shrub with grayish green leaves. Cylindrical panicles of creamy white flowers, pink tinged, in summer, followed by fig-shaped fruit. Can stand hot dry summers. Deciduous in summer in dry areas. Zones 7–10.

Aesculus × *carnea*

Aesculus × *carnea*

syn. *Aesculus rubicunda*

RED HORSE CHESTNUT

↔15 ft (4.5 m) ↑30 ft (9 m)

Hybrid of *A. hippocastanum* and *A. pavia,* thought to have originated in Germany. Erect panicles of deep reddish pink flowers with yellow blotches in spring. Better suited to warm climates than other species. **'Briotii'** (syn. *A. hippocastanum* **'Briotii'**) has bigger and darker flowers. Zones 6–9.

Aesculus chinensis

CHINESE HORSE CHESTNUT

↔35 ft (10 m) ↑90 ft (27 m)

Native to northern China, common tree in temple grounds. Cylindrical panicles of white flowers, up to 18 in (45 cm) long, in summer. Quite slow growing in cultivation, best suited to areas with hot summers and cold dry winters. Zones 6–9.

Aesculus 'Dallimorei'

↔25 ft (8 m) ↑40 ft (12 m)

A graft hybrid of *A. hippocastanum* and *A. flava*, with dark green leaves, downy beneath. Flowers in summer, on erect panicles, up to 8 in (20 cm) long, white to cream with a maroon spot. Zones 5–9.

Aesculus 'Dallimorei'

Aesculus flava

syn. *Aesculus octandra*

SWEET BUCKEYE, YELLOW BUCKEYE

↔35 ft (10 m) ↑90 ft (27 m)

An attractive species that is native to central and eastern USA. Leaflets, which have downy veins, color yellow and orange shades in autumn. Erect panicles of yellow flowers are seen in summer. Hybrids of the species can occur in a variety of colors. A. f. f. vestita has downy young twigs and undersides of leaves. Zones 4–9.

Aesculus hippocastanum

COMMON HORSE CHESTNUT, EUROPEAN HORSE CHESTNUT, HORSE CHESTNUT

↔70 ft (21 m) ↑100 ft (30 m)

Handsome spreading tree from a limited area of Greece, Albania, and Bulgaria. Best suited to parks and large gardens. It has erect panicles of white flowers with yellow to red basal blotches in late spring, followed by round prickly fruits known commonly as conkers. Is tolerant of pollution. Of the cultivars, **'Baumannii'** has a rounded crown and showy, white, doubleflowers; and **'Pyramidalis'** has a pyramidal growth habit. Zones 6–9.

Aesculus indica

INDIAN HORSE CHESTNUT

↔70 ft (21 m) ↑100 ft (30 m)

Tree from northwestern Himalayas, Tends to be low-branching or even multi-stemmed. Young leaves are bronze-pink. Flowers are white, tinged yellow-red, in pyramidal panicles up to 15 in (38 cm) long, in early to mid-summer. **'Sydney Pearce'** is a sturdy cultivar. Zones 6–9.

Aesculus parryi

PARRY'S BUCKEYE

↔3–10 ft (0.9–3 m)
↑3–10 ft (0.9–3 m)

Xerophytic shrub from the dry hills of northern Baja California, Mexico. Thick branches, sparse small leaves, short sprays of flowers after leaves fall as summer dry season sets in. Only North American west coast species apart from *A. californica.* Zones 9–11.

Aesculus hippocastanum

Aesculus parviflora

BOTTLEBRUSH BUCKEYE

↔15 ft (4.5 m) ↑10 ft (3 m)

A graceful shrub growing in woodland areas of southeastern USA. Leaves downy beneath, buff-colored when young. Slender panicles of white summer flowers with protruding pink stamens. Best in areas with hot humid summers. A. p. f. serotina, leaves less downy, bluish green. Zones 6–10.

Aesculus pavia

syn. *Aesculus splendens*

RED BUCKEYE

↔10 ft (3 m) ↑15 ft (4.5 m)

From woodlands on coastal plains of eastern USA. Shrub or small tree. Leaves reddish in autumn. Crimson flowers on short erect panicles in early summer. **'Atrosanguinea'**, deep red flowers. Zones 6–10.

AFROCARPUS

The 6 or so species of this African genus of conifers, of the podocarp or plum-pine (Podocarpaceae) family, were formerly included in *Podocarpus*. In their native habitats they are tall forest trees with massive trunks, seen in mountainous regions of central, eastern, and southern Africa. At up to 250 ft (75 m) high, *A. usambarensis* is one of Africa's tallest trees. All have attractive bark that peels off in flakes or strips. Leaves are leathery and narrow. Male (pollen) and female (seed) organs are on different trees; female cones have a relatively thin stalk with a single, usually larger seed with a thick juicy outer layer. CULTIVATION: These slow-growing trees suit parks and avenues in warm-temperate and subtropical climates with adequate rainfall. Plant in deep, well-drained, reasonably fertile soil. They are affected by few pests or diseases and require little shaping. Propagation normally from seed, sown fresh after removing the fleshy coating.

Afrocarpus falcatus

Afrocarpus falcatus

syns *Nageia falcata, Podocarpus falcatus*

OUTENIQUA YELLOWWOOD

↔25–50 ft (8–15 m)
↑60–200 ft (18–60 m)

One of South Africa's largest trees. In cultivation reaches 30–50 ft (9–15 m). Peeling and flaky bark, purplish brown to paler red-brown. Fine dense foliage, drab green. Female trees covered in pale yellow "fruit" in summer–autumn. Zones 9–11.

AGAPANTHUS

AFRICAN LILY, LILY-OF-THE-NILE

This southern African genus consists of 10 species of fleshy-rooted perennials of the onion (Alliaceae) family. Long, strappy, fleshy leaves form dense clumps of evergreen or deciduous foliage. Tall flower stems with heads of tubular to bell-shaped flowers, usually blue, are held above the foliage. Flowers of evergreens appear over a long season in frost-free climates, and in summer elsewhere. Their narrow, rather upright habit makes them ideal border plants, but old yellowing foliage should be removed. Dwarf forms are superb in large rockeries or containers. The name agapanthus is derived from the Greek *agape*, meaning love, and *anthos*, meaning flower. Agapanthus is therefore the flower of love, though the reason for the name is unclear—perhaps one needs to grow it to know? CULTIVATION: Easily grown in any well-drained soil in sun or half-sun. Will withstand drought and poor soil but better flower production with good conditions. Slugs and snails often damage young foliage. Propagate by division in winter or raise from seed.

Agapanthus africanus

syn. *Agapanthus umbellatus*

AFRICAN LILY, BLUE AFRICAN LILY, LILY-OF-THE-NILE

↔24–36 in (60–90 cm)
↑18–24 in (45–60 cm)

A compact species from Western Cape in South Africa. Leaves are evergreen, 12–15 in (30–38 cm) long. Flower stems extend to 24 in (60 cm) with 1–2 in (2.5–5 cm) long, purple-blue, tubular flowers. Of the cultivars, **'Albus'** has white flowers; and **'Sapphire'** has deep blue flowers. Zones 8–11.

A

Agapanthus praecox cultivar

Agapanthus inapertus

DRAKENSBERG AGAPANTHUS, DROOPING AGAPANTHUS

↔ 40–50 in (100–130 cm)
↕ 40–50 in (100–130 cm)

Deciduous species from southeastern South Africa forming dense clump of blue-tinted leaves up to 27 in (70 cm) long. Pendulous, bright purple blue, sometimes white, tubular flowers on stems up to 5 ft (1.5 m). **A. i. subsp. hollandii,** especially tall stems and flared flowers. **A. i. subsp. pendulus** (syn. *A. pendulus*), light blue flowers, conspicuous protruding stamens. Zones 7–10.

Agapanthus praecox

↔ 40–50 in (100–130 cm)
↕ 40 in (100 cm)

Evergreen, fleshy, bright green leaves to 27 in (70 cm) long. Wide-opening pale to mid-blue flowers on stems to 36 in (90 cm) tall. Most widely cultivated species in warm-temperate gardens. A. p. subsp. orientalis, smaller than the species, forms dense foliage clumps with tightly packed heads of small bright blue flowers. Zones 8–11.

Agapanthus Hybrid Cultivars

↔ 12–30 in (30–75 cm)
↕ 15–48 in (38–120 cm)

Variable group of largely undetermined parentage, ranging from plants suitable for large gardens to those for rockeries or tubs. Mainly easily grown in areas with not too severe winters. Cultivars include: **'Baby Blue'**, a dwarf cultivar with bright blue flowers on 12–16 in (30–40 cm) tall stems; **'Black Pantha'**, purple-blue flowers opening from black buds, 5 ft (1.5 m) tall; **'Cloudy Days'**, white flowers, lavender to blue at base, 32 in (80 cm) tall; **'Elaine'**, upright, vigorous, deep purple-blue flowers on 4 ft (1.2 m) high stems; **'Ellamae'**, bright violet-blue flowers on stems to 5 ft (1.5 m) tall; **'Henryi'**, dwarf, narrow leaves, white flowers on 18 in (45 cm) tall stems; **'Lilliput'**, dwarf, dark blue flowers on 18 in (45 cm) tall stems; **'Loch Hope'**, large heads of dark blue flowers, 4 ft (1.2 m) high stems, late-flowering; Midnight Blue/**'Monmid'**, compact, deep purple-blue flowers on 16 in (40 cm) tall stems; **'Peter Pan'**, dwarf, mid-blue flowers on 12 in (30 cm) high stems; **'Queen Anne'**, bright blue flowers on 24 in (60 cm) tall stems; **'Queen Mum'**, white flowers shading to lavender at base, 40 in (100 cm) tall; **'Rancho White'**, white tubular flowers on stems to 18 in (45 cm) tall; **'Snowball'**, white flowers, 12 in (30 cm) tall; **'Storm Cloud'**, intense purple-blue flowers on 4 ft (1.2 m) high stems; and **'Tinkerbell'**, leaves edged cream, pale blue flowers on 16 in (40 cm) tall stems. Zones 7–11.

AGAPETES

syn. *Pentapterygium*

Allied to *Vaccinium* in the heath (Ericaceae) family, this genus consists of over 90 species of low, often creeping or scrambling shrubs native to tropical and subtropical Asia, the Malay Archipelago, Pacific islands, and Australia. Found in mountain rainforests, many grow as epiphytes. Leaves are mostly leathery and new growth is colored pink, red, or orange. Emerging singly or in small sprays, flowers are tubular and rather waxy, often 5-angled or 5-ribbed. CULTIVATION: Most can be grown outdoors in sheltered positions in a mild frost-free climate. Some of the Himalayan species will cope with some frost, but are best planted under trees. Plant in a well-drained spot in acidic humus-rich soil. Conservatory plants prefer a peaty medium in a large pot or hanging basket, and good light with regular watering and misting. Propagation is easiest by layering, although cuttings can also be used.

Agapetes 'Ludgvan Cross'

↔ 5 ft (1.5 m) ↕ 3 ft (0.9 m)

Hybrid of *A. incurvata* and *A. serpens.* Leaves to 1½ in (35 mm) long. Pink flowers with darker chevron markings and red calyces. Generally similar to *A. serpens* but with larger leaves and lighter-colored flowers. Zones 8–11.

Agapetes 'Ludgvan Cross'

Agapetes serpens

↔ 7 ft (2 m) ↕ 3 ft (0.9 m)

Widely cultivated, this evergreen shrub has arching reddish stems arising from a central rootstock. Along the stems 5-sided, tubular, red flowers with darker chevron markings open late winter. Often grown in hanging baskets. Zones 9–11.

AGASTACHE

GIANT HYSSOP, MEXICAN HYSSOP

There are 20 species of very aromatic perennials in this genus, which is a member of the mint (Lamiaceae) family. They are native to North America, China, and Japan where they grow in dry scrub and fields. Leaf shape varies from pointed oval to almost triangular or lance shaped, the margins being shallowly to finely toothed. Flowers may be red, orange, rose, violet, blue, or white, typically tubular with two lips. They are borne in densely packed whorls on spikes or narrow panicles in summer and are very popular with bees. Some species are used in herbal medicines and teas. CULTIVATION: Grow in a well-drained soil in a sunny position. Most species tolerate some frost but the more tender ones should be given a warm sheltered site in cooler climates or be grown as annuals. Can be susceptible to fungal diseases in summer. Propagate from seed or cuttings.

Agastache aurantiaca

ORANGE HUMMINGBIRD MINT

↔ 24 in (60 cm)
↕ 18–30 in (45–75 cm)

Bushy perennial found from southern USA to Mexico. Pointed, oval to lance-shaped, grayish green leaves. Whorls of orangey pink tubular flowers, on spikes, summer–autumn. Zones 7–10.

Agastache cana

HUMMINGBIRD PLANT, MOSQUITO PLANT

↔ 12–18 in (30–45 cm)
↕ 20–24 in (50–60 cm)

Woody-based perennial from southern USA. Slightly downy triangular or pointed oval leaves. Crushed foliage is said to repel insects. Flower spikes, to 12 in (30 cm) long, bear whorls of rose-colored tubular flowers. **'Heather Queen'** ★ has bright pink flowers. Zones 7–11.

Agastache foeniculum

syns *Agastache anethiodora, A. anisata*

ANISE HYSSOP

↔ 18–24 in (45–60 cm)
↕ 20–32 in (50–80 cm)

Very aromatic plant from North America. Smells of aniseed when foliage is brushed or crushed. Leaves triangular to pointed oval with toothed margins, downy beneath. Short, densely packed flower spikes bear small violet-blue flowers. Zones 8–10.

Agastache mexicana

MEXICAN GIANT HYSSOP, MEXICAN HYSSOP

↔ 18 in (45 cm) ↕ 24 in (60 cm)

From Mexico. Upright perennial with creeping roots. Lance-shaped, serrated edged leaves. Flower spikes, to 12 in (30 cm) long, bear deep pink to crimson flowers. Can be grown as an annual. Zones 9–11.

Agastache pallida

PALE GIANT HYSSOP

↔ 12–18 in (30–45 cm)
↕ 30–50 in (75–130 cm)

Found in Arizona, USA, and neighboring parts of Mexico. Woody-based perennial. Leaves triangular to pointed oval with coarsely toothed margins. Flower spikes 8–15 in (20–38 cm) long, bear crowded whorls of tubular flowers with reddish purple calyces and rose-colored petals. **A. p. var. pallida** (syn. *A. barberi*) grows to around 24 in (60 cm) tall and has shorter flower spikes. Zones 8–10.

Agastache rugosa 'Honeybee Blue'

Agastache, Hybrid Cultivar, 'Blue Fortune'

Agastache rugosa

HUO XIANG, KOREAN MINT, WRINKLED GIANT HYSSOP

☼ ❄ ↔ 24 in (60 cm)
↕ 24–48 in (60–120 cm)

From China and Japan, this erect perennial has coarsely toothed ovate leaves that have hairy undersides. The leaves are used for seasoning meat, as a tea, and in Eastern medicine. In summer, short compact spikes bear small tubular flowers of violet to rose. The **Honeybee Series,** which offers compact plants in selected color strains, includes **'Honeybee White'** and **'Honeybee Blue'** (**'Licorice Blue' is often said to be the prior/correct name for this**). Zones 7–11.

Agastache rupestris

LICORICE MINT, SUNSET HYSSOP, THREADLEAF GIANT HYSSOP

☼ ✱ ↔ 18 in (45 cm)
↕ 18–36 in (45–90 cm)

A very aromatic species found from southwestern USA to northern Mexico. The grayish green thread-like leaves give the plant a feathery look. Leaves may be used in tea. Orange flowers with lavender calyces, creating the "sunset" effect of its common name, are borne in summer. **'Sunset'** is a slightly shorter cultivar. Zones 5–9.

Agastache Hybrid Cultivars

☼ ❄ ↔ 1–3 ft (0.3–0.9 m)
↕ 2–6 ft (0.6–1.8 m)

The crossing of several species has resulted in a range of hybrid cultivars of varying heights and colors. Cultivars include: **'Apricot Sunrise'**, grayish green foliage and spikes of orange flowers; **'Blue Fortune'**, bluish purple flowers; **'Firebird'**, flowers of coppery orange tones; **'Tangerine Dreams'**, similar to 'Apricot Sunrise' but a taller plant; and **'Tutti Frutti'**, with grayish green leaves and flowers of raspberry red. The **Dryspell** cultivars are a range of Australian-raised drought-tolerant plants and include orange, pink, and salmon flower colors. Zones 7–10.

AGATHOSMA

These 135 heather-like shrubs and subshrubs belong to the rue (Rutaceae) family, and are native to the southwestern Cape in South Africa. They are 15–24 in (38–60 cm) tall and slightly less in spread. The plant is densely covered with small narrow leaves, often rolled at the edges. The small 5-petalled flowers are in axillary clusters or umbels, ranging from white through to red-mauve and occasionally yellow. The whole plant is aromatic.
CULTIVATION: These plants thrive in neutral to acid, humus-rich, sandy soil with added grit in full sun. In cool-temperate regions grow in containers, putting outdoors in summer. Need moderate watering in the growing season and feeding with a balanced fertilizer once a month. Reduce watering as the weather becomes colder. Overwinter in frost-free conditions. Propagation is from seed in spring, in lime-free compost with added grit, or from ripe cuttings in summer.

Agathosma ovata

OVAL-LEAF BUCHU

☼ ❄ ↔ 18 in (45 cm) ↕ 18 in (45 cm)

From the Cape region of South Africa. Leaves ½ in (12 mm) long. Small pinkish lilac flowers in small clusters in leaf axils on the newer wood of branch tips. Zones 9–10.

AGAVE

CENTURY PLANT

A genus containing about 225 species, 50 subspecies, and varieties of rosette-shaped, succulent, monocarpic plants in the asparagus (Asparagaceae) family. They are found from southwest USA to Mexico, Central America and the Caribbean, into Colombia and Venezuela. The genus name comes from the Greek *agavos* (stately or noble). Most species take decades to bloom, hence the common name, though many flower within 8–25 years in ideal conditions. After blooming they usually set seeds and some produce offsets or bulbils on the inflorescence. The leaves usually terminate in a strong sharp spike, and mostly have spiny teeth on the margins. Most species produce basal offsets to ensure survival when the mother plant dies after flowering. Native American peoples have long used agaves for food, fibers, soap, beverages, and medicines. In many tropical areas they are grown to produce sisal for rope, twine, and bags. In Mexico, they are used to make the popular beverages pulque and tequila.
CULTIVATION: Grow in rich well-drained soil. Propagate from seed, offsets, or bulbils. Most benefit from a rest in winter; many need protection from frost.

Agave americana

☼ ❄ ↔ 7–15 ft (2–4.5 m)
↕ 17–30 ft (5–9 m)

From northeastern Mexico. Highly variable, medium to large, hardy species with curving blue-gray leaves. Have 10–20 leaves, 5–8 ft (1.5–2.4 m) long, lance-shaped, toothed, flat to guttered, hard, often turned down with age. Inflorescence 17–50 ft (5–15 m) long with 15 to 35 branches. Numerous, yellow, funnel-shaped flowers. A. a. var. marginata has yellow or white variegated stripes on the leaf margins. A. a. **'Cornelius'**, compact form with broad yellow margins on leaves; **'Mediopicta'** ★, yellow variegated mid-stripe on leaves; **'Mediopicta Alba'** ★, white variegated mid-stripe on the leaves. Zones 8–11.

Agave angustifolia

☼ ❄ ↔ 7–8 ft (2–2.4 m)
↕ 10–17 ft (3–5 m)

Highly variable species, widespread from Mexico through to Costa Rica. Almost spherical to cylindrical growth habit. Numerous, straight, rigid leaves, tapering toward the tip, 20–60 in (50–150 cm) long, light green to gray-green, toothed. Inflorescence 10–17 ft (3–5 m) long, branched, producing bulbils. Flowers green to yellow. A. angustifolia var. marginata is a variegated form. Zones 9–11.

Agave attenuata ★

☼ ❄ ↔ 24–60 in (60–150 cm)
↕ 3–7 ft (0.9–2 m)

From just a few habitats in Mexico. Brittle, almost flat, rounded, lime-green to bluish green leaves, 10–28 in (25–70 cm) long, lacking teeth and terminal spine. Inflorescence an arching spike, 7–15 ft (2–4.5 m) long. Displays pale yellow flowers and offsets. **'Boutin Blue'** ★ is a distinctly blue-gray cultivar. Zones 9–11.

Agave celsii

syn. *Agave mitis*

☼ ❄ ↔ 28 in (70 cm) ↕ 5–8 ft (1.5–2.4 m)

From eastern Mexico. Medium to large species forming large clumps with age. Leaves apple green to blue-gray, 12–24 in (30–60 cm) long, soft, succulent, curving upward. Margins slightly wavy, with small reddish brown teeth, closely spaced. Inflorescence a spike, 5–8 ft (1.5–2.4 m) long. Flowers greenish with tinge of lilac. Zones 9–11.

Agave chiapensis

☼ ❄ ↔ 20–40 in (50–100 cm) ↕ 7 ft (2 m)

From Chiapas, Mexico. A medium rosette, solitary to clustering, making a short stem. Leaves dark green, 14–20 in (35–50 cm) long, thick, smooth, flat to slightly concave. Margins slightly wavy, with small dark brown teeth. Inflorescence a spike, 7 ft (2 m) tall. Flowers yellow, tinged red. Zones 9–11.

Agave americana 'Mediopicta Alba'

A

Agave chrysantha

GOLDENFLOWER CENTURY PLANT

↔4–6 ft (1.2–1.8 m)
↑15 ft (4.5 m)

Native to Arizona, USA, where it occurs at elevations up to 6,000 ft (1,800 m). Forms a single rosette of long blue green leaves to 3 ft (0.9 m) long, edged with fierce spines. After many years it produces a spectacular branching golden-yellow inflorescence. Zones 8–11.

Agave colorata ★

↔4–6 ft (1.2–1.8 m)
↑7–10 ft (2–3 m)

An attractive small plant from Sonora, Mexico. Leaves with wavy edges, prominent cross-bands of color, 10–24 in (25–60 cm) long, gray-blue, rough, with strong bud imprints on both sides of the leaves. Leaf margins are indented between strong brown teeth. Inflorescence is 7–10 ft (2–3 m) long, often arched, with 15–20 branches. Flowers are bright yellow. Zones 9–11.

Agave dasylirioides

↔24–36 in (60–90 cm)
↑5–7 ft (1.5–2 m)

From Morales, Mexico. Small, usually solitary, species with atypically thin, scarcely succulent leaves. Leaves 16–24 in (40–60 cm) long, bluish green, lacking teeth, with 1 mm wide yellow-green margin. Inflorescence an arching spike, 5–7 ft (1.5–2 m) tall. Flowers greenish yellow with pink filaments and yellow anthers. Zones 9–11.

Agave deserti

↔16–24 in (40–60 cm)
↑8–15 ft (2.4–4.5 m)

From southern California and southwestern Arizona, USA, and northern Sonoran Desert areas of Mexico. Simple to clumping, with narrow bluish green to gray leaves, 6–16 in (15–40 cm) long. Small, sharp, marginal teeth. Inflorescence 8–15 ft (2.4–4.5 m) tall, branched. Flowers bright yellow. Zones 9–11.

Agave deserti, in the wild, Baja, California

Agave desmettiana

↔24–32 in (60–80 cm)
↑7–10 ft (2–3 m)

From Cuba. Urn-shaped plant with smooth, arched, toothless leaves, 20–24 in (50–60 cm) long. Inflorescence 7–10 ft (2–3 m) tall, with 20–25 compact branches. Flowers pale yellow. Zones 9–12.

Agave filifera ★

↔28 in (70 cm) ↑7–8 ft (2–2.4 m)

This densely clumping species is from central southern Mexico. Numerous leaves, dark to mid-green, with clear white leaf bud imprints, margins lacking teeth but bearing many white hairs or filaments. Leaves straight to incurving, 6–8 in (15–20 cm) long. Inflorescence a spike, 7–8 ft (2–2.4 m) tall. Flowers greenish with purple tinge. Zones 8–11.

Agave geminiflora

syn. *Agave boscii*

↔24–32 in (60–80 cm)
↑10–15 ft (3–4.5 m)

From a restricted area of Nayarit State in Mexico. Large solitary species with 100 to 200 long, thin, flexible, dark green leaves, 20 in (50 cm) long, bearing white filaments on margins lacking teeth. Inflorescence a spike, 10–15 ft (3–4.5 m) tall. Flowers in pairs, yellow, tinged red. Zones 7–11.

Agave ghiesbreghtii

↔20–28 in (50–70 cm)
↑10–15 ft (3–4.5 m)

Suckering species found from southern Mexico to Guatemala. Leaves dark green, 12–16 in (30–40 cm) long, stout, half-rounded, curving upward. Thick white to gray leaf margins bearing many straight to curved teeth. Inflorescence is a spike, 10–15 ft (3–4.5 m) tall. Flowers greenish purple. Zones 9–12.

Agave 'Kichiokan'

↔24 in (60 cm) ↑10 ft (3 m)

A neat, symmetrical, slowly offsetting cultivar, possibly of *A. potatorum*, but with shorter more compact leaves and larger more brightly colored teeth on leaf margins. **'Kichiokan Variegated'** is a variegated form with ½–¾ in (12–18 mm) wide bands of yellow on the leaf margins. Zones 9–11.

Agave lechuguilla

SHIN DAGGER

↔8–12 in (20–30 cm)
↑8–17 ft (2.4–5 m)

Widespread, low-growing, densely clumping species from southern New Mexico and Texas, USA, and Chihuahua Desert areas of Mexico south to Hidalgo State. Leaves light to yellowish green with darker striations, straight, upright, concaved, 10–20 in (25–50 cm) long, forming a narrow rosette. Thin, gray, horny leaf margins bear irregularly spaced, downward-pointing teeth. Inflorescence a spike, 8–17 ft (2.4–5 m) tall. Flowers yellow with tinges of purple. Zones 8–11.

Agave macroacantha ★

↔12–24 in (30–60 cm) ↑6 ft (1.8 m)

From Oaxaca and Puebla, Mexico. Small, symmetrical, clustering species with stout blue-gray leaves, 10–15 in (25–38 cm) long, flat on upper surface, convexed below. Teeth 3–6 mm long, irregularly spaced along margin. Inflorescence upright, 10 to 14 branches. Flowers green to purple. Zones 10–12.

Agave mckelveyana

↔12–20 in (30–50 cm)
↑7–10 ft (2–3 m)

From central western Arizona, USA. Small, narrow-leafed, heavily toothed, dull gray-green species. Leaves straight or slightly wavy, margins with low tubercles. Teeth widely spaced, to ¼ in (6 mm) long, downward-pointing with red tips. Inflorescence 7–10 ft (2–3 m) tall, 10 to 20 branches. Flowers yellow. Zones 7–11.

Agave murpheyi

↔27–32 in (70–80 cm)
↑10–15 ft (3–4.5 m)

From central Arizona, USA. Medium-sized gray-green to yellow-green species. Leaves have some cross-banding, strong leaf bud imprints, flat at base, concaved at tips, 20–28 in (50–70 cm) long. Teeth small, brown, regularly spaced. Inflorescence branched, 10–15 ft (3–4.5 m) tall, usually producing a few seed pods and many bulbils. Flowers yellow-green, purple tinge. Zones 8–11.

Agave ocahui

↔20–40 in (50–100 cm) ↑10 ft (3 m)

From Sonora, Mexico. Solitary highly prized species, rarely producing offsets or bulbils, usually grown from seeds. Symmetrical rosette of small, smooth, dark green, dagger-shaped leaves with narrow brownish red to gray margins that detach from the older leaves. Leaves 10–20 in (25–50 cm) long. Inflorescence a 10 ft (3 m) tall spike. Flowers yellow. Zones 9–11.

Agave palmeri

↔40–48 in (100–120 cm)
↑10–17 ft (3–5 m)

From southeast Arizona and southwest New Mexico, USA, and Sonora and Chihuahua, Mexico. Usually solitary medium-sized species, variable size and leaf form. Leaves bluish green to pale green, long, tapering to a point, stiff, incurving, 14–30 in (35–75 cm) long, toothed margins. Inflorescence 10–17 ft (3–5 m) tall, 8 to 12 branches. Flowers white, reddish bud. Zones 8–11.

Agave parryi ★

syn. *Agave patonii*

↔20–28 in (50–70 cm)
↑12–20 ft (3.5–6 m)

Compact solitary to suckering species from southeastern Arizona and southwestern New Mexico, USA, and Durango and Chihuahua, Mexico. Tight rosette of 100 to 150 leaves, 10–16 in (25–40 cm) long, straight to slightly rounded, ending in a distinctly sharp tip. Leaves smooth, rigid, flat to slightly concave, overlapping, light

Agave parryi

Agave ocahui

gray to blue-green, toothed margins. Inflorescence 12–20 ft (3.5–6 m) tall, 20 to 30 branches. Flowers yellow, tinged red. **A. p. var. huachucensis,** larger and more densely foliaged than the type, growing up to 5 ft (1.5 m) wide. **A. p. var. truncata,** more attractive form of this species with particularly short, rounded leaves. **A. p. subsp. neomexicana** (syn. *A. neomexicana*), leaves rolled inward, flowers may be yellow or orange. Zones 7–11.

Agave parviflora

☼ ❄ ↔ 6–8 in (15–20 cm)
↑ 3–7 ft (0.9–2 m)

From southern Arizona, USA, and the northern Sonoran Desert regions of Mexico. Neat symmetrical species, solitary or with few offsets. Leaves marked with thick white leaf bud imprints, filaments on margins. Leaves 2–4 in (5–10 cm) long. Inflorescence a spike, 3–7 ft (0.9–2 m) tall. Flowers yellow. Zones 8–11.

Agave potatorum

☼ ❅ ↔ 3–8 ft (0.9–2.4 m) ↑ 15 ft (4.5 m)

From Puebla and Oaxaca, Mexico. Symmetrical plant with whitish gray-green leaves, deeply indented along margins, bearing large tubercles from which widely spaced, hooked, red-brown teeth arise. A. p. var. verschaffeltii ★ is distinguished by its whiter color and bigger tubercles on the leaf margins. Zones 9–11.

Agave salmiana

MAGUEY DE PULQUE

☼ ❅ ↔ 10–15 ft (3–4.5 m)
↑ 15–35 ft (4.5–10 m)

A very large, variable, offsetting species, widespread in central Mexico, especially in the States of San Luis Potosi, Hidalgo, and Michoacan. Strong, wide, gray-green, upwardly curving leaves, 3–7 ft (0.9–2 m) long, strongly keeled at the ends, toothed margins. A. s. var. ferox ★ (syn. *A. ferox*), graceful urn shape; leaves thick, shiny, green, with strong leaf bud imprints and wavy warty margins. Zones 9–11.

Agave schidigera

☼ ❅ ↔ 40–60 in (100–150 cm)
↑ 7–12 ft (2–3.5 m)

Native to Chihuahua, Durango, Hidalgo, Zacatecas, San Luis Potosi, and smaller adjacent Mexican States. A solitary to non-suckering species. Leaves 12–20 in (30–50 cm) long, lacking teeth, straight to slightly incurving. Inflorescence is a spike, 7–12 ft (2–3.5 m) tall. Flowers greenish yellow with a tinge of purple. Zones 9–11.

Agave schottii

SHIN DAGGER

☼ ❄ ↔ 40–60 in (100–150 cm)
↑ 5–8 ft (1.5–2.4 m)

From southern Arizona and southwestern New Mexico, USA, and Sonoran Desert States of Mexico. Small profusely clumping species. Leaves few, narrow, straight to slightly incurving, 8–16 in (20–40 cm) long, yellow-green, occasionally filamented. Marginal teeth absent. Inflorescence a spike, 5–8 ft (1.5–2.4 m) tall. Flowers yellow, fragrant. Zones 8–11.

Agave seemanniana

syn. *Agave caroli-schmidtii*

☼ ❄ ↔ 24–36 in (60–90 cm)
↑ 7–10 ft (2–3 m)

Found from Chiapas, Mexico, to Costa Rica. Broad blue-green to gray leaves with widely spaced, spine-tipped teeth. Yellow flowers on a branched inflorescence up to 10 ft (3 m) tall. **A. s. subsp. pygmaea,** rosette only 12 in (30 cm) wide. Zones 9–11.

Agave shawii

☼ ❅ ↔ 40–60 in (100–150 cm)
↑ 7–15 ft (2–4.5 m)

From the coastal areas of northwestern Baja California, Mexico. It is occasionally solitary but usually clustering. Leaves light to dark green, slightly rough, flat to concave. Margins wavy to warty, smooth or bearing a thick horny edge. Teeth straight to hooked, red-brown, ¼–¾ in (6–18 mm) long. Inflorescence 7–15 ft (2–4.5 m) tall, 10 to 15 branches. Flowers greenish with a purple calyx. Zones 9–11.

Agave sisalana ★

☼ ❅ ↔ 10–20 ft (3–6 m)
↑ 17–20 ft (5–6 m)

This profusely offsetting sterile hybrid, of cultivated origins, is thought to have originated in Mexico. Leaves gray-green, stiff, sword-like, 36–60 in (90–150 cm) long, lacking marginal teeth. Leaves terminate in a stout reddish brown spine. Inflorescence 17–20 ft (5–6 m) tall, with 10 to 15 branches, producing many bulbils after flowering. Flowers greenish yellow with an unpleasant odor. Zones 9–11.

Agave stricta

☼ ❅ ↔ 40 in (100 cm) ↑ 5–8 ft (1.5–2.4 m)

From Tehuacan, Mexico. Attractive clustering species. Produces hundreds of pencil-thick, straight to upward-curving, dark green, toothless leaves, 10–20 in (25–50 cm) long, tipped with a very sharp, sturdy terminal spine. Inflorescence a spike, 5–8 ft (1.5–2.4 m) tall. Flowers red to purplish. A. s. f. nana is a dwarf, with heads rarely reaching more than 8–12 in (20–30 cm) in diameter. Zones 9–11.

Agave toumeyana ★

☼ ❄ ↔ 24–32 in (60–80 cm)
↑ 5–8 ft (1.5–2.4 m)

Limited habitat in central Arizona, USA. Small clustering rosette, 40 to 70 stiff thin leaves, 8–12 in (20–30 cm) long, lacking teeth, but with attractive white leaf bud imprints on both surfaces. Leaf margins bear white to gray hairs or filaments. Inflorescence a spike, 5–8 ft (1.5–2.4 m) tall. Flowers yellowish green. A. t. subsp. bella has more leaves, up to 100, and grows to only half the size. Zones 7–11.

Agave utahensis

☼ ❄ ↔ 10–16 in (25–40 cm)
↑ 5–8 ft (1.5–2.4 m)

Variable in size and color throughout its habitat, which includes Utah, Arizona, Nevada, and California, USA. Usually small and clumping, with gray-green leaves, 6–12 in (15–30 cm) long. Marginal teeth, hooked, weak, gray, with distinctive ring at base. Inflorescence 5–8 ft (1.5–2.4 m) tall, branched or a spike. Flowers yellow. A. u. subsp. kaibabensis, attractive solitary form with bright green leaves and gray-white teeth; A. u. var. eborispina, long, cream-colored, wavy, papery terminal spine; A. u. var. nevadensis, smaller than type, bluish green to blue-gray leaves, with larger teeth and longer terminal spine. Zones 7–11.

Agave utahensis subsp. *kaibabensis*

A

Agave victoria-reginae ★

↔ 20–28 in (50–70 cm)
↕ 10–15 ft (3–4.5 m)

Easily recognized, small to medium-sized, solitary species from Coahuila, Durango, and Nuevo Leon, Mexico. Has a dense, symmetrical, tightly packed rosette of hard, dark green, triangular leaves, 6–8 in (15–20 cm) long, marked with thick white lines or leaf bud imprints. **'Variegata'**, with distinctive yellow leaf margins, has recently been renamed as 'Golden Princess'. Zones 9–11.

Agave vilmoriniana

OCTOPUS AGAVE

↔ 5 ft (1.5 m) ↕ 10–17 ft (3–5 m)

From southern Sonora, Sinaloa, Durango, Jalisco, and Aguascalientes, Mexico, where it forms dense colonies on canyon walls. Never offsetting, this species is usually propagated from bulbils. It has many long, incurving, light green to pale green, almost cylindrical leaves which lack marginal teeth and taper evenly to a point bearing a flexible terminal spine. Inflorescence a raceme, 10–17 ft (3–5 m) tall, with yellow to white flowers and bulbils. Zones 9–11.

Agave xylonacantha

↔ 4 ft (1.2 m) ↕ 10–20 ft (3–6 m)

From the Sierra Madre Mountains of Nuevo Leon, Tamaulipas, San Luis Potosi, and Hidalgo, Mexico. Flat to incurving, sword-shaped, green to yellow-green leaves with a pale mid-stripe, 14–24 in (35–60 cm) long. Leaf margins brownish white, highly irregular, scalloped or wavy, warty, bearing up to 3 sharp, hooked, or straight teeth. Inflorescence a spike, 10–20 ft (3–6 m) tall. Flowers yellow-green to pale yellow. Zones 9–11.

AGERATINA

SNAKEROOT

A genus of around 250 species of daisy (Asteraceae) family perennials that are widespread in the Americas, particularly Mexico. The foliage may consist of pairs of simple narrow leaves but some species have broader, lobed or scalloped-edged leaves. The stems are often purple-red-tinted and this can extend to the foliage. The flowers, typically white, pink, or cream, are clustered in heads and open in summer to early autumn. Ray florets are usually very narrow, turning the flowerhead into a fluffy plume. CULTIVATION: Easily grown in any well-drained, moisture-retentive soil in full sun. Some can be invasive. Propagate from seed, basal cuttings in spring, or division of well-established clumps.

Ageratum houstonianum **'Blue Horizon'**

Ageratina altissima

syn. *Eupatorium rugosum*

↔ 3–6 ft (0.9–1.8 m)
↕ 3–6 ft (0.9–1.8 m)

From northeastern North America. Perennial herb with slightly hairy stems. Leaves opposite, elliptical to sword-shaped, grayish-green to purplish-green, slightly hairy, toothed. Flat-topped, rounded clusters of white flowers, borne at stem tips in late summer. **'Braunlaub'**, young foliage tinted with brown, brown-tinged flowers. Zones 4–9.

AGERATUM

FLOSS FLOWER

Found in tropical Americas, including the West Indies, this genus of 43 species of annuals, perennials, and shrubs is a member of the daisy (Asteraceae) family. Best known for the annual bedding species, *A. houstonianum,* the genus is characterized by flowerheads in which the ray florets are tubular filaments rather than petal-like, creating a fine feathery effect. Size varies considerably with the species, but most of the garden forms are compact and have hairy or felted leaves, often with toothed edges. The name *Ageratum* comes from the Greek *a* (without) and *geras* (age), and refers to the long-lasting qualities of the flowers. CULTIVATION: Plant in full sun in gritty well-drained soil that remains moist during the flowering season. Most perennial and shrubby species can tolerate only light frosts and may be grown outdoors only in very mild areas. Raise annuals from seed, usually sown in spring; propagate perennials from half-hardened cuttings.

Ageratum houstonianum

↔ 6–20 in (15–50 cm)
↕ 6–30 in (15–75 cm)

Annuals from Central America and West Indies. Pointed oval to poplar-shaped, downy, tooth-edged, dull green leaves to nearly 4 in (10 cm) long. Large dense or open heads of blue or lavender flowers. Garden forms include pink and white flowers. Popular cultivars include: **'Azure Pearl'**, 12 in (30 cm) tall, mid-blue flowers; **'Blue Danube'**, up to 6 in (15 cm) tall mound forming blue flowers; **'Blue Horizon'**, 24–30 in (60–75 cm) tall, purple-blue flowers; **'Blue Lagoon'**, 8 in (20 cm) tall, neat, rounded, blue flowers; **'Blue Mink'** ★, 12 in (30 cm) tall, light dusky blue flowers; **'Everest Blue'**, blue flowerheads on 26 in (65 cm) stems; **'High Tide Blue'**, 16 in (40 cm) tall, mid-blue, vigorous, lush foliage; **'Pacific'**, 8 in (20 cm) tall, purple-blue flowers; and **'Red Top'**, 24–28 in (60–70 cm) tall, bushy purple-red flowers. There are several seedling strains of uniform size but varying flower, including the **Artist Series,** dense 8–12 in (20–30 cm) mounds, heavy flowering, blue and purple shades; and the **Hawaii Series,** neat, rounded plants around 8 in (20 cm) tall in pink, white, and shades from pale to dark blue. Zones 10–12.

AGLAIA

This genus in the mahogany (Meliaceae) family contains over 100 species, found from southern Asia to northern Australia and islands of the west Pacific. They are mostly evergreen with pinnate leaves, the leaflets are not very numerous, and the young growths are often covered in small whitish or brownish scales. Flowers are small but numerous, in loose panicles, and are followed by globular fruits with a tough skin and one or two large seeds. Only one species, *A. odorata,* is grown as a garden plant for its sweet-scented flowers and attractive foliage, and even this is little known outside East Asia. CULTIVATION: Tough, fairly long-lived plants, they are easily grown in tropical and subtropical climates, preferring a sunny but sheltered position and a plentiful supply of water through summer. *A. odorata* is frequently grown in pots or tubs, flowering freely at a small size. Can propagate from cuttings, or fresh seed if available.

Aglaia odorata

Aglaia odorata

MOCK LIME, RICEGRAIN FLOWER

↔ 8 ft (2.4 m) ↕ 6–10 ft (1.8–3 m)

Evergreen shrub native to Southeast Asia. Spreading, multi-stemmed habit. Glossy foliage, each leaf consisting of 5 leaflets. Pale yellow, fragrant flowers. Plants may bear male or female flowers or both together, so fruits are not always produced. Zones 10–12.

AGONIS

This small genus consists of 12 evergreen species growing naturally in temperate regions of southwest Western Australia. The most widely grown, *A. flexuosa,* is the only tree, but it is the lower-growing cultivars of this species that are more popular for gardens. All have white or pink flowers. Like other members of the myrtle (Myrtaceae) family, the leaves contain aromatic oil, released when the leaves are crushed. The fibrous bark is a feature of the genus. CULTIVATION: An adaptable, almost pest-free genus, it is suited to full sun in a wide range of well-drained soils

Agonis flexuosa, **in the wild, Walpole, Western Australia**

and climates, although some species can be damaged by frost. While tip pruning can be done at any time for bushier growth, the trees will also respond to pruning after flowering. Propagate from seed or cuttings, though cultivars only come true if cuttings are taken.

Agonis flexuosa ★

PEPPERMINT TREE, WILLOW MYRTLE

↔15 ft (4.5 m) ↑30 ft (9 m)

The mature willow myrtle has a graceful dome shape and weeping habit. Attractive white flowers resemble the tea-tree. Cultivars are more popular for garden use, including: **'After Dark'**, red new growth maturing deep purple-red, 15 ft (4.5 m) tall; **'Midnight Shadow'**, deep purple-bronze to red foliage, grows to 10 ft (3 m); **'Nana'**, to around 10 ft (3 m); and dwarf form **'Weeping Wonder'**, to 3 ft (0.9 m). **'Belbra Gold'** and **'Variegata'**, dainty variegated foliage forms. Zones 9–11.

AGROSTIS

BENT GRASS, BROWN TOP

A cosmopolitan genus of some 120 species of evergreen annuals and perennials of the grass (Poaceae) family, many spread by runners (stolons). While hardiness varies, the few cultivated species are mostly frost hardy and valued as lawn grasses. Untrimmed, they develop into dense mounds of very fine leaves and from late summer produce numerous inflorescences.

CULTIVATION: When cultivated as lawn, bent grass needs to be kept growing steadily with frequent watering and feeding. It is prone to fungal diseases and will suffer if the soil is alkaline. Annual aeration and dethatching is recommended.

Agrostis stolonifera

CREEPING BENT GRASS

↔12–24 in (30–60 cm)
↑8–16 in (20–40 cm)

Gray-green foliage and short feathery inflorescence. Spreads by runners. Good for golf courses but too high-maintenance for domestic lawns. May be mown short. Considered a weed in many areas. Zones 3–10.

AICHRYSON

Found on both sides of the Straits of Gibraltar and the Azores, Canary Islands, and Madeira, this stonecrop (Crassulaceae) family genus comprises 15 species of annuals, perennials, and subshrubs that are often monocarpic (die after flowering). Their stems are branched and carry a scattering of leaves along the branches, as well as loose rosettes at the tips. Some species have rather succulent leaves, while those of others are thin. Sprays of small, yellow-green, starry, 7 to 12-petalled flowers appear during the warmer months, the season varying with the species.

CULTIVATION: Tolerant of only light frosts, but otherwise easily grown in a bright sunny position with gritty well-drained soil. Although succulent, they appreciate water during the growing season but may be dried off entirely for winter. Provide some shade in very hot summer areas. Propagate from seed or cuttings, depending on the plant type.

Aichryson laxum

↔20 in (50 cm) ↑12 in (30 cm)

Annual or biennial from the Canary Islands. Upright branching stem with ½ in (12 mm) long, pale to dark green, sometimes purple-marked leaves irregularly along the stems and in terminal rosettes. Flowers in summer. Zones 9–10.

AJANIA

A genus of 30 perennial herbs or shrubs in the daisy (Asteraceae) family, native to central and eastern Asia. Racemes of button-like flowerheads, in a radial pattern, appear in autumn. Spread by underground rhizomes.

CULTIVATION: Hardy plants that adapt to exposed positions or partial shade. Need well-drained, moderately fertile soil, which should be kept moist. Propagate from seed or by division.

Ajania pacifica

syn. *Chrysanthemum pacificum*

PACIFIC GOLD AND SILVER CHRYSANTHEMUM

↔8–12 in (20–30 cm)
↑12–18 in (30–45 cm)

Drought-tolerant perennial from far-eastern Russia and northern Japan, with clusters of yellow button-like flowerheads. Scalloped felt-like leaves with silver undersides. Zones 6–10.

Aichryson laxum

AJUGA

BUGLE

Members of the mint (Lamiaceae) family, the 40-odd, low, spreading annuals and perennials in this genus occur throughout temperate Eurasia, Africa, and Australia, and are widely naturalized elsewhere. Many spread by fleshy stems, others self-layer as they grow. Leaves are in whorls on narrow angular stems. Conical, short-stemmed, upright flowerheads with small, often purple-blue flowers appearing from axils of leaf bracts, bloom mainly from late spring into summer. Use as a quick ground cover around small shrubs or in containers, but take care to control their spread. The common bugle *(A. reptans)* has had several uses in herbal medicine, including as an astringent and to stop blood flow from injuries.

CULTIVATION: Most grow very freely in any well-drained soil and are excellent ground covers for harsh conditions. Some are rather invasive and need to be cut back routinely. Propagation of the perennials is usually by division or from self-rooted layers; annuals from seed.

Ajuga genevensis

BLUE BUGLE, UPRIGHT BUGLE

↔12–16 in (30–40 cm)
↑12–16 in (30–40 cm)

Native to Europe. Creeping perennial with oblong leaves on long stalks.

Ajania pacifica

Upper leaves tinged with blue. Bright blue flowers, borne on leafy spikes, in spring–summer. Zones 6–9.

Ajuga pyramidalis

PYRAMID BUGLE

↔12–24 in (30–60 cm)
↑6–8 in (15–20 cm)

Mat-forming European perennial with rosettes of dark green, finely toothed leaves to 4 in (10 cm) long. Leafy pyramidal flowerheads with mauve-blue flowers backed by purple-bronze bracts. **'Metallica Crispa'** has wavy-edged purple-bronze foliage with a metallic sheen. Zones 6–10.

Ajuga reptans

↔12–48 in (30–120 cm) or more
↑4–8 in (10–20 cm)

A temperate Eurasian native. Vigorous, sometimes invasive, forms a carpet, spreading by runners. Foliage often purple tinted. Flowers in blue to purple shades, sometimes pink. Cultivars include: **'Atropurpurea'**, deep purple-bronze foliage, dark flowers; **'Black Scallop'**, lush, very dark purple-red foliage, deep purple-blue flowers; **'Braunherz'**, very dark, glossy, purple-bronze leaves; **'Burgundy Glow'**, gray-green leaves with reddish markings; **'Burgundy Lace'**, purple-bronze, cream, and green variegated foliage; **'Catlin's Giant'**, large bronze-green leaves and tall flower spikes; **'Jungle Beauty'**, vigorous with large deep green leaves, bright purple-blue flowers; **'Jungle Bronze'**, vigorous upright grower with large, wavy-edged, bronze leaves; **'Multicolor'** (syns 'Rainbow', 'Tricolor'), cream, pink, and green foliage; **'Pink Elf'**, compact plant with deep pink flowers; **'Pink Surprise'**, bronze, gray, and green variegated foliage, bronze in winter, pink flowers; and **'Purple Torch'**, bronze foliage, pink flowers. Zones 5–10.

Ajuga reptans 'Catlin's Giant'

AKEBIA

CHOCOLATE VINE

Found in the small chocolate-vine (Lardizabalaceae) family, which includes some rather unusual plants, this genus from temperate East Asia is composed of just 4 species of evergreen and deciduous twining vines. The extent of foliage loss depends on the degree of winter cold. Leaves are composed of several oval leaflets, the number varying with species. Flowers open in spring, are unisexual, and, while not showy, are distinctive as they occur in panicles and for their color, which ranges from bright maroon to purple-brown. If cross-pollinated, pulpy, sausage-like, blue to purple fruits follow the flowers and are edible, though insipid.
CULTIVATION: Preferring cool shaded conditions with moist humus-rich soil, *Akebia* species are undemanding and in suitable conditions can be vigorous growers that need frequent trimming. Propagate from seed that has been stratified for 4 weeks or from softwood to half-hardened summer cuttings.

Akebia quinata

Alangium platanifolium

Alcea rosea

Akebia quinata

↔ 20 ft (6 m) ↑ 10 ft (3 m)

From Korea, Japan, and nearby parts of China. Leaves with 5 leaflets to 2 in (5 cm) long. Vanilla-scented, maroon flowers; males very small, females about 1 in (25 mm) wide. Plants that fruit well need support to hold the weight. Zones 5–10.

ALANGIUM

This genus consists of about 20 species of small to large trees, shrubs and a few climbers ranging from Japan and China through Southeast Asia to eastern Australia and Fiji, outlying occurrence in tropical Africa. It is a member of the dogwood (Cornaceae) family. Most species are evergreen but a few East Asian species are deciduous, with foliage coloring in autumn. The leaves are arranged spirally on slender twigs and strongly veined. Rather inconspicuous white flowers with narrow recurving petals hang in small clusters from leaf axils. The fruits are small olive-shaped drupes.
CULTIVATION: The deciduous species are frost hardy to varying degrees and like much the same conditions as the smaller maples *(Acer)*. The evergreen species are rainforest plants and enjoy moist, sheltered, frost-free locations. Propagate from seed, sown fresh after removing fruit flesh.

Alangium platanifolium

↔ 6 ft (1.8 m) ↑ 15 ft (4.5 m)

A deciduous species from Japan and Korea, with a low-branching habit. Leaves similar to *Platanus,* with 3 to 5 shallow lobes, turn yellow in autumn. Late spring flowers and fruit similar to those of *A. chinense.* Zones 8–10.

Alchemilla erythropoda

ALBUCA

Most of the 30 species of bulbous plants in this genus, a member of the hyacinth (Hyacinthaceae) family, are native to southern Africa. Only a few are suitable for cultivation. Leaves range from 3 in (8 cm) to 4 ft (1.2 m) long and may be flat or keeled. Flowers, 6-petalled, are yellow or greenish white, in loose racemes on tall stems. Fruiting capsule has many black seeds.
CULTIVATION: Suitable for outdoor cultivation only where frosts are light, but can be grown in a conservatory or greenhouse. Grow in full sun in light free-draining soil, in a sheltered position if light frosts might occur. Keep moist, and provide weak liquid fertilizer regularly when in full growth. Propagate from offsets or seed.

Albuca bracteata

syn. *Ornithogalum longibracteatum*

FALSE SEA ONION, SEA ONION

↔ 20–48 in (50–120 cm)
↑ 24–48 in (60–120 cm)

Native to Cape region of South Africa. Strappy light green leaves to 24 in (60 cm) long. Flower stems over 40 in (100 cm) high, flowers small, green-striped, white, largely enclosed within bracts, in early summer. Zones 9–10.

Albuca nelsonii

↔ 3 ft (0.9 m) ↑ 2–5 ft (0.6–1.5 m)

South African species. Pointed bright green leaves to 4 ft (1.2 m) long. Tall stems carry slightly scented white flowers with a green or reddish median stripe on each petal. Zones 9–11.

ALCEA

HOLLYHOCK

A member of the mallow (Malvaceae) family, this genus contains about 60 species of biennials and short-lived perennial herbs native to central and southwestern Asia. Some are naturalized around the Mediterranean. Flowers, to 4 in (10 cm) across and borne on stems to 7 ft (2 m) tall in summer, have 5 petals and may be pink, purple, yellow, or white. Stamens form a prominent central column, usually yellow. A quintessential English cottage garden style plant.
CULTIVATION: Grow in a sunny position in rich soil, moist but well drained. Stake plants on exposed sites and water in dry spells. Rust is a problem, and it is best to renew plants each year. Propagate from seed sown in late summer or early spring.

Alcea rosea

syn. *Althaea rosea*

HOLLYHOCK

↔ 2–3 ft (0.6–0.9 m)
↑ 2–8 ft (0.6–2.4 m)

Cultivated and naturalized in many places but thought to originate from Turkey or Asia. Rounded leaves have 3 to 7 lobes. Flowers single or double, to 4 in (10 cm) across, shades of pink, purple, yellow, and white. Wide range of cultivars and seed lines. **Chater's Mix,** fully double flowers in a wide color range; **Halo Series,** single flowers in all colors, with contrasting center color; and **'Nigra',** very dark, almost black flowers. Plants sold as *A. ficifolia* are a more robust, often taller, strain of *A. rosea.* Zones 3–10.

ALCHEMILLA

BEAR'S FOOT, LADY'S MANTLE, LION'S FOOT

A widespread rose (Rosaceae) family genus of around 300 species of clump-forming soft-stemmed perennials from Eurasia, Africa, and Central and South America. Foliage, on fine stems that often self-layer, is hand-shaped with rounded lobes, covered in fine hairs. Sprays of tiny yellow-green flowers are borne from late spring. *Alchemilla* comes, via the Arabic name *alkemelych,* from *alchimia* (alchemy), a reference to the fanciful idea that the silvery dewdrops that form on the leaves might be added to recipes for gold. It has featured in herbal medicine, mainly to encourage healing but also in "elixirs of youth."
CULTIVATION: Cultivated species are temperate-zone plants that prefer cool, moist, well-drained conditions with shade from the hottest sun. Propagation usually by division when dormant, but can be raised from seed.

Alchemilla erythropoda

↔ 12–24 in (30–60 cm)
↑ 8 in (20 cm)

Spreading plant found throughout the Balkans, Carpathians, and Caucasus. Leaves hairy, deeply cut, toothed, gray-green, 7 to 9 lobes. Pale green flowers, on sometimes purple-red stems, to 8 in (20 cm) long, in summer. Zones 4–9.

Alchemilla glaucescens

↔ 12–24 in (30–60 cm)
↑ 8 in (20 cm)

Low spreading plant, found from Ireland to western Russia. Rounded, hairy, 7- to 9-lobed, toothed, blue-green leaves. Pale green flowers in summer. Zones 4–9.

Alchemilla mollis ★

LADY'S MANTLE

↔ 12–32 in (30–80 cm)
↑ 12–20 in (30–50 cm)

Mounding spreading species found from Romania to Greece and Iran. Toothed leaves, finely hairy above, densely hairy below. Sprays of yellow-green flowers in summer. Zones 4–9.

Alchemilla xanthochlora

syn. *Alchemilla vulgaris*

↔ 16–24 in (40–60 cm)
↑ 12–20 in (30–50 cm)

Mounding and spreading European species. Yellow-green, kidney-shaped, toothed, 9- to 11-lobed leaves, hairless above, hairy below. Yellow-green flowers in summer. Zones 5–9.

ALKANNA

This is a genus of about 30 frost-hardy annuals and perennials found from southern Europe to Iran, and belonging to the borage or forget-me-not (Boraginaceae) family. Has branching terminal inflorescences with a long tubular corolla and a downy ring in the centre, and smooth-edged, hairy leaves. Fruits are elongated calyces.

CULTIVATION: They prefer rich warm soil in an open sunny position. Propagate from seed.

Alkanna tinctoria

ALKANET, DYER'S BUGLOSS

↔ 12–36 in (30–90 cm)
↑ 12–36 in (30–90 cm)

Perennial from central and southern Europe. Bright purplish blue flowers to ½ in (12 mm) wide with funnel-shaped corolla. Bristly, smooth-edged, linear to egg-shaped leaves to 3 in (8 cm) long. Extensive root system and a hairy angular stem. Zones 5–8.

ALLAMANDA

This genus, a member of the dogbane (Apocynaceae) family, consists of around 12 evergreen shrubs, including both upright and semi-climbing species. They are tropical American natives and are lush, colorful, and flamboyant. The large, glossy, deep green leaves are the perfect foil to the flowers, usually a deep golden yellow. The flowers appear mainly in summer and autumn and are trumpet-shaped with a widely flared throat and 5 large, overlapping petals.

CULTIVATION: Protection from frost is paramount and a moist subtropical to tropical climate is best, though it is possible to grow allamandas in very sheltered areas in cooler zones. For a prolific flower display give them rich well-drained soil and plenty of summer moisture. They also do well in conservatories but watch out for mealy bugs, scale insects, and mites. Propagation is usually by half-hardened cuttings.

Allamanda cathartica

CLIMBING ALLAMANDA, COMMON ALLAMANDA, GOLDEN TRUMPET

↔ 10 ft (3 m) ↑ 17 ft (5 m)

From South America. A vigorous climber with whorls of glossy leathery leaves. Bears bright yellow trumpet-shaped flowers, up to 5 in (12 cm) across, in summer. The seed capsules are prickly. **'Grandiflora'**, very large flowers in profusion; **'Hendersonii'**, smaller flowers with orange markings in throat; and **'Nobilis'**, larger, more flaring flowers. Zones 10–12.

Allamanda schottii

syn. *Allamanda neriifolia*

BUSH ALLAMANDA

↔ 6 ft (1.8 m) ↑ 6 ft (1.8 m)

South American species. Glossy deep green leaves, bright golden yellow flowers streaked with light orange, large green seed pods. Zones 11–12.

ALLIUM

CHIVE, GARLIC, LEEK, ONION, ORNAMENTAL ONION

A genus of around 700 species of bulbous perennials and biennials of the amaryllis (Amaryllidaceae) family. Famous for their taste and pungency, many are vital ingredients in the world's cuisine. Some, especially garlic, have a long history in herbal medicine and folklore, and the ornamental species are not without an air of mystery too. In Europe, *A. moly* was thought to be protection against demons, and Homer's Ulysses used its "magical properties" to enter Circe's lair. Foliage may be fine and grassy, strappy or hollow and tubular. Flowers, often brightly colored, are usually borne in rounded heads on long stems.

CULTIVATION: Most thrive in fairly light soil in a sunny well-drained position. Ample water is needed during foliage growth and flowering, but then they can dry off. Propagate using offsets and bulbils, or from seed.

Allium acuminatum

HOOKER'S ONION, ORNAMENTAL ONION, PINK WILD ONION, TAPERTIP ONION

↔ 3 in (8 cm) ↑ 4–12 in (10–30 cm)

From the Rocky Mountains, USA. Perennial herb. The ½ in (12 mm) long green leaves wither before flowers bloom in late spring–early summer. Flowers are pinkish purple and urn-shaped. Zones 4–9.

Allium aflatunense

↔ 12–24 in (30–60 cm)
↑ 3–5 ft (0.9–1.5 m)

Chinese species with 6 to 8, short, faintly aromatic, blue-green, tubular leaves per bulb. Foliage dies before the flower stems develop in late summer, carrying 4 in (10 cm) wide spherical heads of massed, tiny, dark-veined, lilac flowers. Zones 8–10.

Allium ampeloprasum

KURRANT, LEVANT GARLIC, WILD LEEK

↔ 12–24 in (30–60 cm)
↑ 2–6 ft (0.6–1.8 m)

Occurs in various forms from Ireland and southern England to Iran and North Africa. Flat, rough-edged, gray-green leaves to 20 in (50 cm) long, 4–10 per bulb. Spherical 2–4 in (5–10 cm) wide heads of hundreds of pink to red flowers, initially enclosed by papery bracts. The **Porrum Group** (syn. *A. porrum*) comprises the leeks, of which there are numerous cultivars. **'Colossal'** and **'Unique'** are long-stemmed, self-blanching, quick-maturing cultivars typical of garden leeks. Zones 6–9.

Allium caeruleum

↔ 6–12 in (15–30 cm)
↑ 8–24 in (20–60 cm)

Found from central Asia to southern Siberia. Grassy, 3-angled, blue-green leaves to 3 in (8 cm) long, 2 to 4 per bulb. Tiny blue to light purple flowers in spherical heads around 1 in (25 mm) wide. Zones 6–9.

Allium carinatum

KEELED GARLIC

↔ 6–12 in (15–30 cm)
↑ 12–24 in (30–60 cm)

Found from central and southern Europe to Russia and Turkey. Grassy leaves to 8 in (20 cm) long, 2 to 4 per bulb. Up to 30 purple-pink flowers in heads 1–2 in (25–50 mm) wide. Small bulbils develop around the flowerhead. ***A. c.* subsp. *pulchellum*** has purplish flower stems and does not produce bulbils. Zones 7–10.

Allium cernuum

LADY'S LEEK, NODDING ONION, WILD ONION

↔ 6–12 in (15–30 cm)
↑ 12–27 in (30–70 cm)

Found from southern Canada to northern Mexico. Grassy, flattened, bright green leaves to 8 in (20 cm) long, 4 to 6 per bulb. In summer, heads of 30 to 40 white, pink, or

Allium ampeloprasum, Porrum Group, 'Colossal'

purple-red flowers. **'Hidcote'** is a cultivar with 18 in (45 cm) tall flower stems and heads of nodding purple-pink flowers. Zones 6–10.

Allium cratericola

CASCADE ONION, CRATER ONION, VOLCANIC ONION, WILD GARLIC

↔ 8–12 in (20–30 cm)
↑ 6–8 in (15–20 cm)

Native to volcanic screes of western USA. Narrow to strappy, sometimes red-tinted leaves, 2 per bulb. In summer, heads of white to pale pink flowers, deeper pink in bud. Zones 7–9.

Allium cristophii ★

STAR OF PERSIA

↔ 8–12 in (20–30 cm)
↑ 8–20 in (20–50 cm)

Found in central Asia and parts of Iran and Turkey. Narrow to broad blue-green leaves, downy undersides, 2 to 7 per bulb. Strong-ribbed flower stem with rounded head of small, starry, purple flowers. Zones 7–10.

Allium carinatum subsp. *pulchellum*

Allium cyaneum

↔ 5–10 in (12–25 cm)
↑ 5–10 in (12–25 cm)

A perennial clump-forming bulb from China. Grassy foliage with very narrow leaves, 2 mm wide. Clusters of 10 to 12 small blue or purplish flowers, nodding, appear in late spring. Zones 5–9.

Allium cyathophorum

↔ 12 in (30 cm)
↑ 10–15 in (25–38 cm)

Perennial clump-forming bulb from northwestern China. Leaves 12–15 in (30–38 cm) long, bell-shaped. Purplish red flowers bloom in a loose umbel in late spring. Zones 5–9.

Allium fistulosum

JAPANESE BUNCHING ONION, JAPANESE LEEK, WELSH ONION

↔ 8–12 in (20–30 cm)
↑ 20–24 in (50–60 cm)

Unknown in the wild. Hollow leaves to 12 in (30 cm) long, 2 to 6 per bulb, used in salads or cooked. In summer, small heads of green flowers on tall stems, sometimes forming bulbils. Zones 5–9.

Allium flavum

SMALL YELLOW ONION

↔ 4–6 in (10–15 cm)
↑ 8–12 in (20–30 cm)

Found in southern Europe from France to Greece. Fine, cylindrical, blue-green leaves to 8 in (20 cm) long, few per bulb, often drying before flowering. Heads of scented bright yellow flowers in summer. Zones 7–10.

Allium geyeri

GEYER'S ONION

↔ 4–6 in (10–15 cm)
↑ 8–20 in (20–50 cm)

Native to western USA. Fine, chive-like, grassy leaves to 8 in (20 cm) long. In spring, heads of 10 to 15, white to soft pink, bell-shaped flowers. Zones 5–10.

Allium giganteum

GIANT ALLIUM

↔ 12–20 in (30–50 cm)
↑ 3–6 ft (0.9–1.8 m)

From central Asia. Strappy gray-green leaves to 3 ft (0.9 m) long and 4 in (10 cm) wide at the base. In spring, large near-spherical heads of many tiny purple-pink flowers, less commonly pale pink or white. Zones 7–9.

Allium hollandicum

↔ 8–12 in (20–30 cm)
↑ 32–40 in (80–100 cm)

East Asian species often confused with

Allium fistulosum

A. aflatunense in cultivation. Faintly aromatic, tubular, blue-green leaves, usually dried off by the time the dense rounded heads of starry purple-pink flowers appear. **'Purple Sensation'** has near-spherical heads of deep purple flowers. Zones 7–9.

Allium howellii

↔ 6–8 in (15–20 cm)
↑ 12–20 in (30–50 cm)

Species from California, USA, with few grassy blue-green leaves that wither before the wiry flower stems develop fully. White to cream flowers edged with pink, in loose heads. Drought and heat tolerant. Zones 8–10.

Allium hyalinum

GLASSY ONION

↔ 6–10 in (15–25 cm)
↑ 8–20 in (20–50 cm)

Species from California, USA, with flat narrow leaves, 8–20 in (10–50 cm) long. From late spring it bears heads of 10 to 30 starry flowers, usually white, sometimes pale pink. The plant commonly cultivated as *A. h.* var. *praecox* is now classified as *A. praecox*. Zones 8–10.

Allium karataviense

↔ 8–20 in (20–50 cm)
↑ 4–12 in (10–30 cm)

Central Asian species with broad, strappy, gray-green leaves, often with a metallic purple sheen. Short sturdy stems with large heads of tiny, starry, white to pale mauve flowers with darker mid-veins. **'Ivory Queen'** has short stems with pale green to cream flowers. Zones 7–9.

Allium macranthum

↔ 12 in (30 cm)
↑ 10–12 in (25–30 cm)

A clump-forming perennial bulb from China and Tibet. Mid-green strap-shaped leaves. Deep bell-shaped plum-purple flowers appear throughout summer. As many as 20 flowers per umbel. Zones 4–6.

Allium rosenbachianum 'Michael Hoog'

Allium moly

GOLDEN GARLIC

↔ 8–12 in (20–30 cm)
↑ 8–12 in (20–30 cm)

European species with strappy blue-green leaves, 1 to 3 per bulb. Flower stems fairly short and sturdy with heads of loosely clustered golden yellow flowers from late spring. **'Jeannine'**, slightly larger heads of especially bright flowers. Zones 7–9.

Allium narcissiflorum

↔ 4–8 in (10–20 cm)
↑ 6–15 in (15–38 cm)

Found around the French Maritime Alps. Narrow, flat, grassy, gray-green leaves to 6 in (15 cm) long, 3 to 5 per bulb. In summer, loose heads of 5 to 8 nodding, bell-shaped, pale pink to purple flowers. Zones 8–9.

Allium neapolitanum

DAFFODIL GARLIC, FLOWERING ONION, NAPLES GARLIC

↔ 6–12 in (15–30 cm)
↑ 8–20 in (20–50 cm)

Found around the Mediterranean, North Africa, and into western Asia. Narrow, blue-green, grassy leaves to 12 in (30 cm) long, 2 per bulb. Leaves are usually withered by the time the flowers open in late spring. The plant has pure white flowers in loose heads around 3 in (8 cm) wide. Zones 8–10.

Allium nigrum

↔ 4 in (10 cm) ↑ 36 in (90 cm)

A Mediterranean bulb with broad, strap-shaped, shiny leaves. Flowers are curved and white with a green stripe that gives a green cast to the broad umbel, open in early summer. There is a black ovary in the center of each flower. Zones 7–9.

Allium oreophilum

↔ 6–8 in (15–20 cm)
↑ 4–8 in (10–20 cm)

Found in the Caucasus region and Central Asia. Has narrow blue-green leaves that extend beyond the height of the flower stem. Bright pink to purple bell-shaped flowers, in loose heads, are seen in spring–early summer. Zones 7–9.

Allium paradoxum

FEW-FLOWERED LEEK

↔ 4–8 in (10–20 cm)
↑ 6–12 in (15–30 cm)

Found from the Caucasus to Iran. Each bulb has a single leaf, 8–12 in (20–30 cm) long × 1 in (25 mm) wide, with a prominent keeled midrib. In early spring white flowers open, 1 to 10 per head, followed by prolific bulbils. ***A. p.* var. *normale*** grows to 12 in (30 cm) tall, with heads of around 10 white flowers and no bulbils. Zones 7–9.

Allium platycaule

↔ 8–12 in (20–30 cm)
↑ 4–6 in (10–15 cm)

Native to mountains of western USA. Leaves are blue-green, usually flat to the ground, growing to 8 in (20 cm) long, 2 per bulb. Showy short-stemmed heads of tiny, starry, deep pink flowers are seen in spring–summer. Zones 6–9.

Allium regelii

↔ 12–20 in (30–50 cm)
↑ 32–40 in (80–100 cm)

Found in semi-desert areas of central Asia. Broad, strappy, coarse-edged, green leaves to 20 in (50 cm) long, 2 to 4 per bulb. Stems with up to 6 whorls of pale pink, sometimes purple flowers. Zones 7–10.

A

Allium rosenbachianum

☼ ❄ ↔12–20 in (30–50 cm)
↑24–40 in (60–100 cm)

Central Asian species with broad-based, strappy, blue-green leaves to 12 in (30 cm) long, 2 to 4 per bulb. In spring, strong-ribbed flower stems with 4 in (10 cm) wide heads of purple, rarely white, flowers. '**Michael Hoog**' has large heads of purple flowers; '**Purple King**' has blue-green leaves and dark purple flowers with white stamens. Zones 7–10.

Allium roseum

ROSY GARLIC

☼ ✱ ↔3 in (8 cm) ↑24 in (60 cm)

From Southern Europe, North Africa, and Asia Minor. Perennial bulb. Leaves thin, similar to chives. Rose-white flowers in spring. Multiplies quickly from bulbils. Zones 5–9.

Allium schoenoprasum

CHIVES

☼/◐ ✱ ↔4–12 in (10–30 cm)
↑6–20 in (15–50 cm)

Widespread in northern temperate zones. Fine, grassy, hollow foliage is aromatic and a popular culinary garnish. Rounded heads of small, bell-shaped, pink flowers in summer. '**Black Isle Blush**', up to 12 in (30 cm) tall, with mauve flowers that are deep blush pink at the center; '**Forescate**', strong grower to 20 in (50 cm) tall, with gray-green leaves and deep purple-pink flowers; '**Pink Perfection**', up to 12 in (30 cm) tall, with many heads of bright pink flowers; and '**Silver Chimes**', gray-green foliage and white flowers. Zones 5–10.

Allium senescens

GERMAN GARLIC

☼/◐ ✱ ↔12–20 in (30–50 cm)
↑8–24 in (20–60 cm)

This native of temperate Eurasia has broad-based gray-green leaves, 8–12 in (20–30 cm) long, 4 to 9 per bulb. In summer and autumn it displays many-flowered heads to 2 in (5 cm) wide with cup-shaped lavender-pink flowers. ***A. s.* var. *calcareum*** has blue-green leaves and long-petalled flowers. Zones 5–9.

Allium siculum

syn. *Nectaroscordum siculum*

☼/◐ ✱ ↔4 in (10 cm) ↑40 in (100 cm)

Native of limestone areas of France and Italy. Linear leaves, deeply keeled. Flowers in loose, open umbels, bell-shaped, cream and green, flushed purple-red at base. Seed pods decorative and erect. Adaptable but invasive in some conditions. ***A. s.* subsp. *dioscoridis***, off-white flowers, flushed greenish purple. Zones 5–9.

Allium sphaerocephalon

ROUND-HEADED LEEK

☼/◐ ✱ ↔12–20 in (30–50 cm)
↑24–36 in (60–90 cm)

Found through Europe from England to the Caucasus, in North Africa, and the Middle East. Hollow leaves to slightly over 12 in (30 cm) long, 2 to 6 per bulb. In summer, cone-shaped flowerheads with many tiny purple-red flowers, sometimes followed by bulbils. Zones 5–9.

Allium stellatum

GLADE ONION, PRAIRIE ONION

☼/◐ ✱ ↔1–2 in (2.5–5 cm)
↑18 in (45 cm)

Perennial from central North America. Its 2 to 6 green flat leaves die back at flowering time. Blooms summer–autumn; flowers pinkish rose. *Stellatum* means starry and describes the flowers. Naturalizes easily. Zones 5–9.

Allium unifolium

☼ ❄ ↔8–12 in (20–30 cm)
↑16–24 in (40–60 cm)

Native to western USA. Narrow, flattened, blue-green leaves with a conspicuous central channel/midrib. Leaves to 12 in (30 cm) long, 1 per bulb. In spring and summer, rounded heads of pink to deep lavender-pink bell-shaped flowers. Zones 8–10.

Allium Hybrid Cultivars

☼ ❄ ↔6–12 in (15–30 cm)
↑18–48 in (45–120 cm)

Among the many cultivated hybrids are: '**Beau Regard**', large near-spherical heads of starry steel blue to purple flowers on stems to 3 ft (0.9 m) tall; '**Gladiator**', large rounded heads of lilac to purple flowers on stems to 4 ft (1.2 m) tall; and '**Globemaster**', gray-green leaves, large heads of violet-blue flowers on 24–36 in (60–90 cm) stems, excellent cut flower. Zones 7–9.

ALLUAUDIA

All 8 species of *Alluaudia* are endemic to the arid southern and southwestern tip of Madagascar. They are members of the Didiereaceae family. All the species are sought-after collector plants and are still rare in cultivation. In habitat they start life as small xerophytic shrubs but most species eventually become tree-like, forming dense forests in which lemurs are often found. Because of their heavily spined bodies, alluaudias resemble cacti and are in fact distant relatives. Unlike most cacti, however, alluaudias are covered in small fleshy deciduous leaves during their growing period. The local habitats of many *Alluaudia* species are currently threatened by subsistence farming, and the spread of sisal plantations (for rope and twine) and eucalypt plantations (for wood products). Both male and female flowers appear on the same plant and are often borne in huge numbers from the ends of mature branches.

CULTIVATION: *Alluaudia* species are easily grown from seeds but are more usually raised from cuttings that have been dried out for a week or two. They thrive in a rich well-drained soil and may grow rapidly when planted in the ground.

Alluaudia procera ★

☼ ❅ ↔7–10 ft (2–3 m)
↑35–50 ft (10–15 m)

This is the most common species of *Alluaudia* in cultivation. Wood from this tree-like species is used for housing, fencing, boxes, and firewood. The greenish yellow flowers are produced on massive racemes bearing hundreds of blooms. Zones 9–11.

ALNUS

ALDER

Alnus, of the birch (Betulaceae) family, is an essentially Northern Hemisphere genus. Of the 25 alder species only 2 extend across the equator. All are deciduous or semi-evergreen. In the wild, alders are fast-growing pioneer trees of disturbed ground. Alders mostly have darker brownish or blackish bark, with leaves usually larger and slightly thicker than birches; leaf margins vary from smooth and wavy to jaggedly toothed, winter buds sticky and aromatic. The flowers are tiny and arranged in catkins; the male is long and thin, while the female is short and barrel-shaped.

CULTIVATION: The various species in the genus are easily grown in their appropriate climate. Sapling growth is often very fast but they mature early and are sometimes not very long lived. Many are able to thrive in soils of low fertility and poor drainage, aided by nitrogen-fixing fungi in the roots. Propagation is normally from seed, which may need stratification over winter and should not be covered, as germination is stimulated by light. Some cultivars require grafting.

Alnus cordata

ITALIAN ALDER

☼ ❄ ↔20 ft (6 m) ↑50 ft (15 m)

From southern Italy, Sardinia, and Corsica. A vigorous, narrow tree which has deep green, broadly rounded, shiny leaves that are held horizontally. Male catkins are yellowish, found on branch ends. Female seed cones follow, in groups of three. Tolerant of all soils, and at home even in boggy conditions. Can be invasive in cold moist climates. Zones 6–10.

Alnus glutinosa

BLACK ALDER, COMMON ALDER

☼ ✱ ↔35 ft (10 m) ↑60 ft (18 m)

From Europe to Siberia and North Africa. Deciduous tree, may reach 30 ft (9 m) in cultivation. Leaves dark green, rounded, shallowly toothed. Buds and twigs sticky. Male catkins dull purple to yellow. Female catkins purple to burgundy to green to brown. Cultivars include: '**Imperialis**', with an open habit; and '**Laciniata**', vigorous with dissected leaves. Zones 4–8.

Alnus glutinosa

Alnus incana subsp. *tenuifolia*

Alnus incana

GRAY ALDER

↔30 ft (9 m) ↑70 ft (21 m)

Found in the Caucasus and the mountains of Europe. Hardy and vigorous, well suited to cold wet conditions. Bark smooth gray. Young shoots and undersides of leaves covered in gray down. A. i. subsp. tenuifolia (syn. *A. tenuifolia*), from British Columbia, Canada, to California, USA, is smaller with red and downy young shoots that are soon smooth; buds also downy, leaves dark green, downy veins and undersides. Cultivars include: A. i. '**Aurea**', foliage and branches yellowish; '**Laciniata**', leaves divided in narrow lobes; and '**Pendula**', attractive weeping form. Zones 3–9.

Alnus japonica

JAPANESE ALDER

↔25 ft (8 m) ↑80 ft (24 m)

Native to Japan and eastern Asia. Densely leafy tree. Narrow pointed leaves, dark glossy green, finely toothed. Male catkins erect. Zones 4–9.

Alnus rubra

syn. *Alnus oregona*

OREGON ALDER, RED ALDER

↔30 ft (9 m) ↑50 ft (15 m)

From the canyons and riverbanks of North America. Fast growing tree, pyramidal crown, somewhat pendulous habit. Young shoots dark red, new leaves have reddish brown down, turning dark green above and blue-gray beneath. Zones 4–9.

Alnus serrulata

HAZEL ALDER, SMOOTH ALDER

↔8 ft (2.4 m) ↑12 ft (3.5 m)

Shrubby species from eastern USA. Closely related to *A. incana*. Sticky buds, blunt-ended, finely toothed oval leaves. Zones 3–9.

ALOCASIA

Comprising 70 species, this genus of the arum (Araceae) family occurs in a variety of habitats, from lowland rainforests to swamps, roadsides, and mountain regions from tropical southern Asia, Indonesia, Malaysia, New Guinea, and Australia, to islands of the Pacific. The species are perennial, evergreen, very small to massive herbs, even tree-like, with corms, runners, or aboveground stems. Leaves are several with sheathing leaf stalk, simple, broadly or narrowly arrowhead-shaped, with entire or deeply lobed margins, but usually heart-shaped at the base. The major veins are often strikingly prominent in some species. Inflorescences are borne at or near the apex of the leafy plant, 2 or more together, the spathes constricted, the spadix in 4 parts, lowermost female, then sterile, then male, then a sterile appendage. The female flower has no petals or sepals, consisting only of the single-celled ovary and stigma. Male flowers consist of 3 to 8, stalkless, narrow anthers united into a pyramid shape. Fruit is a globular berry containing several seeds. CULTIVATION: Propagate from seed and stem cuttings or by division of

Alocasia × *amazonica*

fleshy stem. All species require warm moist conditions in shady sheltered locations, and are grown in greenhouses and conservatories in all regions but the tropics.

Alocasia × *amazonica*

↔20–40 in (50–100 cm)
↑40–60 in (100–150 cm)

A hybrid of *A. lowii* and *A. sanderiana*, its origins are unknown. Leaves to 24 in (60 cm) long × 12 in (30 cm) wide, arrowhead-shaped, upperside dark green, midrib yellow-greenish white, other veins silvery white. Underside dull purple, major veins green-white. Leaf stalk green, 45 cm long. '**Magnifica**', more intensely silver coloration on uppersurface, all purple below; '**Randall**', larger in all parts. Zones 11–12.

Alocasia macrorrhizos

syns *Alocasia indica, A. macrorrhiza*

ELEPHANT'S EAR, GIANT TARO

↔7–8 ft (2–2.4 m)
↑15–17 ft (4.5–5 m)

Massive, fleshy-stemmed, perennial herb with stout trunk to 15 ft (4.5 m) tall, occurring naturally in Sri Lanka, India, and western tropical Asia, widely cultivated in many other tropical regions. Leaf stalks to 7 ft (2 m) long, green, blades broadly arrowhead-shaped, 40–50 in (100–130 cm) long, almost as wide, main veins not as prominent as in other species. Spathes yellow-green, fruiting spathe green. Zones 11–12.

ALOE

This genus, of the asparagus (Asparagaceae) family, comprises about 350 species of evergreen succulent plants found through southern and tropical Africa to Madagascar and the Arabian Peninsula. They range from low-growing grass-like perennials to trees, shrubs, and climbers. Succulent leaves grow in rosettes or spirals at the stem or branch tips, usually lance-shaped and toothed or spiny. Red or yellow tubular flowers are borne in racemes, often umbel-like, in late winter or spring. With striking form and brilliant flowers, aloes are popular landscaping plants in warm dry areas and many can be grown to good effect in containers.

CULTIVATION: Aloes require warm, dry, and well-drained conditions. They can tolerate soils of low fertility. Most prefer full sun although some smaller species do well in partially shaded situations. In cool-temperate climates they are suitable for greenhouse culture, and potted plants can be moved outdoors during the summer months. Propagation is by seed or, more easily, from stem cuttings or offsets.

Aloe arborescens ★

KRANTZ ALOE

↔6 ft (1.8 m) ↑10 ft (3 m)

From the bush and open forest in southern Africa. Leaves toothed, blue-green, curved and tapering, up to 2 ft (0.6 m) long, in rosettes at the branch ends. Spikes of orange to red flowers are seen in winter. This species is suitable for growing in coastal areas. Zones 9–11.

Aloe aristata ★

LACE ALOE, TORCH PLANT

↔24 in (60 cm) ↑20 in (50 cm)

From southern Africa. Dense clusters of stemless rosettes with incurved, 4 in (10 cm) long, white-spotted green leaves tapering to a filament-like tip. White spines and soft white teeth. Inflorescences to 20 in (50 cm) tall, often branched. Red 1½ in (35 mm) long flowers from late spring. Zones 9–11.

Aloe brevifolia ★

↔20–32 in (50–80 cm)
↑20 in (50 cm)

Native to South Africa. Dense clusters of 4 in (10 cm) wide rosettes of short, tightly packed, blue-green, soft-spined leaves. Unbranched, 16 in (40 cm) tall, unbranched inflorescences of short, green-tipped, red flowers are borne in summer. Zones 8–11.

Aloe capitata

↔40–48 in (100–120 cm)
↑24–40 in (60–100 cm)

From Madagascar. Single rosette of red-tinted leaves to 20 in (50 cm) long, edged with red teeth. Inflorescences branched, with bell-shaped yellow flowers. Zones 10–12.

Aloe arborescens

Aloe × spinosissima

Aloe chabaudii

↔3–5 ft (0.9–1.5 m)
↕2–5 ft (0.6–1.5 m)

From South Africa to Zambia. Rosettes of thick, fleshy green leaves, red-brown edges and teeth. May have short trunk. Inflorescences with red-brown flowers in winter. Zones 9–11.

Aloe claviflora

CANNON ALOE, KRAALAALWYN

↔3–7 ft (0.9–2 m) ↕5 ft (1.5 m)

From South Africa. Rosettes clustered, up to 24 in (60 cm) wide, with upright gray-green leaves to 18 in (45 cm) long, edged with widely spaced large teeth. Horizontal inflorescences to 24 in (60 cm) tall, branched, with pinkish red to orange flowers, in spring–summer. Zones 9–11.

Aloe dorotheae ★

↔3–7 ft (0.9–2 m)
↕20–32 in (50–80 cm)

From Tanzania. Clump-forming species with short suckering stems and loose rosettes of narrow, red-brown, fiercely toothed leaves to 10 in (25 cm) long. In winter, usually unbranched upright inflorescences with 1¼ in (30 mm) long, green-tipped, yellow to red flowers. Zones 10–11.

Aloe excelsa

↔3 ft (0.9 m) ↕30 ft (9 m)

From southeastern areas of Africa, this aloe forms a single trunked tree, often clothed with dead leaves, topped by a large rosette of broad, channelled leaves. Spikes of orange to deep red flowers, on stems up to 3 ft (0.9 m) long, in late winter. Zones 9–11.

Aloe ferox ★

BITTER ALOE, CAPE ALOE

↔5–10 ft (1.5–3 m) ↕7–17 ft (2–5 m)

From South Africa's Cape region, this aloe is tree-like, with heads of broad, fleshy, red-tinted, sometimes spiny leaves to 40 in (100 cm) long, edged with strong red-brown teeth. Branched inflorescences with spikes of orange-red and golden yellow flowers, 1½ in (35 mm) long, are seen from late winter. A. f. var. candelabrum (syn. *A. candelabrum*) has neatly branched stems, inflorescences that are more heavily branched, and leaf tips that are slightly rolled. Zones 9–11.

Aloe globuligemma

↔3–5 ft (0.9–1.5 m) ↕3 ft (0.9 m)

From southern Africa. Clumps of a few stemless or short-stemmed rosettes with brown-toothed, white-edged, blue-green leaves to 20 in (50 cm) long. Upright, branching inflorescences, flowerheads held horizontally. Flowers 1 in (25 mm) long, yellow to cream with red base, opening from red buds, in winter. Zones 9–11.

Aloe humilis

syn. *Aloe virens*

↔20–32 in (50–80 cm)
↕20 in (50 cm)

From southern Africa. Clumps of stemless rosettes. Dark green fleshy leaves to 8 in (20 cm) long, edged with fierce teeth. Red flowers on branching inflorescence to 16 in (40 cm) high. Zones 10–11.

Aloe littoralis

↔6 ft (1.8 m) ↕17 ft (5 m)

Found from South Africa to Angola. Tree-like with unbranched stem to over 12 ft (3.5 m) tall with head of thick gray- to blue-green leaves, up to 24 in (60 cm) long, edged with fierce brown teeth. Branched inflorescences up to 5 ft (1.5 m) high, with 1½ in (35 mm) long pink to orange-red flowers from autumn. Zones 9–12.

Aloe maculata ★

syn. *Aloe saponaria*

SOAP ALOE, ZEBRA ALOE

↔24–60 in (60–150 cm)
↕40 in (100 cm)

From southern Africa. Clumps of short-stemmed rosettes with fleshy green leaves, light-spotted in bands. Teeth green to brown. Orange flowers on branching inflorescences in spring and summer. **'Commutata'** has dusky red flowers in spring. Zones 9–11.

Aloe perfoliata

syns *Aloe distans, A. mitriformis*

↔4–20 ft (1.2–6 m)
↕24–40 in (60–100 cm)

Native to Northern and Western Cape regions of South Africa. Low, spreading stems that strike root and grow to around 10 ft (3 m) long, ascending at tips. Yellow-toothed blue-green leaves to 8 in (20 cm) long, sometimes white-spotted. Branched inflorescences to 24 in (60 cm) tall, with tubular, dusky red to scarlet flowers in summer. Zones 9–11.

Aloe plicatilis ★

FAN ALOE

↔7 ft (2 m) ↕15 ft (4.5 m)

From the Cape region in South Africa. Grows into a well-branched shrub to 5 ft (1.5 m) tall in cultivation. Terminal leaves, arranged in 2 ranks of 12 to 16, dull green, flat, with rounded tips and minute teeth. Red flowers in winter. Zones 9–11.

Aloe polyphylla ★

↔16–32 in (40–80 cm)
↕30 in (75 cm)

Native of Lesotho. Short-stemmed rosettes with spirals of light-toothed, purple-edged, gray-green leaves to 12 in (30 cm) long. Branched inflorescences to 24 in (60 cm) high, with 2 in (5 cm) long, red to orange-pink flowers, in spring. Zones 8–10.

Aloe speciosa

↔3–10 ft (0.9–3 m)
↕7–15 ft (2–4.5 m)

From South Africa. Shrubby or tree-like. Branched or unbranched trunk and terminal rosettes of red-brown-toothed, fleshy, blue-green leaves up to 32 in (80 cm) long. Unbranched 20 in (50 cm) high inflorescence of striking 1¼ in (30 mm) long, greenish-white flowers with protruding stamens, opening from red buds, in winter. Zones 9–11.

Aloe spicata

↔4 ft (1.2 m) ↕5 ft (1.5 m)

From South Africa. Often solitary rosettes with a stem up to 40 in (100 cm) tall with unmarked green leaves to 24 in (60 cm) long, edged with green or brown teeth. Tall, unbranched, upright inflorescences with kniphofia-like head of yellow and orange flowers in winter. Zones 9–11.

Aloe × spinosissima ★

↔24–48 in (60–120 cm)
↕40 in (100 cm)

Hybrid of *A. humilis* and *A. arborescens*. It forms clumps of stemless or short-stemmed rosettes of narrow, recurved, soft-toothed, green leaves. Unbranched, upright inflorescences of orange-red flowers in winter. Zones 9–11.

Aloe striata ★

CORAL ALOE

↔4–7 ft (1.2–2 m) ↕3 ft (0.9 m)

A native of South Africa's Cape region. Spreading branching stems with rosettes of broad, flat, toothless leaves, usually blue-gray with faint longitudinal stripes and reddish edges, to 20 in (50 cm) long. Branching inflorescences to 40 in (100 cm) tall with dull to bright red flowers from winter. A. s. subsp. karasbergensis has green-veined, white-edged leaves and many-branched inflorescences of green-tipped pink flowers. Zones 9–11.

Aloe striatula

BASUTO KRAAL ALOE

↔3 ft (0.9 m) ↕6 ft (1.8 m)

Species found in rocky places in Eastern Cape and Lesotho in southern Africa. Well-branched, terminal rosettes, downward curving, bright green, glossy leaves with white toothed edges. Conical flowerheads red to yellow in summer. Zones 8–11.

Aloe vera ★

syn. *Aloe barbadensis*

↔24–48 in (60–120 cm)
↕32 in (80 cm)

Believed to be originally native to southern Arabia or nearby parts of Africa, this well-known species has become widely naturalized in the Mediterranean and tropical Africa. Forms clumps of stemless or suckering rosettes of light-spotted, narrow, fleshy, dark green leaves up to 12 in (30 cm) long. Yellow 1¼ in (30 mm) long flowers on few-branched inflorescences in summer. Valued for its sap's medicinal properties. Zones 10–12.

A

ALONSOA

MASK FLOWER

This genus of 12 perennial herbs or shrubs, which is a member of the figwort or foxglove (Scrophulariaceae) family, is native to the western tropical Americas. The flowers are on terminal racemes, with each flower composed of 5 petals and a short tube, held on a long stalk. The fruit is in the form of a capsule containing many small seeds.
CULTIVATION: These species prefer rich well-drained soil. Pinch out the growing shoots to encourage a bushy growth habit. Make sure to protect the plants from aphids. Propagate from seed in spring.

Alonsoa meridionalis

syn. *Alonsoa warscewiczii*

MASK FLOWER

↔ 24–36 in (60–90 cm)
↕ 18–24 in (45–60 cm)

Perennial herb or shrub native to Peru; may be grown as an annual. Bright red or orange flowers, rarely white, through summer–autumn. Slender, branching, red stems, and oval-shaped, toothed, reddish-green leaves. Zones 9–11.

ALPINIA

GINGER LILY

The 200 species of fleshy-stemmed perennials in this genus, which belongs to the ginger (Zingiberaceae) family, are native to tropical regions of Asia, Australia, and some Pacific islands where they grow on forest margins. Lance-shaped leaves are arranged in 2 ranks along reed-like stems from 3–12 ft (0.9–3.5 m) tall depending on the species. The usually showy and long-lasting inflorescences range from pale to brilliant colors. The true flowers are often enclosed at first within colorful bracts. Although generally grown for their flowers or foliage, some species are used in cooking and for their essential oils.
CULTIVATION: In warm climates grow in sun or half-sun in fertile moist soil. Most species will withstand a little frost but must have 4 to 5 months of uninterrupted growth to flower, so in cool climates start earlier indoors or grow under glass in bright filtered light, water plentifully and maintain high humidity. Propagate from seed or by division.

Alpinia zerumbet

Alstroemeria ligtu

Alpinia calcarata

INDIAN GINGER, SNAP GINGER

↔ 2–3 ft (0.6–0.9 m)
↕ 3–6 ft (0.9–1.8 m)

Native to China and India. Glossy narrow leaves to 12 in × 1 in (30 cm × 2.5 cm). The horizontal inflorescence is about 4 in (10 cm) long. White flowers have yellow interiors heavily veined with reddish maroon. Autumn-flowering. Zones 8–12.

Alpinia zerumbet

syns *Alpinia nutans, A. speciosa*

PINK PORCELAIN LILY, SHELL GINGER

↔ 2–3 ft (0.6–0.9 m)
↕ 6–10 ft (1.8–3 m)

From eastern Asia and New Guinea. Most widely grown species. Glossy leathery leaves. Pendulous inflorescence to 16 in (40 cm) long. Pale pink or white bracts at first enclose yellow and red flowers borne in spring and summer. **'Variegata'**, leaves variegated with pale yellow stripes. Zones 9–11.

ALSTROEMERIA

LILY OF THE INCAS, PERUVIAN LILY

A genus of around 50 species of fleshy-rooted perennials, the type genus for the Alstroemeriaceae family. Found in South America, often at altitude, they are known for their long-lasting beautifully marked flowers but notorious for their vigorous roots and self-sowing. At least one of the species, *A. psittacina*, is considered a weed in some areas. Foliage is mid-green, usually lance-shaped, and slightly twisted. It is carried on tall stems that terminate in many flowered heads of 6-petalled lily-like blooms that occur in many shades. The genus was named by Linnaeus after one of his pupils, Claus von Alstroemer (1736–1794), who around 1753 sent seeds of the plant to Linnaeus from Spain, where it had recently been introduced.
CULTIVATION: Though rather frost tender—the roots should be insulated with mulch—these species are easily grown in any sunny position with moderately fertile well-drained soil that can be kept moist during the flowering season. Propagate by division when dormant, or from seed.

Alstroemeria ligtu

ST MARTIN'S FLOWER

↔ 16 in (40 cm) ↕ 24 in (60 cm)

Summer-flowering species from Chile and Argentina. Leaves to 3 in (8 cm) long. Flowers white through creamy yellow and lavender to magenta, usually with yellow throat and darker flecks. Flower clusters of 2 to 3 blooms in heads of up to 8 clusters. Zones 8–10.

Alstroemeria psittacina

syn. *Alstroemeria pulchella*

↔ 16–20 in (40–50 cm)
↕ 28–36 in (70–90 cm)

This Brazilian species has leaves up to 3 in (8 cm) long, and heads of red-flushed green flowers with maroon flecks, borne in summer. **'Royal Star'** (syn. 'Variegata') is a cultivar with cream edged and/or striped leaves. Zones 8–10.

Alstroemeria Hybrid Cultivars

↔ 12–24 in (30–60 cm)
↕ 18–30 in (45–75 cm)

Alstroemerias hybridize freely, and in recent years the range has increased enormously as plant breeders around the world have capitalized on these easily grown plants' use as cut flowers. Many of these cultivars are hybrids between *A. ligtu, A. haemantha* and *A. aurea.* Popular hybrids include: **'Aimi'**, 24 in (60 cm) tall, pink-blushed pale creamy yellow flowers with deep brown flecks; **'Amanda'**, white-flushed pink flowers with green petal tips and dark flecks; **'Apollo'**, 3 ft (0.9 m) tall, white flowers with deep yellow center and brown flecks; **'Belinda'**, soft yellow flowers with darker center and brown flecks; **'Blue Heaven'**, 3–4 ft (1–1.2 m) tall, lavender blue flowers with pale center and red-brown flecks; **'Blushing Bride'**, 3 ft (0.9 m) tall, white flowers with faint pink blush; **'Evening Song'**, 3 ft (0.9 m) tall, deep magenta flowers with yellow throat and dark flecks; **'Friendship'**, 3 ft (0.9 m) tall, soft yellow flowers with deep brown markings and a darker center, and hint of purple at the petal tips; **'Fuego'** ★, 5–6 ft (1.5–1.8 m) tall, fiery red flowers with small yellow throat; Ilona/**'Stalona'**, soft orange-red flowers with creamy yellow throat and dark flecks; Irena/**'Statiren'**, white-flushed pink flowers with near-red mid-stripe and dark flecks; **'Marina'**, 20–30 in (50–75 cm) tall, magenta-pink flowers with small yellow throat and dark flecks; **'Marissa'**, 3 ft (0.9 m) tall, rose pink flowers lightening to cream mid-petal with yellow throat and dark flecks; **'Napoli'**, magenta-purple flowers with faint yellow throat and dark flecks; **'Odessa'**, 3–4 ft (1–1.2 m) tall, white flowers flushed and tipped deep red-pink, with yellow throat and red flecks; Olga/**'Stalog'**, white flowers with yellow center and red flecks; **'Orange Gem'**, 3 ft (0.9 m) tall, orange flowers with golden yellow throat and dark flecks; **'Orange Glory'**, 3 ft (0.9 m) tall, deep orange flowers with dark markings and golden throat; Queen Elizabeth The Queen Mother/**'Stamoli'**, brown-marked cream flowers flushed with pink; Rebecca/**'Stabec'**, 3 ft (0.9 m) tall, cream flowers with deep pink

A

blotches, yellow center and dark flecks; **'Red Beauty'**, 3 ft (0.9 m) tall, with black-flecked, red-orange flowers with yellow-throats, **'Romy'**, 4–5 ft (1.2–1.5 m) tall, white flowers with yellow center and red flecks; **'Tessa'**, 30 in (75 cm) tall, brown-flecked red flowers with small yellow center; **'Yellow Friendship'**, black-flecked bright yellow flowers.

The **Little Miss Series** are dwarf plants, 6–12 in (15–30 cm) tall, with large flowers, strong stems and a long flowering period. They include: **'Little Miss Olivia'**, soft cream with pale yellow throat and red-brown flecks; **'Little Miss Roselind'**, deep pink with yellow center; **'Little Miss Sophie'**, cream with red markings and broad pink mid-stripe; and **'Little Miss Tara'**, deep pinkish red with small golden center and dark flecks.

The Dutch-raised **Princess Series** is a range of compact hybrids that grow 12–18 in (30–45 cm) tall and are long flowering because they are sterile. They are ideal as potted plants. This series includes: Princess Daniela/**'Stapridani'**, pale yellow in color with dark flecks; Princess Ivana/**'Staprivane'**, deep rose pink; Princess Monica/**'Staprimon'**, red-throated, pink-marked, cream flowers; Princess Morana/**'Staprirana'**, pale cream with orange markings; Princess Oxana/**'Staprioxa'**, magenta pink; Princess Pamela/**'Stapripame'**, mauve-pink; Princess Sissi/**'Staprisis'**, deep pink with yellow markings; and Princess Zavina/**'Staprivina'**, salmon pink with yellow throat and dark flecks. Zones 7–10.

ALTERNANTHERA

CHAFF FLOWER, COPPERLEAF, JOYWEED

A genus of about 200 low, compact, trailing or erect, aquatic, annual or perennial herbs from tropical to subtropical Americas belonging to the amaranth (Amaranthaceae) family. Spikes of small flowers with bracts but no petals. Often grown for their brightly colored foliage, which is smooth-edged or densely toothed. Named for their alternate infertile anthers.

CULTIVATION: Adaptable to most soils, they do best in a protected, warm, sunny position in rich soil with frequent watering. Regularly clip plants to a height of 2½–4 in (6–10 cm) for border displays. In cooler climates plants should be lifted after first frosts. Propagate by division or from cuttings taken in late summer or spring.

Alternanthera bettzichiana

CALICO PLANT

↔2–3 ft (0.6–0.9 m) ↕2–3 ft (0.6–0.9 m)

An annual or short-lived perennial from Brazil. Erect habit, narrow spoon-shaped leaves of khaki to yellow, with red to purple markings. **'Brilliantissima'** is a variety with vivid red leaves. Zones 10–12.

ALTHAEA

This genus is a member of the mallow (Malvaceae) family and contains 12 species of annual and perennial herbs native to western Europe and central Asia. They grow in moist or marshy ground at low altitudes. The rounded leaves are lobed to varying degrees. The 5-petalled flowers are no bigger than 1½ in (35 mm) across and have prominent tubes of fused stamens. They are borne in racemes or panicles in summer. *Althaea* is closely related to the true hollyhock, *Alcea,* but is much less showy.

CULTIVATION: Well suited to "wild" gardens. Grow in rich moist soil in a sunny position. Propagate by division or from seed in spring.

Althaea officinalis

MARSH MALLOW, WHITE MALLOW

↔4 ft (1.2 m) ↕4–7 ft (1.2–2 m)

From Europe, naturalized in eastern USA. A rather lax plant with hairy, grayish, 3- to 5-lobed leaves. The small flowers are pale pink or white with purplish red tubes of fused stamens. The popular confectionery marshmallow was originally made from the roots of this plant. Zones 3–10.

ALYOGYNE

Once included within the genus *Hibiscus*, the 4 species that make up this genus, of the mallow (Malvaceae) family, are distinctive, evergreen, Australian shrubs which, despite their delicate silky blooms, are native to the drier regions of the western half of the continent. Leaves are variable; in some species they are entire, in others palmately lobed. They are fast growing and, as though to make up for their short-lived single blooms, usually in pinks or mauves, they flower profusely over a long period.

CULTIVATION: *Alyogyne* species are hardy plants for non-humid areas. Most are able to survive frost. They do best planted in full sun and can survive in all soil types but appreciate good drainage. Pruning is sometimes necessary to control the plant's shape. Propagation is from easily struck cuttings or from seed.

Alyogyne huegelii ★

BLUE HIBISCUS

↔3–6 ft (0.9–1.8 m) ↕3–6 ft (0.9 m–1.8 m)

This is a popular species, because it is both hardy and fast growing. Flowers pale mauve to purplish with overlapping petals set against pale green, slightly felty, and deeply lobed leaves. Prune late summer after flowering. **'Delightfully Double'**, double flowers with petaloid center; **'Monterey Bay'** and **'Santa Cruz'** are popular cultivars. Zones 9–10.

AMARANTHUS

There are about 60 species of weedy annuals and short-lived perennials in this genus, which is a member of the amaranth (Amaranthaceae) family. They have a worldwide distribution, often being found in wasteland areas. Species range from tall to prostrate, with long, often drooping, tassels of small red or green flowers. Individual flowers are either male or female and may be borne on separate plants. Some species are cultivated as leaf or grain crops in tropical areas, while those with dramatic flowers or colorful foliage are popular in the ornamental garden and for floristry.

CULTIVATION: *Amaranthus* species are easily grown in well-drained fertile soil in full sun. Protect tall varieties from strong wind. In cooler climates sow seed under glass in early spring and plant out after danger of frosts has passed. In warmer areas seed can be sown outdoors later in the season.

Amaranthus caudatus

LOVE-LIES-BLEEDING, TASSEL FLOWER, VELVET FLOWER

↔24 in (60 cm) ↕36–48 in (90–120 cm)

Native to Peru, Africa, and India, this annual or short-lived perennial has dull green leaves, as well as drooping crimson-purple tassels, up to 12 in (30 cm) long, in summer. **'Green Tails'** has long greenish yellow tassels; **'Viridis'** (syn. 'Green Thumb') has long-lasting vivid green tassels. Zones 8–11.

Amaranthus cruentus

syn. *Amaranthus paniculatus*

PRINCE'S FEATHER, PURPLE AMARANTH, RED AMARANTH

↔30 in (75 cm) ↕36–60 in (90–150 cm)

An annual species native to the Americas, with oval to lance-shaped leaves, that can be used as a vegetable. It has greenish to red tassels, erect or drooping, up to 24 in (60 cm) long. The seeds are reddish brown to black. **'Golden Giant'** has golden seed heads. Zones 8–11.

Althaea officinalis

Amaranthus cruentus

Alyogyne huegelii

A

Amaranthus hypochondriacus

CEREAL GRAIN AMARANTH

↔ 24 in (60 cm) ↕ 4 ft (1.2 m)

From southern USA, Mexico, India, and China. An annual species with green to purplish leaves and erect spikes of tiny deep crimson flowers. Grown as a cereal crop in South America. '**Green Thumb**' has upright spikes of green flowers. '**Pygmy Torch**' grows to 12 in (30 cm) high, with densely packed crimson flowerheads. Zones 8–11.

Amaranthus tricolor

CHINESE SPINACH, JOSEPH'S COAT, TAMPALA

↔ 30 in (75 cm) ↕ 24–36 in (60–90 cm)

From Africa and Asia, this bushy annual is grown as a leaf vegetable or, in varieties which have colorful foliage, for its ornamental value. Appearing in summer, the flower spikes are green or red. There are several varieties that have colored top growth, the best known being '**Joseph's Coat**', with red and gold upper leaves. Zones 8–11.

Amelanchier canadensis

Amelanchier laevis

AMARYLLIS

BELLADONNA LILY, JERSEY LILY, MARCH LILY, NAKED LADIES

This once large genus has now been reduced to just one species, an autumn-flowering bulb native to South Africa. It is the type genus for the amaryllis (Amaryllidaceae) family. Belladonna means "beautiful lady" and is a reference to the legend of Amaryllis, a beautiful shepherdess who appeared in the works of Virgil. Dormant for most of the warmer months, sturdy red-tinted flower stems begin to appear from late summer and grow quickly to as much as 24 in (60 cm) tall. They are topped with heads of flowers in shades from very pale pink to deep magenta. Long strappy leaves soon follow, persisting till late spring. CULTIVATION: Plant the bulbs with their tops exposed in a warm sunny location and water well from late summer to encourage good flower production. Like most of the summer-dormant African bulbs, belladonna lily can withstand considerable drought when the foliage is absent. Propagation is usually by division of established clumps once the foliage dies back.

Amaryllis belladonna

↔ 12–20 in (30–50 cm) ↕ 24 in (60 cm)

From South Africa's Cape region, this species forms clumps of glossy mid-green leaves to 20 in (50 cm) long. Foliage dies back from spring. In late summer mildly scented, funnel-shaped, 4 in (10 cm) long flowers in heads of 6 or more start to open. Cultivars include: '**Capetown**', deep pink; '**Johannesburg**', pale pink, white center; '**Major**', deep pink, fragrant; and '**Purpurea**', purple-pink. Zones 8–10.

Amaryllis belladonna

AMELANCHIER

SERVICEBERRY

Amelanchier, a member of the rose (Rosaceae) family, consists of 30 or so species of deciduous shrubs and small trees from North America (including Mexico), with one species in China, and another in Europe and Turkey. All have smallish oval or elliptical leaves with finely toothed margins. Flowers, each with 5 white narrow petals, are borne in small sprays; the small hawthorn-like fruit have sepals at the apex. The fruits ripen to blue-black and are edible. Some make attractive ornamentals.
CULTIVATION: These are mostly woodland plants preferring moist sheltered sites, while some species do well at the edge of a pond or stream. Effective planted against a backdrop of darker foliage. Prone to the same pests and diseases as apples, pears, and hawthorns, including the dreaded fireblight. Propagation normally from seed, germination being aided by cold stratification, or by layering of low branches or suckers. Cultivars are often grafted.

Amelanchier alnifolia

syn. *Amelanchier florida*

ALDERLEAF SERVICEBERRY, JUNEBERRY, SASKATOON SERVICEBERRY

↔ 12 ft (3.5 m) ↕ 3–6 ft (0.9–1.8 m)

North American species found on banks of rivulets or on sheltered mountainsides. Leaves rounded, toothed mainly in the upper half, around 1 in (25 mm) long. Flowers in late spring–early summer, dark purple edible fruit. A. a. var. semiintegrifolia (syn. *A. florida*), thicket-forming deciduous shrub or small tree from southern Alaska to northern California. Zones 3–9.

Amelanchier arborea

syn. *Amelanchier canadensis of gardens*

DOWNY SERVICEBERRY

↔ 30 ft (9 m) ↕ 60 ft (18 m)

From eastern USA, the tallest-growing species, smaller in cultivation. Narrow rounded crown. Silver-gray smooth bark, rougher with age. Leaves abruptly pointed, turn red or yellow in autumn. Flowers in early spring. Small purple-black fruit. Zones 4–9.

Amelanchier canadensis

syn. *Amelanchier oblongifolia*

JUNEBERRY, SERVICEBERRY, SHADBLOW SERVICEBERRY

↔ 10 ft (3 m) ↕ 25 ft (8 m)

This eastern North American species is an upright suckering shrub or small tree mainly from boggy ground. Woolly new leaves, spring flowers in upright sprays, juicy blue-black fruits are about ½ in (12 mm) in diameter. Cultivars include '**Glenn Form**' and '**Sprizam**'. Zones 5–9.

Amelanchier × *grandiflora*

APPLE SERVICEBERRY, SERVICEBERRY

↔ 35 ft (10 m) ↕ 25 ft (8 m)

This hybrid between *A. arborea* and *A. laevis*, the two tallest North American species, has given rise to several ornamental cultivars: '**Ballerina**' ★ (syn. *A. lamarckii* 'Ballerina'), spreading, up to 20 ft (6 m) tall, with bronze new leaves, masses of large flowers; and '**Rubescens**', flowers flushed with pink, opening from darker pink buds. Zones 4–9.

Amelanchier laevis

syn. *Amelanchier canadensis of gardens*

ALLEGHENY SERVICEBERRY, SARVIS TREE

↔ 25 ft (8 m) ↕ 25 ft (8 m)

Found mainly in the Appalachian mountains of eastern USA, extending into Canada. Bronzy purple slightly downy new leaves, and sweet, juicy, blue-black fruit. Flowers appear as the leaves unfold in late spring. Zones 4–9.

AMORPHOPHALLUS

This fascinating genus of the arum (Araceae) family of some 170 species occurs in tropical regions from West Africa eastwards to Polynesia. Most species are found in disturbed vegetation, in open savannahs, and limestone outcrops, very few in dense forests. Altitude ranges from sea level to 9,840 ft (3,000 m), and they flower with the onset of the wet season. All are terrestrial herbaceous perennials with underground tubers or fleshy stems.

Plants may be small to massive, with a single leaf, rarely 2, produced from the stem and usually lasting only one season. The leaf stalk is generally cylindrical, ranging from green to purple, or blotchy. Inflorescences vary in shape, size, and color, but are composed of a spadix encircled by a spathe. Being pollinated by various bees or flies, the inflorescences emit odors that can be pleasant or disgusting to the human nose.
CULTIVATION: Propagate from seed or by division of fleshy stems or branching tubers. Some succeed in temperate climates but most require warmth and regulated wet and dry periods to flower. Too much moisture in the leafless stage can cause rotting.

Amorphophallus bulbifer ★

↔ 5 ft (1.5 m) ↕ 3 ft (0.9 m)

Occurs in India, Bangladesh, Bhutan, and Nepal. Has a tuber to 6 in (15 cm) in diameter, producing 1 to 2 leaves, leaf stalk smooth, fleshy, dark green, mottled with whitish pink spots. Inflorescence stalk 4–27 in (10–70 cm) long, spathe oval to boat-shaped, 12 in (30 cm) long, outside grayish green with blackish green spots, inside at base dark pink, paler towards the top. Spadix about same length as spathe. Zone 12.

Amorphophallus bulbifer

Anaphalis triplinervis 'Sommerschnee'

AMSONIA

BLUE STAR

Found from southern Europe, through temperate Asia including Japan, and in North America, this genus of the dogbane (Apocynaceae) family has some 20 species of perennials and subshrubs characterized by milky sap and simple narrow leaves. Flowers, though small, are an unusual shade of blue and mass in heads above the foliage. While not spectacular, most species are distinctive, adding something different to the perennial border.
CULTIVATION: Prefer a climate with distinct seasons. Most are easily cultivated in a quite sunny position with well-drained soil kept moist in growing season. Propagate perennials by division during dormancy or as growth starts. Those with firmer stems will also grow from summer cuttings.

Amsonia ciliata

↔ 30–48 in (75–120 cm)
↕ 12–36 in (30–90 cm)

From southeast USA. Clumps of upright stems, downy when young. Leaves narrow, lance-shaped, 1–2 in (25–50 mm) long. Heads of mid-blue flowers through summer. Zones 7–10.

Amsonia tabernaemontana

BLUE DOGBANE, BLUE STAR

↔ 36–48 in (90–120 cm)
↕ 36 in (90 cm)

Clump-forming perennial of eastern USA. Upright green stems, simple lance-shaped leaves to 3 in (8 cm) long. Heads of pale blue flowers in mid-spring–late summer. Zones 4–9.

ANAGALLIS

PIMPERNEL

This primrose (Primulaceae) family genus includes 20 species, over much of the globe, especially temperate zones. Soft-stemmed, low, spreading plants, mostly biennials or perennials, behaving as annuals in cold climates. Leaves small and simple. Small brightly colored flowers, pink, red, or blue. Some may be weeds, but are not invasive. Scarlet pimpernel (*A. arvensis*) is famous for inspiring Baroness Orczy's novel of the French Revolution.
CULTIVATION: Grow in a sunny spot with moist well-drained soil. Cultivated species easily maintained by pinching to shape; not invasive. Propagate from seed, base cuttings, or by layers.

Anchusa azurea 'Loddon Royalist'

Anagallis monelli

BLUE PIMPERNEL

↔ 12–20 in (30–50 cm)
↕ 12–20 in (30–50 cm)

Mediterranean native, small shrub. Dark green leaves. Flowers single but abundant, bright blue, red-tinted undersides. **'Pacific Blue'** ★, compact, dark blue flowers; **'Phillipii'**, low grower, bright blue flowers. Zones 7–10.

ANAPHALIS

PEARLY EVERLASTING

This daisy (Asteraceae) family genus consists of around 100 species of perennials that may be upright, low and bushy, or trailing. Though found across northern temperate zones and on tropical mountains, a feature common to all is that the foliage and stems are covered with a fine white to gray hair. Leaves are simple, linear to lance-shaped, attached to stems without stalks. Flowerheads form dense downy heads, and while they lack ray florets, papery white bracts create a similar effect. Cut flowers last well but are not that attractive, the plants being grown as much for their foliage.
CULTIVATION: Mostly very hardy. Plant in full sun with gritty well-drained soil kept moist in summer. Dry winter conditions are preferable. Cut back hard in spring to encourage strong new growth. Propagate from seed, base cuttings, or by division.

Anaphalis margaritacea

PEARLY EVERLASTING

↔ 16–24 in (40–60 cm)
↕ 32–40 in (80–100 cm)

Widespread in northern temperate areas. Leaves gray-green above with white hair below. In summer, flowerheads are clustered in corymbs up to 6 in (15 cm) wide with opalescent bracts. Zones 3–9.

Anaphalis triplinervis

↔ 16–20 in (40–50 cm)
↕ 32–36 in (80–90 cm)

This is a central Asian species, found from Afghanistan to southwest China, which has spatula-shaped gray-green leaves that grow to 4 in (10 cm) long. It has dome-shaped heads of white flowerheads in summer. Valuable in a herb or mixed border, forming clumps quickly. One cultivar, **'Sommerschnee'**, grows up to 30 in (75 cm) in length and has bright silvery white flowers. Zones 5–9.

ANCHUSA

ALKANET, BUGLOSS

Classified in the borage or forget-me-not (Boraginaceae) family, this genus includes some 35 species of biennials and perennials from Europe, western Asia, and Africa. They are strong growers, usually clump-forming, with upright stems and simple, pointed, elliptical leaves that can be quite large at the base of the clump. Heads of small 5-petalled flowers in shades from pale blue to purple open through late spring and summer. Some species were once used in herbal medicines but are now largely out of favour. Likewise, the red dye that can be extracted, formerly used as a hair coloring, is now seldom seen.
CULTIVATION: Species thrive in most conditions except very poor soil, deep shade, or drought. Ample feeding and mulching in winter and water in the growing season promotes flowering. Perennials may be divided in winter or very early spring; annuals or biennials must be raised from seed, preferably sown in autumn so young plants can start growth early in spring.

Anchusa azurea

syn. *Anchusa italica*

↔ 32 in (80 cm) ↕ 4 ft (1.2 m)

Perennial native to the Mediterranean region and western Asia. Bristly red-tinted stems with lower leaves to 12 in (30 cm) long. Flowers blue to purple, ½ in (12 mm) wide. Cultivars include: **'Dropmore'**, tall, deep purple-blue flowers; **'Loddon Royalist'** ★, compact and bushy, large deep blue flowers; and **'Opal'**, compact, grayish foliage, light blue flowers. Zones 3–9.

Anchusa capensis

↔ 16 in (40 cm) ↕ 20 in (50 cm)

Hairy biennial from South Africa with narrow lance-shaped leaves to 5 in (12 cm) long. White-centered bright blue flowers through summer. Treated as a spring-sown annual where summers are long. Zones 9–11.

Andromeda polifolia

Anemone blanda

Anemone coronaria

ANDROMEDA

Two fully hardy, low-growing, evergreen shrub species make up this genus of the heath (Ericaceae) family, found growing in the acid peat bogs of the Northern Hemisphere. The somewhat leathery, smooth-edged, small oblong leaves form a deep green background to the white or tiny, pink, bell-like flowers held in terminal clusters during spring.
CULTIVATION: *Andromeda* species require an acid soil where constant moisture is assured, and are best grown in peat beds, shady woodlands, or rock gardens. They can be propagated by suckers, layering, or from softwood cuttings.

Andromeda polifolia

BOG ROSEMARY, MARSH ANDROMEDA

↔ 22 in (55 cm)
↑ 4–18 in (10–45 cm)

A variable growing shrub, either erect or prostrate, it has small, pointed, oblong leaves with clusters of bell-like flowers in spring or early summer. Cultivars include: **'Alba'**, a low-growing prostrate shrub with pure white flowers; **'Compacta'**, compact growth habit, pink flowers; and **'Macrophylla'**, with larger leaves and pink flowers. Zones 2–9.

ANEMONE

WINDFLOWER

Widespread in temperate regions of both hemispheres, this buttercup (Ranunculaceae) family genus encompasses some 120 species of perennials. Their roots may be tuberous, fleshy-stemmed or fibrous, and develop into clumps of finely divided foliage. Bowl-shaped flowers, single or in small clusters, sit on wiry stems well above the foliage. Most species flower in spring shortly after the foliage appears, but some continue into early summer and a few bloom in autumn. The name is derived most likely from the Greek *anemos* (wind), though some say it comes from Naamen, a variation on Adonis. Legend says it was his blood that gave *A. coronaria* its red flowers.
CULTIVATION: The wood anemones prefer woodland conditions with dappled shade, but most species thrive in a sunny border with moist well-drained soil. Propagation is by division in winter when dormant, or from seed in the case of strains grown as annuals.

Anemone blanda

↔ 6–12 in (15–30 cm)
↑ 4–8 in (10–20 cm)

Found from southeastern Europe to the Caucasus region. Strong fleshy stems and ferny base leaves. From late winter, 1–1¾ in (25–40 mm) wide white, blue, mauve, or pink flowers. **'Atrocaerulea'** (syn. 'Ingramii'), deep blue flowers; **'Radar'**, white-centered deep magenta-pink flowers; **'White Splendour'**, tall grower, large white flowers, pink-tinted inside. Zones 5–9.

Anemone canadensis

↔ 12–16 in (30–40 cm)
↑ 12–16 in (30–40 cm)

Summer-flowering North American species with woody rootstock. Finely cut pinnate foliage and simple, often green-tinted, creamy white flowers to 1 in (25 mm) wide. Zones 3–9.

Anemone coronaria

FLORIST'S ANEMONE, WIND POPPY, WINDFLOWER

↔ 8–16 in (20–40 cm)
↑ 16–24 in (40–60 cm)

Tuberous-rooted native of southeastern Europe and northern Mediterranean. Finely divided ferny base foliage and simple leaves on flower stems. Large spring flowers in most shades except yellow. Parent of many cultivars and a large range of garden hybrids, such as the Mona Lisa Series, which grow to 24 in (60 cm) tall with flowers to 4 in (10 cm) wide in all colors; and **Harmony Mix**, 2 in (5 cm) wide flowers in all colors on stems to 20 in (50 cm) tall. Zones 8–10.

Anemone hupehensis

↔ 16–40 in (40–100 cm)
↑ 20–36 in (50–90 cm)

Fibrous-rooted, late summer- to autumn-flowering species from China and Japan. Coarsely toothed, lightly downy, 3-part foliage. Upright branching flower stems with large flowers, usually white but often in pink shades. Fluffy seedheads follow. A. h. var. japonica has stocky flower stems and many-petalled flowers. **'Prinz Heinrich'** is an *A. h.* var. *japonica* cultivar around 32 in (80 cm) tall, forming large clumps with deep pink flowers. A. h. **'Hadspen Abundance'** is a popular cultivar, to 24 in (60 cm) tall, flowers with alternating light and dark pink petals. Zones 6–9.

Anemone × *hybrida*

↔ 20–48 in (50–120 cm)
↑ 32–60 in (80–150 cm)

Garden hybrids of uncertain origin but certainly with *A. vitifolia* and *A. hupehensis* var. *japonica* in their background. Similar to *A. hupehensis* but capable of growing to 5 ft (1.5 m) tall and with infertile flowers. **'Géantes des Blanches'**, 4 ft (1.2 m) tall, large, white, semi-double flowers; **'Honorine Jobert'** ★, 4 ft (1.2 m) tall, large, white, single flowers with pale pink reverse; and **'Margarete'**, 3 ft (0.9 m) tall, pale pink double flowers. **'September Charm'** (syn. *A. hupehensis* 'September Charm'), 30 in (75 cm) high, has tall, pale pink flowers, often drooping. Zones 6–9.

Anemone multifida

↔ 8–16 in (20–40 cm)
↑ 6–24 in (15–60 cm)

North American species with woody rootstock and 3- to 5-part downy leaves divided into narrow lobes. Flowers white, cream, or red, up to ¾ in (18 mm) wide, throughout the warmer months. Formerly misidentified as *A. magellanica*. Zones 3–9.

Anemone narcissiflora

↔ 8–16 in (20–40 cm)
↑ 12–16 in (30–40 cm)

Found across the temperate Northern Hemisphere. Finely divided, downy, 5-part base leaves and simpler foliage on flower stems. Flowers are around 1 in (25 mm) wide in heads of up to 8, usually white but variably colored. Zones 3–9.

Anemone nemorosa

WINDFLOWER, WOOD ANEMONE

↔ 6–16 in (15–40 cm)
↑ 4–12 in (10–30 cm)

This is a fleshy-stemmed, spring-flowering, European native usually found in woodlands. Leaflets are in threes, coarsely toothed, and/or finely divided. Flowers are around 1 in (25 mm) wide, usually white in the wild but garden forms come in a range of mauve and pink shades. **'Allenii'**, 8 in (20 cm) tall, nodding dusky blue flowers with purplish reverse; **'Pallida'**, 6 in (15 cm) tall, pale creamy yellow flowers and dark foliage; **'Robinsoniana'**, 8 in (20 cm) tall, lavendar flowers with pale reverse; **'Vestal'**, 6 in (15 cm) tall, with small, white, double flowers. Zones 5–9.

Anemone pavonina

ANEMONE OF GREECE

↔ 12–16 in (30–40 cm)
↑ 12 in (30 cm)

Clump-forming tuberous species native to the Mediterranean region. Three-part base foliage deeply divided and ferny, bright green. In spring, 2–4 in (5–10 cm) wide flowers in a range of colors. Allow to dry off after flowering. This species is the parent of several cultivars and hybrids. Zones 8–10.

Anemone ranunculoides

BUTTERCUP ANEMONE

↔ 6–12 in (15–30 cm)
↑ 6 in (15 cm)

Fleshy-stemmed European woodland species that flowers in late winter to early spring. Its leaves are trifoliate, deeply cut and divided, often deep green. Flowers are bright yellow and not more than ¾ in (18 mm) wide. Zones 4–9.

Anemone rivularis

↔ 12–20 in (30–50 cm)
↑ 27–36 in (70–90 cm)

Fibrous-rooted Himalayan species

Anemone sylvestris

that forms clumps of short-stemmed, trifoliate, toothed base leaves up to 6 in (15 cm) wide. In late spring–summer, it bears heads of white flowers on long stems. Petals are blue-tinted on the reverse side. Likes damp soil. Zones 7–9.

Anemone sylvestris

SNOWDROP ANEMONE, SNOWDROP WINDFLOWER

↔6–20 in (15–50 cm) ↕6–12 in (15–30 cm)

A spreading fleshy-stemmed European species that is found to occur in a range of conditions from lowland woods to subalpine regions. The species has deeply divided, deep green, hand-shaped leaves and, appearing from late spring, scented white flowers that are up to 3 in (8 cm) wide, often slightly drooping. These are followed by fluffy seed heads. Cultivars include: **'Elise Fellman'** (syn. 'Flore Pleno'), a compact plant with double flowers; and **'Grandiflora'**, which has large pendulous flowers. Zones 4–9.

Anemone tomentosa

GRAPELEAF ANEMONE

↔20–32 in (50–80 cm) ↕3 ft (0.9 m)

This woody-rooted Chinese species is similar to *A. hupehensis*. It has large leaves, usually trifoliate but sometimes entire, with coarsely toothed edges and downy undersides. Flowers, which appear in early summer, are white or pale pink and mildly scented. They are borne singly or in pairs. Zones 3–9.

Anemone trullifolia

↔12–16 in (30–40 cm) ↕12 in (30 cm)

A woody-rooted species from the Himalayas. It features rounded toothed base leaves, as well as upper leaves that often have shallow lobes. Small heads of graceful soft mauve-blue or white flowers are seen in summer. Zones 5–9.

Anemone virginiana

↔12–20 in (30–50 cm) ↕12–24 in (30–60 cm)

This woody-rooted species comes from central and eastern USA. Base leaves with 3 to 5 parts, deeply divided, and ferny. From late spring, sprays of 1 in (25 mm) wide green-tinted white flowers appear on branching stems. Zones 4–9.

ANEMONELLA

Native to eastern North America, the single species in this genus, of the buttercup (Ranunculaceae) family, is a perennial herb with smooth tuberous roots. In spring, 2 to 5 flowers appear on thin stalks, with 5 to 10 sepals and numerous spreading, petal-like, white stamens but no corolla.

CULTIVATION: Heat tolerant but hardy to cold temperatures, preferring shade. Soil should be humus-rich and moist. Plant from containers in early spring, and water until established. Requires little maintenance thereafter and can be cut to ground level in winter. Propagate from seed when fresh or by division every 3 to 5 years in autumn.

Anemonella thalictroides

CROWFOOT, RUE ANEMONE

↔3–6 in (8–15 cm) ↕4–10 in (10–25 cm)

This tuberous-rooted perennial comes from eastern North America. It has delicate 3-lobed leaflets and single white to pale pink flowers. A. t. f. rosea has pale pink flowers; **'Oscar Schoaf'** (syns 'Rosea Plena', 'Schoaf's Double Pink') also with pale pink flowers. A. t. **'Betty Blake'**, has cream flowers. Zones 4–8.

ANETHUM

DILL

A genus of 2 species of annual or biennial herbs of the carrot (Apiaceae) family. Only *A. graveolens* is commonly cultivated and is used (foliage and seeds) as a garnish or as flavoring. It is similar in appearance to its close relative, fennel. Dill flowers attract many species of butterflies and can be used in wildflower gardens. Dill is used medicinally for indigestion or flatulence, often given to babies with colic.

CULTIVATION: Easily grown in a sunny well-drained position that is not too dry in summer. Though plants can be raised from seed and then transplanted, it may be easier to prepare a patch of soil and cast seed over it, lightly raking it in afterward.

Anethum graveolens

↔12–20 in (30–50 cm) ↕24–32 in (60–80 cm)

Strongly aromatic southwest Asian annual with long, finely divided, ferny leaves, the individual leaflets being almost hair-like. Summer-borne heads of tiny yellow flowers are followed by the well-known seeds. Zones 8–10.

ANGELICA

A genus of about 50 species belonging to the carrot (Apiaceae) family, occurring over much of the temperate Northern Hemisphere; some biennial, some perennial, including monocarpic species. Most are grown as ornamentals for their bold foliage, but others are cultivated for herbal uses. Large, often bipinnate leaves, deeply divided, sometimes glossy, and usually with toothed edges. Foliage grows from a stout rootstock. In summer compound flowerheads (umbels) of tiny white, cream, green, pink, or red flowers appear. Angelica has had many uses: as a vegetable, for making herbal tonics and medicines, and candied.

CULTIVATION: Plant in deep humus-rich soil with ample moisture. Will grow well in full sun but foliage is usually lusher with some shade. True perennial species may be divided but annual and monocarpic species are raised from seed, best very fresh.

Angelica pachycarpa

Angelica gigas

↔7 ft (2 m) ↕3–7 ft (0.9–2 m)

Strong-stemmed biennial from Korea, Japan, and northern China. Very large red-tinted leaves. Purple-red stems topped with red flowerheads from late summer. Zones 5–9.

Angelica pachycarpa

↔4 ft (1.2 m) ↕24 in (60 cm)

A near-evergreen perennial that is often confused with *A. angelica* but is very different and purely ornamental. Very glossy bipinnate leaves to over 12 in (30 cm) long with toothed leaflets. Small green flowers quickly turn to seed heads that are best removed to encourage lush foliage. Zones 8–10.

ANGELONIA

There are about 30 species of sub-shrubs or perennials in this plantain (Plantaginaceae) family genus. Native to central and southern America, they grow in damp open spaces. Leaves are usually small and simple. The short, 5-lobed, tubular flowers are mauve, blue, or white and are produced for much of the year. In cool and temperate climates these plants are usually treated as annuals.

CULTIVATION: Grow in a sunny position in a moist but well-drained light soil. Indoors they require bright filtered light in a potting mix with added organic matter and should be kept moist. Propagate from seed or softwood cuttings, or by division.

Angelonia angustifolia

↔12 in (30 cm) ↕18 in (45 cm)

From Mexico and West Indies. Small pointed leaves with serrated edges, and racemes of mauve to violet flowers in summer. The **Angelface, Archangel,** and **Serena** series are mixed color seedling strains, while **'Alba'**, white flowers, **'Purple'**, **'Purple and White'**, and **'Rose Pink'** indicate single colors. Zones 9–11.

Angelonia angustifolia 'Rose Pink'

Anguloa uniflora

× *Angulocaste* Rosemary

Anigozanthos flavidus, in the wild, Walpole, Western Australia

ANGULOA

TULIP ORCHID

These orchids (family Orchidaceae) come from mountainous regions of Venezuela, Colombia, Ecuador, Peru, and Bolivia, and are closely related to *Lycaste*, with fat pseudobulbs and large, thin, pleated leaves. The waxy, 3–4 in (8–10 cm) wide, tulip-shaped flowers do not open fully and are solitary on erect stalks from the base of the pseudobulb in spring and summer, coinciding with new growth. CULTIVATION: These plants require a cool to intermediate growing environment. Because their roots must not dry out during the growing season, they are best suited to containers. Water well when in active growth.

Anguloa clowesii

↔ 12–24 in (30–60 cm)
↕ 16–24 in (40–60 cm)

Native to Colombia and Venezuela. Arguably the most popular species in cultivation. It has bright lemon to golden yellow highly perfumed flowers. Zones 10–11.

Anguloa hohenlohii

↔ 12–24 in (30–60 cm)
↕ 16–24 in (40–60 cm)

From Venezuela. Often seen incorrectly labelled in collections as *A. ruckeri*. The blooms are deep bronze-red on the inside and pale greenish brown on the outside. Zones 10–12.

Anguloa uniflora

↔ 12–24 in (30–60 cm)
↕ 16–24 in (40–60 cm)

From Venezuela, Colombia, Ecuador, Peru, and Bolivia. Somewhat variable in color, with a white to creamy base, finely to coarsely spotted in pink. Some clones appear dark pink. Often confused with the closely related *A. virginalis*. Zones 10–11.

× ANGULOCASTE

A hybrid between the sympodial orchid genera *Anguloa* and *Lycaste*, and likewise a member of the orchid (Orchidaceae) family. Species have fat pseudobulbs and large, thin, pleated leaves. The waxy flowers are solitary on erect stalks from the base of the pseudobulb in spring and summer, coinciding with new growth. The color and shape of the blooms can vary considerably, depending on the genetic makeup of the hybrid. CULTIVATION: They are cool- to intermediate-growing epiphytes or semi-terrestrials best grown in pots, as roots must not dry out in the growing season. Heavy feeders when in active growth, they need copious watering.

× *Angulocaste* Jupiter × *Anguloa hohenlohii*

↔ 24–36 in (60–90 cm)
↕ 16–24 in (40–60 cm)

An unregistered hybrid that shows the heavy *Anguloa* influence with its upward-facing tulip-shaped blooms. Zones 10–11.

× *Angulocaste* Rosemary

↔ 24–36 in (60–90 cm)
↕ 16–24 in (40–60 cm)

Hybrid between *A.* Sanderae and *Lycaste* Balliae. It has a strong *Lycaste skinneri* influence, with *Lycaste macrophylla* and *Anguloa clowesii* also in its ancestry. Zones 10–11.

ANIGOZANTHOS

KANGAROO PAW

This genus contains 11 species of evergreen sword-leafed perennials of the bloodroot (Haemodoraceae) family, all of which are confined naturally to southwestern Australia. The foliage is dark green and varies from grassy to iris-like. Spikes or panicles of intriguingly furry tubular blooms are borne on stems 1–6 ft (0.3–1.8 m) tall, usually in warmer months. Flowers are around 1¼ in (30mm) long and occur in green and warm shades of gold, pink, red, and russet brown, depending on the species. The flower stems last well when cut and many new varieties have been developed with the florist trade in mind.

CULTIVATION: Plant in a sunny position with perfect drainage. Better if watered well in the growing season but will tolerate drought. Blackened foliage signals ink disease, which can be very damaging, as can slugs and snails. Propagation in gardens is mostly by careful division. Species may be raised from seed.

Anigozanthos flavidus

GREEN KANGAROO PAW, TALL KANGAROO PAW

↔ 3 ft (0.9 m) ↕ 10 ft (3 m)

Summer-flowering perennial with green leaves to 3 ft (0.9 m) long. Flowering stems smooth, green, to 10 ft (3 m). Hairy, tubular flowers are green or yellow-green, with red, orange, or pink populations or individuals in a few locations. Its habitat is moist stream banks, edges of wetlands, and roadside drains in wooded and forested regions of southern and southwestern Australia on sandy and gravelly soils. Zones 9–11.

Anigozanthos rufus

RED KANGAROO PAW

↔ to 20 in (50 cm)
↕ 20–40 in (50–100 cm)

Leaves green, 8–16 in (20–40 cm) long, smooth, margins rough. Flowering stems branched, densely woolly-hairy, red, flowers similar. Flowering spring–summer. Occurs in seasonally wet sandy soils along south coast of Western Australia. Zone 9.

Anigozanthos Hybrid Cultivars

↔ 8–30 in (20–75 cm)
↕ 1–6 ft (0.3–1.8 m)

Many of the 12 species of kangaroo paw have been used in deliberate breeding programs since the 1970s, and there are now many attractive cultivars being offered to the gardening public, that are easy to grow, and in a wide range of climates. The species most commonly used in hybridizing has been *A. flavidus,* a species that occurs in moist conditions along stream banks and in cultivation is tolerant of "wet feet." Cultivars include: **'Autumn Sunrise'** ★, orange flowers in late spring–summer; **'Big Red'**, many red flowers; **'Copper Charm'**, tall scapes of orange flowers in spring; **'Dwarf Delight'**, red hairs on yellow-green flowers; **'Hickman's Delight'**, dark green leaves, dark red flowers; **'Joey Calypso'**, golden yellow flowers, dwarf, only 16 in (40 cm) high; **'Joey Lipstick'**, red flowers, 16 in (40 cm) high; **'Little Jewel'**, glossy green evergreen leaves, red flowers in spring; **'Mini Red'**, compact plant, dense clusters of red flowers; **'Patricia'**, red-brown flowers in spring; **'Pink Joey'**, pale, purplish pink flowers; **'Rampaging Roy Slaven'**, orange-red flowers, broad leaves, strong growing; **'Red Cross'**, large deep burgundy-colored flowers with a yellow spot at the base; **'Regal Claw'**, red to orange flowers over most of the year; **'Ruby Jools'**, leaves semi-deciduous, flowers red-green; **'Space Age'**, red flowers; **'Spence's Spectacular'**, red-brown flowers, deciduous leaves; **'Sue Dixon'**, flowers red near base merging to yellow-green near lobes; **'Velvet Harmony'**, very dark, woolly, purplish flowers. The **Bush Gems Series** comes in a wide variety of colors: **'Bush Haze'**, tall, hairy stems, bright yellow flowers; **'Bush Heritage'**, green flowers, densely covered in reddish brown hairs; **'Bush Nugget'**, golden yellow flowers; **'Bush Revolution'**, brilliant vermillion flowers on stems to over 6 ft (1.8 m) high; **'Bush Ruby'**, red flowers; **'Bush Volcano'**, striking orange and red flowers, profuse. Zones 9–11.

ANTHEMIS

DOG FENNEL

Although this genus, along with many others in the daisy (Asteraceae) family, has been revised, it still contains around 100 species. These aromatic perennials and small shrubs are found mainly in the Mediterranean region and western Asia. Their leaves are usually very finely divided, sometimes gray-green or silvery, and form a base

foliage clump with the yellow or white, rarely mauve, daisy flowers held above it. Most cultivated species are now grown purely as ornamentals, but the flowers of *A. tinctoria* were once used to make dye and some species are being investigated for the medicinal properties of their essential oils and other extracts.
CULTIVATION: *Anthemis* species are hardy, and easily grown in moist, fertile, well-drained soil in full sun. Cut back after flowering for bushiness. May be short-lived but easily propagated from cuttings and seed; some perennials may be divided.

Anthemis marschalliana

↔ 12–20 in (30–50 cm)
↑ 12 in (30 cm)

From northeast Turkey and the Caucasus. Ground-covering perennial with silky, ferny, gray-green leaves. In summer it is covered with small lemon yellow daisies. Zones 7–9.

Anthemis punctata

↔ 12–20 in (30–50 cm)
↑ 16–24 in (40–60 cm)

Found in Europe, the Mediterranean islands, and North Africa. Woody-based perennial with silky, white, pinnate leaves to around 4 in (10 cm) long. Abundant white flowerheads in summer. A. p. subsp. cupaniana ★ from Sicily has silver-gray foliage and is a vigorous grower. Zones 7–9.

Anthemis tinctoria

DYER'S CHAMOMILE, YELLOW CHAMOMILE

↔ 20–40 in (50–100 cm)
↑ 24–36 in (60–90 cm)

Shrubby perennial found from Europe to western Asia. Short finely divided leaves, usually light green and faintly hairy, sometimes downy. Masses of golden flowerheads throughout warmer months. **'E. C. Buxton'** (syn. 'Mrs E. C. Buxton'), 18 in (45 cm) tall with soft yellow daises; **'Golden Rays'**, 24 in (60 cm) tall with bright yellow flowers; **'Sauce Hollandaise'**, 24 in (60 cm) tall, vigorous, masses of yellow-centered cream daises; **'Wargrave Variety'** (syn. 'Wargrave'), stems to 3 ft (0.9 m) tall with dark green leaves and lemon yellow flowers. Zones 6–9.

ANTHRISCUS

A genus of about 12 species consisting of annuals, biennials, and herbaceous perennials from Europe, North Africa, and Asia, some of which have become weedy in other countries. They have soft feathery foliage and the flat heads of tiny white flowers typical of the carrot (Apiaceae) family. Some species have marginal ornamental value in the wild type garden, but because of their self-sowing tendencies they need to be planted with discretion.
CULTIVATION: Any well-drained but moisture-retentive soil in sun or half-sun will suit. Propagation is from fresh seed, usually self-sown.

Anthemis tinctoria 'Golden Rays'

Antirrhinum majus, 'Chimes Pink'

Antigonon leptopus

Anthriscus cerefolium

CHERVIL

↔ 10–12 in (25–30 cm)
↑ 20–24 in (50–60 cm)

This annual plant from Europe and western Asia is grown as a food flavoring and tends to bolt in hot dry weather. Sow seed every few weeks to ensure continuous crops and expect it to germinate in 2 to 3 weeks, and be ready to harvest in about 6 weeks. Zones 7–10.

ANTIGONON

A Mexican and Central American genus comprising 3 species of quick-growing perennial vines of the knotweed (Polygonaceae) family. Evergreen in mild climates if the roots can be insulated with mulch. Can be grown in areas with light frosts that do not freeze the soil to any depth. Forming a dense canopy, the vines are smothered throughout the warmer months in floral racemes that derive most of their color, usually bright pink, from the sepals that surround the tiny flowers. The racemes terminate in a tendril that aids climbing. Three-angled fruits follow the flowers.
CULTIVATION: Plant in a sunny well-drained position and water well during summer. Frequent feeding encourages strong growth and heavy flowering. Pinch back to keep compact and remove spent flowers to prolong blooming. Propagate from seed or summer base cuttings, or by division of the tubers in early spring.

Antigonon leptopus

CHAIN OF LOVE, CONFEDERATE VINE, CORAL VINE, MEXICAN CREEPER

↔ 20 ft (6 m) ↑ 15 ft (4.5 m)

Strong-growing tuberous-rooted Mexican climber that will cover almost any support. Pointed, heavily veined, elongated, heart-shaped leaves around 4 in (10 cm) long, with strongly frilled margins. Minute flowers enclosed by coral pink to red heart-shaped sepals. Zones 10–12.

ANTIRRHINUM

SNAPDRAGON

Found in temperate Northern Hemisphere areas, this genus of around 40 species of annuals, perennials, and subshrubs belongs to the plantain (Plantaginaceae) family. The best known are the garden annuals, beloved of children for the way the mouth of the flower opens and closes with squeezing, hence the common name. Most species are compact, forming a low mound of simple rounded to lance-shaped leaves, sometimes with a gray-green tint. Flowering stems develop from late spring and carry heads of the familiar lobed blooms. Snapdragon seed is rich in oil, which in former times was extracted and used like olive oil.
CULTIVATION: These species grow best in a fertile, moist, humus-rich soil in full sun. The Mediterranean species are reasonably drought tolerant but need moisture to flower well. Rust diseases can cause problems in humid conditions. Propagation is from seed, though the perennial species will grow from cuttings of non-flowering stems.

Antirrhinum majus

↔ 6–20 in (15–50 cm)
↑ 12–60 in (30–150 cm)

Southwest European perennial, usually treated as annual. Upright bushy habit, dark green, elliptical leaves. Flowers in upright racemes, usually pink in wild but cultivated in most colors except blue. Popular seedling series include dwarf **Candelabra Series** and **Chimes Series;** trailing **Candy Showers Series** for hanging baskets; mid-height **Sonnet Series;** and slightly taller, often double-flowered **Madame Butterfly Mix** and **Liberty Series.** Zones 7–10.

Antirrhinum molle

↔ 6–8 in (15–20 cm)
↑ 8–16 in (20–40 cm)

Native to Portugal and northeastern Spain. Downy elliptical leaves, flowers pale pink or white with yellow throat and downy exterior. **'Avalanche'** is a white-flowered cultivar with a small yellow patch on lower lip. Zones 7–10.

Antirrhinum sempervirens

☼/◐ ❄ ↔ 6–8 in (15–20 cm)
↑ 8–16 in (20–40 cm)

A Pyrenean native with 1–3 in (2.5–8 cm) long, often downy leaves. Small flowers, usually under 1 in (25 mm) long, white or cream with yellow throat and small mauve patch on upper lip, often purple-veined. Zones 6–10.

APIUM

CELERIAC, CELERY

A member of the carrot (Apiaceae) family, this genus of 20 biennial plants with fleshy bulbous roots originates from Europe and temperate Asia. Pinnate leaves and white flowers in compound short-stalked or stalkless umbels. Fruits are small, ribbed, elliptical to oval seeds.
CULTIVATION: Frost tolerant, drought tender. Plant seedlings 10–12 in (25–30 cm) apart in light, moist, well-drained soil enriched with organic matter, in a protected sunny position. Propagate from seed.

Apium graveolens

CELERY, WILD CELERY

☼ ❄ ↔ 12–18 in (30–45 cm)
↑ 24–36 in (60–90 cm)

Strongly aromatic perennial from southern Europe. Whitish flowers, in compound umbels arranged in panicles, in summer–autumn. Fruits small, ribbed, elliptical to oval seeds. Leaf segments, to ½–2 in (12–50 mm) long, lance-shaped, and toothed or lobed, on thick, long, grooved stalks. A. g. var. dulce (celery), erect leaves with closely overlapping enlarged leaf stalks, popular garden vegetable; A. g. var. rapaceum (celeriac), grossly swollen taproot, shortened edible leaves; **'Brilliant'**, European, early maturing; A. g. var. secalinum (leaf celery), strong-flavored fragrant leaves on thin rounded stalks, used in soups and stews. A. g. **'Tricolor'** has glossy green leaves tinted bronze at first, edged with cream and a silver central stripe; Zones 5–10.

Apium graveolens

APTENIA

HEARTLEAF ICEPLANT, HEARTS AND FLOWERS

This South African genus in the iceplant (Aizoaceae) family contains just 2 species—both small, spreading, branching shrubs with fleshy succulent leaves covered in minute protuberances that give the leaves a texture as though they were dusted with fine sugar crystals. The bright light green leaves are rounded to heart-shaped, tapering to a broad point. Established plants may have a wide spread but are easily controlled. Small, purple-pink, daisy-like flowers, solitary or in 3s, appear at the stem tips in summer. The small, green, fleshy fruits redden as they mature.
CULTIVATION: Surprisingly hardy if kept dry in winter, these little succulents make a bold splash of color and thrive in any sunny well-drained position. Their spreading habit makes them ideal for rockeries, as small-scale ground covers, or in hanging baskets. Will withstand prolonged drought but will not flower until watered. Propagate from seed or cuttings; may self-layer.

Aptenia cordifolia ★

☼/◐ ❄ ↔ 16–40 in (40–100 cm)
↑ 2 in (5 cm)

Native to the Eastern Cape region of South Africa. Heart-shaped leaves to 1 in (25 mm) long and wide. Intense magenta flowers. **'Red Apple'**, an especially vigorous form, possibly a hybrid, can be invasive; **'Variegata'**, small cream-edged leaves. Zones 9–11.

AQUILEGIA

COLUMBINE, GRANNY'S BONNET

This buttercup (Ranunculaceae) family genus is made up of about 70 species found over much of the temperate and subarctic Northern Hemisphere. Fine-stemmed, often blue-green foliage reminiscent of maidenhair fern fronds emerges from a woody rootstock. Flowering stems usually reach above the foliage and carry spurred, bell-shaped, often pendulous flowers. Some are short-flowering, others bloom through much of late spring and summer. Various species were used medicinally by Native North Americans. The name aquilegia is derived from the Latin *aquila* (eagle) and *lego* (to gather), suggesting that the curved nectaries or spurs resemble the closing talons of an eagle.
CULTIVATION: An adaptable genus, with species suitable for woodland, rockeries, and perennial borders. The general preference is for a cool-winter climate and a place in half-sun with cool, moist, humus-rich, well-drained soil. Often attracts aphids. Some species can be divided when dormant but propagation is usually from seed. May self-sow, can be invasive.

Aptenia cordifolia 'Red Apple'

Aquilegia alpina

ALPINE COLUMBINE

◐ ❄ ↔ 6–18 in (15–45 cm)
↑ 8–30 in (20–75 cm)

Very variable European alpine species. Flowers are straight-spurred, pendulous, usually blue-tipped with white. Cultivars in shades from white through blue to purple. Suitable for rockeries. Zones 5–9.

Aquilegia atrata

BLACK COLUMBINE

◐ ❄ ↔ 12 in (30 cm) ↑ 18 in (45 cm)

Southern European alpine with sticky foliage. Small nodding flowers, maroon to almost black with golden stamens and hooked spurs. Zones 4–9.

Aquilegia caerulea

BLUE COLUMBINE, ROCKY MOUNTAIN COLUMBINE

☼/◐ ❄ ↔ 8–16 in (20–40 cm)
↑ 8–24 in (20–60 cm)

From high woodlands and mountains of western USA. Large, spreading flowers. White to cream petals, blue or pink sepals, long spurs. Zones 3–9.

Aquilegia dichroa

Aquilegia canadensis

CANADA COLUMBINE, MEETING HOUSES, ROCK BELLS, WILD COLUMBINE

◐ ❄ ↔ 12–20 in (30–50 cm)
↑ 12–30 in (30–75 cm)

Found over much of eastern North America. Soft yellow, red-spurred flowers on many-branched, wiry stems. Prefers rockery or woodland conditions. Flowers popular with hummingbirds. Zones 2–10.

Aquilegia chrysantha

GOLDEN COLUMBINE

◐ ❄ ↔ 12–32 in (30–80 cm)
↑ 32–36 in (80–90 cm)

Found in southern USA. Vigorous tall stems and large bright yellow flowers with long curved spurs, slightly paler in color. Several cultivars available, including double-flowered, white, and very tall. Zones 3–10.

Aquilegia dichroa

◐ ❄ ↔ 8–20 in (20–50 cm)
↑ 12–30 in (30–75 cm)

Native to Portugal and neighboring northwestern Spain. Paired trifoliate leaves with divided and toothed leaflets. The hook-spurred flowers, appearing in spring and summer, are soft purple-blue all over except for white petal tips. Zones 7–9.

Aquilegia flabellata

◐ ❄ ↔ 6–12 in (15–30 cm)
↑ 8–18 in (20–45 cm)

This species comes from Japan and nearby temperate Asia. It is a small compact plant with pronounced blue-green leaves and 1 or 2 flowers per stem. Petals white to cream; sepals and short, curved spurs, soft mauve-blue. Makes a superb rockery plant. Zones 3–9.

Aquilegia formosa

WESTERN COLUMBINE

◐ ❄ ↔ 12–20 in (30–50 cm)
↑ 20–36 in (50–90 cm)

From western USA, this species has a graceful open habit with many small, orange-red, short-spurred flowers on each of its stems. A number of cultivars are available, including dwarf, and widely hybridized. Zones 3–9.

Aquilegia longissima

◐ ❄ ↔ 8–10 in (20–25 cm)
↑ 30–36 in (75–90 cm)

A narrow upright plant from New Mexico and western Texas, USA. It displays upward-facing bright yellow flowers, with sepals lighter in color and sometimes red-tinted. Long narrow spurs are evident. Zones 8–10.

Aquilegia canadensis

Aquilegia, McKana Group

☼/◑ ✱ ↔ 12–20 in (30–50 cm)
↕ 32–48 in (80–120 cm)

Hybrids between several North American species covering a wide color range. Most of the hybrids in the group are tall upright plants with long-spurred flowers and contrasting colors of corolla and sepals. Zones 3–10.

Aquilegia olympica

◑ ✱ ↔ 8–12 in (20–30 cm)
↕ 12–24 in (30–60 cm)

From the Caucasus and western Asia. Nodding flower with white petals and blue to pink or pale purple sepals with curved spurs. Zones 5–9.

Aquilegia viridiflora

GREEN-FLOWERED COLUMBINE

☼/◑ ✱ ↔ 12 in (30 cm)
↕ 20 in (50 cm)

Perennial, often short-lived, native to northern temperate East Asia. In late spring–summer it bears slightly scented purple-brown and green flowers clustered in nodding heads. **'Chocolate Soldier'**, popular cultivar that differs little from the species. Zones 3–10.

Aquilegia vulgaris

☼/◑ ✱ ↔ 8–18 in (20–45 cm)
↕ 12–36 in (30–90 cm)

This much-cultivated species is found over most of Europe. It has ferny foliage and flowers with hooked spurs in white and shades of blue, mauve, and red, including double-flowered forms. The wild species is seldom seen in gardens but there are many cultivars. Single-flowered cultivars include: **'Heidi'**, 24 in (60 cm) tall, purple-red-stemmed, nodding, soft pink flowers; **'Hensol Harebell'**, 24 in (60 cm) tall with short-spurred, mauve-blue flowers; and **'Nivea'** (syn. 'Munstead White'), 36 in (90 cm) tall with foliage that is gray-green and flowers of pure white. Double-flowered cultivars can be divided into the following groups. **Flore Pleno Group** has elongated flowers with rounded petals, and includes: **'Graeme Iddon'**, a tall cultivar with white flowers which has spawned a range of double-flowered forms; **'Rougham Star'**, 24 in (60 cm) tall flowers, white inner petals, mauve-blue outer petals and sepals. **Stellata Group** has star-shaped double flowers with radiating pointed petals, and includes **'Black Barlow'**, 24 in (60 cm) tall with deep purple to near black flowers; **'Blue Barlow'**, 30 in (75 cm) tall with double blue flowers; **'Nora Barlow'** ★, 32 in (80 cm) tall with soft green, white, and pink pompon-like flowers; **'Rose Barlow'**, 32 in (80 cm) tall with mid-pink and cream flowers. **Vervaeneana Group**, marbled green and gold foliage and variable flower color. Zones 3–10.

Aquilegia Hybrid Cultivars

☼/◑ ✱ ↔ 12–24 in (30–60 cm)
↕ 18–36 in (45–90 cm)

Aquilegias have been so widely hybridized, particularly among the American species, that there are now hybrids in almost any conceivable size and flower color. A. **'Crimson Star'** has large, red-spurred cream flowers, 24 in (60 cm) tall. The Butterfly Series, includes **'Brimstone'**, cream and soft yellow, and **'Holly Blue'**, white to pale mauve petals, powder blue sepals. The **Songbird Series** has a compact foliage clump, 24 in (60 cm) flower stems with large flowers in many shades, including: **'Bluebird'**, very large flowers, white petals, soft blue sepals; **'Cardinal'**, white petals with pink markings, dark red sepals; **'Dove'**, pure white; **'Goldfinch'**, bright yellow; **'Redwing'**, white to cream petals, deep red sepals; and **'Robin'**, white to pale pink petals, dusky deep pink sepals. The State Series includes **'Alaska'**, pure white flowers; **'Colorado'**, semi-double, mauve and white petals with purple sepals; **'Florida'**, yellow petals, creamy white sepals; **'Kansas'**, bright yellow petals, vivid red sepals; and **'Louisiana'**, creamy white petals, deep red sepals. Zones 4–10.

ARACHNIODES

Genus of about 40 ferns from the shield-fern (Dryopteridaceae) family, closely related to *Polystichum* and *Dryopteris*, and native to East Asia, Malaysia, and New Zealand. These plants have a short- to long-creeping scaly rhizome and the fronds are deltoid or ovoid, often leathery, widened at the base, with bipinnate or more divided pinnules. The name comes from the Greek *arachnion,* meaning spider's web.

Aquilegia vulgaris, Flore Pleno Group, 'Graeme Iddon'

Aralia elata

CULTIVATION: Easily grown in semi-shaded situations in well-drained loamy soil with plenty of moisture. Propagate from spores or by division of rhizomes.

Arachniodes simplicior ★

syn. *Arachniodes aristata 'Variegata'*

EAST INDIAN HOLLY FERN, VARIEGATED SHIELD FERN

◑/● ✱ ↔ 18–48 in (45–120 cm)
↕ 12–32 in (30–80 cm)

This slow-growing fern with long-creeping rhizomes comes from subtropical to temperate Japan and China. Glossy, green, pinnate, evergreen fronds are triangular, with a prominent yellowish streak on each side of the midrib. Zones 6–9.

ARALIA

From the ivy (Araliaceae) family, this genus of trees, shrubs, and herbaceous perennials consists of around 40 species mostly from Southeast Asia and North, Central, and South America. Most are deciduous and nearly all have large compound leaves. Flowers are small, numerous, usually cream, carried in umbels arranged in panicles terminating the branches, followed by black fruits. Some species have prickly stems, and suckering can occur. Roots and bark of several species are used in traditional medicine, and young *A. cordata* shoots are an important vegetable (udo) in Japan, used like celery.

CULTIVATION: All species known in cultivation will tolerate at least light frosts, but most need a warm humid summer for best growth. Prefer deep reasonably fertile soil and shelter from strong winds. Though shade tolerant, they grow and flower better in sun. Propagate from seed, which for tree species may need cold stratification, or from root cuttings or basal suckers.

Aralia cordata

JAPANESE SPIKENARD, UDO

☼/◑ ❄ ↔ 8 ft (2.4 m) ↕ 8 ft (2.4 m)

Vigorous herbaceous perennial from Japan, Korea, and nearby parts of China. Huge compound leaves with rounded, finely toothed, 6 in (15 cm) long leaflets. Blanched young stems used as a vegetable in Japan. Large panicles of cream flowers in summer; black fruit. Zones 6–10.

Aralia elata

JAPANESE ANGELICA TREE

◑ ✱ ↔ 30 ft (9 m) ↕ 40 ft (12 m)

Native to Japan, often tall shrub spread by root suckers, with prickly corky trunk. Bipinnate leaves, to 4 ft (1.2 m) long, yellow-purplish in autumn. Large panicles of near-white flowers in late summer. **'Aureomarginata'**, yellow leaf margins, turning to creamy white; **'Variegata'** ★ (syn. 'Albomarginata'), white leaf margins. Zones 4–9.

A

ARBUTUS

This small genus contains about 8 to 10 species of small evergreen trees belonging to the heath or erica (Ericaceae) family, which are known as strawberry trees due to their strawberry-like fruit. They occur in the Mediterranean region, western Asia, and southwestern USA, with a few species in Central America and Mexico. All have attractive bell-shaped flowers and red or yellow fruit of little economic value, and in some cases have red or cinnamon-colored, stringy, peeling bark. Height varies from about 10 to 20 ft (3–6 m).
CULTIVATION: *Arbutus* like a well-drained soil, preferably free of lime, and an open sunny position protected from cold winds. Most species are tolerant of sustained cold winters. Little pruning is required. Propagation is by half-hardened cuttings taken in autumn or winter; scions can also be top-grafted on seedling understocks. Seeds can be sown in spring.

Arbutus menziesii ★

MADRONA, MADRONE, PACIFIC MADRONE

☼ ❄ ↔30 ft (9 m) ↑30 ft (9 m)

From Pacific coast of northern USA. Spreading, shrubby in form. Bright brick red bark peels to reveal a green new layer. White flowers, held in drooping clusters. Fruit orange-red. Not recommended for wet-summer climates. Zones 7–10.

Arbutus unedo

IRISH STRAWBERRY TREE, STRAWBERRY TREE

☼ ❄ ↔20 ft (6 m) ↑25 ft (8 m)

Occurring in the Mediterranean region and Ireland, this tree has red stringy bark, often arranged in a spiral fashion. Flowers are white, flushed with pink, in autumn–winter. Fruits, ripening green to orange-red to bright red, are edible though quite bland to the taste. This tree is tolerant of pollution. A. u. f. rubra grows to 4–6 ft (1.2–1.5 m) tall. A. u. '**Compacta**' is a smaller form, '**Elfin King**' is a small bushy form, and '**Oktoberfest**' is a pink-flowered form. Zones 7–10.

ARCTOSTAPHYLOS

There are about 50 species in this genus of mostly evergreen small shrubs and trees in the heath or erica (Ericaceae) family. The genus is found only in North America, except for 2 species from the alpine-arctic regions of the Northern Hemisphere. They have reddish brown ornamental bark, smooth, or peeling in flakes. Leaves are alternate, smooth, or toothed. Flowers are in terminal racemes or panicles of tiny bells or urn-shaped, white or pink. Fruits spherical. Leaves of *A. uva-ursi* used in Russia as a tea; in the UK has been used as a urinary antiseptic since the thirteenth century.
CULTIVATION: They need lime-free soil. In pots water freely and feed in the growing season. Withhold water and fertilizer from western North American species in summer. Put seed in boiling water for 15–20 seconds before sowing in autumn with protection against frosts. Layer prostrate species in autumn. Plant half-hardened cuttings in summer. Mostly disease-free except for leaf spot.

Arctostaphylos alpina

syn. *Arctostaphylos alpinus*

ARCTIC BEARBERRY, BLACK BEARBERRY

☼/◐ ❄ ↔8 in (20 cm) ↑6 in (15 cm)

Native to Northern Hemisphere heaths. Deciduous creeping shrub, finely serrated, lance-shaped leaves, bright red in autumn. Axillary racemes of flowers, white, flushed pink, in late spring, red-purple berries. Zones 1–8.

Arbutus menziesii

Arctostaphylos bakeri

syn. *Arctostaphylos stanfordiana subsp. bakeri*

BAKER'S MANZANITA

☼/◐ ❄ ↔3–6 ft (0.9–1.8 m) ↑2–8 ft (0.6–2.4 m)

Rare species from chaparral of Sonoma County, California, USA. Erect to spreading shrub with smooth red bark, small dark green leaves, and small pink flowers in late winter–early spring. '**Louis Edmunds**' is a selected clone of upright form with wine red trunks and dense gray-green foliage. Zones 8–10.

Arctostaphylos columbiana

HAIRY MANZANITA

☼ ❄ ↔6–12 ft (1.8–3.5 m) ↑6–20 ft (1.8–6 m)

Shrub or small tree from northern California, USA, to British Columbia, Canada. Peeling purplish brown bark, white-bristled twigs, ovate leaves to 2 in (5 cm) long. White to pinkish flowers in nodding clusters, in late spring–early summer. Zones 7–9.

Arctostaphylos densiflora

☼/◐ ❄ ↔6 ft (1.8 m) ↑5 ft (1.5 m)

Native to Sonoma County, California, USA. Procumbent shrub with dark red to nearly black, smooth bark. Flowers small short panicles, white with a tinge of pink. Leaves glossy, mid-green, and elliptical. '**Emerald Carpet**', a dense ground cover up to 12 in (30 cm) high; '**Howard McMinn**', denser than the species. Zones 8–10.

Arctostaphylos edmundsii

Arctostaphylos manzanita

Arctostaphylos edmundsii

LITTLE SUR MANZANITA

☼ ❄ ↔4–10 ft (1.2–3 m) ↑6–36 in (15–90 cm)

A rare species from near Monterey on the coast of California, USA. Its mat-like form has made it a popular landscape plant. Some forms mound up with age, others quite prostrate, rooting along branches. Leaves small, rounded, glossy, dark green. Dull pinkish flowers in spring. Brownish fruit in summer. Zones 8–10.

Arctostaphylos glauca

BIGBERRY MANZANITA

☼ ❄ ↔20 ft (6 m) ↑20 ft (6 m)

A large shrub, or small tree, that is native to California, USA. Has red-brown bark, and dull grayish green leaves up to 1½ in (35 mm) long, elliptic to ovate in shape. Flowers are white or pink, followed by a sticky brown fruit. Zones 8–10.

Arctostaphylos hookeri

MONTEREY MANZANITA

☼ ❄ ↔4–15 ft (1.2–4.5 m) ↑6–48 in (15–120 cm)

This is a coastal species that is found from San Francisco Bay to near Monterey, California, USA, often on dunes. Forms extensive dense mat, mounding with age. Leaves small, shiny green. Flowers white to pink, in winter–spring. Fruit shiny red, in summer. A. h. subsp. franciscana (Franciscan manzanita), mat-forming, from San Francisco Peninsula, is extinct in the wild but preserved in cultivation; A. h. subsp. hearstiorum (Hearsts' manzanita), quite prostrate, rooting along stems, leaves under ½ in (12 mm) long; A. h. subsp. montana (Tamalpais manzanita), more erect or mounding form, to 6 ft (1.8 m) high. A. h. '**Monterey Carpet**' is a compact cultivar. Zones 8–10.

Arctostaphylos manzanita

MANZANITA

☼ ❄ ↔10 ft (3 m) ↑15 ft (4.5 m)

From California and Oregon, USA, this species forms dense thickets. Its bark is red to brown, tending to peel. Its leaves are leathery, hairy, oval, and green to gray-green in color. Deep pink flowers are seen in early spring. White fruit, ripening to red-brown, is produced in autumn. An attractive addition to a mixed border. **'Doctor Hurd'**, upright cultivar that reaches 15 ft (4.5 m) in height. Zones 8–10.

Arctostaphylos × media

↔ 8 ft (2.4 m) ↑ 12 in (30 cm)

Natural hybrid between *A. columbiana* and *A. uva-ursi*. Usually prostrate but may send up erect shoots. Leaves to 1 in (25 mm) long. Flowers white or pinkish, in spring. Zones 7–9.

Arctostaphylos uva-ursi

BEARBERRY, KINNIKINICK

↔ 20 in (50 cm) ↑ 4 in (10 cm)

A native of the cool-temperate regions of the Northern Hemisphere, this species has white flowers flushed pink, followed by red fruit. The leaves form part of a traditional smoking mixture in North America and are often used for herbal tea in Europe. **'Massachusetts'** is a vigorous mat-former, building to 12 in (30 cm) high and spreading to as much as 15 ft (4.5 m) across; **'Vancouver Jade'** has glossy leaves, a vigorous habit, and good ability to resist diseases; and **'Wood's Red'** is a dwarf cultivar with pink flowers, large shiny red fruit, and red young shoots. Zones 4–9.

Arctostaphylos Hybrid Cultivars

↔ 5–15 ft (1.5–4.5 m) ↑ 6 in–10 ft (15 cm–3 m)

Nearly all these hybrids originated in the wild or as accidental crosses in gardens. They range from low mat-forming plants to tall shrubs. **'Indian Hill'**, possibly a form of *A. edmundsii*, makes an extensive mat of glossy bright green foliage, new shoots an attractive bronze color, white flowers in winter; **'John Dourley'** ★, of uncertain classification, mound-forming shrub, foliage dense, bluish green, with bronze new growths, pale pink flowers; 'Pacific Mist', mat-forming to mound-forming shrub with pink young branches, narrow gray-green leaves, white flowers; 'Sunset', densely mounding shrub, dark red branches, deep gray-green foliage, bright new growths, pink flowers. Zones 8–10.

ARCTOTIS

AFRICAN DAISY

Found from the southern tip of Africa northward to Angola and sometimes confused with *Gazania*, this daisy (Asteraceae) family genus consists of around 50 species of low spreading annuals and perennials that often produce masses of large and brightly colored flowerheads. The leaves are simple, usually lance-shaped and frequently have felted undersides. For much of the year in mild climates the foliage is topped by 1–4 in (2.5–10 cm) wide flowers in a range of colors. Modern strains cover most of the spectrum except blue. The name *Arctotis* comes from the Greek and means "bear's ear," a rather obscure reference to the resemblance of the flower scales to a bear's ear.

CULTIVATION: They thrive in light well-drained soil and full sun. They are drought tolerant but will flower more heavily if watered well in the growing season. Propagate from seed, though perennial species grow readily from cuttings of non-flowering stems.

Arctotis acaulis

↔ 12–40 in (30–100 cm) ↑ 6–12 in (15–30 cm)

Clumping rosette-forming perennial. Wavy, lobed, or toothed leaves to 8 in (20 cm) long, green above, white hair below. Flowerheads to 4 in (10 cm) wide, ray florets mainly in yellow, orange, or red shades, disc florets deep purple. **'Magenta'**, long-stemmed purple-red flowers. Zones 8–10.

Arctotis × hybrida

↔ 8–20 in (20–50 cm) ↑ 8–16 in (20–40 cm)

This species has mainly *A. venusta × A. fastuosa* parentage. They are compact plants, usually with silvery foliage and are often treated as annuals in cool climates. It has many popular named cultivars and seedling strains, including: **'Flame'** ★, with bright orange flowers; **'Mahogany'**, deep red-brown flowers; and **'Red Devil'**, bright red. Zones 9–11.

Arctotis stoechadifolia

AFRICAN DAISY, BLUE-EYED AFRICA DAISY

↔ 18 in (45 cm) ↑ 18–24 in (45–60 cm)

An annual from South Africa. Gray-green oblong leaves. Daisy-like disk flowers, in various bright colors; blooms from summer through to autumn if deadheaded. Can be used in dry sandy soil, withstands drought. Zones 9–10.

ARDISIA

Over 250 species of evergreen shrubs and small trees make up this primrose (Primulaceae) family genus, occurring in the tropics and subtropics of all continents except Africa. They occur mainly in high-rainfall mountain areas. Leaves are simple with margins sometimes toothed or crinkled, crowded at the ends of branchlets. A common feature is translucent brownish spots or streaks in the leaves, more easily seen in species with thinner leaves. The small flowers are mostly star-shaped, borne in stalked umbels among the outer leaves; the 5 petals are often patterned with tiny spots. Fruits are small one-seeded berries.

Arctotis × hybrida 'Flame'

CULTIVATION: Most are shade-loving plants and prefer humid conditions protected from the wind. Soil should be well-drained, humus-rich, and moisture-retentive. Indoor plants should be kept away from hot sunny positions. They can be cut back near the base, resulting in renewal by vigorous shoots. Propagation is usually from seed; cuttings can also be used.

Ardisia crenata

CORAL ARDISIA, CORALBERRY

↔ 18 in (45 cm) ↑ 6 ft (1.8 m)

This species occurs wild in southern Japan, China, and the eastern Himalayas. Side branches in tiers form a bushy head of dark green foliage. White starry flowers in umbels, in spring–summer. Coral red fruits persist into winter. Zones 8–11.

Ardisia japonica

↔ unlimited ↑ 12 in (30 cm)

Native to Japan and China, this groundcover has leaves in whorls of 3 in (8 cm), glossy, dark-green with saw-toothed margins. White to pale pink flowers in summer. Fruits pink to red. **'Nishiki'**, a variegated cultivar with irregular cream margins, translucent pink on new leaves. Zones 7–10.

ARENARIA

SANDWORT

This genus of about 160 low-growing, largely perennial, woody herbs and some annuals from the pink (Caryophyllaceae) family grows naturally across the temperate Northern Hemisphere. They are ideal as rock-garden plants and compact ground covers. The branching stems bear masses of dense, often hairy, linear to circular foliage that grows in opposite pairs. Abundant, small, star-like flowers, normally white and 5-petalled, grow in cymes or solitary on slender stalks. Their shallow root system can make them drought sensitive. Fruit is a cylindrical or ovoid capsule with 6 lobes. The genus derives its name from the Latin for sand, *arena*, referring to a preference for sandy soils.

Arenaria montana

CULTIVATION: Most of the species in this family need partial shade and protection from hot afternoon sun, especially in hot climates. They will tolerate poor soils, but the soil should be moist, sandy, and well drained. Shallow roots will require mulching or frequent watering around, but not over, the plant. Propagate by division, from seed in autumn or spring, or from softwood cuttings in early summer.

Arenaria montana

↔ 9–24 in (23–60 cm) ↑ 4–6 in (10–15 cm)

This vigorous perennial comes from southwestern Europe. It has loose mats of narrow, gray-green, hairy leaves to 1½ in (35 mm) long. White flowers, 15–18 mm across, are solitary or in few-flowered cymes in spring–early summer. **'Avalanche'** is more profuse, with larger white flowers. Zones 4–8.

Argyranthemum, HC, Butterfly/'Ulyssis'

Arisaema sikokianum

ARGYRANTHEMUM

From the Canary Islands and Madeira and often treated as perennials, the 24 members of this genus, of the daisy (Asteraceae) family, are evergreen shrubs. Popular in gardens and as cut flowers, there are numerous cultivars, most with "double" or "semi-double" flowerheads, over a long season. All are shrubs that branch low, with brittle stems and crowded leaves from coarsely toothed to deeply dissected. Leaves have a slightly aromatic, bitter smell when bruised. Long-stalked flowerheads borne in groups of 2 to 5. CULTIVATION: Marginally frost hardy, in cold climates these shrubs need to be brought under shelter in winter. Prefer a temperate climate with a distinct cool winter. Cutting-grown plants can be raised to flowering size in 6 months, so can be treated as annuals. Soil should be very well drained and not too rich, sunny position needed. Pinch out young plants to shape. Propagate from tip cuttings at any time, preferably in autumn for spring and summer display.

Argyranthemum frutescens

syn. *Chrysanthemum frutescens*

MARGUERITE, MARGUERITE DAISY

↔3 ft (0.9 m) ↑3 ft (0.9 m)

The original wild form of this Canary Islands native is a low spreading shrub with leaves dissected into a few narrow segments. Single white flowerheads, golden yellow centers, for much of year. Most recent cultivars have generally been included in this species, but are in fact of hybrid origin, with other species in parentage. Zones 9–10.

Argyranthemum Hybrid Cultivars

↔18–36 in (45–90 cm)
↑12–30 in (30–75 cm)

Though many references have included all *Argyranthemum* cultivars under the species *A. frutescens*, it seems clear that most present-day cultivars are of hybrid origin. Apart from *A. frutescens*, likely parent species include *A. foeniculaceum* and *A. maderense*. Single cultivars include: **Butterfly/'Ulyssis'**, a compact cultivar with rich yellow single flowers; **'California Gold'** ★, having a dwarf habit with large golden yellow blooms, with leaf segments few and broad; **'Cornish Gold'**, yellow flowers, darker centers; **'Donnington Hero'**, low and spreading with coarsely lobed leaves and neat white flowers; **'Gill's Pink'**, with pale pink rays, deeper at the base, and broad leaf lobes; **'Jamaica Primrose'**, a tall cultivar with pale to mid-yellow blooms; and **'Petite Pink'**, pink flowers. Doubles include: **'Blizzard'**, with rather tangled white rays and some disc florets showing. The anemone-form or semi-double group includes: **'Mary Wootton'**, an older cultivar with a pale pink center; **'Tauranga Star'**, having white rays, slightly quilled, with a white "button" grading with a pale gold center; and **'Vancouver'**, similar to **'Mary Wootton'** but with a bright pink domed central "button" and paler rays like the spokes of a wheel. Zones 9–10.

ARISAEMA

This is a genus of about 150 tuberous perennials in the arum (Araceae) family. The plants are found in Africa, North America, and Asia, usually in shade or woodland. Their ornamental leaves and stems and bizarre flowers make them interesting in gardens. The leaves may be compound or divided, and the stems are often mottled in pink to purplish shades. Large hooded flower spathes may be yellow, green, brown, red, or pink; they can also be striped or mottled. They surround the spadix, a central column of small true flowers that can be short and club-like or long and drooping. Orange-red berries form on the spadix. CULTIVATION: Grow frost-tolerant species in shelter, part-shade, or woodland in cool peaty soil. Give protective mulch in winter, guard from slugs. Greenhouse-grown tropical species need a deep pot in a mix of leaf mold, grit, and slightly acid loam. Propagate from seed or by division of tubers.

Arisaema amurense

↔12 in (30 cm) ↑12 in (30 cm)

From northern Asia. One or two leaves with 5 radiating leaflets on dull purple stems. Upright spathe striped purple and green over white. Spring-flowering. **A. a. subsp. robustum** (syn. *A. robustum*), very similar but sturdier and stronger growing. Zones 5–9.

Arisaema candidissimum ★

↔18 in (45 cm) ↑12 (30 cm)

From western China. Single large trifoliate leaf with mottled pinkish brown stem, emerging with or after flower in early summer. Pale pink-striped spathe with long tip. Flowers slightly scented. Zones 6–10.

Arisaema consanguineum

↔12 in (30 cm) ↑36 in (90 cm)

From Himalayas and central China. Single leaf of 11 to 20 radiating leaflets to 16 in (40 cm) long. Spathe has long slightly drooping point, green and purple with narrow stripes. Flowers appear in early summer. Zones 7–10.

Arisaema kishidae

↔12 in (30 cm) ↑12 in (30 cm)

Native to Japan. Stocky species with 2 leaves of several flaring leaflets, sometimes marked silver. Spathe brownish mauve, striped and hooded. Spring-flowering. Zones 5–9.

Arisaema ringens

syn. *Arisaema praecox*

↔12 in (30 cm) ↑12 in (30 cm)

From Japan, China, and Korea. Has two leaves each with 3 broad leaflets. Spathe is small, green and purple with white stripes, and remains in a curled position enclosing the spadix. Flowers are seen in early spring. Zones 7–10.

Arisaema serratum

syn. *Arisaema japonicum*

↔24 in (60 cm) ↑36 in (90 cm)

From northeastern Asia. Two leaves with several leaflets on mottled purple stems. Slender hooded spathe, green or purple, sometimes striped white. Spring-flowering. Zones 5–9.

Arisaema sikokianum

↔18 in (45 cm) ↑18 in (45 cm)

From Japan. Two leaves with 3 to 5 leaflets with toothed margins. Upright spathe has a purple exterior, paler and striped inside. Spadix prominent, white, club-shaped. Flowers in early summer. Zones 5–9.

Arisaema speciosum

COBRA LILY

↔18 in (45 cm)
↑24–36 in (60–90 cm)

Native to Nepal and southwestern China. A single leaf with large leaflets flushed red at the margins. Mottled purple stems. Large hooded spathe, dark purple with white stripes. Spadix has a long thread-like appendage. Flowers appear in early summer. Zones 8–10.

Arisaema taiwanense

↔18 in (45 cm) ↑36 in (90 cm)

From Taiwan. A single leaf with several umbrella-like leaflets and mottled stems. Purplish brown mottled spathe, hooded, with a long thread-like appendage. White spadix, club-shaped. Zones 6–9.

Arisaema tortuosum

☀ ❄ ↔ 18 in (45 cm) ↑ 36 in (90 cm)

Native to the Himalayan region. Two or three leaves with several leaflets. Spathe is green. Spadix with long thread-like twisted appendage. Flowers appear in early summer. Zones 7–10.

Arisaema triphyllum

INDIAN TURNIP, JACK-IN-THE-PULPIT

☀ ❄ ↔ 18 in (45 cm)
↑ 12–24 in (30–60 cm)

From eastern North America. Has two leaves with 3 pointed leaflets. Spathe hooded, green to purple, striped green or white. Summer-flowering. Zones 4–9.

ARISARUM

This genus of 3 species of tuberous perennials is a member of the arum (Araceae) family and is native to the Mediterranean and Atlantic islands. The arrowhead-shaped leaves are borne on a long stalk. The green or purplish flower spathe is usually level with or just below the foliage and is hooded, enclosing the spadix (central column of true flowers).

CULTIVATION: Grow *Arisarum* species in a humus-rich moist soil in shade or half-sun. In areas with very heavy frosts, provide a protective mulch in winter. Propagation is by division of tubers when dormant or from seed in spring.

Arisarum proboscideum

MOUSE PLANT

☀ ❄ ↔ 10 in (20 cm) ↑ 8 in (20 cm)

From Italy and Spain. Its glossy arrow-shaped leaves almost conceal the hooded chocolate-brown spathes, which have a curling tail-like appendage, hence the common name. Flowers over a long period in spring. Zones 7–10.

ARISTEA

This iris (Iridaceae) family genus is made up of about 50 mainly evergreen species of fleshy-stemmed perennials found in Africa from the tropics to South Africa and Madagascar. They have upright sword-shaped leaves, in some species over 24 in (60 cm) long, in fans resembling those of the irises. The 6-petalled flowers, borne on branching stems with somewhat flattened segments, occur in shades of blue, lavender, and purple, and are short-lived, each bloom lasting only a day or so. The flowering season ranges from late winter to summer, depending on the species.

Arisarum proboscideum

CULTIVATION: Tolerant of only light frosts, most *Aristea* species prefer to grow in a position in sun or half-sun with a light but humus-rich, moist, well-drained soil. Although plants can be divided, they resent disturbance, so they are usually propagated from seed, which may be sown in autumn in frost-free areas, otherwise in spring.

Aristea capitata

syn. *Aristea major*

☼/◑ ❄ ↔ 24–36 in (60–90 cm)
↑ 3–5 ft (0.9–1.5 m)

Native to southwestern Cape region of South Africa. Blue-green leaves, 3–4 ft (0.9–1.2 m) long. Rootstock can form a short trunk. Densely packed clusters of soft blue flowers to 1½ in (35 mm) wide, in summer. Zones 9–10.

Aristea ecklonii

☼/◑ ❄ ↔ 18–32 in (45–80 cm)
↑ 18–32 in (45–80 cm)

A South African species. Arching leaves to 24 in (60 cm) long. Loose open panicles of 1 in (25 mm) wide bright blue to magenta flowers in late spring–summer. Zones 8–11.

ARISTOLOCHIA

BIRTHWORT, DUTCHMAN'S PIPE

This genus contains about 300 species ranging from vigorous climbers to perennials, both deciduous and evergreen, found throughout tropical and temperate regions. It is a member of the birthwort (Aristolochiaceae) family. Stems are usually thick and fissured, and leaves vary from entire to

Aristolochia macrophylla

lobed, often being heart-shaped. The flowers, which trap pollinating insects, have bladder-like bases and weird, contorted, tubular shapes. They range from under 3 in (8 cm) to giants of 20 in (50 cm) and many have an offensive smell. Flowers are mottled in shades of brown, pink, purple, and ivory. The common name, birthwort, comes from the herbal use of some species as an aid to childbirth.

CULTIVATION: Many of the vigorous climbers are hardy only to 23°F (–5°C) and better suit the greenhouse in cooler areas. Where suitable, grow outdoors in sun or half-sun in a rich well-drained soil. Climbers require support and can be pruned in late winter. Propagate from softwood cuttings or seed or by division.

Aristolochia fimbriata

☼/◑ ❄ ↔ 10 ft (3 m) ↑ 7–10 ft (2–3 m)

From Brazil, a climber with round to heart-shaped leaves with prominent, pale, netted veining. Small, curving, tubular flowers, fringed edges, greenish brown outside and purplish brown with yellow markings inside. Zones 10–11.

Aristolochia gigantea

☼/◑ ❄ ↔ 15 ft (4.5 m) ↑ 30 ft (9 m)

From Panama and Brazil. Vigorous climber with triangular leaves, downy below. Very large flowers with bladder-like base and flaring lips of mottled chocolate-purple and ivory can be up to 20 in × 14 in (50 cm × 35 cm). Summer-flowering. Zones 10–11.

Aristea capitata

Aristolochia grandiflora

PELICAN FLOWER

☼/◑ ❄ ↔ 6 ft (1.8 m) ↑ 10 ft (3 m)

Native to Central America and West Indies. Deep green heart-shaped leaves. Very large contorted flowers with bladder-like base and lip with long narrow appendage. Mottled in purple, green, and cream. Summer-flowering. Zones 10–11.

Aristolochia littoralis

syn. *Aristolochia elegans*

CALICO FLOWER

☼/◑ ❄ ↔ 15 ft (4.5 m) ↑ 20 ft (6 m)

Native to Brazil. Naturalized in Central America and southern USA. Can be weedy in warm climates. Vigorous climber with heart-shaped leaves, grayish green beneath. Flowers have bladder-like bases with almost round lips. Mottled in chocolate purple and ivory. Summer-flowering. Zones 9–11.

Aristolochia macrophylla

syns *Aristolochia durior, A. sipho*

DUTCHMAN'S PIPE

☼/◑ ❄ ↔ 20 ft (6 m) ↑ 30 ft (9 m)

From eastern USA. Vigorous climber with very large heart-shaped leaves. Small, tubular, green flowers are mottled with pink, brown, and ivory. Flowers arise from the leaf axils in summer and are hidden by the foliage. Zones 6–9.

Armeria maritima 'Bloodstone'

Aronia arbutifolia

Arrhenatherum elatius

ARMERIA

SEA PINK, THRIFT

Armeria was the Roman name for *Dianthus* and was given to this genus because of a supposed resemblance, also reflected in the common name, "sea pink." However, *Armeria* comes from a different family, the leadworts (Plumbaginaceae), not the carnations. The genus comprises around 80 species of herbaceous and shrubby perennials from Eurasia, North Africa, and the American Pacific coast. They form clumps of simple linear leaves, above which rounded heads of tiny flowers with colorful bracts are held in spring and summer. The name "thrift" is applied in the sense of the meaning "to thrive," as the plant grows in harsh conditions.
CULTIVATION: They occur in a wide range of environments and are easily cultivated, being especially at home in rockeries. Most are hardy and prefer moist well-drained soil and a position in full or half-sun. Propagate from seed or cuttings, or by the careful division of well-established clumps.

Armeria maritima

☼/◑ ✱ ↔ 8–16 in (20–40 cm)
↑ 8–12 in (20–30 cm)

This mounding perennial or subshrub is found across the northern temperate zone. It has grassy deep green leaves to 4 in (10 cm) long. Flower stems grow to 12 in (30 cm) tall with 1 in (25 mm) wide heads of white, pink, or red flowers. A. m. subsp. californica, from California, USA, mounds to 6 in (15 cm) high and has lavender-pink flowerheads on short stems. A. m. **'Bee's Ruby'** has vivid magenta flowers; **'Bloodstone'** ★ has 8 in (20 cm) stems with deep magenta to red flowers; **'Corsica'** has a dense clumping habit and small heads of brick red flowers; **'Isobel Burdett'** has deep pink flowerheads on 8 in (20 cm) stems; **'Rubrifolia'** has very dark black-red leaves and deep magenta flowers; **'Vindictive'**, has deep pink flowers on 6 in (15 cm) stems. Zones 4–10.

Armeria pseudarmeria

☼ ❄ ↔ 16–40 in (40–100 cm)
↑ 8–16 in (20–40 cm)

This dwarf subshrub or woody-based perennial is a native of coastal Portugal. Has fine grassy leaves around 1 in (25 mm) long. Flower stems are tall compared to the plant, with white to deep pink flowerheads to 2 in (5 cm) wide. **'Rubra'** is a red-flowered cultivar; and **'Westacre Beauty'** has soft pink flowers. Zones 8–10.

ARONIA

CHOKEBERRY

This genus of deciduous shrubs from woodlands of eastern USA contains 2 species and a naturally occurring hybrid. Of the rose (Rosaceae) family, it is closely allied to *Photinia*—in fact current opinion suggests it should be in that genus, though this has not gained wide acceptance. The shrubs are of compact size bearing white or pale pink spring blossoms that are followed by small berry-like fruits of red, purple, or black which give rise to the common name of chokeberry. The foliage colors attractively in autumn in shades of red and crimson.
CULTIVATION: These shrubs are well suited to informal plantings and woodland edges. They need deep, moist, well-drained soil and will grow in semi-shade or sun. Sunnier sites encourage better fruiting and autumn coloring. The shiny black cherry and pear slug can cause unsightly damage to the foliage but can be controlled with a carbaryl or pyrethrin preparation. Propagate from half-hardened cuttings, layering, removal of suckers, or seed sown in autumn.

Aronia arbutifolia

syn. *Photinia pyrifolia*

AMELANCHIER, RED CHOKEBERRY

◑ ✱ ↔ 5 ft (1.5 m) ↑ 6 ft (1.8 m)

Shrub with downy young branches and clusters of small white to pale pink flowers in spring. Berries bright red, persisting into winter. **'Brilliantissima'** is an aptly named cultivar, with vivid red autumn leaves. Zones 4–9.

Aronia melanocarpa

syn. *Photinia melanocarpa*

BLACK CHOKEBERRY

◑ ✱ ↔ 7 ft (2 m) ↑ 3 ft (0.9 m)

A small shrub, producing suckering growth from its base. Flowers and foliage are similar to *A. arbutifolia* but the leaves are not downy. Berries ripen to shiny black. It is more tolerant of dry soils. **'Autumn Magic'** ★ has crimson-purple autumn foliage. Zones 4–9.

ARRHENATHERUM

OAT GRASS

This genus, a member of the grass (Poaceae) family, consists of 6 perennials native to Europe, northern Africa, and northern and western Asia. The panicles are narrow, with flat 2-flowered spikelets. The stalk bases are sometimes swollen into bulbous or pear-shaped structures. The leaves are flat and strap-like, with usually hairless sheaths.
CULTIVATION: These species grow well in both partial shade and full sun. Soil should be dry to moist. Propagate from seed.

Arrhenatherum elatius

BULBOUS OAT GRASS, FALSE OAT, FRENCH RYE, OAT GRASS, ONION COUCH, STRIPED TUBER OAT GRASS, TUBER OAT GRASS

☼/◑ ✱ ↔ 6–8 in (15–20 cm)
↑ 18–60 in (45–150 cm)

Tussock-forming grass from Europe. The raceme is lance-shaped to oblong, lustrous, tinged with purple, containing spikelets of whitish flowers, in summer. Its finely hairy pale green leaves, up to 16 in (40 cm) long × ½ in (12 mm) wide, turn light tan to brown in winter. A. e. subsp. bulbosum has chains of bulb-like swellings at the bases of its stems; **'Variegatum'** is a loosely tuft-forming, herbaceous, perennial grass with a swollen basal stem and hairless gray-green leaves with ivory white margins. Zones 4–9.

ARTEMISIA

This genus of about 300 species of evergreen herbs and shrubs is spread throughout northern temperate regions with some also found in southern Africa and South America. It is a member of the daisy (Asteraceae) family but they bear small dull white or yellow flowerheads without ray florets. The beauty of these plants lies in their attractive foliage, which is well dissected and of palest gray to silver. The plants are frequently aromatic. Tarragon, the popular culinary herb, is a member of this genus.
CULTIVATION: These shrubs are ideal for hot dry areas as most can withstand considerable drought. They should be grown in full sun in well-drained soil. Their silvery leaves provide an attractive foliage contrast in borders, and when clipped some species can be used as a low hedge. Prune quite hard in spring and lightly clip at flowering time if the flowers are not wanted. Propagation is usually from softwood or half-hardened cuttings in summer.

Artemisia absinthium

ABSINTHE, COMMON WORMWOOD, OLD MAN

☼ ✱ ↔ 36 in (90 cm) ↑ 36 in (90 cm)

From temperate areas of Europe, Asia, and North America. Shrubby species with finely divided, silky, gray leaves. Aromatic. Insignificant tiny flowers in summer. **'Lambrook Mist'**, very finely divided silky leaves; **'Lambrook Silver'** ★, a more compact shrub. Zones 4–10.

Artemisia arborescens

SHRUB WORMWOOD

☼ ❄ ↔ 5 ft (1.5 m) ↑ 5 ft (1.5 m)

Attractive Mediterranean species that grows into a rounded shrub of 5 ft (1.5 m). Finely divided silver foliage, aromatic. More frost tender than most species but its cultivar **'Faith Raven'** is much hardier. Zones 8–11.

A

Artemisia californica

CALIFORNIA SAGEBRUSH

☼ ❄ ↔5 ft (1.5 m) ↑5 ft (1.5 m)

Native to California, USA. Found in poor and sandy coastal soils. Grows into a densely branched shrub with fine, gray, thread-like leaves. Pleasant aroma. Young branches are white. Zones 8–11.

Artemisia dracunculus

syns *Artemisia dracunculina, A. dracunculoides, A. glauca*

DRAGON SAGEWORT, TARRAGON

☼ ✱ ↔3 ft (0.9 m)
↑2–5 ft (0.6–1.5 m)

Wild forms of tarragon range from European Russia through Central Asia and across the Pacific to western North America, extending down the Rockies as far as northern Mexico. Erect herbaceous perennial spreading by rhizomes. Leaves narrow, pointed, dull green to somewhat bluish. Flowers in tiny brownish heads in summer. A. d. var. inodora, Russian tarragon, representative of wild forms, is a more vigorous grower but has little flavor. It has been misnamed *A. dracunculoides*. A. d. **'Sativa'**, French tarragon, is a clone selected for its intense aromatic flavor, renowned for uses as a culinary herb; must be propagated by cuttings or division. Zones 5–9.

Artemisia lactiflora

WHITE MUGWORT

☼ ✱ ↔24 in (60 cm) ↑5 ft (1.5 m)

From China. A perennial species forming clumps of green divided leaves. Tall showy plumes of tiny cream flowers in mid-summer. Requires more moisture than most species. Mahogany stems and purplish green foliage are a feature of the **Guizhou Group**. Zones 4–10.

Artemisia ludoviciana

syns *Artemisia gnaphalodes, A. purshiana*

CUDWEED, SILVER WORMWOOD, WESTERN MUGWORT, WHITE SAGE

☼ ✱ ↔36 in (90 cm) ↑36 in (90 cm)

Native to USA. Perennial herb with white downy stems and narrow, silvery gray, aromatic foliage. Sprays of tiny grayish white flowers in summer. A. l. subsp. mexicana var. albula has lance-shaped leaves, white and hairy. A. l. **'Silver Queen'**, to 18 in (75 cm) with finely cut silvery leaves; **'Valerie Finnis'**, to 24 in (60 cm), broader leaves, silvery white. Zones 5–10.

Artemisia 'Powis Castle' ★

☼ ❄ ↔4 ft (1.2 m) ↑2 ft (0.6 m)

Similar to *A. arborescens* but its habit is more sprawling, with woody stems usually lying on the ground. This attractive plant is possibly a hybrid between *A. arborescens* and the herbaceous *A. pontica*. Zones 7–10.

Artemisia schmidtiana

☼ ✱ ↔18 in (45 cm)
↑12–24 in (30–60 cm)

Native to Japan. Fleshy-stemmed perennial that forms clumps of finely cut, silky foliage. Aromatic. **'Nana'** (syn. 'Silver Mound') is a dwarf form to 4 in (10 cm) high and 12 in (30 cm) wide, with silvery foliage. Zones 4–9.

Artemisia stelleriana

BEACH WORMWOOD, DUSTY MILLER, OLD WOMAN

☼ ✱ ↔18 in (45 cm)
↑18–24 in (45–60 cm)

Evergreen fleshy-stemmed perennial from northeastern Asia and eastern USA. Heavily felted gray-white leaves, deeply lobed. Sprays of tiny yellow flowers in summer. **'Boughton Silver'** and **'Mori'** are white-leafed prostrate forms. Zones 3–9.

ARTHROPODIUM

A small genus in the asparagus (Asparagaceae) family of about 12 species of evergreen or deciduous fleshy-stemmed perennials found mostly in Australia and New Zealand. Plants form clumps of linear leaves ranging from small and grass-like to long and strap-shaped. The flowers, ranging from white to pale mauve and violet, have 6 flaring petals with fuzzy yellow and purple stamens. They are borne in panicles.

CULTIVATION: In warm areas grow in well-drained soil in sun or half-sun. Where frosts are worse, choose a warm sheltered site or grow in a greenhouse. Protect from slugs and snails. Propagate from seed or by division.

Arthropodium cirratum

Arthropodium candidum

☼/◐ ❄ ↔10 in (25 cm) ↑12 in (30 cm)

Native to New Zealand. Deciduous species with narrow grass-like leaves. Small, starry, white flowers, held above foliage, in late spring to summer. Zones 8–11.

Arthropodium cirratum

RENGARENGA, ROCK LILY

☼/◐ ❄ ↔24 in (60 cm)
↑20–30 in (50–75 cm)

Variable evergreen species, native to New Zealand. Fleshy strap-shaped leaves, to 24 in (60 cm) long, may have bluish green overtones. Flowering stems bear airy panicles of starry white flowers, in early to mid-summer. **'Matapouri Bay'**, large heads of white flowers held well above the foliage; **'Te Puna'**, strong grower, to 30 in (75 cm) high and wide, lush foliage. Zones 9–11.

ARUM

Found from western Europe to the Himalayas and centered around the Mediterranean, this genus contains about 26 species of tuberous-rooted perennials, commonly known as lilies but actually of the arum (Araceae) family, of which it is the type genus. Lustrous dark green leaves, sometimes with lighter marbling, tend to be arrowhead-shaped and usually die away in summer or autumn. Inflorescence consists of a spathe ranging from green to yellow, dull purple or almost black with a cream to purplish spadix. Clustered berries, usually bright orange-red, follow flowers. The unpleasant scent and dark purple-red color of many arums mimics rotting flesh, attracts pollinating flies—unpleasant but effective.

CULTIVATION: *Arum* species are best grown in half-sun in a temperate climate with cool humus-rich soil that remains moist over summer. Propagate by division when the plants are dormant, though new stocks can be raised from seed.

Arum italicum

◐/● ✱ ↔12–16 in (30–40 cm)
↑10–12 in (25–30 cm)

From southern and western Europe and North Africa. Leaves arrowhead-shaped, glossy deep green, often lighter marbled, 6–12 in (15–30 cm) long, dying back in late spring. Large pale green spathe, deep cream spadix. **'Marmoratum'** ★ has pale leaf veins and gray-green mottling. Zones 6–10.

Artemisia absinthium

A

Asclepias tuberosa

ARUNCUS

GOAT'S BEARD

This genus is a member of the rose (Rosaceae) family and contains 2 or 3 species of deciduous perennials native to northern temperate and subarctic regions. They are grown for their large fern-like leaves and for the plumes of tiny cream flowers held well above the attractive foliage in summer. CULTIVATION: These fully frost hardy plants are suitable for "wild" gardens, woodland plantings, and borders. Grow in moist soil in half-sun. Propagate by division in autumn or early spring, or from seed sown in autumn.

Aruncus aethusifolius

↔16 in (40 cm) ↑16 in (40 cm)

From Korea. Compact-clump forming species. Deeply divided pinnate leaves to 10 in (25 cm) long. Panicles of tiny cream flowers in summer. Zones 3–9.

Aruncus dioicus

syns *Aruncus sylvester, A. vulgaris, Spiraea aruncus*

GOAT'S BEARD

↔4 ft (1.2 m) ↑2–6 ft (0.6–1.8 m)

From a wide area of Europe and northern Asia. Imposing plant forming large clumps of pinnately divided leaves. Panicles of cream flowers, up to 20 in (50 cm) long, in summer. Weed in much of Australia. Zones 3–9.

ASCLEPIAS

MILKWEED

This American and African genus of the dogbane (Apocynaceae) family comprises over 100 species, including annuals, perennials, subshrubs, and shrubs. The shrubs are usually upright, many-branched plants with simple, narrow, elliptical to lance-shaped leaves. They produce heads of small 5-petalled flowers followed by seed pods, sometimes oddly shaped, tightly packed with small seeds, each with a small parachute of silky down. All parts of the plants exude a milky sap if cut, hence the name. CULTIVATION: Easily grown in light, well-drained soil in full sun, milkweeds will, however, have more luxuriant foliage and will flower more heavily if well-fed and watered. They grow readily and quickly from seed, and can be treated as annuals or short-lived perennials. Trim to shape, not into bare wood, as plants can be slow to recover from harsh pruning.

Asclepias curassavica

BASTARD IPECACUANHA, BLOOD FLOWER, BUTTERFLY WEED, SCARLET MILKWEED, SILKWEED, SWALLOW WORT

↔24 in (60 cm) ↑36 in (90 cm)

Native to tropical America. Weedy in many areas. Short-lived evergreen subshrub. Narrow leaves to 6 in (15 cm) long. Flowerheads of small bright red flowers with a central yellow ruff. The poisonous sap has an emetic effect. '**Silky Gold**' has deep orange-yellow flowers. Zones 8–11.

Asclepias incarnata

↔24 in (60 cm) ↑4 ft (1.2 m)

From USA. A weedy perennial that can be invasive. Narrow lance-shaped leaves on thick stems. Rose pink flowers in summer. Erect pointed seed heads. Zones 3–9.

Asimina triloba

Asclepias speciosa

DAVIS MILKWEED, SHOWY MILKWEED

↔24–36 in (60–90 cm) ↑24–36 in (60–90 cm)

From western to central USA, invasive in some States. Bushy hairy perennial with large oval leaves. Small starry flowers, pink to light purple and white, borne in spherical clusters, to 3 in (8 cm) across. Zones 2–9.

Asclepias tuberosa ★

BUTTERFLY WEED, PLEURISY ROOT

↔12 in (30 cm) ↑24–36 in (60–90 cm)

Native to eastern and southern USA. Woody-based perennial herb. Narrow lance-shaped leaves on crowded stems. Heads of yellow, orange, or vermilion flowers. Pointed seed head to 6 in (15 cm) long. Zones 3–9.

ASIMINA

This genus of 7 or 8 evergreen or deciduous shrubs or trees from eastern North America is a member of the custard-apple (Annonaceae) family. Generally frost hardy, most species tolerate temperatures of 5°F (–15°C) or lower. White or purple, nodding, bell-shaped flowers appear in small clusters. The fruit is pleasant tasting. CULTIVATION: They will grow in moist well-drained soil in sun or semi-shade, though affected by long dry periods. Respond well to pruning and shaping and can be used for hedging, though this reduces flowers and fruit.

Asimina triloba

PAWPAW

↔20 ft (6 m) ↑30 ft (9 m)

From eastern and central North America. Leaves oval, pointed, and narrow, up to 10 in (25 cm) long. Reddish brown pendulous flowers, around 2 in (5 cm) wide, in spring. Edible fruits ripen to yellowish brown in autumn. '**Prolific**', heaving fruiting, early ripening; '**Rebecca's Gold**', heavy fruiting, late ripening; '**Sunflower**', large, heavy fruiting, late ripening; '**Taylor**', small fruit, late ripening; and '**Wells**', with golden orange flesh. Zones 5–10.

ASPARAGUS

syns *Myrsiphyllum, Protasparagus*

Asparagus

A genus of about 300 perennial herbs, shrubs, or climbers that grow from a tuberous rhizome. Mostly from Africa and Asia, they belong to the asparagus (Asparagaceae) family. Leaves are small, scaly, and often spiny. Cladophylls (flattened stems that function as a leaf) are green and often needle-like. The green, yellow, or white flowers are small and inconspicuous. Fruit is a round berry. CULTIVATION: These plants prefer rich moist soils in a protected position with filtered sunlight. Propagate by division of crowded roots or from seed. Edible asparagus (*A. officinalis*) is grown from 1-year-old crowns planted in mid- to late winter, spaced 12 in (30 cm) apart, in heavily mulched rows 4–6 ft (1.2–1.8 m) apart. Harvest when spears are 6–10 in (15–25 cm) tall by breaking off at ground level. Full production in 2 to 3 years after planting; plants can produce for up to 25 years.

Asparagus densiflorus

syn. *Protasparagus densiflorus*

ASPARAGUS FERN, EMERALD FERN, FOXTAIL SHRUB, SPRENGER ASPARAGUS

↔36 in (90 cm) ↑30–36 in (75–90 cm)

Evergreen trailing shrub, with thick tuberous roots, native to subtropical South Africa. No leaves but needle-like branchlets or cladophylls on green or brown wiry, spiny stems. Small white flowers in spring and summer on axillary racemes. Small bright red berries in winter. '**Compactus**' (syn. 'Nanus'), compact form with shorter branches, denser tighter growth; '**Deflexus**', wider cladophylls with metallic tint; '**Myersii**' (foxtail fern), fern-like appearance, dark green cladophylls, upright lateral branches; '**Sprengeri**' (syn. *A. sprengeri*), scrambling woody-stemmed plant, small white flowers, small red berries. Zones 7–11.

Asparagus setaceus

syns *Asparagus plumosus, Protasparagus plumosus*

ASPARAGUS FERN, PLUMOSA FERN LILY

↔24 in (60 cm) ↑12–48 in (30–120 cm)

This species is a twining climber from southern and eastern Africa. Smooth, woody or wiry, green stems and strong thorns. Small white flowers. Red to black berries. Bright or dark green tiny cladophylls, in clusters of 8–20, in a single plane, on branchlets arranged in a flat triangular spray. Varieties include: **'Cupressoides'**, compact, pyramid-shaped; **'Nanus'**, compact, upright habit, shorter crowded cladophylls; **'Pyramidalis'**, roughly pyramidal in shape; and **'Robustus'**, strongly growing form. Zones 9–11.

ASPHODELINE

This genus is a member of the grass tree (Xanthorrhoeaceae) family. It has 18 to 20 species of fleshy-stemmed perennial or biennial herbs native to southern Europe where they grow on rocky slopes and in scrubby areas. They are clump-forming plants with grayish green linear leaves to 12 in (30 cm) long, sometimes with slightly serrated margins. The flowers are about 1¼ in (30 mm) across and are borne in spring and summer. They have 6 flaring petals, yellow or white tinged pink, and are scented in some species.

CULTIVATION: Useful plants for the border, rockery, or for naturalizing. Grow in a moderately fertile soil in full sun. Propagate from seed or by division of clumps.

Asphodeline lutea ★

JACOB'S ROD, KING'S SPEAR, YELLOW ASPHODEL

↔ 12 in (30 cm) ↕ 36–48 in (90–120 cm)

From the Mediterranean. Narrow silvery leaves to 12 in (30 cm) long. Fragrant yellow flowers, borne on stiff spikes, in late spring–summer. Decorative seed pods. Zones 7–10.

ASPHODELUS

There are 12 species of clump-forming, swollen-rooted perennials in this genus, which is a member of the grass tree (Xanthorrhoeaceae) family. The species are found from the Mediterranean to the Himalayas growing in scrub and on rocky slopes. Their leaves are linear, up to 24 in (60 cm) long, and may be flat or cylindrical. The flowers have 6 whorled tepals and are white or pink with green or brown veining. Flowering stems vary in length, from 7 ft (2 m) tall in one species, to non-existent in another, which flowers within the basal rosette.

CULTIVATION: *Asphodelus* is best grown in a moderately fertile soil in a position that receives full sun. Some of the species, such as the low-growing *A. acaulis,* are better suited to the rockery as they require sharp drainage. Propagation is from seed or by division.

Asphodeline lutea

Asphodelus aestivus

↔ 24 in (60 cm) ↕ 40 in (100 cm)

This species is native to the Canary Islands and Mediterranean regions. It has long, flat, basal leaves, and flowering stems with short side branches. Its flowers are starry white, with a central brown stripe on each petal. It is a spring-flowering species. Zones 7–10.

Asphodelus albus

↔ 24 in (60 cm) ↕ 36 in (90 cm)

Native to southern and western Europe and northern Africa, this species has linear leaves that are up to 24 in (60 cm) long. Flowering stems, 12–36 in (30–90 cm) tall, bear white to pale pink flowers, with a pinkish brown stripe on each petal, in spring. Zones 6–10.

ASPIDISTRA

Found from the Himalayas to Japan, the 8 species in this genus are evergreen perennials of the asparagus (Asparagaceae) family. Spreading from thick rhizomes, they form clumps of tough, deep green, elliptical to lance-shaped leaves that emerge directly from the ground on a strong leaf stalk, either singly or in small clusters. Small, purple-red to brown, bell- to urn-shaped flowers open from spring. They are stemless and occur near ground level where they often pass unnoticed.

CULTIVATION: Aspidistra species are easily grown outdoors in a mild temperate climate, preferring a shady spot with warm, moist, well-drained soil. In suitable conditions they spread well, making an excellent large-scale ground cover.

Asphodelus aestivus

Aspidistra elatior

Asplenium bulbiferum

Aspidistra elatior

BAR ROOM PLANT, CAST-IRON PLANT

↔ 16–36 in (40–90 cm) ↕ 16–24 in (40–60 cm)

A much-loved species native to China. Veined overarching leaves to 24 in (60 cm) long emerge singly. Flowers bell-shaped, vary from cream with purple spots to overall purple. Popular house plant. **'Shooting Stars'** is a cultivar with white-flecked foliage. Zones 7–10.

ASPLENIUM

SPLEENWORT

A genus of over 600 ferns found in tropical and subtropical climates and belonging to the spleenwort (Aspleniaceae) family. Short rhizomes are covered with massed roots, hairs, and scales. Fronds, often leathery, grow mostly from a single crown, forming a fountain-like structure.

CULTIVATION: Plant *Asplenium* species in freely draining organically rich soil in a moist, shady, humid spot; some can stand dry spells. Tropical species need frost protection. Apply slow-release and liquid fertilizers when growing. Propagate from spores or by detaching plantlets formed on fronds of some species.

Asplenium bulbiferum

HEN AND CHICKEN FERN, MOTHER SPLEENWORT

↔ 24–48 in (60–120 cm) ↕ 24–48 in (60–120 cm)

Terrestrial or epiphytic fern from New Zealand and Australia. Short-creeping to suberect rhizome and arching, membranous, pinnate fronds to 48 in (120 cm) across. Flattened, grooved, green to brown stems, to 12 in (30 cm) long. Zones 9–11.

Asplenium nidus

BIRD'S-NEST FERN

↔ 18–60 in (45–150 cm) ↕ 18–60 in (45–150 cm)

This large fern has a wide distribution, ranging from East Africa through tropical Asia to northern Australia and the Pacific as far as Hawaii. Nest-like rosette of simple, erect, sword-shaped fronds to 5 ft (1.5 m) long. The leathery, glossy green fronds are held on short, scaly, black, suberect stems to 2 in (5 cm) long. Variable, with some lobed forms. A. n. var. plicatum has narrow, dark green, pleated, convoluted fronds. Zones 10–12.

Asplenium scolopendrium

syn. *Phyllitis scolopendrium*

HART'S TONGUE FERN, SCOLLIES

↔ 8–24 in (20–60 cm)
↕ 8–24 in (20–60 cm)

Robust clump-forming fern, globally distributed through north temperate regions. Scaly rhizomes. Strap-like fronds, to 24 in (60 cm) long, on short stems. Grows naturally on alkaline or acid soils but prefers lime in cultivation. Numerous cultivars, including: **'Crispum Bolton's Nobile'**, broad fronds to 18 in (45 cm) long; **'Crispum Speciosum'**, sharply tapered fronds sometimes with yellow stripes; **'Cristatum'**, fronds divided many times, each ending in a spreading crest; **'Kaye's Lacerated'**, broad irregularly lobed fronds to 8 in (20 cm) long. **Zones 4–10.**

Asplenium trichomanes

COMMON SPLEENWORT, MAIDENHAIR SPLEENWORT

↔ 3–16 in (8–40 cm)
↕ 3–16 in (8–40 cm)

Small terrestrial fern from temperate regions of the Northern Hemisphere, as well as New Zealand and southern Australia. Erect rhizomes. Neat rosettes of spreading, leathery, dark green, pinnate fronds, to 16 in (40 cm) long, with spherical leaflets in pairs. Stiff brownish purple or black stems. A. t. subsp. quadrivalens, larger leaflets than species, almost rectangular, tolerates alkalinity. **Zones 2–6.**

ASTER

MICHAELMAS DAISY

Found across the temperate Northern Hemisphere and into South America, this group of herbaceous perennials of the daisy (Asteraceae) family used to contain around 250 species. However, many of the more widely cultivated of these have now been reclassified in the genus *Symphyotrichum*. Most asters are upright plants that often sprawl under the weight of their foliage and flowers. They usually have simple linear to lance-shaped leaves, sometimes hairy and/or serrated. A few flower in spring but most in late summer and autumn, with large heads of small to medium-sized daisies in a range of colors. The ancient Greeks believed that asters repelled snakes and were an antidote to their venom.

CULTIVATION: Mostly frost tolerant, preferring well-drained soil that stays moist in the growing season. A sunny, airy, open position ensures maximum flowering and minimum mildew, a problem in humid conditions. Cut back hard after flowering. Propagate by winter division or from spring softwood cuttings.

Aster alpinus

ALPINE ASTER

↔ 8–32 in (20–80 cm)
↕ 4–10 in (10–25 cm)

Spreading, sometimes mounding perennial from mountains of southern Europe. Simple spatula- to lance-shaped base foliage. In spring and summer, masses of short-stemmed daisies, to slightly under 2 in (5 cm) wide, in white and all shades of pink, mauve, and purple. **Zones 3–9.**

Aster amellus

↔ 12–20 in (30–50 cm)
↕ 24–27 in (60–70 cm)

Upright Eurasian perennial. Faintly downy stems, green lance-shaped leaves around 2 in (5 cm) long. In autumn, terminal clusters of 2 in (5 cm) wide daisies, violet pink in the wild. Cultivars include: **'Framfieldii'**, 24 in (60 cm) tall, lilac blue flowers; **'Jacqueline Genebrier'**, 12 in (30 cm) tall, small bright pink flowers; **'King George'**, 24 in (60 cm) tall, gray-green leaves, purple flowers; **'Sonia'**, deep pink flowers; and **'Veilchenkönigin'**, 16 in (40 cm) tall, dense heads of small deep violet flowers. **Zones 5–9.**

Aster divaricatus

↔ 12–20 in (30–50 cm)
↕ 24 in (60 cm)

Perennial native to eastern USA. Unusual, elongated, heart-shaped leaves to 4 in (10 cm) long. Summer and autumn, sprays of dark-stemmed, small, white daisies held above foliage. **Zones 4–9.**

Aster × *frikartii*

↔ 16–24 in (40–60 cm)
↕ 20–30 in (50–75 cm)

Garden hybrid between *A. amellus* and *A. thomsonii*. Upright perennial with dark green, elongated, lance-shaped base leaves. In autumn, branching sprays of 2 in (5 cm) wide daisies in shades of lavender and purple-blue. **'Mönch'**, 16 in (40 cm) tall, and **'Wunder von Stäfa'**, 30 in (75 cm) tall, are two cultivars with lavender-blue flowers. **Zones 4–9.**

Aster × *frikartii* 'Mönch'

Astilbe chinensis 'Visions'

Aster sedifolius

syn. *Aster trinervius*

↔ 20 in (50 cm) ↕ 3 ft (0.9 m)

Upright, bushy, summer-flowering perennial found from Nepal through China to Japan. Irregularly toothed lance-shaped leaves to 4 in (10 cm) long, large branching sprays of 1 in (25 mm) wide white flowers. A. s. subsp. ageratoides, compact subspecies, narrow leaves, several cultivars with lavender-pink flowers. **Zones 7–9.**

ASTILBE

FALSE SPIRAEA

Found mainly in temperate East Asia, this perennial genus of the saxifrage (Saxifragaceae) family includes just 12 species which have been extensively selected and hybridized. Their toothed pinnate or bipinnate leaves sprout directly from rhizomes and soon form a large foliage clump. Long-stemmed plumes of tiny flowers appear in spring and summer, in white and all shades of pink, mauve, and red. Though astilbe plumes are thought of as bright and showy, the name actually means "without brilliance," from the Greek *a* (without) and *stilbe* (brilliance). This is because, while the flowerheads are bright, each flower is, on its own, tiny and rather dull.

CULTIVATION: Astilbes are not drought tolerant nor do they thrive in the hot summer sun. Instead they prefer moist, humus-rich, woodland soil and dappled sunlight. They often thrive around pond margins but also tolerate being in well-drained soils.

Astilbe × *arendsii*

↔ 12–32 in (30–80 cm)
↕ 2–6 ft (0.6–1.8 m)

This group of garden hybrids involves several parent species. Both flowers and foliage are highly variable. Popular named forms include: **'Anita Pfeifer'**, 24 in (60 cm) tall, finely divided foliage and feathery sprays of pink flowers; **'Brautschleier'** (syn. 'Bridal Veil'), 30 in (75 cm) tall, white flowers, early-flowering; **'Bumalda'**, 24 in (60 cm) high, white flowers with a faint pink blush, bronze foliage; **'Fanal'** ★, 24 in (60 cm) tall, dark, red-tinted foliage, deep red flowers; **'Federsee'**, sprays of deep pink flowers to 24 in (60 cm) tall; **'Gertrud Brix'**, 24 in (60 cm) tall, deep red flowers, bronze foliage; **'Gloria'**, 27 in (70 cm) tall, deep pink flowers; **'Hyazinth'**, bright green foliage, lilac-pink flower sprays to 36 in (90 cm) high; **'Irrlicht'**, purple-tinted foliage and white flower sprays to 24 in (60 cm) high; '**Mainz**', 24 in (60 cm) tall, deep rose-pink flowers; '**Rosa Perle**' (syn. 'Pink Pearl'), 30 in (75 cm) tall, silvery to pink flowers; **Showstar Group**, dwarf seedling strain in a mixed color range; '**Spinell**', 36 in (90 cm) tall, orange-red flowers; '**Venus**', bright green foliage, sprays of pink flowers to 36 in (90 cm) high; '**Weisse Gloria**', 36 in (90 cm) tall, sprays of white flowers; and '**William Reeves**', 24 in (60 cm) tall, deep pinkish red flowers. Zones 6–9.

Astilbe chinensis

syn. *Astilbe rubra*

◐ ✱ ↔ 12–20 in (30–50 cm)
↑ 20–27 in (50–70 cm)

Native to China and Japan. Foliage with large and coarsely toothed leaflets. Flowerheads short-stemmed with strongly upright plumes. Several natural varieties, including: A. c. var. davidii, bronze young leaves and purple-pink flower plumes to 7 ft (2 m) tall; A. c. var. pumila, just 10 in (25 cm) tall, with green foliage and dense plumes of deep pink flowers; and A. c. var. taquetti '**Superba**', with magenta flowers on brown stems to 4 ft (1.2 m) tall. A. c. '**Visions**' is a typically compact cultivar with 18 in (45 cm) tall, honey-scented, deep pink to red flower sprays and bronze foliage. Zones 5–9.

Astilbe × *crispa*

◐ ✱ ↔ 8–12 in (20–30 cm)
↑ 8–12 in (20–30 cm)

Hybrid group of uncertain origins established by the German breeder Arends. Mainly dwarf plants with broad deeply cut leaflets, and bronze young foliage. '**Perkeo**' is the common form and has deep pink flowers in plumes to 8 in (20 cm) long. Zones 6–9.

Astilbe japonica

◐ ✱ ↔ 3 ft (0.9 m) ↑ 2–3 ft (0.6–0.9 m)

Endemic to Japan, known in gardens chiefly by its cultivars and hybrids. Leaves bi- or tripinnate, flowers white, in pyramidal panicles up to 8 in (20 cm) long in late spring–early summer. Zones 5–9.

Astilbe koreana

syn. *Astilbe grandis*

◐ ❄ ↔ 16–20 in (40–50 cm)
↑ 24 in (60 cm)

Southern Korean species with finely divided ferny foliage. Bright pink buds open to white or very pale pink flowers borne on airy, arching panicles. Zones 7–9.

Astilbe, Hybrid Cultivar, 'Red Sentinel'

Astilbe simplicifolia

◐ ❄ ↔ 8–16 in (20–40 cm)
↑ 12–16 in (30–40 cm)

Compact Japanese species. Foliage often simple, glossy, ovate, lobed, but sometimes more deeply divided. Starry white flowers in narrow upright plumes. Several cultivars, including: '**Bronze Elegance**', 12 in (30 cm) tall, pinkish red flowers on red stems; and '**Hennie Graefland**', 16 in (40 cm) tall, soft pink flowers, bronze foliage. Zones 7–9.

Astilbe thunbergii

◐ ❄ ↔ 12–20 in (30–50 cm)
↑ 20–24 in (50–60 cm)

Early-flowering Japanese species with sharply toothed pinnate foliage, broad olive to bronze-green leaflets, sometimes downy. Flowers small but densely massed, opening white and ageing to pink. Zones 7–9.

Astilbe Hybrid Cultivars

◐ ✱ ↔ 3 ft (0.9 m) ↑ 2–3 ft (0.6–0.9 m)

These cultivars have *A. japonica* as a major part of their heritage. '**Betsy Cuperus**', 36 in (90 cm), tall, arching panicles of soft pink flowers; '**Deutschland**', 20 in (50 cm) tall, bright green foliage, pure white flowers; '**Europa**', 24 in (60 cm) high, pale pink flowers; '**Montgomery**', 30 in (75 cm) tall, red flowers, red-tinted foliage; '**Red Sentinel**', 24–36 in (60–90 cm) high, bronze leaves, open sprays of red flowers on red stems; and '**Straussenfeder**' (syn. 'Ostrich Feather'), 36 in (90 cm) high, salmon pink to soft red flowers in arching sprays. Zones 6–9.

ASTILBOIDES

A genus of the saxifrage (Saxifragaceae) family containing only one species, a herbaceous perennial once included in the genus *Rodgersia*. It comes from China and differs from its former relatives mainly in its leaf shape. It is grown for its huge leaves and racemes of tiny white flowers that occur in summer.
CULTIVATION: It grows best in moist soils in a cool sheltered spot and is usually seen at its best near water. It bears very little resemblance to the genus *Astilbe* after which it was named. Propagation is from seed or by division when dormant.

Astilboides tabularis

syn. *Rodgersia tabularis*

● ❄ ↔ 40–60 in (100–150 cm)
↑ 40–60 in (100–150 cm)

This impressive perennial has huge, bright green, circular leaves to 36 in (90 cm) across with the stem attached to the center. Above the foliage are its large fluffy heads of tiny white flowers, produced in summer. Zones 7–10.

ASTRANTIA

MASTERWORT, PINCUSHION FLOWER

Primarily European, this genus of 10 species of perennials also occurs westward to Asia, often in alpine meadows or woodlands. Belonging to the carrot (Apiaceae) family, they bear their small pastel-toned flowers in small dome-shaped heads (umbels). The true flowers are often less showy than the surrounding papery bracts. The foliage, which forms a basal clump and spreads by runners, is

Astrantia major

hand-shaped, with 3 to 7 toothed lobes. The name *Astrantia* probably comes from the star (aster) shaped flowerheads, but a more fanciful explanation is that it is derived from *ostrutium*, a corruption of *struthio*, an ostrich. The reference is unclear but perhaps the taxonomist thought the flowerheads resemble ostrich plumes.
CULTIVATION: Apart from an intolerance of prolonged dry conditions, grows freely in any cool-temperate garden with moderately fertile free-draining soil. Foliage may be lusher in shade, a consideration with variegated cultivars, but they usually flower best in at least half-sun. Propagate by division when dormant or from seed, which needs stratification.

Astrantia major

GREATER MASTERWORT

◐ ✱ ↔ 16–24 in (40–60 cm)
↑ 24–32 in (60–80 cm)

From central and eastern Europe. Leaves with 3 to 7, broad, toothed lobes. Floral bracts white through red, often green tinted or veined. A. m. subsp. involucrata, has long narrow bracts creating a lacy flowerhead; '**Moira Reid**', very large green-tipped white bracts, pink-tinted early blooms, 30 in (75 cm) tall; and '**Shaggy**', green-tipped white flowers and deeply divided leaves, 30 in (75 cm) tall. A. m. var. rosea has green-tinted pale pink inflorescences, 30 in (75 cm) tall. A. m. '**Rubra**' ★, deep purple-red inflorescence, 24 in (60 cm) tall; '**Ruby Wedding**', dark wine red flowers through summer, 30 in (75 cm) tall; '**Sunningdale Variegated**', variably marked cream and green variegated foliage and pink-flushed white flowerheads, 30 in (75 cm) tall. Zones 6–9.

Astrantia maxima

◐ ✱ ↔ 20–24 in (50–60 cm)
↑ 27–36 in (70–90 cm)

Large leaves with 3 to 5 finely toothed lobes. Pink flowerheads, lighter center, bracts fused to create a ruff rather than "petals." Zones 6–9.

A

Athyrium filix-femina

Aubrieta, Hybrid Cultivar, 'Doctor Mules'

ATHAMANTA

There are 15 species of perennial herbs in this genus, which is a member of the carrot (Apiaceae) family. They are native to the Mediterranean and temperate Eurasia where they grow in scree and other mountain habitats. They have long tap roots and form clumps of finely divided foliage. Their umbels of small flowers are white, occasionally yellow.

CULTIVATION: The tall species are suitable for the wild garden where they can be grown in any well-drained soil in full sun. They dislike winter wet. The alpine species can be grown in troughs or the cool greenhouse. Propagation is from seed or by division in spring.

Athamanta turbith

syn. *Athamanta mathioli*

CANDY CARROT

☼ ✱ ↔15 in (38 cm) ↑24 in (60 cm)

From central Europe. Clumps of finely divided fern-like foliage. Umbels of small white flowers in summer. Zones 6–9.

ATHYRIUM

A member of the cliff fern (Woodsiaceae) family, this genus comprises more than 100 widely variable terrestrial fern species. They are from temperate to tropical regions, and feature short and erect to creeping rhizomes with scales entire to toothed, and brown to black in color. Their fronds are leathery to membranous, often brittle.

CULTIVATION: Most of the species in this genus prefer well-drained, acidic, organically rich loams, with organic mulch applied, in shade or filtered sun. Tropical species are frost tender. Protect from wind, slugs, and snails. Maintain abundant moisture, including water sprayed on foliage in hot weather. Easily propagated from spores or plantlets. Species with multiple crowns or creeping rhizomes can be divided.

Athyrium filix-femina

LADY FERN

☀/✹ ✱ ↔3–7 ft (0.9–2 m)
↑2–5 ft (0.6–1.5 m)

Graceful, easily grown, clumping fern from northern temperate zones in India, China, Japan, North Africa, Canada, North America, Mexico, and Peru. Short-creeping to erect rhizomes. Spreading or arching pinnate fronds, to 3 ft (0.9 m) long, thin-textured and leathery. Smooth frond stalks are green to purple in color. Deciduous in colder regions. This species has over 300 cultivars, including **'Clarissima'**, a graceful uncrested fern, to 40 in (100 cm); **'Frizelliae'** (tatting fern), with ball-shaped leaflets along the midrib; **'Glomeratum'**, with curious ball-like masses of leaflets on slender fronds; **'Magnificum Capitatum'**, frond alone crested, leaflets not crested; **'Minutissimum'**, dwarf form with fronds 4–6 in (10–15 cm) long; **'Vernoniae'**, crimson frond stalks, broadly triangular blades with strongly ruffled overlapping leaflets, ending in a tassel; **'Victoriae'**, crested fronds, to 40 in (100 cm) tall, branched at base to form crosses. Zones 3–9.

Athyrium niponicum

syn. *Athyrium brevisorum*

☀/✹ ✱ ↔20–24 in (50–60 cm)
↑12–14 in (30–35 cm)

Fully frost-hardy fern from East Asia with a short-creeping reddish brown rhizome. Arching pinnate fronds with yellow-colored stems. **A. n. var. pictum** (Japanese painted fern), new fronds metallic gray suffused with red or blue. A. n. **'Pictum Crested'** (painted lady fern), purplish red midrib suffusing into a silver-gray and aquamarine-green lamina. Zones 4–9.

Athyrium otophorum

JAPANESE PLUM FERN

☀/✹ ✱ ↔5–24 in (38–60 cm)
↑12–18 in (30–45 cm)

Fern from East Asia (China, Japan, and Korea) with short-creeping, clump-forming, erect rhizomes. Dark green 2-pinnate fronds, to 18 in (45 cm) long, on red to purple stems. Leaflets in 8 to 10 pairs with toothed or lobed pinnules. A. o. var. okanum, stems and midribs purple-red, fronds yellowish green. Zones 4–9.

AUBRIETA

AUBRETIA

Found from Europe to Central Asia, the 12 evergreen cushion or mat-forming perennials of this genus are members of the cabbage (Brassicaceae) family. Indispensable for rockeries and also a colorful addition to flower borders or spilling over banks, they smother themselves in flower in spring and early summer, becoming carpets of tiny, 4-petalled, purple, mauve, or white blooms. The foliage is small and simple, usually dull gray-green and finely downy, often with small lobes or teeth. Named after Claude Aubriet (1668–1743), a French botanical artist, the name was corrupted to aubretia, which became the common name.

CULTIVATION: Hardy in most temperate zones, aubretias prefer gritty, well-drained, alkaline soil in full or half-sun and, while requiring moisture during the flowering season and appreciative of an occasional light dressing of lime, they are otherwise undemanding. Although perennial, aubretias can be grown as an annual or sheared back hard after flowering to renew their foliage. Propagate from seed or heeled cuttings.

Aubrieta deltoidea ★

ROCK CRESS

☼/☀ ❄ ↔12 in (30 cm) ↑3 in (8 cm)

Found in southwest Europe, especially around the Aegean Sea. Leaves diamond-shaped, smooth edged or with 2 to 6 conspicuous teeth. Pale lavender through magenta to purple flowers up to 1 in (25 mm) in diameter. Zones 7–10.

Aubrieta Hybrid Cultivars

☼ ❄ ↔8–24 in (20–60 cm)
↑3–6 in (8–15 cm)

Garden hybrids are derived from several species. They are difficult to place regarding parentage, but probably all have *A. deltoidea* in their background. All are mat-forming, but otherwise highly variable. Popular named forms include: **'Argenteovariegata'**, with silver-edged leaves and purple flowers; **'Blue Cascade'**, strongly trailing habit, may mound to 6 in (15 cm) high, purplish blue flowers; **'Blue King'**, mauve-blue flowers in abundance; **'Bressingham Pink'**, clusters of large, pink, double flowers; **'Campbellii'**, mauve-blue double flowers; **'Doctor Mules'**, neat, compact habit with attractive violet-blue flowers; **'Hendersonii'**, low spreader with purple flowers, well suited to rock walls and banks; **'Novalis Blue'**, bright mauve-blue flowers; and **'Rokey's Purple'**, which produces deep purple flowers well into summer. Zones 7–10.

AUCUBA

This genus of dioecious plants in the tassel tree (Garryaceae) family originates from the Himalayas and eastern Asia. It contains 3 or 4 species of evergreen shrubs or small trees, frequently used in garden situations, as they tolerate deep shade. Spotted forms most popular. The glossy leaves are lanceolate, smooth or serrate, and grow in an alternate arrangement along the branches. Flowers, either green or maroon, are in leaf axils or at the ends of terminal shoots and are of different sexes on different plants. Fruit are red, orange, or whitish yellow.

CULTIVATION: *Aucuba* grows best in moist soil but will tolerate dry conditions in heavier shade. The variegated forms need dappled shade or protection from sun to prevent their leaves scorching. Cut back in spring. If grown in containers, use a rich, moisture-holding potting mix and slow-release fertilizer during the summer months. Propagate from seed in spring, or take half-hardened cuttings in summer.

Aucuba japonica

JAPANESE AUCUBA, JAPANESE LAUREL

✹ ❄ ↔6 ft (1.8 m) ↑6 ft (1.8 m)

Evergreen shrub from Japan. Glossy green leaves, purplish flowers, red berries. Cultivars include: **'Crotonifolia'**, a strongly gold-variegated cultivar; **'Gold Dust'**, female, variegated leaves; **'Picturata'**, large central splash of gold on each leaf; **'Rozannie'**, a self-fruiting form; **'Salicifolia'**, female, narrow long-pointed leaves; **'Sulpharea Marginata'**, bright yellow leaf margins on new growth, become pale green in summer; and **'Variegata'** ★, gold variegated, preferring deep shade. Zones 7–10.

AURINIA

A genus of 7 species of perennials and biennials of the cabbage (Brassicaceae) family, found from central Europe to Turkey. They are small carpeting plants with silver-gray hairy leaves. Heads of small bright yellow or white flowers open from spring, often almost hiding the foliage.

CULTIVATION: Best suited to a cool-temperate climate where frosts are not severe, these are superb plants for rockeries or alpine troughs. They prefer full sun and need perfectly drained gritty soil, kept moist in spring and early summer. All may be propagated from seed, which often self-sows, and the perennials can also be grown from self-layered pieces or by taking small tip cuttings.

Aurinia saxatilis

syn. *Alyssum saxatile*

BASKET OF GOLD, YELLOW ALYSSUM

↔ 16–24 in (40–60 cm)
↑ 8–12 in (20–30 cm)

Central and southeastern Europe. Low, carpeting perennial with small silver-gray leaves. Sprays of pale to bright yellow flowers from spring. Hardiest species by far. **'Citrina'** is heavy-blooming, bright yellow flowers; and **'Compacta'** has golden flowers on 8 in (20 cm) high stems. Zones 3–9.

Azara microphylla

Aurinia saxatilis 'Compacta'

Azorella trifurcata

Averrhoa carambola

AVERRHOA

An East Asian genus of 2 species of evergreen trees, of the wood-sorrel (Oxalidaceae) family. Foliage is pinnate, composed of quite large leaflets. Flowers, white to red or purple with white markings, are carried in short inflorescences, followed by 5-angled edible fruit, to 5 in (12 cm) long.

CULTIVATION: Easily cultivated, other than requiring tropical or subtropical conditions. Thrive in warm sheltered positions with moist well-drained soil and high humidity. The plants are attractive ornamentally as well as for their fruit. Propagate from seed, or grow fruiting cultivars from grafts or aerial layers.

Averrhoa carambola ★

CARAMBOLA, FIVE-CORNER, STAR FRUIT

↔ 10 ft (3 m) ↑ 20 ft (6 m)

Very attractive small fruit tree for tropical gardens. Leaflets blue-green on undersides, to 4 in (10 cm) long. Sensitive to touch and light, folding at night or if handled. Pretty pink flowers appear much of year. Edible fruit, yellow-green to orange. Several grafted selections are available, including: **'Arkin'**, heavy cropping; **'Kary'**, more cold tolerant; and **'Kembangan'**, very sweet fruit. Zones 11–12.

AZARA

One of temperate South America's most popular gifts to horticulture, this willow (Salicaceae) family genus of 10 species of evergreen trees and shrubs has attractive foliage, graceful growth habits, and easy culture. Mostly native to Chile, their foliage varies in size but is generally glossy and leathery. Each main leaf is appended with one or two smaller "accessory leaves." Flowers tend to be golden yellow, small, fluffy pompons without petals. Fleshy fruits follow.

CULTIVATION: Most species will tolerate repeated light frosts but are damaged by severe cold. They do not tolerate extreme heat and generally prefer a temperate climate with cool moist soil. Otherwise, they are easy-care plants that, while inclined to become rather open and leggy with age, can be kept compact with routine trimming or pinching back. Propagate by seed or half-hardened cuttings.

Azara microphylla

VANILLA TREE

↔ 15 ft (4.5 m) ↑ 25 ft (8 m)

Commonly grown tree from Chile and Argentina. Small leaves on frond-like branches, creating a ferny or pinnate spray. Vanilla-scented, tiny, dull yellow flowers in spring, red fruit. **'Variegata'**, golden variegated, attractive foliage plant. Zones 8–10.

Azara serrata ★

↔ 8 ft (2.4 m) ↑ 12 ft (3.5 m)

From Chile. Shrub with sharply toothed foliage and golden flowers that open later than other azaras. With age can become rather sparse, so best to trim and shape when young. Zones 8–10.

AZORELLA

This carrot (Apiaceae) family genus of about 70 species of perennials occurs naturally in Andean South America, New Zealand, and the subantarctic islands. They are cushion-forming evergreen perennials that develop into hummocks of bright green foliage. In spring and early summer, tiny heads of greenish cream to bright yellow, rarely pink, flowers are seen.

CULTIVATION: Although found over a wide latitude range, they tend to prefer a cool-temperate climate where the frosts are not severe, occurring at high altitudes in their northerly range and descending as the latitude rises to the south. Either full or half-sun will do. Plant in gritty, very free-draining soil, but do not allow to dry out for long periods. Superb plants as ground covers for large rockeries or cascading down banks and stone walls.

Azorella trifurcata

syn. *Azorella nivalis*

↔ 2–7 ft (0.6–2 m)
↑ 4 in (10 cm)

From Chile and Argentina. Usually compact mound of gray-green to bright deep green, leathery leaves, but can spread in ideal conditions. Yellow-green to yellow flowerheads from late spring. **'Nana'** is very compact with smaller leaves. Zones 6–9.

B

B

BACOPA

WATER HYSSOP

A plantain (Plantaginaceae) family genus of up to 100 species of aquatic annual or perennial creeping plants found in marshy areas throughout the tropical and subtropical zones. They mostly have rounded, rather fleshy leaves and small, white to mauve-blue, 5-petalled flowers. There has been some confusion in cultivation between this genus and *Sutera*. *S. cordata* is still often sold under the name *Bacopa*.
CULTIVATION: Most often cultivated as ornamentals in small ponds or as aquarium plants. Some species have local medicinal uses. Propagation is usually by division or from cuttings. Seed germinates freely if available.

Bacopa caroliniana

syn. *Bacopa amplexicaulis*

BLUE HYSSOP, LEMON BACOPA

↔20 in (50 cm) ↑4 in (10 cm)

Found in southeastern USA. Fleshy, bright-green, lemon-scented leaves, become reddish in sun. Blue flowers in summer–autumn. Zones 9–10.

Baileya multiradiata, in the wild, Joshua Tree National Park, California, USA

Baptisia australis

BAILEYA

This small genus from western North America is part of the daisy (Asteraceae) family. It comprises just 3 species of annuals and perennials; one, *B. multiradiata*, is sometimes grown for a bright splash of color in summer and autumn, especially in arid areas. *Baileya* species have opposite pairs of hairy, gray-green, pinnate leaves and have an open habit, rarely growing to more than 12–16 in (30–40 cm) tall. Their cosmos-like yellow flowerheads are held clear of the foliage on long stems, appearing from early summer and continuing until the first frosts.
CULTIVATION: *Baileya* plants thrive in semi-desert conditions and, although sometimes considered weeds, they are one of the most reliable and colorful summer annuals for arid gardens. Plant in full sun and water only to get plants established or if dry conditions persist. Remove spent flowerheads to prolong blooming. Propagate from seed, which may be sown in-situ or started under cover and transplanted.

Baileya multiradiata

DESERT BAILEYA, DESERT MARIGOLD, PAPER DAISY, WILD MARIGOLD

↔4–12 in (10–30 cm) ↑8–20 in (20–50 cm)

Native to southern USA and Mexico. Short-lived perennial with grayish green foliage. Bright yellow flowers, 2 in (5 cm) across and resembling marigolds, are borne from spring to autumn. Needs perfect drainage to prevent rotting. Zones 7–10.

Bartlettina sordida

BAMBUSA

BAMBOO

This genus in the family Poaceae contains about 120 species of giant grasses from low elevations of tropical and subtropical Asia, tropical America, Africa, and northern Australia. The name comes from the Malay word *bambu*. From 15 ft (4.5 m) to 80 ft (24 m) in height, they have smooth cylindrical stems grown from rhizomes, in loose to dense compact clumps. Stems (called culms) are mostly hollow, except at the nodes (rings). From the higher nodes wiry lateral branches emerge bearing leaves. Large pale scale-leaves sheath young stems, but are cast off as the culms mature. Flowering is rarely seen. The "timber" is used to construct Asian houses, boats, bridges, fences, and furniture.
CULTIVATION: Vigorous growers requiring a tropical or subtropical climate. Several species are frost hardy. Plant in deep, fertile, loamy soil with ample water in summer in a sheltered but sunny position. Propagate from offsets buried in soil; flood, mulch, and feed well when new growth shows.

Bambusa multiplex

syn. *Bambusa glaucescens*

HEDGE BAMBOO

↔10 ft (3 m) ↑35 ft (10 m)

From southern China. Crowded deep green culms up to 1½ in (35 mm) in diameter, erect then arching at the top. Leaves small, bluish green undersurface. Mature plants produce arching flowering branches every few years. Used in weaving, as windbreak, and as ornamentals. **'Alphonse Karr'** ★, green-striped gold culms forming broad-headed clump; **'Fernleaf'**, to 20 ft (6 m) tall; **'Riviereorum', to 6 ft (1.8 m) tall; 'Silverstripe'**, pale stripes on new leaves and stems. Zones 8–12.

Bambusa oldhamii

OLDHAM BAMBOO

↔20–40 ft (6–12 m) ↑60 ft (18 m)

Native to southern China and Taiwan. Open clump of straight upright culms 24 in (60 cm) thick, bright green with white bloom, ageing to yellow. Grown for edible shoots, hedging, paper pulp, and as ornamental. Zones 9–12.

BAPTISIA

FALSE INDIGO, WILD INDIGO

Belonging to the pea-flower subfamily of the legume (Fabaceae) family, this genus contains about 17 species of perennial herbs native to the USA. They grow in sand, gravel, and other poor soils in dry woodlands and open areas. Plants have a shrubby habit, spreading or erect, to 7 ft (2 m) tall, with trifoliate leaves. Spikes of lupin-like flowers are white, yellow, or purplish blue. Once used in dye-making as a substitute for true indigo.
CULTIVATION: Grow plants in full sun in deep well-drained, neutral or slightly acidic soil. Most species grow happily in poorly nourished soils. Stake tall plants in exposed positions. Propagate by division or from seed.

Baptisia alba

syn. *Baptisia lactea*

ATLANTIC WILD INDIGO, PRAIRIE FALSE INDIGO, WHITE FALSE INDIGO

↔3 ft (0.9 m) ↑2–3 ft (0.6–0.9 m)

Native to central and eastern region of USA. Erect bushy perennial with bluish green foliage. Upright spikes of pea-like flowers creamy white, often with purple markings, in summer. Erect seed pods. **'Pendula'**, similar to species but with drooping seed pods. Zones 5–9.

Baptisia australis

syn. *Baptisia caerulea*

BLUE FALSE INDIGO

↔4 ft (1.2 m) ↑2–4 ft (0.6–1.2 m)

Native to central and eastern USA, but threatened in some states. Upright or spreading bushy perennial with bluish green foliage. Spikes of purplish blue flowers in summer. Erect, inflated dark gray seed pods can be dried for floral arrangements. Zones 5–9.

BARTLETTINA

Found in tropical and Central America and Mexico, this daisy (Asteraceae) family genus comprises 23 species of evergreen shrubs and small trees. They form a dense, many-branched crown with young stems that are usually covered with fine hairs. The leaves are lance-shaped to oval, often with toothed edges; the

corymbs or panicles of crowded small flowerheads, which occur in a variety of shades, appear at different seasons, depending on species.
CULTIVATION: Most species grow extremely freely and may be somewhat invasive. Plant in moist well-drained soil with a position in full sun or partial shade. If necessary, trim to shape after flowering. Propagate from seed or half-hardened cuttings.

Bartlettina sordida

syns *Bartlettina megalophylla, Eupatorium megalophyllum, E. sordidum*

↔7 ft (2 m) ↑10 ft (3 m)

A very vigorous shrub from Mexico. Young stems covered with red hairs; leaves oval with toothed edges, to 4 in (10 cm) long. Fragrant violet flowers in corymbs that open throughout the warmer months. Zones 10–11.

BASSIA

A genus of 26 densely branching, shrubby annuals or perennials belonging to the amaranth (Amaranthaceae) family. *Bassia* plants are are found in warm-temperate parts of the Northern Hemisphere. One species is grown for its foliage. Leaves are usually narrow and smooth-edged, and the flowers are normally inconspicuous spikes. Fruits are achenes (small, dry, single-seeded fruits). The plants are toxic to livestock and produce allelopathic compounds inhibiting the growth of nearby plants.
CULTIVATION: Sow seed in spring where plants are to grow, in a wide range of soils, including saline. Propagate from seed or cuttings.

Bassia scoparia

syns *Kochia scoparia, K. trichophylla*

BELVEDERE, BURNING BUSH, FIREBALL, FIRE-BUSH, FIREWEED, KOCHIA, SUMMER CYPRESS

↔8–60 in (20–150 cm) ↑8–60 in (20–150 cm)

Annual originally from temperate Asia, now naturalized through Europe and North America. Narrow flat leaves, normally mid-green, turning purple-red in late summer. Small inconspicuous flower clusters same color as leaves. With maturity, plant breaks off at base and rolls in tumbleweed fashion, dispersing seed. Zones 8–11.

BAUHINIA

This genus of around 300 species, many confined to the tropics, occurs in all continents (except Europe) and larger tropical islands. They belong to the caesalpinia subfamily of the legume (Fabaceae) family and include shrubs, climbers, and small to medium-sized trees, many deciduous. A characteristic feature is the compound leaf consisting of only 2 broad leaflets, their inner edges often fused. Flowers have 5 petals, borne in the leaf axils or in terminal sprays. Seed pods are slightly woody and flattened. Bauhinias are ornamental trees and shrubs, but some are used in traditional medicine or as a source of fiber; a few have edible seeds.
CULTIVATION: Easily cultivated in warm climates, though often slow growing. Species from tropical climates with a long dry season do not grow or flower well in wetter climates. Deep rooted, they do not like being transplanted, but will often tolerate hot exposed positions and hard dry soils. Few grow well in shade. Propagate from seed; half-hardened cuttings can also be taken.

Bauhinia galpinii

Bauhinia × blakeana

HONG KONG ORCHID TREE

↔15 ft (4.5 m) ↑30 ft (9 m)

This hybrid, probably between *B. purpurea* and *B. variegata*, is the floral emblem of Hong Kong. Leaves broad, reliably evergreen. Flowers purple-red, slightly scented, 4–6 in (10–15 cm), in autumn–winter. Zones 10–12.

Bauhinia corymbosa

PHANERA

↔10 ft (3 m) ↑20 ft (6 m)

From southern China. Climbing plant with deeply bilobed rounded leaves. Young shoots reddish brown. Very showy terminal racemes of densely packed, small, fragrant, pale pink flowers in summer. Zones 10–11.

Bauhinia galpinii

syn. *Bauhinia punctata*

PRIDE OF DE KAAP, SOUTH AFRICAN ORCHID BUSH

↔8 ft (2.4 m) ↑10–20 ft (3–6 m)

A horizontally branching evergreen shrub or scrambling climber from South Africa. Leaves rounded with 2 distinct lobes, paler undersides. Flowers light to brick red, in summer–autumn. Fruits woody, persistent, flattened, green-brown pods. Lightly prune after flowering. Zones 9–11.

Bauhinia variegata

BUTTERFLY BUSH, ORCHID TREE

↔25 ft (8 m) ↑25 ft (8 m)

From tropical foothills of Himalayas through to Malay Peninsula, small tree with short trunk and spreading canopy. Semi-deciduous in warm areas, fully in cool areas. Orchid-like flowers, pale to deep pink. White form also seen. Zones 9–10.

Bauhinia × blakeana

Beaucarnea recurvata

BEAUCARNEA

The 20 species of evergreen trees and shrubs that make up this genus in the asparagus (Asparagaceae) family are found in arid regions ranging from northeastern Mexico to Nicaragua. The trunks become bulbous and swollen and have thick corky bark. The leaves are long, linear, and often grass-like. It is several years before they commence flowering, when large panicles of tiny white flowers are carried.
CULTIVATION: Outdoor cultivation is only possible in warm, dry, and frost-free areas. In cooler areas plants can be grown in greenhouses or as indoor pot plants. Too much water in winter can cause the stem to rot. Propagation is from seed or offsets in spring.

Beaucarnea recurvata ★

syn. *Nolina recurvata*

PONYTAIL PALM

↔6–8 ft (1.8–2.4 m) ↑25 ft (8 m)

Native of east-central Mexico. Popular indoor plant and dramatic landscaping feature. Narrow strap-like leaves, up to 3 ft (0.9 m) long, from single bulbous trunk. Slow growing, branching occurs as it ages. Panicles of tiny white flowers, followed by pinkish fruit. Zones 9–11.

Begonia coccinea

BEGONIA

Found through the tropics and subtropics but most diverse in the Americas, this group of around 900 species of perennials, shrubs, and climbers is the type genus of the family Begoniaceae. Very diverse, they may be fibrous- or rhizome-rooted or tuberous, with foliage emerging from the rootstock or held on cane-like stems. Leaves vary in color, texture, and shape but are often lobed and finely hairy. Flowers are also variable; often a single female flower is surrounded by 2 or more males. CULTIVATION: Mostly frost tender, they are treated as annuals outdoors or grown indoors in cool climates. Plants prefer a bright but not sunny position with fertile, cool, moist, soil rich in humus. Water and feed well. Watch for fungal diseases. Propagate by division or from offsets, leaf cuttings, or seed, depending on type.

Begonia coccinea

ANGEL-WING BEGONIA

↔ 24 in (60 cm) ↑ 48 in (120 cm)

Fibrous-rooted Brazilian species. Stems sturdy, upright, succulent. Lush green, pointed, wing-shaped leaves, to 6 in (15 cm) long, red undersides. Large racemes of bright red flowers in spring. Zones 10–12.

Begonia fuchsioides

FUCHSIA BEGONIA

↔ 20 in (50 cm) ↑ 36 in (90 cm)

Fibrous-rooted Venezuelan species. Succulent upright stems. Toothed, pointed, wing-shaped leaves, to 2 in (5 cm) long, bright green above, red-tinted below. Pendulous sprays of pink to red 1¼ in (30 mm) wide flowers in winter. Zones 10–12.

Begonia grandis

EVANS' BEGONIA, HARDY BEGONIA

↔ 12–18 in (30–45 cm)
↑ 24 in (60 cm)

From China and Japan. Perennial with loose sprays of flower clusters over large clump of leaves. Green leaves heart-shaped, thick, succulent, ruby red veins on lower surfaces. Flowers

Begonia, Cane-like Group, 'Looking Glass'

pink, in drooping cymes, appear in late summer–autumn. **'Heron's Pirouette'** starts blooming in early summer and continues to autumn. Zones 6–9.

Begonia sutherlandii

↔ 20–36 in (50–90 cm)
↑ 8–32 in (20–80 cm)

Tuberous-rooted trailing or semi-climbing herbaceous species from South Africa and Tanzania. Leaves toothed, lance-shaped, to 6 in (15 cm) long; red stems, edges, undersides, and veins. Pendulous clusters of orange to red flowers up to 1 in (25 mm) wide in summer. Zones 8–11.

Begonia Hybrid Cultivars

Begonia is such a large genus and many of the species interbreed so freely that over the years countless hybrids have been introduced. These largely fall into eight quite clear-cut groups. While there are several subgroups, we concentrate here on the main divisions.

CANE-LIKE GROUP

↔ 20–32 in (50–80 cm)
↑ 2–6 ft (0.6–1.8 m)

Tall upright stems. Leaves, usually wing-shaped, vary in size, texture, and color; may be deeply lobed, feathery; often silvery or red-tinted. Small red, pink or salmon flowers in sprays. **'Bubbles'**, fragrant pink flowers, spotted leaves; **'Honeysuckle'**, fragrant pink flowers; **'Irene Nuss'** ★, coral pink flowers, bronze leaves; **'Looking Glass'**, pink flowers, leaves silvery above, red underneath; **'Orange Rubra'**, orange flowers, mid-green leaves. Zones 9–11.

RHIZOMATOUS GROUP

↔ 12–30 in (30–75 cm)
↑ 6–8 in (15–20 cm)

Grow from spreading or upright rhizomes. Short- to long-stemmed, often fleshy leaves, to 12 in (30 cm) wide. Leaf shape, texture, and color variable, often red-tinted undersides and wavy edges. Flowers few to many, mostly pink. Cultivars include **'Munchkin'**, and **'Tiger Paws'**. Zones 9–11.

SEMPERFLORENS GROUP

↔ 12 in (30 cm) ↑ 12 in (30 cm)

Small bushy perennials, usually treated as bedding annuals. Bright green or red, glossy, waxy leaves. Small, white, pink, or red flowers, usually single. Suit cool, fairly moist summers. **All Round Series**, bronze or green foliage; **Alfa Series**, vigorous plants, bronze foliage, including **'Alfa Pink'**; **Ambassador Series**, compact with mid-green foliage; **Cocktail Series**, single flowers, bronze foliage; **Expresso Series**, bronze foliage, including **'Expresso Scarlet'**; **Inferno Series**, vigorous and resilient, including **'Inferno Apple Blossom'**; **Lotto Mixed**, all colors, large and vigorous; **Prelude Series**, early blooming, rich green foliage; and **Senator Series**, early blooming, bronze foliage. Zones 9–11.

SHRUB-LIKE GROUP

↔ 18–48 in (45–120 cm)
↑ 12–36 in (30–90 cm)

Bushy plants; leaves variably sized, colored, and textured, hairy or smooth, often red-veined. Flowers usually pink or cream, sometimes red or white, usually small and clustered. **'Cockatoo'**, pinkish red flowers; **'Ginny'**, dark green leaves, pink flowers; **'Red Amigo'**, scarlet flowers; **'Richmondensis'** ★, lush green leaves, pink, red, or white flowers; **'Thurstonii'**, green leaves, red undersides, pink flowers. Zones 9–12.

THICK-STEMMED GROUP

↔ 12–18 in (30–45 cm)
↑ 12–18 in ((30–45 cm)

Strong fleshy-stemmed plants, often quite tall. Variably colored leaves, more than 6 in (15 cm) long, deeply toothed, lobed, or smooth-edged. Small flowers, usually white or pink, sometimes scented. Cultivars include: **'Boomer'**, bronze leaves, white flowers; and **'Gryphon'**, light gray-green and dark green foliage, white flowers. Zones 9–12.

TRAILING OR SCANDENT GROUP

↔ 18–36 in (45–90 cm)
↑ 6–12 in (15–30 cm)

Low spreading plants with lax stems. Usually grown in hanging baskets but sometimes climbing. Leaves usually

Begonia, Semperflorens Group, 'Prelude Bicolor'

Begonia, Shrub-like Group, 'Red Amigo'

small to medium-sized, smooth or hairy, often dark green. Sprays of small flowers are white, pink, or red and often scented. Cultivars include: **'Crackling Fire Pink'**, compact, vivid hot pink flowers; and **'Inferno'**, abundant fiery orange-red flowers. Zones 9–12.

TUBEROUS GROUP

↔ 12–20 in (30–50 cm)
↑ 12–32 in (30–80 cm)

This group of plants grow from large flat tubers, producing short, heavy, succulent stems carrying large, often hairy leaves. There is a huge range of flower types and colors, including many that resemble roses. They are suitable for indoor or outdoor cultivation, flowering mainly from mid-summer to frost. **'Coppelia'**, large crimson-edged white flowers; **'Fairylight'**, pink-edged white flowers; **'Roy Hartley'**, large salmon pink flowers. The **Non-Stop Series** and **Pin-up Series** ★ include a variety of attractive plants. Zones 8–10.

BELLEVALIA

The 40 species of spring-flowering bulbs that make up this asparagus (Asparagaceae) family genus are found from Portugal to northeastern

B

Bellevalia romana

Afghanistan. They are closely related to the grape hyacinths *(Muscari)* and many species could easily be mistaken for them. Foliage ranges from fine and grassy to strappy. Although each bulb produces few leaves, typically 3 to 6, some species that form clusters of bulbs can produce quite large clumps of foliage. The small, tubular, funnel-, bell-, or urn-shaped flowers are borne in heads on upright stems usually held clear of the foliage. Flowers are often in pale blue to purple shades or white. CULTIVATION: Tolerant of moderate frosts and at home in a mild-temperate climate, these interesting bulbs thrive in rockery conditions and alpine troughs. Plant in a bright but not sunny position with gritty, humus-rich, well-drained soil kept moist in spring. Propagate by root division when dormant.

Bellevalia paradoxa

syns *Bellevalia pycnantha, Muscari paradoxum of gardens*

↔ 12 in (30 cm) ↑16 in (40 cm)

Found from eastern Turkey to Iran and Armenia. Broad dark green leaves, sometimes blue-tinted, 3 per bulb. Flower stem to 16 in (40 cm) tall, with dense heads of small, dark purple, urn-shaped flowers. Zones 7–9.

Bellevalia romana

syn. *Hyacinthus romanus*

↔ 12 in (30 cm) ↑12 in (30 cm)

From southern France. Probably the most widely cultivated species. Fleshy bright green leaves to 12 in (30 cm) long. Green- to soft brown-tinted cream flowers slightly more than ¼ in (6 mm) long. Zones 7–9.

BELLIS

BELLIS DAISY, BRUISEWORT, LAWN DAISY

This European and Mediterranean genus of 7 species of annual and perennial daisies (family Asteraceae) includes the common daisy *(B. perennis)*, which is the little white flower often seen on lawns. The genus name is derived from the Latin *bellus*, meaning pretty, and although wild species are sometimes weeds, cultivated forms are indeed attractive. They have much larger flowerheads with many more ray florets and a wider color range than wild plants. *Bellis* plants form flat rosettes of spoon- to kidney-shaped leaves and carry their flowerheads on individual stems. The leaves and extracts have been used in herbal medicines to treat wounds and for their unique anti-inflammatory properties. CULTIVATION: Best in cool-temperate climates in a sunny or part-shaded open position with good air movement and soil that remains moist during the growing season. White rust and mildew can occur in humid conditions. The fancy cultivars are propagated by division, others from seed.

Bellis perennis

BELLIS DAISY, ENGLISH DAISY

↔ 4–8 in (10–20 cm) ↑2–4 in (5–10 cm)

Originally from temperate Eurasia; now naturalized in most temperate zones. Leaves 1–2 in (25–50 mm) long, broad, spatula-shaped. White flowers, sometimes tinted pink, with yellow centers, from late winter. **'Dresden China'**, very compact, soft pink, double flowers. The **Pomponette Series** was developed from the pink-flowered dwarf **'Pomponette'** to include white and a wide range of pink and red shades. **'Rob Roy'** is a robust plant with tall flower stems and red double flowers. Zones 4–10.

BERBERIDOPSIS

This group of two species of evergreen climbing shrubs is the type genus for their family, the Berberidopsidaceae. One of the species is from Australia. The other more widely cultivated species is from South America, mainly Chile; it is very rare in the wild and may even be extinct. The shrubs can be trained to 15 ft (4.5 m) in height, with a similar spread, and are grown for their ornamental foliage and sprays of pendent pink to scarlet flowers, in summer–early autumn. CULTIVATION: These plants grow best in moist woodland, in acid to neutral soil. They dislike hot summers, and prefer a sheltered site in partial shade with root protection in winter. While moisture is essential, good free drainage is also needed. Propagate from seed in spring, half-hardened cuttings in late summer, or layered trailing branches in autumn. In areas prone to hard frost, grow in a greenhouse.

Berberidopsis corallina

CORAL PLANT

↔ 5–8 ft (1.5–2.4 m) ↑15 ft (4.5 m)

Evergreen climber native to Chile. Heart-shaped to oval dark green leaves sometimes end in tiny spines. Flowers rounded, dark red, ½ in (12 mm) in diameter, on 2 in (5 cm) long scarlet stalks, in summer–autumn. Zones 8–9.

BERBERIS

BARBERRY

This Berberidaceae family genus consists of more than 450 species of evergreen and deciduous shrubs, mainly seen across the Northern Hemisphere, with a smaller group in the South American Andes. They are variable in size, with spines on their branches, and are generally cultivated for the ornamental value of their leaves, flowers, and berries. Plants are used to make dye for cloth, leather, wood, and hair. All of the plant parts are supposed to cause mild stomach upsets if eaten. *B.* × *stenophylla* has become a serious pest in New Zealand. Many North American botanists now include all of the *Mahonia* species in *Berberis*. CULTIVATION: *Berberis* will grow in most well-drained to fairly heavy soils. Tropical African species prefer rocky soil in mountainous areas. Plants can be grown in full sun or partial shade but autumn color is better in full sun. Propagate from softwood cuttings in early summer, or half-hardened cuttings later in summer. Seed will often not come true. Site with care as branch spines can be hazardous.

Berberis × *carminea*

↔ 8 ft (2.4 m) ↑5 ft (1.5 m)

A hybrid of *B. aggregata* and *B. wilsoniae*. Leaves are egg-shaped, dull gray-green. Flowers yellow, arranged in clusters of 10 to 16 blooms per panicle, in late spring–early summer. Fruits red or orange, in dense clusters. **'Barbarossa'**, showy bright red fruits; **'Pirate King'**, **dense foliage.** Zones 6–9.

Berberis × *gladwynensis*

↔ 4 ft (1.2 m) ↑3–6 ft (0.9–1.8 m)

Evergreen garden hybrid, hardly known outside the USA. **'William Penn'** ★ is the cultivar normally found, forming a broad mound to 4 ft (1.2 m) tall; shiny dark green leaves 1 in (25 mm) long, turn bronzy red in winter. Zones 6–9.

Bellis perennis

Berberidopsis corallina

B

Berberis × *ottawensis* f. *purpurea*

Berberis thunbergii f. *atropurpurea*

Bergenia crassifolia 'Perfecta'

Berberis koreana

KOREAN BARBERRY

☼ ❄ ↔5 ft (1.5 m) ↑5 ft (1.5 m)

From Korea, a compact deciduous shrub with spines encircling the stem. Leaves oblong to egg-shaped, serrated edges, 2½ in (6 cm) long, color in autumn. Flowers yellow, in clusters; glossy red berries. Zones 4–9.

Berberis × *ottawensis*

HYBRID PURPLE BARBERRY

☼ ❄ ↔8 ft (2.4 m) ↑8 ft (2.4 m)

A cross between *B. thunbergii* and *B. vulgaris*. Leaves mid-green, egg-shaped. Flowers pale yellow, in clusters, in spring. Fruits egg-shaped red berries. ***B.*** × ***o.*** **f.** ***purpurea***, purple-red foliage; **'Superba'** (syn. 'Purpurea'), new growth almost bronze. ***B.*** × ***o.*** **'Silver Miles'**, dark purplish red leaves marked silvery gray. Zones 5–10.

Berberis × *stenophylla*

☼ ❄ ↔15 ft (4.5 m) ↑10 ft (3 m)

Parents of this vigorous evergreen shrub are *B. darwinii* and *B. empetrifolia*. Leaves narrow, elliptical, ¾ in (18 mm) long, dark green above, bluish green beneath. Flowers deep yellow, in late spring. Fruits black with blue bloom. **'Corallina Compacta'**, grows to height and spread of 12 in (30 cm); **'Crawley Gem'**, rounded form, red flowers; **'Irwinii'**, golden yellow flowers; and **'Lemon Queen'** (syn. **'Cornish Cream'**), creamy white flowers. Zones 6–9.

Berberis thunbergii

JAPANESE BARBERRY

☼ ❄ ↔8 ft (2.4 m) ↑3 ft (0.9 m)

Native to Japan, deciduous shrub with compact foliage and rounded shape. Leaves egg-shaped, smooth, fresh green above, bluish green beneath. Flowers pale yellow, can be tinged red, in racemes, in mid-spring. Fruits glossy red. Often used for hedging. ***B. t.*** **f.** ***atropurpurea***, purple-red stems and leaves. ***B. t.*** **'Golden Ring'**, red-purple leaves, narrow yellow margins; **'Helmond Pillar'**, to 5 ft (1.5 m) tall, dark red foliage; **'Red Chief**, to 6 ft (1.8 m) tall, pink-variegated leaves; **'Rose Glow'** ★, red-purple foliage flecked with white. Zones 4–9.

BERGENIA

PIGSQUEAK

Found in Asia, from Afghanistan to Mongolia, this genus of the saxifrage (Saxifragaceae) family is made up of 8 species of perennials. Large leathery leaves sprout from tough, woody, fleshy stems. Leaves are broad, often light green, and usually at least 8 in (20 cm) long. They are complemented by long-stemmed heads of 5-petalled flowers in spring. Species most often have pink flowers but garden forms occur in white and shades of pink, red, and mauve. Named for the eighteenth-century German botanist, Karl August von Bergen, the genus is commonly known as pigsqueak because of the sound that is made when the wet leaves are rubbed between one's fingers. CULTIVATION: For lush foliage, plant in cool moist conditions in part-shade in soil rich in humus. Plants in full sun often flower well but at the expense of their leaves, which burn. Excellent in large rockeries. Propagation is by division after flowering.

Bergenia ciliata

HAIRY BERGENIA, HEARTLEAF

◐ ❄ ↔32 in (80 cm) ↑12 in (30 cm)

Himalayan native. Densely hairy, dark green, rounded leaves to 12 in (30 cm) long. Pink-tinted white flowers to 2 in (5 cm) wide on 12 in (30 cm) high stems. Zones 7–10.

Bergenia crassifolia

syn. *Bergenia cordifolia*

HEARTLEAF SAXIFRAGE, PIGSQUEAK

◐ ❄ ↔16–32 in (40–80 cm) ↑12 in (30 cm)

Tough evergreen perennial from Siberia and Mongolia. Rounded, toothed-edged leaves to 8 in (20 cm) long on strong petioles. Bright pink flowers on red stems from late winter. Old leaves often develop red tones in autumn. **'Beethoven'**, white to pale pink flowers, red calyces and stems; **'Perfecta'**, red-tinted foliage, very tall flower stems; **'Purpurea'**, purple-tinted winter foliage, red flowers on tall stems; **'Red Start'**, bronze leaves, magenta to cerise flowers. Zones 3–10.

Bergenia purpurascens

◐ ❄ ↔20–48 in (50–120 cm) ↑12–18 in (30–45 cm)

From eastern Himalayas. Leaves to 10 in (25 cm) long, purple-tinted, hair-fringed, often shallowly toothed. Pendulous deep pink to maroon flowers on red stems. Early-blooming. Zones 4–9.

Bergenia Hybrid Cultivars

☼/◐ ❄ ↔16–32 in (40–80 cm) ↑8–16 in (20–40 cm)

Mainly derived from *B. cordifolia* and *B. crassifolia* and generally resembling the former in size and leaf shape. Need some sunlight for the best leaf color. Cultivars include: **'Abendglut'** (syn. 'Evening Glow'), compact, wavy-edged red-tinted foliage, purple-red semi-double flowers; **'Ballawley'** (syn. 'Delbees'), glossy leaves, purple-tinted in winter, red flowers; **'Bressingham White'**, pure white flowers; **'Eroica'**, bronze- to purple-tinted foliage, purple-red flowers; **'Morgenröte'** (syn. 'Morning Blush'), large bronze green leaves and deep purple-red flowers; **'Rosi Klose'**, dark green leaves, pink flowers; **'Silberlicht'** (syn. 'Silver Light'), large leaves, white flowers ageing to pink; and **'Sunningdale'**, bronze-to red-tinted winter foliage, deep lavender-pink flowers. Zones 3–9.

BERGERA

Belonging to the rue (Rutaceae family), this genus consists of a single species of evergreen shrub or small tree from tropical Asia, until recently accepted as part of the genus *Murraya*. It differs in its longer pinnate leaves, smaller flowers in larger corymbs, and dark bluish fruit. The leaves and flowers contain essential oils with a unique aroma, valued in cooking and perfumery in India and Asian countries. CULTIVATION: It is easily grown in frost free, warm-temperate to tropical climates, in any moderately fertile, well-drained soil, in a protected position. Propagate from seed or half-hardened cuttings.

Bergera koenigii

syn. *Murraya koenigii*

CURRY LEAF, CURRY TREE

☼ ❄ ↔12 ft (3.5 m) ↑15 ft (4.5 m)

Evergreen tree from Asia. Aromatic leaves, leaflets with long pointed tips, finely serrated edges. Small, white or yellow-tinted, fragrant flowers, in corymbs from branch tips, in spring. Blue-black berries. Zones 10–12.

BERLANDIERA

GREEN EYES

This genus of around 12 species of daisy (Asteraceae) family perennials occurs in southern North America and is known in cultivation through 2 or 3 species with unusually colored or

B

scented flowers. They form dandelion-like basal clumps of bright green to blue-green, deeply lobed, toothed leaves that may die away over winter or simply be reduced to smaller rosettes. Some species develop more upright and woody stems clothed with similar leaves. Summer flowerheads are borne on long, upright, wiry stems and usually have bright yellow ray florets with contrastingly colored disc florets. Flowers sometimes have a scent rather like chocolate.
CULTIVATION: Easily grown, hardy, and drought-tolerant once established, most species prefer to grow in full sun in light, gritty, free-draining soil with a little extra humus. Water in summer but otherwise keep dry. Propagate from seed or by careful root division in late winter.

Berlandiera lyrata

BROOCH FLOWER, CHOCOLATE FLOWER, LYRE-LEAF GREEN EYES

☼ ❄ ↔12 in (30 cm) ↑12 in (30 cm)

Native to southern USA and Mexico. Perennial with light green lyre-shaped leaves. Yellow fine-rayed daisies are borne year round. The flowers have dark centers and are heavily scented with a chocolate-like fragrance. Their green cup-like bracts persist after flowering, providing further interest. Zones 8–11.

BESCHORNERIA

Native to Mexico, the 7 perennial rosette-forming species in this genus resemble agave and belong to the same asparagus (Asparagaceae) family. The genus differs from *Agave* in that the stamens are shorter than the perianth segments. Leaves are up to 5 ft (1.5 m) long, lance- to sword-shaped, fleshy and bluish green, with rough margins. Surrounded by colorful bracts, flowers are clustered in racemes or panicles to 7 ft (2 m) or more tall. The 6 erect perianth segments are broadest toward the tips and are green tinged red, while the 6 stamens have delicate filaments and versatile

Bergera koenigii

Berlandiera lyrata

Beta vulgaris, Cicla Group, 'Rhubarb Chard'

anthers. The ovary is inferior, with 3 compartments and a slender style. The fruit is a capsule with many seeds. The leaves provide a soap substitute, and the flowers of some species are edible.
CULTIVATION: Most are frost tender, requiring full sun and needing greenhouse protection in cool regions. Propagate from seed, from suckers, or by division.

Beschorneria yuccoides

☼ ❄ ↔7 ft (2 m) ↑4–6 ft (1.2–1.8 m)

Dense clump of gray-green to blue-green sword-shaped leaves to more than 24 in (60 cm) long. Arching deep pink- to red-stemmed inflorescence with green flowers within large pinkish red bracts. Zones 9–11.

BETA

BEET

A member of the amaranth (Amaranthaceae) family, this genus contains one biennial species with 2 main forms. One is grown for its roots (beets), the other for its leaves (chards). Wild forms are often found on the Mediterranean coastline, western Europe, and parts of Asia growing at the high-tide mark. Leaves small and glossy to large and crinkly or puckered. Insignificant flowers are followed by knobbly seeds in profusion. Leaves of both forms are edible. Roots were used as a food source from the sixteenth century.
CULTIVATION: Beets favor light well-drained soil, not too rich. Chards prefer rich moist soil. Grow from seed.

Beschorneria yuccoides

Beta vulgaris

BEET

☼ ❄ ↔27 in (70 cm) ↑27 in (70 cm)

The original wild or sea beet (also classified as *B. v.* subsp. *maritima*) is a perennial growing on seashores of Europe, North Africa, and western Asia. All cultivated beets are believed to be derived from it, including beetroot, sugar beet, fodder beets such as mangel-wurzel, chard, and spinach beet. They have often been treated as all falling within *B. v.* subsp. *vulgaris*, but this is now regarded as a wrong application of the concept of subspecies. Rather they should be divided among the following cultivar groups:

Cicla Group (syn. *B. v.* var. *cicla*, *B. v.* var. *flavescens*): Includes spinach beets, closest to wild beet with slender green leaf stalk and flat blade, but also chards or silver beets with larger leaves puckered to varying degree, stalk and midrib broad, white or colored, root not swollen. **'Bright Lights'** ★ (syns 'Five Colour Mix', 'Rainbow'), stems in shades of red, orange, yellow, pink, and white, or are bicolored; **'Bright Yellow'**, yellow stems and green crinkly leaves; **'Lucullus'**, huge, crinkly or puckered, glossy, green leaves, and wide white midrib and veins; **'Mostruosa'**, refined Italian strain with broad, bright green, puckered leaves; **'Rhubarb Chard'** ★, crimson stalks and dark green crinkly leaves, midribs can be used as substitute for asparagus or celery.

Betula lenta

BETULA

BIRCH

This genus gives its name to the birch family, Betulaceae, and consists of about 60 deciduous small shrubs or tall trees occurring throughout temperate and arctic zones of the Northern Hemisphere. Tree trunks are often marked in different shades; in many species the outer layer of bark peels off. Wood is used for timber; sap and leaves are used medicinally, as food or drink, or as dye-stuff. Pendulous male catkins and erect female catkins are carried on the same tree in early spring. Leaves are mid- to dark green, ovate in shape, with indented margins. Beautiful ornamental trees.
CULTIVATION: Birches are hardy trees, withstanding extreme cold and exposure to wind. Best in well-drained fertile soil, with some moisture and full sun or light shade. Take softwood cuttings in summer, half-hardened cuttings in autumn. Birches are susceptible to fungi such as *Armillaria melea* and *Piptoporus betulinus*; the latter, specific to the birch family, will destroy the tree.

Betula alleghaniensis ★

syn. *Betula lutea*

YELLOW BIRCH

☼ ❄ ↔30 ft (9 m) ↑80 ft (24 m)

Native to USA and Canada. Peeling yellow or gray bark; young shoots aromatic. Leaves yellow-green, coarsely toothed, to 6 in (15 cm) long. Male catkins 4 in (10 cm) long, erect female catkins. Zones 4–9.

Betula lenta

BLACK BIRCH, CHERRY BIRCH, SWEET BIRCH

☼ ❄ ↔40 ft (12 m) ↑50 ft (15 m)

Native to eastern North America. Bark crimson, becomes scaly and gray ageing to black. Leaves egg-shaped, chartreuse, 4 in (10 cm) long, autumn color. Male catkins pendulous 3 in (8 cm). Female catkins erect. Zones 3–9.

B

Betula papyrifera, in the wild, USA

Betula nigra

RIVER BIRCH, TROPICAL BIRCH

↔15 ft (4.5 m) ↑30 ft (9 m)

Deciduous tree from along rivers in eastern USA. Bark white, smooth then thin flaking plates of cream, salmon, and pale brown. Dark and furrowed with age. Tolerates heat and dryness. **'Heritage'**, peeling cream to pale brown bark; **'Little King'**, dwarf cultivar, to 10 ft (3 m) tall. Zones 4–9.

Betula papyrifera

CANOE BIRCH, PAPER BIRCH, WHITE BIRCH

↔30 ft (9 m) ↑60 ft (18 m)

North America. Deciduous. White papery bark peeling to orange-brown. Light canopy allows sunlight through. Tolerates cold and drought. Zones 2–8.

Betula pendula

EUROPEAN SILVER BIRCH, EUROPEAN WHITE BIRCH

↔35 ft (10 m) ↑80 ft (24 m)

A deciduous tree that comes from northern Europe. It is commonly found on poor soils. The foliage turns clear yellow in autumn. Beautiful winter silhouette, arching habit, and white bark. Trunk blackens with age. Adaptable to confined spaces. **'Dalecarlica'** (weeping birch), with dissected foliage; **'Fastigiata'**, an erect tree to 70 ft (21 m); **'Laciniata'**, loses leaves earlier in autumn than species; **'Purpurea'**, with thin pendulous branches; **'Tristis'**, narrowly conical habit; **'Youngii'** ★, usually sold as a grafted tree with a strongly weeping head. Zones 2–8.

Betula platyphylla

↔40 ft (12 m) ↑70 ft (21 m)

Native to Siberia, northeastern China, Korea, and Japan. Bark pure white. Leaves chartreuse, 4 in (10 cm) long, egg-shaped with serrated margins. Male catkins to 3 in (8 cm) long; female catkins to 1¼ in (3 cm) long. Zones 4–9.

Betula pumila

AMERICAN DWARF BIRCH

↔3 ft (0.9 m) ↑3 ft (0.9 m)

Erect shrub native to northeastern America. Twigs densely hairy. Leaves green, whitish beneath, roughly serrated, rounded or egg-shaped to 1¼ in (30 mm) long. Catkins to 1 in (25 mm) long, in spring. Zones 2–8.

Betula utilis

HIMALAYAN BIRCH, WHITEBARK

↔30 ft (9 m) ↑60 ft (18 m)

Native to Himalayas and China. Bark pink to orange-brown with white bloom, peels in thin flakes. Leaves dark green, to 5 in (12 cm) long, egg-shaped, unevenly serrated, tapering, turn yellow in autumn. Male catkins 5 in (12 cm) long, female catkins erect. **B. u. var. jacquemontii** (**syn.** *B. jacquemontii*), from Kashmir and Nepal, with white bark; **'Grayswood Ghost'**, brilliant white bark, glossy leaves; **'Jermyns'**, reddish brown bark, ages to white; **'Silver Shadow'**, white bark and deep green leaves. Zones 7–9.

BIDENS

BEGGAR'S TICK, BURR MARIGOLD, PITCHFORKS, SPANISH NEEDLES, STICK TIGHT, TICKSEED

This genus of about 200 annual and perennial species belongs to the daisy (Asteraceae) family. It has a worldwide distribution, with its largest numbers in temperate and tropical Africa and America. The few ornamental forms are used as annual bedding plants. The many common names of the genus come from the sticking hooks on the seeds, which help them to become dispersed over wide areas.

CULTIVATION: These plants require little more than a sunny well-drained site with reasonable moisture-retentive soil. Plant after frosts in very cold climates. Propagate from seed or by division of the perennial forms.

Bidens ferulifolia

Bidens ferulifolia

APACHE BEGGARTICKS

↔12–18 in (30–45 cm) ↑24–36 in (60–90 cm)

From Arizona (USA), Mexico, and Guatemala. Annual or perennial with ferny foliage. Golden wide-rayed daisies, about 1¼ in (30 mm) across, from late summer to autumn. **'Golden Goddess'** and **'Goldmarie'** are improved selections. **'Golden Eye'**, **Goldie/'Innbid'**, and **'Peters Goldteppich'** ★ are lower trailing cultivars. **'Flair'** is low and bushy, suits hanging baskets. Zones 8–11.

BIGNONIA

This genus belongs to the trumpet-vine (Bignoniaceae) family. It formerly contained a large number of species, but reclassification at one time reduced it to just 1 species. Recently a few have been returned to the genus. Most are strong-growing climbers with simple or pinnate leaves and clusters of sometimes large trumpet-shaped flowers.

CULTIVATION: Grow in well-drained fertile soil in full sun or part-shade. In cooler climates grow in the greenhouse, with protection from the hottest summer sun. Cut back previous season's growth by two-thirds in early spring. Mealybugs can be serious pests. Propagate from seed or by layering.

Bignonia capreolata

CROSS-VINE, QUARTER VINE, TRUMPET FLOWER

↔10 ft (3 m) ↑10–30 ft (3–9 m)

From southeastern USA. Vigorous summer-flowering vine, climbs by tendrils. Leaves opposite, deep green. Showy heads of flaring trumpet flowers 2 in (5 cm) long, deep orange to scarlet with darker throat. **'Tangerine Beauty'**, orange flowers with yellow throats. Zones 7–9.

BILLARDIERA

This Australian pittosporum (Pittosporaceae) family genus is made up of around 25 species of evergreen shrubs and small vines. Most have simple, narrow, elliptical leaves, often aromatic when crushed. The flowers are small, usually tubular or a widely flared bell shape, mostly pale yellow,

Billardiera heterophylla

mauve, or blue. Fleshy edible berries follow and can be quite showy, ripening to bright purple or magenta in some species.

CULTIVATION: Plant in a sunny or partly shaded position. The soil should be well-drained, and the plants will be more vigorous if watered well during the growing season. Trim as necessary to keep compact. Propagate from half-hardened cuttings or, in the case of the vines, from layers.

Billardiera heterophylla

syns *Sollya fusiformis, S. heterophylla*

AUSTRALIAN BLUEBELL, BLUEBELL CREEPER

↔3–5 ft (0.9–1.5m)
↕5–7 ft (1.5–2 m)

Twining climber native to Western Australia. Narrow, aromatic, mid- to dark green leaves. Can take time to fill out. Intense blue flowers hang in groups, in summer. Can be invasive. ***B. h.* subsp. *parviflora*** has smaller, deeper blue flowers. ***B. h.* 'Alba'** has creamy white flowers. Zones 9–11.

BISMARCKIA

Endemic to Madagascar, this genus in the family Arecaceae has a single species, a fairly large fan palm with a solitary stout trunk topped by a crown of large fronds. These are roughly circular and divided to about half their depth into stiffly radiating segments. Male and female flowers in panicles on separate trees. Tiny male flowers on curving crimson spikes, female flowers on sparser yellowish spikes. Fruits are date-sized, with a single large seed.

CULTIVATION: Widely grown in tropics and subtropics. Best with a distinct dry season, but tolerates cooler and moister regions if planted in a hot sunny position. Propagate from fresh seed with the flesh stripped off; germination requires a container at least 12 in (30 cm) deep to accommodate the downward-growing cotyledon.

Bismarckia nobilis

Bistorta officinalis

Bismarckia nobilis ★

syn. *Medemia nobilis*

↔12 ft (3.5 m) ↕60 ft (18 m)

Attractive palm, trunk gray, slightly rough. Fronds large, pale bluish green, on a thick stalk about 6 ft (1.8 m) long, split into an inverted Y-shape at the base. Brown fruits. Zones 10–12.

BISTORTA

BISTORT, KNOTWEED

This genus in the knotweed (Polygonaceae) family has taken many species from *Polygonum* and *Persicaria*, as their classification has become better determined. These plants are evergreen or deciduous perennials, found over much of the Northern Hemisphere. They are mainly low, spreading plants with wiry stems, simple leaves, and tiny flowers crowded into dense terminal spikes, mostly in white to pink shades.

CULTIVATION: Although very easily grown, sometimes too easily, as they can be invasive, most will do best if shaded from the hottest summer sun and given ample moisture. Propagation is by division, or from softwood or half-hardened cuttings or layers, which may strike naturally.

Bistorta bistortoides

syn. *Persicaria bistortoides*

AMERICAN BISTORT, SMART WEED

↔8–20 in (20–50 cm)
↕8–20 in (20–50 cm)

Perennial herb from moist to wet sub-alpine meadows in northwest USA. Sword-shaped to elliptical leaves, 4–10 in (10–25 cm) long, arising from central base on winged stalks. Leafless flower stems also arise from central base. White to pinkish white, small, 5-petalled flowers in spike-like, dense, terminal racemes in summer. Zones 3–5.

Bistorta officinalis

syn. *Persicaria bistorta*

BISTORT, EASTER LEDGES, SNAKEWEED

↔6–30 in (15–75 cm)
↕6–30 in (15–75 cm)

Perennial from northern Europe and northern and western Asia. Stout rootstock; wavy, triangular, oval or oblong leaves, 4–8 in (10–20 cm) long, with rounded tips and flattened bases, borne on winged stalks. Dense cylindrical spikes of white or rose pink flowers in summer. Eaten as blood-purifying vegetable in parts of Britain, and in Lake District as traditional Easter dish known as "Yarby" or herb pudding. **'Superba'** (syn. 'Superbum'), dense spikes of soft pinkish red flowers. Zones 3–7.

Bistorta vaccinifolia

syn. *Persicaria vaccinifolia*

↔20–36 in (50–90 cm)
↕6–7 in (15–18 cm)

Trailing, slightly woody, deciduous ground cover from Himalayas. Leaves to 1 in (25 mm) long, often turning attractive colors before shedding. Small spikes to 3 in (8 cm) long of tiny pink flowers in late summer. Zones 7–10.

Bistorta vivipara

syn. *Persicaria vivipara*

ALPINE BISTORT, SERPENT GRASS

↔2–12 in (5–30 cm)
↕2–12 in (5–30 cm)

Tufting perennial species widely distributed throughout Northern Hemisphere from temperate regions to Arctic Circle. Erect stems emerge from thick, bulb-like rootstock. Leaves narrow, dark green, sword-shaped, 1–4 in (2.5–10 cm) long; leaf margins are rolled, lower leaves have long stalks. Slender terminal spikes, 1–4 in (2.5–10 cm) long, of white to pale pink flowers with burnt red tips, lower flowers replaced by purplish-brown bulbils in summer. Zones 2–7.

Blechnum spicant

BLECHNUM

A genus of 200 terrestrial or epiphytic ferns in the Blechnaceae family, most native to Australasia and Southeast Asia and from Mexico to southern South America. A single species, *B. spicant*, is widely distributed in cooler parts of Northern Hemisphere. Erect or running fleshy stems covered in glossy brown scales. New fronds often red, bronze, or pink. Upright fronds, glossy and thick, pinnate or deeply and pinnately lobed, dark green in some species, lighter green in softer species. Fertile fronds, carrying continuous linear spore-bodies parallel to midrib, are narrower and more erect than spreading sterile fronds.

CULTIVATION: Mostly frost tender or half-hardy only; prefer slightly acidic, moist, humus-rich soil in a protected dense shade. Propagate from spores on constantly moist sphagnum moss.

Blechnum spicant

DEER FERN, HARD FERN, LADDER FERN

↔12–18 in (30–45 cm)
↕12–18 in (30–45 cm)

Low-growing tufted fern from North America, Europe, and temperate Asia. Rhizome short-creeping, erect, stout. Spreading, lance-shaped, leathery, dark green sterile fronds, 6–8 in (15–20 cm) long and about 1½ in (35 mm) across, with up to 60 pairs of closely set leaflets. The fertile fronds are taller, up to 30 in (75 cm) long. **'Cristatum'**, compact form reaching 4–8 in (10–20 cm) high, with crested frond tips. Zones 5–9.

B

BLETILLA

CHINESE GROUND ORCHID

This genus in the family Orchidaceae contains about 10 species of deciduous sympodial terrestrial orchids from temperate regions of China, Taiwan, and Japan. They are dormant in autumn and winter, blooming with the flush of new growth in early spring.

CULTIVATION: They require a well drained, but rich, potting mixture that retains moisture, and also can be grown in the garden. They can be grown in semi-shade to full sun, and appreciate regular watering in spring and summer. Caterpillars can often disfigure the leaves, particularly the young shoots after their dormant period. They will withstand cold winters, however, the new growth needs to be protected from any late heavy frosts.

Bletilla striata

☼/◐ ✱ ↔ 12–48 in (30–120 cm)
↑ 12–24 in (30–60 cm)

A hardy species, frequently grown as a garden plant, often without the owner knowing it is an orchid! Up to eight 2 in (5 cm) wide pale pink to rose-purple (rarely white) blooms that resemble a small *Cattleya* flower. There is also a form with a variegated leaf. Zones 6–11.

BOLTONIA

FALSE CHAMOMILE

A genus of about 8 species of tall perennials in the daisy (Asteraceae) family, the plants are found in central and eastern USA and northeastern Asia, where they grow in moist soils. Their upright leafy stems bear masses of daisy-like flowers in late summer and autumn. The flowers have a yellow eye and are white, pink, mauve, or purple.

CULTIVATION: Showy and easily grown in borders or "wild" gardens, these plants can be cultivated in any moderately fertile soil in full sun or part-shade. Stake in exposed positions. Regular division will maintain vigor. Propagate by division or from seed.

Boltonia asteroides

☼ ✱ ↔ 5 ft (1.5 m) ↑ 3–5 ft (0.9–1.5 m)

Clump-forming perennial from eastern USA. Leaves narrow, to 4 in (10 cm) long. Erect leafy stems bear masses of starry white daisies in late summer–autumn. ***B. a.*** **var.** ***latisquama***, taller plant with large mauve daisies. ***B. a.*** **'Snowbank'**, strong grower to 7 ft (2 m) tall, white daisies. Zones 4–10.

Bletilla striata

BOMBAX

This distinctive genus of large tropical deciduous trees, a member of the mallow (Malvaceae) family, consists of around 20 species from tropical Africa, southern Asia, and northern Australia. They grow around rock outcrops or along river valleys. Trunks are thick and straight, with tiered branches, often buttressed at the base. Bark is often armed with conical prickles. Leaves are compound with 5 or more leaflets attached to a common stalk. Appearing on leafless branches in the dry season, the large flowers have 5 tongue-shaped red, white, or yellow petals and a central mass of stamens. Large fruits split when ripe to release oily seeds embedded in white hairs.

CULTIVATION: *Bombax* species are easily grown in the tropics; plants prefer a sheltered site, deep, fertile, well-drained soil, and subsoil moisture. Fast growing when young; can be short lived if attacked by termites and other insects. Propagate from fresh seed or tip cuttings, planted in the wet season.

Bombax ceiba

syn. ***Bombax malabaricum***

SILK COTTON TREE

☼ ❄ ↔ 30–40 ft (9–12 m) ↑ 60 ft (18 m)

This widespread Asian species is a broadly spreading, heavy-limbed tree. Trunk prickly when young. Flowers profuse, deep scarlet, appear in the tropical dry season (spring). In Asia, young leaves and flowers used as vegetables; fiber obtained from the bark. Zones 10–12.

BORAGO

BORAGE, TAILWORT

Part of the borage (Boraginaceae) family, this genus is made up of just 3 species of annuals or short-lived perennials from Europe that are usually used in the herb garden or wilder spots where their self-seeding tendencies won't be a problem. The leaves are rough to touch and the summer flowers are usually a rich blue. The flowers are much loved by bees, and can be eaten in salads. The aromatic young leaves can also be eaten.

CULTIVATION: Any moisture-retentive soil in sun or half-sun will suit. Propagation is from self-sown seed that will need to be thinned out.

Borago officinalis f. *alba*

Bougainvillea × ***buttiana*** 'Barbara Karst'

Borago officinalis

BORAGE

☼ ✱ ↔ 12–36 in (30–90 cm)
↑ 20–24 in (50–60 cm)

Vigorous, self-seeding, upright annual. rough leaves to 10 in (25 cm) long. Large open heads of rich blue flowers in summer to 1 in (25 mm) across. ***B. o.*** **f.** ***alba***, white-flowered form that comes true from seed as long as it is not near blue forms. Zones 5–10.

Borago pygmaea

syn. ***Borago laxiflora***

◐ ❄ ↔ 10–12 in (25–30 cm)
↑ 10–12 in (25–30 cm)

Short-lived open-growing perennial. Rough leaves to 6 in (15 cm) long. Bright blue flowers in summer. Usually not as invasive as *B. officinalis*. Zones 7–11.

BORONIA

Noted for its sweet fragrance, early spring blooms, and aromatic foliage, this genus is a member of the rue (Rutaceae) family and consists of approximately 100 species of small to medium-sized, compact, evergreen shrubs, nearly all from Australia. They have simple or pinnate leaves and small 4-petalled flowers that may be open and star-shaped or bell-like with overlapping petals. Flowers come in a range of colors from white, pink, and bluish mauve to red, yellow, yellow-green, and brown. Some species can be short lived.

CULTIVATION: Locate boronias in sheltered positions with the protection of other plants in sun or part-shade. The soil should be well drained with a fairly high organic content; avoid drying out. If growing in pots, ensure that the potting mix does not contain added fertilizers with high phosphorus levels. The flowers generally last well when picked. After flowering, up to one half of the plant can be removed to prolong life and improve bushiness. Propagation is from half-hardened tip cuttings.

Boronia crenulata

Bougainvillea × ***buttiana*** 'Coconut Ice'

Boronia crenulata

◐ ❄ ↔ 3 ft (0.9 m) ↑ 3 ft (0.9 m)

From Western Australia. Upright bushy habit. Aromatic leaves. Masses of pink star-like flowers, in late winter–summer. Attractive plant for a rock garden. Grows best in filtered shade, in a well-drained position with some moisture. Also useful for growing beneath taller shrubs. Zones 9–10.

BOUGAINVILLEA

The 14 species of this South American genus in the four-o-clock (Nyctaginaceae) family, seen in warm-temperate to tropical regions as spectacular climbers, are really scrambling shrubs and usually remain

B

fairly compact or behave as ground covers if left free-standing. Leaves are thin, sometimes downy, and broadly elliptical with pointed tips; stems are protected by long narrow thorns, found at the leaf axils. Foliage is evergreen or deciduous, depending on the species and climate. True flowers, in groups of 1 to 3, are tubular, creamy white to yellow, and around 1 in (25 mm) wide, largely hidden by brightly colored petal-like bracts. The genus is named for the French explorer Louis Antoine de Bougainville (1729–1811).

CULTIVATION: Bougainvilleas will not tolerate heavy or repeated frosts. They prefer light well-drained soil, a sunny position, and will perform better if watered well in summer but not overfed. Bougainvilleas can withstand the heavy pruning necessary to keep the plants shrub-like. Propagate by taking firm cuttings in summer.

Bougainvillea × *buttiana*

↔10–20 ft (3–6 m) ↑17 ft (5 m)

Hybrid between *B. glabra* and *B. peruviana*. It has broad leaves to more than 4 in (10 cm) long with a downy midrib. The bracts are small but densely packed. This cross originated in Trinidad around 1900 and is named after the original cultivar 'Mrs Butt'. Among the many popular hybrid cultivars are: **'Afterglow'**, 8–15 ft (2.4–4.5 m) high, pink suffused orange, fairly sparse foliage; **'Barbara Karst'**, 12–20 ft (3.5–6 m) high, vigorous, red in full sun, deep carmine-pink in part-shade; **'Brilliant Variegated'**, 4–6 ft (1.2–1.8 m) tall, mounding shrub, gray-green and silver variegated foliage, red-brown bracts; **'Coconut Ice'**, 12–15 ft (3.5–4.5 m) high, irregularly marked pink and white bracts; **'Enid Lancaster'** (syns *B.* 'California Gold', 'Hawaiian Glow', 'Sunset', *B.* × *b.* 'Golden Glow'), 12–15 ft (3.5–4.5 m) tall, soft yellow bracts age to gold; **'Killie Campbell'** (syns *B.* 'Green Light', 'Rose Amber'), 12–15 ft (3.5–4.5 m) tall, trailing habit, long-flowering, large bracts open orange-red and age to magenta; **'Lady Mary Baring'**, 12–15 ft (3.5–4.5 m) high, quick-growing, yellow bracts; **'Louise Wathen'** (syn. *B.* 'Orange King'), 15–20 ft (4.5–6 m) high, long stems, copper-orange bracts, tender; **'Mahara'** (syns *B.* 'Manila Red', 'Princess Mahara'), 12–15 ft (3.5–4.5 m) tall, dark green foliage, purple double bracts; **'Mrs Butt'** (syn. *B.* 'Crimson Lake'), 12–15 ft (3.5–4.5 m) high, crimson red, needs heat to flower well; **'Purple Queen'**, 4–8 ft (1.2–2.4 m) tall, bushy, deep purple bracts; **'Rainbow'**, pinkish red bracts that develop various pink tones with age; **'Raspberry Ice'** (syn. *B.* 'Raspberry Ice'), 3–4 ft (0.9–1.2 m) high, bushy, red new growth becomes green with cream to golden edges, vivid magenta bracts, good ground cover or for hanging baskets; **'Rosenka'**, 4–8 ft (1.2–2.4 m) high, golden yellow ageing to soft pink, with large papery bracts; and Texas Dawn/**'Monas'** (syns *B.* 'Purple King', 'Robyn's Glory'), 12–15 ft (3.5–4.5 m) high, large clusters of purple-pink bracts. Zones 9–12.

Bougainvillea glabra

PAPER FLOWER

↔15 ft (4.5 m) ↑10–12 ft (3–5 m)

Native to Brazil, this summer-flowering species features dark green foliage with few hairs. The leaves can reach up to 5 in (12 cm) long. When trained as a climber it can grow to a height or spread of up to 30 ft (9 m). The flower bracts are white to magenta. **'Alba'**, pure white bracts; **'Cypheri'**, deep pink bracts; **'Magnifica'**, masses of short-lived purple bracts; **'Sanderiana Variegated'**, mauve bracts, gray-green and cream variegated foliage. Zones 10–12.

Bougainvillea peruviana

↔12 ft (3.5 m) ↑10–20 ft (3–6 m)

This compact species is native to Peru, Colombia, and Ecuador. The leaves measure up to 4 in (10 cm) long. Slender thorns in leaf axils. The crinkly bracts are pale magenta in color. **'Mary Palmer Special'**, 15–20 ft (4.5–6 m) tall, magenta-pink bracts. Zones 10–12.

Bougainvillea spectabilis

syn. *Bougainvillea brasiliensis*

↔15 ft (4.5 m) ↑12 ft (3.5 m)

Vigorous species from Brazil. Velvety leaves up to 4 in (10 cm) long. Panicles of pink to purple bracts, in spring. Stems have vicious curved thorns. **'Thomasii'** (syn. **'Rosea'**), 15–20 ft (4.5–6 m) high, vigorous climber, deep reddish pink bracts. Zones 10–12.

Bougainvillea Hybrid Cultivars

↔5–20 ft (1.5–6 m) ↑2–20 ft (0.6–6m)

There are many hybrid bougainvilleas with obscure parentage. As might be expected, they are a variable lot covering most sizes and colors. Popular hybrids include: **'Alexandra'**, 15–20 ft (4.5–6 m) high, vigorous, deep magenta-purple; **Bambino Bougs**, range of compact dwarfs, many named cultivars, suit pots or borders; **'Betty Hendry'** (syn. 'Indian Maid'), 8–15 ft (2.4–4.5 m) high, long-flowering, red with occasional purple and yellow flecks; Camarillo Fiesta/**'Monle'**, 15–20 ft (4.5–6 m) high, small leaves with magenta and copper bracts; **'Cherry Blossoms'** (syns *B.* 'Bridal Bouquet', 'Limberlost Beauty'), 7 ft (2 m) tall, compact, slow-growing, white bracts tinted pink, double; **'Closeburn'** (syns 'Helen Johnson', 'Temple Fire', 'Tom Thumb'), 3–5 ft (0.9–1.5 m) high, spreading shrub, good in containers, coppery red bracts; **'Crimson Jewel'**, 2–4 ft (0.6–1.2 m) tall, spreading trailing shrub, ideal for ground cover or hanging basket culture, deep pinkish red bracts; Don Mario/**'Monio'**, 12–15 ft (3.5–4.5 m) high, purple-red bracts; **'Elizabeth Doxey'** (syns 'Apple Blossom', 'Jamaica White', 'Madonna'), 12–15 ft (3.5–4.5 m) tall, white bracts; **'Elsbet'**, 8–12 ft (2.4–3.5 m) high, shrubby with dark leaves and small deep purple bracts; **'Hawaiian White'**, 15–20 ft (4.5–6 m) high, vigorous, white bracts with green veining; **'Isabel Greensmith'**, 12–15 ft (3.5–4.5 m) tall, orange to coppery red bracts; **'Jamburi'**, 15–20 ft (4.5–6 m) tall, vigorous, purple-red to red bracts;

Bougainvillea glabra

B., Hybrid Cultivar, 'Elizabeth Doxey'

B., Hybrid Cultivar, 'Sundance'

'James Walker', 15–20 ft (4.5–6 m) tall, vigorous, deep magenta, large bracts; **'Juanita Hatten'**, 8–15 ft (2.4–4.5 m) high, deep purple-pink bracts; **'La Jolla'**, 3–6 ft (0.9–2 m) high, compact shrub, bright red bracts; **'Lavender Queen'**, 12–15 ft (3.5–4.5 m) high, soft purple bracts; **'Miss Manila'** (syn. 'Tango'), 12–15 ft (3.5–4.5 m) high, pinkish red bracts; **'Oo-La-La'**, 4–8 ft (1.2–2.4 m) high, shrubby growth with deep magenta bracts; **'Pink Tiara'**, 8–15 ft (2.4–4.5 m) high, pale pink bracts, long-flowering; **'Purple Robe'**, 12–15 ft (3.5–4.5 m) tall, large, bright purple-pink bracts; **'Rubyana'**, 15–20 ft (4.5–6 m) tall, vigorous, dark foliage, purple-pink bracts; **'San Diego Red'** (syn. Scarlett O'Hara'), 12–15 ft (3.5–4.5 m) high, massed bright scarlet bracts ageing to magenta, bronze young growth; **'Southern Rose'**, 12–15 ft (3.5–4.5 m) high, bright pink bracts; **'Sundance'**, 8–12 ft (2.4–3.5 m) tall, orange-pink bracts; Tahitian Dawn/**'Monari'**, 15–20 ft (4.5–6 m) tall, vigorous, gold bracts ageing to pink; Torch Glow/**'Pixie'**, (syns 'Pink Pixie', 'Smartipants'), 3–6 ft (0.9–2 m) tall, shrubby, vivid magenta-pink bracts at the stem tips. The **Spectoperuviana Group** includes **'Mary Palmer', 12–15 ft (3.5–4.5 m) tall, with** both pink and white bracts; **'Mary Palmer's Enchantment'**, 15–20 ft (4.5–6 m) tall, very vigorous, pure white bracts. Zones 9–12.

BOUTELOUA

GRAMA GRASS

Found from southern USA and West Indies to Central and South America, this genus of 39 annual or perennial grasses belongs to the family Poaceae. Features clusters or clumps of stiff slender flower stems. Panicles of flowers have one or many branches of delicate, stalkless, "mosquito-like" spikelets on wiry stems, in summer. Leaves with flat or folded blades arise from a central base.

CULTIVATION: Propagate from seed; any garden soil; open sunny position.

Bouteloua curtipendula

SIDEOATS GRASS

↔ 12–18 in (30–45 cm) ↑ 24–32 in (60–80 cm)

Grass native to temperate areas from Canada to Argentina. Panicles of flowers with 30 to 80 branches; 1 to 12 spikelets, each to ½ in (12 mm) long, per branch. Bluish green, rough or slightly hairy leaf blades, to ¼ in (6 mm) wide. Zones 4–9.

Bouteloua gracilis ★

syns *Bouteloua oligostachya, Chondrosum gracile, C. oligostachyum*

BLUE GRAMA, MOSQUITO GRASS, NAVAJITA AZUL, NAVAJITA COMUN

↔ 12 in (30 cm) ↑ 24 in (60 cm)

Grass from plains of southern Canada, USA, and Mexico. Dense arching panicles of flowers with 1 to 4 branches; 1 to 12 spikelets, each to ¼ in (6 mm) long, per branch. Narrow, wispy, sometimes hairy leaf blades, rough to touch. **'Lovington'**, flowers purple fading to yellow. Zones 8–10.

BOUVARDIA

This genus, reaching from southern North America to northern South America, includes several evergreen shrubs among its 30 or so species, and belongs to the madder (Rubiaceae) family. *Bouvardia* tend to be rather sprawling, weak-stemmed plants that need support to keep them upright. Their leaves are not large but they are a pleasant shade of deep green and are usually glossy. The long-tubed flowers are the main attraction. The brighter colors are visually striking, while those in lighter shades or white are fragrant and popular as cut flowers.

CULTIVATION: *Bouvardia* species tolerate light frost only and need a mild climate with rich well-drained soil to flower well. They are best in partial shade and also perform well as greenhouse and conservatory plants. Although inclined to be straggly, light trimming helps to keep them compact and bushy.

Bouvardia ternifolia

↔ 3 ft (0.9 m) ↑ 3 ft (0.9 m)

Soft-stemmed evergreen shrub native to Arizona, Texas, and Mexico. Clustered in corymbs, the tubular flowers are a vivid red. There are several cultivars with flowers in various pink and red shades. Zones 9–11.

Brachyscome iberidifolia 'Blue Star'

BRACHYSCOME

syn. *Brachycome*

DAISY

A popular genus of annuals, perennials, and subshrubs in the daisy (Asteraceae) family. There are 90 to 100 species in the genus, with many cultivars. They occur throughout Australia from coastal to alpine habitats. Leaves are small, bright green, and generally multi-lobed, divided, and/or toothed. Plants can form mats or be suckering or rounded compact bushes. Flowers are a typical daisy type in shades of pink, mauve, blue, purple, lemon, and white, generally with yellow centers. These daisies are popular in rock gardens, pots, hanging baskets, on banks, and at the front of garden borders. Some cultivars have arisen by chance but others are the result of deliberate breeding programs to improve color selections and the size of the flowers.

CULTIVATION: Any well-drained soil in either full or half-sun will do; some plants are more drought/frost tolerant than others. Propagation is from seed, with named cultivars propagated from cuttings or by division.

Bouvardia ternifolia, in the wild, Vera Cruz, Mexico

Brachyscome iberidifolia

SWAN RIVER DAISY

↔ 8–12 in (20–30 cm) ↑ 2–16 in (5–40 cm)

Erect annual daisy with pinnate leaves. Flowers 1 in (25 mm) in diameter in blue, purple, or white throughout spring–summer. Can be frost tender. **'Blue Mist'**, attractive blue flowers; **'Blue Star'** ★, purple-tinted flowers with quilled petals, lightly scented. Zones 9–11.

Brachyscome Hybrid Cultivars

↔ 18 in (45 cm) ↑ 18 in (45 cm)

These hybrids, mostly of *B. angustifolia* and *B. iberidifolia*, are compact heavy-flowering plants. **'Blue Haze'**, compact, low growing, mauve-blue flowers; **'City Lights'**, mounding form with large light lavender-blue flowers; **'Just Jayne'**, compact plant that does sucker, bearing white to pale pink flowers in autumn; **'Lemon Twist'**, spreading ground cover, soft yellow flowers; **'New Amethyst'**, fine foliage, small dark purple flowers in spring–autumn; **'Strawberry Mousse'** has reddish mid-green foliage, spoon-shaped lobed leaves, and bright pink flowers; **'Toucan Tango'** (syn. 'Ultra'), lacy foliage, violet-blue flowers year round; **'Valencia'**, mauve-pink flowers 1½ in (35 mm) in diameter, year round in tropics. Zones 9–11.

Brahea armata

Brahea brandegeei

Brassica juncea, Japonica Group, 'Mizuna'

BRAHEA

syn. *Erythea*

HESPER PALM

This genus of 12 species of attractive small to medium-sized fan palms in the family Arecaceae is from Mexico and Central America. They are usually grown for their striking appearance and beautiful foliage. Mostly from dry rocky habitats, in open woodland and low scrub, most species have a rough-surfaced single trunk topped by a compact crown of fronds. The flattened frond stalks are often edged with spines. The frond blades are fan-shaped. Flowering branches emerge from the frond bases, gracefully arching. The white to yellowish flowers are tiny, crowded densely onto spike-like branchlets. Olive-shaped fruits ripen to blue-black; some are edible.

CULTIVATION: They are sun-loving palms, easily grown in most warm-temperate to subtropical climates, best where summers are hot and dry. Most will tolerate light frosts. Best in well-drained moderately fertile soil with adequate subsoil moisture. Trim away the dead fronds. If left untrimmed the dead fronds form a thatch or "skirt" beneath the crown. Propagate from seed; early growth is often slow but may speed up after a trunk shows beneath the fronds.

Brahea armata ★

syn. *Erythea armata*

BLUE HESPER PALM, HESPER PALM

↔10 ft (3 m) ↑25 ft (8 m)

From the Baja California peninsula of western Mexico. Fronds stiff, pale blue-gray. Trunk stout. Flowering branches to 15 ft (4.5 m) long, arching in a complete semicircle and held well clear of the foliage. Tiny cream flowers attract numerous insects. Zones 9–11.

Brahea brandegeei

syn. *Erythea brandegeei*

BRANDEGEE HESPER PALM, SAN JOSE HESPER PALM

↔15 ft (4.5 m) ↑40 ft (12 m)

From steep canyons in southern Baja California, near San Jose del Cabo, Mexico. Trunk brownish, slender, tapering upward. Fronds pale green, drooping, partly hiding the flowering branches. Collected in 1900 by the California botanist Brandegee. **'Elegans'** (syn. *Erythea* 'Elegans'), dwarf form, usually under 5 ft (1.5 m) tall. Zones 9–12.

Brahea edulis

syn. *Erythea edulis*

GUADALUPE PALM

↔20 ft (6 m) ↑30 ft (9 m)

From the remote Mexican island of Guadalupe, growing in steep ravines running up from the seashore. Trunk thick. Fronds pale green with brownish woolly hairs. Shorter flowering branches thick, woolly, bearing greenish white flowers. Edible brown-black fruit. Zones 9–12.

BRASSICA

The cabbage and its relatives are in the family Brassicaceae. The genus contains around 30 species, and a large number of cultivars have been derived from a few of these. The wild species occur mainly in Europe and temperate Asia. They are annuals, biennials, and perennials, depending on climate and how they are treated. The brassicas are best known for their leaves (cabbages, kale, Asian greens), their flowering parts (broccoli, cauliflower, brussels sprouts), their seeds (rape/ canola), their stems (kohlrabi), or their roots (turnip, swede). The leaves are generally large and waxy with a whitish bloom; flowers are usually yellow but sometimes white. Flowering times depend on the age of the plant and climate. The cabbage family has been utilized by humans for more than 3,000 years.

CULTIVATION: Brassicas like a well-drained moist soil that has been enriched with well-rotted manure. Those grown for their leaves appreciate added nitrogen. Propagate from seed throughout the year, depending on the variety.

Brassica juncea

BROWN MUSTARD, CHINESE MUSTARD, KAI TSOI, MUSTARD GREENS

↔8–40 in (20–100 cm) ↑8–40 in (20–100 cm)

Annual species, native to southern and eastern Asia, long cultivated as a leaf vegetable and for mustard seed. Leaves green, red, or purple, smooth or puckered, smooth-edged or toothed. Racemes of light yellow flowers. Numerous cultivars. **'Red Giant'** (syn. *B. j.* var. *rugosa*), cool-season annual, 24 in (60 cm) long crinkled leaves in shades of green, purple, and maroon can be cooked like spinach.

Brassica oleracea, Acephala Group cultivar

Japonica Group (syn. *B. j.* var. *multiceps*): This group is very hardy, usually growing throughout winter. The leaves are used raw (especially when young) or cooked, salted, and pickled; **'Mizuna'** ★ is a quick-growing green leaf vegetable, with a peppery taste. Zones 9–11.

Brassica oleracea

WILD CABBAGE

↔12 in (30 cm) ↑16 in (40 cm)

Western European annual or perennial. Ancestor of cabbage, broccoli, cauliflower, kale, and brussels sprouts. Forms woody stem with dense head of overlapping blue-green leaves. Differs from cultivated types mainly in its coarsely lyrate or pinnate leaf shape. Sprays of yellow flowers in summer.

Acephala Group: Non-heading brassicas, both ornamental and edible; **'Blue Ridge'**, edible kale with dark blue-green leaves and full curl on all leaves; **'Red Peacock'**, dwarf ornamental kale with pinky red center and deeply cut leaves; **'Redbor'**, hardy, high-yielding edible kale; **'White Peacock'**, similar to 'Red Peacock' but white; **'Winterbor'** ★, vigorous edible kale with finely curled, thick, blue-green leaves.

B

Breynia disticha

BREYNIA

Belonging to the phyllanthus (Phyllanthaceae) family, the 25 or so species in this genus of evergreen shrubs and small trees range from Australia and the Pacific Islands northward to Southeast and East Asia. Often suckering from the roots, they have delicate twigs and small oval leaves arranged alternately and tending to form 2 rows. Leaves often turn black before falling. Inconspicuous greenish flowers, both male and female on the same plant, appear in the leaf axils followed by small, flattened, white, red, or black berries. Few of the species have found their way into home gardens.

CULTIVATION: Only the snow bush *(B. disticha)* is grown as an ornamental. Use as a border shrub in tropical and subtropical gardens; in cooler climates, grow indoors in pots or plant out for summer in bedding schemes or patio tubs. Prefers a sunny but sheltered spot and well-drained soil. Propagate from cuttings. Other species may be grown from seed and are used where local native plants are appropriate.

Breynia disticha

syns ***Breynia nivosa, Phyllanthus nivosus***

SNOW BUSH

↔3 ft (0.9 m) ↑4 ft (1.2 m)

From islands of western Pacific, sends up additional stems from roots if given room. Ovate leaves, 1 in (25 mm) long, spotted white or cream, or some all green, others all white. **'Roseopicta'**, pink new growth, many leaves pink-flushed, has largely replaced white-spotted form in gardens. Zones 10–12.

BRIZA

QUAKING GRASS, SHIVERGRASS

This genus of 12 annual or perennial grasses belongs to the family Poaceae. The genus name comes from the Greek word *brizo* (to be sleepy or nodding), referring to the delicate nodding panicles of flower spikelets that appear in summer. The leaves are flat and strap-like, while the spikelets consist of overlapping florets. *Briza* plants can become invasive in suitable climates. The flowers are ideal for dried arrangements.

Briza maxima

Broussonetia papyrifera

CULTIVATION: Propagate from seed. Plant seeds direct where they are to grow, in full sun, in well-drained cultivated soil raked to a fine tilth.

Briza maxima

GREAT QUAKING GRASS

↔8 in (20 cm) ↑24 in (60 cm)

Annual grass from Mediterranean area. Nodding panicles of 7 to 20 heart-shaped straw-colored or slightly purplish spikelets, in summer. Flat leaves up to 8 in (20 cm) long. **'Rubra'**, flower bracts tinted red-pink, edged with white. Zones 7–10.

Briza media

QUAKING GRASS, TREMBLING GRASS

↔18 in (45 cm) ↑24 in (60 cm)

From Europe and Asia. Ornamental grass with flat mid-green foliage. In early summer tiny light green spikelets appear, shaking in the slightest breeze, hence the common names; turn beige when mature. Does best in poor soils. Zones 7–10.

BROUSSONETIA

From the mulberry (Moraceae) family, *Broussonetia* consists of 8 species of deciduous trees and shrubs with milky sap, from tropical and eastern Asia; 1 species is endemic to Madagascar. Deeply lobed leaves are broad, heart-shaped, with toothed edges. Small male and female flowers are borne on separate trees, males in long catkins, females in globular heads. Male flowers expel pollen explosively, visible as tiny spurts of white dust. Small fleshy fruits are clustered on a globular fruiting head. Inner bark fiber has been used for making paper and cloth.

CULTIVATION: Only the more cold-hardy species from East Asia are known in cultivation. Moderately frost tolerant, they prefer hot humid summers. They adapt to tropical and subtropical climates, as well as inner-urban pollution. Heavy pruning creates vigorous resprouting. Propagate from cuttings of short shoots taken in summer; seed can be used if available.

Broussonetia papyrifera

PAPER MULBERRY

↔30 ft (9 m) ↑50 ft (15 m)

From China and Japan. Polynesian "tapa" cloth is made from bark. Young branches softly hairy. Leaves variably lobed or unlobed to 8 in (20 cm). Male catkins whitish, female purplish. Fruiting heads red. Zones 6–12.

BRUGMANSIA

This genus in the Solanaceae family contains 5 species of small trees or shrubs native to South America, particularly the Andes. Seeds hallucinogenic. All plant parts poisonous; all have woody stems. Grown for their tubular or funnelform flowers, drooping, not erect as in *Datura*. Flowers fragrant, with 2- to 5-lobed cylindrical calyx. Fruits ovoid or elliptical.

CULTIVATION: Brugmansias need a sunny protected position with no more than light frost. Moderately fertile, free-draining soil is suitable. Plants are best trained to a single trunk by removing any competing leaders; branchlets should be shortened annually in late winter or early spring. Propagation is from soft-tip cuttings taken in spring or summer, or hardwood cuttings in autumn or winter; use hormone rooting powder.

Brugmansia arborea

syn. ***Brugmansia cornigera***

↔5–8 ft (1.5–2.4 m) ↑15 ft (4.5 m)

Small evergreen tree from Ecuador and northern Chile, seldom seen in gardens. Leaves irregularly alternate. Flowers white, solitary, with extended green tip, in summer–autumn. Fruits green, ovoid, with numerous seeds. **'Knightii'** (syn. *B.* × *candida* 'Double White'), off-white double flowers, gray-green leaves. Zones 10–12.

Brugmansia arborea

B

Brugmansia aurea
syn. *Brugmansia pittieri*
GOLDEN ANGEL'S TRUMPET
↔15 ft (4.5 m) ↑15 ft (4.5 m)
Native to Central Colombia and Ecuador, on Andean Mountains slopes. Small evergreen tree, short trunk, broad leafy crown. Leaves mid-green, paler beneath. Flowers drooping, solitary, yellowish green, in late summer. The fruits are ovoid berries. Zones 10–12.

Brugmansia × *candida*
ANGEL'S TRUMPET
↔6 ft (1.8 m) ↑10 ft (3 m)
This hybrid between *B. aurea* and *B. versicolor* is sometimes labelled *B. knightii.* Small evergreen tree from Ecuador. Leaves bright green, paler below. Flowers greenish white, fragrant at night, appear in summer–autumn. Fruit a green capsule. '**Grand Marnier**', peach-colored flowers. Zones 10–12.

Brugmansia 'Charles Grimaldi'
↔4 ft (1.2 m) ↑6 ft (1.8 m)
Cross between '**Doctor Seuss**' and '**Frosty Pink**'. Leaves large. Flowers long, widely flared, fragrant, salmon pink to yellow-orange, in autumn–spring. Compact plant flowers heavily, does well in containers. Zones 10–12.

Brugmansia × *insignis*
syn. *Brugmania sanguinea 'Rosea'*
↔8–10 ft (2.4–3 m) ↑12 ft (3.5 m)
Developed from crossing *B. suaveolens* and *B. versicolor*, a multi-stemmed shrub resembling *B. suaveolens.* Flowers slender, tubular, flared petals, white ageing to pink or apricot. '**Betty Marshall**', compact growth habit, white flowers; '**Jamaica Yellow**', pale yellow blooms. Zones 9–10.

Brugmansia sanguinea ★
RED ANGEL'S TRUMPET
↔12 ft (3.5 m) ↑12 ft (3.5 m)
Small tree native to Colombia, Ecuador, and Peru, often seen as shrub. Leaves long. Flowers solitary, with persistent calyx. Corolla yellowish, turning orange-scarlet. Fruits ovoid, smooth skinned. '**Inca Queen**', long orange-red flowers with yellow interior. Zones 9–11.

Brugmansia suaveolens
ANGEL'S TRUMPET
↔10 ft (3 m) ↑15 ft (4.5 m)
Southeastern Brazil. Leaves soft, dark green. Single flowers, calyx green, corolla white, narrowly funnelform, with 3 pale green ribs. Fruits narrowly ellipsoidal, green, smooth. Zones 10–12.

BRUNFELSIA
Found from Central America to subtropical South America, this genus in the nightshade (Solanaceae) family includes some 40 species of mainly evergreen shrubs and trees. Most have fragrant, large, simple, long-tubed, 5-petalled flowers, notable for their progression of color changes. White, mauve, and purple are the usual colors. The leaves are usually simple pointed ovals in lush, deep green tones. All species contain potent alkaloids; generally highly toxic, but still used in some local medicines.
CULTIVATION: While very frost tender, *Brunfelsia* presents no cultivation difficulties in suitably mild climates. Any sunny or partly shaded position with moist well-drained soil will do. They are not drought tolerant but grow well in containers if watered routinely. Indoor potted specimens are prone to mites and mealybugs. Propagate from soft or half-hardened tip cuttings.

Brunfelsia pauciflora

Brunfelsia bonodora
syns *Brunfelsia australis, B. latifolia*
YESTERDAY, TODAY, AND TOMORROW
↔4–6 ft (1.2–1.8 m) ↑5–8 ft (1.5–2.4 m)
As the name *bonodora* suggests, this plant has sweetly scented flowers. They appear through warmer months, open purple, then age to mauve and white over three days, hence common name. Zones 10–12.

Brunfelsia grandiflora
↔7 ft (2 m) ↑3–7 ft (0.9–2 m)
Found from Venezuela to Bolivia. Shrub or small tree with slender arching branches. Rather leathery pointed leaves, narrow to oval, dark green above. Clusters of flowers, purple with white centers. Zones 10–12.

Brunfelsia pauciflora
syn. *Brunfelsia calycina*
↔5 ft (1.5 m) ↑8 ft (2.4 m)
Pauciflora means sparsely flowered, inappropriate for this heavy-flowering often semi-deciduous shrub from Brazil and Venezuela. Large flowers open purple-blue then age through pale mauve to white. Dwarf cultivars, such as '**Floribunda**' ★ and '**Floribunda Compacta**', and larger-flowered forms such as '**Macrantha**' are widely available. Zones 10–12.

BRUNNERA
This genus of 3 species of fleshy-stemmed herbaceous perennials of the borage (Boraginaceae) family comes from temperate Eurasia. The species are closely related to the forget-me-nots and resemble them in flower. Sprays of tiny blue or white flowers appear in spring. However, the rounded to heart-shaped leaves of *Brunnera* are far larger than those of the common forget-me-nots and, as the garden forms are often variegated, the foliage is easily as much a feature as the flowers. The genus was named after Samuel Brunner (1790–1844), a Swiss botanist.
CULTIVATION: These plants are most at home in a temperate climate with cool summers. Extremely hardy and easily grown in woodland conditions with dappled sunlight and moist, humus-rich, well-drained soil. Established clumps of cultivars may be divided near the end of the dormant period, otherwise the seed germinates freely. *Brunnera* species often self-sow and naturalize.

Brunnera macrophylla

Brunnera macrophylla
↔16–32 in (40–80 cm) ↑20 in (50 cm)
A Eastern European perennial with finely hairy, broad, heart-shaped leaves to 6 in (15 cm) long on 8 in (20 cm) stalks. Soft blue flowers are held above the foliage on 20 in (50 cm) stems. '**Hadspen Cream**', one of several variegated cultivars, cream-spotted light green leaves, blue flowers; '**Jack Frost**', silver-gray leaves with dark green veins and margin, blue flowers. Zones 3–9.

BUCHLOE
BUFFALO GRASS
A genus containing 1 species of grass from the family Poaceae, native to North America. The grayish green sparsely hairy leaves arise from a prostrate modified stem or runner, forming tufts. Branched racemes of male flowers, to 8 in (20 cm) long, contain spikelets in 2 rows on 1 side of a central stem. Female flowers appear in short spikes enclosed by leaves.
CULTIVATION: Propagate by division of runners or from seed. Can be planted in any garden soil in an open sunny position.

Buchloe dactyloides
BUFFALO GRASS
↔3–4 in (8–10 cm) ↑4–6 in (10–15 cm)
Low-growing perennial grass from American prairies used widely for ornamental lawns, forming finely textured turf of soft blue-green, which turns gold in autumn. Spreads by surface runners and seed. Zones 3–5.

BUDDLEJA

The name of this genus of deciduous, semi-deciduous, and evergreen plants from the Americas, Asia, and South Africa can be spelt either buddleja or buddleia. The genus is part of the foxglove or figwort (Scrophulariaceae) family and consists of about 100 species, of which a few shrubby or tree-like ones are garden grown. There are also some decorative cultivars that are grown for their profuse, small, fragrant flowers that are held in large panicles. The leaves are, with the exception of *B. alternifolia*, paired and opposite. The plants are tough, undemanding, quick growing and salt tolerant. They are also sun loving and vigorous and, if given shelter, can be grown in climates considerably cooler than those found in their native habitats.

CULTIVATION: Basic requirements include sunlight, good drainage, fertile soil, and, from the gardener's point of view, regular pruning. Some plants show a mild preference for chalky and limy soils. Propagate from half-hardened cuttings in summer.

Buddleja alternifolia ★

FOUNTAIN BUDDLEJA

↔ 15 ft (4.5 m) ↑ 15 ft (4.5 m)

Deciduous shrub native to northwest China. Leaves small, green above, whitish beneath. Flowers fragrant, misty mauve, attract butterflies, in late spring–early-summer. Remove the flowering stems in summer. **'Argentea'**, mauve flowers, fine growth of silvery hairs on leaves. Zones 5–9.

Buddleja crispa

↔ 15 ft (4.5 m) ↑ 15 ft (4.5 m)

From the Himalayas. A deciduous bushy upright shrub, arching habit. Leaves dark oval, new shoots woolly white. Fragrant mauve flowers in long whorled panicles, in spring–summer. Prune in winter. Zones 7–10.

Buddleja davidii

BUTTERFLY BUSH

↔ 17 ft (5 m) ↑ 10–17 ft (3–5 m)

Native to rocky riversides in central and western China. Tough deciduous plant with many garden-grown cultivars. Quick vigorous growth, bushy habit, arching stems. Fragrant mauve flowers in panicles. Long pointed leaves, dark green above, woolly white beneath. Can be invasive in parts of the west. ***B. d.* var. *nanhoensis***, to 5 ft (1.5 m) tall and wide. ***B. d.* 'Black Knight'**, royal purple flowers; **'Dartmoor'**, red-purple flowers on fan-like flowering stems ; **'Empire Blue'**, steely violet-blue flowers, orange eye; **'Harlequin'**, cream-edged leaves; **'Nanho Blue'**, lavender-purple flowers; **'Nanho Purple'**, rich purple flowers; **'Royal Red'**, purple-red flowers; **White Profusion'**, white flowers, golden eye. Zones 4–10.

Buddleja fallowiana

↔ 10 ft (3 m) ↑ 10 ft (3 m)

Deciduous Chinese species; arching stems. Leaves lance-shaped, dark gray-green. Flowers fragrant, pale lavender with orange centers, in large panicles, in summer–early autumn. ***B. f.* var. *alba***, creamy white flowers with orange eye. Zones 8–9.

Buddleja globosa

ORANGE BALL TREE

↔ 10 ft (3 m) ↑ 10–20 ft (3–6 m)

Semi-evergreen tree native to Argentina and Chile. The leaves are dark green above, wrinkled, woolly white on the undersides; the young stems are silvery white. Flowers are scented, orange-yellow, in clusters, in late spring–early summer. Prune when flowering finishes. Zones 7–9.

Buddleja lindleyana ★

↔ 12 ft (3.5 m) ↑ 12 ft (3.5 m).

Semi-deciduous shrub from the scrub of eastern Asia. Leaves sage green, pointed, carried on square sage-like stems. Flowers curved, tubular, purple, on long, tapering, upright spikes. Has naturalized in southeast USA. Zones 7–9.

Buddleja 'Lochinch'

↔ 8–10 ft (2.4–3 m)
↑ 10–15 ft (3–4.5 m)

Garden hybrid between *B. davidii* and *B. fallowiana*, with gray felted leaves and panicles of summer-blooming, sweetly scented, violet-blue flowers with a tiny orange eye. Zones 6–9.

Buddleja nivea

↔ 8 ft (2.4 m) ↑ 10 ft (3 m)

Vigorous, upright, deciduous shrub from China. Leaves narrow, dark green above, woolly white down beneath. Downy panicles of violet-blue flowers. Zones 7–9.

Buddleja 'Pink Delight'

syn. ***Buddleja davidii* 'Pink Delight'**

↔ 7 ft (2 m) ↑ 5–7 ft (1.5–2 m)

Grayish green arching foliage. Flowers are deep pink, fragrant, on racemes 12–15 in (30–38 cm) long, in late summer–early autumn. Zones 7–10.

Buddleja × weyeriana

↔ 12 ft (3.5 m) ↑ 15 ft (4.5 m)

Deciduous hybrid between *B. davidii* and *B. globosa*. Leaves dark, lance-shaped. Flowers bobble-like clusters, scented, orange-yellow shaded with lilac. **'Golden Glow'**, soft purple buds, profusion of apricot flowers in open panicles; **'Honeycomb'**, pale yellow flowers; **'Sungold'**, dense heads of bright yellow flowers with orange centers. Zones 6–9.

Buddleja davidii 'Black Knight'

Buddleja lindleyana

Buddleja globosa

BULBINE

This diverse group of about 35 species from South Africa and Australia belongs to the grass tree (Xanthorrhoeaceae) family. While the Latin word *bulbine* means a bulb, only a few species possess this feature. The larger species have succulent grass-like leaves and flower spikes that can reach 20 in (50 cm) or more in height. There are also several miniature species with attractive leaves; several of these resemble other succulent genera, such as *Aloe* and *Haworthia,* and will die down completely in the dormant period. Numerous flowers in all species, yellow or orange, borne on upright inflorescences. Some species have healing properties and are used externally to treat wounds, burns, and itches, or internally for diarrhea, convulsions, and urinary infections.

CULTIVATION: *Bulbine* species are easy to cultivate in rich, well-drained, but well-watered soil. Can be propagated from seed, but usually raised by dividing old plants.

Bulbine frutescens

syn. ***Bulbine caulescens***

↔ 24 in (60 cm) ↑ 24 in (60 cm)

Branching subshrub from south coast of South Africa north into Mozambique. Leaves light green, linear, semi-cylindrical, 8–10 in (20–25 cm) long. Inflorescence to 24 in (60 cm), bearing 40 to 50 yellow flowers. **'Hallmark'** (syn. *B. caulescens* **'Hallmark'**), compact form, shorter inflorescence, orange flowers. Zones 9–11.

BUTIA

BUTIA PALMS

This genus of small to medium-sized palms in the family Arecaceae comprises 8 species from subtropical and warm-temperate regions of eastern South America. They all have a large spindle-shaped bract around the flowering panicle in bud. Fronds arch from the trunk, consisting of 2 rows of thick narrow leaflets. The stout trunk is clothed by old frond stalks; when shed with age they leave a closely ringed gray surface. Sweet-scented cream to purplish flowers appear on stiff springy spikes; flowering branch bursts through a slit in the bract before the flowers open. The fruits are edible, and can be fermented to make a kind of wine. CULTIVATION: Widely grown as landscape subjects in warm-temperate climates, they tolerate hot exposed environments. Deep-rooted, they tolerate dry topsoil, but are readily transplanted at any age. When trimming old fronds, bases should be cut at an even length to preserve the neat pattern on the trunk. Propagation is from seed, but germination may take some months.

Butia capitata ★

BUTIA PALM, JELLY PALM

↔15 ft (4.5 m) ↑20 ft (6 m)

From southern Brazil, Uruguay, and northern Argentina. Fronds recurving, grayish, to 10 ft (3 m) long. Large cream bracts, pale yellow to reddish flowers, in late spring–early summer. Fruits ripen in summer or autumn of the following year. Zones 8–11.

BUXUS

BOX

A member of the family Buxaceae, the genus *Buxus* has most of its 50 or so species in the West Indies and Central America; there are also species through eastern Asia, the Himalayas, Africa, and Europe. All are evergreen shrubs or trees with simple smooth-edged leaves arranged in opposite pairs. Small greenish or yellowish flowers are borne in the leaf axils. Fruits are small capsules. Mostly used as garden and landscape plants, the close-grained yellowish wood is also used for woodcut engraving, and for small turned and carved objects such as buttons and chess pieces. The leaves and twigs are poisonous to livestock. CULTIVATION: The smaller-leafed species are popular in cool-climate gardens. They are valued for their dense fine-textured foliage, hardiness, and ability to take frequent trimming and shaping. They grow in most soil types, including chalk, as long as there is reasonable drainage. Propagation is usually from cuttings, but seed also germinates readily.

Bulbine frutescens 'Hallmark'

Butia capitata

Buxus balearica

Buxus balearica

BALEARIC BOX

↔8 ft (2.4 m) ↑15 ft (4.5 m)

From the Balearic Islands and nearby parts of Spain and Algeria. It has more erect conical growth habit and larger thicker leaves than *B. sempervirens.* Can grow to 30 ft (9 m) under ideal conditions. Zones 8–11.

Buxus harlandii ★

↔3 ft (0.9 m) ↑3 ft (0.9 m)

Low bushy shrub from southern China. Leaves shiny, dark green, similar size to *B. sempervirens* but narrower in proportion. Many plants grown under this name are in fact forms of *B. microphylla.* Zones 8–11.

Buxus microphylla

CHINESE BOX, JAPANESE BOX, KOREAN BOX

↔7 ft (2 m) ↑8 ft (2.4 m)

East Asian species with a number of forms and cultivars. It is more the differences in frost tolerance than features that are important. Wild forms have slightly brownish green leaves, ¾ in (18 mm) long. Flowers greenish yellow, in spring. **B. m. var. japonica, dense upright shrub, slow-growing to 8 ft (2.4 m) high; 'Green Beauty'**, deep green foliage; **'Morris Midget'**, low-growing with yellow-green leaves. **B. m. 'Compacta'**, dwarf with dense foliage; **'Curly Locks'**, pale green leaves and twisted shoots; **'Faulkner'**, compact with red-brown stems; **'Green Jade'**, egg-shaped pale green leaves, grows to 24 in (60 cm) high; **'Green Pillow'**, small rounded leaves crowded on dwarf mound to 12 in (30 cm) high. Zones 6–10.

Buxus sempervirens

COMMON BOX, ENGLISH BOX

↔5–15 ft (1.5–4.5 m)
↑5–30 ft (1.5–9 m)

Widespread in Europe, western Asia, and northwestern Africa. Native to British Isles. Leaves to 1 in (25 mm) long; leaf apex may be pointed, blunt, or slightly notched. Greenish cream flower clusters, in late spring. **'Argenteovariegata'** (syn. 'Argentea'), delicate gray-green leaves with narrow cream margin; **'Elegantissima'**, mid-green leaves with creamy white margins; **'Graham Blandy'**, narrow columnar growth habit; **'Handsworthiensis'**, unusually large leaves, good for hedging; **'Latifolia Maculata'**, pale gold juvenile leaves, yellow-variegated when mature; **'Marginata'**, misshapen leaves with yellowish band around upper margin; **'Memorial'**, symmetrical form, grows to about 2 ft (0.6 m); **'Suffruticosa'**, dense erect habit, small leaves; **'Vardar Valley'** ★, dense mound-forming shrub, mid-to dark green leaves. Zones 5–10.

Buxus, Sheridan Hybrids

↔18–24 in (45–60 cm)
↑18–24 in (45–60 cm)

From North America, these cultivars have originated from crosses between forms of *B. sempervirens* and *B. microphylla* var. *koreana*. They are mostly dense compact shrubs. **'Green Gem'**, globular form, with rich green foliage; **'Green Mountain'**, conical form, with slightly darker foliage. Zones 5–10.

Buxus sinica

CHINESE BOX, KOREAN BOXWOOD

↔2–12 ft (0.6–3.5 m)
↑3–20 ft (0.9–6 m)

Shrub or small tree from eastern China and Korea and once regarded as variety of *B. microphylla.* Occurs in many varieties covering wide size range. Glossy light green leaves to 1¼ in (30 mm) long. ***B. s.* var. *insularis*** (syn. *B. microphylla* var. *koreana*), slow-growing, with small but fragrant green-yellow flowers; **'Justin Brouwers'**, dense mound with small, narrow, deep green leaves; **'Pincushion'** (syn. *B. microphylla* 'Cushion'), dwarf cushion-forming shrub with dull green rounded leaves; **'Tide Hill'**, dwarf to 12 in (30 cm) tall; **'Winter Gem'** (syn. *B. microphylla* 'Winter Gem'), hardy, foliage remains green during winter. Zones 6–10.

Buxus, Sheridan Hybrid, 'Green Mountain'

C

Caccinia macranthera var. *crassifolia*

CACCINIA

This small genus contains 6 species of multi-stemmed herbaceous perennials, placed in the borage (Boraginaceae) family, and found in a wide range of open habitats in mountainous regions of western and central Asia. Hairy stems arise from a stout rootstock, with a base and stem leaves of varying shapes, but usually simple and not hairy. Inflorescences are terminal, with many bluish star-like flowers. CULTIVATION: Not commonly cultivated. Propagate from seed.

Caccinia macranthera

↔ 36 in (90 cm) ↑ 24 in (60 cm)

The most widespread and most extensively grown species. Gray-green oblong to lance-shaped leaves closely spaced along the stems. Blue-purple flowers from late spring–summer. Requires a well-drained gritty soil. ***C. m.*** **var. *crassifolia*** has blue-green leaves. Zones 5–9.

CAESALPINIA

Occurring in the tropics and many warm-temperate regions (mainly in the Americas), *Caesalpinia* belongs to the cassia subfamily of the legume (Fabaceae) family, and consists of around 150 species of evergreen and deciduous trees, shrubs, and scrambling climbers. *Caesalpinia* species all have bipinnate leaves, with numerous leaflets. Hooked prickles on branches and leaves are common, mainly on the climbers. Flowers are in spikes, terminating the branches. Many species have yellow flowers; most have 5 petals, and protruding stamens of often contrasting color. The pods can be flattened and smooth, or swollen and spiny, containing hard seeds.

CULTIVATION: These plants are readily cultivated in warm climates. Many *caesalpinias* tolerate exposed seashores, arid climates, or poorly drained soil. Some of the ornamental shrub and tree species prefer deeper well-drained soils and a sunny but sheltered position. Propagation is usually from the seed, pre-treated to penetrate the hard coat. *C. gilliesii* can be grown from cuttings.

Caesalpinia gilliesii

syn. *Poinciana gilliesii*

BIRD-OF-PARADISE SHRUB

↔ 4–8 ft (1.2–2.4 m) ↑ 10 ft (3 m)

From northern Argentina and Uruguay. Evergreen or may be deciduous in dry winter climate. Ferny leaves, numerous small leaflets. Flowers are pale yellow, in erect spikes. Showy red stamens to 3 in (8 cm) long. Zones 6–11.

Caesalpinia pulcherrima

syn. *Poinciana pulcherrima*

BARBADOS PRIDE, PEACOCK FLOWER

↔ 6–12 ft (1.8–3.5 m) ↑ 10 ft (3 m)

Of uncertain origin, from tropical America or Asia. Long-stalked showy flowers, varying in color, bright scarlet to pink, gold or pale yellow, or may be red and gold. Stamens like cat's whiskers. Flowers all year. Zones 9–12.

CALADIUM

ANGEL WINGS, ELEPHANT EARS

This genus of 7 species of deciduous tuberous perennials from tropical America belongs to the arum (Araceae) family. They are grown for their stunning leaves, which are attractively splashed or veined with white or brilliant shades of pink and red. These large leaves, up to 18 in (45 cm) long, are arrow- or heart-shaped and are held above the stalks. Although the plants bear arum-like flowers, these are not considered to be of ornamental significance.

CULTIVATION: *Caladium* thrive particularly well in tropical and warm climates. Grow outdoors in a moist but well-drained fertile soil, in a shady position. In colder climates grow in pots indoors or in the conservatory. Use a moist, free-draining, coarse potting mix, and place in bright but not direct sunlight. Maintain a high level of humidity. Water and feed regularly until the leaves fade in autumn, then allow the plants to dry out for dormancy. The first leaves to appear each year may not show the colorful markings.

Caesalpinia gilliesii

Caladium bicolor 'Scarlet Pimpernel'

Caladium bicolor

syns *Caladium* × *hortulanum*, *C. marmoratum*, *C. picturatum*

ANGEL WINGS, ELEPHANT EARS

↔ 12 in (30 cm) ↑ 24 in (60 cm)

From the Amazon region of Brazil. Leaves large, green, arrow-shaped, irregularly splashed with varying amounts of white, pink, and red. Extensively bred to produce an extremely wide range of color forms, including: **'Carolyn Whorton'**, with bright pink blotches, red veining, dark green at edges; **'Festiva'**, transparent red with green veining; **'Fire Chief'**, crimson heart, red veining, green margins; **'Kathleen'**, bright salmon heart, green margins; **'Lord Derby'**, transparent rose, dark veins, green margins; **'Mrs F. M. Joyner'**, white flushed with pink, dark red veins, and light green margins; **'Red Flash'**, bright red heart, red veining, dull green margins; **'Red Frill'** ★, deep red center becoming darker red toward the green margins; **'Rosebud'**, pink heart fading to white, pink veining, green margins; **'Scarlet Pimpernel'**, red heart, red veining, cream to light green margins; **'White Christmas'**, white with green veining; and **'White Queen'**, white with crimson veins. Zones 10–12.

Calamagrostis × *acutiflora* 'Stricta'

CALAMAGROSTIS

REED GRASS

A genus of around 250 species in the grass (Poaceae) family that is fairly widespread throughout temperate zones of the Northern Hemisphere. Only a few species are of ornamental value and those that are in cultivation are mainly hybrids or selected forms. Some can be quite invasive. Their upright form and fluffy flowerheads that can be dried make them dramatic feature plants in the garden.

CULTIVATION: They prefer moist to damp soils in a sunny aspect. Propagate from seed; cultivars should be divided at the end of winter.

Calamagrostis × *acutiflora*

FEATHER REED GRASS

↔ 36–40 in (90–100 cm) ↑ 5–7 ft (1.5–2 m)

Clump-forming herbaceous hybrid between *C. arundinacea* and *C. epigejos* that arose naturally in Europe and is basically sterile. **'Karl Foerster'**, strongly erect, long plumes, lasts well into winter; **'Overdam'** ★ has variegated silver foliage; **'Stricta'** is a vertical form bearing feathery flowers in summer. Zones 4–10.

Calamagrostis brachytricha

syn. *Calamagrostis arundinacea*

↔ 20–40 in (50–100 cm) ↑ 40 in (100 cm)

Found in temperate regions of central to East Asia. Channeled leaves to ½ in (12 mm) in diameter. Panicles from mid-summer, to slightly over 6 in (15 cm) long, tinted purple. Zones 7–9.

Calamagrostis foliosa

FEATHER REED GRASS, LEAFY REED GRASS

↔ 8–20 in (20–50 cm) ↑ 6–16 in (15–40 cm)

Californian species with broad leaves. Panicles to 6 in (15 cm) long. Both foliage and flowers light green turning straw colored with purple tints. **'Zebrina'**, young leaves horizontally banded in green and yellow. Zones 7–9.

Calamintha sylvatica subsp. *ascendens*

Calamintha sylvatica

COMMON CALAMINT

↔ 20 in (50 cm) ↑ 24 in (60 cm)

An aromatic, mint-scented native of central and southern Europe. Deep, slightly glossy green, heavily veined, pointed oval leaves to 1½ in (35 mm) long, with shallowly toothed edges. Whorls of ½ in (12 mm) long, pink to purple flowers produced in summer. ***C. s.* subsp. *ascendens*** has strong peppermint aroma, purple flowers, and grows to around 12 in (30 cm) tall. Zones 7–10.

Calendula officinalis

Calibrachoa, HC, 'Colorburst Violet'

C., HC, Million Bells Cherry Pink/'Sunbelchipi'

C., HC, Million Bells Lemon/'Sunbelkic'

CALAMINTHA

CALAMINT

This mint (Lamiaceae) family genus is made of 7 species of sometimes shrubby perennials found in the northern temperate zones excluding East Asia. The foliage is evergreen in mild climates but in cool winters plants may die back to a basal clump. Their aromatic pointed oval leaves are often slightly glossy and have toothed edges. Flower stems develop in summer and carry tubular pink to mauve flowers in the leaf axils near their tips. Calamint has had a long history of medicinal use but these days this is usually restricted to just a simple infusion of the leaves, which makes a refreshing tea.

CULTIVATION: Hardiness varies, though most species will tolerate quite severe frosts. Plant in a bright but not baking position with moist, humus-rich, well-drained soil. Some species have vigorous rhizomes and can be slightly invasive. Propagate by division, or from basal cuttings or seed.

Calamintha grandiflora

LARGE-FLOWERED CALAMINT

↔ 3–4 ft (0.9–1.2 m)
↑ 2 ft (0.6 m)

Native to southern Europe and North Africa. Bushy plant with spreading rootstock. Dark green, downy, toothed leaves to 3 in (8 cm) long. Flowers are 1½ in (35 mm) long, pink to mauve, and borne singly or up to 5 in a cluster. **'Variegata'** (syn. 'Fornsett Form'), compact, rarely exceeds 12 in (30 cm). Zones 5–10.

Calamintha nepeta

LESSER CALAMINT

↔ 3–5 ft (0.9–1.5 m) ↑ 32 in (80 cm)

Spreading rhizome-rooted perennial found from Britain to southern Europe. Downy gray-green stems and leaves, to 1¼ in (30 mm) long. They are strongly aromatic. Pink to mauve flowers, ½ in (12 mm) long, with up to 15 in a cluster. Zones 6–10.

CALENDULA

A genus of about 20 species of annual and perennial herbs in the daisy (Asteraceae) family. They are found around the Mediterranean area and Atlantic Islands where they are often found growing on disturbed ground, particularly *C. officinalis*, which is a widespread garden escapee. All have alternate simple leaves; some of these are aromatic. The cheerful yellow or orange daisies appear for long periods throughout the year. *C. officinalis* has been used for many centuries for a range of culinary and medicinal purposes. The common name marigold is today also associated with some *Tagetes* species.

CULTIVATION: Very easily grown in any well-drained soil in full sun. Sow seed *in situ* or under glass in spring in cooler areas, or earlier in warmer areas. Successive sowings and deadheading will result in a display over many months, from spring to autumn in cooler areas and throughout the year in warm ones.

Calendula arvensis

FIELD MARIGOLD

↔ 12 in (30 cm) ↑ 12 in (30 cm)

From southern Europe, a branched annual species with slightly downy oblong leaves. The yellow or orange daisies to 1 in (25 mm) in diameter are carried from spring–autumn. Zones 6–10.

Calendula officinalis ★

COMMON MARIGOLD, POT MARIGOLD, SCOTCH MARIGOLD

↔ 12–18 in (30–45 cm)
↑ 12–24 in (30–60 cm)

Originally from southern Europe but widely naturalized. Bushy annual with slightly downy leaves. Orange or yellow daisies to 3 in (8 cm) diameter from spring–autumn. **Bon Bon Series**, to 12 in (30 cm), a mix of apricot, yellow, and orange; **'Dwarf Gem'**, to 12 in (30 cm), double, large, apricot, yellow, and orange daisies; **Fiesta Gitana Group** ★, to 12 in (30 cm), a mix of cream, yellow, orange, and bi-colors; **'Greenheart Orange'**, orange petals and a green centre; **'Orange Salad'**, petals are a saffron substitute; **Kablouna Series**, short ray florets and prominent quilled centers, mixed yellow, orange, and apricot; **Pacific Beauty Series**, tall-stemmed, yellow, orange, and apricot; **'Radio'**, orange flowers, quilled petals resembling cactus-type dahlia. Zones 6–10.

CALIBRACHOA

syn. *Petunia (in part)*

Genus in the nightshade (Solanaceae) family, *Calibrachoa* is closely related to *Petunia* and its 25 species are found across much the same region of South America, from southern Brazil across to Peru and Chile; one species, *C. parviflora*, extends north to southern USA. Indeed all species were classified under *Petunia* until a Dutch geneticist who was involved in petunia breeding discovered major differences in chromosomes between this group and other *Petunia* species, corresponding to external differences and breeding behavior. The name *Calibrachoa* goes back to 1825 and honors a Mexican professor of pharmacy, Antonio de la Cal y Bracho. They are weak evergreen perennials and subshrubs, mostly sprawling or prostrate with leaves under 1 in (25 mm) long. Flowers are smaller than in most petunias, under 1 in (25 mm) across and short-tubed, arising from leaf axils in continuous succession. In the 1990s the Japanese biotechnology firm Suntory (famous for whiskey) began breeding *Calibrachoa*, though which species they used it is difficult to discover, and released the first of the patented **Million Bells Series**. Many strains followed with a wider range of colors and more compact or trailing habits. All are clonal, produced mainly by tissue culture; they flower almost continuously with adequate light and warmth.

CULTIVATION: They will tolerate light frosts and thrive in sun or semi-shade. Mostly grown in pots or baskets; can be treated as annuals or short-lived perennials. Plant in a free-draining medium and apply weak fertilizer at intervals throughout the growing season, pinch back the longer shoots to increase the number of flowers. Water only when the soil is almost dry. Propagate from tip cuttings but be aware that propagation for sale may infringe plant patents.

Calibrachoa Hybrid Cultivars

↔ 12–24 in (30–60 cm)
↑ 3–8 in (7–20 cm)

Valued for their low mounding or trailing habit and profusion of small flowers, mid-spring–late autumn or virtually year-round in warm climates. **Million Bells Series** are yellow-throated flowers in shades from white to lemon, pink, red, and purple, mounding to 6 in (15 cm). **Trailing Million Bells Series** are only 3 in (8 cm) or so high, spilling over edges of baskets or planter boxes. The **Superbells Series** are also trailers, though a little larger, up to 8 in (20 cm) high. Flowers in the **Colorburst Series** come in cherry, red, rose and violet. Flowers of the German-bred **Minifamous Series** (syn. Selecta Series) include some rich colors, especially oranges, reds, and yellows, and also bicolors. The **Liricashower Series** include strong reds and yellows as well as pastels, with flat open blooms. Zones 8–11.

C

CALLIANDRA

This genus in the mimosa subfamily of legume (Fabaceae) family consists of around 200 species, the majority occurring in South and Central America and the West Indies. Mostly shrubs or small trees, they have bipinnate leaves, long-stamened flowers in globular heads or elongated spikes. Flower colors range from white and pink to deep crimson, attracting hummingbirds which pollinate these plants in the wild. Seed pods are rigid and flattened. Most calliandras come from regions that are warm but dry, or at least with a pronounced dry season. Many species are frost tender. Calliandras are useful landscape subjects, providing year-round color as well as a screen of feathery foliage. CULTIVATION: Tough adaptable shrubs where climate is suitable, tolerating hard dry soils and moderately exposed positions. Most species adapt well to clipping into compact forms and can be used for hedges. Propagate from seed, or from cuttings taken in winter from short lateral branches.

Calliandra californica

↔ 3 ft (0.9 m) ↑ 4 ft (1.2 m)

A native of Baja California, Mexico, this plant is often used in desert style gardens. The tough wiry branches are dotted for much of the year with small tassel-like heads of bright crimson flowers. Zones 9–11.

Calliandra emarginata

↔ 20 ft (6 m) ↑ 10 ft (3 m)

Native of southern Mexico and Central America, often confused with the better known *C. haematocephala.* Semi-scrambling habit, large leaflets, large "powderpuff" heads of pink to crimson flowers. Semi-prostrate when planted in an open area. Zones 10–12.

Calliandra emarginata

Calliandra eriophylla

FAIRY DUSTER, MOCK MESQUITE

↔ 36 in (90 cm) ↑ 36 in (90 cm)

Extending from Mexico to the far south of western USA. Crooked prickly branches, fine feathery leaves, profuse wispy heads of pale red flowers in late winter–early spring. Used in desert style gardens. Zones 7–11.

Calliandra haematocephala

BLOOD-RED TASSEL FLOWER, POWDERPUFF TREE

↔ 20 ft (6 m) ↑ 10 ft (3 m)

From northern South America. Flowers pink to scarlet or deep red, densely crowded into globular heads at branch tips, most of the year, autumn–winter in cooler areas. Shelter from strong winds. Zones 10–12.

Calliandra houstoniana

↔ 7 ft (2 m) ↑ 10 ft (3 m)

From southern Mexico and adjacent Central America. Open habit, leaves bipinnate, numerous tiny bright green leaflets. Flowers in terminal spike-like clusters, with showy red stamens, in summer–autumn. Zones 10–12.

Calliandra surinamensis

PINK-AND-WHITE POWDERPUFF

↔ 10 ft (3 m) ↑ 10 ft (3 m)

From northern South America. Showy powderpuff flowerheads, white to pale mauve, most of the year. Vase-shaped habit, with arching branches, and small clustered leaves. Drought tolerant. Zones 10–12.

Calliandra tweedii ★

syn. *Inga pulcherrima*

RED TASSEL FLOWER

↔ 6 ft (1.8 m) ↑ 6 ft (1.8 m)

This native of Uruguay and southern Brazil grows best in a warm-temperate climate without seasonal rainfall. Multi-stemmed fresh green foliage has tiny crowded leaflets. The deep scarlet flowerheads appear in spring–autumn. Can be cut back hard, or trimmed to a dense hedge. Zones 9–11.

Calliandra tweedii

CALLICARPA

BEAUTY BUSH

This genus has about 140 species of trees and shrubs, both deciduous and evergreen, belonging to the mint (Lamiaceae) family. They occur from the tropics to warm-temperate regions around much of the globe. They are close allies of the verbenas, which shows in their simple conspicuously veined and toothed leaves and their spring-borne heads, or cymes, of tiny flowers. The main attraction of most species, however, is the fruit that ripens in late summer and autumn. Individual drupes are often very small, but massed together create a long-lasting display and are very distinctively colored. CULTIVATION: Hardiness varies with the species, some tolerate little or no frost, others are very tough. *Callicarpa* seldom has any cultivation difficulties, thriving in any moist well-drained soil in sun or partial shade. Prune after fruit has fallen and propagate from half-hardened cuttings.

Callicarpa americana

AMERICAN BEAUTY BERRY, AMERICAN BEAUTY BUSH

↔ 7 ft (2 m) ↑ 10 ft (3 m)

Found in southern USA and parts of the West Indies. Leaves to 8 in (20 cm) long, downy undersides. Violet flowers followed by densely clustered bunches of magenta drupes that usually last well into winter. *C. a.* var. *lactea* is a white-fruited cultivar. Zones 5–10.

Callicarpa bodinieri

↔ 8 ft (2.4 m) ↑ 10 ft (3 m)

From central and western China. Deciduous. Toothed leaves to 8 in (20 cm) long, turn golden in autumn. Flowers lilac. Fruits violet-purple, small but profuse. The heavy fruiting variety *C. b.* var. *giraldii* and its cultivar, **'Profusion'** ★, are more commonly cultivated. Zones 6–9.

Calliandra eriophylla

Callicarpa dichotoma

PURPLE BEAUTY BERRY, PURPLE BEAUTY BUSH

↔ 4 ft (1.2 m) ↑ 4 ft (1.2 m)

From China and Japan, deciduous with toothed oval leaves, pink flowers followed by small violet-purple drupes. Can be temperamental with good and bad years. **'Issai'** and **'Purpurea'** are attractive cultivars. Zones 6–10.

Callicarpa japonica

JAPANESE BEAUTY BERRY, JAPANESE BEAUTY BUSH

↔ 5 ft (1.5 m) ↑ 6 ft (1.8 m)

Deciduous shrub native to China and Japan. Leaves up to 8 in (20 cm) long, very finely toothed margins, tapering to a point. Flowers pale pink, fruit pink to violet-purple. **'Leucocarpa'** has white fruits. Zones 7–10.

Callicarpa rubella

BEAUTY BERRY, CHINESE BEAUTY BUSH

↔ 3 ft (1 m) ↑ 3 ft (1 m)

From tropical and subtropical East Asia. Semi-deciduous shrub. Leaves pale yellowish green to 5 in (12 cm) long. Flowers are pink, and followed by purple-red drupes. Both flowers and fruiting heads are covered in fine hairs that gradually wear away. Zones 9–11.

Callicarpa rubella

Callicarpa americana

CALLIRHOE

POPPY MALLOWS

A genus of 9 species of deep-rooted annuals and perennials, belonging to the mallow (Malvaceae) family, and found in prairies and grasslands of the USA and Mexico. The leaves are alternate, deeply lobed, green to gray-green, thick to rough textured. The flowers are cup-shaped, and borne singly or in clusters in the upper leaf axils, their colors range from red through to purple and magenta.
CULTIVATION: Well-drained sandy loam produces better growth than heavier soils. They have a good low temperature tolerance, but full sun is required. Both annuals and perennials are propagated from seed, and perennials from softwood cuttings.

Callirhoe involucrata

BUFFALO ROSE, LOW POPPY MALLOW, PRAIRIE POPPY MALLOW, PURPLE POPPY MALLOW, WINE CUPS

↔ 12–24 in (30–60 cm)
↑ 6–12 in (15–30 cm)

Low-growing sprawling perennial with swollen taproot that comes from inland USA. Naturalized elsewhere. The stems are prostrate, hairy, to 6 in (15 cm) long. Leaves 3 to 7, lobed, 1–2 in (25–50 mm) long. Magenta to cerise flowers with white centers are borne on long erect stems from late spring–summer. Zones 5–8.

CALLISTEMON

BOTTLEBRUSH

This Australian genus of about 30 species of highly ornamental evergreen shrubs and small trees in the myrtle (Myrtaceae) family has a large range of hybrids and cultivars. The leathery, linear or lanceolate leaves are arranged spirally around the stem. Often new growth is richly colored, usually pink or bronze. Blooming in spring, summer, and autumn, the showy together in terminal spikes, form cylindrical bottlebrush-like heads. Round woody seed capsules crowd into a cylindrical group along the stem. Nectar-feeding birds are attracted to the flowers. The larger species are suitable as small street trees in mild climates.
CULTIVATION: Most callistemons prefer moist, well-drained, slightly acid soil in a sunny position; some are only marginally frost tolerant. All respond well to pruning in the final days of flowering to promote bushier growth. Propagate species from seed. Selected forms and cultivars are grown from half-hardened tip cuttings.

Callistephus chinensis

Callistemon citrinus 'Burgundy'

Callistemon citrinus

syn. *Callistemon lanceolatus*

SCARLET BOTTLEBRUSH

↔ 10 ft (3 m) ↑ 10 ft (3 m)

From eastern Australia. Shoots pink and silky. Bright red flowers in spring–autumn. Tolerates moderate coastal exposure and poor drainage. **'Burgundy'**, dark red bottlebrush flowers; **'Jeffersii'**, dwarf to 6 ft (1.8 m) tall, red-purple flowers, lemon-scented leaves; **'Splendens'** (syn. 'Endeavour'), broader leaves, masses of large, brilliant red flowers; **'White Anzac'**, white bottlebrush flowers. Zones 8–11.

Callistemon Hybrid Cultivars

↔ 5–10 ft (1.5–3 m)
↑ 6–20 ft (1.8–6 m)

Callistemons hybridize readily and in recent decades many outstanding hybrid cultivars have been named. All must be propagated from tip cuttings to retain the characteristics of the selected clone. Notable examples include: **'Harkness'**, light green leaves, brilliant red flowers; **'Hot Pink'**, intense magenta pink flowers; **'Injune'**, gray-green leaves, light pink flowers; **'Little John'** ★, dwarf to 3 ft (0.9 m) high, blue-green leaves, dark red flowers; **'Matthew Flinders'**, compact dwarf, bright red flowers; **'Mauve Mist'**, narrow leaves, spikes of mauve-pink flowers; **'Reeve's Pink'**, grows to 10 ft (3 m) high, pink flowers. Zones 9–11.

CALLISTEPHUS

CHINA ASTER

The sole species in this genus is an annual daisy (family Asteraceae) from China. However, despite being just one species, it has been developed into an array of garden varieties, which have flowers in white and all shades of pink, mauve-blue, red, and purple in both single- and double-flowered styles, all of which last well when cut. It is naturally a sturdy upright plant, though dwarf forms are available. The name is from the Greek *kallos* (beautiful) and *stephanus* (crown) and is a reference to the flowers.
CULTIVATION: Plant in the full sun with moist well-drained soil and feed occasionally with liquid fertilizer. Err on the cautious side with feeding or you may produce foliage at the expense of flowers. Raise from seed. Spring sown seed begins flowering by early summer and if the sowing is staggered a succession of bloom results.

Callistephus chinensis

↔ 8–12 in (20–30 cm)
↑ 12–36 in (30–90 cm)

Dark green, pointed oval leaves to over 3 in (8 cm) long, with coarsely toothed edges. Flowerheads are 2–4 in (5–10 cm) across, borne singly on long stems. **Milady Series Mixed**, strong-growing and bushy yet compact series growing to around 10 in (25 cm) tall, available in a wide color range. Zones 8–11.

CALLUNA

There is only one species in this genus belonging to the erica (Ericaceae) family. It is native to north and western Europe to Siberia, Turkey, Morocco, and the Azores. The height and spread of this small shrub is 2 ft (60 cm) on average, but this can vary greatly in some of the 500 or more cultivars. The leaves grow in overlapping pairs, arranged oppositely, along the stems, and look more like scales. The leaves are dark green, usually turning reddish or tinged with purple in winter. *Calluna* differs from *Erica* in that the corolla is hidden by the calyx. Produces pink to purplish pink flowers from summer to late autumn.
CULTIVATION: This plant prefers acid soil in an open well-drained position in full sun. Stems can be layered in spring and detached once rooted, or cuttings of half-hardened wood can be taken in mid-summer.

Calluna vulgaris

syn. *Erica vulgaris*

HEATHER, LING

↔ 30 in (75 cm) ↑ 24 in (60 cm)

Native to acid heathland. Flowers are tubular or bell-shaped racemes, single or double, ranging from white to pink to purple in mid-summer–late autumn. Leaves of cultivars range from pale yellow to gray-green to dark bottle green. **'Annemarie'**, double pink flowers on long racemes; **'Beoley Gold'**, yellow foliage, and single white flowers on shorter racemes; **'Blazeaway'** ★, red foliage in winter; **'County Wicklow'**, semi-prostrate, with double pale pink flowers in long racemes; **'Dark Beauty'**, neat bush, double dark crimson-red flowers; **'Darkness'**, dark red flowers; **'Firefly'**, rust-colored summer foliage, turning dull dark red in winter, deep mauve flowers; **'Gold Haze'**, light gold foliage, white flowers; **'Kinlochruel'**, bright green foliage, turning bronze in winter, long racemes of double white flowers; **'Multicolor'**, neat bush, copper foliage often tinged red or orange, mauve flowers; **'Radnor'**, bright green foliage, double pink flowers; **'Silver Queen'**, silver-gray foliage, pale mauve-tinted white flowers; **'Wickwar Flame'**, golden foliage, turning red for the winter months, and mauve-pink flowers. Zones 4–9.

Callistemon, Hybrid Cultivar, 'Injune'

Calluna vulgaris 'Silver Queen'

Calochortus albus

Calochortus luteus

CALOCEDRUS

Genus of 2 or 3 evergreen species, in the cypress (Cupressaceae) family, native to Thailand, Vietnam, Myanmar, southwest China, and western North America. Its name comes from the Greek *kalos* meaning beautiful and *kedros* meaning cedar. A handsome tree; a good ornamental, with the conical form the most popular. The overlapping leaves are arranged in crossed pairs in 2 rows along the stems. Male cones are borne singly and female cones are up to 1 in (25 mm) long, and have 6, sometimes 8, scales in pairs; only the center pair is fertile. The crown shape varies with climatic conditions. The timber is used for shingle tiles.
CULTIVATION: These plants are best suited to moderately fertile soil in full sun although they will tolerate partial shade. Half-hardened cuttings can be taken in summer and seed should be grown in containers with protection from winter frosts.

Calocedrus decurrens

INCENSE CEDAR

☼ ✱ ↔30 ft (9 m) ↑120 ft (36 m)

Native to western North America. Bark flakes off as it ages. Leaves glossy dark green with a triangular tip, are closely pressed to the stem. Cylindrical cones ripen to red-brown. Foliage of cultivar **'Aureovariegata'** is marked with yellow blotches, and smaller than others in the species. **'Compacta'** ★, globe-shaped, sometimes columnar, and very densely branched. In winter its branches turn brown. Zones 5–9.

CALOCHORTUS

CAT'S EAR, FAIRY LANTERNS, MARIPOSA

This genus of about 60 species of hardy bulbous perennials belongs to the lily (Liliaceae) family. Natives of North America, they grow in perfectly drained areas in grassland, scrub, and forest, and from low to high altitudes. The base of the leaves is sword-shaped. The flowers vary greatly—some are dainty, others flamboyant; they may be pendulous and globe-shaped or upright and open. All have 2 distinct whorls of 3 colorful outer sepals and 3 inner petals. At the base of each petal is a nectar gland, which is often prominently displayed. Flowers are colored white, yellow, orange, red, or purple, and are often marked with red or chocolate brown.
CULTIVATION: Cultivation requirements vary due to the different de-mands of species from a wide variety of habitats. Difficult to grow. In general, they require a sheltered position in full sunlight or half sun and a gritty soil with excellent drainage. They are averse to humidity, preferring wet-winter dry-summer climates.

Calochortus albus

WHITE FAIRY LANTERN, WHITE GLOBE LILY

◐ ✱ ↔6 in (15 cm) ↑6–24 in (15–60 cm)

Native to central California. Small, nodding, goblet-shaped flowers on branching stems. Flowers cream, occasionally flushed pink, with a deep red-brown spot inside, from spring–early summer. Zones 5–9.

Calochortus amabilis

DIOGENES LANTERN, GOLDEN GLOBE TULIP

☼ ✱ ↔6 in (15 cm) ↑8–12 in (20–30 cm)

Comes from northwestern California. Branching stems of nodding goblet-shaped flowers of deep yellow. Outer petals spreading and triangular, inner petals with fringed edges and folding over each other. Zones 5–9.

Calochortus amoenus

ROSE FAIRY LANTERN, SIERRA GLOBE TULIP

◐ ✱ ↔6 in (15 cm) ↑18 in (45 cm)

From central and southern California. Similar to *C. albus* but shorter. The nodding flowers of deep rose pink or purple form on slender stems from spring–summer. Flowers narrowly bell-shaped or more globose. Zones 5–9.

Calochortus luteus

GOLD NUGGETS, YELLOW MARIPOSA TULIP

☼ ✱ ↔6 in (15 cm)
↑8–20 in (20–50 cm)

From central California. Slender stems carry open bell-shaped flowers of clear yellow, up to 3 in (8 cm) wide, usually with a brown spot at the base of each petal. Flowers appear in spring and early summer. Nectar gland is crescent-shaped. Zones 5–9.

Calochortus monophyllus

☼ ✱ ↔6 in (15 cm) ↑4–8 in (10–20 cm)

Native to northern California and Oregon. A small slender species with branching stems of upright, open, yellow, bell-shaped flowers in spring. The petals are covered in fine hairs. Zones 5–9.

Calochortus splendens

☼ ✱ ↔6 in (15 cm) ↑8–24 in (20–60 cm)

From western USA. Bears upright bell-shaped flowers on leafy branching stems. The flowers are pale pink, with slightly hairy petals, a purple spot at the base, and contrasting bluish purple anthers. Zones 5–9.

Calochortus superbus

PROUD MARIPOSA

☼/◐ ✱ ↔6 in (15 cm)
↑16–24 in (40–60 cm)

Native to California. Bears bell-shaped white or cream flowers, streaked with purple, each petal with a maroon spot at the base surrounded by yellow. The outer petals are lance-shaped, the inner petals rounded and slightly hairy. The nectar gland is prominent and V-shaped. Flowering in late spring. Zones 5–9.

Calochortus umbellatus

OAKLAND STAR TULIP

◐ ✱ ↔6 in (15 cm) ↑4–6 in (10–15 cm)

Rare Californian species. Dainty, up-right, open flowers. white or cream, sometimes flushed pink, purple markings on petal bases; carried on umbels for long periods in spring. Zones 5–9.

CALODENDRUM

This genus comprising a single evergreen species in the rue (Rutaceae) family is from the coastal region of South Africa. The name comes from the Greek *kalos*, meaning beautiful, and *dendron*, meaning tree, which aptly describes this majestic tree. It has a spreading crown and is often used in parks and large gardens or as a street tree in the more temperate regions of the Southern Hemisphere and warmer regions of North America.

Calodendrum capense

CULTIVATION: *Calodendrum* prefers an open full sun position where its crown can develop unhindered. Grow in a reasonably fertile, well-composted and well-drained position where water is assured, especially in its initial growth period. Hardy to light frost when mature, it requires protection in early years when grown in marginal areas.

Calodendrum capense

CAPE CHESTNUT

☼ ❄ ↔30 ft (9 m) ↑30 ft (9 m)

Bright mid-green leaves dotted with oil glands. Flowers pink clusters, protruding stamens, and recurved petals dotted with oil glands, which transmit the light and make the flowers appear to glow in the sunlight in spring–summer. Zones 9–11.

CALOTHAMNUS

NET BUSH, CLAW FLOWER

One of the many Australian myrtle (Myrtaceae) family genera, these 40 species of evergreen shrubs are native to Western Australia. They are notable for their one-sided flower spikes and flowers with stamen filaments fused into broad straps. This has given the genus the common name net bush or, when the filaments are more entirely fused and curved, claw flowers. The flowers usually occur in late winter and spring. The foliage is needle-like, varying in length with the species.
CULTIVATION: Net bushes need a light, gritty, well-drained soil. They are drought tolerant and hardy to light frosts once established, needing moisture and shelter when young. Tip prune as the old wood is slow to shoot. Propagate by seed or soft to half-hardened tip cuttings, preferably from non-flowering stems.

Calothamnus quadrifidus

Calothamnus quadrifidus

COMMON NET BUSH, ONE-SIDED BOTTLEBRUSH

↔ 8 ft (2.4 m) ↑ 8 ft (2.4 m)

Upright, heavily branched shrub. Flattened needle-like leaves to 1¼ in (30 mm) long. Flower spikes bright red, with stamens in bundles of 4, to 8 in (20 cm) long. Cultivars include yellow-flowered, dwarf, and gray-green-foliaged forms. Zones 9–10.

CALOTIS

BURR DAISIES

Consisting of 26 species, 2 in southeastern Asia and 24 in Australia, this genus of annual and perennial herbs and small shrubs occurs in a variety of habitats and soils, and is placed in the daisy (Asteraceae) family. The simple or variously divided leaves are smooth, hairy, green, or gray-green. Flower-heads are daisy-like, borne singly or in clusters, terminal or axillary, in white, pink, blue, or yellow colors. The fruits are in globular burr-like heads. *Calotis* is closely related to the genus *Brachyscome*, which is more common in cultivation because its fruiting heads are not burr-like.
CULTIVATION: These plants prefer a sunny position in well-drained soil. They are propagated from seeds and from cuttings, which germinate and strike readily.

Calotis cuneifolia

BINDI-EYE, BLUE BURR DAISY

↔ to 3 ft (0.9 m)
↑ 8–16 in (20–40 cm)

Multi-stemmed hairy perennial common across mainland Australia. Leaves wedge-shaped, green, 1¾ in (40 mm) long, with bases sheathing stem. Blue, whitish or mauve flowerheads, ¾–1 in (18–25 mm) in diameter, throughout year, mostly during spring. Reddish fruit. Zones 8–9.

CALTHA

This buttercup (Ranunculaceae) family genus contains 10 species of herbaceous perennials, widespread in temperate regions of both hemispheres. Often very much like buttercups in general appearance, they have fleshy, bright to deep green, kidney- to heart-shaped leaves on sturdy leaf stalks and develop into mounding clumps of foliage. Flowers white to pale yellow or gold; although petal-less, their 5 or more petal-like sepals give them a buttercup-like appearance. Double-flowered forms common. Flowering season varies with species. Once used medicinally—named verrucaria because of supposed ability to cure warts—now considered too toxic for such purposes.
CULTIVATION: They are mostly very frost tolerant with a preference for damp soil and partly shaded conditions, though ordinary well-drained humus-rich garden soil in a woodland environment is perfectly acceptable. Their roots spread readily, though not nearly as aggressively as those of some of their buttercup cousins. Most easily propagated by division.

Caltha leptosepala

↔ 12 in (30 cm) ↑ 12 in (30 cm)

Attractive heart-shaped leaves. Silver-white flowers in spring. Zones 6–9.

Caltha palustris

syn. *Caltha polypetala*

KING CUP, MARSH MARIGOLD

↔ 16–24 in (40–60 cm)
↑ 12–24 in (30–60 cm)

Widespread in the northern temperate zone. Upright or spreading habit with kidney-shaped leaves, 4–8 in (10–20 cm) wide. Bears bright golden yellow flower-heads on upright stems. Several double-flowered cultivars with rounded heads, including **'Flore Pleno'** and the dark-leafed **'Monstrosa'**. Zones 3–9.

Caltha scaposa

↔ 12 in (30 cm) ↑ 6 in (15 cm)

From the Himalayas and western China. Low spreading habit with long-stemmed, heart-shaped, deep green leaves to 1½ in (35 mm) long, sometimes finely toothed. Deep yellow flowers in summer. Zones 6–9.

Calotis cuneifolia

CALYCANTHUS

Resembling magnolias, but in the allspice (Calycanthaceae) family, the aromatic deciduous shrubs of this temperate East Asian and North American genus of up to 6 species have similar characteristics. They grow to around 10 ft (3 m) tall with a considerable spread, have large elliptical leaves and strappy, many-petalled flowers in late spring and summer. Although the flowers are sometimes small and have rather dull colors, they are borne on the new growth and stand out well.
CULTIVATION: Although difficult to propagate from cuttings (layering or seed being preferred), allspice are not difficult to grow. They prefer cool moist soil with ample summer water in sun or half-sun. The flowers do not last well in low humidity.

Calycanthus fertilis

syn. *Calycanthus floridus* var. *glaucus*

ALLSPICE

↔ 7 ft (2 m) ↑ 10 ft (3 m)

Native to southeastern USA. Leaves glossy, deep green, to 6 in (15 cm) long. Mildly fragrant purple-red to brown flowers, to 2 in (5 cm) wide. Cultivars include the dwarf **'Nanus'** and **'Purpureus'**, which has purple-tinted foliage. Zones 6–10.

Calycanthus floridus

CAROLINA ALLSPICE, STRAWBERRY SHRUB

↔ 7 ft (2 m) ↑ 10 ft (3 m)

Native of southeastern USA. Leaves large, oval, dull mid-green. Bright red to dark red-brown fragrant flowers, up to 2 in (5 cm) wide. Zones 5–9.

Calycanthus occidentalis

Caltha palustris 'Flore Pleno'

Calycanthus occidentalis ★

CALIFORNIAN ALLSPICE, SPICE BUSH

↔ 7 ft (2 m) ↑ 10 ft (3 m)

From California, similar to *C. fertilis*, with slightly larger leaves, and reddish flowers fading to yellow with age. Large-flowered forms, with blooms up to 3 in (8 cm) wide, most often seen in garden centers. Zones 7–10.

CALYLOPHUS

This genus of 6 species from North America belongs to evening-primrose (Onagraceae) family and is closely allied to *Oenothera*. Herbaceous or subshrubby perennials, rarely annual, flowering in first year from seed. Stems are erect to almost creeping, bearing entire to serrated leaves. Flowers, borne in the upper axils, are hardly different in any obvious way from those of some *Oenothera* species; they open in early morning or from mid-afternoon until dusk, wilting after 1½ to 2 hours. The 4 greenish yellow sepals are often marked red or purple; the 4 reflexed yellow petals often redden on withering. Capsules are cylindrical, 4-angled, and contain many seeds in 2 rows in each of the 4 compartments.
CULTIVATION: Annuals are propagated from seed, as are perennials, which can also be increased by division of softwood cuttings from spring growths. As they have a tap root, take care when transplanting them to sunny well-drained sites in the garden.

Calylophus serrulatus

syns *Calylophus drummondianus*, *Oenothera serrulata*

BUSH SUNDROPS, DWARF SUNDROPS, PLAINS YELLOW PRIMROSE

↔ 12–24 in (30–60 cm)
↑ 12–24 in (30–60 cm)

Perennial from southern Canada, central and southern USA. Green leaves toothed in upper half. Flowers, opening pale to bright yellow in the morning and fading to apricot by next day, are 1 in (25 mm) across, from late spring–summer. Stamens are two lengths. Zones 3–9.

Calylophus serrulatus

CAMASSIA

CAMAS, QUAMASH

This genus consists of 5 species of bulbs in the asparagus (Asparagaceae) family, native mainly to western North America. The name *Camassia* comes from the Native American name, which is usually transliterated as quamash. The meaning of the name is unclear but what is known is that the bulbs are edible and were included in the diet of the native peoples. As garden plants they are tough and adaptable and one species, *C. leichtlinii*, has been extensively developed into garden forms. These plants have long narrow leaves and in late spring and early summer produce heads of 6-petalled flowers atop strong stems, rather reminiscent of some of the *Agapanthus*.
CULTIVATION: Mostly very frost hardy and easily grown in any fertile, well-drained soil that does not dry out. Plant in full or half-sun. May be raised from seed but then take up to 5 years to bloom, and because most garden plants are cultivars, division when dormant during winter is preferred.

Camassia cusickii

↔ 24–48 in (60–120 cm)
↕ 24–36 in (60–90 cm)

From northeastern Oregon. Blue-green leaves, 16–32 in (40–80 cm) long. Racemes of pale blue flowers with yellow anthers make up around half the height of flower stems. Flowers to 2 in (5 cm) wide. Zones 5–9.

Camassia leichtlinii

↔ 20–60 in (50–150 cm)
↕ 24–48 in (60–120 cm)

Found from British Columbia in Canada to California, USA. Rather stiff green leaves to 24 in (60 cm) long. Short racemes on tall stems. Flowers creamy white to lavender-blue. **'Semiplena'**, semi-double cream to yellow flowers. ***C. l.* subsp. *suksdorfii*** is a widespread blue-flowered subspecies, of which **'Alba'** is a white-flowered cultivar and **'Blauwe Donau'** ('Blue Danube') has dark blue flowers. Zones 3–9.

Camassia quamash

CAMASH, CAMOSH, SWAMP SEGO

↔ 16–40 in (40–100 cm)
↕ 12–32 in (30–80 cm)

Found over much of western USA. Slightly blue-green leaves to 20 in (50 cm) long. Flower racemes about one-third of the flower stem length. Pale blue to deep violet, rarely white flowers to over 2 in (5 cm) wide. Zones 5–9.

CAMELLIA

A member of the Theaceae family, the camellia genus has nearly 300 species, native to the coast and mountain regions of east Asia. They are evergreen shrubs or small trees, popular in gardens for their ornamental qualities. A few are also grown commercially for the teas made from their leaves. There are innumerable cultivars. Camellias bear short-stalked flowers and bloom during the colder months. A number of flower forms, sizes, and subtle and more flamboyant petal markings are recognized. Petal colors range between shades of white, yellow, pink, rose red, dark red, scarlet, purple-red and puce. Camellias are suitable for planting in formal or woodland settings, and for hedging, edging, topiary, and espalier.
CULTIVATION: While it is usual to choose and plant camellias in late autumn and winter, it is important to withhold nutrition and additional water during this time. Acid to neutral well-drained soils, shaded or semi-shaded positions, dry winters and wet summers suit the majority. Propagation is by grafting, or from cuttings in late summer to winter.

Camellia crapnelliana

↔ 15 ft (4.5 m) ↕ 25 ft (8 m)

Native of southwestern China. Bark is distinctive, smooth, and cinnamon red. Oval leaves glossy, dark green above, pale beneath, and heavily veined. Solitary large flowers with wavy, irregular, white petals, yellow stamens, in autumn. Large, round, brown seed pods. Zones 8–11.

Camellia forrestii

↔ 6–8 ft (1.8–2.4 m)
↕ 6–8 ft (1.8–2.4 m)

Shrub or small tree native to southern China and northern Vietnam. Semi-glossy, pointed oval leaves to 3 in (8 cm) long. Flowers small, white, mildly fragrant, in spring. Zones 9–10.

Camellia granthamiana

↔ 6 ft (1.8 m) ↕ 12 ft (3.5 m)

From southern China. Buds brown; large, single, creamy, flowers, slightly reflexed petals, in early winter. Long puckered leaves, heavily veined, shiny. Open spreading growth. Zones 8–11.

Camellia grijsii

↔ 8 ft (2.4 m) ↕ 10 ft (3 m)

From eastern and central China. Leaves oval, dark green, finely toothed. Flowers fragrant, small, white, lobed petals, yellow stamens. Resembles *C. sasanqua*, but flowers in winter and early spring. Zones 8–11.

Camellia hiemalis

↔ 6 ft (1.8 m) ↕ 10 ft (3 m)

Known only in cultivation, may be a hybrid. Leaves dark green, flowers white or pale pink, lobed irregular petals, in winter–spring. **'Bonanza'**, semi-double peony-form flowers, deep pink to red petals; **'Chansonette'**, brilliant pink petals with hints of lavender; **'Shishigashira'**, compact plant, flowers rose pink to red, semi-double, petals slightly fluted; **'Shôwa-no-sakae'**, Japanese cultivar, semi-double flowers; **'Sparkling Burgundy'**, peony-formed flowers, dark cerise petals. All suitable for espaliering. Zones 7–10.

Camellia japonica

COMMON CAMELLIA

↔ 25 ft (8 m) ↕ 30 ft (9 m)

Shrub or small tree found on several Chinese, Korean, Taiwanese, and Japanese islands. Single flowers, red or puce-pink, mildly scented. Leaves broadly oval, pointed, glossy above, paler, duller, and lightly spotted beneath. Variable sized fruit. Appearance and tolerance variable in wild. Well-known variation is apple camellia, ***C. j.* var. *macrocarpa***, with large, red, apple-like fruit.

Cultivars of *C. japonica* are most popular; over 2,000 display different flower forms, colors, petal markings, growth habits, preferences, and tolerances. Leaves glossy, neat, elliptical. Most grow into neat dense shrubs and, ultimately, small trees. They flourish in suitable climates and soils, in shaded or semi-shaded positions, and sheltered in cold climates. Well-draining neutral to acid soil is essential. **'Adolphe Audusson'**,

Camassia cusickii

Camassia leichtlinii

Camellia forrestii

Camellia grijsii

Camellia japonica 'Alba Plena'

Camellia lutchuensis

semi-double dark red flowers; **'Alba Plena'**, double with snow white, symmetrical, overlapping petals; **'Akashigata'** (syn. 'Lady Clare), semi-double rich rose-pink flowers; **'Alexander Hunter'**, rich crimson flowers; **'Berenice Boddy'**, large, semi-double, pink flowers; **'Betty Ridley'**, sturdy bush, mid-pink, formal double flowers; **'Black Magic'**, semi-double, deep black-red flowers, fast-growing bush; **'Bob Hope'**, dark red semi-double flowers with yellow stamens; **'Bob's Tinsie'**, upright compact growth habit, small, bright red, anemone-form flowers; **'Bokuhan'** (syn. 'Tinsie'), miniature anemone-form flowers, red outer petals, dense boss of white petaloids, small leaves, moderately sun tolerant; **'Brushfield's Yellow'**, anemone-form, pale creamish white flowers; **'Coquettii'**, formal double, or incomplete double, red flowers; **'Debutante'**, large, pale rose, informal double flowers; **'Dona Herzilia de Freitas Magalhaes'**, purple-violet flowers; **'Elegans'** (syn. 'Chandleri Elegans'), pink flowers—has given rise to several breeding programs; **'Elegans Champagne'**, big creamy petals; **'Elegans Supreme'**, deep pink ruffled flowers; **'Elegans Variegated'**, pink flowers with white blotches; **'Fire 'n' Ice'**, semi-double to double, bright red, often white fleck in center; **'Gloire de Nantes'**, semi-double to incomplete double mid-pink flowers; **'Grand Prix'**, semi-double vivid red flowers; **'Janet Waterhouse'**, white, double, perfectly symmetrical flowers; **'Jupiter'**, formal double red flowers; **'Lady Loch'**, veined, whitish pink, peony-form flowers; **'Lavinia Maggi'**, white petals, streaked light and dark pinkish red; **'Masayoshi'** (syn. 'Donckelaeri'), rich pinkish red double flowers, whitish blotches on petals; **'Miss Charleston'**, upright form, intense red flowers; **'Modern Art'**, petaloid double, white overlaid pink, deep pink flecks, sectors, and stripes; **'Mrs D. W. Davis Descanso'**, upright habit, semi-double flowers of softest pink; **'Night Rider'**, compact shrub, semi-double, very dark red flowers; **'Nuccio's Cameo'**, coral pink flowers; **'Nuccio's Carousel'**, medium-sized, semi-double, pink flowers; **'Nuccio's Gem'**, early blooming; **'Nuccio's Jewel'**, formal double, star-shaped flowers, shaded pink petals; **'Nuccio's Pearl'**, blush white petals tipped in shades of orchid pink; **'Roma Risorta'**, flowers with pink and red striped petals; **'Rubescens Major'**, glowing rose red, veined petals, dark, glossy leaves; **'Tama-no-ura'**, dark red, petals edged in white, upright yellow stamens; **'Tomorrow'**, prize-winning plant bred in America, large informal double flowers, pink petals and petaloids with deeper pink markings, early blooming (this strong floriferous plant has produced other cultivars, among them **'Tomorrow's Dawn'**, an informal double, with deep pink flowers); **'Tricolor'**, with semi-double flowers, the petals white with rose-red markings; and **'Twilight'**, with large light blush pink flowers that fade to silvery white. The **Higo Group** camellias, a popular Japanese form of *C. japonica*, are not a separate species; they have flat flowers, with profuse flared stamens, gold, pink, or red, and come in single and semi-double forms. Petals solid, blotched, or striped. Zones 8–10.

Camellia lutchuensis

↔ 8 ft (2.4 m) ↑ 8 ft (2.4 m)

From Taiwan and Japan. Open pendulous habit. Small, scented, white flowers in winter. Leaves small, dark, russet-colored new growth. Sienna brown buds. **'Fairy Blush'**, single, fragrant, pink-toned flowers; **'Quintessence'**, low, spreading habit, very pale pink single flowers, scented. Zones 8–10.

Camellia reticulata 'Captain Rawes'

Camellia maliflora

↔ 4 ft (1.2 m) ↑ 7 ft (2 m)

Thought to be a Chinese species, now believed to be of garden origin. Leaves small, dense, mid-green. Flowers two-toned, pink, peony-form, appear in winter. In cold climates espalier against a sheltered wall. Zones 8–10.

Camellia nitidissima

syn. *Camellia chrysantha*

GOLDEN CAMELLIA

↔ 8 ft (2.4 m) ↑ 10 ft (3 m)

From northern Vietnam and south-western China. Pale bark; leaves leathery, large, conspicuously veined, pale green, with bronze new growth. Flowers golden yellow, in winter–spring. Zones 9–11.

Camellia oleifera

syn. *Camellia drupifera*

OIL CAMELLIA, OIL TEA

↔ 12 ft (3.5 m) ↑ 20 ft (6 m)

Slow-growing species from southeastern Asia. Forms a dense shrub, eventually a small tree. In China, a clear thin oil is extracted from its seeds, which is used for cooking and in cosmetics. Single scented flowers, white petals long, lobed, and slightly twisted. Used in the breeding of cold-hardy camellias. **'Lushan Snow'** is an attractive cultivar. Zones 6–10.

Camellia pitardii

↔ 12 ft (3.5 m) ↑ 20 ft (6 m)

Native of southern China. Leaves lance-shaped, saw-toothed. Flowers shades of delicate pale pink, rose pink, or white, with conspicuous bright red-pink stamens that fade to white. Attractive species used in tubs, mixed shrubberies, bonsai, and breeding programs. Cultivars include: **'Fairy Bouquet'**, soft pink flowers; **'Gay Pixie'**, rich pink flowers; **'Moonbeam'**, upright habit, pink flowers; **'Nicky Crisp'**, light to mid-pink, semi-double, erect growth habit; **'Snippet'**, has pale pink notched petals, used as an edging plant and is particularly suitable for bonsai; **'Sprite'**, attractive flowers with soft salmon pink petals. Zones 8–10.

Camellia purpurea

↔ 3–7 ft (0.9–2 m) ↑ 10–17 ft (3–5 m)

Small tree from Yunnan Province, China. Thick elliptical leaves, 6–8 in (15–20 cm) long. Closely related to *C. sinensis*. Dark red flowers, 1¾–2½ in (4–6 cm) across. Fruits purple and green. Zones 8–10.

Camellia reticulata

↔ 15 ft (4.5 m) ↑ 30 ft (9 m)

Tough open species from western China. Flowers rose pink, in noticeably velvety bracts. Leaves net-veined and toothed, and duller, darker, and narrower than those of *C. japonica*. Long-lived plant, can adopt tree-like form and grow to 30 ft (9 m), but is usually shorter in cultivation. Many handsome cultivars carry distinctive leaves of parent plant and can in time develop parent's tree-like stance, size, and open habit. Today, cultivars of *C. reticulata* are sometimes referred to as Yunnan camellias. *C. r.* **f.** ***simplex*** is wild form. *C. r.* **'Arch of Triumph'**, huge, peony-form, loose flowers, rose red petals, glowing yellow stamens; **'Bright Beauty'**, soft light red blooms; **'Buddha'**, rose pink, semi-double, very large flowers; **'Captain Rawes'**, irregular, semi-double, carmine flowers; **'Change of Day'**, semi-double pale pink flowers, yellow stamens; **'Cornelian'**, large, white-blotched, red flowers, leaves can be variegated; **'Dark Jewel'**, rich red peony-form flowers; **'Dayinhong'** (syn. 'Shot Silk'), an old Chinese cultivar bearing prolific, large, peony-form flowers composed of wavy ruby pink petals; **'Dr. Clifford Parks'**, bright red, informal double, vigorous upright growth; **'Highlight'**, semi-double, scarlet blooms, yellow stamens; **'Ida Cossom'**, attractive pink blooms; **'Lasca Beauty'**, dense, bushy growth, mid-pink semi-double flowers; **'Mandalay Queen'**, dark green foliage, pinkish red flowers; Narrow-leafed Shot Silk/ **'Liuye Yinhong'**, willowy appearance, narrower leaves; **'Nuccio's Ruby'**, semi-double ruby red flowers; **'Otto Hopfer'**, dark pink flowers, stamens tipped gold; **'Red Crystal'**, scarlet flowers, golden stamens; **'Zipao'** (syn. 'Purple Gown'), old Chinese cultivar, deep purple buds, opening into large wine red flowers, pin-striped in red. Zones 8–11.

Camellia rosiflora

↔ 2–3 ft (0.6–0.9 m) ↑ 3–7 ft (0.9–2 m)

Spreading evergreen shrub, native to China. Soft rose pink to reddish pink, funnel-shaped flowers with 6 to 9 petals up to 1 in (25 mm) across. Elliptical leaves, 3 in (8 cm) long, dark green above, paler beneath. Zones 8–10.

Camellia rusticana 'Otome'

Camellia saluenensis

Camellia rusticana

syns *C. decumbens, C. japonica subsp. rusticana*

SNOW CAMELLIA

↔ to 2 m ↑ to 4 m

Occurs only in montane forests and woodlands of western Honshu (Japan) above 2,300 ft (700 m). It is similar to *C. japonica*, but its flowers are pink, not red, and its petiole is shorter and hairy. Although quite cold-tolerant, it has not been used much in breeding programs. **'Botanyuki'**, pale cream flowers; **'Otome'**, full pale pink flowers. Zones 7–9.

Camellia salicifolia

↑ 7–10 ft (2–3 m) ↔ 4–7 ft (1.2–2 m)

Small tree from China and Taiwan, named for similarity of its weeping habit to willow *(Salix)*. White flowers, singly or in pairs, with 5 to 6 oval petals, to ¾ in (18 mm) across. Very narrow elliptical leaves, 2–4 in (5–10 cm) long, serrated. Branches and leaf undersides furry. Zones 9–11.

Camellia saluenensis

↔ 4–15 ft (1.2–4.5 m)
↑ 4–15 ft (1.2–4.5 m)

Native to southwestern China. Open, branching, flowers single, white, sugar pink, red, wavy lightly lobed petals, in late–early spring. Crowded, elongate, oval leaves, dark green with blunt tips. Used for bonsai, woodlands, breeding frost-hardy camellias. Zones 7–10.

Camellia sasanqua 'Narumigata'

Camellia sasanqua

↔ 5 ft (1.5 m) ↑ 10–25 ft (3–8 m)

From Japan. Straggling, woodland, tree-like shrub. Leaves very shiny, dark green. Flowers scented, single, white or pale pink, in autumn. **'Cotton Candy'**, tall, spreading, free-flowering plant with soft, clear pink, semi-double flowers and ruffled petals; **'Crimson King'**, blooms early, deep pink-red semi-double flowers; **'Jean May'**, upright habit, attractive, double, pink flowers; **'Kanjiro'**, semi-double, bright cerise pink, branch tips slightly weeping; **'Mikunikô'**, early bloomer, single rose pink flowers with mauve tonings; **'Mine-no-yuki'**, early bloomer, abundant snow white flowers; **'Misty Moon'**, upright habit and large, wavy, rounded petals of pale lavender-pink; **'Narumigata'**, white flower petals with curled pinkish red edges. Australia has produced the **Paradise Series** of sasanqua camellias. Their small to medium-sized informal double flowers are profuse and fluffy. Of the cultivars, **'Plantation Pink'** has a tall spreading habit making it especially suitable for hedging or espalier; it bears a profusion of flat, bright pink, single flowers that are beautifully formed. **'Red Willow'** has rose pink petals, muted at the center, with a willowy habit. Zones 8–11.

Camellia transnokoensis

Camellia sinensis

syn. *Thea sinensis*

TEA

↔ 10 ft (3 m) ↑ 8–20 ft (2.4–6 m)

Probably originating in China, grown commercially for the production of tea for centuries. Flowers small, single, long-stalked, often in pairs, pronounced yellow stamens, usually rounded white petals. Most of the tea drunk in the Western world is made from C. s. var. assamica (Assam tea), which has smooth-edged, thin, tapering leaves. Grows to 50 ft (15 m) but is usually hedged to a height that is convenient for picking. C. s. var. sinensis (Chinese tea), from which unfermented green teas are made, has long, narrow, crinkly leaves and a bushy appearance to about 20 ft (6 m). C. s. **'Blushing Bride'** is an attractive cultivar. Zones 8–11.

Camellia transnokoensis

↔ to 7 ft (2 m) ↑ to 25 ft (8 m)

Tall shrub or small tree found on the slopes Mt Noko in Taiwan at an altitude of 8,000 ft (2,400 m) in montane vegetation. Small, white, stalkless flowers, less than 10 mm across, borne singly in the leaf axils. The leaf buds are not hairy, a feature that distinguishes this species from *C. nokoensis*. **'Sweet Jane'** is an attractive cultivar with many overlapping petals in two shades of pink. Zones 8–11.

Camellia tsaii

↔ 15 ft (4.5 m) ↑ 30 ft (9 m)

From southern China, Myanmar, and northern Vietnam. Spreading pendulous habit. Prolific, miniature, white flowers in winter. Long, glossy, dark green leaves, paler undersides, wavy margins. Zones 8–11.

Camellia × *vernalis*

↔ 6–12 ft (1.8–3.5 m) ↑ 15 ft (4.5 m)

The derivation of this small group is unclear; it is distinguished from the cultivars of *C. sasanqua,* which it closely resembles, by its tolerance of cold and its mid-winter and mid-spring flowering. **'Egao'** has pink semi-double flowers; the blooms of **'Ginryû'** have delicate white petals with ruffled edges, sometimes with a pink tinge; **'Shibori-egao'** has white-blotched pink-petalled flowers; **'Star Above Star'**, layered reflexed petals arranged in an apparently random manner; **'Yuletide'** blooms have clear bright scarlet petals. Zones 7–10.

Camellia vietnamensis

↔ to 7 ft (2 m) ↑ to 25 ft (8 m)

Native to Vietnam and neighboring regions of China, occurring in lightly wooded areas. Small tree, related to *C. sasanqua*. Leaves up to 4 in (10 cm) long. Flowers greenish white, 5 to 7 petals, up to 1¾–2½ in (4–6 cm) across. Capsules red to yellow. Zones 9–11.

Camellia × *williamsii*

↔ 4–10 ft (1.2–3 m)
↑ 7–15 ft (2–4.5 m)

Hybrids of *C. japonica* and *C. saluenensis*, first developed in UK in 1930s. Said to be most easily grown and free flowering of all camellias. They can endure cold climates and winter-wet root runs better than many others. Leaves duller, paler than *C. japonica*. Flowers mostly in shades of silvery sugary pink. Award-winner **'Anticipation'** has deep pink flowers to 4 in (10 cm) across; **'Brigadoon'**, semi-double pink flowers; **'Donation'**, light pink with darker pink-veined petals, thrives in cooler climates; **'Dreamboat'**, formal double, lavender-pink, slightly deeper petal edges; **'Elsie Jury'**, created in New Zealand, pale pink, producing large frilly blooms to 5 in (12 cm) in diameter; **'Francis Hanger'**, single white flowers; **'George Blandford'**, early flowering, lavender-pink semi-double flowers; **'Golden Spangles'**, single red flowers, variegated leaves; **'J. C. Williams'**, pink flowers over a flowering season that lasts longer than usual; **'Joan Treharne'**, mid-pink double flowers; **'Jubilation'**, informal double pink flowers, long golden stamens; **'Jury's Yellow'**, white outer petals around dense boss of creamy yellow petaloids; **'Les Jury'**, compact and bushy, bright red double flowers; **'Margaret Waterhouse'**, vigorous plant, well-formed, sugar pink, semi-double flowers with rounded petals; **'Mary Christian'**, rich pink petals surrounding mass of golden stamens; **'Saint Ewe'**, single vivid pink flowers, lustrous leaves; **'Shocking Pink'**, tall bushy shrub, which bears bright pink, irregular, ruffled petals in an irregular semi-double formation; **'Water Lily'**, upright shrub, bearing formal double rose pink flowers with pointed petals. Zones 8–10.

Camellia yunnanensis

☀ ❄ ↔7 ft (2 m) ↑20 ft (6 m)

From southern China. Bears prolific, single, white flowers with prominent yellow stamens during late summer–autumn. Leaves dark green on top, paler beneath, smooth and finely toothed. Zones 8–11.

Camellia Hybrid Cultivars

☀ ❄ ↔3–20 ft (0.9–6 m)
↑3–20 ft (0.9 m–6 m)

Most of the popular hybrids have been bred to withstand particular conditions, notably cold wet winters, exposure to sunlight or marginal soil conditions, as well as for their attractive appearances. **'Adorable'** has an upright habit and formal double pink flowers; **'Fragrant Pink Improved'** has miniature, deep pink, fragrant flowers, open spreading habit, long flowering season, red new growth; **'Francie L'**, semi-double pink to red flowers; **'Freedom Bell'**, upright habit, semi-double red flowers; **'Inspiration'** has abundant semi-double pink flowers, petals sometimes with ruffled edges; **'Ole'**, has dark pink buds that open to salmon pink flowers; **'Salutation'**, notched silvery pink petals, long yellow stamens, large semi-double flower formation. **'Satan's Robe'**, upright glossy shrub, flowers large, semi-double carmine petals, golden stamens; **'Snow Drop'**, small distinctive gray-green foliage, with miniature white flowers occasionally flushed with pale pink. The camellias of the **Winter Series**, which bloom during the colder months, were bred in Maryland, USA, to withstand the cold conditions and give color to the garden. **'Winter's Charm'**, an upright shrub, has medium-sized, semi-double flowers composed of orchid pink petals and petaloids; **'Winter's Fire'**, single, open, puce-pink petals surrounding pronounced yellow stamens; **'Winter's Rose'** bears flowers with the palest of pink serrated petals arranged in a semi-double fluffy-looking formation. The Australian-bred **Wirlinga Series** produces an amazing number of miniature, often clustered flowers over quite prolonged periods. **'Wirlinga Belle'** has single, soft pink, medium-sized flowers, and an open growth habit; **'Wirlinga Cascade'**, a seedling from 'Wirlinga Belle' bears single pink flowers; **'Wirlinga Gem'**, abundant tiny pale pink flowers. Zones 8–10.

Camellia, Hybrid Cultivar, 'Ole'

Camellia × *williamsii* 'Anticipation'

CAMPANULA

This large genus of about 300 species of hardy annual, biennial, and perennial plants belongs to the bellflower (Campanulaceae) family. It contains a number of popular and beautiful garden plants. Many are native to Mediterranean areas, the Balkans, and Caucasus region. Some are from North America and temperate Asia. Their growth habit is ground-hugging and clump-forming, or erect and branching. A few species are invasive. Leaves are usually alternately arranged. Flowers are in shades of blue, mauve, pale pink, and white. They range from large drooping bells to delicate open stars, and are borne on panicles, spikes, or singly. With such variety there is a *Campanula* that is suitable for any rock garden, border, woodland, or "wild" garden situation. CULTIVATION: Most species grow easily in any reasonably fertile well-drained soil in sun or half-sun. Some alpine species require grittier soil and dislike winter wet. Propagate from seed, basal cuttings or by division.

Campanula carpatica

syn. *Campanula turbinata*

CARPATHIAN BELLFLOWER, TUSSOCK BELLFLOWER

☀/☀ ❄ ↔12–16 in (30–40 cm)
↑6–12 in (15–30 cm)

From the Carpathian Mountains. Low-growing perennial forming a thick clump of small bright green leaves. In summer the plant is covered with pale blue or white, upward facing, open cup-shaped flowers, 1–2 in (2.5–5 cm) across: *C. c.* f. ***alba*** has white flowers. *C. c.* **'Blaue Clips'**, blue flowers; **'Blue Moonlight'**, very open flowers, light grayish-blue; **'Chewton Joy'**, light blue petals edged with deeper blue. Zones 3–9.

Campanula chamissonis

syn. *Campanula dasyantha subsp. chamissonis*

☀ ❄ ↔8–12 in (10–30 cm)
↑2–6 in (5–15 cm)

From eastern Asia, Aleutian Islands, and Alaska. Low-growing perennial with fleshy stems and small spoon-shaped glossy leaves. Blue bell-shaped flowers are streaked with white and carried on individual stems through summer. **'Superba'** has larger flowers. Zones 3–9.

Campanula cochlearifolia

syn. *Campanula pusilla*

FAIRIES' THIMBLES

☀ ❄ ↔10 in (25 cm) ↑3 in (8 cm)

Creeping fleshy-stemmed perennial from the European Alps. Forms tight clumps of small rounded leaves. Bell-shaped pale lavender-blue flowers hang from wiry stems for long periods over summer. *C. c.* var. ***alba*** has white flowers; the *C. c.* **Baby Series** includes **'Blue Baby'**, prolific, pale blue flowers; **'Bavaria Blue'**, a very compact plant with dark blue flowers; **'Elizabeth Oliver'**, with double pale blue flowers. Zones 6–9.

Campanula garganica

syn. *Campanula elatines var. garganica*

☀ ❄ ↔6–12 in (15–30 cm)
↑6 in (15 cm)

Native to Italy. This low-growing perennial forms tight clumps of small light green leaves. Bears masses of small, starry, light blue flowers on lax panicles, for long periods in summer. **'Dickson's Gold'** (syn. 'Aurea') has golden foliage. Zones 5–9.

Campanula glomerata

CLUSTERED BELLFLOWER

☀ ❄ ↔12–24 in (30–60 cm)
↑12–36 in (30–90 cm)

Perennial species native to Europe and Asia, from England to Siberia. Forms clumps by suckering. Bristly stems, purplish blue flowers in terminal spherical heads and also in leaf axils. Long flowering period over summer. *C. g.* **var. *acaulis***, very dwarf plants, stemless flowers at the base of the rosette. *C. g.* **'Nana'** and **'Purple Pixie'** are smaller with deep purple flowers; **'Superba'**, large robust plant with deep purple flowers. Zones 4–9.

Campanula garganica 'Dickson's Gold'

Campanula isophylla

FALLING STARS, ITALIAN BELLFLOWER, STAR OF BETHLEHEM

☀ ❄ ↔12–18 in (30–45 cm)
↑6 in (15 cm)

From northern Italy, trailing perennial with small heart-shaped leaves. It is smothered in 1 in (25 mm) wide, starry, mid-blue flowers in summer. Suitable for hanging baskets. Protect from winter wet. **'Alba'**, white flowers; **'Stella Blue'**, mid-blue flowers; **'Stella White'**, clear white flowers. Zones 7–9.

Campanula laciniata

☀ ❄ ↔12 in (30 cm) ↑24 in (60 cm)

From Crete and Greece. Erect branching biennial or perennial with basal rosettes. Finely cut lance-shaped leaves. Wide cup-shaped blue flowers, borne in large crowded racemes in summer. Zones 8–10.

Campanula lactiflora

MILKY BELLFLOWER

☀ ❄ ↔2 ft (0.6 m) ↑3–5 ft (0.9–1.5 m)

From the Caucasus region, an upright perennial with well-branched, leafy, arching stems. Its milky blue bell-shaped flowers are borne in wide showy panicles in summer. **'Alba'** bears white flowers; **'Loddon Anna'**, soft pinkish white flowers; **'Macrantha'**, large violet-purple flowers; **'Prichard's Variety'**, violet-blue flowers on slightly smaller plant. Zones 5–9.

Campanula laciniata

C

Campanula lasiocarpa

↔ 6–12 in (15–30 cm)
↑ 4–6 in (10–15 cm)

From North America, Siberia, and Japan. Tufted perennial with small broad leaves. Upward facing, open, bell-shaped flowers of violet-blue are borne singly in summer. Best suited to rock gardens or pot culture. Zones 4–9.

Campanula latifolia

GIANT BELLFLOWER, GREAT BELLFLOWER

↔ 2 ft (0.6 m) ↑ 3–5 ft (0.9–1.5 m)

Found throughout Europe and east to Kashmir. Leafy perennial with stiff unbranched stems. Slightly velvety, broad, pointed leaves with serrated edges. Pale purplish blue, bell-shaped flowers borne along the stems for long periods during the summer. *C. l.* var. ***macrantha*,** large flowers of deep violet-blue. **'Alba'**, large white flowers. Zones 4–9.

Campanula latiloba

syn. *Campanula grandis*

↔ 18 in (45 cm)
↑ 24–36 in (60–90 cm)

Native to Siberia. Clumping perennial forms basal rosettes of narrow pointed leaves. Crowded spikes of open, deep lavender-blue, cup-shaped flowers in summer. **'Hidcote Amethyst'**, lilac-pink flowers. Zones 4–9.

Campanula longistyla

↔ 12–18 in (30–45 cm)
↑ 6–18 in (15–45 cm)

From the Caucasus region. Upright biennial or perennial. Lower leaves oval, forming basal rosettes. Upper leaves lance-shaped, spikes of nodding, bell-shaped flowers of deep violet in summer. Zones 5–9.

Campanula medium

CANTERBURY BELLS, CUP AND SAUCER

↔ 12 in (30 cm)
↑ 24–36 in (60–90 cm)

Native to southern Europe. Biennial, with basal rosettes of soft, hairy, lance-shaped leaves. Showy bell-shaped flowers, with recurved rims, on leafy stems in summer, in shades of white, pink, or blue. Popular for use as cut flowers. Several seed strains available. **'Calycanthema'**, calyx is petal-like, forming "saucer" below cup-shaped flowers. Zones 8–10.

Campanula persicifolia

PEACH-LEAFED BELLFLOWER, WILLOW BELLFLOWER

↔ 18 in (45 cm)
↑ 24–36 in (60–90 cm)

Native to Europe, eastern Asia, and northern Africa. Perennial, forming rosettes of narrow wavy-edged leaves. Open, blue, 2 in (5 cm) wide, bell-shaped flowers, are borne on showy stems in summer. This long-flowering plant has many single and double cultivars, including: **'Bennett's Blue'** (syn. 'Wortham Belle'), pale blue double flowers; **'Boule de Neige'**, large, double, white flowers; **'Chettle Charm'**, single white flowers edged with blue; **'Fleur de Neige'**, large, white, open, cup-shaped flowers; and **'Planiflora'** (syn. 'Nitida'), dwarf form to 8 in (20 cm) high, wide mid-blue flowers. Zones 4–9.

Campanula portenschlagiana

syn. *Campanula muralis*

↔ 18–24 in (45–60 cm)
↑ 6 in (15 cm)

From southern Europe. A vigorous alpine perennial with small heart-shaped leaves. It is smothered through the summer months with erect starry flowers of lavender-blue. **'Resholdt's Variety'** produces deep vivid blue flowers. Zones 4–9.

Campanula poscharskyana

SERBIAN BELLFLOWER

↔ 18–24 in (45–60 cm)
↑ 6–8 in (15–20 cm)

A native of Croatia. This vigorous alpine perennial is similar to related species, *C. portenschlagiana*, but it has a more refined appearance. Bears starry flowers, lavender to violet, in summer–autumn. Spreads rapidly in rock gardens. **'Blue Gown'**, large mid-blue flowers; **'Blue Waterfall'**, vigorous and free-flowering, dark blue flowers with lighter centers cascade outward from plant; **'E. H. Frost'** bears milky white starry flowers; **'Erich G. Arends'** has blue flowers; **'Lisduggan Variety'**, lavender-pink flowers; **'Multiplicity' ★**, double lavender-blue flowers; **'Stella'**, bright blue flowers. Zones 6–9.

Campanula punctata

syn. *Campanula nobilis*

↔ 18 in (45 cm) ↑ 12 in (30 cm)

From Siberia and Japan. A somewhat invasive perennial forming clumps of pointed heart-shaped leaves. Tubular, pendulous, bell-shaped flowers, to 3 in (8 cm) long, cream, flushed with pink and spotted inside with red. ***C. p.* f. *rubriflora*,** narrow cream flowers tinged pink to purple, heavily spotted with red inside. ***C. p.* 'Cherry Bells'**, cherry red with paler edging. Zones 6–9.

Campanula pyramidalis

CHIMNEY BELLFLOWER

↔ 2 ft (0.6 m) ↑ 4–7 ft (1.2–2 m)

From Europe. Short-lived clumping perennial usually grown as biennial. Broad, pointed, serrated-edged leaves. Tall branching stems of densely packed open bell-shaped flowers in pale blue or white in summer. Best grown in the conservatory in cooler areas. Zones 8–10.

Campanula raddeana

↔ 12 in (30 cm) ↑ 12 in (30 cm)

From the Caucasus region. Tufted perennial with small, glossy, dark green, heart-shaped leaves. Sprays of drooping, violet-purple, bell-shaped flowers on upright stems in summer. Zones 6–9.

Campanula rapunculoides

↔ 24 in (60 cm) ↑ 36 in (90 cm)

Native to Europe. Robust, invasive perennial forming large patches of serrated nettle-like leaves. Tall stems of nodding bell-shaped flowers in shades of blue to violet in summer. Best suited to the wild garden. Zones 4–9.

Campanula rapunculus

RAMPION

↔ 24 in (60 cm)
↑ 24–36 in (60–90 cm)

A biennial from Europe, northern Africa, and Siberia. The oval leaves are pointed. The small pale blue or white bell-flowers are borne on leafy stems in summer. The thick taproots and leaves can be used as salad vegetables. Zones 4–9.

Campanula rotundifolia

BLUEBELL, HAREBELL

↔ 10–18 in (25–45 cm)
↑ 6–12 in (15–30 cm)

Found throughout much of the Northern Hemisphere, this fleshy-stemmed perennial has heart-shaped leaves forming rosettes. Dainty bell-shaped flowers, white to deep blue, on slender stems during summer. Buds are upright but flowers hang when opened. Zones 3–9.

Campanula takesimana

↔ 18 in (45 cm) ↑ 24 in (60 cm)

From Korea, a rather invasive fleshy-stemmed perennial. Forms basal rosettes of large leaves. Bears tall stems of long, drooping, tubular bellflowers in summer. Flowers creamy white to lilac-pink on the outside, and spotted maroon inside. **'Beautiful Trust'** (syn. 'Beautiful Truth'), drooping spidery petals, pure white; **'Elizabeth' ★**, prolific and long flowering. Blooms have a dull purplish pink exterior and maroon spotted interior. Zones 4–9.

Campanula trachelium

COVENTRY BELLS, NETTLE-LEAFED BELLFLOWER, THROATWORT

↔ 12 in (30 cm) ↑ 24 in (60 cm)

Native to Europe, northern Africa and Siberia. Bristly perennial with serrated-edged pointed leaves. Fine, hairy, bluish purple, tubular bell-flowers, borne on dense leafy panicles in summer: ***C. t.* subsp. *athoa*** comes from Greece and Turkey; stalkless flowers. ***C. t.* var. *alba*** produces white flowers. Zones 4–9.

C. latifolia var. *macrantha* 'Alba'

Campanula medium

Campanula portenschlagiana

Campanula vidalii

syn. *Azorina vidalii*

↔12 in (30 cm)
↑12–20 in (30–50 cm)

A fleshy evergreen perennial with narrow shiny leaves growing toward the branch tips. In late summer stems of waxy, pale pink, bell-shaped flowers are held above the foliage. Zones 10–11.

Campanula Hybrid Cultivars

↔6–36 in (15–90 cm)
↑12–48 in (30–120 cm)

Bellflowers are naturally variable. Many hybrids and cultivars have been produced in a range of sizes, colors, and flower forms. **'Birch Hybrid'**, extremely free-flowering with lavender-blue flowers; **'Blue Wonder'**, double powder blue flowers in summer; **'Burghaltii'**, stems of hanging bellflowers turning unusual grayish mauve as they age; **'Joe Elliott'**, low tufted perennial with large, open, mid-blue flowers; **'Kent Belle'**, large, hanging, deep violet-blue flowers; **'Mystic Bells'**, massed mid-blue flowers on erect wiry stems; **'Wonder Bells Blue'**, lilac-blue double flowers. Zones 5–9.

Campanula, Hybrid Cultivar, 'Kent Belle'

Campanula punctata

CAMPSIS

TRUMPET CREEPER, TRUMPET VINE

This genus contains 2 species of flamboyant climbing plants, members of the trumpet-vine (Bignoniaceae) family. One is native to China and Japan and the other is native to North America where it is a weed in some places. These vigorous deciduous vines have aerial roots to help them climb and long leaves with 7 to 11 broadly lance-shaped leaflets that are serrated along the margins. The large orange or red trumpet-shaped flowers have widely flaring lobes and are borne in clusters in summer and autumn.

CULTIVATION: Grow *Campsis* species over walls or fences in a well-drained soil in full sun. In cool climates grow in a warm sheltered position to encourage greater flowering. *C. grandiflora* should be tied to a sturdy support, as it produces relatively few aerial roots, and *C. radicans* will also benefit from additional support. Prune hard in late winter–early spring to contain plants within their allotted space. Propagation is from cuttings, layering, or seed.

Campsis grandiflora

syns *Bignonia chinensis, B. grandiflora, Campsis chinensis, Tecoma chinensis, T. grandiflora*

CHINESE TRUMPET CREEPER, CHINESE TRUMPET VINE

↔8–15 ft (2.4–4.5 m) ↑25 ft (8 m)

From Japan and China. Vigorous climber with few aerial roots. Orange to red trumpet-shaped flowers, 3–4 in (8–10 cm) long, borne from summer–autumn on large loose panicles to 20 in (50 cm) long. **'Morning Calm'**, deep peach with yellow interior. Zones 7–11.

Campsis grandiflora

Campsis radicans

syns *Bignonia radicans, Tecoma radicans*

COW-ITCH, TRUMPET CREEPER

↔8–15 ft (2.4–4.5 m) ↑35 ft (10 m)

From southeastern USA. Invasive in some States. Becomes rampant in rich soil. Climbs with aerial roots. Orange or red trumpet-shaped flowers, borne in terminal clusters during summer, are a little smaller than those of *C. grandiflora*. ***C. r.* f. *flava*** has deep bright yellow flowers. Zones 4–10.

Campsis × *tagliabuana*

syns *Bignonia tagliabuana, Tecoma hybrida, T. intermedia*

↔8–15 ft (2.4–4.5 m) ↑17 ft (5 m)

This hybrid of *C. grandiflora* and *C. radicans,* a robust vine, climbs with its aerial roots. Bears loose panicles of orange-scarlet trumpet-shaped flowers, in summer. **'Madame Galen'**, large flaring flowers in rich salmon shades. Zones 6–10.

CANARINA

A genus of 3 species in the bellflower (Campanulaceae) family, 1 endemic to the Canary Islands, the other 2 native to tropical East Africa. All have thick tuberous roots and are herbaceous climbers, in and near a range of forest habitats. Leaves are opposite, smooth or lobed. Pendent flowers bell-shaped, with 6 reflexed petal lobes, borne singly or in small clusters in upper leaf axils.

CULTIVATION: Propagate from seed and stem cuttings. Allow plants to dry out after they die down in the summer months. Water and feed when new growth appears in autumn.

Canarina canariensis

syn. *Canarina campanula*

BICACARO, CANARY BELLFLOWER

↔3 ft (0.9 m) ↑5 ft (1.5 m)

Canary Islands summer-deciduous climber with fleshy branching stems. Leaves arrow-shaped, lobed near base, green to gray-green, 1¾–3 in (4–8 cm) long, margins finely serrated. Orange-red flowers with darker veins, 1¼–½ in (3–6 cm) long, borne singly in upper leaf axils from late winter–late spring. Zones 9–11.

Campsis radicans f. *flava*

CANNA

CANNA LILY, INDIAN SHOT

Found throughout the New World in tropical and subtropical areas and widely naturalized elsewhere, there are just 9 species making up the only genus of their family, the Cannaceae. They are vigorous plants with strong, upright, reed-like pseudostems that sprout from rhizomes and which bear long lance-shaped leaves. Heads of lily-like flowers—usually in shades of yellow, tangerine, and red, either as solid colors or in patterns—appear throughout the growing season. The common name Indian shot comes from the story that the hard black seeds were sometimes substituted for buckshot. They are certainly hard enough for this but are so light that their range would have been extremely limited.

CULTIVATION: Although they are often tropical in origin most can withstand light frosts as dormant roots if well insulated with mulch. Plant in full sun in moist, humus-rich, well-drained soil and feed well. Propagation of selected forms is by division in early spring. Seeds will often self-sow but rarely result in superior plants.

Canna glauca

↔12–36 in (30–90 cm)
↑4–6 ft (1.2–1.8 m)

This species, native to tropical America, has bluish green pointed leaves up to 20 in (50 cm) long, and large pale yellow flowers in summer. Zones 8–12.

Canna indica

syn. *Canna edulis*

INDIAN SHOT, QUEENSLAND ARROWROOT

↔20–32 in (50–80 cm)
↑4–7 ft (1.2–2 m)

Widespread in the tropics. Leaves to 20 in (50 cm) long, often purple-tinted. Flowerheads upright, usually simple but sometimes branched. Red to orange flowers, rarely pink, often with contrasting spots, to slightly over 2 in (5 cm) wide. Zones 8–12.

Canarina canariensis

Canna iridiflora

Canna, Hybrid Cultivar, 'Tropicana'

Cantua buxifolia

Canna iridiflora

☼/◐ ❄ ↔20–32 in (50–80 cm)
↑10 ft (3 m)

Found from Costa Rica to Peru. These plants have banana-like blue-green leaves to 4 ft (1.2 m) long. They bear simple or few-branched heads of semi-pendent, long-tubed, deep pink to orange flowers. Many plants cultivated under this name are now thought to be the hybrid *C.* × *ehemanii*, of which *C. iridiflora* is one parent. Zones 8–12.

Canna Hybrid Cultivars

☼/◐ ❄ ↔3 ft (0.9 m)
↑3–7 ft (0.9–2 m)

Large range of garden hybrids with complex and often uncertain parentage. The names *C.* × *generalis* and *C.* × *orchioides* have been used for these plants in the past. Ranging in size from 20 in (50 cm) dwarfs to over 7 ft (2 m) tall. Wide range of flower colors and forms. **'Durban'**, 4 ft (1.2 m) tall, with yellow-striped purple-red leaves, bright red flowers; **'Erebus'**, 6 ft (1.8 m) tall, silvery blue-green leaves, salmon pink flowers; **'Lucifer'** ★, 30 in (75 cm) high, dark foliage and yellow-edged red flowers; **'Minerva'**, 5 ft (1.5 m) tall, white and green striped foliage, yellow flowers opening from red buds over a long season; **'Pink Sunburst'**, 3 ft (0.9 m) high, pink-tinted yellow and green striped leave and salmon pink flowers; **'Red King Humbert'**, 7 ft (2 m) tall, bronze foliage and blood red flowers; **'Roi Humbert'**, 7–8 ft (2–2.4 m) tall, deep bronze foliage, orange-red flowers, sometimes yellow-marked; **'Striata'** (syn. 'Pretoria'), 6 ft (1.8 m) tall, leaves banded in light and dark shades of green, orange-pink flowers; **'Tropicanna'**, 7 ft (2 m) tall, vivid purple-red and yellow-orange striped foliage, bright orange flowers; **'Tropicanna Black'**, deep purple-red foliage, vivid red flowers, 7 ft (2 m) tall; **'Tropicanna Gold'**, 7 ft (2 m) tall, yellow-striped foliage, yellow and orange flowers. Zones 8–12.

CANTUA

South American genus, of the phlox (Polemoniaceae) family, mainly Peruvian. About 6 species of evergreen or semi-deciduous shrubs; all have, at one time or another, been used as garden plants. The flowers are long tubes with widely flared throats, carried in pendulous clusters, usually at branch tips.
CULTIVATION: *Cantua* is best grown in moist, humus-enriched, well-drained soil. A position in full sun will yield the best flower display, though if necessary the shrub will tolerate light shade and still flower satisfactorily. Regular pruning will result in more compact growth. Cutting back main branches and overly long side shoots also encourages flower-bearing new growth, producing heavier flowering and better foliage cover next season. Propagate from tip cuttings or fresh seed, which germinates well at around 65°F (18°C).

Canna, Hybrid Cultivar, 'Erebus'

Cantua buxifolia ★

MAGIC FLOWER, SACRED FLOWER OF THE INCAS

☼ ❅ ↔8 ft (2.4 m) ↑12 ft (3.5 m)

From the mountains of Peru, Bolivia, and northern Chile. Flowers 3 in (8 cm) long, deep pink to purple, early spring or in warm areas year round. The epithet "sacred" comes from its use by Inca priests. **'Hot Pants'** is a popular North American cultivar. Zones 9–11.

CARDAMINE

BITTER CRESS, CUCKOO FLOWER, LADIES SMOCK, MEADOW CRESS

Genus of about 150 species of annuals and tuberous or fleshy-stemmed herbaceous perennials belonging to the cabbage (Brassicaceae) family, formerly known as Cruciferae. Cosmopolitan in distribution, they are found mainly in the Northern Hemisphere. Some are pernicious weeds, others are dainty woodland and damp meadow plants with attractive foliage and flowers.
CULTIVATION: Most of the ornamental species prefer humus-rich soil shaded by deciduous plants. Propagate from seed or by division of rhizomes when dormant.

Cardamine laciniata

syns *Cardamine concatenata, Dentaria laciniata, Rorippa laciniata*

CUT-LEAFED TOOTHWORT, PEPPER ROOT

◐/● ❄ ↔12 in (30 cm)
↑8–12 in (20–30 cm)

Short-lived North American perennial from Quebec south to Florida. Mid-green deeply cut leaves. Flowers appear in early spring in shades of white, lavender, and pink. Zones 3–8.

Cardamine pratensis

CUCKOO FLOWER, LADIES SMOCK, MEADOW CRESS

● ❄ ↔16–24 in (40–60 cm)
↑16–24 in (40–60 cm)

Well-known and loved species found growing in meadowland in many parts of Europe. Forms rosettes of compound leaves topped by spikes of ¾ in (18 mm) wide pure white flowers in spring. **'Flore Pleno'**, a lilac double-flowered form. Zones 4–9.

CARDIOCRINUM

GIANT LILY

Found from the Himalayas to Japan. This lily (Liliaceae) family genus has just 3 species of bulbs that develop rapidly after winter dormancy, producing a clump of large, fleshy, heart-shaped leaves from which emerge tall flower stems that are usually in bloom before the summer solstice. Flowers are funnel-shaped, sometimes fragrant, and usually clustered near stem tips. Large seed pods follow. Giant lilies are equally impressive as foliage plants.
CULTIVATION: Best suited to woodland conditions in temperate climates where winters are not severe. Plant in fertile, moist, humus-rich, well-drained soil in bright shade or dappled sunlight. The bulb dies after flowering but produces several offsets. These bloom within 3 to 4 years and are a quicker way of securing flowers than raising seedlings, which can take 5 to 7 years to reach flowering age.

Cardiocrinum giganteum ★

HIMALAYAN GIANT LILY

◐/● ❄ ↔3–5 ft (0.9–1.5 m)
↑7–15 ft (2–4.5 m)

From Himalayan region to Myanmar and China. Leaves to 18 in (45 cm) long and nearly as wide. Leafy flower stems, very sturdy at the base, with fragrant, purple-red striped or flecked cream flowers, up to 8 in (20 cm) long. ***C. g.* var. *yunnanense*** from western and central China has green-tinted flowers. Zones 7–9.

CAREX

SEDGE

A large genus of about 1,000 species of deciduous or evergreen grass-like perennials that belong to the sedge (Cyperaceae) family. They inhabit damp and boggy ground, and are found throughout the world, both indigenously and naturalized. Many are native to northern temperate regions. Plants range from low-growing and tufted to tall and tussock-forming. The grass-like leaves may be flat, folded, or rolled and in various shades of green, red, and brown. They often have sharp cutting edges and some have curling tips. The tiny flowers are insignificant in most species and carried on spikes, with male and female flowers that are borne separately on the same plant.

CULTIVATION: Very easy-care plants that are suitable for growing in problem wet areas, beside ponds, or in other moisture-retentive soils. Some species are invasive. A number are suitable for pot culture. Grow in full sun or half-sun. Propagate by division or seed.

Carex buchananii

↔18–24 in (45–60 cm) ↕24–30 in (60–75 cm)

Native to New Zealand. An upright, rather stiff, tufted plant with narrow, rolled, reddish brown leaves that have curling blond tips. Zones 7–10.

Carex comans

↔24–30 in (60–75 cm) ↕12–16 in (30–40 cm)

Native to New Zealand. A drooping sprawling plant with fine narrow leaves that curl at the tips. The foliage color varies considerably from reddish brown to shades of gray and green. The tips are often blond. **'Frosted Curls'** ★, swirling mound of palest green or straw-colored foliage with curling blond tips. Zones 7–10.

Carex conica

↔12–22 in (30–55 cm) ↕10–20 in (25–50 cm)

From Japan and South Korea. This tufted plant has flat dark green leaves that spill outward from the clump. Blade sheaths are brownish purple. **'Snowline'** (syns 'Hime-kan-sige', 'Variegata'), dark green leaves edged with white. Zones 7–10.

Carex elata

TUFTED SEDGE

↔3 ft (0.9 m) ↕3 ft (0.9 m)

Native to Europe, as far east as the Caucasus, and northern Africa. Dense tussock plant which spreads rapidly in wet places. The leaves are folded with a flat tip, and are bluish green with brownish yellow sheaths. **'Aurea'** (commonly known as Bowles golden sedge), golden leaves with green margins. Zones 7–10.

Carex flagellifera

↔20 in (50 cm) ↕20 in (50 cm)

A native of New Zealand, this dense tufted plant, has arching foliage. The narrow leaves with cutting margins, vary in color from shiny green to bronze and brown. The flowering stems elongate across the ground as they mature. Zones 7–10.

Carex grayi

MACE SEDGE, MORNING STAR SEDGE

↔30 in (75 cm) ↕30 in (75 cm)

From eastern North America. Upright clump-forming plant with broad flat pale green leaves. The spiky seed heads resemble a mace and are popular in floral decoration. Zones 7–10.

Carex morrowii

↔30 in (75 cm) ↕30 in (75 cm)

Native to Japan. Tufted plant forming an upright clump of rather untidy appearance. The thick, broad, deep green, glossy leaves have rough margins. It is usually seen in one of its cultivated forms such as **'Expallida'** (syn. 'Variegata'), leaves striped with white. Zones 8–10.

Carex grayi

Carex muskingumensis

PALM SEDGE

↔24–36 in (60–90 cm) ↕24–36 in (60–90 cm)

Native to North America. Dense tufted plant spreading by fleshy stem. Narrow, pointed, light green leaves are slightly arching to sprawling and arise along stems giving a palm-like effect. Zones 4–10.

Carex nigra

↔12–24 in (30–60 cm) ↕8–24 in (20–60 cm)

Found throughout Europe. Tussock-forming plant with narrow bluish green leaves with cutting edges. The dark purplish flower spikes are frequently dried and used in floral arrangements. Zones 5–10.

Carex oshimensis

↔18 in (45 cm) ↕12 in (30 cm)

Tufted evergreen with dark green leaves. **'Evergold'** (syn. *C. siderosticha* 'Variegata') has leaves striped in gold and white. Zones 5–10.

Carex spissa

↔24 ft (0.6–1.2 m) ↕3–4 ft (0.9–1.2 m)

Native to southern California. Upright clump of broad bluish gray leaves which intensify in color during summer. The flower spikes turn from gold to tan, providing contrast with the foliage. Zones 6–10.

Carex elata 'Aurea'

Carex nigra

Carex testacea

↔24 in (60 cm) ↕24 in (60 cm)

From New Zealand. Densely tufted plant with fine, narrow, arching leaves varying in color from green to golden brown, often with orangey green tips. The flowering stem elongates across the ground as it matures. Zones 8–10.

CARISSA

This genus of around 20 species of evergreen shrubs and small trees, in the dogbane (Apocynaceae) family, is found throughout tropical and subtropical Africa, Asia, and Australia. Many are densely branched and spiny, and useful for hedging; they have glossy green foliage, and clusters of fragrant, pure white, 5-petalled, long-tubed flowers. Fruit is edible. A few, small enough for house or greenhouse, may be kept in pots for some years.

CULTIVATION: Usually drought tolerant once established, most *Carissa* species prefer to be moist throughout the growing season. They thrive in warm frost-free areas in a position with well-drained soil and full sun. Prune to shape as necessary, or shear hedges after flowering or after fruiting if the fruit is required. Propagate from seed or cuttings. The stems yield a milky sap when cut, and cuttings should be allowed to dry before inserting in the soil mix.

Carissa macrocarpa

AMATUNGULA, NATAL PLUM

↔10 ft (3 m) ↕7–10 ft (2–3 m)

A widely cultivated species from South Africa with forked spines. Rounded deep glossy green leathery leaves, redden in bright light. Flowers white to 2 in (5 cm) wide. Red to purple-red fruit. **'Boxwood Beauty'** ★, compact moulding habit; one form with cream-edged leaves is available. Zones 10–12.

Carissa macrocarpa

C

Carnegiea gigantea, in the wild, Superstition Mountains, near Phoenix, Arizona, USA

Carpenteria californica

CARNEGIEA

This genus of a single species belongs to the cactus (Cactaceae) family. Native to northern Mexico and southwestern USA. Slow growing, plants around 50 ft (15 m) in the wild are rare and over 100 years old. It may only flower when it reaches a height of 12 ft (3.5 m); it does not do well in cultivation. Heavy fines and strict regulations have stopped the practice of taking it from the wild for "desert gardens." Used in ceremonies by Native Americans.
CULTIVATION: It is not hardy; in frost areas grow in a warm greenhouse. Grow in full light, but shade from full sun. After winter rest, during which time it must not be watered, mist a few times, then start watering moderately; when in growth, water freely. Feed with a low nitrogen fertilizer (tomato fertilizer) monthly, reduce water and stop feeding in early autumn. Outdoors in frost-free areas it should be grown in low humus, alkaline, well-drained soil.

Carnegiea gigantea

SAGUARO CACTUS
↔10 ft (3 m) ↑50 ft (15 m)
Produces between 12 and 24 ribs, sometimes more; areoles grow from the tops of ribs, non-flowering areoles, with up to 30 spines gray or brown, to 3 in (8 cm) long. White funnel-shaped flowers, followed by egg-shaped fruit in autumn. Zones 9–11.

CARPENTARIA

This single-species genus from the palm (Arecaceae) family consists of a feathery leafed tree native to tropical northern Australia. Panicles of creamy white flowers are produced from spring to summer.
CULTIVATION: This palm grows best in well-drained soil with abundant water during dry periods, especially when young. It is easily propagated from freshly collected seed, germinating in 1 to 3 months. Seedlings resent disturbance and can be difficult to transplant, but they are easier when they are mature.

Carpentaria acuminata ★

CARPENTARIA PALM, THORA, YIRRGI YIRRGI
↔20–25 ft (6–8 m)
↑25–50 ft (8–15 m)
Solitary fast-growing palm, with tall, narrow, erect, smooth, whitish gray trunk, 5–6 in (12–15 cm) across, ringed with scars and slightly enlarged at the base. It has a prominent crown of feathery pinnate leaves, to 12 ft (3.5 m) long, with drooping tips. White flowers, oval bright scarlet fruit maturing in summer; the pulp irritates the skin. Australian Aboriginals eat the tender new growth or "cabbage". Zones 11–12.

CARPENTERIA

This genus contains a single species of evergreen shrub from the hydrangea (Hydrangeaceae) family, which has a very limited natural range in central California on rocky mountain slopes. It has narrow glossy green leaves, lightly felted beneath. The fragrant white flowers resemble those of *Philadelphus* (mock orange) to which it is related.
CULTIVATION: *C. californica* requires a sunny site and a light, moisture-retentive, well-drained soil. It can be pruned to maintain a more compact form. Propagation is by seed sown in spring or autumn, or by cuttings which can be difficult to root.

Carpenteria californica

TREE ANEMONE
↔8 ft (2.4 m) ↑8 ft (2.4 m)
A beautiful shrub. The flowers are pure white with 5 to 7 overlapping petals, prominent yellow stamens, to 2½ in (6 cm) across, in early summer. Zones 6–10.

CARPHALEA

This genus, belonging in the large madder (Rubiaceae) family, contains 10 species of evergreen shrubs, 6 confined to Madagascar, the remainder to tropical Africa, and 1 endemic to the island of Socotra off the Horn of Africa. They have leathery smooth-edged leaves arranged in opposite pairs and colorful flowers in dense terminal panicles. Each flower has 4 large sepals, the much smaller petals are united into a slender tube flaring at the mouth into 4 small lobes. The sepals persist into the fruiting stage and act as wings, enabling the small dry fruits to be carried by the wind.
CULTIVATION: Only one species is in cultivation, becoming popular in tropical and warm-temperate gardens for its colorful flowers or, rarely, grown in heated conservatories in cool climates. It requires a sheltered position, strong light, and fertile well-drained soil. Propagate from cuttings or seed.

Carphalea kirondron

FLAMING BEAUTY
↔3 ft (0.9 m) ↑6 ft (1.8 m)
Native to western Madagascar. Irregular form with glossy dark green foliage. Flowers in dense terminal clusters, brilliant red sepals, 1 longer than the other 3, darker red petal tube, pure white lobes, sepals persist for many months. Zones 10–12.

CARPINUS

HORNBEAM
This genus in the birch (Betulaceae) family contains about 35 deciduous trees and shrubs found throughout the temperate regions of the Northern Hemisphere. Commonly known as hornbeams, they are appealing trees at all times of year. The leaves have prominent parallel veining and color well in autumn. In spring they bear pendulous yellow male catkins and separate female catkins, which are erect at first. The fruiting clusters in autumn are surrounded by leafy bracts and in winter an attractive branch pattern is revealed.
CULTIVATION: Hornbeams will grow in most soils and are very suitable trees for parks and specimen plantings. *C. betulus* is a popular species for pleaching and hedging. Hornbeams are propagated from seed sown in autumn and cultivars are grafted.

Carpinus betulus

COMMON HORNBEAM, EUROPEAN HORNBEAM
↔60 ft (18 m) ↑80 ft (24 m)
From Turkey, across Europe to southeastern England. Trunk gray, fluted. Pointed oval leaves to 4 in (10 cm) long with serrated margins, prominent veining, turn yellow or orange in autumn. Yellow catkins are borne in spring. **'Fastigiata'** ★, columnar; **'Fielder's Tabular'**, light green leaves. Zones 5–9.

Carpinus betulus 'Fastigiata'

Carphalea kirondron

Carthamus tinctorius

Carpinus caroliniana

AMERICAN HORNBEAM, BLUE BEECH, IRONWOOD, MUSCLEWOOD

↔50 ft (12 m) ↑40 ft (12 m)

Native to moist woods and river-banks in eastern North America. Similar to *C. betulus* but often shrubby. Leaves turn to deep shades of orange and scarlet in autumn. Zones 5–9.

Carpinus cordata

↔50 ft (15 m) ↑50 ft (15 m)

Native to Japan. Scaly furrowed bark and broadly columnar shape. The leaves are slightly heart-shaped at base; finely pointed tip, prominent veins. Yellowish catkins in spring. Zones 5–9.

Carpinus japonica

JAPANESE HORNBEAM

↔50 ft (15 m) ↑50 ft (15 m)

From the woods and thickets of Japan. Gray fissured bark. The leaves are irregularly toothed with close-set prominent veins; they color well in autumn. Zones 5–9.

Carpinus orientalis

ORIENTAL HORNBEAM, TURKISH HORNBEAM

↔15–20 ft (4.5–6 m) ↑50 ft (15 m)

Native to southeastern Europe and Turkey. Sometimes a low scrubby bush, generally a small tree or large shrub. Its glossy dark green leaves have doubly toothed margins. Zones 5–9.

CARTHAMUS

A genus of 14 species of thistle-like annuals and perennials of the daisy (Asteraceae) family. Found mainly around the Mediterranean and in western Asia, one species, the common *C. tinctorius*, has a much wider distribution and has long been cultivated as a source of yellow and red dyes. Other species are seldom grown as they tend to become invasive. They are upright plants with stems that branch near the top to make a bushy clump of foliage. The leaves tend to be simple or pinnate with spine-tipped teeth. The whole plant is covered in fine downy hairs. Thistle-like heads with yellow, gold, pink, or violet ray florets appear in summer. Spiny bracts surround the base of the flowerheads.

CULTIVATION: They are easily grown in any sunny position with light, gritty, well-drained soil. Sometimes used as a quick filler in annual or perennial borders, they are more likely to be seen as a field-grown commercial crop or as a weed on waste ground.

Carthamus tinctorius

FALSE SAFFRON, SAFFLOWER

↔16–20 in (40–50 cm) ↑24–40 in (60–100 cm)

Lower leaves may be simple or pinnate, sometimes spiny; those on flower stem usually simple and spine-tipped. Flowerheads yellow, gold to orange or red, rarely white. Seeds are an important source of oil used in cooking oils and margarine manufacture. **'Orange Gold'** has intensely golden-yellow flowerheads. Zones 4–10.

CARUM

There are about 30 species of biennials and perennials in this genus, which belongs to the carrot (Apiaceae) family. They are found in temperate to subtropical regions. Their finely divided leaves are often aromatic and bear umbels of small white to pink flowers. The most commonly grown species is *C. carvi* (caraway), which grows in meadowland and naturalizes on wasteland. It is usually grown as a flavoring herb but its tap root is sometimes cooked in the manner of parsnips.

CULTIVATION: Grow in full sun in deep, fertile, well-drained soil. Propagate from seed sown *in situ* as plants dislike transplanting. Harvest the seed of *C. carvi* as its color begins to darken.

Carum carvi

CARAWAY

↔12–18 in (30–45 cm) ↑24 in (60 cm)

From Europe and western Asia, naturalized in the USA. Attractive biennial with fine feathery foliage. Umbels of small white to pinkish flowers in summer. Primarily grown for its aromatic licorice-flavored seeds. Zones 3–10.

CARYA

syn. *Hicoria*

This genus, belonging to the walnut (Juglandaceae) family, consists of about 25 species, the majority of which come from eastern North America, with some from Vietnam and China. These large deciduous trees have both functional male and female organs present on the one plant. The gray-brown bark becomes scaly with age. The pinnate leaves are alternate with serrated-edged leaflets. Male inflorescence is a pendent branched catkin; female inflorescence is a terminal spike with up to 20 individual flowers. The fruit is a drupe. Commercially valuable for pecan nuts, and hard wood, used for tools and sports equipment. Transplanting is difficult as they resent disturbance. Most hickories are valuable as ornamentals, making majestic trees, coloring well in autumn.

CULTIVATION: *Carya* seedlings develop a long tap root very early, so plant when young into deep, fertile, humus-rich but well-drained soil. Sow seed into a seed bed as soon as it is ripe. If growing in a pot, use one that is extra deep. Use good loam with added leafmold; cultivars require winter grafting.

Carya aquatica

WATER HICKORY

↔40 ft (12 m) ↑70 ft (21 m)

Native to southeastern USA. The bark is light brown and the leaves have up to 13 individual lance-shaped leaflets, 5 in (12 cm) long. The fruit is egg-shaped. Zones 6–9.

Carya aquatica

Carya cordiformis

syns *Carya amara, Juglans cordiformis*

BITTERNUT HICKORY, SWAMP HICKORY

↔50 ft (15 m) ↑80 ft (24 m)

From eastern North America. The smooth pale gray bark develops narrow, deep, scaly ridges with age. Buds yellow, flattened, hairy, in winter. Leaves have up to 9 pinnate leaflets, and 5 large terminal leaflets. Grows best in moist ground. Zones 4–9.

Carya floridana

SCRUB HICKORY, SCRUB PECAN

↔10–17 ft (3–5 m) ↑20–25 ft (6–8 m)

Native to southeastern USA. Rather untidy, many-branched, small tree. Pinnate leaves with 5 distinct, finely toothed leaflets. Nuts are edible but not highly prized. Considered a weed in some areas. Zones 7–10.

Carya glabra

HOGNUT BROOM HICKORY, PIGNUT HICKORY

↔70 ft (21 m) ↑80 ft (24 m)

Found throughout eastern USA. Bark gray and narrowly ridged. Mid-green leaves with 5 to 7 individual lance-shaped leaflets to 12 in (30 cm) long. Thin-shelled nuts egg-shaped. Zones 4–9.

Carya illinoinensis

syns *Carya olivaeformis, Juglans illinoinensis*

PECAN

↔70 ft (21 m) ↑100 ft (30 m)

Native to the southern and central USA and northern Mexico. Grows best in deep alluvial soil. Scaly gray bark, mid-green leaves, with up to 17 lance-shaped leaflets. Pecan nuts are an important crop exported worldwide. Some 500 cultivars are available: **'Pawnee'** and **'Lucas'** are early ripeners. Zones 6–11.

Carya laciniosa

BIG SHELLBARK HICKORY

↔35 ft (10 m) ↑100 ft (30 m)

From eastern USA. Bark peels in 3 ft (0.9 m) long curving plates. Leaves reach 18 in (45 cm) long with 5 to 7 leaflets. Fruit oval, 2 in (5 cm) long. Good timber tree. Zones 4–9.

Carya myristiciformis

NUTMEG HICKORY

↔25 ft (8 m) ↑70 ft (21 m)

Native to southern USA and Mexico. Bark dark brown, new shoots have glossy yellow scales. Leaves, green leaflets, broadly oval, white underside, terminal leaflet larger. Nut egg-shaped, rust colored with a hard grooved shell. Zones 9–11.

Carya ovata

Carya ovalis

RED HICKORY, SWEET PIGNUT

↔ 30 ft (9 m) ↑ 70 ft (21 m)

Originating in eastern USA. Young downy shoots open to form leaves consisting of up to 7 leaflets, terminal leaflet largest at 5 in (12 cm). Fruit will split at the base when it is ripe. Zones 6–9.

Carya ovata

syns *Hicoria ovata, Juglans ovata*

LITTLE SHELLBARK HICKORY, SHAGBARK HICKORY

↔ 70 ft (21 m) ↑ 80 ft (24 m)

From eastern USA. Gray to brown peeling bark. Leaves are mid-green, with 5 leaflets, turning golden yellow in autumn. Fruit edible, splitting when ripe. Cultivars often hybrids with *C. cathayensis* or *C. laciniosa*. Zones 4–9.

Carya texana

BLACK HICKORY

↔ 25 ft (8 m) ↑ 50 ft (15 m)

This is a native of central USA from Arkansas to Texas. The furrowed bark is dark ginger brown. The leaves are mid-green, with up to 7 lance-shaped leaflets. The fruit is round, and splits at the base when it is ripe. Zones 6–9.

CARYOPTERIS

This genus now placed in the mint (Lamiaceae) family was previously included in the verbena family. It occurs in eastern Asia, from the Himalayas to Japan, and contains about 6 species of deciduous flowering shrubs with slender cane-like stems. The name, derived from the Greek, refers to the winged nut-like fruit. Most species have opposite, simple, toothed leaves, often aromatic and grayish. Their flowers, which are borne in late summer, are mainly blue, mauve, or white in axillary or terminal panicles.

CULTIVATION: *Caryopteris* species prefer an open sunny position and thrive in cool-temperate regions, ideally in a fibrous loamy soil with free drainage. They flower on the current season's growth and should be pruned moderately in late winter or early spring to promote new growth. Propagation is by soft-tip or firm leafy cuttings between spring and early autumn; dormant hardwood cuttings from winter prunings can also be used.

Caryopteris incana

Caryopteris × *clandonensis*

BLUE MIST SHRUB, BLUE SPIRAEA

↔ 5 ft (1.5 m) ↑ 5 ft (1.5 m)

A hybrid between *C. incana* and *C. mongolica*. Erect, slender, vase-shaped shrub. Leaves downy, serrated. Deep blue to violet-blue flowers, in dense cymes, in late summer. **'Arthur Simmonds'**, purple-blue flowers; **'Dark Night'** ★, low growing form with dark blue flowers; **'Heavenly Blue'**, bright mauve-blue flowers, compact; **'Worcester Gold'**, mauve-blue flowers. Zones 5–9.

Caryopteris incana

syn. *Caryopteris mastacanthus*

BLUE SPIRAEA, BLUEBEARD

↔ 5 ft (1.5 m) ↑ 5 ft (1.5 m)

A native of China and Japan. Small showy shrub. Grayish, serrated, pointed leaves, slender arching stems. Heads of spiraea-like powder-blue flowers in tiers along the stems in late summer. Zones 7–10.

CARYOTA

FISHTAIL PALM

Caryota consists of 12 species, in the palm (Arecaceae) family, ranging through tropical Asia. Most species are single-stemmed; a few multi-stemmed. Large bipinnate fronds divide into segments along either side of a midrib, with triangular or wedge-shaped leaflets, reminiscent of a fishtail. Flowering occurs at maximum stem height, the first flowering panicle bursts from the sheathing base of the topmost frond and bears flowers and fruit. Over several years panicles emerge from the stem in lower positions until at the base of the trunk, then with fruiting over, single-stemmed plants die. Panicles have cream flowers crowded on drooping spikes. Pink to purple fruits follow. Sugary sap may be fermented for a sort of wine or beer.

CULTIVATION: All are fine ornamental palms and most thrive equally well in frost-free climates, with adequate soil moisture. In hot climates growth is very fast, individual stems are short lived, becoming ragged and untidy with age. Propagation is from seed.

Caryota cumingii

↔ 10 ft (3 m) ↑ 30 ft (9 m)

From the Philippines. Single-stemmed trunk 12 in (30 cm) in diameter, marked with prominent rings. Fronds large, with leaflets less drooping than other species. Flowering panicles are massive, sheathed in prominent bracts as they emerge. Zones 11–12.

Caryota mitis ★

CLUSTER FISHTAIL PALM

↔ 10 ft (3 m) ↑ 20 ft (6 m)

Widely cultivated. Narrow clump of stems. Fronds 6–10 ft (1.8–3 m) long, crowd together forming a luxuriant crown. Flowering panicles; a mass of scented cream flowers opening from green buds. Fruit dark red. Needs moist fertile soil. Zones 10–12.

Caryota no ★

GIANT FISHTAIL PALM

↔ 20 ft (6 m) ↑ 80 ft (24 m)

From Borneo. Fronds up to 15 ft (4.5 m) long and two-thirds as wide, fan out stiffly. Trunk to 24 in (60 cm) in diameter. Flowering panicles to 8 ft (2.4 m) long. Fruit blackish. Zones 10–12.

Caryota obtusa ★

INDIAN FISHTAIL PALM

↔ 12–20 ft (3.5–6 m) ↑ 15–20 ft (4.5–6 m)

Clustering palm of open forests from temperate to tropical India and Thailand. Very broad, smooth, grayish, single trunk marked with leaf scars. Large, bipinnate, dark green leaves, up to 10 ft (3 m) long. Cream flowers on a 12 in (30 cm) long stalk, which emerges from leaves. Mature fruit rounded, dull red to black. **'King Kong'**, light green leaves. Zones 9–12.

Caryota ochlandra

Caryota ochlandra

syn. *Caryota maxima*

CHINESE FISHTAIL PALM

↔ 10 ft (3 m) ↑ 25 ft (8 m)

Native to southern China. Single-stemmed, trunk 6 in (15 cm) in diameter. Fronds along the trunk. Crowded, drooping, narrow leaflets. Flowering panicles 6 ft (1.8 m) high or more. Fruit deep red. Will survive light frosts. Zones 9–12.

Caryota urens ★

FISHTAIL PALM, TODDY PALM

↔ 15 ft (4.5 m) ↑ 30 ft (9 m)

Cultivated in southern Asia as a source of sugar. Adapts to seasonally dry climates. Trunk 12 in (30 cm) in diameter, chalky white. Fronds with crowded, narrow, drooping leaflets. Flowering panicles 10 ft (3 m) long. Red fruit. Zones 10–12.

CASSIA

Once a very large genus of perennials, annuals, subshrubs, shrubs, and trees, Cassia has been revised in recent years and, while still containing well over 100 species, it is now a far more consistent grouping of plants in the cassia subfamily of the legume (Fabaceae) family. Found in tropical areas of the world, the shrubs and trees in the genus are mainly evergreen. Pinnate, sometimes hairy leaves; bright yellow or pink flowers, borne singly, in small clusters, or in panicles. Flowers often appear over a long season and are followed by bean-like seed pods.

CULTIVATION: Hardiness varies with species, few tolerate repeated frosts. General preference for a mild climate, moist well-drained soil, full or

Cassia fistula

half-sun. Propagation usually from seed, which should be soaked in warm water prior to sowing. Some cassias will grow from half-hardened cuttings.

Cassia brewsteri

LEICHHARDT BEAN

↔ 12 ft (3.5 m) ↑ 40 ft (12 m)

Native to Queensland, Australia. Spreading tree or shrub. Blackish bark. Leaves pinnate, with 4 to 12 lance-shaped leaflets, about 3 in (8 cm) long. Yellow-orange flowers in drooping racemes, in spring. Cylindrical woody pods. Zones 10–12.

Cassia fistula

GOLDEN SHOWER TREE, INDIAN SENNA

↔ 20 ft (6 m) ↑ 60 ft (18 m)

Native to tropical Asia. Deciduous to semi-evergreen. Smooth gray bark, often irregular branching. Leaves pinnate, leaflets in 3 to 8 pairs. Flowers vivid yellow, scented, pendulous racemes, in summer. Dark brown seed pods. Zones 10–12.

Cassia javanica

syn. *Cassia nodosa*

PINK SHOWER, RAINBOW SHOWER

↔ 10 ft (3 m) ↑ 50 ft (15 m)

From Southeast Asia, popular tropical garden tree. Pinnate leaves composed of up to 34 long, narrow, drooping leaflets. Flowers are over 2 in (5 cm) wide in racemes, color variable, buff through pink to crimson. Zones 11–12.

Cassia × *nealiae* ★

RAINBOW SHOWER

↔ 20–30 ft (6–9 m)
↑ 25–50 ft (8–15 m)

Handsome deciduous flowering tree, a hybrid between yellow-flowered *C. fistula* and pink-flowered *C. javanica* raised around 1916 in Hawaii. Flowers vary from cream to orange and red. Official tree of the City and County of Honolulu. The commonest cultivars are pale yellow-white **'Queen's Hospital White'** and **'Wilhelmina Tenney'**, odorless yellow flowers. **'Lunalilo Yellow'**, fragrant yellow flowers. Propagation is from cuttings. Zones 10–12.

CASSIOPE

This genus of 12 species of small evergreen shrubs is closely related to the heaths and heathers (Ericaceae). Found mainly in northern Europe and northern Asia with outliers in the Himalayas and western North America, they are very much cool-temperate to cold climate plants, with a few species ranging into the Arctic. They seldom exceed 8 in (20 cm) high and have tiny leaves arranged in 4 distinct rows on wiry whipcord stems. The flowers, which appear mainly in spring, are small, usually bell-shaped, and carried singly, though often in large numbers, on fine stems.
CULTIVATION: Cassiopes prefer moist well-drained soil that is rich in humus and slightly acidic. They are not drought tolerant plants and need ample summer moisture. Very frost hardy, they prefer a climate with distinct seasons with a cool moist summer. They are best shaded from the hot summer sun. Trim lightly if necessary. Propagate from self-layered stems or by taking cuttings.

Cassiope 'Edinburgh'

↔ 8–10 in (20–25 cm)
↑ 10–12 in (25–30 cm)

This hybrid between *C. fastigiata* and *C. tetragona* is a strong upright form with dark scaly foliage and clusters of tiny urn-shaped flowers. Zones 4–8.

Cassiope lycopodioides

↔ 10 in (25 cm) ↑ 3 in (8 cm)

A native of mountains of Japan, northeastern Asia, and Alaska. Resembles a clubmoss *(Lycopodium)*. Flat sprawling habit, minute leaves. Flowers, nodding, around ¼ in (6 mm) wide, carried on 1 in (25 mm) long stems. Zones 3–8.

Cassiope 'Medusa'

Cassiope 'Medusa'

↔ 8 in (20 cm) ↑ 10 in (25 cm)

This *C. fastigiata* × *C. lycopodioides* hybrid is a very compact plant. It prefers cool moist conditions. Quite vigorous, forms a clump of dark green heather-like foliage. The flowers are white, with red-tinted calyces and leaf stalks. Zones 4–9.

Cassiope mertensiana

↔ 10 in (25 cm)
↑ 6–12 in (15–30 cm)

Upright or spreading shrub found in mountainous regions of western North America. Leaves tightly pressed to the stem. Small, white, bell-shaped flowers in spring. **'Gracilis'**, a mound-forming cultivar. Zones 5–9.

Cassiope 'Muirhead'

↔ 8–10 in (20–25 cm)
↑ 6–8 in (15–20 cm)

This cross between *C. wardii* and *C. fastigiata* has a low spreading habit, classical scaly foliage, and masses of tiny white flowers. Zones 4–8.

Cassiope tetragona

↔ 8 in (20 cm) ↑ 4–12 in (10–30 cm)

Upright or sprawling shrub from northern Europe and nearby Arctic regions. Tiny downy leaves. Flowers bell-shaped, white, often with a hint of pink, ¼ in (6 mm) long, on ½ in (12 mm) stems. Zones 3–8.

Cassiope lycopodioides

CASTANEA

Belonging to the beech (Fagaceae) family, this is a small genus of about 12 species of sweet chestnuts native to temperate regions of the Northern Hemisphere, from North America across Europe and into eastern Asia. In habit they range from low suckering shrubs to tall trees. Several species are of economic importance, being grown for their sweet-tasting edible nuts, which are enclosed in a spiny whorl of bracts. The taller species are also valued for their use as ornamental trees in parks and large gardens, especially for their spectacular yellowish green drooping male catkins.
CULTIVATION: Sweet chestnuts prefer a well-drained and slightly acid soil; adequate rainfall is essential. Most are frost hardy down to Zones 4 or 5. Propagation is usually from seed which should be sown as soon as it is ripe; selected clones can be reproduced by grafts onto 1- or 2-year-old understocks, in early spring.

Castanea mollissima

CHINESE CHESTNUT

↔ 35 ft (10 m) ↑ 40 ft (12 m)

Native to central and eastern China and Korea. Ovate or oblong, coarsely serrated, short-stalked leaves, coarse white hair beneath. Widely cultivated in China for its edible nuts. Resistant to chestnut blight. Highly valued as an ornamental. **'Pendula'**, an attractive cultivar. Zones 5–9.

Castanea pumila

ALLEGHENY CHINKAPIN, CHINQUAPIN

↔ 20 ft (6 m) ↑ 15 ft (4.5 m)

Large suckering shrub from eastern and southern areas of USA. Downy young shoots, young leaves white and furry on the undersides. **'Ashei'**, the coastal chinquapin, has less densely spiny bracts than the species. Zones 6–9.

Castanea mollissima

C

Castanea sativa

Castilleja exserta

Castanea sativa

syn. *Castanea vesca*

CHESTNUT, SPANISH CHESTNUT, SWEET CHESTNUT

↔ 40 ft (12 m) ↑ 60 ft (18 m)

Native of the high forest areas of southern Europe and western Asia. Fast-growing deciduous tree. Glossy, dark green, coarsely serrated leaves, lighter and slightly furry beneath. Yellow-green catkins, in mid-summer. Edible nuts are a popular delicacy, "marrons glacés." **'Albomarginata'** has creamy white margins to the leaves; **'Glabra'**, very large dark green leaves; and **'Variegata'** (syn. 'Aureomarginata') has yellow borders to the leaves. Zones 5–9.

Castanea Hybrid Cultivars

↔ 30 ft (9 m) ↑ 30 ft (9 m)

There are many hybrid chestnuts; they generally have heavier crops of larger nuts than species cultivars. Most of the best forms have *C. sativa* in their parentage. **'Colossal'** *(C. sativa × C. crenata)* produces 14 to 18 nuts/lb (0.5 kg); **'Nevada'** *(C. sativa × C. crenata)* has a yield of 15 nuts/lb and is a good pollinator for 'Colossal'; **'Schrader'**, a good cropper of unknown parentage; and **'Skioka'** *(C. mollissima × C. sativa)*, produces a heavy crop of small nuts, around 35 nuts/lb. Zones 6–9.

CASTILLEJA

INDIAN PAINTBRUSH, PAINTED CUPS, PRAIRIE FIRE

Named after the eighteenth-century Spanish botanist Domingo Castillejo, and well-known as a strikingly vivid feature of southwest USA, this broom-rape (Orobanchaceae) family genus of around 200 species of annuals and perennials is widespread through the Americas and Eurasia. Usually low growing but upright in habit, their foliage tends to be downy and rather a dull green. Tufted flowerheads appear in spring and summer and it is not the flowers that are colorful but their calyces and the bracts that surround them. Native American legend says that the plants are the discarded tools of a brave warrior who sought painting guidance from the spirits and was given brushes loaded with paints colored to capture the sunset.
CULTIVATION: They are rarely seen in gardens because they are often semi-parasitic, taking nourishment via the roots of certain shrubs and grasses. Usually left to be appreciated in the wild, they can be cultivated if the seed is sown around appropriate host plants, such as *Alnus*, *Symphoricarpos*, *Festuca*, and *Aster*.

Castilleja angustifolia

DESERT PAINTBRUSH

↔ 8 in (20 cm) ↑ 16 in (40 cm)

Perennial from Nevada, Utah, and Idaho. Small light green to gray-green leaves, finely hairy. Small yellow flowers largely enclosed by pink to red bracts. Zones 4–9.

Castilleja coccinea

INDIAN PAINTBRUSH, SCARLET PAINTBRUSH

↔ 12 in (30 cm) ↑ 12–14 in (30–35 cm)

From the North American East Coast to the Rocky Mountains in Canada and USA, south to northern Florida. Annual or biennial species with basal rosette leaves and small greenish yellow flowers. Crimson bracts give good color and are more prominent than the flowers. Attracts hummingbirds. Use in a meadow garden. Zones 4–9.

Castilleja exserta

PURPLE OWL CLOVER

↔ 6–8 in (15–20 cm) ↑ 8 in (20 cm)

Perennial found from central California to northern Mexico. Few hairy basal leaves and upright spikes with small snapdragon-like cream to pale yellow flowers almost entirely enclosed by bright purple-pink bracts. Zones 7–10.

Castilleja rhexifolia × *C. sulphurea*

↔ 8 in (20 cm) ↑ 12 in (30 cm)

Where distributions of *C. rhexifolia* and *C. sulphurea* overlap in the Rocky Mountains, they often form extensive hybrid populations. Range of flower colors from cream to yellow to dusky pink and deeper mauve. Zones 4–8.

Castilleja talamancensis

↔ 12 in (30 cm) ↑ 24 in (60 cm)

Perennial from the mountains of Costa Rica where it is found in boggy conditions at 10,000 ft (3,000 m). Hairy dull green leaves. Red or yellow bracts enclosing yellow flowers, in spring–summer. Zones 8–9.

CATALPA

This genus of 11 species of small to medium deciduous trees, belonging to the trumpet-vine (Bignoniaceae) family, occurs in North America, the West Indies, and southwestern China. They are attractive trees, with a tropical appearance from their large long-stalked leaves. They bear upright panicles of 2 in (5 cm) long, bell-shaped flowers, followed by hanging bean-like seed capsules up to 30 in (75 cm) in length. The genus name is a corruption of the North American Indian name for the plant.
CULTIVATION: *Catalpa* make excellent specimen trees and are good for street planting. They should be sheltered from wind to protect the large leaves. A sunny site with rich, moist, well-drained soil provides the most suitable conditions. Young trees may require protection from late frosts and should be trained to a single trunk. The species are propagated from seed sown in autumn and the cultivars from softwood cuttings taken in late spring or early summer.

Catalpa bignonioides

BEAN TREE, INDIAN BEAN TREE, SOUTHERN CATALPA

↔ 40 ft (12 m) ↑ 50 ft (15 m)

Found at streamsides and in low woods in southeastern USA. The leaves are large, with heart-shaped bases, and have an unpleasant smell when they are crushed. They bear large erect panicles of bell-shaped white flowers, marked with yellow and purple, in summer, and large bean-like pods. **'Aurea'** ★, a fine form with velvety golden leaves. **'Nana'**, a small shrub to 6 ft (1.8 m) high, seldom bears flowers. Zones 5–10.

Catalpa bungei

↔ 25 ft (8 m) ↑ 30 ft (9 m)

Native of northern China. A small tree. Leaves triangular, with a long central tip. Flowers rosy pink to white with purple spots, in summer. Seed capsule may grow up to 20 in (50 cm) in length. Zones 5–10.

Catalpa bungei

Catananche caerulea

Catalpa × *erubescens*

↔50 ft (15 m) ↑50 ft (15 m)

This is a cultivated hybrid between *C. bignonioides* and *C. ovata*. A broad spreading tree. Large leaves to 12 in (30 cm) long and 10 in (25 cm) across. Fragrant white flowers, purple and white markings, forming dense panicles, in summer. Seed capsules up to 15 in (38 cm) long. **'Purpurea'** has shoots and young leaves that emerge purple-black, becoming dark green. Zones 5–10.

Catalpa fargesii

↔40 ft (12 m) ↑60 ft (18 m)

From open mountain areas of western China. Wide leaves taper to a fine point, bronze when young. Flowers rosy pink, marked with yellow and purple, in dense clusters, in summer. Slender seed pods to 30 in (75 cm) long. Zones 5–10.

Catalpa speciosa

NORTHERN CATALPA, SHAWNEE WOOD, WESTERN CATALPA

↔90 ft (27 m) ↑120 ft (36 m)

From riverbanks, damp woods, and swamps of central southern USA. Rather like *C. bignonioides* but has larger leaves. White flowers are larger, less dense, appearing a few weeks earlier. Considered to be less showy. Zones 5–10.

CATANANCHE

CUPID'S DART

This small genus, belonging to the daisy (Asteraceae) family, contains 5 species of annual or perennial herbs found in countries bordering the Mediterranean. Inhabit dry grassy areas. Leaves usually long and narrow and arise at base of clump. Flowering stems are thin and wiry, bearing cornflower-like flowers of blue, white, or yellow. Bracts below the flowers are transparent and papery, often with a silver tinge. Both common and botanical names refer to the ancient use of the sap in the making of aphrodisiacs.

CULTIVATION: *C. caerulea* is usually the only species seen in cultivation. Grow in full sun in any well-drained soil. It tends to be short-lived as a perennial, especially when grown in heavy clay and can be treated as an annual. Plants propagated from seed will flower in the first year. Propagation can also be by division in winter.

Catananche caerulea

BLUE CUPIDONE, BLUE SUCCORY, CUPID'S DART

↔12–18 in (30–45 cm) ↑24–30 in (60–75 cm)

Native to southwestern Europe and northern Africa. Low clumps of narrow, lance-shaped, grayish green leaves, sometimes with a few long teeth. Delicate stems of blue to mauve flowers, like cornflowers in color and appearance, in summer. **'Major'** has flowers of deep blue. Zones 7–10.

CATHARANTHUS

Although related to the common periwinkle *(Vinca)*, the 8 annuals and perennials of this genus, in the dogbane (Apocynaceae) family, are less hardy and tolerate little or no frost. All Madagascan natives, they are bushy plants with simple elliptical leaves on semi-succulent stems. Flat, 5-petalled flowers, mainly in pink and mauve shades, appear at the stem tip and leaf axils. Considered a weed in the tropics and subtropics, the commonly cultivated species *C. roseus* is a perennial often grown as a greenhouse plant or summer bedder in temperate gardens. Naturally highly toxic, it is the source of vinca alkaloids, used to treat lymphocytic leukemia and Hodgkin's Disease.

CULTIVATION: Very easily grown in sun or part-shade, periwinkles are drought tolerant but flower more heavily with summer moisture. Pinch back to encourage bushiness. In cool areas where winter frost would be fatal, bring indoors or discard and replace in spring. Propagate from seed or half-hardened summer cuttings.

Catharanthus roseus

Catharanthus roseus

syn. *Vinca rosea*

MADAGASCAR PERIWINKLE, ROSE PERIWINKLE

↔16 in (40 cm) ↑24 in (60 cm)

Upright perennial from Madagascar. Glossy deep green leaves with pale midrib, to 2 in (5 cm) long. Mauve-throated, soft pink to red, 5-petalled flowers, with red "eye." **'Albus'**, white flowers; **'Blue Pearl'**, 18 in (45 cm) tall, white-centered lavender-blue to mauve flowers; **'Blush Cooler'**, very pale pink flowers, light red center, one of the compact, 12 in (30 cm) tall, heavy-flowering **Cooler Series**; **'Pacifica Punch'**, deep pink flowers with slightly darker center, one of the 18 in (45 cm) tall **Pacifica Series**; **'Parasol'**, white flowers to 2 in (5 cm) wide, with red "eye"; the very heat-tolerant **Pretty Series**; and **'Stardust Orchid'**, cream-centered deep pink flowers, up to 16 in (40 cm) tall. Zones 11–12.

CEANOTHUS

CALIFORNIAN LILAC

This genus of about 50 species of mostly evergreen, ornamental, flowering shrubs is a member of the buckthorn (Rhamnaceae) family. Mainly native to western North America, some are found in eastern USA, and from Mexico south to Guatemala. They tolerate drought, heat, and cold provided the soil is free draining. In habit they range from low, spreading, ground cover plants to tall shrubs. Most are quick growing but they may also be short lived. The flowers range from powder blue to deep purple, some having white or cream flowers. The peak flowering season for *Ceanothus* is early in the summer months.

CULTIVATION: *Ceanothus* will grow in most soils, preferring a position in sun. Most prefer dry-summer climates and are quite wind-tolerant. Tip prune the young plants; the adult plants require little pruning apart from removing spent flowerheads and wayward shoots. *Ceanothus* resent disturbance. Species can be propagated from seed, and soft tip or firm hardwood cuttings can be taken between spring and early autumn.

Ceanothus arboreus

Ceanothus americanus

MOUNTAIN-SWEET, NEW JERSEY TEA

↔2–3 ft (0.6–0.9 m) ↑2–3 ft (0.6–0.9 m)

Small, deciduous shrub, found in eastern and central North America. Slender leaves, believed to have been used as a tea substitute during the American Civil War. Dense panicles of dull white flowers in mid-summer. Zones 5–9.

Ceanothus arboreus

CATALINA MOUNTAIN LILAC, TREE CEANOTHUS

↔12 ft (3.5 m) ↑20 ft (6 m)

From the southern Californian coast, vigorous, wide-spreading, smaller in cultivation. The ovate leaves are downy beneath, and larger than in other species. The pale blue and fragrant flowers appear in abundant panicles, in spring. **'Mist'** ★, paler flowers, gray-blue in color, carried in long spikes. **'Trewithen Blue'** is an improved selection, widely planted, which has large panicles of fragrant deep blue flowers. Zones 7–9.

Ceanothus crassifolius

HOARY LEAFED CEANOTHUS

↔7–12 ft (2–3.5 m) ↑7–12 ft (2–3.5 m)

From southern California and Mexico. Evergreen shrub with open branching habit. Pale gray or brown bark, downy twigs. Small leathery leaves with coarsely toothed margins rolled under, olive green above, white hairs below. Umbel-like heads of white flowers in spring. Zones 8–10.

Ceanothus cuneatus

BUCKBRUSH WEDGELEAF CEANOTHUS

↔5–7 ft (1.5–2 m) ↑6–10 ft (1.8–3 m)

Found from Oregon, USA, to northern Baja California, Mexico. Densely branched, spreading, evergreen shrub with glossy wedge-shaped leaves. Dense cymes of blue-tinted flowers appear in spring. Blue-flowered ***C. c.* var. *rigidus*** (Monterey ceanothus) is just one of several localized varieties, and it has a small-leafed white-flowered cultivar known as **'Snowball'**. Zones 8–10.

C

Ceanothus maritimus

Ceanothus prostratus var. *occidentalis*

Ceanothus delilianus 'Gloire de Versailles'

Ceanothus delilianus

↔5 ft (1.5 m) ↑5 ft (1.5 m)

Strong-growing, deciduous shrub, a hybrid between *C. americanus* and *C. coeruleus*. Broadly oval bright green leaves, panicles of soft blue flowers throughout the summer. One of the parents of the popular "French hybrids." Cultivars include **'Gloire de Versailles'** and **'Topaze'**. Zones 6–9.

Ceanothus divergens

CALISTOGA CEANOTHUS

↔4 ft (1.2 m) ↑3 ft (0.9 m)

Semi-prostrate evergreen species. Spine-toothed bright green leaves, gray undersides. Rather rigid branches covered with racemes of deep blue flowers in spring. Zones 7–9.

Ceanothus diversifolius

PINE-MAT

↔3–6 ft (0.9–1.8 m)
↑4–12 in (10–30 cm)

From California. Evergreen shrub with long flexible branches forming low clumps. Small pale bluish green leaves, hairy beneath. Tiny heads of white to pale blue flowers from spring–early summer. Zones 8–10.

Ceanothus fendleri

↔3–6 ft (0.9–1.8 m)
↑1–7 ft (0.3–2 m)

From southwestern USA and Mexico. Evergreen shrub, usually prostrate. Densely branched and spiny. Shoots and leaves downy. Small umbel-like clusters of bluish white flowers in early summer. Zones 5–10.

Ceanothus gloriosus

POINT REYES CREEPER

↔12 ft (3.5 m) ↑12 in (30 cm)

Occurring naturally on the central Californian coast. Prostrate shrub with dark green, glossy, toothed leaves. Clusters of lavender-blue flowers, in spring. *C. g.* var. ***exaltatus***, erect shrub to 6 ft (1.8 m) high; *C. g.* **'Anchor Bay'**, very dense foliage and mauve-blue flowers. Zones 7–9.

Ceanothus griseus

CARMEL CEANOTHUS

↔10 ft (3 m) ↑10 ft (3 m)

Native to hills of central California, shrub, with dark green leaves, gray beneath. Pale lilac-blue flowers in spring. New growth is arching. *C. g.* var. ***horizontalis*** is a low-growing form with a spreading habit; **'Diamond Heights'**, a form of 'Yankee Point', produces golden leaves blotched with dark green; **'Hurricane Point'** has fast growing, light blue flowers; **'Yankee Point'** ★ has bright blue flowers. Another form, *C. g.* **'Kurt Zalnik'**, discovered clinging precariously to an eroding cliff face, has extremely dark blue blooms, a height to 3 ft (0.9 m), and a spread of 15 ft (4.5 m). **'Santa Ana'** has a spreading habit and bears deep blue flowers. Zones 8–10.

Ceanothus hearstiorum

↔6 ft (1.8 m) ↑12 in (30 cm)

From California. Previously thought a hybrid, now given species status. Prostrate, spreading, evergreen shrub. Small puckered leaves. Mid- to violet-blue flowers in small clusters from late spring–early summer. Zones 8–10.

Ceanothus impressus

SANTA BARBARA CEANOTHUS

↔10 ft (3 m) ↑10 ft (3 m)

Spreading evergreen shrub. The leaves are small, and deeply veined. The flowers are deep blue, and borne in small thin clusters, in spring. One of the hardiest evergreen species. Zones 8–10.

Ceanothus integerrimus

DEER BRUSH

↔3–7 ft (0.9–2 m) ↑3–7 ft (0.9–2 m)

Large semi-evergreen shrub with dull sea green leaves. Flowers in pale blue panicles in mid-summer. Zones 6–9.

Ceanothus × *lobbianus*

↔4 ft (1.2 m) ↑4 ft (1.2 m)

A natural hybrid between *C. dentatus* and *C. griseus*. Upright, relatively compact, densely branched, evergreen shrub. Toothed dark green leaves, hairy beneath. Flowers clear bright blue, borne in rounded panicles in late spring. Zones 8–10.

Ceanothus maritimus

MARITIME CEANOTHUS

↔36 in (90 cm) ↑12 in (30 cm)

From coastal areas of California. A mat-forming evergreen shrub. Small coarsely toothed leaves with margins rolled under, glossy dark green above, white hairs beneath. Flowers pale mauve to dark blue, in small round clusters, in spring. Zones 8–10.

Ceanothus oliganthus

↔3–7 ft (0.9–2 m)
↑3–10 ft (0.9–3 m)

From southern California. Evergreen shrub or small tree. Young branches hairy and tinged red. Leaves dark green and slightly hairy above, paler and hairier beneath. Small loose heads of dark blue to purple flowers in spring. *C. o.* var. ***orcuttii*** has pale blue flowers; *C. o.* var. ***sorediatus*** has pale to dark blue flowers. Zones 8–10.

Ceanothus ovatus

INLAND CEANOTHUS, REDROOT

↔36 in (90 cm)
↑24–36 in (60–90 cm)

A dense deciduous shrub from New England to central USA. Summer foliage is shiny green, no autumn coloring. Dry seed capsules turn bright red in summer. Small white flowers. Zones 4–9.

Ceanothus papillosus

WART LEAF CEANOTHUS

↔3–10 ft (0.9–3 m)
↑3–17 ft (0.9–5 m)

From California. Evergreen shrub with lax downy branches. Narrow, oblong, dark green leaves, to 2 in (5 cm) long, hairy with prominent wart-like bumps. Pale to dark blue flowers in clusters either terminally or along branches, in spring. *C. p.* var. ***roweanus*** (Mt Tranquillon ceanothus, Rowe ceanothus) has narrower blunter leaves. Zones 8–10.

Ceanothus prostratus

MAHALA MATS, SQUAW CARPET

↔8 ft (2.4 m) ↑3 in (8 cm)

From high mountainous areas of Oregon and California, differing from other ceanothus in being subalpine. Creeping evergreen shrub making a dense mat, stems often rooting as they grow. Leaves toothed, dark green; flowers pale lavender-blue, in spring. *C. p.* var. ***occidentalis*** has wavy-edged wedge-shaped leaves. Zones 6–9.

Ceanothus pumilus

SISKIYOU-MAT

↔7 ft (2 m) ↑8 in (20 cm)

From northern California and southwestern Oregon. Prostrate evergreen shrub. Hairy twigs. Leaves small, leathery, white hairs beneath. Produces small umbel-like clusters of white, mauve, or blue flowers in spring. Zones 7–10.

Ceanothus spinosus

GREEN BARK CEANOTHUS, RED-HEAT

↔7–12 ft (2–3.5 m)
↑7–20 ft (2–6 m)

From California and Mexico. Large evergreen shrub or small tree, smooth olive green bark, ascending spiny branches. Leathery, glossy, green leaves. White to pale blue flower clusters, to 6 in (15 cm) long, spring. Zones 8–10.

Ceanothus thyrsiflorus

BLUE BRUSH, BLUEBLOSSOM, CALIFORNIAN LILAC

↔20 ft (6 m) ↑20 ft (6 m)

Large shrub or small tree, fast growing, evergreen. Leaves dark green; flowers blue in dense clusters in early summer. Prune lightly after flowering. *C. t.* var. ***repens***, a prostrate spreading shrub. Zones 7–9.

Ceanothus × *veitchianus*

↔10 ft (3 m) ↑10 ft (3 m)

From California, a natural hybrid of uncertain origin. Large evergreen shrub with small, glossy, wedge-shaped leaves with black tips. Lilac-blue flowers in early summer. Hardy and free flowering. Zones 7–9.

Ceanothus Hybrid Cultivars

↔4–12 ft (1.2–3.5 m)
↑6 in–15 ft (15 cm–4.5 m)

Ceanothus species hybridize readily making classification difficult. Popular landscaping plants, the hybrid cultivars have various growth habits and flower color, although the predominant shade is blue. **'A. T. Johnson'**, free-flowering, rich blue, fuzzy flowers in spring; **'Autumnal Blue'**, hardy floriferous evergreen, sky blue flowers in late summer–autumn, leaves bright glossy green; **'Blue Cushion'**, rich blue flowers; **'Blue Mound'**, small to medium shrub, glossy green finely toothed leaves, bright blue flowers, in late spring–early summer; **'Blue Jeans'**, shrub to 8 ft × 8 ft (2.4 m × 2.4 m), clips readily for hedging; powder blue flowers; **'Blue Sapphire'**, small free-flowering shrub, chocolate colored foliage, royal blue flowers; **'Burkwoodii'**, dense, compact, bushy shrub, bright blue flowers in late summer–autumn; **'Cascade'**, evergreen, powder blue flower clusters on long stalks, in spring; **'Concha'**, dense medium-sized shrub with arching branches, narrow dark green leaves, deep blue flowers; **'Dark Star'**, fragrant cobalt blue flowers; **'Delight'**, exceptionally hardy, with bright blue flowers in long panicles, in spring; **'Edwardsii'**, fast-growing tall shrub, deep blue flowers in dense clusters, in late spring, leaves glossy deep green, clear green beneath; **'Frosty Blue'**, dense dark green foliage, spiky clusters of deep blue flowers frosted with white; **'Gentian Plume'**, large open panicles of dark blue flowers in spring and autumn; **'Italian Skies'**, vigorous evergreen, deep blue flowers in late spring; **'Joyce Coulter'**, clusters of blue flowers; **'Julia Phelps'** ★, purple-red buds opening to deep mauve flowers; **'Pershore Zanzibar'** (syn. 'Zanzibar'), pale gold and dark green variegated foliage; **'Pin Cushion'**, a compact shrub with an arching habit; **'Puget Blue'**, an American-raised hybrid, bearing deep blue flowers in late spring–summer; **'Ray Hartman'**, dark green leaves, hairy gray beneath, clusters of bright blue flowers; **'Snow Flurries'**, pure white flowers in late summer–early autumn. Zones 7–10.

CEDRONELLA

This genus, a member of the mint (Lamiaceae) family, contains a single species of perennial herb native to the Canary Islands. It is grown primarily for its aromatic foliage, which is used in herbal teas and potpourri. The spiky small pale flowers are of less consequence but nonetheless attractive.
CULTIVATION: In cool areas grow in pots in the conservatory or treat as an annual outdoors. Elsewhere grow in a sunny position in well-drained soil. Propagation of *Cedronella canariensis* is from seed or cuttings.

Cedronella canariensis

syn. *Cedronella triphylla*
BALM OF GILEAD, CANARY BALM
↔ 1–3 ft (0.3–0.9 m) ↑ 2–4 ft (0.6–1.2 m)

Found on the Canary Islands. This is a somewhat shrubby perennial with trifoliate leaves comprised of fresh green lance-shaped leaflets. These leaves, when rubbed or crushed, release a strong balsamic scent. The spikes of the small tubular two-lipped flowers are pale pink to lilac. Zones 9–11.

CEDRUS

TRUE CEDAR

The Roman poet Virgil (70–19 BC) said of the cedar, "with the oil whereof the ancients anointed their books, to keep them from being worm-eaten." *Cedrus* come from widely separated regions in northwest Africa, Cyprus, Turkey, Lebanon, and the western Himalayas. They are large long-lived trees from the pine (Pinaceae) family, with needle-like leaves arranged spirally on the leading shoots at the branch tip; crowding on the short lateral shoots to form neat rosettes. Both the male and female cones are large and conspicuous; the seeds feature interesting papery wings. All the cedars are somewhat similar in appearance, and are sometimes treated as varieties or subspecies of a single species, or 2 species *(C. libani* and *C. deodara)*. The classification that is favored by gardeners recognizes the 4 species described here.
CULTIVATION: Cedars are fairly frost hardy but cannot be grown in the more severe northern climates. They adapt to a range of soil types, if the soil is of moderate depth and fertility, and there is subsoil moisture available. These trees do not normally require any pruning to keep them in good shape. Planting out is best done when still at a small size. Propagation is from seed except for the cultivars, which must be grafted.

Cedrus atlantica

syn. *Cedrus libani subsp. atlantica*
ATLANTIC CEDAR, ATLAS CEDAR
↔ 30 ft (9 m) ↑ 80 ft (24 m)

From the Atlas and Rif Mountains of Morocco and Algeria. Young trees are conical with stiff erect leading shoots, ageing to broad-headed. The needles are crowded on the short shoots into tight neat rosettes. Foliage varies from rather bluish to green. **'Aurea'**, with distinctive golden yellow-tipped foliage. The **Glauca Group** are particularly blue and are usually grafted trees. **'Glauca Pendula'** ★ has an extraordinary form, requiring support of the long branches from which foliage sweeps to the ground. **'Pendula'** is a striking clone with all growths completely pendulous, forming a curtain of bluish gray foliage, hanging down to 10 ft (3 m) or more. Zones 6–10.

Cedrus deodara

Cedrus brevifolia

syn. *Cedrus libani subsp. brevifolia*
CYPRUS CEDAR
↔ 20 ft (6 m) ↑ 50 ft (15 m)

Not well known in cultivation, native to the southern mountains of Cyprus. A small tree, very short grayish green needles, mostly under ½ in (12 mm) long. Zones 6–10.

Cedrus deodara

DEODAR, DEODAR CEDAR
↔ 30 ft (9 m) ↑ 200 ft (60 m)

Native to the western Himalayas from Afghanistan to western Nepal, this is the largest of the cedars. It has a spire-like crown with lower branches resting on the ground. Leading shoots are drooping with soft green needles. Seed cones are barrel-shaped. **'Aurea'** has pale yellowish new growth, changing to darker lime green. Zones 7–10.

Cedrus libani

CEDAR OF LEBANON
↔ 90 ft (27m) ↑ 150 ft (45 m)

In Lebanon the famous cedars now grow only on Mt Lebanon. Young trees, narrowly conical in form, with stiff leading shoots and grayish green leaves. Old trees have massive horizontally spreading limbs. **'Golden Dwarf'** (syn. 'Aurea-Prostrata') is a dwarf form. Zones 5–10.

Cedronella canariensis

Cedrus atlantica

C

CEIBA

syn. *Chorisia*

About 10 species of tropical American deciduous trees make up this genus in the mallow (Malvaceae) family. *Ceiba* species are tall stout-trunked trees with smooth bark often armed with large conical prickles. Leaves are compound with leaflets radiating from the end of leaf stalk. Flowers are cream to yellow, pink, or red, and carried in loose panicles toward branch tips. The fruit is a large green capsule enclosing seeds buried in cottonwool-like hairs called kapok, once used for stuffing pillows.
CULTIVATION: They thrive in lowland tropics or in subtropical regions; best in climates with a summer rainfall and a distinct dry season, in deep, well-drained, alluvial soils and a reasonably sheltered position. Early growth is fast, full height attained in only 10 to 20 years. Propagate from freshly gathered seed or half-hardened cuttings in summer.

Ceiba pentandra

syn. *Eriodendron anfractuosum*

KAPOK TREE

↔80 ft (24 m) ↑230 ft (70 m)

Regarded in Africa as the tallest native tree. High open canopy, massive trunk, large buttresses. Cream to dull yellow or pink flowers on pendent stalks from bare branch tips before the new leaves. Elongated pods about 6 in (15 cm) long. Zones 11–12.

CELOSIA

COCKSCOMB, WOOLFLOWER

Found in the tropics of Asia, Africa, and the Americas, this genus of around 50 species of annuals and perennials belongs to the amaranth (Amaranthaceae) family. The name *Celosia* comes from a Greek word, *keleos*, meaning burning, which is a very appropriate reference to the flame-like color and shape of the flowerhead. *C. argentea* var. *cristata*, an annual, is the only widely cultivated species and it has been developed into many variably flowered and colored seedling strains. Upright plants, some are up to 6 ft (1.8 m) tall, though most are far smaller. They have simple lance-shaped leaves up to 6 in (15 cm) long and tiny vivid yellow, orange, or red flowers massed in upright plumes or combs (cristate).
CULTIVATION: Although as an annual it can be grown far outside its natural tropical range, *Celosia* needs ample warmth to perform well. Plant in fertile well-drained soil in full sun and water well. Raise from seed.

Celosia argentea var. *cristata*, Plumosa Group, 'Venezuela'

Celosia argentea

↔16–24 in (40–60 cm)
↑3–7 ft (0.9–2 m)

Quick-growing annual widespread in the tropics. Leaves lance-shaped to 6 in (15 cm) long. Tiny white flowers in upright spikes to 3 in (8 cm) long. Usually seen as ***C. a.* var. *cristata;*** cultivated forms available with green, purple, or red foliage and many flower colors and styles. Divided into groups: **Childsii Group**, rounded to globose flowerheads; **Cristata** or **Cockscomb Group**, flowerheads terminal, flattened and broad, resembling a rooster's comb; **Plumosa Group**, upright plumes of flowers, not always terminal, though axillary flowerheads usually smaller than terminal; **'Apricot Brandy'**, 14 in (35 cm) tall, orange plumes, green foliage; **'Forest Fire'**, 24 in (60 cm) tall, vivid red plumes, red foliage; **'Castle Mix'**, compact and heavy-flowering, available in wide color range and with green or red-tinted foliage, usually with color name, such as **'Pink Castle'**, or **'Yellow Castle'**; **'New Look'**, 14 in (35 cm) tall, branching habit, red plumes, red foliage; **'Venezuela'**, crimson flowers; **Pyramidalis Group**, flowerheads broad-based, tapering evenly to a point, often included with Plumosa Group. Zones 11–12.

Celtis occidentalis

Celosia spicata

Celosia spicata

↔12 in (30 cm)
↑24–36 in (60–90 cm)

Summer-flowering annual. Narrow upright flowerheads, usually in silvery metallic shades of pink or yellow. Zones 10–12.

CELTIS

Occurring in all continents and many larger islands, the large, mainly tropical and mainly evergreen genus *Celtis*, consists of over 100 species. Belonging to the hemp (Cannabaceae) family, the genus has the characteristic leaf shape with usually toothed edges and asymmetric base. Flowers are greenish and inconspicuous, male and female separate on the one tree. Small berry-like fruit with thin but sugary flesh concealing a hard stone; in most species they ripen to black or dark brown, greedily eaten by birds. Some species become troublesome weed trees when cultivated outside their native lands.
CULTIVATION: Vigorous growers, they adapt well to tough environments such as urban streets and parks, tolerating a wide range of soil conditions. The deciduous species make fine shade trees. Propagate from seed, which in the case of temperate species should be cold-stratified for 2 to 3 months before sowing in spring; germination is often erratic.

Celtis laevigata

syn. *Celtis mississippiensis*

SUGAR HACKBERRY, SUGARBERRY

↔60 ft (18 m) ↑80 ft (24 m)

Native to southeastern USA. Deciduous species with smooth dark gray bark. Leaves thin, hairless, very one-sided at base, finely tapered at the apex, with teeth in upper part. Fruit is orange, ripening to purple-black, in autumn. Zones 6–11.

Celtis occidentalis

AMERICAN HACKBERRY

↔60 ft (18 m) ↑60 ft (18 m)

Widely distributed in northern USA. Deciduous, low-branching; smooth, gray, bark, developing rows of corky pustules, becoming dark and closely furrowed with age. Leaves are broad, toothed, pale yellow in autumn. Fruit ripens red to dark purple in autumn. **'Prairie Pride'**, dense bushy crown. Zones 3–10.

Celtis reticulata

syn. *Celtis douglasii*

NETLEAF HACKBERRY

↔25 ft (8 m) ↑25 ft (8 m)

From the mountains of western USA and Mexico, this deciduous species is similar to *C. occidentalis*. Pea-sized orange-red fruits. Native Americans mixed the pounded fruit with animal fat and cornmeal as a food item. Zones 6–10.

Celtis sinensis

syn. *Celtis japonica*

CHINESE HACKBERRY, CHINESE NETTLE-TREE

↔50 ft (15 m) ↑60 ft (18 m)

Occurring in eastern Asia. Deciduous or semi-evergreen. Broad irregular canopy. The bark is relatively smooth, leaden gray. The leaves are glossy dark green above, olive green beneath, with toothed edges. Small, globe-shaped, summer fruits ripen from yellow to orange to black. Zones 7–12.

CENTAUREA

CORNFLOWER, KNAPWEED, STAR THISTLE

Widespread in temperate zones, this daisy (Asteraceae) family genus contains around 450 species of annuals, perennials, and subshrubs. A variable lot, most are readily identifiable by their thistle-like flowerheads, which emerge from an egg-shaped receptacle known as an involucre. Flowerheads often have distinctly different inner and outer florets, with the outer having 5 longer petals. Flower colors include white, yellow, pink, blue, and mauve. Plant size varies; common features are pinnately lobed foliage, often silver-gray, and an upright habit. Some species have been used to treat wounds; named after the Greek mythological centaur, half-horse, half-man, famed for his healing powers. CULTIVATION: Plant in full sun, in light well-drained soil. Good ventilation will lessen any mildew problems. Annuals can be raised from seed; perennials also propagated by division or from softwood cuttings of non-flowering stems.

Centaurea americana

↔ 12–20 in (30–50 cm)
↕ 32–40 in (80–100 cm)

Annual from south-central and southeastern USA. Sparsely toothed, lance-shaped, green leaves to 4 in (10 cm) long. Flowerheads white to pale mauve or purple. Zones 4–10.

Centaurea cineraria ★

syn. *Centaurea gymnocarpa*

DUSTY MILLER

↔ 12–24 in (30–60 cm)
↕ 20–36 in (50–90 cm)

From western and southern Italy. Perennial sometimes treated as an annual. Very decorative silver-gray pinnate leaves, Flowerheads purple-pink. Zones 7–10.

Centaurea cyanus

BACHELOR'S BUTTON, BLUEBOTTLE, CORNFLOWER

↔ 8–16 in (20–40 cm)
↕ 12–36 in (30–90 cm)

Annual or biennial from temperate Eurasia. Narrow green to blue-green leaves, sometimes silvery when young. Flowerheads are usually blue in the species but garden forms include white and a wide range of pink and blue shades. The flowering season is from late spring to summer; deadheading will prolong flowering. **'Blue Diadem'**, large, ruffled, double, deep blue heads; and the **Florence Series**, a dwarf strain, which grows to around 14 in (35 cm) high and covers a wide color range. Zones 2–10.

Centaurea cyanus

Centaurea dealbata

PERSIAN CORNFLOWER

↔ 16–24 in (40–60 cm)
↕ 32–40 in (80–100 cm)

Caucasian and northern Iranian perennial. The pinnate leaves, to 8 in (20 cm) long, are green above with gray furry undersides. Pink to purple flowerheads are borne in summer. **'Steenbergii'**, large vigorous cultivar with attractive deep pink flowerheads. Zones 3–9.

Centaurea hypoleuca

syn. *Psephellus hypoleucus*

↔ 12–18 in (30–45 cm)
↕ 16–24 in (40–60 cm)

Perennial found from Turkey to northern Iran. Variably shaped foliage, green and sparsely hairy above, grayish covering of hair below. Pink to purple-red flowerheads. **'John Coutts'**, large deep purple-pink flowerheads. Zones 5–9.

Centaurea macrocephala

GLOBE CORNFLOWER

↔ 20–24 in (50–60 cm)
↕ 32–40 in (80–100 cm)

Erect perennial native to the Caucasus region. Green lance-shaped leaves covered with minute silvery hairs. Large yellow flowerheads. Zones 3–9.

Centaurea montana

MOUNTAIN BLUET, PERENNIAL CORNFLOWER

↔ 12–40 in (30–100 cm)
↕ 24–32 in (60–80 cm)

Perennial from mountains of Europe. Spreads by rhizomes and may form large clump of broad, green, lance-shaped leaves, sometimes pinnate at base. Flowerheads violet to purple-blue. **'Alba'**, low-growing, white flowers. Zones 3–9.

Centaurea macrocephala

Centaurea simplicicaulis

↔ 12–27 in (30–70 cm)
↕ 12–20 in (30–50 cm)

Low mounding perennial from the Caucasus region and western Asia. Spreads by rhizomes to form a clump of whorls of green to gray-green leaves with silver-gray hairs below. Deep pink flowerheads. Zones 4–9.

CENTRADENIA

There are 4 to 5 species of evergreen perennials or subshrubs in this genus, native to Central America and Mexico, which belongs to the meadow-beauty (Melastomataceae) family. Leaves are simple and opposite with well-defined veining, somewhat velvety, and often red-flushed beneath. Small pink or mauve flowers are borne in panicles either terminally or along the branches. CULTIVATION: In cool areas grow in the conservatory or greenhouse in filtered light in a well-drained sandy loam. Water well during the growing season. In warm areas grow outdoors in a well-drained soil in sun or half-sun. Pinch out growing tips to maintain a dense habit. Propagate from seed or cuttings.

Centradenia inaequilateralis

↔ 12 in (30 cm) ↕ 12 in (30 cm)

Native to Mexico. Broadly oval leaves, slightly hairy, tinged with red beneath. Pink flowers in winter. **'Cascade'** has a weeping habit. Suitable for pots and hanging baskets. Zones 10–11.

CENTRANTHUS

This genus consists of 12 species of annual and perennial subshrubs of the honeysuckle (Caprifoliaceae) family from Europe and the Mediterranean, of which only one, *C. ruber,* is widely cultivated. Forming clumps of upright stems with simple, lance-shaped, blue-green leaves and topped with inflorescences of tiny honey-scented flowers, the species can be 2–5 ft (0.6–1.5 m) tall. The flowers are most often a dusky crimson shade but may be white or pink. Although known as valerian and allied with the valerian (Valerianaceae) family, none of the species has the medicinal properties found in true valerian *(Valeriana officinalis).* CULTIVATION: They are very easily grown in any sunny well-drained position. Alkaline soil is preferred but not essential. Plants are drought tolerant and very adaptable. To prevent seeding, cut back flower stems as soon as they fade. *C. ruber* is inclined to self-sow and is considered a weed in parts of New Zealand.

Centranthus angustifolius

Centranthus angustifolius

NARROW-LEAFED VALERIAN

↔ 20–27 in (50–70 cm)
↕ 20–32 in (50–80 cm)

Southern European native with narrow, bright green, lance- to spatula-shaped leaves. Basal leaves are lobed and more rounded. Spring and summer heads of small lavender-pink flowers with conspicuous lower lobes. Zones 7–10.

Centranthus ruber

JUPITER'S BEARD, RED VALERIAN

↔ 16–27 in (40–70 cm)
↕ 32–40 in (80–100 cm)

Found in Europe, North Africa, and western Asia. Blue-green oval to lance-shaped leaves, are sometimes finely toothed, to 3 in (8 cm) long. Tiny, fragrant, deep rose pink to red flowers massed in upright heads. **'Albus'** has white flowers. Zones 6–10.

Centradenia inaequilateralis 'Cascade'

Centranthus ruber

CEPHALANTHUS

This genus, belonging to the madder (Rubiaceae) family, and comprised of only 10 or so species of deciduous or evergreen shrubs and trees has a wide distribution, occurring in temperate to tropical parts of Africa, Asia, and the Americas. They are commonly known as buttonbushes because their very small flowers are borne in rounded button-like heads that are sometimes backed by small bracts. Firm top-shaped fruits follow. The leaves vary in size and shape but are usually a deep green, often tinted with red, especially on the veins, midribs, or stalks.
CULTIVATION: Hardiness varies de-pending on where the species has come from, with those from the tropics withstanding little or no frost, while the ones that are native to North America are very cold tolerant. All species of *Cephalanthus* adapt well to garden con-ditions and thrive in any moist well-drained soil with a position in full or half-sun. Trim if necessary and propa-gate from seed or cuttings.

Cephalanthus occidentalis

BUTTONBUSH

↔ 10 ft (3 m) ↑ 20 ft (6 m)

Evergreen or deciduous, depending on winter frosts; shrub or small tree, found in damp soil near lakes or streams. Pointed elliptical to lance-shaped leaves. White to cream lightly scented flowerheads in summer. Zones 5–11.

CEPHALARIA

There are about 65 species of annual and perennial herbs in this genus, belonging to the honeysuckle (Caprifoliaceae) family. Found from Europe to central Asia and Africa, they are often called giant scabious because of their resemblance to the

Cephalocereus senilis

Cephalanthus occidentalis

closely related *Scabiosa* genus. Plants form clumps of toothed or divided leaves from which arise tall flowering stems. Tight spherical heads open into overlapping ruffs of mostly white to yellow florets reminiscent of daisies. The seed heads are also attractive, being round with soft bristles and a honeycombed appearance.
CULTIVATION: Grow in full sun in moderately fertile, well-drained, but moisture-retentive soil. Most species are suitable for naturalizing in the wild garden. Propagate from seed or by division.

Cephalaria gigantea

GIANT SCABIOUS

↔ 24–48 in (60–120 cm)
↑ 4–8 ft (1.2–2.4 m)

From the Caucasus region and Siberia. Robust perennial with large, dark green, pinnate leaves. Tall branching stems of creamy yellow flowers in summer. *Cephalaria gigantea* needs plenty of room to spread in the border. Zones 4–9.

CEPHALOCEREUS

This genus contains 5 species belonging to the cactus (Cactaceae) family. Many attempts have been made to classify the columnar cacti of Mexico. No doubt further reclassification will occur as research, including DNA testing, throws more light on the true relationship between *Cephalocereus* and related genera, *Carnegia, Lemaireo-cereus, Mitrocereus, Neobuxbaumia, Neodawsonia, Pachycereus,* and *Piloso-cereus*. The genus was established in 1838, its name is derived from the Greek, *cephale* meaning head, with reference to the pseudocephalium—the area of thick wool and bristles normally found on the northern side of mature stems, through which flowers are produced in summer.
CULTIVATION: *Cephalocereus* species are easy to cultivate in a mineral-rich well-drained soil. They may be raised from seed or from cuttings that have been dried out for a week or two. Rest in winter.

Cephalocereus columna-trajani

syn. *Cephalocereus hoppenstedtii*

↔ 16 in (40 cm) ↑ 25–35 ft (8–10 m)

From Puebla, Mexico. Spectacular columnar cactus, forms large stands that look like a forest of telegraph poles. Ribs 15 to 25, areoles woolly, especially at the growing tip. Spines 5 to 8 centrals, 2½–3 in (6–8 cm) long, grayish, 15 to 20 white radials. Pseudocephalium is usually about 3 in (8 cm) wide and up to 7–10 ft (2–3 m) long on the northern side of mature stems. Flowers 3 in (8 cm) wide, white to yellow. Zones 9–11.

Cephalocereus senilis

OLD MAN CACTUS, OLD MAN OF MEXICO

↔ 12–16 in (30–40 cm) ↑ 50 ft (15 m)

From Hidalgo, Guanajuato, and the Metztitlan Valley of Mexico. This is a very popular and easily recognized cactus because of the distinctive long, twisted, gray or white spines that cover the stem of the plant and give it its species name, *senilis* meaning aged, because it looks like a bearded old man. The plants are solitary or branched from the base, slow growing, and can eventually reach over 40 ft (12 m) in the wild. Ribs 20 to 30. Spines strong, 1 to 5 grayish white centrals, 20 to 30 white hair-like radials, thin, twisted. Pseudo-cephalium on side of mature branches, later covering growing point. Bell-shaped flowers, apricot, 3–4 in (8–10 cm) wide. The seed pods are oval. Zones 9–11.

CEPHALOPHYLLUM

This genus of about 30 species of leaf-succulents from western South Africa and southern Namibia belongs to the ice-plant (Aizoaceae) family. Closely related to *Argyroderma*, whose species usually have solitary flowers and differ in the structure of their fruit capsules. The plants are low and creeping, rarely erect and shrubby. In cross-section the leaves are triangular near the tip and rounded near the base. Flowers are rarely solitary and petals are yellow, purple, or white in various combinations, the stamens often of a contrasting color. Capsules (called "tumble fruits") in some species become detached and, as they are blown over the land, disperse the seeds.
CULTIVATION: Grow outside in regions with no winter rainfall, or in a greenhouse in temperate regions. Need full sun, low humidity, and infrequent watering (none at all in winter). Propagate from seed or cuttings allowed to dry before rooting.

Cephalophyllum alstonii

↔ 20 in (50 cm) ↑ 4 in (10 cm)

From Namibia and Western Cape region of South Africa. Spotted, gray-green, cylindrical leaves to nearly 3 in (8 cm) long. Vivid red flowers with purple-red stamens, to 3 in (8 cm) wide. Zones 9–11.

Cephalophyllum alstonii

Cephalophyllum subulatoides

Cephalophyllum diversiphyllum

syn. *Cephalophyllum loreum*

↔ 20 in (50 cm)
↕ 4–6 in (10–15 cm)

From Western Cape region. The leaves are green, to 4 in (10 cm) long, roughly cylindrical but with flattened base and tapered, in rosettes. Yellow flowers with red-tinted undersides, and very large. The seed pods open to reveal an intricate internal structure. Zones 9–11.

Cephalophyllum 'Red Spike'

↔ 20 in (50 cm) ↕ 6 in (15 cm)

Another species from South Africa's Western Cape region. The narrow, blue-gray, cylindrical leaves grow to over 3 in (8 cm) long. Vivid red-pink flowers, stamens with purple tint. Zones 9–11.

Cephalophyllum subulatoides

↔ 20 in (50 cm) ↕ 6 in (15 cm)

From southwest Cape region. Leaves tapered, cylindrical, green to gray-green with red spots and becoming red-tinted in sun, especially at the tips, to nearly 3 in (8 cm) long. Purplish to purple-red flowers to $1\frac{3}{4}$ in (40 mm) in diameter. Zones 9–11.

Cephalophyllum tricolor

↔ 20 in (50 cm) ↕ 6 in (15 cm)

From Western Cape region. Finely spotted, pale green to gray-green, tapered, cylindrical leaves to around 3 in (8 cm) long. Flower petals yellow with purple-red base, stamens and underside of petal tips red, to 2 in (5 cm) wide. Zones 9–11.

CEPHALOTAXUS

PLUM YEW

This interesting genus of conifers consists of 6 or more species, mostly found in China. In foliage features they resemble the yews *(Taxus)* but on female plants the ovules and the plum-like seeds that develop from them are crowded onto stalked head-like cones. On male plants the pollen cones are likewise crowded into small knob-like heads. The genus is now placed in a separate family, Cephalotaxaceae. All species are shrubs or small trees with flaky brown or reddish bark, often multi-stemmed and suckering from ground level.

CULTIVATION: Tough flexible plants that adapt to a wide range of soils and climates, they tolerate exposed positions as well as partial shade, preferring a climate with adequate steady rainfall throughout the year. They are excellent for hedging as they withstand frequent trimming. Propagation is easily achieved from cuttings, preferably taken from leading shoots. Cold stratification is normally used to germinate seed in a nursery.

Cephalotaxus fortunei

FORTUNE'S PLUM YEW

↔ 10 ft (3 m) ↕ 20 ft (6 m)

Introduced to Britain in 1849 by Scottish plant explorer Robert Fortune. Whorled branches; linear, gently curved, finely pointed leaves, 2 white bands beneath, arranged in 2 rows. Oval seeds ripen to glossy purplish brown. Zones 7–10.

Cephalotaxus harringtonia

JAPANESE PLUM YEW

↔ 10 ft (3 m) ↕ 15 ft (4.5 m)

A spreading shrub, sometimes a small tree. Branches occur alternately, olive green leaves, arranged in 2 rows, narrowed at the tip. Seeds similar to those of *C. fortunei*. ***C. h.* var. *drupacea*** ★, with short stiff leaves, rows arranged in a neat V-shape. ***C. h.* 'Fastigiata'** has erect branches densely crowded into a column. Zones 6–10.

CERASTIUM

A genus of about 100 species in the pink (Caryophyllaceae) family. Mostly annuals or perennials, the majority are vigorous carpeting ground covers or tufting plants; many are classed as weeds. Mainly found in Europe and North America, their range is from temperate to arctic zones. Generally the leaves are small and are often hairy giving a silvery appearance. The flowers are usually small and white. *Cerastium* are popular in rock gardens or massed at the front of borders.

CULTIVATION: A well-drained soil in full sun is a must for these plants. Some species can cope with poor or rocky soils. Propagate from seed, division of plants, or from cuttings.

Cerastium arvense

FIELD/LARGE-FLOWERED/MEADOW OR PRAIRIE CHICKWEED, STARRY CERASTIUM

↔ 40 in (100 cm)
↕ 6–10 in (15–25 cm)

Perennial from North America. Linear leaves. Large mats of bright white flowers. Zones 6–11.

Cerastium boissieri

syn. *Cerastium boissierianum*

↔ 8–16 in (20–40 cm)
↕ 6–8 in (15–25 cm)

European species, found particularly in Spain. Hairy white leaves. White flowers. Does well in sunny dry rock crevices. Zones 6–11.

Cephalotaxus fortunei

Ceratostigma griffithii

Cerastium candidissimum

Ceratostigma willmottianum

Cerastium candidissimum

SNOW-IN-SUMMER

↔ 40 in (100 cm)
↕ 4–6 in (10–15 cm)

A rampant perennial ground-covering plant. Its narrow silvery leaves are $\frac{1}{2}$–$1\frac{1}{4}$ in (12–30 mm) long. The small white flowers appear in spring–summer. Zones 6–11.

Cerastium macranthum

↔ 4–8 in (10–20 cm)
↕ 2–8 in (5–20 cm)

From Turkey. Tufting perennial occurring in grassland. White flowers are borne in spring–summer. Zones 6–11.

Cerastium tomentosum

SNOW-IN-SUMMER

↔ 40 in (100 cm)
↕ 4–6 in (10–15 cm)

In the broad sense, this species ranges widely through mountains of Europe and western Asia, but many botanists have separated from it more narrowly defined species, for example *C. candidissimum*. A vigorous mat-former, this species has whitish-woolly foliage. Profuse heads of starry white flowers, up to 1 in (25 mm) wide, are borne in spring–summer. Zones 6–11.

CERATOSTIGMA

From the leadwort (Plumbaginaceae) family, a genus of 8 species of herbaceous perennials or small evergreen or deciduous shrubs, all but one native to the Himalayas or China. Grown for their intense blue, 5-petalled, flat flowers, borne in terminal clusters from summer to autumn, when the small-leafed foliage becomes red or bronze depending on the intensity of the colder weather.

CULTIVATION: These low-growing plants are best grown in moist well-drained soil in full sun. Frost-tender; lightly prune to promote a dense compact bush—but remember that they flower on current season's growth. Will re-shoot if killed back by winter frosts.

Ceratostigma griffithii

↔ 7 ft (2 m) ↕ 3 ft (0.9 m)

Evergreen shrub, low multi-branched habit, densely foliaged mounded shape. Terminal clusters of blue flowers in late summer–autumn, when the mid-green leaves turn red. Zones 7–10.

Ceratostigma plumbaginoides ★

syn. *Plumbago larpentiae*

↔ 12 in (30 cm) ↕ 18 in (45 cm)

Herbaceous perennial, slender upright stem. Spreading from rhizomes, makes a useful ground cover. Cornflower blue flowers at the ends of red stems, in summer–autumn. Leaves turn red with colder weather. Zones 6–9.

Ceratostigma willmottianum

CHINESE PLUMBAGO

↔ 5 ft (1.5 m) ↕ 3 ft (0.9 m)

Deciduous shrub with an open low-branching habit. Mid-green leaves, pale to bright-blue flowers throughout summer–autumn. The foliage turns rich bronze tones in autumn. **'Forest Blue'**, elliptical leaves, deep blue flowers; **'Summer Sky'**, pale blue flowers, contrast well with red calyces. Zones 7–10.

C

CERCIDIPHYLLUM

Sole member of the Cercidiphyllaceae family, and closely allied to the magnolia family, this genus is represented by 2 species, and includes the largest deciduous native tree species in China and Japan. A distinctive elegant habit of horizontally held branches and heart-shaped leaves that color well—red, pink, and yellow—in autumn are the most notable characteristics of the species. Commonly it is found with the trunks forked low to the ground, which makes it vulnerable to damage in strong winds.

CULTIVATION: A sheltered position is essential to avoid disfigurement from drying winds and late spring frosts. Regular summer moisture is required and preferably rich soils. Propagate from seed after first subjecting to cold. Cuttings are readily struck in the late spring to early summer in cool and moist conditions.

Cercidiphyllum japonicum

KATSURA TREE

☼ ✱ ↔35 ft (10 m) ↑60 ft (18 m)

Elegant horizontal branch structure, vibrant autumn foliage. Smaller in cultivation. Leaves bluish green (reddish when unfolding), change to smoky pink, yellow, red in autumn, exude a pungent aroma reminiscent of burnt sugar. *C. j.* var. *sinense* has velvety hairs beneath the leaves. *C. j.* f. *pendulum* ★ has weeping branches. Zones 6–9.

Cercidiphyllum magnificum

syn. *Cercidiphyllum japonicum var. magnificum*

☼ ✱ ↔10–15 ft (3–4.5 m) ↑10–25 ft (3–8 m)

From Japan. Tree are frequently multi-stemmed, with smooth bark until very mature. Large rounded leaves with heart-shaped base and toothed margins. Purplish red on opening, becoming darkly bluish green in summer and coloring to a bright gold in autumn. Zones 6–9.

CERCIS

This small genus of 6 or 7 deciduous trees and shrubs in the cassia subfamily of the legume (Fabaceae) family, found in North America, eastern Asia, and Europe, is grown for the showy spring flowers. The leaves are alternate and mostly broadly ovate; the flowers are pea-flower-like, with 5 petals in a squat calyx, usually borne on bare stems before or with the early leaves. The fruit is a flat legume with a shallow wing along the edge.

Cercidiphyllum japonicum

CULTIVATION: *Cercis* species prefer a moderately fertile soil that drains well, and exposure to the sun for most of the day. All species frost hardy. Shape to select main leader but little regular pruning required after that. Propagate from fresh seeds; pre-soak in hot water to soften coat. Take half-hardened cuttings in summer or early autumn.

Cercis canadensis

EASTERN REDBUD, REDBUD

☼ ✱ ↔30 ft (9 m) ↑30 ft (9 m)

Widely distributed in the USA. Variable with short main trunk, or multi-stemmed, rounded crown. Flowers have dark red-brown sepals, rose pink petals, in late winter–early spring. Fruits reddish brown in summer. **'Alba,'** similar with white flowers. **'Forest Pansy'** has burgundy-colored foliage and pink flowers. Zones 5–9.

Cercis chinensis

CHINESE REDBUD

☼ ✱ ↔20 ft (6 m) ↑20 ft (6 m)

From central China, and similar to *C. canadensis*, but with shorter leaf stalks. Flowers deep rosy purple in late winter–early spring. Not suitable for cold areas. Zones 6–9.

Cercis occidentalis

CALIFORNIA REDBUD, WESTERN REDBUD

☼ ✱ ↔12 ft (3.5 m) ↑15 ft (4.5 m)

Small tree or large shrub from western USA. Leathery rounded leaves, green with paler undersides. Clusters of rose pink flowers in spring. Excellent for dry-summer climates. Zones 5–9.

Cercis racemosa

☼ ❄ ↔20 ft (6 m) ↑30 ft (9 m)

Native to China, flowers pink, drooping clusters, but not on young trees, freely produced in spring. Introduced by E. H. Wilson in 1907. Zones 7–10.

Cercis canadensis

Cercis siliquastrum

JUDAS TREE

☼ ✱ ↔35 ft (10 m) ↑35 ft (10 m)

Native to the Mediterranean region, flowering ornamental. Heart-shaped to kidney-shaped leaves. Flowers rosy purple, crowding the bare branches, in early spring. Purple-tinted seed pods persist in late summer. *C. s.* f. *albida*, white flowers; **'Bodnant'**, deep purple-red flowers. Zones 6–9.

CERINTHE

HONEYWORT

This mainly European genus from the borage (Boraginaceae) family has 10 species of small mounding annuals, biennials, and perennials. Most have simple, short-stemmed, elliptical to spatula-shaped leaves, often blue-tinted, sometimes with an oily sheen and/or small glands known as tubercles. Flowers are tubular, 5-lobed, carried in small clusters, usually in spring–early summer. They cover quite a wide color range, including interesting metallic blue to purple shades, and often the bracts that partially enclose them develop similar colors. As the common name honeywort suggests, the flowers are rich in nectar and very popular with bees.

CULTIVATION: Hardy and suitable for any temperate climate, honeyworts prefer to be kept dry in winter and should be grown in fairly light well-drained soil, preferably with extra humus. Plant in full or half-sun and deadhead frequently to encourage repeat flowering. Propagate the annuals from seed and the perennials from seed or basal cuttings or by division.

Cerinthe glabra

☼/◑ ✱ ↔12–20 in (30–50 cm) ↑20 in (50 cm)

Biennial or perennial from southern and central Europe. Basal foliage long-stemmed and elliptical to 5 in (12 cm) long, upper leaves and those on flower stems smaller, tending to heart-shaped. Flowers to ½ in (12 mm) long, yellow, purple-red base or band. Zones 5–10.

Cerinthe major

☼/◑ ❄ ↔16–24 in (40–60 cm) ↑16–24 in (40–60 cm)

Annual to biennial native to southern Europe. Blue-green foliage developing purple tints on flower stems. Basal leaves oval to spatula-shaped to 2 in (5 cm) long, often with tubercles. Purple or maroon flowers, to 1¼ in (30 mm) long, purplish bracts. *C. m.* var. *purpurea*, a natural variety, purple-blue bracts. *C. m.* **'Purpurascens'**, intense steel blue bracts. Zones 7–10.

Cerinthe major 'Purpurascens'

Cestrum elegans

CESTRUM

This genus, belonging to the nightshade (Solanaceae) family, consists of around 180 species all from tropical America. They are evergreen or decidu-ous woody shrubs or small trees, and have mostly simple alternate leaves, usually narrow with smooth margins. The tubular to funnel-shaped flowers are borne in clusters; and they are often very fragrant and in some species night-scented. The flowers are followed by small mostly blackish or reddish berries, these and all other parts of the plant should be considered poisonous. Some species have been classified as weeds *(C. parqui)*. They are mostly frost tender.
CULTIVATION: Most grow easily in full or half-sun and moderately fertile soil with adequate watering in summer. Where frosts occur, these plants can be grown against a sunny wall for protection. In colder areas they may be grown in a greenhouse. Plants respond well to pruning; pinch back to encourage bushy growth. Propagation is from soft-tip cuttings.

Cestrum aurantiacum

ORANGE CESTRUM
☼ ❄ ↔6 ft (1.8 m) ↕10 ft (3 m)
Native to tropical America, an evergreen or semi-deciduous rambling shrub that requires regular pruning. Smooth light green leaves, slightly hairy new growth, unpleasant smell when crushed. The orange flowers, in clusters at the ends of the stems, appear in spring–summer. Fleshy white berries. Zones 8–12.

Cestrum × *cultum*

PURPLE CESTRUM
☼ ❄ ↔6 ft (1.8 m) ↕10 ft (3 m)
This is a cross between *C. elegans* and *C. parqui*. Ovate to lance-shaped leaves. Densely flowering terminal panicles, similar to *C. elegans*; single tubular flowers resemble *C. parqui*, although pink to violet in color. Zones 8–12.

Cestrum elegans

syn. *Cestrum purpureum*
☼ ❄ ↔8 ft (2.4 m) ↕10 ft (3 m)
From Mexico. Strong-growing shrub, arching branches, ovate-oblong to lance-shaped, hairy, olive green leaves give off a disagreeable odor when crushed. Tubular-shaped red to purple flowers, in dense panicles, in summer–autumn. Succulent, globular, purple-red berries. **'Smithii'** has orange-red flowers. Can be invasive. Zones 8–12.

Cestrum 'Newellii'

RED CESTRUM
☼ ❄ ↔10 ft (3 m) ↕10 ft (3 m)
Arching branches. Dark green leaves, narrowly ovate to elliptical, hairy both sides, emit an unpleasant smell when crushed. The rich crimson unscented flowers are present most of the year. Berries are small, round, and dark red. Zones 8–11.

Cestrum nocturnum

NIGHT-SCENTED JESSAMINE
☼ ❄ ↔10 ft (3 m) ↕10 ft (3 m)
Evergreen shrub from the West Indies. Pale greenish yellow tubular flowers, which as the species name suggests, give off a strong night fragrance, in summer–late autumn. Flowers have no scent in daylight. Ovoid berries ripen green to white. Leaves are somewhat succulent, and bright green with paler color on the reverse. Zones 9–11.

Cestrum parqui

GREEN CESTRUM
☼ ❄ ↔10 ft (3 m) ↕10 ft (3 m)
From Chile. Suckering shrub. The leaves are linear, and lance-shaped to elliptic, with an unattractive smell. Large racemes of yellow-green to bright yellow tubular, night-scented flowers, most of the year. Violet-brown berries. This species is considered a troublesome weed in mild areas. Zones 8–12.

CHAENOMELES

FLOWERING QUINCE, JAPANESE QUINCE, JAPONICA

This genus, which belongs to the rose (Rosaceae) family, has 3 species of spiny deciduous shrubs, native to the high-altitude woodlands of Japan and China. Their early red, pink, or white flowers appear before the leaves on last year's wood and are highly valued for their beauty. The leaves are alternate, serrate, oval, and deep green. The flowers, which usually have 5 petals, unless double, are cup-shaped and appear from late winter to late spring, singly or in small clusters. The roughly apple-shaped, rounded, green fruit turns yellow when ripe; it is aromatic and used in jams and jellies.
CULTIVATION: Generally, well-drained moderately fertile soil, in sun or half-sun will give best results. Grow against a south wall in colder climates. A good ornamental, it can also be used as a hedging plant. Half-hardened cuttings can be obtained in summer or later in autumn. Seed can be sown in autumn in containers with protection from winter frosts or in a seed bed in the open ground.

Chaenomeles × *californica*

☼/◐ ✱ ↔5 ft (1.5 m) ↕6 ft (1.8 m)
A hybrid between *C. cathayensis* and *C.* × *superba*. Leaves mid-green, lance-shaped, 3 in (8 cm) long. Flowers are 2 in (5 cm) in diameter, pink to pale red, in spring. Fruit 2½ in (6 cm) long. Zones 5–10.

Chaenomeles cathayensis

☼/◐ ✱ ↔10 ft (3 m) ↕10 ft (3 m)
Native to China. Small tree to large sparsely branched shrub. The branches are spiny, the leaves shiny, mid-green, and lance-shaped, with toothed edges and red velvety undersides. Flowers in clusters, white, pink flushed, in early–mid-spring. Green scented fruit, 6 in (15 cm) long. Zones 5–10.

Chaenomeles 'Hime'

☼/◐ ✱ ↔6 ft (1.8 m) ↕8 ft (2.4 m)
Vigorous tall hybrid with bright red single flowers that have contrasting golden yellow anthers. Zones 5–9.

Chaenomeles japonica

JAPANESE FLOWERING QUINCE
☼/◐ ✱ ↔6 ft (1.8 m) ↕3 ft (0.9 m)
From Japan. This species has an uncommon, open twiggy habit with spiny branchlets. Flowers are orange-scarlet, with prominent cream stamens, and appear in late winter–early spring. The fragrant fruit, which turns green to dull yellow when ripe, is used for making jelly. Zones 6–9.

Chaenomeles speciosa

syns *Chaenomeles lagenaria, Cydonia speciosa*

CHINESE FLOWERING QUINCE, FLOWERING QUINCE, JAPONICA
☼/◐ ✱ ↔15 ft (4.5 m) ↕10 ft (3 m)
Native to China. This common shrub has produced numerous cultivars with white, salmon, pink, or red flowers, which can be single, semi-double, or double. It has thicket forming, spiny suckering stems and showy flowers, in winter. The aromatic fruit ripens to a green-yellow. **'Geisha Girl'** is an apricot double-flowered form. Some cultivars are hybrids with *C. japonica*, including: **'Nivalis'**, which has snow white flowers; **'Phylis Moore'**, which has pale pink flowers; **'Toyo-nishiki'**, which has pink and white flowers on the same branch, and sometimes produces a branch of red flowers as well. Zones 6–9.

Chaenomeles × *superba*

☼/◐ ✱ ↔6 ft (1.8 m) ↕5 ft (1.5 m)
Hybrid of *C. japonica* and *C. speciosa*, garden origin. Leaves are 2½ in (6 cm) long, oval to oblong-shape, lustrous mid-green. Spring flowers, white, pink, orange to orange-scarlet. Fruit to 3 in (8 cm) long, and aromatic when ripe. **'Cameo'** ★ has fleshy pink flowers; **'Crimson and Gold'**, scarlet blooms with yellow anthers; **'Crimson Beauty'**, crimson flowers; **'Glowing-ember'**, orange-red blooms; **'Nicoline'**, large dark red flowers, **'Rowallane'**, bright red with yellow anthers. Zones 6–10.

Chaenomeles cathayensis

Chaenomeles japonica

C

CHAMAECYPARIS

Genus in the cypress (Cupressaceae) family consisting of some 8 species from North America and eastern Asia. It is distinguished from true *Cupressus* by its small cones and short branches which have small leaves arranged in pairs and flattened to the stems of the branchlets. Foliage becomes more scale-like as it ages. Pollen and seed cones are borne on the same tree. Rice grain-sized pollen cones in huge numbers; seed cones about ⅓ in (8 mm) or less in diameter release the small winged seeds as soon as they mature (in contrast to *Cupressus*, in which unopened seed cones may persist for years). Several of the many ornamental cultivars are used for hedging. The timber has many uses including house interiors, fences, and matches. Contact with the foliage can cause skin allergies in some people. CULTIVATION: This genus is lime and air-pollution tolerant but will grow better in neutral to acid soil. Propagate from half-hardened cuttings taken in summer or seed sown in autumn or spring. Early trimming is necessary. Named cultivars should be grafted in late winter or early spring.

Chamaecyparis lawsoniana

LAWSON CYPRESS, OREGON CEDAR, PORT ORFORD CEDAR

↔10–15 ft (3–4.5 m) ↑100 ft (30 m)

Native to western North America. The foliage is bright green to blue-green; some cultivars have yellow foliage. Red male flowers in early spring. Grayish cones ripen to rusty brown. **'Chilworth Silver'** is a slow growing with bluish gray juvenile foliage; **'Columnaris'** has narrow pale gray foliage, and grows to 30 ft (9 m) high; **'Intertexta'**, with slightly weeping branches and gray-green foliage; **'Nana'**, yellow foliage to 6 ft (1.8 m); **'Pembury Blue'**, silver-blue foliage; **'Stardust'**, medium-sized slow-growing conical tree. Other popular cultivars include: **'Broomhill Gold'**, **'Ellwoodii'** ★, **'Elwood's Pygmy'**, **'Gnome'**, **'Lanei Aurea'**, **'Minima Aurea'**, **'Minima Glauca'**, **'Stewartii'**. Zones 4–9.

Chamaecyparis obtusa

syn. *Cupressus obtusa*

HINOKI CYPRESS

↔20 ft (6 m) ↑60 ft (18 m)

Native to Japan. A slow-growing tree, larger in the wild. Highly valued for landscaping. Bark thick rusty colored. Leaves opposite, deep green above, striped with silvery white beneath. Foliage aromatic when crushed. Male cones yellow in the spring. Rounded seed cones ripen to orange-brown. **'Crippsii'** (syn. 'Crippsii Aurea') has golden-yellow foliage; **'Coralliformis'**, to 8 ft (2.4 m) tall, dark green leaves; **'Nana Aurea'**, golden foliage; **'Nana Gracilis'**, conical tree up to 10 ft (3 m) high; **'Spiralis'**, lush bright green foliage. Zones 5–10.

Chamaecyparis pisifera

syn. *Cupressus pisifera*

SAWARA CYPRESS

↔15 ft (4.5 m) ↑75 ft (23 m)

Native of southern Japan, larger in the wild. Rusty brown bark. Foliage mid-green, white markings beneath. Male cones very small, tawny; seed cones round, black-brown. **'Boulevard'**, to 30 ft (9 m) tall, blue-green foliage; **'Filifera Aurea'**, golden yellow leaves; **'Filifera Aurea Nana'**, a dwarf form; **'Squarrosa'** (syn. 'Squarrosa Veitchii'), soft young foliage, deep green to blue-green. Other popular cultivars include: **'Gold Spangle'**, **'Golden Mop'**, **'Nana Variegata'**, **'Plumosa Aurea Nana'**, **'Plumosa Juniperoides'**, **'Plumosa Nana'**, and **'Squarrosa Sulphurea'**. Zones 5–10.

Chamaecyparis thyoides

ATLANTIC WHITE CEDAR, COAST WHITE CEDAR, WHITE CYPRESS

↔12 ft (3.5 m) ↑50 ft (15 m)

East coast USA. Bark gray-brown. Leaves pointed, dark green, fan-shaped sprays. Small yellow male cones, seed cones purplish black. Tolerates moist to wet conditions. **'Andelyensis'**, blue-green foliage; **'Ericoides'**, purplish brown winter foliage; **'Heatherbun'** ★, dwarf form; **'Rubicon'** (syn. 'Red Star'), has feathery frosted green foliage, turning bright to deep purple in winter. Zones 4–9.

Chamaecyparis lawsoniana 'Intertexta'

CHAMAEDOREA

Chamaedorea, belonging to the family Arecaceae, is of the larger genera of palms with over 100 species. They are attractive, small, understory palms which adapt to cultivation, especially as indoor plants. Native to tropical America, they include both clumping and single-stemmed palms. Fronds are either pinnate (feather palms) or undivided. Flowers are of different sexes on different plants, very small and fleshy, and borne on spikes. As small single-seeded fruits ripen, fruit color contrasts with that of the spike. CULTIVATION: These tropical palms adapt well to frost-free warm-temperate climates. A few will tolerate light frosts. Some are quite sun-hardy in a humid climate, but most grow best in filtered light in a sheltered spot. Soil should be moderately fertile with a high organic content and the surface mulched with leaves. If grown indoors they need good light, though not direct sunlight. Feed regularly in summer with a dilute high-nitrogen fertilizer. Propagate from seed.

Chamaedorea elegans ★

syns *Collinia elegans, Neanthe bella*

PARLOR PALM

↔36 in (90 cm) ↑6 ft (1.8 m)

From highland rainforests of southern Mexico and Guatemala. Stems single with knobbly protuberances. Short deep green fronds, crowded. Small yellow flowers, on panicles. Female panicles turn orange-red. Pea-sized black fruit. **'Bella'** ★, crown of fronds only 12 in (30 cm) wide. Zones 10–12.

Chamaedorea ernesti-augusti

↔18 in (45 cm) ↑3 ft (0.9 m)

From southern Mexico to Honduras. Single-stemmed, wedge-shaped fronds, undivided, with a broad notch at the apex. The male plants have tiny red flowers, the females a spike of greenish flowers, turning bright orange. Small black fruit. Zones 10–12.

Chamaedorea linearis

syns *Chamaedorea megaphylla, C. poeppigiana, C. polyclada*

↔7 ft (2 m) ↑8–20 ft (2.4–6 m)

Native to the Andes at both low and high altitudes. Single pale green trunk. Spreading dark green fronds with drooping leaflets. Multi-branched inflorescence of white flowers. Red fruits to 1 in (25 mm) on female plants. Zones 10–12.

Chamaedorea microspadix

↔10 ft (3 m) ↑8 ft (2.4 m)

From southeastern Mexico. Clump of spreading, thin, bamboo-like stems. Fronds crowded, matt green broad leaflets. Flower panicles, females green, bearing bright scarlet fruits to ½ in (12 mm) in diameter. One of the most sun-hardy species. Zones 8–11.

Chamaedorea plumosa ★

↔5–8 ft (1.5–2.4 m) ↑10–12 ft (3–3.5 m)

Medium-sized rainforest palm from southern Mexico, with slender solitary trunk, up to 2½ in (6 cm) thick, and crown of 5 to 9 finely divided feathery leaves with 120 to 170 irregularly arranged, thin leaflets. Separate male and female plants. Round fruit is black when mature. Fresh seed germinates in 2 to 4 months. Zones 9–12.

Chamaedorea microspadix

Chamaedorea radicalis

syn. *Chamaedorea pringlei*

↔ 4–6 ft (1.2–1.8 m)
↑ 4–6 ft (1.2–1.8 m)

Widely cultivated slow-growing palm from Mexico. Horizontal, sometimes erect, solitary, suckering trunk, 4 to 8 arched, thick, leathery, deep green leaves, about 36 in (90 cm) long, with straight narrow leaflets. Enlarged terminal leaflets resemble fishtails. Separate male and female plants. Erect flower stalks, with yellowish orange flowers. Round orange to red fruit. Zones 8–12.

Chamaedorea seifrizii

↔ 3 ft (0.9 m) ↑ 10 ft (3 m)

Native to Yucatan, Mexico. Multi-stemmed species, stiff ascending fronds, regularly spaced narrow leaflets. Short flowering branches emerge below the fronds; female plants bear pea-sized black fruit on orange spikes. Zones 11–12.

CHAMAEMELUM

CHAMOMILE

There are 4 species of annual and perennial herbs in this genus, which belongs to the daisy (Asteraceae) family. They are native to Europe and to the Mediterranean where they grow in light sandy soils. The fern-like foliage is aromatic, having a sharp apple scent when crushed or trodden on. The typical daisy flowers are white with yellow centers. *C. nobile* is the commonly grown species, cultivated both for its aromatic foliage and its medicinal qualities. It is often used as a lawn plant and the leaves and flowers have long been made into a tea, taken as a calmative and for complaints such as headache and indigestion.
CULTIVATION: Grow in full sun in well-drained soil. For lawns, place plants about 6 in (15 cm) apart and water frequently until established. Cut regularly. Propagate from seed or by rooted divisions.

Chamaemelum nobile

syn. *Anthemis nobile*

CHAMOMILE

↔ 12 in (30 cm) ↑ 4–12 in (10–30 cm)

Sprawling perennial from western Europe. Very aromatic fern-like foliage. Small white daisies with yellow centers in summer. **'Treneague'** is a non-flowering cultivar particularly suitable for lawns. Zones 4–10.

CHAMAEROPS

There is only a single, rather variable species in this genus of fan palms, in the family Arecaceae, and native to far southern Europe, North Africa, and the eastern Mediterranean. Usually multi-stemmed, single-stemmed forms are known. The trunks of most wild plants are so short that fronds appear to spring from the ground, but in cultivation they may develop trunks of up to 15 ft (4.5 m). Fronds are small, divided into stiffly radiating segments; the stalks are armed with spines. The short flowering branches bear male and female flowers on different plants. Male flowers are yellow, conspicuous, and crowded onto flattened spikes. The females are sparser, greenish, and develop dull orange or tan fruits.
CULTIVATION: These plants require a temperate climate with warm summers, and will not thrive in the tropics. Plant in an open sunny position in well drained soil. Well suited to large pots or tubs for use in sunny conservatories or terraces. Propagation is normally from seed, large clumps can be divided with difficulty, if necessary.

Chamaerops humilis ★

MEDITERRANEAN FAN PALM

↔ 12 ft (3.5 m) ↑ 15 ft (4.5 m)

Fronds vary in size, color, and depth of division between segments. Forms with bluish foliage are sometimes found. ***C. h.* var. *argentea*** (syn. *C. h.* var. *cerifera*), stunning bluish foliage. Zones 8–10.

Chamaerops humilis

Chamaemelum nobile

CHAMBEYRONIA

From New Caledonia, only 2 species belong to this genus of feather palms in the family Arecaceae. They are medium-sized palms with solitary straight trunks topped by a smooth crownshaft consisting of the sheathing bases of the fronds. The blade of each large frond is composed of broad well-spaced leaflets in 2 rows along a strongly recurved midrib. Short-flowering branches emerge from the trunk just below the crownshaft, bearing fleshy flowers on thick curved spikes. Male and female flowers arranged in groups, female flanked by a pair of males. The fruits are fairly large and egg-shaped.
CULTIVATION: Prized by palm collectors for the striking coloration of the new fronds, they thrive best in humid, subtropical, coastal climates in moist organic soil well mulched with leaf litter. Provide shelter from strong sun and wind when young. Propagation is only from fresh seed, which may take some months to germinate.

Chambeyronia macrocarpa

syn. *Chambeyronia hookeri*

↔ 10 ft (3 m) ↑ 30 ft (9 m)

Occurring in dense rainforest, with high rainfall. Strongly ringed trunk. Fronds to 8 ft (2.4 m) long. New fronds, 1 or 2 each year; translucent pale bronze to deep reddish bronze. Spectacular combination. Zones 10–12.

CHASMANTHE

There are 3 species of cormous plants in this genus, which belongs to the iris (Iridaceae) family. Native to South Africa and closely related to *Crocosmia* and *Tritonia*. The sword-shaped leaves are arranged in fans. They flower in late winter to spring, bearing spikes of yellow, orange, or red tubular flowers. May, in sunny well-drained situations, prove moderately frost tolerant.
CULTIVATION: Easily grown in warm climates where they clump quickly and can become weedy. Grow in a warm sunny position in a well-drained soil. Propagate from seed or from offsets.

Chasmanthe floribunda

Chasmanthe aethiopica

syn. *Chasmanthe vittigera*

AFRICAN CORN FLAG

↔ 5–7 in (12–18 cm)
↑ 16–27 in (40–70 cm)

From coastal South Africa. Grows from large corms that are renewed annually. The bright green lance-like leaves are arranged in fans, forming dense clumps. Bright vermilion-red flowers, held in single file on straight thrusting stems, in winter–early spring. Nectar enjoyed by honey-eating birds. Zones 9–11.

Chasmanthe floribunda

↔ 12 in (30 cm) ↑ 2–4 ft (0.6–1.2 m)

From Western Cape, South Africa. A fan of sword-shaped leaves often with a silky sheen. Orangey red flowers with yellow striping, arranged in 2 rows on stems to 4 ft (1.2 m) tall, in winter and spring. Zones 9–11.

CHASMANTHIUM

Native to eastern USA and Mexico, this genus of 6 perennial species is a member of the grass (Poaceae) family. *C. latifolium* is the only species that is usually grown in gardens. It is valued both for its attractive flowerheads, suitable for drying, and for its pleasing bright green foliage that colors well before dying back.
CULTIVATION: Plant in moist soil in full or half-sun. Propagate from seed or by division in late winter.

Chasmanthium latifolium

syn. *Uniola latifolia*

NORTH AMERICAN WILD OATS, SEA OATS, SPANGLE GRASS

↔ 12–16 in (30–40 cm)
↑ 36–40 in (90–100 cm)

Does not grow near the sea as one of the common names suggests, but in woodlands and along streams from Texas to New Jersey. Broad bright green leaves turn to rich colors in autumn. Drooping heads of oat-like flowers can be dried. Zones 4–11.

C

CHEILANTHES

CLOAK FERN, LIP FERN

This genus is made up of 180 small, evergreen, terrestrial or rock-inhabiting ferns, all from the maidenhair-fern (Adiantaceae) family, and widely distributed in drier climates and deserts throughout temperate and tropical regions. They are compact, and short- to long-creeping, and produce reclining or erect rhizomes, and wiry brown to black stalks. The rigidly spreading, pinnate or bipinnate, leathery, often heavily scaly fronds have numerous fine divisions. Some species adapt by shrivelling during droughts then expanding when they are rehydrated.

CULTIVATION: They can be difficult to grow and propagate. Minimize damage from moisture fluctuations by planting near large rocks and avoid wetting foliage. Many species prefer full sun (excessive shade causes weak growth); early morning and late afternoon sun are preferable. They have adapted to cold winters. Propagate from spores or by division.

Cheilanthes fendleri

FENDLER'S LIP FERN

↔ 1–2 in (2.5–5 cm) ↕ 6–12 in (15–30 cm)

This small fern is an inhabitant of southern USA and Mexico. It grows from a long-creeping rhizome. The arched, scaly, polished, thin, brown stalks can be up to 7 in (18 cm) long. The oval- to sword-shaped, glistening, bright green blades are up to 6 in (15 cm) long, and have narrow, oblong to triangular, bead-like segments with white or brown scales underneath. Zones 6–10.

CHILOPSIS

Belonging to the trumpet-flower (Bignoniaceae) family, in which it is most closely allied to *Catalpa*, this genus consists of a single species of evergreen shrub or small tree native to arid regions of southwestern USA and western Mexico. It has brittle cane-like branches and very narrow leaves. Short sprays of showy trumpet-shaped flowers terminate the branches, each flower somewhat 2-lipped at its mouth. Fruits are pendulous pencil-like capsules packed with very light winged seeds.

CULTIVATION: *Chilopsis* comes from a warm climate with a very hot dry atmosphere and although fairly frost hardy, will not thrive in cool humid climates. A warm sunny position and deep, well-drained, sandy soil suit it best. It is readily propagated from cuttings, though seed can also be used.

Chilopsis linearis

Chilopsis linearis

DESERT WILLOW

↔ 8 ft (2.4 m) ↕ 10–20 ft (3–6 m)

Usually a shrub, can become a tree under suitable conditions. Downy twigs, grayish green leaves to 4 in (10 cm) or longer. Flowers 1½ in (35 mm) long, almost as wide, deep rose pink to white, darker spots in the throat. **'Burgundy'** ★, deep red-purple flowers; **'Hope'**, white flowers with light yellow center. Zones 6–11.

CHIMAPHILA

PIPSISSEWA, PRINCE'S PINE

This genus of 4 or 5 species from the temperate Northern Hemisphere extending to the high mountains of tropical America, belongs to the heath (Ericaceae) family. They are evergreen perennials to 12 in (30 cm) tall. The slender, often creeping stems, sometimes branched, bear whorls of leathery toothed leaves. The stalked cluster of pendulous flowers is flat-topped or like a raceme. Flowers have 5 round, hollowed, white or pink to red petals. Fruit is a capsule with 5 compartments, splitting open at top to release seeds.

CULTIVATION: These plants are difficult to cultivate, but established plants can be grown in damp, shady, sandy soils in rock gardens or woodland edges. Damage to the far-spreading root systems can be fatal. They can be propagated by very careful division or from seeds sown on damp sphagnum moss, though germination is erratic and success infrequent. Some are of medicinal significance.

Chimaphila umbellata

PIPSISSEWA, SPOTTED WINTERGREEN

↔ 24 in (60 cm) ↕ 5–12 in (12–30 cm)

From cooler regions of Eurasia and North America. Stems branching below ground, shoots erect with whorls of few toothed, obovate leaves. Inflorescence long-stalked with 3 to 10 red or pink to white flowers in summer. Used for treating bladder problems. Zones 5–9.

CHIMONANTHUS

From China. There are 6 species in this deciduous or evergreen genus within the allspice (Calycanthaceae) family. Grown for their ornamental value, their scented flowers can be used dried, like lavender, to fragrance linen. Leaves are arranged opposite in pairs and appear after the flowers in spring.

CULTIVATION: In colder areas they benefit from a sheltered position. This may also protect the early flowers from frost damage. In less cold areas they make a good specimen shrub in the open garden and fit in well in a shrub border, needing full sun in fertile free-draining soil. Propagate by cuttings in summer. Sow seed in a position protected from winter frost as soon as it is ripe, but seed-raised plants will take 5 to 10 years or more to flower.

Chimonanthus nitens

↔ 8 ft (2.4 m) ↕ 6–10 ft (1.8–3 m)

Native to China, great screening plant. Evergreen shrub. Glossy green leaves, opposite, smooth-edged. Solitary, star-like, yellowish white flowers, slightly fragrant, in autumn. Zones 7–9.

Chimonanthus nitens

Chimonanthus praecox

syns *Chimonanthus fragrans*, *Meratia praecox*

JAPANESE ALLSPICE, WINTERSWEET

↔ 10 ft (3 m) ↕ 12 ft (3.5 m)

Native to China. Deciduous shrub. Lance-shaped leaves, glossy green with a rough surface, turn pale yellow in autumn. Fragrant flowers on second-year bare wood, sulfur yellow to pale yellow, purple or brown stain on inner petals, in winter. **'Grandiflorus'** ★ has deep yellow flowers, larger than the species, up to 2 in (5 cm) in diameter. **'Parviflorus'** has small pale yellow flowers. Zones 6–10.

CHIONANTHUS

This genus in the olive (Oleaceae) family consists of more than 100 species of evergreen and deciduous trees and shrubs mostly from tropical regions of the world but with a few in eastern Asia and eastern USA. Leaves are smooth-edged and are arranged opposite each other on the branches. The white 4-petalled flowers are borne in terminal panicles, and are followed in autumn by a purple-blue fruit with a single seed. The bark is used medicinally.

CULTIVATION: Some species tolerate alkaline soil; others prefer a neutral or acid soil and a position in full sunlight. Wood must be ripened by the sun for a good flower set. Sow seed as soon as it is ripe in autumn, ensuring it is protected from winter frosts. Germination is slow, up to 18 months.

Chionanthus retusus ★

CHINESE FRINGE TREE

↔ 10 ft (3 m) ↕ 15–30 ft (4.5–9 m)

Native to China and Taiwan. Deciduous shrub or small tree. Bark deeply grooved or peeling. Glossy, bright green, egg-shaped leaves, white downy undersides. Panicles of fragrant white flowers in summer. Blue-black fruit. Grows in alkaline soil. Zones 6–10.

Chionanthus retusus

C

Chionanthus virginicus

FRINGE TREE

↔10 ft (3 m) ↑12–25 ft (3.5–8 m)

Native to eastern USA. Shrub or small tree. Leaves egg-shaped, dark green, glossy, to 8 in (20 cm) long. Fragrant white flowers in pendent panicles. Blue-black fruit about ½ in (12 mm) in size. Needs acid soil, will tolerate neutral soil. **'Angustifolius'** ★ has narrower leaves, while the leaves of **'Latifolius'** are broadly egg-shaped. Zones 4–10.

CHIONOCHLOA

SNOW GRASS

This small genus contains about 19 species of perennial grasses in the grass (Poaceae) family. Except for one species found in Australia, they are all native to New Zealand where they grow in alpine and subalpine areas. They are generally tall tussock-forming plants with arching foliage and graceful flowerheads.
CULTIVATION: Easily grown in gritty well-drained soil in full sun. Most species are at least frost hardy but in cool areas some perform better in a hot sheltered position. Propagate from seed or by division.

Chionochloa flavicans

↔3 ft (0.9 m) ↑3–5 ft (0.9–1.5 m)

From coastal areas of the North Island, New Zealand. Clumps of green weeping leaves. Arching flower stems to 5 ft (1.5 m) tall. Silky pale green plumes age to cream and fawn. Zones 8–10.

Chionochloa flavicans

Chionochloa rubra

RED TUSSOCK GRASS

↔3 ft (0.9 m) ↑3–5 ft (0.9–1.5 m)

Clumping grass found throughout New Zealand from the central North Island southward. Narrow weeping leaves, up to 6 ft (1.8 m) long, in red shades from brownish green to copper. Loose open flower panicles held above the foliage, initially red-tinted but soon becoming bleached. Zones 7–10.

CHIRANTHODENDRON

This genus of a single evergreen tree species from southern Mexico and Guatemala is part of the mallow (Malvaceae) family. It is closely allied to *Fremontodendron* and hybrids between the 2 genera have been raised (× *Chiranthofremontia). Broad leaves are cordate and shallowly 3- to 7-lobed. Flowers are borne singly on the branches, each opposite a leaf; they have no petals, only a leathery bell-shaped calyx from which emerges a group of 5 stamens with filaments fused into a tube and extremely large claw-like anthers. Form and position of the flowers adapts them for pollination by perching birds and bats. Resembling human hands, they were held in awe by Mexico's ancient peoples. Capsules contain many black seeds.
CULTIVATION: Cultivated in Mexico before the Spanish conquest as objects of religion, elsewhere they have been grown mainly in botanical collections, though becoming more widely grown in California in recent times. Coming from tropical highlands they tolerate very light frosts, but are rather slow-growing. A sheltered but warm position with fertile, well drained soil is best. Propagate from freshly gathered seed.

Chiranthodendron pentadactylon

MEXICAN HAND TREE

↔30 ft (9 m) ↑30–50 ft (9–15 m)

Native to Mexico and Guatemala, usually large shrub or small tree, smaller in cultivation. Large, 5-lobed, palmate leaves, clusters of red-brown cup-shaped flowers in warmer months. Five-angled seed pods. Zones 9–11.

Chiranthodendron pentadactylon

× *CHITALPA*

The sole species in this genus of the trumpet-vine (Bignoniaceae) family is an intergeneric hybrid of *Catalpa bignonioides* and *Chilopsis linearis*. Although closely related and of North American origin, these 2 species do not meet in the wild, *Catalpa* being found in the moist regions of eastern and southern USA while *Chilopsis* is native to the arid southwestern region of the USA and nearby parts of Mexico.
CULTIVATION: In comparison to its *Catalpa* parent, this hybrid is moderately frost tolerant, and is undemanding, thriving in any reasonably deep and fertile well-drained soil that does not dry out entirely in summer. Young trees can be pruned to shape and established plants benefit from light trimming and thinning in winter or very early spring. Propagate from winter hardwood cuttings, from summer half-hardened cuttings, or by budding onto *Catalpa* rootstocks.

× *Chitalpa tashkentensis*

↔20 ft (6 m) ↑20–40 ft (6–12 m)

Deciduous tree. Leaves matt mid-green, fuzzy undersides. Flowers bell-shaped, to 1 in (25 mm) long, white or pink, in erect racemes, at branch tips. **'Pink Dawn'** ★ is lower, with a spreading crown and pink flowers. Zones 6–11.

CHLOROPHYTUM

This genus in the asparagus (Asparagaceae) family contains about 215 species of fleshy-stemmed perennials native to tropical and subtropical regions of Africa, Asia, and 1 species extending to northern Australia. They range in height from 4–24 in (10–60 cm), with linear to lance-shaped leaves arising from the rootstock. Small white flowers are borne in loose sparse panicles, and in some species the flowering stems form new plantlets.
CULTIVATION: A few species are cultivated for their foliage. The most commonly seen is the popular house plant *C. comosum*. In warmer areas where outdoor cultivation is possible grow in light shade in well-drained soil. Can be grown as a ground cover. Indoor plants need bright indirect sunlight and watering well when in full growth.

Choisya 'Aztec Pearl'

Chlorophytum laxum 'Bichetii'

↔8–12 in (20–30 cm)
↑8–12 in (20–30 cm)

The species ranges from tropical Africa to Southeast Asia and northern Australia. Fleshy-rooted perennial with linear leaves striped creamy white. Small white flowers are borne in loose panicles. Zones 10–12.

CHOISYA

This genus within the rue (Rutaceae) family has about 8 species of evergreen shrubs that are native to southwest USA and Mexico. These are attractive ornamental shrubs with aromatic palmate foliage and scented, white, star-shaped flowers.
CULTIVATION: Most grow well in full sun in fertile well-drained soil. Propagation is from half-hardened cuttings rooted in summer.

Choisya 'Aztec Pearl'

↔8 ft (2.4 m) ↑8 ft (2.4 m)

Hybrid of *C. dumosa* var. *arizonica* and *C. ternata*. Has fine narrow leaflets of *C. dumosa* var. *arizonica*, abundant white flowers of *C. ternata*. Strongly aromatic shrub, lush dark green foliage. Flowers open from pale pink buds in spring–early summer. Zones 8–10.

Choisya dumosa

MEXICAN ORANGE, STAR-LEAF MEXICAN ORANGE

↔3–4 ft (0.9–1.2 m)
↑4–5 ft (1.2–1.5 m)

Bushy evergreen shrub native to Arizona, New Mexico, and Texas, USA. Palmate leaves with 5, short, narrow, bright green, leaflet-like lobes, aromatic when crushed. Starry white flowers appear throughout warmer months. ***C. d.* var. *arizonica*** (syn. *C. arizonica*), from Arizona, has 3–5 longer leaf lobes; ***C. d.* var. *mollis*** (syn. *C. mollis*), from New Mexico has 5–10 leaf lobes, often gray-green when mature. Zones 6–10.

C

Choisya ternata

Choisya ternata

MEXICAN ORANGE, MEXICAN ORANGE BLOSSOM

☼ ❄ ↔6 ft (1.8 m) ↑6 ft (1.8 m)

Evergreen Mexican shrub. Glossy 3-lobed leaves. White, starry, fragrant flower clusters in spring; second flush in late summer. Lightly prune after flowering. Shelter from winds. Tolerates summer dryness once established. Good drainage essential. Sundance/ 'Lich' ★, pale gold foliage, becoming more greenish on ageing, needs light shade. Zones 8–10.

CHONDROPETALUM

Genus of rushes native to South Africa and closely related to the more widely grown *Restio* (family Restionaceae). They have the typically grassy foliage of most reeds, ranging in size from 8 in (20 cm) to over 7 ft (2 m) tall. The large species have a long history of use as a thatching material. Found mostly in the Western Cape region in damp low-lying areas among proteas, leucospermums, and ericas, they are part of the distinctive vegetation known as "fynbos." Flowers are very small but borne in large, if not especially attractive heads; male and female flowers occur on separate plants. Male flowerheads are open panicles reminiscent of grasses, female flowers are more tightly packed and protected by bracts.

CULTIVATION: Plant in an open position and water and feed well in sum-mer. Although *Chondropetalum* occurs naturally in damp ground, in cultivation well-drained soil is preferable. The plants do not always withstand division and propagation from seed tends to be more successful.

Chondropetalum tectorum

☼/◐ ❄ ↔3–5 ft (0.9–1.5 m) ↑5 ft (1.5 m)

Forms a dense clump of fine, green, grassy stems. Female plants tend to have a more olive coloration, especially in summer when carrying their short bronze flowerheads. Male flowerheads are loose, open, slightly arching, and buff-colored. Zones 9–11.

CHORIZEMA

A genus of 18 species, all but one native to southwest Australia, *Chorizema* consists of evergreen shrubs or twiners, many of which also grow as ground cover. They are members of the pea-flower subfamily of the legume (Fabaceae) family with massed short racemes of pea-flowers, often in combinations of vividly contrasting colors. The flowering season varies with the species. The foliage is also variable and may be heart-shaped, narrow or lobed, with or without toothed edges, and sometimes aromatic.

CULTIVATION: The general preference of *Chorizema* species is for light well-drained soil and a position in full sun or partial shade. While prolonged wet conditions are not tolerated, these plants will appreciate an occasional deep watering in summer. Propagation is from seed, which needs to be soaked before sowing, or from half-hardened cuttings.

Chorizema cordatum ★

HEART-LEAFED FLAME PEA

☼/◐ ❄ ↔4 ft (1.2 m) ↑4 ft (1.2 m)

Widely cultivated species from southern Western Australia. Foliage heart-shaped, with small teeth. Flowers orange and yellow standard, deep pink to red keel. Best in well-drained soil, with a little shade, pinch back to keep compact. Zones 9–11.

Chorizema cordatum

Chondropetalum tectorum

CHRYSANTHEMUM

syn. *Dendranthema*

Although once referred to as *Dendranthema*, the florists' chrysanthemum is now correctly known under its old name. There are about 40 species in the genus, mainly from East Asia. In China, where it has been cultivated for over 2,500 years, the chrysanthemum was used medicinally and for flavoring, as well as for ornament. The Japanese adopted it and frequently use it in their art as a symbol of longevity and happiness. The annual species are referred to *Xanthophthalmum* and are mainly used for summer bedding or as fillers in borders of perennial flowers.

CULTIVATION: Florists' chrysanthemums prefer a heavier richer soil and will tolerate some shade. Pinch back when young and disbud to ensure the best flower show. Annual species are raised from seed; the florists' forms by division when dormant or from half-hardened summer cuttings.

Chrysanthemum × *grandiflorum*

syn. *Dendranthema* × *grandiflorum*

FLORISTS' CHRYSANTHEMUM

☼/◐ ❄ ↔18–36 in (45–90 cm) ↑1–5 ft (0.3–1.5 m)

Encompassing a large group of hybrids, chrysanthemums are available from florists throughout the year; under garden conditions they are autumn-flowering, with their flowering season ranging from a few weeks before the equinox until the first frosts. Although they tend to have similar lobed aromatic leaves, chrysanthemums occur in wide range of plant sizes and flower types and are classified in groups based on flower characteristics. Categorization varies around the world, but United States National Chrysanthemum Society Standards are probably the most straightforward, recognizing the following 13 classes.

1. **Irregular incurved**: Very large ball-shaped heads, with incurving florets, the lower ones often loose and irregular, creating a skirt. Popular hybrids include: **'Palisade'**, **'Gold Creamest'**, and **'Shamrock'**.

2. **Reflexed**: Medium sized to large heads, regular, downward curving florets, overlap neatly like scales or feathers. Included in this class are **'Euro'**, **'Fiji'**, and Robin/**'Yorobi'**.

3. **Regular incurved**: Heads 4–6 in (10–15 cm) wide, near-spherical flowers, neat, regular, upward-curving florets. Includes **'Heather James'**.

4. **Decorative**: Compact, rather flattened heads, distinct but short ray florets, no visible disc florets. Includes most of those known as spray chrysanthemums. Usually over 18 in (45 cm) tall. **'Fortune'**, yellow, mid-season; **'Margaret'**, mid-pink with salmon center; **'Salmon Margaret'**, all-over salmon pink; **'Wendy'**, light orange to bronze. Other popular decoratives include: Barbara/ **'Yobarbara'**, **'Red Headliner'**, **'Storm King'**, Sundoro/**'Yosun'**, and **'Wildfire'**.

5. **Intermediate incurved**: Similar to irregular incurved but with smaller flowerheads, still around 6 in (15 cm) wide. Includes **'Primrose Allouise'** and **'Royal Touch'**.

6. **Pompon**: Small, densely petalled, spherical heads ranging from 1–4 in (2.5–10 cm) in diameter. Usually under 18 in (45 cm) tall. Popular hybrids include: **'Carillon'**, **'Cheers'**, **'Ping Pong'**.

C. × *g.*, 7., 'Tiger'

C. × *g.*, 9. Spoon, 'Dublin'

C. × *g.*, 11. Spider, 'Mixed Spider'

C. × *g.*, 13., 'Harlekijn'

C. × *g.*, 8. Anemone, 'Sunny Le Mans'

7. **Single and semi-double:** Simple heads, often very large, visible and clearly defined disc florets surrounded by one or more rows of ray florets. Singles sometimes known as 'daisies'. **'Amber Enbee Wedding'**, semi-double, soft orange-brown; **'Buckeye'**, single, red, mid-season; **'Golden Megatime'**, bright yellow single to semi-double; **'Tiger'**, single, very small, bronze, mid-season; **'Tracy'**, semi-double, white, mid-season. Other hybrids in this group include: **'Megatime'**, **'Poser'**, and **'Splendor'**.

8. **Anemone:** Basically semi-double in structure with a clearly defined halo of outer ray florets but smaller ray florets clustered and mounding at the center, and concealing the disc. Includes **'Pennine Marie'**, vivid pink, to 3 ft (0.9 m) tall; **'Pennine Oriel'**, creamy white, to 3 ft (0.9 m) tall; and **'Yellow Pennine Oriel'**, bright yellow, to 3 ft (0.9 m) tall. Other hybrids include: **'Day's End'**, **'Powder Puff'**, **'Score'**, and **'Sunny Le Mans'**.

9. **Spoon:** Semi-double heads, clearly defined disc florets. Ray florets long, narrow, broaden to spoon shape at tips. Other cultivars include: **'Citrine'**, yellow flowers, **'Seminole'**, pink flowers.

10. **Quill:** Large, regularly shaped heads, long, straight tubular florets open at tips. Includes **'Pennine Flute'**, soft mid-pink.

11. **Spider:** Long, drooping, tubular florets, either narrow or broad, and often coiled or recurved at the tips. Popular hybrids include: **'Dusky Queen'**, **'Mixed Spider'**, and **'Yellow Knight'** ★.

12. **Brush or Thistle:** Very narrow, often twisted florets, lower of which stand out at right angles from stem.

13. **Unclassified:** Catch-all grouping covering blooms yet to be formally classified or not falling into any other categories. **'Max Riley'**, yellow flowers early in the season; **'Pink Gin'**, light pink flowers; **'Roy Coopland'**, bronze blooms; **'Satin Pink Gin'**, pink flowers; **'Yellow John Hughes'**, yellow incurved flowers.

Chrysanthemum weyrichii

Many other cultivars include: **'Angora'**, **'Apricot Shoesmith Salmon'**, **'Beacon'**, Bravo/**'Yabravo'**, **'Bronze Cassandra'**, **'Bronze Fairie'**, **'Cherry Nathalie'**, **'Dark Red Mayford Perfection'**, **'Eastleigh'**, **'Flo Cooper'**, **'George Griffiths'**, **'Golden Cassandra'**, **'Harlekijn'**, **'Lemon Fiji'**, **'Madeleine'**, **'Mancetta Bride'**, **'Mavis'**, **'Myss Madi'**, **'Pennine Alfie'**, **'Pennine Lace'**, **'Pennine Signal'**, **'Rose Mayford Perfection'**, **'Rynoon'**, **'Salmon Fairie'**, **'Southway Swan'**, **'Touché'**, **'Weldon'**, and **'Yvonne Arnaud'**. Zones 5–10.

Chrysanthemum weyrichii

syn. *Dendranthema weyrichii*

MIYABE DAISY

☼/◐ ✱ ↔ 16–24 in (40–60 cm)
↕ 4 in (10 cm)

Spreading ground cover perennial native to Japan. Sometimes considered synonymous with *C. zawadskii*, its leaves are fleshy, glossy, bright green on purple-tinted stems; those near base of stems rounded, 5-lobed, becoming pinnate nearer tips. Short-stemmed 1½ in (40 mm) wide flowerheads with white or pink ray florets in summer–autumn. **'Pink Bomb'** and **'White Bomb'** are heavy-flowering selections with pink and white flowers respectively. Zones 4–9.

Chrysanthemum zawadskii

syn. *Chrysanthemum* × *rubellum*, *Dendranthema zawadskii*

☼ ✱ ↔ 20–40 in (50–100 cm)
↕ 24 in (60 cm)

Found from the Urals to central and northern Russia. Rhizome-rooted perennial forming clump of densely foliaged upright stems. Leaves finely hairy, pinnate with lobes sometimes toothed, to 1½ in (40 mm) long. Flowerheads white, pink, or purple, to slightly over 2 in (5 cm) wide, borne singly or in groups of up to 5. *C. z.* var. *latilobum*, larger in all parts, grows to 3 ft (0.9 m) tall. *C. z.* **'Clara Curtis'** ★ has many bright pink flowerheads; **'Lady Clara'**, deep pink flowers; **'Mary Stoker'**, soft yellow flowers. Zones 3–9.

CHRYSOCEPHALUM

Australian daisy (Asteraceae) family genus established with the breaking up of *Helichrysum, Helipterum,* and *Leptorhynchos,* currently composed of some 6 species of perennials and subshrubs. They are small, spreading plants, which form wide mounds of fine stems with ½–2 in (12–50 mm) long, narrow, finely hairy, gray-green to blue-green leaves. *Chrysocephalum* means yellow head and they do indeed have papery yellow flowerheads, particularly in summer and autumn. The heads, although not large—around ½ in (12 mm) wide—are abundant and quite showy.

CULTIVATION: Hardiness and cultivation requirements vary; most species can be treated as annuals and do best in a bright position with light gritty soil with average summer moisture. They are effective when grown in con- tainers if trimmed and deadheaded routinely. Propagate from seed or from small cuttings; some species produce suckers or natural layers that can be removed and then grown on.

Chrysocephalum semipapposum

syn. *Helichrysum semipapposum*

CLUSTERED EVERLASTING, YELLOW BUTTONS

☼ ❄ ↔ to 5 ft (1.5 m) ↕ to 32 in (80 cm)

Spreading herbaceous to woody perennial, found in a wide variety of habitats in all States of Australia. Woody rootstock produces hairy stems with narrow, clustered, grayish, hairy leaves, up to 2½ in (6 cm) long. Tiny yellow flowers are borne in heads to ½ in (12 mm) in diameter, in terminal clusters of up to 100 heads. Zones 8–10.

Chrysocephalum semipapposum

CHRYSOGONUM

Part of the daisy (Asteraceae) family, this genus contains only one species—a low perennial herb native to eastern USA. It makes a good ground cover for partly shaded borders and along the edges of woodlands. *C. virginianum* has 2 selections—the northern one is taller and more upright, the southern one is more prostrate. In hot summers, it flowers from mid-spring to early summer. Farther north, flowering occurs from spring to early summer. It also flowers sporadically during the summer months.

CULTIVATION: Moist well-drained soil and partial to full shade are the ideal conditions. Propagate by division in early spring or early autumn; it also self-sows. Self-sown seedlings may be transplanted to desired location. It has no serious insect or disease problems.

Chrysogonum virginianum

GOLDEN STAR, GREEN AND GOLD

◐/● ✱ ↔ 24 in (60 cm)
↕ 6–10 in (15–25 cm)

Coarse hairy leaves have a serrated margin; the flowers are yellow with 5 slightly notched petals, 1–1½ in (25–35 mm) wide. Will grow in colder areas provided it gets good snow cover. Zones 5–9.

CHRYSOLEPIS

CHINQUAPIN, GOLDEN CHESTNUT

This genus, belonging to the beech (Fagaceae) family, is native to the western USA and, depending on current botanical opinion, is composed of 2 species or a single rather variable species. The leaves are leathery ovals with pointed tips. When young the foliage and new growth are covered in fine golden hairs and scales, but these soon wear to a thin surface coating, though the undersides of the leaves retain their hairs. The red-brown bark is also an attraction. Catkins of tiny flowers are followed by clusters of nut cases, each containing an edible nut.

CULTIVATION: Chinquapin does best in dry-summer climates. These plants prefer acid soil in a well drained position in sun or partial shade. Pruning is seldom necessary. Propagate by sowing fresh seed, which often germinates better with scarification.

Chrysolepis chrysophylla ★

☼/◐ ✱ ↔ 30 ft (9 m) ↕ 30 ft (9 m)

Yellow-green flowers, summer-borne catkins. Clusters of small warty nut cases. Nuts take about 15 months to ripen, revealing the red-brown nut within. Zones 6–9.

C

Chrysothamnus nauseosus, in the wild, Grand Canyon, Arizona, USA

CHRYSOTHAMNUS

RABBIT BRUSH

This genus of around 16 species of shrubs or subshrubs, native to western North America, belongs to the daisy (Asteraceae) family. They grow in very dry conditions in a variety of habitats from plains to canyons and hillsides, and quickly colonize disturbed ground. Ranging from about 12 in (30 cm) to 7 ft (2 m) tall, they are multi-branched with narrow aromatic leaves. Some contain a latex in their sap. Small yellow or white flowers, usually lacking rays, are borne in dense clusters in summer and autumn.
CULTIVATION: Grow in full sun in a light well-drained soil. Propagate from seed or cuttings.

Chrysothamnus nauseosus

syn. *Ericameria nauseosa*

↔ 12–36 in (30–90 cm)
↑ 12–60 in (30–150 cm)

Native to western and central USA. Variable well-branched shrub; woolly stems contain a small amount of latex. Narrow grayish green leaves with unpleasant smell. Rayless yellow flowers in summer–autumn. ***C. n.* var. *graveolens,*** less woolly stems, greener leaves. Zones 6–9.

Chrysothamnus viscidiflorus

STICKY-LEAFED RABBIT BRUSH

↔ 12–36 in (30–90 cm)
↑ 12–36 in (30–90 cm)

Found from western USA east to Nebraska. Rounded deciduous shrub with whitish bark. Narrow leaves often twisted in appearance. Plants are covered with rayless yellow daisies in summer–autumn. Zones 6–9.

CIBOTIUM

This genus of 15 species of the tree fern (Dicksoniaceae) family, allied to *Dicksonia,* has a scattered distribution, occurring in Mexico, Central America, Hawaii, and parts of tropical and subtropical Asia. The trunk is often upright and tree-like, but in some species may grow horizontally before turning upward. The fronds are very finely divided and the crown and trunk are usually very fibrous and hairy.
CULTIVATION: Some species will tolerate light frosts, but most prefer moist warm-temperate to subtropical conditions. They should be planted in full shade or with shade from the hottest sun in constantly moist humus-enriched soil, and watered well in summer or during dry spells. Propagate by removing basal shoots, from freshly cut lengths of trunk, or from spores.

Cibotium glaucum

HAPU, HAWAIIAN TREE FERN

↔ 6–10 ft (1.8–3 m)
↑ 6–15 ft (1.8–4.5 m)

Large slow-growing tree fern from Hawaii. Erect trunk to 15 ft (4.5 m) tall and 12 in (30 cm) thick, covered with lustrous yellowish brown hairs. Arching, oval- to sword-shaped, leathery, slightly glossy fronds, 3–6 ft (0.9–1.8 m) long. Narrow leaflets with long, narrow, serrated tips, on stalks covered with dark hairs. Zones 9–11.

CIRSIUM

With around 250 species this is one of the largest genera in the thistle tribe of the daisy (Asteraceae) family. Most occur in the Mediterranean region and in central and east Asia, but there are also many in North America, principally in the west. Mostly very prickly plants, they include some of the world's most widespread and troublesome weeds, for example *C. vulgare* (spear thistle). Biennials or perennials, in their first season they form a rosette of spreading leaves edged with spine-tipped teeth, and often with needle-like spines on the leaf surfaces as well. Flowering stems

Cirsium japonicum 'Rose Beauty'

are usually branched into many flowerheads, each consisting of a goblet-shaped receptacle of bristly bracts crowned by a dense group of pink to purple (rarely cream) disk florets. Ray florets are lacking, as in all members of the thistle tribe.
CULTIVATION: A few species have been grown as ornamentals but in most countries the importation of additional species is now prohibited due to the likelihood of their becoming weeds. Easily grown in any good soil in full sun, they are propagated by root division or seed; early sowing can give flowers in the same year.

Cirsium japonicum

JAPANESE THISTLE

↔ 2–4 ft (0.6–1.2 m)
↑ 3–5 ft (0.9–1.5 m)

From China, Japan and Korea. Perennial branching into numerous erect, slender stems terminating in 1–2 in (25 mm–5 cm) wide pink to purple flowerheads from late spring–autumn. **Beauty Series** are sold as seed, are less spiny, and good as cut flowers. **'Early Pink Beauty'**, flowers pale pink; **'Rose Beauty'**, reddish pink. Zones 5–9.

Cirsium rivulare

↔ 2 ft (0.6 m) ↑ 5 ft (1.5 m)

From central Europe. Perennial with branching rootstock, broad deep green leaves, multiple erect, slender stems terminating in tight clusters of several lilac to purple flowerheads, opening in succession through summer. **'Atropurpureum'**, deep reddish purple heads. Zones 5–9.

Cirsium rivulare 'Atropurpureum'

CISTUS

A genus of about 20 species in the rock-rose (Cistaceae) family. All are small to medium-sized, evergreen, flowering shrubs found throughout the Mediterranean region. They grow on sun-baked stony hillsides. In cultivation they become very adaptable long-flowering ornamentals, ideal for difficult dry sites. The leaves are opposite, mostly dark green or whitish, and in some species exude a sticky resin called ladanum or labdanum, which is used in the manufacture of incense and perfume. The flowers, which are individually short-lived, have 5 broad petals, white, pink, mauve, or reddish purple, often blotched, and with prominent yellow stamens.
CULTIVATION: All *Cistus* species revel in a hot sunny position and will grow in most soils provided drainage is good. They thrive in all climates of the Mediterranean type. Young plants should be tip pruned; pinch back older plants after flowering. Seeds can be sown in spring. Short cuttings from non-flowering sideshoots can be taken in autumn.

Cistus × *aguilarii*

↔ 3–5 ft (0.9–1.5 m)
↑ 3–7 ft (0.9–2 m)

Naturally occurring hybrid of *C. ladanifer* and *C. populifolius* found in southwestern Europe and northern Africa. Lance-shaped leaves are bright green with prominent veins. White saucer-shaped flowers, to 3 in (8 cm) across, with fluffy yellow stamens. **'Maculatus'**, maroon blotch at base of each petal. Zones 8–10.

Cistus × *aguilarii*

Cistus heterophyllus

Cistus albidus

☼ ❄ ↔4 ft (1.2 m) ↑3 ft (0.9 m)
Widely distributed through southwestern Europe and North Africa. Dense shrub. Leaves whitish, white downy twigs. Flowers pale rose-lilac with a yellow center. Zones 7–9.

Cistus × argenteus

☼/◐ ❄ ↔3 ft (0.9 m) ↑3–7 ft (0.9–2 m)
This is a garden hybrid between *C. laurifolius* and *C. × canescens* (*C. albidus × C. creticus*). The bush is upright-growing, with leaves that are small and gray-green, and it bears white or pink flowers, which open to over 2 in (5 cm) wide. Blooms throughout the summer months. Cultivars include: **'Peggy Sammons'**, purple-pink flowers; **'Paper Moon'**, pure white flowers; **'Stripey'**, white flowers with irregular stripes and sectors colored pink; **'Silver Pink'**, pink flowers. Zones 7–10.

Cistus × canescens

☼ ❄ ↔8 ft (2.4 m) ↑6 ft (1.8 m)
This is a hybrid between *C. albidus* and *C. creticus*. The leaves are dark green, hairy, and pointed. The flowers, which are borne in summer, are pink to magenta, marked with a yellow stain at the base of each petal. ***C. × c.* f. *albus*** has grayish foliage and white flowers. Zones 8–10.

Cistus creticus

syn. *Cistus incanus subsp. creticus*
HAIRY ROCK ROSE, ROCK ROSE
☼ ❄ ↔3 ft (0.9 m) ↑3 ft (0.9 m)
Found in the eastern Mediterranean from Corsica and Italy eastward. Stems hairy, leaves, whitish green beneath. Flowers purple, flushed yellow at petal bases. ***C. c.* subsp. *incanus*** (syn. *C. incanus*), less wavy margins, no yellow on petal bases. ***C. c.* var. *tauricus***, purple-pink flowers. Zones 7–9.

Cistus heterophyllus

☼ ❄ ↔3 ft (0.9 m) ↑3 ft (0.9 m)
From northwestern Africa and Spain. Erect densely branching shrub. Hairy leaves are dark green above, paler and prominently veined beneath. Purplish pink saucer-shaped flowers, 2–2½ in (5–6 cm) in diameter, yellow basal spot. Zones 8–10.

Cistus × hybridus

syn. *Cistus × corbariensis*
☼ ❄ ↔4 ft (1.2 m) ↑3 ft (0.9 m)
Hybrid of *C. populifolius* and *C. salviifolius*. Leaves downy, 2 in (5 cm) long, deep green, oval, toothed, pale beneath. Red buds in some clones, white flowers, yellow basal spots. Zones 7–10.

Cistus ladanifer

GUM CISTUS
☼ ❄ ↔5 ft (1.5 m) ↑5 ft (1.5 m)
Native to North Africa and the southwestern Mediterranean. Leaves dark green, whitish, furry beneath, exuding ladanum. Flowers up to 4 in (10 cm) in diameter, white with a brownish crimson blotch, bright yellow stamens. ***C. l.* subsp. *sulcatus***, previously called *C. palhinhae*, low-growing, compact, shiny sticky leaves, white flowers. ***C. l.* 'Blanche'**, deep green glossy leaves, grayish beneath, white flowers; **'Paladin'**, glossy green leaves, paler beneath, large white flowers with dark red basal blotches; **'Pat'**, large flowers, up to 5 in (12 cm) across, white with maroon basal blotches. Zones 8–10.

Cistus laurifolius

LAUREL-LEAFED ROCK ROSE
☼ ❄ ↔6 ft (1.8 m) ↑6 ft (1.8 m)
Found naturally in southwestern Europe. Leaves leathery, dark green above, gray to brown, furry beneath. Overlapping petals white, suffused with yellow at the base, stamens dark yellow. Zones 7–10.

Cistus libanotis

☼ ❄ ↔36 in (90 cm) ↑36 in (90 cm)
Native to southwestern Spain and nearby parts of Portugal. Leaves downy, sticky, to 1 in (25 mm) long, rolled edges. White flowers, 1 in (25 mm) wide. Zones 8–10.

Cistus libanotis

Cistus × hybridus

Cistus populifolius

☼ ❄ ↔6 ft (1.8 m) ↑6 ft (1.8 m)
From the Iberian Peninsula and France. Dark green leaves, small, hairy, heart-shaped. White flowers, yellow basal blotches, in summer. Zones 6–10.

Cistus × pulverulentus

☼ ❄ ↔6 ft (1.8 m) ↑2 ft (0.6 m)
Hybrid between *C. albidus* and *C. crispus*, often sold in nurseries under the name **'Sunset'** ★. Dwarf compact shrub bearing gray-green leaves with undulating margins. Bright pink flowers. Zones 8–10.

Cistus × purpureus

☼ ❄ ↔5 ft (1.5 m) ↑4 ft (1.2 m)
Hybrid between *C. ladanifer* and *C. creticus*. Sticky young stems, dark green leaves, grayish hairs beneath. Pink to magenta summer flowers, to 2 in (5 cm) wide, conspicuous dark red basal spots. ***C. × p.* f. *holorhodos***, pink unblotched flowers. ***C. × p.* f. *stictus***, pale pink flowers with blotches. ***C. × p.* 'Alan Fradd'**, albino sport. Zones 7–10.

Cistus salviifolius

SAGE-LEAFED ROCK ROSE
☼ ❄ ↔30 in (75 cm) ↑30 in (75 cm)
First cultivated in sixteenth century. Leaves slightly aromatic, wrinkled, rough, downy, dark gray-green upper surface, whitish gray undersurface. Flowers borne singly or in groups of 2 or 3, with crepe-like white petals, suffused with yellow at their base. **'Prostratus'**, prostrate form. Zones 7–10.

Cistus ladanifer

Cistus × purpureus

Cistus × skanbergii

☼ ❄ ↔3 ft (0.9 m) ↑3 ft (0.9 m)
Discovered in Greece, Cyprus, and neighboring islands. A naturally occurring hybrid between *C. monspeliensis* and *C. parviflorus*. Light pink flowers in large sprays. Leaves have downy undersides. Zones 8–10.

Cistus Hybrid Cultivars

☼ ❄ ↔3–6 ft (0.9–1.8 m) ↑2–5 ft (0.6–1.5 m)
Hybrid cultivars that cannot readily be assigned such names as *C. × dansereaui*, *C. × pulverulentus*, and *C. × purpureus* include: **'Grayswood Pink'**, with pink flowers and **'Snow Fire'**, vigorous and hardy, with white flowers bearing deep red blotches. Zones 7–9.

CLADRASTIS

Native to China, Japan, and eastern USA, these 5 species of deciduous trees in the pea-flower subfamily of the legume (Fabaceae) family are cultivated mainly for their flowers, which are carried in wisteria-like racemes opening from early summer, followed by flat seed pods. The pinnate leaves have fine hairs on the undersides of the leaflets. They are known as yellowwoods, and the heartwood is used for gunstocks with carved detailing.

CULTIVATION: Yellowwoods tolerate a wide range of soils provided drainage is good. They will not withstand extremes of drought or waterlogging, but are otherwise easily grown in any sunny position protected from strong winds. Propagate from seed or winter hardwood cuttings.

Cladrastis kentukea

syn. *Cladastris lutea*
YELLOWWOOD
☼ ❄ ↔30 ft (9 m) ↑25–40 ft (8–12 m)
Native to eastern USA. Bright green leaves, 7 to 11 oval leaflets, golden yellow in autumn. Fragrant white flowers, 12 in (30 cm) long racemes, in early summer. Narrow, 3 in (8 cm) long, brown seed pods. Zones 3–9.

Cladrastis kentukea

CLARKIA

FAREWELL TO SPRING, GODETIA

This genus of 33 species of annual herbs belongs to the evening-primrose (Onagraceae) family. The majority are native to western North America, where they grow in dry open areas in forests and grasslands. They are cultivated for their showy funnel-shaped flowers, which occur in shades of pink, red, purple, and sometimes yellow and white. The petals are often splashed with red or white. Flowering occurs from late spring to summer. The flowers are long-lasting and are very popular for floral display.

CULTIVATION: Grow in full sun in low to moderately fertile well-drained soil. All *Clarkia* species dislike hot humid conditions, so in warmer areas seed should be sown in autumn so that the plants will flower before the summer heat becomes intense. In cooler areas sow in early spring.

Clarkia amoena

syns *Clarkia grandiflora, Godetia amoena*

SATIN FLOWER

☼ ❄ ↔ 12 in (30 cm) ↑ 24 in (60 cm)

Showy species from northern California, USA. Densely packed spikes of cup-shaped flowers of pink to lavender, sometimes darkening at the base or shading to white, centers usually splashed with dark red. **'Grandiflora'** (syn. 'Whitneyi'), flowers up to 4 in (10 cm) across in shades of rose, pink, lavender, red, and white. Zones 7–10.

Clarkia amoena

Clarkia unguiculata

Claytonia perfoliata

Clarkia pulchella

☼ ❄ ↔ 12 in (30 cm)
↑ 12–18 in (30–45 cm)

Found from the Rocky Mountains to the Pacific Coast. Compact species bearing frilly funnel-shaped flowers of bright pink to lavender, sometimes with white or purple veining. Double forms of mixed colors are most commonly grown. Zones 7–10.

Clarkia unguiculata

syn. *Clarkia elegans*

☼ ❄ ↔ 12 in (30 cm)
↑ 24–30 in (60–75 cm)

From California. Commonly grown species with many cultivars, often frilly or double. Flowers, about 1 in (25 mm) across, in wide color range extending through pink, purple, and red shades, also yellow and white. Zones 7–10.

CLAYTONIA

PURSLANE, SPRING BEAUTY

Found mainly in the western parts of North America, this genus of the purslane (Montiaceae) family also includes representatives from South America, Asia, Australia, and New Zealand among its 15 species of succulent perennials. They are small plants with fleshy tap roots, from which develop basal rosettes of small leaves that sometimes surround the stems, an effect more apparent on the upright flowering stems. The flowers are white, 5-petalled, and usually very small. While sometimes solitary, they usually occur in small clusters but even then are not large enough to be showy. All parts of the plants are edible and are often used as salad vegetables.

CULTIVATION: Very hardy and easily grown in most temperate climates; some species are moderately invasive. While sometimes used as a salad herb, *Claytonia* species are seldom deliberately cultivated but are instead harvested from the wild. Most soils are suitable, and the plants may be raised from seed or by division.

Claytonia perfoliata

MINER'S LETTUCE

☼/◐ ❄ ↔ 20 in (50 cm) ↑ 12 in (30 cm)

Spreading Californian perennial with fleshy, round, bright green leaves surrounding the stems. Small white flowers appear in spring. Eaten by nineteenth-century Californian gold miners to combat scurvy. Zones 6–9.

Claytonia virginica

FAIRY-SPUDS, SPRING BEAUTY

● ❄ ↔ 12 in (30 cm)
↑ 8–12 in (20–30 cm)

From eastern North America. Low-growing, deciduous, perennial herb. Occurs mainly in moist shaded woodland. Narrow succulent leaves up to 6 in (15 cm) long. Racemes of pink-tinged, red-veined, white, 5-petalled flowers appear in early spring. Tubers were once used as a food source by Native Americans. **'Lutea'**, orangey yellow flowers. Zones 4–8.

CLEMATIS

LEATHER VINE, TRAVELLER'S JOY, VIRGIN'S BOWER

A genus of over 200 species, in the buttercup (Ranunculaceae) family, encompassing a huge range of forms. *Clematis* species are mainly climbing or scrambling but sometimes shrubby or perennial, deciduous or evergreen, flowering at any time in any color, occurring in both northern and southern temperate zones and at higher altitudes in the tropics. Leaves may be simple or pinnate. Flowers are nearly always showy, with 4 to 8 petal-like sepals. Fluffy seed heads follow. The common name virgin's bower comes from a German legend that Mary and Jesus sheltered under a clematis during their flight into Egypt from the massacre of the innocents.

CULTIVATION: The general rule is that the foliage should be in the sun while the roots are kept cool and moist. Incorporate plenty of humus-rich compost before planting, and water well. Clematis wilt disease is a problem in many areas. Propagate from cuttings or layers. Species may be raised from seed, but sex will be undetermined before flowering.

Clematis alpina ★

☼/◐ ❄ ↔ 5 ft (1.5 m)
↑ 8–10 ft (2.4–3 m)

Deciduous climber from Europe and northern Asia. Paired trifoliate leaves, serrated, lance-shaped leaflets 2 in (5 cm) long. Blue to mauve flowers, white stamens, in spring–early summer. Zones 5–9.

Clematis chrysocoma

Clematis aristata

AUSTRALIAN CLEMATIS

☼/◐ ❄ ↔ 6 ft (1.8 m)
↑ 10–20 ft (3–6 m)

Evergreen climber native to southeastern Australia. Long-stemmed leaves with 3 leaflets, are sometimes toothed. Panicles of 1 in (25 mm) wide, starry, white flowers are produced from late spring to mid-summer. Zones 9–11.

Clematis armandii

☼/◐ ❄ ↔ 7–10 ft (2–3 m)
↑ 20–30 ft (6–9 m)

Vigorous evergreen climber, from central and western China. Leaves with 3 glossy, dark green, leathery leaflets to 6 in (15 cm) long, bronze-green when young. Clusters of white flowers, sometimes faintly pink-tinted, in early spring. Flowers may smell slightly of urine. **'Apple Blossom'**, pink buds opening white; **'Snowdrift'** ★, white, waxy, fragrant flowers in cascading panicles. Zones 8–10.

Clematis × *aromatica*

☼/◐ ❄ ↔ 3–5 ft (0.9–1.5 m)
↑ 5–7 ft (1.5–2 m)

Hybrid between *C. flammula* and *C. integrifolia*. Upright deciduous subshrub; leaves with 3 to 5 short leaflets. Deep violet flowers, white stamens, in summer–autumn. Despite the name, there is little scent in foliage or flower. Zones 4–9.

Clematis chiisanensis

☼/◐ ❄ ↔ 5 ft (1.5 m) ↑ 10 ft (3 m)

Korean deciduous climber. Toothed, heavily veined, trifoliate leaves. Simple nodding, pink-tinted, cream flowers with 4 sepals recurved at tips. **'Lemon Bells'**, pale yellow flowers; **'Love Child'**, large cream flowers over a long season (blooms on both old and new wood); **'Monika'**, deep pink flowers with cream center. Zones 4–9.

Clematis aristata

Clematis chrysocoma

☼/◑ ❄ ↔4–6 ft (1.2–1.8 m)
↑7–15 ft (2–4.5 m)

Deciduous climber from southwestern China. Trifoliate leaves; pointed oval leaflets, sometimes serrated, 1–2 in (2.5–5 cm) long. In summer–autumn 2 in (5 cm) wide, pink-tinted, white flowers are borne on long, downy, brown stems. Zones 7–10.

Clematis cirrhosa ★

syn. *Clematis calycina*

☼/◑ ❄ ↔6 ft (1.8 m)
↑10–15 ft (3–4.5 m)

Native to southern Europe and Mediterranean region. Evergreen climber; paired trifoliate leaves, small lobed leaflets. In winter–early spring, small clusters of pendulous cream flowers, sometimes spotted purple-red. ***C. c.* var. *balearica*,** fragrant flowers, always spotted. ***C. c.* var. *purpurascens* 'Freckles' ★**, large-flowered, long-stemmed. Zones 7–10.

Clematis coactilis

☼/◑ ❄ ↔12–32 in (30–80 cm)
↑8–16 in (20–40 cm)

Deciduous shrub from the Appaachian Mountains of eastern USA. Green lance-shaped leaves. Small, pendulous, bell-shaped, white flowers, sometimes green- or purple-tinted. Silky hairs on flower stems and buds. Zones 7–10.

Clematis crispa

BLUE JASMINE, CURLFLOWER, MARSH CLEMATIS

☼/◑ ✱ ↔3 ft (0.9 m) ↑8 ft (2.4 m)

Deciduous climber from southeastern USA. Leaves to 8 in (20 cm) wide; up to 7 leaflets. Pendulous, bell-shaped, summer flowers, singly or in clusters, strongly reflexed pale pink to lavender-blue sepals. Zones 5–10.

Clematis × durandii

☼/◑ ✱ ↔5 ft (1.5 m)
↑6–8 ft (1.8–2.4 m)

Hybrid between *C. × jackmanii* and *C. integrifolia*. Deciduous climber; glossy, pointed, oval leaves, to 6 in (15 cm) long. Deep violet-blue flowers, cream to yellow stamens, in summer–autumn. Zones 5–10.

Clematis montana var. *wilsonii*

Clematis × eriostemon

☼/◑ ✱ ↔6 ft (1.8 m) ↑8 ft (2.4 m)

Probably hybrid with *C. viticella*, usually classified under *C. × eriostemon*. Large violet flowers. Zones 6–10.

Clematis florida

☼/◑ ❄ ↔5 ft (1.5 m) ↑15 ft (4.5 m)

Deciduous or part evergreen climber from Japan and China. Paired trifoliate leaves, 2 in (5 cm) long leaflets, sometimes toothed. Flowers 3 in (8 cm) wide, often green-tinted, white stamens, violet anthers, in summer. ***C. f.* var. *flore-pleno*,** double flowers, white, striped green; ***C. f.* var. *sieboldiana*** (syn. 'Bicolor'), white flowers, purple-red stamens. ***C. f.* Pistachio/'Evirida'**, large white flowers sometimes flushed pale green, red stamens. Zones 7–10.

Clematis heracleifolia

☼/◑ ✱ ↔2–5 ft (0.6–1.5 m)
↑3–6 ft (0.9–1.8 m)

Sprawling, scrambling, woody-based, herbaceous perennial from central and northern China. Lightly downy trifoliate leaves, irregularly toothed leaflets, to 2½ in (6 cm) long. Clusters of dusky, purple-blue, tubular flowers with 4 flared and reflexed sepals, summer–autumn. **'Blue Dwarf'**, 12–24 in (30–60 cm) high and wide, pale blue flowers; **'New Love'**, very compact with dark purple-blue flowers, lighter inside, fragrant. Zones 3–9.

Clematis integrifolia

☼/◑ ✱ ↔3–5 ft (0.9–1.5 m)
↑3 ft (0.9 m)

Deciduous perennial or subshrub found from Europe to central Asia. Simple, 3–4 in (8–10 cm) long, lance-shaped leaves with downy undersides. Pendulous, flattened, bell-shaped flowers, to 4 in (10 cm) wide, deep violet-blue. Zones 3–9.

Clematis macropetala

Clematis florida var. sieboldiana

Clematis × jouiniana

☼/◑ ✱ ↔7–15 ft (2–4.5 m)
↑7–15 ft (2–4.5 m)

Hybrid between *C. tubulosa* and *C. vitalba*. Sprawling, semi-climbing, partly evergreen, woody-based perennial. Compound leaves, 3 to 5 coarsely toothed leaflets. Clusters of fragrant flowers from late summer, opening white, ageing to pale pink or blue. **'Praecox'**, vigorous cultivar with pale blue flowers. Zones 4–9.

Clematis lanuginosa

☼/◑ ✱ ↔4–8 ft (1.2–2.4 m)
↑7–10 ft (2–3 m)

Chinese deciduous climber. Leaves simple or trifoliate, leaflets to 4 in (10 cm) long. Large flowers, white to pale lavender, in groups of up to 3, in warmer months. Zones 6–9.

Clematis lasiantha

CHAPARRAL CLEMATIS, PIPESTEM CLEMATIS

☼/◑ ❄ ↔8–15 ft (2.4–4.5 m)
↑10–17 ft (3–5 m)

Evergreen climber, western USA. Trifoliate leaves, toothed to lobed leaflets, to 2 in (5 cm) long. Long-stemmed, downy, white flowers, 1 in (25 mm) wide, autumn. Zones 8–10.

Clematis macropetala

☼/◑ ✱ ↔5–10 ft (1.5–3 m)
↑3–10 ft (0.9–3 m)

Deciduous climber from northern temperate Asia. Paired trifoliate leaves, toothed or lobed leaflets, to 1½ in (35 mm) long. Downy dusky blue flowers, spring–early summer; 4 sepals, though cultivars often double-flowered. Zones 5–9.

Clematis recta

Clematis montana

☼/◑ ✱ ↔10–20 ft (3–6 m)
↑15–25 ft (4.5–8 m)

Vigorous, spring-flowering, deciduous climber found from the Himalayas to central China. Deep green trifoliate leaves with toothed leaflets to 4 in (10 cm) long. In spring, massed large sprays of white to pale pink flowers. ***C. m.* var. *glabrescens*,** very vigorous variety with mauve-pink flowers; ***C. m.* var. *grandiflora*,** very vigorous variety, to 40 ft (12 m) tall, bears white flowers; ***C. m.* var. *rubens* ★**, bronze new growth, large pink flowers; ***C. m.* var. *sericea*** (syns *C. chrysocoma* var. *sericea*, *C. spooneri*), downy young stems and reverse of sepals, white flowers in profusion; ***C. m.* var. *wilsonii*,** large sprays of tiny white flowers, fragrant. Zones 6–9.

Clematis paniculata

☼/◑ ❄ ↔10–30 ft (3–9 m)
↑17–30 ft (5–9 m)

From New Zealand. Tough climber, dioecious, evergreen, flowering in spring to early summer; large panicles of scented white flowers. Zones 7–10.

Clematis patens

☼/◑ ✱ ↔5–10 ft (1.5–3 m)
↑10–15 ft (3–4.5 m)

Vigorous climber from Japan and nearby parts of China. Pinnate leaves with 3 to 5 leaflets up to 4 in (10 cm) long. Flowering occurs from spring to early summer; white through mauve to blue flowers borne singly at tips of stems, purple-brown stamens. Zones 6–9.

Clematis recta

☼/◑ ✱ ↔3–4 ft (0.9–1.2 m)
↑3–5 ft (0.9–1.5 m)

From southern and central Europe. Summer-flowering erect perennial, sprawls as gains height. Pinnate foliage, 5 to 7 blue-green leaflets. Small white flowers in large panicles. Zones 3–9.

Clematis terniflora

Clematis tubulosa Alan Bloom/'Alblo'

Clematis rehderiana

☼/◐ ❄ ↔ 8–15 ft (2.4–4.5 m)
↕ 17–25 ft (5–8 m)

Deciduous climber from western China. Pinnate leaves to over 8 in (20 cm), 7 to 9 leaflets. Fine golden hairs on foliage and stems. Small light yellow to yellowy green flowers in summer–autumn. Zones 7–10.

Clematis tangutica

☼/◐ ❄ ↔ 8–12 ft (2.4–3.5 m)
↕ 7–10 ft (2–3 m)

Climber from Mongolia and north-western China. Bright green pinnate leaves, toothed and/or lobed leaflets. Deep yellow bell-shaped flowers from late summer, lantern-shaped if sepals remain unfurled. Zones 5–9.

Clematis terniflora

syn. *Clematis mandshurica*

☼/◐ ❄ ↔ 6–10 ft (1.8–3 m)
↕ 7–15 ft (2–4.5 m)

Japanese perennial that can be upright but usually becomes a mass of tangled scrambling stems. Deep green pinnate leaves with 3 to 5 leaflets to 4 in (10 cm) long, semi-evergreen in mild areas. Panicles of massed greenish white flowers in autumn. Zones 6–10.

Clematis texensis

☼/◐ ❄ ↔ 3–7 ft (0.9–2 m) ↕ 7 ft (2 m)

Scrambling shrubby perennial from southwestern USA. Blue-green pinnate leaves, 4 to 8 rounded leathery leaflets to 3 in (8 cm) long. Unusual, small, urn-shaped flowers on long stems, borne singly, in shades from brick to cherry. Zones 5–10.

C., HC, Texensis Group, 'Etoile Rose'

Clematis tibetana

☼/◐ ❄ ↔ 17–25 ft (5–8 m)
↕ 17–25 ft (5–8 m)

Found in Himalayan India, Nepal, and Tibet. Very finely divided, deep green, ferny foliage. Thickly textured, soft primrose yellow, bell-shaped to starry flowers. ***C. t.* subsp. *vernayi*** (syn. *C. orientalis* of gardens), very coarsely textured, pale yellow to brown flowers. Zones 6–10.

Clematis × *triternata*

☼/◐ ❄ ↔ 10–15 ft (3–4.5 m)
↕ 10–15 ft (3–4.5 m)

Garden hybrid between *C. flammula* and *C. viticella*. Simple or pinnate foliage, with smooth-edged, lance-shaped leaflets to 3 in (8 cm) long. Masses of small, starry, pale lavender flowers in summer. **'Rubromarginata'**, produces a heavy crop of white flowers edged and tipped with soft purple to wine red. Zones 6–9.

Clematis tubulosa

syn. *Clematis heracleifolia var. davidiana*

☼/◐ ❄ ↔ 3 ft (0.9 m) ↕ 3 ft (0.9 m)

Clusters of mauve-blue, mildly fragrant flowers. **Alan Bloom/'Alblo'**, very compact, light purple-blue flowers, often with 5 sepals. Zones 6–9.

Clematis viticella

☼/◐ ❄ ↔ 5 ft (1.5 m)
↕ 7–12 ft (2–3.5 m)

Woody-stemmed deciduous climber from southern Europe. Trifoliate leaves, lance-shaped, lobed leaflets, somewhat downy, to 2½ in (6 cm) long. Nodding, long-stemmed, bell-shaped, blue, mauve, and purple-red flowers, in summer–autumn. **'Purpurea Plena Elegans'** has large, deep violet to purple, double flowers. Zones 6–10.

C., HC, Forsteri Group, 'Early Sensation'

Clematis Hybrid Cultivars

☼/◐ ❄ ↔ 5–15 ft (1.5–4.5 m)
↕ 4–20 ft (1.2–6 m)

The many large-flowered hybrid clematis are broadly classified into 9 groups that vary in growth habit and flowering style depending on parentage. There is also a large range of ungrouped hybrids of indeterminate parentage. Clematis hybrids are now often grouped by flower size and pruning requirements (this varies, as some flower on new growth, others on old wood) rather than on parentage, which is often obscure. Zones 5–9.

ATRAGENE GROUP

This group combines the hybrids formerly listed as *C. alpina* and *C. macropetala* cultivars, as well as those of the other species in the *Clematis* subgenus *Atragene*. They flower in spring to early summer on the old growth. The flowers are nodding, ften have long tepals, and may have petaloid centers, creating a semi-double to double effect. **'Frances Rivis'** (syn. 'Blue Giant'), dusky blue, white petaloid center; **'Helsingborg'**, dusky purple-blue flowers, similarly colored stamens; **'Jacqueline du Pré'**, pink flowers, pale sepal edge, lighter inside, pink stamens; **'Markham's Pink'** (syn. 'Markhamii'), light to mid-pink, double flowers; **'Pink Princess'**, semi-double, pale pink, outer sepals with darker flush; **'Propertius'**, semi-double, scented, purplish pink in bud, opening to pale lavender; **'Snowbird'**, white flowers, double, narrow, slightly curled sepals; **'White Columbine'**, nodding white flowers; **'White Swan'**, large white flowers, greenish yellow center, double.

FORSTERI GROUP

This is a group of evergreen hybrids between several New Zealand species, notably *C. paniculata*, *C. marmoraria*, and *C. forsteri*. Most are low-spreading, though some are more vigorous climbers. Flowers are usually white with hints of green; hardiness varies with parentage, though most survive well in zone 8. The group includes: **'Avalanche'**, over 10 ft (3 m), pure white flowers; **'Early Sensation'**, around 5 ft (1.5m) high, greenish white flowers; **'Lunar Lass'**, low spreader, small greenish white flowers, lobed toothed leaves; **'Moonbeam'**, wiry stems to 5 ft (1.5m) tall, starry, creamy flowers, lobed leaves.

INTEGRIFOLIA GROUP

This relatively small group of cultivars is derived from *C. integrifolia* and related species. The most immediately obvious feature is that they are sprawling or scrambling plants. They will climb but lack the tendrils of other *Clematis*. The flowers are quite variable, ranging from small nodding bells to large flat blooms. **'Arabella'**, upward-facing flat flowers, purple blue with slightly darker bar; **'Blue Bird'**, long mauve-blue sepals, creamy white double center; **'Blue Boy'**, mauve-blue flowers; **'Juuli'**, mauve-blue flowers, 5 sepals, low-growing, often less than 4 ft (1.2 m) tall; **'Rooguchi'**, nodding, purple, bell-shaped flowers, lighter sepal edge.

MONTANA GROUP

This group is composed of cultivars and hybrids of *C. montana* and related species. They flower in spring, before or as the new foliage develops. They have simple 4-sepalled flowers, mainly in pink shades, cream, or white. Young foliage is often bronze-tinted. **'Elizabeth'**, very pale pink flowers, vanilla scented; **'Freda'**, deep pink flowers, pale central bar; **'Jenny'**, semi-double, white, tinted and edged pink; **'Marjorie'** ★, semi-double with petal-like stamens, cream overlaid with orange-pink and copper; **'New Dawn'**, white with pink central bar; **'Rosebud'**, semi-double, pink, scented; **'Snowflake'**, pure white flowers; **'Tetrarose'** ★, very large deep pink flowers, strong growing, lush foliage.

TEXENSIS GROUP

This is a group of sprawling semi-climbing shrubs that can be trained to climb or left to form bushy mounds. They may also be cut back each year as herbaceous perennials. The flowers, usually bell-shaped, bloom in summer on new growth. The group includes: **'Duchess of Albany'**, wide-open bell-shaped to starry flowers, deep pink, lighter at the edges; **'Etoile Rose'**, nodding, bell-shaped, rose pink flowers; **'Gravetye Beauty'**, upward-facing bell-shaped flowers becoming starry, wine red ageing to soft magenta.

VITICELLA GROUP

These are vigorous climbers that grow 8–20 ft (2.4–6 m) tall. They flower on new growth, but in short intense bursts rather than over a longer season like the former Lanuginosa and Jackmanii hybrids. Flowers may be single or double, seldom over 5 in (12 cm) wide, often smaller. Viticella hybrids include: **'Alba Luxurians'**, loose open flowers, creamy white, green mid-stripes or patches, dark stamens; **'Etoile Violette'**, deep purple flowers, creamy to yellow stamens; **'Lady Betty Balfour'**, strong-growing deep violet-blue flowers, creamy yellow stamens; **'Madame Julia Correvon'**, large flowers, deep red, sepals slightly twisted, cream stamens; **'Minuet'**, creamy white flowers, edged and tipped lavender-pink, cream stamens; **'Polish Spirit'**, purple flowers, red anthers; **'Purpurea Plena Elegans'** ★, dusky reddish purple double flowers, very distinctive color and shape; **'Venosa Violacea'**, large white flowers, veins and broad edges of deep purple, cream stamens, purple anthers; **'Ville de Lyon'** ★, deep pink flowers, yellow stamens.

LARGE-FLOWERED GROUPS

The Early and Late Large-flowered Groups are the result of attempting to rationalize the many hybrids of the former Jackmanii, Florida, Lanuginosa, and Patens groups. They are primarily differentiated by whether their first flowers are borne on the old (previous season's) wood or the new spring growth. Early-flowering forms will often flower again on the new growth, but double-flowered forms usually have single flowers in their later flush.

EARLY LARGE-FLOWERED GROUP

'Andromeda', semi-double, white with a pink bar; **'Arctic Queen'**, white, double flowers, often very large; **'Bees' Jubilee'**, light pink flowers with deep pink markings, yellow stamens; **'Belle of Woking'**, pale mauve-pink, very full double; **'Blue Ravine'**, big mauve-blue flowers with faint purple-red markings, purple-red stamens; **'Carnaby'**, pale mauve with darker mauve-pink bar; **'Charissima'**, large cerise flowers, flushed with pale pink, ageing to very pale pink with cerise stripe, cerise stamens; **'Crystal Fountain'**, lavender blue, double, fountain-like cascade of pale stamens; **'Doctor Ruppel'**, deep pink flowers with carmine markings, yellow stamens; **'Elsa Späth'**, blue-purple flowers, purple stamens, red anthers; **'Fireworks'**, mauve flowers, pink-red markings; **'General Sikorski'**, mauve blue, faint dark bar, can exceed 8 in (20 cm) diameter; **'Gillian Blades'**, white flowers, may have blue blush, wavy edges; **'Henryi'**, very large white to cream flowers with up to 8 sepals, brown stamens; **'Hybrida Sieboldii'** (syn. 'Ramona'), large, pale, lavender-blue flowers, purple-red stamens; **'Jan Pavel II'** (syn. 'John Paul II'), cream with light pink bar, dark anthers; **'Josephine'** ★, lavender-pink with narrow dark bar, very full double, later flowers petaloid-centered; **'Lasurstern'**, large blue flowers, wavy-edged, narrow sepals, cream stamens; **'Lawsoniana'**, large light blue to purplish flowers, pale stamens; **'Lord Nevill'**, purple-blue flowers, wavy edges, cream stamens, red anthers; **'Marie Boisselot'** (syn. 'Madame le Coultre'), vigorous grower, pale pink flowers ageing to white, cream to pale brown stamens; **'Minister'**, light mauve-blue, double, purple-red anthers on later single flowers; **'Miss Bateman'**, white flowers, pale green bar when first open, red anthers; **'Mrs Cholmondeley'**, large lavender flowers, narrow sepals, light brown stamens; **'Mrs N. Thompson'**, purplish flowers with red markings; **'Nelly Moser'**, large lilac-pink flowers with wine red stripes, brown stamens; **'Niobe'**, deep red flowers, yellow stamens; **'Phyllis Diller'**, mid-pink with darker bar, double, flowers up to 10 in (25 cm) wide; **'Richard Pennell'**, purple-blue flowers, red stamens, yellow anthers; **'Silver Moon'**, silvery lilac flowers, yellow stamens; **'The President'**, purple-blue flowers, reddish stamens; **'Wada's Primrose'**, cream with pale yellow stamens; **'Warszawska Nike'** (syn. 'Warsaw Nike'), deep reddish purple, very heavy-flowering; **'Will Goodwin'**, light lavender-blue flowers, cream to green stamens.

LATE LARGE-FLOWERED GROUP

'Aotearoa', deep violet to purple, flowers to 5 in (12 cm) wide; **'Comtesse de Bouchaud'**, large pink flowers, cream stamens, very popular; **'Gipsy Queen'**, 6 in (15 cm) wide with purple flowers striped wine red; **'Huldine'**, pure white, hint of a faint pink bar; **'Jackmanii'**, semi-pendulous deep purple flowers, 4 widely spaced sepals, cream stamens; **'Jackmanii Superba'**, deep purple flowers, purple mid-stripe, cream stamens; **'Madame Baron-Veillard'**, lavender-pink flowers, pointed sepals, white stamens; **'Perle d'Azur'**, lavender-blue flowers, yellow stamens; **'Prince Charles'**, mauve-blue, slightly darker bar; **'Romantika'**, deep purple with contrasting pale anthers.

Clematis, Hybrid Cultivar, Viticella Group, 'Madame Julia Correvon'

C., HC, Early Large-flowered Group, 'Fireworks'

Clematis, HC, Late Large-flowered Group, 'Perle d'Azur'

CLEOME

SPIDER FLOWER

This largely tropical and subtropical group of around 150 species of annuals and perennials forms the type genus for its family, the Cleomaceae. The commonly grown species are upright summer annuals. Their large palmate leaves have fine-toothed edges and stems that are sometimes spiny. Their 4-petalled flowers have long, protruding, filament-like stamens and are carried in apical heads with the filaments facing outward, hence the name spider flower. Some species, such as *C. lutea* from western North America, yield a yellow dye. In the USA *Cleome* has long been associated with US president Thomas Jefferson's famous garden at Monticello.

CULTIVATION: In areas with a warm summer the annuals are easily grown in any sheltered sunny position with moist, fertile, free-draining soil. Deadheading the flowers encourages longer blooming. With the exception of a few species, the perennials will not tolerate frost and need at least subtropical conditions. Propagate from spring-sown seed.

Cleome sesquiorygalis

syns *Cleome hassleriana, C. houtteana, C. spinosa*

SPIDER FLOWER

☼/◐ ❄ ↔ 20 in (50 cm) ↕ 5 ft (1.5 m)

Upright annual from southern Brazil, Paraguay, and northern Argentina. Palmate leaves with 5 to 7 finely toothed hairy leaflets to over 4 in (10 cm) long. Flowers clustered in terminal heads, petals to 1¼ in (30 mm) long with long filaments. In white and many shades of pink to purple. Several seedling strains and named forms, such as **'Helen Campbell'** (syn. 'White Queen'), one of the Queen Series, with varieties named after their flower color, such as **'Cherry Queen'**, **'Mauve Queen'**, **'Pink Queen'**, **'Purple Queen'**, **'Rose Queen'**, **'Ruby Queen'**. Zones 10–12.

Cleome sesquiorygalis

CLERODENDRUM

GLORY BOWER

This genus of about 400 evergreen or deciduous small trees, shrubs, and climbers, traditionally placed in the family Verbenaceae, is now assigned to the mint (Lamiaceae) family. They are found mostly in tropical and subtropical regions of Asia and Africa. Their simple leaves are opposite or whorled. They are grown for their summer terminal panicles of showy violet or red flowers. Some species are used in traditional medicine, others make ideal pot plants, and the climbers are ideal for trellis cultivation. The fruit is a drupe or berry. CULTIVATION: *Clerodendrum* species prefer light to medium well-drained soils, rich in humus, in a protected partly shaded to sunny position. Water freely in the growing season. The stems of young plants may require support, and sucking insects such as mites, mealybugs, or whitefly can pose a problem. Propagation is from seed sown in spring or from cuttings of half-hardened wood taken during winter or summer.

Clerodendrum bungei

GLORY FLOWER

↔ 8 ft (2.4 m) ↑ 8 ft (2.4 m)

Found in southern China and northern India. Evergreen aromatic shrub, thicket of suckering stems. Leaves triangular, toothed-edged, dark green with purple overtones. In summer, 6 in (15 cm) wide heads of strongly scented pale pink to purple-red flowers are produced. Zones 8–10.

Clerodendrum chinense

syn. *Clerodendrum philippinum*

HONOLULU ROSE, SPANISH JASMINE

↔ 7 ft (2 m) ↑ 10 ft (3 m)

Evergreen shrub from southern Japan and China. Angular stems and downy, toothed, pointed, oval to trangular leaves to 10 in (25 cm) long. Flower clusters to 4 in (10 cm) long, blooms white, cream, to red, with 1 in (25 mm) long tube. Considered invasive in Hawaii. The cultivar **'Pleniflorum'** has emphasized, semi-double, rose-like flowers. Zones 10–12.

Clerodendrum floribundum

LOLLY BUSH

↔ 10 ft (3 m) ↑ 20 ft (6 m)

Deciduous tree from China. Erect branching habit, smooth oval leaves. Fragrant white flowers with long tubes, 1¼ in (30 mm) long, pinkish calyces, in spikes, blackish purple berries. Zones 10–12.

Clerodendrum floribundum

Clerodendrum trichotomum, in fruit

Clerodendrum glabrum

WHITE CAT'S-WHISKERS

↔ 20 ft (6 m) ↑ 40 ft (12 m)

Small tree or shrub from Africa, multi-branched habit. Glossy, dark green, pointed, smooth leaves, opposite or whorled. Scented white or pink flowers, in dense terminal cymes. White to yellow fruit. Zones 10–12.

Clerodendrum minahassae

TUBE FLOWER TREE

↔ 10 ft (3 m) ↑ 17 ft (5 m)

Small evergreen tree with deep green, veined, pointed, elliptical leaves to 8 in (20 cm) long. Starry pale pink flowers with long petals and tube to 4 in (10 cm) long. After flowering, calyces turn bright red with small central black fruit. ***C. m.* var. *brevitubulosum*,** flowers with short tubes about 1 in (25 mm) long. Zones 10–12.

Clerodendrum speciosissimum

JAVA GLORY BEAN, MATA AJAM

↔ 4 ft (1.2 m) ↑ 6 ft (1.8 m)

A native of Java. Erect shrub. Large oval leaves to 12 in (30 cm) in length. Vivid red flowers, in panicles to 8 in (20 cm) long. Corolla around 1½ in (35 mm) long, in summer. Purplish blue fruit. Ideal container plant. Zones 10–12.

Clerodendrum splendens

↔ 7 ft (2 m) ↑ 7 ft (2 m)

Scrambling or climbing tropical African shrub with lush, dark green, smooth-edged, broad, pointed, oval leaves to over 6 in (15 cm) long and sprays of many bright red flowers. Zones 10–12.

Clethra arborea

Clerodendrum thomsoniae

BLEEDING HEART VINE

↔ 15 ft (4.5 m) ↑ 15 ft (4.5 m)

Vigorous, twining, evergreen climber from tropical West Africa. Smooth-edged, pointed, oval leaves to over 6 in (15 cm) long. Many-bloomed clusters of flowers with white calyces and dark red corolla, a striking contrast. Red to black fruit follow. Zones 10–12.

Clerodendrum trichotomum

↔ 15 ft (4.5 m) ↑ 15 ft (4.5 m)

From China and Japan. Downy leaves, heads of long-tubed, scented, white flowers in late summer. Flowers backed by pink calyces, darkening as the fruit matures. Purplish blue drupes. ***C. t.* var. *fargesii*,** new leaves bronze colored. Zones 8–10.

CLETHRA

This genus of about 60 species of deciduous small trees or shrubs in the family Clethraceae is widely distributed from southern USA to Central and South America and Asia, with one species native to Madeira. They are grown for their white fragrant flowers, often borne in long racemes or panicles, which resemble lily-of-the-valley flowers. Some of the species have attractive peeling bark, and the flowers are followed by numerous tiny seed capsules. CULTIVATION: Being closely related to the erica family, clethras like a lime-free soil and a moist sheltered spot, with some shade from taller trees. They can be propagated from seed, cuttings, or layers.

Clethra acuminata

CINNAMON CLETHRA, WHITE ALDER

↔ 12 ft (3.5 m) ↑ 12 ft (3.5 m)

Large shrub from southeastern USA. Racemes of scented creamy white flowers in late summer. Mid-green elliptical leaves have attractive golden tones in autumn. Zones 6–9.

Clethra alnifolia

SUMMERSWEET CLETHRA, SWEET PEPPER BUSH

↔ 6 ft (1.8 m) ↑ 6 ft (1.8 m)

Species native to eastern North America. Fragrant white flowers, in erect terminal racemes to 6 in (15 cm) long, in late summer. **'Paniculata'**, terminal panicles of white flowers; **'Rosea'** ★, buds and flowers tinged with pink. Zones 4–9.

Clethra arborea

LILY-OF-THE VALLEY TREE

↔ 20 ft (6 m) ↑ 25 ft (8 m)

From Madeira, densely foliaged. Long terminal panicles of scented white flowers. Needs mild conditions to thrive. **'Flora Plena'**, double flowers. Zones 9–10.

Clethra barbinervis

JAPANESE CLETHRA

↔ 10 ft (3 m) ↑ 10 ft (3 m)

From mountainous woodlands of Japan, larger in the wild. Peeling rusty brown bark. Dark green leaves, prominently veined, attractive autumn color. Scented white flowers appear in terminal racemes from summer–autumn. Shoots arch outward. Zones 8–9.

CLIANTHUS

This genus now consists of just one (or possibly two) New Zealand species. (It previously included the Australian plant known as Sturt's desert pea, now classified in *Swainsona.*) *Clianthus,* a member of the pea-flower subfamily of the legume (Fabaceae) family, grows into a somewhat sprawling evergreen shrub, with pinnate leaves and large red flowers in early summer. CULTIVATION: When grown in cool-temperate climates *C. puniceus* needs the protection of a sunny wall or greenhouse to prosper. In warmer areas it should be grown in sun or partial shade where protection is available from strong winds and heavy frosts. It requires well-drained soil and should be watered during dry periods. Light pruning will encourage bushier growth. Snails and slugs find the foliage very appealing and are serious pests. Propagation is from seed sown in spring or half-hardened cuttings taken in summer.

Clianthus puniceus

Clianthus puniceus ★

KAKA BEAK, PARROT'S BILL

↔6 ft (1.8 m) ↕6 ft (1.8 m)

Rare in its native habitat, the northern North Island of New Zealand. Branches clothed with attractive fern-like leaves. Red flowers, shape reminiscent of the beak of the kaka (native parrot). Easy to propagate, fast growing, can be short-lived. **'Albus'**, attractive white-flowering form that grows true from seed. Zones 8–11.

CLITORIA

A genus of 60 species of annual and perennial climbers, woody shrubs, and scramblers, placed in the pea-flower subfamily of the legume (Fabaceae) family. All species occur in mostly tropical regions; the Americas have 49, the remainder are from Africa and Asia. A few species are protected by State legislation in parts of the USA. Others have been planted extensively for stock feed and forage crops in many countries, where some have now become naturalized and are troublesome weeds. All species have pinnate leaves with an uneven number of leaflets, one terminating the leaf. Flowers are pea-shaped, but the largest petal is held downward, in contrast to most other genera in this subfamily, and colors are blue, white, or pinkish. CULTIVATION: Propagate from seed soaked overnight in water or from cuttings, which strike readily.

Clitoria ternatea

ASIAN PIGEONWINGS, BLUE PEA, BUTTERFLY PEA

↔4 ft (1.2 m) ↕to 70 ft (21 m)

Fast-growing evergreen (deciduous in some climates) climber/scrambler. Leaves pinnate, 5 to 9 oval to oblong leaflets, to 1¼ in (30 mm) long. Solitary flowers on long stalks, largest petal bright blue, whitish, yellowish at base, 1¼–¾ in (30–40 mm) long. Pod flat, to 5 in (12 cm) long, seeds round, flattened. Flowers throughout year. Zones 10–12.

CLOEZIA

This is a genus of 6 species of evergreen shrubs and small trees in the myrtle (Myrtaceae) family, allied to *Metrosideros*. All *Cloezia* species are endemic to New Caledonia. They have small to medium-sized opposite leaves with entire margins, often arranged in 4 ranks; small white or yellow flowers are carried in groups of few to many at branch tips; they have 4 or 5 petals alternating with sepals that in some species are of similar length and color to the petals. Fruits are small capsules. *Cloezia* species grow in open shrublands on poor, often boggy soils.
CULTIVATION: Although *Cloezia* species are found mostly in the wild and are scarcely known in cultivation, they include some species with considerable potential as ornamental shrubs. Acid soils with high organic content should suit them. Propagate from seed.

Cloezia buxifolia

↔3 ft (0.9 m) ↕5 ft (1.5 m)

Erect bushy shrub found along boggy stream banks among dense sedges and other shrubs. Leaves ¼ in (6 mm) or less long, thick and rounded, in 4 ranks; flowers clustered in upper leaf axils, golden yellow, in autumn–winter. Zones 10–11.

CLYTOSTOMA

There are 9 species of evergreen vines in this genus, which belongs to the trumpet-vine (Bignoniaceae) family. They are native to tropical America. The leaves are compound with 2 leaflets. Clusters of flaring trumpet-shaped flowers, usually pink, are borne terminally or along the branches from spring to summer. The large seed pods are bristly or spiny.

Cloezia buxifolia

CULTIVATION: In warm climates grow over walls and fences in full sun in well-drained soil and protect from strong winds. In cool climates grow in pots in the glasshouse and protect from direct sun when at its hottest. Propagate from cuttings or seed.

Clytostoma callistegioides

syns *Bignonia callistegioides, B. speciosa, B. violacea*

ARGENTINE TRUMPET VINE, VIOLET TRUMPET

↔20 ft (6 m) ↕10 ft (3 m)

Attractive climber, native to Argentina and southern Brazil. Dark green glossy leaves, bronzed when young. Flaring trumpet-shaped flowers, to 3 in (8 cm) long, lilac-pink with purple veining and soft creamy centers. Zones 10–11.

COBAEA

About 20 species of perennial climbers belong to this genus of the phlox (Polemoniaceae) family. They are native to Mexico and tropical South America. Plants have alternate lobed leaves and climb with tendrils. Cup-shaped flowers are bright green, violet, or purple, borne singly along the stems. The commonly grown species *C. scandens* has become naturalized in many warm areas.
CULTIVATION: Grow in a moisture-retentive but well-drained soil in a sunny position protected from strong winds. *C. scandens* grows rapidly and can be treated as an annual in cool climates or grown in the conservatory. Propagate from seed or cuttings.

Clytostoma callistegioides

Cobaea scandens

CATHEDRAL BELLS, CUP AND SAUCER VINE, MEXICAN IVY

↔5–10 ft (1.5–3 m) ↕20–25 ft (6–8 m)

From Mexico. Vigorous vine with wide cup-shaped flowers to 2 in (5 cm) long. Color varies from white to deep purple. "Saucer" in the common name refers to the open calyx below the flower; ***C. s.* f. *alba*** has white or creamy green flowers. Zones 9–11.

COCCOLOBA

A genus of about 150 mostly evergreen trees, shrubs, or vines in the knotweed (Polygonaceae) family from tropical and subtropical America. They have alternate, entire, leathery leaves, often quite large. The immature leaves are normally a different shape to the mature leaves and are larger. Spikes or racemes of small greenish white flowers are followed by a fleshy grape-like fruit, which is technically a small nut enclosed in the swollen floral remains. Some species are grown ornamentally for their foliage. The fruit is used for making jellies.
CULTIVATION: Light or sandy well-drained soils are preferable, in an open sunny position, with ample watering, particularly in dry weather. Pruning is unnecessary except to maintain shape. Propagation is from seed, by cuttings of ripe wood in spring or of half-hardened wood in autumn, or by layering.

Coccoloba uvifera

JAMAICAN KING, PLATTER LEAF, SEA GRAPE

↔10 ft (3 m) ↕20 ft (6 m)

Native of tropical America. Erect, branching, evergreen tree. Leaves are mid-green, leathery, and heart-shaped, with reddish veins. Bears racemes of fragrant white flowers in summer, followed by grape-like edible fruit, green, ripening to reddish purple. Zones 10–12.

Coccoloba uvifera

C

C

Coccothrinax spissa

Cocos nucifera 'Panama Tall'

Colchicum agrippinum

COCCOTHRINAX

SILVER PALM, THATCH PALM

Native to tropical regions of the West Indies, Mexico, Honduras, the Bahamas, and Florida, USA, this genus in the palm (Arecaceae) family consists of 14 or more species of normally solitary, graceful, slender, medium-sized palms. Their fan-like palmate fronds have broad blades divided into long radiating segments that are glossy dark green above and silvery beneath. As the fronds die and fall away, they leave behind a layer of fibers that wear away, leaving a ringed trunk exposed. These palms are salt and wind tolerant, and are ideal, if slow-growing, ornamental plants for coastal tropical climates.
CULTIVATION: They prefer an open, sunny, or partially protected position in a very well-drained soil, with adequate water in dry periods. Propagate from seed, which germinates within 2 to 6 months, depending on species.

Coccothrinax argentata ★

syns *Coccothrinax fragrans, C. jamaicensis, C. proctorii, C. readii*

FLORIDA SILVER PALM, SILVER PALM

☼ ❄ ↔8 ft (2.4 m) ↑25 ft (8 m)

Native of Florida, USA, and the Bahamas. Solitary palm with smooth gray trunk. Small fan-like leaves, glossy light yellow-green above, silvery white beneath. Fragrant white flowers, purplish black fruits. Zones 10–12.

Coccothrinax crinita ★

OLD MAN PALM, THATCH PALM

☼ ❄ ↔7 ft (2 m) ↑30 ft (9 m)

From tropical Cuba. Trunk 8 in (20 cm) in diameter, with long, brown, fine, woolly fibers. Fan-like fronds, to 6 ft (1.8 m) across, divided into segments, drooping blades, 30 in (75 cm) long, shiny green above, dull gray beneath. Zones 10–12.

Coccothrinax miraguama

syn. *Coccothrinax scoparia*

MIRAGUAMA

☼ ❄ ↔7 ft (2 m) ↑15 ft (4.5 m)

Native of Cuba. Elegant palm, trunk 6 in (15 cm) in diameter, covered in long fibers. Glossy, rigid, dark green leaves, silvery and hairy beneath, to 6 ft (1.8 m) across, 28 segments to 24 in (60 cm) long, short slender leaf stalks. Zones 10–12.

Coccothrinax spissa

GUANO, SWOLLEN SILVER THATCH

☼ ❄ ↔10–17 ft (3–5 m) ↑15–25 ft (4.5–8 m)

From the island of Hispaniola (Dominican Republic and Haiti). Solitary palm with stout trunk, upper part swollen. Sparse crown with rounded deeply divided leaves on long stalks that arch with age. Small bright purple fruit. Zones 10–12.

COCOS

This genus in the palm (Arecaceae) family contains just one species, found in coastal regions of all tropical seas worldwide, growing to a height of 100 ft (30 m) in good conditions. The terminal head carries pinnate fronds. The 3-petalled flowers, seen only in the tropics, are produced in panicles from the leaf axils, followed by the coconuts, encased in thick fibrous husks. In tropical islands all parts of this tree are used: the trunks and fronds for building and weaving; the fiber for matting, rope, and soil-less composts; the flesh of the nut for food and drink; the endosperm for cosmetics; the oil for margarine and soap. The residue is used for cattle feed.
CULTIVATION: Coconuts can be grown successfully outdoors only in the tropics. In subtropical conditions they will not bear fruit. They grow best in coastal lowlands and on seashores. Coconuts will thrive if watered and fed moderately in the growing season. Grow in moist, well-drained, humus-rich soil in full sun. For container growing, provide an open mixture with coarse sand added.

Cocos nucifera

COCONUT PALM

☼ ⚘ ↔10–20 ft (3–6 m) ↑100 ft (30 m)

Large palm, single trunk swollen at the base, often leaning away from the prevailing wind. Bright green pinnate fronds, 20 ft (6 m) long. Fragrant yellow flowers. Fruit covered with a thick husk, green ripening to yellow or orange-red. **'Malay Dwarf'** ★, a widely grown strain with heavy crops of large golden-yellow nuts; **'Nino'**, a dwarf cultivar, will grow to 10 ft (3 m); **'Panama Tall'**, stately tall cultivar. Zone 12.

CODONOPSIS

BONNET BELLFLOWER

A bellflower (Campanulaceae) family genus of around 30 species of herbaceous perennials that will climb on structures but prefer to scramble through surrounding vegetation. They have wiry, often twining stems and simple light-textured leaves of variable shape. The flowers are nodding, bell-shaped, with conspicuous calyces, and although fairly large they are often a pale blue-green color that merges well with the foliage, making for a less than showy flower display. These are interesting plants, though not exactly spectacular, and those who pursue that interest and turn the bells upward will often be rewarded by finding brightly colored nectaries and veins within.
CULTIVATION: They are mostly very hardy and easily grown in any temperate climate with reasonable summer rainfall. Bonnet bellflowers prefer woodland conditions with dappled light and cool, moist, humus-rich, well-drained soil. It is best to try to remove the tangle of dry foliage and stems after it has died off, otherwise it may become very untidy. Propagate by division when dormant, or raise from seed.

Codonopsis clematidea

◐ ✱ ↔20–60 in (50–150 cm) ↑32 in (80 cm)

Perennial from central Asia. Erect when young but eventually sprawling. Slightly downy, 1 in (25 mm) long leaves tinted blue-green. In summer, very pale blue bell-shaped flowers, orange and black markings within. Zones 4–9.

COLCHICUM

AUTUMN CROCUS, MEADOW SAFFRON, NAKED LADIES

A genus of around 45 species of corms that is the type genus for the family Colchicaceae. They are found from eastern Europe to North Africa and eastwards to China. They are not related to the true crocuses, but the name autumn crocus is an apt description of the habit and appearance of many of the species. The plants are dormant and leafless in summer. The flowers have 6 petals, in 2 whorls, and start to appear from early autumn before the foliage develops, or in spring. Double-flowered forms are available. Colchicum species are famous as the source of the cancer treatment drug colchicine, a mutagen that affects cell division. Colchicine is sometimes used to produce new plant cultivars.
CULTIVATION: Hardy, adaptable, and great favorites of rock garden enthusiasts, the autumn crocuses thrive in zones with distinct seasons. Some need a hot dry summer to flower well but most are happy in any fertile well-drained soil in full or half-sun. They also do well in containers.

C

Colchicum agrippinum

☼/◐ ✱ ↔4–8 in (10–20 cm)
↕4–6 in (10–15 cm)

From Greece and southwestern Turkey. Possibly a natural *C. variegatum* × *C. autumnale* hybrid. Upright blue-green leaves to 6 in (15 cm) long, sometimes wavy-edged. In autumn, before the foliage, white-tubed purple-pink flowers, mottled white. Purple anthers. Zones 5–9.

Colchicum autumnale

☼/◐ ✱ ↔6–16 in (15–40 cm)
↕6–10 in (15–25 cm)

Late summer- to autumn-flowering species from western and central Europe. Long, white-tubed, purple-pink flowers, yellow anthers. Later, narrow to broad lance-shaped leaves to 14 in (35 cm) long. **'Alboplenum'**, white double flowers; **'Album'**, small white flowers; **'Plenum'**, lavender-pink double flowers. Zones 5–9.

Colchicum cilicicum

☼/◐ ✱ ↔6–16 in (15–40 cm)
↕6–12 in (15–30 cm)

Native to Turkey, Syria, and Lebanon. Large lavender-pink to purple flowers on strong white stems. Yellow anthers. Bright green leaves to 16 in (40 cm) long emerge in spring. Zones 6–9.

Colchicum parnassicum

☼/◐ ❄ ↔6–16 in (15–40 cm)
↕6–10 in (15–25 cm)

Native to Greece. Less hardy, but otherwise identical to *C. autumnale,* except for more arching foliage and details of membrane covering the corm. Zones 8–10.

Colchicum speciosum

☼/◐ ✱ ↔6–16 in (15–40 cm)
↕4–8 in (10–20 cm)

Found from northern Turkey westward to Iran and northward to Russia. In autumn, pale-centered bright mauve-pink flowers with sturdy stems. Golden-yellow anthers. In spring, broad, bright green, slightly arched leaves to 10 in (25 cm) long. **'Album'**, large, green-throated, white flowers. Zones 6–9.

Colchicum cilicicum

Colchicum 'The Giant'

☼ ✱ ↔8 in (20 cm) ↕10 in (25 cm)

Large white-mottled lilac-pink flowers on strong stems, in autumn. Probably a hybrid with *C. bivonae.* Zones 6–9.

Colchicum 'Waterlily' ★

☼ ✱ ↔8 in (20 cm) ↕8 in (20 cm)

Large and very fully double flowers on fairly short stems. Probably a hybrid with a *C. autumnale* cultivar. Zones 6–9.

COLEONEMA

All of these 8 species of evergreen shrubs in the rue (Rutaceae) family are native to South Africa, most of them confined to Western Cape Province. All have small heath-like leaves on fine twigs and small starry flowers in winter and spring, sometimes repeating in summer. The foliage is slightly aromatic. They make useful small hedges if pruned regularly after flowering when young and brought slowly to the required height. They are often referred to as *Diosma*, which is a separate but related genus.

CULTIVATION: A position in full sun is preferred, with a free-draining rather sandy soil. Avoid exposure to strong winds, as they tend to dislodge the surface roots and blow the plants over. These species are not recommended for cold climates. Seeds germinate freely, but may result in plants of uncertain flowering quality; soft-tip cuttings taken in late summer or autumn give true results.

Coleonema album

syn. *Diosma alba*

WHITE BREATH OF HEAVEN, WHITE CONFETTI BUSH

☼ ❄ ↔6 ft (1.8 m) ↕5 ft (1.5 m)

Densely leafed evergreen shrub, bun-shaped with age. Leaves very small, bright green when young, darker with age; aromatic when bruised. White flowers, solitary or in small clusters, from late winter–early spring. Brown fruit. Prune regularly. Zones 9–10.

Colchicum speciosum 'Album'

Coleonema pulchellum

syn. *Coleonema pulchrum of gardens*

☼ ❄ ↔36–48 in (90–120 cm)
↕24–60 in (60–150 cm)

From South Africa. Well-foliaged shrub, slender branches, soft, needle-like, aromatic leaves. Masses of tiny, starry, pink flowers in late winter–spring. Number of dwarf forms: **'Pinkie'**, compact, very floriferous, dark pink flowers, darker pink center stripes on petals; **'Sunset Gold'** ★, widely grown dwarf form, pale yellow foliage, intensifies to a deep golden yellow in late summer–autumn if grown in a semi-exposed position. Other dwarf forms include: **'Compactum'**, **'Nanum'** and **'Rubrum'**. Zones 9–11.

COLLETIA

ANCHOR PLANT

This genus of 17 thorny shrubs in the buckthorn (Rhamnaceae) family, covered in spines and often with thickened and flattened branches, is native to temperate regions of South America. They are cultivated for their ornamental value, their spines making them particularly useful for boundary planting. Leaves are non-existent or very small and short-lived, while the small, scented, bell-shaped or tubular, usually yellowish or white flowers, appear singly or in clusters, normally from summer to early autumn. The fruit is a leathery 3-lobed capsule.

CULTIVATION: They prefer light to medium, sandy, well-drained soils in a protected but sunny position. Propagation is from seed or by cuttings of half-hardened wood taken in autumn.

Coleonema pulchellum 'Pinkie'

Colletia paradoxa

Colletia paradoxa

syn. *Colletia cruciata*

ANCHOR BUSH

☼ ❄ ↔8 ft (2.4 m) ↕6 ft (1.8 m)

Native of Uruguay and southern Brazil. Slow-growing deciduous shrub. Covered with flattened triangular spines in place of leaves. All plant parts bluish green in appearance. Fragrant yellowish white flowers appear in summer–early autumn. Zones 8–9.

COLOCASIA

A genus of 6 species of tuberous perennials belonging to the arum (Araceae) family. They are native to tropical Asia, where they grow in naturally moist areas. Some are widely naturalized in other tropical and warm-temperate regions. The leaves, which can be very large, are arrow- or heart-shaped with prominent veins. The typical arum flower spike consists of a fleshy spike of minute flowers surrounded by a white to yellow spathe. In tropical areas the roots of *C. esculenta* are a staple food cooked in a variety of ways. Elsewhere they are grown for the ornamental quality of their leaves.

CULTIVATION: In suitably warm climates grow *Colocasia* species in a fertile moisture-retentive soil, watering well in dry spells. If grown as a crop, plant at 24 in (60 cm) spacings and top-dress monthly with a high-potash fertilizer. The tubers are ready for harvesting after approximately 8 months. In temperate climates grow under glass with high humidity and water well.

Colocasia esculenta

syn. *Colocasia antiquorum*

COCOYAM, DASHEEN, TARO

☼ ❄ ↔3–6 ft (0.9–1.8 m)
↕3–6 ft (0.9–1.8 m)

From tropical eastern Asia. Widely grown throughout tropical regions as a food crop. Prominently veined dark green leaves to 24 in (60 cm) long, arrow- or heart-shaped, with sturdy stems supporting them from below. Cultivars grown ornamentally include **'Black Magic'**, purplish black leaves; **'Fontanesii'**, dark purple stems, dark green leaves with purple veins. Zones 8–12.

Colocasia esculenta 'Fontanesii'

Colutea arborescens

COLUTEA

The 30-odd species of leguminous deciduous shrubs and small trees in this genus in the pea-flower subfamily of the legume (Fabaceae) family occur naturally in Africa and Europe eastward to Central Asia. They are wiry-stemmed, sometimes spiny, and have pinnate or trifoliate leaves, usually composed of very small leaflets. The small racemes of yellow to orange pea-like flowers appear from spring to autumn and are quite attractive. The pods become very inflated and balloon-like and may be colored, translucent, glossy, or hairy. They are worth growing as novelties; children love the pods because of the noise they make when burst by squeezing.
CULTIVATION: Most *Colutea* species are moderately to very frost hardy and grow in a wide range of soils with good drainage. They thrive in inland gardens and grow well near the coast. Plant in full sun for the best flower and pod production. Regular tip pinching and thinning will help to keep plants compact. Propagate from seed or from cuttings taken in summer.

Colutea arborescens

BLADDER SENNA

☼ ❄ ↔10 ft (3 m) ↑15 ft (4.5 m)

Native to southern Europe. Leaves 6 in (15 cm) long, 5 to 7 pairs of leaflets. Small yellow and orange-red flowers in late spring. Pods to 3 in (8 cm) long, bright green, developing red tints, becoming translucent when mature. **'Bullata'**, compact form with small puckered leaflets; **'Variegata'**, cream-edged leaves. Zones 5–10.

Colutea × media

☼ ❄ ↔10 ft (3 m) ↑10 ft (3 m)

Hybrid between *C. arborescens* and *C. orientalis*. Leaves 2–4 in (5–10 cm) long, composed of 6 to 12 small gray-green leaflets. Flowers light red-brown to orange. Red-tinted 2 in (5 cm) long seed pods. **'Copper Beauty'** ★, orange-yellow flowers, red-brown pods. Zones 6–10.

COMPTONIA

Native to eastern North America and found from Nova Scotia to Georgia, the sole species in this genus of the wax-myrtle (Myricaceae) family is a small, suckering, deciduous shrub that eventually develops into a many-stemmed thicket. It has pleasantly aromatic foliage which, although more lobed than pinnate, is rather ferny, hence the common name sweet fern. It blooms in spring and early summer, when it produces male and female flowers on separate catkins. The catkins are a red-brown shade, as is the down that coats the young leaves.
CULTIVATION: An inhabitant of fields and woodlands, sweet fern prefers moist, well-drained, humus-enriched, slightly acidic soil and a position in full sun or partial shade. The older wood should be thinned out occasionally to encourage fresh young shoots and maintain the plant's vigor. Propagate by seed, by layering, or by removing rooted suckers.

Comptonia peregrina ★

SWEET FERN

☼/◐ ❄ ↔8 ft (2.4 m) ↑5 ft (1.5 m)

Leaves 2–4 in (5–10 cm) long, narrow, deeply lobed almost to the midrib. Catkins flower in late spring; male catkins slightly longer than female. Female catkins last longer and enlarge as their seeds ripen. Zones 4–9.

CONGEA

This genus, consisting of about 7 species from Southeast Asia, belongs to the nettle (Lamiaceae) family. They are scrambling shrubs, often forming tangled masses of stems over other shrubs and small trees, with entire, simple, opposite leaves. Flowers are usually borne in a terminal panicle of small condensed cymes, each cyme surrounded by 3 conspicuous colored bracts that can be highly ornamental. The leathery fruit contains a single seed.
CULTIVATION: *Congea* species are grown in full sun and need support and plenty of space. In temperate regions they need to be planted in large pots and kept under glass, or they can be grown in the greenhouse border, requiring a rich loam with additional leafmold. Propagation is best done from seed, or from softwood or half-hardened cuttings.

Congea tomentosa

SHOWER ORCHID

☼ ✢ ↔20–40 ft (6–12 m)
↑10–30 ft (3–9 m)

From Thailand and Burma. Large shrub with long scrambling branches, densely mounding over fences or trees. Leaves to 8 in (20 cm) long, usually with hairy undersides. Heads of small white flowers, surrounded by woolly-surfaced white to pink or mauve bracts to 1 in (25 mm) long. Zones 11–12.

CONOCLINIUM

MISTFLOWER

A genus of 3 rhizome-rooted perennials of the daisy (Asteraceae) family, found in the eastern USA, the Caribbean, and Mexico. They are low and spreading to shrubby and have fairly large leaves, usually oval and sometimes downy. The flowerheads do not have ray florets but have elongated disc florets that create fluffy *Ageratum*-like flowerheads, usually in shades of powder blue, violet, or white. The hazy effect gives the genus its common name. For much of the growing season the plants make a low spreading foliage mound, but from late summer they produce upright flower stems that bloom until cut back by the first frosts. The flowers are attractive to butterflies.
CULTIVATION: Their hardiness varies with the species, but they are easily grown in sun or partial shade with a preference for moist but well-drained humus-rich soil. They will tolerate drought but do not flower well. Propagate by division when dormant. Seeds germinate freely.

Comptonia peregrina

Conoclinium dissectum

syn. *Conoclinium greggii*

☼/◐ ❄ ↔36 in (90 cm) ↑24 in (60 cm)

Found in Arizona, New Mexico, and Texas in USA, and northern Mexico. Leaves elliptical, sometimes downy, textured, veined, to 3 in (8 cm) long. Heads of filamentous, powdery, mauve-blue flowers from late summer. Zones 7–10.

CONRADINA

There are 7 species of low-growing shrubs in this genus of the mint (Lamiaceae) family. Native to southeastern USA, where they grow in areas with sandy soil. The narrow leaves are opposite and clustered. The 2-lipped tubular flowers are in shades of purple and are borne along the stems.
CULTIVATION: In warm areas grow in a sunny position in well-drained soil. In cooler areas grow in the glasshouse or conservatory in direct sunlight. Propagate from seed or cuttings.

Conradina verticillata

CUMBERLAND FALSE ROSEMARY

☼ ❄ ↔18–24 in (45–60 cm)
↑6–15 in (15–38 cm)

From Kentucky and Tennessee. Low spreading shrub with branches rooting along ground. Soft, needle-like, aromatic foliage. Tubular flowers, ½ in (12 mm) long, lavender, lower lip spotted with purple. Zones 7–10.

Conradina verticillata

CONSOLIDA

LARKSPUR

A Eurasian buttercup (Ranunculaceae) family genus of around 40 species that are very much the annual cousins of the delphiniums, with which they were once grouped. Larkspurs grow 18–36 in (45–90 cm) tall and have fine feathery foliage, and about half their height is taken up with the upright, sometimes branching heads of their 5-petalled flowers. While most of the myriad many-colored modern strains are developments of *C. ambigua*, the seeds of other species are available. Pretty in the garden, they also make excellent cut flowers. The name comes from the Latin *consolidare*, meaning to make whole, and referring to the medicinal use of the plant to heal wounds. The juice of the leaves has also been used in herbal tonics, but parts of the plant, especially the seeds, are poisonous.
CULTIVATION: Plant in fertile well-drained soil in full sun. *Consolida* species thrive under most conditions and will often self-sow, although the flowers of wild seedlings rarely amount to much. They may need staking. Raise from seed.

Consolida ajacis

syns *Consolida ambigua, Delphinium ajacis*

LARKSPUR

↔6–12 in (15–30 cm)
↑32–40 in (80–100 cm)

Mediterranean native with lacy finely cut foliage in basal clumps and wiry upright stems carrying heads of many spurred flowers in shades of blue, pink, or white. Garden forms occur in wide color range and include double flowers. **Giant Imperial Series**, including **'Giant Imperial Blue Spire'**, **'Giant Imperial Pink Perfection'**, and **'Giant Imperial White King'**, has double flowers covering the entire color range with long spikes that last well and keep their color when dried. The **Seven Dwarfs Series** has tightly packed 8–10 in (20–25 cm) flower spikes in all colors. Zones 8–11.

Consolida ajacis 'Giant Imperial Blue Spire'

Consolida regalis

↔8–12 in (20–30 cm)
↑20 in (50 cm)

From Europe and the Caucasus. Branching stems, leaves narrowly segmented, hairy. Flowers blue, pink, or white. Used to produce dyes: blue from flowers, green from the foliage. **Cloud Series**, such as white-flowered **'Snow Cloud'**, have stocky branching flower stems. Zones 9–11.

CONVALLARIA

LILY-OF-THE-VALLEY

Lily-of-the-valley has been cultivated since at least 1000 bc, which is not surprising considering its unique and intense fragrance and the ease with which it grows. Belonging to the asparagus (Asparagaceae) family, the sole species in the genus is a low spreading perennial found over much of the northern temperate zone. Its vigorous rhizomes can colonize a large area and in spring produce bright green lance-shaped leaves and short-stemmed white flowerheads of bell-shaped blooms (a form with pale pink flowers is available), followed by red berries. Seventeenth-century herbalists recommended lily-of-the-valley to strengthen the heartbeat, although it is dangerously toxic, and the plant does indeed contain glycoside compounds used in modern heart medications.
CULTIVATION: Plant in dappled shade in deep, moist, well-drained soil. A cool winter is required for proper dormancy. The rhizomes, known as pips, are somewhat invasive in loose soil. Propagate by division.

Convallaria majalis

C. ajacis 'Giant Imperial White King'

Convallaria majalis

↔12–40 in (30–100 cm)
↑4–8 in (10–20 cm)

Fragrant waxy flowers in spring–early summer. ***C. m.* var. *rosea***, small pale pink flowers, not as vigorous as white-flowered species. *C. m.* cultivars with variegated foliage include: **'Albostriata'**, dark leaves with white to cream longitudinal stripes; **'Aureovariegata'** (syn. 'Striata'), gold stripes; **'Aureo-marginata'**, cream- to yellow-edged leaves; **'Hardwick Hall'**, broad leaves with pale margins; **'Prolificans'**, unusually shaped flowers. Zones 3–9.

CONVOLVULUS

This is the name genus of the family Convolvulaceae and comprises around 100 species of twining climbers, soft-stemmed shrubs, and herbaceous perennials from many temperate regions. The leaves are mostly narrow and thin textured. The widely flared funnel-shaped flowers bloom in succession over a long period.
CULTIVATION: Most *Convolvulus* species are hardy plants adaptable to a range of soils and situations, but all prefer a sunny position. Trim shrubby species regularly to encourage density of growth. They are easily propagated from cuttings.

Convolvulus althaeoides

↔3–5 ft (0.9–1.5 m)
↑3–5 ft (0.9–1.5 m)

Perennial trailer or low climber from southern Europe. Gray-green heart- to arrowhead-shaped leaves, often lobed. In summer inflorescences of 1 to 5 funnel-shaped pink to magenta flowers, to 1½ in (35 mm) wide.

Convolvulus sabatius

C. a.* subsp. *tenuissimus has covering of fine silvery hairs, narrowly lobed leaves, usually bears flowers singly. Zones 8–10.

Convolvulus cneorum

SILVERBUSH

↔2 ft (0.6 m) ↑2 ft (0.6 m)

From the Mediterranean. Bun-shaped shrub, dense weak stems. Silvery, thin, narrow, silky leaves. White to pale pink flowers, darker pink stripes, flared, funnel-shaped, in spring–summer. Requires free drainage, good air circulation. Suited to coastal gardens, tolerates summer dryness. Zones 8–10.

Convolvulus lineatus

↔20–40 in (50–100 cm)
↑2–10 in (5–25 cm)

Spreading, sometimes mounding perennial found from France to southern Russia and Greece. Stems and narrow elliptical leaves covered in fine silky hairs. Flowers in leaf axils, borne singly or in small clusters, soft pink, in summer. Zones 7–9.

Convolvulus sabatius ★

syn. *Convolvulus mauritanicus*

↔24–60 in (60–150 cm)
↑8–12 in (20–30 cm)

Low spreading perennial or subshrub from Italy and North Africa. Trailing stems, fine-haired, gray-green, oval leaves to 1½ in (35 mm) long. Groups of 1 to 3 flowers in the leaf axils, pale mauve to purple, sometimes pink, to 1 in (25 mm) wide. Zones 8–10.

Convolvulus tricolor

↔12–32 in (30–80 cm)
↑20–40 in (50–100 cm)

Found through southern Europe and in North Africa. Annual or short-lived perennial shrub or small climber. Small, pointed, oval leaves. Flowers up to 2 in (5 cm) wide, borne singly in the leaf axils, in blue shades, often with a yellow throat. **Ensign Series** has brightly colored flowers with contrasting markings, such as **'Blue Ensign'**, white-edged, yellow-throated, deep blue flowers. Zones 8–10.

Convolvulus tricolor

Copernicia macroglossa

COPERNICIA

CARANDA PALM, WAX PALM

Native to tropical and subtropical regions of the West Indies and South America, this palm (Arecaceae) family genus consists of 24 or 25 species. They may be solitary or clumping, and may range from dwarf species to tall spectacular trees. The trunk, which may be covered with the bases of old fronds, or scarred, or occasionally bare, is often swollen at its base. The fan-like palmate fronds are stiff, deeply divided, and often spiny, the dead fronds remaining on the plant and creating a "petticoat" below the living fronds. All species have ornamental value, while one, *C. prunifera*, is grown commercially for the carnauba wax harvested from the leaves.
CULTIVATION: *Copernicia* species prefer an open sunny position in well-drained soil, although they will cope with half-sun. Propagation is from seed, which takes 3 to 10 months to germinate, according to species, but seedling growth is slow.

Copernicia alba

CARANDA, CARANDAY

↔12–25 ft (3.5–8 m) ↑25–100 ft (8–30 m)

Native to South America. Slender palm with rounded crown of stiff palm-shaped leaves. Long leaf stalks are spiny. Flowering spikes, to 6 ft (1.8 m) long, arise within the foliage. Zones 9–11.

Copernicia baileyana ★

YAREY, YAREY HEMBRA

↔10 ft (3 m) ↑40 ft (12 m)

An impressive palm, native of Cuba. Frond stalks to 4 ft (1.2 m) in length, covered with spines. Large crowded crown. Huge, deeply segmented, bright green, fan-shaped fronds. Zones 10–12.

Copernicia macroglossa ★

CUBAN PETTICOAT PALM, JATA DE GUANBOCA

↔10 ft (3 m) ↑20 ft (6 m)

Spectacular palm from Cuba. Spiral crown, closely packed fronds. In older plants, a "petticoat" covers the trunk to ground level. Glossy green fronds, almost no stalks, deeply divided, about 64 stiff, pointed, spiny segments. Zones 10–12.

Copernicia prunifera ★

CARNAUBA

↔12 ft (3.5 m) ↑40 ft (12 m)

From northeastern Brazil. Grown for its versatile wax. Large rounded crown, hard patterned trunk, lower portion covered in persistent leaf bases. Fan-like fronds divided into segments hang from deeply toothed leaf stalks. Zones 10–12.

COPROSMA

This genus belongs to the large family Rubiaceae, which includes *Coffea*, the coffee plant. It comprises about 90 species of evergreen shrubs and small trees from Australia, New Zealand, and Pacific regions. There is a wide variation in habit from erect to creeping; leaves range from minute to large. Inconspicuous male and female flowers grow on separate plants. The berries on the female can give a pretty display in summer and autumn.
CULTIVATION: Adaptable plants tolerating a wide range of situations and soils, *Coprosma* species are usually best in full sun and well-drained conditions. Some are suited to harsh coastal conditions; others are useful for ground cover, hedging, and shelter. In cool-temperate climates they are barely hardy and require overwintering in the greenhouse. If a display of berries is required, male and female plants must be grown together. Propagation is from seed, which is best sown fresh, or from half-hardened cuttings taken in autumn.

Coprosma repens

MIRROR BUSH, TAUPATA

↔12 ft (3.5 m) ↑20 ft (6 m)

From New Zealand coastal areas. Very glossy, thick, dark green, oblong leaves. Berries orangey red. Excellent plant for warm coastal gardens. **'Marble Queen'** ★, leaves speckled white; **'Painter's Palette'**, very glossy leaves of red, cream, yellow, green, and chocolate brown; **'Picturata'**, glossy leaves variegated cream; **'Variegata'**, cream-edged, shiny green leaves; **'Yvonne'**, very glossy dark green and chocolate brown leaves, intensifying in color during winter. Zones 9–11.

Coprosma repens 'Variegata'

CORDIA

This genus in the family Boraginaceae comprises about 300 deciduous or evergreen trees or shrubs that are native to tropical regions of Central and South America, Africa, and Asia. They have terminal flowerheads or spikes of bell-shaped or tubular white or orange flowers, and alternate simple leaves; the fruit is a drupe.
CULTIVATION: They like moist, well-drained, peaty soils, in an open sunny position. Pruning is not usually needed. Propagate in winter to spring from ripe seed, or from cuttings.

Cordia boissieri

TEXAS OLIVE

↔8 ft (2.4 m) ↑8 ft (2.4 m)

Found in Texas and New Mexico, USA, and nearby parts of Mexico. Evergreen shrub, with leaves that are elliptical to ovate, dull green on the upper surface, downy on the underside. Large, white, yellow-centered flowers bloom in summer. This species will not tolerate prolonged wet, cold conditions. Zones 8–11.

Cordia parvifolia

LITTLE LEAF CORDIA

↔3–6 ft (0.9–1.8 m) ↑3–10 ft (0.9–3 m)

Semi-deciduous shrub from northern Mexico, with small, grayish, serrated-edged leaves. Bears clusters of crepe-textured white flowers in summer. Zones 9–11.

COREOPSIS

TICKSEED

Found in the Americas, especially in southwestern USA and Mexico, the 80-odd annuals and perennials (rarely shrubs) in this genus belong to the daisy (Asteraceae) family. They are compact plants that flower profusely, providing spectacular summer color. Most are shrubby plants, 2–4 ft (0.6–1.2 m) tall, with narrow, sometimes lobed leaves. The flowers are usually golden yellow, though garden forms occur in a variety of shades. The tips of the ray florets are often toothed as if cut with pinking shears. The flowers of some species yield a golden orange dye. Both the common name tickseed and the Greek word coreopsis (bug-like), from which the proper name is derived, refer to the appearance of the small black seeds.
CULTIVATION: Plant in a sunny position in light well-drained soil. *Coreopsis* species flower better with summer moisture but are quite drought tolerant. All can be raised from seed, and the perennials will also grow from divisions or small basal cuttings from non-flowering stems.

Cordia boissieri

Coreopsis auriculata

↔24 in (60 cm) ↑5 ft (1.5 m)

Spring-blooming perennial from southeastern USA. Leaves to over 4 in (10 cm) long, entire or with 1 to 2 small lobes. Flowerheads to 2 in (5 cm) wide, yellow, with about 8 ray florets. **'Nana'**, to around 10 in (25 cm) tall, with dark foliage and orange-gold flowers; **'Zamfir'**, 16 in (40 cm) tall, distinctive rolled (quilled) ray florets, golden yellow. Zones 4–10.

Coreopsis gigantea

↔32 in–4 ft (80 cm–1.2 m) ↑7–10 ft (2–3 m)

Vigorous fleshy-stemmed shrub from California, USA. Doubly pinnate leaves to 8 in (20 cm) long with very narrow leaflets. Long-stemmed yellow flowerheads to over 3 in (8 cm) across. Summer-flowering. Zones 8–10.

Coreopsis rosea 'American Dream'

Coreopsis lanceolata 'Sterntaler'

Coreopsis grandiflora

↔ 12–20 in (30–50 cm)
↑ 24 in (60 cm)

Bushy perennial from central and southern USA. Leaves to 4 in (10 cm) long; lower leaves often entire, upper tending toward pinnate. From late spring, long-stemmed flowerheads to slightly over 2 in wide, with around 8 ray florets. In wild, colors range from pale yellow to gold. **'Calypso'**, 14 in (35 cm) tall, cream variegated foliage, small red spots on ray florets; **'Early Sunrise'**, 18 in (45 cm) tall, gold double flowers; **'Kelvin Harbutt'**, up to 36 in (90 cm) tall, golden yellow flowerheads with red-brown disc florets. Zones 7–10.

Coreopsis lanceolata

↔ 12–16 in (30–40 cm)
↑ 24 in (60 cm)

Tough perennial from central and southeastern USA. Leaves to 6 in (15 cm) long, usually entire, rarely with shallow basal lobes, lance-shaped to linear. Yellow flowerheads to 2½ in (6 cm) wide, usually with around 8 ray florets, in summer. A weed in Australia. **'Baby Gold'**, 16 in (40 cm) tall, golden flowers; **'Baby Sun'** (syn. 'Sonnenkind'), 12 in (30 cm) tall, gold flowers; **'Sterntaler'**, 16 in (40 cm) tall, gold flowers, ray florets with bronze-red basal blotch. Zones 3–9.

Coreopsis rosea

↔ 12 in (30 cm) ↑ 24 in (60 cm)

Summer- to early autumn-flowering annual or short-lived perennial found in northeastern USA and southeastern Canada. Small compound leaves, sometimes with very narrow lobes. Flowerheads around 1 in (25 mm) wide on 4 in (10 cm) long stems, white to pale red ray florets, yellow disc florets. **'American Dream'**, to around 12 in (30 cm) tall, many small pink flowerheads. Zones 8–10.

Coreopsis 'Sunray' ★

↔ 12–16 in (30–40 cm)
↑ 20 in (50 cm)

Compact bushy plant with entire and pinnate foliage, bright green, leaflets often narrow. Glowing yellow double flowers from late spring. Often listed as a *C. grandiflora* cultivar. Zones 7–10.

Coreopsis tinctoria

↔ 16–24 in (40–60 cm)
↑ 4 ft (1.2 m)

Summer-flowering annual found over much of North America. Leaves usually narrow and entire, sometimes pinnate, to 4 in (10 cm) long. Many small flowerheads, ray florets yellow, reddening at base, disc florets red-brown. **'Mahogany Midget'**, 12 in (30 cm) tall, all-over red-brown flowerheads; **Quills and Thrills Series**, in-rolled (quilled) ray florets in range of red and yellow combinations; **'Roulette'**, red ray florets in-rolled to show yellow-buff undersides. Zones 6–10.

Coreopsis verticillata

↔ 16 in (40 cm) ↑ 36 in (90 cm)

Upright perennial from southeastern USA. Sticky doubly pinnate leaves, 3 leaflets per section, may be very narrow, to 2½ in (6 cm) long. Bright yellow flowerheads to 2 in (5 cm) wide, in summer. **'Golden Gain'**, 20 in (50 cm), narrow leaf segments, bright yellow flowers; **'Grandiflora'** (syn. 'Golden Shower'), 24 in (60 cm) tall, large bright yellow flowers; **'Moonbeam'**, 20 in (50 cm) tall, soft yellow flowers; **'Zagreb'**, 12 in (30 cm) tall, pale gold flowers. Zones 6–10.

CORNUS

DOGWOOD

There are about 65 species of deciduous and evergreen trees, shrubs, and herbs in this genus of the family Cornaceae, nearly all from eastern Asia, North America, and Europe. A few are ornamental, garden-grown for their autumn leaf color, colored winter stems or their branches covered in blankets of "flowers," composed of large petals or wide decorative bracts surrounding small insignificant flowers. Other species are bractless. The simple oval leaves are usually opposite. The fleshy fruits have stones.

CULTIVATION: They need sun or semi-shade, good drainage, and a fertile neutral to acid soil. Those grown for their winter stem color are best grown in full sun and cut back in early spring. Propagate the multi-stemmed species by layering of sucker growths, from hardwood cuttings taken in summer or autumn, or from seed cleaned and cold-stratified for at least 3 months. The large-bracted species can be raised from seed (also stratified), from half-hardened cuttings in summer, or by grafting.

Cornus alba

RED-BARKED DOGWOOD, TARTARIAN DOGWOOD

↔ 10 ft (3 m) ↑ 10 ft (3 m)

Deciduous spreading shrub, native of eastern Asia. Forms dense thickets. Blood red young stems in winter. Dark green oval leaves, colorful autumn tones. Clusters of creamy flowers in late spring. Small, white, blue-tinted fruits.**'Argenteomarginata'**, cream- to white-edged leaves; **'Aurea'**, light greenish gold foliage; **'Gouchaltii'**, white and red variegations; Ivory Halo/**'Bailhalo'**; **'Kesselringii'**, black-purple stems, red and purple autumn leaves; **'Sibirica'** ★, glowing coral red stems; **'Sibirica Variegata'**, deep green leaves edged with creamy white. Zones 4–9.

Cornus alba 'Argenteomarginata'

Cornus alternifolia

GREEN OSIER, PAGODA DOGWOOD

↔ 20 ft (6 m) ↑ 20 ft (6 m)

Native of eastern North America. Deciduous bushy shrub or small tree. Branches in irregular whorls, forming flat horizontal tiers. Tapering, pointed, mid-green leaves turn red and purple-red in autumn. Star-like whitish cream flowers appear in early summer. Small blue-black fruits. **'Argentea'** has white variegations on the leaves. Zones 3–9.

Cornus amomum

SILKY DOGWOOD

↔ 10 ft (3 m) ↑ 10 ft (3 m)

From North America. Vigorous, compact, deciduous shrub. Dark green leaves, turn red in autumn, reddish brown down on the undersurfaces, hang from purplish stems. Young shoots, purplish, downy. White flowers in late spring. Purplish fruits. Zones 5–9.

Cornus canadensis

BUNCHBERRY, CREEPING DOGWOOD

↔ 36 in (90 cm)
↑ 4–6 in (10–15 cm)

Found from Greenland to Alaska. Hardy, low, deciduous perennial, spreading by rhizomes. Whorls of ovate to lance-shaped leaves, vivid red autumn color. Large white bracts around flowerheads. Red edible fruit. Likes cool moist conditions. Zones 2–8.

Cornus capitata

BENTHAM'S CORNEL, HIMALAYAN DOGWOOD

↔ 30 ft (9 m) ↑ 30 ft (9 m)

Bushy evergreen or semi-evergreen tree from China and the Himalayas. Minute flowers, cream to lemon yellow sky-facing bracts in late spring–early summer. Pendent, rose to apricot, pink-tinted fruits. Leathery, oval, gray-green leaves, paler underneath. Tolerates sheltered coastal conditions. Zones 8–10.

Cornus controversa

GIANT DOGWOOD, TABLETOP DOGWOOD

↔ 50 ft (15 m) ↑ 60 ft (18 m)

Native of Japan and China. Large deciduous tree. Horizontally spreading branches, well-separated tiers. White, upturned, flattish flowerheads. Fruits blue-black. Oval pointed leaves, glossy dark green above, downy beneath, turn red and purple in autumn. Chalk and lime tolerant. **'Pagoda'**, abundant white flowers; **'Variegata'**, broad, streaked, creamy white margins on drooping leaves. Zones 5–8.

C

Cornus 'Eddie's White Wonder'

☼ ✱ ↔15 ft (4.5 m) ↕15 ft (4.5 m)
A hybrid between *C. florida* and *C. nuttallii*, deciduous upright tree or shrub, pendulous outer branches. Dramatic, large, white flowers in spring. Autumn foliage brilliant orange, red, and purple. Zones 5–9.

Cornus florida

FLOWERING DOGWOOD
☼/◐ ✱ ↔25 ft (8 m) ↕30 ft (9 m)
Native to eastern and central USA. Highly ornamental spreading tree. Leaves slightly twisted, oval, pointed, dark green, paler undersides, orange, red, yellow, and purple in autumn. Bracts white to pink in late spring–early summer. Berries red, remaining through winter. ***C. f.* subsp. *urbiniana***, from mountains of eastern Mexico, has yellow-pink bracts; ***C. f.* f. *rubra***, rosy pink bracts. ***C. f.* 'Apple Blossom'**, pale pink bracts; **'Cherokee Chief'**, dark rose red bracts; **'Pink Flame'**, pink-edged bracts. Zones 5–9.

Cornus kousa

CHINESE DOGWOOD, JAPANESE FLOWERING DOGWOOD, KOUSA DOGWOOD
☼ ✱ ↔15 ft (4.5 m) ↕25 ft (8 m)
From Japan, China, and Korea. Deciduous. Glossy wavy-edged leaves, oval and pointed, turn bronze-crimson in autumn. Profuse green flowers in summer. Creamy white bracts, edged with red. Pink- or red-tinted fruits. Grows poorly in shallow chalky soils. ***C. k.* var. *chinensis*** ★, paler smooth-edged leaves. Zones 5–8.

Cornus nuttallii

Cornus officinalis

Cornus florida

Cornus macrophylla

☼ ✱ ↔20 ft (6 m) ↕25 ft (8 m)
Deciduous tree from the Himalayas, China, and Japan. Glossy leaves, creamy white flowers, late summer. Blackish blue fruits. Zones 6–9.

Cornus mas

CORNELIAN CHERRY
☼ ✱ ↔20 ft (6 m) ↕25 ft (8 m)
Native of southern Europe, tolerates drought and exposure. Short-stemmed leaves, oval, pointed, shiny, deeply veined, mid-green, turn reddish purple in autumn. Flowers yellow, on the previous year's bare wood, from mid-winter to early spring. Kidney-shaped fruit. **'Aurea'**, yellow juvenile leaves; **'Aureoelegantissima'**, leaves with yellow and pink margins; **'Macrocarpa'**, large, glossy, red fruit; **'Variegata'**, leaves with white margins. Zones 5–9.

Cornus nuttallii

CANADIAN DOGWOOD, MOUNTAIN DOGWOOD
☼ ❄ ↔40 ft (12 m) ↕60 ft (18 m)
From northwestern USA and adjacent Canada. Oval leaves, dark green, turn yellow and scarlet in autumn. Flowers small; large, flat, irregular, white bracts, flushed with pink, in late spring and early autumn. Orange-red fruits. Grows poorly in shallow chalky soils. **'Gold Spot'**, as leaves mature, they become randomly splotched with patches of yellow. Zones 7–9.

Cornus officinalis

JAPANESE CORNELIAN CHERRY
☼ ✱ ↔15 ft (4.5 m) ↕15 ft (4.5 m)
Spreading deciduous shrub, similar to *C. mas*. Brown flaking bark. Brilliant yellow flowers, on bare stems, in late winter. Bright red edible fruits, richly colored autumn foliage. Zones 6–9.

Cornus, Stellar Series, Ruth Ellen/'Rutlan'

Cornus pumila

DWARF RED-TIPPED DOGWOOD
☼ ✱ ↔7 ft (2 m) ↕8 ft (2.4 m)
Deciduous, slow-growing, mound-forming shrub of unknown origin. White flowers, in large long-stemmed clusters, in summer. Zones 5–9.

Cornus sanguinea

BLOODWING DOGWOOD, COMMON DOGWOOD, EUROPEAN DOGWOOD
☼ ✱ ↔10 ft (3 m) ↕15 ft (4.5 m)
A native of Europe. Deciduous shrub. Red-green shoots. Bears white scented flowers in loose clusters, blue-black fruit. Red-purple autumn foliage. **'Midwinter Fire'**, bright red winter stems; **'Winter Beauty'** ★, red shoots in winter. Zones 6–9.

Cornus sericea

syn. *Cornus stolonifera*
AMERICAN DOGWOOD
☼ ✱ ↔7 ft (2 m) ↕6 ft (1.8 m)
Native of eastern North America. Deciduous suckering shrub. Oval to lance-shaped green leaves turn orangey red in autumn. White flowers in late spring–early summer are followed by green-tinged white fruit. ***C. s.* subsp. *baileyi*** (syn. *C. baileyi*), non-suckering downy shoots, reddish brown in winter, young leaves and flower stalks woolly. Cultivars include ***C. s.* 'Flaviramea'**, white star-shaped flowers, late spring–early summer; **'Isanti'**, dwarf form, abundant white flowers; **'Sunshine'**, striking yellow and green leaves. Zones 2–9.

Cornus Stellar Series

☼ ✱ ↔15 ft (4.5 m) ↕20 ft (6 m)
This series of *C. kousa* × *C. florida* hybrids was developed at Rutgers University in New Jersey, USA. Deciduous trees bear large flower bracts in spring, followed by red fruits. Autumn foliage bright red. Cultivars include: Aurora/**'Rutban'**; **'Constellation'** (syn. 'Rutcan'); Ruth Ellen/**'Rutlan'**. Zones 5–9.

Corokia × *virgata* 'Yellow Wonder'

COROKIA

This small genus of 4 evergreen shrubs is one of just two genera in the silver leaf (Argophyllaceae) family. Three species are native to New Zealand; the fourth is a rare Australian species. The habit and leaf form vary between the species, but all bear small starry flowers in early summer, followed by orange, yellow, or red berries. CULTIVATION: These shrubs will grow in sun or semi-shade and in soils with a reasonable level of fertility. The site should be well drained. Both *C. cotoneaster* and *C. macrocarpa* are tolerant of dry conditions. Light pruning will maintain a compact shape. Propagation of the species is from seed, which is best sown fresh, or from half-hardened cuttings taken in spring. The cultivars are propagated from cuttings only.

Corokia buddlejoides

KOROKIO
☼/◐ ❄ ↔7 ft (2 m) ↕10 ft (3 m)
From the northern North Island of New Zealand. Erect slender habit. Leaves lance-shaped, leathery, olive green above, silvery gray beneath. Small yellow flowers. Berries bright to dark red or almost black. Zones 8–10.

Corokia cotoneaster

WIRE NETTING BUSH
☼/◐ ❄ ↔10 ft (3 m) ↕10 ft (3 m)
From New Zealand. Tangled wiry branches, silvery sheen when young. Sparse foliage. Starry yellow flowers. Red to yellow berries. Good hedging plant when clipped. Zones 8–11.

Corokia macrocarpa

☼ ❄ ↔10 ft (3 m) ↕12 ft (3.5 m)
Native to the Chatham Islands of New Zealand. Shrub or small tree. Dark green, leathery, lance-shaped leaves, with silvery undersides. Flowers yellow. Red berries. Good for dry sites. Zones 8–10.

Corokia × *virgata*

☼ ❄ ↔ 6 ft (1.8 m) ↑ 6 ft (1.8 m)

A natural hybrid of *C. buddlejoides* and *C. cotoneaster*. Cultivars form well-branched shrubs, with different leaf colors, more showy displays of berries. **'Bronze King'**, bronze foliage; **'Cheesemanii'**, small dark green leaves; **'Frosted Chocolate'**, chocolate brown leaves; **'Red Wonder'** ★ and **'Yellow Wonder'**, starry yellow flowers and red or yellow berries. Zones 8–10.

CORONILLA

There are about 20 species of annuals, perennials, and shrubs, some evergreen and some deciduous, in this genus in the pea-flower subfamily of the legume (Fabaceae) family. Native to Europe, Africa, and Asia, their habitat ranges from open woodland to dry scrub and grassland. *C. valentina* grows on cliffs, and is useful for erosion control. The leaves of *Coronilla* are usually pinnate; pea-like flowers are borne in umbels, with some species being fragrant.

CULTIVATION: They need shelter from cold winds and winter frosts, and do best in full sun in well-drained moderately fertile soil. Propagate by cuttings in summer or autumn, or from freshly ripened seed.

Coronilla valentina

☼ ❄ ↔ 5 ft (1.5 m) ↑ 2–5 ft (0.6–1.5 m)

Native to southern Portugal, Spain, and southern Europe to Croatia. Evergreen shrub. Bright green leaves, up to 13 egg-shaped leaflets. Bears bright golden yellow fragrant flowers in late winter–summer, again in autumn. Narrow seed pods about 2 in (5 cm) long. ***C. v.* subsp. *glauca*,** more compact, leaves more blue-green, flowers may be lighter yellow. **'Citrina'**, pale yellow blooms. Zones 9–10.

CORREA

A member of the rue (Rutaceae) family, this is an Australian genus of 11 species, all of which hybridize readily. Often found in cool, moist, shaded positions, some are also able to tolerate coastal situations in full sun. Handsome evergreen shrubs, *Correa* species respond well to cultivation. Most species flower from winter to spring. Some have bell-shaped flowers; others are tubular with protruding stamens.

CULTIVATION: They prefer friable, well-drained, fertile loams. Not recommended for hot humid summer climates. Tip pruning immediately after flowering will improve plant form and density.

Correa alba

☼/◐ ❄ ↔ 6 ft (1.8 m) ↑ 3 ft (0.9 m)

From coastal southern Australia. Vigorous evergreen shrub. Attractive green leaves, with round, fragrant, furry undersurfaces. Small, white, starry flowers from winter–spring. Salt and drought tolerant, this species grows best in well-drained sandy loam. Zones 8–10.

Correa backhouseana

☼ ❄ ↔ 6 ft (1.8 m) ↑ 6 ft (1.8 m)

From Tasmania, Australia. Dense evergreen shrub. Leaves oval, dark green. Cream-green flowers with golden brown edges, winter–spring. Tolerates front-line coastal situations. Zones 8–9.

Correa baeuerlenii

CHEF'S-CAP CORREA

☼/◐ ❄ ↔ 6 ft (1.8 m) ↑ 6 ft (1.8 m)

From New South Wales, Australia. Evergreen shrub, pendulous flowers, usually greenish yellow, distinctive "chef's cap," in autumn–spring. Likes cool, moist, protected areas. Zones 8–10.

Correa pulchella ★

☼/◐ ❄ ↔ 3 ft (0.9 m) ↑ 3 ft (0.9 m)

Small evergreen shrub from South Australia. Leaves smooth, elliptical to lance-shaped. Tubular red, salmon pink, or pink flowers from autumn–spring. Zones 8–10.

Coronilla valentina subsp. *glauca*

Correa backhouseana

Correa reflexa

NATIVE FUCHSIA

☼/◐ ❄ ↔ 1–7 ft (0.3–2 m) ↑ 2–6 ft (0.6–1.8 m)

Tidy but variable shrub from Queensland and southern Australia. Leaves can be oval, narrow, or heart-shaped, and smooth to rough and hairy. Tubular, pendulous, flowers, rich red with green or yellow tips, in spring. **'Fat Fred'** ★, inflated red flowers with greenish yellow tips. Zones 8–10.

Correa Hybrid Cultivars

◐ ❄ ↔ 2–4 ft (0.6–1.2 m) ↑ 18 in–6 ft (45 cm–1.8 m)

Several cultivars and hybrids of uncertain origin have become popular with gardeners. Compact and heavy flowering. **'Canberra Bells'**, compact, yellow-tipped red flowers, named for the centenary of Canberra in 2013; **'Dusky Bells'** ★, deep dusky pink to soft red flowers; **'Ivory Bells'**, white to cream flowers; **'Mannii'**, long, tubular, red flowers; **'Marian's Marvel'**, very pendulous clusters of pink flowers, green at base; **'Ray's Tangerine'**, soft orange flowers. Zones 9–10.

CORTADERIA

PAMPAS GRASS

This genus of about 25 species of grasses belongs to the Poaceae family. With the exception of one New Guinea species, *Cortaderia* are native to South America and New Zealand, where they grow in a range of habitats from grassy plains to mountains. They are dense tussock-forming grasses growing to 10 ft (3 m) or more. Their long, stiff, flat leaves are crowded at the base, and the leaf margins range from rough to very sharp. In flower they are a stunning sight, with tall, showy, erect or arching plumes of tiny flowers that are white, pale pink, or pale gold.

Correa, Hybrid Cultivar, 'Dusky Bells'

CULTIVATION: Most *Cortaderia* species are at least frost hardy, and can be grown as lawn specimens, in the garden border, by water, and for low shelter or hedging. Grow in a sunny situation in any well-drained reasonably fertile soil. Cut or burn out dead material annually. Propagate from seed or by division.

Cortaderia richardii

TOETOE GRASS, TOITOI

☼ ❄ ↔ 2–3 ft (0.6–0.9 m) ↑ 4–10 ft (1.2–3 m)

Clump-forming tussock-like grass, native to New Zealand. Long, narrow, arching, strap-like, soft green leaves, with sharply serrated edges and shiny undersides. Tall arching plumes of pale yellow-gold, usually drooping flowers, carried on long stalks, up to 10 ft (3 m) long, extending beyond the leaves, from early summer to autumn. Zones 7–9.

Cortaderia selloana

syns *Arundo selloana, Cortaderia argentea*

PAMPAS GRASS

☼ ❄ ↔ 4–6 ft (1.2–1.8 m) ↑ 5–25 ft (1.5–8 m)

Large durable grass from southern South America. Narrow, arching, rough-surfaced leaves, forming dense fountain-like clumps. Silvery white oblong flower panicles, to 4 ft (1.2 m) long, tinged red or purple, in autumn. Regarded as a weed in Australia, New Zealand, and California, USA. **'Albolineata'** (syn. 'Silver Stripe'), compact, slow-growing, with white-edged leaves; **'Aureolineata'** (syn. 'Gold Band'), hardy, compact, with leaves broadly edged with rich yellow, later deep gold; **'Bertinii'**, dwarf form, to 3 ft (0.9 m); **'Pumila'** (dwarf pampas grass), hardy dwarf form, up to 3–4 ft (0.9–1.2 m), narrow bluish green foliage; **'Rosea'**, long plumes tinged pink; **'Sunningdale Silver'**, sturdy, large, wind resistant, with dense white plumes to 12 ft (3.5 m); **'Violacea'**, flower panicles tinted violet. Zones 7–11.

Cortaderia richardii

Corybas pruinosus

CORYBAS

HELMET ORCHID

This deciduous orchid (Orchidaceae) family genus consists of about 100 temperate species from Southeast Asia to Australia, the Pacific Islands, and New Zealand. Many of the Australian representatives are known as helmet orchids, and are pollinated by fungus gnats. Most of these small-flowered single-leafed species occur in heavily shaded moist areas in mountain forests, often in association with sphagnum moss. The solitary flowers are sensitive to minor variations in humidity, and will quickly collapse if the air becomes too dry.

CULTIVATION: There are a number of colony-forming *Corybas* species that are relatively easy to cultivate, bring into flower, and multiply, as long as their basic requirements are met. Two of the most important aspects are high humidity and cool temperatures. They are best grown in a well-drained mix containing a high proportion of peat moss (for moisture) and coarse sand (for drainage). They become dormant in summer and revert to small, white, pea-sized tubers; at this time the pots should be allowed to dry out. They are best repotted every year or two, with the dormant tubers repositioned 1¼ in (30 mm) below the soil surface. Some *Corybas* species can be grown in terrariums. Most flower in autumn and winter.

Corybas pruinosus

↔ 1–1¼ in (25–30 mm)
↑ ½–1½ in (12–35 mm)

From coastal New South Wales, Australia. Flowers, dark red markings. Blooms in winter only a few weeks after the ground-hugging leaf emerges from dormancy. Zones 10–11.

CORYDALIS

While many of the 300-odd species of annuals and perennials in this poppy (Papaveraceae) family have long been cultivated, *Corydalis* boomed in popularity in the late 1980s, when the blue-flowered *C. flexuosa* and its cultivars became widely available.

Corydalis elata

Mainly confined to the northern temperate zones, the perennials spread by rhizomes or tubers to form clumps of ferny, often blue-green foliage. Their flowers are borne in racemes and are tubular, with 4 tiny petals and a long spur. The flowers are showy, combining well with the delicate foliage. The name comes from the Greek *korudallis* (lark), because the spurred flower resembles the bird's foot.

CULTIVATION: Mostly very hardy, preferring temperate climates with distinct seasons. Woodland or rockery conditions are best, with moist, cool, humus-rich, well-drained soil. If soil remains moist, they will grow in full sun, though part-shade is preferable. Propagate by division or from seed.

Corydalis cashmeriana

↔ 12–32 in (30–80 cm)
↑ 10 in (25 cm)

Late spring–summer-flowering perennial from the Himalayas. Bright green ferny foliage with leaflets to 1 in (25 mm) long. Bright blue flowers, conspicuously spurred, ½–1 in (12–25 mm) long, in racemes of up to 8 blooms. Zones 5–9.

Corydalis cava

↔ 6 in (15 cm) ↑ 6 in (15 cm)

Perennial from central Europe. Hollow tuber, and lacks basal foliage. Leaves dissected, 2 per stem. Violet or white flowers borne in racemes of 10 to 20 in early spring. Zones 6–9.

Corydalis cheilanthifolia

↔ 20–40 in (50–100 cm)
↑ 10 in (25 cm)

Perennial found in central China. Loose rosettes of short-stemmed, ferny, olive green leaves up to 18 in (45 cm) long. In spring, racemes of bright yellow flowers, ½ in (12 mm) long, on stems up to 18 in (45 cm) tall. Zones 6–9.

Corydalis turtschaninovii

Corydalis elata

↔ 20–24 in (50–60 cm)
↑ 16–20 in (40–50 cm)

Perennial native to China. Bushy upright habit, blue-green foliage. Blue flowers continue into summer. Flowers mildly fragrant. Zones 5–10.

Corydalis flexuosa

↔ 12–32 in (30–80 cm)
↑ 12 in (30 cm)

Perennial from southwestern China. Blue-green leaves die after flowering. Bright blue flowers, mildly scented, spurred, to 1 in (25 mm) long, spring to early summer. **'Bronze Leaf'**, leaves purplish, especially at tips, light blue flowers; **'China Blue'**, deep blue flowers; **'Père David'**, bright blue flowers to 2 in (5 cm) long; **'Purple Leaf'**, deep blue flowers, purplish foliage. Zones 5–9.

Corydalis nobilis

↔ 16–32 in (40–80 cm)
↑ 24–32 in (60–80 cm)

Perennial from northern China and Siberia. Coarse, ferny blue-green leaves up to 12 in (30 cm) long. In spring, racemes of short-spurred pale yellow flowers, 1 in (25 mm) long, with purple-brown tips. Zones 5–9.

Corydalis solida

FUMEWORT

↔ 8–12 in (20–30 cm)
↑ 10 in (25 cm)

Perennial originating from temperate Eurasia, with paired, deeply divided, trifoliate leaves. Racemes of up to 20 flowers in spring, graduating in color from lavender through pale red to purple with darker tips. **'George Baker'**, deep pink to red flowers. Zones 5–9.

Corydalis tomentella

↔ 12–20 in (30–50 cm)
↑ 12 in (30 cm)

Chinese perennial with ferny, down-covered, gray-green leaves. In late spring–summer, upright racemes of bright yellow flowers with yellow-green tips. Zones 6–9.

Corydalis wilsonii

Corydalis turtschaninovii

↔ 16–32 in (40–80 cm)
↑ 16–20 in (40–50 cm)

Perennial from northern China and Siberia. Blue-green ferny or aquilegia-like leaves. Bright blue flowers in spring. Extracts of the tubers widely used in herbal remedies, mainly for their analgesic properties. Zones 5–9.

Corydalis wilsonii

↔ 12–32 in (30–80 cm)
↑ 12–16 in (30–40 cm)

Chinese perennial with bright green to bronze-green, finely divided, ferny leaves to 4 in (10 cm) long. In spring, small racemes of bright yellow flowers with yellow-green tips. Zones 7–9.

CORYLOPSIS

Native to the eastern Himalayas, China, Taiwan, and Japan, this genus in the family Hamamelidaceae contains about 10 species of deciduous shrubs and small trees. The young branches are downy; the egg-shaped blunt-toothed leaves are light to dark green and appear in spring after the fragrant yellow flowers. The fruit, a woody capsule about ½ in (12 mm) wide, contains 2 shiny black seeds.

CULTIVATION: All prefer acid soil and need moist, fertile, well-drained woodland conditions. Propagate from freshly ripened seed in autumn, protected against winter frosts, or take softwood cuttings in summer.

Corylopsis glabrescens

FRAGRANT WINTER-HAZEL

↔ 15 ft (4.5 m) ↑ 15 ft (4.5 m)

Native to Korea and Japan. Open spreading shrub. Leaves oval and dark green, heart-shaped base, pointed tip, blue-green undersides, turn yellow in autumn. Pendent racemes of light yellow fragrant flowers, reddish green bracts, in spring. Zones 6–9.

Corylopsis pauciflora

BUTTERCUP WINTER-HAZEL

↔ 8 ft (2.4 m) ↑ 8 ft (2.4 m)

Native to Taiwan and Japan. Leaves 3 in (8 cm) long, bronze in spring, maturing to bright green. Pendent racemes of fragrant yellow flowers before foliage in early spring. Hairless fruit in autumn. Zones 7–9.

Corylopsis sinensis ★
syn. *Corylopsis willmottiae*
CHINESE WINTER-HAZEL
↔ 15 ft (4.5 m) ↕ 15 ft (4.5 m)
Erect spreading shrub, native to China. Oblong or slightly egg-shaped leaves, green above, blue-green below, to 5 in (12 cm) long. Pendent racemes of yellow flowers, velvety bracts, in mid-spring–early summer. *C. s.* var. *clavescens* f. *veitchiana* (syn. *C. veitchiana)*, more upright, smooth leaf stems, broader pale lemon flowers. Zones 6–9.

Corylopsis spicata
SPIKE WINTER-HAZEL
↔ 10 ft (3 m) ↕ 6 ft (1.8 m)
Native to Japan, spreading shrub. Egg-shaped tapering leaves, dark green above, grayish below. Pendent racemes of bright yellow flowers, red anthers, felted floral bracts, in spring. Zones 6–9.

CORYLUS
Known as filberts, hazelnuts, cobnuts, and cobs, there are about 15 species of deciduous suckering shrubs and trees in this genus in the birch (Betulaceae) family, some garden grown. The flowers, both the long flouncing male catkins ("lambs' tails") and the inconspicuous female flowers, appear on last year's bare wood, the same plant carrying both sexes. Catkins are usually visible by late winter and fluff out in spring, when the female flowers appear. The husked edible nuts ripen in autumn. CULTIVATION: They are easily grown in rich moist soils in full sun or part-shade. Propagate from detached suckers, mounding up soil beforehand to promote root growth. Early summer softwood cuttings are also used, treated with hormone powder. Seeds require cold stratification for about 3 months for germination. Nut production may require a different cultivar for pollination.

Corylopsis glabrescens, in spring

Corylus americana
syn. *Corylus calyculata*
AMERICAN FILBERT, AMERICAN HAZELNUT
↔ 10 ft (3 m) ↕ 10 ft (3 m)
Deciduous shrub from eastern North America. Similar in habit and form to *C. avellana*, but oval leaves larger. Nuts enclosed in long husks. Catkins can be 3 in (8 cm) long. Zones 4–8.

Corylus avellana
COBNUT, EUROPEAN HAZELNUT
↔ 15 ft (4.5 m) ↕ 15 ft (4.5 m)
Native of Europe, western Asia, North Africa. Thicket-like shrub. Coarse mid-green leaves turn yellow in autumn. Long pale yellow catkins in winter on bare branches; red female flowers in early spring. Nuts half covered in ragged husks. 'Aurea', greenish yellow leaves; 'Contorta', dense slow-growing shrub of twisted branches. Zones 4–8.

Corylus colurna
syn. *Corylus byzantina*
TURKISH HAZEL
↔ 25 ft (8 m) ↕ 80 ft (24 m)
Native of western Asia. Leaves veined, bluntly pointed, lightly lobed, turn yellow in autumn. Yellow catkins in late winter. Distinctive deeply fringed husks, cork-like corrugations on bark. Thrives in continental climates—hot summers, cold winters. Zones 4–8.

Corylus cornuta
syn. *Corylus rostrata*
BEAKED FILBERT
↔ 10 ft (3 m) ↕ 10 ft (3 m)
Deciduous shrub from North America. Erect stems. Oval, lobed, serrated leaves. Catkins reach 1¼ in (30 mm) in length. Nuts with long tubular husks. *C. c.* var. *californica* grows to about 25 ft (8 m) high, bears shorter husks, longer catkins. Zones 4–8.

Corylus colurna

Corylus americana

Corylus avellana 'Contorta'

Corylus maxima
FILBERT
↔ 15 ft (4.5 m) ↕ 30 ft (9 m)
Native of southern and eastern Europe and western Asia. Vigorous bushy shrub or small tree. Leaves large, heart-shaped, mid-green, new growth covered in sticky hairs. Large brown nuts, elongated lobed husks. 'Purpurea', young leaves coppery purple tint, fade to leathery greenish purple in summer. Zones 5–9.

CORYNOCARPUS
The 4 species of this genus in the family Corynocarpaceae are tall, evergreen, forest trees. They are found on some western Pacific islands and in New Zealand and Australia. Their simple leathery leaves are arranged alternately on the branches, and they bear tiny flowers in terminal panicles. These are followed by smooth-skinned plum-like fruits. CULTIVATION: The New Zealand *Corynocarpus* species, *C. laevigata*, is the one that is usually seen in cultivation. It requires a warm site in a rich soil with adequate moisture, particularly when it is young. It should be propagated from seed, which is best sown fresh.

Corynocarpus laevigata
KARAKA
↔ 25 ft (8 m) ↕ 50 ft (15 m)
Forest tree, found throughout both islands of New Zealand. Densely foliaged, with large, leathery, oblong leaves of a glossy dark green. Oval orange fruits ripen in autumn. The kernels of the fruits are poisonous. Zones 9–11.

Corynocarpus laevigata

CORYPHA
This group of tall erect members of the palm (Arecaceae) family has stout trunks and very large fan-shaped fronds. It comprises about 6 species, occurring in tropical regions from Asia to Australia. After 30 to 50 years a mature palm produces a burst of millions of individual flowers at the top of the trunk; when the fruits that follow ripen, the whole palm dies. They make outstanding features for large gardens and parks, and in tropical countries the leaves, fruits, and stems have traditional uses. CULTIVATION: In subtropical and tropical climates, grow in well-drained organically rich soil with regular water during the warmer months. Propagate from fresh seed.

Corypha umbraculifera ★
TALIPOT PALM
↔ 35–50 ft (10–15 m)
↕ 40–80 ft (12–24 m)
From Sri Lanka and India. Giant palm with fan-shaped fronds to 17 ft (5 m) across. The spectacular inflorescences, 20–25 ft (6–8 m) long, are the largest of any palm. Zones 11–12.

Corypha utan
syn. *Corypha elata*
BURI PALM, FAN-LEAFED CABBAGE PALM
↔ 12–15 ft (3.5–4.5 m)
↕ 50–75 ft (15–23 m)
Widely cultivated slow-growing palm from Bengal, Myanmar, the Philippines, Indonesia, and northern Australia. Trunk spirally ringed and furrowed. Crown of massive, rounded, fan-shaped fronds, to 20 ft (6 m), 80 to 100 segments, with black toothed margins. Round fruit, greenish to brown. Huge plume, about 10–25 ft (3–8 m) long, of strong-smelling white flowers. Zones 11–12.

C

COSMOS

MEXICAN ASTER

This genus of the daisy (Asteraceae) family is found in the Americas from the tropics to the warm temperate zones. It comprises 26 species, including both annuals and perennials, of which 3 are commonly grown. The common annual cosmos *(C. bipinnatus)* has fine feathery foliage and showy, large, wide-open flowers with 8 ray florets. It is available in many colors and in varieties, from dwarf to 6 ft (1.8 m) tall. The common perennial species have broader leaves and smaller flowers than the annual *C. bipinnatus*, but are interesting for their colors and scents. Native Americans treated the young tops of *C. sulphureus* as a vegetable.

CULTIVATION: Annuals should be planted out only when all danger of frost has past; perennials tolerate occasional moderate frosts. Plant in full sun with moist, well-drained soil. Do not overfeed or the plants may become top-heavy; they may need staking anyway. Propagate the annuals from seed and the perennials from basal cuttings.

Cosmos atrosanguineus ★

CHOCOLATE COSMOS

☼/◐ ❄ ↔ 20–40 in (50–100 cm) ↑ 12–24 in (30–60 cm)

Summer-flowering Mexican perennial. Dark green pinnate leaves to 6 in (15 cm) long, segments sometimes serrated. Long-stemmed, 1–1¾ in (25–40 mm) wide, dark red to almost black flowerheads. As its common name suggests, this species has a distinctive chocolatey fragrance, sometimes varying to vanilla. Zones 8–10.

Cosmos bipinnatus

☼/◐ ❄ ↔ 2–4 ft (0.6–1.2 m) ↑ 4–7 ft (1.2–2 m)

Annual native to Mexico and southern USA. Ferny pinnate leaves to over 4 in (10 cm) long, with very fine narrow leaflets. Flowerheads large and long-stemmed. Pink to lavender flowers in the wild, but many garden forms and seedling strains. **'Candystripe'**, 24 in (60 cm) tall, white with red stripes; **'Dazzler'**, 4 ft (1.2 m) tall, bright crimson; **'Double Click Cranberries'**, 3 ft (0.9 m) tall, fully double, deep pink; **'Double Take'**, 4 ft (1.2 m) tall, semi-double, pink and white; **'Picotee'**, 30 in (75 cm) tall, white to pale pink flushed and edged deep pinkish red; **Sensation Series**, 3–4 ft (1–1.2 m) tall, in wide color range, sold mixed or in single colors such as the red **'Sensation Radiance'**; **Sonata Series**, 24–36 in (60–90cm) tall, simple, daisy-like flowers in pink and white shades, single colors such as **'Sonata White'** or mixed; **'Sweet Dreams'**, 30–36 in (75–90 cm), soft pink flowers with darker center. Zones 7–11.

Cosmos sulphureus

☼/◐ ❄ ↔ 32 in–4 ft (80 cm–1.2 m) ↑ 5–7 ft (1.5–2 m)

Annual found from northern South America to Mexico. Pinnate, sometimes faintly hairy leaves to 14 in (35 cm) long. Flowerheads deep yellow through orange to red. Several seedling strains. **'Bright Lights'**, to 4 ft (1.2 m) tall, a mix of yellow, orange and red shades; **'Cosmic Yellow'**, to 24 in (60 cm) tall, bright yellow single and semi-double flowers; **Ladybird Series**, 12–16 in (30–40 cm) tall, pale yellow to deep red, available individually or mixed; **'Sunny Red'**, 12–16 in (30–40 cm) tall, bright red. Zones 7–11.

Cosmos sulphureus 'Cosmic Yellow'

COTINUS

SMOKE BUSH

This genus contains 3 species of deciduous trees or shrubs found in North America and across southern Europe to central China. It belongs to the same family (Anacardiaceae) as *Rhus* and, like members of that genus, has been known to cause contact dermatitis. *Cotinus* are valuable garden plants, and have a long season of interest. In summer myriads of tiny flowers are borne on long panicles, giving a hazy effect to the plant; hence the common name of smoke bush. In autumn their broadly oval leaves deepen in color to shades of red, yellow, and orange.

CULTIVATION: Smoke bushes will grow in a wide range of soils and climatic conditions but are best in a well-drained site in full sun. As with many trees from cool-temperate climates, richer autumn colors are achieved in areas where winters are cold. Prune to remove dead wood or to shorten long straggly branches. Propagation is from seed sown in autumn or from hardwood cuttings taken in late summer.

Cotinus coggygria

syn. *Rhus cotinus*

EURASIAN SMOKEBUSH, SMOKE BUSH, VENETIAN SUMACH

☼ ✱ ↔ 15 ft (4.5 m) ↑ 15 ft (4.5 m)

Found from southern Europe to central China. A rounded bush with broadly oval leaves. Numerous plume-like panicles, tiny bronze-pink flowers, fading to grayish purple in summer. Cultivars with purplish leaves include: **'Royal Purple'** ★, dark red-purple leaves; **'Velvet Cloak'**, deep reddish purple leaves, turning entirely red in autumn. Zones 6–10.

Cotinus 'Flame'

syn. *Cotinus coggygria 'Flame'*

☼ ❄ ↔ 17–20 ft (5–6 m) ↑ 17–20 ft (5–6 m)

A hybrid cross between *C. coggygria* and *C. obovatus,* resembling the first parent in leaf form but similar to the second in its somewhat tree-like habit. Large, fluffy, gray flowerheads in summer and brilliant scarlet autumn color. Zones 6–10.

Cotinus 'Grace'

☼ ✱ ↔ 15 ft (4.5 m) ↑ 20 ft (6 m)

Hybrid between *C. coggygria* 'Velvet Cloak' and *C. obovatus*. Reddish purple leaves, flower plumes grayish, enhancing the hazy smoke-like effect. Zones 5–10.

Cotinus obovatus

syns *Cotinus americanus, C. cotinoides, Rhus cotinoides*

AMERICAN SMOKE TREE, CHITTAMWOOD

☼ ✱ ↔ 20 ft (6 m) ↑ 30 ft (9 m)

Native to central and southern USA. Foliage colors brilliantly in autumn. Similar to *C. coggygria*, but flowering display less spectacular. Tree-like, broad conical form. Zones 5–10.

COTONEASTER

From the rose (Rosaceae) family, a genus of about 200 species of evergreen, semi-evergreen, or deciduous shrubs and trees from the northern temperate areas. Leaves rounded to lance-shaped, simple, smooth-edged and arranged alternately. Small flowers are white, sometimes flushed pink or red, with 5 petals, and are borne singly or in cymes. They are followed by red-black or red fruits with rather dry flesh and 2 to 5 nutlets. Grown for their profuse flowers and fruit, they can also be used as hedging plants and as attractive specimens.

CULTIVATION: Cotoneasters grow well in moderately fertile well-drained soil. Dwarf evergreens and deciduous plants fruit better in full sun, while taller evergreens grow well in part-shade. In exposed situations they may need protection from cold drying winds. Propagate by taking half-hardened cuttings of evergreen species in late summer, and of deciduous species in early summer.

Cotoneaster adpressus

CREEPING COTONEASTER

☼ ✱ ↔ 5 ft (1.5 m) ↑ 12 in (30 cm)

From western China. A low-growing deciduous shrub, which develops roots wherever it touches the ground. Egg-shaped leaves turn red in autumn. White flowers with reddish petal edges. Bright red fruit in autumn. Zones 4–9.

Cotinus 'Grace'

Cotoneaster apiculatus

CRANBERRY COTONEASTER

☼ ✱ ↔8 ft (2.4 m) ↑3 ft (0.9 m)

Deciduous shrub, native to Sichuan Province in China. Shiny mid-green leaves, rounded, short points, wavy edges, slightly hairy undersurfaces, turn red in autumn. Solitary red to white flowers in summer. Red fruit. Zones 4–9.

Cotoneaster atropurpureus

☼/◐ ✱ ↔8–10 ft (2.4–3 m)
↑20–40 in (50–100 cm)

Often confused with *C. horizontalis,* with its similar herringbone branch arrangement and semi-prostrate habit. Small white flowers in spring, followed by little red berries and brightly colored autumn leaves. '**Variegatus**' has white-edged leaves that turn red and pink in autumn. Zones 4–9.

Cotoneaster conspicuus

syn. *Cotoneaster conspicuus var. decorus*

☼ ✱ ↔8 ft (2.4 m) ↑5 ft (1.5 m)

Native to western China. Densely branched, mound-forming, evergreen or semi-evergreen shrub. Deep green lance-shaped to oblong leaves, spirally arranged. White flowers, sometimes grouped in cymes, in summer. Glossy red fruit. Zones 6–9.

Cotoneaster dammeri

syn. *Cotoneaster humifusus*

☼ ✱ ↔6 ft (1.8 m) ↑8 in (20 cm)

Native to the Hubei region of China. Prostrate evergreen shrub. The shiny green oblong leaves are strongly veined. White flowers, solitary or grouped in cymes, are borne in early summer, followed by scarlet fruit in autumn. Zones 5–10.

Cotoneaster adpressus

Cotoneaster franchetii

Cotoneaster dielsianus

☼ ✱ ↔8 ft (2.4 m) ↑8 ft (2.4 m)

Native to China. Loosely branching shrub, semi-evergreen in milder climates but deciduous in colder regions. The leathery egg-shaped leaves have hairy undersides, and develop red coloring in autumn. Small cymes of up to 7 pinkish white flowers appear in summer, followed by glossy deep red fruit. Zones 5–10.

Cotoneaster franchetii

☼ ✱ ↔10 ft (3 m) ↑10 ft (3 m)

Native to western China. Evergreen, sometimes semi-evergreen, erect shrub. Lustrous, bright green, oval leaves with felty undersides. Generous cymes of pink-tinted white flowers, in summer. Egg-shaped orange-red fruit. Zones 6–10.

Cotoneaster frigidus

HIMALAYAN TREE COTONEASTER

☼ ✱ ↔30 ft (9 m) ↑30 ft (9 m)

Species native to the Himalayas. Deciduous large shrub or small tree with peeling bark. Egg-shaped dull green leaves have wavy edges. Sprays of profuse white flowers are seen throughout summer. Fruit is red. '**Cornubia**' (syn. *C.* × *watereri* 'Cornubia'), dark green lance-shaped leaves turn rich bronze in winter; '**Fructu Luteo**', creamy yellow fruit; '**Notcutt's Variety**', large leaves, dark green in color. Zones 6–9.

Cotoneaster frigidus 'Cornubia'

Cotoneaster serotinus

Cotoneaster horizontalis

ROCK COTONEASTER, ROCKSPRAY COTONEASTER

☼ ✱ ↔5 ft (1.5 m) ↑3 ft (0.9 m)

From western China. Deciduous, herringbone-like branching. Elliptical to rounded tiny leaves, dark green, glossy, color in autumn. Flesh pink flowers in late spring. Scarlet fruit. Zones 4–9.

Cotoneaster 'Hybridus Pendulus'

☼ ✱ ↔6 ft (1.8 m) ↑6 ft (1.8 m)

Of garden origin. Evergreen to semi-evergreen shrub, with elliptical deep green leaves. Cymes of white flowers in summer. Grafted onto an upright stem of tall-growing species, makes a decorative standard; fruits resemble a red waterfall in winter. Zones 6–9.

Cotoneaster lacteus

syn. *Cotoneaster parneyi*

☼ ✱ ↔12 ft (3.5 m) ↑12 ft (3.5 m)

Evergreen shrub from China. Arching branches. Leathery oval leaves, dark green above, felty beneath, deep veins. Creamy white flowers in summer. Red fruit persist in winter. Zones 6–11.

Cotoneaster linearifolius

syn. *Cotoneaster microphyllus var. thymifolius of gardens*

☼ ✱ ↔3 ft (0.9 m) ↑3 ft (0.9 m)

Native of Nepal. Dwarf evergreen shrub. Tiny, narrow, glossy, dark green leaves with gray undersides. Pink buds open to white flowers in early summer. Dark pink fruit. Zones 6–9.

Cotoneaster lucidus

HEDGE COTONEASTER

☼/◐ ✱ ↔6–10 ft (1.8–3 m)
↑6–10 ft (1.8–3 m)

Native to Siberia and northern Asia. Upright, round-topped, deciduous shrub, slender spreading branches. Leaves dark green in summer, yellow and red in autumn. Small pink-white flowers in late spring, followed by round blue-black fruit. Zones 3–7.

Cotoneaster microphyllus

☼ ✱ ↔3 ft (0.9 m) ↑3 ft (0.9 m)

Native to the Himalayas. Prostrate evergreen shrub, dense mound. Thick leaves, egg-shaped, glossy deep green, hairy coating beneath when young. Tiny white flowers in spring–summer. Crimson fruit. Zones 5–10.

Cotoneaster multiflorus

☼ ✱ ↔15 ft (4.5 m) ↑15 ft (4.5 m)

From northwestern China. Deciduous shrub or small tree. Arching branches with weeping tips, relatively thin hairless leaves. White flowers, red fruit. Zones 5–9.

Cotoneaster salicifolius

syn. *Cotoneaster floccosus of gardens*

☼ ✱ ↔15 ft (4.5 m) ↑15 ft (4.5 m)

Naturally occurring in China. Variable species with slim, graceful, bowed branches. Lance-shaped deeply veined leaves, pointed, white felty undersides. Large corymbs in summer. Round, red, persistent fruit. '**Exburyensis**', white flowers in early summer, followed by pinkish yellow fruit in winter; '**Herbstfeuer**' (syn. 'Autumn Fire'), low spreading habit, red fruit; '**Repens**', a prostrate form; '**Rothschildianus**' (syn. *C.* × *watereri* 'Rothschildianus'), vigorous, evergreen, spreading shrub, clusters of white flowers in summer, followed by lemon yellow fruit. Zones 6–10.

Cotoneaster serotinus

syn. *Cotoneaster glaucophyllus var. serotinus*

☼ ✱ ↔12 ft (3.5 m) ↑30 ft (9 m)

Native to western China. Large evergreen shrub or tree. Egg-shaped leaves with dark green upper surfaces and gray felty hairs beneath, becoming hairless with age. White flowers in large corymbs, in summer. Bright red fruit. Zones 6–11.

Cotoneaster simonsii

☼ ✱ ↔6 ft (1.8 m) ↑8 ft (2.4 m)

Found naturally in northern India and the eastern Himalayas. Deciduous or semi-evergreen shrub. Egg-shaped deep green leaves, paler with bristly hair on the undersurfaces. Pink-tinged white flowers, single or in cymes, in summer. Orange-red fruit. Zones 5–9.

Cotoneaster sternianus

☼/◐ ✱ ↔5–7 ft (1.5–2 m) ↑10 ft (3 m)

From Tibet, northeastern India, and Myanmar borders. Semi-evergreen with stiff, upright, fan-shaped growth. Dark green leaves, to 1¾ in (40 mm) long, with downy white undersides. Cluster of 7 to 15 red-tinted white flowers. Pale red fruit. Zones 6–9.

Cotoneaster × *watereri*

☼ ✱ ↔15 ft (4.5 m) ↑15 ft (4.5 m)

Of garden origin, a 3-way cross between *C. frigidus*, *C. salicifolius,* and *C. rugosus*. Evergreen shrub or small tree, bowed branches. Leaves egg-shaped, dark green, veined upper surfaces, felty undersides. White flowers in cymes in summer. Round, red, persistent fruit. '**John Waterer**' is the original clone, and there are numerous cultivars. Zones 6–10.

Cotyledon orbiculata

COTYLEDON

This formerly large stonecrop (Crassulaceae) family genus of succulents has been extensively revised, and now contains around a dozen species of evergreen, often rather woody-stemmed shrubs from South Africa. The leaves vary widely in shape, from flat and rounded to elongated and cylindrical, but are always fleshy and succulent, sometimes with a powdery white surface bloom of wax. The flowers, usually yellow, orange, or red, have 5 recurved petal-like sepals, are bell-shaped, and are borne in heads on strong stems that hold them well clear of the foliage. Flowers appear throughout the year, most abundantly in late spring.

CULTIVATION: Tolerant of light frosts, *Cotyledon* species do best in mild climates with relatively dry winters. Plant in full sun or half-sun with gritty very free-draining soil. Routine deadheading and removal of old branches and dried leaves will keep plants tidy and flowering profusely. Propagation is from seed, cuttings, or offsets.

Cotyledon orbiculata ★

↔ 20 in–4 ft (50 cm–1.2 m)
↑ 1–5 ft (0.9–1.5 m)

Bushy, often quite densely branched shrub. Leaves variable, rounded to elongated, to over 4 in (10 cm) long, seldom hairy, pale green to silver-gray, with a powdery coating. Orange to red flowers, ½ in (12 mm) long, often densely clustered. Can be invasive in favorable climates. ***C. o.*** **var.** ***oblonga,*** wavy-edged bright silver-gray leaves; ***C. o.*** **f.** ***variegata,*** mid-green leaves with large pale sectors. Zones 9–11.

Cotyledon tomentosa ★

BEAR'S PAW

↔ 12–27 in (30–70 cm)
↑ 12–20 in (30–50 cm)

Shrub branching near ground level. Thick fleshy leaves,1 in (25 mm) long, dense silver-gray to gray-green hairs, vestigial brown teeth. Short flower stems. Orange-red to yellow flowers, around ½ in (12 mm) long, often downy. ***C. t.*** **f.** ***variegata,*** cream patches on foliage, usually around edges. Zones 10–11.

CRAMBE

The 20 species of annuals and perennials of this mainly Eurasian genus are classified in the cabbage (Brassicaceae) family, which is quite appropriate, as the name *Crambe* comes from a Greek word for cabbage. They are vigorous plants that produce large leaves on fleshy stems, usually in loose rosettes. The foliage varies with the species, and may be dark green and glossy or blue-gray with a powdery bloom. In summer upright sprays of small, honey-scented, 4-petalled, white or yellow flowers appear. The flower stems usually considerably exceed the height of the foliage.

CULTIVATION: They are easily grown in any temperate climate that does not experience extremes of winter cold or summer heat. Allow plenty of room for the spread of the foliage and flowerheads. Plant in moist, cool, well-drained soil in full or half-sun. Water and feed well until after flowering. Propagation is by division or from seed.

Crambe cordifolia

Crambe cordifolia ★

COLEWORT

↔ 3–7 ft (0.9–2 m)
↑ 5–6 ft (1.5–1.8 m)

Perennial native to the Caucasus region. Leaves heart-shaped to lance-shaped, up to 14 in (35 cm) long, dark glossy green, puckered surface, toothed edges. Huge billowing inflorescence of tiny white flowers. Zones 6–9.

CRASPEDIA

A genus of about 16 species of annuals and perennials in the daisy (Asteraceae) family. They grow all over Australia, from coastal to alpine regions, in moist grasslands and swamps. Leaves are usually bright green and often covered in hairs, giving a woolly appearance. Flowers bloom in spring or summer and look like small balls on long stems, usually yellow but sometimes orange.

CULTIVATION: Species from moist to wet areas need extra water; otherwise grow in a well-drained soil in full sun. Propagate from seed or by division.

Craspedia glauca

syn. *Craspedia uniflora*

BILLY BUTTONS

↔ 12 in (30 cm)
↑ 12–20 in (30–50 cm)

Woolly light green leaves in a rosette formation. Globular yellow flowers on 12 in (30 cm) long stems in spring–summer. Zones 9–11.

Craspedia globosa

syn. *Pycnosorus globosus*

↔ 12–16 in (30–40 cm)
↑ 18–24 in (45–60 cm)

Larger than *C. glauca*; gray grass-like leaves. Orangey flowers, ¾–1¼ in (18–30 mm) wide, are borne on 40 in (100 cm) tall stems, in spring–summer. This species tolerates waterlogging. Zones 9–11.

CRASSULA

This genus in the stonecrop (Crassulaceae) family has some 300 species of succulent annual, biennial, and perennial herbs and small shrubs. A few are found in Asia, Europe, Madagascar, Australia, and North America, but most are native to southern Africa. Leaves are usually opposite, fleshy, and vary in size, texture, color, and shape. Red, pink, green, or white, funnel- or star-shaped flowers, occasionally tubular, are sometimes carried singly but are more often in cyme-like branches.

CULTIVATION: Cultivated as ornamentals, *Crassula* species are best grown in full sun, but will also grow in half-sun. Grow in well-drained average soil with added humus, or in pots in cactus compost. In areas with frost, they should be grown under glass. Water sparingly in winter. Propagate from stem cuttings or set single leaves in soil from spring to mid-summer. Sow seeds in cactus compost with added sharp sand.

Crassula atropurpurea

↔ 12 in (30 cm)
↑ 6–18 in (15–45 cm)

Erect or domed subshrub from Namibia and South Africa's Western Cape. Variable; leaves red-tinted in sun, obovate to lanceolate.Tiny cream to pinkish flowers. ***C. a.*** **var.** ***anomala*** (syn. *C. anomala*) ★, compact, leaves obovate, flattened. Zones 9–11.

Crassula barklyi

RATTLESNAKE TAIL

↔ 8–12 in (20–30 cm)
↑ 2–4 in (5–10 cm)

Found from South Africa to Namibia. Clustered stems to 3 in (8 cm) long, with tiny olive leaves, overlapping like scales, often edged with hairs. Cream flowers, large in comparison, in small clusters in winter. Zones 9–11.

Crassula capitella

↔ 16 in (40 cm)
↑ 8–16 in (20–40 cm)

Perennial from coastal southern South Africa. Spirally arranged, red-tinted, sometimes hairy, pointed, lance-shaped leaves, ½–4 in (12 mm–10 cm) long, initially growing in basal rosettes, then elongating into woody stems. Spikes of small, pink-tinted, white flowers appear in late summer. ***C. c.*** **subsp.** ***thyrsiflora,*** smooth leaves edged with fine hairs, flower sepals sometimes finely toothed. Zones 9–11.

Crassula atropurpurea var. *anomala*

Crassula deceptor

↔ 12–20 in (30–50 cm)
↑ 6 in (15 cm)

Low, spreading, branching perennial, from South Africa. Silver-gray, powder-coated, thick, fleshy leaves to ½ in (12 mm) long, arranged in 4 rows, pressed tightly into stems. Heads of very small cream to buff flowers are produced in summer. Zones 9–11.

Crassula exilis

↔ 6–12 in (15–30 cm)
↑ 3–6 in (8–15 cm)

Variable species from Namibia and South Africa's Western Cape. Sprawling perennial. Thin brownish stems, rosettes of small, elliptical to lanceolate, olive green leaves with darker purplish spots and white-fringed edges; many short leafy clusters of white to pink flowers in summer. ***C. e.* subsp. *cooperi***, denser habit, leaves thin; ***C. e.* subsp. *schmidtii*** (syn. *C. schmidtii*), plumper leaves, flowers bright reddish pink in larger clusters. Zones 9–11.

Crassula hemisphaerica

ARAB'S TURBAN

↔ 12–20 in (30–50 cm)
↑ 8 in (20 cm)

Low spreading perennial, native to South Africa. Rosettes of tightly spiralled, bristle-edged, gray-green to deep green leaves to 2 in (5 cm) long. Rosettes may elongate into short stems. Spikes of tiny, cream, tubular flowers are produced in spring. Zones 9–11.

Crassula lactea

TAILOR'S PATCH

↔ 12–20 in (30–50 cm)
↑ 16–24 in (40–60 cm)

From Eastern Cape, South Africa. Shrubby perennial, spreading or scrambling stems, green, pointed, hard-edged leaves to nearly 3 in (8 cm) long. White flowers, undersides sometimes pink in autumn. Zones 9–11.

Crassula ovata

Crassula multicava ★

↔ 3–10 ft (0.9–3 m)
↑ 12–16 in (30–40 cm)

From South Africa. Thin, rounded, gray-green leaves to 2½ in (6 cm) long, on short, upright or spreading, sometimes branching stems. Rounded inflorescence of tiny, red-tipped, white to cream flowers, in autumn. Zones 9–11.

Crassula muscosa

MOSS CYPRESS, WATCH-CHAIN CYPRESS

↔ 20–40 in (50–100 cm)
↑ 8–32 in (20–80 cm)

From South Africa, Namibia, and Lesotho. Tiny, overlapping, gray-green leaves on short scrambling stems, creating an effect like thickened clubmoss or cypress foliage. Inconspicuous inflorescences of up to 8 yellow-green flowers in summer. Zones 9–11.

Crassula namaquaensis

↔ 12–24 in (30–60 cm)
↑ 4–6 in (10–15 cm)

Spreading and mat-forming, with small, fleshy, hairy, bead-like, blue-green to grayish leaves. Small terminal heads of cream flowers, black anthers, in summer. ***C. n.* subsp. *comptonii,*** leaves more pointed in outline, round in section, smaller flowers with yellow anthers. Zones 9–11.

Crassula ovata ★

syns *Crassula arborescens of gardens, C. argentea of gardens, C. portulacea*

DOLLAR PLANT, JADE TREE

↔ 2–4 ft (0.6–1.2 m)
↑ 3–6 ft (0.9–1.8 m)

Native to most of South Africa. Upright branching shrub, thick stems and peeling bark. Fleshy rounded leaves, usually shiny dark green with red or pale green edges. Heads of pink-tinted white flowers in winter–early spring. **'Crosby's Compact'** (syn. 'Crosby's Dwarf'), low compact habit, rarely exceeding 12 in (30 cm) high, red-tinted foliage; **'Hobbit'**, compact habit with thickened almost cylindrical, to thin slightly curled leaves, often with red tints; **'Hummel's Sunset'** ★ (syn. 'Sunset'), vivid red leaves suffused with yellow and orange; **'Tricolor'**, bold cream-variegated foliage suffused with bright pink. Zones 10–11.

Crassula perfoliata var. *minor*

Crassula perfoliata

↔ 18–36 in (45–90 cm)
↑ 2–4 ft (0.6–1.2 m)

Variable species of wide distribution in southern Africa. Subshrub, branching from base. Typical form has 4-ranked, channeled, long-tapering, gray-green leaves to 6 in (15 cm) long. White, pink, or red summer flowers in large, dense, terminal corymb. ***C. p.* var. *falcata*** (syns *C. falcata, C. p.* var. *minor*), from Eastern Cape, flatter, sickle-shaped, mealy-whitish leaves turned on edge and flattened into one plane, brilliant red flowers. Zones 9–11.

Crassula plegmatoides

↔ 8–12 in (20–30 cm)
↑ 4–6 in (10–15 cm)

From Namaqualand, South Africa. Spreading perennial with short stems densely covered with small, fleshy, almost globular, gray-green leaves. Open, somewhat hairy heads of cream flowers. Zones 9–11.

Crassula pyramidalis

↔ 4–8 in (10–20 cm)
↑ 4–10 in (10–25 cm)

From Northern Cape, South Africa. Short, sometimes branching stems with tiny, pointed, oval leaves arranged in groups of 4, stacked to make a square-sectioned column. Few-flowered terminal heads of small white to cream blooms, in spring. Zones 9–11.

Crassula radicans

RED CARPET

↔ 24 in (60 cm)
↑ 4–6 in (10–15 cm)

Prostrate perennial from South Africa. Spreading, branching stems and lance-shaped, red-edged, green leaves to over ½ in (12 mm) long. Small terminal heads of white flowers, followed by reddish brown seed heads. Zones 10–11.

Crassula rupestris ★

BEAD VINE, BUTTONS ON A STRING

↔ 6–12 in (15–30 cm)
↑ 8–20 in (20–50 cm)

Shrubby perennial from South Africa and Namibia. Short stems with slightly overlapping, thick, red-tinted, olive green, pointed, tiny, oval leaves. Tiny, red-tinted, white flowers in rounded heads. ***C. r.* subsp. *commutata,*** dense, upright, bushy; ***C. r.* subsp. *marnieriana,*** low, spreading, leaves partly fused, larger flower heads. Zones 9–11.

Crassula tecta

↔ 6–12 in (15–30 cm)
↑ 8 in (20 cm)

South African perennial with low branching stems. Thick, blunt-tipped, lance-shaped leaves, covered with light gray hairs and glands. Sprays of cream flowers in autumn. Zones 9–11.

Crassula Hybrid Cultivars

↔ 2–10 in (5–25 cm)
↑ 2–8 in (5–20 cm)

Grown mostly for their brightly colored, variably textured and shaped foliage, and wide range of shapes and sizes. **'Baby's Necklace'** ★, small, bead-like, purplish red-edged leaves surrounding upright stems, sprays of tiny cream flowers; **'Buddha's Temple'** ★, hybrid of *C. pyramidalis,* rosettes of thin, upward-curved, gray-green leaves tiered like a pagoda roof, pale cream flowers; **'Campfire'**, narrow bright green leaves, broadly edged and flushed vivid red, sprays of tiny cream flowers; **'Coralita'**, rosettes of fleshy, curly, gray-green leaves, heads of pink flowers on red-tinted stems; **'Fernwood'**, tight rosettes of small bright green leaves, sprays of light yellow flowers from late winter; **'Frosty'**, small green leaves edged and highlighted with silver-gray, sprays of tiny cream flowers; **'Moonglow'** ★, thick, fleshy, gray-green leaves on short upright stems, soft orange flowers; **'Morgan's Beauty'** ★ (syn. 'Morgan's Pink'), mounding rosettes of fleshy, flat, gray-green leaves to 2 in (5 cm) long, showy, soft pink flowers open from glowing pink buds and age to red; **'Pagoda Village'**, purple-red-edged bronze-green leaves, tiered like pagoda roof, sprays of tiny, pink-tinted, cream flowers, upright stems; **'Pastel'**, small, thick, pale green leaves, short upright stems, sprays of tiny, white to pink-tinted, cream flowers; **'Pink Pagoda'**, thin upright stems, sprays of pale pink or red flowers, reddish seed heads; **'Springtime'**, broad-based, fleshy, bright green leaves on short stems in clusters, sprays of tiny, pink-tinted, cream flowers in summer. Zones 9–11.

C

Crataegus 'Autumn Glory'

Crataegus × *lavalleei*

Crataegus crus-galli

Crataegus punctata

CRATAEGUS

HAWTHORN

This genus within the rose (Rosaceae) family contains around 200 species from temperate Eurasia and North America. Most are large thorny shrubs or small trees. The deep green leaves are alternate, simple or lobed, some toothed. The white to pink flowers, carried singly or in corymbs, have 5 sepals and/or petals. Nutlets with a fleshy edible covering follow. These fruit can be black, yellow, or bluish green, but the majority are red. C. laevigata and C. monogyna have been used as hedging plants for centuries. CULTIVATION: Grow in sun or partial shade in any soil. Bud cultivars in summer or graft them in winter. Sow seeds when ripe in a position that is protected from winter frosts. Germination may take up to 18 months.

Crataegus arnoldiana

ARNOLD HAWTHORN

☼ ✱ ↔30 ft (9 m) ↑30 ft (9 m)

Native of northeastern USA. Small tree. Oval, lobed, toothed leaves are dark green above, paler beneath. Scented white flowers in spring. Bright red fruit with 3 to 4 seeds. Zones 5–10.

Crataegus 'Autumn Glory'

☼ ✱ ↔10 ft (3 m) ↑10 ft (3 m)

Possibly a hybrid of *C. laevigata.* Deciduous shrub. Glossy leaves with 3 to 5 rounded blunt-toothed lobes. Produces clusters of large white flowers in early summer, followed by oval red fruit in autumn, persisting into winter. Zones 5–10.

Crataegus crus-galli

COCKSPUR THORN

☼ ✱ ↔35 ft (10 m) ↑30 ft (9 m)

Native to eastern USA. Small flat-topped tree with long curved thorns. Shiny, dark green, egg-shaped leaves. Foliage turns red in autumn. Large corymbs of small white flowers appear in spring. Deep red fruit persists throughout winter. ***C. c.-g.* var. *salicifolia,*** narrow lance-shaped leaves. Zones 5–9.

Crataegus laciniata

syn. *Crataegus orientalis*

☼ ✱ ↔20 ft (6 m) ↑20 ft (6 m)

Native to southeastern Europe and western Asia. Thorny shrub or tree. Leaves are deeply lobed, dark green, growing to 2 in (5 cm) long, with a covering of silvery white hairs. Clusters of white flowers appear in summer, and are followed by large red fruit. Zones 6–9.

Crataegus laevigata

syn. *Crataegus oxyacantha of gardens*

ENGLISH HAWTHORN, MAY, WHITE THORN

☼ ✱ ↔25 ft (8 m) ↑25 ft (8 m)

Native to most of Europe and the far northwest of Africa. Thorny tree with egg-shaped leaves that are a glossy mid-green in color, lobed and toothed, with paler green undersides. White or pink flowers appear in corymbs in spring, followed by red fruit. Often grown as a hedge, and very ornamental cultivars may be used as specimen trees. **'Paul's Scarlet' ★**, double deep pink flowers; **'Plena,'** double white flowers, becoming pink-tinged with age; **'Rosea Flore Pleno'**, double pink flowers. Zones 5–9.

Crataegus × *lavalleei*

syn. *Crataegus carrierei*

LAVALLEE HAWTHORN

☼ ✱ ↔20 ft (6 m) ↑20 ft (6 m)

Of garden origin, from France. Cross between *C. crus-galli* and *C. pubescens.* Semi-evergreen in warmer climates. Leaves are elliptical to oval in shape, toothed, glossy green; develop good autumn color. White flowers, red stamens, in early summer. Long-lasting red fruit. Zones 6–10.

Crataegus × *media*

☼/◐ ✱ ↔5–7 ft (1.5–2 m) ↑8–10 ft (2.4–3 m)

Hybrid between *C. monogyna* and *C. laevigata.* Similar to *C. laevigata,* apart from minor foliage details and slightly flattened spherical rather than ovoid fruit. **'Gireoudii'**, spreading tree, broad crown. Zones 5–9.

Crataegus monogyna

HAWTHORN, MAY, QUICKTHORN

☼ ✱ ↔25 ft (8 m) ↑25 ft (8 m)

Native to Europe. Thorny hawthorn, a common wild hedge. Leaves broadly egg-shaped, dark green upper surface, paler green downy undersides. Small clusters of white flowers, pink-tinged. Dark red, single-seeded fruit. **'Biflora'**, the Glastonbury thorn, flowers in mid-winter, a second time in spring; **'Stricta'**, columnar habit, spreads to 12 ft (3.5 m). Zones 4–9.

Crataegus nitida

GLOSSY HAWTHORN

☼ ✱ ↔25 ft (8 m) ↑30 ft (9 m)

A dense, rounded, deciduous shrub from Ohio to Missouri and Arkansas. Leaves dark green, lustrous above, paler below, turning orange to red in autumn. Small white flowers appear in mid-spring, followed by dull red fruit, which may remain until the next spring. Zones 4–6.

Crataegus persimilis 'Prunifolia'

syn. *Crataegus* × *prunifolia*

☼ ✱ ↔25 ft (8 m) ↑20 ft (6 m)

Large deciduous shrub or small tree, now considered a cultivar of a distinct species. Dense foliage, thorny branches. Serrated-edged oval leaves to 3 in (8 cm) long, bright red tones in autumn. Flowers white, pink anthers, in corymbs. Red fruit. **'Prunifolia Splendens'**, more vigorous, larger leaves and flower clusters. Zones 5–9.

Crataegus phaenopyrum

syn. *Crataegus cordata*

WASHINGTON HAWTHORN.

☼ ✱ ↔30 ft (9 m) ↑30 ft (9 m)

Native to southeast USA. Thorny tree. Leaves sharply toothed, broadly egg-shaped, lobed, shiny green, good autumn color. White flowers in summer; glossy, vivid, red fruit, persisting until spring. **'Fastigiata'**, narrow upright habit. Zones 5–10.

Crinum bulbispermum

Crataegus pseudomelanocarpa

syn. *Crataegus pentagyna subsp. pseudomelanocarpa*

☼ ✱ ↔10–17 ft (3–5 m) ↑15–20 ft (4.5–6 m)

Species from the Balkan Peninsula. Source of a herbal medicine. White flowers in summer. Zones 6–11.

Crataegus punctata

DOTTED HAWTHORN

☼ ✱ ↔30 ft (9 m) ↑30 ft (9 m)

Native to eastern USA. Thorny tree. Broadly egg-shaped, dark green leaves, toothed, downy undersides. White flowers, pale pink anthers, in hairy corymbs. Red fruit with pale speckles. **'Ohio Pioneer' ★**, popular ornamental tree, brick-red fruit. Zones 4–9.

Crataegus schraderiana

☼ ✱ ↔20 ft (6 m) ↑20 ft (6 m)

Native to Greece and the Crimean Peninsula. Deciduous round-headed tree. Leaves to 2 in (5 cm) long, 5 to 9 deep toothed lobes, deep green, covered by a fine gray down. Flowers in corymbs, white, ½ in (12 mm) wide. Plum-colored fruit. Zones 6–9.

CRINUM

There are about 130 species of evergreen and deciduous bulbous plants in this genus, which belongs to the amaryllis (Amaryllidaceae) family. They are found in tropical and subtropical zones, usually in coastal

Crinum moorei

Crinum × powellii 'Album'

areas. The bulbs are large and the leaves broad and long, to 3 ft (0.9 m) or more. Thick flowering stems support large trumpet-shaped flowers with flaring lobes, narrow and spidery in some species. The flowers may be white or in shades of pink or rose, and are often fragrant.
CULTIVATION: In cool areas grow in pots in the conservatory or greenhouse. Elsewhere grow in a sheltered sunny or semi-shaded position in well-drained soil. Bulbs dislike being transplanted and take time to become established. Propagate from seed and offsets. Seed-grown plants take 3 years to flower.

Crinum americanum
FLORIDA SWAMP LILY, SOUTHERN SWAMP CRINUM
↔ 24–36 in (60–90 cm)
↑ 18–30 in (45–75 cm)

From southern USA. Large short-necked bulbs. Leaves to 4 ft (1.2 m) long. Flowering stems bear 3 to 6 creamy white flowers tinged with green or purple. Prominent flaring stamens are red or pink. Zones 9–11.

Crinum asiaticum
POISON BULB
↔ 3 ft (0.9 m) ↑ 3–5 ft (0.9–1.5 m)
From tropical Asia. Large long-necked bulbs. Very leafy plant with broad bluish green leaves to 4 ft (1.2 m) long. Thick flowering stems bear heads of 20 to 30 fragrant white flowers with narrow spidery petals and long red stamens. ***C. a.* var. *sinicum*** (syn. *C. pedunculatum*), from Australia and some Pacific Islands, has larger leaves and taller flowering stems. Zones 10–12.

Crinum bulbispermum
syn. *Crinum longifolium*
↔ 3 ft (0.9 m) ↑ 3 ft (0.9 m)
A South African species. Large long-necked bulb. Tidy, channeled, arching leaves. Large, funnel-shaped, fragrant flowers in white, or in shades of pink, with a red streak on each petal. Zones 7–10.

Crinum erubescens
↔ 3 ft (0.9 m) ↑ 3 ft (0.9 m)
From tropical America. Aquatic species with large bulb. Thick, fleshy, strap-shaped leaves. Large, fragrant, trumpet-shaped flowers with flaring lobes, borne in heads of 4 to 12. Flowers purplish red with a white throat. Zones 10–11.

Crinum 'Ellen Bosanquet'
↔ 2–3 ft (0.6–0.9 m)
↑ 2–3 ft (0.6–0.9 m)
A hybrid of *C. moorei* and *C. zeylanicum*. Tidy foliage with soft slightly arching leaves. Heads of large, trumpet-shaped, rose red flowers in summer. Zones 7–12.

Crinum moorei
↔ 4–5 ft (1.2–1.5 m)
↑ 4–5 ft (1.2–1.5 m)
From South Africa. Extremely large long-necked bulb. Long, broad, rather untidy deciduous leaves. Tall flowering stems bear 6 to 12 fragrant, pale pink, trumpet-shaped flowers in summer. Zones 8–11.

Crinum × powellii
↔ 4 ft (1.2 m) ↑ 4 ft (1.2 m)
A hybrid of *C. moorei* and *C. bulbispermum*, of garden origin. Large long-necked bulb. Broad, upright, channeled leaves. Trumpet-shaped flowers of pink or white on tall stems in clusters of 8 to 10. **'Album'**, pure white flowers. Zones 7–10.

CROCOSMIA
FALLING STARS, MONTBRETIA
The iris (Iridaceae) family species in this genus come from the grasslands of tropical and South Africa. Their handsome appearance, trouble-free lifestyles, vivid flowers, and erect lance-like leaves make them popular in cultivation. The leaves reach heights of 24–40 in (60–100 cm) and form dense clumps. They can be pleated and/or ribbed, and vary from pale green to mid-green to a brownish shade. The funnel-shaped flowers are held on long, wiry, often branching stems and appear in mid- to late summer. The plants are fully dormant in winter. The corms are disc-like, ivory white, and about 2½ in (6 cm) in diameter.
CULTIVATION: Sun, water, reasonably good drainage, and the regular division of overcrowded corms are the principal requirements of these tough but very attractive plants.

Crocosmia aurea
↔ 24–32 in (60–80 cm)
↑ 32–40 in (80–100 cm)
From streambeds, wet woodlands, and shady gorges. Tolerates shade. Flowers, held in double rows on erect sometimes branched spikes, range between burnt orange and chrome yellow. Leaves are papery and pale green. Zones 7–9.

Crocosmia × crocosmiiflora
↔ 20–24 in (50–60 cm)
↑ 20–24 in (50–60 cm)
Robust hybrid between *C. aurea* and *C. pottsii*. Pale green leaves, arching branching flower stems. Sunny protected situations suit it best. Invasive in mild wet climates. **'Emily McKenzie'** (syn. 'Lady McKenzie'), grows to 24 in (60 cm), mid-green leaves, generous branched spikes of nodding dark orange flowers splashed with red; **'Solfatare'** (syn. 'Solphatare'), popular hybrid dating from the 1890s, elegantly branched arching stems, yellow petals, smoky bronze papery leaves. Zones 5–10.

Crocosmia masoniorum
↔ 32–40 in (80–100 cm)
↑ 3–4 ft (0.9–1.2 m)
Robust plant from a mountainous habitat. Pleated mid-green leaves and single, spraying, arching stems of red-orange flowers. Best in mild climates and on moist sandy soils. **'Rowallane Yellow'**, yellow flowers. Zones 7–10.

Crocosmia pottsii
↔ 32–36 in (80–90 cm)
↑ 32–36 in (80–90 cm)
Grows in the wild beside and in streambeds. Needs similarly damp rocky environment in cultivation. Flowers are orange-red. Zones 7–9.

Crocosmia Hybrid Cultivars
↔ 12–24 in (30–60 cm)
↑ 18–36 in (45–90 cm)
Many colorful, carefully selected, new and old named cultivars of much mixed parentage. Most bred for cool wet climates. All produce dense leaf clumps and a generous supply of summer flowers. **'Citronella'** (syn. 'Golden Fleece'), grows to 24 in (60 cm) high, mid-green leaves, yellow flowers with red-brown markings; **'Lucifer'**, flowers earlier than most, large rich red flowers; **'Norwich Canary'**, orange buds open to bright yellow flowers with orange petal reverse; **'Star of the East'** ★, very large, light-centered, apricot pink to light orange flowers, color more intense at petal tips. Zones 7–10.

C

CROCUS
A genus of around 80 species of small, herbaceous, lily-like perennials in the iris (Iridaceae) family, found in a range of habitats from sea level to subalpine regions of central and southern Europe, northern Africa, central Asia, and western China. All have subterranean corms, from which inflorescences arise. Leaves are similar in shape but produced at different times: autumn-flowering species are leafless at flowering, growth returning in spring; spring-flowering species have leaves at flowering, and fruit is produced before winter. Flowers have a long tube originating from the top of the corm and terminating in a colorful, tall, 6-segmented "flower." The ovary that forms the fruit is at the base of the floral tube. Seeds develop in the 3-celled capsular fruits.
CULTIVATION: Most species grow over some years into compact clumps around 4–6 in (10–15 cm) in diameter. Plant bulbs 4 in (10 cm) apart or in widely spaced groups of more crowded bulbs. Propagate from seed, which germinates readily. Young seedlings should be kept in containers for 2 years before planting out. Soils and aspect vary with the species.

Crocosmia masoniorum

Crocus ancyrensis

↔ 3 in (8 cm) ↕ 2 in (5 cm)

Yellow-flowered species found in open rocky places in oak scrub and pine woods in central and northern Turkey at 2,620–5,250 ft (800–1,600 m) altitude. Leaves, 2 to 6, as long as the 1 to 3 flowers. Requires well-drained, alkaline, gritty soil. Flowers from late winter to summer. Zones 6–8.

Crocus angustifolius

syn. *Crocus susianus*

↔ 4 in (10 cm) ↕ 2 in (5 cm)

From southwestern Russia. Flowers 1 to 2, yellow, striped or blotched purplish brown on outer floral segments. Leaves 3 to 6, as long as flowers, gray-green. Flowers from late winter–early spring. Cultivated in Europe for over 300 years. Zones 5–8.

Crocus banaticus

syns *Crocus byzantinus, C. iridiflorus*

↔ 3 in (8 cm) ↕ 4 in (10 cm)

From Romania, northeastern former Yugoslavia, and Ukraine. Flowers solitary, segments lilac to purple, inner ones smaller than outer ones, appearing in autumn; 1 to 3 leaves in spring. Zones 6–8.

Crocus chrysanthus

syns *Crocus annulatus, C. croceus, C. skorpilii*

↔ 4 in (10 cm) ↕ 2 in (5 cm)

Found in a range of habitats from Albania, Bulgaria, Greece, Macedonia, Serbia, Romania, and Turkey. Variable spring-flowering species, flowers fragrant, pale yellow to orange-yellow, sometimes striped bronze or purple on outer segments. Leaves 3 to 7, various lengths, gray-green. Many selections and hybrids, particularly with *C. biflorus*, now in cultivation. **'Blue Pearl'** ★, flowers white, yellow throat, pale lilac-blue outer segments; **'E. A. Bowles'**, flowers deep lemon yellow, outer segments with bronze-green bases; **'Ladykiller'**, flowers white, deep purple markings on outer segments. Zones 6–8.

Crocus corsicus

syn. *Crocus insularis*

↔ 3 in (8 cm) ↕ 3–4 in (8–10 cm)

Found in scrub and rocky hillsides in Corsica, this species has 1 to 2 flowers, sometimes fragrant, lilac inside, outer segments lilac, buff, or yellow, from late winter to early summer. Leaves, 2 to 4 in number, as long as flowers, dark green. Zones 7–9.

Crocus etruscus

↔ 3 in (8 cm) ↕ 3 in (8 cm)

From Italy. Flowers 1, rarely 2, from late winter–spring, pale lilac-blue, outer segments creamy to buff. Leaves 2 to 4, shorter than flower, to ¼ in (6 mm) wide, green. Zones 6–8.

Crocus goulimyi

↔ 3 in (8 cm) ↕ 4 in (10 cm)

Found in limestone soils in southern Greece. Flowers 1 or 2, fragrant, pale to deep lilac-purple, inner segments paler, throat white, hairy, in autumn. Leaves 4 to 6, shorter than flowers, green. Zones 7–8.

Crocus imperati

syns *Crocus incurvus, C. neapolitanus, C. suaveolens*

↔ 3 in (8 cm) ↕ 4 in (10 cm)

From Italy. Flowers 1 or 2, mid- to deep purple inside, outer segments buff-colored on exterior with purple stripes, from late winter–early spring. Leaves 3 to 6, equal to or longer than flowers, glossy green. Zones 7–8.

Crocus kotschyanus

syn. *Crocus zonatus*

↔ 4 in (10 cm) ↕ 3 in (8 cm)

Variable species from Russia, Turkey, Syria, and Lebanon. Flowers 1 to 2, sometimes fragrant, white or bluish lilac, parallel veins darker, throat white or yellowish, sometimes hairy, in autumn. Leaves 4 to 6, not present at flowering, green. Corms upright or lying on side. Zones 6–8.

Crocus medius

syn. *Crocus nudiflorus*

↔ 5 in (12 cm) ↕ 3 in (8 cm)

From northern Italy and southeastern France. Flowers 1 to 2, lilac to deep purple, darker veins at base of segments, in autumn. Leaves 2 to 3, well after flowering, green with white stripe. Zones 6–8.

Crocus ochroleucus

↔ 3 in (8 cm) ↕ 2 in (5 cm)

From southern Syria, Lebanon, and Israel. Flowers 1 to 5, creamy white, throat, lower part of segments pale to deep yellow, hairy, from late autumn–winter. Leaves 3 to 7, appearing when flowers open, deep green. Zones 7–8.

Crocus pulchellus

↔ 4 in (10 cm) ↕ 4–5 in (10–12 cm)

From moist habitats and deciduous oak/pine woodlands and scrub in southern former Yugoslavia, Bulgaria, Greece, and Turkey. Large-flowered species, flowers 1 to 2, fragrant, pale lilac to mid-blue with darker veins, throat deep yellow, from late summer–late autumn. Leaves 3 to 5, form long after flowering, green. Zones 6–8.

Crocus sativus

SAFFRON CROCUS

↔ 4 in (10 cm) ↕ 2 in (5 cm)

An ancient source of dye and herbal medicine, saffron has been grown for centuries. A pound (450 g) of dried saffron takes 70,000 flowers, making it the world's most expensive spice. Sterile, it reproduces only by vegetative means. Thought to be a selection from wild populations of *C. cartwrightianus*, a species from Greece. *C. sativus* has larger floral segments and styles, from which dye is produced. Flowers 1 to 5, fragrant, pale to deep lilac-purple or white, veins darker, in autumn. Leaves 7 to 12, normally present at flowering, gray-green. Zones 6–8.

Crocus serotinus

↔ 4–6 in (10–15 cm)
↕ 2–4 in (5–10 cm)

From Portugal. Autumn-flowering species, with 3 to 4 grass-like leaves that emerge with flowers. White to mauve flowers, sometimes veined purple, orange stigma. ***C. s.* subsp. *salzmannii*,** pale lilac flowers with yellow throats. Zones 6–9.

Crocus sieberi

↔ 3 in (8 cm) ↕ 2–3 in (5–8 cm)

From the Balkan Peninsula and Crete. Variable species, differences being in flower color and distribution. Hybrids occur where 2 subspecies abut; some have been selected for cultivation. Flowers 1 to 3, fragrant, white, purplish on exterior of outer segments, from spring–summer. Leaves 4 to 7, equal in length to flower, green. **'Bowles White'**, selection with white

Crocus serotinus subsp. *salzmannii*

Crocus vernus

Crocus tommasinianus

flowers, throat golden yellow; **'Hubert Edelsten'**, inner floral segments white, outer segments lilac-purple; ***C. s.* subsp. *sublimis* 'Tricolor'**, narrow floral segments, each with 3 color bands, yellow throat, then white, then lilac-purple. Zones 6–8.

Crocus speciosus

↔3 in (8 cm) ↕4–6 in (10–15 cm)

From Russia, northern Iran, and Turkey. Widespread variable species. Flowers 1 to 2, fragrant, lilac-blue, darker veins present, exterior of segments often with silvery flush, throat whitish, in autumn. Leaves 3 to 5, emerging long after flowering, dark green. Zones 6–8.

Crocus tommasinianus ★

↔3 in (8 cm) ↕3–4 in (8–10 cm)

From Yugoslavia, Hungary, and Bulgaria. Flowers 1 to 2, in early spring, pale lilac to purple, often silvery or buff-colored on exterior segments, sometimes with darker purple on ends of segments, throat white. Leaves 3 to 4, equal in length to flowers, green with prominent longitudinal stripe. Zones 6–8.

Crocus vernus

DUTCH CROCUS

↔4 in (10 cm) ↕4–5 in (10–12 cm)

Most common *Crocus* species, found over much of Europe from Iberian Peninsula to western Russia. Flowers 1 to 2, in early spring, purple, lilac, white, striped darker in some populations. Leaves 2 to 4, mostly shorter than flowers, green. Many cultivars have been selected. Zones 6–8.

Crocus speciosus

CROTALARIA

RATTLEBOX

This predominantly African tropical and warm-temperate genus in the pea-flower subfamily of the legume (Fabaceae) family contains around 600 species, including many evergreen shrubs notable for their racemes of showy pea-flowers, often in strong yellow tones. Conspicuous seed pods follow the flowers, and as they ripen the seeds within rattle, hence the common name "rattlebox," and also the scientific name, which comes from krotalon, Greek for a castanet. The leaves may be simple or trifoliate, and can vary from soft and pliable to leathery, depending on the species.

CULTIVATION: Although some species tolerate light frosts, a warm climate, or at least a good hot summer, is essential to ensure heavy flowering. Flowering is mainly in late spring, though trimming after the first flush of flowers can encourage a second crop. Propagate from half-hardened cuttings or by sowing fresh seed, which should be soaked first.

Crotalaria agatiflora ★

BIRD FLOWER, CANARY-BIRD BUSH

↔5 ft (1.5 m) ↕10 ft (3 m)

From the higher altitude regions of eastern Africa. Leaves trifoliate, light green, soft-textured leaflets. Flowers in terminal racemes up to 15 in (38 cm) long, bright yellow, but often have a greenish hue. Tolerates light frosts. Can be invasive. Zones 9–11.

Crotalaria cunninghamii

BIRDFLOWER

↔3 ft (0.9 m) ↕3–7 ft (0.9–2 m)

From central Australia, often growing on desert dunes. Erect shrub, leaves simple, oval to oblong with blunt or notched tip, covered in silvery hairs. Spikes of 1½ in (35 mm) long greenish-yellow flowers with darker purplish stripes, in winter–spring or after rains. Zones 9–11.

Crotalaria cunninghamii

Crotalaria retusa

RATTLEWEED

↔24 in (60 cm) ↕4 ft (1.2 m)

West Indian perennial. Leaves dull mid-green, simple elongated ellipses to 3 in (8 cm) long. Yellow flowers, suffused and marked with red, in terminal racemes. Hard blunt-tipped seed pods. This species is considered invasive and a vector for mosaic viruses. Zones 10–11.

CROWEA

This small Australian genus is part of the rue (Rutaceae) family. Of its 3 species, all evergreen shrubs, the 2 from southeastern Australia are the showiest and are the parents of several cultivars. These small rounded shrubs have linear gray-green leaves and star-shaped flowers in white or shades of pink.

CULTIVATION: *Crowea* species grow naturally as understory shrubs in light dappled shade, but can withstand full sun provided they are planted in reasonably moist, well-drained, open soil with a mulch of leaf litter or similar organic matter. A light tip prune after flowering will ensure compact growth.

Crowea exalata ★

↔12–60 in (30–180 cm) ↕18–36 in (45–90 cm)

Extended flowering period, from spring into winter. Starry 5-petalled flowers, white to deep pink. Many forms selected, hybrids bred for cultivation, including prostrate or low spreading varieties. Zones 9–10.

Crowea saligna

↔3 ft (0.9 m) ↕3 ft (0.9 m)

Rounded shrub, small linear leaves, slightly recurved margins, prominent midrib. Star-like pink flowers, to 1½ in (35 mm) across, from autumn–winter. Good cut flower. Zones 9–10.

CRYPTANTHUS

Commonly known as earth stars, these plants are members of the pineapple (Bromeliaceae) family. They are generally small and flattened, with an irregular star shape. The triangular leaves are stiff and broad and of many colors, often with crossbands or longitudinal stripes. There are 2 main groups. One has no flower stem and the flowerhead nestles in the center of the plant; there is male dominance in the flowers in the center but female dominance in the outer flowers. The other group has similar flowers throughout the flowerhead, which is on a short stem. The petals are white for both groups. Found from eastern to southern Brazil, earth stars grow in the ground or on rocks, under the protection of trees or bushes. There are over 50 *Cryptanthus* species, of which only half are generally grown in cultivation. They are propagated from offsets that generally appear on the top of the plant from between the leaves. These usually fall off and are easily rooted. The plants are self-sterile, making it difficult to set seed at species level. However, they are very promiscuous, and there are many hybrids—some 400 to date. Because of the small number of species in the hybridizing program, many hybrids look similar.

CULTIVATION: Earth stars need more moisture than most bromeliads, and protection in the winter. They are best grown in shallow pots, and are recommended for indoor culture and for greenhouse conditions in cool-temperate areas, or outdoors with protection from direct continuous sunlight and extremes of rain in warm-temperate, subtropical, and tropical areas. Water when potting mix is dry. Fertilizer extra to that already incorporated in good quality potting mix is not necessary. Propagate from offsets.

Cryptanthus acaulis

↔6 in (15 cm) ↕2 in (5 cm)

The most common and most hardy of the genus; can survive 32°F (0°C). Plant more circular in general shape than the more usual oval. Leaves triangular, to 4 in (10 cm), a scurfy green, sometimes reddish. Zones 9–10.

Cryptanthus beuckeri

↔8 in (20 cm) ↕2 in (5 cm)

Plant with few radiating leaves, which are of a different type to those of most members of the genus and are best described as paddle-shaped with a long handle. They are whitish but tinged with red and spotted with dark green. Need very warm conditions; can be grown in a terrarium. Zones 10–12.

Cryptanthus bivittatus

↔10 in (25 cm) ↕2 in (5 cm)

Plant is regular in shape, resembling an open star. Leaves dark green with 2 broad, longitudinal, white or pinkish stripes. The center of **'Starlite'** (syn. 'Starlight') is cream to light pink instead of dark green; **'Pink Starlite'**, center stripe dark green, rest of leaf hot pink. These colors will be achieved if the plant is given the best possible planting and growing conditions. Zones 10–12.

Cryptanthus Black Mystic Group

↔ 10 in (25 cm) ↑ 2 in (5 cm)

Medium-sized plant, irregular diamond shape. Deep black leaves with silver markings. Grow in low light to achieve the blackness. Zones 10–12.

Cryptanthus fosterianus

↔ 16 in (40 cm) ↑ 2 in (5 cm)

Narrow oval plant, irregular in shape. Leaves to 12 in (30 cm) long, thick and fleshy, wavy along the edges, coloring maroon with wavy gray crossbands. Zones 10–12.

Cryptanthus × *roseus* 'Marian Oppenheimer'

↔ 4 in (10 cm) ↑ 2 in (5 cm)

Created by radiation experimentation, probably of *C. acaulis*. Small plant, light gray-green leaves with bright pink edges, sometimes pink stripes. There are wide-leafed and narrow-leafed forms. Zones 10–12.

Cryptanthus 'Rainbow Star'

↔ 10 in (25 cm) ↑ 8 in (20 cm)

Named *C. bromelioides* var. *tricolor* in 1953, but in 2001 found to be incorrectly identified; common name, rainbow star, then became official cultivar name. Variegated plant with leaves striped in green, white, and pink. Under optimum conditions can grow up to 16 in (40 cm) high and wide. Two forms, one stiffer leafed than the other; both require similar growing conditions. Best allowed to offset freely; when settled into a large clump it will flower. Zones 10–12.

Cryptanthus zonatus

↔ 12 in (30 cm) ↑ 2 in (5 cm)

Oval plant, irregular in shape. Leaves grow to 8 in (20 cm) long and are thick, fleshy, wavy along edges, mainly green, with wavy, shiny, gray crossbands. Zones 10–12.

CRYPTOMERIA

This single-species genus belonging to the swamp cypress (Taxodiaceae) family has numerous cultivars, which are also prized as garden plants. An evergreen from Japan and China, it is a densely clothed conifer with reddish brown fibrous bark and a straight trunk that forms buttresses as it matures. The pollen-bearing male cones, held in clusters at the tips of the branches, release their pollen in spring, while the persistent female seed-bearing cones, held further along the branches, can take up to 10 months to ripen.
CULTIVATION: This long-lived species prefers deep, moist, rich soil in a full sun position. It can be propagated from fresh seed, but cultivars need to be grown from cuttings.

Cryptanthus × *roseus* 'Marian Oppenheimer'

Cryptomeria japonica

JAPANESE CEDAR, SUGI

↔ 20 ft (6 m) ↑ 90 ft (27 m)

Narrow, conical shape. Dense adult foliage in forward-growing spirals. Branches tiered, outer branchlets slightly pendulous. **'Araucarioides'**, dark green leaves; **'Bandai-sugi'**, dwarf form; **'Compressa'**, dwarf form with purple-brown winter foliage. **Elegans Group**: **'Elegans'** ★, fast growing, purplish winter foliage; **'Nana'**, low growing; **'Vilmoriniana'**, to 12 in (30 cm) high; **'Yoshino'**, to 50 ft (15 m) high. Zones 7–11.

CRYPTOTAENIA

This genus of 6 species from the north temperate zone and the mountains of tropical Africa belongs to the carrot (Apiaceae) family. The plants are perennials with strong taproots or rhizomes. Leaves are pinnate, sometimes reduced to 3 broad leaflets. The erect inflorescences are irregularly branched into loose umbels of tiny flowers, which soon give way to small flattened fruits. *C. japonica* is grown in Japan for its strongly flavored young leaves, which are used as a salad vegetable.
CULTIVATION: *Cryptotaenia* species are easily grown in any good garden soil in full sun; they usually self-seed freely. For the tenderest leaves the plants should be kept well watered and regularly fertilized. Sow seed or plant root divisions in spring.

Cryptotaenia canadensis

HONEWORT, WHITE CHERVIL

↔ 20–27 in (50–70 cm)
↑ 3 ft (0.9 m)

Found in North America, Asia and Europe. Perennial, often short-lived and treated as an annual. Leaves to 4 in (10 cm) long, toothed, lance-shaped leaflets. Loose heads of tiny white flowers in summer. Zones 3–9.

Cryptotaenia japonica

Cryptotaenia japonica

syn. *Cryptotaenia canadensis* subsp. *japonica*

JAPANESE PARSLEY, MITSUBA

↔ 16–27 in (40–70 cm)
↑ 24–40 in (60–100 cm)

Perennial, sometimes evergreen, from Japan, where it is used as a vegetable. Very similar to *C. canadensis* (many consider them synonymous), but leaflets usually broader and more closely spaced, plant more compact. ***C. j.* f. *atropurpurea***, deep purple-red leaves, stems with pale pink flowers opening from red buds. Zones 4–10.

CTENANTHE

This genus in the arrowroot (Marantaceae) family contains about 15 species of evergreen perennials. They are native to Costa Rica and Brazil, where they grow on damp forest floors and in scrub. Arising from rhizomes, stems are single or branching, with leaves arising from sheaths at the nodes. The leaves are leathery, oblong, pointed, usually matt, often with colored markings.
CULTIVATION: In suitably warm climates grow in a shady sheltered position. In temperate climates they are cultivated as indoor plants. Grow in bright filtered light. During active growth, water moderately and apply liquid fertilizer fortnightly. Propagate by division or from cuttings.

Cryptomeria japonica 'Yoshino'

Ctenanthe dasycarpa

Ctenanthe burle-marxii

↔ 12–18 in (30–45 cm)
↑ 18 in (45 cm)

From Brazil. Leaves to 6 in (15 cm) long, pale green, with sickle-shaped darker markings above and dark purple beneath. Leaf sheaths also tinged purple. Zones 10–12.

Ctenanthe dasycarpa

↔ 5–10 ft (1.5–3 m)
↑ 3–5 ft (0.9–1.5 m)

From medium-altitude rainforests of Costa Rica, Panama, and Colombia. Spreads by rhizomes forming dense patch. Paddle-shaped glossy green leaves on slender stalks; inflorescences shorter, branched into spikes of white to pale yellow flowers between greenish yellow bracts. Zones 11–12.

Ctenanthe lubbersiana ★

↔ 18–24 in (45–60 cm)
↑ 18–24 in (45–60 cm)

From Brazil. Widely branching stems with narrow oblong leaves, deep green with yellow variegation above, pale green beneath. Zones 10–12.

Ctenanthe oppenheimiana

syn. *Maranta lubbersiana*

NEVER NEVER PLANT

↔ 24–36 in (60–90 cm)
↑ 36 in (90 cm)

From eastern Brazil. Bushy plant with leathery oblong leaves to 16 in (40 cm) long, green, with silvery marking above and deep red beneath. **'Tricolor'**, dark green with irregular creamy yellow markings. Zones 10–12.

CUNILA

There are 15 species of perennial herbs and shrubs in this genus, which is a member of the mint (Lamiaceae) family. They are native to North and South America. The stems and leaves are aromatic, the leaves sometimes spotted purple. The flowers are tubular and 2-lipped, the lower lip being larger and wider, with 3 lobes. CULTIVATION: Easily grown in well-drained soil in full sun. Propagate by division or cuttings, or from seed.

Cunila origanoides

DITTANY

↔9–18 in (23–45 cm) ↕9–18 in (23–45 cm)

A somewhat straggly perennial from eastern USA. Square branching stems, small, pointed, oval leaves. Purple or lavender tubular flowers in loose heads. Yields oil of dittany, a fragrant medicinal oil. Zones 6–10.

CUNNINGHAMIA

This genus belonging to the swamp cypress (Taxodiaceae) family includes just 2 species, one from central China, the other from Taiwan. They are evergreen conifers that can grow to 150 ft (45 m) tall, though they seldom reach that height in cultivation. The narrow leaves are flattened and sharply pointed, deep green above but with bluish white bands on the undersides, and arranged in double rows along the branchlets. The fibrous red-brown bark is reminiscent of the sequoia (*Sequoiadendron giganteum*).
CULTIVATION: Both *Cunninghamia* species are rather frost tender for conifers, *C. lanceolata* being the hardier. They are not fussy about soil type as long as it is reasonably fertile and the drainage is good. Young plants will tolerate light shade and eventually grow to see the sun. Propagate from seed or cuttings.

Cunninghamia lanceolata

CHINA FIR, CHINESE CEDAR

↔20 ft (6 m) ↕70 ft (20 m)

From central to southern China. Spirally arranged deep green leaves, to 3 in (8 cm) long. Cones, sticky while green, to 1½ in (35 mm) in diameter, carried at the branch tips. **'Glauca'** ★, blue-tinted foliage. Zones 7–10.

Cunninghamia lanceolata

CUNONIA

This genus, which is the name genus of the family Cunoniaceae, contains 15 species of evergreen shrubs and trees from New Caledonia, and one species in South Africa. They have lustrous, deep green, pinnate leaves in opposite pairs, with striking spoon-shaped stipules sheathing the growing tips. The bottlebrush-like racemes of fragrant white to cream or red flowers can turn an unsightly brown as they die, and are best removed at this time.
CULTIVATION: Although most species are frost tender, they are not difficult to grow. They prefer moist, fertile, well-drained soil and a position in full sun. If necessary they will tolerate poor soil and, once established, can withstand considerable periods of drought. Young plants can be pruned to a single trunk to make them tree-like; otherwise, a light trim after flowering will keep them compact. Propagate from seed or half-hardened tip cuttings.

Cunonia capensis

BUTTERKNIFE BUSH, SPOON BUSH

↔15 ft (4.5 m) ↕50 ft (15 m)

South African species. Smaller in cultivation, often a large shrub. Foliage deep green, bronze-tipped new growth, pinnate leaves of 5 to 7 leaflets, each up to 4 in (10 cm) long. Racemes of cream flowers, in late summer–autumn. Zones 9–11.

CUPHEA

This large genus in the loosestrife (Lythraceae) family consists of about 250 species of annuals, evergreen perennials, and low-growing shrubs from Central and South America. They have flexible leafy stems and small opposite or whorled leaves. They are grown for their masses of irregularly shaped tubular flowers, produced over a long period—almost the whole year. In warm climates they are easy to grow in average garden conditions.

Cunonia capensis

CULTIVATION: *Cuphea* species are fairly frost tender, and do best in full sun or light shade, in well-drained moist soil, with protection from strong winds. Occasional tip pruning from an early age will encourage compact growth. Propagation is from seed or from tip cuttings.

Cuphea caeciliae

↔24–36 in (60–90 cm) ↕12–24 in (30–60 cm)

Spreading or mounding shrub from Mexico. Lax branches; pointed elliptical leaves, 2–3 in (5–8 cm) long. Tubular flowers, orange at base, deepening to orange-red at tips. Zones 10–12.

Cuphea hyssopifolia

FALSE HEATHER, MEXICAN HEATHER

↔15 in (38 cm) ↕18 in (45 cm)

This small rounded shrub is native to Mexico and Guatemala. Small, dark green, narrow, pointed leaves, on thin stems with soft hairs. Purplish pink or white 6-petalled flowers are borne in small axillary racemes, in late spring–summer. This species can be invasive in subtropical climates. Zones 9–12.

Cuphea ignea

CIGAR FLOWER, CIGARETTE PLANT, FIRECRACKER PLANT

↔30 in (75 cm) ↕24 in (60 cm)

Bushy subshrub from Mexico and Jamaica. Bright green, oval, pointed leaves. Thin, orange-red, tubular flowers, tipped white, touch of black, borne freely almost year-round, with peak flowering from late spring–autumn. Zones 10–12.

Cuphea llavea

BAT-FACED CUPHEA

↔2 ft (0.6 m) ↕2 ft (0.6 m)

From Mexico, continuously flowering perennial or subshrub. Lance-shaped leaves to 1¼ in (30 mm) long. Purple-tipped red, 1 in (25 mm) wide flowers, at stem tips. **Flamenco Series,** flowers in red and pink shades. Zones 9–12.

Cuphea × *purpurea*

Cuphea micropetala

↔30 in (75 cm) ↕30 in (75 cm)

From Mexico. Rounded shrub. Dense, flexible, leafy branchlets, bright green lance-shaped leaves. Terminal leafy racemes of narrow tubular flowers, golden yellow to orange-red, tipped with greenish yellow, through summer–autumn. Zones 9–11.

C

Cuphea × *purpurea*

↔18 in (45 cm) ↕18 in (45 cm)

Bushy subshrub, garden hybrid between *C. llavea* and *C. procumbens*. Dark green, lance-shaped, pointed leaves. Narrow, tubular, deep pink to purplish red flowers, from late spring–autumn. Zones 9–11.

CUPRESSUS

CYPRESS

Originating in the warmer temperate regions of the Northern Hemisphere, this genus in the cypress (Cupressaceae) family comprises about 13 species of evergreen coniferous trees or shrubs. They are cultivated in mild climates for their dense compact crowns and bold symmetrical outlines. The tall, elegant, long-lived *C. sempervirens* is a famous feature of the gardens of Italy. The tiny, scale-like, closely overlapping leaves vary in character and color; they may be soft to the touch or rather coarse, and are often aromatic. They will withstand regular trimming, and are widely planted for large hedges and windbreaks, as ornamental specimens, and as avenue trees. The small female cones have woody scales, are rarely over 1¾ in (4 cm) long, and are usually persistent.
CULTIVATION: *Cupressus* species tend to grow well in any well-drained fertile soil, preferably in full sun. Place each in a roomy well-spaced position to enable the plant to develop its symmetrical shape naturally and to avoid unsightly fungal disease. Propagate from seed in spring or from cuttings in late summer.

Cupressus arizonica

ARIZONA CYPRESS

↔15 ft (4.5 m) ↕40 ft (12 m)

From Arizona and Mexico. Evergreen conifer, at first densely conical, becomes broadly columnar. Bark gray-brown and stringy. Blue-green foliage, white markings beneath. Cones up to 1 in (25 mm) in diameter. Drought tolerant. ***C. a.* var. *glabra*,** smooth bark; **'Blue Ice'** ★**,** attractive silvery blue foliage. ***C. a.* var. *stephensonii*,** smooth, reddish, peeling bark, blue-green foliage. Zones 7–9.

C

Cupressus funebris

Cupressus macrocarpa

× *Cuprocyparis leylandii*

Cupressus cashmeriana

BHUTAN CYPRESS, KASHMIR CYPRESS

↔20 ft (6 m) ↑30 ft (9 m)

Wild stands of this species have been discovered in Bhutan, solving the mystery of its origin. Narrowly conical habit, ascending branches, long pendulous sprays of aromatic blue-gray branchlets. Unstable, prone to wind damage. Prefers warm sheltered site, regular moisture. *C. c.* var. *darjeelingensis* has soft silvery green foliage. Zones 9–11.

Cupressus funebris

syn. *Chamaecyparis funebris*

CHINESE WEEPING CYPRESS, COFFIN CYPRESS

↔25–30 ft (8–9 m) ↑70–80 ft (21–24 m)

Elegant conical tree from China, once prized for its timber, which was used to make coffins. Makes a charming feature tree, with its gray-green foliage and pendulous branchlets, which have shoots all in one plane. Zones 8–10.

Cupressus gigantea

syn. *Cupressus torulosa* var. *gigantea*

TSANGPO CYPRESS

↔30–35 ft (9–10 m) ↑120 ft (36 m)

Native of southwestern China. Strikingly narrow, very upright tree. Foliage bluish green and angled, diamond-shaped in cross-section. Cones are very small and usually measure well under 1 in (25 mm) long. Zones 8–10.

Cupressus goveniana

GOWEN CYPRESS

↔10 ft (3 m) ↑20 ft (6 m)

Shrub or small tree from California, USA. Conical crown becomes ovoid with age. Grayish brown flaking bark. Bright to dark green leaves, aromatic, maroon-tipped when young. Clusters of rounded female cones persist on the tree for several years. Zones 7–10.

Cupressus guadalupensis var. *forbesii*

TECATE CYPRESS

↔10–17 ft (3–5 m) ↑35–40 ft (10–12 m)

Small slender tree from California, USA, with an irregular outline. Bright green foliage. Flaking bark in varying shades from rich brown to reds. Zones 8–11.

Cupressus lusitanica

CEDAR OF GOA, MEXICAN CYPRESS

↔20 ft (6 m) ↑40 ft (12 m)

From the mountains of western Mexico. Vigorous conifer with a spreading habit. Red-brown bark, peeling in strips. Broad crown of pendulous deep green foliage. A good tree for windbreaks. Cones are round and blue-gray. **'Brice's Weeping'**, attractive cultivar with weeping branches. Zones 8–10.

Cupressus macrocarpa

MONTEREY CYPRESS

↔35 ft (10 m) ↑100 ft (30 m)

Fast-growing evergreen conifer found in Monterey, California, USA. Rare in the wild. Spreading open habit. Thick red to brown or gray bark. Leaves small, scaly, yellowish green, aromatic. Tolerates strong winds and salt-laden air. **'Brunniana Aurea'**, upright conical tree, golden foliage, lemon verbena scent; **'Coneybearii Aurea'**, fine, drooping, golden foliage; **'Donard Gold'**, upright, conical tree, gold-tipped leaves; **'Greenstead Magnificent'**, dense, low, almost prostrate mound of blue-gray foliage becomes even bluer in shade; **'Horizontalis'**, large horizontally spreading tree, grown for hedging, especially the gold form **'Horizontalis Aurea'**. Zones 7–9.

Cupressus montana

syn. *Cupressus arizonica* var. *montana*

SAN PEDRO MARTÍR CYPRESS

↔10–20 ft (3–6 m) ↑20–60 ft (6–18 m)

Known only from the highest parts of the rugged Sierra San Pedro Martír in northern Baja California, Mexico, in forests of pine and fir on rocky ridges. Closely allied to *C. arizonica*, but cones open to release seeds as soon as mature. Zones 8–10.

Cupressus sargentii

SARGENT CYPRESS

↔15 ft (4.5 m) ↑80 ft (24 m)

A species from the coastal forests of California,USA. Deeply fissured stringy bark, heavy branches. Leaves are reduced to mere scales, not very resinous. Cones are around 1 in (25 mm) long. Zones 8–10.

Cupressus sempervirens

MEDITERRANEAN CYPRESS, PENCIL PINE

↔15 ft (4.5 m) ↑50 ft (15 m)

From the Mediterranean region and southern Europe. Strongly upright habit. Fast growing when young, forming attractive spires of dark green. Persistent cones are shining green, ripening red-brown to dull gray with age. **Stricta Group**, very narrow form; **'Swane's Gold'** ★, Australian cultivar, golden foliage. Zones 8–10.

Cupressus torulosa

BHUTAN CYPRESS, HIMALAYAN CYPRESS

↔15 ft (4.5 m) ↑60 ft (18 m)

From below 9,000 ft (2,700 m) in the Himalayas. Strongly upright conical habit, broad-spreading at base in cool climates, narrower in warm areas. Cones small, purplish, marble-like. Suited to windbreaks. **'Nana'**, dwarf form, bright green foliage. Zones 8–9.

× *CUPROCYPARIS*

This group of hybrids between *Xanthocyparis* and *Cupressus* within the cypress (Cupressaceae) family are fast-growing, evergreen, coniferous trees. Fine dark green branchlets are arranged in flattened sprays. Egg-shaped male cones are yellow, the round female cones at first green, turning brown as they ripen. The crosses were made in the late nineteenth century, and 5 of the 6 have been named. They are probably the most frequently planted shelter belt trees in Britain and northern Europe, and will grow to a height of 70 ft (21 m) or so over a period of 25 years.

CULTIVATION: Best in deeply dug, fertile, well-drained soil in full sun, but can be grown in partial shade. Propagate by taking cuttings in late summer from half-hardened wood. As hedging, trim back early in establishment, ideally 2 or 3 times a year.

× *Cuprocyparis leylandii*

syns *Cupressocyparis leylandii, Cupressus leylandii*

LEYLAND CYPRESS

↔15 ft (4.5 m) ↑120 ft (36 m)

Cross between *Cupressus macrocarpa* and *Xanthocyparis nootkatensis*. Flattened, slightly drooping sprays of dark green leaves with a gray sheen. **'Castlewellan'** ★ (syn. 'Galway Gold'), young foliage golden yellow, bronze-green with age; **'Harlequin'** (syn. 'Variegata'), foliage creamy white variegations; **'Naylor's Blue,'** blue-gray foliage; **'Stapehill'**, dense columnar tree. Zones 5–10.

CUSSONIA

Found in tropical and southern Africa and the Comoros Islands, this genus in the ivy (Araliaceae) family has 20 species of evergreen and deciduous shrubs and trees. They are characterized by large snowflake-shaped compound leaves, in spiral rosettes at the branch tips. They produce large candelabra-like heads of small white to yellow blooms and small, soft, red to black drupes.

CULTIVATION: Most need a warm frost-free climate and ample moisture in summer. Plant in a sheltered position in full sun in moist well-drained soil. They also grow well in containers, but can be very top-heavy, and are inclined to tip over. Propagate from seed.

Cussonia paniculata

HIGHVELD CABBAGE TREE

↔7 ft (2 m) ↑12 ft (3.5 m)

Found at moderate altitudes. Large shrub or small tree. Thick corky bark, thin trunk, topped with a head of

Cussonia sphaerocephala

long-stemmed, spine-tipped, blue-green leaves. Many-branched heads of flowers in summer, held well clear of the foliage. Zones 9–11.

Cussonia sphaerocephala
FOREST CABBAGE TREE
↔12 ft (3.5 m) ↑30 ft (9 m)
From the forests of Kwazulu-Natal in South Africa, and Swaziland. Similar to *C. spicata,* but has larger flowerheads and slightly denser foliage rosettes. Withstands very light frosts; not as hardy as *C. spicata*. Zones 9–11.

Cussonia spicata
COMMON CABBAGE TREE
↔12 ft (3.5 m) ↑30 ft (9 m)
Native of southern and eastern Africa and the Comoros Islands. Widely grown species. Thickened rather succulent trunk, develops multiple trunks with age. Much-divided leaves, carried on heavy stems. Large flowerheads in spring–summer. Zones 9–11.

CYCAS
There are about 60 slow-growing woody-stemmed species in this genus of primitive ancient plants in the cycad (Cycadaceae) family. They resemble palms but are not related. Almost all are from tropical and subtropical habitats. Long pinnate fronds are borne in annual flushes; some tropical species are leafless in the dry season. Male and female organs are found on separate plants; pollen in elongated cones at stem apex; seeds on leaf-like, often woolly scales, at first clustered at stem apex but left as "skirt" around stem after next flush of fronds emerges. A few species are garden grown.
CULTIVATION: Full sun and good drainage is required, but cycads can tolerate periods of drought. Propagate from seed or by removing and rooting dormant buds, which can be taken from the mature plant's trunk.

Cycas armstrongii
syn. *Cycas media var. inermis*
↔6 ft (1.8 m) ↑15 ft (4.5 m)
From sandy open forests of northern Australia. Trunk dark gray to black, covered in ovate leaf-stem scars. Soft, feathery, glossy leaves, yellowish green, age to dark green. Separate male and female cones. Fruits globular, yellowish green, blue powdered. Zones 11–12.

Cycas bougainvilleana
↔12 ft (3.5 m) ↑15 ft (4.5 m)
Found in the Solomon Islands and eastern New Guinea. Fronds up to 8 ft (2.4 m) long. Broad, 12 in (30 cm) long leaflets, glossy waxy coating. Hybridizes naturally with other species in its native range. Zones 11–12.

Cycas circinalis ★
SAGO CYCAD, SAGO PALM
↔15 ft (4.5 m) ↑15 ft (4.5 m)
Native of southern Asia, India, and the islands of the Pacific. Forms multiple, cylindrical, gray-brown trunks, crowned with bright green glossy fronds to 10 ft (3 m) long, hooked midrib. Large shiny seeds, yellow and mahogany red. Zones 10–12.

Cycas media ★
NUT PALM, ZAMIA PALM
↔10 ft (3 m) ↑15 ft (4.5 m)
Native of northern Australia. Thick trunk, dark, clearly marked with triangular leaf-stem scars. Stiff dark green fronds, bright yellowish green when young, armed with yellow spines. Male cones yellowish brown. Female cones globular. Fruits ripen orange. Zones 10–12.

Cycas revoluta ★
JAPANESE SAGO CYCAD
↔6 ft (1.8 m) ↑10 ft (3 m)
From Japan. Slow-growing, long-lived. Single, straight, cylindrical trunk, several trunks or a branching trunk. Narrow stiff fronds, narrow, dark, shiny leaflets. Attractive orange fruits in feathery husks. Good indoors or in sheltered courtyards. Zones 9–12.

Cycas bougainvilleana

Cycas rumphii ★
syn. *Cycas thouarsii*
↔10–12 ft (3–3.5 m)
↑20–30 ft (6–9 m)
Cycad from Indonesia, New Guinea, and the Pacific Islands. Arching, glossy, bright green leaves, to 6–8 ft (1.8–2.4 m) long, 150 to 200 narrow sickle-shaped leaflets, to 12 in (30 cm) long, paler beneath, swollen or slightly curved edges. Cylindrical to oval male cones, yellow to brown. Long, narrow, hairy female cones. Zones 9–11.

Cycas taitungensis
↔5–10 ft (1.5–3 m)
↑10–15 ft (3–4.5 m)
Cycad from Taiwan with occasionally branching trunk. Light green, hairy, young leaves, semi-rounded crown of numerous, spreading, glossy, dark green leaves, 3–6 ft (0.9–1.8 m) in length, growing from spiny stalks, and 200 to 400 narrow leaflets that diminish into spines toward the base of their parent leaf. The male cones are narrow, erect, oval, and orange to brown in color; the female cones are rounded, hairy, and covered with soft spines, with a prominent spine at the top. Zones 8–10.

CYCLAMEN
ALPINE VIOLET, PERSIAN VIOLET, SOWBREAD
Distinctive in leaf and flower, the 19 species in this genus in the primrose (Primulaceae) family are tuberous perennials found in Europe in hills and mountains around the Mediterranean Sea and in western Asia. From their flattened tubers, heart-shaped gray-green to blue-green leaves emerge, often patterned silver-gray. They bear one downward-facing flower per stem, in white or pink through purple to red, with large reflexed petals.
CULTIVATION: The tubers need perfect drainage. Add a little grit and fibrous compost, and plant the tuber with its top at or just above soil level. Most prefer dappled shade. Propagate from seed, as established clumps flower better if left undivided.

Cyclamen africanum

Cyclamen africanum
↔8–12 in (20–30 cm)
↑6 in (15 cm)
Perennial from Algeria. Kidney- to heart-shaped leaves, scalloped lobes, toothed edges. Dark green leaves, fine silver and pale green markings above, pale green below. Flowers pale to deep pink, 1 in (25 mm) wide, fragrant, on narrow stems, in autumn. Zones 9–10.

Cyclamen balearicum
↔6–8 in (15–20 cm)
↑3 in (8 cm)
From the Balearic Islands and southern France. Dark green leaves, silver-gray marbling, scalloped shallow-toothed edges, purple-red undersides. Small, fragrant, soft pink or pink-veined white flowers, in spring. Zones 8–10.

Cyclamen cilicium
↔6–8 in (15–20 cm)
↑3–4 in (8–10 cm)
From southwestern Turkey. Forms a neat clump of rounded heart-shaped leaves with toothed edges, green with silver-gray markings above, purple-red below. White to pale pink flowers, flushed deep pink, in autumn. Slightly twisted petals. Zones 7–9.

Cyclamen coum
syn. *Cyclamen atkinsii*
↔6–12 in (15–30 cm)
↑4 in (10 cm)
From southeast Europe, the Caucasus, and the Middle East. Silver-gray and dark green-patterned, rounded, heart-shaped leaves, to just over 2 in (5 cm) long, with purple-red undersides. Small flowers, white, pink, or purple-pink, darker at base, mainly in late winter–spring. The **Pewter Group** is a selection of cultivars with leaves strongly marked with silver-gray, including: **'Maurice Dryden'**, green-edged silver leaves, white flowers; **'Tilebarn Elizabeth'**, silver leaves with narrow green edges, light pink flowers. Zones 6–9.

Cyclamen coum

C

Cyclamen hederifolium

Cyclamen hederifolium

syn. *Cyclamen neapolitanum*

↔6–12 in (15–30 cm)
↑4 in (10 cm)

Found from southern Europe to Turkey. Leaves from small to large, 2–6 in (5–15 cm) long, smooth-edged or serrated, overall dark green or patterned silver-gray, green, or purple-red on undersides. Small light pink flowers, color deepening at center, in late summer–early winter. Often flowers with no foliage present. Zones 6–9.

Cyclamen persicum

↔6–12 in (15–30 cm)
↑6–8 in (15–20 cm)

Native to the eastern Mediterranean, including Crete, Cyprus, and other islands, and also Libya. Variably colored and marked, heart-shaped leaves to over 4 in (10 cm) long, serrated edges. White, mauve, or pink flowers, darker centers, in winter–spring. The florists' cyclamen was developed from this species. Zones 9–10.

Cyclamen purpurascens

syn. *Cyclamen europaeum*

↔6–12 in (15–30 cm)
↑4–6 in (10–15 cm)

Central and eastern European species. Round leaves, bright to deep green, with variable silver-gray markings, red-tinted below, smooth or finely toothed edges. Small strong-scented flowers in pink shades, rarely white, in late summer. **Silver Leafed Group** has strongly marked foliage. Zones 7–11.

Cyclamen repandum

↔6–12 in (15–30 cm)
↑4–6 in (10–15 cm)

Found around and on islands of the central and eastern Mediterranean. Broad, heart-shaped, dark green leaves, 2–5 in (5–12 cm) long, conspicuously scalloped and toothed, variable silver-gray markings above, purple-red below. Fragrant white to magenta flowers, reddening at the center. Zones 7–10.

Cyclamen persicum

Cynara cardunculus

CYMBOPOGON

This genus of 56 species of perennial grasses belongs to the Poaceae family. They are found in tropical and subtropical Asia, Africa, and Australia. The plants form into clumps, and have rather coarse leaves. Many species have aromatic foliage. The tiny flowers are borne in airy panicles.

CULTIVATION: Grow in moisture-retentive well-drained soil in full sun. In cooler areas grow indoors in pots, maintaining moderate humidity. Propagate from seed or by division.

Cymbopogon citratus

LEMON GRASS

↔1 ft (0.3 m) ↑3–5 ft (0.9–1.5 m)

Native to southern India and Ceylon. Clumps of green to bluish green leaves with roughened margins. The strongly lemon-scented foliage is widely used as a flavoring in southeastern Asian cooking. Zones 9–11.

CYNARA

There are 10 species of perennial herbs in this genus, which belongs to the thistle tribe of the daisy (Asteraceae) family. They are native to the Mediterranean, northwestern Africa, and the Canary Islands. The plants resemble giant thistles; they have large leaves with pointed lobes, sometimes spiny, and tall heads of thistle-like flowers. They are cultivated for their imposing presence in ornamental gardens, and also for the immature flowerheads and young stems of some species, which may be eaten as vegetables.

CULTIVATION: Grow in full sun in a well-drained soil, sheltered from strong winds. Allow plenty of space for the large heavy leaves to develop. Propagate by seed or division.

Cynara cardunculus

CARDOON

↔4–8 ft (1.2–2.4 m)
↑4–8 ft (1.2–2.4 m)

Native to Mediterranean regions. Statuesque plant with thick, pointed-lobed, grayish green leaves to 5 ft (1.5 m) long. Large, purple, thistle-like flowers stand above the foliage in summer. Grown ornamentally, young stems can be cooked as a vegetable. *C. c.* var. *scolymus* (syn. Scolymus Group), known as globe artichoke, more compact plant, fatter head, florets less showy; popularly grown as a vegetable, with immature flowerheads harvested and cooked. Zones 7–11.

CYNODON

A genus of 8 species of tropical and subtropical grasses, well-represented in southern Africa, and belonging to the family Poaceae. They have strong creeping stems that root at the nodes as they spread and can also grow upward. The stems interweave and form a dense mat, made more impenetrable by their flat-bladed leaves. Small clusters of flower spikes form at the stem tips, but they are not showy and are unlikely to be seen when the grasses are used for lawns or routinely grazed pastures. The vigor of these grasses is both their appeal and their curse, as when they escape from cultivation they can be very invasive. An oft-quoted statistic claims that if the maximum logarithmic growth rates were sustained for a year, a patch measuring 10 feet square (3 meters square) would spread to cover 50 percent of the land surface of the world.

CULTIVATION: Most cultivated species and forms are tolerant of moderate frosts but will suffer in prolonged periods of frost. Plant in full sun to ensure dense growth, and water well in summer. Feed, aerate, and dethatch in spring. The plants are sometimes raised from seed, but more commonly planted as ready-to-lay rolls, or "plugs," of stolons.

Cynodon dactylon

BAHAMA GRASS, BERMUDA GRASS

↔unlimited ↑2–6 in (5–15 cm)

Widespread species, found in warm temperate to tropical zones. Vigorous spreading grass forming dense turf. Tough stems up to 12 in (30 cm) long, broad-bladed leaves to 6 in (15 cm) long, often gray-tinted. Dense 2 in (5 cm) long flower spikes from late summer. **'U-3'**, tough, coarse-bladed cultivar, suitable only for high-traffic lawns or pasture, not for fine turf. Zones 8–12.

Cynodon × *magennisii*

MAGENNIS BERMUDA GRASS

↔unlimited ↑2–4 in (5–10 cm)

This natural *C. dactylon* × *C. transvaalensis* hybrid is similar to *C. dactylon*, but is slightly less hardy, with finer leaf blades. It is better suited as fine turf grass. **'Santa Ana'**, is popu-lar for tough lawns and sports fields. Many fine-leafed selections have been developed for golf courses, including the very fine **'Tifgreen'**, the slightly coarser and more erect **'Tifway'**; and **'Tifdwarf'**, which has dense growth and very short, fine leaves, ideal for greens. Zones 7–12.

Cymbopogon citratus

Cynodon dactylon

CYNOGLOSSUM

HOUND'S TONGUE

This genus in the borage (Boraginaceae) family is made up of around 55 species of annuals, biennials, and perennials, found mainly in the temperate zones. They have simple, elongated, elliptical to lance-shaped leaves, often densely covered with fine hairs, that form a basal foliage clump. Upright flower stems emerge from the clump, branching into racemes of small 5-petalled flowers, usually in vivid blue shades. The flowers appear mainly in summer. The common name, hound's tongue, refers to the shape and texture of the leaves.

CULTIVATION: Hardiness varies with the species, though most will tolerate quite severe short frosts, if not prolonged freezing. Perfect drainage is essential and summer moisture will improve flowering, so incorporate extra grit and humus. Deadhead the plants frequently to prolong the flowering season. Taller types may need to be staked or tied back. *Cynoglossum* species make ideal subjects for border planting. Hound's tongues can be raised from seed; the perennials can also be propagated from basal cuttings.

Cynoglossum amabile

CHINESE FORGET-ME-NOT

☼/◑ ❄ ↔ 12 in (30 cm)
↕ 20–24 in (50–60 cm)

Biennial from temperate East Asia. Oval to lance-shaped basal leaves to 8 in (20 cm) long, often finely hairy. Sprays of white, pink, or blue flowers, ¼ in (6 mm) wide. **'Firmament'**, dwarf cultivar, gray-green leaves and slightly pendulous bright blue flowers. Zones 7–10.

Cynoglossum grande

☼/◑ ❄ ↔ 12–20 in (30–50 cm)
↕ 24–32 in (60–80 cm)

Perennial native to western North America. Long-stemmed basal leaves to 6 in (15 cm) long, sparsely hairy above, densely hairy below. Showy sprays of deep blue to purple-blue flowers. Zones 8–10.

Cynoglossum nervosum

HAIRY HOUND'S TOOTH

☼/◑ ❄ ↔ 24 in (60 cm)
↕ 24–30 in (60–75 cm)

This bushy upright perennial is native to the Himalayas. The oblong green leaves have short stiff hairs; the flowers are an intense blue, like that of forget-me-nots; they appear in late spring and last for about 4 weeks. Soil must be well drained. This species is highly suitable for a woodland setting, or for a very informal garden. Zones 4–9.

CYPERUS

Around 600 species of annual and perennial sedges from all but the coldest parts of the world make up the type genus for the family Cyperaceae. Perhaps best known as the source of our earliest form of paper, papyrus. *Cyperus* includes other locally useful species that provide thatch and fuel, as well as graceful highly ornamental species and several invasive weeds. From a clump of grassy basal foliage, *Cyperus* sedges produce strongly upright flower stems topped with flowerheads, usually on umbels with leafy bracts. It is their interesting appearance, combined with the light airy foliage and bracts, that give the ornamental species their appeal.

CULTIVATION: Hardiness varies widely, subtropical and tropical species often being intolerant of frost. Otherwise, cultivation is straightforward. Plant *Cyperus* species in a bright position with moist, humus-rich soil and water well in summer. Many species will grow in damp to boggy conditions or even in shallow to quite deep water, though most are equally at home in well-drained soil. Propagate from seed or by division.

Cyperus albostriatus

☼/◑ ❄ ↔ 12 in (30 cm) ↕ 24 in (60 cm)

South African species with many narrow leaves up to 20 in (50 cm) long, with 3 conspicuous pale veins. Flower stems, with broad, leafy, white-lined bracts, do not extend much above the height of the foliage. Will grow in wet soil. Zones 9–12.

Cyperus involucratus

syn. *Cyperus alternifolius subsp. flabelliformis*

☼/◑ ❄ ↔ 24–40 in (60–100 cm)
↕ 3–5 ft (0.9–1.5 m)

Widespread in Africa. Short basal foliage clump and numerous 3-sided flower stems topped with many bracts to 16 in (40 cm) long, with rays to a little over 4 in (10 cm) long. Considered invasive in some areas. **'Variegatus'** ★, foliage with longitudinal cream striping. Zones 9–12.

Cyperus longus

Cyperus longus

GALINGALE

☼/◑ ❄ ↔ 12–36 in (30–90 cm)
↕ 3–5 ft (0.9–1.5 m)

European and North American native with few glossy basal leaves and strong, stiffly upright, 3-angled, aromatic stems topped with drooping heads of long bracts and attractively contrasting brown flowerheads. Will grow in up to 12 in (30 cm) of water. Zones 6–9.

Cyperus papyrus

EGYPTIAN REED, PAPYRUS

☼/◑ ❄ ↔ 5–10 ft (1.5–3 m)
↕ 7–17 ft (2–5 m)

Vigorous, clump-forming, African species, with few or no basal leaves but many strong, deep green, 3-sided stems topped with dense umbels each of 100 or more drooping spikelet stalks. Will grow in water. *C. papyrus* is the "bulrush" of the Old Testament story of Moses. Zones 9–12.

CYPRIPEDIUM

LADY'S SLIPPER

This deciduous genus in the orchid (Orchidaceae) family consists of about 50 sympodial species found in North and Central America, Europe, and Asia. One of the rarest of terrestrial genera, they are protected, and should not be removed from the wild under any circumstances.

CULTIVATION: In cool to temperate climates, these herbaceous perennials can be grown in pots or in the garden, in soils rich in decayed leaf matter. They will not grow in subtropical or tropical climates.

Cypripedium formosanum

◑ ❄ ↔ 4–12 in (10–30 cm)
↕ 4–10 in (10–25 cm)

From Taiwan. Mountain-dwelling species, dislikes warm temperatures. Easy to grow in cool climates. Pair of attractive, fan-like, wavy leaves, and single pale pink flower up to 3 in (8 cm) across with darker markings and large inflated lip. Zones 6–9.

Cyperus involucratus

Cypripedium formosanum

Cyrilla racemiflora

CYRILLA

This genus, comprising a single variable species from southeastern USA to northern South America, is a member of the family Cyrillaceae. It is a shrub or small tree, the leaves are simple, entire, spirally arranged but tending to be grouped at the end of each season's growth. Flowers are in racemes arising from the leaf axils and are comprised of 5 sepals, 5 petals, and 5 stamens. The fruit is a small capsule with 1 seed in each of its 2 compartments.

CULTIVATION: *Cyrilla* species tend to grow best in full sun, in rich, moist, slightly acid or neutral soil. Propagation is from freshly obtained seed, from softwood or root cuttings in spring, or from half-hardened cuttings in summer.

Cyrilla racemiflora

BLACK TITI, LEATHERWOOD

↔3–8 ft (1–2.4 m)
↕3–30 ft (1–9 m)

Variable shrub or small tree, ranging from Virginia in eastern USA south to the West Indies and eastern South America. Northern forms are deciduous, southern are evergreen. Leaves to 4 in (10 cm) long, leathery, turning orange-crimson. Flowers tiny, white, in whorled racemes to 6 in (15 cm) long, from previous year's wood, in summer. Zones 5–11.

CYRTANTHUS

FIRE LILY

There are 47 evergreen or deciduous bulbous plants in this genus in the amaryllis (Amaryllidaceae) family. They are found in tropical and southern Africa, where they grow in a range of habitats, from damp and bushy to near desert conditions. Leaves form at the base of a loose rosette and are linear or strap-shaped. The flowers, upright or pendulous, are usually borne in umbels on strong stems. They are funnel-shaped with flaring lobes. Some are fragrant. Colors range from red and yellow to white.

CULTIVATION: In warm areas can be grown in a sheltered situation with dappled shade, in well-drained sandy soil, but are best suited to pot culture. In cool areas grow under glass in indirect bright light. Water thoroughly and feed weekly when in growth. Propagate from seed or offsets.

Cyrtanthus brachyscyphus

DOBO LILY

↔12–18 in (30–45 cm)
↕12–18 in (30–45 cm)

Evergreen species from South Africa. Narrow linear leaves. The bright reddish orange tubular flowers are narrow and pendulous, in clusters of 6 to 8. Zones 9–11.

Cyrtanthus elatus ★

syns *Cyrtanthus purpureus, Vallota speciosa*

GEORGE LILY, SCARBOROUGH LILY

↔12 in (30 cm) ↕18 in (45 cm)

An evergreen species from South Africa. Tall flower stems bear heads of 6 to 9 upright trumpet-shaped flowers of brilliant red. A popular cut flower. Zones 9–11.

Cyrtanthus elatus

Cyrtanthus falcatus

↔12 in (30 cm) ↕12 in (30 cm)

From KwaZulu-Natal. Deciduous species, leaves appearing after the flowers in spring. The flowers are pendulous, pinkish red and yellow, blooming in clusters of 6 to 10. Zones 9–11.

Cyrtanthus mackenii

IFAFA LILY

↔12 in (30 cm) ↕12 in (30 cm)

From eastern Cape Province. A dainty plant with grass-like foliage, bearing fragrant, tubular, white or yellow flowers, narrow and curving, to 2 in (5 cm) long. *C. mackenii* blooms for long periods in spring–summer. Zones 9–11.

CYRTOMIUM

This small genus of 15 to 20 fast-growing terrestrial or rock-inhabiting evergreen ferns from Hawaii, East Asia to South Africa, and Central to South America, is part of the shield-fern (Dryopteridaceae) family. The plants produce erect densely scaly rhizomes. Broad, firm, pointed, pinnate fronds, with pointed mostly sickle-shaped leaflets with smooth or irregular margins, appear on short tufted stalks. The genus name comes from the Greek *kyrtoma,* meaning arch, and refers to veins that form arch-like patterns in some species.

CULTIVATION: These ferns are easily grown in light sandy soil or mix that is kept moist to dry. Give them abundant water in summer, less in winter. They tolerate drier air than most ferns. They grow best in medium to high light, but keep them out of direct sunlight in summer. They propagate easily from spores in sandy peat in high humidity.

Cyrtanthus falcatus

Cyrtomium falcatum

Cyrtomium falcatum

HOLLY FERN

↔24–36 in (60–90 cm)
↕24–36 in (60–90 cm)

Medium-sized fern with erect rhizomes from India to East Asia, naturalized elsewhere in the Northern Hemisphere. Stems to 16 in (40 cm) long, very dark green and glossy pinnate fronds, 8–24 in (20–60 cm) long, usually with 3 to 11 pairs of short-stalked, oval, thick, leathery leaflets, covered with reddish brown scales when young. **'Butterfieldii'** (Butterfield holly fern), margins coarsely serrated; **'Cristatum'** (syn. 'Mayi'), crested frond tips; **'Rochfordianum'** (Rockford holly fern), segment margins deeply etched, like those of a holly leaf. Zones 6–11.

Cyrtomium fortunei

↔12–24 in (30–60 cm)
↕12–24 in (30–60 cm)

Medium-sized highly variable fern from southern and eastern China to Japan and Korea, with erect rhizomes. Stalks to 12 in (30 cm) long. Broadly sword-shaped fronds with 10 to 26 pairs of narrow pale green to gray-green leaflets with serrated margins, and covered with hair-like scales when young. Zones 5–9.

CYSTOPTERIS

Commonly known as bladder or brittle fern, this member of the cliff-fern (Woodsiaceae) family contains 18 species of delicate deciduous ferns, occurring mostly in the northern temperate zone in rocky situations. Its scientific name comes from the Greek *kustis* (cystis), meaning bladder, and *pteris,* meaning fern; the bladder reference is to the inflated indusium (transparent membrane covering the spores). It is difficult to distinguish between the different species.

CULTIVATION: Grow in shaded moist conditions, such as shady rock gardens or rocky banks. A neutral to slightly alkaline soil is preferred. Propagate from spores or bulblets, or vegetatively by rhizome division. No serious diseases or insect problems.

Cystopteris bulbifera

BERRY BLADDER FERN

☀ ✱ ↔24 in (60 cm)
↕12–24 in (30–60 cm)

From Newfoundland, Canada, to Georgia, USA. Perennial fern distinguished by hairy lacy fronds, wider at the base than the tip. Reproduces by dropping small bulblets that form on the edges and undersides of the arching fronds. Found in the wild in rocky habitats, often on moist shady rock faces. Zones 3–9.

CYTISUS

BROOM

This genus of about 50 species from the pea-flower subfamily of the legume (Fabaceae) family consists of mainly evergreen shrubs. They are native to Europe, with a few in western Asia and North Africa, and vary from small prostrate shrubs to small trees. All the *Cytisus* species have typical pea-flowers; the main flowering season is late spring or summer. The plant's broom-like twiggy growths are sometimes almost leafless. The fruit is a flattened legume with small hard-coated seeds. These species are highly valued ornamentally for their extreme hardiness and their showy flowers.
CULTIVATION: Brooms need a free-draining soil, slightly acidic, fairly low in fertility. A sunny position gives the best display of flowers. Spent flowers and shoots should be removed after flowering, plus some of the older shoots, to encourage new growth from the base. The typical arching habit of the plant should be maintained. Most *Cytisus* species can be propagated from short-tip cuttings of ripened current year's growth, taken in late autumn or early winter.

Cytisus albus

syn. *Chamaecytisus albus*

PORTUGUESE BROOM

☼ ✱ ↔2 ft (0.6 m) ↕3 ft (0.9 m)

Native to southwest European coast of southern Portugal. Leaves 1 in (25 mm) long, leaflets covered in fine hairs. Flowers white to pale yellow, in terminal heads, from summer to autumn. Low-growing forms make attractive rock garden plants. Zones 6–10.

Cytisus ardoinoi

☼ ✱ ↔10–24 in (25–60 cm)
↕10–24 in (25–60 cm)

Native of maritime Alps in southern France. Low, mat-forming, shrub, arching stems, leaves deciduous, trifoliate. Bright yellow flowers, in leaf axils, in spring–summer. Zones 6–9.

Cytisus × *beanii*

☼ ✱ ↔30 in (75 cm) ↕12 in (30 cm)

A hybrid of garden origin between *C. ardoinoi* and *C. purgans*. Dwarf deciduous shrub. Leaves trifoliate, small, hairy. Arching sprays of golden yellow flowers in spring. Zones 6–9.

Cytisus decumbens

PROSTRATE BROOM

☼ ✱ ↔30 in (75 cm) ↕6 in (15 cm)

Native to southern Europe. Gray-green hairy oval leaves. Covering of bright yellow flowers in mid-spring to early summer. Zones 5–9.

Cytisus hirsutus

syn. *Chamaecytisus supinus*

☼ ✱ ↔3 ft (0.9 m) ↕3 ft (0.9 m)

Deciduous species. Often upright, though densely branched prostrate forms are more common in cultivation. Flowers in clusters, brown-speckled, yellow-tipped, in summer. Great spillover plant for rock gardens. Zones 6–10.

Cytisus × *kewensis*

☼ ✱ ↔5 ft (1.5 m) ↕18 in (45 cm)

Hybrid between *C. ardoinoi* and *C. multiflorus*. Semi-prostrate habit, trailing stems. Masses of creamy yellow flowers in early summer. Zones 6–9.

Cytisus hirsutus

Cytisus × *kewensis*

Cytisus multiflorus

syn. *Cytisus albus*

PORTUGUESE BROOM, WHITE SPANISH BROOM

☼ ✱ ↔8 ft (2.4 m) ↕10 ft (3 m)

Erect shrub, native to Spain, Portugal, and parts of North Africa. Leaves simple, narrow in the upper part of the plant, becoming trifoliate lower down. Clusters of white flowers appear along the stems in early to mid-summer. Zones 6–10.

Cytisus × *praecox*

☼ ✱ ↔5 ft (1.5 m) ↕4 ft (1.2 m)

Group of hybrids between *C. multiflorus* and *C. purgans*. Compact habit, profusion of flowers. **'Albus'**, white flowers; **'Warminster'**, grows to about 5 ft (1.5 m) tall, deciduous, stems arching outward, flowers usually held in long sprays on the outer stems, heavily perfumed. Zones 6–9.

Cytisus purpureus

syn. *Chamaecytisus purpureus*

☼ ✱ ↔24 in (60 cm) ↕18 in (45 cm)

Native of southeastern Europe and Balkans. Deciduous species, densely branched. Flowers pale pink to crimson, with dark central blotch, in late spring–summer. Marvelous plant for large rock gardens. ***C. p.* f. *albus***, white flowers. Zones 6–10.

Cytisus scoparius

COMMON BROOM, SCOTCH BROOM

☼ ✱ ↔7 ft (2 m) ↕7 ft (2 m)

Widely grown medium-sized shrub. Almost leafless, bears golden yellow flowers, mostly solitary, in the upper leaf axils in early summer. Brownish streaks on the standards, keels yellow, anthers orange-red. Can be invasive. **'Cornish Cream'**, creamy white flowers. Zones 5–9.

Cytisus supranubius

TENERIFE BROOM

☼ ❄ ↔10 ft (3 m) ↕10 ft (3 m)

Medium-sized shrub, native to the Canary Islands. Small trifoliate leaves on blue-gray branches. Fragrant flowers in leaf axils, white tinged with rose, in spring. Zones 7–10.

Cytisus Hybrid Cultivars

☼ ✱ ↔3–6 ft (0.9–1.8 m)
↕3–8 ft (0.9–2.4 m)

Usually originating from *C.* × *praecox* or *C. scoparius*. **'Boskoop Ruby'**, small rounded shrub, abundant red flowers; **'Burkwoodii'** ★, vigorous bushy shrub, pink flowers, crimson wings yellow-edged; **'Firefly'**, yellow standards, wings stained bronze; **'Fulgens'**, late flowering, dense compact habit, orange-yellow flowers, deep crimson wings; **'Hollandia'**, cream flowers, backs of standards and wings pink, late spring–mid-summer; **'Lena'**, compact free-flowering shrub, red standards, red wings yellow-edged, pale yellow keels; **'Luna'**, creamy yellow, red-tinted flowers, wings yellow, keels lemon yellow; **'Minstead'**, derived from *C. multiflorus*, mauve-tinged white flowers, wings flushed deeper mauve; **'Porlock'**, semi-evergreen shrub, racemes of fragrant creamy yellow flowers in spring. Zones 5–9.

Cytisus scoparius, in spring

D

DACTYLORHIZA

MARSH ORCHID

The deciduous terrestrial orchid genus from the family Orchidaceae consists of about 35 sympodial species native to Europe, northern and western Asia, and North America. They are orchids of the grasslands, frequently found growing in moist situations in bogs and drainage patterns. Most of the variable species have green leaves that are heavily spotted with maroon, and long 2-pronged tubers from which the plant grows. Flower color mostly confined to a range of pink tones, with blooms supplemented by finer and darker spotting over the segments. CULTIVATION: In cool to temperate climates, these herbaceous perennials can be grown in pots or in the garden in soils that are rich in decayed leaf matter. Although the members of this genus are quite frost hardy, they do appreciate protection from the most severe frosts. Constant moisture is required throughout the warmer months, but the plants must be kept drier in winter. They will not grow in subtropical or tropical climates. Propagation is by division.

Dactylorhiza elata

syn. *Orchis elata*

ROBUST MARSH ORCHID

↔ 6 in (15 cm) ↑ 24 in (60 cm)

A native of Europe. This plant has plain, unspotted, green leaves. The spikes are crowded with large deep violet flowers during the summer. Zones 6–9.

Dactylorhiza foliosa

MADEIRAN ORCHID

↔ 4–10 in (10–25 cm) ↑ 12–27 in (30–70 cm)

A European species prolific on the Portuguese island of Madeira. Forms large colonies when well cultivated. Densely flowered from spring–summer, pink to purple species with unspotted leaves. Zones 6–9.

Dactylorhiza fuchsii

syn. *Orchis fuchsii*

COMMON SPOTTED ORCHID

↔ 4–10 in (10–25 cm) ↑ 8–24 in (20–60 cm)

European species. Likes slightly alkaline, limestone soils. Summer flowering species, often confused with the closely related *D. maculata*. **'Cruickshank'**, mauve to purple flowers; **'Rachel'**, white flowers. Zones 6–9.

Dactylorhiza incarnata

syn. *Orchis icarnata*

EARLY MARSH ORCHID

↔ 4–10 in (10–25 cm) ↑ 8–24 in (20–60 cm)

A widespread European species, which bears smaller flowers than many in the genus. Up to 40 pale to mid-pink blooms, ¾ in (18 mm) tall, in spring–summer. Zones 5–9.

Dactylorhiza urvilleana

↔ 4–10 in (10–25 cm) ↑ 10–32 in (25–80 cm)

From Europe. Slender, with about 4 or 5 stem-clasping leaves produced along inflorescence that bears up to 90 lilac to purple blooms on robust specimens, in spring–summer. Zones 5–9.

DAHLIA

Genus named after Swedish botanist Andreas Dahl (1751–89). Around 30 species of tuberous-rooted perennials in daisy (Asteraceae) family. From Mexico to as far south as Colombia; in dwarf forms to tree-sized species that can grow to over 20 ft (6 m) high in one season. Most are immediately recognizable, with similar pinnate to tripinnate foliage, hollow cane-like stems and bright flowerheads. Wild species usually have single blooms; garden forms show many styles and colors. CULTIVATION: Full sun or partial shade with moist, fertile, humus-rich, well-drained soil. Do not crowd, good air circulation lessens risk of mildew. Tops die with first frosts, but provided soil does not freeze or become waterlogged, tubers can be left in ground for winter. Elsewhere, lift tubers, store in dry sand or sawdust in a frost-free place. Propagate small bedding strains from seed; divide tubers or take basal cuttings.

Dahlia coccinea

↔ 2–4 ft (0.6–1.2 m) ↑ 7–10 ft (2–3 m)

From Mexico to Guatemala. One of main parents of garden dahlias. Dark green, often purple-tinted, tripinnate leaves, toothed, pointed oval leaflets. Clusters of 2 to 3 flowerheads, ray florets yellow through red to purple-red in summer–autumn. Zones 8–11.

Dahlia imperialis

TREE DAHLIA

↔ 7–15 ft (2–4.5 m) ↑ 17–25 ft (5–8 m)

From Guatemala to Colombia. Huge bamboo-like stems. Many-flowered cluster of pink to lavender flowerheads. Blooms autumn–winter, and often cut by frost before flowering in temperate climates. Zones 8–11.

Dahlia merckii

↔ 3 ft (0.9 m) ↑ 7 ft (2 m)

Mexican species. Leaves often finely divided and red-tinted. Clusters of delicate, upright or semi-pendulous, white to purple flowerheads from late summer. Zones 8–10.

Dahlia pinnata

↔ 20–36 in (50–90 cm) ↑ 5–7 ft (1.5–2 m)

From Mexico. Found in the parentage of most garden dahlias. Purple-tinted leaves, divided into 3 to 5 sometimes downy segments. Flowers from late spring with clustered flowerheads in a range of colors except red. Zones 8–11.

Dactylorhiza foliosa

Dactylorhiza incarnata

Dahlia imperialis

Dahlia tenuicaulis

☼/◐ ❄ ↔3–7 ft (0.9–2 m)
↑10–15 ft (3–4.5 m)

Found in Mexico. A tree-like species in the manner of *D. imperialis* but smaller and earlier flowering. Leaves are often bipinnate, with toothed, pointed, oval leaflets. Flowerheads, lilac pink to near magenta, form in large clusters, with short rounded ray florets, summer–autumn. Zones 9–11.

Dahlia Hybrid Cultivars

☼ ❄ ↔1–3 ft (30–90 cm)
↑1½–3 ft (0.5–0.9 m)

Although breeders are currently trying to introduce other species into the mix, virtually all of our modern garden dahlias are *D. coccinea* × *D. pinnata* hybrids. This cross first appeared in Madrid, Spain, in 1789, not long after dahlias arrived in Europe from Mexico. Since that time, hybridizers have been able to produce a huge and remarkably dazzling range of garden plants in all manner of hues and striking combinations of colors.

As with other genera that have been developed into a wide range of cultivars and hybrids, dahlias are divided into groups. These are based on the flower type, although gardeners need to also consider plant size and weather resistance when making selections. Large cultivars with huge intricate flowers are undoubtedly spectacular but rarely do well in open gardens exposed to the wind. Most dahlias reach their peak of bloom after the longest day and continue to flower until frost or winter cold intervenes. Zones 8–11.

The dahlia groups are as follows.

Dahlia, HC, 1. Single-flowered, 'Yellow Hammer'

Dahlia, HC, 2. Anemone-flowered, 'Brio'

1. SINGLE-FLOWERED

This group comprises cultivars with simple wide-open single flowerheads. These are usually small, and are often treated as summer bedding annuals. Larger forms may have 2 rows of ray florets but the disc florets are always present and clearly visible. Typical single-flowered cultivars include: 'Best Bett' (syn. 'Mystic Spirit'), soft orange-yellow flowers, purple-bronze foliage; **'Coltness Gem'**, dwarf bedding strain available in several colors; 'Happy Single Wink', deep pink, red center, purple bronze foliage, one of the Happy Single Series; 'Knockout' (syn. 'Mystic Illusion'), bright yellow, purple-bronze foliage; and **'Yellow Hammer'**, bedding form with yellow flowers and nicely contrasting bronze-green foliage.

2. ANEMONE-FLOWERED

Flowerheads have 1 or 2 rows of outer ray florets, sometimes slightly incurved, with densely packed, similarly colored, tubular disc florets that often give the flowerhead a mounded center. 'Blue Bayou', lavender-pink ray florets with contrasting purple-red disc florets; **'Brio'**, orange scarlet with large group of disc florets, short reflexed rays; 'Eileen C', orange-red ray florets, disc florets shading to lighter orange at the tips; 'Garden Show', ray florets white with variable red flushing, disc florets yellow at the tips, lighter and flushed red toward the center; and **'Miss Saigon'**, dull orange to pink disc florets, reflexed pale pink rays.

Dahlia, HC, 4. Waterlily, 'Fürst Pückler'

Dahlia, HC, 5. Decorative, 'Arabian Night'

Dahlia, HC, 6. Ball, 'Black Pearl'

3. COLLERETTE

Collerette flowerheads have 1 or 2 outer rows of flat ray florets, an inner row of short ray-like disc florets called the "collar," and a clear center or anther-bearing disc florets. **'Clair de Lune'**, yellow with a pale collar, is typical of the form; 'Inver Splash', light yellow with variable pinkish red flecks, stripes, and sectors; 'Pale Tiger', light orange with darker orange outer ray florets; and 'Rural Lady', bright red with a red-flushed white collar.

4. WATERLILY

Fully double flowerheads with relatively few broad ray florets. They may be flat to slightly involute or revolute. (Involute florets are rolled along their length from underside to upperside; revolute florets are rolled the opposite way: upperside to underside.) This produces rather flat blooms lacking the high center that is characteristic of most double dahlias. Popular waterlily cultivars include: **'Fascination'**, deep pink, semi-double flowers, dark foliage; 'Figurine', beautiful soft pink lightening toward the center, color and form genuinely reminiscent of a waterlily; **'Fürst Pückler'**, deep pinkish red, yellow flushed; **'Glorie van Heemstede'**, bright yellow double flowers; **'Nepos'**, white and lavender; 'Taratahi Ruby', all-over intense glowing orange-red; and **'Vanessa'**, pale to deeper pink.

5. DECORATIVE

Double style, with no central disc, and broad, flat or slightly involute florets making a rounded head. In some classifications this group is subdivided into formal (very even petals that are neatly arranged) and informal (more open and less regular). The flowers are classified as giant, large, medium, small, or miniature depending upon their size. Giant flowers do not, however, necessarily mean giant plants: some of the largest flowers are borne on relatively small plants. Some examples include: **'Akita'**, dark red flushed with yellow; **'Arabian Night'**, a deep black-red turning red, and lightening with age; **'Audacity'**, an unusual combination of maroon with a light golden yellow center; **'Clarion'**, bright yellow flowers, with very dark, black-red foliage; **'Doris Duke'**, apricot-pink shade deepening at the center; **'Fiaker'**, light purple; **'Formby Perfection'**, with magenta to lavender flowers; and **'Orange Sun'**, bright orange flowers, flushed with red. Other cultivars include: 'Croydon Masterpiece', soft orange to coral, old favorite from 1948; 'Edinburgh', deep burgundy with broad white floret tips; 'Grayval Esther', soft pink deepening at center; **'Hamari Gold'**, giant flowers of deep golden amber; **'Hamilton Lillian'**, yellow- to apricot-pink; **'Hulin's Carnival'**, red, splashed white; **'Jennie'**, white to cream with a yellow center, flushed and edged with deep pink, fringed edges; **'Kelvin Floodlight'**, enormous bright yellow, fully double flowers; 'Kotare Buttermilk', large pure white flowerheads; 'Mom's Special', white turning to lavender-pink at the edges, variable lavender-pink flecks and stripes; **'My Valentine'**, soft light red; **'Pearl of Heenstede'**, pale pink, double flowers on thin stems; **'Peter'**, deep rose pink; **'Purple Joy'**, deep purple-red, darkening at the center; 'Rhanna Tammy', opens deep gold and ages to a buff orange tone; **'Stefan Bergerhof'**, bright orange; **'Suffolk Punch'**, deep purple; **'Tartan'**, white with deep purple markings; **'Ted's Choice'**, a deep purple-pink; **'Zingaro'**, cream with a yellow center, edged and flushed with a deep red-pink; and **'Zorro'**, with huge deep red flowers.

6. BALL

Ball-shaped flowerheads are globular but may be slightly flattened on top. The ray florets are broad, rounded at the tips and involute for half their length. They are divided by flower size into miniature, up to 4 in (10 cm) in diameter; small, 4–6 in (10–15 cm) in diameter; medium, 6–8 in (15–20 cm) in diameter; and large, over 8 in (20 cm) across. Popular ball cultivars include: 'Amira', deep magenta, long stems; 'Barbarry Ideal', bright coral, shading slightly toward orange at center of florets; **'Black Pearl'**, deep maroon, almost black at center; **'Boy Scout'**, deep pink with a darker center; **'Charles Dickens'**, small pink flowers; **'Kathryn's Cupid'**, soft orange-pink double flowers; 'Riverlea Summerwine', deep purple-red; and **'Wootton Cupid'**, with dark pink flowers.

D

Dahlia, HC, 7. Pompon, 'Aurwen's Violet'

Dahlia, HC, 8. Cactus, 'Friquolett'

Dais cotinifolia

7. POMPON

Flowerheads nearly spherical. Similar to the ball style but with smaller flowers that give the impression of more tightly packed florets. Florets are involute for their entire length. Typical pompon cultivars include: **'Aurwen's Violet'**, bright purple; 'Chick A Dee', deep wine red with variable white and pink markings, usually at lower edges or center; 'Hallmark', opens very pale pink, deepens with age; 'Jomanda', overall coral to orange-red; 'Kasasagi', picotee effect, yellow edged with orange-red; **'Linos '**, bright yellow almost orange center; **'Lollipop'**, pinkish to mauve, outer ray florets ageing to pale pink; **'Mini Pompon Orange'**, orange, turning reddish in center; 'Moorplace' (syn. 'Moor Place'), deep burgundy purple, densely packed florets; **'Night Queen'**, deepest black-red; and **'White Aster'**, evenly shaped, white flowers.

8. CACTUS

Fully double flowerheads with long quilled ray florets and no central disc. The quilling extends for at least half the length of the floret. Both cactus and semi-cactus forms are further subdivided into large- and small-flowered types and are available in a wide range of colors. Some popular cultivars include: **'Alfred Grille'**, yellow-centered turning deep pink to light red at the tips; **'Border Princess'**, with small orange and yellow flowers; 'Canaries', yellow center, light orange outer ray florets; **'Feuerwerk'**, a bright red with very narrow ray florets like a starburst firework in keeping with its name; **'Friquolett'**, fiery red with white tips; **'Hillcrest Royal'**, intense deep purple-red fully double flowers, with a strong quilted effect; 'Nuit d'Ete' (syn. 'Summer Night'), darkest black-red; 'Oreti Rebel', deep purple pink with pale tips; **'Park Princess'**, bright pink with a yellow center, super reliable and often mass planted for effect;

Dahlia, HC, 9. Semi-cactus, 'Aspen'

'Villandry', salmon pink shading to yellow at center; and **'Wagschal's Goldkrone'**, golden yellow to light orange blooms.

9. SEMI-CACTUS

Not semi-double-flowered cactus forms, but fully double flowers with broad-based ray florets that are quilled for less than half their length. They may be straight or incurving. Popular cultivars include: **'Aspen'**, white, somewhat twisted ray florets, yellowing toward the center; **'Color Magic'**, creamy yellow with irregular sectors, flakes and flecks of deep pink; **'Elga'**, deep mauve with long ray florets; **'Engelhardt's Jubiläum'**, deep golden yellow to light orange; **'Explosion'**, white to cream blooms with purple-red markings and center; **'Fürsten Elizabeth von Bismarck'**, cerise flowerheads; **'Golden Charmer'**, a golden yellow to pale orange; **'Goldener Reiner'**, golden yellow to light orange; 'Grand Finale', reddish purple suffused and tipped with lavender-pink; 'Grayval Sunkist', deep yellow suffused with coral to light orange tones; **'Hamari Accord'**, a soft but bright yellow; **'Herzdame'**, orange, reddening at the tips, edges and center; **'Magic Moment'**, white, very full flowerheads; **'My Love'**, white blooms with a hint of yellow at the center; 'Nenekazi', bright yellow center passing through pink at mid-floret to deeper lavender at tips; **'Royal Wedding'**, orange and yellow; **'So Dainty'**, broad apricot-pink ray florets, with dark edges; 'Sultan', orange with irregular bright red flecks, stripes, and sector;**'Vulcan'**, orange-red with lighter tips; **'Wittemann's Best'**, bright red; and **'Wootton Impact'**, which bears flowers that are classic bronze in color.

10. MISCELLANEOUS

This is a catch-all group for the leftover species of dahlia that do not really fit in the other groups. They are subdivided into several small groups that have too few cultivars to justify a special group of their own. This group includes the very dwarf miniature cultivars. 'Freya's Thalia', crimson, deepening slightly at center; **'Jescot Julie'** is a burnt orange, plum purple, orchid-flowering miniature; **and 'Marie Schrugg'**, dark red and miniature.

11. FIMBRIATED

These dahlias feature fully double flowers with no central disc. The florets may be flat, rolled, or twisted, but have a cut or pinked effect at the tips, creating a fringed edge. **'Anna Mari'**, white center turning to purple-pink at the tips; **'Intombi Yum'**, soft yellow with a little pink at floret tips; **'Show 'n' Tell'**, intense orange-red with yellow tips; **'Tahoma Moonshot'**, bright yellow center with red exterior to quills; and **'Tioga Dawn'**, white shading to pink edges, deep pink center.

12. STAR

As the name suggests, these dahlias have flowerhead with just a few widely spaced inward- or outward-rolled ray florets around a central disc. **'Amy's Star'**, pale pink with deep purple-pink rolled floret edges; **'Honka'**, light yellow, very spidery effect, scented; **'Tahoma Hope'**, pure white; and **'Willie Willie'**, white to pale pink with darker pink rolled edges.

13. DOUBLE ORCHID

The double orchid style has revolute florets with no visible central disc. The inner florets are often very narrow, while the outer florets may be broader and less rolled. **'Alloway Candy'**, mid-pink, lighter center; **'Christie Galah'**, bright pink with light center to each floret; **'Pink Giraffe'**, partly rolled florets, white with deep pink horizontal stripe effect; and **'Santa Claus'**, fire engine red, edged in white.

14. PEONY

Peony dahlias have two or more rows of ray florets but still have a clearly visible center of fertile, non-petaloid disc florets. The ray florets are flat or only slightly rolled. **'Bishop of Llandaff'**, vivid red *Cosmos*-like flowerheads and deep red-tinted foliage; **'Chic'**, golden yellow, deeper at center on first opening; **'Elvira'**, all-over shocking pink; and **'Stillwater Raspberry'**, deep pink transitioning gradually to a white center.

DAIS

This genus consists of 2 species of evergreen or semi-deciduous shrubs or small trees belonging to the daphne (Thymelaeaceae) family. They are found in South Africa and the island of Madagascar where they grow in the moist frost-free margins of wooded regions. One species is widely grown in warmer climate gardens as an evergreen; it is commonly known as the pompon tree for its showy clusters of small pink flowers.

CULTIVATION: Mature plants can withstand light frost, but are best planted in a sunny position with some protection from surrounding shrubs. They thrive in well-drained fertile loam covered with an organic mulch to retain moisture during summer months. Propagate from seed in spring or from half-hardened cuttings.

Dais cotinifolia ★

POMPON TREE

↔ 10 ft (3 m) ↕ 10 ft (3 m)

This species is found in South Africa and Madagascar. Compact, rounded, evergreen shrub. Deciduous in cooler situations. Reddish bark, slightly scented pink flowerheads on the tips of branches in summer. Blue-green foliage. Zones 9–11.

DALEA

INDIGO BUSH

This genus, comprising about 160 species from North, Central, and South America, most diverse in Mexico and the Andes, is a member of the pea-flower subfamily of the legume (Fabaceae) family. They are small trees, shrubs, or herbs. Shoots, including the flowers, are dotted with tiny glands. The leaves are pinnate, sometimes reduced to only 3 leaflets. Flowers, in terminal racemes or spikes, are yellow, purple, or white, sometimes bicolored with the standard (upper petal) of a color contrasting with that of the wings and keel. Seed pods are egg-shaped in outline, flattened, with 1 or 2 kidney-shaped seeds.

CULTIVATION: Most are best restricted to native plantings and grow well in well-drained soils in full sun. Not recommended for wet-winter climates. They are propagated from seed.

Dalea frutescens

Dalea frutescens

BLACK DALEA

↔ 4 ft (1.2 m) ↕ 3 ft (0.9 m)

From south-central USA, and northern Mexico; spreading semi-deciduous shrub with lower branches resting on ground and taking root. Leaves to 1 in (25 mm) long. Profuse display of bright rose-purple and white flowers, in short spikes, in autumn. Selected forms have been promoted. Zones 7–10.

Dalea greggii

↔ 6 ft (1.8 m) ↕ 18 in (45 cm)

Widespread in Mexico, extending into southern Texas and New Mexico, USA. Low mounding subshrub with long trailing and rooting stems, small leaves, spikes of rose-purple flowers, in spring– summer. Zones 8–11.

Dalea purpurea

syn. *Petalostemon purpureum*

PURPLE PRAIRIE CLOVER, VIOLET PRAIRIE CLOVER

↔ 18 in (45 cm) ↕ 18–36 in (45–90 cm)

Erect multi-stemmed perennial that is found in drier tall-grass prairie in nearly all interior States of USA and southern Canada. Leaves up to 2 in (5 cm) long, with 5 leaflets. Flowers bright purple, in dense spikes surrounding a cone of buds, in summer. Zones 4–10.

DANAE

There is just one species of fleshy-stemmed evergreen perennial in this genus, which belongs to the asparagus (Asparagaceae) family. It is found in forests from northern Iran to southwestern Asia. Each year new shoots emerge in the manner of asparagus, to which it is related. The plant is primarily grown for its attractive foliage, the tiny cream flowers being of little significance. The flowers are followed by small orange-red berries.

CULTIVATION: This species is easily grown in moisture-retentive soil in either full sun or part-shade. Propagate by division.

Dalea greggii

Daphne caucasica

Danae racemosa

syn. *Danae laurus*

ALEXANDRIAN LAUREL

↔ 3–4 ft (0.9–1.2 m) ↕ 3–4 ft (0.9–1.2 m)

Shrubby perennial annually sending up shoots from rhizomes. The flexible, arching stems are reminiscent of a small bamboo. Pointed oval leaves, attractive glossy green. Zones 6–9.

DAPHNE

Renowned for its fragrance, this genus in the daphne family (Thymelaeaceae) includes 50 or so evergreen and deciduous shrubs, extending from Europe and North Africa to temperate and subtropical Asia. Forming neat compact bushes, many of them make excellent rockery plants. The leaves are usually simple with smooth-edged, blunt-tipped, elongated ovals, either thin and dull green or thick, leathery, and slightly glossy. Individually flowers are small, usually in shades of white, cream, yellow, or pink, and carried in showy rounded heads that are sometimes highly scented. Drupes follow the flowers and are sometimes colorful.

CULTIVATION: Daphnes generally prefer moist, cool, humus-rich, well-drained, slightly acid soil. If camellias and rhododendrons do well in your garden, so should daphnes. Once established, daphnes resent disturbance, so avoid damaging the surface roots by cultivation. Use mulch to suppress weeds. Small-leafed species prefer bright conditions; those with larger leaves are happier shaded from the hottest sun. Propagate from seed or by cuttings or layers.

Daphne bholua

↔ 4 ft (1.2 m) ↕ 10 ft (3 m)

Native to the eastern Himalayas. There are deciduous and evergreen forms. Strongly scented white flowers, tinged with pink, develop from deep pink buds, in winter–spring. Drupes ripen to black. They are known as paper daphnes as paper and ropes were once made from the bark. **'Gurkha'** is both hardy and deciduous. Zones 7–10.

Daphne × *burkwoodii*

BURKWOOD DAPHNE

↔ 5 ft (1.5 m) ↕ 5 ft (1.5 m)

Hybrid between *D. cneorum* and *D. caucasica*. Twiggy, densely foliaged, evergreen or semi-evergreen bush. Matt mid-green foliage. Small, fragrant, pink flowers, in spring. **'Carol Mackie'**, variegated foliage form, more colorful when not in flower. Zones 5–9.

Daphne caucasica

↔ 5 ft (1.5 m) ↕ 6 ft (1.8 m)

Deciduous species from the Caucasus and western Asia. Leaves light green above, glaucous undersides. Flowers, white and fragrant, borne in clusters of around 20, on short lateral shoots. Red or black drupes. Zones 6–9.

Daphne × *burkwoodii*

Daphne cneorum 'Ruby Glow'

Daphne odora

Daphne genkwa

Dasylirion acrotrichum

Daphne cneorum

GARLAND DAPHNE, GARLAND FLOWER, ROCK DAPHNE, ROSE DAPHNE

↔ 24 in (60 cm) ↑ 8 in (20 cm)

Near-evergreen Eurasian species. Dense twiggy shrub. Massed heads of small, fragrant, bright pink flowers in spring. Requires excellent drainage, shelter from hot summer sun, and some winter chilling. Worth trying in a rockery or alpine trough. **'Eximia'** ★, sturdier than the species; **'Ruby Glow'**, rich red flowers. Zones 4–9.

Daphne genkwa

LILAC DAPHNE

↔ 5 ft (1.5 m) ↑ 5 ft (1.5 m)

Deciduous shrub from China. The young foliage is coppery with new stems covered in fine down. Bears large, lavender, slightly fragrant, delicate flowers, in spring. Propagation difficulties keep *D. genkwa* a fairly rare plant. Zones 5–9.

Daphne odora

WINTER DAPHNE

↔ 5 ft (1.5 m) ↑ 5 ft (1.5 m)

Native of China and Japan. Evergreen shrub with deep green leaves. Bears fragrant clusters of fleshy, pale pink flowers, from mid-winter. Not long-lived. Replace every 8 to 10 years. ***D. o.* f. *rosacea,*** white and pink flowers; **'Rubra'**, dark reddish pink flowers, less fragrance. ***D. o.*** var. *variegata* **'Aureomarginata'**, yellow-edged leaves, hardier and easier to grow than the species. Zones 8–10.

Daphne tangutica

↔ 5 ft (1.5 m) ↑ 6 ft (1.8 m)

Native to northwestern China. Evergreen shrub with small gray-haired leaves. Densely crowded clusters of small, fragrant, rosy purple flowers, reminiscent of lilac *(Syringa),* in spring–summer. Small red fruits. **Retusa Group**, dark green leaves, small, fragrant, purplish red flowers. Zones 6–9.

Daphne × *transatlantica*

↔ 3–4 ft (0.9–1.2 m) ↑ 3–4 ft (0.9–1.2 m)

A hybrid between *D. caucasica* and *D. collina.* Neat, compact, evergreen shrub. Leaves narrow, thick, with blunt, rounded tips. Clusters of small, very fragrant white flowers opening from pink buds, long-flowering. **'Eternal Fragrance'**, flowers almost year-round; **'Summer Ice'**, cream-edged leaves. Zones 5–9.

DAPHNIPHYLLUM

From the Himalayas, China, Japan, Korea, and Southeast Asia as far as New Guinea, this genus of about 15 evergreen shrubs or trees, in the family Daphniphyllaceae, has inconspicuous petal-less flowers borne in clusters in leaf axils, in the late spring or early summer. Members of the genus are dioecious, requiring both male and female plants for reproduction. Male flowers are purplish red, female flowers are green, and leaves are simple and leathery. Fruit is a single-seeded drupe, usually bluish black. Valued mostly for their ornamental year-round foliage.
CULTIVATION: Moist, well-drained, slightly acid, mulched soils are preferred, as well as a sheltered position with some shade. The plants are relatively free of serious pests. Propagation is from seed.

Daphniphyllum macropodum

syn. ***Daphniphyllum himalaense subsp. macropodum***

FALSE DAPHNE

↔ 10–25 ft (3–8 m) ↑ 10–30 ft (3–9 m)

From China, Japan, and Korea. Dark, glossy, leathery, rhododendron-like alternate leaves, with long red stalks. Specimen plant, or suitable for screen or hedge. Zones 6–11

DARMERA

syn. ***Peltiphyllum***

A genus of one species from western North America belonging to the saxifrage (Saxifragaceae) family. Large her-baceous perennial, found along stream sides and in damp woods, grown for its dramatic foliage and early flowers. Re-commended for bog garden or fernery.
CULTIVATION: Plant in moist to wet soils, rich in organic matter, in a cool sheltered site. Propagate by division of established clumps, although raising from seed is an option if sown fresh.

Darmera peltata

syn. ***Peltiphyllum peltatum***

↔ 3–10 ft (0.9–3 m) ↑ 5–7 ft (1.5–2 m)

Herbaceous perennial with rounded heads of tiny pink flowers prior to foli-age in very early spring. Huge leaves soon follow like bright green umbrellas. Dwarf form also grown. Zones 6–10.

DASYLIRION

From southern USA and Mexico, this genus of 18 species is made up of evergreen perennials. *Dasylirion*, in the asparagus (Asparagaceae) family, is closely related to *Beaucarnea.* Single trunk topped with a head of linear leaves that in some species are over 3 ft (0.9 m) long and with edges often spiny-toothed. From among the foliage emerges a tall spike, bearing a vast number of creamy white flowers. Male and female flowers occur on separate plants, usually in the summer.
CULTIVATION: As with most dry-country plants, *Dasylirion* species demand good drainage and full sun. They tolerate light to moderate frosts but suffer if kept wet and cold for prolonged periods. Soil should be light and gritty, though a little extra humus is appreciated. Propagate from seed.

Dasylirion acrotrichum

↔ 5 ft (1.5 m) ↑ 10–20 ft (3–6 m)

Mexican species. The leaves are light green, very narrow, edges with teeth and hooked spines. Inflorescence usually upright to 12 ft (3.5 m) tall. Zones 8–11.

Dasylirion longissimum

syn. ***Dasylirion quadrangulatum***

MEXICAN GRASS TREE, TOOTHLESS SPOON

↔ 6–8 ft (1.8–2.4 m) ↑ 5–25 ft (1.5–8 m)

Mounding, grass-like, succulent, evergreen perennial from eastern Mexico. A spray of stiff, arching, narrow, 4-angled, strap-like leaves, forms billowing grassy head. Insignificant white flowers tinged with green, on erect spikes to 20 ft (6 m) tall. Grow in sheltered position, with support when in flower. Zones 8–11.

Dasylirion wheeleri ★

DESERT SPOON, SOTOL

↔ 3 ft (0.9 m) ↑ 12–25 ft (3.5–8 m)

Found in arid parts of southeastern Arizona and Texas, USA. Leaves blue-green, viciously spiny. Flower spike is very tall. Zones 7–11.

DATURA

This genus of 11 species from southern North America but now widely naturalized in much of the world, belongs to the nightshade (Solanaceae) family. Annual plants with erect flowers and dry capsular fruit, compared with *Brugmansia* (the "daturas" of warm-climate gardens), which have drooping flowers and fleshy fruit. Leaves simple, smooth-edged, or with wavy margins, spirally arranged. The short-lived

flowers arise from leaf axils or forks in the branches. Flowers are tubular or funnel-shaped, usually white though sometimes blotched purple, occasionally yellow or violet. Fruit is a usually spiny short-stalked capsule with 2 compartments, splitting irregularly. Like species of *Brugmansia*, they contain powerful alkaloids, which can be highly toxic, though they have been used as hallucinogens by Native Americans.
CULTIVATION: *Datura* demand good drainage and heavy watering rather than light and often. They are ideal in tubs. Propagate from seed in full sun after frost has finished.

Datura inoxia

syn. *Datura meteloides*

ANGEL'S TRUMPET, DOWNY THORN APPLE, INDIAN APPLE

↔36 in (90 cm) ↕36 in (90 cm)

From Central America. Annual with large, downy, oval leaves. Fragrant flowers, upward-facing, tubular, flaring, white, sometimes flushed pink, and round spiny fruits. **'Evening Fragrance'**, very fragrant selected form. Zones 8–11.

Datura stramonium

COMMON THORN APPLE, JAMESTOWN WEED, JIMSON WEED

↔3–6 ft (0.9–1.8 m) ↕3–6 ft (0.9–1.8 m)

Annual from the Americas, widely naturalized elsewhere. Coarsely toothed leaves with an unpleasant odor when crushed. Tubular flowers, white or purple. Spiny fruits. This extremely poisonous plant contains a hallucinogen. Zones 7–11.

DAVIDIA

The only species in this genus of the dogwood (Cornaceae) family, a deciduous tree, was introduced from China by the French missionary Armand David in the 1890s and the genus was subsequently named after him. *D. involucrata* is native to southwestern China where it grows in damp mountain woods. A handsome tree, with a broadly conical outline and attractive foliage, flowering bracts, and fruit.
CULTIVATION: *D. involucrata* makes an excellent specimen tree although it does have a tendency to branch at a low level so corrective pruning should be carried out to ensure a good straight trunk develops. It requires deep, rich, moist soil; sheltered site. Flowers when tree is about 10 years old. Propagation best from fresh seed, dry seed has much reduced germination rate.

Davidia involucrata ★

DOVE TREE, GHOST TREE, HANDKERCHIEF TREE

↔30 ft (9 m) ↕60 ft (18 m)

Leaves aromatic, toothed margins, heart-shaped bases, downy beneath, taper to a long point. Spherical heads of tiny true flowers surrounded by 2 large, white ornamental bracts of unequal size, in late spring, with the new leaves. Plum-like fruit ripens to purple-brown. ***D. i.* var. *vilmoriniana***, more commonly seen, with leaves smooth beneath. Zones 6–9.

Davidia involucrata

Datura inoxia 'Evening Fragrance'

DELOSPERMA

Found mainly in southern Africa but also spread through eastern Africa to Saudi Arabia, this genus, a member of the iceplant (Aizoaceae) family, is composed of over 150 species of annuals, biennials, and perennials that often have a low spreading habit and can become shrubby. Most have a thickened, somewhat tuberous, central stem known as a "caudex," from which emerge fine stems clothed in succulent cylindrical leaves. The daisy-like flowers are usually small, but are exceptionally bright and abundant. Most species flower in late spring.
CULTIVATION: Intolerant of repeated hard frosts, otherwise undemanding, easily grown in any gritty free-draining soil that can be kept moist during the flowering season. Ideal for covering dry banks and rock walls, often naturalizing in crevices. Propagate from seed, cuttings, or by layering, either natural or deliberately encouraged.

Delosperma aberdeenense

↔20 in (50 cm)
↕4–8 in (10–20 cm)

From South Africa. Small, spreading, slightly mounding, densely branched shrub. Pale pink to magenta flowers. Zones 7–10.

Delosperma ashtonii

↔20 in (50 cm)
↕6–8 in (15–20 cm)

From South Africa. Thick dark green leaves. Clump-forming and slow to spread. Large purple-pink flowers. Zones 5–10.

Delosperma brunnthaleri

↔20 in (50 cm)
↕12–16 in (30–40 cm)

From South Africa. Multi-branched small shrub. Pink or yellow flowers. Zones 8–10.

Delosperma crassuloides

↔24 in (60 cm) ↕2 in (5 cm)

From the Drakensberg mountains of eastern South Africa, this mat-forming plant has densely crowded, oblong, green leaves. Scattered pink flowers. Zones 9–11.

Delosperma lehmannii

↔20 in (50 cm)
↕6–8 in (15–20 cm)

From South Africa. Low spreader with thick, gray-green, keeled leaves reminiscent of *Carpobrotus*. Soft yellow flowers. Zones 9–11.

Delosperma sutherlandii

↔24–32 in (60–80 cm)
↕6–20 in (15–50 cm)

From South Africa. Low and spreading or shrubby. The leaves are glandular and sometimes edged with fine hairs. The flowers are bright lavender-pink to magenta. Zones 5–11.

Delosperma Hybrid Cultivars

↔18–36 in (49–90 cm)
↕2–4 in (5–10 cm)

Many species hybridize naturally or produce forms with distinctive foliage or flowers. Several have been developed into garden plants, including: **'Album'**, low spreader with incandescent white flowers; **'Oberg'**, prostrate and spreading gray-green foliage, flowers open pale pink from darker buds, ageing to white; **'Ruby Star'**, low spreader with small purple flowers through summer. Zones 9–11.

Delosperma aberdeenense

Delosperma brunnthaleri

Delosperma lehmannii

DELPHINIUM

Sometimes known as larkspur, although that name is best reserved for its relatives in the genus *Consolida*. A member of the buttercup (Ranunculaceae) family, *Delphinium* consists of around 250 species of annuals, biennials and perennials. Most species form a basal clump of finely divided or lobed foliage, from which develops an upright spike bearing long-spurred, 4-petalled flowers backed by 5 sepals that sometimes become bract-like. Plant sizes vary markedly with the species: the smaller species may not exceed 12 in (30 cm) tall, while the fancy hybrids can grow to over 7 ft (2 m). Flower colors vary, but *Delphinium* is best known for the intense blue flowers it often produces. CULTIVATION: Best in an open airy position that lessens the risk of mildew. However, the more exposed the location, the more important it is that the plants are staked to prevent damage from the wind. Plant in moist, humus-rich, fertile soil and water well while in flower. Propagate from seed or basal cuttings, or by division.

Delphinium barbeyi

☼/◐ ❄ ↔ 6–16 in (15–40 cm)
↕ 12–40 in (30–100 cm)

This perennial is native to the Rocky Mountains, USA. Clump of downy basal foliage. Leaves with 5 main lobes further divided or toothed. Strong upright flower stems. Dark blue flowers in summer, yellowish hairs on petals. Zones 5–9.

Delphinium × *belladonna*

☼/◐ ❄ ↔ 6–20 in (15–50 cm)
↕ 12–40 in (30–100 cm)

Perennial hybrid crosses between *D. elatum* and *D. grandiflorum.* Compact, sometimes dwarf, with finely divided dark green foliage. Flowers to 1¼ in (30 mm) wide. Many selected forms, which include: **'Bellamosum'**, intensely dark blue flowers; **'Blue Sensation'**, bright mid-blue flowers; and **'Cliveden Beauty'**, light sky blue flowers. Zones 3–9.

Delphinium cardinale

☼/◐ ❄ ↔ 8–20 in (20–50 cm)
↕ 3–7 ft (0.9–2 m)

A short-lived perennial, sometimes annual or biennial, from California, USA. It has dark green, finely divided, basal foliage. The wiry upright flower stems hold widely spaced red flowers, with yellow centers, in the summer. Zones 8–10.

Delphinium, HC, 'Sungleam'

Delphinium elatum

☼/◐ ❄ ↔ 8–20 in (20–50 cm)
↕ 2–6 ft (0.6–1.8 m)

Summer-flowering Eurasian perennial. Downy or hairy leaves and 5 to 7 lobes toothed or further divided. Strong upright flower stems, dense racemes of blue flowers, in summer. Zones 3–9.

Delphinium grandiflorum

syn. *Delphinium chinense*

☼/◐ ❄ ↔ 12–24 in (30–60 cm)
↕ 12–40 in (30–100 cm)

Perennial from temperate East Asia. Low bushy foliage clump, very finely divided, bright green leaves. Racemes of vivid blue flowers, sometimes quite tall and upright, usually short and lax. Popular forms include: **'Blue Butterfly'**, masses of deep blue flowers on short stems; and **'Tom Pouce'**, with bright gentian blue flowers. Zones 3–9.

Delphinium nudicaule

☼/◐ ❄ ↔ 8–16 in (20–40 cm)
↕ 12–24 in (30–60 cm)

Perennial from California, USA. Short-lived, sometimes annual or biennial. The leaves are coarsely lobed, secondary divisions fine, downy, dull green. It has wiry flower stems with widely spaced, orange-red flowers marked yellow on upper lips, from late spring. Zones 8–10.

Delphinium semibarbatum

syn. *Delphinium zalil*

☼/◐ ❄ ↔ 6–12 in (15–30 cm)
↕ 20–30 in (50–75 cm)

From Iran and central Asia. Short-lived perennial, sometimes annual or biennial. Forms a small clump of finely cut deep green foliage. Wiry flower stems bear small bright yellow flowers. Zones 6–9.

Delphinium grandiflorum 'Tom Pouce'

Delphinium × *belladonna*

Delphinium Hybrid Cultivars

☼ ❄ ↔ 1½–3 ft (0.5–0.9 m)
↕ 4–7 ft (1.2–2 m)

Extensively selected and hybridized to produce the Elatum Group, which includes: **'Albert Shepherd'**, medium height, light blue with pink flush and buff center; **'Angela Harbutt'**, medium to tall, pinkish mauve; **'Blue Dawn'**, medium to tall, bright deep blue with white eye; **'Blue Lagoon'**, medium to tall, pure dark blue with light eye; **'Blue Nile'**, low-growing, clear mid-blue with contrasting white center; **'Bruce'**, tall, deep violet-purple with lavender to gray eye; **'Cassius'**, medium height, mid-blue often suffused with mauve, black center; **'Claire'**, low-growing, pale pink to nearly white at the center; **'Conspicuous'**, medium height, mauve with large brown center; **'Constance Rivett'**, medium height, pure white; **'Cupid'**, short, blue with white eye; **'Emily Hawkins'**, tall and strong-growing, lavender suffused with blue, buff center; **'Fanfare'**, tall, pale silvery mauve, early flowering; **'Faust'**, tall, intense almost metallic deep blue with hint of purple; **'Fenella'**, medium height, bright pure blue with black center; **'Gillian Dallas'**, medium height, gray-blue with white center, late flowering; **'Giotto'**, medium height, purple-blue with a mustard center; **'Harlekijn'**, deep violet, semi-double with blackish center; **'Kathleen Cooke'**, medium height, mid-blue with white eye; **'Langdon's Royal Flush'**, medium height, dusky pink with white center; **'Loch Leven'**, low-growing, light blue with white eye; **'Lord Butler'**, low-growing, soft mid-blue with white eye, compact and heavy flowering; **Magic Fountain Series** ★, seedling strain, in a wide color range; **'Michael Ayres'**, medium height, deep pinkish violet with dark center; **'Mighty Atom'**, short semi-double, deep mauve, late flowering; **'Min'**, medium height, lavender with dark veining. The **New Century** hybrids, to over 4 ft (1.2 m) tall, come in a wide range of colors. **'Our Deb'**, mid-sized, soft pink with a dark eye; **'Rosemary Brock'**, medium height, soft mid-pink with a buff center; **'Sandpiper'** ★, tall, white with black center; **'Spindrift'**, medium height, flower variable, usually a turquoise shade but sometimes also with blue or pink flowers; **'Sungleam'**, medium height, creamy yellow with yellow eye; **'Thamesmead'**, short to medium, gentian blue with black eye; **'Tiddles'**, medium height, semi-double, dusky mauve; and **'Walton Gemstone'**, of medium height, pale lavender blue with white eye. Zones 3–9.

DENDROMECON

This genus contains just one species of evergreen shrub, which is native to California, the USA, and Mexico where it grows on the dry rocky chaparral. It belongs to the poppy (Papaveraceae) family and the relationship can be seen in the single yellow flowers that are borne in summer.

CULTIVATION: These plants require winter protection in climates with severe frosts. When grown outdoors, it will not survive severe winters and must be given a warm sheltered site in a well-drained, gritty soil that is not too rich. The shrub dislikes root disturbance and care should be taken at planting time to reduce transplant shock. Propagation is from half-hardened cuttings taken in summer, but these can be difficult to strike.

Dendromecon rigida

TREE POPPY

↔ 10 ft (3 m) ↕ 10 ft (3 m)

Stiff gray-green leaves. which account for its species name. Pure yellow, 4-petalled poppy flowers of a simple beauty, in summer. ***D. r.* subsp. *harfordii*** has thicker stems and leaves than the species, and slightly smaller yellow flowers. Zones 8–10.

DENNSTAEDTIA

CUP FERN

A genus of about 70 medium to large terrestrial or epiphytic ferns in the bracken (Dennstaedtiaceae) family, found in most warm-temperate to tropical regions except Europe. Creeping, branching, woody rhizomes; generous, finely divided, triangular foliage.

CULTIVATION: Creeping habit makes *Dennstaedtia* species unsuited to container cultivation. They prefer moist to dry, well-drained, acidic soil, in full to partial shade. Propagate from spore, or by division of rhizomes in spring.

Dennstaedtia punctilobula

HAY-SCENTED FERN

↔ 5–15 ft (1.5–4.5 m) ↕ 2–3 ft (0.6–0.9 m)

Deciduous fern with creeping rhizomes from eastern North America. Large colonies form a carpet. Lacy, triangular or sword-shaped, light green fronds, with notched pinnules, sticky to the touch, and smelling like hay when bruised. Finely downy stalks, with scattered hairs on frond midribs. Zones 3–9.

DESCHAMPSIA

HAIR GRASS

Charming genus of about 50 species of grasses in the grass (Poaceae) family. Clump-forming and can be herbaceous or evergreen. Found in temperate to cold regions, and many interesting clones have been selected by growers, mainly in Germany. Grown for their graceful foliage and airy flowerheads.

CULTIVATION: Will grow in any good garden soil in sun or light shade.

Dendromecon rigida

Dennstaedtia punctilobula

Clean out old spent flower stems in early spring to allow for new growth. Propagate from seed, but named clones must be divided in early spring.

Deschampsia cespitosa

syn. *Aira cespitosa*

TUFTED HAIR GRASS, TUSSOCK GRASS

↔ 4–5 ft (1.2–1.5 m) ↕ 5–7 ft (1.5–2 m)

An attractive grass native to North America, Asia, and Europe. Fine, rich, evergreen foliage above which billows soft masses of tiny flowers in summer. ***D. c. subsp. holciformis,*** darker green foliage. ***D. c.* var. *vivipara*,** drooping plants that take root. Numerous clones that include: ***D. c.*** **Bronze Veil/'Bronzeschleier'**, bronze flowers and considered a good form; **'Daybreak'**, pink-tinted young spring foliage; **Golden Pendant/ 'Goldgehänge'**, slightly pendulous yellow flowers; **Gold Dust/'Goldstaub'**, flowers that open yellow; and **Golden Dew/'Goldtau'**, yellow-green flowers. Zones 5–10.

Deschampsia flexuosa

COMMON HAIR GRASS, CRINKLED HAIR GRASS, WAVY HAIR GRASS

↔ 6–8 in (15–20 cm) ↕ 27–36 in (70–90 cm)

Found in Eurasia and the Americas. Very fine, wavy, thread-like, green to olive leaves. Fine wiry flower stems with branching, spray-like, pink-tinted inflorescence. Zones 5–9.

DESFONTAINIA

This genus, part of the Columelliaceae family, comprises a single species of evergreen shrub, found growing in the Andes from Colombia to Tierra del Fuego. In the north it grows in cool mountain forests, while further south it is found at sea level. An attractive shrub with brilliant orange and yellow flowers that stand out against its dark glossy foliage. Well suited to the conditions enjoyed by rhododendrons.

Deschampsia cespitosa

CULTIVATION: *Desfontainia* needs a cool moist climate and an acid soil that is moisture retentive and rich in humus. It should have a partially shaded, sheltered position; water well in dry spells. Propagate from seed or half-hardened cuttings in summer.

Desfontainia spinosa ★

↔ 10 ft (3 m) ↕ 10 ft (3 m)

Bushy slow-growing shrub. Tubular flowers scarlet to orange with yellow tips, in summer–autumn. Cherry-sized fruits. Zones 8–9.

DESMODIUM

A member of the pea-flower subfamily of the legume (Fabaceae) family, this genus from warm-temperate and tropical regions contains about 450 species. Most are scrambling perennials, others are deciduous or evergreen shrubs. Genus is characterized by its pink, purple, blue, or white flowers, trifoliate leaves, and fruits that break into single-seeded segments upon maturity. These segments have small hooked bristles that attach them to any passing furry animal or to human clothing, thereby aiding dispersal. Some species from warmer regions are weedy, but some of the shrubby species from cooler origins are attractive garden plants.

CULTIVATION: Propagate from seed in spring, or from cuttings. Sunny well-drained sites are preferred, and species from the warmer areas will need green- house shelter in cooler locations.

Desmodium canadense

SHOWY TICK-TREFOIL

↔ 12 in (30 cm) ↕ 4–6 ft (1.2–1.8 m)

From southern Canada to Virginia in south, and Oklahoma, USA, in west. Perennial with long, oval, green leaves; spikes of pink to lavender, pea-flowers cluster at top of stalk in mid-summer. Can be invasive. Zones 5–9.

Desfontainia spinosa

D

Deutzia compacta

DEUTZIA

Widely cultivated for its ornamental members, this genus of the hydrangea (Hydrangeaceae) family contains 60 species of deciduous and evergreen shrubs, mainly from temperate Asia with a toehold in Central America. Most commonly grown deutzias are spring flowering and deciduous. They have pointed oval to lance-shaped leaves in opposite pairs, often with serrated edges, and heads of small, starry, 5-petalled, white, cream, or pink flowers usually held clear of the foliage.

CULTIVATION: Most very frost hardy; mainstay of temperate gardens. Shelter from strong winds. Prune and thin after flowering to maintain framework of strong branches. Propagate from seed or half-hardened summer cuttings.

Deutzia compacta

☼ ✱ ↔7 ft (2 m) ↑6 ft (1.8 m)

Himalayan deciduous species. Narrow, pointed leaves, with fine branches that cascade somewhat. Leaves dark green upper surfaces, pale undersides, toothed edges, covering of fine hairs. Flowers white, in small heads. Zones 6–9.

Deutzia crenata

☼ ✱ ↔8 ft (2.4 m) ↑8 ft (2.4 m)

Similar to *D. scabra,* deciduous shrub from Japan and southeastern China. Slightly arching stems, hairy leaves, finely toothed edges. White flowers on racemes, in the spring. ***D. c.* var. *nakaiana,*** dwarf, to 12 in (30 cm high); **'Nikko'**, white flowers, dark foliage. Zones 6–9.

Deutzia × *elegantissima*

☼ ✱ ↔5 ft (1.5 m) ↑5 ft (1.5 m)

Derived from *D. purpurascens* and *D. sieboldiana,* of garden origin. Ovate to oblong-ovate leaves, uneven sharp teeth. Cymes of pink flowers, in early summer. Cultivars include: **'Fasciculata'**, with white to pale pink flowers, deep pink in bud; and **'Rosealind'** ★, compact white flowers with a pink tinge. Zones 5–9.

Deutzia × *elegantissima* 'Fasciculata'

Deutzia gracilis

SLENDER DEUTZIA

☼ ✱ ↔3–6 ft (0.9–1.8 m) ↑3–6 ft (0.9–1.8 m)

One of the main parents of hybrid deutzias, from Japan. Spreading shrub, mounded form. Slender erect shoots arch at the ends. Narrow leaves bright green, ovate to lance-shaped, pointed at the ends. Narrow panicles of pure white flowers, in mid-spring–early summer. Zones 5–9.

Deutzia × *kalmiiflora*

☼ ✱ ↔5 ft (1.5 m) ↑5 ft (1.5 m)

Hybrid between *D. parviflora* and *D. purpurascens,* of garden origin. Open shrub with arching branches. Finely toothed, mid-green, narrowly oval leaves. Upright panicles of cup-shaped flowers, deep pink outside, paler inside, early to mid-summer. Zones 5–9.

Deutzia × *magnifica*

☼ ✱ ↔7 ft (2 m) ↑6 ft (1.8 m)

Of uncertain parents, possibly between *D. crenata* and *D. longifolia,* hybrid shrub with strong upright growth. Ovate to oblong-shaped leaves, finely toothed margins, gray and felt-like beneath. Dense panicles of single or double white flowers, in early summer. Zones 5–9.

Deutzia × *rosea*

☼ ✱ ↔3 ft (0.9 m) ↑3 ft (0.9 m)

Dwarf shrub, hybrid of *D. gracilis* and *D. purpurascens.* Ovate to oblong lance-shaped, finely serrated, dark green leaves. Short terminal panicles of flowers, pale pink inside, purplish outside. **'Campanulata'**, white flowers in dense panicles; **'Carminea'**, pale pink flowers, purplish on outside. Zones 5–9.

Deutzia scabra

FUZZY DEUTZIA

☼ ✱ 7 ft (2 m) ↑10 ft (3 m)

Native to Japan and China. Arching shoots; broadly ovate, rough, dark green leaves. Dense cylindrical panicles of honey-scented, white or pink-tinged, bell-shaped flowers terminate the branches, in early to mid-summer. Attractive peeling brown to orange bark. **'Candidissima'**, pure white double flowers; **'Pride of Rochester'**, very large, double white flowers tinged pinkish purple. Zones 5–9.

Deutzia setchuenensis

☼ ✱ ↔5 ft (1.5 m) ↑6 ft (1.8 m)

From western China. Ovate leaves, densely haired beneath, with fine forward-pointing teeth. Loose clusters of white flowers in summer. More often cultivated is ***D. s.* var. *corymbiflora*,** larger flower clusters, peeling pale brown bark with age. Zones 5–9.

DIANELLA

A member of the daylily (Hemerocallidaceae) family, this genus of evergreen perennials comprises some 20 species from Australia, New Zealand, and Pacific Islands. One tropical species *(D. ensifolia)* extends to mainland Asia as far as China, Japan, and India, and to East Africa and Madagascar. *Dianella* are herbaceous plants with fibrous roots, often with underground rhizomes. The stems are creeping or erect, bearing a terminal fan of leaves. The leaves are grass-like, in 2 ranks, sheathing at the base and often with the edges folded and fused together (like an iris leaf) but only in the lower part. Inflorescence is a loose panicle with flowers on nodding stalks. The flowers have perianth segments, in 2 whorls of 3, blue to white, sometimes tinged green or purple. Fruit is a pale blue to dark purple-blue, spherical or egg-shaped berry. Seeds are black and shiny.

CULTIVATION: In warmer regions they are grown in borders or wild plantings; elsewhere best under glass. Some will tolerate temperatures down to 20°F (–7°C) or even lower, others are frost tender. Tolerate light shade. Easily propagated by division or from seed.

Dianella caerulea

BLUE FLAX-LILY, BLUEBERRY LILY

☼ ❄ ↔20–60 in (50–150 cm) ↑to 7 ft (2 m)

Tufted-forming perennial with much-branched, stout, underground rhizomes. Occurs from New Guinea south to Tasmania, on the eastern side of the Great Dividing Range on mainland Australia. Leaves are flat with margins slightly recurved and finely toothed. Inflorescences are longer than leaves, each with 3 to 30 flowers, ranging in color from deep blue to yellow-green or cream, appearing throughout spring–summer. Fruits globular, blue to purplish berries. D. c. var. cinerascens, gray-green to silvery foliage; 'Cassa Blue', striking blue-green foliage; 'Little Jess', dense, clumping, 16 in (40 cm) tall. Zones 9–12.

Dianella tasmanica

syns *Dianella archeri, D. densa, D. hookeri*

BLUE FLAX-LILY, TASMANIAN FLAX-LILY

☼ ❄ ↔12 in (30 cm) ↑40 in (100 cm)

Tufted perennial, rarely forms clumps. Occurs in Australia, in forests from northern inland New South Wales south to the alpine country and Tasmania, ranging from sea level to 3,940 ft (1,200 m) altitude. Leaves up

Dianella tasmanica

to 40 in (100 cm) long, green, inflorescences may exceed the leaves in length. Blue flowers in spring–summer. Large globular berries, bluish purple, containing many black shiny seeds. Many new cultivars, including: 'Lime Splice', lime green foliage; 'Little Devil', red new growth; 'Rainbow', red new growth, mature to yellow, green, and cream variegated; 'Splice', pink new growth, mature foliage has yellow-green striping; 'Tasred', foliage has strong red tones in winter. Zones 9–10.

DIANTHUS

CARNATION, PINK

The 300 or so species in this genus are tufting or spreading perennials largely from the Eurasian region. *Dianthus* belongs to the pink (Caryophyllaceae) family. Most have narrow, somewhat grassy, blue-green leaves emerging directly from a dense basal clump or on wiry spreading stems. The foliage color is a perfect foil for the flowers, which in the species are simple 5-petalled structures often powerfully fragrant, with a spicy scent. Flower stem length varies greatly. The common flower color is pink, but the common name, pinks, refers to the ragged petal edges, which appear as if cut with pinking shears. Most species flower from late spring.

CULTIVATION: Plant in a bright, open position in moist, well-drained, humus-rich soil. Most appreciate a little lime and need regular feeding to prevent center of clump from dying out. Propagate from seed or small basal cuttings known as "slips," or by division.

Dianthus alpinus

↔ 6–12 in (15–30 cm)
↑ 4–6 in (10–15 cm)

Short-lived perennial from European Alps. Leaves dark green, grassy. Flowers borne singly, deep pinkish red with darker spots and white eye, pinked, in late spring. **'Joan's Blood'**, maroon-centered deep red flowers. Zones 3–9.

Dianthus arenarius

↔ 6–12 in (15–30 cm)
↑ 12 in (30 cm)

Northern and eastern European perennial forming a dense tufted mound of short, narrow, green leaves. Flowers on wiry stems, usually borne singly, white to pale pink, pinked. Zones 3–9.

Dianthus barbatus ★

SWEET WILLIAM

↔ 6–12 in (15–30 cm)
↑ 12–24 in (30–60 cm)

Short-lived, southern European perennial usually grown as an annual. Makes clump of lance-shaped leaves. Pinked flowers clustered in heads. Seedling strains available in many colors and patterned forms, such as **Auricula-eyed Group**, which has a contrasting colored ring near the center; and **Indian Carpet Mix**, 6 in (15 cm) high, many colors and patterns, often with a contrasting central ring. Zones 4–9.

Dianthus barbatus, Auricula-eyed Group

Dianthus carthusianorum

syn. *Dianthus tenuifolius*

CARTHUSIAN PINK

↔ 6–12 in (15–30 cm)
↑ 16–24 in (40–60 cm)

Mounding tufted perennial of southern and central Europe. Light green grassy foliage sheathed for much of length. Heads of small pink to purple flowers, rarely white, pinked. Zones 3–9.

Dianthus caryophyllus

CARNATION

↔ 8–16 in (20–40 cm)
↑ 20–32 in (50–80 cm)

Perennial from Mediterranean region. Leaves sheathed, gray-green to blue-green, on wiry spreading stems. Flower-heads on upright, sometimes spindly stems, strongly fragrant. Wild plants have pink flowers, garden forms many colors. **Knight Series**, named for color: **'Crimson Knight'**, **'White Knight'**, and **'Yellow Knight'**. Zones 8–10.

Dianthus chinensis

CHINESE PINK, RAINBOW PINK

↔ 8–16 in (20–40 cm)
↑ 12–20 in (30–50 cm)

Biennial from temperate East Asia, treated as a summer annual. Erect growth habit, range of flower colors in pink and red shades, green to gray-green leaves. **Edwardiana Series** has frilly single to fully double flowers, wide color range. Zones 7–10.

Dianthus deltoides

MAIDEN PINK

↔ 6–12 in (15–30 cm)
↑ 8–16 in (20–40 cm)

Eurasian perennial, forming carpet, sometimes mounding, of small green to blue-green leaves with spreading narrow-leafed stems around the edge. Flowers, usually borne singly, in pink shades, often with dark central spotting, pinked. Cultivars include: **'Albus'**, white flowers; and **'Brilliancy'**, deep crimson flowers. Zones 3–9.

Dianthus gratianopolitanus

syn. *Dianthus caesius*

CHEDDAR PINK

↔ 8–16 in (20–40 cm)
↑ 6–8 in (15–20 cm)

A mat-forming perennial native to central and western Europe. The older leaves can be small and very densely packed. The fragrant pink to crimson flowers, are usually borne singly, and are pinked. **'Baker's Variety'** bears semi-double pinkish purple flowers; **'Flore Pleno'** has semi-double pink flowers. Zones 3–9.

Dianthus monspessulanus

syn. *Dianthus sternbergii*

↔ 12–20 in (30–50 cm)
↑ 12–24 in (30–60 cm)

Perennial from mountains of eastern and southern Europe. Spreading habit with wiry stems and narrow blue-green to green foliage. Flowers in groups of up to 7, pink or white, fragrant, with deeply cut petals, in summer. Zones 4–9.

Dianthus plumarius

PINK

↔ 8–16 in (20–40 cm)
↑ 6–14 in (15–35 cm)

Perennial from eastern and central Europe. Forms loose tuft of blue-green foliage. Flowers pink or white, often with darker markings or center. Parent of most of the garden pinks; crossed with *D. caryophyllus* to produce perpetual-flowering carnations. **Rainbow Loveliness Series**, deeply pinked petals, all colors; **Sonata Series**, fully double flowers, all colors. Zones 3–9.

Dianthus carthusianorum

Dianthus monspessulanus

Dianthus spiculifolius

Dianthus superbus var. *longicalycinus*

D., HC, Annual Bedding, Melody Series, 'Melody Pink'

D., HC, Perennial, Perpetual-flowering, Fancy, 'Cheerio'

Dianthus, Hybrid Cultivar, Perennial, Pink, Fancy, 'Rendez-vous'

D., HC, Annual Bedding, Floral Lace Series, 'Floral Lace Violet'

D., HC, Perennial, Perpetual-flowering, Fancy, 'Hi-lite'

D., HC, P, Perpetual-flowering, Self, 'Moutarde'

D., HC, P, Pink, Self, 'Valda Wyatt'

Dianthus spiculifolius

☼/◑ ✱ ↔6–12 in (15–30 cm)
↑8–12 in (20–30 cm)

Mat-forming tufted perennial from the eastern Carpathian Mountains. Narrow basal leaves, upper leaves smaller. Scented, deeply cut, pink flowers (occasionally white), borne singly or in clusters. Zones 6–9.

Dianthus subacaulis

☼/◑ ✱ ↔6–8 in (15–20 cm)
↑2–4 in (5–10 cm)

A perennial from the mountains of southwestern Europe. Forms densely tufted clumps of deep green foliage. Deep pink flowers are borne singly, with smooth or pinked edges. ***D. s.*** **subsp.** ***brachyanthus*** develops into a densely foliaged dome. Zones 5–9.

Dianthus superbus

☼/◑ ✱ ↔12–20 in (30–50 cm)
↑20–30 in (50–75 cm)

Strong-growing Eurasian perennial with spreading stems. Flowers borne singly, with pink to purple-pink, highly scented, deeply cut almost jagged petals. D. s. var. longicalycinus, mauve to light purple flowers with elongated calyx. Zones 4–9.

Dianthus Hybrid Cultivars

☼/◑ ❄ ↔6–12 in (15–30 cm)
↑8–15 in (20–28 cm)

Like other genera with a long garden history that have been extensively hybridized, the many carnations and pinks and their cultivars are divided into groups based on growth habit and flower color and style. Zones 8–10.

ANNUAL BEDDING DIANTHUS

Although sometimes really perennial, these small plants are grown as annuals. In many ways they resemble sweet William *(D. barbatus)*, but they are available in a wider range of sizes and growth forms, including some suitable for hanging baskets. Popular annual dianthus include: the **First Love Series**; the **Floral Lace Series,** masses of small flowers with pinked edges; and the **Melody Series**, similar to First Love but taller, mainly single-colored in pink shades and white.

PERENNIAL DIANTHUS

Perennial dianthus were among the first plants to be cultivated in European gardens. In medieval times they were grown for their medicinal and flavoring properties as well as for their scent. Since then, countless hybrids have been raised, either as garden plants or for the cut-flower trade. Today we recognize three main groups of dianthus hybrids that are further divided, primarily by flower type.

BORDER CARNATIONS

Tall growers that are derived from *D. caryophyllus*. Flowers are usually strongly scented, often fully double, with or without pinked edges. They bloom mainly in spring and early summer, and are divided as follows:

Fancies: Flowers are basically one color but with flecks, spots, or small sectors of one other color, such as **'Brookham Fancy'**, which is yellow with pink flecks.

Selfs: Flowers are all one color, such as the soft pink **'Cathlene Hitchcock'**; the vivid red **'Fiery Cross'**; the soft yellow **'Golden Cross'**; and the dusky mauve **'Grey Dove'**.

Clove-scented: Flowers are strongly scented, color may be variable, such as the red-striped white **'Candy Clove'**.

Picotees: One base color edged with another color, such as the purple-edged white **'Eva Humphries'**. The edging width is variable.

PERPETUAL-FLOWERING CARNATIONS

These are the tallest carnations, often with flower stems that need staking or tying. Not hardy to repeated severe frosts, and best grown in mild climates for their year-round flowering.

The rare Malmaison carnation is a diploid form with especially strong foliage and flower stems, and very intense clove perfume. **'Duchess of Westminster'**, large cream flowers, is the most widely grown Malmaison.

Perpetuals are widely cultivated as greenhouse plants for florists. Popular forms, which are all doubles unless stated otherwise, include:

Fancies: 'Bright Rendez-vous', a creamy white, with soft pink lacing; **'Cheerio'**, pinkish white and red; **'Crimson Tempo'**, rich red; **'Havana'**, red and yellow; **'Impulse'**, creamy white, deep pinkish red; **'New Tempo'**, pinkish white and red; **'Rendez-vous'**, white laced with deep pink; **'Tempo'**, white with fine red lacing, a few red sectors; **'Tundra'**, yellow laced with light red; **'Yellow Rendez-vous'**, soft yellow laced with deep pink.

Selfs: 'Delphi', white; **'Mambo'**, bright yellow; **'Moutarde'**, yellow; **'Pink Dona'**, shades of pink ; **'Prado'**, creamy pale green; **'Raggio di Sole'**, orange.

Spray carnations: These flowers are usually slightly smaller but they have 5 to 6 per stem. **'Fiorella'** is yellow and red; **'Ibiza'**, yellow; and **'Kortina'**, purple-red.

PINKS

Developed from *D. plumarius* but often crossed with other species and hybrids. The most common cross is with the perpetual-flowering carnations, which gave rise to the Allwoodii Pinks. Their flowers may or may not be fragrant but nearly always have pinked edges.

Fancies: 'Dad's Favourite' (syn. 'Dad's Favorite'), white flowers, maroon lacing and center, double; **'Gran's Favourite'**, white with pinkish red lacing, double; **'Red Ensign'**, deep pink, white lacing;

'Sugar Plum', ruffled double, mid pink with broad, dark "eye," strong scent.

Selfs: 'Becky Robinson', deep pink; **'Bovey Belle'**, purple, double; **'Carmine Letitia Wyatt'**, deep pink, semi-double, good scent; **'Devon Pride'**, bright pink; **'Dwarf Helen'**, pink, double; **'Inglestone'**, bright pink; **'Lemsii'**, small pink flowers; **'Letitia Wyatt'** ★, bright pink, double, strong scent; **'Lionheart'**, red, sometimes lighter edges, single, fragrant; **'Neon Star'**, bright purple-pink, single, strong scent; 'Passion', cherry red, double, good scent; **'Valda Wyatt'**, pink, double, fragrant; **'Whatfield Cancan'**, soft pink, frilled double flowers, fragrant; **'White Joy'**, white, and sometimes flushed pale pink, double.

Allwoodii Pinks: Usually *D. plumarius* × *D. alpinus* hybrids. **'Whatfield Ruby'**, vivid crimson flowers.

Bicolors: 'Coconut Sundae', white with red "eye," semi-double, strong scent; **'Cranmere Pool'**, white to pale pink, deep red center, double; **'Doris'** ★, light pink with purple-red center, double; **'Houndspool Ruby'** (syn. 'Ruby Doris'), deep pink with crimson center, double, sport of 'Doris'; **'Monica Wyatt'**, pink with red center, double; **'Peach Mambo'**, cream with soft orange-pink center, double; **'Rose Monica Wyatt'**, deep pink with red center, double.

Old-Fashioned Pinks: Usually forms of *D. plumarius* but are sometimes hybrids or just varieties of indeterminate origin that have been so long cultivated that their history is forgotten. **'Candy Floss'**, (syn. 'Devon Flavia'), mid-pink, darker "eye," double, very fragrant; **'Earl of Essex'**, deep pink, double flowers; the well-known, very fragrant, white double **'Mrs Sinkins'**; and the pink semi-double **'Pike's Pink'** are typical examples.

DIASCIA

TWINSPUR

Until the 1970s few gardeners were aware of *Diascia*, a South African genus of around 50 species of annuals and perennials, belonging to the foxglove (Scrophulariaceae) family. They have since grown in popularity for borders and rockeries, especially in areas where the winters are mild. They are generally low mounding or spreading plants with upright or semi-trailing stems and small oval to elliptical leaves with toothed edges. The mauve, pink, or soft orange flowers are tiny but showy, because they are massed in racemes at the stem tips. The flowers have 4 small lobes, 2 short-spurred nectaries, a large lower lip, and are produced mainly in the summer.

CULTIVATION: Plant in a bright open position with good air movement, and well-drained humus-rich soil that is kept moist throughout the flowering season. Pinch back to keep the plants bushy, and deadhead regularly to encourage continued blooming. Propagate from seed or from cuttings, as appropriate for the growth form.

Diascia barberae

☼/◐ ❄ ↔ 12–16 in (30–40 cm)
↑ 12 in (30 cm)

From the Drakensberg region of South Africa and Lesotho. Perennial with upright or sprawling habit. Flowers are bright pink, with conspicuous spurs and small yellow patch, edged and spotted maroon. **'Blackthorn Apricot'**, low growing but spreading, bright, apricot-pink to soft orange flowers; **'Fisher's Flora'**, heart-shaped leaves and dark-centered flowers with two yellow spots; **'Ruby Field'**, deep pinkish red flowers. Zones 8–10.

Diascia integerrima

☼/◐ ❄ ↔ 48 in (120 cm) ↑ 18 in (45 cm)

Spreading perennial, widespread in eastern South Africa. Gray-green leaves, sometimes smooth-edged. Open spikes of dark-centered, mauve-pink flowers with conspicuous downward-curved spurs. **'Coral Canyon'**, a more upright habit, more distinctly pink flowers. Zones 8–10.

Diascia Hybrid Cultivars

☼ ❄ ↔ 12–24 in (30–60 cm)
↑ 8–18 in (20–45 cm)

The species tend to interbreed freely, when cultivated and produce many intermediate hybrids. Hybridizers, in particular Hector Harrison of England, have been quick to promote these selected forms. Those that are currently available include: Coral Belle/**'Hecbel'**, which has narrow, slightly glossy leaves, coral red flowers, and is semi-trailing and good in baskets; **'Joyce's Choice'**, with heart-shaped leaves, and apricot-pink flowers; **'Langthorn's Lavender**, with pretty pink-mauve flowers; **'Lilac Belle'**, small leaves, and light purple flowers with a conspicuous lower lip; Little Dancer/**'Pendan'**, small heart-shaped leaves, vivid pink flowers, very good in baskets; Redstart/**'Hecstart'**, coral pink to red flowers; **'Rupert Lambert'** ★, deep pink, to around 10 in (25 cm) tall and twice as wide, blooms from summer through to autumn; **'Salmon Supreme'**, light salmon pink flowers with darker spots; Sydney Olympics/ **'Hecsyd'**, light salmon pink flowers, compact and heavy-flowering; and **'Twinkle'**, dark foliage, purple-pink flowers, trailing habit, good in baskets. Zones 8–10.

DICENTRA

BLEEDING HEART

This genus of around 20 species of annuals and perennials from North America and Asia belongs in the poppy (Papaveraceae) family, though the resemblance may not be obvious. Most have roots adapted as storage organs, as tap roots, rhizomes, or tubers. The foliage, ferny and often finely cut, disappears for winter, but redevelops quickly with the arrival of spring, the larger species often making noticeable daily growth. The flowers have 4 petals, the outer pair creating a pouched structure that largely envelopes the inner pair. The pendulous flowers appear in spring, and are borne in clusters on stems rising above the foliage, mostly in white, pink, or cream shades.

CULTIVATION: These species prefer a cool moist soil that is humus-rich, fertile, and well drained. They thrive in woodlands and perennial borders, and the smaller forms also do well in rockeries. Best lightly shaded from hottest sun. Propagate from seed or basal cuttings, or by division.

Dicentra cucullaria

DUTCHMAN'S BREECHES

☼/◐ ✱ ↔ 20–40 in (50–100 cm)
↑ 12–16 in (30–40 cm)

Perennial from eastern North America. Leaves green, lacy, fern-like, with blue-green undersides, finely divided. Small flowers, heart-shaped but inner petals protruding, white or pink, tipped yellow. Flowers look like upside-down bloomers. May cause dermatitis in some people. Zones 5–9.

Dicentra eximia

STAGGERWEED, TURKEY CORN

☼/◐ ✱ ↔ 20–40 in (50–100 cm)
↑ 12–26 in (30–65 cm)

Perennial found over much of the USA. Blue-green leaves are finely divided. Sprays of pink or white heart-shaped flowers. The plant is somewhat toxic to stock, hence the common name, staggerweed. Zones 5–9.

Dicentra formosa

syn. *Dicentra eximia of gardens*

WILD BLEEDING HEART

☼/◐ ✱ ↔ 20–40 in (50–100 cm)
↑ 12–26 in (30–65 cm)

A perennial native to western North America. Ferny leaves with blue-green undersides. Panicles up to 30 flowers, most commonly deep pink, sometimes yellow, and rarely white. *D. formosa* and *D. eximia* have been confused in cultivation and it now appears that even in the wild they may be one quite variable species. **'Aurora'**, gray-green leaves, white flowers; **'Bacchanal'**, gray-green foliage, pinkish red flowers; **'Bountiful'**, light blue-green leaves, deep pink flowers; **'Langtrees'**, very compact, blue-green leaves, pink-tinted cream flowers; **'Luxuriant'** ★, blue-green foliage, deep cherry pink to red flowers; **'Stuart Boothman'**, blue-green leaves with narrow leaflets, deep pink flowers on short stems; and **'Zestful'**, with light blue-green foliage and deep purple-pink flowers. Zones 4–9.

Dicentra formosa 'Luxuriant'

Dichondra argentea 'Silver Falls'

DICHONDRA

A member of the morning glory (Convolvulaceae) family, this is a genus of up to 10 species of low, spreading perennials that have a widespread distribution in the warm temperate zones. They have small leaves, usually almost round to kidney-shaped. The flowers are very small and can pass unnoticed.
CULTIVATION: Most species are easily grown in well-drained soil. Water requirements differ with origin but most want ample summer moisture. Feed occasionally. Propagate from seed, cuttings, or layers, which often strike naturally.

Dichondra argentea

SILVER PONYSFOOT

↔ 24–60 in (60–150 cm)
↑ 1–3 in (2.5–8 cm)

Native to southwestern USA and Mexico. Spreading, cascading habit ideal for hanging baskets. Long-stemmed, kidney-shaped leaves, 1 in (2.5 cm) wide, covered in silvery felting. Tiny, insignificant flowers. **'Silver Falls'**, metallic silvery foliage, very long stems. Zones 9–10.

DICHORISANDRA

This genus of about 25 species from Central and South America belongs to the spiderwort (Commelinaceae) family that includes the well-known *Tradescantia*. All are perennials, sometimes becoming shrubby, with soft stems and glossy green leaves, sometimes striped with cream or purple. The small flowers are borne in dense terminal spikes and are blue or purple.
CULTIVATION: *Dichorisandra* species are best grown in shady or only partly sunny, sheltered positions in moist soil. They are somewhat frost tender but in cold climates plants can be overwintered in a greenhouse. Propagation is from division or from cuttings taken in summer.

Dichorisandra thyrsiflora

Dichorisandra thyrsiflora

BLUE GINGER

↔ 3 ft (0.9 m) ↑ 3–10 ft (0.9–3 m)

Native of northern South America. Dark green glossy leaves. Produces terminal clusters of purple-blue flowers, on stems that can reach 10 ft (3 m) high, depending upon the growing conditions. Zones 9–12.

DICHROA

This is a temperate to subtropical Asian genus from the family Hydrangeaceae of possibly 13 species of shrubs, resembling the closely related *Hydrangea*. The name is derived from *di* (2 or twice) and *chroma* (color), and refers to the often 2-toned flowers. They have bright mid- to deep green leaves, pointed oval in shape with toothed edges. Heads of flowers rather like lacecap hydrangeas appear at various times, depending on the species, and eventually develop into a mass of tiny dry seed capsules.
CULTIVATION: This is an easily grown, adaptable genus for mild-temperate gardens. Most species prefer moist humus-enriched soil in partial shade and are reasonably frost hardy—to around 18°F (–8°C)—but are best with a little overhead protection such as under trees or eaves, which protect winter-flowering species from frost. Propagate from the seed or from half-hardened cuttings taken in summer or early autumn.

Dichroa febrifuga

↔ 5–8 ft (1.5–2.4 m)
↑ 5–8 ft (1.5–2.4 m)

Found from the Himalayas through China to Japan and southward to the mountains of Indonesia. Similar to hydrangea, but evergreen. Lavender to bright blue flowers, from autumn–spring. Wonderful plant for a partly shaded area, winter color. Zones 8–10.

Dichroa versicolor

↔ 6 ft (1.8 m) ↑ 7 ft (2 m)

A native of northern Myanmar. Large pointed oval leaves of rich dark green have an almost quilted surface. Heads of small deep blue flowers are produced for long periods. In alkaline soil the flowers will be mauve or pink. Zones 8–10.

DICKSONIA

This genus belonging to the family Dicksoniaceae of tree-ferns consists of around 30 species, occurring in the South Pacific, tropical America, and parts of Southeast Asia. The trunks are covered in the lower part by a dense mass of fibrous roots, and in the upper part by overlapping frond stalks, which persist after the fronds are shed with age. The fronds are large and arching, and bipinnately divided into narrow, deeply lobed, parallel leaflets. The spore clusters on the undersides of the fronds are protected by a leaf cap, appearing as rows of tiny green balls along leaflet edges.
CULTIVATION: *Dicksonia* species are best grown in a moist well-drained soil in part- to full shade with protection from the wind. In cold climates, they grow best in greenhouses and conservatories. Propagation is usually from spores, or from offsets of the trunks. Some species transplant easily, or plants can even be re-established from the cut-off upper half of the trunk, as long as this is well covered by fibrous roots.

Dicksonia antarctica ★

SOFT TREE FERN, TASMANIAN TREE FERN

↔ 12 ft (3.5 m) ↑ 20 ft (6 m)

A native of southeastern Australia, from Tasmania north to Queensland, with attractive fronds, tripinnate. The trunk is a dark brown-black, densely fibrous, and upright. This species is an

Dichroa versicolor

excellent plant for tubs. Shower the trunks to keep them moist in hot dry weather. Zones 8–10.

DICLIPTERA

Genus of about 150 annual and perennial herbs and shrubs, belonging to the acanthus (Acanthaceae) family, and native to tropical and warm-temperate regions. Stems are usually 6-angled. Flowers are borne in terminal clusters with 2-lipped tubular corollas, expanding toward the throat.
CULTIVATION: Easily grown in average well-drained soils in full sun and will tolerate some shade and drought. Suited to containers or hanging baskets. Propagate from seed or cuttings.

Dicliptera suberecta

syns *Jacobina suberecta, Justicia suberecta*

HUMMINGBIRD PLANT, KING'S CROWN

↔ 18–24 in (45–60 cm)
↑ 18–24 in (45–60 cm)

Perennial subshrub from Uruguay. Slender, velvety, gray foliage on erect or arching stems. Two-lipped, rusty reddish orange, tubular flowers, in summer–autumn. These blooms attract hummingbirds. Zones 7–11.

DICTAMNUS

BURNING BUSH, DITTANY

This genus in the rue (Rutaceae) family contains only one species, a herbaceous perennial with a woody base found from southwestern Europe through to Asia. The leaves are compound, composed of up to 6 pairs of leaflets, and showy flowers are produced in spikes above the foliage in summer. All parts of the plant can make you ill if ingested, and it exudes a volatile gas that in hot weather can be ignited without harm to the plant, hence one of its common names.
CULTIVATION: This plant likes a sunny aspect in a well-drained but moist humus-rich soil and may take many years to build up into a large flowering clump. Propagate from seed, which takes a long time, or by dividing large established clumps.

Dicliptera suberecta

Dictamnus albus

Dictamnus albus

☼ ✱ ↔ 20–24 in (50–60 cm)
↑ 16–36 in (40–90 cm)

Clumping plant with spikes of white flowers in summer above bright green foliage. Due to its wide distribution, several variants have been named, though the only one currently recognized is ***D. a.* var. *purpureus*,** pink flowers veined with purple. ***D. a.* 'Roseus'**, pale pink flowers. Zones 3–10.

DICTYOSPERMA

Although widely grown throughout the tropics for its ornamental value in landscaped gardens and as a container plant, this genus of one palm (family Arecaceae) is close to extinction in its native Mascarene Islands (Mauritius, Réunion, and Rodrigues) in the southern Indian Ocean. The arching pinnate leaves grow to 10 ft (3 m) long. Large fragrant flowers are grouped in large clusters of 3s, with 1 female and 2 male blooms. Fruit are small, purplish black, bullet-shaped berries.

CULTIVATION: This palm can withstand strong winds, but is not drought tolerant and prefers high humidity in moist rich soils. Best suited to warm coastal areas, in bright sunny situations. Propagate from seed, which germinates in 2 to 4 months.

Dictyosperma album

Dictyosperma album ★

HURRICANE PALM, PRINCESS PALM

☼ ✢ ↑ 60 ft (18 m) ↔ 20 ft (6 m)

An attractive tall palm with graceful crown, gray-ringed trunk, and swollen base. Feather-shaped fronds, yellow midrib, flowers reddish. Attractive pot plant when young. ***D. a.* var. *aureum*,** prominent yellow stripe beneath the leaflets, indistinct veins; ***D. a.* var. *conjugatum*,** shorter with larger trunk, and long fringes hanging from leaf tips. Zones 10–12.

DIERAMA

AFRICAN HAREBELL, ANGEL'S FISHING ROD, WAND FLOWER

From the high grasslands of southern Africa and Ethiopia, these perennial plants in the iris (Iridaceae) family form almost evergreen clumps of grassy gray-green foliage. Of the 40-plus species only a few are common in cultivation. The pendulous funnel-shaped flowers, in shades of wine red, pink, mauve, purple, and white, are held on long, graceful, arching, wiry stems and appear some time between early and mid-summer. The corms, which are replaced annually, reproduce themselves one on top of another. However, although these multitudinous corms often seem overcrowded, they are best left to sort themselves out as disturbance can be resented.

CULTIVATION: Open sunny sites and deep, rich, moist but well-drained soils suit best, but keep well watered during early growth. Propagate from seed or by division. Some forms of *Dierama* become weedy.

Dierama pulcherrimum

☼ ❄ ↔ 12 in (30 cm) ↑ 5 ft (1.5 m)

Tough, graceful species from South Africa. Flowers bell-shaped, colors variable, commonly magenta pink, madder pink, rich sugary pinks, and deep purples. **'Album'**, pure white form. Zones 7–10.

DIERVILLA

Native to North America, this genus of 3 species of deciduous shrubs in the woodbine (Caprifoliaceae) family is similar to *Weigela* but have smaller yellow flowers. Their suckering roots are useful for soil stabilization.

CULTIVATION: *Diervilla* species are frost hardy and will grow in full sun or partial shade in a well-drained soil. They should be cut back in late winter or early spring to encourage the new flowering growth. Propagation is best from cuttings.

Diervilla rivularis

BUSH HONEYSUCKLE, GEORGIA BUSH HONEYSUCKLE

☼/◐ ✱ ↔ 36–48 in (90–120 cm)
↑ 24–36 in (60–90 cm)

A spreading, suckering, slow-growing, deciduous shrub found from southeastern USA. The leaves are dark green, oval- to sword-shaped, and slightly hairy; finely hairy branches. It produces crowded heads of lemon yellow to reddish yellow trumpet-shaped flowers, in terminal panicles, during summer. **'Morton'** (syn. 'Summer Stars'), a densely-branched dwarf selection. Zones 3–9.

Dierama pulcherrimum

Diervilla sessilifolia ★

SOUTHERN BUSH HONEYSUCKLE

☼ ✱ ↔ 5 ft (1.5 m) ↑ 5 ft (1.5 m)

Found in southeastern USA. Leaves have reddish veins. Good autumn foliage color. Sulfur yellow flowers, generally in pairs, during the summer. Zones 4–9.

DIETES

A genus consisting of 6 species of evergreen clumping plants, which belongs to the iris (Iridaceae) family, 5 from southern Africa and the other from Lord Howe Island, Australia. The flowers, produced in summer, are held above the leaves and are flat, lacking the upward-pointing petals of an iris. They make strong bold feature plants. The flowers individually only last a day or two, but the flowering season can last most of the summer.

CULTIVATION: Although these plants are able to endure only very light frosts, in all other respects they are very tough, and will tolerate sun or deep shade, poor soils, and dry conditions. Propagate from seed. Although *Dietes* can be divided, they tend to resent disturbance and will need some care to help them re-establish.

Dietes bicolor

☼/✹ ✱ ↔ 24–36 in (60–90 cm)
↑ 32–36 in (80–90 cm)

Well-known species from the East Cape, South Africa. The long, arching, deep green, strap-like leaves are overtopped by flat lemon flowers with contrasting, brown, basal blotches. Zones 9–11.

Dietes grandiflora

syn. *Dietes iridioides 'Johnsonii'*

WILD IRIS

✹ ✱ ↔ 20–27 in (50–70 cm)
↑ 20–27 in (50–70 cm)

Found in the forests of South Africa. Broader leaves than *D. bicolor*, white flowers marked with yellow and brown blotches. Zones 9–11.

Diervilla rivularis 'Morton'

D

Dietes, Hybrid Cultivar, 'Orange Drops'

Dietes iridioides

AFRICAN IRIS, CAPE IRIS, FORTNIGHT LILY

↔ 12–24 in (30–60 cm)
↕ 18–24 in (45–60 cm)

Erect, wiry stems to 24 in (60 cm). Flower with 3 iris-like blue standards and 3 white falls, yellow centers, in summer. Flowers last one day, open in morning, closed by early afternoon. **'White Tiger'**, white-edged gray-green foliage. Zones 9–10.

Dietes Hybrid Cultivars

↔ 24 in (60 cm) ↕ 30 in (75 cm)

The most popular hybrids take their names from their central colors. **'Lemon Drops'**, resembles *D. bicolor* in habit and size but has darker leaves, flowers are cream with yellow basal spot; and **'Orange Drops'**, similar to *D. grandiflora,* but smaller with narrower leaves, white to cream flowers have orange basal spot. Zones 8–11.

DIGITALIS

FOXGLOVE

Common in gardens, particularly in traditional herbaceous borders, and in the wild, usually as garden escapees, the genus *Digitalis*, once confined to Eurasia and North Africa, now occurs throughout most temperate regions of the world. It is a member of the plantain (Plantaginaceae) family and is made up of around 20 species of biennials and perennials that are quite similar to one another. They form a basal clump of rather coarse, often elliptical, heavily veined leaves, from the center of which emerge upright flower stems carrying smaller leaves, and many downward-facing, 4-lobed, bell-shaped flowers that open progressively upwards along the spike, thus ensuring a long flowering period. Most flower from late spring into summer, in pink, lavender, purple, yellow, cream, or white. All parts of the foxglove are toxic if swallowed; contact with the leaves may irritate the skin; deer and rabbits avoid eating them. Once widely used in the production of heart stimulant drugs that are now mostly synthesized.

CULTIVATION: Easily cultivated in most temperate areas. Plant in moist, humus-rich soil, water well in spring, and while in flower. Biennials must be raised from seed, but perennials will also grow from basal offshoots.

Digitalis ferruginea

RUSTY FOXGLOVE

↔ 12–20 in (30–50 cm)
↕ 48 in (120 cm)

Biennial or short-lived perennial from southern Europe and western Asia. The basal leaves are deep green, sometimes hair-fringed, and narrow. The flowers that occur along most of the stem length are golden brown to rusty red. Zones 7–10.

Digitalis × *fulva*

↔ 20–24 in (50–60 cm)
↕ 40 in (100 cm)

A natural hybrid between *D. grandiflora* and *D. purpurea*, found in southern Europe. Its leaves are finely downy and toothed. It has narrow spikes of white to pale yellow-green flowers. Zones 7–9.

Digitalis grandiflora

syn. *Digitalis ambigua*

LARGE YELLOW FOXGLOVE

↔ 20–24 in (50–60 cm)
↕ 40 in (100 cm)

European biennial or short-lived perennial. Lush dark green leaves, toothed edges, downy undersides, leafy flower stems. The flowers are pale yellow with darker veining. **'Carillon'**, to 24 in (60 cm) tall, primrose yellow flowers. Zones 4–9.

Digitalis 'John Innes Tetra'

↔ 12–16 in (30–40 cm)
↕ 24 in (60 cm)

Perennial tetraploid hybrid *(D. grandiflora* × *D. lanata)*; lush foliage, compact stocky growth, large, gold and brown marked yellow flowers. Zones 6–10.

Digitalis laevigata

↔ 18 in (45 cm) ↕ 36 in (90 cm)

Southern European perennial. Narrow, leathery, finely toothed leaves. Flowers yellow to pale orange, purplish veining, white lower lip, often sparse. Zones 7–10.

Digitalis lanata

GRECIAN FOXGLOVE

↔ 20–24 in (50–60 cm)
↕ 40 in (100 cm)

Biennial or short-lived perennial from Turkey and northeastern Greece. Narrow, downy, lance-shaped leaves. Strong upright flower stems, dull white to buff flowers, brown veining, pale lower lip. Zones 6–9.

Digitalis obscura

Digitalis parviflora

Digitalis lutea

STRAW FOXGLOVE

↔ 16–24 in (40–60 cm)
↕ 24–40 in (60–100 cm)

A native of Europe and North Africa. The leaves are dark green, hairless, and finely to heavily serrated. Produces abundant flowers of soft yellow or white. Zones 4–9.

Digitalis mertonensis

STRAWBERRY FOXGLOVE

↔ 16–20 in (40–50 cm)
↕ 20–30 in (50–75 cm)

Widely grown perennial garden hybrid *(D. grandiflora* × *D. purpurea)* providing the best of *D. purpurea*—large, downy, pinkish red to purple-pink flowers—with none of its vices of invasiveness and top-heavy growth. Compact plant with lush foliage and tightly packed flowers. Zones 4–9.

Digitalis obscura

WILLOW-LEAFED FOXGLOVE

↔ 16–24 in (40–60 cm)
↕ 24 in (60 cm)

Perennial or woody-based subshrub from Spain, with narrow slightly glossy leaves and flower stems that are wiry and not always upright. Flowers are yellow to red-brown with orange to red markings. Zones 7–9.

Digitalis parviflora

CHOCOLATE FOXGLOVE

↔ 16–20 in (40–50 cm)
↕ 24–36 in (60–90 cm)

Perennial from northern Spain. Dense foliage rosette of lance-shaped shallowly toothed leaves. Abundant flower spikes and flowers. Deep red-brown flowers with light base, purple-tinted lower lip. Zones 7–9.

Digitalis purpurea

COMMON FOXGLOVE

↔ 12–32 in (30–80 cm)
↕ 5–6 ft (1.5–1.8 m)

Biennial from western Europe and now widely naturalized, often considered a weed. Forms a dense clump of hairy basal leaves. Strongly upright flower stems with many pink, purple, or white flowers, heavily spotted within, borne from early summer. Natural forms include: ***D. p.* subsp. *heywoodii***, from southern Spain and Portugal, silvery foliage, white and cream flowers, cultivars with these characters are placed in the **Heywoodii Group**; ***D. p.* f. *albiflora***, flowers often free of throat markings. ***D. p.* Excelsior Group**, flowers surrounding the stem, in a mix of colors; **'Sutton's Apricot'** produces creamy salmon pink flowers. Zones 4–9.

Digitalis thapsi

↔ 12 in (30 cm)
↕ 16–24 in (40–60 cm)

Perennial found from central Spain to eastern Portugal. Leaves puckered and toothed, covered in fine golden hairs. Downy, pale-throated, red-spotted, purple flowers. **'Spanish Peaks'**, soft rose pink flowers. Zones 7–9.

DIMOCARPUS

syn. *Euphoria*

This is a small genus of 5 species in the soapberry (Sapindaceae) family closely allied to *Litchi* (lychee), occurring from Southeast Asia to Australia. All are trees with large pinnate leaves, a heavy crown, and small flowers borne in large dense terminal panicles. A characteristic is the fleshy edible aril surrounding the seeds inside the almost leathery skin of the fruit, which is smooth by comparison with the rough checkered skin of the lychee fruit.

CULTIVATION: Propagation is from seed sown soon after hardening since the seeds lose viability quite quickly. Rich sandy loams and protection from frost are preferred.

Dimocarpus longan

syn. *Euphoria longan*

LONGAN

↔20 ft (6 m) ↑40 ft (12 m)

Native to Southeast Asia. Cultivated for its fruit. Heavily foliaged branches, alternate pinnate leaves. Flowering in spring, fruit ripens in summer. Prefers tropical regions, but can grow where heavy frosts do not occur. ***D. l.* subsp. *malesianus*** varies little from the typical trees. Zones 11–12.

DIMORPHOTHECA

This genus of 7 species of annuals, perennials, and subshrubs belongs to the daisy (Asteraceae) family. They are native to southern and tropical Africa. Stems may be upright or sprawling and the leaves simple or divided, sometimes scented. They flower prolifically from spring to late summer. The typical daisy flowers have white or yellow rays that are purplish blue or coppery beneath, creating an attractive contrast.

CULTIVATION: Grow in full sun in a well-drained soil. In cooler areas the protection of a hot sunny wall will promote flowering. Propagate annuals from seed; others from seed or cuttings.

Dimorphotheca sinuata

syn. *Dimorphotheca aurantiaca of gardens*

NAMAQUALAND DAISY

↔12 in (30 cm) ↑12–18 in (30–45 cm)

Native to South Africa. Annual with narrow coarsely toothed leaves. The dark-centered daisies come in a range of colors from white to orange, including some pastel shades. Zones 9–11.

Dimocarpus longan

Dioon spinulosum

Dimorphotheca sinuata

DIOON

This genus of tree-like cycads in the zamia (Zamiaceae) family is made up of 10 species found in Mexico and Central America. Palm-like in appearance, with upright trunks, ringed with the scars of old leaf bases, and frond-like leaves, their name is derived from the Greek and means "two eggs," a reference to their paired seeds. Cycads are ancient plants that do not bear true flowers, instead reproducing by means of pollen cones and seed cones, rather like conifers. The female or seed cones are often very large and woolly.

CULTIVATION: Frost tender, not tolerant of prolonged drought, *Dioon* is best grown in moist, well-drained, humus-rich soil in sun or partial shade. Water well during the warmer months. Restrict pruning to removing old trunks with untidy or dead foliage. Propagate from seed or by removing rooted offsets that develop at the base.

Dioon edule ★

MEXICAN FERN PALM

↔5 ft (1.5 m) ↑6 ft (1.8 m)

Commonly cultivated species from Mexico. Fronds upright, gray-green, glaucous when young. Female cones contain edible seeds. Zones 9–11.

Diospyros virginiana 'John Rick'

Dipelta floribunda

Dioon spinulosum ★

↔10 ft (3 m) ↑30 ft (9 m)

From Mexico. Slender trunk. Near-erect to arching fronds, woolly coating on emerging, wearing away with age. Sharp spines tip the aromatic dark green leaflets, which have distinctive blue tint when young. Zones 9–11.

DIOSPYROS

EBONY, PERSIMMON

This genus in the ebony (Ebenaceae) family of some 475 species of evergreen and deciduous, tender and hardy, tropical and temperate shrubs and trees is a very diverse group of plants. Some have considerable economic importance, either for their timber or their fruit, while others are attractive ornamentals. Their foliage is usually quite simple and the leaves of the deciduous species can be very colorful in autumn. The flowers are unisexual, and to ensure better fruit production it helps to have several trees for cross-pollination. The fruits range from small fleshy berries to the pear-like persimmons.

CULTIVATION: With such a large and diverse genus it is difficult to generalize about cultivation requirements. What can be said is that only a few species will tolerate prolonged drought and most prefer moist well-drained soil that is reasonably fertile. Propagation is from seed or by root cuttings or grafting.

Diospyros virginiana

AMERICAN PERSIMMON, PERSIMMON

↔10 ft (3 m) ↑50 ft (15 m)

Native to eastern USA, deciduous tree, simple oval leaves color well in autumn. Small, edible, yellow fruit. Timber used for making golf woods. **'John Rick'** ★, old-established fruiting cultivar grown for superior eating qualities. Zones 5–9.

DIPELTA

This genus belonging to the woodbine (Caprifoliaceae) family of 4 deciduous shrubs from China is closely related to *Weigela*. Pinkish or purplish, tubular, bell-shaped flowers, in singles or in clusters of up to 8, appear in spring or early summer. Generally grown for their ornamental value, some are also used in traditional Chinese medicine.

CULTIVATION: Frost resistant, drought tender, *Dipelta* species are adaptable to a wide range of soils but do better in a protected position. Propagate from softwood cuttings taken in summer, by layering or from seed sown in spring.

Dipelta floribunda ★

ROSY DIPELTA

↔10 ft (3 m) ↑8 ft (2.4 m)

Native of central and western China. Branches, broad spreading, long arching. Hanging clusters of fragrant, tubular, bell-shaped white flowers, flushed with a shell pink, yellow or orange throat, in spring. Zones 6–9.

D

DIPLAZIUM

Genus of around 400 species of mostly tropical ferns, worldwide in their distribution, that is part of the cliff fern (Woodsiaceae) family. They are ground-dwelling ferns with short or long rhizomes, sometimes forming a short erect trunk. The frond stalks are usually blackish and the fronds are broad and much divided; ultimate leaflets are toothed. On fertile fronds the dark spore-patches (sori) are linear and follow the veins, often arranged in a fan-like manner. In some species plantlets are produced on the frond tips.
CULTIVATION: In the wild these plants grow in moist soil, sometimes in the quite deep shade of the forest understory. They prefer very humid conditions and a spongy growing medium with a high organic content. Some of the species adapt easily to cultivation but others resent disturbance. Propagate from the spores or by division of the rhizomes.

Diplazium pycnocarpon

syn. *Athyrium pycnocarpon*

GLADE FERN, NARROW-LEAFED SPLEENWORT, SILVERY SPLEENWORT

↔ 4 ft (1.2 m)
↑ 24–36 in (60–90 cm)

From eastern Canada to southeastern USA. Deciduous fern. Forms rosettes. Green arching fronds are silvery, light green in spring, darkening in summer then turning russet before dying back. Zones 3–9.

DIRCA

LEATHERWOOD

This genus in the daphne (Thylemaeaceae) family consists of 2 deciduous shrubs, both native to North America. They have tough flexible branches, simple alternate leaves, and fruit which is a small red or greenish drupe with 4 segments. The insignificant yellow flowers have no petals and open in spring before leaves appear. All parts of the plant are poisonous and if touched may cause skin irritation. The fruit has a narcotic effect.
CULTIVATION: Leatherwoods need exposure to full sun to achieve their best habit but will also grow in shade. They are quite hardy and grow best in a well-drained moist soil. Propagation is from seed or by layering.

Dirca occidentalis

WESTERN LEATHERWOOD

↔ 4–6 ft (1.2–1.8 m)
↑ 4–6 ft (1.2–1.8 m)

From California, USA. Rare shrub with attractive yellow foliage in autumn. It is similar to *D. palustris* but has smaller leaves and stalkless flowers. Bears yellow tubular flowers, with long protruding stamens, in groups of 3 to 4, in spring. Zones 7–10.

Dirca palustris

LEATHERWOOD, ROPEBARK, WICOPY

↔ 6 ft (1.8 m) ↑ 6 ft (1.8 m)

From east coast USA and Canada, a slow-growing, dense, rounded, deciduous shrub. Yellowish branches, fibrous, gray, tough, leathery bark. Leaves 3 in (8 cm) long. Clusters of insignificant flowers in leaf axils, before leaves, in spring. Fruit a green to red oval-shaped drupe, with a single seed. Zones 4–9.

DISANTHUS

This genus belonging to the witchhazel (Hamamelidaceae) family contains a single deciduous shrub, with alternate leaves and inconspicuous flowers, that is native to China and Japan. The fruit are dehiscent capsules containing several, shiny, black seeds.
CULTIVATION: Frost resistant but drought tender, *Disanthus* species prefer a cool, moist, rich, acid or peaty soil in a protected sunny position, in conditions similar to rhododendrons and azaleas. Propagate from seed, which takes 2 years to germinate, or from cuttings taken in summer and struck under glass, or by layering.

Disanthus cercidifolius

Disanthus cercidifolius ★

↔ 10 ft (3 m) ↑ 20 ft (6 m)

From mountainous areas of China and Japan. Long leaf stalks, luxuriant, heart-shaped, bluish green leaves, turning maroon, red, and orange in autumn. Curious, inconspicuous, deep purple flowers, spidery petals, in late autumn. Zones 7–9.

DISPORUM

FAIRY-BELLS

This genus, comprising 10 species from Southeast Asia and Japan, belongs to the autumn-crocus (Colchicaceae) family. They are perennial plants with rhizomes, the leaves spiraly arranged, lanceolate to ovate. The usually pendulous flowers occur in few-flowered umbels or are solitary. The red or bluish black fruit is a berry. American species, once included here, are now referred to the genus *Prosartes*.
CULTIVATION: They grow best in part-shade in well-drained but moisture-retentive neutral to acid soils with plenty of organic matter. Propagate by division in spring or from fresh seed.

Disporum uniflorum

Disporum sessile

JAPANESE FAIRY BELLS

↔ 12–24 in (30–60 cm)
↑ 12–24 in (30–60 cm)

Spreading perennial from Japan. Lance-shaped leaves. Small, green to white, drooping, lily-like flowers, tips tinged green, singly or in clusters of 1 to 3, in spring. Bluish black fruit in late summer. **'Variegatum'**, leaves broadly striped with cream. Zones 4–8.

Disporum uniflorum

syns *Disporum flavens, D. flavum*

YELLOW FAIRY BELLS

↔ 12–24 in (30–60 cm)
↑ 12–24 in (30–60 cm)

Upright clump-forming perennial from central to northeastern China and Korea. Pale yellow, lily-like flowers, from spring. Dark black berries in late summer. Zones 4–9.

DISTICTIS

Genus of 9 evergreen woody-stemmed climbers, from Mexico and the West Indies, belonging to the trumpet-vine (Bignoniaceae) family. Terminal racemes or panicles of colorful, tubular to trumpet-shaped, occasionally scented flowers in spring to summer. Branches are hexagonal with tendrils that cling to surfaces. Fruit is a 2-valved capsule containing winged seeds.
CULTIVATION: Grow in full sun in fertile, moist, well-drained soil. Not suited to hot humid conditions or cold or dry inland areas but withstands light frost. Propagate from half-hardened cuttings in growing season, or by layering in early spring.

Distictis buccinatoria

syns *Bignonia cherere, Phaedranthus buccinatorius*

MEXICAN BLOOD TRUMPET

↔ 10–20 ft (3–6 m)
↑ 6–15 ft (1.8–4.5 m)

Vigorous, evergreen, perennial climber or creeper from Mexico. Fast growing. Purple-red, large, tubular to funnel-shaped flowers, corolla about 3 in (8 cm) long, yellow in the throat and covered with minute yellow hairs. **'Mrs Rivers'**, late-flowering, dark mauve-pink, golden yellow throat. Zones 9–11.

DODECATHEON

AMERICAN COWSLIP, SHOOTING STARS

A charming genus of some 14 species of small rosette-forming herbaceous perennials belonging to the primrose (Primulaceae) family, native to North America. They produce several flowers per stem, in spring, with fully reflexed petals like those of a cyclamen.
CULTIVATION: Grow naturally in moist meadows and mountain pastures and so need similar garden conditions. Will not thrive in humid or tropical areas. Usually grow best in a cool rock garden or pot. Propagate from freshly sown seed; division in late winter, just before they break dormancy, is also possible.

Dodecatheon dentatum

↔6–12 in (15–30 cm)
↕4–16 in (10–40 cm)

Found from Washington and Oregon through Idaho to Arizona, USA. Leaves oblong to lance-shaped, bright green, sometimes with finely toothed margins. White flowers, turned-back petals, yellow anthers, from spring–early summer. Zones 5–9.

Dodecatheon hendersonii

MOSQUITO-BILLS, SAILOR'S CAP

↔6–12 in (15–30 cm)
↕8–15 in (20–38 cm)

From California, USA. Deep green, fleshy, oval leaves. Flowers in heads of 2 to 3. Pinkish purple turned-back petals, yellow anthers. Zones 6–9.

Dodecatheon meadia

syn. *Dodecatheon pauciflorum*

AMERICAN COWSLIP, EASTERN SHOOTING STAR, SHOOTING STAR

↔12 in (30 cm)
↕8–18 in (20–45 cm)

From eastern USA. Oblong leaves, and flowers in heads of 10 to 20, turned-back petals usually purple, cream to white base, may be pink or white. ***D. m.* f. *album***, white-flowers. Zones 3–9.

DODONAEA

A genus in the soapberry (Sapindaceae) family of about 70 species of evergreen shrubs or small trees found in tropical and temperate regions, mostly in Australia, quite often in arid and semi-arid areas. Commonly known as hopbush; early European settlers substituted fruits of some species for hops in brewing. Male and female flowers mostly on separate plants. Flowers small and insignificant; it is the highly colored, inflated, winged capsules that form the attraction of these plants.
CULTIVATION: Frost tender, they do best in a moderately fertile well-drained soil in full sun. Some species withstand extended dry periods. Tip pruning will maintain bushy growth. Propagate from tip cuttings taken in summer.

Dodonaea viscosa

HOPBUSH

↔5 ft (1.5 m) ↕10 ft (3 m)

A fast-growing evergreen tree from Australia, New Zealand, Pacific islands, tropical America, and southern Africa. Shiny, light green, sticky foliage. Bears masses of green winged fruit capsules in summer, hardening to a papery light brown. Best with regular trimming. ***D. v.* subsp. *angustifolia***, narrow, wavy-edged leaves. **'Purpurea'** ★, a sought-after form distinguished by its purple-red foliage and capsules. Zones 9–11.

DOMBEYA

This is a large genus of about 225 species occurring from Africa to the Mascarene Islands, with 190 species in Madagascar alone. It is a member of the mallow (Malvaceae) family. All are evergreen, deciduous, or semi-deciduous shrubs or trees with simple, alternate, broad, often lobed leaves, and often with conspicuous stipules at the base of the leaf stalk. Flowers, in axillary or terminal panicles, often densely packed and very showy, are 5-petalled, white, pink, or red in color. The fruits are small and often hairy capsules.
CULTIVATION: Only a few species from the summer rainfall regions of southern Africa are cultivated, in warm-temperate and subtropical localities with adequate moisture in summer. A well-drained, fertile soil in full sun or part-shade is required. Some species are only just frost hardy for short periods. Propagate from seed in spring, or by cuttings in summer.

Dombeya burgessiae

PINK DOMBEYA, PINK WILD PEAR

↔7 ft (2 m) ↕10 ft (3 m)

From northeastern South Africa and Zimbabwe. Dense multi-stemmed shrub branching from ground level. Leaves large, hairy, lobed. Pink flowers in late autumn–winter. Fruits mature in winter–spring. Zones 9–12.

Dombeya cacuminum

↔20 ft (6 m) ↕40 ft (12 m)

Upright, evergreen tree native to open woodlands of Madagascar. Large leaves, maple-like, shiny. Flowers large, in pendent clusters, deep pink to red. Zones 10–12.

Dombeya wallichii

↔10 ft (3 m) ↕15 ft (4.5 m)

Evergreen tree originating from East Africa and Madagascar. Leaves large. Large deep pink to red flowers, in dense clusters, in winter–spring. One of the parents of widely grown hybrid *D.* × *cayeuxii* ★. Zones 10–12.

DORONICUM

LEOPARD'S BANE

There are about 35 species of perennial herbs, native to Europe, southwestern Asia, and Siberia, in this genus in the daisy (Asteraceae) family. They grow from tubers or rhizomes, producing clumps of oval to heart-shaped basal leaves. In spring, brilliant yellow daisies are borne on stems either singly or in small groups. Both rays and central discs are yellow.
CULTIVATION: Grow *Doronicum* species in part-shade in moderately fertile soil that is moisture retentive but well drained. Suitable for wild and woodland plantings. These plants are not suitable for hot climates. Propagate by division in autumn.

Doronicum columnae

↔24 in (60 cm) ↕12 in (30 cm)

From Europe and western Asia. Woodland perennial. Slightly hairy, heart-shaped leaves, scalloped edges. Yellow, sunflower-like flowers from spring– early summer. May die back in mid-summer. Zones 4–8.

Doronicum orientale

syn. *Doronicum caucasicum*

↔12 in (30 cm)
↕12–24 in (30–60 cm)

Native to the Caucasus, Lebanon, and southern Europe. A fleshy-stemmed perennial forming clumps of oval leaves. The bright yellow daisies, finely rayed, are carried singly on tall slender stems, in spring. **'Magnificum'** ★, large flowers. Zones 5–9.

Dodonaea viscosa 'Purpurea', seed capsules

Dombeya burgessiae

Distictis buccinatoria

Dodecatheon meadia

Doronicum orientale

D

DOROTHEANTHUS

LIVINGSTONE DAISY

This genus of 6 species of succulent annuals, belonging to the iceplant (Aizoaceae) family, is confined to South Africa. Spreading or mounding plants with thickened leaves that have a crystalline surface, creating a sugar-coated look. Flowers are daisy-like, often very abundant, in a range of colors, mainly shades of pink or white but also yellow, orange, red, and purple. Mostly ephemeral, these subdesert plants can race into growth with the arrival of rain. In frost-free climates, the plants may grow at any time but in temperate areas they are mainly summer-flowering.
CULTIVATION: Plant in spring in a bright sunny position to ensure maximum flowering time. Soil should be light, gritty, and well-drained, but the plants do need occasional water when flowering. Deadhead frequently for continued bloom. In cooler climates, sow seed under glass in winter or spring. Propagate from seed.

Dorotheanthus bellidiformis

↔ 8–16 in (20–40 cm)
↑ 2–6 in (5–15 cm)

From South Africa. Low spreading plant. Red-tinted stems, fleshy gray-green leaves, rough textured surface. Daisy-like flowers in mainly pink to purple shades but also white. Garden forms with yellow and multi-colored flowers may be *D. bellidiformis* × *D. gramineus* hybrids. Zones 9–11.

DORYANTHES

Genus of 2 species of large perennial herbs, in own family, Doryanthaceae, occurring in woodlands, open forests, and rocky hillsides on sandy or gravelly, well-draining soils in eastern Australia. Leaves are lance-shaped, pointed with an appendage at the apex. Flower stalks can exceed the leaves in length by 2 to 3 times. Flowers are in terminal heads, each large, red, and with 6 equal segments. Fruits are 3-celled capsules. Plants are long-lived in cultivation and were grown in the UK as early as 1800.
CULTIVATION: Propagation is usually from seeds, but flowering could be up to 10 years from germination. Division of clumps, or from suckers, will produce flowering plants sooner.

Doryanthes excelsa

GIANT LILY, GYMEA LILY, ILLAWARRA LILY

↔ 10 ft (3 m) ↑ 8–20 ft (2.4–6 m)

Found in woodlands on sandy soils in the central coast region of New South Wales, Australia. Leaves are bright or slightly yellowish green, generally stiff and erect. Flower stalk, up to 20 ft (6 m) long, terminating in a dense head of many red flowers, in spring–summer. Each flower contains large quantities of nectar, presumably as a bird-attractant to effect pollination. Dark colored capsules. Zones 9–11.

Doryanthes palmeri

SPEAR LILY

↔ 3–10 ft (0.9–3 m)
↑ 3–10 ft (0.9–3 m)

From northern New South Wales and southern Queensland, Australia, on skeletal soils on rocky hillsides. Leaves long, bright green, lance-shaped, with a cylindrical appendage at apex. Flower stalks up to 17 ft (5 m) long, usually not erect, but tending to arch, with brownish flowers, during spring. Capsules greenish. Zones 10–12.

DRACOCEPHALUM

Genus, in mint (Lamiaceae) family, containing about 45 species of annuals, perennials, and dwarf shrubs. Most are found in Europe and Asia, some in northern Africa, and USA. Leaves opposite and simple with toothed or indented margins. Flowers usually deep blue or violet-blue, borne in whorls on spikes, terminally and on branching stems. They are tubular and 2-lipped, lower lip having 3 lobes and upper lip 2 lobes. Some species are aromatic.
CULTIVATION: Full sun, fertile well-drained soil. Grow perennials from cuttings or division, annuals from seed.

Doryanthes excelsa, in the wild, New South Wales, Australia

Dracocephalum ruyschiana

↔ 12–18 in (30–45 cm)
↑ 12–24 in (30–60 cm)

Perennial from central Europe and Russia. Upright stems, narrow leaves. Whorls of 2 to 6 flowers, blue to violet, occasionally pink or white, in dense terminal spikes, in summer. Zones 3–9.

DRIMYS

This genus is one of 5 which make up the small family Winteraceae, origins of which date back to earliest evolution of flowering plants in the age of dinosaurs. It consists of 6 species of evergreen shrubs and small trees occurring in South America and higher mountains of Mexico and Central America. Another 20 to 40 species from Australasia and Southeast Asia have often been included in *Drimys*, but most recent evidence supports their being separated into the separate genus *Tasmannia*. Simple leathery leaves, without teeth or lobes, arranged spirally and clustered towards end of season's growth, new leaves often red. Star-shaped white or cream flowers are carried in umbel-like clusters in spring. Bark is aromatic with a hot, pepper-like taste. From its first discovery by Europeans it was believed to be an effective treatment for scurvy. It thrives in a sheltered position.
CULTIVATION: Most species are not fully frost hardy and at best tolerate down to 14°F (–10°C) for short spells. Grow in sun or partial shade in moist but well-drained fertile soil. Propagate by taking half-hardened cuttings in summer or sowing seed into pots as soon as it is ripe in autumn, with protection against winter frosts.

Dracocephalum ruyschiana

Drimys winteri

Drimys winteri ★

syn. *Wintera aromatica*

WINTER'S BARK

↔ 30 ft (9 m) ↑ 50 ft (15 m)

Aromatic tree, from Mexico, Chile, and Argentina. Lustrous, dark-green, lance-shaped leaves, pale blue-white beneath. Flowers fragrant, creamy white, in umbels of 20 individual blossoms, in spring–early summer. Zones 8–9.

DROSANTHEMUM

Found in South Africa and Namibia, this genus of succulents in the iceplant (Aizoaceae) family is made up of about 90 species of perennials, many trailing, the others mounding or shrubby. The leaves are succulent, cylindrical in section, covered in tiny protuberances and often small. Attraction lies largely in its dense carpeting habit and weight of bloom. Flowers seldom very large but incredibly abundant, frequently making a solid mass of color, in white or any shade of pink, purple, yellow, orange, or red, usually from late spring.
CULTIVATION: Hardiness varies; mostly intolerant of repeated frosts. Plant in open sunny position in gritty, very free-draining soil with a little extra humus.

Drosanthemum speciosum

Water when in flower, otherwise allow to survive on natural rainfall. Propagate from seed or cuttings or by layering.

Drosanthemum speciosum ★

↔40 in (100 cm) ↕24 in (60 cm)

From Cape region, South Africa. Shrub with upright branching stems. Leaves have crystalline surface. Flowers deep orange-red, occasionally purplish, green center, large, many-petalled, plumed effect. Zones 9–11.

DRYAS

MOUNTAIN AVENS

A small genus of 3 species, all evergreen mat-forming shrubs from Arctic and Northern Hemisphere alpine regions, belonging to the rose (Rosaceae) family. They produce comparatively large, white or lemon flowers in summer, well clear of the foliage, followed by large fluffy seed heads. The botanical name comes from that of the Greek mythological wood nymph to whom the oak was sacred, and alludes to the oak-shaped foliage.

CULTIVATION: These shrubs prefer a sunny moist aspect in non-tropical climates in a rock garden or between pavers. Their mat-forming habit and copper-colored leaves in winter make them ideal ground covers over small bulbs. Propagate by division, from cuttings or freshly sown seed.

Dryas octopetala ★

MOUNTAIN AVENS

↔over 40 in (100 cm) ↕3–4 in (8–10 cm)

Northern European species. Glossy oak-shaped leaves, white reverse turns coppery in winter. White flowers, in summer. Fluffy seed heads. Zones 3–9.

Dryas × suendermannii

↔over 40 in (100 cm) ↕3–5 in (8–15 cm)

Hybrid between *D. drummondii* and *D. octopetala* that arose in cultivation. Pale, creamy yellow, slightly nodding flowers, in summer. Zones 3–9.

DRYOPTERIS

BUCKLER FERN, SHIELD FERN, WOOD FERN

Part of shield-fern (Dryopteridaceae) family, this genus is made up of about 200 species found in temperate forests, fields, and wet areas of the Northern Hemisphere. This genus contains the largest number of good ferns for ornamental gardening. The green foliage looks attractive with its upright arching fronds. These ferns work well when planted in mixed borders with most herbaceous plants. Many species have scaly tips to the fronds that can be dramatically beautiful in the spring as they begin to unravel.

CULTIVATION: Mostly deciduous but in mild areas will retain their foliage. An easy to cultivate, resilient fern group that will grow in poor dry soils, with little natural light. Propagate from spores as soon as they harden.

Dryas octopetala

Dryopteris affinis

GOLDEN MALE FERN

↔27–36 in (70–90 cm) ↕36 in (90 cm)

Deciduous fern from Europe, including the UK, and parts of Asia. Very upright fronds appear in spring, initially a brown-green, changing to a lush rich green as the fronds unravel. **'Crispa Gracilis'**, dwarf evergreen, fronds have very congested leaflets (tight foliage) with dark green tonings on the tips; **'Cristata Angustata'**, elegant fern with slim, graceful, long, arching, crested fronds; **'Pinderi'**, uncrested mid-green fronds that narrow to very sharp point. Zones 6–8.

Dryopteris carthusiana

syn. *Dryopteris maderensis*

NARROW BUCKLER FERN

↔12 in (30 cm) ↕24 in (60 cm)

Delicate-looking fern from Europe producing tufts of pale, lime green, lance-shaped fronds. Creeping, ground-covering habit. Enjoys damp, grows well in boggy areas. Zones 6–10.

Dryopteris × complexa

↔36 in (90 cm) ↕36 in (90 cm)

Hybrid of *D. affinis* × *D. filix-mas*. Medium to large, semi-evergreen fern, similar to *D. affinis*, with upright fronds that reappear in spring, initially brown-green, changing to mid-green as they mature. Winter dormant in cool areas. Zones 4–9.

Dryopteris cristata

COMMON SHIELD FERN, CRESTED WOOD FERN, NARROW SWAMP FERN

↔36 in (90 cm) ↕18–30 in (45–75 cm)

From Europe and northern Asia and eastern North America. Erect fern with green, narrow, lance-shaped fronds with short, widely spaced, tilted leaflets. Spores held on undersides of fronds. Good in very damp areas. Will be evergreen in Zones 6 and 7. Zones 3–7.

Dryopteris filix-mas

Dryopteris cycadina

syn. *Dryopteris atrata*

SHAGGY SHIELD FERN

↔18 in (45 cm) ↕24 in (60 cm)

From Japan, China, Taiwan, and northern India. Long, dark green, distinctive, narrow fronds, serrated margins. Black stems support these in an arching habit. Needs well-drained soil. Zones 8–10.

Dryopteris dilatata

syn. *Dryopteris austriaca*

BROAD BUCKLER FERN

↔36 in (90 cm) ↕48 in (120 cm)

Vigorous fern from northern, western, and central Europe. Forms rosettes of broad dark green fronds. Easily grown, tolerates some sun. **'Crispa Whiteside'** (Whiteside's broad buckler fern), only reaches 24 in (60 cm) high, fronds paler green in color ruffled crispy look. Zones 5–8.

Dryopteris erythrosora

AUTUMN FERN

↔16 in (40 cm) ↕24 in (60 cm)

From Asia. Shiny triangular fronds, rosy pink in spring, changing to bronze and eventually deep green as season progresses. Reliable, striking, and easy to grow. Usually deciduous. Zones 6–9.

Dryopteris filix-mas

MALE FERN

↔24 in (60 cm) ↕48 in (120 cm)

From Europe and North America. Mass of lance-shaped green fronds ap-pear in spring. Spreads along ground with rhizomes. Prefers part-shade and neutral to acid soil. Plant ceases growth in autumn, may become deciduous over winter. **'Barnesii'**, a very tall fern with large, sparsely clothed, arching fronds, prefers a light dry soil, perfect in dry shade; **'Crispa'**, dwarf compact plant with sturdy, heavily crested, frilly fronds; **'Crispa Cristata'**, crested pale lime green, very frilly fronds; **'Cristata'**, foliage lightly crested, frond tips very frilly; **'Depauperata'**, compact fern with pretty, ruffled, dense, green foliage along each frond; **Grandiceps Group**, frond tips have a heavy terminal crest, a very vigorous and clumping fern; **'Grandiceps Wills'**, a striking plant, frond tips have large fluffy crests, vigorous and tolerant fern once established; **'Linearis Cristata'**, dwarf fern, dark green foliage, short narrow fronds, plant has a very delicate appearance but is very tough. Zones 4–8.

Dryopteris marginalis

LEATHER WOOD FERN, MARGINAL WOOD FERN

↔ 20 in (50 cm) ↑ 10 in (25 cm)

From Quebec, Canada, to Kansas, USA. A robust evergreen fern. The short rhizomes produce groups of up-right, blue-green, lance-shaped fronds. Perfect for shady hillsides. Zones 9–11.

Dryopteris sieboldii

JAPANESE WOOD FERN

↔ 20 in (50 cm) ↑ 20 in (50 cm)

From Japan. Distinctive fern with glossy green palmate fronds. Broad lance-shaped leaves; each frond has 5 to 7 leaflets. Reliable once established. Zone 7–10.

Dryopteris wallichiana

WALLICHS WOOD FERN

↔ 24–32 in (60–80 cm)
↑ 24–48 in (60–120 cm)

A deciduous fern from the Himalayas. The mature fronds are dark green, yellow-green when young. Produces a strong flush of fronds in the spring. Forms an open tussock-like plant with a small trunk. This species is easy to grow. Zones 8–11.

DUDLEYA

A genus of some 40 species of rosette-forming perennials from southwestern USA and western Mexico. Members of the stonecrop (Crassulaceae) family, they are closely allied to *Echeveria*, in which genus they were once included. Many have gray or gray-green foliage, often with a powdery white bloom. The foliage withers with age but may remain attached. The flower stems tend to be upright, sometimes branching, and carry many small 5-petalled flowers, usually in spring. Old plants often have rosettes that have developed thickened stems or short trunks

CULTIVATION: Although many species tolerate moderate frost, they need mild winters as they tend to grow during the cooler months. Usually do best when placed in full sun but may need a little shade inland. Water in autumn and spring but otherwise keep dry. Rotting is the most common cause of failure, so be sure to plant in gritty free-draining soil. Propagate from seed, or offsets, or by division.

Dudleya anthonyi

↔ 32–40 in (80–100 cm)
↑ 40 in (100 cm)

Found in northern Baja California, Mexico, and offshore islands. This species bears red-tinted green leaves with a white bloom turning opaque white in dry season. The flowers are red with a yellow base. Zones 9–12.

Dudleya attenuata

↔ 16–24 in (40–60 cm)
↑ 12–16 in (30–40 cm)

Native to California, USA, and Baja California, Mexico. A low-growing plant with narrow, cylindrical, powdery, gray- to blue-green leaves in open rosettes. Yellow flowers on branching stems. ***D. a.* subsp. *orcuttii***, white flowers, tinted with pink. Zones 8–11.

Dudleya anthonyi

Dudleya viscida

Dudleya candelabrum

Duranta erecta

Dudleya caespitosa

↔ 16–24 in (40–60 cm)
↑ 24 in (60 cm)

From coastal California as far north as southern Oregon, USA. Bears gray-green to yellow-green, somewhat keeled leaves in short-stemmed, clumping, rather open rosettes. The flowers are yellow to red. Zones 9–11.

Dudleya candelabrum

↔ 14 in (35 cm) ↑ 14 in (35 cm)

A native of California, USA, including some of the islands. This plant usually forms a single short-stemmed rosette of powdery gray-green leaves. Many small, soft yellow flowers are borne on stocky flower stems. Zones 9–11.

Dudleya farinosa

↔ 16–20 in (40–50 cm)
↑ 8–12 in (20–30 cm)

From the coast of California north to Oregon, USA. Branching at base to form a clump of small, powder-coated, blue-green rosettes that develop strong red tints in the sun. Flower stems usually short, with bright yellow flowers. Zones 9–11.

Dudleya greenei ★

↔ 16–24 in (40–60 cm)
↑ 12–16 in (30–40 cm)

From California, USA, including some of the islands. Clusters of powdery, bronze-tinted, blue-green rosettes. Flower stems tall compared to rosette size, pale yellow flowers. Zones 8–11.

Dudleya pulverulenta

CHALK LETTUCE

↔ 20 in (50 cm) ↑ 40 in (100 cm)

Native to California, USA, and Baja California, Mexico. Usually solitary rosette. Leaves broad, yellow-green with powdery white bloom. Sturdy flower stems with branching heads of red flowers. Zones 9–11.

Dudleya virens

↔ 20–32 in (50–80 cm)
↑ 12 in (30 cm)

From coastal chaparral of southern California, USA. Narrow, flattened, gray-green leaves in rosettes on short stems, yellow-green flowers. D. v. subsp. hassei, from Santa Catalina Island. Pointed, powdery, cylindrical leaves in open rosettes. Pale green flowers. Zones 9–11.

Dudleya viscida

↔ 24 in (60 cm) ↑ 24 in (60 cm)

From southern California, USA. Clusters of short-stemmed rosettes with narrow dark green leaves, aromatic, sticky. Pink-tinted white flowers. Zones 9–11.

DURANTA

Genus in the vervain (Verbenaceae) family, 30 species or so of hard-wooded ornamental shrubs from tropical and subtropical regions of the Americas, from southern USA to Mexico and Brazil. Evergreen, except in cold climates, with blue, white, or violet flowers, in terminal or axillary racemes, or panicles. Summer flowers followed by decorative but poisonous fruit in autumn and winter. Only one species commonly grown.

CULTIVATION: Will grow in most sub-tropical and frost-free temperate areas in fertile well-drained soil and full sun. They can be grown as small trees on a single trunk or pruned to make a small or medium-sized shrub.

Propagate from soft-tip cuttings in spring, or from firm-wood leafy cuttings in autumn.

Duranta erecta

syns *Duranta repens, Duranta plumieri*

GOLDEN BEAD TREE, GOLDEN DEW DROP, PIGEON BERRY

↔8 ft (2.4 m) ↑15 ft (4.5 m)

A small evergreen tree from tropical America. Can behave as a scrambling climber. Drooping branches with sharp spines. Inflorescences of 5 to 12 racemes, each with up to 30 lavender-blue flowers, with purplish calyx, in early to mid-autumn. Fruits enclosed within persistent calyces, turn glossy yellow in early autumn. **'Alba'**, white flowers; **'Geisha Girl'**, compact, heavy-flowering, weeping stems; **'Variegata'**, leaf margins creamy yellow. Zones 9–12.

Duranta stenostachya

BRAZILIAN SKY FLOWER

↔4–5 ft (1.2–1.5 m) ↑4–6 ft (1.2–1.8 m)

Evergreen shrub from tropical Brazil. Oblong to sword-shaped leaves, slightly toothed. Clusters of fragrant, tubular, medium, blue-lilac to purple flowers, in summer. Contrasting orange-yellow berries. Zones 9–11.

DYAKIA

Monotypic monopodial orchid genus (family Orchidaceae) from Borneo that was previously included within genus *Ascocentrum*. It differs by its floral structure, as well as its flat leaves (they are strongly channeled in *Ascocentrum*). CULTIVATION: These epiphytes are quite compact and need warm to hot, moist conditions throughout the year, and grow best in either small pots or cork mounts. Propagate by division.

Dyakia hendersoniana ★

syn. *Ascocentrum hendersoniana*

↔2½–6 in (6–15 cm) ↑3–8 in (8–20 cm)

From Borneo. In warmer months, year-round in tropics, this species has upright, densely packed spikes, vivid rose to magenta flowers with a contrasting white labellum. Zones 11–12.

DYCKIA

A genus of over 120 species in the pineapple (Bromeliaceae) family, mostly from Brazil, Argentina, and neighboring countries, with only a few in cultivation. These clump-forming plants on rocks or in the ground. Leaves are triangular, usually green and very succulent, with mostly weak teeth on the edges. The generally long flower stems do not emerge from the plant's center, which means the plant does not die after flowering as with most other Bromeliaceae. The flowerhead is sometimes single, sometimes open-branched, each branch having many well-spaced yellow to orange flowers. CULTIVATION: Grow in well-drained sandy soil mix, in greenhouses or conservatories, in cool-temperate areas, or outdoors in warm-temperate, subtrop-ical, and tropical areas. Water when potting mix is dry. Do not over-fertilize. Propagate from seed or offsets.

Dyckia choristaminea

↔8 in (20 cm) ↑10 in (25 cm)

From southern Brazil. Small clump-forming plant, with small, narrow, light green leaves, with fairly long supple teeth. Flowerhead almost globular, with yellow flowers, pointing upward. Delightfully scented. Ideal size for pot culture. Zones 9–11.

Dyckia remotiflora

↔16 in (40 cm) ↑40 in (100 cm)

From southern Brazil to Argentina. Slow clump-forming plant. Narrow, triangular, dark green leaves. Flower-head is a single stem with a few yellow flowers scattered on all sides. Mainly grown in open rockeries. Zones 9–11.

DYMONDIA

From South Africa, single species genus in the daisy (Asteraceae) family. Forms a ground-hugging, evergreen mat with large, stemless, yellow flowers summer–autumn. It was named after a South African botanist, Margaret Dymond: her surname was used for the genus, her first name to denote the species. CULTIVATION: Prefers a sunny aspect in moist to dry soils, and will tolerate only very slight frosts. Ideal ground covers over small bulbs or to grow between pavers. Propagate by division.

Dymondia margaretae

↔20–40 in (50–100 cm) ↑1¼–1¾ in (30–40 mm)

From South Africa. Evergreen, mat-forming plant that roots down as it expands. Narrow, gray-green, scalloped leaves, white reverse, slightly exposed as leaf edges curl in, giving a variegated look. Yellow daisies among the leaves through warmer months. Zones 8–11.

DYPSIS

syns *Chrysalidocarpus, Neodypsis*

This genus of feather-leafed palms in the family Arecaceae consisting of 140 species, all native to Madagascar except for 2 species on the Comoros Islands, and one on Pemba Island, Tanzania. Growth forms range from tiny undergrowth palms with pencil-thick stems and grass-like fronds, to quite massive palms that tower above the forest canopy. Stems solitary or clustered. Fronds are basically of feather type, some species have fronds that fork into two lobes; others a very few broad leaflets, and many plume-like fronds. Usually smooth crownshaft. Flowering panicles, below frond bases, bear small green, cream, or yellow (rarely red) flowers. Fruits are single-seeded drupes. CULTIVATION: Needs vary greatly; no species is frost tolerant. Some of more robust species thrive outdoors and are very sun hardy; more delicate species require shade and humidity. Most can be grown as indoor plants as long as light levels are not too low. Propagation is normally from seed, although the clumping *D. lutescens* can be divided.

Dypsis decaryi

syn. *Neodypsis decaryi*

THREE-CORNERED PALM, TRIANGLE PALM

↔6 ft (1.8 m) ↑20 ft (6 m)

From the far south of Madagascar. Fronds arranged in 3 vertical ranks, bluish gray, recurved tips. Sheaths and lower parts of frond stalks coated in rusty brown fur when young, ageing to gray. Thick, closely ringed trunk. Great for patio tubs and planter boxes. Zones 10–12.

Dypsis lutescens

syns *Areca lutescens, Chrysalidocarpus lutescens*

BUTTERFLY PALM, GOLDEN CANE PALM

↔6 ft (1.8 m) ↑20 ft (6 m)

From east coast of Madagascar. Forms compact clumps of yellow-green stems branching above ground, slender crownshaft. Fronds recurved, stalks and midribs, yellow-orange. Branched flowering panicles, tiny yellow flowers. Oval yellow fruit. Zones 10–12.

Dyakia hendersoniana

Dyckia choristaminea

Dymondia margaretae

Dypsis lutescens

E

ECCREMOCARPUS

CHILEAN GLORY FLOWER

This genus, comprising 5 species of evergreen or herbaceous tendril climbers from South America, belongs to the trumpet-vine (Bignoniaceae) family. Grown for their brightly colored lopsided trumpets, produced in abundance throughout the warmer months, and often used as quick cover plants, as they will hide almost anything in one growing season.

CULTIVATION: These plants prefer moist but well-drained soil in a sunny site sheltered from strong winds. Grow on wire-up fences, over arches, or through large shrubs and small trees. Can be treated as annuals in frost-prone areas. Propagate from seed; in frost-prone areas plant out young plants as soon as possible after frosts. In warmer climates they can self-sow and become invasive.

Eccremocarpus scaber

CHILEAN GLORY FLOWER

↔7–10 ft (2–3 m) ↑10–15 ft (3–4.5 m)

From Chile and Peru. Fast-growing climber, and virtually the only species grown. Soft green compound leaves. Clusters of yellow, orange, or red tubular flowers, 1½ in (35 mm) long, in late spring–summer. Orange is the color of the wild form and the color most commonly cultivated. Zones 8–10.

Echeveria elegans

ECHEVERIA

This genus of about 150 species of rosette-forming succulents in the stonecrop (Crassulaceae) family is found mainly in Mexico, with a few from Central America. It was named after Atanasio Echeverria Codoy, an eighteenth-century Spanish botanical artist. Though superficially similar to, and sometimes confused with *Sempervivum*, *Echeveria* are generally far less frost hardy but more drought tolerant than their European cousins. Apart from a few species that are shrubby or more leafy and perennial-like, all form spiraling rosettes of flattened but fleshy, pointed, spoon-shaped leaves. The flowers, usually appearing in spring and early summer, are borne on short stems, either along the stem or in branching heads, and are simple, 5-petalled, bell-shaped structures, often in shades of pink, red, yellow, or orange.

CULTIVATION: Most *Echeveria* species prefer full sun and mild winters with only light frosts. They may require some shade in very hot inland areas. Plant in light, gritty, very free-draining soil. Water in spring and when they are flowering, but otherwise keep dry, especially in winter. Propagate from seed or offsets, or by division.

Echeveria colorata

Echeveria agavoides

Echeveria agavoides ★

↔8–12 in (20–30 cm) ↑6–8 in (15–20 cm)

This species forms clumps of small short-stemmed rosettes with red-edged light gray-green to blue-green leaves, to 3 in (8 cm) long. The forked inflorescence bears ½ in (12 mm) long orange-pink flowers, which are yellow inside. ***E. a.* f. *cristata*** has rosettes with many small leaves in rows across the center; ***E. a.* var. *corderoyi*** (syn. *E. a.* 'Red Edge') produces rosettes with numerous small leaves and an inflorescence with 3 branches and smaller flowers. Zones 8–11.

Echeveria chihuahuaensis

↔12 in (30 cm) ↑10 in (25 cm)

Forms clusters of many small rosettes. The leaves are blue-green with a white bloom and reddish tips, and are 1¾ in (40 mm) long. The inflorescence can be simple or branched, and up to 8 in (20 cm) tall. It bears yellow-centered red flowers that are ½ in (12 mm) long. Zones 9–11.

Echeveria colorata

↔20 in (50 cm) ↑16 in (40 cm)

Rosettes of upright, red-tinted, pale blue-green leaves with a white bloom. Red-orange flowers. Zones 9–11.

Echeveria derenbergii

↔8–16 in (20–40 cm) ↑6 in (15 cm)

Short branching stems carry many small rosettes with red-edged pale blue-green leaves, to just under 2 in (5 cm) long. Inflorescence to 4 in (10 cm) long, with sparse, red-tipped, golden yellow, ½ in (12 mm) long flowers. Zones 9–11.

Echeveria elegans ★

MEXICAN SNOWBALL, WHITE MEXICAN ROSE

↔12–16 in (30–40 cm) ↑6–8 in (15–20 cm)

Forms clusters of short-stemmed densely foliaged rosettes, 4 in (10 cm) in diameter, with pale gray-green leaves, to 2¾ in (65 mm) long, that are coated with a white powder. Simple 4–6 in (10–15 cm) long inflorescence with as many as 10 golden-centered deep pink flowers. **'Kesselringii'** produces globular rosettes of blue-gray leaves. Zones 9–11.

Echeveria gibbiflora

↔20 in (50 cm) ↑48 in (120 cm)

Forms open rosettes, to 20 in (50 cm) in diameter, on unbranched stems, to 12 in (30 cm) tall. Leaves are broad, purple-tinted, wavy-edged, powdery, pale blue-green, to 14 in (35 cm) long. The branching inflorescence, to 36 in (100 cm) tall, has soft, brown-centered, red flowers that are backed by lavender calyces through the autumn–winter. ***E. g.* var. *carunculata*** has pale leaves, heavily distorted and covered with protuberances; ***E. g.* var. *metallica*** has silvery gray foliage with a metallic sheen. Zones 9–11.

Echeveria gigantea ★

↔20 in (50 cm) ↑5–7 ft (1.5–2 m)

Winter-flowering species with loose open rosettes, to 16 in (40 cm) across, on unbranched stems, to 20 in (50 cm) tall. Leaves purple-edged, pale green, spatula-shaped, to 8 in (20 cm) long. Branching inflorescence, to 7 ft (2 m) tall, with deep pink-red flowers, over ½ in (12 mm) long. **'Dee'**, rosettes with broad blue-green leaves ageing red in sun. Zones 10–12.

Echeveria × *gilva*

GREEN MEXICAN ROSE

↔ 12–16 in (30–40 cm) ↑ 14 in (35 cm)

Hybrid of *E. agavoides* and *E. elegans.* Short branching stems with densely foliaged rosettes, to 6 in (15 cm) across. Green leaves, to a little over 3 in (8 cm) long, with crystalline surface and translucent edges. Branching inflorescence, up to 10 in (25 cm) tall, with small yellow-topped pink flowers. Zones 9–11.

Echeveria harmsii

syn. *Oliveranthus elegans*

↔ 12 in (30 cm) ↑ 12–16 in (30–40 cm)

Shrubby plant with branching stems and small open rosettes clustered at the tips, finely hairy throughout. Narrow green leaves with red edges, to 2 in (5 cm) long. Produces simple inflorescences, to 8 in (20 cm) long, with few red flowers with yellow tips and interior. Zones 9–11.

Echeveria × *imbricata* ★

↔ 12–16 in (30–40 cm) ↑ 12–16 in (30–40 cm)

Short-stemmed cup-shaped rosettes, to 10 in (20 cm) wide, with broad but thin gray-green to silver-gray leaves. Branching inflorescences with yellow-centered deep pink flowers, to ½ in (12 mm) long. Zones 9–12.

Echeveria leucotricha ★

↔ 20–40 in (50–100 cm) ↑ 24 in (60 cm)

Shrubby plant with branching red-tinted stems. Open rosettes with few, finely hairy, red-tipped, broadly strappy, gray-green leaves, to over 24 in (60 cm) long. Simple or slightly branched leafy inflorescence, to 16 in (40 cm) tall, with up to 15 red-edged orange flowers, ¾ in (18 mm) long. Zones 9–11.

Echeveria peacockii

Echeveria nodulosa ★

↔ 12–20 in (30–50 cm) ↑ 16 in (40 cm)

A shrubby species with leafy branching stems, to 8 in (20 cm) tall. The loose open rosettes have narrow, thickened, red-edged and keeled, light blue-green leaves, up to 2 in (5 cm) long. They produce inflorescences to 12 in (30 cm) long, with up to 12 yellow-centered and edged, orange-red flowers. Zones 9–11.

Echeveria pallida

↔ 16–24 in (40–60 cm) ↑ 24–40 in (60–100 cm)

Clusters of short-stemmed, loose, open, 8–10 in (20–25 cm) wide rosettes with broad, spoon-shaped, light-textured, pale green leaves, to 6 in (15 cm) long. Inflorescence, 24–36 in (60–90 cm) tall, with pink flowers during winter. Zones 9–11.

Echeveria peacockii ★

↔ 12–24 in (30–60 cm) ↑ 12 in (30 cm)

Clusters of powdery pale blue-gray rosettes, each to 6 in (15 cm) across. Leaves to 2½ in (6 cm) long, red-edged and tipped. Inflorescence to 10 in (25 cm) tall, with up to 20 soft orange to pinkish red flowers. Zones 9–11.

Echeveria leucotricha

Echeveria, Hybrid Cultivar, 'Fire Light'

Echeveria potosina

↔ 12–16 in (30–40 cm) ↑ 6–8 in (15–20 cm)

Clusters of short-stemmed densely foliaged rosettes, 4 in (10 cm) across. Powdery pale gray-green leaves, often maroon-tinted, to 2¾ in (65 mm) long. Simple 4–6 in (10–15 cm) long inflorescence, up to 10 golden-centered deep pink flowers. Zones 9–11.

Echeveria pulvinata

CHENILLE PLANT, PLUSH PLANT

↔ 12–20 in (30–50 cm) ↑ 12–16 in (30–40 cm)

Branching stems forming dense mounding clusters of small rosettes with many finely downy, red-tinted, green to blue-green leaves, about 2 in (5 cm) long. Inflorescence, 8–12 in (20–30 cm) long, with up to 15 red-edged golden yellow to orange flowers from mid-winter. **'Ruby'**, velvety-textured red leaves. Zones 9–11.

Echeveria runyonii

↔ 12–20 in (30–50 cm) ↑ 12 in (30 cm)

Clusters of usually stemless rosettes, to 8 in (20 cm) across, with spoon-shaped powdery gray-blue leaves, about 3 in (8 cm) long. Short forked inflorescence with ¼ in (18 mm) long coral pink flowers. **'Topsy Turvy'** ★, narrow leaves curled downward at the edges and up at the tips. Zones 8–11.

Echeveria sayulensis

↔ 16–20 in (40–50 cm) ↑ 12–16 in (30–40 cm)

Shrubby species, low-spreading stems. Densely foliaged, 10 in (25 cm) wide rosettes of pointed blue-green leaves with red edges, to 6 in (15 cm) long. Branched inflorescence, up to 14 in (35 cm) long, up to 30 yellow-centered pink flowers in winter. Zones 9–11.

Echeveria secunda ★

↔ 12 in (30 cm) ↑ 12 in (30 cm)

Mounded clusters of densely foliaged short-stemmed rosettes. The leaves are thick, keeled, blue-green with maroon edges, to about 3 in (8 cm) long. The simple inflorescence, to 12 in (30 cm) long, bears up to 15 yellow-centered pale orange to red flowers. ***E. s.* var. *glauca***, thin pale blue-gray leaves; ***E. s.* var. *pumila***, small narrow leaves. Zones 8–11.

Echeveria, HC, Galaxy Series, 'Nebula'

Echeveria setosa

MEXICAN FIRECRACKER

↔ 12–16 in (30–40 cm) ↑ 8–12 in (20–30 cm)

Small clumping species, which forms 4–6 in (10–15 cm) wide rosettes of 2 in (5 cm) long green leaves covered with fine white hairs, becoming bristly with age. The inflorescence is 12 in (30 cm) long, with up to 10 red-tipped yellow flowers. Zones 9–11.

Echeveria Hybrid Cultivars

↔ 4–18 in (10–45 cm) ↑ 6–24 in (15–60 cm)

Many species hybridize freely, and garden hybrids are available in a wide range of sizes, flower colors, and growth forms. **'Arlie Wright'**, large gray leaves flushed with pink, heavily crimped edges, and a single rosette, to 16 in (40 cm) across; **'Dondo'**, an *E. dehrenbergii* × *E. setosa* hybrid, rosettes of gray-blue leaves with scalloped and pointed tips, golden yellow flowers; **'Fire Light'** ★, rosette of broad leaves, blue-green rapidly ageing to deep glossy red, with frilled edges; **'Kirchneriana'**, massed 4 in (10 cm) wide pale powdery blue-gray rosettes, narrow leafy stems with small heads of orange-tipped yellow flowers in spring; **'Lace'**, similar but with more complexly frilled leaves; **'Morning Light'** ★, clusters of small blue-green rosettes edged with pink; **'Powder Blue'** ★, light blue-green rosettes, to 6 in (15 cm) across, light orange flowers; **'Princess Lace'**, pale green rosettes, to 12 in (30 cm) across, with the edges red and heavily crimped; **'Pulv-oliver'**, a shrubby *E. pulvinata* × *E. harmsii* hybrid, to 20 in (50 cm) tall, with small open rosettes of red-tinted, downy, light green leaves and soft orange flowers; **'Set-oliver'** ★, an *E. harmsii* × *E. setosa* hybrid with rosettes of downy, thickened, red-tinted, light green leaves and orange-red flowers on 16 in (40 cm) tall inflorescences; **'Violet Queen'** ★, clusters of 6 in (15 cm) wide, pink-edged, pale blue-green rosettes. The **Galaxy Series** are similar to 'Pulv-oliver' and 'Set-oliver', and bear flowers in a range of brilliant orange-reds with varying amounts of yellow on the petal tips. Zones 9–11.

Echinacea purpurea

ECHINACEA

CONEFLOWER

This genus, comprising 9 species of summer-flowering perennials, some of which grow as tall as 7 ft (2 m), be-longs to the daisy (Asteraceae) family. Found in eastern USA and closely allied to *Rudbeckia* and *Helianthus*, they spread by rhizomes and after a few years can colonize large areas, though they are not difficult to control. The foliage is simple, usually lance-shaped, and sometimes toothed. The flowerheads are large and have relatively few ray florets, often deep purple-pink and downward facing, around a prominent, often dark, central cone of disc florets. The dried rhizomes and roots of coneflowers are widely used as an ingredient in herbal medicines; they are thought to fortify the immune system's power to ward off infection.

CULTIVATION: Coneflowers grow very freely in temperate gardens, thriving in an open sunny position with well-drained humus-rich soil that is kept moist in summer. Staking is sometimes required, as they can grow quite tall. Propagate from seed or basal cuttings, or by division; they may self-sow.

Echinacea pallida

PALE CONEFLOWER, PALE PURPLE CONEFLOWER

↔ 12–24 in (30–60 cm)
↑ 24–36 in (60–90 cm)

From midwestern USA. Easy-to-grow perennial. Narrow dark green leaves with parallel veins. Petals narrower than those of *E. purpurea*. Pale to dark purple ray flowers with dark centers in early spring–mid-summer; attractive to birds and butterflies. These plants are good in a naturalized area or wild garden. ***E. p.* var. *angustifolia*** (syn. *E. angustifolia*) has deep pink to light purple ray florets, often drooping. Zones 3–10.

Echinacea purpurea

syn. *Rudbeckia purpurea*

PURPLE CONEFLOWER

↔ 20–40 in (50–100 cm)
↑ 20–48 in (50–120 cm)

Forms clump of quick-growing strongly upright stems. Leaves broad, toothed, deep green, pointed oval to lance-shaped, to 6 in (15 cm) long. Reflexed magenta-purple ray florets, to 3 in (8 cm) long, form around orange-brown disc florets opening from dark buds. *E. purpurea* is the species most widely used in herbal medicines. **'Magnus'** ★, with large, intensely colored flowerheads; **'White Lustre'**, about 32 in (80 cm) tall, white ray florets have dark centers; **'White Swan'** ★, compact, 20 in (50 cm) tall, with white flowerheads. Zones 3–10.

ECHINOCACTUS

This genus in the cactus (Cactaceae) family, as now understood, comprises just 5 species native to Mexico and southwestern USA. Globular in growth habit for many years, with prominent spiny ribs and a woolly crown, most eventually become columnar, though none grow to any great height. In cultivation they are favored for their slow growth and symmetry. The flowers are usually in shades of yellow or pink, and tend to be short and not very spectacular, though they bloom for a long time in summer.

CULTIVATION: Tolerant of occasional light frosts but inclined to rot in damp conditions, especially in winter. Plant in light, very gritty, free-draining soil. Water in summer but otherwise keep dry. Most grow best in full sun but some may need light shade in hot in-land areas. Offsets are few but can be propagated; otherwise, raise from seed.

Echinocactus grusonii

GOLDEN BARREL CACTUS, MOTHER-IN-LAW'S CHAIR

↔ 32 in (80 cm) ↑ 50 in (130 cm)

From central Mexico. Stems usually solitary, globular for many years. The crown is very woolly. Offsets rare. Up to 40 ribs with closely spaced areoles bearing many yellow spines, to 2 in (5 cm) long. The flowers are yellow, brown at the tip, a little over 2 in 5 cm) long, and clustered around the crown. Zones 9–12.

Echinocactus platyacanthus

↔ 36 in (90 cm) ↑ 8 ft (2.4 m)

From central and northern Mexico. Solitary stem, spherical when young, becoming columnar and very sturdy. Up to 60 ribs when mature, edged with strong spines, to 3 in (8 cm) long. Yellow-green flowers, 2 in (5 cm) long, 3 in (8 cm) across. Zones 9–11.

Echinocactus polycephalus

↔ 12–24 in (30–60 cm)
↑ 12–24 in (30–60 cm)

From northwestern Mexico and southwestern USA. Clumps of spherical to short cylindrical stems, each to 8 in (20 cm) in diameter, with numerous 2–3 in (5–8 cm) long curved spines interwoven to form a dense matrix. Flowers are 2 in (5 cm) long, 2 in (5 cm) across, and yellow with faint pink stripes. Zones 9–11.

ECHINOCEREUS

HEDGEHOG CACTUS

This genus comprises about 60 species of cacti (family Cactaceae) found in Mexico and southern USA. The name comes from the Greek *echinos*, a hedgehog, and Latin/Greek *cereus*, a candle or taper, referring to the commonly occurring combination of densely packed spines and showy flowers. Most form clumps of cylindrical stems, which are sometimes elongated and may spread across the ground or clamber over low objects. The flowers form near the top of the stem, often developing from woolly areoles. Most open in spring or summer, and are usually large in comparison to the plant and often brightly colored or strikingly marked.

CULTIVATION: Hardiness varies, but none will tolerate repeated hard freezes. Plant in light, gritty, very free-draining soil; keep dry in winter. Best grown in full sun, though in inland continental areas they may need shade from the hottest summer sun. Propagate from seed, offsets, or from stem cuttings.

Echinocereus brandegeei

↔ 3–7 ft (0.9–2 m)
↑ 8–12 in (20–30 cm)

From Baja California, USA. Clusters of spreading stems, to 36 in (100 cm) long, 2½ in (6 cm) in diameter. Stems with up to 10 ribs and a dense covering of flattened spines, to 4 in (10 cm) long. Dark-centered magenta flowers, to 3 in (8 cm) long, during the summer. Zones 10–11.

Echinocereus cinerascens

syn. *Echinocereus chlorophthalmus*

↔ 20–40 in (50–100 cm)
↑ 12–24 in (30–60 cm)

From eastern and northeastern Mexico. A clustering, somewhat spreading, species. Narrow stems, usually about

Echinocactus platyacanthus

Echinacea pallida var. angustifolia

Echinocactus grusonii

Echinocereus fendleri var. *kuenzleri*

12 in (30 cm) long, with many fine spines, to over 1¾ in (40 mm) long. The flowers are magenta with a white to yellow-green throat, to 4 in (10 cm) across. Zones 9–11.

Echinocereus engelmannii ★

STRAWBERRY HEDGEHOG CACTUS

↔ 12–20 in (30–50 cm)
↑ 12–20 in (30–50 cm)

From the western USA–Mexico border region. Clustering, upright, narrow, cylindrical stems with ribs densely covered with fine spines, to over 2 in (5 cm) long. The flowers are magenta to lavender, to 3½ in (9 cm) across, and appear in summer. Zones 6–11.

Echinocereus fendleri

↔ 8–20 in (20–50 cm)
↑ 8–20 in (20–50 cm)

From the western USA–Mexico border region. Clusters of narrow, upright, cylindrical stems with many ribs and sometimes pronounced tubercles. The spines are short and the areoles widely spaced. Flowers, usually magenta with a darker center, sometimes light pink or white, to 4 in (10 cm) across, in summer. The fruit is red. ***E. f.* var. *kuenzleri***, stout spines, and very large flowers. Zones 6–11.

Echinocereus knippelianus

PEYOTE VERDE

↔ 4–6 in (10–15 cm)
↑ 4–6 in (10–15 cm)

From the mountains of northeastern Mexico. Short spherical stems, often solitary, with a few broad indistinctly defined ribs and sparse, small, woolly areoles with 3 short spines. Many-petalled flowers, 2½ in (6 cm) across, in white, pink or purple, in spring–early summer. Zones 9–11.

Echinocereus rigidissimus

Echinocereus stramineus

Echinocereus maritimus

↔ 3–7 ft (0.9–2 m)
↑ 8–16 in (20–40 cm)

From northwestern Mexico. Branching spreading stems forming wide mounds. Stem segments, to 12 in (30 cm) long, 2 in (5 cm) in diameter, with up to 10 sharply defined ribs edged with many spines, to 2½ in (6 cm) long. Yellow flowers tinted red, becoming orange, to 2½ in (6 cm) across, in summer. Zones 9–11.

Echinocereus pectinatus ★

↔ 6–16 in (15–40 cm)
↑ 14 in (35 cm)

From southwestern USA and northern Mexico. Clusters of spherical to short cylindrical stems, rarely branched, to 5 in (12 cm) in diameter, with 12 or more ribs carrying many light brown interlacing spines, to 1 in (25 mm) long. The flowers are green-centered white or pink to red-brown, to about 4 in (10 cm) in diameter, and appear in summer. ***E. p.* var. *dasyacanthus*** (syn. *E. dasyacanthus*) bears yellow or white flowers. Zones 5–11.

Echinocereus pentalophus ★

LADY FINGER CACTUS

↔ 20 in–7 ft (50 cm–2 m)
↑ 8–12 in (20–30 cm)

Found from eastern Mexico to Texas, USA. Clustering, narrow, sometimes sprawling, cylindrical stems with few ribs and a mix of spines ranging from very short to ½ in (6 cm) long. Stems often red-tinted in sun. Deep pink flowers with a white to yellow-green throat, to 6 in (15 cm) across, in summer. Zones 7–11.

Echinocereus reichenbachii ★

↔ 8–20 in (20–50 cm)
↑ 16 in (40 cm)

Found from northeastern Mexico to Texas, USA. Usually clustering spherical to short cylindrical stems with over 10 indistinctly defined ribs bearing many tubercles with short pale spines. Floral tubercles woolly. Many-petalled pink to purple flowers, to over 5 in (12 cm) across. Zones 7–11.

Echinocereus rigidissimus ★

↔ 4 in (10 cm) ↑ 8 in (20 cm)

From northwestern Mexico to Arizona, USA. Solitary cylindrical stem, rarely branched, with 15 or more ribs bearing woolly tubercles, often pink-tinted, with many small spines held flat to the stem. White-centered pink to crimson flowers, to 3 in (8 cm) across, in early summer. Zones 9–11.

Echinocereus stramineus

↔ 16 in–7 ft (40 cm–2 m)
↑ 12–18 in (30–45 cm)

From the western USA–Mexico border region. Forms dense colonies of up to several hundred narrow cylindrical stems with up to 17 ribs largely hidden below many needle-like spines, some to nearly 4 in (10 cm) long. The bright magenta funnel-shaped flowers, 3–5 in (8–12 cm) across, appear during mid-summer. Zones 8–11.

Echinocereus subinermis

↔ 6–12 in (15–30 cm)
↑ 8–10 in (20–25 cm)

From northwestern Mexico. The stems are solitary or few, clustered, dark gray-green to blue-green, with up to 11 clearly defined ribs bearing starry clusters of usually short stout spines. The yellow flowers, to 4 in (10 cm) long and 5 in (12 cm) across, appear in summer. Zones 9–11.

Echinocereus triglochidiatus ★

CLARET CUP

↔ 8–20 in (20–50 cm)
↑ 12–16 in (30–40 cm)

From the western USA–Mexico border region. Stems solitary or clumping, ovate to cylindrical, with about 10 ribs bearing woolly areoles with short radial spines around a central spine to nearly 2¾ in (7 cm) long. Long-tubed bright red flowers, to over 2 in (5 cm) across, in summer. ***E. t.* var. *gurneyi***, compact form from the Chihuahuan desert grasslands; ***E. t.* var. *melanacanthus*** (syn. *E. coccineus*) are found among mountain pines, forming mounds of up to several hundred small stems. Zones 7–11.

Echinocereus viereckii

↔ 12–24 in (30–60 cm)
↑ 12 in (30 cm)

Native to Mexico, low alpine species, with clusters of deep green branching stems that are initially upright then spreading, with spiny tubercles. The plants produce many large, deep pink to magenta flowers with pale centers during the summer months. Zones 9–11.

Echinocereus viridiflorus

↔ 4–12 in (10–30 cm)
↑ 2–5 in (5–12 cm)

From southwestern USA. Clusters of short ovate to cylindrical stems with up to 12 ribs largely hidden beneath many fine needle-like spines. The many-petalled, yellow-green, citrus-scented flowers, to 1¼ in (30 mm) diameter, appear during the summer. ***E. v.* subsp. *davisii***, a dwarf variety, often has solitary, stems, and is only 1 in (25 mm) tall. Zones 4–11.

ECHINOPS

GLOBE THISTLE

This genus, comprising about 120 species of thistle-like perennials found from Europe eastward to central Asia and southward to the mountains of Africa, is from the daisy (Asteraceae) family. The leaves are spine-tipped and usually deeply lobed, and may be simple or have up to 3 large leaflets. The flowers, appearing in summer–early autumn, are small, mostly white to mauve-blue, borne in spherical heads without ray florets, and backed by often spiny basal bracts, which are sometimes colored though smaller and far less colorful than those of the similar-looking but otherwise unrelated *Eryngium*. The flowerheads are sometimes dried but tend to disintegrate rather quickly.
CULTIVATION: These are mostly very hardy plants and easily grown in any temperate climate garden with a moderately fertile, well-drained soil. Best grown in a fairly open position to reduce the risk of mildew. Propagated mainly from seed but easily divided in the late winter.

Echinops bannaticus

↔ 24 in (60 cm)
↑ 48 in (120 cm)

This species is found from Greece to the Czech Republic. It has an upright stem; finely hairy leaves, which are angularly lobed almost to the midrib, with a few narrow spines; and downy stems. The gray-blue flowerheads, to 2 in (5 cm) across, are lighter in bud. **'Blue Globe'**, dark blue flowerheads, 2½ in (6 cm) across; **'Taplow Blue'**, bright steel blue flowerheads. Zones 3–9.

Echinops bannaticus 'Taplow Blue'

Echinops exaltatus

☼/◑ ✱ ↔ 20–32 in (50–80 cm)
↑ 5–7 ft (1.5–2 m)

Found from Italy to Poland and southwestern Russia. A vigorous plant, which forms a dense basal foliage clump, and produces tall flower stems. The leaves are light green, and deeply angularly lobed, with a few short spines. The white to pale gray flowerheads are 2½ in (6 cm) in diameter. Zones 3–9.

E

Echinops humilis

☼/◑ ✱ ↔ 12 in (30 cm) ↑ 12 in (30 cm)

Found from central Asia to Siberia and northwestern China. Forms a dense low clump of narrow-lobed spiny leaves, to 3 in (8 cm) long, with fine white hairs. Light steel blue flowerheads, to 1¾ in (40 mm) across. Zones 3–9.

Echinops ritro

☼/◑ ✱ ↔ 16–24 in (40–60 cm)
↑ 12–24 in (30–60 cm)

Eurasian species. The leaves are finely hairy, narrow, triangular, deeply lobed, with small spines. The flowerheads are deep steel blue to purple, rarely white, to nearly 2 in (5 cm) wide. ***E. r.* subsp. *ruthenicus*** (syn. *E. ruthenicus)*, leaves with small spines and white woolly hair on undersides, steel blue flowerheads; ***E. r.* 'Blue Glow'** bears large light blue flowerheads. Zones 3–9.

Echinops sphaerocephalus

☼/◑ ✱ ↔ 16–32 in (40–80 cm)
↑ 3–7 ft (0.9–2 m)

Native to southern and central Russia. The downy deeply lobed leaves have short spines and white hair on the undersides. Bears white to pale ash gray flowerheads, to over 2 in (5 cm) across. Zones 3–9.

ECHINOPSIS

syns *Chamaecereus, Helianthocereus, Lobivia, Trichocereus*

EASTER LILY CACTUS, SEA URCHIN CACTUS

The species in this South American cactus genus (family Cactaceae) en-compass a wide range of forms, from small, cylindrical, and clustering to tree-like with strong branching trunks. The genus has been expanded in recent years to include the species formerly placed in *Lobivia* and *Trichocereus*, and it now comprises up to 120 species. Most have cylindrical stems with clearly defined ribs, and some also have tubercles bearing areoles with conspicuous and often quite fierce spines. Some species have spectacular, long-tubed, funnel-shaped flowers that are large in comparison to the plant. These are known as Easter lily cacti because they may be in bloom as early as Easter in the Northern Hemisphere, though their main flowering season is early to mid-summer. Some species are night-blooming, with attractive, fragrant, white flowers, while others are day-blooming, with unscented flowers that occur in various shades of red, pink, yellow, or orange.

CULTIVATION: As with most cacti, plant in full sun/half-sun in very free-draining, light, gritty soil and water well in summer but keep dry during the winter months. Most species will tolerate only occasional light frosts. Propagate from offsets where it is appropriate, from stem cuttings of the branching types, or from seed.

Echinops ritro

Echinopsis backebergii

Echinopsis huascha

Echinopsis backebergii

syns *Echinopsis wrightiana, Lobivia wrightiana*

☼ ✱ ↔ 4–8 in (10–20 cm) ↑ 6 in (15 cm)

From Peru and Bolivia. Forms clusters of dark gray-green spherical stems with up to 15 ribs bearing short curved spines. Produces pink to violet flowers, to 4 in (10 cm) in diameter, often exceeding the stem width, in summer. Zones 10–12.

Echinopsis chamaecereus

syns *Chamaecereus silvestris, Lobivia silvestrii*

PEANUT CACTUS

☼ ✱ ↔ 12 in (30 cm) ↑ 4 in (10 cm)

From Argentina. Mat-forming, with freely branching cylindrical stems, to 12 in (30 cm), and numerous lateral stems, 1–4 in (20–100 mm) long. Low ribs and tiny spines on stems. Orange-red flowers, to 2 in (5 cm) across, in early summer. Zones 9–11.

Echinopsis ferox

syn. *Trichocereus ferox*

☼ ✱ ↔ 8–12 in (20–30 cm) ↑ 8 in (20 cm)

From Bolivia and northern Argentina. Unbranched stem is usually solitary, and spherical, with up to 30 spiraled ribs. The areoles are slightly over 1 in (25 mm) apart, carrying up to 12 radial spines, 2½ in (60 mm) long, and about 3 to 4 curved central spines, to 6 in (15 cm) long. The white or pale pink flowers are up to 4 in (10 cm) across. Zones 9–11.

Echinopsis formosa ★

syn. *Trichocereus randallii*

☼ ✱ ↔ 8–16 in (20–40 cm)
↑ 20 in–5 ft (50 cm–1.5 m)

From western Argentina. Stem usually solitary, initially spherical, becoming cylindrical, with up to 35 ribs and central spines to nearly 3 in (8 cm) long. Short-tubed yellow, orange, or red flowers, to about 3 in (8 cm) across. Zones 9–11.

Echinopsis hertrichiana

syns *Lobivia incaiaca, L. hertrichiana*

☼ ✱ ↔ 6–12 in (15–30 cm)
↑ 6–16 in (15–40 cm)

From Peru. The stems are often solitary, spherical, becoming columnar and clustered with great age. Up to 22 deep ribs with small woolly areoles and few spines to 1¼ in (30 mm) long. Bright red flowers, about 2 in (5 cm) long and across. Zones 10–12.

Echinopsis huascha ★

syns *Lobivia huascha, Trichocereus andalgalensis*

☼ ✱ ↔ 24 in (60 cm) ↑ 24 in (60 cm)

From Argentina. The stems are clustering, cylindrical, upright, sprawling, branching, to 2 in (5 cm) in diameter. Up to 17 ribs and many fine needle-like spines, to 3 in (8 cm) long. The floral areoles are densely hairy, opening to bright orange-red or yellow flowers, to 4 in (10 cm) long and 3 in (8 cm) across. Zones 9–11.

Echinopsis litoralis

☼ ✱ ↔ 3–7 ft (0.9–2 m)
↑ 3–7 ft (0.9–2 m)

A native of Chile. This shrubby species forms spreading clumps of upright and sprawling branching stems, to slightly over 4 in (10 cm) in diameter, with 15 or more ribs and spines, to 1 in (25 mm) long. The white flowers are sometimes tinted maroon, to nearly 6 in (15 cm) long. Zones 10–11.

Echinopsis maximiliana

syn. *Lobivia caespitosa*

☼ ✱ ↔ 6–12 in (15–30 cm) ↑ 4 in (10 cm)

Native to southern Peru and northern Bolivia. Clusters of flat-topped spherical stems, to 2 in (5 cm) wide with up to 17 ribs ridged with tubercles bearing central spines, to nearly 3 in (8 cm) long. Red flowers, to 3 in (8 cm) wide, with orange centers. Zones 10–12.

Echinopsis, Hybrid Cultivar, 'Arizona'

Echinopsis oxygona ★

syn. *Echinopsis multiplex*

↔12–24 in (30–60 cm)
↕12 in (30 cm)

From southern Brazil and northern Argentina. Clusters of spherical to short cylindrical stems, to 6 in (15 cm) in diameter, with up to 15 ribs bearing spines to 1 in (25 mm) long. Green-tubed red flowers, to 10 in (25 cm) long and 4 in (10 cm) across, appear in summer. Cristate forms are common. Zones 9–11.

Echinopsis pentlandii

syns *Echinocactus pentlandii, Lobivia boliviensis, and many others*

↔12–16 in (30–40 cm)
↕6–8 in (15–20 cm)

From southern Peru and northern Bolivia. Clusters of ovoid to spherical stems, to over 4 in (10 cm) in diameter, with about 15 ribs ridged with tubercles bearing 1–4 in (25–100 mm) long central spines. Yellow, orange, red, or magenta flowers, about 2 in (5 cm) long and wide. Zones 10–11.

Echinopsis schickendantzii

syn. *Trichocereus schickendantzii*

↔5–10 in (12–25 cm)
↕12 in (30 cm)

From western Argentina. Shrubby species forming wide clumps of low-branching cylindrical stems, about 2 in (5 cm) in diameter, 14 to 18 ribs, and small spines. Funnel-shaped white flowers, to about 8 in (20 cm) across. Zones 9–12.

Echinopsis spachiana ★

syn. *Trichocereus spachianus*

GOLDEN TORCH CEREUS

↔40 in (100 cm) ↕5–7 ft (1.5–2 m)

From Argentina. Shrubby species, tall cylindrical stems, each to 4 in (10 cm) in diameter, branching at the base, and 10 to 15 ribs with sturdy spines, to 2 in (5 cm) long. White flowers, to 10 in (25 cm) long and 6 in (15 cm) across. Zones 9–12.

Echinopsis Hybrid Cultivars

syns × *Chamaelobivia Hybrid Cultivars,* × *Lobivopsis Hybrid Cultivars*

↔6–12 in (15–30 cm)
↕6–18 in (15–45 cm)

Most *Echinopsis* hybrid cultivars have been bred for their large flowers and glowing colors and are derived from the large-flowered day-blooming species, including some formerly classified under *Lobivia.* Some such hybrids were thus treated as bigeneric hybrids. **'Arizona'** produces crowded, large, funnel-shaped flowers, with apricot shading to yellow centers, and ageing dull pinkish; **'Chico Mendes'** forms a compact mounding plant, with flowers to 5 in (13 cm) across, opening almost flat; the petals are broad, and pinkish orange with deeper pink at the edges; **'Samantha Smith'** has clustering short stems, and bears large flowers of apricot shading to a deeper color in the center. Zones 9–12.

ECHIUM

This genus comprises about 60 species in the borage (Boraginaceae) family, a large proportion of which are endemic to the Canary Islands and Madeira. Some of these endemics are shrubs or giant biennials. The remaining species are found in parts of the Mediterranean region, through western Asia, and in parts of Africa. These are nearly all smaller annuals, biennials, or perennials, generally beginning as a rosette of narrow leaves clothed in stiff hairs. Bell-shaped flowers, usually blue, pink, purple, or reddish, are borne in branched, usually erect, spikes in spring and summer.

CULTIVATION: The shrubby species of *Echium* thrive best with only moderate amounts of fertilizer and water. The herbaceous species can be fertilized and watered more liberally. All do best in full sun. The species that are from the Canary Islands are less frost hardy than the European species. They are usually propagated from seed, but cuttings may be taken in spring or summer. These plants have a tendency to self-seed in mild climates, so they must be positioned carefully.

Echium amoenum

Echium amoenum

↔12–18 in (30–45 cm)
↕12–24 in (30–60 cm)

From Europe. This seldom grown perennial species bears blood red flowers. Zones 7–9.

Echium candicans ★

syn. *Echium fastuosum*

PRIDE OF MADEIRA

↔6 ft (1.8 m) ↕6 ft (1.8 m)

Native to the Canary Islands and Madeira. A thick-stemmed, soft-wooded, evergreen shrub, with large densely hairy leaves, to 10 in (25 cm) long. Clusters of about 8 blue flowers with protruding pink to lilac-purple stamens, are borne in a spiky panicle, in early spring–early summer. May naturalize in cool climates. Zones 9–10.

Echium plantagineum

syn. *Echium lycopsis*

PATERSON'S CURSE, PURPLE VIPER'S BUGLOSS

↔12–18 in (30–45 cm)
↕18–36 in (45–90 cm)

Hairy-leafed annual or biennial from Europe; often weedy elsewhere, and especially in Australia, where it is known as Paterson's curse. The pinkish red buds, are borne in spikes, opening to intense reddish or violet blue tubular flowers, to 1¼ in (30 mm) long, in late spring–summer. **'Blue Bedder'** (syn. *E. vulgare* 'Blue Bedder'), shorter form. Zones 8–10.

Echium candicans

Echium plantagineum 'Blue Bedder'

Echium vulgare

BLUE WEED, VIPER'S BUGLOSS

↔18–24 in (45–60 cm)
↕18–24 in (45–60 cm)

From Europe and western Asia. Biennial usually grown as an annual. Often confused with *E. plantagineum* but bristlier and with smaller flowers. Branching spikes of intense violet-blue flowers, to ¾ in (18 mm), in summer. Zones 7–10.

EDGEWORTHIA

This genus of 2 or 3 rather similar species in the daphne (Thymelaeaceae) family is named for Michael Pakenham Edgeworth (1812–81), a part-time botanist, plant collector, and employee of the East India Company. They are heavily wooded shrubs with large, elongated oval, mid-green leaves; when young the leaves have prominent midribs and a felty coating. The bark contains a very strong fiber and is naturally papery, and has been used for the production of paper pulp. The structure and fragrance of the flowerheads, which open in late winter to spring, reveal the close relationship between this genus and *Daphne.*

CULTIVATION: *Edgeworthia* are best suited to moist, well-drained, humus-enriched soil in part-shade. They are moderately frost hardy plants, but are likely to be severely damaged if struck by a late frost after the young foliage has started to develop. Propagate from half-hardened cuttings, by air-layering, or from seed.

Edgeworthia chrysantha ★

PAPER BUSH

↔6 ft (1.8 m) ↕8 ft (2.4 m)

A native of China. Deciduous shrub with sparse growth and very heavy branches, which produces attractive new foliage. The globose heads of short, fragrant, tubular flowers are bright yellow, ageing to creamy white, at the end of winter, and are followed by dry drupes. Some botanists regard *E. papyrifera* and *E. chrysantha* as one species. Zones 8–10.

Edgeworthia chrysantha

Elaeagnus angustifolia

ELAEAGNUS

This genus of 30 to 40 species of deciduous and evergreen shrubs or small trees belonging to the oleaster (Elaeagnaceae) family is from Asia and southern Europe; North America has a single species. Valuable as hedges and windbreaks, especially in coastal areas. Some species have spiny branches. Leaves may be simple or alternate, green or variegated, often covered beneath and sometimes above with silvery or brown scales. Abundant tubular or bell-shaped flowers are borne on the lower side of the upper twigs. Flowers are small, whitish or cream, sometimes strongly fragrant. The red, brown, or yellowish fruit is edible. CULTIVATION: These plants tolerate a wide range of soil types, the exception is shallow chalk soils, and they like adequate summer water and a position in full sun. They should be pruned lightly to promote a dense leafy habit; hedges should not be close-clipped. Propagate from seed, which germinates readily if sown as soon as ripe, or from soft-tip or semi-hardwood cuttings; cultivars should be grown from cuttings.

Elaeagnus angustifolia

OLEASTER, RUSSIAN OLIVE

☼ ✱ ↔20 ft (6 m) ↑25 ft (8 m)

From temperate western Asia. Large, spiny, deciduous shrub or small tree. Silvery gray willow-like leaves, similar to those of the willow-leafed pear *(Pyrus salicifolia)*; the leaves of young plants are broad and hairy. Fragrant yellowish flowers are borne in mid-summer. ***E. a.* var. *caspica,*** striking form with tapered leaves and silvery new growth. Zones 2–9.

Elaeagnus commutata

syn. *Elaeagnus argentea*

SILVERBERRY

☼ ✱ ↔8 ft (2.4 m) ↑15 ft (4.5 m)

Found in North America occurring in poor prairie soils. Suckering shrub with red-brown shoots and silvery leaves. The fragrant flowers, silvery outside, yellow within, are borne in the late spring to early summer. Small, oval, silvery fruit. Zones 2–9.

Elaeagnus × *ebbingei*

syn. *Elaeagnus* × *submacrophylla*

☼ ✱ ↔12 ft (3.5 m) ↑12 ft (3.5 m)

Hybrid of garden origin between *E. macrophylla* and *E. pungens*. Dense, fast-growing, hardy, evergreen shrub with glossy dark green leaves, silvery beneath, to 4 in (10 cm) long. Silver-scaled, fragrant, creamy white flowers in autumn. Orange-red fruit with silver freckles follow in spring. **'Gilt Edge'** ★, deep green leaves with bright golden yellow margin; **'Limelight'**, silvery young leaves becoming light green with golden yellow variegation in the center, though many revert as the plant grows older. Zones 6–9.

Elaeagnus macrophylla

☼ ❄ ↔12 ft (3.5 m) ↑10 ft (3 m)

From Korea and Japan. Large spreading shrub. Broadly ovate leaves covered in silvery scales on both surfaces, upper surface becoming green. Fragrant silvery flowers in autumn. Red scaly fruit. Zones 7–10.

Elaeagnus multiflora

☼ ✱ ↔10 ft (3 m) ↑10 ft (3 m)

From China and Japan. An evergreen wide-spreading shrub. Leaves green on upper surface, silvery beneath. Fragrant creamy white flowers, on red-brown new shoots, in spring. Most attractive in mid- to late summer when covered with oblong, oxblood red, edible fruit. Zones 5–9.

Elaeagnus pungens

SILVERBERRY

☼ ❄ ↔20 ft (6 m) ↑15 ft (4.5 m)

From Japan. Evergreen shrub suitable for hedging. Main branches spiny and horizontal. Leaves oval, glossy green above, silvery white beneath, with scattered, brown, glandular dots. Small clusters of creamy white flowers with brown dots in autumn. Fruit reddish brown with silvery white spots. **'Aurea'**, leaves with a bright yellow margin of irregular width; **'Goldrim'**, deep glossy leaves with a bright yellow margin; **'Maculata'**, spectacular form with a large, yellow, central patch on each leaf and a dark green margin, though it can revert; **'Variegata'**, large shrub, leaves with a thin creamy yellow margin. Zones 7–10.

Elaeagnus pungens 'Aurea'

Elaeagnus × *ebbingei* 'Limelight'

Eleocharis acicularis

Elaeagnus umbellata

syn. *Elaeagnus crispa*

AUTUMN OLIVE

☼ ✱ ↔30 ft (9 m) ↑30 ft (9 m)

From China, Korea, and Japan. Strong-growing shrub. New shoots are golden brown, thorny. Leaves soft green, wavy-edged, silvery beneath. Fragrant yellow-white flowers are borne in late spring–early summer. Small, rounded, silvery bronze fruit ripens to pale red speckled with white in autumn. Zones 3–9.

ELEOCHARIS

SPIKE RUSH

There are about 150 species of annual or perennial rush-like plants in this genus in the sedge (Cyperaceae) family. Found throughout the world in bogs, shallow water, and damp places. True leaves are reduced or non-existent, and the plants comprise cylindrical stems bearing spikelets of tiny flowers at their tips. Height ranges from a few inches to 5 ft (1.5 m) or more. CULTIVATION: Easily grown in bog gardens and shallow ponds, or on pond margins, in sun or part-shade. In Asia, *E. dulcis* (water chestnut) is grown like rice as a crop in flooded fields. Propagate from seed or by division.

Eleocharis acicularis

HAIR GRASS, NEEDLE SPIKE RUSH, SLENDER SPIKE RUSH

☼/◐ ❄ ↔6–12 in (15–30 cm) ↑2–12 in (5–30 cm)

Found throughout North America, Europe, and Asia. Perennial with thin mat-forming runners. Narrow cylindrical stems bearing compressed pointed spikelets of tiny flowers in late summer–autumn. Zones 7–10.

ELEUTHEROCOCCUS

This genus of about 30 mostly deciduous prickly shrubs or trees native to southern and eastern Asia belongs to the ivy (Araliaceae) family and sometimes has a sprawling habit. The leaves are pinnate, consisting of 3 to 5 leaflets. Small flowers appear from late spring to autumn in umbels of 5, followed by black or purplish

black drupes. They are cultivated mainly for the ornamental value of their foliage and sometimes for use in traditional herbal medicine.
CULTIVATION: A sunny position is preferred, in well-drained sandy or loamy soil. Propagate from seed sown in spring, or divide roots or separate suckers in autumn.

Eleutherococcus sieboldianus ★

↔8 ft (2.5 m) ↑10 ft (3 m)
Native to eastern China. A shrub with slender, arching, cane-like branches. Bears solitary umbels of greenish white flowers in late spring–early summer. The black fruit is ⅓ in (8 mm) in diameter. Zones 4–9.

ELYMUS

WHEAT GRASS, WILD RYE

A genus comprising about 150 species of grasses in the family Poaceae, few of which are usually considered ornamental. They include running and clumping species, and inhabit such diverse habitats as steppes, dunes, and woodland in temperate regions of the Northern and Southern Hemispheres. Most species flower in summer.
CULTIVATION: All noteworthy species are fully frost hardy and require nothing more than a sunny aspect and a moisture-retentive soil. Propagation is usually by division in early spring.

Elymus canadensis

BLUE WILD RYE, CANADA WILD RYE, MOUNTAIN WILD RYE, WESTERN WILD RYE

↔24–36 in (60–90 cm)
↑36–60 in (90–150 cm)
Found from North Carolina to Alaska, USA. Drought-tolerant, ornamental, perennial grass. Wheat-like greenish flowerheads; seed plumes turning gold in mid- to late summer. Delicate-looking but tough; good in a wild garden or as a ground cover, providing winter interest. Zones 3–9.

Embothrium coccineum

Elymus magellanicus

Elymus magellanicus

syns *Agropyron magellanicum, A. pubiflorum*

BLUE WHEATGRASS, MAGELLAN WHEATGRASS

↔36–40 in (90–100 cm)
↑40–60 in (100–150 cm)
A native of South America. This spectacular mountain plant is probably the most attractive member of this genus. The semi-evergreen clumps of intense silver-blue foliage are topped with narrow heads of flowers that start out the same color, later turning to a parchment shade. Zones 6–9.

EMBOTHRIUM

This genus in the protea (Proteaceae) family is now considered to be represented by a single species, with regional forms, from Chile and the adjacent Andean region of Argentina. The rather upright tree is spectacular when in flower in late spring and early summer; its profusion of orange-scarlet tubular flowers are best appreciated from above.
CULTIVATION: An open sunny position with free-draining soil will reduce this plant's inclination to legginess. Protect from frost. With plentiful moisture, it grows quickly, producing a worthwhile display within a decade, but its life expectancy may not exceed 25 years. Can be propagated from seed, cuttings, or basal suckers.

Embothrium coccineum

CHILEAN FIRE BUSH

↔20 ft (6 m) ↑40 ft (12 m)
This native of Chile is an upright evergreen tree with glossy leathery leaves. It produces brilliant orange-scarlet flowers. In cultivation, treat as a tall shrub; prune after flowering to encourage flowering at eye level. The hardiest *Embothrium* is reputed to be 'Ñorquincó' ★, introduced in the 1920s by Harold Comber from the Ñorquincó Valley in the province of Neuquén, Argentina; its flower clusters are closely crowded on branches. Zones 8–9.

Emilia sonchifolia

EMILIA

There are about 24 species of rather sparse annual herbs in this genus, belonging to the daisy (Asteraceae) family. They are found throughout Polynesia, India, and tropical Africa. Their foliage is reminiscent of sow thistles, and the finely rayed flowers, which are borne singly or in small corymbs, are in bright shades of purple, scarlet, yellow, or orange.
CULTIVATION: *Emilia* species are easily grown in most soils in the full sun; plant close together for the best effect. Propagate from seed.

Emilia sonchifolia

FLORA'S PAINTBRUSH, TASSEL FLOWER

↔6–10 in (15–25 cm)
↑6–20 in (15–50 cm)
From tropical Asia and Africa. This annual produces rosettes of lyre-shaped leaves, sometimes bluish green. The tassel-like flowers bloom in shades of scarlet, brilliant orange, or yellow in summer. Zones 9–11.

EMMENOPTERYS

A genus of 2 deciduous trees from China and Southeast Asia belonging to the madder (Rubiaceae) family. The oval leaves are opposite and smooth-edged, and the fruit is a winged capsule. Panicles of funnel- or bell-shaped flowers are borne at the branch tips in summer. They are valuable as specimen trees.

Empetrum nigrum

Emmenopterys henryi

CULTIVATION: These trees prefer a sunny position in medium loam but will tolerate clay soils. Propagate from seed or from softwood cuttings grown under glass in summer.

Emmenopterys henryi

↔40 ft (12 m) ↑40–80 ft (12–24 m)
From central and western China, Myanmar, and Thailand. Deciduous tree with rough dark gray bark and gray or purple branchlets. Leaves to 8 in (20 cm) long; young growth reddish bronze. Panicles of white or yellow bell-shaped flowers in summer. Zones 6–9.

EMPETRUM

Exposed windswept sites across the cool-temperate regions of the Northern Hemisphere (and also the southern Andes and the Falkland Islands in the South Atlantic) are home to this genus of 2 heath-like, intricately branched, evergreen shrubs belonging to the family Ericaceae. Low growing and carpeting in habit. Very small solitary flowers appear in the leaf axils, and the fruit is a small, juicy, berry-like drupe containing up to 9 hard white seeds. The shrubs are grown for both their ornamental value and their edible fruit.
CULTIVATION: The two *Empetrum* species prefer moist lime-free soil in an open sunny position; they are ideal for the rock garden in cooler climates. Propagate from seed sown in spring or from cuttings.

Empetrum nigrum

BLACK CROWBERRY, CRAKE BERRY, CURLEW BERRY, MONOX

↔15 in (38 cm) ↑12 in (30 cm)
From the USA, northern Europe, and Asia. Spreading, heath-like, evergreen shrub resembling a miniature fir tree. Decumbent branches. Short needle-like leaves on stems with long woolly hairs. Loose clusters of purplish red flowers in late spring–early summer. Edible fruit, glossy, blackish purple. Zones 3–8.

E

Encelia farinosa

ENCELIA

Genus of about 15 species of perennials and low shrubs, native to arid regions of southwestern USA, Mexico, Peru, and Chile, and belonging to the daisy (Asteraceae) family. Foliage often aromatic; daisies bright orange or yellow.

CULTIVATION: Grow in full sun in deep sharply drained soil. Useful plants for dry areas; they dislike winter wet. In cold climates they can be grown in the greenhouse. Propagate from seed or cuttings.

Encelia farinosa

BRITTLE-BUSH, INCIENSO

↔ 36 in (90 cm) ↑ 36 in (90 cm)

From southwestern USA and Mexico. Aromatic shrub with silvery foliage. Bears orange-yellow daisies with yellow or reddish brown centers in spring. Zones 8–11.

ENCEPHALARTOS

This African genus belonging to the zamia (Zamiaceae) family consists of around 100 species of slow-growing cycads, the majority from southern Africa. There are both male and female plants. They prefer dry winters and summer rainfall. The pinnate fronds are often long and straight or arching, the leaflets are without a midrib and often spiny-toothed. Some develop a stout trunk, but suckering is common in those with underground cylindrical stems. Female plants have spectacular large seed cones with colorful fleshy seeds, maturing mostly in summer to autumn. Male pollen cones are usually smaller. The name comes from the Greek *en*, within, *cephale*, head, and *artos*, bread, referring to the starchy inner part of the trunk of some species, which is used as a staple food (sago) in some areas.

CULTIVATION: All species require well-drained soil. Species with blue-toned leaves are generally more tolerant of full sun, dry conditions, and heat; those with softer green leaves do best in filtered shade, with more regular watering. Propagate from seed or offsets.

Encephalartos altensteinii ★

PRICKLY CYCAD

↔ 12 ft (3.5 m) ↑ 15 ft (4.5 m)

From South Africa. Very slow-growing cycad. The trunk forms clumps from basal suckers. Stiff, glossy, green leaves; narrow leaflets with 1 to 3 prickles on each margin. Large yellow seed cones with red fruits. The trunks are a source of sago. Zones 10–11.

Encephalartos friderici-guilielmi ★

syn. *Zamia friderici-guilielmi*

WOOLLY CYCAD

↔ 10 ft (3 m) ↑ 17–20 ft (5–6 m)

Native to South Africa's Eastern Cape Province, occurring on rocky sites in grassy and shrubby habitats. Leaves to 5 ft (1.5 m) long; narrow leaflets, not lobed and with a few teeth on lower margin, to 7 in long and ⅓ in wide (18 cm × 8 mm). Male cones, yellow and shaped like elongated egg. Broader female cones and seeds also yellow. Species name is Latinized form of Friedrich Wilhelm, a nineteenth-century king of Prussia. Zones 9–11.

Encephalartos horridus

EASTERN CAPE BLUE CYCAD

↔ 3 ft (0.9 m) ↑ 3 ft (0.9 m)

From South Africa. Cycad with a very stiff growth habit and distinctly glaucous foliage. Most of the stem grows below ground. Fronds arching, to 3 ft (0.9 m) long; leaflets tipped with fierce spines. Cones are a warm buff shade. Zones 9–11.

Encephalartos natalensis

NATAL CYCAD, THOUSAND HILLS CYCAD

↔ 8 ft (2.4 m) ↑ 20 ft (6 m)

From southern KwaZulu-Natal, South Africa. Sturdy trunk. Glossy light or bright green leaves, to 10 ft (3 m) long; leaflets do not overlap and usually lack prickles. Cones in clusters, and woolly when young. Zones 10–12.

ENKIANTHUS

This genus from the heath (Ericaceae) family consists of about 10 species of mainly deciduous, rarely evergreen, shrubs found from the Himalayas to Japan. The leaves are elliptical or ovate. The plants flower from mid-spring through to early summer, producing umbels or racemes of white, pink, or red urn- or bell-shaped flowers at the ends of the branches.

CULTIVATION: Ornamental shrubs growing on the edge of woodlands or in woodland conditions, preferring full sun or light shade and moist, well-drained, humus-rich, acid to neutral soil. Propagate from half-

Encephalartos altensteinii

Encephalartos horridus

hardened cuttings taken during summer, by air-layering in autumn, or from seed sown in the winter or early spring. The best propagation medium is peat with lime-free sharp sand.

Enkianthus campanulatus

REDVEIN ENKIANTHUS

↔ 15 ft (4.5 m) ↑ 15 ft (4.5 m)

From the mountains of Honshu in Japan. Deciduous species with whorled branches. Leaves dull green and elliptic with a sharp tip and toothed margins, turning deep red in autumn. Flowers in drooping corymb-like racemes of creamy bells with red or pink veining in late spring–early summer. ***E. c.* var. *palibinii*** has dark red flowers. ***E. c.* 'Albiflorus'**, cream flowers; **'Donardensis'**, larger red flowers than the species; **'Red Bells'** ★, to 10 in (25 cm) tall, with red autumn leaves, and red flowers in pendent clusters. Zones 6–9.

Enkianthus cernuus

↔ 8 ft (2.4 m) ↑ 8 ft (2.4 m)

From Honshu in Japan. A deciduous shrub with bright green leaves, ovate to elliptic, with toothed margins, pointed tips, and brown downy veins beneath. Good autumn color. Pendent racemes of white flowers in late spring–summer. ***E. c.* f. *rubens*** has deep red flowers. Zones 6–9.

Enkianthus campanulatus

Enkianthus chinensis

↔ 6 ft (1.8 m) ↑ 12 ft (3.5 m)

A native of northern Myanmar and China. This deciduous shrub has leaves of mid-green, elliptical to oval, with toothed margins, which turn a good autumn color. The racemes of creamy yellow flowers with pink veins and rosy lobes appear in late spring. Zones 6–9.

Enkianthus perulatus

↔ 7 ft (2 m) ↑ 7 ft (2 m)

From Japan. Produces attractive shiny red young shoots. Oval, toothed leaves with downy midribs beneath, mid-green, turning bright red in autumn. Small drooping umbels of white flowers, in mid-spring. Zones 6–9.

ENSETE

Members of the banana (Musaceae) family, to which this genus belongs, are really giant, tree-like, perennial herbs. *Ensete* is a genus of 7 species of bananas found in tropical Asia and Africa, and is closely related to the banana genus *Musa*. The large solitary trunk or pseudostem is composed of the sheathing bases of the huge leaves, the blades of which are easily frayed by strong winds. Flowers are carried in large pendulous inflorescences at the end of arching stems and develop into small, dry, inedible bananas containing hard seeds.

CULTIVATION: All species of *Ensete* are easy to grow; these ornamental forms do not require nearly as much warmth as their edible relatives. The plants will survive all year in a mild frost-free climate; otherwise, treat them as annuals. Plant in moist, rich, well-drained soil in full sun or part-shade. These plants are usually propagated from seed, though it is sometimes possible to remove and strike basal suckers with roots.

Ensete ventricosum

ABYSSINIAN BANANA, ETHIOPIAN BANANA

↔ 15 ft (4.5 m) ↑ 30 ft (9 m)

African species with a huge crown of leaves, up to 20 ft (6 m) long, with a strong purple tint and a purple-red midrib. **'Maurelii'**, large, broad, red-tinged leaves. Zones 9–12.

EPIGAEA

A genus of 3 small, prostrate, evergreen shrubs in the heath (Ericaceae) family. Their distribution is interesting, with one species each from North America, Japan, and Turkey. Among the hardiest broadleaf evergreens, they make charming additions to a rockery in a cool temperate climate. The leaves are pointed oval with a heart-shaped base, usually deep green and glossy, sometimes red-tinted in winter. Clusters of tiny, bell-shaped, erica-like flowers appear in spring at the branch tips and in the leaf axils.
CULTIVATION: Although requiring some sunlight to flower well, these are cool climate plants that appreciate being shaded from the hottest sun and freedom from drought. Plant in cool, moist, humus-rich soil in dappled sunlight and water well in summer. Unless the seed is required, remove the spent flowers and trim any lanky shoots to keep the plant tidy. Propagation can be from the seed, which is very fine, or from small tip cuttings, and also by air-layering.

Epigaea repens

MAYFLOWER, TRAILING ARBUTUS

↔ 12–24 in (30–60 cm)
↑ 4–8 in (10–20 cm)

A native of North America, with a low spreading habit. The leaves are 1–3 in (25–75 mm) long and half as wide. The racemes of 4 to 6 sweetly scented white to pale pink flowers are about ½ in (12 mm) long. Zones 2–9.

EPILOBIUM

WILLOW HERB

Genus of about 200 species of annuals, perennials and subshrubs, found in temperate climates around the world, some weedy and the majority of little ornamental value. Mostly rhizomatous, leaves opposite, usually 4-ranked. Flowers mostly pink or white, borne in succession in upper leaf-axils, with long calyx tube and 4 petals, these often notched. Fruit a slender capsule releasing tiny plumed seeds like the lightest thistledown, carried by wind. One small group of species from western North America has evolved a more shrubby habit and scarlet flowers; attractive rock garden plants, these were often treated as the distinct genus *Zauschneria.*
CULTIVATION: Best suited to wild gardens or areas where they can spread freely. Grow in full sun in moisture-retentive soil. Alpine species need perfect drainage and protection from the hottest sun. Propagation is from seed or cuttings.

Ensete ventricosum 'Maurelii'

Epilobium angustifolium

syn. *Chamerion angustifolium*

FIREWEED, FRENCH WILLOW, GREAT WILLOW HERB, ROSEBAY WILLOW HERB

↔ 3–8 ft (0.9–2.4 m)
↑ 3–8 ft (0.9–2.4 m)

Found throughout the Northern Hemisphere. Invasive vigorous perennial. Willowy stems of narrow alternately arranged leaves. Racemes of pink or purplish pink flowers in summer–early autumn. Zones 3–9.

Epilobium canum

syns *Zauschneria californica, Z. californica subsp. mexicana, Z. cana*

CALIFORNIA FUCHSIA, ZAUSCHNERIA

↔ 3–7 ft (0.9–2 m)
↑ 1–3 ft (0.9–2.4 m)

Ranging from Oregon and Wyoming to southern California and New Mexico, USA, and northwestern Mexico. Variable semi-deciduous shrub or subshrub spreading by rhizomes, foliage gray-green; brilliant scarlet funnel-shaped flowers 1–2 in (2.5–5 cm) long, petals same shade as calyx, summer–autumn. **'Solidarity Pink'**, reddish pink flowers. ***E. c.* subsp. *latifolium*** (syn. *Zauschneria californica* subsp. *latifolia*), leaves broader, less grayish. Zones 8–10.

EPIMEDIUM

BARRENWORT, BISHOP'S HAT, BISHOP'S MITRE, HORNY GOAT WEED

A genus of 44 species at present, and still growing. Of this number, 36 have been discovered since 1975. Both evergreen and deciduous, they are clumping to slightly running perennials in the barberry (Berberidaceae) family that are found mainly in Asia but extend to the Mediterranean. They have attractive foliage, which is often their biggest asset, and the dainty spring flowers occur in a range of colors, often with long curved spurs. In China the dried roots are thought to cure male sexual dysfunction.
CULTIVATION: Most species prefer a cool shaded aspect under deciduous trees in humus-rich soil; many are quite drought tolerant once established. Propagate by division in late winter.

Epilobium angustifolium, in the wild, Grand Teton National Park, Wyoming, USA

Epilobium canum 'Solidarity Pink'

Epimedium grandiflorum

Epimedium acuminatum

↔ 36–40 in (90–100 cm)
↑ 10–18 in (25–45 cm)

From China. Evergreen. Leaves with 3 long tapered leaflets per leaf, bronze brown when young, turning green with age. Flowers with long, spurred, white sepals with purple petals, are ¾ in (18 mm) across, borne on fine arching stems, in spring and often well into the summer. Zones 5–9.

Epimedium alpinum

↔ 12–32 in (30–80 cm)
↑ 10–12 in (25–30 cm)

From southern Europe. More or less evergreen, with 5 to 9 spiny-edged leaflets that are bronze in winter. The flowers are small, spurless, about ½ in (12 mm) across, and dusty cherry red with a cream center. Zones 5–9.

Epimedium × *cantabrigiense*

↔ 12–18 in (30–45 cm)
↑ 12–24 in (30–60 cm)

Of garden origin. Heart-shaped evergreen leaves, downy beneath, with a few marginal spines. Stems of dainty red and pale yellow flowers in spring. Zones 5–9.

Epimedium davidii

↔ 16–20 in (40–50 cm)
↑ 10–12 in (25–30 cm)

From western China. Evergreen; the 3 leaflets are bright green in summer. Long-spurred lemon yellow flowers, to ¼ in (18 mm) across. Zones 5–9.

Epimedium franchetii

↔ 36–40 in (90–100 cm)
↑ 10–18 in (25–45 cm)

From China. The foliage is very like *E. acuminatum*, but the long spurred flowers are a soft pale yellow throughout. **'Brimstone Butterfly'**, yellow flowers. Zones 5–9.

Epimedium grandiflorum

↔ 8–12 in (20–30 cm)
↑ 8–12 in (20–30 cm)

From Japan, China, and Northern Korea. Widespread more or less deciduous species with heart-shaped leaves and a clumping habit. Small spurred flowers in shades of white, yellow, pink or purple. More selected clones than any other species. **'Lilacinum'**, lilac flowers; **'Lilafee'**, magenta flowers; **'Rose Queen'** ★, deep pink flowers with white-tipped spurs. Zones 5–9.

E

Epimedium × *perralchicum*

↔ 20–24 in (50–60 cm)
↑ 14–16 in (35–40 cm)

Hybrid between *E. perralderianum* and *E. pinnatum* subsp. *colchicum* that was discovered at Wisley Gardens in the UK. Forms large solid clumps of evergreen foliage, bronze when young, and has sprays of bright yellow spurless flowers. **'Frohnleiten'**, German selection with spikier foliage and larger flowers. Zones 7–9.

Epimedium perralderianum

↔ 20–24 in (50–60 cm)
↑ 14–16 in (35–40 cm)

From northern Africa. Slowly spreading evergreen with a slowly spreading habit. Leaves with 3 toothed leaflets, bronze ageing to green. Yellow flowers with short brown spurs. Zones 7–9.

Epimedium pinnatum

↔ 8–12 in (20–30 cm)
↑ 8–12 in (20–30 cm)

From northern Iran. Slowly spreading evergreen. Spiny-edged leaves. Yellow flowers, ¾ in (18 mm) across, with tiny brown spurs. ***E. p.* subsp. *colchicum***, most commonly grown form, with less spiny foliage and a tighter clumping habit. Zones 6–9.

Epimedium × *rubrum*

↔ 10–12 in (25–30 cm)
↑ 10–12 in (25–30 cm)

Clump-forming garden hybrid between *E. alpinum* and *E. grandiflorum* with pointed spiny-edged leaves that are reddish when young and also in winter. Crimson and soft lemon flowers with short spurs, ¾ in (18 mm) across. Zones 5–10.

Epimedium sempervirens

↔ 10–12 in (25–30 cm)
↑ 10–12 in (25–30 cm)

From Japan and Korea. An evergreen species similar to *E. grandiflorum*. Rich green leaves, bronze at first. Small, white, spurred flowers. Zones 7–9.

Epimedium pinnatum subsp. *colchicum*

Epimedium × *setosum*

↔ 16–20 in (40–50 cm)
↑ 8–12 in (20–30 cm)

Species native to Japan. The leaves are bronze-tinged, slightly furry to start, when they are young. It bears small white flowers that are more or less spurless. Zones 7–9.

Epimedium × *versicolor*

↔ 10–12 in (25–30 cm)
↑ 10–12 in (25–30 cm)

Range of evergreen clump-forming garden hybrids between *E. grandiflorum* and *E. pinnatum* subsp. *colchicum*. The spiny-edged leaves are often richly colored with bronze when young. The flowers have short spurs that do not exceed the length of the calyx. The cultivar, **'Neosulphureum'**, produces soft lemon flowers; **'Sulphureum'** has bright yellow flowers with slightly longer spurs. Zones 5–9.

Epimedium × *warleyense*

↔ 24–32 in (60–80 cm)
↑ 16–20 in (40–50 cm)

A garden hybrid between *E. alpinum* and *E. pinnatum* subsp. *colchicum* bred by the famous Miss Ellen Willmott in about 1909 at her equally famous property, Warley Place, in Essex, UK. This species forms sizeable open clumps. The flowers, which are spurless, are burnt orange with a yellow center. The new foliage is an attractive bronze color. Zones 5–9.

Epimedium × *youngianum*

↔ 10–12 in (25–30 cm)
↑ 8–12 in (20–30 cm)

Hybrids between *E. diphyllum* and *E. grandiflorum* with usually spineless leaflets that are attractively bronzed when young. The small spurless flowers can be white through to rose pink. **'Niveum'**, charming cultivar with white flowers, richly colored new foliage. Zones 5–9.

EPISCIA

This genus, comprises 9 species from tropical America, belonging to the African violet (Gesneriaceae) family. They are epiphytic or terrestrial, sometimes subshrubby, herbs and are exceptional in the family in having runners. The leaves are opposite, often colored, and in equal or unequal pairs; when unequal the smaller one is often deciduous. The flowers are borne in stalked racemes in the leaf axils, and may be clustered or solitary. The calyx has 5 green or colored sepals, which are sometimes joined at the base. The corolla is funnel-shaped with 5 spreading lobes, which may be smooth-edged or have fringed margins. The fruit is a 2-valved capsule containing many elliptical seeds.

CULTIVATION: In temperate areas they need greenhouse culture and are often grown in hanging baskets, but in the tropics they can be grown as ground cover or used in bedding schemes. These plants are difficult to overwinter in the poor light of temperate regions, but can be readily propagated from cuttings, which root easily, or from seed. Many hybrids have been raised.

Episcia cupreata 'Acajou'

Epimedium sempervirens

Episcia cupreata

CARPET PLANT, FLAME VIOLET

↔ 12–24 in (30–60 cm)
↑ 8–12 in (20–30 cm)

Native to Central and South America (southern Mexico to Ecuador). Evergreen creeping perennial. Leaves oval, brown to dark green, wrinkled, downy, to 3½ in (9 cm) long, flecked with copper and purple underneath. Clusters of scarlet flowers with a yellow ring, throat sometimes spotted with purple, in summer. Good plants for hanging baskets. **'Acajou'**, lighter-colored leaves with silvery markings; **'Chocolate Soldier'**, very large brown leaves with a silvery gray center band; **'Country Cowgirl'**, silvery green pebble-textured leaves with copper-green margins; **'Metallica'**, copper leaves marked with silver, red flowers; **'Silver Sheen'**, bright copper-green margins, yellow, lilac, or red flowers; **'Tetra'**, large orange-red flowers with wavy lobes, orange-yellow inside; **'Tropical Topaz'**, bright yellow flowers. Zones 10–12.

Episcia dianthiflora

syn. *Alsobia dianthiflora*

LACE-FLOWER VINE

↔ 18–36 in (60–90 cm)
↑ 8 in (20 cm)

This species is found from southern Mexico to Costa Rica. It is a low-growing evergreen perennial with leaves of dark green, which are toothed, elliptical to oval-shaped, to 1¾ in (40 mm) long, and often veined with purple-red. The solitary, pearly white, tubular flowers, borne in summer, are spotted with purple at the base, with their rounded petals conspicuously fringed. Zones 10–12.

Episcia Hybrid Cultivars

↔ 32–40 in (80–100 cm)
↑ 8–20 in (20–50 cm)

Episcia species interbreed quite freely, which has resulted in many hybrid cultivars appearing in cultivation. The best of these tend to be compact plants that flower heavily and often have interesting marked foliage. **'Chocolate**

Episcia, Hybrid Cultivar, 'Toy Silver'

'n' Cherries', very dark bronze foliage, yellow-dotted bright red flowers; **'Star of Bethlehem'**, dark bronze leaves with red undersides, distinctive bright pink flowers with a broad white margin; **'Toy Silver'**, a very dwarf cultivar, with leaves of dark green, heavily marbled and veined with silver-gray, bright red flowers. Zones 10–12.

EPITHELANTHA

This genus of beautiful diminutive plants in the cactus (Cactaceae) family comprises just 2 species, one of which has 5 subspecies, and is found in the Chihuahua Desert regions of Arizona, New Mexico, and Texas, USA, and Coahuila, San Luis Potosi, and Nuevo Leon, Mexico. They resemble the genus *Mammillaria* but bear flowers on the ends of the tubercles rather than between them. The genus name is derived from two Greek words, *epi* (on) and *thelos* (nipple), referring to the plant's tubercles. The spines and growth habit vary. The plants contain hallucinogenic chemicals and are occasionally ingested by the shamans of native tribes as part of their diagnostic rituals when healing the sick.
CULTIVATION: Not easily grown, be-cause these plants do not like compost or wet feet. They need sandy, loamy, well-drained, mineralized soil. Withhold water in winter and again in mid-summer. Propagate from seed or from cuttings that have been dried out for a week or two.

Epithelantha micromeris

↔ 2½ in (6 cm)
↑ ¾–1¾ in (18–40 mm)

From eastern Arizona, New Mexico, and western Texas, USA, and northern Mexico. Small, neat, solitary to clustering, white to grayish white plants with a depressed growing tip. No central spine but 20 to 25 white radial spines, 1/8–½ in (3–12 mm) long. Pink to white flowers in summer. Red seed pods. ***E. m.* subsp. *unguispina***, similar to the type species but usually clustering with age and with a distinct, slightly curved, black-tipped central spine. Zones 7–10 .

EQUISETUM

HORSETAIL, SCOURING-RUSH

This genus of about 25 unusual, rush-like, flowerless, perennial herbs from the scouring-rush (Equisetaceae) family is found worldwide, except in Australia and New Zealand. All species consist of clumps of erect, cylindrical, jointed, bamboo-like stems. The leaves are minute and are usually reduced to a ring of black or brown teeth at the stem nodes, but are sometimes longer, thin, straggly, and wiry. The spore-bearing cones are located at the tips of the stems. These plants resemble a horse's tail; they are called "scouring-rush" because early American settlers used them for cleaning pots. They are also used in Japanese flower arrangements.
CULTIVATION: Plant around water features such as marshes, using garden soil or potting mix kept moist and well drained; pots may be stood in water. Propagate from spores or by division of rhizomes, burying the stem segments directly in the soil.

Equisetum arvense

COMMON HORSETAIL, FIELD HORSETAIL

↔ 12–18 in (30–45 cm)
↑ 16–24 in (40–60 cm)

This species is found across Europe, North America, Asia, and Greenland. A very hardy perennial with irregularly spaced dense whorls of sterile green stems, to 24 in (60 cm) tall, prostrate or erect, slightly rough, and furrowed. Short-lived, light brown, branching stems are smooth and fertile. The fine foliage is feathery and bright green. Zones 2–9.

Equisetum giganteum

GIANT HORSETAIL

↔ 18–24 in (45–60 cm)
↑ 9–12 ft (2.7–3.5 m)

Native to the American tropics. This is a vigorous, colonizing, rush-like perennial. The erect green stems, 1 in (2.5 cm) in diameter, have thin dark brown or black bands at the nodes and lean on surrounding plants for support. Zones 10–12.

Equisetum giganteum

Equisetum telmateia

GIANT HORSETAIL

↔ 12–24 in (30–60 cm)
↑ 20 in–6 ft (0.5–1.8 m)

Native to Eurasia, north Africa, and northern North America. Perennial. Erect, finely grooved, ivory white or pale green, sterile stems, to 6 ft (1.8 m) tall, with smoothly ridged nodes and whorls of numerous simple, rough, feathery branches. Can be too invasive for domestic gardens. Zones 5–10.

ERAGROSTIS

LOVE GRASS

This genus of about 250 species of clumping annuals or perennials, belonging to the grass (Poaceae) family, is native to tropical and subtropical North and South America, South Africa, and Australia. The leaves are narrow, and can be either rolled or flat, with glandular sheaths. The flowerheads are open or form dense panicles of closely overlapping 2- to many-flowered spikelets.
CULTIVATION: These plants are drought tolerant and prefer a sunny position in well-drained sandy soil, but will also tolerate heavy clay. Propagate most species from seed and some by division of the rhizomes.

Eragrostis curvula

AFRICAN LOVE GRASS, WEEPING LOVE GRASS

↔ 9–12 in (22–30 cm)
↑ 3–4 ft (0.9–1.2 m)

From South Africa. Clumping, tufted, perennial grass. Simple narrow leaves, to 12 in (30 cm) long, rough to the touch, green in summer, becoming yellow to bronze in winter. Erect flower stalks in summer–autumn. Zones 7–10.

Eragrostis curvula

ERANTHEMUM

Native to tropical regions in Asia and within the acanthus (Acanthaceae) family, this genus consists of about 30 shrubby perennial herbs and evergreen shrubs with opposite simple leaves. They produce dense branched spikes or panicles of flowers with slender tubular corollas in the spring.
CULTIVATION: All species thrive in light, rich, medium loams in a semi-shaded or protected position provided they have ample moisture. Propagate from cuttings of younger wood taken in the spring.

Eranthemum pulchellum

syn. ***Eranthemum nervosum***

BLUE SAGE

↔ 3 ft (0.9 m) ↑ 4 ft (1.2 m)

From India. Evergreen shrub. Slightly toothed, prominently veined, glossy, green leaves, 4–8 in (10–20 cm) long. Feathery flower spikes, about 3 in (8 cm) long, bear tubular vivid blue flowers, 1¼ in (30 mm) across, with deep purple throats and green, papery, pointed bracts. Zones 10–12.

ERANTHIS

WINTER ACONITE

In the wild these small tuberous plants from the buttercup (Ranunculaceae) family are found in the damp deciduous woodlands of Europe and Asia, where their golden flowers do much to enliven bleak late-winter landscapes. In similar cool, damp, summer-shady situations they colonize and extend their territory. The cupped flowers, each held on a single stem, are encircled with pronounced green "ruffs."
CULTIVATION: Transplant in early spring while the plants are in leaf; they can be temperamental if transplanted when dry during the summer months. Aphids and birds can cause damage. Grow in moisture-retentive soil, with plenty of winter sun. Propagate by dividing the tubers or from seed.

Eranthemum pulchellum

E

Eranthis hyemalis

E

Eranthis hyemalis

↔3–4 in (8–10 cm)
↑3–4 in (8–10 cm)

From southern France to Bulgaria; now naturalized over a far wider range. The brilliant golden flowers, like buttercups, often appearing before snow-melt, held on short curved stems. Stems elongate and straighten as the flower develops from a diameter of ¼ in (6 mm) to about 1 in (25 mm) across. Basal leaves emerge after the flowers fade, and are bright green, lobed, and circular. Plant beneath deciduous trees in alkaline soils. Zones 5–8.

Eranthis × *tubergenii* 'Guinea Gold'

↔3–4 in (8–10 cm)
↑4–8 in (10–20 cm)

A tough, vigorous, but sterile hybrid, product of *E. hyemalis* and *E. cilicica*. Given the right conditions, it quickly expands into decent-sized clumps. The flamboyant flowers are yellow, large, and held above bronzed "ruffs." Zones 5–8.

EREMOPHILA

This genus of about 200 species belongs to the foxglove (Scrophulariaceae) family and is a native of mainland Australia, with most species occurring in semi-arid and arid areas. They are evergreen shrubs or small trees, often with felted or resinous leaves, stems, and floral parts. The 2-lipped tubular flowers, on short to long stalks emerging from the leaf axils, are variously lobed and may be white, yellow, violet, purple, pink, or red, and sometimes have a spotted interior. The fruits are berry-like drupes, the seed enclosed in a tough corky or fibrous layer. Popular as ornamental shrubs in drier regions, and many thrive in alkaline soils. Some are available as grafted plants, making those species from dry areas easier to grow in the higher-rainfall areas. Many *Eremophila* species are attractive to nectar-feeding birds.
CULTIVATION: Marginally frost hardy, most species do not like moist humid conditions. They prefer a position with excellent drainage in an open sunny area with plenty of air movement. Regular light pruning encourages vigorous growth. These plants are propagated most readily from half-hardened cuttings; in fact, germination is only practicable if the seed is first extracted from the tough inner fruit layer, and the sowing medium is treated thoroughly with a fungicide.

Eremophila glabra

COMMON EMU BUSH, FUCHSIA BUSH

↔3–10 ft (0.9–3 m) ↑5 ft (1.5 m)

Occurring throughout arid and semi-arid regions of Australia. Prostrate or erect evergreen shrub with narrow mid-green to grayish leaves. The orange, yellow, red, or green tubular flowers are borne for much of the year. **'Murchison River'** ★, compact plant, soft silvery gray foliage, bright red flowers. Zones 9–11.

Eremophila maculata

SPOTTED EMU BUSH

↔3–10 ft (0.9–3 m)
↑3–8 ft (0.9–2.4 m)

Occurs across the length and breadth of mainland Australia. Compact dense shrub with gray-green leaves, to 2 in (5 cm) long; young leaves often downy. Red, purple, pink, or yellow flowers, often spotted with darker blotches, in autumn–spring. **'Aurea'**, a compact habit to about 3 ft (100 cm), with light green leaves, yellow flowers; **'Carmine Star'**, low shrub, to 20 in (50 cm) high, purplish young branches, carmine flowers, the insides paler and with prominent carmine spots; **'Pink Beauty'**, 10–12 ft (3–3.5 m) tall, bears profuse bluish pink flowers, 1½ in (35 mm) across, in late winter. Zones 9–11.

Eremophila maculata

Eremophila nivea

Eremophila mitchellii

BUDDA, FALSE SANDALWOOD

↔12 ft (3.5 m) ↑30 ft (9 m)

Native to inland northern New South Wales and Queensland, Australia. This resinous aromatic shrub or small tree has shiny linear leaves to 2½ in (6 cm) long. The small, lightly perfumed, bell-shaped flowers are white to creamy pink with lightly spotted throats, 2 to 3 in each leaf axil, in spring and again in autumn. Zones 9–11.

Eremophila nivea

↔5 ft (1.5 m) ↑5 ft (1.5 m)

From Western Australia's "wheatbelt," east of Perth. A beautiful silvery gray shrub. Erect stems covered in dense white hairs. Small, velvety gray, linear leaves. Tubular lilac flowers, borne in upper leaf axils, in winter–spring. Dislikes humidity; best in an open sunny position. An excellent container plant. Zones 9–11.

EREMURUS

DESERT CANDLE, FOXTAIL LILY

This genus of 40 to 50 species of fleshy-stemmed perennials belongs to the grass tree (Xanthorrhoeaceae) family. They are native to western and central Asia, where they grow in dry areas among rocks and in grassland. These statuesque plants form basal clumps of strap-shaped leaves and send up flower spikes to 10 ft (3 m) tall. The white, pink, or yellow flowers are borne in tapering spikes and resemble small starry lilies. Their prominently protruding stamens give the spike a soft fluffy appearance.
CULTIVATION: Grow in a rich, well-drained, sandy soil in sheltered position in full sun. Stake taller species. Protect from winter wet with mulch; remove before new growth emerges. Protect new growth from slugs and snails. Propagate from seed or divide carefully, avoiding damage to the fragile roots.

Eremurus robustus

Eremurus himalaicus

↔30 in (75 cm)
↑36–48 in (90–120 cm)

From Afghanistan and northwestern Himalayas. One of the first species to flower in early summer. Narrow strap-shaped leaves. Bears dense heads of white, starry, lily-like flowers with protruding stamens in the late spring–summer. Zones 3–9.

Eremurus robustus

↔36–48 in (90–120 cm)
↑7–10 ft (2–3 m)

Native to Tajikistan, Kyrgyzstan, and Afghanistan. Vigorous species with leaves to 4 ft (1.2 m) long, often deciduous before flowering. Very showy densely packed spikes of pink flowers marked with brown and green in summer. Zones 6–9.

Eremurus stenophyllus

↔24–36 in (60–90 cm)
↑36–60 in (90–150 cm)

Found in central Asia and the western Himalayas. Bears dense tapering spikes of clear yellow flowers in summer. The flowers fade to orangey brown, giving a two-toned effect. Zones 5–9.

Eremurus Hybrid Cultivars

↔24–40 in (60–100 cm)
↑4–7 ft (1.2–2 m)

Most Eremurus hybrids originate from the cross *E.* × *isabellinus* (*E. olgae* × *E. stenophyllus*), which has resulted in a number of free-flowering hybrid groups in white and various shades of pink, amber, orange, and yellow. **'Cleopatra'** ★, deep orange flowers; **Erfo Hybrids**, to 5–6 ft (1.5–1.8 m) tall, pastel flowers; **Highdown Hybrids**, richly colored, flower in summer: **'Himrob'**, pink flowers, late-flowering; **Ruiter Hybrids**, to 7 ft (2 m), brightly colored: **'Moneymaker'**, yellow flowers ageing to orange; **Shelford Hybrids**, to 4 ft (1.2 m), richly colored flowers in early summer. Zones 5–9.

ERICA

HEATH, HEATHER

This large genus gives its name to the heath (Ericaceae) family. It consists of about 750 species of evergreen shrubs, ranging from small subshrubs to trees, the great majority endemic to the Cape region of South Africa, the remainder scattered throughout East Africa, Madagascar, the Atlantic Islands, the Mediterranean region, and Europe. Habitats include wet and dry heathland and moorland. Most are only half-hardy; the European species are more frost hardy. The small linear leaves are linear with rolled edges, whorled, rarely opposite. The flowers are bell-shaped or tubular, in all colors except blue. Briar pipes are made from the woody root burls of *E. arborea*. Some species yield a yellow dye. CULTIVATION: The winter-flowering heathers are lime tolerant and will grow in neutral and alkaline soil, while the summer-flowering ones like acid soil; both grow in neutral soil. Feed container-grown plants monthly during the growing season and give them plenty of water, reducing both feed and water during the dormant season. Propagation is from half-hardened cuttings taken from mid- to late summer or by air-layering in spring. The successful germination of some of the South African Cape heaths is helped by smoke treatment.

Erica arborea

BRUYERE, TREE HEATH

↔ 10 ft (3 m) ↑ 15 ft (4.5 m)

Native to southwest Europe, through the Mediterranean, and in the higher mountains of east Africa. This upright shrub has dark green leaves, grooved beneath. It bears pyramidal racemes of gray-white, scented, bell-shaped flowers in late spring. ***E. a.*** **var.** ***alpina***, a smaller shrub, with dense cylindrical racemes of white flowers; ***E. a.*** **'Albert's Gold'**, carries golden leaves all year round, white flowers; **'Estrella Gold'**, compact yellow-green foliage, young growth is bright yellow, white flowers. Zones 7–10.

Erica australis

SOUTHERN HEATH, SPANISH HEATH

↔ 3 ft (0.9 m) ↑ 6 ft (1.8 m)

A species native to Portugal, western Spain, and Tangiers. An upright open shrub, with leaves of dark green, linear, and grooved beneath. The reddish pink tubular or bell shaped flowers, are borne in umbel-like racemes on the previous year's wood, in late spring–early summer. Cultivars bloom in different colors: **'Mr Robert'** produces white flowers; **'Riverslea'**, lilac-pink flowers. Zones 8–10.

Erica canaliculata

↔ 4 ft (1.2 m) ↑ 6 ft (1.8 m)

From Western and Eastern Cape in South Africa. Erect shrub. Mid-green linear leaves in whorls; undersurfaces paler green, hairy. Produces whorls of 3 white to pale pink flowers at the ends of the branchlets in winter–spring. Zones 8–10.

Erica canaliculata

Erica carnea 'Pirbright Rose'

Erica cinerea 'Cindy'

Erica carnea

syn. *Erica herbacea*

ALPINE HEATH, SNOW HEATH, WINTER HEATH

↔ 22 in (55 cm) ↑ 12 in (30 cm)

From the Alps, northwest Italy, the northwest Balkans, and eastern Europe. Low-spreading shrub. Dark green linear leaves in whorls of 4. Bears purple-pink flowers in winter–spring. Tolerates some lime. **'Ann Sparkes'**, rose pink flowers, golden foliage with bronze tips; **'Challenger'**, green foliage, magenta flowers; **'December Red'**, deep pink flowers that turn red; **'Foxhollow'**, ro-bust shrub, lime green leaves, pinkish white flowers; **'Kramer's Rubin'**, blackish green foliage, flowers a dull deep pink; **'March Seedling'**, flowers into late spring; **'Myretoun Ruby'** (syn. 'Myreton Ruby'), pink flowers deepening to crimson; **Pink Spangles'**, deep pink flowers; **'Pirbright Rose'**, compact form, rose pink flowers; **'R. B. Cooke'**, mid-green leaves, pink flowers turning mauve; **'Springwood White'**, vigorous, bright green foliage, abundant white flowers; **'Winter Beauty'**, compact, masses of deep pink flowers. Zones 5–9.

Erica cinerea

BELL HEATHER

↔ 30 in (65 cm) ↑ 24 in (60 cm)

From western Europe. Compact low-growing shrub. Bottle green leaves with rolled-under edges in whorls of 3. Racemes of urn-shaped flowers, at stem tips, in summer–early autumn, colors ranging from white to pink to purple. Cultivars include: **'Alba Major'**, mid-green foliage, white flowers; **'Alba Minor'**, dense habit, with profuse white blooms; **'Alice Ann Davies'**, a vigorous spreader, with long spikes of dark pink blooms; **'Altadena'**, chartreuse foliage; **'Atrorubens'**, profuse bright rose purple flowers; **'Atrosanguinea'**, bright reddish purple flowers; **'C. D. Eason'**, broadly spreading low shrub, erect sprays of rose purple flowers; **'Cindy'**, dwarf, almost prostrate, with tight clusters of rose purple flowers; **'Fiddler's Gold'**, leaves turning from gold to red in winter, lilac-pink flowers; **'Flamingo'**, vigorous, spreading, bright rose pink flowers; **'Golden Drop'**, mat-like habit, lilac-pink flowers; **'Katinka'**, dark green foliage, black-purple flowers; **'Mrs E. A. Mitchell'**, fine dark green foliage, dark red flowers; **'Pink Ice'**, dwarf shrub, bearing soft rose pink flowers; **'Plummer's Seedling'**, mound-forming, deep pinkish red flowers; **'Prostrate Lavender'**, semi-prostrate, compact, lavender-pink flowers fading to white; **'Purple Beauty'**, dwarf cultivar, dense heads of rose-purple flowers; **'Startler'**, broadly spreading, with erect sprays of bright rose flowers; **'Vivienne Patricia'**, lax spreading habit, and mauve-pink flowers; and **'Wine'**, spreading, semi-prostrate, dense spikes of rose pink blooms. Zones 5–9.

Erica cruenta

Erica × *darleyensis* 'Margaret Porter'

Erica cruenta

BLOOD RED HEATH

↔ 27 in (70 cm) ↑ 3 ft (0.9 m)

Native to the southwest Cape region of South Africa. This upright sparsely branched shrub carries dark green leaves in whorls of 3. Blood red tubular flowers held on the ends of lateral branches, prolonged flowering period. Hardy species. Prune regularly in first 2 years to promote growth. Zones 9–10.

Erica × *darleyensis*

DARLEY DALE HEATH

↔ 24 in (60 cm) ↑ 12 in (30 cm)

Crosses between *E. carnea* and *E. erigena* of garden origin. Vigorous bushy shrub. Mid-green lance-shaped leaves. Racemes of various-colored flowers, depending on the cultivar, in winter–early spring. Likes well-drained soil. **'Darley Dale'**, pink flowers and cream-tipped leaves in spring; **'Ghost Hills'**, light green cream-tipped leaves; **'Jenny Porter'**, pinkish white flowers, pale cream-tipped foliage; **'Kramers Rote'**, bronze-green foliage, magenta flowers; **'Margaret Porter'**, lilac-pink flowers over a long season; **'Silberschmelze'**, silver-white flowers, foliage tinged red in winter. Zones 6–9.

Erica glandulosa

Erica melanthera

Erica rubens

Erica erigena

syns *Erica hibernica, E. mediterranea*

IRISH HEATHER

↔3 ft (0.9 m) ↑8 ft (2.4 m)

Found in Ireland, southwest France, Spain, Portugal, and Tangiers in northwest Africa. An upright shrub with brittle stems. Dark green linear leaves. The racemes of urn-shaped, honey-scented, lilac-pink flowers appear in winter–spring. Cultivars include: **'Golden Lady'**, golden yellow foliage, white flowers; **'Irish Dusk'**, gray-green foliage, rose pink flowers in the late autumn–spring; **'Superba'** ★ (syn. 'Mediterranea Superba'), mid-green foliage, strongly scented pale pink flowers; **'W. T. Rackliff'**, mid-green foliage, abundant white flowers in spring. Zones 7–9.

Erica glandulosa

↔36 in (90 cm) ↑24 in (60 cm)

Native to the Cape region of South Africa. Sprawling shrub. Light green linear leaves with glandular hairs in whorls of 4. Clusters of pinky orange tubular flowers, borne at branch tips, in autumn–spring. Zones 9–10.

Erica × *griffithsii*

↔24 in (60 cm)
↑18–36 in (45–90 cm)

Hybrids between *E. manipuliflora* and *E. vagans* come under this name, combining the vigor of the first with the dense growth and early flowering of the second. **'Heaven Scent'**, compact form, dark gray-green foliage, long sprays of scented lilac flowers in mid-summer–mid-autumn. Zones 6–9.

Erica × *hiemalis*

FRENCH HEATHER

↔24 in (60 cm) ↑24 in (60 cm)

Parents and origin unknown. Upright, fairly dense. Light green leaves, whorls of 4. Tubular flowers, white with pink shading, in autumn–winter. Zones 8–10.

Erica lusitanica

syn. *Erica codonodes*

PORTUGUESE HEATH, SPANISH HEATH

↔3 ft (0.9 m) ↑5–10 ft (1.5–3 m)

Native from the west of the Iberian Peninsula to southwest France. Has naturalized in southern England, New Zealand, and Australia. Whorls of 3 or 4 mid-green linear leaves. Racemes of tubular flowers, pink in bud, opening to white, during winter–spring. Grows best in acid soil. Can be invasive. **'George Hunt'**, yellow leaves, white flowers. Zones 8–10.

Erica mammosa

↔6 ft (1.8 m) ↑5 ft (1.5 m)

From the Western Cape, South Africa. Dark green lance-shaped leaves in whorls of 4. Tubular flowers in spring–summer, colors ranging from white or green through to pink and dark red. **'Jubilee'**, pink flowers. Zones 9–10.

Erica manipuliflora

syn. *Erica verticillata of gardens*

↔3 ft (0.9 m) ↑3 ft (0.9 m)

Found in southeastern Italy and the Balkans. Mid-green, linear, pointed leaves in whorls of 3. Bears rose pink flowers, in irregular racemes on the previous year's wood, in the summer–autumn. **'Aldeburgh'**, scented lilac-pink flowers; **'Korcula'**, long sprays of pink-tinged white flowers. Zones 8–10.

Erica melanthera

↔18 in (45 cm) ↑24 in (60 cm)

From the Western Cape, South Africa. Erect shrub. Tiny dark green leaves in whorls of 3. Pendent pale pink to deep red blooms with black anthers extending outside the cup in spring to early summer. Zones 8–10.

Erica rubens

RED HEATH

↔3–5 ft (0.9–1.5 m)
↑3–5 ft (0.9–1.5 m)

From the Cape region of South Africa. Evergreen shrub. Slender reddish stems. Tiny, dark green, cylindrical leaves in groups of 4. Spikes with masses of tiny, pink to deep red, tubular flowers, borne at stem tips. Zones 7–9.

Erica scoparia

BESOM HEATH

↔3 ft (0.9 m) ↑6 ft (1.8 m)

From southwest France, Spain, the Canary Islands, and north Africa. An erect shrub. Dark green linear leaves in whorls of 3 or 4. Racemes of small bell-shaped flowers, brownish red tinged green, in summer. Zones 8–10.

Erica × *stuartii*

↔18 in (45 cm) ↑10 in (25 cm)

From western Ireland. This is a naturally occurring hybrid of *E. mackayana* and *E. tetralix*. Most forms are very similar to *E. mackayana* except for minor floral details. **'Irish Lemon'** has lemon-tipped young foliage, mauve flowers; **'Irish Orange'** produces orange young foliage maturing to green, and soft pink flowers. Zones 8–10.

Erica tetralix

CROSS-LEAFED HEATH

↔20 in (50 cm) ↑12 in (30 cm)

From the UK, France, and the Iberian Peninsula. Dwarf spreading. Gray-green lance-shaped to linear leaves, silver undersides, whorls of 4. Umbels of pale pink urn-shaped flowers, at stem tips, in summer–autumn. Prefers moist soil. **'Alba Mollis'**, silvery foliage, white flowers; **'Con Underwood'**, gray-green leaves, purple-red flowers; **'Pink Star'**, dark pink upright flowers. Zones 3–9.

Erica vagans

CORNISH HEATH, WANDERING HEATH

↔30 in (75 cm) ↑30 in (75 cm)

From the UK, Ireland, western France, and Spain. Dark to mid-green linear leaves in whorls of 4 or 5. Racemes of cylindrical or bell-shaped flowers that range from white to pink and mauve, in mid-summer–mid-autumn. Prefers a well-drained soil. **'Lyonesse'**, white flowers with light brown anthers, bright green foliage; **'Mrs D. F. Maxwell'**, compact habit, vivid rose pink flowers; **'Saint Keverne'**, bright pink flowers; **'Valerie Proudley'**, yellow foliage, white flowers. Zones 5–9.

Erica × *veitchii*

↔26 in (65 cm) ↑6 ft (1.8 m)

Of garden origin, this species is a cross between *Erica arborea* and *E. lusitanica.* Linear mid-green leaves. The young branches are covered with downy hairs. Produces racemes of lightly scented white flowers in the spring. **'Exeter'** bears masses of white scented flowers in spring; **'Gold Tips'**, golden yellow young shoots maturing to green, tolerates some alkalinity in the soil; **'Pink Joy'**, pale pink flowers. Zones 8–10.

Erica versicolor

↔3 ft (0.9 m) ↑10 ft (3 m)

From Western Cape in South Africa. Erect shrub. Mid-green linear leaves in whorls of 3. Racemes of tubular flowers, red with green to yellow tips, in whorls of 3 in autumn–winter. Zones 9–11.

Erica verticillata

↔3 ft (0.9 m) ↑3 ft (0.9 m)

From South Africa's Cape Peninsula. A bushy erect shrub, believed to be extinct in the wild. Linear green leaves in whorls of 4 to 6. Clusters of purple-pink, finely hairy, tubular flowers in summer. Zones 9–10.

Erica × *williamsii*

↔18 in (45 cm) ↑30 in (75 cm)

This hybrid is a cross between *E. tetralix* and *E. vagans* that occurred in the wild in Cornwall in the UK. It produces racemes of rose pink bell-shaped flowers in the summer to late autumn. **'P. D. Williams'**, with yellow-tipped new growth and pink flowers. Zones 5–9.

ERIGERON

FLEABANE

This genus of about 200 species of annuals and perennials belongs to the daisy (Asteraceae) family. They are found throughout temperate regions,

Erigeron formosissimus

Erigeron karvinskianus

Erigeron pulchellus

Erinus alpinus

particularly in North America, and grow in a variety of habitats. Their daisy flowers usually have numerous narrow rays in shades of white, pink, or lavender, occasionally yellow. Cultivars extend the color range. Plant habits vary from the very low alpine species, suitable for a rock garden, to robust larger-flowered species growing to 30 in (75 cm) or more. They flower profusely, often over a long season. CULTIVATION: Apart from the alpine species, which benefit from protection in winter and need very good drainage, most are easily grown in full sun in any reasonable soil. Propagate from seed or by division.

Erigeron formosissimus

☼ ✱ ↔ 18 in (45 cm) ↑ 18 in (45 cm)

From the Rocky Mountains, USA. Perennial. Clumps of narrow oblong leaves. Heads of blue, pink or white daisies with yellow centers in summer. Zones 6–9.

Erigeron glaucus

BEACH ASTER, SEASIDE DAISY

☼ ✱ ↔ 12–24 in (30–60 cm) ↑ 6–12 in (15–30 cm)

From western USA. A somewhat succulent straggly perennial, with broadly oval leaves. It bears large gold-centered daisies with lilac to violet rays in the late spring to early summer. **'Arthur Menzies'**, compact form, pink daisies; **'Rose Purple'**, pink-purple daisies. Zones 3–10.

Erigeron karvinskianus

syn. *Erigeron mucronatus*

MEXICAN DAISY, SANTA BARBARA DAISY

☼ ❄ ↔ 24–60 in (60–150 cm) ↑ 12–24 in (30–60 cm)

From highlands of southern Mexico, Central America, and Venezuela. This perennial forms mounds of small toothed leaves on slender stems. Airy masses of small, white to pink, yellow-centered daisies are produced all year round in frost-free areas, from spring to autumn in colder regions. Popular ground cover, but sometimes a weed. Zones 8–11.

Erigeron peregrinus

WANDERING DAISY, WANDERING FLEABANE

☼ ✱ ↔ 16–24 in (40–60 cm) ↑ 16–24 in (40–60 cm)

From western North America. This perennial daisy has narrow oblong or spoon-shaped leaves, to 8 in (20 cm) long. White to purple flowers with yellow centers, solitary or in groups, in summer. Zones 2–9.

Erigeron pulchellus

ROBIN'S PLANTAIN

☼ ✱ ↔ 8–16 in (20–40 cm) ↑ 6–16 in (15–40 cm)

This species is a native of North America. It is a biennial or short-lived perennial with creeping rhizomes. The leaves are spoon-shaped leaves. The dainty pale pink or pale purple daisies with yellow centers appear in summer. Zones 4–9.

Erigeron 'Rosa Jewel'

☼ ✱ ↔ 16–24 in (40–60 cm) ↑ 18–30 in (45–75 cm)

An attractive cultivar with bright pink flowers, which is similar to *E. speciosus*. Zones 3–9.

Erigeron speciosus

☼ ✱ ↔ 16–24 in (40–60 cm) ↑ 18–30 in (45–75 cm)

From northwestern USA. Popular perennial. Prolific blue daisies with yellow centers in summer. *E. s.* var. *macranthus*, slightly larger flowers. There are many cultivars in shades of pink and blue: **'Rosa Jewel'** ★ (syn. 'Pink Jewel'), bright pink flowers; **'Quakeress'**, light mauve-pink flowers. Zones 3–9.

ERINUS

This genus, comprising just 2 species of perennials from North Africa, the Pyrenees, and the Alps, belongs to the plantain (Plantaginaceae) family. They have small, spirally arranged, slightly sticky leaves, and the inflorescences are racemes, borne at the stem tips. The flowers are shortly tubular, expanding at the mouth into 5 spreading petals. The fruit is a capsule with many seeds. Grown as alpines, these perennials are short-lived, but they self-seed in the rock garden. CULTIVATION: Easily grown in sun or part-shade in well-drained soil in the garden or in troughs, but also on walls or soft porous rock and in cracks in paving. They can be grown from fresh seed sown directly in the ground; protect from winter frosts. Many cultivars breed true from seed; others must be propagated from softwood cuttings taken in spring.

Erinus alpinus

ALPINE BALSAM, FAIRY FOXGLOVE

☼ ✱ ↔ 6 in (15 cm) ↑ 4 in (10 cm)

Cushion-forming herb. Leaves to 1 in (25 mm) long, soft, oblanceolate to wedge-shaped, with toothed or wavy margins, covered with sticky hairs. Abundant purple or white flowers late spring and summer. **'Doktor Hähnle'**, deep crimson flowers; **'Mrs Charles Boyle'**, pink flowers. Zones 4–9.

ERIOBOTRYA

This genus belonging to the rose (Rosaceae) family consists of about 10 species of evergreen trees and shrubs found from the eastern Himalayas to Southeast Asia and China. They are all tough plants with dull green, leathery, strongly veined leaves, felted underneath. The felted buds held at the branch tips develop into scented creamy flower clusters in the autumn. The showy, fragrant, fleshy, edible fruits are sweet, soft, and juicy at full ripeness. The best known species is the loquat, *E. japonica,* which is both edible and decorative, but attracts birds and fruit fly. CULTIVATION: These plants prefer subtropical conditions; although they are generally drought-tolerant, they need abundant moisture in winter to produce good fruit. All except strongly alkaline soils are suitable. Seedlings are easily propagated but variable, often producing fruit with large seeds and minimal flesh, but grafted selected varieties are available. Self-sown seedlings are common and the trees survive with little care.

Eriobotrya japonica

LOQUAT

☼ ❄ ↔ 15 ft (4.5 m) ↑ 20 ft (6 m)

Long cultivated in Japan but native to central China. The common name derives from the Cantonese name, *lo kwat.* Evergreen tree valued for its luscious fragrant fruit in early spring. The leaves are large, dull green, and lance-shaped, with prominent veins and woolly undersides, occurring mostly at the branch tips. Flowers (usually self-fertile) developing from woolly buds in autumn. Zones 8–11.

Eriobotrya japonica

Eriogonum grande 'Rubescens'

ERIOGONUM

WILD BUCKWHEAT

Genus from western North America in the knotweed (Polygonaceae) family. which includes about 150 annuals, perennials, and small evergreen shrubs of varied habit, most of which grow from a basal rosette of leaves. Small flowers appear in dense clusters or umbels, and the fruit is a 3-angled achene. *Eriogonum* species are good rockery or background plants for drier gardens and are also grown for cut and dried flower arrangements.

CULTIVATION: Adaptable to a wide range of climates, they will grow in sun or part-shade in a well-drained, preferably sandy, soil. They require plenty of water in warm conditions but need to be drier in winter. Remove spent flowerheads. Propagate from seed sown in spring or from cuttings. The root clumps of perennial species may be divided.

Eriogonum arborescens

SANTA CRUZ ISLAND BUCKWHEAT

☼/◐ ❄ ↔5 ft (1.5 m) ↑5 ft (1.5 m)

From California, USA. Peeling bark. Narrow near-linear leaves with slightly rolled edges and felted undersides. White to pale pink flowers, in downy inflorescences 2–6 in (5–15 cm) wide, in early summer–autumn. Good cut flower. Zones 9–10.

Eriogonum fasciculatum

CALIFORNIA BUCKWHEAT

☼ ❄ ↔4 ft (1.2 m) ↑3 ft (0.9 m)

From Utah, Nevada, and California, USA, and Baja California, Mexico. Spreading shrub with upright stems at its center. Leaves dark green to gray, hairy on upper surfaces, with white-felted undersides. White to pale pink flowers ageing to red-brown in spring–autumn. **'Theodore Payne'** ★, prostrate form. Zones 7–11.

Eriogonum flavum

YELLOW BUCKWHEAT

☼ ❄ ↔7–10 in (18–25 cm) ↑4–9 in (10–22 cm)

From western Canada and the northern Rocky Mountains region of the USA. Low-growing perennial herb, woody at base. Mat-forming rosettes of oval-shaped grayish green leaves, to 4 in (10 cm) long, slightly hairy above and densely woolly underneath. Umbels of lemon yellow flowers are sometimes tinged with red, in the early summer. Zones 3–9.

Eriogonum giganteum

SAINT CATHERINE'S LACE

☼ ❄ ↔10 ft (3 m) ↑8 ft (2.4 m)

From the Santa Barbara Islands off southern California, USA. A rounded evergreen shrub, with a central trunk, and oval, leathery, grayish white leaves. The flat clusters of woolly flowerheads, to 12 in (30 cm) across, appearing in summer, are white slowly fading to rusty red. Zones 9–11.

Eriogonum grande

syn. *Eriogonum latifolium subsp. grande*

☼ ❄ ↔20–36 in (50–90 cm) ↑18–24 in (45–60 cm)

Native to California, USA. Rare, low-growing, shrubby perennial. Curling oblong to oval leaves, to 4 in (10 cm) long, with dense white down underneath. The flat-topped heads of white to pale pink flowers appear in summer– early autumn. **'Rubescens'**, a lower, more sprawling, form, with large leaves, and big clusters of rose pink flowers. Zones 8–10.

Eriogonum parishii

☼ ❄ ↔18–24 in (45–60 cm) ↑12–18 in (30–45 cm)

Native to southern California and Arizona, USA, and the mountains of northern Baja California, Mexico, this

Eriogonum parishii

species grows in denuded areas in gritty soils. It is an annual with a small basal rosette. The inflorescence, a mist-like mass of fine stalks with minute reddish flowers, appears in the late summer–autumn. Zones 8–11.

Eriogonum umbellatum

SULFUR FLOWER

☼ ❄ ↔3–4 ft (0.9–1.2 m) ↑6–18 in (15–45 cm)

From northwestern USA and southwestern Canada. This variable, low-spreading, perennial herb has rosettes of spatula-shaped, purplish-tinged, stalked leaves, finely hairy underneath, in winter. Bears loose ball-like clusters of bright sulfur yellow or cream flowers in summer. Zones 6–10.

Eriogonum wrightii

BASTARD SAGE, SHRUBBY WILD BUCKWHEAT, WRIGHT'S BUCKWHEAT

☼ ❄ ↔1–5 ft (0.3–1.5 m) ↑3–24 in (7–60 cm)

From southwestern USA and adjacent Mexico. Low branched perennial or shrub. Small elliptical to sword-shaped leaves with fine white hairs underneath. Tight heads of white or pink flowers, arranged in a spike, on stalks to 10 in (25 cm) tall, in summer. ***E. w.* var. *subscaposum***, from dry rocky Californian mountain sites, prostrate, mat-forming. Zones 6–10.

ERIOPHYLLUM

In the daisy (Asteraceae) family, this genus comprises 13 species of annual or perennial herbs or subshrubs from western North America. They usually grow in dry, exposed, rocky regions. Perennial species are generally small, closely branched, and woody at the base. Stems and leaves are often woolly. The cheerful yellow flowers are held above the foliage. Rather short-lived; their hardiness varies with the species. Many are attractive to butterflies.

CULTIVATION: Grow in full sun in well-drained soil and water moderately. Easily propagated from seed or from cuttings, or by division.

Eriophyllum lanatum

GOLDEN YARROW, OREGON SUNSHINE, WOOLLY SUNFLOWER

☼ ❄ ↔24 in (60 cm) ↑12–24 in (30–60 cm)

From southern California, USA, to northern British Columbia and the Rocky Mountains in Canada. This is a subshrub perennial with blue-gray woolly leaves. The long-lasting, star-shaped, daisy-like flowers appear in mid-spring–late summer; deadhead for a second flowering. Drought tolerant. Zones 5–9.

ERODIUM

HERONSBILL, STORKSBILL

Genus in the geranium (Geraniaceae) family, including 60 species of perennials and a few annuals and subshrubs. They are found in sunny rocky areas in mountainous regions of Europe, Asia, Australia, and South America. Some are mat-forming, others are erect, growing to 20 in (50 cm) tall. The leaves are lobed or pinnately divided, often finely and ornately, sometimes silvery gray. The charming 5-petalled flowers resemble cranesbill geraniums but have 5 rather than 10 stamens. Some species carry male and female flowers on separate plants. The flowers are pink, red, purple, blue, yellow, or white, and often veined or stained with darker tones. The common names refer to the elongated tapering seed vessels.

CULTIVATION: Grow small species in rockeries, pots, or a greenhouse; taller plants are ideal in borders. Heronsbills need full sun and well-drained slightly alkaline soil. Propagate annuals from seed; perennials from seed or cuttings, or by division.

Erodium absinthoides

syns *Erodium armenum, E. haradjianii*

☼ ❄ ↔12 in (30 cm) ↑8 in (20 cm)

From southeastern Europe and Asia Minor. Perennial. Grayish green ferny foliage. Male and female flowers on separate plants. White, pink, or violet starry flowers, to ¾ in (18 mm) across, in spring–summer. Zones 6–9.

Erodium absinthoides

Erodium cheilanthifolium
syn. *Erodium petraeum subsp. crispum*
☼ ✱ ↔ 12 in (30 cm) ↕ 6 in (15 cm)
From Spain and Morocco. Perennial. Low clumps of finely divided grayish leaves. Flowers are dainty white to pale pink flowers with purplish veins and blotches, to ¾ in (18 mm), in spring–summer. Zones 6–9.

Erodium chrysanthum
☼ ❄ ↔ 12–16 in (30–40 cm)
↕ 4–6 in (10–15 cm)
From Greece. Low tufts of ferny silvery leaves. Male and female flowers on separate plants. Saucer-shaped creamy lemon flowers, to ¾ in (18 mm) across, in summer. Zones 7–10.

Erodium × *kolbianum* ★
☼ ✱ ↔ 8 in (20 cm) ↕ 6 in (15 cm)
Hybrid of garden origin. Fern-like bluish-gray foliage. The sprays of small flowers, vary in color from white to pale rose. **'Natasha'** ★, white flowers, which are heavily veined and marked with maroon. Zones 6–9.

Eryngium alpinum

Erodium 'Pickering Pink'
☼ ❄ ↔ 8 in (20 cm) ↕ 4 in (10 cm)
A hybrid cultivar with fern-like slightly silvery foliage. The flowers are two-toned, white beneath and pink above, marked with darker veins and blotches. Zones 7–10.

Erodium reichardii
ALPINE GERANIUM
☼ ❄ ↔ 10 in (25 cm)
↕ 1–2 in (25–50 mm)
From Majorca and Corsica. This mat-forming species has small, crinkled, scallop-edged leaves. It produces delicate white flowers with pink veins, to ½ in (12 mm) across, in summer. **'Charm'**, white flowers. Zones 7–10.

Erodium × *variabile*
☼ ❄ ↔ 10 in (25 cm)
↕ 6–12 in (15–30 cm)
These hybrids of *E. corsicum* and *E. reichardii* that are intermediate between the parents. **'Bishop's Form'**, deep pink flowers with reddish veins; **'Derek'** (syn. *E. reichardii* 'Derek'), very compact, with deep pink flowers; **'Flora Pleno'**, small, pale or deep pink, double flowers; **'Roseum'**, pink flowers veined with crimson. Zones 7–10.

Eryngium × *oliverianum*

Erodium chrysanthum

ERYNGIUM
Belonging to the carrot (Apiaceae) family, this genus of well over 200 species of annuals, biennials, and perennials is found throughout most of the temperate world. Although the flower stems often carry rudimentary leaves, the foliage, which can be very spiny, is almost entirely basal, often forming a large clump. Unlike most umbellifers, with their open airy flowerheads, the flowerheads of *Eryngium* are thistle-like, with the flowers clustered in a central cone surrounded by spiny bracts, often in shades of metallic blue or silver gray. Flowerheads and foliage last well when cut and have a certain charm when dried. Summer is the main flowering season for this genus.
CULTIVATION: Their hardiness varies with different species, though most will tolerate at least moderate frosts. Although some are drought tolerant, most are comfortable in a moist well-drained soil with regular watering during the growing season. Propagate by division or from the seed, which germinates readily.

Eryngium alpinum
☼/◐ ✱ ↔ 24 in (60 cm) ↕ 24 in (60 cm)
From western France to the Balkans. This perennial has long-stemmed leaves, which are deeply lobed, spiny, triangular to heart-shaped, and up to 6 in (15 cm) long. The purple-blue flowerheads are surrounded by a large feathery ruff of spiny, 2½ in (6 cm) long, metallic purple-blue bracts. The cultivar **'Blue Star'** grows to 30 in (75 cm) tall, and has bracts more blue than purple. Zones 6–9.

Eryngium amethystinum
AMETHYST SEA HOLLY
☼/◐ ❄ ↔ 20 in (50 cm) ↕ 28 in (70 cm)
Found around the Adriatic to Sicily. Perennial. Leaves to 6 in (15 cm) long, palmately lobed and further divided into narrow spine-tipped segments. Many near-spherical purple-blue flowerheads surrounded by narrow, spiny, purple-tinted bracts, to 2 in (5 cm) long. Zones 7–9.

Eryngium bourgatii
☼/◐ ✱ ↔ 16 in (40 cm) ↕ 16 in (40 cm)
Native to Spain and the Pyrenees. Perennial forming low clump of foliage. Leaves much-divided, spiny, rounded, to 3 in (8 cm) across. Branching inflorescence of many flowerheads, to over ½ in (12 mm) in width, with up to 12 narrow light mauve-blue bracts, not always spiny. **'Oxford Blue'**, attractive silver-blue flowerheads and bracts. Zones 5–10.

Eryngium giganteum
MISS WILLMOTT'S GHOST
☼/◐ ✱ ↔ 32 in (80 cm) ↕ 5 ft (1.5 m)
This species is native to the Caucasus. A perennial with long-stemmed leaves that are triangular in shape, up to 6 in (15 cm) long, deeply toothed, and spiny. It produces a green to silvery mauve-blue flowerhead, surrounded by up to 10 large, spiny, silver-white bracts. Zones 6–9.

Eryngium 'Jos Eijking'
☼/◐ ✱ ↔ 16 in (40 cm)
↕ 24–32 in (60–80 cm)
Dutch perennial hybrid of uncertain parentage. It forms a compact clump of deeply lobed spiny basal foliage. Striking bright metallic blue flowerheads and similarly colored, narrow, spiny bracts. Zones 6–9.

Eryngium × *oliverianum*
☼/◐ ✱ ↔ 20–24 in (50–60 cm)
↕ 24–40 in (60–100 cm)
Garden hybrid between *E. alpinum* and possibly *E. giganteum*. Perennial with long-stemmed, spiny, toothed leaves, rounded to heart-shaped, with 3 lobes on basal leaves. Bright metallic blue flowerheads, to 1¾ in (40 mm) across, with up to 15 narrow, spiny, purple bracts. Zones 5–9.

Eryngium pandanifolium
☼/◐ ❄ ↔ 20–24 in (50–60 cm)
↕ 7–8 ft (2–2.4 m)
Native to Brazil, Argentina, Uruguay, and Paraguay. Perennial, which forms a basal clump of narrow serrated leaves and many strongly upright, branching flower stems with many small heads of small-bracted purple flowers. *E. p.* var. *lasseauxii*, white flowerheads, the most commonly grown. Zones 8–10.

Eryngium planum
☼/◐ ✱ ↔ 24 in (60 cm)
↕ 40 in (100 cm)
The native habitat of this species ex-tends from central Europe to central Asia. Perennial. Leaves dark green, oval, with spine-tipped lobes. Many small purple-blue flowerheads with up to 8 spiny narrow bracts, to 1 in (25 mm) long. Zones 4–9.

Eryngium variifolium

Eryngium serra

☼/◐ ❄ ↔ 40 in (100 cm) ↑ 7 ft (2 m)

From Brazil and Argentina. Perennial forming a basal clump of spine-edged sword-shaped leaves, to 24 in (60 cm) long. Strongly upright flower stems with many small white flowerheads, each with up to 9 tiny greenish white bracts. Zones 8–11.

Eryngium × *tripartitum*

☼/◐ ❄ ↔ 24–32 in (60–80 cm) ↑ 48 in (120 cm)

Natural hybrid perennial of unknown parentage. Leaves dark green, trifoliate, with spine-tipped, coarsely toothed, lance-shaped segments. Blue-green flower stems with metallic blue flowerheads, less than ½ in (12 mm) across, and up to 9 narrow blue-green bracts, to about 1 in (25 mm) long. Zones 5–9.

Eryngium variifolium

☼/◐ ❄ ↔ 16–20 in (40–50 cm) ↑ 20–30 in (50–75 cm)

Native to North Africa. An evergreen perennial forming a thistle-like basal rosette of white-marbled, dark green, toothed leaves. Flowerheads are purple-blue, to 1 in (25 mm) across, with up to 7 narrow, spiny, white-centered bracts. Zones 7–9.

Eryngium yuccifolium

BUTTON SNAKEROO, RATTLESNAKE MASTER

☼/◐ ❄ ↔ 5 ft (1.5 m) ↑ 6 ft (1.8 m)

From eastern and central USA. Perennial species with basal clump of sword-shaped fiercely spiny leaves, to 36 in (100 cm) long. Strong, upright flower stems bear white to blue flowerheads, to 1 in (25 mm) across, and up to 10 bracts, to ½ in (12 mm) long. Zones 4–9.

ERYSIMUM

syn. *Cheiranthus*

WALLFLOWER

A genus in the cabbage (Brassicaceae) family, comprising some 80 species of sometimes shrubby annuals and perennials, now includes many species formerly classified under *Cheiranthus*. The narrow green to blue-green leaves with shallow lobes are unremarkable, but the 4-petalled flowers are brightly colored, often fragrant, and frequently appear over a long season. In mild climates the bushy forms flower all year round. The hybrids come in many colors.

CULTIVATION: Although most species of *Erysimum* are very hardy, they prefer a temperate climate with distinct seasons. Plant in moist humus-rich soil and water well during the flowering period. Often quite drought tolerant, but these plants will flower more abundantly with regular watering, feeding, trimming, and deadheading. Propagation of annual species is by seed; perennials can be propagated from seed, from small cuttings of non-flowering stems, or sometimes by division.

Erysimum bicolor

syn. *Cheiranthus bicolor*

☼/◐ ❄ ↔ 24 in (60 cm) ↑ 36 in (90 cm)

Found in the Canary Islands and Madeira. A shrubby perennial with pointed, toothed, lance-shaped leaves. The scented flowers of this species appear from spring onward, opening cream to orange-brown and ageing to mauve. Zones 9–10.

Erysimum cheiri

syn. *Cheiranthus cheiri*

WALLFLOWER

☼/◐ ❄ ↔ 16 in (40 cm) ↑ 24 in (60 cm)

A native of southern Europe. This shrubby perennial is usually cultivated as a biennial. The foliage is narrow and deep green; the lower leaves to 8 in (20 cm) long, becoming smaller higher up. Produces large heads of yellow and/or orange flowers. The cultivated forms, which are most likely hybrids, include: **'Cloth of Gold'**, a deep golden yellow; **Fair Lady** (quite often called **My Fair Lady**) **Strain**, to 18 in (45 cm) tall, offering blooms in a range of pastel shades; **'Fire King Improved'**, growing to 16 in (40 cm) tall, with brilliant orange-red flowers; **'Harpur Crewe'**, yellow double flowers; **Prince Series**, stocky, to 18 in (45 cm) tall, in a wide color range and usually given a color name, for example, **'Prince Primrose Yellow'**. Zones 7–9.

Erysimum kotschyanum

☼/◐ ❄ ↔ 6–8 in (15–20 cm) ↑ 2–4 in (5–10 cm)

This species is a native of Turkey. It is a small tufted perennial, which makes dense mats of narrow, toothed, light green leaves less than ½ in (12 mm) long. It produces long, small, yellow to pale orange flowers in the summer. Zones 6–10.

Erysimum mutabile

syn. *Cheiranthus mutabilis*

☼ ❄ ↔ 18–24 in (45–60 cm) ↑ 18–32 in (45–80 cm)

Long-flowering perennial or subshrub from Canary Islands and Madeira. Woody base. Narrow, sometimes bluish leaves to 3 in (8 cm) long. Flowers open yellow to buff and age to purple. Blooms year-round in mild areas. **'Winter Joy'**, reliable winter-flowering cultivar. Zones 8–10.

Erysimum pulchellum

☼/◐ ❄ ↔ 12–16 in (30–40 cm) ↑ 16–24 in (40–60 cm)

From Eurasia. Perennial. Whorls of toothed spatula-shaped leaves. Golden yellow flowers from spring. The cream variegated form **'Variegatum'** is more common than the species. Zones 6–9.

Erysimum Hybrid Cultivars

☼/◐ ❄ ↔ 24 in (60 cm) ↑ 24–36 in (60–90 cm)

These bushy hybrids are of uncertain parentage but may be hybrids between *E. bicolor* and *E. perofskianum*. Though not long-lasting, they are easily propagated and flower virtually continuously. The best known, **'Bowles' Mauve'** ★ (syn. 'E. A. Bowles'), produces masses of small mauve-purple flowers; **'Gold Shot'**, 18 in (45 cm) tall, golden yellow flowers; **'Sunlight'**, yellow-flowered low spreader, about 4 in (10 cm) tall, and probably with *E. helveticum* and/or *E. kotschyanum* in its background; **'Wenlock Beauty'**, with flowers magenta and ageing to mauve; **'Winter Cheer'**, two-tone orange and light purple flowers. Zones 7–10.

ERYTHRINA

CORAL TREE

A member of the pea-flower subfamily of the legume (Fabaceae) family this genus of over 100 mainly tropical deciduous or semi-evergreen trees, perennials, and shrubs is distributed globally in warm-temperate to tropical regions. Stems, branches, and even the leaflet midribs may be armed with conical or curved prickles. The compound leaves have 3 broad leaflets and inflorescences are erect to drooping racemes of showy tubular to bell-shaped flowers with the upper petal longer than the other petals. Flowers in deciduous species usually precede leaves. The fruits are elongated pods, narrowed between the seeds. They are grown as an ornamental summer shade tree. Some species have medicinal properties; others may be poisonous. The seeds are used to make necklaces.

CULTIVATION: Species of *Erythrina* prefer a warm dry climate and thrive in sandy, moist, but well-drained soils in sunny exposed positions in coastal environments. They are easily propagated from seed sown in spring and summer, and from cuttings of growing wood; the rootstock of herbaceous species may be divided. While fairly free of pests, mites can be a problem in drier weather.

Erysimum cheiri, 'Fair Lady Strain'

Erythrina acanthocarpa

Erythrina zeyheri

Erythrina acanthocarpa

TAMBOOKIE THORN

↔ 6 ft (1.8 m) ↕ 6 ft (1.8 m)

From the Cape region of South Africa. A deciduous stiff shrub with many thorny stems with bluish green leaflets arising from a large underground root. The clusters of showy, pea-flower-like, scarlet blooms are tipped with green in late spring–early summer. Prickly bean-like pods. Zones 9–11.

Erythrina × *bidwillii* ★

HYBRID CORAL TREE

↔ 10 ft (3 m) ↕ 12 ft (3.5 m)

Originated in Australia as a garden hybrid between *E. crista-galli* and *E. herbacea*. A deciduous shrub suited to drier gardens. The pale to mid-green trifoliate leaves, to 4 in (10 cm) long, on prickly stems. Striking dark red flowers with the upper petal to 2 in (5 cm) long, in threes, in spring–early summer. Zones 9–11, or as occasional die-back perennials in zones 8-11.

Erythrina crista-galli

COCKSPUR CORAL TREE, COMMON CORAL TREE

↔ 12–40 ft (3.5–12 m) ↕ 30 ft (9 m)

Native to Brazil. A deciduous species sometimes found as a gnarled old tree with considerable character. If lopped annually, very large red flower clusters appear in spring–summer. *E. crista-galli* can be grown as a potted greenhouse plant in cooler climates; it should be pruned heavily in the late autumn. Zones 9–11, or as occasional die-back perennials in zones 8-11.

Erythrina herbacea

CARDINAL SPEAR, CHEROKEE BEAN, CORAL BEAN, EASTERN CORAL BEAN

↔ 2–6 ft (0.6–1.8 m) ↕ 4–10 ft (1.2–3 m)

From southeastern USA and Mexico. Perennial herb; sometimes a shrub or small tree. The triangular leaflets are held on prickly leaf stalks. Racemes of deep scarlet flowers with the upper petal to 2 in (5 cm) long in summer–autumn. Leathery pods of scarlet seeds. Zones 8–10.

Erythrina humeana

DWARF ERYTHRINA, NATAL CORAL TREE

↔ 7 ft (2 m) ↕ 12 ft (3.5 m)

Native to eastern South Africa and Mozambique. A deciduous shrub or small tree with light gray prickly bark and dark green shiny leaflets. Slender dense racemes, to 20 in (50 cm) long, of scarlet-red, tubular, pea-flower-like blooms, borne at the branch tips, in summer. Bean pods are black or purple. Zones 9–11.

Erythrina crista-galli

Erythronium californicum 'White Beauty'

Erythrina × *sykesii*

syn. *Erythrina indica of gardens*

CORAL TREE

↔ 30 ft (9 m) ↕ 50 ft (15 m)

Deciduous tree of uncertain origin, first appearing in Australia and New Zealand. Squat trunk with ascending branches armed with hooked prickles. Large scarlet pea-flowers, in winter–spring. Very brittle; sheds limbs when windy. Tolerates poor soil and salt-laden air. Easily grown from branches or even wood chips. Zones 9–11.

Erythrina variegata

syn. *Erythrina indica*

CORAL TREE, INDIAN CORAL BEAN, TIGER'S CLAW

↔ 30 ft (9 m) ↕ 30–60 ft (9–18 m)

Widespread along coastlines of tropical Asia, the Indian Ocean, and the western Pacific. Deciduous tree with thick large-prickled branches, grayish green furrowed bark. Large heart-shaped leaflets. Dense clusters of scarlet or crimson pea-flowers, occasionally white, borne at branch tips, in winter. **'Parcellii'**, leaves variegated with light green and yellow. Zones 11–12.

Erythrina zeyheri

PLOUGHBREAKER, PRICKLY CARDINAL

↔ 30 in (75 cm) ↕ 3 ft (0.9 m)

From eastern South Africa. Small very prickly shrub, dying back to large, woody, underground rootstock in autumn and winter. Ovate to diamond-shaped leaflets, thorny beneath, noticeably veined. Racemes of tubular red flowers in mid-summer. Non-hairy woody seed pods, red seeds. Zones 8–10.

ERYTHRONIUM

DOGTOOTH VIOLET, TROUT LILY

A member of the lily (Liliaceae) family, this genus of bulbs is found in the wild in North America, Asia, and across Europe, some species growing in a wide variety of habitats. The flowers, held well above the leaves, hang down, with distinctive, recurved, pointed petals. The shiny leaves fan outward and, in many varieties, are mottled, flecked, or spotted with silver, brown, maroon, or bronze. This striking feature begins to fade as the season progresses.

CULTIVATION: Most thrive in cool damp climates and dappled shade, but those from western North America can, if shaded, tolerate hot dry summers. None like humid heat; majority dislike disturbance. Plant in autumn, always keeping bulbs moist, about 2 in (5 cm) below the surface. Protect from slugs. To propagate, divide as leaves wilt, replanting immediately, or sow fresh seed in rich moisture-retentive soil.

Erythronium albidum

BLONDE LILIAN, WHITE DOGTOOTH VIOLET

↔ 3–6 in (8–15 cm) ↕ 6–12 in (15–30 cm)

From central North America. Long green leaves, rarely mottled. Flowers 1–2 in (2.5–5 cm) long, gleaming white with some yellow, in mid- to late spring. Plant then goes dormant. Eventually forms drifts. Zones 3–9.

Erythronium americanum

ADDER'S TONGUE, AMBERBELL, AMERICAN TROUT LILY, YELLOW ADDER'S TONGUE

↔ 3–6 in (8–15 cm) ↕ 4–10 in (10–25 cm)

From eastern North America. Mottled maroon-purple leaves. Single, nodding, yellow, bell-shaped flowers in early spring. Plant goes dormant in early summer. Eventually forms drifts. Zones 3–9.

Erythronium californicum

FAWN LILY

↔ 6 in (15 cm) ↕ 10 in (25 cm)

From California, USA. Vigorous clump-forming plant found on the north-facing slopes of coastal pine forests. It has mid-green leaves, lightly patterned in purplish green. Flowers, sometimes 3 per stem, appear in spring. The petals are creamy white with brownish to yellow staining on the petal reverse and at the base. Will tolerate some heat. **'White Beauty'** (syn. *E. revolutum* 'White Beauty') is easily grown, with glossy lettuce-green leaves marbled with dark green. It puts on a glamorous show during the spring. The flowers have white petals suffused with a clear cream at their center, and the basal ring is flecked with maroon. Zones 4–9.

Erythronium dens-canis

DOG'S TOOTH VIOLET

↔ 6 in (15 cm) ↕ 6–8 in (15–20 cm)

From cool-temperate Europe and Asia. A variable plant, with white, pale pink, rose pink, or lilac flowers, to 1½ in (35 mm) across, held individually on straight stems, in spring–early summer. These have protruding purple or blue anthers. The leaves are long and mid-green, sometimes mottled or splotched with chocolate brown, purple-green, lettuce green, or silver, and sometimes plain. The common name derives from the elongated fang-like shape of the bulb. *E. dens-canis* can be grown through thin grass. Zones 3–9.

Erythronium hendersonii

Erythronium helenae

↔ 4 in (10 cm)
↑ 6–15 in (15–38 cm)

This species is found on wooded, scrub-covered, moist, volcanic slopes in northwestern California and Mt. St. Helens in Washington, USA. Flowers have white to cream petals, darkening at the center, and cream anthers in the spring. Leaves are green, mottled with chocolate brown. Requires good drainage and a dryish winter. Zones 4–9.

Erythronium hendersonii

TROUT LILY

↔ 4 in (10 cm)
↑ 6–15 in (15–38 cm)

From the pine forests of southwestern Oregon and northwestern California, USA. Flowers are several to a single stem, in spring and mid-summer. Petals dark or pale lilac-pink; anthers and flower centers purple. Leaves dark green, marbled. Requires good drainage and a dry summer. Zones 4–9.

Erythronium oregonum

↔ 10 in (25 cm) ↑ 10 in (25 cm)

From North America. This very variable species is similar in appearance to *E. californicum,* but the stamens have thread-like filaments. The dark green leaves are mottled with brown. The petals are creamy white, with yellow at the base, and the anthers a bright yellow. Produces several flowers per stem in spring. Zones 4–9.

Erythronium 'Pagoda'

↔ 8 in (20 cm)
↑ 6–12 in (15–30 cm)

This is a vigorous decorative hybrid, with glossy, deep green, mottled leaves. The sulfur yellow flowers have deep yellow anthers emerging from a highly visible dark central ring. Each stem bears 3 to 4 blooms, during the spring. Zones 4–9.

Erythronium revolutum

Erythronium revolutum

TROUT LILY

↔ 6 in (15 cm) ↑ 6–8 in (15–20 cm)

From North America. A dainty variable species. The flowers, 3 to 4 per stem, appear in spring. The petals are cyclamen pink, the stamens protruding, cream, spreading, and recurved. The leaves are deep green, marbled, and slightly wavy. There are many named selections. **'Pink Beauty'** produces deep lavender-pink petals. Zones 4–9.

Erythronium tuolumnense

↔ 8 in (20 cm)
↑ 8–15 in (20–38 cm)

Native to the open evergreen forests of central California, USA. The flower production of *E. tuolumnense* is sometimes sparse, with 3 or 4 small flowers per stem in spring. The bright yellow petals are sometimes veined in green, the anthers are yellow. The leaves are plain, pale to mid-green, and are modestly waved at the margins. This species will tolerate hot dry conditions, but it must have shade throughout the summer months. Zones 4–9.

ESCALLONIA

This group of about 60 species of mostly evergreen shrubs and small trees is the type genus for its family, the Escalloniaceae, They are native to temperate regions of South America, and found mainly on hill slopes or exposed coasts in the Andes region. Free-flowering over a long season, they bear panicles or racemes of small white to pink or red flowers with 5 separate petals, though these are usually pressed together in the lower half to form an apparent tube. Leaves are usually small and toothed, sometimes glandular and aromatic. The fruits are small globular capsules that shed fine seed.

CULTIVATION: Not all species are hardy in cold inland areas but most can be grown successfully in exposed coastal gardens. These plants are lime tolerant and drought resistant, and they thrive in almost any well-drained soil in full sun. Prune immediately after flowering, but in cold climates delay this until the early spring. Propagation is from soft-tip cuttings taken in the spring or semi-hardwood tips taken in the autumn.

Escallonia bifida

syn. *Escallonia montevidensis*

WHITE ESCALLONIA

↔ 10–20 ft (3–6 m)
↑ 15–30 ft (4.5–9 m)

From Uruguay and southern Brazil. Small tree. Leaves finely toothed, larger than most species; dark green and slightly shiny on the upper surface, with a whitish midrib, paler beneath. Panicles of sweetly honey-scented white flowers, borne at branch tips, in early to mid-autumn. Zones 8–10.

Escallonia × *exoniensis*

↔ 12 ft (3.5 m) ↑ 15–20 ft (4.5–6 m)

Hybrid of two Chilean species *E. rosea* and *E. rubra*. Strong erect shoots from the base. Young stems are glandular. The leaves are dark lustrous green above, paler beneath. Loose panicles of blush pink to white flowers appear at the tips of branches, in mid-spring to late autumn. **'Frades'**, crimson flowers. Zones 8–10.

Escallonia rubra

syns *Escallonia microphylla, E. punctata*

↔ 15 ft (4.5 m) ↑ 15 ft (4.5 m)

From Chile. Variable shrub. Parent of many hybrids. Aromatic leaves. Loose panicles of deep pink to red flowers in mid-summer. ***E. r.* var. *macrantha*,** rose-crimson flowers set among glossy aromatic leaves; **'C. F. Ball'**, seedling of *E. rubra* var. *macrantha* raised in Scotland, grows to 10 ft (3 m) tall, large aromatic leaves, crimson flowers, excellent for coastal areas; ***E. r.* 'Crimson Spire' ★**, erect habit and bright crimson flowers; **'Woodside'**, low-growing, small leaves, good rock-garden plant. Zones 8–10.

Escallonia × *exoniensis*

Escallonia rubra

Escallonia virgata

↔ 6 ft (1.8 m) ↑ 6 ft (1.8 m)

From Chile. Small-leafed deciduous shrub. Parent of many hybrids. Arching reddish branches. Bright, glossy, green leaves. Racemes of white flowers, borne in leaf axils, in summer. Zones 8–10.

Escallonia Hybrid Cultivars

↔ 6–12 ft (1.8–3.5 m)
↑ 5–10 ft (1.5–3 m)

The most popular hybrids are derived mainly from *E. rubra* and *E. virgata* and originated in the UK and Ireland in the first half of the twentieth century. Most were raised in the Slieve Donard Nursery in County Down, Ireland. **'Apple Blossom'**, suitable for hedging, to 8 ft (2.4 m), short racemes of pink and white flowers; **'Donard Beauty'**, rich rose red flowers, free-flowering, large leaves, aromatic when crushed; **'Donard Radiance'**, bushy plant, rounded, glossy, dark green leaves, to 1¾ in (40 mm) long, clusters of rich pink tubular flowers in summer; **'Donard Seedling'**, vigorous, slightly arching, with oval, deep green, glossy leaves, to 1 in (25 mm) long, clusters of pink-stained white flowers all summer; **'Gold Brian' ★**, bright golden yellow foliage, deep pink flowers; **'Iveyi'**, upright shrub, good for hedging, very dark green glossy leaves, to 2½ in (6 cm) long, dense clusters of white flowers in summer; **'Langleyensis'**, large spreading shrub with oval dark green leaves, to 1 in (25 mm) long, and masses of almost flat bright cerise flowers in summer; **'Peach Blossom'**, medium-sized, and similar in habit to 'Apple Blossom', clear peach pink

Escallonia, HC, 'Pride of Donard'

flowers; '**Pink Pixie**', 32 in (80 cm) high and wide, deep pink flowers; '**Pride of Donard**', racemes of brilliantly rose-colored, somewhat bell-shaped flowers, larger than those of most other species, borne at the branch tips, from mid-summer onward; and '**Slieve Donard**', medium-sized, compact, very hardy, with small leaves and panicles of apple-blossom-pink flowers. Zones 8–10.

ESCHSCHOLZIA

CALIFORNIA POPPY

Native to western North America and now widely naturalized, this genus in the poppy (Papaveraceae) family is made up of about 8 annuals and short-lived perennials. It was named in 1820 for Johann Friedrich Eschscholtz (1793–1831), the leader of the Russian expedition on which it was first collected, in 1816. (The "t" in his name was somehow lost in the transcription.) The seeds were among the many David Douglas took to England. They have fine-feathery foliage, often a rather grayish green, and in summer produce masses of bright golden yellow 4- to 8-petalled poppies that only open on sunny days. Modern seed strains come in many flower colors; the flowers are followed by long seed capsules.

CULTIVATION: Very easily grown in any sunny position with light, gritty, very well-drained soil. Often self-sows and naturalizes, especially in gravel riverbeds. Most are very frost hardy and tolerate poor soil. Propagate from seed, which is best sown directly where it is required to grow.

Eschscholzia caespitosa

TUFTED CALIFORNIA POPPY

↔ 10 in (25 cm) ↑ 10 in (25 cm)

From northern California and Oregon, USA. Annual. The leaves are very finely divided, feathery, green to blue-green. Bright yellow flowers, 2 in (5 cm) across. '**Sundew**', to 6 in (15 cm) tall, lemon yellow flowers. Zones 7–10.

Eschscholzia californica

CALIFORNIA POPPY

↔ 8–16 in (20–40 cm) ↑ 8–24 in (20–60 cm)

From western USA and northern Baja California, Mexico. Now a weed in parts of Australia. Annual or short-lived perennial. Leaves variable but usually finely divided, feathery, blue-green. Flowers to over 2 in (5 cm) across, usually orange but often yellow, rarely cream or pink. Seedling strains in many colors and forms, including double flowers. '**Dali**', interesting soft apricot-colored cultivar with two rows of petals; **Jelly Beans Mix**, semi-double flowers, mainly warm shades; '**Peach Sorbet**', semi-double, peach to soft apricot tones; '**Red Chief**', striking red flowers; '**Summer Sorbet**', rose pink shading to cream center, ruffled petals. Zones 6–10.

Eschscholzia lobbii

FRYING PANS

↔ 12 in (30 cm) ↑ 12 in (30 cm)

From California's Central Valley, USA. Annual. Sticky green foliage and stems. Leaves finely divided and grass-like. Bright yellow flowers, to 2 in (5 cm) across. Similar to *E. caespitosa;* often sold under that name. Zones 7–10.

ESPOSTOA

A genus of 16 beautiful columnar cacti from Bolivia, Ecuador, and Peru that belong to the family Cactaceae. The genus was named in honor of the early twentieth-century Peruvian botanist, Nicholas Esposto. The plants are shrubby to columnar and bear a long lateral cephalium on mature branches. Young plants are often clothed in a dense web of white wool, which protects them from their extremely harsh desert environment. The cylindrical branches bear many ribs. The night-blooming flowers are usually creamy white to reddish. The seed pods are spherical, juicy, and red to green, and may be naked or covered in tufts of hair. The genus now includes all former species of *Thrixanthocereus* and *Pseudoespostoa* and some species of *Facheiroa*.

CULTIVATION: Easily grown in rich well-drained soil; withhold water in winter to avoid root rot. Grows faster in open ground than in pots. Propagate either from seed or from cuttings dried out for a week or two.

Eschscholzia californica

Espostoa melanostele

Espostoa lanata ★

COTTON BALL CACTUS, OLD MAN OF THE ANDES

↔ 3–10 ft (0.9–3 m) ↑ 7–25 ft (2–8 m)

Found from southern Ecuador to northern Peru. One of the most popular of all cacti. Columnar to shrubby, the erect stems clothed in pure white wool, especially noticeable on seedlings. Ribs 20 to 25; central spines sparse, to 2 in (50 mm) long, often absent, radials numerous, short. Cephalium of light gray to brown wool, to 15 ft (4.5 m) long; this is used in Peru to stuff pillows. The purple funnel-shaped flowers are 1¼ in (30 mm) across, and the pear-shaped seed pods are plum-colored. Zones 9–11.

Espostoa melanostele

↔ 40–60 in (100–150 cm) ↑ 7 ft (2 m)

From northern to central Peru. These shrubby plants branch from the base. Ribs 20 to 35, with dense white to brown hair. Spines white or yellow, the central ones becoming black, to ½ in (12 mm) long. Cephalium white, yellow, or brown, to 28 in (70 cm) long. White bell-shaped flowers, to 2½ in (6 cm) long, 2 in (5 cm) across, appear in summer. Spherical green to red seed pods. Zones 8–11.

Espostoa senilis ★

↔ 3–7 ft (0.9–2 m) ↑ 7–15 ft (2–4.5 m)

A native of Ancash in Peru. Shrubby to tree-like plants. The branches are gray-green, covered with brownish white hairs. Ribs 16 to 18. The 1 to 3 central spines are brown, to 1¼ in (30 mm) long; the 60 or more radial spines are white, ½ in (12 mm) long. Purple flowers, to 2½ in (6 cm) long, 1¾ in (40 mm) across. Spherical green seed pods, ¾ in (18 mm) in diameter. Zones 9–11.

EUCALYPTUS

Most of the approximately 800 species of this large genus of evergreen trees are endemic to Australia; a few are found in New Guinea and southeastern Indonesia, with one *(E. deglupta)* re-stricted to the southern Philippines and eastern New Guinea. This genus be-longs to the myrtle (Myrtaceae) family and is noted for its aromatic leaves dotted with oil glands. Species vary in size from immense forest trees to the small multi-stemmed shrubs collectively called mallees. The distinctive bark types of these plants give rise to many of the common names. Most species have 2 distinctive types of foliage: opposite juvenile leaves and alternate adult leaves. The flowers have numerous fluffy stamens, which may be white, cream, yellow, pink, or red; in bud the stamens are enclosed in a cap known as an operculum, which is composed of the fused sepals or petals or both. As the

Eucalyptus cinerea

Eucalyptus cordata

stamens expand, the operculum is forced off, splitting away from the cup-like base of the flower; this is one of the main features that unites the genus. The fruit is a woody capsule. Eucalypts are cultivated in many parts of the world and used for many purposes. Their flowers are rich in nectar; some species are among the world's finest honey plants. In a recent reclassification over 100 species have been split off from *Eucalyptus* to form the genus *Corymbia,* including a few well known as ornamentals, such as the Western Australian red-flowering gum and the lemon-scented gum.

CULTIVATION: The great majority of species are fast growing and long lived, and once established require very little artificial watering or fertilizer. They are best suited to semi-arid or warm-temperate regions. Frost hardiness varies between species, as does the need for moist or dry conditions. Some of the Western Australian mallees dislike summer humidity. Most species can be shaped by pruning or cut back heavily if desired. Propagation is from seed, which germinates readily.

Eucalyptus cinerea

ARGYLE APPLE, SILVER DOLLAR TREE

↔ 30 ft (9 m) ↑ 50 ft (15 m)

From southeastern Australia. Fairly short trunk. Dense spreading crown. Juvenile foliage circular, silvery gray;

Eucalyptus grandis

adult foliage often absent. Small white flowers in early summer. Moderately fast growing; retains lower branches to near ground level. Zones 8–11.

Eucalyptus cordata

SILVER GUM

↔ 10 ft (3 m) ↑ 60 ft (18 m)

From Tasmania, Australia. The smooth white bark is mottled with green and purplish patches. The attractive, silvery gray, heart-shaped juvenile leaves, to 4 in (10 cm) long, often persist on more mature trees. A profusion of creamy white flowers is produced in the spring. Fast-growing. Cut foliage from this species is used for floral decoration. Zones 8–9.

Eucalyptus grandis

FLOODED GUM

↔ 30–50 ft (9–15 m) ↑ 200 ft (60 m)

From the coastal districts of eastern Australia. Straight shaft-like trunk with a short stocking of persistent fibrous bark at the base, and smooth powdery white bark above. The adult leaves are narrow and dark green. This eucalypt bears clusters of small white flowers in winter. It is a fast-growing tree, successful in plantation forests. Zones 9–12.

Eucalyptus gunnii

CIDER GUM

↔ 25 ft (8 m) ↑ 80 ft (24 m)

Found in the highlands of Tasmania, Australia. The smooth gray-pink to reddish brown bark is shed in late summer. The juvenile leaves are glaucous, gray-green, rounded, and stem-clasping. When adult, the leaves become narrow and stalked. Small creamy white flowers are borne in spring– summer. This species is popular in the UK and the USA for its cut foliage. Zones 7–9.

Eucalyptus jacksonii

RED TINGLE

↔ 35–60 ft (10–18 m) ↑ 200 ft (60 m)

One of Western Australia's largest trees. Trunk up to 15 ft (4.5 m) in diameter, with brownish stringy bark persisting to the small branches, Dense canopy of glossy bright green leaves. Small white flowers in summer. Zones 9–10.

Eucalyptus leucoxylon

SOUTH AUSTRALIAN BLUE GUM, YELLOW GUM

↔ 20–40 ft (6–12 m) ↑ 100 ft (30 m)

Woodland tree from southeastern South Australia and western Victoria. Single straight trunk with smooth creamy yellow or bluish gray bark, shedding in irregular flakes. The narrow gray-green adult leaves hang vertically. The profusion of white, cream, pink, or red flowers, hang in pendulous clusters of 3, in late autumn to spring; they are attractive to nectar-feeding birds. Pink- and red-flowered forms are often sold under the name **'Rosea'**. Zones 9–11.

Eucalyptus ligustrina

PRIVET-LEAFED STRINGYBARK

↔ 20 ft (6 m) ↑ 25 ft (8 m)

From eastern Australia. Mallee or small tree. Stringy bark persisting on trunk and main branches, shedding in flakes on smaller branches. The adult leaves are lance-shaped, glossy green, to 3 in (8 cm) long; the juvenile leaves are much smaller. Winter flowering, producing a mass of creamy white flowers. Zones 9–11.

Eucalyptus macrocarpa

MOTTLECAH

↔ 12 ft (3.5 m) ↑ 6–12 ft (1.8–3.5 m)

From Western Australia. Mallee shrub with the largest flowers and fruit of any of the eucalypts. Stems, new bark, and buds powdery gray. Leaves are broadly ovate, silvery gray, thick-textured, and stem-clasping. Showy deep pink to red flowers in late winter–spring. Woody seed capsules, to 4 in (10 cm) wide. Best in winter-rainfall areas. Zones 9–10.

Eucalyptus mannifera

BRITTLE GUM

↔ 30 ft (9 m) ↑ 70 ft (21 m)

Widespread in southeastern Australia. Powdery white, cream, or gray bark, smooth to ground level, turning reddish before shedding in patches. Open canopy of narrow, gray-green, drooping leaves. The clusters of small white flowers are borne through summer and autumn. This is an attractive street tree. **'Little Spotty'**, dense bushy form to around 25 ft (8 m) tall. Zones 8–10.

Eucalyptus marginata

JARRAH

↔ 40 ft (12 m) ↑ 120 ft (36 m)

From the southwestern corner of Western Australia. Straight trunk with rough, reddish brown to gray, fibrous bark. Dense canopy of dark green, pointed, lance-shaped leaves, to 5 in (12 cm) long. Showy clusters of nectar-rich creamy white flowers in spring. One of Australia's most important hardwood trees. Zones 9–10.

Eucalyptus megacornuta

WARTY YATE

↔ 10 ft (3 m) ↑ 40 ft (12 m)

From the Ravensthorpe Range in Western Australia. An ornamental tall shrub or a small tree with an open crown and dull green sickle-shaped leaves. Smooth gray bark mottled with red and green. The specific epithet *megacornuta* refers to the large, horn-like, warty bud caps. Showy yellow-green flowers in spring. Zones 9–11.

Eucalyptus melliodora

YELLOW BOX

↔ 35–50 ft (10–15 m) ↑ 100 ft (30 m)

From eastern Australia. Bark variable, usually rough and fibrous on trunk and lower branches, smooth and white on upper parts. Adult leaves grayish green, to 6 in (15 cm) long. Profuse sweetly scented, white or, rarely, pink flowers in summer. Valued as an ornamental shade tree and for honey. Zones 9–11.

Eucalyptus microcorys

TALLOWWOOD

↔ 40 ft (12 m) ↑ 60–180 ft (18–55 m)

From eastern Australia. Distinctive soft, fibrous, reddish brown bark. Dense spreading crown. Thin-textured dark green leaves. Showy clusters of creamy white flowers in winter–early summer. Yields valuable hardwood. Excellent shade and shelter tree. Zones 10–12.

Eucalyptus neglecta

OMEO GUM

↔ 25 ft (7.5 m) ↑ 60 ft (18 m)

From the mountains of south-eastern Australia. Upright tree to 60 ft (18m). Bark is stringy and light orange with pungent 4–5 in (10–12.5 cm) ovate leaves with a distinct blue cast. Somewhat less likely than other spp to lean away from shade, and tolerates the heat of the south-eastern USA. Zones 7–10.

Eucalyptus nicholii

NARROW-LEAFED BLACK PEPPERMINT

↔ 20–40 ft (6–12 m) ↑ 50 ft (15 m)

From eastern Australia. Fast-growing. Relatively short trunk, fibrous brown bark. Compact crown. Pendulous, fine, sickle-shaped, blue-green leaves. Small white flowers in autumn. Zones 8–11.

Eucalyptus parvula

syn. *Eucalyptus parvifolia*

SMALL-LEAFED GUM

↔ 10–20 ft (3–6 m)
↑ 15–25 ft (4.5–8 m)

From southeastern New South Wales, Australia, occurring in a small area of tablelands above 3,000 ft (900 m) on somewhat boggy soils. Small bushy tree, often branching near ground level, with a broad umbrella-shaped crown. Grayish bark, shedding in strips, exposing smooth gray to pinkish surface. Juvenile leaves opposite, stalkless, oval, green, to 1¾ in (4 cm) long, often persisting well into the crown; adult leaves to about 3 in (7 cm) long. The inflorescences, which carry 7 small white flowers, appear in the summer. Zones 8–10.

Eucalyptus pauciflora

SNOW GUM, WHITE SALLY

↔ 20 ft (6 m) ↑ 60 ft (18 m))

From the mountains of southeastern Australia. Short trunk with smooth, mottled, light gray, white, or yellowish bark, shedding in irregular patches. The adult leaves are shiny, leathery, blue-green, to 8 in (20 cm) long. Profuse nectar-rich white blossoms in spring–summer. E. p. **subsp.** niphophila (syn. E. niphophila), commonly known as the alpine snow gum, occurring above 5,000 ft (1,500 m) in the Snowy Mountains of New South Wales and Victoria; low-branching habit; attractive bark that sheds to leave a smooth white or gray surface with patches of orange, red, yellow, and olive green; shiny blue-green leaves; glaucous buds and fruit. Zones 8–10.

Eucalyptus perriniana

SPINNING GUM

↔ 10–20 ft (3–6 m)
↑ 20–40 ft (6–12 m)

From subalpine areas of southeastern Australia. Mallee-like small tree. Bark sheds to leave a smooth whitish gray surface with pale brown and green patches. Juvenile leaves powdery gray, fused into disk around twig; adult leaves dull gray-green, lance-shaped. Profuse creamy white flowers in summer. Juvenile leaves popular as cut foliage for floral arrangements. Zones 8–10.

EUCHARIS

AMAZON LILY

Found from Guatemala to Bolivia, this is an Amaryllis (Amaryllidaceae) family genus of up to 20 species of evergreen bulbs known for the showy, tall-stemmed flowers. They have large, strong-stemmed, deeply veined leaves, up to 20 in (50 cm) long and 8 in (20 cm) wide. The flowers, which are white, often yellow-green-centered, and fragrant, have a fancied resemblance to daffodils and are borne in heads on stems up to 32 in (80 cm tall), blooming intermittently through the year.

CULTIVATION: Warm conditions are required and frost is not tolerated. Plant in a bright position out of direct sun, in moist, compost-rich soil and feed when in growth. They grow well in pots. Propagation is usually be removing offsets from established bulbs.

Eucharis amazonica

↔ 10–16 in (25–40 cm)
↑ 24–36 in (60–90 cm)

Found from Central America to Ecuador. Bold, deep green foliage creates a hosta-like effect. Flowers white with a central cup that has green markings. Zones 11–12.

Eucharis × *grandiflora*

↔ 10–16 in (25–40 cm)
↑ 24–36 in (60–90 cm)

From Columbia and Ecuador. A natural hybrid between *E. moorei* and *E. sanderi*, but very similar in all respects to *E. amazonica*, with which it is often confused in cultivation. Zones 11–12.

EUCOMIS

PINEAPPLE LILY

These plants, which grow from large, ovate, shiny, greenish purple bulbs, gain their common name from the flowering stem's pineapple-like topknot. Mainly from the summer-rainfall eastern parts of southern Africa, they are members of the asparagus (Asparagaceae) family. The broad leaves are glossy and can be plain or flecked; they appear with the flowers and form a basal rosette. Many tiny star-shaped flowers cluster around a single semi-erect stem in cylindrical formation. These striking plants lend themselves to greenhouse culture and are popular in cut-flower arrangements. In consequence, they are seen at many times of the year, but when left to themselves, they bloom in late summer to early autumn. There are numerous strains and cultivars, in a variety of sizes, shapes, and shades, and new ones appear regularly.

CULTIVATION: The major requirements of these plants are rich, well-drained soil, a dry dormancy, and a moist growth period. Propagate from seed sown in spring or from offsets taken during the winter dormancy.

Eucomis autumnalis

WHITE PINEAPPLE LILY

↔ 24 in (60 cm)
↑ 10–18 in (25–45 cm)

From eastern South Africa, widespread. Leaves broad, wavy-edged, green, to 18 in (45 cm) long. Flower stems upright, not lax, with 6 in (15 cm) long racemes of white flowers ageing to yellow-green in mid-summer–early autumn. There are several subspecies with widely varying foliage and flowers. Zones 8–11.

Eucomis bicolor

↔ 12–24 in (30–60 cm)
↑ 12–24 in (30–60 cm)

From eastern-central South Africa. Grows wild in wet meadows and on stream banks. Bears slightly ragged pendent flowers with green-white petals, sometimes marked with purple, and maroon-flecked stems in late summer. The leaves are undulating and oblong. This plant needs plenty of water during growth. Zones 7–9.

Eucomis comosa

↔ 16 in (40 cm)
↑ 12–24 in (30–60 cm)

Highly variable species from Eastern Cape and KwaZulu-Natal, South Africa. The leaves are wavy-edged. The flowers with green or whitish, pink or reddish, brown-purple or deep purple petals appear in late summer–early autumn. Some selections have purple leaves, but mid-green is more common, often with spotted undersides. Zones 6–10.

Eucalyptus microcorys

Eucalyptus perriniana

Eucharis × *grandiflora*

Eucomis autumnalis

EUCOMMIA

This genus consists of a single species of deciduous tree from China with simple alternate leaves and petal-less flowers that appear in spring before or with the foliage. The fruit is a winged nutlet, to 1½ in (35 mm) long. A form of rubber can be extracted from the tree, which is also valued in herbal medicine and as a specimen tree in the larger garden. *Eucommia* is the sole member of the family Eucommiaceae, the affinities of which have long been in doubt; current thinking is that its closest allies are *Aucuba* and *Garrya.*
CULTIVATION: Frost resistant and drought tender, it prefers sandy, light to medium, well-drained soil in an open sunny position. Propagate from seed, or from cuttings of young wood under glass.

Eucommia ulmoides

GUTTA-PERCHA TREE

↔ 25 ft (8 m) ↑ 60 ft (18 m)

From central China. Broadly domed crown. The leathery, toothed, oval leaves, to 3–6 in (8–15 cm) long, resemble elm leaves. Insignificant solitary flowers appear before or with the new leaves. Zones 5–10.

Eucommia ulmoides

EUONYMUS

This genus belonging to the spindle-tree (Celastraceae) family consists of over 175 species of evergreen, semi-evergreen, or deciduous shrubs, trees, and climbers native to Asia, Europe, North and Central America, and the island of Madagascar; there is also a single Australian species. Not all are frost hardy. Stems and branches are often 4-sided. The leaves may be toothed or smooth-edged. The small flowers may be yellow, green, white, or red-brown, and are borne singly or in cymes in the leaf axils from late spring to early summer. The fruit is a distinctive capsule with 3, 4, or 5 compartments, each containing one large seed surrounded by a usually red or orange aril. The capsule splits open to reveal a paler, often pink, interior that contrasts with the brightly colored aril. Parts of the plant can cause stomach upsets or even severe poisoning if they are eaten.
CULTIVATION: They tolerate all types of soil, but *E. alatus* is especially good in alkaline soil. Grow in well-drained soil in sun or part-shade. Evergreen species need shelter from drying cold winds and slightly more moisture in the soil. Variegated forms perform better in full sun. Propagation is from seed, or from nodal cuttings taken from deciduous plants in summer or from evergreen plants in early summer to mid-autumn.

Euonymus americanus, fruit

Euonymus japonicus 'Bravo'

Euonymus alatus

BURNING BUSH, CORKBUSH, WINGED SPINDLE TREE

↔ 10 ft (3 m) ↑ 6 ft (1.8 m)

Found from northeastern Asia to central China and Japan. Dense, deciduous, bushy shrub with corky wings on branches. Leaves ovate to elliptical, dark green, with toothed margins, turning red in autumn. Pale green flowers in summer. Fruit is pale red, 4-lobed, and has bright orange seeds. **'Compactus'**, a dwarf compact shrub, with winged corky branches, scarlet to purple foliage in winter; **'Nordine'**, large orange leaves in winter, abundant fruit; **'Timber Creek'**, vigorous, with arching branches and broad recurving leaves that color brilliant scarlet in autumn. Zones 3–9.

Euonymus grandiflorus

Euonymus americanus

STRAWBERRY BUSH, WAHOO

↔ 6 ft (1.8 m) ↑ 8 ft (2.4 m)

From eastern USA. Deciduous upright shrub. The deep green ovate to lance-shaped leaves with scalloped margins, are somewhat wrinkly, lasting well into late autumn. The red-tinged green flowers appear in summer. Pink 3- to 5-lobed fruit with yellow-tinged white seeds. Zones 6–9.

Euonymus bungeanus

syn. *Euonymus maackii*

↔ 15 ft (4.5 m) ↑ 20 ft (6 m)

From China and Korea. Deciduous or semi-evergreen shrub or tree. Arching slender shoots; leaves pale green, ovate to elliptic, with finely toothed margins and pointed tips, turning pink and yellow in autumn. Small cymes of yellow flowers. Pink-tinged yellow fruit with bright orange arils. ***E. b.* var. *semipersistens,*** semi-evergreen foliage; and ***E. b.* 'Pendulus'** has elegant pendulous branches. Zones 4–9.

Euonymus europaeus

EUROPEAN EUONYMUS, EUROPEAN SPINDLE TREE, SPINDLE TREE

↔ 8 ft (2.4 m) ↑ 20 ft (6 m)

Found from Europe to western Asia. Deciduous shrub or small tree. Green branches; leaves elliptic, scalloped, with pointed tips. Small cymes of 5 to 7 yellow to green flowers in spring. Pink to red 4-lobed fruit with white seeds and orange arils. ***E. e.* f. *albus*,** white fruit. ***E. e.* 'Aucubifolius'**, white variegated foliage; **'Red Cap'**, bright red fruit, persisting on bare winter branches; **'Red Cascade'** ★, often a small tree, good autumn color, persistent orange-red fruit. Zones 3–9.

Euonymus fortunei

syns *Euonymus hederaceus, E. radicans*

WINTERCREEPER EUONYMUS

↔ 3–10 ft (0.9–3 m)
↑ 1–10 ft (0.3–3 m)

From China. Evergreen ground-cover shrub or root-clinging climber; as a climber, can reach 15 ft (4.5 m) high. Green branches with fine warts. Leaves oval or elliptic, toothed, with pointed tips. Greenish yellow flowers in summer. White fruit, orange arils. ***E. f.* var. *vegetus*,** spreading, bushy, stiff branches, thick dull green leaves. ***E. f.* 'Canadale Gold'**, leaves, marginal bands of yellow; **'Coloratus'**, green foliage turns purple-red in winter; **'E.T.'**, prostrate form, rounded leaves with pinkish cream margins; **'Emerald Gaiety'**, green leaves with white margins tinged pink in winter; **'Emerald 'n' Gold'**, leaves with yellow margins tinged pink in winter; **'Harlequin'**, leaves grayish green, streaked and marbled with cream or white, frequently throwing entirely cream leaves; **'Kewensis'**, prostrate form, tiny leaves; **'Minims'**, procumbent, rooting along branches, 2 in (5 cm) high; **'Niagara Green'**, deep green leaves, new growth lime green; **'Sheridan Gold'**, yellowish green young foliage; **'Silver Queen'**, bushy shrub or spreading climber, leaves, broad white margins tinged pink in winter; **'Sunspot'**, semi-prostrate, weak arching branches, leaves with large cream or yellow blotch mainly on basal half. **'Variegatus'** an older variegated cultivar. Zones 5–10.

Euonymus grandiflorus

↔ 10 ft (3 m) ↑ 15 ft (4.5 m)

Found in northern India and western China. Semi-evergreen. The leaves are dark green, variable, but usually lance-shaped to elliptic, with pointed tips, finely toothed margins. Bears cymes of green to yellow flowers and light pink fruit with black seeds and scarlet arils. Zones 9–10.

Euonymus hamiltonianus

YEDDO EUONYMUS

↔ 20 ft (6 m) ↑ 20 ft (6 m)

Found from the Himalayas to Japan. Deciduous small tree or shrub. Leaves are oblong to lance-shaped with short pointed tips. Red-tinged white flowers in summer. Pink fruit. ***E. h.* subsp. *sieboldianus*** (syns. *E. sieboldianus, E. yedoensis*) similar to the species but leaves are longer and pointed, the fruit almost round, 4-lobed, and pink, with blood red seeds and orange arils. ***E. h.* 'Red Elf'** fruits well; fruit and seeds dark pink with red arils. Zones 4–9.

Euonymus japonicus

EVERGREEN EUONYMUS

↔ 6–12 ft (1.8–3.5 m)
↑ 12 ft (3.5 m)

Found in Korea, China, and Japan. An evergreen, dense, bushy shrub or small tree that grows larger in the wild than in cultivation. Leaves are dark green, oval to oblong, tough, and

Eupatorium cannabinum

Euphorbia amygdaloides 'Purpurea'

Euphorbia avasmontana

leathery. Produces flattened cymes of green flowers during summer. Rounded pink fruit contains white seeds and orange arils. **'Albomarginatus'**, dark green leaves with narrow white margins; **'Bravo'**, leaves deep green streaked gray-green with broad yellow margins; **'Emerald 'n' Gold'**, dwarf form with compact foliage, and pale yellow leaves with green central zone; **'Microphyllus Aureovariegatus'**, deep green leaves with narrow yellow margins; **'Ovatus Aureus'**, leaves blotched and streaked yellow. Zones 7–10.

Euonymus occidentalis

☼ ✱ ↔ 10 ft (3 m) ↑ 15 ft (4.5 m)

From western North America. Deciduous shrub or small tree. Leaves lance-shaped to ovate, finely toothed, with pointed tips. Small cymes of purple- to brown-tinged flowers. Red-purple fruit. Zones 5–9.

EUPATORIUM

A genus of around 40 species of perennials and few shrubs of the daisy (Asteraceae) family, found through the temperate regions of the Northern Hemisphere. All the species of *Eupatorium* have whorled or opposite leaves on simple or branched stems, the stems terminating in corymbs or panicles of small flowerheads. The fruit is plumed, like thistledown. The foliage of some species is still used in traditional herbal remedies, and an infusion made from the leaves and flowers was once used to treat fevers. The flowers are attractive to butterflies.

CULTIVATION: These plants require a sunny position in well-drained but moist fertile soil. Growing tips can be pinched back to encourage compact growth. Propagate in spring from seed or cuttings of green wood, or by dividing root clumps when the plant is dormant; protect from frosts.

Eupatorium cannabinum

HEMP AGRIMONY

☼/◐ ❄ ↔ 3–5 ft (0.9–1.5 m) ↑ 5–6 ft (1.5–1.8 m)

Vigorous clumping herbaceous perennial found over much of Europe. Leaves mid- to dark green, toothed and sometimes lobed. Dense feathery heads of near-petal-less, dusky pink flowers, in summer–autumn. Zones 5–9.

Eupatorium perfoliatum

BONESET, THOROUGHWORT

☼ ✱ ↔ 3–5 ft (0.9–1.5 m) ↑ 3–5 ft (0.9–1.5 m)

From southeastern USA. Perennial herb, with leaves opposite, wrinkled, toothed, to 8 in (20 cm) long. Large compound heads of 10 to 40 white flowers, often tinged with purple, in late summer–autumn from the second year. Zones 3–4.

EUPHORBIA

This large genus of about 2,000 species of annuals, perennials, shrubs, and trees, both evergreen and deciduous, is distributed throughout the world. It gives its name to the large and diverse family Euphorbiaceae. *Euphorbia* alone takes in a very diverse range of forms and natural habitats, from spiny and succulent cactus-like species occurring mainly in hot dry areas to leafy perennials from cool-temperate climates. All *Euphorbia* species contain a poisonous milky sap which can cause severe irritation if it comes in contact with the skin and, if rubbed into the eyes, will sometimes bring on temporary blindness. The sap has purgative qualities. The true flowers are tiny, with separate male and female forms attached to a smooth cup-like structure, or cy-athium (plural: cyathia). Cyathia are generally accompanied by bracts, which may be larger and are often colored, such as the scarlet bracts of poinsettia (*E. pulcherrima*). These cyathia and bracts may be arranged in repeatedly branched inflorescences and sometimes form large flowerheads. The flowering times of many species are rainfall dependent; in temperate climates with even rainfall, the likely flowering time is from late spring to mid-summer.

CULTIVATION: Provide similar growing conditions to the *Euphorbia* plant's particular natural habitat. In cool-temperate climates, most succulent and subtropical species will require greenhouse protection; some will grow in dry rock gardens. Avoid the toxic sap when pruning and disposing of branches. Some species can only be propagated from seed, others can be grown from stem-tip cuttings or by division of the plants.

Euphorbia amygdaloides

WOOD SPURGE

☼/◐ ❄ ↔ 24–40 in (60–100 cm) ↑ 20–32 in (50–80 cm)

A native of temperate Eurasia. This species is a spreading, mounding, leafy perennial. The soft stems are densely foliaged with spatula-shaped leaves, to over 3 in (8 cm) long; they are often purple-tinted and have a slight sheen. The sprays of showy yellow-green flowerheads are produced throughout the spring and summer. ***E. a.* var. *robbiae***, more robust dark foliage and spreading rosettes. Stems and foliage of ***E. a.* 'Purpurea'** are strongly tinted with purple-red, new growth is red-wine colored. Zones 7–10.

Euphorbia antisyphilitica

CANDELLILA

☼/◐ ❄ ↔ 24 in (60 cm) ↑ 40 in (100 cm)

Native to southwestern USA. Succulent shrub with many narrow, upright, spineless, gray-green stems, often purple-tinted at the nodes, which in spring–early summer bear short-lived, 2 in (5 cm) long, red leaves and cream flowerheads stained purple to red. Flowers open from red buds. Zones 8–11.

Euphorbia avasmontana

☼/◐ ❄ ↔ 40–60 in (100–150 cm) ↑ 7 ft (2 m)

From Namaqualand and Namibia. This succulent shrub has from 5- to 7-angled, upright, sturdy branching stems, the angles edged with opposite pairs of fierce, stiff, ½ in (12 mm) long spines, sometimes red. The yellow-green flowers occur in small heads. This is a rare species in cultivation. Zones 9–11.

Euphorbia 'Blackbird' ★

BLACKBIRD SPURGE

☼/◐ ❄ ↔ 18–24 in (45–60 cm) ↑ 18–20 in (45–50 cm)

E. amygdaloides × *E. martinii* hybrid with purple-red new growth and dark purple-green foliage. Flowerheads and bracts are bright greenish yellow, held above foliage on red stems creating great contrast. Zones 6–10.

Euphorbia candelabrum ★

☼ ❄ ↔ 8–30 ft (2.4–9 m) ↑ 20–60 ft (6–18 m)

From southern to northeastern Africa. Succulent species, smaller in cultivation. Segmented branches arch upward, bearing small rust-colored spines. Leaves triangular; short lived. Golden green flowerheads. Sap once used to poison tips of arrowheads. Zones 9–11.

Euphorbia characias

Euphorbia dregeana

Euphorbia caput-medusae ★

MEDUSA'S HEAD

↔48 in (120 cm) ↑12 in (30 cm)

From South Africa. Succulent shrub. Many spreading, tubercle-studded, cylindrical stems radiating from a central caudex, like the snakes on Medusa's head. Stems broaden at the tip, bearing tiny, often short-lived, linear leaves. Unusual cream flowerheads with fimbriated snowflake-shaped cyathia. Zones 9–10.

Euphorbia characias

↔5 ft (1.5 m) ↑6 ft (1.8 m)

Various forms from the Mediterranean region and southern Europe. Perennial subshrub or shrub with soft stems. Narrow, elliptical, gray-green leaves. The heads of up to 20 small purple-green or yellow flowers, are backed by conspicuous yellow-green whorled bracts, usually in late winter–early summer. The yellow-green-flowered *E. c.* subsp. *wulfenii* ★, with its various cultivars, is more widely cultivated than the species; **'Bosahan'**, selected from a garden in Cornwall, UK, is a variegated plant, with pale yellow flowers; **'Humpty Dumpty'**, compact, around 3 ft (0.9 m) high, purple-red flowers, lime green bracts; **'John Tomlinson'**, has 16 in (40 cm) long heads of bright yellow-green flowers; **'Silver Swan'**, cream-edged leaves, also variegated bracts; **'Tasmanian Tiger'**, broad cream to yellow leaf margins. Zones 8–10.

Euphorbia franckiana

Euphorbia cooperi ★

TRANSVAAL CANDELABRA TREE

↔6 ft (1.8 m) ↑15 ft (4.5 m)

From southern and eastern Africa. Succulent tree with upwardly arching segmented branches, usually pentagonal in shape. Pairs of buff-colored spines accentuate margins. Small yellowish flowers arise between them usually in autumn–spring. Zones 9–11.

Euphorbia corollata

FLOWERING SPURGE, TRAMP'S SPURGE, WILD HIPPO, WILD IPECAC

↔12 in (30 cm)
↑12–36 in (30–90 cm)

From eastern North America. An erect perennial, with alternate oblong leaves, turning red in autumn. Slender stem exudes milky juice, which may irritate the skin. Small white flowers in early summer–early autumn. Zones 4–9.

Euphorbia cornigera

↔24 in (60 cm) ↑30 in (75 cm)

From the Himalayas. Perennial shrub. Red stems; the red-tinted dark green leaves have a pale, almost white, midrib. Showy bright yellow-green flowerheads in early summer. Zones 6–9.

Euphorbia cyathophora

syn. *Poinsettia cyathophora*

FIRE ON THE MOUNTAIN, MEXICAN FIRE PLANT, PAINTED LEAF

↔20 in (50 cm) ↑20 in (50 cm)

From southeastern USA and neighboring Mexico. Evergreen shrub, with upright stems. Leaves variable, narrow to spatula-shaped, toothed or smooth-edged. The bright red flowerheads, surrounded by leafy bracts, appear in summer. Zones 9–11.

Euphorbia cyparissias

CYPRESS SPURGE

↔24 in (60 cm) ↑16 in (40 cm)

Widespread in Europe. Perennial, which spreads by rhizomes, forming a clump of narrow stems with narrow green leaves, 1¾ in (40 mm) long, which sometimes redden in sun or drought. Yellow-green inflorescence surrounded by mauve- to red-tinted feathery bracts in late spring to mid-summer. **'Fens Ruby'**, carries bright red bracts, near yellow flowerheads, very compact. Zones 4–9.

Euphorbia griffithii 'Fireglow'

Euphorbia 'Diamond Frost'

↔12–36 in (30–90 cm)
↑12–36 in (30–90 cm)

Short-lived perennial treated as a summer annual. Forms a mound of bright green foliage topped with masses of white-bracted flowers. Zones 9–11.

Euphorbia dregeana

↔4 ft (1.2 m) ↑7 ft (2 m)

From Namaqualand and Namibia. Succulent shrub. Stems spineless and upright, branching, and pale green. The leaves are small and short-lived. It bears inconspicuous inflorescences of yellow-green flowers. Zones 9–11.

Euphorbia dulcis

PURPLE SPURGE

↔12 in (30 cm) ↑12 in (30 cm)

Found in Europe. *E. dulcis* is a rhizomatous perennial. The leaves are narrow, downy, to just under 3 in (8 cm) long, and often purple-tinted. The yellow-green, sometimes red-tinted, inflorescence is surrounded by feathery purple-red bracts in summer. The cultivar, **'Chameleon'**, has strongly purple-tinted leaves, and its bracts are especially colorful and showy in summer. Zones 6–9.

Euphorbia franckiana

↔40 in (100 cm) ↑40 in (100 cm)

From South Africa. Succulent shrub. Stems branching, segmented, usually acutely 3-angled, blue-green, edged with paired ½ in (12 mm) long spines. Yellow-green inflorescences, inconspicuous except that they occur between spine pairs, in spring–early summer. Zones 9–11.

Euphorbia grantii

syns *Euphorbia umbellatum*, *Synadenium grantii*

AFRICAN MILKBUSH, GRANT'S MILKBUSH

↔4 ft (1.2 m) ↑12 ft (3.5 m)

Erect succulent shrub native to tropical Africa, often smaller in cultivation. Fleshy light green leaves, finely toothed margins, spirally arranged near ends of stems. Small, bowl-shaped, deep red flowers in autumn. Zones 9–12.

Euphorbia griffithii

↔36 in (90 cm) ↑36 in (90 cm)

From the Himalayas. Widely grown and usually a perennial, it can become shrubby in mild climates. The leaves are narrow, to 5 in (12 cm) long, dark green, and tinted pink to orange. The flowerheads, with vivid orange-red bracts in summer, develop coppery tones with age. **'Fireglow'**, vivid red bracts. Zones 5–10.

Euphorbia lathyris

CAPER SPURGE, MYRTLE SPURGE

↔ 40 in (100 cm)
↑ 40–60 in (100–150 cm)

From Europe, northwest Africa, and western Asia. Biennial, which is usually considered a weed. Upright and fairly weak stems; fleshy blue-green leaves in 4 ranks. Unspectacular, rather open, yellow-green flowerheads in the warmer months, followed by caper-like but poisonous seed heads. Zones 6–10.

Euphorbia ledienii

↔ 5 ft (1.5 m) ↑ 7 ft (2 m)

From South Africa. Succulent, often clumping, shrub. The stems are cactus-like, branching, segmented, 4- to 7-angled, blue-green, and edged with paired short spines. The inconspicuous yellow-green flowerheads are most usually seen in spring–early summer and are followed by red seed capsules. Zones 9–11.

Euphorbia × *lomii*

GIANT CROWN OF THORNS

↔ 40 in (100 cm) ↑ 40 in (100 cm)

This species is a garden hybrid between two Madagascan species, *E. lophogona* and *E. milii*. It is very like the common crown of thorns, *E. milii*, but generally shorter, with broader stems. Densely prickly; light green leaves, to 6 in (15 cm) long, are red-tinted in the sun. The salmon to red flowerheads and bracts occur at any time except during periods of severe drought. The **Somona Range** includes various flower colors, such as the pale pink **'Merle'** and the cerise **'Rosemarie'**. Zones 10–12.

Euphorbia marginata

GHOST WEED, SNOW ON THE MOUNTAIN

↔ 20 in (50 cm) ↑ 40 in (100 cm)

Native to North America. An annual, which is usually cultivated in gardens in low-growing forms. It produces a dense mound of light green, soft, downy leaves, to 3 in (8 cm) long, edged in white, sometimes entirely white at the top of the plant. White bracts in summer. Contact with the sap can cause severe dermatological problems. Zones 4–10.

Euphorbia × *martinii*

↔ 3 ft (0.9 m) ↑ 3 ft (0.9 m)

A hybrid between *E. amygdaloides* and *E. characias*. This variable plant can closely resemble either of its parents. An unusual plant, less predictable than the parent species. **'Ascot Rainbow'**, yellow-edged foliage and bracts, red-tinted young growth; **'Rudolph'**, purple-red foliage, bright red new growth. Zones 7–10.

Euphorbia schillingii

Euphorbia mellifera

HONEY SPURGE

↔ 7 ft (2 m) ↑ 6 ft (1.8 m)

From Madeira. Rare shrubby species. The leaves are mid-green and lance-shaped, with prominent whitish central veins. The clusters of tiny greenish flowers with very small bronze-green floral bracts occur at the ends of the stems, in spring–summer. *Mellifera* means honey-bearing, and refers to the flowers' scent, which is attractive to bees. Zones 8–11.

Euphorbia milii ★

CROWN OF THORNS

↔ 2–8 ft (0.6–2.4 m)
↑ 1–3 ft (0.3–0.9 m)

From Madagascar. Erect or scrambling shrub, sparsely foliaged, bright green leaves near branch tips. Stems prickly. Tiny yellow flowers with bright red floral bracts appearing intermittently for long periods. ***E. m.* var. *splendens*** (syn. *E. splendens*), commonly cultivated, mound of tangled branches to 2 ft (60 cm), pinkish red bracts; ***E. m.* f. *lutea*** ★, cream bracts. Zones 9–11.

Euphorbia myrsinites ★

CREEPING SPURGE, DONKEY TAIL

↔ 20 in (50 cm) ↑ 10 in (25 cm)

From Eurasia. Clump-forming perennial with sprawling stems. Leaves spiraled, finely toothed, pointed, fleshy, blue-green, to 1¾ in (40 mm) long. Bright green cyathia with chrome yellow bracts in spring. ***E. m.* subsp. *myrsinites*** (syn. *E. pontica*) is more compact than the species. Zones 6–10.

Euphorbia palustris

↔ 40 in (100 cm) ↑ 40 in (100 cm)

From Europe. This clump-forming perennial is very like the better-known *E. polychroma* but is somewhat larger. It has wiry stems, and narrow elliptical leaves, to over 2 in (5 cm) long, often red-tinted in the sunlight. The light green to bright yellow densely clustered flowerheads appear in spring–summer. Zones 6–9.

Euphorbia trigona

Euphorbia polychroma

syn. ***Euphorbia epithymoides***

CUSHION SPURGE

↔ 24 in (60 cm) ↑ 24 in (60 cm)

From Eurasia. Clump-forming perennial. Fine stems, with bright green, elliptical, velvety leaves, to about 2 in (5 cm) long. Bright yellow-green, sometimes red-tinted, flowerheads in spring–summer. **'Major'**, compact form, produces chrome yellow flowerheads. Zones 6–9.

Euphorbia rigida

↔ 24 in (60 cm) ↑ 16 in (40 cm)

Found from southwestern Europe to the Caucasus. Evergreen perennial. Clustered clumps of upright blue-green stems; similarly colored, fleshy, lance-shaped leaves, notched at the tips. Bright yellow-green flowerheads in summer. Zones 7–10.

Euphorbia schillingii

↔ 5 ft (1.5 m) ↑ 4 ft (1.2 m)

From Nepal. Shrubby perennial. Leaves are narrow, bright green, elliptical, and to 3 in (8 cm) long. The showy yellow-green flowerheads with rounded green bracts, borne at stem tips, occur in summer. Zones 7–9.

Euphorbia seguieriana

↔ 32 in (80 cm) ↑ 20 in (50 cm)

From central Europe to Pakistan and Siberia. Woody-based perennial. Forms clump of blue-green stems; similarly colored, pointed, linear leaves, up to 1¾ in (40 mm) long. Large heads of yellow-green cyathia and yellow bracts in summer. ***E. s.* subsp. *niciciana*** has a slightly more spreading habit and less crowded flowerheads. Zones 5–9.

Euphorbia sikkimensis ★

↔ 36 in (90 cm) ↑ 36 in (90 cm)

From the eastern Himalayas. Rhizome-rooted perennial with upright stems and narrow elliptical leaves, up to 4 in (10 cm) long, and often red-tinted. Attractive pink new growth. Orange-red flowerheads in summer. Zones 6–9.

Euphorbia spinosa

↔ 20 in (50 cm) ↑ 8 in (20 cm)

From the Mediterranean region. Low-mounding shrub. Small blue-green leaves enclosed in an interlaced thicket of wiry branches. Yellow-green flowerheads in spring–summer. Zones 7–10.

Euphorbia tirucalli

FINGER TREE, MILK BUSH, PENCIL BUSH, PENCIL TREE, RUBBER HEDGE

↔ 7–12 ft (2–3.5 m)
↑ 15–30 ft (4.5–9 m)

From tropical and southern Africa, and also found from India east to Indonesia. A large shrub or small tree with dense crown of succulent, pale green, cylindrical branches. Small, short-lived, lance-shaped leaves. The insignificant flowers appear in spring–early summer. Can be invasive. Zones 10–12.

Euphorbia tithymaloides

syn. ***Pedilanthus tithymaloides***

↔ 2 ft (0.6 m) ↑ 6 ft (1.8 m)

Originally from the West Indies and southern USA. Succulent shrub can be evergreen or deciduous. Has fleshy erect stems zigzagging at each node, mid-green boat-shaped leaves, and small, reddish green, tubular flowers with red bracts, borne in summer. **'Variegatus'**, commonly grown form, green leaves variegated white and red. Zones 9–10.

Euphorbia triangularis

↔ 6 ft (1.8 m) ↑ 60 ft (18 m)

From southern Africa. Large succulent tree. The upright angular branches are ridged and segmented, with extremely thorny margins. The small leaves soon drop from the branches. Zones 9–11.

Euphorbia trigona

↔ 12–24 in (30–60 cm)
↑ 3–8 ft (0.9–2.4 m)

From Namibia. Succulent cactus-like shrub. Branches all erect, 3-cornered, dark green mottled with white, with vertical ranks of spoon-shaped leaves and short reddish brown spines. Often seen as a house plant. **'Green Angel'** ★, stems and leaves always plain green; **'Red Devil'** ★, attractive cultivar with red leaves. Zones 9–11.

Euryale ferox

Euryops pectinatus

Eustoma grandiflorum 'Forever Blue'

EURYALE

This genus, comprising just one species found from northern India to China and Japan, belongs to the waterlily (Nymphaeaceae) family. It is a very large, perennial, aquatic plant with a massive rhizome. The leaves are round, strongly ribbed, and very prickly, with the stalk attached under the middle of the blade. Flowers consist of 4 sepals and numerous petals, which are shorter than the sepals. The fruit is a prickly berry with many seeds. Plants resemble the tropical American *Victoria*, but the leaves have flat, rather than upturned, margins and the flowers are smaller, with all the stamens fertile.
CULTIVATION: Often grown as an annual in tropical greenhouses, where it is raised from seed sown immersed in water at 70–73°F (21–23°C).

Euryale ferox

↔ 5 ft (1.5 m) ↑ 3 ft (0.9 m)

Leaves 2–5 ft (0.6–1.5 m) across. Up-per surface puckered, dull green, with sparse prickles; lower surface reddish, with prominent spongy veining densely armed with prickles. Summer flowers often do not open, remaining more or less submerged. Flower stalks and calyx prickly. Sepals green; petals red to purple or lilac. Cultivated for 3,000 years by the Chinese for its edible rhizomes and seeds (fox nuts), now sold in Indian markets roasted and "puffed" like wheat. Zones 8–11.

EURYOPS

There are about 100 species of evergreen shrubs, perennials, and annuals in this genus, a member of the large daisy (Asteraceae) family. The majority are native to South Africa. They are attractive plants with lobed or finely divided green to grayish green leaves and bright yellow daisy flowers borne over a long period. Easily grown in a wide range of conditions, *Euryops* can withstand some frost, are drought tolerant, and suitable for coastal planting.
CULTIVATION: Deep free-draining soil in full sun is best. Grow against a warm wall or in a greenhouse or conservatory in cool-temperate climates. Prune after flowering to maintain a compact form. Propagate from seed or half-hardened or softwood cuttings.

Euryops acraeus

syn. *Euryops evansii*

↔ 36 in (90 cm)
↑ 12–36 in (30–90 cm)

Compact plant with small, narrow, silvery gray leaves. Bright yellow daisies, to 1½ in (35 mm) across, in spring–summer. Short-lived in damp climates; requires perfect drainage. Ideal plant for the rock garden. Zones 7–10.

Euryops chrysanthemoides

syn. *Gamolepsis chrysanthemoides*
PARIS DAISY

↔ 5 ft (1.5 m) ↑ 4 ft (1.2 m)

Popular, easily grown plant, particularly in warm climates. Well foliaged with deeply lobed dark green leaves. Yellow daisies, 2 in (5 cm) across, borne on slender stalks above the foliage, in winter–spring. Zones 9–11.

Euryops pectinatus

GOLDEN DAISY BUSH, GRAY-HAIRED EURYOPS

↔ 5 ft (1.5 m) ↑ 4 ft (1.2 m)

Fern-like foliage, deeply cut, downy, gray leaves. Bright yellow daisies are held well above the foliage, in spring–summer. Seldom without flowers in warm climates. Zones 8–11.

EUSTOMA

LISIANTHUS, PRAIRIE GENTIAN, TEXAS BLUEBELL

Formerly classified as *Lisianthus* and still sold under that name, these long-stemmed gentian relatives (family Gentianaceae) are widely cultivated for cut flowers. There are 3 species in the genus, consisting of annuals or short-lived perennials found from southern USA to northern South America. Form clumps of fleshy oval to narrowly elliptical leaves, in summer producing showy 5- to 6-petalled, funnel- to bell-shaped flowers, up to 2 in (5 cm) wide. Some species carry flowers singly, but the cultivated plants have many-flowered stems up to 24 in (60 cm) long with blooms in a wide range of colors and in double-flowered forms. Lisianthus means bitter flower, and refers to the taste; the flowers were used medicinally by Native Americans.
CULTIVATION: Usually cultivated as annuals. Slow-growing, they need prolonged warm conditions to flower well. Plant in full or half-sun with fertile, moist, well-drained soil. The heavy flower stems are best staked. May be propagated by cuttings but better if raised fresh from seed.

Eustoma grandiflorum ★

syns *Eustoma russellianum*, *Lisianthus grandiflorus*

↔ 20 in (50 cm)
↑ 24–32 in (60–80 cm)

Annual or short-lived perennial from southern USA and Mexico. Upright blue-green stems; fleshy, blue-green, pointed oval leaves, to 3 in (8 cm) long. Heads of bell-shaped flowers, to 2½ in (6 cm) across. Many seedling strains, such as the **Echo** mixed color strain, to 24 in (60 cm) tall, in lilac-, blue-, pink-, yellow-, and white-flowered forms as well as picotee-edged; the **Heidi Series**, to 18 in (45 cm) tall, in many colors; the **Mermaid Series**, including the early-flowering dwarf **'Lilac Rose'**, with light purple-pink single flowers; and individual named varieties, such as **'Forever Blue'**, to 12 in (30 cm) tall, with large purple-blue flowers. Zones 9–11.

EUTERPE

ASSAI PALM, MANACO

This genus of feather-leafed palms (family Arecaceae) consists of 7 species from tropical America, though up to 30 species have formerly been distinguished. Single-trunked or clustered, medium to large, with crowns of rather few pinnate fronds, their elongated basal sheaths forming a smooth crownshaft; the leaflets droop gracefully, with finely tapering tips. The inflorescences appear in continuous succession from the trunk below the crownshaft; their branchlets have a dense covering of short soft hairs. The branchlets bear numerous small flowers in groups of one female flanked by two males. The smooth-coated, almost spherical, fruits contain a single seed. The vegetative buds, a single one terminating each trunk, are the principal source of palm-hearts, sometimes called "millionaire's salad" because their removal kills the trunk; but these palms are now grown rapidly in plantations and canned palm-hearts are sold quite cheaply.
CULTIVATION: These palms are native to lowland rainforests and mountain forests and swamps. Fast growing, but because they require high humidity and temperatures they are really only suitable for tropical gardens, not for greenhouses in temperate regions. Propagate from seed.

Euterpe edulis ★

JUÇARA PALM, PALMITO, YAYIH

↔ 12–18 ft (3.5–5.5 m)
↑ 20–40 ft (6–12 m)

From coastal regions of Brazil and ad-jacent parts of Argentina and Paraguay. Slender, usually solitary, palm with a smooth green crownshaft. Finely divided fronds with 120 to 150 pendulous leaflets. Purple flowers are followed by clusters of small, round, dark purple fruit. It is generally agreed that *E. edulis* yields the best-tasting palm-hearts. Zones 11–12.

Euterpe oleracea

ASSAI PALM, AÇAÍ, MANAC, NAIDI, PINOT

↔ 12–18 ft (3.5–5.5 m)
↑ 20–60 ft (6–8 m)

Native to lower Amazon region of Brazil and far northern South America and west to Colombia. Clumping palm with several tall slender trunks and crown of drooping feathery fronds, which emerge from a reddish crownshaft. The juicy blackish-purple fruit is the basic ingredient of the sweet drink açaí, a staple of the Amazon's estuary region, and this species of palm also provides the major source of the palm-hearts used in the canning industry. Zones 11–12.

EUTROCHIUM

Until recently part of *Eupatorium*, this daisy (Asteraceae) family genus of 5 species of herbaceous perennials is native to North America. Distinguished from *Eupatorium* by the leaves, which are in opposite pairs, rather than in groups of 3. Leaves are pointed elliptical to lance-shaped, and finely toothed. Flowers are very small but massed in flat-topped corymbs, white to pink, mainly late summer–autumn. CULTIVATION: Very easily grown in a bright position with well-drained soil. Best with ample summer moisture and in large borders with room for it to develop properly. Propagate by division.

Eutrochium purpureum

syn. *Eupatorium purpureum*

JOE PYE WEED, TRUMPET WEED

↔6–10 ft (1.8–3 m) ↑6–10 ft (1.8–3 m)

Perennial from eastern USA. Large whorls of elliptical leaves that are finely toothed, with a purplish tinge. Inflorescence consists of half-rounded panicle with 5 to 15 flowerheads, purple or pale pink to greenish yellow or rose-purple, in late summer–autumn. Zones 3–9.

EVOLVULUS

This genus of about 100 species comes mostly from tropical and other warm parts of the Americas. It belongs to the bindweed (Convolvulaceae) family. These plants are annuals, perennials, or subshrubs, often creeping but never climbing. The leaves are small, simple, and often narrow. The inflorescences are borne in the leaf axils or at the ends of the stems, each with one to several flowers with 5 small sepals. The corolla is funnel-shaped to flat, blue or pink to white, and has a lobed to smooth margin. The dry seed capsule is spherical to ovate in shape and contains 1 to 4 small seeds. CULTIVATION: These plants thrive in well-drained soil in full sun. Propagate by root division or from cuttings; the shorter-lived species are readily raised from seed.

Euterpe edulis

Evolvulus glomeratus

Evolvulus glomeratus

syn. *Evolvulus pilosus of gardens*

↔24–36 in (60–90 cm) ↑10–18 in (25–45 cm)

From Brazil and some neighboring countries. Evergreen perennial. Dense mound of foliage emerging from mass of rhizomes; leaves gray-green with soft silky hairs. Long succession of brilliant blue flowers with a small white eye, 1 in (25 mm) across, in the spring–autumn, wilting after noon in hot weather. Sold under the names **'Blue Daze'**, **'Hawaiian Blue Eyes'**, and **'Sapphire'**, but these are doubtfully distinct as cultivars. Often grown in hanging baskets. Zones 9–11.

EXACUM

There are about 25 species of tender annuals, biennials, and perennials in this genus, which belongs to the gentian (Gentianaceae) family and is native to the Old World tropics. The leaves are opposite, oval or elliptic, and often stalkless. Clusters of flowers, sometimes fragrant, are borne on leafy stems. The flowers consist of a narrow tube flaring to 5 flattened petal lobes with protruding yellow stamens. CULTIVATION: Popular in temperate regions as pot plants for the house or conservatory. Grow in well-drained but moist potting mix in a well-lit position. These plants can also be grown outdoors as a bedding annual but they are suitable for permanent outdoor cultivation only in humid tropical and subtropical areas. Propagate from seed.

Exacum affine

GERMAN VIOLET, PERSIAN VIOLET

↔12 in (30 cm) ↑12–18 in (30–45 cm)

A native of the island of Socotra at the mouth of the Red Sea. An annual or short-lived perennial with pointed oval leaves. Small fragrant flowers, ranging in color from sky blue to pale and deep violet, are borne from spring through to autumn. Zones 10–12.

EXOCHORDA

PEARL BUSH

This genus consists of 4 or 5 species of deciduous shrubs, within the rose (Rosaceae) family, native to northeast and central Asia. Some botanists now prefer to combine these into a single variable species, for which the name *E. racemosa* takes priority. They are all attractive spring-flowering shrubs, many with arching branches that become festooned with waxy white flowers, which are borne in racemes in the leaf axils or at the branch tips. The leaves are simple and alternate. CULTIVATION: Easy to cultivate, they prefer moderately fertile well-drained soil in a cool-temperate climate with well-defined seasons, and a sheltered position in full sun. They may become chlorotic in chalk soils. Prune basal shoots by about one-third in late winter; remove spent flower clusters after flowering. Seeds germinate readily when sown in spring in a warm humid atmosphere. Soft-tip or half-hardened cuttings taken in summer or autumn can be rooted under cover; or use hardwood cuttings from winter pruning.

Exacum affine

Exochorda giraldii

↔10 ft (3 m) ↑10 ft (3 m)

From northwestern China. Large free-flowering shrub, arching, spreading habit. Green leaves with red veins. White flowers, in late spring. ***E. g.* var. *wilsonii*** is more upright, with flowers to 2 in (5 cm) in diameter. Zones 5–9.

Exochorda × *macrantha*

PEARL BUSH

↔10 ft (3 m) ↑7 ft (2 m)

This strong-growing hybrid between *E. korolkowii* and *E. racemosa* closely resembles *E. racemosa*. The abundant racemes of pure white flowers occur in late spring. **'The Bride'** ★, compact shrub, to 6 ft (1.8 m) high, with a slightly weeping habit and arching branches covered with large white flowers in spring. Zones 5–9.

Exochorda racemosa

syn. *Exochorda grandiflora*

COMMON PEARL BUSH, PEARL BUSH

↔10 ft (3 m) ↑10 ft (3 m)

A native shrub of northeastern China. Dense spherical shape when mature, with many erect arching shoots from the base. Flower buds are like miniature white pearls and open to pure white, waxy, slightly fragrant flowers. Zones 4–9.

Exochorda serratifolia

KOREAN PEARL BUSH

↔7 ft (2 m) ↑8 ft (2.4 m)

From Korea and nearby parts of China. A shrub of upright habit. Serrated leaves with downy undersides, 3 in (8 cm) long. Loose racemes of flowers, 1½ in (35 mm) across, in early spring. Zones 5–9.

Exochorda giraldii

F

F

FAGUS

BEECH

This genus gives its name to the family Fagaceae, which also includes oaks and chestnuts. The genus consists of about 10 species of deciduous trees, native to Europe and the British Isles, and also found through temperate Asia and North America, China, and Japan, with branches to ground level and smooth light green leaves. Horizontally held limbs produce layers of foliage that protect the smooth silvery gray trunks from sunburn. In late autumn to winter, foliage turns golden brown or coppery red before falling. Buds are distinctly sharp-pointed, held at an angle to the stem. Prickly fruits release 2 triangular nuts. Splendid hedged beeches are found throughout Europe.

CULTIVATION: Grow in well-drained reasonably fertile soil in wind-sheltered gardens. Summer moisture is necessary until trees become established. They handle moderate air pollution. Propagate from seed sown when fresh, or use grafted cultivars.

Fagus grandifolia

Fagus crenata

JAPANESE BEECH

☼ ✱ ↔20 ft (6 m) ↑30 ft (9 m)

From Japan, important deciduous tree of temperate areas. Bark gray. Leaves oval, pale green on underside, wavy furry margins when young. Veins beneath, also furry. Zones 6–9.

Fagus grandifolia

AMERICAN BEECH

☼ ✱ ↔35 ft (10 m) ↑80 ft (24 m)

From eastern USA and Canada, deciduous straight-trunked tree, which develops a spreading crown in the open. Does not perform well in cooler summers. Often produces suckers. Zones 4–8.

Fagus sylvatica

COMMON BEECH, EUROPEAN BEECH

☼ ✱ ↔50 ft (15 m) ↑100 ft (30 m)

From Europe and southern England. Deciduous tree, elegant, strongly veined foliage, graceful habit, provides dense shade. Trunk straight, smooth gray bark. Autumn foliage gold to orange to brown. Prickly fruits. **F. s. f fastigiata**, deep green with gold; F. s. f. heterophylla **'Aspleniifolia'**, narrow long-pointed leaves; F. s. f. pendula, weeping beech, pendulous thick branches; F. s. f. tortuosa, twisted branches. Also F. s. **'Albomarginata'**, variegated leaves; **Cuprea Group**, copper colored; **'Dawyck'**, upright tree resembling Lombardy poplar; **'Dawyck Gold'**, gold-tipped foliage; **'Dawyck Purple'**, purplish foliage; **Purpurea Group** ★, soft green turning purple; **'Purpurea Pendula'**, weeping foliage; **'Quercina'**, prickly pale copper nuts; **'Riversii'** ★, color intensifies to almost black; **'Tricolor'**, slow growing, pink margins, white-blotched green leaves. Zones 5–9.

FARFUGIUM

A genus of only 2 species in the daisy (Asteraceae) family, from East Asia. These handsome plants are evergreen perennials with large, deep green, kidney-shaped leaves and clusters of yellow daisies from autumn to winter.

CULTIVATION: Hardy and easily grown in temperate zones in cool, moist, humus-rich soil. Will grow in damp areas but prefer woodland conditions with good drainage. Full sun is tolerated, but foliage will become lusher in partial shade. Good indoor pot plants in colder climates. Propagation is by division in late winter and spring.

Farfugium japonicum

syn. *Ligularia tussilaginea*

☀ ❄ ↔24–40 in (60–100 cm) ↑24–40 in (60–100 cm)

Native to Japan, evergreen herbaceous perennial. The only species usually cultivated. Large, kidney-shaped, rich green leaves. Yellow flowers, widely spaced rays, in winter. **'Argenteum'**, leaves edged with white; **'Aureomaculatum'** ★ (leopard plant), irregular yellow spots on leaf; **'Crispatum'** (syn. 'Cristata'), green leaves, crumpled crested edges. Zones 8–11.

FARGESIA

This Himalayan bamboo genus is a member of the grass (Poaceae) family. It contains just 4 species, but there are also several cultivated varieties. Most species are fairly compact, and are clumping, not running, and hence non-invasive. Stems are fine and well foliaged, forming a dense impenetrable clump, very useful as a screen or barrier. Flowers seldom appear on garden specimens, which is just as well because the plants die after flowering. Of ornamental value.

CULTIVATION: Tolerant of heavy frosts and easily grown in mild temperate climates in moist, humus-rich, well-drained soil in full sun or shade. The only maintenance required is to thin out old canes as necessary. Propagate by division, or from seed if available.

Fargesia murielae ★

syns *Sinarundinaria murielae, Thamnocalamus spathaceus*

UMBRELLA BAMBOO

☼ ✱ ↔2–4 ft (0.6–1.2 m) ↑10–12 ft (3–3.5 m)

This hardy bamboo from west and central China is an important food of the giant panda. Narrow apple green leaves, long-drawn-out apex. Jointed culms, ½ in (12 mm) diameter, yellowish green, fade to yellow. **'Harewood'**, dwarf form; **'Jumbo'**, taller, wider foliage; **'Simba'**, to 6 ft (1.8 m) high; **'Thyme'**, 5 ft (1.5 m) high. Zones 5–10.

Fargesia nitida

syn. *Sinarundinaria nitida*

FOUNTAIN BAMBOO

☼ ✱ ↔2–4 ft (0.6–1.2 m) ↑10–12 ft (3–3.5 m)

From central China. Purplish culms to ½ in (12 mm) wide, branching in 2nd year, persistent purplish green sheaths. Cascades of narrow, rough, dark green, tapered leaves. **'Anceps'**, narrower foliage, more open habit; **'De Belder'**, shorter, purple culms; **'Eisenae'**, up-right, purple culms; **'McClure'**, reaches 18 ft (5.5 m) high; **'Nymphenburg'**, narrow foliage. Zones 5–10.

× *Fatshedera lizei*

× *FATSHEDERA*

Originating in France, this is a cross between Atlantic ivy *(Hedera hibernica)* and Japanese fatsia *(Fatsia japonica)* and belongs to the ivy (Araliaceae) family. Unusual, sprawling, evergreen shrub, sometimes climbing. Flowers are insignificant and sterile, so it is very much a foliage plant.

CULTIVATION: Easily grown in moist well-drained soil in partial or full shade. Tolerates neglect provided the plants remain moist. With a somewhat rangy habit, × *Fatshedera* needs regular pinching back to keep it compact and a support to keep it upright. As it is sterile it must be propagated from cuttings, though it sometimes self-layers.

× *Fatshedera lizei*

☀/☀ ❄ ↔8 ft (2.4 m) ↑6 ft (1.8 m)

Multi-stemmed shrub. Leaves deeply lobed, hand-shaped, bright glossy green. Produces small heads of greenish white flowers, in autumn; these are best removed because flies pollinate them. **'Annemeike'** has yellow leaves; **'Variegata'**, cream-edged leaves. Zones 7–11.

FATSIA

This genus within the ivy (Araliaceae) family contains only 3 evergreen species of large-leafed small trees and shrubs from moist coastal woodlands of South Korea, Japan, and Taiwan. They tend to sucker from the base, producing a fuller shrub; unwanted stems can be removed. Tolerant of

Fatsia japonica

Felicia fruticosa

pollution and salt spray and moderately frost hardy. Variegated cultivars are less frost tolerant. Good indoor and conservatory plants with ornamental leaves, and good specimen plants for courtyards and terraces.
CULTIVATION: They like moisture-retentive soil in sun or part shade. In warm climates they can be grown under trees. In shade, they tolerate dry nutrient-deficient soil, but do better in more fertile soil. In colder areas, they need the protection of a wall or similar shelter. Under glass and in pots, they need a loam-based compost, regular feeding, and watering during growing season. Propagate from seed sown in autumn, from cuttings, or by air-layering.

Fatsia japonica

syns *Aralia japonica, A. sieboldii*

FATSIA, JAPANESE ARALIA

☼/◐ ❄ ↔ 6–12 ft (1.8–3.5 m)
↕ 6–12 ft (1.8–3.5 m)

Native to South Korea and Japan. Leaves dark green, glossy, 7 to 11 lobes, mostly toothed, palmately lobed. Rounded flowerheads of creamy white flowers, in late summer–autumn. Fruit green, ripening black by the spring. **'Aurea'**, yellow variegations; **'Marginata'**, leaves gray-green, white margins, deeply lobed; **'Moseri'** ★, more compact, vigorous, larger leaves; **'Variegata'**, leaf lobes deeply edged with cream tips. Zones 8–11.

FELICIA

This is a genus of about 80 species of annuals, perennials, subshrubs, and shrubs in the daisy (Asteraceae) family, mostly evergreen. Most are from South Africa, with a few from eastern Africa and Arabia. Preferring open, sunny, low-humidity areas, most species need frost-free conditions. They are grown for their mainly blue flowerheads with yellow disc florets. Mauve, pink, and white forms are also available, as are some new cultivars. The shrubby forms are popular as annual container and patio plants, and will overwinter in a greenhouse in colder areas.
CULTIVATION: They grow outdoors in moderately fertile soil, but prolonged damp conditions can kill them. In containers they need a loam-based compost with added grit for drainage. Propagate from seed sown in spring, or by taking stem-tip cuttings in summer and overwintering in frost-free conditions.

Felicia amelloides

syns *Agathaea coelestis, Felicia aethiopica*

BLUE DAISY, BLUE MARGUERITE

☼ ❄ ↔ 24 in (60 cm)
↕ 16–24 in (40–60 cm)

Summer-flowering South African subshrub, trailing and/or upright stems. Fine-haired leaves light green. Solitary flowers, vivid yellow disc florets, light to dark blue ray florets. **'Blue Eyes'**, deep blue flowers; **'Santa Anita'**, heavy flowering, hardier. Zones 9–10.

Felicia fruticosa

☼ ❄ ↔ 36 in (90 cm) ↕ 36 in (90 cm)

Evergreen shrub, native to South Africa. Linear leaves densely packed. Ray florets pink, purple, or white, with yellow disc. Fruits are hairy. Lengthy flowering season through spring–summer; can be extended by deadheading. Zones 9–11.

FEROCACTUS

BARREL CACTUS

This is a genus of 29 species of barrel-shaped cacti (family Cactaceae) from the semi-arid areas of southwestern USA and Mexico, especially Baja California. The name refers to the strong stout spines, which are often savagely hooked. *Ferocactus* is distinguished from the closely related genus *Echinocactus* by the absence of wool at the growing tip. Most are solitary, a few branch, and some form mats and grow to massive proportions.

Felicia amelloides

Ferocactus alamosanus subsp. *reppenhagenii*

Stems are spherical to columnar to barrel-shaped. Ribs range from few to many, often very deep and prominent. The large areoles usually have glands, which secrete nectar that is attractive to ants and other insects. Flowers form near the growing tip and are short, funnelform or bell-shaped, with prominent scales. Seed pods are oval to spherical, dry or juicy at maturity.
CULTIVATION: Relatively easy to grow in rich, very well-drained, predominantly mineral soil, with moderate watering in warmer months but a distinct rest in winter. For good spination, full sun and low humidity are essential. Being mainly solitary, they are almost invariably raised from seed.

Ferocactus alamosanus

☼ ❄ ↔ 12 in (30 cm) ↕ 40 in (100 cm)

From Mexico. Usually solitary, densely spined, with 12 to 20 ribs, narrow, sharply pointed, blunt, or rounded. Spines yellow, needle-like, central, 8 to 12 radials. Flowers funnelform, greenish yellow. Seed pods oval. F. a. subsp. reppenhagenii, 12 to 18 ribs, merging areoles. Zones 9–11.

Ferocactus cylindraceus

Ferocactus cylindraceus

syns *Ferocactus acanthodes, F. lecontei, F. tortulispinus*

CALIFORNIA BARREL CACTUS, COMPASS CACTUS

☼ ❄ ↔ 20 in (50 cm) ↕ 10 ft (3 m)

From southern California, Nevada, Utah, and Arizona, USA, and Baja California and Sonora, Mexico. Solitary, spherical to cylindrical, 20 to 30 ribs with tubercles, slightly wavy ribs with transverse creases. Spines are white, yellow, red, or gray; 10 centrals, 4 to 12 radials. Flowers are bell-shaped, red, yellow, or orange. Seed pods are yellow. ***F. c.* subsp. *lecontei***, straight central spines, never hooked, closely pressed against stem. Winter dry. Zones 7–11.

Ferocactus glaucescens

Ferocactus latispinus

F

Ferocactus emoryi

syn. *Ferocactus covillei*

↔3 ft (0.9 m) ↑8 ft (2.4 m)

From central Arizona, USA, and Sonora, Sinaloa, and Baja California Sur, Mexico. Solitary, spherical to cylindrical, light to bluish green with 15 to 30 ribs, distinctly tuberculed when young. Spines whitish to reddish; 1 central, 7 to 9 radials. Flowers funnelform, mahogany red to red, tinged with yellow. Seed pods oval. *F. e.* subsp. *rectispinus*, smaller stems, 21 ribs. Zones 9–11.

Ferocactus glaucescens ★

↔20 in (50 cm) ↑18 in (45 cm)

From Hidalgo, Mexico. Solitary to many-stemmed, with slightly depressed tops, distinctly powdery pale bluish gray-green, 12 to 17 ribs, no tubercles, long merging areoles. Spines awl-shaped, yellow, 1 central, 6 to 7 radials. Flowers bell-shaped, yellow. Seed pods spherical, whitish or yellowish. Zones 9–11.

Ferocactus gracilis

FIRE BARREL CACTUS

↔12 in (30 cm) ↑5 ft (1.5 m)

From Baja California, Mexico. Solitary, spherical to cylindrical, deep green, 16 to 24 ribs, slightly tuberculed. Spines red with yellow tips; 7 to 13 centrals, 4 main centrals, 8 to 12 radials. Flowers funnelform, red. Seed pods oval, yellow. *F. g.* subsp. *coloratus*, rarely reaches 40 in (100 cm), widest central spine often over ¼ in (6 mm) in diameter. Zones 9–11.

Ferocactus herrerae

syn. *Ferocactus wislizenii var. herrerae*

↔18 in (45 cm) ↑7 ft (2 m)

From Sinaloa, Sonora, and Durango, Mexico. Solitary, with 13 deep, spiraling, deeply tuberculed ribs. Spines variable with age; 6 centrals, several radials. Flowers funnelform, yellow with red mid-stripes, to 2½ in (6 cm) long and wide. Seed pods oval, yellow-green. Zones 9–11.

Ferocactus histrix

↔32 in (80 cm) ↑48 in (120 cm)

From central Mexico. Solitary, flattened spherical to short cylindrical, with large, depressed, woolly stem tip, 20 to 40 ribs, areoles almost merging. Spines strong, yellow, becoming gray with age; 1 to 4 centrals, 6 to 9 radials. Flowers bell-shaped, yellow. Seed pods fleshy, yellow. Zones 9–11.

Ferocactus latispinus ★

↔16 in (40 cm) ↑12 in (30 cm)

From much of central Mexico. Solitary, light green, spherical to flattened, 20 or more deep tuberculed ribs. Spines reddish to yellowish to white; 4 centrals, 5 to 15 radials. Flowers funnelform, purplish pink or yellow, densely overlapping, fringed bracts. Seed pods oval, covered with scales. Zones 9–11.

Ferocactus robustus

↔7 ft (2 m) ↑3 ft (0.9 m)

From southeastern Puebla, Mexico. Distinctive species, usually grows in large clumps of spherical to club-shaped deep green stems, about 8 deep tuberculed ribs with widely spaced areoles. Spines can be reddish, purplish, or tan, with 4 to 7 centrals, erect, straight, and 10 to 14 radials, upper similar to centrals, lower bristle-like, white. Flowers are yellow, funnelform. Seed pods are spherical, yellow, and fleshy. Zones 9–11.

Ferocactus wislizeni ★

ARIZONA BARREL CACTUS, CANDY BARREL CACTUS

↔32 in (80 cm) ↑10 ft (3 m)

From central and southern Arizona, southern New Mexico, southwest Texas, USA, and northwest Mexico. Solitary giant, 20 to 30 ribs, barely tuberculed, widely spaced areoles when young, merging with age. Spines variable, white to red to gray, 4 centrals; 12 or so radials. Flowers funnelform, yellow to yellowish orange. Seed pods oval, green, turning yellow when ripe. The native Seri peoples of Mexico have used the spines as fishhooks, the flesh to make candies, and the dried floral remains as a dye for face paint. Zones 9–11.

Festuca californica

Festuca glauca 'Blauglut'

FESTUCA

FESCUE

A genus of some 300 species in the grass (Poaceae) family, widespread throughout the world. Mostly small unassuming plants, they are valued ornamentally for their sometimes distinctively colored foliage and showy flower plumes; and commercially and practically as some of the finest lawn grasses available, especially for high-quality, low-traffic lawns. The leaves are usually folded around the midrib, in some species making the foliage very fine and hair-like. The flowerheads, which usually exceed foliage in height, are feathery and open.

CULTIVATION: While hardiness varies, most are at home in temperate zones and thrive in most soils with minimal attention, though few will tolerate prolonged poor drainage. Plant in full sun or partial shade. As lawn grasses, they appreciate annual dethatching and aeration. Green year-round, but in hot conditions take care to water well and do not mow too closely. Propagate by dividing established clumps, or raise from seed.

Festuca longifolia

Festuca amethystina

LARGE BLUE FESCUE, TUFTED FESCUE

↔10 in (25 cm) ↑18 in (45 cm)

From central and eastern Europe. Tussock-forming perennial grass with soft gray-green foliage. Flower spikes appear, bearing small violet-green flowers, in early summer. Zones 4–9.

Festuca californica

CALIFORNIA FESCUE

↔24 in (60 cm) ↑24–36 in (60–90 cm)

From California, USA. Foliage green to bright blue; blue forms take on purplish tones once frosts commence. Pale creamy green flower spikes, in summer. **'Serpentine Blue'** ★ (blue California fescue), rich silvery foliage, red-purple autumn tones, not good in shade. Zones 5–9.

Festuca filiformis

FINE-LEAFED SHEEP'S FESCUE, HAIR FESCUE

↔8 in (20 cm) ↑15 in (38 cm)

North American species with short, very fine, green to blue-green, hair-like leaves. Panicles of green or light purple flowers, on wiry stems, in summer. Zones 4–9.

Festuca glauca

BLUE FESCUE, GRAY FESCUE

↔10 in (25 cm) ↑12 in (30 cm)

Found throughout Europe. Densely tufted evergreen grass. Smooth blue-green leaves surround crown of plant. Creamy flower spikes appear from mid-summer, sitting well above the foliage. **'Blaufuchs'** ★ (syn. Blue Fox), intense powder blue leaves, fade to cream at tips; **'Blauglut'** (syn. Blue Glow), clump-forming, intense silver-blue foliage; **'Elijah Blue'**, soft powdery blue foliage, very compact; **'Seeigel'** (syn. Sea Urchin), very fine, upright, spiky, blue-green leaves, very compact. Zones 4–10.

Festuca idahoensis

↔ 12 in (30 cm) ↑ 15 in (38 cm)

From western Canada and northwestern USA, densely tufted, longer living species than *F. glauca*. Tends not to die out in center. Foliage blue-green to silver-blue. Creamy flower spikes appear in summer. Tolerant of wet conditions. Zones 3–8.

Festuca longifolia

HARD FESCUE

↔ 16 in (40 cm) ↑ 24 in (60 cm)

Widespread in almost all northern temperate zones. Popular pasture and lawn grass. Bright green leaves. Buff-colored panicles of flowers, on tall wiry stems, in summer. Does best in cool climates. Zones 5–9.

Festuca ovina

SHEEP'S FESCUE

↔ 16 in (40 cm) ↑ 24 in (60 cm)

Tussock-forming species, very widespread in northern temperate zones. Sometimes used in lawns. Fine blue-green leaves with similarly-colored panicles of flowers, on tall wiry stems, in summer. Zones 5–9.

Festuca pratensis

MEADOW FESCUE, WESTERN FESCUE

↔ 16 in (40 cm) ↑ 24 in (60 cm)

Quick-growing species, widespread in northern temperate zones, and especially in western North America. Fine foliage and summer-flowering panicles, which are golden brown when dry. Occasionally may be used in pastures, but considered a potentially invasive weed in many areas. Zones 5–10.

Festuca valesiaca

WALLIS FESCUE

↔ 6 in (15 cm) ↑ 6 in (15 cm)

This tight, clump-forming, dwarf grass species from central Europe has soft powdery blue foliage. The bluish white flower spikes are held above foliage, in mid-summer. This plant needs well-drained soils, and is ideal in rockeries but not in hot situations. Zones 5–9.

Festuca varia

↔ 15 in (38 cm) ↑ 22 in (55 cm)

Southern European alpine species, aromatic hair-like foliage and downy, violet-tinted, blue-green panicles of flowers. *F. v.* **subsp.** ***scopari***, downy, blue tips. Zones 5–9.

FICUS

FIG

Although this genus is in the mulberry (Moraceae) family, its flower and fruiting stages differ from those of the rest of this family. Fig species come in many variations, from climbers and creepers to large shrubs and very large trees. Many fig species of tropical forests display the "strangler" growth habit, some also develop "curtains" of aerial roots, or even the "banyan" growth form. *Ficus* species have a milky sap, and a large stipule enclosing the tip of each twig and leaving a ring-like scar when it falls. Leaves vary from tiny to huge, with variable shape. Many species shed their leaves in the tropical dry season. The "fruits" (figs) also vary greatly in size, and can be eaten by birds or mammals.

CULTIVATION: *F. carica* can cope with occasional frosts down to about 21°F (–6°C); other species tolerate light frosts only if protected when small. Figs are vigorous growers, and will quickly outgrow a small garden. Propagate from seed, from cuttings, or by air layering. *F. carica*, the edible fig, is the most easily propagated species.

Ficus benghalensis

BANYAN

↔ 75–400 ft (23–120 m) ↑ 30–40 ft (9–12 m)

Southern Asian fig, widespread in India. Vastly spreading; a single tree may produce hundreds, sometimes thousands, of trunks, creating its own mini forest. Broad, stiff leaves, shiny deep green; stalkless figs, ripen to orange. A sacred tree of Hinduism, special in Indian folklore. **'Krishnae'**, similar proportions, inrolled cup-shaped leaves. Zones 11–12.

Ficus benjamina

BENJAMIN FIG, BENJAMIN TREE, WEEPING FIG

↔ 50 ft (15 m) ↑ 80 ft (24 m)

Tropical Asian species, popular foliage plant. Small glossy leaves, pointing downward, narrowing abruptly at apex. Figs deep reddish tan. *F. b.* **var.** ***nuda*** (syn. *F. b.* var. *comosa*), robust, broad-spreading limbs, non-drooping branchlets, leaves abruptly narrowed at tip, orange figs. *F. b.* **'Exotica'** ★, thinner, more finely pointed leaves; **'Golden Princess'**, leaves tinged lemon yellow; **'Pandora'**, small thin leaves, wavy margins; **'Starlight'**, similar to **'Variegata'**, leaves cream-edged gray-green flecked. Zones 10–12.

Ficus carica

EDIBLE FIG

↔ 15–30ft (4.5–9 m) ↑ 35 ft (10 m)

Cultivated over 5,000 years ago in western Asia, origins are obscure. Deciduous tree, spreading rounded canopy. Smooth silvery-gray bark. Leaves 3- to 5-lobed, toothed edges. Tiny flowers. Purple-brown fruit. Used for dried figs. Prefers a climate with long warm summers, dry atmosphere, on soils of low to medium fertility. **'Black Genoa'** ★, large tree, profuse dull purple fruits, very sweet dark red flesh; **'Brown Turkey'**, prolific, pink-fleshed, brown-skinned figs, flavor sweet but slightly insipid; **'White Adriatic'**, tall grower, pale greenish brown figs, tasty deep pink flesh. Most zones 8-12; some performing and fruiting in zone 6. Inquire locally.

Ficus elastica

INDIA-RUBBER TREE, RUBBER TREE

↔ 40–100 ft (12–30 m) ↑ 40–100 ft (12–30 m)

Tropical Asian fig, once renowned as an important source of rubber, or "caoutchouc," tapped from trees in Bangladesh and Assam in India. In the mid-twentieth century, it became the archetypal indoor plant. Large tree, numerous aerial roots draped from its branches. **'Decora'** ★, broad, glossy, bronze-tinted leaves, large reddish buds at apex; **'Doescheri'**, leaves irregularly edged cream, center marbled gray; **'Schrüveriana'**, leaves peppered with dark green, new leaves flushed red; **'Variegata'**, variegated leaves of deep green and cream. Zones 11–12.

Ficus benghalensis

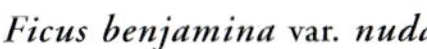

Ficus benjamina var. *nuda*

Ficus benjamina

Ficus carica

Ficus glumosa

F

Ficus glumosa

BERGVY, MOUNTAIN FIG

↔25–60 ft (8–18 m) ↕17–30 ft (5–9 m)

Slow-growing deciduous tree from South Africa. Large vigorous root system, short upright trunk, bark mottled yellow and gray. Green oval-shaped foliage. Leaves and branches covered with yellowish hairs. Figs, borne in the axils without stems, turn yellow with age. Zones 7–9.

Ficus lutea

syns *Ficus nekbudu, F. vogelii, F. zuluensis*

NEKBUDU, VOGEL'S FIG, ZULU FIG

↔40 ft (12 m) ↕60 ft (18 m)

Found throughout most of Africa south of the Sahara, and on Madagascar and other Indian Ocean islands. Large strangler fig, very wide rounded crown. Evergreen leaves; small orange to red figs, crowded along branch ends. Zones 11–12.

Ficus lyrata

FIDDLE-LEAF FIG

↔30 ft (9 m) ↕30 ft (9 m)

From rainforests of central Africa and tropical west Africa. Bushy-crowned erect tree; large stiff leaves resemble a violin body. Green figs, hidden under the leaves. Popular pot plant in the 1950s and 1960s. Zones 9–12.

Ficus macrophylla

MORETON BAY FIG

↔130 ft (40 m) ↕80–100 ft (24–30 m)

From Australia's east coast; rapid growth, dramatic trunk buttresses, large canopy. Large dark green leaves, glossy, thick. Purple figs. *F. m* subsp. *columnaris,* known as banyan, occurs offshore on Lord Howe Island, forming subsidiary trunks and a spreading canopy over endemic palm, *Howea forsteriana*. Zones 9–11.

Ficus pumila

CREEPING FIG

↔unlimited ↕10–30 ft (3–9 m)

From China and Japan, self-clinging evergreen climber. Small, flat, heart-

Ficus lutea

shaped leaves. Vigorous, thick, non-clinging branches with age, with large fleshy leaves. Large, purplish green, barrel-like figs develop on old plants. **'Dorthe'**, green leaves, cream centers; **'Minima'**, smaller leaves; **'Sonny'**, cream leaves, green centers. Zones 8–11.

Ficus religiosa

BO TREE, PEEPUL TREE, SACRED FIG

↔25 ft (8 m) ↕30–40 ft (9–12 m)

Native to the mountains of Southeast Asia and the Himalayan foothills; this species is significant for its rôle in Buddhist philosophy. Strangling fig, normally deciduous in monsoonal climates. Pale gray-barked trunk, spreading branches. Leaves heart-shaped, apex drawn out into a long slender point. Zones 9–12.

Ficus rubiginosa

PORT JACKSON FIG, RUSTY FIG

↔35–70 ft (10–21 m) ↕30–80 ft (9–24 m)

From the east coast of Australia. Evergreen tree, forms a broad dome. Massive buttressed trunk, smooth gray limbs, sprouting aerial roots. Thick, leathery, oval leaves, dark green with rusty or pale olive felted reverse. Figs yellowish green, warty, ripen in autumn. A gold-variegated form is available. Zones 9–11.

Ficus thonningii

syn. *Ficus petersii*

COMMON STRANGLER FIG, COMMON WILD FIG, GEWONE WILDEVY

↔10–40 ft (3–12 m) ↕20–60 ft (6–18 m)

Evergreen fig native to South Africa. Variable size and habit, can be tall tree, strangler fig, or rock fig. Vigorous invasive root system. Hairy figs borne in leaf axils, on short stalks or none. Timber used for furniture and implements. Zones 7–9.

Filipendula vulgaris

FILIPENDULA

DROPWORT, MEADOWSWEET

This genus of about 10 species of tuberous clump-forming perennials belongs to the rose (Rosaceae) family. They are native to northern temperate regions, where they are usually found growing in damp habitats. These tall attractive plants have large pinnately or palmately divided leaves, and bear plumes of tiny white or pink flowers. Some species have been used in herbal medicine for centuries. Salicin, an ingredient in aspirin, was discovered in *F. ulmaria* in 1839. The name aspirin is in part derived from *Spiraea*, the genus in which *Filipendula* was once included.

CULTIVATION: Grow in part-shade in moist humus-rich soil that does not dry out in summer. Propagate from seed or by division.

Filipendula purpurea

↔18 in (45 cm) ↕36–48 in (90–120 cm)

Native to Japan. Stems and leaf stalks often purple. Stiff, palmate, dark green leaves. Plumes of small deep pink to purplish red flowers, in summer. Zones 6–9.

Filipendula rubra

QUEEN OF THE PRAIRIE

↔2 ft (0.6 m) ↕3–7 ft (0.9–2 m)

From eastern USA. Vigorous perennial, forming large clumps of deeply divided foliage. In summer, tall stems of peachy pink flowers are borne in plumes. **'Venusta'** ★ (syn. 'Magnifica'), deep rose flowers. Zones 2–9.

Filipendula ulmaria

MEADOWSWEET, QUEEN OF THE MEADOWS

↔12–18 in (45–60 cm) ↕24–48 in (60–120 cm)

From Europe and Western Asia. Large divided leaves, dark green, hairy beneath. Plumes of creamy white fragrant flowers borne in summer. **'Aurea'**, golden foliage; **'Rosea'**, soft pink flowers; **'Variegata'**, leaves with central yellow stripe. Zones 3–9.

Filipendula vulgaris

syn. *Filipendula hexapetala*

DROPWORT

↔18 in (45 cm) ↕24–36 in (60–90 cm)

From Europe and northern and central Asia. Tuberous with deeply cut fern-like leaves. Small white flowers, often tinged reddish purple, borne in feathery heads, in summer. Zones 3–9.

FOENICULUM

FENNEL

A culinary herb, and in many areas a weed of waste ground, fennel belongs to the carrot (Apiaceae) family. It is an aromatic biennial or perennial from Europe and the Mediterranean region. It forms a clump of erect hollow stems with feathery foliage made up of many hair-like deep green to bronze leaflets. Heads of small yellow flowers appear through summer, then dry to become similarly shaped pale brown seed heads. Despite its scent and flavor, it is not a plant for small gardens, as it has invasive tendencies.

CULTIVATION: It will grow in most soils and climates, from cool-temperate to subtropical, in moderately fertile soil and a little summer moisture, but a rich well-drained soil and good water will impart a more delicate flavor. Propagate from seed; perennial forms will also grow from divisions.

Foeniculum vulgare

FENNEL

↔18–36 in (45–90 cm) ↕3–7 ft (0.9–2 m)

From Europe and the Mediterranean region, naturalized elsewhere. Hollow-stemmed aromatic perennial, soft, fine, green, fern-like foliage smelling of aniseed. Umbels of small yellow

Foeniculum vulgare 'Purpureum'

Forsythia × *intermedia* 'Arnold Giant'

Forsythia ovata 'Tetragold'

Forsythia suspensa

Forsythia, HC, 'New Hampshire Gold'

flowers in summer. *F. v.* var. ***azoricum*** (Florence fennel, Finocchio), smaller annual grown as a vegetable for its swollen basal stem, eaten fresh or cooked; **'Perfection'** and **'Zefo Fino'**, slow to grow. *F. v.* **'Purpureum'** (syns 'Bronze', 'Purpurascens') has dark purplish maroon to bronze foliage. Zones 5–10.

FORESTIERA

A genus of some 15 species from the Americas, especially southwest North America, in the olive (Oleaceae) family. Usually dioecious deciduous small trees or shrubs. Short-stalked leaves are opposite, with smooth to minutely toothed margins. Inflorescences are racemes or clusters in leaf axils on previous season's growth, sometimes maturing before the leaves. Flowers are small, with green petals or none. Fruit is a single-seeded black drupe.

CULTIVATION: They need full sun and well-drained soil. Propagate from half-hardened cuttings or seed. They have little ornamental value.

Forestiera pubescens ★

syn. ***Forestiera neomexicana***

DESERT OLIVE, NEW MEXICAN PRIVET

☼ ✱ ↔8 ft (2.4 m) ↑10 ft (3 m)

Deciduous shrub from southwestern USA. Small, smooth, green leaves, turn yellow in autumn. Insignificant yellow flowers appear in spring before the leaves. Clusters of small, bluish black fruits. Zones 6–10.

FORSYTHIA

This small genus of about 7 species of deciduous shrubs is a member of the olive (Oleaceae) family. They occur mainly in eastern Asia, with one species in southeastern Europe. The simple opposite leaves color in autumn. The yellow flowers appear before, or with, the new leaves in spring. Those species that are semi-pendulous can be trained over a support as wall plants.

CULTIVATION: They are frost hardy and easy to cultivate in well-drained fertile soil in an open sunny position, with adequate water in summer, and winter temperatures below freezing to induce flowering. Flowers are borne on overwintered year-old shoots; remove older shoots when flowering has finished to make room for new shoots that arise from the base of the plant. Propagate from soft-tip cuttings taken in summer, or hardwood cuttings taken in winter. Some species are self-layering and can be increased in this way in late winter.

Forsythia giraldiana

☼ ✱ ↔12 ft (3.5 m) ↑12 ft (3.5 m)

From northwestern China. Shrub with open arching habit. One of the earliest in this genus to flower. Gray-green leaves. Pale yellow blooms, in late winter. Zones 5–9.

Forsythia × *intermedia*

BORDER FORSYTHIA

☼ ✱ ↔7 ft (2 m) ↑15 ft (4.5 m)

This shrub has an erect spreading habit and is a hybrid between *F. suspensa* var. *sieboldii* and *F. viridissima*. It has a single basal trunk, and ascending, arching branches. The leaves are oval-shaped, sharply toothed on the upper half, with reddish stalks. Lemon yellow blooms are solitary or in 2- to 6-flowered racemes and appear on 1- and 2-year-old branches during spring. **'Arnold Giant'**, large, nodding, rich yellow flowers; **'Goldzauber'**, brilliant yellow flowers appear before leaves; **'Lynwood'**, prolific large flowers, broad petals; **'Spectabilis'**, upright, outwardly arching shrub, flowers large, golden yellow. Zones 5–9.

Forsythia ovata

EARLY FORSYTHIA, KOREAN FORSYTHIA

☼ ✱ ↔8 ft (2.4 m) ↑5 ft (1.5 m)

Compact, bushy, early-flowering species from Korea. Leaves dark green, ovate. Golden yellow flowers, in early spring. **'Tetragold'**, raised in Holland, dense habit, larger flowers appear earlier. Zones 5–9.

Forsythia suspensa

GOLDENBELLS, WEEPING FORSYTHIA

☼ ✱ ↔10 ft (3 m) ↑12 ft (3.5 m)

From China. Slender drooping branches. Autumn foliage dull yellow. Flowers solitary or in small clusters, golden yellow, in spring. *F. s.* var. ***fortunei***, vigorous form, more upright habit; *F. s.* var. ***sieboldii***, almost prostrate, rarely taller than 3 ft (0.9 m), spreads by self-layering. Zones 4–9.

Forsythia viridissima

GOLDEN BELLS, GREEN STEM FORSYTHIA

☼ ✱ ↔10 ft (3 m) ↑10 ft (3 m)

From China. Cane-like branches grow from base into hemispherical bush. Long narrow leaves, smooth, dark green, rather shiny, maroon in autumn. Clusters of yellow flowers in leaf axils appear before leaves, calyx purple shaded. **'Bronxensis'**, dwarf form, primrose-colored flowers. Zones 5–9.

Forsythia Hybrid Cultivars

☼ ✱ ↔10 ft (3 m) ↑5–10 ft (1.5–3 m)

Hardy and colorful, they include: **'Arnold Dwarf'** ★, light green foliage; **'Happy Centennial'**, bright yellow flowers; **'Maluch'**, profuse flowers with new leaves; **Marée d'Or/'Courtasol'**, heavily branched dwarf, prolific yellow-gold flowers; **'Meadow Lark'**, heavy flowering, buds very hardy; **'New Hampshire Gold'**, yellow flowers, in early spring; **'Northern Gold'**, shiny bright green leaves, golden yellow flowers; **'Northern Sun'**, strong-growing shrub, clear yellow flowers, in spring. Zones 4–9.

FOTHERGILLA

Mainly from southeastern USA, this genus of 2 deciduous shrubs belongs to the witchhazel (Hamamelidaceae) family. Spikes of petal-less flowers appear in spring before the leaves, their long white stamens creating a bottlebrush effect. Autumn foliage forms a brilliant display of crimson, orange, and yellow.

CULTIVATION: Slow growing, they need moist, well-drained, humus-rich soil. Full sun gives best autumn color. Propagate from seed, best sown fresh, from softwood cuttings in summer, or by layering.

F

Fothergilla gardenii

Fothergilla major

Fouquieria diguetii

Fothergilla gardenii ★

DWARF FOTHERGILLA

☼ ✱ ↔3 ft (0.9 m) ↕3 ft (0.9 m)

Southeastern USA, from North Carolina to Alabama. Spreading shrub, oval leaves, irregularly toothed, fragrant white flowers. '**Blue Mist**', glaucous blue foliage. Zones 5–9.

Fothergilla major

LARGE FOTHERGILLA

☼ ✱ ↔6 ft (1.8 m) ↕5–10 ft (1.5–3 m)

From the Allegheny Mountains of eastern USA. Slow growing erect habit. Leaves dark green above, glaucous beneath. Good autumn color. Fragrant white flower spikes, pinkish tinge, in late spring–early summer. '**Mount Airy**', scented, white, bottlebrush-like flowers, red autumn foliage. Zones 5–9.

FOUQUIERIA

This genus of 11 species of woody or succulent, spiny, deciduous shrubs and small trees occurs in arid regions in the southwest of North America, such as Baja California, Mexico. It is a member of the ocotillo (Fouquieriaceae) family. Small bright green leaves emerge after the irregular rains of those regions. All species have spines along stems and branches. Some grow as columnar unbranched stems up to 50 ft (15 m) tall. Red, purple, cream, or yellow tubular flowers are produced at tips of branches or stems after rain, usually in spring, followed by capsules containing winged seeds.

CULTIVATION: They require full sun, in climates similar to those where they occur naturally. Too much rain, or over-watering, can be fatal. Since all species are frost tender when young, propagate from seed or cuttings in late spring to summer.

Fouquieria diguetii

TALL OCOTILLO

☼ ❄ ↔6 ft (1.8 m) ↕7 ft (2 m)

Occurs in Sonoran Desert of southern California, USA, and in Mexico in Baja California and northwest. Short, but definite, trunk, erect branches. Panicles of red tubular flowers, in late winter–early spring. Zones 9–11.

Fouquieria splendens ★

OCOTILLO

☼ ❄ ↔6 ft (1.8 m) ↕30 ft (9 m)

From arid regions of northern Mexico, and southern California, New Mexico, and Texas, USA. Many-branched shrub; long, cylindrical, gray-green, spiny stems. Small green leaves appear after rain, falling during long dry periods. Panicles of bell-shaped bright red flowers, in early spring–summer. Zones 7–11.

FRAGARIA

STRAWBERRY

This genus of 12 perennials, a member of the rose (Rosaceae) family, is found in northern temperate zones and in Chile. Many botanists now believe that the distinction between *Fragaria* and the large, diverse genus *Potentilla* is artificial, and that the strawberries should be included in *Potentilla*. It is likely that this reclassification will be generally accepted in the future. Among the most widely grown of the small fruits, strawberries are tough adaptable plants that spread by runners. The leaves grow in groups of 3, and are heart-shaped to rounded, with toothed edges. Clusters of pretty, white, 5-petalled flowers precede the familiar fruits, which may be red, white, yellow, pink, or orange. The fruits are unusual in that they carry their seeds on the outside.

CULTIVATION: Hardy in temperate zones in all but the coldest winters, strawberries need moist, fertile, well-drained soil, water to swell the fruit, and sun to ripen it. Planting atop mounds ensures good drainage and, combined with mulching, helps to keep the fruit dry. Covers of netting to keep the birds away from the fruit are almost essential. Propagation is usually by layering, using either natural layers or runners, pegged down until the roots establish.

Fragaria chiloensis

BEACH STRAWBERRY

☼/◐ ✱ ↔20 in (50 cm) ↕6 in (15 cm)

From North and South America. Short thick leaves, hairy undersides. White flowers, rose-colored edible fruit with white flesh. Called "beach strawberry" because it grows naturally in coastal areas. Zones 4–10.

Fragaria vesca

WILD STRAWBERRY

☼/◐ ✱ ↔12 in (30 cm) ↕2 in (5 cm)

From European woodland regions. Compact rosettes of dark green leaves on ground-hugging plant. Flowers white; dark red, sweet, edible fruits in summer. '**Alexandra**', smaller red berries, very sweet, plant habit slightly smaller than species; '**Fructo Albo**' (white wild strawberry), creamy white edible fruits, in summer. Zones 5–9.

Fragaria Hybrid Cultivars

☼/◐ ✱ ↔8–60 in (20–150 cm) ↕2–6 in (5–15 cm)

These are popular mainly for their ground-covering abilities, although some do produce edible fruits. The most popular hybrid cultivars include: '**Darselect**', large, firm, bright red berries; '**Lipstick**', ornamental variety, dark green leaves, deep pink flowers, small fruit; Pink Panda/'**Frel**', dark green, heavily veined, palmate foliage, sterile pink flowers, no fruit; '**Rosie**', ground-covering habit, sterile variety, rosy red flowers. Zones 5–9.

FRANCOA

BRIDAL WREATH

This Chilean genus is sometimes treated as comprising 5 species, but recent studies treat it as having the single variable species *F. sonchifolia*, the type form for its family, the Francoaceae. This summer-flowering perennial has rosettes of foliage and long-stemmed, many-flowered sprays of small pink and white blooms. Leaves are pointed, oval to lance-shaped in outline, but with large lobes that often effectively make them pinnate. The upper leaf surface is bristly and the underside is conspicuously veined. The wiry flower stems, with their tiny 4-petaled flowers, create an airy effect.

CULTIVATION: Hardy in temperate areas where winter frosts are light and infrequent. Easily grown in any well-drained soil that does not dry out in summer. Plant in a bright position. Most often propagated by division or from small basal cuttings.

Francoa sonchifolia

syns *Francoa glabrata, F. ramosa*

☼/◐ ❄ ↔18–24 in (45–60 cm) ↕24 in (60 cm)

From Chile. Rosettes of soft, hairy, spoon-shaped leaves. Unbranched flowering stems bear spikes of white or pink flowers with darker spotting, in summer. Zones 7–10.

Francoa sonchifolia

Fragaria chiloensis

Fragaria, Hybrid Cultivar, 'Rosie'

FRANGULA

A genus of up to 30 species of evergreen and deciduous shrubs of the buckthorn (Rhamnaceae) family that were until recently classified under *Rhamnus.* They occur through the northern temperate zones and are quick-growing, usually about as wide as they are high, have rounded, deeply veined leaves, small, white to cream flowers in sprays in the leaf axils, followed by small red to black berries.
CULTIVATION: Very easily grown in sun or part-shade with moist well-drained soil. Some species are invasive and have become weeds away from their natural range. Propagation is from seed, which is best stratified, semi-ripe cuttings, or by layers.

Frangula californica

syn. ***Rhamnus californica***

COFFEEBERRY

↔10 ft (3 m) ↑12 ft (3.5 m)

Evergreen to semi-evergreen upright shrub from western USA. Red new growth, shiny green leaves. Clusters of pale greenish yellow flowers, in late spring–early summer. Round red berries, ripen to black. Zones 7–10.

FRANKLINIA

This is a monotypic genus in the camellia (Theaceae) family. Probably every franklinia in cultivation today is a direct descendant of seeds collected in 1765 in Georgia, USA, and named after Benjamin Franklin. The species has not been seen in the wild for over 200 years. *Franklinia* is closely related to *Gordonia,* with which it is sometimes merged, but differs in being deciduous, and having almost stalkless flowers. Fruit is a large woody capsule containing two flattened seeds.
CULTIVATION: *Franklinia* will tolerate a slightly alkaline soil, but likes plenty of organic material; a sheltered aspect with some morning sun is preferred. Propagate from fresh seed.

Franklinia alatamaha ★

FRANKLIN TREE, FRANKLINIA

↔12 ft (3.5 m) ↑20 ft (6 m)

From the Altahama River region in Georgia, USA. Attractive, small, upright, deciduous tree. The glossy bright green leaves color scarlet in autumn. The single camellia-like flowers, pure white with a central bunch of yellow stamens, appear in late summer–autumn. Zones 7–10.

FRAXINUS

ASH

This genus in the olive (Oleaceae) family consists of 65 species. Most

Fraxinus americana 'Autumn Purple'

Fraxinus species are deciduous trees, but the genus also includes a few evergreens. They are mainly from temperate Europe, Asia, and North America, although a few species are found in the tropics. Their leaves are opposite and pinnate. Racemes of small, usually insignificant flowers are borne terminally or in the leaf axils, appearing before the leaves, in spring; flowers are unisexual or bisexual. They harden into single-seeded winged fruits. The timber is used for sports equipment and tool handles, and the bark is used medicinally. The foliage is utilized as cattle fodder in Scandinavia. *F. chinensis* is the source of "Chinese insect white wax," and *F. ornus* is cultivated in southern Italy for manna syrup.
CULTIVATION: Most grow well in moist loam and make good specimen trees in large gardens. They tolerate coastal salt air, exposed positions, urban pollution, alkaline soil, and heavy clay. Most species prefer alkaline soil. Propagate by sowing seed after stratifying. Cultivars can be grafted in spring, or they may be budded onto seedling stock of the same species in summer.

Fraxinus americana

WHITE ASH

↔50 ft (15 m) ↑80 ft (24 m)

Native to eastern North America, columnar tree with spreading crown. Leaves pinnate, dark green, with 5 to 9 lance-shaped leaflets. **'Autumn Blaze'**, purple color in autumn; **'Autumn Purple'** ★, autumn foliage colored red to deep crimson; **'Rose Hill'**, dark green leaves, turning bronze-red in autumn. Zones 4–10.

Fraxinus angustifolia

syn. ***Fraxinus rotundifolia***

NARROW-LEAFED ASH

↔40 ft (12 m) ↑80 ft (24 m)

Closely allied to *F. excelsior,* occurs wild in Mediterranean region and western Asia. Typical race *(F. a.* subsp. *angustifolia)* is restricted to southern Europe and northwestern Africa. Vigorous tree, ascending branches, darkish furrowed bark. The leaves have 7 to 13 rather narrow leaflets, arranged in whorls of 3. The winter buds are large and dark brown. ***F. a.* subsp. *oxycarpa*** (syn. *F. oxycarpa)* occurs in southeastern Europe and Caucasus region, only 5 to 7 leaflets per leaf, bands of hairs on undersides; ***F. a.* subsp. *syriaca*** (syn. *F. syriaca* 'Desert Ash'*)*, occurs in Turkey, Syria, and Iran, smaller bushier tree, blackish bark, very thick knobbly twigs, leaves in whorls of 3 or 4. ***F. a.* 'Elegantissima'**, small tree, light green leaves; **'Lentiscifolia'**, leaflets more widely spaced on longer common stalk; **'Raywood'** (claret ash), vigorous, erect, narrow in habit, dark wine red autumn foliage. Zones 6–10.

Fraxinus excelsior 'Pendula'

Fraxinus dipetala

↔10 ft (3 m) ↑15 ft (4.5 m)

From California, USA. Angular branches, red-tinged new growth, turning gray. Up to 7 pairs of leaflets on leaves, oval, smooth, or scalloped edges, pale green above, reticulate veining below. Showy white flower panicles appear with leaves, in late spring. Zones 6–10.

Fraxinus excelsior

COMMON ASH, EUROPEAN ASH

↔60 ft (18 m) ↑100 ft (30 m)

Native to Europe. Gray branches, prominent black buds, in winter. Dark green leaves with 11 pairs of leaflets, turn bright yellow in autumn. Flower panicles appear before leaves, in spring. Fruits winged, pendent, remaining after leaves fall. ***F. e.* f. *diversifolia*** (one-leafed ash), leaves usually a single large leaflet; ***F. e.* 'Aurea Pendula'**, pendulous golden branches; **'Eureka'**, bright green leaves with serrated edges; **'Jaspidea'**, yellow shoots in winter, yellow new growth, yellow leaves in autumn; **'Pendula'**, weeping branches. Zones 4–10.

Fraxinus latifolia

syn. ***Fraxinus oregona***

OREGON ASH

↔50 ft (15 m) ↑80 ft (24 m)

Valuable timber tree from western North America. Deciduous species. Leaves with 9 leaflets, egg-shaped with pointed tips, dark green above, lighter and downy underneath, turn yellow in autumn. Panicles of flowers on previous year's wood. It is closely related to *F. pennsylvanica.* Zones 5–10.

F

Fraxinus velutina, in the wild, in Zion National Park, Utah, USA

Fraxinus nigra

BLACK ASH, SWAMP ASH

↔25 ft (8 m) ↑50 ft (15 m)

Upright deciduous tree, native to North America. Leaves dark green, 11 stalkless leaflets, lance-shaped, small-toothed edges, curved upward, downy brown veins; underside paler green. Fruit oblong, winged. **'Fallgold'**, vigorous, non-fruiting, good yellow autumn color. Zones 7–10.

Fraxinus ornus

FLOWERING ASH, MANNA ASH

↔40 ft (12 m) ↑50 ft (15 m)

Native to southern Europe and southwestern Asia. Leaves with 7 leaflets, paler beneath, rather hairy midribs. Showy, dense panicles of fragrant white flowers, in late spring. Fruit narrow, winged. Sugary substance secreted when bark is damaged. **'Arie Peters'**, creamy flowers. Zones 6–10.

Fraxinus pennsylvanica

GREEN ASH, RED ASH

↔70 ft (21 m) ↑70 ft (21 m)

Robust tree from North America. Olive green leaves, 9 lance-shaped leaflets, smooth or toothed edges, pointed tips, sunken midrib. Flowers appear on old wood, followed by winged fruit. **'Marshall's Seedless'**, vigorous, non-fruiting, dark green leaves; **'Patmore'**, strongly erect, glossy leaves, oval crown, does not fruit; **'Summit'** ★, pyramidal when young, becoming upright, autumn leaves deep yellow. Zones 4–10.

Fraxinus uhdei

EVERGREEN ASH, SHAMEL ASH

↔15 ft (4.5 m) ↑25 ft (8 m)

Semi-evergreen to evergreen upright tree from Mexico and Central America. Rounded canopy. Leaves dark green, lance-shaped to oblong, toothed, hairless, 7 leaflets. Flowers in dense panicles. Thrives in warmer moist conditions. **'Tomlinson'**, small upright tree, reaches 12 ft (3.5 m) in 10 years. Zones 8–11.

Fraxinus velutina

ARIZONA ASH, DESERT ASH, VELVET ASH

↔30 ft (9 m) ↑30 ft (9 m)

Native to southwestern USA and northwestern Mexico. Dull green leaves, 7 lance-shaped to oval, toothed leaflets, leathery, hairy felting beneath. ***F. v.* var. *coriacea*,** from southern California, leaves thicker and almost hairless; ***F. v.* var. *glabra*,** doubtfully distinct from *F. v.* var. *coriacea*; ***F. v.* var. *toumeyi*,** longer-stalked, narrower leaflets, gray-green upper surfaces stay velvety until late summer. ***F. v.* 'Fan-Tex'**, handsome tree, larger dark green leaves, non-fruiting. Zones 7–10.

FREESIA

syn. *Anomatheca*

This genus is a member of the iris (Iridaceae) family and consists of 6 species of corms found in southern and central Africa. They are mainly small plants, forming clumps of simple narrow leaves, usually with a prominent midrib. In the warmer months they produce sprays of small, 6-petalled, sometimes fragrant flowers on wiry, often branching stems, held above the foliage. These plants are not showy, but make an attractive display where left to naturalize.

CULTIVATION: Freesias, which are undemanding plants, are easily grown in any sunny position with moderately fertile well-drained soil. Provided the soil does not freeze to the depth of the corm, they can be left in the ground to overwinter; otherwise store dry in a frost-free place. Propagation is usually by breaking up established clumps while the plants are dormant. Freesias are easily raised from seed, and sometimes they will self-sow.

Freesia alba

syns *Freesia lactea, F. refracta var. alba*

↔3 in (8 cm) ↑4–6 in (10–15 cm)

Vigorous old garden inhabitant of confused nomenclature and possibly muddled ancestry. Strongly perfumed, prolific, small flowers. Petals variable; common coloration is cream splashed in onion-skin colors of gold, brown, purple, bronze, and rose. Stems short. Prefers dry summers, sharp drainage, and poor soils. Zones 9–11.

Freesia laxa

syn. *Anomatheca laxa*

SCARLET FREESIA

↔8–12 in (20–30 cm) ↑12–16 in (30–40 cm)

From South Africa and Mozambique. Forms clumps of grassy leaves. Bears flowers in shades of pink to purple-red, sometimes white or pale blue. Self-sows. **'Joan Evans'**, only 6 in (15 cm) tall, with pale-centered pink flowers. Zones 8–11.

Freesia laxa

Freesia, HC, Royal Crown Series

Freesia Hybrid Cultivars

FLORIST'S FREESIAS

↔6–12 in (15–30 cm) ↑12–20 in (30–50 cm)

This group of cultivars and hybrids has a complex parentage involving several known parents, such as *F. alba, F. corymbosa, F. leichtlinii, F. refracta*, and possibly a few others. They cover a wide range of plant sizes and flower colors, and vary greatly in the intensity of their fragrance. Popular hybrid cultivars in the pink double-flowered range include: **'Aphrodite'**; mixed-color seedling strains such as **'Parego's Blue'**, blue tones; **'Parego's Red'**, pink to red; **Royal Crown Series**, pink, yellow throats; **'Super Emerald'**, shades of green. Zones 8–11.

FREMONTODENDRON

FLANNEL BUSH

There are 3 species of evergreen shrubs in this genus from southwestern North America, which is a member of the mallow (Malvaceae) family. Flannel bushes have showy golden yellow to orange blooms of 5 petal-like sepals. The stems, flower buds, and seed capsules, and the undersides of the leaves, are covered with fine bronze bristles that give rise to the common name of flannel bush.

CULTIVATION: These shrubs require a warm, sunny, sheltered site, and in cool-temperate climates should be grown under the protection of a wall, although they will withstand some frost. Poor dry soils suit them best, as

Fremontodendron californicum

Fremontodendron mexicanum

rich soils produce an excess of foliage rather than flowers and can be a factor in reducing the plant's life span. Too much moisture and root disturbance are other reasons why flannel bush plants are fairly short-lived. Propagate from seed, or from softwood or half-hardened cuttings.

Fremontodendron californicum

FLANNEL BUSH, FREMONTIA

↔ 15 ft (4.5 m)
↕ 12–25 ft (3.5–8 m)

Found in the Sierra Nevada range of California, USA. Leaves variable, almost round to a pointed oval shape, dull green, roughened by tiny hairs. Flowers appear in flushes during spring–summer, bright yellow, often with orange tones on their backs. Zones 8–10.

Fremontodendron decumbens

syn. ***Fremontodendron californicum* subsp. *decumbens***

PINE HILL FLANNEL BUSH

↔ 10 ft (3 m) ↕ 2 ft (0.6 m)

Extremely rare and endangered species in the wild, found only within a mile of the summit of one hill in the Sierra Nevada range in southwestern USA. Low spreading shrub, flowers coppery in color, borne up to 9 months of the year. Zones 8–10.

Fremontodendron mexicanum

MEXICAN FLANNEL BUSH, MEXICAN FREMONTIA, SOUTHERN FLANNEL BUSH

↔ 12 ft (3.5 m) ↕ 20 ft (6 m)

Native to Mexico's Baja California Peninsula and the San Diego area, USA; rare. Grows in chaparral and woodland. More tender than *F. californicum*. Golden yellow flowers, partly hidden by foliage, over many months, from spring. Zones 9–11.

Fritillaria acmopetala

Fremontodendron Hybrid Cultivars

↔ 10–15 ft (3–4.5 m)
↕ 12–20 ft (3.5–6 m)

Hybrids between *F. californicum* and *F. mexicanum* have largely proved superior to either of their parents, being more vigorous, with a heavier crop of larger flowers. Popular hybrids include: **'California Glory'**, vigorous shrub, large yellow flowers; **'Ken Taylor'** low grower, bright orange-yellow flowers; **'Pacific Sunset'**, vigorous, almost tree-like, bright yellow flowers with elongated petal tips. Zones 8–10.

FRITILLARIA

FRITILLARY

This genus of natives from the Mediterranean, Asia, and America contains about 100 species of perennial, herbaceous, bulbous plants that are members of the lily (Liliaceae) family. They are increasingly popular with domestic gardeners, who value them for their unusual coloring, delicate appearance, interesting formations, and odd, almost mechanical markings. The majority bloom in spring. The flowers are usually bell-shaped and somewhat pendent. Their scent is sometimes less than pleasing. The botanical name comes from the Latin *fritillus* (dice box), referring to the neat checked markings that some species bear on their petals and to the shape of the capsules.

CULTIVATION: The origin of each individual species is an important pointer. Many are seriously fussy about their needs, and the moisture levels, soil types, climate, and altitude of the original habitat should be taken into account in cultivation. Propagate from purchased bulbs (avoid if dried out), from bulb scales, from basal "rice-grain" bulbets, or from seed.

Fritillaria agrestis

Fritillaria acmopetala

↔ 1¾–2 in (4–5 cm)
↕ 16–18 in (40–45 cm)

Found in vineyards and grain fields across western Asia and the eastern Mediterranean. Flowers are usually solitary, petals pale, shiny, green-yellow with chocolate-purple blotches. Leaves alternate, linear, gray-green. Prefers fertile well-drained soil. Less demanding than many. Zones 7–10.

Fritillaria agrestis

syn. ***Fritillaria biflora* subsp. *agrestis***

STINK BELL

↔ 1¾–2 in (4–5 cm)
↕ 12–16 in (30–40 cm)

Found on grassy, lightly treed hills of coastal California, USA. Leaves yellowish green, linear, broad and clustered at base, then fine and alternate. Flowers white with sulfur yellow veining, or murky purple-brown, petals recurved, in spring. Their scent is unpleasant. Prefers a heavy moisture-retentive soil, hot dry summers, winter and spring rainfall; resents disturbance. Zones 6–9.

Fritillaria biflora

BLACK FRITILLARY, MISSION BELLS

↔ 1¾–2 in (4–5 cm)
↕ 10–16 in (25–40 cm)

From coastal grasslands of California, USA. Basal leaves are glossy green. Flowers with variable petals, glossy, commonly dark brown with lime green shading and/or checking, 1 to 6 per stem, appearing from early to mid-spring. Prefers full sun, shelter from rain, sharp drainage, winter and spring rainfall, and hot dry summers. Zones 7–9.

Fritillaria glauca 'Goldilocks'

Fritillaria bucharica

↔ 1¾–2 in (4–5 cm)
↕ 8–12 in (20–30 cm)

Found on cliffs and rocky slopes at altitude in northeastern Afghanistan and central Asia. Leaves profuse, linear, in basal pairs, then alternate. Stems of 3 to 4 flowers, petals white with hint of green. Prefers good drainage, dry dormancy. Well suited to container culture. Zones 5–9.

Fritillaria camschatcensis

BLACK SARANA, ESKIMO POTATOES

↔ 1¾–2 in (4–5 cm)
↕ 8–16 in (20–40 cm)

Widespread through northwestern America and northern Japan, in moist open woods and subalpine meadows. Leaves glossy, light green, lance-like, held in whorls. Stems bear 2 to 3 flowers, grape-like, rich dark purple-brown petals with interior sheen, in late spring–early summer. Prefers humus-rich moisture-retentive soil and cool damp summers. Zones 4–9.

Fritillaria glauca

SISKIYOU LILY

↔ 1¾–2 in (4–5 cm)
↕ 4–6 in (10–15 cm)

Found on rocky screes from California to Oregon, USA. Leaves are mostly basal, widely linear, with bluish bloom. Flowers largish, open bell-shaped, solitary; petals waxen, yellow, sometimes with markings. Stamens protruding, yellow. Prefers deep, moist, stony soil. **'Goldilocks'**, low-growing selection, golden yellow petals. Zones 6–8.

Fritillaria graeca

↔ 1¾–2 in (4–5 cm)
↕ 2½–8 in (6–20 cm)

Found on exposed rocky habitats in southern Greece, Albania, and Yugoslavia. The leaves are broad at the base, mid-green, and clustered around the stem. The flowers are solitary or paired, in broad, heavy, pendent bells, appearing in late spring–early summer; petals slightly incurving, green and red, often with central stripe. Prefers fertile soil, good drainage, dry dormancy. The robust ***F. g.* subsp. *thessala*** is the most common form in cultivation. Zones 7–9.

Fritillaria imperialis

Fritillaria meleagris

Fritillaria imperialis

CROWN IMPERIAL, TEARS OF MARY

↔ 16 in (40 cm)
↕ 36–48 in (90–120 cm)

Widespread from southern Turkey to Kashmir. Leaves mid-green, glossy, in whorls. Flowers large, bright, clustered at top of upright stems, appearing in late spring. Scent unpleasant, fox-like. Petals yellow, lemon yellow, orange, or red, commonly orange. Prefers a fertile well-drained soil. **'Aureomarginata'**, margins of leaves lemon yellow; **'Lutea'**, yellow petals. Zones 4–7.

Fritillaria meleagris

GUINEA HEN FLOWER, LEPER LILY, SNAKES HEAD FRITILLARY/LILY

↔ 1¾–2 in (4–5 cm)
↕ 7–8 in (18–20 cm)

Variable protected species, rare in the wild, found in grassy flood plains from southern England to western Russia. Leaves alternate, long, sharply pointed, gray-green. Flowers square-shouldered bells, sometimes paired, appearing in mid-spring; petal color variable, distinctly checked maroon, dark purple, and/or murky pink. Prefers fertile well-drained soils and damp summers. ***F. m.* var. *unicolor* subvar. *alba***, white petals; ***F. m.* 'Aphrodite'**, white petals with green veining. Zones 4–9.

Fritillaria michailovskyi

↔ 2 in (5 cm) ↕ 4–8 in (10–20 cm)

From the alpine slopes of Turkey. Leaves alternate, lance-shaped, mid-green. Stems bear 1 to 7 flowers, broadly bell-shaped, appearing in early summer; petals glossy deep purple-brown with distinctive lower band of yellow. Prefers gritty soil, cold winters, cool summers. Zones 7–9.

Fritillaria persica

↔ 3 in (8 cm) ↕ 4–36 in (10–90 cm)

Robust variable species with changeable nomenclature. Found in the eastern Mediterranean region and inland, on rocky slopes and along the edges of cornfields. Leaves numerous, gray, alternate, lance-like. Flowers appear in conical raceme of 7 to 20 heads, lasting several weeks, in spring; petals narrow, bell-shaped, plum-purple with gray bloom. Prefers deep, damp, fertile soil, protected from both late frosts and sun. **'Adiyaman'**, darker petals. Zones 5–9.

FUCHSIA

There are about 100 species of small or medium-sized trees and spreading or climbing shrubs in this genus, which is a member of the evening primrose (Onagraceae) family. Almost all species are from South and Central America, but a few are native to New Zealand and Tahiti. They are evergreen or deciduous, with foliage growing in whorls, alternate or opposite. Flowers bloom in terminal clusters or from leaf axils and are usually tubular and pendent, often bicolored. The flowers are followed by edible berries, usually with many seeds. In their native habitat, the American species are pollinated by hummingbirds. CULTIVATION: Most fuchsias are frost tender, and even the few fully hardy forms may die down to ground level in a severe winter. Fuchsias planted in the garden do best in fairly fertile

Fuchsia boliviana

moist soil with good drainage in full sun or partial shade. Feed regularly during flowering. Propagate species from seed and cuttings; raise cultivars from cuttings only, using softwood cuttings in spring or half-hardened cuttings in late summer.

Fuchsia × *bacillaris*

↔ 2–4 ft (0.6–1.2 m)
↕ 3–7 ft (0.9–2 m)

This erect or spreading shrub comes from Mexico and is a hybrid of *F. microphylla* and *F. thymifolia*. The leaves are finely toothed and sword-shaped to oval. The flowers are solitary, with a tube, and have narrow rose pink to red sepals and deep red elliptical petals, appearing in summer–autumn. Rounded, glossy, black fruit. Zones 7–9.

Fuchsia boliviana

↔ 3–4 ft (0.9–1.2 m) ↕ 12 ft (3.5 m)

This species occurs naturally in South America from northern Argentina to Peru; it has become naturalized in Colombia and Venezuela. Erect shrub or small tree. Dark green leaves in whorls of 3, pale gray felty veining on undersides. Terminal flowers, tubes pale to dark pink, sepals pale pink to red, scarlet petals, appearing in summer–autumn. Fruit is edible. ***F. b.* var. *alba*** ★, white tubes, sepals with light red marks at bases. Zones 9–11.

Fuchsia denticulata

syn. *Fuchsia serratifolia*

↔ 3 ft (0.9 m) ↕ 8 ft (2.4 m)

Native to Peru and Bolivia. Peeling bark. Leaves are large, lance-shaped or oval, with toothed edges and a pointed tip and base, shiny or matt dark green above, paler and heavily veined underneath. Flowers are pink

Fuchsia magellanica

to light red, tipped with green and white, petals orange to vermilion. Glossy green to purple-red fruit, in summer. Zones 9–11.

Fuchsia fulgens ★

↔ 30 in (75 cm) ↕ 5 ft (1.5 m)

Native to Mexico. Toothed heart-shaped leaves, red above, undersides paler, flushed with red. Small flowers with red sepals tinged yellow-green towards the tips and a bright red corolla. Fruit oblong, deep purple. Zones 11–12.

Fuchsia magellanica

LADIES' EARDROPS

↔ 6 ft (1.8 m) ↕ 10 ft (3 m)

Originating in Chile and Argentina, naturalized elsewhere. Erect vigorous shrub; older branches have flaking bark. Leaves are elliptical to egg-shaped and tinted red underneath. Flowers have red tubes, dark red sepals, a purple corolla, and appear in summer–late autumn. Fruits are oblong and crimson in color. Makes a colorful hedge in mild winter areas; **'Riccartonii'** is commonly used for hedging in Ireland and islands around Britain. ***F. m.* var. *gracilis*** (syn. *F. m.* var. *macrostemma*), small leaves, abundant, very pendent, small flowers, deep scarlet calyx, purple petals; ***F. m.* var. *molinae***, name used for pale-pink-flowered variants in cultivation; ***F. m.* var. *pumila***, to 12 in (30 cm) high, red and blue flowers. ***F. m.* 'Versicolor'**, gray-green leaves, tinted silver, small deep red flowers. Zones 7–10.

Fuchsia microphylla

SMALL-LEAFED FUCHSIA

↔ 2–5 ft (0.6–1.5 m)
↕ 2–15 ft (0.6–4.5 m)

Bushy shrub or climber found from Mexico to Panama. Leaves opposite, lance-shaped, pointed tip and base, toothed or smooth edges. Flowers with white to red-purple tubes, sepals, and petals, in summer. Zones 9–11.

Fuchsia procumbens

TRAILING FUCHSIA

↔3 ft (0.9 m) ↑6 in (15 cm)

Native to New Zealand. Evergreen, prostrate, spreading shrub. Leaves small, heart-shaped. Small upward-facing flowers, greenish to pale orange tubes, purple-tipped green sepals, no petals, appearing in summer. Fruit bright red, persistent. Good rock-garden plant. Zones 8–11.

Fuchsia splendens

↔2 ft (0.9 m) ↑8 ft (2.4 m)

Terrestrial or epiphytic shrub from Mexico to Costa Rica. Leaves heart-shaped, toothed edges, green above, paler, flushed red and veined beneath. Flower tube rose pink, sepals green with red base, petals olive green. Fruit green to purple, warty. Zones 8–11.

Fuchsia thymifolia

↔20 in (50 cm) ↑36 in (90 cm)

From Mexico to northern Guatemala; larger in the wild. Leaves oval to egg-shaped, sometimes with a toothed edge, finely hairy both above and underneath. Flowers solitary, tube green-white to pink, sepals and petals in the same colors, ageing to dark purple, in summer–autumn. Fleshy black-purple fruits. Zones 8–11.

Fuchsia triphylla

HONEYSUCKLE FUCHSIA

↔2 ft (0.6 m) ↑6 ft (1.8 m)

Native to the West Indies; much smaller in cultivation. Leaves opposite, in whorls of 3 or 4; oval or lance-shaped, sometimes finely toothed, dull dark green upper surfaces and paler undersurfaces, which are often tinged with silvery purple. Flowers are all-over orange to coral red; fruit is shiny reddish purple. **'Billy Green'**, rose pink flowers, light green leaves. Zones 11–12.

Fuchsia vulcanica

syn. *Fuchsia canescens*

↔2–7 ft (0.6–2 m)
↑4–12 ft (1.2–3.5 m)

Strong upright shrub from Colombia and Ecuador. Whorls of 3 or 4 narrow elliptical leaves. Flowers at ends of branches with deep scarlet tube, purplish base, scarlet corolla. Zones 8–10.

Fuchsia Hybrid Cultivars

↔18–36 in (45–90 cm)
↑1–7 ft (0.3–2 m)

Over 8,000 fuchsia cultivars have been recorded, with about 2,000 still in cultivation. Most are derived from *F. magellanica, F. fulgens,* and *F. triphylla.*

Fuchsia triphylla 'Billy Green'

Fuchsia vulcanica

Fuchsia, HC, 'Coachman'

Fuchsia, HC, 'Mrs Popple'

Some cultivars, the "hardy" types, can withstand winter in Zone 7. These include: **'Abbé Farges'**, semi-double flowers, cherry red tube and sepal, rose-lilac corolla; **'Constance'**, bushy, tube pale pink, sepals pale pink, green-tipped corolla, mauve base tinted pink; **'Hawkshead'**, tube and sepals white with green, corolla white; **'White Pixie'**, yellow red-veined leaves, red tube and sepal, corolla white, veined with deep pink.

Other hybrids include: **'Brookwood Belle'**, prolific, double medium-sized flowers, deep cerise tube, sepals and corolla white, flushed pale pink; **'Cecile'**, trailer, double, frilly mauve corolla, fully reflexed pink sepals; **'Coachman'**, coral pink sepals, reddish orange corolla; **'Dark Secret'**, white tube and sepal partly enclose deep purple double corolla; **'Display'**, large flowers, pink-red calyx, corolla deeper rose pink, long stamens; **'Dollar Princess'**, medium-sized double flowers, small cerise tubes, reflexed cerise sepals, small purple corollas, deep pink at base; **'Genii'**, bright yellow foliage, small single, red and mauve flowers; **'Golden Marinka'**, later flowering form, trailing habit, variegated red-veined leaves, medium-sized single blooms, rich red tube and sepals, darker red corolla; **'Heidi Ann'**, medium-sized double blooms, crimson-cerise tube and sepals, bright lilac corolla; **'Jack Shahan'**, weeping form, large single blooms, pale pink; **'La Campanella'**, semi-double, white tube, white sepals tinted pink, corolla imperial purple; **'Lena'**, medium-sized semi-double blooms, flesh pink tube, flesh pink sepals shading darker, tipped green, corolla purple, fading toward base; **'Lord Beaconsfield'**, trailer, dusky pinkish-red tube and sepals, corolla darker but similar color, single; **'Machu Picchu'**, velvety foliage, light coral tube and sepal, pale at extremities, orange-pink corolla, single; **'Margaret Pilkington'**, white sepals, reddish purple tube; **'Mrs Popple'**, trailer, red tube and sepals, purple corolla, single; **'Prosperity'**, medium-sized double flowers, crimson tube, crimson sepals, pink corolla, veined rose red; **'Sleigh Bells'**, large, flared skirt-style single, short white tube, reflexed white sepals, pink at base, white corolla; **'Sunray'**, gray-green, cream, and pink variegated foliage, small red and purple single flowers; **'Thalia'**, triphylla hybrid, orange all over, long tube, short sepals, small corolla; **'Tiptop'**, round buds, sealing wax red short tube and sepals, deep purple corolla, single; **'Voodoo'**, very large double flowers, bright red tube and sepals, deep purple corolla; and **'Walz Jubilteen'**, upward-facing, pale pink tube and sepals, dusky coral pink corolla, single. Zones 9–11.

FURCRAEA

syn. *Fourcroya*

Up to 20 species have been credited to this genus of evergreen succulents in the asparagus (Asparagaceae) family from Central and South America and the West Indies, but there may be far fewer. Like agaves, they have rosettes of sword-like leaves, ending in a spine and usually with prickly edges. The flowers have a shorter tube and more spreading petals. A trunk may develop below the rosette, and lateral shoots sprout from the plant base or the trunk. An inflorescence ends the life of a rosette, but may take several decades to appear; some are extremely tall. After flowering, the inflorescence usually develops aerial plantlets that eventually fall and take root.

CULTIVATION: These are among the toughest of plants, and in warm climates will grow and multiply with no attention at all. They have become invasive in some tropical countries. In cold climates they can be grown under glass, but they require a lot of space at maturity. Propagate from offsets, aerial plantlets, or seed.

Furcraea foetida

syn. *Furcraea gigantea*

GIANT CABUYA

↔5–10 ft (1.5–3 m)
↑5–22 ft (1.5–7 m)

Found in northern South America as well as the Caribbean. Rosettes of bright green, sword-shaped leaves grow to 6 ft (1.8 m) long, sometimes edged with short spines. Flower stem to over 20 ft (6 m) tall carries hundreds of fragrant, greenish cream flowers. **'Mediopicta'** (syn. 'Striata'), spineless leaves are strongly variegated in shades of green, cream, and gray-green. Zones 9–12.

Furcraea parmentieri

syns *Furcraea bedinghausii, F. roezlii*

↔4–7 ft (1.2–2 m)
↑4–10 ft (1.2–3 m)

Succulent perennial from Mexico. Has rosettes of bluish sword-shaped leaves with soft tips, forming a ball that eventually develops a trunk. Inflorescences of green flowers appear on tall stems. Zones 8–10.

Furcraea selloa

↔4–7 ft (1.2–2 m)
↑4–7 ft (1.2–2 m)

Succulent perennial from Mexico and Guatemala. Forms dense rosettes of 30 to 40 bright green leaves, with horny spines along the edges. Faintly scented white flowers flushed with green. *F. s.* f. *marginata*, white or yellow leaf edges. Zones 8–10.

G

GAILLARDIA

BLANKET FLOWER, FIREWHEEL

Named in 1786 for a French botany patron, Gaillard de Charentonneau (sometimes given as Marentonneau), this genus of around 30 species of annual, biennial, and perennial daisies (family Asteraceae) occurs mainly in southern Canada, USA, and Mexico. The common name of blanket flower comes from a Native American legend of a blanket maker whom the spirits rewarded with an ever-blooming blanket of flowers on his grave. Appropriately then, the small plants are covered in summer and autumn with 2–4 in (5–10 cm) wide flowerheads. The ray florets are typically red at the center with a yellow outer half. Garden forms occur in a range of warm tones.

CULTIVATION: Hardiness varies, though *Gaillardia* plants are so easily cultivated that replacing any winter casualties is no problem. Plant in a sunny open position with gritty well-drained soil that remains moist during the growing season. Deadhead on a regular basis. Propagate from seed or basal cuttings, or by division.

Gaillardia × grandiflora 'Burgunder'

Gaillardia pulchella

Gaillardia aristata

↔32 in (80 cm) ↑20 in (50 cm)

Perennial widespread in western North America. Very hairy stems and leaves, with basal leaves to 8 in (20 cm) long. Narrow lance-shaped leaves may have small basal lobes and/or toothed edges. Flowerheads to 4 in (10 cm) wide with ray florets to more than 1 in (25 mm) long, yellow or yellow with red base; disc florets usually same color as base of ray florets. **'Arizona Sun'**, forms a neat mound, abundant orange-red flowerheads with broad yellow edges. Zones 6–10.

Gaillardia × grandiflora

↔40 in (100 cm) ↑24 in (60 cm)

Garden hybrid between *G. aristata* and *G. pulchella*. Very similar to *G. aristata* but often slightly larger and generally more vigorous, hardier, and heavier flowering. **'Burgunder'** (syn. 'Burgundy'), deep red flowers; **'Dazzler'**, 12 in (30 cm) tall, red ray florets tipped golden yellow; **'Indian Yellow'**, bright golden yellow flowers; Goblin/**'Kobold'** ★, 16 in (40 cm) tall, red ray florets with yellow border. Also seedling strains, such as **Gaiety** and **Royal Monarch** hybrids and double-flowered forms in mixed red and gold shades. Zones 5–10.

Gaillardia pulchella

↔16 in (40 cm) ↑24 in (60 cm)

Hairy annual found in northeastern Mexico and neighboring parts of eastern and central USA. Leaves to over 3 in (8 cm) long, sometimes lobed and/or toothed. Flowerheads around 2½ in (6 cm) wide, ray florets yellow, red, or red with yellow tips.

Galanthus elwesii

Selected forms include: **'Lollipop'**, to 18 in (45 cm) tall, interesting combination of yellow, red, and orange; **'Razzledazzle'**, double flowerheads to 3 in (8 cm) wide; **'Red Plume'**, 12–18 in (30–45 cm) tall, red double flowers; and **'Yellow Plume'**, 12–18 in (30–45 cm) tall, yellow double flowers. Zones 8–10.

GALANTHUS

SNOWDROP

Probably the most welcome harbinger of spring, this normally late winter-flowering Eurasian genus of 15 bulbs in the amaryllis (Amaryllidaceae) family also includes a few species that bloom in autumn. The narrow grassy leaves usually break through shortly after mid-winter and are soon joined by short flower stems, each carrying one mildly scented, pendulous, white, 6-petalled flower. The name *Galanthus* comes from the Greek *gala* (milk) and *anthos* (a flower) and refers to the flower color. The inner 3 petals are short and green-tipped, and double-flowered forms are available. Flowering is often brief but occurs when most welcome. According to Christian legend, the snowdrop first bloomed to coincide with the Feast of Purification on February 2, known as Candlemas Day.

CULTIVATION: Snowdrops grow best in cool-temperate climates and thrive in woodland or rockery conditions, preferring dappled shade and moist humus-rich soil. Can be propagated from seed, but they usually multiply quickly enough so that division after the foliage dies back is more practical. Do not let the bulbs dry out.

Galanthus nivalis

Galanthus elwesii

GIANT SNOWDROP

↔4 in (10 cm) ↑4–6 in (10–15 cm)

Robust plant with honey-scented winter flowers, to 1¼ in (3 cm) long, with 2 green markings on each inner petal, flaring in sunshine. Broadly oblong gray-green leaves, sometimes twisted. Zones 6–9.

Galanthus ikariae ★

↔4 in (10 cm) ↑4–6 in (10–15 cm)

Highly variable species found from the Aegean to the Caucasus region. Broad, glossy, bright green leaves, up to 6 in (15 cm) long. Flowers to 1¼ in (30 mm) long, with large green marking at petal tips, from late winter–early spring. Zones 6–9.

Galanthus nivalis

COMMON SNOWDROP, ENGLISH SNOWDROP

↔4 in (10 cm) ↑6–8 in (15–20 cm)

Small European species with flat, narrow, blue-green leaves to slightly under 4 in (10 cm) long. Flowers small, slightly scented, with green petal tips and central markings. **'Flore Pleno'**, very small, with beautiful white double flowers finely detailed in lime green. Zones 4–9.

GALIUM

BEDSTRAW, CLEAVERS, WOODRUFF

A widespread madder (Rubiaceae) family genus of around 400 species of often sprawling annuals and perennials. Includes a few useful species and some rather persistent weeds. Plants are characterized by weak angular stems that spread through surrounding growth and may adhere to it by sticky coatings and/or fine hooked hairs. The small bright green leaves are sometimes in opposite pairs but more often in distinct whorls at intervals. Tiny white or yellow flowers, either solitary or in small clusters, appear in the leaf axils and at the stem tips. Woodruff *(G. odoratum)*, by far the most attractive species, is widely used herbally and as a flavoring.

CULTIVATION: Hardiness varies; most thrive in temperate climates. Easily grown in any well-drained soil in full sun or half-sun. Mostly propagated from seed; perennials also by division.

Galium odoratum

syn. *Asperula odorata*

SWEET WOODRUFF, WOODRUFF

↔36 in (90 cm) ↑18 in (45 cm)

Carpet-forming perennial from Europe and North Africa, with erect, square-sectioned stems and all parts aromatic. Stiff, narrow, slightly prickly, elliptic leaves, to 2 in (5 cm) long, and with rough margins, in neat whorls of 6 to 8. Fragrant white flowers, 1½ in (35 mm) across, with deeply lobed corollas, in terminal clusters, in spring–summer. Zones 3–9.

GALVEZIA

A genus of 6 species of shrubs in the plantain (Plantaginaceae) family from the California islands to Peru. These scrambling ground covers have simple elliptical to ovate leaves, rarely more than 2 in (5 cm) long. Flowers, in summer, are reminiscent of those of some of the shrubby sages *(Salvia)*, occurring in terminal racemes and with 2 lips that remain almost closed. Hummingbirds have the knack of getting into the blooms and pollinate them while probing for nectar.
CULTIVATION: Best in full sun if grown near the coast, but needing some shade in hot inland areas, these are drought-tolerant plants that need little or no additional water once established. They prefer light gritty soil and demand perfect drainage. Versatile plants, they can be grown as ground covers, espaliered against fences, or allowed to trail from hanging baskets. Propagate from seed or by taking half-hardened cuttings from non-flowering stems.

Galvezia juncea

BAJA BUSH SNAPDRAGON

↔3–8 ft (0.9–2.4 m) ↑3 ft (0.9 m)

Spreading evergreen shrub native to Baja California, Mexico. Thin, arching, reed-like stems, small dark green leaves, often almost leafless. Bright red flowers, 1 in (25 mm) diameter, at tips of branches throughout the year. Zones 9–10.

GARDENIA

This genus from the madder (Rubiaceae) family consists of around 250 species, from tropical Africa, Asia, and Australasia. Mostly evergreen shrubs or small trees, with opposite or whorled, shiny, simple, deep green leaves. Fragrant large flowers, tubular to funnel-shaped, white or yellow, produced singly or in few-flowered cymes. Fruit is a leathery or fleshy berry. Useful landscape subjects, wonderful container plants. Some species are used to scent tea; others to treat influenza and colds in modern Chinese herbalism. A yellow dye was made from the fruits.
CULTIVATION: Most are fairly adaptable shrubs tolerant of sun or semi-shade, and do best in a well-drained, humus-rich, acidic soil. Gardenias are surface rooted, responding well to regular mulching with good quality compost, fertilizer, and adequate summer watering. In cool climates grow in a heated greenhouse, as most gardenias are frost tender. Propagate from seed or leafy tip or half-hardened cuttings in late spring and summer.

Gardenia jasminoides

syn. *Gardenia augusta*

CAPE JASMINE, COMMON GARDENIA

↔5 ft (1.5 m)
↑5–8 ft (1.5–2.4 m)

Native of southeastern China and Japan. Bushy habit; elliptic to obovate, glossy, dark green leaves. Strong fragrance, white, wheel-shaped flowers, in summer. Cultivars include: **'Aimee Yoshiba'**, lush foliage, semi-double flowers to 5 in (12 cm) wide; **'August Beauty'**, lush green foliage, white flowers; **'Florida'** ★, to about 3 ft (0.9 m) tall with white flowers; **'Four Seasons'**, dense, compact growth, flowers through the year; **'Gold Magic'** ★, primrose yellow double flowers, compact; **'Grandiflora'**, larger leaves, pure white flowers; **'Professor Pucci'**, formal rosebud double flowers, good scent; **'Radicans'**, spreading low growth with rooting stems, smaller foliage, plentiful semi-double white flowers; **'Veitchii'**, upright yet compact shrub with small, highly scented, double white flowers. Zones 10–11.

Gardenia thunbergia

STARRY GARDENIA

↔7 ft (2 m) ↑12 ft (3.5 m)

Occurs in the humid forests of South Africa. Upright shrub or small tree. Smooth gray bark. Glossy dark green leaves with wavy margins. Fragrant, white or cream, solitary flowers, spoke-like petals at the end of a long tube, in summer. Zones 9–11.

GARRYA

This genus of about 18 evergreen trees or shrubs belongs to the silk-tassel (Garryaceae) family. They are grown for their tough leathery leaves and dis-tinctive pendulous catkins of inconspicuous flowers without petals. Male and female flowers are borne on separate plants from winter to early summer, while the fruit of the female plant consists of clusters of round, dry, dark, 2-seeded berries, borne from summer to autumn. Native to western North America and the West Indies, they are valued for their ornamental qualities and durability in warmer climates.
CULTIVATION: Well suited to salty coastal environments and tolerant of pollution, *Garrya* species prefer a sunny sheltered position but can cope with a wide range of soil types. Most dislike humid summers. Avoid transplanting. They are propagated from cuttings of half-hardened wood, or by layering, and from seed.

Garrya elliptica ★

CATKIN BUSH, COAST SILKTASSEL, SILKTASSEL BUSH

↔6 ft (1.8 m) ↑8–12 ft (2.4–3.5 m)

Native of southwestern USA, from Oregon to California. Glossy, oval, gray-green to matt green leaves, undulating margins, dense woolly coating underneath. Long grayish green male catkins, in winter–spring. Smaller female catkins, abundant clusters of oval-shaped dark purple fruit. **'Evie'** has catkins up to 12 in (30 cm) long; **'James Roof'** is a stronger male form with larger leaves and catkins than the species. Zones 8–10.

Garrya veatchii

↔7 ft (2 m) ↑10 ft (3 m)

Evergreen shrub native to southwest USA. Downy leaves to 3 in (8 cm) long. Male catkins to 4 in (10 cm) long, in spring. Female catkins to 2 in (5 cm) long, in summer. Zones 8–9.

Galvezia juncea, in the wild, Baja California, Mexico

Gardenia thunbergia

Gardenia jasminoides 'Radicans'

Garrya veatchii

Gaultheria mucronata 'Coccinea'

GAULTHERIA

SNOWBERRY, WINTERGREEN

This genus, named after Canadian botanist Jean-Francois Gaultier, contains some 170 species of evergreen shrubs, ranging from the Americas to Japan and Australasia. Belonging to the heath (Ericaceae) family, these tough bushes have leathery foliage and prefer temperate to cool climates. They are often found in mountainous areas, where their bright, relatively large fruits stand out among the short alpine vegetation. Flowers tend to be bell-shaped and pendulous. Fruit may be small and fairly dry or a fleshy berry, depending on the species. Many species are quite aromatic, often highly so, especially the fruit.
CULTIVATION: Frost hardiness varies with the species, the toughest being among the large broadleafed evergreens. They prefer moist, well-drained, humus-rich, slightly acidic soil with ample summer moisture. The exposure preference also varies with the species, though few do well in full shade. Propagate from seed, or from half-hardened cuttings or layers, which will often form naturally where the stems remain in contact with the ground.

Gaultheria mucronata

syn. *Pernettya mucronata*
↔ 4 ft (1.2 m)
↑ 18–60 in (45–150 cm)

Native of Argentina and Chile. Strongly branched suckering shrub, young stems often bright pinkish red, densely covered with small deep green leaves, sharp pointed tips. White or pale pink flowers in late spring. Fruit large, white, shades of pink and red. **'Alba'**, white fruit; **'Bell's Seedling'**, crimson fruit; **'Coccinea'**, scarlet fruit; **'Crimsonia'**, crimson fruit; **'Mulberry Wine'**, maroon to purple fruit; **Snow White/'Sneeuwwitje'**, red-speckled white fruit; **'Wintertime'**, long-lasting white fruit. Zones 6–10.

Gaultheria shallon

Gaura lindheimeri 'Siskiyou Pink'

Gaultheria nummularioides

↔ 10 in (25 cm) ↑ 4 in (10 cm)

Tiny summer-flowering shrub, native of the Himalayan region. Neat hummock of densely interwoven twigs. Small, rounded, somewhat wrinkled leaves, dull green upper surfaces, finely hairy undersides. White to pale pink flowers borne singly, hidden within the foliage. Fruit blue-black in color. Zones 8–10.

Gaultheria procumbens

CHECKERBERRY, TEABERRY, WINTERGREEN
↔ 36 in (90 cm) ↑ 6 in (15 cm)

Attractive shrub from eastern North America. Deep green glossy leaves to 2 in (5 cm) long. Racemes of white to pale pink flowers, in summer. Red fruit, to ½ in (12 mm) wide; source of the pungent liniment used for muscle or joint problems. **'Macrocarpa'**, compact form, abundant fruit. Zones 4–9.

Gaultheria shallon

SALAL, SHALLON
↔ 5 ft (1.5 m) ↑ 5 ft (1.5 m)

Found in western North America, from California to Alaska. Spreading shrub takes root along prostrate branches. Broad oval leaves to 4 in (10 cm) long. Tiny white to deep pink flowers, carried in conspicuous red-stemmed racemes near the stem tips, in late spring. Red fruit ripens to black. Zones 5–9.

GAURA

The name *Gaura* comes from the Greek *gauros*, meaning superb, and while not really superb in the sense of being spectacular, the cultivated species of the 21 annuals and perennials in this North American genus are well worth growing. Members of the evening-primrose (Onagraceae) family, they generally form a clump of irregularly shaped basal leaves from which emerge wiry stems bearing graceful, airy, 4-petalled, white to soft pink flowers. The stems may be more than 36 in (90 cm) tall and appear throughout the warmer months. In recent years *Gaura* has become very popular and various pink-flowered and dwarf cultivars are now available.
CULTIVATION: *Gaura* species prefer full sun with light, gritty, well-drained soil. While drought-tolerant, they flower better with summer moisture. Deadhead routinely and cut back hard after flowering. Propagate from seed in autumn and spring, or from basal cuttings in summer.

Gaura lindheimeri

↔ 40 in (100 cm)
↑ 48–60 in (120–150 cm)

Vigorous heavy-flowering perennial from Texas and Louisiana, USA. Forms a clump of upright stems with narrow, elliptical, toothed leaves up to 4 in (10 cm) long. Sprays of pink-tinted white flowers to over 1 in (25 mm) wide, upper petals large and wing-like, in spring–summer. **Butterfly Collection**, several cultivars in varying pink shades; **'Corrie's Gold'**, variegated foliage edged in golden yellow; **'Karalee Petite'**, 24 in (60 cm) tall, deep pink flowers; **Passionate Series**, range of cultivars with pink flowers and generally dark foliage; **'Siskiyou Pink'**, bright pink flowers; and **'Whirling Butterflies'**, 24 in (60 cm) tall, very heavy-blooming, large flowers. Zones 5–9.

GAZANIA

TREASURE FLOWER

The 16 species of annuals and perennials in this daisy (Asteraceae) family genus are found mainly in South Africa, with 1 species extending the range to the tropics. They are low, near-evergreen, clump-forming plants with simple, narrow, lance-shaped, sometimes downy leaves with paler undersides. Their flowers, which appear throughout the warmer months, are large, brightly colored, often interestingly marked, and always showy. While the species usually have yellow or orange flowers, garden forms are available in a large color range. The name *Gazania* comes from Theodore of Gaza (1398–1478), who translated the botanical texts of Theophrastus from Greek into Latin.
CULTIVATION: Apart from being somewhat frost tender and resenting wet winters, they are easily grown in any open sunny position with gritty very free-draining soil. They appreciate additional humus but will grow in poor dry soils. Propagate by division, or from basal cuttings or seed.

Gazania rigens

Gazania linearis

☼ ❄ ↔24 in (60 cm) ↑6 in (15 cm)

A tough woody-based perennial, with narrow lance-shaped leaves, smooth or near-pinnately lobed, green above, woolly white beneath. Flowerheads to 3 in (8 cm) wide, ray florets yellow, disc florets brown. **'Colorado Gold'** has all-yellow flowerheads. Zones 7–11.

Gazania rigens

TREASURE FLOWER

☼ ❄ ↔40 in (100 cm) ↑8 in (20 cm)

Perennial with fleshy stems that strike root as they spread, forming large leafy clump. Leaves to over 4 in (10 cm) long, smooth-edged or near-pinnately lobed, deep green to bronze above, white hair below. Long-stemmed flowerheads to 3 in (8 cm) wide, ray florets orange with black base, disc florets yellow or reddish orange. ***G. r.* var. *uniflora***, small flowerheads, yellow ray florets, and silvery foliage. ***G. r.* 'Variegata'**, foliage variegated with gold or cream, orange flowers. Zones 9–11.

Gazania Hybrid Cultivars

☼ ❄ ↔20 in (50 cm) ↑4–6 in (10–15 cm)

Gazanias naturally flower in a wide range of colors and hybridize freely, so there is now a wide variety of garden forms, sizes, and flower colors. **'Aztec'**, soft silvery gray foliage, white ray florets shading to purple-brown at the center; **'Aztec Queen'**, yellow ray florets with red-brown base; **'Blackberry Ripple'**, buff ray florets with purple mid-stripe; **'Bronze Gnome'**, compact, bronze double flowers; **'Christopher Lloyd'**, ray florets light red, darkening near center, green base; **'Cookei'**, silvery gray foliage, burnt orange petals shading to taupe toward center; **'Copper King'**, large copper-red flowers; **'Cream Dream'**, silver-gray foliage, cream ray florets with green base; **'Fiesta Red'**, rusty red ray florets with orange base; **'Michael'**, dark foliage, yellow ray florets with black base; **'Moonglow'**, golden double flowers. Also available as mixed color seedling strains, such as the early-flowering **Chansonette Series**, the compact **Daybreak Series** and **Mini-star Series**, and the gray-leafed **Talent Series**. Zones 9–11.

GEIJERA

A member of the rue (Rutaceae) family, this genus contains 8 species occurring in New Guinea, eastern Australia, and New Caledonia. Of the 5 endemic Australian species, 2 occur in rainforests and the other 3 in various habitats, even relatively arid regions. All are small to medium trees reaching 80 ft (24 m) tall when growing in rainforest. The flowers are small, no more than ¼ in (6 mm) across and they are borne in terminal panicles. They are followed by small brown fruits of 2 to 4 compartments, each containing a glossy black seed.

CULTIVATION: The different species come from natural habitats ranging from semi-arid inland plains to drier types of coastal rainforest, but the inland species adapt well to moister climates. All prefer reasonably fertile soil. Propagation is from fresh seed, which may germinate quite erratically.

Geijera parviflora

Gelsemium sempervirens

Geijera parviflora ★

WILGA

☼ ❄ ↔35 ft (10 m) ↑40 ft (12 m)

Small tree occurring in drier inland regions of all Australian states except Tasmania and Western Australia. Pendulous narrow leaves. Creamy white flowers, in spring. Propagation is not easy, as seed is often difficult to obtain. Grown successfully in other countries. Zones 8–11.

GELSEMIUM

CAROLINA JASMINE, YELLOW JESSAMINE

Gelsomino is the Italian name for jasmine, and the 3 twining evergreen vines in this genus resemble yellow-flowered jasmines, but they're not even in the same family. *Gelsemium* is in its own false jasmine (Gelsemiaceae) family, while *Jasminum* is related to the olives (Oleaceae). Found in North and Central America and Southeast Asia, they have simple, pointed, oval leaves, around 2 in (5 cm) long, and grow slowly but steadily to cover a large area. The flowers are mildly scented, small, yellow trumpets borne in clusters. As might be expected of a genus related to the strychnine and curare trees, *Gelsemium* is highly poisonous.

CULTIVATION: Suitable as a ground cover and for container cultivation, as well as for training over trellises and walls. While tolerant of moderate frosts, they grow and flower better in a mild climate. Plant in a sunny position with fertile, moist, well-drained soil. Trim back if necessary. Propagate from half-hardened cuttings or seed.

Genista aetnensis

Genista pilosa

Gelsemium sempervirens ★

☼/◐ ❄ ↔20 ft (6 m) ↑20 ft (6 m)

Found from southern USA to Guatemala. Jasmine-like, glossy green, 2 in (5 cm) long, pointed elliptical leaves. Sprays of scented, 1 in (25 mm) long, yellow flowers followed by dark fruits. **'Pride of Augusta'** has double flowers. Zones 8–11.

GENISTA

syns *Chamaespartium, Echinospartium*

About 90 species belong to this genus within the pea-flower subfamily of the legume (Fabaceae) family. Most are deciduous but some appear evergreen because of their flat green branchlets. Native to Europe and the Mediterranean to western Asia, these shrubs or small trees tolerate all types of soils; most grow on rocky hillsides. Leaves are alternate, simple, or consist of 3 leaflets; branches can be nearly leafless.

CULTIVATION: Full sun is necessary and not all plants are fully frost hardy. Grow half-hardy plants in a well-ventilated greenhouse. They need a light well-drained soil to flower well. Sow seed in pots as soon as ripe, in autumn or spring, and protect from winter frosts until plants are ready for transplanting. Propagation also from half-hardened cuttings in summer.

Genista aetnensis

MOUNT ETNA BROOM

☼ ❄ ↔25 ft (8 m) ↑25 ft (8 m)

Native to Sardinia and Sicily, Italy. Upright shrub, weeping branches, narrow leaves only on young shoots, dropping off as the branches age. Fragrant, yellow, pea-like flowers on the pendent shoots, throughout summer–autumn. Zones 8–10.

Genista lydia

DWARF GENISTA, GENISTA

☼ ❄ ↔36 in (90 cm) ↑24 in (60 cm)

Native to the eastern Balkans. Deciduous prostrate shrub, smaller in the wild. Blue-green leaves, long and narrow or elliptic in shape. Short racemes of golden yellow flowers in late spring–early summer. Flat non-hairy fruit. Zones 7–9.

Genista pilosa

GENISTA, SILKY WOADWAXEN, SILKY LEAF WOADWAXEN

☼ ❄ ↔15 in (38 cm) ↑15 in (38 cm)

Native to western and central Europe. Deciduous shrub, prostrate or erect in habit. Leaves narrow, dark green above, pale undersides. Golden yellow flowers in racemes, in late spring to early summer. Densely hairy seed pods. **'Goldilocks'**, to 24 in (60 cm) tall and much wider; **'Vancouver Gold'** ★, a spreading mound, dark green leaves, golden flowers. Zones 5–9.

Genista sagittalis

Gentiana makinoi

Gentiana septemfida

Geranium bohemicum

Geranium × *cantabrigiense*

Geranium farreri

Genista sagittalis

WINGED BROOM

↔ 36 in (90 cm) ↑ 6 in (15 cm)

Prostrate shrub, native to southern and central Europe; appears evergreen, but is not. Winged branchlets. Leaves lance-shaped, hairy undersides. Golden flowers in terminal racemes, in late spring–early summer. Silky fruit. Zones 4–9.

Genista tinctoria

COMMON WOADWAXEN, DYER'S GREENWEED

↔ 3 ft (0.9 m) ↑ 3 ft (0.9 m)

Native to Europe and western Asia. Variable in form and habit, deciduous shrub has no spines, can grow 6 ft (1.8 m) tall. Bright green leaves, elliptic or lance-shaped. Golden flowers on upright racemes, in summer. Used to produce dyes. **'Flore Pleno'**, dwarf form with double flowers; **'Golden Plate'**, clear yellow flowers, spreading compact shape, weeping branches; **'Royal Gold'**, more erect, with flowers carried in panicles. Zones 2–9.

GENTIANA

GENTIAN

A genus of around 250 widely distributed species of annuals, biennials, and perennials, and the type genus for its family, the Gentianaceae. Although ranging from tiny tufted alpine plants to species with 24 in (60 cm) long flower stems, most form a compact clump of simple pointed leaves, sometimes in rosettes. The trumpet- or bell-shaped flowers may be borne singly among the foliage or clustered on upright or overarching stems. Not all gentians have blue flowers, many are white, cream, yellow, or purple. Some gentians have medicinal uses and the name honors Gentius, King of Illyria, who in 180 BC was cited by Pliny as having discovered these properties. Modern herbalists use root extracts to treat anaemia and some gentians are also used as a flavoring.

CULTIVATION: Gentians prefer a climate with distinct seasons and grow best in full sun/half-sun with moist, well-drained, humus-rich soil, perhaps with a little dolomite lime. The small species thrive in rockeries. Propagate by division or from seed.

Gentiana makinoi

↔ 16 in (40 cm) ↑ 24 in (60 cm)

Summer-flowering Japanese species. Basal leaves to around 2 in (5 cm) long. Upright leafy stems bearing 1¼ in (30 mm) long, dark-spotted, blue, bell-shaped flowers at the stem tips and in leaf axils. Zones 6–9.

Gentiana paradoxa

↔ 12 in (30 cm) ↑ 8 in (20 cm)

Summer- to autumn-flowering Eurasian perennial with wiry stems and narrow foliage, spreading to form a small mounding clump. Long-lobed, bell-shaped, mid-blue to light purple flowers, to more than 1¼ in (30 mm) long. Zones 6–9.

Gentiana septemfida ★

↔ 16 in (40 cm) ↑ 12 in (30 cm)

Summer- to autumn-flowering western and central Asian perennial with spreading sometimes upright stems. Paired pointed oval leaves to 1¾ in (40 mm) long. Clusters of light-spotted, bright blue, bell-shaped flowers, to 1¾ in (40 mm) long. ***G. s.* var. *lagodechiana***, solitary flowers. Zones 3–9.

GENTIANOPSIS

FRINGED GENTIAN

Gentian-like in appearance, these plants are closely related to the true gentians (family Gentianaceae) and were once included in the genus. However, all but 1 of the 25 species that make up this North American and Eurasian genus are summer-flowering annuals and biennials, not perennials like the majority of gentians. They are usually upright, with strong angular stems bearing opposite pairs of variably shaped leaves. The widely flared tubular flowers are 4-petalled, clustered or solitary, frequently with finely fringed edges, usually blue to purple-blue, and often long-stemmed.

CULTIVATION: Hardy and easily grown in most temperate areas that aren't very dry in summer. Although some species are natural bog plants, in cultivation they prefer well-drained, moist, humus-rich soil. Full sun is best in cool climates, otherwise shade from hottest summer sun. Propagate from seed sown in spring; biennials can also be sown in early autumn.

Gentianopsis crinita

syn. *Gentiana crinita*

GREATER FRINGED GENTIAN

↔ 18 in (45 cm) ↑ 36 in (90 cm)

Annual or biennial from eastern USA. Erect branching stems; oval to lance-shaped leaves. Fringed flowers, bright blue, up to 2 in (5 cm) across, borne in late summer–autumn. Zones 3–9.

GERANIUM

CRANESBILL

The plants often called geraniums in fact belong in the genus *Pelargonium*. While both genera are in the geranium (Geraniaceae) family, true geraniums are a very different group of some 300 species of perennials and subshrubs, sometimes evergreen, that are widespread in temperate zones. Their leaves, usually palmately lobed, with toothed lobes, are often finely hairy. They bloom in summer and have simple, flat, 5-petalled flowers in pink or purple-blue shades, less commonly white or purple-black. The flowers develop into long narrow fruits. The name *Geranium* comes from the Greek *geranos* (crane), referring to the fruit's resemblance to the shape of a crane's bill. *G. robertianum* (commonly known as Herb Robert) and others have a long history in herbal medicine for a wide range of ailments and uses.

CULTIVATION: Most species are hardy and will grow in a range of conditions, preferring full sun or half-sun and moist humus-rich soil. The rhizomes can be invasive. Propagate from seed, cuttings, or by division. May self-sow.

Geranium albanum

↔ 20 in (50 cm) ↑ 8 in (20 cm)

From the Caucasus region and Iran. Basal leaves rounded, divided into 7- to 9-toothed palmate lobes, to 2 in (5 cm) wide. Magenta-veined pink flowers to 1 in (25 mm) wide, with blue stigma. Zones 7–9.

Geranium bohemicum

↔ 24 in (60 cm) ↑ 18 in (45 cm)

Freely self-sowing annual to short-lived perennial from central Europe. Finely hairy, deeply lobed and cut, maple-like, palmate leaves. Flowers small, cup-shaped, light mauve with purple veins, clustered mainly near the stem tips. Zones 6–9.

Geranium × *cantabrigiense*

↔ 24 in (60 cm) ↑ 8 in (20 cm)

A low spreading *G. macrorrhizum* × *G. dalmaticum* hybrid. Aromatic, bright green, rounded leaves, to 3 in (8 cm) wide, divided into 7 toothed lobes. Flowers to 1 in (25 mm) wide, pink or white with pink center. **'Biokovo'**, pink-flushed white flowers; **'Cambridge'**, deep pink to magenta flowers. Zones 5–9.

Geranium cinereum

↔ 20 in (50 cm) ↑ 6 in (15 cm)

Found in southern Europe and Turkey. Spreading perennial, rosettes of 5- to 7-lobed gray-green leaves, to 2

Geranium himalayense

Geranium ibericum subsp. *jubatum*

Geranium macrorrhizum 'Czakor'

Geranium maderense

in (5 cm) wide. Small heads of often dark-veined white to deep pink flowers, to 1 in (25 mm) wide. **'Purple Pillow'**, very compact habit, striking funnel-shaped purple-red flowers. Zones 5–9.

Geranium farreri

☼/◐ ✱ ↔16 in (40 cm) ↑4 in (10 cm)

Spreading alpine species from western China. Sprawling stems radiate from central tap root and take root. Leaves kidney-shaped, 7 palmate divisions, lobed and toothed, lower leaves to 2 in (5 cm) wide. Flowers solitary, rounded, mauve-pink, to more than 1¼ in (30 mm) wide, wavy edges. Zones 4–9.

Geranium gracile

☼/◐ ❄ ↔24 in (60 cm) ↑16 in (40 cm)

Found in the wild from Turkey to Iran. Thickened, partly emergent rootstock. Leaves wrinkled, hairy, light green, 5- to 7-lobed, toothed, to 4 in (10 cm) wide. Few long-stemmed, dark-veined, mauve-pink flowers. Keep dry in winter. Zones 7–9.

Geranium harveyi

syn. *Geranium sericeum*

☼/◐ ❄ ↔30 in (75 cm) ↑4 in (10 cm)

Spreading ground cover from the Ecuadorian Andes. Rosettes of finely hairy silver-gray leaves, 5 deeply toothed lobes, to 1¾ in (40 mm) wide. Funnel-shaped white to light pink flowers. Zones 7–9.

Geranium himalayense

☼/◐ ✱ ↔40 in (100 cm)
↑18 in (45 cm)

Found from northern Afghanistan to Nepal. Spreading habit with hairy stems and leaves. Basal leaves to 8 in (20 cm) wide, 7-lobed and toothed, upper leaves considerably smaller. Airy sprays of deep purple-blue flowers, to more than 2 in (5 cm) wide, often pink- or white-centered. **'Baby Blue'**, compact habit, vivid bright blue flowers; **'Gravetye'** (syn. 'Alpinum'), intense blue flowers, red-tinted autumn foliage; **'Plenum'** (syn.'Birch Double'), compact habit, small leaves, purple-blue double flowers. Zones 4–9.

Geranium ibericum

☼/◐ ✱ ↔30 in (75 cm) ↑16 in (40 cm)

Sprawling perennial from Turkey, the Caucasus region, and northern Iran. Leaves bright green, to 4 in (10 cm) wide, 9- to 11-lobed, toothed. Small heads of dark-veined purple-blue flowers to over 1¾ in (40 mm) wide. ***G. i.* subsp. *jubatum*** differs only in having hairs on the flower stems. Zones 6–9.

Geranium incanum

☼/◐ ❄ ↔40 in (100 cm)
↑40 in (100 cm)

Evergreen South African species, with branching main stems; long-stemmed, aromatic, bright green leaves, sometimes paired, finely cut into 5 narrow toothed lobes, downy white undersides. Airy sprays of long-stemmed, light-centered, magenta flowers to over 1¼ in (30 mm) wide. Zones 8–11.

Geranium macrorrhizum

☼/◐ ✱ ↔40 in (100 cm) ↑20 in (50 cm)

Spreading perennial native to southern Europe. The leaves are 4–8 in (10–20 cm) wide, with 5 to 7 lobes, toothed and further divided. Densely clustered heads of pink to purple-red flowers. **'Album'**, white flowers with red-tinted sepals; **'Bevan's Variety'**, small leaves, bright magenta flowers; **'Czakor'**, low-growing, magenta flowers with dark sepals; **'Ingwersen's Variety'**, light glossy green leaves, pale pink flowers. Zones 4–9.

Geranium maculatum

☼/◐ ✱ ↔40 in (100 cm)
↑27 in (70 cm)

Bushy North American perennial found from Manitoba to Kansas. Basal leaves to 8 in (20 cm) wide, upper leaves to 4 in (10 cm) wide, 5- to 7-lobed, further divided and toothed. Heads of upward-facing deep pink flowers, to 1¾ in (40 mm) wide. Zones 4–9.

Geranium × *oxonianum* 'Rose Clair'

Geranium maderense

☼/◐ ❄ ↔60 in (150 cm) ↑60 in (150 cm)

This native of Madeira is regarded as the largest geranium. Shrubby habit with rosettes of deeply lobed and divided leathery leaves, to 12 in (30 cm) wide, long purple-tinted stalks. Large, hairy, purple-stemmed flowerheads with many dark-veined deep pink to magenta flowers, to 1¾ in (40 mm) wide. Zones 9–11.

Geranium × *magnificum*

☼/◐ ✱ ↔40 in (100 cm)
↑20 in (50 cm)

Garden hybrid between *G. ibericum* and *G. platypetalum*. Leaves bright green, to 4 in (10 cm) wide, 9- to 11-lobed, toothed; hairy stems. Heads of dark-veined purple flowers to more than 1¾ in (40 mm) wide. Zones 5–9.

Geranium nodosum

☼/◐ ✱ ↔32 in (80 cm) ↑12 in (30 cm)

Clump-forming perennial native to the mountains of southern Europe. Leaves glossy, with shallow lobes, toothed. Lower leaves to 8 in (20 cm) wide, as small as 2 in (5 cm) wide elsewhere. Upright heads of purple flowers to more than 1 in (25 mm) wide, notched petal tips. Zones 6–9.

Geranium × *oxonianum*

☼/◐ ✱ ↔48 in (120 cm)
↑24 in (60 cm)

Hybrid between *G. endressii* and *G. versicolor*. Spreads to cover large area. Leaves with 5 fairly shallow lobes,

Geranium palmatum

2–4 in (5–10 cm) wide, sometimes larger. Masses of dark-veined light pink flowers to 1 in (25 mm) wide. ***G.* × *o.* f. *thurstonianum*,** deep purple-pink flowers, thin petals. ***G.* × *o.* 'A. T. Johnson'**, pale silvery pink flowers; **'Claridge Druce'**, vigorous, hairy stems, dark leaves, deep pink flowers; **'Rose Clair'**, small with purple to pink flowers; **'Sherwood'**, starry flowers with very narrow pale pink petals; and **'Wargrave Pink'**, a vigorous grower, clusters of small leaves, many soft orange-pink flowers. Zones 5–9.

Geranium palmatum

☼/◐ ❄ ↔24 in (60 cm) ↑40 in (100 cm)

Evergreen perennial, sometimes short-lived, native to Madeira. Compact for a while but eventually develops woody stem. Rosettes of long-stemmed, lobed, finely divided leaves, to 14 in (35 cm) wide. Large terminal heads of starry red-pink flowers, to 2 in (5 cm) wide, cream anthers. Zones 9–11.

Geranium phaeum

Geranium platypetalum

Geranium pratense 'Mrs Kendall Clark'

Geranium sanguineum 'Max Frei'

Geranium phaeum

BLACK WIDOW

☼/◐ ✱ ↔16 in (40 cm) ↕32 in (80 cm)

Upright, bushy, European perennial with 9-lobed leaves, large at the base, much smaller higher up the plant. Heads of 1 in (25 mm) wide flowers, mauve, maroon, to dark purple-red, sometimes near-black. **'Album'** ★, large white flowers; **'Lily Lovell'**, large purple flowers. Zones 5–9.

Geranium platypetalum

☼/◐ ✱ ↔16 in (40 cm) ↕12 in (30 cm)

A clumping perennial from the Caucasus region, Turkey, and northern Iran. Strong rootstock bearing hairy-stemmed, light green, 7- to 9-lobed and toothed leaves, 4–8 in (10–20 cm) wide. Densely clustered heads of dark-veined deep mauve-pink flowers, to nearly 2 in (5 cm) wide. Zones 6–9.

Geranium pratense

MEADOW CRANESBILL

☼/◐ ✱ ↔40 in (100 cm) ↕48 in (120 cm)

Sturdy spreading perennial found from central Europe to western Himalayas. Upright stems, leaves 4–8 in (10–20 cm) wide, 7 to 9 deep pinnate lobes, toothed. Flowerheads crowded to rather open, blue flowers to 2 in (50 mm) wide. **'Mrs Kendall Clark'**, pale flowers with translucent veins; **'Splish-splash'**, pale flowers randomly sectored and flecked with light purple-blue. Zones 5–9.

Geranium psilostemon

☼/◐ ✱ ↔16–24 in (40–60 cm) ↕24–40 in (60–100 cm)

Upright slightly spreading perennial from northeastern Turkey. Leaves 2–8 in (5–20 cm) wide, deeply lobed, and further divided. Erect heads of black-centered magenta flowers, to over 1¼ in (30 mm) wide. Zones 6–9.

Geranium pyrenaicum

☼/◐ ❄ ↔24 in (60 cm) ↕24 in (60 cm)

Evergreen, finely hairy, late-flowering perennial from southern Europe. Rounded 5- to 9-lobed leaves, to 4 in (10 cm) wide. Airy sprays of mauve to purple-pink flowers, to ¾ in (18 mm) across. Zones 7–9.

Geranium renardii

☼/◐ ✱ ↔16 in (40 cm) ↕8 in (20 cm)

Clump-forming perennial from Caucasus region. Leaves to 4 in (10 cm) wide, rounded, 5-lobed, toothed. Heads of flat, ¾ in (18 mm) wide, violet-veined, white to lavender flowers, notched petal tips. Zones 6–9.

Geranium × *riversleaianum*

☼/◐ ❄ ↔24 in (60 cm) ↕4 in (10 cm)

Garden hybrid between *G. endressii* and *G. traversii*. Low spreading habit with small, 7-lobed, bronze green leaves. Open heads of dark-veined, funnel-shaped, pink flowers, to more than 1¼ in (30 mm) wide. **'Mavis Simpson'**, light-centered flowers; **'Russell Prichard'**, deep pink flowers, sharply toothed leaves. Zones 7–10.

Geranium robustum

☼/◐ ❄ ↔24 in (60 cm) ↕40 in (100 cm)

South African subshrub with woody base, upright stems and silver-gray, hairy, 2 in (5 cm) wide leaves, 3 to 7 finely cut lobes. Clustered heads of light-centered purple flowers, to more than 1¼ in (30 mm) wide. Zones 8–11.

Geranium sanguineum

BLOODY CRANESBILL

☼/◐ ✱ ↔16 in (40 cm) ↕8 in (20 cm)

Low, slowly spreading, bushy Eurasian perennial. Leaves 2–4 in (5–10 cm) wide, 5- to 7-lobed, further divided. Many flowers, borne singly, magenta to purple-red, to over 1¼ in (30 mm) wide. ***G. s.* var. *striatum*** is small plant with dark-veined soft pink flowers, of which **'Splendens'** is taller form. *G. s.* Alan Bloom/**'Bloger'**, small leaves, compact habit, deep magenta flowers; **'Album'**, white flowers; and **'Max Frei'**, similar to Alan Bloom/'Bloger' but darker foliage, longer flower stems. Zones 5–9.

Geranium soboliferum

☼/◐ ✱ ↔16 in (40 cm) ↕8 in (20 cm)

Perennial; eastern Russia and northeastern China. Clustered basal leaves, 2 in (5 cm) wide, 7 narrow toothed lobes. Flowers rose-purple, to 1¼ in (30 mm) wide; dense heads. Zones 6–9.

Geranium subcaulescens

syn. *Geranium cinereum* var. *subcaulescens*

☼/◐ ✱ ↔12 in (30 cm) ↕10 in (25 cm)

From higher mountains of Greece, Albania and Macedonia, growing among limestone rocks. Compact perennial, smallish deep gray-green leaves. Flowers 1½ in (35 mm) or more wide, mostly vivid magenta with a darker center though paler pink and white forms also known. **'Splendens'**, petals bright purple-red with darker veining. Zones 5-9.

Geranium sylvaticum

◐ ✱ ↔40 in (100 cm) ↕27 in (70 cm)

Native to Europe and northern Turkey, usually growing in moist places. Leaves finely hairy, 2–8 in (5–20 cm) wide, 7 to 9 deep lobes, further divided and toothed. Dense heads of usually mauve-blue but sometimes white to magenta flowers, to 1¼ in (30 mm) wide. **'Album'**, pure white flowers; **'Mayflower'**, purplish blue flowers with pale centers. Zones 4–9.

Geranium wallichianum

☼/◐ ❄ ↔24 in (60 cm) ↕6 in (15 cm)

Spreading mountain perennial found from northeastern Afghanistan to Kashmir. Paired, 3- to 5-lobed, deeply divided and toothed leaves, about 3 in (8 cm) wide, often long-stemmed. Bowl-shaped, light-centered, magenta or light purple flowers, to over 1¼ in (30 mm) wide. **'Buxton's Variety'** ★ (syn. 'Buxton's Blue') has a prostrate habit and light-centered bright mauve-blue flowers. Zones 7–10.

Geranium wlassovianum

☼/◐ ✱ ↔20 in (50 cm) ↕12 in (30 cm)

Shrubby perennial from northeastern temperate Asia. Leaves rounded, downy, short-stemmed, divided into 7 coarsely cut pinnate lobes, to 6 in (15 cm) wide at the base, smaller higher up the plant. Airy heads of dark-veined pale magenta to deep purple flowers, to more than 1½ in (35 mm) wide. Zones 3–9.

Geranium Hybrid Cultivars

☼/◐ ❄ ↔24–48 in (60–120 cm) ↕8–36 in (20–90 cm)

Geraniums tend to sport readily and interbreed freely, so there are many garden forms in assorted sizes and flower colors. Popular cultivars include: **'Ann Folkard'**, trailing habit, yellow-green foliage, magenta flowers with dark-center; **'Ballerina'**, red-veined purple-pink flowers, notched petal tips; **'Frances Grate'**, a cross between the South African species *G. incanum* and *G. robustum*, silvery foliage, reddish purple flowers; **'Johnson's Blue'** ★, 18 in (45 cm) tall, bushy to semi-trailing habit, bright blue to purple-blue flowers; **'Nimbus'**, 16 in (40 cm) tall, glossy foliage, starry purple flowers; **'Patricia'**, spreading, rather open habit with black-centered magenta-pink flowers; **'Philippe Vapelle'**, 16 in (40 cm) tall, large leaves, densely foliaged, dark-veined lavender blue flowers; **'Pink Spice'**, trailing, dark bronze foliage, small pink flowers; **'Rambling Robin'**, mounding, spreading habit, lavender-blue flowers; **Rozanne/'Gerwat'**, to 20 in (50 cm) tall, variegated foliage, large violet-blue flowers; and **'Sue Crûg'**, bushy habit, mauve-pink flowers, with darker centers and veins. Zones 6–9.

GERBERA

BARBERTON DAISY, TRANSVAAL DAISY

Some 40 species of daisy (Asteraceae) family perennials comprise this genus, best known for its winter-flowering South African representatives; other species occur in western and southern Asia. Resembling highly sophisticated dandelions, they have a basal rosette of deeply lobed and softly toothed spatula- to lance-shaped leaves, and from the center of the rosette emerge strong flower stems, each bearing one large daisy head. Available in a wide color range and double flowers. The botanical name honors Traugott Gerber, a German botanist who traveled in Russia and died in 1743.

CULTIVATION: Gerberas are tender but can tolerate light frosts if kept barely moist in winter. Plant in full sun with deep, light, humus-rich soil with added grit for drainage. Popular as a house plant and cut flower. Propagate from seed or by careful division after flowering.

Gerbera jamesonii ★

BARBERTON DAISY

↔30 in (75 cm) ↑27 in (70 cm)

Native to South Africa and Swaziland. Doubtful if the original wild forms are still in cultivation except in native gardens in South Africa. Long-stemmed, deep green, dandelion-like leaves with coarse lobes and finely hairy undersides. Leaves can be more than 24 in (60 cm) long but usually considerably smaller. Flowerheads long-stemmed, to 4 in (10 cm) wide, usually in yellow, orange, or red shades. Zones 8–11.

Gerbera Hybrid Cultivars

↔12 in (30 cm) ↑8-18 in (20-45 cm)

Breeding of gerberas began at the end of the nineteenth century with the crossing of *G. jamesonii* and *G. viridiflora* in Cambridge, England. Most later cultivars are derived from this cross. Breeding was directed to producing long-stemmed blooms in a range of colors and varying degrees of doubleness, chiefly for the cut-flower industry, until short-stemmed seed-raised strains were developed for sale as flowering pot plants in the 1980s. Such plants produce a long succession of large flowerheads through much of the year, in both pastel and strong colors, but they generally do not make satisfactory garden plants. **Dwarf Pandora Series**, large single blooms on short stems, in a mix of reds, oranges, yellows, pinks, and whites, usually 3 to 6 open at any one time; **Fantasia Double Series**, very large double blooms with quilled central florets, in a range of soft colors; **Garvinea Series**, improved hardiness and vigor; **Happipot Series**, large blooms in vivid shades, deep green leaves. Zones 9–11.

GEUM

AVENS

This genus in the rose (Rosaceae) family, consisting of around 40 species and perennials, is widely distributed in the temperate regions. Known as avens, which was the Roman name for the plant, they are either rosette-forming or spread by rhizomes or runners, with their finely hairy pinnate or lobed leaves arising directly from the roots. From late winter to late summer, depending on the species, they produce flower stems bearing showy flowers that resemble tiny single roses, usually in bright shades of yellow, orange, pink, or red. Bristly dry fruits follow. Tincture of avens, an ingredient in some herbal medicines, is a mild sedative.

CULTIVATION: The small species are popular for rockeries, while larger forms suit perennial borders. Plant in a sunny position with moist well-drained soil that does not become compacted. Propagate by division when dormant, or raise from seed.

Gerbera Hybrid Cultivar

Geum chiloense

syn. *Geum quellyon*

↔20 in (50 cm) ↑30 in (75 cm)

Heavy-flowering Chilean perennial that has been extensively developed in cultivation. Long leaves divided into many toothed 1 in (25 mm) lobes. Erect flower stems with sprays of bright red flowers. **'Werner Arends'** (syn. 'Borisii') has many light orange-red semi-double flowers. Zones 5–9.

Geum chiloense 'Werner Arends'

Gerbera Hybrid Cultivar

Geum rivale

INDIAN CHOCOLATE, WATER AVENS

↔30 in (75 cm) ↑12 in (30 cm)

Eurasian and North American native forming a small clump and spreading by rhizomes. Slightly pendulous heads of creamy yellow flowers within downy purple-red calyces. Leaves to 12 in (30 cm) long, pinnate, with 7 to 13 toothed leaflets. **'Leonardii'** (syn. 'Leonard's Variety'), soft orange-red flowers. Zones 3–9.

Geum triflorum

LION'S BEARD, OLD MAN'S WHISKERS, PRAIRIE SMOKE, PURPLE AVENS

↔16 in (40 cm) ↑16 in (40 cm)

As the common names suggest, the ferny leaves of this North American species, to 6 in (15 cm) long, are gray-green and sometimes very downy. Flower stems to 16 in (40 cm) tall, with clusters of small, maroon-tinted, yellow flowers. Zones 6–9.

Geum Hybrid Cultivars

↔to 36 in (90 cm) ↑24 in (90 cm)

Geums hybridize freely, and although many garden forms can be traced to *G. chiloense*, some have more complicated parentage and are classified separately. Popular hybrids include: **'Beech House Apricot'**, flower stems to 8 in (20 cm) tall, light yellow to apricot flowers; **'Coppertone'**, pale apricot flowers; **'Fire Opal'**, 30 in (75 cm), semi-double orange-red flowers; **'Lady Stratheden'**, 24 in (60 cm), bright yellow double flowers; **'Mrs J. Bradshaw'** ★, 24 in (60 cm), bright red semi-double flowers; **'Starker's Magnificum'**, flower stems to 16 in (40 cm), flowers soft orange-pink; **'Tangerine'**, very compact, 5 in (12 cm) flower stems, bright orange flowers. Zones 6–9.

Geum, HC, 'Beech House Apricot'

GILLENIA

A North American genus of 2 species of rhizome-rooted perennials in the rose (Rosaceae) family. They form shrubby clumps of upright, arching, branching stems bearing stemless trifoliate leaves with toothed leaflets that turn orange in autumn. Loose sprays of 5-petalled flowers appear from spring into summer, with calyces that last long after the flowers have fallen, enlarging and reddening as the small seed heads develop. Root extracts are sometimes used medicinally but are potentially dangerous.

CULTIVATION: *Gillenia* species are very hardy but best protected from hot sun. They are easily grown in woodland conditions with dappled light and moist, humus-rich, well-drained soil. Propagate from seed, which should be stratified, or by dividing established clumps as they enter or leave dormancy in autumn or spring.

G

Gillenia trifoliata

BOWMAN'S ROOT, INDIAN PHYSIC

◐ ❄ ↔48 in (120 cm) ↑48 in (120 cm)

Found in eastern North America, from Ontario to Georgia. Leaves with serrated pointed oval leaflets to nearly 3 in (8 cm) long. Flowers to 1 in (25 mm) wide, white, sometimes pink- or purple-tinted. Zones 4–9.

GINKGO

A primitive genus containing a single species and given its own family, Ginkgoaceae, *Ginkgo* is quite different from all other conifers. Fossil records show it to be very ancient. Now unknown in the wild, it was certainly grown in China in the eleventh century; some specimens are believed to be well over 1,000 years old. The foliage resembles that of the maidenhair fern, hence the common name. Pollination is achieved by motile spores, a feature unknown among the higher plants, but normal among ferns. Male and female organs are carried on separate trees. The fruits are edible, nutritious, and are a source of various medicinal substances.

CULTIVATION: This attractive tree prefers hot summers but tolerates a range of conditions, including atmospheric pollution, giving it potential as a street tree. Plant in well-draining soil in full sun. Propagate from seed or half-hardened summer cuttings.

Ginkgo biloba

GINKGO, MAIDENHAIR TREE

☼ ❄ ↔25 ft (8 m) ↑100 ft (30 m)

Deciduous, very long lived, crown only developing fully after the first 100 years. Fronds fan-shaped, parallel veins spreading out from the stalk. Male flowers, pendulous short-stalked catkins. Fruit yellow-green, unpleasant odor when decaying. Foliage turns a beautiful golden yellow in autumn. **'Aurea'**, yellow leaves in summer; **'Autumn Gold'** ★, broadly conical in shape, leaves turn gold in autumn; **'Fastigiata'**, an erect male cultivar that grows to 30 ft (9 m) in height; **Pendula Group** members have nodding branches; **'Princeton Sentry'**, narrow growth habit, yellow autumn coloring; **'Saratoga'**, dense rounded form, deeply cut leaves; **'Tremonia'**, strongly erect form, very narrow crown; **Variegata Group** members have bold streaks of whitish yellow on the leaves. Zones 3–10.

Ginkgo biloba

GLADIOLUS

SWORD LILY

Think of the genus *Gladiolus,* and large-flowered hybrids, derived mainly from South African species, come to mind. But this genus in the iris (Iridaceae) family includes around 180 species of corms found from Europe to western Asia and South Africa, many quite different from the showy hybrids. Those with less colorful flowers are sometimes scented. The name *Gladiolus* comes from the Latin *gladius* (sword).

CULTIVATION: A good rule of thumb is to plant the corms at 4 times their own depth. Plant in full sun with light well-drained soil. In cold areas corms will survive outdoors if planted below freezing depth, otherwise lift and store dry for winter. *Gladiolus* produce tiny cormlets and propagation is simply a matter of grow-ing these cormlets on.

Gladiolus communis **subsp.** ***byzantinus***

Gladiolus communis

☼/◐ ❄ ↔12 in (30 cm) ↑40 in (100 cm)

Southern European native. Narrow leaves to around half of the flower stem length. Flowerheads usually with 2 to 3 branches, up to 20 red- or white-marked pink flowers. ***G. c.*** **subsp.** ***byzantinus*** ★ has long, pink-marked, purple-red flowers on less branching stems. Zones 6–10.

Gladiolus murielae

syns *Acidanthera bicolor, Gladiolus callianthus*

☼/◐ ❄ ↔20 in (50 cm) ↑40 in (100 cm)

From mountains of tropical east Africa. Compact clump of upright, broad, spear-shaped leaves to 20 in (50 cm). Many erect flower stems with solitary or paired, fragrant, white flowers with maroon blotch, in late summer–autumn. Zones 8–10.

Gladiolus tristis

MARSH AFRIKAANER

☼/◐ ❄ ↔12 in (30 cm) ↑24 in (60 cm)

South African species. Narrow leaves, thickened midrib, often twisting at tips. Up to 20 often widely spaced cream to yellow flowers, sometimes marked purple or maroon, on wiry stems, from spring. Scented in evening. Zones 7–10.

Gladiolus Hybrid Cultivars

☼ ❄ ↔12 in (30 cm) ↑2–5 ft (0.6–1.5 m)

It is estimated that some 10,000 *Gladiolus* hybrids have been raised. They are divided into groups with similar characteristics. The classifications vary in different parts of the world but most recognize just 3 main styles. Hardiness varies with the hybrids, though most will withstand overwintering in the ground provided the soil does not freeze to corm depth.

Gladiolus murielae

GRANDIFLORUS GROUP
The common gladioli seen in gardens with their showy flowers belong to this group. They are sometimes subdivided by the size of the flower.

Small-flowered: Flowers less than 3 in (8 cm) across, such as **'Goldfinch'**, 24 in (60 cm) tall, yellow ruffled flowers.

Medium-flowered: Flowers to 3–4 in (8–10 cm) across, such as **'Candyman'**, 27 in (70 cm) tall, pink flowers; **'Green Woodpecker'**, soft yellow-green flowers, contrasting red throat; **'Lady Lucille'**, to 32 in (80 cm) tall, light-centered pink flowers, over 20 blooms per stem; **'Midnight Moon'**, 32 in (80 cm) tall, dark purple-blue flowers marked with white; **'Shiloh'**, cream-edged deep pink with red blotch; **'Sundoro'**, to 30 in (75 cm) high, yellow flowers with red markings; **'Sunsport'**, 27 in (70 cm) tall, yellow and creamy ivory, more than 20 blooms per stem; and **'Tahiti Sunrise'**, to 27 in (70 cm) tall, yellow-throated straw-colored flowers, pink-edged.

Large-flowered: Reaching 40–48 in (100–120 cm) tall with flowers to 6 in (15 cm) across, such as **'Doris Darling'**, with long-stemmed heads of up to 25 ruffled pink flowers; **'Her Majesty'**, white-throated mauve to lavender flowers; **'Madison Avenue'**, orange-red flowers; **'Nova Lux'**, lemon yellow flowers; **'Peerless'**, intense deep red, regarded as the standard for the color; and **'Saxony'**, with yellow-throated apricot flowers.

G, HC, Grandiflorus Group, 'Her Majesty'

Giant-flowered: Around 48 in (120 cm) tall, flowers over 6 in (15 cm) across, such as **'Amsterdam'**, pure white flowers; and **'Dream's End'**, yellow-centered apricot flowers. Zones 9–11.

NANUS GROUP
Also known as **Miniature Hybrids**. Up to 36 in (90 cm) but often less than 24 in (60 cm) tall, with dense heads of flowers to 2 in (5 cm) across. Popular forms include: **'Charm'**, pink flowers with chartreuse blotches; and **'Nymph'**, pale pink flowers with dark edges and cream marks. Zones 8–10.

PRIMULINUS GROUP
Seldom exceed 24 in (60 cm) tall. Very narrow leaves. Single wiry stem of small flowers with a conspicuously hooded upper petal. Forms often seen include: **'Frank's Perfection'**, spaced bright red flowers; **'Lady Godiva'**, white flowers; and **'Pegasus'**, yellow flowers tipped with red. Zones 8–10.

GLANDULARIA

VERBENA, VERVAIN

This genus now includes many of the annual and low, spreading species formerly included in *Verbena*. It is a member of the vervain (Verbenaceae) family, and its species are found through the warmer parts of the Americas. They range from small, clumping annuals, through spreading ground covers, to perennials with erect flower stems to 24 in (60 cm) tall. The leaves are usually finely hairy, often with shallowly scalloped or toothed edges and divided.

CULTIVATION: Easily grown in a sunny spot with moist, well-drained soil. The trailers are excellent bank or hanging basket plants. Feed lightly during the growing season. Mildew can be a problem in humid climates. Propagate from seed, cuttings, or layers.

G., HC, Grandiflorus Group, 'Nova Lux'

Glandularia bipinnatifida

syn. *Verbena bipinnatifida*

☼ ✱ ↔36 in (90 cm) ↑12 in (30 cm)

Bristly-stemmed perennial, native to North America. Forms masses of finely divided hairy leaves. Small lavender, pink, or purple flowers, notched petals, in summer. Zones 3–9.

Glandularia canadensis

syn. *Verbena canadensis*

CREEPING VERVAIN, ROSE VERVAIN

☼ ✱ ↔16 in (40 cm) ↑8 in (20 cm)

From North America. Semi-prostrate perennial rooting at nodes. Leaves toothed, deeply divided. Small showy heads of fragrant rosy pink to purple flowers, in spring–autumn. Zones 4–9.

Glandularia gooddingii

syn. *Verbena gooddingii*

☼/◐ ❄ ↔24 in (60 cm) ↑24 in (60 cm)

Erect or spreading perennial from Mexico and southern USA. Pinnate leaves. Bluish purple, lavender, or pink flowers, in summer. Zones 9–11.

Glandularia Hybrid Cultivars

☼ ❄ ↔24–40 in (60–100 cm) ↑12–24 in (30–60 cm)

Fragrant perennials flowering from summer to autumn. **'Homestead Purple'**, vigorous, trailing, dark green foliage, purple flowers; **'Imagination'**, violet-blue flowers; **Lanai Series**, range of low, spreading cultivars, all colors; **'Peaches and Cream'**, peach and cream flowers; **'Quartz Burgundy'**, dwarf form, deep wine red flowers with tiny white eyes; **'Quartz Scarlet'**, vigorous, scarlet flowers; **'Sissinghurst'**, mat-forming, magenta pink flowers, can be invasive; **'Sister Ann'**, vigorous, pale and deep pink flowers; **Tapien Series**; low-growing, long-blooming, heat-resistant forms in blue, violet-blue, lavender, and pink; **Temari Series**, trailing, long-flowering, dense mats of fern-like foliage, large flowerheads in pink, burgundy, blue, and scarlet. Zones 7–10.

GLAUCIDIUM

This genus in the buttercup (Ranunculaceae) family contains just 1 species, a rhizome-rooted summer-flowering perennial from Japan. It forms a small clump of stiffly upright stems to around 12 in (30 cm) high that carry pairs of kidney- to heart-shaped leaves with 7 to 11 pointed and toothed palmate lobes. The flowers are borne on separate taller stems, each with 1 flower subtended by 2 small leaves. The flowers occur in pastel shades of mauve and lavender, have 4 petal-like sepals, are around 3 in (8 cm) wide, and open from late spring.

CULTIVATION: Hardy and easily grown in a moist cool-temperate climate. Intolerant of prolonged heat, drought, or low humidity and best sheltered from wind. Propagate from seed sown in spring after stratification or by dividing established clumps in late winter or early spring before growth recommences.

Glaucidium palmatum

Glaucidium palmatum

◐/✹ ✱ ↔20 in (50 cm) ↑18 in (45 cm)

Leaves to 8 in (20 cm) wide, deep green, heavily veined, sharply lobed. Cup-shaped flowers on stems to 18 in (45 cm) tall. White-flowered ***G. p.* var. *leucanthemum*** (syn. 'Album'), more widely cultivated than species. Zones 6–9.

GLAUCIUM

HORNED POPPY, SEA POPPY

This poppy (Papaveraceae) family genus of around 25 species of annuals, biennials, and perennials is found from Europe to North Africa, central and western Asia, often in coastal areas. Similar in appearance to poppies but clearly differentiated by the long horn-shaped seed capsules that follow the flowers. Most species have blue-green leaves, toothed and often pinnately lobed, in a basal rosette. Upright, sometimes branching, flower stems with small leaves emerge from the rosette in summer, and carry 4-petalled flowers, usually 2–4 in (5–10 cm) wide, in warm shades of yellow, orange, or red. The stems exude orange latex when cut.

CULTIVATION: These plants are hardy to moderate frosts and very easily grown in any temperate climate with reasonably warm summers. Plant in full sun with light, rather gritty, free-draining soil. Most species, even the perennials, are raised from seed and may self-sow, though rarely invasively.

Glaucium flavum f. fulvum

Glaucium flavum

YELLOW-HORNED POPPY

↔16 in (40 cm) ↑40 in (100 cm)

Biennial or short-lived perennial from Europe, North Africa, and Middle East. Finely hairy, pinnately lobed, toothed, blue-green leaves. Branching stems with bright yellow or orange flowers, to 2 in (5 cm) wide. Very narrow curved seed pods. *G. f.* f. ***fulvum,*** grayish foliage, orange-yellow flowers. Zones 7–10.

GLEDITSIA

LOCUST

There are 14 species of deciduous trees in this genus from the cassia subfamily of the legume (Fabaceae) family, native to North and South America, central and eastern Asia, Iran, and parts of Africa. All have fern-like, pinnately or bipinnately arranged leaves, and stout, sometimes branching, thorns on the trunk and branches. Flowers are insignificant and followed by seed pods of varying lengths. In some species the pods contain a sweet pulp. CULTIVATION: Plants grow best in sun, in moderately fertile soil that is moisture retentive, and may require frost protection when young. However, they are generally very tough, tolerating a range of soils and climates and are pollution resistant. Species are propagated from seed sown in autumn, while cultivars are grafted or budded.

Gleditsia triacanthos

HONEY LOCUST, THORNLESS HONEY LOCUST

↔70 ft (21 m) ↑150 ft (45 m)

Common in cultivation. Native of central and eastern USA. Fern-like foliage bright green, turning clear bright yellow in autumn. Thorns up to 12 in (30 cm). *G. t.* f. ***inermis*** is thornless—nearly all cultivars of honey locust derived from it. **'Elegantissima'**, compact, almost shrub-like, fine foliage, very slow-growing, rarely exceeds 15 ft (4.5 m) tall; **'Emerald Cascade'**, weeping tree, dark emerald green foliage turns bright yellow in autumn; **'Halka'**, fast-growing thornless selection, high, rather narrow crown; fine yellow color in autumn; **'Marando'**, dwarfed cultivar with spreading twisted branches; **'Moraine'** ★, tall, shapely, thornless tree, broadly spreading lower branches, dense ferny foliage; **'Rubylace'**, dark red young foliage, bronzing as it ages; **'Shademaster'**, broad-crowned upright tree, deep green leaves persisting late in autumn; **'Skyline'**, symmetrical outline, developing a broadly conical crown, dark green leaves, golden yellow in autumn; **'Sunburst'**, bright yellow young leaves becoming lime green as season progresses. Zones 3–10.

Gleditsia triacanthos f. inermis 'Sunburst', in spring

GLORIOSA

CAT'S CLAW, CLIMBING LILY, FLAME LILY, GLORY LILY

This genus from the autumn-crocus (Colchicaceae) family presently consists of a single, highly variable, tuberous, perennial species from tropical Africa and Asia. The climbing scrambling plant ascends by means of glossy emerald leaves that taper into coiling clinging tendrils. The showy single flowers, which appear in late summer and autumn, are held on short stems that emerge from the leaf axils. Petals are recurved, widely separated, and bright yellow, red, or purple. Bicolors are common. All plant parts are toxic.
CULTIVATION: Glory lilies require good drainage and full sun to half-sun. Plant the large, red-brown, fang-shaped tubers in a horizontal position, taking great care as they are dangerously brittle. Water plentifully when in growth and liquid feed with weak solution every 2 weeks.

Gloriosa superba

CLIMBING LILY, CREEPING LILY, GLORY LILY

↔12–20 in (30–50 cm) ↑6–8 ft (1.8–2.4 m)

Tuberous perennial vine with 1 to 4 slender, scrambling, bright green stems, native to tropical Africa and Asia. Soft, oval- to spear-shaped, glossy, bright green leaves, 2–3 in (5–8 cm) long, with tendrils, 1¼–2 in (3–5 cm) long, at leaf tips. Flowers are solitary, yellow, red, purple, or bi-colored, 1¾–4 in (4–10 cm) long, on long stalks, from summer–autumn. Many cultivars including: **'Citrina'**, with yellow flowers striped with maroon; **'Grandiflora'**, with large golden yellow flowers; **'Rothschildiana'** ★, with bright red or scarlet petals fading to garnet and purple, yellow near the base and at margins, completely recurved, undulating; and **'Simplex'**, with deep orange and yellow flowers. Zones 9–12.

GLOTTIPHYLLUM

This genus of around 60 species from the Karoo and Cape regions of South Africa belongs to the iceplant (Aizoaceae) family. They are compact succulent plants with semi-prostrate forking stems. Leaves are very fleshy, tongue-shaped or cylindrical, sometimes of different lengths, in 2 or 4 ranks, bright glossy green or whitish, sometimes tinged purple. The single yellow flowers, sometimes stalked, are borne in summer.
CULTIVATION: These succulent plants are easily grown in low-fertility compost as long as it is well drained; little watering is required. Too much water or too many nutrients lead to lush watery leaves that are prone to damage from handling, rots, and winter cold. Plant in full sun and keep completely dry from late summer until spring. Propagate from seed or cuttings, allowing them to dry out well before rooting.

Glottiphyllym linguiforme

Glottiphyllym linguiforme

syns *Mesembryanthemum linguiforme, M. lucidum, M. scalpratum*

↔8 in (20 cm) ↑3–5 in (8–12 cm)

Mat-forming perennial with pairs of curved, glossy, fleshy, apple green, unequal leaves, 2–2½ in (5–6 cm) long, with a rounded tip. Golden yellow flowers, 3 in (8 cm) wide, in autumn. Zones 9–11.

GLYCERIA

MANNA GRASS, MEADOW GRASS, SWEET GRASS

A genus of 16 species of perennial marsh grasses (family Poaceae) that will grow in shallow water. Distribution is widespread throughout the northern temperate zones and temperate regions of South America, Australia, and New Zealand. They spread by rhizomes, from which develop reed-like stems bearing long, strappy, succulent leaves. Large flower plumes, often purple-tinted, develop in summer, followed by edible small seeds.
CULTIVATION: Sweet grass species are mostly frost hardy and easily grown in any temperate climate. Plant in full sun with moist humus-rich soil. Although

Gloriosa superba 'Rothschildiana'

Glyceria maxima var. *variegata*

naturally adapted to damp conditions, they will grow well enough in regular garden soils if they are kept moist. Useful as marginal pond plants and for stabilizing easily eroded stream banks. Propagate from seed or by division.

Glyceria maxima

syns *Glyceria aquatica, Molinia maxima, Poa aquatica*

REED MEADOW GRASS, REED SWEET GRASS

↔ unlimited ↑ 1–8 ft (0.3–2.4 m)

Spreading, rhizomatous, perennial grass, native to temperate Europe and Asia, from the British Isles to Japan. Forms large stands of erect stems, unbranched. Narrowly strap-shaped leaves, to 24 in (60 cm) long, with a central ridge. Panicles of creamy greenish flowers, sometimes with purplish or purplish green tones, appear in summer. ***G. m.* var. *variegata*** (reed manna grass, striped manna grass), cream-striped green leaves tinged with pink toward the base. Zones 3–5.

GOMPHRENA

Native to tropical parts of the Americas and Australia, the 90-odd annuals and perennials in this genus are members of the amaranth (Amaranthaceae) family. However, unlike the long pendulous flower tassels of many amaranths, *Gomphrena* flowers are borne in small, usually upright, heads. The cultivated species form bushy mounds with leaves that are simple narrow oblongs in opposite pairs. The stems are finely hairy, the leaves less so. The flowerheads are borne on wiry stems and held just above the foliage. Each head is a short plume of many tiny flowers, usually creamy yellow, mauve, or pink in the species, with cultivated forms available in most colors.

CULTIVATION: Outside the tropics these plants are treated as summer annuals; they need long warm summers to flower well. Plant in moist humus-rich soil and water well, but do not overfeed. Propagate from seed.

Gomphrena globosa

Gomphrena globosa

BACHELOR'S BUTTON, GLOBE AMARANTH

↔ 18 in (45 cm) ↑ 24 in (60 cm)

From Panama and Guatemala. Bushy annual with slightly hairy pointed leaves. Flowers papery and round, resembling a clover flower, white through to red, purple, and yellow, borne in summer. **'Lavender Lady'**, lavender-colored flowers; **'Strawberry Fields'**, flowers of scarlet to crimson. Zones 7–11.

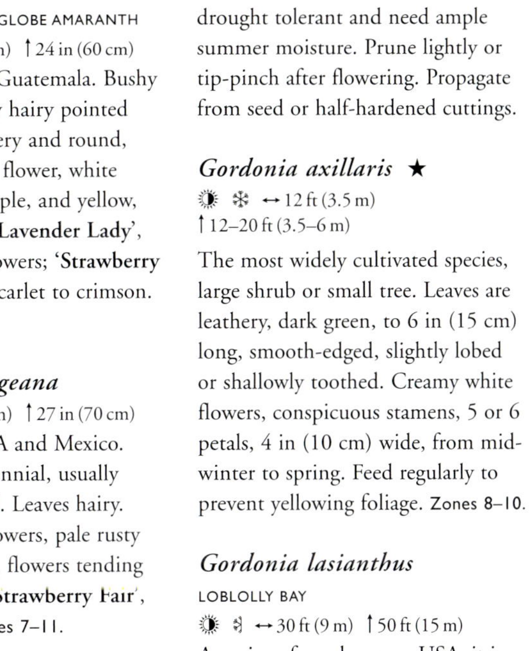

Gomphrena haageana

↔ 20 in (50 cm) ↑ 27 in (70 cm)

From southern USA and Mexico. Well-branched perennial, usually grown as an annual. Leaves hairy. Spherical papery flowers, pale rusty red. **'Amber Glow'**, flowers tending to orange shades; **'Strawberry Fair'**, redder flowers. Zones 7–11.

GORDONIA

Found in East Asia and the warmer temperate parts of North America, this genus of some 70 species of evergreen trees and shrubs is from the camellia (Theaceae) family. *Gordonias* are impressive plants with lush deep green foliage and beautiful flowers. Some species provide the added bonus of flowering in winter, though frost may destroy the flowers. Their flowers are usually white or cream with golden stamens and closely resemble the blooms of a single-flowered camellia.

CULTIVATION: The large deep green leaves suggest a preference for shade, but, as with camellias and rhododendrons, they need some sun to flower well. Shade from the midday summer sun is best. The soil should be humus-rich, friable, slightly acidic, and well drained—in other words, a woodland soil. Gordonias are not drought tolerant and need ample summer moisture. Prune lightly or tip-pinch after flowering. Propagate from seed or half-hardened cuttings.

Gordonia axillaris ★

↔ 12 ft (3.5 m)
↑ 12–20 ft (3.5–6 m)

The most widely cultivated species, large shrub or small tree. Leaves are leathery, dark green, to 6 in (15 cm) long, smooth-edged, slightly lobed or shallowly toothed. Creamy white flowers, conspicuous stamens, 5 or 6 petals, 4 in (10 cm) wide, from mid-winter to spring. Feed regularly to prevent yellowing foliage. Zones 8–10.

Gordonia lasianthus

LOBLOLLY BAY

↔ 30 ft (9 m) ↑ 50 ft (15 m)

A native of southeastern USA, it is more commonly around 25 ft (8 m) tall in cultivation. It has a narrow upright habit and shallowly serrated, deep green, glossy leaves. Although evergreen, older leaves develop red tones before finally falling. Flowers white, to 3 in (8 cm) wide, appear in summer. Zones 8–11.

Gordonia axillaris

GRAPTOPETALUM

These 12 species of succulent perennials native to Paraguay and Mexico to Arizona, USA, belong to the stonecrop (Crassulaceae) family. They form rosettes of fleshy leaves. The flowerheads are cymes bearing flowers with 5 spreading petals that are fused toward the base.

CULTIVATION: *Graptopetalum* species are easily grown in light to medium very well-drained soil in an open sunny position. Propagation is from seed, from stem or leaf cuttings, or by division of the offsets.

Graptopetalum amethystinum

LAVENDER PEBBLES

↔ 3–5 in (8–12 cm)
↑ 4–6 in (10–15 cm)

Clumping succulent perennial from Mexico. Forms rosettes of thick, blunt, rounded, blue-gray leaves, to 3 in (8 cm) long, with an amethyst tinge. Stout erect stems become prostrate with age. The terminal clusters of creamy white, bell-shaped flowers have red markings, and are ½–1 in (12–25 mm) across, appearing in spring–summer. Zones 9–11.

Graptopetalum paraguayense ★

GHOST PLANT, MOTHER OF PEARL PLANT

↔ 5–12 in (12–30 cm)
↑ 4–12 in (10–30 cm)

Small succulent perennial from Mexico. Stout stem forms rosettes, to 6 in (15 cm) across, at stalk ends. Thick, stiff, oval to wedge-shaped, whitish gray leaves, with a pinkish cast, 1½–2 in (3.5–5 cm) long, ridged undersurface. Young leaves pale purple. Terminal flowerhead, to 6 in (15 cm) tall, with up to 6 white star-shaped flowers, red-spotted, to ¾ in (18 mm) across, appear from late winter–early spring. ***G. p.* subsp. *superbum*** has succulent leaves with an eye-catching purplish gray bloom. Zones 8–11.

Graptopetalum amethystinum

G

Graptophyllum pictum

× *Graptoveria,* Hybrid Cultivar, 'Debbi'

G

GRAPTOPHYLLUM

Occurring in Australia, New Guinea, and the southwestern Pacific, this is a genus of 10 species of tall shrubs or small trees in the acanthus (Acanthaceae) family, several of which are popular as house plants. It has a tropical and subtropical distribution in a range of habitats from rainforest margins to rocky hillsides. All have curved tubular flowers in various shades of red, as well as opposite and attractive glossy leaves; some species have unfriendly spines on the stems or leaves.

CULTIVATION: These plants will grow in sun or part-shade on a range of well-drained soils, but flower better in full sun. They are mostly frost tender and require a warm climate if they are to be grown outdoors. Propagate from fresh seed, if obtainable, or from cuttings of 2- to 3-year-old shoots.

Graptophyllum pictum

CARICATURE PLANT

↔ 30 in (75 cm) ↑ 6 ft (1.8 m)

From New Guinea. Leaves elliptical, glossy, deep green. Flowers in terminal spikes of red to purple, in summer. Various color forms include leaves all purple-bronze, others green marked with white, yellow, pink, or purple, in blotches or stripes of many shapes and sizes. Propagate cultivars from cuttings to ensure color. Zones 10–12.

× GRAPTOVERIA

These hybrid succulent perennials are members of the stonecrop (Crassulaceae) family and are the result of crossing species of *Echeveria* with species of *Graptopetalum*. The diversity of growth-form, leaf shape, and coloring found in both parent genera is perpetuated in their hybrids, so it is difficult to generalize about their appearance; most could be mistaken for echeverias. Breeding has mostly been directed toward colorful foliage.

CULTIVATION: Plant these succulents in full sun or light shade in a sandy well-drained soil. Tip prune after flowering. Propagate from stem or leaf cuttings or by division of offsets.

× *Graptoveria* Hybrid Cultivars

↔ to 18 in (45 cm) ↑ 12 in (30 cm)

The partnership of *Echeveria* and *Graptopetalum* has given rise to many hybrid cultivars, including: **'Accolade'**, compact, pale bluish green leaves, edged red; **'Debbi'**, low-growing, rosette-forming succulent with rich pink paddle-shaped leaves; **'Dusty'**, long, narrow, dusky pink leaves, forms a stem; **'Fanfare'**, yellow flowers, rosettes of long narrow leaves with blue-gray bloom; **'Huth's Pink'** ★ (syn. 'Douglas Huth'), flat rosette of pink leaves, which forms stems; **'Kameri'**, short, thick, pointed, pearly pink and white leaves, forms stems; **'Margaret Reppin'**, compact rosette, dull green with pink blush, edges ending in long points, of clumping habit; **'Nausicaa'**, very small, green, clumping rosette, red tips; **'Purple Dream'**, small crowded rosettes, deep purple to red leaves; **'Rapeco'**, compact rosette, leaves short, pointed, bluish green; **'Rose Queen'**, compact rosette, leaves short, pointed, dusky pink; and **'Spirit of '76'** ★, compact bright powdery pink rosette. Zones 9–11.

GREVILLEA

This genus in the protea (Proteaceae) family is represented by around 340 species. Most are native to Australia, with some found in New Guinea, New Caledonia, Vanuatu, and Sulawesi. Naturally occurring Australian forms have been selected and hybrid cultivars developed with huge horticultural potential. They range from prostrate ground covers to tall trees. Distinctive, colorful flower clusters come in 3 basic forms—spider-like, toothbrush-like, and large brushes. Many are rich in nectar, which makes them attractive to insects, birds, and animals (especially Australian marsupials), all of which are pollinators. They are found in a wide climatic range and are tolerant of extremes. Some are short lived but spectacular, others have unique flower clusters, and some have a strong sweet fragrance.

CULTIVATION: Most grevilleas prefer an open sunny position and free-draining loams, and many perform best in phosphorus-deficient soils. Propagate from half-hardened cuttings; seed also germinates well but is often difficult to obtain; some of the species that are difficult to grow have responded well to grafting onto stocks of vigorous species such as *G. robusta*; this technique has also been used to produce weeping standard specimens.

Grevillea banksii

BANKS'S GREVILLEA, RED SILKY OAK

↔ 7 ft (2 m) ↑ 10–30 ft (3–9 m)

Variable dense shrub or slender tree, native to coastal Queensland, Australia. Long leaves, very deeply divided, smooth, silky both sides, prominent midvein. Large nectar-rich brush flowers, red or white, with pink and apricot forms, long flowering period, spring peak. Annual light pruning, avoid old wood. ***G. b.* var. *forsteri***, silvery leafed shrub to 10 ft (3 m), red or cream flowers over a long period. Zones 9–11.

Grevillea lanigera ★

WOOLLY GREVILLEA

↔ 4 ft (1.2 m) ↑ 5 ft (1.5 m)

Native to southeastern Australia. Variable shrub, sometimes prostrate and suckering. Narrow, occasionally fleshy leaves, soft silvery felting. Flowers all year, with a flush of spider clusters of pink, red, orange, or yellow in winter–spring. Prefers well-drained soils in cooler areas, dislikes humidity. Zones 8–10.

Grevillea lanigera

Grevillea lavandulacea

LAVENDER GREVILLEA

↔ 3 ft (0.9 m) ↑ 3 ft (0.9 m)

Compact shrub from southern Australia, a parent of several hybrid cultivars. Gray-green needle-like foliage, plentiful spider flower clusters of pink-red. Variations in leaf texture, habit, and flower color common. Do not crowd, avoid summer watering. Zones 8–10.

Grevillea rosmarinifolia

ROSEMARY GREVILLEA

↔ 6 ft (1.8 m) ↑ 6 ft (1.8 m)

From southeastern Australia, variable, dense or open shrub. Dark green needle-like foliage. Abundant spider flower clusters, in winter–summer, from cream to pale or deep pink. Prefers well-drained sandy loams, moisture in winter. Zones 8–9, or 8–10, depending on cultivar.

Grevillea victoriae

ROYAL GREVILLEA

↔ 6 ft (1.8 m) ↑ 6 ft (1.8 m)

Hardy adaptable shrub from southern Australia. The leaves are simple, oval or narrowly so, with a leathery texture, shiny uppersurface, and silky underside. Pendent spider-like flower clusters of red, orange, yellow, or pink, in spring–summer. Generally long-lived, reliable feature or screen plant. Zones 8–10.

Grevillea Hybrid Cultivars

↔ 4–15 ft (1.2–4.5 m)
↑ 6 in–20 ft (15 cm–6 m)

Most hybrids fall into 3 groups, each derived from a limited range of parent species but with none shared between the groups. A few hybrids can be placed in a "miscellaneous" group.

Grevillea banksii

G, HC, Banksii Group, 'Sylvia'

G, HC, Rosmarinifolia Group, 'Scarlet Sprite'

G., HC, Toothbrush Group, 'Fanfare'

G., HC, Miscellaneous Group, 'Long John'

BANKSII GROUP

The main parent species of these attractive and very popular hybrids is *G. banksii* from the east coast of Australia, but the cultivars can be subdivided into 2 groups: those whose other parent is *G. bipinnatifida,* and those bred from taller-growing tropical and subtropical species such as *G. pteridifolia* and *G. sessilis.* All have leaves dissected into narrow segments and dense bottlebrush-like spikes of flowers, which are crowded toward the upper side of the spike. **'Coconut Ice'**, a shrub to 7 ft (2 m) tall, has bright green foliage, red-pink flowers; **'Honey Gem'**, a shrub to 15 ft (4.5 m) has tall, dark green fern-like leaves, prolific orange or yellow flower clusters; **'Mason's Hybrid'** (syn. 'Ned Kelly'), a fast-growing hardy shrub to 6 ft (1.8 m), similar to 'Robyn Gordon', paler orange blooms, ferny light green foliage, orange-red flower clusters all year; **'Misty Pink'**, is a silvery shrub to 10 ft (3 m) tall, long pink flower clusters with cream tips; **'Moonlight'**, an upright shrub to 10 ft (3 m) tall, has ferny olive green foliage, long creamy flower clusters; **'Parfait Crème'**, a dense shrub to 10 ft (3 m) high and wide, has creamy yellow to caramel flowers; **'Robyn Gordon'**—the most widely planted grevillea—is a shrub to 6 ft (1.8 m) tall, with ferny foliage, spectacular clusters of bright pinkish red flowers; **'Sandra Gordon'**, a shrub to 15 ft (4.5 m) tall, bright yellow flowers; **'Superb'**, similar to 'Robyn Gordon', apricot-pink tint to flowers; **'Sylvia'**, a shrub to 10 ft (3 m) tall, has rosy pink flower clusters with cream tips; **'Winter Sparkles'**, winter-flowering shrub to 20 ft (6 m) tall, has yellow-orange flowers. Zones 9–12.

ROSMARINIFOLIA GROUP

Most of the earliest hybrids belonged to this group, derived from *G. rosmarinifolia*, *G. juniperina* and their allies with small smooth-edged leaves and flowers in the characteristic spider flower clusters. It includes most Clearview and Poorinda hybrids. Some cultivars in this group hybridize freely and their progeny may become invasive. **'Canberra Gem'**, a 6 ft (1.8 m) tall shrub, dark green needle foliage, cerise flowers; **'Clearview David'**, a dense shrub to 8 ft (2.4 m) tall, with prickly leaves, and bright red spider flowers; **'Clearview Robyn'**, a shrub to 6 ft (1.8 m) tall, blue-green needle leaves, vibrant cerise spider flowers; **'Crosbie Morrison'**, a dense shrub to 5 ft (1.5 m) tall, with gray-green leaves, and pink-red spider flowers; **'Evelyn's Coronet'**, an erect shrub to 6 ft (1.8 m) tall, with silvery, woolly, pink spider flowers; **'Firecracker'**, dense, compact bush, yellow-tipped red flowers; **'Noellii'**, may not be a hybrid but merely a compact form of *G. rosmarinifolia* with a neat bushy growth habit; **'Penola'**, gray leaves and an abundance of red and cream blooms; **'Poorinda Beauty'**, a 3 ft (0.9 m) tall shrub, with needle foliage, dense clusters of orange-red flowers; **'Poorinda Constance'**, dense shrub with soft foliage to 8 ft (2.4 m) high, red flowers; **'Poorinda Firebird'**, a shrub to 6 ft (1.8 m) high, with abundant scarlet spider flower clusters; **'Poorinda Leane'**, dense soft-foliaged shrub to 8 ft (2.4 m) tall, orange flowers; **'Poorinda Rachel'**, a shrub to 3 ft (0.9 m) tall, with oval leaves, and orange-red flowers; **'Poorinda Stephen'**, a shrub to 3 ft (0.9 m) tall, with silvery oval leaves, and large dark red spider flower clusters; and **'Poorinda Vivacity'**, a shrub to 3 ft (0.9 m) tall, with broad oval foliage, tight orange-red spider flower clusters. Other cultivars include **'Poorinda Queen'**, **'Poorinda Rondeau'**, **'Poorinda Tranquillity'**, and **'Scarlet Sprite'**. Zones 8–12.

TOOTHBRUSH GROUP

These hybrid cultivars are derived from a large group of species, mainly from southeastern Australian, with the "toothbrush" type of flower spike, in which the flowers are densely crowded and all turned upward to form an elongated brush; often they are bent sharply backward as well. The leaves of both species and hybrids range from simple and smooth-edged to toothed, lobed, or dissected into narrow segments. The plants range from quite prostrate to tall and erect. **'Boongala Spinebill'** ★, very adaptable spreading shrub to 8 ft (2.4 m) tall, cascading branches, new ferny foliage coppery red, deep crimson toothbrush flower clusters; **'Bronze Rambler'**, vigorous ground cover with a spread of 15 ft (4.5 m), dissected leaves, bronze tint on new growth, purplish flowers; **'Brookvale Letitia'**, tall shrub to 15 ft (4.5 m) high, orange and red hairy flowers; **'Fanfare'** (syn. 'Austraflora Fanfare'), prostrate, spreading to about 17 ft (5 m), spring to summer inflorescences are dark red with pink styles; **'Ivanhoe'** ★, dense foliage, dense habit, and vigorous growth to 10 ft (3 m) tall and 15 ft (4.5 m) across, red flowers. Zones 9–12.

MISCELLANEOUS GROUP

This group includes: **'Deuagold'**, wide leaves, yellow flowers, *G. rhyolitica* hybrid; **'Granya Glory'**, to 2 ft (0.6 m) high, creamy and rosy flowers; **'Long John'**, shrub to 10 ft (3 m) tall, red and pink flowers; **'Merinda Gordon'**, to 10 ft (3 m) tall, deep pink to red flowers; **'Orange Marmalade'**, to 8 ft (2.4 m) tall, leaves smooth-edged and silky hairy on the undersurface, flowers orange; **'Pendant Clusters'** (syn. 'Austraflora Pendant Clusters'), creamy yellow flowers with deep red styles; **'Poorinda Ensign'**, less than 3 ft (0.9 m) tall, leaves smooth edged, densely clustered bright pink flowers; **'Sid Reynolds'**, shrub to 8 ft (2.4 m) tall, pale reddish pink flowers; **'Winpara Gem'**, shrub to 7 ft (2 m) tall, reddish flowers; and **'Winter Delight'**, spreading mound, 20 in (50 cm) high, gray-green leaves, red and white flowers, in winter–spring. Zones 9–12.

GREYIA

This South African genus of 3 species of deciduous shrubs is a member of the Melanthiaceae family. Notable for its striking flowers and unusual foliage, the leaves resemble those of a regal pelargonium, being rounded, lobed, and around 3 in (8 cm) wide. They occur mainly at the tips of heavily wooded branches and redden before dropping in autumn. The flowers are bright red and have an unusual structure: 5 petals fused to a fleshy central disc, from which protrude 10 long stamens. They are clustered in racemes up to 6 in (15 cm) wide.

CULTIVATION: Best grown in a hot sunny position, *Greyia* species prefer mild climates but will tolerate light frosts. Soil should be fairly fertile and well drained. Water well in summer but allow plants to dry off as they approach winter dormancy. Propagate from seed or half-hardened cuttings in late spring or summer.

Greyia sutherlandii

NATAL BOTTLEBRUSH

↔7 ft (2 m) ↑15 ft (4.5 m)

Large shrub; branches very heavy at base. Bright red flowerheads at tips of bare branches, in late winter–early spring. Deeply lobed leaves follow, an attractive feature through summer, coloring in autumn. Zones 9–11.

Greyia sutherlandii

GRINDELIA

GUM PLANT, ROSIN WEED, TAR WEED

Found in the drier regions of western North America and South America, this daisy (Asteraceae) family genus is made up of some 60 species, mostly annuals and perennials with a few shrubs. They have wiry stems with simple leaves covered with small resin glands that make them sticky to touch. The stems exude resin when cut, which dries to form a white deposit that is often a conspicuous feature on the stems and leaves. Yellow daisy-like flowerheads appear mainly in summer. Extracts of the leaves of some California species have been used medicinally, mainly for bronchial complaints.

CULTIVATION: Hardiness varies considerably with the species, but most are at home in a temperate climate with only light to moderate frosts. Plant in full sun with light, gritty, free-draining soil. They can be propagated from seed or spring to summer cuttings. Because of the woody base, division is seldom practical.

Grindelia camporum

↔40 in (100 cm) ↑60 in (150 cm)

Annual or short-lived perennial native to California, USA. Upright, quite open growth habit. Very resinous toothed leaves to 3 in (8 cm) long. Flowerheads to over 1½ in (35 mm) wide, with up to 35 recurved ray florets. Zones 8–10.

Grindelia stricta

PACIFIC GRINDELIA

↔40–60 in (100–150 cm)
↑8–36 in (20–90 cm)

Perennial from western North America. Upright or spreading habit. Leaves deep green, oblong to spatula-shaped, usually minutely toothed, around 4 in (10 cm) long. Bright yellow flowerheads to 2 in (5 cm) wide, with up to 35 narrow recurved ray florets. ***G. s.* subsp. *venulosa*,** low and spreading, 2 in (5 cm) long leaves. Zones 8–10.

Grindelia stricta

GRISELINIA

This group of 7 evergreen trees and shrubs is the type genus for its family, the Griseliniaceae; 5 of the species are native to Chile and southeastern Brazil and 2 to New Zealand. Generally plants of coastal areas, they have large, glossy, leathery leaves. The tiny yellow-green flowers are unisexual, with male and female flowers borne on separate trees.

CULTIVATION: *Griselinia* species are grown for their attractive shiny foliage and are particularly useful for providing screens, shelter, and hedging. They are invaluable in coastal areas, being very tolerant of salt winds, and will grow in most well-drained soils in sun or part-shade. In very cold areas they are best given a warm sheltered site or grown in a conservatory. Pruning should be carried out in summer. Propagation is easiest from half-hardened cuttings in autumn, as seed can be difficult to germinate.

Griselinia littoralis

BROADLEAF, KAPUKA, PAPAUMA

↔15 ft (4.5 m) ↑25 ft (8 m)

Found throughout New Zealand. Leathery oval leaves, very glossy, bright green. Panicles of tiny flowers, in spring. Small purplish fruits on female trees. Attractive cultivars, foliage variegated in creamy yellow are often available; these include **'Dixon's Cream'** and **'Variegata'**. Zones 8–11.

Griselinia lucida

AKEPUKA, PUKA

↔15 ft (4.5 m) ↑15 ft (4.5 m)

In the wild this New Zealand species starts life as an epiphyte. Puka forms a wide-spreading tree, branches close to the ground. Large oval leaves, uneven sides, to 8 in (20 cm) long, very glossy rich green above, paler undersides. **'Variegata'** ★ has variegated leaves. Zones 9–11.

Griselinia littoralis

GUNNERA

There are 40 to 50 species of fleshy stemmed perennials in this genus, which belongs to its self-named family, the Gunneraceae. They are native to Australasia, South Africa, South America, and the Pacific. Species range from tiny ground huggers to spectacular giants of 7 ft (2 m) or more. Grown for their foliage, which may be round to oval, heart-shaped or deeply lobed, with or without toothed margins. Tiny greenish yellow or red flowers are borne on spikes in summer, and followed by red, orange, yellow, or white berries.

CULTIVATION: Excellent plants for waterside planting, the larger species being quite dramatic. Grow in moisture-retentive soils in full sun. Cover the crowns of large species with a protective mulch in winter. Propagate from seed or by division.

Gunnera insignis

POOR MAN'S UMBRELLA

↔10 ft (3 m) ↑7 ft (2 m)

From Central America. Rounded, rough-textured leaves, 3–5 ft (0.9–1.5 m) across, lobed, spiny beneath. Reddish flowers on tall spikes. Zones 8–10.

Gunnera manicata

syn. *Gunnera brasiliensis*

GIANT RHUBARB

↔10–15 ft (3–4.5 m)
↑6–10 ft (1.8–3 m)

Spectacular species from South America. The leaves are rhubarb-like, to 7 ft (2 m) or more across, sharply toothed, spiny beneath. Tiny greenish red flowers on erect spikes 3–6 ft (0.9–1.8 m) tall. Zones 7–9.

Gunnera manicata

Gunnera prorepens

↔12–18 in (30–45 cm)
↑2–4 in (5–10 cm)

Mat-forming stoloniferous perennial from New Zealand. Small, round-toothed, ovate leaves, bronze to purplish green. Male and female flowers on separate plants; the female plants bear short spikes of dense red berries after flowering. Zones 8–10.

Gunnera tinctoria

syns *Gunnera chilensis, G. scabra*

↔8 ft (2.4 m) ↑6 ft (1.8 m),

From Chile. Similar to *G. manicata* but of smaller and more compact habit. Leaves up to 5 ft (1.5 m) across. Flowering spikes, with redder flowers and fruit than *G. manicata,* are about 2 ft (0.6 m) tall. Zones 7–9.

GUSTAVIA

This genus of 41 evergreen trees from the brazilnut (Lecythidaceae) family is native to wet tropical Central and South America. Leaves are clustered at the ends of the branches, and showy flowers are carried in terminal or axillary racemes. The berry-like fruit contains a nut or kernel.

CULTIVATION: Moist, rich, well-drained soils; hot damp conditions. Propagate from seed or by layering.

Gustavia augusta

syn. *Gustavia marcgraaviana*

↔7 ft (2 m) ↑20 ft (6 m)

Native to northeastern South America. Evergreen shrub or small tree, stiff erect habit. Coarse paddle-shaped leaves, to 18 in (45 cm) long, finely toothed edges. Large showy flowers, 6

Gunnera tinctoria

Gustavia augusta

Guzmania, Hybrid Cultivar, 'Caroline'

in (15 cm) or more in diameter, camellia-like white to pink petals, most of the year. Tolerates quite severe dry seasons. Zones 10–12.

GUZMANIA

This genus of about 200 usually epiphytic species, few of which are in cultivation, and over 200 hybrids belongs to the bromeliad (Bromeliaceae) family. These plants are found mainly in the high rainforests of Ecuador and Colombia and also in Central America and the West Indies. They grow up to 40 in (100 cm) high and wide but are mostly smaller, with green, spineless, strap-like leaves, sometimes finely lined or cross-banded on the undersides, forming an open rosette. The flower stem is usually conspicuous and the flowerhead is globular to cylindrical, with side branches and flowers on all sides. Beneath each branch or flower there are generally brilliant colored bracts in yellow to orange to red shades. Petals are white or yellow.
CULTIVATION: Recommended for indoor culture if in flower, for greenhouse or conservatory in cool-temperate areas, or outdoors with protection from continuous sunlight and excessive heat in warm-temperate, subtrop-ical, and tropical areas. Prefers a damp atmosphere and a constant temperature 68–86°F (20–30°C). Water when potting mix is dry. Do not over-fertilize. Propagate from seed or offsets.

Guzmania Hybrid Cultivars

☀ ❄ ↔ 10–24 in (25–60 cm)
↕ 18–36 in (45–90 cm)

Most of these cultivars show a strong influence of *G. lingulata* and have a similar growth habit, but usually with more brilliantly colored and larger inflorescence bracts. **'Amaranth'**, green leaves with brownish lines on the undersides, intense raspberry-purple flower bracts, petals white; **'Attila'**, dark green rosette, red bracts, yellow flowers; **'Caroline'**, bright green rosette, pinkish red bracts; **'Cherry'**, leaves reddish green with faint striping at the base, vibrant cherry red bracts, yellow flowers. **'Cherry Smash'**, **'Grand Prix'** ★, **'Grapeade'**, **'Orangeade'**, and **'Samba'** are similar but have different-colored bracts. Some forms also have variegated leaves. Zones 9–12.

GYMNOCARPIUM

These 5 deciduous terrestrial ferns from the cliff-fern (Woodsiaceae) family are native to Europe, North America, and Asia. The slender, creeping, and freely branching rhizomes are covered with scales and bristles. Scales cover the bases of the erect frond stalks, which darken in color toward the base. The thin, papery, pinnate, triangular fronds arise singly or in masses.
CULTIVATION: These plants prefer low to medium light in moist garden soil or potting mix. Propagate by division or from spores.

Gymnocarpium dryopteris

COMMON OAK FERN

☀ ✻ ↔ 9–15 in (22–38 cm)
↕ 9–15 in (22–38 cm)

From Europe, temperate Asia, and North America. Spreading blackish rhizomes with brown fibrous scales. Broadly triangular, chartreuse fronds, on erect, slender, shiny, straw-colored stalks, usually single but often in masses, 3–15 in (8–38 cm) tall. Zones 2–9.

GYMNOCLADUS

A member of the cassia subfamily of the legume (Fabaceae) family, this genus of 2 to 5 deciduous trees allied to *Gleditsia* occurs across warm-temperate regions of North America and eastern Asia. They have bipinnate leaves and separate male and female plants with flowers in short terminal panicles. The fruit is a large woody pod containing flat, hard, glossy seeds. The fruit of *G. dioica* was used by early American settlers as a substitute for coffee. Native Americans cooked and ate the seeds.
CULTIVATION: Adaptable to most soil types in an open sunny position, these trees are drought and frost tolerant. Propagation is from seed.

Gymnocladus dioica ★

CHICOT, KENTUCKY COFFEE TREE

☼ ✻ ↔ 12 ft (3.5 m) ↕ 75 ft (23 m)

Native to central and eastern North America. Coarsely textured bark, thick branchlets, young twigs light gray, almost white. Large bipinnate leaves, 8 to 14 oval leaflets, pink, turning yellow in autumn. Dull greenish white flowers, in racemes, in summer. Thick, succulent, reddish brown or maroon fruit. *G. d.* var. *folio-variegata*, variegated foliage; *G. d.* 'Variegata', variegated cream foliage. Zones 4–8.

GYPSOPHILA

BABY'S BREATH

Related to the pink (Caryophyllaceae) family, the 100-odd annuals and perennials in this genus occur naturally in temperate Eurasia. They can be spreading mat-forming plants studded with pink or white blooms, or upright shrubby species with billowing heads of tiny flowers. Leaves simple linear to lance-shaped, sometimes rather fleshy and often blue-green. *G. paniculata* and its cultivars are very popular cut flowers. The common name comes from the sweet scent of the flowers.
CULTIVATION: *Gypsophila* means lime-loving, but most species are happy in any neutral to slightly alkaline soil that is fertile, moist, and well-drained. Mat-forming species are superb rockery plants. Plant in full sun. Larger types will often rebloom if cut back after their first flush. Propagate from basal cuttings or seed.

Gypsophila cerastioides

☼/◐ ✻ ↔ 8 in (20 cm) ↕ 3 in (8 cm)

Mat-forming perennial from the Himalayas. Small, downy, gray-green leaves with small sprays of pink-veined white or mauve flowers to over ½ in (12 mm) wide. Zones 5–9.

Gypsophila paniculata

BABY'S BREATH

☼/◐ ✻ ↔ 48 in (120 cm)
↕ 48 in (120 cm)

Rhizome-rooted perennial found from central Europe to central Asia. Forms a bushy clump of narrow blue-gray leaves to 3 in (8 cm) long, often hidden below billowing panicles massed with tiny white or pink flowers. **'Bristol Fairy'** ★, the most widely grown form, has relatively large white double flowers. Zones 4–9.

Gypsophila repens

☼/◐ ✻ ↔ 24 in (60 cm) ↕ 4 in (10 cm)

Mat-forming perennial from the mountains of central and southern Europe. Narrow, pointed oval, blue-green leaves to more than ½ in (12 mm) long. Sprays of up to 25 tiny, white, pink, or mauve flowers. **'Rosa Schönheit'** (syn. 'Rose Beauty'), rose pink flowers. Zones 4–9.

Gymnocarpium dryopteris

Gymnocladus dioica

Gypsophila repens

H

H

HABRANTHUS

This genus of about 10 bulbous perennials from Central and South America belongs to the amaryllis (Amaryllidaceae) family. The solitary, trumpet-shaped flowers, which appear after rain in summer and autumn, are held at an angle from their straight stems. The leaves are semi-erect, narrow, and linear. Some species are evergreen and some deciduous. The name comes from the Greek *habros,* meaning graceful—which they are. CULTIVATION: Give these plants sharp drainage and a sandy loam. Apply a weak liquid feed while in growth and keep slightly moist while dormant. Propagation is best done from offsets or from fresh ripe seeds kept at 61°F (16°C).

Habranthus robustus

syn. *Zephyranthes robusta*

↔ 4 in (10 cm)
↕ 8–12 in (20–30 cm)

Robust, invasive in appropriate conditions. Flowers open funnel-shaped, solitary or paired, 2½ in (6 cm) across, in summer. Petals rose pink fading to almost white. Leaves deep green, finely linear with a visible midrib, appearing after flowers and persisting until late spring. Zones 8–10.

Habranthus tubispathus

↔ 3 in (8 cm) ↕ 6–10 in (15–25 cm)

Robust, invasive in appropriate conditions. Flowers small, funnel-shaped, produced in succession throughout summer. Petals coppery red, orange, or yellow. Leaves appear after flowers and persist until late spring. **'Rosea'**, dark pink petals. Zones 8–10.

Habranthus robustus

HACQUETIA

This genus of a single species in the carrot (Apiaceae) family inhabits lowland to alpine woods in Europe. It is a herbaceous clumping perennial with cut foliage and clusters of tiny yellow flowers surrounded by green bracts, looking like large green-petalled flowers. This charming plant shows little obvious connection to the carrot. CULTIVATION: A moist humus-rich soil under deciduous trees and shrubs or in a cool rock garden will suit. Propagate from seed or root cuttings, or by careful division.

Hacquetia epipactis

↔ 6–12 in (15–30 cm)
↕ 5–6 in (12–15 cm)

Widespread throughout Europe. Bright green-bracted flowerheads with tiny yellow flowers, to 1¾ in (40 mm) across, in early spring. Glossy green leaves, to 2½ in (6 cm) long, have 3 wedge-shaped leaflets and only reach maturity after flowering. **'Thor'**, cream variegated form whose variegation extends into floral bracts. Zones 6–9.

HAKONECHLOA

A grass (Poaceae) family genus, it comprises one ornamental species and numerous cultivars. This slow-spreading, rhizomatous, perennial grass is found on wet rocky cliffs in the mountains of the Tokaido district of southeast Honshu, Japan. The linear to lance-shaped blades grow to 12–36 in (30–90 cm) tall, and in mid- to late summer small airy inflorescences appear between the leaves, which turn orange to bronze in autumn. A number of attractive variegated forms exist whose variegation is affected by siting and climatic conditions: in deep shade, yellow variegation is lime green; in partial shade in warm regions, the yellow parts turn a strong gold-yellow; grown in full sun in cool summer climates, yellow variegation bleaches to creamy white.
CULTIVATION: Frost-hardy.
Prefers moist, humus-rich, well-drained soil. Grow in full or half-sun, depending on climate. It requires shade in hot dry areas. Generally disease free, it can be propagated by division in spring.

Hacquetia epipactis 'Thor'

Hakonechloa macra

HAKONE GRASS, JAPANESE FOREST GRASS, URAHAGUSA

↔ over 24 in (60 cm)
↕ to 24 in (60 cm)

Slender, arching, green leaves with wiry stems form loose cascading mounds. Provides dramatic textural contrasts, particularly planted in drifts. Orange- to red-flushed autumn foliage persists into winter. Green-leafed form is more cold hardy (Zone 4), sun and drought tolerant, and faster growing than cultivars, which both reach 12 in (30 cm) high. **'Alboaurea'**, mostly off-white and yellow variegated leaves with green, and red- to pink-flushed autumn foliage; **'Aureola'**, golden yellow leaves and thin green stripes, pinkish red tints in autumn. Zones 6–11.

HALESIA

SILVERBELL

This is a genus of 4 or 5 species of deciduous shrubs or small trees in the storax (Styracaceae) family, indigenous to China and eastern North America. Predominantly found in moist deciduous woodlands, these plants have graceful and attractive spring flowers. Individually the flowers are simple, small white bells, but massed together, moving on the breeze, they have an instant appeal. Winged fruits appear in autumn. The leaf is usually a simple mid-green ellipse, to 5 in (12 cm) long. CULTIVATION: At home in a moist humid environment sheltered from strong winds. They are cool-climate plants but need a hot summer for best display of flowers. Soil should be well drained and slightly acidic. Confine pruning to trimming shape. Propagate from seed or summer cuttings.

Halesia carolina

syn. *Halesia tetraptera*

CAROLINA SILVERBELL, SILVERBELL, SNOWDROP TREE

↔ 25–30 ft (8–10 m) ↕ 25 ft (8 m)

From southeastern USA. Spreading crown. Most commonly cultivated species. Heavy flowering, in spring, with the tree smothered in pendulous clusters of white or pink-flushed bells which, by autumn, develop into 4-winged fruit. Foliage develops yellow tones, in autumn. Zones 3–9.

Halesia carolina

Halesia diptera

TWO-WING SILVERBELL

↔ 30 ft (9 m) ↕ 20 ft (6 m)

Native to southeastern USA along the Gulf coast region. Most commonly a large shrub, sometimes attains tree-like proportions. Leaves to 4 in (10 cm) long, edged with minute teeth, downy when young. Flowers less than 1 in (25 mm) wide, white with downy calyces, in clusters of 3 to 6, followed by 2-winged fruits. Zones 6–9.

Halesia monticola

MOUNTAIN SILVERBELL, MOUNTAIN SNOWDROP TREE

↔ 20 ft (6 m) ↕ 30 ft (9 m)

From southern Appalachian mountains of eastern USA. Wide-spreading crown. White flowers in clusters of 2 to 5 blooms, followed by 4-winged fruit. *H. m.* f. *rosea*, pale pink flowers. Some botanists now treat this species as a subspecies of *H. carolina.* Zones 4–9.

HALIMIUM

There are about 12 species of evergreen shrubs and subshrubs in this genus of the rock-rose (Cistaceae) family. They are native to the Mediterranean region and western Asia in dry open forest thickets and sandy and rocky scrubland. These gray-leafed plants resemble *Cistus* (rock rose), for which they are often mistaken. CULTIVATION: Mild winters and warm summers are the ideal conditions for cultivation. *Halimium* species grow in full sun in sandy, moderately fertile soil with protection from cold and drying winds. For best results, grow in pots or a rock garden border. In areas with wet winters, extra sharp drainage needs to be provided or the plants need to be protected from over-saturation. Grow from seed in spring in a heated tray or take half-hardened cuttings in late summer.

Halesia diptera

Halimium, Hybrid Cultivar, 'Sarah'

Halimium atriplicifolium

↔3 ft (0.9 m) ↑5 ft (1.5 m)

Upright shrub native to Spain and Morocco. Leaves elliptic with silvery scales, 3 distinctive veins. Bright yellow flowers, with or without a reddish brown spot, in late spring–early summer. Zones 8–9.

Halimium lasianthum ★

syn. *Halimium formosum*

↔4 ft (1.2 m) ↑3 ft (0.9 m)

Bushy erect shrub from Spain and Portugal. Gray foliage. Clusters of yellow flowers, with a dark red basal spot, from leaf axils, in spring–early summer. ***H. l.*** **subsp. *alyssoides***, compact shrub, native to southwestern Europe; egg- to lance-shaped leaves, dark green above, white hairy undersides; small yellow flowers, in cymes from the axils or tips of branches, in late spring–early autumn. ***H. l.*** **subsp. *formosum***, has slightly larger flowers with a distinct rust red basal spot. ***H. l.*** **'Concolor'**, no basal spot; **'Sandling'**, bright maroon basal spot. Zones 8–9.

Halimium ocymoides

syn. *Cistus algarvensis*

↔3 ft (0.9 m) ↑3 ft (0.9 m)

Erect, compact, bushy shrub from southwestern Europe. Leaves are lance- to egg-shaped, gray-green, with white down. Golden yellow flowers, each petal with a deep maroon spot, arise from terminal panicles, in early–late summer. Zones 8–9.

Halimium Hybrid Cultivars

↔3 ft (0.9 m) ↑3 ft (0.9 m)

Shrubs with spreading habit. **'Sarah'**, bright yellow blooms with brown centers; **'Susan'**, more compact than *H. ocymoides* with broader leaves, often with semi-double yellow flowers, in summer. Zones 8–9.

HAMAMELIS

A small genus of 5 or 6 species of deciduous winter-flowering shrubs or small trees in the witch hazel (Hamamelidaceae) family, found in eastern North America and eastern Asia. They are characterized by spider-like, yellow or reddish, perfumed flowers, with crinkled strap-shaped petals, clustered on the bare branches from mid-winter to early spring. Foliage often provides attractive autumn color. Fruit is a horned capsule containing 2 shiny black seeds. CULTIVATION: Witch hazels grow mainly in the shade of light woodland, prefer some shade from the midday sun, and like a cool moist climate. The best flowers are borne on strong, young, 1 to 3-year-old shoots that have not been shortened. Cutting for indoor decoration makes way for new shoots. Seeds can be collected before they are discharged and sown at once, but germination may take a year or more. Layers can be put down in winter and lifted the following winter.

Halimium lasianthum

Hamamelis × intermedia cultivar

Hamamelis 'Brevipetala'

syn. *Hamamelis mollis 'Brevipetala'*

↔10–15 ft (3–4.5 m) ↑10–17 ft (3–5 m)

Probably a hybrid, not a form of *H. mollis.* Has short, curled, rich yellow petals with a brown-red center. Scented blossoms in dense clusters along bare stems in winter. Zones 6–9.

Hamamelis × intermedia

HYBRID WITCH HAZEL

↔12 ft (3.5 m) ↑12 ft (3.5 m)

Hybrid between *H. japonica* and *H. mollis*, large shrub. Leaves, to 6 in (15 cm) long, turn yellow in autumn. Flowers have crimped petals, creamy, red, and apricot. **'Arnold Promise'** ★, dense clusters of dark yellow flowers; **'Diane'**, red flowers, with leaves that color well in autumn; **'Jelena'**, vigorous spreading habit, large broad leaves, flowers yellow suffused with copper red, foliage turning orange, red and scarlet; **'Pallida'**, clear sulfur or lemon yellow flowers with no trace of other colors. Zones 4–9.

Hamamelis japonica

JAPANESE WITCH HAZEL

↔12 ft (3.5 m) ↑15 ft (4.5 m)

Large spreading shrub or small tree. Short stout trunk, rigid branches. Leaves become shiny and smooth when mature. Flowers small to medium, with crimpled petals. **'Sulphurea'**, large spreading shrub, ascending branches, small to medium flowers, pale sulfur yellow in color. Zones 4–9.

Hamamelis mollis

CHINESE WITCH HAZEL, WITCH HAZEL

↔12 ft (3.5 m) ↑15 ft (4.5 m)

Native of central and eastern China. Leaves mid-green, downy above, gray-green beneath, turning deep golden yellow, in autumn. Perfumed flowers in axillary clusters, 1 to 2-year-old wood, golden yellow straight petals; calyx yellow-brown, 4 spreading sepals chocolate brown inside. Zones 4–9.

Hamamelis virginiana ★

syn. *Hamamelis macrophylla*

COMMON WITCH HAZEL, WITCH HAZEL

↔8–12 ft (2.4–3.5 m) ↑12–15 ft (3.5–4.5 m)

Native to northeastern USA down to the Lawrence Valley and into Virginia. Leaves dark green, shiny above, paler beneath. Flowers in small clusters in upper axils, yellow in color, in autumn before leaves fall, sometimes partly obscured. Zones 7–9.

Hedera colchica 'Dentata'

Hedychium coccineum

Hedychium greenii

H

HEDERA

IVY

A well-known genus of 11 species of evergreen climbers from Europe, Asia, and northern Africa that will cling by aerial roots to almost any surface. These plants, members of the ivy (Araliaceae) family, are used to clothe walls and grow up trees, as well as being efficient ground covers. They will grow in a wide range of soils and climates, and can become quite weedy outside their native habitats. The foliage usually changes shape to an adult form when it can no longer grow any taller, and cuttings taken from this wood will produce a shrubby form. The flowers are small, borne in clusters, and of little interest to all but their fly pollinators. The berries that follow are usually black.
CULTIVATION: Ivy will grow in almost any soil that is not waterlogged, in aspects from heavy shade to full sun, or in pots as indoor plants. Propagate from cuttings, which strike easily at almost any time of the year.

Hedera colchica

BULLOCK'S HEART IVY, COLCHIC IVY, PERSIAN IVY

↔20–60 ft (6–18 m) ↑20–35 ft (6–10 m)

Large-leafed species found from northern Iran to the Caucasus. Strong self-clinging climber. Foliage is rich deep green, leathery and generally unlobed, to 5 in (12 cm) long. Cultivars include: **'Dentata'**, very large unlobed leaves to 9 in (22 cm) long, bright green on purple-flushed stems; **'Dentata Variegata'**, one of the boldest ivies grown, mottled gray-green leaves with wide, irregular, yellow edges; **'Sulphur Heart'** (syn. 'Paddy's Pride'), rich green leaves, irregular yellow and light green central splashes. Zones 6–10.

Hedera hibernica

syn. *Hedera helix subsp. hibernica*

ATLANTIC IVY, IRISH IVY

↔unlimited ↑25–35 ft (8–10 m)

Not restricted to Ireland but native to much of western Europe. Widely grown as a vigorous ground cover or climber. Differs from *H. helix* in its larger leaves, to 3½ in (9 cm) long, with 5 lobes. Zones 6–10.

Hedera nepalensis

HIMALAYAN IVY, NEPAL IVY

↔unlimited ↑10–17 ft (3–5 m)

Found from Afghanistan east to Assam. Rich green, leathery, spearhead-shaped leaves with irregular shallow lobes. Makes a good wall cover with its orange berries, although these are rarely produced in colder climates. **'Marbled Dragon'** has gray-green veins. Zones 6–10.

HEDYCHIUM

GARLAND LILY, GINGER LILY

This genus is a member of the ginger (Zingiberaceae) family and includes some 40 species of perennials with heavy rhizomes from which emerge strong cane-like pseudostems with large leaves reminiscent of those of canna lilies. Found naturally in tropical Asia, the Himalayan region, and Madagascar, they have naturalized elsewhere and have become troublesome at times, one species being a serious pest in northern New Zealand. Ginger lilies are grown mainly for their colorful and fragrant flowerheads, in which are clustered many slender-tubed flowers with protruding anthers. The flowers appear in summer and are mainly yellow or pink shades. Several of the species are known to be used in Indian Ayurvedic medicines.
CULTIVATION: They are mostly tolerant of very light frosts and capable of reshooting from the rootstock. Plant in sun or shade with fertile, moist, humus-rich, well-drained soil. Cut back the spent flower stems and any old, unproductive canes to encourage fresh growth. Propagate by division or from seed.

Hedychium coccineum

RED GINGER LILY, SCARLET GINGER LILY

↔2–5 ft (0.6–1.5 m) ↑7–10 ft (2–3 m)

An autumn-flowering Himalayan native with very narrow leaves to 20 in (50 cm) long. Heads of pink, orange, or red flowers with similarly colored lower lip and filaments. **'Tara'** has large spikes of orange flowers. Zones 7–12.

Hedychium coronarium

BUTTERFLY LILY, GARLAND FLOWER, WHITE GINGER

↔2–5 ft (0.6–1.5 m) ↑10 ft (3 m)

Spring-flowering Indian species with leaves to 24 in (60 cm) long by a little over 4 in (10 cm) wide. Heads of very fragrant white flowers with yellow-green markings. **'F. W. Moore'** has soft yellow-brown flowers with orange markings. Zones 7–12.

Hedychium densiflorum

↔3–7 ft (0.9–2 m) ↑17 ft (5 m)

Summer-flowering Himalayan native, probably the tallest species in genus. Narrow leaves to 16 in (40 cm) long and dense spikes of deep orange flowers with red filaments. **'Assam Orange'**, small form with very fragrant orange-brown flowers. Zones 8–11.

Hedychium greenii

↔32–48 in (80–120 cm) ↑7 ft (2 m)

Summer-flowering native of Bhutan. Very narrow leaves to 10 in (25 cm) long and bright red flowers in 5 in (12 cm) long spikes. Sometimes forms bulbils in the leaf axil near flowerheads. Zones 8–12.

HEDYSCEPE

UMBRELLA PALM

This genus of a single palm species in the Arecaceae family is native to Lord Howe Island in the southwest Pacific Ocean. Its solitary trunk has a prominent crownshaft and distinctive white rings. The pinnate fronds are recurved, smooth above, with slightly hairy leaflet margins underneath. Branched clusters of up to 3 egg-yellow flowers are followed by dull red elliptical fruit, to 2 in (5 cm) long, containing a single seed. The botanical name comes from the Greek *hedys*, meaning sweet, and *scepe*, meaning covering.
CULTIVATION: This good wind-resistant coastal and container palm requires well-drained soil with year-round moisture and shelter from full sun for the first 5 years. Propagate from seed, which will germinate erratically from 5 to 19 months.

Hedyscepe canterburyana ★

BIG MOUNTAIN PALM, UMBRELLA PALM

↔6–8 ft (1.8–2.4 m) ↑15–30 ft (4.5–9 m)

Medium-sized, slow-growing, slim palm. Slender gray-ringed trunk, to 5 in (12 cm) in diameter, light bluish green cylindrical crownshaft. Compact dense crown of short, silvery, curved, dark green, arching fronds, 5–7 ft (1.5–2 m) long, divided into numerous erect, stiff, upward-pointing leaflets, densely arranged in a V-shape. Clusters of cream flowers, followed by large, bright red, oval-shaped fruit. Zones 8–10.

HELENIUM

SNEEZEWEED

These are known as sneezeweed not because they cause allergies, but from the use by Native Americans of the powdered flowers of some species to make snuff. They also used the genus medicinally and an alkaloid extract, helanalin, is part of modern chemotherapy. This mainly North American genus in the daisy (Asteraceae) family contains about 40 species of annuals, biennials, and perennials. Most species form an upright foliage clump and have simple lance-shaped leaves, usually covered with fine hairs. From mid-summer into autumn they produce large flowerheads with a central cone of disc florets and large often slightly drooping ray florets. Yellow and orange to red shades are most common.

CULTIVATION: Hardiness varies but most are very frost tolerant. Plant in a sunny, open position in moist, well-drained soil. Routine deadheading prolongs flowering; alternatively use as a cut flower to encourage repeat flowering. Propagate by division, or from basal cuttings or seed.

Helenium autumnale

SNEEZEWEED

☼ ✱ ↔3 ft (0.9 m) ↑5 ft (1.5 m)

North American perennial making a dense clump of stems with narrow, usually serrated, leaves to 6 in (15 cm) long topped with many 2 in (5 cm) wide, bright yellow to golden flowerheads each with up to 20 reflexed ray florets. **'Sunshine Hybrid'** is a seedling strain with yellow, orange, red-brown, and red flowers in a range of color patterns. Zones 3–9.

Helenium autumnale

Helenium, Hybrid Cultivar, 'Waldtraut'

Helenium Hybrid Cultivars

☼ ✱ ↔40 in (100 cm) ↑40 in (100 cm)

These hybrids mostly have *H. autumnale* somewhere in their parentage. They are heavy-flowering plants usually more compact than the species. Popular forms include: **'Moerheim Beauty'**, red-brown to red flowers, strongly downward-angled ray florets; Pipsqueak/**'Blopip'**, 18 in (45 cm) tall, yellow ray florets and red-brown disc florets; **'Waldtraut'** ★, burnt orange and gold flowers; **'Wyndley'**, gold to tawny brown ray florets, brown disc florets. Zones 5–9.

HELIANTHEMUM

ROCK ROSE, SUN ROSE

Related to *Cistus*, the 110 or so evergreen and semi-evergreen shrubs and subshrubs in this genus, in the rock-rose (Cistaceae) family, are less widely grown but have a wider natural range: Eurasia, North Africa, and the Americas. Relatively low mounding, short-lived plants, foliage is often hairy, giving it a gray-green coloration. Flowers re-semble tiny single roses, and are individually short-lived but appear over much of late spring and summer. They are usually in bright shades of yellow, orange, red, or pink, with bright yellow stamens massed at the center.

CULTIVATION: They need full sun for their flowers to develop and open properly and suit sunny borders, rock gardens or large containers such as alpine troughs. Soil should be rather gritty and free draining. Keep moist in summer, dry in winter. Trim lightly after flowering to shape and encourage vigor. Propagation is from seed; hybrids and cultivars should be propagated by cuttings or by removing rooted pieces from established plants.

Helianthemum nummularium

syn. *Helianthemum chamaecistus*

COMMON SUN ROSE, SUN ROSE

☼ ✱ ↔24 in (60 cm) ↑20 in (50 cm)

Widely cultivated species, parent of many hybrids and cultivars. Leaves dark green above, gray-green, felted below. Flowers bright yellow, orange or red shades, any color except purple or blue, in late spring–summer. ***H. n.* subsp. *glabrum*** (syn. *H. nitidum*), from central and southwest Europe, fewer foliage hairs, slightly downy margins, orange-yellow flowers. Zones 5–10.

Helianthemum Hybrid Cultivars

☼ ✱ ↔18–36 in (45–90 cm) ↑6–12 in (15–30 cm)

Alpine and rock garden enthusiasts have produced many hybrids in a broad color spectrum. Most have *H. nummularium* somewhere in their background. **'Ben Heckla'**, bronze-gold flowers; **'Ben Hope'**, light foliage, red flowers with orange centers; **'Ben Ledi'**, dark green leaves, deep rose flowers; **'Ben Vane'**, terracotta flowers; **'Ben Vorlich'**, orange flowers; **'Butter and Eggs'**, creamy yellow; **'Dazzler'**, dark green foliage, deep red flowers; **'Fire Dragon'**, gray-green leaves, orange-red flowers; **'Golden Queen'**, large bright yellow flowers; **'Henfield Brilliant'** ★, gray-green leaves, dark red flowers; **'Jubilee'**, double primrose yellow flowers; **'Mrs C. W. Earle'**, double scarlet flowers; **'Orange Surprise'**, orange flowers; **'Raspberry Ripple'**, deep reddish pink flowers tipped with white; **'Rhodanthe Carneum'**, silvery gray leaves, orange-centered pink flowers; **'Rose Queen'**, rose pink flowers; **'Sudbury Gem'**, grayish green leaves, deep pink flowers with red centers; **'The Bride'**, silver-gray foliage, white flowers; **'Wisley Pink'**, silver-gray foliage with light pink flowers; **'Wisley Primrose'**, gray-green foliage and primrose yellow flowers; **'Wisley White'**, gray foliage with white flowers. Zones 6–10.

Helianthemum, HC, 'Butter and Eggs'

Helianthemum, HC, 'Mrs C. W. Earle'

Helianthemum, HC, 'Rhodanthe Carneum'

HELIANTHUS

SUNFLOWER

Sunflowers are so called not so much for the shape of the bloom as for the way the flowerhead turns to follow the sun. This genus of 70 annuals and perennials in the daisy (Asteraceae) family is from the Americas and is best known for the common or giant sunflower *(H. annuus)*, an annual daisy that grows to over 6 ft (1.8 m) tall and which is both popular as an ornamental and widely grown commercially for its seeds and the oil extracted from them. Other species are smaller and tend to have lance-shaped rather than heart-shaped leaves. Most have bristly stems. The flowers are held above the foliage and are nearly always yellow. Double-flowered forms are common.

CULTIVATION: Plant in a sunny, open position with fertile, moist, well-drained soil. Mildew can be a problem but usually only when the plants are past their best. Propagate annuals from seed and perennials also by division and from basal cuttings.

Helianthus angustifolius

SWAMP SUNFLOWER

↔2–3 ft (0.6–0.9 m) ↑7 ft (2 m)

Biennial or short-lived perennial from eastern USA. Narrow, hairy, lance-shaped leaves to 8 in (20 cm) long. Flowerheads with golden ray florets around a purple-brown disc, to 2 in (5 cm) wide, from early autumn. Zones 6–9.

Helianthus annuus

COMMON SUNFLOWER

↔2–4 ft (0.6–1.2 m) ↑10–17 ft (3–5 m)

Quick-growing annual native to USA. Broad, bristly, toothed, pointed heart-shaped leaves to 16 in (40 cm) long. Flowerheads to 12 in (30 cm) wide from mid-summer, ray florets golden yellow around a purple-brown disc. Many cultivars, including: 'Coconut Ice', ray florets cream, white at edges, 6 ft (1.8 m) tall; Harlequin Series, mixed shades of deep pink, orange, yellow, and red-brown, 5 ft (1.5 m) tall; **'Italian White'**, 5 ft (1.5 m) tall, very pale yellow flowers; 'Music Box', mixed color seedling strain with 2-tone ray florets, 30 in (75 cm) tall; **'Ring of Fire'**, 5 ft (1.5 m) tall, flower 5 in (12 cm) wide, yellow and red ray florets; **'Ruby Eclipse'**, 6 ft (1.8 m) tall, red-tinted primrose ray florets, red at base, no pollen; **'Sunrich Orange'**, 5 ft (1.5 m) tall, bright orange ray florets, no pollen; **'Teddy Bear'**, 3 ft (0.9 m) tall, fully double, golden yellow flowers 5 in (12 cm) wide. Zones 4–11.

Helianthus atrorubens

DARK-EYE SUNFLOWER

↔2 ft (0.6 m) ↑7 ft (2 m)

Perennial native to southeastern USA. Basal clump of broad, hairy, toothed leaves, from which emerge, in summer, upright flower stems with smaller leaves and flowerheads to 4 in (10 cm) wide. Golden to light orange ray florets around purple-brown disc. Zones 7–10.

Helianthus debilis

↔2 ft (0.6 m) ↑7 ft (2 m)

Annual native to the Gulf of Mexico region, USA. Leaves broadly lance-shaped to 6 in (15 cm) long, smooth-edged or deeply toothed, hairy or hairless. Flowerheads to 2½ in (6 cm) wide, yellow ray florets around a maroon disc in summer. Zones 7–11.

Helianthus decapetalus

THIN-LEAF SUNFLOWER

↔2 ft (0.6 m) ↑7 ft (2 m)

Perennial native to south-central and southeastern USA. Forms a bushy clump of coarsely hairy, lance-shaped lower leaves to 8 in (20 cm) long. From mid-summer flowerheads to over 3 in (8 cm) wide. Ray and disc florets yellow. Zones 5–9.

Helianthus giganteus

GIANT SUNFLOWER

↔3 ft (0.9 m) ↑15 ft (4.5 m)

Perennial found from Canada to southern USA. Leaves to 8 in (20 cm) long, shallowly toothed and finely hairy, pointed oval to lance-shaped. From mid-summer, 3 in (8 cm) wide flowerheads with yellow ray florets around yellow-brown disc. Zones 4–9.

Helianthus maximilianii

↔2–3 ft (0.6–0.9 m) ↑7–10 ft (2–3 m)

Perennial found from Texas to southern Canada. Forms a bushy base of 8 in (20 cm) long, often shallowly toothed, blue-green, lance-shaped leaves. Yellow flowerheads to 4 in (10 cm) wide in autumn. Zones 4–9.

Helianthus × *multiflorus*

↔2 ft (0.6 m) ↑7 ft (2 m)

Garden hybrid between *H. annuus* and *H. decapetalus*. Perennial with coarsely hairy, lance-shaped lower leaves to 8 in (20 cm) long. Flowerheads to nearly 5 in (12 cm) wide, often double, sometimes with no disc florets from late summer until first frosts. **'Capenoch Star'**, 5 ft (1.5 m) tall, soft yellow flowerheads; **'Loddon Gold'**, 5 ft (1.5 m) tall, golden yellow, double flowerheads. Zones 5–9.

Helianthus salicifolius

↔2–4 ft (0.6–1.2 m) ↑10 ft (3 m)

Perennial native to south-central USA. Drooping, slightly hairy, narrowly lance-shaped leaves to 8 in (20 cm) long. Flowerheads to 3 in (8 cm) wide, yellow ray florets around a dark disc, in autumn. **'Golden Pyramid'**, 5 ft (1.5 m) tall, has a double row of yellow ray florets. Zones 4–9.

Helianthus tuberosus ★

JERUSALEM ARTICHOKE

↔5 ft (1.5 m) ↑10 ft (3 m)

Tuberous perennial that is found from Canada through to southeastern USA. Coarsely hairy, toothed, lance-shaped or pointed oval leaves to 12 in (30 cm) long. Flowerheads yellow, to 4 in (10 cm) wide, in autumn. Tubers edible. Zones 4–9.

Helianthus salicifolius

Helianthus annuus 'Teddy Bear'

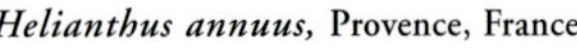

Helianthus annuus, Provence, France

Helianthus, Hybrid Cultivar, 'Sunny'

Helianthus annuus 'Ring of Fire'

Helianthus Hybrid Cultivars

↔3–4 ft (0.9–1.2 m)
↕4–7 ft (1.2–2 m)

These hybrid cultivars are robust hardy plants popular with gardeners. **'Monarch'**, 6 in (15 cm) wide flowerheads, double row of golden ray florets; **'Moonshadow'**, 4 ft (1.2 m) tall, near-white ray florets; **'Newcutt Gold'**, rich yellow flowers; **'Sunbeam'**, 5 ft (1.5 m) tall, golden ray florets, outer disc florets yellow around a green center; **'Sunny'**, double row of bright yellow blooms; **'Vanilla Ice'**, 5 ft (1.5 m) tall, starry, 4 in (10 cm) wide flowerheads, creamy yellow ray florets around a dark disc. Zones 5–10.

HELICHRYSUM

Revision by botanists in recent years has reduced the number of species in this genus, which once stood at around 500. A member of the daisy (Asteraceae) family, it is perhaps best known for its perennials, though it also includes a few shrubby species. They have simple, often heavily felted leaves, usually in pale green to gray-green shades. Tiny flowers, usually quite heavily clustered and conspicuous, lack ray florets or petals but have white to yellow, pink, or purple papery bracts around each flowerhead.

CULTIVATION: Most species tolerate drought once established. Plant in full sun with light, gritty, very well-drained soil. Their frost hardiness varies, but few will tolerate prolonged cold; if wet at the same time, they tend to rot before they are killed by frost. Any trimming or shaping should be done in spring. Propagation is from seed (some species self-sow freely), or layers can be pegged down at any time. Half-hardened tip cuttings strike well in both summer and autumn.

Helictotrichon sempervirens

Helichrysum petiolare 'Limelight'

Helichrysum petiolare

LICORICE PLANT, LIQUORICE PLANT

↔5 ft (1.5 m) ↕12–18 in (30–45 cm)

This winter-flowering South African native is a spreading shrub that forms a mounding ground cover. It has a long soft stem and rounded leaves to over 1¼ in (30 mm) long. Leaves and stems covered in pale gray down. Small, dull white flowerheads loosely clustered. **'Limelight'**, distinctive pale yellow-green foliage; **'Variegatum'**, gray and cream variegated leaves. Zones 9–11.

HELICTOTRICHON

OAT GRASS

This grass (Poaceae) family genus includes some 60–100 perennial species, mostly native to dry hillside meadows and woodland margins in temperate Eurasia but also found in other temperate regions. These tussock-forming grasses can reach 3–7 ft (0.9–2 m) in height, with slender culms and flat, folded or rolled-back blades. Erect or nodding panicles of flowers are produced in summer. *H. sempervirens* is the major ornamental species and makes a superb specimen, border mixer and container plant. The name *Helictotrichon* is derived from the Greek *heliktos* (twisted) and *thrix* or *trichos* (hair or bristle), referring to the shape of the awn.

CULTIVATION: Most prefer full sun and well-drained soil and are quite drought tolerant, depending on native habitat. They flower best if spring-time conditions are cool and steadily moist, and are sparsely flowering in hot humid climates. Avoid root rot by providing good drainage and mulch in climates where temperatures drop below 5°F (–15°C).

Heliopsis helianthoides var. *scabra*

Helictotrichon sempervirens ★

syns *Avena candida, A. sempervirens*

BLUE OAT GRASS

↔36 in (90 cm) ↕24 in (60 cm)

Clump-forming western Mediterranean native found on dry rocky hillsides. Produces dense tufts of erect vivid silver-blue foliage that is evergreen in mild climates. Straw-colored inflorescences on slender, arching, 24 in (60 cm) long stems, in late spring. **'Pendula'**, heavy blooming, inflorescences more nodding; **'Robusta'**, rust-resistant for humid climates; **'Saphirsprudel'**, bright steely blue, fairly rust-resistant foliage. Zones 4–9.

HELIOPSIS

FALSE SUNFLOWER, OX-EYE

Native to North America, this genus of 13 species of loosely branched, erect, perennial herbs is a member of the daisy (Asteraceae) family. Flowerheads of bright yellow daisy-like flowers are produced from mid-summer to autumn, over a long period. The name *Heliopsis* means "resembling the sun."

CULTIVATION: Fully frost hardy, these plants are ideal for herbaceous borders. They prefer full sun and average soil kept moist throughout summer. Some staking may be needed. Propagate from seed or divide clumps periodically in spring or autumn.

Heliopsis helianthoides

EVERLASTING SUNFLOWER, FALSE SUNFLOWER, SMOOTH OX-EYE

↔12–24 in (30–60 cm)
↕24–60 in (60–150 cm)

Perennial found from Ontario, Canada, to Florida and Mississippi, USA. Smooth, oval- to sword-shaped, coarse-toothed, mid-green leaves, to 6 in (15 cm) long. Numerous terminal flowerheads of yellow daisy-like flowers, to 3 in (8 cm) across, on stems to 10 in (25 cm) long. ***H. h.* var. *scabra***, double orange-yellow flowers, very rough stems and leaves; **'Incomparabilis'**, single orange-yellow flowers; **'Light of Loddon'**, double bright golden orange flowers, to 48 in (120 cm) high. Zones 3–9.

Heliopsis Hybrid Cultivars

↔12–24 in (30–60 cm)
↕4 ft (1.2 m)

These are all perennials with mid-green leaves. **'Goldgefieder'** (ox-eye), late-flowering, 48–60 in (120–150 cm) tall, with double golden daisy-like flowers; Loraine Sunshine/**'Helhan'**, dwarf, variegated, loosely branched form, 16–30 in (40–75 cm) long, white leaves with green veins and large, golden yellow, daisy-like flowers. Zones 3–9.

HELIOTROPIUM

A member of the borage family (Boraginaceae), this is a genus of about 250 species of annuals, perennials, subshrubs, and evergreen shrubs, from tropical and warmer temperate climates around the world. Some species are locally important for medicinal purposes, and others are significant ornamentals. The fragrant flowers can be white, yellow, blue, or purple.

CULTIVATION: Most of the species prefer fertile free-draining soils, summer moisture and shelter from cold. Full sun to filtered light is their favored habitat. Where frosts occur, the most sheltered position in the garden must be selected. Prune moderately immediately after flowering to encourage new shoots. Propagate from soft-tip cuttings in spring or summer or half-hardened cuttings in autumn to winter in a warm and moist situation.

Heliotropium arborescens

Helleborus argutifolius

Helleborus cyclophyllus

Helleborus foetidus

Helleborus orientalis subsp. *guttatus*

H

Heliotropium arborescens

CHERRY PIE, COMMON HELIOTROPE

↔20 in (50 cm) ↑3 ft (0.9 m)

From highlands of Peru, Ecuador, and Bolivia. Spreading, evergreen bun-shaped shrub. Narrow oval leaves dark and shiny above, paler reverse. Abundant sweetly perfumed mauve to purple flowers, from early spring to late summer. Cultivars are good for use in borders or pots, and include: **'Aurea'**, pale lime green to bright yellow foliage; **'Black Beauty'** ★, very dark purple-black flowers; **'Chatsworth'**, purple flowers, strongly scented; **'Fragrant Delight'**, dark purple flowers, also strongly scented; **'Iowa'**, dense, upright habit, purple-tinted foliage, large clusters of fragrant dark purple flowers; **'Lord Roberts'**, compact growth, violet flowers; **'Marine'**, bushy and compact growth, purple-blue flowers; and **'Princess Marina'**, dark violet-blue flowers. Zones 9–12.

Heliotropium curassavicum

↔24 in (60 cm) ↑16 in (40 cm)

Annual to short-lived perennial from the American tropics and subtropics. Forms a mounding and spreading bush with fleshy stems and foliage. Narrow lance-shaped, light green leaves to 2 in (5 cm) long. Terminal inflorescences to 4 in (10 cm) wide, opening cream, ageing to purple. Zones 10–12.

HELLEBORUS

LENTEN ROSE, WINTER ROSE

This genus of 15 species of buttercup (Ranunculaceae) family perennials was a favorite of Gertrude Jekyll and she used it extensively in her garden at Munstead Wood. Found in the temperate zone from Europe to western China, they are mainly low-growing plants with short-stemmed, often toothed, palmate foliage emerging direct from a rhizome. The simple, 5-petalled, bowl-shaped flowers appear from mid-winter into spring and occur in unusual shades of green, dusky pink, and maroon as well as white. At the center of the flower are prominent greenish nectaries and yellow stamens.

CULTIVATION: Most prefer woodland conditions with deep, fertile, humus-rich, well-drained soil and dappled shade. Some of the smaller types are well suited to rock gardens. Many are near-evergreen but benefit from having old foliage removed when dormant. Propagate by division or from seed, which may require 2 periods of stratification. Naturalizes in suitable climates.

Helleborus argutifolius

syns *Helleborus corsicus, H. lividus subsp. corsicus*

↔24–40 in (60–100 cm) ↑40 in (100 cm)

Winter- to spring-flowering plant native to islands of Corsica, France, and Sardinia, Italy. Evergreen, leathery trifoliate leaves with soft-spined and toothed leaflets to 8 in (20 cm) long, sometimes gray-green. Large heads of green flowers to 2 in (5 cm) wide. **'Janet Starnes'**, compact habit, foliage mottled cream; **'Pacific Frost'**, mottled cream, pink, and green foliage. Zones 7–10.

Helleborus × *ballardiae*

↔12–16 in (30–40 cm) ↑12 in (30 cm)

Hybrid between *H. niger* and *H. lividus*. Leaves with 3 to 9 segments to 6 in (15 cm) long, blue-green with silvery veins, semi-evergreen. Pale green, white, or pink flowers, to over 2½ in (6 cm) wide, in winter. Zones 5–9.

Helleborus cyclophyllus

↔24–32 in (60–80 cm) ↑16 in (40 cm)

Found from Greece to Albania and Bulgaria. Deciduous leaves with 8 to 11 leaflets, rarely up to 25, largest to 8 in (20 cm) long, hairy undersides. In winter, stems to 20 in (50 cm) long with yellow-green flowers. Zones 7–9.

Helleborus foetidus

BEAR'S FOOT, STINKING HELLEBORE, STINKWORT

↔24–40 in (60–100 cm) ↑24–32 in (60–80 cm)

Evergreen found from Britain to Hungary. Foliage is pungent if crushed. Dark green leaves with 5 to 13 narrow leaflets, longest to 8 in (20 cm), toothed. Green flowers, often red-tinted, bell-shaped, 1 in (25 mm) wide, on strongly upright stems. **'Green Giant'**, bright green flowers, finely divided foliage; **'Miss Jekyll'**, fragrant flowers, intensity varying with the time of day; **Sierra Nevada Group**, only 12 in (30 cm) high; **Wester Flisk Group**, red-tinted stems and leaves, gray-green flowers. Zones 6–9.

Helleborus × *hybridus*

↔16–24 in (40–60 cm) ↑16 in (40 cm)

Hybrids of *H. orientalis* and other species. **'Banana Split'**, large creamy yellow flowers; **'Blue Spray'**, bell-shaped smoky purple flowers; **'Fred Whitsey'**, white flowers with purple spots and streaks; **'Hades'**, dark-speckled gray-blue flowers; **'Mardi Gras'**, red-blotched white flowers; **'Pleiades'**, dwarf with red-flecked white flowers; **'Southern Belle'**, lavender flowers on tall stems; and **'Trotter's Spotted'**, large purple-spotted white flowers. Zones 5–9.

Helleborus lividus

↔24 in (60 cm) ↑16 in (40 cm)

Evergreen from Mallorca and possibly neighboring Cabrera, Spain. Simple 3-part, deep green, purple-tinted leaves, usually smooth-edged. Flowers from mid-winter, bright green flushed purple to all purple, near flat when open. May rot in cold wet winters. Zones 8–10.

Helleborus multifidus

↔16–32 in (40–80 cm) ↑20 in (50 cm)

Winter- to spring-flowering deciduous species from Italy and Balkans. Leaves much divided. Flowers usually green, to 1½ in (35 mm) wide, but no typical form, instead 3 distinct subspecies: ***H. m.* subsp. *bocconei***, with flowers to nearly 3 in (8 cm) wide; ***H. m.* subsp. *hercegovinus***, with narrow, lacy leaflets, rarely very finely divided into up to 100 leaflets, maximum recorded is 185; and ***H. m.* subsp. *istriacus***, with purple-tinted flowers. Zones 6–9.

Helleborus niger

CHRISTMAS ROSE

↔12–20 in (30–50 cm) ↑12 in (30 cm)

Winter- to spring-flowering evergreen from Alps of northern Italy to southern Germany. Deep green, leathery, serrated leaves with 5 to 9 broad leaflets, to 8 in (20 cm) long. White flowers on strong stems, sometimes flushed pink. H. n. subsp. macranthus, large flowers, blue-green

Helleborus × hybridus cultivar

leaves with soft-spined leaflets. H. n. **'Potter's Wheel'**, white flowers to 4 in (10 cm) wide; **'White Magic'**, dark-stemmed white flowers, pink-tinted with age. Zones 3–9.

Helleborus × nigercors

◐/● ❄ ↔24 in (60 cm) ↑24 in (60 cm)

Hybrid between *H. niger* and *H. argutifolius*. Leaves evergreen, large, gray-green, 3 to 7 leaflets coarsely toothed and often soft-spined. Heads of large blue-green-tinted white flowers from mid-winter. Zones 7–10.

Helleborus orientalis ★

LENTEN ROSE

◐/● ✱ ↔16–24 in (40–60 cm) ↑16 in (40 cm)

Semi-evergreen winter-flowering species from northern Turkey and Greece and around the Black Sea. Leaves with 7 to 9 coarsely serrated leaflets, longest to 10 in (25 cm). Flowers variable, from pure white to red-black forms, often dark-spotted. ***H. o.* subsp. *orientalis***, white flowers, sometimes green tinted; ***H. o.* subsp. *abchasicus***, red to purplish flowers, ***H. o.* subsp. *a.*, Early Purple Group** (syn. *Helleborus atrorubens*), flowers greenish purple, nodding; and ***H. o.* subsp. *guttatus***, white flowers, usually dark-spotted. **'Jet Black'**, deep purple-black flowers, dark foliage; **Lady Collection**, named cultivars, e.g., 'Blue Lady', in a range of colors, including yellow; **'Tutu'**, petaloid center, semi-double, pale pink suffused with dark spotting. Zones 5–9.

Helleborus × sternii

◐/● ❄ ↔12–32 in (30–80 cm) ↑12–32 in (30–80 cm)

Variably sized semi-evergreen hybrid between *H. argutifolius* and *H. lividus*. Leaves dark gray-green, sometimes lighter veined and/or purple-tinted, smooth-edged or spiny. Heads of green flowers from winter, often flushed pink or purple. **'Clifton'**, foliage heavily gray marbled, dusky pink flowers. Zones 7–9.

Helleborus viridis

GREEN HELLEBORE

◐/● ✱ ↔24 in (60 cm) ↑16 in (40 cm)

Deciduous plant native to western Europe, including Britain. Usually just 2 leaves divided into 7 to 13 toothed leaflets with downy undersides. Bright green, sometimes red-veined flowers, usually carried singly, from late winter. Zones 6–9.

Helleborus Hybrid Cultivars

◐ ✱ ↔12–32 in (30–80 cm) ↑10–18 in (25–45 cm)

Over the last 20 years many hybrid hellebores have been developed, including: **'Angel Glow'**, blue-green foliage, pink flowers, green tones with age; **'Ivory Prince'**, compact, extremely heavy blooming, flowers open greenish white, ageing to pink then green; **'Moonshine'**, spreading, *H. niger*-style habit and foliage, yellow-green flowers; **'Penny's Pink'**, marbled foliage, erect head of pink flowers, darker edges; **'Winter Sunshine'**, gray-green, pink, and white flowers, ageing red. Zones 5–9.

Heloniopsis orientalis

HELONIOPSIS

There are 4 species of rhizomatous perennials in this genus, which belongs to the bunchflower (Melanthiaceae) family. They are native to Japan, Korea, and Taiwan where they grow in mountain woods and meadows. The oblong to lance-shaped leaves form basal rosettes from which stems of nodding flowers arise from spring to summer. Flowers may be solitary or in loose umbels. They are white, pink or yellow.

CULTIVATION: Grow these species in a rich, moisture-retentive soil in light shade. Protect from cold winds to prevent leaf scorch. Propagation is by division or from seed.

Heloniopsis orientalis

syn. *Heloniopsis japonica*

◐ ❄ ↔8–12 in (20–30 cm) ↑8–12 in (20–30 cm)

From Japan and Korea, this species has oblong leathery leaves that form basal rosettes. The nodding flowers have flaring petals and are borne 2–10 to a stem. They are pink or violet with bluish anthers. ***H. o.* var. *kawanoi*** is a dwarf form, 2–8 in (5–20 cm) high. Zones 7–9.

HEMEROCALLIS

DAYLILY

Daylilies are so-named because each of their funnel- to bell-shaped flowers lasts just one day, though they carry a succession of blooms from late spring until autumn. Once classified with the true lilies, this group of 15 species of rhizome-rooted perennials from temperate East Asia is now part of the grass tree (Xanthorrhoeaceae) family. They form clumps of grassy or iris-like leaves with sometimes branching racemes of 6-petalled flowers in a range of warm yellow, apricot, and red shades. All parts of the plant, especially the buds and flowers, are edible and may be added to salads or used as a

Hemerocallis citrina

colorful garnish. The stamens can be used as a saffron color substitute.

CULTIVATION: They are hardy and easily grown in a sunny or part-shaded position with fertile, moist, well-drained soil. Slugs and snails often badly disfigure the foliage. Take care when siting as the flowers turn to face the sun. Rust disease is a problem in some areas. Propagation is usually by division.

Hemerocallis citrina

☼/◐ ✱ ↔3–7 ft (0.9–2 m) ↑5 ft (1.5 m)

Chinese species with narrow leaves to 4 ft (1.2 m) long. Flower stems are upright, branching from above half-height, bearing up to 50 plus fragrant pale yellow flowers to over 4 in (10 cm) wide. Flowers open at night and stay open for most of the next day. Zones 4–9.

Hemerocallis dumortieri

LEMON LILY

☼/◐ ✱ ↔16–24 in (40–60 cm) ↑16 in (40 cm)

Compact, early-flowering species from Korea and eastern Russia. Very narrow leaves to around 14 in (35 cm) long. Flower stems red-tinted, unbranched, only slightly exceeding foliage height, bearing 2 to 4 fragrant golden flowers to a little over 2 in (5 cm) wide, backed by broad bracts. Zones 4–9.

Hemerocallis fulva

☼/◐ ✱ ↔4–5 ft (1.2–1.5 m) ↑3 ft (0.9 m)

Wild origin uncertain, perhaps China or Japan, but may be a hybrid. Leaves to over 24 in (60 cm) long, strappy. Flower stems usually 2-branched with up to 20, dark-striped, light orange-brown, 3–4 in (8–10 cm) wide flowers. **'Kwanzo'** (syn. 'Kwanzo Flore Pleno'), an early cultivar from 1860, has dark-centered double flowers; **'Kwanzo Variegata'** has the same flowers and creamy white-edged foliage. Zones 4–9.

Hemerocallis lilioasphodelus

Hemerocallis lilioasphodelus

CUSTARD LILY

☼/◐ ✱ ↔ 40–48 in (100–120 cm)
↕ 24–40 in (60–100 cm)

An early-flowering Chinese species characterized by very narrow sickle-shaped leaves to over 24 in (60 cm) long. Wiry, branching flower stems carry up to 12 night-scented, pale yellow flowers to 3 in (8 cm) wide. Zones 4–9.

Hemerocallis middendorffii

☼/◐ ✱ ↔ 20–24 in (50–60 cm)
↕ 18 in (45 cm)

Native to Japan and nearby parts of mainland northeastern Asia. Leaves strappy, to 12 in (30 cm) long. Flower stems unbranched but extending well beyond the foliage, with few fragrant yellow flowers clustered together. Zones 5–9.

Hemerocallis minor

☼/◐ ✱ ↔ 20–24 in (50–60 cm)
↕ 20 in (50 cm)

From Japan and nearby parts of China. Very narrow leaves to 18 in (45 cm) long. Flower stems with 2 or sometimes more branches bearing up to 5 soft yellow flowers to over 2 in (5 cm) wide. Zones 4–9.

Hemerocallis Hybrid Cultivars

☼/◐ ✱ ↔ unlimited
↕ 12–48 in (30–120 cm)

Daylilies hybridize readily, and with such beautiful flowers it should not come as a surprise to find that there are several hundred hybrids and cultivars covering a wide range of flower colors and plant sizes, from miniatures growing only to around 12 in (30 cm) tall to those with 4 ft (1.2 m) flower stems. Some of the most popular or distinctive of these cultivars include: **'Anzac'**, 30 in (75 cm), yellow-centered dark red; **'Baby Betsy'**, 18 in (45 cm), deep cherry red; **'Barbara Mitchell'** ★, 20 in (50 cm), pale creamy apricot pink with yellow-green center; **'Barbary Corsair'**, 16 in (40 cm), purple-red; **'Blue Sheen'**, 24 in (60 cm), purplish blue flowers to

Hemerocallis, Hybrid Cultivar, 'Cartwheels'

Hemerocallis, HC, 'Prairie Blue Eyes'

4 in (10 cm) wide, prominent yellow center; **'Cartwheels'**, 30 in (75 cm), bright yellow, light mid-stripe, large cultivar; **'Charlie Brown'**, 20 in (50 cm), pink to orange with yellow center, large cultivar; **'Cherry Lace'**, 20 in (50 cm), pinkish red with yellow centers; **'Corky'**, 24 in (60 cm) long wiry stems with yellow flowers and brown buds; **'Etched in Gold'**, 24 in (60 cm), apricot with yellowish edging; **'Fabulous Favorite'**, 24 in (60 cm), rusty orange, deep yellow center; **'Franz Hals'**, 28 in (70 cm), red-brown and orange flowers with fine cream mid-stripe; **'Golden Chimes'**, branching stems with small gold flowers, brown buds; **'Green Flutter'**, 20 in (50 cm), greenish yellow, semi-double, late; **'High Lama'**, 36 in (90 cm), large, lavender; **'Hope Diamond'**, scented golden yellow flowers, wide; **'Little Bumble Bee'**, 20 in (50 cm), many small maroon-centered yellow flowers; **'Little Gypsy Vagabond'**, 18 in (45 cm), light yellow with maroon center; **'Little Tawny'**, 20 in (50 cm), rusty orange, heavy-flowering; **'Many Happy Returns'** ★, 16 in (40 cm), pale yellow, long-flowering and heat tolerant; **'Midnight Magic'**, 28 in (70 cm), very dark red; **'Missouri Beauty'**, 36 in (90 cm), green-tinted yellow, ruffled; **'Moonlight Mist'**, 20 in (50 cm), very pale apricot pink; **'Neal Berrey'**, 18 in (45 cm), deep pink shades; **'Nob Hill'**, gold-centered pale pink and lavender flowers; **'Paper Butterfly'**, 28 in (70 cm), mauve-pink with purple and yellow center; **'Pink Flirt'**, 24 in (60 cm), bright pink; **'Prairie Blue Eyes'**, 28 in (70 cm), light purple, large; **'Priscilla's Rainbow'**, 24 in (60 cm), pale apricot with purple and pink band around yellow center; **'Purple Pauper'**, 20 in (50 cm), purple with yellow-green throat, large; **'Stafford'**, 24 in (60 cm), bright red with yellow center, wiry stems; **'Stella d'Oro'** ★, 16 in (40 cm), orange-centered bright yellow flowers over long season; **'Stoke Poges'**, 24 in (60 cm), lilac pink shades, orange-yellow center; **'Thumbelina'**, 14 in (35 cm), small gold flowers, wiry stems. Zones 4–9.

Heptacodium miconioides

HEPTACODIUM

This genus, in the woodbine (Caprifoliaceae) family and allied to *Abelia* and *Kolkwitzia*, consists of 1 species of deciduous shrub from central and eastern China. It has large glossy leaves with 3 longitudinal veins, in opposite pairs on the twigs. Small white flowers are borne in large panicles at branch ends. As the small dry fruits develop, the sepals, inconspicuous in flower, enlarge and turn deep pink, making a display that lasts several months. The species is little known in cultivation outside northeastern USA.

CULTIVATION: This plant likes woodland conditions with moist acid soil and shelter, though not too much shade. Lower twiggy growth should be thinned out in winter. Propagation should be from hardwood cuttings in autumn or half-hardened tip cuttings in summer, from basal suckers, or from seed.

Heptacodium miconioides ★

syn. *Heptacodium jasminoides*

CHINESE HEPTACODIUM, SEVEN SON FLOWER

◐ ✱ ↔ 7–10 ft (2–3 m)
↕ 10–15 ft (3–4.5 m)

Chinese deciduous shrub or small tree, dark green elliptical leaves. Heads of fragrant white flowers, from late summer to the first frosts. Calyces of flowers remain, turning bright rosy red to purple in autumn. Zones 5–9.

HESPERALOE

This agave (Agavaceae) family genus, which contains 3 species of stemless evergreen perennial herbs that form grass-like clumps, is native to southwestern Texas and the Chihuahuan Desert region of northern Mexico. The species produce spreading rosettes of soft, narrow, strap-like leaves with margins that have thread-like appendages. Narrow bell-shaped flowers are produced in sparsely branched racemes or panicles to 1¼ in (30 mm) in diameter. The fruit is a brown capsule.

CULTIVATION: Plant at any time in full sun or half-sun in well-drained rocky gravel or sandy soil. Removing spent flower stalks will prolong blooming. Propagation is from seed or by division of clumps in winter.

Hesperaloe parviflora

FALSE RED YUCCA

☼/◐ ❄ ↔ 24–48 in (60–120 cm)
↕ 24–48 in (60–120 cm)

Clumping succulent perennial native to southwestern Texas. Thick, spreading, leathery, tapering, blue-green leaves, to 48 in (120 cm) long, developing buds at base, margins with fine white threads. Slender flower stalk, up to 40 spikes of nodding rose to rich salmon pink flowers, golden yellow inside, 1¼ in (30 mm) across, in late summer. ***H. p. var. engelmannii***, more bell-shaped flowers; **'Rubra'**, bright red flowers. Zones 7–10.

HESPERIS

This cabbage (Brassicaceae) family genus consists of 60 biennials and short-lived perennials of upright habit. Stems are clothed with oblong leaves and topped with open clusters of 4-petalled flowers in shades of yellow, white, or purple, often sweetly scented, particularly in the evenings. H. matronalis is food for the orange-tip butterfly and a good source of nectar.
CULTIVATION: These plants are suitable for the border or wild garden. They do best in full sun or light shade and prefer a neutral to alkaline soil. Although they tolerate poor soils, they will perform better if the ground is enriched. Propagate from seed, which will usually self-sow, or from cuttings of the sterile double forms.

Hesperis matronalis

DAMASK VIOLET, DAMES VIOLET, SWEET ROCKET

↔16–20 in (40–50 cm) ↕32–36 in (80–90 cm)

Well-known biennial or short-lived perennial from southern Europe through to central Asia. Dark green leaves to 8 in (20 cm) long. Clusters of scented flowers, 1¾ in (40 mm) across, late spring–summer. Forms with both white and lilac, single and double flowers are grown. Zones 3–10.

HETEROCENTRON

syn. *Heeria*

A basically tropical genus of about 27 species in the meadow-beauty (Melastomataceae) family from Central and South America. They are evergreen perennials and ground cover plants. The leaves may be heart-shaped, lance-shaped or pointed oval and are often prominently veined. Showy 4-petalled flowers either in clusters or solitary are produced in shades of white, pink, and mauve to purple, from late summer.
CULTIVATION: In frosty climates they can be grown in a greenhouse and planted out for summer color when the danger of frost is over. In warm regions plant in a moist soil in a sunny aspect as a ground cover or rock garden subject. Propagate from seed or cuttings, or by division.

Heterocentron elegans

syn. *Schizocentron elegans*

CREEPING LASIANDRA, SPANISH SHAWL

↔18–40 in (45–100 cm) ↕3–4 in (8–10 cm)

From Mexico, Guatemala, and Honduras. Mat-forming showy evergreen subshrub with small, pointed, downy leaves often stained purple. Upward-facing, bowl-shaped, magenta to mauve flowers smother the plant in a vivid display in late summer–autumn. Zones 10–12.

HETEROMELES

CALIFORNIA HOLLY, CHRISTMAS BERRY, TOLLON, TOYON

This genus comprises a single species, a native of California that is an evergreen shrub closely related to Photinia. Fruit, which may be red or yellow, small or large, develops from heads of small creamy white flowers and, as the name "Christmas berry" suggests, it ripens around Christmas, or mid-winter, in its home range.
CULTIVATION: Any well-drained soil with a sunny or partly shaded aspect will do. Heat and drought resistant, this species will tolerate poor soils. The bush is usually a neat grower and needs trimming to shape only occasionally. It may be propagated from half-hardened cuttings or seed.

Heteromeles arbutifolia

↔12 ft (3.5 m) ↕12 ft (3.5 m)

Native to the Sierra Nevada foothills of coastal California, USA, to Baja California, Mexico. Simple, oval, mid-green leaves, finely serrated edges. Flowerheads nectar-rich, with a honey-like scent, in summer. A compact, tough plant. Zones 8–10.

HEUCHERA

ALUM ROOT, CORAL BELLS

This genus, a member of the saxifrage (Saxifragaceae) family, consists of around 55 near-evergreen perennials native to North America. It was named after Johann Heinrich von Heucher (1677–1747), professor of medicine at Wittenburg University. The species form a dense clump of basal foliage with rounded to kidney-shaped, toothed leaves on thin wiry leaf stalks. The branching flower stems are also very fine and from late spring to autumn carry sprays of tiny flowers, usually 5-petalled but sometimes petalless. Extracts of the root are strongly astringent and often used in herbal medicines.
CULTIVATION: They are mostly very hardy and adaptable and are suitable for perennial borders or rock gardens, depending on size. Plant in full or half-sun with fertile, moist, humus-rich, well-drained soil. Remove flower stems as they fade. Propagate by division or from seed, sown fresh in early autumn.

Heuchera americana

ROCK GERANIUM

↔16 in (40 cm) ↕18 in (45 cm)

Evergreen North American native with downy, broad, lobed, heart-shaped leaves about 3 in (8 cm) long, sometimes white mottled. Upright flower stems with narrow heads of faintly pink-tinted cream flowers. **'Garnet'**, leaves which are red when young, turning bronze-veined green, developing a red center in winter; **'Lace Ruffles'**, ruffled, silver-mottled leaves, white flowers; **'Persian Carpet'**, silver-marked red to purple-red leaves, buff flowers; **'Pewter Moon'**, silver-veined deep purple-red foliage; **'Pewter Veil'**, purple-red foliage overlaid silver-gray; **'Ring of Fire'**, red-veined green foliage turning pink in winter with pale edges; **'Ruby Veil'**, deep maroon and silver-gray upper leaves with purple-red undersides; **'Velvet Night'**, darkest purple-black leaves overlaid metallic purple. Zones 4–10.

Heterocentron elegans

Heteromeles arbutifolia

Heuchera americana

Heuchera × *brizoides*

Heuchera × *brizoides*

☼/◐ ✱ ↔ 12–18 in (30–45 cm)
↑ 12–30 in (30–75 cm)

A group of hybrids that share *H. sanguinea* as one parent, the other being *H. micrantha*, *H. americana* and perhaps others. They are a mixed group, sharing simple green, lobed, heart-shaped leaves and differing mainly in flower color. Popular forms include: **Bressingham Hybrids**, with graceful, airy flowerheads, available in many shades of pink, red, and white; **'Firefly'**, coral pink, faintly scented; **'Freedom'**, dwarf form, flowers bright pink; **'June Bride'**, white flowers; and **'Snowstorm'**, white-mottled foliage, red flowers. Zones 4–10.

Heuchera hirsutissima

☼/◐ ✱ ↔ 6–8 in (15–20 cm)
↑ 10 in (25 cm)

Evergreen subalpine to alpine species from California. Has a compact habit with rounded, lobed leaves up to 1½ in (35 mm) wide. Stems and leaves are hairy. Flowers cream to pale pink. Zones 6–9.

Heuchera maxima

☼/◐ ✱ ↔ 16–20 in (40–50 cm)
↑ 24 in (60 cm)

Evergreen species from western USA. Rounded, toothed leaves to over 6 in (15 cm) wide, underside veins downy. Pinkish white flowers. Zones 6–10.

Heuchera micrantha

☼/◐ ✱ ↔ 12–16 in (30–40 cm)
↑ 24 in (60 cm)

Western North American species with broad, shallowly lobed, heart-shaped leaves to over 3 in (8 cm) long. Open sprays of small white to cream flowers. *H. m.* var. *diversifolia* **'Palace Purple'**, deep purple-red leaves and stems, small white flowers. Zones 5–9.

Heuchera sanguinea

☼/◐ ✱ ↔ 12–16 in (30–40 cm)
↑ 24 in (60 cm)

Evergreen species native to New Mexico and Arizona, USA. Roughly kidney-shaped leaves to 2 in (5 cm) wide, with irregular lobes and downy

Heuchera maxima

Heuchera sanguinea

undersides. Bright red flowers on stems with a few small leaves. Many former cultivars now listed under *H.* × *brizoides*; those remaining include: **'Brandon Pink'**, bright coral-pink flowers and green and white leaves; **'Northern Fire'**, pinkish red flowers, green leaves, vigorous; **'Singham'**, bright green leaves, hot pink flowers; **'Splendens'**, deep red flowers; and **'Virginalis'**, white flowers. Zones 3–9.

Heuchera Hybrid Cultivars

☼/◐ ✱ ↔ 12–18 in (30–45 cm)
↑ 12–36 in (30–90 cm)

In recent years many *Heuchera* hybrids have been introduced. Breeders have concentrated on providing interesting foliage, often seen as a more important feature than the flowers. Popular hybrids include: **'Amber Waves'**, late 2002 introduction with light golden bronze foliage and deep pink flowers; **'Autumn Haze'**, purple leaves overlaid silver, autumn tones of pink and buff; **'Chocolate Ruffles'** ★, deep bronze-green foliage with purple-brown overtones, white flowers; **'Fireglow'**, red blooms; **'Mint Frost'**, green leaves overlaid silver, cream flowers; **'Monet'**, white-variegated green foliage, red flowers; **'Petite Marble Burgundy'**, compact, silver-marked, purple-red leaves, pinkish flowers; **'Plum Pudding'**, purple-brown leaves with red undersides, cream flowers; **'Red Spangles'**, plain green leaves, bright

Heuchera HC, 'Strawberry Candy'

red flowers; **'Santa Ana Cardinal'** -(*H. maxima* × *H. sanguinea*), tall, rounded bright green leaves, deep pink to red flowers; **'Snow Angel'**, red flowers, white-flecked green foliage; **'Strawberry Candy'**, green leaves overlaid silver, pink flowers; **'Wendy'** ★ (*H. maxima* × *H. sanguinea*), large light green leaves, soft pink flowers. The Canyon Series is a group of compact evergreen hybrids raised by the American breeder Emery. Small, lobed, rounded to heart-shaped leaves, usually deep green, sometimes with a hint of purple. Many tiny flowers in upright, airy sprays. Original varieties include: **'Canyon Delight'**, tall, deep pink to red; **'Canyon Pink'**, bright pink. The Canyon Quartet Series was released in 1993 after Emery's death and includes **'Canyon Bell'**, short stems, bright red; **'Canyon Chimes'**, tall stems, red; **'Canyon Duet'**, bi-color red and white; and **'Canyon Melody'**, smaller plant, pink and white. Zones 5–10.

× *HEUCHERELLA*

A group of garden hybrids in the saxifrage (Saxifragaceae) family that are crosses between the genera *Heuchera* and *Tiarella*. They are sterile hybrids with evergreen maple-shaped leaves that often color well in winter and sprays of tiny dainty pale pink to white flowers on upright stems in late spring.

CULTIVATION: These hybrids are best grown in humus-rich moist soils in cool woodland-type aspects where they make attractive slow-moving ground covers. Propagation is by division.

× *Heucherella alba*

☼/◐ ✱ ↔ 20 in (50 cm) ↑ 12 in (30 cm)

Mid-green divided leaves form tight compact mounds. Creamy white flower spikes sit 16 in (40 cm) above plant, in mid-summer. In winter leaves shrink in size; flush of new leaves in spring. **'Rosalie'**, compact dark green foliage, reddish bronze center, masses of rose pink blooms, for a long time in late spring, ideal woodland plant. Zones 5–9.

× *Heucherella tiarelloides*

☼/◐ ✱ ↔ 18 in (45 cm) ↑ 18 in (45 cm)

Smooth, light green, divided leaves heart-shaped at the base. Each leaf has dark brown marking along the veins when young. Short stems of pink flowers sit above the foliage through spring–summer. Zones 5–9.

× *Heucherella* Hybrid Cultivars

☼/◐ ✱ ↔ 12–16 in (30–40 cm)
↑ 16–20 in (40–50 cm)

Evergreen perennials, striking foliage. **'Bridget Bloom'**, heart-shaped mid-green leaves, heavy brown markings, white flower spikes, spring–autumn; **'Dayglo Pink'**, mid-green leaves, chocolate-colored inlay, purple foliage tones in winter, brilliant pink flowers; **'Kimono'**, tawny flowers, summer–autumn; **'Viking Ship'**, silver leaves in spring, silvery maple-like leaves in summer, coral-pink spires of star-like flowers ascending to 16 in (40 cm). Zones 5–9.

HIBISCUS

GIANT MALLOW, MALLOW, ROSE MALLOW

This genus of over 200 annual or perennial herbs, shrubs or trees in the mallow (Malvaceae) family is widely distributed throughout warm-temperate, subtropical and tropical regions of the world. They are grown mostly for their large dramatic flowers, borne singly or in terminal clusters, usually lasting for just a day. The open bell-shaped flowers appear in a wide variety of colors, and are characterized by a prominent staminal column and a darker coloring in the center. The alternate simple leaves are usually palmate. The fruit is a capsule.

× *Heucherella* Hybrid Cultivar, 'Dayglo Pink'

Hibiscus arnottianus 'Kona Kai'

Hibiscus cisplatinus

Hibiscus lasiocarpus

CULTIVATION: Most species of *Hibiscus* are drought tender and rather frost tender, and prefer a position in full sun in a rich and moist soil. Many will tolerate hard pruning after flowering to maintain shape. Perennials are propagated from seed or by division, while annuals are best grown from seed in the growing position. Shrub types can be propagated from cuttings, by grafting or from seed sown in containers for later transplanting.

Hibiscus × archeri

↔7 ft (2 m) ↑15 ft (4.5 m)
Hybrid between *H. rosasinensis* and *H. schizopetalus*. Large shrub or small tree, evergreen in frost-free climates. Closely resembles *H. rosa-sinensis* in habit and flower, though leaves are larger and more roughly serrated, and flowers crimson to red. Popular garden specimen. Zones 9–11.

Hibiscus arnottianus

HAWAIIAN WHITE HIBISCUS
↔10 ft (3 m) ↑25 ft (8 m)
Fast-growing, erect, branching evergreen shrub or small tree, native to the Hawaiian Islands. Dark green, smooth-edged, oval-shaped leaves. Solitary white or yellow flowers, delicately fragrant, red staminal column. Good hedge plant. **'Kona Kai'**, attractive cultivar. Zones 10–12.

Hibiscus brackenridgei

↔8 ft (2.4 m) ↑10 ft (3 m)
Native of Hawaiian Islands. Sprawling evergreen shrub or small tree. Leaves have 3 to 7 lobes. Flowers have red to yellow calyx and yellow petals, with maroon spot at base. Zones 10–12.

Hibiscus cannabinus

BIMLI, DECCAN HEMP, INDIAN HEMP, KENAF
↔6 ft (1.8 m) ↑12 ft (3.5 m)
Annual or short-lived, shrubby perennial, thought to be from East Indies. Pale yellow, sometimes pale purple flowers in racemes, reddish purple column and center. Leaves prickly, deeply lobed, serrated. Zones 10–12.

Hibiscus cisplatinus

↔4 ft (1.2 m) ↑10 ft (3 m)
Native of southern Brazil, Paraguay, and Argentina, cultivated in Hawaiian Islands. Stout yellow spines, 6 in (15 cm) long leaves, up to 5 lobes. Solitary rose pink flowers, to 3 in (8 cm) long, purple base. Zones 10–12.

Hibiscus coccineus

SCARLET HIBISCUS, SCARLET ROSE MALLOW, SWAMP HIBISCUS
↔2–3 ft (0.6–0.9 m) ↑7 ft (2 m)
From southern USA. Shrub-like herbaceous perennial with 5-petalled crimson flowers, 6–8 in (15–20 cm) across, that appear in early to mid-summer; followed by attractive papery green fruits. Vigorous grower in good conditions. **'Davis Creek'**, robust cultivar. Zones 7–11.

Hibiscus diversifolius

NATIVE HIBISCUS, SWAMP HIBISCUS
↔3 ft (0.9 m) ↑3 ft (0.9 m)
Spreading evergreen shrub, native of tropical Africa, Asia, northern Australia, and tropical Pacific Islands. Stems hairy, serrated palmate leaves. Flowers solitary or in loose terminal heads, from summer–autumn, pale yellow petals, maroon center, purple staminal column. Zones 10–12.

Hibiscus lasiocarpus

syn. *Hibiscus californicus*
ROSE-MALLOW
↔3–5 ft (0.9–1.5 m)
↑4–7 ft (1.2–2 m)
From southern USA and Mexico, this plant has softly hairy, pointed, oval to heart-shaped leaves. The white to pink flowers are 4–6 in (10–15 cm) wide, often with maroon basal spots, and are borne in leaf axils in late summer. Zones 6–9.

Hibiscus moscheutos

COMMON ROSE MALLOW, SWAMP ROSE MALLOW
↔40 in (100 cm) ↑8 ft (2.4 m)
From eastern North America, common from Ohio through to Alabama and Florida, USA. Woody perennial shrub. Lobed leaves, 2–6 in (5–15 cm) long. Large trumpet-shaped flowers in pink and white produced from spring to summer. **'Lord Baltimore'**, large, single, crimson red flowers, to 12 in (30 cm) across; **'Southern Belle'**, compact, to 40 in (100 cm), serrated leaves, deep pink flowers. Zones 5–9.

Hibiscus mutabilis

CONFEDERATE ROSE, COTTON ROSE
↔6–8 ft (1.8–2.4 m)
↑10–15 ft (3–4.5 m)
Native of China. Small, spreading deciduous shrub, or erect, branching small tree. Large palm-shaped leaves, 7 serrated lobes. Double or single flowers, white or pink with darker base and staminal column. **'Plena'**, rounded double flowers that open white and turn a deep rose red. Zones 8–9.

Hibiscus rosa-sinensis

CHINA ROSE, CHINESE HIBISCUS, HAWAIIAN HIBISCUS, ROSE OF CHINA, SHOE BLACK
↔5 ft (1.5 m) ↑8 ft (2.4 m)
Erect, branching evergreen shrub, or small tree to 30 ft (9 m) high. Solitary flowers, variable in color, normally red to dark red, summer–winter. Oval-shaped, serrated, glossy, deep green leaves. Prune straight after winter, before new growth appears. The many hybrid cultivars include: **'Agnes Galt'** ★, tall vigorous shrub, large rose pink flowers; **'Aurora'**, blush pink, pompon-shaped flowers; **'Bridal Veil'**, large pure white flowers with a crape texture; **'Cooperi'**, small, rose pink single flowers, narrow variegated leaves, olive green marbled with red, pink and white, good container plant; **'Crown of Bohemia'**, bushy shrub, medium double flowers, gold with bright orange throat; **'D. J. O'Brien'**, medium, double orange-apricot flowers; **'Eileen McMullen'**, large, deep yellow flowers heavily flushed with crimson; **'Moon Beam'**, bright yellow flowers, crimson throat, strongly reflexed petals. Zones 9–11.

Hibiscus Herbacious Hybrid, 'Lady Baltimore'

Hibiscus Herbacious Hybrid, 'Davis Creek'

Hibiscus schizopetalus

CORAL HIBISCUS, FRINGED HIBISCUS, JAPANESE HIBISCUS, JAPANESE LANTERN

↔6 ft (1.8 m) ↑10 ft (3 m)

Evergreen to semi-deciduous shrub, native to tropical east Africa. Arching, slender, weeping habit, clusters of small, oval-shaped, serrated leaves. Flowers ragged, deeply fringed margins, petals pink or brilliant red, long staminal column, from summer to autumn. Zones 10–12.

Hibiscus sinosyriacus

↔6–10 ft (1.8–3 m) ↑8–12 ft (2.4–3.5 m)

Handsome, vigorous, medium-sized shrub, very similar to *H. syriacus* but with broader, sage green leaves and larger flowers with thicker petals, in autumn. Zones 5–9.

Hibiscus syriacus

BLUE HIBISCUS, ROSE OF SHARON, SHRUB ALTHEA, SYRIAN HIBISCUS

↔6–10 ft (1.8–3 m) ↑8–12 ft (2.4–3.5 m)

Shrub or small tree, native to cool-temperate regions of Asia. Smooth gray branches, leaves with 3 narrow, coarsely toothed triangular lobes. Single or double flowers, petals white, reddish purple or bluish lavender with a crimson base and staminal column. **'Blue Bird'** (syn. 'Oiseau Blue'), gentian blue flowers, lilac-purple centers, grows to about 5 ft (1.5 m); **'Diana'**, single pure white flowers, grows to about 5 ft (1.5 m); **'Hamabo'**, large, light pink single flowers with a red center that radiates at edges into fine red streaks; **'White Supreme'**, semi-double white flowers with a crimson center, rose pink on outside of the petals; **'Woodbridge'**, wine red flowers with darker center, grows to about 6 ft (1.8 m). Other cultivars include: **'Aphrodite'**, **'Boule de Feu'**, **'Lady Stanley'**, **'Lohengrin'**, **'Minerva'**, and **'Red Heart'**. Zones 5–9.

Hibiscus Herbaceous Hybrids

↔2–4 ft (0.6–1.2 m) ↑18 in–5 ft (45 cm–1.5 m)

Perennials derived mainly from *H. moscheutos*. Leaves vary from toothed to deeply lobed. Succession of large, flat to funnel-shaped flowers from upper leaf axils in shades from white or pale pink to dark red, sometimes with darker eye. **'Davis Creek'**, pinkish red flowers; **'Lady Baltimore'**, pink flowers; **'Miss Kitty'**, yellow flowers. Zones 5–10.

HIPPEASTRUM

AMARYLLIS, KNIGHT' S STAR LILY

From the subtropics of Central and South America these bulbous, deciduous, spring-flowering perennials of the amaryllis (Amaryllidaceae) family are grown as pot plants in cooler climates. In the past, 2 single trumpet-shaped heads per stem and petals in red, white, or pink shades were common. Today the range of robust cultivars includes pale translucent yellows, doubles, and stems carrying up to 5 large, outward-facing heads. Leaves are strap-like and mid-green. Stems are straight, stout, and hollow.

CULTIVATION: Grow outdoors in frost-free areas or as greenhouse plants elsewhere. They are heavy feeders and drinkers while in growth, but prior to a dry winter dormancy reduce their foliage and water. The bulbs are large and should be planted with the necks protruding from the soil. They mildly resent root disturbance. Provide total shelter from frost and rain in winter. Propagate from offsets or from fresh ripe seeds kept at 61°F (16°C).

Hippeastrum papilio

BUTTERFLY AMARYLLIS

↔12–16 in (30–40 cm) ↑24 in (60 cm)

From southern Brazil. Flowers 2 to 3 per stem, large, open, star-like. Usually flowers mid-winter–early spring. Petals flamboyant, striped pale green-cream, stained reddish chocolate. The 5 distinctive leaves are dark green, purple at base, strap-like. Zones 9–10.

Hippeastrum vittatum

ST JOSEPH'S LILY

↔12 in (30 cm) ↑36 in (90 cm)

Large, robust plant from the Peruvian Andes. Flowers are wide open stars, 5 to 6 per tall stout stem. Petals in variable arrangement of white with red stripes. Leaves are bright green, and appear after flowers. Likes a crowd, dislikes disturbance. Zones 9–10.

Hippeastrum Hybrid Cultivars

↔12–16 in (30–40 cm) ↑20–36 in (50–90 cm)

When growing *Hippeastrum* hybrid cultivars, the temperature should not be allowed to fall below 55°F (13°C). **'Apple Blossom'**, robust bulb, 20 in (50 cm) high, large flowers, petals white tinged with pink; **'Christmas Star'**, stems with up to 8 brilliant red and white flowers; **'Flamingo'**, large trumpets, red petals; **'Las Vegas'**, bright red with white center stripe; **'Pamela'** ★, 20 in (50 cm) high, robust miniature, free-flowering, small and fine blue-green stems, narrow leaves, flowers up to 5 per stem, perfect shape, petals clear bright red; **'Picotee'**, spectacular but can prove weak, 20 in (50 cm) high, up to 5 large flowerheads per stem, petals white, finely margined in red, flushed green at the base; **'Royal Velvet'**, deep velvety blackcurrant red petals, robust, big firm bulbs and strong stems. Zones 9–12.

HIPPOPHAE

From Eurasia, the Himalayas, and China, these 3 dioecious species belong to the oleaster (Elaeagnaceae) family, growing in coastal dunes and screes on riverbanks in the mountains. All are deciduous large shrubs or small trees, used in gardens for their long-lasting berries and good silver foliage, and make useful coastal windbreaks. The berries can be used in sauces and drinks; the wood is suitable for turning and as a source of yellow dye; and the oil from the wood is used in cosmetics.

CULTIVATION: Best in full sun in well-drained but moist, alkaline to neutral, preferably sandy soil. In dry areas they grow well in clay soil as this retains moisture. For berry production, male and female plants are needed. Propagate by taking half-hardened cuttings in summer or hardwood cuttings in autumn, or from suckers. Sow fresh seed in autumn or after several months' stratification in spring.

Hippeastrum papilio

Hippophae rhamnoides

SEA BUCKTHORN

↔ 20 ft (6 m) ↑ 20 ft (6 m)

Native to western China. Spiny, deciduous. Leaves narrow, linear, gray-green, rough scaly surfaces. Yellow-green female flowers in small racemes, before the leaves. Male flowers, on previous year's growth, tiny spikes. Orange, oval to round fruit. Zones 2–9.

HOMERIA

CAPE TULIP

A member of the iris (Iridaceae) family, this genus consists of 30-plus cormous perennials. Natives of South Africa, where they favor sunny sandy habitats, some species have been declared noxious weeds in parts of Australia. Flowers are bowl-shaped, symmetrical with narrow well-separated petals and, although often short-lived, are borne in succession over an extended period. The plants are winter-growing, spring-flowering, and summer-dormant. Colors range from pink to yellow, and peach. Recent research shows there is no clear distinction between this genus and *Moraea*, and some botanists now place all *Homeria* species under that name.

CULTIVATION: When grown in containers in colder climates, provide shelter from frost and a fast-draining potting mix. Reduce water and nutrition after flowering and store corms in dry, frost-free conditions. Propagate from offsets or from fresh ripe seeds.

Homeria collina

↔ 3 in (8 cm) ↑ 6–14 in (15–35 cm)

From southwestern Cape region of South Africa. Robust, potentially weedy. Flowers are scented, upturned, held well above the foliage. Petals pale yellow, peach-pink, bronze-pink, or sugar pink, darker at the base. Leaves linear, grayish green, often trailing, provide little support to flowers. Stems solitary or sparsely branched. All parts toxic to stock. Zones 9–12.

HOODIA

This genus contains about 17 species of unusual succulent perennials in the milkweed (Asclepiadaceae) family. They are found naturally in arid areas among rocks in southern Africa. These leafless plants have robust, angular, usually grayish green stems up to 40 in (100 cm) tall. The stems are covered in small growths, called tubercles, and hard thorny teeth. The large saucer-shaped flowers are borne near the stem tips in groups of 1 to 5. They are in muted shades of yellow to brown and have an unpleasant smell.

CULTIVATION: In temperate climates grow in the greenhouse in a well-drained potting mix with a mulch of gravel to prevent collar rot. Water sparingly and leave dry in winter. Can be grown outdoors in dry, subtropical, and tropical areas. Propagation is from seed.

Homeria collina

Hoodia bainii

↔ 12 in (30 cm) ↑ 12 in (30 cm)

Stems, to 1½ (35 mm) wide, have spirally arranged tubercles with pale brown spines. Flowers range from bell-shaped to almost flat. They are pale yellow to buff colored with darker veining. Zones 10–12.

HOSTA

PLANTAIN LILY

Hosta, from the agave (Agavaceae) family, was named for Dr Nicholaus Host (1761–1834), the physician to the emperor of Austria. Previously called *Funkia*, the genus was first described by Engelbert Kaempfer in 1712, a Dutch East India Company employee who, in exchange for plants, taught Japanese astronomy and mathematics. Hostas are clump-forming and grown primarily for their large, bold, heart-shaped leaves. In addition to green, blue, and grayish tones, there are cultivars variegated or with yellow-green foliage. The flowers are funnel-shaped and borne in small racemes atop stiff stems. They are usually white, mauve, or purple, appear from mid-summer, and are sometimes scented.

CULTIVATION: Although sun-tolerant cultivars have been raised, hostas prefer shaded conditions with moist, cool, humus-rich, well-drained soil. Water and feed well during the growing season. Propagate by dividing as the first buds show. The young shoots are very vulnerable to slug and snail damage.

Hosta decorata

Hosta crispula

SAZANAMI GIBOSHI

↔ 24 in (60 cm) ↑ 36 in (90 cm)

From Japan, though not known in wild. Deeply veined, pointed oval to lance-shaped leaves to around 10 in (25 cm) long, deep green with white edges, usually twisted with wavy edges rolled around leaf stalk. Pale mauve flowers on tall stem. Zones 6–10.

Hosta decorata

OTAFUKU GIBOSHI

↔ 20 in (50 cm) ↑ 20 in (50 cm)

Japanese species. Rounded leathery leaves to near 6 in (15 cm) long, pointed at the tip, deep green with lighter edges. Flowers light purple, less commonly white. Zones 6–10.

Hosta fluctuans

KURONAMI GIBOSHI

↔ 24 in (60 cm) ↑ 40 in (100 cm)

Japanese species with heavily veined, narrow, twisted leaves to 10 in (25 cm) long, deep green above, gray-green below. Narrow, pale mauve flowers on tall stem. **'Variegated'** has wider leaves with creamy yellow edges. Zones 6–10.

Hosta fortunei

↔ 32–48 in (80–120 cm) ↑ 36 in (90 cm)

Wild status uncertain—it is perhaps Japanese but may be a garden hybrid from Europe. Wavy, deep green, heart- to lance-shaped leaves tapering to a fine point, often variegated. Mauve flowers on leafy stems. Cultivars include: **'Albomarginata'**, large white-edged leaves; **'Albopicta'**, large, thin leaves, light green when young, maturing to green with hint of cream; **'Antioch'**, dark green leaves, yellow edge turning cream; **'Aurea'**, leaves yellow, turning light green; **'Aureo-marginata'**, clearly defined gold-edged leaves; **'Elizabeth Campbell'**, leaves with broad green edge and light green central zone; **'Francee'**, white-edged deep green leaves, slightly puckered; **'Gold Haze'**, like 'Aurea' but slower to turn green; **'Gold Standard'**, green-gold leaves, clearly defined dark green edge; **'Goldbrook Gold'**, yellow-gold leaves; **'Joker'**, gray-green to blue-green leaves; **'Mary Marie Ann'**, bright green edges around a broad yellow-green center; **'Minuteman'**, bright green leaves, with irregular broad white edge; **'North Hills'**, mid-green leaves with an irregular narrow white edge; **'Striptease'**, heart-shaped blue-green leaves with a narrow cream and green central zone; **'Whirlwind'**, mid-green, broad yellow-gold center. Zones 6–10.

Hosta fortunei 'Albopicta'

Hosta fortunei 'Gold Haze'

Hosta hypoleuca

URAJIRO GIBOSHI

↔ 40 in (100 cm) ↑ 16 in (40 cm)

Japanese species with slightly wavy, pointed oval to heart-shaped leaves to 18 in (45 cm) long, blue-green above, very pale beneath. Flowers lavender to white on short, sometimes leafy stem. Zones 6–10.

Hosta kikutii 'Green Fountain'

Hosta montana 'Yellow River'

Hosta nakaiana 'Emerald Scepter'

Hosta plantaginea

H

Hosta kikutii

HYUGA GIBOSHI

☀/☀ ✱ ↔32 in (80 cm) ↑16 in (40 cm)

Japanese native with lustrous deep green, arching, deeply veined, pointed oval leaves to 8 in (20 cm) long. Leafy flower stems with bracts partly enclosing white to cream flowers, sometimes mauve-tinted. **'Green Fountain'** has larger leaves with wavy edges and curved flower stems. Zones 6–10.

Hosta lancifolia

☀/☀ ✱ ↔16–20 in (40–50 cm) ↑18 in (45 cm)

Not known in the wild. Narrow, deep green, lance-shaped leaves to around 6 in (15 cm) long, tapering to a fine point. Flower stems leafy, flowers purple. Zones 6–10.

Hosta longissima

MIZU GIBOSHI

☀/☀ ✱ ↔16–20 in (40–50 cm) ↑20 in (50 cm)

A Japanese species forming a clump of leaves that is held upright or slightly overarching. Leaves are dark green, narrow, tapering to a fine point and extending to over 6 in (15 cm) in length. Zones 6–10.

Hosta minor

KIRIN GIBOSHI

☀/☀ ✱ ↔16 in (40 cm) ↑24 in (60 cm)

Korean species long cultivated in Japan. Clump of small, dark green, pointed oval to heart-shaped leaves to 3 in (8 cm) long. Comparatively tall flower stem with deep mauve flowers. Zones 6–10.

Hosta montana

OBA GIBOSHI

☀/☀ ✱ ↔40 in (100 cm) ↑40 in (100 cm)

Wild status uncertain, though probably Japanese. Broad, deep green to blue-green, heavily veined, sometimes undulating oval leaves tapering to fine point, to 12 in (30 cm) long. Flowers lavender-gray to white, stems leafy. **'On Stage'**, bright gold leaves with irregular green margins; **'Yellow River'**, leaves with a sharply defined yellow edge and flower stems to 24 in (60 cm) tall. Zones 6–10.

Hosta nakaiana

KANZASHI GIBOSHI

☀/☀ ✱ ↔12–16 in (30–40 cm) ↑16 in (40 cm)

Compact low ground cover from Korea and Japan. Long-stemmed, bright green, heavily veined, undulating, heart-shaped leaves to around 2½ in (6 cm) long, pale undersides. Wiry flower stem with bell-shaped mauve flowers. **'Emerald Scepter'**, especially bright green foliage; **'Golden Scepter'**, golden yellow leaves; **'Golden Tiara'**, gold-edged leaves; **'Grand Tiara'**, sport of **'Golden Tiara'** with broader leaves and wider golden edge; **'Platinum Tiara'**, lime green leaves with clearly defined white edge. Zones 6–10.

Hosta nigrescens

KURO GIBOSHI

☀/☀ ✱ ↔3–4 ft (0.9–1.2 m) ↑3–7 ft (0.9–2 m)

Bushy, late-flowering Japanese species. Tall flower stems. Pointed oval leaves to 10 in (25 cm) long, base rolled over the stalk, blue-gray when young, maturing to dark green. Stems leafy, flowers open white from mauve buds. **'Sum and Substance'**, heavy textured, glossy, golden green leaves. Zones 6–10.

Hosta plantaginea

AUGUST LILY, MARUBA

☀/☀ ✱ ↔32 in (80 cm) ↑26 in (65 cm)

Native to China and Japan. Unlike most hostas, grown as much for flowers as foliage. Leaves bright green, wavy, deeply veined, lance-shaped tapering to a fine point, to 10 in (25 cm) long. Flowers white, sometimes mauve-tinted, large and pleas-antly scented. ***H. p.* var. *japonica*** (syn. *H. p.* var. *grandiflora*), taller flower stems with larger flowers. ***H. p.* 'Honey Bells'**, mauve-tinted flowers; **'Venus'**, double flowers. Zones 8–10.

Hosta pulchella

UBUTAKE GIBOSHI

☀/☀ ✱ ↔12 in (30 cm) ↑12 in (30 cm)

Compact rock garden-style species from Japan. Bright green, heart-shaped leaves to 2 in (5 cm) long. Leafy flower stems with mauve often scented flowers, late. **'Kifukurin'** has yellow-edged leaves and purple flowers. Zones 6–10.

Hosta sieboldiana ★

☀/☀ ✱ ↔3–5 ft (0.9–1.5 m) ↑20–24 in (50–60 cm)

Japanese species. Large, fine-pointed, heart-shaped leaves to 20 in (50 cm) long. Leaves usually in striking blue-gray tones with a heavily veined and puckered surface. Flowers white to mauve, on leafy stems. ***H. s.* var. *elegans***, thick, heavily puckered leaves, pearly mauve flowers. ***H. s.* 'Aurora Borealis'**, leaves with bright gold edges, white flowers; **'Big Daddy'**, very large, heavy textured, intensely blue-green leaves; **'Birchwood Parky's Gold'**, light yellow-green leaves, mauve flowers; **'Blue Angel'** ★, very vigorous with huge blue-green leaves, white flowers; **'Bressingham Blue'**, large, undulating leaves, white to pale mauve flowers; **'Crumples'**, pale blue-green with incredibly deeply puckered surface; **'Frances Williams'**, leaves with broad green-gold edges; **'Great Expectations'**, gold leaves with blue-green edges; **'Reversed'**, blue-green leaves, broad white center. Zones 6–10.

Hosta sieboldii

KOBA GIBOSHI

☀/☀ ✱ ↔32 in (80 cm) ↑20 in (50 cm)

Native to Japan and Sakhalin Island. Finely pointed, often undulating and puckered, lance-shaped leaves to 6 in (15 cm) long, deep green with clean white edges. Mauve flowers. ***H. s.* f. *kabitan***, small, green-edged golden leaves. ***H. s.* 'Krossa Cream Edge'**, narrow, cream-edged leaves; **'Wogon'**, bright lime green leaves. Zones 5–10.

Hosta × *tardiana*

☀/☀ ✱ ↔16–20 in (40–50 cm) ↑16 in (40 cm)

Hybrids between *H. sieboldiana* var. *elegans* and *H. tardiflora*. Mainly forming mounding clumps of heavily veined blue-green leaves, sometimes variegated. Flower stems fairly short, flowers cream to pale mauve. **'Brother Ronald'**, dark blue-green leaves to over 6 in (15 cm) long; **'Camelot'**, wide spreading with broad, heart-shaped, intensely blue-green leaves to 8 in (20 cm) long, lavender flowers; **'Devon Blue'**, pointed, gray-marked, blue-green leaves to over 6 in (15 cm) long; **'Halcyon'**, heart-shaped blue-green leaves to 8 in (20 cm) long, many lavender-gray flowers; **'Moody Blues'**, broad, intensely blue-green leaves, pale lavender flowers. Zones 6–10.

Hosta tardiflora

☀/☀ ✱ ↔20 in (50 cm) ↑12 in (30 cm)

A species unknown in the wild, with prominently veined, glossy, olive green, sometimes undulating, lance-shaped leaves to 6 in (15 cm) long. Flower stem to 14 in (35 cm) long but held at around a 45° angle, flowers mauve within cream to purple bracts. Zones 6–10.

Hosta tokudama

TOKUDAMA GIBOSHI

☀/☀ ✱ ↔32–48 in (80–120 cm)
↑18 in (45 cm)

Unknown in the wild, long cultivated in Japan. Broad oval to heart-shaped leaves, puckered surface, bright blue-green, to 10 in (25 cm) long and wide. Flowers lavender-gray to white. ***H. t.* f. *aureonebulosa***, leaves irregular, large central yellow-green area. ***H. t.* 'Love Pat'**, possibly of hybrid origin, heavily textured, deep blue-green leaves, mauvish white flowers. Zones 6–10.

Hosta undulata

SUJI GIBOSHI

☀/☀ ✱ ↔16–20 in (40–50 cm)
↑12 in (30 cm)

This species is unknown in the wild, though it has long been cultivated in Japan. Dark green leaves, narrow central band of creamy white, pointed elliptical to lance-shaped, wavy edged with undulating surface, to nearly 6 in (15 cm) long. Flowers pale purple within greenish white bracts. **'Albomarginata'**, leaves with white edges, wavy but not twisted; **'Variegata'** (syn. *H. u. var. undulata*), leaves with central area cream and 2-tone green; **'Univittata'**, large leaves with a narrow central creamy white zone; and **'White Christmas'**, white leaves with narrow irregular green edge. Zones 6–10.

Hosta ventricosa

MURASAKI GIBOSHI

☀/☀ ✱ ↔24–32 in (60–80 cm)
↑40 in (100 cm)

Chinese species long cultivated in Japan. Deep green, broad, often wavy, heart-shaped leaves to 10 in (25 cm) long. Tall flower stems, light purple flowers. ***H. v.* var. *aureomaculata***, young leaves with bright yellow center. ***H. v.* 'Peedee Elfin Bells'**, pendulous flowers. Zones 6–10.

Hosta venusta

OTOME GIBOSHI

☀/☀ ✱ ↔12 in (30 cm) ↑14 in (35 cm)

Low-growing, spreading, late-flowering native of Korea and Japan. Dark green, pointed oval, short-stemmed leaves under 2 in (5 cm) long, sometimes wavy edged. Mauve flowers. Sun-tolerant, good rock garden plant. Zones 6–10.

Hosta Hybrid Cultivars

☀/☀ ✱ ↔12–60 in (30–150 cm)
↑6–36 in (15–90 cm)

In recent decades hostas have been among plant breeders' favorites, and extensive hybridizing has produced a myriad of foliage forms. Although much effort has gone into producing sun-tolerant forms, most are still better with some shade. **'Allan P. McConnell'**, medium height, dark green with white edge, purple flowers; **'August Moon'**, tall, wavy yellow-gold leaves, lavender flowers; **'Blue Moon'**, low-growing, small blue-green leaves, white flowers; **'Brim Cup'**, tall, puckered, light yellow-green leaves with irregular green center, mauve flowers; **'Candy Hearts'**, tall blue-green leaves, pale mauve flowers; **'County Park'**, tall, broad, flat, mid-green leaves, white flowers; **'Devon Gold'**, medium height, small yellow-green leaves, purple flowers; **'Floradora'**, medium height, neat heart-shaped mid-green leaves, pale mauve flowers; **'Gold Edger'**, low-growing, golden green leaves, white flowers; **'Green Piecrust'**, tall, large mid-green wavy-edged leaves, lavender flowers; **'Ground Sulphur'**, a medium height, low spreader with bright yellow-green leaves; **'Island Charm'**, medium height, small pink-stemmed bright green heart-shaped leaves with yellow center, lavender flowers; **'Julie Morss'**, medium height, yellow-gold leaves with green edges, lavender-pink flowers; **'June'**, medium height, small yellow-centered blue-green leaves, violet flowers; **'King Michael'**, tall, large lustrous mid-green leaves, white flowers; **'Krossa Regal'**, tall, long-stemmed blue-green leaves, white to pale mauve flowers; **'Lady Isobel Barnett'**, tall, very large mid-green leaves with creamy yellow margin, white to pale lavender flowers; **'Medusa'**, medium height, narrow green-edged cream leaves, purple flowers; **'Midwest Magic'**, tall, yellow-green leaves with darker edges, lavender flowers; **'Patriot'**, tall, dark green leaves with broad white edge, violet flowers; **'Paul's Glory'**, medium height, heavily puckered yellow-centered blue-green leaves, lavender flowers; **'Pearl Lake'**, tall, small mid-green leaves, many lavender flowers; **'Pizzazz'**, medium height, broad blue-green leave with thin irregular yellow edges, pale mauve flowers; **'Radiant Edger'**, tall, small mid-green leaves with yellow-green edges, mauve flowers; **'Royal Standard'**, tall, glossy mid-green leaves, fragrant white flowers; **'Ryan's Big One'**, tall, very large puckered blue-green leaves, pale lavender flowers; **'September Sun'**, tall, leaves initially yellow-green becoming green-edged, white flowers; **'Shade Fanfare'**, medium height, puckered white-edged blue-green leaves, pale mauve flowers; **'Summer Music'**, medium height, slightly twisted dark green leaves with white to cream center, pale mauve flowers; **'Tall Boy'**, tall, long-stemmed mid-green leaves, purple flowers on tall stems; **'Torch-light'**, medium height, dark green leaves with broad white edge, lavender flowers; **'Veronica Lake'**, medium height, blue-green leaves with white to light green edges, pale mauve flowers; **'Wide Brim'**, tall, blue-green leaves with creamy yellow edge, mauve flowers; **'Yellow Waves'**, low-growing, small yellow-gold leaves, mauve flowers. Zones 6–10.

Hosta sieboldii

Hosta tokudama 'Love Pat'

Hosta tardiflora

Hosta ventricosa

Hosta, Hybrid Cultivar, 'Floradora'

Hottuynia cordata 'Chameleon'

HOUTTUYNIA

A genus of a single species in the lizard's-tail (Saururaceae) family from East Asia. It is a widely spreading herbaceous perennial with heart-shaped leaves and cones of tiny yellow flowers surrounded by 4 white petal-like bracts. Leaves can be eaten raw or cooked and have a peppery taste. CULTIVATION: Grows well in moist to wet soil and even slightly submerged in water, and is happy in full sun or half-sun. Can become quite invasive and hard to remove, although growing them in pots kept off the ground will control them. Propagate by division.

Houttuynia cordata

↔ over 40 in (100 cm)
↑ 6–12 in (15–30 cm)

Herbaceous plant from swamps and damp margins of China and Japan. Aromatic heart-shaped leaves to 3½ in (9 cm) long, deep green often stained burgundy. White-bracted flower clusters atop red stems from mid-summer onward. Below ground produces thong-like rhizomes. Usually grown in one of its forms, which include: **'Chameleon'** (syns *H. c. 'Court Jester'*, *H. c. 'Tricolor'*, *H. c. 'Variegata'*), slightly less vigorous, leaves broadly edged in yellow and stained red; **'Flore Pleno'**, masses of white bracts arranged like little cones and just as vigorous as the species. Zones 5–10.

HUMULUS

This genus of 2 species in the hemp (Cannabaceae) family consists of herbaceous, climbing, and twining perennials from northern temperate regions. The plants naturalize in trees and woodland areas and can grow up to 70 ft (21 m) in a season. Grown primarily for their attractive foliage, many cultivars have been selected for ornamental purposes. *H. lupulus* is grown for its fruits (hops), used to flavor beer. Spreading via underground suckers, they cover large areas quickly. CULTIVATION: These plants need well-drained, moist, fertile soil. They die back to the ground over winter, and are prone to mildew in the damp. Propagate from semi-hardwood stem cuttings in late summer or by division when plants are dormant.

Humulus lupulus

BINE, COMMON HOP, EUROPEAN HOP

↔ 10–30 ft (3–9 m)
↑ 17–20 ft (5–6 m)

Well-known vigorous herbaceous twiner with rough stems. Source of hops, an indispensable ingredient of beer. Suckers far and wide from its questing rhizomes. Leaves 3- to 5-lobed, to 6 in (15 cm) long. Female plants are festooned with bracted hops in summer. Usually grown in gardens in its golden-leafed form, **'Aureus'**, which varies in color depending on how much light it gets. ***H. l.* var. *neomexicanus*** is a North American form that, apart from its distribution, is almost indistinguishable from the species. Zones 5–10.

HUNNEMANNIA

GOLDEN CUP, MEXICAN TULIP POPPY

This genus belongs to the poppy (Papaveraceae) family and contains one species of perennial that is often grown as an annual. It is native to highland areas of Mexico. Although rather woody at the base, it is of delicate appearance with finely divided bluish gray foliage. The flowers are up to 3 in (8 cm) wide and are clear yellow. CULTIVATION: Grow in full sun in a well-drained soil. It will not tolerate wet conditions. Care should be taken not to disturb the roots on transplanting. Propagate from seed.

Hunnemannia fumariifolia

↔ 10 in (25 cm)
↑ 18–36 in (45–90 cm)

A perennial or annual that has attractive bluish gray filigree leaves. The satiny flowers are clearest yellow and held above the foliage in summer. Zones 8–10.

HYACINTHOIDES

syn. *Endymion*

BLUEBELL

With 3–4 species from western Europe and northern Africa, these vigorous bulbous plants, members of the asparagus (Asparagaceae) family, are well suited to informal naturalistic plantings. The flowers, in the form of elegant pendent bells attached to a single stem, are commonly an azure blue and appear in spring. Some are sweetly fragrant. The leaves are linear to strap- shaped and fleshy. Hybrids between *H. hispanica* and *H. non-scripta* are as common as they are confusing. CULTIVATION: They are best grown in the ground in damp-summer climates or in irrigated beds, placed beneath deciduous trees and shrubs and planted deeply in a humus-rich, moisture-retentive, fairly heavy soil. Give them sun in winter and shade in summer, and moist conditions throughout the year. The plants are robust and fecund and, in appropriate conditions, have considerable weedy potential. Survival time in a vase is brief and the copious syrupy sap can cause skin irritations. The plants are said to be toxic if ingested. Propagate by division (the bulbs lie deep), or from ripe fresh seed.

Hyacinthoides hispanica ★

syns *Endymion hispanicus*, *Scilla campanulata*, *S. hispanica*

SPANISH BLUEBELL

↔ 4–6 in (10–15 cm)
↑ 16–18 in (40–45 cm)

Flowers without fragrance, arranged loosely around a single erect stem, in spring. Petals commonly blue, also lilac-pink and white; anthers blue. Leaves broad, strap-shaped, glossy emerald green, copious, erect but usually prostrate after rain. Clump-forming. Cultivars include: **'Excelsior'**, large-flowered, tall, with violet-blue petals adorned with a stripe; **'La Grandesse'**, with widely spaced, pure white bells. Zones 6–7.

Hyacinthoides italica

syn. *Scilla italica*

↔ 2–6 in (5–15 cm)
↑ 4–8 in (10–20 cm)

Native to southern Europe from Spain to Italy. Bluish violet flowers densely packed, bell-shaped, upward-facing, 6 to 30 per stem, in spring. Leaves linear, dull dark green. Zones 5–9.

Hyacinthoides non-scripta

syns *Endymion non-scriptus*, *Scilla non-scripta*

BLUEBELL, ENGLISH BLUEBELL, WILD HYACINTH

↔ 2–6 in (5–15 cm)
↑ 8–16 in (20–40 cm)

Clump-forming colonizer of damp oak, beech, and chestnut woodlands. Flowers 6 to 10 per stem, narrow bells, scented, arranged in drooping racemes on 1 side of stalk, in spring. Petals commonly azure blue; anthers creamy white. Stem bent like a shepherd's crook. Leaves narrow, glossy dark green. **'Alba'**, common white form; **'Rosea'**, lilac-pink flowers. Zones 5–10.

HYACINTHUS

HYACINTH

There are only 3 species in this bulbous perennial genus, which is in the asparagus (Asparagaceae) family and comes from western and central Asia. However, from these many cultivars have been developed for the cut-flower market and for container culture. Today the most common are the showy cultivars of *H. orientalis*, which can bloom at almost any time of the year. There are 3 basic forms: Dutch hyacinths, which pack their numerous flowerheads tightly around a central stem forming a dense cylinder; Roman hyacinths, which have less numerous flowerheads and a looser arrangement; and the Multiflora Group, which produce several stems of loosely set flowerheads. All are sweetly fragrant and, to greater and lesser extents, lend themselves to container culture and forcing.

Hyacinthoides hispanica 'La Grandesse'

Hyacinthoides italica

CULTIVATION: In gardens, plant in autumn under a light deciduous canopy, in well-drained moderately fertile soil. In containers, use a moisture-retentive mix, plant in autumn, and keep in a cool dark place until roots are well developed, or suspend over water and keep in a cool dark place until the roots are well developed. Bulbs grown over water should be discarded after flowering. Give them sun in winter and shade in summer. Propagate from offsets or fresh ripe seed. Cultivars are encouraged to form offsets by cutting into the base of the bulb.

Hyacinthus orientalis

COMMON HYACINTH

◐/☀ ❄ ↔ 3 in (8 cm)
↑ 8–12 in (20–30 cm)

Flowers in 6 or 7 heads sparsely arranged at angles around a central stem, smallish, dainty, narrowly bell-shaped, waxy, fragrant. Petals blue, blue-mauve, pink, white, and cream. **'Amethyst'**, mauve-violet petals; **'Anna Marie'**, light pink; **'Bismarck'**, lilac with pale margins; **'Blue Jacket'**, navy with purple veins; **'Carnegie'**, compact, pure white, late; **'City of Haarlem'**, primrose yellow, late; **'Delft Blue'**, soft blue flushed with mauve; **'Gipsy Queen'**, salmon orange; **'Hollyhock'**, compact, crimson, double; **'Jan Bos'**, carmine-red; **'King of the Blues'**, rich dark blue; **'Ostara'**, large, deep lavender-blue; **'Violet Pearl'**, carmine-pink with pale margins. Zones 5–9.

Hyacinthus orientalis 'Amethyst'

Hyacinthus orientalis 'Carnegie'

HYDRANGEA

There are about 100 species of deciduous and evergreen shrubs, trees, and climbers in this Hydrangeaceae family genus, native to eastern Asia, North and South America. Leaves are usually large and oval with serrated edges. Flowerheads are comprised of very small fertile flowers surrounded by larger, 4-petalled sterile florets, conical, flat-topped (lacecap) or rounded (mophead). Colors range from white through to red, purple and blue.
CULTIVATION: Hydrangeas grow in a wide range of conditions. However, they will do better in good soil with compost and light feeding. Grow in sun or dappled shade, ensuring they have ample moisture. Grow *H. macrophylla* cultivars to suit the soil pH. Color can be changed by dressing with aluminum sulphate for blue and with lime for red. Prune in late winter, and remove old wood. Propagate from seed sown in spring as well as from tip cuttings in late spring or hardwood cuttings in winter. Cultivars are propagated from cuttings only.

Hydrangea arborescens

SMOOTH HYDRANGEA

☼/◐ ✱ ↔ 8 ft (2.4 m)
↑ 3–12 ft (0.9–3.5 m)

Native to North America, from moist shady sites. Deciduous shrub, open habit, often spreading from suckers. Flat creamy white flowerheads, in summer, numerous tiny fertile flowers surrounded by a few sterile florets.

Hyacinthus orientalis 'Blue Jacket'

Hyacinthus orientalis 'Violet Pearl'

H. a.* subsp. *radiata has deep green leaves. ***H. a.* 'Annabelle'** ★, extremely large white mophead flowerheads; **'Grandiflora'**, slightly uneven mopheads of pure white sterile flowers. Zones 3–10.

Hydrangea aspera

syn. ***Hydrangea villosa***

☼/◐ ❄ ↔ 10 ft (3 m) ↑ 10 ft (3 m)

Native of eastern Asia. Variable deciduous species. Lacecap flowers, held well above foliage, to 10 in (25 cm) wide, pale mauve sterile florets, tiny, bright purplish blue fertile flowers in center. ***H. a.* f. *kawakamii***, pink veined leaves. ***H. a.* subsp. *sargentiana***, large leaves, velvety above, bristly beneath. Flat-topped flowerheads, pinkish white sterile florets surrounding mauve fertile flowers. ***H. a.* 'Mauvette'**, mauve dome-shaped flowerheads to 6 in (15 cm) across; **'Peter Chappell'**, large downy leaves, flat-topped flowerheads of white sterile florets surrounding creamy pink fertile flowers. Zones 7–10.

Hydrangea arborescens 'Annabelle'

Hydrangea aspera f. *kawakamii*

Hydrangea involucrata

☼/◐ ❄ ↔ 6 ft (1.8 m) ↑ 3 ft (0.9 m)

From Japan and Taiwan, rare in cultivation. Broadly oblong leaves, rough, bristly margins. Lacecap flowerheads, to 5 in (12 cm) across, a few white sterile florets around mauve fertile flowers, late summer. **'Hortensis'**, interesting form with showy, double sterile florets of pinkish white, more difficult to cultivate. Zones 7–10.

Hydrangea macrophylla

syn. ***Hydrangea hortensis***

BIGLEAF HYDRANGEA, FLORIST'S HYDRANGEA, GARDEN HYDRANGEA, HORTENSIA

☼/◐ ✱ ↔ 8 ft (2.4 m) ↑ 10 ft (3 m)

Long-cultivated species from coastal areas of Japan, wild form rare in cultivation. Deciduous shrub, large shiny leaves, pinkish blue flat-topped flowers. Many cultivars are popular garden plants. Cultivars usually grow 3–6 ft (0.9–1.8 m) high, divided into two groups: mophead (hortensias) and lacecap. There are more than 500 cultivars of the well-known mophead type, with globular heads of showy sterile florets. Mophead cultivars are suitable for coastal gardens. There are about 20 lacecap cultivars, with flat-topped formation of outer sterile florets, central fertile flowers.

Hydrangea involucrata 'Hortensis'

Hydrangea macrophylla

H. m., Mophead, 'Ami Pasquier'

H. m., Mophead, 'Générale Vicomtesse de Vibraye'

Hydrangea paniculata

H. m., Mophead, 'Enziandom'

H. m., Lacecap, 'Hobella'

MOPHEAD CULTIVARS

'Alpenglühen' ★, medium-sized robust plant, maintaining a rosy red color even in slightly acid soil; **'Altona'**, grows to 6 ft (1.8 m), with pink or blue flowers depending on soil pH; **'Amethyst'**, semi-double flowers and serrated bracts, lavender in acid soil and pale pink in alkaline soil; **'Ami Pasquier'**, medium size, producing rich crimson to purple flowers all summer, leaves turn red in autumn; **'Blue Diamond'**, bright mid-blue flowers, 4 ft (1.2 m) high; **Cityline Series**, group of compact 40 in (100 cm) high and wide cultivars, including **'Cityline Mars'**, pink flowers with broad white edge, **'Cityline Paris'**, deep pinkish red flowers, and **'Cityline Rio'**, flowers open mauve, age to blue; **'Edgy Hearts'** ★, pink flowers with narrow white edge, 4 ft (1.2 m) high; **Endless Summer Series**, early- and long-flowering, wide color range; **'Enziandom'** (syn. 'Gentian Dome'), compact shrub to 5 ft (1.5 m), needing acid soil to produce its stunning gentian blue flowers; **'Générale Vicomtesse de Vibraye'**, medium grower, flowerheads commencing as soft cream, gradually becoming powder blue; **'Hamburg'**, large serrated petals of deep rose to purple or blue, depending on soil pH; **'Jyougasaki'** ★, double flowers, white flushed pink, 5 ft (1.5 m); **'Madame Emile Mouillère'**, growing up to 6 ft (1.8 m), one of the best of the white mopheads; **'Miss Belgium'**, growing to 3 ft (0.9 m), small heads of pink flowers when grown in alkaline soil; **'Montgomery'**, yellow and pink flowerheads; **'Nigra'**, distinctive black stems, small flowerheads from pink to blue depending on soil pH; **'Nikko Blue'** ★, growing to 5 ft (1.5 m), blue flowers; **'Parzifal'**, flowers from deep pink to deep blue, depending on soil type; **'Pia'**, very dwarf form growing slowly to only 2 ft (0.6 m), flowers ranging from pink to red; **'President Doumer'**, rich cherry red flowers in small clusters on top of small, dark green, serrated leaves; **'Soeur Thérèse'**, growing up to 6 ft (1.8 m) tall, a pure white variety that is best grown in shade in order to prevent scorching; **You and Me Series**, range of compact double-flowered cultivars, such as **'Emotion'**, mid-pink flowers, 3 ft (0.9 m) high. Zones 5–11.

LACECAP CULTIVARS

'Fireworks Pink', double, star-shaped, pink florets around outer edge of each flowerhead, in autumn new flowers opening while older ones become green; **'Geoffrey Chadbund'**, flowerheads in shades of magenta; **'Hobella'**, soft pink flowers ageing to green, then to cherry red; **'Lanarth White'**, pure white flowers; **'Libelle'**, stunning heads of white sterile florets surrounding deep blue fertile flowers; **'Lilacina'**, lavender-purple flowerheads; **'Love You Kiss'**, large white flowerheads, each petal with a red margin, red-tinted leaves; **'Mariesii'**, pale pink to light blue flowers; **'Mariesii Variegated'**, cream and gray-green foliage variegations; **'Sea Foam'**, excellent for coastal planting—flowerheads up to 12 in (30 cm) across, consisting of white sterile florets surrounding mauve to blue fertile flowers; **'Twist-n-Shout'**, mauve to mid-pink flowers, repeat blooming, one of the Endless Summer Series. Zones 5–11.

Hydrangea paniculata

PANICLE HYDRANGEA

☼/◐ ❄ ↔10 ft (3 m) ↑6–20 ft (1.8–6 m)

Deciduous species from Japan and southeastern China. Conical flowerheads, densely packed, creamy white sterile and fertile flowers, often create an arching shape, in late summer–autumn. **'Grandiflora'**, creamy white sterile flowers on panicles up to 18 in (45 cm) long; **'Kyushu'**, smaller bush with dainty airy panicles of creamy white sterile and fertile flowers; **'Praecox'**, early-flowering cultivar; **'Tardiva'**, late-flowering cultivar; **'Unique'**, round-ended panicles larger than those of 'Grandiflora'. Zones 3–10.

Hydrangea petiolaris ★

syn. *Hydrangea anomala* subsp. *petiolaris*

◐ ❄ ↔17–35 ft (5–10 m) ↑50 ft (15 m)

Climbing hydrangea from Russia, Korea, Taiwan, and Japan. Attractive dark green leaves; flowers with large lacecap blooms at start of the season. May take several years to bear flowers. Do not prune. Often treated as a subspecies of *H. anomala*. Zones 4–9.

Hydrangea 'Preziosa'

☼/◐ ❄ ↔5 ft (1.5 m) ↑5 ft (1.5 m)

Erect shrub with distinctive reddish stems, red-flushed leaves. Small globular flowerheads change color from creamy white through shades of pink to reddish purple. Zones 6–10.

Hydrangea quercifolia

OAK-LEAFED HYDRANGEA

☼/◐ ❄ ↔8 ft (2.4 m) ↑3–8 ft (0.9–2.4 m)

Deciduous shrub from southeastern USA. Large, lobed, green leaves turn crimson in autumn. Creamy white flowers in summer on conical panicles, to 10 in (25 cm) long, become pinkish in autumn. **'Snow Flake'**, double flowers; **'Snow Queen'**, exceptional autumn foliage colors. Zones 5–10.

Hydrangea serrata

syn. *Hydrangea macrophylla* subsp. *serrata*

☼/◐ ❄ ↔5 ft (1.5 m) ↑3–6 ft (0.9–1.8 m)

Deciduous species from Japan and Korea, closely related to *H. macrophylla*. Flat-topped flowerheads, sterile florets of white, pink, or blue surrounding white or blue fertile flowers, in summer, color changing with age. **'Bluebird'**, neat shrub with lacecap flowers of pale and rich blue, carried for a long time, foliage turning red in autumn; **'Grayswood'**, attractive flowerheads with bluish purple fertile flowers surrounded by sterile florets, changing color to shades of white, pink and crimson. Zones 6–10.

Hydrangea serratifolia

syn. *Hydrangea integerrima*

☼/◐ ❄ ↔7–17 ft (2–5 m) ↑up to 35 ft (10 m)

Woody deciduous climber from Chile. Clings to structures with its sticky aerial roots. Dark green serrated leaves in late spring. Clean white flowerheads in masses in mid-summer. Flowers can be tinged pink. Zones 6–9.

Hydrangea serrata 'Bluebird'

HYDRASTIS

This genus, a member of the buttercup (Ranunculaceae) family, contains only 2 species of low-growing perennial herbs, one native to Japan and the other to eastern North America. The North American species is often grown for the medicinal properties of its roots, and Native Americans used it as a dye. CULTIVATION: It grows best in conditions similar to its natural habitat—the forest floor. Give it a shady position with rich moist soil that has been enriched with leafmold. Add more leafmold or similar organic matter every year. Propagate from seed or by division.

Hydrastis canadensis

EYE ROOT, GOLDENSEAL, GROUND RASPBERRY, INDIAN DYE, JAUNDICE ROOT, ORANGEROOT, TURMERIC, YELLOW PUCCOON

↔ 8 in (20 cm) ↑ 12 in (30 cm)

This perennial woodland herb comes from eastern North America. Each of its stems carries 2 large, serrated, 5-lobed, wrinkled leaves; in spring, small white flowers bloom in the middle of the leaves, and raspberry-like fruit, in the form of a cluster of red berries, follows in summer. Listed as an endangered species. All parts are poisonous. Zones 6–8.

HYMENOCALLIS

syn. *Ismene*

SACRED LILY OF THE INCAS, SPIDER LILY

A genus of 20 or so species of bulbs and perennials from tropical and subtropical Central and South America, in the amaryllis (Amaryllidaceae) family. They are closely allied with *Ismene,* and species have at times been exchanged between the genera. The distinctive flowers have a central narcissus-like staminal cup and long, narrow, recurved, or streamer-like petals. The name comes from the Greek *hymen* (membrane) and *kallos* (beauty), referring to the membrane that unites the stamens. CULTIVATION: The group divides into deciduous and evergreen species. The deciduous ones require a dry dormancy and a sunlit or semi-shaded position, whereas the evergreen species, which have clivia-like leaves, thrive in damp, fertile, shaded soil. Plant with the bulb's neck protruding. Propagation is from offsets or fresh ripe seed. Clumps can be divided in winter.

Hymenocallis littoralis

Hymenocallis × *festalis*

↔ 12–24 in (30–60 cm)
↑ 24–32 in (60–80 cm)

Common in horticulture. Up to 4 flowers at right angles to the stout stem, pure white, fragrant, cup with spidery swept-back outer segments, in late spring in seasonal climates, otherwise spasmodic. Stamens golden. Leaves clump-forming, deciduous, dark green, long and broad. Zones 9–11.

Hymenocallis littoralis

syn. *Hymenocallis americana*

↔ 30–60 in (75–150 cm)
↑ 27–36 in (70–90 cm)

From Central and South America. Flowers 4 to 8 borne in umbel; white, long-tapering streamer-like reflexed petals surround a flattened cup. Leaves evergreen, 48 in (120 cm) long, semi-erect, clump-forming, fleshy, tapering at both ends, bright green. 'Variegata', bright green central stripe on leaves margined with cream. Zones 10–12.

Hymenocallis narcissiflora

SACRED FLOWER OF THE INCAS

↔ 12–24 in (30–60 cm)
↑ 20–24 in (50–60 cm)

From the Peruvian Andes, growing in stony fields to 9,840 ft (3,000 m) above sea level. Flower a long daffodil-like cup, filaments stand out like aeroplane propellers, very fragrant, white with touches of green, held well above foliage. Flower stem emerges from 12 in (30 cm) false stem. Leaves deciduous, strap-like. 'Advance', slightly elongated cup lobes, robust, pure white version of species. Zones 9–11.

Hymenocallis speciosa

Hymenocallis speciosa

↔ 12–24 in (30–60 cm)
↑ 18–20 in (45–50 cm)

From the West Indies. Flowers white, fragrant, open umbels, filaments splayed outward. Anthers protruding, golden. Broad leaves evergreen, glossy, to 24 in (60 cm) long. Zones 10–12.

Hymenocallis 'Sulphur Queen'

↔ 12–20 in (30–50 cm)
↑ 20–24 in (50–60 cm)

Scented hybrid cultivar. Cross between yellow-flowering Peruvian *I. amancaes* and *I. narcissiflora.* Narrow leaves to 20 in (50 cm) long. Very large primrose yellow cup and white filaments. Zones 9–11.

HYMENOSPORUM

Consisting of a single evergreen tree species, this genus in the pittosporum (Pittosporaceae) family is from subtropical areas of Australia's east coast where grows in rainforests. Cultivated for many years for its creamy white flowers, which turn yellow as they age, it is a slender, often open tree with mid-green shiny foliage. CULTIVATION: Although it prefers a spot in full sun, *Hymenosporum* can grow in part-shade but may not flower as profusely. Moist humus-enriched soil will suit this plant as it does not like to be deprived of moisture when conditions are dry. Propagate from seed or cuttings.

Hymenosporum flavum

NATIVE FRANGIPANI

↔ 12 ft (3.5 m) ↑ 30 ft (9 m)

Slender tree. Light foliage coverage, widely spaced horizontal branches bearing shiny deep green leaves. Fragrant cream blossoms ageing to yellow, in spring. Zones 9–11.

HYMENOXYS

BITTERWEED

This North America genus in the daisy (Asteraceae) family contains 28 species of perennials. The genus is closely related to *Helenium,* and several species were formerly placed there. Plants of open, dry areas and prairies, they range from small rosettes to erect plants over 3 ft (0.9 m) tall, with foliage that can be pinnate, linear, or broader and lance-shaped, usually covered with fine hairs. Yellow flowerheads appear in summer to autumn and can be showy. CULTIVATION: The cultivated species are easily grown in any sunny position with light, well-drained soil. Most are very hardy and require no more care than deadheading and cutting back in early winter. Propagation is from seed or by the division of established clumps, and in some cases from basal cuttings.

Hymenoxys hoopesii

syn. *Helenium hoopesii*

↔ 40 in (100 cm) ↑ 40 in (100 cm)

Native to southwestern quarter of USA. Narrow lower leaves up to 12 in (30 cm) long, upper leaves lance-shaped and smaller. Flowerheads to 3 in (8 cm) wide with up to 21 orange ray florets held horizontally. Zones 3–9.

Hymenosporum flavum

HYPERICUM

This group of over 400 species of deciduous and evergreen annuals, herbaceous perennials, shrubs, and trees makes up the type genus for the St. John's-wort (Hypericaceae) family. They occur worldwide in various habitats, and have simple smooth-edged leaves in opposite pairs and usually yellow 5-petalled flowers with a central bunch of many stamens. Some are used locally as medicinal plants. CULTIVATION: Most will thrive in sun or partial shade in good garden soil. *H. calycinum* takes root along its prostrate branches in dry shade, but also does well in partial shade. *H. olympicum* is a good rock-garden plant, and needs sharp drainage. Most North American species prefer damper conditions. Evergreen species are best sheltered from cold drying winds. Propagate by sowing seed in autumn, though seed may not come true. Take softwood cuttings in spring, half-hardened cuttings in summer.

Hypericum androsaemum

TUTSAN

↔3 ft (0.9 m) ↕30 in (75 cm)

Native to western, southwestern Europe, the Mediterranean to the Caucasus. Deciduous shrub, leaves oblong to broadly egg-shaped, mid-green above, paler below. Star-shaped yellow flowers, mid-summer–autumn. Fruits ripen to red and black. Used for cut flowers. Invasive weed in Australia and New Zealand. ***H. a.* f. *variegatum***, variegated pink and white foliage; ***H. a.* 'Albury Purple'**, purple-tinged leaves; **'Dart's Golden Penny'**, bright yellow flowers, long stamens. Zones 6–9.

Hypericum ascyron

syn. ***Hypericum pyramidatum***

GIANT ST JOHN'S WORT, GREAT ST JOHN'S WORT

↔12–30 in (30–75 cm) ↕2–5 ft (0.6–1.5 m)

Native of Asia, Russia, and northeastern North America. Variable perennial with shiny pointed leaves, paler beneath. Starry bright yellow flowers, to 3 in (8 cm) wide, have very prominent stamens. Summer flowering. Zones 3–9.

Hypericum androsaemum

Hypericum beanii

↔6 ft (1.8 m) ↕2–6 ft (0.6–1.8 m)

Native to Yunnan and Guizhou Provinces in China. Vigorous, evergreen bushy shrub. Mid-green leaves, elliptic to lance-shaped, with pale undersides. Golden yellow flowers, bowl- to star-shaped, in summer. Zones 7–10.

Hypericum calycinum

AARON'S BEARD, CREEPING ST JOHN'S WORT, ROSE OF SHARON

↔5 ft (1.5 m) ↕8–24 in (20–60 cm)

Native to parts of Bulgaria and Turkey. Evergreen or semi-evergreen shrub, rooting branches. Elliptic or oblong leaves, dark green above, paler below. Bright yellow flowers, from mid-summer to autumn. Flowers better in light shade—a good ground cover plant for dry shade. Zones 6–9.

Hypericum cerastoides

syn. ***Hypericum rhodoppeum***

↔18 in (45 cm) ↕6–12 in (15–30 cm)

From southern Bulgaria, Greece, and Turkey. Variable perennial, erect or forming loose mats. Small oblong leaves, slightly hairy. Open golden yellow flowers 1 in (25 mm) wide, in summer. Zones 7–10.

Hypericum empetrifolium

↔3 ft (0.9 m) ↕2 ft (0.6 m)

Native to southeastern Europe, Turkey, and Libya. Dwarf, cushion-forming evergreen shrub. Narrow leaves mid-green in whorls of 3. Cylindrical cymes of up to 40 golden yellow star-shaped flowers, in summer. ***H. e.* subsp. *oliganthum*** (syn. *H. e.* var. *prostratum* of gardens), 2 in (5 cm) tall with cymes of 4 to 7 deep yellow flowers. Zones 8–9.

Hypericum 'Hidcote'

↔4 ft (1.2 m) ↕4 ft (1.2 m)

Likely cross between *H.* × *cyathiflorum* 'Gold Cup' and *H. calycinum*. Dense evergreen or semi-evergreen shrub. Leaves dark green, lance-shaped. Large, bowl-shaped, deep yellow flowers, summer–autumn. Zones 7–10.

Hypericum × *inodorum*

↔4 ft (1.2 m) ↕2–7 ft (0.6–2 m)

Natural hybrid between *H. androsaemum* and *H. hircinum* from northwestern Mediterranean. Deciduous shrub, 1–4 in (2.5–10 cm) long, ovate to lance-shaped leaves. Scentless flowers to 1 in (25 mm) wide. Zones 8–10.

Hypericum ascyron

Hypericum calycinum

Hypericum cerastioides

Hypericum kouytchense

syns ***Hypericum grandiflorum*, *H. patulum* var. *grandiflorum***

↔4 ft (1.2 m) ↕6 ft (1.8 m)

From Guizhou Province, China. Semi-evergreen. Leaves dark blue-green. Cymes of up to 11 star-shaped golden yellow flowers, in summer. Red fruit. Showy stamens. Zones 6–10.

Hypericum × *moserianum*

↔24–32 in (60–80 cm) ↕12–16 in (30–40 cm)

Attractive, arching, semi-deciduous garden hybrid with lance-shaped leaves to 2 in (5 cm) long and yellow flowers to 2½ in (6 cm) across throughout summer and autumn. Usually grown in variegated form **'Tricolor'**, which has green leaves broadly edged with yellow and stained pink. Zones 7–10.

Hypericum olympicum

↔15 in (38 cm) ↕10 in (25 cm)

Native to Greece and the southern Balkans. Dwarf deciduous shrub. Oblong, elliptic gray-green leaves, glaucous undersides. Cymes of 5 golden yellow star-shaped flowers, in summer. ***H. o.* f. *uniflorum* 'Citrinum'** has pale citron flowers. Zones 6–10.

Hypericum prolificum

↔5 ft (1.5 m) ↕6 ft (1.8 m)

Loosely branched shrub from central and eastern USA and southern Canada. Leaves narrow, oblong, elliptical or lance-shaped, leaf edges sometimes recurved, undersides, pale waxy bloom. Golden yellow flowers, in summer. Zones 4–9.

Hypericum olympicum

Hypericum 'Hidcote'

Hypericum pseudohenryi

☼ ✱ ↔ 6 ft (1.8 m) ↑ 5 ft (1.5 m)

Native to north Yunnan and central Sichuan Provinces in China. Erect or arching stems. Leaves paler green undersides, with a white bloom. Golden yellow star-shaped flowers, in summer. Young fruit is red. Zones 6–9.

Hypericum 'Rowallane'

☼ ❄ ↔ 4 ft (1.2 m) ↑ 6 ft (1.8 m)

Semi-evergreen shrub, believed to be a chance hybrid between *H. leschenaultii* and *H. hookerianum* 'Charles Rogers'. Leaves egg-shaped, oblong to lance-shaped, dark green above, paler green and crinkly underneath. Rich golden flowers in small cymes, late summer–autumn. Zones 8–10.

HYPOESTES

An acanthus (Acanthaceae) family genus of 40 perennials, subshrubs and shrubs from open woodland regions of Africa, Madagascar, Arabia, tropical Asia, and Australasia. Some decoratively foliaged species are used as indoor plants or grown as annuals in cooler areas; others are valued for their autumn flowers. Evergreen, the leaves are held opposite on upright stems and in some species are velvety to touch. CULTIVATION: Grow in humus-rich well-drained soil. Water freely in summer but keep drier in the cold months when growth is not apparent. These plants do well in part-shade with protection from drying winds. Propagate in spring from seed, or from stem cuttings taken from spring to summer.

Hypoestes aristata

RIBBON BUSH

◐ ❄ ↔ 26 in (65 cm) ↑ 3 ft (0.9 m)

From southern Africa. Evergreen shrubby plant, upright stems. Downy mid-green leaves. Masses of small purple flowers in the upper leaf axils, in autumn. Zones 9–11.

Hypoestes phyllostachya

POLKA-DOT PLANT

◐ ❄ ↔ 30 in (75 cm) ↑ 3 ft (0.9 m)

From Madagascar. Subshrub grown for its pink-speckled green leaves, widely used as an indoor plant in cold areas. Soft tender stems, becoming woody near the base. Tip pruning ensures a well-covered bushy plant. '**Splash**', larger pink markings. Zones 10–12.

HYSSOPUS

This genus in the mint (Lamiaceae) family contains about 10 species of perennials or small shrubs. The opposite leaves are lance-shaped and aromatic. Rather sparse flower spikes bear the 2-lipped tubular flowers. *H. officinalis* has in the past been used in asthma and bronchitis remedies. CULTIVATION: Grow in well-drained soil in a sunny situation. *H. officinalis* can be used as a low hedge. Pinch growing tips to encourage bushiness. Propagate from seed or cuttings.

Hyssopus officinalis

HYSSOP

☼ ✱ ↔ 12 in (30 cm)
↑ 18–24 in (45–60 cm)

From southern and eastern Europe. Naturalized in USA. Variable shrubby perennial with aromatic foliage. Violet to blue flowers carried on thin spikes in late summer. '**Sissinghurst**' has a dwarf, compact habit. Zones 3–10.

HYSTRIX

This genus, of the grass (Poaceae) family, has 9 species in Asia, North America, and New Zealand. These tall upright grasses adapt to a wide range of conditions but do best in part to complete shade. They bloom in early to late summer, and their straw-colored seed heads give summer and autumn interest to a woodland garden. They also mix well with spring ephemerals, filling in when they go dormant. *Hystrix* in Greek means hedgehog or porcupine—the seed heads are said to resemble their quills.
CULTIVATION: Grow in dry to medium moist soil in half-sun to shade. They prefer a sandy loamy soil, though will tolerate a wide variety of soils. They are easily grown from seed and will self-seed in optimum growing conditions.

Hystrix patula

BOTTLEBRUSH GRASS

◐/✱ ✱ ↔ 12 in (30 cm)
↑ 24–60 in (60–150 cm)

From North America. Perennial woodland grass that produces lovely seed heads, which resemble a bottlebrush. Seed heads are green maturing to brown, and are retained well into autumn. Zones 3–9.

Hypoestes phyllostachya

Hypoestes aristata

Hyssopus officinalis 'Sissinghurst'

I

IBERIS

CANDYTUFT

Popular for the bold effect of their massed heads of white, pink, mauve, or purple flowers, the 30-odd annuals, perennials, and subshrubs in this genus in the cabbage (Brassicaceae) family are found from western and southern Europe to western Asia. They usually have simple, small, narrow leaves; when not flowering they form a rounded bush. Their flowerheads open in summer, on short stems holding them clear of the foliage. *Iberis* refers to Iberia, the Roman name for Spain; candytuft means "the tufted plant from Candia," a former name for the island of Crete.

CULTIVATION: Plant in a sunny position with light yet moist, well-drained soil. A light dressing of dolomite lime is appreciated. Deadhead regularly to encourage continuous blooming. Propagate the annuals from seed and the perennials and subshrubs from seed or small cuttings.

Iberis amara

ANNUAL CANDYTUFT

☼/◐ ❄ ↔ 12–20 in (30–50 cm) ↕ 12 in (30 cm)

Western European summer-flowering annual. Small, lance-shaped, sometimes toothed leaves often hidden under massed heads of white, pink, or purple flowers. Sow in succession as blooms are not always long-lasting. Zones 7–11.

Iberis gibraltarica

GIBRALTAR CANDYTUFT

☼/◐ ❄ ↔ 20–24 in (50–60 cm) ↕ 12 in (30 cm)

Evergreen summer-flowering subshrub from Gibraltar. Forms a neat mound of narrow stems with rosettes of small leaves at tips. Heads of white, lavender, or pink-tinted flowers. May be used as annual. Zones 7–10.

Iberis saxatilis

☼/◐ ❄ ↔ 12–20 in (30–50 cm) ↕ 6 in (15 cm)

Small, spreading, evergreen subshrub found from the Pyrenees to Sicily. It has narrow, fleshy, rather succulent leaves, fringed with fine hairs. The heads of white flowers, purple-tinted with age, appear in summer. ***I. s.* subsp. *cinerea*** has silver-gray foliage and stems. Zones 7–10.

Iberis sempervirens

☼/◐ ❄ ↔ 20–24 in (50–60 cm) ↕ 12 in (30 cm)

Spreading evergreen subshrub from southern Europe with small oblong leaves, mainly clustered at stem tips. Flowerheads to 2 in (5 cm) wide, usually white, from spring–summer. **'Flore-Plena'**, compact habit, double flowers; **'Purity'**, to 8 in (20 cm) high; **Snowflake/'Schneeflocke'** ★, low-growing, dark foliage, glowing silvery white flowers; **'Weisser Zwerg'** (syn. 'Little Gem'), compact habit, 6 in (15 cm) high, early white flowers. Zones 7–10.

Iberis sempervirens

Iberis umbellata

☼/◐ ❄ ↔ 16 in (40 cm) ↕ 12 in (30 cm)

Annual from southern Europe. The very narrow lance-shaped leaves are sometimes toothed. Produces purple flowers from spring–summer. The flower colors of **Flash Series** include white, all shades of pink, mauve, red, and purple. Grow from autumn-sown seed in mild areas; summer annual elsewhere. Zones 7–10.

Iberis gibraltarica

ILEX

HOLLY

Widely distributed genus, belonging to the holly (Aquifoliaceae) family, and containing more than 400 species of evergreen or deciduous trees, shrubs, and climbers. Used for its foliage and berries since Roman times, holly has long been associated with Northern Hemisphere festivals celebrating the winter solstice and Christmas. Wood of some species is used for veneers and musical instruments; leaves are used as tea substitutes or in tisanes. Male and female flowers usually grow on separate trees, thus plants of both sexes are required for the production of berries.

CULTIVATION: North American hollies prefer neutral to acid soils, while the Asian and European species will grow in most soils that are moderately fertile, well drained, and humus-rich. Green hollies will also grow in part- or full shade (but not deep shade). Variegated hollies require a position in full sun for best effect. Propagate from half-hardened cuttings in late summer or early autumn. Seed germination may take 2 or 3 years. Tender species need greenhouse protection in winter in colder climates.

Ilex aquifolium 'Aurea Marginata'

Ilex cassine

Ilex decidua

Ilex aquifolium

COMMON HOLLY, ENGLISH HOLLY

↔ 25 ft (8 m) ↑ 40–80 ft (12–24 m)

Occurs over southern and western Europe, North Africa, and western Asia. Glossy dark green leaves, elliptic, spine-toothed edges. The male and female flowers usually borne on separate trees. Berries red, sometimes yellow or orange. The cultivars include: 'Amber', a female cultivar, to 20 ft (6 m) tall, bright green leaves, amber berries; **'Argentea Marginata'**, a female cultivar, with dark green leaves edged in creamy white; **'Argentea Marginata Pendula'** (syn. 'Argentea Pendula'), a weeping female tree with spiny, cream-margined, elliptic leaves; **'Ferox Argentea'**, spiny leaves with cream margins; **'Handsworth New Silver'**, a female clone, with elongated, spiny, cream-edged leaves, dark purple stems; **'J. C. van Tol'**, a broad female tree, with dark green leaves, and scarlet berries; **'Madame Briot'**, a vigorous female form, which has egg-shaped dark green leaves with gold margins, and vivid red fruit; **'Pyramidalis'**, a self-fertile cultivar, yellowish green stems, and spiny bright green leaves; **'Pyramidalis Fructu Luteo'**, a female conical shrub or small tree, with yellow berries; **'Silver Milkmaid'**, a female cultivar, pale green to yellow stems, spiny mid-green leaves with silver-white markings. Other popular cultivars include: **'Aurifodina'**, **'Bacciflava'**, **'Gold Flash'**, **'Golden Milkboy'**, and **'Silver Queen'**. Zones 6–10.

Ilex × *aquipernyi*

↔ 12 ft (3.5 m) ↑ 20 ft (6 m)

Evergreen tree or shrub of garden origin, hybrid between *I. aquifolium* and *I. pernyi*. Elongated glossy green leaves, strong spines. Red berries. **'San Jose'** ★, female form, green leaves with up to 9 spines. Red fruit. Zones 6–10.

Ilex × *attenuata*

TOPAL HOLLY

↔ 6 ft (1.8 m) ↑ 12 ft (3.5 m)

Evergreen conical shrub, natural hybrid between *I. cassine* and *I. opaca*. Light green, egg- to lance-shaped leaves, dark red berries. **'East Palatka'**, female tree, pyramidal, light green leaves with single spine at tip, red berries; **'Foster No. 2'**, heavy fruiting female, conical habit, small dark green leaves, spine at tip, red berries; **'Sunny Foster'**, slow-growing female, narrow in habit, some golden yellow leaves, bright red berries. Zones 7–10.

Ilex cassine

DAHOON HOLLY

↔ 15 ft (4.5 m) ↑ 40 ft (12 m)

Evergreen tree, native to Cuba and southeastern USA. Pointed or rounded, glossy, dark green leaves with pronounced midrib, leaf edges smooth or toothed near the apex. Yellow or red berries. Zones 6–10.

Ilex ciliospinosa

↔ 12 ft (3.5 m) ↑ 20 ft (6 m)

Evergreen upright shrub, native to western China. Narrow, pointed, dull dark green leaves, weakly spined. Red berries. Zones 5–9.

Ilex cornuta

CHINESE HOLLY, HORNED HOLLY

↔ 6–12 ft (1.8–3.5 m)
↑ 6–12 ft (1.8–3.5 m)

Native to China and Korea. A dense, evergreen, rounded shrub. Oblong dark green leaves, variable spines. Large red berries, long-lasting. **'Burfordii'**, free-fruiting, female form, red berries, leaves with terminal spines; **'Dwarf Burford'**, to 8 ft (2.4 m) high, dense habit, dark red berries. Zones 6–10.

Ilex crenata

JAPANESE HOLLY

↔ 12 ft (3.5 m) ↑ 15 ft (4.5 m)

Evergreen shrub or small tree from Korea, Japan, and Sakhalin Island. Small deep green leaves, minutely scalloped. Flowers white; fruit mainly glossy black, sometimes white or yellow. **'Convexa'** (syn. 'Bullata'), female, purple-green stems, abundant black fruit; **'Golden Gem'**, compact female, to 3 ft (0.9 m) high, golden yellow leaves, prefers full sun; **'Helleri'**, spreading female shrub, dark green leaves, black fruit; **'Ivory Tower'**, female, late-ripening white fruit; **'Mariesii'** (syns *I. c.* var. *nummularioides*, *I. mariesii*), very slow growing, dark green leaves, black fruit; **'Shiro Fukurin'** (syns 'Fukarin', 'Snow Flake'), upright female, rounded leaves with cream markings, black fruit; and **'Sky Pencil'**, narrowly columnar female. Zones 6–10.

Ilex decidua

POSSUMHAW, WINTERBERRY

↔ 6–15 ft (1.8–4.5 m)
↑ 6–20 ft (1.8–6 m)

Native to southeastern and central USA. Upright deciduous shrub, rarely a tree. Mid-green leaves, sprout in late spring, oval or egg-shaped, scalloped, crowded on short lateral spurs. Berries orange or red, sometimes yellow, last well into winter. Zones 6–10.

Ilex glabra

GALLBERRY, INKBERRY

↔ 10 ft (3 m) ↑ 10 ft (3 m)

Erect evergreen shrub from eastern North America. Glossy dark green leaves, almost smooth-edged, slightly toothed near the apex. Berries round, black. Shallow rooting. ***I. g.* f. *leucocarpa*** bears white fruit; **'Ivory Queen'** is a popular form. ***I. g.* 'Compacta'** ★, to 4 ft (1.2 m) high, denser foliage than species, black berries. Zones 3–10.

Ilex × *koehneana*

↔ 12 ft (3.5 m) ↑ 20 ft (6 m)

Evergreen shrub or tree, hybrid between *I. aquifolium* and *I. latifolia*. Strongly resembles *I. latifolia*, but more spiny; sometimes wrongly sold as that plant. Zones 7–10.

Ilex × *koehneana*

Ilex latifolia

TARAJO

↔ 12 ft (3.5 m) ↑ 20 ft (6 m)

Evergreen narrow shrub from Japan and China. Glossy dark green leaves, oblong to egg-shaped, smooth-edged or toothed with spines. Flowers greenish yellow, in late spring. Orange-red berries. Zones 7–9.

Ilex × *meserveae*

BLUE HOLLY, HYBRID BLUE HOLLY, MESERVE HOLLY

↔ 10 ft (3 m) ↑ 6–15 ft (1.8–4.5 m)

Of garden origin, a hybrid between *I. aquifolium* and *I. rugosa*. The small, often blue-green are leaves similar to those of *I. aquifolium* but smaller. The red berries are borne on female plants. **'Blue Angel'** is a compact female shrub, slow-growing, to 12 ft (3.5 m) high, with royal purple stems, and blue-green leaves; it is least hardy; **'Blue Boy'**, male, grows up to 10 ft (3 m) high; **'Blue Girl'** is female and produces red berries; **'Blue Maid'** is a dense female shrub with red berries; **'Blue Prince'**, male shrub with lustrous bright green leaves; **'Blue Princess'**, female shrub with prolific red berries. Zones 6–10.

Ilex glabra f. *leucocarpa* 'Ivory Queen'

Ilex opaca 'Old Faithful'

Ilex montana

↔ 10 ft (3 m) ↑ 40 ft (12 m)

Native to eastern USA. Deciduous shrub or small tree. Leaves sharply toothed, lance to egg-shaped. Bears white flowers, red berries. ***I. m.* var. *mollis***, leaves with hairy undersides. Zones 5–9.

Ilex opaca

AMERICAN HOLLY

↔ 35 ft (10 m) ↑ 50 ft (15 m)

From USA. Leaves oblong to elliptic, smooth-edged or spiny, matt green above, yellow-green beneath. White flowers. Red, orange, or yellow berries. ***I. o.* f. *xanthocarpa***, yellow berries. ***I. o.* 'Hedgeholly'**, hardy, compact; **'Morgan Gold'**, golden fruit; **'Old Faithful'**, large berries; less hardy. Zones 5–9.

Ilex pedunculosa

↔ 20 ft (6 m) ↑ 30 ft (9 m)

Evergreen tree found in China, Japan, and Taiwan. The glossy dark green leaves are egg-shaped with pointed tips, smooth-edged and spineless. This species bears white flowers and red fruits. Zones 5–9.

Ilex pernyi

PERNY'S HOLLY

↔ 12 ft (3.5 m) ↑ 30 ft (9 m)

From Gansu and Hubei Provinces in China. Evergreen shrub, smaller in cultivation. Almost stalkless, dark green leaves, triangular to rectangular. Yellow flowers, in late spring, Red berries. Prefers a moisture-retentive soil. Zones 5–10.

Ilex serrata

FINETOOTH HOLLY, JAPANESE WINTERBERRY

↔ 10 ft (3 m) ↑ 15 ft (4.5 m)

Native to Japan and China. Bushy deciduous shrub, purple new twigs. Finely toothed, oval, dark green leaves, downy coating on both surfaces. Pink flowers, small red berries. Zones 5–10.

Ilex verticillata

BLACK ALDER, WINTERBERRY

↔ 15 ft (4.5 m) ↑ 15 ft (4.5 m)

Deciduous shrub from eastern North America. Bright green leaves, obovate or lance-shaped, toothed, fine downy undersides. White flowers, red, yellow, or orange berries. ***I. v.* f. *aurantiaca***, orange berries. ***I. v.* 'Afterglow'**, female shrub, orange-red berries; **'Nana'** (syn. 'Red Sprite'), female shrub, needs early-flowering male for pollination; **'Winter Red'** ★, female shrub, dark green leaves, red berries. Zones 3–9.

Ilex pedunculosa

Ilex vomitoria 'Pendula'

Ilex vomitoria

CAROLINA TEA, YAUPON

↔ 12 ft (3.5 m) ↑ 20 ft (6 m)

Evergreen shrub or small tree, native to southeastern USA and Mexico. Glossy dark green leaves, elliptic to egg-shaped, scalloped edges. White flowers, red berries. **'Nana'**, to 3 ft (0.9 m) high; **'Pendula'**, lax branches, clear red fruit. Zones 6–10.

Ilex Hybrid Cultivars

↔ 5–15 ft (1.5–4.5 m) ↑ 8–20 ft (2.4–6 m)

Hollies have been extensively hybridized over the years. Some of the best cultivars available are: **'China Boy'**, very hardy male pollinator, grows quickly to 8 ft (2.4 m) tall; **'China Girl'**, very hardy, female, evergreen shrub, masses of bright red berries; **'Ebony Magic'**, female clone, evergreen leaves with a wavy margin and up to 22 spines, leaf stems almost black, orange-red berries; **'John T. Morris'**, male form, dark evergreen foliage, a good pollinator; **'Nellie R. Stevens'**, evergreen female, orange-red berries; **'September Gem'**, female evergreen hybrid, narrow dark green leaves, red berries; and **'Sparkleberry'**, deciduous female shrub, bright red berries. Zones 6–10.

ILLICIUM

This genus of over 40 evergreen shrubs and trees in the star-vine (Schisandraceae) family is found in moist shaded areas of India, East Asia, and the Americas. Leaves and flowers are fragrant, and members of the genus supply aromatic oils used in some perfumes. *I. verum* is the source of the Chinese spice, star-anise. These trees were originally included in the same genus as magnolias because of their resemblance to them. Flowers range in color from cream to reddish purple and are followed by star-shaped fruit. Leaves are deep green. The genus name comes from the Latin for "allurement," in reference to the perfume of some species.

Illicium floridanum

CULTIVATION: *Illicium* species will survive in full sun but do best in a sheltered position out of direct sunlight, in a moist, well-drained, acid soil. Propagate from half-hardened cuttings taken in summer or by layering in autumn.

Illicium anisatum

ANISE SHRUB, JAPANESE ANISE, JAPANESE STAR-ANISE

↔ 20 ft (6 m) ↑ 25 ft (8 m)

Conical evergreen shrub from China, Taiwan, and Japan. Aromatic wood, leaves, and bark. Greenish yellow flowers, in mid-spring. Woody fruits are poisonous; the alkaloid concentrated in the seed has been used to kill fish. Variegated form available. Zones 7–11.

Illicium anisatum

Illicium floridanum

syn. *Illicium mexicanum*

FLORIDA ANISE TREE, POLECAT TREE, PURPLE ANISE

↔8 ft (2.4 m) ↑10 ft (3 m)

Aromatic, bushy, evergreen shrub from southeastern States of USA. Slightly furrowed, smooth, dark brown trunk. Slender, leathery, deep green leaves. Showy, star-shaped, reddish purple flowers, from late spring–early summer. **'Album'**, white flowers; **'Halley's Comet'**, large red flowers; **'Variegatum'**, variegated leaves; **'Woodland Ruby'** ★, reddish pink flowers. Zones 8–11.

Illicium henryi

↔10 ft (3 m) ↑25 ft (8 m)

Native of central and western China. Evergreen shrub or small tree. Slender leaves, 6 in (15 cm) long. Cupped flowers, copper to dark red, in late spring. Zones 8–11.

Illicium parviflorum

↔7–10 ft (2–3 m) ↑7–10 ft (2–3 m)

North American species. Foliage strongly scented, bright green. Inconspicuous yellow flowers, about ½ in (12 mm) across. Zones 7–10.

IMPATIENS

BALSAM, BUSY LIZZIE, WATER FUCHSIA

The type genus giving its name to the balsam (Balsaminaceae) family is home to around 850 species of annuals, perennials, and subshrubs found worldwide except in Australasia, South America, and the polar regions. These are generally soft-stemmed plants with simple, pointed, lance-shaped leaves, often with toothed edges. Flowers in many colors appear through the year in mild areas and have 5 petals, an upper standard and the lower 4 fused into 2 pairs, the sepals also partly fused to form a spur. When ripe the seed pods explosively eject their contents at the slightest touch, hence the genus name from the Latin for "impatient." CULTIVATION: Grow the annuals as summer plants in cooler climates outside the recommended zones; perennials need mild winter conditions. Provide shade from the hottest sun and plant in deep, cool, moist, humus-rich soil. Feed well. Propagate annuals from seed, the perennials also by cuttings. Some species self-sow and are slightly invasive.

Impatiens sodenii

Impatiens balsamina

BALSAM

↔12 in (30 cm) ↑27 in (70 cm)

Vigorous upright annual from East Asia. Toothed lance-shaped leaves. Flowers to nearly 2 in (5 cm) wide, clustered, in many colors, mainly pink, mauve to red shades. Conspicuous seed pods burst when ripe. Garden seedling strains include: **Camellia-flowered Series**, large double flowers; and **Tom Thumb Series**, low-growing double-flowered. Zones 10–12.

Impatiens hawkeri

syn. *Impatiens schlechteri*

↔16–40 in (40–100 cm) ↑3–7 ft (0.9–2 m)

Shrubby, continuous-flowering, evergreen perennial from New Guinea and Solomon Islands. Heavy fleshy stems; pointed oval to lance-shaped leaves, toothed, usually red or red-tinted. Long-spurred flowers to over 3 in (8 cm) wide, white, or pink, red, and purple shades. Zones 10–12.

Impatiens New Guinea Hybrids

↔16–40 in (40–100 cm) ↑10–48 in (25–120 cm)

These are usually cultivars of *I. hawkeri* or hybrids with *I. linearifolia*. They generally resemble *I. hawkeri* but are available in many striking combinations of flower and foliage, such as: **Bonita Series**, including **Improved Quepos/'Kimpque'**, bright reddish flowers, dark red-tinted green leaves, and **Sarchi/'Kisar'**, deep magenta flowers, dark green leaves; **Celebration Series, 'Light Lavender II'**, mauve flowers and mid-green leaves; **Celebrette Hot Pink/'Balcebhopi'**, vivid magenta flowers and mid-green leaves; **Paradise Series**, including **Pascua/'Kipas'**, deep pink flowers, mid-green leaves, **Tagula/'Kigula'**, pale pink flowers with red upper petal, dark green leaves, and **Timor/'Kitim'**, deep orange-red flowers, red-tinted bright green leaves; and **'Tango'** ★, bright orange flowers, bronze-green leaves. Zones 10–12.

Impatiens Seashell Yellow/'96–009–7'

↔20 in (50 cm) ↑12 in (30 cm)

American-raised, first commercially available yellow-flowered hybrid, between *I. walleriana* and *I. auricoma*. Compact bushy habit, bright green lance-shaped leaves, yellow flowers in small clusters. **'African Queen'** is a similar cultivar. Zones 10–12.

Impatiens sodenii

↔3–7 ft (0.9–2 m) ↑3–7 ft (0.9–2 m)

Shrubby evergreen perennial from tropical east Africa. Whorls of toothed lance-shaped leaves. Long-stemmed flowers to over 2 in (5 cm) wide, in lavender and pink shades or white, in summer. Zones 10–12.

Impatiens walleriana

syns *Impatiens holstii, I. sultani*

↔8–20 in (20–50 cm) ↑8–24 in (20–60 cm)

Continuous-flowering, shrubby, evergreen, tropical east African perennial; often treated as annual. Fleshy, succulent stems; toothed lance-shaped leaves, often red-tinted. Spurred flat-faced flowers, evenly sized petals; most colors except yellow and blue. **'Blackberry Ice'**, double purple-red flowers; **Candy Box Series**, 16 in (40 cm) tall, full color range, flowers 2 in (5 cm) wide; **Carousel Mix**, rosebud doubles in wide range of colors; **Dazzler Series**, many single flowers in warm pastel shades; **Deco Series**, spreading, single flowers in all shades; **Fiesta Series**, rosebud double flowers in many shades including bicolors; **Garden Leader Series** comes in a wide range of colors; **Ice Series**, white-marked foliage, rosebud double flowers in all shades; **Merlot Series**, bright green foliage, single flowers in all colors; **Super Elfin Series**, very compact, single flowers in all shades; **Tempo Series**, large flowers, compact plants; **'Victorian Rose'**, semi-double deep pink flowers, spreading habit. Propagate double and variegated cultivars from cuttings, the rest from seed. Zones 10–12.

Impatiens, New Guinea Hybrid, Celebration Series, 'Light Lavender II'

INCARVILLEA

This group of 14 species from central and eastern Asia includes annuals and perennials, some of which are slightly woody, and belongs in the trumpet-vine (Bignoniaceae) family. Depending on which species you plant, they can make exotic-looking rock-garden or border plants. The flowers are trumpet-shaped with flared and often undulated edges, and are usually a bright pink to magenta, although yellow forms have been discovered. Most species have a long flowering period, which means that they earn their space; besides the decorative value of the flowers, the foliage is usually also attractive. CULTIVATION: Grow in moisture-retentive but not wet soils in a position sheltered from the hottest afternoon sun. Propagate from fresh seed or by careful division, although established plants resent disturbance.

I. walleriana, Fiesta Series, 'Sunrise'

Impatiens walleriana 'Victorian Rose'

Incarvillea arguta

Incarvillea arguta

↔ 12–16 in (30–40 cm)
↑ 36–40 in (90–100 cm)

Slightly shrubby species from the Himalayas and western China. Compound leaves to 8 in (20 cm) long. The flowers are rich pink, sometimes white, and trumpet-shaped, 1½ in (35 mm) long, and appear in the late spring to autumn. Zones 8–10.

Incarvillea delavayi

↔ 12–16 in (30–40 cm)
↑ 20–24 in (50–60 cm)

Rosette-forming species from western China. Long compound leaves. Up to 10 large rich pink trumpets per stem, to 3 in (8 cm) across, with a yellow throat, held above the foliage, in early to mid-summer. **'Snowtop'**, white with a yellow throat. Zones 6–9.

Incarvillea emodi

↔ 12–16 in (30–40 cm)
↑ 16–20 in (40–50 cm)

Rosette-forming perennial from Afghanistan, Pakistan, and into northern India. Large leaves; stems of deep pink trumpets with a yellow throat, each bloom 2½ in (6 cm) long. Spring-flowering. Zones 7–9.

Incarvillea emodi

Incarvillea mairei ★

↔ 10–12 in (25–30 cm)
↑ 16–20 in (40–50 cm)

Small perennial from China and Nepal. Prominent tap root, wrinkled leaves to 10 in (25 cm) long. Rich deep pink flowers with yellow and white throat, 2½ in (6 cm) across, produced in small numbers per stem. Zones 4–9.

INDIGOFERA

The source of the purple-blue dye indigo, this genus in the pea-flower subfamily of the legume (Fabaceae) family includes some 700 species of perennials, shrubs, and a few trees that are widespread in the tropics and subtropics. Foliage varies but is typically pinnate, often made up of many small leaflets. The flowers are primarily in pink, mauve, and purple shades, carried in long racemes or spikes. They usually open in summer but may occur year-round in mild climates. Small seed pods follow.
CULTIVATION: The shrubby species are usually neat bushes, often deciduous, that vary in hardiness depending on their origins. They generally grow best in full sun with light well-drained soil and ample summer moisture. If necessary, prune after flowering or in late winter. Propagate from seed or half-hardened cuttings. Many species produce suckers that can be replanted.

Indigofera amblyantha

↔ 8 ft (2.4 m) ↑ 6 ft (1.8 m)

Chinese deciduous shrub. Pinnate leaves spread widely on wiry branches, 7–11 leaflets. Racemes of pale pink to red flowers, in the leaf axils, in late spring–autumn. Zones 5–9.

Indigofera decora ★

↔ 4 ft (1.2 m) ↑ 30 in (75 cm)

Widely cultivated, deciduous, spreading, suckering shrub from China and Japan. Leaves to 8 in (20 cm) long, 25–40 leaflets. Large racemes of light pink flowers, in summer. Zones 6–10.

Indigofera decora

Indigofera heterantha

Indigofera heterantha

syn. *Indigofera gerardiana*

↔ 8 ft (2.4 m) ↑ 8 ft (2.4 m)

Deciduous shrub from northwestern Himalayas, widely cultivated species, smaller in cultivation. Densely twiggy plant, short pinnate leaves. Massed racemes of bright pink to light red flowers, in summer. Zones 7–10.

Indigofera kirilowii

↔ 3–6 ft (0.9–1.8 m)
↑ 2–5 ft (0.6–1.5 m)

Deciduous shrub found in Korea, nearby parts of China, and Kyushu, Japan. Pinnate leaves, bright green, 13 leaflets. Smothered in short racemes of rose pink flowers, in spring–early summer. Zones 5–10.

Indigofera tinctoria

↔ 6 ft (1.8 m) ↑ 6 ft (1.8 m)

Most common dye-yielding species, native of Southeast Asia, evergreen shrub. Short pinnate leaves with hairy undersides. Small racemes of pink to light red flowers with a blue keel, through most of year. Zones 10–12.

INDOCALAMUS

A genus of about 30 species of running bamboo in the grass (Poaceae) family, native to China, Japan, and south-east Asia. They have thin culms that branch up to 3 times and large leaves, the foliage in some species so heavy as to make the culms arch over towards the ground. Not commonly grown bamboos, these are elegant plants that will give a tropical look to the garden. They make excellent ground covers or fine erect specimens of pillar-like growth for shady courtyards, or understory planting to specimen trees.
CULTIVATION: The hardier species usually encountered prefer a position in half-sun with humus-rich moist soil, although they are reasonably drought tolerant once established. They spread by underground runners and can become invasive, so a trench or other root barrier may be desirable; they can also be pot grown by the truly nervous. Propagate by division in early spring.

Indocalamus tessellatus

↔ 7–20 ft (2–6 m)
↑ 3–6 ft (0.9–1.8 m)

From central China and Japan. This species has the largest leaves of any hardy bamboo, up to 24 in (60 cm) long by 4 in (10 cm) wide. Arching culms, ½–1 in (12–25 mm) in diameter, give a mound-like habit. ***I. t.* var. *hamadae***, from Japan, to 10 ft (3 m) high, thicker foliage. Zones 8–10.

INULA

Members of this large genus in the daisy (Asteraceae) family are found in a wide range of habitats, from dry mountainsides to moist shaded sites, from Europe through to subtropical Africa and Asia. Most are herbaceous perennials, with some biennials and annuals, the perennial species being those most commonly grown. Some can be invasive. The basal leaves tend to be largest, the leaves reducing in size towards the top of the stems. All have yellow daisy flowers produced mainly in summer. *I. helenium* is often grown in herb gardens for its medicinal properties.
CULTIVATION: Despite the range of habitats from which they originate, most species like a sunny aspect and rich moist soil. The dwarf species are suited to the larger rock garden, while the taller species can be planted in the wilder parts of the garden or amongst other perennials in the border. Propagation is from seed or by division.

Inula helenium

Inula ensifolia

☼ ✱ ↔10–12 in (25–30 cm)
↑16–24 in (40–60 cm)

Bushy, clumping, thin-stemmed perennial from the Caucasus region. Narrow, stalkless, mid-green, bristly leaves, to 4 in (10 cm) long. Masses of yellow daisy flowers. Zones 5–10.

Inula helenium

ELECAMPANE

☼/◐ ✱ ↔3–4 ft (0.9–1.2 m)
↑8–10 ft (2.4–3 m)

Tall, robust, somewhat invasive species from temperate Eurasia. Roots used to make an expectorant. Large hairy lower leaves, to 27 in (70 cm) long, serrated and undulating edges. Spikes of yellow daisy flowers. Zones 5–10.

Inula hookeri

☼ ✱ ↔20–24 in (50–60 cm)
↑24–30 in (60–75 cm)

Clump-forming herbaceous perennial from the Himalayas. Bright green lance-shaped leaves, to 6 in (15 cm) long. Yellow daisy flowers, to 3 in (8 cm) across. Zones 6–10.

Inula magnifica

syn. *Inula afghanica*

☼ ✱ ↔3–5 ft (0.9–1.5 m)
↑5–6 ft (1.5–1.8 m)

Robust, impressive, herbaceous perennial from Caucasus region. Large, deep green, basal leaves, to 10 in (25 cm) long, hairy beneath. Large open clusters of yellow daisies. Zones 6–10.

Inula orientalis

syn. *Inula grandiflora*

☼ ✱ ↔36–40 in (90–100 cm)
↑20–24 in (50–60 cm)

Almost shrubby species from Caucasus region. Smooth-edged leaves, to 5 in (12 cm) long, yellow to brown hairs, densely covered in minute glands. Yellow daisy flowers, to 3 in (8 cm) across. Zones 6–10.

IOCHROMA

These large-leafed evergreen shrubs from Central America and Andean South America have a rather lax habit with long brittle branches. Although there are around 15 species within this genus, only 5 or 6 are generally used in horticulture. The soft foliage of most species is a downy mid-green. In common with other members of the nightshade (Solanaceae) family, the late summer flowers, usually held in clusters of drooping tubular blooms, are in shades of purple, orange, red, or white.

CULTIVATION: These plants need a sunny position with wind protection to ensure their quick-growing soft-stemmed branches are not damaged. Plant in well-drained moisture-retentive soil and ensure they are given ample water during summer. Suitable for pot culture in cooler areas. They can be pruned to shape in early spring without undue loss of blossom. Propagate from cuttings or seed.

Iochroma australe

☼ ❄ ↔7–10 ft (2–3 m)
↑10–15 ft (3–4.5 m)

More or less evergreen shrub from northern Argentina. Leaves to 4 in (10 cm) long. Rich purple-blue, drooping, flared, trumpet-shaped flowers, to 2½ in (6 cm) long, throughout summer–autumn. Zones 8–11.

Iochroma grandiflorum

☼ ❄ ↔6 ft (1.8 m) ↑8 ft (2.4 m)

From Ecuador. Downy green leaves. Large purple flowers, in clusters of 5 or 6, in summer–autumn. Adds an interesting dimension to the warmly sited garden. Zones 9–11.

IPHEION

In the past this genus, a member of the amaryllis (Amaryllidaceae) family, was incorporated in *Brodiaea, Triteleia,* and *Milla,* and some confusion remains in common horticulture. Some botanists have proposed *Ipheion* be merged with *Tristagma.* Native to South America, these bulbous perennials give off a strong smell of stale garlic when the leaves are bruised. The starry flowers are upward-facing and prolific.

CULTIVATION: These easy-going plants thrive in well-drained sunny situations in warm climates, but need protection against frost in cold climates. Keep just moist during dormancy. Propagate from seed in spring or from offsets taken as the foliage dies down.

Ipheion 'Alberto Castillo'

☼ ❄ ↔2 in (5 cm) ↑7–8 in (18–20 cm)

Narrow, gray-green leaves. Fragrant, large, white blooms held on strong flower stems from late winter to late spring. Zones 7–11.

Ipheion uniflorum

syns *Brodiaea uniflora, Tristagma uniflorum, Triteleia uniflora*

SPRING STAR FLOWER

☼ ❄ ↔2 in (5 cm) ↑4–8 in (10–20 cm)

From Argentina and Uruguay. Robust plant with weedy potential. Leaves mat-forming, linear, grassy, gray-green. Flowers starry, prolific, soap-scented, produced in succession over 6–8 weeks, from mid-winter to mid-spring, opening only during sunlit hours. Petals silvery mauve, palest blue, white, with a pronounced midrib. **'Froyle Mill'**, large deep purple petals; **'Wisley Blue'**, a popular pale blue form, bluish petals, darker midrib. Zones 7–11.

Iochroma australe

Ipheion 'Alberto Castillo'

Ipheion uniflorum 'Wisley Blue'

Ipomoea horsfalliae

Ipomoea lobata

I

IPOMOEA

This large and variable genus in the bindweed (Convolvulaceae) family, takes its name from the Greek word for a type of worm, because many of its members are twining climbers; others are annual or perennial herbs, shrubs, and small trees. Widely cultivated in tropical to warm-temperate areas for their showy flowers and vigorous growth, some species, including the sweet potato *(I. batatas)*, have tuberous roots used as food. Bell-shaped to tubular flowers usually open for just 1 day and appear in the leaf axils.
CULTIVATION: *Ipomoea* species prefer full sun and plenty of water in the growing season but will make the best of almost any conditions. Species other than annuals may be propagated from softwood or half-hardened cuttings in summer. Seeds are better started under glass. Make sure these plants have plenty of room and cut back after flowering. They may require support.

Ipomoea cairica

Ipomoea alba

syns *Calonyction aculeatum, Ipomoea bona-nox*

BELLE DE NUIT, MOONFLOWER

↔20–30 ft (6–9 m)
↑10–20 ft (3–6 m)

Found throughout tropical regions. Perennial climber with long-stalked heart-shaped leaves. White saucer-shaped flowers, to 6 in (15 cm) wide, open at night, fragrant. Summer-flowering. Zones 10–12.

Ipomoea batatas

KUMARA, SWEET POTATO

↔10 ft (3 m) ↑10 ft (3 m)

Native to tropical regions. Important food crop with edible tubers, usually grown as a prostrate annual. Leaves oval to heart-shaped, lobed or toothed. Tubers have purple, red, or yellow skins, orange or white flesh. **'Blackie'**, ornamental variety grown for its purple-black foliage; **'Vardaman'**, ornamental dark green foliage, flushed purple when young, orange-fleshed tubers. Zones 9–12.

Ipomoea cairica

syn. *Ipomoea palmata*

↔10 ft (3 m) ↑10 ft (3 m)

From tropical and subtropical regions. Prostrate or climbing plant with tuberous rootstock. Leaves palmately lobed. Funnel-shaped flowers of red, purple, or white, purple interior. Summer-flowering. Zones 9–12.

Ipomoea horsfalliae

CARDINAL CREEPER

↔5–10 ft (1.5–3 m)
↑15–25 ft (4.5–8 m)

Perennial twining climber from the West Indies. The palmate leaves have 3–5 lobes, to 8 in (20 cm) long. Bears large clusters of flared deep pink to purple flowers. Zones 9–12.

Ipomoea indica

syn. *Ipomoea learii*

BLUE DAWN FLOWER, MORNING GLORY

↔10–30 ft (3–9 m)
↑10–30 ft (3–9 m)

Found throughout tropical regions. Vigorous perennial climber regarded as a nuisance weed in some areas. Broadly heart-shaped leaves. Funnel-shaped flowers, produced throughout the year, open dark blue or purple, occasionally white, and fade during the day. Zones 10–12.

Ipomoea lobata

syns *Mina lobata, Quamoclit lobata*

SPANISH FLAG

↔3–6 ft (0.9–1.8 m)
↑10–15 ft (3–4.5 m)

Native to Mexico. A perennial that is often grown as an annual. Variable smooth or deeply lobed leaves. Produces racemes of small, tubular, scarlet flowers, fade to yellow, giving a two-toned effect. Summer-flowering. Zones 9–12.

IIpomoea × multifida

syn. *Ipomoea × sloteri*

CARDINAL FLOWER

↔3–6 ft (0.9–1.8 m)
↑3–10 ft (0.9–3 m)

Of garden origin; hybrid of *I. coccinea* and *I. quamoclit*. Leaves deeply divided, several linear lobes. Funnel-shaped flowers, 1–2 in (25–50 mm) wide, red with white centers, from summer to autumn. Zones 8–12.

Ipomoea nil

↔2–5 ft (0.6–1.5 m)
↑10–15 ft (3–4.5 m)

Found throughout tropical regions. Annual climber with hairy stems. Broadly oval or 3-lobed leaves. Blue funnel-shaped flowers, around 4 in (10 cm) wide, in clusters of 1–5, in summer. **'Chocolate'**, pale chocolate brown flowers; **'Scarlett O'Hara'**, red flowers. Zones 9–12.

Ipomoea purpurea

COMMON MORNING GLORY

↔5–10 ft (1.5–3 m)
↑5–10 ft (1.5–3 m)

Vigorous annual climber originally from Mexico, but now naturalized in many countries and often declared as a weed. Stems hairy, leaves whole to lobed, heart-shaped, 4 in (10 cm) wide. Flowers large, trumpet-shaped, in shades ranging from red through to pink, blue, white, and purple, opening in the morning and lasting only a day, from spring–summer. ***I. p.* var. *diversifolia***, leaves more often 3- to 5-lobed than smooth. Zones 7–11.

Ipomoea tricolor

MORNING GLORY

↔3 ft (0.9 m) ↑10 ft (3 m)

From Mexico and Central America. Annual climber with heart-shaped leaves. Wide funnel-shaped flowers that fade as the day progresses, sky blue, yellow interior base, in summer. **'Heavenly Blue'**, blue flowers, white and yellow throat; **'Minibar Rose'**, rosy crimson, white throat, variegated leaves; **'Tie Dye'**, leaves green, purple, and white. Zones 8–12.

IPOMOPSIS

This genus in the phlox (Polemoniaceae) family, contains 24 species of annuals and perennials that are native to western North America,

Iresine herbstii 'Brilliantissima'

with outlying species found in Florida and temperate South America. Leaves often form a basal rosette and are either smooth or pinnately divided. The tubular flowers, in shades of red, yellow, pink, white, or violet, are borne in loose racemes in spring and summer. CULTIVATION: In cooler climates they can be grown as temporary summer bedding or in the conservatory or greenhouse. Elsewhere, grow in full sun in fertile well-drained soil. Propagate from seed.

Ipomopsis rubra

syn. *Gilia rubra*

STANDING CYPRESS

↔ 18 in (45 cm)
↑ 3–6 ft (0.9–1.8 m)

From South Carolina, Florida and Texas, USA. Erect unbranched perennial or biennial that forms basal rosettes of thread-like leaves. Stems of tubular flowers, scarlet with speckled yellow throats, from summer to autumn. Zones 7–10.

IRESINE

BLOODLEAF

There are about 80 species of annuals, perennials, and subshrubs in this genus, which belongs to the amaranth (Amaranthaceae) family. They are native to the Americas and Australia. The simple leaves are often brilliantly colored with contrasting veins, and it is for this feature that these plants are cultivated. The spikes of small white or green flowers are of little ornamental significance. CULTIVATION: Grow outdoors all year round in tropical and subtropical areas. In cooler regions, grow outside in summer. Plant in well-drained moisture-retentive soil in full sun for best leaf coloring. Can be used in summer bedding schemes and in pots, both indoors and outdoors. Pinch growing tips to maintain bushiness. Propagate from cuttings, seed, or by division.

Iresine herbstii

BEEF PLANT, BEEF STEAK PLANT, BLOOD-LEAF

↔ 12–18 in (30–45 cm)
↑ 18–24 in (45–60 cm)

Native to Brazil. Perennial, often renewed annually in cultivation. Green, purple, or red stems. Pointed oval leaves vary in color from deep purple with pink veins to green with yellow veins. **'Aureo-reticulata'**, red stems, green, gold, and red leaves; **'Brilliantissima'**, rich crimson leaves. Zones 9–12.

IRIS

Iris is the type genus for the family Iridaceae, taking its name from the Greek goddess of the rainbow. The 300-odd species, which are divided into various sections, and scattered over the northern temperate zones, occur in bulbous, rhizomatous, and fibrous-rooted forms. The sword-shaped foliage, often arranged in fans, is sometimes variegated. The flowers have 6 petals, usually in the fleur-de-lis pattern of 3 upright standards and 3 downward-curving falls, which may be bearded, beardless, or crested, and occurring in all colors. Irises have been cultivated for a very long time, since the reign of the Egyptian pharaoh Thutmosis I, around 1500 bc. CULTIVATION: Bog irises need a sunny position at pond margins or in permanently damp soil. Woodland irises thrive in dappled sunlight with moist well-drained soil. Bearded irises need sun and should be dried off after flowering. Rockery irises require a sunny position in moist, perfectly drained, gritty soil. Propagation is usually by division when dormant, less commonly by seed.

Iris bracteata

↔ 6 in (15 cm)
↑ 8–12 in (20–30 cm)

This fleshy-stemmed beardless iris is native to Oregon and California, USA. It is dormant in winter. The plants are sparsely foliaged with thick stiff leaves. Unbranched flowering spikes with sheathing bracts. The large yellow flowers, veined with reddish maroon, appear in the early summer. Zones 7–9.

Iris brevicaulis

syns *Iris foliosa, I. lamancei*

↔ 15–20 in (38–50 cm)
↑ 15–20 in (38–50 cm)

Fleshy-stemmed beardless iris from central USA. Foliage longer than flowering stems. Large blooms, blue to violet; falls have yellow center, usually veined with white and green. Summer-flowering. Zones 7–9.

Iris bucharica

Iris ensata 'Carnival'

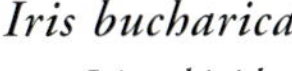

Iris bucharica

syn. *Iris orhioides*

↔ 6 in (15 cm) ↑ 18 in (45 cm)

A native of Russia and Afghanistan. Bulbous iris, which has distinctive, shiny green, channeled leaves that resemble dwarf maize. Creamy flowers, yellow-centered falls, small white standards, in the upper leaf axils, appear in spring. Zones 5–9.

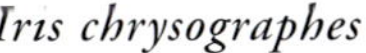

Iris chrysographes

GOLD NET IRIS, GOLD PATTERN IRIS

↔ 12 in (30 cm)
↑ 12–20 in (30–50 cm)

Fleshy-stemmed beardless iris from China, Myanmar, and Tibet. Strappy grayish green leaves. Flowers in late spring–summer, color variable to purple-black, varying amounts of gold streaks on falls. **'Black Knight'**, purple-black flowers. Zones 7–10.

Iris confusa

↔ 24 in (60 cm) ↑ 36 in (90 cm)

Vigorous, clump-forming, crested iris from western China. Fans of flat strap-like leaves on cane-like stems. Branching flower stems bear many small blooms, white, spotted yellow, or mauve, with yellow crests, in spring. **'Martyn Rix'**, ruffled blue flowers. Zones 8–11.

Iris cristata

CRESTED IRIS

↔ 12–20 in (30–50 cm)
↑ 4–5 in (10–12 cm)

Herbaceous woodlander from eastern USA, with exposed, creeping, fleshy stems, and fans of bright green strappy leaves. Blue spring flowers, on stems to height of leaves, with white markings on falls and yellow crests. White-flowered form is also grown. Zones 6–10.

Iris chrysographes 'Black Knight'

Iris ensata 'Flying Tiger'

Iris ensata 'Hekito'

Iris domestica

syn. *Belamcanda chinensis*

BLACKBERRY LILY, LEOPARD LILY

↔ 12 in (30 cm) ↑ 36 in (90 cm)

From eastern Russia to Japan. Short-lived, with deciduous sword-like leaves. Borne on loose spikes in summer, flowers have 6 narrow flaring petals from yellow to orange, usually speckled with crimson. Zones 8–10.

Iris douglasiana

↔ 18 in (45 cm)
↑ 20–32 in (50–80 cm)

Fleshy-stemmed beardless iris from California and Oregon, USA. Loose clumps of dark green ribbed leaves. Branching flower stems. Blooms, in summer, vary in color from cream to deep reddish purple, veining usually in darker tones. Zones 7–9.

Iris ensata ★

syn. *Iris kaempferi*

JAPANESE WATER IRIS, WOODLAND IRIS

↔ 40 in (100 cm) ↑ 36 in (90 cm)

Native to Europe, Asia, and North America. Tall, dark green, strappy, grass-like foliage. Single, occasionally branched stems of flowers vary in color from red, purple, or blue, held well above foliage, in early summer.

Iris ensata 'Rose Queen'

Will grow in shallow water. Not tolerant of dry hot conditions. **'Flying Tiger'**, white flowers, heavily veined in violet; **'Hekito'**, deep blue flowers, yellow signals, white styles, blue-tipped; **'Hue and Cry'**, red-veined plum-red flowers, yellow signals with white margins; **'Rose Queen'**, soft pink flowers, darker veined falls; **'Variegata'**, purple-red flowers, variegated foliage; **'Yaemomiji'**, cerise-purple flowers streaked with white, yellow signals. Zones 5–8.

Iris foetidissima

GLADDON, GLADWYN, ROAST BEEF PLANT, STINKING GLADWYN

↔18–30 in (45–75 cm)
↑18–30 in (45–75 cm)

Vigorous, fleshy-stemmed, beardless iris, native to Europe and north Africa. Glossy, deep green, sword-shaped leaves, distinctive odor when crushed. Spring flowers unspectacular, buff-yellow and dusty dull purple. Large green seed pods split to expose scarlet seeds. **'Variegata'** has boldly white-striped leaves. Zones 6–10.

Iris iberica

Iris forrestii

↔6–8 in (15–20 cm)
↑15–16 in (38–40 cm)

Dainty, narrow-leafed, herbaceous species from China and northern Myanmar. Leaves narrow, glossy, gray-green undersides. Bears yellow flowers, spotted all over with brown, to 2½ in (6 cm) across, in early summer. Moist soil required. Zones 7–10.

Iris × *fulvala*

↔10 in (25 cm)
↑18–30 in (45–75 cm)

Hybrid of *I. fulva* and *I. brevicaulis*, both of which are beardless irises from USA. Purplish red flowers, in summer. Plants require a very moist soil. Zones 7–10.

Iris × *germanica*

↔18–24 in (45–60 cm)
↑24–48 in (60–120 cm)

Rhizomatous bearded iris. Origin uncertain, widely naturalized; possibly from the Mediterranean or an ancient fertile hybrid. Blue, white, and yellow flowers, to 4 in (10 cm) wide, yellow beards. Zones 5–9.

Iris foetidissima

Iris innominata

Iris graminea

syn. *Iris colchica*

↔10 in (25 cm)
↑8–18 in (20–45 cm)

Variable, fleshy-stemmed, beardless iris, found from Spain eastwards to Russia. Narrow grassy leaves. Small purple flowers, 1–2 per stem, often hidden within the foliage, distinctive fruity fragrance, in summer. Zones 5–9.

Iris iberica

↔6 in (15 cm) ↑8 in (20 cm)

Fleshy-stemmed, dwarf, bearded iris from southwestern Asia. Narrow grayish green leaves. Relatively large white flowers, veined with brown, purplish beards, in spring. A difficult garden subject requiring perfect drainage. Zones 6–9.

Iris innominata

↔10 in (25 cm)
↑8–10 in (20–25 cm)

A fleshy-stemmed beardless iris, native to Oregon, USA, with narrow dark green leaves. The slender-petaled flowers vary from cream to purple, with darker veining, and appear in summer. This species is used extensively in breeding the Pacific Coast hybrids. Zones 8–10.

Iris japonica

syns *Iris chinensis, I. fimbriata*

↔18–24 in (45–60 cm)
↑24–32 in (60–80 cm)

Fleshy-stemmed crested iris from central China and Japan. Shiny dark green leaves in fans. Pale lavender flowers with orange markings, ruffled and fringed at margins, borne on branching airy stems, in spring. Zones 8–10.

Iris lacustris

↔4–6 in (10–15 cm)
↑2–3 in (5–8 cm)

Native to North America. Very dwarf, fleshy-stemmed, crested iris. Soft bright green leaves, to 3 in (8 cm) long. Small sky blue flowers, with frilly gold-tipped crests, from late spring to summer. Zones 4–9.

Iris japonica

Iris lazica

↔10–12 in (25–30 cm)
↑10–12 in (25–30 cm)

From northeastern Turkey and Georgia. This evergreen species is related to *I. unguicularis* but has thicker shorter leaves arranged in fans. Soft lavender-blue flowers, white and yellow falls, in late winter–early spring. Zones 8–10.

Iris longipetala

↔12 in (30 cm)
↑12–24 in(30–60 cm)

From western USA. Fleshy-stemmed beardless iris with dark green foliage. Unbranched flower stems carry up to 6 white, blue, or purple blooms; long, narrow, white falls veined with violet, in late spring–summer. Zones 5–9.

Iris milesii

↔10 (25 cm)
↑12–36 in (30–90 cm)

Fleshy-stemmed crested iris from the Himalayas. Bright green ribbed foliage. Frilly lilac-purple flowers, with darker markings, on branched stems, in the summer. Zones 7–9.

Iris missouriensis

↔12 in (30 cm)
↑12–20 in (30–50 cm)

From western North America. This fleshy-stemmed beardless iris is similar to *I. longipetala*. Narrow grayish green leaves. White, blue, or purple flowers, long narrow falls, in late spring to summer. Zones 3–8.

Iris pallida

syns *Iris glauca, I. odoratissima*

DALMATIAN IRIS

↔12 in (30 cm)
↑36–48 in (90–120 cm)

Fleshy-stemmed bearded iris from the European Alps. Stiff, sword-like, bluish green foliage. Large fragrant flowers, blue with yellow beards, in early summer. ***I. p.* subsp. *cengialti*** ★ (syn. *I. cengialti*), greener leaves than species, dark purple flowers. ***I. p.* 'Argentea Variegata'**, white stripes on leaf edges; **'Variegata'**, creamy yellow leaf markings. Zones 5–9.

Iris reticulata 'Blue Veil'

Iris prismatica

☼ ✱ ↔12 in (30 cm)
↑24–32 in(60–80 cm)

Fleshy-stemmed beardless iris, native to eastern USA. Long, bluish green, grassy leaves. Flowers pale violet, veined blue, on wiry stems, in summer. Zones 5–9.

Iris reticulata

☼ ✱ ↔2 in (5 cm) ↑6 in (15 cm)

From the Caucasus region. Variable bulbous iris with very narrow channeled leaves. Solitary stemless flowers, narrow petals, in violet shades with gold markings on falls. **'Blue Veil'** and **'Cantab'** are popular cultivars. Zones 3–9.

Iris × *robusta*

☼ ✱ ↔20 in (50 cm)
↑32–40 in (80–100 cm)

This is a hybrid of *I. versicolor* and *I. virginica*, two of the moisture-loving beardless irises from North America, which has characteristics that are intermediate between the parents. The leaves are dark green and ribbed. The flowers are borne in late spring to early summer, in bluish violet shades. **'Gerald Darby'** produces dark violet flowers, on spikes to 40 in (100 cm) tall. Zones 4–9.

Iris sanguinea

☼ ✱ ↔12–24 in (30–60 cm)
↑24–36 in (60–90 cm)

Native to Siberia, China, Japan, and Korea. Fleshy-stemmed beardless iris similar to *I. sibirica*. Narrow grassy foliage, usually taller than the flowering spike. Unbranched stems bear 2 bluish violet flowers in early summer. ***I. s.* var. *violacea***, narrower leaves, darker purple flowers. Zones 4–9.

Iris setosa

☼ ✱ ↔18 in (45 cm) ↑30 in (75 cm)

Widespread species from Siberia, China, Canada, and Alaska, USA. Fleshy-stemmed beardless iris. Narrow ribbed leaves, may be flushed red at base. Numerous pale bluish purple dark-veined flowers borne on branching spikes, in late spring to summer. Large falls and very small standards give flowers a 3-petalled appearance. ***I. s.* subsp. *interior*** has narrower leaves. Zones 3–9.

Iris tectorum

Iris × *robusta* 'Gerald Darby'

Iris setosa subsp. *interior*

Iris sibirica

☼ ✱ ↔8–24 in (20–60 cm)
↑18–48 in (45–120 cm)

From Europe and northern Asia. Rhizomatous beardless iris. Thin, grassy, bright green leaves. Flowers: up to 5 per stem, each to 3 in (8 cm) wide, purple-blue, dark veins on falls, appear in late spring to summer. Zones 4–9.

Iris spuria

☼ ✱ ↔3–7 ft (0.9–2 m)
↑4–7 ft (1.2–2 m)

From northern and northwestern Iran. Colonizing iris are usually found in damp fields, shallow riverbeds, and even in saline soils. Flowers range in color from pale and dark blues, through to whites, creams, and mauves. Plants need rich warm soils. ***I. s.* subsp. *halophila***, pale to deep yellow flowers, dark green strappy foliage. Zones 6–9.

Iris tectorum

ROOF IRIS

◐ ✱ ↔12 in (30 cm)
↑12–16 in (30–40 cm)

Native to China. Fleshy-stemmed crested iris. Fans of light green leaves. Bluish purple flowers, darker veining appear in early summer. Zones 6–9.

Iris tenax

syn. *Iris gormanii*

◐ ❄ ↔12 in (30 cm) ↑16 in (40 cm)

From western USA. Fleshy-stemmed beardless iris with deciduous foliage. Flowers in white, yellow, blue, and purple shades, on unbranched stems, in early summer. **'Alba'** is a white-flowered form. Zones 8–10.

Iris tenuis

◐ ❄ ↔6 in (15 cm) ↑12 in (30 cm)

Rare native of western USA. Fleshy-stemmed crested iris, like *I. cristata* but taller. Flowers lavender-blue, darker veining, some yellow markings, in late spring. Zones 7–10.

Iris unguicularis

syn. *Iris stylosa*

ALGERIAN IRIS, WINTER IRIS

☼/◐ ❄ ↔16–20 in (40–50 cm)
↑12–15 in (30–38cm)

Evergreen species from Greece, Turkey, western Syria, Algeria, and some of the Mediterranean islands. Grows well in hot dry aspects, producing tough grassy leaves and pale lavender to blue flowers, hidden amongst the leaves, in winter–early spring. Many forms have been selected. **'Alba'** has white flowers with yellow on the falls; **'Mary Barnard'** has deep violet-blue flowers; the flowers of **'Starkers Pink'** are a soft mauve-pink; and **'Variegata'** has deep blue blotching and streaking on soft blue flowers. Zones 7–10.

Iris variegata

syns *Iris lepida, I. leucographa, I. reginae, I. virescens*

☼ ✱ ↔6–10 in (15–25 cm)
↑8–20 in (20–50 cm)

Fleshy-stemmed bearded species from central and eastern Europe. The leaves are dark green, ribbed, and sword-shaped. The yellow flowers, marked with variable veining of blue to reddish brown, appear from spring to summer. Zones 6–9.

Iris tenax 'Alba'

Iris versicolor

Iris, Hybrid Cultivar, Bearded, Standard Dwarf, 'Wow'

Iris, Hybrid Cultivar, Bearded, Standard Dwarf, 'Bibury'

Iris, Hybrid Cultivar, Bearded, Tall, 'In Town'

Iris versicolor

☼ ❄ ↔ 10 in (25 cm)
↑ 8–32 in (20–80 cm)

From eastern USA. Vigorous, water-loving, fleshy-stemmed, beardless iris. Broad, ribbed, green foliage. Many small flowers in bluish purple shades, with darker veining, on branching flower spikes, in summer. Zones 4–9.

Iris virginica

☼ ❄ ↔ 10 in (25 cm)
↑ 8–32 in (20–80 cm)

From eastern USA. Vigorous water-loving beardless iris. Heavily ribbed dark green foliage. Similar to *I. versicolor*, but with unbranched flower spikes. Bluish purple flowers, larger and longer standards, in summer. Zones 4–9.

Iris Hybrid Cultivars

ARILBRED HYBRIDS

☼ ❄ ↔ 12 in (30 cm)
↑ 10–27 in (25–70 cm)

Hybrids of species in the Aril Group and Tall Bearded Iris. Large flowers in a range of purple shades and yellow, with variously colored markings. Flowers in early spring. Require a dry dormant summer season. **'Judean Gem'**, 10 in (25 cm) high, bearded, early season, white flowers, yellow falls with orange-red signals; **'Oyez'**, 24 in (60 cm) high, early season, white flowers, dark purple veins on standards and falls. Zones 3–9.

BEARDED HYBRIDS

☼ ❄ ↔ 12–36 in (30–90 cm)
↑ 8–40 in (20–100 cm)

These hardy perennials are grown from rhizomes. They will survive in most climates but produce more flowers in cooler climates. The upright pale blue-green foliage sits above the ground, and large heads of flowers appear in late spring, ranging in color from blues, purples, and browns through to oranges, whites, and yellows. Flowers have standards and falls, with a distinctive beard on each fall. Do not cover rhizomes with soil, as they will rot and die. These plants need well-drained and fertile soil in full sun. Divide every 5 to 7 years.

Miniature Dwarf Bearded Hybrids: Reaching to less than 8 in (20 cm) high, these are the smallest and earliest-flowering of the bearded hybrids. They produce small flowers, 1½–3 in (35–80 mm) wide, in spring.

Standard Dwarf Bearded Hybrids: These flower well in cool maritime climates. They will reach height of 8–15 in (20–38 cm), will form good clumps, and are reliable garden plants. Flowers appear in late spring. These hybrids need a good cold period through the winter to perform well. **'Bromyard'**, early season, blue-gray standards, blue-purple and ocher falls, blue-gray beards; **'Bibury'**, white to cream flowers; **'Eyebright'**, mid-season, yellow flowers with deep brown lines, creamy yellow beards; **'Flower Shower'**, ruffled flowers in violet and white; **'Honington'**, cream-yellow flowers; **'Quark'**, cream flowers with maroon markings; **'Rain Dance'**, early season, violet-blue flowers, matching violet-blue beards; **'Tirra Lirra'**, mauve flowers; and **'Wow'**, bright yellow flowers with maroon markings.

Intermediate Bearded Hybrids: These hybrids reach 16–27 in (40–70 cm) high. These medium-sized plants bear blooms that are also medium-sized. They will flower well in most areas, the flowers well able to support themselves on their stems. They do well in wind-prone areas, but need full sun. **'Arctic Fancy'**, pure white flowers with purple markings; **'Barocco'**, deep pink to maroon flowers; **'Eye Magic'**, yellow flowers, with red thumbprint on falls; **'Happy Mood'** ★, creamy flowers edged in lavender; **'Maui Moonlight'**, mid-season, rich lemon flowers; **'Mon Ange'**, yellow-veined white flowers; **'Sunny Dawn'**, bright yellow flowers with red beard. Other popular Intermediate Bearded Hybrids include: **'Katie-Koo'**, **'Miss Carla'**, **'Sherbet Lemon'**, and **'Templecloud'**.

Miniature Tall Bearded Hybrids: Sharing a similar flowering season to the Tall Bearded Hybrids, and reaching a similar height to Border Bearded Hybrids, these hybrids produce smaller flowers on wiry stems. **'Bumblebee Deelite'**, flowers have yellow standards, maroon falls edged with yellow; **'Frosted Velvet'**, two-tone flowers with white centers, rich velvet purple falls edged in white.

Border Bearded Hybrids: Flowering at the same time as the Tall Bearded Hybrids, but with somewhat smaller flowers held on stalks 16–27 in (40–70 cm) high. **'Apricot Frosty'**, white flowers, deep apricot falls, apricot beards; **'Batik'**, white-striped purple flowers, yellow beards with white tips; **'Brown Lasso'**, deep butterscotch and yellow flowers, petals edged in pale lavender.

Tall Bearded Hybrids: Well-branched spikes of robust large flowers, may be ruffled or smooth-edged. Can reach height of 27–40 in (70–100 cm). Good for cutting. **'Apricorange'**, orange flowers; **'Berry Sherbet'**, early flowering, pink and violet flowers; **'Blue-Eyed Brunette'**, ruffled bronze flowers, blue beards; **'Breakers'**, mid-blue ruffled flowers; **'Celebration Song'**, late season, pinkish standards, lavender-blue falls; **'Champagne Elegance'** ★, apricot flowers, yellow standards, white falls edged in apricot, with yellow-red beards, large number of blooms; **'Cinderella's Coach'**, pumpkin orange flowers, bright red-tangerine beards, ruffled flowers; **'Cupid's Arrow'**, pink to maroon flowers; **'Dazzling Gold'**, mid-season, yellow and red flowers; **'Designing Woman'**, rosy lilac standards and falls, coral beards, very wavy and ruffled blooms; **'Dusky Challenger'**, large, ruffled, dark black-purple flowers; **'Early Light'**, creamy yellow ruffled flowers; **'Good Morning America'**, mid-season, pale blue flowers; **'Hello Darkness'**, mid-season, rich velvet black flowers; **'Honky Tonk Blues'**, mid-season, blue-violet, heavily washed over a white base, giving a soft blue effect, wide ruffled blooms; **'In Town'**, mid-season, lilac blue standards, with slightly ruffled purple falls; **'Incantation'**, mid-season, bluish standards, pure white falls; **'Jesse's Song'**, white center bleeding into violet, lemon beard, violet edging; **'Joyce Terry'**, early mid-season, yellow standards, white falls, yellow beards; **'June Sunset'**, mid-season, white standards, soft peach-orange falls; **'Mystique'**, early to mid-season, blue standards, purple-blue mid-ribs, deep purple falls, blue beards. **'Silverado'**, mid-season, silvery lavender flowers and beards; **'Stepping Out'**, similar to 'Jesse's Song'; **'Thornbird'**, yellowish standards, greenish brown falls; **'Vanity'**, pink flowers, with salmon pink beards. Other attractive Tall Bearded Hybrids include: **'Bewick Swan'**, **'Meg's Mantle'**, **'Paradise'**, **'Paradise Bird'**, **'Phil Keen'**, **'Precious Heather'**, and **'Sun Miracle'**. Zones 3–9.

Iris, Hybrid Cultivar, Louisiana, 'Newsbrief'

DUTCH HYBRIDS

☼ ✱ ↔ 12–18 in (30–45 cm)
↑ 24–36 in (60–90 cm)

Bulbous irises with large spring blooms in shades of blue and purple, yellow and white. Grown for cut flower trade. **'Blue Diamond'**, dark blue buds open to mid-blue flowers, yellow thumbprints at base of petals; **'Blue Magic'**, deep blue flowers, yellow thumbprints; **'Cream Beauty'**, ivory flowers, gold thumbprints; **'Madonna'**, crisp white, yellow thumbprints; **'Telstar'**, rich purple-blue flowers, golden yellow thumbprints at petal base. Zones 5–9.

LOUISIANA HYBRIDS

☼/◐ ✱ ↔ 3–7 ft (0.9–2 m)
↑ 18–60 in (45–150 cm)

Water plants bred from species from swamps of southeastern USA. Very adaptable to growing in water and also on edges of ponds and rivers. Will grow in ordinary garden soil if given plenty of water. Need to be planted in well-prepared soil, with a good amount of humus. Will grow in full sun or part-shade. Flower spikes vary in height from 14 in (35 cm) to 5 ft (1.5 m). Flowers range in color from pinks, yellows, and blues through to oranges, purples, and browns. **'Green Elf'**, mid-season, chartreuse-green flowers, ageing to cream; **'Marie Caillet'**, ruffled violet-blue flowers, with yellow signals; **'Newsbrief'**, purple-red flowers, paler centers; **'President Hedley'**, early season, dark buttery yellow flowers, areas of brown shading on falls, with yellow-orange signals. Zones 6–9.

ONCOCYCLUS HYBRIDS

☼ ❄ ↔ 40 in (100 cm)
↑ 4–24 in (10–60 cm)

Similar in appearance to the bearded iris, but are smaller in size. Only one flower is borne on each flower stem. A large blotch and dark veining on the flowers are characteristics of this group. They are adaptable to hot dry climates. The large seed heads are produced in the autumn. Zones 7–9.

PACIFIC COAST HYBRIDS

☼/◐ ✱ ↔ 12 in (30 cm)
↑ 10–20 in (25–50 cm)

Hybrids of about 6 iris species from California and Oregon, sometimes known as Pacific Coast Hybrids, with wide color range, from yellow to pink and purple. Long bloom period from spring. **'Broadleigh Carolyn'**, compact white flowers, mauve-purple veining and yellow blotches in eye; **'Broadleigh Medusa'**, rich purple flowers, cream and yellow throats; **'Broadleigh Nancy'**, mid-purple flowers, petals edged in white, white and yellow blotch in eye; **'Broadleigh Rose'**, rich rose pink flowers, yellow and cream blotches in eye; **'Broadleigh Sybil'**, creamy apricot standards, deep rose pink falls. Zones 5–9.

SIBERIAN HYBRIDS

☼ ✱ ↔ 8–24 in (20–60 cm)
↑ 18–48 in (45–120 cm)

This adaptable group of irises is happy in heavy clay soils. Dark green grassy foliage. Flower spikes are taller than the foliage, producing up to 5 flowers on each stem; flowers are usually blue-violet or white. The flowers of **'Annemarie Troeger'** are in 2 shades of blue with white signals; **'Anniversary'** produces ruffled white flowers; **'Caesar's Brother'**, bright blue flowers, yellow signals; **'Harpswell Happiness'**, ruffled white flowers; **'Perry's Blue'**, pale lavender-blue flowers, creamy yellow veined eyes; **'Pink Haze'**, lavender-pink flowers, red-violet veins on falls; **'Ruffles'**, ruffled blue-violet flowers, dark styles; **'White Swirl'**, pure white flowers, yellow blotches at base, rounded flared outer petals. Zones 4–9.

Iris, Hybrid Cultivar, Dutch, 'Blue Diamond'

Iris, HC, Siberian, 'White Swirl'

SPURIA HYBRIDS

☼ ✱ ↔ 18–24 in (45–60 cm)
↑ 30–48 in (75–120 cm)

Tall plants with large flowers in white and yellow to red and purple shades, in spring–summer. **'Shelford Giant'**, 4 ft (1.2 m) tall, mid-season, large lemon and white flowers. Zones 4–9.

ISMELIA

This genus of around 5 species of annuals and short-lived perennials in the daisy (Asteraceae) family, which was established with the break-up of the genus *Chrysanthemum*, may prove to be indistinguishable from *Xanthopthalmum*. Found around the Mediterranean region and on Madeira and the Canary Islands, they are bushy plants with upright stems that sometimes become woody at the base. The foliage is pinnately lobed, sometimes with very narrow lobes, and may be toothed. The daisy-like flowerheads are often brightly colored and appear in abundance.

CULTIVATION: These plants are intolerant of repeated frosts but are otherwise very adaptable in mild climates. Plant in a bright position with light well-drained soil. Water well when in bud and flower, but otherwise keep rather dry. Usually raised from seed, although perennial species may also be propagated from half-hardened stem cuttings.

Ismelia carinata

syns *Chrysanthemum carinatum*, *Ismelia versicolor*

☼/◐ ✢ ↔ 12–16 in (30–40 cm)
↑ 32–40 in (80–100 cm)

Annual of obscure origin, probably from Morocco. Upright stems; bright green, fleshy, pinnately lobed leaves. Flowerheads to 4 in (10 cm) diameter, disc florets dark, ray florets multicolored in yellow, orange, and red tones with light base, in summer–early autumn. **'Court Jesters'**, popular mixed color strain. Zones 10–12.

Iris, Hybrid Cultivar, Pacific Coast, mixed

Ismelia carinata

ISOPLEXIS

Evergreen subshrubs, 3 species, from the Canary Islands and Madeira in the foxglove (Scrophulariaceae) family. Bear upright spikes of flaring tubular flowers in shades of yellow and orange.
CULTIVATION: These showy shrubs grow well in warm-temperate climates; require protection in colder areas. Need moderately fertile soil, full sun or light shade, and plentiful water in summer. Deadhead regularly. Propagate from seed in spring, from softwood cuttings taken in late summer, or basal suckers.

Isoplexis canariensis ★

↔3 ft (0.9 m) ↕4 ft (1.2 m)

Native to Canary Islands. Lance-shaped to oblong leaves, toothed margins, slightly downy. Foxglove-like flower spikes to 12 in (30 cm) long; flowers are orangey yellow to yellowish brown, in summer. Zones 9–11.

Isoplexis sceptrum

↔7 ft (2 m) ↕6 ft (1.8 m)

This species has slightly glossy foliage, and is a native of Madeira. The flower spikes, held well above the foliage, are shorter than those of *I. canariensis*, but are very showy, being well packed with tawny orange flowers. Zones 9–11.

ISOPOGON

The majority of the 35 species in this southern Australian genus of the protea (Proteaceae) family are found in Western Australia. They are attractive evergreen shrubs with tough dissected foliage and showy flowers that form dense globular heads, generally in shades of yellow and pink. The rounded or egg-shaped cone-like fruiting heads are usually borne terminally and persist for a long time, giving some members of the genus the common names of cone bush or drumsticks.

Isoplexis canariensis

Isoplexis sceptrum

CULTIVATION: These plants like full sun and light well-drained soil. Some species are best suited to winter rainfall areas, especially those from Western Australia. Pruning is not usually necessary, except when young to form the basis of a well-branched shrub. Most species will tolerate occasional light frosts. Propagate from cuttings or from seed, which may be slow to germinate.

Isopogon anemonifolius

DRUMSTICKS

↔4 ft (1.2 m) ↕6 ft (1.8 m)

An erect bushy shrub, which is found in eastern Australia. The flat dull green leaves are divided into 3 segments, and then again divided and lobed, with an attractive purplish tinge. The soft yellow flowers form in terminal rounded heads, 1½ in (35 mm) across, and appear in spring to early summer. **'Woorikee 2000'**, dwarf cultivar, with leaves tipped with red, and yellow flowers. Zones 9–11.

ITEA

SWEETSPIRE

Very attractive but not widely cultivated, the 10 evergreen and deciduous shrubs and small trees in this genus present an interesting combination of foliage and flowers. Although they are members of their own distinct sweetspire (Iteaceae) family, their foliage is often more reminiscent of members of the holly (Aquifoliaceae) family. Found naturally in Asia, with a sole eastern North American representative, the evergreens offer dark lustrous leaves throughout the year, while the deciduous species have brilliant autumn foliage color. The catkin-like racemes are not colorful and are really more of a novelty for their contrast with the foliage. Named from the Greek, *itea*, meaning willow, on account of their pendulous catkins.

CULTIVATION: Frost hardiness varies, but the commonly grown species are reasonably tough and will thrive in most well-drained soils with a position in full sun or partial shade. They are, however, not drought tolerant and need ample summer moisture. Propagate from seed or from half-hardened cuttings.

Itea chinensis

CHINESE SWEETSPIRE, SWEETSPIRE

↔6–10 ft (1.8–3 m)
↕6–10 ft (1.8–3 m)

Evergreen shrub, native to western China. Arching branches; leaves deep green, serrated edges, rather holly-like. Narrow clusters of tiny white flowers, on 8 in (20 cm) long racemes. Small brown seed capsules. Zones 7–9.

Itea japonica

↔12–16 in (30–40 cm)
↕12–16 in (30–40 cm)

Attractive deciduous shrub of bushy habit from Japan. Leaves to 1¾ in (4 cm) long. Upward-pointing 2½ in (6 cm) spikes of tiny, fluffy, white, scented flowers, in summer. Foliage turns brilliant colors in autumn. **'Beppu'**, particularly rich autumn color. Zones 6–9.

Itea virginica 'Henry's Garnet'

Isopogon anemonifolius 'Woorikee 2000'

Itea chinensis

Itea virginica

SWEETSPIRE, VIRGINIA WILLOW

↔5 ft (1.5 m) ↕4–10 ft (1.2–3 m)

Deciduous shrub from eastern North America, and the most widely grown species. Forms clump of arching stems, 2–4 in (5–10 cm) long, serrated-edged leaves, develop vivid red and orange tones in autumn. Racemes of tiny honey-scented cream flowers, 2–6 in (5–15 cm) long, erect rather than pendulous. **'Henry's Garnet'** is a well-known cultivar. Zones 5–9.

IXIA

CORN LILY, WAND FLOWER

This South African genus in the iris (Iridaceae) family contains some 50 species of corms with fine grassy foliage, usually quite short in comparison to the wiry, often arching flower stems. The flowers are simple 5- or 6-petaled structures massed in spikes at the stem tips. Often brightly colored, they may also be pale with brighter markings, and occur in some unusual shades including pale blue-green. CULTIVATION: Plant in a sunny position in light well-drained soil. In hot areas the flowers will last longer with a little shade. Water well in spring but allow to dry off after flowering. Propagation is usually from offsets, less commonly from seed.

Ixia maculata

↔6 in (15 cm) ↕8–20 in (20–50 cm)

Variable robust plant with weedy potential. Stems are erect and wiry. Leaves are grassy and untidy, withering quickly after the flowers fade. Numerous large cupped flowers, petals in cream, purple-pink, cherry red, pink, yellow, orange shades, often with a dark eye, as well as stripes and bicolors, spring-flowering. Zones 8–11.

Ixia viridiflora

↔8 in (20 cm)
↕12–24 in (30–60 cm)

Robust species from southwest Cape region, South Africa. Fine grassy leaves to 20 in (50 cm) long. Variable short-lived flowers in open stars, petals sea-green, turquoise, teal, aqua-blue, duck-egg blue, often with a dark central marking, appear from mid-spring. Zones 9–10.

IXIOLIRION

This group of 4 bulbous perennial herbs is the type genus for the Siberian lily (Ixioliriaceae) family, originating from southwest and central Asia. The narrow grassy leaves grow from a central point, forming rosettes. In spring and summer tall slender stems carry umbels or loose racemes of funnel-shaped flowers in blue to violet shades. CULTIVATION: Plant these bulbs in a sheltered sunny position in light, well-drained, sandy soil, allowed to become hot and dry in summer. Propagate from seed or by dividing the bulbs and removing the offsets in autumn.

Ixia maculata

Ixiolirion tataricum

SIBERIAN LILY, TARTAR LILY

↔12–16 in (30–40 cm)
↕10–16 in (25–40 cm)

Bulbous perennial from southwest and central Asia. Narrow, semi-erect, grass-like leaves. Abundant clusters of up to 4 flowers, on 16 in (40 cm) tall stems, blue or purple-blue tepals, darker stripe at center, in spring–early summer. Zones 5–9.

IXORA

JUNGLE FLAME

Common throughout the wet tropics, this genus of about 400 evergreen shrubs and small trees belongs to the madder (Rubiaceae) family. The genus name is from the Portuguese name for the Hindu deity, Siva, to whom the blooms are dedicated. The flowers are usually produced in showy clusters, ranging from scarlet, pink, or yellow to white, and are sometimes fragrant. Attractive glossy leaves and a compact habit makes them suitable for containers or massed plantings. The fruit, a 1- to 2-seeded drupe, mostly red, ripens to black. In addition to the species, there are hybrids and varieties that are of uncertain botanical origin. CULTIVATION: Frost tender, many species will not tolerate a temperature much below 55°F (13°C), and prefer bright indirect sun. The soil should be friable, with added sharp sand and leaf mold. Pinch out the tips when young to encourage branching, and prune older plants after flowering. Propagate from seed in spring, or from half-hardened cuttings, taken from short-jointed non-flowering shoots, in summer.

Ixora coccinea

FLAME OF THE WOODS

↔8 ft (2.4 m) ↕8 ft (2.4 m)

Bushy gently rounded shrub from tropical Asia, mainly India and Sri Lanka. Leaves are glossy, dark green. Small brilliant orange-red flowers, in large round clusters, appear most of the year in the tropics. Zones 11–12.

Ixora javanica

↔8 ft (2.4 m) ↕15 ft (4.5 m)

This shrub or small tree, from Java and the Malay Peninsula, is smaller in cultivation than in its natural habitat. The flowers are red or, less often, pink or orange, and appear in dense clusters. Zones 11–12.

Ixora Hybrid Cultivars

↔12–36 in (30–90 cm)
↕1–6 ft (0.3–1.8 m)

There are numerous *Ixora* hybrid cultivars, most of which are derived from *I. coccinea.* They include: **'Exotica'**, bright red flowers fading to orange, creating a distinctively two-toned flowerhead; **'Frances Perry'**, deep yellow flowers; **'Fraseri'**, vivid salmon pink flowers; **'Herrera's White'**, white flowers; **'Orange Glow'**, bright orange flowers; **'Pink Delight'**, pink flowers; **'Rosea'**, rose pink flowers; **'Sunkist'**, the most common *Ixora* cultivar, a dwarf shrub to 3 ft (0.9 m), small, slender, glossy leaves, and flowers of apricot-yellow, ageing to brick red; **'Sunny Gold'**, orange-amber flowers; **'Thai Dwarf'**, flowers in a range of colors from pink to red, yellow to orange; and **'Thai King'**, orange-red flowers. Other attractive cultivars include: **'Aurora'** and **'Florida Sunset'**. Zones 11–12.

Ixora javanica

JK

JACARANDA

The genus comprises about 50 species of deciduous and evergreen trees and shrubs belonging to the trumpet-vine (Bignoniaceae) family. They are native to the drier areas of tropical and subtropical Central and South America and have elegant, fern-like, bipinnate leaves, some pinnate or simple. Mauve-blue, rarely pink or white, funnel- or bell-shaped flowers in terminal or axillary panicles appear in spring– summer. Widely grown as an avenue tree or lawn specimen. Pretoria, South Africa, is called the jacaranda city.

CULTIVATION: Jacarandas will grow quickly in fertile well-drained soil in full sun. Protect from the wind and frost when young. They are relatively frost hardy once established. Pruning is not necessary for outdoor specimens. Water freely in the growing season and sparingly in winter. They are shallow-rooted heavy feeders, and shrubs planted nearby may suffer. Propagation is from seed in late winter or early spring, and from half-hardened cuttings taken in summer.

Jacaranda mimosifolia

BLUE HAZE TREE, BRAZILIAN ROSEWOOD, FERN TREE, JACARANDA

↔20–35 ft (6–10 m) ↑25–50 ft (8–15 m)

This fast-growing deciduous tree comes from drier areas of South America. Elegant, mid-green, bipinnate foliage, may turn rich yellow in late winter before being shed. From late spring–early summer produces prolific terminal clusters of hanging, bell-shaped, mauve-blue flowers on mostly leafless branches. Disc-shaped red-brown seed pods. **'Variegata'**, green and yellow variegated leaves; **'White Christmas'**, large clusters of white flowers. Zones 10–11.

JASMINUM

JASMINE

Famed for the fragrance of its flowers, this genus, which belongs to the olive (Oleaceae) family, is native to Africa, Europe, and Asia (with a single American species). The genus includes some 200 species of deciduous, semi-deciduous, and evergreen shrubs and woody-stemmed climbers. The foliage is usually pinnate or less commonly trifoliate and varies greatly in color and texture. The flowers, in clusters at the branch tips and leaf axils, are tubular with 5 widely flared lobes. They are most commonly white, white flushed with pink, or yellow, and can be scentless to overpoweringly fragrant.

CULTIVATION: Jasmines vary greatly in their hardiness, depending on their origins, though few will tolerate repeated severe frosts. They are averse to drought, preferring moist, humus-rich, well-drained soil and a position in full sun or partial shade. In suitable climates most species grow rapidly and some can become rather invasive. Readily propagated from seed, cuttings, or layers, which with some low-growing species may form naturally, making them difficult to contain.

Jacaranda mimosifolia

Jasminum nudiflorum

Jasminum sambac

Jasminum angulare

syn. *Jasminum capense*

↔7–10 ft (2–3 m) ↑15–17 ft (4.5–5 m)

From South Africa. Evergreen climber or rambler. Dark green pinnate leaves, 3 to 5 leaflets, with sweetly scented bunches of star-shaped flowers, 1¼ in (30 mm) wide. Flowers cover the plant from mid-summer to late autumn. Zones 10–11.

Jasminum beesianum

↔15 ft (4.5 m) ↑15 ft (4.5 m)

Scrambling or twining, Chinese, deciduous shrub. Simple, 2 in (5 cm) long, lance-shaped leaves in pairs. Small fragrant blooms in 3-flowered clusters, shades of pink from pale to deep rose, in late spring–autumn. Glossy black fruits. Zones 7–10.

Jasminum fruticans

↔10 ft (3 m) ↑10 ft (3 m)

Native to the Mediterranean region and western Asia. Near-evergreen to evergreen shrub. Foliage trifoliate, leathery deep green leaflets. Clusters of up to 5 unscented flowers, in summer, throughout the year in frost-free climates. Zones 8–10.

Jasminum humile

ITALIAN JASMINE, ITALIAN YELLOW JASMINE

↔12 ft (3.5 m) ↑12 ft (3.5 m)

Evergreen or semi-evergreen shrub found naturally from the Middle East to China. Short pinnate leaves, up to 7 leaflets. Clusters of yellow, variably scented flowers, in summer. **'Revolutum'** is a reliably fragrant cultivar with large leaves. Zones 8–10.

Jasminum nudiflorum

WINTER JASMINE

↔10 ft (3 m) ↑10 ft (3 m)

From northern China. Sprawling deciduous shrub. Mass of slightly arched, whippy, green canes, dark green trifoliate leaves. Bright yellow blooms, in winter, when all else is bare. Zones 6–9.

Jasminum officinale

COMMON JASMINE, COMMON WHITE JASMINE, POETS' JASMINE, TRUE JASMINE

↔15 ft (4.5 m) ↑30 ft (9 m)

Found from the Middle East to China. Sprawling, somewhat twining, deciduous shrub, usually trimmed to 8 ft (2.4 m). Slightly downy pinnate leaves, 5 to 9 leaflets. White or very pale pink flowers, fragrant, in early summer–autumn. Several variegated foliage cultivars, such as cream-edged **'Argenteovariegatum'** and gold-blotched **'Aureum'**. Zones 7–10.

Jasminum polyanthum

↔25 ft (8 m) ↑10–17 ft (3–5 m)

Vigorous evergreen climber from southwestern China that twines and tangles through trees, trellises, and other structures. Dark green foliage consists of 5 to 7 leaflets, can have bronze tones in winter. Delicate pink buds appear from late winter and open to white fragrant flowers, ¾ in (18 mm) wide, in spring. Flowers through to mid-autumn. Zones 7–9.

Jasminum sambac

ARABIAN JASMINE, ZAMBAC

↔6 ft (1.8 m) ↑5–12 ft (1.5–3.5 m)

Woody-stemmed evergreen climber, can be treated as a lax shrub. Large simple, not pinnate, leaves, glossy deep green with a heavy texture. Clusters of up to 12 fragrant, waxy, white flowers that age to pale pink, throughout the year. **'Grand Duke of Tuscany'**, double-flowered cultivar. Zones 10–11.

Jasminum × *stephanense*

↔5–10 ft (1.5–3 m) ↑17 ft (5 m)

A *J. beesianum* × *J. officinale* hybrid from southwestern China. Rampant, woody, twining, deciduous climber with soft gray-green foliage that has a dull appearance. Bunches of fragrant pale pink flowers, ¾ in (18 mm) long, in summer–autumn. Zones 8–10.

JATROPHA

This variable genus of the euphorbia (Euphorbiaceae) family comprises some 170 species of succulent perennials and evergreen or deciduous shrubs, rarely trees. All species contain a milky latex that may irritate the skin. They are found in tropical to warm-temperate regions of the world, mainly Central and South America. Leaves are usually palmately lobed, although some are lobeless. Small clusters of purple, yellow, scarlet, or red flowers are borne in summer. All parts of the plant are mildly poisonous, but they are used medicinally in the tropics. One species, *Jatropha curcas,* is being grown commercially for the production of biodiesel.

CULTIVATION: Used in street plantings, borders, and hedges, these plants appreciate a fertile, well-drained, sandy soil and full sun, but most will tolerate part-shade. Frost tender, in temperate zones they can be grown in a warm greenhouse. Half-hardened cuttings should be placed in cool shade to allow the ends of the cuttings to dry before rooting, or propagate from seed in spring or summer.

Jatropha integerrima

syns *Jatropha hastata, J. pandurifolia*

PERENNIAL, SPICY JATROPHA

↔4–8 ft (1.2–2.4 m) ↕10–20 ft (3–6 m)

Spreading evergreen tree, native of Cuba, Hispaniola, and Puerto Rico; may reach 20 ft (6 m) high. This species does best in moist tropical conditions. Leaves variable, ranging from 3-lobed to fiddle-shaped, rich green with bronze undersides. Branched clusters of small, funnel-shaped, 5-petalled, bright rose red flowers in terminal clusters, throughout the year, but predominantly in warmer weather. Seeds and sap are both poisonous. Zones 10–12.

Jatropha integerrima

JEFFERSONIA

syn. *Plagiorhegma*

TWIN LEAF

This genus consists of 2 species of herbaceous perennials in the barberry (Berberidaceae) family, one from North America and the other from northeastern Asia. They are small clump-forming plants with 2-lobed kidney-shaped leaves and dainty cup-shaped flowers in late spring. The genus was named after Thomas Jefferson, third president of the USA.

CULTIVATION: They are woodlanders by nature so like a cool moist aspect under a deciduous canopy in a compost-enriched soil. As they are small plants, care should be taken in siting them in large woodland areas and they may be better cared for in a slightly shaded rock garden. Propagate from seed sown as soon as ripe, or by dividing established clumps.

Jeffersonia diphylla

RHEUMATISM ROOT

↔8 in (20 cm) ↕6–8 in (15–20 cm)

Found from Ontario, Canada, to Tennessee, USA. Leaves to 6 in (15 cm) wide. Flowers are 1 in (25 mm) across and white. Zones 5–9.

Jeffersonia dubia

syn. *Plagiorhegma dubia*

↔6–8 in (15–20 cm) ↕6–8 in (15–20 cm)

From the woods of northeastern Asia. Blue-green leaves to 4 in (10 cm) across. Flowers are pale lavender-blue or rarely white, and 1¼ in (30 mm) across. Zones 5–9.

JOVIBARBA

A small genus of 6 species from the mountains of Europe belonging to the stonecrop (Crassulaceae) family. They are rosetting succulents that are often confused with the better known houseleeks *(Sempervivum),* which in foliage they resemble and in which genus some botanists prefer to place them. The insignificant flowers are 6-petalled and bell-shaped, whereas those of the houseleeks are star-shaped.

Jovibarba hirta var. *neilreichii*

CULTIVATION: These are hardy little succulents, ideal in well-drained poor soil in the rock garden, dry stone walls, troughs, or pots. Remove old rosettes after they have flowered. Propagate by division; some species detach their own rosettes that will then roll away to take root elsewhere.

Jovibarba hirta

syn. *Sempervivum globiferum var. hirtum*

↔10–12 in (25–30 cm) ↕4–6 in (10–15 cm)

From the mountains of central and southeastern Europe. Rosettes to 2 in (5 cm) across. Small flat leaves are narrow or broadly lance-shaped, convex below, green with darker colored tips. Branching heads of small pale yellow flowers are produced in summer. ***J. h.*** var. ***neilreichii***, from the lower Carpathian Mountains, has narrow leaves aranged in open rosettes. Zones 6–10.

JUBAEA

This genus contains a single species of palm, in the family Arecaceae, native to coastal areas of Chile, where wild populations have been greatly reduced by harvesting. Its tall stout trunk has a dense crown of leaves. The sugary sap is made locally into syrup or alcohol.

CULTIVATION: Tolerates short periods of light frost but grow in a conservatory or greenhouse in cool climates. Grow in any reasonable soil in sun or filtered light and give plenty of water when young. Propagation is from fresh seed but germination is slow.

Jubaea chilensis

syn. *Jubaea spectabilis*

CHILEAN WINE PALM, COQUITO PALM

↔25 ft (8 m) ↕80 ft (24 m)

From Chile. Stout trunk, occasionally swollen in the middle. Dense crown; fronds to 15 ft (4.5 m) long, arching or rigid, pinnately arranged leaves. Long-stalked flowers hidden within the leaves. Small, egg-shaped, edible yellow fruits, called coquito. Zones 8–10.

Jubaea chilensis

JUGLANS

The walnuts, a genus of the Juglandaceae family, comprise about 20 species of deciduous trees. They are distributed over the temperate zones of the Americas, southeastern Europe, and Southeast Asia. They have alternate compound leaves and monoecious flowers, borne in spring. The fruit is a hard-shelled nut enclosed in a fleshy green drupe, the kernels being prized as food. Some species produce hard, beautifully grained wood, valued for furniture making; some produce juglose, which can poison apple trees.

CULTIVATION: Walnuts thrive on deep, alluvial, well-drained soil with a high organic content, and an assured water supply, in a cool humid climate. Plantation trees are often severely pruned after 1 year to force strong single trunk growth, then stopped at 12 ft (3.5 m) or so to induce lateral branches; ornamental trees can be treated the same way. Seeds can be collected as soon as ripe in early autumn and stored in cool conditions until sown in early spring.

Juglans ailantifolia

syn. *Juglans sieboldiana*

JAPANESE WALNUT

↔40 ft (12 m) ↕50 ft (15 m)

From Japan. Upright tree, attractive leaves, 11 to 17 leaflets, covered in dark red fine hairs. Bark striped pale and dark gray. Male catkins 6–12 in (15–30 cm) long, female flowers deep red. Fruits covered in an adhesive down. ***J. a.*** var. ***cordiformis*** differs only in the shape of the fruits. Zones 4–9.

Juglans ailantifolia

J K

Juglans major

Juglans regia

Juncus patens

J
K

Juglans californica

☼ ❄ ↔30 ft (9 m) ↑30 ft (9 m)

Native of southern California, USA. Large shrub or small tree, attractive leaves composed of 11 to 15 lanceolate leaflets. Zones 7–10.

Juglans cinerea

BUTTERNUT, BUTTERNUT WALNUT, WHITE WALNUT

☼ ❄ ↔50 ft (15 m) ↑60 ft (18 m)

From New Brunswick, Canada, to Georgia, USA. Fast-growing species, smaller in cultivation. Shoots sticky, leaves oblong, notched edges, hairy, yellow-green. Fruits solitary or in clusters. Can be short-lived. Zones 4–9.

Juglans major

syn. *Juglans elaeopyren*

ARIZONA WALNUT, NOGAL

☼ ❄ ↔30 ft (9 m) ↑50 ft (15 m)

New Mexico to Arizona, USA. Single upright trunk, slender crown. Leaves oblong to lance-shaped, 9 to 13 leaflets. Nuts with dark brown shells. Autumn foliage creamy yellow. Zones 9–11.

Juglans nigra

AMERICAN WALNUT, BLACK WALNUT

☼ ❄ ↔70 ft (21 m) ↑100 ft (30 m)

Native of eastern and central USA and southeastern Canada. Dome-shaped crown, large leaves, 11 to 23 leaflets. Edible nuts dark brown. Grows quickly in warm areas on rich soils, usually slow elsewhere. **'Laciniata'** has finely cut leaves. Zones 4–10.

Juglans regia

ENGLISH WALNUT, PERSIAN WALNUT, WALNUT

☼ ❄ ↔35 ft (10 m) ↑40–60 ft (12–18 m)

Native to southeastern Europe, the Himalayas, and China. Grown for its edible nuts. Bark pale gray. Smooth aromatic leaves, 7 leaflets; young leaves coppery purple turning green as they mature. Cultivars of the **Carpathian Group** are cold hardy, and popular throughout the USA, especially selected commercial clones **'Broadview'** and **'Buccaneer'**. **'Laciniata'** has deeply cut leaflets. Zones 4–10.

JUNCUS

This genus of some 225 species of grass-like plants belongs to the self-named Juncaceae or rush family. Species are of cosmopolitan distribution and are found growing in wet soils such as bogs and water margins. Leaves may be flat, channeled, cylindrical, or reduced to sheaths at the stem bases. The small green or brown flowers are borne in round heads or more open clusters at the stem ends. The plants range from 12 in–5 ft (30 cm–1.5 m) in height. The name *Juncus* is derived from the Latin word meaning to bind, and refers to the use made of the stems for tying.

CULTIVATION: Many *Juncus* species are invasive and few are grown ornamentally. They have some use around large ponds or in wild gardening in wet areas. Grow in full sun or part-shade in heavy wet soil or shallow water. Propagation is from seed or by division.

Juncus effusus

COMMON RUSH

☼ ❄ ↔30 in (75 cm) ↑5 ft (1.5 m)

Stiff, upright, twisted evergreen with rush-like leaves. Stems are rigid but smooth and look like a corkscrew. Tiny brown flowers appear in clusters in autumn, sitting above the foliage. Needs a moist soil. **'Spiralis'** (corkscrew rush) has mounding, curly, sometimes upright stems. Zones 6–9.

Juncus patens

CALIFORNIAN GRAY RUSH

☼/◐ ❄ ↔24 in (60 cm) ↑27 in (70 cm)

Steel blue-gray foliage, upright habit. Inconspicuous flowers appear in summer. Very tolerant to dry soils but will grow in shallow water. **'Carman's Gray'**, silvery gray, stiff, upright foliage, needs little room for roots; **'Elk Blue'**, intense steely blue foliage, wider leaves. Zones 7–10.

JUNIPERUS

This genus consists of some 60 generally slow-growing evergreen trees and shrubs in the cypress (Cupressaceae) family, occurring naturally in the Northern Hemisphere. The larger trees are valued for their timber and all species are long lived, performing particularly well on alkaline soils. Two foliage types are seen: juvenile, which is awl-shaped (needle-like), and adult, which is scale-like and stem-clasping. When crushed, the foliage of most is pungently aromatic. The small, fleshy, berry-like fruits are actually cones that ripen to blue-black or reddish. Usually there are separate male and female plants.

CULTIVATION: Although drought tolerant and tough, these plants are susceptible to fungal attack, needing an open airy situation. Well-drained soils are essential. Regular light pruning maintains shape, but do not cut bare wood. Propagation from fresh seed is best, although named cultivars should be either grafted or grown from a cutting in winter. The new season's terminal growth will also strike readily.

Juniperus ashei

☼ ❄ ↔20 ft (6 m) ↑30 ft (9 m)

From southern USA and Mexico. Slow-growing large shrub, sometimes a small conical tree. Young awl-shaped foliage is sage green maturing to dark green, scale-like. Small, fleshy, aromatic fruits, deep blue when ripe. Zones 8–10.

Juniperus chinensis

CHINESE JUNIPER

☼ ❄ ↔15 ft (4.5 m) ↑30 ft (9 m)

Native to China and Japan. Variable species in habit and size. Blunt-tipped adult foliage, prickly juvenile foliage, both on lower branches and within the tree. Berries small, round, blue-green. ***J. c.* var. *sargentii***, low growing, excellent bonsai subject. ***J. c.* 'Aurea'**, golden adult foliage, yellowish green juvenile leaves, narrow, upright or conical habit, to 20 ft (6 m); **'Blaauw'**, vigorous shrub, to 5 ft (1.5 m), dense sprays of green to gray-blue scale-like leaves; **'Expansa Variegata'**, dwarf spreading shrub to 3 ft (0.9 m), flecked with creamy white sprays; **'Femina'**, good bonsai subject; **'Kaizuka'**, large upright shrub or small tree, spreading branches densely clustered, scale-like bright green foliage; **'Keteleeri'** ★, upright spire of dark green, distinctive spiraled habit of blunt-tipped closely held scales, attractive blue-green berries; **'Mountbatten'**, shrub or small tree, dense columnar habit, gray-green awl-shaped leaves; **'Oblonga'**, rounded shrub, dense branches, inner foliage dark green, awl-shaped and prickly, outer foliage adult and scale-like; **'Olympia'**, of Japanese origin, a small conical tree; **'Parsonii'**, dwarf shrub, wide-spreading sturdy branches eventually mounding to 3 ft (0.9 m) in the center, sage-green scale-like leaves, in dense clustered sprays; **'Shoosmith'**, conical tree, bright green foliage; **'Spartan'**, columnar form,

Juniperus chinensis

Juniperus communis 'Depressed Star'

Juniperus chinensis 'Variegata'

Juniperus flaccida

Juniperus scopulorum 'Blue Arrow'

dark green foliage, considered one of the best of this habit; **'Variegata'**, mostly juvenile foliage on long branchlets when young, then progressively develops adult foliage, at all stages irregularly flecked with creamy yellow or white. Zones 4–9.

Juniperus communis

COMMON JUNIPER

☼ ✱ ↔ 3–15 ft (0.9–4.5 m)
↑ 20 ft (6 m)

Widespread throughout the Northern Hemisphere. Variable evergreen shrub or small tree. In mild situations, narrow-columnar, tendency to spread in colder climates. Silver-backed foliage, needle-like, prickly; fruit (which is used widely for flavorings and gin) green ripening to glossy black with a whitish bloom. ***J. c.* var. *montana*** (syn. *J. c.* 'Nana') very prostrate, slow-growing ground cover, forms a mat of dark green, excellent choice on embankments and coastal cliffs. Numerous cultivars (including prostrate forms) that have been selected for shape, foliage, and color are available. ***J. c.* 'Compressa'**, compact, narrow and slow-growing column to a height of 3 ft (0.9 m); **'Depressa Aurea'** ★, wide-spreading ground cover to approximately 2 ft (0.6 m) in height, foliage dense, slightly ascending, brownish green, becoming more bronze in winter; **'Depressed Star'**, rounded spreading habit, light green foliage; **'Hibernica'** (syn. 'Stricta'), slender column to 10 ft (3 m) in height, dense foliage, prominent silvery reverse; **'Pendula'**, graceful weeping branches. Zones 2–8.

Juniperus flaccida

MEXICAN JUNIPER

☼ ✱ ↔ 20 ft (6 m) ↑ 30 ft (9 m)

From Mexico and Texas, USA. Tree with slender branches weeping at the tips. Bark is scaly. Awl-shaped leaves, gray-green on young plants, becoming brighter, scale-like on mature plants. Small round fruits ripen reddish brown with a white bloom. Zones 5–9.

Juniperus horizontalis

CREEPING JUNIPER, HORIZONTAL JUNIPER

☼ ✱ ↔ 12 ft (3.5 m) ↑ 18 in (45 cm)

Native to northern North America, found on coastal cliffs and stony hillsides. Vigorous ground-hugging shrub with long trailing branches. Leaves gray-green or bluish, often develop a purplish tinge in winter. **'Bar Harbor'**, mat-forming cultivar with blue-green foliage, the tips turning mauve in winter; **'Blue Chip'**, blue-green foliage, variegated with gold; **'Douglasii'**, prostrate form to 2 ft (0.6 m) high, displaying blue-green foliage of both juvenile and adult type, turns purplish in autumn–winter; **'Prince of Wales'**, mat-forming with deep green foliage; **'Repens'**, blue-green foliage; **'Wiltonii'**, blue-foliaged, prostrate, trailing cultivar. Zones 4–10.

Juniperus occidentalis

WESTERN JUNIPER

☼ ✱ ↔ 30 ft (9 m) ↑ 40 ft (12 m)

From the mountains of California, USA. Often shrubby in the wild, tree in protected gardens. Branches with near-horizontal habit, with drooping tips, blue-green scale-like leaves. Small blue-green cones. Zones 5–9.

Juniperus × *pfitzeriana*

syn. *Juniperus* × *media*

☼ ✱ ↔ 5–15 ft (1.5–4.5 m)
↑ 4–10 ft (1.2–3 m)

This name refers to a collection of garden hybrids, derived mainly from *J. chinensis*, which usually have adult and juvenile foliage present simultaneously. Adult foliage is stem-clasping scales, while juvenile foliage is triangular, sharp, protruding. Branches wide spreading and lifted just above horizontal. Dull green, adult, scale-like leaves release unpleasant scent when crushed. Many have white or blue-black fruit, globular to rounded. Vigorous ground covers. **'Golden Sunset'**, low-growing shrub; **'Pfitzeriana Aurea'**, greenish yellow foliage, similar in habit to 'Wilhelm Pfitzer'; **'Wilhelm Pfitzer'**, vigorous, spreading shrub with sturdy ascending branches and pendulous tips, leaves mostly green and scale-like. Ideal ground cover where space is available, shade tolerant. Zones 4–10.

Juniperus procumbens

BONIN ISLAND JUNIPER, CREEPING JUNIPER, JAPANESE GARDEN JUNIPER

☼ ✱ ↔ 12 ft (3.5 m) ↑ 30 in (75 cm)

From western China. Prostrate spreading ground cover, stiff and wiry habit, prickly blue-green leaves. Small berry-like cones, brown-green, each contains 2 to 3 seeds. **'Nana'** has smaller leaves, softer texture, and a more conical habit. Both are excellent for covering embankments. Zones 4–9.

Juniperus rigida

NEEDLE JUNIPER

☼ ✱ ↔ 5–15 ft (1.5–4.5 m)
↑ 2–20 ft (0.6–6 m)

From Japan, Korea, Sakhalin Island, and northern China. Elegant large shrub or small tree with pendulous branchlets. Leaves dark, needle-like, in whorls of 3, prominent white band on uppersurface. Fruit ripens to glossy blue-black. ***J. r.* var. *conferta*** (syn. *J. conferta*), wide-spreading, fast-growing, prostrate ground cover, light green to blue-green foliage, very prickly and dense, small berry-like fruit ripen to brown; **'Blue Lagoon'** and **'Blue Pacific'**, bluer foliage; **'Emerald Sea'**, gray-green foliage; **'Sunsplash'**, green and gold variegated foliage. Zones 4–9.

Juniperus sabina

SAVIN JUNIPER

☼ ✱ ↔ 6–15 ft (1.8–4.5 m)
↑ 2–12 ft (0.6–3.5 m)

Variable, spreading, self-layering ground cover, excellent for binding slopes. Dark green foliage with disagreeable odor when crushed. Leaves awl-shaped on young foliage, scale-like on adult. Fruit is a small, ovoid, blue-black berry with whitish bloom, containing 1 to 3 seeds. ***J. s.* var. *davurica*** (syn. *J. davurica*), variable variety, often erect, occurring naturally throughout northern Asia, gray flaking bark, branches clothed in narrow scale-like leaves. ***J. s.* 'Calgary Carpet'**, bright green foliage, low-growing form; **'Skandia'**, mid-green foliage; **'Tamariscifolia'**, spreading ground cover, green to blue-green foliage. Zones 4–9.

Juniperus scopulorum

ROCKY MOUNTAINS JUNIPER

☼ ✱ ↔ 15 ft (4.5 m) ↑ 30 ft (9 m)

From western North America and Texas, USA. Small tree or shrub with sturdy spreading branches; tightly held, scale-like leaves, light to blue-green. Small round fruits. **'Blue Arrow'**, pencil-shaped, blue-green foliage, **'Blue Heaven'**, blue-green foliage; **'Horizontalis'**, spreading, blue-green foliage; **'Mountaineer'**, bright green foliage; **'Repens'**, prostrate, blue-green; **'Skyrocket'**, very narrow columnar form to 10 ft (3 m) tall, silvery blue foliage, arguably the narrowest of all conifers; **'Tabletop'**, spreading, blue-green foliage; **'Tolleson's Blue Weeping'**, pendulous; **'Wichita Blue'**, conical, blue-gray foliage. Zones 5–9.

Juniperus squamata

HOLLYWOOD JUNIPER, SINGLESEED JUNIPER, SQUAMATA JUNIPER

↔15 ft (4.5 m) ↑2–20 ft (0.6–6 m)

Extremely variable species from central Asia and China. May be a mound-like shrub, a small shrubby tree, or a prostrate ground cover. Bark red-brown and flaky. Dense, juvenile-type, awl-shaped leaves, grayish green to silvery blue-green, upper surface marked pale green or white. **'Blue Carpet'**, spreading form, blue-green foliage; **'Blue Star'**, rounded shrub, very blue, small, dense; **'Chinese Silver'**, medium to large, dense, multi-stemmed shrub, recurved terminal shoots, leaves silvery blue; **'Meyeri'**, open vase shape, several leaders, leaves very blue when young, turn dark green with age. Zones 4–9.

Juniperus virginiana

EASTERN RED CEDAR, PENCIL CEDAR, RED CEDAR

↔12–20 ft (3.5–6 m) ↑40 ft (12 m)

From central and eastern North America. Upright tree, becoming more open with age. Bark reddish brown, peels in long strips. Small, adult, closely held scale leaves with pointed tips, glaucous green, becoming purplish in winter. Fragrant timber traditionally used for the casings of lead pencils. **'Burkii'** ★, narrowly pyramidal habit, blue-foliaged shrub becoming steel-blue in cold winters; **'Manhattan Blue'**, popular pencil-shaped cultivar. Zones 2–8.

Juniperus virginiana 'Manhattan Blue'

Justicia aurea

JUSTICIA

syns *Adhatoda, Beloperone, Drejerella, Jacobinia, Libonia*

This largely tropical and subtropical American genus of the acanthus (Acanthaceae) family encompasses more than 400 species of perennials, subshrubs, and shrubs. The shrubby species are evergreen, their leaves usually simple pointed ovals in opposite pairs, sometimes hairy or with a velvety surface. The flowers are clustered, sometimes in upright panicles at the branch tips, or in looser, more open heads. The true flowers are often small, the flowerheads made colorful and showy by the large bracts.

CULTIVATION: A feature of gardens in warm climates and popular house and greenhouse plants elsewhere, most justicias do not tolerate severe frosts. Some tolerate being frosted to the ground, reshooting in spring, but most need mild winter conditions. Justicias prefer moist well-drained soil in sun or part-shade with shelter from strong winds. Water regularly during the growth period. Keep compact by regular tip pinching or a light trimming after flowering. Propagate from seed or half-hardened cuttings.

Justicia aurea

↔3 ft (0.9 m) ↑3–5 ft (0.9–1.5 m)

From Mexico and Central America. Similar to the better-known *J. carnea*, but the foliage is a slightly lighter green; heads of yellow flowers rather than the pink of *J. carnea*. Flowers in late summer–autumn. Often reshoots if the foliage is cut back by frost. Zones 9–12.

Justicia brandegeeana

syns *Beloperone guttata, Drejerella guttata*

SHRIMP PLANT

↔26 in (65 cm) ↑36 in (90 cm)

From Mexico. Evergreen shrub, curved array of overlapping pink and yellow bracts enclose small white flowers with red markings. Elliptical downy leaves, to 3 in (8 cm) long. **'Fruit Cocktail'**, yellow-green bracts. Zones 9–11.

Justicia californica

syn. *Beloperone californica*

CHUPAROSA HONEYSUCKLE

↔4 ft (1.2 m) ↑3–5 ft (0.9–1.5 m)

Found in the deserts of southwestern North America, shrub differs in being nearly leafless. Mounding stems covered in fine silvery hairs for protection from harsh elements. Small leaves, after the spring rains. Narrow, nectar-rich, red flowers. Zones 9–10.

Justicia carnea

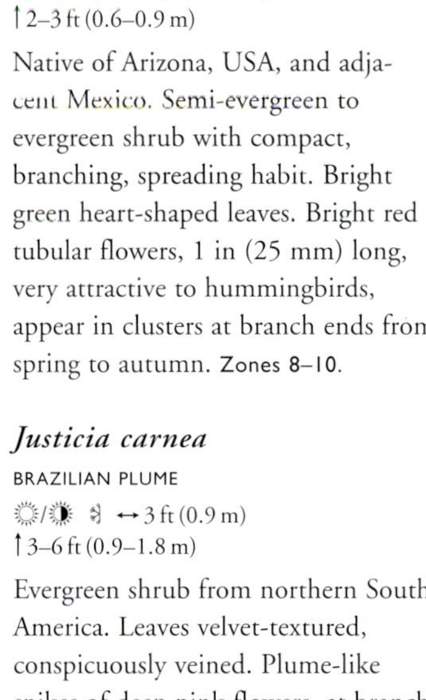

Justicia candicans

syns *Jacobinia ovata, Justicia ovata*

ARIZONA WATER-WILLOW, HUMMINGBIRD BUSH, RED JUSTICIA

↑3–6 ft (0.9–1.8 m) ↑2–3 ft (0.6–0.9 m)

Native of Arizona, USA, and adjacent Mexico. Semi-evergreen to evergreen shrub with compact, branching, spreading habit. Bright green heart-shaped leaves. Bright red tubular flowers, 1 in (25 mm) long, very attractive to hummingbirds, appear in clusters at branch ends from spring to autumn. Zones 8–10.

Justicia carnea

BRAZILIAN PLUME

↔3 ft (0.9 m) ↑3–6 ft (0.9–1.8 m)

Evergreen shrub from northern South America. Leaves velvet-textured, conspicuously veined. Plume-like spikes of deep pink flowers, at branch tips throughout the year, especially late summer. Pinch back when young to keep compact. Zones 10–12.

Justicia rizzinii

syns *Jacobinia pauciflora, Justicia floribunda, Libonia floribunda*

↔10–22 in (25–55 cm) ↑10–22 in (25–55 cm)

One of the hardier justicias, from Brazil, densely twiggy shrub. Small, leathery, oval leaves, which often develop bronze tints in winter, the main flowering season. **'Firefly'**, heavier flowering, scarlet red flowers with glowing golden yellow tips, flared tubes, slightly under 1 in (25 mm) long, in small clusters. Zones 9–11.

Justicia spicigera

syn. *Justicia ghiesbreghtiana*

MEXICAN HONEYSUCKLE, MOHINTLI

↔5 ft (1.5 m) ↑6 ft (1.8 m)

Found from Mexico to Colombia. Upright shrub, deeply veined oval leaves to 6 in (15 cm) long. Leaves with fine down on the underside, smooth upper surface. Flowers up to 1½ in (35 mm) long, through the warmer months, in bright shades of orange to red. Zones 10–12.

KALANCHOE

This genus belonging to the stonecrop (Crassulaceae) family contains about 125 species of succulent shrubs, herbs, and climbers distributed throughout tropical regions of Africa, Madagascar, and parts of Asia. Usually grown for their interesting foliage forms, although the vibrantly colored flowers of *K. blossfeldiana* make it a popular house

plant. Growth habits range from low sprawling subshrubs to tall tree-like plants, with a similar wide variation in leaves, from small to large and glossy to felted.
CULTIVATION: Plants require indoor or greenhouse cultivation in all climates where frost is experienced; grow in a moderately fertile gritty potting mix. Can be grown outdoors in suitable climates in a sunny sheltered position in well-drained soil; keep fairly dry in winter. Propagate by stem or leaf cuttings, or seed sown in spring.

Kalanchoe beharensis

FELT PLANT, GIANT KALANCHOE
↔3 ft (0.9 m) ↕10 ft (3 m)
Tree-like species from Madagascar, smaller in cultivation. Foliage stunning; large, thick, triangular leaves to 12 in (30 cm), heavily felted, silvery gray, light bronze overtones on uppersurface; wavy, uneven, toothed edges. Small, tubular, yellowish flowers seen on mature specimens. **'Oak Leaf'** ★, greenish yellow flowers. Zones 10–11.

Kalanchoe blossfeldiana

FLAMING KATIE
↔16 in (40 cm) ↕16 in (40 cm)
Bushy perennial succulent from Madagascar. Large, round, dark green, fleshy leaves. Heads of tubular scarlet flowers in clusters from early spring. Numerous cultivars, flowers in white, cream, yellow, orange, and red. Free-draining soil. Zones 10–12.

Kalanchoe daigremontiana

syn. *Bryophyllum daigremontianum*
MEXICAN HAT PLANT
↔12 in (30 cm) ↕40 in (100 cm)
From Madagascar. Upright perennial succulent with long, lance-shaped, silver-gray leaves, changing to green as temperatures fall. On leaf edges, plantlets appear that look like "Mexican hats"; these can be separated to produce new plants. Pendulous pale pink flowers in spring. Zones 10–12.

Kalanchoe fedtschenkoi

Kalanchoe delagoensis

syns *Bryophyllum tubiflorum, Kalanchoe tubiflora*
CHANDELIER PLANT
↔12 in (30 cm) ↕40 in (100 cm)
Upright unbranched succulent from Madagascar and South Africa. Cylindrical, long, pale green leaves, irregular red spots and small plantlets on the edge. In winter pink, orange, or yellow pendent flowers in large terminal clusters. Zones 9–12.

Kalanchoe fedtschenkoi

↔12 in (30 cm) ↕20 in (50 cm)
From Madagascar. Upright spreading succulent with thick, fleshy, blue-green, round leaves with serrated edges. Tubular orange to red flowers in panicles in spring. *K. f.* **'Variegata'** ★, blue-gray white-edged foliage, new leaves creamy white, changing to blue-green edged in white. Zones 9–12.

Kalanchoe grandiflora

↔16 in (40 cm) ↕32 in (80 cm)
From southern India. Upright succulent with blue-green oval leaves. Panicles of tubular yellow flowers throughout summer. Zones 11–12.

Kalanchoe marmorata

syn. *Kalanchoe somaliensis*
↔36 in (90 cm) ↕50 in (130 cm)
From northeastern Africa. Sprawling succulent; branches from base of plant. Dusty gray leaves have distinctive brown markings. Panicles of white flowers in summer. Zones 10–12.

Kalanchoe thyrsiflora ★

↔12 in (30 cm) ↕24 in (60 cm)
From southern Africa. Bushy succulent, white-frosted green leaves. Red margins on leaf edges. Tubular, fragrant, yellow flowers in spring. Zones 11–12.

Kalanchoe tomentosa ★

PANDA PLANT
↔7 in (18 cm) ↕15 in (38 cm)
Small erect shrub from Madagascar. Dense rosettes of oblong gray leaves, heavily felted, brown markings near tips. Small yellow–green flowers. Zones 10–12.

KALIMERIS

This genus is made up of 10 perennial herbs native to East Asia; it is part of the daisy (Asteraceae) family. Leaves are alternate and narrowly oval to elliptical. Plants produce clusters of rounded panicles of spreading white ray florets, tinged with purple or violet, and yellow disc florets.
CULTIVATION: Plant in full sun to part-shade. Plants tolerate damp soil, and are suitable for bog gardens and water margins. Propagate from seed.

Kalimeris incisa

syn. *Boltonia incisa*
↔5 ft (1.5 m) ↕1–5 ft (0.3–1.5 m)
Perennial from northeastern Asia. Oblong to spear-shaped, stalkless, smooth, toothed leaves, hairy margins, up to 4 in (10 cm) long. Purple to white flowerheads, in summer–autumn. **'Alba'**, starry, single, white flowers; **'Blue Star'**, starry, single, blue flowers. Zones 3–9.

KALMIA

Genus of 7 species of shrubs in the heath (Ericaceae) family. Most are evergreen. They are native to northeastern USA, a single species occurs in Cuba. They are grown for their attractive foliage and their showy flowers, ranging in color from pale pink to deep red. Leaves are smooth, opposite or alternate, sometimes found in whorls, deep green on the uppersurface, paler beneath, occasionally stalkless. Flowers are generally carried in terminal corymbs. Fruits are small capsules containing very small seeds.
CULTIVATION: Kalmias are at home in slightly acid, peaty soil but resent clay and lime in any form. Adequate water is needed on hot summer days. Dappled shade under tall deciduous trees in a cool moist climate is ideal. Little pruning is necessary apart from the removal of spent flowers. Propagate from seed. Firm tip-cuttings taken in late summer through to winter may be struck; alternatively, simple layers can be set down in autumn and severed a year later.

Kalmia latifolia 'Ostbo Red'

Kalmia angustifolia

SHEEP LAUREL
↔5 ft (1.5 m) ↕3 ft (0.9 m)
From northeastern USA. Dwarf shrub, slowly spreading to dense bush. Smooth leaves ovate-oblong, to ¾ in (18 mm) long. Pinkish red flowers, in mid-summer. All plant parts are poisonous. **'Rubra'**, pinkish red flowers, over a long period; **'Rubra Nana'**, dwarf form, rich garnet red flowers. Zones 2–9.

Kalmia latifolia

CALICO BUSH, MOUNTAIN LAUREL
↔10 ft (3 m) ↕10 ft (3 m)
Dense shrub found from eastern Canada to Gulf of Mexico. Leaves dark green, smooth above, paler beneath, to ½ in (12 mm) long. Flower buds crimped round edge; open to shell pink, purplish markings inside. In cultivation a number of clones have different flower colors, otherwise resembling parent. **'Carousel'**, mid-pink flowers; **'Clementine Churchill'**, rosy pink flowers; **'Elf'**, dwarf with faded pink flowers; **'Minuet'**, pink flowers with purplish margins; **'Myrtifolia'**, pale pink blooms; **'Nipmuck'**, dark red buds open to almost white; **'Olympic Fire'**, rich crimson flowers; **'Ostbo Red'** ★, vivid red buds opening to faded pink; **'Pink Charm'**, crimson flowers; **'Silver Dollar'**, white flowers with red anthers; **'Snow Drift'**, white blooms. Zones 3–9.

Kalmia angustifolia

KENNEDIA

CORAL PEA

A genus of 16 species of evergreen climbers and trailers in the pea-flower subfamily of the legume (Fabaceae) family; all except one are endemic to Australia. The flowers are usually brightly colored and produced in spring and summer, and they usually have a contrasting color at the base of the standard. Flowers are followed by round to flattened pea-style pods. The leaves are composed of 3 leaflets.
CULTIVATION: In nature these plants tolerate drought and poor soils and in near frost-free conditions will do so in gardens as well. They make attractive ground covers or can be grown on fences and arches in full to half-sun. They are usually raised from seed that must be soaked in hot water prior to sowing in spring.

Kennedia coccinea

CORAL VINE

↔ 10 ft (3 m) ↕ 7–10 ft (2–3 m)

From southwestern Western Australia. Fast-growing twiner or ground cover with leathery, green, wedge-shaped leaflets to 3 in (8 cm) long. Bright red pea-flowers with yellow blotches, ¾ in (18 mm) wide, in spring–summer. Zones 9–11.

Kennedia nigricans

BLACK BEAN, BLACK CORAL PEA

↔ 10–15 ft (3–4.5 m) ↕ 17–20 ft (5–6 m)

Extremely vigorous climber from Western Australia. Leaflets to 5 in (12 cm) long. Black pea-flowers with yellow patches, to 1½ in (35 mm) long, in spring–summer. Zones 9–11.

Kennedia rubicunda

DUSKY CORAL PEA

↔ 15 ft (4.5 m) ↕ 10–15 ft (3–4.5 m)

Strong-growing climber from coastal eastern Australia. Leaflets to 6 in (15 cm) long. Deep red flowers with paler blotches, to 1½ in (35 mm) long, in spring–summer. Zones 9–11.

KERRIA

This genus with a single species in the rose (Rosaceae) family is native to China and Japan. Leaves alternate, toothed, egg-shaped, and dark green. It is a low, suckering, deciduous shrub with bright yellow 5-petalled flowers, 2 in (5 cm) across, and graceful cane-like stems with rather sparse but attractive foliage, and makes an interesting addition to a shrub border.
CULTIVATION: *K. japonica* will grow in any moderately fertile soil with free drainage, preferring a sunny or lightly shaded position and a cool moist climate. Several of the older flowering shoots should be removed at the base after flowering each year to make room for new shoots; no further pruning is necessary. It is easily propagated; soft-tip or half-hardened cuttings taken in spring or summer strike readily, or stems can be layered and lifted a year later.

Kerria japonica

↔ 5 ft (1.5 m) ↕ 6 ft (1.8 m)

Found naturally in the mountains of Japan and in southwestern China. Bright green leaves, simple and alternate, 2–4 in (5–10 cm) long, prominent veins, downy beneath, turn yellow in autumn. Deep yellow flowers on short terminal and axillary spurs, in early–late spring. More common form is '**Pleniflora**' (syn. 'Flore Pleno'), fully double flowers, taller, more vigorous; '**Simplex**', single flowers, arching shrub; '**Variegata**', creamy white variegated foliage, low-spreading habit, seldom exceeding 5 ft (1.5 m) in height. Zones 5–10.

Kennedia nigricans

Kerria japonica 'Simplex'

Kirengeshoma palmata

KIRENGESHOMA

A genus of a single species in the hydrangea (Hydrangeaceae) family. A woodland perennial from Japan and Korea with large, maple-like, soft green leaves and drooping thick-petalled flowers, shaped like a shuttlecock, in late summer.
CULTIVATION: Give *Kirengeshoma* a cool shaded aspect, sheltered from wind, in moist humus-rich soil. Propagation is from seed freshly sown or by careful division of established clumps.

Kirengeshoma palmata

↔ 30 in (75 cm) ↕ 48 in (120 cm)

Elegant, arching, herbaceous perennial from Japan and Korea. Leaves to 8 in (20 cm) long on black stems. Pale lemon flowers to 1½ in (35 mm) long, in late summer. Zones 5–9.

KNAUTIA

A genus of some 60 species of annuals and herbaceous perennials within the honeysuckle (Caprifoliaceae) family. They can be found in Europe, the Caucasus region, Siberia, and the Mediterranean in a wide range of habitats, from woods to meadows and rocky hillsides. They have flowers very like those of *Scabiosa* species, consisting of a cluster of small flowers that look like a single bloom. Their open airy habit makes them useful in the border or the wild garden. They are loved by nectar-feeding insects.
CULTIVATION: Grow in any well-drained fertile soil in full sun. Propagation is usually from seed and they will usually self-seed, sometimes to the extent of weediness.

Knautia arvensis

syn. *Scabiosa arvensis*

BLUE BUTTONS, FIELD SCABIOUS

↔ 12 in (30 cm) ↕ 5 ft (1.5 m)

Upright clumping perennial from Europe through to Siberia via Caucasus, Iran, and central Asia. Hairy dull green leaves can be smooth-edged through to indented and up to 10 in (25 cm) long. Flowerheads are 1½ in (35 mm) across and usually a soft lilac-blue. Flowers from mid-summer through to when it becomes too cold. Zones 6–10.

Knautia macedonica

syn. *Scabiosa rumelica*

↔ 20 in (50 cm) ↕ 32 in (80 cm)

Clumping perennial from central Europe. Lyre-shaped leaves at the base to 6 in (15 cm) long; these become smaller and most dissected higher on the stems. Flowerheads up to 1½ in (35 mm) across, from mid-summer, usually a deep purple-red. '**Egyptian Rose**', deep crimson, long-flowering; '**Melton Pastels**', flowers in soft shades of cream through pale pink to soft lavender-blue. Zones 6–10.

KNIPHOFIA

RED-HOT POKER, TORCH LILY

Most of the nearly 70 species in this genus in the grass tree (Xanthorrhoeaceae) family are South African clump-forming perennials with grassy to sword-shaped, often evergreen, foliage that emerges from vigorous rhizomes. They are grown for their spikes of intensely colored, usually orange and/or yellow, flowers, borne mainly from autumn to spring in bottlebrush heads at the top of strong, tall, upright stems. Many hybrids and cultivars in a variety of sizes and flower colors. Named after German professor Johann Hieronymus Kniphof (1704–1763).
CULTIVATION: Hardiness varies, though none will tolerate repeated heavy frosts. Plant in an open sunny position in moist, humus-rich, well-drained soil. Water and feed well during active growth. Most will tolerate salt winds and thrive near the coast. Propagation is usually by division after flowering or from seed.

Kniphofia caulescens

↔ 20 in (50 cm) ↕ 4 ft (1.2 m)

Tough alpine species; evergreen, narrow but thick blue-green leaves on "trunk" to 12 in (30 cm) high. Coppery flower stems and densely packed heads of pink-tinted cream flowers opening from red buds, in late summer–autumn. Zones 7–10.

Kniphofia citrina

↔ 16 in (40 cm) ↕ 36 in (90 cm)

Evergreen perennial. Thick bright green leaves with deep central channel. The flowerheads are rounded, with cream to yellow-green flowers. '**Lime Select**' has bright, very noticeably green-tinted flowers. Zones 8–10.

Kniphofia hirsuta

↔ 12 in (30 cm) ↕ 16 in (40 cm)

Evergreen perennial. Narrow blue-green leaves. Short-stemmed cylindrical heads of orange-red flowers

Knautia macedonica

with lower buds yellow-green. Tolerant of dry conditions; flowers start to open when stem just 4 in (10 cm) tall. **'Traffic Lights'**, green, orange, and red flowers. Zones 8–10.

Kniphofia northiae

☼/◑ ❄ ↔40 in (100 cm) ↑5 ft (1.5 m)

Evergreen perennial. Thick, broader, slightly blue-green leaves with deep central keel; dense cylindrical heads of yellow flowers opening from red buds, from late spring–autumn. Zones 8–10.

Kniphofia praecox

RED-HOT POKER

☼/◑ ❄ ↔20–40 in (50–100 cm) ↑4–5 ft (1.2–1.5 m)

This is a fairly general name for the wild and garden hybrids between *K. uvaria* and/or *K. linearifolia* and *K. bruceae*. Evergreen perennial. The plants have dense basal clumps of narrow leaves that are deeply channeled. The strong upright flower stems bear cylindrical to rounded heads of orange, yellow, or cream flowers, which appear mainly in late summer–winter. Zones 7–10.

Kniphofia pumila

☼/◑ ❄ ↔12–20 in (30–50 cm) ↑20–32 in (50–80 cm)

This compact summer-flowering species is a native of Ethiopia. Evergreen perennial. Grassy foliage and dense cylindrical heads of small yellow to red flowers on short stems. Zones 9–11.

Kniphofia rooperi

☼/◑ ❄ ↔20–24 in (50–60 cm) ↑4 ft (1.2 m)

Evergreen perennial. Thick leaves with conspicuous keels. From late summer, large spherical heads of bright red flowers appear; the lower flowers are often yellow-green. Zones 8–10.

Kniphofia sarmentosa

☼/◑ ❄ ↔24 in (60 cm) ↑36 in (90 cm)

Evergreen perennial. Blue-green leaves and cylindrical heads of pinkish red to orange-red flowers opening from green buds on stocky stems, from mid-summer to autumn. Zones 8–10.

Kniphofia caulescens

Kniphofia thomsonii

☼/◑ ❄ ↔16–24 in (40–60 cm) ↑4 ft (1.2 m)

From Kenya. Usually evergreen. Narrow leaves. Strong flower stems, large cylindrical heads of deep dusky red flowers, yellow-gold at base of head, in mid-summer to autumn. *K. t.* var. *snowdenii* is deciduous. Zones 9–11.

Kniphofia uvaria

☼/◑ ❄ ↔24 in (60 cm) ↑4 ft (1.2 m)

Evergreen perennial. Thick, deeply channeled leaves. Strong flower stems with ovoid heads of yellow-tipped bright orange-red flowers, in late summer–autumn. Parent of many garden hybrids. Zones 5–10.

Kniphofia Hybrid Cultivars

☼/◑ ❄ ↔12–20 in (30–50 cm) ↑2–5 ft (0.6–1.5 m)

Among the best of the many hybrids are: **'Bees' Sunset'**, deciduous, leaves have serrated edges, yellow-orange flowers on dark stems to 3 ft (0.9 m) tall; **'Green Jade'**, evergreen, flowers initially pale cream ageing through cream to white, 5 ft (1.5 m) stems; **'Ice Queen'**, deciduous, green buds open pale yellow and age to off-white, 5 ft (1.5 m) stems; **'Little Maid'**, deciduous, fine grassy leaves, green buds open soft yellow and age to cream, 24 in (60 cm) stems; **'Painted Lady'**, dusky red flowers age to orange-pink, 3 ft (0.9 m) stems; **'Primrose Beauty'**, fine grassy foliage, bright yellow flowers on 24 in (60 cm) stems; **'Royal Standard'**, deciduous, bright yellow flowers open from red buds on stocky 3 ft (0.9 m) stems; **'Sunset'**, orange to red flowers; **'Tetbury Torch'**, broad, slightly blue-green leaves, golden yellow flowers open from orange buds, 3 ft (0.9 m) stems; **'Yellowhammer'**, spring-flowering, bright yellow flowers on 4 ft (1.2 m) stems. Zones 8–10.

Kniphofia northiae

KOELERIA

JUNEGRASS

This genus of about 25 to 35 annual and perennial grasses with narrow leaf blades belongs to the grass (Poaceae) family. They occur in temperate and colder regions of the Northern Hemisphere. The plants produce very dense, cylindrical, spike-like panicles, to 4 in (10 cm) in length, each compressed spikelet with 2 to 8 flowers, on flimsy erect stems.

CULTIVATION: Plant in a sunny position in well-drained soil. Propagate by division in spring or autumn.

Koeleria glauca

LARGE BLUE HAIR GRASS

☼ ❄ ↔24 in (60 cm) ↑24 in (60 cm)

Short-lived, evergreen, herbaceous, tuft-forming, perennial grass from central Europe and Siberia, forming neat low mounds of bright blue ribbed foliage with stems thickened at the base. Panicles of flowers to 4 in (10 cm) long, with spikelets, each up to ¼ in (6 mm) long, in summer. Zones 4–9.

KOLKWITZIA

There is just one species in this genus within the woodbine (Caprifoliaceae) family—an attractive deciduous shrub occurring in the wild among rocky outcrops in the mountainous areas of Hubei Province, China. It is grown in gardens for its floriferous spring show.

CULTIVATION: *Kolkwitzia* grows in full sun in well-drained fertile soil. When planted in very cold areas it needs protection from cold spring winds, but in general it is frost hardy. Propagation is from cuttings taken from young wood in late spring or early summer or from suckers, which can be removed and grown on. Prune after flowering to retain a tidy shape.

Kniphofia sarmentosa

Kniphofia, HC, 'Primrose Beauty'

Kniphofia, HC, 'Little Maid'

Kolkwitzia amabilis

Kolkwitzia amabilis

BEAUTY BUSH

☼ ❄ ↔12 ft (3.5 m) ↑12 ft (3.5 m)

Bushy deciduous shrub; long, upright or arching shoots. Leaves opposite, broadly egg-shaped, tapered, with rounded tip. Corymbs of bell-shaped flowers, white to pink, yellow-marked throats, late spring–early summer. **'Pink Cloud'** ★, slightly larger, deeper pink flowers. Zones 4–9.

L

LABLAB

A genus of a single species in the pea-flower subfamily of the legume (Fabaceae) family, native to Africa but long grown in India, Southeast Asia, Egypt, and Sudan as a vegetable. It must be treated with caution, for most parts of the plant are poisonous; the pods and seeds are edible only after they have been boiled thoroughly. It is a short-lived herbaceous perennial climber, often treated as a half-hardy annual in colder climates. The leaves consist of 3 triangular leaflets; the pea-flowers occur in various colors and are produced throughout summer, followed by edible pods.
CULTIVATION: Grow in a sunny well-drained site when danger of frost is past. Propagate by seed sown in spring.

Lablab purpureus

syns ***Dolichos lablab, Lablab niger***

BANNER BEAN, BLACK BEAN, EGYPTIAN BEAN, HYACINTH BEAN, INDIAN BEAN

↔5–10 ft (1.5–3 m) ↑12–20 ft (3.5–6 m)

Perennial vine from tropical Africa. Purplish stems; alternate divided leaves, 3 broad oval leaflets. Elongated flowerheads of fragrant white, pink, or purple pea-flowers. Flat, often curved, maroon or purplish seed pods. Most plant parts poisonous; pods and seeds edible if well boiled. **'Darkness'**, violet-purple flowers, black seeds; **'Daylight'**, white flowers, white seeds; **'Giganteus'**, larger form, white flowers. Zones 9–12.

Lablab purpureus

+ *LABURNOCYTISUS*

Hybrid between the genera *Laburnum* and *Cytisus*, the + sign indicating a graft hybrid. This particular hybrid arose in the French nursery of M. Jean-Louis Adam around 1825. Adam had been grafting the purple broom, *Cytisus purpureus,* onto stems of the common laburnum, *Laburnum anagyroides,* with the object of producing a long-stemmed broom. Most of the resulting plants turned out as expected, but one produced a branch with flowers of a curious brownish color and foliage intermediate between that of the broom and the laburnum. Adam propagated from this plant, producing plants with characteristics of both the parents, which were then named after him to acknowledge his work.
CULTIVATION: Cultivation requirements are the same as for *Laburnum.* The plants grow well in a cool-temperate climate, preferably with uniform annual rainfall. They require moderately fertile soil with good drainage. Seeds germinate readily if they are soaked in warm water for 24 hours before sowing.

+ *Laburnocytisus adamii*

✱ ↔15 ft (4.5 m) ↑25 ft (8 m).

A variable tree, some branches producing the yellow flowers of the laburnum, others with clusters of purple broom flowers, and yet others with muddy beige flowers, in short racemes. The leaves are 3-palmate and dark green; the leaflets about 2 in (5 cm) long. Pea-like flowers appear in late spring. Zones 5–9.

LABURNUM

A genus of only 2 species of small deciduous trees, allied to *Genista* in the pea-flower subfamily of the legume (Fabaceae) family, found in central and southern Europe. The leaves are trifoliate and alternate. They are widely grown for their long drooping racemes of yellow pea-flowers, produced in spring and early summer. All parts of the plant, especially the seeds, are poisonous.
CULTIVATION: Laburnums grow well in a cool-temperate climate, preferably with uniform annual rainfall; any moderately fertile soil with good drainage will suit them. It may be necessary to carry out some early shaping by way of removing competing leaders, but otherwise very little pruning is required. In larger gardens laburnums are popularly planted to form an arch. The seeds germinate readily if soaked in warm water for 24 hours before sowing. Position where the plants will be sheltered from winter frosts.

Laburnum alpinum

Laburnum alpinum

SCOTCH LABURNUM

✱ ↔25 ft (8 m) ↑25 ft (8 m)

This is a small spreading tree from mountain regions. The leaflets are deep shiny green above, paler and hairy beneath. Racemes of yellow flowers appear in mid-summer. The seed pods are flattened, smooth, and shiny. **'Pendulum'** is a slow-growing form with pendulous branches; **'Pyramidale'** has upright branches. Zones 3–9.

Laburnum × *watereri*

GOLDEN CHAIN TREE, LABURNUM

✱ ↔25 ft (8 m) ↑25 ft (8 m)

This is a hybrid between *L. alpinum* and *L. anagyroides*, which resembles *L. alpinum,* but has leaves and pods that are more densely hairy. Yellow flowers occur in packed racemes. Best-known clonal form, **'Vossii'** ★, has a similar habit to the parent but is more prolific, with longer flower racemes, to 2 ft (0.6 m). Zones 3–9.

LAGERSTROEMIA

CRAPE MYRTLE

Genus in the loosestrife (Lythraceae) family, consisting of 53 species of evergreen or deciduous, small to large trees, occurs from southern and eastern Asia to northern Australia. They have attractive, often peeling bark and simple, variable, usually opposite leaves that in many species provide brilliant autumn color. In summer they bear showy panicles of flowers with crinkled petals and a crape-like texture in differing shades of pink, mauve, and white. For all these reasons, these trees are a popular inclusion in many gardens. The fruit is a capsule. The timber of some species has been used to manufacture bridges, furniture, and railway sleepers.
CULTIVATION: These trees are generally easy to grow, adapting to a wide variety of soils. They grow best in well-drained soil in a sunny position and some tolerate light frosts. Propagate from seed or half-hardened cuttings in summer, or from hardwood cuttings in early winter. Powdery mildew can be a problem, but newer cultivars are more disease resistant.

Lagerstroemia indica

CRAPE MYRTLE

❄ ↔20 ft (6 m) ↑20 ft (6 m)

From China and Japan. Often multi-stemmed deciduous tree, with wide-spreading, flat-topped, open habit when mature. Bark smooth, pinkish

Lagerstroemia indica

gray, mottled. Leaves small, dark green, turning orange-red in autumn. White, pink, mauve, purple, or carmine flowers with crimped petals, in panicles to 8 in (20 cm) long. Zones 7–11.

Lagerstroemia speciosa

syn. *Lagerstroemia flos-reginae*

PRIDE OF INDIA, QUEEN CRAPE MYRTLE

☼ ↔30 ft (9 m) ↕30–50 ft (9–15 m)

Occurring from India and China to Australia. Deciduous tree with attractive, mottled, smooth, gray-yellow, peeling bark. Leaves dark green, shiny, duller beneath, turning coppery red in autumn. Erect panicles of white, mauve, purple, or pink flowers in summer–autumn. Zones 10–12.

Lagerstroemia tomentosa

☼ ↔20–30 ft (6–9 m)
↕45–75 ft (12–23 m)

From tropical Asia. Deciduous tree with erect branching trunk. Oval to sword-shaped green leaves. Dense panicles of white or purple flowers at branch tips. Zones 11–12.

Lagerstroemia Hybrid Cultivars

CRAPE MYRTLE

☼ ❄ ↔8–25 ft (2.4–8 m)
↕15–25 ft (4.5–8 m)

Over recent decades the US National Arboretum, Maryland, has released a series of hybrids between *L. indica* and the Japanese species *L. faurei*, combining the flower size of the first with the hardiness, mildew resistance, and bark color of the second. Their given names allude to Native American peoples, and they include the popular **'Natchez'**, to about 25 ft (8 m) high, cinnamon bark often mottled with cream, white flowers; and **'Tuscarora'**, fast growing, to 25 ft (8 m), dark coral pink flowers. Other cultivars include: **Indian Summer Series**, full range of colors, and dwarf **Chopin** hybrids, such as **'Bourbon Street'**, 32 in (80 cm) tall, pinkish-red flowers, cascading; **'Pixie White'**, 36 in (90 cm) high, pure white blooms; **'Purple Velvet'**, 4 ft (1.2 m) tall, blackish purple flowers; **'World's Fair'**, 30 in (75 cm) tall, deep red flowers. Zones 7–11.

LAGUNARIA

This genus comprising a single species in the mallow (Malvaceae) family, native to Norfolk and Lord Howe Islands, off eastern Australia, and a small stretch of coastal Queensland, Australia, was named after Andres de Laguna, a sixteenth-century Spanish physician and botanist. It is an evergreen tree growing to 50 ft (15 m) or more; there are, however, several distinct geographic forms, differing mainly in the quantity of soft downy hairs occurring on the simple alternate leaves. The flowers are hibiscus-like, with a conspicuous staminal column; the fruit is a leathery capsule. It is useful for park and street planting, especially in coastal area, as it can withstand salt-laden winds.

CULTIVATION: This tree grows best in well-drained fertile soil in a warm-temperate or subtropical climate. It requires little or no pruning. Propagate from seeds sown in spring; they germinate very readily in a warm humid atmosphere.

Lagerstroemia, Hybrid Cultivar, 'Natchez'

Lagunaria patersonia

syn. *Hibiscus patersonius*

NORFOLK ISLAND HIBISCUS, WHITE OAK

☼ ↔15 ft (4.5 m) ↕25–50 ft (8–15 m)

This species was named after William Paterson, who was the second Lieutenant Governor of New South Wales, Australia. Solitary rosy to mauve-pink flowers with golden yellow anthers, are borne in the upper axils, in summer. Contact with the kidney-shaped seeds, enclosed by fine sharp hairs, can cause a skin irritation. **'Royal Purple'** has shiny green leaves and crimson flowers. Zones 10–11.

LAMIUM

DEAD-NETTLE

Type genus for the mint (Lamiaceae) family. This group of about 50 species of low-growing annuals and perennials, which often spreads by rhizomes or runners, occurs naturally in Europe, North Africa, and temperate Asia, but some are also widely naturalized elsewhere and have become weeds. They are known as dead nettles: their opposite pairs of toothed, pointed, heart-shaped leaves resembling those of stinging nettles but lacking the sting. The small flowers, usually yellow, pink, or white, emerge in spring near the stem tips in leafy heads known as verticillasters. Sometimes used in herbal medicines, the leaves can be eaten as a salad vegetable.

CULTIVATION: Very hardy and easily grown in any partly shaded or shaded position in moist, humus-rich, well-drained soil. Variegated forms are common, often needing more light to maintain their color. Propagate at any time from cuttings or by division.

Lagunaria patersonia

Lamium galeobdolon

syns *Galeobdolon luteum, Lamiastrum galeobdolon*

YELLOW ARCHANGEL

◐/● ❄ ↔48 in (120 cm)
↕8–16 in (20–40 cm)

Vigorous, creeping or scrambling, near-evergreen perennial from temperate Eurasia. Leaves narrow, dark green, elliptical to triangular, to over 2 in (5 cm) long, deeply toothed edges. Heads of up to 10 yellow flowers, to ¾ in (18 mm) long, in summer. **'Hermann's Pride'** ★, narrow leaves with silver streaks and spots; **'Silver Angel'**, low spreader but stems initially upright, silver-marked leaves. Zones 6–10.

Lamium maculatum

◐/● ❄ ↔24–60 in (60–150 cm)
↕6–20 in (15–50 cm)

From Europe, western Asia, and North Africa. Spreading, sometimes mounding or scrambling, near-evergreen perennial. Stems long, rooting as they spread, with downy, toothed, pointed oval to triangular, often white-marked leaves, to over 3 in (8 cm) long. Heads of up to 8 widely spaced pinkish red to purple, rarely white, flowers, to ¾ in (18 mm) long, in summer. Many cultivars. **'Album'**, silver blotched leaves, white flowers; **'Anne Greenaway'**, tricolor foliage, silver center outlined in dark green on a yellow-green base, light purple flowers; **'Aureum'**, white-centered yellow-green leaves, pink flowers; **'Beacon Silver'**, silver leaves with a thin green margin, pink to purplish flowers; **'Orchid Frost'**, gray-green leaves edged green, abundant lavender flowers; **'Pink Nancy'**, silver leaves with a thin green margin, pale pink flowers; **'Pink Pewter'**, green leaves overlaid with silver-gray, deep pink flowers; **'White Nancy'**, silver leaves with a thin green margin, white flowers. Zones 4–10.

Lamium maculatum 'Pink Pewter'

Lamium maculatum

Lampranthus aurantiacus 'Sunman'

Lampranthus glaucus

Lamium orvala

↔ 40 in (100 cm)
↑ 40 in (100 cm)

Bushy perennial found from southern to central Europe. Leaves are toothed, pointed oval, to 6 in (15 cm) long. Flowerheads consist of a few pinkish red to purple flowers, ¾ in (18 mm) long, appear in summer. Zones 6–10.

LAMPRANTHUS

This genus of some 155 species belonging to the iceplant (Aizoaceae) family is found from southern Namibia to South Africa's Eastern Cape; there is also one species possibly native to Australia. They are creeping, sometimes erect subshrubs. The succulent leaves are linear to club-shaped, often triangular in section. The flowers are commonly large and brightly colored and produced profusely over long periods in spring–summer, making them useful for summer bedding and containers in temperate regions. A few are frost hardy, and can be grown all year round in sheltered sites. Some species formerly placed here have now been reclassified as *Oscularia*. CULTIVATION: These plants need full sun and thrive in poor well-drained soils. They are very easily propagated from stem cuttings, which can be rooted at almost any time of the year.

Lampranthus aurantiacus ★

syn. *Mesembryanthemum aurantiacum*

ICE PLANT

↔ 8–18 in (20–45 cm)
↑ 6–12 in (15–30 cm)

Succulent perennial with upright stems becoming prostrate with age. Leaves bluish green, tapering, minutely rough and spotted. Bears profuse daisy-like bright yellow or orange flowers in the late spring. **'Sunman'**, golden yellow flowers. Zones 9–11.

Lamprocapnos spectabilis

Lamprocapnos spectabilis 'Alba'

Lampranthus filicaulis

syn. *Mesembryanthemum filicaule*

TRAILING ICE PLANT

↔ 18–36 in (45–90 cm)
↑ 12–24 in (30–60 cm)

Succulent perennial. Weak, delicate, creeping or prostrate stems. Leaves are crowded, tapering, curved, and about 1 in (25 mm) long. Reddish flowers are borne on long stalks. Zones 8–11.

Lampranthus glaucus

NOON FLOWER

↔ 12–24 in (30–60 cm)
↑ 12–24 in (30–60 cm)

Bushy, low-spreading, succulent perennial with roughly dotted, flattened, 3-angled, gray-green leaves, to 1 in (25 mm) long. The soft, sulfur yellow, daisy-like flowers appear in late spring. The fruit is a dry capsule. Zones 9–11.

Lampranthus productus

PURPLE ICE PLANT

↔ 12–24 in (30–60 cm)
↑ 12–24 in (30–60 cm)

Much-branched succulent perennial with narrow leaves, to 1½ in (35 mm) long, covered with fine dots. Groups of 3 or 5 pale rose pink flowers, each 1 in (25 mm) across. Zones 9–11.

Lampranthus roseus

syns *Lampranthus multiradiatus*, *Mesembryanthemum roseum*

↔ 12–20 in (30–50 cm)
↑ 12–20 in (30–50 cm)

Short-lived, erect, shrubby, succulent perennial, sometimes grown as an annual, with slender branches and narrow curved leaves. Clusters of rose pink to reddish violet daisy-like flowers, with a slightly peppery smell, in mid-spring–early summer. Zones 9–11.

Lantana camara var. *crocea*

Lampranthus spectabilis

syn. *Mesembryanthemum spectabile*

ICE PLANT

↔ 20–30 in (50–75 cm)
↑ 6–20 in (15–50 cm)

Prostrate, trailing, succulent perennial. Branching stems, mounding spreading habit. Fleshy, bright green to grayish green, curved leaves with reddish tips, keeled and triangular in section. Profuse glossy, pink to purplish red, daisy-like flowers, 2–3 in (5–8 cm) across, in spring–summer. **'Tresco Apricot'**, apricot flowers; **'Tresco Brilliant'**, magenta flowers; **'Tresco Red'**, fiery red flowers. Zones 9–10.

LAMPROCAPNOS

The sole species in this genus is much better known under its former name of *Dicentra spectabilis*. Probably the most popular of the bleeding hearts, it is now in a genus of its own as part of the poppy (Papaveraceae) family. It is a woodland perennial with beautiful blue-green foliage and arching stems, below which from mid-spring hang graceful, heart-shaped flowers. CULTIVATION: Thrives in moist, compost-rich, well-drained soil in sun to dappled shade. Delicate-looking but tough and adaptable. Propagate from seed, by division, or from basal cuttings of non-flowering stems.

Lamprocapnos spectabilis

syn. *Dicentra spectabilis*

BLEEDING HEART

↔ 20–40 in (50–100 cm)
↑ 40–56 in (100–140 cm)

Perennial from Japan, northeastern China, and Russia's far east. Vigorous grower with leaves coarsely divided. Strongly upright, often red-tinted flower stems carry up to 15 large, pink, heart-shaped flowers with slightly protruding white inner petals. **'Alba'**, pure white flowers. Zones 6–9.

Lantana montevidensis

LANTANA

A small genus of about 150 species evergreen shrubs within the vervain (Verbenaceae) family, these plants are mostly found in tropical America. They have scrambling, somewhat prickly stems, simple opposite leaves, rough on both surfaces, and small flowers grouped in dense flattened or hemispherical heads, with the youngest flowers at the center. CULTIVATION: Lantanas will tolerate quite harsh conditions but are at their best in light fertile soils with free drainage. They flower freely in a sunny open position in a frost-free climate, and although they are generally suitable for coastal areas, they should be given some protection from salt-laden winds. Regular tip pruning when the plants are young will help the formation of a compact shape, but in later years little or no pruning is necessary. Propagate from seed sown in spring or from half-hardened cuttings taken in summer. Soft-tip cuttings can be taken at any time of the year.

Lantana camara

LANTANA

↔ 8–30 ft (2.4–9 m)
↑ 4–12 ft (1.2–3.5 m)

Native to the West Indies and Central America. Evergreen shrub. Flowers in shades ranging from creamy white through yellow, orange and pink to brick red, the heads often appearing bicolored owing to florets ageing to another color. Wild forms are particularly invasive colonizers, and proclaimed as noxious weeds in some warm-climate countries, including some States of Australia. Sterile or near-sterile forms available. ***L. c.* var. *crocea***, golden yellow to orange flowers. ***L. c.* 'Chelsea Gem'**, mainly scarlet, and some orange, flowers; **'Orange Carpet'**, with trailing habit, orange flowers; **'Patriot Dove Wings'**, cascading habit, and pale yellow flowers soon turning white; **'Patriot Rainbow'**, compact, about 16 in (40 cm) wide and high, bicolored florets from deep pinkish red to creamy yellow; **'Schloss Ortenburg'**, multi-colored florets from yellow to orange or pink; **'Variegata'** (syn. 'Lemon Swirl'), pale green cream-edged leaves, yellow flowers. Zones 9–12.

Lantana montevidensis

syn. *Lantana sellowiana*

TRAILING LANTANA

↔ 10 ft (3 m) ↑ 3 ft (0.9 m)

Native to the central eastern region of South America. This species is an evergreen trailing shrub. Leaves are dark green, oblong to lance-shaped, and roughly toothed. The rosy lilac flowers, 1 in (25 mm) across, with a bright yellow flush in the throat, are slightly fragrant, and appear in winter and throughout the year. **'Alba'** is a white-flowered cultivar popular in the USA. Zones 9–11.

LAPAGERIA

This genus consists of a single species of evergreen, climbing, woody plants from Chile that twine up trees, trellises, and fences. They are members of the small family Philesiaceae, allied to the sarsaparilla (Smilacaceae) family. Their upright stems need support to climb up and through structures. If there is no support available, the plant will scramble over the ground. The large, oval, dark green leaves are thick and leathery and have distinctive ribbing along the length of the leaf. The large, pendent, bell-shaped flowers have 3 broad waxy outer segments overlapping the 3 narrower inner ones; they are predominantly a rosy red in wild populations, but cultivars can vary in color from deep crimson red to a range of pinks and creams. There are some reports of yellow forms of *Lapageria*.

CULTIVATION: Sensitive to frost, these plants need to be in a sheltered spot, away from all-day sun in summer. They like a cool area for their roots, and their branches head toward the light, which helps initiate flower bud development. They need free-draining, open, fertile soil, not waterlogged, with a neutral pH. Propagate from seed in spring; it may take up to 7 years for plants to flower from seed, and flower color may vary in seedlings. They can be grown in a greenhouse.

Lapageria rosea 'Angol'

Lapageria rosea

CHILEAN BELLFLOWER, COPIHUE

↔ 3–10 ft (0.9–3 m) ↑ 17 ft (5 m)

Chile's national flower. Leaves, to 5 in (12 cm) long, are held on thin, smooth, rope-like stems. Large rosy red flowers, 4–6 in (10–15 cm) long, are produced in summer–autumn. **'Alba'**, white flowers; **'Angol'** (perhaps more correctly 'Ongol', though usually sold as 'Angol') has especially large salmon pink flowers; **'Collinge'**, striking red-edged white flowers; **'Contulmo'** (syn. 'Sangre del Toro'), deep red, heavy waxy texture; **'Nash Court'** bears soft shell pink flowers, the petals marked with dark red stripy mottling; **'Nuhuelbuta'**; cream suffused violet; **'Quelipichum'**, double flowers, deep pink to light red. Zones 8–10.

LARIX

The larches, members of the pine (Pinaceae) family, comprise the largest genus of deciduous conifers; they are found in northern Europe, over much of Asia from Siberia to as far south as the mountains of northern Myanmar, and in northern North America. They are among the earliest trees to come into leaf in spring, the leaves being carried on both long and short shoots. The upright summer-ripening cones, borne on the shorter shoots, persist on the tree for some time. With age, branches tend to droop in a graceful manner. The leaves are needle-like and usually vivid green, sometimes blue-green in summer, turning butter yellow to old gold in autumn. Some species yield valuable timber that is strong and heavy.

CULTIVATION: Larches are adaptable to most soils, though wet soils are best avoided for all but 1 or 2 species. All larches need plenty of light. Species hybridize readily, both in the wild and in cultivation. Propagation from seed is easily achieved.

Larix decidua 'Pendula'

Larix laricina, in the wild, Ontario, Canada

Larix decidua

syn. *Larix europaea*

EUROPEAN LARCH

↔ 12–20 ft (3.5–6 m) ↑ 165 ft (50 m)

Native to mountains of central and eastern Europe; introduced to Britain around 1600. Conical crown becoming broader with age, with some wide-spreading horizontal as well as erect branches. Bark smooth gray, fissured on old trees, coarsely ridged. Leaves tender light green; mature cones yellowish. **'Corley'**, dwarf spreading tree; **'Pendula'**, strongly weeping habit, usually grafted on 6–8 ft (1.8–2.4 m) standards. Zones 2–8.

Larix kaempferi 'Stiff Weeping'

Larix kaempferi

syn. *Larix leptolepis*

JAPANESE LARCH

↔ 12–20 ft (4.5–6 m) ↑ 100 ft (30 m)

Common in Japan, less common in cultivation, although it withstands atmospheric pollution. Long low branches sweeping out and up, upper branches sweeping upward; scaly rusty brown bark. Leaves gray-green; female flowers pink or cream; cones brown. **'Pendula'** ★ and **'Stiff Weeping'** both have pendulous branches. Zones 4–9.

Larix laricina

AMERICAN LARCH, EASTERN LARCH, TAMARACK LARCH

↔ 12–20 ft (4.5–6 m) ↑ 60 ft (18 m)

Found throughout most of northern North America, growing in sphagnum bogs and swamps. Crown open, often with twisted, hooped branches. Bark pink to reddish brown, finely flaking, not fissured. Leaves are short soft needles turning yellow in autumn. Zones 2–8.

Larix lyallii, in the wild, Yoho National Park, British Columbia, Canada

Larix × marschlinsii 'Varied Directions'

Larix lyallii

☼ ✱ ↔6–15 ft (1.8–4.5 m) ↑40 ft (12 m)

From western North America. A small to medium-sized tree, with densely felted young shoots, and 4-angled grayish green leaves. Twigs are densely woolly; the bark thin, furrowed, and scaly. This species is sometimes listed as a subalpine form of *L. occidentalis*. Zones 2–8.

Larix × marschlinsii

syn. *Larix × eurolepsis*

DUNKELD LARCH, HYBRID LARCH

☼ ✱ ↔20 ft (6 m) ↑90 ft (27 m)

A hybrid between *L. decidua* and *L. kaempferi*. Intermediate between its parents, differing in having yellow, slightly waxy-bloomed shoots and conical cones. The leaves are long, thin, gray-green, to 1½ in (35 mm) long. **'Varied Directions'**, pendulous branches. Zones 2–9.

Larix occidentalis

WESTERN LARCH

☼ ✱ ↔15 ft (4.5 m) ↑180 ft (55 m)

Native to North America. Bark purplish gray, deeply and widely fissured; crown rather open, narrowly conical. Leaves bright green on both surfaces. Cones rich purple in summer, with orange and yellow bracts ripening to purple-brown. Zones 3–9.

Larix sibirica

syn. *Larix russica*

SIBERIAN LARCH

☼ ✱ ↔15 ft (4.5 m) ↑100 ft (30 m)

Native to eastern Russia (Siberia), Mongolia, and China's Xinjiang Province. Attractive red-brown bark, which becomes furrowed and gnarled with age. The branches sweep down, rising at the tips, preventing snow build-up. The leaves are very narrow, soft bright green in spring, turning gold in autumn. Small scaly cones. Zones 1–8.

LARREA

CREOSOTE BUSH

This genus of 5 species of evergreen shrubs, a member of the twinleaf (Zygophyllaceae) family, occurs from South America to southwestern USA. The suckering jointed stems carry opposite compound leaves with leaflets up to ¾ in (18 mm) long. The flowers are solitary, borne at the branch tips, with 5 unequal sepals and clawed, oblong, yellow petals. The rounded fruits are covered with soft fine hairs. A secretion from the leaves, which gives them a varnished look, has a smell resembling creosote, particularly when wet. These bushes also release toxins that restricts the growth of nearby plants. Plant parts are used by local peoples for their medicinal properties, despite their unpleasant taste.

CULTIVATION: All *Larrea* species prefer light, sandy well-drained soil in an open sunny position. Propagation is from seed.

Larrea tridentata

syn. *Larrea divaricata*

COVILLE, CREOSOTE BUSH

☼ ❄ ↔6–10 ft (1.8–3 m) ↑6–12 ft (1.8–3.5 m)

Found from southwest USA to northern Mexico. Straggly, slow-growing, aromatic, evergreen shrub. Dark gray to black bark. Leaves compound, resinous, dark green to yellowish green, with 2 or 3 oblong to spear-shaped leaflets. Profuse tiny yellow flowers, to ½ in (12 mm) across, in spring and autumn. Zones 7–10.

Larrea tridentata

LASTHENIA

This genus of annuals and perennials in the daisy (Asteraceae) family consists of 16 species from the Pacific coast of North America and one from central Chile. Their wild habitats include dunes, saline flats, and grasslands. Leaves are opposite, simple or dissected, smooth-surfaced or sometimes hairy. Showy long-stalked flowerheads, borne at the stem tips, have both ray and disc florets, both usually golden yellow, with the rays broad and rounded, forming a neat ring around the broad domed disc.

CULTIVATION: *Lasthenia* species are drought and frost tolerant, and adaptable to a wide range of soils and positions. Propagate from seed.

Lasthenia glabrata

GOLDFIELDS

☼ ❄ ↔9–18 in (22.5–45 cm) ↑18–24 in (45–60 cm)

From California, USA. Erect annual. Leaves narrow, toothed, fleshy, 2–6 in (5–15 cm) long. Daisy-like flowerheads with golden or lemon yellow ray florets, in summer. Zones 7–10.

Lasthenia glabrata

LATANIA

There are 3 species in this genus of the palm (Arecaceae) family, all endemic to the Mascarene Islands, east of Madagascar. Once more common in drier parts of the islands' coastal regions, they are now rare owing to the clearing of land for agriculture. Each species is confined to one island. They are tall single-stemmed palms with large fan-shaped fronds. The male and female flowers are borne on separate plants, usually during the wet season. Although all 3 species are similar in general appearance, they differ in the coloration of the leaves.

CULTIVATION: The young plants grow quite quickly, but they must be placed in full sun, in well-drained soil, and not exposed to frosts. Propagate from fresh seed, which can take 4 months to germinate after sowing. Seed obtained from plants in cultivation, where there are 2 or 3 species growing near each other, can produce hybrids.

Latania loddigesii ★

BLUE LATAN PALM

☼ ✢ ↔12 ft (3.5 m) ↑25 ft (8 m)

Native to Mauritius, the middle island of the Mascarene group. Glaucous adult fronds with woolly white bases. Fronds over 15 ft (4.5 m). The flowers, on inflorescences to 6 ft (1.8 m), are borne in summer; male and female are similar in size. The fruit, round and fleshy, turns greenish brown when ripe. Zones 10–12.

LATHYRUS

SWEET PEA, VETCHLING, WILD PEA

This genus in the pea-flower subfamily of the legume (Fabaceae) family has far more than just the old-fashioned and popular sweet peas to offer among its 110 species of annuals and perennials. From Eurasia, North America, temperate South America, and the mountains of East Africa, many are climbers, others are low-spreading plants, and some are

Latania loddigesii

shrubby. The climbers support themselves with tendrils growing at the tips of the pinnate leaves, where the terminal leaflets would normally be. The typical pea-flowers occur in many colors, and may be borne singly or in racemes arising from the upper leaf axils.
CULTIVATION: Non-climbing perennials will tolerate partial shade, but otherwise grow them in sunny well-ventilated conditions to lessen the risk of mildew and botrytis. Plant in moist well-drained soil and provide stakes or wires for climbers. Propagate annuals from seed sown in early spring, or in autumn–winter in mild climates, and perennials by division when dormant.

Lathyrus grandiflorus

EVERLASTING PEA, TWO-FLOWERED PEA

☼ ✱ ↔7 ft (2 m) ↑7 ft (2 m)

Found from Sicily to southern Balkans. Climbing perennial. Angled stems; leaves tendril-tipped, with paired 2 in (5 cm) long leaflets. Sprays of up to 4 violet and pink flowers, 1¼ in (30 mm) across, in summer. Zones 6–10.

Lathyrus grandiflorus

Lathyrus latifolius

PERENNIAL PEA

☼ ✱ ↔7 ft (2 m) ↑10 ft (3 m)

Found in central and southern Europe. Climbing perennial. Faintly angled stems; leaves tendril-tipped, with paired 6 in (15 cm) long leaflets. Racemes of up to 15 purple, pink, or white flowers, 1¼ in (30 mm) across, are borne in summer. **'Albus'** (syn. 'Snow White'), pure white flowers; **'Pink Beauty'**, pink and red flowers; **'White Pearl'**, long-lasting white flowers. Zones 5–9.

Lathyrus odoratus

SWEET PEA

☼ ❄ ↔40 in (100 cm) ↑8 ft (2.4 m)

From Italy and the Mediterranean islands. Highly scented annual climber. Angled, somewhat downy stems and paired blue-green leaflets, to over 2 in (5 cm) long. The wild species has ra-cemes of up to 3 violet and purple red flowers in summer. Garden forms are heavier flowering in a very wide range of colors. Sow in autumn in zones 9 and above or in spring in cooler climates. **'Alan Williams'**, buff-pink and white; **'Annie Good'**, pink tonings; **'Anniversary'** ★, white with pink edge; **'Bijou Mix'**, only 12 in (30 cm) tall, many colors; **'Brian Clough'**, orange and white; **'Charlie's Angel'**, blue and lavender; **'Cream Southbourne'**, pale cream; **'Eclipse'**, deep lavender; **'Evening Glow'**, mid-pink and orange; **'Firebird'**, orange-red; **Fragrantissima Mix,** large flowers, all colors, strong fragrance; **'Jill Walton'**, cream and pale pink, darker edge; **'Lilac Ripple'**, white and mauve; **'Midnight'**, deep purple-red; **'Noel Sutton'**, deep blue; **'Sea Wolf'**, lavender; **'Spencer Mixed'**, old favorite, first of the large-flowered mixed color strains; **'Teresa Maureen'**, lavender and cerise, purplish edge; **'Wiltshire Ripple'**, brown-red and white; **'Winner'**, red suffused with orange. Cultivars with small, fragrant, single flowers, often known as **Heirloom** style, include: **'Blanche Ferry'**, pink and white bicolor; **'Cupani'**, compact, with intensely fragrant, purple and red flowers, known since 1699; **'Old Spice Mix'**, very fragrant flowers in wide color range, including bicolor and striped; **'Painted Lady'**, very pale pink and deep cherry red. Zones 8–11.

Lathyrus odoratus 'Charlie's Angel'

Lathyrus odoratus 'Brian Clough'

Lathyrus splendens

PRIDE OF CALIFORNIA

☼ ❄ ↔3–7 ft (0.9–2 m)
↑7 10 ft (2 3 m)

From the mountains of northern Baja California, Mexico. Shrubby, sometimes scrambling, evergreen perennial. Leaves tendril-tipped, with up to 10 leaflets to nearly 3 in (8 cm) long. Racemes of up to 12 violet to purple-red flowers, 1¾ in (40 mm) across. Zones 8–10.

Lathyrus vernus

SPRING VETCH

☼ ✱ ↔24–40 in (60–100 cm)
↑12–24 in (30–60 cm)

From Europe. Often semi-evergreen perennial. Angular stems; leaves with 1 to 2 pairs of leaflets to 4 in (10 cm) long. Long racemes of up to 15 flowers, ¾ in (18 mm) across, initially purple-red, ageing to blue-green, in early spring. **'Alboroseus'**, pink and white flowers; **'Rosenelfe'**, 12 in (30 cm) tall, pale pink flowers. Zones 4–9.

L. odoratus 'Cream Southbourne'

LAURUS

LAUREL

There are just 2 species of evergreen trees and shrubs in this genus, which gives its name to the large and mainly tropical laurel (Lauraceae) family, one found around the Mediterranean region and the other native to the Canary Islands and the Azores. Botanists regard them as relics of the warmer evergreen "laurel forest" believed to have clothed most of Europe before the last Ice Ages. The foliage is leathery, deep green, and aromatic, and the small yellowish flowers arise along the branches in spring.
CULTIVATION: *L. nobilis* is the species commonly seen in cultivation. It is a very adaptable plant, suitable for hedging, topiary, specimen planting, or containers, and tolerates coastal conditions. In cool-temperate climates it is best grown against a warm wall. It requires a sunny site in fertile well-drained soil. Formal shapes and hedging should be trimmed in the summer. Propagate from seed sown in autumn or from half-hardened cuttings taken in summer.

Laurus nobilis

BAY LAUREL, BAY TREE, SWEET BAY, TRUE LAUREL

☼ ❄ ↔6–15 ft (1.8–4.5 m)
↑10–50 ft (3–15 m)

Native to the Mediterranean region, growing in moist rocky valleys. Densely branched small tree or shrub. Leaves glossy, dark green, with slightly wavy margins. Small yellowish flowers; black egg-shaped fruit. The leaves are extremely popular as a culinary herb. **'Aurea'**, yellow leaves. Zones 8–11.

Laurus nobilis

L. angustifolia 'Royal Purple'

LAVANDULA

LAVENDER

The 28 species of evergreen aromatic shrubs and subshrubs in this genus belong to the large mint (Lamiaceae) family, which includes herbs such as sage and rosemary. They occur mainly around the Mediterranean, with a few in western Asia and the Canary and Cape Verde Islands. Their natural habitat is dry and exposed rocky areas. The narrow leaves are usually grayish green, often toothed or in some species pinnately divided. The spikes of small purple flowers vary in their intensity of color and perfume. Cultivated species belong to 3 groups: the hardy **Spica** (English lavender) **Group**, with mostly basal entire leaves and long slender flower-spikes; the slightly more tender **Stoechas Group**, with flower-spikes terminating in a "topknot" of colored bracts; and the tender **Pterostoechas Group**, with pinnately divided leaves. Some of the Spica Group lavenders are cultivated commercially for their aromatic foliage and flowerheads, which are mostly distilled to produce the lavender oil widely used in perfumes, toiletries, and air fresheners.

CULTIVATION: Lavenders are excellent for hot dry sites, containers, hedging, and positions where they can be brushed against to release their aroma. They need well-drained soil, not too fertile. Hardy species are pruned after flowering. All lavenders can be propagated from seed, or from tip cuttings in the spring or half-hardened cuttings in the autumn.

Lavandula dentata

Lavandula × *allardii*

HYBRID LAVENDER

↔ 3 ft (0.9 m) ↑ 3 ft (0.9 m)

Thought to be a cross between *L. dentata* and *L. latifolia.* Vigorous grower. The leaves are gray, relatively wide, and roundly toothed. The long narrow spikes of dark purple flowers, are carried well above the foliage, in summer. Zones 8–11.

Lavandula angustifolia ★

syns *Lavandula officinalis, L. spica, L. vera*

ENGLISH LAVENDER

↔ 4 ft (1.2 m) ↑ 2–3 ft (0.6–0.9 m)

A Spica Group species native to the Mediterranean region. Bushy shrub, with narrow, gray, slightly downy leaves. Fragrant deep purple flower spikes are produced in early summer. *L. angustifolia* does not grow as well in hot humid areas. Cultivars include: **'Alba'**, white flowers; **'Beechwood Blue'**, low-growing and with short-stemmed blue flowers; **'Folgate'**, mid-height, light gray-green foliage, bright blue flowers; **'Hidcote'**, densely packed spikes of purple flowers; **'Imperial Gem'**, narrow gray leaves, deep purple flowers; **'Loddon Blue'**, to 20 in (50 cm) tall, bright silvery gray foliage, deep purple-blue flowers; **'Martha Roderick'**, compact mounding habit, green-gray foliage, bright lavender flowers; **'Munstead'** ★, dwarf variety, popular for edging; **'Princess Blue'**, leaves tending green, pale lavender flowers; **'Rosea'**, pink flower spikes; **'Royal Purple'**, tall, narrow, gray leaves, deep purple flowers. Zones 5–10.

Lavandula dentata

FRENCH LAVENDER, FRINGED LAVENDER, TOOTHED LAVENDER

↔ 5 ft (1.5 m) ↑ 3–5 ft (0.9–1.5 m)

This Stoechas Group species is native to Mediterranean region, Madeira, and Cape Verde Islands. Leaves narrow, grayish green, bluntly toothed; stems slightly downy. Pale purple flower spikes on long stems above foliage. *L. d.* var. *candicans,* grayer in appearance, more downy, with flowers a deeper purple. *L. d.* **'Ploughman's Blue'**, lilac flower spikes on long stems, to 12 in (30 cm), good for hedging and confined to tubs. Zones 9–11.

Lavandula × *intermedia*

Lavandula × *intermedia*

↔ 3 ft (0.9 m) ↑ 3 ft (0.9 m)

Various hybrids between *L. angustifolia* and *L. latifolia* are known by this name. Characteristics are intermediate be-tween the 2 species, flowers paler than *L. angustifolia.* Frequently grown for cut flowers and oil production. **'Gray Hedge'**, attractive silvery gray foliage, purple flowers, popular as hedging plant; **'Grosso'** ★, the cultivar most commonly grown for oil production, fine-leafed, long dark purple flowers; **'Provence'** ★, attractive cultivar popular in the USA; **'Seal'**, vigorous, very free flowering, with pale purple flower spikes. Zones 7–10.

Lavandula lanata

WOOLLY LAVENDER

↔ 3 ft (0.9 m) ↑ 3 ft (0.9 m)

Native to the mountains of southern Spain. The leaves are different from other species in the Spica Group, they are wider, and covered in a whitish gray down. The spikes of purple flowers are held well above the foliage, in the summer. *L. lanata* dislikes humidity. Zones 7–10.

Lavandula latifolia

SPIKE LAVENDER

↔ 4 ft (1.2 m) ↑ 3 ft (0.9 m)

Native to the western Mediterranean regions. Rather like *L. angustifolia*, but with broader grayish green leaves and purple flower spikes carried on long stalks, which are frequently in 3 branches. Flowers later in summer than *L. angustifolia.* Zones 7–10.

Lavandula multifida

↔ 3 ft (0.9 m) ↑ 3 ft (0.9 m)

A Pterostoechas Group species, native to areas of southern Europe and northern Africa. Finely divided fern-like leaves. Soft purple flower spikes, on long, often branched stems, in summer. Lacks the true lavender fragrance. Zones 7–10.

Lavandula pedunculata

syn. *Lavandula stoechas subsp. pedunculata*

BUTTERFLY LAVENDER, FRENCH LAVENDER

↔ 24–32 in (60–80 cm) ↑ 24–32 in (60–80 cm)

Mediterranean native. Leaves gray-green, not toothed, narrow, to 1½ in (35 mm) long. Long-bracted purple flowerheads on tall wiry stems, fragrant. **Ruffles Series** ★, compact plants, shorter bracts, rippled and ruffled, various colors such as **'Blueberry Ruffles'**, blue flowers, lavender bracts; **'Strawberry Ruffles'**, pink flowers and bracts; **'Sweetberry Ruffles'**, lavender flowers and bracts. **'Violet Lace'** (deep pinkish purple) and **'Winter Lace'** (mid-lavender) start early and bloom from winter through summer. Zones 9–11.

Lavandula pinnata

CANARY ISLAND LAVENDER

↔ 3 ft (0.9 m) ↑ 3 ft (0.9 m)

Native to the Canary Islands. This Pterostoechas Group species is lightly covered in fine short hairs. Leaves green to gray, pinnate, with broad lobes. Flowerheads of soft purple spikes, usually branched into 3, in summer. **'Sidonie'**, hybrid thought to have *L. pinnata* as a parent; free flowering in warm climates, bearing deep purple flower spikes on long branching stalks for most of the year from late winter. Zones 9–11.

Lavandula stoechas

FRENCH LAVENDER, ITALIAN LAVENDER, SPANISH LAVENDER

↔ 24 in (60 cm) ↑ 24 in (60 cm)

From the Mediterranean region. Variable species. Leaves fine grayish green. Plump flower spikes of deep purple topped by prominent petal-like bracts in summer. Can become invasive. **'Alba'**, dull white flower spikes; **'Avonview'**, fast growing, 24–32 in (60–80 cm) tall, sterile bracts long and pink, bracts of fertile heads purple with fine green mid-stripe; **'Helmsdale'**, compact, with burgundy-purple flowers; **'Kew Red'**, to 10 in (25 cm) tall, pink flowers; **'Major'**, flowering profusely with spikes of deepest intense purple; **'Marshwood'**, slightly bigger, to 3 ft

(0.9 m), large plump spikes of purple flowers topped with very long mauve bracts; **'Otto Quast'**, popular American cultivar; **'Regal Splendour'**, deep purple flowers, lavender bracts; **'Willow Vale'**, unusual wavy-edged and crinkled purple bracts. Zones 8–11.

LAVATERA

TREE MALLOW

There are 25 species of evergreen or deciduous annuals, biennials, perennials, and softwooded shrubs in this genus within the mallow (Malvaceae) family. Found from the Mediterranean to the northwestern Himalayas, and in parts of Asia, Australia, California, USA, and Baja California, Mexico. The leaves are usually palmately lobed and slightly downy, and most species have attractive hibiscus-like flowers with prominent staminal columns, in colors ranging from white to a rosy purple. *Lavatera* is closely related to *Malva*, and following recent botanical studies several of its species have been reclassified as *Malva* species.

CULTIVATION: Shrubby mallows are suitable for planting in mixed borders, where they will bloom abundantly throughout summer. They should be grown in full sun in light well-drained soil. Too rich a soil will result in an excess of foliage at the expense of flowers. Prune after flowering to prevent legginess. Mallows tend to be fairly short lived; softwood cuttings taken in spring or early summer strike readily and are the usual method of propagation for the shrubby species.

Lavandula pinnata

Lavandula stoechas 'Helmsdale'

Lavatera cachemiriana

Lavatera cachemiriana

TREE MALLOW

☼/◐ ✱ ↔24 in (60 cm) ↑7 ft (2 m)

Semi-evergreen woody perennial. Wiry stems; mid-green ivy-shaped leaves. Silky clear pink flowers appear in mid-summer–early autumn. Zones 6–10.

Lavatera × *clementii*

☼ ❄ ↔6 ft (1.8 m) ↑6 ft (1.8 m)

Popular perennial *Lavatera* hybrids derived from *L. thuringiaca* and *L. olbia*. They tend to be vigorous upright plants that, while sometimes short lived, always bloom reliably and sometimes with spectacular results. **'Barnsley'** ★ bears masses of pale pink flowers, very easy-care; **'Bredon Springs'** ★, attractive deep pink flowers; **'Candy Floss'** (syn. 'Cotton Candy'), very bright pink flowers; **'Kew Rose'**, as for 'Rosea' but to 12 ft (3.5 m) tall; **'Rosea'** is tall, with gray-tinted foliage and dusky pink flowers. Zones 8–10.

Lavatera olbia

TREE LAVATERA, TREE MALLOW

☼ ❄ ↔5 ft (1.5 m) ↑6 ft (1.8 m)

From western Mediterranean regions. True *L. olbia* is rarely cultivated; the plant sold under that name is usually *L.* × *clementii*. Evergreen shrub. Bristly stems; downy lobed leaves; reddish purple flowers. Zones 8–10.

Lavatera thuringiaca

TREE MALLOW

☼ ❄ ↔3–4 ft (0.9–1.2 m) ↑6 ft (1.8 m)

Shrubby evergreen perennial from central Europe. Rose pink flowers for several months from summer–autumn. Zones 8–11.

Lavatera × *clementii* 'Rosea'

Lavatera trimestris 'Ruby Regis'

Lavatera olbia

Lavatera trimestris

ANNUAL MALLOW, REGAL MALLOW, ROSE MALLOW, ROYAL MALLOW

☼ ❄ ↔18–36 in (45–90 cm) ↑24–48 in (60–120 cm)

Bushy easy-to-grow annual native to Mediterranean region. Does not need to be staked. Silky cup-shaped flowers. **'Ruby Regis'**, to 24 in (60 cm) tall, cerise pink flowers; **'Silver Cup'**, 24 in (60 cm) tall, pink flowers. Zones 8–10.

LAYIA

This genus is a member of the daisy (Asteraceae) family, and contains about 15 species of annuals from western USA, found on scrubland, grassy hillsides, and in coastal areas. They develop into bushy plants with narrow, alternate, grayish green leaves that are sometimes pinnate or have toothed edges, and can be aromatic. Showy yellow-centered daisy flowers in white, yellow, or yellow with white petal tips are borne prolifically from spring to summer, and are attractive cut flowers.

CULTIVATION: Grow *Layia* species in full sun in a well-drained soil. These plants dislike hot humid conditions. Propagate from seed sown direct in areas with long hot summers or with protection from frosts in cooler climates.

Layia platyglossa

syn. *Layia elegans*

TIDY TIPS

☼ ❄ ↔10 in (25 cm) ↑18 in (45 cm)

From California. Narrow grayish green leaves. Yellow daisy flowers, 2 in (5 cm) wide, with white-tipped rays, in summer–autumn. Zones 8–11.

LEDEBOURIA

AFRICAN SQUILL

This genus of about 30 species of bulbous perennials from sub-Saharan Africa, Madagascar, and India belongs to the asparagus (Asparagaceae) family. Leaves are basal, sometimes grayish, often striped or spotted red or green. The inflorescence is a simple raceme with inconspicuous bracts, borne at the branch tips. The flowers are small to very small, the 6 outer segments purple or greenish and recurved.

CULTIVATION: Grown mainly for their colored foliage, *Ledebouria* species grow well with cacti and succulents. In temperate climates they grow best in a cool greenhouse in moderately rich compost.

Ledebouria cooperi

syns *Scilla adlamii, S. cooperi*

☼ ❄ ↔2–3 in (5–8 cm)
↕2–4 in (5–10 cm)

Semi-evergreen bulb from South Africa. Leaves fleshy, to 10 in (25 cm) long, green with parallel purple stripes, setting off the spikes of tiny deep purple-pink flowers in mid- to late summer. Zones 8–11.

Ledebouria socialis ★

syns *Scilla socialis, S. violacea*

☼ ❄ ↔2–3 in (5–8 cm)
↕2–4 in (5–10 cm)

From South Africa. Evergreen with exposed bulb. Leaves broad, to 4 in (10 cm) long, gray with deep green blotches, purple beneath. Spikes of tiny, nodding, green bellflowers, on pink stalks, are held above the leaves. Zones 8–12.

Ledebouria cooperi

Ledebouria socialis

LEONOTIS

Comprising 15 species, this genus of softwooded annuals, perennials, and evergreen to semi-deciduous subshrubs in the mint (Lamiaceae) family, with the exception of one widely distributed tropical species, occurs wild in tropical and southern Africa. Opposite pairs of mid-green leaves are borne on upright squarish stems, and in late summer to winter whorls of narrow 2-lipped flowers are arranged densely around the stems.

CULTIVATION: These are warm-climate plants that can be grown under cover in frost-prone areas. They need moderately fertile soil in full sun and ample water in the growing season. The somewhat brittle stems can be cut back in spring. Propagate from seed or from softwood cuttings in summer.

Leonotis nepetifolia

☼ ❄ ↔8–12 in (20–30 cm)
↕3–4 ft (0.9–1.2 m)

From India and Africa; now naturalized in parts of North America. Upright annual. Serrated leaves, to 5 in (12 cm) long. Curved orange trumpet-flowers are borne in winter. Zones 8–11.

Leonotis nepetifolia

Leonotis ocymifolia

Leonotis ocymifolia

syn. *Leonotis leonurus*

LION'S TAIL, WILD DAGGA

☼ ❄ ↔3 ft (0.9 m) ↕8 ft (2.4 m)

Most widely cultivated species of *Leonotis*. Clump-forming subshrub, semi-deciduous or evergreen depending on climate. Upright stems, with bright orange woolly flowers in the late summer to winter. **'Alba'** and **'Harrismith White'**, similar white-flowered plants. Zones 9–11.

LEPECHINIA

This genus comprises about 55 species of trailing to upright, slightly woody perennials in the mint (Lamiaceae) family, occurring mainly in Mexico, Central America, and western South America, with 4 species native to California and 1 to Hawaii, USA. They grow in open to rocky habitats, mostly in mountain regions. They have strongly scented, usually furry, leaves, which are often large and handsome. Spikes of salvia-like flowers, mainly in shades of purple and mauve, may be produced over a very long season; in frost-free climates some species flower all year.

CULTIVATION: These plants require full sun in a well-drained fairly dry site. In frosty climates they can be overwintered in a well-lit greenhouse. Propagate by seed, which will often germinate where it falls, or by cuttings taken in summer.

Lepechinia fragrans

Leptodactylon californicum

Lepechinia fragrans

CHANNEL ISLAND SAGE, FRAGRANT PITCHER SAGE

☼ ❄ ↔3–4 ft (0.9–1.2 m)
↕3–4 ft (0.9–1.2 m)

From southern California's Channel Islands and nearby mainland USA, growing in chaparral on coastal hills; now rare in the wild. An evergreen shrubby perennial. Leaves large, arrow-shaped, aromatic when touched. The light pink-purple flowers in spring–summer are attractive to butterflies. Zones 7–10.

LEPTODACTYLON

This genus, belonging to the phlox (Polemoniaceae) family, comprises 12 species of woody-based subshrubs, shrubs, or perennials native to western North America, extending from British Columbia to California. Their natural habitat is forest and scrubland. Some are of compact habit; others are straggly, usually growing to no more than 40 in (100 cm) high. The narrow leaves may be opposite or alternate and are lobed or palmately divided with rigid pointed tips. Phlox-like flowers of cream, pink, or lilac, usually in dense clusters borne at the stem tips, appear from late winter to summer.

CULTIVATION: Plant in full sun in light, fertile, very well-drained soil, or grow in a container. Transplants can be difficult to re-establish, as these plants dislike root disturbance. Propagate from seed or cuttings.

Leptodactylon californicum

syn. *Navarretia californica*

PRICKLY PHLOX

☼ ❄ ↔24 in (60 cm) ↕24 in (60 cm)

From California, USA. An upright branching shrub. Small, narrow, 5- to 9-lobed leaves with prickly young leaves in axils. Starry phlox-like flowers of pale to bright pink, covering plant, in late winter–summer. Zones 7–10.

LESPEDEZA

This genus is a member of the large pea-flower subfamily of the legume (Fabaceae) family, which includes many edible plants, such as peas and beans. It contains about 40 species of prostrate annuals and perennials and deciduous shrubs, which are found in eastern and tropical Asia, Australia, and eastern USA. The leaves are trifoliate, and the flowers are small but are usually borne in long racemes.

CULTIVATION: Grow in a sunny position in deep, well-drained, fertile soil. In cooler areas these plants need the protection of a warm wall. In spring prune out the dead growth and

Lespedeza japonica

cut back hard to rejuvenate the plant. Propagate from seed or from half-hardened cuttings.

Lespedeza japonica

↔5–10 ft (1.5–3 m)
↑3–8 ft (0.9–2.4 m)

From Japan. An erect semi-evergreen or deciduous shrub, with long arching branches. Compound leaves with elliptic leaflets. Drooping racemes of pure white pea-flowers with a long-pointed calyx form in autumn. Zones 4–9.

Lespedeza thunbergii

THUNBERG BUSH CLOVER, MIYAGINO-HAGI

↔5–10 ft (1.5–3 m)
↑3–8 ft (0.9–2.4 m)

From Japan and China. An erect semi-evergreen or deciduous shrub. Long, wiry, widely spreading, interlacing branches; arching fountain-like habit. Bluish green compound leaves with 3 sharp-tipped leaflets, smooth above, finely hairy beneath. Dense drooping racemes of numerous pea-flowers with rose-purple corollas in late summer–autumn. **'Alba'**, white flowers; **'Albiflora'**, smaller leaflets, small white flowers with violet markings; **'Edo Shindori'**, pink and white flowers; **'Gibraltar'**, profuse lavender pink flowers. Zones 4–9.

LEUCADENDRON

This genus is a member of the protea (Proteaceae) family, comprising approximately 80 diverse evergreen shrubs and small trees. All are from South Africa's Western Cape province and the far west of Eastern Cape, except for 3 species, which are isolated in eastern KwaZulu-Natal. Borne on separate male and female plants in winter to spring, the flowers are in dense heads, the females commonly concealed among rather woody scales, the males in rather looser cone-like structures. The longer bracts surrounding both male and female flowerheads are often colorful, giving each head the appearance of a single "flower." They are sought after as cut

Leucadendron discolor

flowers because of their long vase life. The leaves are simple, often leathery, and spirally arranged. Most species are insect pollinated but a few are wind pollinated. The cone-like fruits yield seed that ripens in summer.

CULTIVATION: The vast majority require perfect drainage, preferring humus-rich, acid, basaltic or sandy loams low in phosphorus. They generally prefer an open, sunny, frost-free position with good air circulation. Propagate from seed sown in autumn, or cuttings, or by grafting or budding.

Leucadendron argenteum

SILVER TREE

↔6–20 ft (1.8–6 m)
↑20–30 ft (6–9 m)

Rare in the wild, occurring on the slopes of Table Mountain, South Africa. Beautiful tree; trunk with whorled branches, smooth gray bark with distinctive horizontal leaf scars. Leaves lance-shaped, to 6 in (15 cm) long, silvery, silky, with a glistening sheen. Female flowers, in silvery cone-like heads with a pinkish tinge, occur in summer. Produces silvery cone-like fruits. Zones 9–10.

Leucadendron discolor

↔6 ft (1.8 m) ↑6 ft (1.8 m)

Species native to the rocky sandstone soils of Table Mountain, South Africa. An erect shrub with leaves broad, oval, and gray-green. The flowerheads form in spring, the male turning bright red with yellow bracts, the female remaining light green. *L. discolor* needs well-drained soil. Excellent as cut flowers. Zones 8–10.

Leucadendron galpinii

↔4 ft (1.2 m) ↑10 ft (3 m)

Endemic to the coastal lowlands of Western Cape. Shrub with linear grayish leaves with a twist. Round, shiny, grayish flower cones, with an unpleasant scent, in spring. Persistent fruit. Zones 8–10.

Leucadendron galpinii

Leucadendron, Hybrid Cultivar, 'Superstar'

Leucadendron Hybrid Cultivars

↔4–8 ft (1.2–2.4 m)
↑4–8 ft (1.2–2.4 m)

Many hybrids have been developed, featuring large showy bracts, a compact growth habit, and interesting foliage. **'Amy'**, compact, red winter bracts turn cream in spring; **'Bell's Sunrise'** (syn. 'Wilson's Wonder'), male, red-flushed creamy yellow bracts, winter; **'Cloudbank Jenny'** (syn. 'Cloudbank Ginny'), male, cream bracts around orange cones; **'Duet'**, most probably an *L. stelligerum* hybrid, red-edged yellow bracts around yellow cones; **'Harvest Girl'**, *L. stelligerum* hybrid, red-edged cream bracts, winter; **'Inca Gold'** ★, large shrub, intense golden yellow bracts, winter; **'Jester'**, cream, pink, and green-variegated foliage, sport of 'Safari Sunset'; **'Pisa'**, *L. floridum* hybrid, silver-haired leaves, yellow bracts around silvery green cones; **'Safari Sunset'** ★, magnificent strong-growing bush, vivid red bracts, colorful young leaves; **'Silvan Red'**, like 'Safari Sunset' but with slimmer bracts; **'Sundance'**, Australian hybrid, bright yellow to gold bracts; **'Superstar'**, wiry-stemmed bush, small red and yellow bracts in winter. Zones 9–11.

LEUCAENA

Belonging to the mimosa subfamily of the legume (Fabaceae) family, the 20-odd species of evergreen trees and shrubs in this genus range from southern Texas, USA, and Mexico to South America as far as Peru. Some are now naturalized throughout the tropics and subtropics. All species have feathery foliage and fluffy globular heads of white flowers. The leaves are bipinnate, with many small leaflets or fewer larger ones. Dark brown pods hang in drooping clusters from the branches.

CULTIVATION: These fast-growing plants thrive in a wide range of soils; routine care is minimal. They respond to pruning or coppicing, which quickly produces regrowth. Widely planted in tropical and subtropical areas as screen or shade trees, or for fodder or green manure; in cool-temperate climates they may be grown under glass. Propagate from the seed, which needs soaking in warm water for 24 hours to soften it before planting, or from half-hardened cuttings.

Leucaena leucocephala

syn. *Leucaena glauca*

LEAD TREE, WHITE POPINAC

↔15 ft (4.5 m) ↑30 ft (9 m)

Vigorous, fast-growing, evergreen tree; abundantly naturalized in the tropics. Gray-green bipinnate leaves; young stems a deep copper color. Fluffy balls of creamy white flowers, on short stalks, in spring. Drooping clusters of dark brown, broad, flat pods in summer. Zones 10–12.

Leucaena retusa

GOLDENBALL, LEAD TREE, LEMONBALL, LITTLE-LEAF LEAD TREE, WAHOO TREE

↔ 15–25 ft (4.5–8 m)
↑ 12–25 ft (3.5–8 m)

From Texas, USA, and northern Mexico. Evergreen shrub or small tree. Flaky cinnamon-colored bark. Compound leaves consisting of 8 to 16 light green leaflets, each with 4 to 8 segments. Globes of bright yellow stamens, in leaf axils, in spring–autumn. Flattened brown seed pods. Zones 7–11.

LEUCANTHEMUM

Somewhat prosaically named from the Greek *leukos,* white, and *anthemon,* flower, this genus from Europe and northern Asia comprises 33 species of annual and perennial daisies (family Asteraceae), most of which do have flowerheads with white ray florets, usually around a central boss of golden disc florets. They have often been in-cluded in the genus *Chrysanthemum*, which botanists now define more narrowly. They form often large clumps of deep green, usually toothed, linear to spatula-shaped leaves. The flowers appear from spring to autumn, de-pending on the species. Garden forms include pompon-centered flowers and various colors, especially among the *L.* × *superbum* hybrids, originally developed by Luther Burbank.
CULTIVATION: Grow in a sunny position in moist well-drained soil. Feeding and watering will result in more luxuriant plants but not necessarily more flowers. Tall types may need staking. Propagate the species from seed, cultivars and hybrids by division or from basal cuttings.

Leucanthemum × *superbum*

syns *Chrysanthemum maximum of gardens, C. superbum*

SHASTA DAISY

↔ 40 in (100 cm)
↑ 48 in (120 cm)

Garden hybrid of *L. maximum* and *L. lacustre*, first developed around 1900 by the Californian plant breeder Luther Burbank and named by him in tribute to snow-capped Mt Shasta in the far north of his State. Many upright flower stems emerging from dense basal clump of dark green, toothed, spatula-shaped leaves, to 8 in (20 cm) long. Flowerheads solitary, to 4 in (10 cm) across, ray florets white, disc florets golden yellow. Many cultivars. **'Aglaia'** ★, white semi-double flowers; **'Becky'**, 3–4 ft (0.9–1.2 m) tall, with large, single, white flowers in spring–

Leucanthemum × *superbum* 'Aglaia'

Leucanthemum × *superbum* 'Snowcap'

summer; **'Cobham Gold'**, creamy yellow double flowers; **'Esther Read'**, feathery semi-double flowers; **'Horace Read'**, 20 in (50 cm) tall, feathery double flowers; **'Marconi'**, very large, double, white flowers; **'Silberprinzesschen'**, 12–15 in (30–38 cm) tall, single white flowers in spring–autumn; **'Snow Lady'**, 12–15 in (30–34 cm) tall, single white flowers in spring–autumn; **'Snowcap'**, 12–15 in (30–38 cm) tall, large, white, single flowers; **'T. E. Killin'**, 3 ft (0.9 m) tall, yellow-centered, white, semi-double flowers; **'Wirral Supreme'**, anemone-centered white flowers. Zones 5–10.

Leucanthemum vulgare

syn. *Chrysanthemum leucanthemum*

OX-EYE DAISY

↔ 24 in (60 cm)
↑ 40 in (100 cm)

From Europe and northern Asia. Perennial forming basal clump of toothed leaves, sometimes pinnately lobed, to 4 in (10 cm) long. Flower stems sometimes branched, with small leaves, flowerheads 1–3 in (2.5–8 cm) across, ray florets white, disc florets yellow, in summer. Zones 3–9.

Leucojum aestivum

LEUCOJUM

SNOWFLAKES

A genus of 20 species of bulbs in the amaryllis (Amaryllidaceae) family, native to Europe, the Middle East, and North Africa. Better suited than the related snowdrops *(Galanthus)* to mild and warm climates. Their overall appearance is similar, the 6 white petals of the nodding flowers at the tops of the slender stems are of equal length; snowdrops have 3 long and 3 short petals. The linear leaves, said to be poisonous to stock, appear either with or before the flowers. The name comes from the Greek *leukos*, meaning white, and *ion*, meaning violet (the latter referring to the faint fragrance).

CULTIVATION: Trouble-free, needing almost no maintenance. Propagate by division of offsets after flowering, or by sowing ripe fresh seed.

Leucojum aestivum

syn. *Leucojum aestivale*

SUMMER SNOWFLAKE

↔ 12 in (30 cm)
↑ 18–22 in (45–55 cm)

Native to damp woods of central and southern Europe. Robust, with strap-like leaves. Flowers delicate-looking, 1 to 5 per stem, white with green markings, sometimes scented; in wet-winter dry-summer climates the flowers appear in winter, in cooler wet-summer climates in summer. **'Gravetye Giant'** ★, equally robust, adaptable, to 30 in (75 cm). Zones 6–9.

Leucojum vernum

SPRING SNOWFLAKE

↔ 12 in (30 cm)
↑ 12–30 in (30–75 cm)

From the shady hillsides and woodlands of higher parts of central Europe; widely naturalized in similar situations. Flowers are large flared bells, 1¼ in (30 mm) across, held singly on straight stems, white marked with green or yellow, in spring. Plant bulbs deeply. Zones 5–8.

LEUCOPHYLLUM

This genus belonging to the foxglove (Scrophulariaceae) family comprises about 12 species of attractive, low-spreading, evergreen shrubs, native to southwestern USA and Mexico. The foliage is pale green to gray-white, owing to the leaves being felted with short white hairs. Showy, lavender to violet, bell- to funnel-shaped flowers are borne singly in the leaf axils in summer; the fruit is capsular.

Leucanthemum vulgare, in the wild, Provence, France

Leucophyllum langmaniae 'Rio Bravo'

CULTIVATION: These slow-growing shrubs are often found in sandy and impoverished soils in a dry climate; they thrive in virtually any soil as long as it is well drained, and are tolerant of salt spray. Grown for their pleasing gray-white foliage and silvery stems, they make undemanding specimens. They prefer a warm, sheltered, sunny spot. Although they may survive at temperatures down to 10°F (–12°C), they require higher temperatures to bloom well. In cooler areas they may be grown under glass. They withstand vigorous pruning. Propagate from seed or from half-hardened cuttings.

Leucophyllum langmaniae

MONTEREY CENIZO, RIO BRAVO SAGE

↔4–6 ft (1.2–1.8 m) ↕3–5 ft (0.9–1.5 m)

From northeastern Mexico and Texas, USA. Dense evergreen shrub. Bright green leaves, spatula shaped, wavy edges. Pale lavender to lavender-blue flowers in summer–autumn. **'Rio Bravo'**, heavy flowering. Zones 8–10.

LEUCOPHYTA

The sole species in this genus in the daisy (Asteraceae) family is an evergreen shrub native to the coasts of southern Australia. Rather reminiscent of lavender cotton *(Santolina chamaecyparissus),* it develops into a dense mound of wiry stems clothed in tiny, almost scale-like, silver-gray leaves. In summer and autumn small, knob-like, white to creamy yellow flowerheads lacking ray florets open from silvery buds.

CULTIVATION: Very much a coastal plant and highly resistant to salt spray, it adapts well to cultivation and can be trimmed as a low border or hedge, good for accenting darker foliage. It dislikes hot humid conditions and appreciates full sun and good air movement. The soil should be light and well drained. While tough and drought resistant, it is short lived and eventually dies out from the center; hard pruning will not rejuvenate it. Light pinching back year round can keep it more compact and vigorous. Propagate by half-hardened tip cuttings.

Leucophyta brownii

syn. *Calocephalus brownii*

CUSHION BUSH

↔3 ft (0.9 m) ↕3 ft (0.9 m)

Intricately branched dome of bright silvery foliage. Inconspicuous yellowish flowerheads, to ½ in (12 mm) across. Western Australian race has longer leaves, to ½ in (12 mm). Zones 9–11.

LEUCOSPERMUM

PINCUSHION

Unlike many plants in related genera of the protea (Proteaceae) family, leucospermums, often referred to as pincushion proteas, owe their beauty to their flowers, in roundish pincushion-like heads with long conspicuous styles. There are approximately 50 species, all evergreen shrubs, and all from a narrow coastal belt in South Africa's Western Cape province, except for a handful in eastern South Africa, one extending to Zimbabwe. The majority are compact shrubs, which flower abundantly in spring. The thick leaves are generally broadest near the tip, which usually has several rather blunt teeth.

CULTIVATION: All require well-drained soil in an open sunny situation. Some species tolerate light frosts; all prefer a dry summer with low humidity. Winter watering is desirable. Pruning is usually unnecessary apart from cutting flowers. Propagate from seed or cuttings or by grafting, which is used for many of the hybrid cultivars.

Leucospermum cordifolium ★

syn. *Leucospermum nutans*

NODDING PINCUSHION

↔6 ft (1.8 m) ↕6 ft (1.8 m)

Popular shrub with an open habit; some cultivars almost prostrate. Gray-green foliage offsetting the apricot, pink, orange, or red flowers in spring; these are valued for their long life in the garden and for floristry. Tolerant of clay soils; frost tender when young. **'Aurora'**, apricot-yellow flowers; **'Copper Glow'**, copper-orange, deepens with age; **'Fire Dance'**, scarlet flowerheads; **'Fireball'**, massed small heads, bright orange-red; **'Yellow Bird'**, bright yellow. Zones 9–10.

Leucophyta brownii

Leucospermum patersonii

↔6 ft (1.8 m) ↕12 ft (3.5 m)

From coastal limestone areas. Large shrub or small tree. Leaves dark green, deeply toothed, red-tipped. Bright orange flowers with scarlet styles in spring–early summer. Tolerant of alkaline soils; good drainage essential. Zones 8–10.

Leucospermum tottum

FIREWHEEL PINCUSHION

↔5 ft (1.5 m) ↕5 ft (1.5 m)

Dense evergreen shrub. The leaves are narrow-elliptical, gray-green, and covered with fine hairs. Produces rounded scarlet flowers with creamy styles in spring–summer. Prefers well-drained gritty soils. Several hybrid cultivars are available, some extending the flowering season into mid-summer. **'Scarlet Ribbon'**, a hybrid of *L. tottum* and *L. glabrum,* compact rounded habit, to 5 ft (1.5 m), frosted appearance, bearing scarlet flowers in late spring. Zones 8–10.

Leucospermum Hybrid Cultivars

↔3–10 ft (0.9–3 m) ↕2–7 ft (0.6–2 m)

Leucospermum readily hybridize and have produced many showy cultivars, including: **'Carnival Red'**, dusky dark red, compact; **'Mardi Gras Ribbons'**, dense growth, golden yellow flowerheads; **'Sincere'**, long-lasting, somewhat flattened, bright light red flowerheads; **'So Cheerful'**, yellow with silvery cream tips, gray foliage. Zones 9–10.

LEUCOTHOE

Found mainly in eastern Asia and the USA, this genus belonging to the heath (Ericaceae) family, as now understood, consists of only 6 species of evergreen and deciduous shrubs. Many more species formerly included in it are now separated as the genus *Agarista.* They usually have simple leathery leaves, dark green with toothed edges; some show a tendency to produce variegated foliage. The deciduous species often color well in autumn. The flowers are small, bell- or urn-shaped, and usually cream to pink. Opening in spring to early summer in racemes or panicles, they can be quite showy.

CULTIVATION: Most species prefer shade from the hottest sun and should be grown in cool, moist, humus-rich soil that is open and well drained. Other than light trimming to shape, pruning is seldom necessary. Propagation from seed is usually slow, so air-layering or half-hardened cuttings are more often used. Some species produce suckers that can be grown on.

Leucospermum cordifolium 'Aurora'

Leucospermum patersonii

Leucospermum tottum 'Scarlet Ribbon'

Leucothoe fontanesiana

Leucothoe racemosa

Lewisia columbiana

Lewisia congdonii

Lewisia cotyledon f. *alba*

Lewisia tweedyi

Leucothoe davisiae

SIERRA LAUREL

↔5 ft (1.5 m)
↑1–6 ft (0.3–1.8 m)

From California's Sierra Nevada, USA. Evergreen, variable in size. Leaves with glossy green uppersurfaces, sparsely toothed edges. Small, white, lily-of-the-valley-like flowers, in erect terminal racemes to 4 in (10 cm) long. Zones 5–10.

Leucothoe fontanesiana

syns *Leucothoe catesbaei, L. walteri*

SWITCH IVY

↔7 ft (2 m) ↑6 ft (1.8 m)

From southeastern USA. Evergreen shrub with arching stems. Leaves, long-pointed to 4 in (10 cm) long, glossy uppersurfaces, toothed edges; red-tinted new growth. White lily-of-the-valley-like flowers, in short racemes, in spring. **'Rainbow'** ★ (syn. 'Girard's Rainbow'), foliage variegated with green, cream, and pink. Zones 5–10.

Leucothoe racemosa

FETTER BUSH, SWEET BELLS

↔5 ft (1.5 m) ↑3–8 ft (1–2.4 m)

From eastern USA. Deciduous shrub. Leaves to 2½ in (6 cm) long, finely toothed edges; autumn foliage often develops yellow, orange, and cherry red tones. Short racemes of white to cream flowers in spring–summer. Zones 5–9.

LEVISTICUM

Genus in the carrot (Apiaceae) family consisting of a single species of tall upright perennial with compound triangular leaves that have a strong celery taste. Grown for its leaves, used in salads, and seeds, used for flavoring. In summer it produces the classic flat flowerheads typical of the carrot family, with tiny green-yellow blooms. The true garden celery *(Apium graveolens* var. *dulce)* is more tender and has taken its place in most kitchens.

CULTIVATION: This plant likes a position in full sun with fertile, moist but well-drained soil. Propagate by freshly sown seed or division in spring.

Levisticum officinale

LOVAGE, LOVE PARSLEY

↔40 in (100 cm) ↑7 ft (2 m)

Native to the Mediterranean region. Umbelliferous perennial. Dark green, leathery, shiny leaves, similar to a carrot's but wider. Flower stalks thick and hollow, yellow flowers. Zones 3–10.

LEWISIA

BITTER ROOT

Named after the North American explorer Captain Meriwether Lewis (1774–1809) of the famed Lewis and Clark expedition of 1806–7, this is a genus of 19 species of exquisite, semi-succulent, evergreen and deciduous, alpine and subalpine perennials in the purslane (Montiaceae) family. They are found in western North America from New Mexico to southern Canada and usually form basal rosettes of fleshy, linear, lance- or spatula-shaped leaves. Their starry many-petalled flowers may be solitary or clustered and are borne at the ends of short wiry stems from mid-spring through to early summer. Yellow, apricot, and pink shades predominate.

CULTIVATION: Most species have deep tap roots and prefer gritty free-draining soil that remains moist in the growing season but is otherwise dry. Plant in full- or half-sun and use gravel mulch around the crown to prevent rotting. Deciduous species generally only reproduce from seed, but evergreens can also be propagated from offsets.

Lewisia brachycalyx

↔8 in (20 cm) ↑4 in (10 cm)

Found from southern Utah to New Mexico, USA. A deciduous species forming basal rosette of broad lance-shaped leaves, to 3 in (8 cm) long. Flowers are solitary, to about 2 in (5 cm) across, with up to 9 petals, white to pale pink with darker pink veins. Zones 5–9.

Lewisia columbiana

↔8 in (20 cm) ↑12 in (30 cm)

Found over much of North America west of the Rockies. Evergreen species with crowded, fleshy, narrow, basal leaves, 1–4 in (25–100 mm) long. Many-flowered heads of pink-veined white to magenta flowers, to 1 in (25 mm) across, with up to 11 petals, in spring-summer. Zones 5–9.

Lewisia congdonii

↔12–20 in (30–50 cm)
↑16–24 in (40–60 cm)

Deciduous California native. Basal clump of broad, strappy, rather fleshy, 2–8 in (5–20 cm) long leaves. Tall flower stem with large lax panicles of many ½–1 in (12–25 mm) wide, purple-veined, pale pink flowers with up to 7 petals. Zones 7–9.

Lewisia cotyledon

↔8 in (20 cm)
↑6–12 in (15–30 cm)

From the area around the California–Oregon State line, USA. Evergreen, loose rosette of spatula-shaped leaves, to over 4 in (10 cm) long, often blue-green and/or pink-tinted, edges often wavy, rarely toothed. Forms panicle of a few to many 7- to 10-petalled flowers, to 1¾ in (40 mm) across, in spring–summer. Flowers usually purple-pink. ***L. c.* f. *alba***, white flowers. Cultivars come in many shades. **Sunset Group**, many shades of yellow, orange, pink, and red; **'White Splendour'**, dark green foliage, pure white flowers. Zones 5–9.

Lewisia longipetala

↔10 in (25 cm)
↑6–12 in (15–30 cm)

Californian evergreen. Rosette of fleshy, often red-edged, narrow leaves, to 5 in (12 cm) long. Purple-pink flowers, to 2 in (5 cm) across, with about 9 petals. Zones 4–9.

Lewisia 'Pinkie'

↔8 in (20 cm)
↑6–8 in (15–20 cm)

Evergreen hybrid between *L. cotyledon* and *L. longipetala.* Resembles compact *L. cotyledon* with slightly narrower leaves. Many broad-petalled apricot pink flowers with dark pink centers. Zones 5–9.

Lewisia rediviva

BITTERROOT

↔8 in (20 cm) ↑4 in (10 cm)

Found over much of subalpine and alpine western North America. Deciduous species forming a dense basal tuft of many narrow leaves, to 2 in (5 cm) long. Flowers solitary, to over 2 in (5 cm) across, with up to 6 petals in pink to purple shades or white. Zones 4–9.

Lewisia tweedyi

☼/◐ ❄ ↔ 8 in (20 cm) ↑ 8 in (20 cm)

From Washington State, USA, and British Columbia, Canada. Evergreen forming small clump of often purple-tinted, broad, lance-shaped leaves, to 3 in (8 cm) long. Up to 8 soft pink or yellow, 7- to 12-petalled flowers, to over 2 in (5 cm) across. Zones 5–9.

LEYCESTERIA

This genus, belonging to the woodbine (Caprifoliaceae) family, consists of 6 species of deciduous or semi-evergreen shrubs, found in western China and the Himalayas as far west as Pakistan. They have small tubular flowers, borne over a long period, with very noticeable colored bracts. The soft berries mature so quickly that they are often carried at the same time as the flowers. In favorable climates these plants, which have a suckering habit, may become invasive weeds.

CULTIVATION: Grow in moderately fertile soil in a sunny or partially shady location, though the flower bracts and fruit color better in full sun. Less hardy species can be overwintered in a greenhouse in colder climates. Propagate from seed in autumn or spring or by taking softwood cuttings in summer.

Leycesteria formosa

Liatris pycnostachya

Liatris spicata 'Floristan'

Leycesteria formosa

HIMALAYAN HONEYSUCKLE

☼ ❄ ↔ 6 ft (1.8 m) ↑ 6 ft (1.8 m)

Native to the Himalayas and western China. Leaves long, dark green, slightly heart-shaped at the base, smooth-edged or slightly toothed, undersurface paler and downy. Whitish flowers with purple bracts, on pendent spikes, in summer–autumn. Fruit ripening deep red-purple to black. A weed in cool moist areas of Australia and New Zealand. Zones 7–10.

LEYMUS

From the northern temperate zones, with one species extending the range to Argentina, this genus comprises about 40 species of spreading and sometimes invasive, perennial, rhizomatous grasses in the family Poaceae. Most *Leymus* species were formerly classified under *Elymus*. Found in a wide range of habitats, but usually in full sun and mostly in dry soils. The foliage is stiff, often silvery blue: the summer flowers held in upright spikes on long stems.

CULTIVATION: Most species are salt tolerant and so can be grown on sand dunes to stabilize them; this can result in weediness in non-native areas.

Leymus arenarius

Provide a sunny well-drained aspect and control spread. Cut down in winter and propagate by division in spring.

Leymus arenarius

syn. *Elymus arenarius*

EUROPEAN DUNE GRASS, LYME GRASS, SEA LYME GRASS

☼ ❄ ↔ 3–7 ft (0.9–2 m) ↑ 12–15 in (30–38 cm)

From Europe. Very vigorous grass with spreading rhizomes. Arching silvery leaves, to 24 in (60 cm) long. Upright spikes of white flowers in summer, turning cream with age. **'Findhorn'**, more compact shorter-growing selection. Zones 6–10.

Leymus condensatus

syn. *Elymus condensatus*

GIANT WILD RYE

☼ ❄ ↔ 3 ft (0.9 m) ↑ 3–7 ft (0.9–2 m)

From North America. Vigorous, semi-evergreen, upright grass; can be dormant in dry summer climates. Gray-green foliage tones in with bluish flower stems, which sit 8 in (20 cm) above foliage in summer months. **'Canyon Prince'** (blue giant wild rye), slow spreading habit, upright bright bluish green foliage, showy creamy blue flowers sitting 24 in (60 cm) above grass. Zones 3–9.

LIATRIS

BLAZING STAR, GAYFEATHER, SNAKE ROOT

Native to eastern North America and growing from corms or modified flattened roots, the 35 species of perennials in this genus of the daisy (Asteraceae) family make a bold splash of color in summer; very easy to grow. They form clumps of simple linear to lance-shaped leaves, sometimes finely hairy, bearing 24–60 in (60–150 cm) tall stems, topped with long, quite un-daisy-like, bottlebrush spikes of filamentous purple-pink flowers. Native Americans used the roots medicinally, and early settlers found that the dried roots repelled clothes moths.

CULTIVATION: While hardiness varies, most species are frost resistant. Wild plants are found along watercourses, though they can be grown in any sunny position in moist, humus-rich, well-drained soil. Place at back of borders to disguise the foliage clump and make use of flower stem's height. Propagate by division or from seed.

Liatris aspera

ROUGH BLAZING STAR

☼/◐ ❄ ↔ 12–20 in (30–50 cm) ↑ 40 in (100 cm)

Found across most of eastern North America. Leaves are narrow, to 6 in (15 cm) long. Spikes of up to 20 purple flowerheads in mid-summer to autumn. Zones 5–10.

Liatris pycnostachya

BUTTON SNAKE ROOT

☼/◐ ❄ ↔ 10–18 in (25–45 cm) ↑ 60 in (150 cm)

Native to southeastern USA. Upright habit. Leaves narrow, sometimes downy, to 4 in (10 cm) long. Densely crowded purple-red flowerheads, in spikes to 12 in (30 cm) long, in mid-summer–autumn. **'Alexander'**, dark green foliage, purple flowerheads. Zones 3–10.

Liatris scariosa

☼/◐ ❄ ↔ 8–12 in (20–30 cm) ↑ 32 in (80 cm)

Native to southeastern USA. Compact, with more foliage and broader leaves than other species. Leaves to 6 in (15 cm) long and 2 in (5 cm) wide. Variably sparse or crowded flower spikes with purple flowerheads from mid-summer to autumn. Zones 3–9.

Liatris spicata ★

BLAZING STAR, BUTTON SNAKE ROOT, GAYFEATHER

☼/◐ ❄ ↔ 10–18 in (25–45 cm) ↑ 60 in (150 cm)

Found across most of eastern USA. Up-right habit. Leaves narrow, sometimes linear, to 8 in (20 cm) long. Dense spikes, to 24 in (60 cm) long, with purple-red flowerheads in mid-summer to autumn. **'Callilepsis Purple'**, 24 in (60 cm) high, dark purple flowerheads; **'Floristan'**, 32 in (80 cm) high, deep violet flowerheads; **'Floristan White'**, 32 in (80 cm) high, white flowerheads; **'Kobold'** (syn. 'Goblin'), 20 in (50 cm) high, dense heads of purple-pink flowers. Zones 3–10.

Libertia formosa

LIBERTIA

The 9 species of perennial rhizomatous plants in this genus, a Southern Hemisphere member of the iris (Iridaceae) family, have a creeping or tufted growth habit and a prolonged flowering season. They occur in eastern Australia, New Zealand, New Guinea, and the Andes of South America. The strap-like leaves are produced in sparse to dense tufts. The flowers, usually white and recognizably iris-like in form, are borne in clusters at the top of straight stems. Often the leaves partially obscure the flowers.
CULTIVATION: The majority of species are quite tolerant of both drought and poor soils; however, most will respond visibly to softer conditions and light feeding. In appropriate climates, with their weed-defeating habit and general vigor, some species may be used for roadside plantings. Propagate in spring by division or from seed.

Libertia formosa

SHOWY LIBERTIA, SNOWY MERMAID
↔24 in (60 cm)
↑18–36 in (45–90 cm)

Chilean species. Clumping perennial. Dark green leaves are narrow, strap-shaped, and leathery. Tall spikes of white or pale yellow flowers in the late spring. Zones 9–10.

Libertia grandiflora

MIKOIKOI, NEW ZEALAND IRIS, TUKAUKI
↔24 in (60 cm) ↑30 in (75 cm)
From New Zealand. Clumping perennial. Leaves green to yellowy green, narrow, leathery. Tall spike of white flowers, in dense clusters, in spring, followed by attractive, yellow, pear-shaped seed capsules. Zones 8–11.

Libertia ixioides

MIKOIKOI, NEW ZEALAND IRIS, TUKAUKI
↔24 in (60 cm)
↑8–12 in (20–30 cm)

From New Zealand. Clumping perennial. Leaves green to orange-brown, narrow, leathery. Spike of white flowers in late spring. Zones 8–11.

Libertia peregrinans

↔20 in (50 cm)
↑15–27 in (38–70 cm)

From New Zealand. Long-running rhizomes; leaves obviously veined, turning orange-brown in cold weather. White flowers with yellow anthers in spring. Needs well-drained soil. Zones 8–10.

LIGULARIA

While some popular species formerly included in this temperate Eurasian genus of the daisy (Asteraceae) family have been reclassified, there are still some 125 species of perennials in *Ligularia*. In spring these vigorous plants soon develop into clumps of long-stalked, broad, basal leaves, usually kidney- to heart-shaped, with toothed edges. In summer and autumn flowering stems develop, ranging from broadly forking panicles of large yellow to orange daisies to tall spike-like racemes of numerous smaller heads, depending on the species.
CULTIVATION: Most species are very hardy. Grow in full sun/half-sun, in deep, fertile, humus-rich soil kept moist through the year. Cut back when flowers and foliage fade. Propagate by division when dormant or from seed.

Ligularia dentata

↔40–60 in (100–150 cm)
↑30–60 in (75–150 cm)

From China and Japan. Vigorous clump-forming perennial with impressive foliage. Leaves rounded to kidney-shaped, deeply toothed, downy undersides, often red-tinted, to 16 in (40 cm) wide. Strong upright flower stems with many gold to orange flowerheads, to 4 in (10 cm) across. **'Desdemona'**, purple-red leaves, orange flowers on stems to 48 in (120 cm). Zones 4–10.

Ligularia przewalskii

Ligularia przewalskii

SHAVALSKI'S LIGULARIA
↔40–48 in (100–120 cm)
↑7 ft (2 m)

Northern Chinese vigorous perennial. Leaves deeply palmately lobed and toothed, basal leaves to 12 in (30 cm) long and wide. Stems dark purple-red. Narrow spikes of many spidery golden yellow flowerheads. Zones 4–9.

Ligularia stenocephala

↔32–40 in (80–100 cm)
↑60 in (150 cm)

Native to Japan, China, and Taiwan. Leaves heart-shaped to triangular, toothed, basal leaves to 12 in (30 cm) long and wide. Stems deep purple-red. Deep yellow flowerheads, to over 2 in (5 cm) across. Zones 5–10.

Ligularia Hybrid Cultivars

↔32–60 in (80–150 cm)
↑3–7 ft (0.9–2 m)

Bred with both foliage and flowers in mind, hybrid ligularias are bold architectural plants ideally suited to moist partly shaded corners, especially near ponds and streams. Hybrids include: **'Gregynog Gold'**, coarsely toothed green leaves, and pyramidal spikes of orange flowers; **'The Rocket'**, dark black-green stems contrasting with numerous bright yellow flowerheads; **'Weihenstephan'**, large deep golden yellow flowerheads; **'Zepter'**, slightly shorter than the species but with more densely crowded golden yellow flowerheads. Zones 5–9.

Ligularia dentata

Ligularia, Hybrid Cultivar, 'The Rocket'

LIGUSTRUM

PRIVET

This genus of about 50 species of both deciduous and evergreen trees and shrubs is part of the olive (Oleaceae) family. Most species are found in the Himalayas and eastern Asia, with one found in Europe and North Africa. All have simple opposite leaves with smooth edges and bear panicles of scented white flowers at the branch or stem tips, followed by small blue-black drupes. In warmer climates the seed is produced in large quantities and is popular with birds, which has resulted in several species invading native vegetation and becoming weeds. *L. japonicum* and *L. ovalifolium* are weeds in the USA and New Zealand; *L. lucidum* and *L. sinense* have become pests in eastern Australia. The varieties with colored foliage can be grown with less risk but are apt to revert.
CULTIVATION: Privets are not particular about soil or exposure to the sun. Seeds can be sown as soon as they are ripe, while the colored forms are best propagated from firm tip cuttings taken in late spring or summer.

Ligustrum japonicum

JAPANESE PRIVET
↔8 ft (2.4 m) ↑10 ft (3 m)
From Japan and Korea. Compact, very dense, evergreen shrub. The leaves are camellia-like, shiny, and olive green. The large panicles of white flowers appear in late summer–early autumn. Useful as a screening or hedging plant. **'Rotundifolium'**, slow growing, to 6 ft (1.8 m) tall, round leaves, to 1½ in (35 mm) in diameter. Zones 7–10.

Ligustrum japonicum 'Rotundifolium'

Ligustrum lucidum 'Excelsum Superbum'

Lilium × *burbankii*

Lilium lancifolium

Ligustrum lucidum

BROAD-LEAFED PRIVET, GLOSSY PRIVET, WAXLEAF PRIVET

↔30 ft (9 m) ↑30 ft (9 m)

From China. Large evergreen shrub or small tree. Leaves long, pointed, shiny, deep green, to 6 in (15 cm) long. Large panicles of white flowers in the autumn. **'Excelsum Superbum'** has pale green leaves edged with yellow; **'Tricolor'** has narrow deep green leaves, predominantly marked with gray-green, edged with pale creamy yellow. Zones 7–11.

Ligustrum obtusifolium

↔10 ft (3 m) ↑10 ft (3 m)

From Japan. Vigorous deciduous shrub, with leaves deep green, oblong, often turning crimson in autumn. Profuse white flowers, in drooping panicles, in late summer. Round black fruit. L. obtusifolium var. regelianum, to 5 ft (1.5 m) tall, leaves slightly smaller, blunter. Zones 3–10.

Ligustrum ovalifolium

CALIFORNIA PRIVET, OVAL-LEAFED PRIVET

↔12 ft (3.5 m) ↑12 ft (3.5 m)

Cultivated for hedging. Leaves shiny, deep green, falling in very cold climates. White flowers in mid-summer. **'Argenteum'**, leaves with creamy white margins; **'Aureum'**, the golden privet, green-centered leaves with wide yellow margins, or all yellow. Zones 5–10.

LILIUM

LILY

Cultivated for over 5,000 years, lilies are undeniably beautiful, and there are about 100 species of these bulbs spread across the northern temperate zone. Type genus for their family, Liliaceae, they are strongly upright plants with leafy aerial stems that die back to the bulb after flowering; the bulbs are composed of many narrow, overlapping, fleshy scales with no outer covering (tunic). The leaves are short, usually linear to lanceolate. The flowers are borne at the stem tips and may be solitary or in umbels or panicles; they may be bell-, trumpet-, or cup-shaped, or have strongly recurved sepals, producing the "turk's-cap" flower shape. They come in all colors, except for blue, and are often spotted or streaked. In common with many other genera with large groups of hybrids, lilies are divided into groups of similar plants. The genus *Lilium* is split into 9 main divisions, to each of which both species and hybrids may be assigned. CULTIVATION: Lilies flower best with sun for at least half the day. They need moist, humus-rich, fertile, well-drained soil. Do not store bulbs dry; use moist sawdust or shredded paper. Propagate from offsets, from detached bulb scales, or from leaf axil bulbils or seed.

Lilium × *burbankii*

↔12–18 in (30–45 cm) ↑3–7 ft (0.9–2 m)

Garden hybrid between *L. pardalinum* and *L. parryi*. Fragrant horizontal flowers with reflexed yellow petals spotted with brown and tipped red, in summer–early autumn. Zones 5–9.

Lilium candidum

MADONNA LILY, WHITE LILY

↔12–18 in (30–45 cm) ↑3–7 ft (0.9–2 m)

Native to the Mediterranean region (Lebanon, Israel, Turkey, Greece); the species held by statues of the Virgin Mary. Up to 20 flowers per stem, pure white trumpets with reflexed tips and a strong fragrance, in summer–early autumn. Unlike most lilies, likes alkaline soil and a sunny aspect. Zones 6–9.

Lilium columbianum

COLUMBIA LILY, COLUMBIA TIGER LILY, OREGON LILY

↔12–18 in (30–45 cm) ↑7–8 ft (2–2.4 m)

From western North America. Lance-shaped leaves in whorls up the stems. Flowers strongly reflexed in turk's-cap fashion, yellow to orange-red spotted with maroon, 3 in (8 cm across, in summer–early autumn. Zones 5–9.

Lilium davidii

↔12–18 in (30–45 cm) ↑3–5 ft (0.9–1.5 m)

Native to western China. Slightly stoloniferous species. Scattered leaves, to 4 in (10 cm) long. Up to 20 un-scented, nodding, turk's-cap flowers, to 3 in (8 cm) across, bright vermilion-red spotted with black, in summer–early autumn. Zones 5–9.

Lilium formosanum

↔12–18 in (30–45 cm) ↑3–7 ft (0.9–2 m)

From Taiwan. Tall elegant species with scattered leaves and up to 10 blooms on each stem, but usually fewer, in summer–early autumn. Flowers are trumpet-shaped, horizontal, 8 in (20 cm) long, strongly scented, white stained purple on the outside. *L. f.* var. ***pricei***, dwarf form, 1 or 2 flowers per stem. Zones 5–11.

Lilium henryi

↔12–18 in (30–45 cm) ↑7 10 ft (2 3 m)

From China. Stems, each holding up to 20 flowers, inclined to lean from the weight. Leaves relatively broad, scattered up the stems. Reflexed turk's-cap flowers, orange spotted with black. Zones 5–9.

Lilium lancifolium

syn. *Lilium tigrinum*

DEVIL LILY, KENTAN, TIGER LILY

↔12–18 in (30–45 cm) ↑3–4 ft (0.9–1.2 m)

From eastern China, Japan, and Korea. Hardy well-known lily, probably an ancient hybrid. Scattered leaves, to 8 in (20 cm) long; black bulbils produced in leaf axils. Turk's-cap flowers, to 8 in (20 cm) across, orange with bold dark purple spots, in summer–early autumn. Zones 4–10.

Lilium longiflorum

EASTER LILY

↔12–18 in (30–45 cm) ↑36–40 in (90–100 cm)

From Japan and Taiwan. Vigorous species. Scattered shiny leaves, to 7 in (18 cm) long. Horizontally held, strongly scented, trumpet-shaped flowers, to 7 in (18 cm) long, white with green central stripes, in summer–early autumn. Zones 5–11.

L

Lilium philippinense

Lilium martagon

MARTAGON, TURK'S CAP

↔ 12–18 in (30–45 cm)
↑ 3–8 ft (0.9–2.4 m)

Native from northwestern Europe to Mongolia. The classic lily in turk's-cap form. Leaves broad, in whorls. Up to 50 flowers per stem, usually far fewer, to 2 in (5 cm) across, dull pink with darker spots, unpleasantly scented, in summer–early autumn. ***L. m.* var. *album*,** pure white flowers; ***L. m.* var. *cattaniae*,** deep wine-red flowers without spots. Zones 4–9.

Lilium nepalense ★

↔ 12–18 in (30–45 cm)
↑ 27–40 in (70–100 cm)

Himalayan. Rare and desirable species. Scattered leaves, to 6 in (15 cm) long. Drooping, flared, trumpet-shaped flowers, 6 in (15 cm) long, usually green-white with a large purple throat, in summer–early autumn. Zones 5–9.

Lilium philippinense

↔ 12–18 in (30–45 cm)
↑ 16–40 in (40–100 cm)

From the Philippines. Deep green scattered leaves, to 6 in (15 cm) long. Up to 6 highly scented trumpets per stem, to 10 in (25 cm) long, white, stained outside with green and red, in summer–early autumn. Zones 9–10.

Lilium pumilum ★

syn. ***Lilium tenuifolium***

CORAL LILY

↔ 12–18 in (30–45 cm)
↑ 15–18 in (38–45 cm)

From eastern Russia, Mongolia, China, and North Korea. Narrow scattered leaves. Up to 30 scented turk's-cap flowers per stem, to 2 in (5 cm) across, bright scarlet, usually without spots, in summer–early autumn. **'Yellow Bunting'**, yellow flowers. Zones 5–9.

Lilium pyrenaicum

↔ 12–18 in (30–45 cm)
↑ 32–40 in (80–100 cm)

From the Pyrenees. Narrow scattered leaves. Up to 12 turk's-cap flowers per

Lilium pyrenaicum

Lilium regale

stem, to 2 in (5 cm) across, bright yellow, black spots, unpleasant smell, in summer–early autumn. Zones 3–9.

Lilium regale

REGAL LILY

↔ 12–18 in (30–45 cm)
↑ 5–7 ft (1.5–2 m)

From China. Scattered leaves, to 5 in (12 cm) long. Up to 20 flowers per stem, flared trumpets, to 6 in (15 cm) long, held horizontally, white inside with purple flushes on the outside, in summer–early autumn. Zones 5–9.

Lilium speciosum

↔ 12–18 in (30–45 cm)
↑ 3–5 ft (0.9–1.5 m)

From China, Japan, and Taiwan. Scattered leaves, to 7 in (18 cm) long. Up to 12 pendent, fragrant, turk's-cap flowers per stem, to 7 in (18 cm) across, usually pale pink, deeper pink toward center, with deep pink spots, in summer–early autumn. ***L. s.* var. *album*,** purple stems, white flowers; ***L. s.* var. *rubrum*,** purple stems, dark carmine flowers, white edges. Zones 6–9.

Lilium Hybrid Cultivars

↔ 12–24 in (30–60 cm)
↑ 30 in–7 ft (75 cm–2 m)

Most garden or florists' lilies are hybrid cultivars, nearly all from generations of breeding from many wild species. The classification of

***Lilium*, HC, 1. Asiatic, 'Connecticut King'**

***Lilium*, HC, 1. Asiatic, 'Avignon'**

***Lilium*, Hybrid Cultivar, 4. American Species, Bellingham Hybrid**

Lilium cultivars below is that used by the *International Lily Register*, kept by the Royal Horticultural Society. Zones 5–9.

1. ASIATIC HYBRIDS

These hybrids, derived from *L. amabile, L. bulbiferum, L. cernuum, L. concolor, L. davidii, L. lancifolium, L. leichtlinii, L. maculatum, L.* × *hollandicum,* and *L. pumilum*, typically have one or a few large trumpet-shaped flowers and occur in a huge range of colors and patterns. Although known as Asiatic, the geographic origins of these often overlap with the Oriental hybrids, and the name should not be taken literally.

The Asiatics are subdivided by their flower form into 3 categories: 1a, upward-facing flowers; 1b, outward-facing; and 1c, pendent.

Popular Asiatic hybrids include: **'Alaska'**, to 48 in (120 cm) tall, white flowers; **'Avignon'**, to 36 in (90 cm) tall, red and orange flowers; **'Belo Horizonte'**, to 48 in (120 cm) tall, deep yellow with heavy red speckling; **'Blackout'**, to 30 in (75 cm) tall, deep red, darkening at center; **'Chianti'**, to 32 in (80 cm) tall, pink flowers; **'Connecticut King'**, to 36 in (90 cm) tall, yellow flowers; **'Corrida'**, to 34 in (85 cm) tall, buff yellow shading to pinkish orange at petal tips; **'Côte d'Azur'**, to 27 in (70 cm) tall, pink flowers; **'Double Strawberry Vanilla'**, to 36 in (90 cm) tall, double, coral to apricot tones, no pollen; **'Dreamland'**, to 36 in (90 cm) tall, yellow flowers; **'Easy Salsa'**, to 48 in (120 cm) tall, deep orange with dark red-brown patch around orange center; **'Golden Stone'**, to 36 in (90 cm) tall, yellow with heavy purple-red speckling; **'Graffiti'**, to 40 in (100 cm) tall, golden yellow with red-brown speckled center; **'Kansas'**, to 48 in (120 cm) tall, soft yellow shading to deep gold at center; **'Lionheart'** ★, to 30 in (75 cm) tall, dark red-brown with golden yellow petal tips and small center; **'Monte Negro'**, to 36 in (90 cm) tall, orange to dark red flowers; **'Montreaux'**, to 48 in (120 cm) tall, pink flowers; **'Navona'**, to 36 in (90 cm) tall, white flowers with yellow-green center; **'Nerone'**, to 6 ft (1.8 m) tall, deep black-red, upward-facing flowers; **'Strawberry Cream'**, to 48 in (120 cm) tall, large deep reddish pink center shading to cream petal tips; **'Vivaldi'**, to 42 in (105 cm) tall, pink flowers.

2. TURK'S-CAP OR MARTAGON HYBRIDS

Hybrids between *L. martagon* and *L. hansonii*, or hybrids with one of those species as a parent. They have large heads of many small to medium-sized pendulous flowers. The mixed color selection known as the

Backhouse Hybrids are the most widely grown lilies of this style. Other hybrids include: **'Chameleon'**, to 36 in (90 cm) tall, soft pink with darker spots; **'Claude Shride'**, to 36 in (90 cm) tall, dark mahogany red; **'Pepper Gold'**, to 36 in (90 cm) tall, soft copper orange with yellow-edged darker spots and thin yellow petal edges; **'Russian Morning'**, to 48 in (120 cm) tall, deep rose red, lighter petal reverse; **'Terry'**, to 36 in (90 cm) tall, soft pink with dense mist of darker spotting.

3. *L. CANDIDUM* HYBRIDS
Hybrids of *L. candidum, L. chalcedonicum,* and a number of other related species, but not *L. martagon.* These plants are typically tall and dark-stemmed, with fragrant, often white to cream, funnel-shaped flowers.

4. AMERICAN SPECIES HYBRIDS
Hybrids between American species, such as *L. canadense, L. maritimum, L. columbianum,* and *L. grayi.* These plants should be quite variable and interesting, but as yet this group is represented by just a few plants, of which the **Bellingham Hybrids**, with brown-spotted red and orange or red and yellow flowers, are the most commonly seen.

5. *L. LONGIFLORUM* AND *L. FORMOSANUM* HYBRIDS
Hybrids between or of these 2 species often have large, green-tinted, white, trumpet-shaped flowers. **'Eyeliner'**, to 36 in (90 cm) tall, white with very fine purple-red edge and central flecks; **'Gizmo'**, to 48 in (120 cm) tall, large white flowers, green stripe down each petal center; **'LanKon'** ★, to 48 in (120 cm) tall, cream to pale pink heavily suffused and spotted burgundy, powerful fragrance; **'Triumphator'**, to 48 in (120 cm) tall, flowers large, deep pink center shading to broad white petal tips, good scent.

6. TRUMPET-SHAPED AND AURELIAN LILIES
Hybrids of *L. henryi* and related species, but not including those species that make up Division 7. This group is subdivided into 4 categories based on flower shape: 6a, trumpet-shaped flowers; 6b, bowl-shaped flowers; 6c, flat flowers with recurved tips; and 6d, strongly recurved flowers.

Popular Division 6 lilies include: **'Beaverton Pentimento'**, to 6 ft (1.8 m) tall, golden yellow with dark spotting; **'Black Dragon'**, to 60 in (150 cm) tall, deep purple-red flowers with white interior; **'Golden Splendor'**, to 60 in (150 cm) tall, upward-facing deep yellow flowers; **'Lady Alice'**, to 60 in (1.5 m) tall, white with large deep gold center and darker spotting; **'Pink Perfection'**, to 60 in (150 cm) tall, very large, fragrant, deep magenta flowers.

7. ORIENTAL HYBRIDS
Hybrids of *L. auratum, L. speciosum, L. japonicum,* and *L. rubellum.* Includes hybrids between these species and *L. henryi* but not with Trumpet or Aurelian hybrids. Subdivided into 4 categories based on flower shape: 7a, trumpet-shaped flowers; 7b, bowl-shaped flowers; 7c, flat flowers; and 7d, strongly recurved flowers. Popular Oriental hybrids include: **'Acapulco'**, to 36 in (90 cm) tall, mauve flowers; **'Alliance'**, to 48 in (120 cm) tall, pink flowers with dark mid-stripe and pale edges; **'Brasilia'**, to 40 in (100 cm) tall, light pink flowers, edged and flushed deep lavender-pink, scented; **'Canberra'**, to 32 in (80 cm) tall, deep pink, small yellow center; **'Cartouche'**, to 48 in (120 cm) tall, reddish pink flowers with dark mid-stripe and pale edges; **'Casa Blanca'**, to 54 in (135 cm) tall, white flowers; **'Expression'** ★, to 36 in (90 cm) tall, white flowers; **'Mambo'**, to 36 in (90 cm) tall, deep rose red with near-black spotting; **'Miss Lucy'**, to 48 in (120 cm) tall, white to pale pink, suffused and edged deeper pink, no pollen; **'Muscadet'**, to 27 in (70 cm) tall, white, flushed pale pink flowers with red spots; **'Pesaro'**, to 36 in (90 cm) tall, deep pink flowers with pale center; **'Rio Negro'**, to 48 in (120 cm) tall, deep purple red with pale edges to recurved petals; **'Siberia'**, to 48 in (120 cm) tall, pure white flowers; **'Sissi'**, to 36 in (90 cm) tall, pink flowers; **'Sorbonne'**, to 48 in (120 cm) tall, deep pink flowers with pale edges; **'Star Gazer'**, to 36 in (90 cm) tall, pink flowers with red flecks and pale edges; **'Woodriff's Memory'**, to 36 in (90 cm), purplish-pink flowers with a yellow mid-stripe.

8. OTHER HYBRIDS
Miscellaneous hybrids not classified elsewhere, such as: **'Virginia'**, 24–36 in (60–90 cm), white flowers greenish yellow at center. **LA Hybrids** appeared in the 1990s, so named because they combined *L. longiflorum* with Asiatic Hybrids; they include: **'Glossy Wings'**, to 36 in (90 cm) tall, strong salmon-pink flowers; **'Royal Fantasy'**, to 36 in (90 cm) tall, creamy yellow scented flowers; **'Royal Present'**, to 36 in (90 cm) tall, coral pink shading to yellow center; **'Royal Sunset'**, to 30 in (75 cm) tall, orange petals tipped scarlet, finely spotted; **'Wiener Blut'** ★, to 30 in (75 cm) tall, tomato-red flowers, major commercial cut flower. More recent still are the Orienpet (Oriental × Trumpet) hybrids that offer improved drought-resistance and interesting color combinations, such as: **'Anastasia'**, to 48 in (120 cm) tall, pale pink shading to deeper center, dark central petal stripe; **'Belladonna'**, to 48 in (120 cm) tall, bright chrome yellow, huge flowers; **'Caravan'**, to 60 in (150 cm) tall, golden yellow with large red center, scented; **'Miss Libby'**, to 60 in (150 cm) tall, buff yellow with large red center and red-brown petal stripe; **'Nymph'**, to 48 in (120 cm) tall, pale pink with deep pink basal blush on each petal; **'Scheherazade'**, to 6 ft (1.8 m) tall, large flowers, deep pinkish red fading to cream at edges and tips, light scent; **'Silk Road'** ★, to 6 ft (1.8 m) tall, huge flowers, deep rose pink fading to white at tips and edges, strong scent.

9. SPECIES
The species as they occur in the wild, including the many natural subspecies and varieties. In this book the species all have their own entries.

L., HC, 7. Oriental, 'Alliance'

L., HC, 7. Oriental, 'Cartouche'

Lilium, Hybrid Cultivar, 8. Other, LA, 'Wiener Blut'

L., HC, 8. Other, 'Virginia'

L., HC, 8. Other, LA, 'Royal Sunset'

Limonium brassicifolium

Limonium perezii

Limonium sinuatum

Linaria maroccana cultivar

LIMONIUM

SEA LAVENDER, STATICE

Genus of about 150 species of mainly summer-flowering annuals, perennials, and small shrubs in the leadwort (Plumbaginaceae) family, widely distributed around the world, but with the main concentration in southern Europe and North Africa. The name comes from the Greek *leimon,* meadow, referring to the fact that many species occur in salt marshes (or salt meadows). Most are low-growing, forming mounds of basal leaf rosettes. The leaves vary in size and tend to be lance- or spatula-shaped. Flowers are minute but showy, borne in billowing sprays held well clear of the foliage on branching wiry stems, in white, cream, and mauve to purple shades. The flowers are still widely sold as "statice," and are popular for dried flower work.
CULTIVATION: Many *Limonium* species are somewhat frost tender, thriving in coastal conditions, with a preference for sheltered sunny locations and light, well-drained, yet moist soil. If the flowers are not cut for indoor use, they should be removed, as allowing the plants to set seed can shorten their life. Propagate from seed or root cuttings, or by division, depending on the plant type.

Limonium brassicifolium

↔ 12 in (30 cm) ↑ 16 in (40 cm)
From Canary Islands. Perennial with woody rhizome producing winged stems and 4–12 in (10–30 cm) long, broad, pointed oval leaves. Panicles of many single-flowered spikes with purple calyces and a white corolla. Zones 9–11.

Limonium perezii

↔ 20 in (50 cm) ↑ 27 in (70 cm)
From Canary Islands. Subshrub with broad oval leaves, to 6 in (15 cm) long. Flower stems downy. Large heads of flowers, deep purple calyces, creamy yellow to white corolla. Zones 9–11.

Limonium platyphyllum

syn. *Limonium latifolium*
↔ 24 in (60 cm) ↑ 32 in (80 cm)
Found from southeastern to central Europe. Vigorous summer-flowering perennial. Leaves narrow, spatula-shaped to elliptical, sparsely downy, usually about 10 in (25 cm), sometimes to 24 in (60 cm) long. Rounded billowing panicles of pale violet flowers. Zones 5–10.

Limonium sinuatum

syn. *Statice sinuata*
↔ 16 in (40 cm) ↑ 16 in (40 cm)
Native to the Mediterranean region. Summer-flowering perennial, often short-lived and treated as an annual. All parts downy. The leaves are pinnately lobed, lance-shaped, 1–4 in (2.5–10 cm) long. Flower stems are winged, with many short compact spikes of papery flowers. Wild species has lavender, pink, or white flowers; cultivars come in many colors. Can become invasive. **'Art Shades'**, pastel tones, most colors; **California Series**, bright tones, most colors; **'Forever Gold'**, deep golden yellow flowers. Zones 9–11.

LINARIA

SPURRED SNAPDRAGON, TOADFLAX

From the plantain (Plantaginaceae) family, this genus encompasses about 150 species of annuals and perennials found in Europe (mainly around the Mediterranean) and temperate Asia. A few North American species formerly included in *Linaria* are now placed in the genus *Nuttallanthus.* Toadflaxes are closely related to snapdragons, with similar but smaller flowers. They are easy to cultivate but stop flowering in hot weather. For best effect, plant in masses, as the individual plants are wispy. The name is derived from the Greek *linon,* flax, because of the similarity in foliage.
CULTIVATION: Grow *Linaria* species in full sun or partial shade in well-drained soil. Cut perennials down to ground level in autumn. Propagate annuals and perennials from seed; perennials also by division and from cuttings. Sow seed outdoors in late autumn or early spring (even when snow is still on ground) or indoors. Seed germinates in about 2 weeks and flowering starts about 8 weeks later. Annuals also self-seed.

Linaria maroccana

ANNUAL TOADFLAX, BUNNY RABBITS, MOROCCO TOADFLAX
↔ 6–12 in (15–30 cm)
↑ 8–10 in (20–25 cm)
From Morocco; naturalized in northeastern USA. Annual. Leaves narrow, grass-like, alternate. Profuse tiny snapdragon-like flowers in white, yellow, pink, red, and dark blue to purple shades in the early summer. **'Fairy Bouquet'**, flowers ranging from lavender, purple, and pink to crimson; **'Fantasy Blue'**, dwarf form, compact habit, will grow year-round in mild climates; **'Northern Lights'**, faintly violet-scented, jewel-like, bicolored flowers in pink, red, yellow, and purple; **Soda Pop Series**, magenta-rose, blue, or pink flowers. Zones 9–11.

Linaria purpurea

PURPLE TOADFLAX
↔ 6–12 in (15–30 cm)
↑ 20–36 in (50–90 cm)
From southern Europe. Narrow bushy perennial. Slender gray-green leaves. Bright blue-purple flowers with white stripes in mid-summer–early autumn. **'Canon Went'**, tall, with grayish foliage and soft pink flowers. Zones 5–10.

Linaria triornithophora

THREE-BIRDS-FLYING
↔ 24 in (60 cm) ↑ 36 in (90 cm)
From Spain and Portugal. Perennial. Foliage gray-green, toxic if ingested. Pale lavender and yellow spurred flowers, carried on long stems and grouped in 3s with the long spurs pointing downward, like the tails of perching birds, in late spring–late summer. Zones 7–10.

LINDERA

This genus in the laurel (Lauraceae) family consists of about 80 species of deciduous and evergreen trees and shrubs, all from East Asia except for 3 from North America. They have an open habit and aromatic alternate leaves, smooth-edged or 3-lobed. The leaves color in autumn on deciduous species. Heads of star-shaped yellow flowers, in spring, in the leaf axils, followed by clustered berry-like fruits. Leaves of the North American species have been used to make a type of tea.
CULTIVATION: Suitable for a woodland or other informal garden, in a shady position when young. All species transplant well and will survive in ordinary, somewhat acidic, soil. Established trees require little or no care but may be pruned if they become ungainly. Propagate from seed sown when fresh; if the seed must be stored, do not allow it to dry. Otherwise propagate from cuttings taken in summer or by air-layering.

Lindera obtusiloba

Lindera obtusiloba

☼ ✱ ↔25 ft (8 m) ↕30 ft (9 m)

From East Asia. Branches gray-yellow, sometimes flushed with purple. Aromatic leaves turning pale gold in the autumn. Produces tiny, yellow-green, star-shaped flowers, in umbels on the previous year's growth, in early spring, before the leaves. Fruit glossy dark red to black. Zones 6–9.

LINUM

FLAX

This genus, which gives its name to the family Linaceae, comprises about 180 species of tender and hardy annuals, biennials, perennials, and subshrubs, with flax, *L. usitatissum*, the important fiber and oilseed plant included among them. Native to temperate or subtropical regions of the world though predominantly from the Northern Hemisphere. They are delicate but easy-to-grow plants. The stems are erect and branching, and the gray-green leaves are simple and narrow. The cup-shaped to funnel-shaped 5-petalled flowers are carried in branched clusters at the stem tips, lasting only one day. Colors vary with the variety but are mostly shades of blue or yellow, less commonly red, pink, or white. However, they are produced in great numbers throughout the summer.

CULTIVATION: For the best flowering effect, grow in well-drained humus-rich soil in full sun. Provide shelter in cool climates. Annuals and perennials are easily raised from seed or from cuttings of named varieties. Plant out perennials in autumn or early spring; sow annual species in early autumn or spring. Thin seedlings as needed.

Linum grandiflorum

FLOWERING FLAX

☼ ❄ ↔12 in (30 cm)
↕15–18 in (38–45 cm)

From Algeria. Annual. Slender stems; narrow, pointed, pale green leaves. Single, clear rose to purple, saucer-shaped flowers, 1½ in (35 mm) across, in early–late summer. **'Bright Eyes'**, to 15 in (38 cm) tall, white flowers, 2 in (5 cm) across, with a carmine eye; **'Rubrum'** (scarlet flax), to 12 in (30 cm) tall, brilliant crimson flowers. Zones 7–10.

Linum narbonense

☼ ✱ ↔12–18 in (30–45 cm)
↕12–24 in (30–60 cm)

From southern Europe. Perennial. Leaves gray-green, narrow. Blue cup-shaped flowers 1–1¼ in (25–30 mm) across, with white eye, in late spring–autumn. Usually dies back in winter but may be evergreen in mild climates. **'Heavenly Blue'**, more compact, with ultramarine flowers. Zones 5–9.

Linum perenne

PERENNIAL BLUE FLAX

☼ ✱ ↔12 in (30 cm)
↕12–18 in (30–45 cm)

From Europe. Vigorous but short-lived perennial. Many sky blue flowers, 1 in (25 mm) across, in early–late summer. Self-seeds freely. Zones 4–9.

LIQUIDAMBAR

SWEET GUM

In the sweet-gum (Altingiaceae) family, this genus comprises 4 species of tall deciduous trees found in North and Central America, East Asia, and Turkey. The meaning of the name is much as it appears, liquid amber, referring to the resin, known as storax, exuded by the winter buds. The trees have an attractive conical or rounded form, and the palmately lobed leaves are similar to those of maples but arranged spirally on the twig instead of in opposite pairs. In autumn the foliage changes color dramatically to shades of orange, red, and purple. Spring flowers are greenish and inconspicuous, in small spherical heads, but the brown fruiting heads that follow are spiky and decorative. *L. styraciflua* has a number of cultivars selected for autumn color.

CULTIVATION: These are large trees requiring plenty of room to develop; their site should be chosen carefully, as they dislike being transplanted. They require a sunny situation in deep rich soil with plenty of moisture. Propagate from seed sown in autumn or softwood cuttings taken in summer, or by air-layering.

Liquidambar formosana

CHINESE LIQUIDAMBAR, FORMOSAN GUM

☼ ❄ ↔30 ft (9 m) ↕60 ft (18 m)

From mountains of east, central, and southern China, Taiwan, northern Vietnam, Laos, and South Korea. Straight-trunked tree, grayish white bark, fissures with age. Leaves broad, 3-lobed, with serrated margins, downy beneath. Inconspicuous greenish yellow flowers; spiky fruits. Zones 8–11.

Linum grandiflorum 'Rubrum'

Liquidambar orientalis

ORIENTAL SWEET GUM, TURKISH LIQUIDAMBAR

☼ ❄ ↔15 ft (4.5 m) ↕25–50 ft (8–15 m)

From southwestern Turkey. Broad crown; bark thick, orangey brown, cracking into small plates. Leaves 5-lobed, smaller than other species, turning orange in autumn. Zones 8–11.

Liquidambar styraciflua

LIQUIDAMBAR, SWEET GUM

☼ ✱ ↔35 ft (10 m) ↕70 ft (21 m)

Native to eastern USA, with separate occurrence in highlands of southern Mexico and Central America. Most commonly cultivated liquidambar. Bark dark grayish brown, deeply furrowed. Leaves large, 5 to 7 tapering lobes, coloring brilliantly in shades of orange, red, and purple in autumn. Cultivars selected for their autumn colors include: **'Burgundy'**, deep red; **'Festival'**, yellow, peach, pink; **'Lane Roberts'**, deep reddish purple; **'Palo Alto'**, orange and red; **'Worplesdon'**, orangey yellow and purple. Other cultivars include: **'Aurea'**, yellow-striped leaves; **'Gold Dust'**, gold and green leaves turning red and pink in autumn; **'Golden Treasure'**, leaves with yellow margins; **'Gumball'**, grafted dwarf form and rounded shape; **'Oakville Highlight'**, very narrow form, ideal for avenues; **'Rotundiloba'** ★, leaves with rounded lobes; **'Variegata'**, leaves splashed with yellow; **'Ward'** (syn. 'Cherokee'); near-sterile, no fruit litter. Zones 8–11.

Liquidambar orientalis

Liquidambar styraciflua

LIRIODENDRON

Genus in the magnolia (Magnoliaceae) family believed to consist of a single species native to North America until a second similar species was found in central China in 1875. Both form quite tall, fast-growing, deciduous trees with long straight trunks and unusually shaped 4-lobed leaves that turn a translucent yellow in autumn. The greenish bell-shaped flowers have a tangerine tint at petal bases. They somewhat resemble a tulip; hence the common name, tulip tree. Capsule-like fruit follow. Hybrids between the 2 species are in cultivation.
CULTIVATION: Tulip trees grow best in fertile soil, in a cool climate in partial shade, with protection from drying winds. Some shaping of the plant in the early stages to establish a single trunk may be necessary. Propagate from seed sown in a position protected from winter frosts. Cultivars may be apical-grafted in early spring onto 1- or 2-year-old seedling understocks.

Liriodendron tulipifera, in spring

Liriodendron chinense

CHINESE TULIP TREE

☼ ❄ ↔ 35 ft (10 m) ↑ 80 ft (24 m)

Widely scattered through mountains of China, Taiwan, and northern Vietnam; still rare in cultivation in the West. Broad, columnar, fast-growing tree. Leaves deep green, smoother than those of the other species. Cup-shaped flowers, green outside, yellow-green veins inside, in spring. Zones 8–10.

Liriodendron tulipifera

NORTH AMERICAN TULIP TREE, TULIP TREE

☼ ❄ ↔ 40 ft (12 m) ↑ 100 ft (30 m)

Found east of Mississippi River, USA, from Gulf States up to St Lawrence River and Great Lakes. Leaves quite large. Solitary flowers, 6 petalled, yellow-green with orange-yellow blotch at base, in spring. **'Aureomarginatum'**, yellow-edged leaves; **'Fastigiatum'** ★, upright columnar habit; growing only about half height of type. Zones 4–10.

Liriope muscari 'Monroe White'

Liriope spicata, border plant in foreground

LIRIOPE

LILY TURF

This small genus in the asparagus (Asparagaceae) family, comprising 5 or 6 species of evergreen or semi-evergreen frost-hardy perennials, is closely related to *Ophiopogon*. From acid-soil woodland habitats in East Asia. Tough, mat-forming, trouble-free plants, which soon establish a dense fibrous root system and in some species develop nutrient-storing fleshy tubers. Grass-like leaves, arching, linear, and dense. Flowers, clustered and grape-like on blunt stems, usually showy for extended late summer period, followed by black, berry-like seeds.
CULTIVATION: Grow in shade in mild climates; allow more sun in cold climates. Propagate by division or by fresh ripe seed sown in a sandy medium.

Liriope muscari

☼/◑ ❄ ↔ 18–24 in (45–60 cm)
↑ 8–24 in (20–60 cm)

Native to China, Taiwan, and Japan. Woodland plant; drought-tolerant, tough, sturdy, evergreen, spreading ground cover. Leaves narrow, grass-like, glossy deep green, mat-forming. Dense, bead-like, steely deep lavender flowers, held on blunt spikes, in late autumn. **'Big Blue'**, blue-green foliage, blue flowers, up to 20 in (50 cm) high; **'Christmas Tree'**, large form, resplendent flowers; **'Evergreen Giant'**, 20 in (50 cm) high and wide; **'John Burch'**, large flowers on tall spikes, wide leaves with a yellow-green central stripe; **'Majestic'**, to 16 in (40 cm), narrow leaves, violet flowers; **'Monroe White'**, numerous white flowers, requires full shade; **'Silver Midget'**, white-edged leaves, 8 in (20 cm) high; **'Variegata'**, leaves margined in yellow. Zones 4–10.

Liriope spicata

☼/◑ ❄ ↔ 18 in (45 cm) ↑ 10 in (25 cm)

From China and Vietnam. Drought-tolerant evergreen ground cover. Leaves glossy, dark, dense, mat-forming. Pale lavender flowers in late summer. **'Silver Dragon'**, compact, to about 8 in (20 cm) tall, narrow dark leaves silver striped, pale purple flowers. Zones 5–10.

LITHOCARPUS

Genus of about 300 oak-like evergreen trees in the beech (Fagaceae) family found on mountain slopes of East and Southeast Asia and New Guinea, with one species from western USA. Leathery leaves spirally arranged but crowded toward the ends of seasonal growths, smooth-edged or toothed. Tiny flowers are borne on stiff catkins near branch tips in spring, females close to catkin bases, males above. Seeds (acorns) mature in the second year. *Lithocarpus* differs from *Quercus* in that the male catkins are erect rather than pendulous and the acorns are crowded onto spikes.
CULTIVATION: Most enjoy cool, moist winters and dry summers. Plant in moderately fertile acid to neutral soil in full sun or part-shade. Shelter from cold drying winds in cooler climates. Propagate from seed, sown in autumn.

Lithocarpus densiflorus

TANBARK OAK

☼ ❄ ↔ 40 ft (12 m) ↑ 100ft (30 m)

From northern California and southern Oregon, USA. Smaller in open positions. Bark thick, furrowed, red-brown. Young shoots woolly white; leaves stiff, leathery, toothed, prominently veined, with rusty hairs on the undersides, turning a leaden hue with age. Tiny whitish male flowers. Egg-shaped acorns. *L. d.* var. *echinoides*, to 10 ft (3 m) high, leaves smaller, less toothed, than species. Zones 7–9.

LITHODORA

Genus in the borage (Boraginaceae) family of 7 species of low hairy shrubs or subshrubs, native to western and southern Europe, North Africa, and Asia Minor. Plentiful, deep dark green, simple leaves are about 1 in (25 mm) long and evergreen in most conditions when grown within the zone range, though they are susceptible to frost burn. Covered with many small vibrant blue or purple flowers in late spring or early summer. Low-growing habit makes them ideal for ground covers, rockeries or at the front of borders.
CULTIVATION: Grow in well-drained acid soil in full sun to partial shade; can become leggy in too much shade. Propagate from seed in spring or from tip cuttings in mid- to late summer.

Lithodora diffusa

syns *Glandora diffusa, Lithospermum diffusum*

☼/◑ ❄ ↔ 24–36 in (60–90 cm)
↑ 6–12 in (15–30 cm)

From France, Spain, and Portugal. Creeping plant, green linear leaves, blue flowers in mid-spring–early summer. With age, it ceases producing foliage and flowers in center. **'Grace Ward'**, low-creeping form, bright azure flowers; **'Heavenly Blue'** ★, petals edged with brilliant white; **'Star'**, petals edged with clear white. Zones 7–9.

Lithocarpus densiflorus var. *echinoides*

LOBELIA

While the small mounding annuals often seen edging flower borders are well known, *Lobelia* is a large, enormously variable, and widespread genus of the self-named lobelia (Lobeliaceae) family, encompassing over 350 species of annuals, perennials, and shrubs, including some amazing megaherbs from the mountains of East Africa. Other than the annuals, with their massed summer display of blue, white, or pink flowers, cultivated lobelias are mainly perennials from the Americas, most of which form a basal clump of simple leaves, from which emerge upright flower stems bearing spikes of tubular 5-lobed flowers, the lower 3 lobes enlarged. *Lobelia* species were used medicinally by Native Americans; the Cherokee of the eighteenth century reputedly had an infallible lobelia-based cure for syphilis.
CULTIVATION: Requirements vary but most *Lobelia* species prefer a sunny position with moist well-drained soil. Tall types may need staking. Propagate the annuals from seed sown in spring and the perennials by division or from basal cuttings.

Lobelia erinus

Lithodora diffusa 'Star'

Lobelia cardinalis

Lobelia cardinalis

CARDINAL FLOWER

☼/◐ ✱ ↔12–16 in (30–40 cm) ↑36 in (90 cm)

North American short-lived perennial forming a clump of upright stems with often red-tinted, narrow, pointed oval to lance-shaped leaves, to 4 in (10 cm) long. Long spikes of bright red flowers, to over 1 in (25 mm) wide, from summer to autumn. Zones 6–9.

Lobelia erinus

BEDDING LOBELIA, EDGING LOBELIA

☼/◐ ❄ ↔12–16 in (30–40 cm) ↑8 in (20 cm)

South African, small, long-flowering perennial usually treated as an annual. Dense mounding habit; fine stems; small, often purple-tinted, deep green leaves, roughly oval, toothed. Masses of small pale-centered flowers, blue, mauve, purple. **Cascade Series**, for hanging baskets; **'Kathleen Mallard'**, mounding, with deep blue double flowers; **'Mrs. Clibran'**, mounding, with dark blue flowers; **Palace Series**, dwarf and heavy flowering, for borders and pots; **'Periwinkle Blue'**, trailer, bright blue flowers; **Regatta Series**, trailer, mixed colors; **Royal Jewels** seed mix, flowers in blue, mauve, and purple-red shades. Zones 8–11.

Lobelia laxiflora

Lobelia × *gerardii* 'Tania'

Lobelia × *gerardii*

syn. *Lobelia* × *speciosa*

☼/◐ ❄ ↔20–24 in (50–60 cm) ↑60 in (150 cm)

Garden hybrid between *L. cardinalis* and *L. siphilitica*. Vigorous perennial forming a clump of upright stems with pointed oval to elliptical leaves, to 6 in (15 cm) long, mainly crowded at base. Large heads of white-marked pink or violet to purple flowers. **'Bee's Flame'**, bronze foliage, red flowers; **'Cherry Ripe'**, dark green leaves, red flowers; **Compliment Series**, seedling strain, blue or red flowers; **'Fan Scarlet'**, green foliage, purple-red flowers; **'Queen Victoria'** ★, deep red foliage and stems, bright red flowers; **'Russian Princess'**, green foliage, green flowers. **'Tania'**, red-tinted foliage, deep magenta flowers; **'Vedrariensis'**, red-tinted foliage, purple flowers. Zones 7–10.

Lobelia laxiflora

TORCH LOBELIA

☼/◐ ❄ ↔4 ft (1.2 m) ↑3 ft (0.9 m)

From southern Arizona, USA, through the Mexican highlands to Colombia, occurring in oak and pine forests. Variable species with shrubby habit. Leaves pointed, lance-shaped. Long-stalked tubular flowers, scarlet with yellow tips, in summer. Zones 8–11.

Lobelia richardsonii

☼/◐ ✢ ↔24–36 in (60–90 cm) ↑6 in (15 cm)

Of unknown origin, possibly only a form of *L. erinus*; plants sold as *L. ricardii* are possibly the same. Trailing perennial with wiry stems, small purple-tinted leaves, bright blue flowers in spring–autumn. May be grown as an annual, but from cuttings as it does not set viable seed. Zones 10–11.

Lobelia siphilitica

BLUE CARDINAL FLOWER

☼/◐ ✱ ↔16 in (40 cm) ↑24 in (60 cm)

From eastern USA. Bushy perennial with mainly basal foliage. Leaves pointed oval to lance-shaped, toothed, to 4 in (10 cm) long. Flower stems upright, with long spikes of deep blue flowers, to 1 in (25 mm) across, in summer–autumn. Zones 5–9.

Lobelia tupa

☼ ❄ ↔3 ft (0.9 m) ↑6 ft (1.8 m)

From Chile, growing in sandy hills near the sea. Attractive leaves lightly felted, grayish green. Terminal spikes of scarlet or brick-red flowers in summer–autumn. Zones 8–10.

LOBULARIA

ALYSSUM, BEDDING ALYSSUM

Genus of 5 species of annuals and perennials in the cabbage (Brassicaceae) family from the northern temperate zones. Small mounding plants with simple linear to lance-shaped leaves, sometimes with fine silvery hairs. Tiny, often sweet-scented flowers in warmer months, in rounded heads. Garden forms in white and shades of primrose, apricot, mauve, and purple.
CULTIVATION: Hardy, easily grown in sun in light free-draining soil. Water to encourage flowering, but plants often remain more compact and less likely to fall apart from center if kept dry. Propagate from seed, or the seed may be broadcast; often self-sows.

Lobularia maritima

BEDDING ALYSSUM

☼ ❄ ↔8–16 in (20–40 cm) ↑10 in (25 cm)

Widespread in northern temperate zones. Annual or short-lived perennial forming a compact mound of narrow dull green leaves, about 1 in (25 mm) long. Tiny flowers in massed rounded heads. Species usually white- to cream-flowered; garden forms in several sizes and colors. **'Carpet of Snow'**, to 4 in (10 cm) high, pure white flowers; Easter Bonnet Series, to 6 in (15 cm) high, compact mounding habit, in white and pink to purple shades; **'Snow Crystals'**, to 8–10 in (20–25 cm) high, large white flowers. Zones 7–10.

Lobularia maritima 'Snow Crystals'

L

Lomandra longifolia, in the wild, Washpool National Park, New South Wales, Australia

Lonicera × brownii 'Dropmore Scarlet'

Lonicera chaetocarpa

Lonicera × heckrottii 'Gold Flame'

Lonicera nitida

Lonicera pileata 'Moss Green'

LOMANDRA

MAT-RUSH

The 50 species in this genus in the asparagus (Asparagaceae) family are, with a few exceptions, confined to Australia. They are evergreen, clump-forming, rush-like perennials or subshrubs with tiny flowers produced in spikes or panicles usually held low down amongst the leaves. The flowers are usually creamy white to lemon yellow, and the panicles are not particularly showy. Mat-rushes are used for soil stabilization, providing a habitat for small animals such as lizards.

CULTIVATION: Once cultivated only by native plant enthusiasts or as roadside plantings owing to their drought tolerance, *Lomandra* has recently enjoyed a huge increase in popularity as new cultivars have been introduced. Because dead foliage builds up in the clumps, prune to the ground and de-thatch every so often. Propagate from fresh seed or by dividing established clumps.

Lomandra confertiflora

SMALL MAT-RUSH

↔10–36 in (25–90 cm)
↕16–36 in (40–90 cm)

From coast to foothills of southeastern Australia. Leaves up to 24 in (60 cm) long, but very narrow. Flowers creamy yellow on stiff stems. **'Lime Wave'**, long, fine, light green leaves; **'Little Con'**, compact, dense foliage, 12 in (30 cm) high and wide; **'Seascape'**, blue-gray leaves to 20 in (50 cm) long, arching; **'Silver Grace'**, silver-gray foliage, 20 in (50 cm) high; **'Tilga'**, very fine green leaves, airy. Zones 8–11.

Lomandra filiformis

WATTLE MAT-RUSH

↔8–16 in (20–40 cm)
↕16–24 in (40–60 cm)

Found in eastern Australia from Adelaide to Cape York. Leaves stiff, up to 18 in (45 cm) long and ¼ in (6 mm) wide, olive green to blue-green. Flowers yellow, small, widely spaced on wiry stem. **'Mondra'**, compact, tufting, bright green, 8 in (20 cm) high and wide; **'Savanna Blue'**, blue-green leaves, 12 in (30 cm) high and wide. Zones 8–12.

Lomandra longifolia

BASKET GRASS, SPINY-HEADED MAT-RUSH

↔30–36 in (75–90 cm)
↕20–40 in (50–100 cm)

From Eastern Australia. Sedge-like perennial forming large tussocks. Leaves stiff, flat, with several points at each tip. Narrow panicle of dense clusters of small, fragrant, creamy yellow flowers with straw-colored spiny bracts, held in foliage, in the spring to early summer. **'Tanika'**, fine, overarching foliage, 24 in (60 cm) high and wide. Zones 8–12.

LONICERA

HONEYSUCKLE

Honeysuckles, belonging to the woodbine (Caprifoliaceae) family, are often regarded as somewhat untidy second-class climbers, but in the right place they are among the easiest and most rewarding plants. Occurring widely throughout the Northern Hemisphere though chiefly in temperate Eurasia, the 180-odd species in the genus en-compass climbers, ground covers, and shrubs, both evergreen and deciduous, most of them very hardy. The foliage usually consists of opposite pairs of smooth-edged leaves, often somewhat leathery. The flowers, sometimes highly fragrant, vary in size; most are tubular at the base but divided at the mouth into 5 petals frequently arranged in 2 lips, an upper lip of 4 fused petals and a lower lip of a single petal. The fruit is an ornamental berry relished by birds, usually backed or partially enclosed by bract-like calyces that may color slightly.

CULTIVATION: Although honeysuckles are tough adaptable plants that thrive in most conditions, they are generally best grown in rich, moist, humus-enriched, well-drained soil in full sun to partial shade. They can be raised from seed, though most are easily grown from layers or half-hardened cuttings. Cultivars and hybrids must be propagated from cuttings.

Lonicera × brownii

SCARLET TRUMPET HONEYSUCKLE

↔8 ft (2.4 m) ↕10 ft (3 m)

Garden-raised deciduous or semi-deciduous *L. sempervirens × L. hirsuta* hybrid, resembling *L. sempervirens,* with paired blue-green leaves. Whorls of pale orange to red unscented flowers in the late spring to early summer. **'Dropmore Scarlet'**, strong growing, with larger leaves, long-tubed bright red flowers in mid-summer–autumn. Zones 5–9.

Lonicera caprifolium

ITALIAN HONEYSUCKLE

↔10 ft (3 m) ↕20 ft (6 m)

From Europe and western Asia. Usually seen as climber but can be grown as ground cover. Oval leaves in pairs. Whorls of very fragrant, pink-tinted creamy yellow flowers, to 2 in (5 cm) long, in spring–summer. Orange-red fruit. Zones 5–9.

Lonicera sempervirens

Lonicera chaetocarpa

↔ 6 ft (1.8 m) ↑ 6 ft (1.8 m)

From China. Deciduous shrub. Young stems, also leaf undersides, bristly. Cream long-tubed flowers, single or in pairs, in summer. Red fruit backed by red-tinted calyces. Zones 5–9.

Lonicera fragrantissima

WINTER HONEYSUCKLE

↔ 8 ft (2.4 m) ↑ 6 ft (1.8 m)

From China. Shrubby, fragrant, evergreen or deciduous plant. Leaves dull green. Small, strongly scented, cream flowers, borne in pairs in leaf axils along the arching twigs, in winter–spring. Red fruit. Zones 5–9.

Lonicera × *heckrottii*

↔ 6 ft (1.8 m) ↑ 15 ft (4.5 m)

Hybrid, possibly between *L. sempervirens* and *L.* × *americana*. A sprawling deciduous climber with paired oblong to elliptical leaves, purplish when young, maturing to blue-green. Whorls of yellow-throated deep pink flowers in late spring–summer. Red fruit. **'Gold Flame'**, dark green leaves, purple-red flowers, which are bright yellow inside. Zones 5–9.

Lonicera hildebrandiana

GIANT BURMESE HONEYSUCKLE

↔ 15–40 ft (4.5–12 m)
↑ 15–60 ft (4.5–18 m)

Vigorous evergreen twining climber from northern parts of Myanmar and Thailand and neighboring parts of southern China. Strong stems, leathery, deep green to bronze-green, paired leaves to over 6 in (15 cm) long. Clustered, tubular, cream to yellow, powerfully fragrant flowers to 4 in (10 cm) long, in summer–autumn. Zones 9–12.

Lonicera involucrata

TWINBERRY

↔ 3 ft (0.9 m) ↑ 3 ft (0.9 m)

Found from Mexico through western USA to southern Canada. Deciduous shrub grown for its fruit, deep purple berries backed by large purple-red bracts. Leaves to 5 in (12 cm) long. Short-tubed, yellow to red, paired flowers in spring. Zones 4–10.

Lonicera × *italica*

↔ 5–10 ft (1.5–3 m) ↑ 10 ft (3 m)

Evergreen vine with variegated leaves of pink, lime green, and cream. The spicy-scented, rose-purple, tubular flowers appear in mid-spring to mid-summer. Zones 5–9.

Lonicera ledebourii

↔ 8 ft (2.4 m) ↑ 6 ft (1.8 m)

From western USA. Deciduous shrub, similar to *L. involucrata*. Long narrow leaves with felty undersides. Orange-yellow flowers in summer. Heart-shaped bracts, reddening as the black berries mature. Zones 6–10.

Lonicera nitida

syn. *Lonicera ligustrina subsp. yunnanensis*

BOX HONEYSUCKLE

↔ 10 ft (3 m) ↑ 12 ft (3.5 m)

From central and southwestern China. Widely grown, shrubby, evergreen honeysuckle. Leaves tiny, dark green, purple toned in winter. Small cream flowers in spring, rarely seen in some climatic zones. Purple-black berries. Dense bushy habit, responds well to pruning; used for hedging, topiary, and borders. **'Hohenheimer Findling'**, very dense and vigorous for quick cover; **'Maigrun'**, small, dense, and bushy, good box *(Buxus)* substitute. Zones 7–10.

Lonicera periclymenum

WOODBINE

↔ 8 ft (2.4 m) ↑ 12 ft (3.5 m)

From Eurasia. Twining, scrambling, deciduous or semi-evergreen shrub. Finely downy young leaves becoming smooth and glaucous when mature. Very fragrant pinkish red flowers with creamy yellow interiors, in whorls of 3 to 5 blooms, in summer. Red fruit. Can become invasive. **'Serotina'**, narrow-leafed cultivar, red berries developing from flowers with purple exteriors. Zones 4–10.

Lonicera pileata

↔ 8 ft (2.4 m) ↑ 2 ft (0.6 m)

From China. Evergreen or semi-deciduous shrub, often prostrate, with neat mounding growth habit. Leaves to 1¼ in (30 mm) long, deep green, rhomboidal in shape. Very small cream flowers, in pairs. Light purple fruit. **'Moss Green'**, low-growing, with bright green leaves. Zones 5–9.

Lonicera sempervirens

TRUMPET HONEYSUCKLE

↔ 10 ft (3 m) ↑ 10–20 ft (3–6 m)

From eastern and southern USA. De-ciduous twining vine with blue-green leaves; scarlet-orange trumpet-shaped blooms with yellow centers, borne on previous year's stems. **'Superba'**, scarlet-orange to scarlet tubular flowers; **'Blanche Sandman'**, semi-evergreen vine, rich orange-red tubular blooms in spring–summer. Zones 4–10.

Lonicera × *tellmanniana*

REDGOLD HONEYSUCKLE, TELLMANN HONEYSUCKLE

↔ 5 ft (1.5 m)
↑ 7–20 ft (2–6 m)

Deciduous, vigorous, twining climber with showy coppery gold flowers in late spring–summer. Zones 6–9.

LOPHOMYRTUS

This genus native to New Zealand belongs to the myrtle (Myrtaceae) family and is closely allied to *Myrtus* itself. It consists of 2 species of small evergreen trees or shrubs, which are grown primarily for their interesting foliage, though with age they also develop attractive dappled or streaked smooth bark. The species hybridize freely. A number of named cultivars are now placed in a group known as *L.* × *ralphii*.

CULTIVATION: Grow in full sun for best leaf coloration, in reasonably fertile well-drained soil. In cool-temperate climates they are best given a warm sheltered site and protection in winter. Prune for hedging or to maintain a dense shrubby form, or to a single trunk as a small tree. Species can be propagated from seed sown in spring but are usually propagated from half-hardened cuttings taken in autumn. *L.* × *ralphii* and its cultivars can only be propagated from cuttings.

Lophomyrtus bullata ★

RAMARAMA

↔ 8 ft (2.4 m) ↑ 8–12 ft (2.4–3.5 m)

Small tree. Leaves small, oval, with puckered surface, greener in shade, developing bronzy purplish tones in sun. Small fluffy cream flowers in summer. Dark reddish purple berries. Zones 9–10.

Lophomyrtus × *ralphii*

↔ 5 ft (1.5 m) ↑ 6 ft (1.8 m)

Hybrid with characteristics intermediate between the 2 parent species, *L. bullata* and *L. obcordata*. Leaves more rounded than those of *L. bullata* and much less puckered; flowers for a longer period over summer. **'Gloriosa'** (syn. *L.* × *ralphii* 'Variegata'), small, light green, rounded leaves variegated with cream and tinged pink; **'Indian Chief'**, dark reddish brown leaves in-tensifying in color during the winter; **'Kathryn'**, purplish red, glossy, oval leaves with a puckered surface; **'Pixie'**, suitable for rock gardens, to 12 in (30 cm) tall, small bronze-green leaves, chocolate-purple when young. Zones 9–11.

Lophomyrtus bullata

Lophomyrtus × *ralphii*

Lophospermum atrosanguineum

Lophostemon confertus

Loropetalum chinense 'Plum Delight'

LOPHOSPERMUM

Native to Mexico, this plantain (Plantaginaceae) family genus is composed of about 10 species of slender, climbing, short-lived, perennial vines. Their leaves are often heart-shaped, sometimes toothed and with a covering of fine hairs. The flowers are trumpet-shaped and in some species their effect is enhanced by large, brightly colored calyces. CULTIVATION: Best in warm bright locations in rich well-drained soil. Often grown in containers, especially hanging baskets. Easily raised from seed but can also be propagated from cuttings of vigorous plants.

L

Lophospermum atrosanguineum

syn. *Rhodochiton atrosanguineum*

PURPLE BELL VINE

↔2 ft (0.6 m) ↑15 ft (4.5 m)

From Mexico. Tender perennial vine often treated as annual. Small flowers hang down on slender stalk. Deep purple-red tubular flower emerges from persistent 4-pointed fuchsia-red calyx, in mid-summer. Zones 9–11.

Lophospermum erubescens

syn. *Asarina erubescens*

CREEPING GLOXINIA, MEXICAN TWIST

↔8 ft (2.4 m) ↑8 ft (2.4 m)

Trailer or climber from Mexico, often grown in hanging baskets. Leaves light green, heart- to lance-shaped, toothed. Flowers trumpet-shaped, to 2 in (5 cm) long, pink to purple-red, in summer. **'Bridal Bouquet'**, white flowers; **'Great Cascade'**, burgundy red flowers. Zones 9–11.

LOPHOSTEMON

This genus is a member of the myrtle (Myrtaceae) family, which includes such important plants as the eucalypts. Its 6 species of evergreen trees are native to Australia and New Guinea. The leaves are spirally arranged and crowded toward the end of the branchlets. The flowers, white, with 5 petals and 5 showy feather-like groups of fused stamens, are grouped in short cymes in the upper leaf axils. The fruit is a woody capsule like that of some *Eucalyptus* species, though *Lophostemon* is not closely related to *Eucalyptus*. CULTIVATION: These trees are popular for street and park planting in warm climates. They should be planted in fertile free-draining soil. They will survive outdoors in regions with very light winter frosts in a warm sheltered site but in cool-temperate climates need greenhouse protection. Propagate from seed sown in spring or autumn. Variegated cultivars are propagated by budding or grafting.

Lophostemon confertus

syn. *Tristania conferta*

BRUSH BOX

↔30 ft (9 m) ↑130 ft (40 m)

Found in east-coastal Queensland and northeastern New South Wales, Australia. Densely foliaged tree, pinkish brown peeling bark. Leaves long-pointed, elliptical, dark green above, olive-green beneath. White flowers, 1 in (25 mm) across, with masses of fluffy stamens, in summer. Yields a valuable, very hard, timber. Zones 10–12.

LOROPETALUM

Botanists have yet to determine whether more species belonging to this genus exist, but currently it is treated as comprising a single species of evergreen dome-shaped shrub or small tree from the woodland regions of the Himalayas, China, and Japan. One of the witchhazel (Hamamelidaceae) family, it is grown for its distinctive flowers and its horizontal branching habit, which makes it easy to train as an espalier or bonsai. The leaves are alternate, simple, and smooth-edged, and the small flowers, borne in tight heads of 3 to 6 flowers in the leaf axils, each have 4 twisted strap-like petals. The fruit is a small nut-like capsule containing 2 seeds. CULTIVATION: This trouble-free plant grows best in fertile, humus-enriched, well-drained soil in a position in full sun where its often widely branching habit can be fully appreciated. As it flowers on the last season's wood, prune after flowering, and only to enhance the shape. Propagate from cuttings taken in summer.

Loropetalum chinense

FRINGE FLOWER

↔8 ft (2.4 m) ↑6–15 ft (1.8–4.5 m)

Bushy shrub. Leaves small, dull green, oval. Slightly perfumed, creamy white, fringed flowerheads in spring. Distinctively bronze-foliaged form *L. c.* f. ***rubrum*** has become popular with gardeners worldwide; sometimes sold as cultivar **'Burgundy'**, it has red new leaves and purple-pink flowers. *L. c.* **'Daybreak Flame'**, deep purple-pink flowers, long petals, burgundy new growth, ageing green; **'Plum Delight'**, purple-red foliage and flowers; **'Plum Gorgeous'**, dark foliage year-round, pink flowers; **'Sizzling Pink'**, red spring foliage and bright pink flowers. Zones 8–11.

LOTUS

Genus of about 150 species of annuals, perennials, and both deciduous and evergreen subshrubs in the pea-flower subfamily of the legume (Fabaceae) family. They are found almost worldwide in open grasslands and rocky places; all but a few species are native to temperate regions of the Northern Hemisphere. The leaves are small and pinnate, often with only 4 or 5 leaflets and sometimes closely hairy, giving them a silvery appearance. The pea-flowers come in a range of colors, from white to yellow, pink, or red, and are borne singly or in clusters in the leaf axils. The most colorful are the several large-flowered species from the Canary Islands and Madeira, with yellow or red flowers adapted to pollination by birds. They are popular in garden borders, the trailing types are suited to hanging baskets or pots. CULTIVATION: Most species prefer well-drained soil in full sun. Propagate from seed or cuttings.

Lotus berthelotii

CORAL GEM, PARROT'S BEAK, PELICAN'S BEAK

↔3–6 ft (0.9–1.8 m) ↑8 in (20 cm)

From the Canary Islands. Popular, trailing, evergreen subshrub. Leaves silvery gray, with needle-like leaflets. Yellow-orange to red flowers, 1½ in (35 mm) long, in spring–summer. Zones 10–11.

Lotus maculatus

syn. *Heinekenia maculata*

FIRE VINE

↔3–6 ft (0.9–1.8 m) ↑8 in (20 cm)

From Canary Islands. Trailing perennial well suited to hanging baskets and pots. Mid-green needle-like leaflets. Bears yellow-tipped red-orange flowers in spring–summer. **'Amazon Sunset'**, long-flowering, with silvery leaves and deep red flowers; **'Gold Flash'**, red-orange flowers; and **'New Gold Flash'**, improved form of 'Gold Flash', abundant red-orange flowers. Zones 10–11.

LUCULIA

This genus in the madder (Rubiaceae) family comprises 5 species of deciduous flowering shrubs and small trees found in elevated forest regions of the Himalayas, from northern India to western China. They are beautiful, fragrant, flowering plants, prized both for their attractive foliage and prolific clusters of pink, red, or white flowers in the form of a slender tube opening to a broad 5-lobed disc. The fruit is a capsule with 2 chambers containing flattened seeds. Although they are technically deciduous, there is no long period of leaflessness, as the new foliage usually appears at about the same time as the old leaves are dropping. CULTIVATION: Tolerating only mild frosts, they prefer a moderate summer temperature and grow well in moderately fertile, moist, well-drained soil with plenty of humus. They need protection from the wind and do not like competition from other roots. Plant in part-shade or full sun; provide adequate water and fertilize regularly from spring to autumn. Prune back old flowering shoots after flowering. In frost-prone areas they may be grown in a cool greenhouse. Propagate from seed in spring or from half-hardened cuttings in summer.

Lotus maculatus 'Gold Flash'

Luculia grandifolia

Luculia grandifolia

☼/◐ ❄ ↔7 ft (2 m) ↑12–20 ft (3.5–6 m)

From elevated forest regions of Bhutan. Leaves large, deep green, elliptic to ovate, prominent reddish purple veins, stalks, and margins. Large clusters of 16 to 20 very fragrant, snow white, tubular flowers in summer. Zones 9–10.

Luculia gratissima

☼/◐ ❄ ↔10–15 ft (3–4.5 m) ↑10–20 ft (3–6 m)

Native to Himalayas. Outstanding free-flowering large shrub or small tree. Leaves ovate-oblong to lance-shaped, dark green. Large trusses of fragrant, slender-tubed, rosy pink flowers, forming a wonderful rounded mass, appear in autumn to mid-winter. Fruit is egg-shaped. Zones 9–10.

Luma apiculata

Luculia gratissima

LUMA

This genus, found in Argentina and Chile, includes just 4 species of densely foliaged, round-headed, evergreen shrubs and trees. Belonging to the myrtle (Myrtaceae) family and closely allied to *Myrtus*, they have small aromatic leaves and 4-petalled white flowers with a central mass of stamens. The flowers usually open in spring and early summer, and are followed by dark berries. The bark can also be an attractive feature, as in some species it peels and is a warm cinnamon tone on the outside and white to pink on the underneath.

CULTIVATION: All species are easily cultivated in any mild climate with adequate rainfall, preferring moist well-drained soil and a position in sun or light shade. Although usually neat growers, they benefit from being lightly trimmed to shape; if allowed to become old and overgrown, they can be rejuvenated with heavy pruning, which is best done over 2 or 3 seasons. Propagate from the seed or half-hardened tip cuttings.

Luma apiculata ★

syns *Myrtus apiculata, M. luma*

PALO COLORADO, TEMU

☼/◐ ❄ ↔20 ft (6 m) ↑20 ft (6 m)

Large shrub or small tree, sometimes exceeding 30 ft (9 m). Attractive, flaking, warm brown bark. Leaves deep olive green, glossy. Small white flowers, comprising over 150 stamens, in spring–summer. Small, dark purple-red fruit. Zones 9–10.

LUNARIA

This genus of 3 species of biennials and herbaceous perennials belongs to the cabbage (Brassicaceae) family. They are best raised in containers or for cut flowers, as they can be somewhat weedy and invasive. They are primarily grown for their silvery flat seed pods, which are used in dried flower arrangements. The botanical name is derived from the Latin *luna*, meaning moon, referring to the shape of the fruit.

CULTIVATION: Grow in full sun or partial shade in light, fertile, moist, well-drained soil. Propagate perennials from seed or by division in autumn or spring. Propagate biennials and annuals from seed in spring. These plants will readily self-seed.

Lunaria annua

HONESTY, MONEY PLANT, MONEYWORT, SILVER DOLLAR

☼/◐ ❄ ↔12 in (30 cm) ↑30 in (75 cm)

From southern Europe. Leaves bright green, alternate, heart-shaped, coarsely serrated. Rosy magenta, white, or violet-purple flowers, with 4 petals, in spring or early summer, followed by circular seed pods covered with a silvery translucent membrane. ***L. a.* var. *albiflora***, white flowers. ***L. a.* 'Variegata'**, variegated crimson flowers. Zones 8–10.

Lunaria rediviva

☼/◐ ❄ ↔24 in (60 cm) ↑36–42 in (90–105 cm)

Native to Europe, *L. rediviva* is a hairy-stemmed perennial that produces somewhat smaller flowers and seed pods than the annual species, but the pale mauve flowers of this species are sweetly scented. Zones 8–10.

LUPINUS

LUPIN, LUPINE

There are about 200 species of annuals, perennials, and evergreen shrubs in this genus in the pea-flower subfamily of the legume (Fabaceae) family from North and South America, southern Europe, and northern Africa, usually in dry habitats. Many have ornamental flowers, borne in showy terminal panicles or racemes. The leaves are palmate, with 5 to 15 leaflets, and the stems are often covered in fine soft down. Many species are grown for horticultural purposes, such as nitrogen fixing and stock fodder, and some seeds are processed for food.

CULTIVATION: Although *Lupinus* species generally tolerate poor dry conditions, they are best grown in full sun in moderately fertile well-drained soil. Propagate from seed or cuttings. The seedlings should be planted out when small, as these plants dislike root disturbance.

Lupinus albifrons

SILVER BUSH LUPINE, SILVER LUPINE

☼ ❄ ↔5 ft (1.5 m) ↑5 ft (1.5 m)

From California, USA. Rounded evergreen shrub, with stems and leaves covered in fine, silky, silvery hairs, giving the plant an attractive gray appearance. Racemes of flowers, from blue to maroon or lavender, in spring–summer. Zones 8–11.

Lunaria annua

Lunaria rediviva

Lupinus arboreus var. *eximius*

Lupinus succulentus

Lupinus, HC, 'Pagoda Prince'

Lupinus arboreus

TREE LUPIN, YELLOW BUSH LUPINE

↔ 4–8 ft (1.2–2.4 m)
↕ 3–7 ft (0.9–2 m)

Native to central coastal California, USA, occurring mostly on seashores. Bushy evergreen shrub. Leaves grayish green, smooth above, woolly hairs beneath. Loose racemes of flowers, usually bright yellow, occasionally blue or lavender, in spring–summer. ***L. a.* var. *eximius***, hairier stems and leaves, yellow and blue flowers. Zones 8–10.

Lupinus chamissonis

↔ 4–10 ft (1.2–3 m)
↕ 2–7 ft (0.6–2 m)

From seashores of California, USA, often occurring on loose dunes. Often mound-forming shrub. Leaves gray to blue-green from dense hairs. Blue flowers, on 4 in (10 cm) long spikes, in mid-spring–mid-summer. Tolerates drought and salt spray. Zones 9–10.

Lupinus perennis

BLUEBONNETS, BLUE LUPINE, SUNDIAL LUPINE, WILD LUPINE

↔ 12 in (30 cm)
↕ 12–24 in (30–60 cm)

From eastern and central USA: Maine to Florida and west to Minnesota. Perennial with spikes of bright blue-purple flowers in late spring. Hairy seed pods propel seeds several feet (about 1 m) away; mature seeds are poisonous. Zones 4–9.

Lupinus polyphyllus

BLUE-POD LUPINE

↔ 20–40 in (50–100 cm)
↕ 24–60 in (60–150 cm)

From mountains of western North America, from British Columbia to California, growing in moist ground. Perennial with thick rootstock, chief ancestor of Russell lupins. Leaves large, basal, long-stalked, up to 17 leaflets, to 6 in (15 cm) long. Dense tapering spikes of very showy flowers, usually blue, often in shades of red, purple, or pink, in early–mid-summer. Zones 5–9.

Lupinus succulentus

ARROYO LUPINE, FOOTHILL LUPINE, HOLLOWLEAF ANNUAL LUPINE

↔ 12–36 in (30–90 cm)
↕ 18–36 in (45–90 cm)

Found in California, USA, and Baja California, Mexico; widespread in disturbed habitats. Annual blooming in late winter–late spring with bright blue-purple flowers. Fragrant and drought tolerant. Excellent in wildflower mixes. Zones 8–11.

Lupinus texensis

TEXAS BLUEBONNET

↔ 12 in (30 cm)
↕ 12–24 in (30–60 cm)

From Texas, USA; the State wildflower. Drought-tolerant annual blooming in early–late spring with dark blue and white flowers. Must be planted in well-drained soil. Zones 7–10.

Lupinus Hybrid Cultivars

↔ 2–5 ft (0.6–1.5 m)
↕ 2–4 ft (0.6–1.2 m)

Perennial lupins were first hybridized in the 1890s, but gained most popularity with the hybrids George Russell developed between 1911 and 1937. Known as the Russell lupins, these laid the foundations for later cultivars of hybrid lupins. Many of these later perennial hybrids are still informally referred to as Russell lupins, and can become invasive. **Band of Nobles Series**: rich colors of blue, purple, intense reds ('The Page'); deep pinks, creamy whites ('Noble Maiden'); and many bicolors ('The Governor', blue and white, 'The Chatelaine', soft pink and white). Other cultivars include: **'Bishop's Tipple'**, to 48 in (120 cm) tall, mauve and lilac flowers with ivory flecks; **'Blue Moon'**, to 18 in (45 cm) tall, late-blooming, tall narrow spikes of mauve-blue and white flowers; **'Candy Floss'**, to 24 in (60 cm) tall, delicate blush-pink and white flowers, becoming deep pink with age; **'Chandelier'**, 36–40 in (90–100 cm) tall, yellow flowers in early summer; **Gallery Series**, compact plants, to 20 in (50 cm) tall, bearing 10 to 12 spikes of red, blue, or pink sweet-pea-like flowers in late spring or early summer; **'My Castle'**, 30–36 in (75–90 cm) tall, bright brick-red blooms; **'Pagoda Prince'**, 36–48 in (90–120 cm) tall, early-blooming, soft lilac to purple and white bicolor flowers; **'Red Arrow'**, to 36 in (90 cm) tall, pure red flowers flecked with yellow, ageing to mulberry; **'Terracotta'**, 36–48 in (90–120 cm) tall, early-blooming, large rusty-colored bells. Zones 3–9.

Lupinus, Hybrid Cultivar, 'Bishop's Tipple'

LYCHNIS

CAMPION, CATCHFLY

Lychnis or *lukhnis* is a Greek word meaning lamp, and this genus of 20 species of biennials and perennials in the pink (Caryophyllaceae) family was given its name in the third century bc by Theophrastus, presumably because of its vivid flowerheads. It is closely allied to *Silene*, and recent studies have thrown some doubt on whether it can be validly distinguished from that genus. (If not, *Silene* is the prior name.) Found in the northern temperate zone, *Lychnis* species are quite variable, often forming large clumps of foliage, sometimes with silver-gray leaves. While their flowers are simple 5-petalled structures, they are brightly colored and showy, occurring in heads usually held well clear of the foliage, and maximizing the color effect.

CULTIVATION: They are mostly very hardy and easily grown in sun or part-shade in moist well-drained soil. The silvery *L. coronaria* prefers fairly dry conditions, but most others can be given routine watering. Deadhead frequently to encourage continuous flowering. Propagate from seed or from basal cuttings or by division, depending on the growth form.

Lychnis × *arkwrightii*

↔ 16–24 in (40–60 cm)
↕ 12–30 in (30–75 cm)

Garden hybrids between *Silene banksia* and *L. chalcedonica*. Sometimes short-lived perennials. Bristly bright to dark green foliage. Small heads of vivid flowers, held above the foliage, in summer. By far the best known is **'Vesuvius'**, to 18 in (45 cm) tall, with dark green to purplish foliage and large, striking, orange-red flowers. Zones 6–10.

Lychnis chalcedonica

syn. *Silene chalcedonica*

MALTESE CROSS

☼/◐ ✱ ↔ 12–16 in (30–40 cm) ↑ 20 in (50 cm)

Upright, bristly, Eurasian perennial. Clump of large, pointed, oval, basal leaves, smaller leaves up flower stems. Heads of up to 50 small bright red flowers in summer; Zones 4–10.

Lychnis coronaria

syn. *Silene coronaria*

DUSTY MILLER, ROSE CAMPION

☼/◐ ✱ ↔ 20–40 in (50–100 cm) ↑ 16–32 in (40–80 cm)

From southeastern Europe. Spreading mounding biennial or short-lived perennial. Stems and foliage with dense silver-gray hairs. Leaves lance-shaped, to about 3 in (8 cm) long, often smaller. Small heads of flowers, usually pink or purple-red. 'Alba', white flowers; 'Atrosanguinea', very light foliage and deep magenta flowers; 'Oculata' ★, red-centered white flowers. Zones 4–10.

Lychnis viscaria

syn. *Silene viscaria subsp. viscaria*

GERMAN CATCHFLY, VISCARIA

☼/◐ ✱ ↔ 16 in (40 cm) ↑ 24 in (60 cm)

Found from Europe to Siberia. Upright perennial, with stems and leaves bristly, and sticky leaf bases. The leaves are elliptical to lance-shaped. The flower spikes are narrow, carrying small mauve to purple-red flowers, in the summer. *L. v.* subsp. *atropurpurea*, deep purple flowers. *L. v.* 'Flore Pleno' (syn. 'Splendens Plena') has bright magenta double flowers; 'Splendens', pale to deep pink single flowers. Zones 4–10.

Lychnis × *arkwrightii* 'Vesuvius'

Lychnis coronaria 'Alba'

LYCORIS

SPIDER LILY

These cousins of the South African genus *Nerine*, often found growing at the edges of cultivated fields in Japan and China, bear a strong resemblance to nerines. A member of the amaryllis (Amaryllidaceae) family, *Lycoris* contains about 18 bulbous perennials, dormant in summer prior to flowering in late summer to early autumn. The spidery flowers have strongly reflexed petals and are showy and elegant, borne in an umbel at the top of a straight stem. The linear leaves emerge from the base of the bulb after the flowers and persist during winter; frost and rain can cause damage. Their name commemorates the beautiful Roman actress who was Mark Antony's mistress.

CULTIVATION: These plants grow best in well-drained fertile soil, in areas with dry summers. If growing in a pot, do not transplant for several years. Withhold water from late spring through to mid-summer.

Lycoris aurea

GOLDEN SPIDER LILY, HURRICANE LILY

☼ ❄ ↔ 18 in (45 cm) ↑ 18–24 in (45–60 cm)

From limestone areas of China and Japan. Leaves fleshy, gray-green. Flowers in golden shades, recurved at tips, petal margins slightly wavy, rather crowded at top of stem. Zones 7–10.

LYSIMACHIA

LOOSESTRIFE

This genus of about 150 species of perennials and subshrubs belonging to the myrsine (Myrsinaceae) family is found over much of Europe and Asia, as well as in North America and South Africa. A few species are low-spreading plants, but most are clump-forming perennials with narrow lance-shaped leaves and upright spikes of small 5-petalled flowers, often in shades of yellow, rarely white or purple-pink. The flowers appear from early summer to autumn.

CULTIVATION: Some species prefer the damp soil of pond margins or stream banks, others thrive in rockeries, but most are perfectly happy in full sun or half-sun in moist well-drained garden soil. Propagate by division or from basal cuttings or layers, depending on the growth type.

Lysimachia ciliata

◐ ✱ ↔ 20 in (50 cm) ↑ 40 in (100 cm)

From North America. Perennial with upright stems and whorls of lance-shaped leaves, to nearly 6 in (15 cm) long. The yellow flowers, solitary or paired, appear in the upper leaf axils, in summer. 'Purpurea', deep purple-red foliage. Zones 4–10.

Lysimachia clethroides

GOOSENECK LOOSESTRIFE

◐ ✱ ↔ 24 in (60 cm) ↑ 40 in (100 cm)

Native to China and Japan. Upright perennial with narrow, finely downy, lance-shaped leaves, to 5 in (12 cm) long. Produces nodding heads of small white flowers, at the stem tips, during summer. Zones 4–9.

Lysimachia congestiflora

◐ ❄ ↔ 8–16 in (20–40 cm) ↑ 6 in (15 cm)

From temperate East Asia. Perennial forming densely foliaged mound of dark green, often red-tinted, pointed oval leaves, topped with clusters of golden yellow flowers in late spring. 'Outback Sunset', yellow-green leaves with a darker central zone. Zones 7–10.

Lycoris aurea

Lysimachia punctata 'Alexander'

Lysimachia ephemerum

◐ ❄ ↔ 16–24 in (40–60 cm) ↑ 40 in (100 cm)

From southwestern Europe. Upright perennial. Opposite pairs of narrow, lance-shaped, gray-green to blue-green leaves, to 6 in (15 cm) long. Terminal spikes of small white flowers, initially curved, becoming erect. Zones 7–10.

Lysimachia nummularia

CREEPING JENNY, MONEYWORT

◐/● ✱ ↔ 24–40 in (60–100 cm) ↑ 2–4 in (5–10 cm)

European low-spreading, sometimes mounding perennial. Leaves light-textured, wavy-edged, rounded, to 1 in (25 mm) wide. Bright yellow flowers, usually solitary, sometimes paired, in leaf axils, in summer. Can become invasive. 'Aurea', bright yellow-green to golden foliage. Zones 4–10.

Lysimachia punctata

◐ ✱ ↔ 16–24 in (40–60 cm) ↑ 40 in (100 cm)

Upright Eurasian perennial. Opposite pairs and/or whorls of downy, finely pointed, lance-shaped leaves, to 3 in (8 cm) long. Terminal heads or spikes of bright yellow flowers, to over ½ in (12 mm) across, in summer. 'Alexander', striking cream-edged foliage. Zones 5–10.

Lysimachia congestiflora 'Outback Sunset'

Lysimachia nummularia 'Aurea'

M

Maackia amurensis subsp. *buergeri*

Mackaya bella

Macleaya microcarpa

MAACKIA

This genus, in the pea-flower subfamily of the legume (Fabaceae) family, contains 8 species of deciduous trees and shrubs native to East Asia. They have attractive pinnately divided leaves made up of 7 to 13 leaflets. Small flowers, usually creamy shades, are borne on short upright racemes, standing above the foliage. *Maackia* species are hardy slow-growing plants, suitable for borders and specimen planting. Showy foliage and late-summer flowering season provide color into autumn. Plants commence flowering at a very young age.
CULTIVATION: Best grown in a fertile well-drained soil in a sunny situation, but will tolerate a wide range of soil types. They transplant quite readily. Do not over-prune. Propagate from seed sown in autumn.

Maackia amurensis

AMUR MAACKIA

☼ ✱ ↔30 ft (9 m) ↑60 ft (18 m)

Shrub or tree, native to China. Well-branched habit, peeling coppery brown bark. Pinnate leaves dark green, to 8 in (20 cm) long. Flowers white with a pale blue tint, on erect crowded racemes, in late summer. ***M. a.* subsp. *buergeri*** ★, downy leaves. Zones 4–10.

MACHAERANTHERA

This genus of 26 annual, biennial, and perennial herbs from the daisy (Asteraceae) family is native to northwestern parts of the USA. Stems rise from a sturdy taproot. They bear alternate, spiny-toothed, divided leaves, with bristly tips. Flowerheads are solitary or numerous and daisy-like with ray florets of bluish violet or purple, and yellow, red, or brown disc florets, in panicles or cymes. The fruit is a cypsela with bristles. The name comes from Greek, *machaira* meaning sword and *anthera*, anthers, referring to the branching habit of its stems.
CULTIVATION: Ideal in borders and as cut flowers. These plants prefer a position in sandy or gravelly soil in full sun. Soil should be well drained but retain moisture. Propagate from seed sown in autumn or early spring.

Machaeranthera tanacetifolia

syn. ***Aster tanacetifolius***

PRAIRIE ASTER, TAHOKA DAISY, TANSYLEAF ASTER

☼ ✱ ↔8–15 in (20–38 cm) ↑12–20 in (30–50 cm)

Upright or sprawling, smooth or slightly hairy annual from western USA. Dense compact foliage, leaves deeply divided. Flowerheads with pinkish purple to bluish purple ray florets, brilliant yellow center, in late spring–early autumn. Zones 2–9.

MACKAYA

This single-species genus is a member of the acanthus (Acanthaceae) family, which also includes the well-known perennial bear's breeches, *Acanthus mollis*. Native to southern Africa, it is an evergreen shrub that grows as an understory plant in forests, often along stream banks. Leaves are very deep green with soft wavy edges and appear all year. Flowers are tubular with wide-open petals, usually mauve. They occur at the ends of branches from spring to autumn.
CULTIVATION: Grow in moist well-drained soil in full sun or partial shade in a sheltered position. Propagate from seed or from half-hardened cuttings in spring.

Mackaya bella ★

☼/◐ ❄ ↔4 ft (1.2 m) ↑8 ft (2.4 m)

South African native shrub; develops a spreading habit over time. Glossy deep green leaves, wavy edges. Tubular flowers, 5 flaring petals, pale mauve with darker veining, in loose spikes at the ends of branches, in spring–autumn. Zones 9–11.

MACLEAYA

PLUME POPPY

This genus from the poppy (Papaveraceae) family includes 2 species of hardy herbaceous perennials, sometimes sold under the name *Bocconia*. These bold, attractive plants can be invasive, forming dense thickets, and spread by means of underground suckers. They have scalloped, deeply lobed, heart-shaped, gray to olive green leaves, 6–8 in (15–20 cm) long. Tiny flowers are borne in large plume-like panicles, 12 in (30 cm) long. The genus is named after Alexander Macleay, a former secretary of the Linnaean Society of London.
CULTIVATION: Plant in autumn or early spring in a sheltered sunny position in deep loamy soil. Remove spent flowerheads and cut down stems in autumn. Soils with high fertility will encourage their invasive nature. Propagate from seed or by division of roots in autumn or early spring. Plants will self-seed.

Macleaya cordata

syn. ***Bocconia cordata***

PLUME POPPY, TREE CELANDINE

☼ ✱ ↔36 in (90 cm) ↑8 ft (2.4 m)

Plume poppy from China and Japan. Lower stem has large deeply lobed leaves, gray-green above, gray-white beneath. Feathery plumes, to 36 in (90 cm) tall, of small, pearly white or pink flowers appear in summer. Zones 3–10.

Macleaya microcarpa

syn. ***Bocconia microcarpa***

☼ ✱ ↔36 in (90 cm) ↑8 ft (2.4 m)

Plume poppy from central China. Similar to *M. cordata*. Leaves grayish green to olive with white undersides, downy. Flowers pink outside, bronze inside, in autumn. Can be very invasive. **'Coral Plume'**, pinker flowers; **'Kelway's Coral Plume'**, showy deep buff to coral flowers. Zones 3–10.

MAGNOLIA

Comprising around 100 species and countless cultivars, this genus within the magnolia (Magnoliaceae) family occurs naturally throughout Asia and North America. Both evergreen and deciduous, the flowers are primitive, and many are fragrant. They are pollinated largely by beetles. The flowers are often seen to advantage on bare limbs before the foliage appears. The fruit is often a cone-like showy cluster, pink or red with colorful seeds, these sometimes suspended on fine threads.
CULTIVATION: Although some species will tolerate lime, most do better in well-drained acid soils rich in manure and humus. Generally fast growing, their fleshy surface roots are easily damaged by cultivation. For this reason they are best left undisturbed. Wind and late frosts can also damage the large flowers. Light shade is generally ideal. Propagate by taking cuttings in summer or sowing seed in autumn. Grafting should be carried out in winter.

Magnolia acuminata

Magnolia champaca

Magnolia acuminata

CUCUMBER TREE

↔ 30 ft (9 m) ↕ 100 ft (30 m)

Deciduous tree from eastern North America, wide-spreading with age. Large oval leaves, undersides blue-green, usually hairy. Flowers metallic green to yellow-green with upright petals, in summer. Unripe fruit resemble cucumbers. ***M. a.* var. *subcordata*** (syn. *M. cordata*) often flowers again in autumn. Zones 4–9.

Magnolia ashei

syn. *Magnolia macrophylla var. ashei*

ASHE MAGNOLIA

↔ 20 ft (6 m) ↕ 30 ft (9 m)

Deciduous tree from moist woods in northwest Florida, USA. Large oval leaves, glaucous, finely hairy beneath, bunched at the ends of the shoots. Flowers white, fragrant, large cups, flushed purple inside, appearing with leaves, in spring. Zones 7–10.

Magnolia campbellii

CAMPBELL'S MAGNOLIA, PINK TULIP TREE

↔ 30 ft (9 m) ↕ 100 ft (30 m)

Tree from Himalayan forests in southwest China to eastern Nepal. Large oval leaves, bronze when young, paler reverse. Huge slightly fragrant flowers, pale to deep pink, before leaves, in late winter–early spring. Seedlings take 30 years to flower, grafted varieties 5 years, using the understock of *M.* × *soulangeana*. ***M. c.* subsp. *mollicomata*,** flowering younger, earlier in season, slightly larger flowers, more cold hardy; **'Lanarth'**, huge cyclamen-purple flowers. ***M. c.* 'Charles Raffill'**, deep rose pink buds opening to rose-purple outside, white-flushed rose-purple inside; **'Darjeeling'** dark rose-purple flowers. Zones 7–9.

Magnolia champaca

syn. *Michelia champaca*

CHAMPACA

↔ 10–20 ft (3–6 m)
↕ 60–100 ft (18–30 m)

Erect evergreen tree from eastern Himalayan foothills, smaller in cultivation. Leaves bright green, shiny above, dull beneath. Cup-shaped flowers, deep yellowish cream, heavily perfumed, in mid-summer–mid-autumn. Fruit pale yellow-green, brown spots. Zones 10–11.

Magnolia dawsoniana

↔ 25 ft (8 m) ↕ 40 ft (12 m)

Deciduous tree or shrub from mountain forests of Sinkiang Province, China. Leaves dark green, paler reverse. Lightly fragrant flowers, white inside, tinged pink outside, fading with age, before leaves, in early spring. Zones 6–9.

Magnolia denudata

JADE ORCHID, LILY TREE, YULAN

↔ 30 ft (9 m) ↕ 30 ft (9 m)

Deciduous tree or shrub revered for its beauty, native to central China. Leaves alternate, green undersides. Flowers white, fragrant, chalice-shaped, symbol of purity, emerge on bare wood before foliage appears, in summer. Flowers within 3 years. **'Forrest's Pink'**, deep pink flowers, pale interior. Zones 6–9.

Magnolia doltsopa

syn. *Michelia doltsopa*

↔ 20 ft (6 m) ↕ 30 ft (9 m)

Mostly evergreen tree, native to western China and eastern Himalayas. Pendulous dark green leaves, brown indumentum. Cup-shaped flowers, white to deep cream, greenish at base, heavy perfume, in late winter–spring. Fruit small, light green, flushed red. **'Rusty'**, thick indumentum on buds; **'Silver Cloud'** ★, profuse white flowers. Zones 9–11.

Magnolia doltsopa

Magnolia figo

syn. *Michelia figo*

BANANA SHRUB, PORT WINE MAGNOLIA

↔ 10 ft (3 m) ↕ 15 ft (4.5 m)

Medium to large shrub from southeastern China. Small, dark green, glossy leaves. Small purple-brown flowers, in spring–summer. Fragrance resembles bananas, pear drops, and vintage port. **'Coco'** (syn. 'Lady of the Night'), large, fragrant, cream flowers with just a little purple red at center. Zones 8–11.

Magnolia fraseri

EAR-LEAFED MAGNOLIA, FRASER'S MAGNOLIA

↔ 30 ft (9 m) ↕ 40 ft (12 m)

Broadly spreading, open-branched, deciduous tree from southeast USA. Young bronze foliage becomes pale green. Fragrant flowers, vase-shaped becoming saucer-shaped, creamy white, green flush to outer petals, in late spring–early summer. Zones 6–9.

Magnolia grandiflora

BULL BAY, GREAT LAUREL MAGNOLIA, SOUTHERN MAGNOLIA

↔ 35 ft (10 m) ↕ 35 ft (10 m)

Evergreen tree from central Florida to North Carolina and west to Texas, USA. Leaves stiff, leathery, deep glossy green, rusty-furry undersides. Large, creamy white, saucer-shaped flowers, fragrant, in early summer. Woody fruits. **'Baby Grand'**, 12 ft (3.5 m) tall, flowers to 5 in (12 cm) wide; **'Exmouth'**, glossy green leaves, rusty-felted beneath, huge fragrant flowers at early age; **'Ferruginea'**, erect form, dense habit, leaf undersides richly red-felted; **'Goliath'**, many huge globular flowers, in mid-summer; **'Greenback'**, no brown indumentum on leaf undersides; **'Kay Parris'**, 15 ft (4.5 m) tall, brightly colored indumentum; **'Little Gem'**, smaller leaves, slightly smaller flowers appear when young; **'Teddy Bear'**, very dense and bushy, 20 ft (6 m) tall, flowers to 8 in (20 cm) wide, continuous blooming. Zones 6–9.

Magnolia × *kewensis*

↔ 25 ft (8 m) ↕ 40 ft (12 m)

Cross between *M. kobus* and *M. salicifolia*. Deciduous large shrub or small tree; mid-green leaves, 5 in (12 cm) long. Flowers cup-shaped, fragrant, white, 5 in (12 cm) across, borne in spring before leaves. Zones 6–11.

Magnolia kobus

KOBUS MAGNOLIA

↔ 30 ft (9 m) ↕ 40 ft (12 m)

From Japan and Korea. Oval leaves dark green, smooth, paler undersides. Lightly fragrant, creamy white flowers, streaked pink at base, in early spring, before foliage. Species considered by some to be represented by forms now named *M.* × *loebneri* and *M. stellata*. ***M. k.* var. *borealis*,** more vigorous, larger leaves, sparser flowers. Zones 4–8.

Magnolia grandiflora

Magnolia laevifolia

Magnolia laevifolia

syn. ***Michelia yunnanensis***

☼/◑ ✱ ↔7–10 ft (2–3 m) ↑12–15 ft (3.5–4.5 m)

Slow-growing shrub or small tree native to China. Brownish velvety covering on young leaves and buds. Leaves variably sized and shaped. Flowers yellowish white, little scent, in late winter–spring. Suitable for containers. **'Scented Pearl'**, 10 ft (3 m) high and wide, strong scent. Zones 7–11.

Magnolia liliiflora

syn. ***Magnolia quinquepeta***

LILY-FLOWERED MAGNOLIA

☼ ✱ ↔15 ft (4.5 m) ↑10 ft (3 m)

Small deciduous tree or large shrub from central China; smaller than other species. Fully hardy. Oval dark green leaves, paler and downy on reverse. Purplish pink, waxy, goblet-shaped, lily-like flowers, to 3 in (8 cm) wide, appear with the foliage, in spring–summer. **'Nigra'**, wine-purple flowers, paler purplish inside. Zones 6–11.

Magnolia × loebneri 'Leonard Messel'

Magnolia × loebneri

LOEBNER MAGNOLIA

☼ ✱ ↔20 ft (6 m) ↑30 ft (9 m)

Variable *M. kobus* and *M. stellata* hybrid. Prolifically flowering deciduous tree or shrub, grown in wide range of soils. Leaves narrow, dark green, long oval-shaped. Flowers large, white, often pink beneath, in spring–summer. **'Leonard Messel'**, spreading tree, deep rose-lilac buds in winter, pink narrow-petalled flowers, white inside; **'Merrill'** ★, attractive white flowers. Zones 4–8.

Magnolia macrophylla

BIGLEAF MAGNOLIA, UMBRELLA TREE

◑ ✱ ↔30 ft (9 m) ↑50 ft (15 m)

Deciduous tree from moist forests of southeast USA. Large oval leaves, thin-textured, glaucous and downy reverse. Cup-shaped creamy yellow flowers, in early to mid-summer. Rounded pink fruit cluster. Zones 4–8.

Magnolia liliiflora 'Nigra', in summer

Magnolia salicifolia

Magnolia stellata 'Pink Star'

Magnolia sieboldii

Magnolia maudiae

syn. ***Michelia maudiae***

☼/◑ ✱ ↔20 ft (6 m) ↑20–35 ft (6–10 m)

Evergreen tree from China. Large, thick, glossy leaves, to 6 in (15 cm) long. Many large, fragrant, cupped, white flowers, sometimes tinged pink, in late winter–spring. Zones 7–11.

Magnolia × proctoriana

◑ ✱ ↔15 ft (4.5 m) ↑20 ft (6 m)

Hybrid between *M. salicifolia* and *M. stellata* originated in the Arnold Arboretum, Massachusetts, USA. Small tree, pyramidal habit. Small narrow leaves, pale green above. Flowers white, pink at base, fragrant, with spreading petals, in early spring. Zones 6–9.

Magnolia pyramidata

PYRAMID MAGNOLIA

☼ ❄ ↔25 ft (8 m) ↑30 ft (9 m)

Uncommon, often multi-trunked deciduous tree from the coastal plain of southeast USA. Leaves rhombic, bronze, becoming pale. Fragrant creamy flowers, in spring. Regarded by some specialists as a variety of *M. fraseri*. Zones 7–9.

Magnolia salicifolia

WILLOW-LEAFED MAGNOLIA

◑ ✱ ↔20 ft (6 m) ↑40 ft (12 m)

Shrub or deciduous tree found growing along banks of streams in mountain oak and beech forests in Japan. Narrow, willow-like, pale green leaves, glaucous beneath; lemon-anise scent from leaves, bark, and wood when bruised. Flowers white, fragrant, before the foliage, in spring. **'Wada's Memory'**, fragrant white flowers. Zones 6–9.

Magnolia sargentiana

◑ ❄ ↔25 ft (8 m) ↑60 ft (18 m)

Beautiful deciduous tree from China. Leaves deep green, glossy, undersides grayish. Flowers purplish pink to white, in spring. ***M. s.* var. *robusta*,** larger, more shrubby plant, earlier flowers. Sometimes regarded as a form of *M. dawsoniana*. Zones 7–9.

Magnolia sieboldii

OYAMA MAGNOLIA, SIEBOLD'S MAGNOLIA

◑ ✱ ↔25 ft (8 m) ↑20 ft (6 m)

Large, spreading, deciduous shrub from Japan, Korea, and southern China, smaller in cultivation. Leaves felty-white beneath. Spot-flowering, pure white, fragrant, nodding blooms, in late spring–late summer. Small pinkish fruits. ***M. s.* subsp. *sinensis*,** broadly oval leaves, felty undersides. The white, cup-shaped, pendulous flowers are strongly lemon-scented, and appear in late spring, with leaves. Large pink fruit. Zones 6–9.

Magnolia × soulangeana

SAUCER MAGNOLIA, TULIP MAGNOLIA

◑ ✱ ↔20 ft (6 m) ↑20 ft (6 m)

Deciduous low-branched tree or large shrub from a cross between *M. denudata* and *M. liliiflora*. Leaves are short, oval, dark green, and glossy. The flowers are erect, white to rose pink, with deeper color beneath, in spring–summer. Flowers appear before the foliage, even on young trees. **'Alexandrina'**, large erect flowers, white inside, flushed rosy purple outside, darker veins; **'Brozzonii'**, very large, elongated, white flowers, pink-purple veins at base; **'Burgundy'**, purple-pink flowers; **'Lennei'**, globular flowers, very concave, thick fleshy petals magenta-purple outside, creamy white inside; **'Lennei Alba'**, ivory white; **'Picture'**, deep maroon to burgundy, fading to white at tips of petals; **'Rustica Rubra'**, deep rosy pink petals outside, fading to pink-white inside on smaller globular flowers. Zones 4–9.

Magnolia sprengeri

SPRENGER'S MAGNOLIA

◑ ❄ ↔25 ft (8 m) ↑40 ft (12 m)

Deciduous spreading tree from China. Leaves dark green, oval, felty undersides when young. Huge fragrant flowers, pale to deep pink, before foliage, in spring. ***M. s.* var. *diva*,** white flowers. Zones 7–9.

Magnolia stellata

STAR MAGNOLIA

◑ ✱ ↔10 ft (3 m) ↑15 ft (4.5 m)

Deciduous rounded shrub from highlands of Honshu Island, Japan. Leaves dark green, oval. Clusters of fragrant ivory white flowers strap-like with curved, reflexed petals, in late winter before foliage. Regarded by some as a variety of *M. kobus* of garden origin. **'Chrysanthemiflora'**, double flowers, white petals, reverse flushed pink; **'Pink Star'**, pale pink almost white flowers; **'Rosea'**, petals pale pink reverse; **'Royal Star'**,

Magnolia × *soulangeana* 'Burgundy'

abundant, double, snow white flowers; **'Waterlily'** ★, larger, more abundant, pale pink petals. Zones 5–9.

Magnolia × *thompsoniana*

☀ ❄ ↔ 20 ft (6 m) ↕ 30 ft (9 m)

Large spreading deciduous shrub developed at Thompson's nursery, London, 1808. Hybrid between *M. tripetala* and *M. virginiana.* Leaves large, glossy green. Foliage is larger than *M. virginiana*, retained into early winter. Flowers large, fragrant, creamy white, in summer. Zones 6–9.

Magnolia tripetala

UMBRELLA MAGNOLIA

☀ ❄ ↔ 35 ft (10 m) ↕ 40 ft (12 m)

Broadly spreading deciduous tree from deep, moist, mountain soils in eastern USA. Foliage dark green above, gray-green and felty beneath. Fragrant, creamy, narrow-petalled flowers, in late spring–early summer. Fruit clusters purplish red. Zones 5–8.

Magnolia × *veitchii*

VEITCH'S MAGNOLIA

☀ ❄ ↔ 15 ft (4.5 m) ↕ 100 ft (30 m)

Deciduous tree of garden origin, vigorous hybrid between *M. denudata* and *M. campbellii.* Leaves bronze-purple, becoming dark green. Flowers upright, vase-shaped, fragrant, pink at base, suffusing to white, in mid-spring before the foliage. Zones 6–9.

Magnolia virginiana

SWAMP LAUREL, SWEET BAY

☀ ❄ ↔ 20 ft (6 m) ↕ 30 ft (9 m)

Adaptable tree or densely branched shrub from coastal swampy areas in USA. Evergreen or deciduous. Glossy leaves, silvery beneath. Richly lemon scented cream or white cup-shaped flowers, in late summer. Zones 6–10.

Magnolia wilsonii

WILSON'S MAGNOLIA

☀ ❄ ↔ 20 ft (6 m) ↕ 20 ft (6 m)

Spreading deciduous shrub from western China. Narrow, elliptical, dark green leaves, paler felty reverse. White flowers, fragrant, saucer-shaped, pendent, spring–early summer. Zones 6–9.

Magnolia Hybrid Cultivars

☼/☀ ❄ ↔ 10–30 ft (3–9 m) ↕ 10–60 ft (3–18 m)

These include: **'Ann'**, deep pink base fading to pale pink on tips; **'Apollo'**, rosy pink buds, rosy red flowers, in spring; **'Betty'**, petals deep rose; **'Black Tulip'**, deep reddish purple, goblet-shaped, 6 in (15 cm) wide flowers; **'Blush'**, lilac pink flowers, fragrant, evergreen; **'Charles Coates'**, scented, creamy white flowers, in spring; **'Elizabeth'**, primrose yellow, fragrant flowers, in late spring, dark green leaves; **'Felix'** ★, deep pink flowers to 12 in (30 cm) wide; **'Freeman'**, dark green, leathery, glossy leaves, fragrant white flowers, in summer; **'Galaxy'**, soft pink flowers with creamy white interior, upright, medium-sized to large, tulip-shaped, before foliage, in early spring; **'Genie'**, intense dark reddish purple; **'George Henry Kern'**, small, strappy-petalled, white to pale pink flowers with a mauve petal reverse; **'Gold Star'**, yellow flowers; **'Golden Joy'**, bright yellow flowers, late; **'Heaven Scent'**, one of the Gresham hybrids known as Svelte Brunettes, beautiful free-flowering, scented, narrow, deep pink, cup-shaped blooms, in early spring; **'Iolanthe'**, mid-pink, very large-flowered Jury hybrid; **'Jane'**, deep pink flowers with deeper vein, in early spring; **'Judy'**, small flowers, sometimes scented; **'Manchu Fan'**, velvety cream flowers; **'Mark Jury'** ★, huge pale pink and white flowers open from velvety buds; **'Mixed Up Miss'**, cream, purple-pink center, fragrant, evergreen; **'Pink Alba Superba'**, deep pink cup-shaped flowers, in spring; **'Pinkie'**, petals pink underneath, white on top; **'Randy'**, very deep pink undersides, triangular shrub or small tree; **'Ricki'**, pale pink flowers, deeper pink undersides, very erect petals; **'Rouged Alabaster'**, creamy flowers, flushed with rose pink; **'Royal Crown'**, flowers dark red to violet with white interior, outside tepals reflexed to resemble crown, in spring; **'Star Wars'**, pink flowers, pale interior, lush foliage; **'Susan'**, pale pink flowers deepening near center, faint ribbing; **'Vulcan'**, cyclamen pink flowers; **'Yellow Bird'**, cream to yellow flowers. Zones 6–9.

Magnolia, Hybrid Cultivar, 'Judy'

MAHONIA

Aptly known as holly grapes, this genus from the barberry (Berberidaceae) family of some 70 species of evergreen shrubs is found in Asia and North America, some species extending into Central America. Leaves are often very spiny and may be trifoliate or pinnate with relatively large leaflets; foliage may be carried alternately, or in whorls, with several changes of color during maturation. Sprays of small yellow flowers, often scented, between spring and early winter. Fruit is usually blue-black edible berries with a grape-like powdery bloom. Botanists have long debated whether *Mahonia* should be maintained as a genus distinct from *Berberis.* Most British and Continental botanists have recognised both genera, while there is a strong school in North America, where the characteristics distinguishing the two groups tend to break down, that prefers to place all species in a broadly defined *Berberis.* Several studies have given support to the latter classification, and while *Mahonia* is recognized here, the debate continues.

CULTIVATION: *Mahonia* species vary in hardiness. Most commonly grown species are temperate-zone plants tolerant of moderate to hard frosts while some tropical Asian species withstand only light frosts. Prefer moist well-drained, fertile soil and rich in humus. Protect from the hottest summer sun. Pruning seldom necessary. Propagate from cuttings, or rooted suckers that often develop at base of established plants.

Mahonia aquifolium

Mahonia aquifolium

OREGON HOLLY GRAPE

☀ ❄ ↔ 8 ft (2.4 m) ↕ 6 ft (1.8 m)

Suckering clump-forming shrub from western North America. Pinnate leaves composed of 5 to 13 spiny holly-like leaflets, dark green in summer, strong red tints in winter. Erect racemes of yellow to golden yellow flowers, in late winter. Purple-black fruit. **'Compacta'**, tiny, round, yellow flowers; **'Green Ripple'**, green rippled leaves. Zones 5–10.

Mahonia dictyota

syns *Berberis aquifolium var. dictyota, B. dictyota*

CALIFORNIA BARBERRY, CHALK-LEAF BERBERIS

☼ ❄ ↔ 2–4 ft (0.6–1.2 m) ↕ 6 ft (1.8 m)

Evergreen shrub from southwest USA. Leaves, 3 overlapping pairs of glossy oval leaflets, serrated, up to 4 spiny teeth on either side. Dark blue flowers, in racemes, in late spring. Zones 7–10.

Mahonia fortunei

☀ ❄ ↔ 3 ft (0.9 m) ↕ 7 ft (2 m)

Chinese shrub, notable foliage. Leaves to 10 in (25 cm) long, dark green leaflets, 4 in (10 cm) long, pale undersides. Leaflets bronze when young, toothed not spiny. Short racemes of bright yellow flowers, in autumn. Zones 7–10.

Mahonia dictyota, berries

Mahonia fortunei

Mahonia fremontii

Mahonia haematocarpa

Mahonia × media 'Arthur Menzies', berries

M

Mahonia fremontii

DESERT MAHONIA

↔7 ft (2 m) ↑12 ft (3.5 m)

Drought-tolerant shrub from southwestern USA and Mexico. Open branching habit. Leaves pale green, strongly glaucous in best forms, 3 to 7 spiny toothed leaflets. Clusters of soft yellow flowers, in summer. Deep yellow to red fruit. Zones 8–11.

Mahonia 'Golden Abundance'

↔3 ft (0.9 m) ↑6–8 ft (1.8–2.4 m)

This is often listed as a cultivar of *M. aquifolium*, but is probably a hybrid. Densely foliaged, glossy holly-like leaves. Bright golden yellow flowers in large clusters, in summer. Purple-blue berries. Zones 6–9.

Mahonia haematocarpa

syn. *Berberis haematocarpa*

↔6 ft (1.8 m) ↑12 ft (3.5 m)

Shrub from southwestern USA. Strong upright stems. Leaves blue-gray, leaflets with 4 spiny teeth each side. Clusters of 6 pale yellow flowers, in late spring. Deep red to purple-red fruit. Zones 8–10.

Mahonia japonica

↔10 ft (3 m) ↑6 ft (1.8 m)

Spreading shrub native to Japan, but cultivated in China and Taiwan. Long leathery leaves, with 19 spiny dark green leaflets. Fragrant bright yellow flowers, held in upright or arching racemes, in late winter. Small blue-black fruit. **Bealei Group**, upright shrub, native to western China, deep olive green leaflets, scented pale yellow flowers, appear in late winter. Zones 6–10.

Mahonia lomariifolia

↔8 ft (2.4 m) ↑10 ft (3 m)

Shrub from Myanmar and western China. Upright stems, whorls of spiny leaves, bronze, maturing to dark green, 20 to 40 spiny leaflets. Erect spikes of fragrant yellow flowers, autumn–spring. Purple-blue fruit. Zones 8–10.

Mahonia × media

↔12 ft (3.5 m) ↑15 ft (4.5 m)

M. japonica and *M. lomariifolia* hybrids. Vigorous upright plants, magnificent foliage, reddens in winter. Erect racemes of yellow flowers, in summer. **'Arthur Menzies'**, striking bright yellow flower spikes; **'Buckland'**, fragrant flowers, long arching racemes; **'Charity'**, tall, flowers in winter; **'Winter Sun'**, horizontal racemes, in autumn. Zones 7–10.

Mahonia nervosa

LONGLEAF MAHONIA

↔36 in (90 cm) ↑36 in (90 cm)

Suckering shrub from northwestern North America. Leaves to 24 in (60 cm) long, 11 to 23 leathery, gray-green leaflets, yellowish undersides, serrated edges. Crowded 8 in (20 cm) racemes of yellow flowers, in late winter. Blue-black fruit. Zones 6–9.

Mahonia nevinii ★

↔6 ft (1.8 m) ↑8 ft (2.4 m)

Shrub from California, USA. Grayish blue-green leaves, 3 to 7 narrow pointed leaflets, 6 spine-tipped teeth on each side, almost white undersides. Small, rather open racemes of light yellow flowers, in spring. Tiny dark red berries. Zones 8–10.

Mahonia pinnata

CALIFORNIAN HOLLY GRAPE

↔6 ft (1.8 m) ↑8 ft (2.4 m)

From California, USA. Shrub closely resembling *M. aquifolium*. Matt mid-green leaves, 5 to 9 leaflets, 13 spines on each side. Foliage reddens in winter, purplish undersides. Clusters of soft yellow flowers, in late winter. Blue-black berries. ***M. p.* subsp. *insularis***, balls of bright yellow flowers near stems. Zones 7–10.

Mahonia pumila

↔36 in (90 cm) ↑20 in (50 cm)

Suckering shrub, native to western USA. Leaves with 5 to 7 spiny leaflets, to 6 in (15 cm) long, light purplish red on new growth, maturing to gray-green. Flowers yellow, hint of blue tone, in small racemes, in spring. Zones 7–10.

Mahonia repens

CREEPING MAHONIA

↔36 in (90 cm) ↑18 in (45 cm)

Suckering shrub from northwest North America. Blue-green leaves, reddening in winter, to 10 in (25 cm) long, 5 leaflets, very spiny. Flowers deep yellow, fragrant, in 3 in (8 cm) racemes, in spring. Blue-black fruit. **'Denver Strain'**, dark green leaves. Zones 6–9.

MAIANTHEMUM

syn. *Smilacina*

FALSE SOLOMON'S SEAL

This genus consists of about 35 species of herbaceous perennials in the asparagus (Asparagaceae) family, the majority from eastern Asia and North America but with a few in the highlands of Central America and one extending across northern Asia and into Europe. They have creeping underground rhizomes and erect or arching, unbranched stems, each bearing 2 to 15 ovate leaves, usually in 2 rows. Plants will grow into clumps or, in some species, into substantial colonies. Small white flowers are borne in spring and summer in terminal panicles or spikes, followed by small red berries. *Maianthemum* is similar in growth habit and foliage to *Polygonatum* (Solomon's seal), except that it has flowers arising from leaf axils. CULTIVATION: All species grow best in moist humus-rich soils in full sun or partial shade under deciduous shrubs and trees. Plants should not be allowed to dry out when in leaf. Propagate by division while dormant, or by sowing seed as soon as ripe.

Maianthemum bifolium

FALSE LILY-OF-THE-VALLEY, MAY LILY

↔40–48 in (100–120 cm)
↑5–6 in (12–15 cm)

This spreading perennial is found from western Europe to Japan. It has upright unbranched stems bearing two heart-shaped leaves to 3 in (8 cm) long. A narrow spike of tiny flowers appears in spring. The taller ***M. b.* subsp. *kamtschaticum*** (syn. *M. dilatatum*), has stems to 14 in (35 cm) high, and leaves to 8 in (20 cm) long. Zones 3–10.

Maianthemum canadense

syn. *Unifolium canadense*

TWO-LEAFED SOLOMON'S SEAL

↔36–40 in (90–100 cm)
↑7–8 in (18–20 cm)

Woodland plant, native to Canada and northern parts of the USA. Leaves oval, 1 to 3 per stem, to 4 in (10 cm) long. Tiny, fragrant, white flowers, on spikes 2 in (5 cm) long, in spring. Zones 1–7.

Maianthemum racemosum

syn. *Smilacina racemosa*

FALSE SOLOMON'S SEAL, FALSE SPIKENARD

↔2–4 ft (0.6–1.2 m)
↑2–3 ft (0.6–0.9 m)

Occurs right across the USA and in parts of northern Mexico. Arching cane-like stems, each with up to 12 pointed oval leaves to 6 in (15 cm) long. Panicles to 6 in (15 cm) long of tiny creamy white flowers, in summer. Red-tinted green berries. Zones 4–10.

MALUS

APPLE, CRABAPPLE

This well-known genus is found in temperate regions right around the Northern Hemisphere. The apples and crabapples comprise a large genus of around 30 species of ornamental and fruiting, small to medium-sized, deciduous trees belonging to the rose (Rosaceae) family. Nearly all have soft green leaves. The fruits are pomes; not all crabapples are edible, some being too bitter for the human palate. The cultivated apple is one of the most widely grown of all edible fruits, and the many species and cultivars of crabapple are valued as floriferous ornamental trees.

CULTIVATION: *Malus* will grow in all cool-temperate regions. Apples and crabapples flower in spring and most cultivated varieties of apple require a cross-pollinator in order to produce fruit. While cultivated apples require careful winter pruning, crabapples, being largely ornamental, need less attention. Propagate by grafting onto a range of apple rootstocks, some of which have the effect of producing a dwarfed plant.

Malus × *adstringens*

☼ ✱ ↔20–40 ft (6–12 m) ↕25–40 ft (8–12 m)

This large spreading tree is a hybrid between *M. baccata* and *M. pumila*. Leaves softly downy beneath. Flowers pinkish, on short stalks. Fruits red, yellow, or green. Susceptible to most apple diseases, often disfigured by scab, rusts, and leaf blights. **'Hopa'** has flowers in varying shades of pink; **'Patricia'** has deep pink flowers with yellow stamens; **'Pink Beauty'** has petals that are almost white with deep pink undersides; **'Radiant'** has deep pink flowers blotched with white; **'Transcendent'** has deep pinkish red buds that open to reveal white flowers. Zones 4–9.

Malus × *arnoldiana*

☼ ✱ ↔15 ft (4.5 m) ↕8 ft (2.4 m)

Garden hybrid between *M. baccata* and *M. floribunda*, both Asian. Large shrub, arching stems, serrated leaves. Clusters of 4 to 6 white flowers, deep pink to red buds, in summer. Small yellow-green fruits. Zones 4–9.

Maianthemum racemosum

Malus × *atrosanguinea*

Malus × *hartwigii* 'Katherine'

Malus × *atrosanguinea*

☼ ✱ ↔20 ft (6 m) ↕20 ft (6 m)

A garden-raised hybrid between *M. halliana* and *M. sieboldii*, this is a spreading shrub or small tree. Waxy-textured serrated leaves, 2 in (5 cm) long. Small purple-red flowers, in summer. Red or red-streaked yellow fruits, less than ½ in (12 mm) wide. Zones 4–9.

Malus baccata

SIBERIAN CRABAPPLE

☼ ✱ ↔40 ft (12 m) ↕40 ft (12 m)

Rounded erect crabapple tree from Siberia. Buds pinkish, opening to single, white, fragrant flowers. Fruits red, sometimes yellow, on long thin stems. Resistant to most apple diseases, vital to modern hybridization programs. ***M. b.* var. *mandshurica***, from Japan and northeastern China, lightly serrated leaves, undersides initially downy, single white flowers, brilliant red fruit; **'Midwest'**, very early in both leaf and flower, larger creamy white flowers. ***M. b.* 'Jackii'**, spreading habit, stouter branches; **'Spring Snow'**, drooping white flowers. Zones 2–9.

Malus coronaria

AMERICAN CRABAPPLE, AMERICAN SWEET CRABAPPLE

☼ ✱ ↔30 ft (9 m) ↕30 ft (9 m)

Large wide-limbed crabapple tree from eastern USA. Buds dark pink, single flowers, fragrant, pale pink to pink-white, salmon pink. Green fruit unpalatable. Susceptible to scab and rust diseases. ***M. c.* var. *angustifolia***, to 30 ft (9 m) high, short trunk, spreading branches, highly fragrant rose-colored flowers, susceptible to disease. ***M. c.* var. *dasycalyx***, Great Lakes crabapple, leaves paler beneath, woolly calyx; **'Charlottae'**, apricot to deep pink buds, light pink semi-double to double flowers. Zones 4–9.

Malus floribunda

JAPANESE FLOWERING CRABAPPLE

☼ ✱ ↔20 ft (6 m) ↕12 ft (3.5 m)

Beautiful crabapple from Japan. Leaves green, serrated, tapered. Buds dark pink to red, opening to single light pink or nearly white flowers, in late spring. Fruits yellow and red, ½ in (12 mm) in diameter. May be affected by powdery mildew. Long cultivated. Zones 4–9.

Malus × *gloriosa*

Malus × *gloriosa*

☼ ✱ ↔8–10 ft (2–3 m) ↕10 ft (3 m)

Hybrid shrub of *M. pumila* 'Niedzwetzkyana' and *M.* × *scheideckeri*. Heavily toothed leaves, red-tinted when young. Purple-red flowers, 1½ in (35 mm) wide. Yellow fruit, ½ in (12 mm) wide, in spring. **'Oekonomierat Echtermeyer'**, pendulous bronze foliage, bright pink-red flowers, red-brown fruit. Zones 4–9.

Malus halliana

☼ ✱ ↔10 ft (3 m) ↕15 ft (4.5 m)

Small tree with loose open habit, from China. Oblong leaves, dark green, often purple-tinted. Red stalks. Flowers bright rose, nodding, in late spring. Fruits purplish, ripening late. Disease resistant. ***M. h.* var. *spontanea***, shorter, smaller whitish flowers, greenish yellow fruits. ***M. h.* 'Parkmanii'**, bronze-green glossy leaves, rosy buds in clusters on long red stalks, flowers double or semi-double, flesh-pink; fruit red to red-purple. Zones 4–9.

Malus × *hartwigii*

☼ ✱ ↔6 ft (1.8 m) ↕12 ft (3.5 m)

A hybrid of garden-raised *M. baccata* × *M. halliana*. This shrub or small tree has dark brown upright stems. The smooth-edged, pointed, oval leaves are 3 in (8 cm) long. Flowers are semi-double, deep pink fading to white, 1½ in (35 mm) across, and appear in spring. They are followed by tiny red-brown fruits. **'Katherine'**, large double flowers open from pinkish white buds, yellowish fruit flushed with red. Zones 4–9.

Malus hupehensis

HUPEH CRABAPPLE, TEA CRABAPPLE

☼ ✱ ↔25 ft (8 m) ↕15 ft (4.5 m)

Open spreading crabapple tree from China and India. Straight upright limbs. Leaves deep green, violet hue when young. Buds pink, opening to single, white, fragrant flowers, in spring. Fruits green-yellow, slight red cheek. Disease resistant. Zones 4–10.

Malus ioensis

IOWA CRABAPPLE, PRAIRIE CRABAPPLE

☼ ❄ ↔20 ft (6 m) ↕20 ft (6 m)

Beautiful crabapple native to midwest USA. Leaves dark green, deeply serrated, yellowish green undersides. Flowers white tinged with pink, fragrant, in spring. Fruits shiny green. Highly susceptible to disease, several more resistant clones have been produced. **'Plena'**, fully double pink flowers; **'Prairifire'** ★, dark pink buds and flowers. Zones 2–9.

Malus kansuensis

☼ ❄ ↔12 ft (3.5 m) ↕15 ft (4.5 m)

Often shrubby, sometimes tree-like species found in northwestern China. Red-brown young shoots, serrated-edged leaves with 3 to 5 lobes. Clusters of 4 to 10 white flowers, ½ in (12 mm) wide, in spring. Tiny yellow to purple-red, rough-surfaced apples. Zones 5–9.

Malus × *micromalus*

☼ ❄ ↔15 ft (4.5 m) ↕15 ft (4.5 m)

This small Japanese tree is a natural hybrid between *M. baccata* and *M. spectabilis*. It has dark brown stems, and waxy serrated leaves that taper to a fine point. Pink blooms, in clusters of 3 to 5 flowers, in spring. Yellow, somewhat pointed fruits, ½ in (12 mm) wide. Zones 4–9.

Malus prunifolia

PEAR-LEAFED CRABAPPLE

☼ ❄ ↔25 ft (8 m) ↕25 ft (8 m)

Several forms occur in northeastern Asia; they vary in fruit size, shape, and color. This small tree has pinkish buds, and single white flowers, in spring, followed by yellow or red fruit. **'Fastigiata'** has profuse white flowers, in late spring. All highly susceptible to disease. Zones 3–9.

Malus × *purpurea*

☼ ❄ ↔25 ft (8 m) ↕20 ft (6 m)

A very early flowering crabapple, this is a hybrid of *M.* × *atrosanguinea* and *M. pumila* 'Niedzwetzkyana'. It has deep green leaves, and dark flowers that fade to pale mauve, in late spring. **'Aldenhamensis'** blooms up to 3 times per season, leaves red-green to bronze-green, buds bright carmine, single and semi-double pinkish red flowers; **'Eleyi'**, deep red-purple foliage, purple to red flowers, subject to leaf diseases; **'Lemoinei'**, a popular red-flowered crabapple. Zones 4–9.

Malus × *robusta*

☼ ❄ ↔12 ft (3.5 m) ↕20 ft (6 m)

Conical-crowned large shrub or small tree, an *M. baccata* × *M. prunifolia* hybrid. Bright green leaves, 4 in (10 cm) long, scalloped edges. Flowers white to pink, in clusters of 3 to 8, in spring. Long-stemmed yellow to red fruits. **'Erecta'**, large white flowers with pink edges. Zones 3–9.

Malus sargentii

SARGENT'S CRABAPPLE

☼ ❄ ↔15 ft (4.5 m) ↕6 ft (1.8 m)

This is a very small, densely branched crabapple. The leaves are broadly oval, sharp-tipped, heavy, bright green, and lobed, with serrated edges. The flowers are white, single, fragrant, and appear in spring. Tiny fruit, crimson to purple, follow the flowers. Disease resistant, blooms in alternate years. **'Rosea'**, deep red-pink buds, white flowers, dark red fruit. Zones 4–9.

Malus × *scheideckeri*

☼ ❄ ↔8 ft (2.4 m) ↕15 ft (4.5 m)

This slow-growing, small, upright tree is a hybrid of *M. floribunda* and *M. prunifolia*. It has coarsely serrated leaves. The flowers are faded rose pink, usually semi-double, in thick clusters on the branches, in late spring. The fruit is slightly ribbed, yellow-orange. Tolerates pruning. **'Exzellenz Thiel'**, pale pink to white flowers; **'Red Jade'**, drooping red fruit. Zones 4–9.

Malus sieboldii

☼ ❄ ↔10 ft (3 m) ↕15 ft (4.5 m)

This slow-growing, small- to medium-size, rounded tree comes from Japan. Lobed or simple leaves. Buds red to carmine, opening to single white flowers, in spring. The fruits are very small, red. Disease resistant. ***M. s.* var. *arborescens***, larger leaves, white flowers, reddish fruit. Zones 4–9.

Malus spectabilis

CHINESE FLOWERING CRABAPPLE

☼ ❄ ↔20 ft (6 m) ↕25 ft (8 m)

Old, spectacular, flowering crabapple, originally from China, but now unknown in the wild. The buds are deep rose red, blush-colored flowers, attractive semi-double to double form or single form, in spring. Fruits yellowish. **'Riversii'**, largest double pink crabapple flowers. Zones 4–9.

Malus sylvestris

COMMON CRAB APPLE, WILD CRAB APPLE

☼ ❄ ↔10 ft (3 m) ↕30 ft (9 m)

From Europe. Small tree with dense rounded crown, dark bark. Some branches are thorny. Flowers are white or pink, followed by sour yellow-green or reddish fruits. Zones 3–9.

Malus tschonoskii

☼ ❄ ↔20 ft (6 m) ↕40 ft (12 m)

This is one of the larger crabapples, and comes from Japan. Sturdy upright habit. Excellent autumn color; green leaves turn purple, orange, bronze, yellow, and crimson. The flowers are white with pink hue, in spring. Fruit insignificant. Susceptible to most apple diseases. Zones 6–10.

Malus × *zumi*

☼ ❄ ↔10 ft (3 m) ↕15 ft (4.5 m)

This small downy-stemmed tree has a pyramidal habit. It is a natural Japanese hybrid of *M. baccata* var. *mandshurica* and *M. sieboldii*. The leaves taper to a fine point, and have scalloped to lobed edges. Pink buds, in spring, then white flowers, 1¼ in (30in mm) wide. Small red fruits. ***M.* × *zumi* var. *calocarpa***, spreading habit, smaller flowers, leaves smooth-edged on fruiting spurs, lobed elsewhere. Zones 5–9.

Malus Hybrid Cultivars

☼ ❄ ↔5–25 ft (1.5–8 m) ↕10–40 ft (3–12 m)

Numerous crabapple cultivars have been raised, many in the USA. Most are grown for floral display, some for decorative fruit, and larger fruit of some can be eaten fresh or as preserves. The parent with the most influence is *M. pumila* 'Niedzwetzkyana', originating from a single tree with red flowers and purple-red new foliage, discovered in central Asia before 1900. Some of the best are: **'Adams'**, to 20 ft (6 m) high, reddish pink flowers, red fruit; **'Adirondack'**, to 12 ft (3.5 m) high, narrow upright tree, buds dark

Malus × *robusta* 'Erecta'

Malus × *purpurea*

Malus sargentii

Malus × *scheideckeri*

Malus, Hybrid Cultivar, 'Adams'

M

carmine, wide-spreading white flowers with traces of pink, fruit red to orange–red; **'Almey'**, deep reddish pink flowers, small fruit; **'Beverly'**, 20 ft (6 m) high, white single flowers, red fruit; **'Brandywine'**, to 20 ft (6 m) high, dome-shaped tree, buds deep rose, double fragrant flowers of rose pink, yellow-green fruit; **'Butterball'**, 25 ft (8 m) high, pinkish white flowers, orange-yellow fruit; **'Centurion'**, very upright, deep pink flowers, purple-red young leaves, small purplish fruit; **'Chilko'**, single purple-pink flowers, vivid red to crimson fruit; **'Christmas Holly'** ★, 15 ft (4.5 m) high, small rounded spreading tree, buds bright red, single white flowers, fruit small, holly-like, bright red, in clusters; **'Cinderella'**, 10 ft (3 m) tall, white flowers, golden fruit; **'Coralburst'**, compact, pink and white, double flowers, orange to red fruit; **'Dolgo'**, white flowers, early-ripening purple-red fruit; **'Fiesta'**, to 15 ft (4.5 m) high, weeping habit, buds carmine, single white flowers in cascades, fruit burnt coral to orange-gold; **'Golden Hornet'**, small, upright, pendulous tree, single white flowers, fruit lime-yellow; **'Gorgeous'**, compact dome-shaped tree, pink buds, single white flowers, fruit crimson to orange-red; **'Hamlet'**, 10 ft (3 m) tall, pink flowers from red buds, red fruit; **'Harvest Gold'**, upright tree, single white flowers, golden fruit, disease resistant; **'John Downie'**, pink buds, single white flowers, fruit large, orange with red cheeks, disease resistant; **'Lancelot'**, 10 ft (3 m) tall, white flowers from pink buds, golden fruit and autumn foliage; **'Madonna'**, 20 ft (6 m) high, compact upright tree, white buds, large, double, fragrant, white flowers, small brown-red fruit; **'Mary Potter'**, 20 ft (6 m) high, dark foliage, bright pink flowers, dark buds, deep red to purple-red fruit; **'Naragansett'**, 12 ft (3.5 m) high, broad crown, buds carmine, single white flowers, pink hue, shiny cherry red fruit, in clusters, disease resistant; **'Pink Perfection'**, sterile cultivar, pink and white double flowers; **'Profusion'**, to 20 ft (6 m) high, upright, wide, spreading tree, leaves purplish to bronze, buds deep red to purple-pink, deep rose pink single flowers, fruit maroon to blood red; **'Red Sentinel'**, early white flowers, red fruit; **'Royal Raindrops'**, deep pink flowers, lobed, purple-red, maple-like foliage, red fruit; **'Royalty'**, 15 ft (4.5 m) high, reddish foliage, purple-red flowers and fruit; **'Sugar Tyme'**, white flowers from pink buds, red fruit, vigorous; **'Tom Matthews'**, purple-red flowers and young foliage, dark leaves, purple-red fruit; **'White Angel'** (syn. 'Inglis'), white flowers, pink buds, small red fruit; **'White Cascade'**, to 15 ft (4.5 m) high, graceful weeping habit, single white flowers, green-yellow fruit, disease resistant; **'Winter Gold'**, to 20 ft (6 m) high, vase-shaped tree, carmine buds, single white flowers, fruit bright lemon yellow. Zones 4–9.

MALVA

MALLOW, MUSK MALLOW

Like the hollyhock, to which it is related, *Malva* is a member of the mallow (Malvaceae) family. These easily cultivated plants are native to Europe, North Africa, and Asia. This genus contains at least 30 species of annuals, biennials, and short-lived herbaceous perennials similar to hollyhocks, but bushier and with smaller leaves. Flowers 5-petalled, single, in shades of white, pink, blue, or purple.

CULTIVATION: Grow in herbaceous or annual borders. They do best in a sunny position but will tolerate partial shade in well-drained soil. Remove spent flowers to encourage a second flowering; cut down to the ground in autumn. Propagate from cuttings or seed in spring. Plants will self-seed.

Malva alcea

↔ 24 in (60 cm) ↑ 40 in (100 cm)

Southern European herbaceous perennial, naturalized in the USA. Deeply lobed light green leaves with toothed edges. Mauve-pink flowers, in mid-summer to mid-autumn. Zone 3–10.

Malvaviscus penduliflorus

Malva moschata

MUSK MALLOW

↔ 18 in (45 cm) ↑ 40 in (100 cm)

European perennial. Narrow, finely cut, mid-green leaves; musky smell when brushed or crushed. Abundant, saucer-shaped, rose-pink flowers, in summer. **'Alba'**, white, bushy branching habit; **'Rosea'**, pink flowers. Zone 3–10.

Malva sylvestris

CHEESES, COMMON MALLOW, HIGH MALLOW

↔ 7–25 ft (2–8 m) ↑ 3 ft (0.9 m)

Biennial or perennial from Europe. Leaves green, alternate, to 4 in (10 cm) long. Flowers rose-purple with dark veins, in early summer to early autumn. **'Primley Blue'**, bluish purple flowers, dark blue veins. Zones 3–9.

MALVAVISCUS

This genus consists of 3 species of Central and South American evergreen shrubs from the mallow (Malvaceae) family. Their broad downy leaves are often lobed. They have unusually shaped flowers, borne singly in the leaf axils or in small clusters at the ends of branches. They are bright orange-red and usually held upright. The long petals stay partly furled, never really opening fully, and from their center emerges a long hibiscus-like column. Small red berries follow the flowers.

CULTIVATION: Although able to withstand the very lightest frosts, these shrubs are best grown in warm subtropical to tropical areas. They thrive in moist, humus-rich, well-drained soil and can be grown in sun or part-shade. Their branches have a tendency to die back and are often attacked by boring grubs, so some pruning, thinning, and trimming is necessary. Propagate from seed or from half-hardened cuttings.

Malva moschata 'Alba'

Malvaviscus arboreus

TURK'S CAP, WAX MALLOW

↔ 10 ft (3 m) ↑ 12–15 ft (3.5–4.5 m)

Shrub from southern Texas and Florida, USA, to Peru and Brazil. Velvety ovate to heart-shaped leaves, may be 3-lobed. Long-stemmed rich red flowers, face upward or slightly bend, in summer. ***M. a.* var. *drummondii***, brilliant reddish orange hibiscus-like flowers, swirled petals never fully open, in late summer–autumn. Zones 8–12.

Malvaviscus penduliflorus

syn. *Malvaviscus arboreus* var. *penduliflorus*

CARDINAL'S HAT, SLEEPING HIBISCUS

↔ 10 ft (3 m) ↑ 12–15 ft (3.5–4.5 m)

Mexican shrub, very similar to more widely grown *M. arboreus*. Less hairy leaves. Larger, pendulous rather than upright, red flowers, in late summer. Zones 11–12.

Malva sylvestris 'Primley Blue'

Mandevilla × *amabilis* 'Alice du Pont'

Mandevilla boliviensis

Mandevilla laxa

Mandevilla sanderi, 'Scarlet Pimpernel'

MANDEVILLA

Central and South American genus in the dogbane (Apocynaceae) family; contains some 120 species of mainly tuberous perennials, subshrubs, and twining vines. Leaves are large, deep green, elliptical to lance-shaped with prominent elongated tips. Trumpet flowers, carried singly or in racemes, often large and sometimes fragrant, throughout the warmer months. They come in white to cream and various shades of pink. More commonly cultivated are the beautiful vigorous vines.
CULTIVATION: Only a few species will tolerate any frost and all prefer a mild to warm climate, dappled sunlight, and moist, humus-rich, well-drained soil. Trim if necessary. All parts exude an irritant milky latex when cut. Feeding produces lush foliage but also rampant growth. Propagate from half-hardened stems in summer, or cuttings.

Mandevilla × *amabilis*

↔15 ft (4.5 m) ↑15 ft (4.5 m)

Vigorous climber, uncertain origins (probably *M. splendens* hybrid). Deeply veined, leathery leaves, 4–8 in (10–20 cm) long. Yellow-throated, dark-centered, pink flowers, in spring. **'Alice du Pont'**, back-cross of *M.* × *amabilis* with *M. splendens* (syn. *M.* × *amoena)*, lush foliage, large deep pink flowers. Zones 11–12.

Mandevilla boliviensis

WHITE DIPLADENIA

↔10 ft (3 m) ↑15 ft (4.5 m)

Twining climber from Bolivia and Ecuador. Broad, glossy, elliptical leaves, tapering to fine point, to 4 in (10 cm) long. White flowers, to 2 in (5 cm) long, with golden centers; up to 7 blooms per raceme, appear in summer. Zones 11–12.

Mandevilla laxa

CHILEAN JASMINE

↔17 ft (5 m) ↑15 ft (4.5 m)

Vigorous semi-evergreen to deciduous climber, native to Argentina. Elliptical leaves taper to fine point, dark green to bronze, downy, sometimes purplish undersides, to 3 in (8 cm) long. White flowers, 2 in (5 cm) wide, strongly scented, especially evenings, in late spring–summer. Zones 9–11.

Mandevilla sanderi

↔17 ft (5 m) ↑17 ft (5 m)

Strong-growing Brazilian climber. Glossy, smooth-surfaced, leathery leaves, 3 in (8 cm) long. Deep pink yellow-throated flowers, to 2 in (5 cm) wide, up to 5 blooms per raceme, in spring. **'My Fair Lady'**, shrubby, 5 ft (1.5 m) high and wide, white flowers; **'Red Riding Hood'**, 10 ft (3 m) high and wide, deep pink; **'Scarlet Pimpernel'**, very deep pink to red flowers. Zones 11–12.

Mandevilla Hybrid Cultivars

↔3–8 ft (0.9–2.4m)
↑4–10 ft (1.2–3 m)

Hybrids bred mainly for heavy flowering and compact growth, suitable for containers, conservatories, and patios, includes: **Aloha Series**, cultivar in pink-red shades from very pale to blackish red; **Fantasy Series**, pink to red shades, also white; **Sun Parasol Series**, cultivars named by flower size, pretty (small), classic (standard), and giant (large), such as **'Giant Crimson'**, red flowers to 4 in (10 cm) wide. Zones 10–12.

MANDRAGORA

MANDRAKE

A genus of 6 species of stemless, rosette-forming, herbaceous perennials in the nightshade (Solanaceae) family. Flowers are held in clusters surrounded by the leaves, followed by fleshy rounded berries. Native to dry areas of the Mediterranean and the Himalayas, they have long been thought to hold magical powers; the deep tap root, which often resembles the torso of a man, is believed to stimulate sexual desire. Many thought that uprooting a mandrake would caused madness as it would scream, so a dog was employed to remove it. The root was tied to the dog's tail.
CULTIVATION: Best suited to a well-drained but moisture-retentive soil in a sunny site. Propagate from fresh seed, or from root cuttings in winter. Dislikes being transplanted.

Mandragora officinarum

DEVIL'S APPLES, LOVE APPLES, MANDRAKE

↔8–10 in (20–25 cm)
↑5–6 in (12–15 cm)

Herbaceous perennial. Rosettes of heavily wrinkled, deep green, lance-shaped leaves, to 12 in (30 cm) long. Clusters of upward-facing greenish white flowers, stained purple, in spring. Poisonous yellow berries. Zones 5–10.

MANFREDA

An asparagus (Asparagaceae) genus of around 30 species of rhizomatous perennials closely allied to *Agave* and the tuberoses *(Polianthes)*. Found from southern USA to Central America, they form a rosette of long, narrow, fleshy leaves, often purple-mottled or marked, sometimes large. A tall flower spike emerges from the rosette, with 6-petalled greenish cream to pink or red flowers that have long, protruding stamens. The flowers often change color over time.
CULTIVATION: Drought-tolerant once established, most thrive in a sunny position with well-drained soil and steady moisture through the growing season. Hardiness varies with the species, but few will tolerate repeated hard frosts. Propagate from seed or offsets.

Manfreda longiflora

syn. *Polianthes runyonii*

↔16–24 in (40–60 cm)
↑10–24 in (25–60 cm)

From Texas, USA, and Mexico. Open rosette with narrow, purple-spotted, succulent leaves often held near flat to ground. Flowers on drooping overarching stem, open near white in evening then age to red by following morning, in autumn. Zones 9–10.

Marrubium vulgare

Manfreda maculosa

SPICE LILY, TEXAS TUBEROSE

↔24–36 in (60–90 cm)
16–27 in (40–70 cm)

Native to southern Texas, USA, and northern Mexico. Forms clumps of fleshy-leafed, purple-spotted, slightly blue-green leaves. Silvery blue flower stem with greenish cream flowers ageing to pink, in summer. Zones 9–10.

MARRUBIUM

HOREHOUND

This is a genus of some 40 species of woolly gray-leafed perennials from Asia, the Mediterranean region, and North Africa. They are members of the mint (Lamiaceae) family, and as such usually feature rounded leaves that have quite a strong smell. They have square stems and 2-lipped pink to mauve flowers. Some species have been used medicinally. They can become invasive.
CULTIVATION: These sun-loving perennials are drought-tolerant and enjoy a dry summer climate. Prune hard each winter to clean up the plant and encourage bushiness. Propagate by division or from spring-sown seed, which is inclined to germinate in an erratic fashion.

Marrubium incanum

syn. *Marrubium candidissimum*

↔24 in (60 cm) ↑20 in (50 cm)

Perennial from Italy and the Balkans. Densely woolly white shoots; gray-green, scalloped, rounded leaves. Dense clusters of pale mauve to nearly white flowers, in summer. Zones 6–10.

Marrubium vulgare

COMMON HOREHOUND, WHITE HOREHOUND

↔ 20 in (50 cm) ↕ 20 in (50 cm)

Native to southern Europe, northern Africa, the Canary Islands, and Asia. Leaves rounded, woolly, gray. Small, 2-lipped flowers, in summer. Poor as a garden plant, weedy outside native areas. Marginally ornamental variegated form exists. Zones 3–10.

MATRICARIA

This genus of 5 species of usually annual herbs belongs to the daisy (Asteraceae) family. Found throughout temperate areas of Europe and Asia, they have upright, branching, leafy stems with alternate, finely divided, light to bright green leaves. The foliage is often aromatic. The freely borne flowers may be single or in clusters and are either yellow and button-like or white daisies with yellow centers. *M. recutita* is used in herbal medicine for a wide range of ailments, including digestive disorders and fevers, and as a calmative. Its aroma and medicinal qualities are similar to that of chamomile but it is more bitter and generally thought to be of inferior quality.

CULTIVATION: These herbs are easily grown in a sunny position in well-drained soil. Propagate from seed, *in situ,* in late summer.

Matricaria recutita

syn. *Matricaria chamomilla*

GERMAN CHAMOMILE, SWEET FALSE CHAMOMILE, WILD CHAMOMILE

↔ 6–20 in (15–50 cm) ↕ 6–20 in (15–50 cm)

A bushy annual, native to Europe and western Asia. It has fine, pinnately divided, aromatic foliage, and small daisy-like flowers, with white ray petals that flex downward, in summer–autumn. Zones 4–10.

Matteuccia struthiopteris

Matthiola incana, Cinderella Series, 'Cinderella White'

Matthiola incana, Vintage Series, 'Vintage Lavender'

MATTEUCCIA

A member of the cliff-fern (Woodsiaceae) family, this genus contains 3 species of hardy deciduous ferns and is native to North America, Europe, and Asia. Fronds are tall, pinnate, with alternate leaflets in soft green. These elegant plants have an arching habit and are most at home in a waterside setting. They are easy to cultivate but have invasive underground stems.

CULTIVATION: Plant from autumn to spring in a slightly shaded, constantly moist spot, in lime-free soil that contains leaf mold. For best results, plant at least 48 in (120 cm) apart. Propagate by dividing the rhizomatous roots in autumn or winter.

Matteuccia struthiopteris

OSTRICH FERN, SHUTTLECOCK FERN

↔ 18–30 in (45–75 cm) ↕ 36–60 in (90–150 cm)

Fern from North America, East Asia, and Europe. Clumps of arching, leathery, pale green fronds. Dark brown spore-bearing fronds in center of clump, develop in summer–late winter and persist up to a year. Zones 3–10.

MATTHIOLA

GILLYFLOWER, STOCK

The genus, a member of the cabbage (Brassicaceae) family, contains 55 mainly temperate Eurasian species of annuals, perennials, and subshrubs. They usually have simple leaves, often gray-green and sometimes toothed. Their flowers, which are 4-petalled and often evening-scented, are borne on upright, often branching stems. There are many garden strains in a wide range of flower forms and colors. Famed for their scent, stocks were once grown for medicinal purposes and a comment attributed to Italian botanist Pierandrea Mattioli, after whom the genus is named, that he grew stock only for "matters of love and lust," suggests the medicine had much to do with the scent.

CULTIVATION: Plant in full sun with moist well-drained soil. A light dressing of lime is beneficial. Taller types need shelter from strong wind or can be supported by staking. Propagate mostly from seed, which can be sown in succession for continuous spring and summer flowering.

Matthiola incana

BROMPTON STOCK

↔ 12 in (30 cm) ↕ 32 in (80 cm)

Woody-based biennial from southern and western Europe. Leaves elliptical, gray-green, downy, 2 in (5 cm) long. Upright spikes, scented purple, pink, or white flowers, in summer. Long seed pods. **'Annua'** (ten weeks stock), matures and flowers in one season; **Cinderella Series**, single-stemmed, most colors; **Katz Series**, double flowers, short spikes, all colors, early; **Lady Series**, biennial, branching, dense spikes, most colors, many double flowers; **Vintage Series**, 6–8 in (15–20 cm), branching, most colors, many doubles. Zones 8–11.

Matthiola longipetala

NIGHT-SCENTED STOCK

↔ 10 in (25 cm) ↕ 20 in (50 cm)

Summer-flowering annual found from Greece and Middle East to Crimean region. Narrow leaves, to 3 in (8 cm) long, toothed or pinnately lobed. Creamy yellow or pink flowers, 1 in (25 mm) across, evening fragrance, in summer. Horned seed pods. ***M. l.* subsp. *bicornis*,** usually double flowers. Zones 8–11.

MAYTENUS

This genus of the spindle-tree (Celastraceae) family, with more than 200 species, occurs in southern Europe, Africa, tropical and eastern Asia, Central and South America, and Australia. Trees, shrubs, or scrambling shrubs, all are evergreen, some with rhizomes. Leaves are simple, smooth-edged or toothed. The small, usually whitish flowers can be bisexual; there may be separate males and females on the same plant or on different plants. The leathery or woody fruits are 2- to 5-celled capsules; in a few species they are fleshy, the seeds partly or wholly surrounded by a fleshy aril. Extracts from some species have been locally used for medicinal purposes.

CULTIVATION: Frost hardiness varies. All species should be grown in a sunny position in well-drained soil. Propagate from seed or cuttings. Since the seeds have only a short viability, they must be sown while as fresh as possible.

Maytenus boaria ★

MAITEN, MAYTEN

↔ 30 ft (9 m) ↕ 70 ft (21 m)

Tree or large shrub from forests in Chile, Argentina, Bolivia, Paraguay, and southern Brazil. Branches upright or pendent, glossy dark green leaves with finely toothed edges. Small, greenish, separate male and female flowers, in spring. Fruits 3- to 5-celled, orange-red, aril red. Zones 8–11.

Maytenus boaria

MAZUS

These 30 species of ground-covering and mat-forming perennials from the lopseed (Phrymaceae) family are found in Asia, Australia, and New Zealand. Foliage color varies from mid- to bright greens through to brown and bronze shades. The prostrate stems hug the ground and new roots form as the plant creeps along. Often found in damp sheltered areas, they creep through and over rocks. The narrow tubular flowers sit up on the mats of foliage in spring and summer. Flowers vary in color from purples and blues through to pale lavender, white, and yellow. Depending on the species, flowers may have a splash of lilac-mauve in the throat, or be marked with white and yellow.
CULTIVATION: These plants prefer full sun, good drainage, and open porous soils. Propagate from half-hardened stem cuttings in summer and autumn.

Mazus radicans

syn. *Mimulus radicans*

↔ 12 in (30 cm) ↑ 2 in (5 cm)

A New Zealand perennial species. Round bronze-brown leaves, 1¼–2 in (3–5 cm) long, with very tight, nearly impenetrable, foliage mats. Flowers, in spring–summer are white, lilac streaked, and 1½–2 in (3.5–5 cm) across. Zones 7–9.

Mazus reptans

↔ 20 in (50 cm) ↑ 2 in (5 cm)

The mid-green, almost glossy leaves of this Himalayan species cover its stems. The flowers are purple-blue, ¾ in (18 mm) wide, with a dark center fleck, appearing in spring–summer. Zones 7–9.

Mazus reptans

M

MECONOPSIS

Mainly native to the Himalayan region, with one notable exception. This genus of more than 40 species from the poppy (Papaveraceae) family, includes annuals, biennials, and perennials, some of which die after flowering. The genus is known for its blue-flowered species, but the other more traditional poppies of yellow, pink, or red are often more easily grown. They form compact mounds of coarsely hairy lower leaves that may be round, pinnately lobed, or deeply toothed. The flowers, carried singly on short stems or in heads on taller stems, open in spring or summer.
CULTIVATION: Most species grow best in woodland conditions in a cool-temperate climate with reliable rainfall. Plant in a sheltered part-shaded position with moist, deep, humus-rich, well-drained soil. Water well in spring and early summer. Propagate from seed.

Meconopsis betonicifolia

BLUE POPPY

↔ 8–20 in (20–50 cm)
↑ 3–6 ft (0.9 m–1.8 m)

Perennial, often short-lived, from Himalayan China. Stems and foliage bristly, golden brown hairs. Oblong, often shallowly serrated leaves, to 12 in (30 cm) long. Open heads of up to 6 bright blue flowers, to 2 in (5 cm) long, in late spring–early summer. ***M. b.* var. *alba***, white flowers. Zones 7–9.

Meconopsis betonicifolia

Meconopsis cambrica var. *aurantiaca*

Meconopsis cambrica

WELSH POPPY

↔ 8–16 in (20–40 cm)
↑ 12–24 in (30–60 cm)

Perennial, native to western Europe. Small clumps of ferny mid-green leaves, to 8 in (20 cm) long. Flowers are solitary, on hairy stems, bright yellow, to 2 in (5 cm) wide, in late spring–summer. Often self-sows freely. ***M. c.* var. *aurantiaca***, orange flowers. Zones 6–10.

Meconopsis grandis

↔ 16–24 in (40–60 cm)
↑ 4 ft (1.2 m)

Himalayan perennial. Foliage and stems have rusty brown hairs. Lower leaves to 12 in (30 cm) long, elliptical, serrated to coarsely toothed. Long-stemmed flowers, in groups of 3 or more, deep blue to purple-blue, in late spring–early summer. Zones 5–9.

Meconopsis horridula

↔ 16 in (40 cm) ↑ 32 in (80 cm)

Often short-lived Himalayan perennial. Very bristly foliage and stems. Leaves elliptical, gray-green, to 10 in (25 cm) long. Long-stemmed flowers in upper leaf axils, solitary or paired, blue to light purple or white, in summer. Zones 6–9.

Meconopsis napaulensis

SATIN POPPY

↔ 20–32 in (50–80 cm)
↑ 6–8 ft (1.8–2.4 m)

The true *Meconopsis napaulensis* is a quite different plant, now known as *M. paniculata*. The plants cultivated under the name *M. napaulensis* are vigorous, strongly upright perennials. Stems and foliage are covered with fine, downy, golden brown hairs. Leaves deeply pinnately lobed, almost to midrib. Red or purple flowers, rarely blue or white, on drooping heads, in spring–summer. Zones 8–10.

Meconopsis napaulensis

Meconopsis punicea

↔ 20–27 in (50–70 cm)
↑ 24–30 in (60–75 cm)

Perennial from Chinese Himalayas. Broad lance-shaped leaves, to more than 14 in (35 cm) long. Bristly flower stems with solitary bright flowers, to nearly 4 in (10 cm) long, in spring–summer. Zones 7–10.

Meconopsis × *sheldonii*

↔ 16–24 in (40–60 cm)
↑ 4 ft (1.2 m)

A garden hybrid between *M. betonicifolia* and *M. grandis*, this plant provides good color and ease of cultivation. Bristly oblong leaves, 6–10 in (15–25 cm) long. The flower stems are leafy, with 1¼ in (30 mm) wide blue flowers in the upper axils, in spring–summer. Zones 6–9.

MEDINILLA

This genus of more than 150 species of evergreen shrubs and climbers, some epiphytic, is from the melastoma (Melastomataceae) family and is native to the rainforests of Africa, Southeast Asia, and the Pacific. They are grown for their ornamental value as their large leaves, conspicuous colorful bracts, and white, rose, and shell pink flowers in panicles or cymes make them showy specimens. Grown over a frame or pergola, the climbing varieties are also very attractive.
CULTIVATION: In humid tropical areas, these plants will grow under shade in fertile well-drained soil. In cooler climates, grow in a greenhouse in containers with added grit and leafmold in good loam soil. If grown under glass, protect from direct sun in summer. Water and feed well during growing season and mist several times daily. Water carefully in winter or cooler months to prevent wilting. Propagate from half-hardened cuttings rooted in a growing medium with added sharp sand.

Medinilla magnifica

Medinilla magnifica

PINK LANTERN, SHOWY MEDINILLA

↔3 ft (0.9 m) ↑3–6 ft (0.9–1.8 m)

Robust epiphytic species, native to the Philippines. Ribbed or winged stems. Large leathery leaves, dark green, pronounced pale veins. Long-lasting flowers, pink to red, in pendulous panicles and basal bracts, in spring–summer. Zones 11–12.

MEGASKEPASMA

The sole species in this genus from the acanthus (Acanthaceae) family is an evergreen shrub from Venezuela. It is a lushly foliaged plant with flowers that are striking in both color and shape. These appear through most of the year. This plant is a must for any warm-climate garden; it is also useful as a plant for large conservatories and greenhouses.

CULTIVATION: This shrub needs warmth, moisture, and humidity to do well. Given the right climate, a humus-rich soil and regular feeding, it is the very epitome of a luxuriant tropical plant. Because its stems are soft and pliable it can be espaliered against a sheltered wall in cooler zones. Propagate from seed or half-hardened cuttings.

Megaskepasma erythrochlamys

BRAZILIAN RED CLOAK

↔4 ft (1.2 m) ↑10 ft (3 m)

Evergreen shrub from Venezuela. Heavily veined, semi-glossy, mid-green leaves. Individual flowers, white or pale pink, on upright, 12 in (30 cm) tall red spikes, almost enclosed by red bracts; showy flowerheads held above foliage. Zones 10–12.

Megaskepasma erythrochlamys

MELAMPODIUM

The 37 annual or perennial herbs and subshrubs in this genus from the daisy (Asteraceae) family are native to the warmer parts of North America and Mexico. They have narrow to oval toothed or simple leaves, and carry heads of daisy-like flowers with white to yellow ray florets and yellow disc florets.

CULTIVATION: These plants are suited to a sunny position in moist well-drained soil. During winter reduce the amount of water given. Can be propagated from seed.

Melampodium divaricatum

syn. *Melampodium paludosum*

BUTTER DAISY, GOLD MEDALLION FLOWER

↔5 ft (1.5 m) ↑5 ft (1.5 m)

Annual herb, from Mexico. Light green oblong leaves on purplish green stems. Solitary, yellow, daisy-like flowers, darker centers, in late spring–early autumn. May self-seed in suitable conditions. **'Showstar'**, golden yellow daisy-like flowers. Zones 10–12.

Melampodium leucanthum

BLACKFOOT DAISY

↔24 in (60 cm) ↑24 in (60 cm)

Short-lived, mound-forming, perennial shrub found from Mexico to Colorado, USA. Leaves smooth or divided into 6 lobes. Honey-scented flowerheads, white to cream ray florets, in spring–autumn. Zones 4–11.

Melampodium divaricatum 'Showstar'

Melinis repens

MELIANTHUS

This genus of 6 species of often leggy shrubs native to South Africa is a member of the honey-flower (Melianthaceae) family. *M. major* is naturalized in India. Tiny flowers borne in erect racemes produce a large quantity of nectar. Vigorous growers, they are often treated like perennials, being cut back severely to shoot again and inhibit their straggling tendencies.

CULTIVATION: Not frost hardy, they grow well in full sun or part-shade in free-draining but moisture-retentive soil. Propagate from seed in spring, softwood cuttings in spring and summer, or rooted suckers in spring.

Melianthus major

HONEY FLOWER

↔3 ft (0.9 m) ↑6–10 ft (1.8–3 m)

Shrub, native to hilly grasslands of South Africa. Large, decorative, pinnate leaves, 20 in (50 cm) long, 17 oval leaflets, toothed, gray-green. Racemes of brick red tubular flowers, in spring–mid-summer. Used in folk medicine. Can be invasive. Zones 8–11.

MELINIS

There are 12 species of annual and perennial grasses in this genus, which belongs to the family Poaceae. The majority of species are native to tropical and southern Africa and Madagascar. One species is found in tropical South America and the West Indies. They grow in open grassland, savannah woodland, and disturbed ground. The shoots are aromatic and the leaf blades narrow, sometimes with fine hairs. The flowers are in spikelets borne in open panicles.

Melianthus major

CULTIVATION: These tropical grasses can be invasive. Easily grown in any soil in sun or light shade in warm and tropical climates. Propagate annuals from seed, and perennials from seed or division of clumps.

Melinis repens

syn. *Rhynchelytrum repens*

BLANKETGRASS, NATAL REDTOP

↔2 ft (0.6 m) ↑3–4 ft (9–1.2 m)

Native to South Africa. Naturalized in the Pacific Islands. Perennial grass with bluish green leaves. Flowering panicles, to 6 in (15 cm) long, purplish at first becoming silvery pink with silky hairs, in summer. Zones 9–12.

MELISSA

BALM

This hardy genus, which belongs to the mint (Lamiaceae) family, contains 3 species of perennial herbs that are native to Europe and central Asia. When the small heart-shaped leaves are crushed, a lemony scent is released. The flower spikes, which appear in summer, bear white or yellow flowers but these are relatively insignificant. The leaves can be infused to make a herbal tea or can be chopped and used in salads and soups. The name *Melissa* comes from a Greek word meaning bee, as these plants are rich in nectar and are very attractive to bees.

CULTIVATION: Grow at the front of borders, along path edges, in herb gardens or containers. Plant in full sun or half-sun in moist but well-drained soil. They may die in soils that are wet in winter. Plants may self-seed. Propagate from seed or cuttings, or by division of roots in spring.

Melissa officinalis

BEE BALM, LEMON BALM

↔18 in (45 cm) ↑24–36 in (60–90 cm)

Herb from Europe. Green, oval, tooth-edged leaves in opposite pairs. Insignificant white tubular flowers, in summer–early autumn. **'Aurea'**, green leaves, gold splotches. Zones 5–9.

Melissa officinalis

MENISPERMUM

MOONSEED

This genus contains 2 species of woody twining vines belonging to the moonseed (Menispermaceae) family and is native to northeastern America and East Asia. These plants are generally grown for their foliage. The leaves are rounded and smooth, similar to a maple leaf. The flowers are small and yellow, appearing in summer. Black fruit, similar to grapes, are produced in autumn. They are highly toxic if ingested. The dried rhizome is used in medicines.

CULTIVATION: Grow these vines in a moderately fertile soil in full or partial sun. Water well in summer. Propagate from seed or cuttings of mature wood.

Menispermum canadense

COMMON MOONSEED, YELLOW PARILLA

☼/◐ ❄ ↔7 ft (2 m) ↑10–15 ft (3–4.5 m)

Vine found in North America from Quebec and Manitoba to Georgia and Arkansas. Dark green foliage, large alternate leaves, 4–10 in (10–25 cm) long. Flowers greenish yellow, followed by black fruit, in summer. Half-moon shaped seeds. Zones 4–8.

M

MENTHA

A genus of 25 species of fragrant and aromatic herbs in the mint (Lamiaceae) family. From Europe, Africa, and Asia, they naturalize in damp moist areas and marginal wetlands. Shallow-rooted plants, they spread easily. They have an upright branching habit and form dense bushy plants from a few inches to 5 ft (1.5 m) high. Stems can travel long distances underground. The flowers sit on the ends of the stems in clusters or in spikes and vary from ¼ in (6 mm) to 4 in (10 cm). Foliage is aromatic. Many are used in teas and food, and for medicinal purposes; some are grown commercially for their essential oils. Species can be evergreen or

Mentha × piperita f. *citrata*

deciduous, depending on conditions and varietal differences.

CULTIVATION: Mints grow in any open, fertile, moist soil, in part-shade or full sun. Propagate by dividing the rhizomes throughout the year; roots will appear in a few weeks. Seed can be sown in spring.

Mentha aquatica

WATER MINT

☼ ❄ ↔3–7 ft (0.9–2 m) ↑3 ft (0.9 m)

Marginal water herb from temperate Eurasia. Strongly scented foliage, serrated dark green leaves on purple upright stems. Small purple flowers, in summer. Zones 7–9.

Mentha spicata 'Crispa'

Mentha suaveolens

Mentha × gracilis

☼ ❄ ↔36 in (90 cm) ↑12 in (30 cm)

Low-growing, ground-hugging plant from temperate Eurasia. Crinkly, dark green, rounded leaves. Tubular lilac flowers, in summer–autumn. Minty, slightly ginger taste. **'Variegata'** (variegated ginger mint), leaves with yellow streaks. Zones 7–9.

Mentha × piperita

PEPPERMINT

☼ ❄ ↔36 in (90 cm) ↑24–36 in (60–90 cm)

Quick-growing upright herb from Europe. Purplish stems. Long, lance-shaped, dark green leaves, serrated edge, intense minty flavor and aroma. Mauve-pink flowers, in summer. Sterile seeds. ***M. × p. f. citrata*** (bergamot mint), rounded toothed leaves are tinged purple, may turn bronze, lilac flowers, strong citrus aroma and flavor, use in fruit salads, can be invasive, best grown in pots; **'Chocolate'** ★ (chocolate mint), leaves with dark brown tonings, delicate chocolate fragrance and taste, used in teas. ***M. × p. 'Variegata'*** (variegated peppermint), leaves with creamy yellow markings. Zones 3–7.

Mentha pulegium

PENNYROYAL

☼/◐ ❄ ↔20 in (50 cm) ↑8–12 in (20–30 cm)

Carpeting, spreading aromatic herb from southwest and central Europe, and the Mediterranean to Iran. Small, dark green, sometimes gray, leaves, flat on stems. Balls of tubular lilac flowers, on top of foliage, in summer–autumn. Oils deter houseflies. Zones 7–9.

Mentha requienii

syn. *Mentha corsica*

CORSICAN MINT

☼/◐ ❄ ↔27 in (70 cm) ↑¾ in (1.8 cm)

Carpeting herb from France and Italy. Tight mats of tiny leaves spread on creeping stems. Dark green foliage, pales in hot sun, very aromatic when rubbed. Tiny heads of lavender-colored flowers, in summer. Zones 7–10.

Mentha spicata

SPEARMINT

☼ ❄ ↔3–6 ft (0.9–1.8 m) ↑4 ft (1.2 m)

Herb from Europe. Mid-green, narrow, pointed leaves, serrated edge. Creeping rhizomes; flowers pale mauve, pink, or white, in summer. **'Crispa'** (curly spearmint), lance-shaped dark green leaves, may be red edge, survives freezing, tall-growing, pale mauve-pink flowers. Zones 3–7.

Menyanthes trifoliata

Mentha suaveolens

syn. *Mentha rotundifolia*

APPLE MINT, WOOLLY MINT

☼ ❄ ↔36 in (90 cm) ↑36 in (90 cm)

Herb from southwestern Europe. Round pale green leaves, fine hairs. Apple-like aroma. Flowers white to pink, in summer. **'Variegata'** (syn. *M. rotundifolia* var. *variegata*) (pineapple mint), leaves gray-green, creamy white streaks, fruity sweet fragrance. Zones 6–9.

Mentha × villosa

BOWLES MINT

☼ ❄ ↔5 ft (1.5 m) ↑3 ft (0.9 m)

Spreading mound-forming mint. There are delicate hairs on the round bright green leaves. Large spikes of pink tubular flowers, in summer. Zones 5–8.

MENYANTHES

This genus of perennial aquatic or marginal herbs is native to Europe and Asia and gives its name to the Menyanthaceae family, of which it is the sole member. Grown for its foliage and fragrant flowers, it has smooth, dark green, compound leaves with elliptic to oval leaflets, with slightly serrated edges. These are carried on sheathed stalks arising from a thick, rooting, creeping then rising rhizome. It carries erect racemes of 10 to 20 short-lived flowers. These are heavily fringed and bearded, 5-petalled, white, flushed with pink.

CULTIVATION: This plant prefers an open, sunny position in shallow water. Keep tidy by removing fading flower-heads and foliage. Propagate from seed or by division of overcrowded clumps in spring.

Mespilus germanica

Menyanthes trifoliata

BOG BEAN, BUCK BEAN, MARSH TREFOIL

↔ 8–12 in (20–30 cm) ↑ 10–16 in (25–40 cm)

From Europe. Smooth, dark green, compound leaves; elliptic to oval leaflets, slightly serrated edges, on sheathed stalks. Erect racemes of short-lived, fringed, white flowers, flushed pink, in summer. Zones 3–9.

MERTENSIA

This genus, found in western Europe, Asia, and North America, is a member of the borage (Boraginaceae) family. It contains about 40 species of hardy herbaceous perennials, although only 4 or 5 are cultivated. Their leaves are usually lance-shaped and hairy. Most species are relatively small and produce terminal panicles of usually blue tubular or bell-shaped flowers in spring. Some species are used in wild or rock gardens.

CULTIVATION: Plant in full sun or half-sun in early spring. These plants prefer moist, well-drained soil, rich in humus. Propagate from seed or by division after flowering.

Mertensia sibirica

SIBERIAN BLUEBELLS

↔ 12 in (30 cm) ↑ 12–18 in (30–45 cm)

Perennial from East Asia, northern China, and Siberia. Light green leaves on long stems. Deep blue-purple funnel-shaped flowers, in spring–early summer. Zones 3–7.

Mertensia simplicissima

syn. *Mertensia asiatica*

OYSTER PLANT

↔ 18 in (45 cm) ↑ 6 in (15 cm)

Perennial from Japan and Korea. Long trailing stems of fleshy silver-gray leaves. Sky blue flowers, in spring–early autumn. Needs well-drained soil. Zones 5–9.

Mertensia virginica

syn. *Mertensia pulmonaroides*

BLUEBELLS, COWSLIP, ROANOKE BELLS, VIRGINIA BLUEBELLS

↔ 12–24 in (30–60 cm) ↑ 12–24 in (30–60 cm)

Perennial from North America. Oval gray-green leaves, 8 in (20 cm) long. Blue-purple flowers, in nodding clusters, in spring. Foliage dies after blooming, so plant among other perennials. Zones 3–9.

MESPILUS

This genus within the rose (Rosaceae) family has just one species, a deciduous tree that grows in mountain woodland and scrubland throughout southeast Europe and southwest Asia. It is a good ornamental shrub or tree with large single flowers that are usually white, sometimes with a pink flush, and good autumn foliage. It is now grown less for its fruit, which is only edible after frost, when it is described as "bletted" (slightly rotted); the high malic acid content is reduced and the sugar increased in this way. Long known in cultivation, it may have been cultivated by the Assyrians and Babylonians, and brought to Great Britain by the Romans.

CULTIVATION: Grows well in any good moisture-retentive soil with shelter from strong winds. Propagate from seed in autumn, or by bud-grafting in late summer. Can also be grafted onto hawthorn to form graft hybrids.

Mespilus germanica

MEDLAR

↔ 25 ft (8 m) ↑ 20 ft (6 m)

A large shrub or small tree from Europe. Thorny branchlets in the wild, but cultivated forms are usually thornless. Leaves alternate, oblong to lance-shaped, toothed, dull green above, felty underneath, red and yellow, in autumn. Profuse apple-blossom-like flowers, in spring. Round, fleshy, brown fruit, too astringent to eat until bletted. '**Breda Giant**', apple-cinnamon flavored fruit; '**Dutch**', good ornamental tree; '**Large Russian**', large pink tinged flowers, spreading crown, large leaves and fruit; '**Nottingham**', good-flavored fruit (an acquired taste); '**Royal**', medium-sized fruit; '**Stoneless**', seedless cultivar, very small fruit. Zones 4–9.

METASEQUOIA

A genus of a single species of conifer in the cypress (Cupressaceae) family, this plant was long thought to be extinct, known only from fossil remains found in China. In 1941 a Chinese botanist visited a village between Hubei and Sichuan and noticed a deciduous conifer known locally as *shuiskan*. It was found the tree was identical to the fossil remains. Seed was collected in 1947 and sent to the Arnold Arboretum in the USA, from where it was distributed to botanic gardens throughout the world. Finally named and described in 1948, it has become a popular ornamental tree both in and outside China. The bark is reddish brown, darkening with age. The leaves are green and flattened and turn reddish brown in autumn.

CULTIVATION: *Metasequoia* species grow rapidly, particularly in a moist but well-drained soil, and have proved hardy and relatively resistant to atmospheric pollution. It is highly regarded as an ornamental for large gardens and parks in cool temperate areas. Propagate from seed.

Metasequoia glyptostroboides ★

DAWN REDWOOD

↔ 20 ft (6 m) ↑ 70 ft (21 m)

Vigorous, quick-growing, deciduous conifer from China. Cinnamon-brown bark. Flattened, linear, larch green leaves, on short branchlets, turn tawny pink and old gold, in autumn. Dark brown cones, pendulous, on long stalks. Larger in the wild. Zones 5–10.

METROSIDEROS

This genus is a member of the large myrtle (Myrtaceae) family, which includes *Eucalyptus* and *Psidium* (guava), and is found in South Africa, the Pacific Islands, Australia, and New Zealand. *Metrosideros* contains 50 species of evergreen shrubs, trees, and woody climbers with simple, often leathery leaves that can be aromatic. Flowers are comprised of numerous stamens and resemble rounded bottle-brushes, usually in shades of red, pink, or white.

CULTIVATION: *Metrosideros* species are best suited to warmer climates, but will grow in any reasonably fertile well-drained soil. *M. excelsa*, in particular, will grow in dry soils of lower fertility and in very exposed coastal conditions. It can be pruned for hedging and used as shelter. In cool climates, plants can be grown in pots, overwintered in a greenhouse and placed outdoors for summer. Propagate from seed sown in spring, or half-hardened cuttings taken in summer.

Metasequoia glyptostroboides

Metrosideros excelsus

Metrosideros excelsus ★

NEW ZEALAND CHRISTMAS TREE, POHUTUKAWA

↔25 ft (8 m) ↑50 ft (15 m)

Shrubby coastal tree from New Zealand. Thick, leathery, oval leaves, dark green above, gray and felted beneath. Red-crimson bottlebrush-like flowers, in early summer. Young trees susceptible to frost. **'Fire Mountain'**, orangey scarlet flowers. Zones 9–11.

Metrosideros kermadecensis

KERMADEC POHUTUKAWA

↔15 ft (4.5 m) ↑20 ft (6 m)

Native to Kermadec Islands, New Zealand. Similar to *M. excelsus*, but with smaller leaves and flowers. It flowers spasmodically year-round. **'Variegatus'**, leaves variegated grayish green, with a wide creamy yellow margin. Zones 9–11.

MICROBIOTA

RUSSIAN CYPRESS, SIBERIAN CARPET CYPRESS

This conifer genus in the cypress (Cupressaceae) family contains just one species. It is common in the mountains of southeastern Siberia above the timber line. It is a small shrub to about 24 in (60 cm) tall, spreading to 5 ft (1.5 m) across, with the male and female cones borne on separate plants.

CULTIVATION: This shrub is quite adaptable to cultivation in milder climates in moist soil. Propagate from seed or cuttings of half-hardened shoots taken in summer.

Microbiota decussata ★

RUSSIAN CYPRESS

↔5 ft (1.5 m) ↑2 ft (0.6 m)

Small shrub from Siberia. Flattened short branches covered in tiny, scale-like, almost triangular, overlapping leaves. Male and female cones at ends of short branches, in summer. Female cones egg-shaped. Foliage can turn bronze in cold winters. Zones 3–9.

MICROLEPIA

The 45 to 50 species of this genus of deciduous, semi-evergreen, or evergreen, rock-dwelling or terrestrial ferns in the bracken (Dennstaedtiaceae) family are found in the tropics and subtropics worldwide. They have creeping underground rhizomes covered with bristles, and dense roots, with the fronds spaced along the rhizome. The fronds are erect or arching, borne on short stalks, with blades divided, thinly textured and slightly hairy, and notched or lobed segments.

CULTIVATION: These ferns are suited to hanging baskets and containers, preferring shade or semi-shade in moist soil. Keep tidy by removing faded fronds. Propagate by division in spring or by spores in summer.

Microbiota decussata

Microlepia speluncae

↔6 ft (1.8 m) ↑3–6 ft (0.9–1.8 m)

Terrestrial tropical fern from southern China. Branching, spreading rhizome. Very large triangular, papery, pinnate fronds, triangular to sword-shaped leaflets, serrated, notched or lobed, sword-shaped to triangular segments, on rough stalks, all year. Zones 11–12.

Microlepia strigosa

↔24 in (60 cm) ↑36 in (90 cm)

Evergreen fern from tropical Asia. Creeping rhizome. Broad, irregularly lance-shaped, pinnate fronds, up to 32 in (80 cm) long, with leaflets up to 8 in (20 cm) long, notched segments, on rough hairy stalks. Zones 11–12.

Microlepia strigosa

MICROSORUM

syns *Microsorium, Phymatosorus*

This genus of 40 to 50 mostly epiphytic ferns from tropical and subtropical Africa, Asia, Australasia, and Polynesia belongs in the polypody (Polypodiaceae) family. Their surface-creeping or climbing rhizomes may be smooth or covered in scales and roots. Fronds arising from the rhizomes are stalked, simple or divided. The genus name is from the Greek *mikros*, "small," and *soros*, "mound," referring to scattered spore bodies of most species.

CULTIVATION: *Microsorum* species refer full sun to half-shade in moist, well-drained soil or fibrous mix. Propagate by division of rhizomes or from spores, from spring.

Microsorum punctatum

syns *Microsorium punctatum, Polypodium polycarpon*

CLIMBING BIRD'S NEST FERN

↔5 ft (1.5 m) ↑40 in 100 cm)

Epiphytic fern of tropical Africa, Asia, Australasia, and Polynesia. Dense ground-covering habit. Woody to fleshy, creeping, scaly, brownish rhizome. Long, simple, smooth, fleshy yet tough, pale to olive green, sword-shaped fronds, in summer. Dot-like spore bodies. Zones 11–12.

MIMETES

One of the many members of the South African protea (Proteaceae) family, this genus is composed of 11 or 12 species of evergreen shrubs, some of which are very endangered. The genus name is from the Greek *mimetes*, which means a mimic, and refers to these plants' resemblance to other species. Usually bearing simple leaves covered with silky hairs, the foliage near the stem tips becomes brightly colored and conceals small tufted flowers in the leaf axils. The plants carry colored bracts most of the year, though they are usually at their most prolific in spring.

CULTIVATION: Like most plants from the protea family, *Mimetes* species grow best in light well-drained soil with an airy position in full sun. They tolerate occasional light frosts but resent prolonged wet and cold conditions, and can suffer from root rots and foliar fungal diseases. They can be trimmed to shape as necessary. Cutting the flowerheads will ensure that they keep their color well. Propagate from seed, as soon as it is ripe, or from half-hardened cuttings in the late summer or autumn.

Microsorum punctatum

Mimetes cucullatus ★

ROOISTOMPIE

↔5 ft (1.5 m) ↕5 ft (1.5 m)

Shrub native to Western Cape, South Africa. The leaves, to 3 in (8 cm) long, are yellow-green. White flowers appear among the leaves, in summer, causing the leaves to redden. The plant maintains its color over a long season, and is popular with the cut-flower trade. Zones 8–11.

MIMULUS

MONKEY FLOWER, MUSK

While it is best known for its annuals and perennials, this mostly American genus belonging to the lopseed (Phrymaceae) family has some 180 species and includes a few shrubs. These are vigorous upright plants with stems covered in fine hairs and sticky glands, which may also be present on the leaves. The flowers form in the leaf axils and are short tubes with widely flared throats. The annuals and perennials often have flowers with vividly contrasting color patterns, but this is less common among the shrubs.
CULTIVATION: In suitably mild climates, the shrubby *Mimulus* are easy to grow, provided they are given full sun and a well-drained soil that remains moist through summer. They are quick growing, inclined to become untidy unless routinely pinched back. They tend to be short lived. Propagate from seed or half-hardened cuttings.

Mimulus aurantiacus

BUSH MONKEY FLOWER

↔3 ft (0.9 m) ↕4 ft (1.2 m)

Upright shrub found in western USA from southern Oregon to California. Narrow, bright to dark green leaves have serrated edges. Stems and foliage have a sticky coating. Flowers are funnel-shaped, yellow, gold, and orange, in spring–summer. Zones 8–10.

Mimulus bifidus

↔12–40 in (30–100 cm)
↕12–40 in (30–100 cm)

Much-branched, sticky, hairy shrub, native to California, USA. Finely toothed spear-shaped leaves. Yellow flowers, bell-shaped corolla, up to 2½ in (6 cm) wide, in spring–summer. Zones 7–9.

Mimetes cucullatus, in the wild, Western Cape, South Africa

Mimulus cardinalis

SCARLET MONKEY FLOWER

↔24–27 in (60–70 cm)
↕32–36 in (80–90 cm)

Vigorous clumping perennial from southern North America. Roots down when a stem touches ground. Stems are sticky. Leaves to 5 in (12 cm) long. Scarlet tubular flowers, in leaf axils, in summer. Zones 6–10.

Mimulus ringens

ALLEGHENY MONKEY FLOWER

↔4–5 ft (1.2–1.5 m)
↕3–4 ft (0.9–1.2 m)

Perennial herb from North America and Europe. Smooth, 4-cornered, narrowly winged stems. Narrow green leaves. Violet-blue tubular flowers, occasionally white or pink, thin throat, on erect stalks, in summer. Zones 3–9.

Mimulus bifidus

Mimulus Hybrid Cultivars

↔12–32 in (30–80 cm)
↕8–36 in (20–90 cm)

Mimulus hybrids are strong and vigorous with a wide range of striking colors to choose from. Popular cultivars include: **'Highland Park'**, varying shades from apricot to tomato red; **'Highland Pink'**, strong red velvet colors with paler undersides; **'Malibu Red'**, larger blooms in rich red; **'Puck'**, clear yellow; and **'Roter Kaiser'**, larger trumpet-shaped blooms in rich red. Zones 3–9.

MIRABILIS

A genus of about 50 species of annuals and tuberous-rooted perennials in the four-o-clock (Nyctaginaceae) family, native to southern North America, Central America, and South America. The leaves are in opposite pairs and are simple and smooth-edged, modified into small bracts below the flower clusters. The flowers are short lived and fragrant, and come in a wide range of bright colors.
CULTIVATION: Grow these plants in a sunny moist aspect in rich soil. In frost-prone areas, lift the tubers of perennials and store as you would dahlias. Propagate annual species from seed sown where it is to grow, or by division of tuberous perennial species.

Mirabilis jalapa

FOUR O'CLOCK FLOWER, MARVEL OF PERU, VIERUURTJIE

↔20–24 in (50–60 cm)
↕20–24 in (50–60 cm)

Widespread in tropical and subtropical regions of the Americas, so widely cultivated and naturalized that its exact origin is uncertain. Bushy herbaceous perennial. Tuberous roots and leaves to 4 in (10 cm) long. Short-lived, flared, trumpet-flowers, 2 in (5 cm) wide, mainly magenta, or yellow, red, or white, striped, in summer. Zones 8–11.

Mimulus, Hybrid Cultivar, 'Puck'

MISCANTHUS

This genus, part of the grass (Poaceae) family, contains about 20 species found from Africa to East Asia. These tufted spreading plants have showy, green, silver, white, and mottled foliage, deciduous or evergreen. They are found in moist areas with free drainage. Commonly referred to as reeds, they have upright clumps of leaves that cascade from rounded upright stems. Masses of tall flowerheads usually appear in late summer through autumn, often remaining on plants through winter. They dry well, holding their form for months, so are ideal for floral work. Autumn tonings, orange, red, yellow, or purple.

CULTIVATION: *Miscanthus* species prefer full sun and moist open soils. Used widely in ornamental gardens as features and for screening. To propagate, divide into small clumps in autumn, or sow seed in containers in spring after frosts. Division is best, as seed is often slow to germinate.

Miscanthus floridulus

AMUR SILVERGRASS

☼ ✱ ↔5 ft (1.5 m) ↑8 ft (2.4 m)

Tall grass plant from Southeast Asia. Deciduous or evergreen. Arching mid-green leaves, silver midribs; silver flower spikes, in autumn. Zones 6–9.

M

Miscanthus oligostachyus

SMALL JAPANESE SILVER GRASS

☼ ✱ ↔32 in (80 cm) ↑40 in (100 cm)

Small compact grass plant from Japan and China. Upright clumping foliage, round stems. Showy creamy white flowers, in autumn. Ideally suited to cooler climates. Zones 5–9.

Miscanthus sinensis

EULALIA, JAPANESE SILVER GRASS

☼ ✱ ↔4 ft (1.2 m) ↑15 ft (4.5 m)

Tall clump-forming grass from Japan and China. Blue-green leaves turn vivid orange–reds and yellows in autumn. Support in windy areas. Flower spikes from silver-pink to reddish purple, in autumn. ***M. s.* var. *condensatus***, taller form, wide leaves with cream central stripe; **'Cabaret'** (Japanese silver grass), wide ribbon-like foliage, creamy white stripes, blush pink flowers, in autumn; **'Cosmopolitan'**, improved form of *M. s.* 'Variegatus', wide, more upright, non-floppy stems and leaves, flowers sit above foliage, in autumn. ***M. s.* 'Gracillimus'** ★ (maiden grass), upright clumps, narrow silver leaves, bright orange foliage, in autumn, **'Kleine Silberspinne'** (silver tower Japanese spider grass), delicate silvery foliage, spider-like flowers, in autumn; **'Morning Light'** ★ (morning light Japanese silver grass), thin, narrow, green leaves, reddish bronze flowers fade to dusty cream; **'Strictus'** (porcupine grass, banded miscanthus), clump-forming, stiff, upright, gold-banded leaves and stems, copper flowers, in autumn fade to cream; **'Variegatus'** (variegated Japanese silver grass), loose, pendulous, green and white-striped foliage; **'Yaku jima'** (Yaku jima Japanese silver grass), delicate fine-textured foliage, compact plant, reddish bronze flowers; **'Zebrinus'** (zebra grass, banded miscanthus), long arching leaves, pale yellow, almost white bands, pinkish bronze flowers above foliage, in autumn. Zones 5–9.

Miscanthus transmorrisonensis

EVERGREEN MISCANTHUS, FORMOSA MAIDEN GRASS

☼ ❄ ↔36 in (90 cm) ↑40 in (100 cm)

Grass from Taiwan. Mounding ground cover. Glossy green, thin, narrow leaves, slight arching habit. Reddish bronze flowers arch over foliage, in late summer–autumn. Zones 7–10.

Miscanthus transmorrisonensis

Miscanthus sinensis 'Variegatus'

Miscanthus sinensis 'Yaku jima'

MITCHELLA

PARTRIDGE BERRY

There are 2 species of trailing, mat-forming, evergreen herbs in this genus belonging to the madder (Rubiaceae) family. One is native to North America and the other to Japan and Korea. They grow naturally in rather sandy soils on wooded hillsides. Dark green leaves are glossy and broadly oval. Small white or pinkish flowers are borne in pairs in summer. They are tubular with flaring lobes and velvety interiors. Although fairly inconspicuous they have a pleasant fragrance. The pea-sized scarlet berries have a noticeable dimple and are edible but have little flavor. They persist on the plant for long periods. The North American species was used by Native Americans in herbal medicine and is still used today.

CULTIVATION: Grow as ground cover in shady areas or in the rock garden in a rich soil, neutral to acid. Propagate from pieces of stem from which roots have emerged, or from seed.

Mitchella repens

☀ ✱ ↔24 in (60 cm) ↑3 in (8 cm)

Trailing prostrate perennial from North America. Roots along the stems. Small rounded leaves, whitish veins. Small pinkish white flowers, in summer. Scarlet berries. Zones 3–9.

MITELLA

BISHOP'S CAP, MITREWORT

A genus of some 20 small, clumping, evergreen perennials in the saxifrage (Saxifragaceae) family from the woods of North America and northeast Asia. Leaves are rounded and hairy, above which they produce spikes of tiny greenish flowers in summer. These plants are dainty but hardly showy.

CULTIVATION: Grow these perennials in moist humus-rich soil in a shaded site. Propagate by division or from seed, which will often self-sow.

Mitella breweri

Mitella breweri

☀ ✱ ↔6 in (15 cm) ↑4–6 in (10–15 cm)

Tiny plant from central North America. Rounded, slightly lobed leaves, to 4 in (10 cm) across. Spikes of tiny green flowers among the leaves, in summer. Zones 5–9.

MOLINIA

MOOR GRASS

There are only 2 species of these deciduous, tuft-forming perennial grasses from temperate Eurasia. Members of the grass (Poaceae) family, they grow in wetland tussock areas. The stiff upright foliage changes color in autumn, adding great contrast. Tall flower spikes sit high above the foliage from late spring to autumn. They are unusual because they are "self-cleaning." When the plants die down in winter, the foliage detaches itself from the plant, unlike most deciduous grasses that hold onto the old foliage through to the next season. This leaves the crown free of any material over the winter months giving a clean look when new growth starts in spring.

CULTIVATION: These plants prefer moist open soils and will grow in sun or shade. Propagate from seed or by division in spring. Division is the best method as it is quick and reliable. The seed may not be true to type and is very slow to germinate.

Molinia caerulea

MOOR GRASS, PURPLE MOOR GRASS

☼/◐ ✱ ↔16 in (40 cm) ↑16 in (40 cm)

Perennial grass, native to Eurasia. Clumping form with slender sword-shaped leaves, slightly arching. Purple flowers appear on spikes above the foliage, in summer. ***M. c.* subsp. *arundinacea***, long, pale gray-green, arching foliage, graceful purple to brown flower spikes, fade to vivid yellow, in late summer, prefers damp, moist, boggy areas. ***M. c.* 'Variegata'** ★ (variegated moor grass), mid-green leaves, creamy yellow to white variegations, upright brown flowers, in summer, slow to establish. **'Moorhexe'** (witch moor grass), pale green foliage, neat clumps, purplish flowers on fine spikes. Zones 5–9.

Molinia caerulea 'Variegata'

MONARDA

BEE BALM, BERGAMOT, HORSEMINT

The genus *Monarda* honors Nicholas Monardes (1493–1588), a Spanish botanist, once physician to Phillip II, who wrote of plants from his long travels. His genus, a member of the mint (Lamiaceae) family, contains 16 species of annuals and perennials from North and Central America. They form large clumps, dying away completely in winter but recovering quickly in spring to form thickets of angled stems, densely clothed in lance-shaped leaves, often red-tinted and hairy, with serrated edges. In summer the top of each stem carries several whorls of tubular flowers backed by leafy bracts. The origin of the common name bee balm is obvious on any sunny day in summer, when bees continuously visit the flowers.

CULTIVATION: Very hardy and easily grown in any open sunny position with moist well-drained soil. Mildew is often a problem in late summer and good ventilation is important. Propagate by division when dormant, or from basal cuttings.

Monarda didyma ★

BEE BALM, OSWEGO TEA

☼/◐ ✱ ↔ 24–40 in (60–100 cm) ↑3–4 ft (0.9–1.2 m)

Perennial from Canada and the USA. Finely downy, often purple-red-tinted, serrated leaves, to 6 in (15 cm) long. Flowerheads 2 in (5 cm) wide, usually red shades, in summer. '**Cambridge Scarlet**', heavy-flowering, bright light red; '**Mahogany**', purple-red flowers, persistent red-brown bracts. Zones 4–9.

Monarda didyma

Monarda, HC, 'Cambridge Scarlet'

Monarda fistulosa

Monarda fistulosa ★

☼/◐ ✱ ↔ 24–40 in (60–100 cm) ↑3–4 ft (0.9–1.2 m)

Perennial found from Canada to Mexico. Very similar to *M. didyma*. Leaves seldom over 4 in (10 cm) long, may be smooth-edged. Flowers lavender to pink, in summer. Zones 4–9.

Monarda punctata

☼/◐ ✱ ↔ 16–24 in (40–60 cm) ↑24–40 in (60–100 cm)

Annual, biennial, or short-lived perennial of USA and northern Mexico. Stems and foliage downy. Leaves lance-shaped, to 4 in (10 cm) long, sometimes serrated. Flowerheads small, pale yellow to pink, greenish cream or purple-tinted bracts, in summer. Zones 6–10.

Monarda Hybrid Cultivars

☼/◐ ✱ ↔ 20–32 in (50–80 cm) ↑20–60 in (50–150 cm)

The 2 most commonly grown species, *M. didyma* and *M. fistulosa*, hybridize freely resulting in excellent garden varieties such as: '**Beauty of Cobham**', 50 in (130 cm) high, lavender-pink flowers; '**Cambridge Scarlet**' ★, large ruby red flowers; '**Croftway Pink**' ★, 40 in (100 cm) tall, bright mid-pink flowers; '**Ruby Glow**', 24 in (60 cm) tall, bright red flowers, red-tinted foliage; '**Scorpion**', 40 in (100 cm) tall, purple-pink flowerheads, purple-red-tinted foliage; '**Vintage Wine**', 27 in (70 cm) high, deep purple-red flowers. Zones 4–9.

MONARDELLA

This genus in the mint (Lamiaceae) family contains 19 species of annual or perennial herbs, often with creeping stems. They are native to western North America, where they grow on dry rocky slopes. The small, smooth or serrated-edged leaves smell strongly of mint. They are often grayish green and hairy to some degree. Round flowerheads of small, tubular, 2-lipped flowers are borne at stem tips in summer and autumn. Usually red, pink, or purple. The foliage of some species is used by Native Americans in herbal teas and medicines.

Monardella odoratissima

CULTIVATION: Grow in full sun in a sandy well-drained soil. Perennial species dislike cold damp soil in winter and can be grown in a cool greenhouse as an alternative. Propagate annuals from seed, and perennials from seed, division, or cuttings.

Monardella macrantha

☼ ❄ ↔ 8 in (20 cm) ↑6 in (15 cm)

Trailing subshrub native to California, USA. Downy stems, small leaves. Spherical heads bear small, tubular, scarlet to yellow flowers, purple calyces, in summer–autumn. Zones 9–11.

Monardella odoratissima

☼ ❄ ↔ 12–24 in (30–60 cm) ↑4–24 in (10–60 cm)

Variable perennial with woody-based prostrate stems from western USA. Small, broadly oval, grayish green leaves, mint odor when crushed. Pale pink to rosy pink flowerheads, to 2 in (5 cm) wide, in summer–autumn. Zones 8–11.

MONOPSIS

Native to tropical, central, and southern Africa, this genus has 18 species of small annual or perennial herbs and is in the bellflower (Campanulaceae) family. Leaves are serrated and small. The solitary flowers appear on slender stalks growing from the leaf axils. They have horizontal calyx tubes with spreading lobes and a lipped corolla.

CULTIVATION: Prefer moist well-drained soil in an open sunny position. Propagate by division or from cuttings taken throughout the year.

Monopsis lutea

GOLDEN LOBELIA

◐ ❄ ↔ 4–5 in (10–12 cm) ↑3–4 in (8–10 cm)

Low-growing evergreen perennial from South Africa. Long trailing stems, up to 3 ft (0.9 m) long. Alternate, shiny, serrated leaves. Yellow flowers, in summer–autumn. Cascading habit suits hanging baskets. Zones 9–11.

Monopsis lutea

MORELLA

WAXBERRY

This genus consists of deciduous and evergreen shrubs and trees in the family Myricaceae, all until recently treated as species of *Myrica*. The 40 or so *Morella* species are mostly tropical, mainly from Africa and the Americas, but there are several from cooler areas as well. All have dark gray or brown, slightly rough bark; leaves are simple, arranged spirally on the twigs, mostly narrow and tapering to the base, often toothed. Flowers are small and of different sexes, which may be on different plants. Fruits are small globular drupes, rough-surfaced and often wax-coated, in many small clusters. The wax, or more correctly a kind of fat, has been used to make candles.

CULTIVATION: *Morella* species vary considerably in hardiness, but are not difficult to cultivate in suitable climates and will thrive in well-drained soil that is not strongly alkaline or prone to prolonged drought. Plant in sun to half-day shade, water well in sun, and trim to shape if necessary. Propagate from seed, layers, or in summer to autumn from half-hardened cuttings.

M

Morella cerifera

syn. *Myrica cerifera*

WAX MYRTLE

↔15 ft (4.5 m) ↑30 ft (9 m)

Large evergreen shrub or small tree native to most of Central America, the West Indies, southern Mexico, and southeastern USA; thrives in shade of other trees. Broad-based lance-shaped leaves. Flowers, small, pale yellow-brown, in summer. Tiny fruits. Grown as adaptable foliage plant. Zones 6–11.

Morina longifolia

Morella pensylvanica

syn. *Myrica pensylvanica*

BAYBERRY, CANDLEBERRY

↔4 ft (1.2 m) ↑6–10 ft (1.8–3 m)

Semi-evergreen to deciduous shrub, native to coastal eastern North America. Spreading suckering growth habit. Lance-shaped leaves, smooth or toothed edges. Tiny pale gray fruit, in summer. Zones 2–8.

MORINA

A genus of 4 species of prickly-leafed evergreen perennials in the honeysuckle (Caprifoliaceae) family; native to eastern Europe and Asia. The leaves are mainly basal, through which appear upright spikes of curved tubular flowers in whorls supported by prickly green bracts.

CULTIVATION: Grow these perennials in a sunny aspect in well-drained but moist soil and protect plants from winter wet. Propagate from seed sown individually in small containers to stop disturbance, or raise from root cuttings in winter.

Morina longifolia

WHORLFLOWER

↔10–12 in (25–30 cm) ↑32–36 in (80–90 cm)

Rosette-forming perennial from the Himalayas. Spine-edged leaves, to 10 in (25 cm) long. Upright flower stem, whorls of curved tubular flowers, to 1¼ in (30 mm) across, white, turning pink with age, in spring–summer. Zones 6–9.

MORUS

MULBERRY

There are about 12 species of deciduous trees and shrubs in this genus belonging to the mulberry (Moraceae) family. Most species are from Asia, a few are from North America and central Africa. The leaves are arranged alternately and are generally heart-shaped with serrated edges. Inconspicuous male and female flowers are borne on separate catkins and are followed by fruits resembling raspberries. The black mulberry *(M. nigra)* has long been cultivated for its edible fruits; leaves of the white mulberry *(M. alba)* provide food for silkworms.

CULTIVATION: Mulberries will grow in any reasonably fertile well-drained soil. Pruning should be done in winter and kept to a minimum as the sap bleeds freely. Propagate from cuttings in spring or autumn, although large pieces of branch (truncheons) up to 5 ft (1.5 m) long can be planted 20 in (50 cm) into the ground.

Morus alba 'Pendula', in spring

Morus alba

WHITE MULBERRY

↔30 ft (9 m) ↑30–50 ft (9–15 m)

Long-cultivated tree native to China. Leaves broadly oval, heart-shaped base, 2- to 3-lobed, coarsely toothed; silkworm food. Greenish male and female flowers, in separate clusters, in early summer. Fruit white, becoming pale pink then red. **'Bungeana'**, dense bright green foliage; **'Pendula'**, weeping form; **'Venosa'**, heavily veined mid-green leaves. Zones 4–10.

Morus nigra

BLACK MULBERRY

↔40 ft (12 m) ↑50 ft (15 m)

Deciduous tree from central or southwestern Asia. Wide dense crown, relatively short trunk, gnarled with age. Broadly oval to heart-shaped leaves, serrated edges, deep green, roughened uppersurface. Greenish flowers, in spring. Edible, juicy, sweet berries ripen to purplish black. Zones 5–10.

Morus rubra

RED MULBERRY

↔40 ft (12 m) ↑50 ft (15 m)

Deciduous tree from eastern USA and southeastern Canada, rarely cultivated. Slightly heart-shaped leaves, sometimes lobed, roughened uppersurface, very downy beneath, coarsely serrated edges. Edible fruits ripen to purple in summer. Zones 5–10.

MUEHLENBECKIA

WIRE VINE

These plants are often twining, scrambling, or forming dense mounds of tangled stems. The common name is appropriate for this genus of around 15 species of evergreen or semi-deciduous subshrubs and shrubs, which is a member of the knotweed (Polygonaceae) family. Examples are found in South America, Australia, New Zealand, and New Guinea, often in hilly country, with some extending into the alpine zone. They are well adapted to harsh windswept conditions, with reduced foliage hidden within the mass of stems. The flowers are very small and clustered in the leaf axils or at the branch tips. Small, 3-sided, nut-like fruit in a fleshy cup follow the flowers.

Morus nigra

CULTIVATION: These plants are tolerant of light to moderate frosts but are not suited to continental climates. The best features of the genus are its ground-hugging habit and resistance to wind. Plant in full sun with light well-drained soil that can be kept moist in summer. Propagate from seed in autumn, or by layers, which often form naturally, or from hardwood cuttings in winter.

Muehlenbeckia complexa

MAIDENHAIR VINE, MATTRESS VINE, NECKLACE VINE, WIRE VINE

↔10 ft (3 m) ↑5–15 ft (1.5–4.5 m)

Dense twining climber from New Zealand. Fine dark purple stems. Tiny bronze-green leaves. Tiny white flowers, in spring. White receptacle, one black nut. Zones 8–10.

MUHLENBERGIA

MUHLY GRASS

A genus of around 160 species of mainly perennial grasses (family Poaceae), most native to warmer parts of North America, with a few in Asia as

Murraya paniculata

well. They are tussock-forming grasses, often making large clumps of fine foliage. They produce numerous long plume-like flowerheads in summer; the small crowded spikelets may be finely awned. They are generally evergreen but foliage may be killed by winter frost or wither in hot summers. CULTIVATION: Most are easily grown in any sunny position with moist well-drained soil. The more tender species may be grown as annuals in colder areas, or potted and moved under cover for winter. Propagate from seed but the best forms must be increased by division.

Muhlenbergia rigens

DEERGRASS

↔ 24–48 in (60–120 cm) ↕ 36–60 in (90–150 cm)

Found across southwestern USA from northern California to western Texas, also northern Mexico; large dense tussocks of fine, spreading, pale green foliage; many slender erect seed heads in summer with crowded small grayish spikelets. Zones 7–10.

MUKDENIA

syn. *Aceriphyllum*

A genus of 2 species in the saxifrage (Saxifragaceae) family from the damp woods of north and northeastern China, and Korea. They are clumping herbaceous perennials with attractive maple-shaped leaves and leafless stalks of tiny, white, bell flowers in spring. CULTIVATION: These plants require a cool moist aspect in well-drained, but never dry, humus-rich soil. Propagate from seed sown when ripe, or by division in late winter before growth starts.

Mukdenia rossii

syn. *Aceriphyllum rossii*

↔ 18 in (45 cm) ↕ 14 in (35 cm)

From South Korea and northeastern China. Lobed leaves, to 6 in (15 cm) long. Panicles of tiny white flowers, above foliage, in spring. Zones 6–9.

MURRAYA

This small genus in the rue (Rutaceae) family is a relative of *Citrus* and consists of about 8 species from tropical Asia to Australia. They are shrubs or trees with pinnate dark green leaves, and white perfumed flowers in large panicles. Fruit are small globe- to egg-shaped berries. CULTIVATION: Most are adaptable and grow best in well-drained mulched soil with added moisture and fertilizer during the growing season. They tolerate full sun to part-shade and perform best in a warm frost-free climate. Responds well to pruning. Propagate from seed or cuttings.

Murraya paniculata

COSMETIC BARK, JASMINE ORANGE, ORANGE JESSAMINE

↔ 10 ft (3 m) ↕ 10 ft (3 m)

Shrub found from Southeast Asia to Australia. Globe-shaped, with many branches. Pinnate leaves pale green, maturing to dark glossy green. Orange blossom-like flowers, white, sweetly perfumed, in spring. Orange to red berries. Zones 10–12.

MUSA

BANANA

There are about 40 species in this genus of evergreen suckering perennials from Asia to Australia. They belong to the banana (Musaceae) family. Leaves are large, paddle-shaped, and smooth-edged. The flowers appear on a spike that can be pendent or erect. The female or hermaphrodite flowers are near the base and the male flowers are near the tip. The fruit can be long, slim, and curved, or stubby, nearly round, sausage-shaped, or cylindrical. CULTIVATION: *Musa* species are found in light woodland and forest margins and will do best in humus-rich fertile soil in full sun, with shelter from wind. In temperate areas where frosts occur, grow in a greenhouse in loam-based compost with added leafmold. Water and feed regularly during the growing months. Propagate by division of suckers, or by seed in spring.

Mukdenia rossii

Musa acuminata

syn. *Musa cavendishii*

BANANA

↔ 8 ft (2.4 m) ↕ 12–20 ft (3.5–6 m)

From Southeast Asia and north Queensland, Australia. Paddle-shaped leaves, mid- to gray-green. Pendent flowers, pear-shaped, yellow, white, or cream, in summer. Edible yellow fruit. 'Dwarf Cavendish' (syn. 'Basrai'), smaller, yellow flowers and purple bracts. Zones 10–12.

Musa basjoo

HARDY BANANA, JAPANESE BANANA

↔ 7–10 ft (2–3 m) ↕ 10–15 ft (3–4.5 m)

Short-trunked, relatively hardy banana once thought to come from the Ryukyu Islands, but now known to be native to southern China. Leaves to 7 ft (2 m) long, fruit inedible, yellow-green, to 4 in (10 cm) long. Will re-shoot if cut down by frost. Zones 9–11.

Musa acuminata

Musa ornata

Musa ornata

FLOWERING BANANA

↔ 6 ft (1.8 m) ↕ 6–10 ft (1.8–3 m)

Ornamental suckering perennial, native to Myanmar and Bangladesh. Waxy green leaves, 6 ft (1.8 m) long. Inflorescences of flowers, orange to yellow, light purple bracts, in summer. Yellow or pink fruit. Zones 11–12.

Musa × *paradisiaca*

syn. *Musa sapientum*

BANANA, PLANTAIN

↔ 8 ft (2.4 m) ↕ 10–20 ft (3–6 m)

An *M. acuminata* and *M. balbisiana* cross. Includes cooking and eating bananas. Leaves large, green, oblong. Fruit yellow, pale pulp, seedless, in summer. Often bags are placed over fruit to aid ripening and give protection. Zones 10–12.

Musa velutina

VELVET BANANA

↔ 3 ft (0.9 m) ↕ 5 ft (1.5 m)

Rhizomatous plant from northeastern India. Dark green leaves, paler undersides, red midrib. Red bracts, white or yellowish flowers, in spring. Pink velvety fruit, splits when ripe. Zones 9–12.

Musa × *paradisiaca*

Musa velutina

MUSCARI

GRAPE HYACINTH

This genus, a member of the asparagus (Asparagaceae) family, contains some 30 species of spring-blooming bulbous perennials. Originally from the Mediterranean basin and southwest Asia. Widely used in woodland gardens and for bedding displays. The flowers, like tiny upside-down bowls, hang in dense clusters from stems, in spring. Lower florets open before those at the top. The foliage is voluminous and can sometimes be untidy.

CULTIVATION: Feed with bone meal in spring. Divide overcrowded clumps while dormant, incorporating fresh soil if replanting in same spot. Propagate from offsets during dormancy, or by seed sown when fresh.

Muscari armeniacum

syn. *Muscari szovitsianum*

↔ 2 in (5 cm) ↑ 8 in (20 cm)

Bulbous perennial. Leaves mid-green, may collapse in rough weather. Flowers in dense racemes, bright blue, pinched white mouths, faintly fragrant, in summer. Needs winter sun. **'Blue Spike'**, large, double, soft blue flowers; **'Cantab'**, vigorous, pale blue flowers, short stalks; **'Valerie Finnis'** ★, pale lavender flowers, in dense showy spirals, dark semi-erect leaves, may be more closely related to *M. neglectum*. Zones 6–9.

Muscari aucheri

syn. *Muscari tubergenianum*

↔ 2 in (5 cm) ↑ 4–6 in (10–15 cm)

Bulbous perennial from Turkey. Leaves mid-green, narrowly spoon-shaped. Flowers in tight racemes, bright blue, pinched white mouths, top flowers often paler and sterile, in early summer. Requires winter sun. Zones 6–9.

Muscari armeniacum 'Blue Spike'

Muscari azureum

syns *Muscari szovitsianum, Pseudomuscari azureum*

↔ 2 in (5 cm) ↑ 4–6 in (10–15 cm)

Bulbous perennial from eastern Turkey. Leaves gray-green. Flowers bright blue with darker stripe, bell-shaped with unconstricted mouths, in early summer. Requires winter sun. Zones 6–9.

Muscari botryoides

↔ 2 in (5 cm) ↑ 4–6 in (10–15 cm)

Bulbous perennial from central and southeastern Europe. Leaves mid-green, narrowly spoon-shaped, semi-erect. Flowers spherical, bright blue, pinched white mouths, in early summer. Requires winter sun. **'Album'**, slender racemes of fragrant white flowers. Zones 6–9.

Muscari latifolium

↔ 2 in (5 cm) ↑ 8 in (20 cm)

Bulbous perennial from southwest Asia. Leaves mid-green, lance-shaped. Blooms, extended urn shape, violet-black, pinched mouths, racemes topped with paler sterile flowers, in early summer. Requires winter sun. Zones 6–9.

Muscari macrocarpum

↔ 4 in (10 cm) ↑ 4–6 in (10–15 cm)

Bulbous Asian perennial requiring good drainage and dry summers. Leaves erect, linear, gray-green. Flowers tubular, greenish yellow opening from brownish purple buds, strongly scented, in spring. Zones 7–10.

MUSSAENDA

This genus contains about 100 species of evergreen subshrubs, shrubs, and climbers, sometimes with twining stems, native to tropical areas of Africa and Asia. It belongs to the madder (Rubiaceae) family. They have pointed elliptical leaves, opposite or in whorls of three. Small tubular flowers, in panicles or clusters throughout the year, are of secondary importance to colorful enlarged sepals that accompany them, often in startling contrast.

CULTIVATION: Plant in a tropical greenhouse in temperate climates. Require direct sunlight and should be watered well in the growing season. In warmer climates can be grown outdoors in sun or part shade, in rich well-drained soil. Propagate from seed sown in spring, or half-hardened cuttings taken in summer.

Mussaenda, Hybrid Cultivar, 'Queen Sirikit'

Muscari latifolium

Muscari macrocarpum

Mussaenda glabra

↔ 7 ft (2 m) ↑ 10 ft (3 m)

Evergreen shrub, native to tropical Asia. Erect or widespreading branches. Leaves thick and shiny. Orange to red flowers, in many-flowered clusters, accompanied by large white sepals, in spring. Zones 10–12.

Mussaenda Hybrid Cultivars

↔ 5–7 ft (1.5–2 m) ↑ 10 ft (3 m)

These hybrids have often been placed under the name *M. philippica* but may have originated from crosses between *M. erythrophylla* and *M. frondosa*. All have colorful enlarged sepals. **'Aurorae'**, bushy shrub to 10 ft (3 m) high, flowers yellow, large, white, pendulous sepals; **'Queen Sirikit'**, salmon pink sepals. Zones 11–12.

MYOSOTIS

FORGET-ME-NOT

A genus of around 100 species of an-nuals, biennials, and perennials of the borage (Boraginaceae) family found in Europe, Asia, Africa, North and South America, Australia, and New Zealand. Most are small tufted plants with simple, usually lance-shaped, leaves that are sometimes grayish and often finely hairy. Their 5-petalled flowers are tiny but quite showy and are usually borne in sprays on short branching stems. Most bloom in spring and early summer and are com-monly white, cream, pink, or various shades of blue and mauve. Legends about the name abound; one attributes it to a lover who, while gathering the flowers, fell into a river and cried "forget-me-not" as he drowned.

CULTIVATION: Easily grown in any position, sunny or shady, that remains moist during summer. Alpine species benefit from a gritty free-draining soil but the others aren't fussy. Propagate perennials by careful division in late winter, otherwise raise from seed, which often self-sows.

Myosotis alpestris 'Alba'

Myosotis alpestris

↔ 16 in (40 cm) ↑ 12 in (30 cm)

Long-flowering temperate Eurasian and North American perennial. Spreading mounding clump; simple, bright green, pointed oval to lance-shaped leaves, to 3 in (8 cm) long. Small sprays of bright to dark blue tiny flowers, in spring. **'Alba'**, white-flowered cultivar. Zones 3–9.

Myosotis scorpioides

↔ 16–40 in (40–100 cm)
↑ 6–18 in (15–45 cm)

European perennial, spreads by rhizomes. Untidy mounding clump of bright green leaves to 4 in (10 cm) long. Tiny pale to mid-blue flowers, white, cream, or pale pink centers, in summer. Zones 3–9.

Myosotis sylvatica

BEDDING FORGET-ME-NOT

↔ 8–16 in (20–40 cm)
↑ 6–16 in (15–40 cm)

A biennial to short-lived perennial, often treated as annual, from Europe and Asia. Bright green leaves, to 4 in (10 cm) long. Open spikes of pale-centered, ¼ in (6 mm) wide flowers, blue or pink, in summer. Cultivars and seedling strains include: **'Blue Ball'**, compact, deep blue flowers; **'Music'**, compact, large deep blue flowers; **'Royal Blue Improved'**, tall, many deep blue flowers; **'Spring Symphony Blue'**, early, bright blue; **Victoria Series**, compact seedling strain, blue, pink, and white flowers. Zones 5–10.

MYRICA

syn. *Gale*

As now understood (following the removal of most species to *Morella*), this genus consists of only 2 species, one widespread in northern Europe, Asia, and North America, the other restricted to the lower slopes of California's Sierra Nevada. It gives its name to the small family Myricaceae. The plants are deciduous low shrubs spreading by suckers, occurring in the wild in boggy ground and along stream banks. Leaves are small, toothed near their tips, aromatic when crushed, and arranged spirally on the reddish twigs. Flowers are small, in groups of catkins appearing before the leaves, of different sexes on different plants but the plants may switch sexes. Fruits are small, dry, flattened drupes with tiny resin dots.

CULTIVATION: Occasionally planted in woodland gardens for its fragrant foliage, though of little ornamental value. Tolerates wet ground but grows equally well in well-drained soil as long as moisture is adequate. Propagate from seed, which should be cold-stratified, or by division of clumps.

Myrica gale

syns *Gale belgica, G. palustris*

BOG MYRTLE, SWEET GALE

↔ 4 ft (1.2 m)
↑ 3–6 ft (0.9–1.8 m)

Deciduous shrub found over a wide range from Europe to Japan and in North America. Leaves, 1–2½ in (2.5–6 cm) wide, toothed. Buff-yellow fruit, in massed spikes, in summer. Grows well in damp soil. Zones 3–9.

MYRRHIS

SWEET CICELY

Containing a single species, an aromatic herbaceous perennial from Europe, this genus is a member of the carrot (Apiaceae) family. It has delicate, ferny, bright green leaves from spring until autumn and flat heads of tiny pure white flowers in summer. It is grown for its sweet-flavored leaves and attractive appearance.

CULTIVATION: Grow *Myrrhis* plants in an open sunny position. Propagate from seed; they can self-sow copiously and become weedy.

Myrrhis odorata

GARDEN MYRRH, SWEET CICELY

↔ 4–5 ft (1.2–1.5 m)
↑ 5–7 ft (1.5–2 m)

Clumping herbaceous perennial from Europe. Fine, ferny, aniseed-flavored leaves, to 18 in (45 cm) long, hollow stems. Tiny white flowers, in flat clusters, in summer. Ridged dark brown seeds. Zones 5–10.

MYRTUS

Although *Myrtus* was once quite a large genus in the myrtle (Myrtaceae) family, the Southern Hemisphere species have now been classified under other genera, including *Lophomyrtus, Luma,* and *Ugni*, leaving only 2 species, both native to the Mediterranean region. These are evergreen shrubs with simple, opposite, dark green leaves and small, fragrant, white flowers produced in summer.

CULTIVATION: Grow these shrubs in a moderately fertile well-drained soil in a mild climate. Normally self-shaping into a rounded bush, they will respond to light tip-pruning in late winter, which produces denser foliage and a more compact habit. They prefer a position sheltered from cold drying winds. Propagate from half-hardened cuttings taken any time between spring and early winter.

Myrtus communis

COMMON MYRTLE, TRUE MYRTLE

↔ 10 ft (3 m) ↑ 10 ft (3 m)

Shrub from the Mediterranean region, popular for topiary. Leaves dark green above, paler beneath, aromatic when crushed. Flowers solitary, in upper axils, white, reddish pink shading on reverse; numerous conspicuous stamens, in spring. Oval purplish berries. ***M. c.* var. *italica*** has an upright habit. ***M. c.* 'Citrifolium'** has cream flowers; **'Compacta'**, dwarf form; **'Variegata'** has leaves with a conspicuous cream margin. Zones 8–11.

Myrtus communis

Myosotis sylvatica

Myrrhis odorata cultivar

N

NAGEIA

This conifer genus in the plum-pine (Podocarpaceae) family consists of 6 species and occurs in the south of India, China, and Japan, in Thailand, the Malay Peninsula, the Philippines, Indonesia, New Guinea, and New Caledonia. They are evergreen trees with broad, lance-shaped, multi-veined leaves, unusual in conifers. In all but one species male and female cones are borne on separate plants.
CULTIVATION: Only *N. nagi* is cultivated. Plants require well-drained soil and water during dry periods. Frost tolerance is minimal. Propagate from seed or cuttings.

Nageia nagi

syn. *Podocarpus nagi*

NAGI

↔ 15 ft (4.5 m) ↑70 ft (21 m)

Native to Japan, China, and Taiwan. Smooth dark brown bark, ageing to gray; almost horizontal branches. Leaves oval or oblong, glossy deep green, with paler undersides and numerous parallel veins. Male cones are single or clustered. The seeds occur singly, bluish green, globular, ripening in late autumn. Zones 8–10.

NANDINA

HEAVENLY BAMBOO, SACRED BAMBOO

Just a single species of small evergreen shrub is contained in this genus. Despite its common name, this plant is a member of the barberry (Berberidaceae) family. It is grown for its colorful foliage and the bright red berries it bears in autumn. Plants are either male or female; some hermaphroditic cultivars are now available.
CULTIVATION: *Nandina* is easily grown in a rich soil that is moist but well drained. Leaf color is more intense when planted in full sun. For the best berry crops, make a group planting to ensure cross-pollination. Leggy older stems can be cut back to the base in summer. Propagate from cuttings taken in summer as seed is difficult to germinate.

Nandina domestica

HEAVENLY BAMBOO

↔ 4 ft (1.2 m) ↑7 ft (2 m)

Native to the region from India to Japan. Erect cane-like stems. Leaves bipinnate or tripinnate, lance-shaped, soft, tinted pinkish red, becoming green and glossy with age, developing yellow, red, and purplish hues in winter. Small creamy white flowers, in summer. Showy red berries. Cultivars include: **'Blush'**, red growth year-round; **'Filamentosa'**, thin green leaves, yellowish edges; **'Firepower'**, compact dwarf shrub, lime green leaves change to pink and cream in winter; **'Flirt'**, dwarf, red growth year-round; **'Gulf Stream'**, compact, leaves coloring light red to scarlet; **'Harbor Dwarf'**, compact ground cover, can be weedy in warmer wet areas; **'Nana'** (syn. 'Pygmy'), rounded dwarf shrub, leaves purple, crimson, orange, and scarlet throughout year, more intense color in winter; **'Nana Purpurea'**, shorter leaves than species, striking autumn color; **'Plum Passion'**, deep purple-red new growth and winter color; **'Richmond'**, heavy crops of brilliant red berries without requiring another plant for cross-pollination; **'Town and Country'**, heavy crop of bright red berries; **'Woods Dwarf'**, low growing, red leaves in winter. Zones 7–10.

Nageia nagi

Nandina domestica

Narcissus bulbocodium

NARCISSUS

DAFFODIL, JONQUIL

Narcissus is part of the amaryllis (Amaryllidaceae) family and includes around 50 species of mainly spring-flowering bulbs found from Europe and North Africa to Japan and Australasia. They have grassy to strap-like leaves, and the flowers almost always have the typical cup- or trumpet-shaped corona backed by 6 petals. Garden forms abound in a range of colors and flower types and are classed according to flower shape and form. There are 13 divisions, listed here under *Narcissus* Hybrid Cultivars. Wild species belonging to Division 13 are listed first as individual entries. The genus name is derived from Greek mythology. When the youth Narcissus spurned the love of Echo, she sought revenge from Aphrodite, who caused him to fall in love with his reflection in a pool. Unable to pull himself away, he eventually wasted away to a flower.
CULTIVATION: Daffodils are mainly very hardy and adaptable, and will thrive in borders, pots, or naturalized in lawns. They prefer full sun/half-sun when in growth, and do well under deciduous trees. Good drainage is important. Water well until the foliage dies off. Propagate by breaking up established clumps.

Narcissus bulbocodium

HOOP-PETTICOAT DAFFODIL

↔ 12 in (30 cm) ↑4–6 in (10–15 cm)

From France, Portugal, and Spain. Fine dark green leaves, more rounded than other *Narcissus*. Bright yellow to soft lemon flowers with flared trumpet, narrow much-reduced petals in same color, in early spring. *N. b.* var. *conspicuus* is a large-flowered rich yellow form. Division 13. Zones 6–10.

Narcissus cyclamineus

↔ 12 in (30 cm) ↑6–8 in (15–20 cm)

From northwestern Portugal and Spain. Dainty little species much used in hybridizing; threatened in the wild. Dark green strappy leaves. Bright yellow flowers with long narrow trumpet, petals reflex right back, in early spring. Division 13. Zones 6–9.

Narcissus jonquilla

JONQUIL

↔ 8 in (20 cm) ↑18 in (45 cm)

From Portugal and Spain. Narrow leaves, 2 to 4 per bulb. Thin flower stems, heads of small bright yellow flowers, seldom more than 1¼ in (30 mm) wide, with tiny cup-shaped corona, often strongly scented, in early spring. Division 13. Zones 4–9.

Narcissus minor

syn. *Narcissus pseudonarcissus subsp. minor*

↔ 4 in (10 cm) ↑8 in (20 cm)

Native to France and northern Spain. Short, upright, gray- to blue-green leaves, often noticeably channeled, 3 to 4 per bulb. Narrow flower stem with solitary, large-cupped, bright yellow flower to 1¾ in (40 mm) wide, in early spring. Corona usually has frilled edge. Division 13. Zones 4–9.

Narcissus obesus

Narcissus × *odorus* 'Plenus'

Narcissus obesus

syn. *Narcissus bulbocodium subsp. obesus*

☼ ✱ ↔12 in (30 cm) ↕7–8 in (18–20 cm)

Hoop-petticoat daffodil from Portugal. Foliage sits almost flat to the ground. Large yellow trumpets to 1 in (25 mm) long, in early spring. Division 13. Zones 6–10.

Narcissus × *odorus*

☼ ✱ ↔12 in (30 cm)
↕14–16 in (35–40 cm)

From southern Europe. Fragrant natural hybrid between *N. jonquilla* and *N. pseudonarcissus* with bright green curved leaves. Bright yellow flowers, 1 to 2 per stem, short trumpet, spreading petals, in early spring. **'Plenus'**, double-flowered, fine leaves; **'Rugulosus'**, more robust form, up to 4 flowers per stem. Division 13. Zones 6–9.

Narcissus poeticus

PHEASANT'S EYE NARCISSUS, POET'S NARCISSUS

☼ ✱ ↔12 in (30 cm)
↕12–20 in (30–50 cm)

From Italy, France, and Switzerland. Erect green leaves, somewhat glaucous. Flowers 2¾ in (7 cm) across, 1 per stem, pure white flat petals, tiny cup-shaped trumpet, yellow with red rim, green center, in late spring. Division 13. Zones 4–9.

Narcissus pseudonarcissus

LENT LILY, WILD DAFFODIL

☼ ✱ ↔12 in (30 cm) ↕8–14 in (20–35 cm)

Widespread European species. Thin, mid-green, erect leaves. Nodding yellow flowers to 2¾ in (7 cm) across, narrow trumpet and twisted petals, appear in early spring. Division 13. Zones 4–10.

Narcissus rupicola

☼ ✱ ↔12 in (30 cm) ↕5–6 in (12–15 cm)

From Spain and Portugal. Pale green leaves, very erect. Highly fragrant yellow flowers to 1¼ in (30 mm) across, shallow-lobed cup, produced singly, in early spring. Division 13. Zones 6–9.

Narcissus tazetta

BUNCH-FLOWERED NARCISSUS, JONQUIL, POLYANTHUS NARCISSUS

☼ ❄ ↔12 in (30 cm)
↕6–20 in (15–50 cm)

Variable species from Mediterranean, naturalized in many places. Mid-green erect leaves, twisted. Sweetly scented flowers, up to 1¾ in (4 cm) across, in clusters of up to 20, white petals, shallow yellow cup, in late winter. ***N. t.* subsp. *aureus*,** yellow petals, orange-yellow cup, very early flowering. ***N. t.* subsp. *lacticolor*** (syn. *N. canaliculatus*), dwarf form of unknown origin, white petals, orange cups. Parent of many cultivars. Division 13. Zones 7–10.

Narcissus triandrus

ANGEL'S TEARS

☼/◐ ✱ ↔12 in (30 cm)
↕5–10 in (12–25 cm)

From Spain and Portugal. Leaves green, strappy, tips often curled. Flowers 2½ in (6 cm) across, cream with open cup-shaped trumpets and reflexed petals, in early spring. Division 13. Zones 4–9.

Narcissus Hybrid Cultivars

Daffodils hybridize freely and are favorites with plant breeders. The widely used Royal Horticultural Society classification system divides the cultivars and hybrids into 13 groups or divisions based on the flower type and parentage.

DIVISION 1: TRUMPET

☼/◐ ✱ ↔12 in (30 cm)
↕12–16 in (30–40 cm)

Large-cupped flowers, with one bloom per stem. The corona (cup) must be at least as long as the perianth segment, that is, the length of the petals. Division 1 hybrids include: **'Attraction'**, creamy white perianth, bright yellow corona; **'Cyclope'**, bright yellow flowers, broad cup; **'Dutch Master'**, overall bright yellow; **'Gold Medal'**, bright yellow flowers, late flowering; **'Honeybird'**, green-tinged yellow perianth, white to cream corona; **'King Alfred'**, typical of group, bright golden yellow blooms; **'Las Vegas'**, pale cream perianth, bright yellow corona; **'Mount Hood'**, white to cream flowers, tall; **'Small Talk'** ★, miniature, all-over bright yellow, 4–6 in (10–15 cm) tall; **'Spellbinder'** ★, soft to brighter yellow blooms with pale center; **'Standard Value'**, soft golden yellow flowers, held aloft on short stems; **'Topolino'**, white perianth, sulfur yellow corona; **'Unsurpassable'**, deep golden yellow blooms, tall, very early flowering; **'W. P. Milner'**, elegant form, flowers open lemon yellow, paling to white with age. Zones 5–10.

DIVISION 2: LARGE-CUPPED

☼/◐ ✱ ↔12 in (30 cm)
↕12–16 in (30–35 cm)

The Division 2 plants are similar to the trumpet-flowered style with one flower per stem but with a smaller cup (corona) that should be shorter than the length of the perianth and at least one-third as long. Popular Division 2 members include: **'Abalone'**, white perianth, with deeper colored corona; **'Ambergate'**, deep yellow perianth, with orange corona; **'Berlin'**, yellow perianth, yellow corona with frilled bright orange edge; **'Billy Graham'**, soft yellow perianth with salmon pink corona; **'Blimey'**, primrose yellow perianth, corona of palest yellow; **'Camelot'** ★, all-over yellow; **'Ceylon'**, yellow perianth, with orange corona; **'Chilli Belle'**, white perianth, with deep pink corona; **'Coquille'**, ivory perianth, orangey pink corona, deeper colored at rim; **'Fortune's Bowl'**, yellow perianth, with rich golden corona; **'Fragrant Breeze'**, cream perianth, with yellow corona, fragrant blooms; **'Golden Aura'**, brilliant yellow perianth, with yellow corona; **'Ice Follies'**, white perianth, with pale yellow corona; **'Just So'**, creamy white perianth, with pinkish corona, deeper colored at rim; **'Modern Art'**, bright yellow perianth, with heavily ruffled orangey corona; **'Passionale'**, rich cream perianth, with ivory corona; **'Precocious'**, petals white, corona coral to orange, flat, semi-double; **'Quasar'**, crisp white perianth, with deep orange-red and pink corona; **'Redhill'**, white perianth, orange-red corona; **'Saint Patrick's Day'**, all-over yellow; **'Salomé'** ★, white perianth, with yellow corona; **'Zampatti'**, very large flowers, cream perianth, yellow and orange-gold corona. Zones 5–10.

Narcissus tazetta

DIVISION 3: SMALL-CUPPED

☼/◐ ✱ ↔12 in (30 cm)
↕12–14 in (30–35 cm)

Small-cupped flowers, with one bloom per stem and a cup length of less than one-third of the perianth length. Division 3 hybrids include: **'Amor'** ★, white perianth, with soft orange corona; **'Barrett Browning'**, white perianth, with orange corona; **'La Stupenda'**, perianth soft yellow with an orange flush, corona orange-red, tall; **'Lough Areema'**, white perianth, with dark-edged greenish-yellow corona; **'Mary MacKillop'**, white perianth, red-edged yellow cup; **'Red Ember'**, deep yellow perianth, with orange-red corona; **'Verger'**, white perianth, with red-edged golden corona. Zones 5–10.

Narcissus, HC, 1. Trumpet, 'Attraction'

Narcissus, HC, 2. Large-Cupped, 'Blimey'

Narcissus, HC, 3. Small-Cupped, 'Amor'

Narcissus, HC, 4. Double, 'Flower Drift'

Narcissus, HC, 8. Tazetta, 'Geranium'

Narcissus, HC, 5. Triandrus, 'Thalia'

Narcissus, HC, 9. Poeticus, 'Actaea'

Narcissus, HC, 6. Cyclamineus, 'Jack Snipe'

Narcissus, HC, 11. Split-Corona, 'Egard'

Narcissus, HC, 7. Jonquilla, 'Trevithian'

DIVISION 4: DOUBLE

☼/◐ ✻ ↔ 12 in (30 cm)
↕ 10–14 in (25–35 cm)

These hybrids can have one or more flowers per stem. The corona or the perianth, or both, may be doubled. Popular doubles include: **'Acropolis'**, white all over except for orange touch at base of corona; **'Bridal Crown'**, fully double, white and pale yellow; **'Candida'**, fully double, cream and pale yellow; **'Cheerfulness'**, fully double, creamy white, yellow center; **'Flower Drift'**, cream perianth, orange-red and yellow double corona; **'Gay Kybo'**, fully double, white perianth, yellow-orange in center; **'Madison'**, white double perianth, golden corona; **'Manly'**, fully double, white and bright yellow; **'Pink Paradise'**, white perianth, pink double corona; **'Rip van Winkle'**, sulfur yellow, corona split and splayed in "dandelion" head effect; **'Sir Winston Churchill'**, white perianth, cream and yellow double corona; **'Tahiti'**, double perianth, yellow split orange corona; **'White Lion'**, fully double, pale yellow; **'Yellow Cheerfulness'**, yellow with some orange on central doubled petals. Zones 5–10.

DIVISION 5: TRIANDRUS

☼/◐ ✻ ↔ 8 in (20 cm)
↕ 6–10 in (15–25 cm)

These plants show clear evidence of *N. triandrus* parentage and usually have two or more pendent flowers per stem with reflexed perianth segments. **'Hawera'**, up to 5 pendulous soft yellow flowers; **'Lapwing'**, white perianth, yellow corona; **'Stint'**, soft yellow, corona slightly darker; **'Thalia'** ★, overall white to cream. Zones 5–10.

DIVISION 6: CYCLAMINEUS

☼/◐ ✻ ↔ 8 in (20 cm)
↕ 8–12 in (20–30 cm)

Hybrids of *N. cyclamineus* parentage with usually one flower per stem and perianth segments strongly reflexed, often almost to the stem. Popular hybrids include: **'Cotinga'**, perianth white, corona salmon pink, slight fragrance; **'Dove Wings'**, soft yellow perianth, deep yellow corona; **'February Gold'**, all-over yellow; **'Jack Snipe'**, cream perianth, yellow corona; **'Jetfire'**, golden yellow perianth, orange corona; **'Kaydee'**, white perianth with buff to salmon pink corona; **'Toby the First'**, petals cream and partly reflexed, bright yellow cup, narrow. Zones 5–10.

DIVISION 7: JONQUILLA

☼/◐ ✻ ↔ 12 in (30 cm)
↕ 12–18 in (30–45 cm)

Plants with *N. jonquilla* parentage evident in their small fragrant flowers, in heads of 1 to 3, sometimes more, with a starry array of perianth segments. Popular jonquils include: **'Bell Song'**, cream to pale yellow perianth, pink corona; **'Bella Estrella'**, perianth white, corona soft sulfur yellow, frilled; **'Quail'**, overall deep golden yellow; **'Sailboat'**, white perianth, slightly swept back, cream to very pale yellow corona; **'Suzy'**, yellow perianth, orange corona; **'Trevithian'**, deep yellow perianth, darker corona. Zones 5–10.

DIVISION 8: TAZETTA

☼/◐ ✻ ↔ 18 in (45 cm)
↕ 12–18 in (30–45 cm)

Hybrids of *N. tazetta* with heads of 3 to 20 clustered, small, often highly scented flowers on sturdy stems. These hybrids include: **'Avalanche'**, white perianth, yellow corona; **'Geranium'**, white perianth, golden orange corona; **'Golden Dawn'**, yellow perianth, gold corona; **'Minnow'**, soft yellow perianth, darker corona; **'Ziva'**, white perianth, cream to pale yellow corona. Zones 5–10.

DIVISION 9: POETICUS

☼/◐ ✻ ↔ 10 in (25 cm)
↕ 12–16 in (30–45 cm)

Hybrids of species belonging to the *N. poeticus* group. Distinctive, usually one flower per stem, with small disc-shaped corona edged in red. Poeticus daffodils include: **'Actaea'** ★, flat white petals, tiny cup-shaped trumpet, bright yellow, edged with red; **'Cantabile'**, white perianth, red-edged yellow-green corona; **'Felindre'**, white perianth, red-edged, green-centered, yellow corona; **'Green Pearl'**, white petals, small white cup with green center, sometimes in Division 3, Small-cupped. Zones 5–10.

DIVISION 10: BULBOCODIUM

☼ ❄ ↔ 4–6 in (10–15 cm)
↕ 4–6 in (10–15 cm)

These daffodils are derived from and generally resemble *N. bulbocodium* and its relatives. Leaves narrow and grassy. One flower per stem, corona predominant part of flower, petals reduced and narrow. These hybrids include: **'Cornish Cream'**, white to cream all over; **'Fyno'**, white shading to cream at base of perianth; **'Golden Bells'**, deep golden yellow all over. Zones 5–10.

DIVISION 11: SPLIT-CORONA

☼/◐ ✻ ↔ 12 in (30 cm)
↕ 12–14 in (30–35 cm)

Unlike most daffodils with fused corona segments, split-corona forms have separate lobes, usually for more than half their length. Popular split-corona daffodils include: **'Articol'**, which has a white perianth with a pale dusky pink double corona; **'Egard'**, a white perianth with soft yellow corona; **'Palmares'**, a cream perianth with pale pink corona; **'Sovereign'**, a white perianth with deep gold to orange corona; **'Tricollet'** ★, very unusual, white perianth, 3-part yellow corona spread flat against petals. Zones 5–10.

DIVISION 12: MISCELLANEOUS

☼/◐ ✻ ↔ 6–12 in (15–30 cm)
↕ 6–16 in (15–40 cm)

Division 12 includes daffodil garden forms that do not fall into any other division—for example, **'Jumblie'**, up to 3 flowers per stem, bright yellow; **'Mesa Verde'**, overall soft greenish yellow, small cup; **'Téte à Téte'**, yellow perianth, cup slightly darker, long, 6 in (15 cm) tall. Zones 5–10.

DIVISION 13: SPECIES/HYBRIDS KNOWN BY BOTANICAL NAMES

☼ ❄ ↔ 4–12 in (10–30 cm)
↕ 4–16 in (10–40 cm)

This group includes the species and hybrids that have not been assigned to other groups. These are listed under their botanical names, such as *Narcissus* × *odorus* 'Rugulosus'.

NASSELLA

This grass (Poaceae) family genus is closely allied to *Stipa*, and contains over 100 mostly perennial, occasionally annual, tussocky grasses from North and South America. Forming small clumps, they have fine leaves, so slender in many species that they are commonly named needlegrass. Unbranched or branched flowering stalks carry spikelets, each of one long-awned floret, with an attractive feathery appearance. CULTIVATION: These grasses prefer full sun, in most well-drained soils. Most growth occurs in cooler weather. As a number of species have become significant weeds outside their natural habitat, care should be taken with their placement. Propagate from seed.

Nassella tenuissima

Nassella cernua

syn. *Stipa cernua*

NODDING NEEDLEGRASS

↔6–10 in (15–25 cm) ↕12–40 in (30–100 cm)

Perennial found from California, USA, to northwestern Mexico. Stiff, smooth, narrow leaves. Flower stalks, with 5 or more nodes, from spring–early summer. Zones 9–11.

Nassella tenuissima

syn. *Stipa tenuissima*

FINE-LEAFED NASSELLA, MEXICAN FEATHER GRASS

↔6–10 in (15–25 cm) ↕20–32 in (50–80 cm)

Perennial from southern USA and northern Mexico. Leaves are narrow, rolled, and stiff. Flower stalks hairy below lower nodes. Dry bracts, panicles of florets appear in spring–early summer. Zones 9–11.

NASTURTIUM

Not to be confused with the flowers commonly called nasturtium, which are actually in the genus *Tropaeolum,* these plants of the cabbage (Brassicaceae) family are mainly semi-aquatic perennials that live along the margins of slow-running water, such as creeks and streams. Their pinnate foliage, which is usually dark- to bronze-green, has a pungent peppery taste and is used as a garnish or vegetable. The small white flowers are not a feature of the genus.
CULTIVATION: Not easy to actively cultivate, but in gardens with natural watercourses they may be successfully introduced by planting at the waterline in a sunny position. Otherwise, try growing in a partly shaded position that can be kept wet.

Nasturtium officinale

syn. *Rorippa nasturtium-aquaticum*

WATERCRESS

↔4–6 ft (1.2–1.8 m) ↕1–4 ft (0.3–1.2 m)

Semi-aquatic perennial found over much of Northern Hemisphere. Foliage develops quickly in spring and should be harvested while young. Regular cutting encourages new growth. Heads of tiny white flowers open from mid-spring. Zones 6–9.

NEILLIA

This genus, in the rose (Rosaceae) family, contains 10 species of deciduous shrubs that are closely related to *Spiraea* and are found in Asia, from the eastern Himalayas to the western side of the Malay Peninsula. They are arching shrubs with prominently veined 3-lobed leaves that color to yellow in autumn. In winter their attractive form, with a zigzag pattern of twigs, is revealed. Slender panicles or racemes of small bell-shaped flowers are borne in spring or summer.
CULTIVATION: Although not widely grown, these shrubs are easily cultivated in all but the driest soils, in full sun or part-shade. After flowering, cut out old stems at ground level to encourage new growth and retain the arching habit. Propagate from seed, from cuttings in summer, or by the removal of suckers in autumn.

Neillia sinensis ★

↔7 ft (2 m) ↕10 ft (3 m)

Native of central China. Deciduous shrub, upright habit. Smooth brown branchlets, bark exfoliates. Lobed leaves, serrated edges, purplish bronze when young. Short terminal racemes of white to pale pink bell-shaped flowers, in spring–summer. Zones 6–10.

NELUMBO

This genus of 2 species of aquatic perennials belongs to the lotus (Nelumbonaceae) family. One species is native to eastern North America, and the other found throughout Asia and in Australia. The round leaves are borne umbrella-like on long stalks, usually above the water. Showy fragrant flowers are also borne on long stalks, often over 36 in (90 cm) tall, in shades of pink, yellow, and white. They are followed by decorative seed heads. Stalks, rootstock, and seeds are all edible, and the viability of the seeds extends to several hundred years.
CULTIVATION: In warm subtropical climates, they can be grown in outdoor ponds. In cool-temperate climates, plant in shallow water or in tubs. Plant rhizomes in baskets or beds of heavy rich soil mix. Grow in calm water in full sun. Propagate by division of rhizomes or from seed.

Nelumbo nucifera

Nelumbo lutea

syn. *Nelumbium luteum*

AMERICAN LOTUS, WATER CHINQUAPIN, YANQUAPIN

↔7 ft (2 m) ↕7 ft (2 m)

From eastern North America. Round bluish green leaves, to 24 in (60 cm) across. Pale yellow flowers, to 10 in (25 cm) wide, in summer. Flat-topped seed heads studded with small holes resemble showerheads. Zones 4–9.

Nelumbo nucifera

syn. *Nelumbium nelumbo*

SACRED LOTUS

↔7 ft (2 m) ↕7 ft (2 m)

Found from Iran to Japan and in Australia. Bluish green wavy-edged leaves on prickly stems. Very fragrant pink or white flowers, to 12 in (30 cm) wide, in summer. Flat-topped seed heads. **'Alba Plena'**, camellia-like white double flowers; **'Carolina Queen'**, large pink flowers, creamy at base; **'Kakadu'**, apricot pink, tall stems; **'Momo Botan'**, smaller with dark pink to rosy red flowers; **'Mrs Perry D. Slocum'**, deep pink flowers, ageing to creamy yellow; **'Paleface'**, white with pink petal tips; **'Rosea Plena'**, double flowers, deep pink with lighter center; **'Sharon'**, large double flowers, pink to red; **'Shiroman'**, large, white, double flowers; **'Speciosum'**, light pink flowers. Zones 9–12.

NEMESIA

Confined to South Africa, this genus in the foxglove (Scrophulariaceae) family includes around 65 species of annuals, perennials, and subshrubs. They form small mounds of toothed linear to lance-shaped foliage. Their flowers, borne in clusters on short stems, have a conspicuous lower lobe, often with a blotch of contrasting color. The annuals, mainly derived from *N. strumosa* and *N. versicolor*, are popular short-lived bedding plants in a wide range of bright colors. While less colorful, the perennials are sometimes mildly scented and are neat plants for borders, rockeries, or pots.
CULTIVATION: Grow *Nemesia* species in a sunny position in any light free-draining soil that is kept moist. Pinch back to keep compact. Sow annuals in succession for continuous bloom. Perennials will tolerate light frosts and grow from cuttings of non-flowering stems. Propagate from seed in late autumn or early spring.

Nemesia caerulea

↔16–24 in (40–60 cm) ↕16–24 in (40–60 cm)

Woody-based perennial from South Africa. Bright green, narrow, lance-shaped leaves, often finely toothed. Heads of small pink to light purple-blue flowers with yellow eye, in summer. Bluebird/**'Hubbird'**, violet flowers with yellow eye. Zones 8–10.

Nemesia denticulata

↔16–20 in (40–50 cm) ↕8–12 in (20–30 cm)

South African species. Rather brittle-stemmed mounding perennial with small bright green leaves. Pleasantly scented mauve to dusky pink flowers, in late spring–summer. Zones 8–10.

Neillia sinensis

Nemesia denticulata

N

Nemesia strumosa

☼/◑ ❄ ↔ 8–16 in (20–40 cm)
↑ 6–20 in (15–50 cm)

Fast-growing mounding annual native to South Africa. Lower leaves to 3 in (8 cm) long, bright green, toothed, with upper leaves much smaller. Produces many small flowers in crowded heads, often in warm shades of yellow-orange and apricot, sometimes purple or white, in summer. **'Blue Gem'**, 8 in (20 cm) tall, bright blue flowers; **'KLM'**, striking, compact, two-tone flowers, dark blue upper petals, white lower petals. Zones 9–11.

Nemesia versicolor

☼/◑ ✢ ↔ 12–20 in (30–50 cm)
↑ 12–20 in (30–50 cm)

Quick-growing herbaceous annual native to South Africa's West Cape with initially upright then mounding habit. Narrow leaves, usually toothed, to 2 in (5 cm) long. Racemes of ½ in (12 mm) wide, blue to light purple flowers, sometimes yellow or white. *N. v.* f. ***compacta*** is a compact form with abundant flowers in many colors and has contributed extensively to today's seedling strains. Zones 11–12.

Nemesia Hybrid Cultivars

☼/◑ ✢ ↔ 8–16 in (20–40 cm)
↑ 6–16 in (15–40 cm)

Many hybrids have been bred to produce early-flowering compact plants in a wide range of colors. They are short-lived but may be sown in succession from spring–late summer. **Berry Delight Series**, compact, fragrant, various colors, including bicolors, such as **'Berries 'n Cream'**, pale pink and purple, and **'Blueberry Ripple'**, bright purple; **'Fleurie Blue'**, low spreader, bright blue flowers; **'Fragrant Cloud'**, to 18 in (45 cm) tall, fragrant pale pink and white flowers; **'Innocence'**, pure white flowers, each with a small yellow throat; **Maritana Series**, low-spreading, heavy-flowering plants, wide color range including bicolors; **Sachet Series**, compact, heavy-flowering, often fragrant plants in single colors, for example **'Blueberry Sachet'**, blue to purple, and **'Vanilla Sachet'**, white; **'Sundrops'** produces a mixed color selection of compact rounded plants in a range of warm tones. Zones 11–12.

NEMOPHILA

There are 11 species of annuals in this genus, which is a member of the borage (Boraginaceae) family. Native to western North America, they have small pinnate leaves on wiry stems, and form spreading mounds of ferny foliage that are smothered in small 5-petalled flowers, usually borne singly in the leaf axils, in late spring and summer. While not spectacular plants, they are graceful and often intriguingly colored, with flowers in various shades and patterns of blue and white. Although the name, coming from the Greek *nemos* (a glade) and *phileo* (to love), suggests a preference for shade, they are most at home in full sun/half-sun.

CULTIVATION: These are superb plants for narrow borders, banks, hanging baskets, and window boxes, where their semi-trailing habit is shown off to advantage. They require moist well-drained soil. Propagation is from seed, which is best sown *in situ*, as once it has germinated, the young plants resent disturbance.

Nemesia, Hybrid Cultivar, Sachet Series, 'Vanilla Sachet'

Nemesia, HC, Sachet Series, 'Blueberry Sachet'

Nemesia, Hybrid Cultivar, 'Fragrant Cloud'

Nemophila maculata

Nemophila menziesii 'Pennie Black'

Nemophila maculata

FIVE SPOT

☼ ❄ ↔ 12–20 in (30–50 cm)
↑ 8–12 in (20–30 cm)

Annual species from central California, USA. Initially upright, later spreading. Soft green pinnate leaves, up to 7 lobes. White flowers, purple blotch near petal tip, in summer. Zones 7–11.

Nemophila menziesii

☼ ❄ ↔ 12–20 in (30–50 cm)
↑ 4–6 in (10–15 cm)

Low spreading annual from California, USA. Ferny light green leaves, up to 11 lobes. The many white-centered mid-blue flowers, sometimes entirely white, appear in summer. *N. m.* **subsp. *atromaria*** has white flowers spotted with purple-black. *N. m.* **'Oculata'** has pale blue flowers with a purple-black center; **'Pennie Black'** has very dark purple-black flowers, edged with white. Zones 7–11.

NEOMARICA

WALKING IRIS

This genus of 15 species of tender rhizomatous perennials is a member of the iris (Iridaceae) family. They are native to tropical America and western Africa. The thick leaves are erect and sword-shaped, with strong veins or ribs, and are arranged in fans. Tall stems bear short-lived, flattened, iris-like flowers, in summer. Outer petals are larger and spreading; the inner 3 petals are upright and reflexed. Some species have fragrant flowers, often marked in contrasting colors. Flower stems sometimes bend to the ground, take root, and spread, hence the common name of walking iris.

CULTIVATION: In suitably warm climates, grow outdoors in a sunny position in well-drained soil. In temperate areas, grow in the greenhouse in a fertile well-drained mix, in bright filtered light or full sun. Propagate by division or from seed.

Neomarica caerulea

syn. *Marica caerulea*

☼ ✢ ↔ 12 in (30 cm)
↑ 24–36 in (60–90 cm)

Rhizomatous perennial, native to Brazil. Leaves mid-green, sword-shaped, erect. Flowers on tall stems, 3–4 in (8–10 cm) wide, pale blue to lilac outer petals, deep blue inner petals, veined and marked yellow, white, and brown, in summer. Flowers rarely last more than one day but are replaced by another. Zones 11–12.

Neomarica gracilis

☼ ✢ ↔ 10 in (25 cm) ↑ 24 in (60 cm)

Native to Mexico and Brazil. Rhizomatous perennial. Strongly ribbed leaves, erect. Flowers about 2½ in (6 cm) wide, white outer petals, bluish inner petals with red and white markings, in summer. Zones 10–12.

NEOREGELIA

These highly variable members of the bromeliad (Bromeliaceae) family range from small tubular plants to large, flat, circular plants. Their leaves are generally strap-like, forming a rosette, and they can be green, silvery green, purplish, banded, spotted, striped in white, cream, or red, or marbled in a number of colors, or even tipped red. In some species the center leaves turn red or reddish blue, sometimes white. The flower stem is short, and the globular flowerhead, with up to 100 flowers, generally nestles in the center of the leaf rosette. This genus contains over 70 species covering 3 groups. The first group come from eastern Colombia and Peru and are not common in cultivation because they are quite difficult to grow. The second group come from southeastern Brazil, have 2–4 in (5–10 cm) long petals and are not common because of their rarity in the wild. The third group also come from southeastern Brazil; they are common and easy to grow, especially in tropical

Neomarica caerulea

to warm-temperate areas. This third group provides most of the nearly 3,000 hybrids listed for this genus. CULTIVATION: Grow *Neoregelia* indoors or in a conservatory or greenhouse in cool-temperate areas, or outdoors with protection from direct sunlight and extremes of rain in warm-temperate, subtropical, and tropical areas. Water when the potting mix is dry. Try to keep the water in the leaf rosette clean. These plants do not require extra fertilizer. Propagate from offsets.

Neoregelia Hybrid Cultivars

↔ 4–40 in (10–100 cm) ↑ 6–20 in (15–50 cm)

Mostly from Australia, Brazil, and USA, these are all easy to grow in warm areas. **'Amazing Grace'**, upright rosette in pale lime green, at flowering the whole plant blushes red in good light; **'Barbie Doll'**, light green leaves, red tips; **'Beef Steak'**, magnificent, symmetrically layered, wide-leafed rosette; **'Blushing Bride'**, center turns bright red on flowering; **'Bobby Dazzler'**, broad rich red leaves, heavy apple green spotting; **'Charm'**, bright wine red leaves, tiny lime green spots; impostors grown from seed have large spotting; **'Chili Verde'**, rich red in center at flowering; **'Chirripo'**, glazed centrally in rich reddish purple; **'Debbie'**, shy bloomer, inner leaves at first almost vertical; **'Empress'**, strap-like green and pink leaves; **'Fireball'**, shy flowering, petals blue; **'George's Prince'**, pale lilac leaves; **'Gespacho'**, wide red leaves with yellow-green markings; **'Green Apple'**, leaves apple green; **'Lambert's Pride'**, leaves with red to orange-red barring; **'Manoa Beauty'**, leaves with unique speckling in yellow-green; **'Medallion'**, inner leaves form dense crested rosette of brilliant red; **'Meyendorffii'**, center turns red at flowering; **'Midnight'**, deep burgundy central leaves, almost black; **'Ounce of Purple'**, dull green leaves covered in tiny purple spots; **'Painted Desert'**, symmetrical rosette of yellow-green leaves, developing more color in strong light; **'Passion'**, chartreuse-green leaves with hot lilac-pink intense areas; **'Perfection'**, yellow-cream central variegation; **'Red of Rio'**, mahogany red with small random green markings; **'Rosella'**, at flowering, green part of leaves turns red; **'Spots and Dots'**, dark red spots, blotches, and wavy lines; **'Takemura Grande'**, greenish plum-colored; **'Vulkan'**, varying darker purple blotches and broken stripes. Zones 11–12.

NEPETA

CATMINT, CATNIP

A member of the mint (Lamiaceae) family, this genus of around 250 mainly temperate Eurasian and North African aromatic perennials is represented in cultivation by just a few species, and one widely grown hybrid group. Commonly grown in herbaceous borders or for edging large beds, they are valued for the hazy effect created by their gray-green foliage and mauve-blue to purple flowerheads. They are mainly low-growing sprawling plants, with small toothed leaves. In summer, the foliage disappears under upright spikes of tiny flowers. Sometimes used in herbal salads and medicines. The origin of the name is unclear but it may be named after the Etruscan city of Nepete.

CULTIVATION: Grow in full sun with light free-draining soil. Pinch back in spring to encourage compact growth and water well. Propagate from seed or cuttings of non-flowering stems.

Nepeta cataria

CATMINT, CATNIP

↔ 40 in (100 cm) ↑ 40 in (100 cm)

Bushy upright species, widely naturalized in Europe. Downy gray-green leaves. Spikes of widely spaced, mauve-spotted, white flowers, in summer. **'Citriodora'**, stems and foliage lemon-scented when crushed. Zones 3–10.

Nepeta × *faassenii* ★

↔ 40 in (100 cm) ↑ 24 in (60 cm)

Often sprawling hybrid of *N. racemosa* × *N. nepetella*. Leaves gray-green to silver-gray, toothed, lance-shaped to pointed oval. Spikes of lavender to purple-blue flowers, in summer. **'Walker's Low'**, mounding habit, lavender-blue flowers. Zones 3–10.

Nepeta grandiflora

↔ 24 in (60 cm) ↑ 24 in (60 cm)

Bushy eastern European species. Leaves toothed, downy, broad-based, pointed oval. Spikes of lavender-blue flowers, in summer. **'Bramdean'**, compact flowerheads; **'Dawn to Dusk'**, gray-green foliage, mauve flowers. Zones 3–10.

Nepeta nervosa

↔ 32 in (80 cm) ↑ 20 in (50 cm)

Native to Kashmir. Initially upright, later sprawling. Narrow lance-shaped leaves, toothed or smooth-edged. Dense upright spikes of purple-blue flowers appear in spring–summer. Yellow-flowered forms occur rarely. Zones 5–10.

Nepeta racemosa

↔ 24 in (60 cm) ↑ 12 in (30 cm)

Found from the Caucasus and northern Iran. Stems spreading. Downy pointed oval leaves. Masses of violet-blue flowers, also downy, are borne in spring–summer. **'Six Hills Giant'**, gray foliage, large sprays of lavender flowers; **'Superba'**, spreading habit, gray foliage, purple-blue flowers. Zones 4–10.

Nepeta sibirica

↔ 40 in (100 cm) ↑ 40 in (100 cm)

Quick-growing shrubby native of Siberia. Leaves sparsely hairy, toothed, dark green. Flowerheads crowded but individual whorls widely spaced, blue to soft purple, in spring–summer. **'Souvenir d'Andre Chaudron'**, very aromatic foliage, lavender-blue flowers. Zones 3–9.

Nepeta racemosa

Neoregelia, HC, 'Painted Desert'

Nepeta tuberosa

↔ 20 in (50 cm) ↑ 32 in (80 cm)

Bushy rhizome-rooted species found in coastal areas from Portugal to Sicily. Pointed oval leaves to 3 in (8 cm) long, finely hairy to densely downy. Small spikes of light purple flowers, with pink to purple-red bracts at base, in summer. Zones 8–10.

Nepeta Hybrid Cultivars

↔ 18–36 in (45–90 cm) ↑ 12–18 in (30–45 cm)

In recent years, a range of hybrids has been introduced, including: **'Dropmore'**, very aromatic gray-green foliage, long flowering season; **'Dryspell Lilac'**, smaller leaves, dusky lilac flowers; **'Lemon Nip'**, light green foliage with citrus aroma, large purple flower spikes; **'Little Trudy'**, very compact, drought tolerant, gray-green foliage. Zones 6–10.

NEPHROLEPIS

BOSTON FERN, FISHBONE FERN, SWORD FERN

Found in the wild in many tropical areas such as Asia, Africa, Central America, and West Indies. This genus of about 40 species belongs to the family Davalliaceae. They are terrestrial or epiphytic with short rhizomes and usually wiry spreading runners. The long tapering fronds bear varying numbers of alternating leaflets and may be erect, arching, or pendulous. Colonies become established quickly and some species are a weedy nuisance in warm countries.

CULTIVATION: These ferns are popular house plants in cool climates. Indoors they need bright filtered light and a humid atmosphere. In warm climates they are unfussy and easily grown in part-shade or sun in a reasonably moist soil, but they can become rampant. Propagate by division or from spores.

Neoregelia Hybrid Cultivars

Nephrolepis cordifolia

Nerine bowdenii

Nerine sarniensis

Nerium oleander

Neviusia alabamensis

Nephrolepis cordifolia

ERECT SWORD FERN, LADDER FERN

↔12–48 in (30–120 cm) ↑12–48 in (30–120 cm)

Native to tropics of the world. Erect or arching fronds, yellowish green to dark green. Blunt-ended, narrow, leathery leaflets. **'Duffii'** (Duff's sword fern), dense fronds, often forked, crowded rounded leaflets; **'Kimberley Queen'**, tolerates more sun; **'Plumosa'**, leaflets with lobed margins. Zones 10–12.

Nephrolepis exaltata

↔36 in (90 cm) ↑36 in (90 cm)

Native to tropics of Africa, Asia, and the Americas. Tufted ferns with long, arching, pale lime green fronds, wavy-edged leaflets. **'Bostoniensis'** (Boston fern), broad lance-shaped fronds, pale lime green, fronds cascade as they mature; **'Bostoniensis Aurea'** (golden Boston fern), lime green-gold; **'Childsii'**, hardy indoor plant, broad pale green fronds that overlap each other; **'Hillii'**, fast-growing, crested double fronds, very adaptable; **'Mini Ruffle'**, miniature, broad triangular-shaped fronds, definite lacy appearance. Zones 10–12.

Nephrolepis falcata

MACHO FERN, WEEPING SWORD FERN

↔5 ft (1.5 m) ↑8 ft (2.4 m)

From Sri Lanka, the Maldives, Myanmar, and southeastern Asia. Long dark glossy green fronds, arching or weeping. Leathery leaflets forked toward tips. Scattered black scales on both surfaces of frond blade. Zones 9–12.

NERINE

GUERNSEY LILY, SPIDER LILY

From southern Africa, this genus in the amaryllis (Amaryllidaceae) family encompasses 23 species of autumn-flowering bulbs that often resemble small-scale versions of *Amaryllis*. Their grassy to strappy leaves may be evergreen or summer-deciduous. Flower stems carry many-flowered heads of long-tubed funnel-shaped flowers, each with 6 widely flared, reflexed, narrow petals. Bright pink and orange-red are the main flower colors and white forms are common. The genus is named for Nereis, a sea nymph of Greek mythology.

CULTIVATION: These plants tolerate moderate frosts, but where the soil freezes they are best grown in pots that can be moved under cover. Plant in full sun/half-sun with the bulb neck exposed. Nerines prefer a light, gritty, well-drained soil, but appreciate extra humus. Keep dry when dormant. Propagate by division, from offsets or seed. May self-hybridize and self-sow.

Nerine bowdenii

↔12 in (30 cm) ↑16–18 in (40–45 cm)

Well-known South African species. Leaves pale to dark green, glossy. Bright pink flowers, wavy edges, in clusters of up to 7, in autumn. Foliage comes up in early winter, after flowering. **'Pink Triumph'**, deep pink flowers. Zones 8–11.

Nerine sarniensis

GUERNSEY LILY

↔6 in (15 cm) ↑16–18 in (40–45 cm)

South African species. Erect leaves, bright green, to 12 in (30 cm) long. Rounded heads of up to 20 brilliant orange-red flowers with wavy-edged petals and prominent stamens, in autumn. ***N. s.* var. *curvifolia* f. *fothergillii* 'Major'**, larger and darker orange-red flowers. Zones 9–11.

NERIUM

OLEANDER

This genus of a single species from North Africa, the Middle East, northern India, and southern China belongs to the dogbane (Apocynaceae) family. It is a long-flowering evergreen shrub or small tree, with simple, smooth-edged, narrow leaves, and yellow, white, pink, and tangerine flowers. Petals are fused into a narrow tube but flaring from the end into a disc or a shallow cup, borne in terminal clusters. Tolerant of salt-laden winds and dry sandy soils; can be invasive.

CULTIVATION: Will grow in almost any type of soil except wet, but like full sun. Tolerant of light frosts if given a sheltered position. For a dense shrubby habit, remove flowering shoots and prune well-established plants in winter every 3 years. As these plants are extremely poisonous, wear protective clothing when pruning and dispose of prunings carefully (do not burn). Propagate from half-hardened cuttings taken in autumn, or seed in spring.

Nerium oleander

↔8 ft (2.4 m) ↑10 ft (3 m)

Evergreen shrub. Many erect shoots rising from base. Leaves dark green above, paler below. Flowers appear in late spring to early autumn, and sporadically until early winter. Many single- and double-flowered cultivars in a wide range of colors. Double cultivars have petals crimped, waved on outer edge. **'Album'**, bears single white flowers; **'Casablanca'**, faded pink flowers, almost white; **'Delphine'**, single dark purplish red flowers; **'Docteur Golfin'**, single, mauve tinged, cherry red flowers; **'Petite Pink'**, dwarf cultivar, pale pink flowers; **'Petite Salmon'**, dwarf cultivar, salmon flowers; **'Splendens'**, deep rose pink double flowers; **'Splendens Giganteum Variegatum'**, creamy yellow edge to leaves. Zones 8–11.

NEVIUSIA

Related to *Kerria*, this genus consists of a single species of deciduous shrub in the rose (Rosaceae) family. It is a threatened species in its native Alabama, USA. It increases in width by means of rooted branches. The white flowers are petal-less, with many prominent stamens.

CULTIVATION: This shrub is suitable for the border or woodland edge. It grows in moderately fertile soils and should be watered well in periods of drought. After flowering, the old and dead wood should be cut out at the base. Propagate from seed or cuttings, or by division.

Neviusia alabamensis

ALABAMA SNOW WREATH

↔5 ft (1.5 m) ↑5 ft (1.5 m)

From southern USA. Suckering plant, forms a wide multi-stemmed shrub. Leaves have serrated edges, downy beneath. Small flowers with a fluffy mass of white stamens, in spring. Zones 5–9.

NICOTIANA

TOBACCO

Famous as the source of tobacco leaf, this genus, which is a member of the nightshade (Solanaceae) family, encompasses over 65 species, the bulk of which are annuals and perennials, most native to tropical and subtropical America, with a smaller number in Australia and the South Pacific. A few species are shrubby in habit, though they tend to be softwooded and short-lived. Their leaves are usually very large and covered with fine hairs, sticky to the touch, and may exude a fragrance when crushed. The flowers are tubular or bell-shaped, usually white or in pastel shades of green, pale yellow, pink, or soft red, and if fragrant their scent is generally released at night.
CULTIVATION: Most tobacco species are marginally frost tolerant. They grow best in warm humid climates that feature ample summer rainfall, in a position that is in full sun or partial shade. The soil should be well drained and reasonably fertile. Propagation is from seed sown in spring, though some species can be successfully grown from cuttings.

Nicotiana alata

syn. *Nicotiana affinis*

FLOWERING TOBACCO, JASMINE TOBACCO

↔ 12 in (30 cm)
↕ 24–36 in (60–90 cm)

Native to South America. Sticky-stemmed perennial often grown as an annual. Large oval leaves. Narrow, tubular, greenish white flowers with flaring starry ends, are produced in summer. They are fragrant and open at night. Zones 4–11.

Nicotiana × sanderae Nikki Series

Nicotiana sylvestris

Nicotiana glauca

MUSTARD TREE, TREE TOBACCO

↔ 6 ft (1.8 m)
↕ 6–12 ft (1.8–3.5 m)

Native from southern Bolivia to northern Argentina. Large blue-green leaves. Cream to yellow-green tubular flowers, to 2 in (5 cm) long, in late summer–autumn. Naturalized in warmer parts of USA. In Australia, there may be restrictions on growing this plant to minimize risk of virus passing to commercial tobacco crops. Zones 8–10.

Nicotiana langsdorffii

↔ 15 in (38 cm) ↕ 5 ft (1.5 m)

From Brazil. Upright tall annual with dark green, deeply veined, ovate leaves. Masses of twiggy flower spikes, lime green tubular-shaped flowers, in summer. Zones 8–11.

Nicotiana mutabilis

↔ 3–6 ft (0.9–1.8 m)
↕ 3–6 ft (0.9–1.8 m)

From Brazil. Tender perennial often treated as annual. Basal foliage clump hidden by airy sprays of long-tubed white flowers, ageing to pink, on stems to 6 ft (1.8 m) high, in summer. Zones 9–12.

Nicotiana × sanderae

↔ 10 in (25 cm)
↕ 15–24 in (38–60 cm)

Garden hybrid between *N. alata* and *N. forgetiana*. Bushy hairy-leafed annual. Slightly crinkled, wavy, dark green, ovate leaves. Fragrant, flaring, tubular flowers, red, purple, and white, open all day. **Avalon Mixed,** 8 in (20 cm) high, bushy, spreading, all colors, including bicolors; **Eau de Cologne Mix,** upright flower stems to 20 in (50 cm) tall, all colors, good scent; **Hummingbird Mix,** 12 in (30 cm) high and wide, all colors; **Nikki Series,** prolonged flowering, red, pink, yellow, and white on stems to 16 in (40 cm) high. Zones 7–10.

Nicotiana sylvestris

↔ 18–24 in (45–60 cm)
↕ 3–5 ft (0.9–1.5 m)

Native to Argentina. Vigorous annual with very large sticky leaves. Tall stems bear terminal panicles of long, white, pendulous flowers, very fragrant, in summer. Zones 8–11.

NIEREMBERGIA

CUPFLOWER

There are about 23 species of annuals, perennials, and subshrubs in this genus, which is a member of the nightshade (Solanaceae) family. They are native to South America where they grow in moist sunny situations. They are slender-stemmed plants, either creeping, spreading, or erect, with small narrow leaves. The showy flowers are open and upward-facing, in shades of blue, purple, or white, often with yellow throats. They are borne for long periods from summer to autumn.
CULTIVATION: Grow in a sunny sheltered position in a gritty moisture-retentive soil. In cold climates grow in pots or as annuals. Plants flower in the first year from seed. Propagate all species from seed, and perennials also by division or from cuttings.

Nierembergia caerulea

syn. *Nierembergia hippomanica*

↔ 8 in (20 cm) ↕ 8–15 in (20–38 cm)

From Argentina. Small, upright, densely branching perennial often grown as an annual. Narrow pointed leaves. Numerous lavender flowers with yellow throats, in summer. **'Purple Robe'**, darker purple flowers with yellow throats. Zones 9–11.

Nierembergia repens

syn. *Nierembergia rivularis*

↔ 18 in (45 cm) ↕ 2 in (5 cm)

Native to South America. A low spreading rhizomatous perennial with spoon-shaped leaves. Flaring white flowers, about 1 in (25 mm) wide, tinged with yellow or pink at base, in summer. Zones 9–11.

Nierembergia scoparia

syn. *Nierembergia frutescens*

TALL CUPFLOWER

↔ 12 in (30 cm)
↕ 18–24 in (45–60 cm)

An upright, densely branched, annual species from South America. Leaves are spoon-shaped, and flaring flowers, white or violet fading to white at the edges, are borne from summer to early autumn. Zones 8–11.

Nierembergia caerulea 'Purple Robe'

NIGELLA

FENNEL FLOWER, LOVE-IN-A-MIST, WILD FENNEL

This genus of about 15 species of annuals, from the Mediterranean region and western Asia, is a member of the buttercup (Ranunculaceae) family. They are all easy to grow and feature fine green foliage with bushy growth. Flower colors are sky blue and mixes of white, blue, pink, purple, mauve, and rosy red. Nigellas bloom profusely and make good cut flowers. Their decorative seed pods and foliage are also used in dried floral arrangements.
CULTIVATION: Grow in full sun/half-sun in any well-drained soil and fertilize once a month with a relatively high phosphorus fertilizer. Deadhead to prolong flowering. Propagate from seed sown directly where it is to grow, since *Nigella* seedlings resent being transplanted. Plants will reseed.

Nigella damascena

LOVE-IN-A-MIST

↔ 10 in (25 cm) ↕ 20 in (50 cm)

European species. Bright green finely cut foliage, somewhat like fennel. Fluffy flowers, in blue, pink, or white. Make successive plantings for blooms all summer. **'Miss Jekyll'**, semi-double, sky blue flowers. Zones 8–10.

NOLINA

This genus in the asparagus (Asparagaceae) family contains approximately 24 species of evergreen perennials related to *Yucca,* native to southern USA, Mexico, and Guatemala. Adapted to very dry climates, most have swollen bases that are conical, spherical, or bottle-shaped, with thick corky bark. The long narrow leaves are fibrous and tough. Flowers, usually blooming on mature plants, are very small, creamy white, and are borne densely on tall panicles. Some species are often split off into the genus *Beaucarnea*.
CULTIVATION: Most will withstand some frost. Grow outdoors in warm dry climates. In cooler regions grow in the greenhouse, in a well-drained mix. Propagate from seed or offsets.

Nigella damascena 'Miss Jekyll'

Nolina bigelovii

BEARGRASS, SACAHUISTA, SAWGRASS

↔3–5 ft (0.9–1.5 m)
↕3–6 ft (0.9–1.8 m)

Native to southwestern USA and Mexico. Slow-growing with rosettes of stiff narrow leaves that shred into fibers at edges. Plant eventually forms branching trunk. Flowering panicles grow to 10 ft (3 m) tall. Flowers creamy white, small and numerous, in summer. Zones 8–11.

Nolina microcarpa

BEARGRASS, SACAHUISTA, SAWGRASS

↔4 ft (1.2 m) ↕5 ft (1.5 m)

From southwestern USA and Mexico. Stemless species, forming dense tufts of arching grass-like leaves with finely toothed margins. Flowering panicles to 7 ft (2 m) tall. Numerous, small, pale cream flowers, in summer. Zones 6–10.

Nolina parryi

PARRY'S BEARGRASS

↔5 ft (1.5 m) ↕5 ft (1.5 m)

Slow-growing species, native to southwestern USA and Mexico. Eventually forms thick stems, with terminal rosettes of narrow leaves. Very like *N. bigelovii* but leaf edges are minutely toothed and do not shred into fibers. Tiny white flowers on ends of long flower stalks, in summer. Zones 8–11.

Nolina parryi, in the wild, Mexico

NUPHAR

This genus is a member of the waterlily (Nymphaeaceae) family. It contains about 25 species of aquatic perennial herbs, native to temperate regions of the Northern Hemisphere, including Spain, southern Italy, and the Mediterranean. They grow in still or slow-moving water and have large oval to round leaves that may be floating, submerged, or held above the water. Floating and emergent leaves are leathery. The rather small flowers are held above the water and have prominent yellow sepals, with smaller yellow petals.

CULTIVATION: Plant rhizomes in baskets containing a rich soil mix. Baskets can be lowered gradually to acclimatize plants to the water depth. Grow in full sun in still water, although *Nuphar* are more tolerant of shade and water movement than *Nymphaea* species. They can be invasive where conditions suit. Propagate from seed or by division.

Nuphar lutea

YELLOW WATERLILY

↔3–8 ft (0.9–2.4 m)
↕3–15 in (8–38 cm)

Widespread species in northern temperate regions. Invasive plant with broadly oval or rounded, floating or emergent, leathery and shiny leaves. Produces small, globular, bright yellow flowers, in summer. Blooms emit a distinct odor. Zones 4–9.

Nuphar polysepala

↔3–8 ft (0.9–2.4 m)
↕3–15 in (8–38 cm)

Native to North America. Broadly heart-shaped dull green leaves, usually floating. Waxy, yellowish green, globular flowers, in summer. Interiors often tinged brownish purple. Zones 4–9.

Nymphaea alba

NYMPHAEA

A genus of aquatic perennials, in the waterlily (Nymphaeaceae) family, and of varied distribution, in ponds over most of the world. About 50 species, split into hardy and tropical groups. Broadly oval or round leaves, with base cleft in 2 lobes. Flowers, with pointed or rounded petals, cover the color spectrum. They may be on stalks above the foliage, or sit at water level. Some are fragrant or night-opening.

CULTIVATION: Hardy water lilies are suitable for permanent pond positions in temperate climates. Tropical plants need a summer water temperature of 65–70°F (18–21°C), and a winter temperature of 50°F (10°C). Plant rhizomes in baskets in a rich soil mix, the water depth varying with plant size. Grow in full sun in still water. Overcrowded plants produce smaller flowers and the foliage lifts above the water. Propagate by dividing rhizomes.

Nymphaea alba

EUROPEAN WHITE LILY

↔3–10 ft (0.9–3 m)
↕3–15 in (8–38 cm)

Species native to temperate Eurasia and northern Africa. Rounded leaves, 12 in (30 cm) across, red when young, becoming dark green. Floating white flowers, to 8 in (20 cm) wide, open during day, in summer. Zones 5–9.

Nymphaea caerulea

syn. *Nymphaea capensis*

CAPE BLUE WATERLILY

↔3–12 ft (0.9–3.5 m)
↕3–15 in (8–38 cm)

From southern and eastern Africa. Round wavy-edged leaves, to 16 in (40 cm) wide. Fragrant blue flowers, held well above foliage, open during day, in spring–summer. **'Colorata'** (syn. *N. colorata*), smaller leaves with overlapping lobes, and smaller, mauve to blue flowers. Zones 10–12.

Nuphar polysepala

Nymphaea gigantea

Nymphaea caerulea 'Colorata'

Nymphaea × *daubenyana*

↔3–6 ft (0.9–1.8 m)
↕3–15 in (8–38 cm)

Hybrid of garden origin. Small, fragrant, light blue flowers held well above the water. New plants arise within the axils of leaves and stalks. Day-opening, in spring–summer. Zones 11–12.

Nymphaea gigantea

AUSTRALIAN WATERLILY

↔3–12 ft (0.9–3.5 m)
↕3–15 in (8–38 cm)

Native to tropical areas of Australia and New Guinea. Large leaves, often up to 24 in (60 cm) in diameter. Day-opening flowers, to 12 in (30 cm) wide, sky blue to purple-blue, prominent yellow stamens, from spring to summer. Zones 11–12.

Nymphaea lotus

EGYPTIAN WATERLILY, LOTUS, WHITE LILY

↔3–12 ft (0.9–3.5 m)
↕3–15 in (8–38 cm)

From Egypt and tropical southeastern Africa. Large, rounded, wavy-edged leaves to 20 in (50 cm) wide. Flowers, to 10 in (25 cm), white, fragrant, usually night-opening, closing the following noon, from spring to summer. Zones 11–12.

Nymphaea nouchali

syn. *Nymphaea stellata*

↔3–12 ft (0.9–3.5 m)
↕3–15 in (8–38 cm)

Native to southern and southeastern Asia. Bright green round or oval leaves, to 6 in (15 cm) wide. Flowers to 5 in (12 cm) wide, open during day, vary from blue to pink or white, in spring–summer. Zones 11–12.

Nymphaea, Hybrid Cultivar, Hardy, 'Colorado'

Nymphaea, HC, Tropical Day-Blooming, 'Margaret Randig'

Nymphaea, HC, Tropical Night-Blooming, 'Trudy Slocum'

Nymphaea odorata

FRAGRANT WATERLILY, POND LILY

↔3–8 ft (0.9–2.4 m)
↕3–15 in (8–38 cm)

From eastern USA. Round dull green leaves to 10 in (25 cm) wide. Fragrant white flowers open during day, in summer. *N. o.* subsp. *odorata,* more robust form from northeastern USA, flowers to 9 in (22 cm) diameter. Zones 3–10.

Nymphaea tetragona

syn. *Nymphaea pygmaea*

PYGMY WATERLILY

↔12–48 in (30–120 cm)
↕3–15 in (8–38 cm)

Found throughout Europe, Asia, and Japan. Small, oval, dark green leaves, dull red beneath. Slightly fragrant flowers, about 2 in (5 cm) wide, white with yellow stamens, in summer. **'Alba'**, small leaves, purple beneath, white flowers. Zones 3–9.

Nymphaea Hybrid Cultivars

Nymphaea hybrids are divided into hardy and tropical hybrids, with the tropical hybrids further divided into day- and night-blooming hybrids.

HARDY HYBRIDS

↔3–8 ft (0.9–2.4 m)
↕3–15 in (8–38 cm)

These hybrids are suitable for cooler climates. Day-blooming flowers are usually held close to water level and include all colors except blue shades. Some are "changeables," which alter their coloring dramatically as they age. **'Charlene Strawn'**, scented yellow flowers held above water; **'Charlie's Choice'**, changeable, apricot-yellow turning to nearly red; **'Colorado'**, salmon, deepening near center; **'Fire Crest'**, scented clear pink flowers with red stamens; **'Gladstoneana'**, large white flowers with gold stamens; **'Gonnère'**, large pure white flowers; **'James Brydon'**, large-cupped, bright red, scented flowers; **'Odorata Sulphurea Grandiflora'**, mottled leaves and large, starry, bright yellow flowers; **'Pink Sensation'**, rich pink flowers held above water; **'Pygmaea Helvola'**, mottled leaves, bright yellow flowers, orange stamens; **'Texas Dawn'**, large yellow flowers; **'William B. Shaw'**, large creamy pink flowers; **'William Falconer'**, blood red flowers with yellow stamens.

The Marliacean hybrids were originated by Joseph Marliac in the mid-nineteenth century. Many of the hardy hybrids he developed are still extremely popular, such as: **'Marliacea Albida'**, white; **'Marliacea Carnea'**, soft pink with yellow stamens; **'Marliacea Chromatella'**, soft yellow; **'Marliacea Ignea'**, deep crimson. Zones 3–10.

TROPICAL DAY-BLOOMING HYBRIDS

↔3–12 ft (0.9–3.5 m)
↕3–15 in (8–38 cm)

These hybrids need a water temperature of 70°F (21°C). Some produce flowers to 15 in (38 cm) wide. All colors, including blue shades, are covered. Flowers are usually held above the foliage. **'Evelyn Randig'**, hot pink flowers; **'General Pershing'**, deep pink fragrant flowers, to 12 in (30 cm) across; **'Margaret Randig'**, deep blue-purple scented flowers; **'Marion Strawn'**, starry, white, fragrant flowers; **'Mrs George H. Pring'**, scented, white, star-shaped flowers, to 10 in (25 cm) across; **'Pamela'**, starry sky blue flowers; **'Panama Pacific'**, deep plum flowers with yellow stamens; and **'Pink Platter'**, open soft pink flowers. Zones 11–12.

TROPICAL NIGHT-BLOOMING HYBRIDS

↔3–12 ft (0.9–3.5 m)
↕3–15 in (8–38 cm)

These plants need a water temperature of 70°F (21°C). Flowers open about dusk and close by the following noon. They are mostly in shades of red, pink, and white. **'Emily Grant Hutchings'**, rich pinkish red cupped flowers, to 12 in (30 cm) wide; **'Mrs George C. Hitchcock'**, large clear pink flowers with orange stamens; **'Red Flare'**, starry, vivid red, scented flowers; **'Rosa de Noche'**, pink flowers with yellow centers; **'Sir Galahad'**, flowers of starry white with yellow stamens; **'Sturtevantii'**, pearly pink scented flowers; and **'Trudy Slocum'**, large, flat, white flowers with yellow stamens. Zones 11–12.

NYSSA

This is a small genus that includes about 5 species of deciduous trees from North America and eastern and southeastern Asia. It is a member of the dogwood (Cornaceae) family. They are all noted for their spectacular foliage in autumn, which ranges in color from soft green, pale yellow, gold to orange, and brown. Most species inhabit moist land on the edges of streams, lakes, and swamps, and are rarely successful on dry soils. The leaves are simple, the flowers are inconspicuous, and the fruits small and bluish. They are named after the water nymph of Greek mythology because of their liking for a reliable water supply.

CULTIVATION: These plants prefer well-drained, moist, fertile soil in full sun or part-shade. Little pruning is required, apart from the removal of competing leaders in the early stages. Propagate from seeds collected as soon as they are ripe in autumn. Sow immediately, before they dry out. Alternatively, they can be propagated from half-hardened cuttings in mid-summer.

Nyssa aquatica

COTTON GUM, TUPELO GUM, WATER TUPELO

↔15 ft (4.5 m) ↕50 ft (15 m)

Native to southeastern USA, rare both in the wild and in cultivation. Erect stems, dome-shaped crown. Leaves ovate-oblong, downy underneath, serrated. Flowers greenish white, in axillary clusters, in summer. Fruit deep mauve. Zones 5–10.

Nyssa sinensis

CHINESE TUPELO

↔30 ft (9 m) ↕40 ft (12 m)

Rare species from China, beautiful small tree or large shrub, open habit. Leaves narrowly ovate, to 6 in (15 cm) long, juvenile foliage red. Leaves turn to almost every shade of red and yellow, in autumn. Zones 7–10.

Nyssa sylvatica ★

BLACK GUM, BLACK TUPELO, SOUR GUM, TUPELO

↔30 ft (9 m) ↕50 ft (15 m)

Native to North America, from Canada to the Gulf of Mexico. Deciduous tree with predominantly horizontal branches. Smooth-edged leaves, shiny dark green, paler beneath; turn various shades of orange, scarlet, and purplish red in autumn. Small bluish black fruits. Thrives in wet marshy conditions. **'Sheffield Park'**, leaves start to color 2 to 3 weeks earlier than type; **'Wisley Bonfire'**, fine autumn coloring, symmetrical form. Zones 3–10.

Nyssa sinensis

Nyssa sylvatica 'Wisley Bonfire'

N

O

OCIMUM

BASIL

This genus encompasses 35 species of annuals and perennials from tropical and subtropical Africa and Asia that are known for their aromatic foliage. These herbs belong to the mint (Lamiaceae) family and are generally erect bushy plants, with a distinctive branching habit and narrow oval to elliptic leaves. Their foliage varies from pale to dark green through to dark red and purple. Whorls of tiny tubular flowers appear on short spikes in summer and vary from white to creamy green. The foliage is used to flavor a range of dishes. These herbs have become favorites with many, and they are often referred to as the summer herb. Basil was probably first cultivated in India, where it is sacred and is dedicated to the gods Vishnu and Krishna.

CULTIVATION: Some basil species may be temperamental to grow. These plants need moist well-drained soil in a warm sunny position to thrive and do not tolerate frost or cold temperatures. Pinch back plants regularly to encourage bushy growth. Propagate from seed in summer for the annual species and from stem cuttings for the perennial species.

Ocimum basilicum

BASIL, SWEET BASIL

↔12 in (30 cm)
↕12–24 in (30–60 cm)

From tropical and subtropical Asia. Upright, erect, bushy annual. Oval mid-green leaves, sometimes slightly serrated around edges, often hairy on topside of leaf. Foliage is used to flavor many dishes. Whorls of creamy white flowers, on short spikes, in summer. Can be invasive, so best grown in pots. Dispose of seed carefully. ***O. b.*** **var. *minimum*** ★, (Greek bush basil) small compact leaves on very tight compact plant, short white flowers in summer, good flavor. ***O. b.*** **'Dark Opal'** (purple leaf basil), dark red-purple, sometimes curly leaves, pale creamy green stems, pale pink flowers; **'Fino Verde Compatto'** (Italian basil), compact plant, small mid-green leaves; **'Lemon Sweet Danny'**, pointed, pale green, lemon-scented foliage, weak plant; **'Mini Purple'**, dwarf compact plant, dark purple foliage, hint of green through leaves; **'Napolitano'**, large, crinkled, lettuce-like leaves; **'Purple Ruffles'**, strongly aromatic, large, purplish, glossy leaves, serrated edges; **'Red Rubin'** ★, a selection from 'Dark Opal', more uniform and compact habit, foliage stays rich red-purple for longer in summer; **'Ruffles'** ★, green foliage, curly and frilly leaf edges; **'Siam Queen'**, bushy, compact plant, long, narrow, fragrant leaves, rosy purple flowers, high foliage yields make it popular in the culinary trade, licorice flavor. Zones 10–12.

Ocimum basilicum 'Dark Opal'

Ocimum basilicum 'Lemon Sweet Danny'

OEMLERIA

This single-species genus, belonging to the rose (Rosaceae) family, consists of a deciduous shrub that is closely related to *Prunus*. It is found in the moist woodlands of North America's west coast. The slender erect branches have oblong, glossy, green leaves that are gray and slightly downy beneath. White male and female flowers are borne on separate plants.

CULTIVATION: Suitable for woodland plantings and shady borders. Grow in good moist soil in a shady situation. Prune after flowering to remove old and dead shoots. Propagate from seed, cuttings, or the removal of suckers.

Oemleria cerasiformis ★

syn. *Osmaronia cerasiformis*

OREGON PLUM, OSO BERRY

↔12 ft (3.5 m) ↕8 ft (2.4 m)

Found along North America's west coast, from British Columbia, Canada, to California, USA. Suckering shrub, smooth gray stems. Spring foliage has a very fresh appearance. Dainty white flowers, in pendulous racemes, scented like almonds, in late winter–early spring. Plum-like fruits ripening to purple on female trees. Zones 6–10.

OENANTHE

This genus in the carrot (Apiaceae) family contains 30 species of perennial herbs. They are native to damp habitats of the Northern Hemisphere and southern Africa. The foliage is usually pinnately divided into small leaflets, and the tiny white flowers are borne on umbels, typical of the family. Some species are very poisonous while, conversely, *O. javanica* is cultivated as a vegetable in Asia.

CULTIVATION: These plants are suitable for naturalizing in wild gardens. Grow in damp fertile soil in full sun/shade. Propagate from cuttings or seed or by division.

Oenanthe javanica

syn. *Oenanthe japonica*

WATER CELERY, WATER DROPWORT

↔12–16 in (30–40 cm)
↕12–16 in (30–40 cm)

Found from India to Japan and into southeastern Asia. Grows in very boggy ground. The divided foliage resembles celery leaves. Umbels of small white flowers in summer. Grown as a leafy vegetable crop in Asia. **'Flamingo'**, variegated form with green, cream, and pink leaves. Zones 9–12.

OENOTHERA

EVENING PRIMROSE

A genus of more than 120 species of annuals, biennials, and perennials in the evening-primrose (Onagraceae) family, found in temperate zones of the Americas. Some have tap roots and tend to be upright, others have fibrous roots and a more sprawling habit. Apart from their use in homeopathic medicines, these plants are grown mainly for their short-lived but pretty summer flowers, which are cup-shaped, 4-petalled, and mainly yellow, sometimes pink, in color. The common name reflects the

Ocimum basilicum 'Purple Ruffles'

Oemleria cerasiformis

predominantly yellow flower color and the fact that many species open from evening or night, sometimes not lasting beyond the following morning. Elongated seed capsules follow.
CULTIVATION: Mostly very hardy, these tough adaptable plants prefer full sun and light, gritty, free-draining soil. Summer watering produces stronger growth, but they will tolerate drought if necessary. Fibrous-rooted species can be divided when dormant, otherwise propagate from seed or basal cuttings. May self-sow and naturalize.

Oenothera 'Crown Imperial'

Oenothera 'Lemon Sunset'

Oenothera acaulis

☼ ✱ ↔16–24 in (40–60 cm)
↑6 in (15 cm)

Chilean biennial or perennial. Spreading clump of often red-tinted stems. Irregularly lobed pinnate leaves. White flowers, ageing to pale pink, to 3 in (8 cm) wide, in summer. Zones 5–10.

Oenothera biennis

COMMON EVENING PRIMROSE

☼ ✱ ↔16–20 in (40–50 cm)
↑5 ft (1.5 m)

Annual or biennial from eastern North America. Basal rosettes of broad lance-shaped leaves, shallowly toothed. Erect flower stems, numerous, 1 in (25 mm) wide, bright yellow flowers open from red-tinted buds, color deepening with age, in summer–autumn. Zones 4–9.

Oenothera caespitosa

FRAGRANT EVENING PRIMROSE, WHITE EVENING PRIMROSE

☼ ✱ ↔24 in (60 cm)
↑4–10 in (10–25 cm)

Low, bushy, mounding perennial from western USA. Loose rosettes of variably sized leaves, narrow lance- to spatula-shaped, shallowly toothed, wavy edges. Fragrant white flowers, to 2½ in (6 cm) wide, in summer. Zones 4–9.

Oenothera 'Crown Imperial'

☼ ❄ ↔12 in (30 cm)
↑16–20 in (40–50 cm)

Hybrid of undeclared parentage. Forms clump of bright green, lance-shaped, basal leaves. Upright flower stems, fritillary-like heads of bright yellow flowers, to over 1¼ in (30 mm) wide, in summer. Zones 7–10.

Oenothera elata

☼ ❄ ↔12 in (30 cm) ↑40 in (100 cm)

North American perennial. Basal rosettes, gray-green, lance-shaped leaves. Upright flower stems; heads of many bright yellow flowers, to 2 in (5 cm) wide, in summer. ***O. e.*** **subsp. *hookeri***, shorter, pale yellow flowers, widely studied due to medically promising extracts. Zones 7–10.

Oenothera fruticosa

☼ ✱ ↔12–16 in (30–40 cm)
↑20–32 in (50–80 cm)

Sometimes short-lived biennial or perennial from eastern North America. Leaves to over 4 in (10 cm) long, lance-shaped, midrib and stems usually red-tinted. Heads of golden yellow flowers, in summer. ***O. f.*** **subsp. *glauca***, broad blue-green leaves, red-tinted when young. ***O. f.*** **'Fyrverkeri'** (syns 'Feuerwerkeri', 'Fireworks'), foliage tinted purple-red, bright yellow flowers. Zones 4–9.

Oenothera 'Lemon Sunset'

☼ ✱ ↔16–32 in (40–80 cm)
↑40 in (100 cm)

Erect hybrid perennial of uncertain parentage. Forms mounding clump of small deep green leaves. Red stems; fragrant flowers, to 4 in (10 cm) wide, light yellow, ageing to deep pink or red, in summer. Zones 5–9.

Oenothera macrocarpa

MISSOURI PRIMROSE, OZARK SUNDROPS

☼ ✱ ↔16–32 in (40–80 cm)
↑8–16 in (20–40 cm)

Spreading, sometimes mounding perennial from south-central USA. Stems initially erect then sprawling; somewhat downy leaves, to 3 in (8 cm) long. Bright yellow flowers, to 4 in (10 cm) wide, in summer. Zones 5–9.

Oenothera perennis

SUNDROPS

☼ ✱ ↔16–32 in (40–80 cm)
↑8–20 in (20–50 cm)

Sprawling, often partly erect perennial from eastern North America. Wiry, sometimes branching stems. Narrow leaves, sparsely hairy, often irregularly toothed. Open heads of bright yellow flowers, in summer. Zones 5–9.

Oenothera speciosa

WHITE EVENING PRIMROSE

☼ ✱ ↔12–24 in (30–60 cm)
↑12–24 in (30–60 cm)

Perennial from southwestern USA and Mexico. Upright mounding habit; rosettes of broad lance-shaped leaves, usually irregularly toothed, sometimes lobed. Flowers open white, ageing to deep pink, in summer–early autumn. **'Alba'**, white flowers; **'Rosea'**, pale pink flowers; **'Siskiyou'**, pale pink to mauve flowers; **'Twilight Primrose'**, light pink to near-white at center, purplish spring foliage. Zones 5–10.

Oenothera versicolor

☼ ✱ ↔16 in (40 cm) ↑24 in (60 cm)

Native range unclear, possibly of garden origin. Upright perennial; red-tinted stems; narrow elliptic leaves taper to a fine point, toothed. Terminal heads of bright orange flowers ageing to red, in summer. Zones 6–10.

Oenothera speciosa 'Siskiyou'

Oenothera speciosa 'Alba'

OLEA

OLIVE

This genus, belonging to the olive (Oleaceae) family, includes some 20 species of evergreen shrubs and trees with a wide distribution in the warm-temperate areas of the world (excluding the Americas). With age, the branches become wonderfully gnarled and twisted. Each leaf is usually a simple narrow ellipse, deep green above and greenish white below. The flowers are massed in panicles. They are followed by the familiar fleshy drupes, each of which contains a hard pit or stone.

CULTIVATION: Olives vary in hardiness, though none are very frost tolerant, especially when young. If grown for their fruit, olives require a climate with distinct seasons. Flowering, cropping, and ripening are invariably best on trees grown in full sun with relatively mild winters and long hot summers that gradually decline into autumn. Olives are tolerant of most soils and are very drought tolerant once established; fertile well-drained soil will yield a better crop. Propagate from seed, heel cuttings, or suckers.

Olea europaea

COMMON OLIVE

↔20 ft (6 m) ↕20–30 ft (6–9 m)

In cultivation since ancient times, evergreen tree from the Mediterranean region. Gnarled branches, fissured bark with age. Leaves leathery, silver undersides. Very long lived. Fruit not edible off the tree, must be processed. ***O. e.* subsp. *cuspidata*** (syns *O. africana, O. cuspidata* and *O. e. subsp. africana*), to 25 ft (8 m) high, makes a good shade tree, self-seeds quite freely, can become invasive; leaves not silvery, pea-sized globular fruit. ***O. e.* 'Frantoio'**, self-fertile, small fruit, top-quality commercial oil cultivar; **'Hardy's Mammoth'**, quick-growing, large edible fruit; **'Kalamata'**, good pickling fruit, medium size; **'Lugano'**, elongated, brownish fruit, good taste, usually preserved in strong brine; **'Manzanillo'** ★, leathery leaves, edible black fruit; **'Mission'**, vigorous cold-hardy cultivar; **'Sevillano'** (syn. 'Spanish Queen'), good fruit, large yield, best pickled. Zones 8–10.

OLNEYA

This single-species genus belongs to the pea-flower subfamily of the legume (Fabaceae) family. The sole member is a tree native to arid regions of southwestern North America. This evergreen tree is short-trunked, often with multiple stems, and a broad spreading crown. In periods of intense cold or drought, it is deciduous. In the wild, new leaves emerge shortly after the clusters of pea-flowers, following spring rains. The seeds are edible once they are roasted. The genus is named for Stephan Olney, a nineteenth century American botanist.

CULTIVATION: This small tree is best grown in full sun in very well-drained soil. Propagate from seed.

Olea europaea

Olneya tesota

DESERT IRONWOOD

↔12–25 ft (3.5–8 m) ↕15–30 ft (4.5–9 m)

Native to southwestern USA and northern Mexico. Broad-crowned tree. Grayish green pinnately divided leaves, to 2 in (5 cm) long. Produces clusters of pink to light purple pea-flowers, in spring. Zones 8–10.

OMPHALODES

NAVELSEED, NAVELWORT

There are about 28 species of annuals, biennials, and perennials in this genus, which belongs to the borage (Boraginaceae) family. They are native to Europe, northern Africa, Asia, and Mexico, where they grow in habitats such as shady rocks and cliffs, damp woodland, or streamsides. The leaves vary from heart-shaped to lance-shaped and may be slightly hairy. The small blue or white flowers are borne in terminal clusters, in spring or early summer, and resemble forget-me-nots. The common and botanical names arise from the seed vessel's apparent resemblance to a navel.

CULTIVATION: Most species prefer a cool, somewhat shaded situation in any moist but well-drained soil high in organic matter. Low-growing species are suitable for rockeries or make excellent ground covers, while taller plants can be grown in the border. Propagate all species from seed in spring. Perennials can also be propagated by division in autumn, but care should be taken as they resent root disturbance.

Omphalodes cappadocica

NAVELWORT

↔12–18 in (30–45 cm) ↕8 in (20 cm)

Native to Turkey. Perennial, forming low clumps of heart-shaped leaves. Small, blue, forget-me-not flowers, in early to mid-summer. **'Cherry Ingram'**, taller vigorous form, deeper blue flowers; **'Starry Eyes'**, darker blue central stripe on each pale petal, creating a starry effect. Zones 6–9.

Omphalodes linifolia

VENUS' NAVELWORT

↔6–10 in (15–25 cm) ↕12–18 in (30–45 cm)

From western Europe. Annual with narrow grayish green leaves. Sprays of slightly scented white flowers, borne profusely in summer. Unlike other members of the genus, should be grown in a sunny situation. Zones 6–9.

Omphalodes verna

BLUE-EYED MARY, CREEPING FORGET-ME-NOT

↔24 in (60 cm) ↕6 in (15 cm)

Native to Europe. Low-growing perennial, suitable for ground cover. Long, creeping, rooting stems; pointed oval to heart-shaped leaves. White-centered, blue, forget-me-not flowers, in spring. Zones 6–9.

ONOCLEA

BEAD FERN, SENSITIVE FERN

This genus contains a single species of deciduous fern which belongs to the cliff-fern (Woodsiaceae) family. It is native to eastern North America

Olea europaea subsp. *cuspidata*

Omphalodes cappadocica 'Cherry Ingram'

and eastern Asia where it grows in damp grassy or woodland areas. Fronds are pale green, often bronze-pink on opening, and sterile and fertile fronds are different in appearance. The common name of sensitive fern arises because the leaflets of the sterile fronds fold together in cold weather. The other common name refers to the bead-like leaflets of the fertile fronds.

CULTIVATION: Grow in damp soil in part-shade. Suitable for waterside and woodland gardens. Can be invasive where conditions suit. Propagate by division or from spores.

Onoclea sensibilis

↔ 24 in (60 cm)
↕ 36 in (90 cm)

From eastern North America and eastern Asia. Spreading fern with triangular, pinnate, sterile fronds to 36 in (90 cm) long. Fertile fronds, to 24 in (60 cm) long, are narrow with bead-like leaflets, and persist over winter. Zones 4–9.

OPHIOPOGON

MONDO GRASS

This is a small genus of 4 species of evergreen perennials from Japan belonging to the asparagus (Asparagaceae) family. They form clumps of grassy leaves and in summer bear small lily-like flowers of white to purple which are followed by blue-black berries. These plants are cultivated for their attractive foliage and are popular both as ground covers and for edging.

CULTIVATION: Grow in full sun or part-shade in moist but well-drained soil. All species will withstand at least short periods of frost but in cooler areas can be treated as bedding or container plants. Propagate from seed or by division.

Ophiopogon japonicus

↔ 18 in (45 cm) ↕ 12 in (30 cm)

Native to Japan; popular species for ground cover. Very narrow, dark green, curving leaves form dense mats. White to pale lilac flowers, on short stems, in summer. **'Kyoto Dwarf'**, very tightly clumped, grows 2–4 in (5–10 cm) high; **'Nana'**, slightly taller, to 5–6 in (12–15 cm) high; **'Silver Dragon'**, dense and compact, several white stripes along length of leaf; **'Silver Edge'**, white variegation, mainly at leaf edge, high rust-resistance; **'Silver Mist'**, white and very dark green variegated foliage. Zones 7–10.

Ophiopogon planiscapus

↔ 18 in (45 cm)
↕ 12–18 in (30–45 cm)

From Japan. Similar to *O. japonicus*; usually seen as cultivar **'Nigrescens'** (syns 'Arabicus', 'Black Dragon', 'Ebony Knight'), commonly known as black mondo grass. Lower growing plant, purple-black foliage. Zones 6–10.

OPUNTIA

PRICKLY PEAR, TUNA

This genus in the cactus (Cactaceae) family contains more than 180 species that grow throughout the Americas, from southern Canada to the most southerly part of South America, and also in the West Indies and Galapagos Islands. They range widely from high-altitude to temperate-region and tropical lowland species. They have stem segments that are highly variable. The flowers are cup- or funnel-shaped and appear in spring and summer, followed by prickly egg-shaped fruits. Some species have become invasive. Most species have bristles that break off; these can cause irritation when they penetrate and stick in the skin.

CULTIVATION: Opuntias do not like having their roots confined. Those grown outdoors do best in sandy, humus-enriched, well-drained soil that is moderately fertile. Frost-hardy species need protection from too much winter wet, and should be grown in full sun under glass, with the light filtered in hot summers. Feed regularly from spring to summer, and reduce or stop watering during winter months. Propagate in spring by sowing pre-soaked seed or by rooting stem segments.

Opuntia aciculata

syn. *Opuntia lindheimeri*

CHENILLE PRICKLY PEAR

↔ 36–60 in (90–150 cm)
↕ 36–60 in (90–150 cm)

Shrubby species native to southwestern USA and northwestern Mexico. The flattened oblong to round stem segments are dotted with tufts of yellowish brown spines and bristles. The flowers are yellow or red, and are borne in spring–summer. Zones 9–11.

Opuntia basilaris ★

BEAVER TAIL CACTUS

↔ 4 ft (1.2 m) ↕ 2–3 ft (0.6–0.9 m)

Perennial cactus, native to southwestern USA and northwestern Mexico. Oblong to rounded fleshy stems are bluish gray, often tinged with red, dotted with tufts of reddish bristles. Purplish red flowers, in summer. Zones 7–11.

Ophiopogon planiscapus 'Nigrescens'

Opuntia macrocentra

Opuntia humifusa

PRICKLY PEAR CACTUS

↔ 36 in (90 cm)
↕ 8–12 in (20–30 cm)

From eastern North America. Forms spreading clumps of fleshy dull green leaves made up of sections that are lightly spiny. Yellow frilly flowers in early summer. Dark red fruit, inedible. Zones 5–10.

Opuntia littoralis

↔ 12–48 in (30–120 cm)
↕ 12–24 in (30–60 cm)

Native to southwestern USA and northwestern Mexico. Sprawling shrub. Flattened oblong to nearly round stem segments, dotted with tufts of yellowish bristles and brown spines. Flowers yellow with red centers, in spring–summer. Red fruit. ***O. l.* var. *vaseyi***, salmon flowers. Zones 9–11.

Opuntia macrocentra

syn. *Opuntia violacea var. macrocentra*

BLACK-SPINE PRICKLY PEAR

↔ 4 ft (1.2 m) ↕ 4 ft (1.2 m)

Native to southwestern USA and northern Mexico. Sprawling shrub. Flat, nearly round, purplish gray stem segments covered with long black spines. Bright yellow flowers, red at base, in spring–summer. Zones 9–11.

Opuntia microdasys ★

↔ 18–24 in (45–60 cm)
↕ 18–24 in (45–60 cm)

From central and northern Mexico. Thicket-forming shrub. Oblong, flattened, green stem segments, to 6 in (15 cm) long, densely dotted with tufts of yellow bristles. Yellow flowers, often tinged red, in spring–summer. **'Albispina'**, darker green segments, white bristles. Zones 8–11.

Opuntia littoralis var. *vaseyi*

Opuntia basilaris

Opuntia phaeacantha

Opuntia phaeacantha

PURPLE-FRUITED PRICKLY PEAR

↔48 in (120 cm)
↑12–36 in (30–90 cm)

Sprawling shrub found across southwestern USA and Mexico. Stem segments flattened. Clusters of fierce 2½ in (6 cm) spines stud surfaces and edges. Bright yellow flowers, often reddish within, in spring or following rain. Pear-shaped purple-red fruits. Zones 7–11.

Opuntia polyacantha

PLAINS PRICKLY PEAR, STARVATION PRICKLY PEAR

↔48 in (120 cm) ↑12 in (30 cm)

Mat-forming cactus found from northern Mexico to Canada. Flattened round stem segments. Clusters of 5 to 10 blue-green spines, 2 in (5 cm) long. The flowers, yellow to yellow-green, appear in spring–summer. Dry, rather spiny, 1 in (25 mm) long fruits. Zones 3–10.

Opuntia stricta

PRICKLY PEAR

↔5 ft (1.5 m) ↑6 ft (1.8 m)

From southeastern USA to northern Venezuela, naturalized in various countries. Erect or prostrate bush. Blue-green oblong to cylindrical stem segments, spines few, curved and flattened, stems sometimes spineless. Yellow flowers, in summer. Rounded purple fruit. Zones 9–12.

Opuntia strigil

↔4–7 ft (1.2–2 m)
↑24–40 in (60–100 cm)

Native to southwestern USA and northern Mexico. Erect or sprawling shrub. Flattened oblong stem segments, dotted with tufts of reddish brown bristles and spines. Creamy white flowers, in spring–summer. Zones 7–11.

ORIGANUM

Found from the Mediterranean region to East Asia and known mainly as a genus of perennials, including some of the best-known culinary herbs, this genus belongs to the mint (Lamiaceae) family. *Origanum* also includes a few subshrubs that can become shrubby in mild climates, though they tend to be short lived. They have aromatic foliage on stems that are often noticeably 4-angled. Their flowers are borne in spikes, usually with conspicuous bracts that enclose the flowers, and may be brightly colored, often in rose shades. CULTIVATION: Most species are very easily grown in any sunny position with light well-drained soil. They can be trimmed to shape and usually need a few damaged stems removed after winter. Hardiness varies with the species, although most will tolerate moderate frosts. Propagate the shrubby species from seed, small half-hardened cuttings, or by layering.

Origanum amanum

↔6 in (15 cm) ↑2–4 in (5–10 cm)

Native to eastern Mediterranean and Turkey. Slow-growing mat-forming plant. Light green heart-shaped leaves. Tubular rosy pink flowers, on whorled spikes, from late summer–autumn. Zones 8–10.

Origanum dictamnus

DITTANY OF CRETE

↔8–12 in (20–30 cm)
↑8–12 in (20–30 cm)

Small, very pretty, Cretan evergreen shrub. Woolly white leaves, in opposite pairs. Drooping heads of pink flowers, enclosed within large pink bracts, in summer. Wonderful plant for a cool greenhouse. Zones 7–10.

Origanum × hybridum

↔12 in (30 cm) ↑8 in (20 cm)

Hybrid between *O. dictamnus* and *O. sipyleum*. Downy, grayish green, oval leaves. Pink flowers, in drooping clusters of bracts, from late summer to autumn. **'Santa Cruz'**, pink to purple flowers held above foliage. Zones 9–11.

Origanum laevigatum

↔18–24 in (45–60 cm)
↑12–24 in (30–60 cm)

Native to Turkey. Upright plant with suckering rootstock. Well foliaged with small oval leaves. Tubular purple flowers, on numerous airy branching stems, from spring into autumn. **'Herrenhausen'**, leaves and shoots flushed purple when young, pale lilac flowers. Zones 8–10.

Origanum × hybridum 'Santa Cruz'

Origanum libanoticum

Origanum libanoticum

↔18–24 in (45–60 cm)
↑24 in (60 cm)

Native to Lebanon. Upright perennial plant with small oval leaves. Produces pendent airy spikes of pink flowers, with deeper pink bracts, in summer. Zones 8–10.

Origanum majorana

syn. *Majorana hortensis*

KNOTTED MARJORAM, SWEET MARJORAM

↔18 in (45 cm) ↑24 in (60 cm)

Native to the Mediterranean region and naturalized widely throughout Europe. Grown for its grayish green leaves, which are used for flavoring many culinary dishes. Stems root readily where they touch the soil. Produces heads of small white to pink flowers, from late summer to autumn. Zones 7–10.

Origanum rotundifolium

↔12 in (30 cm) ↑12 in (30 cm)

From Turkey and the Caucasus region. Subshrub spreading from rhizomes. Small, round, bluish gray leaves. White to pink flowers, held within drooping, overlapping, green bracts with purplish pink tints, in summer–autumn. Zones 8–10.

Origanum scabrum

↔12–18 in (30–45 cm)
↑12–18 in (30–45 cm)

Native to the mountains of southern Greece. Rhizomatous perennial, small oval to heart-shaped leaves. Small pink flowers, in showy, purplish pink, overlapping bracts, in summer. Zones 8–10.

Origanum vulgare

COMMON MARJORAM, OREGANO, WILD MARJORAM

↔12 in (30 cm)
↑12–18 in (30–45 cm)

Variable species found from Europe to Asia. Popular culinary herb with very aromatic foliage and a stronger, more pungent flavor than marjoram. Dark green oval to round leaves. Produces small pink, purple, or white flowers, from summer to autumn. O. v. var. humile is a compact creeping variety with deep green leaves. O. v. **'Aureum'**

Origanum vulgare 'Gold Tip'

Origanum majorana

has small golden leaves; '**Dr Ietswaart**' is low growing with golden leaves; '**Gold Tip**' has leaves that are tipped with yellow; '**Polyphant**' (syn. 'White Anniversary') has leaves edged with creamy white; '**Thumble's Variety**' has large yellowish green leaves. Zones 5–9.

Origanum Hybrid Cultivars

↔ 12–24 in (30–60 cm)
↑ 4–12 in (10–30 cm)

Some hybrids are grown for their globular flowerheads with shell-like pink to red bracts, while others have less showy flowers but attractive aromatic foliage. '**Barbara Tingey**', small, rounded, bluish leaves, flowers green at first, ageing to rosy pink; '**Betty Rollins**', crowded dark green leaves, small pink flowers, in summer; '**Kent Beauty**', small rounded leaves, small pink flowers enclosed within drooping, overlapping, pink and green bracts; '**Norton Gold**', aromatic bright golden foliage in spring, later becoming greenish gold, pinkish purple flowers. Zones 6–9.

ORNITHOGALUM

CHINCHERINCHEE, STAR OF BETHLEHEM

This genus of around 200 species of bulbs, in the asparagus (Asparagaceae) family, is native to Europe, Western Asia, and Africa, which has over 50 species. Some quickly form large clumps of grassy to strappy leaves, sometimes with a prominent midrib, and can be slightly invasive. In spring or summer, upright conical spikes of white to cream flowers appear, sometimes mildly scented, in whorls of 3, usually starry or cup-shaped, with 6 petals. The botanical name comes from the Greek *ornis*, "bird," and *gala*, "milk"—when spread out a flower resembles a white bird.

CULTIVATION: Most European species tolerate moderate frosts; the South African species may need to be lifted for winter. Plant in a sunny open position in any light well-drained soil. Water well when flowering, dry off afterward. Shorter varieties are suitable for rock gardens; taller ones grow well in borders. Most species multiply rapidly; propagate by simple division or from seed. *Ornithogalum* species may self-sow.

Ornithogalum arabicum ★

↔ 24–48 in (60–120 cm)
↑ 16–30 in (40–75 cm)

Native to the Mediterranean region. Heavily-textured leaves to 24 in (60 cm) long. Flower stem to 32 in (80 cm) long; up to 20 large fragrant white or cream flowers, conspicuous black ovaries, from spring to early summer. Zones 9–10.

Ornithogalum candicans

syn. *Galtonia candicans*

↔ 12 in (30 cm)
↑ 48 in (120 cm)

From Free State and KwaZulu-Natal, South Africa, and Lesotho. Strap-shaped leaves to 30 in (75 cm) long. Fragrant, drooping, bell-shaped, white flowers, base tinged green, in late summer. Zones 5–10.

Ornithogalum dubium ★

↔ 12–20 in (30–50 cm)
↑ 8–12 in (20–30 cm)

Native to South Africa. Hair-fringed lance-shaped leaves, to 4 in (10 cm). Crowded heads of orange, red, yellow, or white flowers, on 12 in (30 cm) stems, in winter–spring. Zones 8–10.

Ornithogalum narbonense

↔ 24–48 in (60–120 cm)
↑ 24–36 in (60–90 cm)

Found from Mediterranean to northern Iran. Very narrow leaves, to 32 in (80 cm) long. Flower stems to 36 in (90 cm) tall; heads of many small flowers, white with fine green center stripe, in spring. Zones 7–10.

Ornithogalum umbellatum

STAR OF BETHLEHEM

↔ 20–32 in (50–80 cm)
↑ 20 in (50 cm)

Perennial from Europe and around the Mediterranean. Very narrow leaves, to 12 in (30 cm) long, with pale mid-vein. Broad heads of small, green-striped, white flowers, in spring. Zones 5–10.

Ornithogalum viridiflora

syn. *Galtonia viridiflora*

↔ 12 in (30 cm) ↑ 36 in (90 cm)

From Free State and KwaZulu-Natal, South Africa, and Lesotho. Bluish green leaves to 24 in (60 cm) long. Pale green bell-shaped flowers, flushed white at petal edges, from late summer. Zones 8–10.

ORONTIUM

GOLDEN CLUB

This genus in the arum (Araceae) family contains a single species of aquatic perennial. It is native to streams and shallow lakes and ponds of North America. The oblong leaves may be floating or upright. The narrow yellow spadix is borne on a long white stalk above a small green spathe, which withers and drops at flowering.

CULTIVATION: Grow in large tubs or as a marginal plant in water 4–18 in (10–45 cm) deep. Grow in full sun in a fertile soil mix. Propagate by division or from seed.

Orontium aquaticum

GOLDEN CLUB

↔ 18–24 in (45–60 cm)
↑ 12–18 in (30–45 cm)

Native to eastern USA. Aquatic perennial with leathery oblong leaves, to 12 in (30 cm) long, dark green with a metallic sheen. Erect white flowering stems, to 24 in (60 cm) long, with narrow yellow spadices, in summer. Zones 7–10.

Ornithogalum arabicum

Ornithogalum dubium

Ornithogalum narbonense

Ornithogalum viridiflora

ORTHOSIPHON

Genus of about 40 species found in tropical regions of Africa, Asia, and Australasia, belonging to the mint (Lamiaceae) family. They are mainly softwooded shrubs with simple leaves in opposite pairs that may be smooth-edged or toothed. The elongated tubular flowers with long prominent stamens are borne in spiked whorls for long periods in spring and summer.
CULTIVATION: Frost tender, these plants prefer a protected sunny or shaded spot and a moist, moderately fertile, well-drained soil. Trim excess growth regularly, especially after flowering, to maintain density. Propagation is usually from seed or from cuttings.

Orthosiphon aristatus

CAT'S MOUSTACHE, CAT'S WHISKERS

↔ 36 in (90 cm) ↕ 36 in (90 cm)

Softwooded shrub occurring from Southeast Asia to northern Australia, often found growing near streams. Dark green ovate leaves, with coarsely toothed margins. Whorls of white or pale mauve flowers with long stamens, borne in terminal racemes, in spring–summer. Zones 10–12.

Orthosiphon aristatus

Osmanthus × *burkwoodii*

Orychophragmus violaceus

ORYCHOPHRAGMUS

There are 2 species of annual or biennial plants in this genus from the cabbage (Brassicaceae) family. They have thin, lyre-shaped, pinnate, toothed basal leaves giving way to simple, ovate stem leaves. The simple 4-petalled flowers are violet and borne in clusters in spring.
CULTIVATION: Can be grown in the border in fertile well-drained soil in full sun. Propagate from seed.

Orychophragmus violaceus

↔ 12 in (30 cm) ↕ 20 in (50 cm)

Native to China, where it is eaten as a leaf vegetable. Variable green leaves. Clusters of purple flowers, held above foliage, in spring. Zones 9–11.

OSMANTHUS

Genus of about 15 species of slow-growing evergreen shrubs and small trees in the olive (Oleaceae) family, all native to East Asia, except 1 or 2 in the USA and 1 in the Caucasus region. All have simple opposite leaves, some with spiny margins, and small, 4-petalled white or yellow flowers, often with a strong perfume suggestive of jasmine or gardenia. Round dark blue fruit. They are valued as ornamentals for their attractive foliage and flowers.
CULTIVATION: Require a moderately fertile well-drained soil and a position in full sun, preferably in a cool moist climate. Propagate from half-hardened cuttings taken in summer or winter.

Osmanthus × *burkwoodii* ★

syn. × *Osmarea burkwoodii*

↔ 10 ft (3 m) ↕ 10 ft (3 m)

Hybrid between *O. delavayi* and *O. decorus*; resilient thick-set shrub. Leaves dark glossy green, leathery, finely toothed. Flowers white, very fragrant, produced in profusion, in late spring. Zones 6–9.

Osmanthus delavayi

↔ 8 ft (2.4 m) ↕ 8 ft (2.4 m)

Slow-growing shrub from western China. Strong arching branches. Leaves smooth, dark green above, paler beneath. Flowers white, highly perfumed, in terminal, occasionally axillary, clusters of 5 or 6, in late winter–spring. Purplish black fruits. '**Heaven Scent**', heavy flowering, dense clusters of blooms, strong fragrance; '**Pearly Gates**', compact, flowers early. Zones 7–9.

Osmanthus delavayi

Osmanthus × *fortunei*

↔ 10 ft (3 m) ↕ 10 ft (3 m)

Hybrid between *O. fragrans* and *O. heterophyllus*, compact robust shrub. Leaves large, prominently veined on uppersurface, edged with sharp teeth, sometimes smooth-edged on mature plants. Small, fragrant, white flowers, in autumn. '**San Jose**', cream to orange flowers. Zones 7–11.

Osmanthus fragrans

FRAGRANT OLIVE, SWEET OLIVE, SWEET OSMANTHUS

↔ 20 ft (6 m) ↕ 20 ft (6 m)

Evergreen species occurring naturally in China and Japan. Normally pruned to a 10 ft (3 m) shrub. Leaves smooth dark green above, paler underneath. Tubular flowers pure white, very fragrant, in late winter to mid-summer. The flowers have been used by the Chinese for centuries for making scented tea. ***O. f.* f. *aurantiacus***, has smooth-edged leaves, orange flowers. Zones 7–11.

Osmanthus heterophyllus

HOLLY OSMANTHUS

↔ 12 ft (3.5 m) ↕ 12 ft (3.5 m)

Evergreen shrub or small tree found on the main islands of Japan as well as Taiwan. Leaves oppositely arranged, smooth, dark glossy green. Small, fragrant, pure white flowers, carried in clusters, in autumn–early winter. '**Aureomarginatus**', leaves margined and splashed with broad patches of pale yellow; '**Aureus**', yellow-edged leaves; '**Goshiki**', cream and red-brown variegated leaves; '**Purpureus**', deep purple-green leaves; '**Variegatus**', leaves irregularly margined, marked with creamy white, lighter color often spreading into center. Zones 7–11.

OSMUNDA

This genus of about 10 species of tall, perennial, deciduous or evergreen, clump-forming ferns in the royal-fern (Osmundaceae) family is found in moist woods and shaded roadsides. Native to temperate and tropical areas in East Asia and North and South America, these deep-rooted ferns are attractive, rugged, and adaptable. In autumn, the green fronds turn a soft golden yellow. The fibrous dense roots may be used as a medium for growing epiphytes or orchids and are rich in nutrients. The unfurled young fronds (called croziers) are gathered in spring and are cooked as a delicacy called fiddleheads.
CULTIVATION: Grow in partial shade in damp soil or at the water's edge. Top-dress in spring with rich compost

and remove dead fronds. Propagate by division in autumn or sow spores when ripe. May take some time to recover after dividing.

Osmunda claytoniana

INTERRUPTED FERN

↔24–36 in (60–90 cm)
↑16–40 in (40–100 cm)

Native to eastern North America. Deciduous fronds grow 24–48 in (60–120 cm) long. Stems round in cross-section, sometimes with fuzzy tufts. Fertile leaflets in middle of frond wither away, leaving a space or interruption, hence the common name. Zones 3–9.

Osmunda regalis

LOCUST FERN, ROYAL FERN

↔36 in (90 cm)
↑24–60 in (60–150 cm)

From North, Central, and South America, Europe, and Asia. Large compound leaves. Broadly oval to oblong, bright green fronds make dense rounded clump. Coppery brown and bronze croziers, in spring. **'Purpurascens'**, red to purplish fronds turn green in early summer; **'Cristata'**, leathery green fronds, maturing to rich golden brown. Zones 3–10.

OSTEOSPERMUM

Mainly from southern Africa, genus in the daisy (Asteraceae) family, with some 70 species of annuals, perennials, and subshrubs. Valued for their carpeting of flowers during the warmer months, year-round in mild areas. They are mainly low, spreading or mounding plants with simple, broadly toothed, elliptic to spatula-shaped leaves. The flowerheads are large, with showy ray florets, mainly in pinks and purples, or white. Disc florets are an unusual purple-blue that contrasts with the golden anthers. The name comes from the Greek *osteon*, "bone," *sperma*, "seed," and refers to the hard seeds.

CULTIVATION: Most will tolerate only light frosts and do better in mild climates. Very good coastal plants. They prefer a sunny position with light well-drained soil. Overwatering can lead to straggly growth. Pinch back and deadhead to keep compact. Propagate annuals from seed and perennials from tip cuttings.

Osteospermum ecklonis

↔20–40 in (50–100 cm)
↑20–40 in (50–100 cm)

South African shrub or subshrub. Narrow, downy, lance-shaped leaves, the edges often irregularly toothed. Ray florets white with deep purple-blue undersides, disc florets blue, appearing throughout most of the year. Zones 8–11.

Osteospermum fruticosum

↔20–40 in (50–100 cm)
↑12–24 in (30–60 cm)

Initially upright, then spreading South African perennial. Woody base; broad, irregularly toothed, lance- to spatula-shaped leaves. Ray florets white with purple-pink undersides, disc florets dusky mauve, year round.
Zones 9–11.

Osteospermum jucundum

syn. *Osteospermum barberae of gardens*

↔20–32 in (50–80 cm)
↑12–20 in (30–50 cm)

Spreading, mounding, South African perennial. Narrow lance-shaped leaves, irregularly toothed. Flowerheads over 4 in (10 cm) wide, ray florets mauve-pink to purple, disc florets purple-black, late spring–autumn. ***O. j.* subsp. *compactum***, high-altitude form, compact growth, many small flowers; **'Purple Mountain'** ★, purple-pink ray florets. ***O. j.* 'Blackthorn Seedling'**, purple-pink ray florets. Zones 8–10.

Osmunda regalis

Osteospermum Hybrid Cultivars

↔16–24 in (40–60 cm)
↑8–12 in (20–30 cm)

Osteospermum species hybridize freely, especially in cultivation, and new forms are constantly being introduced. Most are low spreading. Among the most popular are: **'Buttermilk'**, warm buff-yellow petals, with dark reverse; **'Hopleys'**, pink flowers; **'Pink Whirls'** ★, pink ray florets, crimped, dark reverse; **'Pixie'**, dark green leaves, soft pink flowers; **'Silver Sparkler'**, cream-variegated foliage, white flowers; **'Stardust'**, deep pink flowers; **'Sunny Gustav'**, large white flowers; **'Weet-wood'**, white flowers with blue eye; and **'Whirligig'**, gray-green foliage, dusky gray-green flowers, strongly crimped ray florets. There are also seedling strains: the **Nasinga Series**, various colors, some have crimped ray florets; the **Symphony Series**, mainly bright warm colors. Zones 9–11.

Osteospermum jucundum

Osteospermum, HC, Petite Series, 'Pixie'

Osteospermum, HC, 'Stardust'

OSTRYA

HOP HORNBEAM

This genus in the birch (Betulaceae) family contains about 10 species of deciduous trees related to *Betulus* and *Carpinus*. They grow throughout temperate Northern Hemisphere regions in open woodland. The alternate leaves have conspicuous veining and toothed edges, and are often hairy. The male catkins resemble the flowers of hornbeams *(Carpinus)*. The female flowers, on the same tree, develop into catkins that look like those of hops *(Humulus)*, with overlapping bracts.

CULTIVATION: These slow-growing trees are not common in cultivation. They prefer well-drained fertile soil in either sun or shade, and make good specimen trees. Propagate in spring from fresh seed, in pots protected from frosts. Seed which has dried out must be stratified to break dormancy. Graft cultivars onto *Carpinus betulus* rootstocks in the colder months.

Ostrya carpinifolia

HOP HORNBEAM

↔70 ft (21 m) ↑70 ft (21 m)

Native to southern Europe and Turkey. Shoots with a fine growth of hairs. Green leaves with pointed tips and doubly toothed edges, turning golden to pale yellow in autumn. Female flower clusters creamy white at first, turning brown in autumn. Zones 6–9.

Ostrya virginiana ★

EASTERN HOP HORNBEAM, IRONWOOD

↔35 ft (10 m) ↑50 ft (15 m)

From eastern North America. Dark brown bark. The leaves are dark green above, with paler undersides, lance-shaped, double-serrated edges. The yellow male catkins are produced in the spring; female fruit clusters are white at first, ripening to brown. Zones 4–9.

Ostrya carpinifolia

OTATEA

This Central American genus, a member of the grass (Poaceae) family, is composed of 2 species of shrubby bamboos. They have narrow arching stems, with a dense covering of long, thin, soft green leaves crowded near the end of the stems, creating a plume-like or pompon effect. The exposed parts of the stems turn dark brown to black in their second year. Although they spread by runners, they are not invasive and are easily controlled.
CULTIVATION: Unusually for bamboos, *Otatea* species can be rather reluctant to grow well and often develop into rather sparse clumps. While hardy to light frosts and reasonably drought tolerant once established, they prefer warm conditions with summer moisture and do best in fertile humus-rich soil and a position in full sun or part-shade. They are excellent container plants and also grow well around ponds. Propagation is most commonly by division.

Otatea acuminata

↔ 20 ft (6 m) ↑ 25 ft (8 m)

Bamboo found from Mexico to Nicaragua. Forms large clump of very narrow stems. Stems curve gracefully, moving in the breeze. Narrow leaves, to 6 in (15 cm) long, sheaths fall, revealing distinctive white powder below leaf nodes. ***O. a.* subsp. *aztecorum*** (Mexican weeping bamboo) has culms 1½ in (35 mm) in diameter, mostly obscured by prolific, long, narrow leaves. Zones 10–12.

OTHONNA

This genus belonging to the daisy (Asteraceae) family contains about 150 species of perennials or small shrubs of varying habit, ranging from woody to fleshy and succulent, and erect to sprawling. Most are native to arid regions of South Africa. Leaves vary from smooth to dissected, lobed or toothed, and may be leathery or fleshy. The daisy flowers are yellow.
CULTIVATION: In cool-temperate climates grow in the greenhouse in a moderately fertile sandy soil mix. Water sparingly during the growing period. In warm climates grow outdoors in full sun in perfectly drained soil. Propagate from seed or cuttings.

Othonna capensis

LITTLE PICKLES

↔ 12–18 in (30–45 cm)
↑ 3–6 in (8–15 cm)

From South Africa. Low-growing mat-forming succulent. Thick cylindrical leaves, about 1 in (25 mm) long, resemble jellybeans. Small yellow daisies, on thin stems, borne above the foliage, in summer. Good plant for hanging basket. Zones 9–11.

OXALIS

A huge genus occurring worldwide of about 500 species belonging to the wood-sorrel (Oxalidaceae) family. These mainly bulbous plants also inlude evergreen ground-covering perennials, succulents, and shrubs. Many species have clover-shaped leaves that close at night. Flower buds are rolled like an umbrella and open to bowl- or cup-shaped 5-petalled blooms, some species opening only in full sunlight. Some troublesome weeds belong in *Oxalis*, but many species are highly desirable, sometimes difficult-to-keep collector's plants, so careful selection is advised.
CULTIVATION: The bulbous winter-growers like almost frost-free sunny sites, dry in summer. Evergreen and woodland summer-growing species prefer shade and moist soil. Some succulent and shrubby forms, in all but frost-free climates, should be grown as greenhouse plants. Propagation is from seed sown fresh, by division of bulbous and perennial forms, or from cuttings of shrubby species.

Otatea acuminata subsp. *aztecorum*

Oxalis articulata

Othonna capensis

Oxalis enneaphylla

Oxalis acetosella

CUCKOO BREAD, WOOD SORREL

↔ 18–36 in (45–90 cm)
↑ 2–4 in (5–10 cm)

Creeping perennial ground cover from North America, Asia, and Europe. Clover-shaped leaves. White flowers, veined with purple, in summer. ***O. a.* var. *subpurpurascens*** has rose pink flowers with purple veins. Zones 3–10.

Oxalis adenophylla

↔ 5–6 in (12–15 cm)
↑ 3–4 in (8–10 cm)

Lovely clump-forming species from the Andes in Chile and Argentina with fibrous bulbs. Suitable for rockeries. The gray-green leaves have up to 22 leaflets. Pink, occasionally mauve, flowers, veined with purple, are produced in the late spring. Zones 5–9.

Oxalis articulata

↔ 12–16 in (30–40 cm)
↑ 12–16 in (30–40 cm)

Tuberous perennial from Paraguay. Leaves have 3 leaflets, to 1 in (25 mm) across. Bright mauve-pink flowers, ¾ in (18 mm) across, held well above leaves, in summer. Zones 8–10.

Oxalis bowiei

syn. *Oxalis purpurata* var. *bowiei*

↔ 6–8 in (15–20 cm)
↑ 8–10 in (20–25 cm)

Summer-growing species from South Africa. Leaves with 3 leaflets, each to 1 in (25 mm) across. Flowers are bright pink, over 1½ in (35 mm) wide, held well above leaves. Zones 8–11.

Oxalis enneaphylla

SCURVY GRASS

↔ 4–6 in (10–15 cm)
↑ 2½–3 in (6–8 cm)

Native to the Falkland Islands and Patagonia. Branched, slowly spreading, scaly rhizomatous plant. The leaves have up to 20 gray-green pleated leaflets, giving them a crinkled appearance. White to pink flowers, to 1 in (25 mm) across, borne from spring to summer. **'Rosea'** has deep pink flowers. Zones 6–9.

Oxalis hirta

↔ 4–6 in (10–15 cm)
↑ 10–12 in (25–30 cm)

Bushy bulbous species from South Africa. Upright leafy stems; leaflets long and narrow; arranged in 3s but do not have classic clover appearance. Flowers may be mauve through salmon to bright pink, in autumn. Zones 8–10.

Oxalis adenophylla, dark form

Oxalis oregana

RED WOOD SORREL

↔40 in (100 cm)
↕7–8 in (18–20 cm)

Creeping perennial from the woods of western North America. Leaves with 3 mid-green leaflets. Flowers pink through to lilac, sometimes white, to 1 in (25 mm) across, from spring to autumn. Zones 7–10.

Oxalis purpurea

↔12–24 in (30–60 cm)
↕3–4 in (8–10 cm)

Variable, strongly spreading bulbous perennial from South Africa. Leaves green, grayish, even purple, divided into 3 leaflets. Flowers to 2 in (5 cm) across, white, yellow, pink, mauve, or purple, in winter. Many selections available. Zones 8–10.

Oxalis spiralis

Oxalis rubra

↔10–12 in (25–30 cm)
↕15–16 in (38–40 cm)

Tuberous summer-growing perennial from Brazil and Argentina. The leaves with 3 leaflets are green marked with brown. The flowers to ¾ in (18 mm) across, may be white, lilac, pink, or red, in summer. Zones 9–11.

Oxalis spiralis

SPIRAL SORREL

↔12–20 in (30–50 cm)
↕12–20 in (30–50 cm)

Bushy small shrub from Central America. Succulent reddish stems; thick green leaves with 3 leaflets. Small bright yellow flowers, fine red veins, from summer to autumn. ***O. s.* subsp. *vulcanicola,*** velvety leaves, usually flushed red. Zones 9–11.

Oxalis triangularis

↔12–20 in (30–50 cm)
↕8–10 in (20–25 cm)

Summer-growing South American species; branching scaly rhizome. Leaves with 3 triangular leaflets, close at night; foliage deep purple suffused with violet. Slightly nodding soft pink flowers, throughout warmer months. ***O. t.* subsp. *papilionacea*** (syn. *O. regnellii*), bright green triangular leaves, pure white flowers. Zones 8–11.

Oxalis triangularis

Oxalis versicolor

BARBER'S POLE OXALIS, CANDY-CANE OXALIS

↔8–10 in (20–25 cm)
↕3–4 in (8–10 cm)

Lovely winter-growing bulbous species from southern Africa. Neat clumps of fine foliage with 3 narrow leaflets. Flowers pure white, deep pink edges on outsides of petals, in late winter; when closed, rolled petals give effect of barbers' poles. Zones 9–10.

OXYDENDRUM

The single species of deciduous shrub or small tree in this genus, is native to North America, and belongs to the same family as *Rhododendron*, the heath (Ericaceae) family. It has a slender trunk, which is sometimes multi-stemmed, with rusty red fissured bark. In summer, small white flowers appear and in autumn the leaves color vividly before they fall.
CULTIVATION: This plant is suitable for growing as a specimen or in open woodland. Grown in full sun, flowering is better and the autumn colors more intense. It needs an acid soil that is moist but well drained. Plants are slow growing and take time to become established. Propagate from seed in autumn or spring, or softwood cuttings in summer.

Oxydendrum arboreum ★

SORREL TREE, SOURWOOD

↔10 ft (3 m) ↕6–10 ft (1.8–3 m)

From woods and stream banks in eastern USA. Pointed glossy leaves, finely toothed, color vivid shades of red, purple, and yellow, in autumn. Fragrant white flowers, small urn-shaped, on slender spreading racemes at branch tips, in summer. Zones 5–9.

Oxydendrum arboreum

OZOTHAMNUS

From the daisy (Asteraceae) family, this genus includes 50 species that occur in Australia, New Zealand, and New Caledonia. Small-leafed shrubs or subshrubs. The compound inflorescences are composed of a large number of small flowerheads with a few female flowers and enclosed by papery bracts. Colors range from white to yellow to dark pink and various shades between. Most species are hairy to some degree, with several being quite woolly.
CULTIVATION: Neutral to acidic well-drained soils give best results, and most species prefer some shade rather than full sun. Extra water during long dry periods will be necessary. Most species are frost hardy, with those from high altitudes being very tolerant of long periods of snow cover. Propagate from seed, which needs to be fresh, or from cuttings. Seed from high-altitude species will need to be stratified in a refrigerator for a few weeks before being sown.

Ozothamnus diosmifolius

syn. ***Helichrysum diosmifolium***

PILL FLOWER, RICE FLOWER, WHITE DOGWOOD

↔7 ft (2 m) ↕15 ft (4.5 m)

Erect-growing shrub, commonly found from central Queensland to southeastern New South Wales, Australia. Thin dark green leaves, with hairy undersides. Tiny individual flowers, in small heads, ¼ in (6 mm) across; many hundreds of these heads form terminal clusters, in white to pink to red shades, from spring to summer. Widely grown for the cut flower trade. **'Coral Flush'**, bright coral pink flowers; **'Just Blush'**, mauve-pink flowers; **'Radiance'**, long-blooming, white flowers open from pink buds; **'Winter White'**, white flowers, mainly autumn–winter. Zones 9–11.

Ozothamnus diosmifolius

P

Pachycereus marginatus

Pachycereus schottii

PACHYCEREUS

Genus of 9 species of large, tree-like cacti, family Cactaceae, all found in Mexico, with some straying into southern USA. They are upright plants, branching either at the base or further up the main stem. Shrubbier species may form clumps of unbranched stems. Stem ribbing is sharply angled, with clearly defined spine-bearing areoles along the ridges. The nocturnal flowers, usually white or in shades of pink, are tubular, around 2–3 in (5–8 cm) long, with protruding anthers.

CULTIVATION: As for all cacti, the soil should be very gritty and free draining, and the plants should receive sun for at least half the day. Some species will tolerate the occasional light frost, but in general they are warm climate plants. Moisture is appreciated in summer, but wet conditions in winter can lead to rotting. Propagate from seed or, with the unusual cultivars, by grafting.

Pachycereus marginatus ★

MEXICAN FENCE POST CACTUS

↔3–8 in (8–20 cm)
↑10–17 ft (3–5 m)

From Mexico. Stout, vertical, columnar branches are used as living fences. Recognized by its 4 to 7 almost triangular ribs that bear elongated white to gray areoles. Spines yellow to gray, 1 to 3 centrals, 5 to 9 radials. Flowers funnelform, red to pink. Fruit spherical, with detachable spines and wool. Zones 10–12.

Pachycereus schottii

syn. *Lophocereus schottii*

GARAMBUYO, SENITA, SINITA

↔2–4 in (5–10 cm)
↑3–10 ft (0.9–3 m)

From USA and Mexico. Tree-like to shrubby, with up to 100 yellow-green branches. Upper sections of flowering stems bear a distinctive mat of bristly gray spines, 2–40 in (5–100 cm) long. Spines 1 to 3 centrals, thin, gray, 3 to 15 radials, also gray. Flowers nocturnal, funnel-form, white to pink. The seed pods are spherical, red with red pulp. **'Monstrosus'** ★ (syn. *Lophocereus schottii* f. *monstrosus*), completely spineless and lacks distinct ribs. Branches are irregularly bumpy. Zones 10–12.

PACHYPHRAGMA

This genus consists of a single species in the cabbage (Brassicaceae) family, found from northeastern Turkey to the Caucasus. It is a round-leafed perennial with spikes of small pure white flowers in spring. The foliage stays attractive throughout the growing season. *Pachyphragma* is closely allied to *Thlaspi*, possibly not distinct from it.

CULTIVATION: *Pachyphragma* makes an attractive, weed-smothering, slow-growing ground cover in lightly shaded aspects in humus-rich and moisture-retentive soils. Propagate from seed sown in autumn or from basal stem cuttings in late spring.

Pachyphragma macrophyllum

Pachyphragma macrophyllum

syns *Cardamine asarifolia, Thlaspi macrophyllum*

↔28–36 in (70–90 cm)
↑12–16 in (30–40 cm)

Herbaceous woodlands perennial with large, rounded, rich green leaves to 4 in (10 cm) across. Open spikes of pure white flowers, to ¾ in (18 mm) across, late winter–spring. Zones 7–9.

PACHYSANDRA

Commonly known as spurge, *Pachysandra* belongs to the box (Buxaceae) family and contains 5 species of low-growing shrubby or creeping perennials native to North America and East Asia. Some are deciduous, some are semi-evergreen or evergreen, depending on the climate. They are used for ground cover in shady places and although slow to get started they are reliable once established. They spread by underground runners and have the advantage of being able to grow over tree roots. They have a compact growth and attractive tidy foliage, growing in whorls at the tip of the stem. The flowers are insignificant but scented and appear in the spring. The name *Pachysandra* comes from the Greek *pachys*, thick, and *andros*, man, referring to the thick stamens.

CULTIVATION: Ideal conditions for these plants include shade, in moist slightly acidic soil, with organic matter incorporated. If too much light is admitted to their growing area, the foliage will turn yellow and they will not grow well. Propagate by division or from cuttings in summer.

Pachysandra procumbens

ALLEGHENY PACHYSANDRA, ALLEGHENY SPURGE

↔12–18 in (30–45 cm)
↑6–12 in (15–30 cm)

From eastern Kentucky to Florida and Louisiana, USA. Deciduous in colder areas, semi-evergreen or evergreen elsewhere. The leaves are dull green, tinged gray; and may be mottled with brown or gray colorings. Small white or pinkish flowers. Zones 5–9.

Pachysandra terminalis

Pachystachys lutea

Pachysandra terminalis

JAPANESE PACHYSANDRA, JAPANESE SPURGE

↔18 in (45 cm)
↑8–12 in (20–30 cm)

Native to Japan. The leaves are a shiny dark green with slightly toothed edges. The flowers are small and white. Withstands heavy shade and tree roots. **'Green Spike'** is a popular cultivar; **'Variegata'** has green and gray-green leaves variegated with creamy white. Zones 5–10.

PACHYSTACHYS

The 12 species of evergreen perennials and shrubs in this genus, a member of the acanthus (Acanthaceae) family, are native to tropical America. They are closely related to *Justicia* with similar showy, terminal flower spikes. The tubular flowers are 2-lipped and have large overlapping bracts. The opposite leaves are quite large with a wrinkled surface due to their prominent veining.

CULTIVATION: In cool climates these are indoor or greenhouse plants, but in warm humid areas they can be grown outside. They will require a fertile, moist but well-drained soil in a semi-shaded situation. Propagation is best done from softwood cuttings taken in summer.

Pachystachys coccinea

CARDINAL'S GUARD

↔2 ft (0.6 m) ↑7 ft (2 m)

Shrub, native to northern South America, naturalized in the West Indies. Oval leaves to 8 in (20 cm) long. Terminal spikes of bright red flowers with large green bracts, most of the year. Zones 10–12.

Paeonia anomala var. *intermedia*

Paeonia cambessedesii

Pachystachys lutea

GOLDEN CANDLES

↔ 20 in (50 cm) ↕ 36 in (90 cm)

Native to Peru. Shorter narrower leaves than *P. coccinea*. Long flowering season, with terminal spikes of showy golden yellow bracts that hold white tubular flowers. Zones 10–12.

PAEONIA

PEONY

This genus of 30 or so species is a member of the peony (Paeoniaceae) family. It is named after Paeon, who was physician to the gods in Greek mythology. Most of the species are herbaceous perennials native to temperate parts of the Northern Hemisphere. There are also shrubs and subshrubs known as tree peonies, which have persistent woody stems, brilliantly colored flowers, and highly decorative foliage. Recent revisions of the genus have seen several familiar names, such as *P. mlokosewitschii,* disappear from the species list, as they have been amalgamated into other species.

CULTIVATION: Peonies are best suited to deep fertile soils of basaltic origin, heavily fed annually with organic matter; soils should not be allowed to dry out in summer. Protection from strong winds and scorching sun is essential, and some protection from early spring frost. The only pruning that is necessary is the removal of spent flowerheads and dead or misplaced shoots. Propagate from seed, which can be slow and difficult, or by division of herbaceous peonies, or by apical grafting of tree peonies, with the graft union being buried 3 in (8 cm) below soil level.

Paeonia anomala

↔ 24 in (60 cm) ↕ 24 in (60 cm)

From western Mongolia and central China to Siberia and Russian steppes. Biternate, finely divided, dark green leaves, fine hairs on main veins, bluish green beneath; foliage orange in autumn. Single crimson flowers with slightly undulating petals in early summer. ***P. a.* var. *intermedia,*** differs in having furry carpels; ***P. a.* subsp. *veitchii*** (syn. *P. veitchii*), bronze-green leaves, deep pink flowers. Zones 4–9.

Paeonia cambessedesii

MAJORCAN PEONY

↔ 24 in (60 cm) ↕ 24 in (60 cm)

From the Balearic Islands. Leathery, ovate leaves with purple-suffused veining, wavy margins; reddish stems. Flowers single, deep rose to magenta, darker veins, in spring. Requires protection in winter. Zones 8–9.

Paeonia × *chamaeleon*

↔ 20 in (50 cm) ↕ 20 in (50 cm)

Naturally occurring hybrid between *P. mlokosewitschii* and *P. caucasica*, from mountains of Georgia. Oval leaflets are bluish green. Flowers variable in color, from pink to creamy yellow, in late spring. Zones 6–9.

Paeonia davurica

↔ 40 in (100 cm) ↕ 40 in (100 cm)

Late spring-flowering Caucasian and western to central Asian species that is composed of 5 subspecies that encompass some very popular peonies formerly regarded as species in their own right, such as ***P. d.* subsp. *lagodechiana*** (syns *P. d.* subsp. *mlokosewitschii, P. mlokosewitschii*) from Caucasus, with blue-green foliage and primrose yellow flowers; and ***P. d.* subsp. *wittmanniana*** (syn. *P. wittmanniana*) from Iran, Turkey, Azerbaijan, and Georgia, with bronze young foliage and cream to pale yellow flowers. Zones 4–9.

Paeonia delavayi

MAROON TREE PEONY

↔ 5 ft (1.5 m) ↕ 7 ft (2 m)

From western China. Deciduous suckering shrub. Dark green leaves large, deeply cut, bluish green below. Saucer-shaped flowers, dark red, deep gold anthers, in spring. Pod-like fruits with colored sepals. ***P. d.* var. *lutea*** (syn. *P. lutea*), lemon yellow, single flowers in mid-spring. ***P. d.* var. *ludlowii*** (syn. *P. l.* var. *ludlowii*), larger than *P. d.* var. *lutea*, less divided leaves, more open flowers, to 5 in (12 cm) across, profuse in early spring. Zones 6–9.

Paeonia lactiflora

syn. *Paeonia albiflora*

CHINESE PEONY

↔ 24 in (60 cm) ↕ 24 in (60 cm)

Native to steppes and scrub of Siberia, Tibet, and China. Erect stems, lobed, pointed leaves, good autumn color. Two or more scented white flowers per stem, to 4 in (10 cm) diameter, early–mid-summer. A parent of thousands of cultivars and hybrids. Easy to grow in well-drained soil; tolerates winter temperatures to –22°F (–30°C). Cultivars mostly taller, to 40 in (100 cm), include: **'A La Mode'**, scented white flowers, petals shiny, serrated, up to 4 blooms per stem, mid-spring; **'Angel Cheeks'**, double pink flowers; **'Barrington Belle'**, deep red outer petals, gold-edged pink or deep red, petal-like staminodes (narrow inner petals); very free flowering; **'Bowl of Beauty'**, large, rose pink, rounded outer petals, mass of creamy staminodes, early–mid-summer; **'Carrara'**, tall, white outer petals, mass of white staminodes; **'Cora Stubbs'**, tall, pale lilac outer petals, cream and pale pink petaloids; **'Dawn Pink'**, large, single pink, in late spring; **'Duchesse de Nemours'**, sweetly scented, double cream flowers flushed pale yellow toward center; **'Globe of Light'**, petals almost white-edged, becoming bright pink toward center, free flowering, early summer; **'Haku-Gah'**, white flowers; **'Heirloom'** ★, fully double pale pink; **'Helen'**, old cultivar, single pink flowers; **'Kelway's Supreme'**, scented, single or semi-double blush pink flowers, very free flowering, late spring–mid-summer; **'Miss America'**, beautiful, large, semi-double, scented, pure white flowers flushed creamy yellow at center, spring; **'Moonstone'**, large flowers, blush pink fading to white; **'Nellie Shaylor'**, red flowers; **'Peppermint'**, double flowers, open-ing blush pink, fading to white, cream flush at center, outer petals with crimson streak, early summer; **'Pillow Talk'**, fully double, outer petals rose pink, pale yellow staminodes surround pink center, late spring; **'Pink Lemonade'**, anemone- or double-flowered, pink and yellow petals; **'Pink Princess'** (syn. 'Pink Dawn'), rather crinkled petals, pale pink outer edge, fading to white at center; **'Reine Wilhelmine'**, fully double, scented, rose pink flowers, fine carmine markings in center, very free flowering, in the early summer; **'Requiem'**, spicy-scented, single blush cream flowers, free flowering, late spring; **'Sarah Bernhardt'**, fully double, scented, large, rose pink flowers fading to blush on outer edges, early to mid-summer; **'Sorbet'**, fully double, rose pink outer petals surrounding ring of finely fringed cream petals enclosing pink center, early–mid-summer; **'White Wings'**, scented, purple-streaked buds opening to pure white single flowers, mid-summer. Zones 6–9.

Paeonia delavayi var. *lutea*

Paeonia lactiflora 'Requiem'

Paeonia × *lemoinei*

↔ 6 ft (1.8 m) ↕ 6 ft (1.8 m)

Name of a group of cultivars originating as crosses between *P. lutea* and *P. suffruticosa,* inheriting the strong yellow coloring of *P. lutea,* usually flushed red in the center or colors blended giving shades of orange. **'Roman Child'**, semi-double yellow flowers, dark red blotches at petal bases; **'Souvenir de Maxime Cornu'** (syns 'Kinshe', 'Souvenir de Professeur Maxime Cornu'), large, fully double, yellow flowers, soft orange at the center, red margins. Zones 6–9.

Paeonia × *lemoinei* 'Roman Child'

P

Paeonia mollis

Paeonia officinalis 'Rosea Plena'

Paeonia mascula

MALE PEONY

↔24 in (60 cm)
↑24–36 in (60–90 cm)

Variable species from forests of southern Europe. Large, spreading clumps. Dark green ovate leaves, bluish green below. Single flowers, 5 in (12 cm) wide, usually deep rose red or pink, sometimes magenta or white, mid- to late spring. Good autumn color. Once used in medicines. ***P. m.* subsp. *arietina***, from Turkey and eastern Europe, leaves biternate, narrowly elliptic, light or dark green, bluish green below, red or pink single flowers; **'Mother of Pearl'**, large, pale pink, single; **'Northern Glory'**, single, carmine; **'Purple Emperor'**, single, magenta; **'Rosy Gem'**, single, rosy pink. ***P. m.* subsp. *russoi*,** shorter, from Mediterranean islands and central Greece; mid-green oval leaflets, purple below, purplish stems; flowers single, deep pink, in mid-spring. Zones 8–9.

Paeonia mollis

↔18 in (45 cm) ↑18 in (45 cm)

Dwarf peony believed to originate in Russia. Deeply cut blue-green leaves. Small red or white flowers, 3 in (8 cm) in diameter, on very short stems, in late spring. Zones 6–9.

Paeonia obovata

↔24 in (60 cm) ↑24 in (60 cm)

Found in mountain woods and scrub in Siberia, China, Japan, and Korea. The lower leaves are biternate with obovate leaflets which increase in size after flowering. The single, 2½ in (6 cm) diameter, rose purple flowers, open in mid-spring–early summer. ***P. o.* var. *alba*** is a white-flowered form. Zones 7–9.

Paeonia suffruticosa 'Mountain Treasure'

Paeonia officinalis

FEMALE PEONY

↔24 in (60 cm)
↑15–24 in (38–60 cm)

Native to Europe. Most famous of all peonies, cultivated from ancient times for its medicinal properties. Lower leaves dark green, biternate, deeply cut into narrow segments. The single flowers, 5 in (12 cm) across, are magenta to deep red. **'Rosea Plena'**, double, bright pink; **'Rubra'**, an old cultivar, single, deep red; **'Rubra Plena'** (syn. 'Memorial Day'), very vigorous, with double flowers, deep red. Zones 8–9.

Paeonia rockii

syn. *Paeonia suffruticosa 'Joseph Rock'*

ROCK'S VARIETY

↔3 ft (0.9 m) ↑7 ft (2 m)

From northern Sichuan, southern Gansu, and Qinghai Provinces, China. A sought-after tree peony which has woody stems and coarsely toothed, bipinnate, bright green leaves. It produces single white flowers, with notched petals, distinguished by a deep purple central blotch. **'Fen He'**, pink flowers. Zones 7–10.

Paeonia suffruticosa

MOUTAN, TREE PEONY

↔7 ft (2 m) ↑7 ft (2 m)

Found from northwestern China west to Bhutan. A freely branching upright shrub, with smooth mid-green leaves variously cut and lobed, with bluish green undersides. Large, sometimes double, white, pink, yellow, or red flowers, solitary, petals fluted, frilled on the edges, in mid-spring. Cultivar flowers in various shades of red, pink, white, and violet, with a purplish blotch near the base; some are slightly fragrant. **'Godaishu'**, white flowers, semi-double; **'Hiro-no-yuki'**, large, semi-double, white flowers; **'Louise Mouchelet'** produces pale pink flowers; **'Mountain Treasure'**, white flowers, purplish blotches at petal bases; **'Shin-Shium-Ryo'**, yellow flowers; **'Yellow Heaven'**, yellow flowers; **'Zenobia'**, rich magenta blooms. Zones 4–9.

Paeonia tenuifolia

↔20–27 in (50–70 cm)
↑20–27 in (50–70 cm)

Dainty herbaceous species found from southeastern Europe to the Caucasus. Finely dissected feathery leaves and single, blood red, bowl-shaped flowers to 3 in (8 cm) across, with yellow stamens, in spring. **'Plena'** is a full double red selection. Zones 8–9.

Paeonia Hybrid Cultivars

↔30–36 in (70–90 cm)
↑30–36 in (70–90 cm)

The breeding of herbaceous peonies was greatly enhanced by the introduction from China in the mid-eighteenth century of *P. lactiflora,* bringing, among other qualities, an attractive fragrance and the ability to produce double flowers. Among the best of the countless hybrid cultivars are: **'America'**, with large, single, scented, scarlet flowers; **'Avant Garde'**, single flowers, pale pink petals with darker veins; **'Blaze'**, beautiful, single, red flowers with golden yellow centers, an early-flowering hybrid; **'Buckeye Belle'**, unusual semi-double flowers, very dark red, rather crinkled petals; **'Burma Ruby'**, a hybrid between *P. lactiflora* and *P. peregrina,* with single red flowers, an important cultivar for breeding; **'Claire de Lune'**, large single flowers of palest yellow, early spring; **'Coral Charm'**, profuse, large, semi-double, coral peach flowers, in spring; **'Defender'**, single blooms of rich crimson, very lightly scented, early-flowering; **'Early Windflower'**, a hybrid between *P. emodi* and *P. veitchii* with small, single, white flowers, in early spring; **'Fairy Princess'**, single red flowers, in mid-spring; **'Flame'**, single, orange-tinted, bright red flowers, in mid-spring; **'Gauguin'**, large, single, long-lasting yellow flowers with red center, early spring-flowering; **'Hakuo-jisi'** (syns 'King of White Lion', 'White Tailed Lion'), a Japanese tree peony, double white flowers flushed purple toward the center; **'Honor'**, single deep pink flowers; **'Moonrise'**, single flowers open pale yellow, ageing to an attractive rich cream color, blooms appear mid-season; **'Nymph'**, single flowers of delicate pink, shading to yellow at the center; **'Paula Fay'**, semi-double, bright pink, scented flowers flushed with white in the center; **'Pink Hawaiian Coral'**, scented, semi-double, smallish coral pink flowers with white stripe on the outer petals, spring-flowering; **'Prairie Moon'**, very beautiful, single to semi-double, pale yellow flowers, early spring-blooming; **'Red Charm'**, a hybrid between *P. lactiflora* and *P. officinalis* 'Rubra Plena', with fully double, deep red, ruffled petals, early spring-flowering; **'Salmon Surprise'**, single salmon pink flowers; **'Sanctus'**, hybrid between *P. lactiflora* and *P. officinalis,* attractive single white flowers; **'Scarlett O'Hara'**, a hybrid between *P. lactiflora* and *P. officinalis,* single bright red flowers, in early spring; **'Vesuvian'**, smaller-growing hybrid with deep, dark red flushed purple, almost black flowers, finely divided leaves, showing good autumn color; and **'Yellow Dream'** large scented double flowers of rich yellow, mid-season. Zones 6–9.

Paeonia, Hybrid Cultivar, 'Red Charm'

PANDANUS

The evergreen screw pines, with about 700 species in the family Pandanaceae, are found in east Africa, Madagascar, tropical Asia, the Pacific Islands, and northern Australia, in various habitats. Most are tree-like often with trunks supported by stilt roots. Stems are commonly branched with terminal rosettes of long, leathery, strap-like, spiny-toothed, parallel-veined leaves arranged in distinct spirals. Male and female flowers borne in dense spikes on separate plants. Resembling a pineapple, the woody or fleshy fruiting heads of compound drupes, many edible after cooking, can be red, pink, or yellow. Leaves and roots used by local communities for weaving baskets, mats, ropes, and fishing nets. CULTIVATION: These plants need full sun and moist well-drained soil in warm humid environments. Propagate from seed, soaked for 24 hours before sowing, or from offsets or rooted suckers.

Pandanus tectorius, in the wild, Kauai, Hawaii, USA

Pandanus tectorius

syns *Pandanus odoratissimus, P. pedunculatus*

BEACH SCREW PINE, PANDANG

↔ 10–20 ft (3–6 m)
↑ 12–25 ft (3.5–8 m)

Most widely distributed *Pandanus* species, occurring on coasts and islands of the Pacific and Indian Oceans, as far as Hawaii to the east, Sri Lanka to the west, Okinawa (Japan) to the north, and New South Wales, Australia to the south. Short trunk, supported by strong stilt roots and broadly spreading branches. Leaves have spiny edges and midribs on undersides. Male flowers cream, sweetly scented, in dense spikes among large white bracts, at various times of year. Fruiting heads up to 8 in (20 cm) long, the segments very variable but usually with grooved sides, ripening deep red. Several variegated forms belong here, some originally named as species; they rarely if ever produce fruit. **'Baptistii'** (syn. *P. baptistii*), dwarf, trunk under 3 ft (0.9 m), arching spineless leaves with yellow stripes; **'Sanderi'** (syn. *P. sanderi*), compact, to 12 ft (3.5 m), leaves rather small with fine striping of paler green and gold; **'Variegatus'**, leaves with broad gold stripes, purple-brown spines, apex thread-like; **'Veitchii'** (syn. *P. veitchii*), like 'Variegatus', but leaves striped cream, spines green to yellow, tips not thread-like. Zones 10–12.

Pandanus utilis

COMMON SCREW PINE

↔ 15 ft (4.5 m) ↑ 40–60 ft (12–18 m)

Many-branched Madagascan tree. Stiff, blue-green leaves arranged in spirals, red spines. Aerial roots help buttress tree. Inflorescences carry masses of minute creamy white flowers. Rounded compound fruits of woody drupes, edible when fully ripe. Zones 10–12.

PANDOREA

A small genus consisting of 6 species and several cultivars in the trumpet-vine (Bignoniaceae) family. This genus has been classified as *Bignonia* and *Tecoma* in the past. These woody evergreen climbers, which are grown for their flowers and foliage, are native to Australia, New Caledonia, Malaysia, and New Guinea, where they grow from sea level up to 9,840 ft (3,000 m). Leaflets are usually green and glossy, and the plant climbs by using tendrils. Flowers are 5-petalled, tubular, fragrant, and usually white, cream, buff, or pink. An excellent choice for pergolas, archways or trellises. The genus name comes from the Greek legend of Pandora's box, referring to the box-like seed capsules.
CULTIVATION: These warm climate plants grow best in moist well-drained soil in full sun. Prune after flowering. Propagate from seed, cuttings or layers.

Pandorea jasminoides

syns *Bignonia jasminoides, Tecoma jasminoides*

BOWER-OF-BEAUTY, BOWER PLANT

↔ 8–15 ft (2.4–4.5 m) ↑ 17 ft (5 m)

Vigorous twining climber with glossy bright green leaflets. White flowers with hot-pink throats produced in abundance on large panicles from spring–summer. Prefers rich moist soil. **'Alba'**, pure white-flowering form; **'Charisma'**, yellow variegated form, pink flowers with crimson throat; **'Funky Bellz'**, mid-pink flowers with pale throat; **'Jazzy Bellz'**, white flowers with magenta to red throat; **'Lady Di'** (syn. 'Snow Queen'), white flowers with creamy yellow to orange-yellow throat; **'Rosea'**, pink flowers with deep pink throat; **'Rosea Superba'**, pink flowers, throat spotted purple. Zones 9–11.

PANICUM

CRAB GRASS, PANIC GRASS

A genus of about 470 species of grasses belonging to the family Poaceae. They can be annual or perennial, evergreen or deciduous, and are native to the tropics as well as North America and Europe. Only a few species are considered to be ornamental, but those are admired for their light and airy looks. Some are valued as fodder crops.
CULTIVATION: *Panicum* species that are likely to be used in gardens all prefer a sunny aspect in fertile, well-drained, but moist soil. Perennial species are propagated by division in early spring, and annuals from seed sown in spring

Panicum miliaceum

BROOM CORN MILLET, HOG MILLET, MILLET

↔ 8–10 in (20–25 cm)
↑ 36–40 in (90–100 cm)

An annual species from Europe and Asia. It is grown mainly for its seeds that can be fed to birds. These plants are reasonably ornamental, with upright clumps of bright green arching leaves and sprays of soft fluffy flowerheads in summer. A form with purple leaves and flowerheads is also grown. Zones 5–9.

Panicum virgatum

SWITCH GRASS

↔ 27–32 in (70–80 cm)
↑ 36–40 in (90–100 cm)

Clumping herbaceous grass found from Canada to Central America. Bright green narrow leaves to 24 in (60 cm) long. Bears open, drooping, fluffy panicles with tiny purple-green flowers, in autumn, these turn straw-colored as they mature. **'Heavy Metal'**, has more erect blue-gray leaves, pink inflorescences; **'Warrior'** is a tall form with foliage turning red-brown as it dies. Zones 5–10.

Panicum virgatum

PAPAVER

POPPY

This widespread group of around 50 species of annuals and perennials gives its name to the poppy (Papaveraceae) family. Today we associate poppies with war remembrance days, though it was Homer, the ninth-century bc Greek poet, who first linked the hanging poppy bud with a dying soldier. From basal rosettes of usually finely lobed often hairy leaves emerge bristly upright flower stems, each with one nodding bud, rarely 2 or 3. The flowers most often have 4 crape-like petals around a central ovary topped with a prominent stigmatic disc. Red is a common color, though the range is huge.
CULTIVATION: Most are very hardy and prefer a sunny position with light, moist, and well-drained soil. Propagate perennial poppy cultivars by root cuttings, otherwise raise from seed.

Papaver alpinum

ALPINE POPPY

↔ 8–16 in (20–40 cm)
↑ 10 in (25 cm)

Variable summer-flowering perennial from mountains of southern Europe, possibly conglomerate of closely related species. Forms basal clump of finely divided, downy, gray-green to blue-green leaves. Orange, yellow, or white flowers borne singly. ***P. a.* subsp. *rhaeticum*** (syn. *P. rhaeticum*), smaller plant, yellow to orange flowers. Zones 5–9.

Papaver alpinum

Papaver anomalum

↔ 8–12 in (20–30 cm)
↑ 16 in (40 cm)

Summer-flowering perennial from China, forming clump of blue-green pinnate leaves to 4 in (10 cm) long. Wiry stems with orange-brown hairs. Solitary, narrow-petalled orange flowers to 1½ in (35 mm) wide. Zones 7–10.

Papaver atlanticum

↔ 8–12 in (20–30 cm)
↑ 18 in (45 cm)

Summer-flowering perennial from Morocco. Broad, hairy, lance-shaped leaves, coarsely toothed or lobed. Flowers usually solitary but stems sometimes forked, light orange to red. **'Flore Pleno'** has orange double flowers on stocky stems. Zones 6–10.

Papaver bracteatum

↔ 16–36 in (40–90 cm)
↑ 32–40 in (80–100 cm)

Summer-flowering perennial from the Caucasus and western Asia. Forms clump of pinnate, gray-green to light green basal leaves. Flowers bright red with maroon basal blotches, on white-haired stems. Zones 5–10.

Papaver commutatum

↔ 16 in (40 cm) ↑ 16 in (40 cm)

Summer-flowering annual native to western Asia. Leaves, to 6 in (15 cm) long, are sometimes shallowly lobed. The flowers are red with black basal blotches, 2 in (5 cm) wide. **'Lady Bird'** is slightly taller, with bright red flowers liberally splashed with black. Zones 8–10.

Papaver × *hybridum*

ROUGH POPPY

↔ 6–10 in (15–25 cm)
↑ 8–20 in (20–50 cm)

Naturally occurring hybrid. Eurasian annual with finely divided pinnate leaves to 4 in (10 cm) long. Bright red flowers with a purple blotch at the base of the petals. Zones 6–9.

Papaver nudicaule

syn. *Papaver croceum, P. miyabeanum*

ARCTIC POPPY, ICELAND POPPY

↔ 8–12 in (20–30 cm)
↑ 12–16 in (30–40 cm)

Perennial, native to subarctic regions, flowering in spring–summer. Often treated as an annual. Pinnate leaves, often light blue-green, hairy. Bears solitary long-stemmed flowers to 3 in (8 cm) wide, in many colors; wild forms usually white, yellow, or orange. *P. n.* var. *croceum*, orange to orange-red flowers. *P. n.* **'Pacino'**, yellow flowers on stocky stems; mixed-color seedling strains include: **'Meadhome's Strain'**, producing a range of bright warm colors; and **'Artist Mixed'** in soft pastel tones. Zones 2–10.

Papaver orientale

ORIENTAL POPPY

↔ 12–20 in (30–50 cm)
↑ 24–40 in (60–100 cm)

This is a summer-flowering western Asian perennial. Forms a sturdy clump of bristly, pinnate, often blue-green leaves to 10 in (25 cm) long. The flower stems are usually leafy on the lower half. The flowers are solitary, to 4 in (10 cm) wide, red, orange, or pink, often darker blotched. There are many cultivars of *P. orientale*. **'Black and White'** has large white flowers with a black center; **'Cedric Morris'** ★, very hairy leaves and dark-blotched soft pink flowers; **'Coral Reef'**, soft coral pink flowers to 8 in (20 cm) wide; the **Goliath Group** are sturdy plants, and have very large flowers in bright colors with dark centers, such as **'Beauty of Livermere'**, deep red with small black blotches; **'Mrs Perry'**, large salmon pink flowers with dark blotches; **'Patty's Plum'** ★, purplish red, dusky edges, dark center; **'Princess Victoria Louise'**, ruffled apricot pink flowers with dark blotches. Zones 3–9.

Papaver rhoeas

CORN POPPY, FIELD POPPY, FLANDERS POPPY

↔ 12–16 in (30–40 cm)
↑ 36–48 in (90–120 cm)

Vigorous, hardy, summer-flowering annual from Old World temperate zones. Pinnate leaves to 6 in (15 cm) long. Bristly flower stems, solitary bright red flowers to 3 in (8 cm) wide, sometimes with black basal blotch. Mixed color strains include: **'Angel's Choir'**, ruffled doubles in delicate pastel blends; **'Mother of Pearl'**, unusual pastel mauves, pink, red, gray tones, often subtly blended; and **'Shirley Mixed'**, single or double flowers in range of colors. Zones 5–9.

Papaver rupifragum

↔ 8–12 in (20–30 cm)
↑ 18 in (45 cm)

Perennial, native to Spain. Tufted clump of finely divided, downy, pinnate leaves 4 in (10 cm) long. Solitary flowers to 3 in (8 cm) wide, dusky shade of red-brown, late spring–summer. Zones 7–10.

Papaver somniferum

OPIUM POPPY

↔ 12–24 in (30–60 cm)
↑ 3–4 ft (0.9–1.2 m)

Vigorous summer-flowering annual from southeastern Europe and western Asia. Leaves light blue-green, heavy textured, deeply cut with jagged teeth. Strong, leafy flower stems. Flowers 4 in (10 cm) wide, white, mauve, or purple, sometimes with a dark basal blotch. The conspicuous seed pods are the source of opium. *P. s.* var. *paeoniflorum*, deep blue-green leaves, peony-like maroon-black double flowers. *P. s.* **'Black Peony'** ★, double, deep blackish red; **'Cherry Glow'**, deep red with black basal blotches; **'Hen and Chickens'**, lavender flowers, large seed pod surrounded by small pods; **'Seriously Scarlet'**, scarlet red with purple-black basal blotches, frilled petal edges; **'Violetta Blush'**, peony-style full double, mauve; **'White Cloud'**, tall, white double flowers. Zones 7–10.

PARIS

A genus of more than 20 species of rhizomatous perennials in the honey-flower (Melanthiaceae) family, found in woodlands from Europe across to eastern Asia. Erect stems from extremely slow-growing rhizomes. A whorl of leaves surrounds the unusual flowers at the top. These appear in summer, with spidery or lance-shaped petals, often in shades of green.
CULTIVATION: Grow in a cool aspect with moist not wet humus-rich soil. Propagate from seed, which can take 2 years or more to germinate, or by division of old clumps when dormant.

Paris polyphylla

syn. *Daiswa polyphylla*

↔ 8–12 in (20–30 cm)
↑ 36–40 in (90–100 cm)

Slow-growing perennial found from the Himalayas to Myanmar and Thailand. Upright stems topped with up to 12 lance-shaped leaves to 7 in (18 cm) long. Flowers consist of up to 8 narrow green sepals, thread-like yellow petals, and a purple ovary. If cross-pollinated, the plant produces large green pods that contain red seeds. *P. p.* var. *yunnanensis* f. *alba* has white filament-like petals.
Zones 6–9.

PARKINSONIA

syn. *Cercidium*

A member of the cassia subfamily of the legume (Fabaceae) family, this genus of 12 evergreen or deciduous trees and shrubs is found in warmer arid regions of North America. It has narrow leaves and racemes of yellow flowers. The fruit is a flattish pod containing numerous seeds.
CULTIVATION: *Parkinsonia* species prefer rich well-drained soils in a protected position. Propagate from seed, which should be scarified for successful germination.

Parkinsonia aculeata

JERUSALEM THORN, PALO VERDE

↔ 20 ft (6 m) ↑ 30 ft (9 m)

Found on ephemeral watercourses of southwest USA and Mexico, naturalized in many countries. Spiny shrub or tree, drooping branches, pinnate leaves in pairs, with 25 pairs of leaflets. Clusters of yellow flowers in spring. Long narrow seed pods.
Zones 9–11.

Papaver commutatum

Papaver nudicaule 'Meadhome's Strain'

Papaver orientale, Goliath Group, 'Beauty of Livermere'

Paris polyphylla

Parkinsonia florida

syn. *Cercidium floridum*

PALO VERDE

↔25 ft (8 m) ↑25 ft (8 m)

Deciduous tree, native to southwestern USA and northwestern Mexico. Leafless most of year, pendulous foliage appears in spring, soon falls. Yellow flowers, to ¾ in (18 mm) wide, in spring. Seed pods to 3 in (8 cm) long. Zones 9–11.

PARROTIA

This genus of a single species in the witchhazel (Hamamelidaceae) family is native to northern Iran and Azerbaijan, where it is found in the forests south and southwest of the Caspian Sea. It was named after Dr F. W. Parrot, a German plant collector who travelled through the Middle East in the early nineteenth century. It is grown mainly for its beautiful leaf color, especially in spring and autumn. It is a useful small tree for street planting and a very suitable species for parks and gardens in cool climates, where the foliage colors brilliantly. CULTIVATION: Any moderately fertile soil with free drainage is suitable, including chalk soils; exposure to full sun is desirable. Propagation is usually from seed, which should be collected just before being expelled from the capsules, and sown immediately, taking up to 18 months to germinate. Softwood cuttings taken in summer are sometimes used.

Parkinsonia aculeata

Parrotia persica, in spring

Parrotia persica

IRON TREE, PERSIAN IRONWOOD, PARROTIA, PERSIAN WITCH HAZEL

↔20 ft (6 m) ↑25–40 ft (8–12 m)

Small deciduous tree, short trunk with flaking bark. Leaves simple, alternate, leathery, shallowly toothed, and pale lettuce-green; crimson, scarlet, orange, and yellow tones in autumn. Flowers small, bright red stamens, green calyx, enclosed in a bract of dark brown hairy scales, in late winter–spring. 'Pendula' ★, with drooping branches, slowly develops into a dome-shaped mound. Zones 5–9.

PARROTIOPSIS

This genus belonging to the witchhazel (Hamamelidaceae) family consists of a single deciduous small tree reaching 20 ft (6 m) high. Native to the Himalayas, it has hairy young shoots and toothed, ovate to rounded leaves 3 in (8 cm) long. The large flowerheads, about 2 in (5 cm) in diameter, are made up of densely packed yellow stamens surrounded by large, white, petal-like bracts. The fruit is an egg-shaped 2-beaked capsule. CULTIVATION: Moderately frost hardy, this is a beautiful species which requires a sunny, protected site and grows best in fertile, moist but well-drained soil. Propagation is from cuttings in the summer or from seed during autumn.

Parrotiopsis jacquemontiana

↔15 ft (4.5 m) ↑20 ft (6 m)

Slightly toothed ovate leaves turn shades of yellow in autumn. Produces attractive, creamy white and yellow flowerheads over a long period, in spring–early summer. Zones 5–9.

PARTHENOCISSUS

A genus of 10 species of deciduous tendril-producing climbers in the grape (Vitaceae) family from East Asia and North America. Grown for their attractive foliage and, in most species, their self-clinging habit, which makes them ideal to clothe walls. The leaves are either maple-shaped or divided into leaflets, and usually develop brilliant colors before they shed. The flowers are tiny and green, and, like the small black berries, have no ornamental value.
CULTIVATION: They will grow in any moderately fertile soil in sun or part shade. Propagate from cuttings at almost any time or by removing rooted layers. Can also be raised from seed.

Parthenocissus henryana

CHINESE VIRGINIA CREEPER, SILVER VEIN CREEPER

↔20 ft (6 m) ↑30–35 ft (9–10 m)

Lightly self-clinging species from China with 5 leaflets, to 5 in (12 cm) long, green above with a slightly purple reverse and white veins when grown in shade, the veins fading in sunlight. In autumn, the leaves turn brilliant red with white veins. Zones 7–10.

Parthenocissus inserta

↔30 ft (9 m) ↑30–35 ft (9–10 m)

North American species with leaves divided into 5 leaflets to 5 in (12 cm) long that color intensely before shedding. Differs from the true Virginia creeper, *P. quinquefolia,* in having tendrils without suction cups and slightly thicker foliage. Zones 3–10.

Parthenocissus quinquefolia

syn. *Vitis quinquefolia*

VIRGINIA CREEPER

↔30 ft (9 m) ↑40–50 ft (12–15 m)

Fast-growing self-clinging climber from North America, Mexico, and Cuba. Suction cups on tendrils, 5 leaflets to 5 in (12 cm) long, turn brilliant scarlet before shedding. *P. q.* var. *engelmannii* has smaller leaves. Zones 3–10.

Parthenocissus tricuspidata

BOSTON IVY, JAPANESE CREEPER

↔20 ft (6 m) ↑50–70 ft (15–21 m)

Strongly self-clinging species from China, Japan, and Korea with maple-shaped leaves to 8 in (20 cm) long, usually with 3 lobes although juvenile plants usually have leaves divided into 3 leaflets. Leaves sit almost like slates, one overlapping the other to the very top of any support, turning brilliant colors before shedding. 'Veitchii' ★, slightly smaller leaves that turn dark plum before shedding. Zones 4–10.

PASSIFLORA

PASSIONFLOWER

Type genus for its family, Passifloraceae, the 500-odd species of passionflowers are mainly evergreen tendril-climbing vines from tropical America, though there are a few shrubby species and the range does extend to Asia and the Pacific Islands. Grown mainly for their flowers and fruit, the great vigor of passionflowers makes them superb plants for covering unsightly objects. The flowers have an unusual structure, with a tubular calyx of 5 conspicuous sepals, usually 5 petals of the same size and color as the sepals, a corona of anthers, and 3 styles on an extended central tube. Fruits of many species are mildly to quite poisonous, though others are edible and quite delicious.
CULTIVATION: Most *Passiflora* species are frost tender and prefer a warm climate in full or half-sun with deep, moist, humus-rich, well-drained soil. Feed and water well. Trim to shape and remove any frosted foliage in spring. Some species are very vigorous and may be considered local weeds, for example *P. caerulea* is banned from sale in New Zealand. Propagate from seed or cuttings, or by layering.

Parthenocissus quinquefolia

Passiflora alata

Passiflora amethystina

Passiflora alata

↔ 8–20 ft (2.4–6 m) ↑ 20 ft (6 m)

Vigorous climber from Amazonian Brazil and Peru. Winged stems, simple pointed oval leaves to 6 in (15 cm) long, edges may be finely toothed. Flowers, scented, to 5 in (12 cm) wide, deep red petals, purple and white banded filaments, in summer. Ovoid to pear-shaped, edible, yellow fruit to 4 in (10 cm) long. Zones 10–12.

Passiflora amethystina

syn. *Passiflora violacea of gardens*

↔ 3–6 ft (0.9–1.8 m) ↑ 10 ft (3 m)

Found from central Bolivia to northern Argentina. Autumn-flowering, with 3-lobed leaves to 5 in (12 cm) long. Flowers to 4 in (10 cm) wide, deep violet-pink, radiating white filaments. Zones 9–11.

Passiflora × *belotii*

syn. *Passiflora* × *alatocaerulea*

↔ 6–15 ft (1.8–4.5 m)
↑ 15 ft (4.5 m)

Summer- to autumn-flowering garden hybrid between *P. alata* and *P. caerulea.* Shallowly winged stems and smooth-edged 3-lobed leaves. Flowers, to 4 in (10 cm) wide, mauve-blue and white petals and many radiating purple and white banded filaments around a yellow-green center. Zones 9–11.

Passiflora caerulea

BLUE PASSIONFLOWER

↔ 6–15 ft (1.8–4.5 m)
↑ 30 ft (9 m)

From Brazil and Argentina. Tolerant of repeated frosts, though partly

Passiflora caerulea

Passiflora citrina

Passiflora racemosa

deciduous in cold. Broadly palmate leaves, 3 to 9 lobes, often with toothed edges. Flowers to over 4 in (10 cm) wide, petals mostly creamy white, many radial purple and white banded filaments around a greenish center, in summer–autumn. **'Constance Elliot'**, creamy white flowers. Zones 7–10.

Passiflora citrina

↔ 15 ft (4.5 m) ↑ 15 ft (4.5 m)

Relatively recently discovered native of Honduras and Guatemala. Simple, downy, deeply veined, dark green, elliptical to bilobed leaves to 4 in (10 cm) long. Flowers yellow-green to bright yellow, 1½ in (35 mm) wide, throughout the year. Zones 10–12.

Passiflora coccinea

RED GRANADILLA, RED PASSIONFLOWER

↔ 12–30 ft (3.5–9 m)
↑ 12 ft (3.5 m)

Vigorous summer-flowering climber from tropical South America. Deep green, heavily textured, toothed elliptical leaves to 6 in (15 cm) long. Long-tubed flowers to 5 in (12 cm)

Passiflora incarnata

wide, bright red with dark filaments around a pale pink to white center. Fruit yellow to orange, sometimes mottled, to 2 in (5 cm) long. Zones 10–12.

Passiflora edulis

GRANADILLA, PASSIONFRUIT, PURPLE GRANADILLA

↔ 8–15 ft (2.4–4.5 m)
↑ 15 ft (4.5 m)

Strong summer-flowering climber from Brazil. Glossy, 3-lobed leaves to 4 in (10 cm) long. White flowers with white and purple banded filament. Ovoid edible fruit to around 3 in (8 cm) long, becoming purple-black and wrinkled when ripe. ***P. e.* f. *flavicarpa*** has golden yellow fruit, hybrids between these 2 forms include: **'Lacey'** and **'Purple Gold'** ★, which have large, light purple fruit; **'Fredrick'** has red fruit. ***P. e.* 'Edgehill'**, large purple-black fruit; **'Kahuna'**, pale purple fruit; **'Nelly Kelly'**, vigorous, heavy crop of sweet, purple fruit; **'Panama Gold'**, large golden yellow fruit; **'Panama Red'**, very large, red-skinned fruit, excellent flavor; **'Red Rover'**, large red fruit. Zones 10–12.

Passiflora foetida

LOVE-IN-A-MIST, RUNNING POP

↔ 3–6 ft (0.9–1.8 m)
↑ 6–10 ft (1.8–3 m)

Summer- to autumn-flowering climber from tropical South America and the Caribbean. Light-textured dark green leaves, 3- to 5-lobed, to around 3 in (8 cm) long and similarly sized mauve-pink flowers with long, pale filaments. Bristly, yellow to red, mildly poisonous fruits follow. Invasive weed in some tropical areas. Zones 10–12.

Passiflora incarnata

MAY APPLE, MAY POPS, WILD PASSIONFLOWER

↔ 6–15 ft (1.8–4.5 m)
↑ 6 ft (1.8 m)

Vigorous climber from eastern USA. Evergreen in mild areas, dies back to ground in cold conditions, but regrows up to 15 ft (4.5 m) in summer. Leaves 3-lobed, to 6 in (15 cm) long and wide, with toothed edges and blue-green undersides. Lavender and white flowers to 3 in (8 cm) wide followed by ovoid, 2 in (5 cm) long fruit. Zones 6–10.

Passiflora manicata

RED PASSIONFLOWER

↔ 8–15 ft (2.4–4.5 m)
↑ 10 ft (3 m)

Native to Colombia and Peru. Leaves toothed, 3-lobed, around 3 in (8 cm) long and slightly wider, downy undersides. Flowers with pale green sepals, bright red petals, mauve-blue and white banded filaments. Green ovoid fruit to 2 in (5 cm) long. Zones 9–11.

Passiflora mollissima

BANANA PASSIONFRUIT, CURUBA

↔ 8–15 ft (2.4–4.5 m)
↑ 15 ft (4.5 m)

Very vigorous climber from northern South America. Leaves to 4 in (10 cm) long, 3-lobed, downy, usually with serrated edges. Long-tubed bright mid-pink flowers, filaments reduced to small protuberances. Edible, yellow, ovoid fruit to 3 in (8 cm) long. Zones 9–11.

Passiflora quadrangularis

GIANT GRANADILLA

↔ 10–20 ft (3–6 m)
↑ 50 ft (15 m)

Very vigorous climber from tropical South America. Pointed oval leaves, deep green, leathery, to 8 in (20 cm) long. Flowers dusky gray-pink, with many twisted blue, white, purple-red banded filaments, to 5 in (12 cm) wide. Edible, bright yellow, ovoid fruit to 12 in (30 cm) long. Zones 10–12.

Passiflora racemosa

RED PASSIONFLOWER

↔ 6–15 ft (1.8–4.5 m)
↑ 15 ft (4.5 m)

Brazilian species with pointed oval to 3-lobed leaves to 4 in (10 cm) long and wide. Large pendulous racemes of bright red, rarely white, flowers to nearly 4 in (10 cm) wide, short white filaments. Zones 10–12.

Passiflora reflexiflora

↔ 4–8 ft (1.2–2.4 m)
↑ 6–10 ft (1.8–3 m)

Naturally found in Ecuador. Leaves 3-lobed with 1 long central lobe and 2 small lobes held at right angles to the midrib. Long-tubed magenta flowers, with petals becoming strongly reflexed, and much-reduced filaments. Zones 10–12.

Passiflora × *violacea*

syn. *Passiflora* ≥ *caeruleoracemosa*

↔6–15 ft (1.8–4.5 m) ↑20 ft (6 m)

Summer-flowering hybrid of *P. caerulea* and *P. racemosa*. Dark green palmate leaves, 5 deep lobes. Deep purple-pink flowers with darker filaments. Best known form is mauve-pink **'Eynsford Gem'** with white filaments. Zones 9–11.

Passiflora vitifolia

↔6–15 ft (1.8–4.5 m) ↑15 ft (4.5 m)

Spring- to summer-flowering species from Central and northern South America. Grape-like, glossy, 3-lobed, toothed leaves to 6 in (15 cm) long and wide, often red tinted. Flowers to 4 in (10 cm) wide, with strongly reflexed, narrow, bright red petals and short white filaments. These are followed by small yellow to red fruits. Zones 10–12.

Passiflora Hybrid Cultivars

↔6–15 ft (1.8–4.5 m) ↑6–12 ft (1.8–3.5 m)

There are many hybrid passionflowers, often based on *P. caerulea* to increase their hardiness, though some frost-tender hybrids have been raised specifically for tropical gardens. **'Amethyst'** has 3-lobed leaves to 4 in (10 cm) wide, and blue flowers with purple-blue filaments and center; **'Bluebird'**, blue flowers; **'Coral Sea'**, coral-pink flowers; **'Debby'**, 3-lobed leaves, white flowers, many purple and white banded filaments; **'Incense'**, 5-lobed leaves, fragrant deep purple flowers with many fine, frilly filaments; **'New Incense'**, ('Incense' back-crossed with *P. cincinnata*) preferable to the older hybrid due to its greater vigor and disease resistance; **'Sunburst'**, large pointed oval leaves, and camphor-scented golden orange flowers. Zones 8–12.

PATRINIA

Genus of 15 perennial herbs in the honeysuckle (Caprifoliaceae) family from temperate Asia and northern Europe, inhabiting damp rocky crevices in mountain areas. They have erect stems and divided or deeply lobed leaves. Panicles up to 4 in (10 cm) across, of small yellow or white flowers with very short corolla tubes, with 5 spreading lobes, appear from early to late summer. The fruit is an achene. The dried roots of *P. scabiosifolia* are valued in traditional Chinese medicine as a diuretic.

CULTIVATION: These plants may be useful for damp shady spots. They prefer full shade to partial shade in poor soil that is kept consistently moist. Propagate *Patrinia* species from seed in spring, or by division in spring and autumn.

Patrinia scabiosifolia

SCABIOUS PATRINIA, VALERIAN

↔18–24 in (45–60 cm) ↑3–6 ft (0.9–1.8 m)

Perennial herb from temperate East Asia. Sparsely leafed stems grow from a central mound. Divided, deeply toothed, oblong to oval-shaped foliage and open, terminal panicles of yellow flowers over long period in summer. Zones 5–8.

PAULOWNIA

This group of about 6 species of deciduous trees makes up the type genus for the paulownia (Paulowniaceae) family. They have handsome leaves that in some species are very large in the juvenile stage, and bear large panicles of flowers in spring. Paulownias have been cultivated in China for more than 3,000 years, both for their strong light timber, and for their attractive flowers; the bark, wood, leaves, flowers and fruit all have medicinal uses. They are characterized by their extremely rapid growth rate.

CULTIVATION: Paulownias do best in a moderately fertile and free-draining soil with adequate summer water. Protection from wind is important, especially in the early stages when the large leaves are easily damaged. Although quite hardy, dormant flower buds can be damaged by late frosts. The young trees are sometimes pruned back to 2 or 3 basal buds in order to encourage the vigorous growth of a single trunk. Propagation is from the seed, or from root cuttings.

Paulownia fortunei

POWTON, WHITE-FLOWERED PAULOWNIA

↔40 ft (12 m) ↑60 ft (18 m)

Found mainly in the Yangtze delta area of China. Tall tree, straight-trunked, with a rounded crown. The flowers open before the leaves appear, in upright terminal panicles, 4 in (10 cm) long, white to cream, mauve or soft violet. Zones 6–10.

Paulownia tomentosa

EMPRESS TREE, HAIRY PAULOWNIA, PRINCESS TREE

↔30 ft (9 m) ↑50 ft (15 m)

Native to northern and central China, Korea, and Japan. Medium-sized tree, broad spreading crown. Pinkish lilac flowers in upright terminal panicles, 50 to 60 flowers in each panicle. Heart-shaped leaves are downy, pale green maturing darker green, and turning yellow-brown, in autumn. **'Lilacina'**, lilac-purple flowers, hairy on the outside, pale lemon yellow on the inside; **'Sapphire Dragon'**, prominent clusters of creamy buff flowers. Zones 5–10.

PEDIOMELUM

A genus of about 25 species of perennials and subshrubs in the pea-flower subfamily of the legume (Fabaceae) family, 20 of them occurring in the USA and centered mainly in the prairie states with some spilling over into Canada or Mexico, the remainder Mexican. They have often been treated as species of *Psoralea*. All have thickened roots, in some quite swollen and starchy; stems are short; leaves are palmately divided into 3 to 7 leaflets. Flowers are white to blue or purple, in short dense spikes arising from leaf axils. Stems, leaves, floral bracts, and calyces are in most species covered in woolly or silky hairs. Pods are hairy, like small *Lupinus* pods.

CULTIVATION: Not often cultivated, they prefer a sunny position and deep well-drained soil of reasonable fertility. Growth is likely to be rather slow. Propagation is normally by seed, although it may be possible to divide the rootstock in some species.

Pediomelum esculentum

syn. *Psoralea esculenta*

INDIAN BREADROOT, POMME DE PRAIRIE, PRAIRIE TURNIP

↔12–20 in (30–50 cm) ↑12–20 in (30–50 cm)

Perennial found in most of the prairie states of central USA, from Wyoming to Louisiana, and in Canada's Saskatchewan province. Turnip-like roots, up to 3 in (8 cm) thick and 6 in (15 cm) long. Stems and leaves hairy; leaves with 5 narrow leaflets. Flowers dark purple-blue ageing almost white, in dense spike to 4 in (10 cm) long, in late spring–summer. Zones 2–9.

Passiflora, Hybrid Cultivar, 'New Incense'

Passiflora, Hybrid Cultivar, 'Coral Sea'

Paulownia tomentosa 'Sapphire Dragon'

P

PELARGONIUM

STORKSBILL

Most of the 250 species of annuals, perennials, and subshrubs in this genus of the geranium (Geraniaceae) family come from South Africa, a few from the rest of Africa, Australia, and the Middle East. Foliage is variable but often light green, rounded or hand-shaped, with conspicuous lobes, fine hairs and darker blotches. Some have succulent leaves. Flowers are simple 5-petalled structures, often massed and/or brightly colored, making a spectacular show. The name is from the Greek *pelargos,* stork, which refers to the shape of the seed pod.

CULTIVATION: Tolerant of light frosts only, many pelargoniums are treated as annuals in areas with cold winters. Plant most species in full sun in light well-drained soil. Drought tolerant once established. Ideal in coastal conditions. Propagate annuals and species from seed; perennials and shrubs from cuttings.

Pelargonium abrotanifolium

SOUTHERNWOOD GERANIUM

↔ 24 in (60 cm) ↑ 20 in (50 cm)

Bushy South African subshrub. Finely divided, aromatic, gray-green leaves to 1 in (25 mm) wide. Flowers a little over ½ in (12 mm) wide, in clusters of up to 5, white or pink, in spring–summer. Zones 9–11.

Pelargonium abrotanifolium

Pelargonium crithmifolium

Pelargonium endlicherianum

Pelargonium cordifolium ★

↔ 40 in (100 cm) ↑ 40 in (100 cm)

South African spring- to summer-flowering subshrub. Hairy stems and foliage. Leaves to over 2 in (5 cm) wide, 3- to 5-lobed, toothed, with pale undersides. Head of up to 8 purple, 1¼ in (30 mm) wide flowers, upper petals broad, lower petals linear. Zones 9–11.

Pelargonium crispum

LEMON-SCENTED GERANIUM

↔ 36 in (90 cm) ↑ 30 in (75 cm)

South African aromatic shrub. Small, 3-lobed leaves, crinkled edges. Pink flowers, dark markings, ¾ in (18 mm) wide. Foliage has a strong lemon scent when crushed. *P. crispum* is the parent of a number of cultivars with small fragrant leaves. **'Major'**, larger leaves; **'Minor'**, upright habit with tiny leaves; **'Peach Cream'**, pink flowers, subtle scent of peaches; **'Variegatum'**, cream-edged foliage. Zones 9–11.

Pelargonium crithmifolium

SAMPHIRE-LEAFED GERANIUM

↔ 12–20 in (30–50 cm) ↑ 20 in (50 cm)

Summer- to autumn-flowering South African and Namibian species with thick succulent stems and fleshy, gray-green, pinnate leaves to 6 in (15 cm) long. Heads of up to 8 starry white to pale pink flowers with reddish basal blotch, to over ½ in (12 mm) wide. Zones 10–11.

Pelargonium echinatum

CACTUS GERANIUM, SWEETHEART GERANIUM

↔ 20 in (50 cm) ↑ 20 in (50 cm)

A summer-dormant, tuberous, spring-flowering subshrub, native to western South Africa. The erect succulent stems have spiny leaf bases and a basal clump of short-lived pointed oval leaves to over 2 in (5 cm) long, with downy undersides. *P. echinatum* produces heads of up to 8 starry white or purple flowers with dark purple basal blotches. Zones 10–11.

Pelargonium endlicherianum

↔ 8–16 in (20–40 cm) ↑ 10–14 in (25–35 cm)

Rhizome-rooted, summer-flowering, Turkish perennial with leaves that are mostly basal, hairy, rounded, to over 2 in (5 cm) wide, with 5 shallow lobes. Produces heads of 5 to 15 fragrant light magenta flowers with large upper petals and very small or absent lower petals. Zones 9–10.

Pelargonium graveolens

ROSE-SCENTED GERANIUM

↔ 26 in (65 cm) ↑ 4 ft (1.2 m)

This shrub, native to South Africa, is possibly a hybrid. Erect stems. The rounded, deeply divided leaves release a strong scent of rosewater when they are crushed. The foliage and young stems are covered with fine hairs. The clusters of small, purple-veined pink flowers, appear in summer. **'Lady Plymouth'** produces compact growth with cream-edged strongly scented foliage, which is often used in floral decorations. Zones 9–11.

Pelargonium odoratissimum

APPLE GERANIUM

↔ 24 in (60 cm) ↑ 12 in (30 cm)

Low-spreading, spring- to summer-flowering perennial, native to South Africa. *P. odoratissimum* has fragrant leaves, apple-scented, rounded, pale green, and toothed, to around 1½ in (35 mm) wide. The branching flower stems carry heads of up to 10, ½ in (12 mm) wide, red-marked white flowers. Zones 9–11.

Pelargonium peltatum

IVY-LEAFED GERANIUM

↔ 8 ft (2.4 m) ↑ 8 ft (2.4 m)

Sprawling, scrambling, climbing, continuous-flowering, woody-stemmed South African perennial. Succulent rounded leaves, 5 triangular lobes, often zonally marked. Short-stemmed heads of up to 9 flowers. Zones 9–11.

Pelargonium, HC, Ivy-leafed, 'Evka'

Pelargonium quercetorum

↔ 12 in (30 cm) ↑ 16 in (40 cm)

Summer- to autumn-flowering perennial from Turkey and northern Iraq. Forms a small basal clump of rounded, 5- to 9-lobed, mid-green leaves to slightly more than 2 in (5 cm) wide. Wiry upright flower stems carry deep pink flowers. Zones 6–10.

Pelargonium sidoides

UMCKALOABO

↔ 12–30 in (30–75 cm) ↑ 12–20 in (30–50 cm)

Summer-flowering subshrub from South Africa. Sprays of small, deep blood red flowers and rounded gray-green leaves. Thickened roots enable it to reshoot after fire. Subject of much attention for medicinal properties in treating bronchitis, throat infections, and inflammation. Zones 9–10.

Pelargonium suburbanum

↔ 12–24 in (30–60 cm) ↑ 6–8 in (15–20 cm)

Winter- to summer-flowering, sprawling South African subshrub with small, deeply lobed, light green leaves and large, magenta, rarely white, flowers held just above the foliage on short stems. Upper petals large, lower petals small and narrow. Zones 9–11.

Pelargonium tomentosum

↔ 40 in (100 cm) ↑ 20 in (50 cm)

Spring- to summer-flowering South African perennial developing into a low, spreading clump of velvety, peppermint-scented, 3- to 5-lobed, rounded leaves to a little under 3 in (8 cm) wide. Erect flower stems with heads of up to 15 white flowers to over ½ in (12 mm) wide. Upper petals purple-marked, lower petals long and narrow. Zones 9–11.

Pelargonium tricolor

↔ 8–20 in (20–50 cm) ↑ 8–16 in (20–40 cm)

Small, spreading, evergreen perennial or subshrub native to southern Africa.

P. HC, Angel, 'Captain Starlight'

P., Hybrid Cultivar, Dwarf, 'Brackenwood'

P., HC, Scented-leafed, 'Lara Ballerina'

P., HC, Regal, 'Rimfire'

P., Hybrid Cultivar, Unique, 'Bolero'

P., HC, Zonal, 'Pagoda'

Downy gray-green foliage. Pansy-like 2-tone flowers appear on the plant for much of the year. Zones 9–10.

Pelargonium Hybrid Cultivars

↔ 8–40 in (20–100 cm)
↑ 6–60 in (15–150 cm)

Pelargonium species interbreed freely; the first hybrids appeared soon after the plants entered cultivation. The parentage of these early crosses is long-lost, but their legacy lives on in a range of hybrid groups of mostly compact plants with large showy flowers.

Ivy-Leafed Hybrids: These are derived mainly from *P. peltatum* and, for the great majority, it is questionable whether any other species enters into their parentage. They show a large range of growth forms, from extensive scramblers to very compact miniatures. They are very hardy for outdoor planting, and are tolerant of humidity and damp soil. **'Balcon'**, compact plants for containers, range includes pink, red, and lilac; **'Barbe Bleu'** produces deep purple double flowers ageing to deep red; **'Crock-etta'** has light veined leaves and white flowers with red markings; **'Evka'** has white-edged foliage with bright red flowers; and **'Mutzel'** has gray-green and white variegated leaves, and flowers of bright red.

Angel Hybrids: Similar to Regal Hybrids but are usually only 12 in (30 cm) tall or less. They do not produce double flowers. **'Angel's Perfume'**, pretty pansy-like pink and maroon flowers, lemon-scented foliage; **'Captain Starlight'**, 10 in (25 cm) tall, upper petals purple-red, lower petals pink-flushed white; **'Oldbury Duet'**, attractive hybrid with bright green leaves rimmed with white, upper petals burgundy with mauve markings, lower petals shades of mauve; **'Quantock Marjorie'**, 12 in (30 cm) tall, upper petals purple-red, lower petals very pale pink; **'Quantock Matty'**, 16 in (40 cm) tall, upper petals deep purple, lower petals pink-flushed white; **'Quantock Rita'**, 10 in (25 cm) tall, upper petals maroon, lower petals pink-flushed white; **'Quantock Star'**, 12 in (30 cm) tall, upper and lower petals dark red with broad pale pink margin; **'Spanish Angel'**, 12 in (30 cm) tall, upper petals purple-red edged with mauve, lower petals mauve with maroon blotch and veins; **'The Culm'**, upper petals of royal purple feature a delicate mauve edging, lower petals lavender pink with deeper pink markings; **'Tip Top Duet'**, 12 in (30 cm) tall, upper petals maroon, lower petals lavender.

Dwarf Hybrids: Resembling Zonal Hybrids in their foliage and stature, these small plants often have fully double blooms, which is the main point of difference from the Angel Hybrids. Flower display tends to be damaged by rain and they are best used in pots and window boxes. **'Beryl Reid'**, 6 in (15 cm) tall, pink flowers, darker blotch; **'Brackenwood'**, 8 in (20 cm) tall, salmon pink double flowers; **'Brenda'**, mid-pink flowers, red blotch; **'Brookside Flamenco'**, 6 in (15 cm) tall, vivid pink double flowers; **'Hope Valley'**, 8 in (20 cm) tall, golden yellow leaves, pink double flowers; **'Little Alice'**, 6 in (15 cm) tall, deep green leaves, dark salmon pink flowers; **'Orion'**, 8 in (20 cm) tall, orange-red double flowers; **'Redondo'**, 8 in (20 cm) tall, large red double flowers.

Regal Hybrids: These, also known as Martha Washington Hybrids, are around 20 in (50 cm) tall, though plant size ranges from dwarfs under 12 in (30 cm) tall through to shrubs of 4 ft (1.2 m) or more. Flowers large and reminiscent of evergreen azaleas; may be single or double and occur in a huge range of colors and patterns. **'Askham Fringed Aztec'**, frilly white flowers with red veining; **'Australian Mystery'**, cut-edged upper petals, magenta with lighter veining, lower petals white with magenta veining and blotch; **'Bert Pearce'**, large, frilly, pink flowers with red veining; **'Bosham'**, pink with dark purple-red upper blotch and magenta veining; **'Cherry Orchard'**, bright red with lighter center and dark red upper veining; **'Doris Hancock'**, bright light purple-pink; **'Eileen Postle'**, many-flowered heads of bright mid-pink with purple-red upper blotch; **'Harbour Lights'**, bright pink with pink-edged, dark-blotched, light red upper petals; **'Joan Morf'**, white flushed mid-pink with red upper blotch; **'Kimono'**, lavender-pink with white throat, deep magenta veining; **'Lara Susan'**, single, pale pink-edged purple-red upper petals, near white lower petals with small purple-red blotch; **'Lavender Sensation'**, lavender-pink with purple-red upper blotch; **'Lord Bute'**, simple single flowers, unusual colors, dark maroon with narrow bright pink edge; **'Rembrandt'** ★, purple edged with mauve-pink; **'Rimfire'**, black-red with red to pink edge; **'Rosmaroy'**, bright pink, pale red upper blotch, lower spotting; **'Springfield Black'**, dark purple-red, lighter center; **'Super Spot-on-bonanza'**, white flecked and sectored bright orange-red; **'Virginia Louise'**, pale pink, blotched deeper pink.

Scented-leafed Hybrids: Grown mainly for the aroma of their foliage, though their flowers can be very showy. **'Camphor Rose'**, minty camphor scent, small lavender flowers; **'Copthorne'**, showy magenta-centered pink flowers, cedar-scented foliage; **'Lara Ballerina'**, sharp citrus scent, white to pale pink flowers flushed with purple-red; **'Lara Starshine'**, mild citrus scent, many small, deep pinkish red flowers; **'Pink Champagne'**, dwarf habit with green and gold foliage, bright pink double flowers.

Unique Hybrids: These are woody-based perennials and most of them have *P. fulgidum* parentage, which shows in the large pinnately lobed leaves. Foliage is aromatic; flowers are large. **'Bolero'**, vivid pink flowers with darker center, single; **'Mystery'**, red flowers with darker blotch; **'Scarlet Unique'**, rich red flowers, aromatic velvety leaves; **'Shrubland Pet'** (syn. 'Shrubland Rose'), dwarf form, rose-red petals, deeper colored toward petal edges.

Zonal Hybrids: These are mainly of *P. inquinans* × *P. zonale* parentage with many now classified as *P.* × *hortorum*. They have a low bushy habit with succulent stems and light green, rounded to kidney-shaped, shallowly lobed leaves with dark zonal markings, to 4 in (10 cm) across. The heads of brightly colored flowers, to nearly 1 in (25 mm) wide, are held above the foliage on upright stems throughout the warmer months, year-round in frost-free areas. Many cultivars and seedling strains, including: **'Dolly Vardon'**, attractive tricolored leaves, red and green with creamy white edges, red single flowers; **'First Yellow'**, green leaves, primrose yellow flowers; **'Mrs Pollock'**, green leaf center, bordered with maroon, red, and yellow, orange-red flowers; **'Mrs Wren Improved'**, green leaves, white-edged orange-red flowers; **'Occold Shield'**, yellow leaves with red center, red flowers; and **'Retah's Crystal'**, variegated leaves, large soft pink flowers. Stellar forms have narrow, pointed petals and more sharply lobed foliage. These include: **'Annsbrook Gemini'**, leaves with dark red-brown central zone, bright pink double flowers with red flecks; **'Bird Dancer'**, very dark foliage, spidery salmon pink single flowers; **'Grandad Mac'**, dark foliage, orange-pink double flowers; **'Laura Parmer'**, dwarf habit, dark foliage, mid-pink single flowers; **'Mrs Pat'**, golden brown leaves with dark central zone, salmon pink single flowers; **'Pagoda'**, strongly marked foliage, pale pink double flowers; **'Red Cactus'**, green foliage, starry bright red flowers with long petals; **'Vancouver Centennial'**, red leaves with light green edges, small, bright magenta, single flowers. Zones 9–11.

PELLAEA

CLIFF BRAKE

This genus of 80 small to medium-sized, rock-loving ferns from the maidenhair-fern (Adiantaceae) family is found mostly in tropical to warm-temperate regions and has creeping or short rhizomes. Divided fronds are carried on dark or black stems, with small broad leaflets, with spore-bodies carried in bands along the frond margins. The genus is named from the Greek *pellos*, dusky, referring to the bluish gray leaves of some species.
CULTIVATION: Cliff brakes prefer a rich, well-drained, slightly alkaline soil, in a partially or fully shaded protected position with high humidity. Propagate from spores or by division.

Pellaea rotundifolia

ROUNDLEAF FERN

↔ 15–18 in (38–45 cm)
↑ 12–18 in (30–45 cm)

Fern from New Zealand and Australia with creeping stout rhizomes. Narrowly oblong, dull dark green fronds, 6–12 in (15–30 cm) long, with narrowly oblong to nearly circular, minutely serrated leaflets carried on stems to 6 in (15 cm) tall, which are covered with rust-colored scales. Zones 9–12.

PELTANDRA

ARROW ARUM

The 3 aquatic, rhizomatous, perennial herbs in this arum (Araceae) family genus inhabit the bogs and marshes of eastern North America and are grown for their decorative foliage. They have simple, arrowhead-shaped leaves on long, sheathed stalks, and tiny, unisexual flowers borne on spikes, carried on stalks the same length or longer than the leaf stalks, and enclosed by undulating spathes with overlapping margins. The fruit is a berry.
CULTIVATION: Arrow arums thrive in full or half-sun in damp, acidic soil adjacent to water, or in water up to 12 in (30 cm) deep. Propagate by division in spring or from seed, which should be stratified prior to sowing.

Peltandra virginica

GREEN ARROW ARUM, TUCKAHOE

↔ 12–36 in (30–90 cm)
↑ 12–36 in (30–90 cm)

From swamps and marshes of eastern and southeastern USA. Large, glossy, dark green leaves, 12–36 in (30–90 cm) long, in spring, clustered on succulent stalks, 18–36 in (45–90 cm) long. Narrowly opening yellowish green spathe, up to 8 in (20 cm) long, edged with white or yellow, enclosing an erect, whitish green flower spike, followed by green berries in late summer–autumn. Zones 5–9.

PELTOPHORUM

Consisting of 8 species of evergreen or deciduous trees from the cassia subfamily of the legume (Fabaceae) family, this genus occurs in the tropical savannah and coastal forests of Africa, Asia, the Americas, and northern Australia. Some species have been harvested for timber, others widely planted as ornamentals. The glossy green leaves are bipinnate, up to 18 in (45 cm) long, the ultimate leaflets being in 15 pairs, each about ½ in (12 mm) long. Prominent terminal panicles up to 24 in (60 cm) long bear many fragrant yellow flowers, with crinkly edges to the petals. Brown fruit pods contain several seeds.

Peltophorum pterocarpum, Thailand

Peltophorum africanum

CULTIVATION: Like most legumes, propagation is from seed which requires pre-treatment such as soaking in boiling water or scarification of the seed coat. These plants are only suitable for the tropics. Young plants require some shelter when first planted, but when established, full sun and well-drained moist soils are necessary.

Peltophorum africanum

↔ 20 ft (6 m) ↑ 40 ft (12 m)

Common semi-deciduous species of tropical Africa, south to northern South Africa, and Namibia. Leaves bipinnate, 7 pairs of leaflets, 20 pairs of ultimate leaflets. Bright yellow flower, in summer. Dark brown, flat, leathery seed pods. Zones 11–12.

Peltophorum pterocarpum

YELLOW FLAME TREE

↔ 30 ft (9 m) ↑ 50 ft (15 m)

Found in tropical India, Southeast Asia, Malay Archipelago, New Guinea, and Australia's "Top End." Medium-sized tree, with spreading branches. Leaves consist of bipinnate leaflets, 10 to 20 pairs. Terminal panicles of numerous fragrant yellow flowers, in summer. Flat, brown, leathery pods. Zones 11–12.

PENIOCEREUS

From southwestern USA, northern Mexico, and Central America, this genus of 18 species of shrubby, prostrate or climbing plants with thickened or tuberous roots belongs to the family Cactaceae, and includes species formerly placed in *Cullmannia, Neoevansia, Nyctocereus,* and *Wilcoxia.* Made up of thin often weedy-looking stems to 15 ft (4.5 m) high, the branches of some species have downy or velvety skin. Stems are always ribbed but rarely have tubercles. Spines are often conspicuous, usually even in shape and size, occasionally flattened against the stem. Large often white flowers with spiny pericarpels open by day or night, mostly borne laterally, occasionally terminally. Seed pods are spherical to pear-shaped, red, with deciduous spines.
CULTIVATION: Grow in a rich well-drained soil. Propagate from seed or cuttings dried out for a week or two. Rest in winter to avoid rotting underground stems.

Peniocereus greggii

ARIZONA QUEEN OF THE NIGHT, SWEET POTATO CACTUS

↔ 20 in (50 cm) ↑ 10 ft (3 m)

From southwestern USA and Mexico. Shrubby plant with a stem ½–¾ in (12–18 mm) in diameter, branching only occasionally. Large, white, nocturnal flowers, 6–8 in (15–20 cm) long, on stems arising from large tuberous roots to 24 in (60 cm) in diameter. Seed pods red and oval. Zones 8–11.

PENNISETUM

A genus of about 80 clump- or mat-forming, rhizomatous or stoloniferous, annual or perennial grasses from the family Poaceae, native to tropical, subtropical, and warm-temperate regions of Eurasia, Africa, Arabia and Australasia. They have round, hollow, prostrate to erect and tufted stems with solid swollen nodes, and alternate, narrow, strap-like, flat leaves rising from a central base as well as from the stems. The cylindrical or rounded, feathery, spike-like flowerheads grow at the ends of stems or from leaf axils, and contain clusters of up to 4 sword-shaped to oblong spikelets, minute bisexual flowers with 3 stamens and 2 stigmas, appearing in late summer and autumn. Fruit is an achene-like grain. Some species are cultivated for ornamental and foodcrop value. The genus is named from the Latin *penna*, feather, and *seta*, bristle, referring to the plant's feathery bristles.
CULTIVATION: They prefer moist, well-drained soil with either full sun or light shade. Propagate species from seed and hybrids by division in spring.

Pennisetum setaceum

Pennisetum setaceum 'Burgundy Giant'

Pennisetum alopecuroides ★

syn. *Pennisetum japonicum*

CHINESE PENNISETUM, FOUNTAIN GRASS, SWAMP FOX-TAIL GRASS

↔ 18–24 in (45–60 cm) ↑ 4–5 ft (1.2–1.5 m)

Clump-forming, upright, perennial grass, found from eastern Asia to northwestern Australia. Solitary, terminal, yellowish green to dark purple, cylindrical to narrowly oblong flowerheads, to 8 in (20 cm), with spikelets with purplish anthers and long bristles. Leaves to 24 in (60 cm) long, rough to the touch. **'Black Lea'**, 30 in (75 cm) tall, green foliage, very dark black-tinted flowerheads; **'Cassian'**, to 4 ft (1.2 m) tall, light brown foxtail-shaped flowerheads contrast with foliage, which turns gold with reddish tints in autumn; **'Hameln'**, clump-forming to 20 in (50 cm) high, with buff-colored flowerheads, golden leaves in autumn; **'Little Bunny'**, very compact form, to 18 in (45 cm) tall, with heads of whitish green flowers; **'Moudry'**, dark purple to black flowerheads, shiny dark green leaves, turning golden yellow then beige in autumn; **'Nafray'**, dense, compact growth habit; **'Purple Lea'**, vigorous grower, purple-pink-tinted flowerheads. Zones 5–9.

Pennisetum orientale

ORIENTAL FOUNTAIN GRASS, TALL TAILS

↔ 3–4 ft (0.9–1.2 m) ↑ 5–6 ft (1.5–1.8 m)

Rhizomatous perennial grass, native from central and southwestern Asia to northwestern India, which forms upright, arching clumps of slightly rough, green leaves to 4 in (10 cm) long. Loose, hairy flowerheads, to 6 in (15 cm) long, with 2 to 5 pinkish spikelets. Zones 8–10.

Pennisetum setaceum

FOUNTAIN GRASS

↔ 24–36 in (60–90 cm) ↑ 3–5 ft (0.9–1.5 m)

A clumping, perennial grass native to tropical Africa, southwestern Asia, and Arabia, annual in cooler climates. It has an erect slender stem and very narrow, rough, rigid leaves, 8–26 in (20–65 cm) long. The feathery, erect or inclined flowerheads, to 12 in (30 cm) long, are tinged with pink to purple, and contain 1 to 3 purplish spikelets in summer. **'Atrosanguineum'** has burgundy foliage and its soft reddish purple, nodding flower plumes appear in summer; **'Burgundy Giant'** has broad burgundy leaves, to 1 in (25 mm) wide, and whitish pink flowers on stalks to 4 ft (1.2 m) long, bright green in summer, and turning golden brown in autumn. Zones 9–10.

Pennisetum villosum ★

syn. *Pennisetum longistylum*

FEATHERTOP

↔ 18–24 in (45–60 cm) ↑ 2–4 ft (0.6–1.2 m)

A slowly spreading perennial grass, grown as an annual in cooler climates, and a native of northeastern tropical Africa. It forms loosely clumped, spreading mats. Sheathed leaves with bluish green blades, 2–16 in (5–40 cm) long. Solitary, compact, plumed, cylindrical to almost spherical flower spikes are 2–5 in (5–12 cm) long, with long, feathery bristles, and tinged with tawny brown to purple spikelets. This species self-seeds prolifically and can be invasive. Zones 8–10.

PENSTEMON

This genus of around 250 species of perennials and subshrubs in the plantain (Plantaginaceae) family is found from Alaska to Guatemala, with one straggler in cool-temperate Asia. Some are mat-forming, some shrubby, but most form clumps of simple linear to lance-shaped leaves in opposite pairs. Their flowers, borne mainly in summer on upright terminal spikes reminiscent of foxgloves *(Digitalis)*, are tubular to bell-shaped, with 2 upper lobes and 3 larger lower lobes. Native Americans used parts of several species in herbal medicines, primarily for pain relief and to control bleeding.

CULTIVATION: Because some species and garden forms are frost tender, considerable work has recently been put into producing hardy hybrids. Gardeners in cold winter areas should look for these. Plant in full or half-sun with moist well-drained soil. Alpine and southwestern species often prefer gritty soil but others like added humus. Propagate by division or from cuttings of non-flowering stems. The species may be raised from seed.

Penstemon alamosensis

ALAMO BEARDTONGUE

↔ 12 in (30 cm) ↑ 27 in (70 cm)

Summer-flowering perennial from the mountains around New Mexico/Texas border, USA. Pointed, silvery to blue-gray, lance-shaped leaves to about 3 in (8 cm) long. Wiry stems with narrow heads of downy, bright red, ½–1 in (12–25 mm) long flowers. Zones 8–10.

Penstemon ambiguus

↔ 16–20 in (40–50 cm) ↑ 24 in (60 cm)

Shrubby summer- to autumn-flowering perennial from alpine areas of western and southwestern USA and nearby parts of Mexico. Very narrow, finely toothed leaves to 2 in (5 cm) long. Open panicles of ½–1 in (12–25 mm) long flesh pink flowers, ageing to white. Zones 3–9.

Penstemon angustifolius

↔ 12–16 in (30–40 cm) ↑ 12 in (30 cm)

Summer-flowering perennial found in central USA from South Dakota to Colorado. Forms a tufted mound of fleshy, narrowly lance-shaped leaves to 3 in (8 cm) long. The wiry flower stems have small heads of ½–¾ in (12–18 mm) long pink flowers, ageing to mid-blue. Zones 3–9.

Penstemon azureus

↔ 8–12 in (20–30 cm) ↑ 12–20 in (30–50 cm)

From California, USA, this species is a late summer-flowering perennial with narrowly lance-shaped blue-green leaves to over 2 in (5 cm) long. Thin stems support small heads of narrow purple-blue or bright blue flowers to 1¼ in (30 mm) long. Zones 8–10.

Penstemon barbatus

BEARDLIP, CORAL PENSTEMON

↔ 12–20 in (30–50 cm) ↑ 40 in (100 cm)

Sturdy, strong-stemmed, summer-flowering perennial from Colorado, Arizona, and New Mexico, USA. Narrow lance-shaped leaves to around 3 in (8 cm) long and heads of pink to red flowers to 1½ in (35 mm) long, with extended upper lobes. **'Coccineus'**, bright red flowers; **'Elfin Pink'** is 14 in (35 cm) tall with bright pink flowers; **'Rose Elf'**, 14 in (35 cm) tall, deep pink flowers; **'Schooley's Yellow'**, 24 in (60 cm) tall with bright yellow flowers. Zones 3–9.

Penstemon campanulatus

↔ 8–12 in (20–30 cm) ↑ 12–24 in (30–60 cm)

Late spring- to early summer-flowering perennial from the mountains of Mexico and Guatemala. The leaves are narrow, toothed, and lance-shaped, to nearly 3 in (8 cm) long. Inflorescences of funnel- to bell-shaped, deep pink to purple flowers to 1 in (25 mm) long. Zones 9–10.

Penstemon cardwellii

↔ 20 in (50 cm) ↑ 8 in (20 cm)

Found in the low coastal ranges of Washington and Oregon, USA. Summer-flowering perennial forms low clump of short upright stems with 1 in (25 mm) long, blue-green, spatula-shaped leaves. The flowers are bright purple, and large in comparison to the plant size, nearly 1½ in (35 mm) long. Zones 5–9.

Pennisetum setaceum 'Atrosanguineum'

Pennisetum villosum

Penstemon azureus

Penstemon digitalis 'Husker Red'

Penstemon centranthifolius

SCARLET BUGLER

↔ 12–20 in (30–50 cm)
↑ 4 ft (1.2 m)

This late spring- to early summer-flowering perennial, a native of Baja California, Mexico, and California, USA, has erect stems with blue-green, lance- to spatula-shaped leaves to 4 in (10 cm) long. Inflorescences of narrow, tubular, bright red flowers around 1¼ in (30 mm) long. Zones 9–11.

Penstemon davidsonii

↔ 20–24 in (50–60 cm)
↑ 4 in (10 cm)

Low, spreading, summer-flowering perennial from western USA. Forms a mat of fine stems with ½ in (12 mm) long elliptical leaves, studded with short inflorescences of bright pink flowers around 1 in (25 mm) long. Zones 6–9.

Penstemon digitalis

FOXGLOVE BEARDTONGUE

↔ 12–24 in (30–60 cm)
↑ 5 ft (1.5 m)

Summer-flowering perennial from central USA. Strongly upright stems clothed in glossy, purple-tinted, blue-green leaves, 4–6 in (10–15 cm) long. The top 4–12 in (10–30 cm) of stems is composed of panicles of purple-pink flushed white flowers to around 1¼ in (30 mm) long. **'Husker Red'** has deep purple-red foliage, especially on new growth. Zones 3–9.

Penstemon eatonii

EATON'S FIRECRACKER

↔ 8–16 in (20–40 cm)
↑ 24 in (60 cm)

Late summer-flowering perennial from western USA. Forms a clump of fairly short, upright stems but with large

Penstemon laevis

Penstemon newberryi

lance-shaped basal leaves to over 6 in (15 cm) long, the upper leaves are much smaller. Small-branched heads of 1 in (25 mm) long bright red flowers. Zones 4–9.

Penstemon fruticosus

SHRUBBY PENSTEMON

↔ 20 in (50 cm) ↑ 16 in (40 cm)

Spring- to summer-flowering perennial from western USA. Forms a bushy clump of mostly erect stems with lance-shaped leaves to 2 in (5 cm) long, sometimes finely toothed. Heads of lavender to purple flowers around ¾ in (18 mm) long. Zones 4–9.

Penstemon grandiflorus

LARGE BEARDTONGUE

↔ 12–20 in (30–50 cm)
↑ 40 in (100 cm)

Found in central USA from North Dakota to Texas. Summer-flowering perennial with 1–4 in (2.5–10 cm) long, leathery, rounded, blue-green leaves. Inflorescences are up to 12 in (30 cm) long, with 1½ in (35 mm) long, lavender to pale blue flowers. **'Prairie Snow'**, 24 in (60 cm) tall, is a heavy-blooming white-flowered cultivar. Zones 3–9.

Penstemon heterophyllus

FOOTHILLS PENSTEMON

↔ 8–12 in (20–30 cm)
↑ 12–20 in (30–50 cm)

This is a shrubby summer-flowering Californian perennial. Narrow, dark green to blue-green leaves to 2 in (5 cm) long. Fairly short heads of lavender-pink to bright blue flowers around 1¼ in (30 mm) long. **'Blue Bedder'** ★ has compact, bright blue flowers; **'Heavenly Blue'**, dark mauve-blue to blue flowers. Zones 8–10.

Penstemon parryi

Penstemon hirsutus

↔ 8–12 in (20–30 cm)
↑ 16–32 in (40–80 cm)

Clump-forming, late summer-flowering perennial from eastern North America. The stems are erect, with toothed, lance-shaped leaves, 2–4 in (5–10 cm) long with downy uppersurfaces. The flowers are slightly pendulous, around 1 in (25 mm) long, purple with white-edged lobes. **'Pygmaeus'** is a 6 in (15 cm) tall cultivar with purple flowers. Zones 3–9.

Penstemon isophyllus

↔ 40 in (100 cm) ↑ 27 in (70 cm)

Spring-flowering Mexican perennial with purple-tinted stems initially spreading, then upright. The leaves are leathery and lance-shaped with slightly rolled edges, to 1½ in (35 mm) long. The inflorescence to 12 in (30 cm) long, bears 5-lobed, white-haired, red flowers to 1½ in (35 mm) long. Zones 9–11.

Penstemon laevis

SOUTHWESTERN BEARDTONGUE

↔ 16 in (40 cm) ↑ 20 in (50 cm)

Summer-flowering perennial native to western North America. Lance-shaped 2–3 in (5–8 cm) long leaves and spikes of rather widely spaced, bulbous, large-lobed mauve flowers to over 1 in (25 mm) long. Zones 5–9.

Penstemon newberryi

MOUNTAIN PRIDE

↔ 20–32 in (50–80 cm)
↑ 6–12 in (15–30 cm)

From California and Nevada, USA. Spreading, mat-forming, summer-flowering perennial. Finely toothed, pointed oval leaves about 1 in (25 mm) long. Short upright stems with heads of narrow, tubular, pinkish red flowers to 1¼ in (30 mm) long. Zones 6–9.

Penstemon palmeri

SCENTED PENSTEMON

↔ 16–24 in (40–60 cm)
↑ 32–55 in (80–140 cm)

Erect summer-flowering perennial from western USA. Pointed oval leaves to 6 in (15 cm) long, teeth tipped with small spines. Large, showy, scented heads of bulbous white flowers marked and flushed deep pink to red, to over 1¼ in (30 mm) long. Zones 5–9.

Penstemon parryi

↔ 16–24 in (40–60 cm)
↑ 12–24 in (30–60 cm)

Erect, short-stemmed, spring-flowering perennial from southern Arizona, USA. Broad, blue-green, lance- to spatula-shaped leaves to 3 in (8 cm) long. Short-branched racemes of funnel-shaped, ¾ in (18 mm) long, magenta flowers. Zones 8–10.

Penstemon pinifolius

↔ 16–24 in (40–60 cm)
↑ 16 in (40 cm)

Woody-based summer-flowering perennial native to Arizona and New Mexico, USA, and nearby parts of Mexico. Very narrow filament-like leaves with heads of bright red, 1 in (25 mm) long flowers. **'Mersea Yellow'** is an 8 in (20 cm) tall cultivar with bright yellow flowers. Zones 5–10.

Penstemon procerus

SMALL-FLOWERED PENSTEMON

↔ 12–16 in (30–40 cm)
↑ 6–16 in (15–40 cm)

Clump-forming summer-flowering perennial from northwestern North America. The stems are slender with broad, dark green, lance-shaped leaves to over 2 in (5 cm) long. The short-branched inflorescences of ½ in (12 mm) long carry white-centered lavender-blue and purple-pink flowers. ***P. p.* var. *tolmiei*** is just 4 in (10 cm) tall, with bright lavender-blue flowers. Zones 3–9.

Penstemon procerus var. *tolmiei*

Penstemon spectabilis

↔ 16–20 in (40–50 cm)
↕ 32–48 in (80–120 cm)

Strongly erect, early summer-flowering perennial native to California, USA, and northern parts of Baja California, Mexico. The coarsely toothed, green to blue-green, pointed oval to lance-shaped leaves to 4 in (10 cm) long, often partly or entirely encircle the stems. It produces short-branched heads of narrow, white-centered light purple flowers to over 1¼ in (30 mm) long. Zones 7–10.

Penstemon strictus

STIFF BEARDTONGUE

↔ 12–16 in (30–40 cm)
↕ 32 in (80 cm)

Clumping summer flowering perennial from the mountains of southwestern USA. Long-stemmed spatula-shaped basal leaves to over 3 in (8 cm) long, upper leaves linear to lance-shaped. Narrow heads of large-lobed, 1¼ in (30 mm) long violet to purple-blue flowers. Zones 3–9.

Penstemon superbus

↔ 20–32 in (50–80 cm)
↕ 5–6 ft (1.5–1.8 m)

Vigorous, erect, summer-flowering Mexican perennial with blue-green, leathery, pointed oval leaves to 6 in (15 cm) long, sometimes partly or entirely encircling the stems. Short-branched heads of whorls of many large-lobed bright red flowers to 1½ in (35 mm) long. Zones 9–11.

Penstemon venustus

LOVELY PENSTEMON

↔ 16–32 in (40–80 cm)
↕ 16–32 in (40–80 cm)

Late spring- to early summer-flowering subshrub found from Washington and Oregon to Idaho, USA. The leaves are finely toothed and lance-shaped, to over 4 in (10 cm) long, and it produces panicles of 1¼ in (30 mm) long, violet to purple flowers with hair-fringed lobes. Zones 5–9.

Penstemon virens

Penstemon virens

↔ 16–32 in (40–80 cm)
↕ 8–16 in (20–40 cm)

Mat-forming summer-flowering perennial species from Colorado, USA. Finely toothed or smooth-edged leaves to 4 in (10 cm) long; 3–6 in (8–15 cm) long inflorescences of large-lobed, ½ in (12 mm) long violet-blue and purple flowers. Zones 4–9.

Penstemon watsonii

↔ 12–16 in (30–40 cm)
↕ 12–24 in (30–60 cm)

Clump-forming, summer-flowering perennial from the mountains of Colorado, Utah, and Nevada, USA. Leaves pointed oval to lance-shaped, 1–2 in (25–50 mm) long, and sometimes finely toothed. Inflorescence with small branches, the flowers violet with occasional white markings, funnel-shaped and slightly over ½ in (12 mm) long. Zones 3–9.

Penstemon Hybrid Cultivars

↔ 8–16 in (20–40 cm)
↕ 24–48 in (60–120 cm)

Formerly listed under *P.* × *gloxinioides*, these hybrids have a complex parentage largely lost in the mists of time, though it is likely that *P. hartwegii* and *P. cobaea* were major influences. Modern hybrids are bred with large flowers, compact habit, bright colors, and frost tolerance as the main objectives and have proved to be among the most reliable performers in the perennial border. **'Alice Hindley'**, 4 ft (1.2 m) tall, white-centered mauve flowers; **'Andenken an Friedrich Hahn'** (syn. 'Garnet'), 32 in (80 cm) tall flowers, paler at first, becoming purple-red; **'Apple Blossom'**, 32 in (80 cm) tall, small pink-tipped white flowers; **'Burgundy'**, 4 ft (1.2 m) tall, deep purple-red; **'Chester Scarlet'** ★, 32 in (80 cm) tall, bright red with darker throat stripes; **'Countess of Dalkeith'**, 36 in (90 cm) tall, white-throated deep purple flowers; **'Hewell Pink Bedder'**, 32 in (80 cm) tall, gray-green foliage, reddish pink flowers; **'Hidcote Pink'**, 36 in (90 cm) tall, gray-green foliage, deep pink flowers with darker throat markings; **'Maurice Gibbs'**, 36 in (90 cm) tall, purple-red with white throat; **'Myddleton Gem'**, 30 in (75 cm) tall, vivid pinkish red with white throat; **'Osprey'**, 36 in (90 cm) tall, large-lobed pink flowers with white throat; **'Peace'**, 24 in (60 cm), narrow pink and white flowers; **'Pennington Gem'**, 36 in (90 cm), deep pink with red-marked white throat; **'Raven'**, 36 in (90 cm), purple-red with white throat; **'Rich Ruby'**, 36 in (90 cm) tall, purple-red with darker throat; **'Schoenholzeri'** (syn. 'Firebird'), 36 in (90 cm) tall, deep red; **'Stapleford Gem'**, 36 in (90 cm), violet and light purple tones; **'White Bedder'**, 27 in (70 cm) tall, 1930s seedling strain with compact habit and white flowers, sometimes pink in bud. Zones 6–10.

Penstemon, Hybrid Cultivar, 'Rich Ruby'

PENTAGRAMMA

A North American genus of the brake fern (Pteridaceae) family. The two species are small ferns that may be evergreen in cool moist climates but which are capable of surviving periods of drought by drying up and becoming dormant. They recover quickly after rain. The fronds are pinnate, and the undersides are often covered with spore capsules.
CULTIVATION: Plant in a moist position that is reasonably bright but not exposed to hot sun. These ferns are not spectacular, but are understated plants that reward a closer look. Propagation is from spores or by division.

Pentagramma triangularis

syns *Gymnogramma triangularis, Pityrogramma triangularis*

GOLDENBACK FERN

↔ 8–16 in (20–40 cm)
↕ 4–12 in (10–30 cm)

Small semi-evergreen fern, inhabiting rocky slopes and crevices in North America, from California to Alaska. Divided, broadly triangular to pentagonal, dark to mid-green fronds, to 7 in (18 cm) long, with narrow leaflets and rounded segments, on stiff, very dark brown stems, about twice the length of the frond, with a white, yellow, or orange powdery appearance underneath. Fronds curl up in drought, rejuvenating when rain comes. Zones 6–10.

Pentas lanceolata 'Butterfly Blush'

PENTAS

Mainly biennials and perennials, the 30 to 40-odd species in this genus of the madder (Rubiaceae) family from tropical parts of Arabia, Africa, and Madagascar also include a few shrubs. They have 3–8 in (8–20 cm) long ovate to lance-shaped leaves and small flowers in showy terminal heads. Flowers occur in all shades of pink, white, purple, mauve, and red. Removing the spent flowers extends the flowering season. Dry seed heads follow the flowers.
CULTIVATION: All are tender and will not tolerate frosts or prolonged cold conditions. Cultivated outdoors in the tropics and subtropics, they are treated as house or greenhouse plants elsewhere. They are not drought tolerant and need plenty of moisture while actively growing and flowering. Plant in a moist, fertile, humus-rich, well-drained soil and keep stem tips pinched back to ensure a compact habit. Propagate from seed or half-hardened cuttings, which strike quickly.

Pentas lanceolata

STAR CLUSTER

↔ 3 ft (0.9 m) ↕ 6 ft (1.8 m)

Found from Yemen to tropical east Africa, smaller in cultivation. Velvety leaves dark green. Large heads of flowers, white through shades of pink to magenta to lavender-blue, in summer. **'New Look Red'** ★ has scarlet flowers; **'New Look Rose'**, deep pink flowers; **'Stars and Stripes'**, white and cream variegated foliage, red flowers. The Butterfly Series includes **'Butterfly Blush'**, **'Butterfly Cherry Red'**, and **'Butterfly Light Lavender'**; and the **Lava Series** includes cerise, pink, white, and rose colors. Zones 10–12.

Pentas lanceolata 'New Look Rose'

PERICALLIS

CINERARIA

This genus of 14 species of perennials and shrubs in the daisy (Asteraceae) family, mostly Canary Island natives, is known mainly for its fancy-flowered hybrids. With soft, bristly or hairy leaves, some of the species carry their flowers singly but the cultivated plants produce large heads of daisies. Pink to purple is the predominant flower color in the wild, but the hybrids occur in a wide range of shades. The name is from Greek *peri,* around, and *kallos,* beauty, referring to the circle of showy ray florets.

CULTIVATION: Cinerarias prefer temperate climates; in cool areas treat as summer annuals or winter-flowering indoor plants. They like shade in summer but need more light in winter. Plant in humus-rich, cool, moist, well-drained soil. Usually propagated by seed, but the shrubby types will grow from cuttings.

Pericallis × *hybrida*

CINERARIA

↔16–40 in (40–100 cm)
↑16–32 in (40–80 cm)

Perennial hybrids mainly between *P. lanata* and *P. cruenta* parents, ranging from small mounding plants to taller, more open, shrubby forms. The preferred compact types have downy, angular heart-shaped leaves with toothed edges, sometimes purplish undersides; flowerheads clustered, often densely, in many colors. Zones 9–11.

PERILLA

A genus of 6 annual herbs in the mint (Lamiaceae) family, found naturally in Asia from India to Japan. Tight dense spikes of tiny flowers with a 5-toothed, bell-shaped calyx, and a 5-lobed corolla tube that is shorter than the calyx. Opposite pairs of leaves are often variegated or colored; those of some species are used in Oriental cuisine. Fruit consists of 4 joined nutlets.

Pericallis × *hybrida*

CULTIVATION: Space plants about 12 in (30 cm) apart, in rich but well-drained soil and full sun to light shade. Sow seeds outdoors in warm soil; the seeds require light to sprout. Deadhead to prevent invasive self-sowing.

Perilla frutescens

BEEFSTEAK PLANT, CHINESE BASIL, WILD SESAME

↔18–24 in (45–60 cm)
↑24–40 in (60–100 cm)

An erect, finely hairy, annual herb that resembles basil. Native species of the Himalayas and eastern Asia. Forms spikes, up to 4 in (10 cm) long, of small, white, pink, or reddish flowers with a corolla to 4 mm across, in the late summer to autumn. The leaves, which are green or purple or sometimes speckled with purple, are often wrinkled, and are broadly oval, heavily serrated, pointed, and 1½–5 in (3.5–12 cm) long, with a scent resembling cinnamon. *P. f.* var. *crispa* (syn. *P. f.* var. *nankinensis*) is an attractive plant, with extra-crinkled bronze or dark purplish brown leaves. Zones 8–11.

Perilla frutescens var. *crispa*

Perovskia atriplicifolia

PEROVSKIA

A genus of 7 species belonging to the mint (Lamiaceae) family. They are deciduous subshrubs or perennials from central Asia and the Himalayas. They are grown for their deeply toothed grayish foliage and large sprays of small blue flowers that are produced in late summer and autumn.

CULTIVATION: These hardy plants require little more than a sunny well-drained position and a heavy pruning each winter. Propagate from softwood or semi-hardwood cuttings.

Perovskia atriplicifolia

RUSSIAN SAGE

↔18–36 in (45–90 cm)
↑30–60 in (75–150 cm)

Clump-forming deciduous perennial, from Iran, Afghanistan, and western Pakistan. Upright stems. Grayish green, coarsely toothed to lobed leaves, 2–2½ in (5–6 cm) long, pungent when crushed. Narrow spikes, 12 in (30 cm) or longer, of tubular, tiny, blue to lavender flowers in late summer–autumn. Zones 5–9.

Perovskia Hybrid Cultivars

↔18–36 in (45–90 cm)
↑24–48 in (60–120 cm)

Thought to be hybrids of *P. atriplicifolia* and *P. abrotanoides*: **'Blue Haze'**, leaves hardly lobed; **'Blue Mist'**, light blue flowers, blooms earlier in the season; **'Blue Spire'** ★, darker, violet flowers in large panicles and deeply cut leaves; **'Filigran'**, finely dissected, almost fern-like leaves; **'Little Spire'**, sturdy, compact form; **'Longan'**, upright habit and compact. Zones 5–9.

PERSICARIA

KNOTWEED

A large and somewhat confused genus of between 50 and 80 species in the knotweed (Polygonaceae) family, found around the world. Many species are alternatively listed in the genera *Polygonum, Bistorta, Tovara, Antenoron,* or *Aconogonon.* Some are annuals, but most cultivated species are creeping perennials or occasionally subshrubs. Some can be quite weedy under ideal growing conditions. Many are grown for their attractive foliage; some are cultivated for their upright or drooping spikes of small flowers, which are usually pink turning to red as they age.

CULTIVATION: Most like a moist to very moist soil, in full sun to partial shade. Propagate by division or from softwood cuttings in spring.

Persicaria affinis

syns *Bistorta affinis, Polygonum affine*

↔20–24 in (50–60 cm)
↑8–10 in (20–25 cm)

Evergreen creeping perennial from the Himalayas. Upright stems clothed with leaves to 6 in (15 cm) long that turn bronze in frost-prone areas in winter. Produces tight upright spikes of tiny pink flowers in late summer, turning brown in winter. **'Darjeeling Red'**, larger leaves, flowers that open pink and turn red; **'Superba'**, vigorous form, producing large spikes of tiny pink flowers that turn red and then brown. Zones 3–10.

Persicaria amplexicaulis

syns *Bistorta amplexicaulis, Polygonum amplexicaule*

KNOTWEED, MOUNTAIN FLEECE

↔3–4 ft (0.9–1.2 m)
↑3–4 ft (0.9–1.2 m)

Upright perennial, native to Himalayas. Forms large, dense, bushy, slowly spreading clumps from woody rootstock. Stem-clasping, oval to sword-shaped, pointed leaves, 3–10 in (8–25 cm) long, heart-shaped at base and downy underneath, on long stalks. Dense, bottlebrush-like, erect flower spikes, 3–6 in (8–15 cm) long, of tiny rose red to purple or white flowers from early summer to early autumn. 'Firetail', low-growing form with bright crimson flowers. Zones 4–9.

Persicaria capitata

syn. *Polygonum capitatum*

KNOTWEED

↔6–12 in (15–30 cm)
↕3–6 in (8–15 cm)

Spreading perennial, native to the Himalayas. Dense, trailing, stalked heads of pink to red flowers from summer–autumn. Silvery grayish green heart-shaped or oval leaves, 1–2 in (25–50 mm) long, with intricate, purplish maroon, V-shaped bands, on hairy, glandular, rooting and creeping stems, to 12 in (30 cm) long. Best treated as an annual in cooler climates; can become invasive in warmer regions. **'Magic Carpet'**, fast-growing, compact, creeping form, to 4 in (10 cm) high. Zones 5–10.

Persicaria microcephala

↔5–7 ft (1.5–2 m)
↕40–48 in (100–120 cm)

Spreading, open-habited, herbaceous species from China. Green spearhead-shaped leaves to 7 in (18 cm) long, marked with bronze and pewter. Open heads of tiny white flowers at the tips in summer–autumn. **'Red Dragon'**, spectacular form with burgundy red leaves marked with pewter and chocolate brown. Zones 5–10.

Persicaria orientalis

syn. *Polygonum orientale*

KISS-ME-OVER-THE-GARDEN-GATE, ORIENTAL PERSICARY, PRINCE'S FEATHER

↔15–18 in (38–45 cm)
↕36–60 in (90–150 cm)

Sturdy annual, native to eastern and southeastern Asia and northern Australia, naturalized in North America. Lush, oval, bronze-green leaves, 4–8 in (10–20 cm) long, with soft fine hairs, on stout branching stems. Dense, drooping, many-branched spikes of bead-like, rose-purple, pink, or white flowers, in late summer–early autumn, lasting until frost. Self-seeds. Zones 8–10.

Persicaria amplexicaulis

Persicaria tenuicaulis

syns *Bistorta tenuicaulis, Polygonum tenuicaule*

↔8–16 in (20–40 cm)
↕4–10 in (10–25 cm)

Slow-growing, mat-forming, deciduous or semi-evergreen perennial native to Japan. Short dense spikes of tiny, bell-shaped, fragrant, white flowers appear in late spring–summer. Triangular, oval or elliptical, light or dark green leaves, 1¼–3 in (3–8 cm) long, on narrowly ridged stalks growing from a central, thick, trailing rootstock. Zones 4–6.

Persicaria virginiana

syn. *Polygonum virginianum*

↔32–60 in (80–150 cm)
↕24–48 in (60–120 cm)

Large perennial with mounding habit, found from Himalayas to Japan, and also in northeastern USA. Leaves pointed oval in shape, growing to 6 in (15 cm) long, tapering to a fine tip, downy to bristly, with dark markings. Narrow spikes of minute, pink-tinted, greenish white flowers, in late summer. **'Painter's Palette'**, variegated foliage combining cream with yellow, green, and red-brown patches. Zones 5–9.

PETASITES

BUTTERBUR, SWEET COLTSFOOT

A genus of about 15 species of herbaceous perennials from Europe, Asia, and North America in the daisy (Asteraceae) family. All have kidney-shaped leaves on upright stems and clusters or spikes of smallish flowers that are sometimes sweetly scented before the foliage emerges in spring. Some species are found in damp mountain meadows, but most are from swamps or damp soil in woods. They provide good ground cover in damp sites and make attractive poolside plants, but some can be quite invasive. In Japan, one species is used to make a condiment.

CULTIVATION: Grow in a humus-rich moist to wet soil in a sheltered site with morning sun or shade. Propagate by division while dormant.

Persicaria microcephala 'Red Dragon'

Petasites frigidus

↔36–40 in (90–100 cm)
↕6–10 in (15–25 cm)

Northern European species. Heart-shaped leaves are serrated around the edges and may be slightly lobed. The flowers grow in open spikes and are yellow-white or reddish. Zones 5–10.

Petasites japonicus

↔10–17 ft (3–5 m)
↕40–48 in (100–120 cm)

From China, Japan, and Korea. Huge kidney-shaped leaves grow to 32 in (80 cm) across, on a stem 40 in (100 cm) tall, or more. ***P. j.* var. *giganteus*,** even larger-leafed form; **'Nishiki-buki'**, which is sometimes called 'Variegata', streaks of variegated yellow. Zones 5–10.

PETREA

BLUE BIRD VINE

This genus of 30 evergreen, woody-stemmed, twining climbers, shrubs, or small trees, belonging to the vervain (Verbenaceae) family, is native to tropical America and the West Indies. They have simple, opposite, leathery leaves and long racemes of blue, purple, violet, or white flowers, growing from leaf axils or at the ends of branches. The narrow, bell-shaped corolla tubes have 5 flared and rounded lobes and 4 stamens. The fruit is a drupe.

CULTIVATION: Plant in full sun in fertile well-drained soil, and water regularly—less when not in growth. Plants may require support. Thin out crowded spring growth and protect against sucking insects. Propagate in sumer from semi-ripe tip cuttings, or from seed.

Petrea arborea

Petrea arborea

BLUE PETREA, TREE PETREA

↔10–12 ft (3–3.5 m)
↕20–25 ft (6–8 m)

Evergreen shrub or small tree with a climbing habit; native to northern South America and the West Indies. Slender gray branches covered with pores. Pairs of thinly textured, elliptical, grayish green leaves, to 6 in (15 cm) long, without stalks or on short stalks. Blue flowerheads, erect or nodding, finely hairy, 2–6 in (5–15 cm) long. **'Broadway'**, white flowers. Zones 10–12.

Petrea volubilis

PURPLE WREATH, QUEEN'S WREATH, SANDPAPER VINE

↔10–20 ft (3–6 m)
↕20–60 ft (6–18 m)

Evergreen woody vine or subshrub with intertwining pale brown to ash gray branches covered with pores. Native to Central America and the West Indies. Rough-textured leaves, about 8 in (20 cm) long, are dark green, oblong or elliptical, lighter green underneath. Erect or drooping cylindrical flowerheads, 3–12 in (8–30 cm) long. Flowers have a lilac calyx with lobes longer than the tube, and an indigo to amethyst corolla with a densely hairy tube. Dead flowers fall to the ground, rotating like helicopter blades. **'Albiflora'**, white flowers. Zones 10–12.

PETRORHAGIA

A genus of 25 to 30 erect, annual or perennial herbs belonging to the pink (Caryophyllaceae) family, native to temperate Eurasia, especially the eastern Mediterranean to southern Asia. They grow from tap roots, and their leaves are sheathed at the base with narrow sword-shaped blades that have 3 prominent veins. They bear terminal heads of few to several flowers with bracts and 5 fused, smooth, or minutely hairy sepals, and a prominent cylindrical corolla tube with 5 rounded, sometimes lobed, petals. Fruits are egg-shaped capsules with 4 chambers containing many blackish brown to black seeds. Some species grow in rock fissures, and this is reflected in the genus name, from two Greek words: *petros* (rock); *rhagas*, (chink).

CULTIVATION: Grow in rock gardens and banks, in full sun or part-shade, in well-drained sandy soil. Propagate from seed in spring or autumn (they self-seed readily in appropriate conditions), or by division in spring.

Petroselinum crispum 'Krausa'

Petrorhagia saxifraga

syns *Kohlrauschia saxifraga, Tunica saxifraga*

COAT FLOWER, SAXIFRAGE PINK

↔ 12–24 in (30–60 cm)
↑ 4–16 in (10–40 cm)

Mat-forming perennial from Turkey and southern and central Europe. Erect tuft-forming stems and narrow, ridged, smooth-edged, pointed leaves. Delicate loosely flowered cymes of cup-shaped flowers with short-clawed pale pink or white petals and darker veins, in summer. **'Alba'**, white flowers; **'Alba Plena'**, double white flowers; **'Lady Mary'**, to 3 in (8 cm) tall, soft pink double flowers; **'Pleniflora Rosea'**, low-growing form, pink double flowers; **'Rosea'**, light pink flowers; **'Rosette'**, compact form, pink double flowers. Zones 4–6.

PETROSELINUM

PARSLEY, ROCK PARSLEY, ROCK SELINEN

A genus of 3 annual or biennial tap-rooted herbs, these are members of the carrot (Apiaceae) family, and are native to temperate Eurasia. They have erect or spreading, branching stems and divided foliage. The compound leaf blades are broadly oblong, triangular, or oval, with toothed or lobed leaflets, often ornately curled. In late summer to autumn compound umbels of small greenish yellow or reddish flowers appear, followed by flat, ribbed, oval seeds. *P. crispum* is a widely cultivated culinary herb, which can become weedy; the leaves, roots, and seeds also have many medicinal purposes. The genus was named by Dioscorides, a herbalist of ancient Greece, from the words *petros* (rock) and *selinon* (celery).

CULTIVATION: Sow seeds after last frosts in early spring to autumn in moist well-drained garden soils in an open, sunny position, about 6–8 in (15–20 cm) apart in rows 12 in (30 cm) apart. Cut back frequently to maintain vigor. Plants last 2 years and will need to be replanted but may also self-seed. Otherwise, propagate from seeds soaked in warm water before planting to promote germination.

Petroselinum crispum

syns *Petroselinum hortense, P. sativum*

CURLY PARSLEY, PARSLEY

↔ 9–36 in (22–90 cm)
↑ 12–36 in (30–90 cm)

Biennial herb, native to Europe and western Asia. Erect or spreading stems. Grown widely for the culinary and medicinal value of its foliage. Dark to bright green, aromatic, edible leaves are mostly triangular, deeply divided, with toothed or deeply cut oval segments, sometimes flat, often curling. Terminal umbels of many small greenish yellow flowers appear, mostly above the leaves. There are many cultivars and varieties of garden parsley, with a wide variety of growth habits, leaf forms, and flavor strength. **'Afro'**, tall upright form, tightly curled dark green leaves; **'Champion Moss Curled'**, curled, finely cut, deep green leaves; **'Clivi'**, neat dwarf form; **'Darki'**, very cold-tolerant form, tightly curled very dark green leaves; **'Forest Green'**, strong-flavored variety; **'Italian Plain Leaf'**, plain, flat, deeply cut, dark green leaves; **'Krausa'**, triple-curled leaves; **'New Dark Green'**, very compact hardy form, emerald green leaves; **'Paramount'**, hardy vigorous form, dense, very dark green, closely curled leaves; ***P. c.* var. *neapolitanum*** (Italian parsley), flat uncurled leaves; ***P. c.* var. *tuberosum*** (Hamburg parsley, turnip-rooted parsley), thick, fleshy, edible root. Zones 7–9.

PETUNIA

Known mainly for the showy annual and perennial hybrids classified as *Petunia* × *hybrida*, this tropical South American genus from the nightshade (Solanaceae) family includes some 35 species of annuals, perennials, and shrubs. The genus is closely allied to tobacco *(Nicotiana)*, and its name is derived from Tupian Indian *petun*, "tobacco." Most are low spreading plants with soft, downy, rounded leaves and large funnel-shaped flowers with 5 fused lobes. Cultivated varieties occur in virtually every color, but lack the fragrance of some of the species.

Petunia × *hybrida*, Wave Series, 'Pink Wave'

CULTIVATION: Plant in full sun in moist, humus-rich, well-drained soil. Flowers are vulnerable to water spray and wet weather, although modern types are sturdier. Most are raised from seed; the more reliably perennial forms all grow well from cuttings.

Petunia axillaris

LARGE WHITE PETUNIA

↔ 16–24 in (40–60 cm)
↑ 12–20 in (30–50 cm)

Annual from Argentina, Uruguay, and southern Brazil. Sticky, short-haired, thin leaves with rounded tips. Conical white or creamy yellow flowers, night-scented, to 2 in (5 cm) long and wide, in summer. Zones 10–12.

Petunia × *hybrida*

↔ 8–40 in (20–100 cm)
↑ 4–16 in (10–40 cm)

Garden hybrids, mostly between *P. axillaris* and *P. integrifolia*. Generally low, spreading, short-lived perennials treated as annuals and raised from seed; they are often sold as mixed color strains. **'Colorwave'** is a distinct cultivar propagated vegetatively. *Petunia* × *hybrida* forms are sometimes grouped in classes such as Grandiflora (large flowers), Milliflora (small flowers, compact habit), and Multiflora (many flowers, spreading habit). Popular forms include: **'Black Cat'**, velvety black flowers; **Carpet Series**, mounding bushes in many colors; **Celebrity Series**, compact, heavy-flowering, several color mixes; **Daddy Series**, shades of pink and purple, large flowers, veins in contrasting colors; **Fantasy Series**, very compact, many small flowers, good container plant; **Frills and Spills Series**, frilly double flowers in all colors, trailing plants; **Giant Victorious Series**, all-double flowers, huge color range including bicolors and picotees; **Marco Polo Series**, double-flowered, mainly pinks, mauves, and purples; **Mirage Series**, large single flowers, often light colors, striking contrasting dark veins; **'Orchid Picotee Mixed'**, double flowers, mainly darker shades, white petal edges; **'Phantom'**, black petals with yellow central bar; **Supercascade Series**, compact but with trailing habit, wide color range; **Supertunia Series**, dense, low, spreading plants, wide color range; **Surfinia Series**, mainly purples, pinks, and blues; **Wave Series**, mounding bushes, large flowers. Zones 9–10.

Petunia integrifolia

Phacelia campanularia

Petunia integrifolia

↔ 16–24 in (40–60 cm)
↑ 12–20 in (30–50 cm)

Annual or short-lived perennial from Argentina. Sticky, downy, elliptical leaves, leaf stalks roughly equal in length; long-tubed violet flowers with purple-pink interior, to nearly 2 in (5 cm) wide, summer. Zones 8–10.

PHACELIA

SCORPION WEED

This genus of about 150 glandular, hairy, annual, biennial, or perennial herbs is a member of the borage (Boraginaceae) family, and originates from North and South America. The plants grow from thick tap roots. They have alternate leaves, divided or smooth-edged, and they bear dense terminal heads of white to purple flowers, which have a narrow 5-lobed calyx and an open to spreading bell-shaped corolla with lobed petals. The fruits are oblong or spherical capsules containing one to many brownish seeds with a pitted or furrowed appearance. The genus name comes from the Greek *phakelos* (cluster)—a reference to the dense flowerheads. The bristly hairs of this plant may cause severe dermatitis, and some species can become invasive and weedy.

CULTIVATION: Propagate both annual and biennial species in spring, sowing seed where plants are to grow in full sun in fertile well-drained soil. Tall species may need to be supported. Perennial species can also be propagated by division.

P

Phacelia campanularia

syn. *Phacelia minor* var. *campanularia*

CALIFORNIA BLUEBELL, DESERT BLUEBELL, WILD CANTERBURY BELL

↔ 6–24 in (15–60 cm) ↑ 6–24 in (15–60 cm)

Annual herb from sandy or gravelly dry or desert regions of southern California, USA. Simple, short-haired, erect stems; stiffly hairy, elliptical to oval, toothed leaves. Loose clusters of dark blue bell-shaped flowers with tubular to broadly bell-shaped corollas to 1½ in (35 mm) across, spotted with white, in early spring. Hairy glandular calyx lobes; oval, fine-haired, beaked fruits containing 40 to 80 pitted seeds. Zones 7–10.

Phacelia ixodes

↔ 8–24 in (20–60 cm) ↑ 8–24 in (20–60 cm)

Densely glandular and hairy annual from California, USA, and Baja California, Mexico. Erect sparsely branched stem, and lobed or compound, oval, toothed leaves. Bears flowers with oval calyx lobes and white to rose-colored bell-shaped corolla, in spring. The oblong fruits contain 10 to 18 brownish pitted seeds. Zones 6–9.

PHAEDRANASSA

QUEEN LILY

This genus of 7 bulbous herbaceous perennials belonging to the amaryllis (Amaryllidaceae) family is native to dry and barren zones of the South American Andes from Peru to the southern parts of Colombia. They are dormant in winter, and produce narrow to broadly oblong leaves on stalks after the flowers bloom. Their drooping umbels consist of narrow tubular or funnel-shaped to cylindrical flowers with narrow, spreading lobes. CULTIVATION: They prefer full sun or part-shade and rich well-drained soil. Water sparingly in winter, and apply fertilizer high in potash during summer. Propagate from seed, or by division of offsets in spring.

Phaseolus coccineus

Phaedranassa dubia

Phaedranassa dubia ★

↔ 12–18 in (30–45 cm) ↑ 12–18 in (30–45 cm)

From the Peruvian Andes. Unusual stalked leaves, heads of waxy, tubular, purplish pink to reddish flowers, 2 in (5 cm) long or more, tipped with green, from spring–summer, on stalks up to 18 in (45 cm) tall. Zones 6–8.

PHASEOLUS

BEAN

This is a genus of about 20 annual or perennial, usually climbing herbs belonging to the pea-flower subfamily of the legume (Fabaceae) family. They are native to the Americas, with several species grown widely as food crops. All have compound leaves, with 3 smooth-edged or lobed leaflets and sickle-shaped flower buds, which grow from the leaf axils and open as loose racemes of pea-flowers with persistent bracts. The fruits are narrow oblong pods, often flattened. The fruits contain several oval or flattened seeds.

CULTIVATION: Perennial species are often grown as annuals, sown and harvested during frost-free months. Grow in humus-rich well-drained soil in full sun, providing support for stems of climbing varieties. Water freely during growth and propagate from seed in autumn or spring.

Phaseolus coccineus

DUTCH CASE-KNIFE BEAN, SCARLET RUNNER BEAN

↔ 24 in (60 cm) ↑ 4–6 ft (1.2–1.8 m)

Tall, twining, perennial vine, native to tropical Americas. Grown as an annual. Compound leaves with broad oval to heart-shaped leaflets, to 5 in (12 cm) long. Long racemes of many bright scarlet flowers appear in spring. Pods, to 12 in (30 cm) long, contain black seeds, to 1 in (25 mm) long, mottled with red. *P. c.* var. ***albonanus***, bushy form, white seeds. *P. c.* var. ***rubronanus***, erect form, red flowers. *P. c.* **'Albus'**, white seeds and flowers; **'Painted Lady'** ★, red and white flowers. Zones 8–10.

PHELLODENDRON

This is a genus of 10 species of deciduous trees from temperate East Asia, which belong to the rue (Rutaceae) family. Notable for their aromatic foliage and corky bark, these trees have large pinnate leaves composed of broad, often glossy leaflets. The flowers are small and yellow-green in color and are carried in panicles, followed by small, black, fleshy fruits. The autumn foliage, however, is often bright yellow and can be quite spectacular in some years.

CULTIVATION: Most species in this genus need a climate with seasons that are well differentiated, and a cool winter is important to ensure proper dormancy. On the other hand, they handle hot summers and harsh sun with ease, though the foliage is easily damaged by strong winds. They seem to thrive in any well-drained soil with a position in full sun. Plants may be propagated from seed, from cuttings, by layering, or by grafting.

Phellodendron amurense ★

AMUR CORK TREE

↔ 40 ft (12 m) ↑ 50 ft (15 m)

Found in northern China. Corky pale gray bark. Strongly aromatic leaves composed of 9 to 13 broad leaflets, dark glossy green upper sides, blue-green undersides, turning yellow in autumn. Panicles of small yellow-green flowers are borne in early summer. Clusters of fruit held erect above the foliage. Zones 3–9.

Phellodendron lavallei

↔ 35 ft (10 m) ↑ 30 ft (9 m)

Native of central Japan. Thick corky bark, young shoots with a rusty coating. Leaves to 15 in (38 cm) long, with 5 to 13 light green pointed leaflets, undersides covered in fine hairs. Flowers from early summer. Zones 6–9.

Phellodendron lavallei

Phellodendron sachalinense

↔ 35 ft (10 m) ↑ 25 ft (8 m)

Found in Korea, Sakhalin (an island between Russia and Japan), and western China. Bark thin, shallowly channeled, deep brown. Spreading crown of matt mid-green leaves, 8–12 in (20–30 cm) long. Colors well in autumn. Good shade tree. Zones 3–9.

PHILADELPHUS

MOCK ORANGE

Occurring within the hydrangea (Hydrangeaceae) family, this genus from temperate regions of Central and North America, southeast Europe, the Himalayas, and Asia includes 60 or so species of mainly deciduous shrubs. They usually have peeling bark. They are frequently grown for ornamental purposes, but are also cultivated for their scented double or single flowers, as specimen shrubs in woodland, or in a shrub border.

CULTIVATION: They grow well in full sun or partial shade, or in deciduous open woodland in moderately fertile well-drained soil, but flower better in full sun. If grown in pots, a loam-based compost is best, and regular feeding and watering are necessary throughout the growing season. Propagate from softwood cuttings taken in summer or hardwood cuttings taken in autumn and winter.

Phellodendron sachalinense

P

Philadelphus delavayi

↔8 ft (2.4 m) ↑10 ft (3 m)

Native to western China and northern Myanmar. Deciduous upright shrub. Leaves narrow, egg-shaped, toothed, with a pointed tip, larger on non-flowering shoots, dense flattened hair on undersides. Saucer-shaped flowers, white and fragrant, 9 per raceme, in early summer. Zones 6–9.

Philadelphus incanus

↔6 ft (1.8 m) ↑12 ft (3.5 m)

Erect shrub native to the Hubei and Shaanxi Provinces in China. Branches hairy when young, peeling with age. Leaves oval to elliptical, larger on non-flowering shoots. White blooms in racemes of up to 11 individual flowers, in late summer. Zones 5–9.

Philadelphus lewisii

INDIAN ARROWWOOD, LEWIS MOCK ORANGE, LEWIS SYRINGA

↔10 ft (3 m) ↑10 ft (3 m)

State flower of Idaho, USA. Arching shrub native to the west of North America. Leaves bright green, egg-shaped, margins occasionally finely toothed. Racemes carrying 5 to 11 mildly scented flowers appear in early summer. Zones 5–9.

Philadelphus mexicanus

MEXICAN MOCK ORANGE

↔8 ft (2.4 m) ↑15 ft (4.5 m)

Native to Guatemala and Mexico. Evergreen climbing shrub. Pendulous branches, long bristles on current growth, egg-shaped leaves may have toothed margins. Bears rose-scented lemony white flowers, often solitary, in summer. Zones 9–10.

Philadelphus mexicanus

Philadelphus microphyllus

↔3 ft (0.9 m) ↑3 ft (0.9 m)

Native to southwestern USA. Erect deciduous shrub. Bark peels second year, new growth is felty. Small, mid-green, shiny, smooth-edged leaves. Cross-shaped, scented, white flowers, in early–mid-summer. Zones 6–9.

Philadelphus pubescens

MOCK ORANGE, SYRINGA

↔7 ft (2 m) ↑15 ft (4.5 m)

Native to southeastern USA. Egg-shaped pointed leaves are bristly and hairy on the undersides. White flowers carried in racemes of 5 to 11 blooms appear in early summer. Zones 6–9.

Philadelphus subcanus

↔8 ft (2.4 m) ↑20 ft (6 m)

Shrub native to southwestern China. Upright habit, peeling bark on mature branches only. Leaves are fine-toothed on flowering shoots, deeply toothed on non-flowering wood. Racemes of white, fragrant flowers, slightly cup-shaped, in early summer. ***P. s.* var. *magdalenae,*** shorter, with smaller leaves and flowers. Zones 6–9.

Philadelphus Hybrid Cultivars

↔6 ft (1.8 m) ↑5 ft (1.5 m)

Most early hybrid cultivars were created by the French plant breeder Pierre Lemoine, and were crosses of *P. coronarius* and *P. microphyllus*, often grouped as *P.* × *lemoinei.* The influence of *P. inodorus* and *P. insignis* prompted the new hybrid names *P.* × *cymosus* and *P.* × *polyanthus*, respectively. Crosses between earlier hybrids and *P. coulteri* were grouped under *P.* × *purpureomaculatus*. Finally, a group emerged in which *P. pubescens* showed its influence, under the name *P.* × *virginalis*. **'Avalanche'**, an early Lemoine hybrid, upright growth to 6 ft (1.8 m), scented white flowers; **'Beauclerk'**, a later English hybrid, height and spread of 8 ft (2.4 m), large, fragrant, single, cup-shaped, white flowers, pink-tinged centers, early–mid-summer; **'Belle Etoile'**, *P.* × *purpureomaculatus* hybrid, purple-red central splash on flowers, sweet pineapple-like fragrance; **'Boule d'Argent'**, *P.* × *polyanthus* hybrid, compact slightly arching shrub to 5 ft (1.5 m) tall and spread, double or semi-double flowers, in summer; **'Bouquet Blanc'**, *P.* × *cymosus* hybrid, profuse semi-double flowers; **'Buckley's Quill'**, to 6 ft (1.8 m), upright shrub, fragrant double flowers in early–mid-summer, up to 30 long quill-like petals per flower; **'Dame Blanche'**, Lemoine hybrid, cream colored semi-double flowers; **'Fimbriatus'**, Lemoine hybrid, compact fine-cut petal edges; **'Glacier'**, *P.* × *virginalis* hybrid, compact shrub to 5 ft (1.5 m) in height and spread, fragrant double white flowers, mid-summer; **'Innocence'**, Lemoine hybrid, to 10 ft (3 m), yellow foliage, fragrant, white, single or semi-double flowers, summer; **'Manteau d'Hermine'**, Lemoine hybrid, to 30 in (75 cm) high, creamy double flowers, summer. Other *P.* × *virginalis* types include: **'Minnesota Snowflake'**, double white flowers; **'Natchez'**, single flowers; **'Rosace'**, *P.* × *cymosus* hybrid, semi-double flowers; **'Schneesturm'**, *P.* × *virginalis* hybrid, pure white double flowers; **'Sybille'**, *P.* × *purpureomaculatus* hybrid, to 4 ft (1.2 m), purple patches in the center of single white flowers; **'Virginal'** (the original member of the *P.* × *virginalis* group), fragrant double white flowers carried in loose heads. Zones 5–9.

Philadelphus, Hybrid Cultivar, 'Rosace'

PHILODENDRON

This genus, a member of the arum (Araceae) family, consists of around 500 species from tropical America and the West Indies. They are mainly epiphytic clinging vines with aerial roots, but the genus also includes some shrubby and almost tree-like species. The large glossy leaves may be smooth-edged, variously lobed, or deeply divided in a feather-like pattern. The flowers are insignificant and without petals; they are held on a flower spike. Plant parts are poisonous, and contact with the sap may cause skin irritation. Suitable species can make attractive landscape plants in warm climates. Many are used as indoor plants.

CULTIVATION: Philodendrons do best in the tropics and subtropics, requiring a moist, well-drained, humus-rich soil with generous watering in the growth phase. Many species are tolerant of low light and should be grown in dappled shade. Propagate from seed, from cuttings, or by layering.

Philodendron bipinnatifidum

Philodendron bipinnatifidum

syn. *Philodendron selloum*

TREE PHILODENDRON

↔10 ft (3 m) ↑10 ft (3 m)

Native to southeastern Brazil, this is a large tree-like shrub with stout aerial roots. Spectacular, shiny, deep green leaves, up to 3 ft (0.9 m) long, deeply divided, lobed, broadly ovate, and somewhat arrow-shaped at their bases; the leaf stalks are as long as the leaves. The spathes are green to purplish red on the outside, red-edged cream on the inside. Zones 10–12.

Philodendron Hybrid Cultivars

↔7 ft (2 m) ↑7 ft (2 m)

Hybridizing between various species has produced range of cultivars, usually with emphasis on compact habit and foliage color, including: **'Autumn'**, narrow, undivided leaves pass through orange shades; **'Congo'**, compact with lush, undivided heart-shaped leaves; **'Imperial Gold'**, orange-red new growth, then orange and green; **'Imperial Green'**, dense, lush, vivid green foliage; **'Imperial Red'**, bright red new growth, long bronze-green leaves; **'Rojo Congo'**, red-tinted dark foliage form of 'Congo'; **'Xanadu'**, lush heart-shaped foliage with curled drip-tip, also **'Golden Xanadu'** with yellow-green foliage. Zones 10–12.

PHILOTHECA

WAX FLOWER

A genus of about 45 species of evergreen shrubs of the rue (Rutaceae) family, endemic to Australia. They have very aromatic young stems and foliage covered in oil glands. The leaves are usually a simple narrow elliptical shape. The flowers are small and starry, 5-petalled, white to mauve, with a waxy texture. Spring to early summer is the main blooming season but flowers appear all year.

CULTIVATION: Most are easily grown in moist, humus-rich, well-drained soil. They will flower most heavily in sun but the foliage is better with a little shade. May be pruned hard or sheared as a hedge. Propagation is from half-hardened cuttings, which strike freely.

Philotheca myoporoides 'Profusion'

Philotheca myoporoides

syn. *Eriostemon myoporoides*

LONG-LEAF WAX FLOWER

☼/◐ ❄ ↔5–7 ft (1.5–2 m)
↕4–6 ft (1.2–1.8 m)

Native to Victoria, New South Wales, and southern Queensland, Australia. Stems and foliage a distinctive light green shade with tiny warty oil glands, spicy aroma. White flowers in abundance, open from pink buds, year-round. **'Bournda Beauty'**, very compact form; **'Galaxy'**, abundant flowers in open clusters; **'Moon Shadow'**, yellow leaf margins; **'Profusion'**, popular long-flowering cultivar with short-stemmed flowers. Zones 9–10.

PHLEBODIUM

This genus of 4 evergreen or semi-evergreen ferns belongs to the polypody (Polypodiaceae) family. Native to tropical America and the West Indies, they have thick, fleshy, creeping rhizomes sheathed with rust-colored to gold scales, and smooth, oval, divided fronds, leathery or papery in texture, on jointed stems. The genus name comes from the Greek *phlebodes,* meaning full of veins, and refers to the many veins on the fronds.

CULTIVATION: *Phlebodium* species like a rich, well-drained, moist soil in half-sun to shade, with regular watering and protection from frost. They are suited to cultivation in pots or hanging baskets, and are propagated from spores or by division.

Phlebodium aureum

syn. *Polypodium aureum*

HARE'S FOOT FERN, RABBIT'S FOOT FERN

◐ ✢ ↔24–36 in (60–90 cm)
↕24–36 in (60–90 cm)

Widespread and variable evergreen epiphytic fern, found on palm trunks or tree limbs in tropical and subtropical regions of Mexico and West Indies. Thick creeping rhizomes covered with golden yellow hairs. Deeply divided fronds, oval to triangular, to 40 in (100 cm) long.

Phlebodium aureum var. *areolatum* 'Mandanum'

Large narrow or strap-shaped leaflets vary in color from grayish green and silvery green to an intense powdery-looking blue-green, often with undulating margins. Leaflets turn purplish in cold weather. There are several cultivars with highly crested or wavy-edged fronds that are a metallic gray-blue in color, including: ***P. a.* var. *areolatum***, erect, smooth, leathery fronds; **'Mandanum'**, leaflets curved and wavy; **'Mayi'**, ruffled and fringed leaflets. Zones 10–12.

PHLOMIS

This is a genus of about 100 low growing shrubs, subshrubs and herbs in the mint (Lamiaceae) family. These species are widely distributed through Europe and Asia, from the Mediterranean regions to China. Most have felted leaves and tubular flowers, which are borne in whorls along the stems. The flowers have 2 lips at their tips, the upper lip being hooded over the lower one; they may be yellow, cream, pink, mauve, or purple in color.

CULTIVATION: Most *Phlomis* species are quite frost hardy, and are best planted in exposed sunny positions where the felted leaves can dry out quickly after rain. They are drought tolerant, to the point at which they generally resent receiving too much water in summer. Propagation is from seed, or else from tip cuttings from non-flowering shoots.

Phlomis bovei

☼ ❄ ↔36 in (90 cm) ↕36 in (90 cm)

Native to Algeria and Tunisia. Upright hairy-stemmed perennial with long heart-shaped leaves with puckered upper surface and very hairy beneath; purplish pink flowers are borne in well-spaced whorls. ***P. b.* subsp. *maroccana***, native to Morocco, is taller and has larger flowers. Zones 9–11.

Phlomis fruticosa

Phlomis cashmeriana

☼ ❄ ↔36 in (90 cm) ↕36 in (90 cm)

Robust plant with very woolly stems, native to Kashmir and the western Himalayas. Narrow oval leaves are downy, with white undersides. Pale lilac flowers, held in crowded whorls, appear in summer. Zones 8–11.

Phlomis chrysophylla

☼ ❄ ↔3 ft (0.9 m) ↕4 ft (1.2 m)

Small evergreen subshrub, native to Lebanon. Erect branching stems and broad oval leaves, which are covered in golden down when young and fade to a yellowish gray as they mature. The bright golden yellow flowers are borne in whorls in the leaf axils, in summer. Zones 7–10.

Phlomis 'Edward Bowles'

☼ ❄ ↔36 in (90 cm) ↕36 in (90 cm)

Robust hybrid subshrub. Pointed oval leaves, up to 6 in (15 cm) long, have wrinkled surfaces. Whorls of sulfur yellow flowers appear in summer. Zones 7–11.

Phlomis fruticosa

JERUSALEM SAGE

☼ ❄ ↔30 in (75 cm) ↕30 in (75 cm)

Evergreen shrub from the Mediterranean region. Leaves green and felty; bright yellow flowers, in summer. Tolerates coastal conditions. Prune vigorously, to half its size, in autumn. Zones 7–10.

Phlomis italica

☼ ❄ ↔12 in (30 cm) ↕12 in (30 cm)

Subshrub from the Balearic Islands, Spain. The leaves are narrow and oblong, and have white hairs. The flowers, which are borne in well-spaced whorls of 6 in summer–autumn, have grayish white calyces and are pink or pale lilac in color. Zones 8–11.

Phlomis russeliana

Phlomis lanata ★

☼ ❄ ↔20 in (50 cm) ↕20 in (50 cm)

Native to Crete, Greece. Small shrub with golden hairy stems. The small oblong leaves and flower calyces are very woolly. The orange-yellow flowers are carried in whorls of 2 to 10 blooms, in summer. Zones 8–11.

Phlomis purpurea

☼ ❄ ↔24 in (60 cm) ↕24 in (60 cm)

From Spain and Portugal. Woolly-stemmed plant with narrow, wrinkled, leathery, grayish green leaves that have very hairy undersides. Downy purple to pink flowers are borne in whorls in summer. Zones 8–11.

Phlomis russeliana

☼ ❄ ↔24 in (60 cm) ↕36 in (90 cm)

Native to just a small area of western Syria, but common in cultivation. It is a small shrub with long-stemmed heart-shaped leaves that are covered with fine hairs, especially on the undersides. It bears spikes of pale yellow hooded flowers in summer. It does not thrive in prolonged wet conditions. Zones 7–9.

Phlomis tuberosa

☼ ✱ ↔36 in (90 cm) ↑36 in (90 cm)

Tuberous-rooted deciduous perennial, from central Europe to central Asia. Lightly hairy, pointed oval leaves to 10 in (25 cm) long. Whorls of purple to pink flowers, more crowded near the stem ends, in summer. Zones 6–10.

Phlomis viscosa

☼ ❄ ↔3–4 ft (0.9–1.2 m) ↑3–4 ft (0.9–1.2 m)

Native to southwestern Asia and Turkey. Well-branched shrub, sometimes confused with the perennial *P. russelliana,* which is often misnamed *P. viscosa*. Hairy leaves to 6 in (15 cm) long, and whorls of 12 to 20 yellow flowers in summer. Zones 8–11.

PHLOX

This North American genus of 67 annuals and perennials belongs in the phlox (Polemoniaceae) family. All types have similar terminal heads of small bell-shaped flowers with long widely flaring tubes, but growth habits differ markedly. Annual species tend to be small mounding bushes; the ground-hugging rock phlox has tiny leaves; trailing forms have long stems and suit hanging baskets; and border phlox species are upright and bushy, often with plenty of foliage. *Phlox* is Greek for "flame"—a very appropriate epithet for the annual, rock, and border types, with their vivid bursts of incandescent color.

CULTIVATION: All phlox species prefer well-drained soil that can be kept moist; annual and rock phlox need full sun; border and trailing forms will take part shade. Border phlox need good ventilation to prevent late-season mildew. Propagate by seed, by division, or from cuttings.

Phlox divaricata subsp. *laphamii* 'Chattahoochee'

Phlox carolina 'Bill Baker'

Phlox douglasii 'Crackerjack'

Phlox adsurgens

WOODLAND PHLOX

☼/◐ ✱ ↔12–20 in (30–50 cm) ↑4–6 in (10–15 cm)

From western USA, a spreading perennial, stem tips sometimes partly erect. Oval leaves, ½–1 in (12–25 mm) long. Open flowerheads of pink to purple blooms, to 1 in (25 mm) wide, in late spring–summer. Zones 6–10.

Phlox bifida

SAND PHLOX

☼/◐ ✱ ↔12–16 in (30–40 cm) ↑4–8 in (10–20 cm)

Tufted perennial from central USA. Rather sparse hairy leaves, elliptical to near-linear. Drooping downy inflorescences of honey-scented, starry, white to lavender flowers with notched petals, spring–summer. Zones 6–10.

Phlox drummondii

Phlox paniculata

Phlox carolina

THICKLEAF PHLOX

☼/◐ ✱ ↔16–24 in (40–60 cm) ↑4 ft (1.2 m)

Upright clump-forming perennial from eastern USA. Leaves leathery, glossy, narrow, lance-shaped, sometimes linear. In spring–early summer, large showy heads of pink or purple flowers, to 1 in (25 mm) wide. **'Bill Baker'**, 18 in (45 cm) tall, compact, large pink to mauve flowers. Zones 5–10.

Phlox divaricata

BLUE PHLOX, WILD SWEET WILLIAM

☼/◐ ✱ ↔24–40 in (60–100 cm) ↑12–18 in (30–45 cm)

Spreading low-clump-forming perennial from central North America. Wiry stems, pointed oval to narrow lance-shaped leaves. In spring, small heads of lavender-pink, mauve, or white flowers to 1½ in (40 mm) wide. ***P. d.* subsp. *laphamii* 'Chattahoochee'** ★, 6 in (15 cm) tall, lavender flowers with red eye. Zones 4–9.

Phlox douglasii

☼/◐ ✱ ↔12–20 in (30–50 cm) ↑2–6 in (5–15 cm)

Perennial from northwestern USA; usually mat-forming, but sometimes stem tips ascend slightly. Fine downy stems with very narrow hair-fringed leaves. Flowers in showy, tightly clustered heads, mainly in deep pink, red, mauve, and purple, in spring–early summer. **'Boothman's Variety'**, 3 in (8 cm) tall, dark-centered lavender flowers; **'Crackerjack'**, neat compact habit, magenta flowers; **'Kelly's Eye'**, pale pink flowers, purple-red center; **'Red Admiral'**, mounding to 4 in (10 cm) high, crimson flowers; **'Rosea'**, silvery pink flowers. Zones 5–10.

Phlox drummondii

☼/◐ ✱ ↔8–16 in (20–40cm) ↑6–16 in (15–40 cm)

Annual native to Texas, USA, now widely established as a wildflower. Upright, sometimes sprawling stems with pointed oval to narrow lance-shaped leaves. Showy heads of small flowers, bright lavender to purple-red, often with notched petals, in summer. Mixed color seedling strains include **Beauty Series**, many colors, including yellow; **Brilliancy Series**, wide color range; **Buttons and Bows Series**, mainly bright colors, often with contrasting eye; **Intensia Series**, dense, compact, heavy-flowering, wide color range; **Phlox of Sheep Series**, primrose-centered pastel shades, including yellow, orange-red, and apricot; **Tapestry Series**, wide range of pastel shades with contrasting eye color, fragrant. Zones 6–10.

Phlox maculata

MEADOW PHLOX, WILD SWEET WILLIAM

☼/◐ ✱ ↔16 in (40 cm) ↑27 in (70 cm)

Erect rhizome-rooted perennial native to eastern USA. Thick, lustrous, dark green leaves, usually pointed oval in shape, sometimes linear. Densely packed heads of pink, violet, or white flowers, often with purplish centers, appear in summer. **'Alpha'**, fragrant lavender pink flowers; **'Omega'**, fragrant white flowers with deep violet centers. Zones 5–10.

Phlox nana

SANTA FE PHLOX

☼/◐ ✱ ↔12–20 in (30–50 cm) ↑6–10 in (15–25 cm)

Small, bushy, mounding perennial from southwestern USA. The leaves are very narrow and lance-shaped. The long-tubed flowers are solitary or in small clusters, to ¾ in (18 mm) wide, in shades of pink and purple, blooming in late spring–summer. **'Mary Maslin'** has distinctive red flowers featuring yellow centers. Zones 8–10.

Phlox nivalis

TRAILING PHLOX

☼/◐ ✱ ↔12–24 in (30–60 cm) ↑4–12 in (10–30 cm)

Subshrub from southeastern USA. Usually has a spreading habit, but is sometimes partly erect. The leaves are lance-shaped. The downy flowerheads appear in spring and consist of 3 to 6 blooms. The flowers may be pink or white, and often have notched petals. Zones 6–10.

Phlox paniculata

BORDER PHLOX, SUMMER PHLOX

☼/◐ ✱ ↔16–40 in (40–100 cm) ↑24–48 in (60–120 cm)

Vigorous eastern USA perennial. Forms thick clumps of upright stems with pointed oval to lance-shaped leaves, often toothed, sometimes downy. Large rounded flowerheads, usually pink, lavender, and purple, in summer. **'Brigadier'**, dark foliage, apricot pink flowers; **'Europa'**, honey-scented white flowers, scarlet eye; **'Eva Cullum'**, dark pink flowers, deep pink center; **'Eventide'**, mauve-blue flowers; **'Fujiyama'** ★, white flowers; **'Le Mahdi'**, purple-blue flowers; **'Mother of Pearl'**, pale silvery pink flowers; **'Prospero'**, lavender to light purple flowers; **'Starfire'**, deep red flowers; **'Tenor'**, scarlet flowers; **Volcano Series**, good mildew resistance, wide

P

color range; **'White Admiral'**, pure white; **'Windsor'**, white flowers suffused lavender blue. Zones 4–10.

Phlox pilosa

PRAIRIE PHLOX

↔ 12–20 in (30–50 cm)
↕ 24 in (60 cm)

Clump-forming perennial from Texas, USA. Leaves linear to lance-shaped. Large heads of pink to purple or white blooms, in spring. Zones 5–10.

Phlox × procumbens

↔ 12–32 in (30–80 cm)
↕ 4–8 in (10–20 cm)

Garden hybrid of *P. stolonifera* and *P. subulata*. Spreading, sometimes partly erect clump of broad lance-shaped leaves. Many lax heads of purple-pink flowers to ¾ in (18 mm) wide, from mid-spring. Zones 4–9.

Phlox stolonifera

↔ 20–40 in (50–100 cm)
↕ 6–10 in (15–25 cm)

Mounding perennial native to south-eastern USA. Spreads by underground runners. Broad, pointed, oval leaves. Lax heads of about 6 violet to purple flowers, 1 in (25 mm) wide, in spring. **'Blue Ridge'**, glossy foliage, bright mid-blue flowers. Zones 4–9.

Phlox subulata

MOSS PHLOX, MOUNTAIN PHLOX

↔ 12–20 in (30–50 cm)
↕ 2–4 in (5–10 cm)

Prostrate mat-forming perennial from eastern USA. Small, narrow, pointed leaves. Only a few blooms per head, but densely clustered; flowers usually pink to lavender or white, often with notched petals, in spring–early summer. **'Bonita'**, glossy leaves, bright pink flowers; **'Emerald Blue'**, compact habit, bright green foliage, mid-blue flowers; **'Emerald Pink'**, compact habit, bright green foliage, vivid pink flowers; **'Late Red'**, purple-red flowers; **'McDaniel's Cushion'**, bright pink flowers; **'Scarlet Flame'**, very compact, deep purple-red flowers. Zones 3–9.

PHOENIX

This genus in the palm (Arecaceae) family consists of around 17 species, mostly from tropical and subtropical Africa, Madagascar, the Grecian island of Crete, the Canary Islands, and Asia. They are solitary or clustered feather-leafed palms. Male and female plants are separate. They have long pinnate leaves, lower leaflets on each frond reduced to stiff sharp spines. Panicles of small, 3-petalled, often yellow

Phlox subulata 'Emerald Blue'

flowers are followed by yellow, orange, green, brown, or red to black fruits with 1 seed. They are widely grown as landscape specimens, street plantings, or container plants. Some produce dates and palm sugar.

CULTIVATION: Most species are fairly adaptable and tolerant of poorer drier soils in full sun as long as drainage is good, but better results are achieved from increased watering and more productive soils. Propagate from seed, or from suckers from suckering varieties. Remove old fronds carefully.

Phoenix canariensis ★

CANARY ISLAND DATE PALM

↔ 30 ft (9 m) ↕ 70 ft (21 m)

From the Canary Islands. Spreading crown, and thick trunk covered in old frond base scars. Large, arching, green fronds to 20 ft (6 m), sharply spined at the base. Cream to yellow flowers in drooping panicles, many orange fruits. Can be massive and set lots of seed; dispose of seeds carefully. Zones 9–11.

Phoenix dactylifera

DATE PALM, EDIBLE DATE

↔ 30 ft (9 m) ↕ 70 ft (21 m)

Commercial date palm cultivated for at least 5,000 years. Graceful spreading crown, gray-green fronds, lower leaflets reduced to spines. The sweet edible fruits are produced only in hot dry climates. Excellent coastal plant. Commercially developed varieties have superior fruits. Zones 9–12.

Phoenix roebelenii ★

DWARF DATE PALM

↔ 8 ft (2.4 m) ↕ 10 ft (3 m)

Popular, elegant, small palm from Laos. Solitary rough trunk clothed with the remains of old frond stalks. Attractive, arching, deep green fronds, leaflets silvery beneath, lower leaflets reduced to sharp spines. Panicles of cream flowers, small, egg-shaped, black, edible fruits. Zones 10–12.

***Phormium cookianum*, in the wild, Te Mata Peak, Hawkes Bay, New Zealand**

Phoenix canariensis

Phormium tenax 'Purpureum'

PHORMIUM

FLAX LILY, NEW ZEALAND FLAX

Phormium is a genus of only 2 species of large evergreen perennials in the family Phormiaceae, and is restricted to New Zealand. The leaves are long and fibrous, and in summer the plants produce large candelabras of upright curved flowers, dripping nectar that is highly attractive to birds. Glossy decorative seed pods follow. The foliage was traditionally used to make rope, and the dried seed heads are often used for decoration.

CULTIVATION: Give these plants a sunny spot in moisture-retentive soil; in frosty climates, cover them in winter. Propagate from seed, or by division of the colored leaf or dwarf clones in early spring.

Phormium cookianum

syn. *Phormium colensoi*

NEW ZEALAND MOUNTAIN FLAX

↔ 7–8 ft (2–2.4 m)
↕ 7–7½ ft (2–2.2 m)

Arching leaves to 5 ft (1.5 m) long, and yellow-green flowers with thick petals, followed by glossy brown seed pods that are curled and pendulous. ***P. c.* subsp. *hookeri* 'Cream Delight'** has narrow creamy yellow bands toward the edges of the leaves and broader bands further in; 'Tricolor' is an old clone whose leaves have irregular bands of creamy yellow and fine red edges. Zones 8–11.

Phormium tenax

NEW ZEALAND FLAX, NEW ZEALAND HEMP

↔ 7–10 ft (2–3 m)
↕ 10–15 ft (3–4.5 m)

Large impressive species with upright leaves to 10 ft (3 m) long, usually gray-green in the wild forms of the species. Flowers are upright, waxy, red-brown trumpets, followed by upright black seed heads. **'Purpureum'**, dark green leaves. Zones 8–10.

Phormium Hybrid Cultivars

↔ 1–6 ft (0.3–1.8 m)
↕ 1–6 ft (0.3–1.8 m)

The 2 *Phormium* species hybridize readily, both in the wild and in cultivation. There are a large number of cultivars available, in dwarf to tall sizes, with weeping or erect foliage, and in a range of colors and variegations. Cream and green striped cultivars include: **'Duet'**, to 3 ft (0.9 m); **'Tricolor'**, to 4 ft (1.2 m); and **'Yellow Wave'**, to 3 ft (0.9 m). Variegated cultivars in tones of pink, red, and bronze include: **'Rainbow Maiden'** (syn. 'Maori Maiden') and **'Sundowner'**, both erect forms, and **'Evening Glow'** and **'Pink Panther'**, both weeping forms. Cultivars with dark purple to black foliage include: **'Bronze Baby'** and **'Tom Thumb'**, dwarf forms, and **'Black Prince'** and **'Dark Delight'**, taller weeping forms. Zones 8–11.

Photina × *fraseri* 'Red Robin'

PHOTINIA

This genus in the rose (Rosaceae) family consists of around 60 species of evergreen and deciduous shrubs and trees, most from the Himalayas to Japan and Sumatra, Indonesia. The leaves are often strikingly colored when young, especially in spring. The flowers are small, mostly white, with 5 petals, and grow in dense, flattish, clustering panicles along the shoots or at their tips. The fruits are small pomes, usually red. The evergreen species are cultivated for their strikingly colored foliage and are popular plants for hedging; the deciduous species are more reliable than the evergreens in flowering, and in autumn their foliage can be attractively colored.
CULTIVATION: Most *Photinia* species are fairly adaptable, with good drainage being a key requirement. For best results, plant in a well-drained fertile soil in a sunny position. Prune to promote dense growth, particularly when used as hedging plants. Propagate from seed or cuttings.

Photinia beauverdiana

↔20 ft (6 m) ↑30 ft (9 m)
Deciduous spreading tree native to western China. Narrow obovate to lance-shaped dark green leaves, small-toothed margins, turn orange-red, in autumn. New growth purple-brown. Clustering panicles of small white flowers, in late spring. Egg-shaped orange-red fruits. Zones 6–9.

Photinia davidiana

syn. *Stransvaesia davidiana*
↔20 ft (6 m) ↑25 ft (8 m)
From western China. Large evergreen shrub or small tree. Leaves leathery, elliptical to inversely lance-shaped, dark green; older leaves may color red in autumn. Clustering panicles of small white flowers, in summer. Small, red, hanging, persistent fruits. Zones 7–10.

Photina beauverdiana

Photinia × *fraseri*

FRASER PHOTINIA
↔15 ft (4.5 m) ↑15 ft (4.5 m)
Hybrid between *P. glabra* and *P. serratifolia*, developed at Fraser Nurseries in Alabama, USA. Large shrub, many stems, leathery dark green leaves, finely serrated margins, new leaves bronze to bright red. Small white flowers in panicles, in spring. **'Red Robin'** ★, compact cultivar from New Zealand with shiny red new growth; **'Robusta'**, widely grown for its flushes of brilliant red new growth, which are encouraged by repeated trimming. Zones 8–10.

Photinia glabra

JAPANESE PHOTINIA
↔12 ft (3.5 m) ↑15 ft (4.5 m)
From Japan. Small tree with narrow-domed crown, bright red new leaves that mature to green. Small white flowers in clustering panicles bloom in summer. The small, fleshy, red drupes ripen to black and persist throughout winter. **'Rubens'**, popular for hedging in cool climates. Zones 7–10.

Photinia prunifolia

↔12 ft (3.5 m) ↑15 ft (4.5 m)
From Vietnam; resembles P. glabra, but has numerous small black dots on the undersides of the leaves. Flowers are somewhat larger than those of *P. glabra*. Zones 7–10.

Photinia serratifolia

syn. *Photinia serrulata*
CHINESE HAWTHORN
↔25 ft (8 m) ↑30 ft (9 m)
Native of China. Small tree, leathery oblong leaves, saw-toothed margins. Young copper-red foliage ages to dark green. Small white flowers in clustering panicles, in spring. Many red berries. Zones 7–10.

Photinia villosa

syn. *Pourthiaea villosa*
ORIENTAL PHOTINIA
↔15 ft (4.5 m) ↑15 ft (4.5 m)
Native to China, Korea, and Japan. Deciduous tree or large shrub, often vase-shaped. Downy young shoots. Elliptical to obovate dark green leaves, sharply serrated, bronze when young, yellow, orange, and red in autumn. Panicles of small white flowers, in spring. Red fruits. Zones 4–9.

PHUOPSIS

This genus in the madder (Rubiaceae) family contains one mat-forming finely hairy perennial, native to the Caucasus region of Asia. It has whorls of narrow sword-shaped leaves and clusters of tiny pink flowers with 5 lobes.
CULTIVATION: Suited to rock gardens and banks, *Phuopsis* prefers full sun or part-shade in moist well-drained soil. Propagate by division in spring, from semi-ripe cuttings in summer, or from seed in autumn; it may self-seed in the right conditions.

Phuopsis stylosa

syn. *Crucianella stylosa*
CROSSWORT
↔8–12 in (20–30 cm)
↑8–12 in (20–30 cm)
Low-growing herb forming a mat of wiry ground-hugging stems. Whorls of small, coarse, pale green or grayish leaves, terminating in rounded heads of tiny pink flowers in late spring–early summer. **'Purpurea'** (syn. 'Rubra'), purplish red flowers. Zones 7–8.

PHYGELIUS

This genus of evergreen subshrubs from South Africa is in the foxglove (Scrophulariaceae) family. It consists of only 2 species, which have been crossed to produce numerous hybrids. They are often grown as herbaceous perennials where winters fall below freezing. The soft green leaves grow on erect stems and hold pendent, fuchsia-like, tubular flowers in warm tones throughout late summer. When grown as a perennial, the suckering or running rootstock can form attractive clumps 3 ft (0.9 m) in diameter.
CULTIVATION: Given fertile, moist, humus-enriched soil, these plants will thrive in a morning sun position in warmer climates, but need the protection of a wall or a similar warm spot to minimize frost damage in cold climates. They are fleshy-leafed plants that dislike dry conditions, so they should be well watered throughout summer. Propagation is from cuttings taken in summer.

Phygelius aequalis

↔3 ft (0.9 m) ↑3 ft (0.9 m)
A suckering shrub, or herbaceous perennial in colder climates. Upright stems, soft bright green foliage, dusky pink tubular flowers. **'Trewidden Pink'**, soft flesh pink flowers; **'Yellow Trumpet'**, dense bushy habit with leaves and flowers larger than those of its parent. Zones 8–10.

Phygelius capensis ★

CAPE FIGWORT, CAPE FUCHSIA
↔22 in (50 cm) ↑6 ft (1.8 m)
Well-clothed suckering shrub. Soft green leaves, lance-shaped. Masses of orange tubular flowers with distinctive recurved lobes. Zones 8–10.

Phygelius × *rectus*

↔4 ft (1.2 m) ↑4 ft (1.2 m)
A cross of garden origin between *P. aequalis* and *P. capensis*. Compact suckering shrub. Dark green leaves, upright stems. Masses of pendent tubular flowers. **'African Queen'**, pale red flowers; **'Moonraker'**, creamy yellow flowers; **'Salmon Leap'**, deeply lobed orange blooms. Zones 8–10.

Phygelius aequalis

PHYLA

FROGFRUIT

A genus of 15 perennial herbs, creeping or mat-forming, in the vervain (Verbenaceae) family, and native to warm-temperate to subtropical Central and South America. Sprawling or erect branches arise from a stem with runners. The hairy leaves are opposite or clustered. Solitary or paired flower-heads grow from the leaf axils, with many small flowers with oval to wedge-shaped bracts, a compressed membranous calyx with 2 to 4 teeth, and a straight or slightly curved corolla tube with 2 or 4 lobes. Fruits are pairs of nutlets with 2 compartments.
CULTIVATION: Most are salt-tolerant and make good ground covers, grown in full sun or part-shade, in moist but well-drained soil. Propagate by division in spring or autumn.

Phyla nodiflora

CAPEWEED, MATGRASS, TURKEY TANGLE

↔3–6 ft (0.9–1.8 m)
↑1¼–6 in (3–15 cm)

Vigorous salt-tolerant perennial herb. Leaves oblong to spatula-shaped, green or grayish green, to 3 in (8 cm) long, margins serrated toward the tips, on stems covered with fine furry hairs. Flowerheads, to 1 in (25 mm) long, of slightly hairy blooms with green or violet bracteoles and white, reddish, or lilac corollas with a yellow eye, in spring–summer. Zones 9–10.

Phyla nodiflora

Phylica plumosa

PHYLICA

Primarily native to South Africa, this genus in the buckthorn (Rhamnaceae) family has around 150 species of evergreen shrubs. A few are cultivated for their flowerheads, long lasting when cut. Leaves are dark green with lighter undersides, usually with a coating of silky silvery hairs. The true flowers are often petal-less or with fine filamentous petals, and are usually nearly enclosed by large feathery bracts or surrounded by white woolly hairs.
CULTIVATION: Plant in light, gritty, well-drained, slightly acidic soil and full sun. They tolerate high humidity, but their foliage suffers in prolonged rain. Coastal conditions suit them. Added humus and water will give lusher foliage, but a looser habit and fewer flowers. Prune by removing spent flowers and general tidying. Propagate from seed or half-hardened cuttings from non-flowering stems.

Phylica plumosa

syn. *Phylica pubescens*

FLANNEL FLOWER

↔3 ft (0.9 m) ↑3–6 ft (0.9–1.8 m)

South African shrub. Hairy buff bracts enclose tiny white flowers. Plant densely covered with fine hairs, deep green foliage shows through. Flowerheads mature in early winter. Long lasting cut flower. Zones 9–11.

× *PHYLLIOPSIS*

This hybrid genus of small evergreen shrubs, of garden origin, results from crosses between *Phyllodoce* and *Kalmiopsis*, members of the heath (Ericaceae) family. Plants have shiny brown bark, small, lustrous, dark green, oblong to oval leaves with rounded tips, and elongated racemes, on short red stalks, of flowers with 5 slightly hairy sepals and a reddish purple, bell-shaped, 5-lobed corolla, in spring.
CULTIVATION: × *Phylliopsis* plants prefer part-shade and peaty acidic soil. Trim back after flowering to maintain compact habit, and propagate from half-hardened cuttings in late summer.

× *Phylliopsis,* Hybrid Cultivar, 'Sugar Plum'

× *Phylliopsis* Hybrid Cultivars

↔8–12 in (20–30 cm) ↑12 in (30 cm)

Small shrubs suitable for containers or rock gardens. '**Coppelia**', large pinkish lilac flowers, cup-shaped,; '**Pinocchio**', compact form; '**Sugar Plum**', candy pink blooms. Zones 3–9.

PHYLLOSTACHYS

This is the largest and best known genus of running bamboos (family Poaceae), consisting of 50 or more species ranging from the eastern Himalayas to Japan, most native to China. They are medium to tall, with widely spaced culms arising from deep long-running rhizomes, so that they spread rapidly when conditions suit. The culm internodes are flattened or shallowly grooved on one side, and each lower node bears just 2 lateral branches, though there may be a third smaller branch. Foliage is not very distinctive, and flowers are rare and inconspicuous. The genus includes species for edible shoots, as well as many used in Asia for building, furniture, fishing-rods, umbrella handles, and similar items.
CULTIVATION: Although ornamental, they spead aggressively. Some are very frost hardy, and when grown near their cold limit they remain fairly compact, though vigorous spreaders in warmer climates. Their spread can be contained by inserting concrete, steel, or plastic barriers in the soil to a depth of about 24 in (60 cm), or by cutting a deep bench on the downhill edge of a stand. Smaller species can be grown in tubs or planter boxes; water generously. They are not choosy about soil, as long as they have ample moisture in summer. They are readily propagated from excavated lengths of rhizome, each with several culm bases, planted in spring and kept well watered.

Phyllostachys aurea

FISHPOLE BAMBOO, GOLDEN BAMBOO

↔20–40 ft (6–12 m)
↑25 ft (8 m)

From south-eastern China. Culms smooth olive-green to quite yellowish, depending on exposure to sun, the stronger ones 1–1½ in (25–40 mm) thick but usually mixed with many smaller ones, making dense bushy stands; bases of culms with crowded, often crooked nodes. Versatile species, tolerating dry air, suitable for screens or even for indoor use where light is adequate; can be kept trimmed to a small size. '**Holochrysa**', whole culm bright yellow, turning a transient red in first season (in full sun); '**Flavescens Inversa**', dark green culms, contrasting bright yellow groove; '**Koi**', golden culms, prominent green groove. Zones 7–11.

Phyllostachys aureosulcata

Phyllostachys aureosulcata

CROOKSTEM BAMBOO, YELLOW GROOVE BAMBOO

↔25–50 ft (8–15 m)
↑25 ft (8 m)

Vigorous spreader from north-eastern China. Matt green culms with broad yellow groove in the cultivated form. Slightly rough to the touch, sometimes slightly zigzagging between lower nodes. Straight and upright in warm climates, inclined to bend over in cooler areas. Wind tolerant, ideal for roof tops and containers. '**Aureocaulis**', young culms sulfurous yellow, flushed crimson where facing sun, older culms dark yellow; '**Harbin**', like '**Aureocaulis**' but with narrow green stripes on internode, excellent when planted with '**Harbin Inversa**', its opposite, green internode with narrow yellow stripes; '**Spectabilis**', bright golden-yellow culms with green groove. Zones 6–11.

Phyllostachys bambusoides

JAPANESE TIMBER BAMBOO

↔20–60 ft (6–18 m)
↑40–70 ft (12–21 m)

One of the largest timber bamboos, valued for construction due to its thick, straight, strong culms, up to 6 in (15 cm) in diameter. Native to China, but long cultivated in Japan. Slower to mature and later shooting than P. vivax, which it resembles. Ornamental cultivars, mostly 25 ft (8 m) or smaller, include: '**Allgold**', rich golden culms; '**Castillon**', like '**Allgold**' but with green groove and stronger apricot-variegated foliage; '**Castillon Inversa**', reverse of '**Castillon**' with randomly variegated foliage; '**Kawadana**', green culm subtly striped white and finely white-striped foliage, requires dappled sun; '**Richard Haubrich**', apricot-striped foliage; '**Marliac**', corrugated internodes. Zones 7–11.

Phyllostachys nigra

Phyllostachys flexuosa

Physalis ixocarpa 'Indian Strain'

Physalis philidelphica 'Purple de Milpa'

Phyllostachys dulcis

SWEETSHOOT BAMBOO

↔30–60 ft (9–18 m)
↑25–40 ft (8–12 m)

Vigorous bamboo of uncertain wild origin. Spreads strongly even in cooler regions. Fresh green culms arch up to the light, growing to 3 in (8 cm) in diameter; internodes often compact with prominent nodes on leaning face, giving skeletal effect. New shoots very sweet, hence the common name. Zones 7–10.

Phyllostachys edulis

syns *Phyllostachys heterocycla, P. pubescens*

MAO ZHU, MOSO, MOUSOU CHIKU

↔30–100 ft (9–30 m)
↑40–75 ft (12–22 m)

Believed native to Japan, but long cultivated in China. Most important bamboo for edible shoots, canned in large quantity; also valued as a timber bamboo. Culms up to 7 in (18 cm) in diameter though 3–4 in (8–10 cm) is more usual, clothed in dense hairs when young, pale matt green ageing to deep yellowish; long branches and fine leaves give a plume-like appearance. **'Bicolor'**, golden culms with green groove; **'Gold Stripe'**, only 20 ft (6 m) tall, culms and foliage striped golden; **'Heterocycla'**, smaller-growing with some lower nodes crooked due to slanted nodes; **'Spring Beauty'**, small, delicate, fine-white-striped variegation prominent in spring; **'White Stripe'**, like 'Gold Stripe' but striped white. Zones 6–10.

Phyllostachys flexuosa

ZIG-ZAG BAMBOO

↔10–20 ft (3–6 m)
↑8–15 ft (2.4–4.5 m)

Gracefully arching, dark green, aerial stems, fast growing. Leaves dark green, becoming golden in the sun. Aerial stems become almost black with age; may show white powdering at the nodes. Zones 6–10.

Phyllostachys nigra ★

BLACK BAMBOO

↔20–50 ft (6–15 m)
↑25–50 ft (8–15 m)

From China, but long cultivated in Japan. Original wild plants are not as black as the commonly grown form. New culms are green but soon develop brown stippling that transforms them to black; this happens more rapidly in full sun. Probably the most popular bamboo species; its color is unique among running bamboos. **'Bory'**, like 'Henon' but developing brown cloud-like markings; **'Henon'**, larger culms, blue-gray in shade or golden green in sun; **'Megurochiku'**, like 'Henon' but groove matures to dark brown. Zones 7–10.

Phyllostachys vivax

ELEGANT BAMBOO, VIVAX BAMBOO

↔20–60 ft (6–18 m)
↑30–60 ft (9–18 m)

From eastern China. Similar to P. bambusoides, but more cold hardy and faster to establish. Culms to 4 in (10 cm) in diameter but thin-walled, susceptible to wind damage, and yielding poor-quality timber. **'Aureocaulis'**, glossy pale yellow culms with random green stripes; **'Huangwenzhu'**, green culms with yellow groove; **'Huanwenzhu Inversa'**, reverse of **'Huanwenzhu'**, yellow culm with green groove. Zones 6–10.

PHYSALIS

GROUND CHERRY, HUSK TOMATO

This genus in the nightshade (Solanaceae) family consists of about 80 erect, bushy, or sprawling annual and rhizomatous perennial herbs. It is widely distributed, especially in the Americas, but also in temperate Eurasia and Australia. Alternate simple or divided leaves, sometimes roughly opposite and often in groups of 2 or 3, grow from erect or straggling stems, sometimes woody at the base. Nodding, mostly solitary flowers, on short stalks or none, grow from the leaf axils, with widely bell-shaped to open, blue, yellowish, or white corollas. The bell-shaped calyx has 5 lobes and enlarges into a papery husk enclosing the spherical, 2-celled, greenish, yellowish, orange, or purple fruits, which contain many spherical to kidney-shaped seeds. The husks split open as fruits ripen in late summer to autumn. Unripe berries may be toxic to humans and livestock, although those of some species are edible and are used in preserves, pickles, and Mexican salsa dishes. Named from the Greek *physa* (bladder), referring to the enlarged calyx.

CULTIVATION: Sow seed in autumn or early spring and plant out seedlings of annual species in a warm, sunny, exposed or part-shaded position, in fertile well-drained soil. Perennials can be propagated by division of rhizomes or from tip cuttings in spring.

Physalis alkekengi

ALKEKENGI, BLADDER CHERRY, CHINESE LANTERN, WINTER CHERRY

↔12–24 in (30–60 cm)
↑12–24 in (30–60 cm)

Perennial growing from long, creeping, underground rhizomes. Native to central and southern Europe, and from western Asia to Japan. Erect, leafy, finely glandular, hairy stems. Mid-green triangular to oval leaves, to 5 in (12 cm) long. Inconspicuous drooping flowers, calyx expanding to 2 in (5 cm) across as it encloses the fruit, yellow to cream corolla, red to scarlet berries, in late summer. **'Gigantea'** (syn. 'Monstrosa'), larger growing, larger fruits. Zones 4–6.

Physalis ixocarpa

MEXICAN GROUNDCHERRY, STRAWBERRY TOMATO, TOMATILLO

↔3–4 ft (0.9–1.2 m)
↑3–4 ft (0.9–1.2 m)

Annual herb from Mexico and southern USA, grown as a culinary seasoning; possibly not distinct from *P. philadelphica*. Simple or toothed sword-shaped to oval leaves, to 3 in (8 cm) long. Flowers bowl-shaped to bell-shaped, yellow corollas, 5 brown or purple central spots, twisting blue or yellow anthers. Sticky yellow to purple berry almost fills the purple-veined yellow calyx when mature. **'Indian Strain'**, attractive cultivar. Zones 8–10.

Physalis peruviana

syn. *Physalis edulis*

CAPE GOOSEBERRY, GOLDEN BERRY, TEPAREE

↔2–3 ft (0.6–0.9 m)
↑2–6 ft (0.6–1.8 m)

Herbaceous spreading perennial, from Peru and Chile. Widely introduced elsewhere. Branches ribbed, spreading, often purplish; leaves nearly opposite, randomly toothed, velvety, pointed, mid-green, heart-shaped to oval, 2½–6 in (6–15 cm) long; flowers inconspicuous, bell-shaped, yellow, with 5 dark purple-brown markings, in summer. Purple-green hairy calyx becomes a straw-colored husk enclosing glossy, smooth-skinned, orange-yellow fruit; juicy pulp contains many tiny yellowish seeds. Fruits eaten fresh or stewed, canned, used in jams, sauces, and preserves; worn as jewelry in Peru; used as a diuretic and anti-asthmatic in Colombia, and as a poultice or enema in South Africa. Zones 8–10.

Physalis philadelphica

syn. *Physalis subglabrata*

JAMBERRY, PURPLE GROUND CHERRY, TOMATILLO

↔18–24 in (45–60 cm)
↑24–40 in (60–100 cm)

From Mexico. Cultivated widely as a food crop. Smooth-edged, toothed, oval to broadly sword-shaped leaves, 1½–4 in (3.5–10 cm) long; flowers with a green calyx, yellow-veined, enlarging to 2 in (5 cm) to enclose the yellow to purple edible berry; open yellow corollas marked with purplish brown. **'Purple de Milpa'**, small, purple, acidic fruits. Zones 7–10.

Physocarpus amurensis

PHYSOCARPUS

NINEBARK

From North America and temperate northeastern Asia, the 10 deciduous shrubs in this genus in the rose (Rosaceae) family have showy flowerheads, foliage that is attractive in spring, and sometimes in autumn, and flaking bark. Most have conspicuously veined lobed foliage like that of raspberry or blackberry. Flowers are white or pale pink, small, massed in flat corymbs. Inflated fruits with 3 to 5 lobes ripen in late summer.

CULTIVATION: They are best grown in full sun in fertile well-drained soil that remains moist through summer. They are not fussy, but dislike lime; foliage exposed to drought becomes desiccated and brown. The plants form thickets of stems; thin these and cut back the remaining growth after flowering. Propagate from seed or half-hardened cuttings.

Physocarpus amurensis

↔ 7 ft (2 m) ↕ 10 ft (3 m)

From Korea and China. Leaves, 3 to 5 pointed lobes, serrated edges, deep green above, almost white, below, fine hairs. Flowers white, pinkish streaks, in corymbs to 2 in (5 cm) wide, in late spring–early summer. Zones 5–9.

Physocarpus capitatus

↔ 8 ft (2.4 m) ↕ 10 ft (3 m)

Upright shrub native to western parts of North America. Leaves, felted coating beneath, to 3 in (8 cm) long, deeply lobed. Fine display of large rounded corymbs of tiny cream flowers, in spring–early summer. Zones 6–10.

Physocarpus monogynus

MOUNTAIN NINEBARK

↔ 4 ft (1.2 m) ↕ 4 ft (1.2 m)

From central USA. Spreading bush, forming a thicket of arching stems. Toothed, rounded leaves to 2 in (5 cm) long, 3 to 5 lobes. Flat heads of small white flowers, around 2 in (5 cm) wide, in spring–summer. Zones 5–9.

Physocarpus opulifolius 'Diablo'

Physocarpus opulifolius

COMMON NINEBARK, NINEBARK

↔ 15 ft (4.5 m) ↕ 10 ft (3 m)

From central and eastern North America, most widely grown species in the genus. Leaves usually 3-lobed, light green, with toothed margins. Corymbs of flowers, commonly white, but may be pink-tinged or entirely pink, in late spring–early summer. ***P. o.* var. *intermedius*** (syn. *P. intermedius*), compact form around 5 ft (1.5 m) tall, slightly smaller leaves, more densely packed heads of flowers; ***P. o.* 'Dart's Gold'** ★, low-growing golden yellow foliage, pink-tinted white flowers; **'Diabolo'**, burgundy foliage; **'Luteus'**, golden new growth, ageing to deep green, then bronze; **'Nanus'**, dense covering of small deep green leaves. Zones 2–9.

PHYSOSTEGIA

FALSE DRAGON HEAD, OBEDIENT PLANT

A member of the mint (Lamiaceae) family, this North American genus has 2 species of upright perennials, one widely cultivated. They normally form a clump of unbranched stems bearing simple, dark green, toothed, narrow, elliptical to lance-shaped leaves. In summer to autumn flowerheads of many 5-lobed tubular to bell-shaped blooms, mainly pink and purple, develop at most stem tips. It is often known as "obedient plant" because the flowers stay in place when twisted.

CULTIVATION: They are hardy, and are easily grown in full or half-sun in moist well-drained soil. They spread by rhizomes that can become invasive, but provided the clumps are broken up occasionally this causes few problems. Propagate by division.

Physostegia virginiana

OBEDIENT PLANT

↔ 12–20 in (30–50 cm) ↕ 32–48 in (80–120 cm)

Vigorous perennial from eastern USA, forming clumps of upright stems with narrow, toothed, lance-shaped leaves. Narrow conical flower spikes to 8 in (20 cm) long, with downy, tubular, purple-pink flowers to 1¼ in (30 mm) long, in summer–autumn. **'Alba'**, white flowers; **'Rose Queen'**, pink flowers; **'Rosea'**, large light pink flowers; **'Summer Snow'**, white flowers; **'Variegata'**, white-edged gray-green leaves; **'Vivid'**, bright purple-red flowers. Zones 5–10.

Physostegia virginiana 'Rose Queen'

PICEA

SPRUCE

About 45 species and many cultivars make up this genus of resinous evergreen conifers in the pine (Pinaceae) family, from cool latitudes or high altitudes in the Northern Hemisphere. Most are large symmetrical trees, favoring deep, rich, acidic, well-drained soils in mountainous areas. The foliage is green, blue, silver, or gray, and consists of needle-like leaves on short, persistent, peg-like shoots. The large cones are pendulous at maturity.

CULTIVATION: Some are slow growing, but all are wind-firm, and taller species make good windbreaks in large gardens and parks. They tolerate a range of soils and climates, but dislike mild areas or polluted atmospheres. Smaller cultivars are suitable bonsai subjects. Propagation is from seed or, for cultivars, firm cuttings or grafting.

Picea abies

COMMON SPRUCE, NORWAY SPRUCE

↔ 20 ft (6 m) ↕ 200 ft (60 m)

Native to southern Scandinavia and parts of Europe. Columnar habit, slow-growing, smaller in cultivation. Thick reddish brown bark, spreading branches, 4-sided dark green leaves. Light brown cones, erect at first, becoming pendulous, to 8 in (20 cm) long. There are many ornamental cultivars, some of which are: **'Clanbrassiliana'**, very slow-growing dwarf selection, 5 ft (1.5 m) tall with a spread of 8 ft (2.4 m), dark green foliage; **'Cranstonii'**, sparse irregularly branched form; **'Cupressina'**, broadly conical habit, 60 ft (18 m); **'Echiniformis'**, slow-growing dwarf form, long prickly foliage; **'Gregoryana'**, rounded dwarf form to 30 in (75 cm) in diameter; **'Humilis'**, slow-growing compact dwarf form to less than 18 in (45 cm) tall, small deep green leaves; **'Little Gem'**, very slow-growing, flat-topped, dwarf shrub; **'Maxwellii'**, short thick branches to 12 in (30 cm) long, bright green foliage, good for rock gardens and borders; **'Nidiformis'** (bird's nest spruce), outward-spreading branches forming a nest-shaped central depression, bright green young shoots in spring, grows to 5 ft (1.5 m) in diameter; **'Pendula'**, drooping branches; **'Procumbens'**, slow-growing, flat-topped, spreading bush with densely layered branches to 3 ft (1 m) across. Others include: **'Pumila'**, **'Pyramidalis'**, **'Gracilis,'** and **'Repens'**. **'Reflexa'** is mat-forming to 12 ft (3.5 m) wide, young shoots point upwards at first, then relax into a typically pendulous habit; **'Tabuliformis'** has horizontal prostrate branches. Zones 2–9.

Picea abies 'Cranstonii'

Picea engelmannii

Picea pungens Glauca Group

Picea breweriana

BREWER'S SPRUCE, WEEPING SPRUCE

↔15 ft (4.5 m) ↑120 ft (36 m)

From North America. Horizontal whorled branches from which hang "streamers" of blunt-tipped, flattened, blue-green leaves. Often slender under crowded conditions. Prefers freedom from competition. Zones 2–8.

Picea engelmannii

ENGELMANN SPRUCE

↔15 ft (4.5 m) ↑150 ft (45 m)

North American evergreen, dense columnar-pyramidal habit. Leaves sharp-pointed, 4-angled, gray-blue. Cylindrical pendulous cones green flushed with purple. Zones 1–8.

Picea glauca

DWARF ALBERTA SPRUCE, WHITE SPRUCE

↔12–20 ft (3.5–6 m) ↑80 ft (24 m)

Slow-growing evergreen conifer from Canada, grown commercially for paper making. Bright green shoots in spring; 4-angled, aromatic, needle-like leaves, on drooping branchlets. Small narrow cones. *P. g.* var. *albertiana* **'Alberta Globe'**, mound-forming conifer, to 12 ft (3.5 m); **'Conica'** ★, slow-growing to a perfect conical form, fine blue-green foliage, deepening with age to gray-green, widely regarded as one of the best dwarf conifers, reaching only 6 ft (1.8 m) in height. *P. g.* **'Alberta Blue'**, blue-green foliage; **'Densata'**, slow-growing form, blue-green needle-like leaves; **'Echiniformis'** and **'Nana'**, dwarf forms; **'Rainbow's End'**, conical form, attractive yellow young growth. Zones 1–8.

Picea jezoensis

YEZO SPRUCE

↔25 ft (8 m) ↑120 ft (36 m)

From Japan and northeast Asia. Branches with upturned tips sweep to ground level. Gray bark fissured with age, shed in plates. Flat dark green leaves, glaucous beneath. Small cylindrical cones crimson when young, maturing to rich brown. Zones 8–10.

Picea likiangensis

LIJIANG SPRUCE

↔20 ft (6 m) ↑100 ft (30 m)

From Sichuan Province, China. Variable evergreen conifer, sturdy straight trunk with thick deeply furrowed bark. Overlapping sharply pointed leaves; shorter and more spreading leaves in 2 rows lower down. Young cones generally violet-purple. Zones 7–10.

Picea mariana

AMERICAN BLACK SPRUCE

↔10 ft (3 m) ↑60 ft (18 m)

From the USA. Pyramidal evergreen conifer. Whorled branches, narrow, blue-green, blunt-tipped leaves. Many small persistent purple-brown cones. Distinctive densely hairy shoots. **'Doumetii'**, broader-leafed than the species; **'Nana'**, more rounded dwarf form. Zones 1–8.

Picea meyeri

MEYER SPRUCE

↔4–17 ft (1.2–5 m) ↑10–40 ft (3–12 m)

Evergreen from northwestern China. Purplish gray bark, falling in thick chunks. Upswept branches, blue or bluish green leaves, to 1¼ in (30 mm) long, pale brown cones with rounded striped scales. Zones 4–7.

Picea obovata

SIBERIAN SPRUCE

↔20 ft (6 m) ↑200 ft (60 m)

Resembles *P. abies*. Leaves 4-sided, dark green, bluntly pointed, whitish lines on each side. Pendulous, cylindrical, shiny, brown cones; pinkish catkins, in spring. Young shoots covered with fine red-brown hairs. Zones 1–8.

Picea omorika

SERBIAN SPRUCE

↔20 ft (6 m) ↑100 ft (30 m)

From Bosnia and Serbia. Elegant evergreen, narrow pyramidal form. Fast-growing, drooping branches upturned at the ends. Flattened, blunt-tipped, needle-like, bright green leaves, grayish beneath. **'Nana'**, dwarf form, rounded to conical. Zones 4–9.

Picea orientalis

CAUCASIAN SPRUCE

↔20 ft (6 m) ↑100 ft (30 m)

From sheltered sites in the Caucasus and Turkey. Upright, pyramidal, slow-growing, evergreen conifer. Pendulous branches to ground level. Short glossy green leaves. Short, pendulous, purplish cones. Brick red flower catkins, in spring. **'Aureospicata'**, upward-curving branches; **'Connecticut Turnpike'**, shorter denser cultivar. Zones 3–9.

Picea pungens

COLORADO BLUE SPRUCE

↔20 ft (6 m) ↑100 ft (30 m)

Evergreen pyramidal conifer from western USA. Gray bark. Horizontal branches bear stiff, sharp, needle-like, blue-green leaves. Most cultivars fall into the **Glauca Group** with paler blue-gray foliage, such as **'Compacta'**, silvery green foliage; steel blue-foliaged form, slower growing than species, drought hardy; **'Glauca Compacta'**, silvery blue-foliage. Other Glauca Group cultivars include: **'Globosa'**, **'Hoopsii'**, **'Koster'**, and **'Moerheimii'**. They are usually propagated by grafting, but seedlings of the blue-foliaged cultivars are also sometimes available. Zones 2–10.

Picea rubens

AMERICAN RED SPRUCE

↔20 ft (6 m) ↑70 ft (21 m)

From North America, often at high altitudes. Evergreen pyramidal conifer. Slender branches, scaly red-brown bark. Grass green leaves, twisted and crowded, on the uppersides of shoots. Short cylindrical cones purplish green, glossy brown at maturity. Zones 4–8.

Pieris 'Forest Flame'

Picea sitchensis

ALASKA SPRUCE, SITKA SPRUCE

↔25 ft (8 m) ↑100 ft (30 m)

From the west coast of North America. Broadly conical evergreen conifer, widely planted for timber. Narrow stiff leaves, green above, silvery beneath, tips sharply pointed. Favored Christmas tree. Zones 4–8.

Picea smithiana

syn. *Picea morinda*

WEST HIMALAYAN SPRUCE

↔20 ft (6 m) ↑75 ft (23 m)

Elegant, pyramidal, evergreen conifer from northern India. Horizontal branches, cascading foliage. Needle-like, finely pointed, dark green leaves surround the branches. Pendulous, shiny, brown-purple cones. Highly ornamental. Zones 6–8.

Picea spinulosa

EAST HIMALAYAN SPRUCE, SIKKIM SPRUCE

↔25 ft (8 m) ↑200 ft (60 m)

From the Himalayas. Evergreen conifer, scaly plated bark. Pendulous branches, crowded, irregular, overlapping, flattened leaves with sharp tips, upper-surface dark green, 2 whitish bands on underside. Cones green, cylindrical, glossy brown when mature. Zones 4–8.

PIERIS

This genus belonging to the heath (Ericaceae) family comes mainly from subtropical and temperate regions of the Himalayas. Widely cultivated and extensively hybridized, the best known of the 7 species are common garden plants and popular evergreen shrubs for gardens in temperate climates, but the genus also includes a vine and some shrubby species from the eastern regions of the USA and from the West Indies. Typically, the leaves are simple pointed ellipses, often with serrated edges, and the flowers are bell-shaped, downward-facing, and carried in panicles. They usually open in spring, and are sometimes scented.

CULTIVATION: Like most members of the erica family, *Pieris* species prefer

Pieris japonica 'Bert Chandler'

P

Pieris japonica 'Variegata'

cool, moist, well-drained soil with ample humus. A position in full sun yields more flowers; light shade results in lusher foliage. Heavy pruning is seldom required as the the plants are naturally tidy; light trimming and pinching back is all that is necessary. Propagate from half-hardened cuttings or by layering.

Pieris floribunda

FETTER BUSH

↔7 ft (2 m) ↕6 ft (1.8 m)

From southeastern USA. Pointed serrated-edged leaves to 3 in (8 cm) long. Flowers white, ¼ in (6 mm) long, carried in showy panicles, in spring. Flowerheads differ from those of the Asian species, being stiffer and held more erect. Zones 5–9.

Pieris 'Forest Flame'

↔6 ft (1.8 m) ↕12 ft (3.5 m)

Hybrid between *P. formosa* 'Wakehurst' and *P. japonica*. Strongly upright shrub, can be kept compact by pruning. Panicles of white flowers, in spring. Young foliage bright red, changing to pink, then cream, then pale green, then dark green. Zones 6–9.

Pieris japonica

syn. *Pieris taiwanensis*

JAPANESE PIERIS, LILY-OF-THE-VALLEY BUSH

↔8 ft (2.4 m) ↕8–10 ft (2.4–3 m)

This species now includes *P. taiwanensis*, found in Japan, Taiwan, and eastern China. Leaves, pink to bronze when young, ageing to dark green. Floral racemes erect or drooping, flowers usually white, in spring. **'Bert Chandler'**, light pink new growth turning yellow, then green; **'Christmas Cheer'**, early white and pink flowers; **'Debutante'**, white flowers in erect racemes; **'Karenoma'**, red-brown new growth; **'Little Heath'**, dwarf form, white-edged leaves; **'Mountain Fire'** ★, reddish new leaves; **'Purity'**, white flowers; **'Red Mill'**, bright red new growth, long-flowering; **'Robinswood'**, green leaves, yellowish green edges, bright red new growth; **'Sarabande'**, compact, white flowers, in winter; **'Valley Valentine'**, purple-red flowers, crimson buds; **'Variegata'**, cream and green foliage, young leaves pink-tinted; **'Whitecaps'**, white flowers. Zones 6–10.

PILOSOCEREUS

This is a genus of around 45 species of shrubby or tree-like cacti in the family Cactaceae, found from Florida, USA, through Central America and the Caribbean, to tropical South America. They have a stocky ribbed trunk that with age becomes deeply furrowed, studded with often woolly areoles. Spines are clustered, some 3 in (8 cm) long. Flowers open at night, developing from exceptionally hairy areoles. They are tubular to bell-shaped, usually white or in pastel shades, and last only a day. The fruits are fleshy and green to purple. CULTIVATION: These large cacti grow well in sun or partial shade. Drought tolerant, they appreciate regular moisture during the growing and flowering seasons, and light well-drained soil with a little extra humus. Some tolerate light frosts, but most grow best in mild frost-free areas. The large tree-like species may be pruned. Propagate from seed or from cuttings of young stems. Allow the cut end to dry before inserting in soil.

Pinus albicaulis 'Nana'

Pinus aristata

Pilosocereus leucocephalus

syns *Cephalocereus maxonii, C. palmeri, C. sartorianus*

OLD MAN CACTUS, OLD MAN OF MEXICO

↔7–10 ft (2–3 m) ↕7–17 ft (2–5 m)

From Mexico, Guatemala, and Honduras. Tree-like plant, branching from below. Stems upright, green to bluish, with 7 to 12 ribs. Spines brownish, becoming gray with age, 1 central and 8 to 12 radials. Flower-bearing areoles on the upper parts of stems produce white wool. Flowers funnel-shaped to bell-shaped, pink to white. Seed pods green to purple. Zones 9–12.

PINELLIA

A genus of 6 species in the arum (Araceae) family that come from wooded regions of China, Korea, and Japan. They are summer-growing tuberous perennials that have handsome leaves and strange usually green flowers consisting of a slightly hooded spathe with a long curving spadix. CULTIVATION: Grow *Pinellia* species in a semi-shaded aspect in moisture-retentive soil. Propagate from seed sown as soon as it is ripe, or by division of tubers when dormant. Some species produce tiny bulbils where the stem and leaf meet.

Pinellia cordata

↔4–6 in (10–15 cm) ↕4–6 in (10–15 cm)

Chinese species. Deep green spearhead-shaped leaves marked with white, and with purple undersides. It produces a single bulbil where the stem joins the leaf. Flowers are held at same level as the leaf and are green throughout. Zones 6–10.

PINUS

PINE

This very variable genus of conifers in the pine (Pinaceae) family has around 110 species, found throughout Europe, Asia, northwestern Africa, North and Central America, and the West Indies. They grow in a range of climates and conditions, from tropical equatorial forests to the extreme cold at the edge of the Arctic Circle. Predominantly large trees, only a couple of species are shrubs. The leaves are needle-like, and may be quite small to as long as 18 in (45 cm). They are generally found in bundles of 3 or 5, with never more than 8 in a group. The seed cones vary in shape, color, and dimension. The genus includes some of the world's most important timber species. CULTIVATION: Most can easily withstand cold and extended dry periods, and also tolerate a range of soils, although they must have full sun. Some species are popular for bonsai. Propagation of the species is from seed; the cultivars are grafted.

Pinus albicaulis

WHITEBARK PINE

↔20 ft (6 m) ↕30 ft (9 m)

Native to the mountains of southwestern Canada and northeastern USA. Evergreen tree, larger in the wild. Bark smooth and white, turns gray and separates with age. Spreading ascending branches, short yellow-green needles. Small persistent cones. Dwarf cultivars include **'Flick'**, **'Nana'**, **'Noble's Dwarf'**. Zones 4–8.

Pinus aristata

ROCKY MOUNTAIN BRISTLECONE PINE

↔15 ft (4.5 m) ↕15 ft (4.5 m)

Small tree from mountainous and subalpine western USA. Slow growing, irregularly shaped, dense crown of short, resin-flecked, 2 in (5 cm) long leaves. Cones have a brittle prickle. Some specimens have been dated at around 2,500 years old. Zones 4–8.

Pinus attenuata

KNOBCONE PINE

↔20 ft (6 m) ↕50 ft (15 m)

Naturally occurring in rocky mountainous soils in Oregon and California, USA. Medium tree, narrow pointed crown, horizontal to ascending branches. Groups of 3 yellow-green leaves. The large woody cones can remain unopened on the tree for decades. Zones 7–10.

P

Pinus bungeana

Pinus densiflora

Pinus canariensis

Pinus banksiana

JACK PINE

☼ ✱ ↔20 ft (6 m) ↕60 ft (18 m)

Native to southern Canada and northeastern USA. Straight tree, irregular in outline, short twisted leaves growing in pairs. Light brown cones slightly curved. The species is grown and harvested for pulpwood, power poles, and railway ties, and is planted for land rehabilitation and for commercial trade in Christmas trees. Zones 2–8.

Pinus bungeana

LACEBARK PINE

☼ ✱ ↔20 ft (6 m) ↕60 ft (18 m)

Multi-trunked tree from northwestern China. Rare in cultivation. Stiff leaves give off the smell of turpentine when crushed. Cones small and egg-shaped. Gray-green peeling bark, splotched white and brown. Zones 5–9.

Pinus canariensis

CANARY ISLAND PINE

☼ ❄ ↔25 ft (8 m) ↕130 ft (40 m)

From the Canary Islands. Straight solid main trunk, dense oval crown of 6–12 in (15–30 cm) needles that tend to droop. Attractive dark reddish brown bark, shiny, brown cones. Naturalized in Australia and South Africa. Zones 9–11.

Pinus cembra

AROLLA PINE, SWISS STONE PINE

☼ ✱ ↔15 ft (4.5 m) ↕30 ft (9 m)

From central Europe. Narrowly conical to almost columnar in shape, branching from ground level up. Densely foliaged with stiff 3 in (8 cm) needles, dark green and twisted. Small cones on very old trees. **'Chlorocarpa'**, popular cultivar. Zones 4–8.

Pinus contorta

LODGEPOLE PINE, SHORE PINE

☼ ✱ ↔25 ft (8 m) ↕75 ft (23 m)

Tall tree native to western North America, from Alaska to Mexico. Variable in habit, generally tall, straight, conical. Dense, stiff, dark green needles, small, asymmetrical, orange-brown cones. Zones 5–9.

Pinus densiflora

JAPANESE RED PINE

☼ ✱ ↔20 ft (6 m) ↕70 ft (21 m)

Tree from Japan, Korea, and China. Open irregular crown. Green leaves, 5 in (12 cm) long, growing in tufts at ends of branches. Bark reddish brown, cones dull brown. **'Pendula'** ★, vigorous, semi-prostrate; **'Umbraculifera'**, very slow-growing, shaped like an umbrella. Zones 4–9.

Pinus edulis

NUT PINE, ROCKY MOUNTAIN PINYON

☼ ✱ ↔20 ft (6 m) ↕25 ft (8 m)

Found on dry mountain slopes in southwestern USA and Mexico. Small tree with a rounded crown. Short, stiff, blue-green leaves. Small, symmetrical cone, edible nuts. Zones 5–9.

Pinus leiophylla

Pinus elliottii

SLASH PINE

☼ ❄ ↔25 ft (8 m) ↕100 ft (30 m)

From southeastern USA. Straight central leader, often free of lower branches to a considerable height. Leaves 8 in (20 cm) long. Cones caramel colored, bark sheds in thin flakes. This species is an important timber tree, valued for its strong heavy wood. Zones 7–11.

Pinus flexilis

LIMBER PINE

☼ ✱ ↔20 ft (6 m) ↕40 ft (12 m)

Small to medium tree from western North America. Dense conical shape when young, broadening out with age. Short dark green needles, yellow-brown cones. Some specimens have been dated at over 1,600 years old. Zones 4–7.

Pinus glabra

SPRUCE PINE

☼ ❄ ↔20 ft (6 m) ↕100 ft (30 m)

Found in southeastern USA, particularly on the coastal plain. Dark gray bark, almost smooth at first but roughening with age. Narrow open crown, medium-sized leaves. Small reddish brown cones often remain on the tree for several years. Tolerates shade. Zones 9–11.

Pinus jeffreyi

JEFFREY PINE

☼ ✱ ↔25 ft (8 m) ↕200 ft (60 m)

Occurs in western regions of North America from Oregon, USA, to Baja California, Mexico. Straight-trunked tree, irregular outline. Large red-brown cones, 8 in (20 cm) long needles. New growth and bark aromatic. Important timber tree. Zones 6–9.

Pinus koraiensis

KOREAN PINE

☼ ✱ ↔20 ft (6 m) ↕90 ft (27 m)

From southeastern China, northern Korea, and central Japan. Narrow conical outline when young, rounded with age; smaller in cultivation. Rough bluish needles, 4 in (10 cm) long. Not widely cultivated. Zones 3–9.

Pinus lambertiana

SUGAR PINE

☼ ❄ ↔20 ft (6 m) ↕150 ft (45 m)

Occurs from central Oregon, USA, to northern Baja California, Mexico. Extremely tall tree; has been known to reach a height of 216 ft (65 m). Narrow irregular crown. Needles stiff, sharp, bluish. Pendulous cones, 20 in (50 cm) long, on long stalks. Valuable timber species. Zones 7–9.

Pinus leiophylla

SMOOTH-LEAF PINE

☼ ❄ ↔15 ft (4.5 m) ↕50 ft (18 m)

From southeastern Arizona, southwestern New Mexico, USA, and Mexico. Small to medium tree, irregular narrow crown. Gray-green needles. Small, symmetrical, egg-shaped cones, in pairs on short stems. Will sprout from a cut stump. Zones 7–10.

Pinus longaeva

ANCIENT PINE, GREAT BASIN BRISTLECONE PINE

☼ ✱ ↔15 ft (4.5 m) ↕60 ft (18 m)

From the dry subalpine peaks of western USA. Famous for its longevity with ages of over 5,000 years recorded. Small stiff leaves, medium-sized cones. Often crooked in form. Zones 5–8.

Pinus monticola

WESTERN WHITE PINE

☼ ✱ ↔20 ft (6 m) ↕100 ft (30 m)

Growing in northwestern North America, from Canada to California and eastward to Montana, USA. Large tree, narrow crown, solid straight main trunk. Foliage dense, leaves to 4 in (10 cm) long. Narrow cylindrical cones. Valuable timber. Zones 4–9.

Pinus mugo

DWARF MOUNTAIN PINE, MUGO PINE, SWISS MOUNTAIN PINE

☼ ✱ ↔12 ft (3.5 m) ↕25 ft (8 m)

From the mountains of central Europe. Small tree, often shrub-like, windswept habit. Long, bright green, needle leaves growing in pairs. Cones small, dark brown. Favorite for bonsai cultivation, containers, and rock gardens. Many forms tolerant of a wide range of soils. **'Green Candles'**, dense shrub; **'Honeycomb'**, very compact rounded form, yellowish foliage; **'Paul's Dwarf'**, tiny needle-like leaves; **Pumilio Group**, low-growing, can be invasive in cool high-rainfall areas. **'Slowmound'**, tiny

P

needle-like leaves; '**Tannenbaum**', very erect symmetrical form with a pointed leader; '**Teeny**', attractive dwarf form. Zones 2–9.

Pinus muricata

BISHOP PINE

↔ 20 ft (6 m) ↕ 30 ft (9 m)

Occurs in western USA, and Baja California and Isla Cedros, Mexico; fairly rare in the wild. Small tree, open rounded crown, flat-topped with age. Needles green, bluish in the northern populations. Glossy red-brown cones stay on tree for decades. Zones 8–10.

Pinus nigra

AUSTRIAN PINE, BLACK PINE, CORSICAN PINE

↔ 25 ft (8 m) ↕ 120 ft (36 m)

Variable species, naturally occurring in southern Europe. Straight central trunk, silvery gray. Stiff needles 6 in (15 cm) long, cones light brown, glossy. Important timber tree, naturalized in New Zealand and parts of the USA. '**Hornibrookiana**', dwarf cultivar forming a compact mound. Zones 4–9.

Pinus palustris

LONG-LEAF PINE, PITCH PINE

↔ 15 ft (4.5 m) ↕ 100 ft (30 m)

From southeastern USA. Open crown, straight trunk. Long leaves to 18 in (45 cm), clustered at branch tips. Brown cones have short thorns. Seedlings look like a tuft of grass before trunk develops. Zones 7–10.

Pinus parviflora

JAPANESE WHITE PINE

↔ 20 ft (6 m) ↕ 80 ft (24 m)

From Japan. Smaller in cultivation; slow growing. Dense rounded crown; stiff, curved, blue-green leaves. Oval to cylindrical red-brown cones. '**Adcock's Dwarf**', to 30 in (75 cm). Zones 4–9.

Pinus pinea

ROMAN PINE, STONE PINE, UMBRELLA PINE

↔ 20 ft (6 m) ↕ 80 ft (24 m)

From southern Europe and Turkey. Flat-topped conifer; leaning trunk; fissured reddish gray bark. Needles bright green, in pairs. Rounded cones, shiny, brown, resinous. Large edible seeds known as "pine nuts." Drought tolerant once established. Zones 8–10.

Pinus ponderosa

PONDEROSA PINE, WESTERN YELLOW PINE

↔ 20 ft (6 m) ↕ 130 ft (40 m)

From western North America. Conical open crown; solid straight trunk; fissured pale yellow bark. Stiff pointed leaves to 10 in (25 cm) long. Prickly brown cones to 6 in (15 cm) long. Used for timber. Zones 3–9.

Pinus pumila

Pinus parviflora

Pinus pumila

DWARF SIBERIAN PINE, JAPANESE STONE PINE

↔ 10 ft (3 m) ↕ 10 ft (3 m)

Dwarf, often creeping shrub found in extremely cold regions of northeastern Asia. Glossy, dense, twisted needles. Oval cones 2 in (5 cm) long, dark when young, maturing to yellow-brown. Many cultivars. Zones 5–9.

Pinus radiata

syn. *Pinus insignis*

MONTEREY PINE, RADIATA PINE

↔ 25 ft (8 m) ↕ 100 ft (30 m)

From coastal central California, USA, and Guadalupe and Cedros Islands off Mexico. Tall tree; straight trunk, irregular open crown. Leaves 3–6 in (8–15 cm) long. Cones asymmetrically conical, 5 in (12 cm) long. Very important timber tree in Australia, New Zealand, and Chile. Zones 8–10.

Pinus resinosa

RED PINE

↔ 20 ft (6 m) ↕ 100 ft (30 m)

From northeastern USA and south-eastern Canada. Trunk straight, crown narrow oval. Reddish brown bark. Sharp pointed leaves to 5 in (12 cm) long. Symmetrical oval to conical cones 2 in (5 cm) long. Timber tree. Zones 2–8.

Pinus rigida

NORTHERN PITCH PINE

↔ 20 ft (6 m) ↕ 100 ft (30 m)

From northeastern USA and southeastern Canada. Smaller in cultivation. Multiple trunks, irregular outline, flattened top. Stiff spread-out leaves. Cones curved, light brown, 3 in (8 cm) long, in clusters. Sprouts from the trunk and base after fire. Zones 4–8.

Pinus sylvestris, in the wild, Scotland

Pinus sabiniana

DIGGER PINE, GRAY PINE

↔ 20 ft (6 m) ↕ 70 ft (21 m)

From California and Oregon, USA. Open irregular crown. Forked trunk, often free of branches for quite some height. Drooping gray-green leaves. Heavily spiked cones bear edible seeds. Drought-tolerant. Zones 7–11.

Pinus serotina

POND PINE

↔ 35 ft (10 m) ↕ 70 ft (21 m)

From swamps and poor marshy soils of southeastern USA, from Alabama to New Jersey. Open crown of straight leaves, 8 in (20 cm) long. Cones light brown, symmetrical, almost round, with small spines. Zones 3–9.

Pinus strobus

EASTERN WHITE PINE, WHITE PINE

↔ 20 ft (6 m) ↕ 165 ft (50 m)

From southeastern Canada and northeastern USA. Straight trunk, irregular crown of horizontal branches. Leaves blue-green; pendulous cones. '**Banzai Nana**', bright green foliage; '**Fastigiata**', upcurved branches; '**Horsford**', compact, rich green foliage; '**Pendula**', weeping branches; '**Prostrata**', low spreading habit; '**Radiata**', dwarf form, light green foliage. Zones 3–9.

Pinus sylvestris

SCOTCH PINE, SCOTS PINE

↔ 20 ft (6 m) ↕ 100 ft (30 m)

Across Europe and northern Asia. Round-crowned tree, straight trunk, smaller in cultivation. Pairs of bluish green leaves. Gray-green symmetrical cones 2½ in (6 cm) long. Valuable for timber and as Christmas trees. *P. s.* var. ***lapponica***, smaller leaves and cones; *P. s.* var. ***mongolica***, leaves up to 4 in (10 cm) long; *P. s.* '**Argentea**' (syn. 'Edwin Hillier'), silver-blue foliage; '**Fastigiata**', narrow erect habit, to 25 ft (8 m) tall; '**Moseri**', dwarf form, yellowish needles; '**Saxatilis**', low growing, dark green leaves; '**Troopsii**', appealing foliage; '**Watereri**', bluish leaves, slow growing, eventually reaching 12–15 ft (3.5–4.5 m) tall, can be invasive in cool high-rainfall areas. Zones 2–9.

Pinus taeda

Pinus tabuliformis

CHINESE RED PINE

↔ 20 ft (6 m) ↕ 80 ft (24 m)

From temperate montane areas, central and northern China. Broad-crowned, flat-topped with age, needles crowded at branch tips. Buff, oval, symmetrical cones, small prickle. Zones 5–10.

Pinus taeda

LOBLOLLY PINE

↔ 25 ft (8 m) ↕ 100 ft (30 m)

Leading timber tree, southeastern USA. Dense oval crown, straight trunk, lower half often free of branches. Twisted bright green leaves, oval to conical cones 4 in (10 cm) long. Zones 7–11.

Pinus thunbergii

JAPANESE BLACK PINE

↔ 20 ft (6 m) ↕ 130 ft (40 m)

Tall tree from Japan and South Korea. Irregular outline, single main trunk often curved. Dense dark green leaves, small oval cones. Popular for bonsai and Japanese-style gardens. Cultivars include '**Majestic Beauty**' and the attractive '**Tsukasa**', both compact and hardy. Zones 5–9.

Pinus virginiana

SCRUB PINE, VIRGINIA PINE

↔20 ft (6 m) ↑50 ft (15 m)

From eastern USA. Leaves in pairs, red-brown, oval to conical, symmetrical cones. Variable species in the wild, often open-crowned and contorted. Dense, conical, young trees are grown in plantations for sale as Christmas trees. Zones 4–9.

Pinus wallichiana

BHUTAN PINE, BLUE PINE, HIMALAYAN PINE

↔20 ft (6 m) ↑150 ft (45 m)

Very tall tree with a conical crown, naturally occurring in the Himalayas. Blue-green leaves reach 8 in (20 cm) long, frequently arching or drooping. Cones very long, thin and cylindrical, hanging from the tips of the branches. Zones 6–9.

Pinus yunnanensis

YUNNAN PINE

↔30 ft (9 m) ↑50 ft (15 m)

From temperate montane areas of southwestern China. Conical outline becomes flat with age. Leaves pendulous, thin, to 12 in (30 cm). Cones pale brown to red-brown, oval to egg-shaped, in groups of 3. Zones 8–10.

PISONIA

A genus of trees, shrubs, and climbers, this member of the four-o-clock (Nyctaginaceae) family occurs widely in tropical regions of the world, with the bulk of the species occurring in the Americas. *P. grandis,* found on most of the island groups in the Indian and Pacific Oceans, forms dense thickets on coral cays. The leaves are smooth-edged, opposite or alternate or whorled, the flowers are unisexual or bisexual in axillary or terminal inflorescences. The fruits are various shapes, but all are sticky and trap insects and small animals. Various bird species disperse the fruits that stick to their feathers.

CULTIVATION: Propagate from very fresh seed. Cuttings are also successful. There are a few leaf color variants in cultivation and these must be propagated in this manner to remain true.

Pisonia umbellifera 'Variegata'

Pisonia umbellifera

BIRDLIME TREE

↔15 ft (4.5 m) ↑80 ft (24 m)

Widespread species from the islands of Réunion and Mauritius to Asia, Australia, and New Zealand. The leaves are elliptical, dark green and shiny, crowded toward the ends of the branches. Small, scented, whitish flowers, produced in axillary or terminal clusters, in winter–spring. Elongated sticky fruits. **'Variegata'**, yellow and green leaves. Zones 9–10.

PISTACIA

This small genus in the cashew (Anacardiaceae) family consists of around 9 species from the Mediterranean region, eastern and southeastern Asia, Central America, and southern USA. They are mainly deciduous trees with compound, mostly pinnate leaves terminated by a pair of leaflets, and panicles of small-petalled flowers. The flowers are followed by peppercorn-like fruits produced on the female plants; male plants are separate. Some species are important for their oils and edible seeds, while others make fine ornamental trees with colorful autumn foliage. Most species originated in dry, warm-temperate regions.

CULTIVATION: Most species are fairly adaptable and grow best in a well-drained moderately fertile soil in full sun. Propagate from seed, cuttings, budding, or grafting.

Pistacia chinensis

CHINESE PISTACHIO

↔15 ft (4.5 m) ↑25–50 ft (8–15 m)

Deciduous tree from China and Taiwan. Mostly pinnate leaves, 10 to 12 leathery dark green leaflets, turn shades of orange, red and yellow, in autumn. Panicles of inconspicuous reddish flowers, in summer. Small bluish fruit. Popular street and shade tree. Zones 7–10.

Pistacia chinensis

Pistacia terebinthus

CYPRUS TURPENTINE, TEREBINTH TREE

↔15 ft (4.5 m) ↑25 ft (8 m)

Deciduous, large shrub or tree, native to the Canary Islands, Portugal to Turkey, and North Africa. Leaves pinnate, 12 semi-glossy, aromatic, green leaflets. Panicles of flowers, in spring–early summer. Reddish purple fruit. Zones 9–10.

PITTOSPORUM

This genus consists of about 200 species of evergreen trees and shrubs in the family Pittosporaceae. They are found in Africa, southern and eastern Asia, Australia, New Zealand, and the Hawaiian Islands, USA. The foliage is usually glossy with leaves arranged alternately or in whorls. The small flowers, 5-petalled, may be cup-shaped or reflexed, single or in clusters, some have a sweet fragrance. Capsules contain seeds with a sticky coating. Some species are useful for shelter and hedging, borders or containers. Can be clipped for formal situations and to keep the foliage dense.

CULTIVATION: Most species will grow in sun or part-shade in any well-drained soil. In cool-temperate climates they may require the protection of a sunny wall, or they can be grown in the conservatory or greenhouse. Propagation is from seed, which germinates erratically, or from half-hardened cuttings taken in summer or autumn. Cultivars are propagated from cuttings only.

Pittosporum crassifolium

KARO

↔8 ft (2.4 m) ↑10–20 ft (3–6 m)

Robust New Zealand species, withstands coastal conditions. Dark green leaves, thick and leathery, white hairy coating beneath. Flowers, small, dark red, and noticeably fragrant in the evening, in early summer. Down-covered fruits, shiny black seeds. Zones 9–11.

Pittosporum tenuifolium

KOHUHU

↔15 ft (4.5 m) ↑15–20 ft (4.5–6 m)

Variable species, native to New Zealand, usually a large shrub. Dense foliage; thin, slightly leathery, oblong leaves with wavy edges. Small flowers, reflexed petals, dark red, almost black, in spring, strong honey fragrance. Capsules turn black on maturity. **'Deborah'**, grayish green leaves with creamy margins flushed pink; **'Eila Keightley'** (syn. 'Sunburst'), rounded leaves with central yellow variegations; **'Golden Sheen'**, bright yellow-green leaves; **'Green Pillar'**, bright green foliage, narrow and erect; **'Irene Paterson'**, slower-growing form with almost white leaves speckled pale green; **'Ivory Sheen'**, white-edged gray-green leaves; **'James Stirling'**, blackish red branchlets, silvery green leaves; **'Marjory Channon'**, popular cultivar in USA; **'Mellow Yellow'**, yellow-centered dark green leaves; **'Screenmaster'**, quick growing, light green leaves, suits hedging; **'Silver Sheen'**, gray-green foliage; **'Silver Song'**, columnar, silver-gray leaves, quick growing; **'Stirling Mist'**, white-edged light green to gray-green leaves; **'Tom Thumb'**, dwarf variety with foliage that ages to dark purple; **'Variegatum'**, cream-edged green leaves; **'Warnham Gold'**, light green leaves that change to creamy yellow and gold. Zones 9–11.

Pittosporum crassifolium

Pittosporum tenuifolium

Pittosporum tobira

JAPANESE PITTOSPORUM, TOBIRA

↔7 ft (2 m) ↑20 ft (6 m)

Erect bushy shrub that is native to China and Japan. Leathery oblong leaves, dark glossy green, have rolled edges. Orange-scented flowers, flaring petals creamy white, lemony yellow with age, in spring–early summer. **'Miss Muffet'**, dense, compact form, grown mainly for foliage; **'Nanum'**, bright green leaves; **'Variegatum'**, tolerates coastal conditions, leaves have irregularly marked white margin; **'Wheeler's Dwarf'**, compact miniature to about 24 in (60 cm) high. Zones 8–11.

PLATANUS

PLANE TREE

This genus in the plane (Platanaceae) family consists of about 8 species from the northern temperate zone, including Eurasia, North America, and Mexico. These deciduous trees have inconspicuous spring flowers; globe-shaped fruits on hanging stalks; large, alternate, palmately lobed, simple leaves; and ornamental, flaking, mottled bark. They are useful large shade trees and are widely planted as street trees. Many species are highly tolerant of compacted soils and air pollution and will grow well in both temperate and cool climates.

CULTIVATION: Most species are adaptable, as can be seen by the many cases of street trees in less than optimal conditions, but they perform best on deep, productive, alluvial soils with a consistent water source, such as a permanent stream, in full sun. Pruning is not essential, though it is desirable in the early years if a single trunk is to be established. Propagate from seed, cuttings, or by layering.

Platanus × *hispanica*

syns ***Platanus* × *acerifolia*, *P.* × *hybrida***

LONDON PLANE

↔60 ft (18 m) ↑100 ft (30 m)

Believed to be a hybrid between *P. occidentalis* and *P. orientalis*, it has a rounded pyramidal form. Gray to light brown bark, variable bright green leaves, usually 5-lobed. Fruits small. Tolerates heat, drought and pollution. **'Pyramidalis'**, upright cultivar with coarse bark, leaves 3-lobed, often slightly toothed. Zones 4–9.

Platanus occidentalis

AMERICAN PLANE, BUTTON-BALL, BUTTONWOOD, SYCAMORE

↔70 ft (21 m) ↑150 ft (45 m)

Native to USA and Canada. Very tall deciduous tree, broad open crown, spreading branches. Attractive flaking bark, 3 to 5 bright green shallow-lobed leaves. Single hanging nutlets, sometimes in pairs. Timber used for furniture and pulp. Zones 4–9.

Platanus orientalis

ORIENTAL PLANE

↔90 ft (21 m) ↑100 ft (30 m)

Large, spreading, deciduous tree from southeastern Europe to western Asia. Huge trunk with mottled, brown, gray and greenish white bark. Dark green leaves, palmately lobed. Inconspicuous flowers, in early spring. Clusters of 2 to 6 globe-shaped fruit. ***P. o.* var. *insularis***, bright green leaves, toothed lobes; hairy fruits. Zones 5–9.

Platanus racemosa

ALISO, CALIFORNIA PLANE, CALIFORNIA SYCAMORE, WESTERN SYCAMORE

↔75 ft (23 m) ↑100 ft (30 m)

Large, strong-growing, deciduous tree, from southern California, USA, and Mexico. Dark green leaves, 3 to 5 deep lobes, downy undersides. Clusters of 2 to 7 bristly hanging fruits turn brown when mature. Zones 7–10.

PLATYCLADUS

At times put in the genus *Thuja*, this genus, in the cypress (Cupressaceae) family, is now considered distinct. It contains only 1 species, an evergreen coniferous tree featuring flattened spray-like branchlets of lightly aromatic foliage. Native to Korea, China, and northeastern Iran, it is rarely seen outside eastern Asia in its typical form, but rather as one of its numerous cultivars. These generally have a more rounded low-branching habit and are highly ornamental and dependable. Many are suitable for hedging. Dwarf varieties are excellent in rock gardens or containers and as a low border.

CULTIVATION: Grow this fully hardy genus in a moist well-drained soil in a sunny position protected from strong winds. Prune lightly in spring. Propagate from seed or cuttings.

Platycladus orientalis

syn. ***Thuja orientalis***

CHINESE ARBOR-VITAE

↔15 ft (4.5 m) ↑40 ft (12 m)

Small conical tree, upward-curving branches. Small, mid-green, scale-like leaves in flattened vertical sprays. Fleshy, ovoid, female cones, ripen to a waxy silvery sheen. **'Aurea Nana'** ★, dense oval shape to 3 ft (0.9 m) high, creamy yellow foliage darkens to a rich green, in autumn–winter; **'Balaton'**, soft light green foliage; **'Elegantissima'**, compact conical bush to 15 ft (4.5 m) tall, golden yellow foliage develops bronze tones, winter; **'Meldensis'**, dwarf rounded bush to 3 ft (0.9 m), with soft blue-green foliage, purplish toning, winter; **'Rosedalis'**, to 5 ft (1.5 m) tall, fine soft foliage, changes from bright yellow in spring to sea green in summer, has purplish tones in winter. Zones 6–11.

PLATYCODON

BALLOON FLOWER, CHINESE BELLFLOWER

The sole species in this genus in the bellflower (Campanulaceae) family is a vigorous herbaceous perennial found in Japan and nearby parts of China. It forms a clump of bold, lance-shaped leaves with toothed edges. The flowers open from enlarged, balloon-like buds and are cup- to bell-shaped, white, pink, or blue, with 5 broad lobes. Double-flowered and dwarf forms are common. *Platycodon* root, used in traditional Chinese medicine, is being studied for its mutagenic effects on tumors.

CULTIVATION: A perennial species suitable for a distinctly seasonal temperate climate. Plant in sun or part-shade in moist, humus-rich, well-drained soil. Slow to establish, but long lived and very hardy. May be raised from seed; cultivars are propagated by division.

Platycodon grandiflorus

BALLOON FLOWER, CHINESE BELLFLOWER

↔24 in (60 cm) ↑27 in (70 cm)

Broad lance-shaped, toothed leaves held whorled around sturdy, usually upright, sometimes sprawling stems. Bell-shaped blue, purple, white, or pink flowers open from inflated buds in summer. **'Apoyama'**, low growing, large deep lavender flowers; **'Fuji Blue'** ★, erect habit, flowers large, blue; **'Fuji White'**, pure white flowers; **'Perlmutterschale'** (syn. 'Mother of Pearl'), large pale pink flowers; **'Sentimental Blue'**, dwarf habit, large mauve-blue flowers. Zones 4–9.

P

Platanus orientalis

Platanus racemosa

Platycladus orientalis

Platycodon grandiflorus 'Apoyama'

PLATYSTEMON

CALIFORNIAN POPPY, CREAMCUPS

This monotypic genus belongs to the poppy (Papaveraceae) family and contains a rather variable annual herb native to the western USA where it grows in open grassy areas, often emerging after fires. It may be erect or spreading and has narrow oblong leaves to 3 in (8 cm) long. The attractive open flowers are 6-petalled with prominent stamens. They may be cream, yellow or two-toned, with the cream petals having yellow basal spots or tips. They are borne singly on short hairy stems in summer.
CULTIVATION: Grow at the front of the border in a sunny position in well-drained soil. Propagate from seed sown in the position they are to flower and when germinated thin to about 4 in (10 cm) spacing.

Platystemon californicus

↔ 4 in (10 cm) ↕ 12 in (30 cm)

From California and Arizona, USA. Annual with hairy grayish green leaves. Pale yellow or cream 6-petalled flowers are individually short-lived but profuse in summer. Zones 8–10.

PLECTRANTHUS

Over 200 species of annuals, perennials, and shrubs make up this large genus of herbaceous, semi-succulent, or succulent plants in the mint (Lamiaceae) family. They come from Africa, Asia, Australia, and the Pacific Islands. Most are grown for their attractive evergreen foliage and ease of growing, either in the garden, in pots, or as hanging basket specimens in greenhouses, where necessary. Although individual tubular flowers are usually insignificant, the massed flower display provided by the spikes is a captivating feature of the genus.
CULTIVATION: Many of these undemanding plants can be grown as ground covers in lightly shaded areas in warmer climates or as easy-care specimens for pot or basket. Others of shrub-like proportions can be grown in a warm sheltered position. Any fertile soil or potting mix will suit. Provide ample water during growing season. They are quite rapid growers; the succulent stems are easily pruned and can be used for propagating.

Plectranthus ambiguus

LARGE-FLOWERED PLECTRANTHUS

↔ 16 in (40 cm) ↕ 27 in (70 cm)

Low-growing, evergreen perennial suits ground cover, container, or basket growth, with stems that root freely as they touch the ground. Fragrant, green, hairy foliage. Erect heads of small, unusually narrow, mauve to dark purple flowers, in spring. Zones 9–10.

Plectranthus argentatus

↔ 36 in (90 cm) ↕ 36 in (90 cm)

Spreading shrub from Australia. Silvery gray, softly felted, slightly hairy leaves, one of the few silver-leafed plants to endure damp shade. Lilac flowers held in the branch tips. Regularly tip prune to keep bushy. **'Silver Shield'**, 24 in (60 cm) high, leaves large, downy, silver-gray. Zones 10–11.

Plectranthus ciliatus

↔ 4 in (10 cm) ↕ 2–4 in (5–10 cm)

Straggling herb or shrub from eastern South Africa, spreads by runners. Hairy trailing stems; opposite pairs of shining, hairy leaves, to 5 in (12 cm) long, purple underneath, dotted with glands. Raceme-like flowerheads, tiny flowers, white corolla tube, 2-lobed upper lip, purple dots inside lower lip, in winter–autumn. Fruit dark brown nutlets. Zones 9–11.

Plectranthus ecklonii

↔ 3 ft (0.9 m) ↕ 5 ft (1.5 m)

Bushy South African shrub, mid-green tapering leaves, prominent veining. Pale lilac flowers in tightly packed up-right clusters, in autumn. Zones 9–11.

Plectranthus forsteri

↔ 10 ft (3 m) ↕ 3–8 ft (0.9–2.4 m)

From eastern Australia and nearby Pacific Islands. Sprawling, aromatic perennial herb, hairy straggling stem, to 40 in (100 cm) long. Serrated, oval, hairy leaves. Small pale to mid-blue or mauve flowers. **'Marginatus'** (syn. 'Variegatus'), white flowers, leaves variegated with cream. Zones 8–10.

Plectranthus madagascariensis

MADAGASCAR SPUR FLOWER

↔ 18 in (45 cm) ↕ 4–6 in (10–15 cm)

Sprawling, evergreen, perennial ground cover from Mozambique, Madagascar, and South Africa. Hairy stem, to 40 in (100 cm) long, roots freely where it touches the ground. Slightly succulent, oval to nearly round, toothed, green or variegated, fragrant leaves, to 2 in (5 cm) long. Solitary or branching heads to 5 in (12 cm) long, of white, mauve, or purple flowers, often dotted with red glands. **'Variegated Mintleaf'** (syn. *P. coleoides* 'Variegatus'), fragrant, variegated foliage. Zones 10–11.

Plectranthus neochilus

FLY BUSH, LOBSTER FLOWER, SKUNK LEAF

↔ 24 in (60 cm) ↕ 18 in (45 cm)

Sprawling succulent perennial from southern Africa. Mat-forming branches, succulent highly fragrant leaves with prominent veins, strong garlic-like smell when crushed. Flowerheads distinctly 4-sided, to 4 in (10 cm) long. Blue 2-lipped flowers emerge from large overlapping bracts, most of summer. Zones 8–11.

Plectranthus verticillatus

SWEDISH IVY

↔ 12 in (30 cm) ↕ 12 in (30 cm)

Succulent, sprawling, perennial herb from Southeast Asia, Swaziland, and Mozambique. Leaves oval to rounded, toothed, to 1½ in (35 mm) long, on smooth or slightly hairy stems, to more than 40 in (100 cm) long. Heads, singly or in pairs of cymes, of 1 to 3 white to pale mauve flowers, speckled with purple, without stalks. Zones 9–11.

PLEIOBLASTUS

A genus, in the grass (Poaceae) family, of about 20 species of mainly small-growing running bamboos from Japan and China. Leaves lance-shaped. Over the years many attractive variegated clones have been selected, many of which are still grown as species because they haven't been properly classified.
CULTIVATION: Prefers well-drained but moist rich soil in full or half-sun. Variegated clones need sun to keep their color. Most are best pruned to ground level each spring. Propagate by division in spring.

Pleioblastus fortunei

syns *Arundinaria pygmaeus, Pleioblastus pygmaeus*

DWARF FERN-LEAFED BAMBOO, KE OROSHIMA, PYGMY BAMBOO

↔ 60 in (150 cm) ↕ 16 in (40 cm)

Dwarf suckering species long cultivated in Japan but of uncertain origin. Leaves to 1¾ in (40 mm) long, mid-green, usually slightly downy. ***P. p.* var. *distichus*** is taller, to 40 in (100 cm), with leaves to 2½ in (6 cm) long. Zones 6–10.

Pleioblastus variegatus

syns *Arundinaria fortunei, A. variegata*

CHIGO-ZASA, DWARF WHITE-STRIPED BAMBOO

↔ 40–60 in (100–150 cm) ↕ 28–40 in (70–100 cm)

Upright form from Japan with upright leaves to 6 in (15 cm) long, boldly striped with white. Long cultivated in Japan, obviously a selection of an as yet unidentified green-leafed species. Zones 5–10.

PLUMBAGO

LEADWORT

There are about 15 species of annuals, perennials, and shrubs in this genus, which is a member of the leadwort (Plumbaginaceae) family. They are widely distributed throughout the tropics and subtropics. They have simple light to mid-green leaves and can become rather sparsely foliaged and twiggy if not trimmed. Their main attraction is their flowers, which appear throughout the warmer months. Carried on short racemes, they are very narrow tubes tipped with 5 relatively large lobes. The flowers come in white or various shades of pink and blue.

Plectranthus ambiguus

Plectranthus ecklonii

Plectranthus neochilus

Plumbago auriculata

CULTIVATION: The taller shrubby species can be trained as climbers if grown against a wall. The shorter forms do well in containers. Plumbagos are not fussy about soil, as long as it is moist and well drained. Prune them in late winter to thin out the summer's congested growth and remove any frost-damaged wood. Plant in full sun; propagate from seed, half-hardened cuttings, or by layers.

Plumbago auriculata

syn. *Plumbago capensis*

CAPE LEADWORT, PLUMBAGO

↔7 ft (2 m) ↑15 ft (4.5 m)

Native to South Africa. Tough vigorous shrub with long arching stems. Profuse pale blue flowers are produced throughout the warmer months. **'Alba'** has white flowers; **'Escapade Blue'** has light blue flowers; **'Royal Cape'** ★ has darker blue flowers. Zones 9–11.

Plumbago indica

↔3 ft (0.9 m) ↑5 ft (1.5m)

Sprawling shrub or subshrub from Southeast Asia, popular in subtropical and tropical gardens. Long spikes of deep pink, pale red or purple-red flowers, warmer months, intermittently at other times. Zones 10–12.

PODOCARPUS

Widely distributed in warm-temperate areas of the Southern Hemisphere to tropical zones of eastern Asia and Japan, this genus in the plum-pine (Podocarpaceae) family consists of around 100 species of evergreen trees and shrubs. They have simple, usually spirally or alternately attached leaves that are mostly flat and narrow. The male and female plants are usually separate. The female flowers turn into round drupe-like fruits, often on a fleshy red or purple receptacle. Most species are useful landscape subjects and can be utilized as specimen trees, shrub borders or hedging plants in streets, parks, golf courses, or larger gardens in mild areas; some species are valued as timber trees.

Plumbago indica

CULTIVATION: Most *Podocarpus* species prefer a well-drained soil in a sunny position protected from cold strong winds. Once established, they will tolerate extended dry periods. Propagate from seed, preferably fresh, or from cuttings.

Podocarpus macrophyllus

KUSAMAKI, LOHAN PINE

↔20 ft (6 m) ↑60 ft (18 m)

Native to China and Japan. Outer branches droop. Dark green, leathery, linear to lance-shaped leaves, bluish green below. Fruits on succulent purplish red stalk. **'Maki'**, more compact, smaller leaves. Zones 7–11.

PODOPHYLLUM

MAY APPLE

This genus of 7 perennial herbs from the barberry (Berberidaceae) family, native from eastern North America to eastern Asia and the Himalayas, grows from stout rhizomes. Large, palm-shaped, lobed leaves, on long stalks, and groups of single or several, overlapping, ruff- or parasol-like flowers with 6 to 9 petals, rise on erect stems, to 16 in (40 cm) tall. The fruit is a large, fleshy, egg-shaped berry. Native Americans made an extract from the rhizomes of *P. peltatum*, to treat intestinal worms and for use as a laxative.

CULTIVATION: Most may apples prefer a shady position, often in wet or marshy ground. Propagate by division or from seed.

Podophyllum difforme

syn. *Dysosma difformis*

↔20 in (50 cm) ↑8 in (20 cm)

Western Chinese species. Leaves have 5 to 8 lobes with a marbled cyclamen-like pattern and cream and purple-brown central markings, maturing to light green. Up to 5 flowers per cluster, dark purple-red or less commonly pink, followed by plum-like fruits. Zones 6–10.

Podocarpus macrophyllus

Podophyllum hexandrum

HIMALAYAN MAY APPLE

↔16 in (40 cm) ↑16 in (40 cm)

Native to western China and the Himalayas. Leaves to 10 in (25 cm) across, with 3 to 5 lobes, each tipped with a further 3 lobes, and often flushed with reddish bronze. Solitary, erect terminal flowers appear before the leaves mature, with 6 white to rose pink petals, in spring, followed by red fruit. Zones 4–9.

Podophyllum peltatum

AMERICAN MANDRAKE, DEVIL'S APPLE, HOG APPLE, INDIAN APPLE, MAY APPLE

↔24 in (60 cm) ↑24 in (60 cm)

From the woodlands of eastern USA south to Texas. A single, round, simple, forked stem and only 2 leaves, to 12 in (30 cm) across, with 3 to 5 lobes, finely hairy underneath. Flowering stem with 2 to 3 leaves or leafless, with solitary, nodding, fragrant flowers with white or rose pink petals, with toothed points, in spring. Fruit is a single berry, greenish yellow, occasionally red, with pulpy flesh; it ripens in late summer, the only part of the plant not poisonous. Zones 4–9.

PODRANEA

This genus is made up of 2 evergreen, twining, climbing shrubs, members of the trumpet-vine (Bignoniaceae) family and natives of South Africa, grown for their foxglove-like flowers. They have divided leaves and terminal, pyramid-shaped flowerheads. The fruit is a long capsule or pod containing winged seed. *Podranea* is an anagram of the closely related *Pandorea*.

CULTIVATION: Grow in full sun in any fertile, well-drained soil. Plants may need support. Propagate by striking half-hardened cuttings in summer or from seed sown in spring.

Podranea ricasoliana

syns *Pandorea brycei, P. ricasoliana, Tecoma ricasoliana*

PINK TRUMPET VINE

↔20 ft (6 m) ↑12–20 ft (3.5–6 m)

Fast-growing, climbing shrub with slender twining stems and compound leaves with 5 to 11 smooth-edged, green leaflets. Loose clusters of pale pink, fragrant, funnel-shaped flowers, to 2½ in (6 cm) across, striped with red, appear from spring to autumn. Zones 10–11.

Podophyllum difforme

Podranea ricasoliana

Polemonium caeruleum Brise d'Anjou/'Blanjou'

POLEMONIUM

JACOB'S LADDER, SKY PILOT

A genus of 25 erect or spreading or rhizomatous annual or sometimes short-lived perennial herbs from the phlox (Polemoniaceae) family, native from temperate to Arctic regions of the Americas, Europe, and Asia. Plants have pinnate leaves with simple or divided leaflets, with or without stalks. Heads of 5-lobed, tubular, bell- or funnel-shaped flowers, in blue, purplish, white, or yellow, grow from the leaf axils or at the ends of sprawling or erect stems. Egg-shaped to spherical fruit contain 3 to 10 brown or black seeds per compartment.
CULTIVATION: They grow well in sun or part-shade in rich, well-drained, moist, loamy soil. Propagate by division in autumn or early spring, or from seed sown in autumn or winter.

Polemonium boreale

syns *Polemonium macranthum, P. nudipedum, P. richardsonii*

ARCTIC POLEMONIUM, NORTHERN JACOB'S LADDER

↔ 3–12 in (8–30 cm)
↕ 3–12 in (8–30 cm)

Erect, hairy or glandular perennial, growing naturally in crevices and rocky slopes in central Asia. Erect stems and leaves mostly from a central base, with 13 to 23 oval leaflets. Terminal heads of bell-shaped flowers, blue, violet, or white, about ½ in (12 mm) across, in summer. Zones 3–8.

Polemonium caeruleum

CHARITY, GREEK VALERIAN, JACOB'S LADDER

↔ 12–20 in (30–50 cm)
↕ 12–36 in (30–90 cm)

Hairy and glandular perennial, found from northern and central Europe and northern Asia. Leaves to 16 in (40 cm) long; 11 to 27 sword-shaped to oblong leaflets, growing from central base. Loose heads of flowers with blue, occasionally white, widely bell-shaped

Polemonium boreale

corollas, with oval lobes, in late spring–summer. ***P. c.* subsp. *caeruleum*,** heads of many blue flowers, with stamens protruding beyond the corolla. ***P. c.* 'Blue Dove',** pale blue flowers; **'Brise d'Anjou'** ★, stunning variegated form; **'Lambrooke Mauve',** 18 in (45 cm) high, purple-blue flowers. Zones 3–9.

Polemonium carneum

↔ 4–24 in (10–60 cm)
↕ 4–24 in (10–60 cm)

Clump-forming, minutely hairy, erect perennial, native to western USA from California to Oregon. Erect or sprawling, hollow, angular stems and leaves with 5 to 21 elliptical to oval, green leaflets. Loose clusters of 3 to 7 flowers with bell-shaped, lilac, pink, or yellow corollas, ½–1 in (12–25 mm) long, on short stalks, in early summer, followed by fruit. Zones 4–6.

Polemonium pulcherrimum

SHOWY POLEMONIUM, WESTERN SKY PILOT

↔ 20–24 in (50–60 cm)
↕ 20–24 in (50–60 cm)

Vigorous, erect, clumping, deciduous perennial, growing naturally from slender, branching rhizomes on moist to dry, often rocky slopes in northwestern North America. There are 4 to 10 sprawling or erect stems, covered with soft hairs. Leaves grow from a central base, with 9 to 37 bright green, oval leaflets covered in fine hairs. Dense, glandular clusters of flowers with a bell-shaped, blue, violet, or white corolla, surrounded

Polemonium reptans

by 2 leaf-like bracts, yellow inside, on stalks to 1 in (25 mm) long, in late spring–summer. Zones 4–7.

Polemonium reptans

ABSCESS ROOT, CREEPING JACOB'S LADDER, GREEK VALERIAN

↔ 12–27 in (30–70 cm)
↕ 8–27 in (20–70 cm)

Erect or spreading perennial, native to eastern USA. Fleshy roots and many erect, smooth, hollow, branching, herbaceous, greenish stems, sometimes with a reddish tinge, growing from a small crown. Leaves to 8 in (20 cm) or more long, with 7 to 19 elliptical to oval, dull green leaflets, silvery green underneath. Loose panicles, with bracts of drooping flowers with a densely glandular, bell-shaped calyx and a smooth, lilac to light blue, funnel-shaped corolla, in spring–early summer. Roots traditionally used by Native Americans for a variety of ailments from bronchitis to snakebite. **'Blue Pearl'** grows to 10 in (25 cm) high, with blue flowers. Zones 4–7.

Polemonium viscosum

SKUNK POLEMONIUM, SKY PILOT, STICKY POLEMONIUM

↔ 16 in (40 cm) ↕ 16 in (40 cm)

Perennial, native to northwestern North America. Erect, angular, hollow stems, and densely glandular leaves, to 8 in (20 cm) long, with many tiny, lobed leaflets, mostly growing from a central base. Dense heads of drooping, blue to violet flowers, with tubular or funnel-shaped corollas, in late spring–summer. Zones 3–5.

POLIANTHES

This Mexican genus in the asparagus (Asparagaceae) family comprises 13 species of strongly rhizomatous perennials forming clumps of linear to lance-shaped, sometimes strappy basal leaves, from which emerge upright flower stems bearing several pairs of very fragrant, waxy flowers backed by leafy bracts. The flowers of the commonly grown *P. tuberosa*, cultivated for the perfume and florist trades, last

Polianthes tuberosa

well when cut. Introduced to Europe in the sixteenth century, *P. tuberosa* was cultivated by local tribespeople and is not known in the wild.
CULTIVATION: These plants are best grown in a mild climate. Summer-flowering outdoors, but can be forced into bloom at any time indoors. Plant in a sunny, sheltered position in fertile, moist, humus-rich, well-drained soil. Although perennial, they flower only once. Propagate by removing the strongest side-shoots before discarding spent crowns, or from seed.

Polianthes tuberosa

TUBEROSE

↔ 20 in (50 cm) ↕ 48 in (120 cm)

Mexican perennial. Forms basal clump of narrow, strap-like, green to gray-green leaves. Racemes of fragrant, funnel-shaped, waxy, white flowers to 2 in (5 cm) long, with 6 widely flared lobes, on erect stems, in summer–autumn. **'The Pearl',** strongly scented, white, double flowers. Zones 9–10.

POLYALTHIA

This genus of around 100 species of shrubs or trees belongs to the custard-apple (Annonaceae) family. It is widespread in tropical regions, particularly in Southeast Asia, with a few species occurring in Australia. They have large glossy leaves that have very fine oil dots and are aromatic when crushed. Borne singly or in clusters on older leafless wood, the open star-like flowers have 6 to 8 petals. Decorative clusters of succulent berry-like fruit follow.
CULTIVATION: All species demand warm, frost-free conditions. They prefer moist, humus-rich, well-drained soil in full sun or part-shade. Water liberally during dry periods. Propagate from fresh seed or cuttings.

Polyalthia longifolia

INDIAN WILLOW

↔ 3–10 ft (0.9–3 m) ↕ 50 ft (15 m)

Occurring naturally in Sri Lanka. The form usually seen in streets and parks in tropical Asia has a striking columnar form, with short side branches right down to the base. The wild trees have a much more open growth form. Pendulous, bright green, elliptic leaves. Small greenish yellow flowers in axillary clusters, in summer. Zones 11–12.

POLYGALA

Covering over 500 species of almost every growth form, except tall trees, this genus, a member of the milkwort (Polygalaceae) family, is very widespread. The foliage ranges from small and linear to large and oval but is usually simple with smooth edges. The flowers have a pea-flower-like structure with distinct wings and a keel, which usually has a feathery tuft unique to polygalas. The flowers, carried in clusters or racemes, come in a range of colors, with purple and pink dominant, and are followed by small seed pods.

CULTIVATION: While frost hardiness varies, most prefer a light well-drained soil with a position in sun or partial shade. The European and American alpine species are ideal subjects for pots or troughs. The shrubby species can be trimmed or pruned to shape, spring usually being the best time as it ensures the speediest recovery. Propagate from seed, layers, or cuttings.

Polygala chamaebuxus

↔ 15 in (38 cm) ↕ 2–6 in (5–15 cm)

Tiny spreading shrublet from the mountains of central Europe. Long, elliptical, leathery, glossy leaves. White-winged, yellow-keeled, pea-flowers. Popular for troughs, alpine houses, and well-drained rock gardens. *P. c.* var. ***grandiflora*** has purple-winged flowers. Zones 6–9.

Polyalthia longifolia

Polygala × *dalmaisiana*

Polygala virgata

Polygala × *dalmaisiana*

↔ 3 ft (0.9 m) ↕ 3–10 ft (0.9–3 m)

Evergreen shrub, garden hybrid between *P. oppositifolia* and *P. myrtifolia*; neat, compact if trimmed occasionally. Mid-green, 1 in (25 mm) long leaves. Magenta to pale purple flowers, most of the year. Zones 9–11.

Polygala myrtifolia

↔ 3–6 ft (0.9–1.8 m) ↕ 6 ft (1.8 m)

South African evergreen shrub. Elliptic to oblong, mid-green leaves, often develop purplish tints, in winter. Small clusters of pale-tufted purple-pink flowers most of the year. Trim to keep compact. Zones 9–11.

Polygala virgata

CAPE PURPLE BROOM

↔ 5 ft (1.5 m) ↕ 5–10 ft (1.5–3 m)

South African deciduous or semi-evergreen shrub. Small narrow leaves shed early. Flowers purple-pink in racemes to 6 in (15 cm) long. Small seed pods. Can become weedy, suits coastal conditions. Zones 9–11.

POLYGONATUM

SOLOMON'S SEAL

There are approximately 50 species in this genus, which is a member of the asparagus (Asparagaceae) family. They are found in the temperate zones of the Northern Hemisphere. Most of these easy-to-grow herbaceous perennials are fully hardy. The taller species have graceful arching stems, attractive leaves, and carry the delicate flowers in small pendulous clusters from the upper leaf axils. Small blue-black berries often follow the flowers. There is one dwarf variety that is perfect for rock gardens. The plant spreads by slow-growing underground rhizomes. Plant in a woodland garden with hostas, hellebores, wild ginger, ferns, or astilbe.

CULTIVATION: Plant in a shady or partly shady position in a rich, moist, peaty soil. Propagate from seed or divide the rhizomes in spring or autumn. Cut the stems down to soil level in late autumn. Mulch annually with leaf mold.

Polygonatum cirrhifolium

↔ 24 in (60 cm) ↕ 7 ft (2 m)

From China. Whorls of long thin leaves, coiled at tips. Narrow, tubular, pink to purple flowers with tips sometimes differently colored, in late spring–early summer; red berries in autumn. Zones 6–9.

Polygonatum × *hybridum*

syn. *Polygonatum multiflorum of gardens*

↔ 12–24 in (30–60 cm) ↕ 36 in (90 cm)

White, green-tipped, bell-shaped flowers hang from arching stems in late spring–early summer. Oval green leaves turn a buttery yellow color in autumn. Easy to grow in almost any soil. Protect the roots from the sun. Zones 3–9.

Polygonatum odoratum

syn. *Polygonatum officinale*

ANGULAR SOLOMON'S SEAL

↔ 24 in (60 cm) ↕ 36 in (90 cm)

From Europe, northern Iran, Siberia, and Japan. Grows in woods, in limestone. Flowers mid-spring–early summer. **'Flore Pleno'** ★, attractive double flowers; **'Variegatum'**, leaf margins and tips edged white. Zones 3–9.

POLYPODIUM

POLYPODY

A genus of about 75 deciduous, semi-evergreen or evergreen, epiphytic, rock-dwelling, or terrestrial ferns in the polypody (Polypodiaceae) family, from temperate regions of the Northern Hemisphere. They have stemmed, simple or divided fronds, with yellow spore-bodies on the backs of veins, and grow from creeping scaly rhizomes. The fronds dry up and fall in summer, but new fronds appear with autumn rain. The genus name comes from the Greek words *polys*, many, and *pous*, foot, referring to the much-branching rhizomes.

CULTIVATION: Polypody prefer a fibrous, well-drained soil but cope with heavy clay or gravel kept moist, particularly in winter, in part-shade. Propagate from spores in late summer, or by division of clumps or rhizomes in spring.

Polygonatum cirrhifolium

Polypodium californicum

Polypodium californicum

CALIFORNIA POLYPODY

↔ 20 in (50 cm) ↕ 40 in (100 cm)

Summer-deciduous, creeping, perennial fern naturally inhabiting moist rock crevices in California, USA. Arching, deeply divided, oblong to triangular, green fronds, to 12 in (30 cm) long and 6 in (15 cm) wide, on straw-colored stems to 8 in (20 cm) high. Zones 7–10.

Polypodium glycyrrhiza

syn. *Polypodium vulgare* var. *occidentale*

LICORICE FERN

↔ 12–24 in (30–60 cm)
↕ 12–24 in (30–60 cm)

Epiphytic, colonizing, summer-deciduous fern grows on wet mossy logs and rocks on the western coast of North America, from Alaska to California. Named for its perennial licorice-flavored rhizomes, which Native Americans used medicinally and for food flavoring. Rhizomes are shallow, branching, yellowish green, roundish, up to ¼ in (6 mm) thick. Thinly textured, sword-shaped to elliptical, light green fronds, to 14 in (35 cm) long, with 10 to 20 offset pairs of notched pointed segments, on straw-colored stems. Zones 6–9.

Polypodium scouleri

COAST POLYPODY, LEATHERY POLYPODY

↔ 36 in (90 cm) ↕ 15 in (38 cm)

Evergreen fern, native to the west coast of North America, from British Columbia to California. Rigid, thickly textured, glossy, leathery, oval to triangular, deep green fronds, to 16 in (40 cm) long, with up to 14 pairs of narrow, spreading segments with smooth-edged or notched margins, on smooth stems to 4 in (10 cm) high. Zones 8–10.

Polypodium triseriale

Polypodium triseriale

syn. *Serpocaulon triseriale*

ANGLE-VEIN FERN

↔ 16–24 in (40–60 cm)
↑ 16–24 in (40–60 cm)

Fern from the West Indies, Central America, and northern South America. Herbaceous or leathery, divided fronds, to 24 in (60 cm) long. Spreading, narrow, strap-shaped leaflets on lustrous, straw-colored to reddish brown stems to 14 in (35 cm) long. Zones 9–10.

Polypodium vulgare

ADDER'S FERN, COMMON POLYPODY, GOLDEN MAIDENHAIR, WALL FERN

↔ 10–12 in (25–30 cm)
↑ 10–12 in (25–30 cm)

Evergreen fern, widely distributed through North America, Europe, Africa, and East Asia, suited to rock gardens. It grows from creeping, brownish, scarred rhizomes covered with copper-brown scales. Arching or erect, smooth, thinly textured, sword-shaped to oval, leathery, herringbone-like fronds, to 12 in (30 cm) long, with closely set, horizontal or spreading segments carried on straw-colored stems. Zones 3–5.

POLYSTICHUM

HOLLY FERN, SWORD FERN

A genus of more than 175 evergreen, semi-evergreen, or deciduous terrestrial ferns, widely distributed throughout the world. Members of the shield-fern (Dryopteridaceae) family, they grow from stout, woody, densely scaly, erect or sprawling rhizomes. Tufted, thin to leathery fronds are divided pinnately to tripinnately into toothed leaflets with a tapered base, with rounded spore-bodies underneath, carried on straw-like, densely scaly stems. The genus is named from the Greek *polys*, many, and *stichos*, a row or file, a reference to the regular rows of spore.

CULTIVATION: These ferns prefer part-shade and moist, well-drained, soil with plenty of organic matter. Propagate by division in spring or from spores sown in summer.

Polystichum aculeatum

Polystichum acrostichoides

CHRISTMAS FERN, DAGGER FERN

↔ 18–24 in (45–60 cm)
↑ 18–24 in (45–60 cm)

Evergreen fern from wooded slopes of North America. One of its common names reflects the resemblance of its leaf segments to Christmas stockings. Compact, sometimes branched rhizome covered with brownish orange scales, has long fibrous roots. Narrowly sword-shaped fronds, 8–30 in (20–75 cm) long, with 20 to 35 finely toothed, dark green leaflets per side, with hair-like scales underneath and a densely scaly midrib. Native Americans used the rhizomes to make a tea to treat chills, fevers, pneumonia, and to induce vomiting. Zones 3–9.

Polystichum aculeatum

HARD SHIELD FERN, PRICKLY SHIELD FERN

↔ 18–24 in (45–60 cm)
↑ 18–24 in (45–60 cm)

Variable evergreen or semi-evergreen fern from Europe has rigid, sword-shaped, leathery fronds, 12–36 in (30–90 cm) long, with up to 50 toothed leaflets per side. Fronds are yellowish green in spring, maturing to dark glossy green, carried on short brown stems. **Densum Group**, densely massed fronds; **'Pulcherrimum'**, sharply edged, delicate, dark green fronds. Zones 4–8.

Polystichum andersonii

ALASKAN HOLLY FERN, ANDERSON'S HOLLY FERN, ANDERSON'S SWORD FERN

↔ 24–30 in (60–75 cm)
↑ 24–30 in (60–75 cm)

Evergreen fern, native to northwestern North America. Fronds, sword-shaped to elliptical, 16–36 in (40–90 cm) long, with numerous, narrowly triangular, deeply toothed leaflets. Zones 4–8.

Polystichum braunii

Polystichum braunii

syn. *Aspidium braunii*

BRAUN'S SWORD FERN, EASTERN HOLLY FERN, SHIELD FERN

↔ 24–36 in (60–90 cm)
↑ 24–36 in (60–90 cm)

Semi-evergreen fern from moist woodlands of North America and temperate Eurasia. Arching, dark green, glossy, soft, oblong to sword-shaped, twice-cut fronds, with 30 to 40 leaflets per side, with oval to triangular, finely toothed and slightly hairy segments, on thick stems. The stalks, midribs, and undersides of fronds are covered in light brown scales, with few small spore-bodies underneath. Zones 4–8.

Polystichum californicum

syn. *Aspidium californicum*

CALIFORNIAN SHIELD FERN

↔ 20–30 in (50–75 cm)
↑ 20–30 in (50–75 cm)

Fern from woods, streambanks and rocky open slopes of western North America, from California to British Columbia. A naturally occurring hybrid between *P. munitum* and *P. dudleyi*. Sword-shaped fronds, 8–30 in (20–75 cm) long, numerous leaflets, on brown stems. Zones 7–9.

Polystichum dudleyi

↔ 20–30 in (50–75 cm)
↑ 20–30 in (50–75 cm)

Fern from moist forests of California, USA. Oblong, narrowly oval or sword-shaped fronds, 10–30 in (25–75 cm) long, with serrated leaflets. Zones 7–9.

Polystichum falcinellum

↔ 18–24 in (45–60 cm)
↑ 18–24 in (45–60 cm)

Evergreen fern from eastern North America and the North Atlantic island of Madeira. Stems covered with glossy brown scales. Sword-shaped, leathery fronds are 12–60 in (30–150 cm) long, with numerous toothed leaflets. Zones 5–10.

Polystichum munitum

syn. *Aspidium munitum*

GIANT HOLLY FERN, WESTERN SWORD FERN

↔ 36–48 in (90–120 cm)
↑ 36–48 in (90–120 cm)

Evergreen fern, native from south east Alaska to Baja, California, and into the Rockies, with rigid, erect or arching, linear or sword-shaped, leathery, dark green fronds, forming a crown from an erect or sprawling rhizome. Fronds, 20–48 in (50–120 cm) long, have up to 40 spiny-toothed leaflets on each side, with large, circular, orange spore-bodies underneath. Zones 4–9.

Polystichum polyblepharum

HOLLY FERN, TASSEL FERN

↔ 48 in (120 cm) ↑ 48 in (120 cm)

Evergreen or semi-evergreen fern from South Korea and Japan. Narrowly oblong to oval, deep green, slightly lustrous fronds, which unfurl in a normal manner. They are clothed with white scales, then flip backward in a lax droop or tassel habit. They are 12–32 in (30–80 cm) long, have leaflets with oblong to oval, overlapping leaflets. The fronds are densely scaly on the underside, and are carried on stout brown stalks. Zones 5–9.

Polystichum setiferum

SOFT SHIELD FERN

↔ 18–24 in (45–60 cm)
↑ 18–24 in (45–60 cm)

Evergreen or semi-evergreen fern, from southern, western, and central Europe. Soft, sword-shaped, mid-green fronds, 12–48 in (30–120 cm) long, with up to 40 leaflets per side, carried on stalks that are covered with pale orange to brown scales. Bulbils form on frond midribs. **Cristatum Group**, crested, dark green, frilly fronds. **Divisilobum Group ★**, large, very frilly, light green fronds; group includes **'Divisilobum Densum'**, delicate-looking fern; and **'Herrenhausen'**, leathery, dark green fronds with pointed leaflets. **Plumosodivisilobum Group** with compact soft fronds, includes

Polystichum falcinellum

'Plumosum Densum', slightly smaller version with frilly lace-like fronds. **'Pulcherrimum Bevis'**, elongated crested tips on ends of fronds; **Rotundatum Group**, fronds with rounded leaflets; **'Wakeleyanum'**, narrow fronds, with leaflets forming cross-pattern across midrib. Zones 5–9.

Polystichum × *setigerum*

syn. *Polystichum alaskense*

ALASKAN HOLLY FERN

↔ 18–24 in (45–60 cm) ↑ 18–24 in (45–60 cm)

Evergreen fern, naturally occurring hybrid of *P. braunii* and *P. munitum*, native to western North America from Alaska to British Columbia. Pointed, diamond-shaped fronds, 10–36 in (25–90 cm) long, deeply lobed, sword-shaped leaflets, carried on pale brown stems. Zones 3–8.

Polystichum tsus-simense

syn. *Aspidium tsussimense*

Korean rock fern, tsu-shima holly fern

↔ 12–16 in (30–40 cm) ↑ 6–18 in (15–45 cm)

Clump-forming, evergreen or semi-evergreen fern, native to northeastern Asia, with thin, gently tapering, broadly sword-shaped to oval, dull green fronds, with distinctive black veining, 8–16 in (20–40 cm) long. Oval, finely toothed leaflets are carried on pale green to straw-colored stems covered with black to brown scales. Zones 6–9.

PONTEDERIA

A genus of 5 perennial, aquatic or marginal herbs, members of the pickerel-weed (Pontederiaceae) family, from the east of North and South America and the Caribbean. Erect or prostrate stems grow from a branching, often submerged rhizome, with smooth-edged, sword-shaped, dark green leaves on long stalks. Spikes of small tubular flowers, usually blue with 3 lobes, the largest lobe spotted with yellow. The genus is named for eighteenth-century Italian botanist, Guilio Pontedera.

CULTIVATION: Plant them in full sun in ponds and bog gardens, in water 8–12 in (20–30 cm) deep. Propagate in spring by division or from seed.

Pontederia cordata

PICKEREL RUSH, PICKEREL WEED, WAMPEE

↔ 27 in (70 cm) ↑ 48 in (120 cm)

Deciduous, perennial, marginal water plant found mostly on the east of North America and the Caribbean. Dense cylindrical spikes, 1–6 in

Pontederia cordata

(2.5–15 cm) long, of blue to white flowers, to ¾ in (18 mm) in diameter, are carried on erect stalks, to 14 in (35 cm) tall, in late summer. Zones 2–5.

POPULUS

ASPEN, POPLAR

About 35 species of poplars or aspens in this genus, deciduous trees that range over much of the temperate Northern Hemisphere. They are in the willow (Salicaceae) family. Many poplars have deltoid-shaped leaves, but foliage shapes, sizes, and textures vary widely. Tiny flowers on pendulous catkins appear before foliage. Small capsules follow, often filled with cotton-like down. Male and female catkins are usually on separate trees.

CULTIVATION: Poplars prefer a position in full sun in deep, moist, well-drained soil. Short-lived, seldom exceeding 60 years before becoming rotten. They have vigorous invasive root systems and some can sucker heavily, which often makes them a problem near drains and paving. Prune to shape; propagate from winter hardwood cuttings.

Populus alba

BOLLEANA POPLAR, SILVER POPLAR, WHITE POPLAR

↔ 40 ft (12 m) ↑ 80 ft (24 m)

Vigorous tree from Europe and North Africa to central Asia. Can become a weed. Young stems and leaves are covered with downy white hairs, uppersurface becoming deep green with age. Leaves broad-based, egg-shaped, with coarsely toothed edges. Cultivars include the chalky white **'Nivea'**; the weeping **'Pendula'**; and the upright **'Raket'** (syn. 'Rocket'). Zones 3–10.

Populus balsamifera

BALSAM POPLAR, TACAMAHAC

↔ 25 ft (8 m) ↑ 80 ft (24 m)

Northern North American and Russian species, notable for the fragrant resin that coats its young twigs, buds and new foliage, giving bronze coloration. This wears away to glossy mid-green color below. Leaves roughly egg-shaped. Zones 3–8.

Populus × *canadensis*

CANADIAN POPLAR, CAROLINA POPLAR, HYBRID POPLAR

↔ 35 ft (10 m) ↑ 80 ft (24 m)

Hybrid between *P. deltoides* and *P. nigra*. Leaves egg-shaped to triangular, sparsely toothed edges, leaf stalks red. **'Aurea'**, new growth golden; **'Eugenei'**, tall columnar habit, new growth bronze; **'Robusta'**, dense foliage, strongly upright columnar habit; **'Serotina'**, male form with conical habit coming into leaf late. Zones 4–9.

Populus × *canescens*

GRAY POPLAR, TOWER POPLAR

↔ 40 ft (12 m) ↑ 100 ft (30 m)

Natural hybrid between *P. alba* and *P. tremula*. Rounded crown of large triangular to oval leaves, toothed at edges, felted beneath. Yellow-gray bark, scarred and fissured. Zones 4–9.

Populus alba

Populus deltoides

COTTONWOOD, EASTERN COTTONWOOD

↔ 60 ft (18 m) ↑ 100 ft (30 m)

From eastern half of North America. Leaves, deltoid, coarse-toothed edges. Buds, new shoots, and leaves covered in balsam-scented resin. Zones 2–10.

Populus fremontii

ALAMILLO, FREMONT COTTONWOOD, WESTERN COTTONWOOD

↔ 40 ft (12 m) ↑ 100 ft (30 m)

Western North American tree. Stocky trunk, rounded head of yellow-green, broad-based, deltoid leaves, tapering to a point, toothed. Female trees shed masses of seed "cotton." Zones 7–10.

Populus grandidentata

BIGTOOTH ASPEN

↔ 30 ft (9 m) ↑ 60 ft (18 m)

From eastern North America. Leaves on shorter older twigs very sharply toothed, on younger longer shoots, more ovoid, with wavy rather than toothed edges. Short branches that form a narrow rounded crown. Zones 3–9.

Populus heterophylla

BLACK COTTONWOOD, SWAMP POPLAR

↔ 25 ft (8 m) ↑ 50–80 ft (15–24 m)

From eastern USA. Short branches forming a narrow rounded head, buds and young foliage coated in resin. Leaves egg-shaped, toothed. Female trees shed copious quantities of down-covered seeds. Zones 4–9.

P

Populus nigra

BLACK POPLAR, THEVES POPLAR

↔ 60 ft (18 m) ↑ 100 ft (30 m)

Native to Europe, North Africa, and western Asia. Round-headed, with a thick trunk, deeply fissured, knotted and gnarled, gray bark. Triangular to diamond-shaped leaves, develop brilliant yellow tones, in autumn. **'Italica'**, broadly columnar up to 100 ft (30 m) high, orange young twigs, more intense autumn color; **'Lombardy Gold'** has bright golden yellow foliage from summer through autumn. Zones 2–10.

Populus nigra

Portulaca grandiflora, Sundial Series, 'Sundial Fuchsia'

Portulacaria afra

Populus tremuloides ★

AMERICAN ASPEN, QUAKING ASPEN, TREMBLING ASPEN

↔30 ft (9 m) ↑50 ft (15 m)

North American tree, foliage moves in the slightest breeze. Slender, upright, with yellow-gray bark. Leaves broad, glossy, dark green, serrated edges, glaucous undersides, turn yellow in autumn. Zones 1–9.

Populus trichocarpa

BLACK COTTONWOOD

↔35 ft (10 m) ↑80–120 ft (24–36 m)

Tree that is native to western North America, with furrowed dark gray bark, brittle branches. Leaves leathery, shallowly toothed, dark glossy green above, pale brown to nearly white, beneath, turning yellow, in autumn. Female trees shed copious amounts of "cotton." **'Fritz Pauley'**, a male cultivar. Zones 7–10.

PORTULACA

PURSLANE

This genus of some 40 species occurring in the warmer parts of the world belongs to the purslane (Portulacaceae) family. They are mostly succulent herbs, usually with tuberous roots. Leaves are flat or cylindrical, opposite or spirally arranged, usually with hairs in their axils, though these are absent in Australian species (subgenus *Portulacella*). Flowers are solitary or in heads, surrounded by a whorl of bracts formed by the upper leaves, the Australian species with distinct stalks. There are 2 sepals and usually 5 pink, purple, or yellow petals, which open in direct sun and close in shade. There are 8 to many stamens. The fruit is a small conical capsule, opening when the top falls off to release the many small seeds. The various species are often very difficult to distinguish. Some are grown as ornamentals, some for eating.

CULTIVATION: They are easily grown from seed in well-drained soils in sunny but sheltered positions.

Portulaca grandiflora

syn. *Portulaca pilosa subsp. grandiflora*

ELEVEN-O'CLOCK, GARDEN PORTULACA, MOSS ROSE, ROSE MOSS, SUN PLANT

↔6–12 in (15–30 cm) ↑6–12 in (15–30 cm)

Slow-growing annual, native to Brazil, Argentina, and Uruguay. Partially prostrate or climbing stem, to 12 in (30 cm) long, reddish twigs and alternate, thick, fleshy, lance-shaped, cylindrical, pale green leaves. Single or double flowers of rose, red, purple, lavender, yellow, or white, often striped, open only in sunlight. **'Sundance'**, semi-double flowers remain open most of the day. Other popular cultivars include: **'Double Mix'**, **'Margarita Rosita'**, the **Sundial Series**, and **'Tutti Frutti Mix'**. Zones 8–10.

PORTULACARIA

In a single-species genus of its own, this ornamental, evergreen, multi-branched, succulent belongs to the purslane (Portulacaceae) family and is native to South Africa. The branches are often held horizontally and develop twists to create a plant that has great character even when young. The leaves are less than 1 in (25 mm) long and rounded, with a smooth, glossy green surface. Clusters of pale pink flowers open from late spring and are followed by 3-lobed pink fruit (rarely seen in cultivation).

CULTIVATION: Suitable for mild almost frost-free gardens, especially near the coast, this succulent shrub is an ideal plant for arid areas, well-drained raised beds or for growing in large containers. It prefers light gritty soil and a position in full sun or light partial shade. Thinning the branches to emphasize the plant's tree-like character can be very effective, otherwise light trimming is all that is required to keep it tidy. Propagate from seed or cuttings in summer.

Portulacaria afra

CHINESE JADE PLANT, ELEPHANT BUSH, ELEPHANT'S FOOD, SPEKBOOM

↔5 ft (1.5 m) ↑10 ft (3 m)

An attractive shrub with bright green glossy foliage that contrasts well with the dark purple-brown of the branches. It produces an abundance of small pink flowers. Zones 9–11.

POSOQUERIA

This is a genus of some 12 species of evergreen shrubs or trees belonging to the madder (Rubiaceae) family. They come from tropical America and the West Indies, are frost-tender, and are grown for their attractive and very fragrant, white or red, exceptionally long, tubular flowers. These are often borne in profusion and continue to open throughout spring. The flowers each have 5 spreading petal lobes and are borne in large crowded clusters at branch tips. Large glossy leaves are smooth-edged and arranged in opposite pairs. Fruit is a plum-sized, fleshy, yellow berry containing several seeds.

CULTIVATION: They require a humus-enriched well-drained soil in a warm sheltered position in full sun or partial shade. Propagate from half-hardened cuttings taken in late summer.

Posoqueria latifolia

BRAZILIAN OAK

↔15 ft (4.5 m) ↑6–20 ft (1.8–6 m)

From Mexico to South America and the West Indies. Bushy, evergreen, shrub or small tree. Glossy, green leaves, prominent veins. Pure white, heavily perfumed, tubular flowers, in dense terminal clusters, in spring. Edible yellow fruits. Zones 10–12.

POTENTILLA

This is a large genus of some 500 species in the rose (Rosaceae) family from the Northern Hemisphere. While most are herbaceous perennials, the shrubby species are exceptionally useful as small ornamentals, being very hardy, thriving in most soils, in sun and in partial shade. The flowers are like small single roses, and are produced over a long period, from spring throughout summer and in some species well into autumn.

CULTIVATION: Prefer a fertile well-drained soil. Cultivars with orange, red, or pink flowers tend to fade in very strong sunshine and should be given a position where they receive some shade in the hottest part of the day. Propagation is usually from seed in autumn or cuttings in summer.

Potentilla alba

WHITE CINQUEFOIL

↔10 in (25 cm) ↑10 in (25 cm)

Vigorous, low-growing, spreading, mat-forming, perennial herb from central, southern, and eastern Europe. Sprays of 5 white, single flowers, to 1 in (25 mm) in diameter, appear in spring–summer. Dark green lower leaves are palm-shaped with 5 oblong leaflets, to 2½ in (6 cm) long, with toothed tips; stem leaves smaller, simple or divided into leaflets, silvery silky at first. Zones 3–9.

Potentilla atrosanguinea

syns *Potentilla argyrophylla var. atrosanguinea*, *P. leucochroa*

RED CINQUEFOIL

↔36 in (90 cm) ↑36 in (90 cm)

Clump-forming perennial herb from grassland and thickets of the Himalayas and western China. Branching stems with few branches. Forms a mound of semi-evergreen leaves with 3 elliptical to oval, toothed, silky leaflets, each up to 3 in

Posoqueria latifolia

P

(8 cm) long, with white hairs underneath, carried on long stems. Loose clusters of deep red to reddish purple, orange, or yellow flowers, to 1½ in (35 mm) across, usually with dark "eyes," on slender stalks, in late summer–early autumn. Zones 3–9.

Potentilla aurea

syns *Potentilla chrysocraspeda, P. halleri, P. ternata*

↔ 12 in (30 cm) ↑ 12 in (30 cm)

Rounded, mat-forming, perennial herb with woody base, native to grassland and thickets of the European Alps and the Pyrenees. Hand-shaped leaves with 5 oblong leaflets with silver hairs along the margins and veins, toothed at tips, and growing from a central base; smaller leaves on stems. Loose clusters of few golden yellow flowers, with deeper orange centers, in spring–summer. Zones 3–9.

Potentilla cinerea

syns *Potentilla arenaria, P. subacaulis, P. tommasiniana*

↔ 4 in (10 cm) ↑ 2–4 in (5–10 cm)

Dwarf, clump-forming perennial herb from dry, stony grasslands of temperate central, eastern, and southern Europe. Sprawling stems densely covered with fine gray hairs and rooting where they touch the ground. Compound leaves have 3 to 5 narrow, toothed, grayish green leaflets, to 1 in (25 mm) long. Heads of up to 6 pale yellow flowers, to 1 in (25 mm) in diameter, in summer. Zones 3–9.

Potentilla cinerea

Potentilla neumanniana 'Nana'

Potentilla fruticosa var. *dahurica*

Potentilla fruticosa

CINQUEFOIL, POTENTILLA, SHRUBBY CINQUEFOIL

↔ 5 ft (1.5 m) ↑ 5 ft (1.5 m)

Distributed widely through Northern Hemisphere. Dense shrub with striking yellow flowers, summer–autumn. Small palmately arranged leaves with 5 to 7 narrow leaflets. P. f. var. dahurica up to 20 in (50 cm), white, sometimes yellow, disc-shaped flowers. P. f. **'Daydawn'**, yellow flowers tinged with pink; **'Katherine Dykes'**, lemon yellow flowers; **'Ochraleuca'**, lemony white flowers; **'Primrose Beauty'**, rich cream flowers; **'Tangerine'** ★, orange flowers. Zones 3–9.

Potentilla nepalensis

CINQUEFOIL

↔ 12–24 in (30–60 cm) ↑ 12–24 in (30–60 cm)

Easily grown, freely flowering, clump-forming, perennial herb, originating in grassland and thickets of the western Himalayas. Numerous, slender, erect, leafy, branching, purple stems. Oval, coarsely toothed, palm-shaped, strawberry-like leaves with 5 leaflets, 1¼–3 in (3–8 cm) long on tall stalks, grow from a central base. Long, branching panicles of pink, purplish red, or crimson flowers, with 5 petals, in summer. **'Miss Willmott'** ★ (syn. 'Willmottiae'), freely flowering dwarf form, salmon pink flowers, darker pink center and veining. Zones 5–8.

Potentilla neumanniana

syns *Potentilla crantzii, P. tabernaemontani, P. verna*

SPRING CINQUEFOIL

↔ 6–12 in (15–30 cm) ↑ 3–4 in (8–10 cm)

Prostrate, mat-forming, evergreen, perennial herb with a sprawling, woody stem, from temperate northern, western, and central Europe. Spreads rapidly by runners to form dense ground cover. Spicily scented, strawberry-like, shiny, hand-shaped, deep green leaves, usually with 5 leaflets, occasionally 3, up to 1½ in (35 mm) long, with toothed tips. Small clusters of up to 12 buttery yellow, 5-petalled flowers, in spring, on stalks growing from the leaf axils. **'Nana'** (syn. *P. verna* 'Nana') grows to 3 in (8 cm) high with vivid green leaves and gold flowers. Zones 5–8.

Primula auricula 'Alicia'

Potentilla × *tonguei*

↔ 12–20 in (30–50 cm) ↑ 6–10 in (15–25 cm)

This perennial herb is a hybrid of garden origin, a cross between *P. anglica* and either *P. nepalensis* or *P. nevadensis*. Sprawling, non-rooting stems and compound leaves, with 3 to 5 narrowly oval, coarsely toothed leaflets. Flowers with an apricot corolla and carmine red eye, in summer. Zones 3–5.

PRIMULA

COWSLIP, POLYANTHUS, PRIMROSE

This widespread, mainly Northern Hemisphere, perennial genus gives its name to the family Primulaceae. The name comes from the word *primavera*, which is Italian for "spring," and it is as spring-flowering woodland plants that primroses are best known. Most primulas form basal rosettes of heavily veined leaves from which emerge the flower stems, sometimes with just a single bloom, but often with a large terminal head or several well-shaped whorls of flowers. Various species, especially the cowslip *(P. veris)*, have been used medicinally and are known to be astringent and mildly sedative.

CULTIVATION: Most *Primula* species prefer dappled shade in woodland gardens and moist, humus-rich, well-drained soil. So-called bog primroses like damper conditions and often naturalize along streams. Propagate from seed or by dividing thriving clumps when dormant.

Primula alpicola

↔ 10–16 in (25–40 cm) ↑ 16–36 in (40–90 cm)

Native to the Himalayas. Genuine bog primroses, prefer wet peaty soil. Toothed elliptical leaves. Flowers white, yellow, mauve, purple, to 1 in (25 mm) wide, atop stems with powdery white coating, in late spring–early summer. Zones 6–9.

Primula amoena

syn. *Primula elatior subsp. meyeri*

↔ 12 in (30 cm) ↑ 8 in (20 cm)

Native to the Caucasus region. Leaves elliptical to spatula-shaped, often red-tinted, with downy undersides; heads of up to 10 lavender to purple, ½–1 in (13–25 mm) wide flowers, in early spring. Zones 5–9.

Primula auricula

↔ 6–16 in (15–40 cm) ↑ 4–8 in (10–20 cm)

Spring-flowering species native to the mountains of southern Europe. Foliage and stems with dusty coating, clump-forming. Leaves fleshy, light green, rounded to broad lance-shaped, usually toothed; heads of few to many flat, ½–1 in (12–25 mm) wide flowers on 6 in (15 cm) high stems, in the wild most often yellow or purple-red with yellow center, some with a white band. Large number of cultivars: **'Alicia'**, dark purple-red with broad lighter margin; **'Beatrice'**, purple with mauve border and cream center; **'Butterwick'**, red-brown, golden yellow center; **'C. W. Needham'**, dark purple-blue, yellow-green center; **'Dales Red'**, red with heavy powdery white coating and white band, yellow center; **'Hawkwood'**, red with white edge and band, yellow center; **'Jeannie Telford'**, purple-red with mauve edge, cream center; **'Lavender Lady'**, light purple, white center; **'Lucy Locket'**, buff yellow, cream center; **'Rowena'**, maroon with lavender edges, yellow center and white band; **'Sirius'**, coffee-colored with purplish red markings, yellow center; **'Spring Meadows'**, cream with yellow-green center, light green edges; and **'Trouble'**, pinkish beige double flowers. Zones 3–9.

Primula bulleyana

☀/☀ ✱ ↔12–27 in (30–70 cm)
↑24 in (60 cm)

Native to southwestern China. Leaves toothed and tapering to narrow base. Flower stems with up to 7 whorls of golden yellow to orange flowers, borne in late spring–early summer. Zones 6–9.

Primula Candelabra Hybrids

☀/☀ ✱ ↔12–20 in (30–50 cm)
↑24–36 in (60–90 cm)

Mainly hybrids between *P. bulleyana* and *P. beesiana;* they are often listed as *P.* × *bulleesiana*. Foliage resembles the parents. Tall, erect stems with several whorls of flowers, may be sterile. Wide range of colors as named cultivars, such as **'Inverewe'** ★, bright orange-red flowers, sterile; or mixed color seedling strains, such as **Sunset Shades**. Zones 6–9.

Primula capitata

☀/☀ ✱ ↔12–18 in (30–45 cm)
↑10–15 in (25–38 cm)

From the Himalayas. Stems and undersides of foliage powdery white. Leaves coarsely toothed. Sturdy, erect flower stems, somewhat flattened heads of many small, violet to purple flowers, in late spring–early summer. Zones 5–9.

Primula denticulata

DRUMSTICK PRIMULA

☀/☀ ✱ ↔10–18 in (25–45 cm)
↑8–12 in (20–30 cm)

Found from the mountains of Afghanistan to Myanmar. Overwinters as a conical bud, producing rounded heads of mauve to purple-red flowers in spring, rarely white, with or before the new leaves. The flower stems and undersides of the toothed leaves are downy white. Zones 5–9.

Primula denticulata

Primula florindae

☀/☀ ✱ ↔8–16 in (20–40 cm)
↑36 in (90 cm)

Native to Tibet. Long-stemmed, broad pointed oval, toothed leaves. Tall sturdy flower stems carry open heads of up to 40 scented yellow flowers, in late spring–early summer. There are several probably hybrid groups such as **Keillour Group** (hybrids with *P.* × *walton*ii), which produce flowers in oranges, reds, and several yellow tones. Zones 6–9.

Primula frondosa

☀/☀ ✱ ↔6–10 in (15–25 cm)
↑6 in (15 cm)

This small spring-flowering species is native to the Balkan region. The stems and foliage have a heavy coating of white powder. The spatula-shaped leaves have coarsely toothed edges, and reach up to 4 in (10 cm) long. Flower stems to 5 in (12 cm) tall carry attractive mauve-pink flowers, ½ in (12 mm) wide. Zones 5–9.

Primula bulleyana

Primula japonica

☀/☀ ✱ ↔12–24 in (30–60 cm)
↑18 in (45 cm)

A clump-forming plant native to Japan. It has broad, coarsely toothed, spatula-shaped leaves to 10 in (25 cm) long. The flower stems bear up to 6 whorls of white, pink, magenta to red flowers, to ¾ in (18 mm) wide, in late spring–early summer. **'Postford White'**, white flowers with pink eye; **'Valley Red'**, bright pinkish red flowers. Zones 5–9.

Primula kisoana

☀/☀ ✱ ↔8–18 in (20–45 cm)
↑8 in (20 cm)

From Japan. Downy, rounded, lobed and coarsely toothed leaves to 6 in (15 cm) long, often considerably smaller. Flower stems carry heads of up to 6 deep pink to mauve flowers, 1 in (25 mm) wide, in spring. **'Alba'** is white-flowered form. Zones 6–10.

Primula marginata

☀/☀ ❄ ↔4–10 in (10–25 cm)
↑5 in (12 cm)

From the Cottian Alps on the border between France and Italy. Coarsely toothed, leathery, spatula-shaped leaves with powdery edges. Short stems with heads of up to 20 funnel-shaped flowers, lavender to purple-blue, in spring. **'Linda Pope'** (probably a hybrid with *P. allionii*), very powdery foliage, white-centered mauve flowers. Zones 7–9.

Primula Pruhonicensis Hybrids

POLYANTHUS

☀/☀ ✱ ↔6–16 in (15–40 cm)
↑4–12 in (10–30 cm)

Complex group of garden and natural hybrids involving combinations of *P. elatior, P. juliae, P. veris,* and *P. vulgaris*, ranging from very small, long-lived rock-garden types, such as **'Wanda'** (purple-red flowers) to the large showy hybrid polyanthus (usually mixed color seedling selections, such as the **Crescendo**, **Kaleidoscope**, **Pacific Giants**, and **Rainbow Series**), which are often treated as annuals. There are also named single-flowered hybrids; rosebud-double-flowered types ("double primroses"); hose-in-hose, appearing to have two blooms sleeved one within the other, and "gold-" or "silver-laced" forms with light-edged brownish black flowers. Popular single-flowered forms include: **'Dorothy'**, pale yellow flowers; **'Guinevere'** (syn. 'Garryard Guinevere'), bronze-green leaves, white flowers with red stems and sepals; **'Iris Mainwaring'**, mauve-blue suffused with pink; **'Old Port'**, deep purple-red; **'Schneekissen'**, dark green foliage, pure white flowers; and **'Velvet Moon'**, very dark foliage, deep velvet red flowers. Double primroses include: **'April Rose'**, deep red flowers; **Bon Accord Series**, a series of doubles mainly named by color, such as **'Bon Accord Purple'**; **'Ken Dearman'**, apricot-pink suffused with yellow, deep pink buds; and **'Sunshine Susie'**, bright yellow to gold flowers. Zones 7–9.

Primula × *pubescens*

☀/☀ ✱ ↔10 in (25 cm) ↑6 in (15 cm)

Hybrid between *P. auricula* and *P. hirsuta*. Leaves often powdery, toothed, usually quite rounded, to 4 in (10 cm) long. Flowers to over 1 in (25 mm) wide, in small, short-stemmed heads, most shades, except darker blue tones. **'Boothman's Variety'** (syn. 'Carmen'), white-centered deep crimson flowers; **'Harlow Car'**, large cream flowers; **'Wharfedale Buttercup'**, sulfur yellow. Zones 5–9.

Primula pulverulenta

☀/☀ ✱ ↔20 in (50 cm) ↑36 in (90 cm)

Native to China. Coarsely toothed leaves to 12 in (30 cm) long. The tall flower stems, candelabra-like, have several whorls of purple-red flowers with dark red centers; flowers are up to 1 in (25 mm) wide and appear in late spring–summer. **Bartley hybrids**, typically dark-centered pink-red flowers, also include some darker colors. Zones 6–9.

Primula rosea

☀/☀ ✱ ↔6–15 in (15–38 cm)
↑4–6 in (10–15 cm)

From the northwest Himalayas. The glowing deep pink flowers appear before the foliage, or before it is fully expanded. The leaves are toothed, developing slowly, and are often flushed bronze when immature. Heads of up to 12 flowers, with the petal tips notched, appear in spring. **'Grandiflora'** has large flowers on stems to more than 6 in (15 cm) tall. Zones 6–9.

Primula sieboldii

☀/☀ ✱ ↔12–24 in (30–60 cm)
↑12 in (30 cm)

Native to Japan and nearby parts of temperate mainland Asia. The leaves are very coarsely toothed with an indented heart-shaped base. The flowers are white, pink, or purple, and are borne in small heads to just above foliage height, in late spring–

summer. **'Blush Pink'** ★ has bright pink flowers with hint of apricot; **'Cloth of Mist'** has pale lavender flowers; **'Mikado'** has dark purple-pink flowers. Zones 5–9.

Primula sikkimensis

↔10–24 in (25–60 cm) ↕12–36 in (30–90 cm)

Native to Nepal and the Chinese western Himalayas. Dark green, serrated to toothed leaves. Partly pendulous flowers, white to yellow and funnel-shaped, borne in heads atop sturdy erect stems, in late spring–early summer. Zones 6–9.

Primula veris

COWSLIP

↔16 in (40 cm) ↕12 in (30 cm)

Eurasian species. Leaves smooth-edged to coarsely toothed, 2–8 in (5–20 cm) long, undersides sometimes downy. Downy flower stems, heads of up to 16 fragrant yellow flowers, in late spring–early summer. ***P. v.* subsp. *columnae*,** pointed oval leaves with downy white undersides; ***P. v.* subsp. *macrocalyx*,** large hairy calyces, larger flowers, rounded leaves. Zones 5–9.

Primula vialii

↔6–16 in (15–40 cm) ↕8–16 in (20–40 cm)

Western Chinese species. Narrow, downy, toothed leaves, 4–12 in (10–30 cm) long. Strong flower stems with cylindrical heads of small purple-pink flowers topped with a conical cap of overlapping red buds, in summer. Zones 7–10.

Primula vialii

Primula vulgaris

ENGLISH PRIMROSE, PRIMROSE

↔6–16 in (15–40 cm) ↕4–6 in (10–15 cm)

European species. Leaves toothed, sometimes coarsely, undersides often faintly downy. Fragrant pale yellow flowers, 1¼ in (30 mm) wide, emerge at ground level on thin stems, in spring. Extensively hybridized. P. v. subsp. sibthorpii, very compact, light mauve-pink flowers. **P. v. 'Blaue Auslese'** (syn. 'Blue Selection'), lavender blue flowers; **'Quaker's Bonnet'**, lavender pink flowers. Zones 6–9.

PRITCHARDIA

This is a genus of around 25 species of tropical fan palms, in the family Arecaceae, native to the Pacific Islands. They are grown for their impressive, large, flat fronds that are divided only about halfway to the midrib and have a neat pleated appearance. These palms, which may reach up to 70 ft (21 m) in height, have a smooth, slender, columnar trunk with grooved rings. They produce small, cream to orange, bell-shaped flowers in spikes or panicles at the base of the crown, usually in summer. These are followed by small dark brown to black fruits.
CULTIVATION: Frost tender, *Pritchardia* species require a warm humid climate and prefer humus-enriched well-drained soil in full sun with some protection from the midday sun when young. Propagate from seed.

Pritchardia gaudichaudii

syn. *Pritchardia martii*

↔6–10 ft (1.8–3 m) ↕20–30 ft (6–9 m)

A colony-forming palm from the Hawaiian Islands, suits coastal conditions. Large, stiff, pleated fronds, bright green, to 3 ft (0.9 m) across, covered with white wool when young. Spherical, shiny fruit. Zones 11–12.

Primula veris

Pritchardia hillebrandii

LELO PALM, LOULOU

↔12–20 ft (3.5–6 m) ↕15–25 ft (4.5–8 m)

Solitary, unarmed fan palm from the Hawaiian Islands with fan-shaped, bluish green fronds with stiff leaflets with a waxy coating, carried on bluish green stems that are densely woolly underneath. Shiny, bluish black, spherical fruit. Zones 10–12.

Pritchardia pacifica ★

FIJI FAN PALM

↔15 ft (4.5 m) ↕30 ft (9 m)

Probably originally native to Tonga. Fan palm with very wide, lush, long-stemmed, pleated fronds, dense foliage head, rain-shedding skirt. Insignificant heads of yellow flowers. Fruit blackens when ripe. Zones 11–12.

Pritchardia thurstonii

↔12 ft (3.5 m) ↕25 ft (8 m)

Occurring in large colonies on one of the Fijian island groups. Slender palm, fan-shaped pleated leaves. Inflorescences to 8 ft (2.4 m) long hang below the leaves, yellow flowers. Dark red globular fruits. Zones 11–12.

PROSOPIS

Native mainly to tropical and warmer arid parts of North and South America, with a few in Africa and Asia, this genus of some 40 species of shrubs and trees is closely related to *Mimosa* and belongs to the mimosa subfamily of the legume (Fabaceae) family. They have spiny branches and bipinnate leaves with numerous pairs of tiny olive green leaflets. Fragrant, nectar-rich, greenish white to dull yellow flowers are borne in axillary spike-like catkins. The elongated, pale yellow, bean-like pods are a valuable source of food. The pods and young shoots are also valued as livestock feed in hot climates with very little rainfall. The aromatic timber gives off a slightly sweet smoke and is used for barbecues and smoking foods.
CULTIVATION: These fast-growing, tough plants are easily grown in a warm dry climate. They prefer deep well-drained soil in full sun. Although most species tolerate only light frosts, they are extremely drought-resistant and provide welcome shade in arid regions. Propagate from seed or half-hardened cuttings.

Pritchardia hillebrandii

Prosopis glandulosa

HONEY MESQUITE

↔25 ft (8 m) ↕30 ft (9 m)

From southern USA and northern Mexico. Large deciduous shrub or small tree. Spiny stems, bipinnate leaves. Fluffy yellow flowers, nectar-rich, in racemes, in spring–summer. Pale yellow linear pods. A prohibited plant in some countries. ***P. g.* var. *torreyana*** (syn. *P. juliflora* var. *torreyana*), smaller with shorter leaves. Zones 8–11.

Prosopis pubescens

syns *Strombocarpa odorata, S. pubescens*

CREOSOTE BUSH SCRUB, SCREWBEAN, SCREWBEAN MESQUITE, TORNILLO

↔17 ft (5 m) ↕17–30 ft (5–9 m)

From southwestern USA and northwestern Mexico, Deciduous shrub or tree often with a twisted trunk; branches covered with narrow spines. Compact crown of feathery light green leaves, 5 to 9 pairs of narrow, elliptical to oblong, hairy leaflets to ½ in (12 mm) long. Spike-like racemes, to 3 in (8 cm) tall, of small, slightly hairy cream or yellow flowers with fused petals from spring–autumn. Unusual, tightly coiled, yellow seed pods covered with minute hairs, containing oval or egg-shaped seeds that are used for food and as a coffee substitute. Zones 8–11.

Prosopis glandulosa var. *torreyana*

Prostanthera ovalifolia 'Variegata'

Prosopis velutina

syn. *P. glandulosa subsp. velutina*

VELVET MESQUITE

↔15–40 ft (4.5–12 m) ↕15–40 ft (4.5–12 m)

Large shrub or medium-sized tree from southwestern USA and northwestern Mexico. Smooth dark brown bark; spine-covered velvety branches. Narrow, dull green, compound leaves with 2 to 3 leaflets, each with 15 to 20 pairs of minor leaflets with finely hairy surfaces. Clusters of small pale yellow to yellow-green flowers, appear in late spring–early summer, sometimes again in autumn. Slender brown pods ripen in mid- to late summer. Zones 8–11.

PROSTANTHERA

This Australian genus of around 100 species of evergreen shrubs belongs to the mint (Lamiaceae) family, noted for its Mediterranean culinary herbs, such as mint, sage, basil, and rosemary. Most species have highly aromatic opposite leaves on squarish stems and produce masses of spring and summer flowers, usually in shades of blue, mauve, or purple, sometimes white or red, and rarely yellow. The tubular flowers are irregular, usually 2-lipped and 3-lobed, often in clusters encircling the upper part of the stem. These plants are short lived in garden situations, but prostantheras are extremely fast growing and flower well, even when quite small.
CULTIVATION: They require a warm climate, excellent drainage and thrive in a sheltered position. As many species prefer some shade, they can be planted beneath the light overhead cover of trees with open foliage. Tip prune from an early age and immediately after flowering to ensure compact bushy growth and a pleasing shape. Propagate from half-hardened tip cuttings taken in summer.

Prostanthera ovalifolia

PURPLE MINT BUSH

↔6 ft (1.8 m) ↕6 ft (1.8 m)

Shrub from eastern Australia. Aromatic oval leaves, 1½ in (35 mm) long. Mass of purple or mauve flowers, darker spotted throats, in spring. **'Variegata'**, leaves with yellow edges. Zones 9–11.

PRUNELLA

syn. *Brunella*

HEAL ALL, SELF-HEAL

These 7 semi-evergreen, spreading, sprawling perennial herbs belong to the mint (Lamiaceae) family and are native to temperate Eurasia, North Africa, and North America. The plants' creeping, grooved, and slightly hairy stems sometimes take root at lower nodes. Opposite leaves with generally smooth-edged blades are on stalks from the base of the plant or from the stems. Heads of densely whorled groups of 4 to 6 bluish violet or purplish red, tubular to bell-shaped flowers, with an erect, hooded, 2-lipped corolla with 3 lobes, are borne on stubby stalks surrounded by leaf-like bracts. Fruit, egg-shaped nutlet.
CULTIVATION: They grow well in sun or shade in dry to moist, well-drained soil, and are suited to rock gardens and shaded areas. Propagate from seed or by division in spring.

Prunella grandiflora

BIGFLOWER, LARGE SELF-HEAL, SELF-HEAL

↔12–24 in (30–60 cm) ↕12–24 in (30–60 cm)

European mat-forming herb. Woody branching stems; tiny, oval to sword-shaped leaves, scalloped edges. Showy heads of off-white, pale blue, or purple flowers, with deep violet lips, in summer. **'Loveliness'** ★, has pale lilac flowers; **'Pink Loveliness'**, has pink flowers. Zones 4–9.

Prunella grandiflora 'Loveliness'

Prunella laciniata

↔9–12 in (22–30 cm) ↕9–12 in (22–30 cm)

From southwestern and central Europe. Lobed or divided leaves, to 3 in (8 cm) long, densely covered with fine hairs. Spikes of ¾ in (18 mm) wide yellowish white, sometimes rose pink or purple, flowers in spring–summer. Zones 6–9.

PRUNUS

This widely grown genus is naturally widespread throughout the northern temperate regions of the world and mountain parts of Africa and includes a range of shrubs and trees, mostly deciduous. A rose (Rosaceae) family member, it is best known for the edible stone fruits (cherries, plums, apricots, peaches, and nectarines) and their ornamental flowering cousins. The leaves are usually simple pointed ellipses, often with serrated edges, sometimes brilliant autumn colors. Flowers are 5-petalled, carried singly or in clusters, and range in color from white through to dark pink, followed by fleshy fruit with a single seed enclosed in a hard stone. It is possible that in a few years this large genus may be broken into several smaller genera, such as *Amygdalus* (almonds), *Cerasus* (cherries), and *Laurocerasus* (cherry laurels).
CULTIVATION: Although hardiness varies with the species, most need some winter chilling to flower and fruit properly. Wind protection is important. Most species prefer cool, moist, well-drained soil that is both fertile and rich in humus. Correct pruning techniques are important for the fruiting varieties. Propagate the species from seed, the fruiting forms by grafting, and the ornamentals by grafts or, in some cases, from cuttings.

Prunella laciniata

Prunus americana

AMERICAN PLUM, AMERICAN RED PLUM, GOOSE PLUM, HOG PLUM, WILD PLUM

↔12 ft (3.5 m) ↕25 ft (8 m)

Eastern and central North American tree with spiny branches, peeling dark brown bark. Leaves to 4 in (10 cm) long, white flowers. Small, yellow-fleshed, red to plum-blue fruit. Zones 3–9.

Prunus × amygdalo-persica

FLOWERING ALMOND

↔20 ft (6 m) ↕20 ft (6 m)

Hybrid between *P. dulcis* and *P. persica*. Highly ornamental flowers; inedible green fruits. **'Pollardii'**, regarded as the typical form, large bright pink flowers, in late winter before the foliage expands. Zones 4–9.

Prunus avium

GEAN, MAZZARD, SWEET CHERRY, WILD CHERRY

↔20 ft (6 m) ↕50 ft (15 m)

The main parent of edible cherries. A deciduous Eurasian tree with serrated-edged leaves. Flowers white, massed in small clusters, open before the new leaves. Purple-red fruit. **'Asplenifolia'**, deeply cut leaves; **'Cavalier'**, an eating cherry, with medium-sized to large fruit, black, very sweet, produced early to mid-season; **'Plena'** (syn. 'Multiplex'), peeling bark, orange-red autumn foliage, white double flowers. Zones 3–9.

Prunus campanulata

TAIWAN CHERRY

↔25 ft (8 m) ↕30 ft (9 m)

Deciduous tree from Taiwan and southern Japan. Leaves large, doubly serrated, color in autumn. Flowers, deep cerise, pendulous in clusters, open before the foliage. Small purple-black fruits. Flowers in winter in mild climates. **'Felix Jury'**, deep magenta-cerise flowers, early. Zones 7–10.

Prunus caroliniana

CAROLINA LAUREL-CHERRY, WILD ORANGE

↔ 20 ft (6 m) ↑ 40 ft (12 m)

Found in southern USA. Evergreen tree, glossy, elliptical, smooth-edged leaves, cream flowers, densely massed in racemes, in spring. Small, shiny, black fruit. Used for hedging and utility plantings. Zones 7–11.

Prunus cerasifera

CHERRY PLUM, FLOWERING PLUM, MYROBALAN

↔ 30 ft (9 m) ↑ 30 ft (9 m)

Eurasian species found in many cultivated varieties. Deciduous, large shrub or a small tree. Leaves, bronze tinted, fairly small, veins on their undersides, hairy. White flowers, small yellow to red fruit. *P. c.* subsp. ***divaricata***, lax habit, bears smaller, yellow flowers. *P. c.* **'Hessei'**, shrubby, with light green foliage, and snow white flowers; **'Lindsayae'**, reddish young foliage maturing to green, pale pink flowers; **'Newport'**, shrubby in habit, with bronze foliage, small, white to pale pink flowers; **'Nigra'** has deep purple-black foliage; **'Pendula'** has weeping growth habit; **'Pissardii'** has red to purple leaves, white flowers opening from pink buds, plum-red fruit; **'Thundercloud'**, a tall cultivar with deep bronze foliage, pink flowers. Zones 4–10.

Prunus cerasifera

Prunus dulcis

Prunus cerasus

SOUR CHERRY

↔ 15 ft (4.5 m) ↑ 20 ft (6 m)

Found from southeastern Europe to India. Large deciduous shrub or small tree. Small, deep green, glossy leaves, finely serrated edges. Long-stemmed umbels of small white flowers, in spring. Fruit resembles sweet cherries. Zones 3–9.

Prunus × *cistena*

PURPLE-LEAFED SAND CHERRY, RED-LEAF PLUM

↔ 6 ft (1.8 m) ↑ 8 ft (2.4 m)

Hybrid between *P. cerasifera* 'Atropurpurea' and *P. pumila.* Slow-growing shrub with lustrous, bronze-tinted leaves with serrated edges. White flowers develop into small, dark purple-red fruits. Zones 3–9.

Prunus cyclamina

CYCLAMEN CHERRY

↔ 20 ft (6 m) ↑ 30 ft (9 m)

From central China. Leaves, coarsely serrated, heavily veined, 3 in (8 cm) long, tapering abruptly to a point. Flowers, in clusters of 4, long-stemmed, deep rose pink, fringed edges, in spring. Small red fruits. Zones 6–9.

Prunus davidiana

DAVID'S PEACH

↔ 30 ft (9 m) ↑ 30 ft (9 m)

Deciduous Chinese tree. Young branches upright, whippy, dark green leaves, very small, tapering point, sharp teeth. White or pale pink flowers, in late winter–spring. Yellow furry edible fruit. Zones 4–9.

Prunus × *domestica* 'Bühlerfrühwetsch'

Prunus laurocerasus 'Etna'

Prunus × *domestica*

EUROPEAN PLUM, PLUM

↔ 15 ft (4.5 m) ↑ 30 ft (9 m)

The common plum has been grown since ancient times, a hybrid, probably between *P. spinosa* and *P. cerasifera* subsp. *divaricata.* Leaves to 4 in (10 cm) long, flowers white, soft-fleshed yellow or red-skinned fruit. **'Angelina Burdett'** (syn. 'Angelina'), early fruiting, light red skin, yellow flesh; **'Bühlerfrühwetsch'**, from Germany, purple-skinned; **'Coe's Golden Drop'**, mid-season, yellow skin, yellow flesh; **'Hauszwetsch'** and **'Mount Royal'**, purple-skinned; **'President'**, mid- to late season, large, purplish blue skin, yellow flesh; **Reine Claude Group** (syn. **Greengage** Group), mid season, greenish yellow skin, yellow flesh, largely self-fertile. Zones 5–9.

Prunus dulcis

ALMOND

↔ 15 ft (4.5 m) ↑ 20–30 ft (6–9 m)

Species native to eastern Mediterranean and North Africa. Deciduous tree with 5 in (12 cm) long narrow leaves with finely serrated edges. Large white to deep pink flowers, followed by edible kernels. **'Alba Plena'** has white double flowers; **'Macrocarpa'** has large pale pink flowers; **'Roseoplena'** has pink double flowers. Zones 7–10.

Prunus glandulosa

DWARF FLOWERING ALMOND

↔ 5 ft (1.5 m) ↑ 5 ft (1.5 m)

Lovely deciduous shrub from China and Japan. Densely branched, rather narrow leaves, finely serrated edges. Smothered in deep pink to red flowers, in spring. Dark red fruits. Prune to near ground level after flowering to encourage strong growth, with heavy flowering next season. **'Alba Plena'** has white double flowers; **'Sinensis'** has large leaves, pink double flowers. Zones 4–9.

Prunus hortulana

HORTULAN PLUM

↔ 15 ft (4.5 m) ↑ 20–30 ft (6–9 m)

Deciduous tree from central USA. Leaves yellow-green with a slight gloss, fine hairs, serrated edges. Dark brown branches with peeling bark. Flowers white, in umbels of 2 to 5 blooms. Edible red or yellow fruit. Zones 6–9.

Prunus ilicifolia

HOLLY-LEAFED CHERRY, ISLAY

↔ 20 ft (6 m) ↑ 25 ft (8 m)

A densely branched evergreen shrub or small tree that is native to California. Leathery, glossy, green, holly-like leaves with spiny edges. Small creamy white flowers massed in racemes. Red, sometimes yellow fruit. Zones 9–11.

Prunus laurocerasus

CHERRY LAUREL, LAUREL CHERRY

↔ 30 ft (9 m) ↑ 20 ft (6 m)

Popular hedging plant. Evergreen Eurasian shrub or small tree. Lustrous deep green leaves. Racemes of tiny creamy white flowers in spring, followed by small black fruits. Cut back hard in late spring or early summer. **'Etna'**, finely toothed shiny leaves; **'Zabeliana'**, low-growing, to 3 ft (0.9 m) high with a greater spread, narrow pale green leaves. Zones 7–10.

Prunus lusitanica

PORTUGAL LAUREL

↔ 30 ft (9 m) ↑ 20 ft (6 m)

Superficially similar to *P. laurocerasus,* this plant is native to the Iberian Peninsula. Evergreen with large, glossy, deep green leaves. Flowers later than *P. laurocerasus,* racemes of cream flowers. Fruit deep purple to near-black shade. *P. l.* subsp. ***azorica,*** the Azores cherry laurel, shrubby, rarely exceeding 12 ft (3.5 m) tall, smaller leaves, shorter racemes. Zones 7–10.

Prunus maackii ★

AMUR CHOKE CHERRY, MANCHURIAN CHERRY

↔ 25 ft (8 m) ↑ 50 ft (15 m)

From Korea and nearby parts of China, smaller in cultivation. Small cream flowers in racemes, in spring. Purple-tinted leaves, peeling papery bark, light orange-red shade. Small black fruit. Zones 2–9.

Prunus mandshurica

MANCHURIAN APRICOT

↔ 25 ft (8 m) ↑ 15–20 ft (4.5–6 m)

From northeastern China and Korea. Small, spreading, rounded tree. Beautiful, single, pinkish flowers, in spring, before leaves emerge. Green leaves turn yellow to reddish in autumn; yellow rounded fruit in autumn. Zones 3–9.

Prunus maritima

BEACH PLUM, SAND PLUM

↔ 7 ft (2 m) ↑ 6 ft (1.8 m)

From eastern USA. Deciduous shrub, dark green leaves, pale undersides, dark bark. White flowers, in pairs or small clusters, spring. Fruit purple, red or yellow, edible. **'Eastham'**, large fruit; **'Hancock'**, early-ripening. Zones 3–9.

Prunus sargentii

Prunus serrulata

Prunus, Hybrid Cultivar, 'Amanogawa'

Prunus mume

JAPANESE APRICOT, MEI

↔25 ft (8 m) ↑20–30 ft (6–9 m)

Early flowering deciduous tree from China. Rounded crown of leaves to 4 in (10 cm) long. Flowers, more than 1 in (25 mm) wide, soft fragrance, dusky rose pink. Yellow fruit. **'Beni-chidori'** has small, deep pink, fragrant, double flowers; **'Dawn'** has large, light pink, double flowers, blooming late; **'Geisha'** has dusky pink, semi-double, fragrant flowers, blooming very early; **'Pendula'** is a small weeping plant with single pale pink flowers, appearing early in spring. Zones 6–10.

Prunus munsoniana

WILD GOOSE PLUM

↔20 ft (6 m) ↑25 ft (8 m)

Native of central USA. Deciduous tree, young stems red. Lustrous, deep green leaves, finely serrated edges. Small clusters of white flowers, in spring. Bright red fruit, edible but bitter. Zones 6–9.

Prunus pensylvanica

PIN CHERRY, RED CHERRY

↔30 ft (9 m) ↑30 ft (9 m)

Deciduous North American tree. Conspicuously toothed leaves to 4 in (10 cm) long. Tiny white flowers, in clusters of up to 8 blooms, in spring. Tiny red fruits. Zones 2–9.

Prunus pumila

SAND CHERRY

↔30 in (75 cm) ↑30 in (75 cm)

Hardy small shrub from northeastern USA; sometimes prostrate. Green-gray leaves, 1½ in (35 mm) long, serrated near tips, blue-tinted below. Clusters of white flowers in spring. Small, dark red, edible fruits. *P. p.* var. *depressa*, prostrate habit, narrow leaves, bluish white undersides. Zones 2–9.

Prunus sargentii

SARGENT CHERRY

↔35 ft (10 m) ↑50 ft (15 m)

Native to Japan, smaller in cultivation. Red-toothed leaves, 4 in (10 cm) long. Clusters of large, frilly, dusky pink flowers. Small red cherries. Zones 4–9.

Prunus, Sato-zakura Group

JAPANESE FLOWERING CHERRY

↔30 ft (9 m) ↑20–40 ft (6–12 m)

Large group, composed mainly of hybrids, probably derived from *P. serrulata*, ornamentals grown for early–mid-spring flower display. **'Alborosea'**, white to pink double flowers; **'Kanzan'** (syn. 'Sekiyama'), strongly upright growth when young, clusters of bright pink double flowers, vivid autumn foliage; **'Kiku-shidare'** (syn. 'Cheal's Weeping Cherry'), pendulous growth, pink double flowers; **'Ojochin'** (syn. 'Senriko'), flat-topped tree, semi-double, white to very pale pink; **'Okumiyako'** (syn. 'Shimidsu-sakura'), flat-topped tree with large, white, double flowers from pink buds; **'Shirotae'** (syn. 'Mt Fuji'), massed, large, single to semi-double, white flowers, golden autumn foliage; **'Ukon'**, pale green, semi-double flowers. Zones 5–9.

Prunus serotina

BLACK CHERRY, CAPULIN, RUM CHERRY

↔30 ft (9 m) ↑100 ft (30 m)

Deciduous North American tree. Glossy, mid-green, finely serrated leaves, lighter beneath, over 3 in (8 cm) long. White flowers, in short pendulous racemes, in spring. Small near-black fruit. Zones 3–9.

Prunus serrulata

JAPANESE FLOWERING CHERRY

↔15 ft (4.5 m) ↑12–30 ft (3.5–9 m)

Small deciduous tree, native to China. Leaves to over 4 in (10 cm) long. White flowers, to 1¼ in (30 mm) wide, in spring. Small black fruit. **'Pink Cloud'**, pink flowers. Zones 5–9.

Prunus subcordata

OREGON PLUM, PACIFIC PLUM

↔10 ft (3 m) ↑15 ft (4.5 m)

Deciduous shrub naturally found throughout western North America, can reach 25 ft (8 m) in height in the wild. Small, serrated-edged leaves, furrowed, gray-brown bark, flakes off in scales. Flowers white, ¾ in (18 mm) wide, in small clusters, in spring. Purple-red or yellow fruit. Zones 7–10.

Prunus subhirtella

SPRING CHERRY

↔25 ft (8 m) ↑50 ft (15 m)

Broad, deciduous tree naturally found in Japan, smaller in cultivation. Serrated leaves to 3 in (8 cm) long. Appearing before the foliage, the small flowers are white or pink. Tiny purple-black fruit. **'Autumnalis'**, early-flowering, white flowers with a hint of pink; **'Autumnalis Rosea'**, attractive pink flowers; **'Fukubana'**, early-flowering, attractive double pink flowers; **'Pendula'**, long-lived, weeping habit; **'Pendula Rosea'**, weeping habit, pink flowers; **'Stellata'**, clusters of starry, single, pink flowers. Zones 5–9.

Prunus tomentosa

DOWNY CHERRY, MANCHU CHERRY, NANKING CHERRY

↔8 ft (2.4 m) ↑8 ft (2.4 m)

Shrub from Himalayas with downy young stems. Puckered deep green leaves slightly over 2 in (5 cm) long, fluffy undersides. White to pale pink flowers, 1 in (25 mm) wide, carried singly or in pairs. Downy red fruit. Zones 2–8.

Prunus triloba

DWARF FLOWERING ALMOND, FLOWERING PLUM, ROSE TREE OF CHINA

↔12 ft (3.5 m) ↑12 ft (3.5 m)

From China. Pale pink flowers, semi-or fully double, open before or with leaf buds. Leaves 2½ in (6 cm) long, often 3-lobed. Red fruit with downy skin is rather unreliable, but can make a good show in some years. **'Multiplex'**, soft pink flowers. Zones 5–9.

Prunus virginiana

COMMON CHOKE CHERRY, CHOKE CHERRY

↔12 ft (3.5 m) ↑12 ft (3.5 m)

Large deciduous shrub or small tree from North America. Leaves 3 in (8 cm) long. Racemes of small white flowers, in spring. Zones 2–9.

Prunus × *yedoensis*

TOKYO CHERRY, YOSHINO CHERRY

↔30 ft (9 m) ↑40 ft (12 m)

Hybrid between *P.* × *subhirtella* and *P. speciosa*. Upright tree with spreading crown. Deep green, serrated leaves, turn vivid orange and red, in autumn. Racemes of scented white flowers, in spring. Tiny black fruit. **'Shidare-yoshino'** ★ has weeping branches and profuse snow white flowers. Zones 5–9.

Prunus Hybrid Cultivars

↔12–30 ft (3.5–9 m) ↑15–40 ft (4.5–12 m)

In addition to the species cultivars and the Sato-zakura cherries, there are hybrids that are not grouped, such as: **'Accolade'**, flat-topped tree, slightly weeping, semi-double flowers, mid-pink; **'Amanogawa'**, erect tree, single white to very pale pink flowers, mauve-tinted petal reverse, scented; and **'Okame'**, bright pink, very heavy-flowering, upright tree. Zones 6–9.

PSEUDOBOMBAX

Found in tropical America, this genus of some 20 species of deciduous trees is in the mallow (Malvaceae) family. The leaves may be simple or hand-shaped and are usually clustered at the branch tips. The flowers appear before the leaves and open from cylindrical buds. They have 5 narrow petals that peel back to reveal a mass of brightly colored stamens. The woody seed capsules that follow the flowers contain seeds embedded in downy fibers.

CULTIVATION: Although tropical in origin, some species adapt well to rather cooler conditions and can be grown in frost-free warm-temperate gardens with shelter from cool breezes. Plant in moist, humus-enriched, well-drained soil in a sunny or partly shaded position. Dry conditions are tolerated during the leafless period before flowering Prune or trim after flowering. Propagate from seed.

Pseudobombax ellipticum

SHAVING BRUSH TREE

↔20–30 ft (6–9 m) ↑30–50 ft (9–15 m)

Deciduous tree, found from Mexico to Guatemala; the only commonly cultivated species. Long-stemmed hand shaped leaves, up to 6 in (15 cm) long. Appearing before the foliage, downy buds open to reveal the bright pink flowers. Yellow-brown fruits, up to 6 in (15 cm) long. Zones 10–12.

PSEUDOFUMARIA

A genus of 2 species of herbaceous perennials of the poppy (Papaveraceae) family. Until recently members of the genus *Corydalis,* they are small clump-forming plants found in southern Europe. Their foliage is finely divided and lobed, green to blue-green. The small, tubular flowers with flared tips are held in clusters on wiry stems that extend just beyond the foliage.
CULTIVATION: Very easily cultivated in any moist, well-drained soil in partial shade. In a suitable climate they can grow too well and may be invasive. Propagation is from seed or by division.

Pseudofumaria alba

syn. *Corydalis ochroleuca*

↔12–32 in (30–80 cm) ↑8–16 in (20–40 cm)

Native to Balkans. *Aquilegia*-like foliage strongly blue-green, flowers very pale yellow to cream, yellow throat, ½ in (12 mm) long, in spring to early summer. Zones 5–9.

Pseudofumaria lutea

syn. *Corydalis lutea*

↔12–32 in (30–80 cm) ↑8–16 in (20–40 cm)

From Italy and Switzerland. Blue-green foliage and bright yellow flowers throughout the warmer months. Very tough and adaptable. Zones 3–9.

PSEUDOGYNOXYS

This is a genus of 13 perennial shrubs or climbers, native mainly to tropical South America. They are members of the daisy (Asteraceae) family. They have alternate leaves and solitary or many radiate heads or clusters of pale to deep orange or red, daisy-like flowers.
CULTIVATION: *Pseudogynoxys* species prefer a sunny position in moist, moderately fertile, well-drained soil. Water sparingly when not actively growing. Propagate from seed.

Pseudogynoxys chenopodioides

syn. *Senecio confuses*

MEXICAN FLAMEVINE, ORANGEGLOW VINE

↔10 ft (3 m) ↑12–17 ft (3.5–5 m)

Moderately bushy, evergreen, twining climber from Mexico to Honduras and Colombia, cultivated for its brightly colored orange flowers, attractive to butterflies, bees and hummingbirds. Smooth, thick, alternate, narrowly oval, toothed, light green leaves, up to 3 in (8 cm) long. Few radiate heads of fragrant bright orange flowers fading to red, mainly in summer, at branch ends or growing from the leaf axils. Zones 9–11.

PSEUDOLARIX

The sole species in this genus, part of the pine (Pinaceae) family, is a larch-like deciduous conifer from eastern China, with leaves larger and strappier than true larches. Young foliage is bright green but changes to fiery hues of yellow, orange, and red-brown before falling with the first hard frosts.
CULTIVATION: Although hardy to quite severe frosts, young plants may be damaged by very early or late freezes. Plant in deep, fertile, humus-rich, well-drained soil with sun or morning shade. Trees that are too shaded will develop poor autumn color. Naturally upright and conical, this tree needs little pruning, other than to lightly shape or tidy. Propagation is usually from seed.

Pseudolarix amabilis

GOLDEN LARCH

↔25 ft (8 m) ↑100 ft (30 m)

Upright conifer has deeply fissured, warm red-brown bark. Leaves to 2 in (5 cm) long, in whorls on short sideshoots. Female cones, purplish, to 3 in (8 cm) long, persist on the tree after shedding their seed. 'Nana' ★, 3 ft (0.9 m) tall with a spreading habit, one of several dwarf cultivars. Zones 6–9.

Pseudogynoxys chenopodioides

PSEUDOMUSCARI

Closely related to the grape hyacinths *(Muscari),* this genus of about 7 species of spring-flowering bulbs is part of the asparagus (Asparagaceae) family. They occur naturally in southern Europe and western Asia. They have narrow, strappy leaves, usually just a few per bulb, and their tiny blue to purple flowers, urn-shaped in bud, flared on opening flowers, are clustered in conical heads atop fleshy stems.
CULTIVATION: Most are easily grown in gritty, humus-rich soil that can be kept moist. Shade from the hottest sun. They do well in rockeries or pots under alpine house conditions. Propagate from seed or by dividing established clumps.

Pseudomuscari forniculatum

syn. *Bellevalia forniculata*

↔8 in (20 cm) ↑12 in (30 cm)

Native to northeastern Turkey, where it grows in permanently damp meadows. Narrow leaves, flower stems to 12 in (30 cm) tall. Purple-blue flowers ¼ in (6 mm) long, in early spring. Zones 7–9.

PSEUDOPHOENIX

CHERRY PALM

These 4 solitary palms are members of the family Arecaceae, and are native to the West Indies and southern Florida. They often have swollen trunks, a prominent swollen crownshaft, and sparse crown of few feathery fronds. Separate male and female flowers ap-pear in the same head, followed by the fruit, which is a 2- or 3-lobed drupe. The genus is named from the Greek *pseudo*, false, and *phoenix*, a date palm.
CULTIVATION: Cherry palms will adapt to most well-drained soils, in a sunny position, and will tolerate some neglect. Propagate from seed, which remains viable for up to 2 years.

Pseudophoenix sargentii

BUCCANEER PALM, FLORIDA CHERRY PALM, SARGENT'S PALM

↔8–12 ft (2.4–3.5 m) ↑10–25 ft (3–8 m)

Slow-growing palm from southern Florida and the West Indies. Slender, tapering trunk, sparse crown of long arching fronds. Regularly arranged, stiff, dark green leaflets, gray or silvery underneath. Clusters of yellow flowers are followed by dense, erect, branching bunches of cherry red to orange-scarlet, pear-shaped fruit. ***P. s.* subsp. *saonae*** produces heavier, larger fruit and has hanging rather than erect flowerheads. Zones 10–11.

P

Pseudofumaria alba

Pseudolarix amabilis

Pseudophoenix sargentii

PSEUDOTSUGA

DOUGLAS FIR

There are 6 to 8 species of coniferous trees within this genus in the pine (Pinaceae) family. All are evergreen forest trees from western North America, Mexico, Taiwan, Japan, and China. They are major timber trees used for power poles, railway sleepers, plywood, and wood pulp and are also a source of Oregon balsam. Some trees reach 300 ft (90 m) in height in their native habitat, but this is rare in cultivation. The foliage and cones are frequently used as Christmas decorations, as the foliage sheds its needles less readily than other species. The linear leaves grow radially on the shoots. The female cones have 3-pronged bract scales protruding from between the cone scales; the cylindrical male cones are smaller. CULTIVATION: These hardy trees prefer colder climates and will grow in any well-drained soil in full sun. Propagate the species from seed in spring, or graft cultivars in late winter.

Pseudotsuga menziesii

syns *Pseudotsuga douglasii, P. taxifolia*

DOUGLAS FIR

↔ 15–30 ft (4.5–9 m) ↑ 80–150 ft (24–45 m)

Native to North America, from British Columbia to California. Fast growing, long lived. Bark has corky plates, deep fissures developing with age. Narrow leaves, dark blue-green above, 2 white bands beneath, juvenile foliage apple-green in spring. Female cones, produced on mature trees. ***P. m.* var. *glauca***, glaucous blue leaves, smaller cones; ***P. m.* 'Densa'** and **'Fletcheri'** are dwarf forms. Zones 4–9.

PSORALEA

As now understood this is a genus of around 20 species of evergreen shrubs and subshrubs from southern Africa in the pea-flower subfamily of the legume (Fabaceae) family. Many other species were formerley included in *Psoralea* but are now distributed among at least 4 other genera. Leaves are mostly small and crowded, simple or compound (trifoliate or pinnate), characteristically dotted with tiny black glands. Flowers are borne prolifically, in short dense spikes and are mostly blue, purplish or white; small grayish pods follow. CULTIVATION: Cold-hardiness varies, though few will tolerate any but the lightest frosts. They prefer light but reasonably moist well-drained soil; will flower best in full sun. Propagate from seed or from half-hardened cuttings.

Psoralea pinnata

Psoralea pinnata

AFRICAN SCURF-PEA, BLUE PEA BUSH

↔ 7 ft (2 m) ↑ 6–10 ft (1.8–3 m)

South African shrub. Leaves with 5 to 11 narrow deep green leaflets, often with fine hairs. Clusters of violet to bright blue flowers with white wings, in late spring–summer. Able to thrive in low-nutrient soils; has become a weed in parts of southern coastal Australia. Zones 9–11.

PTELEA

Despite looking rather more like lilacs than oranges, and bearing sycamore-like fruits, the 11 deciduous shrubs or small trees in this North and Central American genus are *Citrus* relatives, and belong to the rue (Rutaceae) family. This is only apparent in the aromatic oil glands of the leaf, which is usually trifoliate, with a dominant central leaflet flanked by a smaller one on each side. The leaves often become bright yellow in autumn. The small white to pale green flowers are scented and clustered together in conspicuous cymes. They appear first in spring or early summer, then sporadically later. Small, 2-seeded, winged fruit, a little like hop seeds, follow. CULTIVATION: Species from southern USA and northern Mexico are a little tender. Otherwise, most are adaptable and easily grown in any well-drained soil in sun or partial shade. In areas with hot summers, some shade from the afternoon sun is advisable. Propagate from seed, layers, or grafts.

Ptelea trifoliata

COMMON HOP TREE

↔ 12 ft (3.5 m) ↑ 25 ft (8 m)

From eastern USA, west to Rocky Mountains and south to northern Mexico. Leaves mid-green, 3 leaflets, semi-glossy, paler undersides, slightly notched edges. Pale green flowers, in early summer. Fruit to 1 in (25 mm) wide. ***P. t.* subsp. *angustifolia***, 12 ft (3.5 m) high, downy foliage, blue-green undersides, fruit with reduced wings. ***P. t.* 'Aurea'**, yellow-green foliage; **'Glauca'**, blue-green foliage. Zones 5–10.

PTERIDIUM

BRACKEN, BRAKE

This genus of the bracken (Dennstaedtiaceae) family occurs worldwide, except for arctic and arid regions. Botanists disagree about the number of species: some argue that all bracken plants fall within such a narrow range of variation that only one species (*P. aquilinum*) can be recognized, though divided into varieties; others recognize a number of species, most with large geographical ranges that do not overlap. Fronds tough, triangular, much-divided, arising from deeply buried, long-running, repeatedly branched rhizomes; one plant can form a patch 50 ft (15 m) or more across. Spores are borne in continuous bands along curled-under margins of frond segments, but reproduction from spores seems rare as plants spread so effectively by rhizomes. Fronds are frost-killed in autumn and new ones emerge in spring. Bracken is often seen as a weed because of its aggressive spread and difficulty of removal. Farmers dislike it because it smothers pastures and is toxic to livestock, but it is part of a healthy natural ecosystem and provides shelter to birds and other wildlife. Some hunter-gatherer societies eat the starchy rhizomes. CULTIVATION: Deliberate cultivation is rarely attempted; management of bracken is usually the requirement. It is resistant to many herbicides. The most successful removal method from grassed areas is continual cutting; this eventually depletes its food reserves.

Pteridium aquilinum

↔ 30–60 ft (9–18 m) ↑ 2–8 ft (0.6–2.4 m)

Common bracken of Europe, Asia, Africa, and temperate North America. Fronds hairy beneath to varying degrees, more so when young, bipinnate with primary divisions regularly spaced and evenly tapering, the secondary divisions deeply and fairly regularly lobed. ***P. a.* var. *latiusculum*** is the race from eastern North America, while ***P. a.* var. *pubescens*** is widespread in western North America. Zones 3–10.

Pseudotsuga menziesii 'Fletcheri'

Ptelea trifoliata

PTERIS

BRAKE, DISH FERN, TABLE FERN

This is a genus of about 300 semi-evergreen or evergreen terrestrial ferns, native to tropical and subtropical regions and part of the brake (Pteridaceae) family. The plants have erect or creeping, scaly or hairy rhizomes and deciduous, arching, divided fronds on slender, erect, grooved stems. Spore-bodies are carried in hair-like structures along the frond margins. *Pteris* is Greek for fern, referring to the feathery fronds.
CULTIVATION: Brakes can grow in sun or shade, depending on the species, in moist peaty soil. Propagate by division in spring or from spores sown in summer.

Pteris argyraea

SILVER BRAKE

↔ 20–40 in (50–100 cm)
↑ 3–6 ft (0.9–1.8 m)

Evergreen fern native to the tropics. Erect or short-creeping rhizome, covered with papery brown scales. Green fronds with a broad, silvery white center line and narrow, oblong leaflets, 6–12 in (15–30 cm) long. Zones 10–12.

Pteris cretica

CRETAN BRAKE, RIBBON FERN

↔ 12–20 in (30–50 cm)
↑ 12–20 in (30–50 cm)

This evergreen or semi-evergreen fern is native to tropical regions of the Old World. It grows from slender, erect or short-creeping rhizomes. The fronds are oval or rounded, to 12 in (30 cm) long, with 1 to 5 pairs of simple or finger-like, forked, narrow, olive green leaflets, 4–8 in (10–20 cm) long, on slender, straw-colored stems. **'Albolineata'** ★ has wider leaflets with a broad white stripe; **'Mayi'** is up to 12 in (30 cm) high and has crested frond tips; and **'Wilsonii'** has crested bright green fronds that give the plant a fan-like appearance. Zones 10–12.

Pteris cretica

Pteris ensiformis

syn. *Pteris crenata*

SWORD BRAKE

↔ 8–12 in (20–30 cm)
↑ 8–12 in (20–30 cm)

This slender fern is found from the Himalayas to Japan, the Philippines, Polynesia, and tropical Australia. It has dark green fronds, 6–12 in (15–30 cm) long, with slightly compound terminal leaflets and 4 to 5 pairs of lateral leaflets cut into 2- to 6-toothed oval lobes, grayish white around the midribs. **'Arguta'**, to 20 in (50 cm) tall, has dark green fronds with central silvery white markings. Zones 10–12.

Pteris vittata

↔ 12–20 in (30–50 cm)
↑ 12–20 in (30–50 cm)

An evergreen fern that inhabits moist rocky sites in tropical and temperate regions of Europe, Africa, Asia, and Australasia. It grows from a stout, short-creeping rhizome and is well-suited to being grown in containers. The fronds are mid- to dull green, thickly textured, elongated, oblong, 8–40 in (20–100 cm) long, and have narrow leaflets that can be either smooth or covered with brown scales. Zones 9–11.

PTEROCARYA

There are 10 deciduous trees in this genus, which belongs to the walnut (Juglandaceae) family, and these are found from the Caucasus to the temperate areas of East Asia and Southeast Asia. They are commonly known as wingnuts because of their fruits, which have a wing either side of a small hard shell that contains a single seed. The effect is something like the winged fruit of a sycamore, though the trees are more closely related to walnuts. The leaves are pinnate and can be quite large, sometimes with more than 20 leaflets up to 4 in (10 cm) long. The foliage seldom shows much autumn color. In spring, long bract-studded catkins of tiny green flowers open, developing into strings of winged nutlets that become brown as they ripen.
CULTIVATION: Most species are tolerant of quite severe frosts and will thrive in any reasonably fertile, moist, well-drained soil with a position in full sun. Propagate from seed, suckers, or cuttings.

Pterocarya stenoptera var. *brevifolia*

Pterocarya fraxinifolia

CAUCASIAN WINGNUT

↔ 60 ft (18 m) ↑ 80 ft (24 m)

Found from the Caucasus to northern Iraq. Dark deeply furrowed bark, leaves to 15 in (38 cm) long, with up to 11 to 21 leaflets. Catkins yellow-green shade. Zones 7–9.

Pterocarya × *rehderiana*

↔ 60 ft (18 m)
↑ 50–100 ft (15–30 m)

Raised in 1908 at New York's Arnold Arboretum. A hybrid between *P. fraxinifolia* and *P. stenoptera*, vigorous, quick-growing. Leaves 10 in (25 cm) long, with up to 21 leaflets. Long pendulous catkins, borne in spring. Zones 6–9.

Pterocarya rhoifolia

JAPANESE WINGNUT

↔ 60 ft (18 m)
↑ 70–100 ft (21–30 m)

Japanese tree. Leaves with up to 21 leaflets, 4 in (10 cm) long. Young stems and leaflets have fine downy hairs that wear off with time. Zones 6–9.

Pterocarya stenoptera

↔ 40 ft (12 m) ↑ 70 ft (21 m)

Chinese species notable for leaves to 15 in (38 cm) long with up to 23 leaflets; new foliage is downy. A fine tan down covers young twigs. Catkins often longer than the leaves. *P. s.* var. ***brevifolia*** has fewer leaflets, making a shorter leaf. Zones 7–9.

Pterostyrax hispida

PTEROCEPHALUS

These 25 or more compact annual or perennial herbs and small shrubs are members of the teasel (Dipsacaceae) family and native from the Mediterranean to eastern Asia. They are grown for their bristly flowers and feathery seed heads, and are suited to rock gardens. Flattened, disc-shaped flowerheads appear in summer, on long stalks, and are surrounded by narrow bracts; the outermost flowers have 2 lips and are larger than those in the center.
CULTIVATION: Plant in a sunny position in well-drained soil. Avoid areas that are wet in winter. Propagate from softwood or semi-ripe cuttings in summer, from fresh seed sown in autumn, or by division in spring. This plant self-seeds readily.

Pterocephalus dumetorum

syn. *Pterocephalus canus*

↔ 3–4 in (8–10 cm)
↑ 3–4 in (8–10 cm)

Native to dry rock crevices in Iran and Turkey. Leaves oblong to elliptical, smooth-edged, finely hairy. Flower-heads of yellow flowers are at least 1 in (25 mm) across, and appear in summer. Zones 4–9.

PTEROSTYRAX

The 3 species of deciduous shrubs or trees in this genus, belonging to the storax (Styracaceae) family, are native to eastern Asia. Leaves alternately arranged, serrated edges; numerous long open panicles of small flowers.
CULTIVATION: These are quick-growing plants that should be given a deep, rich, acid soil in a sheltered position in sun or semi-shade. Plants can be pruned after flowering to retain their shape. Propagate from seed or half-hardened cuttings.

Pterostyrax corymbosa

↔ 20 ft (6 m) ↑ 40 ft (12 m)

Spreading shrub or tree from Japan. Dark green leaves, bristly toothed margins. Small, fragrant, white, bell-shaped flowers, in panicles, in spring. Zones 6–10.

Pterostyrax hispida ★

EPAULETTE TREE

↔ 20 ft (6 m) ↑ 25 ft (8 m)

Found from Japan and China. Large leaves, finely serrated edges. Panicles of fragrant creamy white flowers to 8 in (20 cm) long, in summer. Small green and bristly fruit. Zones 6–10.

Ptilotus exaltatus

PTILOTUS

MULLA MULLA

Genus of about 100 annual or perennial herbs and shrubs in the amaranth (Amaranthaceae) family, native mainly to arid inland areas of Australasia. They bear dense shaggy spikes or heads of flowers with membranous bracts; the outer part is a tube of 5 segments.

CULTIVATION: Prefer an open sunny position in well-drained, composted, relatively dry, sandy soil. Propagate from cuttings or from seed sown in spring; germination can be difficult.

Ptilotus exaltatus

PINK MULLA MULLA, TALL PUSSY-TAILS

↔ 40 in (100 cm) ↑ 40 in (100 cm)

Erect, sturdy, bushy annual or perennial, native to mainland Australia. Thick, undulating, oblong to sword-shaped, bluish green leaves with pointed tips, tinged with red, to 3 in (8 cm) long. Feathery, conical to cylindrical spikes, to 6 in (15 cm) long, of lilac to pink flowers, sometimes white, from winter–summer. Suited to container growth. **'Joey'** ★, 16 in (40 cm) high, vivid pink plumes; **'Phoenix'**, 20 in (50 cm) high, purple-red-tinted foliage, soft pink plumes. Zones 9–11.

Pulmonaria longifolia 'Bertram Anderson'

Ptychosperma macarthurii

PTYCHOSPERMA

These 30 solitary or clump-forming, feathery palms belong to the family Arecaceae and are native to northern Australia, New Guinea, the Solomon Islands, and Micronesia. They have slender, smooth, ringed trunks and distinct crownshafts. Gracefully curved, divided fronds have slender pointed leaflets, jagged or smooth-edged at the tips. Flowers are spirally arranged in groups of 3. The fruit is small, egg-shaped or elliptical, and sometimes beaked, containing a single furrowed seed. The genus is named from the Greek *ptychos*, wrinkled, and *sperma*, seed.

CULTIVATION: These palms need warmth and humidity, in a shaded position when young, in moist, well-drained and composted soil. Propagate from seed, which takes 6 to 12 weeks to germinate.

Ptychosperma elegans ★

syn. *Seaforthia elegans*

Seaforthia palm, solitaire palm

↔ 10–12 ft (3–3.5 m)

↑ 12–50 ft (3.5–15 m)

This fast-growing palm is found in northeastern Australia. It has a gray, solitary trunk, and a woolly green crownshaft. There are relatively few, arching, bright green leaves, to 8 ft (2.4 m) long, and these have regularly arranged leaflets to 24 in (60 cm) long, toothed or notched at tips. They are carried on long stems emerging from under the crownshaft. The large branching clusters of fragrant greenish white flowers are followed by large clusters of decorative, bright red, spherical to oval, berry-like fruit. Zones 10–11.

Pulmonaria rubra 'Bowles' Red'

Ptychosperma macarthurii ★

syn. *Actinophloeus macarthurii*

MacArthur palm

↔ 6–12 ft (1.8–3.5 m)

↑ 15–25 ft (4.5–8 m)

Densely clumping evergreen palm, native to New Guinea and northeastern Australia, common in tropical gardens. Gray trunk; green woolly crownshaft. Small crown of dark green, arched fronds, reaching up to 6 ft (1.8 m) long, with regularly arranged, broad leaflets with toothed tips. Branching sprays of yellowish flowers, appear on stems emerging from below the crownshaft, mostly in summer, growing into long pendulous clusters of bright red fruits. Zones 10–11.

PULMONARIA

LUNGWORT

Starting into growth at the first sign of spring, this genus of 14 temperate Eurasian perennials of the borage (Boraginaceae) family overcomes its rather unappealing name by being indispensable for woodland, perennial border, and rock-garden cultivation. Their simple, long-stemmed, lance-shaped leaves are sometimes white spotted and can grow to a considerable size. The first flowers, while welcome, are sparse but, as spring warms further, the plants carry larger heads of small 5-petalled blooms. Blue is the usual color, though white and pink forms are common. "Wort" is a word often attached to plants that have been used for medicinal purposes.

CULTIVATION: Lungworts are very hardy and need a temperate climate with distinct seasons. They can be grown in full sun, but are best cultivated in moist, humus-rich, well-drained soil, in a partly shaded position. Propagate by division, or from basal cuttings or seed.

Pulmonaria saccharata 'Mrs Moon'

Pulmonaria longifolia

↔ 48 in (120 cm)

↑ 16 in (40 cm)

European species. Forms clump of narrow, often white-spotted, dark green leaves to 20 in (50 cm) long. Heads of tightly clustered mauve to purple-blue flowers in late winter–late spring. ***P. l.* subsp. *cevennensis*** is smaller, with foliage blotched silver-white and violet-blue flowers. ***P. l.* 'Bertram Anderson'**, especially narrow, heavily white-spotted leaves, purplish blue flowers. Zones 6–9.

Pulmonaria officinalis

JERUSALEM SAGE

↔ 16–24 in (40–60 cm)

↑ 12 in (30 cm)

European perennial, usually flowering well into spring when foliage is well expanded. Leaves pointed elliptical, white-spotted, to around 6 in (15 cm) long; mauve through blue to purple-red flowers in tightly clustered heads. **'Blue Mist'** and **'White Wings'**, popular cultivars. Zones 6–9.

Pulmonaria rubra

↔ 20–40 in (50–100 cm)

↑ 12–18 in (30–45 cm)

Native to Europe. Leaves often spotted white or silver-gray. Small heads of light red flowers, sometimes mauve tinted, on flower stems that tend to be erect, in spring–early summer. **'Bowles' Red'**, white-spotted leaves, red-pink flowers; and **'David Ward'**, creamy white-edged leaves, red-pink flowers. Zones 6–9.

Pulmonaria saccharata

JERUSALEM SAGE

↔ 16–32 in (40–80 cm)

↑ 12–16 in (30–40 cm)

From northern Italy, flowers after foliage is well developed. Spring leaves are small, lance-shaped, spotted, summer leaves are larger. Flowers are white, or shades of mauve to purple or purple-red. **Argentea Group**, silver-mottled leaves, mauve-blue flowers; **'Dora Bielefeld'**, white- or lighter green-spotted leaves, mauve-pink flowers; **'Janet Fisk'**, silver-spotted and marbled leaves, purple flowers opening from red buds; **'Leopard'**, white-spotted leaves, purplish pink flowers; and **'Mrs Moon'**, white-spotted leaves, red-tinted mauve flowers. Zones 3–9.

Pulmonaria vallarsae

◐/● ✱ ↔ 20–40 in (50–100 cm)
↑ 12–18 in (30–45 cm)

Northern Italian species. Forms clump of finely hairy, often white-spotted or variegated leaves. First flowers appear with new growth, red-tinted buds opening to purple flowers, in early spring–early summer. Zones 6–9.

Pulmonaria Hybrid Cultivars

◐/● ✱ ↔ 16–40 in (40–100 cm)
↑ 8–16 in (20–40 cm)

Lungworts hybridize freely, in the wild and in cultivation, and there are many widely grown hybrids, often of indeterminate parentage. Modern forms tend to have showy variegated foliage and short flower stems. **'Benediction'**, silver-flecked leaves, mauve-blue flowers; **'Beth's Pink'**, has broad spotted leaves, mauve-pink flowers; **'Blue Pearl'**, small rounded leaves, light blue flowers; **'High Contrast'**, silver-gray leaves with irregular green edges, flowers deep pink ageing to purple-blue; **'Lewis Palmer'**, white-spotted leaves, purple-blue flowers; **'Margery Fish'** ★, silver-mottled foliage, pink flowers ageing to blue; **'Purple Haze'**, white-spotted leaves, purple flowers; **'Roy Davidson'**, long silver-spotted leaves, light blue flowers; **'Silver Streamers'**, large silver-gray leaves with ruffled edges, pink flowers darkening with age; **'Sissinghurst White'**, large white-spotted leaves, and white flowers, produced early in the season; **'Smoky Blue'**, dark green white-spotted leaves, purplish blue flowers; and **'Trevi Fountain'**, silver-spotted leaves, open sprays of deep blue flowers. Zones 6–9.

PULSATILLA

PASQUE FLOWER

These beautiful Eurasian and North American relatives of the anemones race into growth in early spring. They are members of the buttercup (Ranunculaceae) family. Clumps of ferny leaves, silvery in most species from a dense covering of fine hairs. Long-stemmed, very graceful, cup- or bell-shaped flowers in a wide color range. Carried singly, they have 5 to 8 petals and a prominent boss of golden stamens. *Pasque* is an old French word for Easter, when the plants usually flower. The significance of the proper name, taken from Latin *pulso,* "to strike," is obscure, possibly referring to the drooping buds turning upward as they open.

CULTIVATION: Pasque flowers need a seasonal temperate climate. They grow well in woodland conditions but are at their best in rock gardens with sun or part-shade, in gritty, humus-rich, well-drained yet moist soil. Propagate by division when dormant, or raise from seed.

Pulsatilla patens

EASTERN PASQUE FLOWER

☼/◐ ✱ ↔ 8–12 in (20–30 cm)
↑ 6–10 in (15–25 cm)

From northern Europe to Siberia and Alaska, USA. Leaves lightly hairy, heavy textured, less finely divided than most silvery species. Flowers quite late, purple shades, sometimes with yellow tint, rarely white, stems silky. Zones 4–9.

Pulsatilla pratensis

☼/◐ ✱ ↔ 16 in (40 cm) ↑ 12 in (30 cm)

Found through most of Europe. Entirely covered with dense, silky, silvery hairs. Foliage very finely divided. Pendent, narrow bell-shaped flowers, to 1½ in (40 mm) wide, mauve to deep purple. ***P. p.*** subsp. ***bohemica*** has small, very dark purple flowers. Zones 5–9.

Pulsatilla vulgaris

syn. *Anemone pulsatilla*

PASQUE FLOWER

☼/◐ ✱ ↔ 8–16 in (20–40 cm)
↑ 8–15 in (20–38 cm)

From Britain through Europe to Ukraine. Covered in fine, silky, silvery hairs. Very finely divided feathery foliage. Mauve to purple flowers usually upward-facing, open bell-shaped. **'Alba'**, white flowers; **'Papageno'** (syn. *P. v.* subsp. *grandis* 'Papageno'), mixed color strain, shades include apricot and purple-black; **'Rubra'**, red flowers. Zones 5–9.

Pulsatilla vulgaris

PUNICA

This genus in the loosestrife (Lythraceae) family contains only 2 species, both small, deciduous, fruiting trees native to the Mediterranean region, North Africa, Iran, and Afghanistan. They have simple lance-shaped leaves, scarlet flowers, and reddish yellow apple-shaped fruits. They are quite hardy, tolerating quite low temperatures as well as sustained high temperatures with low humidity, but need hot dry summers for fruit to ripen.

CULTIVATION: They respond to a well-aerated coarsely textured soil, preferably enriched with organic matter. Lightly prune current year's growth in late winter to retain a dense leafy habit. Propagate from seed sown in spring, or from soft-tip or half-hardened cuttings between spring and autumn.

Punica granatum

COMMON POMEGRANATE

☼ ❄ ↔ 15 ft (4.5 m) ↑ 25 ft (8 m)

Small tree, broad domed crown, lateral shoots thorny. Leaves opposite, broadly lance-shaped, reddish in spring, then bright green; turn yellow in autumn. Flowers with 5 to 8 bright scarlet petals, many stamens, late spring–late summer. Orange-red fruit, jelly-like crimson pulp. **'Nana'**, dwarf form, up to 3 ft (0.9 m) high; **'Nochi Shibari'**, North American cultivar; **'Wonderful'**, double-flowered form, fruit said to taste of wine. Zones 8–11.

Punica granatum (bonsai)

Puschkinia scilloides

PURSHIA

This genus, in the rose (Rosaceae) family, consists of 2 species of shrubs or small trees native to western North American regions that are warm but dry, or with a pronounced dry season. They have gray-green leaves with 3 to 5 lobes and slightly toothed or rolled-under edges. Small, white to light yellow, 5-petalled, tubular flowers are produced at the ends of the previous season's growth.

CULTIVATION: They are moderately frost hardy, but resent winter-wet soil. Grow in a warm sheltered position with excellent drainage. Propagate from seed or by layering.

Purshia tridentata

ANTELOPE BUSH

☼ ✱ ↔ 6 ft (1.8 m) ↑ 10 ft (3 m)

From the dry interior of western USA. Erect shrub, wide-spreading branchlets. Glossy, green, wedge-shaped leaves to 1 in (25 mm) long, white, bristly beneath. Tiny creamy yellow flowers, in spring–summer. Zones 5–11.

PUSCHKINIA

From Turkey, this single-species genus in the asparagus (Asparagaceae) family is related to *Scilla.* Strap-shaped leaves from tubular base. Flowers striped, pale, in clusters on slender stems.

CULTIVATION: Plant the bulbs under deciduous shrubs in part-shade in well-drained soil. Plant in autumn, 3 in (8 cm) deep and the same distance apart. They shouldn't be disturbed for several years. When flowering lessens, dig the bulbs up after the foliage has ripened. Small bulbs require a cool spot where they will not become too hot and dry in summer. Bulbs can be detached for propagation.

Puschkinia scilloides ★

STRIPED SQUILL

☼/◐ ✱ ↔ 3 in (8 cm)
↑ 2–4 in (5–10 cm)

Two green leaves at base, from which a stalk emerges in early spring bearing fragrant, white to pale blue, bell-shaped flowers with a darker blue stripe in the center of each of 6 petals. ***P. s.*** var. ***libanotica***, slightly smaller flowers. Zones 4–8.

P

PUYA

More than 200 species, mainly from the Andes of South America, make up this ground-dwelling genus in the bromeliad (Bromeliaceae) family, most of them preferring colder conditions than other bromeliads. Many are large plants forming trunks, and are not often seen in private gardens; they are popular in botanic gardens in subtropical areas. One species reaches a height of 35 ft (10 m) in flower; the smallest species reaches only 3 in (8 cm) high. They form rosettes of green, narrow-triangular leaves, generally with large spines along the edges. The flowerheads may be cylindrical or pyramidal and branched, and the flowers are generally large and showy.
CULTIVATION: Recommended for greenhouse, conservatory or outdoor cultivation in cool temperate areas; some species will adapt to warmer areas if kept on the dry side. Water when potting mix is dry. Extra feeding may speed up their slow-growing habit. Propagation is by seed or from offsets of most species.

Puya berteroniana

☼ ❄ ↔7 ft (2 m) ↑15 ft (4.5 m)
From central Chile. Forming a trunk with age. Leaves green, narrow-triangular, strongly toothed edges, forming a dense rosette. Flower stem stout, to 10 ft (3 m). Flowerhead to 40 in (100 cm) long and 20 in (50 cm) wide, up to 100 side branches, each carrying about 15 large blue-green flowers. Upper part of branches without flowers. Zones 8–11 .

Puya berteroniana

Puya venusta

Puya venusta

☼ ❄ ↔20 in (50 cm) ↑40 in (100 cm)
From coastal Chile. Clump-forming, branching plant. Leaves gray-green, narrow-triangular, toothed-edged, forming dense rosette. Flower stem stout, bright red. Flowerheads reddish, like pine cones, end of some branches, flowers deep violet. Zones 8–9.

PYCNANTHEMUM

syn. *Koellia*

AMERICAN MOUNTAIN MINT

This genus of 21 smooth or hairy, perennial herbs in of the mint (Lamiaceae) family, is native to eastern North America, and has erect, simple or branched stems and opposite, smooth-edged, mint-scented leaves on short stalks. Simple or branching flowerheads of compact clusters, on stalks, usually with a pair of leaf-like bracts and a corolla tube expanding to form 2 lips, appear from summer to autumn, followed by smooth or finely hairy fruit. Genus is named from the Greek *pyknos*, dense, and *anthos*, flower, referring to the densely crowded flowers. It is sometimes used for flavoring teas.
CULTIVATION: Mountain mints prefer open, sunny positions and are adaptable to most soil conditions. Propagation is from seed or cuttings.

Pycnanthemum virginianum

syn. *Pycnanthemum lanceolatum*

WILD HYSSOP

☼ ✱ ↔40 in (100 cm) ↑40 in (100 cm)
Upright, stiff, many-branched herb with short, leafy branches; narrow to sword-shaped, serrated, tapering leaves to 2½ in (6 cm) long. Flat-topped heads of fragrant, pink and white flowers, in mid- to late summer. All plant parts emit a strong, mint-like aroma when crushed. Zones 3–7.

Pycnostachys urticifolia

PYCNOSTACHYS

Native to tropical and southern Africa, these 40 or so species of perennials and soft-wooded shrubs are grown for their dense terminal spikes of 2-lipped deep blue flowers. Members of the mint (Lamiaceae) family, they have squarish stems and opposite or whorled leaves that are often aromatic when bruised.
CULTIVATION: These plants need a warm, frost-free climate and are best suited to fertile, moist but well-drained soil in full sun. In cool areas they are grown in the greenhouse or conservatory, with a plentiful supply of water during the growing season. Propagate from seed or cuttings.

Pycnostachys urticifolia

☼ ✢ ↔4 ft (1.2 m) ↑8 ft (2.4 m)
Soft-wooded shrub with erect branching stems. Oval leaves, 5 in (12 cm) long, toothed edges. Tubular deep blue to purple flowers in dense terminal spikes, to 4 in (10 cm) long, summer–autumn. Zones 9–12.

PYRACANTHA

FIRETHORN

This small genus in the rose (Rosaceae) family consists of 9 species of mostly spiny shrubs, from eastern Asia and southeast Europe. They have simple leaves that are often toothed on the margins, and whitish flowers in corymbs are produced at the ends of branches. The flowers are followed by masses of red, orange, or yellow fruit, which persist into winter. Most species perform best in cool, moist climates, where they are useful landscape subjects for the shrubbery or used as espalier specimens or for hedging. *Pyracantha* species can naturalize in favorable areas.
CULTIVATION: Most are fairly adaptable shrubs tolerating exposed sites in full sun. They perform best in a fertile well-drained soil. Pruning is not essential but may be helpful to control size; hedges can be pruned from early to mid-summer. Watch for fireblight, scab and wilt problems. Propagate from seed or cuttings.

Pyracantha angustifolia

Pyracantha, Hybrid Cultivar, 'Mohave'

Pyracantha angustifolia

NARROW-LEAFED FIRETHORN, ORANGE FIRETHORN

☼ ❄ ↔12 ft (3.5 m) ↑12 ft (3.5 m)
Native to southwest China. Spiny bushy shrub, horizontal branches, dark green shiny leaves, gray and furry beneath. Dense corymbs of small white flowers, in mid-summer. Yellow to deep orange berries. Zones 7–10.

Pyracantha coccinea

EUROPEAN FIRETHORN, SCARLET FIRETHORN

☼ ✱ ↔15 ft (4.5 m) ↑15 ft (4.5 m)
From southern Europe, Turkey, and the Caucasus. Dense shrub. Shiny, dark green, ovate to lance-shaped, toothed leaves, new growth finely downy. Small white flowers. Attractive scarlet berries on downy stalks. **'Lalandei'** ★, strong growth habit, reaching up to 20 ft (6 m) tall, with glossy bright orange-red fruits. Zones 5–9.

Pyracantha koidzumii

TAIWAN FIRETHORN

☼ ❄ ↔12 ft (3.5 m)
↑12–15 ft (3.5–4.5 m)
Native to Taiwan. Many-branched species with reddish, downy, young stems becoming smooth and purplish with age. Leaves dark green, glossy above, paler below. Small white flowers in corymbs, in summer. Fruit is a berry, in variable colors, sometimes orange-scarlet. Zones 7–10.

Pyracantha Hybrid Cultivars

↔6–10 ft (1.8–3 m) ↑5–10 ft (1.5–3 m)

Spreading shrubs which make good hedges and suit shrub borders. **'Golden Charmer'**, vigorous arching shrub with long branches, finely toothed glossy green leaves, rounded orange-yellow fruits; **'Golden Dome'**, mound of arching branches, white summer flowers, small deep yellow fruits; **'Harlequin'**, variegated form, attractive pink-flushed leaves, cream margins; **'Mohave'**, dense medium-sized shrub, dark green leaves, masses of persistent bright orange-red fruits; **'Orange Charmer'** can be trimmed as a free-standing shrub from 3–8 ft (0.9–2.4 m) tall, long-lasting orange-red berries; **'Orange Glow'**, dense, vigorous shrub, bright orange-red fruits persist into winter; **'Shawnee'**, spiny shrub, dense-branched, widely spreading at base, masses of white flowers, yellow to light orange fruits; **'Sparkler'**, variegated form, slightly tender, leaves strikingly mottled, white, becoming pink-tinged in autumn; **'Watereri'**, compact yet vigorous shrub, covered in summer with white flowers, bright red fruits. Zones 5–9.

PYROSTEGIA

These 4 evergreen, woody-stemmed, tendril climbers belong to the trumpet-vine (Bignoniaceae) family. Native to the tropical Americas, they are grown for their showy flowers. They have angled branches and compound leaves with 2, sometimes 3, oval leaflets, with or without a terminal tendril, and clusters, at the ends of branches, of flowers with curved, tubular corollas with protruding stamens. The genus is named from the Greek *pyr*, fire, and *stege*, a roof, referring to the flower shape and crimson-orange color.

CULTIVATION: *Pyrostegia* species grow best in full sun in fertile well-drained soil. These attractive climbers require support. Propagate from half-hardened cuttings taken in summer.

Pyrostegia venusta

syn. *Pyrostegia ignea*

FLAME VINE, GOLDEN SHOWER, ORANGE TRUMPET CREEPER, TANGO POI

↔20 ft (6 m) ↑20–30 ft (6–9 m)

Fast-growing, vigorously branching climber, native to Brazil, Paraguay, Bolivia, and northeastern Argentina. Smooth, papery or leathery leaflets, to 4 in (10 cm) long, blunt tips. Terminal clusters of orange flowers appear in autumn–spring. Zones 8–10.

PYRUS

PEAR

Widely distributed through Europe and Asia, this genus of about 20 species is related to the apple *(Malus)* and belongs to the rose (Rosaceae) family. It comprises mostly deciduous trees of small to medium size, some thorny, with simple leaves that sometimes color to yellow and red in autumn. Flowers are mostly white, and are followed by fruits, edible in some species, that vary in size and shape. The ornamental species are deep-rooted, tolerant of drought and reasonably tolerant of atmospheric pollution. Fruiting forms require a cross-pollinator to set fruit.

CULTIVATION: Pears will grow in most moderately fertile soils and prefer cool-temperate climates. Pruning of the ornamental species is seldom necessary. They can be propagated from seed sown very fresh, but clonal forms are propagated by grafting to keep them true to type.

Pyrus calleryana

CALLERY PEAR

↔40 ft (12 m) ↑40 ft (12 m)

From southeastern China, Korea, Japan, and Taiwan. Ornamental tree, branches thorny. Glossy green leaves turn red, in late autumn. Flowers, white, unpleasant scent. Small pitted brown fruit on slender stalks. **'Bradford'**, non-thorny selected form, dark red autumn color, flowers heavily in spring; **'Chanticleer'/Glen's Form** ★, rich scarlet autumn color, similar but much narrower in form. Zones 5–10.

Pyrus communis

CALLERY PEAR, COMMON PEAR, GARDEN PEAR

↔20 ft (6 m) ↑50 ft (15 m)

Medium-sized tree with rounded or oval, glossy, green leaves. Thorny branches covered in white blossoms, in spring. Large, edible, sweet-tasting fruit. Has been in cultivation for centuries. Over 1,000 named cultivars have been raised. **'Beurré d'Anjou'**, very old French cultivar, a late bearer, smooth green fruit, slight red cheek or all red, flesh is sweet and juicy; **'Cascade'**, heavy bearer, almost globular fruit, bright red, some yellow showing through, white flesh is sweet and juicy; **'Clapp's Favourite Liebling'**, small fruit, very juicy delicious flavor; **'Conference'**, large pear, with a long neck, brown skin, yellow-green showing through, sweet juicy flesh faintly pink-tinged; **'Doyenné du Comice'** ★ (syn. 'Comice'), old French pear, with many variants, fruit smooth-skinned, ripening to pale green, sweet creamy flesh, very juicy and aromatic; **'Gellerts Butterbine'**, greenish yellow fruit, bronze-orange cheek; **'Red Bartlett'**, bright red fruit; **'Williams' Bon Chrétien'** (syn. 'Bartlett'), bright green with a slight red cheek, ripening yellowish, very juicy and deliciously flavored. Zones 2–9.

Pyrostegia venusta

Pyrus kawakamii

syn. *Pyrus calleryana var. calleryana*

EVERGREEN PEAR

↔30 ft (9 m) ↑30 ft (9 m)

From Japan. Evergreen shrub or small tree, thorny branches. Attractive, glossy, green, oval leaves around 4 in (10 cm) long. White flowers in small clusters, in late winter. Tiny, rounded fruit. Zones 8–10.

Pyrus nivalis

SNOW PEAR

↔20 ft (6 m) ↑30 ft (9 m)

Native to southern Europe. Small tree, thornless ascending branches. White flowers in racemes as the young leaves open in spring. Smooth-edged oval or egg-shaped leaves. Small rounded fruits yellowish green. Suitable tree for small gardens. Zones 5–9.

Pyrus pashia

HIMALAYAN PEAR

↔25 ft (8 m) ↑40 ft (12 m)

From the Himalayas and western China. Small round-headed tree. Finely toothed leaves, sometimes 3-lobed. Flowers pink-flushed in the bud, opening white with red anthers. Fruits rounded, brown with paler speckles. Zones 5–9.

Pyrus salicifolia

SILVER PEAR, WILLOW-LEAFED PEAR

↔15 ft (4.5 m) ↑25 ft (8 m)

From the Caucasus. Small graceful tree with slender drooping branches. Narrow willow-like leaves, silvery when young, turn grayish green and shiny uppersurface as they age. Flowers creamy white. Small brown pear-shaped fruit. **'Pendula'** is smaller with fully pendulous branches; **'Silver Cascade'**, silvery gray foliage. Zones 4–9.

Pyrus ussuriensis

MANCHURIAN PEAR, MONGOLIAN PEAR, USSURIAN PEAR

↔20 ft (6 m) ↑50 ft (15 m)

From northeastern China, Korea, and northern Japan. Sometimes used in street plantings. Yellowish green leaves ovate or rounded, bristle-toothed, turn crimson-bronze, in autumn. Broad corymb of white flowers, in early spring. Fruits greenish brown ripen in autumn–winter. Zones 4–9.

Pyrus ussuriensis

Pyrus communis

QR

QUERCUS

OAK

This large genus of some 600 species, both evergreen and deciduous, is a member of the beech (Fagaceae) family. Most are trees, a few are shrubs, widely distributed throughout the Northern Hemisphere. Many are large trees that live to a great age; their timber has long been valued for ship-building, fine furniture, and paneling. Fruits (acorns) are partly enclosed in a cup. All have simple leaves, often toothed or deeply lobed, in some turning to spectacular tones of red or yellow-brown in autumn. Male and female flowers are carried on separate catkins on the same tree, usually in early spring. CULTIVATION: Oaks grow well in deep alluvial valley soils; only some of the Mediterranean and western North American species are tolerant of poor dry soil. Most enjoy cool moist conditions. Some early pruning may be needed to help establish a single straight trunk. Seeds, sown as soon as ripe in summer or autumn, germinate readily; cultivars and sterile hybrids are usually grafted in late winter or early spring.

Quercus agrifolia

CALIFORNIA LIVE OAK, COAST LIVE OAK

↔35 ft (10 m) ↑40 ft (12 m)

From California and Mexico. Evergreen tree or large shrub, branched almost to the ground. Smooth black bark, roughens with age. Leaves oval or rounded, hard-textured, edged with spine-tipped teeth, smooth undersides. Acorns half-enclosed in cups. Zones 8–10.

Quercus alba

AMERICAN WHITE OAK, STAVE OAK, WHITE OAK

↔100 ft (30 m) ↑100 ft (30 m)

Large deciduous tree from southeastern Canada and eastern USA. Straight, often massive trunk, spreading branches, broad canopy of foliage. Bark dark gray. Oval leaves deeply and irregularly lobed, soft green when young, turning purple-crimson in autumn. Acorns held in shallow scaly cups. Zones 3–9.

Quercus bicolor

SWAMP WHITE OAK

↔40 ft (12 m) ↑80 ft (24 m)

Found growing naturally in southeastern Canada and eastern USA. Matures into a well-developed trunk, with ascending branches. Bark is pale gray with thick ridges that are blackish gray. Leaves are egg-shaped, shallowly lobed, shiny green, grayish and felted on the undersides. Acorns in clusters. Zones 4–10.

Quercus coccinea

SCARLET OAK

↔40 ft (12 m) ↑70 ft (21 m)

From eastern and central USA. Deciduous tree with wide-spreading branches. Leaves oblong or elliptic, shiny dark green above, paler beneath, a few leaves turn bright deep red, later whole crown colors, in autumn. Acorns in shallow cups. **'Splendens'**, larger leaves, more reliable autumn color. Zones 2–9.

Quercus alba

Quercus ellipsoidalis

NORTHERN PIN OAK

↔40 ft (12 m) ↑70 ft (21 m)

From central and southern USA. A deciduous tree with a spreading habit. Leaves deeply lobed, turn a deep crimson-purple in autumn. Closely resembles *Q. palustris*, but has ellipsoidal acorns. Zones 5–10.

Quercus falcata

SOUTHERN RED OAK, SPANISH OAK

↔35 ft (10 m) ↑80 ft (24 m)

Deciduous tree from southern USA. Bark thick, nearly black, deeply furrowed. Leaves egg-shaped to ovate, shallowly 3-lobed or deeply 5- to 7-lobed, dark green above, pale gray-green, woolly beneath. Acorns nearly stalkless. ***Q. f.* var. *pagodifolia***, bark smoother, becoming scaly with age, larger leaves. Zones 8–10.

Quercus kelloggii

CALIFORNIAN BLACK OAK

↔40 ft (12 m) ↑60–90 ft (18–27 m)

From California and Oregon, USA. Medium-sized to large deciduous tree with a large, open, globe-like crown. Bark is thick, divided by deep furrows into wide ridges. Leaves are deeply lobed, bristle-toothed, shiny yellow-green above, paler, usually hairy beneath. Acorns are carried on short stalks. Zones 7–10.

Quercus laurifolia

LAUREL OAK

↔60 ft (18 m) ↑60 ft (18 m)

From eastern USA. A medium-sized, semi-evergreen tree, dense rounded habit. Bark thick, nearly black, deeply furrowed. Leaves are glossy green, oblong or egg-shaped, smooth-edged, occasionally shallowly lobed. Acorns are stalkless or nearly so. Zones 5–11.

Quercus macranthera

CAUCASIAN OAK, PERSIAN OAK

↔40 ft (12 m) ↑90 ft (27 m)

Native to the Caucasus region and northern Iran. Fast-growing tree, becomes deciduous with age. Bark purplish gray. Leaves large, broadly ovate, strongly lobed. Twigs, winter buds, and leaf undersurfaces clothed with pale gray velvety down. Acorns held in scaly cups. Zones 6–10.

Quercus macrocarpa

BURR OAK, MOSSYCUP OAK

↔40 ft (12 m) ↑120 ft (36 m)

Found in northeastern and central North America from Nova Scotia, Canada, to Texas, USA. Large deciduous tree, massive trunk, spreading branches. Bark coarsely ridged, scaly, gray-brown. Leaves egg-shaped, conspicuously lobed. Young shoots and leaf undersurfaces covered in pale down. Acorns large, cup with long recurved scales. Zones 4–9.

Quercus muehlenbergii

CHINQUAPIN OAK, YELLOW CHESTNUT OAK, YELLOW OAK

↔40 ft (12 m) ↑100 ft (30 m)

Deciduous tree found in central and southern USA. Grayish bark fissured vertically. Leaves oblong to lanceolate, coarsely toothed, yellow-green above, pale and downy beneath; turn to rich reds and crimsons in autumn. Acorns half-enclosed in a scaly cup. Zones 5–9.

Quercus agrifolia

Quercus coccinea

Quercus macrocarpa

Quercus virginiana (with *Tillandsia usneoides* in trees), Louisiana, USA

Quercus nigra

WATER OAK

↔40 ft (12 m) ↑50 ft (15 m)

Broad-domed deciduous tree native to southern USA. Bark dark gray, develops scaly ridges. Leaves on slender stalks, egg-shaped, variously lobed, glossy deep green, persisting until winter. Acorns enclosed in shallow cups. Zones 6–10.

Quercus palustris

PIN OAK, SWAMP OAK

↔60 ft (18 m) ↑100 ft (30 m)

Native of southeastern Canada and eastern USA. Large, dense, deciduous tree, slender branches droop at their extremities. Bark silver-gray becoming purplish gray with age. Leaves deeply lobed, shiny green; turn scarlet in autumn, persist until winter. Acorns held in shallow hairy cups. **'Green Pillar'**, very narrow form. Zones 3–10.

Quercus phellos

WILLOW OAK, WILLOW-LEAFED OAK

↔40 ft (12 m) ↑100 ft (30 m)

A large deciduous tree with slender branches, native to eastern USA. Bark smooth, gray, becoming fissured with age. Leaves narrow, willow-like, glossy green on the uppersurfaces, turning yellow and orange tones in autumn. Small acorns are enclosed in shallow cups. This species requires lime-free soil. Zones 5–10.

Quercus pontica

ARMENIAN OAK, PONTINE OAK

↔15 ft (4.5 m) ↑20 ft (6 m)

A shrub or a small tree that is native to Armenia and the Caucasus region. The leaves are large, oval to egg-shaped, strongly ribbed and toothed, with a yellow stalk and midrib; the whole leaf turns warm rich red tones in the autumn months. The ovoid acorns are enclosed in shallow gray cups. Zones 6–10.

Quercus prinus

syns *Quercus michauxii, Q. montana*

BASKET OAK, SWAMP CHESTNUT OAK

↔60 ft (18 m) ↑100 ft (30 m)

From southeastern Canada and eastern USA. Deciduous tree, large spreading branches. Bark dark red-brown to black, deeply fissured. Egg-shaped to oblong leaves, yellow-green, lustrous above, paler, finely hairy beneath; turn rich yellow in autumn. Acorns half-enclosed in hairy cups. Zones 3–9.

Quercus robur

COMMON OAK, ENGLISH OAK, PEDUNCULATE OAK

↔70 ft (21 m) ↑100 ft (30 m)

Native of Europe, western Asia, and North Africa. A large and long-lived, deciduous tree. Bark pale gray, closely fissured into short, narrow, vertical plates. Leaves shallowly lobed. Long-nosed acorns in shallow cups. May be invasive in cooler climates. ***Q. r.* subsp. *pedunculiflora*,** native to Greece, Turkey, and the Caucasus region, leaves with fewer lobes, bluish undersides. ***Q. r.* f. *fastigiata*,** columnar habit. ***Q. r.* 'Concordia'**, the golden oak, leaves suffused with golden yellow; **'Pendula'**, drooping branches. Zones 3–10.

Quercus rubra

syn. *Quercus borealis*

NORTHERN RED OAK, RED OAK

↔70 ft (21 m) ↑100 ft (30 m)

Deciduous tree from eastern Canada to Texas, USA. Broad head, horizontal branches. Bark smooth, silvery gray, can become brown-gray with age. Leaves large, oval to egg-shaped, lobed, turn red then red-brown to yellow and brown on old trees before falling. Dark red-brown acorns, on short stalks, in shallow scaly cups. **'Schrefeldii'**, more deeply lobed leaves, lobes overlapping. Zones 3–9.

Quercus shumardii

SHUMARD OAK

↔40 ft (12 m) ↑100 ft (30 m)

Native of the prairie states of central USA. Large deciduous tree, wide-spreading crown. Bark thick, furrowed. Leaves 5- to 7-lobed, toothed, dark green above, paler below; turn red or golden brown in autumn. Acorns in a thick shallow cup. Q. s. var. schneckii, smoother bark, less deeply lobed leaves. Zones 5–9.

Quercus virginiana

LIVE OAK

↔35 ft (10 m) ↑70 ft (21 m)

From southeastern USA, Mexico, and Cuba. Wide-spreading evergreen. Bark charcoal gray, fissured. Twigs downy, leaves elliptic or oblong, leathery, smooth-edged, glossy dark green above, grayish to whitish hairs below. Acorns singly or in clusters. Used for ship-building and posts. Zones 7–11.

RANUNCULUS

BUTTERCUP

The type genus for the buttercup (Ranunculaceae) family, this widespread group encompasses some 400 species of annuals, biennials, and perennials, many of which are cultivated, others are admired in the wild, and some are despised as invasive weeds. The foliage varies markedly, though pinnate, glossy, leathery, kidney-shaped leaves predominate. The flowers too are often glossy and commonly have 5 petals. Most species produce yellow flowers but cultivated forms occur in many different colors. *Ranunculus* is Latin for little frog, a name given by the Roman Pliny due to the wet conditions in which wild buttercups are often found growing.

CULTIVATION: Buttercups are very hardy and will grow in a wide range of conditions, but generally prefer to have their roots kept cool and moist. Many species have strong rhizomes that can be invasive, so take care to plant where they can be controlled. Bedding ranunculus "corms" can be lifted and stored dry. Propagate by division or from seed. Mildew can be a problem in autumn.

Ranunculus asiaticus

↔8–12 in (20–30 cm) ↑18 in (45 cm)

Rhizome-rooted southern Eurasian perennial. Finely divided, ferny, basal leaves; hairy upright flower stems. Large, often double flowers, in late spring–summer, mainly in yellow to red shades in the wild, but cultivated forms are available in many colors. Often sold as mixed color strains, such as **Bloomingdale Series**, 8 in (20 cm) tall, fully double flowers and compact habit, wide color range excluding mauve to purple shades; and **Tecolote Hybrids**, 18 in (45 cm) tall, very large double flowers, all colors except blue. Zones 8–10.

RAOULIA

SCABWEED

Found in screes or open rocky places from sea level to alpine areas throughout New Zealand, these 20 to 30 species of tiny-leafed, cushion- or mat-forming, evergreen perennials or subshrubs belong to the daisy family (Asteraceae). Their leaves are green or silvery in appearance, caused by minute silky hairs. Flowers are tiny, disc-like and pale white, cream, or yellow. The largest cushion-forming species are known as vegetable sheep because from a distance these plants look like sheep sitting down! Many botanists now regard *Raoulia* as an unnatural group and propose that some of the species should go into a distinct genus, *Psychrophyton*.

CULTIVATION: *Raoulia* species will do well in pots, troughs, or rock gardens. Grow in moist well-drained soil in full sun. Propagate from seed or sections of the mat (rooted stems).

Raoulia australis

syn. *Raoulia lutescens*

COMMON MAT DAISY, GOLDEN SCABWEED

↔12 in (30 cm) ↑½ in (12 mm)

From New Zealand's South Island. A mat-forming perennial that layers itself as it creeps. Tiny leaves, gray or silver. Yellow flowers, 5 mm wide, in summer. Zones 7–9.

Ranunculus asiaticus

RATIBIDA

CONEFLOWER

This genus in the daisy (Asteraceae) family contains 5 biennial or perennial species that are found throughout North America, from Ontario, Canada, through to New York, Minnesota, South Dakota, Nebraska, south to Georgia and Texas, USA, and northern Mexico. These plants are stiff and erect, with deeply cut leaves covered with rigid hairs. Flowerheads are similar to those of *Rudbeckia* species but have fewer ray florets and a round or cylindrical central disc, unlike the flat disc of the *Rudbeckia* flowerheads. The crushed seed heads have an aromatic anise scent. The genus was named by wanderer-botanist Constantine Rafinesque-Schmaltz (1773–1840), who often assigned unexplained names to plants.

CULTIVATION: Use in casual settings, in native flower gardens, or cottage gardens. Grow in full sun in a very well-drained soil. Propagate from seed, which will self-sow.

Ratibida columnifera

LONG-HEAD CONEFLOWER, MEXICAN HAT, PRAIRIE CONEFLOWER

↔18 in (45 cm) ↑24 in (60 cm)

Perennial found from North America to Mexico. Hairy gray-green leaves. Flowers bright yellow or brown-purple, in drooping rays, in summer to autumn. Floral disc is cylindrical or columnar, and brown. Zones 4–9.

Ratibida pinnata

GRAY-HEAD CONEFLOWER, PRAIRIE CONEFLOWER, YELLOW CONEFLOWER

↔12–18 in (30–45 cm) ↑48 in (120 cm)

A perennial from eastern North America. Leaves lance-shaped, blue-green and toothed. Yellow ray flowers, rounded brown disc, from mid-summer to early autumn. Zones 3–8.

RAVENALA

This genus belonging to the strelitzia (Strelitziaceae) family consists of a solitary species from Madagascar, a clump-forming tree with trunks resembling those of palm trees. The top third of the stem is clothed in old leaf bases. The new leaves resemble those of the banana; when wind-blown they become split and frayed. The spathes are boat-shaped and enclose small flowers, which are followed by edible seeds. Originally from rainforest areas, this species is grown as an ornamental in many tropical and subtropical regions of the world, being admired for its striking

Ratibida columnifera, Chihuahua, Mexico

form, foliage, and spathes. The common name traveler's tree comes from the ability of the flower bracts and leaf sheaths to hold water, which is believed to provide travelers with an emergency supply.

CULTIVATION: Grow in moist, fertile, well-drained soil in a sunny position with protection from frosts and high winds. Propagate from seed or from rooted suckers.

Ravenala madagascariensis

TRAVELER'S PALM, TRAVELER'S TREE

↔7–15 ft (2–4.5 m) ↑30 ft (9 m)

From Madagascar. Palm-like tree with many trunks, and a fan-shaped crown. Bright green paddle-shaped leaves, in 2 opposite rows, long leaf stalks. Clusters of white flowers, in summer. Fruit capsules contain edible seeds. Zones 10–12.

REBUTIA

syns *Aylostera, Weingartia*

These 40 evergreen, low-growing, simple or clustering cacti from the family Cactaceae are native to the mountains of Bolivia and northwestern Argentina. The small stems, 4 in (10 cm) in diameter or less, are lightly ribbed or with a warty surface, and have weak spines, with the radial and central spines often similar. Funnel-shaped flowers, which emerge from the lower part of the stem, are mostly yellow to red or white, with a sometimes bristly or scaly, slender, curved corolla, opening in daylight. The genus is named after P. Rebut, a nineteenth-century French cactus dealer.

CULTIVATION: *Rebutia* species prefer a gritty, well-drained, slightly acidic soil in an open sunny position. Propagate from seed less than 12 months old or by dividing offsets.

Ravenala madagascariensis

Rebutia aureiflora

syn. *Mediolobivia aureiflora*

↔3–8 in (8–20 cm) ↑2 in (5 cm)

A clustering globular cactus from northwestern Argentina. Warty stems, often tinged with red, 3 to 4 central spines, smaller radial spines. Broadly funnel-shaped yellow flowers, usually with a white throat and a paler tube, are borne in summer. ***R. a.* var. *rubelliflora***, over 10 radial spines, 1 darker central spine, and deep orange flowers. Zones 9–12.

REHMANNIA

CHINESE FOXGLOVE

This genus of up to 9 species of herbaceous perennials in the plantain (Plantaginaceae) family is native to the woods and hills of China. They are grown for their large exotic-looking flowers which are produced over a prolonged period. These blooms are usually a magenta-pink with patterns of brown and yellow in the throat. The foliage is heavily serrated and hairy to sticky.

CULTIVATION: Grow these perennials in moisture-retentive but not wet, humus-rich soil in a spot that receives lots of light but not the very hottest sun. Propagate from seed, or from stem cuttings early in the growth cycle, or more usually by division.

Rehmannia angulata

syn. *Rehmannia piasezkii*

↔12–16 in (30–40 cm) ↑8–12 in (20–30 cm)

From central China; similar to *R. glutinosa.* Stemless leaves. Trumpet-flowers, 2½ in (6 cm) long, magenta, in spring–early summer. Very rarely grown in true form; the name is often incorrectly used for *R. elata* in horticulture. **'Beverley Bells'**, pink flowers. Zones 8–10.

Rehmannia elata

syn. *Rehmannia angulata of gardens*

CHINESE FOXGLOVE

↔20–32 in (50–80 cm) ↑40–60 in (100–150 cm)

Vigorous suckering perennial from China. Lobed hairy leaves, to 10 in (25 cm) long, in basal foliage. Slightly drooping trumpet-flowers, to 4 in (10 cm) long, heavily spotted in throat, in late spring–summer. Zones 8–10.

Rehmannia glutinosa

↔12–16 in (30–40 cm) ↑8–12 in (20–30 cm)

A native of northern China. Strongly suckering habit. Scalloped basal leaves, to 4 in (10 cm) long. Trumpet-flowers, 2 in (5 cm) long, classic magenta color, darker markings inside trumpet, yellow-brown lips, in spring. Zones 8–10.

RHAMNUS

There are more than 125 species within this genus in the buckthorn (Rhamnaceae) family. Mostly prickly evergreen or deciduous shrubs or trees, they are found throughout the Northern Hemisphere, as well as Brazil, eastern Africa, and South Africa, in woodland and heathland areas. The simple dark green leaves can be smooth-edged or toothed. The flowers are insignificant; some are fragrant. Green, blue-green, and yellow dyes are made from some species, while others are used medicinally, or wood is used commercially for turning. Cultivated for ornamental foliage and decorative berries.

CULTIVATION: Depending on the species, these shrubs or trees prefer moist to very dry conditions in full sun or part-shade, in moderately fertile soil. Some species tolerate alkaline soil and coastal sites.

Rehmannia angulata

Propagate by sowing seed in autumn, as soon as it is ripe, giving protection from winter frosts; or from softwood cuttings of deciduous species in early summer. Half-hardened cuttings can be taken from evergreen species in summer and layering can be done in autumn or spring.

Rhamnus alaternus

ITALIAN BUCKTHORN

↔12 ft (3.5 m) ↑15 ft (4.5 m)

An evergreen shrub, native to the Mediterranean and Caucasus regions. Leathery leaves are dark green and shiny. Small yellow-green flowers, in late spring–early summer. Fruit ripens to black, in late summer. Tolerates dry soil conditions, pollution, and salt-laden air. **'Argenteovariegata'** (syn. 'Variegata'), slightly less hardy than the species, leaves with marbled grayish green center and prominent white leaf edges. Zones 7–10.

Rhamnus crocea

REDBERRY

↔7 ft (2 m) ↑6 ft (1.8 m)

Native to Baja California, Mexico, and north to southwestern Oregon, USA. Evergreen spreading shrub with thorny twigs. Leaves are glossy, egg-shaped to elliptic, with slightly toothed edges. Small flower clusters are followed by red fruit. Zones 7–11.

Rhamnus crocea

Rhaphiolepis indica

RHAPHIOLEPIS

There are up to 10 species of evergreen shrubs in this genus of the rose (Rosaceae) family, allied to *Photinia*. Originating in East and Southeast Asia, these plants do not bear spines or thorns; they have leathery deep green leaves and clusters of white or pink flowers in spring, often blooming again in autumn. Flowers are followed by blue-black berries highly attractive to some birds, which can distribute the seeds.

CULTIVATION: Considered tough low-maintenance plants that are suitable for seaside planting, these shrubs can withstand quite hard pruning, which makes them ideal for hedges. Plant them in full sun in reasonable soil topped up with an organic mulch into which branches can be layered to produce further plants. The soil should be forked over as little as possible as the plants resent root disturbance. In addition to layering, the plants can be propagated from cuttings or seed.

Rhaphiolepis × *delacourii*

HYBRID INDIAN HAWTHORN

↔8 ft (2.4 m) ↑6 ft (1.8 m)

This name is applied to a number of plants intermediate in character between *R. indica* and *R. umbellata*. The first were deliberate crosses made by a M. Delacour at Cannes shortly before 1900. Cultivars from these crosses include: **'Coates' Crimson'**, slow growing, glossy green leaves, dark pink flowers from spring to summer; **'Spring Song'**, light pink flowers held for a long time; and **'White Enchantress'**, a dwarf form with small white flowers. Zones 8–11.

Rhaphiolepis indica

INDIAN HAWTHORN

↔8 ft (2.4 m) ↑8 ft (2.4 m)

From southern China. Leathery leaves serrated, narrow, pointed, dark green above, olive green beneath. Pinkish brown new growths. Pink-tinted white flowers in clusters, at ends of branches, in spring. Invasive in warm-temperate climates. **'Ballerina'**, pink flowers, reddish autumn foliage; Springtime/ **'Monme'**, small pink flowers, bronzy new growth. Zones 8–11.

Rhaphiolepis umbellata

↔7 ft (2 m) ↑6 ft (1.8 m)

Dense mound-like shrub from coastal areas of southern Japan and Korea. Broad, thick, grayish green leaves, rounded tip, recurved edges. Bunches of white perfumed flowers, in spring to early summer, spasmodically into winter in warmer areas. Blue-black berries. **'Minor'** ★, dwarf form with smaller leaves and flowers. Zones 8–11.

RHAPIS

This genus in the family Arecaceae consists of 12 species of small multi-stemmed palms found in higher rainfall areas of subtropical and tropical regions of southern China and across Southeast Asia. They have a clumping habit, with bamboo-like stems and fan-shaped fronds that are deeply divided into finger-like segments. Rhapis palms are mostly dioecious, so both male and female plants are needed for seed production. Small, bowl-shaped, creamy yellow flowers are produced in panicles. The fruit is berry-like. Highly valued in horticulture, most species are long-lived landscape specimens in the garden; they are also used as a screen, or as tub or indoor plant.

CULTIVATION: Most members of the genus are fairly adaptable, tolerating full sun to semi-shade and bright positions indoors. In full sun, some bleaching of the leaves may occur. Grow in fertile well-drained soil protected from strong winds and frost. Humid conditions favor growth. Propagate from seed, which can be slow, or by division.

Rhaphiolepis × *delacourii*

Rhapis excelsa

LADY PALM, RHAPIS PALM

↔8–15 ft (2.4–4.5 m) ↑10 ft (3 m)

Native to southern China, one of the most popular species in the genus. Multi-stemmed fan palm. Slender stems covered in brown interwoven fibers. Light green fronds, 5 to 8 stiff segments with blunt tips. Bowl-shaped cream flowers, in summer. Excellent tub plant. **'Variegata'**, leaves with a white stripe. Zones 9–12.

Rhapis humilis

SLENDER LADY PALM

↔10 ft (3 m) ↑15 ft (4.5 m)

A native of southern China. Forms a spreading clump; numerous slender stems covered in interwoven brown fibers. Thin dark green fronds divided into many drooping segments with pointed tips. Propagate by division. Excellent indoor plant. Zones 9–12.

RHEUM

RHUBARB

This genus of 50 robust perennials includes several ornamental foliage plants as well as the popular edible rhubarb. *Rheum* belongs to the knotweed (Polygonaceae) family and species are native to a wide area of temperate Asia. Their large leaves, which are often wavy-edged or palmately lobed, are borne on stout stalks and form basal clumps. The small greenish white or red tinged flowers are wind-pollinated and borne in large panicles on strong upright stems.

CULTIVATION: Ornamental species of *Rheum* make excellent feature plants with their architectural foliage and stately flowering spikes. They will do best when grown in sun or part-shade in a rich, deep, moisture-retentive but well-drained soil. Propagate from seed or by division. Edible rhubarb should be planted at a 30–36 in (75–90 cm) spacing in a deeply cultivated soil with plenty of compost added. The plants require plenty of moisture but should be well-drained. Rhubarb cultivars are propagated by division of the crown.

Rhapis excelsa

Rheum australe

syn. ***Rheum emodi***

HIMALAYAN RHUBARB, RED-VEINED PIE PLANT

☼/◐ ✱ ↔5 ft (1.5 m) ↑5 ft (1.5 m)

From Himalayas. Leaves rounded or broadly oblong, prominently veined, and with wavy margins. Stout red-tinged flowering stalks, dense clusters of small white to red flowers, in summer. Zones 6–9.

Rheum × hybridum

syns ***Rheum ≥ cultorum, R. rhabarbarum of gardens***

RHUBARB

☼ ✱ ↔3–6 ft (0.9–1.8 m) ↑3 ft (0.9 m)

Hybrid of unclear origin grown for culinary use in Europe since the 1700s. Stout edible stalks, large, wavy-edged, triangular leaves. Cultivars differ in flavor, degree of stalk color, and productive season. **'Cherry'**, thick red stalks; **'MacDonald'**, brilliant red stalks; and **'Victoria'**, thick green stalks shaded red near base. Zones 6–10.

Rheum palmatum

☼/◐ ✱ ↔5 ft (1.5 m)
↑5–8 ft (1.5–2.4 m)

Majestic plant native to northwestern China. Deeply lobed and toothed leaves, to 40 in (100 cm) wide, purplish red when young. Fluffy panicles of small pink flowers, on tall stems, in summer. ***R. p.* var. *tanguticum***, even more robust with very deeply lobed leaves. ***R. p.* 'Atrosanguineum'**, cerise flowers, leaves open vivid red; and **'Bowles' Crimson'**, leaves crimson beneath. Zones 6–9.

Rheum palmatum

RHODANTHE

STRAWFLOWER

This genus in the daisy (Asteraceae) family, one of several in the complex *Helichrysum* group, was extensively revised in the early 1990s and is now considered to be exclusively Australian. The 40 species in the genus are annuals, perennials, and small shrubs with simple, narrow, light green to silver-gray leaves. They are rather sprawling plants grown for their long-lasting show of flowers, which are made colorful by dry papery bracts enclosing the yellowish flowerheads. Some species have long-stemmed flowerheads that last well when cut. Some are ephemeral plants native to desert regions, remaining in the ground as seeds for many years ready to burst into a carpet of bloom with the arrival of rain.

CULTIVATION: Hardiness varies, but most *Rhodanthe* species are surprisingly tough and are ideal for dry banks or rockeries. Plant in full sun with light, gritty, very free-draining soil. They are tolerant of poor soil. Propagate from seed or cuttings. Some will self-layer.

Rhodanthe anthemoides

syn. ***Helipterum anthemoides***

☼/◐ ❄ ↔12–20 in (30–50 cm)
↑4–8 in (10–20 cm)

Wiry-stemmed evergreen perennial from southeastern Australia. Narrow, pointed, gray-green leaves, less than ½ in (12 mm) long. Clusters of 1 in (25 mm) wide, papery, white, daisy-like flowerheads, from spring to summer. **'Paper Baby'**, compact habit, red buds open to white flowers; **'Paper Cascade'**, near prostrate, cascading habit for spilling over banks, hanging baskets; **'Paper Star'**, an especially heavy flowerer with a compact habit, superb rockery plant; **'Sunray Snow'**, upright and bushy. Zones 9–10.

Rhodanthe chlorocephala

syn. ***Helipterum roseum***

☼ ❄ ↔8–12 in (20–30 cm)
↑12–24 in (30–60 cm)

Annual from southwestern Australia; usually erect or rounded. The narrow gray-green leaves are around 1 in (25 mm) long. Flowerheads 1–2 in (25–50 mm) wide, white to pink papery bracts around a conspicuous soft yellow disc, from late spring to early summer; winter-flowering in mild areas. ***R. c.* subsp. *rosea***, flowerheads with bright pink ray florets; ***R. c.* subsp. *splendida***, white flowerheads, to 2½ in (6 cm) wide, with many ray florets. Zones 9–11.

Rhodanthemum hosmariense

Rhodanthe floribunda

syn. ***Helipterum floribundum***

☼ ❄ ↔2–12 in (5–30 cm)
↑3–12 in (8–30 cm)

Annual found over much of drier inland Australia. Compact bushy habit with tiny gray-green leaves. After rain it can form a carpet of white flowerheads, to over 2 in (5 cm) wide. Zones 9–11.

RHODANTHEMUM

A mainly alpine Eurasian and North African genus of some 15 to 20 species that was established with the revision of *Chrysanthemum* in the 1960s to 90s, and belongs to the daisy (Asteraceae) family. These shrubby perennials have ferny, usually silver-gray foliage, sometimes in whorls or loose rosettes, and develop into dense mounds. In spring and early summer they are covered in wiry-stemmed flowerheads with white ray florets, often pink-tinted, around a yellow disc. In mild areas flowers occur less heavily throughout the year.

Rhodanthe anthemoides 'Paper Star'

CULTIVATION: Although generally frost tolerant, few species will withstand prolonged cold, damp winter conditions. They are best grown in an alpine house or dry winter climate. Plant in full sun or half-sun in gritty free-draining soil with a little added humus. Water in summer and feed very lightly. Propagate from seed or from small basal cuttings of non-flowering shoots.

Rhodanthemum gayanum

syns ***Chrysanthemum gayanum, C. mawii, Pyrethropsis gayana***

☼ ❄ ↔24–40 in (60–100 cm)
↑8–12 in (20–30 cm)

A low-growing perennial subshrub, native to Algeria and Morocco. Forms a dense spreading cushion of lacy, finely divided, dark green, glossy foliage. Abundant, bright pink, daisy-like flowers with yellow to burgundy centers, in winter–spring. Zones 8–10.

Rhodanthemum hosmariense

syns ***Chrysanthemum hosmariense, Pyrethropsis hosmariensis***

MOROCCAN DAISY

☼ ❄ ↔12–16 in (30–40 cm)
↑4–8 in (10–20 cm)

Spreading, drought-resistant, bushy perennial herb from Morocco's Atlas Mountains. Forms compact cushion of finely cut silvery gray leaves. Scaly, decorative floral buttons in winter open to white daisy-like flowers with yellow centers, from spring to autumn, with scattered blooms through year. **'Flamingo'**, bright pink flowers. Zones 9–10.

RHODODENDRON

syn. ***Ledum***

AZALEA, RHODODENDRON

This very diverse genus of 800 or more species of mostly evergreen and some deciduous shrubs is widely distributed across the Northern Hemisphere, with the majority growing in temperate to cool regions. Particular concentrations occur in western China, the Himalayas and northeastern Myanmar, while the so-called "tropical" Vireya rhododendrons grow mostly at higher

Rhodanthe chlorocephala

altitudes throughout tropical southeastern Asia, as far south as the northern tip of Australia, with more than 200 species occurring on the island of New Guinea alone. Deciduous azalea species are scattered across cooler Northern Hemisphere climates, notably in Europe, China, Japan, and North America. Rhododendrons vary in form from tiny, ground-hugging, prostrate and miniature plants adapted to exposed conditions to small trees, often understory species in the forests of mountainous areas. Many species grow at high altitudes of 3,000 ft (900 m) or more and some can grow as epiphytes in the branches of trees or on rock faces. As members of the heath (Ericaceae) family, they are closely related to heathers (*Erica* and *Calluna* species), *Pieris*, and strawberry trees (*Arbutus* species) and have similar growing requirements. Some rhododendrons have solitary flowers but most bear terminal racemes, known as "trusses," of up to 24 or more spectacular blooms, in a wide palette of colors including whites, pinks, reds, yellows, and mauves, excluding only shades of pure blue. Flowers may be a single color but are often multi-colored, with spots, stripes, edging, or a single blotch of a different color or shade in the throat of the flower. With the exception of some Vireya species and hybrids, fragrant rhododendrons are always white or very pale pink. Blooms vary in size and shape but are generally campanulate (bell-shaped), with a broad tube ending in flared lobes, and usually single. Flowers with double petals do occur, particularly among the evergreen azaleas, which may also be "hose-in-hose," when the calyx is enlarged and the same color as the petals.

Most rhododendrons flower from early spring (early season) to early summer (late season), although some bear spot flowers briefly in autumn, and Vireya rhododendrons can flower at various times during the year, often in winter. Deciduous azaleas flower in spring on bare branches, usually just before new leaf growth starts to emerge. The fruit is a many-seeded capsule, normally woody but sometimes soft, and sometimes bearing wings or tail-like appendages designed to aid transportation.

The genus is divided into 2 botanically distinct groups known as lepidotes and elepidotes, and these groups are subdivided further into the various rhododendron types. Plants from one group may not breed with plants from the other, thus limiting the options for hybridizers. The leaves, and sometimes the flowers and other parts, of lepidote rhododendrons are covered with scales, which is thought to aid transpiration. This group includes many of the cool-climate evergreen plants, including the Vireya rhododendrons. The rest of the genus, the elepidote rhododendrons, with no scales on leaf or flower parts, includes the remaining cool-climate evergreen plants and the evergreen and deciduous azaleas, which are normally rather more compact plants with 5 stamens rather than the more usual ten. Azaleas were originally classified as a separate genus but are now regarded as botanically part of the *Rhododendron* genus. Vireya rhododendrons can be grown in just about any climate as long as protection from frost is provided. Many are well suited to growing in hanging baskets and containers. The nectar of some species and some flower parts are poisonous and care should be taken when handling the flowers.

CULTIVATION: Establishing an ideal growing environment before planting is the key to success with rhododendrons. Many of the problems likely to afflict them in the home garden can be minimized by maintaining soil quality and ensuring adequate ventilation. All prefer acidic soils between pH 4.5 and 6, that is high in organic matter and freely draining. A cool root run is essential and is best achieved by applying a deep mulch of organic material that also helps to reduce moisture loss and control weed growth, while minimizing disturbance of the delicate roots. Many rhododendrons, particularly those with larger leaves, prefer a shaded or semi-shaded aspect. They are ideally suited to planting under deciduous trees, allowing winter sun and summer shade. While most prefer some protection from wind, sun, and frost, many others are tolerant of these conditions and some are well suited to exposed rock gardens.

Evergreen rhododendrons may be propagated by taking tip cuttings of new growth in spring, while decid-uous azaleas are best grown from hardwood cuttings taken in winter. Plants may be grown from seed but germination and development is slow, and plants grown from the seed of hybrids are unlikely to be the same as their parents. Layering enables new plants to be created from low-hanging branches pinned to the ground and covered in a moist organic medium such as sphagnum moss. Plants which are difficult to propagate and establish by other means can be grafted onto the roots of stronger plants with more vigorous root systems. Regular pruning of rhododendrons is not necessary other than as required to control size, maintain shape, and to remove any damaged or diseased material, while some species and hybrids actually resent unnecessary pruning. Culti-vated rhododendrons are normally more compact and attain only about half the height of similar plants growing in the wild. The growing habit of all species and hybrids varies widely according to the amount of shade the plant receives.

Rhododendron aberconwayi

↔4 ft (1.2 m) ↑6 ft (1.8 m)

From western China. Freely flowering, upright, evergreen shrub. Thick, smooth, glossy, dark green, elliptic leaves. Delicate, saucer-shaped, pale rose flowers, to 1½ in (35 mm) long, crimson or purple spots, in trusses of 5 to 12 blooms, in late spring–early summer. Zones 7–9.

Rhododendron alabamense

ALABAMA AZALEA

↔5 ft (1.5 m) ↑5 ft (1.5 m)

Deciduous azalea from southern USA; rarely grown. Masses of dazzling white, lemon-scented, funnel-shaped flowers, distinctive yellow blotch, with new spring growth of hairy pale gray-green leaves. Zones 7–9.

Rhododendron albrechtii

Rhododendron albrechtii

↔4 ft (1.2 m) ↑7 ft (2 m)

Deciduous azalea, native to central and northern Japan. Compact shrub. Whorls of 5 finely toothed leaves, gray hairy coating underneath. Openly bell-shaped, reddish purple flowers, in trusses of 3 to 5 blooms, in mid- to late spring. Zones 5–8.

Rhododendron anagalliflorum

↔24–48 in (60–120 cm) ↑8 in (20 cm)

A tiny Vireya species from New Guinea, with a prostrate creeping habit. Whorls of tiny delicate leaves are covered with a textured mass of scales. Solitary, miniature, bell-shaped, red or pinkish flowers. Ideal subject for containers or hanging baskets. Zones 10–11.

Rhododendron arborescens

↔8 ft (2.4 m) ↑10 ft (3 m)

Deciduous azalea, native of woodlands of the Appalachian region of eastern USA. Fragrant flowers white or pink, funnel-shaped, open with or after bright green obovate leaves. Zones 4–8.

Rhododendron atlanticum ★

COAST AZALEA

↔36 in (90 cm) ↑36 in (90 cm)

Compact deciduous azalea occurs on the USA east coast. Highly fragrant, white, funnel-shaped flowers, a distinctly cylindrical tube, flushed with purple or pink, open with or just before the bright bluish green foliage. 'Seaboard', white flowers with a pink corolla tube. Zones 6–9.

Rhododendron atlanticum

Rhododendron augustinii

Rhododendron campanulatum

Rhododendron calophytum

Rhododendron concinnum

Rhododendron augustinii

↔ 2–10 ft (0.6–3 m) ↑ 3–20 ft (0.9–6 m)

Compact, freely flowering, variable, evergreen shrub from China. Elliptic leaves, hairy beneath. Flowers mauve-blue to purple, greenish spots; funnel-shaped, in trusses of 2 to 6 blooms, mid- to late season. Zones 6–9.

Rhododendron auriculatum

↔ 15 ft (4.5 m) ↑ 30 ft (9 m)

Evergreen shrub or tree from western China. Large oblong-oblanceolate leaves, whitish brown hairs underneath. Fragrant, funnel-shaped, white flowers, in loose trusses of 7 to 15 blooms, in mid-spring. Zones 6–9.

Rhododendron austrinum

FLORIDA AZALEA

↔ 10 ft (3 m) ↑ 10 ft (3 m)

A rarely grown, freely flowering, deciduous azalea from southeastern USA. Fragrant, funnel-shaped, creamy yellow to golden yellow, orange or red flowers, with distinctive long protruding stamens, bloom before or as the downy leaf shoots open. Zones 6–9.

Rhododendron barbatum

↔ 20 ft (6 m) ↑ 20 ft (6 m)

Evergreen species from the Himalayas. Smooth, peeling, mahogany-colored bark. Long stiff bristles on young shoots; dark green, glossy, elliptic to oblong leaves, to 8 in (20 cm) long, pale mat green undersides. Brilliant scarlet or blood red, or occasionally pure white, fleshy flowers, up to 3 in (8 cm) long, in very compact rounded trusses of 10 to 20 blooms, in early spring. Zones 7–9.

Rhododendron barbatum

Rhododendron bureavii

↔ 10 ft (3 m) ↑ 20 ft (6 m)

Evergreen shrub from southwestern China. Elliptic foliage covered with pink to rusty red hairs. Bell-shaped white flowers, to 2 in (5 cm) wide, sometimes flushed pink, occasionally spotted purple, produced in late spring. **'Ardrishaig'** bears pale pink flowers that are flushed with darker pink, with red spotting. Zones 6–9.

Rhododendron burmanicum

↔ 5 ft (1.5 m) ↑ 8 ft (2.4 m)

Compact, abundantly flowering, evergreen shrub from slopes of Mt Victoria in Myanmar. White, creamy yellow, or greenish yellow, funnel-shaped flowers, in trusses of 4 to 6 blooms, in late spring. Flowers and dark green foliage densely covered with scales. Zones 9–10.

Rhododendron calendulaceum ★

FLAME AZALEA

↔ 10 ft (3 m) ↑ 10 ft (3 m)

Originating in southeastern USA, this attractive deciduous azalea is a densely branched shrub, The slightly fragrant, funnel-shaped, orange, red, or yellow flowers, to 2 in (5 cm) wide, open with the leaves, in late spring. Zones 5–8.

Rhododendron callimorphum

↔ 8 ft (2.4 m) ↑ 10 ft (3 m)

Evergreen shrub from southwestern China. Broad, almost circular, leaves. Bell-shaped, white, pink, or rose flowers, to 2 in (5 cm) in length, sometimes with purple spots, held in trusses of 5 to 8 blooms, in late spring. Zones 7–9.

Rhododendron calophytum

↔ 20 ft (6 m) ↑ 15 ft (4.5 m)

Native of China, evergreen small tree, shorter in cultivation. Long, dark green, smooth leaves curl and droop in colder weather. White or pink bell-shaped flowers, with purple basal blotch, early to mid-season. Zones 6–9.

Rhododendron calostrotum

↔ 36 in (90 cm) ↑ 27 in (70 cm)

A prostrate mat-forming, evergreen species that is distributed across the Himalayas, western China, as well as northern Myanmar and India. Shiny dark green leaves are almost circular. The magenta, rose-crimson, or sometimes pink and purple flowers, are carried in trusses of 1 to 5 blooms, in late spring. ***R. c.* subsp. *keleticum*** produces abundant purplish crimson flowers, about 1½ in (35 mm) across, widely funnel-shaped, densely spotted with crimson, in trusses of 2 or 3, late in the season, and has leaves with brown or fawn scales on the undersides. ***R. c.* 'Gigha'** is a compact, freely flowering cultivar that bears rosy crimson blooms. Zones 6–9.

Rhododendron campanulatum

↔ 15 ft (4.5 m) ↑ 15 ft (4.5 m)

From the Himalayas, a shrub or small tree which varies widely in form and height. Smooth leaves, undersides densely covered with brown woolly hairs. Bell-shaped flowers, lavender-blue or white to pale mauve, with purple spots, in trusses of 6 to 12 blooms, in spring. Zones 5–8.

Rhododendron campylogynum

↔ 30 in (75 cm) ↑ 18 in (45 cm)

Ideal for rock gardens, creeping evergreen shrub from eastern India and northeastern Myanmar. Dark green leaves, distinctive white or silvery hairy undersides. Nodding creamy white or bright pink flowers, in delicate trusses of 1 to 3 blooms, in late spring to summer. Zones 7–9.

Rhododendron canadense

RHODORA

↔ 36 in (90 cm) ↑ 36 in (90 cm)

Native of woodlands in eastern North America. Dull bluish green elliptic to oblong leaves, hairy coating beneath. Broadly bell-shaped flowers, 5-lobed, rose-purple, occasionally white, in late spring. Zones 3–8.

Rhododendron canescens

FLORIDA PINXTER AZALEA, PIEDMONT AZALEA, SWEET AZALEA

↔ 8 ft (2.4 m) ↑ 15 ft (4.5 m)

Deciduous azalea native to eastern USA, from North Carolina southward and west to Oklahoma. Oblong to lance-shaped leaves. Scented pink flowers, funnel-shaped, before or with leaves, in spring. White- or magenta-flowered forms occur. Zones 6–10.

Rhododendron catawbiense ★

CATAWBA RHODODENDRON, MOUNTAIN ROSEBAY

↔ 10 ft (3 m) ↑ 10 ft (3 m)

From eastern USA; robust evergreen similar in form to *R. ponticum.* Glossy dark green leaves, broadly elliptic to obovate. Funnel-shaped faintly spotted flowers, lilac-purple, in compact trusses of 15 to 20 blooms, in late spring–early summer. Important parent of many frost-hardy hybrids. Zones 4–9.

Rhododendron cephalanthum

↔ 4 ft (1.2 m) ↑ 4 ft (1.2 m)

Variable evergreen shrub found in western China and upper Myanmar. Young shoots are densely bristly; aromatic, oblong leaves, smooth above, scaly underneath. Trusses of about 8 white or pink tubular flowers, up to ¾ in (18 mm) long, in spring. Zones 7–9.

Rhododendron cinnabarinum

↔ 7 ft (2 m) ↑ 10 ft (3 m)

Evergreen species from the Himalayas and northern Myanmar. Roundish, glaucous, green leaves. Waxy, red to deep orange, narrowly bell-shaped flowers, trusses of 3 to 9 blooms, mid- to late season. Zones 6–9.

Rhododendron concinnum

↔6–10 ft (1.8–3 m)
↑6–20 ft (1.8–6 m)

Vigorous evergreen shrub or small tree from western China. Smooth dark green leaves, scaly above, gray-brown scales underneath. Purple or reddish purple, funnel-shaped flowers, scaly on the outside, in trusses of 2 to 8, in mid- to late spring. **Pseudoyanthinum Group**, ruby red flowers. Zones 7–9.

Rhododendron cumberlandense

syn. *Rhododendron bakeri*

CUMBERLAND AZALEA

↔3–8 ft (0.9–2.4 m)
↑3–8 ft (0.9–2.4 m)

From Kentucky, Virginia, Tennessee, Georgia, and Alabama, USA. Compact deciduous shrub ranging from dwarf to medium height. Branches rather horizontal in habit. Funnel-shaped flowers in red, yellow, or orange shades appear in early to mid-summer. Zones 5–7.

Rhododendron dauricum

↔8 ft (2.4 m) ↑8 ft (2.4 m)

From northern latitudes in East Asia, from eastern Siberia to Japan. Evergreen straggly shrub, scaly young shoots, densely scaly dark green leaves, hairy beneath. Widely funnel-shaped flowers, pink or violet-pink, singly or in pairs, early season. Zones 5–8.

Rhododendron davidsonianum

↔7 ft (2 m) ↑7 ft (2 m)

Upright open shrub from western China. Lance-shaped leaves have deep scaly undersides. Flowers are carried in trusses of 2 to 6 blooms, funnel-shaped, usually white or white suffused with pink, may be pink or lavender, flecked with red or green, and appear in mid- to late spring. Zones 7–10.

Rhododendron decorum

↔8 ft (2.4 m) ↑20 ft (6 m)

Native of western China, northeastern Myanmar, and Laos. Evergreen shrub or small tree, with large smooth leaves, to 8 in (20 cm) long. Scented, white to pale pink, funnel-shaped flowers, carried in trusses of 8 to 12 blooms, late in season. *R. d.* subsp. *diaprepes* has larger leaves and flowers. Zones 7–9.

Rhododendron degronianum

↔7 ft (2 m) ↑8 ft (2.4 m)

Evergreen species from central and southern Japan. Shiny, dark green, deeply veined leaves, fawn-colored felt-like hairs underneath. Pink, rose, reddish, or white, bell-shaped flowers, carried in trusses of 6 to 15 blooms, mid- to late season. Although a slow grower, the low-growing, spreading form *R. d.* subsp. *yakushimanum* (syn. *R. yakushimanum*) is sought-after and used extensively in developing compact hybrids; from the island of Yakushima, it has glossy dark green leaves with distinctive recurved margins, and produces compact trusses of 8 to 12 rose-colored buds and pink flowers. Zones 7–9.

Rhododendron davidsonianum

Rhododendron durionifolium

↔4–7 ft (1.2–2 m)
↑5–10 ft (1.5–3 m)

A Vireya species, native to Borneo, which is mostly epiphytic in the wild. Pointed elliptic leaves, to 6 in (15 cm) long, with a heavy covering of waxy scales. It bears loose trusses of up to 35 orange to red tubular flowers, up to 1¼ in (30 mm) long, mainly in late summer. Zones 10–11.

Rhododendron edgeworthii

↔6 ft (1.8 m) ↑6 ft (1.8 m)

Evergreen species from the Himalayas, upper Myanmar, and southwestern China. Deeply textured, wrinkled leaves, brown hairy coating, scales beneath. Fragrant, white, funnel-shaped flowers, occasionally flushed with pink, in trusses of 2 to 3 flowers, mid-season. Zones 9–10.

Rhododendron elliottii

↔8 ft (2.4 m) ↑10 ft (3 m)

Evergreen shrub or small tree from northeastern India. Bright red flowers, very late, fleshy, narrowly bell-shaped, in trusses of 9 to 15 blooms. Young glandular shoots covered with hairs, dark green glossy leaves. Zones 9–10.

Rhododendron facetum

↔8 ft (2.4 m) ↑30 ft (9 m)

Closely related to *R. elliottii*; freely flowering evergreen shrub or tree from western China and northeastern Myanmar. Mat green leaves. Flowers deep pink to scarlet, narrowly bell-shaped, in trusses of 8 to 15 blooms, very late in season. Zones 8–9.

Rhododendron falconeri

↔30 ft (9 m) ↑40 ft (12 m)

A native of the Himalayas, and one of the finest rhododendrons. An evergreen plant with brown flaking bark. Large, wrinkled, dark mat green leaves are white with a reddish hairy coating underneath. Fragrant, creamy white to pink or pale cream, bell-shaped flowers, held in large trusses of 12 to 25 blooms, mid- to late season. R. f. subsp. eximium has a more persistent hairy coating under the leaves, and is regarded by some as a separate species, *R. eximium*. Zones 9–10.

Rhododendron fastigiatum

↔36 in (90 cm) ↑36 in (90 cm)

Prostrate or cushion-forming, alpine, evergreen shrub, from the western Chinese province of Yunnan. Scaly, glaucous, gray leaves. Bright, widely funnel-shaped, lavender or bluish purple flowers, bloom in trusses of 2 to 5, mid- to late season. **'Blue Steel'**, bluish green leaves. Zones 6–9.

Rhododendron ferrugineum

ALPINE ROSE

↔5 ft (1.5 m) ↑6 ft (1.8 m)

Native of the European Alps and the Pyrenees. Small, rounded, evergreen shrub. Bristly, dark green, elliptic leaves, edges rolled under, undersides densely covered with reddish brown scales. Crimson-purple to deep pink flowers, very late in the season. Other forms include: **'Album'**, white flowers; **'Coccineum'**, crimson flowers; and **'Glenarn'**, deep rose pink flowers. Zones 4–8.

Rhododendron falconeri

Rhododendron flammeum

FLAME AZALEA

↔3 ft (0.9 m) ↑6 ft (1.8 m)

Freely flowering deciduous azalea from eastern states of USA, from Georgia to South Carolina. Compact shrub, slender branches. Scarlet flowers open with leaves, late spring to early summer. Rare in cultivation. Zones 10–11.

Rhododendron fletcherianum

↔3–5 ft (0.9–1.5 m)
↑3–5 ft (0.9–1.5 m)

This neat rounded shrub is native to southwestern China and Tibet. The bristly, deep green to olive green, pointed oval leaves, up to 2 in (5 cm) long and often with a wavy edge, turn an attractive bronze color in winter. The small bright yellow flowers are produced in clusters, from early spring. Zones 7–10.

Rhododendron formosum

↔3–5 ft (0.9–1.5 m)
↑5–7 ft (1.5–2 m)

A densely foliaged shrub, native to Taiwan. The pointed narrowly elliptic leaves, to 3 in (8 cm) long, have scaly undersides. Trusses of 10 to 20 widely flared, dark-spotted white to pale pink funnel-shaped flowers, up to 2 in (5 cm) long, are often late-flowering. ***R. f.* var. *formosum*** is a compact form with bristly young growth and leaf edges; **Iteaphyllum Group** has very narrow leaves and white to soft pink flowers. Zones 8–10.

Rhododendron forrestii

↔48 in (120 cm) ↑4 in (10 cm)

Native to western China and northeastern Myanmar. Creeping, prostrate, evergreen shrub. Leaves leathery, dark green, purple-red beneath. Bright scarlet tubular-campanulate flowers, singly or in pairs, mid- to late season. Used in breeding programs. ***R. f.* subsp. *papillatum*** has narrow leaves, light brown beneath; **'Scarlet Runner'** bears scarlet flowers. ***R. f.* Repens Group** is a dwarf form with a creeping habit, leaves extensively veined, and red flowers; **'May Day'** produces scarlet flowers. Zones 8–9.

Rhododendron fulvum

Rhododendron glischrum

Rhododendron impeditum

Rhododendron fortunei

☀ ✱ ↔ 8 ft (2.4 m) ↑ 15 ft (4.5 m)

A species that is widespread in its native eastern China. An evergreen, broadly upright, sometimes spreading shrub or tree. Rough grayish brown bark, reddish, bluish, or purplish leaf stalks. Fragrant, pale pink, rose, lilac to white, bell-shaped flowers, held in trusses of 6 to 12 blooms, late in the season. ***R. f.* subsp. *discolor***, abundant pink flowers, late season; ***R. f.* Houlstonii Group**, soft pink to light purple flowers, mid-season. Zones 6–9.

Rhododendron fulvum

☀ ❄ ↔ 5–12 ft (1.5–3.5 m) ↑ 25 ft (8 m)

Evergreen rounded shrub or small tree, smaller in cultivation, from western China and northeastern Myanmar. Brownish hairs cover young growth and dark green leaves. White, pink, or mauve bell-shaped flowers, dark crimson basal blotch, trusses of 3 to 15 blooms, early to mid-season. Zones 7–9.

Rhododendron glischrum

☀ ❄ ↔ 10 ft (3 m) ↑ 25 ft (8 m)

Evergreen shrub or tree, native of western China and upper Myanmar. Rough greenish gray bark. Sticky leaf buds and flower buds. Dark or yellowish green leaves, bristly underneath. Trusses of 10 to 15 plum-rose, pink, or white, bell-shaped flowers, crimson blotch, early in the season. Zones 7–9.

Rhododendron griersonianum

☀ ❄ ↔ 8 ft (2.4 m) ↑ 8 ft (2.4 m)

Evergreen species from western China and northeastern Myanmar. Rough brown bark. Smooth leaves, heavy hair beneath. Deep red buds, bright geranium-scarlet, deep pink, or crimson flowers, in trusses of 5 to 12 blooms, late season. Zones 8–9.

Rhododendron griffithianum

☀ ❄ ↔ 10 ft (3 m) ↑ 60 ft (18 m)

Himalayan evergreen tree species with open habit. Flaking peeling bark and smooth oblong leaves. Fragrant flowers, white, shades of pale pink, even yellowish, carried in trusses of 3 to 6 blooms, in mid- to late season. Zones 8–9.

Rhododendron groenlandicum

syn. *Ledum groenlandicum*

LABRADOR TEA

☀/☀ ✱ ↔ 3 ft (0.9 m) ↑ 3 ft (0.9 m)

From Greenland and northern parts of North America; larger in the wild. Young branches covered in rusty colored hairs. Leaves elliptic to oval, dark green, with rusty hairs underneath. Clusters of white flowers, borne at the branch tips, in late spring–summer. Zones 2–8.

Rhododendron haematodes

☀ ❄ ↔ 5 ft (1.5 m) ↑ 5 ft (1.5 m)

Evergreen shrub from western China and northeastern Myanmar. Young shoots densely bristly; mature leaves matted with fawn to reddish brown hairs underneath. Fleshy, tubular-campanulate, scarlet to deep crimson flowers, late spring–early summer. R. h. subsp. chaetomallum, bristly young shoots and leaf stems. Zones 7–9.

Rhododendron hanceanum

☀ ❄ ↔ 24 in (60 cm) ↑ 12–18 in (30–45 cm)

A small western Chinese shrub. Scaly, dark green, lance-shaped leaves with pale undersides. Slightly scented, small, cream to pale yellow blooms, in many-flowered, 1 in (25 mm) long trusses, in spring. Makes a neat addition to a rockery or alpine garden. Zones 7–10.

Rhododendron hippophaeoides

☀ ✱ ↔ 5 ft (1.5 m) ↑ 5 ft (1.5 m)

Compact evergreen shrub from western China, well suited to the rock garden. Pale gray-green oblong leaves, with creamy yellow scales on the undersides. Delicate, funnel-shaped, lavender-blue or purplish blue flowers, in trusses of 3 to 8 blooms, mid- to late season. Zones 6–9.

Rhododendron hyperythrum

☀ ❄ ↔ 6 ft (1.8 m) ↑ 8 ft (2.4 m)

Evergreen species from Taiwan. Smooth young shoots, dark green elliptic leaves. White or pink funnel-shaped flowers, sometimes with red spots, mid- to late season. Zones 8–9.

Rhododendron impeditum

☀ ✱ ↔ 12 in (30 cm) ↑ 12 in (30 cm)

Compact, ground-covering evergreen, western China. Dense, shiny, dark green, scaly foliage. Violet to purple funnel-shaped flowers, small trusses of 1 to 3 blooms, mid-season. Zones 4–8.

Rhododendron indicum

INDIAN AZALEA, JAPANESE EVERGREEN AZALEA

☀ ✱ ↔ 24 in (60 cm) ↑ 36 in (90 cm)

Originating in southern Japan, this variable evergreen species is densely branched and has a low, sometimes prostrate, habit. It features a mass of shiny dark green foliage. Red broadly funnel-shaped flowers, singly or in pairs, are produced in spring. **'Balsaminiflorum'** is a dwarf form with salmon red double flowers; **'Macranthum'** is a compact shrub with orange-red flowers. Zones 6–9.

Rhododendron johnstoneanum

☀ ❄ ↔ 8 ft (2.4 m) ↑ 15 ft (4.5 m)

A native of northern India with smooth, peeling, reddish brown bark. Hairy-edged leaves are scaly on the undersides. Funnel-shaped flowers, slightly fragrant, creamy white, often flushed pink or purple, in trusses of up to 5 blooms, in spring. **'Demi-John'**, white flowers flushed with yellow-green; **'Double Diamond'**, pale yellow double flowers; **'Rubeotinctum'**, white and pink stripes on each petal. Zones 7–9.

Rhododendron keiskei

☀ ✱ ↔ 36 in (90 cm) ↑ 24 in (60 cm)

This variable evergreen species from Japan forms a low-growing, creeping, twiggy mat, more erect in shade. Bronze young shoots, dark or olive green hairy leaves, lower surfaces pale green. Creamy to pale yellow funnel-shaped flowers, carried in trusses of 2 to 6 blooms, in spring. **'Ebino'**, a freely flowering dwarf form with pale yellow flowers. Zones 5–8.

Rhododendron kiusianum

KYUSHU AZALEA

☀ ✱ ↔ 36 in (90 cm) ↑ 36 in (90 cm)

A parent of the Kurume Group of azaleas, this evergreen species from Kyushu, Japan is deciduous at higher altitudes. it is a much-branched, often prostrate shrub with small hairy leaves. The funnel-shaped flowers, in trusses of 2 to 3 blooms, rose-purple, purple, red, pink, or sometimes white, are produced in late spring. **'Mountain Gem'**, bears rose-purple flowers. Zones 6–9.

Rhododendron lacteum

☀ ❄ ↔ 12 ft (3.5 m) ↑ 12 ft (3.5 m)

Evergreen shrub or small tree found naturally in western China. Leaves have hairy undersides. Large, bell-shaped, cream flowers, sometimes flushed with pink, up to 2 in (5 cm) long, in large compact trusses of 15 to 30 blooms, in spring. Prefers a well-sheltered position. Zones 7–9.

Rhododendron laetum

☀ ⚘ ↔ 4 ft (1.2 m) ↑ 10 ft (3 m)

Native of northwestern New Guinea, Vireya species more compact in cultivation. Broad elliptic leaves. Large funnel-shaped flowers of pure golden yellow, ageing to red, orange, or salmon, held in open trusses of 6 to 8 blooms, autumn to spring. Zones 10–11.

Rhododendron johnstoneanum

Rhododendron lindleyi

Q R

Rhododendron lepidostylum

◐ ✱ ↔5 ft (1.5 m) ↑3 ft (0.9 m)

From western China. Evergreen low spreading shrub. Bluish green young foliage, leathery leaves, edges rolled downward, bristles and golden scales underneath. Flowers solitary or in 2s or 3s, funnel-shaped, clear yellow, in late spring. Zones 6–9.

Rhododendron leucaspis

◐ ❄ ↔4 ft (1.2 m) ↑4 ft (1.2 m)

Shrub from western China. Compact, rounded, evergreen. Hairy elliptic leaves. Flowers bell-shaped, milky white, often tinged pink, singly, in 2s, or threes. Very early flowers, protect from late winter frosts. Zones 7–9.

Rhododendron lindleyi

◐ ❄ ↔6 ft (1.8 m) ↑8 ft (2.4 m)

Evergreen shrub found as an epiphyte among rocks in the Himalayas region. Elliptic leaves. Large, scented, tubular, funnel-shaped flowers, 3 in (8 cm) long, white or white tinged with pink, with a yellow blotch, in trusses of 3 to 6 blooms, from late spring to early summer. Zones 9–10.

Rhododendron loranthiflorum

◐ ✢ ↔3 ft (0.9 m) ↑6 ft (1.8 m)

Vireya species from the islands around New Guinea, with distinctive, rust-colored, scaly young leaf shoots. The fragrant, creamy white, tubular flowers, carried in trusses of 4 to 5 blooms, are produced in autumn–spring. Zones 10–11.

Rhododendron luteiflorum

syn. *Rhododendron glaucophyllum var. luteiflorum*

○/◐ ✱ ↔18–32 in (45–80 cm) ↑12–36 in (60–90 cm)

This alpine species from northern Myanmar has aromatic, pointed oval to lance-shaped, olive green leaves, around 1 in (25 mm) long. Nodding, yellow-green to yellow, 1 in (25 mm) long flowers, in trusses of 3 to 6 blooms, in mid-spring. Zones 6–9.

Rhododendron loranthiflorum

Rhododendron lutescens

◐ ❄ ↔15 ft (4.5 m) ↑20 ft (6 m)

From western China, straggly habit, gray or brown flaking bark. Bright bronze-red young foliage in spring, show of color in autumn. In late winter to early spring, small, delicate, pale yellow, funnel-shaped flowers with long elegant stamens are held in trusses of 1 to 3 blooms. Zones 7–9.

Rhododendron luteum

PONTIC AZALEA

◐ ✱ ↔8 ft (2.4 m) ↑12 ft (3.5 m)

Widely grown deciduous azalea from eastern Europe, used extensively in breeding programs. Foliage colors red, orange, and purple in autumn. Tubular, funnel-shaped, clear yellow flowers, in trusses of 7 to 12 blooms, before the leaves in spring. Zones 5–9.

Rhododendron macabeanum

◐ ❄ ↔20 ft (6 m) ↑50 ft (15 m)

Evergreen from northeastern India. Shiny mature leaves, white or fawn hairy coating beneath. Bell-shaped, pale or greenish lemon yellow flowers, deep red or purple blotch, in trusses of 12 to 20 blooms, in spring. Zones 8–9.

Rhododendron macgregoriae

◐ ✢ ↔7 ft (2 m) ↑15 ft (4.5 m)

Shrub or small tree, most widespread of New Guinea's Vireya rhododendrons. Leaves with scaly undersides. Flowers light yellow to dark orange or red, narrow corolla tube, in trusses of 8 to 15 flowers, winter. Zones 10–11.

Rhododendron macrophyllum

◐ ✱ ↔12 ft (3.5 m) ↑12 ft (3.5 m)

Robust evergreen shrub from western North America. Dark green leaves, paler undersides, smooth-edged. Bell-shaped flowers, white to pink with yellow spots, in trusses of 9 to 20 blooms, late season. Zones 6–9.

Rhododendron maddenii

◐ ❄ ↔8 ft (2.4 m) ↑25 ft (8 m)

From the Himalayas, southwestern China, Myanmar, and Vietnam. Leaves smooth, thick, brownish, hairy below, heavy scaling. Large funnel-shaped flowers, white, often flushed pink or purple, yellow basal blotch, trusses of 1 to 11 blooms, late spring. Zones 9–10.

Rhododendron makinoi

◐ ❄ ↔7 ft (2 m) ↑8 ft (2.4 m)

An evergreen shrub from Japan. Long, narrow, dark green mature leaves, smooth on the uppersurfaces, brown woolly coating on undersides. Trusses of 5 to 8 funnel-shaped flowers, pink or rose, with or without red spots, in late spring. Zones 8–9.

Rhododendron mallotum

◐ ❄ ↔12 ft (3.5 m) ↑20 ft (6 m)

Evergreen shrub or small tree from western China and northeastern Myanmar. Young leaf shoots and thick, stiff, leathery leaves have a gray or brown hairy coating. Trusses of up to 20 tubular bell-shaped, red or crimson flowers, early spring. Zones 7–9.

Rhododendron maximum

GREAT LAUREL RHODODENDRON, ROSEBAY RHODODENDRON

◐ ✱ ↔7 ft (2 m) ↑6 ft (1.8 m)

Compact, spreading, evergreen shrub from eastern North America. Smooth leaves, fine hairy coating underneath. Bell-shaped flowers white to pinkish purple with yellow-green spots, in late spring–early summer. **'Summertime'**, white flowers, tips of petals flushed reddish purple. Zones 3–8.

Rhododendron megeratum

Rhododendron megeratum

◐ ❄ ↔15 in (38 cm) ↑15–30 in (38–75 cm)

Found growing naturally in northeastern India, northeastern Myanmar, and western China. A very early-flowering, evergreen, prostrate species. The small almost circular leaves have a whitish hairy coating on the undersides. It produces broad, bell-shaped, creamy white to yellow flowers. Zones 9–10.

Rhododendron minus

◐ ✱ ↔3–5 ft (0.9–1.5 m) ↑3–5 ft (0.9–1.5 m)

Small evergreen from North America. Pointed elliptic leaves, densely scaly below. Flowers usually scaly, white to pink or mauve, in trusses of 6 to 12 blooms, in mid-spring. **Carolinianum Group**, dark green leaves, dense scales below; pink or pale rose-purple flowers, in summer. Zones 4–9.

Rhododendron molle

DECIDUOUS AZALEA

◐ ❄ ↔4 ft (1.2 m) ↑4 ft (1.2 m)

This small deciduous azalea is native to eastern China. The funnel-shaped flowers are a golden yellow or orange color with a large greenish blotch, in trusses of 6 to 12 blooms; they open with or before the mid-green leaves, in mid-spring. ***R. m.* subsp. *japonicum*** (syn. *R. japonicum*), from Japan, yellow or orange flowers, one parent of the Mollis group of hybrids. Zones 7–9.

Rhododendron mucronulatum

KOREAN RHODODENDRON

◐ ✱ ↔3 ft (0.9 m) ↑6 ft (1.8 m)

Straggly deciduous shrub from eastern Russia, northern and central China, Mongolia, Korea, and Japan. Elliptic to lance-shaped leaves. Funnel-shaped bright mauve-pink flowers, protruding stamens, blue anthers, in spring, before the foliage. **'Alba'** has white flowers; **'Cornell Pink'** ★, large clear pink flowers; **'Crater's Edge'**, deep pink flowers; **'Mahogany Red'**, wine red flowers tinged bronze. Zones 4–8.

Rhododendron nuttallii

◐ ❄ ↔20 ft (6 m) ↑35 ft (10 m)

From the Himalayas, western China, northern Myanmar, and northern India. Evergreen large shrub or small tree. Purplish brown bark, crimson-purple young growth, wrinkled leaves. Creamy white bell-shaped flowers, deep yellow throat, in trusses of 7 blooms, mid- to late spring. Zones 9–10.

Rhododendron occidentale

Rhododendron × *obtusum*

KURUME AZALEA

↔ 36 in (90 cm) ↑ 36 in (90 cm)

Naturally occurring hybrid between *R. kiusianum* and *R. kaempferi,* from Japan. Twiggy, sometimes prostrate shrub. Bright green leaves, preceded by densely bristly brown leaf shoots. Bright red, scarlet, or crimson funnel-shaped flowers, in trusses of 1 to 3 blooms, in late spring. Zones 6–9.

Rhododendron occidentale

WESTERN AZALEA

↔ 5 ft (1.5 m) ↑ 5 ft (1.5 m)

Variable deciduous, azalea from western USA. Bright green foliage turns bronze, then scarlet, crimson, or yellow in autumn. Fragrant, white or light pink, funnel-shaped flowers, deep yellow blotch, in mid-spring. Zones 6–9.

Rhododendron orbiculare

↔ 10 ft (3 m) ↑ 10 ft (3 m)

An evergreen from western China. Rounded bright green leaves, deeply notched bases. Rose to deep red bell-shaped flowers, up to 2½ in (6 cm) long, in trusses of 7 to 10 blooms, in spring. Zones 6–9.

Rhododendron orbiculatum

↔ 36 in (90 cm) ↑ 36 in (90 cm)

This compact Vireya rhododendron comes from the island of Borneo. It has thick rounded leaves. The large, delicate, orchid-like flowers, white or silvery pink, are held in loose trusses

Rhododendron periclymenoides

of up to 5 blooms. This species makes a good specimen for hanging baskets and containers. Zones 10–11.

Rhododendron pachysanthum

↔ 3 ft (0.9 m) ↑ 4 ft (1.2 m)

Compact, rounded, evergreen shrub from Taiwan. Dark green leaves have dense brownish hair on the undersides. New growth felted all over with pale brownish hairs. Trusses of 8 to 10, sometimes 20, bell-shaped white flowers, densely spotted with crimson, in spring. Zones 7–9.

Rhododendron pemakoense

↔ 24 in (60 cm) ↑ 24 in (60 cm)

Native to southwestern China. A prostrate, dwarf, densely branched, evergreen rhododendron. Foliage has dense covering of golden or dark brown scales. The pinkish purple to purple-mauve or violet-pink, bell-shaped, hairy flowers, carried singly or in pairs, are produced in spring. Zones 6–9.

Rhododendron racemosum

Rhododendron pentaphyllum

↔ 4 ft (1.2 m) ↑ 4 ft (1.2 m)

Native of central and southern Japan. Deciduous azalea, prefers a moist sheltered position. Leaves clustered in whorls of 5 at branch tips, coloring in autumn. Rose pink, bell-shaped flowers, borne singly or in pairs, before the foliage, in spring. Zones 7–9.

Rhododendron periclymenoides

syn. *Rhododendron nudiflorum*

PINXTERBLOOM AZALEA

↔ 8 ft (2.4 m) ↑ 10 ft (3 m)

Deciduous azalea from eastern North America. Trusses of 6 to 12 fragrant funnel-shaped flowers, white, pale pink, or violet-red, with distinctive long stamens and a long corolla tube, open just before or with the bright green leaves, in late spring. Zones 3–9.

Rhododendron prinophyllum

MOUNTAIN PINK, ROSESHELL AZALEA

↔ 6–10 ft (1.8–3 m)
↑ 6–15 ft (1.8–4.5 m)

Deciduous azalea found from Quebec in Canada southward to northern central USA. Small oblong leaves, hairy undersides. Clusters of 5 to 9 funnel-shaped flowers, in pink shades, with a dark blotch, open with the leaves, in late spring. Zones 4–9.

Rhododendron protistum

↔ 15 ft (4.5 m) ↑ 100 ft (30 m)

Evergreen species from western China and northern Myanmar; usually a tall shrub in cultivation. Young shoots, dense, yellowish gray, hairy coating; dark green leaves. Large trusses of 20 to 30 bell-shaped creamy white flowers, flushed with rose, in late winter to early spring. Protect in cooler areas. Zones 9–10.

Rhododendron prunifolium

↔ 4 ft (1.2 m) ↑ 6 ft (1.8 m)

Deciduous azalea, allied to *R. calendulaceum*, native to a limited area of Alabama and Georgia, USA. Smooth leaves, often edged with tiny hairs. Heads of rich scarlet flowers, about 1½ in (35 mm) wide, in late spring. Zones 6–9.

Rhododendron quinquefolium

FIVE-LEAF AZALEA

↔ 4–8 ft (1.2–2.4 m)
↑ 8–25 ft (2.4–8 m)

Deciduous azalea from central Japan. Oval-shaped leaves, in whorls of 4 to 5, at ends of branches. Pure white flowers with green spots appear in late spring. **'Five Arrows'**, white flowers spotted with olive green. Zones 6–8.

Rhododendron racemosum

↔ 5 ft (1.5 m) ↑ 5 ft (1.5 m)

Widely variable evergreen shrub from western China with smooth leathery leaves. Funnel-shaped flowers, white to pale pink, held in trusses of up to 6 blooms, are produced in spring. **'Forrest'**, dwarf form, pink flowers; **'Glendoick'**, taller, with deep pink flowers; **'Rock Rose'**, bright purplish pink flowers. Zones 5–8.

Rhododendron saluenense

↔ 18–60 in (45–150 cm)
↑ 18–60 in (45–150 cm)

Native to northeastern Myanmar and western China. A robust, prostrate, variable, evergreen shrub. Shiny, dark green, aromatic leaves. Funnel-shaped flowers, deep pinkish purple, in trusses of 2 to 5 blooms, in spring. Zones 6–9.

Rhododendron schlippenbachii

ROYAL AZALEA

↔ 15 ft (4.5 m) ↑ 15 ft (4.5 m)

This prevalent deciduous azalea from Korea and far eastern Russia has light green foliage, in whorls at the ends of the branches, which turns bronze in autumn. The widely funnel-shaped star-like flowers, pale pink or white, open with or shortly after the leaves, in late spring. Zones 4–8.

Rhododendron scopulorum

↔ 8 ft (2.4 m) ↑ 15 ft (4.5 m)

This native of southwestern China is smaller in cultivation than in the wild. Dark green grooved leaves, pale green and scaly underneath. Fragrant, white or apple blossom pink, widely funnel-shaped flowers, in trusses of 2 to 7 blooms, crinkled margins, yellowish blotch, scaly, mid- to late season. Zones 9–10.

Rhododendron sinogrande

↔ 30 ft (9 m) ↑ 50 ft (15 m)

An evergreen understory tree from western China and northern Myanmar, one of the largest rhododendrons. Long, dark green, heavily wrinkled leaves; silvery white, pale brown, or tan coating underneath. Creamy white or yellow flowers, held in trusses of 15 to 30 blooms, appear in mid-spring. Zones 8–9.

Rhododendron smirnowii

TURKISH RHODODENDRON

↔15 ft (4.5 m) ↑12 ft (3.5 m)

Robust evergreen species from northeastern Turkey and adjacent Georgia. Dense, white, woolly hairs cover ovaries, young leaf growth, and undersides of mature leaves. Funnel-shaped flowers, pink with yellow spots, in trusses of 10 to 12 flowers, late season. Zones 4–9.

Rhododendron stenopetalum

↔3–5 ft (0.9–1.5 m) ↑3–6 ft (0.9–1.8 m)

A Japanese evergreen azalea, with pointed elliptic leaves, 1 in (25 mm) long, hairy. Deep pink to purple-red flowers, to 1½ in (35 mm) wide. **'Linearifolium'** (syn. *R. linearifolium*), the spider azalea, very narrow strappy leaves and petals. Zones 8–10.

Rhododendron strigillosum

↔10 ft (3 m) ↑12 ft (3.5 m)

A native of western China. Evergreen bushy shrub or small tree. Bristly young leaf shoots, bright green leaves. Brilliant crimson narrowly bell-shaped flowers, in trusses of 8 to 12 blooms, early season. Zones 8–9.

Rhododendron sutchuenense

↔20 ft (6 m) ↑30 ft (9 m)

From western China. Large, umbrella-shaped, evergreen shrub, smaller in cultivation. Smooth dark green leaves. Widely bell-shaped flowers, pale pink to pale mauve, in open trusses of 10 blooms, in late winter to early spring. Zones 6–9.

Rhododendron tephropeplum

↔3–8 ft (0.9–2.4 m) ↑3–8 ft (0.9–2.4 m)

From the Himalayas and northeastern India and Myanmar. Compact evergreen shrub; scaly brown bark. Dark green shiny leaves, scaly underneath. Trusses of 3 to 9 dark or pale rose, pink, or crimson-purple flowers, in spring. Spreading forms suited to rock gardens. Zones 8–9.

Rhododendron thomsonii

↔2–20 ft (0.6–6 m) ↑2–20 ft (0.6–6 m)

Variable evergreen species found in the Himalayas, clinging to steep, rocky, exposed sites. Reddish brown, fawn, or pinkish bark. Thick, leathery, rounded leaves. Bell-shaped flowers, rich blood red or deep crimson, darker spots, in trusses of 6 to 13 blooms, in spring. Zones 6–9.

Rhododendron tomentosum

syn. *Ledum palustre*

CRYSTAL TEA, MARSH LEDUM, WILD ROSEMARY

↔3 ft (0.9 m) ↑1–4 ft (0.3–1.2 m)

Widespread across northern and central Europe, northern Asia, and northern North America. Spreading or erect evergreen shrub. Young shoots covered in red-brown hairs; dark green leaves with incurved edges. Clusters of white flowers, borne at branch tips, in late spring–early summer. Zones 2–8.

Rhododendron trichanthum

syn. *Rhododendron villosum*

↔8 ft (2.4 m) ↑8 ft (2.4 m)

Evergreen rhododendron from western China, 20 ft (6 m) high in the wild. Leaf shoots densely covered with bristles. Purple funnel-shaped flowers, in trusses of 3 to 5 blooms, late in the season. Sheltered position. Zones 7–9.

Rhododendron sutchuenense

Rhododendron trichostomum

↔3 ft (0.9 m) ↑5 ft (1.5 m)

Highly variable evergreen shrub from western China; normally a compact, often tiny, twiggy, intricately branched, miniature bush. Aromatic, narrow, stiff, leathery, dark green leaves. Tiny flowers white, pink, or deep rose, in spherical trusses of 8 to 20 blooms, in late spring. Zones 7–9.

Rhododendron ungernii

↔10 ft (3 m) ↑3–20 ft (0.9–6 m)

Native to northeastern Turkey and Georgia. Evergreen shrub or small tree, flaking brown bark. Large dark green leaves; dense, woolly, white coating on undersides and shoots. White funnel-campanulate flowers, in trusses of 12 to 30 blooms, in summer. Zones 5–9.

Rhododendron vaseyi

PINK-SHELL AZALEA

↔15 ft (4.5 m) ↑15 ft (4.5 m)

Deciduous azalea from eastern North America. Shiny dark green leaves. Trusses of 4 to 8 funnel-shaped flowers, rose pink, pale pink, or white, with orange-red or red spots, open before the leaves in late spring. Zones 4–9.

Rhododendron viscosum

SWAMP AZALEA, SWAMP HONEYSUCKLE

↔8 ft (2.4 m) ↑8 ft (2.4 m)

This compact deciduous azalea is native to eastern and central North America. New leaf growth is yellowish or grayish brown. Dark green leaves have paler undersides. Funnel-shaped white flowers, spicy fragrance, held in trusses of 4 to 9 blooms, in late spring to early summer, after new leaves appear. Zones 4–9.

Rhododendron wardii

↔15 ft (4.5 m) ↑25 ft (8 m)

This evergreen shrub from western China has grayish brown bark. The leathery, dark green, rounded leaves are pale green and glaucous underneath. Saucer-shaped pale yellow or bright yellow flowers, in loose trusses of 5 to 14 blooms, are produced in late spring. Zones 7–9.

Rhododendron thomsonii

Rhododendron williamsianum

↔4 ft (1.2 m) ↑5 ft (1.5 m)

Evergreen shrub, native to western China. Bristly young shoots, rounded leaves, reddish glands underneath. The bell-shaped flowers, pale pink with darker spots, appear in 2s or 3s, in spring. Zones 7–9.

Rhododendron wiltonii

↔15 ft (4.5 m) ↑15 ft (4.5 m)

This evergreen species from western China has olive green shiny leaves that have a dense, cinnamon-colored, hairy coating on the undersides. Bell-shaped flowers, white to pink, held in trusses of 6 to 10 blooms, appear in spring. Zones 6–9.

Rhododendron yedoense

KOREAN AZALEA, YODOGAWA AZALEA

↔36 in (90 cm) ↑36 in (90 cm)

Deciduous or semi-deciduous azalea species from Korea. Compact densely branched shrub, foliage turning rich orange and crimson in autumn. The fragrant, double, funnel-shaped, lilac-purple flowers, held in trusses of 2 to 4 blooms, are produced in late spring. Originally named from this double-flowered cultivated form, wild plants were subsequently named ***R. y.* var. *poukhanense*** ★, and feature single pale to deep pink flowers. Zones 5–8.

Rhododendron yunnanense

↔10 ft (3 m) ↑12 ft (3.5 m)

This evergreen shrub from northeastern Myanmar and western China is deciduous in cooler conditions. It has narrow leaves and scaly branchlets. Abundant, white, pale pink, rose pink, rose-lavender, or lavender, funnel-shaped flowers, densely spotted with red, green, or yellow, in trusses of 3 to 5 blooms, are borne in late spring. Zones 7–9.

Rhododendron Hybrid Cultivars

Rhododendron hybrids are cultivated as ornamental plants, valued for their masses of colorful flowers and year-round foliage in great diversity of form; some are also sought-after for their attractive textured bark and rich fragrance. The new leaf shoots of evergreen rhododendrons often form attractive perpendicular "candle-sticks," while mature leaves vary enormously in size. The foliage of deciduous azaleas progresses through the growing season from bright green shoots in spring to bronze in summer, followed by rich reds to yellows in autumn before falling.

Rhododendron, Hybrid Cultivar, Hardy Small, 'Blue Tit'

Rhododendrum, Hybrid Cultivar, Hardy Small, 'Carmen'

Rhododendron, Hybrid Cultivar, Hardy Medium, 'Anah Kruschke'

HARDY SMALL HYBRIDS

☀ ✱ ↔ 12–40 in (30–100 cm)
↑ 12–40 in (30–100 cm)

The hardy small hybrids are a variable group, ranging from those derived from tiny alpine species and best suited to rockery cultivation to dense mounding bushes with large leaves and upright flower trusses. **'Blue Crown'** has deep lilac-blue or violet flowers with a lighter center blotched with magenta, held in trusses of 20 blooms, mid- to late season; **'Blue Tit'**, small leaves, abundant grayish blue flowers; **'Bric-à-Brac'**, small, rounded, downy leaves, small white flowers with faint pink markings on upper lobes, contrasting chocolate-colored anthers; **'Carmen'**, a dwarf form, less than 12 in (30 cm) high, deep red bell-shaped flowers, in trusses of 2 to 5 blooms, in early to mid-season; **'Chikor'**, soft yellow flowers, delicate foliage which turns to red in winter; **'Cilpenense'**, shiny deep forest green foliage, blush pink bell-shaped flowers with a deeper pink shading, early in the season; **'Creeping Jenny'** (syn. 'Jenny'), bright red funnel-campanulate flowers, held in large loose trusses of 5 to 6 blooms, early to mid-season; **'Curlew'**, abundant soft yellow flowers with green-brown markings; **'Dora Amateis'** bears pure white fragrant flowers, lightly spotted with green, held in trusses of 3 to 6 blooms, in early to mid-season; **'Elizabeth'** has bright red funnel-campanulate flowers, in loose trusses of 6 to 8 blooms, early to mid-season; **'Ginny Gee'** bears dark pink flowers shading to shell pink, with white stripes, carried in trusses of 4 to 5 blooms, in early to mid-season; **'Jingle Bells'** produces orange flowers with a red throat that fade to yellow, mid-season; **'Lemon Mist'**, small, bright greenish yellow, funnel-shaped flowers in trusses of 2 to 3 blooms, early to mid-season; **'May Day'**, cerise or light scarlet funnel-shaped flowers in loose trusses of 8 blooms, in early to mid-season; **'Nancy Evans'**, buds red, flowers yellow, orange-tinted, leathery rounded leaves; **'Paprika Spiced'**, light buff yellow flowers, orange-red throat and spotting, rounded trusses, mid-season; **'Prostigiatum'**, dwarf shrub, tiny grayish green leaves, rich deep purple flowers, in trusses of 2 to 3 blooms, in mid- to late season; **'Ptarmigan'**, delicate foliage, densely scaly underneath, broadly funnel-shaped white flowers, in terminal clusters of several trusses of 2 to 3 blooms, in early to mid-season; **'Ramapo'**, pinkish violet flowers, early to mid-season, almost circular leaves with distinctive deep metallic hue in winter; **'Ruby Hart'**, dark blackish red flowers, in loose trusses of 7 blooms, early to mid-season; **'Scarlet Wonder'**, bright cardinal red bell-shaped flowers with wavy edges, in trusses of 5 to 7 blooms, mid-season; **'Snow Lady'**, dark green hairy leaves, white flowers with dark anthers, early to mid-season. Zones 6–9.

HARDY MEDIUM HYBRIDS

☀ ✱ ↔ 2–6 ft (0.6–1.8 m)
↑ 3–6 ft (0.9–1.8 m)

The medium-sized hybrids are the plants best suited to general cultivation and this size range is where most hybridizers have placed the emphasis of their development programs. Consequently this group encompasses hundreds of beautiful plants that bloom in the full color range over the entire flowering season. **'Alison Johnstone'**, bluish gray waxy foliage, cream flowers initially, changing to a delicate light apricot-pink, in trusses of 9 blooms, early to mid-season; **'Anah Kruschke'**, conical trusses of lavender to purple-red flowers, late spring; **'Arthur Bedford'** (syn. 'A. Bedford'), red-stemmed glossy green leaves, flowers light mauve with darker lobes, marked with deep rose to almost black, in domed trusses of 16 funnel-shaped blooms; **'Arthur J. Ivens'**, rose pink bell-shaped flowers; **'Award'**, fragrant white flowers with light yellow flare, margins shaded with pink, in ball-shaped trusses of 14 blooms, mid-season; **'Black Magic'**, intense dark red, mid-season to late, lustrous foliage; **'Blue Diamond'**, deep lilac-blue flowers, early to mid-season; **'Bow Bells'**, cup-shaped light pink flowers, in loose trusses of 4 to 7 blooms, early to mid-season; **'C. I. S.'**, twisted leaf tips, orange-yellow flowers, bright orange-red throat, in trusses of about 11 blooms, mid-season; **'C. P. Raffill'**, deep orange-red to red flowers, in large rounded trusses, late in season; **'Canary'**, deeply veined leaves, bright lemon yellow flowers, in tight trusses, early to mid-season; 'Cary Ann', deep pink to rose red flowers, mid-season, dark foliage; 'Chevalier Felix de Sauvage', deep coral pink with darker throat, early to mid-season, long heavily veined leaves; **'Christmas Cheer'**, mid-pink and white flowers, small trusses, very early; **'Creamy Chiffon'**, salmon-orange buds, creamy yellow double flowers, in mid- to late season; **'Crossbill'**, small, tubular flowers, yellow flushed with apricot, early in season; **'Dido'**, soft salmon shading to coral, frilled petals, many crowded trusses, mid-season to late; **'Fabia'**, unusual red to tangerine orange shading, mid-season, also grex with several cultivars, such as terracotta-colored 'Fabia Roman Pottery'; **'Fireman Jeff'**, bright blood red flowers, bright red calyx, in compact trusses of 10 blooms, mid-season; **'Flora Markeeta'**, coral pink buds open to ivory white flowers, flushed with coral, fringed with bright pink, in rounded trusses of 10 blooms, early to mid-season; **'Florence Mann'**, one of the best "blue" rhododendrons in milder climates with deep lavender-blue or lavender-violet flowers, early to mid-season; **'Furnivall's Daughter'**, bright pink flowers with a cherry blotch, in conical trusses of 15 blooms, mid-season; **'Golden Star'**, mimosa yellow flowers, with 7 wavy lobes, in ball-shaped trusses of up to 13 blooms, in mid- to late season; **'Goldflimmer'**, striking variegated foliage, mauve flowers, late in season; **'Hallelujah'** ★, massed trusses of large, deep rose red flowers, mid-season, lush dark foliage; **'Helene Schiffner'**, pure white flowers with faint yellow to brown markings, in upright, dome-shaped trusses; **'Horizon Monarch'**, light yellow flowers open from orange-red buds, mid-season, lush foliage; **'Hotei'**, canary yellow bell-shaped flowers with a darker throat, in round trusses of 12 blooms, mid-season; **'Humming Bird'**, deep pink to red bell-shaped flowers, in loose trusses of 4 to 5 blooms, early to mid-season; **'Lady Clementine Mitford'** (syn. 'Lady C. Mitford') has glossy green foliage covered with silver hairs when young, soft peach-pink flowers, darker at the edges, slight yellow eye, mid- to late season; **'Letty Edwards'**, pale pink buds opening to pale primrose yellow flowers, in rounded trusses of 9 to 11 blooms, mid-season; **'Markeeta's Prize'**, leathery dark green leaves, scarlet-red flowers, in trusses of 12 blooms, mid-season; **'Matador'**, dark orange-red tubular flowers, in trusses of 8 blooms, early to mid-season; **'Midnight'**, dark green glossy foliage, very deep magenta-mauve flowers, blackish throat, heavily spotted with dark red on upper lobe, in rounded trusses of 16 blooms, mid- to late season; **'Moonstone'**, creamy yellow, pink, or cream, bell-shaped flowers, flushed with pink, in loose trusses of 3 to 5 blooms, early to mid-season; **'Mount Everest'**, apricot flowers, yellowish inside; **'Mrs A. T. de la Mare**, large, white, upright flowers with a faint green blotch, in large dome-shaped trusses of 12 to 14 blooms, mid-season; **'Mrs Betty Robertson'** (syn. 'Mrs Betty Robinson'), soft creamy yellow flowers with red speckled upper petal, in upright dome-shaped trusses, mid-season; **'Mrs E. C. Stirling'**, slightly ruffled, pink, medium-sized blooms, mid-to late season; **'Mrs Furnivall'**, widely funnel-shaped light rose pink flowers, paler at the center, with conspicuous deep sienna blotch, in large trusses, mid- to late season; **'Mrs T. H. Lowinsky'**, near-white flowers, pink in bud, with striking orange-brown blotch, late; **'Naomi'**, large trusses of fragrant pale pink flowers, mid-season, one of a grex including large-leafed 'Naomi Astarte' and deep pink-flowered 'Naomi Pink Beauty'; **'Olin O. Dobbs'**, striking deep purple-red flowers, dark blotch, waxy texture, mid-season, dark foliage; **'PJM'**, small, rounded, aromatic leaves, green in summer, turning mahogany in winter, bright lavender-pink flowers, early in season; **'President Roosevelt'**, strongly variegated leaves, frilled flowers white flushed red with bold red edging, in medium-sized conical trusses early to mid-season; **'Purpureum Elegans'**, bluish purple flowers marked green or brown, in dense rounded trusses, mid- to late season; **'Ring of Fire'**, soft yellow flowers shading to broad coral red edge, mid-season to late, dense, well-foliaged; 'Rubicon' ★, glowing red flowers in tight, rounded trusses, early to mid-season, lush heavily veined foliage; **'Russautinii'**, masses of lavender-blue flowers with a darker eye, in trusses of 2 to 5 blooms, early to mid-season; **'Seta'**, very narrow, bell-shaped flowers of white with bold margins of rose pink, early in the season, over a long period; **'Tally Ho'**, clear orange-red flowers, in compact trusses, late in the season; **'The Hon. Jean Marie de Montague'** (syn. 'Jean Mary Montague'), thick emerald green leaves, large bright scarlet flowers, in dome-shaped trusses of 10 to 14 blooms, in mid-season; **'Unique'**, strong pink buds open to subtle apricot-pink flowers on medium-sized trusses, early- to mid-season; **'Vanessa Pastel'**, pointed mossy green leaves, brick red flowers, changing to apricot then to deep cream, with a bronze-yellow throat, in trusses, mid- to late season, a pinker variety is also available; **'Winsome'**, reddish winter buds open to rosy cerise flowers, in mid-season; **'Yellow Hammer'**, small, light green, and scaly leaves, very deep yellow tubular flowers, in trusses of 3 blooms, early to mid-season. Zones 6–9.

HARDY TALL HYBRIDS

☀ ❄ ↔5–17 ft (1.5–5 m)
↑6–35 ft (1.8–10 m)

Many of the taller hybrids will eventually become tree-like, though they take many years to reach such proportions. While they undoubtedly demand more space, few sights are more spectacular than a large rhododendron in full bloom. **'Alice'** takes some years before producing large conical flower trusses of pale rose or frosty pink flowers, mid-season; **'America'**, dark purple-red flowers, mid-season to late, extremely hardy; **'Anna Rose Whitney'**, large mid-green leaves, upright trusses of deep pink flowers; **'Auguste van Geert'**, large reddish purple flowers, in generous trusses, early in the season; **'Beauty of Littleworth'**, pure white flowers, spotted with dark purple markings, in very large trusses of 16 to 19 blooms, mid-season; **'Bernstein'**, old gold flowers with vivid coral-red flare; **'Betty Wormald'**, pastel pink flowers, paler center and light purple spotting, in huge dome-shaped trusses, late season; **'Bibiani'**, deep bright blood red flowers, in dense rounded trusses of 14 blooms, early in season; **'Boddaertianum'** (syn. 'Croix d'Anvers'), lavender-pink buds opening as white flowers, dark purple blotch, crimson ray, in compact rounded trusses of 18 to 22 blooms, mid-season; **'Brigitte'**, purple flowers, reddening toward the center, green blotch; **'Broughtonii'**, rosy crimson flowers, darker spots, in large pyramid-shaped trusses of 20 blooms, mid-season; **'Caractacus'**, purplish red flowers, lighter shading toward center; **'Carita'**, rich green leaves, pink buds open to primrose yellow flowers; **'Cornubia'**, blood red flowers, in large conical trusses, early season; **'Crest'** (syn. 'Hawk Crest'), bright primrose yellow flowers, slightly darkening around throat, in large dome-shaped trusses, mid-season; **'Cunningham's White'**, white flowers, yellowish green at center; **'David'**, deep red bell-shaped flowers, white anthers and frilly margins, in loose trusses, early to mid-season; **'Everestianum'**, rosy lilac flowers, spotted in throat, frilled edges, in compact rounded trusses of about 15 blooms, mid- to late season; **'Fastuosum Flore Pleno'**, deep green foliage, medium-sized, semi-double, mauve flowers, in loose trusses, mid- to late season; **'Fire Bird'**, glowing salmon red flowers, bright yellow anthers, in large trusses, mid- to late season; **'Fusilier'**, bright orange-red flowers, in medium-sized trusses, mid- to late season; **'Gill's Crimson'**, bright blood red long-lasting flowers, in tight rounded trusses, early to mid-season; **'Gomer Waterer'**, pure white flowers open from slightly rose pink-tinged buds, mid- to late season; **'Janet Blair'**, light pink, golden throat markings, frilled petals, mid-season to late, lush slightly in-rolled leaves; **'Lady Chamberlain'**, slender willowy branches, bluish green new foliage, fleshy, tubular, trumpet-shaped flowers, bright orange to salmon pink, in drooping trusses of 3 to 6 blooms, mid- to late season; 'Lady Rosebery', tubular flowers, deep reddish pink and salmon tones, mid-season, glossy aromatic foliage; **'Lem's Monarch'**, deep pink buds open white with broad pink edge, large trusses, mid-season, impressive foliage; **Loderi**, grex of many large-leafed, fragrant, pink-flowered cultivars, including near-white-flowered 'King George', pale pink 'Horsham', and mid-pink 'Pink Diamond'; **'Loder's White'**, slightly fragrant flowers, white, edged with pale lilac, tinge of yellow in throat, in large conical trusses, mid-season; **'Mrs Charles E. Pearson'**, lush deep green foliage, pale pinkish mauve flowers edged with lavender, heavy chestnut spotting, in very large conical trusses, mid- to late season; **'Mrs G. W. Leak'**, startling bright pink flowers, deep reddish carmine blotch, crimson markings, in large, compact, conical trusses, early to mid-season; **'One Thousand Butterflies'** ★, shades of lavender-pink, dark edges and throat, massed large trusses, mid-season to late; **'Phyllis Korn'**, cream with golden-brown throat blotch, mid-season, densely foliaged; **'Pink Pearl'**, mid-pink buds open pale pink, open trusses, very prolific, tree-like when mature; **'Red Admiral'**, glowing red bell-shaped flowers, early in season; 'Sappho', white with large near-black blotch, bold contrast, mid-season to late; **'Scintillation'**, pastel pink flowers, yellowish brown flare in the throat, in large trusses of about 15 blooms, mid-season; **'Sir Charles Lemon'**, pure white flowers faintly spotted in the throat, in large rounded trusses, early to mid-season; **'Souvenir de Doctor S. Endtz'**, rose pink buds open to rich pink widely funnel-shaped flowers, marked with a crimson ray, in domed trusses of 15 to 17 blooms, mid-season; **'Susan'**, lavender flowers, fading to nearly white, dark margins, purple spots, rounded trusses of about 12 blooms, mid-season; **'Taurus'**, long-lasting deep green leaves, large trusses of bright red flowers, with faint black spotting; **'Trewithen Orange'**, sea-green foliage, tubular deep orange-brown flowers, in loose pendulous trusses, mid-season; **'Trude Webster'**, slightly twisted glossy leaves, clear pink flowers, spotting on upper lobe, mid-season; **'Van Nes Sensation'** ★, deep lavender-pink buds opening pale pink, large flowers in large trusses, mid-season; **'Viennese Waltz'**, light salmon shading to pale center, frilled, early to mid-season; **'White Gold'**, white flowers, deep golden brown blotch, mid-season to late, sun-sensitive foliage. Zones 6–9.

R., HC, Hardy Tall, 'Betty Wormald'

Rhododendron, Hybrid Cultivar, Hardy Tall, 'Fastuosum Flore Pleno'

Rhododendron, Hybrid Cultivar, Vireya, 'Cristo Rey'

R., Hybrid Cultivar, Yak, 'Golden Torch'

R., HC, Deciduous Azalea, Ghent, 'Pucella'

VIREYA HYBRIDS

↔ 12–60 in (30–150 cm)
↕ 18–72 in (45–180 cm)

Extending the range of the genus *Rhododendron* into the Southern Hemisphere, these tropical Southeast Asian species enjoyed great popularity in Victorian times and are now back in vogue, with many new hybrids appearing recently. Part of their appeal lies in their vivid coloration, with fragrance and non-seasonal flowering completing the package. **'Alisa Nicole'**, cerise pink bell-shaped flowers; **'Aravir'**, beautifully fragrant, soft, white, tubular flowers, in domed trusses of 7 to 10 blooms; **'Bold Janus'**, very large, lightly perfumed flowers of apricot edged with pink; **'Coral Flare'**, large coral pink flowers in trusses of 3 to 7 blooms, throughout the year; **'Craig Faragher'**, damask pink or mauve tubular flowers, lobes of pale cyclamen pink, in trusses of 6 to 8 blooms; **'Cristo Rey'**, brilliant orange flowers with yellow center; **'Dresden Doll'**, waxy, heavily veined, lime green leaves, deep salmon pink flowers with cream throat; **'Esprit de Joie'**, large, fragrant, soft rose pink flowers with creamy throat, in trusses of 4 to 6 blooms; **'Great Scent-sation'**, large, highly fragrant, bell-shaped, carmine pink flowers; **'Hari's Choice'**, generous vivid crimson flowers in very full trusses; **'Iced Primrose'**, beautifully fragrant, very large, creamy primrose flowers, with a faint hint of pastel green in throat; **'Liberty Bar'**, red flowers, in trusses of 10 to 15 blooms, flowering throughout year; **'Little One'**, tiny mandarin-pink flowers, in trusses of 2 to 3 blooms, appear for up to 3 months; **'Littlest Angel'**, petite, waxy, and deep red flowers in trusses of 4 blooms; **'Nancy Miller Adler'**, very glossy foliage, soft blush pink flowers; **'Ne Plus Ultra'**, waxy foliage, bright red, tubular, funnel-shaped flowers, in trusses of 8 to 14 blooms; **'Niugini Firebird'**, medium-sized trumpet flowers, bright red with glowing orange throat; **'Popcorn'**, trusses of 10 to 14 pale cream flowers with white lobes; **'Princess Alexandra'**, open trusses of tubular, medium-sized, slightly flared flowers of white, sometimes with a blush of pale pink; **'Scarlet Beauty'**, bright scarlet-orange flowers, deep yellow throat, mid-red lobes; **'Simbu Sunset'**, large, bicolored, funnel-shaped flowers, brilliant orange with buttercup yellow center, in trusses of 4 to 6 blooms; **'Sir George Holford'**, orange-yellow flowers, in trusses of 8 to 10 blooms; **'Souvenir de J. H. Mangles'**, very full trusses of soft coral red flowers; **'Sweet Amanda'**, large, fragrant, tubular, pale yellow flowers in trusses of 5 to 8 blooms; **'Sweet Wendy'**, abundant, perfumed, light orange flowers; **'Triumphans'** has glowing scarlet-crimson flowers, in trusses of 8 to 14 blooms, from winter to early spring; **'Tropic Fanfare'**, trusses of 8 to 10 bright pink waxy flowers; **'Tropic Tango'**, delicate flowers of soft tangerine; **'Wattlebird'** (syn. 'Wattle Bird'), loose trusses of 7 to 9 large, open, flared, bell-shaped flowers, bright clear golden yellow. Zones 10–12.

YAK HYBRIDS

↔ 2–5 ft (0.6–1.5 m)
↕ 1–6 ft (0.3–1.8 m)

"Yaks" are hybrids in which the dominant parent is *Rhododendron degronianum* subsp. *yakushimanum*. They are low growing and very hardy, with attractive foliage and abundant flowers, usually in combinations of pink and white. **'Bashful'**, camellia pink flowers, deeper shades of rose, reddish brown blotch, early in season; **'Doc'**, rose pink flowers with deeper rims and spots on the upper lobes, in rounded trusses of 9 blooms, in mid-season; **'Dopey'** has glossy, red, bell-shaped flowers, paler toward edges, dark brown spots on the upper lobes, in spherical trusses of 16 blooms, in mid-season; **'Golden Torch'** has soft yellow flowers, in compact trusses of 13 to 15 blooms, in mid- to late season; **'Grumpy'**, orange buds open as creamy flowers tinged with pink, in rounded trusses of 11 blooms, in mid-season; **'Hoppy'**, white flowers with greenish speckling appear in ball-shaped trusses of 18 blooms, in mid-season; **'Hydon Dawn'**, flowers with pink frilled petals, fading to the edges, with reddish brown spots, in large, compact, and rounded trusses of 14 to 18 blooms, in mid-season; **'Percy Wiseman'** has pink funnel-shaped flowers fading to white, with a pale yellow center and orange spots, in trusses of 14 blooms, mid-season; **'Peste's Blue Ice'**, deep purplish pink flowers, fading to very pale purple, lightly spotted with green, in trusses of 21 blooms, in mid-season; **'Polaris'** has abundant pinkish purple flowers, with lighter shading at the center; **'Renoir'**, deeply bell-shaped rose pink flowers with a white throat and crimson spots, in rounded trusses of 11 blooms, in mid-season; **'Surrey Heath'**, rose pink flowers with a lighter center bloom, in mid-season; **'Titian Beauty'** bears turkey red flowers, in mid-season. Zones 7–9.

DECIDUOUS AZALEA HYBRIDS

Deciduous azaleas are multi-stemmed from the ground, never forming a central trunk. The leaves have a thin texture, and the large, often sticky, winter buds contain both the flowers and the spring foliage flush. Flowers of deciduous azaleas are trumpet-shaped, flaring from a narrow tube, and are predominantly in shades of cream to salmon, yellow, orange, and scarlet. Deciduous azaleas bloom in spring with or before the new leaves; if they are to flower well, they require a climate with fairly cold winters.

GHENT HYBRIDS

↔ 3–6 ft (0.9–1.8 m)
↕ 5–8 ft (1.5–2.4 m)

These very hardy hybrids were bred in the early 1800s in the Belgian city of Ghent, starting with the American species *Rhododendron calendulaceum* and *R. periclymenoides*. Large bushes flower in late spring to early summer, with large trusses of relatively small flowers, up to 2 in (5 cm) in diameter, often fragrant, with long tubes, mostly single, but occasionally double. There are numerous cultivars: **'Altaclarense'**, white flowers with an orange blotch; **'Coccineum Speciosum'**, bright orange-red flowers, attractive autumn foliage; **'Corneille'**, double cream flowers, petals pink tinged on reverse, colorful autumn foliage; **'Daviesii'**, fragrant white flowers with a yellow flare; **'Gloria Mundi'**, orange and yellow flowers; **'Nancy Waterer'**, large golden yellow flowers, pleasantly scented; **'Narcissiflorum'**, double yellow flowers, shaded darker at the center and on petal reverse; **'Phoebe'**, double deep yellow flowers; **'Pucella'**, pink flowers with a bright orange blotch; **'Vulcan'**, deep red flowers with an orange blotch. Zones 5–9.

MOLLIS HYBRIDS

↔ 5–7 ft (1.5–2 m)
↕ 5–8 ft (1.5–2.4 m)

Created from crosses between *Rhododendron molle*, *R. molle* subsp. *japonicum*, and the earlier Ghent hybrids, the numerous Mollis azaleas were developed in the Netherlands and Belgium from the 1860s and 1870s. Large hardy shrubs, to 8 ft (2.4 m) in height, with single flowers, 2 in (5 cm) wide, sometimes fragrant, appearing from mid-spring in strong colors including creams, yellows, oranges, and reds. Difficult to propagate from cuttings, so often sold as variable seedlings, best selected for purchase when in flower. **'Anthony Koster'**, yellow flowers; **'Apple**

Blossom', light pink flowers; **'Babeuff'**, glowing salmon-orange flowers; **'Carat'**, red-dish orange flowers, orange blotch; **'Christopher Wren'**, large flowers of brilliant yellow with a strong orange blotch; **'Dr M. Oosthoek'**, vivid reddish orange flowers, lighter blotch; **'Esmeralda'**, red buds open to orange flowers; **'Hortulanus H. Witte'**, orange-yellow flowers with an orange blotch; **'Hugo Koster'**, orange flowers; **'J.C. van Tol'**, flowers apricot-pink; **'Koningin Emma'**, orange flowers; **'Koster's Brilliant Red'**, reddish orange flowers; **'Koster's Yellow'**, orange-yellow flowers with an orange blotch; **'Saturnus'**, bright orange-red flowers, petals red-tingd on reverse; **'Spek's Brilliant'**, large trusses of bright orange-red flowers; **'Spek's Orange'**, deep orange buds open to orange-red flowers; **'Winston Churchill'**, orange-red flowers. Zones 6–9.

OCCIDENTALE HYBRIDS

☼/◐ ❄ ↔6–10 ft (1.8–3 m)
↑6–10 ft (1.8–3 m)

Developed in England in early twentieth century from *R. occidentale* and Mollis hybrids. Usually a broad spreading shrub to about 8 ft (2.4 m) tall. White or pale pink fragrant flowers, to 3 in (8 cm) wide, open after leaves in mid-spring. Most characterized by deep yellow blotch on flowers. Slow-growing, the most heat-, drought-, and humidity-tolerant of all deciduous azaleas. **'Bridesmaid'**, white flowers, yellow blotch; **'Coccinto Speciosa'**, densely packed rounded clusters of deep orange flowers; **'Delicatissimum'**, pink-flushed white to cream flowers, orange flare; **'Exquisitum'**, frilled, fragrant, pale pink flowers, orange flare, darker reddish buds; **'Graciosa'**, pale orange-yellow flowers, flushed pink; **'Magnifica'**, white to yellow flowers flushed pink, yellow flare; **'Superba'**, frilled pink flowers, apricot blotch. Zones 7–10.

RUSTICA FLORE PLENO HYBRIDS

☼/◐ ✱ ↔4–6 ft (1.2–1.8 m)
↑6–8 ft (1.8–2.4 m)

The double-flowering Ghent and Mollis hybrids were crossed in Belgium in the late nineteenth century to produce the Rustica Flore Pleno hybrids, which have double flowers. **'Byron'**, white flowers flushed pink; **'Freya'**, pale pink flowers flushed salmon pink; **'Norma'**, red buds opening to bright rose pink flowers; **'Phideas'**, pink buds opening to cream flowers flushed pink; **'Ribera'**, rose pink flowers with a yellow throat. Zones 5–9.

Rhododendrom, Hybrid Cultivar, Deciduous Azalea, Mollis, 'Christopher Wren'

Rhododendron, Hybrid Cultivar, Deciduous Azalea, Occidentale, 'Coccinto Speciosa'

Rhododendron, Hybrid Cultivar, Deciduous Azalea, Rustica Flore Pleno, 'Norma'

OTHER DECIDUOUS AZALEA HYBRIDS

☼/◐ ✱ ↔5–8 ft (1.5–2.4 m)
↑5–8 ft (1.5–2.4 m)

The American-bred Lights Group, probably the most widely grown of the many American-raised deciduous azalea groups, are very hardy, with abundant small flowers, and include: **'Apricot Surprise'**, vigorous, with golden yellow flowers from orange-pink buds; **'Golden Lights'**, golden yellow flowers; **'Northern Lights'**, fragrant pale to deep pink flowers; and **'White Lights'**, white flowers with yellow markings. Other deciduous azalea hybrids include: **'Antilope'**, fragrant moderate pink flowers with darker median lines and a faint yellow blotch; **'Arpège'**, fragrant vivid yellow flowers, tube flushed yellowish pink; **'Rosata'**, broad upright shrub, fragrant pink flowers with darker ribs; and **'Soir de Paris'**, fragrant light pink flowers with an orange blotch and darker lines. Zones 5–9.

EVERGREEN AZALEA HYBRIDS

Like deciduous azaleas, the evergreen azalea hybrids are multi-stemmed plants. The leaves are of 2 types: spring leaves that surround the flower-heads and are crowded at the ends of the previous year's shoots; and summer growth flush that produces longer leaves, more widely spaced on the branchlet. Flowers are widely funnel-shaped, in shades from white to pink, red, and purple, often bicolored. Most of these azaleas flower well in warmer temperate climates where winter frost is mild or even absent.

R., HC, Deciduous Azalea, Other, 'Antilope'

Rhododendron, Hybrid Cultivar, Evergreen Azalea, Indica, Belgian, 'Albert Elizabeth'

INDICA HYBRIDS

☼/◐ ❄ ↔1–12 ft (0.3–3.5 m)
↑1–10 ft (0.3–3 m)

The most widely grown azaleas in temperate climates, the Indica hybrids were first developed as Christmas-flowering container plants intended for a short life indoors. The breeders developed the plants for flower qualities over landscaping attributes, so in general they are not very hardy. They were developed from *Rhododendron simsii*, originally in Belgium, but breeding continues today worldwide. They are reasonably fast-growing medium-sized shrubs. Flowers are normally large and single, but there are also numbers of double, semi-double, and hose-in-hose types, in strong colors. Zones 8–11.

BELGIAN INDICA HYBRIDS

☼/◐ ❄ ↔3–6 ft (0.9–1.8 m)
↑2–5 ft (0.6–1.5 m)

One of the first evergreen azaleas to arrive in Europe from Asia was the tender species *R. simsii*. Its willingness to be forced into bloom in winter quickly endeared it to the Belgian flower growers, who from the mid-nineteenth century developed hundreds of hybrids. Although damaged by repeated frosts, these spectacular, compact, heavy-flowering plants are among the most widely grown azaleas. **'Advent Bells'** (syns 'Adventglocke', 'Chimes'), strong purple-red, semi-double, cup-shaped flowers; **'Albert Elizabeth'**, pale pink flowers, darker pink edges, olive green spotting in throat; **'Alphonse Anderson'**, pale pink flowers with darker blotch; **'Comtesse de Kerchove'**, soft pink, medium-sized, double flowers edged with white; **'Elsa Karga'**, glowing red double flowers; **'Eri Schaume'**, coral pink double flowers edged with white; **'Gretel'**, compact growth, white, medium-sized, double flowers edged with deep cerise; **'Haeren's Saumona'** (syn. 'California Sunset'), moderate red flowers with edges fading to pink; **'Helmut Vogel'**, long-flowering shrub, vivid purplish red semi-double or double flowers; **'James Belton'**, white to pale pink flowers, darker pink stamens; **'Kelly's Cerise'**, purplish red semi-double to double flowers; **'Leopold Astrid'**, large, frilled, double, white flowers bordered with rose red; **'Only One Earth'**, ruffled, semi-double, hose-in-hose flowers, bright red to deep purplish pink; **'Orchidiflora'**, semi-double pink flowers; **'Osta'**, very large, single, blush pink to white flowers with red throat, also comes in a red-flowering form; **'Red Wing'**, long-flowering, ruffled hose-in-hose deep red blooms, compact sun-tolerant shrub. Zones 8–11.

Rhododendron, Hybrid Cultivar, Evergreen Azalea, Indica, Rutherford, 'Purity'

Rhododendron, Hybrid Cultivar, Evergreen Azalea, Indica, Southern, 'Fielder's White'

Rhododendron, Hybrid Cultivar, Evergreen Azalea, Kaempferi, 'Double Beauty'

Rhododendron, Hybrid Cultivar, Evergreen Azalea, Kaempferi, 'Sunrise'

RUTHERFORD INDICA HYBRIDS

↔ 4–8 ft (1.2–2.4 m)
↑ 3–8 ft (0.9–2.4 m)

The Rutherford hybrids were bred in the 1920s in the USA as short-lived greenhouse plants for the florist trade. Many are hose-in-hose and have ruffled or frilled petals, in colors which include reddish orange, pinks, purples, and white. Larger than the Belgian hybrids, they usually reach 3–8 ft (0.9–2.4 m) in height. **'Constance'**, vigorous bushy growth habit to 3 ft (0.9 m) high, purplish pink single to hose-in-hose flowers, darker markings; **'Dorothy Gish'**, orange-salmon, semi-double, hose-in-hose flowers; **'Firelight'**, bright red flowers; **'Gloria USA'**, semi-double hose-in-hose flowers, salmon pink or white, red throat, white petal margins; **'Louise J. Bobbink'**, usually purplish red, occasionally light pink, semi-double, hose-in-hose flowers, lighter throat, edged white; **'Purity'**, snow white flowers; **'Rose King'**, deep rose pink semi-double flowers; **'Rose Queen'**, deep purplish pink, semi-double, hose-in-hose flowers, white throat, darker blotch; **'White Gish'**, compact, to 3 ft (0.9 m) high, white, semi-double, hose-in-hose flowers, greenish yellow markings; **'White Prince'**, white, semi-double, hose-in-hose flowers, red throat, sometimes flushed pink. Zones 9–11.

SOUTHERN INDICA HYBRIDS

↔ 6–12 ft (1.8–3.5 m)
↑ 5–10 ft (1.5–3 m)

Bred in the USA, the Southern Indica azaleas refined the characteristics of the earlier Indica hybrids to produce vigorous sun-tolerant plants which are hardier than the Belgian hybrids. They are early flowering, usually with single flowers, 2 in (5 cm) wide, in shades of pink, red, and dark purple; the flowers are sometimes striped. There are no hose-in-hose forms in this group. **'Brilliantina'** (syn. 'Brilliant'), deep pink flowers with purple-red blotch; **'Concinna'**, deep rose-violet flowers; **'Duc de Rohan'**, salmon flowers with a rose throat; **'Fielder's White'**, white flowers, greenish tinge in throat; **'Formosa'**, deep purple-red flowers with darker blotch; **'George Lindley Taber'**, white with purple-pink flush and spotted throat; **'Glory of Sunninghill'**, large, single, orange-red flowers; **'Iveryana'**, white with red-flecked throat and faint pink flush; **'Mucronatum'**, profuse clusters of large, fragrant, widely funnel-shaped, white or occasionally pink flowers; **'Pink Lace'**, light pink single flowers with a rose throat, white-edged petals; **'Pride of Dorking'**, brilliant carmine or deep pink flowers, bronze-red and orange forms also available; **'White Lace'**, plain white flowers. Zones 8–11.

KAEMPFERI OR MALVATICA HYBRIDS

↔ 3–7 ft (0.9–2 m)
↑ 2–8 ft (0.6–2.4 m)

The late spring- or early summer-flowering Kaempferi or Malvatica hybrids were developed in the Netherlands in the 1920s by crossing the hardy *Rhododendron kaempferi* with *R.* 'Malvaticum', a garden plant of unknown origin. The large flowers are mostly single, but occasionally double or hose-in-hose, and tend to fade in full sunlight. Kaempferi hybrids typically grow to around 4 ft (1.2 m) in height with a spread of around 5 ft (1.5 m). Cultivars include: **'Blue Danube'** with strong purplish pink flowers, deep purplish red midribs, and deep red blotches; **'Cleopatra'**, upright shrub, deep pink flowers; **'Double Beauty'**, pink hose-in-hose flowers, mid-season; **'Fedora'**, deep purplish pink flowers; **'John Cairns'**, orange-red flowers; **'Othello'**, red flowers; **'Orange King'**, reddish orange flowers; **'Sunrise'**, reddish orange flowers. Zones 6–10.

GABLE HYBRIDS

↔ 3–7 ft (0.9–2 m)
↑ 4–8 ft (1.2–2.4 m)

Bred in the USA from various species and hybrids to produce a fully frost-hardy group, many of these hybrids have showy double flowers. **'Herbert'**, frilled, hose-in-hose, vivid reddish purple flowers, darker blotch; **'James Gable'**, with red hose-in-hose flowers, darker blotch; **'Louisa Gable'**, double flowers, salmon pink; **'Rosebud'**, double soft pink flowers; **'Stewartsonian'**, bright red flowers, rich red winter foliage. Zones 6–10.

VUYK HYBRIDS

↔ 3–7 ft (0.9–2 m)
↑ 2–8 ft (0.6–2.4 m)

The Vuyk hybrids were developed in the 1920s from original Kaempferi hybrids and are very similar to them but are more compact in habit. While some Mollis azalea parentage was initially suggested, this now seems unlikely. **'Beethoven'**, bright mid-pink flowers; **'Palestrina'**, snow white flowers, light green throat; **'Vuyk's Rosyred'**, deep pink-red flowers; **'Vuyk's Scarlet'**, vivid red flowers. Zones 6–10.

KURUME HYBRIDS

↔ 2–4 ft (0.6–1.2 m)
↑ 2–4 ft (0.6–1.2 m)

The Kurume hybrids were introduced to the West by the noted plant-hunter Ernest H. Wilson, working on behalf of the Veitch Nursery in England. His selection, known as Wilson's Fifty, was drawn from plants which had been cultivated for several centuries in Japan, and were believed to be crosses between *Rhododendron kaempferi*, *R. kiusianum*, and *R.* × *obtusum*. Large, normally single flowers, in shades of pink or white, appear early to mid-season in a wide range of strong colors, including pinks, reds, and purples. They are occasionally striped or "freckled," and sometimes hose-in-hose, flowering abundantly. The plants are hardy, slow growing, usually up to about 3 ft (0.9 m) high, occasionally up to about 5 ft (1.5 m), and with age they can spread to be much larger than this. They are best planted in fully exposed positions. **'Anniversary'**, a shrub with compact growth to 2 ft (0.6 m) high, light to pale purplish pink hose-in-hose flowers; **'Emily Knights'**, bright red flowers, crinkled star-shaped petals; **'Fairy Queen'** (syn. 'Aioi'), small, semi-double, hose-in-hose, almond-blossom pink flowers; **'Hatsu Giri'**, vivid reddish purple flowers, pink spotting in the throat; **'Hinomayo'**, strong purplish pink flowers; **'Iroha Yama'**, white flowers, pale lavender at edges; **'Kasane Kagaribi'** (syn. 'Rositi'), shrub with low, dense, spreading growth, yellowish to salmon pink flowers; **'Kirin'**, bright pink hose-in-hose flowers, early, low, spreading bush; **'Kumo-no-Ito'** (syn. 'Suga no Ito'), strong pink hose-in-hose flowers, darker center; **'Kure-no-yuki'**, white hose-in-hose flowers; **'Mother's Day'**, dense low-growing bush that produces abundant cherry red colored flowers; **'Osaraku'** (syn. 'Penelope'), small single flowers, soft lavender or light purple; **'Seikai'** (syn. 'Madonna'), white, semi-double, hose-in-hose flowers; **'Seraphim'** (syn. 'Tancho'), small, single, hose-in-hose flowers, blush pink edged with rose; **'Sherwood Red'**, orange-red single flowers; **'Shin Utena'** (syn. 'Santoi'), white flowers flushed with strong yellowish pink; **'Show Girl'**, small hose-in-hose flowers, a bright salmon-orange; **'Takasago'** (syn. 'Cherryblossom'), white hose-in-hose flowers, flushed with deep red or pale pink and with dark spots; **'Vida Brown'**, pink-red hose-in-hose flowers; **'Waka Kayede'** (syn. 'Red Robin'), a sun-tolerant shrub that produces strong red flowers; **'Ward's Ruby'**, featuring blood red flowers, is less hardy than other Kurume azaleas. Zones 7–10.

SATSUKI HYBRIDS

☼/◐ ❄ ↔24–48 in (60–120 cm) ↕12–36 in (30–90 cm)

Introduced to the West in the early 1900s, these late-flowering low-growing plants have been cultivated for centuries in Japan, and most likely originate from crosses between *R. indicum* and *R. eriocarpum* or *R. simsii*. In Japan they are valued for their landscaping qualities and were also traditionally used for bonsai and container cultivation. They are normally small spreading bushes up to 3 ft (0.9 m) in height. The Gumpo series of dwarf plants is useful in rockeries. **'Banzai'**, white flowers flushed with pink; **'Benigasa'**, deep orange red; **'Daishuhai'**, white with a broad red edge; **'Gumpo'**, large white flowers, petals wavy-edged; **'Gumpo Lavender'**, large, single, lavender flowers; **'Gumpo Pink'**, ruffled, single, pink flowers edged with white; **'Gumpo Salmon'**, ruffled salmon pink flowers; **'Gumpo Stripe'**, white flowers with mauve-red stripes and flecks; **'Gumpo White'** frilly white flowers; **'Gyoten'**, single flowers, up to 3 in (8 cm) across, pale pink with white edges, yellowish blotch and often with random red or white stripes; **'Hitoya-no-Haru'**, large lilac-pink flowers, olive green spotting in throat; **'Joga'**, white to pale pink with purple-red spotted throat; **'Kunpu'**, pale pink, wavy-edged, single flowers, 2½ in (6 cm) across; **'Mansaku'**, salmon pink flowers, rounded wavy petals; **'Nani-Wagata'**, abundant white flowers; **'Osakazuki'**, smallish, deep pink, single blooms, darker blotch in throat; **'Otome'**, white and pink flowers; **'Shiko'**, deep lavender pink shading to pale center; **'Shin-Kyo'**, light salmon pink flowers, **'Shinnyo-no-Hikari'**, white flowers, green throat; **'White Shiko'**, white flowers with green blaze. Zones 7–11.

INTERGROUP HYBRIDS

☼/◐ ✱ ↔3–6 ft (0.9–1.8 m) ↕2–6 ft (0.6–1.8 m)

These hybrids include crosses between the various other groups of azalea hybrids, as well as plants bred from later species introductions, and plants which do not neatly fall into any particular category. ***R.* × *pulchrum*** (syn. *R.* 'Phoeniceum') was introduced into the West from China as *Azalea indica* in the early nineteenth century, but in fact is a hybrid between *R. indicum* and *R.* 'Mucronatum', and known only as a garden plant in China and Japan, where it has been cultivated for centuries. Its very large single flowers are purplish red or violet-rose on a very tough shrub which grows to about 6 ft (1.8 m) high. **'Chippewa'**, dwarf spreading plant, pink flowers; **'Dew Drop'** (syn. 'Nuccio's Dew Drop'), blush pink to white single to semi-double flowers, flushed with green, pink spots in throat; **'Dogwood'** and **'Dogwood Red'**, sun-tolerant plants, red flowers edged with white or pure red, greenish throat; **'Dogwood Variegated'**, bright salmon pink flowers streaked white; **'Easter Delight'**, abundant, clear purple, tubular flowers, tolerates full sun; **'Fascination'**, large, single, pink flowers, red edging on petals; **'Gloria Still'**, compact bush to 2 ft (0.6 m) high, variegated light pink and white flowers in large trusses; **'Jeanne Weeks'**, buds resemble rosebuds, open as strong purplish pink hose-in-hose flowers; **'Orange Delight'** (syn. 'Mrs John Ward'), shrub with low dense growth to 30 in (75 cm) high, very large bright reddish orange flowers; **'Summerland Chiffon'**, light pink double flowers; **'Summerland Mist'**, ruffled, semi-double, white flowers; **'Swashbuckler'**, reddish flowers, red blotch, stamens, and pistil; **'Sweetheart Supreme'**, shrub with spreading habit, deep or salmon pink, frilled, semi-double, hose-in-hose flowers, darker blotch; **'Teena Maree'**, semi-double hose-in-hose flowers, salmon or yellowish pink; **'Tokay'**, best when fully mature, purplish pink flowers, lighter blotch. Zones 6–10.

GLENN DALE HYBRIDS

☼/◐ ❄ ↔5–10 ft (1.5–3 m) ↕4–8 ft (1.2–2.4 m)

The Glenn Dale hybrids are also included in the Intergroup category. Bred in the USA from the 1930s, they combine the large flowers of the Southern Indica hybrid azaleas with cold hardiness and a later flowering season, from spring to summer. They range in form from low-growing dwarf plants to open bushes that are 8 ft (2.4 m) or more in height. Large spectacular flowers can be of a solid color, striped or speckled, semi-double or double in form, and they often have frilled petals. **'Alight'**, strong purple-pink flowers, lighter center, mid-season; **'Aphrodite'**, light purplish pink flowers with a darker blotch, mid-season; **'Ben Morrison'** ★, brownish red, darker throat, broad white edge; **'Bonanza'**, vivid purplish red flowers, darker blotch, mid-season; **'Chanticleer'**, purple flowers; **'Corydon'**, early-flowering shrub, strong purplish pink flowers, a few darker blotches, and overlapping lobes; **'Dimity'**, white single flowers with purplish red flecks; **'Festive'**, white with irregular deep pink flecks and sectors; **'Firedance'**, large, double, glowing rose red flowers; **'Gaiety'**, light purplish pink flowers, darker blotch, early to mid-season; **'Martha Hitchcock'**, white flowers edged with lilac; **'Revery'**, medium, single, rose pink flowers; **'Romance'**, double hose-in-hose flowers, rich purplish pink; **'Saffrano'**, white flowers flushed with yellowish green on upper lobe, mid-season; **'Tanager'**, vivid purplish red flowers, darker blotch. Zones 7–10.

RHODOTYPOS

The sole species in this genus is a deciduous shrub native to China and Japan. A member of the rose (Rosaceae) family, it is cultivated mainly for its spring flowers and, to a lesser extent, for the black berries that ripen over summer and last well into winter. The serrated foliage is a fresh green throughout the warmer months and sometimes develops slight red or yellow colors in autumn.

CULTIVATION: *Rhodotypos scandens* is frost hardy and easily cultivated in most temperate areas in sun or partial shade. It prefers a well-drained humus-rich soil and ample summer moisture, which will also result in a better fruit crop. It is best to prune this plant in winter after the last berries have fallen. Propagate from stratified seed, layers, or hardwood cuttings in winter, or half-hardened cuttings in summer.

Rhodotypos scandens ★

syn. *Rhodotypos kerrioides*

☼ ✱ ↔6 ft (1.8 m) ↕8 ft (2.4 m)

Deciduous shrub from China and Japan. Several upright or slightly arching stems, 1–2 in (25–50 mm) wide. Rose-like, 4-petalled, white flowers at branch tips, in spring. Calyces remain after flowers fall, partially enclosing developing fruit. Zones 5–9.

Rhododendron, Hybrid Cultivar, Evergreen Azalea, Kurume, 'Kumo-no-Ito'

Rhododendron, Hybrid Cultivar, Evergreen Azalea, Intergroup, 'Tokay'

Rhodotypos scandens

Rhus glabra 'Laciniata'

RHUS

SUMAC

There are about 200 species of deciduous or evergreen trees, shrubs and climbers in this genus within the cashew (Anacardiaceae) family. Widely distributed throughout the temperate and subtropical regions of the world, they are used to produce laquer, dyes, tannin, wax, and drinks. *Rhus* species are mainly grown in the garden for their good autumn color, interesting foliage, and fruit, which can persist on the tree into winter and often drop off only when the new leaves appear.

CULTIVATION: *Rhus* species grow in full sun in moderately fertile, moist but free-draining soil with shelter from the wind. Propagate from root cuttings in winter, half-hardened stem cuttings in late summer or divided root suckers taken when the plant is dormant. Seed can be sown in autumn. Feed and water well during growing season; do not feed in winter and water sparingly.

Rhus aromatica

FRAGRANT SUMAC, LEMON SUMACH, POLECAT BUSH

☼ ✱ ↔5 ft (1.5 m) ↑3–5 ft (0.9–1.5 m)

Native to eastern North America. Suckering deciduous shrub. Palmate leaves, oval toothed leaflets, aromatic. Small yellow flowers on panicles, in spring. Round red fruit. **'Gro-Low'** ★, to 2 ft (0.6 m) high, fragrant deep yellow flowers. Zones 3–9.

Rhus chinensis

CHINESE GALL, NUTGALL

☼ ❄ ↔15 ft (4.5 m) ↑20 ft (6 m)

Erect deciduous tree, native to Japan and China. Leaves compound, mid-green, 3 to 7 oblong leaflets, scalloped edges, turn red in autumn. White conical clusters of flowers, in late summer–early autumn. Rounded scarlet fruit. Zones 8–11.

Rhus lancea

Rhus copallina

syn. *Rhus copallinum*

DWARF SUMAC, MOUNTAIN SUMACH, SHINING SUMAC

☼ ✱ ↔5 ft (1.5 m) ↑5 ft (1.5 m)

From eastern North America. Erect deciduous shrub. Dark green pinnate leaves, 15 lance-shaped leaflets, winged stalks. Yellowish green flowers on upright panicles, in summer. Rounded red fruit. Foliage turns red in autumn. *R. c.* var. *latifolia* (prairie flame sumac), compact male form, reddish orange autumn foliage. Zones 5–9.

Rhus glabra

SCARLET SUMAC, SMOOTH SUMAC, VINEGAR TREE

☼ ✱ ↔8 ft (2.4 m) ↑8 ft (2.4 m)

Bushy deciduous shrub, native to North America and Mexico. Bronze-colored stems, whitish bloom, pinnate leaves, deep blue-green leaflets, turn rich red in autumn. Dense upright panicles of greenish red flowers, in summer. Rounded, crimson, hairy fruits. **'Laciniata'**, finely cut leaves. Zones 2–9.

Rhus lancea

KAREE, WILLOW RHUS

☼ ❄ ↔25 ft (8 m) ↑25 ft (8 m)

Evergreen tree that is native to South Africa. Leaves dark green above, paler beneath, with 3 lance-shaped leaflets, sometimes with toothed edges. Tiny yellow-green flowers appear in late summer. Fruit is glossy brown. Zones 9–11.

Ribes aureum

Rhus microphylla

CORREOSA, DESERT SUMAC, SCRUB SUMAC

☼ ❄ ↔4–6 ft (1.5–1.8 m) ↑6–10 ft (1.8–3 m)

From southern USA and northern Mexico. Rounded deciduous shrub. Compound leaves with up to 9 leaflets; usually evergreen but can shed leaves in cold or dry conditions. Tight spikes of tiny white flowers, in spring. Tiny orange-red fruit. Zones 8–11.

Rhus trilobata

syn. *Rhus aromatica subsp. trilobata*

SKUNKBUSH SUMAC, THREE-LOBE SUMAC

☼ ✱ ↔10 ft (3 m) ↑8 ft (2.4 m)

Deciduous shrub from western and central USA and northern and central Mexico. Hairy new growth. Leaves with 3 toothed leaflets. Clusters of light green flowers, in spring. Round red fruit. Zones 5–9.

Rhus typhina

STAGHORN SUMAC, STAG'S HORN SUMAC

☼ ✱ ↔15 ft (4.5 m) ↑15 ft (4.5 m)

Deciduous tree or shrub from eastern North America. Can reach 30 ft (9 m) high in the wild. Pinnate leaves, up to 31 dark green leaflets, turn flame red in autumn. Green-yellow flowers, in summer. Felty red fruit. **'Dissecta'**, finely divided leaves. Zones 3–9.

RIBES

CURRANT

Mainly from the northern temperate regions, with some species native to South America, this genus of around 150 species of shrubs is in the gooseberry (Grossulariaceae) family. Some are ornamental; others are grown for their fruit. They are usually deciduous, with twiggy or wiry stems. Usually with 3 to 5 lobes, leaves often have scalloped or toothed edges and bristly hairs. Flowers are small, sometimes in racemes, followed by often bristly, many-seeded, frequently edible berries. Some species are important commercial or home garden crops.

CULTIVATION: Some are not self-fertile and must be planted in groups to ensure good fruiting. Apart from this, and the need for some winter chilling, most are easily grown, requiring little more than a well-drained soil, moisture in summer, and some shade from the very hottest summer sun. Rust or mildew can cause problems with some species, but disease-resistant cultivars are often available. Propagate from seed or cuttings, or by layering.

Ribes alpinum

ALPINE CURRANT, MOUNTAIN CURRANT

☼ ✱ ↔3 ft (0.9 m) ↑3–6 ft (0.9–1.8 m)

Deciduous shrub found over much of Europe and extending to North Africa and Russia. Smooth purple-red stems, leaves usually 3-lobed. Erect racemes of tiny yellow-green flowers, in spring. Bitter red fruit. **'Aureum'**, yellow-green young growth; **'Green Mound'**, non-fruiting low-growing form; **'Pumilum'**, low and spreading with small leaves; **'Schmidt'**, slower growing, smaller than the species. Zones 2–9.

Ribes aureum

GOLDEN CURRANT, GOLDEN FLOWERING CURRANT

☼ ✱ ↔6 ft (1.8 m) ↑6 ft (1.8 m)

From western USA and northwestern Mexico. Upright deciduous bush. Leaves 3-lobed, coarsely toothed. Pendent racemes of strongly scented yellow flowers, in spring. Fruit purple-black. *R. a.* var. *gracillimum*, unscented red-tinted flowers, yellow fruit. Zones 2–9.

Ribes cereum

SQUAW CURRANT

☼ ✱ ↔3 ft (0.9 m) ↑3–6 ft (0.9–1.8 m)

Smooth-stemmed deciduous shrub from western USA. Rounded to kidney-shaped leaves, 3 to 5 lobes, downy, shallowly toothed edges. Short pendent racemes of flowers, white, pale green, or light yellow, in spring. Shiny red fruit. Zones 5–9.

Ribes indecorum

WHITE-FLOWERED CURRANT

☼ ❄ ↔3–7 ft (0.9–2 m) ↑7–8 ft (2–2.4 m)

Deciduous shrub from California, USA. Downy shoots and lobed leaves similar to *R. sanguineum*. White flowers in drooping spikes, in early spring. Downy fruit. Zones 8–10.

Ribes inerme

WHITE-STEMMED GOOSEBERRY

☼ ✱ ↔5 ft (1.5 m) ↑3–6 ft (0.9–1.8 m)

Deciduous shrub that is native to USA. Small leaves with 3 to 5 rounded lobes, edged with blunt teeth. Small clusters of greenish flowers with pink or white petals, in late spring. Fruit purple-red, edible. Some thorns. Zones 6–9.

Ribes malvaceum

CHAPARRAL CURRANT

☼ ❄ ↔6 ft (1.8 m) ↑6 ft (1.8 m)

Deciduous shrub that is native to California, USA, similar to the far better known *R. sanguineum*. Hairy stems, downy dull green leaves, felting beneath. Pink flowers on pendulous racemes, in mid-winter to spring. Zones 7–10.

Ribes nigrum

BLACKCURRANT

☼ ✱ ↔6 ft (1.8 m) ↑7 ft (2 m)

Deciduous shrub, native to Eurasia. Upright multi-stemmed habit. Stems downy when young, leaves with 3 to 5 lobes, downy beneath. Downy pendent racemes of red-centered yellow-green flowers, in spring. Fruiting and foliage cultivars include: **'Ben Connan'**, attractive award-winning cultivar; **'Ben Lomond'**, late large fruit; **'Black Beauty'**, popular American cultivar; **'Boskoop Giant'**, vigorous form, large fruit; **'Coloratum'**, variegated foliage; **'Jet'**, large dark fruit. Zones 5–9.

Ribes malvaceum

Ribes nigrum 'Ben Connan'

Ribes odoratum

BUFFALO CURRANT, CLOVE CURRANT, GOLDEN CURRANT

☼ ✱ ↔6 ft (1.8 m) ↑6 ft (1.8 m)

From central USA. Spice-scented leaves, 3 to 5 lobes, toothed edges. Pendent racemes of sweetly scented yellow flowers, in spring–early summer. Edible black fruit. **'Xanthocarpum'**, orange-yellow berries. Zones 5–9.

Ribes oxyacanthoides

MOUNTAIN GOOSEBERRY, NORTHERN GOOSEBERRY

☼ ✱ ↔27 in (70 cm) ↑18–32 in (45–80 cm)

Deciduous shrub found in northern USA and Canada. Slender bristly stems with thorns. Glossy, dark green, heart-shaped leaves, 5 deep lobes. Paired or single, greenish white to light mauve flowers, in spring. Edible purple-red berries. Zones 2–8.

Ribes rubrum

syns *Ribes sativum*, *R. silvestre*, *R. spicatum*

NORDIC CURRANT, REDCURRANT

☼/◐ ✱ ↔32–60 in (80–150 cm) ↑5–7 ft (1.5–2 m)

Smooth-stemmed shrub found from Scandinavia to eastern China. Leaves are 3- to 5-lobed, to 4 in (10 cm) in diameter, with undersides sometimes downy. Upright to pendulous racemes of small red-flushed green flowers appear in early summer. Translucent red fruit. **'Macrocarpum'**, large-fruited; **'Red Lake'**, vigorous pest- and disease-resistant cultivar; **'White Grape'**, pale yellow to cream fruit. Zones 3–9.

Ribes sanguineum

FLOWERING CURRANT, WINTER CURRANT

☼ ✱ ↔10 ft (3 m) ↑10 ft (3 m)

Deciduous shrub from western USA. Branches warm red-brown. Leaves dark green, 3 to 5 lobes, downy beneath. Pendent racemes of soft pink to red flowers, in spring, before the leaves appear. Fruit deep blue-black with a white bloom. ***R. s.* var. *glutinosum***, pink flowers, leaves less downy than the species; **'Joyce Rose'**, rich pink flowers. Popular cultivars include: ***R. s.* 'Brocklebankii'**, clear pink scented flowers; **'Claremont'**, developed recently by the University of British Columbia in Canada, almost white flowers, ageing to deep pink; **'Elk River Red'** ★, blooms bright rose red, very early in season, can become weedy; **'Inverness White'**, greenish white flowers in long sprays; **'King Edward VII'**, compact, with deep pink flowers; **'Plenum'**, red double flowers; **'Pulborough Scarlet'**, red flowers; **'Spring Showers'**, pink flowers, bright green foliage; and **'Tydeman's White'**, white flowers. Zones 6–10.

Ribes speciosum

FUCHSIA-FLOWERED CURRANT

☼ ❄ ↔10 ft (3 m) ↑12 ft (3.5 m)

From California, USA. Evergreen bushy upright shrub. Thorny stems, small smooth leaves, 3 to 5 lobes, toothed edges. Flowers bright red, pendulous, with long red stamens, singly, pairs, or groups of 3, in summer. Fruit bristly and red. Zones 8–10.

Ribes uva-crispa

GOOSEBERRY

☼ ✱ ↔36 in (90 cm) ↑36 in (90 cm)

Found through Europe to North Africa and the Caucasus region. Thorny many-branched bush. Leaves small, heart-shaped, 3 to 5 lobes, downy undersides. Green flowers. Bristly green fruit. Makes excellent tarts, pies, and jams. Fruit of some cultivars ripen to yellow or red. Cultivars include: **'Crown Bob'**, **'Leveller'** ★, and **'Roaring Lion'**. Zones 5–9.

Ribes speciosum

Ribes viburnifolium

☼ ❄ ↔5 ft (1.5 m) ↑5 ft (1.5 m)

Native to California, USA. Smooth-stemmed evergreen shrub. Stems droop and take root. Leaves strongly aromatic, with a turpentine scent. Small erect racemes of pink flowers, in spring. Red fruit. Zones 8–10.

RICINUS

This single-species genus, a member of the euphorbia (Euphorbiaceae) family, comes from northeast Africa but has naturalized throughout the tropical regions. It is considered a prized annual in many cold-climate gardens (but a weed in warmer regions), and is grown for its deeply lobed, and often colored, leaves.

CULTIVATION: *Ricinus communis* requires fertile soil with ample organic matter added to ensure moisture retention and free drainage. This plant's brittle stems need to be protected from winds and frost. When grown from seed care must be taken as the seed coats, and other parts of the plant, are extremely toxic.

Ricinus communis

CASTOR BEAN PLANT, CASTOR OIL PLANT

☼ ❄ ↔3 ft (0.9 m) ↑5–15 ft (1.5–4.5 m)

Fast-growing evergreen shrub from northeast Africa; can grow to 40 ft (12 m) high in the wild. Somewhat brittle stems; distinctive, lobed, green leaves. Smaller growing cultivars include: **'Cambodgensis'**, purple-black stems, dark purple leaves; **'Red Spire'**, red stems, bronze-green foliage; **'Zanzibarensis'**, taller, with large white-veined green leaves. Zones 9–12.

Ricinus communis

Ribes rubrum

ROBINIA

The 20 or so species of deciduous trees and shrubs in this genus, in the pea-flower subfamily of the legume (Fabaceae) family, are found mainly in eastern USA. They bear pendulous racemes of white, cream, pink, or lavender pea-flowers, followed by flat seed pods. Leaves are pinnate, often quite large; some species have vivid yellow autumn colors. Stems may have fierce thorns.
CULTIVATION: These tough adaptable plants grow quickly and tolerate most soils provided they are well drained. They are, however, rather brittle, with branches that are prone to break or tear in strong winds. It is best to prune when young to establish a strongly branched structure. Some species sucker freely and the suckers can be used for propagation, otherwise they are propagated from stratified seed or cuttings. Special growth forms are usually grafted.

Robinia hispida

ROSE ACACIA
↔10 ft (3 m) ↕10 ft (3 m)
Large shrub from southeastern USA, dense and bushy, suckering. Branches covered in red bristles. Leaves with 7 to 15 leaflets, dark green above, gray-green below, bristles at tips. Flowers magenta to purple, in small racemes, in late spring. *R. h.* var. *fertilis* (syn. *R. fertilis*), blue-green foliage, deep pink flowers. Zones 4–10.

Robinia hispida

Robinia pseudoacacia

BLACK LOCUST, FALSE ACACIA
↔35 ft (10 m) ↕50 ft (15 m)
Most widely grown robinia, parent of many cultivars, native to eastern and central parts of the USA. Thorny stems, red-tinted when young. Leaves with 19 bright green leaflets. White to cream flowers, in racemes, in summer. **'Appalachia'**, narrowly erect form; **'Aurea'**, greenish yellow spring foliage; **'Bessoniana'**, thornless rounded form; **'Coluteoides'**, rounded, compact, closely crowded leaflets; **'Frisia'**, bright golden foliage, thornless, few flowers; **'Inermis'**, thornless, upright habit; **'Tortuosa'**, twisted branches; **'Umbraculifera'**, rounded, dense foliage. Zones 3–10.

Robinia × *slavinii*

↔10 ft (3 m) ↕15 ft (4.5 m)
Shrubby hybrid between *R. kelseyi* and *R. pseudoacacia*. Foliage deep green and pinnate; rose pink racemes in spring. **'Hillieri'**, tree-like growth habit, pink flowers with distinct mauve tint. Zones 5–9.

RODGERSIA

The 6 large perennial species of this genus are members of the saxifrage (Saxifragaceae) family. Found naturally among the woodlands and streamsides of temperate Asia, they have a preference for damp conditions. They have large pinnate leaves with toothed edges and are grown primarily as foliage plants. Their astilbe-like plumes of tiny flowers are also attractive, although they are quite short lived. Foliage develops quickly in spring, and the flowers, which are white, cream, or pink in color, open at about the time the leaves reach their maximum size. The genus was named for American Rear Admiral John Rodgers (1812–82), who from 1852–56 led a botanical expedition in the western Pacific region.
CULTIVATION: Plant in part- or full shade in cool, moist, humus-rich soil. Although preferring constant moisture, rodgersias are not happy in stagnant boggy conditions and often do better alongside moving water rather than ponds. Propagate from seed or divide when dormant.

Rodgersia aesculifolia

↔3–7 ft (0.9–2 m)
↕5–7 ft (1.5–2 m)
Native to China. Large palmate leaves, to over 16 in (40 cm) long, reminiscent, as the Latin name suggests, of horse chestnut *(Aesculus)* foliage. White flowers, in dense panicles, to 24 in (60 cm) long, in summer. Zones 5–9.

Rodgersia pinnata

↔3–7 ft (0.9–2 m)
↕32–48 in (80–120 cm)
Native to southwestern China. Leaves partly pinnate, with 5 to 9 dark green, deeply veined leaflets, to 8 in (20 cm) in length. Deep pink to red, rarely white flowers, in long-stemmed panicles held well clear of foliage, in summer. **'Rosea'**, deep pink flowers; **'Superba'** ★, bronze- to purple-tinted foliage, large panicles of pink flowers. Zones 6–9.

Rodgersia podophylla

↔3–7 ft (0.9–2 m)
↕32–48 in (80–120 cm)
Native to Japan and Korea. Broad palmate leaves, usually 5-lobed, to over 12 in (30 cm) long and wide, with lobes at tips. Foliage reddens in autumn, sometimes brilliantly. White flowers, in heads to 12 in (30 cm) long, borne in summer. Zones 6–9.

Rodgersia sambucifolia

↔24–48 in (60–120 cm)
↕24–36 in (60–90 cm)
From China. Pinnate leaves, to over 12 in (30 cm) long, with up to 11 deeply veined, finely hairy, dark green leaflets. Flat-topped, often rather open panicles of white to light pink flowers, in summer. Zones 6–9.

ROLDANA

This genus of bushy daisies from Central America includes some 50-odd species and is a member of the daisy (Asteraceae) family. While many are annuals or perennials, the genus also includes a few shrubs. The leaves are usually large and rounded to hand-shaped with shallow lobes, dark green on top and often considerably lighter on the undersides. The leaves and young stems are covered with fine hairs that can sometimes be dense enough to become felted. The flowers, which are most commonly bright yellow, are carried in corymbs and occur throughout the year if the climate is mild enough.
CULTIVATION: Many species are frost tender, though the hardiest of them will withstand light frosts and relatively cool winters. They prefer moist, well-drained, fertile soil and flower best if grown in full sun. The foliage, however, is often more luxuriant with some shade. Propagate from seed or cuttings in general, but in some cases by division.

Roldana petasitis

syn. *Senecio petasitis*
↔6–10 ft (1.8–3 m)
↕6–10 ft (1.8–3 m)
From Central America. Grown as perennial or annual. Leaves with 7 or more pointed lobes, densely felted beneath. Yellow daisy flowers in flat-topped corymbs or in spikes, in winter. Zones 9–11.

Rodgersia podophylla

Roldana petasitis

Q R

ROMNEYA

This is a genus of only 2 species in the poppy (Papaveraceae) family, native to western North America and Mexico, both with glaucous stems and deeply cut leaves. The flowers are large, 6-petalled, white and poppy-like, with a central mass of golden yellow stamens. Romneyas are sometimes difficult to establish but once settled they spread quickly by underground stems, so should be allowed plenty of space.

CULTIVATION: These plants thrive in a warm sunny position and are quite frost hardy. They prefer a fertile and well-drained soil and resent being transplanted. Propagation is from seed or from cuttings.

Romneya coulteri

Rosa acicularis

Rosa banksiae normalis

Romneya coulteri

CALIFORNIA TREE POPPY

↔7 ft (2 m) ↕8 ft (2.4 m)

From southern California, USA. Small to medium-sized shrubby perennial. Persistent stems. Leaves silvery gray, finely cut. Flowers solitary, buds smooth, slightly conical, opening to large white flowers, crumpled crape-like petals, in late summer to mid-autumn. **'Butterfly'**, smaller flowers, pure white ruffled petals; **'White Cloud'**, large white flowers, silvery gray leaves. Zones 7–10.

ROSA

ROSE

The genus *Rosa* is one of the most widely grown and best loved of all plant genera around the world. It belongs to the large rose (Rosaceae) family, which includes a wide range of favorite fruiting plants such as apples, plums, and strawberries as well as ornamentals. Since ancient times roses have been valued for their beauty and fragrance as well as for their medicinal, culinary, and cosmetic properties. There are between 100 to 150 species of rose, which range in habit from erect and arching shrubs to scramblers and climbers. The majority of species are deciduous and most have prickles or bristles. They are found in temperate and subtropical zones of the Northern Hemisphere; none are native to the Southern Hemisphere. The pinnate leaves are usually comprised of 5 to 9, but sometimes more, serrated-edged leaflets. Flowers range from single, usually 5-petalled, blooms to those with many closely packed petals. They are borne singly or in clusters. Many are intensely fragrant. The majority of species and old garden roses flower only once but most of the modern cultivars are repeat-blooming. Rose fruits (hips or heps) are very rich in vitamin C. They are usually orangey red, but can be dark, and can be very decorative. They may be small and in clusters or single large fruits. Roses have been bred for many centuries and are divided into a number of recognized groups. The old garden roses were originally bred from a handful of species and include groups such as Gallica and Alba. In the late eighteenth century the repeat-flowering China rose *(R. chinensis)* arrived in Europe and subsequent cross-breeding extended the number of Old Rose groups further. The Tea Roses, also repeat-flowering, followed in the nineteenth century, and fifty years later a Frenchman bred the first Hybrid Tea, heralding the start of modern rose breeding. Hybrid Tea, Polyantha, Floribunda, and Shrub Roses proliferated in the twentieth century. While most of the species and Old Roses are in shades of pink, red, purple, or white, modern rose-breeding programs have seen the color range increase to include shades of yellow and orange.

CULTIVATION: Roses can be grown in separate beds or mixed borders, in formal and informal settings, as ground covers, climbing up arches and pergolas, scrambling up trees, as hedging, and in containers. Such is the popularity of roses that numerous books are devoted to their cultivation. Roses generally require a site that is sunny for most of the day, as shade inhibits flowering. They should not be overcrowded and there should be good air movement around the plants, factors that help reduce the risk of disease. Roses will grow in most well-drained medium-loamy soils in which compost or organic manure has been incorporated. When planting, the point at which the plant is grafted should be about 1 in (25 mm) below the soil. Granular or liquid rose fertilizer can be applied once or twice a year from spring. Plants should be watered well in dry periods and a mulch will help to conserve moisture in summer. Roses that flower more than once should be deadheaded to encourage further blooms. Roses should be pruned to maintain strong healthy growth, a good shape, and to let light into the plant. A number of pruning regimes are promoted for different rose groups, but recent research has shown that a simple "tidying up" of dead wood and pruning for size may be just as effective. Most pruning is done when the plants are dormant in winter. Fungal diseases such as rust, black spot, and mildew can be a problem, particularly in humid areas. Insect pests can also be troublesome, the most common being aphids. Others include spider mites, thrips, leafhoppers, froghoppers, and scale. Fungicidal and insecticidal sprays, both chemical and organic, are available to combat these problems. Roses planted in a position previously occupied by another rose can suffer rose sickness—to prevent this a generous amount of the old soil should be removed and replaced with a fresh supply. Most roses are very hardy and indeed benefit from a period of winter cold, but some of the old Tea Roses are a little tender and are better suited to warm-temperate climates. In warm areas roses often grow much larger than their cool-climate counterparts and can be more prone to problems caused by mild winters not killing off pests and diseases. Propagation in commercial quantities is usually from budding, but the gardener can take hardwood cuttings in autumn or softwood cuttings in summer. While hybrid plants will not come true from seed, the species can be propagated in this way. Seeds will need to be stratified before planting.

Rosa acicularis

↔4 ft (1.2 m) ↕6 ft (1.8 m)

Widespread species, found throughout northern areas of Europe, Asia, and America. Lax shrub, densely packed bristles of varying lengths, grayish green foliage. Mildly fragrant, single, deep pink flowers, in summer. Hips are bright red, pear-shaped. Zones 2–9.

Rosa arkansana

PRAIRIE ROSE

↔20 in (50 cm) ↕24–48 in (60–120 cm)

Native to central USA. Small suckering shrub. Erect branches very bristly, leaves shiny green. Single, mildly fragrant blooms, from pink to red, in summer. Round, small, red hips. Zones 4–9.

Rosa banksiae

BANKSIAN ROSE

↔30 ft (9 m) ↕30 ft (9 m)

Near-evergreen in mild climates, once-flowering climbing rose from western and central China. Leaves with 3 to 5 leaflets. Massed sprays of small white flowers, in spring–early summer. ***R. b. banksiae***, double, white, scented flowers; ***R. b. lutea*** ★, yellow double flowers; ***R. b. normalis***, thornless form, fragrant ivory white flowers. Zones 7–10.

Rosa blanda

HUDSON BAY ROSE, MEADOW ROSE, SMOOTH ROSE

↔3 ft (0.9 m) ↕3–7 ft (0.9–2 m)

Erect brown-stemmed shrub found in eastern and central North America. It is similar to *R. canina*. Few prickles near base, dull green leaves. Mildly fragrant, single, mid-pink flowers in summer. Ovoid to pear-shaped hips, red in color. Zones 3–9.

Rosa californica

↔6 ft (1.8 m) ↕7 ft (2 m)

Species common west of the Sierra Nevadas in the USA south to Baja California, Mexico. Stems bear stout prickles; leaves are mid-green. Single, slightly fragrant, pink flowers, in clusters, appear in summer. Round hips are orangey red. ***R. c. plena*** has grayish green leaves; semi-double, more strongly scented than the species, and the flowers are deeper pink. Zones 5–10.

Rosa moyesii fargesii

Rosa fedtschenkoana

Rosa foetida bicolor

Rosa glauca

Rosa nitida

Rosa chinensis

CHINA ROSE

↔8 ft (2.4 m) ↑20 ft (6 m)

From China. Variable species, from dwarf shrub to climber. Lustrous leaves, 3 to 5 leaflets. Flower color varies from red and pink to white, single, in summer; cultivars can have semi-double flowers. Hips greenish brown to scarlet. This species brought repeat-flowering into modern rose breeding. Plants from central China that are believed to be the original wild form have been known as ***R. c. spontanea***, a vigorous climbing form. Zones 7–10.

Rosa davidii

↔8 ft (2.4 m) ↑10 ft (3 m)

Deciduous shrub, found throughout western and central China. Arching stems, red-tinged prickles, wrinkled leaves. Single flowers in clusters, in summer, soft pink, mildly fragrant. Flagon-shaped orangey red hips. Zones 6–10.

Rosa eglanteria

syn. *Rosa rubiginosa*

BRIAR ROSE, EGLANTINE, SWEET BRIAR

↔10 ft (3 m) ↑10 ft (3 m)

Deciduous shrub from Europe and western Asia. Arching prickly stems, apple-scented leaves. Small, single, pink, fragrant flowers, in summer. Ovoid orangey red hips. Best in wild garden or as hedgerow plant. Considered a weed in Australia, New Zealand, and North America. Zones 4–10.

Rosa elegantula

syns *Rosa farreri, R. persetosa*

↔8 ft (2.4 m) ↑3–7 ft (0.9–2 m)

Dense suckering shrub, native of northwestern China. Fern-like foliage, grayish green, turns purple and crimson shades in autumn. Small single flowers, white to rose pink, in summer. **'Persetosa'** (threepenny-bit rose) has stems thickly covered in red bristles. Zones 6–10.

Rosa fedtschenkoana

↔3–8 ft (0.9–2.4 m)
↑3–8 ft (0.9–2.4 m)

Species native to mountain areas of central Asia. Vigorous suckering shrub. Prickles tinged pink, leaves grayish green. Single white flowers, prominent yellow stamens, mildly fragrant, in summer–autumn. Pear-shaped hips, bristly, orangey red. Zones 4–10.

Rosa foetida

AUSTRIAN BRIAR, AUSTRIAN YELLOW

↔6 ft (1.8 m) ↑3–10 ft (0.9–3 m)

An erect shrub that is native to Asia, with large blackish thorns, bright green leaves. Single flowers, deep yellow with prominent stamens, which give off an unpleasant aroma, in summer. Round red hips. ***R. f. bicolor*** (Austrian copper rose) has coppery orange flowers; ***R. f. persiana*** (Persian yellow rose) has double yellow flowers. Zones 4–10.

Rosa foliolosa

↔36 in (90 cm)
↑18–36 in (45–90 cm)

Small suckering shrub, native of southeastern USA, with relatively thornless, narrow leaflets. Single bright pink flowers, slightly scented, appear in summer. Small round hips, bright red. Tolerant of wet soils. Zones 6–10.

Rosa gallica

FRENCH ROSE, RED ROSE

↔4 ft (1.2 m) ↑4 ft (1.2 m)

Ancient rose native to southern, central, and eastern Europe. Low suckering shrub. Lightly bristled, leathery dark green leaves. Mildly fragrant flowers, usually single, soft to deep pink, prominent light yellow stamens. Small ovoid hips, brick red. Species not as well known as its 2 forms: ***R. g. officinalis*** ★ (apothecary's rose or Provins rose), slightly smaller, with quite large, semi-double, heavily perfumed, crimson flowers, can become weedy. ***R. g. versicolor*** (syn. 'Rosa Mundi'), sport of *R. g. officinalis*, identical except for its striped white, pink, and crimson flowers. Zones 5–10.

Rosa glauca

syn. *Rosa rubrifolia*

REDLEAF ROSE

↔6 ft (1.8 m) ↑6 ft (1.8 m)

Deciduous shrub, native to Europe. Arching stems dark purplish red when young, leaves bluish gray. Flowers starry-petalled, deep pink fading to white near center, in summer. Ovoid hips, purplish red. Zones 3–10.

Rosa gymnocarpa

WOOD ROSE

↔7 ft (2 m) ↑3–10 ft (0.9–3 m)

North American native. Slender plant with moderately thorny stems, small rounded leaflets. Small, single, pale pink flowers appear in summer. Pear-shaped hips are red and shiny. Zones 6–10.

Rosa hugonis

syn. *Rosa xanthina f. hugonis*

↔6 ft (1.8 m) ↑7 ft (2 m)

Chinese species; very similar to *R. xanthina*. Differs from *R. xanthina* in having broader leaflets and primrose yellow flowers to well over 2 in (5 cm) wide. Zones 5–10.

Rosa laevigata

CHEROKEE ROSE

↔20 ft (6 m) ↑30 ft (9 m)

From warm-temperate and subtropical East Asia, naturalized in southeastern USA; shrubby if cut back hard. Evergreen foliage, leathery, glossy, deep green leaflets, toothed edges. Flowers large, single, white to cream, fragrant, in summer. Bristly orange-red hips. Zones 7–10.

Rosa marretii

↔4 ft (1.2 m) ↑6 ft (1.8 m)

Upright shrub, native to far eastern Russia on the Pacific coast. Purplish stems, mid-green leaves. Flowers mid- to pale pink, in small clusters, in summer. Hips round and red. Zones 6–9.

Rosa moyesii

↔10 ft (3 m) ↑10 ft (3 m)

Deciduous shrub from western China. Stout erect stems, scattered thorns, dark green leaves. Single deep red flowers, in summer. Pendulous, flagon-shaped, orange-red hips. ***R. m. fargesii***, reddish pink flowers. Zones 5–10.

Rosa mulliganii

↔7–10 ft (2–3 m)
↑10–15 ft (3–4.5 m)

Vigorous shrub, native to China. Purplish gray young shoots and leaves. Single white flowers, scented, in small clusters, in summer. Showy, small, round, red hips. Zones 4–9.

Rosa nitida

↔4 ft (1.2 m) ↑3 ft (0.9 m)

Suckering shrub, native to eastern North America. Slender prickly stems, small fern-like leaves, turning crimson in autumn. Small, single, fragrant, deep pink flowers, in summer. Dark scarlet hips. Suitable for a ground cover. Zones 3–10.

Rosa nutkana

↔7 ft (2 m) ↑6–10 ft (1.8–3 m)

Vigorous rose, native to western North America. Almost thornless purplish brown stems, dark grayish green leaves. Fragrant single flowers, medium pink, in summer. Small, round, red hips. ***R. n. hispida***, fragrant pink flowers. Zones 4–10.

Rosa palustris

SWAMP ROSE

☼ ✱ ↔6 ft (1.8 m) ↑4–7 ft (1.2–2 m)

Deciduous shrub from eastern North America, grows in wet boggy conditions. Erect suckering habit, reddish stems, mid- to dark green leaves. Single deep pink flowers, in summer. Small red hips. Zones 4–10.

Rosa pisocarpa

CLUSTER ROSE

☼ ✱ ↔4 ft (1.2 m) ↑3–7 ft (0.9–2 m)

Deciduous shrub from western North America. Arching stems, small leaves, bristly at base. Small single flowers in clusters, rosy pink, in summer. Small, bright red, shiny hips. Zones 6–10.

Rosa pomifera

syn. *Rosa villosa*

APPLE ROSE

☼ ✱ ↔4 ft (1.2 m) ↑6 ft (1.8 m)

From central and southern Europe and Turkey. Deciduous shrub. Branches stiff, straight, scattered thorns, downy gray-green leaves. Single deep pink, fragrant, flowers, in summer. Large, round, red, bristly hips. Zones 5–10.

Rosa rugosa

BEACH ROSE, JAPANESE ROSE, RAMANAS ROSE

☼ ✱ ↔5–8 ft (1.5–2.4 m) ↑5–8 ft (1.5–2.4 m)

Vigorous deciduous shrub, native to Japan and eastern Asia. Stout prickly stems. Dark green leaves, wrinkled surface. Scented single flowers, light to deep pink, in summer–autumn. Round rich red hips. ***R. r. alba***, large white flowers opening from pink buds, large tomato red hips; ***R. r. rubra***, single deep pink-purple flowers. Zones 2–10.

Rosa setigera

syn. *Rosa rubifolia*

PRAIRIE ROSE

☼ ✱ ↔10 ft (3 m) ↑7–15 ft (2–4.5 m)

Trailing shrubby species from North America. Long arching stems, scattered thorns, deep green leaves. Clusters of single deep pink flowers, ageing to white, in summer. Round hips, bristly, red to greenish brown. Zones 4–10.

Rosa spinosissima

syn. *Rosa pimpinellifolia*

BURNET ROSE, SCOTCH BRIAR

☼ ✱ ↔4 ft (1.2 m) ↑3–7 ft (0.9–2 m)

Small suckering rose found over a wide area of Europe and Asia. Well branched, prickly stems, coarse fern-like leaves. Single creamy white flowers, in spring. Small, round, black, shiny hips. ***R. s. altaica***, beautiful pure white flowers, prominent yellow stamens. Zones 4–10.

Rosa stellata

syn. *Hesperhodos stellata*

DESERT ROSE

☼ ✱ ↔36 in (90 cm) ↑36 in (90 cm)

Deciduous shrub from hot southwestern areas of the USA. Forms a dense spiny thicket. Light green wedge-shaped leaflets, small, slightly hairy. Single rich pink flowers, in midsummer. Flower buds and red hips covered with soft spines. ***R. s. mirifica***, flowers range from pink to purplish red. Zones 6–10.

Rosa virginiana

VIRGINIA ROSE

☼ ✱ ↔5 ft (1.5 m) ↑5 ft (1.5 m)

Erect, sometimes suckering shrub native to eastern North America. Leaves shiny green, coloring well in autumn. Flowers single deep pink blooms, with prominent yellow stamens, in midsummer. Round red hips. Zones 3–10.

Rosa wichurana

syn. *Rosa lucieae var. lucieae*

MEMORIAL ROSE

☼ ✱ ↔20 ft (6 m) ↑6 ft (1.8 m)

Dense spreading shrub or short climber from eastern Asia. Trailing stems bear stout thorns, glossy green foliage almost evergreen. Clusters of single, fragrant, white flowers, in summer. Small, dark red, oval hips. Species much used in breeding programs. Regarded by some as doubtfully distinct from *R. luciae*. Zones 5–10.

Rosa woodsii

WESTERN WILD ROSE

☼ ✱ ↔5 ft (1.5 m) ↑3–7 ft (0.9–2 m)

Native to North America. Stiffly branching shrub. Stems purplish brown when young, very prickly. Foliage colors well in autumn. Mid-pink single flowers, in small clusters, in summer. Bright red hips. ***R. w. ultramontana***, from northwestern USA and adjacent areas of Canada, smaller flowers than the typical variety. Zones 4–10.

Rosa spinosissima

MODERN ROSES

The term "Modern Roses" is somewhat misleading as a number of them were being developed in the latter half of the 1800s, at the same time as some of the Old Rose groups. Modern Roses are best characterized by their mainly repeat-flowering qualities, their floriferousness, and the yellow and orange shades that have been introduced. The crossing of Hybrid Tea (Large-flowered) Roses and Polyantha Roses resulted in the Floribunda (Cluster-flowered) Roses; others have followed, most recently the Ground Cover Roses and David Austin's English Roses. A breeding program initiated by the Canadian Department of Agriculture in the early 1900s has produced some very hardy roses, some tolerant to Zone 1, notably the Explorer Series, named after explorers of Canada. The Modern Roses are divided into major categories based on habit—Bush, Shrub, Climbing, Miniature, and Ground Cover.

BUSH ROSES

The Bush Roses usually have a tidy habit, the biggest growing no more than 5 ft (1.5 m) tall. They have a long flowering season and are suitable for growing as bedding plants and in borders. The complex crossing and re-crossing of the various groups can make classification difficult, with some Hybrid Tea Roses bearing flowers in quite large clusters, and taller-growing Floribunda Roses being more shrub-like.

FLORIBUNDA (CLUSTER-FLOWERED) ROSES

☼ ✱ ↔3–6 ft (0.9–1.8 m) ↑4–7 ft (1.2–2 m)

These Bush Roses resulted from the crossing of the small cluster-flowered Polyantha Roses and the Hybrid Tea Roses. The individual blooms, while usually smaller than those of the Hybrid Tea Roses, are borne in large crowded clusters, and the flowers are usually flatter when fully open. The majority are double or semi-double. **'Amber Queen'**, quite large, cup-shaped, clear amber-yellow flowers; **'Apricot Nectar'**, cupped golden-apricot flowers, well-scented; **'Betty Boop'** ★ (syn. 'Centenary of Federation'), highly fragrant single blooms of creamy white to yellow, shading to red toward petal edges; **'Brass Band'** ★, lightly scented blooms in dark and light apricot shades; **'Chinatown'**, long-stemmed fragrant blooms of rich bright yellow with pink highlights at petal edges; **'City of Belfast'**, large clusters of scarlet-red blooms; **'City of London'**, very fragrant, cupped, double flowers of soft pink fading to blush; **'Dancing Pink'**, deep pink, lighter center, semi-double; **'Dearest'**, very fragrant, large, salmon pink flowers open to reveal prominent yellow stamens; **'Dicky'** (syn. 'Anisley Dickson'), lightly scented, orange-pink, double flowers; **'Easy Does It'** ★, fragrant, soft orange and pink blend; **'Ebb Tide'**, purple-red, strong clove scent, old-fashioned-style double; **'Elizabeth of Glamis'** (syn. 'Irish Beauty'), named for the UK's Queen Elizabeth the Queen Mother, very fragrant well-shaped flowers of clear

Rosa setigera

Rosa virginiana

Rosa stellata mirifica

Rosa, MR, Floribunda, 'Amber Queen'

Rosa, Modern Rose, Floribunda, 'Hannah Gordon'

Rosa, Modern Rose, Hybrid Tea, 'Fragrant Cloud'

Rosa, Modern Rose, Hybrid Tea, 'Irish Gold'

salmon pink; **'Fabulous'**, pure white, semi-double, strong scent, dark glossy foliage; **'Fragrant Delight'**, strong perfume, large flowers in soft salmon-orange shades; **'Frensham'**, vigorous rose, deep red semi-double flowers; **'Gavnø'** (syn. 'Buck's Fizz'), high-centered soft orange blooms; **'Glad Tidings'**, velvety dark red blooms; **'Gold Badge'** ★, large, rich yellow, double flowers; **'Greensleeves'**, unusual pale green, faint pink overlay, semi-double; **'Hannah Gordon'** (syn. 'Raspberry Ice'), creamy white petals suffused with deep pink at edges; **'Hot Cocoa'**, rusty red-brown, mild scent; **'Iceberg'** ★ (syns 'Fée des Neiges', 'Schneewittchen'), large clusters of pure white flowers; **'Julia Child'**, deep golden yellow, fragrant, lush dark foliage; **'Katherine Loker'**, bright yellow, mildew-resistant; **'Ketchup and Mustard'** ★, red with yellow petal reverse, outstanding bicolor contrast; **'Lilac Charm'**, almost-single rose, large petals of pale lilac, prominent red stamens; **'Lilli Marleen'**, large, velvety, deep red flowers; **'Liverpool Echo'**, salmon pink, mildly scented; **'Livin' Easy'** ★ (syn. 'Fellowship'), fiery orange-red blooms; **'Ma Perkins'**, large cupped flowers in shades of clear pink and salmon; **'Margaret Merril'**, very fragrant, large, white flowers with a hint of pink at center; **'Mariandel'** ★, vivid red semi-double flowers with a mild fragrance; **'Matangi'**, one of a number of so-called "hand-painted" roses that appear to be brushed with secondary colors, bright orangey vermilion with a silvery white central eye and petal reverse; **'Matilda'** (syn. 'Seduction'), large, white, double flowers, petals delicately edged with pink; **'Moody Blues'**, unusual mauve to light purple shade, fragrant; **'Old Master'**, red, edges and center pale pink to white, semi-double; **'Picasso'**, "hand-painted" rose, flowers brushed with deep pink, carmine, and silvery white; **'Pinnacle'**, red shading to pale pink at center; **'Prima'** (syn. 'Many Happy Returns'), semi-double flowers of palest pink; **'Purple Tiger'**, reddish purple shading to mauve with irregular dark flecks and sectors, strong scent; **'Queen Elizabeth'**, long pointed buds open to large, high-centered, clear pink blooms; **'Radox Bouquet'** (syn. 'Rosika'), very fragrant cupped blooms of soft rose pink; **'Rosemary Rose'**, camellia-like flowers of deep pinkish red, in large clusters with distinctive maroon foliage; **'Serendipity'**, deep yellow, strong scent, lush dark foliage; **'Sexy Rexy'** ★, large clusters of soft salmon pink camellia-like flowers; **'Sheila's Perfume'** ★, very fragrant yellow flowers edged with red; **'Southampton'** (syn. 'Susan Ann'), apricot flowers flushed with orange and red; **'Sunsprite'** (syns 'Friesia', 'Korresia'), rounded buds open to very fragrant double flowers of bright yellow; **'Sweet Dream'** ★, double blooms of soft apricot-orange; **'Trumpeter'**, flowers of brilliant scarlet-orange. Zones 4–10.

HYBRID TEA (LARGE-FLOWERED) ROSES

☼ ✱ ↔3–6 ft (0.9–1.8 m)
↕5–8 ft (1.5–2.4 m)

This group has become the most popular of all roses and thousands have been bred. They are generally sturdy plants, growing to about 3 ft (0.9 m) in height, with an upright bushy habit and mid- to dark green, often glossy leaves. The very large flowers are usually double or semi-double and borne singly or in clusters. They have elegant long-pointed buds and when open retain the high center, to varying degrees, as the outer petals reflex. The Hybrid Tea Rose usually acknowledged as the first is 'La France', bred in 1867. Only a very small selection of the vast numbers available is included here. **'Abbeyfield Rose'**, rich deep pink double flowers; **'Alec's Red'**, plump black-red buds open to double well-perfumed flowers; **'Alexander'**, lightly scented, double, vermilion blooms; **'Black Beauty'**, very deep red, mild fragrance; **'Blackberry Nip'**, deep magenta to purple, fragrant, vigorous erect growth; **'Brandy'**, large, sweetly perfumed, apricot flowers; **'Carina'**, fragrant double blooms of rosy pink; **'Christian Dior'**, bright mid-red, long-flowering, mild fragrance; **'Congratulations'**, high-centered clear rose pink flowers on long stems; **'Dainty Bess'**, light pink, red stamens, spicy scent, large single flowers; **'Deep Secret'** (syn. 'Mildred Scheel'), very dark, deep crimson-red flowers, velvety-textured, very fragrant; **'Double Delight'**, very fragrant creamy pink flowers, darkening to cherry red at edges; **'Elina'** ★ (syn. 'Peaudouce'), lemony yellow flowers fading to cream at edges; **'Erotica'**, deep red, strong fragrance; **'Fragrant Cloud'** (syns 'Duftwolke', 'Nuage Parfumé'), highly perfumed coral red flowers; **'Hi Ho Silver'**, unusual silvery mauve-gray shade, strong scent; **'Indian Summer'**, fragrant double blooms in orange shades; **'Ingrid Bergman'** ★, named for the actress, has deep red velvety blooms, long lasting, good for picking; **'Irish Gold'** (syn. 'Grandpa Dickson'), very prickly plant, elegant lemony yellow flowers; **'Just Joey'** ★, large coppery orange flowers that pale to soft pink at edge of petals; **'Kronenbourg'** ★, deep pinkish red, buff petal undersides, mild fragrance; **'La France'**, high-centered, well-perfumed, silvery pink flowers; **'Lady Rose'**, high-centered bright salmon and orange flowers emerge from long pointed buds; **'Love'**, high-centered scarlet flowers, silvery white reverse on petals; **'Lovely Lady'**, fragrant, double, rosy pink flowers emerge from long buds; **'Loving Memory'** (syns 'Burgund 81', 'Red Cedar'), high-centered bright crimson blooms on long stems; **'Midas Touch'**, bright deep yellow, musk scent; **'Mme Butterfly'**, very fragrant soft pink flowers emerge from long buds; **'Mrs Oakley Fisher'**, single deep buff-yellow flowers, prominent amber stamens; **'Moonstone'** ★, lightly scented, large, white flowers, highlighted with shades of soft pink; **'National Trust'**, large, high-centered, bright red flowers; **'New Zealand'** ★ (syn. 'Aotearoa New Zealand'), soft pink fragrant flowers open from long pointed buds; **'Olympiad'** ★, brilliant red, velvety, double flowers, delicately scented; **'Pascali'**, considered one of the best whites, long, nearly thornless stems topped with ivory white flowers; **'Paul Shirville'** (syn. 'Heart Throb'), perfumed, high-centered, pink flowers with a hint of salmon; **'Peace'**, probably the most famous and popular Large-flowered Rose of all, large pale yellow flowers suffused with creamy pink; **'Perfume Delight'**, cupped deep pink flowers, very fragrant; **'Pot o' Gold'**, bright yellow blooms touched with gold, very fragrant; **'Precious Platinum'** (syns 'Opa Pötschke', 'Red Star'), bright red high-centered flowers with a velvety sheen; **'Pristine'**, long pointed buds open to reveal large, shapely, white flowers flushed with pale pink; **'Purple Passion'**, pinkish purple, fruity scent; **'Remember Me'**, coppery orange flowers; **'Royal William'**, large, rich red, velvety blooms; **'Savoy Hotel'**, fully double soft pink flowers, deeper colored on petal reverse, lightly scented; **'Shot Silk'**, globular silky-petalled blooms of salmon pink with a yellow base; **'Silver Jubilee'**, silvery pink and apricot flowers with a deeper colored reverse; **'Simply The Best'**, golden yellow, apricot, and soft orange blend, strong scent; **'Sunblest'** (syn. 'Landora'), rich yellow flowers emerge from slim buds; **'Sutter's Gold'**, deep yellow flowers flushed with orange and pink; **'Tiffany'**, pale pink, deeper center, full double, strong scent; **'Touch of Class'** (syn. 'Maréchale LeClerc'), long-stemmed high-centered flowers, shades of cream, coral, and salmon pink; **'Valencia'** ★, fragrant, apricot-yellow, double blooms; **'Veteran's Honor'**, dark dusky red, fruity scent; **'White Lightnin'**, vigorous plant, well-scented pure white flowers; **'White Wings'**, white, red stamens, large single. Zones 4–10.

PATIO (DWARF CLUSTER-FLOWERED) ROSES
☼ ✱ ↔18–36 in (45–90 cm)
↑18–30 in (45–75 cm)

The roses in this more recent group are the result of much cross-breeding between Polyanthas, Miniatures, and Floribunda Roses, and classification of them can be difficult. They are usually bushier and slightly taller than the Miniatures, around 2 ft (0.6 m) tall, and most resemble the Floribunda Roses with all parts proportionately smaller. They are suitable for beds and borders as well as for patios and growing in containers. Some popular examples of this group are: **'Anna Ford'**, which bears long pointed buds opening to cup-shaped deep orange flowers with a yellow eye; **'Boys' Brigade'**, single crimson flowers with paler eye; **'Brass Ring'** (syn. 'Peek-a-Boo'), deep peachy orange buds opening to peach and pale apricot, fading to pink at edges; **'Dainty Dinah'**, soft coral red flowers on a spreading plant; **'Festival'**, carrying clusters of striking deep red flowers, semi-double; **'Queen Mother'** ★, delicate pink semi-double flowers; and **'Rexy's Baby'**, an offspring of the Floribunda Rose 'Sexy Rexy', which produces pale pink flowers deepening to salmon pink at the center. Zones 4–11.

POLYANTHA ROSES
☼ ✱ ↔24–36 in (60–90 cm)
↑24–36 in (60–90 cm)

Introduced in 1875, only a few of these small roses are still available, usually growing to about 2 ft (0.6 m) tall. They are very hardy, withstanding the winter cold of northern Europe, and very free flowering, with small pompon-like flowers covering the plants for months. **'Baby Faurax'**, small, amethyst-violet, pompon flowers; **'Cameo'**, semi-double blooms in shades of salmon and coral pink; **'Gloire du Midi'**, orange-red blooms; **'Mlle Cécile Brünner'**, profuse shell pink flowers open from long pointed buds; **'Mevrouw Nathalie Nypels'**, pink semi-double flowers, sweet fragrance; **'Nypels Perfection'**, semi-double blooms in shades of pink; **'Phyllis Bide'**, small, double, opens buff yellow and pink, ages to pale pink; **'Pinkie'**, cupped, semi-double, very fragrant rosy pink flowers; **'The Fairy'**, large crowded clusters of small, very double, clear pink flowers smother the plant constantly throughout summer; **'White Cécile Brünner'**, slightly fragrant, double, white flowers with yellow centers; **'White Pet'** (syn. 'Little White Pet'), sometimes classed as a Floribunda Rose, small, pompon-like, white flowers, with a pink tint in the bud; **'Yesterday'**, purple-pink double blooms emerge from dark buds. Zones 3–10.

SHRUB ROSES

Shrub Roses, usually bigger and more vigorous than Bush Roses, range from 4–10 ft (1.2–3 m) in height. Flower formation varies considerably and some cultivars flower only once in the season. Suitable for specimen or shrubberies and mixed borders, and some can be trained as small climbers or pillar roses.

HYBRID RUGOSA ROSES
☼ ✱ ↔5–10 ft (1.5–3 m)
↑2–7 ft (0.6–2 m)

The Hybrid Rugosa Roses are a distinctive group with stout bristly branches and rather coarse wrinkled leaves that often color to buttery yellow in autumn. These roses are tough and healthy plants, ranging from 2–7 ft (0.6–2 m) in height. Many have very fragrant flowers; blooms range in formation from single to double, in shades of pink and crimson, with a few white and yellow. As a group they span the eras of Old and Modern Roses, with plants being bred from the late 1800s to the present day. **'Agnes'**, dense bush, bearing very fragrant, creamy yellow, double flowers; **'Blanc Double de Coubert'**, vigorous, with heavily perfumed semi-double flowers of purest white; **'Dr Eckener'**, very large, heavily perfumed, semi-double flowers in soft shades of pale yellow and coppery rose, fading to pale pink; **'Fimbriata'** (syns 'Dianthiflora', 'Phoebe's Frilled Pink'), small, white, double flowers, frilled petal edges resembling *Dianthus*; **'Frau Dagmar Hartopp'**, large, single, silvery pink flowers, sometimes darker; **'Hansa'**, fragrant, double, pink-purple flowers; **'Henry Hudson'** (one of the Explorer Series), hardy to Zone 1, fragrant white flowers, tinged with pink; **'Martin Frobisher'** (Explorer Series), hardy to Zone 1, fragrant soft pink flowers; **'Purple Pavement'**, purple-red, double, very fragrant, showy yellow to deep red hips; **'Roseraie de l'Haÿ'**, dense and vigorous bush, with large, semi-double, extremely fragrant flowers of rich crimson-purple; **'Scabrosa'**, modern introduction with large, single, cerise flowers; **'Souvenir de Philémon Cochet'**, fully double flowers, white with pale pink center; **'Thérèse Bugnet'**, large fragrant flowers, up to 4 in (10 cm) in diameter, opening reddish pink, maturing to light pink; and **'Vanguard'**, large, double, apricot-pink to salmon flowers, which are highly aromatic. Zones 3–10.

MODERN SHRUB ROSES
☼ ✱ ↔4–8 ft (1.2–2.4 m)
↑4–8 ft (1.2–2.4 m)

These roses are a miscellany of plants bred from a variety of different parents and they do not have a definitive characteristic. They vary in size and growth habit and the flowers range through all colors and from single to double. **'Adelaide Hoodless'**, hardy to Zone 1, semi-double clear red flowers in clusters of up to 35 blooms; **'Anna Zinkeisen'**, double flowers of ivory white, lemon tones at base; **'Berlin'**, semi-double flowers of rich red, paling at center, prominent yellow stamens; **'Bonica'** ★ (syn. 'Bonica 82'), long arching stems of double light pink flowers, rather frilled petals; **'Canary Bird'** (syn. *R. xanthina* 'Canary Bird'), fragrant, single, canary yellow flowers, prominent stamens; **'Cantabrigiensis'** (syn. *R.* × *cantabrigiensis*), large pale primrose flowers; **'Cerise Bouquet'**, semi-double deep pink-red flowers; **'Champlain'** (from the Explorer Series), slightly fragrant, dark red, velvety flowers, hardy to Zone 2; **'Eddie's Jewel'**, repeat-flowering form; **'Flower Carpet'** ★, semi-double rich pink flowers with light scent, also available with yellow, white, light pink, coral, or red flowers; **'Fred Loads'**, large, almost-single, bright salmon pink flowers on large trusses; **'Fritz Nobis'**, once-flowering shrub, large double flowers of light pink to soft salmon; **'Geranium'** ★, more compact habit, good display of larger hips; **'Golden Wings'**, single pale primrose yellow flowers, prominent gold stamens; **'Goldstern'**, large golden yellow blooms emerge from elegant, long, pointed buds; **'J. P. Connell'**, hardy to Zone 2, clusters of 3 to 8 lemon yellow flowers fade to cream; **'Lavender Dream'**, clusters of flattish lilac-pink flowers, may be slightly fragrant; **'Nevada'**, almost-single white flowers, up to 4 in (10 cm) across, prominent yellow stamens; **'Phantom'**, slightly fragrant saucer-shaped flowers, rich deep red petals, bright yellow stamens; **'St John's Rose'** (syns *R.* × *richardii, R. sancta*), dark green leaves, single flowers, mildly fragrant, clear delicate pink; an ancient hybrid, its flowers have been found in Egyptian tombs; **'Sally Holmes'** ★, large, creamy white, single flowers open from soft apricot-pink buds; and **'Westerland'**, fragrant, apricot, double blooms.

Rosa, Modern Rose, Patio, 'Anna Ford'

Rosa, Modern Rose, Polyantha, 'White Cécile Brünner'

Rosa, Modern Rose, Modern Shrub, 'Déclic'

Rosa, MR, MS, English, 'Charles Rennie Mackintosh'

Rosa, Modern Rose, Floribunda Climbing, 'Climbing Diablotin'

Rosa, MR, MS, Hybrid Musk, 'Danaë'

Rosa, Modern Rose, Hybrid Tea Climbing, 'Albertine', sport

Rosa, Modern Rose, Rambler, 'Trier'

English Roses: These roses are also classed as Modern Shrub Roses. In the early 1960s Englishman David Austin began a breeding program that crossed Old and Modern Roses. English Roses, as they are now known, have become very popular, combining as they do the flower forms and fragrance of Old Roses with the growth habits, repeat-flowering ability, and wider color range of Modern Roses. They range from 3–7 ft (0.9–2 m) in height. Most are well perfumed. A large number are now available, including: **'Abraham Darby'** ★, large, orange-pink, fully double flowers; **'Charles Rennie Mackintosh'**, fragrant blooms open rose pink, age to lilac-pink; **'Constance Spry'**, the first of the group, lax plant, large, cupped, soft pink flowers, myrrh-like fragrance also found in some other English Roses, in late spring–summer; **'Gertrude Jekyll'**, very fragrant, rich pink, very double flowers; **'Golden Celebration'** ★, highly fragrant, deep yellow, double flowers in summer–autumn; **'Graham Thomas'**, long-stemmed, rich yellow, double flowers, sweetly scented; **'Jubilee Celebration'**, salmon pink with pale petal reverse, strong fruity scent; **'Jude the Obscure'**, strongly scented yellow blooms; **'Mary Rose'**, rich rose pink flowers; **'Winchester Cathedral'**, fragrant white blooms; and **'Windrush'**, large semi-double flowers, pure soft lemon, prominent yellow stamens, very sweetly perfumed.

Hybrid Musk Roses: Although placed correctly under the mantle of Modern Shrub Roses, this group is often thought of as "Old." The first Hybrid Musk Rose was introduced in 1913 by Rev. Joseph Pemberton and most of this group were bred by him. The name Hybrid Musk relates to the fragrance, which is inherited very indirectly from the musk rose *(R. moschata)*. The plants have a shrubby habit, often with dark green leaves and purplish stems, and a long flowering season when they bear clusters of single to double flowers. Their popularity is undiminished and most are still available today. Growing 4–8 ft (1.2–2.4 m) tall, they make very good specimen or shrubbery plants in the garden. **'Belinda'** ★, mid-pink flowers, often highlighted with white at petal base; **'Buff Beauty'**, double apricot blooms age to buff-yellow; **'Cornelia'**, small, double, very pale pink flowers with orange base, musk-like fragrance; **'Danaë'**, double blooms open rich yellow, age to white; **'Erfurt'**, fragrant semi-double blooms of pink, shaded yellow toward petal base; **'Moonlight'**, one of the first Hybrid Musk Roses to be introduced, clusters of almost-single creamy white flowers, prominent yellow stamens; **'Mozart'**, a large white eye accents the rich pink single flowers; **'Penelope'**, semi-double blooms of palest pink that age to white; and **'Prosperity'**, large clusters of double white flowers on long arching stems. Zones 4–10.

CLIMBING ROSES

Modern climbing roses are usually long-flowering and not quite as rampant as the early introductions. They encompass a huge range of colors and frequently have double flowers. Non-rambling climbers are most often produced from Bush Rose sports and some popular Bush Roses, such as 'Iceberg', also occur in climbing forms.

FLORIBUNDA CLIMBING ROSES

☼/◐ ❄ ↔ 8–15 ft (2.4–4.5 m)
↕ 10–20 ft (3–6 m)

Frequently the most satisfying of the climbers because their smaller flowers are more weather resistant while being just as showy as the larger-flowered forms. Also, their whippy stems are less inclined to break under the weight of blooms and are more easily trained. **'Climbing Diablotin'**, small, rich red, semi-double flowers; **'Climbing Iceberg'**, lightly scented, white, double blooms; **'John Cabot'** (Explorer Series), hardy to Zone 1, fragrant red-pink flowers; **'Santa Catalina'**, slightly scented semi-double flowers of palest pink; **'Sparkling Scarlet'**, semi-double blooms of vivid scarlet, fruity fragrance; **'William Baffin'** (Explorer Series), hardy to Zone 1, slightly fragrant red flowers in clusters of as many as 30 blooms. Zones 5–9.

HYBRID TEA CLIMBING ROSES

☼/◐ ❄ ↔ 7–17 ft (2–5 m)
↕ 7–17 ft (2–5 m)

Hybrid Tea climbers have the same fancy double and large single flowers as their bushy cousins. They tend to have heavier, less pliable stems than other climbers and need support to prevent weather damage and to ensure long-lasting displays. **'Albertine'**, fragrant, pink to salmon, double flowers; **'Compassion'** ★, fragrant, apricot-pink, double flowers; **'Dublin Bay'** ★, fragrant, rich red, double flowers; **'Fourth of July'** ★, variable red, pink, and white combinations of flecks, stripes, and sectors; **'Golden Showers'**, large double flowers of bright light yellow, paling with age; **'New Dawn'** ★, large, fragrant, double blooms of palest pink; **'Pierre de Ronsard'** ★, lightly scented, large, double blooms of ivory suffused with pink. Zones 5–9.

RAMBLER ROSES

☼/◐ ❄ ↔ 10–25 ft (3–8 m)
↕ 10–25 ft (3–8 m)

Often very thorny plants, Rambler Roses, which are principally of *R. wichurana* or *R. multiflora* parentage, differ from other Climbing Roses in not only elongating their stems, but also producing many vigorous new basal shoots each year. This results in a clump of cane-like stems. Pruning is mainly cutting out the older and less productive stems. Ramblers are usually once-flowering. **'Albéric Barbier'**, lightly scented, ivory, double blooms, color deepening toward center; **'American Pillar'**, rose pink with large white center, single; **'Bobbie James'**, highly perfumed, semi-double, cupped blooms in ivory white, prominent bright yellow stamens; **'Bonfire'**, pink-red double blooms; **'Excelsa'**, white-centered crimson double blooms; **'François Juranville'**, salmon pink double flowers, tinged yellow near center, fruity fragrance; **'May Queen'**, double rose pink blooms, fruity fragrance; **'Rambling Rector'**, highly fragrant, white, semi-double blooms; **'Sander's White Rambler'**, small, white, double flowers, fruity fragrance; **'Seagull'**, fragrant, snow white, double flowers, lustrous golden yellow stamens; **'Super Elfin'**, orange-red blooms; **'Thalia'**, small, pure white, double blooms; **'Trier'**, semi-double blooms of ivory, deepening to pale golden yellow toward center; **'Veilchenblau'**, semi-double blooms of violet-pink with white markings, fruity fragrance. Zones 5–9.

MINIATURE ROSES

Among the more recent large groups to be developed, Miniature Roses of the style we know today first appeared in the late 1930s. Their tiny flowers are perfect replicas in miniature of those of the large bushes. What they lack in scent, they more than make up for in intricate beauty.

CLIMBING MINIATURE ROSES

↔ 3–7 ft (0.9–2 m)
↑ 3–12 ft (0.9–3.5 m)

There are a few small climbers, but Climbing Miniatures are frequently only miniature in their flowers, and produce a tremendous display. The dividing line between Polyanthas and Climbing Miniatures can be difficult to discern. **'Nozomi'**, taller plant, small, single, starry flowers of pearly pink; **'Warm Welcome'** ★, small scented blooms of orange-red. Zones 4–11.

MINIATURE ROSES

↔ 12–18 in (30–45 cm)
↑ 8–24 in (20–60 cm)

True Miniature Roses grow only 8–24 in (20–60 cm) high and are perfect miniature replicas of the Bush Roses, with tiny leaves and dainty buds and flowers. They are useful for edging borders and make very good container plants. Some roses classed as Miniatures are somewhat taller, but bear small flowers and leaves. **'Air France'** (syns 'American Independence', 'Rosy Meillandina'), double flowers of clear rose pink; **'Autumn Splendour'** ★, light fruity fragrance, large, double, yellow-orange flowers, deeper coloring at petal edges intensifies with age; **'Baby Darling'**, double apricot flowers; **'Baby Love'** ★, small, single, buttercup yellow flowers, prominent stamens; **'Cachet'** ★, large, unscented, white blooms; **'Cider Cup'**, rich apricot double blooms, lightly scented; **'Cinderella'**, pearly white flowers lightly flushed with pink; **'Fairy Tale'**, small, delicately perfumed, pink flowers, mature to pale pink; **'Gentle Touch'**, small, soft pink, double flowers, lightly scented; **'Gourmet Popcorn'** ★, lightly scented, semi-double, snow white flowers; **'Holy Toledo'**, double flowers of apricot-orange; **'Hot Tamale'**, striking pink-orange flowers, either singly or in clusters; **'Hula Girl'**, long pointed buds open to deep salmon pink flowers; **'Irresistible'** ★, fragrant double blooms, almost pure white, becoming pink-tinged toward center; **'Little Red Devil'**, well-perfumed, double, deep red flowers; **'Loving Touch'**, long pointed buds open to fragrant high-centered flowers in apricot tones; **'Magic Carrousel'** ★, double flowers, creamy white, petals red-edged; **'My Valentine'**, high-centered deep red flowers; **'Party Girl'** ★, fragrant, soft apricot-yellow, double blooms; **'Pink Bells'**, bright mid-pink, double, trailing, often trained as weeping standard; **'Pride 'n' Joy'**, profuse orange blooms, fruit-like perfume; **'Red Ace'** (syns 'Amanda', 'Amruda'), velvety deep red blooms; **'Rosina'** (syns 'Josephine Wheatcroft', 'Yellow Sweetheart'), semi-double blooms of clear yellow; **'Rosmarin'**, slightly fragrant double flowers range in color from pale pink to pale red, depending on air temperature; **'Si'**, pale pink, exquisite tiny double flowers; **'Snow Carpet'**, small, very double, white flowers; **'Sweet Magic'**, orange semi-double blooms; **'Tapis Jaune'**, profuse, double, yellow, small flowers. Zones 4–11.

GROUND COVER ROSES

↔ 5–12 ft (1.5–3.5 m)
↑ 12–24 in (30–60 cm)

Some sprawling Shrub Roses are classed as Ground Cover Roses. With their lax spreading habit they are useful for growing on banks and cascading over low walls, as well as for covering large areas of ground. More recent breeding has led to the introduction of a number of plants that are very long flowering and have a densely foliaged habit. **'Bassino'**, single cupped flowers of brilliant scarlet; **'Diamant'**, rich orange-red double blooms; **'Eyeopener'**, single bright red flowers with white eye; **'Pink Bells'**, lightly scented double flowers of rich pink; **'Pretty in Pink'**, scented pink blooms; **'Rosy Cushion'**, soft pink almost-single blooms, taller plant; **'Sommermärchen'**, lightly scented rich pink flowers. Zones 4–10.

OLD (HERITAGE) ROSES

Under the umbrella term "Old Roses" fall a number of groups containing roses that, through deliberate breeding, have similar characteristics to each other. Some of the oldest groups, such as Gallica, contain roses that have been cultivated for centuries, while other groups, like Bourbon, are the product of nineteenth-century breeding. The term "Old Rose" is a misnomer as some Old groups contain plants bred more recently, and the term is often used in reference to shrubs such as the Hybrid Musks (included here under Modern Roses), which are of twentieth-century origin. Many people consider that it is a rose's attributes rather than its date of introduction that earn it the title of "Old." Some of the Old Rose groups, such as the Teas, include a number of climbing plants and there are also Old groups of climbers and ramblers, like the Noisettes.

OLD NON-CLIMBING ROSES

For as long as roses have been cultivated gardeners have been improving on the wild species. Old Non-climbing Roses, which include such groups as the China Roses, Damask Roses, and Gallica Roses, may be once-flowering and limited in color range but they more than make up for those failings with delicate tones, unusually shaped flowers, and fragrance that combine to conjure up a bygone era.

ALBA ROSES

↔ 6–10 ft (1.8–3 m)
↑ 6–8 ft (0.6–2.4 m)

This is a very hardy group of Old Roses that have light bluish green foliage and very fragrant pale-colored flowers that are usually double or semi-double. They flower only once during mid-summer. Most varieties grow 6–8 ft (1.8–2.4 m) tall. **'Alba Maxima'** (syns 'Bonnie Prince Charlie's Rose', 'Jacobite Rose', 'White Rose of York'), vigorous shrub, large, pure white, double flowers; **'Celestial'** (syn. 'Céleste'), heavily perfumed, semi-double flowers of soft pink; **'Chloris'** (syn. 'Rosée du Matin'), ancient rose, comparatively thornless, darker leaves, double soft pink flowers; **'Félicité Parmentier'**, smaller shrub, flat double flowers, salmon pink, fading to pale pink; **'Great Maiden's Blush'**, vigorous shrub dating back to the fifteenth century or earlier, large, very double, blush pink flowers; **'Königin von Dänemark'** ★ (syn. 'Queen of Denmark'), smaller double flowers of a deeper pink than other Albas; **'Mme Plantier'**, rather flat, double, white flowers, buds often tinged reddish pink; **'Maiden's Blush'** fragrant, creamy white to very light pink, double flowers. Zones 4–10.

BOURBON ROSES

↔ 5–8 ft (1.5–2.4 m)
↑ 4–7 ft (1.2–2 m)

The first Bourbon Rose was a hybrid between *R. chinensis* and a Damask Rose that occurred naturally on the Ile de Bourbon. The majority are shrubs of 4–7 ft (1.2–2 m); a few of climbing habit; highly perfumed, and many with repeat-flowering characteristics. The flowers may be semi-double or double, often cupped or with a quartered arrangement of petals. In humid areas they are susceptible to fungal diseases. **'Boule de Neige'**, globular, double, white blooms, sometimes with reddish purple tinge on petal edges; **'Commandant Beaurepaire'**, double flowers striped in shades of crimson, pink, purple, and white; **'Gros Choux d'Hollande'**, medium-sized, fragrant, pink flowers opening from rounded red buds; **'Honorine de Brabant'**, light pink cupped flowers, faint rose spotting on inner surfaces; **'Louise Odier'**, vigorous bush, very double bright rose pink flowers; **'Mme Isaac Pereire'**, one of the most heavily perfumed, large very double flowers of magenta-rose; **'Mme Pierre Oger'**, cupped, double, translucent silvery pink flowers; **'Queen of Bourbons'** (syn. 'Bourbon Queen'), semi-double, cupped, rose pink flowers, in summer; **'Reine Victoria'**, slender bush, cupped double flowers, silky textured, lilac-pink; **'Souvenir de la Malmaison'**, double flowers, flattened and quartered, palest flesh pink, quickly pulped by wet weather. Its sport, **'Souvenir de St Anne's'**, a semi-double form with prominent yellow stamens, survives bad weather; **'Zéphirine Drouhin'**, no thorns, rich pink, semi-double, fragrant flowers. Zones 6–10.

Rosa, Modern Rose, Miniature, 'Tapis Jaune'

Rosa, MR, Ground Cover, 'Sommermärchen'

Rosa, Old Rose, Alba, 'Alba Maxima'

Rosa, OR, Bourbon, 'Mme Isaac Pereire'

Rosa, Old Rose, Centifolia, 'Fantin-Latour'

Rosa, Old Rose, Damask, 'Blush Damask'

CENTIFOLIA ROSES

☼ ✱ ↔ 4–8 ft (1.2–2.4 m)
↕ 2–8 ft (0.6–2.4 m)

Many roses in this group are centuries old. Centifolia means "one hundred leaves" and refers to the crowded petals that form the large flowers. Centifolias, "rose of the painters,"often feature in works by the Old Masters. The flowers come in shades of pink as well as white and, occasionally, purplish magenta shades. They generally flower only once in early summer. Bushes, often prickly and coarse with quite lax growth, vary in height from 2–8 ft (0.6–2.4 m). Smaller cultivars produce proportionally smaller blooms. **'Cabbage Rose'** (syn. 'Provence Rose'), rose of complex hybrid parentage, known in Europe since before 1600, grayish green leaves, deep pink flowers, very double and cupped, strong sweet perfume; **'Fantin-Latour'**, highly fragrant, soft pink, double blooms; **'Gros Choux d'Hollande'**, bright mid-pink, very fragrant; **'Petite de Hollande'**, small, scented, double blooms of rose pink; **'Petite Lisette'**, to 3 ft (0.9 m) tall, small, very fragrant, pink pompon flowers; **'Reine des Centfeuilles'**, fragrant pink flowers, up to 2½ in (6 cm) across; **'Rose de Meaux'**, to about 2 ft (0.6 m) high, small pink slightly frilly flowers, resemble those of *Dianthus;* **'The Bishop'**, flowers slightly earlier than most, purplish magenta blooms; **'Tour de Malakoff'**, tall lax bush, very fragrant purplish magenta blooms fade to lilac. Zones 5–10.

Rosa, Old Rose, China, 'Archduke Charles'

Rosa, Old Rose, Gallica, 'Tuscany'

CHINA ROSES

☼ ❄ ↔ 3–6 ft (0.9–1.8 m)
↕ 3–6 ft (0.9–1.8 m)

When the first China Roses were introduced to Europe in the eighteenth century, their repeat-flowering characteristic was seized on by breeders who welcomed this new source with this attribute. Generally China Roses are low growing with airy, often spindly growth, and are rather sparsely foliaged. The flowers are usually quite small and semi-double or double in shades of pink, with some crimson and flame tints. Fragrance is usually light. **'Archduke Charles'**, pink to crimson flowers mature to a deeper shade, banana-scented; **'Comtesse du Caÿla'**, loosely semi-double, scented flowers in flame shades; **'Gloire des Rosomanes'**, hardy rose, large, cup-shaped, semi-double, pink to crimson flowers, in spring–autumn; **'Green Rose'** (syn. 'Viridiflora') bears green leaf-like sepals with red-brown serrated edges, rather than colored petals; **'Le Vésuve'**, large slightly fragrant flowers, can be pink or red, depending whether grown in sun or shade; **'Louis XIV'**, scented almost-double flowers of a rich deep crimson, yellow stamens; **'Mutabilis'** ★, taller with single yellow flowers opening from buff red-streaked buds and changing in color through shades of pink and soft crimson; **'Old Blush'** (syns 'Common Monthly', 'Parsons' Pink'), one of the first China Roses, semi-double silvery pink flowers; **'Sophie's Perpetual'**, few thorns, scented mid-pink flowers, darker pink shading on some outer petals. Zones 7–10.

R., OR, HP, 'Baron Girod de l'Ain'

DAMASK ROSES

☼ ✱ ↔ 5–8 ft (1.5–2.4 m)
↕ 3–7 ft (0.9–2 m)

Crusaders returning from the Middle East took the first Damask Roses back to Europe. Often untidy bushes, they grow 3–7 ft (0.9–2 m) tall, prickly, and with rather downy grayish leaves; the majority flower only once in spring or summer. The flowers are double or semi-double in paler shades of pink and white. Most are very fragrant, and Damask Roses have long been cultivated for making perfume. **'Autumn Damask'** (syn. 'Quatre Saisons'), highly fragrant mid-pink blooms; **'Blush Damask'**, profuse summer-borne flowers, mid-pink in center, lighter pink towards outer petals; **'Celsiana'**, clusters of semi-double clear pink flowers; **'Gloire de Guilan'**, very double flowers, flattened and quartered when fully open; **'Ispahan'**, longer flowering variety, intensely perfumed, clear pink, double flowers; **'Mme Hardy'**, very double white flowers, petals arranged around a green "button" eye; **'Rose de Rescht'**, deep pink double flowers; **'Summer Damask'**, clusters of very fragrant, semi-double, pink flowers; **'York and Lancaster'**, unusual rose, semi-double flowers that can be white, blush pink, or two-toned. Zones 5–10.

GALLICA ROSES

☼ ✱ ↔ 4–6 ft (1.2–1.8 m)
↕ 4–6 ft (1.2–1.8 m)

This group are mostly compact plants growing to 4–6 ft (1.2–1.8 m) tall. Foliage is usually dark green, not very prickly. Most bear sweetly perfumed double or semi-double flowers in shades of pink or magenta-purple. They flower only once in spring or summer. **'Belle de Crécy'**, fragrant, rich pink and purple, double blooms; **'Belle Isis'**, double flowers, flattened when fully open, of clear flesh pink, fading to white near edges; **'Cardinal de Richelieu'**, scented, dark red-purple, double flowers; **'Charles de Mills'** ★, very fragrant, rich purple, double flowers with a quartered arrangement of the petals; **'Complicata'**, tall vigorous shrub, large single flowers of bright pink, paler at center, large stamens; **'Duc de Guiche'**, fragrant, deep pink-purple, double blooms; **'Duchesse d'Angoulême'**, summer-borne, semi-double to double, mid-pink flowers, highly fragrant; **'Duchesse de Montebello'**, small, fully double, very fragrant flowers of soft pink; **'Officinalis'**, deep pink, semi-double, strong fragrance; **'Président de Sèze'**, scented double flowers, magenta to cerise at center, shading to lilac-pink at outer petals; **'Tuscany'**, extremely old and attractive variety, purple-red double flowers, prominent yellow stamens, **'Tuscany Superb'**, fragrant purple-red flowers; **'Versicolor'**, white to pale pink with irregular deep pink flecks, stripes, and sectors, fragrant. Zones 5–10.

HYBRID PERPETUAL ROSES

☼ ✱ ↔ 3–6 ft (0.9–1.8 m)
↕ 4–7 ft (1.2–2 m)

Becoming prominent during the reign of Queen Victoria, this group has a complex parentage involving several rose groups, including Bourbons and Chinas. Growing 4–7 ft (1.2–2 m) tall, they are repeat flowering, and bear large, double, usually fragrant blooms in shades of pink to red. **'Baron Girod de l'Ain'**, crimson flowers, petals edged in white; **'Baroness Rothschild'**, pink, very large, heavily scented flowers; **'Baronne Prévost'**, deep pink flowers, flattened when open; **'Champion of the World'**, large, pink, scented, double blooms; **'Comtesse Cécile de Chabrillant'**, rare rose, fragrant pink flowers; **'Frau Karl Druschki'** (syns 'Reine des Neiges', 'Snow Queen', 'White American Beauty'), globular white blooms; **'Général Jacqueminot'**, fragrant, purple-red, double blooms on long stems; **'Henry Nevard'**, rich red, highly fragrant, double flowers, up to 30 petals each; **'Marchesa Boccella'** ★, fragrant double flowers, pink, almost white on outer petals; **'Maurice Bernardin'**, clusters of large, rich red, fragrant blooms; **'Paul Neyron'**, vigorous, mid-pink, cupped, fragrant flowers, up to 50 petals each; **'Reine des Violettes'**, sweetly scented purple to violet flowers; **'Souvenir du Docteur Jamain'**, deep ruby red semi-double flowers; **'Sydonie'**, quartered mid-pink flowers; **'Ulrich Brunner Fils'**, red buds, fragrant, cupped, pinkish red flowers. Zones 5–10.

MOSS ROSES

☼ ✱ ↔5–8 ft (1.5–2.4 m)
↕3–7 ft (0.9–2 m)

The first Moss Rose occurred as the sport of a Centifolia. They are named for the mossy growth that arises on stems and buds. The degree and type of mossing varies, some being hard and prickly, others soft and downy. A small group, not widely grown, it is similar to the Centifolias, with large, double, fragrant blooms, flowering once in spring or summer. **'Alfred de Dalmas'** (syn. 'Mousseline'), semi-double creamy pink flowers; **'Catherine de Würtemberg'**, rare rose, slightly scented, rich pink flowers; **'Comtesse de Murinais'**, flattened double flowers open soft pink, fade to white; **'Gloire des Mousseux'**, large light pink flowers; **'Henri Martin'**, deep pink-red semi-double blooms; **'Mme Louis Lévêque'**, warm pink silky-petalled flowers, double, cupped; **'William Lobb'**, semi-double purplish magenta flowers. Zones 5–10.

PORTLAND ROSES

☼ ✱ ↔3–5 ft (0.9–1.5 m)
↕2–4 ft (0.6–1.2 m)

A small group closely allied to the Damasks and Gallicas, foliage usually resembles one or the other. 'Autumn Damask' has given them the popular repeat-flowering characteristic. Small shrubs to 4 ft (1.2 m) tall, most bear fragrant double flowers in shades of pink to red. **'Comte de Chambord'**, mid-pink, very full double, strong fragrance; **'Duchess of Portland'** (syn. 'Portland Rose'), single or semi-double cerise-red flowers; **'Mme Knorr'**, large, heavily perfumed, rich pink, double flowers; **'Rose du Roi'**, heavily scented, rich red, double flowers. Zones 5–10.

SCOTS ROSES

☼ ✱ ↔5–8 ft (1.5–2.4 m)
↕3–7 ft (0.9–2 m)

This group became prominent early in the nineteenth century when a breeding program began from seedlings of a malformed *R. spinosissima*. Scots Roses are quite tough plants, 3–7 ft (0.9–2 m) in height, with fern-like foliage and prickly stems. The flowers range from single to double in white and cream shades to yellow, and from light to deepest pink and red. Most flower only once in spring or summer. The hips are all unusually dark in color, a blackish maroon when fully ripe. **'Aïcha'**, vigorous grower, large, semi-double, fragrant, yellow flowers; **'Andrewsii'** (syn. 'Andrew's Rose'), large, semi-double to double, mid-pink flowers, often cream toward the petal base; **'Double White Burnet'**, highly fragrant white flowers, can be semi-double to double in form; **'Dunwich Rose'**, soft yellow single flowers, prominent yellow stamens; **'Falkland'**, fragrant, semi-double, cupped blooms of lilac-pink fading to white; **'Karl Förster'**, lightly scented, creamy white, double flowers, prominent stamens when fully open, and repeat flowering; **'Single Cherry'**, thorny stems, deep red single flowers, bright yellow stamens; **'Stanwell Perpetual'**, arching bush, grayish green foliage, very fragrant double flowers of soft pink (paler with age), long flowering season; **'William III'**, fragrant semi-double flowers of rich maroon, becoming lighter with age. Zones 4–10.

SWEET BRIAR ROSES

☼ ✱ ↔5–10 ft (1.5–3 m)
↕4–8 ft (1.2–2.4 m)

The apple-scented foliage of this group is inherited from its *R. eglanteria* parent and is its main distinguishing feature. The majority are large, rather untidy bushes, which are best suited for planting in hedgerows or wild gardens. The flowers are usually single or semi-double, and occur in shades of pink to deep red and white. **'Amy Robsart'**, prolific flower bearer, almost-single, highly fragrant, deep pink blooms; **'Lady Penzance'**, most strongly scented foliage of the group, single coppery pink flowers, prominent stamens; **'Magnifica'**, dense scented foliage that can be pruned to form a hedge, and crimson semi-double flowers; **'Manning's Blush'**, densely foliaged, large, fully double, white flowers flushed with pink; **'Meg Merrilies'**, extremely vigorous and prickly rose, deep pink to bright crimson, semi-double, scented flowers. Zones 4–10.

TEA ROSES

☼ ❄ ↔3–6 ft (0.9–1.8 m)
↕3–7 ft (0.9–2 m)

Tea Roses arrived in Europe from Asia in the early nineteenth century. Their name is thought to come from being shipped on boats carrying tea rather than for a tea scent. With their repeat-flowering ability and the yellow coloring of some, they, together with the Chinas, revolutionized rose breeding. The foliage is large and glossy on plants ranging from 3–7 ft (0.9–2 m) tall. Their double flowers often have long pointed buds. Flower color varies from creamy yellows and white through to shades of pink and red. They grow better in warmer climates. **'Agnes Smith'**, free-flowering, flowers rose pink in cooler weather, turning paler in hotter months; **'Catherine Mermet'**, high-pointed buds opening to light salmon pink; **'Duchesse de Brabant'** (syns 'Comtesse de Labarthe', 'Comtesse Ouwaroff'), free flowering, cupped, double, pink flowers; **'Francis Dubreuil'**, velvety, dark red, double flowers; **'Freiherr von Marschall'**, rich red, ageing to deep pink, fragrant, double flowers; **'Lady Hillingdon'**, long, pointed, deep yellow buds open to loose, semi-double, buff-yellow flowers; **'Marie van Houtte'**, cream to pale yellow overlaid with pink, mild scent; **'Mme de Tartas'**, lightly scented double blooms of blush pink; **'Mrs Reynolds Hole'**, fragrant, rich purple-pink, double flowers; **'Monsieur Tillier'**, rosy pink with salmon tonings, double flowers with darker shading; **'Niphetos'**, double white flowers opening from creamy buds; **'Perle des Jardins'**, very double, often quartered, sulfur yellow flowers; **'Rosette Delizy'**, light pink to pale yellow petals, darker pink veins; **'Safrano'**, apricot and yellow on opening, ageing to pale buff, strong scent; **'Souvenir d'un Ami'**, double flowers in shades of deep rose pink to salmon. Zones 7–11.

Rosa, Old Rose, Moss, 'William Lobb'

Rosa, Old Rose, Portland, 'Rose du Roi'

Rosa, Old Rose, Scots, 'Aïcha'

MISCELLANEOUS OLD GARDEN ROSES

☼/◐ ✱ ↔20–48 in (50–120 cm)
↕2–6 ft (0.6–1.8 m)

In some instances the parentage of Old Roses is hard to establish or the plants simply do not seem to fit any particular category. This miscellaneous group is a mixed lot, though that in no way lessens their beauty. **'Duplex'** (syn. 'Wolley Dodd's Rose'), repeat-flowering, semi-double blooms; **'Dupontii'**, plentiful grayish green leaves, sweetly perfumed single flowers, clear creamy white; **'Empress Josephine'**, grayish green leaves, fragrant double flowers dark pink with darker veining, flushed with lilac and purple; **'Fortuniana'**, of garden origin in China, dark green leaves, large, scented, double flowers creamy white; **'Harison's Yellow'** (the yellow rose of Texas), of garden origin in the USA, said to have been carried west by the pioneers and planted wherever they stopped, small double flowers, deep clear yellow; **'Mermaid'**, fragrant, single, pale yellow blooms; **'Polliniana'**, white flowers, sometimes flushed palest pink; **'The Garland'**, scented semi-double blooms of pink, light yellow, and white. Zones 6–9.

Rosa, Old Rose, Miscellaneous, 'Dupontii'

Rosa, Old Rose, Tea, 'Francis Dubreuil'

ROYSTONEA

ROYAL PALM

This genus in the family Arecaceae consists of about 10 species of single-stemmed palms, the majority from the humid tropical Caribbean Islands and surrounding coastal regions. These pinnate or feather-leafed palms have a prominent crownshaft. Many species have smooth gray-white trunks that may be swollen in the middle or base. Panicles of small, white, cup-shaped flowers appear from just below the crownshaft, followed by round, often deep purple berries. Most come from fertile low-lying forest areas near the sea, that are sometimes swampy. These palms make useful landscape subjects in the tropics and subtropics, where they are popularly used to line roads and paths or as specimen plantings. CULTIVATION: *Roystonea* palms give best results in a moist, well-drained, fertile soil in full sun. They are moderately tolerant of seaside conditions. The genus is self-pollinating, and can be propagated from seed.

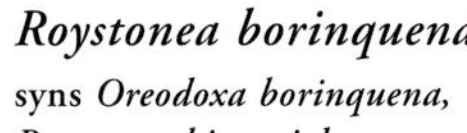

Roystonea borinquena

syns *Oreodoxa borinquena, Roystonea hispaniolana*

PUERTO RICAN ROYAL PALM

↔15–20 ft (4.5–6 m) ↑50–60 ft (15–20 m)

Very fast growing palm from the West Indies. Grayish brown trunk, swollen above middle, about 24 in (60 cm) diameter at base. Huge crown of arching, feathery, divided, bright green leaves, up to 10 ft (3 m) long and 6 ft (1.8 m) across, with 2 crowded rows of leaflets with divided tips, up to 40 in (100 cm) long. Densely crowded clusters of yellow flowers emerge below the crownshaft, in summer. Pale brown oblong fruit, flat on one side. Zones 10–11.

Roystonea oleracea

CARIBBEAN ROYAL PALM

↔20 ft (6 m) ↑130 ft (40 m)

Occurs along Caribbean coast of South America and on Lesser Antilles islands of the West Indies. Grayish trunk swollen at base, bright shiny green crownshaft, dark green fronds held in one plane, appear flat. Zones 11–12.

Roystonea oleracea

Rubus odoratus

Rubus parviflorus

Roystonea regia ★

syn. *Roystonea elata*

CUBAN ROYAL PALM

↔20 ft (6 m) ↑80 ft (24 m)

Native to Cuba, southern Florida, Bahamas, southeastern Mexico, Belize, and Honduras. Attractive, smooth, whitish trunk, often thickened in the middle. Green feathery fronds, to 20 ft (6 m) long, plume-like, above long green crownshaft. Pendulous inflorescence of small white flowers. Purple-black fruits. Zones 10–12.

RUBUS

There are more than 250 species of climbing, low-growing, or upright shrubs, often with prickles on stems and leaves, within this genus from the rose (Rosaceae) family. Found throughout the world, some are cultivated for their ornamental value and as a use-ful food source, others are regarded as weeds. Most species have biennial stems or canes, which means they produce fruit only on second-year wood; leaves on first and second year's growth are often a different shape. CULTIVATION: The wide distribution of this genus means it has a variety of habitats. Most species thrive in fertile, humus-rich, moist, free-draining soil. Many grow in full sun to light shade, and some grow in deeper shade under deciduous trees. Propagate by dividing suckering species in spring or take half-hardened cuttings from evergreen species, or softwood or hardwood cuttings from deciduous species, or layer. Grow from stratified seed in spring.

Rubus calycinoides

syns, *R. fockeanus of gardens, R. hayatae-koidzumii, R. rolfei*

↔3–7 ft (0.9–2 m) ↑4 in (10 cm)

Taiwanese, evergreen, low-growing, spreading shrub. Dark green, 3- to 5-lobed leaves, wrinkled edges, heart-shaped base, paler and often woolly undersides. Solitary white flowers, in summer. Round red fruit. Zones 8–11.

Rubus odoratus

PURPLE-FLOWERING RASPBERRY, THIMBLEBERRY

↔8 ft (2.4 m) ↑8 ft (2.4 m)

From eastern North America. Deciduous erect shrub, vigorous arching stems, peeling bark. Toothed leaves, 5 lobes, hairy undersides. Fragrant lilac-pink flowers, in summer–autumn. Flat reddish orange fruit. **'Albus'**, white flowers. Zones 3–9.

Rubus parviflorus

SALMON BERRY, THIMBLEBERRY

↔10 ft (3 m) ↑15 ft (4.5 m)

Naturally found in North America. Robust deciduous shrub, upright stems, peeling bark, no prickles. New growth furry, leaves mostly 5-lobed, edges unevenly toothed. White flowers, in corymbs, in summer. Red fruit. Zones 3–9.

Rubus spectabilis

SALMONBERRY

↔6 ft (1.8 m) ↑6 ft (1.8 m)

Native to North America. Deciduous shrub, upright stems, tiny thorns. Leaves have 3 egg-shaped leaflets. Pink to purple solitary flowers, in spring. Egg-shaped pale orange to yellow fruit. Can become invasive. ***R. s.* var. *franciscanus***, coastal form from California with hairier leaves. Zones 5–9.

Rubus tricolor

↔8–15 ft (2.4–4.5 m) ↑24 in (60 cm)

Native to western China. Low-growing evergreen or semi-evergreen shrub, bristly stems. Shiny, dark green leaves, 3-lobed, felty white beneath. White saucer-shaped flowers, singly or in sparsely flowered terminal racemes, in summer. Edible red fruit. Zones 7–9.

RUDBECKIA

BLACK-EYED SUSAN, CONEFLOWER

North American genus of 15 species of perennials in the daisy (Asteraceae) family. Popular in gardens for great hardiness, ease of cultivation, and valuable late-season flower display. Most are fairly bulky plants, over 4 ft (1.2 m) tall, and carry masses of large golden yellow daisies, usually with dark brown to black disc florets. Available in dwarf, double-flowered, and variously colored forms. They flower from late summer until cut back by frost. Linnaeus named *Rudbeckia* to honor Olaus Rudbeck (1660–1740), a professor at Uppsala University, who employed the young Linnaeus as a tutor for his 24 children! CULTIVATION: Plant in a sunny open position with moist well-drained soil. Deadhead to encourage continued blooming. Mildew can occur but usually only late in the season. Propagate by division, from basal cuttings or seed.

Rudbeckia fulgida

BLACK-EYED SUSAN, ORANGE CONEFLOWER

↔24–48 in (60–120 cm) ↑40 in (100 cm)

Perennial from southeastern USA. Lance-shaped leaves, to over 4 in (10 cm) long, often bristly. Flowerheads to nearly 3 in (8 cm) wide, ray florets yellow to orange, disc florets dark purple-brown, in summer–autumn. Several natural varieties, including: ***R. f.* var. *deamii***, 24 in (60 cm) tall, hairy pointed oval leaves; ***R. f.* var. *speciosa***, 36 in (90 cm) tall, hairy elongated lance-shaped leaves; and ***R. f.* var. *sullivantii***, 36 in (90 cm) tall, pointed oval leaves often downy, flowerheads to 4 in (10 cm) wide; **'Goldsturm'**, to 24 in (60 cm) tall, slightly larger flowerheads. Zones 4–9.

Rudbeckia 'Herbstsonne'

syn. *Rudbeckia 'Autumn Sun'*

↔3 ft (0.9 m) ↑6 ft (1.8 m)

Vigorous *R. nitida* hybrid, strongly erect habit. Flowerheads to well over 4 in (10 cm) wide, yellow ray florets around a tall, yellow-green cone, in summer–autumn. Zones 3–10.

Rudbeckia hirta

BLACK-EYED SUSAN

↔32–48 in (80–120 cm) ↑5–7 ft (1.5–2 m)

Biennial or short-lived perennial, native to central USA. Dwarf forms often treated as annuals. Narrow, 4 in (10 cm) long, lance-shaped leaves, toothed. Flowerheads to nearly 4 in (10 cm) wide, ray florets yellow, disc florets purple-brown, in summer–autumn. **'Becky Mix'**, 10 in (25 cm) tall, mixed color dwarf seedling strain with yellow-, orange-, and red-flowered forms; **'Cherry Brandy'** ★, 24 in (60 cm) tall, deep red, very dark

Rudbeckia hirta

center; **'Irish Eyes'** ★, olive green disc florets; **'Kelvedon Star'**, 30–36 in (75–90 cm) tall, yellow ray florets with black markings on inner half, very distinctive; **'Marmalade'**, 18 in (45 cm) tall, golden orange ray florets; **'Rustic Dwarfs'**, 24 in (60 cm) tall, warm shades of gold, orange, terracotta, and red-brown; **'Toto'**, 10 in (25 cm) tall, golden yellow ray florets, large deep purple-brown disc florets. Zones 4–9.

Rudbeckia laciniata

CUT-LEAF CONEFLOWER

↔3–7 ft (0.9–2 m) ↑7–10 ft (2–3 m)

Vigorous North American perennial. Leaves deeply lobed to pinnate, tending toward blue-green, often with hairy undersides. Flowerheads to over 5 in (12 cm) wide, ray floret yellow, disc florets yellow-green, in late summer–autumn. **'Goldquelle'** (syn. 'Gold Drop'), 30 in (75 cm) tall, large, yellow, fully double flowerheads; **'Hortensia'** (syn. 'Golden Glow'), 6 ft (1.8 m) tall, yellow double flowerheads. Zones 3–9.

Rudbeckia maxima

↔24–40 in (60–100 cm) ↑3–5 ft (0.9–1.5 m)

Perennial found in central and southern USA. Leaves diamond- to lance-shaped, to over 4 in (10 cm) long. Flowerheads to around 3 in (8 cm) wide, golden yellow ray florets, prominent green and brown central disc, in late summer. Zones 7–10.

Rudbeckia nitida

↔32–48 in (80–120 cm) ↑5–7 ft (1.5–2 m)

North American perennial. Leaves to 6 in (15 cm) long; deeply lobed, almost to midrib. Flowerheads to 4 in (10 cm) wide, ray florets yellow, disc florets yellow-green, in late summer–autumn. Zones 3–9.

Ruellia macrantha

Rudbeckia occidentalis

↔32–48 in (80–120 cm) ↑5–7 ft (1.5–2 m)

Perennial from western USA. Pointed oval leaves, to over 4 in (10 cm) long, sometimes toothed. Flowerheads to over 3 in (8 cm) wide, yellow ray florets, central cone brown-black, to over 2 in (5 cm) high, in summer. **'Green Wizard'**, no ray florets but elongated bright green sepals around a large near-black disc. Zones 7–10.

Rudbeckia triloba

BROWN-EYED SUSAN

↔24–40 in (60–100 cm) ↑3–5 ft (0.9–1.5 m)

Perennial from eastern central USA. Leaves 3- to 7-lobed, to over 4 in (10 cm) long, bristly. Flowerheads to about 3 in (8 cm) wide, ray florets golden yellow, disc florets brown to purple-black, in summer. Zones 5–9.

RUELLIA

Mostly from tropical and subtropical regions, with a few species in temperate North America, this is a genus containing some 150 species of evergreen perennials and soft-stemmed shrubs, belonging to the acanthus (Acanthaceae) family. They are grown either indoors or out for their showy funnelform flowers, usually red, pink, or mauve, that may occur singly, or in dense terminal panicles or axillary clusters. The smooth-edged, oblong to lance-shaped leaves have prominent veins. CULTIVATION: Although some species from temperate America are quite frost hardy, most need a warm climate and a fertile, moist, well-drained soil in part-shade. In cooler areas they are grown indoors or in a greenhouse. Water-potted specimens adequately during the growing season and keep just moist during winter. Trim excess growth regularly and especially after flowering to maintain density of foliage. Propagate from seed or softwood cuttings in spring.

Ruellia brittoniana

syns *Ruellia angustifolia, R. simplex*

COMMON RUELLIA

↔18–24 in (45–60 cm) ↑24–36 in (60–90 cm)

Upright evergreen perennial shrub from Mexico and southwestern USA. Purple fleshy stems; lower branches drooping over with age and taking root. The narrow, sword-shaped, serrated, dark green leaves have prominent purple veins. The funnel-shaped, purple or blue, petunia-like flowers, 2 in (5 cm) long, in leaf axils, last from mid-spring until the first autumn frosts. *R. brittoniana* dies back in winter and self-seeds aggressively. **'Alba'** (syn. 'Clean White Katie'), a low-growing form, up to 8 in (20 cm) high, white flowers throughout summer; **'Chi Chi'**, 24–36 in (60–90 cm) tall, pale pink flowers throughout summer; **'Katie'** (dwarf blue bells), low-growing form, 6–8 in (15–20 cm) high, purple flowers all summer; **'Texas Blue'**, up to 10 in (25 cm) tall, purple summer flowers. Zones 8–11.

Ruellia macrantha

CHRISTMAS PRIDE

↔20 in (50 cm) ↑6 ft (1.8 m)

This short-lived species is native to Brazil. Erect stems, rounded crown of hairy, dark green, oval to lance-shaped leaves. Large, deep pink, trumpet-shaped flowers, with spreading rounded lobes and darker veins, in winter. Zones 10–12.

Ruellia makoyana

MONKEY PLANT, TRAILING VELVET PLANT

↔15–18 in (38–45 cm) ↑6–12 in (15–30 cm)

Perennial native to Brazil. This species has a spreading habit with trailing branching stems. Variegated velvet-textured leaves are 2–3 in (5–8 cm) long, veined with white above and purple underneath. Brilliant reddish purple trumpet-shaped flowers, up to 2 in (5 cm) across, growing from leaf axils, appear all year round, but mostly from the autumn through to spring. Zones 10–12.

Ruellia peninsularis

DESERT RUELLIA

↔4–5 ft (1.2–1.5 m) ↑4–5 ft (1.2–1.5 m)

From southern half of Baja California peninsula and coastal Sonora state, northwest Mexico. Fast-growing evergreen shrub; rounded habit. Whitish gray stems; small glossy green leaves. Deep blue-purple flowers, 1 in (25 mm) in diameter, in spring–early summer, with occasional flowering throughout year. Zones 10–11.

RUMEX

DOCK, SORREL

This genus of some 200 species of annuals, biennials, and often taprooted perennials belongs to the knotweed (Polygonaceae) family. Its members are found worldwide, in most countries with temperate climates. The leaves are usually basal and the normally small flowers are produced in terminal racemes or spikes. The seeds are enclosed in a papery membrane that allows them to float. Although some species are ornamental and some are edible, this genus also includes some dreadfully weedy species that have hitchhiked around the world with human travelers.

CULTIVATION: Most species do best in a deep, fertile, and moist to even damp soil in full sun. Propagation is usually from seed, which will often self-sow; root cuttings are another option.

Rumex sanguineus

BLOODY DOCK, RED-VEINED DOCK

↔ 12–36 in (30–90 cm)
↑ 20–40 in (50–100 cm)

Clumping species from Europe, southwest Asia, and northern Africa. Dark stems, lance-shaped leaves, to 6 in (15 cm) long, beetroot red veins. Panicles of tiny green flowers, in early to mid-summer. Brown seeds. Zones 6–10.

Rumex scutatus

BUCKLER-LEAFED SORREL, FRENCH SORREL, GARDEN SORREL

↔ 12–16 in (30–40 cm)
↑ 16–18 in (40–45 cm)

Hardy clump-forming perennial native to Europe, western Asia, and northern Africa. Bright green spearhead-shaped leaves. Spikes of tiny green flowers, in summer. Brown seeds. Edible, and used in the famous sorrel soup. Zones 6–10.

Rumex vesicarius

syn. *Acetosa vesicaria*

ROSY DOCK

↔ 6–8 in (15–20 cm)
↑ 8–10 in (20–25 cm)

Annual species from northern Africa and southwest Asia. Fleshy spearhead-shaped leaves, to ¾ in (18 mm) long. Produces tiny deep pink flowers, in panicles, in late spring. Bladder-like, rose pink, conspicuous fruits. A weed in arid southern Australia. Zones 6–10.

RUMOHRA

This genus of 50 species of terrestrial or epiphytic ferns is sometimes placed in the haresfoot-fern (Davalliaceae) family, and sometimes in the shield-fern (Dryopteridaceae) family. Native to the Southern Hemisphere, they have creeping rhizomes covered in brown scales from which, at irregular intervals, they produce their large, finely divided, leathery fronds. They are often seen growing on the trunks of tree ferns in their native haunts.

Rumex vesicarius (foreground)

CULTIVATION: In all but almost frost-free climates these ferns make good indoor or greenhouse subjects. Given an aspect in light shade and a humid atmosphere with moist but not wet soil they will make quite large colonies. Propagation is by careful division of the rhizomes or by raising spores.

Rumohra adiantiformis

IRON FERN, LEATHER FERN, LEATHERLEAF FERN, SEVEN WEEKS FERN

↔ 36–60 in (90–150 cm)
↑ 20–60 in (50–150 cm)

From tropical to temperate climates in Southern Hemisphere. Long-running brown rhizomes; fronds variable in size depending on conditions, to 24 in (60 cm) long, deep green with leathery triangular leaflets. Zones 10–11.

RUSCHIA

This large genus of about 400 perennial species, from the drier parts of southern Africa, belongs to the iceplant (Aizoaceae) family. The plants are succulent shrubs or ground covers, with dark reddish brown internodes, some branches bearing spines derived from sterile parts of the flowerheads. Leaves in a pair are free to united, the free parts 3-angled to round in cross-section. Flowers may be solitary or in branched flowerheads; they have pink, purple, or sometimes white petals.

CULTIVATION: They need full sun and thrive in poor well-drained soils. Propagate from stem cuttings, which can be rooted at almost any time of year.

Ruschia caroli

Ruschia dichroa

Ruschia caroli

PURPLE DEW PLANT

↔ 12–18 in (30–45 cm)
↑ 8–12 in (20–30 cm)

Succulent ground-covering perennial from coastal western South Africa. Leaves up to 4 in (10 cm) long. Purple flowers, up to 1 in (25 mm) across, in early spring–summer. Zones 10–11.

Ruschia dichroa

ICE PLANT

↔ 12–16 in (30–40 cm)
↑ 8–12 in (20–30 cm)

Succulent perennial from coastal western South Africa. Leaves up to 2½ in (6 cm) long. Purple, white, or pink flowers, 1¾ in (4 cm) across, in summer. Zones 10–11.

Ruschia perfoliata

↔ 12–20 in (30–50 cm)
↑ 6–12 in (15–30 cm)

Succulent, perennial, cushion-forming ground cover, native to South Africa. Wiry branching stems. Fleshy thick leaves with sharp tips, sheathed at stems and united at base. Solitary, terminal, purple to pink, daisy-like flowers, 1 in (25 mm) wide, in early spring–summer. Zones 10–11.

Ruschia pulvinaris

↔ 10–18 in (25–45 cm)
↑ 4–10 in (10–25 cm)

Low growing, spreading, succulent subshrub from the mountains of South Africa. Small, fleshy, toothed, bluish green leaves. Red to rose pink daisy-like flowers, in summer. Zones 6–9.

RUSCUS

Genus of about 6 species of evergreen subshrubs from the Mediterranean region belonging to the family Ruscaceae. These plants form clumps, spreading slowly by underground rhizomes. Their leaves are more correctly called "cladodes," which are flattened stems that function as a leaf. The real leaf is a small protuberance on the surface of the cladode, from whence emerge the tiny greenish or white starry flowers. These are followed by red pea-sized fruits if both male and female plants are present. Some forms appear to be hermaphroditic. In former times, butchers used bunches of one species to sweep down their chopping blocks, hence the common name of butcher's broom.

Ruscus aculeatus

CULTIVATION: These hardy plants are good in dry shade. Grow in well-drained soil in full sun to half-sun. Propagate from seed or by division.

Ruscus aculeatus

BUTCHER'S BROOM

↔ 40 in (100 cm)
↑ 30–40 in (75–100 cm)

Native to southern Europe and the Mediterranean region. Clumping subshrub spreading by rhizomes. Small, oval-shaped, dark green, leathery cladodes, ¾–1¼ in (18–30 mm) long, with prickly tips. Bright red berries appear in summer–winter. Zones 6–10.

Ruscus hypoglossum

↔ 40 in (100 cm)
↑ 18–26 in (45–65 cm)

From southern Europe and elsewhere in the Mediterranean region. Clumping subshrub that spreads by rhizomes. Cladodes are oval-shaped, mid-green, to 4 in (10 cm) long. Arching stems. The green flowers and red fruit are borne on a cladode under a tongue-like leaf. Zones 7–11.

Ruspolia hypocrateriformis

RUSPOLIA

The 4 species of evergreen shrubs in this genus, which is a member of the acanthus (Acanthaceae) family, are native to Africa. They have oval opposite leaves and bear spikes or panicles of flowers in shades of red or yellow with flaring petal lobes.
CULTIVATION: In cool climates, species of *Ruspolia* make attractive flowering shrubs for the conservatory or greenhouse where they should be shaded during the hottest part of the day. In very warm and tropical climates, grow outdoors in a humus-rich soil. Propagate from softwood cuttings taken in late spring.

Ruspolia hypocrateriformis

↔3 ft (0.9 m) ↕3 ft (0.9 m)
Small shrub from tropical and southern Africa; semi-trailing habit. Smooth leaves, to 3 in (8 cm) long. Tubular flowers, deep reddish pink, darker throat, in showy terminal panicles, over many months. Zones 10–12.

RUSSELIA

This genus of about 50 evergreen subshrubs and shrubs found from Mexico to Colombia is a member of the plantain (Plantaginaceae) family. The commonly grown species has arching stems, but *Russelia* species vary in habit and may be erect, arching, or spreading. They also vary in foliage, some species having much-reduced, scale-like leaves, others having heart-shaped leaves up to 4 in (10 cm) long. The flowers, however, are more distinctive, being flared pendulous tubes that appear through much of the year.
CULTIVATION: These plants are marginally frost tender and perform best in a mild climate. They flower most heavily when grown in full sun, and they prefer a gritty well-drained soil that can be kept moist in the warmer months. Trim lightly to encourage a neat bushy habit. Propagation is usually from cuttings or by removing self-rooted layers.

Russelia equisetiformis

CORAL PLANT
↔8 ft (2.4 m) ↕5 ft (1.5 m)
Native to Mexico. Arching weeping stems, leafless or nearly so, leaves reduced to small scales, closely held to wiry green stems. Small, bright red, tubular flowers, throughout the year. Great spillover plant for a wall or a bank. Zones 9–12.

RUTA

This genus of 8 species belongs to the rue (Rutaceae) family. Mostly subshrubs, some species can become shrubby in mild climates. The genus, found throughout temperate Eurasia, is the source of several herbs that since ancient times have been used both medicinally and in the manufacture of beverages. The foliage is a grayish blue-green and finely divided. Small yellow flowers in cymose heads appear in the summer and are followed by rather insignificant greenish seed heads.
CULTIVATION: These plants are very easily grown in any well-drained soil, preferably in full sun. Established plants may be trimmed to shape, but hard pruning is seldom necessary. Propagation is from seed or from half-hardened cuttings.

Ruta graveolens ★

COMMON RUE, HERB OF GRACE, RUE
↔15 in (38 cm) ↕20 in (50 cm)
Subshrub or shrub from southern Europe. Glaucous stems and leaves, finely divided foliage, rounded to lance-shaped leaflets, wavy edges. Heads of tiny greenish yellow flowers, in summer. *R. graveolens* has a strong, but rather musty, fragrance. During the Middle Ages, carrying sprigs of rue was believed to protect one from catching lice and diseases. Treat this species with caution as it is toxic and can become weedy. Several foliage cultivars include: **'Jackman's Blue'** ★, very glaucous form; **'Variegata'**, creamy white-edged foliage. Zones 5–9.

Russelia equisetiformis

Ruta graveolens

Ruttya fruticosa 'Scholesii'

Ruttya fruticosa

RUTTYA

Genus in the acanthus (Acanthaceae) family containing 3 species of evergreen shrubs that are native to tropical areas of eastern Africa. They have oval opposite leaves and bear colorful tubular flowers on short spikes.
CULTIVATION: In tropical and subtropical climates these plants are easily grown in a fertile well-drained soil, and are ideal for shrub borders. In cooler climates they make attractive flowering plants for the greenhouse or conservatory. Young plants should be pinched out to encourage bushiness. Propagation is from seed or from half-hardened cuttings.

Ruttya fruticosa

JAMMY-MOUTH
↔5 ft (1.5 m) ↕12 ft (3.5 m)
Bushy shrub native to eastern Africa. Leaves are oval. Flowers, which appear over several months, are in terminal spikes, with the petals fused into 2 lips; they are orangey red, the lower lip marked by a dark brown blotch. **'Scholesii'** ★, yellow flowers, the lower lip marked with a black blotch. Zones 10–12.

Q R

S

Sabal palmetto

Sabal uresana

SABAL

PALMETTO

This genus in the palm (Arecaceae) family consists of around 16 species found from southeastern USA to South America, the West Indies, and Bermuda. They mostly have tall erect trunks, but some species are stemless; some have old frond bases remaining, others are clean. All species have fan-shaped fronds that are deeply divided. The small cream flowers are bisexual, and are borne in long sprays growing from between the leaves; they are followed by small berries. The leaves of some species are used for making baskets, hats, and matting; the trunks are used to produce furniture and wharf piles. Most palmetto palms are found growing in swampy areas in the subtropics and tropics.

CULTIVATION: Most *Sabal* species are fairly adaptable palms that tolerate a range of soils, from wet to dry, as well as sandy; they even tolerate light frost. The best cultivation results, however, come from planting in a well-drained fertile soil in full sun, with adequate watering in the growth phase. Propagation is from seed.

Sabal bermudana

BERMUDA PALMETTO

↔10 ft (3 m) ↕40 ft (12 m)

Native to Bermuda, smaller in cultivation than the species. Fronds to 10 ft (3 m) wide, 24 in (60 cm) segments, central section around 12 in (30 cm) wide, undivided. Zones 8–11.

Sabal causiarum

PUERTO RICO HAT PALM

↔20 ft (6 m) ↕50 ft (15 m)

From West Indies islands of Anegada, Hispaniola, and Puerto Rico. Tall, stout, gray trunk. Heavy crown of bright green, sometimes dull blue-green fan-like fronds to 10 ft (3 m) wide. White flowers in sprays. Small, spherical, black fruits. Zones 9–12.

Sabal mexicana

MEXICAN PALMETTO, OAXACA PALMETTO, RIO GRANDE PALMETTO

↔12 ft (3.5 m) ↕60 ft (18 m)

Adaptable species from Texas, USA, and Mexico. Thick trunk, crown of light green fronds. Blades have deeply divided thread-like filaments. Inflorescence of small, white, fragrant flowers. Large black fruits. Zones 9–12.

Sabal minor ★

DWARF PALMETTO, SCRUB PALMETTO

↔12 ft (3.5 m) ↕10 ft (3 m)

From southeastern USA. May form large clump of fronds at ground-level, or above-ground trunk. Large, stiff, blue-green fronds, narrow segments. Flower stalk grows from clump, extending well above foliage. Zones 7–11.

Sabal palmetto ★

CABBAGE PALM, PALMETTO

↔15 ft (4.5 m) ↕80 ft (24 m)

From southeastern USA. Mature trunk bare. Large crown of twisted green to blue-green fan fronds, divided into segments, deeply lobed, thread-like filaments between. Inflorescences of small white flowers. Glossy brown to black fruits. Zones 8–12.

Sabal uresana

SONORAN PALMETTO

↔10 ft (3 m) ↕25 ft (8 m)

Eye-catching palm from Mexico. Large bluish green fan fronds, deeply divided into spreading segments; juvenile leaves bluer. Inflorescence as long as fronds. Brown fruits. Zones 8–12.

SACCHARUM

syn. *Erianthus*

This genus contains around 40 species of clumping or rhizomatous perennial grasses in the family Poaceae. Native to tropical and warm temperate regions worldwide, they grow by riversides and in rich soils in valleys. Their strong, cane-like, jointed stems are green to violet, with exposed roots near the base. Their long flat leaves are arranged in 2 ranks, and the tiny flowers are borne in attractive fluffy panicles. One species, *S. officinarum,* is a major crop from which several products are made, including sugar cane, rum, molasses, and wax. The genus is also host to a parasite, *Aeginetia indica*, which has purple flowers.

CULTIVATION: In cool temperate climates grow in the greenhouse in beds or large containers of rich damp loam. In warm regions grow outdoors in rich moist soil in full sun. These plants can be invasive in ideal conditions. Propagate from seed, or, more usually, from stem cuttings.

Sabal causiarum

Saccharum ravennae

syn. *Erianthus ravennae*

PLUME GRASS, RAVENNA GRASS

↔40 in (100 cm) ↕10–15 ft (3–4.5 m)

Upright, decorative, dominant grass from southern Europe. Green leaf blades with a white stripe. Silver plumes, in late summer, turning gray with maturity. Do not plant in heavy clay soils. Zones 5–9.

SAGINA

PEARLWORT

This Northern Hemisphere genus contains approximately 20 species of annual and perennial, ground-covering, mat-forming plants, which grow on rocky outcrops. Members of the pink (Caryophyllaceae) family, many of the species in this genus are garden weeds, and can be extremely difficult to eradicate because of their highly developed reproductive system. Their fine linear leaves are arranged in pairs, and they quickly form dense mats of growth that cover both soil and rocky areas.

CULTIVATION: Pearlworts do not like prolonged periods of hot dry weather; they prefer low temperatures and cool free-draining soils, with full sun or part-shade. Some of the golden forms of pearlwort will die if temperatures exceed 86°F (30°C). These plants can be propagated very easily, either from seed in spring or by division at any time of year.

Sagina subulata

GOLDEN PEARLWORT

↔12 in (30 cm) ↕1 in (25 mm)

Mat-forming perennial from central Europe. The plants have soft foliage, and form dense ground-covering mounds, which bear solitary white flowers in summer. **'Aurea'**, lime green to canary yellow foliage. Zones 4–7.

Sagina subulata

S

SAGITTARIA

ARROWHEAD

This genus of some 30 mostly perennial species is distributed throughout the world, but particularly in the Americas. It belongs to the family Alismataceae. *Sagittaria* species are aquatic plants, usually with flowers of a single sex on the same plant. Some have rhizomes or runners; many have tubers, which are sometimes edible. The leaves are smooth-edged, and are borne below, on, or above the water. The flowerheads are erect, floating, or submerged, in racemes or panicles, rarely umbel-like. The 3-petalled flowers are white, sometimes with a pink spot. Fruits are compressed achenes, with a conspicuous dorsal wing and sometimes lateral wings.
CULTIVATION: They are grown as marshy garden or pond-edge plants. They can also be grown in deep fast-flowing water, and will tolerate light shade. Weighted tubers thrown into water to 24 in (60 cm) deep will grow well. Propagate by division in spring.

Sagittaria graminea

☼ ✱ ↔12 in (30 cm) ↕20 in (50 cm)

Cormous aquatic perennial from eastern USA. Narrow, strap-like, submerged leaves, emergent leaves being wider and pointed. Upright flowering stems bear whorls of white 3-petalled male flowers above small, green, petal-less female flowers. ***S. g.* var. *platyphylla***, flowers have longer beaks. Zones 6–12.

SALIX

OSIER, WILLOW

This large genus in the willow (Salicaceae) family consists of around 400 species, most from cold and temperate Northern Hemisphere regions. The genus consists of trees through to creeping shrublets, mostly deciduous, with leaves often lance-shaped and toothed. The small flowers are usually insect-pollinated and are borne in a catkin, and male and female flowers often appear on separate trees. The capsular fruits contain wind-dispersed hairy seeds. Many willows are widely grown for their timber, used for basketry and cricket bats. The bark has been used medicinally, as it contains salicin, from which aspirin is derived. They are valued ornamentally, particularly the weeping species, which are attractive when planted near water.
CULTIVATION: Most are fairly adaptable if adequately watered during growth and the soil is well drained, not swampy. Propagate from seed, by layering, or from cuttings, which root easily even up to branch size.

Salix amygdaloides

Salix acutifolia

CASPIAN WILLOW, SHARP-LEAFED WILLOW

☼ ✱ ↔30 ft (9 m) ↕25 ft (8 m)

Shrubby willow, found from Russia to temperate East Asia. Gray bark, contrasting red-brown young twigs. Leaves narrow, dark green, bluish undersides. Conspicuous, silky, white catkins, in spring. **'Blue Streak'**, dark branches, powdery blue-white bloom; **'Pendulifolia'**, tree-like, to 20 ft (6 m) tall, pendulous branches. Zones 5–9.

Salix alba

WHITE WILLOW

☼ ✱ ↔30 ft (9 m) ↕80 ft (24 m)

Broadly columnar tree, native to western Asia and Europe. Drooping branch tips, dark gray deeply fissured bark. Narrow lance-shaped leaves, silky and white when young; dark green above, bluish green beneath with age. Thin catkins, with leaves, in spring. **'Vitellina'**, bright yellow young shoots prominent in winter. Zones 2–10.

Salix amygdaloides

PEACH-LEAFED WILLOW

☼ ✱ ↔25 ft (8 m) ↕70 ft (21 m)

Tree, native to western North America. Young growth is smooth and yellow or reddish brown. The oval to lance-shaped leaves have finely serrated margins, are bluish or grayish green beneath, and downy when young. Female catkins to 4 in (10 cm). Zones 5–10.

Salix babylonica

PEKING WILLOW, WEEPING WILLOW

☼ ✱ ↔35 ft (10 m) ↕40 ft (12 m)

Native to northern China; brought to Middle East via trade routes, then to Europe in the 1700s. Most planted trees belong to single female clone. Long vertically pendulous branches; leaves tapering to long fine point, finely toothed, smooth, bluish-gray beneath. Non-weeping ancestral Chinese trees are named ***S. b.* f. *pekinensis*** (syn. *S. matsudana*). They include: **'Crispa'**, slow-growing, leaves twisted or spirally curled; **'Navajo'** (syn. *S. matsudana* 'Navajo'), broad, umbrella-shaped dense crown, very large; **'Tortuosa'** (syn. *S. matsudana* 'Tortuosa'), contorted shape, upright in habit, twigs twisted and curled, used in floristry; **'Umbraculifera'** (syn. *S. matsudana* 'Umbraculifera'), broad rounded habit. Zones 5–10.

Salix caprea

FLORIST'S WILLOW, PUSSY WILLOW

☼ ✱ ↔10–20 ft (3–6 m) ↕15–35 ft (4.5–10 m)

Small tree or shrub, occurs naturally from Europe to northeastern Asia. Elliptical to oblong leaves, slightly glossy, dark green above, gray and felted below, dull yellow in winter. Plump silky male catkins, in spring, harvested for decorations. **'Pendula'** (Kilmarnock willow) has weeping branches, yellow-brown shoots, and gray male catkins. Zones 5–10.

Salix daphnoides

VIOLET WILLOW

☼ ✱ ↔20 ft (6 m) ↕35 ft (10 m)

Vigorous erect tree or shrub, native to Europe and central Asia to the Himalayas. Plum-colored bloom on young shoots. Long narrow leaves, glossy dark green above, bluish green below. Small, broad, silky male catkins, in late winter–spring. Zones 5–10.

Salix caprea

Salix discolor

AMERICAN PUSSY WILLOW

☼ ✱ ↔15 ft (4.5 m) ↕25 ft (8 m)

Shrub or small tree native to North America. Purplish brown shoots, downy at first. Oval leaves taper at both ends, bright green above, bluish gray beneath. Catkins appear before leaves, to 3 in (8 cm) long, in late winter–spring. Zones 2–9.

Salix elaeagnos

HOARY WILLOW, ROSEMARY WILLOW

☼ ✱ ↔20 ft (6 m) ↕20 ft (6 m)

Shrub or small tree, native to central Europe, Turkey, and southwestern Asia. Twigs gray and downy, becoming smooth, reddish yellow to brown. Dark green leaves, long, narrow, and felted white beneath. Catkins appear before leaves, in spring. ***S. e.* subsp. *angustifolia***, shrubby, creeping stems, thin narrow leaves, dark green above, silky gray beneath. Zones 4–9.

Salix exigua

COYOTE WILLOW

☼ ✱ ↔10 ft (3 m) ↕12 ft (3.5 m)

Tall erect shrub from North America. Long flexible stems, downy, becoming slender and smooth. Leaves silvery light green, narrow, silky at first. Oval catkins on long leafy stalks. Zones 2–9.

Salix 'Flame'

FLAME WILLOW

☼ ✱ ↔20 ft (6 m) ↕20 ft (6 m)

Large shrub or round-headed small tree, most likely a hybrid of *S. alba*. Young branches bright red. Leaves lance-shaped, downy when young, turn bright yellow, in autumn, contrasting with red twigs. Prune in spring to encourage bright new growth. Zones 5–9.

Salix babylonica f. *pekinensis*

Salix gracilistyla 'Melanostachys'

Salix hookeriana

Salix gracilistyla

ROSEGOLD PUSSY WILLOW

☼ ✱ ↔10–15 ft (3–4.5 m) ↕10–15 ft (3–4.5 m)

Shrub native to eastern Asia. Oblong leaves 4 in (10 cm). Catkins before leaves, late winter; male catkins red, later orange, then yellow, female catkins silky gray. **'Melanostachys'** ★ (syn. *S. melanostachys*), more upright male form; black catkins explode with red-tipped yellow stamens. Zones 6–10.

Salix hastata

HALBERD WILLOW

☼ ✱ ↔7 ft (2 m) ↕5 ft (1.5 m)

Dense erect shrub native to mountainous areas of central Europe and northeastern Asia. Twigs become purple in second year. Leaves variable, oblong to slightly rounded, dull green above, glaucous beneath. Small plump catkins appear with leaves, in spring. **'Wehrhahnii'**, attractive silvery catkins. Zones 6–9.

Salix helvetica

SWISS WILLOW

☼ ✱ ↔3 ft (0.9 m) ↕2–5 ft (0.6–1.5 m)

Shrub from European alpine regions. Forms a small spreading mound of densely interlaced twigs, larger in cultivation than the species. Red-brown stems, glossy green leaves with serrated edges and downy undersides. Smothered in small silver-gray catkins, in spring. Zones 5–9.

Salix nigra

Salix hookeriana

☼ ✱ ↔3 ft (0.9 m) ↕3 ft (0.9 m)

Shrub native to northwestern North America. Prostrate habit. Branches occasionally shiny reddish brown in color. Leaves broadly oval, covered with whitish down when young, smooth, dark green above, bluish green beneath. Catkins on short leafy stalks. Zones 6–9.

Salix integra

DAPPLED WILLOW, JAPANESE WILLOW

☼ ✱ ↔12 ft (3.5 m) ↕10–15 ft (3–4.5 m)

Slender shrub from Japan and Korea; like *S. purpurea,* but leaves lighter shade of green. Drooping, purplish branches. Slender catkins before leaves. **'Hakura Nishiki'**, pink leaf buds and stems, light green leaves, flecked pink and white. Zones 6–10.

Salix irrorata

ARIZONA WILLOW

☼ ✱ ↔10 ft (3 m) ↕10 ft (3 m)

Shrub from southwestern USA. Green shoots become smooth and purplish yellow with a waxy bloom in winter. Narrow leaves glossy green above, glaucous beneath. Red anthers of male catkins age to yellow. Zones 5–10.

Salix laevigata

POLISHED WILLOW, RED WILLOW

☼ ✱ ↔25 ft (8 m) ↕50 ft (15 m)

Tree from southwestern USA. Smooth red to yellow-brown shoots. Serrated-edged leaves, light green above, glaucous below. Catkins to 4 in (10 cm) long, with leaves. Zones 5–10.

Salix lindleyana

☼ ✱ ↔30 in (75 cm) ↕2 in (5 cm)

Alpine species found in the Himalayas. Low creeping plant forms dense mats of small, green, rosemary-like leaves on reddish stems. Leaves turn attractive yellow in autumn. Tiny catkins appear with leaves. Ripened seed like white cotton wool. Zones 5–10.

Salix lucida

SHINY WILLOW

☼ ✱ ↔15 ft (4.5m) ↕25 ft (8 m)

North American tree. Glossy leaves, yellowish brown twigs. Slender pointed leaves, shiny green, paler beneath. Golden catkins appear at same time as leaves, in spring. Zones 2–9.

Salix miyabeana

☼ ✱ ↔7–15 ft (2–4.5 m) ↕10–20 ft (3–6 m)

Ornamental species native to Japan; resembles *S. purpurea*. Narrow leaves to 7 in (18 cm) long. Small inconspicuous catkins. Branches have light gray bark. Zones 6–10.

Salix nakamurana

☼ ✱ ↔36 in (90 cm) ↕12 in (30 cm)

Slow-growing dwarf shrub, native to Japan. The stout arching stems eventually form a mound. Leaves are large in relation to plant size, light green, almost round, with silvery hairs. Catkins also silvery. Zones 6–10.

Salix nigra

BLACK WILLOW

☼ ✱ ↔15 ft (4.5 m) ↕10–30 ft (3–9 m)

North American large shrub or small tree. Rough bark, yellowish twigs. Narrow, pointed, pale green leaves with finely serrated margins. Catkins on short downy shoots appear with leaves in spring. Zones 4–10.

Salix pentandra

BAY WILLOW, LAUREL WILLOW

☼ ✱ ↔30 ft (9 m) ↕50 ft (15 m)

Shrub or tree native to a wide area of Europe, naturalized in eastern USA. Aromatic dark green foliage, glossy brownish green twigs, yellow buds. Male catkins bright yellow, with foliage, in spring. Zones 5–10.

Salix irrorata

Salix purpurea

ALASKA BLUE WILLOW, ARCTIC WILLOW, PURPLE OSIER WILLOW

☼ ✱ ↔15 ft (4.5 m) ↕15 ft (4.5 m)

Graceful shrub or small tree, native from Europe to northern Africa, central Asia, and Japan. Arching purplish shoots, narrow oblong leaves, bluish green above, paler beneath. Red catkins, becoming purplish black, appear in spring before leaves. **'Nana'** (syn. *S. purpurea* f. *gracilis*), compact cultivar, gray-green leaves, thin shoots; **'Pendula'**, thin pendulous branches. Zones 5–10.

Salix repens

CREEPING WILLOW

☼ ✱ ↔5 ft (1.5 m) ↕8 in–5 ft (20 cm–1.5 m)

Creeping shrub from Europe, Turkey, southwestern Asia, and Siberia. Downy shoots become smooth. Small tapering leaves, green above, silvery below. Small catkins, spring. Zones 5–10.

Salix × *rubens*

☼ ✱ ↔25 ft (8 m) ↕35 ft (10 m)

Naturally occurring hybrid between *S. alba* and *S. fragilis*, native to central Europe. Olive twigs tinged yellow or red. Lance-shaped leaves, bright green above, glaucous beneath. Cylindrical catkins to 2 in (5 cm). Zones 6–10.

Salix × *sepulcralis*

☼ ✱ ↔40 ft (12 m) ↕40 ft (12 m)

Hybrid between *S. alba* and *S. babylonica*, of garden origin. Habit and foliage similar to but slightly less weeping than *S. babylonica*. Fissured bark. Slender catkins similar to *S. alba*. **'Chrysocoma'** (syn. *S. alba* 'Tristis'), broadly weeping, thin golden twigs, bright green leaves. Zones 6–10.

Salix nakamurana

Salix repens

Salix sericea

SILKY WILLOW

↔5–10 ft (1.5–3 m) ↑12 ft (3.5 m)

Shrub native to eastern USA. Gray bark, slender shoots, tinged purple. Lance-shaped leaves to 4 in (10 cm) long, silky beneath. Catkins appear before leaves, in spring. Zones 7–10.

Salix taxifolia

↔7–10 ft (2–3 m) ↑10–15 ft (3–4.5 m)

Shrub from southern North America and Mexico. Narrow leaves, branches slightly furry. Both male and female catkins inconspicuous. Zones 8–10.

Salix udensis

↔10 ft (3 m) ↑17 ft (5 m)

Shrub native to Japan and eastern Russia. Narrow lance-shaped leaves, dark green above, bluish green and slightly hairy beneath, sometimes with wavy edges. Small cylindrical catkins, in early spring. '**Sekka**', upright branches. Zones 5–9.

SALPIGLOSSIS

A genus of 2 species of annuals or short-lived perennials in the nightshade (Solanaceae) family. Natives of the southern and central Andes, they are small upright plants with alternate, simple linear to elliptical, dark green leaves with finely toothed edges. The stems and foliage are rather sticky to the touch. The flowers are funnel-shaped, 5-lobed; they are borne singly in the leaf axils near the stem tips, and are strikingly colored and patterned. Seedling strains in a range of sizes and colors are widely available. Named from the Greek *salpinx* (a trumpet) and *glossa* (a tongue), in reference to the flower shape.

CULTIVATION: Treated as an annual, *Salpiglossis* species are best grown in an area with cool moist summer conditions. Plant in a sunny position with fertile, moist, well-drained soil, and water well. In mild almost frost-free regions these species can be overwintered. They are usually propagated by seed sown in situ.

Salpiglossis sinuata, Festival Strain

Salpiglossis sinuata

PAINTED TONGUE

↔8–12 in (20–30 cm) ↑16–24 in (40–60 cm)

Annual, biennial, or short-lived perennial, usually treated as annual. Narrow, dark green, sticky leaves to 4 in (10 cm) long, often toothed, sometimes lobed. Heads of funnel-shaped flowers to 2 in (5 cm) wide, yellow to reddish purple, darker veins and markings. Mixed color seedling strains include: **Bolero Hybrids**, 12 in (30 cm) tall, wide color range; **Casino Mixed**, 12 in (30 cm) tall, wide color range with contrasting veining; **Emperor Royal Series**, 24 in (60 cm) tall, large petunia-like flowers, conspicuously veined; **Festival Strain**, dark red-maroon flowers. Zones 8–11.

SALVIA

SAGE

The largest genus in the mint (Lamiaceae) family, *Salvia* contains annuals, perennials, and softwooded evergreen shrubs. They grow in habitats from coastal to alpine; over half the 900 or so species are native to the Americas. The leaves are opposite and carried on squared hairy stems, and are aromatic when crushed. The flowers are tubular, with the petals split into 2 straight or flaring lips. Colors may be shades of blue to purple and pink to red, as well as white and some yellows.

CULTIVATION: The shrubby sages grow in a range of soil types but dislike heavy wet soils. Most do best in full sun; all require a well-drained situation. Prune in spring to remove straggly, bare, and frost-damaged stems. Propagate most shrubby species from softwood cuttings taken throughout the growing season. Seed of all species can be sown in spring.

Salvia bulleyana

Salvia africana-lutea

syn. *Salvia aurea*

BEACH SAGE, BROWN SAGE, GOLDEN SAGE

↔3 ft (0.9 m) ↑3–5 ft (0.9–1.5 m)

Stiff well-branched shrub from coastal areas of South Africa. Small, aromatic, grayish green leaves. Whorls of large yellow flowers, fading to orangey brown, in summer–autumn. Prominent greenish brown calyces. '**Kirstenbosch**', dwarf cultivar. Zones 9–11.

Salvia apiana

BEE SAGE, CALIFORNIA WHITE SAGE

↔3 ft (0.9 m) ↑4 ft (1.2 m)

Shrub from southwestern California, USA. Silvery covering of fine hairs. Leaves very aromatic. White or pale lavender flowers grow in loose whorls above foliage, in spring. Zones 9–11.

Salvia argentea

↔24–40 in (60–100 cm) ↑24 in (60 cm)

Perennial from southern Europe. Large, woolly, silvery-looking leaves, to 40 in (100 cm) long, grow on basal rosette of foliage. Tall candelabra-like stems of white flowers produced in second year. Zones 8–11.

Salvia blepharophylla

EYELASH-LEAFED SAGE

↔20–27 in (50–70 cm) ↑8–12 in (20–30 cm)

Mexican mat-forming perennial, spreads by runners. Tiny hairs along margins of glossy green oval leaves; orange-red flowers in early summer–late autumn. Zones 9–11.

Salvia buchananii

syn. *Salvia bacheriana of gardens*

BUCHANAN'S SAGE

↔12 in (30 cm) ↑12–20 in (30–50 cm)

Clumping perennial, most probably originating from Mexico. Lovely, rich, glossy, oval leaves ¾–2 in (18 mm–5 cm) long. Velvety hot magenta flowers appear mainly from summer to autumn. Zones 10–11.

Salvia canariensis

Salvia bulleyana

syn. *Salvia flava var. megalantha*

↔16–24 in (40–60 cm) ↑20–40 in (50–100 cm)

Compact low-growing species from China. Bright green crinkled foliage. Yellow flowers with purplish brown lower lip and bright green calyx, in summer. Zones 9–11.

Salvia cacaliifolia

CACALIA SAGE

↔12–20 in (30–50 cm) ↑36 in (90 cm)

Suckering perennial from Central America. Bright green arrowhead-like leaves. Royal blue flowers with green calyx. Blooms year round in mild climates, in mid-summer to autumn in cooler climates. Zones 10–11.

Salvia canariensis

CANARY ISLAND SAGE

↔3 ft (0.9 m) ↑4–7 ft (1.2–2 m)

Shrub native to the Canary Islands. The stems are covered in dense white hairs, and the soft arrowhead-shaped leaves are grayish green and hairy. The lilac-pink flowers emerge from showy purplish red calyces, in spring–summer. '**Alba**', pink calyces, white flowers. Zones 9–11.

Salvia candidissima

↔20–40 in (50–100 cm) ↑20–40 in (50–100 cm)

Subshrub from Greece, Turkey, and northern Iran. Wide silvery basal foliage, bright white flower spikes, 20 in (50 cm) long, mid-spring. Zones 8–11.

Salvia castanea

↔24 in (60 cm) ↑36 in (90 cm)

Perennial from the Himalayas. Basal clump of narrow oval leaves with serrated margins and long stalks. Spikes of maroon-purple tubular flowers, 24 in (60 cm) long, tinged yellow below, in summer. Hardy. Zones 7–11.

Salvia castanea

Salvia darcyi

Salvia clevelandii

Salvia chamaedryoides

syn. *Salvia chamaedryfolia*

GERMANDER SAGE

↔ 12–20 in (30–50 cm)
↑ 12–24 in (30–60 cm)

Suckering evergreen perennial from Mexico. Small silvery leaves, sky blue flowers, white throat markings, in spring–autumn. Zones 8–11.

Salvia chiapensis

CHIAPAS SAGE

↔ 16–24 in (40–60 cm)
↑ 16–24 in (40–60 cm)

Perennial from Mexico. Glossy olive green leaves to 3 in (8 cm) long. Cerise-pink flowers, velvety green calyces. Long-flowering in mild climates. Zones 9–11.

Salvia clevelandii

CALIFORNIA BLUE SAGE, CLEVELAND SAGE

↔ 15–26 in (38–65 cm)
↑ 24–48 in (60–120 cm)

Shrub from California's dry chaparral. Aromatic, oval to lance-shaped, gray-green leaves, with toothed edges and wrinkled upper surfaces. Erect flower spikes, whorls of fragrant, lavender-blue, rarely white, flowers, in summer. **'Winifred Gilman'** ★, drought-tolerant, very dark flowers. Zones 8–10.

Salvia farinacea 'Victoria Blue'

Salvia greggii

Salvia coccinea

syn. *Salvia coccinea var. pseudococcinea*

TEXAS SAGE, TROPICAL SAGE

↔ 20–32 in (50–80 cm)
↑ 40 in (100 cm)

Annual or short-lived shrub from tropical South America; in mild climates may be perennial, elsewhere treated as annual. Mostly triangular, hairy, green leaves, scalloped margins. Flowers usually scarlet, may be red, pink, or white. **Hummingbird Mixed**, compact, flowers in white, red, or pink shades; **'Lady in Red'**, slightly smaller, red flowers. Zones 9–12.

Salvia confertiflora

↔ 24–40 in (60–100 cm)
↑ 40 in (100 cm)

Woody-based perennial from Brazil. Toothed, pointed, oval leaves to 8 in (20 cm) long, with tan to red-brown covering of hairs, especially on undersides; unpleasant scent when crushed. Flowerheads to 12 in (30 cm) long, bearing up to 15 downy deep red flowers, in summer. Zones 9–10.

Salvia daghestanica

syn. *Salvia canescens var. daghestanica*

DWARF SILVER-LEAF SAGE

↔ 8–12 in (20–30 cm)
↑ 12–18 in (30–45 cm)

Silver-leafed perennial from southern Russia. Violet-lavender flowers, in summer. Zones 5–8.

Salvia darcyi

syn. *Salvia oresbia*

↔ 4 ft (1.2 m) ↑ 3–4 ft (0.9–1.2 m)

Large clumping perennial from Mexico. Spreads slowly by runners. Flowers bright red with purplish green calyces, produced on spikes 12–24 in (30–60 cm) long, in summer–autumn. Zones 9–11.

Salvia coccinea

Salvia discolor

ANDEAN SILVER SAGE

↔ 32–40 in (80–100 cm)
↑ 32–40 in (80–100 cm)

Perennial from Peru. White, wiry, sprawling stems. Attractive leaves are green on top, silver beneath. Dark purple to navy blue flowers with green calyces and silver bracts, appear in late summer–early autumn. Zones 9–11.

Salvia dorisiana

FRUIT-SCENTED SAGE, PEACH SAGE

↔ 36 in (90 cm)
↑ 36–48 in (90–120 cm)

Hairy heavily branched plant from Honduras. Long velvety leaves. Spikes of bright pink loosely tubular flowers, 2 in (5 cm) long, in winter. Flowers and leaves scented; flowers attract hummingbirds. Zones 10–12.

Salvia elegans

PINEAPPLE SAGE

↔ 3 ft (0.9 m) ↑ 6 ft (1.8 m)

Shrub from high mountain regions of Central Mexico and Guatemala. Crushed leaves have a distinctive pineapple aroma. Shorter habit in cold areas. Leaves soft and downy, with finely serrated edges. Narrow scarlet-red flowers in well-spaced whorls, in spring–autumn. Attracts hummingbirds. **'Scarlet Pineapple'** (syn. *S. rutilans*), stronger pineapple scent, larger flowers. Zones 8–11.

Salvia farinacea

MEALY SAGE

↔ 24 in (60 cm)
↑ 36–48 in (90–120 cm)

Popular perennial, often treated as an annual, from Texas and New Mexico, USA. Leaves oval, green and glossy. Flowers at ends of stems in shades of blue, purple, or white, and dusted with a flour-like substance. **'Strata'**, shorter habit, blue flowers, mealy white stem and calyces; **'Victoria'**, blue flowers, blue stems and calyces; **'Victoria Blue'**, shorter habit, flowers deeper blue, larger. Zones 9–11.

Salvia fulgens

CARDINAL SAGE

↔ 30 in (75 cm) ↑ 48 in (120 cm)

Subshrub, native of Mexico. Woody-stemmed and shrubby in mild climates. Ovate to poplar-shaped leaves, cleft at base, toothed edges, downy undersides. Bright red flowers, 2 to 6, on spikes, in summer. Zones 9–10.

Salvia gesneriiflora

↔ 10 in (25 cm) ↑ 26 in (65 cm)

Shrub or subshrub found from Mexico to Columbia. Dense mound of hairy, somewhat wrinkled, ovate leaves with toothed edges. Orange-red flowers, 2 in (5 cm) long, resembling those of *Columnea* species. Flower spikes to 8 in (20 cm) long appear in summer–autumn. **'Tequila'**, large shrub, scarlet flowers, black calyx. Zones 8–11.

Salvia glutinosa

JUPITER'S DISTAFF

↔ 20 in (50 cm) ↑ 40 in (100 cm)

Small deciduous shrub from Europe and western Asia. Hairy spear-shaped leaves grow to 5 in (12 cm) long. The sticky flowers are pale yellow dotted with maroon on upper lip, with green calyces, and appear in early summer. Zones 6–10.

Salvia greggii

AUTUMN SAGE

↔ 12–36 in (30–90 cm)
↑ 12–36 in (30–90 cm)

Variable species native to Texas, USA, and Mexico. Hybridizes freely with related *S. microphylla*. Small leathery leaves, usually smooth. Flowers usually red or shades of pink, purple, and white, in summer–late autumn. Cultivar names **'Alba'**, **'Iced Lemon'**, **'Peach'**, and **'Raspberry Royale'** reflect flower colors. The **Sierra Series** are dense, shrubby plants around 24 in (60 cm) tall in a range of flower colors. Zones 7–11.

Salvia guaranitica ★

syns *Salvia ambigens, S. concolor*

ANISE-SCENTED SAGE

↔ 16–27 in (40–70 cm)
↑ 4–5 ft (1.2–1.5 m)

South American perennial, suckering lightly to form large clumps. Flowers borne on 10 in (25 cm) long spike, true blue with green calyces, early summer–autumn. **'Black and Blue'**, shorter, less spreading, blue flowers, almost black calyces; **'Blue Enigma'**, shorter, earlier flowering, deep blue flowers, green calyces; **'Costa Rica Blue'**, tall cultivar, violet-blue flowers, yellow-green calyces. Zones 8–11.

Salvia hians

↔24 in (60 cm) ↕24–40 in (60–100 cm)

Perennial from Kashmir and Pakistan. Basal green foliage, leaves to 10 in (25 cm) long. Flowers soft violet with brownish red calyx, in whorls on tall branching stems, in summer. Zones 7–11.

Salvia indica

↔24 in (60 cm) ↕24–36 in (60–90 cm)

Perennial from the Middle East. Gray leaves with scalloped margins form mound of basal foliage. Tall spikes of purple flowers with white markings on bottom lip, spring. May die down during warmer months. Zones 8–11.

Salvia involucrata

ROSELEAF SAGE

↔5 ft (1.5 m) ↕5 ft (1.5 m)

Perennial from Mexico. Some wood at base. Purplish green leaves. Beetroot red flowers and calyces in summer–autumn. **'Bethellii'**, more compact, sometimes suckering, large heart-shaped leaves, flowers sugar pink. Zones 8–11.

Salvia × jamensis

↔27–40 in (70–100 cm) ↕27–40 in (70–100 cm)

Shrubby hybrid. A cross between *S. microphylla* and *S. greggii*, generally with glossy green oval leaves. Flowers occur in a range of solid colors, including reds, pinks, oranges, apricots, and yellows, also some bi-colored forms, in summer–autumn. **'Cinega de Oro'**, pale yellow flowers. Zones 9–11.

Salvia lavandulifolia

syn. *Salvia officinalis subsp. lavandulifolia*

SPANISH SAGE

↔18 in (45 cm) ↕18 in (45 cm)

From Spain and southern France. Builds some wood at base. Narrow grayish white leaves, scented like rosemary. Sparse short spikes of small pale lavender blue flowers, early summer. Zones 6–10.

Salvia leucantha

MEXICAN BUSH SAGE, VELVET SAGE

↔3 ft (0.9 m) ↕3 ft (0.9 m)

Spreading shrub, native to Mexico and tropical America. Stems very woolly. Soft, narrow, wrinkled leaves, dull green, thickly felted beneath. Spikes of white or purple flowers extend from showy, velvety, purple calyces, in late summer. **'Midnight'** (syn. 'Purple Velvet'), stunning purple flowers and calyces; **'Santa Barbara'**, compact, heavy flowering over long season; **'Velour Pink'**, bright pink flowers on 40 in (100 cm) stems; **'Velour White'**, white flowers. Zones 9–11.

Salvia leucophylla

CHAPARRAL SAGE, GRAY SAGE, PURPLE SAGE

↔3 ft (0.9 m) ↕5 ft (1.5 m)

Well-branched shrub native to hot, dry, stony hillsides of California, USA. Attractive, whitish gray, hairy leaves. Whorls of pinkish purple flowers on pinkish stems, in autumn. **'Figuero'**, smaller, drought tolerant, silvery foliage; **'Point Sal Spreader'** ★, prostrate form, grayer leaves. Zones 8–11.

Salvia mexicana

MEXICAN SAGE

↔7 ft (2 m) ↕10 ft (3 m)

Vigorous grower native to Mexico. Smooth to slightly hairy leaves, almost heart-shaped, mid-green to grayish green. Spikes of deep purple flowers emerge from large green calyces, held well above foliage, in autumn. **'Black Sepals'**, deep green leaves with dark stems and calyces; **'Limelight'**, chartreuse stems and calyces. Zones 9–11.

Salvia microphylla

LITTLE-LEAFED SAGE

↔3 ft (0.9 m) ↕4 ft (1.2 m)

Variable species, widespread in its native southern USA and Mexico. Slightly hairy serrated-edged leaves give off a blackcurrant-like aroma when crushed. Flowers variable in color, shades of pink, red, and deep purple, in summer–autumn. S. m. var. microphylla, crimson flowers, heavily blooming; **'La Foux'** , shrubby, glossy green, oval leaves, hot pink to red flowers with purple stems and calyces. S. m. **'Coral'**, deep salmon pink flowers; **'Huntington Red'**, bright scarlet flowers; **'Kew Red'**, deep red flowers; **'La Trinidad Pink'**, compact, bright pink to magenta flowers; **'Newby Hall'**, vivid deep scarlet flowers; **'Pink Blush'**, magenta-pink flowers; **'San Carlos Festival'**, continual display of crimson flowers. Zones 8–11.

Salvia lavandulifolia

Salvia munzii

MUNZ'S SAGE, SAN MIGUEL SAGE

↔3–5 ft (0.9–1.5 m) ↕3–7 ft (0.9–2 m)

Shrubby perennial from California, USA. Scented foliage. Spikes of lavender blue flowers with green calyces, in spring. Cold and drought tolerant. Zones 8–11.

Salvia nemorosa

BALKAN CLARY, STEPPE SAGE

↔12–24 in (30–60 cm) ↕24–36 in (60–90 cm)

Perennial from Europe to central Asia. Simple, oval to oblong, wrinkled, green leaves. Racemes of mauve to purple flowers, sometimes white to pink, summer–autumn. intensely blue flowers, tall, upright; **'Lubecca'** (syn. *S. × superba* 'Lubecca'), dwarf cultivar, gray-green leaves, tall spikes of mauve flowers with rich burgundy bracts, in spring; **'Ostfriesland'** (syn. 'East Friesland'), vivid violet-blue flowers, slightly taller than 'Lubecca', in late spring. Zones 5–10.

Salvia involucrata

Salvia officinalis ★

COMMON SAGE, GARDEN SAGE

↔36 in (90 cm) ↕30 in (75 cm)

Perennial shrub native to Spain, the Balkans, and northern Africa; naturalized in southern Europe. White hairy stems, oblong grayish green leaves, upper wrinkled, white-haired beneath, aromatic. Flowers white to pink and purple shades, in summer. Used for centuries for medicinal and culinary purposes. **'Berggarten'** ★, rounded leaves, flowers less often; **'Extrakta'**, high-yielding medicinal oil; **'Icterina'**, attractive variegated leaves edged in pale yellow; **'Minor'**, dull green leaves, small violet-purple flowers; **'Purpurascens'**, reddish purple leaves; **'Purpurascens Variegata'**, purple leaves, splashed with white to cream; **'Purpurea'**, mauve flowers, purple leaves; **'Tricolor'**, dull green leaves edged with yellow and salmon pink. Zones 5–10.

Salvia pachyphylla

BLUE SAGE, MOUNTAIN DESERT SAGE, ROSE SAGE

↔40 in (100 cm) ↕40 in (100 cm)

Small evergreen shrub native to California, USA. Fragrant gray leaves. Large flowers borne in tight bunches, pink with hint of blue, with lavender bracts, in summer. Zones 5–11.

Salvia officinalis 'Minor'

Salvia × jamensis

Salvia patens

Salvia patens

GENTIAN SAGE

↔ 12–24 in (30–60 cm) ↑ 12–24 in (30–60 cm)

Perennial from Mexico. Dies back to tubers in winter. Oval green leaves to 8 in (20 cm) long. Bears spikes of gentian blue flowers, in pairs, 12 in (30 cm) long, with green calyces, in summer–autumn. **'Cambridge Blue'**, sky blue flowers. Zones 8–11.

Salvia pratensis

MEADOW CLARY, MEADOW SAGE

↔ 12 in (30 cm) ↑ 36 in (90 cm)

Perennial of meadows across Europe. Basal clump of rich green wrinkled leaves with irregular margins. Violet flowers (also blue, pink, and white forms), brown calyces, green bracts, in spring. **Haematodes Group** (syn. *S. haematodes*), large erect sprays of pale lilac-blue flowers with reddish brown stems, in summer; **'Indigo'**, superb indigo blue flowers, in early summer. Zones 4–10.

Salvia przewalskii

↔ 12–24 in (30–60 cm) ↑ 12–24 in (30–60 cm)

Chinese species forming basal clump of yellow-green foliage. Some leaves grow to 12 in (30 cm) long. Flowers purplish red with reddish brown calyces, borne on much-branched stems, in summer. Zones 8–11.

Salvia regla

MOUNTAIN SAGE

↔ 3 ft (0.9 m) ↑ 4 ft (1.2 m)

Shrub found in Texas, USA, and Mexico. Erect woody habit, upper stems dark red-brown. Leaves roughly triangular with wavy edges. Large bright scarlet-red flowers, in autumn. **'Royal'**, tubular orange flowers; **'Huntington'**, orange-red flowers, tolerates hot dry conditions. Zones 8–11.

Salvia splendens 'Vista Salmon'

Salvia roemeriana

CEDAR SAGE

↔ 12 in (30 cm) ↑ 12 in (30 cm)

Small perennial from Arizona and Texas, USA, and Mexico. Rounded, geranium-like, green leaves. Bright red flowers borne on 8 in (20 cm) long stalks, in summer. Zones 8–11.

Salvia sclarea

CLARY SAGE, CLEAR EYE

↔ 36 in (90 cm) ↑ 36–48 in (90–120 cm)

Perennial or biennial from southern Europe. Leaves are heart-shaped and puckered, 9–12 in (22–30 cm) long. Candelabra of small white-lilac or pale blue flowers are borne in prominent rosy pink or mauve bracts, in early summer. Long-blooming species with a strong musky aroma. **'Turkestanica'** ★, larger bluish or pinkish white flowers, violet bracts tinged with green. Zones 4–9.

Salvia sonomensis

CREEPING SAGE, SONOMA SAGE

↔ 3–7 ft (0.9–2 m) ↑ 12 in (30 cm)

Mat-forming perennial from California, USA. Leaves variable in shape and color, from long and narrow to short and round, green, yellow-green or gray-green. Flowers on short stalks, in various shades of lavender. **Dara's Choice'**, slightly taller, more mounding, taller flower spikes, violet flowers, blue-green calyces. Zones 8–11.

Salvia spathacea

CRIMSON SAGE, HUMMINGBIRD SAGE, PITCHER SAGE

↔ 12–36 in (30–90 cm) ↑ 12–36 in (30–90 cm)

Suckering perennial from California, USA. Forms large mats. Large spear-shaped leaves. Flowers crimson-pink, prominent reddish black calyces and bracts, borne on tall stems, in early spring–summer. **'Powerline Pink'**, larger than the species, taller flower stems, pink flowers. Zones 8–11.

Salvia splendens

SCARLET SAGE

↔ 8–32 in (20–80 cm) ↑ 8–48 in (20–120 cm)

Variable perennial, often treated as an annual. Many-branched. Oval green leaves, serrated margins. Flowers are usually red; many cultivars in other colors. **'Empire Purple'**, deep reddish purple flowers; **'Red Arrow'**, bright red with dark green foliage; **'Red Riches'** (syn. 'Ryco'), early-blooming, vivid scarlet flowers, dark green leaves; **'Scarlet King'**, traditional bedding variety, big dense spikes of scarlet flowers, dark green foliage; **Sizzler Series**, compact foliage, early-flowering, long-lasting, flowers burgundy, lavender, pink, red, salmon, white, and bicolored; **'Vanguard'**, compact, early flowering, dark leaves, red flowers; **'Vista Salmon'**, compact, well-branched, dark green leaves, well-packed spikes of salmon flowers, pink inner petals. Zones 9–11.

Salvia × *superba*

↔ 12–24 in (30–60 cm) ↑ 12–27 in (30–75 cm)

Hardy perennial hybrid between *S.* × *sylvestris* and *S. villicaulis*, of European origin. Many cultivars. Upright flower spikes in a range of colors, in summer. Zones 5–10.

Salvia × *sylvestris*

↔ 20–40 in (50–100 cm) ↑ 20–40 in (50–100 cm)

Very hardy and widespread European perennial. Small, narrow, green leaves with stalks and scalloped margins. Flowers usually purple. **'Blauhügel'** (syns 'Blue Hills', 'Blue Mount'), deep blue flower spikes on low plants to 15 in (38 cm) high; **'Mainacht'** (syn. 'May Night'), midnight violet flowers, in early spring; **'Tänzerin'**, erect, deep violet flower spikes to 32 in (80 cm) long. Zones 5–10.

Salvia spathacea

Salvia uliginosa

BOG SAGE

↔ 3 ft (0.9 m) ↑ 3–6 ft (0.9–1.8 m)

Perennial from Brazil, Uruguay, and Argentina. Clump-forming, spreading by underground runners. Yellowish green lance-shaped leaves are carried on erect stems. Whorls of small sky blue and white flowers appear in late summer–autumn. Needs moist soil. Zones 9–11.

Salvia verticillata

LILAC SAGE

↔ 32 in (80 cm) ↑ 40 in (100 cm)

Perennial, widespread in Europe and western Asia; naturalized in North America. Leafy clump of hairy, pale green leaves. Branched inflorescences of whorls of lavender-violet flowers with green calyces, in summer. **'Alba'**, white flowers and lime green calyces; **'Purple Rain'**, slightly smaller than the species, dusky purple flowers and violet calyces. Zones 6–10.

Salvia viridis

syn. *Salvia horminum*

ANNUAL SAGE, PAINTED SAGE, PURPLE-TOP

↔ 12 in (30 cm) ↑ 12–24 in (30–60 cm)

Slender annual found from the Mediterranean across to Crimea, Ukraine. Tiny flowers bloom in the leaf axils; petal-like top bracts are purple, pink, or white with darker veining. Grow plants massed for best effect. **'Tricolor Mixed'**, improved form with blue, pink, or cream bracts. Zones 8–10.

Salvia wagneriana

syns *Salvia albopileata, S. tonduzii*

WAGNER SAGE

↔ 4 ft (1.2 m) ↑ 3–10 ft (0.9–3 m)

Shrub-like perennial from Central America. Yellowish green leaves. Flowers vary from red to pink and pale pink, with colored bracts and calyces, autumn–winter. Zones 10–11.

Salvia, Hybrid Cultivar, 'Plum'

Salvia Hybrid Cultivars

↔ 16–48 in (40–120 cm) ↕ 20–60 in (50–150 cm)

Salvia hybrids have been developed from a wide range of species—some are known crosses, others chance seedlings—and are a diverse group. They are grown mainly for their flowers, but many cultivars also have attractive or unusual foliage. Many are probably perennial, but are often treated as annuals, especially in cold climates. **'Costa Rica Blue'**, vibrant green heart-shaped leaves and bright blue flowers; **Heatwave Series**, pink, salmon, purple, or white, heat- and drought-tolerant, long-flowering; **'Hot Lips'**, white, red, and red/white flowers on the same plant; **'Indigo Spires'** ★, deep violet flowers, double white bee-line, lower lip, dark purple calyces; **'Maraschino'**, cherry red flowers on sprawling plant, long-flowering; **'Phyllis's Fancy'**, white flowers, bluish tinge, calyces purple, long-flowering; **'Plum'**, flowers bright magenta, calyces deep reddish purple; **'Purple Majesty'**, flowers and calyces rich dark purple, growing in spikes 10 in (25 cm) long; **'Wendy's Wish'**, bushy, spikes of pink flowers, pink-tinted calyces. Zones 6–10.

SAMBUCUS

ELDER, ELDERBERRY

This genus from the world's temperate areas encompasses around 25 species of perennials, shrubs, and small trees that are mostly deciduous, from the muskroot (Adoxaceae) family. Some are ornamental, others invasive weeds. Both flowers and fruits are used for making wines, jams, and jellies; the foliage is sometimes used medicinally. Elders have pinnate leaves, and the umbel-like heads of small white to creamy yellow flowers develop into quick-ripening berries, which are usually red to black.

CULTIVATION: Elders are not difficult to grow, and some species are only too easily cultivated; think twice before deliberately introducing *S. nigra* to your garden. They are not fussy about soil type as long as the ground remains fairly moist in summer, nor are they worried by brief periods of waterlogging in winter. Most species are very frost hardy, and will reshoot even when cut to the ground by frost. Prune trees to shape as necessary, and propagate from seed or cuttings.

Sambucus canadensis

AMERICAN ELDER, AMERICAN ELDERBERRY, SWEET ELDER

↔ 12 ft (3.5 m) ↕ 8–12 ft (2.4–3.5 m)

Deciduous shrub from eastern North America, sometimes suckering. Leaves usually have 7 leaflets with serrated edges, and may be smooth or rather woolly on the undersides. Cream flowers in summer, tiny purple-black berries. **'Goldfinch'**, lime green foliage, leaflets with incised edges, reddish young leaves. Zones 3–9.

Sambucus canadensis

Sambucus nigra

BLACK ELDER, EUROPEAN ELDER

↔ 10–20 ft (3–6 m) ↕ 8–30 ft (2.4–9 m)

Deciduous shrub or small tree from Europe, North Africa, and western Asia. Self-sows and suckers freely. This species is a weed in many areas, but is cultivated for its edible flowers and fruits. Leaves have 3 to 9 dark green leaflets with serrated edges. Large heads of scented white flowers, in spring–early summer. Purple-black berries. **'Aurea'**, golden yellow foliage; **'Aureomarginata'**, paler variegated foliage, berries grow on pink stems; **'Black Beauty'**, dark purple-red foliage, pink flowers; **'Black Lace'**, very fine filigree foliage, purple-red, flowers pale pink; **'Guincho Purple'**, deep green leaves turn very dark purple; **'Laciniata'**, deeply dissected leaflets; **'Marginata'**, gold- to cream-edged foliage; **'Nana'**, loosely rounded form; **'Pulverulenta'**, cream and green mottled foliage and musk-scented flowers; **'Viridis'**, pale green flowers and fruits. Zones 5–10.

Sambucus racemosa

EUROPEAN RED ELDER, RED ELDERBERRY

↔ 12 ft (3.5 m) ↕ 12 ft (3.5 m)

Deciduous shrub found through most of temperate Eurasia, from the UK to Japan. Leaves divided into 5 leaflets with coarsely serrated edges. Panicles of pale green to cream flowers appear in spring–early summer, followed by clusters of very small red berries. **'Plumosa Aurea'**, dissected yellow foliage; **'Sutherland Gold'**, deeply dissected golden foliage, turning copper-colored in spring (does best in partial shade, but can be grown in complete shade); **'Tenuifolia'**, dwarf, deeply cut foliage, purple new growth. Zones 4–9.

Sandersonia aurantiaca

SANDERSONIA

A genus consisting of a single species of scrambling to climbing tuberous perennial, which is a member of the autumn-crocus (Colchiacaceae) family. Now rare in its native South African habitat of KwaZulu-Natal, the species is widely cultivated in gardens and for the cut-flower trade. It was named for John Sanderson (1820–91), honorary secretary to the Horticultural Society of Natal, and bears some similarities to the equally strange and surprising *Gloriosa rothschildiana* (glory lily).

CULTIVATION: Grow in full sun in a free-draining mix to which some well-rotted garden humus has been added. Poor soils are tolerated, and may even be preferable. Water well, and apply weak liquid feed every 10 days during the growth phase. Provide support for the climbing stems. Propagate from offsets in autumn, or by sowing ripe seed in a sandy mix in late winter.

Sandersonia aurantiaca ★

syn. *Sandersonia koetjape*

CHINESE LANTERN LILY, CHRISTMAS BELLS

↔ 8 in (20 cm) ↕ 40 in (100 cm)

Deciduous perennial, tuberous and scrambling to climbing. Leaves are a soft green, growing alternately along the stems; tips often develop into tendrils by which the plant scrambles. Flowers are lantern-shaped, glowing golden orange, pendent, on downturned stalks, in summer. Zones 9–11.

SANGUINARIA

BLOODROOT, RED PUCCOON

This genus belonging to the poppy (Papaveraceae) family consists of a single species, found only in eastern North America. The plant is a hairless perennial that grows in woodlands. It has a branching rhizome, usually with a single palmately incised leaf. The small, white, starry flowers appear early, unfurling to reveal their rounded scalloped shape. The fruit capsules open from the middle to both the base and the apex. The many seeds have a juicy aril that is attractive to ants, which then help to disperse the seeds. This plant is an ephemeral and will die down by mid-summer—so mark its location. It will eventually spread to make a good woodland ground cover. The plant contains alkaloids, and has been used medicinally as an emetic.

CULTIVATION: Grow *Sanguinaria* in half-sun or shade in rich moist soil, and keep well watered. Prefers a damp shaded area, where it can be left to spread. Sow seed when ripe, or divide rhizomes when the plant is dormant.

Sanguinaria canadensis

Sanguinaria canadensis 'Multiplex'

Sanguinaria canadensis
BLOODROOT, RED PUCCOON

↔ 4 in (10 cm) ↑ 8 in (20 cm)

Perennial woodland plant from North America. Large green-gray leaves with deep indentations. White or pinkish flowers, 1 per stalk, in spring. Ephemeral, dies back in mid to late summer. Both **'Flore Pleno'** and **'Multiplex'** (syn. 'Plena') have showy double white flowers. Zones 2–8.

SANGUISORBA
syn. *Poterium*

BURNET

This genus, comprising about 10 species of shrubs and rhizomatous perennials found in temperate parts of Eurasia, North America, and the Canary Islands, is a member of the rose (Rosaceae) family. The spirally arranged leaves, divided into many leaflets with toothed edges, have a fern-like quality. The flowers are small, either unisexual or hermaphroditic, green, white, or pink, stalkless, and arranged in dense heads at the ends of stems, resembling bottlebrushes. The calyx tube has 4 petal-like lobes, and there are no petals. There are 4, rarely 12, stamens, and a single carpel. The fruits are leathery achenes. These plants are grown for their flower spikes and foliage. The rootstock has astringent qualities and was used to stop bleeding. Some species, such as *S. minor*, the salad burnet, have edible leaves.

CULTIVATION: Most *Sanguisorba* species are plants of damp meadowland, needing moist rich soils that do not dry out in summer. They are propagated by division in spring, or from seed sown in autumn or spring.

Santolina chamaecyparissus

Sanguisorba canadensis
CANADIAN BURNET, GREAT BURNET

↔ 24–36 in (60–90 cm)
↑ 48–60 in (120–150 cm)

Clump-forming perennial from Newfoundland, Canada, through Michigan, and south to Georgia, USA. Bright green compound leaves with small regular indentations on edges. White bottlebrush-like flowers, in late summer. Zones 4–8.

Sanguisorba officinalis
BURNET BLOODWORT, GREAT BURNET

↔ 24–36 in (60–90 cm)
↑ 30–36 in (75–90 cm)

Clump-forming perennial from temperate Eurasia. Medium green leaves, sometimes eaten when young. Deep red or dark purple flowers appear in summer. Zones 4–8.

SANSEVIERIA
BOWSTRING HEMP, MOTHER-IN-LAW'S TONGUE

A genus consisting of over 50 species of perennial plants in the asparagus (Asparagaceae) family, all native to tropical and southern Africa and the East Indies. The thick fibrous leaves generally form a rosette, either lying nearly flat on the ground or stiffly upright up to 5 feet (1.5 m) tall. The flowers are held in a cluster or panicle on simple stems. The fiber from the leaves of *Sansevieria* species is traditionally used for making mats, rope, and bowstrings. These plants are generally cultivated for their decorative leaves, which may be variegated or mottled. They are important indoor plants in temperate climates.

CULTIVATION: Sansevierias are not tolerant of frost, and they need shade from the afternoon sun, and only moderate water during the summer months. Keep dry in winter. Propagation is either by division of offsets or from leaf cuttings.

Santolina rosmarinifolia

Sansevieria cylindrica
CYLINDER SNAKE PLANT

↔ 5 ft (1.5 m) ↑ 16 in (40 cm)

Native to southern tropical Africa. Long, arching, leathery leaves, cylindrical in section, forming low mound. Flowers white, flushed with pink, in raceme to 24 in (60 cm) long, held on stiff stem, in summer. Zones 10–11.

SANTOLINA

This Mediterranean genus from the daisy (Asteraceae) family has some 18 species of largely similar evergreen shrubs that form low hummocks. The slender stems are crowded with narrow leaves that have finely toothed or lobed margins. They are often clothed in silvery hairs, as are the leaf stalks. Clusters of button-like flowerheads, usually bright yellow, appear in summer.

CULTIVATION: Fully to moderately frost hardy, these shrubs thrive in a warm sunny position and are ideal for dry banks and as border plants. They need perfect drainage and do not like overly wet winters, but are not fussy about soil type as long as it is reasonably loose and open. *Santolina* species respond well to regular trimming to keep the bushes neat and compact. It is also advisable to remove the dead flowerheads, as they are not attractive once they have dried. They can be propagated from small cuttings or by removing self-rooted layers.

Santolina chamaecyparissus
LAVENDER COTTON

↔ 4 ft (1.2 m) ↑ 24 in (60 cm)

Shrub from coastal southern Spain to the Adriatic region. Bright silvery gray foliage, almost white when young. Clusters of ½–¾ in (12–18 mm) wide flowerheads, early summer. ***S. c.* var. *nana***, smaller, 12–24 in (30–60 cm) tall. ***S. c.* 'Lemon Queen'**, soft yellow flowerheads; **'Pretty Carol'**, to 16 in (40 cm) tall. Zones 7–10.

Santolina rosmarinifolia
GREEN SANTOLINA

↔ 36 in (90 cm)
↑ 12–24 in (30–60 cm)

Bushy shrub native to southwestern Europe. Sparsely downy linear leaves have fine narrow teeth that are very closely spaced. Clusters of ¾ in (18 mm) wide bright yellow flowerheads, in mid-summer. **'Morning Mist ★'**, compact form; **'Primrose Gem'**, light lemon flowers. Zones 7–10.

SANVITALIA

This genus of 7 species extends from southwestern USA through Central America to northwestern South America, and belongs to the daisy (Asteraceae) family. They are small ornamental shrubs or low-growing perennials or annuals. Leaves are opposite, with sheathing bases, and may be smooth-edged or lobed. The flowers resemble daisies. Outer florets have orange to yellow to white rays; disc florets are usually a deep purple.

CULTIVATION: Garden species are usually annuals, and are suited to an open sunny position in well-drained good soil. Propagate from seed sown in situ in spring or autumn.

Sanvitalia procumbens
CREEPING ZINNIA

↔ 12 in (30 cm)
↑ 6–8 in (15–20 cm)

Low spreading annual from southwestern USA and Mexico. Forms mats of hairy mid-green leaves. Many bright yellow to orange daisies with purple-black centers, in summer. **'Aztec Gold'**, bright yellow daisies, green centers; **'Gold Braid'**, double golden daisies; **'Mandarin Orange'**, bright orange flowers, black centers. Zones 6–11.

Sanvitalia procumbens

SAPINDUS

There are about 13 species in this tropical and subtropical genus, most from the Americas and Asia. These evergreen and deciduous trees, shrubs and climbers belong to the soapberry (Sapindaceae) family. They are grown mostly as ornamental and shade trees. They have alternate simple or pinnate leaves, which in some species color attractively to shades of yellow in autumn. They bear clusters of small 5-petalled flowers with prominent hairy stamens in summer, and these are followed by a crop of fleshy berry-like fruits. These berries are rich in saponins (glycosides that foam in water solution), and are used to yield a soap substitute in some countries.
CULTIVATION: Most species are fairly adaptable, and will tolerate poor soil as long as it is well drained. They prefer a sheltered sunny position. Propagate from seed or cuttings.

Sapindus drummondii

WESTERN SOAPBERRY, WILD CHINA TREE

↔30 ft (9 m) ↕50 ft (15 m)

Deciduous tree from harsh dry habitats of southern USA and Mexico. Spreading canopy of pinnate leaves, 18 mid-green leaflets, turn golden yellow in autumn. Small white flowers in panicles at ends of branches in summer. Rounded orange-yellow fruits. Zones 8–10.

Sapindus mukorossi

CHINESE SOAPBERRY

↔20 ft (6 m) ↕40–80 ft (12–24 m)

Deciduous tree found from India eastward through China to Japan. Large pinnate leaves. White flowers bloom in panicles at the ends of branches in summer. The yellow to orange-brown fruits used as a soap substitute; the black seeds used for beads. Zones 8–11.

Sapindus saponaria

FALSE DOGWOOD, SOAPBERRY, WING-LEAFED SOAPBERRY

↔20 ft (6 m) ↕30 ft (9 m)

Evergreen tree from tropical America. Pinnate leaves to 12 in (30 cm) long. White flowers in panicles to 6 in (15 cm) long, in summer. Glossy, orange-brown, saponin-rich fruits, used locally as soap. Zones 10–12.

SAPONARIA

SOAPWORT

This genus belonging to the pink (Caryophyllaceae) family contains some 20 species of temperate Eurasian annuals and perennials that contain saponin, a glycoside that forms a soapy colloidal solution when mixed with water. The roots in particular were once used as soap, and the extract is sometimes used in detergents and foaming agents. That use aside, these are pretty little plants. They are mainly low-growing, ranging from tufted mounds to fairly wide-spreading ground covers. They have blue-green linear to spatulate leaves, sometimes toothed, and in summer they are smothered in heads of small, starry, 5-petalled, pink flowers.
CULTIVATION: Mainly very hardy and easily grown, they do best spilling over banks or in perennial borders or rockeries with gritty, moist, humus-rich, free-draining soil. They will tolerate slightly alkaline soil. Propagate from cuttings or seed, or by layering.

Saponaria ocymoides

ROCK SOAPWORT

↔12–20 in (30–50 cm) ↕6–12 in (15–30 cm)

Summer-flowering, mound-forming, alpine perennial found from Spain to the Balkans. Small, downy, lance-shaped leaves. Clusters of deep pink flowers, less commonly red or white, ½ in (12 mm) wide. **'Rubra Compacta'** ★, dense mounding habit, deep crimson flowers. Zones 3–10.

Saponaria officinalis

BOUNCING BET, SOAPWORT

↔20–40 in (50–100 cm) ↕12–24 in (30–60 cm)

Perennial found over much of Europe. Large billowing mound of wiry stems, green to gray-green, with pointed oval leaves to ½ in (12 mm) long. Heads of 5 or more flowers to 1 in (25 mm) wide, pale to bright pink, sometimes red or white, in late summer–autumn. **'Rosea Plena'**, tall, with pink double flowers; **'Rubra Plena'**, double flowers, crimson at opening, ageing to deep pink. Zones 4–10.

Saponaria × olivana

↔8 in (20 cm) ↕2 in (5 cm)

A dwarf cushion-forming hybrid, probably between *S. caespitosa* and *S. pumilio*, perhaps with some *S. ocymoides* influence. Dense low mound, tiny green to gray-green leaves. Smothered in pink flowers, ¾ in (18 mm) wide, in late spring. Zones 3–10.

Saponaria pumilio

↔8 in (20 cm) ↕2–4 in (5–10 cm)

Small, tufted, summer-flowering perennial native to the Carpathians and the Alps. Dense, very narrow, short leaves forming a slightly mounded carpet studded with solitary or paired purple-pink, rarely white, flowers to ¾ in (18 mm) wide. Zones 6–10.

SARCOBATUS

Native to western North America, the sole species is the type for its genus and family, the Sarcobataceae. It is a dense spiny shrub with arching branches and narrow fleshy leaves. Male and female flowers appear on the same plant, and both are usually small, with the male flowers forming catkin-like spikes. The enlarging calyx of the female flowers develops into a leathery fruit with a broad papery wing toward the middle.
CULTIVATION: Moderately frost hardy, this species grows best in a warm sheltered position in full sun and a well-drained soil. Propagation is from seed.

Sarcobatus vermiculatus

GREASEWOOD

↔7 ft (2 m) ↕6 ft (1.8 m)

Rounded spreading shrub with arching branches. Narrow, fleshy, gray-green leaves to 1½ in (35 mm) long. Spikes of male flowers up to 1¼ in (30 mm) long. The hard yellow wood is used for fuel. Zones 5–10.

SARCOCOCCA

CHRISTMAS BOX, SWEET BOX

This genus within the box (Buxaceae) family consists of evergreen monoecious shrubs cultivated for their ornamental value. Their natural habitats are damp woods and dense forests in western China, the Himalayas, and the mountains of Southeast Asia. The male flowers can be recognized by their visible anthers, while the female flowers grow below the male flowers.
CULTIVATION: They grow best in neutral to alkaline soil, with plenty of humus added. Once established, they will tolerate drier conditions in shade. They can be grown in full sun, but will then need more moisture. Most will tolerate a variety of conditions, as well as years of negligence and air pollution. Propagation is from seed, by division of suckering species, or by taking half-hardened cuttings in late summer. Hardwood cuttings can be taken in winter and propagated in an area protected from winter frosts.

S

Sapindus mukorossi

Saponaria ocymoides

Sarcobatus vermiculatus, in summer

Sarcococca confusa

↔7 ft (2 m) ↑7 ft (2 m)

Attractive evergreen shrub, origin unknown. Leathery, dark green, elliptical to lance-shaped leaves with pale undersides. Clusters of cream flowers, female form very fragrant, in mid-winter. Bright red berries turn black when ripe. Zones 6–10.

Sarcococca hookeriana

↔6 ft (1.8 m) ↑5 ft (1.5 m)

Evergreen thicket-forming often suckering shrub native to China. Lance-shaped deep green leaves. Clusters of scented white flowers, males with deep pink anthers, in late autumn to winter. Black fruits. ***S. h.* subsp. *humilis*** ★, ground cover, shiny bluish black fruit. ***S. h.* var. *digyna***, slender leaves, off-white anthers. ***S. h.* 'Purple Stem'**, young magenta shoots, pink-tinted flowers. Zones 6–10.

Sarcococca ruscifolia

↔3 ft (0.9 m) ↑3 ft (0.9 m)

Thick bushy suckering shrub native to western China and the Himalayas. Glossy, deep green, broadly lance-shaped leaves. Clusters of creamy white perfumed flowers in winter. Dark red fruits. Zones 8–10.

Sarcococca saligna

↔3 ft (0.9 m) ↑3 ft (0.9 m)

Suckering, evergreen, thicket-forming shrub native to the Himalayas from Nepal to Afghanistan. Narrow, lance-shaped, pale green leaves. Male flowers green, female flowers greenish white, in winter–early spring. Egg-shaped dark purple fruits. Zones 7–10.

Sarcococca ruscifolia

SARITAEA

The single species in this genus, which belongs to the trumpet-vine (Bignoniaceae) family, is found in Ecuador and Colombia. The plant is a liane. The stems are almost round in cross-section, and are marked with longitudinal stripes. The leaves have 2 leaflets and a further 2 leaflet-like appendages at the base of the leaf stalk, plus a tendril at the tip. The large often showy flowers in shades of purple to red and rose pink are borne in panicles along or at the ends of the branches. Their nectar is collected by the male bees of the tropical genus *Euglossa*, which pollinate the flowers by brushing against the pollen and transferring it. The calyx is tubular, with an unlobed margin. The corolla is a tubular bell-shape, and is hairy inside around the bases of the stamens. The fruit is a long flattened capsule containing 2 winged seeds.

CULTIVATION: These plants prefer bright filtered light and well-drained moisture-retaining soil with plenty of humus; keep moist. Propagate from cuttings or seed.

Saritaea magnifica

syns *Arrabidaea magnifica, Bignonia magnifica*

↔8–15 ft (2.4–4.5 m) ↑25 ft (8 m)

Evergreen climber with 2-part leathery leaves and oblong leaflets to 4 in (10 cm) long. Narrow, tubular, rosy purple flowers, flaring petals, showy heads, in summer. Zones 10–12.

Saritaea magnifica

SASA

Sasa is the Japanese word for bamboo, and this genus has 60 species of small to medium-sized bamboos native to southeastern Russia, southern China, northern Japan, and Korea. Members of the grass (Poaceae) family, they have running rhizomes and arching culms, and the stems have a waxy white bloom at the nodes. The broad finely toothed leaves wither in winter; those of *S. veitchii* create ornamental white margins of "false parchment," which lowers leaf maintenance yet still suppresses competition from weeds and protects buds from severe cold. The tropical appearance of these plants is illusory: when weighed down with snow, the thin flexible culms protect against severe cold winds.

CULTIVATION: Grow in a damp rich soil in part-shade. *Sasa* species spread rapidly, so careful siting is necessary, or the plants can be confined in a large container. Propagate in spring by coiling the mature rhizomes into pots and covering them with potting compost. Tidy plants by clearing away disheveled culms at the end of winter.

Sasa palmata

↔10–20 ft (3–6 m) ↑7 ft (2 m)

Native to Japan. Vigorous spreading species forms thick hedge. Stems may be streaked with purple. Palm-like foliage, long tapering leaves, bright shiny green all year, yellow midrib. **'Nebulosa'**, brown cloud-like markings on mature culms. Zones 7–11.

Sasa veitchii

KUMA ZASA

↔10–20 ft (3–6 m) ↑5 ft (1.5 m)

From Japan. Ground-covering foliage tolerates dark dry locations. Stems purple-lined, glaucous. Short tapering leaves wither in winter to broad, papery, white margins. Zones 6–11.

Sasa veitchii

SASAELLA

This genus of around 10 species of bamboo from Japan belongs to the grass (Poaceae) family. It differs from the related *Sasa* in having multiple thinner canes and smaller narrow leaves on near-horizontal branches. The leaves are quite heavily textured, and often have longitudinal stripes or bands, as do the leaf sheaths. The widely cultivated colourful variegated forms are often low-growing and used as ground cover or ornamental shrubs.

CULTIVATION: Tolerant of fairly heavy frosts and able to grow in most exposures, they prefer warm humid summers and thrive in humus-rich soil. All species spread quite quickly through running roots, especially in moist loose soil, and can become invasive. Propagate by division whenever conditions are not extreme.

Sasaella masamuneana

syn. *Sasa masamuneana*

↔3–10 ft (0.9–3 m) ↑3–7 ft (0.9–2 m)

Very fine canes, narrow leaves to 8 in (20 cm) long, purple-lined sheaths. Rarely cultivated. Attractive 12–24 in (30–60 cm) tall cultivars include **'Albostriata'**, creamy striped leaves ageing to yellow; **'Aureostriata'**, golden yellow striped leaves. Zones 7–10.

SASSAFRAS

This genus includes just 3 species in the laurel (Lauraceae) family. They are deciduous trees with a rather scattered distribution, occurring in temperate East Asia and eastern North America. They have been cultivated for their aromatic oils, which repel pests and so are valuable in the furniture industry. *Sassafras* leaves may be smooth-edged

Sassafras albidum

S

or lobed, are downy on their undersides, and sometimes develop vivid autumn colors. Racemes of tiny, petal-less, yellow-green flowers appear in spring with the developing leaves, and are followed by blue-black drupes. CULTIVATION: They are reasonably frost hardy. They prefer deep, fertile, well-drained soil, and will grow in sun or part-shade. They tend to produce multiple trunks, and pruning can be directed to encourage this habit or to produce a single-trunked tree, as the situation dictates. Propagate from seed, suckers, or root cuttings.

Sassafras albidum

SASSAFRAS

↔30 ft (9 m) ↑50 ft (15 m)

North American tree, may be many-trunked. Oval leaves, up to 3 lobes, dark green, downy undersides, turn gold and red in autumn. Elegant shape. The underbark is the source of sassafras oil. Zones 5–9.

SATUREJA

SAVORY

This genus of highly aromatic, small shrubs belonging to the mint (Lamiaceae) family, is native to dry stony hillsides in the Mediterranean, the woods of North America, and the Himalayas. Four-angled, woody stems bear small, hairy, round to oval leaves. Pale lilac to white flowers are borne in whorls on upright spikes throughout spring and summer. These are valuable plants for the rock garden and dry walls, and they attract bees and butterflies. It is a very fragrant herb, and the leaves of some species are used for herbal tea or as a seasoning. CULTIVATION: Grow in any fertile well-drained soil. These plants require only minimal water through summer. Some species self-seed. Propagation is generally from cuttings or by removal of rooted shoots.

Satureja montana

Satureja hortensis

SUMMER SAVORY

↔8 in (20 cm) ↑8 in (20 cm)

Annual from southern Europe. Erect hairy stems, long pointed leaves. Dense spikes of mauve to white flowers, in whorls, appear in spring–summer. Aromatic, it is widely used in cooking. Zones 5–9.

Satureja montana

WINTER SAVORY

↔12 in (30 cm)
↑20–36 in (50–90 cm)

Semi-evergreen shrublet from southern Europe and northern Africa. Small, highly fragrant, oblong leaves. Bears whorls of pale lilac flowers in summer. Leaves similar in flavor and scent to thyme *(Thymus vulgaris)* used for seasoning meat and vegetables. Zones 4–8.

SAURURUS

LIZARD'S TAIL

This genus of just 2 species—one from eastern Asia, one from eastern North America—gives its name to the lizard's-tail (Saururaceae) family. They are tall, erect, rhizomatous, perennials that grow in bogs. The leaves are undivided and spirally arranged. The leaf-base is kidney- to heart-shaped, and the stipules are joined to the stalk. The flowerhead is a dense raceme on the sides of the ends of branches. The ivory to white fragrant flowers are small, without sepals or petals, and have 6, rarely 8, stamens. They produce no nectar, but have a faint scent. The round fruit is warty with just a single seed. CULTIVATION: These are plants for bog gardens or damp woodlands. They are propagated by division, or from seed sown in pots kept moist.

Saururus cernuus

LIZARD'S TAIL

↔36 in (90 cm)
↑12–18 in (30–45 cm)

Water plant from eastern USA. Forms small colonies by underground runners. Leaves are arrow- or heart-shaped. Bottlebrush-like flower spikes arch above foliage. Bead-like seeds resemble lizard's tail. Zones 5–10.

Saururus cernuus

SAXIFRAGA

This genus in the saxifrage (Saxifragaceae) family is very extensive, comprising a wide range of perennial, annual, or biennial ground-hugging plants, many of which are alpines. They are found throughout much of the temperate and subarctic zones of the Northern Hemisphere, with outposts in places such as Ethiopia, Mexico, and the Arctic. There are some 480 known species, as well as numerous garden hybrids. The 3 main sections that are of garden interest are the "mossies," "silvers," and Kabschia and Engleria subsections. A major attraction for gardeners is that the plants are not only diverse in themselves but come from a variety of habitats, such as exposed mountains and moist woodlands. CULTIVATION: Being shallow-rooted plants, they require free-draining relatively fertile soil in either sun or part-shade. Propagate by division at any time, or from seed in autumn.

Saxifraga andersonii

↔12 in (30 cm) ↑4 in (10 cm)

Cushion-forming perennial from Nepal and Tibet. Loose rosettes of gray-green leaves. Clear white or pink flowers on 4 in (10 cm) tall stalks, in spring. Zones 6–8.

Saxifraga californica

syns *Heuchera rubescens, Micranthes californica*

↔6 in (15 cm) ↑6 in (15 cm)

Clump-forming tufted perennial from western North America and Mexico. Rounded, kidney-shaped, mid-green leaves. Spikes of pale pink to white bell-shaped flowers, in summer. Zones 4–8.

Saxifraga callosa

syn. *Saxifraga lingulata*

↔8 in (20 cm) ↑10 in (25 cm)

Evergreen perennial from western and eastern Spain, the southwestern alpine areas of Europe, Sardinia, Sicily, and southern Italy. Rosettes of broad, round, silver-gray foliage growing in dense clumps. Star-shaped white flowers, ½ in (12 mm) wide, in early summer. Grows on limestone formations. Zones 7–9.

Saxifraga fortunei

syn. *Saxifraga cortusifolia var. fortunei*

↔12 in (30 cm) ↑20 in (50 cm)

Semi-evergreen to deciduous clump-forming perennial herb, native to Japan. Leaves are kidney-shaped and rounded, to 4 in (10 cm) long, with undersides of foliage frequently dark purple. White flowers appear on 20 in (50 cm) tall stems in late autumn. Zones 6–8.

Saxifraga × *gaudinii*

↔6–12 in (15–30 cm)
↑4–6 in (10–15 cm)

Hybrid between *S. cotyledon* and *S. paniculata*. Forms low spreading clump of small spatula-shaped leaves. Purple-flecked white flowers appear in heads to 6 in (15 cm) tall from late spring. Zones 4–9.

Saxifraga globulifera

↔8–12 in (20–30 cm)
↑6–8 in (15–20 cm)

Mounding perennial found on both sides of the Straits of Gibraltar. Short, leafy, erect stems, and rosettes of small 5-lobed leaves. White flowers to 6 mm wide appear in heads on stems to 6 in (15 cm) long in autumn–spring. ***S. g.* var. *oranensis***, summer-dormant buds on long stalks. Zones 7–10.

Saxifraga callosa

Saxifraga globulifera

S

Saxifraga hartii

Saxifraga oppositifolia

Saxifraga hartii

syn. *Saxifraga rosacea subsp. hartii*

↔ 6–12 in (15–30 cm)
↑ 3–6 in (8–15 cm)

British species, now rare in the wild. Forms densely foliaged bright green cushions with a few trailing stems around the edges. Leaves are up to ¾ in (18 mm) long, cut at tips, usually into 5 segments. Short erect spikes carry heads of small white or pink flowers. Zones 7–9.

Saxifraga oppositifolia

PURPLE MOUNTAIN SAXIFRAGE

↔ 8 in (20 cm) ↑ 1 in (2.5 cm)

Very small, clumping and dense mat-forming perennial herb from arctic-latitude mountains of Europe, western Asia, and North America. Stiff, elliptical, dark green leaves in rosettes. Single, almost stemless, dark red to purple to pale pink flowers in summer. Zones 1–7.

Saxifraga paniculata

syn. *Saxifraga aizoon*

↔ 10 in (25 cm) ↑ 6 in (15 cm)

Mat-forming perennial from Canada, Norway, Greenland, and Iceland. Rosettes of narrow gray-green leaves, 2½ in (6 cm) long, lime-encrusted margins. Creamy white to pink flowers, in early summer. Zones 1–6.

Saxifraga spathularis

ST PATRICK'S CABBAGE

↔ 6–8 in (15–20 cm)
↑ 8–12 in (20–30 cm)

Summer-flowering species from Ireland, Spain, and Portugal. Clumped rosettes of rounded, 1–2 in (25–50 mm) long, leathery, bright green leaves, coarsely toothed edges. Sprays of tiny pinkish purple flowers in spring. Zones 5–9.

Saxifraga, Hybrid Cultivar, 'Purple Robe'

Saxifraga stolonifera

syn. *Saxifraga sarmentosa*

MOTHER OF THOUSANDS, STRAWBERRY BEGONIA

↔ 12 in (30 cm) ↑ 16 in (40 cm)

Perennial from East Asia. Rounded, kidney-shaped, mid- to dark green, serrated leaves form dense mounds of foliage. Tall loose stems of white flowers, 16 in (40 cm) long and spotted with red or yellow, in summer. **'Eco Butterfly'**, golden yellow leaves, green centers; **'Harvest Moon'**, moon-shaped golden green to reddish leaves; **'Tricolor'**, leaves edged in tones of red, white, and/or pink. Zones 5–10.

Saxifraga umbrosa

↔ 12 in (30 cm) ↑ 12 in (30 cm)

Clump-forming perennial from the Pyrenees. Green foliage grows in stiff rosettes. Loose panicles of rose pink flowers, 10 in (25 cm) long, spotted with some irregular red blotches, appear in late spring–early summer. Zones 1–5.

Saxifraga × *urbium*

syn. *Saxifraga umbrosa 'London Pride'*

LONDON PRIDE

↔ 18–36 in (45–90 cm)
↑ 12 in (30 cm)

Of garden origin, a quick-growing ground covering perennial with large rosettes of spoon-shaped, leathery, dark green leaves. Arching stems of small pale pink flowers in summer. **'Aureovariegata'**, gray-green and gold variegated leaves. Zones 6–7.

Saxifraga Hybrid Cultivars

↔ 6–18 in (15–45 cm)
↑ 3–12 in (8–30 cm)

Saxifraga species hybridize freely in the wild, and many garden plants are of indeterminate parentage. Nevertheless, their more carefully bred brethren are attractive little plants, at home in rock and alpine gardens. **'James Bremner'**, 6 in (15 cm) tall, creamy white flowers; **'Purple Robe'**, dense foliage cushion, many 4–6 in (10–15 cm) tall sprays of purple-pink flowers; **'Southside Seedling'** dark green spoon-shaped leaves in rosettes, arching panicles of white saucer-like flowers; **'Stansfieldii'** (syn. *S. stansfieldii*), tiny rosettes, soft zpink flowers in spring; **'Tumbling Waters'** (syn. *S. longifolia* 'Tumbling Waters'), dark green rosettes of foliage, and arching racemes of star-shaped white flowers; **'Whitehill'**, gray-green foliage with crusty white edges, white flowers on stems to 12 in (30 cm) tall. Zones 6–9.

SCABIOSA

SCABIOUS

An unpleasant sounding name, *Scabiosa* is derived from *scabies*, a Latin word for scurf or mange, which was said to be relieved by rubbing with the leaves of these plants. A member of the teasel (Dipsacaceae) family, the genus comprises around 80 species of annuals and perennials found in Europe, parts of Africa, and Japan. Most species form a spreading basal clump of light green to gray-green, rounded to lance-shaped leaves with deeply incised notches or lobes. A few species have an erect or branching habit. The flowers are individually tiny, but occur in rounded to flattened composite heads on stems held clear of the foliage. White and pale yellow to soft pink or powder blue and mauve are the usual colors.

CULTIVATION: They are hardy and easily grown in any sunny position in fertile, moist, free-draining, slightly alkaline soil. Propagate annuals from seed and perennials from seed and basal cuttings, or by division.

Scabiosa atropurpurea

EGYPTIAN ROSE, MOURNFUL WIDOW, SWEET SCABIOUS

↔ 16–30 in (40–75 cm)
↑ 16–36 in (40–90 cm)

Annual, biennial, or short-lived perennial herbs from southern Europe. Basal cluster of light green to gray-green, lobed or toothed leaves to 6 in (15 cm) long, upper leaves shorter and more deeply lobed, almost pinnate. Flowerheads crimson to deep purple-black, fragrant, to 2 in (5 cm) wide, in summer–early autumn. **'Blue Cockade'**, 36 in (90 cm) tall, rounded, deep blue, double flowerheads; **'Chile Black'**, 24 in (60 cm) tall, deep black-red flowers with minute flecks of lavender; **'Crimson Clouds'**, 16 in (40 cm) tall, purple-red flowers, profuse; **'Peter Ray'**, 24 in (60 cm) tall, large purple-black flowerheads; **'Salmon Queen'**, 36 in (90 cm) tall, deep salmon pink to light red double flowers. Zones 8–10.

Scabiosa caucasica

↔ 16–18 in (40–45 cm)
↑ 20–36 in (50–90 cm)

Perennial from the Caucasus region. Leaves gray-green to blue-green, basal foliage lance-shaped, large, smooth-edged; upper leaves lobed almost to midrib. Powder blue flowers bloom in heads to 3 in (8 cm) wide, in summer–autumn. **'Alba'**, white flowers; **'Bressingham White'**, white flowers; **'Clive Greaves'** ★, pale lavender blue flowers; **'Fama'**, bright blue flowers; **'Floral Queen'**, tall, vigorous, light blue flowers; **'Miss Willmott'**, tall, cream flowers; **'Nachtfalter'**, dark purple flowers; **'Pink Lace'**, bright pink flowers. Zones 4–10.

Scabiosa columbaria

↔ 16 in (40 cm) ↑ 24 in (60 cm)

Biennial or short-lived perennial from temperate Eurasia and North Africa. Stems and foliage gray-green, woolly; basal leaves smooth-edged to deeply lobed, upper leaves pinnate, often further divided. Lavender to purple-blue flowerheads to 1¾ in (40 mm) wide, summer. ***S. c.* var. *ochroleuca***, 36 in (90 cm) tall, primrose flowerheads. ***S.c.* 'Butterfly Blue'**, 28 in (70 cm) tall, lavender blue; **'Pink Mist'**, 24 in (60 cm) tall, light pink. Zones 6–10.

Scabiosa columbaria var. ochroleuca

Scabiosa atropurpurea 'Chile Black'

Scabiosa caucasica 'Clive Greaves'

Scabiosa graminifolia

↔12–20 in (30–50 cm)
↕16 in (40 cm)

Southern European perennial. Short grassy leaves with dense covering of fine silver-gray hairs. Flowers lavender to purple-pink, flowerheads to 1¾ in (40 mm) wide, summer. **'Pinkushion'**, deep pink flowers. Zones 7–10.

Scabiosa incisa

↔20–24 in (50–60 cm)
↕24–36 in (60–90 cm)

Perennial from the Cape region of South Africa. Gray-green deeply lobed leaves to 6 in (15 cm) long at plant base, upper leaves smaller. Large deep pink to lavender blue flowerheads in spring–early summer. Zones 7–10.

Scabiosa lucida

↔12–20 in (30–50 cm)
↕12 in (30 cm)

Low spreading perennial from central Europe. Deeply divided, hairy, dark green to silvery leaves. Lavender-pink to purple-red flowerheads to 1¾ in (40 mm) wide, summer–autumn. **'Rosea'**, pale pink flowers. Zones 5–10.

Scabiosa stellata

STARFLOWER

↔8–12 in (20–30 cm)
↕18 in (45 cm)

Annual found all the way around the Mediterranean. Short, toothed, gray-green, ferny, pinnate leaves. White flowers in heads over 1 in (25 mm) wide. Flowers fall, leaving enlarged calyces on the long-lasting heads, in summer. **'Drumstick'**, 12 in (30 cm) tall with rounded heads of light blue flowers and copper-colored calyces; **'Paper Moon'**, white to pale blue with bronze calyces. Zones 8–11.

SCADOXUS

BLOOD LILY

A member of the amaryllis (Amaryllidaceae) family, this genus of 9 perennial species comes from the tropical regions of Africa and the Arabian Peninsula. These plants are closely related to species belonging to the genus *Haemanthus,* to which they bear a striking resemblance, and they also share the common name, blood lily. However, *Scadoxus* species are distinguished by the form and arrangement of their leaves, which do not have obvious mid-veins and are arranged in a rosette. Moreover, *Scadoxus* has fleshy-stemmed bulbs, not true bulbs.

CULTIVATION: Plant bulbs in full sun or part-shade in fertile well-drained soil, with top of bulb above ground. When grown in containers, keep slightly damp while dormant in winter, and water well during their summer growth phase. In frost-prone areas, grow in the greenhouse. Propagate from seed or offsets in spring.

Scadoxus multiflorus

syn. *Haemanthus multiflorus*

BLOOD LILY

↔24 in (60 cm) ↕20 in (50 cm)

Perennial from southern Africa. Large bulb. Almost evergreen, large fresh-green leaves, lance-shaped to oval, growing in an upright arching rosette. Flowers glowing salmon-red, large rounded heads of star-shaped florets, narrow petals, whiskery stamens, in summer. ***S. m.* subsp. *katherinae*** ★ (syn. *Haemanthus katherinae*), wavy undulating leaves. ***S. m.* 'Koning Albert'** (syn. *Haemanthus* 'King Albert'), coral-red flowers. Zones 9–11.

Scadoxus multiflorus subsp. *katherinae*

SCAEVOLA

This genus from the Goodeniaceae family contains nearly 100 plants from Australia and islands in the Indian and Pacific Oceans, and includes shrubs, subshrubs, and perennials. Many have a ground-hugging habit, and provide reliable ground cover in temperate areas. The leaves of most are small, somewhat succulent, often hairy, and usually carried on short, often brittle stems. The foliage is covered in fan-shaped flowers in varying shades of blue, sometimes white, over a long period from mid-winter onwards.

CULTIVATION: Full sun and freely draining soil are the main requirements. Many species are resistant to salt spray, making them ideal plants for coastal sites, but they do need a frost-free position. Propagate from cuttings taken in the warmer months.

Scaevola aemula

↔20–60 in (50–150 cm)
↕6–16 in (15–40 cm)

Perennial from southern and eastern Australia. Variable, usually prostrate habit; oblong, wedge-shaped, toothed leaves. Pale mauve-blue fan-shaped flowers, 1¼ in (30 mm) wide, along stems, in spring–summer. **'Aussie Salute'**, low, spreading, purple-blue flowers; **'Blue Fan'**, purple-blue, trailing; **'Blue Wonder'**, and **'New Wonder'**, more vigorous and upright; **'Bombay Blue'** and **'Bombay Pink'**, densely branched trailers; **'Edna Walling Fan Tastic'**, purple-blue flowers, very profuse; **'Fan Magic Spellbinder'**, wide-spreading, long-flowering; **Fandango Series**, more erect and bushy, purple and blue shades, and white; **'Purple Fanfare'**, large flowers over most of year; **'Superclusters'**, up to 7 ft (2 m) wide; **'Zig Zag'**, trailer with striking blue and white flowers. Zones 9–11.

Scaevola aemula 'New Wonder'

Scaevola albida

WHITE FAN FLOWER

↔16–36 in (40–90 cm)
↕4–8 in (10–20 cm)

From South Australia. Small carpeting subshrub with rounded, fleshy, bright green, elliptical leaves around ½ in (12 mm) long. Flowers are white or blue to mauve shades. **'Karwarra Pink'**, bright pink flowers; **'Mauve Carpet'** and **'White Carpet'**, prostrate, ideal for hanging baskets; **'Mauve Clusters'** ★, mauve-pink flowers. Zones 9–11.

SCHAUERIA

This member of the acanthus (Acanthaceae) family has 8 species of evergreen shrubs and subshrubs, native to Brazil, and grown for their spikes of narrow tubular flowers; the bristly calyces give a brush-like appearance.

CULTIVATION: Outdoors in tropical climates, plant in a rich moist soil. In cool climates they are suitable for the conservatory or greenhouse, but need shading during the hottest part of the day. Propagate by softwood cuttings.

Schaueria flavicoma

↔24 in (60 cm) ↕36 in (90 cm)

Erect subshrub from Brazil. Glossy green leaves, with prominent pale veins and midribs. Narrow, soft yellow, tubular flowers with downy to bristly yellow-green calyces grow in dense spikes on ends of branches. Zones 10–12.

Schaueria flavicoma

Scaevola aemula 'Purple Fanfare'

SCHEFFLERA

syns *Brassaia, Dizygotheca, Heptapleurum*

This large genus in the ivy (Araliaceae) family consists of around 900 species, occurring in tropical and subtropical regions throughout the world, usually in moist environments, with the majority found from Southeast Asia to the Pacific Islands. Mostly shrubs, trees, scrambling climbers, or epiphytes, they have leaves composed of usually rounded leaflets of similar sizes and arranged in whorls held on a long stalk. Small flowers are produced in umbels, panicles, racemes, or spikes, and are followed by small black or purple fruits. Cultivated for their ornamental foliage, they are suitable for the garden in frost-free climates, or they can be used as pot plants, both indoors and outside.

CULTIVATION: Most are fairly adaptable, tolerating full sun to semi-shade. They prefer a well-drained moderately fertile soil with adequate moisture during periods of growth. Propagate from seed, which is sown as soon as it is ripe, or from cuttings, or by aerial layering.

Schefflera actinophylla

syn. *Brassaia actinophylla*

OCTOPUS TREE, QUEENSLAND UMBRELLA TREE

↔ 12 ft (3.5 m) ↑ 30 ft (9 m)

Rainforest shrub or tree from New Guinea and northern and northeastern Australia. Many trunks, glossy light green leaflets. Radiating spikes of small red flowers on ends of branches in late summer–early spring. Fruits reddish black. Zones 10–12.

Schefflera actinophylla

Schefflera arboricola

Schefflera arboricola

DWARF UMBRELLA TREE, HAWAIIAN ELF SCHEFFLERA

↔ 3 ft (0.9 m) ↑ 3–5 ft (0.9–1.5 m)

From Taiwan. Rounded shrub with palmate leaves, 7 to 11 glossy bright green leaflets. Small yellowish flowers appear on panicles near branch tips in spring–summer. Golden berries. Popular house plant. **'Jacqueline'**, leaves irregularly splashed with pale yellow. Zones 10–12.

Schefflera digitata

PATE

↔ 8 ft (2.4 m) ↑ 10 ft (3 m)

New Zealand shrub or tree. Young branches and leaflet stalks reddish purple. Leaves have 7 to 10 oblong leaflets with finely serrated margins. Margins, veins, and midribs tinged with red. Panicles of tiny greenish white flowers in summer. White to purple berries. Zones 10–12.

Schefflera elegantissima

ARALIA, FALSE ARALIA

↔ 10 ft (3 m) ↑ 50 ft (15 m)

Tree native to New Caledonia, smaller in cultivation. The juvenile stage is unbranched and well-foliaged, the leaves consisting of 7 to 11 long, narrow, deeply serrated leaflets. The lustrous dark green leaflets become wider and more broadly toothed with maturity. Black berries. Zones 10–12.

Schefflera umbellifera

Schefflera umbellifera

BASTARD CABBAGE TREE, FOREST CABBAGE TREE

↔ 25 ft (8 m) ↑ 30 ft (9 m)

Tree native to southern and southeastern Africa. Older specimens have dense rounded crowns and fissured resinous bark. Leaves comprising 5 oblong leaflets are crowded near branch tips on long stalks. Panicles of small yellowish green flowers. Black berries. Zones 10–12.

SCHINUS

Found in Central and South America, this genus from the cashew (Anacardiaceae) family includes some 30 species of evergreen shrubs and trees. They are notable for their attractive pinnate leaves, sometimes weeping branches, and their sprays of brown-red drupes. The fruits develop from racemes of tiny flowers—usually white, yellow-green, or pale pink—that open in spring or summer. There are separate male and female flowers, and these may occur on the same plants or on different plants.

CULTIVATION: Hardiness varies with the species, though no *Schinus* species is extremely frost tolerant and many are quite frost tender, preferring a warm climate. Most species are very drought tolerant once established, and are best grown in well-drained soil in full sun. Propagation is from seed or cuttings.

Schinus molle

PEPPER TREE

↔ 50 ft (15 m) ↑ 50–60 ft (15–18 m)

Spreading, evergreen tree from South America. Drooping branches, finely divided, pinnate leaves. Small yellow-white flowers, in spring. Clusters of pea-sized red berries. Street tree in southern Europe; can prove weedy in some conditions. *S. m.* var. ***areira*** (syn. *S. areira*), semi-weeping, dark green leaves have aromatic resin; pink to red-brown berries; drought and heat tolerant. Zones 9–11.

Schinus molle var. *areira*

SCHIZANTHUS

POOR MAN'S ORCHID

This Chilean genus of 12 species of annuals and biennials is a member of the nightshade (Solanaceae) family, although the relationship is not an obvious one. The cultivated species are small upright plants around 12 in (30 cm) tall, with soft, green, ferny foliage, often covered with fine hairs. Flowers are borne in branching panicles that are held above the foliage. They are beautifully marked and shaped, with a prominent lower lip, hence the common name, poor man's orchid. Modern strains are available in a wide range of colors and sizes. The genus name is derived from the Greek *schizo* (divide) and *anthos* (flower), referring to the plant's deeply divided corolla.

CULTIVATION: They are intolerant of cold, but are easily grown as annuals where summer temperatures are warm and consistent. Elsewhere they are best treated as greenhouse pot plants. Grow in a bright position in fertile, moist, well-drained soil. Raise from seed, with several sowings to ensure continued flowering. Pinch out growing tips when young to make bushy.

Schizanthus pinnatus

↔ 8–16 in (20–40 cm) ↑ 8–20 in (20–50 cm)

Annual with bushy habit and lance-shaped, usually lobed, light green leaves. Tightly clustered heads of flat flowers, lobes almost evenly sized, in summer–autumn. White-throated deep pink flowers with yellow and black central markings. Garden forms come in many colors. Zones 9–11.

Schizanthus × *wisetonensis*

↔ 12 in (30 cm) ↑ 12–20 in (30–50 cm)

Garden hybrid annual of *S. pinnatus* × *S. grahamii* parentage. Several cultivars resembling *S. pinnatus* in foliage and habit. Flowers in various colors, including white, pink to purple-brown, and blue. Zones 9–11.

Schizanthus × *wisetonensis*

SCHIZOPHRAGMA

This genus of 2 deciduous ornamental woody climbers in the hydrangea (Hydrangeaceae) family is native to woodlands and cliffs of China, Korea, and Japan. Both species climb by means of short, adhesive, aerial roots. Leaves are attractive, pointed, few- to many-toothed, sometimes turning yellow in autumn. Bark flakes off older branches. Flowerheads consist of flat clusters of tiny fertile flowers and a ring of sterile, showy, outer florets, typically creamy white. The fruits are capsules. The vines can eventually grow very large, but can be slow to establish. They can be grown up trees, but need support until they develop their rootlets.

CULTIVATION: Rich well-drained soil is ideal but these plants will grow in nearly any soil. They tolerate a wide range of light conditions, including shade, but flower best in full sun if the roots are shaded. Propagate from softwood cuttings in early to mid-summer, or from half-hardened cuttings in late summer. Few pest or disease problems.

Schizophragma hydrangeoides

JAPANESE HYDRANGEA VINE

↔10 ft (3 m) ↕30 ft (9 m)

Deciduous, woody, self-clinging climber native to Korea and Japan. Pointed, toothed, dark green leaves. Flat clusters of creamy white flowers to 10 in (25 cm) wide, tiny fertile inner flowers, teardrop-shaped outer ones, in summer. **'Moonlight'**, blue-green foliage, pewter markings and deep green veins; **'Roseum'**, pale pink flowers intensifying to rose. Zones 5–9.

Schoenoplectus lacustris

SCHOENOPLECTUS

This genus of some 50 tufted or creeping annuals or perennials found throughout the world belongs to the sedge (Cyperaceae) family. Perennial species are found in deep to shallow water, annuals in seasonal wet depressions. Leaves are usually represented merely by a sheath, less often by a strap-like blade. The reddish brown summer flowerheads are generally held on long slender stems, and usually comprise a few to many spikelets, each containing numerous flowers. The fruits are achenes. Many species are used for basketry and mat-making in various parts of the world.

CULTIVATION: They are easily grown in full sun or shade in any moist soil. Some may become invasive, so care should be taken if growing them in non-native areas. Easily propagated by division or raised from seed.

Schoenoplectus lacustris

syn. *Scirpus lacustris*

BULRUSH, CLUBRUSH, TULE

↔3–4 ft (0.9–1.2 m)
↕3–10 ft (0.9–3 m)

Grass-like annual or perennial, found throughout Europe, Asia, Africa, and northern South America. Slow-spreading, clump of circular rush-like stems. Dense rust-colored flowerheads made up of over 100 spikelets, in summer–autumn. Leaves used for making mats and baskets. S. l. subsp. tabernaemontani, shorter stems; its cultivar **'Zebrinus'**, less vigorous, usually less than 5 ft (1.5 m) tall, bands of yellow to ivory on stems. Zones 4–11.

Sciadopitys verticillata

SCIADOPITYS

This remarkable conifer genus is part of the swamp cypress (Taxodiaceae) family and consists of a single species of evergreen tree endemic to the mountains of Japan. The most striking attribute of *Sciadopitys* is its foliage, as it features 2 kinds of leaves: brown scale-leaves arranged spiraly on elongated intervals of stem, and long, green, leaf-like needles radiating in dense whorls of up to 30 at the end of each interval. Male and female cones are borne on the same tree. The seed cones are like small pine cones, and have broad thin scales recurving at their tips.

CULTIVATION: Plants are easily grown in cool climates as long as rainfall is adequate and summers are warm and humid. They prefer a reasonably sheltered position and deep fertile soil. Growth is slow but steady. Propagation is normally from seed, though germination is poor unless seeds are stratified and then chilled for 3 months before sowing.

Sciadopitys verticillata

JAPANESE UMBRELLA PINE, UMBRELLA PINE

↔20 ft (6 m) ↕70 ft (21 m)

Conifer tree, smaller in cultivation, habit neat, conical, branches to ground level. Young plants grown in shade are more elongated. Rich brown bark peels in vertical strips. Whorls of deep glossy green leaves. Zones 6–9.

SCILLA

BLUEBELL, SQUILL

A genus of up to 90 species of bulbs of the asparagus (Asparagaceae) family, *Scilla* species are found from western Europe to Japan and in parts of Africa. They form clumps of grassy or strappy bright green leaves, and some, for example *S. peruviana*, can cover a large area. Long flower stems carry conical heads of small, star-shaped, sometimes fragrant flowers. Flowering time varies with the species but is usually spring. While species often have mauve to purple flowers, cultivars occur in a wide color range. Extracts of squill bulbs have a long history of medicinal use, mainly as diuretics and expectorants.

CULTIVATION: They are mostly hardy and easily grown in full or half-sun with moist, humus-rich, well-drained soil. When the clumps become large, lift and divide as the foliage dies back in autumn. They can be raised from seed, but take longer to flower.

Scilla forbesii

Scilla bifolia

TWO-LEAFED SQUILL

↔3 in (8 cm)
↕3–6 in (8–15 cm)

From Europe. Each bulb produces 2, occasionally 3, green elongated leaves. Small deep blue-violet flowers, appear with leaves, in early spring. Zones 4–8.

Scilla forbesii

syn. *Chionodoxa forbesii*

FORBES' GLORY OF THE SNOW

↔2–3 in (5–8 cm)
↕3–8 in (8–20 cm)

From mountains of western Turkey. Bears a few sparse leaves that reach 3–10 in (8–25 cm). Erect stems carry up to 12 downturned flowers. Slightly recurved petals, about ¾ in (18 mm) wide, are intensely blue with white central markings. Bulging white tubes. There are several cultivars, including the well-known large but pale **'Pink Giant'**. Zones 4–9.

Scilla hyacinthoides

HYACINTH SCILLA

↔12 in (30 cm) ↕36 in (90 cm)

Rare bulb from the Mediterranean. Strap-shaped green leaves. Strong stems each carry up to 100 small, violet-blue, star-shaped flowers, in mid-spring. Zones 8–11.

Scilla liliohyacinthus

PYRENEAN SQUILL

↔4 in (10 cm)
↕4 in (10 cm)

From France and Spain. Leaves broad, strap-like, mid-green, lustrous. Flowers pale violet, deep purple anthers, mid- to late spring. Zones 6–8.

Scilla liliohyacinthus

Scilla natalensis

Scilla peruviana

Scilla luciliae
syn. *Chionodoxa luciliae*
GLORY OF THE SNOW
↔2–3 in (5–8 cm) ↕4–6 in (10–15 cm)
From mountains of western Turkey. Soft violet-blue flowers, small white central zone, 2–3 per stem. Leaves, often slightly recurved, reach 3–8 in (8–20 cm) long. **'Alba'**, white petals; **'Gigantea'**, larger blue form to 8 in (20 cm) high; **'Rosea'**, pinkish petals. Zones 4–9.

Scilla natalensis ★
syn. *Merwilla plumbea*
BLUE SQUILL
↔20 in (50 cm) ↕36 in (90 cm)
From South Africa. Short dark green leaves. Long-lasting, graceful, starry, blue plumes of flowers, 50 to 100 per stalk, in spring–summer. Zones 7–10.

Scilla peruviana
CUBAN LILY, HYACINTH-OF-PERU
↔18 in (45 cm) ↕12 in (30 cm)
From the Mediterranean. Broad-pointed, shiny, green leaves, fleshy stems. Rounded cushion of indigo-blue star-shaped flowers in mid-spring–early summer. ***S. p.* var. *venusta***, from Tunisia, mauve-blue flowers, leaves lie flat. Zones 8–11.

Scilla ramburei
↔4 in (10 cm) ↕6 in (15 cm)
From Spain and Portugal. Has 3 to 6, narrow, bright green curled, grass-like, leaves, and flattish nodding inflorescences of violet-blue flowers, ½–¾ in (12–18 mm) wide, spring. Robust, salt tolerant. Zones 7–10.

Scrophularia auriculata 'Variegata'

Scilla sardensis
syn. *Chionodoxa sardensis*
LESSER GLORY OF THE SNOW
↔2–3 in (5–8 cm) ↕4–6 in (10–15 cm)
From mossy woodlands in western Turkey. Rich blue flowers with small white "eyes." Up to 12 on each red-brown stem. Neat, channeled, dark green leaves, erect and spreading. Zones 4–9.

Scilla siberica
BLUE SQUILL, SIBERIAN SQUILL
↔3 in (8 cm) ↕6 in (15 cm)
From Russia and southwest Asia. Strap-like, glossy, bright green leaves. Bright blue star-shaped flowers in groups of 3 to 5 per stem, in early spring. **'Spring Beauty'**, large blue flowers, taller. Zones 2–8.

Scilla tubergeniana ★
syn. *Scilla mischtschenkoana 'Tubergeniana'*
↔4 in (10 cm) ↕5 in (12 cm)
Naturally found in Iran and Russia. Cup-shaped white or pale blue flowers with deep blue veins borne in early spring. Shiny strap-like leaves follow flowers. Good in shady rock gardens. Zones 5–7.

SCROPHULARIA
FIGWORT
The members of this large genus of some 200 species in the foxglove (Scrophulariaceae) family are mainly perennials, with some being subshrubs. Often marsh-dwellers, they come mostly from temperate parts of the Northern Hemisphere, although some species are found as far south as Central America. The stems are 4-angled; their leaves may be either simple or compound, and either alternate or opposite. The flowers are usually small, like tiny, fat, inflated foxgloves *(Digitalis)* with a lower lip, in bronze, copper, or dull red. Few species are of garden merit, and some are garden weeds. Some species were once thought to cure scrofulous tumors.
CULTIVATION: Most grow well in moist humus-rich soil in dappled shade; some are aquatic. Propagation is by seed sown in situ, or from basal cuttings taken in spring.

Scrophularia auriculata
syn. *Scrophularia aquatica*
WATER BETONY, WATER FIGWORT
↔36–48 in (90–120 cm) ↕36–48 in (90–120 cm)
Vigorous marginal aquatic species native to western Europe. Slightly toothed opposite leaves to 10 in (25 cm) long. Open sprays of tiny, rounded, reddish brown flowers, drooping lip, yellowish green interior, in summer. **'Variegata'**, leaves, bold white edges. Zones 5–10.

SCUTELLARIA
HELMET FLOWER, SKULLCAP
This genus of about 300 species of annuals and perennials belongs to the mint (Lamiaceae) family. They are found mostly in temperate Northern Hemisphere regions, where they grow in scrub, open woodland, and grassland. The roots are often rhizomatous, and the plants are erect or sprawling, ranging from 6 in (15 cm) to 4 ft (1.2 m) high. The leaves are opposite and simple, sometimes pinnate or toothed. The 2-lipped tubular flowers emerge from hooded calyces, which give the genus its common names. The blue, white, or yellow flowers appear in summer singly, in pairs, or on the ends of spikes. A number of species are grown ornamentally, and some are used in herbal medicine for their anti-spasmodic properties.
CULTIVATION: Plant taller species in borders and smaller species at the edges of borders or in rock gardens. Grow in full sun in any reasonable soil. Water well in dry summers. Propagate from seed or by division.

Scutellaria alpina
↔18 in (45 cm) ↕6–10 in (15–25 cm)
Sprawling perennial found in mountains from southern Europe to Siberia. Often roots at nodes. Mats of small oval leaves. Small flowers in crowded racemes, purple to pale pink, often with yellow on lower lip, in late spring to early summer. ***S. a.* subsp. *supina***, soft lemon-colored flowers. ***S. a.* 'Arcobaleno'**, bluish purple to white, rose, and pale yellow flowers, contrasting colors on lower lip. Zones 5–9.

Scutellaria baicalensis
↔8 in (20 cm) ↕16 in (40 cm)
Sprawling plant found from Siberia to Japan. Stems often suffused with purple. Small, narrow, slightly hairy leaves. Dense heads of velvety tubular flowers, purple with a white lower lip, in summer. Zones 5–9.

Scutellaria barbata
↔8 in (20 cm) ↕12–16 in (30–40 cm)
Annual or perennial from China, India, and Japan. Small oval or lance-shaped leaves. Blue tubular flowers along stems in spring–autumn. Used in Chinese herbal medicines; currently being researched as anti-cancer drug. Zones 5–9.

Scutellaria incana
DOWNY SKULLCAP
↔24 in (60 cm) ↕24–48 in (60–120 cm)
Bushy perennial native to eastern North America. Leaves grayish green, covered with minute hairs, oval, to 3 in (8 cm) long. Dense panicles of velvety purplish blue flowers appear on ends of stems in summer–autumn. Zones 4–9.

Scutellaria indica
↔12 in (30 cm) ↕6 in (15 cm)
Low-growing mat-forming perennial native to Japan, Korea, and China. Small, rounded, grayish green leaves, shallow toothed margins. Pale purplish blue flowers in dense racemes in summer. ***S. i.* var. *parvifolia*** ★, dark green leaves, relatively large lavender-blue flowers. Zones 5–9.

Scutellaria indica var. *parvifolia*

Scutellaria alpina 'Arcobaleno'

S

Scutellaria orientalis

☼ ❄ ↔ 6–10 in (15–25 cm)
↑ 12–18 in (30–45 cm)

Subshrub forming a low mound, native to southeastern Europe. Small oval leaves, dark green above, woolly gray beneath. Dense racemes of lemon yellow flowers, sometimes tinged or spotted with red. Zones 7–10.

SEDUM

STONECROP

This is a very diverse group of succulent species from the stonecrop (Crassulaceae) family, with many hybrids. Of Northern Hemisphere origins, with over 300 species they vary enormously in foliage and form. Some are shrubby, with flattened, oval, gray-green leaves; others are trailing, with succulent jellybean-like leaves; and some form very compact mats. Most produce small heads of tiny, bright yellow, 5-petalled flowers in summer and autumn. The autumn-flowering types have been reclassified, mainly to the genera *Hylotelephium* and *Rhodiola*. Their name is derived from the Latin *sedo* (to sit), referring to their low spreading habit. Some species have been used medicinally and as salad vegetables. Some, such as *S. spectabile*, are grown for their flowers; others, such as *S. rubrotinctum*, for their colorful plant bodies.

CULTIVATION: Plant in full sun in gritty well-drained soil. Most appreciate water at flowering time, but are otherwise drought tolerant. Propagate by division, from cuttings, or from seed, depending on the growth type.

Sedum acre

STONECROP, WALL PEPPER

☼ ✱ ↔ 12–24 in (30–60 cm)
↑ 2–4 in (5–10 cm)

Perennial native to Europe and North Africa. Spreading, slightly mounding mats of fine stems clothed with tiny, light green, overlapping, triangular leaves, often red-tinted in sun. Heads of small bright yellow flowers at ends of stems in summer. **'Aureum'**, creamy yellow foliage variegations. Zones 5–10.

Sedum aizoon

☼ ❄ ↔ 20 in (50 cm) ↑ 16 in (40 cm)

Summer-flowering succulent native to temperate northern Asia. Upright stems, fleshy, toothed, 2–3 in (5–8 cm) long, lance-shaped leaves. Flat heads of golden yellow flowers, over ½ in (12 mm) wide. Zones 7–10.

Sedum album ★

☼ ✱ ↔ 8–20 in (20–50 cm)
↑ 2–4 in (5–10 cm)

Spreading mat-forming perennial from temperate regions of Eurasia and North Africa. Leaves ¼–¾ in (6–18 mm) long, often red-tinted, narrow and cylindrical. Heads of tiny white flowers appear during summer. **'Coral Carpet'**, 2 in (5 cm) high cultivar, pink-tinted leaves, light pink flowers. Zones 6–10.

Sedum borissovae

☼ ❄ ↔ 12 in (30 cm) ↑ 2–4 in (5–10 cm)

Evergreen mat-forming perennial herb spread by runners, native to Ukraine. Spreading branching stems, minute overlapping leaves. Forked heads of tiny pale yellow flowers in summer. Zones 7–10.

Sedum hispanicum

Sedum cauticolum

syn. *Hylotelephium cauticolum*

☼ ✱ ↔ 8–20 in (20–50 cm)
↑ 4–6 in (10–15 cm)

Spreading ground cover, native to Japan. Wiry stems. Rounded, sometimes sparsely toothed, gray powder-coated, red-tinted leaves to 1 in (25 mm) long. Dense heads of small pink to near-red flowers in summer–early autumn. Zones 4–10.

Sedum confusum

☼ ❄ ↔ 12–16 in (30–40 cm)
↑ 12–24 in (30–60 cm)

Shrubby species of obscure origin, probably Mexican. Fleshy, shiny, bright green, lance-shaped leaves, 1–1½ in (25–35 mm) long. Small rounded heads of bright yellow flowers in spring. Zones 8–11.

Sedum dasyphyllum

☼ ❄ ↔ 8–16 in (20–40 cm)
↑ 2–4 in (5–10 cm)

Cushion-forming perennial from around the Mediterranean region, with some apparently natural forms found in southwestern parts of the USA. Spreading pink-tinted stems. Tiny overlapping leaves, grayish to bluish green. Few-flowered heads of tiny, pink-tinted, white flowers in summer. Zones 8–11.

Sedum dendroideum

☼ ❄ ↔ 12–16 in (30–40 cm)
↑ 6–12 in (15–30 cm)

Spring-flowering Mexican subshrub. Usually one main stem and many side branches that are tipped with rosettes of bright green spatula-shaped leaves to 1½ in (35 mm) long. Airy panicles of tiny yellow flowers appear in spring. Zones 8–11.

Sedum aizoon

Sedum borissovae

Sedum ewersii

syn. *Hylotelephium ewersii*

☼ ✱ ↔ 16–30 in (40–75 cm)
↑ 6–12 in (15–30 cm)

Perennial found from the Himalayas to Mongolia. Low spreading habit, branching stems. Broad blue-green leaves to 1 in (25 mm) long, smooth-edged or toothed. Dense heads of tiny purple-red flowers appear in summer–autumn. Zones 5–9.

Sedum hidakanum

syn. *Hylotelephium pluricaule*

☼ ❄ ↔ 12–24 in (30–60 cm)
↑ 4–6 in (10–15 cm)

Perennial from coastal areas of eastern Siberia. Forms clump of spreading stems with opposite pairs of small, rounded, gray-green leaves. Tiny purple-red flowers, densely clustered in small heads, in summer. Zones 7–10.

Sedum hispanicum

☼ ❄ ↔ 12–24 in (30–60 cm)
↑ 4–6 in (10–15 cm)

Low spreading annual to short-lived perennial from southern Europe to Iran. Wiry stems with small, narrow, fleshy, blue-green leaves, red-tinted in sun. Small heads of pink-tinted white flowers in summer. Zones 7–10.

Sedum kamtschaticum

KAMCHATKA STONECROP

☼ ❄ ↔ 16–24 in (40–60 cm)
↑ 4–12 in (10–30 cm)

Succulent native to Japan. Spreading by rhizomes. Low branching stems. Fleshy, coarsely toothed, deep green, lance-shaped leaves, under 2 in (5 cm) long. Flattish flowerheads of golden yellow blooms in summer. ***S. k.* var. *ellacombeanum***, pale yellow flowers. ***S. k.* 'Variegatum'**, creamy white- and pink-variegated mid-green leaves, golden yellow flowers. Zones 7–10.

Sedum kamtschaticum

Sedum lucidum

↔ 12–20 in (30–50 cm) ↑ 12–18 in (30–45 cm)

Mexican evergreen subshrub. Low, spreading, branching stems. Leaves thick, fleshy, silver-green to bright green, pointed oval in shape, 1–2 in (25–50 mm) long. Flowerheads of many small white blooms in late winter–spring. Zones 9–11.

Sedum lydium ★

↔ 6–12 in (15–30 cm) ↑ 2–4 in (5–10 cm)

Small tufted to cushion-forming Turkish perennial. Stems root as they spread, and bear ¼ in (6 mm) long, fleshy, red-tipped leaves. Heads of many tiny, pink-tinted, white flowers in summer. Zones 9–11.

Sedum mexicanum

MEXICAN STONECROP, MEXICAN SEDUM

↔ 18–36 in (45–90 cm) ↑ 3–6 in (8–15 cm)

Despite name, origins are unclear. Narrow, fleshy, bright green leaves on trailing stems form dense foliage carpet. Abundant tiny yellow-green flowers from late spring. Although succulent, it prefers moist soil and part shade. Ideal for hanging baskets. **'Gold Mound'**, striking yellow foliage. Zones 9–11.

Sedum moranense

↔ 12–16 in (30–40 cm) ↑ 4–6 in (10–15 cm)

Mexican perennial. Forms a bushy hummock of many wiry stems that are densely covered with minute bright green leaves. White flowers, sometimes red-tipped, around ¼ in (6 mm) wide, singly or in small clusters, in summer. Zones 9–11.

Sedum moranense

Sedum lucidum

Sedum morganianum ★

BURRO'S TAIL, DONKEY'S TAIL

↔ 4 ft (1.2 m) ↑ 20 in (50 cm)

Evergreen perennial of obscure origin, probably Mexican. Widely cultivated as hanging basket plant. Long trailing stems, and densely crowded, spiraly arranged, pointed cylindrical, blue-green leaves. Small long-stemmed flowerheads of pink blooms appear in spring–summer. Zones 9–11.

Sedum niveum

↔ 20–24 in (50–60 cm) ↑ 2–4 in (5–10 cm)

Perennial native to southwestern California, USA. Mainly prostrate, short erect stems. Small rosettes of tiny, fleshy, pointed leaves. Flowers white, pink veins, to ½ in (12 mm) wide, few per head, in summer. Zones 8–10.

Sedum oreganum

↔ 12–16 in (30–40 cm) ↑ 6 in (15 cm)

Spreading North American perennial. Succulent, green, club-shaped leaves to ¾ in (18 mm) long, red-tinted in autumn. Small yellow flowers, singly or in flat heads, in summer. Zones 6–10.

Sedum praealtum ★

↔ 16–24 in (40–60 cm) ↑ 12–24 in (30–60 cm)

Surprisingly hardy shrub of Mexican origin. Shiny green, lance- to spatula-shaped leaves to over 2 in (5 cm) long. Large panicles of bright yellow flowers in summer. ***S. p.* subsp. *parvifolium***, compact habit, small leaves. Zones 6–10.

Sedum oreganum

Sedum rubrotinctum

Sedum rubrotinctum

↔ 12–24 in (30–60 cm) ↑ 10 in (25 cm)

Mounding evergreen subshrub of obscure origin, probably Mexican. The arching stems root where they touch ground. The leaves are thick and cylindrical, blunt-tipped, mid-green in color, red-tinted in sunlight. Loose heads of pale yellow flowers appear in spring. **'Aurora'** ★, pale yellow-green leaves with a strong red tint. Zones 9–11.

Sedum rupestre

syn. *Sedum reflexum*

↔ 12–20 in (30–50 cm) ↑ 8–15 in (20–38 cm)

Spreading, somewhat mounding evergreen perennial native to central and southern Europe. Woody stems are crowded with small, narrow, fleshy, light blue-green leaves. Flowerheads of tiny bright yellow blooms appear in summer. Zones 7–10.

Sedum sediforme

↔ 12–24 in (30–60 cm) ↑ 8–24 in (20–60 cm)

Evergreen perennial herb from the Mediterranean region. Grows in a mounding hummock of woody-based stems. Leaves are small, fleshy, and lance-shaped. Erect flowering stems bear flowerheads of pale greenish yellow to gold flowers in summer. Zones 8–11.

Sedum sieboldii

syn. *Hylotelephium sieboldii*

↔ 12–20 in (30–50 cm) ↑ 4 in (10 cm)

Low spreading perennial from Japan. Leaves to ¾ in (18 mm), rounded, fleshy, long, gray- to blue-green, often tinted purple or red. Dense heads of tiny pale pink flowers in autumn. **'Mediovariegatum'** ★, broad cream centered leaves; **'Variegatum'**, cream-mottled blue-green leaves. Zones 7–10.

Sedum niveum

Sedum spathulifolium ★

↔ 24 in (60 cm) ↑ 6 in (15 cm)

Clump-forming perennial from western North America. Spreads by long runners. Spatula-shaped fleshy leaves, often coloring to bronzy red, mainly clustered in rosettes at stem tips. Tiny flowers, bright yellow, in late spring–early summer. **'Cape Blanco'**, silver-gray leaves; **'Purpureum'**, foliage tinged purple-red. Zones 7–10.

Sedum spectabile ★

syn. *Hylotelephium spectabile*

ICE PLANT

↔ 16–32 in (40–80 cm) ↑ 27 in (70 cm)

Perennial from Korea and nearby parts of China. Erect thickened stems, opposite pairs or whorls of fleshy, toothed, elliptical leaves, 2–4 in (5–10 cm) long. Large 3-branched heads of small pink to red flowers in late summer–autumn. **'Brilliant'** ★, pink flowers; **'Iceberg'**, white flowers, sometimes tinted with pink; **'Indian Chief'**, deep pink to purple-red flowers. Zones 6–10.

Sedum spurium

↔ 12–20 in (30–50 cm) ↑ 6 in (15 cm)

Evergreen mat-forming perennial or subshrub, found from the Caucasus region to northern Iran. Spreading branches; opposite pairs of rounded, fleshy, toothed leaves, red-tinted in sunlight. Heads of small purple-red flowers, rarely white or pink, on erect stems, in summer. **'Dragon's Blood'**, reddish pink flowers, sometimes red-tinged leaves; **'Variegatum'**, leaves edged pink and cream. Zones 7–10.

Sedum telephium

syn. *Hylotelephium telephium*

LIVE-FOREVER, ORPINE

↔ 24–32 in (60–80 cm) ↑ 24 in (60 cm)

Perennial found from eastern Europe to Japan. Erect thickened stems; fleshy, toothed, pointed oval leaves, 1–3 in (2.5–8 cm) long. Showy heads of many purple-red flowers in late summer. ***S. t.* subsp. *maximum* 'Atropurpureum'**, deep purple-red foliage and red flowers. ***S. t.* 'Matrona'**, stems tinted with red, very pale pink flowers; **'Mohrchen'**, deep red flowers, purple-red foliage. Zones 6–10.

Sedum treleasei

SILVER SEDUM

☼ ❄ ↔12–16 in (30–40 cm)
↑12 in (30 cm)

Mexican evergreen subshrub. Upright, branching habit. Succulent, upcurved, cylindrical to almost bead-like, pale blue-green leaves to ¾ in (18 mm) long. Long-lasting panicles of tiny soft yellow flowers in spring. Zones 8–10.

Sedum Hybrid Cultivars

☼ ❄ ↔12–24 in (30–60 cm)
↑12–24 in (30–60 cm)

Several popular interspecies garden hybrids are placed in the subgenus *Hylotelephium*; these are mainly autumn flowering, though the foliage is attractive throughout the growing season. **'Herbstfreude'** (syn. 'Autumn Joy') (*S. telephium* × *S. spectabile*) has blue-green foliage and salmon pink flowers ageing to bronze; **'Ruby Glow'** (*S. cauticolum* × *S. telephium*), purple-green foliage, often pink-edged, deep red flowers; **'Vera Jameson'** ('Ruby Glow' × *S. telephium* subsp. *maximum* 'Atropurpureum'), purple foliage, light pink flowers. Zones 6–10.

SEMIAQUILEGIA

This genus, belonging to the buttercup (Ranunculaceae) family, contains 7 species of low perennial plants closely related to *Aquilegia*. They are native to Asia, where they grow in high mountain grassland and scrub in damp conditions. The lacy foliage resembles that of maidenhair fern *(Adiantum)*, with leaves comprised of 3 leaflets. The nodding flowers are in shades of pink, red, and purple, often plump with many petals, but lacking the spurs typical of *Aquilegia* species.

CULTIVATION: Suitable for the rock garden, they should be grown in full sun to half-sun. They require a moist but well-drained soil. Propagate from seed or by division.

Semiaquilegia ecalcarata

☼/◐ ❄ ↔8–10 in (20–25 cm)
↑12 in (30 cm)

Perennial native to western China. Clumps of deeply divided ferny foliage, often with a purplish tinge. Nodding cup-like flowers, pink to purple, in loose panicles, in summer. Zones 6–9.

SEMIARUNDINARIA

This genus of bamboos is from Japan and contains 6 species, also found wild in China. This leptomorph bamboo is considered a natural bigeneric cross between *Phyllostachys* and *Pleioblastus*. Members of the grass (Poaceae) family, they are usually running plants but tend to be more clumping in cooler climates. The stems are comparatively short-lived, so should be regularly removed as they age to keep the plant tidy. The stems usually have 3 short principal branches and up to 7 branches at each node. Although they are regarded as shrubs, *Semiarundinaria* species can reach up to 40 ft (12 m) tall.

CULTIVATION: Plant in moist but not wet soils in partially shaded woodland situations. These plants are not particularly fussy about soil type, but they tend to prefer a humus-rich acid soil. Propagation is by division of the rhizomes in early spring.

Semiarundinaria fastuosa

syn. *Arundinaria fastuosa*

NARIHARA BAMBOO

☼/◐ ❄ ↔7–10 ft (2–3 m)
↑20–30 ft (6–9 m)

Erect clumping to running bamboo from Japan. Slender green stems, with purple-brown stripes in direct sun. Leaves to 6 in (15 cm) long, most numerous toward tops of stems. *S. f.* var. ***viridis***, bushier growth habit, with narrower, non-fading, dark green leaves, easily propagated. Zones 7–10.

SEMPERVIVUM

HENS AND CHICKENS, HOUSELEEK

This genus in the stonecrop (Crassulaceae) family, containing about 40 species of perennials, comes from the mountains of central and southern Europe and eastward to Turkey and Iran, where it grows in rocks and crevices. The thick fleshy leaves may be dull or glossy, and are sometimes covered in a soft down of hairs. They form a flat crowded rosette and spread by offsets, in time becoming a dense tight mat. White, yellow, red, or purplish flowers are held in a cluster on stout fleshy stems in summer. Mainly grown for their colorful decorative leaves, these plants are excellent for rock gardens and pots.

CULTIVATION: These plants require sandy well-drained soil and dry conditions. Smaller species prefer to nest tightly in narrow crevices, while the larger species need a soil that is richer in humus. *Sempervivum* species are easily propagated from offsets, and they hybridize readily.

Semiaquilegia ecalcarata

Sempervivum arachnoideum ★

COBWEB HOUSELEEK

☼ ❄ ↔5–10 in (12–20 cm)
↑5 in (12 cm)

From the Pyrenees and the Carpathian mountains. Forms dense rosettes of green or reddish leaves, their pointed tips connected by fine, cobweb-like, white hairs. Bright rose red flowers appear in summer. *S. a.* subsp. ***tomentosum***, particularly dense leaves with silvery cobwebbing and showy red flowers. *S. a.* **'Cebanse'**, larger rosettes. Zones 5–9.

Sempervivum calcareum

☼ ❄ ↔5–8 in (12–20 cm)
↑2–3 in (5–8 cm)

Native to the Pyrenees, closely related to *S. tectorum*. Rosettes of brown-tipped gray-green leaves. **'Mrs Giuseppi'**, gray-green rosettes, red-tipped leaves darken in winter; **'Sir William Lawrence'** ★, larger more globose rosettes, leaves with prominent reddish tips. Zones 5–9.

Sempervivum arachnoideum 'Cebanse'

Sempervivum ciliosum

☼ ❄ ↔1–2 in (25–50 mm)
↑½–¾ in (12–18 mm)

From the Balkans and northwestern Greece. Somewhat globe-shaped tight rosette of gray-green incurving leaves. Grayish marginal hairs give the plant a furry appearance. Compact heads of starry greenish yellow flowers, in summer. Zones 6–9.

Sempervivum marmoreum

☼ ❄ ↔4 in (10 cm) ↑1–2 in (2–5 cm)

From the Balkans and eastern Europe. Flat open rosettes of reddish to purplish tinged leaves, softly hairy when young, becoming smooth and glossy. Star-shaped mauve flowers with white edges. Many cultivars have more red leaves, **'Brunneifolium'**, pink-brown leaves; **'Rubicundrum'**, red-tipped leaves; **'Rubrifolium'**, bright red-tipped leaves. Zones 5–9.

Sempervivum montanum

☼ ❄ ↔1¼–1¾ in (30–40 mm)
↑¾ in (18 mm)

Native to mountains of Europe. Very variable; forms clustered mats of dense open rosettes, fleshy, softly furry green leaves, many offsets on fine stems. Violet-purple flowers, in summer. *S. m.* subsp. ***stiriacum***, larger, leaves with prominent brown-red tips. Zones 5–9.

Sempervivum marmoreum

Sempervivum calcareum 'Sir William Lawrence'

Sempervivum pumilum

Sempervivum zeleborii

Sempervivum pumilum

☼ ✱ ↔ 1–1¼ in (25–30 mm)
↑ ¾ in (18 mm)

Miniature species from the Caucasus region. Forms small rosettes of finely hairy green leaves. Mauve flowers with white margins, in summer. Zones 5–9.

Sempervivum tectorum ★

HEN AND CHICKENS, ST PATRICK'S CABBAGE

☼ ✱ ↔ 8 in (20 cm) ↑ 3–4 in (8–10 cm)

Found on mountains in Europe from Pyrenees to Balkans; naturalized in UK. Vigorous and variable. Wide flat rosettes of very fleshy green leaves with reddish tips, many offsets on stout reddish stems. Mauve-red flowers in summer. Parent of many cultivars. Zones 5–9.

Sempervivum zeleborii

syn. *Sempervivum ruthenicum*

☼ ✱ ↔ 1½–2 in (35–50 mm)
↑ ¼–¾ in (6–18 mm)

From the Balkans. Produces small dense rosettes with fleshy, downy, slightly incurved leaves, occasionally with purple tips and offsets, on lax short stems. Bears yellow flowers in summer. Zones 6–9.

Sempervivum Hybrid Cultivars

☼/◐ ✱ ↔ 4–16 in (10–40 cm)
↑ 4–8 in (10–20 cm)

Sempervivum species hybridize freely and garden forms vary. Mostly grown for their foliage, a few have showy flowers. **'Booth's Red'**, dense, neat, purplish red rosettes, symmetrically arranged, to over 3 in (8 cm) wide; **'Commander Hay'**, large mound of

Senecio cineraria 'Cirrus'

Sempervivum, HC, 'Reginald Malby'

heavily red-tinted rosettes, each to over 6 in (15 cm) wide; **'Corona'**, many 1 in (25 mm) wide red-tinted rosettes, turning bright red in winter; **'Engle's Rubrum'**, 3 in (8 cm) wide gray-green rosettes heavily tinged with red; **'Hall's Hybrid'**, flat 3 in (8 cm) wide rosettes, flushed with red at the base; **'Raspberry Ice'**, tight symmetrical rosettes, red-tinted, fringed with white hairs; **'Reginald Malby'**, large flat rosettes of deep red-brown tinged leaves; **'Reinhard'**, many small rosettes with deep purple-red leaf tips, showy pink -flowers; **'Virgil'**, 3 in (8 cm) wide gray-green rosettes, flushed purple-blue with darker tips; **'White Eyes'**, central part of rosette yellowish green. Zones 4–10.

SENECIO

There are 1,250 species in this cosmopolitan genus of trees, shrubs, lianes, annuals, biennials, perennials, and some succulent species in the daisy (Asteraceae) family; this is one of the largest genera of flowering plants. The leaves are lobed or smooth-edged, and the daisy-like flowers are usually arranged in clusters, with or without florets. The flowers are usually yellow, but can be purple, white, red, or blue. Many species are toxic to livestock.

CULTIVATION: With such a large genus, cultivation requirements are diverse, so general guidelines only can be given. They grow in either moderately fertile well-drained soil in full sun, or in moderately fertile soil that retains moisture; a few will grow in bogs. Plants grown in pots in colder climates need fertile well-drained soil with added grit and leaf mold. They should be fed and watered moderately during the growing season. Propagation is from seed or cuttings.

Senecio serpens

Senecio cineraria

syn. *Cineraria maritima*

DUSTY MILLER, SEA RAGWORT

☼ ❄ ↔ 16 in (40 cm) ↑ 20 in (50 cm)

Mounding subshrub from southern Europe; naturalized in southern England. Leaves are deeply dissected and lobed, intensely silver-white. Small heads of yellow daisies appear in summer. **'Cirrus'**, rounded-lobed grayish blue leaves; **'Silver Dust'** ★, broad, deeply cut, pewter leaves; **'Silver Lace'**, rounded leaves deeply lobed but less dissected; **'White Diamond'**, finely dissected white leaves, compact habit. Zones 7–10.

Senecio serpens ★

syn. *Kleinia repens*

BLUE CHALKSTICKS

☼ ❄ ↔ 24 in (60 cm) ↑ 12 in (30 cm)

Spreading South African shrub. Narrow, succulent, glaucous leaves with powdery white coating. White flowers in small heads in late spring; best removed to keep plant more lushly foliaged. Zones 9–11.

Senecio vira-vira

syn. *Senecio leucostachys*

DUSTY MILLER

☼ ❄ ↔ 12–24 in (30–60 cm)
↑ 16–24 in (40–60 cm)

Shrubby perennial from Argentina. Covered in dense white hairs. Lacy effect of finely divided, soft, silvery gray leaves. Small, creamy, button-like flowers in summer. Zones 8–11.

SENNA

This genus contains about 350 species of tropical and warm-temperate trees, shrubs, and a few climbers, most from the Ameri-cas, Africa, Australia, and Asia. It is a member of the cassia subfamily of the legume (Fabaceae) family. All species have pinnate leaves, and almost all are evergreen. Most have yellow flowers, a few have pink flowers, but all are very showy when in flower. Many are the source of chemical compounds used medicinally. Fruits are long, flat, or rounded pods. Many species have become invasive weeds in countries where they have escaped cultivation.

CULTIVATION: Many species are frost tender. Grow in well-drained soils in open sunny positions. Species that originate from low-rainfall desert regions appear to be more frost hardy. Propagation is usually from seed, which germinates readily after pre-treatment, or from cuttings.

Senna alata

syn. *Cassia alata*

RINGWORM CASSIA

☼ ✢ ↔ 15 ft (4.5 m) ↑ 30 ft (9 m)

Shrub or tree native to the American tropics; has naturalized elsewhere. Leaves large, to 3 ft (0.9 m) long, 20 pairs of leaflets. Spikes of bright yellow flowers in late summer–early autumn. Green winged pods turn brown as they mature. Zones 10–12.

Senna artemisioides

syn. *Cassia artemisioides*

FEATHERY CASSIA, SILVER CASSIA

☼ ❄ ↔ 7 ft (2 m) ↑ 7 ft (2 m)

Occurs throughout the arid inland of mainland Australia. Many forms. Typical subspecies, round shrub, silvery gray leaves, 2 to 6 pairs of narrow leaflets. Yellow flowers in the leaf axils in spring–autumn. Narrow flat pods. ***S. a.* subsp. *filifolia*** (syns *S. eremophila, S. nemophila*), pinnate leaves, 1 to 4 pairs of very narrow leaflets, leaf stalk flattened. Less frost tolerant than other forms. ***S. a.* subsp. *sturtii***, bright yellow flowers year-round. Zones 9–11.

Senna corymbosa

syn. *Cassia corymbosa*

☼ ❄ ↔ 8 ft (2.4 m) ↑ 10 ft (3 m)

Native to Uruguay and Argentina; naturalized in southern USA. Shrub or small tree with a spreading habit. Long, light green, pinnately divided leaves with oval leaflets. Racemes of golden yellow flowers appear from spring–autumn. Zones 8–11.

Senna didymobotrya

Senna didymobotrya

syn. *Cassia didymobotrya*

↔10 ft (3 m) ↑10 ft (3 m)

Large evergreen shrub, originally from tropical Africa to Southeast Asia, now widely naturalized. Large leaves, leathery leaflets, downy when young. Erect flower spikes, golden yellow flowers emerging from blackish buds. Downy seed pods. Zones 10–12.

Senna hebecarpa

WILD SENNA

↔24 in (60 cm) ↑4–6 ft (1.2–1.8 m)

Well-foliaged perennial native to eastern USA, although endangered in some states. Pinnately divided leaves. Bears large racemes of yellow flowers in summer. Long black seed pods. Zones 4–9.

Senna multijuga

syn. *Cassia multijuga*

↔20 ft (6 m) ↑25 ft (8 m)

Small tree, native to northern South America. Found in open grasslands and forests. Leaves 12 in (30 cm) long, with 40 or more pairs of leaflets. Terminal panicles of small yellow blooms in late summer–autumn. Fruit matures to black. Zones 9–12.

Senna pendula

syns *Cassia bicapsularis of gardens, C. coluteoides*

↔8 ft (2.4 m) ↑10 ft (3 m)

Spreading shrub or small tree from South America. Mature stems have brown corky spots. Light green pinnately divided leaves, oblong leaflets. Showy panicles of yellow flowers in autumn. Drooping cylindrical seed pods. Zones 9–11.

Senna splendida

GOLDEN WONDER

↔8–12 ft (2.4–3.5 m) ↑10–15 ft (3–4.5 m)

Naturally found in Brazil. Spreading shrub or small tree. Slender hanging branches. Glossy pinnately divided leaves with oblong leaflets. Racemes of yellow flowers in autumn. Long drooping cylindrical seed pods. Zones 10–12.

SEQUOIA

This genus from the swamp cypress (Taxodiaceae) family contains a single species of coniferous tree native to the coastal areas of Oregon and California, USA. It is the tallest plant species in the world, with plants in the wild growing to over 360 ft (110 m) high.

CULTIVATION: This tree is suitable only for parks and large gardens, as it can reach 90 ft (27 m) in 20 years under ideal conditions. It does not grow well in cities as it dislikes pollution. Any good well-drained soil will suit it, but it does best in cool humid areas. It will coppice from the stump of a felled tree. Propagate from seed or from heeled cuttings.

Sequoia sempervirens

CALIFORNIA REDWOOD, COAST REDWOOD

↔15–25 ft (4.5–8 m) ↑150 ft (45 m)

Tree develops a conical shape. Bark deeply ridged, reddish brown, very thick, spongy, exfoliating in strips. Dark green yew-like leaves arranged in ranks along stems. Bears small, reddish brown, barrel-shaped cones. **'Adpressa'**, slow-growing dwarf cultivar, grayish green leaves, will reach 90 ft (27 m) tall in about 100 years. Two cultivars have almost horizontal branches: **'Aptos Blue'**, teal foliage with drooping tips, site carefully as it sets abundant seed; **'Soquel'**, greener foliage with curling tips. Zones 8–10.

SEQUOIADENDRON

There is just a single species of coniferous tree in this genus from the swamp cypress (Taxodiaceae) family, which was formerly included in *Sequoia*. It is found in small groves in the Sierra Nevada foothills in California, USA. This species is the largest living organism (though *Sequoia* is taller), with trees acquiring massive bulk; the biggest existing specimen is named "General Sherman," and is estimated to weigh 2,460 tons (2,500 tonnes). It is also one of the longest living trees, with specimens in the range of 1,500 to 3,000 years old.

CULTIVATION: With its great bulk, this tree is suitable only for parks and similar situations. For planting in lines or avenues, trees should be spaced at least 70 ft (21 m) apart. They will grow in a wide range of conditions but dislike pollution. Propagate from seed or cuttings.

Sequoiadendron giganteum

syn. *Wellingtonia gigantea*

BIG TREE, GIANT SEQUOIA, SIERRA REDWOOD

↔20–35 ft (6–9 m) ↑150–165 ft (45–50 m)

Often confused with *Sequoia sempervirens*. Similar conical shape, very thick, reddish brown, spongy bark. Branches curve downward, then up at tips. Leaves compressed, scale-like, spiraly arranged on stems. Cones are larger than those of *Sequoia*. **'Pendulum'**, hanging branches. Zones 7–10.

SERENOA

This genus of palms in the family Arecaceae consists of a single species from southeastern USA, where it forms large colonies, particularly in coastal areas. It is short and has fan-shaped fronds. Branching flowerheads arise from within the foliage.

CULTIVATION: This adaptable palm grows in a range of soils and climates, including coastal areas, where it tolerates salt-laden winds. It does best in warm subtropical areas, and should be grown in a sunny situation. In cool climates it can be grown in pots in the greenhouse. Propagation is from seed.

Serenoa repens ★

SAW PALMETTO

↔7 ft (2 m) ↑3–15 ft (0.9–4.5 m)

Palm with branching prostrate or subterranean trunk, forms dense clumps. Fan-shaped yellowish green to bluish and silvery green fronds are deeply divided into stiff segments, and borne on very thorny stalks. Fragrant cream flowers on branching woolly flowerheads. Zones 8–11.

SERISSA

The sole species in this genus from the madder (Rubiaceae) family is a small, densely branched, evergreen shrub from warm-temperate Southeast Asia. It is a neat little bush with tiny leaves that emit an unpleasant smell when crushed. It produces small white flowers followed by berries, but it is often grown as a foliage plant, as there are several variegated cultivars.

CULTIVATION: Apart from being somewhat frost tender, *Serissa* is quite easily grown. It likes a warm, moist, humid climate and a rich soil with plenty of humus. In areas where the climate does not permit it to be grown outdoors it makes an excellent greenhouse or conservatory plant. Propa-gate from cuttings or from self-layered pieces.

Serissa japonica

syn. *Serissa foetida*

↔18 in (45 cm) ↑18 in (45 cm)

Attractive shrub. White flowers in spring–autumn. **'Flore Pleno'**, very compact bush with double flowers; **'Mount Fuji'**, very compact, leaves edged and striped with white; **'Variegata Pink'**, pink flowers, white-edged leaves. Zones 9–11.

Senna hebecarpa

Sequoiadendron giganteum

Serenoa repens

Serissa japonica, bonsai

Shepherdia argentea

Sidalcea malviflora

Sidalcea oregana

Silene hifacensis

SHEPHERDIA

There are only 3 species of deciduous or evergreen shrubs in this genus from the oleaster (Elaeagnaceae) family. They are native to North America, where they grow on exposed slopes and dry rocky sites. They have simple opposite leaves and bear small petalless flowers; male and female flowers are produced on separate plants. CULTIVATION: These shrubs will grow in a range of conditions, and can tolerate poor dry sites. They like full sun and free-draining soil. Propagation is from seed or cuttings.

Shepherdia argentea ★

BUFFALO BERRY, SILVER BUFFALO BERRY, SILVERBERRY

☼ ✱ ↔12 ft (3.5 m) ↑12 ft (3.5 m)

Well-branched shrub with spiny branches and silvery oblong leaves. Small yellowish white flowers in spring. Female plants produce glossy, red, pea-sized fruits. Zones 2–9.

Shepherdia canadensis

BUFFALO BERRY

☼ ✱ ↔8 ft (2.4 m) ↑8 ft (2.4 m)

Spreading shrub. Leaves dark yellowish green above, white below. Creamy yellow flowers. Fruits are yellow to red. Zones 2–9.

SHORTIA

syn. *Schizocodon*

This genus in the family Diapensiaceae comprises 6 dainty, rhizomatous, clumping, evergreen perennials. Five are native to East Asia, the other to the woodlands of southeastern USA. Their leaves are heart-shaped, rounded, or elliptical, and are toothed and leathery, usually glossy dark green, often turning red in winter. In early spring they bear bell-, trumpet-, or funnel-shaped white to deep pink flowers with toothed or fringed petals. CULTIVATION: All appreciate humus-rich, acidic, moist but well-drained soil and part- to full shade. They are a challenge to grow in dry regions, even with adequate water; regions with cool damp summers are preferred. If available, sow seed when ripe in autumn, or propagate by basal cuttings in early summer or runners in mid-summer. These plants dislike root disturbance.

Shortia galacifolia

syn. *Sherwoodia galacifolia*

OCONEE BELLS

◐ ✱ ↔10 in (25 cm) ↑6 in (15 cm)

Perennial native of southeastern USA. Sizeable clump of roundish glossy green leaves with scalloped edges, bronze-red in winter. Nodding, 1 in (25 mm), rose-flushed white bells, toothed edges, in spring. Zones 6–9.

SIDALCEA

FALSE MALLOW

This genus of about 22 annual and perennial species in the mallow (Malvaceae) family is native to western parts of North America, where these plants grow on lime-free sandy grasslands along stream beds, and in damp mountain meadows. Resembling a small hollyhock *(Alcea rosea)* to which they are related, they have glossy, round, palmately lobed basal leaves and stiffly upright flower spikes that bear stalkless or short-stemmed, white, pink, or purple, open, cup-shaped flowers at the ends. These are popular and charming plants for perennial borders, and many improved varieties are bred for their color and length of flowering. They will flower freely throughout the summer if the spent flower spikes are removed. CULTIVATION: They require a humus-rich free-draining soil in a sunny position, and they may be propagated by division or from seed.

Sidalcea candida

☼ ❄ ↔20 in (50 cm)
↑24–36 in (60–90 cm)

From Utah, New Mexico, Wyoming, and Colorado, USA. The roundish, 7-lobed, glossy leaves grow on long stalks. Branching stems carry white flowers with bluish anthers, in early summer. Parent, with *S. malviflora*, of many modern cultivars. Zones 5–9.

Sidalcea malviflora

CHECKERBLOOM

☼/◐ ✱ ↔16–30 in (40–75 cm)
↑24–40 in (60–100 cm)

Perennial found from Oregon, USA, to Baja California, Mexico. Forms clump of erect stems carrying shallow-toothed 7- to 9-lobed leaves, 1–2 in (25–50 mm) long. Racemes of many 1–2 in (25–50 mm) wide pink to lavender flowers in spring–autumn. Zones 6–10.

Sidalcea oregana

☼ ❄ ↔20 in (50 cm) ↑48 in (120 cm)

From Washington to California and Nevada, USA. Round basal leaves, shallow-lobed, up to 6 in (15 cm) across, stem leaves shiny green and segmented. Small deep pink flowers in dense racemes in summer. Zones 5–9.

Sidalcea Hybrid Cultivars

☼/◐ ✱ ↔16–24 in (40–60 cm)
↑24–32 in (60–80 cm)

These hybrids, which mostly have *S. malviflora* in their parentage, are compact heavy-blooming plants that usually hold their flowers well above the foliage. **'Elsie Heugh'**, triangular ruffled leaves, dainty shell pink flowers; **'Little Princess'**, miniature, compact, soft pink flowers; **'Rose Queen'** ★, deep rose pink flowers on many dense spikes; **'Sussex Beauty'**, particularly large pale pink flowers; **'Monarch'**, taller cultivar, pink flowers. Zones 6–10.

SILENE

CAMPION, CATCHFLY, CUSHION PINK

A large and very varied genus in the pink (Caryophyllaceae) family, *Silene* contains about 500 annuals and perennials widely distributed throughout the Northern Hemisphere and southern Africa. The smaller cushion types, some of them very challenging to grow away from their native habitat, are often used in rock gardens, while some of the taller species are good as garden, hedgerow, or wild garden plants. The flowers are 5-petalled, generally white or shades of pink, and may be solitary or borne in one-sided spikes. Leaves and stems of many are downy and sticky. CULTIVATION: Good drainage is essential for cultivation of these plants, as is a light loamy soil in a sunny position. Propagation is by seed, division, or cuttings.

Silene laciniata

Silene acaulis

CUSHION PINK, MOSS CAMPION

☼ ✱ ↔4 in (10 cm) ↑2 in (5 cm)

Perennial from Eurasia and North America extending into higher mountain regions further south. Forms low, dense, tufted cushion of bright green linear leaves. Solitary deep pink to purple flowers sit just above the foliage. Numerous cultivars. Zones 2–8.

Silene alpestris

syns *Heliosperma alpestre, Silene quadrifida*

☼/◐ ✱ ↔12 in (30 cm)
↑6–12 in (15–30 cm)

From the southern European Alps to the Caucasus region. Low loose cushion of linear-lanceolate leaves. Starry flowers on long stems, white, rarely pink, with cleft or fringed petals, in summer. Zones 5–9.

Silene uniflora

Silene dioica

RED CAMPION

☼/◑ ✱ ↔12 in (30 cm) ↑24 in (60 cm)

Perennial from the woods, rocky hillsides, and cliffs of Europe. Rosettes of downy leaves. Tall, stiff, branching stems carry bright pink, rarely white, flowers, in summer. Double and semi-double forms. Zones 6–10.

Silene fimbriata

☼/◑ ✱ ↔24 in (60 cm) ↑40 in (100 cm)

Perennial from damp woodlands of the Caucasus region. Rosettes of dark green, hairy, oval leaves forming a mound. Open panicles of fringed white flowers with swollen globular calyces, in early summer. Zones 5–8.

Silene hifacensis

syn. *Silene mollissima*

☼ ❄ ↔8 in (20 cm) ↑12 in (30 cm)

Endangered perennial from the Iberian Peninsula. Dense rosettes of oval leaves. Upright, occasionally branched stems bear open panicles of rosy pink flowers with tubular calyces in early summer. Zones 8–10.

Silene laciniata

FRINGED INDIAN PINK, MEXICAN CAMPION

☼ ❄ ↔8 in (20 cm) ↑36 in (90 cm)

From California and New Mexico, USA, and Mexico. Narrow oval leaves to 2 in (5 cm) long. Upright, softly hairy stems bear 1 or 2 large, starry, crimson flowers. Zones 7–10.

Silene schafta

☼ ✱ ↔8 in (20 cm) ↑4 in (10 cm)

Perennial from the Caucasus region. Many upright stems; small, bright green, linear leaves forming loose mat. Bears profuse, star-shaped, rosy magenta flowers with cleft petals, in late summer–autumn. Easily grown rock garden plant. Zones 5–9.

Silene uniflora

syn. *Silene vulgaris subsp. maritima*

BLADDER CAMPION, SEA CAMPION

☼ ✱ ↔4 in (10 cm) ↑4–8 in (10–20 cm)

Native to coasts of western Europe and North Africa. Perennial with gray-tinged oval to spathulate leaves. Upright stems of solitary white flowers with a pronounced inflated calyx like a small bladder, in summer. **'Robin White-breast'** (syn. 'Flore Pleno'), double-flowers. Zones 5–9.

SILPHIUM

This genus, comprising 23 species of coarse-leafed perennials native to central and eastern North America, is in the daisy (Asteraceae) family. The simple to deeply divided leaves are opposite to whorled, the basal ones forming a rosette, those on the inflorescence stalks spiraly arranged. The daisy-like flowerheads are large and have numerous outer rayed florets growing in 2 or 3 rows, white or yellow, while the disc florets are small and yellow. Rather unspectacu-lar plants, they are mostly suited to the wild garden, though their size can impress. CULTIVATION: They grow in full sun or very light shade in any soil not too nitrogen-rich. Seed is the best method of propagation, because the deep root system of larger species makes them difficult to propagate vegetatively.

Silphium laciniatum

COMPASS PLANT

☼/◑ ✱ ↔3–4 ft (0.9–1.2 m) ↑5–10 ft (1.5–3 m)

From central USA. Strongly erect, hairy, fern-like leaves, 4–16 in (10–40 cm) long, aligned north–south. Bears clusters of bright yellow flowerheads, 2 in (5 cm) wide, in summer. It has traditional medicinal and culinary uses. Zones 4–9.

Sinapis alba

Silphium perfoliatum

Silphium perfoliatum

CUP PLANT

☼/◑ ✱ ↔3 ft (0.9 m) ↑5 ft (1.5 m)

Perennial from damp woodlands and prairies of eastern North America. Forms large clump of rough, irregularly toothed, ovate leaves, upper leaves stem-clasping. Stiffly upright stems branching towards top carry single yellow daisy flowers. Zones 5–10.

Silphium terebinthinaceum

PRAIRIE DOCK

☼/◑ ✱ ↔3–6 ft (0.9–1.8 m) ↑7–10 ft (2–3 m)

From southern Canada to southeastern USA. Dense clump of large, long-stemmed basal leaves to over 12 in (30 cm) long, heart-shaped at base, toothed or lobed near tip. Erect red-brown flower stems with summer-borne sprays of 1–2 in (25–50 mm) wide golden flowerheads with many ray florets. Zones 4–9.

SINAPIS

This genus containing 8 species of mostly annual edible herbs in the cabbage (Brassicaceae) family, is native to the Mediterranean region, and is closely related to the genus *Brassica*. The lower leaves form a rosette and the upper leaves are stem-clasping. Racemes of small yellow flowers appear in summer. S. arvensis is a persistent weed of farmland, but is sometimes used for the oil obtained from its reddish brown to black seeds. CULTIVATION: These plants prefer a sandy soil in sun. Raise from seed, avoiding mid-summer sowing as they run to seed when the weather is hot.

Sinapis alba

WHITE MUSTARD

☼ ❄ ↔6 in (15 cm) ↑10–15 in (25–38 cm)

Annual with upright stems branching toward top. Ovate, downy, lobed leaves, bright green, sometimes spotted violet. Up to 50 small yellow flowers per raceme. Young seedlings used as a salad vegetable. Zones 7–11.

SINOCALYCANTHUS

This genus from the family Calycanthaceae is closely related to the allspices *(Calycanthus)* and includes just one species, a deciduous shrub native to central and eastern China. It has variably sized elliptical leaves with a spicy aroma, and it produces miniature camellia-like flowers from mid-spring through to early summer. Hard seed capsules follow. CULTIVATION: Relatively new to cultivation, *Sinocalycanthus* has proved quite hardy and appears to thrive in most well-drained soils. It is best grown in relatively cool conditions with full sun. In areas with hot summers it should be shaded from the hottest afternoon sun. Propagation is from seed or layers.

Sinocalycanthus chinensis

syn. *Calycanthus chinensis*

☼ ✱ ↔4–10 ft (1.2–3 m) ↑6–12 ft (1.8–3.5 m)

Rare in gardens, an ideal shrub for areas with cool moist summers. Lustrous dark green leaves taper abruptly to a point. White to cream camellia-like flowers, pink-tinted yellow centers. Zones 5–9.

Sinocalycanthus chinensis

SINOJACKIA

JACK TREE

A Chinese genus of up to 8 species of deciduous shrubs or small trees of the silverbells (Styracaceae) family. The pointed elliptical to lance-shaped leaves are bright green, with conspicuous veins and finely serrated edges. The foliage usually develops before the small, bell-shaped, white flowers open in mid-spring. Brown seed capsules follow.

CULTIVATION: Relatively new to cultivation in western gardens, but seemingly largely trouble-free in sun or part-shade with moist, well-drained, slightly acid soil. May be pruned lightly. Propagation is from seed or half-hardened cuttings, preferably under mist.

Sinojackia xylocarpa

↔ 7–12 ft (2–3.5 m) ↑ 12–17 ft (3.5–5 m)

Native to Jiangsu Province in eastern China. Leaves around 3 in (8 cm) long, with very finely serrated edges. Flowers white, in clusters of 3–5. **'Linda Carol'**, weeping branches. Zones 7–10.

SISYRINCHIUM

This genus has about 90 species of annuals and perennials from the iris (Iridaceae) family. These plants are native to North and South America, but have also been known to naturalize in other temperate countries. They produce clumps of stiff, upright, linear, or sword-shaped leaves, which arch out into a fan shape. During spring and summer, clusters of trumpet-shaped flowers appear on spikes that hold the flowers just above the top of the foliage.

CULTIVATION: These plants are happy in poor to moderately fertile, well-drained soil in full sun. *Sisyrinchium* species propagate readily from seed and the rhizomatous clumps divide easily in autumn and spring.

Sisyrinchium angustifolium

Sisyrinchium angustifolium

syns *Sisyrinchium bermudiana*, *S. graminoides*

↔ 8 in (20 cm) ↑ 20 in (50 cm)

Tight clump-forming perennial from North America. Rush-like dark green foliage year-round. Stems of dark blue star-shaped flowers, each with distinctive yellow center dot, in summer–autumn. Zones 5–10.

Sisyrinchium californicum

syns *Sisyrinchium boreale*, *S. brachypus*

GOLDEN EYE GRASS

↔ 6 in (15 cm) ↑ 24 in (60 cm)

Semi-evergreen perennial found from California, USA, to British Columbia, Canada. Often short-lived. The linear to sword-shaped gray-green leaves are 4–6 in (10–15 cm) long. The star-shaped yellow flowers, 1 in (25 mm) wide, are held on sturdy stems, in summer. *S. californicum* seeds freely. Zones 8–10.

Sisyrinchium idahoense

syns *Sisyrinchium bellum*, *S. birameum*

CALIFORNIAN BLUE-EYED GRASS

↔ 6 in (15 cm) ↑ 5 in (12 cm)

Semi-evergreen clump-forming perennial occurring from Washington and Idaho to California, USA. Narrow, sword-shaped, dark green foliage. The stiff upright stems support star-shaped violet-blue flowers with yellow throats, in summer. Zones 4–9.

Sisyrinchium palmifolium

YELLOW-EYED GRASS

↔ 16–32 in (40–80 cm) ↑ 20–24 in (50–60 cm)

Large clumping species native to Argentina, Uruguay, and southern Brazil. Long, narrow, strappy, blue-green leaves tapering to fine point. Upright stems carry heads of bright yellow flowers that open in the evening; these appear from late spring. Zones 9–10.

Sisyrinchium idahoense

Sisyrinchium, Hybrid Cultivar, 'Californian Skies'

Sisyrinchium striatum

syn. *Phaiophleps nigricans*

↔ 14 in (35 cm) ↑ 32 in (80 cm)

Clump-forming, upright perennial from Chile and Argentina. Attractive gray-green linear foliage. Sturdy spikes of pale yellow star-shaped flowers push up on stems through the foliage, in summer. **'Aunt May'**, creamy yellow variegated foliage. Zones 8–10.

Sisyrinchium Hybrid Cultivars

↔ 8–12 in (20–30 cm) ↑ 6–14 in (15–35 cm)

Popular garden hybrids have been developed, mainly between the smaller blue-flowered species. They include: **'Biscutella'**, up to 12 in (30 cm) tall, brown-veined yellow flowers in summer; **'Californian Skies'**, mid-blue flowers on stems to 12 in (30 cm) tall, long-blooming; **'Devon Skies'**, grassy foliage, 10 in (25 cm) stems of mauve-blue flowers; **'Quaint and Queer'**, up to 12 in (30 cm), unusual pinkish brown flowers; and **'Sapphire'**, 6 in (15 cm) tall, mauve-blue flowers. Zones 5–10.

SKIMMIA

This genus of 4 slow-growing species belonging to the rue (Rutaceae) family is native to the Himalayas and eastern Asia. They are evergreen shrubs or small trees that will tolerate shade and seaside conditions in cool-temperate regions. The leaves are simple, smooth-edged, and mostly broad and glossy; they are slightly aromatic when crushed due to minute oil cavities. The small flowers are white, yellow or pink-tinged, and borne in short dense clusters at the branch tips. Some species produce male and female flowers on different plants, so both sexes need to be grown in close proximity to ensure the production of the colorful winter-borne berries.

CULTIVATION: They are easily grown in cooler climates in soils that contain plenty of organic matter and have adequate drainage. The plants can be kept trimmed into compact shapes or as hedges. Propagation is best from tip cuttings; seeds can be used but the sex of plants cannot be predicted.

Skimmia japonica

↔ 20 ft (6 m) ↑ 20 ft (6 m)

Dense medium-sized shrub from Japan, shaped like a dome. Leathery leaves, flowers white, fragrant, in panicles, in spring. Clusters of red globular fruits. ***S. j.* subsp. *reevesiana*** bears male and female white flowers; dull pink berries; **'Chilan Choice'**, fragrant flowers, red berries. ***S. j.* 'Cecilia Brown'**, bright green glossy leaves, large clusters of white flowers opening from red buds; **'Fructo Alba'**, cream flowers, small leaves, compact height; **'Kew White'**, narrow glossy leaves, fragrant, cream flowers; **'Nymans'**, many large fruits; **'Robert Fortune'**, pale leaves, dark green edge; **'Rubella'** ★, male cultivar with white flowers, yellow anthers; **'Snow Dwarf'**, small prostrate cultivar with white flowers. Zones 7–10.

Skimmia japonica subsp. *reevesiana* 'Chilan Choice'

SOLANDRA

CHALICE VINE

This genus of 8 species of showy vigorous climbers belongs to the nightshade (Solanaceae) family. They are native to tropical America where they grow in forests, often up buttressed trees near waterways. The alternately arranged simple leaves are usually leathery and shiny. The open trumpet-shaped flowers may be fragrant at night and are usually yellow or white, sometimes with purplish red stripes or markings. Some species were used by the Aztecs and other indigenous groups for their hallucinogenic properties, which are extremely dangerous and capable of causing death.

CULTIVATION: In warm climates, grow against walls and fences or over pergolas in full sun in rich moist but well-drained soil. Grow in the greenhouse in cool-temperate climates. Excessive watering will promote foliage growth at the expense of flowers. Prune to contain size. Propagate from seed or from cuttings.

Solandra maxima

syn. *Solandra hartwegii*

CUP OF GOLD

↔ 10–30 ft (3–9 m) ↕ 20–50 ft (6–15 m)

Rampant climber native to Mexico and Central America. Glossy green oval leaves to 7 in (18 cm) long. The large, golden yellow, funnel-shaped flowers are widely flared, with purple stripes along the center of each lobe. Zones 10–12.

Solandra maxima

Solanum ellipticum

SOLANUM

syns *Cyphomandra, Lycianthes*

Distinguished by the humble potato (*S. tuberosum*) in its many forms, this genus in the nightshade (Solanaceae) family includes some 1,400 species of annuals, perennials, vines, shrubs, and trees with a cosmopolitan distribution, most from tropical America. The trees and shrubs may be deciduous or evergreen and many are armed with thorns. While variable, their flowers are all remarkably similar, being simple, small, 5-petalled structures carried singly or in clusters with a central cone of yellow stamens. Fleshy berries follow the flowers. The berries are usually somewhat poisonous and, because of their conspicuous color, may be attractive to children.

CULTIVATION: Hardiness varies, although a few species are really frost tolerant, most are quite tender. They are generally easily grown in any well-aerated well-drained soil; some have become serious weeds in various parts of the world. Most species prefer sun or partial shade. Propagation is from seed or from cuttings, or in a few cases by division.

Solanum crispum

CHILEAN POTATO VINE

↔ 8–15 ft (2.4–4.5 m) ↕ 10–20 ft (3–6 m)

Evergreen climbing plant native to Chile. Pointed oval to lance-shaped leaves, often wavy margins. Showy, crowded clusters, open, 5-lobed, purplish blue flowers, yellow stamens, in summer. **'Glasnevin'**, hardier, very free flowering. Zones 8–11.

Solanum ellipticum

BUSH TOMATO, VELVET POTATO BUSH, WILD GOOSEBERRY

↔ 3–7 ft (0.9–2 m) ↕ 3–7 ft (0.9–2 m)

Woody-based perennial from inland Australia. Low, hairy, prickly branches. Smooth dark blue-green leaves with prominent veins. Racemes of 3 to 7 purple or blue flowers, yellow centers. Edible greenish fruits. Zones 9–11.

Solanum rantonnetii 'Royal Robe'

Solanum jasminoides

POTATO VINE

↔ 8–15 ft (2.4–4.5 m) ↕ 10–20 ft (3–6 m)

Evergreen Brazilian climber. Vigorous, twiggy-stemmed, well-foliaged. Oval, lance-shaped or lobed leaves. Clusters of long-lasting, starry, white flowers, tinged blue, in summer. **'Album'**, pure white flowers. Zones 9–12.

Solanum melanocerasum

GARDEN HUCKLEBERRY

↔ 18 in (45 cm) ↕ 24 in (60 cm)

Bushy annual probably originating from western tropical Africa. Broadly oval leaves. Small white flowers. Black berries, ¾ in (18 mm) wide, through summer; edible if cooked, Zones 9–12.

Solanum pseudocapsicum

syn. *Solanum capsicastrum*

JERUSALEM CHERRY

↔ 4 ft (1.2 m) ↕ 3–6 ft (0.9–1.8 m)

Evergreen shrub from South America. Dark green leaves, wavy edges. Small white flowers, showy bright orange fruit. Many cultivars, variably colored fruit: cream, yellow, orange, and red. Fruit eaten by birds but poisonous to humans. Zones 9–11.

Solanum pyracanthum

↔ 2–3 ft (0.6–0.9 m) ↕ 3–6 ft (0.9–1.8 m)

Shrubby biennial or perennial from tropical Africa and Madagascar. Rust-colored felted stems. Lobed leaves; eye-catching long orange spines on midrib, which provide effective protection from herbivores. Bluish violet flowers are borne, in dense clusters, in summer. Zones 10–12.

Solanum quitoense

NARANJILLA

↔ 7 ft (2 m) ↕ 7 ft (2 m)

South American shrub, straggly growth habit. All parts have dense covering of fine hairs. Stems and leaves light green, purple toned; leaves angularly lobed. Clusters of white flowers. Tomato-like edible orange fruit, its green pulp makes a refreshing juice Zones 10–12.

Solanum rantonnetii

syn. *Lycianthes rantonnetii*

BLUE POTATO BUSH, PARAGUAY NIGHTSHADE

↔ 7 ft (2 m) ↕ 6 ft (1.8 m)

Grown as scrambling shrub or semi-climber, long-flowering species from Argentina and Paraguay. Leaves, wavy edges. Fragrant purple to violet-blue flowers, in summer. Red fruit. Trim to keep plants compact. **'Royal Robe'**, long-blooming, rich purple flowers. Zones 9–11.

Solanum wendlandii

GIANT POTATO CREEPER, PARADISE FLOWER, POTATO VINE

↔ 5–10 ft (1.5–3 m) ↕ 15 ft (4.5 m)

Evergreen climber native to Costa Rica. Prickly scrambling branches. Glossy pinnate leaves. Lilac-blue flowers, to 2½ in (6 cm) wide, are produced in large showy clusters, in summer. Oval yellowish fruits to 4 in (10 cm) long. Zones 10–12.

SOLEIROLIA

BABY'S TEARS, MIND-YOUR-OWN-BUSINESS

This monotypic genus, comprising an evergreen, mat-forming perennial native to the islands of the western Mediterranean, notably Corsica, and widely naturalized in warm countries, belongs to the nettle (Urticaceae) family. The branches are fine and root at the nodes. The tiny leaves are almost circular and spiraly arranged but appear alternate. The white flowers are pink-tinged, minute, solitary, 4-petalled, and held in the leaf axils.

CULTIVATION: Makes a neat ground cover in greenhouses, especially under staging, and in terraria, for temperate regions. Its invasive habit makes it less welcome in warmer climates. It needs humus-rich well-drained soil but can grow in crevices on almost bare ground, in paving, or against walls; it is intolerant of scorching midday sun. Easily propagated by division.

Soleirolia soleirolii

syn. *Helxine soleirolii*

ANGEL'S TEARS, BABY'S TEARS, MIND-YOUR-OWN-BUSINESS

↔ 2–4 ft (0.6–1.2 m) ↕ 2–4 in (5–10 cm)

Creeping mat-forming perennial from Corsica and nearby islands, widely naturalized in Europe. Can be invasive. Tightly packed, small, rounded, bright green leaves. Tiny 4-petalled flowers, white tinged with pink, are produced in summer. **'Aurea'**, yellowish green leaves. Zones 9–12.

Soleirolia soleirolii

S

Solenostemon scutellarioides 'Crinkly Bottom'

Solenostemon scutellarioides 'Muriel Pedley'

SOLENOSTEMON

This genus in the mint (Lamiaceae) family contains 60 species of shrubby plants native to tropical Africa and Asia. They may be erect, prostrate, or sprawling and are sometimes downy or succulent. Some of the species were previously included in the closely related genera *Plectranthus* and *Coleus*. Species of *Solenostemon* are grown for their colorful foliage that is often strikingly blotched or variegated, the leaves being pointed oval with toothed or scalloped margins. The flowers have little importance for their appearance, and are the typical tubular, 2-lipped flowers of the mint family.
CULTIVATION: In cool temperate climates, grow *Solenostemon* species in the conservatory, as house plants, or outdoors as annual bedding plants. In frost-free areas the plants can remain outdoors. Grow in any reasonable soil or potting mix in direct sunlight. Pinch back the growing tips regularly to maintain the plant's bushy shape and to prevent flowering. Propagation is easy from seed or from cuttings of desired plants.

Solenostemon scutellarioides

syns *Coleus blumei, C. scutellarioides, Plectranthus scutellarioides*

COLEUS, PAINTED NETTLE

☼/◐ ✢ ↔ 12–24 in (30–60 cm)
↑ 12–24 in (30–60 cm)

Shrubby plant from southeastern Asia. Square, semi-succulent, lightly downy stems. Pointed oval, scallop-edged leaves, extremely variable: green, red, purple, white, and yellow combinations. **'Cantigny Royale'**, reddish purple leaves; **'Crimson Ruffles'**, crimson leaves, lighter veins, ruffled margins; **'Crinkly Bottom'**, deep blue-purple leaves, bright green edges; **'Display'**, burnt orange leaves, bright green edges; **Dragon Series**, large serrated-edged leaves, scarlet to purple and black, gold edging; **'Frogsfoot Purple'**, magenta leaves with deep purple edges; **'Jupiter'**, beet red crinkly leaves, edged pale green; **'Kiwi Fern'**, deeply serrated crimson leaves, edged lemon; **'Lemon Dash'**, brilliant green leaves, yellow center; **'Muriel Pedley'**, blood red leaves, splashed yellow, bright green edges; **'Pineapple Beauty'**, deep maroon splashed, golden green leaves; **Rainbow Series**, variegated in greens, creams and purples, irregularly marked leaves of yellow, red, copper, purple, and green, including **'Rainbow Fringed Mix'**, cut frilly edged leaves; **'Solar Eclipse'**, serrated edge; **'Walter Turner'**, red to dark red leaves, bright green edges; **'White Pheasant'**, serrated-edged rich green leaves, pale lemon center; **'Winsley Tapestry'**, highly serrated bright green leaves, beet red center; **'Winsome'**, vivid green leaves, vivid red to black centers. Zones 10–12.

Solidago canadensis

SOLIDAGO

GOLDENROD

Although a few species are found in other temperate regions, this genus of around 100 species of perennials is primarily North American, and belongs to the daisy (Asteraceae) family. These plants form clumps of upright, sometimes branching stems, the upper half of which develops panicles of tiny golden yellow flowers. The leaves may be linear, lance-shaped, or pointed oval, and usually have toothed edges. Often, by the time flowering starts in late summer, many of the lower leaves have withered somewhat. This late-flowering habit was used in the past by Native Americans as a kind of floral calendar, guiding them to when the corn would be ripe for harvest.
CULTIVATION: They are very hardy plants and easily grown in full or half-sun in any position, provided the soil is reasonably fertile, moist, and well-drained. All *Solidago* species will grow in poor soil and withstand drought but will not flower well or reach maximum size with such conditions. Propagate from seed, basal cuttings, or by division. May self-sow.

Solidago californica

CALIFORNIA GOLDENROD

☼/◐ ❄ ↔ 24–32 in (60–80 cm)
↑ 40–48 in (100–120 cm)

Perennial species from southwestern USA east to New Mexico and south to Mexico. The upright stems are coarsely toothed with narrow, pointed oval leaves to over 4 in (10 cm) long. Flowerheads, which are deep yellow and massed in slightly overarching spikes, appear in autumn. Zones 8–10.

Solidago canadensis

☼/◐ ✱ ↔ 40 in (100 cm)
↑ 60 in (150 cm)

Erect species widespread throughout North America. The narrow lance-shaped leaves, to 4 in (10 cm) long, have serrated edges. Short panicles of golden yellow flowers are borne in late summer–autumn. ***S. c.* subsp. *elongata***, minutely bristly stems and leaves. Zones 3–9.

Solidago confinis

YELLOW BUTTERFLY WEED

☼/◐ ✱ ↔ 20–32 in (50–80 cm)
↑ 24–40 in (60–100 cm)

From California and Mexico. Small leaves, compact growth habit. Large golden yellow flowerheads, in late summer–autumn. Hardiness and drought tolerance both excellent. Zones 4–10.

Solidago flexicaulis

ZIGZAG GOLDENROD

☼/◐ ✱ ↔ 24–40 in (60–100 cm)
↑ 100–48 in (100–120 cm)

Eastern North American native perennial. Sparsely hairy, toothed, pointed oval to elliptical leaves to 6 in (15 cm) long. Flowerheads in small clusters on alternate sides up flower stem, golden yellow, 3 or 4 ray florets, in summer–autumn. Zones 4–9.

Solidago rugosa

ROUGH-STEMMED GOLDENROD

☼/◐ ✱ ↔ 40 cm (100 cm)
↑ 60 in (150 cm)

Species from Eastern North America species. Forms densely foliaged basal clump of bristly, toothed, broad lance-shaped leaves to over 5 in (12 cm) long. Bears massed branching, arching panicles of small bright yellow flowerheads, in late summer. **'Fireworks'**, 48 in (120 cm) tall, very heavy flowering, produces starburst-like array of panicles. Zones 3–9.

Solidago Hybrid Cultivars

☼/◐ ✱ ↔ 12–48 in (30–120 cm)
↑ 24–60 in (60–150 cm)

Goldenrods, especially the hardier species from northern North America, interbreed freely, often producing vigorous heavy-flowering hybrids that generally make better garden plants. These include: **'Golden Wings'**, 60 in (150 cm) tall, toothed lance-shaped leaves and feathery bright yellow panicles; **'Goldenmosa'** ★, 40 in (100 cm) tall, with strongly erect cane-like stems and small, overarched, bright yellow plumes; and **'Summershine'**, golden yellow panicles. Zones 4–9.

× *SOLIDASTER*

This is a hybrid genus, arising in cultivation, of a single clump-forming perennial. It is probably a cross between *Solidago canadensis* and *Aster ptarmicoides*, members of the daisy (Asteraceae) family, and was found in 1910 in a nursery in Lyons. It bears tiny daisy flowers from late summer into autumn; they are attractive in the border and make good cut flowers.
CULTIVATION: It grows well in a sunny well-drained border with moist but not wet soils and prefers a non-humid Mediterranean climate. Propagation is by dividing dormant plants throughout the winter or from basal cuttings taken in spring.

× *Solidaster luteus*

syn. × *Solidaster hybridus*
↔ 12–15 in (30–38 cm)
↑ 32–36 in (80–90 cm)
Erect clumping perennial with leaves to 6 in (15 cm) long. Summer sprays of tiny soft yellow daisies. **'Lemore'**, paler yellow flowers. Zones 6–10.

SOPHORA

This widespread genus from the pea-flower subfamily of the legume (Fabaceae) family includes more than 50 species of evergreen, deciduous, or briefly deciduous shrubs and trees. They have pinnate leaves, often composed of many tiny leaflets. The flowers are pea-like, usually cream or yellow, and frequently have a prominent keel; they are carried in racemes or panicles. Spring is the principal flowering season, though the tropical species tend to be less seasonal in their flowering. Woody winged seed pods follow the flowers.
CULTIVATION: While hardiness varies with the species, most adapt well to cultivation and thrive in any well-drained soil with a position in sun or light shade. Propagate from seed, cuttings, or, in some cases, from grafting. The seed is particularly moisture resistant and must be soaked in warm water to soften it before sowing. Its moisture resistance allows the seed to survive prolonged exposure to seawater and this feature accounts for the rather unusual distribution patterns of some *Sophora* species.

Sophora arizonica

ARIZONA MOUNTAIN LAUREL, ARIZONA NECKLACE
↔ 8–10 ft (2.4–3 m)
↑ 10–15 ft (3–4.5 m)
Evergreen, slow-growing, spreading shrub or small tree from Arizona, USA. It has attractive silvery green

Sophora davidii

pinnately divided leaves. Profuse wisteria-like bunches of fragrant violet flowers are produced in spring, and followed by bean-like seed pods, which are thought to be poisonous. Zones 8–10.

Sophora davidii

↔ 10 ft (3 m) ↑ 10 ft (3 m)
Deciduous shrub originating in China. Short leaves, to 20 small leaflets. The flowers are purple-blue with whitish tips to white, and are produced in short racemes at the stem tips, in summer. Zones 6–9.

Sophora secundiflora

FRIJOLITO, MESCAL BEAN, TEXAS MOUNTAIN LAUREL
↔ 15 ft (4.5 m) ↑ 30 ft (9 m)
Evergreen shrub or small tree, native of Texas and New Mexico, USA, and nearby parts of Mexico. Leaves with 3 to 5 pairs of leaflets. Racemes of fragrant violet-blue flowers, wisteria-like, in early spring. Silver-gray seed pods. Zones 8–11.

SORBARIA

This genus, native to Asia, is a member of the rose (Rosaceae) family and is commonly called false spirea as the flowers are similar to *Spiraea*. There are 4 species of deciduous, usually suckering shrubs with pinnate leaves. They produce large panicles of small white flowers in summer followed by masses of small brownish seed capsules that often persist into winter.
CULTIVATION: These plants are grown for both their foliage and their flowers. They prefer a fertile moisture-retentive soil in sun or part-shade and should be planted in a position with protection from strong winds, which may damage the foliage. Cut back in early spring and remove any old or weak branches at ground level. Propagation is by the removal of suckers or from cuttings in summer.

Sorbaria grandiflora

Sorbaria grandiflora

↔ 36 in (90 cm)
↑ 12–36 in (30–90 cm)
Small shrub, native to eastern Siberia. Downy reddish gray shoots, exfoliating bark. Fine pinnate leaves, up to 8 in (20 cm) long. White flowers in flattened clusters, in summer. Zones 5–9.

Sorbaria kirilowii

syn. *Sobaria arborea*
TREE FALSE SPIREA, URAL FALSE SPIREA
↔ 20 ft (6 m) ↑ 17 ft (5 m)
Large, deciduous, spreading, Chinese shrub with slender pointed leaflets. White flowers on long panicles to 12 in (30 cm) in mid-summer. If deadheaded, continues blooming till frosts arrive. Spicy fragrance. Zones 5–7.

Sorbaria sorbifolia

FALSE SPIREA
↔ 10 ft (3 m) ↑ 10 ft (3 m)
Suckering shrub native to Asia, stiff erect stems. Pinnate leaves, finely serrated margins; colorful autumn foliage. White flowers in large plumes, in summer. Zones 2–9.

Sorbaria tomentosa

↔ 15 ft (4.5 m) ↑ 20 ft (6 m)
Wide-spreading, branching, Himalayan shrub. Pinnate leaves, to 21 narrow finely serrated leaflets. Yellowish white flowers, large panicles, in summer. S. t. var. angustifolia (syn. *S. aitchisonii*), purplish brown branches. Zones 6–10.

SORBUS

MOUNTAIN ASH
The 100-odd species of deciduous shrubs and trees in this genus from the northern temperate zones belong to the rose (Rosaceae) family. The foliage is usually pinnate with serrated-edged leaflets, but may be simple and oval to diamond-shaped. Clusters of white or cream, sometimes pink-tinted, spring flowers, somewhat unpleasantly scented, are followed by heads of berry-like pomes that ripen through summer and autumn. Some species develop russet to red toned foliage in autumn.
CULTIVATION: Most *Sorbus* species are very hardy and prefer a cool climate, suffering in high summer temperatures. They are best grown in moderately fertile, deep, humus-enriched soil with ample summer moisture, but adapt well to most conditions. Plant in sun or partial shade, prune to shape in the autumn or winter and propagate from stratified seed or by grafting. Fireblight can cause significant damage.

Sorbus alnifolia

KOREAN MOUNTAIN ASH
↔ 25 ft (8 m) ↑ 50 ft (15 m)
From Japan and Korea. Leaves with heavily serrated edges; orange and red in autumn. Young stems red-brown, bright green young foliage. Flowers white; fruit red or yellow. Zones 6–9.

Sorbus americana ★

AMERICAN MOUNTAIN ASH
↔ 20 ft (6 m) ↑ 20–30 ft (6–9 m)
Sometimes shrubby tree from central and eastern USA. Leaves, 17 bright green leaflets, gray-green undersides, turn yellow, in autumn. Resinous buds, white flowers, in spring. Bright red fruit. Zones 2–9.

Sorbus alnifolia

Sorbaria sorbifolia, in winter

Sorbus aucuparia 'Fructu Luteo'

Sorbus aucuparia

EUROPEAN MOUNTAIN ASH, MOUNTAIN ASH, ROWAN

↔ 20 ft (6 m) ↑ 15–40 ft (4.5–12 m)

This hardy tree is found over much of northern Eurasia. Dark green to bronze pinnate leaves, coarsely serrated leaflets, turning orange and red, in the autumn. Flowers have an unpleasant scent. Bears orange berries, which are both ornamental and a rich source of vitamin C; their juice is used as a flavoring. **'Aspleniifolia'** has deeply cut leaves with hairy undersides; **'Black Hawk'** is an upright, narrow tree; **'Cardinal Royal'** has a very upright habit and dark red fruit; **'Fastigiata'**, a narrow crown, stiff upright shoots, and large fruit; **'Fructu Luteo'**, spreading habit; **'Xanthocarpa'**, golden yellow fruit. Zones 2–9.

Sorbus decora

SHOWY MOUNTAIN ASH

↔ 15 ft (4.5 m) ↑ 30 ft (9 m)

Often small and shrubby tree found in northeastern North America. Leaves, 17 leaflets. Loose white flowerheads, in spring. Clusters of small red fruits. Zones 2–8.

Sorbus forrestii

↔ 20 ft (6 m) ↑ 25 ft (8 m)

Similar species to the commonly grown *S. hupehensis*, but with larger fruit. This is pure white when ripe, and persists well into winter after the leaves have fallen. Zones 7–9.

Sorbus hedlundii

↔ 25 ft (8 m) ↑ 30 ft (9 m)

Very like *S. vestita*, but this species has distinctly silvery undersides to its leaves. Prominent veins on undersides of the leaves are a distinguishing feature. Zones 8–10.

Sorbus × thuringiaca

OAK-LEAFED MOUNTAIN ASH

↔ 25 ft (8 m) ↑ 30–40 ft (9–12 m)

Hybrid between 2 European species, *S. aria* and *S. aucuparia*. Pinnate leaves, finely serrated leaflets. Flowers develop into small red fruits. **'Fastigiata'**, strong upright growth, very dark green foliage; **'Leonard Springer'**, leaves of only 9 to 11 heavily serrated leaflets, red stalks. Zones 6–9.

Sorbus Hybrid Cultivars

↔ 7–15 ft (2–4.5 m) ↑ 10–25 ft (3–8 m)

Sorbus hybrids range in size, including dwarf forms, most seen in gardens are tree-like. Foliage type and fruit color vary, all tend to be heavy cropping, and are often have bright foliage in autumn. **'Coral Beauty'**, strong *S. aucuparia* influence, brilliant orange-scarlet fruits. **'Joseph Rock'**, probable hybrid, 20–30 ft (6–9 m) tall, pinnate leaves, deeply serrated leaflets, turn orange or purple-red, in autumn; flowers white; fruit, initially cream, ripens to golden yellow. **'Pearly King'**, pale pearl pink fruits; **'Sunshine'**, yellow fruit. Zones 6–9.

Sorbus × thuringiaca

SORGHASTRUM

Genus of around 16 species of annual and perennial grasses in the family Poaceae from the American and African tropics. They can form open, rather airy sprays or strong, densely foliaged clumps of long, very narrow leaves, often rolled along the midrib. Large feathery panicles, usually from late summer, are borne on long stems that hold them well clear of the foliage. CULTIVATION: They are easily grown in any reasonably sunny position with moist, well-drained soil. Drought tolerant once established. Hardiness varies with the species. Propagate by seed; perennials will also grow from division.

Sorghastrum nutans

INDIAN GRASS, WOOD GRASS

↔ 16–32 in (40–80 cm) ↑ 5–7 ft (1.5–2 m)

Perennial grass from central and eastern USA. Narrow leaves to 24 in (60 cm) long. Pale to golden brown panicles, to over 12 in (30 cm) long. atop erect, wiry stems, in autumn. Zones 5–10.

SORGHUM

MILLET, SORGHUM

This genus of about 20 quick-growing, broad-leafed, annual or perennial grasses, members of the family Poaceae originates from tropical and subtropical Africa, Asia, and Australia, except for 1 species native to Mexico. The stems are quite robust, usually upright, and form clumps. The leaves have flat or wavy margins in 2 ranks and these overlap the waxy sheaths encircling the stem. Branching, finely hairy, usually upright, conical to oval-shaped panicles of flower spikelets, which yield round bluntly pointed seed, partly covered by glumes. *Sorghum* species are grown for grain and forage and for the sweetening syrup extracted from the stalks of *S. vulgare* var. *saccharatum*. CULTIVATION: Sorghum tolerates a wide range of fertile well-drained soils in an open sunny position. Propagate from seed.

Sorghum bicolor

GREAT MILLET, SORGHUM

↔ 2–3 ft (0.6–0.9 m) ↑ 10–20 ft (3–6 m)

Widely cultivated in warm climates; believed to be of African origin. Narrow strap-like leaves, to 36 in (90 cm) long, white midrib. Large dense panicles, to 24 in (60 cm) long, fertile spikelets to ½ in (12 mm), in summer. Large variously colored grains, which provide the staple diet for the people of many countries. Zones 9–12.

SPARAXIS

HARLEQUIN FLOWER

Under suitable conditions, this South African genus of 6 species of corms in the iris (Iridaceae) family will naturalize and form large drifts. The leaves are grassy to sword-shaped, with prominent ribbing, developing quickly from late winter. They are soon followed by wiry spikes carrying just a few blooms or fan-like sprays of ¾ in (18 mm) wide, 6-petalled, funnel-shaped flowers. These may be white, yellow, or shades of pink to orange and red, usually with a yellow center and contrasting dark colors in the throat. The name comes from the Greek *sparasso*, to tear, referring to the lacerated bracts at the base of the flowers. CULTIVATION: They are not hardy where the soil freezes but otherwise are easily grown in full sun in fertile, moist, well-drained soil. In cold areas, they can be lifted in the autumn and replanted in the early spring for a late flower show. Propagation is from seed or by division.

Sparaxis tricolor ★

VELVET FLOWER

↔ 6–10 in (15–25 cm) ↑ 8–16 in (20–40 cm)

Narrow sword-shaped leaves and 1 to 5 flower stems per corm, each with up to 5 darkly marked, yellow-centered, orange to red flowers to over 1 in (25 mm) wide. Readily naturalizes in suitable climates. Zones 9–10.

Sparaxis tricolor

S

Spartium junceum, Provence, France

Spathodea campanulata

Sphaeralcea ambigua

SPARTINA

CORD GRASS, MARSH GRASS

This genus of 15 perennial species, members of the grass (Poaceae) family, is native to western and southern Europe, the Americas, northwestern and southern Africa, and the South Atlantic islands. These plants grow from rhizomes, with rigid upright stems and tough flat or folded leaves with finely hairy ligules. The flowerheads are stalkless spikelets, held close or spreading out. The name comes from the Greek word *spartine*, a cord, referring to the plant's tough flowering stems.
CULTIVATION: Marsh grasses prefer a position in full sun and thrive in salty coastal marshes and sand flats, but can adapt to any moist soil. Propagate by division or from seed planted in the autumn.

Spartina pectinata

FRESHWATER CORD GRASS, MARSH GRASS, SALT GRASS

↔ 18–24 in (45–60 cm)
↕ 3–10 ft (0.9–3 m)

Aggressively spreading perennial grass native to the wet prairies of North America. Narrow, arching, leathery, flat leaves, to 4 ft (1.2 m) long; change from green to yellow to fawn. Feathery columnar flowerheads, masses of tiny purple flowers, in autumn–winter. **'Aureomarginata'** (syn. 'Variegata') arching olive green leaves, edged with golden yellow, purplish, hanging stamens. Zones 4–5.

SPARTIUM

All but one species in this genus of brooms from the pea-flower subfamily of the legume (Fabaceae) family have now been transferred, most of them to *Genista*. The one remaining species is a deciduous shrub native to the Mediterranean region and southwestern Europe. Leafless for much of the year, but green-stemmed, it produces a few small leaves in spring, usually as it comes into bloom. A yellow dye is extracted from the flowers. Several are considered invasive in western North America.
CULTIVATION: Spanish broom is easily grown in any well-drained soil with a position in full sun. It can be cut back hard after flowering to encourage bushiness. Pruning also helps to prevent excessive self-sowing, which can be a problem if too many seed pods are left to ripen. Propagation is from seeds or from cuttings.

Spartium junceum

SPANISH BROOM

↔ 10 ft (3 m) ↕ 10 ft (3 m)

Many-stemmed shrub, smothered in flowers, in spring–early summer, later in cool climates. Strongly scented, bright yellow, pea-flowers are produced in large racemes on new growth. Flat dark brown seed pods split open when ripe. Zones 8–10.

SPATHODEA

The sole species in this genus from the trumpet-vine (Bignoniaceae) family is an evergreen tree found in the warmer areas of Africa. It has a domed crown, dark green compound leaves, and large bell-shaped flowers with a spathe-like calyx. Flowers are yellow at the base on the outside, becoming bright red near the mouth. They are a bright orange inside, merging to orangey red on the lobes.
CULTIVATION: It is best grown in fertile well-drained soil containing plenty of organic matter, which helps keep the soil moist during hot summers; raised ground is ideal as it allows rapid air drainage. It is frost tender and needs shelter from wind, especially salt-laden wind. The strongest leading shoot should be kept free of competition until the trunk is 7 ft (2 m) or more tall, when the crown may be allowed to develop naturally. Seeds can be sown in spring in a warm environment.

Spathodea campanulata

syn. *Spathodea nilotica*

AFRICAN TULIP TREE

↔ 25 ft (8 m) ↕ 25–35 ft (8–10 m)

Evergreen tree native to tropical central and western Africa. Broad-domed crown. Leaves are compound on short stalks, leaflets are shiny, dark green, paler and dull underneath. Bell-shaped flowers, in racemes, in late spring–mid-summer. Fruit, slender capsule. Zones 11–12.

SPHAERALCEA

syn. *Iliamna*

FALSE MALLOW, GLOBE MALLOW

This genus consists of 60 species belonging to the mallow (Malvaceae) family. Deciduous or evergreen perennials, subshrubs, and shrubs, they are native to the dry, even volcanic, mountain slopes of the warmer areas of North America, South America, and South Africa. The leaves are arranged in spirals, have a variety of shapes, and are usually toothed and downy. The saucer-shaped flowers are red, pale purple, pink, white, orange, or yellow and are produced singly in clusters or inflorescences.
CULTIVATION: Grow *Sphaeralcea* species outdoors in full sun in well-drained moderately fertile soil and provide protection from winter moisture. If grown in pots, provide added grit to loam-based compost and feed and water moderately. Propagate by sowing seed in spring and dividing perennials at the same time. In areas with heavy winter rain, they are best protected in a cool greenhouse as excess wet, rather than cold, often kills the hardier species.

Sphaeralcea ambigua

DESERT MALLOW

↔ 12–24 in (30–60 cm)
↕ 24–36 in (60–90 cm)

Upright shrubby perennial naturally found throughout southern USA and Mexico. Whitish green or yellowish felted stems. Thick, gray, shallowly lobed leaves. Small salmon to orange saucer-shaped flowers, in loose clusters, appear in spring–autumn. Zones 4–9.

Sphaeralcea coccinea

syn. *Malvastrum coccineum*

GLOBE MALLOW, PRAIRIE MALLOW, RED FALSE MALLOW

↔ 6–12 in (15–30 cm)
↕ 6–18 in (15–45 cm)

Well-branched perennial found from southern Canada to Arizona, USA. White or gray felted stems. Pinnately parted leaves, rough-textured, grayish green. Short racemes of orange to red flowers, in summer. Zones 4–9.

Sphaeralcea munroana

↔ 12–27 in (30–70 cm)
↕ 8–36 in (20–90 cm)

Short-lived perennial native to western North America. Felted gray stems. Small, deeply toothed, 5-lobed, hairy leaves. Apricot-pink to red or orange saucer-shaped flowers, in summer. Zones 4–9.

SPIRAEA

BRIDAL WREATH, SPIREA

This genus has about 70 species of mainly deciduous, sometimes semi-evergreen, flowering shrubs in the rose (Rosaceae) family. It is valued for its flowering and foliage qualities. Leaves are simple and alternate, variously toothed and lobed. The genus is found in many northern temperate areas, mainly in eastern and southeastern Asia and in North America.
CULTIVATION: They thrive in most soils, though some grow poorly on chalk, and prefer a sunny position and cool moist conditions. They fall into 2 groups for pruning: those that flower on the current year's growth, which can be hard pruned in spring, and those that flower on the previous year's growth, which should have the old flowering shoots removed just after flowering. Propagation is from soft-tip or half-hardened cuttings during the summer months.

Spiraea alba var. *latifolia*

Spiraea japonica 'Crispa'

Spiraea thunbergii

Spiraea douglasii

Spiraea alba

MEADOWSWEET

↔5 ft (1.5 m) ↑5 ft (1.5 m)

Shrub from eastern North America. Upright or slightly overarching spreading habit. Young stems coated with fine red-brown hairs. Leaves, pointed oblong shape, serrated edges. Large conical panicles of white, rarely pink, flowers, in summer. ***S. a.* var. *latifolia***, noticeably broader leaves. Zones 5–9.

Spiraea 'Arguta'

BRIDAL WREATH

↔4 ft (1.2 m) ↑5–7 ft (1.5–2 m)

Dense shrub. Thin branches, hairless, inversely lance-shaped to oval leaves, smooth edges or a few teeth. Clusters of white flowers along the branches, in spring. Zones 4–10.

Spiraea betulifolia

BIRCHLEAF SPIREA

↔3 ft (0.9 m) ↑3 ft (0.9 m)

A dwarf shrub found in Japan and northeastern Asia. Forms mound of brown hairless shoots, round to egg-shaped leaves. Flowers are white, in closely packed corymbs, appearing in mid-summer. ***S. b.* var. *aemiliana***, to 12 in (30 cm) high, broad rounded leaves. Zones 5–10.

Spiraea × *billardii*

↔7 ft (2 m) ↑7 ft (2 m)

Spreading shrub, hybrid between *S. douglasii* and *S. salicifolia*. Hairy upright stems. Oblong to lance-shaped leaves, sharp teeth, gray downy undersides. Red flowers in densely packed panicles, in summer. **'Triumphans'**, small leaves, slightly downy undersides, flowers deep pink, sometimes hint of purple. Zones 4–10.

Spiraea cantoniensis

REEVES' SPIREA

↔8 ft (2.4 m) ↑6 ft (1.8 m)

Deciduous or semi-evergreen shrub, native to China. Arching hairless branches. Diamond-shaped leaves have glaucous undersides, and are conspicuously toothed or 3-lobed. White flowers are borne in spherical clusters, in mid-summer. **'Flore Pleno'** (syn. 'Lanceata'), double flowers, the most popular form of *S. cantoniensis* in cultivation. Zones 5–11.

Spiraea chamaedryfolia

GERMANDER SPIREA

↔6 ft (1.8 m) ↑6 ft (1.8 m)

Suckering, densely branched shrub found from the eastern Alps to Siberia. Dark green, pointed, oval leaves. Puts on a showy display of small white flowers, in crowded domed clusters, in spring. Zones 5–9.

Spiraea × *cinerea*

GREFSHEIM SPIREA

↔5 ft (1.5 m) ↑5 ft (1.5 m)

Garden hybrid between *S. hypericifolia* and *S. cana*. Small, rather pale green leaves. Branch tips covered with tiny white flowers, a few in leaf axils of lower branches, in spring. **'Compacta'** is under 3 ft (0.9 m) tall, with arching branches; **'Grefsheim'**, early-flowering, with slightly pendulous branches, and narrower leaves. Zones 5–9.

Spiraea decumbens

↔18 in (45 cm) ↑10 in (25 cm)

Low shrublet from the southeastern Alps. Prostrate branches from which wiry flowering stems arise. Small oval leaves, coarsely toothed near the tips. Small white flowers in clusters to 2 in (5 cm) wide, in summer. Zones 5–9.

Spiraea douglasii

WESTERN SPIREA

↔6 ft (1.8 m) ↑6 ft (1.8 m)

Suckering shrub mainly from northwestern USA, and naturalized in parts of Europe. Forms a thicket of red shoots. Oblong leaves have downy gray undersides. Produces purplish pink flowers in panicles, in mid-summer. Zones 4–10.

Spiraea fritschiana

KOREAN SPIREA

↔5 ft (1.5 m) ↑3 ft (0.9 m)

This mounding shrub is a native of Korea. Rather glaucous foliage, develops purplish tones in autumn. Large clusters of white flowers sometimes tinged pink, are borne in summer. Zones 4–9.

Spiraea hypericifolia

↔6 ft (1.8 m) ↑6 ft (1.8 m)

Shrub found from Europe to central Asia. Erect to arching and somewhat downy stems. Small leaves, bluish green, conspicuously veined beneath. Tiny creamy white flowers in small clusters, in spring. Zones 5–9.

Spiraea japonica

JAPANESE SPIREA

↔4 ft (1.2 m) ↑6 ft (1.8 m)

Upright shrub from Japan, China, and Korea. Lance- to egg-shaped leaves. Pink flowers, in clusters, in summer. S. j. var. albiflora, pale green leaves, white flowers. S. j. **'Anthony Waterer'**, purplish red flowers; **'Bullata'**, dwarf slow-growing shrub, deep pinkish red flowers; **'Bumalda'**, dwarf form, leaves can be variegated pink and off-white; **'Crispa'**, purplish pink flowers; **'Dart's Red'**, bright pink flowers; **'Fire Light'**, ovate leaves, purple-pink flowers; **'Gold Charm'**, golden to chartreuse leaves; **'Gold Mound'** ★, golden leaves turn chartreuse; **Golden Princess/'Lise'**, foliage ages from bronze to yellow; **'Goldflame'**, orange autumn leaves, red flowers; **'Limemound'**, leaves initially yellow, becoming lime green, russet in autumn, pink flowers; **'Little Princess'**, pink flowers; **Magic Carpet/ 'Walbuma'**, bronze-red leaves turn chartreuse, pink flowers; **'Monhub'**, dwarf shrub, light green leaves; **'Nana'**, dwarf, dark pink flowers; **'Neon Flash'**, lance-shaped leaves, pink flowers; **'Shirobana'**, red buds open to deep pink and white flowers. Zones 3–10.

Spiraea miyabei

↔3 ft (0.9 m) ↑3 ft (0.9 m)

Small upright shrub, native to Japan. Somewhat angled branches. Pointed oval, deep green leaves. Small white flowers borne in crowded heads, in summer. Zones 6–9.

Spiraea nipponica

NIPPON SPIREA

↔6 ft (1.8 m) ↑6 ft (1.8 m)

This vigorous bushy shrub is native to Japan. The leaves are oval or inversely egg-shaped, with teeth at tip. White flowers borne in clusters at the ends of the branches, in mid-summer. ***S. n.* var. *tosaensis,*** smaller leaves; many sold under this name are the cultivar 'Snowmound'. ***S. n.* 'Halward's Silver'**, smaller form than species, produces abundant white flowers; **'Rotundifolia'**, broader leaves, rather larger flowers than most of other cultivars; and **'Snowmound'**, green leaves, tinted blue. Zones 5–10.

Spiraea prunifolia

BRIDAL WREATH SPIREA, SHOE BUTTON SPIREA

↔7 ft (2 m) ↑7 ft (2 m)

Rounded bush, native to China. Usually grown in the form **'Plena'**, dense shrub with egg-shaped leaves, edged with very small teeth, which turn reddish orange in autumn. Double white flowers, in closely packed clusters, in spring. Zones 4–10.

Spiraea 'Snow White'

SNOW WHITE SPIREA

↔7 ft (2 m) ↑6 ft (1.8 m)

Vigorous shrub, arching branches. Pale green foliage developing attractive yellow tones, in autumn. Smothered in white flowers, in late spring. This cultivar is believed to have originated as a cross between *S. trichocarpa* and *S. trilobata*. Zones 3–9.

S

Spiraea thunbergii

THUNBERG SPIREA

☼ ✱ ↔7 ft (2 m) ↕5 ft (1.5 m)

Shrub, native to China, extensively naturalized in Japan. Thin hairy stems, narrow hairless leaves, toothed margins. White flowers in small clusters, occur in spring. **'Okon'**, early flowering, the pale yellow leaves fading to pale green. Zones 4–10.

Spiraea tomentosa

HARD HACK, STEEPLEBUSH

☼ ✱ ↔7 ft (2 m) ↕7 ft (2 m)

Robust, thicket-forming, upright shrub from eastern USA. Young stems, with brown velvety coating; tooth-edged leaves, downy yellow-gray undersides. Crimson flowers, in dense panicles, in late summer. Zones 4–10.

Spiraea trilobata

THREE-LOBED SPIREA

☼ ✱ ↔4 ft (1.2 m) ↕4 ft (1.2 m)

Spreading shrub, ranging from Central Asia to northern China and Siberia. Dense twiggy habit. Small rounded leaves, coarsely toothed, bluish green. Tight umbels of small white flowers dot branches profusely, in summer. **'Fairy Queen'**, more compact, floriferous, leaves more lobed; **'Swan Lake'**, compact shrub, attracts butterflies. Zones 6–9.

Spiraea × *vanhouttei*

BRIDAL WREATH SPIREA, VAN HOUTTE SPIREA

☼ ✱ ↔4 ft (1.2 m) ↕6 ft (1.8 m)

Robust form, a hybrid shrub between *S. cantoniensis* and *S. trilobata*. Leaves inversely egg-shaped to diamond-shaped, lobed toothed edges. White flowers in dense umbels, in mid-summer. Zones 5–11.

SPOROBOLUS

DROPSEED, RUSHGRASS

This genus of about 100 perennial or annual species, widely distributed and naturalized, belongs to the grass (Poaceae) family. Finely textured, hair-like, medium green leaves, 8–24 in (20–60 cm) long, typically form a dense arching mound, to 15 in (38 cm) tall and 18 in (45 cm) wide. The leaves turn golden to orange in autumn, fading to light bronze in winter. Open branching panicles, 12–27 in (30–70 cm) long, of small stalked spikelets, carry a single fragrant flower with pink and brown tints, on slender stems that rise well above the foliage, from late summer to autumn. Tiny spherical seeds drop from their hulls in autumn. Cultivated as ornamentals and for livestock and wildlife feed.

CULTIVATION: They are slow to establish but easily grown in a wide range of dry to medium-wet, well-drained soils in full sun. They are tolerant to drought. Propagate from seed.

Sporobolus heterolepis

PRAIRIE DROPSEED

☼ ✱ ↔12–16 in (30–40 cm) ↕24–36 in (60–90 cm)

North American prairie grass. Very fine bright green leaves, vivid orange in autumn. Airy, open, buff flower plumes on wiry stems, in summer. Drought tolerant once established. Zones 3–9.

SPREKELIA

This single-species genus in the amaryllis (Amaryllidaceae) family is native to the dry winter/wet spring and summer climates of Central and South America. In cultivation, however, these bulbous perennials seem quite happy to sit in damp but well-drained situations during the winter months. These highly adaptable plants are easily grown and will adjust their lifestyles to many different conditions, thriving on neglect and producing a generous supply of large red flowers in almost frost-free climates.

CULTIVATION: They flower best in well-established clumps and resent root disturbance. In frost-prone climates, *Sprekelia* can be pot-grown, providing the pots are moved into protected conditions during the colder months. When in growth they should be well drained, watered regularly, and given a weak liquid feed every 10 days. Propagate from offsets taken in autumn, and by sowing seeds as soon as they ripen.

Sprekelia formosissima

Sprekelia formosissima ★

AZTEC LILY, JACOBEAN LILY, ST JAMES LILY

☼/◐ ❄ ↔8 in (20 cm) ↕12 in (30 cm)

Winter dormant or almost evergreen depending on conditions. Leaves strap-like, forming dense clumps. Flowers showy, solitary, 6-petalled, 3 upright and 3 pointing downward, dark red to orange-red. Flowering varies between late winter and summer. Zones 7–10.

STACHYS

BETONY, HEDGE NETTLE, WOUNDWORT

About 300 species are in this genus in the mint (Lamiaceae) family, and they range from stoloniferous and rhizomatous perennials through to a few evergreen shrubs. In the wild these plants can be found in a range of situations, from dry mountain areas through to scrub areas, wastelands, meadows, and streamsides, particularly in northern temperate zones. The hairy, soft to touch, lance-shaped sometimes round leaves vary in color from pale silvery grays to greens. Flowers are tubular, sometimes hooded, and vary from red, pink, and purple through to white and yellow. The foliage is often aromatic, lending itself to many uses in the ornamental garden. *S. officinalis,* known then as wood betony, was revered for its curative properties by ancient Greek physicians and in the Middle Ages.

CULTIVATION: *Stachys* species require well-drained open soil in full sun. They will not cope very well in shade or humid areas. Propagate from seed in spring and autumn or softwood cuttings when material is available.

Stachys byzantina

Stachys albotomentosa

☼ ❄ ↔16 in (40 cm) ↕27 in (70 cm)

Low-growing shrubby perennial from Mexico. Distinctly textured, elongated, heart-shaped leaves; the undersides of the foliage and stems covered in fine white down. Produces salmon-orange flowers, in summer. Zones 8–10.

Stachys byzantina

syns *Stachys lanata, S. olympica*

LAMBS' EARS, WOOLLY BETONY

☼ ✱ ↔24 in (60 cm) ↕18 in (45 cm)

Ground-hugging perennial found from the Caucasus region to Iran. Oblong to elliptical gray-green leaves covered in silvery white down. Soft to touch, with upright stems of pink to purple flowers, in late spring–early summer. **'Cotton Boll'** ★ (syn. 'Sheila McQueen'), longer leaves, modified cottonball-like flowers. Zones 4–8.

Stachys citrina

☼ ✱ ↔12 in (30 cm) ↕8 in (20 cm)

This spreading, low-growing, woody perennial is a native of Turkey. Ovate, minutely serrated, delicately downy, soft green leaves. The yellow flowers, to 1 in (25 mm) wide, are borne on spikes, in summer. Zones 5–7.

Stachys citrina

Stachys macrantha

Stachys coccinea

Staphylea bumalda

Stachys coccinea

SCARLET HEDGE NETTLE

↔ 18 in (45 cm) ↑ 24 in (60 cm)

Mounding perennial species found from Arizona and Texas, USA, to Mexico. Ovate to lance-shaped, slightly downy, crinkly, mid-green leaves. Upright stems of scarlet-pink flowers, are produced from mid-spring through to late autumn. Zones 7–9.

Stachys macrantha

syns *Stachys grandiflora, S. spicata*

BIG BETONY

↔ 12–18 in (30–45 cm) ↑ 18–24 in (45–60 cm)

Upright hairy perennial from northeastern Turkey and northwestern Iran. Rosettes of wide, ovate, crinkly, veined, dark green leaves, to 3 in (8 cm) long. The spikes of hooded dark cerise-purple flowers, 1¼ in (3 cm) wide, are produced on erect stems, in summer. The cultivar **'Superba'** has bright cerise-purple flowers. Zones 5–7.

Stachys officinalis

syn. *Stachys betonica*

BISHOP'S WORT, WOOD BETONY

↔ 18–36 in (45–90 cm) ↑ 12–36 in (30–90 cm)

Perennial from Europe. Upright, almost completely hairless, oblong, wrinkled, mid-green leaves to 5 in (12 cm) long. Erect stems of oblong flower spikes carrying purple, reddish pink, or white flowers are produced in early summer–early autumn. **'Alba'**, white flowers; **'Rosea Superba'**, rose pink flowers. Zones 5–8.

Stachys sylvatica

HEDGE WOUNDWORT

↔ 16–48 in (40–120 cm) ↑ 36 in (90 cm)

A creeping perennial from western Asia. Not widely used in gardens owing to its unpleasant smell. Hairy green leaves and stems. White flowers, with reddish purple markings, in summer–autumn. Zones 5–8.

Stachyurus praecox

STACHYURUS

Subject to recent revisions, this genus includes 6 to 10 species of deciduous shrubs and trees from the Himalayan and temperate East Asian region. While generally not spectacular plants and somewhat like *Corylopsis*, though in a different family—the Stachyuraceae—they have the attraction of blooming in late winter and early spring, before or just as the leaves are developing. They produce drooping racemes of small cream to pale yellow flowers at every leaf bud. The leaves are lance-shaped and are usually around 6 in (15 cm) long. CULTIVATION: *Stachyurus* species prefer a humus-rich, well-drained, acidic soil in sun or light shade. They are not hardy in the coldest regions but thrive in areas with distinct yet relatively mild winters. Hard late spring frost may damage the flowers and young leaves. Propagate from seed or from half-hardened cuttings.

Stachyurus praecox

↔ 6–12 ft (1.8–3.5 m) ↑ 6–12 ft (1.8–3.5 m)

Shrub, native of Japan. Branches somewhat tiered, reddish-brown stems bear 6 in (15 cm) long leaves, which color slightly in autumn. Gracefully drooping racemes of small pale yellow flowers, in late winter–early spring, before the foliage. Zones 7–10.

STAPHYLEA

BLADDERNUT

This genus, belonging to the bladdernut (Staphyleaceae) family, of around 11 species of deciduous shrubs and small trees, is found over much of the northern temperate zone. They have large trifoliate to pinnate leaves, and long leaflets with serrated edges tapering to a point. Panicles of pale pink to white flowers are produced at the ends of branches, mainly in spring, followed by the 2- to 3-lobed inflated seed pods that give the genus its common name. The seed pods dry and brown as they ripen. The foliage may develop attractive autumn tones. CULTIVATION: Mostly very hardy, bladdernuts thrive in nearly all well-drained moist soils in full sun or partial shade. The bushes tend to form a thicket, or if pruned after flowering they can be thinned to one or a few main stems and made tree-like. Propagate from seed or summer cuttings; rooted suckers can sometimes be removed and grown on.

Staphylea bumalda

JAPANESE BLADDERNUT

↔ 6 ft (1.8 m) ↑ 7 ft (2 m)

Deciduous shrub, native to Japan. Leaves trifoliate, lance-shaped leaflets, sharply serrated edges, down on underside veins. Panicles of white flowers, in spring. Pods are 1 in (25 mm) wide, 2-lobed. Zones 4–9.

Staphylea colchica

CAUCASIAN BLADDERNUT

↔ 10 ft (3 m) ↑ 10–15 ft (3–4.5 m)

Deciduous shrub from the Caucasus region. Leaves with 3 to 5 glossy green, finely toothed leaflets. Flowers to ½ in (12 mm) wide, white, fragrant. Seed pods are 3-lobed, 3 in (8 cm) across. **'Colombieri'**, ovate, finely serrated, light green leaves. Zones 6–9.

Staphylea holocarpa

CHINESE BLADDERNUT

↔ 10 ft (3 m) ↑ 15 ft (4.5 m)

Chinese native, shrub or tree. Trifoliate leaves, leaflets with hairy undersides. Flowers, in drooping panicles, open white from pink buds. Pods around 2 in (5 cm) wide. Zones 6–9.

Staphylea pinnata

EUROPEAN BLADDERNUT

↔ 15 ft (4.5 m) ↑ 15 ft (4.5 m)

Temperate Eurasian shrub. Leaves with 3, 5, or 7 leaflets taper to a fine point, serrated edges, glaucous undersides. Flowers white, red-tipped sepals, in late spring. Seed pods 1 in (25 mm) wide. Zones 6–9.

Staphylea trifolia

BLADDERNUT, EASTERN BLADDERNUT

↔ 15 ft (4.5 m) ↑ 15 ft (4.5 m)

Shrub from the eastern USA. Leaves trifoliate, 2–3 in (5–8 cm) long leaflets, finely pointed, sharply serrated edges, fine hairs beneath, change color in autumn. White flowers 1½ in (35 mm) wide, borne in short panicles; 3-lobed fruit. Zones 5–9.

STAUNTONIA

Genus of up to 16 species of evergreen and deciduous twining and climbing plants, belonging to the chocolate-vine (Lardizabalaceae) family. From East Asia, these plants are now naturalized in many other countries. Quick-growing and very ornamental plants, they are frequently chosen for their handsome palmate foliage and fragrant bell-like flowers. They are only hardy outdoors in milder areas, tolerating temperatures down to about 15°F (–10°C) when fully dormant. The young growth in spring, however, can be damaged by late frosts. They are cultivated for their edible fruits in some countries, such as Japan.

Stauntonia hexaphylla

CULTIVATION: They require a well-drained, moisture-retentive soil in a sheltered position and grow best if the roots are in a shady position and the top is grown into the sun. Propagate from seed in early spring, but note that seed can take 18 months to germinate.

Stauntonia hexaphylla ★

↔10–17 ft (3–5 m) ↑35 ft (10 m)

Quick-growing climber from South Korea and Japan. Dark green leathery leaves. Fragrant white flowers tinged with violet, appear in spring–summer. Zones 7–11.

STENOCEREUS

A genus of 23 disparate species of columnar to tree-like cactus (Cactaceae) family members from southwestern USA, Central America, the Caribbean, Venezuela, and Colombia. The name comes from the Greek *stenos*, narrow, and refers to the many thin ribs of many of the species. The genus now includes all species previously classified as *Rathbunia* and *Machaerocereus*, and most of *Lemaireocereus*. These plants have stout, cylindrical, mostly green stems with numerous ribs. They may or may not have tubercles and the areoles may be woolly, but a common feature is very strong spines. Flowers are bell-shaped to funnelform, opening at night, lasting into the next day. Pericarpels are short, with many areoles, often spiny. Seed pods are spherical, fleshy, with deciduous spines.
CULTIVATION: Grow in a rich well-drained soil. Propagate from seed or cuttings dried out for a week or two. Rest in winter.

Stenocereus eruca

syns *Lemaireocereus eruca, Rathbunia eruca*

CATERPILLAR CACTUS, CREEPING DEVIL

↔17–20 ft (5–6 m) ↑3–10 ft (0.9–3 m)

Prostrate plant from Mexico. Forms tangled mats of heavily spined dark green stems, 10 to 12 ribs. Spines have 1 to 3 stout, flattened, dagger-shaped, gray centrals, 10 to 15 rounded, whitish radials. Flowers few, nocturnal, salverform, pinkish white to cream. Seed pods spherical. Zones 9–10.

Stenocereus thurberi

syns *Lemaireocereus thurberi, Marshalloceresus thurberi, Rathbunia thurberi*

ORGAN PIPE CACTUS

↔3–15 ft (0.9–4.5 m) ↑3–25 ft (0.9–8 m)

Large cactus from the USA and Mexico. Numerous columnar gray-green branches, 10 to 20 ribs, usually lacking trunk. Spines have 1 to 3 gray centrals, 7 to 9 gray radials. Flowers nocturnal, funnelform, white. Seed pods edible. Zones 9–10.

STENOMESSON

There are about 30 species of bulbous perennials in this genus, which belongs to the amaryllis (Amaryllidaceae) family. Most are uncommon in cultivation. They come from South America where they are found on high rocky slopes and in the meadows of the Andes in Peru, Bolivia, and Ecuador, where snow sometimes provides the protection from frost that these plants require. The genus name comes from the Greek *stenos*, narrow, and *mesos*, middle, referring to the plant's narrow perianth.
CULTIVATION: Easily grown outside in frost-free climates, these plants can be cultivated under glass in colder climates provided temperatures do not fall below 44–50°F (7–10°C). Bulbs should be kept slightly moist when dormant in winter. Propagate from offsets or fresh seed sown ripe in sand.

Stenomesson miniatum ★

↔6 in (15 cm) ↑12–16 in (30–40 cm)

Almost evergreen in some conditions or winter dormant. Leaves dark green, narrow, strap-like. Flowers orange to red, umbels of drooping tubular bells, on straight stalks, in spring–summer. Anthers creamy yellow, protruding. Zones 8–10.

Stenocereus thurberi

STENOTAPHRUM

This genus of 7 annual or perennial mat-forming species is native to tropical or subtropical regions. These members of the grass (Poaceae) family have creeping or rising stems, rooting at the nodes. Short flattened racemes at the ends of stems, growing from the leaf axils, bear spikelets of 2 stalkless flowers on upright or sprawling, solid, flattened stems. The leaves can be thick, flat, or folded, and narrow to sword-shaped. They grow from the stems with a sheath at the base, with the leaf blade held at right angles to the stem. One species, *S. secundatum*, is used widely for lawns in the southern USA.
CULTIVATION: These plants prefer partial shade and moist soil. Propagate from cuttings.

Stenomesson miniatum

Stenotaphrum secundatum

BUFFALO GRASS, GRAMA, ST AUGUSTINE GRASS

↔2–16 in (5–40 cm) ↑2–16 in (5–40 cm)

Hardy creeping perennial grass, native to tropical regions. Widely grown as a warm-season lawn grass. Forms fans of smooth, flat, or folded, narrow, oblong leaves, to 6 in (15 cm) long. Stiff one-sided spikes, to 6 in (15 cm) long, green stalkless spikelets. **'Variegatum'**, leaves striped pale green and ivory, suited to indoor culture. Zones 9–11.

STEPHANANDRA

Genus of 4 species of deciduous shrubs in the rose (Rosaceae) family, allied to *Spiraea*, and native to eastern Asia. Valued for their attractive, soft green, toothed and lobed leaves, which often have rich orange autumn tones. Panicles of white or pale green flowers, shaped like tiny stars, with a profusion of stamens, borne in summer.
CULTIVATION: They will grow in most soils in sun or part-shade, but prefer moist loam. Maintain shape by hard pruning in spring. Propagate in the autumn from cuttings or by division.

Stephanandra chinensis

↔8 ft (2.4 m) ↑10 ft (3 m)

Graceful deciduous shrub, native to China. Attractive, bright green, serrated leaves to 2½ in (6 cm) long, turning yellow-orange in autumn. Smooth pale brown branchlets are crowded with racemes of tiny white flowers. Zones 7–9.

Stephanandra incisa

CUTLEAFED STEPHANANDRA, LACE SHRUB

↔10 ft (3 m) ↑6 ft (1.8 m)

Dense shrub originating in Japan and Korea. Thin angular stems. Egg-shaped, deeply toothed, lobed leaves fade to yellow-green in autumn. Flowers in densely packed panicles, pale green to white, in mid-summer. **'Crispa'** ★, mound-forming dwarf, small wrinkled leaves, ideal ground cover. Zones 4–10.

Stenocereus eruca

Stephanandra incisa 'Crispa'

STEPHANOTIS

This genus of the dogbane (Apocynaceae) family is a group of 5–15 species of twining evergreen vines native to the African tropics. They have leathery elliptical leaves in opposite pairs on strongly twining stems. Flowers occur in heads that develop in the leaf axils and are white or cream and fragrant. Conspicuous seed pods follow and are filled with seed enclosed in fluffy down.
CULTIVATION: Intolerant of frost or drought but easily grown in a warm climate with moist, compost-rich, well-drained soil. Also very popular as greenhouse or conservatory plants, where the scent can be fully appreciated. Propagate from cuttings or layers. May also be raised from seed.

Stephanotis floribunda

BRIDAL VEIL, BRIDAL WREATH, MADAGASCAR JASMINE

↔10–20 ft (3–6 m) ↑6–15 ft (1.8–4.5 m)

Vigorous climber with thick, leathery, elongated oval, dark green leaves to 4 in (10 cm) long. Through summer it bears massed clusters of waxy, white, tubular bell-shaped flowers that are powerfully scented and popular as wedding flowers. Zones 10–12.

Stephanotis floribunda

STERNBERGIA

AUTUMN CROCUS, AUTUMN DAFFODIL

There are 7 to 8 species in this genus of bulbous perennials, which belong to the amaryllis (Amaryllidaceae) family. They come from the sparse woodlands and winter-rainfall climates of southern Europe and central Asia. Often confused with *Crocus*, they can be distinguished by their leaves, which do not bear the pale midrib of the true crocus. The goblet-like flowers, however, are recognizably crocus-like. The majority bloom in autumn. The genus take its name from Count Kaspar von Sternberg (1761–1838), a Austrian botanist and botanical author.
CULTIVATION: They do best when provided with sharp drainage, in summer heat, and a limy soil. While withstanding several degrees of short sharp frost, they are intolerant of wet soggy root conditions in frost-prone climates. In containers, use equal parts of loam, leaf mold, and sand. Water sparingly and only while in growth.

Sternbergia lutea ★

↔3 in (8 cm) ↑6 in (15 cm)

Found from southern Europe to central Asia. Leaves black-green, linear, appear with flowers, persist until spring. Flowers large, bright yellow, goblet-like, in autumn. **S. l. subsp. sicula** (syn. *S. sicula*) is smaller and has more open, starry flowers. Zones 7–9.

Sternbergia lutea

STEWARTIA

Related to and resembling *Camellia* in their flowers, the 9 species in this genus are from the camellia (Theaceae) family. Deciduous trees and shrubs of eastern North America and temperate East Asia, they are cultivated for their spring flowers, bright autumn foliage, and beautifully marked and colored bark, often at its best in winter. The leaves, around 3 in (8 cm) long, are simple and short-stemmed with serrated edges. The flowers, usually white and about 2 in (5 cm) wide, are carried singly or occasionally in clusters of 2 or 3 blooms. The bark often flakes away to reveal a range of colors.
CULTIVATION: Preferring cool, moist, well-drained, humus-rich soil and a position in sun or partial shade, most species are adaptable and will grow well in any position that does not dry out in summer. If it becomes necessary, trim plants after flowering. Propagate from stratified seed or from summer cuttings.

Stewartia malacodendron

SILKY CAMELLIA, VIRGINIA STEWARTIA

↔10 ft (3 m) ↑15–30 ft (4.5–9 m)

Shrub or small tree found in southeastern USA. Young shoots and new leaves rather downy. Leaves with finely toothed edges, downy beneath, color well in autumn. Flowers carried singly, blue-gray anthers on purplish filaments, in summer. Zones 7–9.

Stewartia pseudocamellia

Stewartia monadelpha

TALL STEWARTIA

↔20 ft (6 m) ↑50 ft (15 m)

Tree from Japan and Korea. Red-brown bark flakes to reveal light tones. Downy young shoots, leaves densely hairy on underside veins. Foliage turns vivid pinkish red in autumn. Flowers 1½ in (35 mm) wide, violet anthers. Zones 6–9.

Stewartia ovata

MOUNTAIN STEWARTIA

↔15 ft (4.5 m) ↑15–20 ft (4.5–6 m)

Shrub occurring in southeastern USA. Leaflets with sparsely toothed edges, downy undersides, turn yellow in autumn. Flowers 2 in (5 cm) long. S. o. var. grandiflora, flowers to 5 in (12 cm) wide, purple anthers. Zones 5–9.

Stewartia pseudocamellia ★

JAPANESE STEWARTIA

↔15 ft (4.5 m) ↑20–50 ft (6–15 m)

Widely grown Japanese species. Light reddish brown bark flakes freely, leaves with serrated edges, downy undersides, bright red in autumn. Flowers with frilly-edged petals, golden anthers, in spring. ***S. p.* var. *koreana***, broader leaves and larger flowers. Zones 5–9.

Stewartia pteropetiolata

↔12 ft (3.5 m) ↑20 ft (6 m)

Shrub or small tree, native to southern China and Korea; evergreen in mild winters. Toothed-edged leaves, small wing-like bracts on stalks. Small flowers, jagged-edged white petals, golden anthers, mid- to late summer. Zones 5–9.

Stewartia sinensis

CHINESE STEWARTIA

↔20 ft (6 m) ↑15–30 ft (4.5–9 m)

From China. Flaking red-brown bark. Stems and leaves downy when young, leaves taper to fine point, serrated edges, purple-red in autumn. Fragrant flowers have yellow anthers. Zones 6–9.

Stigmaphyllon ciliatum

STIGMAPHYLLON

A genus in the family Malpighiaceae, of about 100 species of mainly woody climbers, some shrubby, others perennial, mostly from Central and South America and the Caribbean. Twining species wind their stems around their supports. The leaves are usually opposite and smooth-edged. The 5-petalled yellow flowers occur in open sprays. The seeds are attractive, with wings like those of a maple seed.
CULTIVATION: These plants need frost-free conditions in well-drained soil and a sunny aspect. In frost-prone areas grow in a warm greenhouse. Propagation is by cuttings or layering. Seed, if available, should be sown fresh.

Stigmaphyllon ciliatum

GOLDEN VINE

↔10–20 ft (3–6 m) ↑20–25 ft (6–8 m)

Evergreen twining climber found from Belize to Uruguay. Spearhead-shaped rich green leaves. Flowers flat, 1¾ in (4 cm) across, petal edges undulating, rich bright yellow, in late summer–autumn. Zones 10–12.

Stigmaphyllon littorale

↔10–20 ft (3–6 m) ↑20–35 ft (6–10 m)

Tall Brazilian climber. Leaves to 5 in (12 cm) long, variable shape. Open sprays of bright yellow flowers to 1 in (25 mm) across, in late summer–autumn. Zones 10–11.

STIPA

FEATHER GRASS, NEEDLE GRASS, SPEAR GRASS

This is a wide and varied genus in the grass (Poaceae) family, containing about 200 species of tufted evergreen and deciduous grasses. Occurring as native plants on slopes in the world's temperate and warm-temperate regions, some of these pretty grasses are now widely grown in ornamental

S

gardens. Many species formerly included in the genus *Stipa* are now reclassified under other genera such as *Austrostipa* and *Nassella*. *Stipa* species have fine-textured, linear, flat leaves that bear long panicles of feathery, often fluffy flowerheads. Some are grown for floral work, and they are often used in garden perennial borders and for roadside plantings.
CULTIVATION: These grasses need a fertile, medium to light soil in full sun. Trim back deciduous species in winter to ensure good growth the next season. Propagate by division in summer or sow seed in containers in spring.

Stipa arundinacea
NEW ZEALAND WIND GRASS
↔4 ft (1.2 m) ↑3 ft (0.9 m)
Mid-sized New Zealand grass. Light green arching foliage, turns light orange with bronzy tones in sunlight. Spikelets of fluffy green flowers, tinted purple, appear in summer–autumn. Zones 8–10.

Stipa calamagrostis ★
syn. *Stipa lasiogrostis*
↔4 ft (1.2 m) ↑3 ft (0.9 m)
Deciduous perennial grass, native to southern Europe. Forms tufted clump. Linear blue-green leaves arch slightly during the season. Bears creamy silver plumes of nodding feathery flowers, in summer. Zones 7–10.

Stipa gigantea ★
GIANT FEATHER GRASS, GOLDEN OATS
↔4 ft (1.2 m) ↑8 ft (2.4 m)
Striking large perennial grass from Spain and Portugal. Clump of green to gray-green foliage. Large loose panicles of flowers and seeds, in spring, become golden, persist through summer. Zones 6–10.

Stipa splendens
↔4 ft (1.2 m) ↑8 ft (2.4 m)
Deciduous perennial grass from central Asia and Russia. Tufted mounded plant. Dark green leaves, slightly arching habit. Purple-tinted white flower spikes, in large loose panicles held above foliage, in summer. Zones 7–10.

Stokesia laevis 'Purple Parasols'

Stipa arundinacea

Stipa splendens

STOKESIA
STOKES ASTER
The single species in this genus in the daisy (Asteraceae) family has been extensively developed in cultivation and is available in a wide range of plant sizes, flower colors, and forms. A late summer- to autumn- flowering perennial from the southeastern USA, the Stokes aster is an upright plant with 6–8 in (15–20 cm) long leaves and large cornflower-like heads of white, yellow, or mauve to deep purple-blue flowers.
CULTIVATION: Plant in full sun or half-sun in light free-draining soil. Water and feed well. Watch for mildew in late summer. Propagate by division near the end of the dormant period or from seed.

Stokesia laevis
STOKES ASTER
↔8–16 in (20–40 cm)
↑10–30 in (25–75 cm)
Found from South Carolina to Louisiana and northern Florida, USA. Narrow, deep green, lance-shaped leaves, smooth-edged, sometimes spiny-toothed at the base. Flowerheads to 4 in (10 cm) wide, occur solitary or in small clusters, usually mauve to purple. **'Blue Danube'** ★, 16 in (40 cm) tall, deep blue with white center; **'Blue Parasols'**, very large lilac-blue flowerheads; **'Bluestone'**, 10 in (25 cm) tall, bright blue; **'Mary Gregory'**, pale yellow with a darker center; **'Purple Parasols'**, 20 in (50 cm) tall, deep violet-blue flowerheads to over 4 in (10 cm) wide; **'Silver Moon'**, 18 in (45 cm) tall, pure white; **'Wyoming'**, 20 in (50 cm) tall, very dark blue flowers. Zones 6–10.

STRELITZIA
Originating in South Africa, the 4 or 5 species in this genus are large evergreen perennials in the strelitzia (Strelitziaceae) family. Usually treated as shrubs or trees, they are clump-forming and have very long oblong to lance-shaped leaves that are borne on stout stalks. A large bud or spathe borne at the end of the stem is usually held clear of the foliage; from it opens a succession of flowers, each with a long projecting corolla and wing-like sepals, often in a striking range of contrasting colors.
CULTIVATION: They prefer full sun or partial shade, and are tender to all but the lightest frosts. Soil should be well-drained and moist, but most species will tolerate brief periods of drought once established and prefer to be kept on the dry side in winter. Roots are very strong, so take care when siting. Propagate from seed or by removing suckers. Division is possible.

Strelitzia juncea
syns *Strelitzia* × *kewensis* var. *juncea*, *S. reginae* var. *juncea*
↔3–5 ft (0.9–1.5 m) ↑5 ft (1.5 m)
Native to South Africa's Cape region. Thick, rush-like, grayish green leaves lack blades, tapering to point. Orange flowers emerging from beaked bract, like those of *S. reginae*. Zones 10–12.

Strelitzia nicolai
GIANT BIRD OF PARADISE, NATAL WILD BANANA
↔15 ft (4.5 m) ↑30 ft (9 m)
Found in KwaZulu-Natal and Eastern Cape, South Africa. Leaves and leaf stalks often over 4 ft (1.2 m) long. Flowers light greenish to purple-blue, white projecting corolla, open from red-brown spathes, in late spring–early summer. Zones 10–12.

Strelitzia nicolai

Strelitzia reginae
BIRD OF PARADISE
↔3 ft (0.9 m) ↑4 ft (1.2 m)
Widely grown shrubby evergreen perennial. Leaves 12–30 in (30–75 cm) long, stems to 6 ft (1.8 m) tall. Flowers have orange calyces, deep purple-blue corolla, over 4 in (10 cm) long, in winter–spring. **'Kirstenbosch Gold'** and **'Mandela's Gold'** ★, bright yellow calyces. Zones 10–12.

STREPTOSOLEN
This genus from the nightshade (Solanaceae) family is doubtfully distinct from *Browallia*. The single species is from tropical South America. It has a scrambling habit and simple alternate leaves. Popular in warm climates for its spectacular red to orange flowers.
CULTIVATION: Plant in a position in full sun with shelter from cold winds, in a light, fibrous, well-drained soil. This species should be well watered during dry weather. It is intolerant of frost. Frequent tip pruning in the first few years will help develop a densely foliaged bush and, thereafter, regular light pruning after flowering will maintain its shape. Soft-tip cuttings can be taken in late spring or summer, half-hardened cuttings in autumn.

Streptosolen jamesonii
syn. *Browallia jamesonii*
MARMALADE BUSH, ORANGE BROWALLIA
↔5 ft (1.5 m) ↑7 ft (2 m)
Evergreen shrub. Flexible branches, leaves simple, alternate, finely hairy, dark green, paler beneath. Inflorescence, dense panicle, 2 forms: one is a mixture of yellows and reds to orange, the other pure yellow flowers, in early to late spring. Zones 9–11.

Streptosolen jamesonii

Strobilanthes gossypinus

Strongylodon macrobotrys

STROBILANTHES

This genus of more than 250 species of evergreen or deciduous perennials and soft-stemmed shrubs is native to tropical Asia and Madagascar, and belongs to the acanthus (Acanthaceae) family. A few species are grown both indoors and out for their attractive tubular or funnel-shaped flowers, in varying shades of blue and purple. *Strobilanthes* species have colorful purplish foliage; the opposite paired leaves are frequently of unequal size. CULTIVATION: Frost tender, these plants require a warm climate and prefer full sun or semi-shade in well-drained humus-enriched soil. Prune lightly to shape, or clip to form a hedge. The new growth has the most attractive coloring. Propagate from seed, cuttings, or by division.

Strobilanthes anisophyllus

GOLDFUSSIA

↔ 5 ft (1.5 m) ↑ 5 ft (1.5 m)

Bushy shrub native to Assam in northern India. Narrow silvery purple leaves in unequal-sized pairs. Tubular flowers, lavender-blue, 1 in (25 mm) long, ends of branches, in late summer–autumn. Zones 10–11.

Strobilanthes dyerianus

syn. *Perilepta dyeriana*

↔ 3 ft (0.9 m) ↑ 3 ft (0.9 m)

Originally a native of Myanmar. Evergreen shrub grown mostly as an indoor plant for its attractive foliage. Lance-shaped iridescent purple leaves, to 6 in (15 cm) long, toothed edges. Bears short spikes of funnel-shaped, pale blue flowers, above the leaves, in spring–summer. Zones 10–12.

Strobilanthes gossypinus

↔ 20–30 in (50–75 cm)
↑ 3–5 ft (0.9–1.5 m)

Shrubby species native to southern India and Sri Lanka. Green leaves, 2–4 in (5–10 cm) long, lance-shaped, tapering to a fine point, densely coated with cream hairs. Small heads of soft blue to lavender flowers clustered at the stem tip and in the upper leaf axils, in summer. Zones 10–12.

STRONGYLODON

This genus, comprising 12 species of vigorous evergreen or deciduous shrubs or twining climbers, is native to tropical areas from the island of Madagascar eastward to Polynesia but is especially numerous in the Philippines. It belongs to the pea-flower subfamily of the legume (Fabaceae) family. The compound leaves consist of 3 leaflets. Pea-flowers are borne in long, spectacular racemes; the seed pods are large and do not split open at maturity. CULTIVATION: Grow outside in the tropics, in a heated greenhouse in temperate areas. Plants raised from seeds are slow to reach flowering size; air-layering or propagation by cuttings gives quicker results.

Strongylodon macrobotrys

EMERALD CREEPER, JADE VINE

↔ 5–10 ft (1.5–3 m)
↑ 20–40 ft (6–12 m)

Tall woody climber from the Philippines. Dark green 3-part leaves, open pinkish bronze. Large, waxy, claw-like flowers, luminous bluish green or jade, in pendulous racemes, to 40 in (100 cm) long, in spring. Zones 11–12.

STYLOPHORUM

Genus, in the poppy (Papaveraceae) family, containing 3 species of hairy perennials, is native to eastern Asia and eastern North America where they grow in woodlands. When cut they ooze a yellow or red sap. The foliage is attractive, forming basal rosettes of long divided leaves, irregularly lobed and toothed. The stem leaves are much smaller and usually stalkless. Clear yellow or orange 4-petalled saucer-shaped flowers are borne in small clusters in spring. They are followed by narrow cylindrical seed pods covered in fine silvery hairs. The yellow sap from *S. diphyllum* was used by the American Indians in dye making. CULTIVATION: These are woodland plants suitable for shady positions in the garden. Unlike most plants in the poppy family, which resent disturbance, these plants can be readily transplanted, and will grow in any reasonably fertile moist but well-drained soil. Propagate from seed or by division.

Stylophorum diphyllum

CELANDINE POPPY, WOOD POPPY

↔ 12 in (30 cm) ↑ 18 in (45 cm)

Downy perennial native to eastern USA. Leaves deeply and irregularly lobed with scalloped or toothed margins. Simple yellow flowers, to 2 in (5 cm) wide, on delicate stems, in spring. Zones 5–9.

Stylophorum lasiocarpum

CHINESE CELANDINE POPPY

↔ 12 in (30 cm) ↑ 12 in (30 cm)

Perennial native to central and eastern China. Long irregularly lobed and toothed leaves. Clear yellow flowers, in clusters, 4–5 in (10–12cm) wide, in spring. Zones 5–9.

STYPHNOLOBIUM

A genus of 3 or 4 species of deciduous leguminous (Fabaceae family) trees that until recently were included in the genus *Sophora*. They have a widespread natural distribution, occurring in temperate East Asia, plus North and Central America. They have large pinnate leaves and in spring or summer produce sprays of pea-like flowers in cream to mauve shades. Conspicuous elongated seed pods follow. CULTIVATION: Tolerant of most conditions except prolonged drought. Best in full sun with moist well-drained soil. Propagation is from seed, which should be soaked thoroughly before sowing, by hardwood winter cuttings, or half-hardened late summer cuttings.

Styphnolobium japonicum

syn. *Sophora japonica*

CHINESE SCHOLAR TREE, PAGODA TREE

↔ 35 ft (10 m) ↑ 50 ft (15 m)

Deciduous tree from China and Korea, long cultivated in Japan. Smaller in cultivation. Leaves light to mid-green,

Stylophorum diphyllum

16 leaflets, downy undersides. Drooping panicles, 6–10 in (15–25 cm) long, fragrant creamy white flowers, in midsummer. Weeping habit of flowers emphasized in **'Pendula'**, also weeping foliage, usually grafted on upright standard trunk; **'Princeton Upright'** reaches 60 ft (18 m) tall; **'Regent'** ★, white flowers; **'Violacea'**, pale mauve-pink flowers. Zones 5–9.

STYRAX

Found over much of the northern temperate and subtropical zones, this genus gives its name to the storax (Styracaceae) family. It includes some 100 species of deciduous and evergreen shrubs and trees. Foliage is usually a simple rounded leaf with serrated edges, obvious veins, and a pointed tip. The leaves are usually small to medium-sized, but a few species have attractive, large, felted leaves. The flowers, which are usually fragrant, hang in clusters beneath the foliage of the previous season's wood. They are white, occasionally with a flush of pink, and open in spring to be followed by 1- to 2-seeded drupes. CULTIVATION: They prefer a cool moist climate with clearly defined seasons that is not too cold in winter. Hardiness varies with species' native range. Propagate from seed, which often needs stratification to germinate well, or by taking cuttings in summer.

Styphnolobium japonicum

Styrax americanus ★

☼ ❄ ↔ 8 ft (2.4 m) ↑ 10 ft (3 m)

Deciduous shrub from southeastern USA. Gray-brown branches, thinly coated with golden down when young. Dark green leaves usually elliptical, serrated edges, pale, downy undersides. Pendulous clusters, up to 4 flowers, in late spring. Zones 6–10.

Styrax grandifolius

BIG-LEAFED SNOWBELL

☼ ❄ ↔ 15 ft (4.5 m) ↑ 15 ft (4.5 m)

Deciduous large shrub or small tree native to southeastern USA. The leaves are large, and like the young stems and flower buds, have a downy coating. The undersides of the leaves are gray, yellowish elsewhere. Fragrant flowers are produced in racemes in the spring. Zones 8–10.

Styrax japonicus

JAPANESE SNOWBELL, JAPANESE SNOWDROP TREE, SNOWBELL TREE

☼ ❄ ↔ 15 ft (4.5 m) ↑ 20–30 ft (6–9 m)

Deciduous tree from Japan. Lightly branched. Downy young stems. Leaves glossy dark green, shallowly toothed edges. Short pendulous flower clusters, are produced in late spring–early summer. **'Fargesii'**, vigorous cultivar with larger leaves; **'Pink Chimes'**, pale pink flowers. Zones 5–9.

Styrax japonicus 'Fargesii'

Styrax obassia

BIG-LEAFED STORAX, FRAGRANT SNOWBELL

☼ ❄ ↔ 20 ft (6 m) ↑ 35 ft (10 m)

This is a beautiful tree native to Japan. Rounded oval leaves to 8 in (20 cm) long, dark green, very fine serrations, densely downy, beneath. Flowers, carried on 4–8 in (10–20 cm) long racemes, are produced in late spring. Zones 6–10.

SUCCISA

This genus belonging to the teasel (Dipsacaceae) family contains one species of perennial native to Europe, northern Africa, and western Asia, and naturalized in northeastern USA. Its natural habitat is wet grassy places in heath or open forest. The plant forms a basal rosette of oblong to lance-shaped leaves that are lightly downy. Slender flowering stems can be up to 40 in (100 cm) tall. The attractive pincushion flowers are usually dark purple, occasionally pink or white, and appear in late summer to autumn. CULTIVATION: Grow this plant in sun or part shade in moist soil. Suitable for planting informally in wildflower meadows. Mowing meadows should be delayed until late autumn to allow the plants to seed. Propagate by division or from seed.

Succisa pratensis

DEVIL'S BIT SCABIOUS

☼/◐ ❄ ↔ 6–12 in (15–30 cm) ↑ 12–40 in (30–100 cm)

Perennial with short rootstock and basal rosettes of narrow oblong leaves. Stem leaves narrower and sometimes toothed. Flowerheads to 1 in (25 mm) wide, appear from axils of purple-tipped leafy bracts, in summer–autumn. Zones 5–9.

Styrax japonicus

SUTERA

This genus of about 130 perennials and annuals from the foxglove (Scrophulariaceae) family originates from South Africa.They have become well known in recent years as hanging basket plants. Breeders all over the world have been working to produce new colors of these reliable plants. Small, rounded, toothed, green leaves sit on thin stems that hug the ground. Starry white, mauve, lilac, pink, or blue flowers sit face-up on the foliage and the plants can flower for up to 10 months of the year. CULTIVATION: Require free-draining fertile soil and are adaptable to sun and shade. During warmer months they need extra water to keep blooming. Propagate from stem cuttings in autumn or by sowing seed in spring.

Sutera cordata

syn. *Bacopa cordata*

☼ ❄ ↔ 20 in (50 cm) ↑ 3 in (8 cm)

Low-growing, ground covering perennial, pale green leaves all year. Pure white flowers with a delicate yellow eye appear almost year round in warm climates. **'Atlas Lavender'**, large lavender-pink flowers; **'Atlas White'**, large white flowers; **'Blue Showers'**, lilac to pale blue flowers; **'Lavender Showers'**, pale lavender star-shaped flowers; **'Snowflake'**, tiny white flowers in leaf axils; **'Snowstorm'** ★, large white flowers, more compact habit. Zones 9–10.

Succisa pratensis

Sutera cordata

SWAINSONA

Around 50 species of perennials and subshrubs from the pea-flower subfamily of the legume (Fabaceae) family; all but one species in this genus are Australian natives. They are leguminous and have small racemes of ridged pea-flowers, often red or pink, but also occur in mauve- or white-flowered forms. The foliage is pinnate, usually with many small leaflets often gray-green and covered in fine downy hairs. The flowering season varies: some species bloom in winter, others in spring–summer, and those from very arid areas burst into bloom after rain. CULTIVATION: Although some species tolerate very light frosts, most perform best in a mild frost-free climate in full sun. They vary in their soil requirements; those from hot arid areas prefer to be dry over winter, while those from cooler zones require constant moisture. Good drainage is also most important. Propagation is from seed, which needs to be soaked before sowing, or from half-hardened summer cuttings.

Swainsona galegifolia

☼ ❄ ↔ 6 ft (1.8 m) ↑ 24 in (60 cm)

Upright or trailing perennial or softwooded shrub from eastern Australia. Gray- to dark green pinnate leaves, 25 tiny leaflets edged with fine hairs. Pink, mauve, purple, white, reddish purple pea-flowers, appear in spring–summer. Zones 9–11.

SYAGRUS

syn. *Arecastrum*

This genus in the palm (Arecaceae) family consists of 32 species native to South America. Their fronds have a feathery appearance. Trunks may be single or clustered (some species are trunkless) and become smooth and ringed with age. Separate male and female flowers are produced in panicles on the same tree, followed by fibrous fleshy fruit. Some species are a source of palm kernel oil and wax. Most are suitable for growing in tropical and subtropical regions. *S. romanzoffiana* is suited to temperate areas. They may be grown as indoor plants but other palms from different genera are often better suited to indoor cultivation. CULTIVATION: Most are adaptable and very hardy once established. They perform best in a well-drained moderately fertile soil with adequate watering and added fertilizer. They tolerate seaside conditions and will grow in full sun to part-shade. Remove old fronds. Propagate from seed. These palms will transplant readily.

Syagrus romanzoffiana

Syagrus sancona

Syagrus flexuosa

ACUMA, PALMITO DO CAMPO

↔7–15 ft (2–4.5 m)
↑7–15 ft (2–4.5 m)

Solitary-trunked or clumping palm from Brazil. Crown of arching gray fronds. Narrow leaflets arranged in groups of 2 to 4 along stem. Flowering spikes borne within leaves. Zones 10–12.

Syagrus romanzoffiana ★

syns *Arecastrum romanzoffianum, Cocos plumosa*

COCOS PALM, QUEEN PALM

↔25 ft (8 m) ↑50 ft (15 m)

Palm native to Brazil. Gray trunk, thick head of deep green plume-like fronds to 15 ft (4.5 m) long. Cream flowers in panicles. The large heavy bunches of fat, orange, edible fruits, are highly favored by bats and insects. Zones 9–12.

Syagrus sancona

↔20 ft (6 m) ↑20–40 ft (6–12 m)

A rainforest palm native to South America. Single-trunked, with a graceful crown of arching fronds to 12 ft (3.5 m) long. Narrow leaflets arranged in groups of 2 to 4. Zones 10–12.

Symphoricarpos × *chenaultii* 'Hancock'

SYMPHORICARPOS

CORALBERRY, SNOWBERRY

Allied to the honeysuckles *(Lonicera)* the 17 deciduous shrubs in this genus from the woodbine (Caprifoliaceae) family are mainly found in North and Central America, with 1 species from China. They have opposite pairs of usually simple leaves with blunt rounded tips. The small white or pink flowers that appear in spring may be carried singly or in clusters. The fruit is really the dominating feature of most species. The berry-like drupes are near-spherical, and last well into the winter when they stand out clearly on the then leafless stems.

CULTIVATION: Most species are very frost hardy and prefer to grow in a distinctly seasonal temperate climate. They are not fussy about soil type as long as it is well drained, but will crop more freely if fed well and watered during dry spells. Plant in sun or partial shade and prune or trim to shape in winter after the fruit has past its best. Propagation is most often from winter hardwood cuttings.

Symphoricarpos albus ★

COMMON SNOWBERRY, SNOWBERRY

↔4–6 ft (1.2–1.8 m)
↑4–6 ft (1.2–1.8 m)

Shrub with slightly differing varieties over most of North America. Wiry stems, suckering habit. Clusters of small pink flowers, in spring. Berries, pale green at first, ripen to a strikingly pure white. ***S. a.* var. *laevigatus*** (syn. *S. rivularis*) native to western North America, upright habit, forms dense thickets, fruits more heavily than eastern forms. Zones 3–9.

Symphoricarpos × *chenaultii*

CHENAULT CORALBERRY

↔5 ft (1.5 m) ↑6–8 ft (1.8–2.4 m)

This is a garden hybrid between *S. microphyllus* and *S. orbiculatus*. Deciduous shrub, downy young stems, dark green leaves, glaucous, slightly downy beneath. Small spikes of pink flowers near branch tips, in summer. Red-and-white spotted or mottled fruits. **'Hancock'**, low spreading habit, rarely exceeds 20 in (50 cm) high. Zones 5–9.

Symphoricarpos mollis

↔3 ft (0.9 m) ↑3 ft (0.9 m)

From western USA. Compact shrub, velvety new stems and young leaves. Foliage downy on undersides. Inconspicuous pinkish white flowers, in the spring. White berries, ¼ in (6 mm) in diameter. Zones 7–9.

Symphoricarpos orbiculatus

CORALBERRY, INDIAN CURRANT

↔6 ft (1.8 m) ↑6 ft (1.8 m)

From eastern USA and Mexico. Dark green leaves, gray undersides, red tints in autumn. Flowers white, flushed pink, in summer. Small berries ripen from dull white to deep red, various colors on bush at one time. Zones 3–9.

SYMPHYOTRICHUM

MICHAELMAS DAISY

This daisy (Asteraceae) family genus now includes many popular garden plants that were formerly included in the genus *Aster.* There are some 90, mostly North American, species in the genus. They form dense clumps of upright stems clothed with simple linear to lance-shaped leaves, and from late summer through autumn they are topped with heads of small, brightly colored daisies, usually in pink to blue and purple shades.

CULTIVATION: These hardy perennials prefer well-drained soil that can be kept moist during the growing season. They need a sunny open position with good air movement to lessen the risk of mildew when flowering. Cut back to the ground once the stems have dried after flowering. Propagate by winter division or spring softwood cuttings.

Symphyotrichum ericoides

syn. *Aster ericoides*

↔20–32 in (50–80 cm)
↑32–40 in (80–100 cm)

Branching, bushy North American perennial with narrow leaves to 2½ in (6 cm) long. Blooms in summer and autumn with masses of small daisies on leafy flower stems. Many cultivars, of which **'Pink Cloud'**, to 3 ft (0.9 m) tall, with bronze new growth and small pink flowers, is typical. Zones 3–9.

Symphyotrichum laeve

syn. *Aster laeve*

↔2 ft (0.6 m)
↑3–4 ft (0.9–1.2 m)

Upright, autumn-flowering, North American perennial with purple-red stems and blue-green leaves to 5 in (12 cm) long. Branching sprays of lavender to purple flowers. Zones 4–9.

Symphyotrichum lateriflorum

syn. *Aster lateriflorus*

↔2–4 ft (0.6–1.2 m)
↑3–4 ft (0.9–1.2 m)

Upright to spreading, autumn-flowering, North American perennial. Basal leaves to 6 in (15 cm) long. Sprays of pink-centered white to lavender-pink flowers on downy, wiry stems. ***S. l.* var. *horizontalis,*** spreading variety with brown-centered cream flowers. ***S. l.* 'Prince'** is a typical cultivar and grows to 2 ft (0.6 m) tall, with bronze leaves and pink-centered white flowerheads. Zones 3–9.

Symphyotrichum novae-angliae

syn. *Aster novae-angliae*

↔2–4 ft (0.6–1.2 m)
↑4–5 ft (1.2–1.5 m)

Bushy, autumn-flowering perennial from eastern North America. Lance-shaped basal leaves to 5 in (12 cm) long. Dense sprays of yellow-centered soft purple flowerheads up to 1¾ in (4 cm) wide. **'Andenken an Alma Pötschke'**, 4 ft (1.2 m) tall, cerise pink flowers; **'Barr's Pink'**, 4 ft (1.2 m) tall with small, deep pink, double flowers; **'Harrington's Pink'**, 5 ft (1.5 m) tall with small, soft pink, semi-double flowers; **'Hella Lacy'**, 4 ft (1.2 m) tall with violet-blue flowers; **'Purple Dome'**, 18 in (45 cm) dwarf covered in purple flowers. Zones 2–9.

Symphyotrichum novi-belgii

syn. *Aster novi-belgii*

↔24–32 in (60–80 cm)
↑3–4 ft (0.9–1.2 m)

North American perennial similar to *S. novae-angliae* except that it is slightly shorter and its leaves are more noticeably toothed. Over 400 cultivars have been raised and include: **'Coombe Violet'**, 30 in (75 cm) tall, deep purple flowers; **'Ernest Ballard'**, 30 in (75 cm) tall, bright pink, named after famous hybridizer; **'Little Red Boy'**, 24 in (60 cm) tall, masses of bright cerise red flowers; **'Marie Ballard'**, 3 ft (0.9 m) tall, lavender blue, very fully double flowers; and **'Professor Anton Kippenberg'**, 15 in (38 cm) tall, lavender blue flowers. Zones 2–9.

Symphyotrichum oolentangiense

syn. *Aster oolentangiense*

↔2–3 ft (0.2–0.9 m) ↑5 ft (1.5 m)

Upright, summer- to autumn-flowering perennial from eastern North America. Leathery lance- to heart-shaped basal leaves, smooth-edged or toothed, to 5 in (12 cm) long. Sprays of small lavender blue or pink flowers. Zones 5–9.

Symphyotrichum pilosum

syn. *Aster pilosis var. pringlei*

↔3 ft (0.9 m) ↑4 ft (1.2 m)

Autumn-flowering perennial from North America. Fine linear leaves. Airy sprays of tiny white daisies. Species is seldom seen, more commonly grown is cultivar **'Monte Cassino'**, slightly smaller, heavier flowering, popular cut flower. Zones 5–9.

Symphyotrichum novae-angliae 'Andenken an Alma Pötschke'

Symphyotrichum novi-belgii cultivar

Symphyotrichum turbinellum

syn. *Aster turbinellus*

↔3 ft (0.9 m) ↑4 ft (1.2 m)

Branching, multi-stemmed, autumn-flowering perennial from eastern USA. Lance-shaped, 3 in (8 cm) long basal leaves fringed with fine hairs. Flowerheads 1 in (25 mm) wide, pink, singly on stems, in large numbers. Zones 5–9.

SYMPHYTUM

COMFREY, KNITBONE

This genus contains 35 species of hardy perennials belonging to the borage (Boraginaceae) family. Of temperate Eurasian origin, they favor damp woodlands, streamsides, and wasteland. Plants are characterized by vigorous growth and prolific flowering. A basal rosette of coarse tapering leaves emerges from a fleshy tap root. Clusters of small bell-shaped flowers, red-tipped in bud, reddish to blue in bloom, are arranged in 1-sided coils at the tips of branching stems. Hummingbirds are attracted to the flowers. Comfrey has a long history of use in the treatment of bruises and broken bones. If taken internally in quantity, it could be carcinogenic.

CULTIVATION: Comfreys favor damp soil and will grow in full sun or partial shade. They are adaptable to dry conditions where their growth is restrained. They can be grown in full sun in cold climates if the soil is heavy and moisture-retentive. Control and propagate by chopping out extra growth; cut back after blooming.

Symphytum asperum

PRICKLY COMFREY

↔5–7 ft (1.5–2 m) ↑4–5 ft (1.2–1.5 m)

From Europe, the Caucasus region, and Iran. Oval bristly leaves to 10 in (25 cm) long. Tubular flowers to ¾ in (18 mm) long, start pink, ageing to blue or lilac, in summer. Zones 5–10.

Symphytum 'Goldsmith'

Symphytum caucasicum

↔24–32 in (60–80 cm) ↑24–32 in (60–80 cm)

Native to the Caucasus region. Basal leaves mid-green, 10 in (25 cm) long. Flared trumpets of rich blue flowers to ½ in (12 mm) long, in summer. **'Eminence'**, smaller than the species leaves gray tinged, blue flowers produced in early summer. Zones 5–10.

Symphytum 'Goldsmith' ★

syns *Symphytum ibericum* 'Jubilee', *S. i.* 'Variegatum'

↔12–20 in (30–50 cm) ↑10–12 in (25–30 cm)

Spreading bristly perennial. Leaves to 10 in (25 cm) long, irregularly and broadly edged with yellow. Drooping blue and white flowers, to ¾ in (18 mm) long, open from pink buds, late spring–early summer. Zones 5–10.

Symphytum grandiflorum

↔20–24 in (50–60 cm) ↑15–16 in (38–40 cm)

From Europe and the Caucasus region. Bristly leaves to 10 in (25 cm) long. Trumpet shaped flowers open to pale yellow from red-tipped buds, in late spring–early summer. Zones 5–10.

Symphytum 'Hidcote Blue'

↔18–20 in (45–50 cm) 18–20 in (45–50 cm)

Hybrid with leaves to 10 in (25 cm) long. Red buds, pale blue trumpets, to ¾ in (18 mm) long, in late spring–early summer. Zones 5–10.

Symphytum officinale

COMFREY, COMMON COMFREY, ENGLISH COMFREY

↔6 ft (1.8 m) ↑5 ft (1.5 m)

Vigorous plant with rangy habit from temperate Eurasia. Bell-shaped flowers in drooping clusters, rose-purple crimson, mauve crimson, white, in late spring–early summer. **'Variegatum'**, non-invasive, leaf margins white. Zones 3–9.

Symphytum grandiflorum

Symphytum × *uplandicum*

syn. *Symphytum peregrinum*

RUSSIAN COMFREY

↔4 ft (1.2 m) ↑6 ft (1.8 m)

Bristly plant of garden origin, may be a natural hybrid of *S. officinale* and *S. asperum*. Heavy clusters of rose-purple flowers, late spring–late summer. Use as a background plant. Has been used for cattle fodder. **'Variegatum'**, lilac flowers, yellow edged mid-green leaves. Zones 3–9.

SYMPLOCOS

This genus gives its name to the family Symplocaceae. It consists of 250 species of trees and shrubs, some evergreen and some deciduous, occurring in woodlands in Asia, Australasia, and North and South America, in tropical and warm-temperate regions. Their leaves are simple and alternate. Some of the species accumulate aluminum in their tissues and these have yellow-green leaves and blue fruits. Other species have egg-shaped fruits that are black, purple, or white. The flowers are yellow or white and are borne in a variety of inflorescences.

CULTIVATION: Well-drained, acid to neutral soils are required, in a full sun position. The species in cultivation respond well to regular feeding. The frost tolerance varies between species, depending upon the climate of their original habitat. Propagation is from fresh seed or cuttings, both methods are quite reliable.

Symplocos paniculata

SAPPHIRE BERRY

↔15 ft (4.5 m) ↑15 ft (4.5 m)

Deciduous, bushy spreading shrub or small tree from eastern Asia and the Himalayas. Oval, slightly hairy, dark green leaves, toothed margins. Small, white, sweet-smelling flowers in clusters, in late spring–summer. Egg-shaped blue fruits. Zones 7–9.

Symplocos paniculata

SYNTHYRIS

KITTENTAILS

This genus belonging to the plantain (Plantaginaceae) family contains 14 species of perennials from northern and western North America, where they grow in woodland and alpine areas. Closely related to *Veronica*, they are low-growing, rhizomatous, tufted plants. The leathery leaves, which are heart-shaped, kidney-shaped, or deeply cut, become smaller and bract-like on the flowering stems. The flowers are blue or violet-blue with a short tube and 4 erect or spreading lobes.

CULTIVATION: Woodland species will tolerate quite poor soils such as those under deciduous trees but do best in a fertile well-drained soil with added organic matter in light shade. Alpine species require a sunny open site with protection from the hottest summer sun. Propagate from seed or division.

Synthyris missurica

◐/● ✱ ↔12 in (30 cm) ↑16–24 in (40–60 cm)

Tufted perennial native to northern and western North America. Dark green, leathery, heart-shaped to kidney-shaped, toothed leaves. Bright bluish purple tubular flowers in loose spikes are produced in spring–summer. **'Alba'**, white flowers. Zones 3–9.

Synthyris platycarpa

EVERGREEN KITTENTAIL

◐/● ✱ ↔6 in (15 cm) ↑6–12 in (15–30 cm)

Species native to Idaho, USA. Clumps of round leaves to 3 in (8 cm) wide, hairy with round-toothed margins. Flowering stems bear racemes of delicate, fringed blue flowers, in spring. Flattened, heart-shaped, capsular fruit. Zones 4–9.

Synthyris platycarpa

Synthyris missurica

Synthyris reniformis

SPRING QUEEN, SNOW QUEEN

◐/● ✱ ↔4 in (10 cm) ↑2–6 in (5–15 cm)

Species native to moist shady forest habitats in Washington and Oregon, USA. Round to heart-shaped leaves, shallowly lobed, paler beneath. Short racemes of bluish purple flowers, in early spring. Zones 6–9.

Synthyris stellata

● ✱ ↔6 in (15 cm) ↑10 in (25 cm)

Native to Washington and Oregon, USA. Round to heart-shaped deeply toothed leaves with starry appearance. Racemes of bluish purple tubular flowers are borne in spring–summer. Zones 6–9.

SYRINGA

LILAC

This genus, which a member of the olive (Oleaceae) family, is made up of 23 species of vigorous, deciduous, flowering shrubs, most of them native to northeast Asia, with 2 species only in Europe. Of the European species one, *S. vulgaris*, the common lilac, is known to have been grown in the gardens of western Europe since the sixteenth century; today, it is represented by more than 1,500 named cultivars. The plants have simple pointed elliptical to heart-shaped leaves in opposite pairs and produce upright panicles of small 4-petalled flowers, usually in spring. The flowers may be single or double, and occur in conspicuous clusters. Almost all are strongly sweet smelling, although not every cultivar is noted for its fragrance. *Syringa* species are among the most popular of the cool-climate shrubs.

CULTIVATION: Their main requirements are a well-drained soil and a position in sun or light shade; they thrive in a sandy gravelly soil, preferably one that is slightly alkaline, but do not do well in heavy clay. Propagate from seed, but the results may be variable. They can be grown from cuttings of the current year's growth, or by layering.

Syringa × *hyacinthiflora*

Syringa × *chinensis*

CHINESE LILAC

☼ ✱ ↔12 ft (3.5 m) ↑12 ft (3.5 m)

Collective name for group of hybrids between *S. laciniata* and *S. vulgaris*. Upright rounded bushes with slender branches. Medium to dark green oval leaves. Large panicles of flowers, white to pinkish lavender to reddish, highly fragrant, in late spring. **'Saugeana'** ★, reddish mauve flowers. Zones 4–9.

Syringa emodi

HIMALAYAN LILAC

☼ ✱ ↔12 ft (3.5 m) ↑15 ft (4.5 m)

From western Himalayas. Upright branches, leaves oblong to elliptical, half main vein tinged purple. Flowers tinged pinkish mauve in bud, open to white, in early summer. **'Aurea'**, clear golden yellow leaves. Zones 4–9.

Syringa × *hyacinthiflora*

AMERICAN HYBRID LILAC, EARLY FLOWERING LILAC, HYACINTH LILAC

☼ ✱ ↔15 ft (4.5 m) ↑15 ft (4.5 m)

Hybrids of *S. oblata* and *S. vulgaris*. Strong-growing heavy-blooming plants, single or double flowers in early spring. Ovate leaves often reddish bronze, purplish red tones in autumn. **'Blue Hyacinth'**, pale purple to light blue flowers; **'Charles Nordine'**, lilac-pink flowers; **'Laurentian'**, rose pink buds. Zones 4–9.

Syringa × *josiflexa*

☼ ✱ ↔7 ft (2 m) ↑8–10 ft (2.4–3 m)

Hybrid between *S. josikaea* and *S. k.* subsp. *reflexa*. Erect shrub, broadly lance-shaped leaves, magenta flowers in early summer. **'Anna Amhoff'** and **'Elaine'**, both with single white flowers; **'Bellicent'**, perfumed pink flowers; **'Lynette'** and **'Royalty'**, both with single purple flowers. Zones 5–9.

Syringa oblata subsp. *dilatata*

Syringa laciniata

CUT-LEAFED LILAC

☼ ✱ ↔10 ft (3 m) ↑12 ft (3.5 m)

Discovered in the Chinese Province of Gansu in 1915, one of the first of the oriental lilacs to be introduced into the West. Tall shrub, smooth-edged and cut leaves. Pale lavender flowers, small clusters along the branches, in spring. Zones 5–9.

Syringa meyeri

DWARF KOREAN LILAC, MEYER LILAC

☼ ✱ ↔4 ft (1.2 m) ↑5 ft (1.5 m)

Discovered in a garden near Beijing, China, in 1909, unknown in the wild. Low compact shrub, sturdy upright branches. Flowers, small clusters, pale lilac to lilac-purple, sometimes whitish lavender, in spring, repeat late summer to very early autumn. **'Palibin'**, smallest of all lilacs, around 4 ft (1.2 m) high, pinkish lavender flowers; **'Superba'**, deep pink flowers, fade with age, long flowering season. Zones 4–9.

Syringa oblata

BROADLEAF LILAC

☼ ✱ ↔10 ft (3 m) ↑12 ft (3.5m)

Native to China and Korea, like *S. vulgaris*, but flowers in mid-spring. Loose strongly fragrant panicles. ***S. o.* subsp. *dilatata***, heart-shaped leaves, fragrant pale purple flowers. Zones 5–9.

Syringa pekinensis

syn. *Syringa reticulata subsp. pekinensis*

CHINESE TREE LILAC, PEKING LILAC

↔ 12 ft (3.5 m) ↑ 15 ft (4.5 m)

Tall shrub or tree collected in the Beijing area, China, in 1742. Dark green leaves. Tiny flowerheads, creamy white, in mid-summer. Bark peels into papery curls with age. Zones 5–9.

Syringa × *prestoniae*

NODDING LILAC, PRESTON LILAC

↔ 12 ft (3.5 m) ↑ 12 ft (3.5 m)

Garden hybrid between *S. k.* subsp. *reflexa* and *S. villosa*. Dark green leaves, slightly glaucous, faintly downy undersides. Slightly drooping panicles of scented soft pink to light purple flowers, in early summer. **'Desdemona'**, rich purple-pink to blue flowers; **'Elinor'**, purple tinged buds open to mauve flowers; **'James MacFarlane'**, soft pink flowers, spreading habit to over 8 ft (2.4 m) wide. Zones 4–9.

Syringa protolaciniata

syn. *Syringa afghanica*

AFGHAN LILAC

↔ 40–48 in (100–120 cm) ↑ 40–48 in (100–120 cm)

Shrub native to northern Afghanistan and neighboring mountain areas. Dark slender stems, pinnate foliage. Narrow heads of small, fragrant, lavender flowers, in late spring. Zones 6–9.

Syringa pubescens

↔ 12 ft (3.5 m) ↑ 12 ft (3.5 m)

From China. Numerous slender branches. Flowers fragrant, buds, pale purple, mature to pale lilac with pinkish wash. ***S. p.* subsp. *julianae*** (syn. *S. julianae*), downy leaves, especially on undersides. ***S. p.* subsp. *microphylla*** (syn. *S. microphylla*), from western China, slightly shorter leaves, shorter panicles of more pinkish flowers in spring and earlier summer; **'Superba'**, heavy-flowering, slightly darker flowers over long season. ***S. p.* subsp. *patula*** (syn. *S. patula*) from northern China and Korea, larger leaves, purplish new growths; **'Miss Kim'**, darker pink buds. ***S. p.* subsp. *potaninii*** (syn. *S. potaninii*), downy leaves, flowers often very pale. ***S. p.* 'Excellens'**, white flowers, pale flesh pink buds; **'Sarah Sands'**, very pale mauve-pink flowers, more compact clusters. Zones 5–9.

Syringa reticulata

JAPANESE TREE LILAC

↔ 15 ft (4.5 m) ↑ 30 ft (9 m)

Tree lilac native to Japan. Round top. Large plumes of feathery white blooms with their protruding yellow anthers, in summer, contrast well with the dark green foliage. Flowers have strong fragrance. Bark reddish brown, peels on younger branches. **'Ivory Silk'**, abundant ivory flowers, blooms young. Zones 3–9.

Syringa pubescens subsp. *microphylla*

Syringa × *swegiflexa*

↔ 5 ft (1.5 m) ↑ 10 ft (3 m)

Garden hybrid between *S. k.* subsp. *reflexa* and *S. t.* subsp. *sweginzowii* Upright shrub, pointed oval leaves, downy undersides. Slender, pendent, many-flowered, red to dusky pink panicles to over 6 in (15 cm) long, in late spring. Zones 6–9.

Syringa villosa

↔ 12 ft (3.5 m) ↑ 12 ft (3.5 m)

Chinese species discovered in the Beijing mountains. Round-topped dense habit. Leaves oval, broad-elliptic to oblong, hairy. Pink buds, flowers pale lavender tinged pink, in late spring–early summer. Zones 4–9.

Syringa vulgaris

COMMON LILAC, FRENCH HYBRID LILAC

↔ 20 ft (6 m) ↑ 20 ft (6 m)

One of the 2 species native to Europe, with 14 subspecies reflecting geographic variations. Typical form has blue flowers, but cultivars can have deep purple and white flowers. Blooms appear in late spring–early summer.

Single-flowered cultivars include: **'Andenken an Ludwig Späth'**, dark reddish flowers; **'Charles X'**, crimson blooms in conical panicles; **'Congo'**, purple-red flowers, becoming lighter with age; **'Maréchal Foch'**, large bright purplish red flowers; **'Maud Notcutt'**, panicles of white blooms; **'President Lincoln'**, flowers are closest to true blue; **'Primrose'**, pale yellow flowers in small panicles; **'Sensation'**, purplish red blooms with white margins to the petals; **'Vestale'**, white flowers; **'Volcan'**, dark red to purple flowers.

Double-flowered cultivars include: **'Ami Schott'**, medium blue flowers with deeper tones; **'Ann Tighe'**, crimson-purple buds, pink flowers; **'Belle de Nancy'**, purplish red buds opening to pale purple-pink flowers; **'Charles Joly'**, dark purple-red blooms; **'Edith Cavell'**, pale yellow buds opening to white flowers; **'Madame Antoine Buchner'**, reddish pink to mauve flowers; **'Madame Lemoine'**, pale yellow buds opening to snow white flowers; **'Monique Lemoine'**, late-blooming white flowers; **'Mrs Edward Harding'**, deep purplish red flowers, shaded pink; **'Olivier de Serres'**, large panicles of lavender-blue flowers; **'Paul Thirion'**, red-purple buds becoming lovely lilac-pink flowers; **'Victor Lemoine'**, thin panicles of flowers ranging from lavender-pink to lilac-blue in color; and **'William Robinson'**, abundant pale pink flowers. Zones 4–9.

Syringa wolfii

syn. *Syringa formosissima*

↔ 12 ft (3.5 m) ↑ 15 ft (4.5 m)

Tall shrub originally from northeastern China and Korea. Bright green elliptic leaves. Large pyramidal inflorescence, 12 in (30 cm) long, lilac-colored flowers, slightly fragrant, in late spring. Color may vary from pale lavender to darker purple. Zones 4–9.

Syringa wolfii

Syringa vulgaris 'Olivier de Serres'

S

T

TABERNAEMONTANA

This genus of about 100 species of tropical and subtropical evergreen shrubs and small trees belongs to the dogbane (Apocynaceae) family and is grown for its gardenia-like flowers and attractive foliage. Found in the tropics and subtropics around the world, they have large glossy green leaves and waxy, usually white, funnel-shaped flowers with 5 wide-spreading curved petals. Flowers are borne throughout the warmer months and are fragrant, particularly at night. These plants have a milky sap and are recognized by the paired boat- to egg-shaped fruits joined to a common stalk.
CULTIVATION: These warm-climate, frost-tender plants require regular watering. They need good soil that is well-drained but moisture-retentive, in full sun or bright filtered light, and shelter from wind. Plants can be kept neat and bushy by lightly trimming. Propagate from seed or cuttings.

Tabernaemontana divaricata

syns *Ervatamia coronaria, E. divaricata*

CRAPE GARDENIA, CRAPE JASMINE, PINWHEEL FLOWER

↔5 ft (1.5 m) ↑6 ft (1.8 m)

Tropical evergreen shrub found from India to Yunnan Province, China, and parts of northern Thailand. May grow into a small bushy tree. Leathery elliptic leaves. Large, waxy, fragrant white flowers, in small clusters, in summer. Perfume more noticeable at night. **'Flore Pleno'**, double flowers with crowded petals. Zones 11–12.

Tagetes patula

TAGETES

MARIGOLD

All but one of the 50-odd species of this genus in the daisy (Asteraceae) family originates in the American tropics and subtropics. They are mainly upright annuals or perennials with dark green, sometimes aromatic, pinnate leaves with toothed edges. Their flowers are usually yellow or orange, and often daisy-like, with obvious ray and disc florets. In some forms the disc florets are largely hidden. The genus name, referring to the marigold's habit of just popping up from seed, comes from Tages, an Etruscan deity, and grandson of Jupiter, who was said to have sprung from the plowed earth.
CULTIVATION: They prefer a warm sunny position in light, well-drained soil. Water well and feed if the foliage begins to yellow. Deadhead frequently to ensure continuous blooming. Propagate from seed, which is usually started indoors in early spring.

Tagetes lucida

Tagetes tenuifolia 'Starfire'

Tagetes lemmonii

MEXICAN MARIGOLD, PERENNIAL MARIGOLD

↔3–6 ft (0.9–1.8 m)
↑2–5 ft (0.6–1.5 m)

Shrubby perennial marigold with dark green, very finely divided, ferny foliage. Small golden yellow flowerheads appear through winter into spring in mild areas, spring to early summer elsewhere. Zones 9–11.

Tagetes lucida

MEXICAN MINT, SPANISH TARRAGON, SWEET MACE

↔16–32 in (40–80 cm)
↑16–40 in (40–100 cm)

This perennial is naturally found in Mexico and Guatemala. It is woody-based, branching a little way up the stem. The lance-shaped leaves are toothed and pleasantly aromatic. Small bright golden yellow flowerheads are borne in late summer. Can be used as a tarragon substitute. Zones 9–11.

Tagetes patula

FRENCH MARIGOLD

↔6–12 in (15–30 cm)
↑8–20 in (20–50 cm)

Compact bushy annual from Mexico and Guatemala. Pinnate leaves with narrow, toothed, lance-shaped segments. Flowers solitary or in small clusters, usually yellow to orange in wild, in early summer–autumn. Garden forms available in many colors. Zones 11–12.

Tagetes tenuifolia

SIGNET MARIGOLD, STRIPED MARIGOLD

↔12–24 in (30–60 cm)
↑12–32 in (30–80 cm)

Annual found from Mexico to Colombia. Sometimes narrowly upright, usually bushy, with fine branches. The pinnate leaves are many toothed, with narrow lance-shaped segments. Abundant bright yellow flowerheads with short ray florets, in early summer to autumn. **'Starfire'** is a seedling mix which has various shades of yellow, orange, and red. Zones 11–12.

Tagetes, HC, Safari Series,'Safari Queen'

Tagetes Hybrid Cultivars

↔6–12 in (15–30 cm)
↑8–12 in (20–30 cm)

Mainly derived from *T. patula,* these popular border marigolds make ideal summer bedding plants. They are usually marketed as seedling series, in mixed or individual colors; mostly double flowers with few visible ray florets, predominantly in yellow, orange, and red shades. **Antigua Series,** flowerheads up to 3 in (8 cm) wide; **Atlantis Series,** pompon-like flowerheads up to 4 in (10 cm) wide; **Bonanza Series,** crested flowerheads up to 2 in (5 cm) wide; **Boy Series,** crested flowerheads to 1½ in (35 mm) wide; **Crush Series,** flowerheads nearly 4 in (10 cm) wide; **Disco Series,** many single flowers up to 2 in (5 cm) wide; **Durango Series,** semi-double to double, full color mix, to 2½ in (6 cm) wide; **'French Vanilla'** ★, fully double, cream, deep center, 3 in (8 cm) wide blooms on 24 in (60 cm) tall plants; **Gate Series,** double flowerheads up to 3 in (8 cm) wide; **Girl Series,** dwarf, double flowerheads; **Inca Series,** flowerheads reach up to 5 in (12 cm) wide; **'Jolly Jester'**, red petals with yellow striping; **'Lofty Lady'**, bright yellow, double, fragrant, heads to 4 in (10 cm) wide on 3–4 ft (0.9–1.2 m) tall plants; **'Naughty Marietta'** ★, single yellow flowers with red mid-band; **Safari Series,** double flowers to 3 in (8 cm) wide; **Zenith Series,** stocky and heavy foliage, double flowers to nearly 3 in (8 cm) wide. Zones 11–12.

TAIWANIA

The single conifer species in this genus, which belongs to the swamp cypress (Taxodiaceae) family, is related to *Cryptomeria.* It is native to Taiwan, with a variety being found in southwestern China and Myanmar. It is well known for the way the bark peels off in long strips. The foliage is bluish green, forming a rather cone-shaped crown on a very tall tree. The foliage becomes scaly with age and produces male and female cones in shades of brown. On some varieties, the cones can be in shades of gray and green.
CULTIVATION: This species prefers a sheltered sunny position in an acid soil that is moist but well drained. Propagate from seed.

Taiwania cryptomerioides

↔35 ft (10 m) ↑180 ft (55 m)

Tree much smaller in cultivation. Bark exfoliates in strips; conical or columnar crown. Variable bluish green foliage, narrow and pointed on juvenile plants, scale-like on adults. Small brown male and female cones, in summer. *T. c.* var. *flousiana*, from China and Myanmar, cones grayish green stained with maroon. Zones 8–11.

TALINUM

This group of over 40 species of succulent shrubs or herbs from Africa and the Americas forms the type genus of the Talinaceae family. The plants usually have deciduous leaves and branches arising from a perennial tuber or caudex. Leaves are alternate, often irregularly spaced, variously flat to cylindrical, more or less succulent and often soft and limp. Flowerheads are often solitary and usually held at the tips of the stems. The flowers come in various colors and open once, often for only a few hours, some setting seed without opening. The seed pod is a 3-chambered, spherical to oval capsule. Some have established themselves as introduced weeds.
CULTIVATION: These plants are extremely easy to grow in any well-drained soil. Most mature plants will readily set seed, which may germinate in surrounding pots or soil. Underground roots may be raised for display. Propagate from seed.

Talinum paniculatum

JEWELS OF OPAR

↔16–20 in (40–50 cm)
↑40 in (100 cm)

Variable perennial herb found from southern USA to central Argentina, naturalized throughout tropics and subtropics. Leaves elliptical to oblong. Flowerheads weakly branched; flowers small with 5 petals, pink, yellow, or white, in spring–summer. Seed pods yellow. Often a weed. Zones 6–11.

TANACETUM

This genus of about 70 annuals and perennials belonging to the daisy (Asteraceae) family originates in northern temperate regions. It includes plants with diverse foliage and forms that are suitable to grow in a variety of situations, from rock gardens and borders to naturalizing. Foliage is often strongly aromatic, sometimes silvery, and can be fringed, ferny, scalloped, or toothed. Flowers are daisy-like or rayless buttons, produced in a mass on vigorous plants of mounding, upright, or shrubby habit. Flower colors are dominated by yellow, white, and red. The genus name means "immortality," from the Greek, a reference to the flowers' habit of drying without wilting.
CULTIVATION: These plants require well-drained, poor to moderately fertile soil, full sun, and dry growing conditions. Cut back plants after blooming to encourage new growth and to prevent prolific self-seeding of some types. Propagate by division or from seed in spring.

Tanacetum cinerariifolium ★

syns *Chrysanthemum cinerariifolium*, *Pyrethrum cinerariifolium*

DALMATIA PYRETHRUM, INSECT FLOWER, PYRETHRUM

↔12 in (30 cm)
↑12–24 in (30–60 cm)

Perennial from the Balkans. It features finely cut, silvery gray foliage on slender stems. The daisy-like flowers with white rays and a yellow center appear from late summer to autumn. Mulch where winters are severe. It needs hot dry conditions. The source of insecticidal pyrethrum. Zones 6–10.

Tanacetum coccineum

syns *Chrysanthemum coccineum*, *Pyrethrum coccineum*

PAINTED DAISY, PYRETHRUM

↔18 in (45 cm)
↑18–30 in (45–75 cm)

Compact low-growing perennial from southwest Asia and the Caucasus. Fern-like, elliptical to oblong, silver-gray, aromatic foliage. White, pink, or red daisy flowers, yellow eye, in early summer–late autumn. Oils of leaves used to deter pests. **'Brenda'**, bright cerise-pink flowers with yellow eye; **'Eileen May Robinson'**, larger pale pink flowers with soft yellow eye; **'James Kelway'** ★, vibrant crimson-pink flowers. Zones 5–9.

Tanacetum niveum

SILVER TANSY

↔24 in (60 cm) ↑36 in (90 cm)

Superb species from southern and central Europe. Deeply cut, fragrant leaves are a striking silver-gray. Plant forms a mound and bears hundreds of *Chrysanthemum*-like white flowers in late spring–summer. Zones 6–9.

Tanacetum parthenium

syn. *Chrysanthemum parthenium*

FEVERFEW

↔12 in (30 cm) ↑24 in (60 cm)

A short-lived perennial from southern Europe to the Caucasus. Branched sprays with ferny foliage. Flowers with a flat yellow center surrounded by short, stubby, white petals appear in summer. For rock garden, ground cover, or border. **'Aureum'**, bright golden foliage with single yellow-tinted white flowers; **'Santana Lemon'**, yellow button flowers, thinly rayed; **'Snowball'**, tight ivory buttons; **'White Stars'**, white starry flowers. Zones 4–9.

Tanacetum vulgare

GOLDEN BUTTONS, TANSY

↔36–48 in (90–120 cm)
↑36–48 in (90–120 cm)

A perennial from Europe. Creeping roots and finely divided ferny foliage all along the stem. Flower clusters 4 in (10 cm) across, bright yellow, in spring to summer. Strong camphor scent. *T. v.* var. *crispum*, attractive arching foliage. *T. v.* **'Goldsticks'**, longer stems, larger flowers. Zones 4–9.

Tanacetum coccineum

Taiwania cryptomerioides

Tanacetum parthenium (left foreground, right center)

Tanacetum parthenium cultivar

TAXODIUM

This group of 3 species from North America and Mexico form the type genus for the swamp cypress (Taxodiaceae) family. These deciduous or semi-deciduous trees are found growing in or near water. In these swampy conditions mature trees often produce aerial roots known as "knees" or pneumatophores, which allow the roots to breathe. These majestic conical trees bear foliage that resembles that of the yew *(Taxus)*, after which they were named, with fissured peeling bark on buttressed trunks. Both male and female cones are held on the same tree, the small male cones held in pendulous groups, the female ones scattered along the branches.

CULTIVATION: These plants will grow in either a clay or sandy soil as long as it remains relatively moist. They can withstand very low winter temperatures where their foliage color turns to vivid rust tones before the leaves fall to reveal a fine tracery of branches. Propagate from seed, except for cultivars, which need to be grafted.

Taxodium distichum

BALD CYPRESS, SWAMP CYPRESS

↔20 ft (6 m) ↑75 ft (23 m)

This fast-growing tree is from North America. The deeply fissured fibrous bark exfoliates in long strips. Initially conical outline broadens, becomes irregular as the tree matures. Fine leaves light green, in spring, ageing to a deep green before turning rusty red, in autumn. *T. d.* var. ***imbricatum*** (syn. *T. ascendens*), distinctly conifer shape, clasping bright green leaves; **'Nutans'**, initially upright, pendulous tips with maturity. *T. d.* **'Shawnee Brave'**, compact bright green leaves, ideal for hedges. Zones 6–10.

Taxodium distichum

Taxodium mucronatum

Taxodium mucronatum

MEXICAN SWAMP CYPRESS, MONTEZUMA CYPRESS

↔50 ft (15 m) ↑100 ft (30 m)

Tree from Mexico and southern Texas, USA. Evergreen in warmer climates, semi-deciduous in cooler areas. Pendulous foliage very similar to *T. distichum*. Clasping leaves, bright green turning rusty brown in autumn. Cones long, often warty. Zones 8–11.

TAXUS

YEW

This small evergreen conifer genus belonging to the yew (Taxaceae) family, consists of around 7 species, occurring in cool-temperate regions of the Northern Hemisphere and some more tropical mountain regions, including the Philippines and Mexico. Most are small to medium trees, with sharply pointed, linear or slightly sickle-shaped leaves, often with prominent olive green midribs. Most species have separate male and female plants and flower in spring. The single seed found on the female plant is partly clothed in a red fleshy covering (or aril) that is sweet and edible; the rest of the plant, including the seed, is poisonous. The seeds are dispersed by birds. They make useful specimen or hedge plants, and handsome topiary subjects. Slow growing but long lived.

CULTIVATION: Most members of the genus are fairly adaptable in cool regions, tolerating sun or shade, frost, alkaline soils, exposure, and pollution. Propagate these conifers from seed sown as soon as hardened, from cuttings, or by grafting.

Taxus baccata

COMMON YEW, ENGLISH YEW

↔25 ft (8 m) ↑50 ft (15 m)

Slow-growing tree from Europe, North Africa, and western Asia. Very long lived, dense many-branched head. Reddish brown bark, dark green linear leaves, paler yellowish green below. Male cones yellow and scaly. Female flowers on separate plants, in summer. **Aurea Group** (golden yew), golden yellow young growth turning greener with age; **'Dovastonii Aurea'**, male plant, low and spreading, dense foliage; **'Dwarf White'**, low and spreading moderately dense foliage, new growth whitish but soon turning green; **'Fastigiata'** (Irish yew), female plant, dark green leaves; **Fastigiata Aurea Group** (golden Irish yew), smaller than 'Fastigiata', golden yellow leaves; **'Nutans'**, to less than 20 in (50 cm) high, dark green leaves; **'Repandens'**, spreading female, to 36 in (90 cm) high, green leaves; **'Semperaurea'**, male, to 10 ft (3 m) high, ascending branches of bright yellow young growth changing to russet-yellow in winter; **'Standishii'**, female, golden leaves, columnar habit. Zones 5–10.

Taxus chinensis

CHINESE YEW

↔15 ft (4.5 m) ↑20 ft (6 m)

A shrub from China with stiff, sharp, pointed leaves, tapering abruptly at the point. Glossy green leaves, curling outward on top, gray-green below, in 2 ranks. Pollen cones yellowish maturing to brown, appear in summer. Zones 6–10.

Taxus cuspidata

JAPANESE YEW

↔20 ft (6 m) ↑50 ft (15 m)

Erect tree from Japan, normally seen as a shrub in gardens. The horizontal or ascending branches have spiraly arranged, dark green, linear leaves. New shoots are red-brown, fleshy aril red when ripe, in summer. Suitable for hedging and topiary, tolerant of pollution. *T. c.* var. ***nana*** is a low-spreading shrub with dense growth. *T. c.* **'Capitata'**, strong upright foliage; **'Densa'**, female compact form with dark green leaves to 36 in (90 cm) high; **'Densiformis'**, dwarf, to 36 in (90 cm) tall. Zones 4–9.

Taxus × *media*

ANGLO-JAP YEW, HYBRID YEW

↔20 ft (6 m) ↑25 ft (8 m)

A hybrid between *Taxus baccata* and *T. cuspidata*. Tree or shrub suitable for hedging. Linear olive green leaves, prominent white midribs beneath.

Taxus baccata

Taxus cuspidata 'Capitata'

Tecoma capensis

Tellima grandiflora

Ternstroemia japonica

Tecoma stans

Seed partly covered by a scarlet aril, in summer. **'Brownii'**, to 10 ft (3 m) high, dark green leaves, spherical shape; **'Dark Green Spreader'**, a shrub with very dense deep green foliage; **'Everlow'**, a low, rounded, up to 8 ft (2.4 m) high; **'Hatfieldii'**, male columnar form to about 6 ft (1.8 m) high; **'Hicksii'**, columnar habit, dense growth, popular for hedges. **'Nigra'**, compact dark green foliage. Zones 5–9.

TECOMA

syns *Stenolobium, Tecomaria*

YELLOW BELLS

There are 13 species of mostly evergreen trees and scrambling shrubs in this genus belonging to the trumpet-vine (Bignoniaceae) family. They are found from southern Arizona, USA, to Mexico, the West Indies, and as far south as northern Argentina. One species *(T. capensis)*, is native to southern and eastern Africa. Pinnate leaves are borne in opposite pairs in leaflets with toothed edges. Funnel-shaped or narrowly bell-shaped flowers are borne in showy terminal clusters in yellow, orange, or red, with 5 unequal petals. The fruit is a smallish pod splitting into 2 halves.

CULTIVATION: Fine ornamentals for the tropical and subtropical garden. In cool climates they can only be grown as potted shrubs in a greenhouse or conservatory. They like a sunny but sheltered position and reasonably fertile soil with good drainage. Propagate from fresh seed, or from tip cuttings or larger cuttings from the previous year's growth. Suckering species can be divided or layered.

Tecoma capensis

syns *Bignonia capensis, Tecomaria capensis*

CAPE HONEYSUCKLE

↔ 7 ft (2 m) ↑ 10 ft (3 m)

An adaptable shrub, partly climbing habit, from eastern and southern Africa. Glossy green pinnate leaves. Orange-red to scarlet tubular flowers, in racemes at ends of branches, from spring to autumn. Tolerant of salt spray, drought, and wind. **'Aurea'**, golden yellow flowers. Zones 9–12.

Tecoma stans

syns *Bignonia stans, Stenolobium stans*

SHRUBBY TRUMPET FLOWER, YELLOW BELLS, YELLOW ELDER

↔ 10 ft (3 m) ↑ 15–30 ft (4.5–9 m)

Small tree or large open shrub, native to southern USA and Central and South America. Leaves oblong, lance-shaped, toothed, bright green leaflets. Yellow flowers, funnel-shaped, in terminal racemes or panicles, from late winter to summer. Fruit capsules ripen to brown. Zones 9–11.

TELEKIA

This genus, comprising a single species native from central Europe eastward to the Caucasus region, belongs to the daisy (Asteraceae) family. The plant is a coarse perennial herb. Leaves are large and heart-shaped, deeply toothed, and hairy, with long stalks. The large flowerheads have ray florets and form loose terminal corymbs. The receptacle has scales, which persist after flowering. The whorl of bracts is cup-shaped and the bracts are heart-shaped and herbaceous. Ray florets are female, each with a very long, narrow, yellow petal. The dry fruits are linear and flattened.

CULTIVATION: This plant grows wild by streamsides and in wet woodlands up to the subalpine zone. It is easily grown in open or lightly shaded moist places in a garden but can readily become invasive. However, the statuesque forms of the larger ones in cultivation are always impressive. Propagate by division or from seed.

Telekia speciosa

syn. *Buphthalmum speciosum*

OXEYE DAISY, TELEKIA SUNFLOWER

↔ 4–6 ft (1.2–1.8 m) ↑ 4–6 ft (1.2–1.8 m)

A strongly scented perennial found from central Europe to Russia. Coarsely serrated leaves, finely hairy underneath. Clusters of 2 to 8 flowerheads, up to 35 tiny yellow ray florets, in summer. Zones 3–9.

TELLIMA

There is just the one species of perennial herb in this genus which belongs to the saxifrage (Saxifragaceae) family. It is native to western North America, where it is found in cool moist woodland and rocky areas. The plant forms spreading clumps of hairy, heart-shaped or round leaves that are lobed and toothed. They are tinted with purple in some forms. In summer, tall wiry flowering stems bear spikes of small creamy flowers tinged with green and red. The flowers deepen in color as they age.

CULTIVATION: Fringecups are well suited for growing in cool woodland gardens, and in shady borders and rockeries. Grow in a moist humus-rich soil. Propagate by division in autumn or from seed sown in spring.

Tellima grandiflora

FRINGECUPS

↔ 24 in (60 cm) ↑ 24 in (60 cm)

This perennial is found growing from California to Alaska, USA. Clumps of almost round, lobed, hairy, basal leaves, up to 2–4 in (5–10 cm) wide. Delicate flowers with deeply fringed petals appear in summer. **Rubra Group** (syn. 'Purpurea') features rounder, scallop-edged leaves tinted bronze and green flowers fringed with pink. Zones 6–9.

TERNSTROEMIA

This genus of 85 species of evergreen trees and shrubs is a member of the Pentaphylaceae family. These plants are found in Asia, Africa, and the Americas. The large glossy leaves are leathery, sometimes with a serrated edge. The single white flowers are 5-petalled and appear in summer. The seed capsules are red.

CULTIVATION: These plants will grow well in a fertile, humus-rich, acid soil that is moisture retentive but well drained. Pinch out the shoot tips to encourage branching. Propagate from seed or from half-hardened cuttings in late summer.

Ternstroemia japonica ★

syn. *Ternstroemia gymnanthera*

↔ 10 ft (3 m) ↑ 12 ft (3.5 m)

A shrub or small tree, native to Japan. Well-branched; thick, leathery, glossy, oval leaves. Hanging clusters of small white flowers, lightly perfumed, are borne in summer. Round red fruits split to reveal red seeds. **'Variegata'**, dark green leaves marbled with gray, creamy white edges that turn pink in autumn. Zones 8–11.

TETRACENTRON

The single species of deciduous tree in this genus, belonging to the family Trochodendraceae, is found from Nepal to southwestern and central China. It has an attractive form with smooth new shoots revealing oval leaves, sometimes heart-shaped. They have prominent veins and are mid-green changing to deep bluish red in autumn. The flowers are small and yellow and bloom on long spikes. This tree is often cultivated for its ornamental value.

CULTIVATION: This plant requires a moderately fertile soil in a sunny position and with shelter from cold winds. Although quite hardy, young shoots are susceptible to late spring frosts. Propagate from seed or half-hardened cuttings.

Tetracentron sinense

↔ 30 ft (9 m) ↑ 50 ft (15 m)

A tree found from southwestern and central China to Nepal. Dark smooth shoots, pale brownish orange buds. Leaves pointed oval to heart-shaped, prominent veins, bluntly toothed edges, color to a rich blue-red, in autumn. Small yellow flowers on pendulous spikes, in summer. Zones 6–9.

Tetradium daniellii

Tetrapanax papyrifer

Teucrium cossonii

Teucrium fruticans

Teucrium hircanicum

Teucrium pyrenaicum

TETRADIUM

Native to the area from the Himalayas through to East and Southeast Asia, this small genus of about 9 species of deciduous and evergreen shrubs and trees belongs to the rue (Rutaceae) family. They are grown for their aromatic foliage, masses of small sweetly scented flowers, and the generous clusters of fruits. The capsular fruits contain dark red to black seeds and are poisonous in some species.

CULTIVATION: Most species are very frost hardy. To thrive, they need a fertile, moist but well-drained soil in full sun or partial shade. Prune to remove damaged foliage and spent flowerheads. Propagate from seed in autumn, or from cuttings in late winter.

Tetradium daniellii

syn. ***Euodia daniellii***

KOREAN EUODIA

☼ ❄ ↔ 40 ft (12 m) ↕ 50 ft (15 m)

A large tree, native to southwestern China and Korea. The large pinnate leaves are composed of 11 ovate or lance-shaped, glossy, dark green leaflets that turn russet in autumn. Small, white, perfumed flowers in terminal dome-shaped sprays, from late summer to early autumn. Small pear-shaped fruits. Zones 8–10.

TETRAPANAX

The sole confirmed species in this genus, part of the ivy (Araliaceae) family, is a suckering clump-forming evergreen shrub or small tree from Taiwan. Known as rice-paper plant because a type of fine rice paper is made from the pith of its stems, it has large hand-shaped leaves that are felted all over when young, although the covering soon wears from the uppersurfaces to reveal the underlying dark green coloration. Large panicles of creamy white flowers open from heads of woolly buds that develop at the stem tips in autumn.

CULTIVATION: Intolerant of drought or hard frosts, this species prefers to grow in a mild climate, with moist, humus-rich, well-drained soil in a position that is shaded from the hottest summer sun. It will also grow well in sandy soils near the coast. Old stems and spent flowerheads are best removed. Although rice-paper plant will grow from cuttings, these are large and unwieldy, so seed is more commonly used for propagation.

Tetrapanax papyrifer

RICE-PAPER PLANT

☀ ❄ ↔ 15 ft (4.5 m) ↕ 20 ft (6 m)

Evergreen small tree or shrub from Taiwan, can sucker profusely to form large clump. Downy palmate leaves, mainly at stem tips, overlap to form dense foliage canopy. Creamy white flowerheads in autumn. Clusters of purple-black berries. **'Variegata'**, cream-edged leaves. Zones 8–11.

TEUCRIUM

GERMANDER

Members of this genus of about 100 species of herbs, shrubs, and subshrubs, part of the mint (Lamiaceae) family, occur in warm-temperate regions but particularly around the Mediterranean. The shrubs are often colorful flowering plants. All have characteristic squarish stems with opposite leaves that are usually downy or hairy, oval to lance-shaped, and have notched or slightly toothed edges. The summer flowers are borne in whorls on loose stems and are cream, purple, or pink. Some species are attractive to cats.

CULTIVATION: These plants require a sunny position and well-drained soil. They will tolerate the dry heat of the inland but do best in coastal areas. Lightly prune the ends of the branchlets to remove spent inflorescences and stimulate lateral growth immediately after the summer-flowering period. Propagation is best from firm tip cuttings taken in summer.

Teucrium canadense

AMERICAN GERMANDER, WOOD SAGE

☼ ❄ ↔ 24–36 in (60–90 cm) ↕ 24–36 in (60–90 cm)

A perennial, native to North America. Stiff, erect, downy stems; leaves hairy, oval to lance-shaped, with notched edges. Spikes of cream, pink, or purple flowers, to 1 in (25 mm) wide, held in whorls, in summer. Zones 4–9.

Teucrium chamaedrys

GROUND OAK, WALL GERMANDER

☼ ❄ ↔ 24–36 in (60–90 cm) ↕ 12–24 in (30–60 cm)

A woody-based perennial from central and southern Europe but naturalized further north. Small oval leaves have toothed edges, and are shiny green above, downy below. Whorls of pink to purple flowers borne on terminal spikes in summer. Zones 5–10.

Teucrium cossonii

syns *Teucrium gussonei*, *T. majorcum*

☼ ❄ ↔ 24 in (60 cm) ↕ 8 in (20 cm)

Low-growing shrubby perennial from the Mediterranean island of Majorca, Spain. Small, narrow, gray leaves. Whorls of lavender flowers on short leafy spikes, almost year-round in warm climates. Zones 8–11.

Teucrium fruticans

BUSH GERMANDER, SHRUBBY GERMANDER

☼ ❄ ↔ 6 ft (1.8 m) ↕ 4 ft (1.2 m)

Small evergreen shrub native to southern parts of Spain, Portugal, and Italy, as well as North Africa. Stems and undersides of grayish leaves covered in dense white hairs. Flowers pale lilac-blue, in summer. **'Azureum'**, deep blue flowers; **'Silver n Sapphires'**, bright silver-gray foliage, intense blue flowers. Zones 8–10.

Teucrium hircanicum

☼ ❄ ↔ 24 in (60 cm) ↕ 24 in (60 cm)

Woody-based perennial from western Asia and Caucasus region. Soft, green, downy leaves are somewhat wrinkled on uppersurface. Terminal spikes of closely packed whorls of small purple to reddish purple flowers in summer–autumn. Zones 6–9.

Teucrium pyrenaicum

☼ ❄ ↔ 16 in (40 cm) ↕ 3 in (8 cm)

A perennial from the Pyrenees. Forms mats of rounded leaves with notched edges. Dense terminal flowerheads, up to 1 in (25 mm) wide, bear 2-toned purple and cream flowers in summer. Zones 6–9.

Teucrium scorodonia

MOUNTAIN SAGE, WOOD GERMANDER, WOOD SAGE

☼/☀ ❄ ↔ 18 in (45 cm) ↕ 24 in (60 cm)

Downy rhizomatous perennial, native to southern and western Europe. The wrinkled, coarsely toothed, grayish green leaves resemble sage. Small yellowish green flowers borne in terminal spikes, in summer–autumn. **'Crispum Marginatum'**, crimped, frilly-edged, green leaves. Zones 6–10.

THALIA

ALLIGATOR FLAG

This genus of 12 aquatic perennial herbs is a member of the arrowroot (Marantaceae) family, native to the tropical and subtropical Americas and tropical Africa. Growing from thick rhizomes, the overlapping, decorative, blue-green leaves have large oval- to sword-shaped blades that fold upward at night, and long stalks with sheaths at the base. Two ranks of tubular, often waxy flowers are produced in curving

Thalia dealbata

tassel-like branches on long-stalked panicles that extend beyond the leaves. CULTIVATION: These plants grow in water 12–18 in (30–45 cm) deep, or in moist to wet loamy soil in an open sunny position. Propagate by division in spring.

Thalia dealbata

POWDERY ALLIGATOR FLAG, WATER CANNA

↔20–30 in (50–75 cm)
↕3–6 ft (0.9–1.8 m)

Erect perennial, native to southeastern North America, with unbranching stems. The large, textured, grayish green leaves with fine red edges are powdery white underneath. Branching heads of 6-petalled, violet, waxy flowers are borne from late summer to early autumn. Zones 9–11.

THALICTRUM

MEADOW RUE

A member of the buttercup (Ranunculaceae) family, this genus of around 130 species of tuberous or rhizomatous perennials is found mainly in the northern temperate zone. They are upright plants with lacy, pinnate, blue-green leaves that are reminiscent of *Aquilegia* or *Adiantum* (maidenhair fern) foliage. Tall flower stems grow well above the foliage and from late spring to autumn, depending on the species, produce inflorescences of small fluffy flowers. Mainly in pink to mauve shades, but also white and yellow, the petal-less flowers sometimes gain color from their 4 or 5 petal-like sepals. The Romans favored meadow rue as a medicinal plant and also attached superstitions to it.
CULTIVATION: Usually very hardy, these plants are easily grown in temperate climates in full or half-sun in fertile, humus-rich, and well-drained soil. Propagate these perennials by division, as the cultivated plants are mainly selected forms.

Thalictrum aquilegiifolium

FEATHERED COLUMBINE, FRENCH MEADOW RUE

↔20–40 in (50–100 cm)
↕60 in (150 cm)

Multi-stemmed perennial found from Europe to Japan. Blue-green aquilegia- or maidenhair fern-like foliage, leaves to 12 in (30 cm) wide. Panicles of greenish white through pink to purple flowers with inconspicuous sepals, in early summer. Zones 6–9.

Thalictrum delavayi

↔16–24 in (40–60 cm)
↕4–5 ft (1.2–1.5 m)

A perennial native to the Himalayas. Dark-stemmed, blue-green, aquilegia- or maidenhair fern-like foliage. Erect showy heads of purple-pink, rarely white flowers, sepals similarly colored, large and long-lasting, in summer. **'Hewitt's Double'** ★, double flowers, slightly shorter. Zones 7–9.

Thalictrum delavayi

Thalictrum dioicum

EARLY MEADOW RUE

↔12–16 in (30–40 cm)
↕12–30 in (30–75 cm)

Species found in North America, from Ontario, Canada, to Tennessee, USA. Aquilegia-like blue-green foliage; tiny leaflets have deeply scalloped edges. The flowers have pendulous pink filaments below conspicuous pale green, sometimes purple-tinted sepals, said to resemble floating jellyfish, in summer. Zones 4–9.

Thalictrum flavum

FALSE RHUBARB, YELLOW MEADOW RUE

↔16–20 in (40–50 cm)
↕40 in (100 cm)

A perennial found in southwestern Europe and North Africa, with finely divided, blue-green, aquilegia-like, pinnate foliage. Small heads of cream to yellow flowers with inconspicuous sepals, in summer. *T. f.* **subsp. *glaucum*** features intensely blue-green foliage. Zones 6–10.

Thalictrum kiusianum

↔12–20 in (30–50 cm)
↕6–12 in (15–30 cm)

A small species from Japan. Develops into a dense clump of short-stemmed, small, doubly trifoliate, blue-green leaves with 3- to 5-lobed segments. Abundant small heads of white to purple-pink blooms with inconspicuous sepals, in summer. Zones 8–10.

Thalictrum minus

↔20–32 in (50–80 cm)
↕3–5 ft (0.9–1.5 m)

This erect species is found throughout Europe and Asia. Finely divided, blue-green, pinnate leaves. The panicles of yellow, sometimes purple-tinted flowers with inconspicuous sepals, are borne in summer. Zones 6–9.

Thalictrum delavayi 'Hewitt's Double'

Thalictrum rochebruneanum

↔16–20 in (40–50 cm)
↕40 in (100 cm)

From Japan. Finely divided foliage, smooth-edged or lobed leaflets, to over 1 in (25 mm) long. Airy sprays of small pendulous flowers with many yellow filaments and showy purple-pink sepals, in summer. **'Lavender Mist'**, large heads of tiny, bell-shaped, violet flowers. Zones 8–10.

THAMNOCHORTUS

This genus of 34 species of rush-like plants in the family Restionaceae is restricted to South Africa. The stems are green and the leaves are reduced to brown scales up the stems. Their tiny brown flowers are produced in tight heads at the top of the stems and are usually surrounded by brown to golden papery bracts that can be quite showy. Male and female flowers are borne on separate plants; in most cases the sexes look quite different and in earlier times they were often mistaken for different species. These plants are still used for thatching in South Africa.
CULTIVATION: They grow in a sunny site in almost frost-free climates. They enjoy moist, poor, sandy soils but are quite adaptable. Propagate them from smoke-treated seed sown in autumn.

Thamnochortus insignis

DEKRIET, THATCHING REED

↔6–7 ft (1.8–2 m)
↕6–7 ft (1.8–2 m)

This species is from the coastal areas of South Africa. The stiff deep green stems have brown stem-clasping leaf bracts. The tiny brown flowers are surrounded by dark brown floral bracts, larger on the male plants, in summer. Zones 8–10.

Thamnochortus insignis

THELYPTERIS

This genus gives its name to the wood-fern (Thelypteridaceae) family and contains 2 species of terrestrial ferns, 1 of which is native to the Northern Hemisphere, the other from the Southern Hemisphere. They are found in shaded, damp, marshy ground. Their creeping or upright rhizomes are covered with hair-like scales. The divided, sword-shaped or triangular, often glandular, frond blades are covered with fine gray hairs. Circular spore bodies are carried in rows on the undersides of the fronds. Different botanists have widely differing views as to how many species belong to this genus. At one extreme, 2 species are recognized, while acknowledging many other closely related genera. At the other extreme, 900 species are included in the genus. CULTIVATION: These ferns prefer a shaded, protected position in a moist, well-drained, fertile soil. Propagation is from spores.

Thelypteris palustris

syns *Dryopteris thelypteris, Thelypteris thelypteroides*

MARSH FERN

✹ ✱ ↔ 10–18 in (25–45 cm)
↑ 18–24 in (45–60 cm)

Found across temperate USA and Europe, Bermuda, Cuba, and Peru. Long creeping rhizome. Sterile frond blades sword-shaped, to 16 in (40 cm) long, oval segments, on smooth pale green stalks. Fertile fronds to 40 in (100 cm) long, narrower segments, on longer stalks, rows of spore bodies near midvein, in summer. Zones 6–11.

THERMOPSIS

FALSE LUPIN

This genus, which belongs to the pea-flower subfamily of the legume (Fabaceae) family, contains 23 species of rhizomatous perennial herbs, native to North America, Siberia, and parts of Asia. They grow in habitats such as riverbanks and open woods. Attractive 3-part leaves are often silvery. Their nectar-rich, yellow or purple flowers are typical of the pea-flower family. They are borne in spring or summer in dense or loose terminal racemes, often resembling lupins *(Lupinus)*, a fact recognized in the common name applied to several species. CULTIVATION: These plants are suitable for the border or for naturalizing in larger areas. Grow in full sun in any reasonably fertile soil that is moist but well drained. Some species spread rapidly by their rhizomes. Propagate from seed or by division, which must be undertaken carefully as these deep-rooted plants resent disturbance.

Thermopsis villosa

syn. *Thermopsis caroliniana*

CAROLINA LUPIN

☼ ✱ ↔ 2 ft (0.6 m)
↑ 3–5 ft (0.9–1.5 m)

A stout perennial from southeastern USA. Bluish green leaves are downy on the undersides. Yellow flowers are borne in terminal, downy, lupin-like racemes, from spring to summer. Seed pods are silky-hairy. Zones 6–9.

THOMASIA

A genus of around 35 species of evergreen shrubs of the mallow (Malvaceae) family, found mainly in southern Western Australia. Their leaves are usually small and dark green but vary in shape, ranging from near linear to broad and rounded. Some species have larger, lobed leaves. The flowers are starry, usually mauve-pink, and are held clear of the foliage in sprays on wiry stems. CULTIVATION: Many species are difficult to cultivate outside their natural range. They resent high summer humidity, but a few grow well in gardens provided they have gritty well-drained soil with the addition of some well-aged neutral pH compost. Propagate from seed or half-hardened cuttings.

Thomasia grandiflora

LARGE-FLOWERED THOMASIA

☼ ❄ ↔ 3 ft (0.9 m) ↑ 3 ft (0.9 m)

From southwestern corner of Western Australia. Small, narrow, dark green to bright green leaves on fine stems. Showy sprays of bright purple-pink flowers, from late winter. **'Mt. Lesueur'**, vivid magenta flowers. Zones 9–10.

Thomasia solanacea

☼ ❄ ↔ 3–4 ft (0.9–1.2 m)
↑ 3–8 ft (0.9–2.4 m)

From small area around Albany, Western Australia. Leaves light olive shade, lobed, oak-like in shape, up to 1½ in (35 mm) long. Flowers mauve-pink. **'Velvet Star'**, pale flowers, slightly larger, velvety leaves. Zones 9–10.

THRINAX

THATCH PALM

This genus, which is a member of the palm (Arecaceae) family, is made up of 7 species, the majority occurring in Florida, USA, the Caribbean Islands, Mexico, and Belize. Thatch palms are solitary-trunked fan palms with palmately lobed fronds on long unarmed stalks. The small flowers are cup-shaped and self-pollinating, borne in panicles from between the fronds and followed by fruit that is usually white. Members of this genus can be found growing in alkaline soils, from sea level to higher areas near the coast, including woodlands and mountain rainforests. They are very attractive palms, most being suited to tropical and subtropical regions although some are grown in warm-temperate zones. Thatch palms will make very handsome specimens or they can be used in garden bed plantings in combination with other species, or for tub planting. CULTIVATION: These palms will give the best results when they are grown in well-drained soil in a warm sunny position that gives them protection from cold winds. In nature they grow in limestone soils. They are tolerant of salt winds. Propagation of these palms is from seed.

Thrinax parviflora

JAMAICAN FAN PALM, ROYAL PALMETTO

☼ ❄ ↔ 7 ft (2 m) ↑ 10–50 ft (3–15 m)

Variable small to medium palm from Jamaica. Green fan fronds, uneven surface. Fragrant cream to yellow flowers in panicles, in summer. Small white fruit. Zones 10–12.

Thrinax parviflora

Thrinax radiata

Thrinax radiata

FLORIDA THATCH PALM

☼ ❄ ↔ 7 ft (2 m) ↑ 40 ft (12 m)

From the Caribbean to south Florida, USA. Fan fronds deep green, on stalks with base clothed in fibers. Upright panicles of small, white, fragrant, summer flowers. White fruit. Zones 10–12.

THUJA

syn. *Platycladus*

ARBORVITAE, RED CEDAR, WHITE CEDAR

This genus consists of 5 coniferous evergreen trees within the cypress (Cupressaceae) family. Their natural habitat is North America and East Asia, in high rainfall woodland or damp, cold, coastal and lowland plains. The bark is reddish brown and comes off in long vertical strips on mature trees. The leaflets are flattened and scale-like. Solitary male cones grow on the ends of branchlets and the solitary female cones, with 6 to 12 overlapping scales, grow lower down. These are important timber trees as well as being used often for hedging and the greenery for floristry. The aromatic foliage can cause skin allergies. CULTIVATION: Young trees do well in full sun in deep, moist, well-drained soil, but need shelter from cold drying winds. *Thuja* species will survive boggy areas that are too wet for other conifers. Propagate by sowing seed in winter in an area protected from frosts, or by rooting half-hardened cuttings in late summer.

Thuja koraiensis 'Glauca Prostrata'

Thuja plicata

Thuja koraiensis

KOREAN ARBORVITAE

↔ 12 ft (3.5 m) ↑ 30 ft (9 m)

A small tree, native to northeastern China, as well as northern and central Korea. Conical shape with branchlets that often trail. Mid-green scale-like leaves are bright silver below. Female cones have 4 pairs of scales, during summer. **'Glauca Prostrata'**, very low growing with bluish foliage. Zones 5–9.

Thuja occidentalis

AMERICAN ARBORVITAE, EASTERN ARBORVITAE, WHITE CEDAR

↔ 15 ft (4.5 m) ↑ 30–70 ft (9–21 m)

Large conifer, native to eastern North America. Conical form, rounded at the top with dense foliage. Bark hangs in orange-brown strips. Crowded, flattened, dull green branchlets, with grayish green undersides. The female cones have 8 to 10 pairs of smooth scales, in summer. **'Caespitosa'**, round slow-growing shrub, 12 in (30 cm) high; **'Filiformis'**, thin pendent branchlets, grows to 25 ft (8 m) high, golden yellow leaves; **'Golden Globe'**, height and width of 3 ft (0.9 m); **'Nigra'**, grows up to about 30 ft (9 m) high, narrowly conical form with branches down to ground, compact, very dark green foliage that retains its color through winter; **'Ohlendorffii'**, retains juvenile foliage; **'Pyramidalis Compacta'**, a column of fairly dense, compact, bright green foliage to about 12 ft (3.5 m) high but no more than 4 ft (1.2 m) wide, tapering to pointed leader, fast-growing, good for screens and hedges; **'Rheingold'**, pink tints when young, turns golden bronze in cold winters; **'Silver Queen'**, green-yellow foliage; **'Smaragd'**, conical shrub, bright green foliage; **'Tiny Tim'**, dwarf form with rust-colored winter foliage; **'Wintergreen'**, broadly conical; **'Woodwardii'**, compact shrub with light green foliage. Zones 2–10.

Thuja plicata

GIANT ARBOR, WESTERN RED CEDAR

↔ 15 ft (4.5 m) ↑ 70–120 ft (21–36 m)

Tall columnar tree, native to western North America, often with buttressed bole. Flattened horizontal sprays of foliage, mid- to dark green, pale green to gray-white underneath. The female cones have 4 to 5 pairs of scales, each one with a tiny hook, in summer. **'Atrovirens'**, dark green, makes a good compact hedge; **'Aurea'**, narrow conical habit, gold-tipped shoots which soon revert to yellowish green; **'George Washington'**, broadly conical habit with long leading shoot; **'Hillieri'**, dwarf, height and spread of 6–10 ft (1.8–3 m), and bluish green foliage; **'Stoneham Gold'**, young leaves golden, ageing to green; **'Sunshine'**, yellow-green foliage; **'Virescens'**, dark green foliage; **'Zebrina'**, conical, green leaves with yellow stripes. Zones 5–10.

Thuja occidentalis 'Tiny Tim'

Thujopsis dolabrata 'Nana'

Thuja standishii

JAPANESE ARBORVITAE

↔ 20 ft (6 m) ↑ 100 ft (30 m)

A large tree, native to Japan, with split reddish brown bark. The crown is open, broadly conical with irregular branches. Flattened branchlets are green above, white on the undersides. Female cones have 4 pairs of scales, in summer. Zones 6–9.

THUJOPSIS

The single species of conifer tree in this genus is a member of the cypress (Cupressaceae) family and is native to Japan. It resembles the better known *Thuja* but has broader and flatter branchlets which are almost horizontal with tips lifting. The bark is brownish often tending to red. The deep glossy green leaves are larger than those of *Thuja* species, which have silvery undersides. The single species is extremely slow growing.

CULTIVATION: This tree should be planted in a sheltered position in moisture-retentive soil. It is very hardy but must have high humidity. Propagate from seed or cuttings.

Thujopsis dolabrata

DEERHORN CEDAR, FALSE ARBORVITAE, HIBA, HIBA CEDAR

↔ 20 ft (6 m) ↑ 100 ft (30 m)

This conifer is from Japan. Conical crown, almost horizontal branches, upswept at tips. Reddish brown bark exfoliates in strips. Leaves deep glossy green with silvery undersides. Slow growing, just 8 ft (2.4 m) after 5 to 10 years in the garden. **'Nana'**, dwarf, spreading flat-topped bush, grows to about 30 in (75 cm) high. Zones 6–10.

Thuja occidentalis 'Smaragd'

THUNBERGIA

From tropical Asia and Africa, and also found in South Africa and Madagscar, containing around 100 species of annuals, perennials, and shrubs that are members of the acanthus (Acanthaceae) family. They form an enormously varied group with many being vigorous twining climbers, others are shrubby in habit. Their leaves are usually pointed oval to heart-shaped, sometimes lobed or toothed. Flowers occur in a wide color range, but most often yellow, orange, and purple-blue shades, borne singly or in racemes and are generally long-tubed trumpets with 5 large lobes. Named after Carl Peter Thunber (1743–1828), a Swedish physician and botanist employed by the Dutch East India Company.

CULTIVATION: These plants are mostly frost tender or tolerant only of very light frosts. Plant in a warm sheltered position in moist, humus-rich, well-drained soil. Many species are quite drought tolerant but generally perform best with frequent watering and feeding. Propagate from cuttings or seed, rarely by division.

Thunbergia alata

BLACK-EYED SUSAN VINE

↔ 10 ft (3 m) ↑ 10 ft (3 m)

A twining annual or perennial from tropical Africa. Quick-growing, with many long stems. Leaves are heart-shaped, toothed. Flowers numerous, usually orange with near-black throat, sometimes cream to yellow and/or evenly colored, in early summer. Suits hanging baskets. Zones 10–12.

Thunbergia alata

Thunbergia erecta

BUSH CLOCK VINE, KING'S MANTLE

↔7 ft (2 m) ↕6–8 ft (1.8–2.4 m)

Erect freestanding or twining shrub found from tropical western Africa to South Africa. Toothed ovate leaves to 2 in (6 cm) long. In summer, solitary, cream-centered, violet-blue flowers that follow the sun. Zones 10–12.

Thunbergia grandiflora

BENGAL CLOCK VINE, BLUE TRUMPET VINE, SKY VINE, SKYFLOWER

↔15 ft (4.5 m) ↕15 ft (4.5 m)

Vigorous twining perennial, native to northern India. Downy pointed oval leaves, sometimes lobed or toothed. In summer, sky blue to violet flowers, to 3 in (8 cm) wide, occasionally solitary, usually in racemes. Zones 10–12.

Thunbergia gregorii

ORANGE CLOCK VINE

↔6 ft (1.8 m) ↕6 ft (1.8 m)

Perennial twiner from tropical Africa, often cultivated as an annual. Toothed, coarsely hairy, triangular leaves. The flowers are solitary but abundant, bright orange, in summer. Zones 10–12.

Thunbergia mysorensis

↔20 ft (6 m) ↕20 ft (6 m)

A strong-growing, twining, woody-based perennial or shrub from India. Simple, often toothed, narrowly elliptic leaves. Spectacularly long pendulous racemes of yellow and red-brown flowers, in late spring. Zones 10–12.

Thunbergia gregorii

Thunbergia mysorensis

Thunbergia togoensis

Thunbergia togoensis

↔20 ft (6 m) ↕20 ft (6 m)

Vigorous, twining, climbing perennial, native to tropical Africa. Bright green lance-shaped leaves, to 3 in (8 cm) long. In summer, panicles of yellow-centered, intense purple-blue flowers, 3 in (8 cm) wide. Zones 10–12.

THYMUS

THYME

Well known as the source of one of the most widely used culinary herbs, this genus in the mint (Lamiaceae) family is composed of around 350 species of mainly evergreen, aromatic perennials and subshrubs, many of which become quite shrubby. They occur in most parts of Europe, temperate Asia, and northwest Africa but with the highest concentration around the Mediterranean and in the Middle East. Small wiry-stemmed plants, they have tiny, often downy leaves and heads of equally small mauve, pink, or sometimes white flowers that are very attractive to bees. Late spring to mid-summer is the main flowering season.

CULTIVATION: Frost hardiness varies with the species, though most will withstand moderate frosts. Thyme grows best in light, rather gritty soil that has been enriched with humus for moisture retention. Plant in full sun and trim lightly after flowering to keep the plants compact and well-foliaged. Propagate from seed, by removing naturally formed layers, or by taking half-hardened cuttings.

Thymus camphoratus

CAMPHOR THYME

↔8 in (20 cm) ↕8 in (20 cm)

A small woody shrub from western Europe, the western Mediterranean, and southern Portugal. Round, dark green, camphor-scented leaves. Unusual and attractive purplish leafy bracts surround the flowers. Rich rosy pink flowers, in summer. Zones 7–9.

Thymus pulegioides

Thymus polytrichus subsp. *britannicus*

Thymus citriodorus

syns *Thymus* × *citriodorus*, *T. serpyllum* subsp. *citriodorus*

LEMON-SCENTED THYME, LEMON THYME

↔24 in (60 cm) ↕6–12 in (15–30 cm)

Long thought to be garden hybrid between *T. pulegioides* and *T. vulgaris*, DNA research recently revealed it to be distinct species, though wild origins are unclear. Erect subshrub with very fine, twiggy, branching stems and glossy dark green leaves. Dense lavender-pink flowerheads in summer. Strong lemon scent. **'Aureus'**, upright, spreading, with gold-splashed leaves; **'Bertram Anderson'** (golden lemon thyme), gray-green leaves suffused gold, new growth tinged red; **'Lime'**, low, creeping, lime green foliage, white flowers; **'Silver Queen'**, silver-green to cream marbled foliage. Zones 5–10.

Thymus Coccineus Group

↔14 in (35 cm) ↕3–4 in (8–10 cm)

Mat-forming creeper of garden origin, possibly forms of *T. serpyllum*. Tiny dark green leaves. Magenta flowers are borne in terminal clusters, in summer. **'Coccineus Minor'**, dwarf form, tiny leaves and pink flowers. Zones 4–9.

Thymus herba-barona

CARAWAY THYME

↔24 in (60 cm) ↕4 in (10 cm)

Wide-spreading species from Corsica and Sardinia. Carpet of glossy dark green leaves with a spicy scent. Loose clusters of pink-mauve flowers are produced in mid-summer. Makes a useful ground cover. Zones 7–9.

Thymus polytrichus

↔24 in (60 cm) ↕2 in (5 cm)

A tight mat-forming species from southern Europe. Creeping form; dark green oval leaves. Flowers are pale to deep purple splashed with white, in summer. T. p. subsp. britannicus, dark pink flowers on slightly downy foliage; **'Minor'**, dwarf habit, tiny pink and white flowers; **'Thomas's White'** (syn. *T. praecox* subsp. *arcticus* 'Albus'), compact, crisp clear white flowers. Zones 5–9.

Thymus praecox ★

CREEPING THYME

↔24 in (60 cm) ↕2–4 in (5–10 cm)

Mat-forming creeper from southern, western, and central Europe. Tiny, slightly rounded leaves. Mauve-purple flowers, occasionally white, appear in terminal clusters with prominent purple bracts, in summer. **'Albiflorus'** produces white flowers on dark green foliage. Zones 4–9.

Thymus pseudolanuginosus

syn. *Thymus lanuginosus*

WOOLLY MOTHER-OF-THYME, WOOLLY THYME

↔24 in (60 cm) ↕1–3 in (2.5–8 cm)

This species is of unknown origin. It forms a low-spreading mat of woolly leaves. Scentless pink flowers in early summer. Sparse flowering. Must have sharp drainage. Plant between rocks. Zones 5–9.

Thymus serpyllum 'Snow Drift'

Thymus pulegioides

LARGE THYME

↔ 12 in (30 cm) ↕ 10 in (25 cm)

This low-growing spreading subshrub is widely distributed throughout Europe. Pretty, mid-green, fragrant, oval leaves on a compact mounded plant. Pink and purple flowers, from spring to summer. **'Foxley'**, deep pink flowers, large variegated cream and dark green leaves; **'Sir John Lawes'**, cerise-pink flowers on a more compact plant. Zones 4–9.

Thymus serpyllum

CREEPING THYME, MOTHER-OF-THYME, WILD THYME

↔ 36 in (90 cm) ↕ 1–4 in (2.5–8 cm)

Variable, wide, mat-forming perennial found naturally from northern Europe to northwestern Spain. Grows close to ground from woody base. The tiny lavender-purple flowers bloom prolifically, in early summer. **'Annie Hall'**, old reliable cultivar, very early-blooming, fragrant, pink flowers; **'Pink Chintz'**, gray-green leaves, pale pink flowers; **'Rainbow Falls'**, more upright form with gold-splashed deep green foliage, pink mid-summer flowers; **'Russetings'**, bronze-tinted foliage, bright pink flowers; **'Snow Drift'**, pure white flowers over a spreading mat; **'Vey'**, compact form, pale salmon pink flowerheads, darker in bud. Zones 4–9.

Thymus vulgaris

COMMON THYME

↔ 10 in (25 cm) ↕ 12 in (30 cm)

Woody-based perennial or subshrub found naturally around the western Mediterranean. Tiny lance-shaped leaves, downy undersides. White to pinkish purple flowers, in summer–autumn. The thyme most often used in cooking. **'Argenteus'**, silver-edged foliage, contain in pots as it spreads; **'Aureus'**, golden yellow foliage, reddish purple flowers; **'Compactus'**, a dwarf, dense mound of gray-green leaves; **'Erectus'**, upright growth with very aromatic, conifer-like, gray-green needle leaves, white flowers; **'Silver Posie'**, white-edged foliage maintained throughout season, pale pink-mauve flowers. Zones 7–10.

TIARELLA

This genus in the saxifrage (Saxifragaceae) family is made up of 5 perennials, 4 from North America and 1 found from the Himalayas to Japan. They spread by rhizomes or an underground network of thin fleshy stems, forming clumps of lobed heart-shaped leaves with long stalks. The flower stems carry airy open racemes of tiny white and/or pink to red, 5-petalled flowers, in late spring and summer. Foliage and flower stems are covered in fine hairs. *Tiarella* has been crossed with *Heuchera* to produce the intergeneric hybrid × *Heucherella*.

CULTIVATION: They are very hardy, especially the American species, and easily grown in woodlands or perennial borders; spreading but seldom invasive. Plant in half or full shade in humus-rich, moist, well-drained soil. Propagate by division in late winter to early spring or from seed.

Tiarella cordifolia

FOAMFLOWER

↔ 16–20 in (40–50 cm) ↕ 12 in (30 cm)

This perennial is found naturally in eastern North America; spreading by underground stems. Leaves hairy, lobed, toothed, heart-shaped, up to 4 in (10 cm) long. Airy sprays of tiny, often pink-tinted flowers on fine stems, in early summer. **'Major'** has salmon pink flowers that darken with age. Zones 3–9.

Tiarella polyphylla

↔ 16–20 in (40–50 cm) ↕ 12–18 in (30–45 cm)

Species found from the Himalayas to Japan. Toothed, 5-lobed, heart-shaped leaves, to nearly 3 in (8 cm) long and wide. Sturdy purple-red-tinted flower stems with branching sprays of small, pink-tinted, cream flowers, from late spring to early summer. **'Rosea'**, deep pink flowers. Zones 7–9.

Tiarella wherryi

↔ 16–20 in (40–50 cm) ↕ 8–12 in (20–30 cm)

Perennial from North America, closely allied to *T. cordifolia*. Leaves usually have 5 pronounced lobes, reddening in autumn. Racemes of narrow, cream flowers open from base upward from pink to maroon buds, in summer. **'Bronze Beauty'**, red-brown leaves, pink flowers; **'Oakleaf'** ★, leaves dark center and more pronounced lobes, flowers strongly pink-tinted. Zones 5–9.

Tiarella Hybrid Cultivars

↔ 16–20 in (40–50 cm) ↕ 12–18 in (30–45 cm)

The North American foamflowers interbreed freely and intermediate forms are common. Hybridizers have developed these into a range of attractive garden forms, including: **'Crow Feather'**, foliage with a dark central feather marking intensifying in winter, cream to pink flowers on spikes; **'Dark Star'**, bright green leaves with a dark center, pink-tinted white flowers; **'Elizabeth Oliver'**, deep maroon-veined foliage, maroon-tinted flowers; **'Spring Symphony'**, long-lobed, dark-centered leaves, pale pink flowers from dark buds; **'Tiger Stripe'**, dark-veined bronze foliage, reddening in autumn, pink-tinted cream flowers. Zones 6–9.

Tiarella, Hybrid Cultivar, 'Elizabeth Oliver'

TIBOUCHINA

syns *Lasiandra, Pleroma*

GLORY BUSH, LASIANDRA

This large genus belonging to the meadow-beauty (Melastomataceae) family consists of around 350 species, most from tropical South America. They are mostly shrubs or small trees, perennials, and scrambling climbers with large, hairy, prominently veined, simple leaves, oppositely arranged, often on square stems. The large, showy, 5-petalled flowers are violet, purple, pink, or white and may be borne singly or in panicles at the ends of branches followed by capsular fruit containing spiraly curved seeds. They are generally only suitable for warm to hot areas that are frost free, although well-established plants that are properly acclimatized may tolerate light frosts. Tibouchinas make very attractive horticultural subjects.

CULTIVATION: Most are fairly adaptable but perform best in warm areas in a light well-drained soil with a high organic content in full sun with plentiful water during the summer. Protect from strong winds and prune after flowering. Propagate from seed or cuttings taken in late spring or summer.

Tibouchina granulosa

GLORY BUSH

↔ 10 ft (3 m) ↕ 12–35 ft (3.5–10 m)

A large shrub or small tree, native to southeastern Brazil. Thick branching stems, lance-shaped to oblong leaves, shiny dark green, hairy underneath. Variable-colored flowers, violet to rose-purple or pink, in panicles at the ends of branches, in autumn. **'Rosea'** bears smaller purple to rosy magenta flowers. Zones 10–12.

Tibouchina heteromalla

↔ 4 ft (1.2 m) ↕ 3 ft (0.9 m)

This small spreading shrub comes from Brazil. Many erect stems, with broadly ovate velvety leaves, bright green; whitish green and very hairy beneath. Violet flowers, in erect panicles at the ends of branches, from summer to autumn. Zones 10–12.

Tiarella, HC, 'Spring Symphony'

Tibouchina lepidota 'Alstonville'

Tibouchina urvilleana

Tibouchina lepidota

GLORY BUSH

↔ 10 ft (3 m) ↑ 12 ft (3.5 m)

Bushy shrub, native to Ecuador and Colombia, that is taller and more tree-like in its natural environment. Ovate-oblong to oblong lance-shaped leaves are dark green, paler on the undersides. Panicles of violet-purple flowers, with violet-purple stamens, bloom from late summer to early winter. **'Alstonville'**, prolific display of vibrant purple flowers. Zones 10–12.

Tibouchina urvilleana

syns *Lasiandra semidecandra, Tibouchina semidecandra*

GLORY BUSH, PRINCESS FLOWER

↔ 10 ft (3 m) ↑ 15 ft (4.5 m)

Fast-growing shrub from Brazil. Dense rounded form with red hairy stems. Oblong-ovate leaves, dark green with serrated edges. Purple-violet flowers with purple stamens, appear singly or in panicles, in summer. **'Edwardsii'**, similar to the species but with somewhat larger flowers; **'Macrantha'**, large flowers. Zones 9–12.

Tibouchina Hybrid Cultivars

↔ 2–10 ft (0.6–3 m)
↑ 2–20 ft (0.6–6 m)

Tibouchina species interbreed freely. Many showy garden hybrids, including: **'Chameleon'**, to 7 ft (2 m) high and wide, flowers open white and age to deep pink; **'Groovy Baby'**, 32 in (80 cm) high and wide, small bright purple flowers; **'Jules'**, 24 in (60 cm) high and wide, small purple flowers year-round; **'Noeline'** (syn. 'Noelene'), large, to 20 ft (6 m) tall, flowers open near-white and age to mauve-pink; **'Peace Baby'**, 32 in (80 cm) high and wide, white to pale pink flowers, deep pink stamens. Zones 9–12.

Tibouchina, Hybrid Cultivar, 'Noeline'

TIGRIDIA

JOCKEY'S CAP, TIGER FLOWER

This bulbous genus in the iris (Iridaceae) family comprises 23 species found in Mexico and Guatemala. They have sword- to lance-shaped leaves with pronounced longitudinal ribbing. Upright, sometimes-branched flower stems appear from late spring through summer, carrying interestingly shaped and colored blooms with a bold tiger-stripe patterned central cup surrounded by 3 large lobes with 3 small lobes in between. Individual flowers last only one day and occur in a range of shades.

CULTIVATION: Considering their origins, these are surprisingly hardy bulbs that will thrive anywhere the soil does not freeze to bulb depth. Elsewhere they can be lifted for winter and replanted in spring. Propagate from offsets or from seed.

Tigridia pavonia ★

↔ 12–20 in (30–50 cm)
↑ 24–48 in (60–120 cm)

This long-flowering species is native to Mexico. Basal leaves grow 12–20 in (30–50 cm) long. The flower stems are usually about 24 in (60 cm) long, sometimes considerably longer. The flowers are yellow to red with heavily red-marked yellow cup, from spring to summer. Zones 9–10.

TILIA

BASSWOOD, LINDEN

Tilia has been revised down to just 45 species of deciduous trees belonging to the mallow (Malvaceae) family. They occur in eastern and central North America, Europe, as well as most of temperate Asia. They are upright single-trunked trees with a rounded to conical crown of foliage. The bark is silver-gray and smooth and with great age it becomes fissured. The leaf shape is usually oval to heart-shaped with serrated edges, tapering to a fine point. The foliage is usually mid-green but develops vibrant yellow tones in autumn. Small, cream, scented, separate male and female flowers with large bracts are produced in small clusters from late spring. These trees produce conspicuous pale green fruits.

CULTIVATION: These very hardy trees prefer a temperate climate with 4 distinct seasons. They thrive in deep well-drained soil and should be given plenty of moisture in summer. Young trees should be trimmed to shape. Propagate from the copiously produced seed, which needs stratification; from cuttings or layers; or, for special forms, by grafting.

Tilia americana

AMERICAN LINDEN, BASSWOOD

↔ 40 ft (12 m) ↑ 100 ft (30 m)

Broad-crowned tree found in central and eastern North America. Leaves up to 6 in (15 cm) long and almost as broad, with serrated edges, paler green beneath, tapering abruptly to a point. In mid-summer, clustered, pale yellow, fragrant flowers are produced. This species is complex, with many regional variations. ***T. a* var. *caroliniana*** (syns *T. australis, T. caroliniana*), leaves generally smaller, more heavily serrated, blue-green on undersides. ***T. a.* var. *heterophylla*** (syn. *T. heterophylla*), leaves are white-felted on the undersides, sometimes sparsely. ***T. a.* 'Ampelophylla'** has large-lobed leaves; **'Fastigiata'** has a narrow conical habit; **'Macrophylla'** features very large leaves; and **'Redmond'** has a conical growth habit. Zones 3–9.

Tigridia pavonia

Tilia amurensis

AMUR LINDEN

↔ 35 ft (10 m)
↑ 50–100 ft (15–30 m)

This large tree is found naturally in Russia, Korea, and in nearby parts of China. It has very thin bark, and dark green rounded leaves with narrow tips and serrated edges. The flowers are cream, fragrant, borne in clusters, in summer. Very similar to the far more commonly grown small-leafed lime (*T. cordata*). Zones 4–9.

Tilia cordata

LITTLE-LEAF LINDEN, SMALL-LEAFED LIME

↔ 40 ft (12 m)
↑ 80–100 ft (24–30 m)

This wide-crowned tree is found over most of temperate Europe from Wales, UK, to western Russia. Dark green rounded leaves, serrated, taper to a narrow tip. Clusters of 5 to 7 fragrant cream flowers, in summer. **'Greenspire'** ★, strong-growing form with narrow crown; **'Rancho'**, conical habit, glossy leaves. Zones 3–9.

Tilia × *euchlora*

↔ 40 ft (12 m) ↑ 70 ft (21 m)

Hybrid most likely of *T. cordata* × *T. dasystyla* parentage. Arching branches, become increasingly more pendulous with age. Leaves deep glossy green,

Tilia americana var. *caroliniana*

Tilia cordata 'Rancho'

pale blue-green hairy beneath. Cream flowerheads, relatively large, attractive to bees, in summer. Zones 4–9.

Tilia × europaea

syn. *Tilia × vulgaris*

COMMON LIME, EUROPEAN BASSWOOD

↔40 ft (12 m) ↑100 ft (30 m)

This *T. cordata × T. platyphyllos* hybrid is much planted in parks and city avenues. Tall, broad, conical crown, branches well down trunk. Leaves dark green, heart-shaped, hairy underside veins. Yellow autumn color. Cream flowers, in clusters, in summer, attractive to bees. **'Pallida'**, strongly upright growth with pale green leaves, ideal street tree; **'Wratislaviensis'**, golden yellow leaves when young. Zones 5–9.

Tilia japonica

JAPANESE LIME

↔20 ft (6 m) ↑50 ft (15 m)

This tree is found in Japan and nearby parts of China. Small pointed leaves have somewhat glaucous undersides. Fragrant creamy yellow flowers, in summer. Its relatively small size and upright growth habit make it an attractive specimen for avenue planting. Zones 6–10.

Tilia mongolica

MONGOLIAN LIME, MONGOLIAN LINDEN

↔35 ft (10 m) ↑50 ft (15 m)

This native of Mongolia is rare in cultivation. Gray bark becomes fissured and purple-tinted with age. The small leaves have pointed tips and are red-tinted. They mature to dark green, roughly triangular to heart-shaped leaves that have 3 to 5 maple-like lobes and coarse triangular teeth. The cream flowers, 6 to 10 in each cyme, bloom in mid-summer. Zones 3–9.

Tilia japonica

Tilia platyphyllos

BROAD-LEAFED LIME

↔50 ft (15 m) ↑100 ft (30 m)

This dome-shaped tree is found in various forms from western Europe to southwest Asia. Stems are distinctive, very hairy when young. Small clusters of pale yellow flowers are produced in early summer. Fruits persist after the leaves have fallen. It is smaller in cultivation. **'Laciniata'** develops a pretty dome shape, and bears yellow flowers from the crown; **'Orebro'** is shorter and broader, with slightly deeper green foliage. Zones 5–9.

Tilia tomentosa

EUROPEAN WHITE LIME, SILVER LIME, SILVER LINDEN

↔50 ft (15 m)
↑80–100 ft (24–30 m)

A dense conical to dome-shaped tree found in areas around the Black Sea. Rounded heart-shaped leaves, very dark green, coarsely serrated edges, fine gray down beneath. Dull white summer flowers. **'Brabant'**, broadly conical; **'Nijmegen'**, mottled gray bark, heart-shaped leaves. Zones 6–9.

Tilia tomentosa 'Brabant'

Tipuana tipu

TIPUANA

From northern South America, this genus, which is a member of the pea-flower subfamily of the legume (Fabaceae) family, consists of a single species. It is an evergreen tree widely grown for its outstanding floral display and overall attractive appearance. It has a wide flat crown covered in dark green foliage. In spring, the tree bursts into a profusion of deep yellow flowers at the tips of the branches. It has become a favorite shade and avenue tree in subtropical regions of the world. In cool or dry conditions it may be deciduous, but is bare for only a short period.
CULTIVATION: This tree needs a warm climate and a fertile, moist but well-drained soil in full sun. Pruning is rarely necessary, but young specimens may be shaped in late winter. It is sensitive to frost. Propagate from scarified seed in spring, which must be pretreated by rubbing them briefly on sandpaper and soaking in cold water.

Tipuana tipu

syn. *Tipuana speciosa*

PRIDE OF BOLIVIA, TIPU TREE

↔25 ft (8 m) ↑100 ft (30 m)

This fast-growing slender tree from northern South America develops a spreading, slightly flattened crown. Dark green pinnate leaves, composed of 11 to 21 glaucous, green, oblong leaflets. Profuse racemes of orange-yellow flowers, at the branch tips, in spring. Woody winged seed pods. Smaller under cultivation. Zones 9–12.

TITHONIA

MEXICAN SUNFLOWER

This genus is made up of 10 species of annuals, perennials, and shrubs that are native to Mexico and Central America. It is a member of the daisy (Asteraceae) family. Quite shrubby species, they are robust plants, sometimes with hairy stems, and have alternate leaves that are often lobed. They bear large daisy flowers in shades of yellow and orangey scarlet.
CULTIVATION: These plants are useful for providing a bright spot in the garden in late summer and autumn. Grow in a well-drained, moderately fertile soil in full sun. Propagate from seed or from cuttings.

Tithonia rotundifolia 'Torch'

Tithonia rotundifolia

syn. *Tithonia speciosa*

MEXICAN SUNFLOWER

↔2 ft (0.6 m) ↑3–6 ft (0.9–1.8 m)

This annual from Mexico and Central America is a rapidly forming, large, many-branched plant. Velvety-hairy leaves, to 12 in (30 cm) long. Orange ray flowers with tufted yellow centers, from summer to autumn, or first frost. **'Aztec Sun'**, 4 ft (1.2 m) tall, golden flowers; **'Fiesta del Sol'**, an earlier-blooming dwarf, to 3 ft (0.9 m) tall; **'Goldfinger'**, a bushy selection with deep orange flowers; **'Torch'**, orange-red flowers. Zones 9–10.

TOLMIEA

Native to the coastal mountains of western North America, from northern California and north to Alaska, USA, this monotypic genus in the saxifrage (Saxifragaceae) family is a mat-forming herbaceous perennial with shallowly lobed pale green leaves that are sometimes evergreen. Young plants are borne on the leaves where the leaf stalk and leaf blade meet.
CULTIVATION: They prefer neutral to acidic, cool, moist, humus-rich soil in partial to deep shade. Sun can scorch the leaves, particularly the variegated form. They are sometimes grown as a house plant, requiring cool temperatures and filtered light. Propagate by division in spring, or from seed in autumn. Plantlets may also be removed from leaves in mid- to late summer and potted up.

Tolmiea menziesii

PICKABACK PLANT, PIGGYBACK PLANT, THOUSAND MOTHERS

↔3–6 ft (0.9–1.8 m)
↑18–24 in (45–60 cm)

Shade-loving perennial from the west coast of North America. Shallowly lobed leaves, slightly hairy, medium green. Small, inconspicuous, reddish brown flowers are borne on top of 12–24 in (30–60 cm) stems, from late spring to summer. **'Taff's Gold'** (syns 'Maculata', 'Variegata') has leaves splashed with gold in spring; foliage fades somewhat in summer. Zones 6–9.

TORENIA

WISHBONE FLOWER

This is a genus of up to 50 species of low-growing, spreading, bushy annual and perennial plants from tropical parts of Africa and Asia. They have long been part of the foxglove (Scrophulariaceae) family, but their part of it may soon be split off as the Linderniaceae. These plant are noted for their ability to bloom well in both shady and sunny conditions. The toothed oval leaves, to 4 in (10 cm) long, cover the pale creamy green stems. The flowers are pale violet with dark blue-purple lower lips and a yellow throat blotch. A pair of stamens unites at the anthers in a shape resembling the wishbone of a chicken, hence the common name. The flowers generally appear from late spring and finish once the first frosts start. They make excellent edging plants for beds, borders, and shade or woodland gardens, as well as for containers or window boxes.

CULTIVATION: These plants need a warm spot to flourish and will not cope with frost, cold persistent winds, or cold wind-chill factors. They are best grown in consistently moist, organically rich, well-drained soils in part-shade to full sun. Propagate from seed in spring, or once the last of the frosts has finished.

Torenia fournieri

BLUEWINGS, WISHBONE FLOWER

↔ 10 in (25 cm) ↕ 12 in (30 cm)

Small bushy species naturally found in tropical Asia. Pale green lightly serrated leaves, 2 in (5 cm) long, form mounds on stems. Flowers pale purple, from summer to autumn. Ideal hanging basket plant. **'Blue Panda'**, compact habit, lilac-blue flowers; **Clown Series**, mix containing several colors, some with a contrasting rim to each flower. Zones 11–12.

Torenia fournieri 'Blue Panda'

Torenia, HC, 'Duchess Deep-blue'

Torenia, HC, 'Duchess White and Pink'

Torenia Hybrid Cultivars

↔ 10 in (25 cm)
↕ 12–15 in (30–38 cm)

Cultivars expand the range of flower colors to include shades of burgundy, pink, rose, lavender, as well as white. **'Duchess Deep-blue'**, deep purplish blue flowers with orange spotting; **'Duchess White and Blue'** ★, white flowers with very deep blue blotches; **'Duchess White and Pink'**, white flowers with deep magenta markings. Zones 11–12.

TORREYA

This genus consists of 7 species of evergreen coniferous shrubs or trees belonging to the yew (Taxaceae) family. It is native to North America and Asia, and is found in sheltered woodland and moist riverside situations. The species vary from shrubs to trees with a wide-open crown. The leaves are glossy, fine, sharp needles, yew-like, with paler undersides. Some of the leaves will emit a scent when crushed. The fruit is a seed, smooth or furrowed, dull green to purplish in color. *Torreya nucifera*, the kaya nut of Japan, is edible and the oil is used for cooking in that country. The timber of *T. taxifolia* is used for fencing; however, this is an endangered species surviving in the wild in only a few small areas in the States of Florida and Georgia, USA.

CULTIVATION: These plants require shelter from cold or drying winds and grow in moist fertile soil with good drainage in full sun or part-shade. Propagate from half-hardened cuttings in late summer, or sow seed as soon as it is ripe in an area protected from frost. Label well as germination may take up to 2 years.

Torreya californica

Torreya californica

CALIFORNIA NUTMEG, CALIFORNIA NUTMEG YEW

↔ 25 ft (8 m) ↕ 80 ft (24 m)

A tall tree, native to California, USA, only species to adapt to cool seaside climates. Open crown, broadly conical, and somewhat pendulous shoots. Leaves yew-like, dark green needles, paler on the underside, scented when crushed. Greenish purple female cones appear in summer. Zones 7–10.

Torreya nucifera

JAPANESE NUTMEG YEW, KAYA NUT

↔ 25 ft (8 m) ↕ 50–80 ft (15–24 m)

Tree or shrub, native to Japan. Leaves dark green glossy above, blue-white stomatal bands beneath, scented when crushed. Olive green female cones have an edible kernel. Considerably smaller in cultivation. Zones 7–10.

TRACHELIUM

A small genus of 7 species of perennial herbs belonging to the bellflower (Campanulaceae) family, native to Mediterranean regions, and usually found growing in rocky crevices. They range from tiny cushion-forming species to more robust, erect, woody-based plants. Their simple leaves are alternately arranged. The flowers, in shades of purple and white, usually appear in clusters in summer. They are tubular with prominently protruding styles. *T. caeruleum*, which is suitable for border planting, is most commonly seen, flowering from seed in its first year or grown as an annual.

Trachelium caeruleum

CULTIVATION: Grow in a sunny position in reasonably fertile, well-drained soil. The small species, requiring perfectly drained, alkaline soil, are better suited to the rock garden, pots or alpine house. Provide protection from the hottest sun and from winter wet. Propagate from seed or cuttings.

Trachelium caeruleum ★

↔ 18 in (45 cm)
↕ 24–36 in (60–90 cm)

Upright perennial from the Mediterranean. Serrated-edged, pointed, oval leaves. Rounded clusters of tiny, starry, pleasantly perfumed, purple flowers, in summer. Very long protruding styles give flowerheads a soft fluffy appearance. Zones 9–11.

TRACHELOSPERMUM

CONFEDERATE JASMINE, STAR JASMINE

A genus of about 20 species of evergreen climbing and twining plants found originally in woodland areas from Japan to India, and part of the dogbane (Apocynaceae) family. The attractive, glossy, oval leaves are pointed at both ends. The stems will climb over supports and cling to walls and hard surfaces with great ease and abandon. These plants are popular in the ornamental garden for covering fences and pergolas or to clamber up tree trunks. They are used to soften concrete and brick walls and absorb heat in urban landscapes. They work well as ground cover for larger areas and are effectively used in containers and urns, making great indoor or greenhouse specimens. When grown indoors, they will reward with fragrant blossoms if supplied with at least a few hours of sun in winter.

CULTIVATION: These climbers are not particular as to soil but prefer well-drained situations with some organic matter. They will grow happily in sun or shade and require average amounts of water; however, they are somewhat drought tolerant once established. Propagate from half-hardened cuttings in summer.

T

Trachelospermum jasminoides 'Tricolor'

Trachelospermum asiaticum

↔ 10–17 ft (3–5 m) ↑ 20 ft (6 m)

A twining climber from Japan and Korea. The oval, dark green, glossy, leathery-looking leaves can grow up to 2 in (5 cm) long. Very fragrant, star-shaped, white flowers hang in clusters, in summer. Zones 8–10.

Trachelospermum jasminoides ★

syn. *Rhynchospermum jasminoides*

CONFEDERATE JASMINE, STAR JASMINE

↔ 17–25 ft (5–8 m) ↑ 30 ft (9 m)

A twining climber from Korea, Japan, and China, with oval to elliptical, dark green, glossy leaves, up to 4 in (10 cm) long. Masses of very fragrant white flowers appear in clusters, from summer to mid-autumn. This species can be grown as a ground-cover plant. **'Tricolor'** ★, red, yellow, and green foliage; **'Variegatum'** ★, with white-marked dark green foliage that can burn in hot sun. Zones 9–10.

TRACHYCARPUS

Originally found from southern China to the Himalayas, this is a genus of about 6 species grown for their attractive foliage and their cold tolerance. They are members of the palm (Arecaceae) family. The fan-shaped or circular fronds are up to 5 ft (1.5 m) across and divided almost to the base into stiff, narrow, pleated segments. The frond stalks are often armed with stout sharp teeth. The small fragrant flowers are followed by rounded or kidney-shaped dark purple or orange fruit. These palms are slow-growing and long-lived. They will make good indoor plants in areas that experience severe frosts.

CULTIVATION: These palms will grow well in any well-drained soil that is reasonably fertile. They need plenty of water and do best in full sun or part-shade in a position that is sheltered from cold winds, especially when they are young. Potted specimens should be watered moderately during the growing season, much less in cooler weather. Propagate these palms from fresh seed in spring.

Trachycarpus fortunei

Trachycarpus wagnerianus

Trachycarpus fortunei ★

CHINESE FAN PALM, CHINESE WINDMILL PALM, CHUSAN PALM

↔ 12 ft (3.5 m) ↑ 35 ft (10 m)

Widely cultivated cold-tolerant palm from northern Myanmar and central and eastern China. Slender trunk clothed in loose dark brown fibers and old frond bases. Deep green fan-shaped fronds, divided into many segments. Clusters of small yellow flowers, in summer. Bluish fruits. Zones 8–11.

Trachycarpus wagnerianus ★

↔ 8 ft (2.4 m) ↑ 10–20 ft (3–6 m)

Known only in cultivation, this fan palm is probably a form of the far more commonly grown *T. fortunei*. Distinguished by its smaller and stiffer fronds and by the very tightly woven thatch that develops on its trunk. Zones 8–11.

TRACHYSTEMON

RUSSIAN BORAGE

This small genus of only 2 species of herbaceous perennials is a member of the borage (Boraginaceae) family and is native to eastern Europe. They have large bristly leaves very like

Trachystemon orientalis

those of comfrey *(Symphytum)* and bright blue starry flowers in very early spring as the leaves come up. Only *T. orientalis* is in general cultivation.

CULTIVATION: These exceptionally hardy plants do best in light to heavy shade in moist humus-rich soil where they will make large weed-smothering clumps. Propagate by division when dormant. Plants will self-seed.

Trachystemon orientalis

syn. *Borago orientalis*

RUSSIAN BORAGE

↔ 3–7 ft (0.9–2 m)
↑ 2–3 ft (0.6–0.9 m)

A coarse herbaceous perennial from Europe. Paddle-shaped, bristly, green leaves, to 12 in (30 cm) long. Open sprays of bright blue starry flowers with a white center to ¾ in (18 mm) across, in late winter–early spring. Zones 5–10.

TRADESCANTIA

SPIDER LILY, SPIDERWORT

This genus is made up of around 70 species of annuals and perennials from the Americas is a member of the spiderwort (Commelinaceae) family. It includes a few species that, while attractive as garden plants, have become serious pests in some areas. Tuberous or fibrous rooted and often evergreen, they have rather succulent stems and fleshy, pointed elliptical, lance-shaped, or narrow leaves. The clusters of small, 3-petalled flowers, subtended by bracts, appear through the warmer months. They are sometimes very bright magenta, though white, soft pink, and blue to mauve predominate. Variegated and colored foliage forms are common.

CULTIVATION: Most of these plants are tolerant of light to moderate frosts. Some species prefer a sunny aspect and are drought tolerant, but most prefer part-shade and moist well-drained soil. Propagate by division, or from self-struck layers, tip cuttings or seed, depending on the growth form.

Tradescantia, AG, 'Bilberry Ice'

Tradescantia Andersoniana Group

↔ 12–48 in (30–120 cm)
↑ 8–20 in (20–50 cm)

This group includes hybrids of several species, not just one cross. Mainly derived from *Tradescantia virginiana*, it is a selection of mainly clumping hybrids with the narrow foliage and flowering habits of *T. virginiana*. This group is often wrongly called *T.* × *andersoniana*. Popular hybrids include: **'Bilberry Ice'**, blue-green foliage, pale silver-mauve flowers; **'Blue and Gold'** (syn. 'Sweet Kate'), with long, narrow, bright yellow leaves and vivid blue flowers; **'Concord Grape'**, blue-green foliage and deep magenta flowers; **'Innocence'**, bright green foliage, pure white flowers; **'Isis'**, green foliage and bright blue flowers; **'J. C. Weguelin'**, green foliage and striking sky blue flowers; **'Little Doll'**, very compact, bright green foliage, soft mauve-blue flowers; **'Osprey'**, green foliage and flowers white to palest mauve with a mauve-blue center; **'Purple Dome'**, green foliage, deep purple flowers; **'Zwanenburg Blue'**, green foliage, blue to violet flowers. Zones 7–10.

Tradescantia fluminensis

syn. *Tradescantia albiflora*

WANDERING JEW

↔ 24–60 in (60–150 cm)
↑ 12–20 in (30–50 cm)

A somewhat invasive perennial from South America and naturalized in southern USA. Thick succulent stems, closely spaced. Broadly lance-shaped fleshy leaves with lighter central area, to over 3 in (8 cm) long; large white flowers. Cultivated forms occur in wide range of foliage colors and patterns. Zones 9–11.

Tradescantia virginiana

Tradescantia sillamontana

Trevesia palmata

Trichostema lanatum

Tricyrtis hirta

Tradescantia sillamontana

WHITE VELVET

↔ 40 in (100 cm)
↑ 6–32 in (15–80 cm)

A perennial from northern Mexico. Sometimes erect, or spreading and trailing. Fleshy lance-shaped leaves, to nearly 3 in (8 cm) long, purple-red tinted under a dense covering of silky silvery hairs. Small purple-magenta flowers, in summer. Zones 9–11.

Tradescantia spathacea

syn. *Rhoeo discolor*

BOAT LILY, CRADLE LILY, MOSES-IN-HIS-CRADLE

↔ 12–16 in (30–40 cm)
↑ 15 in (38 cm)

A short-stemmed clumping perennial from southern Mexico, Guatemala, and Belize. Rosettes of erect leaves, to 14 in (35 cm) long, broadly spear-shaped, dark green above, purple-red below. Small white flowers in boat-shaped bract near leaf base, all year. **'Vittata'** ★ (syn. 'Variegata'), cream-and-pink striped foliage. Zones 10–12.

Tradescantia virginiana

↔ 20–48 in (50–120 cm)
↑ 12–20 in (30–50 cm)

Mounding spreading perennial from eastern USA. Narrow, rather grass-like leaves. Small heads of white, pink, mauve-blue, or purple flowers with similarly colored bracts, in summer. Widely hybridized to produce a range of garden forms. Zones 7–10.

TREVESIA

The 12 species of shrubs and trees in this genus, which is a member of the ivy (Araliaceae) family, are found from the Himalayas to southern China and Southeast Asia. Often forming dense clumps, they have thick stems that may be prickly. The large palmately lobed leaves are carried in clusters near the branch tips. Large terminal clusters of small creamy flowers are borne in summer.

CULTIVATION: Grown for their handsome foliage, *Trevesia* species require heated greenhouse or conservatory protection in cold climates. In humid tropical areas they will grow in a shrub border, where they'll need a sheltered, and partly shaded site in moisture-retentive, deep, fertile soil. Propagate from seed or softwood cuttings.

Trevesia palmata

↔ 12 ft (3.5 m) ↑ 30 ft (9 m)

Species native from India to southern China and Southeast Asia. Can grow unbranched or can develop into a wide-crowned shrub or tree. Stout thorny stems and unusual palmately lobed leaves. Large clusters of off-white flowers, in spring. Zones 10–12.

TRICHOSTEMA

This genus of 16 species of aromatic annuals and small shrubs is a member of the mint (Lamiaceae) family and is found throughout most parts of North America. They have simple lance-shaped leaves that have a woolly underside. They produce blue, or occasionally pink or white, tubular flowers, which resemble those of the related *Salvia* genus, during most of spring and summer.

CULTIVATION: The shrubby species should be grown in a well-drained soil of medium fertility. In cool climates they are best overwintered in the greenhouse. Propagate these plants from seed sown in spring, or from half-hardened cuttings in autumn.

Trichostema lanatum

BLUE CURLS, WOOLLY BLUE CURLS

↔ 2 ft (0.6 m) ↑ 2–5 ft (0.6–1.5 m)

Shrubby species from California, USA. Dark green lance-shaped leaves, woolly beneath, rolled edges. Woolly, tubular purple-blue flowers on 15 in (38 cm) spikes, in spring–summer. Zones 8–10.

TRICYRTIS

TOAD LILY

A genus of 16 graceful, rhizomatous, woodland perennials in the asparagus (Asparagaceae) family, occurring in moist woodlands and on mountains and cliffs from the eastern Himalayas to the Philippines, and in Japan and Taiwan. Their oblong to lance-shaped, pointed, often glossy and sometimes spotted leaves clasp upright on arching stems. The star-, bell-, or funnel-shaped flowers are terminal or in upper leaf axils and can be pure white, golden yellow, lavender, or purple, usually spotted, with a somewhat waxen or iridescent quality. They usually bloom in late summer and autumn.

CULTIVATION: These perennials need moist, well-drained, humus-rich soil, and part-shade to sun. In warmer areas, they will do best in part- to full shade. Some species may be propagated from seed in autumn. All may be divided in spring when dormant.

Tricyrtis affinis

↔ 24 in (60 cm) ↑ 36 in (90 cm)

Hardy Japanese species. Arching stems and large, broadly oval leaves. White flowers, 1 in (25 mm) wide, speckled purple, are borne from mid-summer to autumn. Prefers full to part-shade. Zones 5–9.

Tricyrtis formosana

syn. *Tricyrtus stolonifera*

FORMOSA TOAD LILY

↔ 18 in (45 cm) ↑ 36 in (90 cm)

Erect species, native to Taiwan, spreading by runners. Green leaves mottled deeper green. Flowers borne mostly in terminal clusters; maroon or brown buds open to white or pale lilac, purple-spotted flowers tinged yellow, in mid-summer to autumn. Zones 5–9.

Tricyrtis hirta

HAIRY TOAD LILY

↔ 24 in (60 cm) ↑ 36 in (90 cm)

Upright species from Japan. Arching stems, slightly hairy, with soft green foliage. White flowers speckled with dark purple, along stems in leaf axils, in early to mid-autumn. **'Myazaki'**, smaller plant, arching habit, slightly larger purple-spotted pink to white flowers; **'Myazaki Gold'**, similar flowers to **'Myazaki'**, with gold-edged leaves. Zones 4–9.

Tricyrtis macrantha

↔ 24 in (60 cm) ↑ 30 in (75 cm)

Graceful species, native to Japan. Arching stems; glossy green, ovate-oblong, bamboo-like leaves. Pendulous bell-like flowers held on brownish, slightly fuzzy stems, lemon yellow with chocolate spots inside, in early autumn. Prefers deep shade and moist soil. Zones 7–9.

Tricyrtis macropoda

syn. *Tricyrtis dilatata*

◐ ✱ ↔ 24 in (60 cm) ↑ 30 in (75 cm)

Handsome species from China. Oblong-ovate leaves on erect stems. Branched inflorescences of lavender flowers with darker purple spots, in mid- to late summer. Zones 5–9.

TRILLIUM

WAKE ROBIN, WOOD LILY

This group of 30 rhizome-rooted, spring-flowering, woodland perennials from North America and temperate Asia is part of the Melanthiaceae family. Ranging from the tiny *T. rivale*, to 2 in (5 cm) high, to species 24 in (60 cm) tall in flower, the genus is remarkably consistent in form. The leaflets are bright green, often mottled and usually broadly oval, tapering to a point. At the center of the 3-leafed cluster is a simple 3-petalled flower that may be white, cream, pink, or deep maroon-red. The common name comes from their early flowering habit—the plant that wakes the robin in spring.

CULTIVATION: Plant in part- or full shade in a cool, moist, humus-rich, well-drained soil. All species die back completely in autumn but race into growth in early spring. Propagate by division or from seed.

Trillium albidum

◐/☀ ✱ ↔ 20 in (50 cm) ↑ 20 in (50 cm)

Species native to western USA, allied to *T. chloropetalum*. Leaves rounded, often silver mottled, making a complete ruff behind the flowers. Flowers fragrant, white with a pink base, with erect, slightly reflexed petals, in early spring. Zones 6–9.

Trillium chloropetalum

◐/☀ ✱ ↔ 20 in (50 cm) ↑ 20 in (50 cm)

Perennial from California, USA. Thick stems; rounded, often maroon-mottled leaves developing rapidly from early spring to form a full ruff behind the flowers. Fragrant, white to greenish white, soft yellow or maroon flowers with slightly reflexed petals, in early spring. T. c. var. giganteum, robust, usually dark red-flowered form, with maroon-mottled foliage. Zones 6–9.

Trillium cuneatum

SWEET BETSY, TOAD SHADE

◐/☀ ✱ ↔ 16 in (40 cm) ↑ 24 in (60 cm)

Variegated species native to southeastern USA. Mottled gray-green and olive foliage said to resemble pattern of a toad's skin. Leaves pointed oval, not quite making a full circle. Flowers burgundy to yellowish green, musk-scented, in early spring. Zones 6–9.

Trillium erectum ★

BETHROOT, BIRTHROOT

◐/☀ ✱ ↔ 20 in (50 cm) ↑ 20 in (50 cm)

Woodland perennial, native to eastern North America. Large, light textured, bright green leaves, sometimes making a complete ruff. Flowers unpleasantly scented, sitting at or slightly above foliage level, dark velvety red, rarely white, narrow petals, in early spring. Zones 4–9.

Trillium flexipes

BENT TRILLIUM

◐/☀ ✱ ↔ 12 in (30 cm) ↑ 16 in (40 cm)

From northern USA. Pointed oval leaves. Distinctive nodding flowers on slender stems, white to pale pink, rarely maroon, petals and sepals reflexed or sometimes nearly horizontal, to 2 in (5 cm) long, in early spring. Zones 4–9.

Trillium grandiflorum

GRAND TRILLIUM, SHOWY TRILLIUM

◐/☀ ✱ ↔ 20 in (50 cm) ↑ 18 in (45 cm)

Late-flowering species from eastern North America. Rounded to pointed oval leaves, sometimes overlapping to form a full circle. Flowers opening white, ageing to pink, with narrow to broad petals to 3 in (8 cm) long, in early summer. *T. g.* f. *roseum* ('Roseum'), flowers pink, ageing to a deep dusky shade. *T. g.* 'Flore Pleno', double flowers. Zones 5–9.

Trillium chloropetalum

Trillium cuneatum

Trillium luteum

WOOD TRILLIUM, YELLOW WAKE ROBIN

◐/☀ ✱ ↔ 18 in (45 cm) ↑ 18 in (45 cm)

Native to southeastern USA. Broad pointed oval, mottled leaves, not overlapping. Yellow to yellow-green, very fragrant flowers with erect petals to over 3 in (8 cm) long, in early spring. Zones 5–9.

Trillium ovatum

WESTERN TRILLIUM, WAKE ROBIN

◐/☀ ✱ ↔ 20 in (50 cm) ↑ 20 in (50 cm)

Erect species, native to Oregon, USA. Conspicuously veined, deep green, pointed oval to rhomboidal leaves. Flowers held above foliage level on erect stems, white petals held almost horizontally, ageing to pink, musk-scented, in early spring. Zones 5–9.

Trillium pusillum

DWARF WAKE ROBIN

◐/☀ ✱ ↔ 6–8 in (15–20 cm) ↑ 6 in (15 cm)

A small woodland species from southeastern USA. Narrow leaflets, to 2 in (5 cm) long, sometimes slightly blue-green. White flowers, nearly horizontal petals to 1 in (25 mm) long, sepals conspicuous, slightly larger, in early spring. Zones 6–9.

Trillium rivale

BROOK WAKE ROBIN

◐/☀ ✱ ↔ 6 in (15 cm) ↑ 4 in (10 cm)

A small species from the Siskiyou Mountains of California and Oregon, USA. Leaves up to 1¼ in (3 cm) long, leaf stems slightly shorter. Flowers are white, held above the foliage, often flushed pink with purple-pink spotting, in early spring. Zones 5–9.

Trillium sessile

TOAD SHADE

◐/☀ ✱ ↔ 12–16 in (30–40 cm) ↑ 12 in (30 cm)

Native to northeastern USA. Elliptical to rounded leaves with dark mottling, often slightly drooping, leaves encircle flower but seldom overlap. Flowers musk-scented, petals deep purple-red, sepals green tinted purple-red, in early spring. Zones 4–9.

Trillium sulcatum

FURROWED WAKE ROBIN, SOUTHERN RED TRILLIUM

◐/☀ ✱ ↔ 20 in (50 cm) ↑ 16 in (40 cm)

A tall species found in central eastern USA. Large, light-textured, bright green leaves, making a complete ruff. Flowers held above the foliage on long stems, red-brown, to around 3 in (8 cm) wide, slightly malodorous, in early spring. Zones 5–9.

Trillium tschonoskii

◐/☀ ✱ ↔ 8–12 in (20–30 cm) ↑ 8 in (20 cm)

This small species is found from the Himalayas to Japan. Resembles *T. kamtschaticum*, forming small clump of short-stemmed pointed oval leaves, to 6 in (15 cm) long. Small greenish white flowers ageing to pink and mauve, in early spring. Zones 5–9.

Trillium flexipes

Trillium ovatum

Trillium pusillum

TROCHODENDRON

This genus, a member of the family Trochodendraceae, contains a single species of evergreen tree or shrub that has attractive tiered branches and is native to Japan, Korea, and Taiwan. The leaves are glossy and bright green and grow spirally near the tips of the stems. The green and petal-less flowers are produced in upright clusters from late spring. The genus name means "wheel tree," which refers to the spoke-like arrangement of the flower stamens. In the wild this plant will often start life as an epiphyte growing on *Cryptomeria japonica*. Its wood resembles that of coniferous trees and it is thought to be a quite primitive plant.

CULTIVATION: Although interesting and attractive, this species is very slow-growing in cultivation. It requires a fertile moisture-retentive soil in part-shade with protection from cold winds. Propagate from seed or half-hardened cuttings.

Trochodendron aralioides

WHEEL TREE

◐ ❄ ↔25 ft (8 m) ↑70 ft (21 m)

A tall tree from Japan, Korea, and Taiwan; in cultivation it will slowly grow to about 15 ft (4.5 m) high. Tiered branches bear simple glossy green leaves in spirals near the stem tips. Upright clusters of 10 to 12 small, green, petal-less flowers, in late spring. Zones 8–10.

TROLLIUS

GLOBE FLOWER

There are approximately 31 species of perennial herbs in this genus, which is a member of the buttercup (Ranunculaceae) family. They are found in almost all northern temperate regions from the Himalayas to Turkey, China, Europe, and North America. The roots are thick and fibrous and the plants form basal tufts or rosettes of palmately lobed and divided leaves with toothed edges. The flowers, often cupped, are up to 3 in (8 cm) wide, and have spirally arranged sepals and petals of white, yellow, or orange, sometimes tinged with red or lilac. They grow in damp sunny meadows and on stream banks, often in heavy soils. The many cultivars of *T.* × *cultorum* have a more refined bushy habit and will fit easily into the garden border.

CULTIVATION: These plants will grow best in full sun or part-shade in permanently moist soil or in boggy areas beside water. Propagate from seed or by division.

Trochodendron aralioides

Trollius chinensis 'Golden Queen'

Trollius chinensis

syn. *Trollius ledebourii*

☀/◐ ❄ ↔18 in (45 cm) ↑36 in (90 cm)

This clumping species can be found growing naturally in northern China. It has deeply lobed and finely toothed leaves. The flowers are bowl-shaped, golden yellow, and have prominent stamens. They are produced on tall stems, held well above the foliage, during summer. **'Golden Queen'** ★, deep orange-yellow flowers. Zones 5–9.

Trollius × *cultorum*

☀/◐ ❄ ↔18 in (45 cm) ↑24–36 cm (60–90 cm)

This group of garden hybrids includes crosses between *T. asiaticus*, *T. chinensis*, and *T. europaeus*. They show characteristics intermediate between the parents with attractive, finely divided foliage and flowers in colors ranging from lemon to orange, in summer. **'Cheddar'**, palest lemon to almost white flowers; **'Feuertroll'**, rich orangey yellow flowers; **'Orange Princess'**, orange flowers tinted with yellow. Zones 5–9.

Trollius europaeus

COMMON GLOBE FLOWER

☀/◐ ❄ ↔18 in (45 cm) ↑24 in (60 cm)

This variable species is found growing naturally in Europe, northern Asia, and far northern North America. Leaves 3- to 5-lobed, much-divided, and toothed. Globular lemon yellow flowers, to 2 in (5 cm) wide, in spring–summer. Zones 5–9.

Tropaeolum majus 'Peach Schnapps'

Trollius × *cultorum* 'Cheddar'

Trollius pumilus

☀/◐ ❄ ↔12 in (30 cm) ↑4–10 in (10–25 cm)

This alpine species is found from the Himalayas eastward to China. It has deeply lobed glossy leaves. Small, open, yellowish orange flowers are borne in summer. Zones 5–9.

TROPAEOLUM

CANARY BIRD VINE, FLAME CREEPER, NASTURTIUM

The type genus for the nasturtium (Tropaeolaceae) family, this group of over 80 species of sometimes tuberous annuals and perennials is found from southern Mexico to the southern tip of South America. Many climb using their twining leaf stalks. Though variable, the leaves are often shield-shaped and tinted blue-green. All have long-spurred 5-petalled flowers in a wide range of mainly warm shades. The name comes from the Greek *tropaion*, "trophy," a term used for the tree trunk on which were hung the shields and helmets of defeated enemies.

CULTIVATION: Hardiness varies considerably in these species. Plant in full sun or half-sun in moist well-drained soil. May need trimming back occasionally. Propagate by division, from basal cuttings or seed.

Tropaeolum ciliatum

◐/● ❄ ↔20 ft (6 m) ↑20 ft (6 m)

Vigorous, climbing, herbaceous perennial from Chile. Leaves mid-green, with 5 to 7 lobes. Bright golden yellow trumpet-shaped flowers have deep red center and veining, in summer. Capable of covering large area in one season. Zones 8–10.

Tropaeolum speciosum

Tropaeolum majus

NASTURTIUM

☀/◐ ❄ ↔10 ft (3 m) ↑10 ft (3 m)

Annual climber or scrambler found from Colombia to Bolivia. Near round, dull green leaves, sometimes shallowly lobed. Flowers to over 2 in (5 cm) wide, long-spurred, in shades of yellow, orange, and red, in summer. Now grown mainly in the form of seed-raised cultivars in various colors, some double-flowered; it is possible that some cultivars are of hybrid origin, with other annual species such as *T. minus* and *T. peltophorum* in their parentage, but breeders have not revealed their history. **Alaska Series** ★, white-variegated foliage, most flower colors; **'Empress of India'**, green to bluish green leaves, vivid red flowers; **Gleam Hybrids**, mixed or individual colors; **'Hermine Grashoff'**, shallowly lobed leaves and orange-red double flowers; **Jewel Series** ★, white foliage variegation, in most flower colors; **'Margaret Long'**, shallowly lobed leaves and golden yellow shading to pink double flowers; **'Peach Melba'**, pale yellow flowers with orange blotch on each petal; **'Peach Schnapps'**, pinkish orange with orange veining on each petal; **'Red Wonder'**, low, slightly spreading, purple-blue leaves, deep red flowers; **Whirlibird Series**, low and spreading, in most flower colors. Zones 9–11.

Tropaeolum peregrinum

CANARY CREEPER

☀/◐ ❄ ↔8 ft (2.4 m) ↑8 ft (2.4 m)

A quick-growing perennial climber from Peru and Ecuador, often treated as an annual. Light green, 5-lobed leaves. Clusters of long-stemmed, 1 in (25 mm) wide, sulfur yellow to gold flowers, cut-edged petals, in summer–autumn. Zones 9–11.

Tropaeolum speciosum

FLAME CREEPER, FLAME FLOWER, FLAME NASTURTIUM

↔ 10 ft (3 m) ↑ 10 ft (3 m)

Perennial climber from Chile. Mid-green to blue-green, palmate, 5- to 7-lobed leaves, often downy. Clusters of brilliant red, 1 in (25 mm) wide flowers, in summer–autumn. Blooms well in shade. Zones 8–10.

Tropaeolum tuberosum

↔ 10 ft (3 m) ↑ 10 ft (3 m)

Tuberous-rooted perennial climber from central Andes. Gray-green leaves. Solitary long-stemmed flowers, spur red, petals golden yellow to red, in summer. The large purple-marked yellow tubers are used as a vegetable in its native range. ***T. t.* var. *lineamaculatum* 'Ken Aslet'**, orange flowers. Zones 8–10.

TSUGA

HEMLOCK SPRUCE

These 10 or 11 evergreen, monoecious, coniferous trees from North America and Asia belong to the pine (Pinaceae) family. It grows in mountainous areas in its southern distribution, and in wet cool coastal areas and plains in the north. Most young trees are shade tolerant. They have flattened linear leaves with whitish silver bands on the undersides. The female cones become pendent as they ripen and drop off in the second year. Grown mainly for its timber and ornamental cultivars.

CULTIVATION: *Tsuga* grows in humus-rich, slightly acid, neutral to marginally alkaline soil in shade to sun. All need moist well-drained soil and shelter from cold winds. In poor dry soil these plants make weedy specimens. Propagate by sowing seed in pots in an area protected from winter frosts, or by rooting half-hardened cuttings in late summer to autumn.

Tsuga canadensis

CANADIAN HEMLOCK, EASTERN HEMLOCK

↔ 30 ft (9 m)
↑ 80–120 ft (24–36 m)

An evergreen tree, native to eastern North America, in cultivation often smaller, multi-stemmed. Gray hairy young shoots, linear leaves arranged in 2 rows. Leaves toothed, mid-green above, silver underneath. Female cones brown, grow on end of branchlets. **'Aurea'**, grows to 25 ft (8 m) tall, young foliage is golden, turning green as it matures; **'Bennett'**, a dwarf cultivar with lighter green leaves; **'Cole's Prostrate'**, low-growing ground cover that reaches up to 12 in (30 cm) tall; **'Gracilis'**, a slow-growing dwarf; **'Jacqueline Verkade'**, dwarf cultivar of globular form; **'Minuta'**, a very compact form; **'Pendula ★'**, a mound-forming slow-growing shrub with pendent branches that reaches 12 ft (3.5 m) in height. Zones 4–9.

Tsuga diversifolia

NORTH JAPANESE HEMLOCK

↔ 25 ft (8 m) ↑ 50 ft (15 m)

Large dense tree from northern Japan; rounded habit. Retains leaves for up to 10 years before shedding. Young branchlets are reddish brown; needles notched; cones dark brown, appearing in summer. Often seen as a shrub in cultivation. Zones 5–8.

Tsuga heterophylla

WESTERN HEMLOCK

↔ 20–30 ft (6–9 m)
↑ 60–120 ft (18–36 m)

A large tree, native to western North America. Horizontal branches have pendent tips, glossy dark green leaves. Egg-shaped female cones. Shade tolerant, needs protection from wind. Timber and bark used commercially. **'Argenteovariegata'**, white young shoots; **'Laursen's Column'**, dwarf, narrow and columnar. Zones 6–10.

Tsuga heterophylla, in the wild, North Cascades National Park, Washington, USA

Tsuga canadensis

Tsuga mertensiana

MOUNTAIN HEMLOCK

↔ 20 ft (6 m) ↑ 50 ft (15 m)

Slow-growing tree, native to western North America. Blue-green leaves, blunt tips. Young cones purple, mature to dark brown, in summer. **'Glauca Nana'**, to 10 ft (3 m) high, silver-gray foliage. Zones 4–9.

TULBAGHIA

SOCIETY GARLIC, WILD GARLIC

This genus, which is a member of the amaryllis (Amaryllidaceae) family, is known for its flowering habit. These bulbous perennials come from summer-rainfall areas in southern Africa, and those in cultivation adapt well to irrigated beds in dry-summer climates. They also pick well, pot well and, generally speaking, lead clumping trouble-free lives. The umbels of starry flowers are held well above the leaves. Many species carry a persistent stale garlic scent when crushed. The flowers of these garden-grown members are dainty to look at and perform well over extended periods, and some will even put on two flowery displays in a single year, depending on the local conditions.

CULTIVATION: Grow in full sun in well-drained soils and water well while in growth. Provide a sheltered spot in cool climates. Propagate from offsets or by sowing fresh ripe seed.

Tsuga mertensiana

Tulbaghia natalensis ★

↔ 6 in (15 cm)
↑ 8–12 in (20–30 cm)

Small perennial from Zimbabwe and South Africa. Leaves linear, light green, with stale garlic scent when crushed. Flowers dark purple or white, slightly fragrant, in early to late summer. Good container specimen. Zones 8–10.

Tulbaghia simmleri

syns *Tulbaghia fragrans, T. pulchella*

PINK AGAPANTHUS, SWEET GARLIC

↔ 10–12 in (25–30 cm)
↑ 20–24 in (50–60 cm)

Bulbous semi-evergreen perennial from South Africa. Comparatively broad gray-green leaves. Clusters of up to 40 scented mauve flowers, from spring to summer. **'Alba'** (syn. *T. fragrans* 'Alba'), pure white form. Zones 8–10.

Tulbaghia violacea ★

↔ 12 in (30 cm)
↑ 12–16 in (30–40 cm)

Vigorous clump-forming plant from South Africa, gray-green foliage. Clusters of up to 20 pink-mauve flowers produced almost year-round where frost is minimal. Whole plant has strong garlic smell when crushed. Can become weed if neglected. **Border Stars Series**, compact, dense, clumping forms in range of flower colors; **'Silver Lace'** (syn. 'Variegata'), slightly smaller variegated form with cream stripes. Zones 8–10.

Tulbaghia simmleri

Tulbaghia violacea

Tulipa hageri

Tulipa praestans

Tulipa iliensis

Tulipa orphanidea, Whittallii Group, cv

T. linifolia, Batalinii Group, 'Bronze Charm'

TULIPA

TULIP

This genus, a member of the lily (Liliaceae) family, contains approximately 100 species of bulbs occurring naturally in northern temperate regions, especially in central Asia. Cultivated for at least 3,000 years, they reached Europe from Turkey in 1554. The Dutch "tulipomania" of the 1630s established tulips in folklore as well as gardens. The foliage is gray-green to blue-green and may be grass-like or quite broad, with contrasting markings. The flowers vary widely. The numerous hybrids and cultivars are divided into 15 groups based mainly on parentage and flower type. *Tulipa* species generally fall into the Miscellaneous Group (Group 15); any exceptions to this rule are indicated in their individual entry. CULTIVATION: Tulips require a temperate climate and winter chilling, preferring a sunny position that does not bake in summer. Plant at around 6 in (15 cm) depth in autumn, watering well once foliage appears. Propagate hybrids and cultivars from offsets; species also from seed.

Tulipa acuminata

HORNED TULIP

☼ ❄ ↔2–4 in (5–10 cm) ↑18 in (45 cm)

A narrow species from Turkey. The gray-green foliage has undulating edges. The narrow, 3–5 in (8–12 cm) long flowers, scarlet and yellowish with curious, narrow, twisted tips, are borne in late spring. Zones 3–8.

Tulipa aucheriana

☼ ❄ ↔2–4 in (5–10 cm)
↑2–4 in (5–10 cm)

Tiny species from Iran and Syria. Charming dwarf plant with strap-like, deep green, almost prostrate leaves with wavy edges. The flowers are star-shaped, 1 to 3 per stem, deep rose pink with a yellow basal blotch, borne in mid-spring. Zones 5–8.

Tulipa clusiana

CANDY-STICK TULIP, LADY TULIP

☼ ❄ ↔2–4 in (5–10 cm)
↑8–12 in (20–30 cm)

From Iran, Iraq, and Afghanistan. Linear gray-green leaves with soft bloom. Flowers open flat and star-shaped, in mid- to late spring. They have white interior, dark blue base, outer petals red-edged white. ***T. c.* var. *chrysantha*** (syn. *T. chrysantha*), bright golden tepals with red or purple-brown exterior. ***T. c.* 'Tubergen's Gem'**, bright yellow flowers with red exterior. Zones 3–8.

Tulipa fosteriana

☼ ❄ ↔4–6 in (10–15 cm)
↑12–16 in (30–40 cm)

Outstanding species from eastern Uzbekistan. Oblong to broadly ovate, glossy green leaves. Faintly scented, vivid scarlet flowers with black basal blotch edged yellow, in early to mid-spring. Mostly used in hybridizing. Group 13. Zones 5–8.

Tulipa greigii

☼ ❄ ↔4–6 in (10–15 cm)
↑6–10 in (15–25 cm)

Small species from central Asia. Lance-shaped to oblong leaves with a soft bloom, mottled and striped purple-brown. Solitary, cup-shaped, scarlet, yellow, or multicolored flowers with black or red blotch on a yellow base, in mid-spring. Group 14. Zones 5–8.

Tulipa hageri

☼/◐ ❄ ↔6–8 in (15–20 cm)
↑6–10 in (15–25 cm)

From the eastern Mediterranean. Each bulb has 2 to 7 grass-like leaves and 3 to 5 wide open, red flowers, contrasting buff exterior, about 2 in (5 cm) wide, in mid-spring. Excellent rockery or alpine-garden plant. Zones 5–9.

Tulipa humilis

syns *Tulipa pulchella, T. violacea*

☼ ❄ ↔2–4 in (5–10 cm)
↑4–6 in (10–15 cm)

Popular variable species from southeastern Turkey, Iraq, and Azerbaijan. Linear gray-green leaves with a soft bloom. Flowers bright rose pink to violet, basal blotches pink, purple to black, yellow, or blue, in early spring. **'Persian Pearl'**, deep magenta with yellow center; **Violacea Group**, deep violet, with pale violet to black center, slightly smaller plants. Zones 3–9.

Tulipa iliensis

☼ ❄ ↔2–4 in (5–10 cm) ↑8 in (20 cm)

Erect species from central Asia, with channeled undulate leaves with a soft bloom. Clusters of 1 to 5 yellow flowers with red and dull green reverse, in early spring. Zones 6–8.

Tulipa kaufmanniana

WATERLILY TULIP

☼ ❄ ↔4–6 in (10–15 cm)
↑6–10 in (15–25 cm)

Broad-flowered species from central Asia. Slightly narrow, wavy-edged, gray-green foliage. Flowers open flat, star-shaped, creamy white with yellow base, outer segments streaked red; also pink, orange, and red forms, often scented, in early spring. Group 12. Zones 3–8.

Tulipa linifolia

☼ ❄ ↔2–4 in (5–10 cm)
↑4–6 in (10–15 cm)

Variable species from central Asia, northern Iran, and Afghanistan. Lance-shaped, undulating, red-edged, grayish green leaves in rosette. Shiny red flowers with cream-edged jet black blotch, in late spring. **Batalinii Group** (syn. *T. batalinii*), single soft yellow to apricot flowers, to 3 in (8 cm) across; **'Bright Gem'**, yellow tinged with orange; **'Bronze Charm'**, yellow with bronze markings; **'Yellow Jewel'**, pink-tinted pale yellow. Zones 5–9.

Tulipa montana

IRANIAN TULIP, MOUNTAIN TULIP

☼/◐ ❄ ↔4–6 in (10–15 cm)
↑2–6 in (5–15 cm)

Small showy species from northern Iran and central Asia. Narrow purple-tinted blue-green leaves, to 6 in (15 cm) long, 3 to 6 per bulb. Comparatively large, bright red, goblet-shaped flowers, in late spring. Zones 6–9.

Tulipa orphanidea

☼/◐ ❄ ↔6 in (15 cm)
↑6–15 in (15–38 cm)

This is a variable species from Turkey. Grass-like leaves, 2 to 7 per bulb. Flowers are orange to red with a contrasting buff exterior, often green- or purple-tinted, 1 to 4 per bulb, in spring. **Whittallii Group** (syn. *T. whittallii*) bears star-shaped flowers, orange to red-brown, with black basal markings inside and greenish tinge outside. Zones 5–9.

Tulipa praestans

☼/◐ ❄ ↔6–8 in (15–20 cm)
↑6–20 in (15–50 cm)

Species naturally found throughout central Asia. Leaves blue-green, 4 to 6 per bulb. Goblet-shaped, bright red flowers to 3 in (8 cm) wide, 1 to 5 per stem, in early to mid-spring. **'Fusilier'**, up to 4 orange-red flowers per stem; **'Unicum'**, similar flowers but distinctive cream-edged foliage. Zones 5–9.

T

Tulipa saxatilis

CANDIA TULIP

☼ ✱ ↔4–6 in (10–15 cm)
↑6–10 in (15–25 cm)

Popular species from Crete, Greece, and western Turkey. Network of thin fleshy stems; linear glossy leaves, occasionally with soft bloom. Flowers pale lilac-pink with large deep yellow blotch, cupped, fragrant, in early spring. **Bakeri Group** (syn. *T. bakeri*), lightly fragrant flowers, deep pink-purple with yellow base, opening flat, 3 or 4 per stem, in early spring; **'Lilac Wonder'**, broad glossy green leaves, up to 4 lavender-pink flowers with a bright yellow center that opens almost flat in the sun. Zones 6–8.

Tulipa sylvestris

☼ ✱ ↔4–6 in (10–15 cm)
↑10–18 in (25–45 cm)

A tall species, naturalized in Europe, Iran, and North Africa. Network of thin fleshy stems. Narrow dark green leaves with a soft bloom. Fragrant flowers, clear yellow, exterior occasionally tinged green or red, petal tips reflexed, in spring. Zones 3–8.

Tulipa tarda

☼/◐ ✱ ↔6–8 in (15–20 cm)
↑4–6 in (10–15 cm)

This small species comes from central Asia. Leaves are narrow, deep green to blue-green. The flowers are small, fragrant, starry, cream to yellow with a maroon- to green-tinted exterior, 1 to 8, rarely to 15, blooms per stem, in spring. Zones 5–9.

Tulipa turkestanica

☼/◐ ✱ ↔6–10 in (15–25 cm)
↑8–10 in (20–25 cm)

Slightly clumping species from central Asia. Narrow blue-green foliage, 2 to 4 leaves per bulb. Small, starry, yellow-centered white to cream flowers, up to 12 per stem, in spring. Flower stem is shorter than foliage. Zones 5–9.

T. saxatilis, Bakeri Group, 'Lilac Wonder'

Tulipa undulatifolia

syn. *Tulipa eichleri*

☼/☀ ✱ ↔6–10 in (15–25 cm)
↑12–20 in (30–50 cm)

Narrow species from Balkans, Turkey, Greece, Iran, and central Asia. Wavy-edged blue-green leaves, fringed with very short hairs. Flower stems wiry, with 1 flower per stem. Bright red flowers, dark central zone, open goblet shape, in late spring. Zones 5–9.

Tulipa urumiensis

☼ ✱ ↔4–6 in (10–15 cm)
↑4–6 in (10–15 cm)

From northwestern Iran and eastern Turkey; naturalizes readily. Mostly subterranean stem; rosettes of linear leaves with soft bloom. Flowers cup-shaped, opening to bright golden yellow star, bronze-streaked reverse, in mid- to late spring. Zones 3–8.

Tulipa vvedenskyi

☼/◐ ✱ ↔6–16 in (15–40 cm)
↑6–8 in (15–20 cm)

Native to central Asia. Undulating, downy, blue-green, sometimes purple-tinted leaves, held near horizontally at ground level. Flowers orange-red, single, with broad buff to pale green exterior mid-stripes, in mid-spring. Zones 3–9.

Tulipa Hybrid Cultivars

☼/◐ ✱ ↔4–12 in (10–30 cm)
↑4–30 in (10–75 cm)

Tulip hybrids are divided into 15 groups according to flower type. The flowers come in a bewildering array of forms and colors and include the Parrot Group with deeply cut petals, Viridifloras with green markings and those with broad splashes or "flames" of a contrasting color. Zones 6–9.

Tulipa tarda

Tulipa vvedenskyi

SINGLE EARLY GROUP (GROUP 1)

Single-flowered, single or multicolored forms 12–18 in (30–45 cm) tall, generally blooming within a month after spring equinox. **'Apricot Beauty'**, apricot-pink suffused soft orange, mild scent; **'Christmas Dream'**, bright pink; **'Christmas Marvel'**, very deep pink with pale edge; **'Christmas Orange'**, dusky orange with broad deep pink flame; **'Diana'**, pure white, mild scent; **'Kiezerkroon'**, a Rembrandt Group look-alike, golden yellow with broad red flame; **'Merry Christmas'**, bright deep red; **'Van der Neer'**, bright purple, in cultivation since 1860.

DOUBLE EARLY GROUP (GROUP 2)

Fully double-flowered forms 12–16 in (30–40 cm) tall, generally blooming within a month after spring equinox. **'Baby Doll'**, golden yellow; **'Double Price'**, lavender-pink; **'Foxtrot'**, pale to mid-pink; **'Monte Carlo'**, bright yellow; **'Montreux'**, cream to yellow, sometimes pink tint; **'Murillo'**, deep pink; **'Orange Nassau'**, deep red with lighter zones; **'Peach Blossom'**, deep pink flamed and flecked with white; **'Verona'**, cream shading to yellow center.

TRIUMPH GROUP (GROUP 3)

These single-flowered hybrids between single early and Darwin tulips, from 15–20 in (38–50 cm) tall, often have contrastingly colored petal edges or flecks, generally bloom after spring equinox. **'Abra'**, red-brown with yellow edges; **'Abu Hassan'**, deep red with a yellow edge; **'African Queen'**, purple-red with feathered white edge; **'Annie Schilder'**, bright orange with darker flame; **'Attila'**, pinkish purple; **'Couleur Cardinal'**, bright red with purple-tinted base; **'Don Quichotte'**, mauve-pink; **'Escape'**, pure red; **'Francoise'**, white, deepening to rich cream at base; **'Happy Generation'**, white with broad red flame and yellow base; **'Ice Follies'**, Rembrandt Group look-alike, white with red flaming; **'Judith Leyster'**, deep pink to light red, pale green-tinted petal center and base; **'Leen van der Mark'**, cherry red with yellow edges ageing to white; **'Meissner Porzellan'**, white with broad feathered pink edge; **'Negrita'** ★, deep purple; **'New Design'**, white with pink edge, white-edged foliage; **'Palestrina'**, salmon pink with green flame; **'Prinses Irene'**, yellow-orange with purple flame; **'White Dream'**, pure white; **'Yokohama'**, bright yellow; **'Zurel'**, white to ivory with purple-red base extending along petal center.

Tulipa, Hybrid Cultivar, Single Early, 'Christmas Dream'

Tulipa, Hybrid Cultivar, Double Early, 'Murillo'

Tulipa, Hybrid Cultivar, Triumph, 'Abra'

Tulipa, HC, Single Late, 'Dreamland'

Tulipa, HC, Darwin Hybrid, 'Ollioules'

Tulipa, Hybrid Cultivar, Darwin Hybrid, 'Golden Parade'

Tulipa, HC, Single Late, 'Douglas Bader'

Tulipa, HC, Lily-Flowered, 'Ballerina'

T., HC, Fringed, 'Blue Heron'

T., HC, Viridiflora, 'Spring Green'

DARWIN HYBRID GROUP (GROUP 4)
Single-flowered hybrids between single late (Group 5) tulips and *T. f osteriana* and/or similar closely related species. They are 20–27 in (50–70 cm) tall, and in cool areas flower more than a month after spring equinox; also called Cottage tulips. **'Ad Rem'** has orange-red blooms with a gold edge; **'American Dream'**, bright orange and cream; **'Apeldoorn'**, deep red with a yellow center; **'Big Chief'**, light red, cream base fades to white along petal center; **'Burning Heart'**, pale to primrose yellow, red to mahogany flame; **'Daydream'**, irregular mix of yellow, orange, and apricot; **'Design Impression'**, deep coral, pale petal tip and edge, pale green-edged leaves; **'Elizabeth Arden'**, orange-pink to red, yellow base; **'Golden Parade'**, deep yellow blooms; **'Gudoshnik'**, blend of yellow and light red; **'Ollioules'**, dark pink with paler edges; **'Olympic Flame'**, Rembrandt Group look-alike, yellow with red flame; **'Pink Impression'**, soft pink ageing to rose with cream edge.

SINGLE LATE GROUP (GROUP 5)
These single-flowered forms, 18–30 in (45–75 cm) tall, usually flower more than a month after spring equinox. **'Black Diamond'**, deep purple-red; **'Bleu Aimable'**, purple suffused with lavender; **'Candy Club'**, pale pink with dark central "kiss;" **'Dordogne'**, soft orange edges, deepening to center; **'Douglas Bader'**, soft pink; **'Dreamland'**, deep pink, light edges, white base; **'Halcro'**, deep red; **'Lily Schreyer'**, bright yellow; **'Maureen'**, pure white; **'Mrs John T. Scheeper'**, massive deep yellow flowers; **'Perestroyka'**, white with purplish red markings; **'Purple Prince'**, light purple; **'Queen of Night'**, deep black-purple; **'Roi du Midi'**, pure golden yellow; **'Sorbet'**, white flowers flamed cherry red; **'Sweet Harmony'**, pale yellow; **'Temple's Favorite'**, orange with slightly darker flame; **'Union Jack'**, Rembrandt Group look-alike, white flowers flamed and edged deep red; **'World Expression'**, white ageing to cream with dark red flame.

LILY-FLOWERED GROUP (GROUP 6)
Long 2-toned flowers tapering at the center to distinct waist. Lily-flowered tulips are 15–24 in (38–60 cm) tall, and have a variable flowering time. **'Aladdin'**, bright red with yellow edge and center; **'Ballade'**, violet edged with white; **'Ballerina'**, orange suffused with red; **'China Pink'**, deep pink with light tips and center; **'Elegant Lady'**, soft gold turning to pink near tips; **'Marilyn'**, white flamed with red; **'Queen of Sheba'**, red with golden orange edge; **'West Point'**, bright golden yellow; **'White Triumphator'**, pure white.

FRINGED GROUP (GROUP 7)
The flowers in this group have fringed edges, with the fringe itself often in a contrasting color to the rest of the flower and usually with a crystalline texture, 18–26 in (45–65 cm) tall. **'Arma'**, deep red with crystalline fringe; **'Blue Heron'**, dusky purple and mauve with white fringe; **'Burgundy Lace'** ★, wine red with crystalline edge; **'Maja'**, bright yellow with crystalline fringe.

VIRIDIFLORA GROUP (GROUP 8)
The tulips in this group are around 12–20 in (30–50 cm) tall and have either strong green coloration in the base or an external flare up the center of each petal. **'Artist'**, salmon suffused with orange and purple, and a green flame; **'China Town'**, dusky light pink, with darker edges and green flame; **'Golden Artist'**, deep golden yellow, red-edged green flame; **'Groenland'**, mid-pink, a narrow green flame with a broad pale pink edge; **'Hollywood'**, red with darker flame; **'Spring Green'**, cream with a narrow green flame; **'Virichic'**, narrow petals, magenta with white-edged green central stripe.

REMBRANDT GROUP (GROUP 9)
Fancy-flowered, often multi-colored tulips with contrasting flares, flecks, and veining, usually on a base color of yellow, red, or white, patterns originating from a viral disease that led to the plants' slow decline; cultivars with such viral patterning are now banned from sale. Members of other groups can show similar color patterns. Modern Rembrandt look-alikes that fall into other groups include: **'Ice Follies'** (Triumph Group); **'Kiezerkroon'** (Single Early Group); **'Olympic Flame'** (Darwin Group); and **'Union Jack'**, (Single Late Group).

PARROT GROUP (GROUP 10)
The hybrids in this group, which commonly reach 18–22 in (45–55 cm) in height, largely result from sports within other groups and are notable for their deeply cut petals, often bi-colored. **'Bird of Paradise'** has deep red flowers edged with gold; **'Black Parrot'**, deep blackish purple; **'Blue Parrot'** is a deep mauve; **'Burgundy Lace'**, deep rose red; **'Estella Rijnveld'**, cream with red flame, sometimes creamy yellow-marked interior; **'Fantasy'**, deep pink with purple-green flame near tips; **'Karel Doorman'**, bright red edged with gold; **'Professor Röntgen'**, orange-red flowers with a green-gold flame; **'Rococo'**, red with chrome yellow to green tones at base; **'Weber's Parrot'**, twisted pale pink petals with a green flame and deep pink edges and tips.

DOUBLE LATE OR PEONY-FLOWERED GROUP (GROUP 11)
This group features very large, fully double flowers that are produced on stems 15–24 in (38–60 cm) tall. Impressive tulips, they usually bloom well after the spring equinox, and

Tulipa, HC, Parrot, 'Blue Parrot'

T., HC, Double Late, 'Allegretto'

include: **'Allegretto'**, red flowers with golden edge; **'Angélique'**, pink flowers with a pale exterior; **'Carnaval de Nice'**, white flowers with narrow red striping; **'Hermione'**, lavender-pink, slightly darker blush, pale center; **'Lilac Perfection'**, lilac deepening to purple center, fragrant; **'Maywonder'**, deep pink; **'Orange Princess'**, a deep orange center, lightening at the edges, tipped with green; and **'Wirosa'**, deep pink blooms with a broad cream edge.

KAUFMANNIANA GROUP (GROUP 12)

This group are very early-flowering cultivars and hybrids of *T. kaufmanniana* growing to around 10 in (25 cm) tall. Flowers open flat and are sometimes known as waterlily tulips; leaves may be plain or mottled; flowers usually bi- or multi-colored in a variety of patterns. **'Ancilla'**, white with orange-red-edged yellow center; **'Heart's Delight'**, pale pink petal edge and interior, light cherry red exterior, **'Shakespeare'**, dusky salmon pink.

FOSTERIANA GROUP (GROUP 13)

Variably sized cultivars and hybrids of *T. fosteriana*, 8–24 in (20–60 cm) tall; foliage may be plain, mottled, or variegated; flowers tend be very boldly colored. **'Analita'**, orange red, cream petal edges and interior, orange-red center; **'Honorose'**, cream to pale yellow with bright yellow center; **'Madame Lefeber'** (syn. 'Red Emperor'), bright red; **'Orange Emperor'**, bright orange blending to yellow base; **'Princeps'**, large bright red flowers; **'Purissima'** (syn. 'White Emperor'), white with creamy yellow center; **'Sweetheart'**, golden yellow, cream petal edges and tips.

GREIGII GROUP (GROUP 14)

Sometimes known as rock or rockery tulips, these cultivars and hybrids of *T. greigii* rarely exceed 12 in (30 cm) tall and are widely grown. They are easily recognizable by their purple-red marbled gray-green foliage, and

Tulipa, HC, Kaufmanniana, 'Ancilla'

commonly simple single flowers in one or two colors. **'Cape Cod'**, orange with gold edge; **'Oriental Splendour'**, deep yellow with red flame; **'Plaisir'**, cream with red flame; **'Red Riding Hood'**, bright red; **'Toronto'** ★, bright salmon to orange; **'Yellow Dawn'**, deep pink with yellow edge.

MISCELLANEOUS GROUP (GROUP 15)

This is a catch-all group for species and their cultivars which are otherwise ungrouped *(see* individual species*)*.

TWEEDIA

This genus in the dogbane (Apocynaceae) family contains a single species of twining or scrambling shrub, native to subtropical South America. It is sparsely branched with softly hairy stems and foliage. Oblong to heart-shaped leaves are up to 10 in (25 cm) long. Starry pale blue flowers are borne in summer and autumn. They are long-lasting when cut.

CULTIVATION: These plants flower from seed in the first year so can be grown as an annual in cool-temperate zones or, alternatively, they can be grown under glass. In frost-free areas grow in full sun in well-drained, moderately fertile soil. Pinch back when young to encourage bushier growth. Propagate from seed or cuttings.

Tulipa, HC, Fosteriana, 'Purissima'

Tweedia caerulea

syn. *Oxypetalum caeruleum*

↔36 in (90 cm) ↑36 in (90 cm)

Twining or scrambling shrub, a native of southern Brazil and Uruguay with lightly hairy grayish green leaves. Flowers starry pale blue, darken to lilac as they age, for long periods from summer. **'Heaven Bow'**, pretty pale blue to lilac flowers, look almost painted. Zones 10–12.

TYPHA

BULRUSH, CAT-TAIL, REED MACE

This genus, comprising some 10 to 12 species found almost throughout the world, makes up the family Typhaceae. These often very large perennials are from marshlands, where they can form extensive stands. The leaves arise from rhizomes and have sheathing bases; the leaf blade is very elongated and linear, flat or concave, with spongy internal tissue. Flowering stems are erect and spear-like, bearing dense cylindrical spikes of tightly packed wind-pollinated flowers. The male and female flowers are separate but on the same plant, the males borne in an upper distinct part, often differently colored. The fruits are tiny and plumed, like thistledown. They are released by disintegration of the female spike and float away on the breeze in vast numbers. The starch-rich rhizomes, and even the pollen, provide emergency food. The leaves are used in matting and chair-seating ("rush") and have been tried for paper-making. The plush formed by the female flowers has been used as a substitute for kapok.

CULTIVATION: Cultivation is easy in any moist soil. They grow in water to 24 in (60 cm) or so deep, although seed germination takes place on damp mudbanks. Except for some of the smallest species, they are too invasive for use as aquatics in any but the largest ponds or artificial lakes. Propagate from seed or by rhizome division.

Tulipa, Hybrid Cultivar, Greigii, 'Toronto'

Typha minima

↔1¼–2 in (3–5 cm) ↑2½–3 in (6–8 cm)

Perennial from Europe, the Caucasus region, and Asia with narrow, sword-shaped, green leaves. Flower stalks shorter than leaves, bearing oblong, dark brown, terminal heads of scaly, finely hairy, upright, catkin-like flowers, in summer. Zones 3–11.

Tweedia caerulea 'Heaven Bow'

T

UV

UGNI

Once included in the genus of the true myrtles *(Myrtus)*, this variable group of approximately 10 species of evergreen shrubs from the temperate Americas is now in a genus of its own within the myrtle (Myrtaceae) family. They have simple oval leaves that are usually tough, leathery, and small. Their flowers are carried singly, in the leaf axils; they have 5 petals and tend to hang downwards. Fleshy berries, sometimes edible, but not particularly flavorsome, follow the flowers and can become very aromatic as they near ripeness.

CULTIVATION: Apart from being a little frost tender when young, the only cultivation problem is a dislike of lime. Grow in cool, moist, humus-rich, well-drained soil in sun or part-shade. An annual trim, after either flowering or fruiting, will keep the growth compact. Propagate from seed, cuttings or by removing naturally formed layers.

Ugni molinae

Ulmus × hollandica 'Modolina'

Ulmus carpinifolia 'Variegata'

Ugni molinae ★

CHILEAN CRANBERRY, CHILEAN GUAVA

↔ 3 ft (0.9 m) ↑ 6 ft (1.8 m)

This is a native of Chile and western Argentina. It is a wiry-stemmed shrub with glossy deep green leaves on red stems. The flowers are cream flushed with pink, with a cluster of 40 to 60 tiny stamens at the center. Flowering time is spring to early summer. Red berries follow the flowers. Zones 8–10.

ULMUS

ELM

There are 45 species of elms (family Ulmaceae). Most are trees, some very large, but a few are shrubs. Although most are deciduous and very hardy, a few are semi-evergreen and not so tough. They occur in northern temperate zones and even extend into the subtropics. They are generally round-headed trees with bark often furrowed or fissured though seldom corky, except on young shoots. Leaves are usually elliptic with conspicuous veins and serrated edges. Flowers are inconspicuous but the papery winged fruits (samaras) that follow can be showy.

CULTIVATION: In the main, elms are tough plants that adapt well to cultivation, growing successfully in a range of soils provided the drainage is good. However, in some areas populations have been decimated by Dutch elm disease, a fungal infection carried by small beetles with wood-boring larvae. Propagate from seed or by grafting.

Ulmus americana 'Columnaris'

Ulmus japonica

Ulmus americana

AMERICAN ELM, WHITE ELM

↔ 100 ft (30 m) ↑ 100 ft (30 m)

Largest of the North American elms. Impressive tree, deep gray furrowed bark, and large leaves that turn bright yellow, in autumn. **'Augustine'**, vigorous grower, columnar habit; **'Columnaris'**, columnar habit. Zones 3–9.

Ulmus carpinifolia

syn. *Ulmus minor*

FIELD ELM, SMOOTH-LEAFED ELM

↔ 70 ft (21 m) ↑ 50–70 ft (15–21 m)

Species native to central and southern Europe, including Britain. Leaves are 2–4 in (5–10 cm) long, with serrated edges, develop golden orange autumn tones. Many cultivars. **'Variegata'**, white-speckled leaves. Zones 5–10.

Ulmus 'Coolshade'

↔ 20–30 ft (6–9 m) ↑ 20–35 ft (6–10 m)

This *Ulmus pumila* and *U. rubra* hybrid is a broad-headed and slow-growing tree that closely resembles *U. pumila*. However, it has a lusher head of foliage. Weeps slightly, so is resistant to snow damage. Zones 3–9.

Ulmus crassifolia

CEDAR ELM

↔ 40 ft (12 m) ↑ 70–100 ft (21–30 m)

Found in southern USA. Young twigs edged with "wings" of bark. Rather stiff leaves, about 2 in (5 cm) long, have toothed edges and downy undersides. Zones 7–10.

Ulmus × hollandica

DUTCH ELM

↔ 80 ft (24 m) ↑ 100 ft (30 m)

This is a naturally occurring hybrid between *U. glabra* and *U. carpinifolia*. Strong, heavily veined, serrated, deep green leaves turn a yellow tone in autumn months. Cultivars include: **'Groenveldt'**, tall, vigorous, and disease-resistant; **'Jacqueline Hillier'**, densely branched, shrubby to around 8 ft (2.4 m) tall; **'Major'**, with a wide-spreading crown and broad leaves; **'Modolina'**, tall and vigorous with a somewhat vase-shaped crown; and **'Vegeta'** (syn. *U.* × *vegeta*), a vigorous grower to 120 ft (36 m) tall. Zones 5–9.

Ulmus japonica

↔ 60 ft (18 m) ↑ 100 ft (30 m)

A large broad-headed tree native to Japan and nearby parts of temperate northeastern Asia. Young stems have corky yellow-brown bark, roughly oval leaves taper abruptly to a point, coarsely toothed edges. Small purplish flowers, pale green fruits. Zones 5–9.

Ulmus parvifolia

CHINESE ELM

↔ 30 ft (9 m) ↑ 70 ft (21 m)

A disease-resistant tree from Japan, Korea, and China, near-evergreen in mild climates. Round crown, smooth flaking bark, fine branches. Mature fruit in autumn. **'Catlin'**, slow grower, gracefully drooping branch tips; **'Frosty'**, compact shrub, white-toothed leaves; **'Hansen'**, vigorous upright growth; **'King's Choice'**, larger bright green leaves, peeling bark, vigorous open growth habit; **'Pendens'**, weeping branches; **'True Green'**, reliably evergreen in mild winters. Zones 5–10.

Ulmus pumila

CHINESE ELM, SIBERIAN ELM

↔ 20–30 ft (6–9 m) ↑ 20–35 ft (6–10 m)

This native of cool-temperate Asia has coarsely textured, serrated leaves that color slightly in autumn. **'Den Haag'**, disease-resistant tall form, with open crown. Zones 3–9.

Ulmus 'Sapporo Autumn Gold'

↔35 ft (10 m) ↑50 ft (15 m)

A hybrid notable for its resistance or tolerance of Dutch elm disease. It has a strongly upright habit when young, eventually develops a broad crown. New spring foliage, soft yellow-green, matures to lime green, golden yellow autumn foliage. Zones 4–9.

UMBELLULARIA

Related to the laurels *(Laurus)*, the sole species in this genus from the family Ulmaceae is an aromatic evergreen tree found in Oregon and California, USA. It has tough leathery leaves and male and female flowers carried on separate flowerheads. The foliage is so strongly aromatic that crushing it in the hand and sniffing it can cause an instant though usually brief headache. It was widely used medicinally by native North Americans. Its timber is quite dense and used in woodturning for mainly ornamental objects or utensils. CULTIVATION: Tolerant of light to moderate frosts and not particularly fussy about the soil type, California laurel grows best in deep, moist, humus-enriched, well-drained soil with a position in full sun or partial shade. Propagate from seed or half-hardened cuttings.

Umbellularia californica

Umbellularia californica

CALIFORNIA LAUREL, HEADACHE TREE

↔35 ft (10 m) ↑50–70 ft (15–21 m)

Densely foliaged spreading crown, scaly red-brown bark. Strongly aromatic, glossy deep green, oval to lance-shaped leaves. Clusters of small yellow flowers open at the branch tips, in spring. Purplish, olive-like berries 1 in (25 mm) long. Zones 8–10.

UNCINIA

HOOK SEDGE

This is a genus of about 40 species of evergreen tuft-forming grasses from southern temperate zones throughout the world, except South Africa. They are members of the sedge (Cyperaceae) family. These grasses are identified by their smooth, cylindrical stems that arch as they mature. They vary in color from rich oranges and reds through to plums, dark browns, and dull greens. Now popular garden specimens, they are often chosen because of their striking year-round foliage color. The flowers appear in summer and the mature seed head spikes are distinctive because they have barb-like hooks on them as they mature. The hooks attach themselves to passing animals and people, which aids in the dispersal of the seed. CULTIVATION: *Uncinia* species need free-draining soils with plenty of natural light, in areas that do not have extreme cold periods. They will not tolerate long periods of wet weather; too much water can kill them. Propagate by division in autumn or by sowing fresh seed in spring.

Uncinia rubra

RED HOOK SEDGE

↔14 in (35 cm) ↑12 in (30 cm)

From New Zealand. Perennial, tuft-forming grass with shiny, red-brown, sharply pointed, narrow, flat leaves all year round. Spikes of dark brown flowers sit just above the foliage in late summer. Zones 8–11.

UVULARIA

BELLWORT, MERRYBELLS

This genus contains 5 species of easy-to-grow herbaceous perennials. For now in the autumn crocus (Colchicaceae) family, they may soon move to the Asparagaceae. From eastern North America, they are found in moist, well-drained, deciduous woodlands. Stems are erect or arching; the lance-shaped leaves are a bright green. Leaves are perfoliate (wrapping around the stem at the base) on all species except *U. sessilifolia*. Yellow bell-shaped flowers dangle from the stem and have long, slender, pointed, slightly twisted petals. Blooms last for 2 to 3 weeks in early spring to mid-summer, depending on species, but foliage remains visible all summer. CULTIVATION: Grow in shade in deep, moist, slightly acid soil. Propagate by dividing clumps in spring or autumn, from ripened seed in late summer, or by transplanting underground stems, which spread easily.

Uvularia grandiflora

Uvularia grandiflora

BIG MERRYBELLS, GREAT MERRYBELLS, LARGE-FLOWERED BELLWORT

↔12–24 in (30–60 cm)
↑12–24 in (30–60 cm)

From Quebec to Ontario, Canada, south to Minnesota, Georgia, Tennessee, and Kansas, USA. Light green foliage, arching stems. Bright yellow, drooping, bell-shaped flowers, mid-spring to early summer. Fruit a small triangular capsule. ***U. g.* var. *pallida***, pale sulfur yellow flowers. Zones 3–9.

Uvularia perfoliata

PERFOLIATE BELLWORT, STRAW BELL, WOOD MERRYBELLS

↔12–18 in (30–45 cm)
↑16 in (40 cm)

From Quebec to Ontario, Canada, south to Florida and Mississippi, USA. Flowers pale yellow from mid-spring to early summer. Zones 3–9.

Uvularia sessilifolia

LITTLE MERRYBELLS, SESSILE BELLWORT, STRAW LILIES, WILD OATS

↔12–18 in (30–45 cm)
↑6–12 in (15–30 cm)

From moist woods from Ontario and New Brunswick, Canada, west to Minnesota, south to Georgia, Arkansas, USA. Flowers pale green-yellow, late spring to early summer. Zones 3–9.

VACCINIUM

BLUEBERRY

This genus of around 450 species of evergreen and deciduous shrubs, small trees and vines includes the blueberries, cranberries, and huckleberries. Members of the heath (Ericaceae) family, they occur over much of the Northern Hemisphere, with a few species found in South Africa. Their main feature is the small but colorful edible fruits. Their flowers can be attractive, usually small, urn-shaped and downward-facing, carried singly or in clusters. The leaves are usually simple, oval to lance-shaped, often pointed at the tip and sometimes serrated around their edges. CULTIVATION: As with most plants of the heath family, *Vaccinium* species prefer cool, moist, humus-rich soil that is acidic and well drained, with shelter from the hottest summer sun. In cultivation the type of conditions preferred by *Camellia* and *Rhododendron* tend to give the best results. Shrubbier species should be pruned to shape: after flowering if the fruit is not required, otherwise at harvest. Propagate from seed, cuttings, layers, and in some cases, by division.

Vaccinium ovatum

Vaccinium ashei

RABBIT-EYE BLUEBERRY

↔7 ft (2 m) ↑3–15 ft (0.9–4.5 m)

Shrub from southeastern USA. Usually deciduous, sometimes near-evergreen in mild winters. Broad, serrated-edged leaves. White to light red flowers, in spring. Edible, ½ in (12 mm) wide, purple-black fruit. Zones 8–10.

Vaccinium corymbosum

BLUEBERRY, HIGHBUSH BLUEBERRY

↔5 ft (1.5 m)
↑3–6 ft (0.9–1.8 m)

Deciduous shrub from eastern USA widely cultivated for its edible fruit. Lance-shaped leaves develop fiery orange tones, in autumn. Flowers, white, sometimes with a red tint, in clusters, in spring. Edible, blue-black berries. **'Earliblue'** is a tall vigorous cultivar with large fruit. Zones 2–9.

Vaccinium ovatum

BOX BLUEBERRY, EVERGREEN HUCKLEBERRY

↔3–5 ft (0.9–1.5m)
↑3–5 ft (0.9–1.5 m)

Evergreen shrub from western North America. Leaves 1 in (25 mm) long, oval, finely serrated edges. Clusters of small white to pale pink flowers, tinted with red, in spring. Fruit is blue-black. Zones 7–10.

Vaccinium parvifolium

RED HUCKLEBERRY, RED WHORTLEBERRY

↔6 ft (1.8 m) ↑6 ft (1.8 m)

Found from Alaska to California, USA. A deciduous shrub with small leaves, 1 in (25 mm) long. Flowers ¼ in (6 mm) wide, green with red tints, in late spring. Translucent, edible, pinkish red berries. Zones 6–10.

Vaccinium Hybrid Cultivars

↔3–6 ft (0.9–1.8 m)
↕2–5 ft (0.6–1.5 m)

There are many popular hybrids and cultivars, some of indeterminate origin. **'Beckyblue'**, red-green stems, medium-sized blue fruit; **'Elliott'**, to 8 ft (2.4 m) tall, with a long-lasting display of orange-red autumn color; **'Lingonberry'**, reddish pink tints; **'Ornablue'**, narrow leaves turn bright red in autumn; **'Sharpeblue'** ★, low-chill tetraploid variety, produces smallish sweet fruit. Zones 2–9.

VANCOUVERIA

This genus is made up of 3 species of herbaceous creeping perennials that are native to the woodlands of northwestern North America. Like Epimedium, they are members of the barberry (Berberidaceae) family and are useful ground covers in shady areas, but they will not do well in dry soil. Their leathery divided leaves grow on wiry stems from crowns arising from branched underground rhizomes. The small and pendulous flowers are held above the foliage. Given ideal conditions they will spread quickly. The genus is named after Captain George Vancouver, an eighteenth-century English naval officer who explored the west coast of North America.

CULTIVATION: Grow in partial shade in cool, moist, organic, acid soil. Additions of leaf mold or humus will ensure success. They will not grow well in areas with hot dry summers. Propagate by dividing the rhizomes in spring or autumn.

Vancouveria hexandra ★

AMERICAN BARRENWORT

↔12 in (30 cm) ↕12 in (30 cm)

Found from Washington to California, USA. Pale green deciduous foliage, similar to maidenhair fern *(Adiantum)*. Drooping white flowers from late spring to early summer. Zones 7–9.

Vancouveria hexandra

VELTHEIMIA

This genus of the asparagus (Asparagaceae) family consists of 2 species that are found on the grassy and rocky hillsides of southern Africa. The huge papery bulbs protruding from the soil's surface are decorative in their own right, as are the glossy undulating leaves, the well-held flowers, and the shimmering papery seed pods that follow the flowers.

CULTIVATION: These plants are easily grown outside in temperate climates and do well in wet-summer areas and in summer-irrigated beds. In other climates they are not so obliging. They resent root disturbance. Propagate by removing and replanting offsets while the plant is dormant, or by sowing fresh ripe seed. Alternatively, mature leaves can be taken from the base of the bulb, set in sand and grown on in a mild even temperature.

Veltheimia bracteata ★

syn. *Veltheimia capensis*

FOREST LILY, TORCH LILY

↔12 in (30 cm)
↕16–18 in (40–45 cm)

This robust, very variable, summer-dormant perennial bears long-lasting flowers in warm coral-red, pinkish purple, or murky white shades. The flowers are held in terminal racemes on straight mottled stems in spring. Decorative seed pods follow. Leaves are dark green, very glossy, forming a decorative rosette. As a container plant, place the bulb with top two-thirds protruding, water sparingly, and feed with a low-strength, low-nitrogen liquid feed when in growth. **'Yellow Flame'** produces pale yellow flowers. *V. capensis* is sometimes listed as a separate species, but is now considered by many to be a form of *V. bracteata.* It bears muted yellow, flesh pink, or murky white blooms, has very wavy leaves, and is smaller and slightly less robust than the common forms. Zones 9–11.

Veltheimia bracteata

VERBASCUM

MOTH MULLEIN, MULLEIN

This genus of some 300 species of annuals, biennials, perennials, and subshrubs in the foxglove (Scrophulariaceae) family includes cultivated plants and many that have become weeds outside their natural temperate Eurasian and North African range. The commonly cultivated species usually form basal rosettes of large elliptic leaves, often heavily veined and sometimes felted. Tall upright flower spikes emerge from the rosettes, carrying massed, small, 5-petalled flowers, usually in white, yellow, or pink to lavender shades. *Verbascum* was described by the Roman writer Pliny as attractive to moths: he called the plants moth mulleins. It also featured as a protection against evil in Greek legends and was used as an everyday medicinal plant to treat a variety of ills.

CULTIVATION: Hardiness varies with the species, but the majority prefer a sunny position with light, gritty, free-draining soil. They can tolerate summer drought but need moisture until after flowering. Propagate by division or from seed, depending on the growth form.

Verbascum chaixii 'Album'

Verbascum blattaria

MOTH MULLEIN

↔12–20 in (30–50 cm)
↕5–6 ft (1.5–1.8 m)

Widely naturalized temperate Eurasian biennial with basal rosettes of downy, toothed, lance-shaped, green leaves, up to 10 in (25 cm) long. Strong, erect, leafy flower stems, with many ¾ in (18 mm) wide, white, sometimes pale yellow or pink flowers. Cultivated forms may have considerably larger flowers. Zones 6–10.

Verbascum bombyciferum

↔24–40 in (60–100 cm)
↕6–8 ft (1.8–2.4 m)

A western Asian summer-flowering biennial that forms large rosettes of broadly oval, wavy-edged, white-felted leaves, to 20 in (50 cm) long. Flower stems to over 6 ft (1.8 m) tall, leafy at the base but leafless from where the flowers start. Stems and buds woolly, sometimes branching, flowers deep yellow, to over 1¼ in (30 mm) wide. **'Polarsommer'** (syn. 'Arctic Summer') is yellow flowered, deriving its name from the especially heavy silver felting on its leaves. Zones 6–10.

Verbascum chaixii

NETTLE-LEAFED MOTH MULLEIN

↔12–24 in (30–60 cm)
↕36–48 in (90–120 cm)

A summer-flowering perennial found from central Europe to Spain and east to Russia. Forms a clump of rosettes of deeply veined, toothed, gray-green to dark green, downy leaves, to 12 in (30 cm) long. Narrow erect flower stems with flowers under 1 in (25 mm) wide, bright yellow with purple-red stamens. **'Album'** ★ grows up to 33 in (85 cm) tall and bears white flowers with mauve stamens. Zones 5–9.

Verbascum olympicum

↔20–40 in (50–100 cm)
↕5–6 ft (1.5–1.8 m)

A Turkish summer-flowering biennial or short-lived perennial that makes a dense basal foliage clump with smooth-edged, lance-shaped, white, woolly leaves, around 12 in (30 cm) long, sometimes more than 24 in (60 cm) long. Branching leafy-based stems with dozens of 1 in (25 mm) wide bright yellow flowers. Zones 6–10.

Verbascum phoeniceum

PURPLE MULLEIN

↔12–16 in (30–40 cm)
↕8–16 in (20–40 cm)

Southern Eurasian summer-flowering biennial or short-lived perennial. Usually one large rosette of sparsely hairy, dark green, wavy-edged or finely toothed, pointed oval leaves, to 6 in (15 cm) long. Simple or few-branched stems with mauve to purple, rarely white, pink, or yellow flowers, around 1 in (25 mm) wide. Zones 6–10.

Verbascum Hybrid Cultivars

☼/◐ ✱ ↔ 12–20 in (30–50 cm)
↑ 12–60 in (30–150 cm)

Moth mulleins hybridize freely, and British breeders in particular have produced a range of hybrids that combine lush velvety foliage with beautifully shaded flowers. Some of the best include members of the **Cotswold Group** such as '**Cotswold Beauty**', to 48 in (120 cm), with buff to apricot-pink flowers, purple-pink anthers; '**Gainsborough**', to 48 in (120 cm), bright yellow flowers, gray felted foliage; '**Mont Blanc**', to 36 in (90 cm), pure white flowers, gray felted foliage; and '**Pink Domino**', to 48 in (120 cm), bright pink with a dark center. Other excellent cultivars include '**Helen Johnson**', 24–32 in (60–80 cm), variable dusky apricot-pink shades, gray-felted foliage; '**Jackie**', to 24 in (60 cm), dusky pink with deep magenta center; '**Letitia**', to 12 in (30 cm), shrubby habit, many bright yellow flowers. Zones 6–10.

VERBENA

VERVAIN

This tropical and subtropical American member of the self-named vervain (Verbenaceae) family has recently been revised, and many of the more commonly cultivated species have been reclassified to the genus *Glandularia*. Those that remain tend to be the taller perennials with slender erect spikes of flowers, mainly in pink to purple tones. Their foliage is often finely hairy, with toothed or shallowly scalloped edges.

CULTIVATION: Grow these plants in a border in full sun in moderately fertile, moist, but well-drained soil. Most can be propagated from half-hardened cuttings, but stocks should be rejuvenated occasionally by raising new seedlings.

Verbena bonariensis

PURPLE TOP, SOUTH AMERICAN VERVAIN, TALL VERBENA

☼ ❄ ↔ 24 in (60 cm)
↑ 3–5 ft (0.9–1.5 m)

South American perennial; also grown as annual. Erect, square, rough stems. Sparsely foliaged, lance-shaped serrated leaves. Tiny purple flowers in flat-topped clusters. Self-sows. Zones 7–10.

Verbena hastata

BLUE VERVAIN, SIMPLER'S JOY

☼ ✱ ↔ 12–24 in (30–60 cm)
↑ 3–5 ft (0.9–1.5 m)

Native to eastern and central USA. Perennial with stiff upright stems and lance-shaped, toothed, and roughened leaves. Small violet-blue flowers in spiky clusters in summer to autumn. Used in herbal remedies. Zones 3–9.

Verbena rigida

syn. *Verbena venosa*

VEINED VERBENA

☼ ❄ ↔ 12 in (30 cm)
↑ 24–36 in (60–90 cm)

Native to South America. Creeping perennial with stiff upright stems bearing stalkless oblong leaves, rough and irregularly toothed. Vivid purple to magenta flowers are borne in clusters in summer. '**Polaris**' has lavender-blue flowers. Zones 8–10.

Verbena stricta

HOARY VERVAIN

☼ ✱ ↔ 30–40 in (75–100 cm)
↑ 30–40 in (75–100 cm)

Perennial from western North America. Upright, stems densely covered with soft, fine hairs. Leaves rough, serrated, elliptic to nearly circular. Compact, upright spikes of deep purple, lavender, or white flowers. Zones 4–8.

VERONICA

This plantain (Plantaginaceae) family genus has recently been considerably enlarged by the return of all of the shrubs and subshrubs formerly classified as *Derwentia, Hebe,* and *Parahebe.* This means that *Veronica* is now a genus of almost 400 species that encompass almost all plant types other than trees. It is difficult to give a general description of such a diverse group but, with the exception of the conifer-like foliage of the "whipcord" species, their leaves tend to be small, oval to lance-shaped, often shallowly toothed, and rarely pinnately lobed. A few species have solitary flowers, but more often many-flowered upright spikes develop in spring and summer. The color range is mainly in the white and pink to purple-blue shades, including some striking deep blue flowers. Probably named in honor of St Veronica, or because the floral markings of some species resemble the marks left on Veronica's sacred handkerchief or veil, with which she wiped Christ's face as he carried the cross.

CULTIVATION: They are mostly very hardy and easily grown in full to half-sun, with moist well-drained soil. Some are superb rock garden plants, others are better suited to borders. Propagate from cuttings or seed, or by self-rooted layers or division.

Veronica austriaca

☼/◐ ✱ ↔ 10–24 in (25–60 cm)
↑ 6–16 in (15–40 cm)

A spreading, late spring- to summer-flowering European perennial with wiry stems, sparsely hairy, narrow lance-shaped, ½ in (12 mm) long leaves, and upright spikes of many bright purple-blue flowers. V. a. subsp. teucrium has broader, more deeply toothed leaves, a parent of the best garden forms, such as '**Crater Lake Blue**' ★, 10 in (25 cm) tall, compact, intense blue flowers; and '**Shirley Blue**', 10 in (25 cm) tall, bright mid-blue flowers. Zones 6–10.

Verbena rigida 'Polaris'

Veronica gentianoides

☼/◐ ✱ ↔ 12–24 in (30–60 cm)
↑ 12–24 in (30–60 cm)

This spreading, summer-flowering, Caucasian and western Asian perennial forms a dense clump of upright stems with narrow, toothed, pointed oval leaves, to nearly 3 in (8 cm) long at the base of the clump. Usually pale blue flowers in erect spikes to 12 in (30 cm) long, in spring and summer. '**Tissington White**' has white flowers; and '**Variegata**' produces pale blue flowers and has attractive cream-variegated foliage. Zones 4–9.

Veronica longifolia

☼/◐ ✱ ↔ 16–30 in (40–75 cm)
↑ 20–48 in (50–120 cm)

Erect summer- to autumn-flowering perennial found over much of continental Europe and widely naturalized in northeastern North America. The foliage is narrow, lance-shaped, and toothed, sometimes sparsely hairy. Basal leaves to over 4 in (10 cm) long, upper leaves much smaller. Terminal flower spikes to 10 in (25 cm) long, with numerous tiny blue to lavender flowers. '**Blauriesin**' (syn. 'Blue Giantess'), to 32 in (80 cm) tall, bright blue flowers; '**Pink Damask**', to 36 in (90 cm) tall, soft pastel pink flowers. Zones 4–9.

Veronica officinalis

COMMON SPEEDWELL, GYPSY WEED

☼/◐ ✱ ↔ 12–20 in (30–50 cm)
↑ 8–20 in (20–50 cm)

This late spring- to early summer-flowering perennial is widespread in Europe. Spreading or upright habit with downy to hairy stems and foliage. Leaves are toothed, broadly oval, ½–2 in (12–50 mm) long. Flowerheads to more than 2 in (5 cm) long, with ¼ in (6 mm) wide lilac flowers. Zones 3–9.

Veronica gentianoides

Veronica pectinata

Veronica perfoliata

Veronica oltensis

↔ 8–12 in (20–30 cm)
↑ 1–2 in (25–50 mm)

This is an alpine perennial from northern Turkey. It develops into a dense-foliaged ground-hugging mat with tiny pinnate leaves that in early summer disappear under clusters of ¼ in (6 mm) wide, pale to bright blue flowers. This species can make a marvelous rock garden specimen. Zones 6–10.

Veronica pectinata

↔ 12–16 in (30–40 cm)
↑ 2–6 in (5–15 cm)

An evergreen southern Eurasian subshrub that flowers from late spring. Makes a mat of hairy, deeply toothed or cut leaves around 1 in (25 mm) long. Racemes, up to 8 in (20 cm) long, form in the leaf axils and carry numerous light-centered deep blue flowers that can reach to nearly ½ in (12 mm) wide. Zones 3–9.

Veronica peduncularis

↔ 8–20 in (20–50 cm)
↑ 2–6 in (5–15 cm)

A late spring- to summer-flowering perennial found in the Caucasus, southern Russia, and western Asia. Forms a carpet of wiry stems with upturned tips and ¼–1 in (6–25 mm) long, dark green, toothed, lance-shaped leaves. Flowers are bright blue, sometimes pink or white, in small racemes. **'Georgia Blue'** has vivid mid-blue flowers. Zones 6–10.

Veronica spicata 'Heidekind'

Veronica perfoliata

syn. *Derwentia perfoliata*

DIGGER'S SPEEDWELL

↔ 20–60 in (50–150 cm)
↑ 12–26 in (30–65 cm)

Occurs in a range of habitats from central New South Wales, generally above 1,640 ft (500 m) altitude, south to eastern and central western Victoria, Australia. Small shrub with woody rootstock. Stems mostly held erect, glaucous, with finely toothed, oval-shaped, leathery leaves, in 2s or 3s at the nodes. Bluish flowers in terminal and axillary spikes, in spring–summer. Grown in Europe since the early 1800s. Can be grown from both seeds and cuttings. Zones 8–9.

Veronica pimeleoides

syn. *Hebe pimeleoides*

↔ 26 in (60 cm) ↑ 18 in (45 cm)

From New Zealand's South Island. Attractive plant for rock gardens. Small shrub, dark purplish branchlets, glaucous leaves, red margins. Flowers bluish purple, in summer–autumn. **'County Park'**, spreading plant with grayish green leaves edged with red and flushing reddish purple in winter; **'Quicksilver'**, particularly small and very glaucous leaves. Zones 7–10.

Veronica pinguifolia

syn. *Hebe pinguifolia*

VERONICA

↔ 30 in (75 cm) ↑ 10 in (25 cm)

From the drier eastern ranges of the South Island of New Zealand. Variable habit in the wild. Cultivated plants are usually low-growing. Stout branches, small thick bluish gray leaves with red margins. Small white flowers rise in dense heads near branch tips, in spring–autumn. **'Pagei'** is an excellent rock garden plant, spreading to 3 ft (0.9 m), with very glaucous leaves and dark purplish branchlets. Zones 6–10.

Veronica, HC, Wiri Series, 'Wiri Charm'

Veronica prostrata

↔ 8–16 in (20–40 cm)
↑ 2–4 in (5–10 cm)

Flowering from late spring to summer, this European perennial forms a small mat of wiry stems with toothed, narrow pointed oval leaves, to 1 in (25 mm) long. Flower spikes in the leaf axils, with many small pale to deep blue flowers. Dainty rock garden plant. **'Heavenly Blue'**, intense bright blue; **'Spode Blue'**, deepest blue; **'Trehane'**, golden leaves and violet-blue flowers. Zones 5–9.

Veronica rakaiensis

syn. *Hebe rakaiensis*

↔ 4 ft (1.2 m) ↑ 3–7 ft (0.9–2 m)

Bushy shrub from the South Island, New Zealand. Short narrow leaves, glossy bright green. White flowers carried in loose racemes 1½ in (35 mm) long, in spring. Zones 6–9.

Veronica repens

CREEPING SPEEDWELL

↔ 12–18 in (30–45 cm)
↑ 2–4 in (5–10 cm)

This low, spreading, late spring- to summer-flowering perennial is from Spain and Corsica. Foliage is bright green to yellow-green, pointed oval, sometimes toothed, less than ½ in (12 mm) long. Flowers are a little over ¼ in (6 mm) wide, pink, white, or blue, solitary or in heads of up to six. Zones 5–10.

Veronica spicata

↔ 12–32 in (30–80 cm)
↑ 12–24 in (30–60 cm)

European summer-flowering perennial forming a clump of erect stems with downy, finely toothed, narrow lance-shaped, 1–3 in (25–80 mm) long leaves. Terminal spikes densely packed with ¼ in (6 mm) wide deep blue flowers. V. s. subsp. incana, velvety silver-gray to white flowers, sometimes classified as distinct species. Its cultivars include: **'Rotfuchs'** (syn. 'Red Fox'), deep reddish pink flowers; **'Silbersee'**, a low spreading foliage carpet, spikes of dark blue flowers; **'Wendy'**, gray-green foliage and an open growth habit. V. s. **'Barcarolle'**, bright pink; **'Heidekind'**, short spikes of purple-red flowers; **'Icicle'**, long spikes of white flowers; **'Rosea'**, deep pink; and **'Sunny Border Blue'**, dark violet-blue flowers over a long season. Zones 3–9.

Veronica Hybrid Cultivars

↔ 1–5 ft (0.3–1.5 m)
↑ 1–5 ft (0.3–1.5 m)

The many attractive *Veronica* cultivars available include: **'Alicia Amherst'**, well-branched shrub to 5 ft (1.5 m) tall, young branchlets, reddish coloring, leaves glossy dark green, deep purple flowers densely packed on spikes up to 2½ in (6 cm) long, from autumn; **'Amy'**, rounded compact shrub growing to 3–5 ft (0.9–1.5 m) tall, dark branchlets, leaves deep purplish bronze when young, older foliage flushed purple in winter, erect spikes of purple flowers in late summer; **'Autumn Glory'** ★, low bushy shrub to 24 in (60 cm) tall with purplish branchlets, dark green leaves, violet flowers on short crowded spikes in mid-summer–autumn; **'Carnea'**, old cultivar, dense spreading shrub to 5 ft (1.5 m) tall, leaves lance-shaped, summer flowers on racemes to 3 in (8 cm) long, rosy purple; **'Edinensis'**, low spreading habit, to 12 in (30 cm) high, 18 in (45 cm) wide, tiny vivid green leaves, semi-whipcord appearance, white flowers slightly tinted with mauve; **'Emerald Green'** (syns 'Emerald Gem', 'Green Globe'), natural hybrid, semi-whipcord appearance, fresh green compact bun shape 8–12 in (20–30 cm) high, small white flowers in summer; **'Fragrant Jewel'**, reaches 5 ft (1.5 m) high, masses of large, fragrant, lavender-purple flowers; **'Hagley Park'**, low, spreading, leaves red-edged, toothed, and round, flowers pinkish lilac in erect sprays in autumn; **'Hebe Jeebies'**, around 40 in (100 cm) high and wide, small elliptical leaves, purple flowers on short spikes mainly in spring; **'Inspiration'**, hybrid with *V. speciosa* parentage, grows into neat shrub about 3 ft (0.9 m) high, dark green shiny leaves, deep purple flowers for long periods, main flush in summer, good shrub for coastal areas; **'Loganioides'**, 10 in (25 cm) tall heath-like whipcord with white flowers; **'Margret'**, 16 in (40 cm) tall, sky blue flowers fading to white in late spring–early summer; **'Marjorie'**, to 5 ft (1.5 m) tall, yellow-green leaves, large mauve-blue flowers fading to white; **'Midsummer Beauty'** (syn. *V.* × *andersonii* 'Midsummer Beauty'), to 6 ft (1.8 m) tall, plum-colored new growth, lilac-purple flowers fading to white; **'Mrs Winder'** (syns 'Waikiki', 'Warleyensis'), spreading rounded shrub about 3 ft (0.9 m) high, leaves flushed red at base, reddish purple in winter, violet flowers in summer; **'Orphan Annie'**, to 3 ft (0.9 m) tall, narrow cream and green variegated foliage, new growth pink, pink early summer flowers; **'Pink Elephant'**, 2 ft (0.6 m) tall, yellow-edged pink-tinged new growth, white summer flowers; **'Temptation'**, to 12 in (30 cm) tall, apple-blossom pink flowers fading to white; **'Wardiensis'**, to 8 in (20 cm) tall, gray-green leaves, white summer flowers; and **'Youngii'** (syn. 'Carl Teschner'), well-branched spreading shrub, 8 in (20 cm) tall, branchlets purplish, small leaves dark green, leathery, deep violet flowers on short spikes in summer. Extensive breeding at Auckland's Botanic Gardens has resulted in the **Wiri Series**, including **'Wiri Charm'**, dense wide shrub, 30 in (75 cm) high, rosy purple flowers in summer; **'Wiri Dawn'**, low spreading plant to 18 in (45 cm) high, light olive green foliage, pale pinkish white flowers; **'Wiri Grace'**, large rounded shrub to 5 ft (1.5 m) tall, long spikes of light purple flowers in summer; **'Wiri Image'**, vigorous shrub to 3 ft (0.9 m) tall, long racemes of violet flowers in early summer Zones 8–11.

VERONICASTRUM

This genus of 2 upright perennials, in the plantain (Plantaginaceae) family, is from northeastern Asia and northeastern North America. The plants have whorls of simple leaves and a terminal raceme of spikes of flowers with a calyx with 4 to 5 lobes, and saucer-shaped corolla with 2 stamens. CULTIVATION: These perennials like moist, humus-rich soil and will grow in full or half-sun. Propagation is from seed, or by division.

Veronicastrum virginicum

syns *Leptandra virginica, Veronica virginica*

BLACKROOT, BOWMAN'S ROOT, CULVER'S ROOT

↔ 1–3 ft (0.3–0.9 m) ↕ 2–6 ft (0.6–1.8 m)

This perennial, native to northeastern America, has whorls of 4 to 7 simple, smooth, sword-shaped, serrated leaves. Dense, slender spikes, to 12 in (30 cm) tall, of tiny pale blue or white flowers in summer. V. v. var. sibiricum, narrow spikes of lilac flowers. V. v. **'Album'**, white flowers; **'Pointed Finger'**, lilac flowers; **'Roseum'**, soft pink flowers. Zones 3–6.

VIBURNUM

This genus in the muskroot (Adoxaceae) family consists of easily grown, cool-climate, deciduous, semi-evergreen or evergreen, shrubby plants that are grown for their pretty flowers, autumnal leaf color, and berries. Most have erect branching stems, paired leaves, a spread about two-thirds their height, and display their small white flowers in dense clusters. (Those plants that resemble the lace-top *Hydrangea* species bear sterile florets at the outer edges of the cluster.) The buds and petals, particularly in cultivars, may be softly colored in tints of pink, yellow, and green. CULTIVATION: Light open positions and light well-drained soils are preferred. Many are drought tender. Prune the evergreens by clipping in late spring and the deciduous species by removing entire old stems after flowering. For a good berry display grow several in the same area. Propagate from cuttings taken in summer, or from seed in autumn.

Viburnum betulifolium

↔ 10 ft (3 m) ↕ 10 ft (3 m)

Upright, arching, deciduous shrub, native to western China. Bark is smooth, purple-brown. Bright green roundly oval leaves, glossy undersides. Tiny white flowers in flat-topped clusters, in early summer. Persistent, glowing, round, red berries. Zones 6–8.

Veronicastrum virginicum 'Pointed Finger'

Viburnum bitchiuense

↔ 10 ft (3 m) ↕ 10 ft (3 m)

Sometimes listed as *V. carlesii* var. *bitchiuense*. Bushy deciduous shrub, native of Korea. Smooth leaves have longer stems, are narrower than *V. carlesii*. Fragrant flowers, in open rounded clusters in early summer, pink on opening, fade to white. Egg-shaped red fruit. Zones 6–8.

Viburnum × *bodnantense*

↔ 7 ft (2 m) ↕ 10 ft (3 m)

Large, upright, deciduous shrub, a hybrid of *V. farreri* and *V. grandiflorum*. Long, oval, mid-green leaves, paler beneath, noticeably veined, color in autumn. Persistent, pinkish white to red, fragrant flowers, in dense clusters on bare wood, in late autumn–early spring. **'Charles Lamont'** large bright pink flowers; **'Dawn'**, distinctive, deep pink, fragrant flowers that fade with age. Zones 7–9.

Viburnum × *burkwoodii*

BURKWOOD'S VIBURNUM

↔ 8 ft (2.4 m) ↕ 8 ft (2.4 m)

Open bushy shrub, an English hybrid of *V. carlesii* and *V. utile*. Evergreen dark leaves, shiny above, felted below, bronze when young, turn yellow. Flowers are produced in rounded clusters, intense fragrance, in early spring, pink in bud, white on opening. **'Anne Russell'**, deciduous, valued for its small size, neat compact habit; **'Park Farm Hybrid'**, featuring red autumnal foliage. Zones 6–9.

Viburnum × *carlcephalum*

FRAGRANT SNOWBALL VIBURNUM

↔ 8 ft (2.4 m) ↕ 8 ft (2.4 m)

Deciduous shrub, a garden hybrid between *V. carlesii* and *V. macrocephalum* f. *keteleeri*. Lustrous leaves redden in autumn. Pink, 6 in (15 cm) wide buds appear in spring, opening to reveal mildly scented pink flowers that lighten with age. Zones 5–9.

Viburnum carlesii

KOREAN SPICE VIBURNUM

↔ 7 ft (2 m) ↕ 8 ft (2.4 m)

From the open scrub of Korea and Japan, a dense, deciduous, rounded shrub. The mid-green leaves, paler beneath, oval shape, bronze-tinted when young, purple-red in autumn. Clustered crimson-pink buds open to reveal pink flowers that fade to white. **'Aurora'** ★ features light acid green young leaves, red buds, and pink flowers; **'Diana'** has bronzed new growth, and red flowers that fade to purple. Zones 9–11.

Viburnum cassinoides

WILD RAISIN, WITHE-ROD

↔ 10 ft (3 m) ↕ 12 ft (3.5 m)

Deciduous shrub from eastern North America, noted for deep bronze new growth and scarlet autumn coloring. Oval leaves thick, dull green, finely toothed. Flowers white or yellowish white, in summer. Red fruit, ripening to deep blue and black. Zones 2–6.

Viburnum × *burkwoodii*

Viburnum carlesii

Viburnum davidii

Viburnum 'Cayuga'

↔ 6 ft (1.8 m) ↕ 6 ft (1.8 m)

Hybrid between *Viburnum carlesii* and *V.* × *carlcephalum*. Leaves develop soft orange tones in autumn. Flowers pleasantly scented, open from pink buds, outer flowers a similar pink shade, those in the center, white. Fruit deep purple-red to black. Zones 8–10.

Viburnum davidii

↔ 4 ft (1.2 m) ↕ 4 ft (1.2 m)

This low-growing, dense, evergreen, mound-forming shrub is from the woods of western China. Glossy green leather-like leaves, 3 distinctive main veins. Small off-white flowers in stiff well-spaced clusters, are produced in late spring. Bright, oblong, midnight blue berries. Zones 8–10.

Viburnum dentatum

ARROWWOOD, SOUTHERN ARROWWOOD

↔ 10 ft (3 m) ↕ 10 ft (3 m)

This dense, deciduous, bushy shrub is found naturally across North America. Stems are erect and branching, leaves broadly oval, coarsely toothed, redden in autumn. Flat clusters of tiny white flowers, from late spring through to early summer. Dark blue oblong fruit. **'Ralph Senior'** has a vigorous bushy habit and large leaves. Zones 2–6.

Viburnum dilatatum

LINDEN VIBURNUM

↔ 8 ft (2.4 m) ↕ 10 ft (3 m)

A deciduous bushy shrub from China and Japan. Large, oval, coarse leaves, roundish, toothed, dark green, good autumn coloring. Tiny, creamy white, star-shaped flowers, in clusters, in late spring or summer. Oval scarlet fruits persist. **'Catskill'**, broad low-growing habit, smaller leaves than the species, good autumn coloring; **'Erie'**, pink fruit, rich autumn colors; **'Iroquois'**, shorter than the species, with reddish yellow fruits. Zones 5–8.

Viburnum lantana

Viburnum 'Eskimo'

Viburnum 'Eskimo'

↔ 4 ft (1.2 m) ↕ 4 ft (1.2m)

Attractive hybrid between *V.* 'Cayuga' and *V. utile*. Dwarf shrub, mounding growth habit. Semi-evergreen, glossy, dark green leaves. Flowers, white opening from pink-tinted buds, small carried in rounded heads. Zones 8–10.

Viburnum farreri

syn. *Viburnum fragrans*

↔ 8 ft (2.4 m) ↕ 10 ft (3 m)

Upright, deciduous shrub, native of northern China. Leaves oval, veined, tapering, bronze when young, red when old. Sweetly scented persistent flowers pale pink or white, appear before the leaves, from mid-autumn to spring. Edible scarlet berries with poisonous stones. Zones 6–9.

Viburnum × *globosum*

↔ 3–4 ft (0.9–1.2 m)
↕ 3–4 ft (0.9–1.2 m)

Evergreen *V. davidii* × *V. lobophyllum* hybrid usually seen as selected form **'Jermyn's Globe'**, neat rounded shrub. Lustrous, leathery, heavily veined, red-stemmed leaves. Heads of massed small white flowers open from red-tinted buds. Small dark blue fruit. Zones 7–10.

Viburnum japonicum

↔ 8 ft (2.4 m) ↕ 8 ft (2.4 m)

Robust evergreen shrub from Japan. Long, leathery, lustrous leaves, oval, dark green above, paler beneath. Tiny, white, strongly scented flowers in clusters, in early summer. Berries red, persist through the winter. Zones 7–9.

Viburnum prunifolium

Viburnum nudum

Viburnum × *juddii*

JUDD VIBURNUM

↔ 7 ft (2 m) ↕ 6 ft (1.8 m)

Deciduous *V. bitchiuense* and *V. carlesii* cross. Bushy spreading habit. Sweetly fragrant, pink budded, white starry flowers in rounded clusters, in mid–late spring. Elongated oval foliage, dull dark green. Zones 5–9.

Viburnum lantana

WAYFARING TREE

↔ 12 ft (3.5 m) ↕ 15 ft (4.5 m)

Robust deciduous shrub or small tree, native of Europe and northwest Asia. Oblong-oval dull green leaves sometimes turn rusty crimson in autumn. Creamy white flowers in terminal clusters, in late spring–early summer. Red oblong fruits mature to black. Grows best on alkaline soils. Darker-leafed **'Mohican'** ★ has reddish orange fruit, maturing to black; **'Versicolor'** has light yellow new leaves ageing to golden yellow. Zone 3–6.

Viburnum lentago

NANNYBERRY, SHEEPBERRY, WILD RAISIN

↔ 10 ft (3 m) ↕ 20 ft (6 m)

Slender, branching, vigorous, deciduous shrub or small tree from North America. Broadly oval, lustrous, dark green leaves, attractive autumn hues. Creamy white, fluffy flowers, similar to elderberry *(Sambucus)* species, in clusters, from spring to early summer. Oval bluish black berries. Zones 2–5.

Viburnum macrocephalum

CHINESE SNOWBALL BUSH/TREE

↔ 15 ft (4.5 m) ↕ 15 ft (4.5 m)

A Chinese species with spreading branches. Showy pompon-like clusters of white flowers, opening from almost luminous green buds, in spring. May be semi-evergreen in mild winters. Dark green oval-oblong leaves, downy on the undersides. V. m. f. keteleeri has attractive lacecap-like flowers. V. m. **'Sterile'**, sterile and berryless, is a popular cultivar for mild-climate gardens. Zones 6–9.

Viburnum nudum

POSSUM-HAW VIBURNUM, SMOOTH WITHE-ROD

↔ 6 ft (1.8 m) ↕ 10 ft (3 m)

Deciduous erect shrub native to eastern USA and Canada. Oval glossy leaves, prominent veins, minutely toothed edges, turn reddish purple in autumn. Flowers white or pale yellow, in summer. Fruit is blue-black. Zones 6–9.

Viburnum odoratissimum

SWEET VIBURNUM

↔ 12–20 ft (3.5–6 m)
↕ 12–20 ft (3.5–6 m)

Evergreen shrub found from southern Japan through southern China to India and northern Myanmar. Oval, mid-green, leathery leaves, 4–6 in (10–15 cm) long. Massed heads of fragrant white to cream flowers, in spring, followed by small red berries, blackening when ripe. **'Emerald Lustre'**, very glossy leaves. Zones 8–11.

Viburnum opulus

COMMON SNOWBALL, EUROPEAN CRANBERRY, EUROPEAN SNOWBALL, GUELDER ROSE

↔ 15 ft (4.5 m) ↕ 15 ft (4.5 m)

Vigorous parent plant to many popular deciduous garden shrubs. Native hedgerow habitat from Siberia to Algeria. Deep green vine-like leaves, paler downy undersides, redden in autumn. Lace-top clusters of white flowers, in early summer. Lustrous, semi-translucent, red fruits. **'Aureum'**, bright yellow spring foliage, yellow-green in summer, easily scorched by sun; **'Nanum'**, dwarf cultivar of dense multi-stemmed habit, to about 2 ft (0.6 m) tall, with small crowded leaves, rarely flowers; **'Notcutt's Variety'**, tall vigorous shrub to about 12 ft (3.5 m) high with fine foliage color in autumn, large red fruits last into winter; **'Roseum'** (syn. 'Sterile'), showy, snowball-like, greenish white flower clusters, in mid-spring with the leaves; **'Xanthocarpum'**, white flowers, mid-green leaves, glossy, partly translucent, yellow berries. Zones 3–9.

Viburnum plicatum

syn. *Viburnum plicatum var. tomentosum*

DOUBLEFILE VIBURNUM, JAPANESE SNOWBALL

↔ 10 ft (3 m) ↑ 8 ft (2.4 m)

From China and Japan. A vigorous, deciduous, spreading shrub with tiered branches. Leaves with pleated surface, bright green in spring, mid-green in summer, burgundy-red in autumn. Profuse flat umbels of small, cream, fertile flowers, in late spring to early summer, ringed by larger, white, sterile flowers. Small red fruits. **'Fireworks'**, reddish black fruits, purple-red autumn foliage; **'Grandiflorum'**, white flowers turn pink; **'Lanarth'**, spreads to 15 ft (4.5m); **'Mariesii'**, horizontal overlapping branches, large flat heads of mainly sterile flowers, rarely fruiting; **'Nanum Semperflorens'** (syn. *V. watanabei*), slow-growing, small flowerheads during the warmer months; **'Pink Beauty'**, white flowers ageing to pink; **'Roseum'**, flowers age from white to deep pink; **'Shasta'**, 7 ft (2 m) tall, deep purple-red autumn foliage, large white flowers followed by dark red fruit; **'Summer Snowflake'**, compact shrub with strongly tiered branches, long-lasting white flowers, purple-red autumn foliage. Zones 4–9.

Viburnum prunifolium

BLACK HAW

↔ 12 ft (3.5 m) ↑ 20 ft (6 m)

Spreading deciduous shrub or small tree from eastern parts of North America. Leaves roundish oval, finely and sharply toothed. Reddish buds open to small, white, flat-topped clusters of flowers, in spring to early summer. Yellow-green berries ripen to blue-black. Zones 3–9.

Viburnum × rhytidophylloides

↔ 15 ft (4.5 m) ↑ 20 ft (6 m)

Of garden origin, a hybrid between *V. rhytidophyllum* and *V. lantana.* Deciduous in cold climates, densely upright shrub or small tree. Long oval leaves, shiny dark green, paler on the undersides. Flowers a dull yellowish to pinkish white, in spring to summer. Red berries ripen to black. Zones 5–9.

Viburnum rhytidophyllum

↔ 8 ft (2.4 m) ↑ 10 ft (3 m)

Stout, upright, fast-growing, evergreen shrub. Long, narrow, wrinkled, veined, leathery, dark green leaves, gray or yellow woolly beneath. Terminal clusters of small, fluffy, yellowish to pinkish white flowers, in early summer. Oval red fruit darkens to black. **'Aldenhamense'**, leaves with sulfur yellow tinges; **'Roseum'**, deep pink flowers turn lighter with age. Zones 6–8.

Viburnum sargentii

SARGENT VIBURNUM

↔ 10 ft (3 m) ↑ 10 ft (3 m)

Large deciduous shrub from Siberia, China, and Japan. Thick, dark gray, fissured, corky bark. Leaves large, long, maple-like, turn yellow-orange and scarlet in autumn. Creamy white lacecap flowers, early summer. Semi-translucent, light red, round berries. **'Onondaga'** has bronze red young growth. **'Susquehanna'** is smaller than the species, with a rounded growth habit. Zones 5–9.

Viburnum setigerum

↔ 7 ft (2 m) ↑ 5–12 ft (1.5–3.5 m)

Deciduous shrub variable in height, depending on climate and clone. Large oblong-oval leaves dark green above, paler, slightly woolly beneath, color well in autumn. Flowers are insignificant. Spectacular, gleaming, golden orange and bright red, oval fruits. Zones 5–9.

Viburnum sieboldii

↔ 15 ft (4.5 m) ↑ 10 ft (3 m)

From Japan. Spreading deciduous shrub. Young growth downy. Large prominently veined leaves, oblong-oval, glossy, dark green above, paler beneath. Panicles of tiny creamy white flowers, in late spring–early summer. Fruits red when young, ripen to black. **'Seneca'**, reaching up to 30 ft (9 m) high, has clusters of white flowers followed by persistent red fruit, ripening to almost black. Zones 4–8.

Viburnum tinus 'Robertson'

Viburnum tinus

LAURUSTINUS

↔ 8–10 ft (2.4–3 m) ↑ 8–10 ft (2.4–3 m)

Native of Mediterranean region. Dense evergreen shrub, popular for centuries as hedging plant. Leaves dark green, glossy, oblong-oval, pointed. Flattened heads of white, pink, or pinkish white flowers, strongly fragrant. Blue-black berries. Several named forms grow in sun or shade, tolerate coastal conditions, and are semi-tolerant of summer drought. **'Anvi'**, compact, deep dusky pink to red flower buds, large flowers; **'Eve Price'**, elongated leaves and light pink flowers; **'Lucidum'**, particularly glossy leaves; **'Purpureum'**, bronzed new growth; **'Robertson'**, small whitish flowers; and **'Variegatum'**, leaves margined in yellow. Zones 7–9.

Viburnum trilobum

syns *Viburnum americanum, V. opulus var. americanum*

AMERICAN HIGHBUSH CRANBERRY, CRANBERRY BUSH

↔ 10 ft (3 m) ↑ 10 ft (3 m)

Deciduous shrubby plant from North America. Dark leaves, broadly oval, deeply serrated, redden in autumn. Showy, flat-topped, white flowerheads, in early summer. Bright scarlet edible berries. **'Bailey Compact'** and **'Compactum'** have attractive autumn foliage; **'Wentworth'**, vigorous cultivar, tolerant of damp soils, very brightly colored long-lasting fruit. Zones 2–8.

Viburnum utile

↔ 5 ft (1.5 m) ↑ 6 ft (1.8 m)

From China. Evergreen, slender, open shrub with dark shiny leaves. Flowers white, in dense rounded clusters, in spring. Oval berries. Zones 7–9.

Viburnum sieboldii

Viburnum wrightii

↔ 10 ft (3m) ↑ 12 ft (3.5 m)

Deciduous shrub from Japan. Broad, bright green, oval leaves turn red in autumn. Flowers white, in flat rayed clusters, in late spring–early summer. Glistening red fruit. Zones 6–8.

VIGNA

This genus, comprising some 150 species native throughout the tropics, but particularly in the Americas, is a member of the pea-flower subfamily of the legume (Fabaceae) family. The plants are erect or twining herbs. They usually have woody or tuberous rootstocks. The leaves have 1 to 3 elliptic to ovate leaflets. The flowers are in racemes or clustered together, often on long stalks. The calyx is 2-lipped. The yellow, blue, or purple corolla has an upper petal generally with 2 to 4 appendages; the inner petals forming the keel are often beaked, the beak can be incurved up to 360 degrees. The pod is cylindrical or flattened, straight or curved. The seeds are often kidney-shaped and sometimes have an aril.

CULTIVATION: These are important pulses and many provide valuable green manure. They are also grown as "bean sprouts." Frost tender. In tropical regions grow in full sun in fertile well-drained soil; in cooler climates grow in the greenhouse. Propagate from seed in spring.

Vigna caracalla

syn. *Phaseolus caracalla*

CORKSCREW FLOWER, SNAIL BEAN, SNAIL FLOWER

↔ 10 ft (3 m) ↑ 12–20 ft (3.5–6 m)

A twining perennial from tropical South America. Finely hairy leaves with 3 oval-shaped leaflets. Fragrant white or yellow flowers, up to 2 in (5 cm) across, with pinkish purple wings. Coiled keel resembles a snail shell. Zones 10–11.

Vigna caracalla

VINCA

PERIWINKLE

This genus of 7 species of evergreen groundcovering perennials found in woodland areas of North Africa, central Asia, and Europe, is part of the dogbane (Apocynaceae) family. These plants are distinctive for their opposite, simple, lance-shaped leaves that cover the slender, often cream or pale green, ground-hugging stems. The foliage varies in color from pale to dark green and many variations occur with attractive variegations. The star-shaped flowers are produced from spring through to late autumn, and will vary in color from dark purple to blue and white.

CULTIVATION: Ideally, these plants like a free-draining light soil with a reasonable level of organic matter. They will spread indefinitely and in some areas they can become invasive if neglected. Plant in sun or shade. The plant spreads by sending out long trailing and rooting shoots, which make new plants. Propagation is easy any time of year by separating the new offshoots or by layering new shoots.

Vinca major

BLUE BUTTONS, GREATER PERIWINKLE

↔ 5–10 ft (1.5–3 m) ↑ 18 in (45 cm)

From western parts of Mediterranean. Mounding plant with dark green leaves, 3½ in (9 cm) long, on arching stems. Rich violet-blue flowers, 2 in (5 cm) across, from early spring to late autumn. **'Variegata'** (syn. 'Elegantissima') has creamy white streaked green leaves. Has become invasive in parts of the western USA. Zones 7–11.

Vinca major

Vinca minor 'Atropurpurea'

Vinca minor

CREEPING MYRTLE

↔ 5–10 ft (1.5–3 m)
↑ 8 in (20 cm)

From Europe, southern Russia, and northern Caucasus. This tight mat-forming, evergreen perennial has dark green leaves, to 2 in (5 cm) long. The star-shaped violet-blue flowers, 1¼ in (3 cm) across, appear from early spring to mid-autumn. It is ideal for hanging baskets. **'Alba'** bears white flowers; **'Argenteovariegata'** (syn. 'Variegata'), creamy white stripes on foliage with pale lavender flowers; **'Atropurpurea'**, dark plum colored flowers; **'Azurea Flore Pleno'**, pale blue, frilly, double flowers; **'Bowles' Variety'**, with pale lavender-blue flowers; **'Gertrude Jekyll'**, a compact plant with plenty of white flowers; **'Illumination'**, variegated leaves, mainly yellow, with some green marking; **'Multiplex'**, double, red wine colored flowers; **'Ralph Shugert'**, deep green leaves outlined in white variegations. Zones 4–9.

Vinca Hybrid Cultivars

↔ 12 in (30 cm) ↑ 16 in (40 cm)

Plants have an upright habit and branch early in the growing season. Quite tolerant of cool wet growing conditions. **'Cooler Raspberry Red'**, dark green leaves and large, overlapping flower petals of bright red with a white eye; **'Merlot Mix'**, large flowers displaying rich shades of burgundy, orchid, rose, and white; **'Pacific Red'**, carmine red; **'Pacific White'**, pure white. Zones 10–11.

VIOLA

HEARTSEASE, PANSY, VIOLET

The type genus for the family Violaceae, *Viola* includes some 500 species of annuals, perennials, and subshrubs found in all the world's temperate zones from the mountains of New Zealand to the subarctic. Most species are small clump-forming plants with lobed, elliptic, kidney- or heart-shaped leaves. All violas have remarkably similarly shaped 5-petalled flowers, with the lower petal often carrying dark markings. White, yellow, and purple predominate but the flowers occur in every color, at least among the garden forms. The plants have been used medicinally in several ways, and also symbolically: *V. tricolor* was a symbol of Athens and was also used by Napoleon.

CULTIVATION: They are mostly very hardy and easily grown in sun or shade. The woodland species prefer a humus-rich soil, while the rock-garden types like something grittier, but most do perfectly well in any moist well-drained soil. Propagation is from seed or basal cuttings or by division, depending on the growth form.

Viola cornuta

BEDDING PANSY, HORNED VIOLET

↔ 8–14 in (20–35 cm)
↑ 6–12 in (15–30 cm)

From the Pyrenees and northern Spain. A late spring- to summer-flowering, rhizome-rooted perennial, initially prostrate then more mounding. Oval, 1 in (25 mm) long, shallowly toothed leaves and spurred, broad-petalled, ¾ in (18 mm) wide, violet flowers with darker veining and yellow center. Alba Group, white-flowered forms of various sizes and degree of color purity; **'Belmont Blue'** (syn. 'Boughton Blue'), 1 in (25 mm) wide lilac flowers; **'Jewel White'**, very compact habit, white flowers to 1¾ in (40 mm) wide; **'Magnifico'**, white flowers with broad mauve border; **'Pat Kavanagh'**, pale lemon yellow, forms large clumps; **'Victoria's Blush'**, mid-pink narrow-petalled flowers. Also many mixed color seedling strains, such as Penny Series and Princess Series. Sorbet Series includes **'Sorbet Black Delight'**, deep velvet inky purple, almost black; and **'Sorbet Coconut'**, pure white with faint yellow center. Zones 7–10.

Viola cornuta, 'Magnifico'

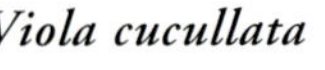

Viola cucullata

syn. *Viola obliqua*

MARSH BLUE VIOLET

↔ 8–16 in (20–40 cm)
↑ 4–6 in (10–15 cm)

This is a North American spring- to early summer-flowering perennial. It develops a low spreading habit and has shallowly toothed, broad, pointed oval to kidney-shaped leaves, to over 3 in (8 cm) wide. The 5-petalled, short-spurred flowers, up to 1¼ in (30 mm) wide, are white washed with mauve to purple, sometimes heavily. Zones 4–9.

Viola jooi

↔ 8–14 in (20–35 cm)
↑ 2–4 in (5–10 cm)

A native of southeastern Europe, this is a spring- to summer-flowering perennial. It has a stemless habit, spreading by runners, with shallowly toothed heart-shaped leaves, to 3 in (8 cm) long, and short-spurred, ½ in (12 mm) wide, dark-streaked, mauve flowers. Zones 5–10.

Viola odorata

SWEET VIOLET

↔ 12–24 in (30–60 cm)
↑ 4–6 in (10–15 cm)

A spring- to early summer-flowering southern and western European perennial that spreads by runners. Its heart-shaped dark green leaves, grow to over 2 in (5 cm) long and wide. The highly fragrant, spurred, 1 in (25 mm) wide flowers are lavender, purple, yellow, or white. Can be weedy. Numerous cultivars are available, with single or double flowers in a range of colors. **'Purple Robe'** ★ has a low spreading habit and masses of deep purple flowers. Zones 7–10.

Viola cornuta 'Jewel White'

Viola sororia

↔6–16 in (15–40 cm)
↑2–6 in (5–15 cm)

Eastern North American spring- to early summer-flowering perennial Leaves broad, rounded, toothed, light-textured, downy, up to 4 in (10 cm) long, often smaller. Light-centered violet flowers, to 1 in (25 mm) wide, less commonly white with purple veining. **'Freckles'**, white flowers heavily purple-spotted; **'Priceana'**, flowers white, deep blue center. Zones 4–9.

Viola tricolor

HEARTSEASE, JOHNNY JUMP-UP, LOVE-IN-IDLENESS

↔6–16 in (15–40 cm)
↑4–14 in (10–35 cm)

A temperate Eurasian spring- to early summer-flowering annual, biennial, or perennial that is usually treated as an annual. It often self-sows and naturalizes. Pointed oval to lance-like, shallowly lobed or toothed leaves and small bi- or multi-colored pansy flowers, often with a face-like pattern. Many cultivars and seedling strains, including: **'Bowles' Black'** (syn. 'E. A. Bowles'), intense velvety black flowers to 1¼ in (30 mm) wide, with small yellow center; **'Czar Bleu'**, pink to purple; and **Tinkerbelle Series**, small flowers in various pure shades and combinations. Zones 4–10.

Viola Hybrid Cultivars

PANSY, VIOLA

↔8–16 in (20–40 cm)
↑6–12 in (15–30 cm)

Annual or short-lived perennial garden hybrids developed from *V. cornuta*, *V. tricolor*, *V. corsica*, and other mainly European species. Mostly neat, slowly spreading clumps of fleshy, dark green, shallowly lobed, ½–2 in (12–50 mm) long, pointed oval to lance-shaped leaves. Flowers variably sized from small to giant styles nearly 3 in (8 cm) wide. Virtually all colors and many beautiful combinations and patterns. Baby Face Series, bi- to multicolored flowers with central "face" markings; Banner Series, vigorous plants with massed display of mainly bright clear colors; Crystal Bowl Series, large flowers, bright pure colors; Delta Series, large flowers, wide color range in pure and bi-color; Dynamite Series, large flowers, pure colors and several multi-tone forms; Fama Series, semi-trailing habit, abundant mid-sized flowers, usually selfs but some pastel blends; Imperial Series, similar colors to 'Antique Shades' but larger flowers, such as **'Imperial Antique Shades'**, large heat-tolerant flowers in delicate pale creams, mauves, peachy apricots, blues, rosy pinks; Joker Series, boldly patterned mid-sized flowers usually combining blue and another color; Panola Series, narrow leaves and abundant small flowers with dark faces; Penny Series, including **'Penny Primrose'**, creamy white upper petals, pale yellow lower petals; **'Penny Violet Flare'**, deep violet petals; **Turbo Series**, hardy plants, bright colors; Ultima Series, fast-growing, large flowers, wide color range, including selfs, blotched and pastel types in lavender, scarlet, yellow, bronze-apricot, pale salmon orange, including Ultima Supreme, compact form bred to withstand very cold temperatures, with mid-sized early-flowering blooms; Universal Series, tolerant of hot and cold weather, 18 prolific bloomers, masses of early-flowering blooms with 13 clear colors, including blue, white, burgundy, orange, purple and yellow, or the typical pansy face; Velour Series, medium to large, velvet-textured flowers in intense shades, often with dark markings. Other cultivars include **'Antique Shades'**, mid-sized, dusky pink and apricot pastel tones; **'Black Moon'**, rich black petals; and **'Elaine Quin'**, deep velvety rosy mauve with cream stripes, giving a marbled effect.

Viola Group, more compact pansies, usually fragrant, flowers often patterned. **'Baby Lucia'**, clear blue blooms, 6 in (15 cm) high mounding plant, heavy bloomer, cold tolerant; **'Etain'**, cream-yellow petals edged with lavender, refreshing scent; **'Fiona'**, sweet scent, creamy white flowers, suffused with lavender-blue; **'Irish Molly'** ★, gold-bronze yellow petals, dark maroon eye; **'Jackanapes'**, lower sections bright yellow, upper chocolate brown; **'Maggie Mott'**, a silvery mauve with creamy center and golden eye; **'Martin'**, violet flowers with a creamy center; **'Masterpiece'**, large ruffled flowers, purple-blue with bronze; **'Molly Sanderson'**, long-lasting, nearly black, velvety flowers with purple veins and a golden eye, green heart-shaped leaves; **'Nellie Britton'**, originally called 'Haslemere', rosy pink; **'Vita'**, small dainty flowers, with delicate lavender-pink petals and a creamy eye.

Viola, HC, 'Elaine Quin'

Violetta Group, similar to Viola Group but smaller, more compact fragrant flowers. **'Dawn'**, pale cream flowers deepening to gold; **'Melinda'**, white with mauve-blue edges and gold centers. Zones 7–10.

VITEX

This unusual genus that encompasses several seemingly very different species is made up of some 250 species of evergreen and deciduous shrubs in the mint (Lamiaceae) family, and has a widespread distribution in the tropical, subtropical, and warm-temperate zones. The foliage is usually digitately divided with up to 7 leaflets, and may be smooth-edged or toothed. The flowers are clustered in panicles, racemes, or cymes, and come in a wide range of colors.

CULTIVATION: As expected of a genus with tropical members, many species of *Vitex* are frost-tender, but some are quite hardy and will tolerate moderate frosts. In general, *Vitex* species prefer to avoid the extremes of soil moisture, being tolerant of neither drought nor waterlogging. Plant them in moist, fertile, well-drained soil and water them well in summer. Most grow best with at least half-sun. Hard pruning is seldom required but trim to shape as necessary. Propagate from seed or cuttings.

Vitex agnus-castus ★

CHASTE TREE

↔15 ft (4.5 m) ↑15 ft (4.5 m)

This aromatic shrub or small tree is found from southern Europe through to western Asia, naturalized in mild areas. The gray-green leaves have 5 to 9 narrow leaflets, and downy undersides. Dusty white panicles of buds open to scented lilac flowers, from summer to autumn. Purple drupes. **'Blushing Spires'**, soft pink flowers; **'Shoal Creek'**, large heads of lavender-blue flowers, very showy. Zones 7–10.

Vitex agnus-castus

Vitex trifolia

ARABIAN LILAC, SIMPLELEAF CHASTETREE

↔12–20 ft (3.5–6 m)
↑15–30 ft (4.5–9 m)

Found from eastern Africa through islands of Indian Ocean and Pacific to Tahiti. Leathery, elliptical, dark green leaves to 4 in (10 cm) long. Terminal spikes of showy purple flowers. Local medicinal uses, extracts used as insect repellents. **'Purpurea'**, purple-red foliage; **'Variegata'**, cream-edged leaves. Zones 10–12.

VITIS

GRAPE

This is a genus of 65 species of woody deciduous vines which are indigenous to the Northern Hemisphere, particularly North America, giving its name to the grape (Vitaceae) family. The vines climb by tendrils; the leaves are mostly simple, toothed or lobed and the bark often peels from the stems in strips. Flowers are small, sometimes fragrant. Berries can be small and unpalatable or large and sweet and are often produced in bunches. There are hundreds of cultivars, particularly of *Vitis vinifera*, the European wine grape. Asian species are primarily grown for their attractive foliage and autumn color.

CULTIVATION: These vines prefer to be cultivated in deep, moderately fertile, well-drained, often chalky, alkaline soil. Full sun and warmth are necessary for best fruit ripening. Most commercial *Vitis vinifera* grapes are grafted onto *Phylloxera*-resistant American species rootstock. Propagate most species from hardwood cuttings in late winter; propagate *V. coignetiae* by layering or from seed.

Vitis californica

CALIFORNIA WILD GRAPE

↔15–30 ft (4.5–9 m) ↑30 ft (9 m)

Native western North American vine with large, rounded to heart- or kidney-shaped, occasionally 3-lobed leaves turning rich red in autumn. Small black fruit enjoyed mainly by birds. **'Roger's Red'**, brilliant red autumn color, gray-green summer foliage; **'Walker Ridge'** more compact, bright red and orange autumn color. Zones 7–9.

WXYZ

Wachendorfia thyrsiflora (at front), Harold Porter National Botanical Garden, South Africa

WACHENDORFIA

This genus of some 25 species of mostly deciduous strappy-leafed perennials from South Africa is a member of the bloodroot (Haemodoraceae) family. The deciduous species have bright red tubers, and both deciduous and the single evergreen species have orange-red roots. The leaves are usually bright green and heavily pleated, with each leaf sheathing the next one in a flat fan arrangement. The flowers are yellow and star-shaped and produced in tall narrow spikes or, in the case of smaller species, in open clusters. These plants are considered to be weeds in southern Australia.
CULTIVATION: In more or less frost-free climates, grow in a sunny moist position; in other areas, protect from frost by growing *Wachendorfia* in large pots which can be overwintered in a greenhouse. Raise from fresh seed or by division in late winter.

Wachendorfia thyrsiflora

↔36–40 in (90–100 cm) ↑7–8 ft (2–2.4 m)

The only evergreen *Wachendorfia.* Strongly pleated, rich green leaves to 40 in (100 cm) long. In early summer it produces tall upright spikes with star-shaped rich yellow flowers to 1¼ in (30 mm) across. Zones 10–11.

WALDSTEINIA

There are 6 species of creeping fleshy-stemmed perennials in this genus, which belongs to the rose (Rosaceae) family. They are native to northern temperate regions where they are inhabitants of woodland areas. Plants form low mats of lobed and toothed leaves that are similar to those of the related strawberry and cinquefoil *(Potentilla).* Their leaves sometimes take on bronze tones in winter. The saucer-shaped 5-petalled flowers are yellow and are carried for long periods in spring and early summer. They are often more prolific on new growth.
CULTIVATION: These plants are suitable for the rock garden, the front of a border or a woodland edge. Their creeping well-foliaged habit makes them useful ground covers. Grow in partial shade in moist but well-drained soils. Where soils remain moist in summer, they can be grown in full sun. Propagate by division of rooted runners or from seed.

Waldsteinia fragarioides

BARREN STRAWBERRY

↔12–20 in (30–50 cm) ↑2 in (5 cm)

Mat-forming species native to eastern USA. Trifoliate bronze-green leaves with toothed, pointed oval leaflets to nearly 3 in (8 cm) long. From spring, clusters of up to 8 yellow, ¾ in (18 mm) wide flowers. Zones 3–9.

Waldsteinia ternata ★

↔24 in (60 cm) ↑6 in (15 cm)

Found from Europe to China and Japan. A vigorous ground-covering plant with dark green, 3-lobed, toothed, somewhat hairy leaves. The flowers, nearly ¾ in (18 mm) wide, are borne in groups of 3 to 7 in spring and summer. Can become invasive. Zones 3–9.

WASHINGTONIA

This genus in the palm (Arecaceae) family consists of 2 species from southwest USA and northwestern Mexico. These single-stemmed robust palms have fan leaves. The trunks are clothed in old leaf bases that hang like a skirt or petticoat. The leaves are deeply lobed with fibrous margins, while the small, bisexual, tube-shaped flowers can be creamy white or creamy apricot-pink, in slender hanging clusters among the leaves. The small fruits are drupes, and each contains a single seed. They come from desert areas where they obtain moisture from springs or streams, and can be seen cultivated in drier parts of tropical and subtropical regions as well as in temperate areas. They are useful for lining roadways and for planting in parklands.
CULTIVATION: These are very hardy and adaptable palms in a well-drained soil. They tolerate full sun, exposed conditions and, once established, drought. Both species grow very tall, so a large garden is a must; dispose of seed carefully, to avoid unwanted proliferation. Decaying foliage can be a fire risk and is best removed. Propagate from seed.

Washingtonia filifera ★

COTTON PALM, PETTICOAT PALM, WASHINGTONIA PALM

↔25 ft (8 m) ↑50 ft (15 m)

Heavy, gray trunk clothed in old leaves. Long spiny leafstalks, gray-green leaves, with thread-like filaments. Panicles of creamy white flowers. Hard blackish drupes. Zones 9–11.

Washingtonia robusta ★

COTTON PALM, MEXICAN WASHINGTONIA PALM, THREAD PALM

↔25 ft (8 m) ↑80 ft (24 m)

Native to northwestern Mexico and California, USA. This species differs from *W. filifera* in having a slender, taller, tapering trunk. Mature fan-shaped leaves brighter green, reddish brown spiny leaf stalks. The cottony threads are inconspicuous or absent on mature plants. Panicles of creamy apricot-pink flowers, in summer. Dark brown drupes. Zones 9–11.

Waldsteinia ternata

WATSONIA

BUGLE LILY

This genus contains 52 species of sun-loving bulbous perennials from South Africa. Members of the iris (Iridaceae) family, they are cormous and clump forming, with the common garden-grown species holding their flowers well above the reed-like foliage. Species that flower in late spring–early summer are dormant during summer months and require wet-winter to dry-summer climates. Those that flower in summer and autumn are either evergreen or winter dormant, requiring damp-summer climates. Those with narrow tubular flowers are thought to be pollinated by honey-eating birds; those with open cupped flowers by bees. There are many cultivars and hybrids, and some confusion exists with the nomenclature. Named for Sir William Watson (1715–1787), a British scientist who helped introduce the Linnaean system of plant classification to the UK.
CULTIVATION: Protect from frost in cold climates. They require sharp drainage, an open sunny position and light liquid feed when grown on very poor soils. Propagate from seed in spring or from offsets just as the plants move into dormancy.

Washingtonia filifera

Washingtonia robusta, in the wild, Mexico

W X Y Z

Watsonia borbonica

Watsonia borbonica

syn. *Watsonia pyramidata*

↔4 in (10 cm) ↕3–7 ft (0.9–2 m)

Leaves narrowly sword-shaped. Flowers are lightly scented, pale or deep pink, appearing in spring–early summer. Corms ¾–1¾ in (18–40 mm) wide. *W. b.* subsp. *ardernei* (syn. *W. ardernei*) is white, occasionally light pink, with flared trumpets, flowering for an extended period in late spring. Can become invasive. Zones 9–10.

WEIGELA

CARDINAL BUSH, WEIGELA

The 10 or 12 species of this genus within the bush honeysuckle (Diervillaceae) family are deciduous long-lived shrubs with opposite oblong to elliptic leaves. Native to eastern Asia, their natural habitat is scrubland and the edges of woods. Cultivated for their bell- or funnel-shaped flowers, produced in late spring and early summer, they have pink, red, white, or sometimes yellow blooms, growing on the previous year's wood.

CULTIVATION: They do well in moist but well-drained fertile soil in sun or partial shade. Remove older branches after flowering to encourage vigorous growth. Propagate by sowing seed in autumn in an area protected from winter frosts or from half-hardened cuttings in summer. Seed may not come true, as weigelas have a tendency to hybridize freely.

Weigela florida

OLD-FASHIONED WEIGELA, WEIGELA

↔8 ft (2.4 m) ↕8 ft (2.4 m)

From East Asia, larger in wild. Oblong leaves, pointed tips, toothed margins, felty undersides. Funnel-shaped dark pink to nearly white flowers, in spring–summer. **'Alexandra'** (syn. 'Wine & Roses'), purple spring foliage becomes almost blackish and glossy in summer, flowers bright rose red, plant compact, under 5 ft (1.5 m) in height; **'Evita'**, low and spreading, deep pink flowers; **'Foliis Purpureis'**, coppery foliage with dark pink flowers, compact habit to 3 ft (0.9 m); **'Java Red'**, purple-tinged foliage, dark pink flowers. Zones 5–10.

Weigela middendorffiana

Weigela hortensis

↔10 ft (3 m) ↕10 ft (3 m)

Japanese native with 4 in (10 cm) long heavily serrated leaves, very downy undersides. Rose pink flowers 1½ in (35 mm) long, in clusters of 3 blooms, in mid-spring–early summer. **'Nivea'**, large white flowers. Zones 7–9.

Weigela japonica

↔10 ft (3 m) ↕10 ft (3 m)

Native to Japan, larger in the wild. Leaves dark green. Spring flowers are solitary or in pairs, white, turning red later. *W. j.* var. *sinica* taller than the species, with light pink flowers, turning a deeper pink. Zones 6–10.

Weigela middendorffiana

↔5 ft (1.5 m) ↕5 ft (1.5 m)

Erect shrub from eastern Asia has vivid green leaves. Solitary or paired blossoms, bell-shaped flowers pale yellow with orange or red throat markings, in summer. Protect from strong winds. Zones 4–10.

Weigela praecox

↔7 ft (2 m) ↕8 ft (2.4 m)

An erect densely branched shrub that is native to Korea, northeastern China, and Japan. Parent of numerous early-flowering cultivars. Leaves are dark green with hairy undersides. Fragrant, pink, funnel-shaped flowers with yellow throats, are produced in late spring–early summer. Zones 5–10.

Weigela Hybrid Cultivars

↔5–8 ft (1.5–2.4 m) ↕5–12 ft (1.5–3.5 m)

Great plants for placing in borders, these are hybrids between a number of *Weigela* species. The range of cultivars to choose from is very extensive with many color possibilities. These include: **'Abel Carrière'**, dark green leaves, bell-shaped pink to red flowers; **'Bristol Ruby'**, carmine red flowers; **'Candida'**, vivid green leaves, bell-shaped white flowers; **'Chameleon'**, around 6 ft (1.8 m) tall, finely serrated mid-green leaves, pastel pink flowers, grows in sun or in part-shade; **'Eva Rathke'**, dark green leaves, funnel-shaped dark purple flowers; **'Florida Variegata'** (syn. *W. florida* 'Variegata'), cream-edged leaves and rich pink trumpets to 1¼ in (30 mm) long; **'Looymansii Aurea'**, yellowish leaves, rich pink flowers with paler pink center, foliage will scorch in hot sun, and lose its color in heavy shade; **'Madame Lemoine'**, pale pink flowers fading to white; **'Minuet'**, 30 in (75 cm) high with coppery oval leaves, bell-shaped magenta flowers; **'Newport Red'** ★ (syn. 'Vanicek'), tall, very hardy, with dark red flowers; **'Praecox Variegata'** (syn. *W. praecox* 'Variegata'), slightly scented pink trumpets with soft yellow center, leaves have creamy yellow margins turning white as they age; and **'Red Prince'**, lushly foliaged, long-lasting dark red flowers. Zones 5–10.

Weigela japonica var. sinica

Weigela, Hybrid Cultivar, 'Newport Red'

Weigela florida

Weigela, HC, 'Looymansii Aurea'

Wisteria brachybotrys 'Shiro-kapitan'

WISTERIA

Often seen covering verandahs and porches and capable of spreading a great distance, the 10 species of twining deciduous vines in this genus belong to the pea-flower subfamily of the legume (Fabaceae) family. They are native to China, Japan, and eastern USA. When young, the pinnate leaves are a soft bronze green but turn light green when mature. The flowers, primarily mauve in the species, occur in long racemes that start to open as the leaves expand. Cultivated forms range from white to various pink and purple tones. Named for Caspar Wistar (1761–1818), an anatomy professor at the University of Pennsylvania, USA.

CULTIVATION: Like *Clematis*, wisterias like their tops in sun and their roots in cool, moist, humus-rich, well-drained soil. These hardy, heavy-wooded, vigorous climbers need sturdy support and routine trimming. Propagate from cuttings or seed, by layering or grafting.

Wisteria brachybotrys

syn. *Wisteria venusta*

SILKY WISTERIA

☼/◐ ❄ ↔30 ft (9 m) ↕30 ft (9 m)

Vigorous Japanese climber with stems twining counterclockwise, densely downy when young. Leaves to 14 in (35 cm) long with 9 to 13, downy, pointed oval leaflets to 4 in (10 cm) long. Pendulous racemes to 6 in (15 cm) long of white, very fragrant, 1 in (25 mm) wide flowers. **'Murasaki Kapitan'** (syn. *W. venusta* 'Violacea'), clockwise-twining with purple-keeled mauve flowers; and **'Shiro-kapitan'** (syn. *W. sinensis* 'Prematura Alba'), like the species but shorter, sometimes pink-tinted racemes. Zones 6–9.

Wisteria floribunda 'Kuchi-beni'

Wisteria floribunda

Wisteria floribunda ★

JAPANESE WISTERIA

☼/● ❄ ↔25 ft (8 m) ↕25 ft (8 m)

Clockwise-twining Japanese climber. Leaves to 14 in (35 cm) long, downy when young, 11 to 19 pointed oval leaflets to 3 in (8 cm) long. Pendulous racemes 16–40 in (40–100 cm) long, fragrant violet, purple, pink, white, or magenta-red flowers to ¾ in (18 mm) wide. **'Alba'** (syn. 'Shîro-nôda'), long racemes with more than 100 faintly scented white flowers; **'Kuchi-beni'**, dark-keeled pale pink flowers in racemes to 18 in (45cm) long; **'Multijuga'** (syn. 'Macrobotrys'), extremely long racemes of light purple flowers; **'Violacea Plena'**, clustered racemes to 16 in (40 cm) long with many lavender and purple double flowers. Zones 5–10.

Wisteria frutescens

AMERICAN WISTERIA

☼/◐ ❄ ↔40 ft (12 m) ↕40 ft (12 m)

Very vigorous clockwise-twining climber native to eastern USA. Leaves to 12 in (30 cm) long, with 9 to 15 pointed oval leaflets around 2 in (5 cm) long. Racemes to 4 in (10 cm) long, often held horizontally or semi-erect; flowers bright purple, mildly scented. **'Amethyst Falls'**, 6 in (15 cm) racemes of purple-blue flowers, mainly spring, also sporadically in summer. Zones 5–9.

Woodwardia fimbriata

Wisteria macrostachya

KENTUCKY WISTERIA

☼/◐ ❄ ↔25 ft (8 m) ↕25 ft (8 m)

Counterclockwise-twining climber found from Louisiana to Illinois, USA. Leaves to 12 in (30 cm) long, with 7 to 11 leaflets, 2 in (5 cm) long, tapering to fine point. Pendulous, 6–12 in (15–30 cm) long racemes of small pale pink and lavender flowers opening from deep pink buds. Zones 5–9.

WOODSIA

CLIFF FERN

Widespread in the northern temperate and tropical zones, this group of some 25 species of ferns is the type genus for the wood fern (Woodsiaceae) family. Most species have short creeping rhizomes that are sometimes adapted for growing over rocks and in narrow crevices. The pinnate fronds, though not very finely divided, rarely grow more than about 16 in (40 cm) long. The more northerly species may be deciduous or have greatly reduced fronds over winter. Many species have scaly red-brown stems and this coating can extend to the fronds, which tend to be slightly downy.

CULTIVATION: Those species that occur naturally on rocky outcrops, growing in crevices, will tolerate fairly sunny conditions, otherwise plant in half-sun or dappled light with moist, humus-rich soil. Water well during the growing season to encourage lush growth. Propagation is usually by division, which is easiest in early spring.

Woodsia × *gracilis*

LAWSON'S CLIFF FERN

◐ ❄ ↔12–20 in (30–50 cm) ↕4–10 in (10–25 cm)

Natural hybrid between *W. alpina* and *W. ilvensis*. Fronds to 8 in (20 cm) long with red scaled stems, scaling sometimes occurring sparsely on fronds, which can have a leathery texture. Zones 4–9.

Woodsia ilvensis

FRAGRANT WOODSIA, RUSTY WOODSIA

◐ ❄ ↔12–20 in (30–50 cm) ↕4–10 in (10–25 cm)

North American and Eurasian species often found growing in rock crevices. Fronds to 10 in (25 cm) long, often smaller, with red-brown scales extending to frond bases and sometimes quite vivid on stems. Zones 1–9.

WOODWARDIA

CHAIN FERN

A mainly North American and Asian genus of some 10 species of ferns of the hard-fern (Blechnaceae) family. The rhizomes may be short and stocky or elongated and creeping, sometimes forming short trunks. The fronds, which are usually long, gracefully arching, and borne in a crown, most often occur in distinctly different fertile (spore-bearing) and sterile forms. Frequently the sterile fronds are simple pinnate structures that are not further divided, though a few species have feathery fronds. The fertile fronds tend to occur toward the center of the crown and are more erect, and often with conspicuous spore-bearing organs (sporangia).

CULTIVATION: They are best grown in humid woodland conditions with humus-rich soil that is well-drained but which remains moist throughout the year. Hardiness varies considerably with the species. The hardier species are mainly deciduous. Propagation is mainly by division in early spring, though in suitable climates these ferns multiply freely from spores.

Woodwardia areolata

NETTED CHAIN FERN

◐/● ❄ ↔20–48 in (50–120 cm) ↕20–40 in (50–100 cm)

Tough deciduous species native to much of North America. Broad, simply divided pinnate sterile fronds to 32 in (80 cm) long. Fertile fronds

Woodwardia unigemmata

erect, slightly longer, with twisted segments often darkened by sporangia. Both frond forms have dark stems. Zones 5–9.

Woodwardia fimbriata

GIANT CHAIN FERN

↔3–7 ft (0.9–2 m) ↑3–7 ft (0.9–2 m)

Evergreen species from California and Arizona, USA. Fronds to 10 ft (3 m) long, frequently smaller. Sterile and fertile fronds do not differ greatly except for obvious sporangia on undersides of fertile fronds. May develop short trunk with age. Zones 8–10.

Woodwardia unigemmata

↔4–8 ft (1.2–2.4 m) ↑24–40 in (60–100 cm)

Evergreen species native to Southeast Asia and the Himalayas with broad, doubly divided fronds to nearly 4 ft (1.2 m) long. Young fronds are often vivid red if they are exposed to sun. Fertile fronds do not differ greatly. Can produce new plantlets at frond tips. Zones 8–12.

XANTHOCERAS

The one species of deciduous shrub or small tree in this genus is native to northern China and is a member of the soapberry (Sapindaceae) family. It has pinnate leaves clustered near the branch tips and bears clusters of 5-petalled flowers. The fruits are thick-walled green capsules resembling the fruit of chestnut trees.
CULTIVATION: Although quite hardy, this species needs a long hot growing season to flower well, so in cooler areas should be given the shelter of a warm wall. Grow in a well-drained fertile soil and prune to maintain a compact shape. Propagate from seed, cuttings or suckers.

Xanthoceras sorbifolium

Xanthoceras sorbifolium ★

↔10 ft (3 m) ↑25 ft (8 m)

Shrub or small tree with wide rounded habit, dark green pinnate leaves, and sharply toothed leaflets. The fragrant white flowers have a crimson blotch at their base, and are borne in sprays, in spring–summer. Zones 6–9.

XEROCHRYSUM

ALPINE EVERLASTING, ORANGE EVERLASTING

A small genus of 6 Australian species, formerly classified in the genus *Bracteantha*. They are members of the daisy (Asteraceae) family. The genus name comes from the Greek *xeros*, dry, and *chrysos*, golden, referring to the dry papery bracts, which are golden yellow in many species.
CULTIVATION: Grow these plants in full sun, in light well-drained soil. Propagate from seed.

Xerochrysum bracteatum

syns *Bracteantha bracteatum, Helichrysum bracteatum*

GOLDEN EVERLASTING, STRAWFLOWER

↔16 in (40 cm) ↑3 ft (0.9 m)

Australian annual or short-lived perennial with often sticky, narrow, pointed lance-shaped leaves to over 4 in (10 cm) long. Flowerheads nearly 3 in (8 cm) wide, deep golden yellow. Garden forms produce flowerheads in many colors, including: **'Bright Bikini'** strain in all shades except blue and mauve; **'Coco'**, pale yellow flowers; **'Dargan Hill Monarch'**, buttery yellow flowers; **Dazette Series**, white, red, orange, or dark orange flowerheads; **'Golden Beauty'**, all-over deep golden yellow; **'Pink Sunrise'**, orange and cream flowerheads, pink buds; **'Princess of Wales'**, compact habit, golden yellow flowerheads; **Sundaze Series**, bronze, yellow, red, or white flowerheads. Zones 9–10.

Xerochrysum bracteatum

Xerochrysum bracteatum 'Golden Beauty'

Xerochrysum bracteatum 'Pink Sunrise'

XYLOSMA

BRUSH HOLLY

A willow (Salicaceae) family genus of around 100 species of evergreen shrubs and trees found in the tropical to warm-temperate zones, mainly in the Northern Hemisphere. They usually have opposite pairs of glossy deep green leaves with finely serrated edges, reminiscent of camellia foliage. Racemes of small, yellow-green, fragrant flowers are followed by purplish berries.
CULTIVATION: Hardiness varies considerably with the species. Plant in sun or partial shade with well-drained soil that can be kept moist during the growing season. Most species can be regularly trimmed, and some are good hedging plants. Propagate from seed or half-hardened cuttings.

Xylosma congestum

SHINY XYLOSMA

↔12–15 ft (3.5–4.5 m) ↑12–20 ft (3.5–6 m)

Large shrub or small tree from Japan. Lustrous, pointed oval, serrated leaves to around 3 in (8 cm) long. Creamy yellow flowers, in spring. Often used for hedging, can be kept trimmed to 8–10 ft (2.4–3 m). Zones 9–10.

Yucca baccata

YUCCA

Native to dry regions of North and Central America and the West Indies, there are about 40 species in this genus within the asparagus (Asparagaceae) family, which include evergreen herbaceous perennials, as well as trees and shrubs. They have a strong bold form and strap- to lance-shaped leaves arranged in rosettes. Bell- to cup-shaped flowers are held on usually erect panicles. The inflorescence of *Y. whipplei* grows to 12 ft (3.5 m) in 14 days. Herbalists and traditional healers make a tea from boiled yucca roots. Native Americans still use parts of the yucca plant for craft tools, and as a dye to color fibers.

CULTIVATION: All *Yucca* species grow best in loamy soil with good drainage, but they will tolerate poor sandy soil. In colder regions it is best to grow the tender species in large pots in loam-based potting compost and overwinter them indoors. Grown outdoors they need good light through summer, a monthly feed and careful watering. *Yucca* species range from frost hardy to frost tender. Propagation is by sowing seed in spring, or by taking root cuttings in winter, or by removing suckers in spring.

Yucca aloifolia

DAGGER PLANT, SPANISH BAYONET

↔10 ft (3 m) ↑25 ft (8 m)

Native to the West Indies, Mexico, and southeastern USA. Slow-growing shrub or small tree. Erect stem simple or branched, stiff, lance-shaped, toothed, gray-green leaves to 20 in (50 cm) long, sharply pointed. Bell-shaped, pendent, white flowers, on erect spikes, in summer to autumn. Fleshy fruit. **'Marginata'** ★, yellow leaf edges, but its spreading habit can pose problems; **'Tricolor'**, leaves striped white or yellow in the center. Zones 7–12.

Yucca brevifolia, **in the wild, Death Valley National Park, California, USA**

Yucca baccata

BANANA YUCCA, BLUE YUCCA, SPANISH BAYONET

↔4 ft (1.2 m) ↑5 ft (1.5 m)

Native to northern Mexico and southwestern USA. Can be single-stemmed or branched, spent leaves persist on the stem. Leaves green with yellow or blue tinges, fine hairs on leaf edges. Bell-shaped flowers, in panicles, cream sometimes tinged purple. Zones 5–11.

Yucca brevifolia

JOSHUA TREE

↔5 ft (1.5 m) ↑30–40 ft (9–12 m)

Found from California to southwestern Utah, USA. Branching habit, bark gray or orange-brown forming plates. Leaves straight and narrow, finely toothed edges. Flower spikes bear unpleasant smelling greenish flowers, tinged with yellow or cream, in the late spring. Zones 6–10.

Yucca elata

PALMELLA, SOAP WEED

↔5 ft (1.5 m) ↑10 ft (3 m)

Found from Arizona to Texas, USA, and Mexico. Suckering shoots, multiple stems covered with dead leaves. New leaves light green, edged with fine hairs. Flower stalk is 6 ft (1.8 m) tall, flowers are creamy white, tinted pink or green. Zones 6–10.

Yucca faxoniana

↔7–10 ft (2–3 m) ↑10–17 ft (3–5 m)

Evergreen perennial shrub from southwestern USA and Mexico. Forms stout upright trunk, to 12 in (30 cm) in diameter. Rosette of stiff pointed leaves, to 3 ft (0.9 m) long, sharply pointed tips, reddish or sometimes black margins with curly threads. Old yellow leaves bend down to form thick thatch. Terminal stalk emerges from the center of the leaf rosette, 3–4 ft (0.9–1.2 m) tall. Creamy white bell-shaped flowers. Reddish seed pods. Zones 6–10.

Yucca glauca, **in the wild, Montana, USA**

Yucca filamentosa **'Bright Edge'**

Yucca filamentosa ★

ADAM'S NEEDLE

↔5 ft (1.5 m) ↑3 ft (0.9 m)

From eastern USA. Usually trunkless, multiple suckering heads of 30 in (75 cm) long, filamentous, blue-green leaves. Flower stems up to 10 ft (3 m) tall bear masses of pendulous cream flowers, in summer. **'Bright Edge'** ★, dwarf cultivar with yellow-edged foliage, creamy flowers tinged with green; **'Golden Sword'** ★, similar but larger; **'Ivory Tower'**, creamy white flowers tinged with green. Zones 6–10.

Yucca flaccida

syn. *Yucca filifera*

↔17–35 ft (5–10 m) ↑17–35 ft (5–10 m)

Branching, evergreen, perennial North American shrub. Dark bluish green, flexible, narrowly sword-shaped leaves, to 22 in (55 cm) long, sharp tips, yellow serrated margins ending in straight threads. Cylindrical heads of creamy white bell-shaped flowers, to 2 in (5 cm) long, from summer–autumn. **'Golden Sword'**, green leaves with yellow margins; **'Ivory'**, freely flowering with spikes of ivory flowers. Zones 4–9.

Yucca glauca

SPANISH BAYONET

↔36 in (90 cm) ↑24 in (60 cm)

From western and central USA. Clump-forming species, blue-green narrow leaves, thin straight filaments along the edges. Flower stalk to 3 ft (0.9 m) tall, bell-shaped off-white flowers, sometimes tinged green or red-brown, in summer. ***Y. g.* var. *tristis*** (syn. *Y. recurvifolia*), leaves sometimes with recurved (weeping) tips. Zones 4–10.

Yucca gloriosa

CANDLE YUCCA, PALM LILY, ROMAN CANDLE

↔6 ft (1.8 m) ↑6–8 ft (1.8–2.4 m)

Found from North Carolina to Florida, USA. Usually unbranched tree-like species. Stiff, thin, lance-shaped, blue-green, age to dark green. White, pendent bell-shaped flowers, sometimes tinged green, pink or purplish red on tall panicles, in summer–autumn. **'Variegata'** ★, leaves with yellow-cream stripes and edges. Zones 7–10.

Yucca whipplei

OUR LORD'S CANDLE

↔4 ft (1.2 m) ↑3 ft (0.9 m)

Stiff-leafed stemless yucca ranges from southwestern USA into Baja California, Mexico. Rosettes of narrow, rigid, blue-green leaves, spiny tips, fine-toothed edges. The flowering panicle grows rapidly to 10–15 ft (3–4.5 m) high, with pendulous, small, white flowers, often green- or purple-tipped, from the late summer to early autumn. Y. w. subsp. parishii is an unbranched race. Zones 8–11.

ZAMIA

This genus in the zamia (Zamiaceae) family consists of more than 55 species, the majority occurring in South, Central, and North America. All have pinnate leaves and cylindrical or tuber-like stems that are usually subterranean but may be above ground. They are fern or palm-like in appearance, with the male and broader female cones borne on separate plants. Many species have highly toxic seeds. The spiraly arranged arching leaves have mostly smooth leaflets, and the margins can be smooth-edged, toothed or bumpy, and spiny in some species. They come from a range of habitats. These plants make useful landscape subjects. Most are best suited to tropical and subtropical regions that are free from frost.

CULTIVATION: Most are fairly adaptable in a well-drained soil. Tolerances vary; the understory types

Yucca gloriosa

with softer lusher foliage usually are best in sheltered, more humid, semi-shaded positions, while the tougher-leafed species from more open habitats can usually tolerate more exposure and sun. Propagate from fresh seed.

Zamia fairchildiana ★

↔5 ft (1.5 m) ↑8 ft (2.4 m)

From Costa Rica and western Panama. Attractive, with upright trunk. Leaves in whorls of 3 to 10, erect, thinly textured, papery green. Leaf stalk densely prickly. Male cones cream to yellow, female yellowish green to light brown. Zones 11–12.

Zamia furfuracea ★

CARDBOARD PALM

↔7 ft (2 m) ↑3 ft (0.9 m)

From Mexico. Broad, hairy, stiff leaflets, attractive small to medium cycad, subterranean stem when young. Forms mound of spreading leaves, olive green leathery leaflets, on spiny stalks. Cones are pink to red. An excellent tub plant. Zones 9–12.

Zamia pumila

GUAYIGA

↔6 ft (1.8 m) ↑5 ft (1.5 m)

From islands of the Caribbean. Short, many-branched, subterranean stems from which emerge 4 to 12 erect dark green leaves with smooth leaf stalks. Cones red to red-brown. Zones 10–12.

ZANTEDESCHIA

ARUM LILY, CALLA LILY

The large calla lily *(Z. aethiopica)* is a plant that polarizes opinions. Some gardeners love it, while others cannot abide its funereal associations. Named after the Italian botanist Giovanni Zantedeschi (1773–1846), this genus in the arum (Araceae) family comprises 6 species of rhizome-rooted perennials from southern Africa, with large, upward-facing, elongated heart-shaped leaves that taper to a long tip and sometimes speckled with translucent spots. The flower spathe is funnel-shaped and also tapers to a tip. The spadix may be enclosed within the spathe or protrude slightly. Although the white form is the best known, modern hybrids cover a wide color range. Both leaves and the flowers are supported by strong stalks. CULTIVATION: Cultivated callas withstand moderate frosts. They lose their foliage in cold winters but may retain some in milder conditions. Some prefer damp almost boggy conditions, but most will grow in full or half-sun in any garden soil that does not dry out. Propagate by division, or from basal offsets or seed.

Zamia furfuracea

Yucca whipplei subsp. *parishii*

Zantedeschia aethiopica

ARUM LILY, CALLA LILY

↔20–60 in (50–150 cm) ↑4–6 ft (1.2–1.8 m)

From South Africa and widely naturalized in mild areas, this evergreen or semi-evergreen species develops large rhizomes and can form impressive clumps of long-stemmed, 12–24 in (30–60 cm) long, arrowhead-shaped leaves. Tall flower stems topped with a white spathe, to 10 in (25 cm) long, around a yellow spadix. Can become invasive. **'Childsiana'** ★, compact, small leaves, pink-tinted flowers last well when cut; **'Crowborough'**, 36 in (90 cm) tall; **'Green Goddess'**, 36 in (90 cm) tall, small greenish spathe, can be invasive. Zones 8–11.

Zantedeschia albomaculata

↔16–24 in (40–60 cm) ↑24–40 in (60–100 cm)

Perennial found from South Africa to tropical eastern Africa. Long-stemmed, white-spotted, arrowhead-shaped leaves, to 18 in (45 cm) long. Sturdy flower stems with cup-shaped spathe, to 5 in (12 cm) long, usually white to cream, sometimes yellow or pink. Spadix pale to deep yellow. Zones 6–11.

Zantedeschia elliottiana ★

GOLDEN CALLA

↔12–18 in (30–45 cm) ↑12–18 in (30–45 cm)

Unknown in the wild and possibly of hybrid origin. Heavily white-spotted, arrowhead-shaped leaves, 8–12 in (20–30 cm) long, deep yellow 4–5 in (10–12 cm) long spathes. Zones 9–11.

Zantedeschia rehmannii

↔12–20 in (30–50 cm) ↑16–20 in (40–50 cm)

Native of South Africa and Swaziland. Narrow, unspotted, lance-shaped leaves, to 16 in (40 cm) long. Flowerheads often held below foliage level. Spathes white, pink, or purple-red, to over 4 in (10 cm) long. **'Superba'**, many deep pink spathes held just above foliage level. Zones 9–11.

Zantedeschia aethiopica 'Green Goddess'

Zantedeschia aethiopica, in the wild, South Africa

Zantedeschia, HC, 'Scarlet Pimpernel'

Zantedeschia Hybrid Cultivars

↔1–5 ft (0.3–1.5 m)
↕1–6 ft (0.3–1.8 m)

Developed through crossing most of the smaller species, these hybrids are generally quite compact. White-spotted leaves, sturdy flower stems with showy spathes. **'Flame'**, 24 in (60 cm), red-flecked yellow spathes deepening with age; **'Hercules'**, 6 ft (1.8 m), giant-sized, white to very pale pink spathes; **'Kiwi Blush'**, 30 in (75 cm), white spathes heavily flushed pink; **'Scarlet Pimpernel'** ★, 18–24 in (45–60 cm), bright red spathes. Zones 9–11.

ZELKOVA

Allied to the elms *(Ulmus)* but not troubled by Dutch elm disease, the 5 deciduous trees in this genus are members of the family Ulmaceae, and are found in China, Taiwan, and Japan, as well as in the Caucasus and Crete, Greece. They have simple, pointed, elliptical leaves with conspicuous veins and heavily serrated edges. The foliage often develops some attractive autumn colors. In some species the bark is an attractive feature, flaking to reveal interesting patterns and colors. The separate male and female flowers are largely inconspicuous, as are the small nut-like fruits.

CULTIVATION: Quite frost hardy, these spreading round-headed trees develop a better shape if sheltered from strong winds when they are young. They also benefit from pruning to encourage a strong single trunk. Plant in deep, fertile, well-drained soil in full sun. Propagation is from seed, from root cuttings of the young potted plants, or by grafting.

Zantedeschia, Hybrid Cultivar, 'Flame'

Zelkova serrata

Zelkova serrata

JAPANESE ZELKOVA

↔50 ft (15 m)
↕60–100 ft (18–30 m)

Widely cultivated, found in Japan, Taiwan, and eastern China. Wide-spreading crown, bark flakes to reveal range of colors and textures. Heavily toothed, veined leaves, fine hairs on underside veins. Foliage turns gold and russet, in autumn. **'Goblin'**, 3 ft (0.9 m) high dwarf cultivar; **'Green Vase'** ★, vase-shaped form, brilliant green foliage; **'Village Green'**, fast-growing, rich green leaves. Zones 5–9.

ZENOBIA

The single species in this genus in the heath (Ericaceae) family is a deciduous or semi-evergreen shrub found in southeastern USA, on open heathland and in pine forest clearings. Notable for beautiful flowers and their pleasant scent. Foliage sometimes develops red tints in autumn.

CULTIVATION: This plant prefers cool, moist, humus-rich, acidic soil conditions. Very frost hardy; prefers partial shade. If necessary trim to shape after flowering. Propagate from seed or summer cuttings. Alternatively, try removing rooted layers or suckers.

Zenobia pulverulenta ★

↔4 ft (1.2 m) ↕3–10 ft (0.9–3 m)

From southeast Virginia to South Carolina, USA. Retains much of its foliage in mild winters, deciduous elsewhere. Narrowly elliptical leaves, light green, covered with a powdery bluish bloom. Heads of bell-shaped, nodding, scented white flowers, in late spring. **'Quercifolia'** retains shallowly lobed foliage seen on juvenile plants. Zones 5–10.

ZEPHYRANTHES

FAIRY LILY, RAINFLOWER, ZEPHYR LILY

This amaryllis (Amaryllidaceae) family genus is composed of around 70 species of bulbs, many of which are known for their ability to quickly come into flower with the arrival of rain after prolonged drought. They occur from southern North America to Argentina, often at quite high elevations. The foliage is usually grassy, and the 6-petalled flowers often resemble rather wide-open crocuses, in yellow, pink, and purple shades or white.

CULTIVATION: Excellent drainage is vital; the bulbs will rot with prolonged damp conditions. However, the bulbs resent being lifted and stored dry. Plant in full sun or light shade, with gritty, free-draining soil. Propagate by dividing established clumps.

Zephyranthes candida

WHITE RAIN LILY

↔6–8 in (15–20 cm)
↕6–8 in (15–20 cm)

From Argentina, Uruguay, Paraguay, and Chile. Fine grassy leaves. White flowers, mainly in autumn. More damp- and cold-tolerant than most others. Zones 8–10.

Zephyranthes carinata

syn. *Zephyranthes grandiflora*

PINK RAIN LILY, ROSEPINK ZEPHYR LILY

↔10–12 in (25–30 cm)
↕8–10 in (20–25 cm)

From Central America. Narrow strappy leaves and pink flowers up to 4 in (10 cm) across, larger than most others, year-round. Does not need a dormant period. Zones 10–12.

Zephyranthes citrina

↔6–8 in (15–20 cm)
↕4–6 in (10–15 cm)

From Mexico. Fine grassy leaves. Short-stemmed, crocus-like, deep yellow flowers. Can bloom several times per year. Zones 9–11.

Zephyranthes rosea

CUBAN ZEPHYR LILY, PINK RAIN LILY

↔6–8 in (15–20 cm)
↕6–8 in (15–20 cm)

Caribbean native with strappy leaves and long-stemmed deep pink flowers, mainly from late summer. Will take light frosts with protection. Zones 10–12.

Zephyranthes candida

ZINNIA

Named for Johann Gottfried Zinn (1727–1759), a German botany professor, this daisy (Asteraceae) family genus of around 20 species of annuals, perennials, and small shrubs is from south-central USA to Argentina, with its center in Mexico. Zinnias have soft light green leaves that range from linear to broadly spatula-shaped, depending on the species. While the flowers of the wild species are typically daisy-like with conspicuous ray and disc florets, modern seed strains are mainly doubles with the disc florets largely hidden or absent. The color range is very wide, though mostly warm tones: yellow, pink, orange, and red to mahogany.

CULTIVATION: They are mostly frost-tender summer annuals that should be grown in a sunny warm position sheltered from drafts. The soil should be moist and well-drained, but zinnias can withstand dry periods. Deadhead frequently to prolong the flowering. Propagate from seed.

Zinnia angustifolia

↔12–20 in (30–50 cm)
↕8–16 in (20–40 cm)

Erect summer-flowering annual from southeastern USA and Mexico. Needle-like to narrow lance-shaped leaves, to 3 in (8 cm) long. Flowerheads have up to 9 bright orange ray florets and orange disc florets, interspersed with dark hairs. **'Classic'**, 12 in (30 cm), white ray florets; **'Coral Beauty'**, 12 in (30 cm), semi-double orange-pink; **'Crystal White'**, 12 in (30 cm), white ray florets; **'Golden Eye'**, 14 in (35 cm), white ray florets deepening to creamy yellow at center; **'Star White'**, 12 in (30 cm), white ray florets arranged around a pure orange disc. Zones 9–11.

Zinnia elegans

syn. *Zinnia violacea*

↔ 8–18 in (20–45 cm)
↑ 8–40 in (20–100 cm)

These are popular garden flowers and some of the newer varieties are disease resistant. The numerous cultivars include: **'Aztek'**, white flowers; **'Canary Yellow'**, 30 in (75 cm) tall, bright yellow flowers; **Crayon Colors Mix**, double flowers, tall, up to 40 in (100 cm), "hot" and "cool" color mixes; **Dreamland Series**, 12 in (30 cm) tall, double flowers, in many colors; **'Envy'**, 30 in (75 cm) tall, light green fully double flowers; **'Giant Purity'**, 30 in (75 cm) tall, fully double white flowers; **'Halo'**, red flowers; **Mammoth Exhibition Series**, 30 in (75 cm) tall, double flowers, large color range; **Oklahoma Series**, 36 in (90 cm) tall, semi-double and fully double flowers, wide color range; **'Polar Bear'**, 30 in (75 cm) tall, pure white double flowers; **Profusion Series**, 12 in (30 cm) tall, single flowers, in red, orange, or white; **'Pulcino'**, 16 in (40 cm) tall, semi-double and fully double flowers, wide color range; **Ruffles Series**, 27 in (70 cm) tall, double flowers in most colors; **Splendor Series**, 24 in (60 cm) tall, fully double flowers in red, pink, orange, or yellow; **Sun Series**, 20 in (50 cm) tall, double flowers, in variety of bright warm colors; **Whirlygig Series**, 24 in (60 cm) tall, double, wide range, contrasting floret tip color. Zones 9–11.

Zinnia angustifolia 'Coral Beauty'

Zinnia angustifolia 'Crystal White'

Zinnia elegans 'Canary Yellow'

Zinnia elegans, 'Aztek'

Zinnia peruviana 'Yellow Peruvian'

Zinnia haageana 'Stargold'

Zinnia grandiflora

PRAIRIE ZINNIA

↔ 24–32 in (60–80 cm)
↑ 12 in (30 cm)

Shrubby summer-flowering perennial from southern USA and northern Mexico. Narrow sparsely hairy leaves, to 1 in (25 mm) long. Very bright 1¾ in (40 mm) wide flowerheads with 3 to 6 broad golden yellow ray florets around an orange-red disc. Zones 9–11.

Zinnia haageana

syn. *Zinnia angustifolia of gardens*

↔ 12–24 in (30–60 cm)
↑ 24 in (60 cm)

This species is an erect, bushy, summer-flowering annual from Mexico. Narrow, sparsely hairy to downy, lance-shaped leaves, to over 1¼ in (30 mm) long. Forms flowerheads with 8 to 9 golden to red-brown ray florets around an orange disc; fully double-flowered forms, such as **'Old Mexico'**, common in cultivation. **'Stargold'**, yellow-orange flowers. Zones 9–11.

Zinnia marylandica

↔ 6–10 in (15–25 cm)
↑ 6–12 in (15–30 cm)

Sterile *Z. angustifolia* × *Z. violacea* hybrid produced by colchicine treatment in 1980s. Compact, disease-resistant, fully double, prolific, and long-flowering. **Zahara Series**, various mixes in wide color range, including bicolors. Zones 9–11.

Zinnia peruviana

↔ 12–16 in (30–40 cm)
↑ 36 in (90 cm)

Fast-growing summer-flowering annual found from southern USA to Argentina. Narrow, bright green, lance-shaped leaves, to nearly 3 in (8 cm) long. Flowerheads borne on broad stems held clear of the foliage, with up to 15 red, dusky tangerine, or yellow ray florets, to 1 in (25 mm) long, around a yellow to purple-black disc. **'Yellow Peruvian'** has yellow flowerheads ageing to gold. Zones 9–11.

ZOYSIA

ZOYSIAGRASS

This genus of 5 creeping, warm season, perennial grasses in the grass (Poaceae) family comes from Southeast Asia. These plants grow from both runners and rhizomes. Leaves are rounded to slightly flattened, stiff, and sharply pointed, with occasional hairs near the base, smooth margins and fine to coarsely textured surfaces. Short, slender, and sheathed terminal spikes or spikelets, each with 1 flower, on short stalks. This genus takes its name from the eighteenth-century Austrian botanist, Karl von Zois.

CULTIVATION: They are normally planted in the late spring and early summer for lawn turf as plugs. Adaptable to most soils in the full sun; they are also shade-tolerant.

Zoysia 'Emerald'

↔ 1–2 in (25–50 mm)
↑ 1–2 in (25–50 mm)

Developed for lawn turf use. Hybrid between *Z. japonica* and *Z. tenuifolia*. Creeping, fast-growing, dark emerald green, perennial grass growing from underground runners. Fine dense texture, cold- and drought-tolerant. Zones 1–9.

Zoysia tenuifolia ★

syn. *Zoysia matrella var. tenuifolia*

KOREAN VELVET GRASS, MASCARENE GRASS

↔ 1–2 in (25–50 mm)
↑ 1–2 in (25–50 mm)

Extremely slow-growing, creeping, ornamental, perennial grass from Southeast Asia. Spreads by underground rhizomes. Low-growing ground cover, forms clumps or mounds. Fine, short, wiry, dark green leaves, to 2 in (5 cm) long. Narrow oblong spikelets of green flowers, to 2 in (5 cm) long, in late summer. Zones 6–10.

Index

Italicized page numbers indicate a photograph or a photograph and reference in the text. Plain page numbers indicate a reference in text only.

A

B

D

E

G

H

N

O

P

Q

R

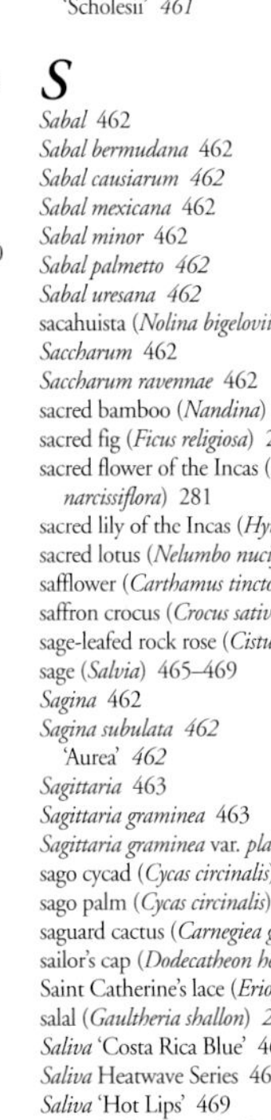

S

T

U

V

W